BUSINESS LAW

THIRD EDITION

JAMES F. MORGAN
Professor of Legal Studies
California State University, Chico

PETER J. SHEDD
Professor of Legal Studies
University of Georgia

ROBERT N. CORLEY
Distinguished Professor Legal Studies Emeritus
University of Georgia

BVT
PUBLISHING
THE PUBLISHER OF AFFORDABLE TEXTBOOKS

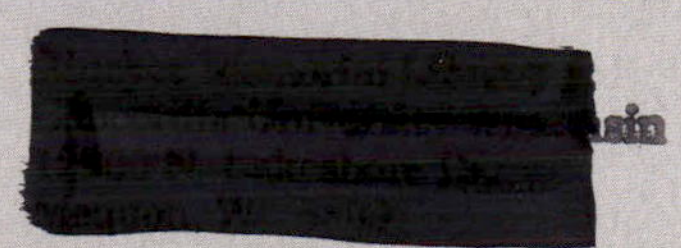

BUSINESS LAW, THIRD EDITION

Some ancillaries, including electronic and print components, may not be available to customers outside the United States.

ISBN: 978-1-60229-995-5

PROJECT DEVELOPMENT MANAGER: Brae Buhnerkemper

PROJECT DEVELOPMENT ASSISTANT: Brandi Cornwell

MANAGING EDITOR: Joyce Bianchini

SENIOR DEVELOPMENT EDITOR: Rhonda Minnema

PHOTO RESEARCHER: Della Brackett

COVER DESIGN: Dan Harvey

ILLUSTRATIONS: Dan Harvey

TYPESETTER: Dan Harvey

TEXT AND COVER PRINTING: World Color, Inc.

SALES MANAGER: Robert Rappeport

MARKETING MANGER: Richard Schofield

PERMISSIONS COORDINATOR: Suzanne Schmidt

ART DIRECTOR: Linda Price

Brief Table of Contents

Table of Contents

Chapter 9 Property: Personal Property, Intellectual Property, and Wills 155

Chapter 10 Property: Real Property, Leases, and Mortgages 181

CHAPTER 27 EMPLOYMENT DISCRIMINATION 525

CHAPTER 28 PARTNERSHIPS 547

CHAPTER 36 LIABILITY OF PARTIES TO NEGOTIABLE INSTRUMENTS 723

Chapter 41 Antitrust Law 857

Preface

Welcome to Business Law, 3rd edition! We believe this edition of the text is worthy of the trust you have placed in us to deliver clearly contemporary aspects of business law in a comprehensive manner appropriate for a variety of learning styles. This book is based on a textbook, written by co-authors Peter Shedd and Robert Corley, which enjoyed strong popularity in university and college classrooms for decades. Using this strong, and tested foundation and adding James Morgan as an author to further update and refine the content, we have created *Business Law* not only to present traditional principles of business law but also to delve into new arenas pertaining to the interaction of law and business appropriate for business leaders of the twenty-first century.

Purpose of the Text

Business Law is written with a realization of the forces that have shaped, and continue to mold, our Legal Studies discipline and with a full understanding of the challenges students face when studying this subject. Therefore, we hope to offer a text that is *contemporary* in approach, *comprehensive* in coverage, and *clearly* presented.

First, we desire to offer a *contemporary* text. Issues associated with globalization, diversity, and the Internet, among others, provide tremendous challenges to members of the business community today. Moreover, within the legal studies discipline, significant changes have occurred recently in a variety of areas—including the laws of bankruptcy, intellectual property, limited liability business structures, negotiable instruments, to name just a few. Transformation is occurring in business and within the legal studies discipline, and we attempt to capture major developments on both fronts within this text.

While we certainly wish to present a contemporary text, we strive also to offer a *comprehensive* legal studies book. Each author has taught business law on university campuses to both undergraduate and graduate students for over two decades. Further, each of us has associated for years with scores of colleagues from across the nation and has participated in numerous legal studies conferences where we have discussed with others the teaching of business law. What do we conclude from our collective experience? One thing for sure: each instructor of a course in business law (or legal environment of business or legal studies in business) has a slightly different (well … sometimes *widely* different) group of topics that they present in a single quarter or semester class. That is the nature of our discipline; and we believe the wide array of topics that might be included in a business law course, the varying emphasis that might be provided to a subject area, and the degree of instructor passion associated with specific legal topics— all enrich the student learning experience.

In *Business Law* we embrace this diversity of approaches to the discipline because students, ultimately, benefit if the instructor can teach a selection of business law topics with which they have a familiarity and that they believe are most relevant to students of business. For example, many of our colleagues desire that their students be most familiar with private law topics, including contracts, torts, partnerships, and corporations. Others hold the position that matters of public law are most critical, so they focus their course on consumer law, environmental law, employment law, and antitrust law. A large number of those who teach business law, not surprisingly, attempt to cover in considerable detail both private law and government regulation topics. The point is, regardless of the topics an instructor selects to cover (in a one quarter, one semester, course, or in a full year course), this text provides comprehensive coverage of the topics generally captured by the terms "business law" and "legal environment of business."

Lastly, we desire to present the subject matter *clearly.* The reader will note that plain language is the norm; and where legal terms are employed, they are defined. Fact-based examples of legal doctrines are used liberally. Also, on average each chapter has at least one visual depiction of the specific subject area being addressed, with the hope of being able to assist those who learn more easily through a diagram, table, or other visual form of presentation.

Further, in terms of readability, we recognize that this text is aimed at students from various levels within a campus community. Some students will be studying selected chapters within the context of a business law or legal environment class as part of the general business curriculum at a community college or university. For the chapters most often used in such a course of study (e.g., Chapter 14 "The Agreement: Offer and Acceptance"), we write at a level that respects the preliminary stage of business education for the most typical reader of such a chapter. For those students near the end of their four-year degree or in graduate school, we offer a more sophisticated presentation for chapters that are often read by those students (e.g., Chapter 37 "Secured Transactions"). For all readers, though, we trust you will find the material presented in a clear fashion.

Pedagogical Design

The chapters in *Business Law* are made up of three basic parts: text, cases, and problems. First, the *text* is written in a style designed for business students and students in related disciplines, introducing them to the legal issues they will face throughout their careers. However, as mentioned above, this text is written without much of the legalese to which law school students become so familiar.

Second, most chapters contain three edited *cases.* These case opinions, included in the judge's actual language, illustrate a point of law discussed in the text. In order to improve readability, the authors have lightly edited the prose in the official opinion of the court, particularly regarding the elimination of citations to many cases and statutes not important for our purposes. The reader will discover each case consists of basic facts (set forth in *italics* for ease of understanding). This portion of the case provides a true-to-life view of business, almost always in a fairly contentious setting. Each case then presents the legal analysis of a judge or justice, allowing the student to experience the legal process as the law is explained and applied.

A further comment or two about the cases included in *Business Law*—while almost all of the cases were decided recently, a small number of judicial opinions are classic cases from prior decades. We feature those cases to illustrate the rich history associated with many legal doctrines we take for granted today. Also, the cases come from both state and federal courts and from all reaches of the United States (there is an occasional case from outside the United States to illustrate how other countries make legal decisions).

Third, *review problems,* including questions and factual scenarios, are included at the end of each chapter. Many students learn best by being able to apply what they have read in a book, so we have crafted various types of learning exercises to allow students to use the legal principles explained in the text.

Numerous aspects of this text were designed to help enhance the "reader-friendly" and "student-centered" nature we hope is conveyed throughout the book. Of particular interest, in this pedagogical sense, are the following items:

- A *Chapter Outline* to provide a detailed list of the subject matter covered
- A *Chapter Preview* to serve as an introductory statement to help students understand how the chapter's topic fits into the overall business transaction
- A *Business Management Decision* to whet students' appetites for the chapter's discussion
- *Marginal Definitions* to reinforce the meaning of key terms and phrases
- A *Case Concepts Review* follows every case with questions to assist students in their comprehension of the case's major points
- A *Chapter Summary* to assist in the review process
- A *Matching Problem* at the outset of the review questions to provide students with a quick method to test their knowledge of key terms and phrases
- Numerous factual-oriented *Review Problems* to allow students to become comfortable in applying their understanding to business transactions.

We are particularly excited about two changes incorporated in this 3rd edition. We have *italicized* significant words, phrases, and sentences throughout the text in an effort to assist the reader in recognizing particularly important aspects of the text. Also, as commented previously, we have added a large number of *visual depictions* of legal principles—sometimes in the form of a diagram showing the relationship between and among principles, sometimes in the form of a chart geared at comparing principles, and sometimes in other forms aimed at further enhancing the learning process.

In addition to these pedagogical devices, *Business Law* includes a detailed set of *appendices.* A glossary for student referral is also provided.

Coverage of Text

The forty-three chapters in *Business Law* are divided into nine distinctive parts. These divisions permit the material to be covered in the order that professors feel best meets their students' needs. We believe this organization provides the flexibility for courses on either the semester or quarter calendar. Also, this structure allows students to have a logical skeleton with which to see the "big picture" of business law along with major divisions of the subject area.

Part I serves as an *introduction to our legal system.* Topics of particular importance include the structure of the courts (Chapter 2), the litigation procedure (Chapter 3), alternatives to litigation (Chapter 4), and the Constitution (Chapter 5). This part can be deleted if the students have had a Legal Environment of Business course, or it can serve as a quick review.

Part II consists of seven chapters discussing some of the *basic legal concepts* that we believe essential for students to understand prior to their coverage of the other topics in this text. Chapter 6 is on criminal law because of the increasing importance of white-collar crime and the problems business managers face as the result of the high crime rate. Chapters 7 and 8 place special emphasis on the various theories that are used to impose tort liability on businesspeople and their organizations. Chapters 9 and 10 introduce the reader to the law of property, including the topics of personal, real, and intellectual property. In a rather unique offering, we include a single chapter (11) that introduces various forms of organizations that can be used to operate business activities and present factors that make one organizational form preferable to the other forms. Finally, Chapter 12 on international business transactions provides students with an appreciation for the growing importance of the globalization of business. As with the chapters in Part I, these seven chapters can be deleted or reviewed quickly if the students have already completed a course in business law or the legal environment of business.

Part III, on *contracts*, is designed to give students an understanding of the basic and traditional concepts of contracts as well as of recent developments from the closely related topic of sales under the Uniform Commercial Code. This Code is included as an appendix, and appropriate sections are referred to in brackets within the text. Also, the impact of the digital age on traditional notions of contract law is explored within this part. After an introductory chapter (13), the next four chapters (14 through 17) discuss the essential requirements for every valid contract. Chapter 18 involves issues of form and interpretation of contracts; and Chapter 19 includes a discussion of contractual performance, along with a presentation of the methods of discharging or excusing the performance of promises. Finally, issues created when third parties become involved in contracts are discussed in Chapter 20.

Part IV consists of three chapters that present additional material on the *sale of goods*. Without repeating the details contained in the chapters on contracts, Chapters 21 and 22 emphasize the provisions of Article 2 of the Uniform Commercial Code necessary to understand formational and operational aspects of sales and leases of goods. Chapter 23 is an in-depth examination of the law of warranties.

Part V contains four chapters on legal principles directed at dealing with *people* within a business environment. Chapter 24 covers the creation, termination, and general principles of the agency relationship. Chapter 25 discusses liability principles associated with an agency relationship from the perspective of the law of contracts and the law of torts. Employment-related concepts follow in the next two chapters, with Chapter 26 examining general employment and labor law subjects and Chapter 27 focusing on discrimination.

Part VI discusses *business organizations* in three stages. These stages are (1) the methods of creating the various forms of organizations, (2) the legal aspects of operating the various forms of organizations, and (3) the law as it relates to dissolution of business organizations. This material is covered in Chapters 28 through 31. Recognizing the explosion in the use of limited liability companies, most of Chapter 31 is devoted to this exciting mechanism for conducting business. Chapter 32, on security regulations, is designed to assist students in their understanding of the government's regulation of corporate securities.

Part VII consists of four chapters devoted to *negotiable instruments*. Chapter 33 serves as an introduction to terminology and to an understanding of the scope of Articles 3 and 4 of the Uniform Commercial Code. Chapters 34 and 35 discuss the basic elements and advantages of negotiable instruments. Chapter 36 concentrates on the liability of the parties involved in the commercial paper transaction.

Part VIII contains three chapters dealing with the law as it relates to *creditors and debtors*. The first chapter (37) examines Article 9 of the Uniform Commercial Code on secured credit transactions. Chapter 38 presents additional laws assisting creditors, emphasizing the complex area of suretyship. Finally, Chapter 39 discusses bankruptcy.

Part IX contains four chapters on the subject of *government regulation of business*. Chapter 40 covers administrative law, with an emphasis on the operation and impact of administrative agencies. The subject of antitrust law is dealt with in Chapter 41. Two areas of comparatively recent vintage, consumer law (Chapter 42) and environmental law (Chapter 43), conclude this part.

Supplements for Instructors

1. Instructor's Manual The Instructor's Manual can be used by the first-time instructor for structuring the course or by the seasoned instructor who simply wants to have another perspective on the materials. Each section of the Instructor's Manual coincides with a chapter in the textbook. The user-friendly format begins by providing a section on the overall purpose of the chapter. Then, a detailed outline of the chapter is presented, including a summary of the principal cases presented in the text. Following the outline, sample answers to the end-of-chapter questions are provided, along with citations to the section or sections of the chapter that provide the rationale for the sample answer. Finally, Internet addresses for additional resources are suggested where appropriate.

2. Test Bank An extensive test bank of approximately 1700 questions is available to instructors in both hard copy and electronic forms. Each chapter consists of a variety of multiple choice, true/false and essay questions.

3. Distance Learning Solutions BVT Publishing is committed to providing the ability to administer tests and quizzes over the Internet. We have a strong relationship with Respondus, whose Course Management Software allows for the creation of randomly-generated tests and quizzes, that can be downloaded directly into a wide variety of course management environments, such as Blackboard, Web CT, Desire 2 Learn, Angel, E Learning and others.

4. PowerPoints These slides, developed by one of the authors, provide an outline of learning objectives/topics for the chapter, a comprehensive framework for each of the legal doctrines addressed in the chapter, and definitions of salient terms employed in the materials. We have crafted the slides to avoid being "busy" with an overabundance of information; instead, they provide a template for lectures and discussions in an "eye-pleasing" format.

5. Customize This Book If you have additional material you'd like to add (handouts, lecture notes, syllabus, etc) or if you would like to simply rearrange and delete content, BVT Publishing's custom publishing division can help you modify this book's content to produce a book that satisfies your specific instructional needs. BVT Publishing has the only custom publishing division that puts your material exactly where you want it to go, easily and seamlessly. Please visit www.bvtpublishing.com or call us at 1-800-646-7782 for more information on BVT Publishing's Custom Publishing Program.

Supplements for Students

BVT Publishing is pleased to provide students with a free, comprehensive online tutorial that can be found at www.bvtstudents.com. This website offers the following:

1. eBook editions Save time, money and paper by purchasing an eBook version of this text directly from our convenient online store, located on our student website.

2. Shopping Cart For the student's convenience and pocketbook, the student website also contains a shopping cart where they have the added option of purchasing the traditional paper textbook directly from the publisher if they prefer.

3. Self Testing Students can test their knowledge of this book's content on our student website. The Self Test questions are designed to help improve students' mastery of the information in the book.

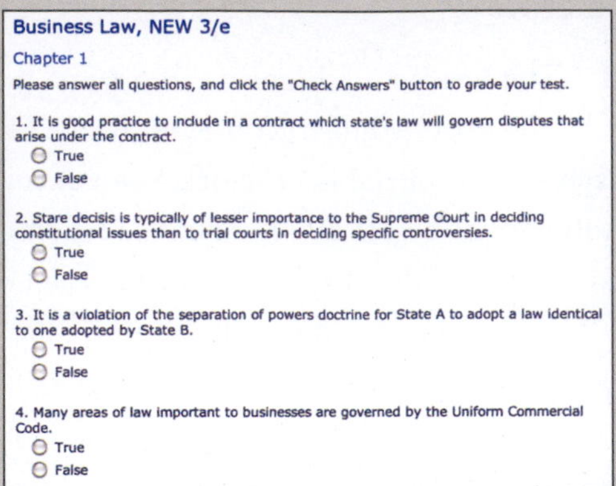

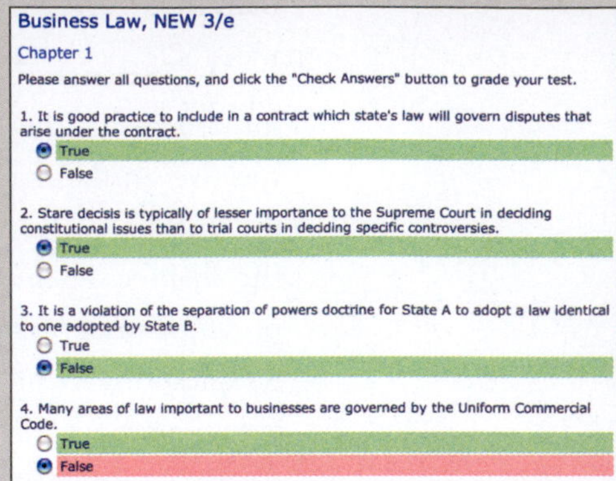

4. Chapter Outlines Chapter outlines are available for students to use either on our website or they can be downloaded directly from our website. They are designed to serve as a helpful outline approach to getting an overview of each chapter's content.

5. Flash Cards We also feature Flash Cards on our student website. The Flash Cards are an easy way for students to spot-check their understanding of common and important Business Law terms, as well as effectively retain the information.

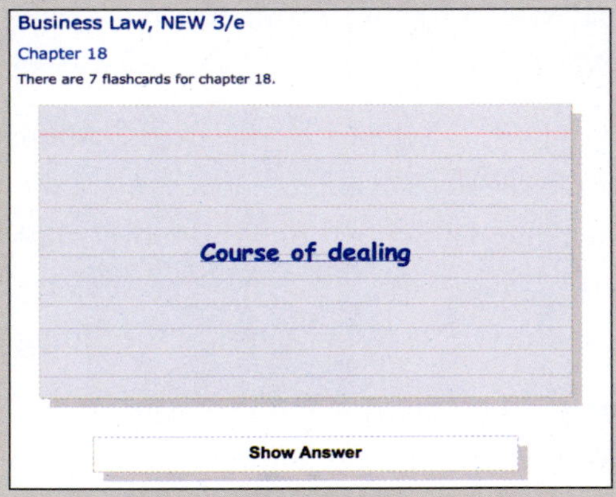

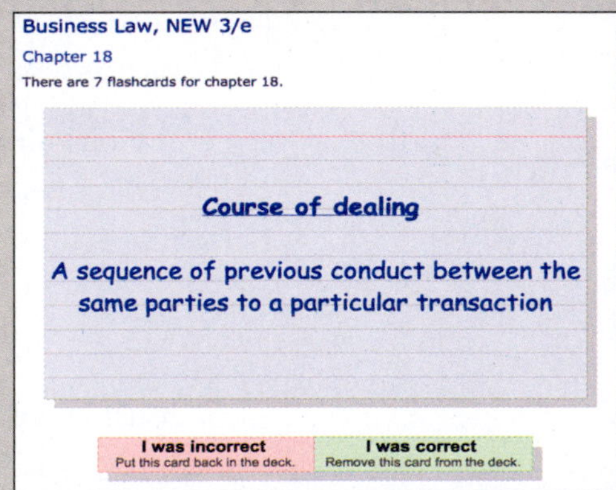

6. Chapter Summaries The Chapter Summaries are another tool designed to give the students an overview of each chapter's content, further aiding the students in content comprehension and retention.

Acknowledgments

We owe to all the dedicated staff at BVT Publishing, including Jason James, Suzanne Morse, Brae Buhnerkemper, and Robert Rappeport, considerable gratitude for their insight in creating the concept for this book and working so tirelessly to make that concept the reality you hold in your hands today. We also wish to express our heartfelt appreciation to our immediate families for the support they have offered during the writing process.

Welcome to *Business Law!* Good luck as you embark on a most fascinating journey!

James F. Morgan
Peter J. Shedd
Robert N. Corley

PART I

INTRODUCTION

Law | 1

CHAPTER OUTLINE

INTRODUCTION TO LAW

1. Definitions of Law
2. Classifications of Legal Subjects

SOURCES OF LAW

3. Court Decisions
4. Basic Constitutional Principles
5. Legislation
6. Interpreting Legislation
7. Uniform State Laws

CASE LAW

8. *Stare Decisis*
9. Problems Inherent in Case Law
10. Rejection of Precedent
11. Conflict of Laws
12. Jurisprudence

LAW AND ETHICS

13. Ethical Conduct
14. Interrelationship Between Law and Ethics

CHAPTER PREVIEW

As you begin your study of business law, two questions arise immediately. What does the term *law* mean? Secondly, how does the law affect the people and organizations engaged in business activities? The search for answers to these two questions forms the basis of this text. By way of introducing our subject matter, this first chapter attempts to answer the first question. The entire text is dedicated to answering the second question.

Perhaps you are asking yourself, "Why should I study business law? Is the legal environment of business really that important?" The answer is clear. Legal concepts, principles, and rules provide the foundation for the conduct of business. The law determines *who* may conduct business, *how* it is to be conducted, and *what sanctions* are to be imposed if its requirements are not met. Thus, knowledge of the law as it relates to business is an indispensable ingredient in any successful business venture.

Now, more than ever before, law affects business decisions. Laws written to solve many of society's problems are directed at business, regulating its activity and its processes. This text attempts to create an awareness of the role of law in business. A sampling of business decisions that probably will be influenced by the law is presented in Figure 1-1.

This text is divided into nine parts. Each examines an important area wherein the law is governing the business transaction. Part I provides a background, an understanding of our legal system. We find out where our laws come from, how they are applied, and how they are changed. There is also a discussion of the role of ethics as an influence on individual and business conduct. Our emphasis is on the various methods of resolving conflicts and controversies. Litigation and arbitration as a substitute for litigation are the major areas of study.

FIGURE 1-1 ■ Sampling of Areas Where Law Influences Business Decisions

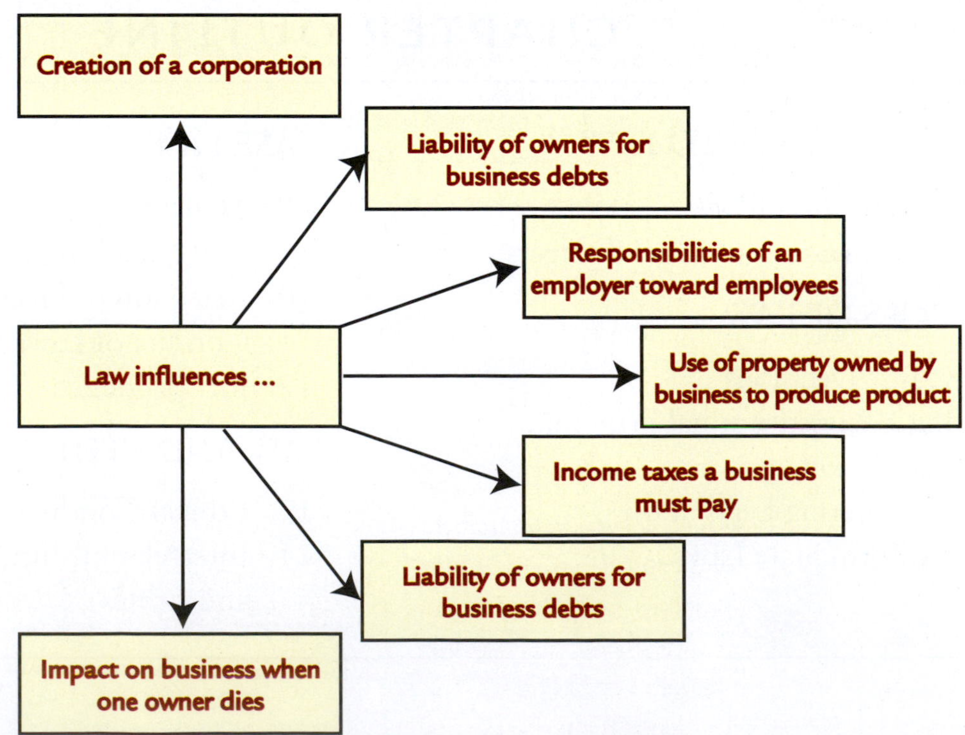

BUSINESS MANAGEMENT DECISION

Your import-export business becomes subject to new legislation regulating international trade transactions. A particular provision of the new law is unclear in its application to your business. You consult your company lawyer for advice. He informs you that he is not sure what the law means.

Should you hire a new lawyer?

INTRODUCTION TO LAW

1. Definitions of Law

In everyday conversation, people use the word law in many different ways, but it is a word that is very difficult to define. In its broad context, it expresses a variety of concepts. Law has been defined as rules and regulations established by government and applied to people in order for civilization to exist. Law and legal theory, however, are far too complex for such a simple definition.

In attempting to define *law,* it is helpful to look at its purposes or functions. A basic purpose of law in a civilized society is to maintain order. This is the prime function of that body of law known as *criminal law.* Another role of law is to resolve disputes that arise between individuals and to impose responsibility if one person has a valid, legal claim against another, as in a suit for breach of contract. It is important that we bear in mind that the law is not simply a statement of rules of conduct but also the means whereby remedies are afforded when one person has wronged another.

In one sense, almost every issue or dispute in our society—political, social, religious, economic—ultimately becomes a legal issue to be resolved by the courts. Thus it can be said that law is simply what the courts determine it to be as an expression of the public's will in resolving these issues and disputes.

In still another sense, *law* has been defined as the rules and principles applied by the courts to decide controversies. These rules and principles fall into three categories:

1. *Legislative law* These are laws, including the federal Constitution and state constitutions, that have been passed by legislative bodies.
2. *Judicial pronouncements* These are legal statements made by courts. They can be interpretations of statutes, or they can be based on common law principles that were created by the courts decades or centuries ago.
3. *Procedural law* Most often this type is the product of the legislative branch, aimed at determining how lawsuits are handled in the courts. These laws include matters such as the rules of evidence and related issues.

Civilization is governed by law.

The first two elements provide the rules of *substantive law* that the courts apply to decide controversies. The third provides the machinery whereby these rules of substantive law are given effect and applied to resolve controversies.

Many legal scholars have defined law in relation to the *sovereign*. For example, Blackstone, the great legal scholar of the eighteenth century, defined law as "that rule of action which is prescribed by some superior and which the inferior is bound to obey." This concept of law as a command from a superior to an inferior is operative in many areas. For example, the tax laws command that taxes shall be paid to the sovereign.

Another view of law is that it is a method of *social control*—an instrument of social, political, and economic change. Law is both an instrument of change and a result of changes that take place in our society. The law brings about changes in our society; society brings about changes in the law. The law—responding to the goals, desires, needs, and aspirations of society—is in a constant state of change. Sometimes the law changes more rapidly than the attitudes of the majority. In this event, the law and our legal system provide leadership in bringing about changes. At other times society is ahead of the law in moving in new directions, and changes in the law are brought about by the people. In the field of ecology, for example, various groups have put pressure on legislators to clean up the air and water. As a result, laws have been enacted requiring devices to be installed to control pollution. Here public pressure resulted in the enactment of laws, and the law was a follower rather than a leader. It is important to note that the law is not static. It is constantly changing, and the impetus for the changes may come from many different sources.

As Oliver Wendell Holmes, Jr., one of the most influential justices to ever serve on the United States Supreme Court, wrote in a famous *Harvard Law Review* article more than one hundred years ago, the law is an "instrument … of business" because it assists members of the business community to *predict the future*. In essence, the law provides stability for the business community. However, for many business leaders today the complexity of the law, especially as it has developed in the United States during the past several decades, creates uncertainty. Consider the following famous case recently decided by the Supreme Court. Portions of the majority opinion, signed by five justices, and a minority opinion, approved by four justices, are presented.

CASE

Susette Kelo et al. v. City of New London, Connecticut, et al.

SUPREME COURT OF THE UNITED STATES

545 U.S. 469 (2005)

The city of New London (hereinafter City) sits at the junction of the Thames River and the Long Island Sound in southeastern Connecticut. Decades of economic decline led a state agency in 1990 to designate the City a "distressed municipality." In 1996, the Federal Government closed the Naval Undersea Warfare Center, which had been located in the Fort Trumbull area of the City and had employed over 1,500 people. In 1998, the City's unemployment rate was nearly double that of the State, and its population of just under 24,000 residents was at its lowest since 1920.

These conditions prompted state and local officials to target New London, and particularly the Fort Trumbull area, for economic revitalization. To this end, respondent New London Development Corporation (NLDC), a private nonprofit entity established some years earlier to assist the City in planning economic development, was reactivated. In January 1998, the State authorized a $5.35 million bond issue to support the NLDC's planning activities and a $10 million bond issue toward the creation of a Fort Trumbull State Park.

The city council approved a redevelopment plan in January 2000, and designated the NLDC as its development agent in charge of implementation. The city council also authorized the NLDC to purchase property or to acquire property by exercising eminent domain in the City's name. The NLDC successfully negotiated the purchase of most of the real estate in the 90-acre area, but its negotiations with the petitioners failed. As a consequence, in November 2000, the NLDC initiated the condemnation proceedings that gave rise to this case.

Petitioner Susette Kelo has lived in the Fort Trumbull area since 1997. She has made extensive improvements to her house, which she prizes for its water view. Petitioner Wilhelmina Dery was born in her Fort Trumbull house in 1918 and has lived there her entire life. Her husband Charles (also a petitioner) has lived in the house since they married some 60 years ago. In all, the nine petitioners own 15 properties in Fort Trumbull—4 in parcel 3 of the development plan and 11 in parcel 4A. Ten of the parcels are occupied by the owner or a family member; the other five are held as investment properties. There is no allegation that any of these properties is blighted or otherwise in poor condition; rather, they were condemned only because they happen to be located in the development area.

In December 2000, petitioners brought this action in the New London Superior Court. They claimed, among other things, that the taking of their properties would violate the "public use" restriction in the Fifth Amendment.

We granted certiorari to determine whether a city's decision to take property for the purpose of economic development satisfies the "public use" requirement of the Fifth Amendment.

MAJORITY OPINION

JUSTICE STEVENS DELIVERED THE OPINION OF THE COURT.

Two polar propositions are perfectly clear. On the one hand, it has long been accepted that the sovereign may not take the property of *A* for the sole purpose of transferring it to another private party *B*, even though *A* is paid just compensation. On the other hand, it is equally clear that a State may transfer property from one private party to another if future "use by the public" is the purpose of the taking; the condemnation of land for a railroad with common-carrier duties is a familiar example. Neither of these propositions, however, determines the disposition of this case.

The disposition of this case, therefore, turns on the question of whether the City's development plan serves a "public purpose." Without exception, our cases have defined that concept broadly, reflecting our longstanding policy of deference to legislative judgments in this field.

Those who govern the City were not confronted with the need to remove blight in the Fort Trumbull area, but their determination that the area was sufficiently distressed to justify a program of economic rejuvenation is entitled to our deference. The City has carefully formulated an economic development plan that it believes will provide appreciable benefits to the community, including—but by no means limited to—new jobs and increased tax revenue. As with other exercises in urban planning and development, the City is endeavoring to coordinate a variety of commercial, residential, and recreational uses of land with the hope that they will form a whole greater than the sum of its parts. To effectuate this plan, the City has invoked a state statute that specifically authorizes the use of eminent domain to promote economic development. Given the comprehensive character of the plan, the thorough deliberation that preceded its adoption, and the limited scope of our review, it is appropriate for us to resolve the challenges of the individual owners not on a piecemeal basis but, rather, in light of the entire plan. Because that plan unquestionably serves a public purpose, the takings challenged here satisfy the public use requirement of the Fifth Amendment.

In affirming the City's authority to take petitioners' properties, we do not minimize the hardship that condemnations may entail, notwithstanding the payment of just compensation. We emphasize that nothing in our opinion precludes any State from placing further restrictions on its exercise of the takings power. Indeed, many States already impose "public use" requirements that are stricter than the federal baseline. Some of these requirements have been established as a matter of state constitutional law, n22 while others are expressed in state eminent domain statutes that carefully limit the grounds upon which takings may be exercised. As the submissions of the parties and their *amici* make clear, the necessity and wisdom of using eminent domain to promote economic development are certainly matters of legitimate public debate. This Court's authority, however, extends only to determining whether the City's proposed condemnations are for a "public use" within the meaning of the Fifth Amendment to the Federal Constitution.

Because over a century of our case law interpreting that provision dictates an affirmative answer to that question, we may not grant petitioners the relief that they seek.

DISSENTING OPINION

JUSTICE O'CONNOR, DISSENTING.

Over two centuries ago, just after the Bill of Rights was ratified, Justice Chase wrote:

> "An Act of the Legislature (for I cannot call it a law) contrary to the great first principles of the social compact, cannot be considered a rightful exercise of legislative authority. A few instances will suffice to explain what I mean. … [A] law that takes property from A. and gives it to B: It is against all reason and justice, for a people to entrust a Legislature with such powers; and, therefore, it cannot be presumed that they have done it." *Calder* v. *Bull*, 3 U.S. 386, 3 Dallas 386, 1 L. Ed. 648 (1798) (emphasis deleted).

Today the Court abandons this long-held, basic limitation on government power. Under the banner of economic development, all private property is now vulnerable to being taken and transferred to another private owner, so long as it might be upgraded—i.e., given to an owner who will use it in a way that the legislature deems more beneficial to the public—in the process. To reason, as the Court does, that the incidental public benefits resulting from the subsequent ordinary use of private property render economic development takings "for public use" is to wash out any distinction between private and public use of property—and thereby effectively to delete the words "for public use" from the Takings Clause of the Fifth Amendment. Accordingly I respectfully dissent.

The petitioners' is an objection in principle: They claim that the NLDC's proposed use for their confiscated property is not a "public" one for purposes of the Fifth Amendment. While the government may take their homes to build a road or a railroad or to eliminate a property use that harms the public, say petitioners, it cannot take their property for the private use of other owners simply because the new owners may make more productive use of the property.

continued

The public use requirement, in turn, imposes a more basic limitation, circumscribing the very scope of the eminent domain power: Government may compel an individual to forfeit her property for the *public's* use, but not for the benefit of another private person. This requirement promotes fairness as well as security.

Where is the line between "public" and "private" property use? We give considerable deference to legislatures' determinations about what governmental activities will advantage the public. However, were the political branches the sole arbiters of the public-private distinction, the Public Use Clause would amount to little more than hortatory fluff. An external, judicial check on how the public use requirement is interpreted, however limited, is necessary if this constraint on government power is to retain any meaning.

Here, in contrast, New London does not claim that Susette Kelo's and Wilhelmina Dery's well-maintained homes are the source of any social harm. Indeed, it could not so claim without adopting the absurd argument that any single-family home that might be razed to make way for an apartment building, or any church that might be replaced with a retail store, or any small business that might be more lucrative if it were instead part of a national franchise, is inherently harmful to society and thus within the government's power to condemn.

■ *Affirmed.*

CASE CONCEPTS REVIEW

1. Economic development projects and community planning have certainly added to the complexity of law for members of the business community. Does the majority opinion recognize sufficiently the role of private property rights in light of the need for bettering the public?
2. The majority opinion gives considerable deference to the power of local and state governments to determine a public use. Is this a good approach for members of the business community?
3. Does the dissenting opinion argue in favor of stability, of relying on the status quo? Why or why not?

2. Classification of Legal Subjects

Substantive law

Laws that regulate and control the rights and duties of persons and are used to resolve disputes

Procedural law

Laws that establish the process by which litigation is conducted

Legal subjects may be classified in a variety of ways. Laws and legal principles are sometimes classified as substantive or procedural. As described above, the law that is used to decide disputes is **substantive law**. The legal procedures that determine how a lawsuit is begun, how the trial is conducted, how appeals are taken, and how a judgment is enforced are called **procedural law**. Substantive law is the part of the law that defines rights; procedural law establishes the procedures by which rights are enforced and protected. For example, assume that A and B enter into an agreement and A claims that B breaches the agreement. The rules that provide for bringing B into court and for the conduct of the trial are rather mechanical, and they constitute procedural law. The enforceability of the agreement and A's right to a remedy are matters of substance. These issues are resolved by the courts applying the substantive law of contracts.

Law is also frequently classified into areas of public and private law. *Public* law includes those bodies of law that affect the public generally. Public law may be further divided into three general categories:

1. *Constitutional law* concerns itself with the rights, powers, and duties of federal and state governments under the U.S. Constitution and the constitutions of the various states.
2. *Administrative law* is concerned with the multitude of administrative agencies, such as the Federal Trade Commission and the National Labor Relations Board.
3. *Criminal law* consists of statutes that forbid certain conduct as being detrimental to the welfare of the state or the people generally and provides punishment for their violation.

Private law is that body of law that pertains to the relationships between individuals in an organized society. Private law encompasses the subjects of contracts, torts, and property. Each of these subjects includes several bodies of law. The law of *contracts*, for example, may be subdivided into the subjects of sales, commercial paper, agency, and business organizations.

The law of *torts* is the primary source of litigation in this country and is also a part of the total body of law in areas such as agency and sales. A *tort* is a wrong committed by one person against another or against another's property. The law of torts is predicated on the premise that, in a civilized society, people who injure other persons or their property should compensate them for their loss.

The law of *property* may be thought of as a branch of the law of contracts, but in many ways our concept of private property contains much more than the contract characteristics. Property is the basic ingredient in our economic system, and the subject matter may be subdivided into several areas, such as wills, trusts, estates in land, personal property, bailments, and many more. Part IX of this text is devoted to a study of property.

Any attempt at classification of subject matter, particularly in the area of private law, is difficult because the law is indeed a "seamless web." For example, assume that an agent or a servant acting on behalf of his or her employer commits a tort. The law of agency, although a subdivision of the law of contracts, must contain a body of law to resolve the issues of tort liability of employer and employee. Likewise, assume that a person is injured by a product he or she has purchased. The law of sales, even though a part of the law of contracts, contains several aspects that could best be labeled a branch of the law of torts. Therefore it is apparent that even the general classifications of contract and tort are not accurate in describing the subject matter of various bodies of law.

TABLE 1-1 ■ Classification of Legal Subjects

Public Law	Private Law
1. Constitutional Law	1. Contracts
2. Administrative Law	2. Torts
3. Criminal Law	3. Property

SOURCES OF LAW

3. Court Decisions

Our law comes from four basic sources: (1) constitutions, (2) legislation, (3) judicial decisions, and (4) the rules, regulations, and decisions of administrative agencies. Assuming that administrative agencies are part of the executive branch of government, our law comes from all three branches. Administrative law is treated in detail in Chapter 40.

Although in this text we study examples of laws from all these sources, you must realize the importance of court decisions. The concept of decided cases as a source of law comes from England. This system of relying on the judiciary is referred to as the **common law**. In the United States, the common-law system is predominant. Since most of the colonists were of English origin, they naturally followed the laws and customs of their mother country.

Common law

That body of law deriving from judicial decisions

Our common-law system, which relies on case precedent as a source of law, must be contrasted with **civil-law** systems, which developed on the European continent. The civil-law countries have codified their laws—reduced them to statutes—so the main source of law in those countries is in the statutes rather than in the cases. In Louisiana, and to some extent in Texas and California, the civil law has influenced the legal systems because of these states' French and Spanish heritage.

Civil law

A system of law based on legislation or codes, as in the European system of codified law

Even in our common-law system, legislation enacted by the federal government and the various state and local governments is an important source of law. Indeed, throughout our nation's history, the importance of legislation in regulating business activities has increased. Nevertheless, court decisions remain a vital source of law because of the difficulty of reducing all laws to writing before issues are addressed in court.

To help manage our complex legal system, the judiciary establishes a general priority among the various sources of law. Constitutions prevail over statutes, and statutes prevail over common-law principles established in court decisions. Courts will not turn to case decisions for law if a statute directly provides an answer to the issue being litigated.

4. Basic Constitutional Principles

In our constitutional system, the Constitution of the United States and the constitutions of the various states provide the basis of our legal system and our supreme law. All other laws must be consistent with them, or they are void. Most state constitutions are modeled after the federal Constitution. They divide state government into executive, legislative, and judicial branches, giving each branch checks and balances on the others. Constitutions also define the powers and functions of the various branches.

The Constitution of the United States and the constitutions of the various states are the fundamental written law in this country. A federal law must not violate the U.S. Constitution. All state laws must conform to, or be in harmony with, the federal Constitution as well as with the constitution of the appropriate state.

Two very important principles of constitutional law are basic to our judicial system. They are closely related to each other and are known as the **doctrine of separation of powers** and the **doctrine of judicial review**.

Separation of powers

The doctrine that the legislative, executive, and judicial branches of government function independently of one another and that each branch serves as a check on the others

Judicial review

The power of courts to declare laws and executive actions unconstitutional

The doctrine of separation of powers results from the fact that both state and federal constitutions provide for a scheme of government consisting of three branches—legislative, executive, and judicial. Separation of powers has both a horizontal and a vertical aspect. The vertical aspect is that there is separation between the federal government and the state government. Each has its own functions to perform. The horizontal aspect of separation of powers ascribes to each branch a separate function and a check and balance on the functions of the other branches. The doctrine of separation of powers implies that each separate branch will not perform the function of the others and that each branch has limited powers.

The doctrine of judicial review is the heart of the concept of separation of powers. This doctrine and the doctrine of supremacy of the Constitution were established at an early date in our country's history in the celebrated case of *Marbury* v. *Madison* (1803). In this case, Chief Justice Marshall literally created for the court a power the founding fathers had refused to include in the Constitution. This is the power of the judiciary to review the actions of the other branches of government and to set them aside as null and void if in violation of the Constitution. In creating this power to declare laws unconstitutional, Chief Justice Marshall stated,

> Certainly, all those who have framed written constitutions contemplated them as forming the fundamental and paramount law of the nation, and consequently, the theory of every such government must be that an act of the legislature, repugnant to the constitution, is void. This theory is essentially attached to a written constitution and is, consequently, to be considered by this court as one of the fundamental principles of our society.

Justice Marshall then decided that courts have the power to review the actions of the legislative and executive branches of government to determine if they are constitutional. This doctrine of judicial review, to some extent, makes the courts the overseers of government and of all aspects of our daily lives.

5. Legislation

Much of our law is found in legislation. Legislative bodies exist at all levels of government. Legislation is created by Congress, state assemblies, city councils, and other local government bodies. The term *legislation* in its broad sense also includes treaties entered into by the executive branch of government and ratified by the Senate.

Statute

A law passed by Congress or the legislative body of a state

Ordinance

Generally speaking, the legislative act of a municipality (A city council is a legislative body, and it passes ordinances that are the laws of the city.)

Code

A collection or compilation of the statutes passed by a legislative body on a particular subject

Legislation enacted by Congress or by a state legislature is usually referred to as a **statute**. Laws passed by local governments frequently are called **ordinances**. Compilations of legislation at all levels of government are called **codes**. For example, we have local traffic codes covering all aspects of driving automobiles, and state laws such as the Uniform Commercial Code that cover all aspects of commercial transactions. The statutes of the United States that attempt to regulate general conduct are known as the U.S. Code.

Legislative bodies have procedural rules that must be followed if a law is to be valid. Among the typical procedural rules are those relating to the way amendments are added to a proposed law, the way proposed statutes are presented for consideration (reading aloud to the members, etc.), and the manner of voting by the members of the legislative body.

Legislation at all levels contains general rules for human conduct. Legislation is the result of the political process expressing the public will on an issue. Courts also play a significant role in the field of statutory law. In addition to their power of judicial review, courts interpret legislation and apply it to specific facts. Courts interpret legislation by resolving ambiguities and filling the gaps in the statutes. By its very nature, most legislation is general, and interpretation is necessary to find the intent of the legislature.

6. Interpreting Legislation

Theoretically, legislation expresses the will or intent of the legislature on a particular subject. In practice, this theory suffers from certain inherent defects. First, it is not possible to express the legislative intent in words that will mean the same thing to everyone. Statutes, by their very nature, are written in general language that frequently is ambiguous.

Second, the search for legislative intent often is complicated by the realization that the legislative body, in fact, had no intent on the issue in question, and the law is incomplete. The matter involved is simply one that was not thought about when the law was passed. Therefore, sometimes the question about legislation concerns not what the legislature intended, but what it would have intended had it considered the problem. Both of these problems result in an expanded role for courts in our legal system.

One technique of statutory interpretation is to examine the *legislative history* of an act to determine the purpose of the legislation or the evil it was designed to correct. Legislative history includes the committee hearings, the debates, and any statement made by the executive in requesting the legislation. Legislative history does not always give a clear understanding of the legislative intent, because the legislature may not have considered many questions of interpretation that confront courts.

Judges use several additional accepted rules of statutory interpretation in determining legislative intent. Many of these rules are based on the type of law being construed. For example, one rule is that criminal statutes and taxing laws should be strictly or *narrowly construed*. As a result, doubts as to the applicability of criminal and taxing laws will be resolved in favor of the accused or the taxpayer, as the case may be. Another rule of statutory construction is that remedial statutes (those creating a judicial remedy on behalf of one person at the expense of another) are to be *liberally construed* so the statute will be effective in correcting the condition to be remedied.

There are also rules of construction that aid in finding the meaning of words used in legislation. Words may be given their plain or *usual meaning*. Technical words are given their technical meaning. Other words are interpreted by the *context* in which they are used. For example, if a general word in a statute follows specific words, the general word takes its meaning from the specific words.

Statutory construction is not always based on the type of statute or the words used. For example, if a statute contains both specific and general provisions, the specific provision controls. A frequently cited rule provides that a thing may be within the letter of the statute and yet not within the statute because it is not within the statute's spirit or within the intention of the makers. This rule allows a court to have a great deal of flexibility and to give an interpretation contrary to the plain meaning. The power of courts to interpret legislation means that in the final analysis, a statute means what the court says it means.

7. Uniform State Laws

Since each state has its own constitution, statutes, and body of case law, there are substantial differences in the law among the various states. It is important to recognize that ours is a federal system in which each state has a substantial degree of autonomy; thus it can be said that there are really fifty-one legal systems—a system for each state plus the federal legal structure. In many legal situations it does not matter that the legal principles are not uniform throughout the country. This is true when the parties to a dispute are *citizens* of the same state and the transaction or occurrence creating the dispute happened in that state; then the controversy is strictly *intrastate* as opposed to one having *interstate* implications. However, when citizens of different states are involved in a transaction (perhaps a buyer in one state contracts with a seller in another), many difficult questions can arise from the lack of uniformity in the law. Assume that a contract is valid in one state but not in the other. Which state's law controls? Although a body of law called *conflict of laws* (see Section 11) has been developed to cover such cases, more uniformity is still desirable.

Two methods of achieving uniformity in business law are possible: (1) having federal legislation govern business law, or (2) having states' legislatures adopt uniform laws concerning at least certain phases of business transactions. A legislative drafting group known as the National Conference of Commissioners on Uniform State Laws uses this latter method. This group of commissioners appointed by the governors of the states tries to promote uniformity in state laws on all subjects for which uniformity is desirable and practical. They accomplish this goal by drafting model acts. After approval by the National Conference, proposed uniform acts are recommended to the state legislatures for adoption.

More than one hundred uniform laws concerning such subjects as partnerships, leases, arbitration, warehouse receipts, bills of lading, and stock transfers have been drafted and presented to the various state legislatures. The response has varied. Very few of the uniform laws have been adopted by all the states. Some states have adopted the uniform law in principle but have changed some of the provisions to meet local needs or to satisfy lobbying groups, so the result has often been non-uniform uniform state laws.

The most significant development for business in the field of uniform state legislation has been the Uniform Commercial Code. It was prepared for the stated purpose of collecting in one body the law that "deals with all the phases which may ordinarily arise in the handling of a commercial transaction from start to finish. ..." The detailed aspects of the Code, as it is often called, make up a significant portion of this text; and sections of the Code are referred to in brackets throughout this text where appropriate. Its provisions are set forth in Appendix B.

The field of commercial law is not the only area of new uniform statutes. Many states are adopting modern procedures and concepts in criminal codes and other uniform laws dealing with social problems. In addition, the past few years have seen dynamic changes in both state and federal statutes setting forth civil procedures and revising court systems. The future will undoubtedly bring many further developments to improve the administration of justice. The trend, despite some objection, is to cover more areas of the law with statutes and to rely less on precedent in judicial decisions, or common law, as a source of law.

CASE LAW

8. *Stare Decisis*

Stare decisis

The doctrine that law should adhere to decided cases and "stand by the decision"

Notwithstanding the trend toward adopting law in statutory form, a substantial portion of our law has its source in decided cases. This case law, or common law, is based on the concept of precedent and the doctrine of ***stare decisis***, which means "to stand by decisions and not to disturb what is settled." *Stare decisis* tells us that once a case has established a precedent, it should be followed in subsequent cases involving the same issues. Judicial decisions create precedent by interpreting legislation and by deciding issues not covered by legislation.

When a court decides a case, particularly on an appeal from a lower-court decision, the court writes an opinion setting forth, among other things, the reasons for its decision. From these written opinions rules of law can be deduced, and these make up the body of case law or common law.

Stare decisis gives both certainty and predictability to the law. It is also expedient. Through the reliance on precedent established in prior cases, the common law has resolved many legal issues and brought stability into many areas of the law, such as the law of contracts. The doctrine of *stare decisis* provides a system so businesspeople may act in a certain way, confident that their actions will have certain legal effects. People can rely on prior decisions and, knowing the legal significance of their action, can act accordingly. There is reasonable certainty as to the results of conduct.

Precedent affects trial courts more than courts of review; the latter have the power to make precedent in the first instance. However, even the appellate courts usually hesitate to renounce precedent. They generally assume that if a principle or rule of law announced in a former judicial decision is unfair or contrary to public policy, it will be changed by legislation. It is important to note that an unpopular court ruling can usually be changed or overruled by statute.

Res judicata

The legal doctrine that once a dispute is litigated and resolved, these parties are forever barred from litigating the same matter again—"the thing has been decided"

The doctrine of *stare decisis* must be contrasted with the concept of ***res judicata***, which means "the thing has been decided." *Res judicata* applies when, *between the parties themselves,* the matter is closed at the conclusion of the lawsuit. The losing party cannot again ask a court to decide the dispute. *Stare decisis* means that a court of competent jurisdiction has decided a controversy and has, in a written opinion, set forth the rule or principle that formed the basis for its decision, so that rule or principle will be followed by the court in deciding subsequent cases involving the same issues. Likewise, subordinate courts in the same jurisdiction will be bound by the rule of law set forth in the decision. *Stare decisis,* then, affects persons who are not parties to the lawsuit, but res *judicata* applies only to the parties involved.

9. Problems Inherent in Case Law

The common-law system as used in the United States has several inherent difficulties. First, the unbelievably large volume of judicial decisions, each possibly creating precedent, places "the law" beyond the actual knowledge of lawyers, let alone laypersons. Large law firms employ lawyers whose major task is to search case reports for "the law" to be used in lawsuits and in advising clients. Today, computers are being used to assist in the search for precedent because legal research involves examination of cases in hundreds of volumes. Because the total body of ruling case law is so extensive, it is obvious that laypersons who are supposed to know the law and govern their conduct accordingly do not know the law and cannot always follow it, even with the advice of legal counsel.

Another major problem involving case law arises because conflicting precedents are often cited to the court by opposing lawyers. One of the major tasks of the court in such cases is to determine which precedent is applicable to the present case. In addition, even today, many questions of law arise on which there has been no prior decision or in areas where the only authority is by implication. In such situations, the judicial process is "legislative" in character and involves the creation of law.

It should also be noted that there is a distinction between precedent and mere *dicta.* As authority for future cases, a judicial decision is coextensive only with the facts on which it is founded and the rules of law on which the decision is actually based. Frequently, courts make comments on matters not necessary to the decision reached. Such expressions, called *dicta,* lack the force of an adjudication and, strictly speaking, are not a precedent the court will be required to follow within the rule of *stare decisis.* **Dicta** or implication in prior cases may be followed if sound and just. In fact, dicta that have been repeated frequently are often given the force of precedent.

Dicta

Statements of the court that are not necessary to decide the controversy before the court

Two additional problems that arise with our common-law, precedent-oriented judicial system are discussed in the next two sections. One acknowledges that courts do not always follow established precedent. The other problem involves which precedent is applicable to a multi-state transaction or occurrence.

10. Rejection of Precedent

The doctrine of *stare decisis* has not been applied in a fashion that renders the law rigid and inflexible. If a court, especially a reviewing court, finds that the prior decision was "palpably wrong," it may overrule and change it. By the same token, if the court finds that a rule of law established by a prior decision is no longer sound because of changing conditions, it may reverse the precedent. The strength and genius of the common law is that no decision is *stare decisis* when it has lost its usefulness or the reasons for it no longer exist. The doctrine does not require courts to multiply their errors by using former mistakes as authority and support for new errors. Thus, just as legislatures change the law by new legislation, courts change the law from time to time by reversing former precedents. Judges, like legislators, are subject to social forces and changing circumstances. As personnel of courts change, each new generation of judges deems it their responsibility to reexamine precedents and adapt them to the present.

The argument is frequently made that changes in the law should be left to the legislative process. If a rule of law does not represent the judgment of society, the people, through the political process, will cause the appropriate legislative body to change it. The argument that an issue is more appropriate for legislative resolution is often unpersuasive. Such an argument ignores the responsibility of courts to face difficult legal questions and to accept judicial responsibility for a needed change in the common law. Courts often meet changing times and new social demands by reexamining outmoded common-law concepts. Many cases produce changes that have a profound effect on social and business relationships. Many judges believe that it is the responsibility of the courts to balance competing interests. They recognize that the common law is judge-made and judge-applied. As a result, case law will be changed when changed conditions and circumstances establish that it is unjust or has become bad public policy. The dynamic quality of the law allows it to grow and meet changing conditions.

Stare decisis may not be ignored by mere whim or caprice. It must have more impact on trial courts than on reviewing courts. It must be followed rather rigidly in daily affairs. In the whole area of private law, uniformity and continuity are necessary. It is obvious that the same rules of tort and contract law must be applied from day to day. *Stare decisis* must take the capricious element out of law and give stability to a society and to business.

In the area of public law, however, especially constitutional law, the doctrine is frequently ignored. As United States Supreme Court Chief Justice John Marshall wrote in *McCullough* v. *Maryland* (1819), "It is a constitution which we are expounding, not the gloss which previous courts may have put on it." Constitutional principles are often considered in relation to the times and circumstances in which they are raised. Public law issues are relative to the times, and precedent is often ignored so we are not governed by the dead. Courts reexamine precedents and adapt them to changing conditions Under a doctrine known as *constitutional relativity,* the meaning of the Constitution is relative to the time in which it is being interpreted. Under this concept, great weight is attached to social forces in formulating judicial decisions. As the goals, aspirations, and needs of society change, precedent changes.

11. Conflict of Laws

Certain basic facts about our legal system must be recognized. First, statutes and precedents, in all legal areas, vary from state to state. Second, the doctrine of *stare decisis* does not require that one state recognize the precedent or rules of law of other states. Each state is free to decide for itself questions concerning its common law and interpretation of its own constitution and statutes. (However, courts will often follow decisions of other states if they are found to be sound. They are considered persuasive authority. This is particularly true in cases involving uniform acts, when each state has adopted the same statute.) Third, many legal issues arise out of acts or transactions that have contact with more than one state. A contract may be executed in one state, performed in another, and the parties may live in still others; or an automobile accident may occur in one state involving citizens of different states.

Thus, courts often face a fundamental question: Which state's *substantive* laws are applicable in a multiple-jurisdiction case when the law differs from one state to the other? The body of law known as **conflict of laws** or choice of laws answers this question. It provides the court with the applicable substantive law in the multi-state transaction or occurrence. The law applicable to a tort is generally said to be the law of the state of place of injury. Thus, a court sitting in state X would follow its own rules or procedure, but it would use the tort law of state Y if the injury occurred in Y.

Conflict of laws

A body of legal principles used to determine the appropriate law to apply to a litigated case when more than one state is involved

The following are several rules used by courts on issues involving the law of contracts:

1. The law of the state where the contract was made
2. The law of the place of performance
3. "Grouping of contacts" or "center of gravity" theory, which uses the law of the state most involved with the contract
4. The law of the state specified in the contract

Many contracts designate the applicable substantive law. A contract provision that provides "This contract shall be governed by the law of the State of New York" will be enforced if New York has at least minimal connection with the contract.

It is not the purpose of this text to teach conflict of laws, but the reader should be aware that such a body of law exists and should recognize those situations in which conflict of laws principles will be used. The trend toward uniform statutes and codes has tended to decrease these conflicts, but many of them still exist. As long as we have a federal system and fifty separate state bodies of substantive law, the area of conflict of laws will continue to be of substantial importance in the application of the doctrine of *stare decisis* and statutory law.

The role of conflict of laws is exhibited in the following case.

CASE

The Estee Lauder Companies Inc., Plaintiff, against Shashi Batra, Defendant

UNITED STATES DISTRICT COURT FOR THE SOUTHERN DISTRICT OF NEW YORK

430 F. Supp. 2d 158 (2006)

SWEET, D.J.

• *Plaintiff Estee Lauder Companies, Inc.("Estee Lauder") has moved by order to show cause for a temporary restraining order and preliminary injunction restraint defendant Shashi Batra ("Batra") from breaching the terms of his Confidentiality, Non-solicitation, and Non-competition Agreement with Estee Lauder the "Non-compete Agreement") and from engaging in employment with N.V. Perricone M.D. Ltd.*

• *On March 13, 2006, Batra filed a complaint in California State Court seeking a declaratory judgment that the Non-compete Agreement was void under California Law. On March 15, 2006, filed its complaint in this court against Batra alleging: (1) breach of Batra's Non-compete agreement and (2) theft of trade secrets.*

Plaintiff Estee Lauder is a corporation organized under the laws of the State of Delaware with its principal place of business located in New York, New York. Estee Lauder is engaged in the business of manufacturing and marketing skin care, makeup, fragrance, and hair care products.

• *Defendant Batra is an individual who resides in San Francisco, California, and did from 2004 until March 10, 2006, when he was employed as a senior executive for two of Estee Lauder's brands, Rodan and Fields ("R+F") and Darphin. On or about March 13, 2006, Batra began employment as the Worldwide General Manager of Perricone.*

At the commencement of his employment, Batra signed an employment agreement with Estee Lauder, which contained confidentiality, non-solicitation, non-competition provisions. In return for signing the agreement (which all Estee Lauder executive employees are required to sign) Batra received a $100,000 signing bonus. In addition, Batra was provided with a compensation package of $300,000 per year, benefits, an automobile allowance, stock options, and bonus eligibility. (Id.) On July 1, 2004, Batra's base salary was increased to $325,000. (Id.) In July, 2005, in conjunction with his new responsibilities for Darphin, Estee Lauder increased Batra's base salary to $375,000.

The non-competition clause, contained in Paragraph 4 of the employment agreement that Batra signed in January 2004, provides as follows:

> You recognize that the Company's business is very competitive and that to protect its [**7] Confidential Information the Company expects you not to compete with it for a period of time. You therefore agree that during your employment with the Company, and for a period of twelve (12) months after termination of you employment with the Company, regardless of the reason for the termination, you will not work for or otherwise actively participate in any business on behalf of any Competitor in which you could benefit the Competitor's business or harm the Company's business by using or disclosing Confidential Information. This restriction shall apply only in the geographic areas for which you had work-related responsibility during the last twelve (12) months of your employment by the Company and in any other geographic area in which you could benefit the Competitor's business through the use or disclosure of Confidential Information.

As a threshold matter, the Court first must determine which state's law controls—New York's or California's—as a court is to apply the choice-of-law rules prevailing in the state in which the court sits governs the choice of law determination.

To determine the appropriateness of the parties' choice of law, New York follows the "substantial relationship" approach, as stated in Restatement (Second) of Conflicts of Law § 187:

> (2) The law of the state chosen by the parties to govern their contractual rights and duties will be applied . . . unless either
>
> (a) the chosen state has no substantial relationship to the parties ... or

> (b) application of the law of the chosen state would be contrary to a fundamental policy of a state which has a materially greater interest than the chosen state ...

Generally, "under New York law ... a contract's designation of the law that is to govern disputes arising from the contract ... is determinative if the state has sufficient contacts with the transaction. However, there is an exception to this rule when "application of the law of the chosen state would be contrary to a fundamental policy of a state which has a materially greater interest than the chosen state." For this exception to apply, "the issue [must be] of such overriding concern to the public policy of another jurisdiction as to override the intent of the parties and the interest of [New York] in enforcing its own policies."

In other words, three conditions must be met in order to override the intent of the contracting parties. First, Batra must establish that in the absence of the choice of law provision, California law would apply. Second, he must demonstrate that the application of New York law would be contrary to a fundamental policy of California. Third, Batra must demonstrate that California has a materially greater interest than New York in the determination of this dispute.

Batra argues, in essence, that irrespective of the presence of the New York forum selection clause in the contract, California law should apply due to the presence of significant contacts in California and to California's strong public policy against the enforcement of non-compete agreements.

For the first element of the inquiry, New York courts employ the "substantial relationship" test. The New York Court of Appeals has addressed the 'substantial relationship' approach and held that while the parties' choice of law is to be given heavy weight, the law of the state with the 'most significant contacts' is to be applied."

The fact that Batra literally carried out many of his duties from California does not overcome the fact that work itself was the management of a New York-based brand with predominantly New York-based employees. Accordingly, while this may be a close call, New York has the most significant contacts.

Because, pursuant to California's fundamental policy against the enforcement of restrictive covenants, non-compete agreements, such as the one at issue in this case, are declared null and void under California law, the enforcement of Batra's agreement by this Court would be contrary to a fundamental policy of California, notwithstanding Estee Lauder's contention that there is no conflict between California's policy and the application of New York law. The Non-compete Agreement would not be enforceable under California law. However, in spite of the fact that the application of New York law would run contrary to the fundamental policy of California, it is concluded that California's interest in this dispute is not materially greater than that of New York and that therefore, New York law shall apply.

Because, as set forth above, the contacts point toward New York, it is concluded that California's interest is not materially greater than that of New York. Just as California has a strong interest in protecting those employed in California, so too does New York have a strong interest in protecting companies doing business here in keeping with:

> New York's recognized interest in maintaining and fostering its undisputed status as the preeminent commercial and financial nerve center of the Nation and the world. That interest naturally embraces a very strong policy of assuring ready access to a forum for redress of injuries arising out of transactions spawned here. Indeed, access to a convenient forum which dispassionately administers a known, stable, and commercially sophisticated body of law may be considered as much an attraction to conducting business in New York as its unique financial and communications resources.

Marine Midland, 223 A.D.2d at 124.

Accordingly, based upon New York's policy of enforcing restrictive covenants that are reasonable in time and scope and given New York's interest in having a predictable body of law that companies can rely on when employing individuals who will have close contact with trade secrets and confidential information, it is concluded that California's interest is not "materially greater" than New York's.

It is concluded that New York law will apply.

CASE CONCEPTS REVIEW

1. Are the public policies of California and New York different regarding non-competition agreements in the employment arena? If so, how; and is one better than another?
2. Might the result have been different if a California court had decided the choice of law issue? Why?

12. Jurisprudence

The study of the philosophy of law is called jurisprudence. There are a number of schools of jurisprudential thought currently acknowledged by legal scholars. Some of the more common include:

(1) *Natural Law* Followers of this school believe that there is a higher law or a group of universal rules that should bind all human behavior. Proponents of natural law believe that these principles apply generally through society, and have applied though the ages. In general, moral principles are more prominent in the thinking of those following natural law precepts than those following other types of jurisprudential thought.

(2) *Positive Law* Followers of this school do not hold to the notion that there is necessarily a moral component to law. Rather, the law is simply a command of government. These commands may be good or evil in terms of morality.

(3) *Legal Realism* Followers of this school believe that the law is really the impact of decisions of those who are charged with administering the law … juries, judges, etc. Therefore, a statute may be interpreted in a variety of ways by judges, for example, and the law is what those judges rule.

(4) *Sociological* Followers of the sociological school believe the law should reflect societal values, which may change over time.

Note that schools of jurisprudential thought may overlap. Also, it is entirely possible that a judge, for example, may adopt sociological school notions to make one determination and positive law precepts to make another determination.

LAW AND ETHICS

13. Ethical Conduct

The law is not the only means of influencing conduct and regulating the behavior of individuals and businesses. Fear of or concern for the consequences of actions is probably as important an influence on behavior as is the law. Between nations, the threat of reprisal by force of arms is more effective in preventing undesirable conduct than is international law. The fact that individuals and businesses fear the economic consequences of conduct is obviously an important influence on behavior. Economists believe that our economy is best understood and regulated when everyone recognizes that people usually act in their own best self-interest. Our competitive economic system is predicated on a belief that decisions made by millions of individuals provide the most effective and efficient allocation of the nation's resources. The law and economic consequences are not the only influences on individual and business decisions.

Today, *individual and institutional ethical standards* and a *sense of responsibility to society* are having an ever-increasing impact on decisions. Almost every publicly held business has adopted a Code of Ethical Conduct for its employees. Professional associations such as the American Bar Association or the American Institute of Certified Public Accountants have adopted ethics codes for their members. There is a federal code of ethics for government employees. While these codes are not "laws," they usually provide for sanctions for noncompliance.

Conduct is also influenced by standards for which there is no sanction for noncompliance. This is sometimes described as obedience to the unenforceable. The late Albert J. Harno, for thirty-five years Dean of the College of Law at the University of Illinois, discussed this influence in a graduation address in 1961. The following excerpt from that address indicates its relationship to law and to free choice:

> Life for most people is a day-to-day affair; it is "numbered by years, days and hours."[1] Men live, seek diversion and comfort, have fleeting glimpses of happiness, are touched by sorrow, and pass from the scene. A few stop to contemplate and to wonder. But now and then there rises from the multitude a prophet, a Plato, an Aristotle,

[1]Guillaume De Salluste du Bartas, Divine Weekes and Workes, second week, third day, part two.

a Jesus of Nazareth, a Beethoven, an Abraham Lincoln, to fashion for us in words, in poetry, in music, and in song, some lasting conception of the eternal verities of life—of the good, the true, and the beautiful—and to formulate for us directives and precepts to guide us on our way.

We live in an age in which materialism and, in many parts of the world, crass materialism prevails. It is a technical age in which men put their faith in mechanized force, in atomic power, missiles, earth satellites, and space ships. We look for guidance and hear only a babel of voices as men give expression to guile, deception, hate, greed, and prejudice. …

But law is not the only force that regulates human conduct. I wish to speak about three areas, or domains, of human action. I am indebted to an Englishman, Lord Moulton,[2] for this classification. The development is my own. The *first* is the area of free choice; the *second*; the domain of obedience to the unenforceable; and *third*, the domain of law.

The first, the domain of free choice, is a limited area. I sometimes wonder if we really appreciate how little freedom of choice we have in making decisions; we are constantly under one pressure or another. If we have an evening to ourselves, we may have a choice of reading... or of going to a movie. We may be able to choose whether we will or will not take sugar in our coffee. But even that choice may be denied to us by doctor's orders.

The second domain, obedience to the unenforceable, is difficult to define. In it there is no law which determines our course of action, and yet we feel that we are not free to choose as we would. It is a very broad area. It covers those actions which we are not compelled to perform but which some inner voice directs us to discharge. It is the realm of kindliness and conscience—the domain of manners, ethics, and morals. It is the realm which recognizes the sway of duty, of fairness, of honest dealings between men, of sympathy, of taste, and of the spirit. It covers all those things that make life beautiful and a good society possible. What other than a call of conscience is it that makes us willing to take part in community enterprises and in matters relating to the public welfare?

It is the realm of tolerance. When men have lost their tolerance for the views and practices of others, they have lost something that is precious to a good society. Tolerance is the premise for some important provisions that have been written into our Constitution—freedom of speech, freedom of worship, freedom of the press.

It is the realm of truth, of ethics, morals, aesthetics, the spiritual, and of those great precepts: Love thy neighbor as thyself; do unto others as you would have them do unto you.

Truly, the full measure of a man can be gauged by the extent to which he gives obedience to these guides to human conduct that are unenforceable. The extent to which its members give credence to these standards is also the measure of the greatness of a

[2]"Law and Manners," Atlantic Monthly, I (July 1924), 134.

> people, of the greatness of a nation. It is through obedience of the people to these precepts that a democratic society is made possible. …
>
> Observe how closely the last two domains, that of obedience to the unenforceable and that of obedience to law, are interrelated. They intertwine and complement each other. Obedience to law in a free society is of the essence, but law observance would come to naught unless the members of that society were also deeply devoted to the precept of obedience to that which they cannot be forced to obey. …
>
> The issue before us is one of values. There are those among us who assert, and with reason, that we have lost our sense of purposeful direction; that we are a drifting people in ideas and ideals; that we are "paralyzed in self-indulgences"; that the impact of technology upon self-government is subjecting "the processes of democracy to a complete change of scale" … it is imperative that we do not permit ourselves to be deflected from the supreme and enduring values. We must fortify our lives and all of our actions with these values and make them a fighting faith.
>
> We must never waiver in our support of the democratic process, in our adherence to the rule of law, and in our fidelity to the enduring values of life. Thus accoutered, the individual can rise above the confusion of the day. To live by these values marks the supreme measure of a man, of a people, of a nation.

Ethics can be thought of within the context of moral behavior, as described above. Many societies stress the concepts of "good and evil," and "right and wrong." Unfortunately, determining what is right or wrong is often difficult. Having a personal ethical construct can serve to guide one through ethical dilemmas.

Today, we often hear about two primary systems of individual ethics. One is based on *duties.* Whether based on *religious standards, philosophical precepts* (for example, the teachings of Immanuel Kant), or *social contract theory* (most often associated with the work of John Rawls), the idea is that ethical standards must conform to moral absolutes. For example, you must always keep your promises. The other system is based on *outcomes.* The most popular form of the outcomes or consequences-based system is *utilitarianism.* Here, the ends justify the means; the directive is often to do the greatest good for the greatest number. In business, for example, this form is represented by the cost-benefit analysis.

14. Interrelationship Between Law and Ethics

Ethics is a term used to describe good behavior. Ethical conduct is based on a commitment to what is right and a rejection of what is wrong. Ethics provides values beyond what the law requires or prohibits. Such values are important if people are to live together peacefully in a free society because a free society depends on people's trust and confidence in each other. Ethical standards supply the foundation on which trust and confidence are built.

Ethics and the law are closely connected and interrelated. Ethical standards are frequently enacted into law or used in court decisions because the law usually reflects society's view of right and wrong. The following case presents well one situation where ethics plays a major role within the legal context.

CASE

In the Matter of Julianne Delio, on Behalf of Daniel Delio v. Westchester County Medical Center, et al.

SUPREME COURT OF NEW YORK, WESTCHESTER COUNTY

510 N.Y.S.2d 415 (1986)

OPINION OF THE COURT:

"Vex not his ghost, O, let his pass! He hates him
That would upon the rack of this tough world
Stretch him out longer."
Shakespeare, King Lear, act V, scene iii

Daniel Delio, age 33, once a fine specimen of a man, is now, according to Dr. Robert Strobos, Director of the Department of Neurosurgery at the Medical Center, in a state of chronic vegetation with neocortical death—and no hope for improvement. This vegetative condition followed cardiac arrest which occurred during a surgical procedure for the repair of an anorectal fistula. A malpractice action has been commenced against St. Agnes Hospital and physicians concerned with that operation. Following the ill-fated operation, Mr. Delio was transferred to the Westchester County Medical Center and has been there since. While there is no respirator attached to Mr. Delio, he does receive nutrition and hydration through a tube connected directly to his stomach. He could live indefinitely in such state as long as nutrition and hydration via the feeding tube were maintained. This opinion by Dr. Strobos was corroborated by Dr. Sidney Carter and Dr. Paul Rosch, who were retained by the court-appointed guardian ad litem, James D. Hopkins, esteemed lawyer and former Judge. Julianne Delio, the wife of Daniel Delio, supported by Mr. Delio's mother, seeks an order authorizing her to direct Westchester Medical Center, or some institution willing to comply with her instructions, to remove the feeding tube, stop all feeding and nutrition, and stop treatment of all type for Daniel Delio.

At a hearing, Julianne Delio, as well as other relatives and friends, all testified that Daniel Delio was a person, who, occasionally in conversation, remarked that he never would want his life prolonged by artificial means if he were in a chronic vegetative state with no hope of recovery. Many of these conversations occurred when the Karen Ann Quinlan case was in the news. Again he made these remarks when his father had a stroke. This testimony was most compelling and satisfies in the mind of this court "the clear and convincing standard" established by the Court of Appeals in cases such as this. The types and number of these conversations, the occasions when they were said, and to whom, all point to a very physical man who, on some occasions, contemplated death, and in particular, dying with dignity.

The question before this court now is whether the law in New York will permit the termination of care, and eventual death, for Daniel Delio in accordance with his previously announced wishes.

Daniel Delio can exist indefinitely in the vegetative state awaiting, perhaps, some future medical breakthrough, where an aged and terminally ill patient cannot. It should be reiterated, however, that at present there is no form of medical treatment that can either cure or improve Mr. Delio's condition.

Not one of the three medical doctors in this case described Daniel Delio as terminally ill. All three indicated that though he lies in an irreversible chronic vegetative state, with no cortical functions, he is otherwise in good health and could live, as just noted, indefinitely if fed through a tube.

In this most difficult area there seems to be but one unanimous conclusion—Legislatures are better suited than courts to balance the various interests involved in determining whether to permit termination of care. The Legislature, possessing as it does the broad plenary power to make laws and regulations for the public health, safety and welfare, are the elected representatives of the people and, as such, reflect the collective will of the people. The Legislature is empowered to define "death" and "homicide" and can prescribe substantive rules and the procedural framework within which courts can decide the merits of each particular case. In that area, the Legislature in New York is found wanting.

My personal sympathies in this human tragedy are with the anguished wife, mother, and relatives of Daniel Delio. Moreover, the prevailing view in our society, as recently reported in the *New York Times*, appears to support the withdrawal of artificial means of prolonging the life of a person in a chronic vegetative state with no hope of recovery. I do not doubt that "for many years physicians and members of patients' families, often in consultation with religious counselors, have in actuality been making decisions to withhold or to withdraw life support procedures from incurably ill patients incapable of making the critical decisions for themselves." However, placing a judicial imprimatur on a decision to terminate the care in this case, in the absence of clear legislative or judicial guidance, is fraught with danger. The undersigned is of the view that judicial activism in cases such as this, can only involve the courts in a yet unsanctioned broad scale policy of euthanasia.

Accordingly, I am constrained to deny the petition to terminate.

■ *Petition denied.*

CASE CONCEPTS REVIEW

1. Why did the court refuse to approve the petition to terminate?
2. Why did the court want guidance from the legislature?
3. Did the judge employ an ethical standard in making the decision presented above? Is the legislature in a better position to meld law and ethics in cases like that presented above?

It is usually recognized that ethical standards go beyond the law. The law provides a floor above which ethical conduct rises. Ethical business conduct normally exists at a level well above legal minimums. Ethical conduct often means doing more than the law requires or less than it allows.

Codes of ethics adopted by government, the professions, trade associations, and businesses should be thought of as internal laws for all persons subject to them. These codes of conscience are based on fairness, honesty, courtesy, self-restraint, and consideration for others. Most provisions only require disclosure of facts to superiors in certain situations. However, some may dictate certain decisions and conduct. They state a collective sense of right and wrong. Codes of conduct, usually, are general statements because the more specific the code, the more difficult it is to obtain acceptance of the principles.

CHAPTER SUMMARY

LAW

Definitions of Law

1. There are many definitions of law, depending on the content and subject matter involved.
2. In some areas, the law is a command from the sovereign.
3. Law is a method of controlling society and implementing change.
4. Law consists of the principles used by courts to decide controversies.

Classifications of Legal Subjects

1. One way to classify laws is by their purpose—substantive versus procedural.
2. Public law versus private law is another common way to distinguish between classifications of laws.

SOURCES OF LAW

Court Decisions

1. Reliance on decided cases as precedents for present controversies is the foundation of our common-law system.
2. Common law must be contrasted with the civil-law system, which relies more on statutory law than on court decisions as a primary source of law.

Basic Constitutional Principles

1. Constitutional principles provide the foundation of our legal system.
2. One of the most important constitutional principles is the doctrine of judicial review.

Legislation

1. Legislation in the form of statutes, codes, and ordinances provides much of our body of law.
2. Courts have a major role to play in interpreting legislation.

Uniform State Laws

1. Uniform state laws such as the Uniform Commercial Code are an attempt to provide uniformity in business transactions throughout the country.

CASE LAW

Stare Decisis

1. This means to stand by decisions and not disturb what is settled.
2. The goal is certainty and predictability.

Problems Inherent in Case Law

1. The volume of cases makes legal research difficult.
2. There are often conflicting precedents that are difficult to apply.
3. Precedent must be distinguished from mere dicta.

Rejection of Precedent
1. Case law may be changed if conditions change or its reasoning is no longer sound.
2. Precedent is given greater weight in private law than in cases involving public law issues.

Conflict of Laws
1. Conflict of laws principles determine the appropriate statutes and case law to be used in litigation involving more than one jurisdiction.
2. A court in one forum may use the substantive law of another to decide a case.

Jurisprudence
1. Jurisprudential schools capture how individuals think about law and its application.

LAW AND ETHICS

Ethical Conduct
1. Along with legal and economic consequences, ethics influences behavior within the business community.
2. Some ethical lapses result in sanctions while others do not.

Interrelationship Between Law and Ethics
1. Ethical standards are frequently enacted into law or used in court decisions.
2. Ethical principles usually go beyond the law.

REVIEW QUESTIONS AND PROBLEMS

1. Give three definitions of law, and give an example of the application of each.
2. Classify the following subjects as public law or private law:
   a. Constitutional law
   b. Contract law
   c. Administrative law
   d. Criminal law
   e. Property law
   f. Tort law
   g. Sales law
   h. Business organization law
3. Compare and contrast the following:
   a. Public law and private law
   b. Civil law and common law
   c. Torts and crimes
   d. Substance and procedure
   e. Case law and legislation
4. Describe three advantages of the common-law (case-law) system.
5. The basic characteristic of the common law is that a case, once decided, establishes a precedent that will be followed by the courts when similar issues arise later. Yet courts do not always follow precedent. Why?
6. *Stare decisis* is of less significance in public-law subjects than in cases dealing with private-law subjects. Why?
7. Why is it necessary for each state to have a system of conflict of laws principles?
8. While in Missouri, Taylor, a resident of Kansas, became involved in an automobile accident with Stewart, a resident of Illinois. With respect to the appropriate substantive law being applied, does it matter whether Taylor sues Stewart in Missouri or Illinois? Why?
9. The courts of Arizona adopted the doctrine of employment at will, meaning that an employer generally can terminate an employee for any reason or no reason at all. ABC Grocery Company management asked Mary, a twenty-five year employee in the accounting department of ABC Grocery, to make certain statements to a grand jury looking into a

contract that existed between ABC Grocery and the local prison. Statements made to the grand jury are under oath. If anyone lies under oath, they commit the crime of perjury. Mary reviews the statement that she is asked to deliver and indicates that there are many aspects of the document that are untrue. ABC Grocery states that either she tells the grand jury what is stated in the document or she is fired. What is the ethical thing for Mary to do? Is it the same action that the law requires? What about Mary facing the possibility of being terminated? Should the law act to protect Mary so that she does not lose her job, i.e., through the creation of an exception to at-will employment?

10. One of Boeing's suppliers offered a Boeing employee a personal discount on a product sold by the supplier. Under the Boeing "Business Conduct Guidelines" and "Policy Implementation Instructions," may the employee accept the discount? Why? Is accepting the discount legal?

Court Systems | 2

CHAPTER OUTLINE

CHAPTER PREVIEW

In our system of government, courts are the primary means to resolve controversies that cannot be settled by agreement of the parties involved. Litigation is the ultimate method for resolving conflict and disagreements in our society. Whether the issue is the busing of school children, the legality of abortions, the enforceability of a contract, or the liability of a wrongdoer, the dispute—if not otherwise resolved—goes to the court system for a final decision.

The basic function of the judge is to apply the law to the facts. The facts are often determined by a jury. If a jury is not used, the judge is also the finder of the facts. The rule of law applied to the facts produces a decision that settles the controversy.

The three great powers of the judiciary come into play as it performs its functions of deciding cases and controversies: (1) the power of judicial review, (2) the power to interpret and apply statutes, and (3) the power to create law through precedent. The extent to which these powers are exercised varies from case to case, but all three are frequently involved.

BUSINESS MANAGEMENT DECISION

You are president of a small business that has seven employees. One of these employees, your bookkeeper, has been called for jury duty. There is a possibility that this employee will be asked to serve on a jury that will hear a three-month-long trial.

Should you require that this employee attempt to be excused from jury service?

Operating the Court System

1. Trial Judges

Numerous persons with special training and skills must operate the court system, which is highly technical. Trial court judges, reviewing court judges (or justices), and professional expertise and responsible citizens are required to serve as jurors if justice is to be achieved.

The trial judge conducts the lawsuit. It is in the trial courts that the law is made alive and its words are given meaning. Since a trial judge is the only contact that most people have with the law, the ability of such judges is largely responsible for the effective function of the law.

The trial judge should be temperate, attentive, patient, impartial, studious, diligent, and prompt in ascertaining the facts and applying the law. This judge is the protector of constitutional limitations and guarantees of the litigants. Judges should be courteous and considerate of jurors, witnesses, and others in attendance on the court, but they should also criticize and correct unprofessional conduct of attorneys.

Judges must avoid any appearance of impropriety and should not act in a controversy in which they or near relatives have an interest. They should not be swayed by public clamor or consideration of personal popularity or be apprehensive of unjust criticism.

2. Reviewing Court Judges and Justices

Members of reviewing courts are also called *judges.* Persons serving on final reviewing courts, such as the Supreme Court of the United States, are called *justices.* The reviewing judges and justices must be distinguished from trial court judges because their roles are substantially different. For example, a reviewing court judge or justice rarely has any contact with litigants. These judges or justices must do much more than simply decide cases; they usually give written reasons for their decisions, so anyone may examine them and comment on their merits. Each decision becomes precedent to some degree, a part of our body of law. Thus the legal opinion of a reviewing judge or justice—unlike that of the trial judge, whose decision has direct effect only on the litigants—affects society as a whole. Reviewing judges or justices, in deciding a case, must consider not only the result between the parties involved but the total effect of the decision on the law. In this sense, they may assume a role similar to that of a legislator.

Because of this difference in roles, the personal qualities required for a reviewing judge or justice are somewhat different from those for a trial judge. The duties of a reviewing judge or justice are in the area of legal scholarship. These individuals are required to be articulate in presenting ideas in writing and to use the written word to convey their decisions. Whereas trial judges, as a part of the trial arena, observe the witnesses and essentially use knowledge gained from their participation for their decisions, reviewing judges or justices spend hours studying briefs, the record of proceedings, and the law before preparing and handing down their decisions.

3. The Jury

In Anglo-American law, the right of trial by jury, particularly in criminal cases, is traced to the famous Magna Carta issued by King John of England in 1215, which stated

> ....that no freeman shall be taken or imprisoned or disseised or outlawed or exiled ... without the judgment of his peers or by the law of the land. ...

In early English legal history, the juror was a witness—that is, he was called to tell what he knew, not to listen to others testify. The word *jury* comes from the French word *juré,* which means "sworn." The jury gradually developed into an institution to determine facts. The function of the jury today is to ascertain facts, just as the function of the court is to ascertain the law.

The Sixth and Seventh Amendments to the United States Constitution guarantee the right of trial by jury both in criminal and civil cases. The Fifth Amendment provides for indictment by a grand jury for capital offenses and infamous crimes. **Indictment** is a word used to describe the decision of the grand jury. A grand jury differs from a petit jury in that the grand jury determines whether the evidence of guilt is sufficient to warrant a trial; the petit jury determines guilt or innocence in criminal cases and decides the winner in civil cases. In civil cases, the right to trial by a jury is preserved in suits at common law when the amount in controversy exceeds $20. State constitutions have similar provisions guaranteeing the right of trial by jury in state courts.

Indictment

A grand jury's finding that it has probable cause to believe there is sufficient evidence to require that the accused be tried and that informs the accused of the offense with which he or she is charged so the accused may prepare a defense

Historically, the jury consisted of twelve persons, but many states and some federal courts now have rules of procedure that provide for smaller juries in both criminal and civil cases. As the following case established, juries consisting of as few as six persons are constitutional.

Historically, too, a jury's verdict was required to be unanimous. Today, some states authorize less than unanimous verdicts. If fewer than twelve persons serve on the jury, however, the verdict in criminal cases must be unanimous.

The jury system is much criticized by those who contend that many jurors are prejudiced, unqualified to distinguish fact from fiction, and easily swayed by skillful trial lawyers. However, the "right to be tried by a jury of his peers" in criminal cases is felt by most members of the bench and bar to be as fair and effective a method as has been devised for ascertaining the truth and giving an accused his or her day in court.

CASE

Colgrove v. Battin

SUPREME COURT OF THE UNITES STATES

413 U.S. 149 (1973)

BRENNAN, J.

Local Rule 13(d) (1) of the District Court for the District of Montana provides that a jury for the trial of civil cases shall consist of six persons. When respondent District Court Judge set this diversity case for trial before a jury of six in compliance with the Rule, petitioner sought mandamus from the Court of Appeals for the Ninth Circuit to direct respondent to impanel a 12-member jury. Petitioner contended that the local Rule (1) violated the Seventh Amendment. The Court of Appeals found no merit in these contentions, sustained the validity of Local Rule 13(d)(1).

The pertinent words of the Seventh Amendment are: "In suits at common law … the right of trial by jury shall be preserved." On its face, this language is not directed to jury characteristics, such as size, but rather defines the kind of cases for which jury trial is preserved, namely, "suits at common law." While it is true that "[w]e have almost no direct evidence concerning the intention of the framers of the seventh amendment itself," the historical setting in which the Seventh Amendment was adopted highlighted a controversy that was generated not by concern for preservation of jury characteristics at common law but by fear that the civil jury itself would be abolished unless protected in express words. Almost a century and a half ago, this Court recognized that "one of the strongest objections originally taken against the Constitution of the United States was the want of an express provision securing the right of trial by jury in civil cases"; but the omission of a protective clause from the Constitution was not because an effort was not made to include one. On the contrary, a proposal was made to include a provision in the Constitution to guarantee the right to trial by jury in civil cases but the proposal failed because the States varied widely as to the cases in which civil jury trial was provided, and the proponents of a civil jury guarantee found too difficult the task of fashioning words appropriate to cover the different state practices. The strong pressures for a civil jury provision in the Bill of Rights encountered the same difficulty. Thus, it was agreed that, with no federal practice to draw on and since state practices varied so widely, any compromising language would necessarily have to be general. As a result, although the Seventh Amendment achieved the primary goal of jury trial adherents to incorporate an explicit constitutional protection of the right of trial by jury in civil cases, the right was limited in general words to "suits at common law." We can only conclude, therefore, that by referring to the "common law," the Framers of the Seventh Amendment were concerned with preserving the right of trial by jury in civil cases where it existed at common law, rather than the various incidents of trial by jury. In short, constitutional history reveals no intention on the part of the Framers "to equate the constitutional and common-law characteristics of the jury."

Consistently with the historical objective of the Seventh Amendment, our decisions have defined the jury right preserved in cases covered by the Amendment, as "the substance of the common-law right of trial by jury, as distinguished from mere matters of form or procedure. …" The Amendment therefore does not "bind the federal courts to the exact procedural incidents or details of jury trial according o the common law in 1791" and "new devices may be used to adapt the ancient institution to present needs and to make of it an efficient instrument in the administration of justice."

Our inquiry turns then to whether a jury of 12 is of the substance of the common law right of trial by jury. Keeping in mind the purpose of the jury trial in criminal cases to prevent government oppression, and, in criminal and civil cases, to assure a fair and equitable resolution of factual issues, the question comes down to whether jury performance is a function of jury size. In *Williams,* we rejected the notion that "the reliability of the jury as a fact finder … is a function of its size," and nothing has been suggested to lead us to alter that conclusion. Accordingly, we think it can not be said that 12 members is a substantive aspect of the right of trial by jury.

There remains, however, the question whether a jury of six satisfies the Seventh Amendment guarantee of "trial by jury." We had no difficulty reaching the conclusion in *Williams* that a jury of six would guarantee an accused the trial by jury secured by Art. III and the Sixth Amendment. Significantly, our determination that there was "no discernible difference between the results reached by the two different-sized juries," drew largely upon the results of studies of the operations of juries of six in civil cases. Since then, much has been written about the six-member jury, but nothing that persuades us to depart from the conclusion reached in *Williams.* Thus, while we express no view as to whether any number less than six would suffice, we can conclude that a jury of six satisfies the Seventh Amendment's guarantee of trial by jury in civil cases.

■ *Affirmed.*

CASE CONCEPTS REVIEW

1. What type of civil case must be tried before a jury under the language of the Seventh Amendment?
2. Why does the Supreme Court conclude that a six-person jury is as reliable as a twelve-person jury?
3. Do you think the same result would occur if the proposed jury consisted of less than six members?

The persons who are selected to serve on trial juries are drawn at random from lists of qualified voters in the county or city where the trial court sits. Most states, by statute, exempt from jury duty those who are in certain occupations and professions, but such exemptions have been reduced or eliminated in recent years in an effort to make jury duty a responsibility of all citizens. Many persons called for jury duty attempt to avoid serving because it involves a loss of money or time away from a job; but because of the importance of jury duty, most judges are reluctant to excuse citizens who are able to serve. Indeed, citizens are encouraged to view the opportunity to serve on a jury as a privilege and obligation of being a part of our constitutional democracy.

COURT SYSTEMS

4. The State Structure

The judicial system of the United States is a dual system consisting of state courts and federal courts. Most states have three levels of court systems: *trial courts,* where litigation is begun; *intermediate reviewing* courts; and a *final reviewing* court. States use different names to describe these three levels of courts. For example, some states call their trial courts the circuit court because in early times a judge rode the circuit from town to town holding court. Other states call the trial court the superior court or the district court. New York has labeled it the supreme court.

Jurisdiction

The court's power or authority to conduct trials and decide cases

Before examining these courts, it is necessary to define **jurisdiction** as it is used in the study of courts. Jurisdiction means the power to hear a case. There are courts in every state of *general jurisdiction.* This means that these courts have the power to hear almost any type of case. In contrast, many courts have limited powers. They can hear only certain types of cases and thus are said to have *limited jurisdiction.* They may be limited as to the area in which the parties live, the subject matter involved, or the dollar amount in the controversy. For example, courts with jurisdiction limited to a city's residents often are called *municipal* courts.

Courts may also be named according to the subject matter with which they deal. *Probate courts* deal with wills and the estates of deceased persons, *juvenile courts* with juvenile crime and dependent children, *municipal* and *police courts* with violators of local ordinances, and *traffic courts* with traffic violations. For an accurate classification of the courts of any state, the statutes of that state should be examined. Figure 2-1 illustrates the jurisdiction and organization of reviewing and trial courts in a typical state.

The *small claims court* is a court whose jurisdiction is limited by the amount in controversy. In recent years, these courts have assumed growing importance. In fact, a popular television program has been created out of this concept. The small claims court represents an attempt to provide a

The small claims court has a limited jurisdiction based on the amount in controversy. The amount of $5,000 is a typical limit. The television show *Judge Judy* was based on the small claims court.

FIGURE 2-1 ■ Typical State Court System

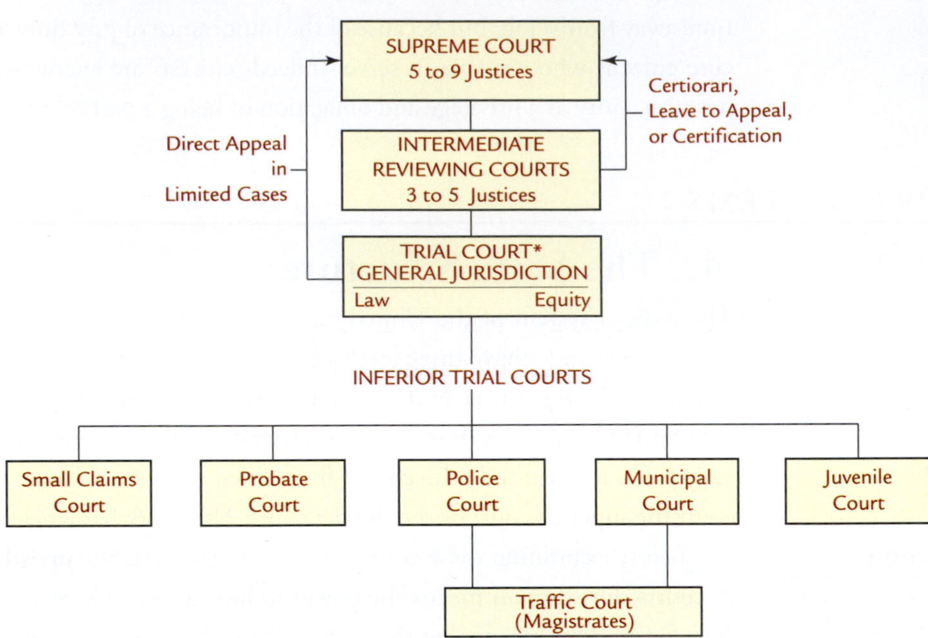

*Commonly called circuit court, district court, or superior court in many states.

prompt and inexpensive means of settling thousands of minor disputes that often include suits by consumers against merchants for lost or damaged goods or for services poorly performed. Landlord-tenant disputes and collection suits are also quite common in small claims courts. In these courts, the usual court costs are greatly reduced. The procedures are simplified, so the services of a lawyer usually are not required. Most of the states have authorized small claims courts and have imposed a limit on their jurisdiction. Some states keep the amount as low as $1,000; others exceed $5,000, but $5,000 is a typical limit.

5. The Federal Structure

The United States Constitution created the Supreme Court and authorizes Congress to establish inferior courts from time to time. Congress has created twelve intermediate United States courts of appeal, plus a special Court of Appeals for the Federal Circuit. This latter special reviewing court, located in Washington, D.C., hears appeals from special courts, such as the United States Claims Court and Contract Appeals, as well as from administrative agencies, such as those by the Patent and Trademark Office. Intermediate reviewing courts are not trial courts, and their jurisdiction is limited to reviewing cases, Congress has also created the United States district courts (at least one in each state) and others to handle special subject matter, such as the Court of Military Appeals. Figure 2-2 illustrates the federal court system and shows the relationship of the state courts for review purposes.

6. Federal District Courts

The district courts are the trial courts of the federal judicial system. They have original jurisdiction, exclusive of the courts of the states, over all federal crimes—that is, all offenses against the laws of the United States. The accused is entitled to a trial by jury in the state and district where the crime was committed.

FIGURE 2-2 ■ **The Federal Court System**

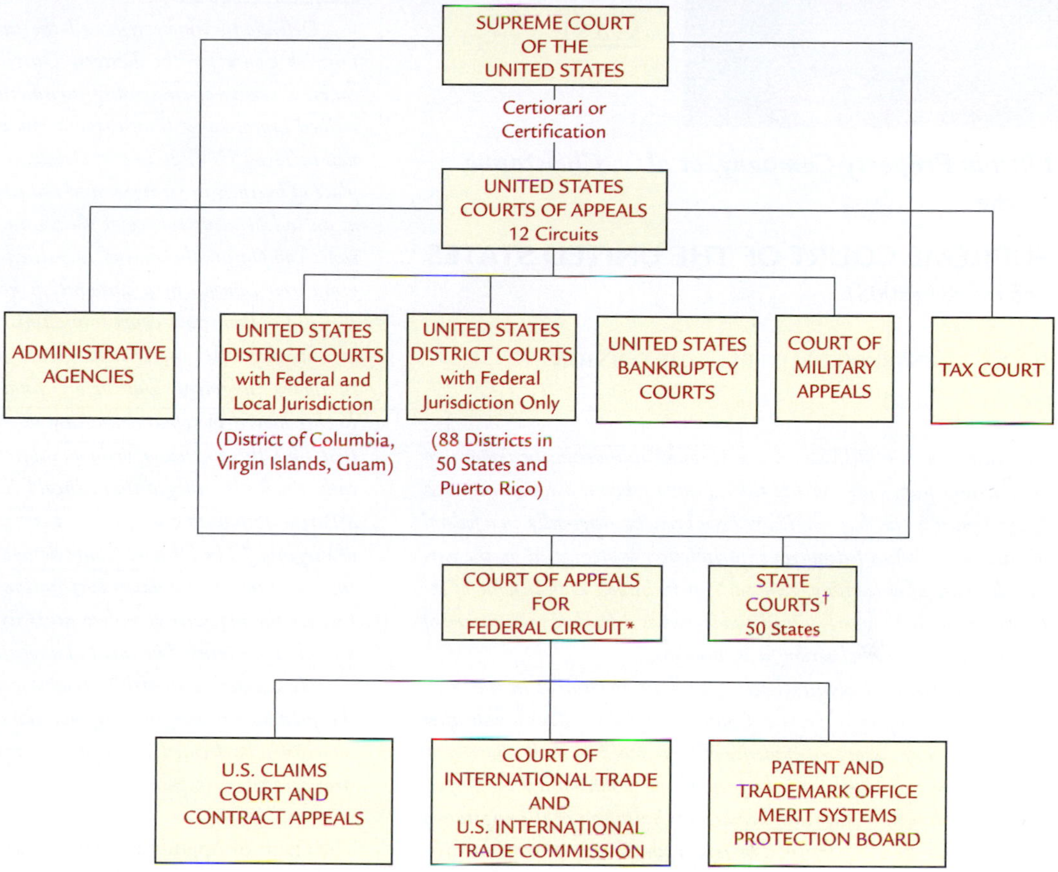

SUPREME COURT OF THE UNITED STATES

Certiorari or Certification

UNITED STATES COURTS OF APPEALS 12 Circuits

ADMINISTRATIVE AGENCIES

UNITED STATES DISTRICT COURTS with Federal and Local Jurisdiction (District of Columbia, Virgin Islands, Guam)

UNITED STATES DISTRICT COURTS with Federal Jurisdiction Only (88 Districts in 50 States and Puerto Rico)

UNITED STATES BANKRUPTCY COURTS

COURT OF MILITARY APPEALS

TAX COURT

COURT OF APPEALS FOR FEDERAL CIRCUIT*

STATE COURTS† 50 States

U.S. CLAIMS COURT AND CONTRACT APPEALS

COURT OF INTERNATIONAL TRADE AND U.S. INTERNATIONAL TRADE COMMISSION

PATENT AND TRADEMARK OFFICE MERIT SYSTEMS PROTECTION BOARD

*Same as other United States courts of appeal.
†Certiorari.

In civil actions, the district courts have jurisdiction only when the matter in controversy is based on either *diversity of citizenship* or a *federal question.*

DIVERSITY OF CITIZENSHIP Diversity of citizenship exists in suits between (1) citizens of different states, (2) a citizen of a state and a citizen of a foreign country, and (3) a state and citizens of another state. For diversity of citizenship to exist, all plaintiffs must be citizens of a state different from the state in which any one of the defendants is a citizen. Diversity of citizenship does not prevent the plaintiff from bringing suit in a state court; however, if diversity of citizenship exists, the defendant has the right to have the case *removed* to a federal court. A defendant, by having the case removed to the federal court, has an opportunity of having a jury selected from an area larger than the county where the cause arose, thus perhaps reducing the possibility of jurors tending to favor the plaintiff.

For the purpose of suit in a federal court based on diversity of citizenship, a corporation is considered a "citizen" both of the state where it is incorporated and of the state in which it has its principal place of business. As a result, there is no federal jurisdiction in many cases in which one of the parties is a corporation. If any one of the parties on the other side of the case is a citizen either of the state in which the corporation is chartered or is doing its principal business, there is no diversity of citizenship and thus no federal jurisdiction.

The following case illustrates the notion of "complete diversity."

Case

Lincoln Property Company, et al. v. Christophe Roche

SUPREME COURT OF THE UNITED STATES

546 U.S. 81 (2005)

Justice Ginsburg delivered the opinion of the Court

This case concerns 28 U.S.C. § 1441, which authorizes the removal of civil actions from state court to federal court when the action initiated in state court is one that could have been brought, originally, in a federal district court. When federal-court jurisdiction is predicated on the parties' diversity of citizenship, removal is permissible "only if none of the parties in interest properly joined and served as defendants is a citizen of the State in which [the] action [was] brought."

Christophe and Juanita Roche leased an apartment in the Westfield Village complex in Fairfax County, Virginia. About a year after moving in, they discovered evidence of toxic mold in their apartment. Expert inspection confirmed the presence of mold, which the inspection report linked to hair loss, headaches, irritation of the respiratory tract, fatigue, and dermatitis. The report stated that spores from toxigenic mold species were airborne in the apartment and had likely contaminated the carpeting and fabric surfaces throughout the dwelling. The Roches moved out of their apartment for the remediation process, leaving their personal belongings in the care of Lincoln, the designated property manager of Westfield Village, and the mold treatment firm.

Some months later, the Roches commenced suit, filing two substantially similar complaints in the Circuit Court for Fairfax County, Virginia. Both complaints asserted serious medical ailments from the Roches' year-long exposure to toxic mold, and sought damages under multiple headings, including negligence, breach of contract, actual fraud, constructive fraud, and violations of Virginia housing regulations. In addition, the Roches alleged loss, theft, or destruction of their personal property (including irreplaceable family keepsakes) during the remediation process. Regarding these losses, they sought damages for conversion and infliction of emotional distress.

In state court, the Roches' complaints named three defendants: Lincoln; INVESCO Institutional, an investment management group; and State of Wisconsin Investment Board, the alleged owner of Westfield Village. The complaints described Lincoln as "a developer and manager of residential communities, including ... Westfield Village." "[A]cting by and through [its] agents," the Roches alleged, Lincoln caused the personal injuries of which they complained.

The Roches state that they preferred to litigate in state court for two principal reasons: Virginia does not permit summary judgment based on affidavits or deposition testimony, and Virginia has not adopted the rule of Daubert v. Merrell Dow Pharmaceuticals, Inc., to assess expert evidence.

Defendants timely removed the twin cases to the United States District Court for the Eastern District of Virginia, invoking that court's diversity-of-citizenship jurisdiction. The notice of removal described Lincoln as a Texas corporation with its principal place of business in Texas, INVESCO as a Delaware corporation with its principal place of business in Georgia, and State of Wisconsin Investment Board as an independent agency of Wisconsin. In their consolidated federal-court complaint, the Roches identified themselves as citizens of Virginia and Lincoln as a corporation headquartered in Texas, just as they did in their state-court complaints.

Six days after the District Court granted defendants' motion for summary judgment, but before final judgment was entered, the Roches moved to remand the case to the state court, alleging for the first time the absence of federal subject-matter jurisdiction. Specifically, the Roches alleged that Lincoln "is not a Texas Corporation, but a Partnership with one of its partners residing in the Commonwealth of Virginia." The District Court denied the remand motion, concluding that Lincoln is a Texas corporation and that removal was proper because the requisite complete diversity existed between all plaintiffs and all defendants. The court of appeals reversed.

We granted certiorari, to resolve a division among the Circuits on the question whether an entity not named or joined as a defendant can nonetheless be deemed a real party in interest whose presence would destroy diversity.

The Court of Appeals correctly identified Lincoln as a proper party to the action, but it erred in insisting that some other entity affiliated with Lincoln should have been joined as a codefendant and that it was Lincoln's obligation to name that entity and show that its joinder would not destroy diversity.

We stress, first, that at this stage of the case the existence of complete diversity between the Roches and Lincoln is not in doubt. The Roches, both citizens of Virginia, acknowledge that Lincoln is indeed a corporation, not a partnership, and that Lincoln is chartered in and has its principal place of business in Texas. Accordingly, for jurisdictional purposes, Lincoln is a citizen of Texas and of no other State. 28 U.S.C. § 1332(c)(1) ("a corporation shall be deemed to be a citizen of any State by which it has been incorporated and of the State where it has its principal place of business").

In the instant case, Virginia plaintiffs Christophe and Juanita Roche joined and served no Virginian as a party defendant. Hence, the action qualified for the removal defendants affected

[No federal law] requires plaintiffs or defendants to name and join any additional parties to this action.

The Roches sued the entity they thought responsible for managing their apartment. Lincoln affirmed that it was so responsible. Complete diversity existed. The potential liability of other parties was a matter plaintiffs' counsel might have assiduously explored through discovery devices. It was not incumbent on Lincoln to propose as additional defendants persons the Roches, as masters of their complaint, permissively might have joined.

■ *Reversed.*

CASE CONCEPTS REVIEW

1. Why do you believe the defendants wanted the case removed from state court to federal court?
2. The Roches wanted to have diversity destroyed so that the case would go back to the state court in Virginia. Their premise was that the defendants should be obligated to prove that there was no entity affiliated with the defendant that was a Virginia entity. The United States Supreme Court disagreed. The defendants here were under no obligation to negate the existence of a potential additional defendant that would destroy diversity. Is this a practical approach to determining diversity for federal jurisdiction purposes? Why?

Jurisdictional Amount If diversity of citizenship is the basis of federal jurisdiction, the parties must satisfy a *jurisdictional amount,* which is $75,000. If a case involves multiple plaintiffs with separate and distinct claims, each claim must satisfy the jurisdictional amount. Thus, in a class-action suit, the claim of each plaintiff must exceed the $75,000 minimum unless changed by statute.

Federal Question In addition to diversity of citizenship, the Constitution, laws, or treaties of the United States may base federal jurisdiction on a federal question that exists if the lawsuit arises out of rights granted. Here there is *NO jurisdictional amount.* These civil actions may involve matters such as bankruptcy, anti-trust, securities regulations, patents, copyrights, trademarks, taxes, elections, the rights guaranteed by the Bill of Rights, and those rights secured to individual citizens by the Fourteenth Amendment. In addition, by statute the district courts have original jurisdiction to try tort cases involving citizens who suffer damages caused by officers or agents of the federal government.

7. The Law in Federal Courts

Our dual system of federal and state courts creates a unique problem in conflict of laws. In all cases, federal courts use their own body of procedural law. In cases involving the U.S. Constitution, treaties, and federal statutes, federal substantive law is used. However, there is no body of federal common law in suits based on diversity of citizenship. *Therefore, federal courts use the substantive law, including conflict of laws principles, of the state in which they are sitting.* Thus, just as the state courts are bound by federal precedent in cases involving federal law and federally protected rights, federal courts are bound by state precedent in diversity of citizenship cases. The following case established this very important principle.

Case

Erie Railroad v. Tompkins

SUPREME COURT OF THE UNITED STATES

304 U.S. 64 (1938)

Brandeis, J.

Tompkins, a citizen of Pennsylvania, was injured on a dark night by a passing freight train of the Erie Railroad Company while walking along its right of way at Hughestown in that state. He claimed the accident occurred through negligence in the operation, or maintenance, of the train; that he was rightfully on the premises as a licensee because he was on a commonly used beaten footpath which ran for a short distance alongside the tracks; and that he was struck by something which looked like a door projecting from one of the moving cars. To enforce that claim he brought an action in the federal court for Southern New York, which has jurisdiction because the company is a corporation of that state. It denied liability; and the case was tried by a jury.

The Erie insisted that its duty to Tompkins was no greater than that owed to a trespasser. It contended, among other things, that its duty to Tompkins, and hence its liability, should be determined in accordance with the Pennsylvania law; that under the law of Pennsylvania, as declared by its highest court, persons who use pathways along the railroad

continued

right of way—that is, a longitudinal pathway as distinguished from a crossing—are to be deemed trespassers; and that the railroad is not liable for injuries to undiscovered trespassers resulting from its negligence, unless it be wanton or willful. Tompkins contended that railroad's duty and liability is to be determined in federal courts as a matter of general law.

The trial judge refused to rule that the applicable law precluded recovery. The jury brought in a verdict of $30,000; and the judgment entered thereon was affirmed by the Circuit Court of Appeals, which held that the question was one not of local but of general law, and that

> *upon questions of general law the federal courts are free, in absence of a local statute, to exercise their independent judgment as to what the law is; and it is well settled that the question of the responsibility of a railroad for injuries caused by its servants is one of general law....*

The Erie had contended that application of the Pennsylvania rule was required, among other things, by section 34 of the Federal Judiciary Act which provides: "The laws of the several States, except where the Constitution, treaties, or statutes of the United States otherwise require or provide, shall be regarded as rules of decision in trials at common law, in the courts of the United States, in cases where they apply."

Because of the importance of the question whether the federal court was free to disregard the alleged rule of the Pennsylvania common law, we granted certiorari.

First, Swift v. Tyson held that federal courts exercising jurisdiction on the ground of diversity of citizenship need not, in matters of general jurisprudence, apply the unwritten law of the state as declared by its highest court; and they are free to exercise an independent judgment as to what the common law of the state is—or should be.

Doubt was repeatedly expressed as to the correctness of the construction given section 34, and as to the soundness of the rule which it introduced. But it was the more recent research of a competent scholar, who examined the original document, which established that the construction given to it by the Court was erroneous.

Second, experience in applying the doctrine of Swift v. Tyson had revealed its defects, political and social; and the benefits expected to flow from the rule did not accrue.

On the other hand, the mischievous results of the doctrine had become apparent. Diversity of citizenship jurisdiction was conferred in order to prevent apprehended discrimination in state courts against those not citizens of the state. Swift v. Tyson introduced grave discrimination by noncitizens against citizens. It made rights enjoyed under the unwritten "general law" vary according to whether enforcement was sought in the state or in the federal court; and the privilege of selecting the court in which the right should be determined was conferred upon the noncitizen. Thus, the doctrine rendered impossible equal protection of the law. In attempting to promote uniformity of law throughout the United States, the doctrine had prevented uniformity in the administration of the law of the state.

Thirdly, except in matters governed by the Federal Constitution or by acts of Congress, the law to be applied in any case is the law of the state. And whether the law of the state shall be declared by its Legislature in a statute or by its highest court in a decision is not a matter of federal concern. There is no federal general common law. Congress has no power to declare substantive rules of common law applicable in a state whether they be local in their nature or "general," whether they be commercial law or a part of the law of torts. There is no clause in the Constitution that purports to confer such a power upon the federal courts.

Thus the doctrine of Swift v. Tyson is, as Mr. Justice Holmes said, "an unconstitutional assumption of powers by the Courts of the United States which no lapse of time or respectable array of opinion should make us hesitate to correct." In disapproving that doctrine we do not hold unconstitutional section 34 of the Federal Judiciary Act of 1789 or any other act of Congress. We merely declare that in applying the doctrine this Court and the lower courts have invaded rights that, in our opinion, are reserved by the Constitution to the several states.

■ *Reversed and remanded.*

CASE CONCEPTS REVIEW

1. Why was Tompkins able to file this lawsuit in a federal district court?
2. Why did Tompkins argue that the federal common law should apply in this case?
3. How does the Supreme Court's decision provide for the same outcome of the litigation regardless of the court system in which the case is filed?

8. Federal Reviewing Courts

Writ of certiorari

The legal document used within the discretion of a reviewing court to decide whether to hear a case, thereby agreeing to review a lower court's decision

As previously noted, there are two levels of federal reviewing courts. Cases decided in the federal district courts are reviewed by the appropriate courts of appeals. In most cases, the decisions of the courts of appeals are final. The Supreme Court may review cases in the courts of appeals if a **writ of certiorari** is granted by the Supreme Court upon a petition of any party before or after a decision in the courts of appeals. The granting of a writ of certiorari to review a judgment of the courts of appeals is within the discretion of the Supreme Court. Only four of the nine justices need to vote in favor of granting a writ of certiorari for the Court to review the merits of a case. Generally, the writ will be granted only to bring cases of significant public concern to the court of last resort for decision.

Prior to 1988, the Supreme Court was required to review certain cases. This mandatory or obligatory jurisdiction extended to certain cases heard by three judges at the district court level and to certain state Supreme Court decisions involving constitutional issues. This mandatory jurisdiction was eliminated almost entirely in 1988 to grant the Supreme Court the total power to control its docket. Today, the Justices of the Supreme Court themselves determine which issues they will allow to be brought before the Court.

Decisions of state courts that could formerly be appealed as a matter of right are now subject to the discretion of the certiorari process. This relieves the Supreme Court of any obligation to review the merits of inconsequential federal challenges to state laws. If there is a significant federal issue of paramount importance, the court may, of course, hear the case.

The 1988 law also transferred most appeals from the Supreme Court to the courts of appeals. However, federal statutes still do authorize a few direct appeals to the Supreme Court. For example, the Antitrust Procedures and Penalties Act of 1974 authorizes a direct appeal to the Supreme Court in civil antitrust cases brought by the government seeking equitable relief where immediate Supreme Court review is found by the trial judge to be "of general public importance in the administration of justice." However, the Supreme Court may decide in its discretion" to "deny the direct appeal and remand the case to the court of appeals." These few statutory kinds of Supreme Court obligatory jurisdiction contribute very little to the Court's workload.

As a virtually all-certiorari court, the Supreme Court will review annually over 5,000 petitions for a writ of certiorari. It can be expected to grant fewer than 150 each year. Today, the law recognizes that the Supreme Court Justices are the best judge of what cases out of the thousands are the most deserving of a hearing on their merits.

LAW AND EQUITY

9. Basic Distinction

Legal remedies
Relief sought from a court, involving monetary damages

Historically, trial courts in the United States have been divided into two parts—a court of law and a court of equity or chancery. The term equity arose in England because the failure of **legal remedies** to provide adequate relief often made it impossible to obtain justice in the king's courts of law. *The only remedy at law was a suit for money damages.*

The Justices of the Supreme Court decide which issues are brought before the Court.

Equitable remedies
Any form of relief that does not involve a request for monetary damages

In order that justice might be done, the person sought **equitable remedies** from the king in person. Because the appeal was to the king's conscience, he referred such matters to his spiritual adviser, the chancellor, who was usually a church official and, in giving a remedy, usually favored the ecclesiastical law.

By such a method, there developed a separate system of procedure and different rules for deciding matters presented to the chancellor. Suits involving these rules were said to be brought "in chancery" or in equity, in contrast to suits "at law" in the king's courts. Courts of equity were courts of conscience, and they recognized many rights that were not recognized by common-law courts. For example, trusts in lands were recognized; rescission was allowed on contracts created through fraud; injunction and specific performance were developed as remedies.

In a few states, courts of equity are still separate and distinct from courts of law. In most states, the equity and law courts are organized under a single court with two dockets—one at law, the other in equity. Whether the case is in equity or at law is determined by the remedy desired. Modern civil procedure laws usually have abolished the distinction between actions at law and in equity. However, pleadings usually must denote whether the action is legal or equitable because, as a general rule, there is no right to a jury trial of an equitable action. The constitutional guarantee to a trial by jury applies only to actions at law.

10. Equitable Procedures

By statute in some states, a jury may hear the evidence in equity cases, but the determination of the jury in these cases is usually advisory only and is not binding on the court. The judge passes on questions of both law and fact and may decide the case based on the pleadings without the introduction of oral testimony. If the facts are voluminous and complicated, the judge may refer the case to an attorney at law, usually called a *master in chancery,* to take the testimony. The master in chancery hears the evidence, makes findings of fact and conclusions of law, and reports back to the judge.

Courts of equity use maxims instead of strict rules of law to decide cases. There are no legal rights in equity, for the decision is based on moral rights and natural justice. Some of the typical maxims of equity are as follows:

- Equity will not suffer a right to exist without a remedy.
- Equity regards as done that which ought to be done.
- Where there is equal equity, the law must prevail.
- Those who come into equity must do so with clean hands.
- Those who seek equity must do equity.
- Equity aids the vigilant.
- Equality is equity.

Decree
The decision of the chancellor (judge) in a suit in equity that, like a judgment at law, is the determination of the rights between the parties

These maxims guide the chancellor in exercising discretion. For example, the clean-hands doctrine prohibits a party who is guilty of misconduct in the matter in litigation from receiving the aid of a court. Likewise, a court of equity may protect one party if the other party does not act in good faith.

The decision of the court of equity is called a **decree**. A judgment in a court of law is measured in damages, whereas a decree of a court of equity is said to be in *personam*—that is, it is directed to the defendant personally, who is to do or not to do some specific thing.

Decrees are either final or interlocutory. A decree is final when it disposes of the issues of the case, reserving no question to be decided in the future. A decree establishing title to real estate, granting a divorce, or ordering specific performance is usually final. A decree is *interlocutory* when it reserves some question to be determined in the future. A decree granting a temporary injunction, appointing a receiver, and ordering property to be delivered to such a receiver would be interlocutory.

Failure on the part of the defendant to obey a decree of a court of equity is contempt of court because the decree is directed not against his or her property, but against his or her person. Any person in contempt of court may be placed in jail or fined by order of the court.

Equity jurisprudence plays an ever-increasing role in our legal system. The movement toward social justice requires more reliance on the equitable maxims and less reliance on rigid rules of law.

CHAPTER SUMMARY

OPERATING THE COURT SYSTEM

Trial Judges

1. Judges conduct the trial. They decide questions of procedure and instruct the jury on the law applicable to the issues to be decided by the jury.
2. Judges supply the law applicable to the facts.
3. Judges find the facts if there is no jury.

Reviewing Court Judges and Justices

1. Judges of intermediate reviewing courts and justices of final reviewing courts decide cases on appeal. The questions to be decided are questions of law.
2. Reviewing courts require more legal scholarship of the reviewing judges and justices than that typically required of the trial judges.

The Jury

1. The jury function is to decide disputed questions of fact.
2. A jury may consist of as few as six persons.
3. Less than unanimous verdicts are possible with twelve-person juries.
4. Excuses from jury duty are more difficult to obtain today.

COURT SYSTEMS

State Structure

1. Each state has a trial court of general jurisdiction and inferior courts of limited jurisdiction.
2. The small claims court is of growing importance because it provides a means of handling small cases without the need for a lawyer.
3. Historically, trial courts were divided into courts of law and courts of equity or chancery.

Federal Structure

1. The Constitution created the Supreme Court.
2. Congress has created thirteen courts of appeals and at least one district court in each state.

Federal District Courts

1. Federal courts have limited jurisdiction. They hear cases based on federal laws (federal question cases) and cases involving diversity of citizenship.
2. Diversity of citizenship cases have a jurisdictional minimum of more than $75,000.
3. For diversity of citizenship purposes, a corporation is a citizen of two states: the state of incorporation and the state of its principal place of business.

The Law in Federal Courts

1. Federal courts use the rules of federal procedure.
2. Federal question cases are decided using federal substantive law.

3. A federal court in a diversity of citizenship case uses the substantive law of the state in which it sits to decide such a case.

Federal Reviewing Courts

1. Courts of appeals decisions are usually final.
2. Most cases in the Supreme Court are there as the result of granting a petition for a writ of certiorari.

LAW AND EQUITY

Basic Distinction

1. Historically, courts of law handled cases involving claims for money damages.
2. Courts of equity or chancery were created where the remedy at law (money damages) was inadequate—for example, suits seeking an injunction or dissolution of a business.

Equitable Procedures

1. There is usually no right to a trial by jury.
2. Sometimes a special appointee, known as a master in chancery, assists with the fact finding.
3. The decision is called a decree.
4. A person may be jailed for violating a decree.
5. Courts of equity use maxims instead of rules of law to decide cases.
6. Use of maxims allows courts to achieve justice.

REVIEW QUESTIONS AND PROBLEMS

1. Why are some controversies excluded from the court system? Give examples of such issues.
2. Why were small claims courts created? Give three examples of typical cases decided in such courts.
3. Jane deposited $400 with her landlord to secure a lease and to pay for any damages to an apartment that she had rented. At the end of the lease, she vacated the apartment and requested the return of the deposit. Although the landlord admitted that the apartment was in good shape, the landlord refused to return the deposit. What should Jane do? Explain.
4. Henry, a resident of Nevada, sued Adam, a resident of Utah, in the federal court in California. He sought $60,000 damages for personal injuries arising from an automobile accident that occurred in Los Angeles, California.

   a. Does the federal court have jurisdiction? Why or why not?
   b. What rules of procedure will the court use? Why?
   c. What rules of substantive law will the court use? Why?

5. For diversity of citizenship purposes, a corporation is a citizen of two states. How do you identify these states?
6. Paul, a citizen of Georgia, was crossing a street in New Orleans when he was struck by a car driven by David, a citizen of Texas. The car was owned by David's employer, a Delaware corporation, which has its principal place of business in Atlanta, Georgia. Paul sues both David and the corporation in the federal district court in New Orleans. Paul's complaint alleges damages in the amount of $100,000. Does this court have jurisdiction? Why?
7. What is the function of a petition for a writ of certiorari or a petition for leave to appeal? Explain.
8. John sues Ivan in a state court, seeking damages for breach of contract to sell a tennis racquet. The trial court finds for Ivan. John announces that he will appeal "all the way to the

Supreme Court of the United States, if necessary, to change the decision." Assuming that John has the money to do so, will he be able to obtain review by the Supreme Court of the United States? Explain.

9. Describe three controversies that would be decided in a court of equity or chancery in states that still distinguish between courts of law and courts of equity.

10. Mario agreed to sell his house to George, but he later changed his mind. George sued Mario for specific performance. Is either party entitled to a jury trial? Why or why not?

Litigation | 3

CHAPTER OUTLINE

CHAPTER PREVIEW

In the preceding chapter, the organization and functions of our courts were introduced. Business leaders should have a basic understanding of the litigation process so that they can effectively work with attorneys on strategies and tactics once litigation has commenced. As a person in business, the main reason you would use the courts is to resolve some dispute. This chapter discusses the role and process of litigation.

BUSINESS MANAGEMENT DECISION

Your company, which operates in Georgia, makes and sells peanut brittle to a distributor in Atlanta that, in turn, sells the peanut brittle in Vermont. A customer in Vermont breaks a tooth on your peanut brittle. This customer files suit in Vermont against you, and a summons is served on you in Georgia. Can you ignore the complaint and summons without risk?

BASIC PRINCIPLES

1. Parties

Plaintiff
The party who files a claim in a court

Defendant
One who answers a complaint

Appellant
The party who appeals from one court to another

Appellee
The party against whom an appeal is filed

In a criminal case, *the people* bring the action against the named defendant. Most civil cases use the term **plaintiff** to describe the party bringing the lawsuit by filing a complaint, and **defendant** describes the party against whom it is brought.

When the result at the trial court level is appealed, the party appealing is usually referred to as the **appellant** and the successful party in the trial court is called the **appellee**. Many jurisdictions, in publishing the decisions of reviewing courts, list the appellant first and the appellee second, even though the appellant may have been the defendant in the trial court.

In most states and in the federal courts, all persons may join in one lawsuit as plaintiffs if the causes of action arise out of the same transaction or series of transactions and involve common questions of law or fact. In addition, the plaintiffs may join as defendants all persons who are necessary to a complete determination or settlement of the questions. In addition, if a defendant alleges that a complete determination of a controversy cannot be made without other parties, that defendant may bring in new third parties as third-party defendants. This procedure is usually followed when someone is liable to a defendant, if the defendant is liable to the plaintiff.

2. Standing to Sue

The requirement that plaintiffs have *standing to sue* arises because of the limited role of courts in our society. The constitution requires that a plaintiff must allege a case or controversy between himself or herself and the defendant if the court is to hear the case. A plaintiff must have a personal stake in the outcome of the controversy, and this stake must be based on some threatened or actual injury resulting from the defendant's action. Without the requirement of "standing," courts would be called on to decide abstract questions of public interest. Such questions are best resolved by the political process.

When the asserted harm is a generalized grievance shared in substantially equal measure by all or a large class of citizens, courts hold that harm alone normally does not grant standing to sue. For example, a taxpayer filed suit challenging the budget of the CIA. The court held that the taxpayer lacked standing to sue. Likewise, a plaintiff must assert his or her own legal rights and not those of some third party. A citizen objected to the army's surveillance of civilians, but the case was dismissed without a showing that the plaintiff was one of the civilians under surveillance.

Standing to sue is in no way dependent on the merits of the plaintiff's contention that particular conduct is illegal. The presence of standing is determined by the nature and source of the plaintiff's claim. For example, a plaintiff-seller acting in good faith has standing to sue a defendant-buyer for breach of contract even though the defendant might have a defense that prohibits the plaintiff's recovery.

As illustrated by the following case, standing can be defined by a statute granting a specific cause of action.

CASE

Domino's Pizza, Inc., et al. v. John McDonald

SUPREME COURT OF THE UNITED STATES

546 U.S. 470 (2006)

JUSTICE SCALIA DELIVERED THE OPINION OF THE COURT

We decide whether a plaintiff who lacks any rights under an existing contractual relationship with the defendant, and who has not been prevented from entering into such a contractual relationship, may bring suit under Rev. Stat. § 1977, 42 U.S.C. § 1981.

Respondent John McDonald, a black man, is the sole shareholder and president of JWM Investments, Inc. (JWM), a corporation organized under Nevada law. He sued petitioners (collectively Domino's) in the District Court for the District of Nevada, claiming violations of § 1981. The allegations of the complaint, which for present purposes we assume to be true, were as follows.

JWM and Domino's entered into several contracts under which JWM was to construct four restaurants in the Las Vegas area, which would be leased to Domino's. At least in part because of the failed contracts, JWM filed for Chapter 11 bankruptcy. While the bankruptcy proceedings were still ongoing, McDonald filed the present § 1981 claim against Domino's in his personal capacity. The gravamen of McDonald's complaint was that Domino's had broken its contracts with JWM because of racial animus toward McDonald, and that the breach had harmed McDonald personally by causing him "to suffer monetary damages and damages for pain and suffering, emotional distress, and humiliation." Domino's filed a motion to dismiss the complaint for failure to state a claim. It asserted that McDonald could bring no § 1981 claim against Domino's because McDonald was party to no contract with Domino's. The District Court granted the motion. The Court of Appeals for the Ninth Circuit reversed.

Domino's filed a motion to dismiss the complaint for failure to state a claim. It asserted that McDonald could bring no § 1981 claim against Domino's because McDonald was party to no contract with Domino's. The District Court granted the motion. It noted that Domino's had "relied on the basic proposition that a corporation is a separate legal entity from its stockholders and officers," and concluded that a corporation may have "standing to assert a § 1981 claim" but that "a president or sole shareholder may not step into the shoes of the corporation and assert that claim personally."

Among the many statutes that combat racial discrimination, § 1981, originally § 1 of the Civil Rights Act of 1866, 14 Stat. 27, has a specific function: It protects the equal right of "all persons within the jurisdiction of the United States" to "make and enforce contracts" without respect to race. The statute currently defines "make and enforce contracts" to "include the making, performance, modification, and termination of contracts, and the enjoyment of all benefits, privileges, terms, and conditions of the contractual relationship."

McDonald argues that the statute must be read to give him a cause of action because he "made and enforced contracts" for JWM. On his reading of the text, "If Domino's refused to deal with the salesman for a pepperoni manufacturer because the salesman was black, that would violate the section 1981 right of the salesman to make a contract on behalf of his principal." We think not. The right to "make contracts" guaranteed by the statute was not the insignificant right to act as an agent for someone else's contracting—any more than it was the insignificant right to act as amanuensis in writing out the agreement, and thus to "make" the contract in that sense. Rather, it was the right—denied in some States to blacks, as it was denied at common law to children—to give and receive contractual rights on one's own behalf.

McDonald's complaint does identify a contractual relationship, the one between Domino's and JWM. But it is fundamental corporation and agency law—indeed, it can be said to be the whole purpose of corporation and agency law—that the shareholder and contracting officer of a corporation has no rights and is exposed to no liability under the corporation's contracts. McDonald now makes light of the law of corporations and of agency—arguing, for instance, that because he "negotiated, signed, performed, and sought to enforce the contract," Domino's was wrong to "insist that [the contract] somehow was not his 'own.'" This novel approach to the law contradicts McDonald's own experience. Domino's filed a proof of claim against JWM during its corporate bankruptcy; it did not proceed against McDonald personally. The corporate form and the rules of agency protected his personal assets, even though he "negotiated, signed, performed, and sought to enforce" contracts for JWM. The corporate form and the rules of agency similarly deny him rights under those contracts.

■ *Reversed.*

CASE CONCEPTS REVIEW

1. Should the court have ignored the corporate form in this case because the corporation had only the one shareholder?
2. Should the civil rights law in question be altered to allow corporations to have standing? Are there any practical problems with that suggestion?

A *class-action* suit is one in which a person files suit on his or her own behalf and on behalf of all other persons who may have a similar claim. For example, a class-action suit may be brought on behalf of all purchasers of a defective product. The number of people who comprise a class is frequently quite large. Class-action suits are popular because they often involve matters in which no one member of the class would have a sufficient financial interest to warrant filing suit. The combined interest of all members of the class not only makes litigation feasible but also often makes it very profitable for the lawyer who handles the suit. Issues associated with standing tend to be quite complex.

THE PLACE OF LITIGATION

3. Jurisdiction

The first requirement in any lawsuit is that it must be brought before a court that has the power to hear the case. This power to hear is known as *jurisdiction,* and it has two aspects: jurisdiction over the subject matter and jurisdiction over the parties.

SUBJECT MATTER In Chapter 2, jurisdiction over the subject matter of a case was defined to mean that a court has authority to resolve the controversy between the parties. For example, a probate court has subject-matter jurisdiction over the issue of a will's validity. However this court lacks *subject-matter jurisdiction* to determine the rights of the parties in a personal-injury case. As previously noted, the amount of money sought by the plaintiff may determine which court has subject-matter jurisdiction. Small claims courts cannot hear cases involving dollar damages over a stated limit.

Every state court system must have a court of general subject-matter jurisdiction. This requirement assures a plaintiff of a forum to have any and every dispute litigated. Some states have created courts of exclusive subject-matter jurisdiction. Probate courts, for example, often are the only courts where parties may bring issues involving wills, estates, guardianships, and similar matters.

PARTIES In addition to having power to hear the subject matter of a case, courts also must have jurisdiction over the parties—the plaintiff and the defendant. A plaintiff voluntarily submits to the jurisdiction of the court when the suit is filed.

Summons

A document issued by a court directing the defendant to appear in court or otherwise respond to the plaintiff's allegations

Jurisdiction over the defendant is accomplished by the service of a **summons** issued by the court. It is delivered to a sheriff or other person, who then serves it on the defendant. Jurisdiction over a defendant, in a limited number of cases, may be obtained by publishing a notice in a newspaper. This method is possible in a suit for divorce or one concerning real estate, something important enough to be written up in a public notice that would be deemed adequate to notify the defendant.

Guardianship of children is reviewed quite often in litigation between parents and families.

Publication may also be accompanied by proper attachment proceedings. In such cases, service by publication brings under the court's jurisdiction all attached property of a nonresident defendant if it lies within the territorial limits of the court. When this technique is employed, the attached property may be used to satisfy any judgment.

Most cases, however, require the actual service of a summons to the defendant to give him or her notice of the suit. Many states allow a summons to be served on any member of the family above a specified age, such as ten years, at the defendant's home. In such cases, a copy is also mailed to the defendant.

4. Long-Arm Statutes

Historically, the jurisdiction of courts to enter judgment against a person required actual personal service of the summons on the defendant in the state in which the suit was brought. This was necessary to give the defendant notice of the suit and an opportunity to defend. Because the jurisdiction of courts was limited to geographical areas such as a state, the power to issue and serve a summons beyond the borders of the state did not exist.

Limiting the jurisdiction of courts to persons physically present in the state is no longer accepted. Personal jurisdiction over nonresidents has been expanded because modern transportation and communication facilities have minimized the inconveniences to nonresident defendants who must defend themselves in courts beyond their home state. There is no longer any logical reason to deny a local citizen a remedy in local courts for an injury caused by a nonresident temporarily present in the state.

The first extension of jurisdiction over nonresidents occurred in auto accident cases. This extension was made by creating a legal "fiction" that resulted in the summons being served within the state whose court issued the summons. This legal fiction was created by the enactment of statutes providing that a nonresident, by using the state highways, automatically appointed a designated state official, usually the secretary of state, as his or her agent to accept service of process. The summons would be served on the secretary of state, who would notify the defendant of the suit; and the defendant was then subject to the power of the court.

These nonresident motorist statutes opened the door for adoption of other statutes called *long-arm statutes,* which further extend the jurisdiction of courts over nonresidents whether they are individuals or corporations. Long-arm statutes typically extend the jurisdiction of courts to cases in which a tort injury has been caused by a nonresident temporarily present in the state. They also usually extend jurisdiction to cases arising out of the ownership of property located within the state. Of course, the conduct of business such as entering into contracts confers jurisdiction. Thus, a nonresident individual or a corporation may be subject to a suit for injuries if either has certain *"minimum contacts"* within the state, as long as the maintenance of the suit does not offend traditional notions of fair play and substantial justice.

What "minimum contacts" and activities are necessary to bring the defendant into a state is a fact question depending on each particular case. Whatever the basis for the action may be, either in contract or in tort, the court can acquire jurisdiction over the defendant if these minimum contacts are present. If there are no minimal contacts, there is no jurisdiction because requiring a defense would be a denial of due process of law.

The advent of the Internet and a host of other technological advances has caused courts to consider carefully the application of long-arm statutes to the many challenging situations that are developing as a result of these changes in the manner in which firms may conduct their business. The following case illustrates how one court addressed a complex issue dealing with the defendant's use of the Web and whether one state's long-arm statute is applicable.

CASE

Butler v. Beer Across America

U. S. DISTRICT COURT FOR THE NORTHERN DISTRICT OF ALABAMA

83 F. Supp. 2d 1261 (2000)

OPINION: JAMES H. HANCOCK

The Court has before it the August 6, 1999 motion of defendants Beer Across America, Merchant Direct, and Shermer Specialties (collectively "Beer Across America") to dismiss the present action for lack of personal jurisdiction.

On June 8, 1999, plaintiff Lynda Butler initiated the present action by filing a complaint in the Circuit Court of Shelby County, Alabama. The complaint asserts a claim under the Civil Damages Act, section 6-5-70 of the Alabama Code, arising from the sale of beer to plaintiff's son, Hunter Butler, by the defendants via the Internet. The Civil Damage Act provides for a civil action by the parent or guardian of a minor against anyone who knowingly and illegally sells or furnishes liquor to the minor. On August 6, 1999 defendants timely removed the action to this Court; removal was based upon diversity of citizenship given that plaintiff is a citizen of Alabama and that the defendants are three related Illinois corporations engaged in the marketing and sale of alcoholic beverages and other, complementary merchandise. Upon removal, the defendants simultaneously moved for dismiss.

Here, the facts are simple. In early April of 1999, plaintiff's minor son, who apparently was left home unsupervised (but with a credit card issued in his name) while his parents vacationed, placed an order for twelve bottles of beer with defendants through Beer Across America's Internet site on the World Wide Web. Under the applicable provisions of the U.C.C., the sale occurred in Illinois. The beer was then shipped to plaintiff's son in Alabama and delivered to the Butler residence by the carrier acting, the entire time, as the agent of the plaintiff's son. The sale was not discovered by plaintiff until she returned home and found several bottles of beer from the shipment remaining in the family's refrigerator.

Together, these facts present the following question: whether personal jurisdiction properly may be asserted by a federal court sitting in diversity in Alabama over a nonresident Illinois defendant in an action arising from a sale made in Illinois solely in response to an order placed by an Alabama resident via the Internet?

Having framed the issue, the Court turns to the multi-part analysis implicated by this question. The first part of the analysis requires a consideration of state law because the reach of a federal diversity court's jurisdictional power over a nonresident defendant may not exceed the limits allowed under state law.

As one arm of the due process analysis, the court initially must determine whether at least minimum contacts exist between the defendant and the jurisdiction. The significant question is whether "the defendant's conduct and connection with the forum State are such that he should reasonably anticipate being haled into court there"?

In addition to minimum contacts, due process mandates a consideration of the fairness in forcing the defendant to litigate in a foreign forum.

Regarding the minimum contacts element of due process analysis, plaintiff asserts that defendants' contacts with the state of Alabama are sufficient for either general or specific jurisdiction. To support general jurisdiction, the plaintiff cites not only the sale to her son but also the defendants' sales (in Illinois) to other Alabama residents as well as the sale of beer to defendants by two Alabama brewers through a non-party Illinois wholesaler. However, the plaintiff has not offered any competent evidence to seriously controvert the defendants' averments that they are not registered to do business in Alabama; that they own no property in the state; that they maintain no offices in the state; that they have no agents in Alabama; that their key personnel have never even visited the state; and that they do not place advertisement with Alabama media outlets (except for what nationally placed advertisements may reach the state) or engage in any other significant promotions targeting the state, which would rise to such a level as would justify an exercise of general jurisdiction by this state's courts. What plaintiff has offered is simply not sufficient to conclude that Beer Across America can be brought before an Alabama tribunal for any claim that any plaintiff may bring.

The fact that many companies have established virtual beachheads on the Internet and the fact that the Internet is now accessible from almost any point on the globe have created complex, new considerations in counting minimum contacts for purposes of determining personal jurisdiction. Jurisdiction is proper when the "defendant clearly does business over the Internet by entering into contracts with residents of other states which 'involve the knowing and repeated transmission of computer files over the Internet. ...'" Jurisdiction is improper, however, when the nonresident defendant has established a passive Internet site, which acts as little more than an electronic billboard for the posting of information. Between those two extremes lies a gray area "where a defendant has a website that allows a user to exchange information with a host computer"; there, the determination turns on the nature of the information transmitted and on the degree of interaction.

Applying these principles to the present case, clearly Beer Across America's site does not even anticipate the regular exchange of information across the Internet, much less provide for such interaction. Rather, it is closer to an electronic version of a postal reply card; the limited degree of interactivity available on the defendants' website is certainly insufficient to satisfy the minimum contacts requirement of due process for this Court to exercise personal jurisdiction over these defendants.

Furthermore, considerations of "fair play and substantial justice" do not support personal jurisdiction over the nonresident defendants in this action.

In conclusion, the Court finds that plaintiff has failed to make a prima facie case of personal jurisdiction over the defendants.

■ *Defendant's motion to dismiss is DENIED and this action is TRANSFERRED to the United States District Court for the Northern District of Illinois.*

CASE CONCEPTS REVIEW

1. What specific facts do you believe influenced the court in making this decision?
2. Is the "active," "passive," and "intermediate" differentiation discussed in the opinion practical? Why?

5. Venue

As previously discussed, the term *jurisdiction* describes the power of the court to hear and adjudicate the case. Jurisdiction includes the court's power to inquire into the facts, apply the law to the facts, make a decision, and declare and enforce a judgment. *Venue* relates to and defines the particular territorial area within the state, out of all those with jurisdiction, in which the case should be filed and tried. Matters of venue are usually determined by statute. In a few states, the subject of venue is covered in the state constitution.

Venue statutes usually provide that actions concerning interests in land must be commenced and tried in the county or district in which the land is located. Actions for the recovery of penalties imposed by statute against public officers must be commenced and tried in the county or district in which the cause of action arose. Suits for divorce must be commenced and tried in the county in which one of the parties resides. All other suits or actions must be commenced and tried in the county in which one or all of the defendants reside or in the county in which the transaction took place or where the wrong was committed. A tort action, for example, may be commenced and tried either in the county or district where the tort was committed or where the defendant resides. If the defendants are nonresidents, and assuming that proper service can be made on them under a long-arm statute, the suit may be commenced and tried in any county the plaintiff designates in his or her complaint.

The judge may change the place of trial at the request of either party when it appears from an affidavit of either party that the action was not commenced in the proper venue. A change of venue may also be requested on the ground that the judge has an interest in the suit or is related to any parties to the action or has manifested a prejudice that would interfere with the conduct of a fair and impartial trial. A change of venue is often requested in criminal trials when the inhabitants of the county are allegedly so prejudiced against the defendant that a fair trial is not possible. The convenience of witnesses and the parties may also justify a change of venue.

Proceedings Prior to Trial

6. Pleadings

A *pleading* is a legal document filed with the court that sets forth the position and contentions of a party. The purpose of pleadings in civil actions is to define the issues of the lawsuit. This is accomplished by each party making allegations of fact and the other party either admitting the allegations or denying them. The procedure begins when the plaintiff files with the clerk of the court a pleading, usually called a **complaint**. In some types of cases, this initial pleading is called a *declaration* or a *petition.* The clerk then issues a summons that, together with a copy of the complaint, is served on the defendant. The summons notifies the defendant of the date by which he or she is required to file a pleading in answer to the allegations of the complaint or to file some other pleading attacking the complaint.

Complaint

The first pleading, a statement of the facts on which the plaintiff rests his or her case and files a lawsuit in court

If the defendant has no legal basis to attack the sufficiency of the complaint, he or she may simply file an entry of appearance or may file an **answer** either admitting or denying each material allegation of the complaint. This answer will put in issue all allegations of the complaint that are denied. A simple entry of appearance is an admission of the truth of all allegations of the complaint.

Answer

The pleading filed by the defendant responding to the plaintiff's complaint

In addition to admissions and denials, an answer may contain affirmative defenses that, if proved, will defeat the plaintiff's claim. The answer may also contain *counterclaims,* causes of action the defendant has against the plaintiff. Upon receipt of the defendant's answer, the plaintiff will, unless the applicable rules of procedure do not so require, file a reply that specifically admits or denies each new allegation in the defendant's answer. These new allegations are those found in the affirmative defenses and counterclaims. Thus the allegations of each party are admitted or denied in the pleadings. Allegations of fact claimed by either party and denied by the other become the issues to be decided at the trial.

Default

The failure of the defendant to file an answer, that allows the court to enter a judgment for the plaintiff

A defendant who fails to answer the allegations of the plaintiff is in **default**, and a court of law may enter a default judgment against him or her. In effect, the defendant has admitted the allegations of the plaintiff. A court of equity would enter a similar order, known as a decree *pro confesso.* A plaintiff who fails to reply to new matter such as a counterclaim is also subject to a judgment or decree by default.

7. Motions Attacking Pleadings

The first pleading (complaint), to be legally sufficient, must allege facts sufficient to set forth a right of action or the plaintiff's right to legal relief. The defendant's attorney, after studying the complaint, may (instead of answering) choose one of several different ways to challenge its legal sufficiency. For example, by motion to the court, the defendant may object to the complaint, pointing out specifically its defects through a *motion to dismiss.* The defendant, through such motion, admits for purposes of argument all the facts alleged in the complaint. The defendant's position is that those facts are not legally sufficient to give the plaintiff the right to what is sought in the complaint. *Such a motion raises questions of law, not questions of fact.* If the court finds that the complaint does set forth facts sufficient to give the plaintiff what is sought, it will deny the motion. Some states require that the complaint state a cause of action. Others require only that the facts alleged establish a right to the relief sought. In either case, it is reversible error to dismiss a complaint that is legally sufficient.

If the motion is denied, the defendant will then be granted time to answer the complaint. Should the defendant fail to do so within the time limit set by the court, a judgment by default may be entered for the plaintiff. If the court finds, however, that the complaint fails to state facts sufficient to give the plaintiff the relief sought, the court will allow the motion and dismiss the suit but will give the plaintiff permission to file an amended complaint. The plaintiff will thus be given an opportunity to restate the allegations in order to set forth a right to recover from the defendant.

In addition to a *motion to dismiss* for failure to allege a valid cause of action, a defendant may also move to dismiss the suit for reasons that as a matter of law would prevent the plaintiff from winning the suit. Matters such as a discharge in bankruptcy, a lack of jurisdiction of the court to hear the suit, or an expiration of the time limit during which the defendant is subject to suit may be raised by such a motion. These are technical matters that raise questions of law for the court's decision.

To expedite litigation, many states require that all motions attacking a complaint be included with an answer to the allegations set forth in the complaint. This requirement reduces the time required for the pleading stage of the litigation.

8. Discovery Procedures

During the pleading stage and in the interval before the trial, the law provides for procedures called *discovery* procedures. Discovery is designed to take surprise out of litigation and to ensure that the results of lawsuits are based on the merits of the controversy rather than on the ability, skill, or cunning of counsel. Discovery procedures prevent a party or a witness from remaining silent about material facts. They ensure that all potential testimony and other evidence are equally available to both parties. With each side fully aware of the strengths and weaknesses of both sides, the second of the avowed purposes of discovery—to encourage settlement of suits and to avoid actual trial—is facilitated. Modern discovery procedures result in the compromise and settlement of most civil suits.

Discovery practices include written questions, called *interrogatories,* answered under oath by the opposite party and compulsory physical examinations by doctors chosen by the other party in personal injury cases. A court may order a *subpoena* that requires the production of statements, exhibits, documents, maps, photographs, and so on. Discovery, typically, also includes *depositions* (oral questioning under oath) of other parties and witnesses and serving of demands (referred to as *requests for admission*) by one party on the other to admit facts under oath. These procedures allow a party to learn not only about matters that may be used as evidence but also about matters that may lead to the discovery of evidence. The fact that evidence is relevant does not always mean that it is subject to discovery. However, the law will deny discovery when other interests, such as trade secrets, may outweigh the needs of a party to litigation.

Just prior to the trial, a *pretrial conference* between the lawyers and the judge will be held in states with modern rules of procedure. At this conference the pleadings, results of the discovery process, and probable evidence are reviewed in an attempt to settle the suit. The issues may be further narrowed, and the judge may even predict the outcome to encourage settlement.

9. Decisions Prior to a Trial

JUDGMENT ON THE PLEADINGS Most states and the federal courts also have procedures known as *motions for judgment on the pleadings,* by which either party may seek a final decision without a trial. In hearings on these motions, the court examines the pleadings on file in the case to see if a genuine material issue of fact remains. If there is no such question of fact, the court will then decide the legal question raised by the facts and find for one party or the other. In such cases, the pleadings alone establish that there is no reason for a trial, and the issues between the parties are pure questions of law.

SUMMARY JUDGMENT If a litigant asks the trial judge to decide a case based on the pleadings plus supporting materials, a *motion for summary judgment* is involved—a procedure created to avoid trials when the facts are not disputed. If the only issue before the court is the legal effect of those facts, this issue can be decided by the court on motion by one of the parties.

Affidavit

A statement of facts reduced to writing, sworn to or affirmed before some officer—usually a notary public—who is authorized to administer oath

Either party may ask the court for a summary judgment. The usual procedure is to attach to the motion the supporting **affidavits** that set forth the facts and to supplement these affidavits with depositions taken during the discovery process (discussed in detail in the preceding section). The opposing party is also permitted to file affidavits and depositions with the court. These affidavits and depositions in effect supply the court with sworn testimony. The court then examines this sworn testimony to see whether there is a genuine issue as to any material fact. If there is no such factual issue, the litigation will be decided on the facts presented to the court.

In most states, a court may render a summary judgment on the issue of liability alone and leave the amount of damages to be decided at the trial. Many of the cases set forth in later chapters of this text were decided by the summary judgment procedure. Remember that a summary judgment will not be granted when there is a disputed question of any material fact. A summary of three of the most common pretrial motions is presented in Table 3-1.

THE TRIAL

10. Jury Selection

Not every case can be settled, even under modern procedures. Some must go to trial on the issues of fact raised by pleadings that remain after the pretrial conference. If the only issues are questions of law, the court will decide the case without a trial by ruling on one of the motions previously mentioned. If the case is at law and either party has demanded a jury trial, the case

TABLE 3-1 ■ Pre-trial Motions

Motion	Description
Motion to Dismiss	Determination based on the complaint whether there is law to support the cause of action
Motion on the Pleadings	Determination as to whether there is a genuine issue as to any material fact based on the pleadings
Motion for a Summary Judgment	Determination as to whether there is a genuine issue as to any material fact based on affidavits and the pleadings

Venire
A panel of potential jurors

Voir dire
The process of questioning prospective jurors to determine their qualifications and biases

Peremptory challenge
An objection raised by a party to a lawsuit rejecting a prospective juror for which no reason need be given for the objection

will be set for trial and a jury empanelled. If the case is in equity or if no jury demand has been made, it will be set down for trial before the court. For purposes of the following discussion, we shall assume a trial before a jury.

The first step of the trial is to select the jury. Prior to calling the case, the clerk of the court will have summoned potential jurors, known as the **venire**. They will be selected at random from lists of eligible citizens, and the appropriate number (six or twelve) will be called into the jury box for the conduct of *voir dire* examination.

In ***voir dire***, the court and attorneys for each party question prospective jurors to determine their fairness and impartiality. Jurors are sworn to answer truthfully and may be challenged or excused for cause, such as bias or relation to one of the parties.

A certain number of **peremptory challenges**, for which no cause need be given, may also be exercised to reject prospective jurors. However, peremptory challenges may not be used in either civil or criminal cases to excuse jurors because of their race or gender. A defendant in either type of case is constitutionally entitled to a jury consisting of a cross-section of the community. The following case illustrates the Supreme Court's commitment to a jury selection process free from racial bias.

Potential jurors are summoned by the court clerk. The jurors are randomly selected and then questioned in order to determine their fairness and impartially.

CASE

Edmonson v. Leesville Concrete Company, Inc.

SUPREME COURT OF THE UNITED STATES

500 U.S. 614 (1991)

KENNEDY, J.

We must decide in the case before us whether a private litigant in a civil case may use peremptory challenges to exclude jurors on account of their race.

Thaddeus Donald Edmonson, a construction worker, was injured in a job-site accident. Edmonson sued Leesville Concrete Company for negligence claiming that a Leesville employee permitted one of the company's trucks to roll backward and pin him against some construction equipment. Edmonson invoked his Seventh Amendment right to a trial by jury.

During voir dire, Leesville used two of its three peremptory challenges to remove black persons from the prospective jury. As impaneled, the jury included 11 white persons and 1 black person. The jury rendered a verdict for Edmonson, assessing his total damages at $90,000. It also attributed 80% of the fault to Edmonson's contributory negligence, however, and awarded him the sum of $18,000.

Indeed, discrimination on the basis of race in selecting a jury in a civil proceeding harms the excluded juror no less than discrimination in a criminal trial. In either case, race is the sole reason for denying the excluded person the honor and privilege of participating in our system of justice.

The Constitution's protections of individual liberty and equal protection apply, in general, only to action by the government. Racial discrimination, though invidious in all contexts, violates the Constitution only when it may be attributed to state action.

Although the conduct of private parties lies beyond the Constitution's scope in most instances, governmental authority may dominate an activity to such an extent that its participants must be deemed to act with the authority of the government and, as a result, be subject to constitutional constraints.

If peremptory challenges based on race were permitted, persons could be required by summons to be put at risk of open and public discrimination as a condition of their participation in the justice system. The injury to excluded jurors would be the direct result of governmental delegation and participation.

Race discrimination within the courtroom raises serious questions as to the fairness of the proceedings conducted there. Racial bias mars the integrity of the judicial system and prevents the idea of democratic government from becoming a reality. In the many times we have addressed the problem of racial bias in our system of justice, we have not questioned the premise that racial discrimination in the qualification or selection of jurors offends the dignity of persons and the integrity of the courts.

The judgment is reversed, and the case is remanded for further proceedings consistent with our opinion.

■ *Reversed and remanded.*

CASE CONCEPTS REVIEW

1. Does it surprise you that this issue would come before the highest court in the land in the 1990s? Why or why not?
2. Does this decision protect the litigating parties' rights to a jury of their peers, or does it protect prospective jurors?

11. Proof

After selecting the jurors, the attorneys make opening statements. An opening statement is not evidence. Its purpose is to familiarize the jury with essential facts that each side expects to prove, so the jury may understand the overall picture of the case and the relevancy of each piece of evidence. After the opening statements, the plaintiff presents his or her evidence.

EVIDENCE *Evidence* is presented in open court by means of examination of witnesses and the production of documents and other exhibits. The party calling a witness questions him or her to establish the facts about the case. As a general rule, a party calling a witness is not permitted to ask *leading questions,* questions in which the desired answer is indicated by the form of the question. After the party calling the witness has completed direct examination, the other party is given the opportunity to cross-examine the witness. Matters inquired about on cross-examination are limited to those that were raised during direct examination. After cross-examination, the party calling the witness again has the opportunity to examine the witness, and this examination is called *redirect examination.* It is limited to the scope of those matters covered on cross-examination and is used to clarify matters raised on cross-examination. After redirect examination, the opposing party is allowed recross-examination, with the corresponding limitation on scope of the questions. Witnesses may be asked to identify exhibits. Expert witnesses may be asked to give their opinion, within certain limitations, about the case, and sometimes experts are allowed to answer hypothetical questions. In the conduct of a trial, *rules of evidence* govern admissibility of testimony and exhibits and establish which facts may be presented to the jury. For example, fair play requires that attorneys not be required to testify on matters told to them in confidence by their clients. Similarly, the existence of insurance coverage for a party is privileged because of the impact that knowledge of the existence of insurance would have on a jury. Jurors might award damages or increase the amount simply because of the ability of an insurance company to pay.

BURDENS OF PROOF The term *burden of proof* has two meanings. It may describe the person with the burden of coming forward with evidence on a particular issue. The party alleging the existence of a certain fact usually has the burden of coming forward with evidence to establish that fact. The more common usage of the term, however, is to identify the party with the burden of persuasion. The party with this burden must convince the trier (judge or jury) on the factual issues. If a party with the burden of persuasion fails to do so, that party loses the issue.

The extent of proof required to satisfy the burden of persuasion varies, depending on the issue and the type of case. There are three distinct levels of proof recognized by the law: (1) beyond a reasonable doubt, (2) preponderance of evidence, and (3) clear and convincing proof. For criminal cases, the burden of proof is described as *"beyond a reasonable doubt."* This means that the prosecution in a criminal case has the burden of convincing the trier of fact, usually a jury, that the defendant is guilty of the crime charged and that the jury has no reasonable doubt about guilt. This burden of proof does not require evidence beyond any doubt, but only beyond a reasonable doubt. A reasonable doubt is one that a reasonable person viewing the evidence might reasonably entertain.

In civil cases the party with the burden of proof will be subject to one of two standards: the preponderance of evidence standard or the clear and convincing proof standard. The preponderance of evidence of the evidence standard is used most frequently in civil cases. It requires that a party convince the jury by a *preponderance of evidence* that the facts are as contended. By preponderance of evidence we mean that there is greater weight of evidence in support of the proposition than there is against it.

The *clear and convincing* proof requirement is used in certain civil situations in which the law requires more than a simple preponderance of evidence but less than proof beyond a reasonable doubt. In a securities law case, proof of fraud usually requires clear and convincing evidence if a plaintiff is to succeed. A slight preponderance of evidence in favor of the party asserting the truth of a proposition is not enough. Unless the evidence clearly establishes the proposition, the party with the burden of proof fails to sustain it and loses the lawsuit.

12. Motions During Trial

A basic rule of evidence is that a party cannot introduce evidence unless it is competent and relevant to the issues raised by the pleadings. A connection between the pleadings and the trial stage of the lawsuit is also present in certain motions made during the trial. After the plaintiff has presented his or her evidence, for example, the defendant will usually make a motion for a **directed verdict**. This motion asks the court to rule as a matter of law that the plaintiff has failed to establish the case against the defendant and that a verdict should be entered for the defendant.

Directed verdict
A decision of the judge that the jury must decide, as a matter of law, in favor of one party and against the other

The court can direct a verdict for the defendant only if the evidence taken in the light most favorable to the plaintiff establishes as a matter of law that the defendant is entitled to a verdict. The defendant argues that the plaintiff has failed to prove each allegation of the complaint. Just as a plaintiff must allege certain facts or have the complaint dismissed, he or she must also have some proof of each essential allegation or lose the case on a motion for a directed verdict. If the plaintiff has some proof of each essential allegation, the motion will be denied. If a reviewing court finds that there was no evidence to support a claim, it may reverse for failure to grant a motion for a directed verdict.

If the defendant's motion for a directed verdict is denied, that party presents the evidence to support the defense. At the conclusion of the defendant's evidence, either party or both of them may make a motion for a directed verdict. If these motions are denied, the plaintiff may bring in rebuttal evidence. When neither party has any additional evidence, the attorneys and the judge retire for a conference to consider the instructions of law to be given the jury.

13. Jury Instructions

The purpose of jury instructions is to acquaint the jury with the law applicable to the case. Since the function of the jury is to find the facts, and the function of the court is to determine the applicable law, court and jury must be brought together in an orderly manner that will result in a decision. This uniting is accomplished by the court's instructing the jury, which acquaints the jury with the law applicable to the case.

To prepare instructions, the court confers with attorneys for both sides. At the conference, the attorneys submit to the court the instructions they feel should be given to the jury. The court examines these instructions and allows each side to object to the other's instructions. A party who fails to submit an instruction on a point of law cannot later object to the failure to instruct on that point. Similarly, the failure to object to an instruction is a waiver of the objection. The court then decides which instructions will be given to the jury. A jury instruction tells the jury that if it finds certain facts, then its verdict should be for the plaintiff. If it fails to find these facts, then the verdict should be for the defendant.

In the federal courts and in some state courts, judges may comment on the evidence while giving instructions. They may indicate the importance of certain portions of evidence, the inferences that might be drawn therefrom, the conflicts, and what statements are more likely to be true than others and why. The judge, however, is duty bound to make clear to the jury that it is not obligated to follow the court's evaluation of the evidence and that it is the jury's duty to determine the facts of the case.

14. Verdicts and Judgments

After the conference on jury instructions, the attorneys argue the case before the jury. The party with the burden of proof, usually the plaintiff, is given an opportunity to open the argument and to close it. The defendant's attorney is allowed to argue only after the plaintiff's argument and is allowed to argue only once. After the arguments are completed, the court gives instructions to the jury. The jury then retires to deliberate. In some states, the jurors take written instructions with them to the jury room. In others, they must remember the instructions.

Verdict
The decision of a jury, reported to the court, on matters properly submitted to the jury for consideration

Upon reaching a **verdict**, the jury returns from the jury room and announces its verdict. There are two kinds of verdicts—general and special. A *general verdict* is one in which the jury makes a complete finding and single conclusion on all issues presented to it. First, the jury finds the facts, as proved by the evidence, then it applies the law as instructed by the court, and finally it returns a verdict in one conclusion that settles the case. Such verdict is reported as follows: "We the jury find the issues for the plaintiff [or defendant, as the case may be] and assess his damages at one hundred thousand dollars." The jury usually does not make separate findings of fact or report what law is applied.

After the verdict is announced, a judgment is entered. A judgment entered by a court of law is similar, in its impact, to a final decree entered by a court in equity.

PROCEEDINGS AFTER THE TRIAL

15. Post-Trial Motions

After the judgment is entered, the losing party starts the procedure of post-trial motions, which raise *questions of law* concerning the conduct of the lawsuit. These motions seek relief such as a new trial or a judgment notwithstanding the verdict of the jury. A *motion seeking a new trial* may be granted if the judge feels that the verdict of the jury is contrary to the manifest weight of the evidence. A *motion for a judgment notwithstanding the verdict* may be granted if the judge finds that the verdict is, as a matter of law, erroneous. To reach such a conclusion, the court must find that reasonable people viewing the evidence could not reach the verdict returned. For example, a verdict for the plaintiff based on sympathy instead of evidence could be set aside.

After the judge rules on the post-trial motion, the losing party may appeal. The right to appeal is absolute if perfected within the prescribed time. All litigants are entitled to a trial and a review, provided that the proper procedures are followed.

Lawsuits usually end by ruling on a motion, either before the trial, during the trial, or after the trial. Motions raise questions of law that are decided by the court. The appeal usually is based on the trial judge's ruling on one of these motions.

16. Appeals

A dissatisfied party—plaintiff or defendant—has a right to appeal the decision of the trial court to a higher court, provided that he or she proceeds promptly and properly. In the case of this first level appeal, sometimes termed an *appeal by right,* the appellate court must grant a hearing and hear the case. Beyond this first level appeal, typically, an appellate court has an option as to whether to take the case. This is called a *discretionary appeal.* For example, since most appeals to the United States Supreme Court are discretionary, that court actually hears less than five percent of the cases that they are asked to review.

APPELLATE PROCEDURE Appellate procedures are not uniform among the states, and the appellant must comply with the appropriate statute and rules of the particular court. Appeals are usually perfected by the appellant's giving *notice of appeal* to the trial court and opposing parties. This notice of appeal must be filed within a statutory time period (usually thirty days) after the trial court has entered a final judgment or order. Failure to file the notice of appeal on time denies the appellate court jurisdiction.

Most states require that within at least ten days after giving notice of appeal the appellant must file an appeal bond, in effect guaranteeing to pay costs that may be charged against him or her on the appeal. This bond permits the appellee (respondent) to collect costs if the appellant loses an appeal.

The statutes usually require that within a specified time after an appeal is perfected, the appellant shall file with the clerk of the appellate court a *transcript,* consisting of a record of the testimony, a copy of the judgment, decree, or order appealed from, and other papers required by rules of the court.

The transcript alone, however, is not enough to present the case to the appellate court. The appellant must prepare and file a *"brief"* that contains a statement of the case, a list of the assignment of errors on which the appellant has based the appeal, and the appellant's legal authorities and argument. The brief contains the arguments on both fact and law by which the attorney attempts to show how the lower court committed the errors alleged.

The appellee files a brief of like character—setting out his or her side of the case with points, authorities, and arguments. By such procedure, the case on the issues raised goes to the appellate court for decision.

ROLE OF APPELLATE COURT The appellate court, on receipt of an appeal by right, will place it on the calendar for hearing. Attorneys will be notified of the time and will be given an opportunity for oral argument. After the oral argument, the court prepares a written opinion stating the applicable law involved and giving the reasons for its decision. If the case has already been heard on appeal, then the next highest court must decide whether to hear the discretionary appeal. If that court grants a hearing, then the court will place the case on the court's calendar.

The court, by its decision, may *affirm* or *reverse* the court below, or the court may *remand* (send back) the case for a new trial. At the end of each published opinion found in the reports, a word or a few words will express the court's decision: affirmed, reversed, reversed and remanded, or whatever the case requires.

The appellate courts basically review the legal rulings made by the trial judge. Very seldom will the jury or judge's factual findings be reversed during the appeals process. Since those at the trial had an opportunity to see and hear the witnesses in person, their determination of the factual situation is presumed to be accurate. In other words, the reviewing court will not disturb the trial court's findings of fact unless such findings are clearly erroneous.

CHAPTER SUMMARY

BASIC PRINCIPLES

Parties

1. The names used to describe the parties in litigation vary depending on the type of lawsuit and the stage of the litigation.
2. Cases on appeal are usually titled in the name of the appellant versus the appellee (respondent).

Standing to Sue

1. A plaintiff must have standing to sue.
2. Standing requires that the plaintiff have an actual stake in the controversy such that all issues will be adequately raised.
3. One person often brings suit on behalf of a class.

THE PLACE OF LITIGATION

Jurisdiction

1. To render a binding decision, a court must have jurisdiction over the subject matter of the litigation and over the parties.
2. Jurisdiction over the defendant is usually obtained by the service of a summons. In some cases, jurisdiction may be obtained by publishing a notice in the newspaper.

Long-Arm Statutes

1. A summons may be served beyond the borders of the state if the state has a long-arm statute. This service is not a denial of due process if the defendant has sufficient contact

with the state issuing the summons such that requiring him or her to defend the lawsuit does not offend our traditional notions of fair play and substantial justice.

2. A plaintiff may file a lawsuit in a state without minimum contact since the plaintiff is voluntarily submitting to the jurisdiction of the court.

Venue

1. *Jurisdiction* is the power to hear a case. The term venue is used to describe the appropriate court among all those with jurisdiction to hear the case.

PROCEEDINGS PRIOR TO TRIAL

Pleadings

1. The term *pleadings* is used to describe papers filed with the court by the parties to create the issues for trial.
2. The plaintiff makes allegations in a complaint, and the defendant answers the complaint by admitting or denying each allegation of the complaint.
3. The answer may contain counterclaims of the defendant, and in some states the plaintiff must file a reply to all new matters raised in the answer.

MOTIONS ATTACKING PLEADINGS

1. Many cases are decided on motions attacking pleadings. The law requires certain minimal allegations; and if each of these allegations is not present, a court may dismiss the complaint.
2. Motions may also be filed during the pleading stage that raise technical matters such as bankruptcy, illegality, or other matters that would indicate that a trial was unnecessary.

Discovery Procedures

1. During the pleading stage and thereafter, the law has several techniques that the parties use to discover facts known by the other.
2. These techniques include the taking of depositions, the furnishing of copies of documents and photographs, serving interrogatories, and compulsory physical examinations.
3. The purpose of discovery is to encourage settlement and to take the surprise element out of litigation.
4. At the close of discovery, the parties and the judge meet at a pretrial conference to finish narrowing the issues for trial and to settle the case, if possible.

Decisions Prior to Trial

1. If during the pleading stage it appears that there is no material fact in dispute, then there is no need for a trial.
2. The court will decide the questions of law raised by the pleadings and other documents on file.
3. This decision may be a judgment on the pleadings, or it may be a summary judgment.

THE TRIAL

Proof

1. In selecting the jury, each party is entitled to challenge any potential juror for cause.

2. In addition, each party is given a specified number of peremptory challenges to reject potential jurors without giving a reason.
3. The parties attempt to prove their factual contentions by introducing evidence in open court. Evidence is presented through questioning of witnesses, with the opposing party being given the right of cross-examination.

Burdens of Proof

1. The term *burden of proof* is used to describe the party that is required to come forward with evidence on a certain point. It is also used to describe the party with the burden of persuasion.
2. The law imposes three levels in satisfying the burden of persuasion. In criminal cases, the burden is beyond a reasonable doubt. In most civil cases, the burden is by a preponderance of greater weight of the evidence. In some special situations, there is a burden between these other two that is known as the clear and convincing proof standard.

Motions During Trial

1. At the close of the plaintiff's case, a defendant will ordinarily make a motion for a directed verdict.
2. The court will grant this motion and order the jury to return a verdict for the defendant if the evidence considered in the light most favorable to the plaintiff will not support a verdict for the plaintiff.
3. The motion will be denied if there is any evidence to support each allegation of the complaint.
4. In cases tried without a jury, either party may move for a finding in his or her favor if the result is not in doubt.

Jury Instructions

1. After the parties have introduced all their evidence, the court instructs the jury on the law applicable to the case.
2. Jury instructions tell the jury that if it finds certain facts, then it should reach a certain result.

Verdicts and Judgments

1. The decision of a jury is known as a verdict.
2. The final decision of the court, based on the verdict, is known as a judgment.

PROCEEDINGS AFTER THE TRIAL

Post-Trial Motions

1. The losing party before the trial judge ordinarily files a post-trial motion. In this post trial motion, the losing party seeks either a new trial or a judgment in its favor notwithstanding the verdict.
2. It is from the ruling on this post-trial motion that the losing party appeals.

Appeals

1. Appeals are costly and time-consuming. The party must obtain a transcript of the proceedings before the trial court and excerpt therefrom the matters to be raised on appeal. A brief must be prepared containing the points to be considered by the reviewing court and a party's legal authorities in support of the appeal.
2. The issues before the reviewing court are essentially questions of law, and great deference is given the findings of fact at the trial level.

Review Questions and Problems

1. Match each term in Column A with the appropriate statement in Column B.

A	B
(1) Plaintiff	(a) The proper court in which to conduct a trial
(2) Venue	(b) When served with a summons, this person is subject to the jurisdiction of the court.
(3) Beyond a reasonable doubt	(c) A person bringing a lawsuit
(4) Long-arm statute	(d) A defendant who seeks damages from a plaintiff
(5) Counterplaintiff	(e) A law that authorizes the service of a summons beyond the border of the state
(6) Preponderance of the evidence	(f) A final decision without a trial because no facts are in dispute
(7) *Voir dire* examination	(g) The removal of a prospective juror for which no cause need be given
(8) Peremptory challenge	(h) The questioning of prospective jurors as to their qualifications of be fair and impartial
(9) Defendant	(i) The burden of proof standard in criminal cases
(10) Summary judgment	(j) The usual burden of proof standard in civil cases

2. The Sierra Club, an organization devoted to the conservation and maintenance of national forests, sued the Secretary of the Interior to prevent federal approval of an extensive skiing development. The secretary asked the court to dismiss the suit on the ground that the plaintiffs lacked standing to sue. What was the result? Why?

3. A paving contractor, incorporated in Delaware with its principal place of business in Indiana, was hired to oil and chip streets in a mobile home park located in Urbana, Illinois. Heavy winds developed during the spraying of oil on the street, and a light film of oil was sprayed on thirty-six mobile homes, doing approximately $500 damage to each. A class-action suit was filed in federal court seeking $18,000 damages. Does the court have jurisdiction? Explain.

4. An accounting firm incorporated in Oregon performed accounting services in California in connection with a merger. A dispute arose later, and the corporation was sued in California. The summons was served in Oregon, as authorized by the California long-arm statute. The accounting firm objected to the jurisdiction of the court. Did the California court have jurisdiction over the defendant? Why?

5. Pauline filed a complaint for divorce against Daniel. The complaint and summons were left with Daniel's secretary at his office while he was out of town. Was Daniel properly served with these process papers? Why?

6. Geraldine's car had been illegally repossessed in Texas by the Baker Bank, a federally chartered national bank located in the state of Tennessee. The National Bank Act requires that Suits against national banks be brought in the county in which the bank is located. Geraldine sued the bank in Texas, and it moved to dismiss, contending that the suit could not be brought in Texas. Should the court grant or deny this motion? Why?

7. Ron sues Walter for personal injuries arising from an automobile accident. Walter was allegedly driving under the influence of alcohol at the time of the accident. An investigation reveals that the list of prospective jurors includes a relative of Ron and the owner of a package liquor store. Walter does not want his case to be tried by a jury that includes these persons. What can he do? Explain.
8. Bruce was killed by the explosion of a steel drum that he was cutting with a circular saw. In a wrongful death action brought by the plaintiff, Pearl, administratrix of his estate, against the defendant, Dorsey Trailers, Inc., the defendant served interrogatories on the plaintiff seeking information concerning the facts and circumstances that supported the plaintiffs claim that the defendant was responsible for the death. The interrogatories requested information about the decedent's medical history, work history, and educational background. In addition, the defendant requested the identities of expert witnesses to be called by the plaintiff and the substance of their testimony. When the plaintiff refused to answer the questions, the defendant asked the trial judge to compel answers to the interrogatories. When the trial judge refused to grant the defendant's request, the defendant appealed. Did the trial judge abuse his discretion in not compelling answers to the interrogatories? Why?
9. Robert borrowed $900,000 on behalf of his company, RRR&G, Inc. Robert signed a promissory note payable to Farmers Bank of Delaware on behalf of the corporation and as a personal guarantor. Farmers Bank had financial difficulty, and as a result it sold many of its notes to the FDIC. Among these notes purchased by the FDIC was the RRR&G note, which was guaranteed by Robert. RRR&G filed for bankruptcy, and the FDIC sued Robert personally for payment of the $900,000 owed. The FDIC presented photocopies of the promissory note and personal guaranty. Robert objected to these copies being admitted as evidence, since they were not the original notes. Should the photocopies be admitted into evidence in lieu of the original note and guaranty agreement? Why?
10. Pat sued Vince for breach of contract. Pat testified that Vince had agreed to work as a salesman for a 10 percent commission. Vince testified that the commission was to be 15 percent. There were no witnesses to the conversation that created the oral contract. Assume that the case is tried before a jury.

    a. Which party has the burden of producing evidence as to the terms of the contract? Why?
    b. Which party has the burden of persuasion?
    c. What standard of proof is required? Explain.
    d. Is it possible for the jury to find for Pat without any corroborating evidence?

    Explain.

Internet Sources

The National Center for State Courts Web site provides access to all state court Web sites. The Center's Courts Web address is:

http://www.ncsconline.org/D_KIS/info_court_web_sites.html

Alternatives for Resolving Controversies | 4

CHAPTER OUTLINE

COMPROMISES

1. Reasons to Settle
2. Mediation

ARBITRATION

3. Advantages
4. Common-Law Arbitration
5. Types of Arbitration Systems
6. General Aspects of Arbitration
7. The Submission
8. The Award
9. Procedures in Arbitration
10. Judicial Review of Arbitration Issues

CHAPTER PREVIEW

In the preceding chapter the process of litigation was described, emphasizing the expense of time and money associated with it. Because litigation often is an inefficient way to resolve business-related disputes, business people look for alternative ways to resolve these disputes. This chapter presents three basic approaches designed to help avoid litigation.

The most common alternative is for the parties to compromise their positions and settle their disagreement, usually through a process of *negotiation.* This method of creating a contract or ending a dispute only involves the parties impacted. If a third person is engaged to assist the parties, then the second approach covered in this chapter, *mediation,* could be quite helpful. The mediation process can be a positive step in accomplishing a settlement because it usually occurs in a non-confrontational environment. Mediation is especially common in a union environment or other situation where it is assumed that the parties will continue to deal with one another. A third important method of resolving disputes is *arbitration.* This process involves the parties submitting their controversy to a nonjudicial body for a binding decision. Today, more and more unresolved business-related disputes are being submitted to arbitration because it usually consumes less time and money than litigation.

BUSINESS MANAGEMENT DECISION

As president of a construction company, you have successfully bid to build a large office building. You realize, from past experience, that issues will arise with the architect and the owner during this construction project.

How do you provide for a resolution of these potential issues?

COMPROMISES

1. Reasons to Settle

Most disputes are resolved by the parties involved, without resort to litigation or to arbitration. Only a small fraction of the disputes in our society end up in court or even in a lawyer's office. Among the multitude of reasons why a negotiated compromise is so prevalent a technique for settling disputes, some may be described as personal and others as economic.

PERSONAL The desire to compromise is almost instinctive. Most of us dislike trouble, and many fear going to court. Our moral and ethical values encourage compromise and settlement. Opinions of persons other than the parties to the dispute are often an influential, motivating force in many compromises, adding external forces to the internal ones that encourage people to settle their differences amicably.

ECONOMIC Compromise and settlement of disputes are also encouraged by the economics of many situations. Lawsuits are expensive to both parties. As a general rule, both parties must pay their own attorney's fees, and the losing party must pay court costs. As a matter of practical economics, the winning party in a lawsuit is a loser to the extent of the attorney's fees, which are often quite substantial.

At least two additional facts of economic life encourage business to settle disputes out of court. First, business must be concerned with its public image and the goodwill of its customers. The motto "The customer is always right" and the influence of the philosophy it represents cannot be underestimated. It often is simply not good business to sue a customer. Second, juries are frequently sympathetic to individuals who have suits against large corporations or defendants who are covered by insurance. Close questions of liability, as well as the size of verdicts, are more often than not resolved against business concerns because of their presumed ability to pay. As a result, business seeks to settle many disputes rather than submit them to a jury for decision.

OBLIGATION OF LAWYERS The duty of lawyers to seek and achieve compromise whenever possible may not be understood by laypersons. In providing services, lawyers devote a substantial amount of their time, energy, and talent to seeking a compromise solution of the disputes involving their clients. In most cases attempts to compromise will be made before resort to the courts. Of all the disputes that are the subject of legal advice, the great majority are settled without resort to litigation. Of those that do result in litigation, the great majority are settled before the case goes to trial or even during the trial. Literally, the attempt of the lawyers to resolve the dispute never ends. It occurs before suit, before and during the trial, after verdict, during appeal, and even after appeal. As long as there is a controversy, it is the function of lawyers to attempt to resolve it.

Lawyers can be very effective in *negotiating* on behalf of their clients. While not all contracts or disputes need to be solved through negotiation skills possessed by attorneys, many businesses will hire lawyers to serve as their negotiator. As the following case illustrates, however, the interactive nature of negotiation may result in a binding agreement, or it may not.

CASE

Burbach Broadcasting Company of Delaware v. Elkins Radio Corporation; Cat Radio Incorporated

UNITED STATES COURT OF APPEALS FOR THE FOURTH CIRCUIT

278 F.3d 401 (2002)

GREGORY, CIRCUIT JUDGE

Burbach Broadcasting brought suit against Elkins Radio for breach of contract and specific performance based on an alleged agreement made between the parties for the purchase of Elkins' radio station assets. The agreement Burbach sought to enforce took the form of a letter of intent, signed by the parties on October 2, 1998. The district court granted judgment on the pleadings, finding that the letter of intent was not binding because it was subject at all times to the negotiation and execution of a mutually agreeable asset purchase agreement, and no such agreement was ever reached by the parties. Burbach contends that the letter of intent contained all the elements of a complete, binding and enforceable contract and that the lack of an asset purchase agreement does not affect Elkins' obligation to sell the assets. It argues that it could waive the provision calling for an asset purchase agreement because the sole purpose of that provision was to protect itself, due to limited information provided by Elkins. In the alternative, Burbach contends that the letter of intent was, at a minimum, a binding agreement obligating the parties to negotiate in good faith towards a final contract. We find that the complaint adequately states a claim on which relief can be granted, and because the parties' intent to be bound cannot be discerned on the face of the pleadings alone, we vacate and remand to the district court for further proceedings.

In September of 1998, Elkins Radio, through its agent, submitted a written offering document to Burbach Broadcasting regarding the sale of Elkins' radio station assets in West Virginia. In the offering, Elkins proposed to sell the station assets for "$3.6 million on terms." The offering stated that Elkins sought the sale due to retirement of its owner.

After numerous discussions and meetings, the parties signed what was termed a "Letter of Intent" on October 2, 1998. The five-page letter was written on Burbach letterhead. Burbach's president, Nicholas Galli, authorized the letter, which was addressed to Richard McGraw, president of Elkins Radio. It was faxed to Richard McGraw at approximately 4:30 p.m. on October 2, 1998, and if Mr. McGraw had not signed it by 5:00 p.m. that same day, it would have become null and void.

One of the last paragraphs in the letter stated: "Upon execution by the parties herein and subject at all times to the terms herein, this Letter of Intent shall be binding on and enforceable by the parties hereto." The letter of intent was to expire by its own terms if an asset purchase agreement was not executed by 5:00 p.m. on October 22, 1998, provided that a party was not in material breach or had not unreasonably caused a delay.

The court dismissed the complaint with prejudice, concluding that the letter of intent was not enforceable as a purchase agreement and that it expired by its own terms when the parties failed to negotiate and execute a mutually agreeable asset purchase agreement. Burbach appeals the decision granting judgment on the pleadings.

continued

Burbach cannot prevail on either theory if the parties did not intend to be bound by the letter of intent. It is fundamental to contract law that mere participation in negotiations does not create a binding obligation, even if agreement is reached on all terms. More is needed than agreement on each detail—the parties must have intended to enter into a binding agreement. The district court ruled on Elkins' motion for judgment on the pleadings that the letter was not intended to be binding on the parties.

We find, due to ambiguous language in the letter, that intent cannot be discerned on the face of this letter of intent. When intent is not clear from the face of a document, whether parties negotiating a contract intended to be bound by a writing or whether they did not intend to be bound until a formal agreement was prepared and signed by them must be determined from the facts and circumstances in each case. For this reason, and because the district court considered some matters outside the pleadings, we remand to the district court for determination, based on a full record, of whether the letter falls into one of the two types of preliminary agreements that can be binding on the parties.

Letters of intent have led to much misunderstanding, litigation, and commercial chaos. Courts have expressed reservation concerning the binding nature of "letters of intent" because, traditionally, the purpose and function of a preliminary letter of intent has been to merely provide the initial framework from which the parties might later negotiate a final binding agreement. Calling a document a "letter of intent" implies, *unless circumstances suggest otherwise,* that the parties intended it to be a nonbinding expression in contemplation of a future contract.

A trial on the merits may be warranted if disputed issues of fact remain. We decline to make an immediate determination of the issue because the record we have before us does not clearly indicate whether summary judgment should be granted or denied.

■ *Vacated and remanded.*

CASE CONCEPTS REVIEW

1. What evidence exists that a contract was formed based on the negotiations? What evidence exists that no contract was formed?
2. How could the letter of intent have been clearer on whether it was a contract?

Lawyers on both sides of a controversy seek compromise for a variety of reasons. A lawyer may view the client's case as weak, either on the law or on the facts. The amount of money involved, the necessity for a speedy decision, the nature of the contest, the uncertainty of legal remedy, the unfavorable publicity, and the expense entailed are some other reasons for avoiding a court trial. Each attorney must evaluate the client's cause and seek a satisfactory—though not necessarily the most desirable—settlement of the controversy. The settlement of disputes is perhaps the most significant contribution of lawyers to our society.

2. Mediation

Mediation

The process involving a third party's efforts to help disputing parties reach a settlement

The term **mediation** describes the process by which a third person assists the parties to a controversy when they seek a compromise. Although a mediator cannot impose a binding solution on the parties, a disinterested and objective mediator is often able to bring about a compromise that is satisfactory to the parties.

The mediation of labor disputes is the function of the National Mediation and Conciliation Service. This government agency, staffed with skilled negotiators, has assisted in the settlement of countless labor disputes. Mediation is playing an expanding role in the relationship between the business community and the consuming public. Better Business Bureaus and others are serving as mediators of consumer complaints and, on occasion, as arbitrators under arbitration agreements. Their efforts have resolved thousands of consumer complaints, in part because they provide some third parties to whom a consumer can turn.

Congress has expressed its support for mediation. The Magnuson-Moss Warranty Act provides that if a business adopts an informal dispute-resolution system to handle complaints about its product warranties, then a customer cannot sue the manufacturer or seller for breach of warranty without first going through the informal procedures. This law does not deny consumers the right to sue, nor does it compel a compromise solution. It simply favors mediation by requiring an attempt at settlement before litigation.

ARBITRATION

3. Advantages

Arbitration

The procedure used, as an alternative to litigation, to submit a dispute to one or more third parties who have authority to impose a resolution to the dispute

There are several advantages to using **arbitration** as a substitute for litigation. For one thing, it is much quicker and far less expensive. An issue can be submitted to arbitration and decided in less time than it takes to complete the pretrial phase of a lawsuit. Then, too, arbitration creates less hostility than litigation, and it allows the parties to continue their business relationship somewhat more peacefully while the dispute is being decided. Arbitration also provides for a decision without resort to a tribunal and allows for a hearing to be conducted without the rigid formality of strict rules of law. Arbitration is favored today because it eases the congestion of court calendars. Finally, under the arbitration process, complex issues can be submitted to an expert for decision. For example, if an issue arises concerning the construction of a building, in arbitration it can be submitted to an architect for decision. Lawyers and other specialists frequently serve as arbitrators, physicians decide issues relating to physical disabilities, certified public accountants deal with those regarding the book value of stock, and engineers decide issues relating to industrial production. A substantial amount of arbitration is also conducted by the academic community, especially in the area of labor relations.

For these reasons, arbitration as a substitute for litigation is becoming increasingly useful to business. Commercial arbitration clauses are being added to many business contracts. The American Arbitration Association will furnish experienced arbitrators for parties in a dispute, and many standard contract clauses provide for submission to this group. Since arbitration costs are deductible business expenses, this speedy, inexpensive solution to conflicts should be carefully considered by business and legal counsel in all possible areas of dispute.

The law may require arbitration for certain cases. For example, some states have passed laws requiring cases involving small dollar claims (less than $15,000) to be arbitrated rather than litigated. These cases are referred to as *statutory-* or *court-annexed arbitrations.* More frequently, contracting patties agree to arbitrate their disputes voluntarily in accordance with a contractual provision to submit a dispute to arbitration rather than litigation. Since the right is based on a contract, the parties are obligated to arbitrate only those issues they have agreed to arbitrate.

4. Common-Law Arbitration

Arbitration was recognized by the common law. It has been the subject of legislation in many states and by the federal government. Arbitration at common law was not a matter of right but was based on an agreement to arbitrate. The agreement to arbitrate was revocable until the time of the final award because it required continued consent of the parties. Thus, a party who felt that the proceeding was not going favorably would frequently withdraw by repudiating the agreement. When this occurred, the other party could sue for breach of contract, but any recovery was limited to the expenses incurred to date in the proceedings.

A distinction existed at common law between an agreement to arbitrate an existing dispute and an agreement to submit future disputes to arbitration. The latter agreement was unenforceable, and a party that refused to arbitrate when a dispute arose had no liability.

5. Types of Arbitration Systems

The various states have taken four distinct approaches to arbitration. A few have not enacted arbitration legislation. In these states, the principles of the common law are applicable. An agreement to arbitrate is revocable, but a final award is enforceable. Other states have enacted statutes that cover only the method of enforcing awards. These states have taken advantage of the cost-savings and time-reduction aspects of arbitration by eliminating the necessity for a suit on an award. In these states, an agreement to arbitrate is revocable, but there is a quick and inexpensive method for enforcing the award, if rendered.

Submission

The act of the disputing parties to refer an issue to the arbitration process (See Section 7)

Award

The decision of the arbitrator (See Section 8)

The majority of states fall into a third category. They have enacted comprehensive arbitration statutes that cover all aspects of **submission**, the **award**, and its enforcement. They also recognize common-law arbitration. An arbitration agreement is revocable if common-law arbitration is being used, but it is not revocable if the statutory method is being used. If a question arises about which method the parties are using, this matter is resolved by reference to the statute. If all the statutory requirements are met in the submission agreement, the arbitration agreement is irrevocable. If any of the statutory requirements for a submission are not met, the arbitration is subject to the common-law principles and the agreement to arbitrate is revocable.

The fourth and final approach to arbitration legislated by some states makes the statutory method exclusive. In these states, the statutory requirements for submission must be met, and all proceedings must comply with the statute. Failure to comply with any portion of the statute renders the agreement and the award, if any, a nullity. Statutory compliance makes the agreement irrevocable and the award enforceable.

6. General Aspects of Arbitration Statutes

The Commissioners on Uniform State Laws have prepared a Uniform Arbitration Act. There is also a Federal Arbitration Act, which covers businesses engaged in maritime and interstate commerce. Both statutes authorize and encourage voluntary arbitration,

Most statutes authorizing voluntary arbitration require a written agreement to arbitrate. Written agreements are required as a corollary of the provision that makes the agreement to arbitrate irrevocable. It should be remembered, however, that in many states failure to follow the statute is not completely ineffective because common-law arbitration procedures may be followed as an alternative.

Consistent with the goal of arbitration to obtain a quick resolution of disputes, most statutes require submission within a stated time after the dispute arises—usually six months. These statutes recognize, too, that arbitration contracts can be rescinded on the same grounds used for any other contract. Fraud, mutual mistake, or lack of capacity would be grounds for avoiding arbitration contracts. Revocation by operation of law is provided for also on the death, bankruptcy, or insanity of a party, or by destruction of the subject matter of the agreement.

While an agreement to submit disputes to arbitration is binding in many circumstances, courts recognize that the parties may waive the right to arbitrate. The following case, dealing with an employment contract, addresses the issue of under what conditions will a court uphold a requirement in the contract mandating the use of arbitration.

7. The Submission

Submission is the act of referring an issue or issues to the arbitration process. The submitted issues may be factual, legal, or both; they may include questions concerning the interpretation of the arbitration agreement. The scope of the arbitrator's powers is controlled by the language of the submission. Doubts concerning whether or not the subject matter of a dispute can be arbitrated are usually resolved in favor of arbitration. When a contract leaves it up to the court to determine whether or not arbitration is possible, an order to arbitrate a particular grievance will not be denied unless it may be said with positive assurance that the arbitration clause is not susceptible to interpretation that covers the asserted dispute.

CASE

Marybeth Armendariz, et al. v. Foundation Health Psychcare Services, Inc.

SUPREME COURT OF CALIFORNIA

24 Cal. 4th 83 (2000)

MOSK, J.

Marybeth Armendariz and Dolores Olague-Rodgers (hereafter the employees) filed a complaint for wrongful termination against their former employer, Foundation Health Psychcare Services, Inc. (hereafter the employer). The complaint and certain documents filed in support of the employer's petition to compel arbitration provide us with the basic factual background of this case. In July and August of 1995, the employer hired the employees in the "Provider Relations Group" and they were later given supervisory positions with annual salaries of $38,000. On June 20, 1996, they were informed that their positions were being eliminated and that they were being terminated. During their year of employment, they claim that their supervisors and coworkers engaged in sexually based harassment and discrimination. The employees alleged that they were "terminated … because of their perceived and/or actual sexual orientation (heterosexual)."

Both employees had filled out and signed employment application forms, which included an arbitration clause pertaining to any future claim of wrongful termination. Later, they executed a separate employment arbitration agreement, containing the same arbitration clause. The clause states in full: "I agree as a condition of my employment, that in the event my employment is terminated, and I contend that such termination was wrongful or otherwise in violation of the conditions of employment or was in violation of any express or implied condition, term or covenant of employment, whether founded in fact or in law, including but not limited to the covenant of good faith and fair dealing, or otherwise in violation of any of my rights, I and Employer agree to submit any such matter to binding arbitration pursuant to the provisions of title 9 of Part III of the California Code of Civil Procedure, commencing at section 1280 et seq. or any successor or replacement statutes. I and Employer further expressly agree that in any such arbitration, my exclusive remedies for violation of the terms, conditions or covenants of employment shall be limited to a sum equal to the wages I would have earned from the date of any discharge until the date of the arbitration award. I understand that I shall not be entitled to any other remedy, at law or in equity, including but not limited to reinstatement and/or injunctive relief."

The employees' complaint against the employer alleges a cause of action for violation of the Fair Employment and Housing Act (FEHA) and three additional causes of action for wrongful termination based on tort and contract theories of recovery. The complaint sought general damages, punitive damages, injunctive relief, and the recovery of attorney fees and costs of suit. The employer countered by filing a motion for an order to compel arbitration.

A. FEHA Claim

Of course, certain statutory rights can be waived, but arbitration agreements that encompass unwaivable statutory rights must be subject to particular scrutiny.

1. **Limitation of Remedies** The principle that an arbitration agreement may not limit statutorily imposed remedies such as punitive damages and attorney fees appears to be undisputed. As stated, the arbitration agreement in this case provides in part, "I and Employer further expressly agree that in any such arbitration, my exclusive remedies for violation of the terms, conditions or covenants of employment shall be limited to a sum equal to the wages I would have earned from the date of any discharge until the date of the arbitration award. I understand that I shall not be entitled to any other remedy, at law or in equity, including but not limited to reinstatement and/or injunctive relief." The employees claim that the agreement compels them to arbitrate statutory claims without affording the full range of statutory remedies, including punitive damages and attorney fees to a prevailing plaintiff, available under the FEHA. We conclude this damages limitation is contrary to public policy and unlawful.
2. **Written Arbitration Award and Judicial Review** The employees argue that lack of judicial review of arbitration awards makes the vindication of FEHA rights in arbitration illusory. All we hold today is that in order for such judicial review to be successfully accomplished an arbitrator in a FEHA case must issue a written arbitration decision that will reveal, however briefly, the essential findings and conclusions on which the award is based. In all other respects, the employees' claim that they are unable to vindicate their FEHA rights because of inadequate judicial review of an arbitration award is premature.
3. **Employee Not to Pay Unreasonable Costs and Arbitration Fees** The employees point to the fact that the agreement is governed by Code of Civil Procedure section 1284.2, which provides that "each party to the arbitration shall pay his pro rata share of the expenses and fees of the neutral arbitrator, together with other expenses of the arbitration incurred or approved by the neutral arbitrator. …" They argue that requiring parties to share the often-substantial costs of arbitrators and arbitration effectively prevents them from vindicating their FEHA rights. Accordingly, consistent with the majority of jurisdictions to consider this issue, we conclude that when an employer imposes mandatory arbitration as a condition of employment, the arbitration agreement or arbitration process cannot generally require the employee to bear any type of expense that the employee would not be required to bear if he or she were free to bring the action in court. This rule will ensure that employees bringing FEHA claims will not be deterred by costs greater than the usual costs incurred during litigation, costs that are essentially imposed on an employee by the employer.

continued

B. Unconscionability and Mandatory Employment Arbitration

Applying the above principles to this case, we first determine whether the arbitration agreement is adhesive. There is little dispute that it is. It was imposed on employees as a condition of employment, and there was no opportunity to negotiate.

Moreover, in the case of pre-employment arbitration contracts, the economic pressure exerted by employers on all but the most sought-after employees may be particularly acute, for the arbitration agreement stands between the employee and necessary employment; few employees are in a position to refuse a job because of an arbitration requirement. While arbitration may have its advantages in terms of greater expedition, informality, and lower cost, it also has, from the employee's point of view, potential disadvantages: waiver of a right to a jury trial, limited discovery, and limited judicial review. Various studies show that arbitration is advantageous to employers not only because it reduces the costs of litigation, but also because it reduces the size of the award that an employee is likely to get, particularly if the employer is a "repeat player" in the arbitration system. It is perhaps for this reason that it is almost invariably the employer who seeks to compel arbitration.

Aside from FEHA issues discussed in the previous part of this opinion, the employees contend that the agreement is substantively unconscionable because it requires only employees to arbitrate their wrongful termination claims against the employer, but does not require the employer to arbitrate claims it may have against the employees. Given the disadvantages that may exist for plaintiffs arbitrating disputes, it is unfairly one-sided for an employer with superior bargaining power to impose arbitration on the employee as plaintiff but not to accept such limitations when it seeks to prosecute a claim against the employee, without at least some reasonable justification for such one-sidedness based on "business realities."

■ *The judgment of the Court of Appeal upholding the employer's petition to compel arbitration is reversed, and the cause is remanded to the Court of Appeal with directions to affirm the judgment of the trial court.*

CASE CONCEPTS REVIEW

1. Should the parties be able to negotiate contractual provisions without interference from the courts? Why or why not?
2. Does the decision of this case effectively prohibit the use of arbitration in any type of employment agreement? Why?

Submission may occur under two circumstances. First, the parties may enter into an agreement to arbitrate an existing dispute. The arbitration agreement serves as the "submission" in this case. Second, the parties may contractually agree to submit to arbitration all issues that *may* arise, or they may agree that either party *may* demand arbitration of any issue that arises. Submission to arbitration under the second circumstance occurs when a demand to arbitrate is served on the other party. This demand may take the form of a notice that a matter is being referred to the arbitrator agreed upon by the parties, or it may be a demand that the matter be referred to arbitration. Merely informing the other party that a controversy exists is not an act of submission nor is it a demand for arbitration.

8. The Award

The decision of the arbitrator, the *award*, is binding on all issues submitted and may be judicially enforced. Every presumption is in favor of the validity of an arbitration award, and doubts are resolved in its favor. The scope of judicial review of an award is limited in most states by statute as well as by the agreement to arbitrate. Any challenge to an award on the ground that the arbitrator exceeded his or her powers is properly limited to a comparison of the award with the submission. Once it is decreed that a matter is can be arbitrated, courts do not decide the issues on the merits.

When the submission does not restrict arbitrators to decide according to principles of law, they may make an award according to their own notion of justice without regard to the law. The scope of judicial review is whether the issues contained in the submission have been decided. An allegation that there is insufficient evidence to support an award or that it is contrary to the evidence does not constitute a ground for vacating an award. Only clear, precise evidence of fraud, misconduct, or other grave irregularity will suffice to vacate an arbitration award. Courts do not reweigh the evidence and make independent findings of fact.

Submissions to arbitration are for determinations based on the ad hoc application of broad principles of justice and fairness in the particular instance. The continuity of the tribunal personnel or operation is not relied on, and predictability is not an objective. Awards do not have, nor is it intended that they should have, the precedent value that attaches to judicial determinations.

9. Procedures in Arbitration Hearings

In the usual arbitration procedure, the parties to the dispute are given notice of the time and place of the hearing. Testimony is given at the hearing; then, the arbitrator or arbitrators deliberate and render a decision. There are no formal pleadings or motions, and the strict rules of evidence used in trials usually are not followed.

The function of the arbitrators is to find a solution to the controversy; and, to that end, they have the power to fashion the remedy appropriate to the wrong. Arbitrators are not bound by principles of substantive law or the rules of evidence, unless the submission so provides. As a result, errors of law or fact do not justify a court in setting aside the decision of the arbitration process. The arbitrator is the sole and final judge of the evidence and the weight to be given it.

Once an issue is submitted for arbitration, questions of law are for the arbitrator. They are no longer open to judicial intervention or to judicial review. Arbitrators are obligated to act fairly and impartially and to decide on the basis of the evidence before them. Therefore, it is misconduct for arbitrators to use outside evidence obtained by independent investigation without the consent of the parties.

10. Judicial Review of Arbitration Issues

One purpose of arbitration is to avoid the time and expense of litigation. Judicial action may be necessary if either party refuses to submit the dispute to arbitration or refuses to carry out the terms of the award. Statutes usually contemplate the following as the procedures to be followed when a party to an arbitration contract refuses to submit the dispute to arbitration as agreed:

1. The aggrieved party may petition the court for an order directing that the arbitration be carried out according to the terms of the agreement. Upon hearing, if the court finds that making the contract to arbitrate or submission to arbitrate is not an issue, the court directs the parties to proceed to arbitrate according to the terms of the agreement.

Judicial action is needed when neither part submits to arbitration.

2. If there is disagreement over the making of the contract or submission, the court will try that issue, either with or without a jury. If it is found that no contract was made, the petition is dismissed. If it is found that a contract to arbitrate or to submit was made and there was a default, the court will issue an order directing the parties to proceed with arbitration according to the contract.

If the parties do submit the issues to arbitration as agreed, or if arbitration is conducted pursuant to a court order, certain judicial proceedings may be necessary in order to enforce the award. Most statutes prescribe the following procedures:

1. After the award is made, it is filed with the clerk of the court. After twenty days, if no exceptions are filed, it becomes a judgment upon which a writ of execution may be issued in the same manner as if a judgment had been entered in a civil action.
2. A dissatisfied party may file exceptions to the award because, for example, (a) the award covered matters beyond the issues submitted, (b) the arbitrators failed to follow the statutory requirements, and (c) fraud or corruption permeated the decision. The court does not review the merits of the decision.
3. Appeals from the judgment may be taken as in any legal action, and such appeals cannot be denied by contractual provisions.
4. If it appears that the award should be vacated, the court may refer it to the arbitrators, with instructions for correction and rehearing.

Note, though, voluntary arbitration is treated differently than mandatory arbitration within the context of judicial review. In order to further the goal of reducing litigation's impact on the court system, an arbitration award created through the *voluntary arbitration* process is

TABLE 4-1 ■ Comparison of Voluntary and Mandatory Arbitration

	Voluntary	Mandatory
Submission	Parties agree in a contract (either before or after a dispute has arisen) that they will arbitrate.	Required by statute or administrative regulation
Process	Varies considerably because of the individual contract nature of the arbitration	Usually quite formal, somewhat like a trial with rules of evidence
Judicial Review	Infrequent, and award is generally final.	More common, de novo review by court

deemed as final. Therefore, judicial review is usually not an option; the arbitrator's decision on factual and legal issues is deemed conclusive. Because the parties have agreed in writing to accept the arbitrator's decision through provisions in the arbitration agreement, any factual or legal error is not subject to review by the court system. Judicial review of voluntary arbitration decisions is limited to the narrow categories of fraud by the arbitrator, arbitrary decisions by the arbitrator (where there is no substantiation for a decision), or a decision is clearly against public policy. Judicial reviews of this type are exceedingly rare.

Regarding *mandatory arbitration*, where parties are required by statute to arbitrate their dispute, judicial review is far more common. If there is an allegation that procedures employed in the arbitration are unconstitutional, for example, a court will conduct a de novo review (as if there was no arbitration) of facts and law. In a similar manner, errors of facts or law conducted by the arbitrator are often taken to court. Usually, too, the losing party will have the right to reject the arbitrator's decision and proceed to trial.

The following case illustrates the role of the courts in reviewing arbitration decisions and applies the rule that arbitration awards will be overturned only in rare situations.

CASE

Greenberg v. Bear, Stearns & Company

UNITED STATES CIRCUIT COURT OF APPEALS FOR THE 2ND CIRCUIT

220 F.3d 22 (2000)

JOHN M. WALKER, JR., CIRCUIT JUDGE

At the time of the events underlying Greenberg's claim, Bear Stearns (a "clearing broker") provided securities clearing services to Greenberg's primary broker, Sterling Foster (an "introducing broker"). According to Greenberg, Bear Stearns violated federal and state securities laws because it knew of and participated in a fraudulent scheme perpetrated by Sterling Foster; sent false and misleading confirmations in connection with this scheme; and failed to send out a required prospectus. We briefly discuss the facts and allegations pertinent to the appeal.

In 1996, Sterling Foster organized the initial public offering ("IPO") for a company called ML Direct. Under an agreement between Bear Stearns and Sterling Foster, the latter requested permission from the former to underwrite this sale. According to Sterling Foster's plan, ML Direct would make a public sale of 1.1 million shares, and Sterling Foster would sell short an additional 2.3 million shares, to be covered by shares it would obtain from existing shareholders. This scheme was fraudulent, alleged the plaintiff, because the prospectus distributed to purchasers of ML Direct stock stated that shares from the selling shareholders were subject to a lock-up agreement for 12 months and that there were "no agreements or understandings ... with respect to release of the securities prior to [this time]." Bear Stearns employees admitted having seen the prospectus, but did not recall reading the sentences about the lock-up. Bear Stearns agreed to clear the transaction.

In September 1996, the IPO and stock sales proceeded as planned. Sterling Foster allegedly reaped an enormous profit at the expense of the selling shareholders by selling shares short and purchasing shares from those shareholders at a significantly lower price. Bear Stearns sent out confirmations to purchasers of ML Direct stock that stated: "Your broker makes a market in this security and acted as principal." The confirmations did not disclose Sterling Foster's short sales or its large profit, nor was a prospectus sent to those who purchased shares.

In May 1997, the petitioner filed a claim with the National Association of Security Dealers ("NASD") against Bear Stearns alleging, among other things, fraud and market manipulation in connection with Bear Stearns's provision of securities clearing services to Sterling Foster. A panel of three arbitrators heard arguments and testimony through extensive briefing and seven days of hearings. The arbitrators first dismissed Greenberg's claim based on Bear Stearns's purported failure to send him a prospectus and thereafter dismissed his remaining claims. On March 9, 1999, the arbitrators issued a written award confirming their decision to dismiss.

On January 18, 1999, Greenberg moved in federal district court to vacate the award on the basis that it "violated public policy and manifestly disregarded the law." In an opinion and award dated August 23, 1999, the district court denied the motion on the grounds that the petitioner had failed to demonstrate manifest disregard of the law in the arbitrators' treatment of his claims. This appeal followed.

The district court held that the petitioner had failed to demonstrate that the arbitral award was rendered in manifest disregard of the law. Review for manifest disregard is "severely limited." In order to vacate an award on these grounds, a reviewing court must find "both that (1) the arbitrators knew of a governing legal principle yet refused to apply it or ignored it altogether, and (2) the law ignored by the arbitrators was well defined, explicit, and clearly applicable to the case." The party seeking vacatur of the award bears the burden of showing manifest disregard under these standards.

The petitioner has failed to meet this very stringent burden with respect to any of his claims against Bear Stearns. First, Greenberg argues that the arbitrators manifestly disregarded federal law in denying his claim that Bear Stearns knew about Sterling Foster's

continued

fraudulent scheme and is, therefore, liable under § 10(b) of the Securities Exchange Act. Knowing participation in a fraudulent scheme may render a participant liable under § 10(b).

In this case, however, Bear Stearns employees testified that they did not know about Sterling Foster's fraud, and thus the arbitrators could reasonably have concluded that Bear Stearns lacked the knowledge required for § 10(b) liability. The petitioner argues that Bear Stearns should be deemed to have knowledge of the fraud because it had the necessary information before it, but it is by no means clear that the doctrine of imputed knowledge applies in this context.

Also, Greenberg contends that Bear Stearns failed to comply with 17 C.F.R. § 230.174, which requires delivery of a prospectus in connection with the sale of newly issued securities. However, the regulation imposes this requirement only on underwriters and dealers, not on clearing brokers, and nothing in the agreement between Bear Stearns and Sterling Foster unambiguously shifted the burden of complying with this requirement onto Bear Stearns.

Finally, Greenberg asserts that Bear Stearns should be held liable as an aider and abettor under New York law because it participated in the fraudulent scheme and provided substantial assistance to Sterling Foster. However, there was ample basis for the arbitrators to conclude that Bear Stearns's participation was insufficient to constitute substantial assistance.

In sum, the arbitrators did not ignore or refuse to apply well-defined and clearly applicable law in rejecting any of the appellant's claims in such a way that would amount to manifest disregard.

Accordingly, we affirm the judgment of the district court.

■ *Affirmed.*

CASE CONCEPTS REVIEW

1. What standard did the court apply in deciding whether to overturn the decision of the arbitration panel?
2. Do you believe that the general rule restricting the ability of a court to overturn an arbitration decision is a good position for our society? Why or why not?

Chapter Summary

COMPROMISES

Reasons to Settle

1. Most disputes in our society are settled without resort to litigation.
2. There are both personal and economic incentives to settle business-related disputes.
3. A major function of lawyers is to negotiate a settlement of controversies.

Mediation

1. Mediation is a process by which a third party assists in reaching a compromise of a dispute.
2. The National Mediation and Conciliation Service is available to mediate labor disputes.

ARBITRATION

Advantages

1. Arbitration is the submission to a person or persons other than a court for a final binding decision of a controversy.
2. Arbitration is less expensive than litigation. It generally takes far less time and allows the parties to remain more amicable than does litigation.

Common-Law Arbitration

1. Such proceedings were based on an agreement of the parties that was revocable until the award.
2. Agreements to arbitrate future disputes were not enforceable.

Types of Arbitration Systems

1. Most states have comprehensive arbitration statutes that encourage arbitration.
2. Agreements that comply with the statute are enforced by courts.

Arbitration Statutes

1. Most statutes require a written agreement to arbitrate.
2. Submission is usually required within six months of the dispute.

Submission

1. The term *submission* is used to describe the action of referring an issue to arbitration.
2. The submission governs the duties and powers of the arbitrators.
3. Submission may result from an agreement to arbitrate all disputes that may arise in the future or from an agreement to arbitrate a particular dispute.

The Award

1. The decision in arbitration is known as an award. Awards may be judicially enforced.
2. If an award is within the power of the submission, a court will not change it because of errors of fact or errors of law.

Procedures in Arbitration Hearings

1. The parties are given notice of the time and place of the hearing.
2. The proceedings are less formal than a trial, and the arbitrators need not follow strict rules of evidence.

Judicial Procedures in Arbitration

1. Litigation is often necessary to enforce an award, which is treated as if it were a judgment of a court.
2. An agreement to arbitrate may also be ordered enforced by courts.
3. There are a few grounds for challenging an award in court.

REVIEW QUESTIONS AND PROBLEMS

1. Match the terms in Column A with the appropriate statement in Column B.

A	B
(1) Mediation	(a) The decision resulting from arbitration
(2) Arbitration	(b) Where arbitration is required by law
(3) Submission	(c) A process whereby a third party assists others in reaching a compromise of a dispute
(4) Award	(d) The decision to arbitrate was based on agreement.
(5) Negotiation	(e) Entity that will provide arbitrators
(6) Judicial review	(f) A process of give and take
(7) American Arbitration Association	(g) The action of referring a dispute to arbitration
(8) Uniform Arbitration Act	(h) Court's power to overrule an arbitrator's decision
(9) Common law arbitration	(i) Attempt to standardize arbitration statutes
(10) Statutory arbitration	(j) The submission of a dispute to one or more persons for a final binding resolution

2. Alexander is involved in a dispute related to his business. He is confident that he is right, and he is considering legal action. List the reasons why it may be financially advantageous to Alexander's business to avoid court and, instead, to compromise and settle for less money than he claims is owed to him.
3. Distinguish between mediation and arbitration.

4. Differentiate between a submission and an award in arbitration.
5. Assume that State X has no arbitration statute. During an arbitration hearing, one party became quite upset at the arbitrator and announced, "This proceeding is over. I am going to court." May the arbitrator go ahead and decide the dispute? Explain.
6. A dispute arose between partners on a construction project. The partnership agreement provided that if the partners were unable to agree on any matter with respect to which a decision was to be made by both partners, the dispute would be submitted to arbitration. One partner asked a court to appoint a receiver for the business. The other insisted on arbitration. How will the dispute be resolved? Why?
7. There was a dispute between an automobile insurance company and its insured concerning value in the loss of a truck. The insurance policy required arbitration of disputes. Each party selected an arbitrator and these two, when unable to agree, selected a third party as umpire. The umpire, without consulting anyone or receiving any testimony, fixed the value of the loss. If challenged, will a court set aside this award? Why or why not?
8. Sara worked as an employee for ABC Company. She signed an employment contract that required her to arbitrate any dispute with her employer. She believes she is being sexually harassed and wants to sue in court. The arbitration agreement says that the employer can choose the arbitrator, that the employee must pay for the arbitration, and that the maximum amount the employee can win are lost wages. Will the contractual provision mandating arbitration be enforced? Discuss.
9. Perry is serving as an arbitrator for the first time and wants to do a great job reaching a proper conclusion. Without telling either party, Perry contacts individuals and solicits information from them regarding the dispute. Has Perry done anything wrong?
10. Under what circumstances will a court review an arbitrator's decision?

Constitutional Foundations for Business Regulation | 5

CHAPTER OUTLINE

CHAPTER PREVIEW

What gives the government the right to regulate the activities of business? To answer this question, we must turn to the document that established our form of governance more than two centuries ago. The drafters of the United States Constitution believed government was necessary. They understood that a successful government should ensure that economic interests are not only protected, but also fostered. Further, the framers of the Constitution looked to create a form of government that not only attempted to serve the needs of society at the time our republican form of government was created, but also looked ahead to meet unanticipated challenges awaiting a fledgling nation.

While the Constitution certainly establishes the political—and in many ways the economic—foundation for this country, the framers of the Constitution also were fearful of government, in general, and of the concentration of government power more specifically. Therefore, the Constitution creates a sophisticated system of limitations on the role of government in our society. To many, the limited role government plays in regulating the business environment is a significant reason for the economic success enjoyed today by business owners and employees. To others, the government has overstepped its constitutional powers and is a major impediment to achieving economic success. To yet others, the government should do more to honor its constitutional duties to regulate business.

A number of constitutional dynamics are addressed in this chapter. The first section presents the federal form of government, looking at how the Constitution disperses power among the three branches of government. The next section examines federalism, an approach to governing that distributes power to both the federal government and to the states. Major limitations on all forms of government are covered in the third section—with particular attention paid to free speech, takings, due process, and equal protection. The chapter concludes with a brief coverage of privacy considerations.

BUSINESS MANAGEMENT DECISION

Carton Company is the largest manufacturer of paper cartons used to hold half-gallons and gallon of milk. Plastic Company dominates the plastic container market, again geared toward providing dairies and milk processors with containers in the half-gallon and gallon sizes. Competition is fierce between the two companies. One advantage of paper cartons is that they are more easily and more cheaply recycled.

Congress passed a law last month that assesses a five-cent per container tax on plastic containers. The author of the bill stated a desire to encourage consumers to use more "Earth-friendly" containers. Plastic Company believes this action of Congress is unconstitutional. Is Plastic Company correct? Why?

1. An Introduction to the Constitution and Government Regulation

The United States Constitution is a masterful document. Created more than two hundred years ago, it continues to be the model for countries throughout the world that wish to create a form of government which rests solidly on principles of federalism and free enterprise. Amended during its history only twenty-seven times, the Constitution has survived, in part, because of the foresight of its authors and in part because of the interpretation given to its wording by members of the judiciary, most importantly the United States Supreme Court, as courts have struggled to apply concepts imbedded in the Constitution to legal controversies.

The Constitution, for purposes of understanding its impact on the regulatory environment of business, serves three principal functions. First, the document *creates the federal government.* It establishes a form of government with three distinct branches (legislative, executive, and judicial). What about administrative agencies? No doubt many from the business community would claim today that administrative agencies are a "fourth branch" of government, but the framers of the Constitution did not expressly provide for administrative agencies. They did, however, provide a means for administrative agencies to be created under this constitutional form of government. The nature of administrative agencies is discussed in Chapter 40.

Next, the Constitution creates a plan for *allocating the regulatory powers of both federal and state governments.* The Constitution states quite specifically those powers that only the federal government possesses (e.g., the power to make war) and those powers that the federal government shares with other forms of government (e.g., the power to tax). Given the strong colonial (state) orientation of the authors of the Constitution, it is not surprising that the Constitution embraces solidly the concept of *federalism.* That is, under the Constitution there are two forms of government: state and federal. At the time of the drafting of the Constitution, it was imagined that states would be the main form of government. So, regulation of business, to the extent necessary, was envisioned to be primarily a matter for the states. Federal regulation was clearly of secondary importance. Today, many would argue the reverse is true: federal regulation, including the regulation of the business environment, is most prominent. Given this dynamic change in the role of the federal government, it is critical for students of business to understand the nature of federalism and consider what is appropriate federal regulation given the malleable concept of federalism.

Finally, the Constitution creates *limitations on the role of government* in regulating the lives of individuals and the efforts of business. These protections largely are embedded in the amendments to the Constitution, primarily the Bill of Rights. Individuals who operate a sole proprietorship or are a partner in a general partnership may be interested to learn that the Constitution provides protection from government overreaching even in their role as a member of the business community. Constitutional safeguards go further; corporations, for example, have significant protections based on the Bill of Rights and other constitutional provisions. Therefore, the power to regulated business is subject to a host of limitations.

THE FEDERAL FORM OF GOVERNMENT

2. Separation of Powers

Separation of powers
Constitutional mandate that requires branches of government, with each branch charged with performing certain functions

In forming the federal government, the authors of the Constitution recognized the dangers associated with having political power concentrated. One method of distributing the power of government is to create branches with unique powers provided to each branch. The **doctrine of separation of powers** is embraced in the Constitution through the creation of three branches of federal government, an approach that is also present in state government.

The first branch of the federal government is *legislative.* Article I of the Constitution establishes a Congress comprised of two houses. The upper house, the Senate, today consists of two senators from each of the fifty states. Recognizing the significance of having state (at the time, colonial) representation, each state—regardless of population—is granted the same number of elected officials in elected officials in the Senate as every other state. Therefore, a strong industrial state would have the same representation as a strong agrarian state. The lower assembly, the House of Representatives, currently has 435 members from the fifty states. Recognizing the importance of having representation based on population, each member of the House of Representatives represents a set number of individuals in the United States. This process generates more than forty representatives from states with large populations and fewer than five representatives for less populated states. While the duties of both houses are quite similar, the Constitution provides that certain powers of each chamber are different from the other. For example, the Senate approves treaties, while the House of Representatives does not vote on treaties. Also, all bills that impact taxation must arise in the House of Representatives and be passed by that chamber of Congress; it is only then that the Senate can consider such measures.

Article II of the Constitution establishes the *executive* branch of the federal government, including powers associated with the presidency, to enforce the laws. Under the power granted by the Constitution, the president, for example, approves acts of Congress and appoints federal judges (with the approval of the Senate). In a host of other areas, the president and other members of the executive branch work with the legislative and judicial branches. However, the need for a single individual to execute particular powers of government is illustrated by the fact that the president is commander-in-chief of the military and the primary architect of the country's foreign affairs policy. In both areas, it is important that one person makes decisions.

The *judicial* branch emanates largely from the provisions of Article III. This provision of the Constitution confers the power to adjudicate disputes to the Supreme Court of the United States and such other lower courts as Congress may establish. Some of these lower courts address general areas of dispute as they interpret the law. In this vein, federal district courts are to be the primary trial courts and the circuit courts of appeal are designated to be the first level of appeal from the district court. This portion of the Constitution also provides the areas in which the federal judiciary may operate. For example, federal courts can hear controversies that arise under the Constitution, federal laws, or treaties of the United States. Also, if a controversy involves a citizen of one state suing a citizen of another state, the federal court system is empowered to hear that case. In addition, the federal judiciary includes courts with specialized roles (e.g., United States Tax Court, United States Bankruptcy Court).

3. Checks and Balances

While the framers of the Constitution recognized the importance of separating powers within the federal government, they also understood the need to establish a system of **checks and balances** among the legislative, executive, and judicial branches. This system creates another means of dispersing the power of government.

Checks and balances

Under the Constitution, the process by which each branch of government restrains the power of another branch

The Constitution provides numerous instances where one branch of government restrains the power of another branch. In the situation where a president has vetoed a bill passed by both the Senate and the House of Representatives, for example, the bill can still become law if both chambers of Congress *override* the veto by a two-thirds vote. Also, the president may be removed from office through the actions of the House and the Senate. Finally, members of the federal judiciary are nominated by the president and confirmed by the Senate.

Another limitation on the power of an individual branch of government is not expressly provided for in the Constitution. In a landmark decision *(Marbury v. Madison),* the United

Judicial review

The doctrine that allows the federal courts to determine whether acts by the federal government or the state governments conform to edicts of the Constitution

States Supreme Court decided in 1803 that the federal courts have the **power of judicial review.** This doctrine empowers the federal courts with the ability to review actions by Congress and by the executive branch to determine whether those actions violate the Constitution. Judicial review also includes the actions of state government—all legislative, executive, and judicial actions of a state must be in conformity with the Constitution. As a result of the concept of judicial review, the United States Constitution is the fundamental law of the land.

The importance of judicial review is considerable in terms of allocation of power. First, it establishes the federal court system and, ultimately the United States Supreme Court, as the final arbiter of what a provision of the Constitution means. Moreover, it allows constitutional provisions to trump actions of the two elected branches of government. So, principles of democratic rule are subservient to the edicts of the Constitution, as interpreted by the Supreme Court. Individuals and business entities are often successful in arguing that an order from the president or an act of Congress violates a right guaranteed under the Constitution. This ability to challenge the constitutionality of an action of government is possible because the federal courts have the power of judicial review.

FEDERALISM

4. Nature of Federalism

A cursory review of one period of United States history is instructive in examining the nature of federalism. Just prior to the Revolutionary War, the thirteen colonies functioned in a largely independent and fractured manner. Each colony had its own government, and each colony paid homage to the Crown of England. Once independence was established, the states perceived a need for a central government. In 1781, the Articles of Confederation created a layer of government that sought to unite the various states, but that entity had severely limited power. Under the Articles of Confederation, states remained the superior governmental entity. Unfortunately, this system was deeply flawed, and within a few years citizens and business interests demanded a new approach. One reason for change related to the growing economy. Many members of the business community desired to have free trade of goods across state borders. Commercial establishments increasingly recognized that markets could be developed beyond the boundaries of their state. However, state legislators, fearing a loss of commerce, erected considerable trade barriers that restrained the growth of a national economy. While the initial call in 1789 was for members of a congress assembled in Philadelphia to simply revise the Articles of Confederation, the delegates instead decided to create a new form of government, based on a document called the Constitution of the United States.

Federalism

Doctrine under which lawmaking is divided between a federal government and a state government

The framers of the Constitution adopted federalism as the central underpinning for the proposed governmental structure. Under **federalism**, government power is divided between two sovereigns: federal and state.

The idea is that one government has power to act in one realm, and the other government acts in the remaining areas appropriate for regulation. Along with the notion of separation of powers, the concept of federalism also ensures that the power of government is distributed.

5. Distribution of Powers

FEDERAL ENUMERATED POWERS In addressing the role of the federal government, the authors of the Constitution expressed their continuing distrust of a central government. The federal government's powers are limited to those *enumerated* in the Constitution; so if a power is not listed, the federal government lacks the ability to regulate in that area. Article I, Section 8, of the Constitution provides a number of areas in which Congress can regulate business, including the power to regulate commerce with foreign nations and between the states, coin money, borrow on behalf of the government, establish bankruptcy laws, and enact laws pertaining to patents and copyrights. Further, most of these enumerated powers are *exclusive to the federal government.* The Tenth Amendment to the Constitution, which provides that those powers "not delegated to the United States by the Constitution, nor prohibited by it to the States, are reserved to the States respectively, or to the people" reinforces the notion of enumerated powers.

Police powers

Government powers, including the areas of public safety, health, welfare, and morals, which are traditionally domains that are regulated by state government

STATE POLICE POWERS Because the authors of the Constitution were familiar with the operation of the colonial (state) form of government, there is little written in the Constitution about the role of state government. Tradition, however, dictates that the states possess **police powers**. The term is read quite broadly, meaning that the states have the authority to regulate public safety, health, welfare, and morals.

The police power of the state provides the avenue that allows state and local governments to regulate business activities. While the framers of the Constitution may have envisioned that principles of federalism would demand that only the states could delve into the arenas of public safety, health, welfare, and morals, few constitutional scholars today believe that the federal government cannot exercise police power in these areas.

CONCURRENT POWERS A great number of powers are exercised by both federal and state governments. These are called *concurrent powers.* Examples include the ability to tax a business and the power of government to spend money. While it is unclear whether the framers of the Constitution envisioned the growth of the federal government into the dominant entity it is today, the history of the United States, primarily during the past one hundred years, illustrates that the boundaries of what is a constitutional expression of federal power are in flux. During a significant portion of the twentieth century, the nation witnessed a growing role of the federal government in regulating the affairs of business. It would not be unusual for actions of Congress, for example, to directly impact areas of business that traditionally would have been the sole purview of state and local governments through the police powers doctrine. Even though business challenged in court the extension of federal government regulation during these years, the federal judiciary was generally supportive of the extension of federal governmental authority. During the past decade or so, however, the United States Supreme Court, in particular, has strengthened state government rights while reducing the extent to which the federal government can regulate, among other areas, business activities.

RELATIONSHIPS AMONG THE STATES Even at the time the Constitution was drafted, individuals and business entities from one state entered into contracts and other relationships with individuals and business entities from another state. In order to facilitate strong working relationships among parties in different states, the Constitution includes two clauses that support the vibrancy of business relationships. The *privileges and immunities clause,* of Article IV, Section 2, guarantees a citizen of one state who engages in important activities in another state is entitled to the same treatment as he/she would receive in his or her home state. Activities within the protection of the privileges and immunities clause include seeking employment in another state, entering into a contractual relationship in another state, or using the courts of another state.

Under this provision of the Constitution, non-citizens of a state may be treated differently from residents only if a substantial reason exists for distinguishing between the two. For example, Wong, Inc. operates a business in Nebraska near the state border with South Dakota. The nearest city to Wong, Inc. that has a waste disposal plant is located in South Dakota. If the State of South Dakota charges nonresidents, including non-resident businesses, a standard fee of $1,000 for use of waste disposal facilities located within the state yet allows residents to use the facilities for free, Wong, Inc. probably would be successful in challenging the action of South Dakota if the business can show there is not substantial reason for treating nonresidents differently from residents of the state of South Dakota.

The *full faith and credit clause* also encourages commerce among individuals and entities located in different states. Located in Article IV, Section I, this provision provides that rights associated with property deeds, contracts, and other legal documents in one state will be honored by all other states. Needless-to-say, if this protection did not exist, business would lack necessary stability because there could be tremendous uncertainty as to whether a determination of legal status in one state would be respected in another state. The full faith and credit clause goes further. It also provides that a state court determination in one state will be honored and enforced in other states. This is an important right to have secured under the Constitution in a society that is increasingly mobile. For instance, GoFlow, Inc. enters into a contractual relationship to provide services to By Gone & Associates, a business located in another state. GoFlow supplies the requested service, but By Gone & Associates fails to pay for the services as required under the contract. If GoFlow secures a court judgment in their home state for damages resulting from the breach of contract, GoFlow can then go to the state where the By Gone & Associates resides and ask a court in that state to assist the business in enforcing the judgment of the court located in the GoFlow's home state.

6. Commerce Clause

Commerce clause
Provision of the Constitution that empowers the federal government with the ability to regulate interstate commerce

The single greatest constitutional clause that fosters federal regulation of business is the **commerce clause**. Among the enumerated powers established in Article I, Section 8 of the Constitution is the provision granting to Congress the power to regulate interstate commerce. The provision provides that Congress may "regulate Commerce with foreign Nations, and among the several States, and with the Indian Tribes."

"ACTIVE" COMMERCE CLAUSE INTERPRETATIONS The ability for the courts to read the commerce clause in an expansive fashion dates back to early interpretations of the Constitution. In

FIGURE 5-1 ■ Distribution of Power to Regulate the Constitution

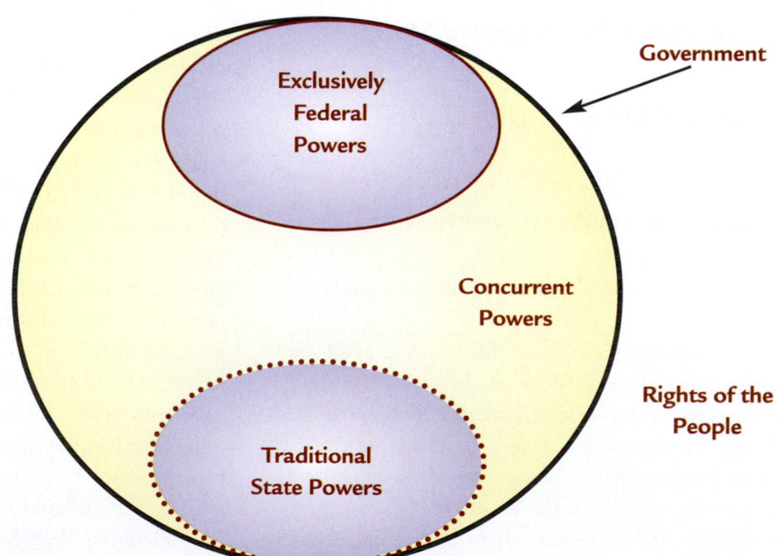

an 1824 case before the United States Supreme Court *(Gibbons v. Ogden),* the court was faced with an interesting dilemma. Some courts had interpreted the phrase "among the several States" to limit the reach of federal action to those transactions that crossed state boundaries; that is, they supported the idea that the federal government could only regulate commerce that was truly *interstate.* The Supreme Court ruled, however, that the federal government could regulate economic activities that are intrastate in nature, as long as the commerce that occurs within in one state *substantially affects or impacts* commerce in other states.

For more than sixty years in the mid-1800s, the courts allowed the federal government considerable sway in regulating businesses whose activities "substantially affected" interstate commerce. From the period 1887-1937, however, the Supreme Court adopted a more conservative view. In a series of decisions during those fifty years, the ability of the federal government to regulate business was curtailed. For example, a manufacturing plant located in Illinois produced goods, all of which were sold to a wholesaler also situated in Illinois. The wholesaler then sold the product to retailers located in numerous other states. Under the more narrow interpretation of the commerce clause prevalent during this time, the manufacturer could not be regulated by the federal government.

In a 1937 decision *(NLRB v. Jones & Laughlin Steel Corp.),* the Supreme Court once again adopted a more expansive view of the commerce clause. In this case, the Supreme Court held that Congress did have the power to regulate labor relations in a manufacturing plant because the product manufactured by the entity was sold across state lines and any reduction of production resulting from a labor strike would have a significant impact on interstate commerce. For almost sixty years, this liberal reading of the commerce clause prevailed, with almost all attempts by Congress to regulate business under the clause succeeding. The classic case presented below illustrates the reach of federal regulation under this view of the commerce clause.

CASE

Heart of Atlanta Motel, Inc. v. United States, et al.

SUPREME COURT OF THE UNITED STATES

379 U.S. 241 (1964)

MR. JUSTICE CLARK DELIVERED THE OPINION OF THE COURT

This is a declaratory judgment action attacking the constitutionality of the Civil Rights Act of 1964.

Appellant owns and operates the Heart of Atlanta Motel which has 216 rooms available to transient guests. The motel is located on Courtland Street, two blocks from downtown Peachtree Street. It is readily accessible to interstate highways 75 and 85 and state highways 23 and 41. Appellant solicits patronage from outside the State of Georgia through various national advertising media, including magazines of national circulation; it maintains over 50 billboards and highway signs within the State, soliciting patronage for the motel; it accepts convention trade from outside Georgia and approximately 75% of its registered guests are from out of State. Prior to passage of the Act the motel had followed a practice of refusing to rent rooms to Negroes, and it alleged that it intended to continue to do so. In an effort to perpetuate that policy this suit was filed.

The appellant contends that Congress in passing this Act exceeded its power to regulate commerce under Art. I, § 8, cl. 3, of the Constitution of the United States. The appellees counter that the unavailability to Negroes of adequate accommodations interferes significantly with interstate travel, and that Congress, under the Commerce Clause, has power to remove such obstructions and restraints.

While the Act as adopted carried no congressional findings, the record of its passage through each house is replete with evidence of the burdens that discrimination by race or color places upon interstate commerce. This testimony included the facts that (1) our people have become increasingly mobile with millions of people of all races traveling from State to State; (2) Negroes, in particular, have been the subject of discrimination in transient accommodations, having to travel great distances to secure the same; (3) often Negroes have been unable to obtain accommodations and have had to call upon friends to put them up overnight; and (4) these conditions had become so acute as to require the listing of available lodging for Negroes in a special guidebook which was itself "dramatic testimony to the difficulties" Negroes encounter in travel.

That Congress was legislating against moral wrongs in many of these areas rendered its enactments no less valid. In framing Title II of this Act, Congress was also dealing with what it considered a moral problem. That fact, however, does not detract from the overwhelming evidence of the disruptive effect that racial discrimination has had on commercial intercourse. It was this burden that empowered Congress to enact appropriate legislation; and, given this basis for the exercise of its power, Congress was not restricted by the fact that the particular obstruction to interstate commerce with which it was dealing was also deemed a moral and social wrong.

The power of Congress over interstate commerce is not confined to the regulation of commerce among the states. It extends to those intrastate activities, which so affect interstate commerce or the exercise of the power of Congress over it, to make regulation of them an appropriate means to the attainment of a legitimate end—the exercise of the granted power of Congress to regulate interstate commerce.

Thus the power of Congress to promote interstate commerce also includes the power to regulate the local incidents thereof, including local activities in both the States of origin and destination, which might have a substantial and harmful effect upon that commerce. One need only examine the evidence which we have discussed above to see that Congress may—as it has—prohibit racial discrimination by motels serving travelers, however "local" their operations may appear.

We, therefore, conclude that the action of the Congress in the adoption of the Act as applied here to a motel which concededly serves interstate travelers is within the power granted it by the Commerce Clause of the Constitution, as interpreted by this Court for 140 years. It may be argued that Congress could have pursued other methods to eliminate the obstructions it found in interstate commerce caused by racial discrimination. This, however, is a matter of policy that rests entirely with the Congress not with the courts. How obstructions in commerce may be removed—what means are to be employed—is within the sound and exclusive discretion of the Congress. It is subject only to one caveat—that the means chosen by it must be reasonably adapted to the end permitted by the Constitution. We cannot say that its choice here was not so adapted. The Constitution requires no more.

■ *Affirmed.*

CASE CONCEPT REVIEW

1. If racial discrimination was not the subject of the federal legislation and a more benign topic was the focus of the regulation, do you believe the author of the opinion would have supported the expansive reach of the commerce clause?
2. What limits, if any, is there on the commerce clause after this case? Is there today any area free of federal government regulation under the reasoning of the case?

Beginning in 1995, the Supreme Court reversed course once. A majority of the justices in recent years have favored limiting the reach of the federal government into the affairs of business. Today, it appears that the Supreme Court does not embrace the view that all commercial activities are within the ambit of the commerce clause. The federal government's power to regulate, under this current view, has limits. As the Supreme Court decides future cases under the commerce clause, members of the business community will better understand the extent of power Congress and other federal governmental officials have to regulate business.

"DORMANT" COMMERCE CLAUSE APPLICATIONS The previous discussion dealing with the "active" aspects of the commerce clause requires that the *federal* government take action, usually in the form of a law passed by Congress. It appears that the writers of the Constitution, however, intended that the federal government have *exclusive power* to regulate interstate commerce. Therefore, the Supreme Court is sensitive to situations where a *state* creates a law or regulation that *burdens* interstate commerce. Realize that in these situations the federal government has not acted. Instead, the Supreme Court has simply looked to the commerce clause of the Constitution and employed it as the means to prevent one state from discriminating against business activities emanating from another state. This aspect of constitutional law is known as the **"dormant" commerce clause.**

"Dormant" commerce clause

Judicially-created doctrine that forbids states from acting in a manner that unreasonably impedes commerce among the states

Just because an out-of-state business is impacted negatively by a law applied to their commercial activities does not mean the law is unconstitutional. Where a state undertakes to regulate business activities in general, businesses in another state may be impacted negatively. As long as in-state and out-of-state businesses are similarly impacted, there is no constitutional violation. If, however, a state law discriminates against out-of-state businesses *and* there is insufficient justification for treating the out-of-state business in a more burdensome manner, then a court will find the law is unconstitutional.

Assume Kentucky requires all trucks operating on its roads to have maximum-sized mud flaps. The federal government and most other states require only medium-sized flaps. Under the Kentucky law, all trucks coming into the state would have to change to the larger mud flaps, then change back to the smaller size upon leaving the state. Interstate commerce would be affected because of the time and costs associated with stopping and changing mud flaps. (Medium-sized mud flaps are preferred by truckers because they do not cause as much drag on the tractor-trailer rigs as do maximum-sized mud flaps.) A court would probably conclude that the "dormant" commerce clause provision is violated because the law impedes interstate commerce, discriminates against out-of-state truckers, and has a negligible impact on safety for those driving on Kentucky roads.

7. Supremacy and Preemption

Where the federal government and a state both regulate the same area of business, does the business have to comply with both sets of laws? Can it choose which it will honor? The doctrines of supremacy and preemption are necessary components of government in order for the principle of federalism to work effectively. The **supremacy clause**, located in Article VI of the Constitution, states that the Constitution, treaties, and federal laws take precedence over state laws.

Supremacy clause
Constitutional provision mandating that federal law is superior to state law

Where both federal and state governments legislate in the same area, the doctrine of *preemption* is employed. In many situations, states already have passed legislation regulating a subject by the time that Congress acts. In such cases, Congress may *expressly preempt* any state regulation. That is, in the language of the legislation, Congress makes clear that under the supremacy clause that it will control all aspects within a particular arena. Congress may, also, include a *"savings clause"* in a specific act that provides states may regulate in the area as long as the state legislation does not impede the intent of Congress. For example, many states have anti-discrimination in employment statutes that provide additional areas of illegal discrimination beyond those included in federal law. Congress in its anti-discrimination laws has included a savings clause. Therefore, any state antidiscrimination statute is legal under the federal preemption doctrine as long as the state antidiscrimination statute is not at variance with federal legislation prohibiting discrimination at work.

The tough cases occur where Congress is unclear as to federal preemption. The courts must attempt, then, to discern the intent of Congress. If other federal laws and regulations suggest that Congress has exercised plenary control over a field, then a court may conclude that even though Congress failed to specify in a more recent act its intent; and a state law impacting that area will be declared unconstitutional because of federal preemption. Where federal legislation is sporadic in a particular area, there probably is insufficient evidence as to the intent of Congress to preempt. In these cases, the courts look to see whether business can reasonably be expected to comply with both federal and state law. If there is a conflict, the state law is deemed unconstitutional under the preemption doctrine, and the business must comply only with the mandates of the federal law.

CHECKS ON THE POWER OF GOVERNMENT

8. Basic Aspects of Constitutional Limitations

The authors of the Constitution exercised caution to create a form of government where the power possessed by government was limited and dispersed. The first Congress remained concerned, though, that the Constitution failed to express unequivocally the rights individuals possessed that would protect them from government interference in their lives, both personal and financial. Congress proposed twelve amendments to the Constitution, of which ten were adopted in 1791. These first ten amendments are known as the Bill of Rights. Many of the rights included in the first ten amendments are applicable to members of the business community, as discussed below. Also, after the Civil War, another important amendment, the Fourteenth Amendment, became part of the Constitution. While earlier in the history of the country courts held that the protections afforded in the Bill of Rights protected citizens only from actions of the federal government, today almost all checks on the power of government apply to actions of both federal and state governments.

State Action Even where a federal action is proper under the commerce clause or where a state's action is appropriate as an exercise of its police power, the government's action may still be unconstitutional because the action violates a limitation of power included in an amendment to the Constitution. These protections necessarily apply only where a law or regulation of the government impacts an individual or entity's right protected by the Constitution. This is called **state action**.

State action

Constitutional protections embedded in selective provisions of amendments to the Constitution that apply only to instances where the government has acted

To avoid confusion, "state" action is action by the state, by the government, without considering whether the statute, for example, is federal or state. The state action requirement compels a judge applying a constitutional right to inquire whether a government (federal, state, or local) is acting. If Jack yells at Joan while Joan is talking, Joan may desire to sue Jack for violating her right of free speech. While the right of free speech is part of the First Amendment, the right is asserted only to actions of the government, not to individuals. Therefore, in Joan's case, there is no state action.

Constitutional Balancing Tests Once state action is found, often based on a law passed by Congress or a state legislature, the next step in the process of deciding whether the action by government is constitutional is to access whether an individual's or a business' right guaranteed under an amendment to the Constitution has been infringed upon. If a right (e.g., freedom of speech) has been impacted, then a court must balance the interests served by the statute, and the nature of the right that is being denied. This balancing process, regardless of the right involved, also changes with time, as society weighs—through the judicial system—the importance of accomplishing important social goals through government action against an individual's or a business' right guaranteed under the Constitution.

For example, during World War II, Japanese-Americans were interred in camps for the duration of the war. While the United States Supreme Court ruled on numerous occasions that the due process and equal protection rights of those held in camps were not violated because the nation

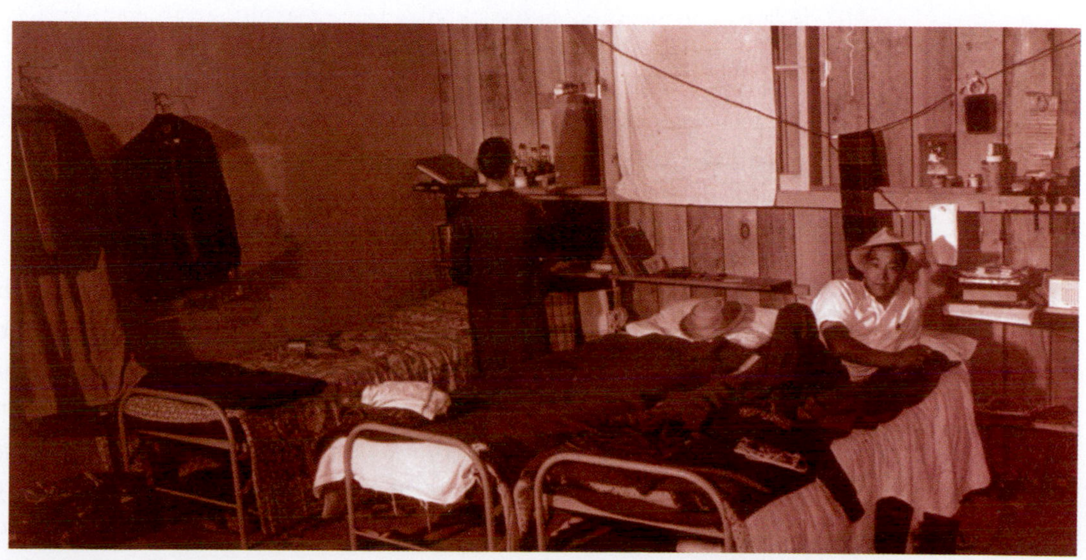

World War II Japanese internment quarters

was at war with Japan, many legal scholars today believe that the Supreme Court today would have found confinement in the internment camps unconstitutional. Simply put, the weighing of the interests by the Supreme Court would have been different today than in the 1940s.

In general, the Supreme Court will adopt one of three approaches to balancing interests in a case involving a right guaranteed under the amendments to the Constitution. When the *strict scrutiny test* is employed, the government must establish that its action *necessarily relates* to a *compelling state interest.* Practically, any governmental action that invokes the strict scrutiny text will be declared unconstitutional because of the very rigorous burden the government must meet in light of the gravity of the constitutional right infringed upon. At the other end of the spectrum, the *rational basis test* is an easy test for the government to meet. If a constitutional charge is made that requires employing the rational basis test, the government must only show that there is a *reasonable relationship* to a *legitimate interest* of the government. With the courts showing almost total deference to legislative or executive branch actions under the rational basis test, an individual or business pursuing a breach of a constitutional right will fail. Between these two tests, the judiciary has fashioned an *intermediate scrutiny test.* Here the results are uncertain. Under this test, the government will win in the face of an allegation of constitutional rights being violated if it can show that the governmental action *substantially relates* to an *important interest* of society. The following figure presents the basic tenets of the three tests.

TABLE 5-1 ■ BALANCING TESTS

Name of Test	Connection	Interest	Result
Strict Scrutiny	Necessarily relates	Compelling	Action by government is probably unconstitutional
Intermediate Scrutiny	Substantially relates	Important	Case-by-case determination
Rational Basis	Reasonably relates	Legitimate	Action by government is probably constitutional

Examples of the application of each of these tests are included in the constitutional clause specific discussions presented below.

9. Freedom of Speech

The First Amendment provides that "Congress shall make no law ... abridging the freedom of speech." Two comments about the words employed in this provision. First, the term "Congress" has been interpreted to include all aspects of the federal government—including, for instance, an action of a member of the executive branch, and all levels of government, including actions of state government. Also, while the authors of the amendment employed the word "no," courts have refused to view this provision as protecting all speech. Courts interpreting the freedom of speech clause have actively balanced the inherently-conflicting interests of an individual or busi-

The First Amendment provides freedom of speech

ness and the government making a judgment as to the constitutionality of an action of the government. This concept will be explored in greater detail below.

The constitutional protection pertaining to freedom of speech certainly stands for the proposition that citizens should be able to criticize their government without fear of being persecuted for their speech. Another justification for fostering freedom of speech relates to the marketplace theory. Under this rationale, individuals and entities should be able to offer their ideas into the public "marketplace" and let principles of free competition control. In this manner, robust protection of free speech allows the best ideas to be recognized.

Restraints on the freedom of speech are necessary. Statutes that attempt to control obscenity, if properly drafted, are constitutional. Also, an individual cannot cry "Fire!" in a crowded theater and expect that the individual's right of free speech will trump an arrest for causing a riot. Thus, the courts recognize that some speech is *unprotected* by the freedom of speech provision contained within the First Amendment, and the government generally has the power to control the *time, place, and manner* of speech. It may be permissible for an individual to use technology to amplify a speaker's voice at a city square, noontime political rally, but the same behavior would be found unconstitutional to use the same technology to broadcast the same message in the middle of a neighborhood at midnight.

Political speech

Entitled to the greatest protection of all speech, it includes speech associated with matters of public interest

POLITICAL SPEECH The principal rationales for the freedom of speech clause of the First Amendment generally pertain to those expressions deemed **political speech**. Because political discourse lies at the heart of a constitutional republic, government attempts to bridle expressions of public interest normally receive the greatest protection when challenged.

Under the *strict scrutiny* test applicable to freedom of speech cases involving political and other noncommercial speech, the government must meet two principal tests before the state action impeding speech will be held constitutional. The first test requires that the restriction on the speech is *necessary.* Also, the government must show a *compelling government purpose* for the restriction. In almost all circumstances, the government will fail to meet its burdens under the strict scrutiny test. Therefore, if an individual is engaged in political speech and the government attempts to curtail that expression by enforcing a statute forbidding, for example the use of certain unsavory words in public, the governmental action will most certainly be declared an unconstitutional act. Corporations and other business entities are deemed to have the same right of free speech in the realm of political and other types of noncommercial speech.

Commercial speech

Speech that relates to a business transaction (Some commercial speech, primarily speech that misleads, receives no protection from the First Amendment. Other types of commercial speech receive an intermediate level of protection.)

COMMERCIAL SPEECH Speech relating to the behavior of business in the commercial world may be deemed **commercial speech** and receive less than the full extent of freedom of speech protection allowed political speech. For a number of decades, the United State Supreme Court deemed commercial speech unworthy of receiving any protection under the First Amendment. In the 1970s, however, the Court recognized that government actions that severely limiting information to consumers may not be of benefit to society. As a result, the Supreme Court grants a limited amount of freedom of speech protection to commercial speech, as long as the speech does not mislead. For commercial speech that misleads (or promotes illegal activity), however, freedom of speech protection simply does not apply. Therefore, advertising and marketing activities may be subject to federal and state laws geared to prevent consumers from being misled.

Where government regulation of commercial speech is not directed at misleading customers, what is the level of protection afforded to the business? The Supreme Court has articulated an *intermediate level of scrutiny*. Under this test, the freedom of speech clause is not violated if: (1) a substantial government interest is furthered by the restriction, (2) the restriction directly advances that interest, and (3) the restriction is no more extensive than necessary. As illustrated in the following case, it is sometimes difficult to categorize speech as political or commercial, and if commercial, whether the speech falls within the type of speech that misleads and therefore deserves no constitutional protection.

CASE

Kasky v. Nike, Inc.

CALIFORNIA SUPREME COURT

27 Cal. 4th 939 (2002)

OPINION BY JUSTICE KENNARD

Plaintiff Marc Kasky is a California resident suing on behalf of the general public of the State of California under Business and Professions Code sections 17204 and 17535. Defendant Nike, Inc. (Nike) is an Oregon corporation with its principal place of business in that state; Nike is authorized to do business in California and does promote, distribute, and sell its products in this state. The individual defendants (Philip Knight, Thomas Clarke, Mark Parker, Stephen Gomez, and David Taylor) are officers and/or directors of Nike.

Nike manufactures and sells athletic shoes and apparel. In 1997, it reported annual revenues of $9.2 billion, with annual expenditures for advertising and marketing of almost $1 billion. Most of Nike's products are manufactured by subcontractors in China, Vietnam, and Indonesia. Most of the workers who make Nike products are women under the age of 24. Since March 1993, under a memorandum of understanding with its subcontractors, Nike has assumed responsibility for its subcontractors' compliance with applicable local laws and regulations concerning minimum wage, overtime, occupational health and safety, and environmental protection.

Beginning at least in October 1996 with a report on the television news program 48 Hours, and continuing at least through November and December of 1997 with the publication of articles in the Financial Times, the New York Times, the San Francisco Chronicle, and the Sporting News, various persons and organizations alleged that in the factories where Nike products are made workers were paid less than the applicable local minimum wage; required to work overtime; allowed and encouraged to work more overtime hours than applicable local law allowed; subjected to physical, verbal, and sexual abuse; and exposed to toxic chemicals, noise, heat, and dust without adequate safety equipment, in violation of applicable local occupational health and safety regulations.

In response to this adverse publicity, and for the purpose of maintaining and increasing its sales and profits, Nike and the individual defendants made statements to the California consuming public that plaintiff alleges were false and misleading. Specifically, Nike and the individual defendants said that workers who make Nike products are protected from physical and sexual abuse, that they are paid in accordance with applicable local laws and regulations governing wages and hours, that they are paid on average double the applicable local minimum wage, that they receive a "living wage," that they receive free meals and health care, and that their working conditions are in compliance with applicable local laws and regulations governing occupational health and safety. Nike and the individual defendants made these statements in press releases, in letters to newspapers, in a letter to university presidents and athletic directors, and in other documents distributed for public relations purposes. Nike also bought full-page advertisements in leading newspapers to publicize a report that GoodWorks International, LLC, had prepared under a contract with Nike. The report was based on an investigation by former United States Ambassador Andrew Young, and it found no evidence of illegal or unsafe working conditions at Nike factories in China, Vietnam, and Indonesia.

Plaintiff alleges that Nike and the individual defendants made these false and misleading statements because of their negligence and carelessness and "with knowledge or reckless disregard of the laws of California prohibiting false and misleading statements."

Nike demurred to the first amended complaint on grounds, among others, that it failed to state facts sufficient to constitute a cause of action against Nike and that the relief plaintiff was seeking is absolutely barred by the First Amendment to the United States Constitution. The individual defendants separately demurred to the first amended complaint on the same grounds.

Although advertising has played an important role in our nation's culture since its early days, and although state regulation of commercial advertising and commercial transactions also has a long history, it was not until the 1970's that the United States Supreme Court extended First Amendment protection to commercial messages. In 1975, the court declared that it was error to assume "that advertising, as such, was entitled to no First Amendment protection."

The federal Constitution accords less protection to commercial speech than to other constitutionally safeguarded forms of expression. For noncommercial speech entitled to full First Amendment protection, a content-based regulation is valid under the First Amendment only if it can withstand strict scrutiny, which requires that the regulation be narrowly tailored (that is, the least restrictive means) to promote a compelling government interest. By contrast, regulation of commercial speech based on content is less problematic." To determine the validity of a content-based regulation of commercial speech, the United States Supreme Court has articulated an intermediate-scrutiny test. The court explained the components of the test this way: At the outset, we must determine whether the expression is protected by the First Amendment. *For commercial speech to come within that provision, it at least must concern lawful activity and not be misleading.* Next, we ask whether the asserted governmental interest is substantial. If both inquiries yield positive answers, we must determine whether the regulation directly advances the governmental interest asserted and whether it is not more extensive than is necessary to serve that interest.

The United States Supreme Court has not adopted an all-purpose test to distinguish commercial from noncommercial speech under the First Amendment, nor has this court adopted such a test under the state Constitution, nor do we propose to do so here. A close reading of the high court's commercial speech decisions suggests, however, that it is possible to formulate a limited-purpose test. We conclude, therefore, that *when a court must decide whether particular speech may be subjected to laws aimed at preventing false advertising or other forms of commercial deception,* categorizing a particular statement as commercial or noncommercial speech requires consideration of three elements: the speaker, the intended audience, and the content of the message.

Here, the first element, a commercial speaker, is satisfied because the speakers, Nike and its officers and directors, are engaged in commerce. Specifically, they manufacture, import, distribute, and sell consumer goods in the form of athletic shoes and apparel.

The second element, an intended commercial audience, is also satisfied. Nike's letters to university presidents and directors of athletic departments were addressed directly to actual and potential purchasers of Nike's products because college and university athletic departments are major purchasers of athletic shoes and apparel. Plaintiff has alleged that Nike's press releases and letters to newspaper editors, although addressed to the public generally, were also intended to reach and influence actual and potential purchasers of Nike's products. Specifically, plaintiff has alleged that Nike made these statements about its labor policies and practices "to maintain and/or increase its sales and profits." To support this allegation, plaintiff has included as an exhibit a letter to a newspaper editor, written by Nike's director of communications, referring to Nike's labor policies practices and stating that "[c]onsumers are savvy and want to know they support companies with good products and practices" and that "[d]uring the shopping season, we encourage shoppers to remember that Nike is the industry's leader in improving factory conditions."

The third element, representations of fact of a commercial nature, is also present. In describing its own labor policies, and the practices and working conditions in factories where its products are made, Nike was making factual representations about its own business operations. In speaking to consumers about working conditions and labor practices in the factories where its products are made, Nike addressed matters within its own knowledge. The wages paid to the factories' employees, the hours they work, the way they are treated, and whether the environmental conditions under which they work violate local health and safety laws, are all matters likely to be within the personal knowledge of Nike executives, employees, or subcontractors. Thus, Nike was in a position to readily verify the truth of any factual assertions it made on these topics.

Because in the statements at issue here Nike was acting as a commercial speaker, because its intended audience was primarily the buyers of its products, and because the statements consisted of factual representations about its own business operations, we conclude that the statements were commercial speech for purposes of applying state laws designed to prevent false advertising and other forms of commercial deception.

As we have explained, to the extent Nike's speech represents expression of opinion or points of view on general policy questions such as the value of economic "globalization," it is noncommercial speech subject to full First Amendment protection. Nike's speech loses that full measure of protection only when it concerns facts material to commercial transactions—here, factual statements about how Nike makes its products.

We conclude, accordingly, that here the trial court and the Court of Appeal erred in characterizing as noncommercial speech, under the First Amendment to the federal Constitution, Nike's allegedly false and misleading statements about labor practices and working conditions in factories where Nike products are made. As the United States Supreme Court has explained, false and misleading speech has no constitutional value in itself and is protected only in circumstances and to the extent necessary to give breathing room for the free debate of public issues. Commercial speech, because it is both more readily verifiable by its speaker and more hardy than noncommercial speech, can be effectively regulated to suppress false and actually or inherently misleading messages without undue risk of chilling public debate. With these basic principles in mind, we conclude that when a corporation, to maintain and increase its sales and profits, makes public statements defending labor practices and working conditions at factories where its products are made, those public statements are commercial speech that may be regulated to prevent consumer deception.

■ *Reversed and remanded.*

CASE CONCEPTS REVIEW

1. Why did the court deem the speech commercial and not political?
2. Why did the court find that the commercial speech was not entitled to any constitutional protections?

10. Takings

Federal and state governments have the power of *eminent domain,* a concept that has roots deep in the common law of England. In order for a society to grow and prosper, the government must be able to claim land for public uses, including parks, roads, and government buildings. A provision in the Fifth Amendment guarantees that where the government takes property for public use, the private owner (whether an individual or an entity) is entitled to *just compensation.* The reach of the takings clause of the Constitution is considerable on a number of fronts.

First, the notion of *property* extends beyond real property. Trade secrets and other intangible property are subject to the provisions of the takings clause, as are rights guaranteed under a contract. Next, governmental action included as a *taking* is also broadly defined. Included are situations where the government simply imposes zoning restrictions or the government allows others to enjoy the use of the property. If Yountville, a city in California, enacts extensive land use regulation on land owned by Ogego Enterprises, the company may be successful in saying that a taking of the land has occurred and it should receive just compensation. In order for Ogego to win, they must show that the governmental action so restricts the company's ability to develop the land that all economic benefit of ownership is ruined or that while some value remains, the government's action is too extreme given the purpose of the regulation. Finally, the taking must be for a *public use.* This term is also broadly construed. The Supreme Court has ruled that public use includes not only purposes that benefit the health, safety, and welfare of the public, but also situations where property is resold to a private entity that plans to develop the land. In other words, it is probably constitutional for property containing a few scattered homes to be taken by the government and sold to private developers who build factories that supply additional employment opportunities and increase the taxes generated from the property. (See the *Kelo* case in Chapter 1.)

11. Due Process

Due process clauses associated with the Fifth Amendment and the Fourteenth Amendment prohibit the government from depriving an individual or a legal entity (including a corporation) of life, liberty, or property without due process of law. As the Supreme Court has interpreted the due process clause embedded in these two amendments to the Constitution, it has developed two complementary doctrines: *procedural due process and substantive due process.*

PROCEDURAL DUE PROCESS This aspect of the Constitution mandates that the government follow specific procedures when it takes completely or denies in part any aspect of life, liberty, or property. Usually, the components of *procedural due process* consist of (1) *notice* that the government is going to act and why, (2) a *hearing* before any governmental action takes place so that the individual or entity with the right has an opportunity to be heard, and (3) an ability to *appeal* the determination made at the hearing. The right to procedural due process extends well beyond situations where the government is infringing on a private property right; it also extends to benefits created by the government, including situations where a driver's license is being revoked or welfare benefits are being curtailed. As a result of the broad coverage of property interests protected under this constitutional right, the precise nature of the protection varies as the nature of an individual's or business entity's interest is balanced against the government's need to take action. Therefore, in a criminal proceeding, the possibility of severe loss of liberty requires that a high level of procedural due process attach. Where a university student at a public institution is charged with academic misconduct, however, fewer protections are necessary because the potential consequences are less harsh.

SUBSTANTIVE DUE PROCESS The underlying rationale associated with procedural due process is that a government action geared toward depriving an individual or an entity of life, liberty, or property must be done in a fair manner. Fairness is also the watchword associated with *substantive due process.* Under this constitutional doctrine, the government act itself must be fair. For many decades, businesses and others used the substantive due process provision to declare many forms of social legislation unconstitutional. Perhaps the most famous case occurred in 1905 when the Supreme Court *(Lochner v. New York)* found the state's attempt to set maximum hours of work for employees violated the employer's fundamental right to contract with its employees. Beginning in 1937, however, the Supreme Court has consistently stated that mere economic legislation should invoke only the *rational basis test* because aspects of economic liberty and associated property rights should be subservient to governmental actions that further the public good. Therefore, the substantive due process clause has little life today when applied to matters of economic regulation.

The substantive due process clause, however, is a vibrant legal theory regarding government actions that impact fundamental rights as opposed to economic rights. The Supreme Court has incorporated in the word *liberty* a significant number of the rights guaranteed under amendments to the Constitution and other rights, although not mentioned in the Constitution, are deemed deep-seated to a society (the most prominent of the latter category is the right to privacy, covered in greater detail in the last section of this chapter.) For example, the Supreme Court has ruled that a two million dollar punitive damages award arising from a controversy justifying only a $4,000 compensatory damage award violated the substantive due process clause. Laws restricting any fundamental right will receive review under the *strict scrutiny test,* meaning that it will be rare that a governmental action that infringes upon a fundamental right protected under the substantive due process doctrine will be found constitutional.

12. Equal Protection

The Fourteenth Amendment provides that the government may not "deny to any person within its jurisdiction the equal protection of the law." As with other constitutional protections, coverage extends to business entities. On the one hand, the doctrine recognizes that in order to perform its functions, government must classify individuals and businesses. A law benefits some groups, some are not affected, and some are harmed. On the other hand, basic principles of justice require that the government treat similarly situated individuals in a similar fashion. Making equal protection decisions require courts to weigh competing interests. The Supreme Court employs the three balancing tests described earlier in the chapter to equal protection cases.

Strict scrutiny test under equal protection

Government action is constitutional under the equal protection clause where legislation necessarily relates to a compelling interest of government.

STRICT SCRUTINY Where government regulation creates a classification system that separates individuals or businesses based on the exercise of a fundamental right or on membership in a suspect class, then the **strict scrutiny test** applies. *Fundamental rights* include the right to vote and the right to engage in interstate travel. A *suspect class* includes race, religion, and national origin. Any classification method directed at a group having a history of being disenfranchised socially or economically will invoke the strict scrutiny test.

Because of the high sensitivity society associates with these two methods of classifying individuals and business entities, the government must meet a very difficult burden before a court will uphold the constitutionality of a government action in light of an equal protection challenge. In order for the regulation to be found constitutional, the classification must be *necessary* to support a *compelling interest* of the government. This strong presumption of unconstitutionality is rarely overcome by the government.

INTERMEDIATE SCRUTINY Where government regulation creates a classification scheme based on sex or gender, the Supreme Court has created the intermediate scrutiny test for determining whether the means (considering the purpose of the legislation and the wording of the legislation) is more important than the ends (classification based on sex or gender that necessarily disenfranchises individuals or businesses). In order for a law to pass muster under the **intermediate scrutiny test**, the government action must *substantially relate* to an *important* government interest.

In practical application, the government may categorize on the basis of sex or gender in some instances, but not in others. The following case illustrates the application of the intermediate scrutiny test within a university environment.

CASE

Mississippi University for Women v. Hogan

SUPREME COURT OF THE UNITED STATES

458 U.S. 718 (1982)

JUSTICE O'CONNOR DELIVERED THE OPINION OF THE COURT.

This case presents the narrow issue of whether a state statute that excludes males from enrolling in a state-supported professional nursing school violates the Equal Protection Clause of the Fourteenth Amendment.

The facts are not in dispute. In 1884, the Mississippi Legislature created the Mississippi Industrial Institute and College for the Education of White Girls of the State of Mississippi, now the oldest state-supported all-female college in the United States. The school, known today as Mississippi University for Women (MUW), has from its inception limited its enrollment to women.

Mississippi maintains no other single-sex public university or college. Thus, we are not faced with the question of whether States can provide "separate but equal" undergraduate institutions for males and females.

In 1971, MUW established a School of Nursing, initially offering a 2-year associate degree. Three years later, the school instituted a 4-year baccalaureate program in nursing and today also offers a graduate program. The School of Nursing has its own faculty and administrative officers and establishes its own criteria for admission.

Respondent, Joe Hogan, is a registered nurse but does not hold a baccalaureate degree in nursing. Since 1974, he has worked as a nursing supervisor in a medical center in Columbus, the city in which MUW is located. In 1979, Hogan applied for admission to the MUW School of Nursing's baccalaureate program. Although he was otherwise qualified, he was denied admission to the School of Nursing solely because of his sex. School officials informed him that he could audit the courses in which he was interested, but could not enroll for credit.

Hogan filed an action in the United States District Court for the Northern District of Mississippi, claiming the single-sex admissions policy of MUW's School of Nursing violated the Equal Protection Clause of the Fourteenth Amendment. Hogan sought injunctive and declaratory relief, as well as compensatory damages.

We begin our analysis aided by several firmly established principles. Because the challenged policy expressly discriminates among applicants on the basis of gender, it is subject to scrutiny under the Equal Protection Clause of the Fourteenth Amendment. That this statutory policy discriminates against males rather than against females does not exempt it from scrutiny or reduce the standard of review. Our decisions also establish that the party seeking to uphold a statute that classifies individuals on the basis of their gender must carry the burden of showing an "exceedingly persuasive justification" for the classification. The burden is met only by showing at least that the classification serves "important governmental objectives and that the discriminatory means employed" are "substantially related to the achievement of those objectives."

Although the test for determining the validity of a gender-based classification is straightforward, it must be applied free of fixed notions concerning the roles and abilities of males and females. Care must be taken in ascertaining whether the statutory objective itself reflects archaic and stereotypic notions. Thus, if the statutory objective is to exclude or "protect" members of one gender because they are presumed to suffer from an inherent handicap or to be innately inferior, the objective itself is illegitimate.

The State's primary justification for maintaining the single-sex admissions policy of MUW's School of Nursing is that it compensates for discrimination against women and, therefore, constitutes educational affirmative action. As applied to the School of Nursing, we find the State's argument unpersuasive.

Mississippi has made no showing that women lacked opportunities to obtain training in the field of nursing or to attain positions of leadership in that field when the MUW School of Nursing opened its door or that women currently are deprived of such opportunities. In fact, in 1970, the year before the School of Nursing's first class enrolled, women earned 94 percent of the nursing baccalaureate degrees conferred in Mississippi and 98.6 percent of the degrees earned nationwide.

Rather than compensate for discriminatory barriers faced by women, MUW's policy of excluding males from admission to the School of Nursing tends to perpetuate the stereotyped view of nursing as an exclusively woman's job. By assuring that Mississippi allots more openings in its state-supported nursing schools to women than it does to men, MUW's admissions policy lends credibility to the old view that women, not men, should become nurses and makes the assumption that nursing is a field for women a self-fulfilling prophecy. Thus, we conclude that although the State recited a "benign, compensatory purpose," it failed to establish that the alleged objective is the actual purpose underlying the discriminatory classification.

■ *The judgment of the Court of Appeals is affirmed.*

CASE CONCEPT REVIEW

1. Describe the equal protection test employed. What are its components?
2. What do you think the author of the opinion thought was the actual reason that the state created the discriminatory classification system?

Intermediate scrutiny test under equal protection

Government action is constitutional under the equal protection clause where legislation is substantially related to an important purpose of government.

RATIONAL BASIS Where government regulation is aimed at social welfare and economic matters, then the courts will apply the **rational basis test** to determine if the equal protection clause is violated. Because the government must only articulate a *legitimate (or rational) reason* for the legislation and establish a *reasonable relationship* between the legislation as worded and the reason for the legislation, most every governmental action challenged under the rational basis means-ends test is found constitutional.

For example, in the "Business Management Decision" presented at the beginning of the chapter, the Plastic Company is challenging an economic regulation. Therefore, the rational basis test applies, and the chances of Plastic Company being able to convince a court that the dissimilar treatment between paper carton manufacturers and plastic container manufacturers violates the equal protection clause is slim.

PRIVACY

13. Privacy Rights

Rational basis test under equal protection

Government action is constitutional under the equal protection clause where legislation is reasonably related to a legitimate purpose of government.

As one justice of the United States Supreme Court remarked in 1928, the right of privacy is "the right to be left alone—the most comprehensive of rights and the right most valued by civilized man." Surprising to many, the Constitution does not expressly provide a right of privacy capable of protecting an individual or a business from intrusions by government. During the 1960s, in a series of controversial decisions, the United States Supreme Court drew from various provisions of the Bill of Rights, in particular the due process clause, and found that a right of privacy was implied by the Constitution. Therefore, even though no amendment establishes such a right, through Supreme Court decisions a right of privacy has been found in matters of contraception, marriage, lifestyle, and, of course, abortion.

With the development of a constitutional right of privacy currently mired in considerable debate and found to be present in only selected areas of life, Congress has acted to protect individual and business privacy interests in some contexts. The *USA Patriot Act,* for instance, enacted within six weeks after the September 11, 2001, terrorist attacks, empowers government officials to monitor communications and access financial and other types of information. Included in the USA Patriot Act are checks on governmental actions to protect privacy interests. For example, a special court was formed to issue warrants for certain types of searches of property, including medical and financial records. As more private information is available, especially on the Internet, Congress and the judiciary will continue to require that privacy rights of individuals be protected.

CHAPTER SUMMARY

An Introduction to the Constitution and Government Regulation

1. The Constitution creates the federal government, establishes the roles of the federal and state governments, and provides limitations on government that protect individuals and businesses from unwarranted intrusions.

THE FEDERAL FORM OF GOVERNMENT

Separation of Powers

1. The doctrine of separation of powers divides the federal government into three branches.
2. The role of the legislative branch is to make the laws, the executive branch enforces the laws, and the judicial branch interprets the laws.

Checks and Balances

1. The system of checks and balances acts to disperse the power of government.
2. The power of judicial review ensures that any act of the federal government or a state government must comply with the Constitution.

FEDERALISM

Nature of Federalism

1. Under federalism, government power is divided between two sovereigns: federal and state.

Distribution of Powers

1. The powers of the federal government, generally, are limited to those listed or enumerated in the Constitution.
2. State police powers are those government functions relating to public safety, health, welfare, and morals.
3. Concurrent powers are those that can be exercised by both federal and state governments.
4. The privileges and immunities clause and the full faith and credit clause both encourage strong working relationships between and among individuals and business located in different states.

Commerce Clause

1. The commerce clause provides that the federal government regulate interstate commerce.
2. The judicially created "dormant" commerce clause doctrine forbids a state from unreasonably restraining interstate commerce.

Supremacy and Preemption

1. The supremacy clause provides that federal law prevails over state law.
2. Federal preemption is the doctrine that delineates where federal and state laws can co-exist and where federal law is superior.

CHECKS ON THE POWER OF GOVERNMENT

Basic Aspects of Constitutional Limitations

1. Constitutional protections apply only to state actions.
2. If a government action is challenged as being unconstitutional, the courts will employ one of three tests to balance the interests of the government against the constitutional right being asserted.

Freedom of Speech

1. Political speech receives a heightened level of protection from government interference.
2. Some commercial speech, primarily speech that misleads, receives no protection from the First Amendment. Other types of commercial speech receive an intermediate level of protection.

Takings

1. The Constitution prohibits the government from taking property unless just compensation is provided.

Due Process

1. Procedural due process references to the process the government must follow when it deprives an individual or entity of life, liberty, or property.
2. Substantive due process questions whether the content of legislation is fair.

Equal Protection

1. The Constitution guarantees that the government may not deny individuals and entities equal protection of the laws.
2. Where government regulation creates a classification system that separates individuals or businesses based on the exercise of a fundamental right or on membership in a suspect class, the *strict scrutiny test* then applies to determine if the equal protection clause is violated.
3. Where government regulation creates a classification scheme based on sex or gender, then the *intermediate scrutiny test* applies.

4. Where government regulation is aimed at social welfare and economic matters, then the courts will apply the *rational basis test.*

PRIVACY

Privacy Rights 1. Although privacy rights are not mentioned in the wording of the Constitution, the United States Supreme Court has fashioned a constitutional right of privacy.

REVIEW QUESTIONS AND PROBLEMS

1. Match each term in Column A with the appropriate statement in Column B.

A	B
(1) Federalism	(a) Under the Constitution, the process by which each branch of government restrains the power of another branch
(2) Separation of powers	(b) A provision of the Constitution that requires courts in one state to honor contracts and court judgments created in another state
(3) Supremacy clause	(c) A provision of the Constitution that provides the federal government with the power to regulate business transactions between and among individuals and businesses located in different states
(4) Judicial review	(d) Communication that relates to a business transaction
(5) Commerce clause	(e) Constitutional mandate that requires branches of government, with each branch charged with performing certain functions
(6) Commercial speech	(f) Government power is divided between two sovereigns
(7) Checks and balances	(g) Protects individuals and businesses from government actions that improperly categorize
(8) Due process clause	(h) The doctrine that allows the federal courts to determine whether acts by the federal government or the state governments conform to edicts of the Constitution
(9) Full faith and credit clause	(i) Constitutional provision mandating that federal law is superior to state law
(10) Equal protection clause	(j) Protects individuals and businesses from government actions that impede the enjoyment of life, liberty, or property

2. Should one branch of the federal government be more powerful than another? What are the benefits associated with a system of government where powers are dispersed among three branches?
3. Imagine that the doctrine of judicial review did not exist within the United States. What would be the ramifications?
4. A software consulting entity offers its service in all fifty states. Would the business prefer to be regulated by state law or federal law? What provisions of the Constitution would provide for federal regulation? What happens if there is a conflict between federal law and state law?
5. California enacted the Wine Fair Dealing Act, which requires out-of-state suppliers of wine to show good cause if they wish to terminate a distributorship. In-state suppliers of wine are exempt from this requirement and can cancel at will. A New York wine supplier sought to end its relationship with a California firm. The California firm, invoking the operative provision of the Wine Fair Dealing Act, objected because the New York firm had not demonstrated good cause for the termination. The New York supplier argues that this provision of California law violates the commerce clause of the United States Constitution. Is the commerce clause violated? Why?
6. Massachusetts passed a law forbidding any public utility from encouraging a pro-nuclear energy position in utility advertisements or in billing information provided to customers. Is the targeting speech protected under the freedom of speech clause? If so, what type of protection does that speech receive?
7. Momma Cass lived all of her eighty years in a home nestled next to a pine grove within fifty feet of a lake and included within the city limits of Elliott Township. The Cass home was in need of repairs, as were a number of homes in neighborhood. The City of Elliott wishes to exercise its eminent domain powers to purchase the Cass home and ones in the neighborhood. The homes would be razed and a new shopping center would be built next to the lake. Is this a proper use of eminent domain powers? How does the Constitution protect the interests of Momma Cass, if at all?
8. Congress wishes to impose regulations on the insurance industry. What test would the United State Supreme Court use to determine whether such regulations would violate the substantive due process rights of insurance companies that would be subject to the regulations? What is the likely outcome of the case?
9. Iowa was looking to increase tax revenues. Racetrack and riverboat gambling establishments were subject to a maximum tax rate of 12 percent, until the Iowa legislature passed a law last year that raises the allowable maximum tax rate on racetrack gambling to 42 percent. Racetrack gambling establishments assert that the new statute violates their equal protection rights. Are they correct? Why?

10. The City of Houghton enacted an ordinance that forbids religious groups from distributing religious materials within the city limits of Houghton unless the distributor was granted a permit. Other types of materials could be distributed without a permit. What concerns do you have about the constitutionality of this ordinance?

Internet Resources:

For an excellent presentation of materials relating to the law-making process and the Constitution, see: http://www.house.gov/house/Educate.shtml

To see high-resolution photographs of the Constitution and other information regarding the Constitution, see: http://www.archives.gov/national-archives-experience/charters/constitution.html

PART II

BASIC LEGAL CONCEPTS

6 Criminal Law and Business

CHAPTER OUTLINE

BASIC CONCEPTS

1. Terminology
2. Classification of Crimes
3. Administrative Crimes
4. White-Collar Crimes
5. Damage Suits

ESSENTIAL ELEMENTS

6. Act and Intent
7. Capacity
8. Corporate Liability
9. Defenses to Criminal Prosecutions

CONSTITUTIONAL PROTECTIONS

10. General Principles
11. The Fourth Amendment
12. The Fifth Amendment
13. The Sixth Amendment
14. The Eighth Amendment

CHAPTER PREVIEW

In this chapter, plus the following six, we present material that should help provide you with essential background to enhance your understanding of the topics presented throughout the rest of this text. The basic concepts covered in Chapters 6 through 12 include crimes, torts, property, business organization forms, and the regulation of international business transactions.

Much of our legal system and our laws are designed to protect us from wrongful conduct. When this conduct is a wrong against society, it is a crime. Criminal conduct usually affects individual persons, and, as noted in the preceding chapter, this effect is, by definition, tortious. Crime also has a tremendous impact on business. The increase in business-related criminal activities during the 1990s, including the debacles associated with Enron and ImClone, among others, should cause each of us to ponder what changes need to be made in our business values and conduct. This chapter introduces a number of topics concerning crime and business.

BUSINESS MANAGEMENT DECISION

You are the production manager for a small manufacturing firm. One product being made involves the use of toxic chemicals. A supervisor reports to you that a small amount of toxic fumes is leaking into your employees' workspace. Upon investigation, you discover that it will cost in excess of $3 million to repair the leak. This dollar figure represents an amount of money that your firm does not have readily available. Further, you discover that no employee has complained of (or possibly even noticed) the leak.

What should you do?

BASIC CONCEPTS

1. Terminology

Conduct is criminal because a *legislative body* (e.g., Congress or a state legislature) has declared it to be *wrongful* and has authorized *punishment* if it occurs. Some crimes, such as murder, have always been considered wrongful by a civilized society. They are said to be *malum in se,* or per se wrongful. That is, they are evil by their vary nature. Other crimes have been created by legislative bodies because of a desire to prevent certain conduct. Such crimes are said to be *malum prohibitum.* For example, gambling is a crime only because a legislature has declared it to be.

The criminal law has developed some terminology separate and distinct from that of civil-law cases. The word *prosecution* is used to describe criminal proceedings, and *prosecutor* is the name usually given to the attorney who represents the people. Although the proceedings are brought on behalf of the people of a given state or the United States, the people are generally not called the plaintiff, as in a civil case. Rather, the case is entitled *U.S. v. John Doe, or State of Ohio v. John Doe.*

In *felony* cases, the usual procedure is for a court to conduct a preliminary hearing to determine if there is sufficient evidence that the accused committed the crime as charged to justify submission of the case to the grand jury. If the court finds there is probable cause, the accused is *bound over* to the grand jury. The grand jury examines evidence against the accused and determines if it is sufficient to cause a reasonable person to believe that the accused probably committed the offense. If this *probable cause* exists, the grand jury *indicts* the accused by returning to the court what is called a *true bill.* If it is the opinion of the grand jury that the evidence is insufficient to indict, then a *no true bill* is returned to the court. Indictment by the grand jury will be discussed with the Fifth Amendment, later in this chapter.

If the crime involved is a *misdemeanor* or if the accused waives the presentment of the case to the grand jury, the prosecution may proceed by filing the charges in a document known as an *information.* Both an indictment and an information serve to notify and to inform the accused of the nature of the charges, so a defense may be prepared.

The technical aspects of the various crimes are beyond the scope of this text; however, it should be recognized that every crime has elements that distinguish it from other crimes. Larceny, robbery, and burglary are crimes with many common characteristics, yet they are legally distinct. Robbery is theft with force; larceny implies no force. Burglary is breaking and entering with intent to commit a felony (usually larceny). One act may be more than one crime, and it is possible to be convicted of more than one crime for any particular act. Many crimes are actually a part of another crime and are known as *lesser included* offenses. An assault would be a lesser included offense of forcible rape.

Criminal cases differ from civil cases in the amount of proof required to convict. In a civil case, the plaintiff is entitled to a verdict if, when weighing the evidence, the scales tip ever so slightly in favor of a plaintiff. The burden is one of preponderance of the evidence. In a criminal case, however, the people or prosecution must prove the defendant's guilt *beyond a reasonable doubt.* Note that the law does not require proof "beyond the shadow of a doubt" or proof that is susceptible of only one conclusion. It does require such a quantity of proof that a reasonable person viewing the evidence would have *no reasonable doubt* about the guilt of the defendant. A summary of basic differences between criminal law and civil law is presented in Table 6-1.

2. Classification of Crimes

One way to classify criminal conduct is by the purpose for which the conduct is prohibited by society. In essence, this classification system seeks to provide protection to certain persons or

TABLE 6-1 ■ Depiction of Foundational Differences Between Criminal Law and Civil Law

	CRIMINAL	CIVIL
Source of Law	Always based on statute	May be used on either statute or common law
Who brings suit?	The state (i.e., government)	Individual or entity that suffered harm
Burden of Proof	Beyond a reasonable doubt	Preponderance of the evidence
Remedy	Punishment (e.g., imprisonment, fine)	Usually damages, but also judicial decree forcing performance or forbidding activity
Nature	Protect society	Provide compensation or other relief

organizations or to protect all of us from deviant behavior. Table 6-2 classifies a number of crimes from the perspective of the *protection* that is to be provided.

TABLE 6-2 ■ Classification of Crimes by Purpose

1. *Protection of the person from hard*
   - Assault and battery
   - Kidnapping
   - Manslaughter
   - Mayhem
   - Murder
   - Sexual crimes (See 3 below)

2. *Protection of property*
   - Arson
   - Blackmail
   - Burglary
   - Embezzlement
   - Extortion
   - Forgery
   - Larceny
   - Robbery

3. *Protection from sexual abuse*
   - Adultery
   - Bigamy
   - Incest
   - Rape
   - Sodomy

4. *Protection of government*
   - Bribery of officials
   - Sabotage
   - Treason

5. *Protection of the courts*
   - Bribery of witnesses, judges, jurors
   - Perjury

6. *Protection of the public interest*
   - Antitrust
   - Disorderly conduct
   - Food and drug laws
   - Gambling
   - Liquor licenses and drunkenness
   - Narcotics
   - Obscenity
   - Pollution

Treason
The offense of attempting by overt acts to overthrow the government of the state to which the offender owes allegiance or of betraying the state into the hands of a foreign power

Felony
A criminal offense that is punishable by death or imprisonment in a penitentiary

Misdemeanor
A criminal offense, less than a felony, that is punishable by fine or jail sentence

A second method used to classify crimes is the *punishment* that the courts can impose on the wrongdoer after the government's prosecutor has proven that the criminal conduct occurred. Historically, upon a person's conviction of a crime, one of the following punishments is imposed by the court: (1) death, (2) imprisonment, (3) fine, (4) removal from office, (5) disqualification to hold and enjoy any office or to vote, or (6) a combination of these punishments. Based on the degree of permissible punishment to be imposed, crimes have been traditionally classified as **treason, felonies**, and **misdemeanors**. Treason against the United States consists of levying war against it or in giving aid and comfort to its enemies. Punishment for treason is often death. *Felonies* are offenses usually defined by statute to include all crimes punishable by incarceration in a penitentiary. Examples are murder, grand larceny, arson, and rape. Crimes of lesser importance than felonies—such as petty larceny, trespass, and disorderly conduct—are called misdemeanors. They are usually defined as any crimes punishable by short imprisonment (less than one year) in the local jail. A fine may also be levied against a person who commits a crime.

Violations of traffic ordinances, building codes, and similar municipal ordinances prosecuted before a city magistrate are sometimes termed *petty offenses* or *public torts* instead of crimes. The distinction is insignificant; because whether they are called crimes or public torts, the result is the same—the party charged may be fined or put in jail or both. Table 6-3 lists typical felonies and misdemeanors.

TABLE 6-3 ■ Classification of Crimes by Punishment

TYPICAL FELONIES (Imprisonment for More Than One Year and/or Fine)	TYPICAL MISDEMEANORS (Jail for Less Than One Year and/or Fine)
Aggravated assault	Rape
Arson	Robbery
Bribery	Battery
Burglary	Disorderly conduct
Embezzlement	Gambling
Forgery	Larceny (petty)
Kidnapping	Prostitution
Larceny (grand)	Public disturbance
Manslaughter	Simple assault
Mayhem	Traffic offenses
Murder	Trespass
Price fixing	

3. Administrative Crimes

Some crimes are said to be *administrative crimes.* Administrative agencies such as the Environmental Protection Agency or the Food and Drug Administration may adopt rules, the violation of which is punishable as a crime. The legislative body by statute declares the violation to be criminal and delegates the power to the agency to adopt the rules and regulations.

In most administrative crimes the statute fixes the penalty for the violation. In a few cases, the statutes not only authorize the agency to create the regulations but also to fix the penalty. For example, a statute may authorize an agency to issue regulations and to set penalties not to exceed a stated fine or time in jail or both. Such statutes may be valid if the punishment is reasonable.

Agencies may not be given the power to conduct the trial, as a general rule. If conduct is criminal, the accused has a right to a trial by jury. Exceptions exist for minor penalties such as revocation or suspension of licenses or levying small fines. Such proceedings may be considered quasi-criminal in the nature of a penalty similar to traffic violations and parking meter fines.

4. White-Collar Crimes

Historically, the criminal law was concerned with acts of violence and the wrongful application of physical force. Murder, arson, rape, burglary, robbery, and other violent crimes affected the business community, but businesses seldom committed them. Today, businesspeople are guilty of hundreds of new crimes, the so-called white-collar or business crimes.

White-collar or *business* crimes are illegal acts committed by guile, deceit, and concealment, rather than by force and violence. Such crimes usually involve attempts to obtain money, property, or services without paying for them or to secure some other business advantage. Such crimes are not limited to executives; they are committed by employees at all levels. Any employee with access to cash may be guilty of **embezzlement** or theft of company property. Salespersons may engage in price fixing in violation of the antitrust laws. Stockbrokers may engage in illegal stock trading, as may officials of companies involved in mergers and acquisitions.

Embezzlement
The fraudulent appropriation by one person, acting in a fiduciary capacity, of the money or property of another

Bernie Madoff pleaded guilty in 2009 to the white-collar crime of bilking investors out of an estimated $65 billion.

Business crime is a significant cost of doing business. Losses from embezzlement and employee theft, including theft through manipulation of computers, probably exceed losses from burglary and larceny. There is evidence that shoplifting by employees exceeds shoplifting by customers. The cost of crime results in higher prices for consumers. Costs include higher insurance premiums as well as the cost of the property stolen.

Fraud in various forms is rampant. The fraudulent use of another's credit card, forgery, obtaining money by false pretenses, and false auto repair bills are everyday occurrences. By statute, all these are crimes. Bribery, kickbacks, and payoffs have become so common that the Securities and Exchange Commission demands that the amounts paid be included in the reports filed by major corporations.

Although business crime does not depend on force or violence, physical injury and even death can be caused by it. Defective products sold in violation of applicable statutes frequently cause injuries. Building code violations may result in fire and injury to persons and property. Some businesses, to compete, buy stolen merchandise or employ illegal aliens. The maintenance of a dangerous workplace may be a crime. In fact, in one case the operators of a business were convicted of murdering an employee who was poisoned by cyanide used on the job.

One reason for the massive amount of white-collar crime is that, in the past, the risk of being caught and sent to prison was slight. White-collar crime has often been considered a legitimate cost of doing business, especially overseas. A business is usually hesitant to prosecute its employees because disclosure would have an adverse effect on the image of the business. Even when there have been successful prosecutions, sentences have been minimal in the light of the economic consequences of the crimes. In many states there are inadequate prison facilities and; as a result, judges often do not send white-collar criminals to prison.

Now that the relation of crime to business has reached crisis proportions (e.g., Worldcom, Enron, Tyco), many people are advocating new approaches in an attempt to alter criminal conduct. Perhaps the most common suggestion is to impose stiff penalties for white-collar crime. Table 6-4 illustrates that Congress has placed an increased emphasis on the criminal penalty. Another recommendation is to improve the internal controls of businesses, so internal theft and wrongdoing are more likely to be discovered. Finally, there is a trend toward punishing corporate officials who commit crimes on behalf of their corporations. A corporate official who fixes prices with competitors in violation of the Sherman Antitrust Act is more likely to go to prison now than in the past, and the

TABLE 6-4 ■ Recent Statutes Strengthening Criminal Sanctions

Antitrust Criminal Penalty Enhancement & Reform Act of 2004	Violation of Sherman Act	$100,000,000 fine for corporations; $1,000,000 and imprisonment for 10 years.
Clean Air Act of 1990	Releasing hazardous air pollutants	$1,000,000 fine for organization plus fifteen years in prison (These penalties double for subsequent offense.)
Sarbanes-Oxley Act (2002) amending the Securities Exchange Act of 1934	Trading securities based on material, non-public information	$25,000,000 fine for organization; $5,000,000 fine for individual plus twenty years in prison.

fine for such conduct has been greatly increased. Today, knowledge about the criminal law, its enforcement, and crime prevention are key elements in business decision making.

5. Damage Suits

In addition to the governmental sanctions of a fine and confinement for a person's criminal conduct, the victim of a crime often seeks to recover dollar damages in a civil lawsuit. The victim's claim is based on the fact that the criminal conduct constitutes a tort. This civil remedy often is a hollow one because many criminals do not have any money with which to pay the damages and there is usually no liability insurance covering criminal conduct.

With respect to white-collar crime, many legislative bodies go farther and enact legislation providing for triple damages for the victims of certain crimes. For example, if a party is convicted of a Sherman Act violation such as price fixing, the conviction creates a prima facie case for triple damages on behalf of all of the victims of the price-fixing conspiracy. Such parties are also entitled to attorney's fees and court costs.

One very important federal law in this regard is known as RICO, the 1970 Racketeer Influenced and Corrupt Organizations Act. Its goal is to combat organized crime by authorizing private parties to file suits for triple damages and attorney's fees when federal laws dealing with various forms of fraud have been violated. Such suits are possible when an individual or a business has twice within a ten-year period violated one of these enumerated federal statutes, which include wire and mail fraud.

The law has had an *unintended impact.* It has not encouraged many suits against organized crime. Rather, it has encouraged suits against accounting firms, brokerage houses, banks, and other businesses. More than 75 percent of all RICO suits involve securities frauds and other types of business fraud. Less than 10 percent involve criminal activity generally associated with organized crime. RICO makes it a crime to: (1) use income obtained from racketeering activity to purchase any interest in a commercial enterprise, (2) acquire or maintain an interest in an enterprise through racketeering activity, (3) conduct or participate in the affairs of an enterprise through racketeering activity, or (4) conspire to do any of the preceding activities. "Racketeering activity" requires an individual commit two offences, including bribery, embezzlement, mail and wire fraud, and securities fraud. No conviction of the "underlying offense" is needed, only proof during the RICO trial that they occurred. The use of the mail or telephone makes access to RICO very easy for any plaintiff alleging fraud in a business transaction. A plaintiff need not prove racketeering injury—only an injury resulting from the illegal act.

RICO cases often involve routine commercial transactions that generally are not considered criminal. For example, RICO has been used by the Federal Deposit Insurance Corporation (FDIC) to recover funds lost in a bank failure. RICO cases have arisen in landlord-tenant disputes, labor relations cases, the sale of land, and, of course, the sale of securities. In 1989, the U.S. Supreme Court found that RICO was applicable to a pattern of bribery utilized by a telephone company to encourage members of a public utilities commission to grant increased rates. The Court reinstated a RICO suit seeking triple damages against the phone company on behalf of the company's customers.

RICO provides both criminal sanctions and civil liability. Criminal fines, for example, may reach $25,000 per violation. A business also may sue for treble damages for injuries caused by a violation of the RICO statute.

ESSENTIAL ELEMENTS

6. Act and Intent

As a general rule, a crime involves a combination of an *act* and *criminal intent.* Criminal intent without an overt act to carry it out is not criminal. If Joe says to himself, "I am going to rob the First National Bank," no crime has been committed. Some act toward carrying out this intent is necessary. If Joe, however, communicates his desire to Frank, who agrees to assist him, then a crime has been committed. This crime is known as **conspiracy**. The criminal act was the communication between Joe and Frank.

Conspiracy

An agreement by two or more persons to commit a crime

Just as a crime requires an act, most crimes also require criminal intent. A wrongful act committed without the requisite criminal intent is not a crime. Criminal intent may be supplied by negligence to the degree that it equals intent. If a person drives a car so recklessly that another is killed, his or her criminal intent may be supplied by the negligent act.

Criminal intent is not synonymous with motive. Motive is not an element of a crime. Proof of motive may help in establishing guilt, but it is not an essential element of a prosecution.

Some crimes are known as *specific intent* crimes. When a crime has a specific intent as part of its definition, that specific intent must be proved beyond a reasonable doubt. In a burglary prosecution, there must be proof of intent to commit some felony, such as larceny, rape, or murder. Also, if a crime is defined in part "with intent to defraud," this specific intent must be proved, as any other element of the crime must be.

The following case discusses the meaning of "willfulness" in the context of a criminal defendant's defense to charges of evading the payment of federal income taxes and failing to file an income tax return. Note that the court accepts one argument but rejects another presented by the defendant.

CASE

Cheek v. U.S.

498 U.S. 192 (1991)

WHITE, J.

Title 26, § 7201 of the United States Code provides that any person "who willfully attempts in any manner to evade or defeat any tax imposed by this title or the payment thereof" shall be guilty of a felony. Under 26 U.S.C. § 7203, "[a]ny person required under this title … or by regulations made under authority thereof to make a return … who willfully fails to … make such return" shall be guilty of a misdemeanor. This case turns on the meaning of the word "willfully" as used in §§ 7201 and 7203.

Petitioner John L. Cheek has been a pilot for American Airlines since 1973. He filed federal income tax returns through 1979 but thereafter ceased to file returns. He also claimed an increasing number of withholding allowances—eventually claiming 60 allowances by mid-1980—and for the years 1981 and 1984 indicated on his W-4 forms that he was exempt from federal income tax.

As a result of his activities, petitioner was indicted for 10 violations of federal law. He was charged with six counts of willfully failing to file a federal income tax return for the years 1980,1981, and 1983 through 1986, in violation of 26 U.S.C. § 7203. He was further charged with three counts of willfully attempting to evade his income taxes for the years 1980,1981, and 1983 in violation of 26 U.S.C. § 7201. In those years, American Airlines withheld substantially less than the amount of tax petitioner owed because of the numerous allowances and exempt status he claimed on his W-4 forms. The tax offenses with which petitioner was charged are specific intent crimes that require the defendant to have acted willfully.

Cheek represented himself at trial and testified in his defense. He admitted that he had not filed personal income tax returns during the years in question. He testified that as early as 1978, he had begun attending seminars sponsored by, and following the advice of, a group that believes, among other things, that the federal tax system is unconstitutional. Some of the speakers at these meetings were lawyers who purported to give professional opinions about the invalidity of the federal income tax laws. Cheek produced a letter from an attorney stating that the Sixteenth Amendment did not authorize a tax on wages and salaries but only on gain or profit. Petitioner's defense was that, based on the indoctrination he received from this group and from his own study, he sincerely believed that the tax laws were being unconstitutionally enforced and that his actions during the 1980–1986 period were lawful. He therefore argued that he had acted without the willfulness required for conviction of the various offenses with which he was charged.

In the course of its instructions, the trial court instructed the jury that if it found that Cheek "honestly and reasonably believed that he was not required to pay income taxes or to file tax returns," a not guilty verdict should be returned.

The District Judge gave the jury an additional instruction. This instruction stated in part that "[a]n honest but unreasonable belief is not a defense and does not negate willfulness," and that "[a]dvice or research resulting in the conclusion that wages of a privately employed person are not income or that the tax laws are unconstitutional is not objectively reasonable and cannot serve as the basis for a good faith misunderstanding of the law defense.". The jury returned a verdict finding petitioner guilty on all counts.

Petitioner appealed his convictions, arguing that the District Court erred by instructing the jury that only an objectively reasonable misunderstanding of the law negates the statutory willfulness requirement. The United States Court of Appeals for the Seventh Circuit rejected that contention and affirmed the convictions. We granted certiorari.

The general rule that ignorance of the law or a mistake of law is no defense to criminal prosecution is deeply rooted in the American legal system. Based on the notion that the law is definite and knowable, the common law presumed that every person knew the law.

The proliferation of statutes and regulations has sometimes made it difficult for the average citizen to know and comprehend the extent of the duties and obligations imposed by the tax laws. Congress has accordingly softened the impact of the common-law presumption by making specific intent to violate the law an element of certain federal criminal tax offenses. Thus, the Court almost 60 years ago interpreted the statutory term "willfully" as used in the federal criminal tax statutes as carving out an exception to the traditional rule.

Willfulness, as construed by our prior decisions in criminal tax cases, requires the Government to prove that the law imposed a duty on the defendant, that the defendant knew of this duty, and that he voluntarily and intentionally violated that duty.

In this case, if Cheek asserted that he truly believed that the Internal Revenue Code did not purport to treat wages as income, and the jury believed him, the Government would not have carried its burden to prove willfulness, however unreasonable a court might deem such a belief. Of course, in deciding whether to credit Cheek's good-faith belief claim, the jury would be free to consider any admissible evidence from any source showing that Cheek was aware of his duty to file a return and to treat wages as income.

It was, therefore, error to instruct the jury to disregard evidence of Cheek's understanding that, within the meaning of the tax laws, he was not a person required to file a return or to pay income taxes and that wages are not taxable income, as incredible as such misunderstandings of and beliefs about the law might be. Of course, the more unreasonable the asserted beliefs or misunderstandings are, the more likely the jury will consider them to be nothing more than simple disagreement with known legal duties imposed by the tax laws and will find that the Government has carried its burden of proving knowledge.

Cheek asserted in the trial court that he should be acquitted because he believed in good faith that the income tax law is unconstitutional as applied to him and thus could not legally impose any duty upon him of which he should have been aware. Such a submission is unsound.

Claims that some of the provisions of the tax code are unconstitutional are submissions of a different order. They do not arise from innocent mistakes caused by the complexity of the Internal Revenue Code. Rather, they reveal full knowledge of the provisions at issue and a studied conclusion, however wrong, that those provisions are invalid and unenforceable. Thus in this case, Cheek paid his taxes for years; but after attending various seminars and based on his own study, he concluded that the income tax laws could not constitutionally require him to pay a tax.

We do not believe that Congress contemplated that such a taxpayer, without risking criminal prosecution, could ignore the duties imposed upon him by the Internal Revenue Code.

We thus hold that in a case like this, a defendant's views about the validity of the tax statutes are irrelevant to the issue of willfulness and need not be heard by the jury; and if they were, an instruction to disregard them would be proper. For this purpose, it makes no difference whether the claims of invalidity are frivolous or have substance. It was, therefore, not error in this case for the District Judge to instruct the jury not to consider Cheek's claims that the tax laws were unconstitutional. However, it was error for the court to instruct the jury that petitioner's asserted beliefs that wages are not income and that he was not a taxpayer within the meaning of the Internal Revenue Code should not be considered by the jury in determining whether Cheek had acted willfully.

continued

For the reasons set forth in the opinion above, the judgment of the Court of Appeals is vacated, and the case is remanded for further proceedings consistent with this opinion.

■ *The judgment of the Court of Appeals is vacated, and the case is remanded for further proceedings consistent with this opinion.*

CASE CONCEPTS REVIEW

1. Cheek purports to have two strongly held beliefs about the application of the Sixteenth Amendment, in particular, and the federal tax laws, in general. How would you state these beliefs?
2. The trial court and court of appeals agreed with each other that a defendant in a criminal tax evasion case must establish "an objectively reasonable misunderstanding" of the law to defeat the government's showing of a "willful" violation. What is meant by the phrase "objectively reasonable misunderstanding?"
3. Why does the Court not accept Cheek's argument that his belief in the tax laws being unconstitutional defeats the showing of "willfulness"?

There is a presumption of intent in crimes that do not require a specific intent. The intent in such crimes may be implied by the facts. In other words, the doing of the criminal act implies the criminal intent. The accused may rebut this presumption, however. The accused is presumed to intend the natural and probable consequences of his or her acts. Thus, if one performs an act that causes a result the criminal law is designed to prevent, one is legally responsible, even though the actual result was not intended. If a robber dynamites a safe and a passerby is killed in the explosion, the robber is guilty of homicide even though he or she did not actually intend to kill the passerby; the robber intended the natural and probable consequences of his or her act.

In some instances, criminal liability may be imposed without fault or without criminal intent. Such crimes are often referred to as *strict liability crimes.* The crime consists of conduct, and the law does not require that the actor have any particular intent or mental state. In effect, the crime consists of conduct that brings about a stated result. It is immaterial whether the conduct is intentional, reckless, or negligent. Usually only a misdemeanor, the conduct is declared to be criminal to discourage it. For example, most liquor and narcotics laws, pure food and drug laws, and traffic laws impose liability without fault. Under these statutes, proof of the state of mind of the accused is not required. Proof of the sale of alcoholic beverages to a minor is a crime, even though the seller did not intend to commit an unlawful act.

7. Capacity

In common law children under the age of 7 were conclusively presumed to lack sufficient mental capacity to form criminal intent. Those over 14 were treated as fully capable of committing a crime. Children between the ages of 7 and 14 were subject to a rebuttable presumption that they could have criminal capacity, but this presumption could be overcome by proof of lack of mental capacity. Many states have changed these ages by statute, and all states have juvenile courts that provide special procedures for crimes involving minors. Juvenile courts usually handle cases involving persons under 18. They attempt to avoid harsh punishment and seek to rehabilitate the juvenile and prevent further criminal conduct. However, most states allow the prosecution to elect to try an offender as an adult for certain serious crimes, such as murder or rape.

8. Corporate Liability

Originally the law was written such that a corporation could not be held criminally liable, since it was incapable of forming criminal intent. Corporations were not liable for the conduct of others, including agents and employees acting within the scope of their employment on behalf of the corporation. Today a corporation is considered a person as the word is used in most criminal statutes, and a corporation may have criminal liability.

Corporate criminal liability may be imposed under the strict liability theory or under the vicarious liability concept. A vicarious liability crime occurs where one person without personal fault is liable for the conduct of another. Some criminal statutes impose criminal liability on a principal for the criminal conduct of its agents and servants. For example, most states have statutes that impose liability on the employer if an agent sells articles short weight or sells liquor to a minor. This vicarious liability is imposed even though the employer may have instructed the employee not to engage in the illegal conduct. Vicarious liability is often imposed on corporations, especially if the activity is performed in part by the board of directors, an officer, or high managerial agent. Lack of criminal intent on the part of the corporate principal is no defense.

The following case addresses the subject of criminal intent regarding a corporate defendant.

CASE

Arthur Andersen, LLP v. United States

SUPREME COURT OF THE UNITED STATES

544 U.S. 696 (2005)

CHIEF JUSTICE REHNQUIST DELIVERED THE OPINION OF THE COURT

As Enron Corporation's financial difficulties became public in 2001, petitioner Arthur Andersen LLP, Enron's auditor, instructed its employees to destroy documents pursuant to its document retention policy. A jury found that this action made petitioner guilty of violating 18 U.S.C. §§ 1512(b)(2)(A) and (B). These sections make it a crime to "knowingly use intimidation or physical force, threaten, or corruptly persuade another person … with intent to … cause" that person to "withhold" documents from, or "alter" documents for use in, an "official proceeding." The Court of Appeals for the Fifth Circuit affirmed. We hold that the jury instructions failed to convey properly the elements of a "corrupt persuasion" conviction under § 1512(b), and therefore reverse.

Enron Corporation, during the 1990's, switched its business from operation of natural gas pipelines to an energy conglomerate, a move that was accompanied by aggressive accounting practices and rapid growth. Petitioner audited Enron's publicly filed financial statements and provided internal audit and consulting services to it. Petitioner's "engagement team" for Enron was headed by David Duncan. Beginning in 2000, Enron's financial performance began to suffer, and, as 2001 wore on, worsened. On August 14, 2001, Jeffrey Skilling, Enron's Chief Executive Officer (CEO), unexpectedly resigned. Within days, Sherron Watkins, a senior accountant at Enron, warned Kenneth Lay, Enron's newly reappointed CEO, that Enron could "implode in a wave of accounting scandals."

On October 10, partner Odom spoke at a general training meeting attended by 89 employees, including 10 from the Enron engagement team. Odom urged everyone to comply with the firm's document retention policy. He added: "'If it's destroyed in the course of [the] normal policy and litigation is filed the next day, that's great … . We've followed our own policy, and whatever there was that might have been of interest to somebody is gone and irretrievable.'" What followed was the substantial destruction of paper and electronic documents.

The parties have largely focused their attention on the word "corruptly" as the key to what may or may not lawfully be done in the situation presented here. Section 1512(b) punishes not just "corruptly persuading" another, but "*knowingly* … corruptly persuading" another. (Emphasis added.) The Government suggests that "knowingly" does not modify "corruptly persuades," but that is not how the statute most naturally reads. It provides the *mens rea*—"knowingly"—and then a list of acts—"uses intimidation or physical force, threatens, or corruptly persuades." We have recognized with regard to similar statutory language that the *mens rea,* at least, applies to the acts that immediately follow, if not to *other* elements down the statutory chain. The Government suggests that it is "questionable whether Congress would employ such an inelegant formulation as 'knowingly … corruptly persuades.'" Brief for United States 35, n. 18. Long experience has not taught us to share the Government's doubts on this score, and we must simply interpret the statute as written.

The parties have not pointed us to another interpretation of "knowingly … corruptly" to guide us here. In any event, the natural meaning of these terms provides a clear answer. Joining these meanings together here makes sense both linguistically and in the statutory scheme. Only persons conscious of wrongdoing can be said to "knowingly … corruptly persuade." And limiting criminality to persuaders conscious of their wrongdoing sensibly allows § 1512(b) to reach only those with the level of "culpability … we usually require in order to impose criminal liability."

The outer limits of this element need not be explored here because the jury instructions at issue simply failed to convey the requisite consciousness of wrongdoing. Indeed, it is striking how little culpability the instructions required. For example, the jury was told

continued

that, "even if [petitioner] honestly and sincerely believed that its conduct was lawful, you may find [petitioner] guilty." The instructions also diluted the meaning of "corruptly" so that it covered innocent conduct.

■ *For these reasons, the jury instruction here was flawed in important respects. The judgment of the Court of Appeals is reversed, and the case is remanded for further proceedings consistent with this opinion.*

CASE CONCEPTS REVIEW

1. What is the *mens rea* required in order for there to be a violation of the statute?
2. How does the court use a common understanding of a word in the opinion? In crafting jury instructions, is it a good idea to use common words? Why?

Moreover, high corporate officials may have liability because of the high standards of conduct imposed on them by some statutes. Such crimes exist to impose strict standards of performance on certain business activities. The punishment imposed in such cases is a fine and in some cases other sanctions, such as the loss of a license to do business.

The officers and directors of a corporation are ordinarily not personally liable for the crimes of the enterprise or their subordinates. Of course, if a corporate official commits a crime that furthers a business interest, the fact that the individual is committing a crime within the scope of business responsibilities will not absolve the individual from criminal liability.

9. Defenses to Criminal Prosecutions

Defendants in criminal cases may avail themselves of a variety of defenses. They may contend that they did not commit the act of which they are accused. They may present an alibi—proof that they were at another place when the crime was committed. They may also contend that if they did the act, it was not done with the requisite intent. There are also many technical defenses used on behalf of persons accused of crimes. Some of them are described in the following paragraphs.

ENTRAPMENT This is a defense commonly raised in certain crimes, such as the illegal sale of drugs. Entrapment means that the criminal intent originated with the police. When a criminal act is committed at the instigation of the police, fundamental fairness seems to dictate that the people should not be able to contend that the accused is guilty of a crime. Assume that a police officer asked Bill to obtain some marijuana. Bill could not be found guilty of illegal possession because the criminal intent originated with the police officer. Entrapment is sometimes described as a positive defense because the accused must, as a basis for the defense, admit that the act was committed.

Immunity
Freedom from the legal duties and penalties imposed on others

IMMUNITY FROM PROSECUTION This is another technical defense. The prosecution may grant **immunity** to obtain a "state's witness." When immunity is granted, the person receiving it can no longer be prosecuted; and thus he or she no longer has the privilege against compulsory self-incrimination. When several persons have committed a crime together, it is common practice for one to be given immunity so evidence is available against the others. The one granted immunity has a complete defense.

INSANITY A person cannot be guilty of a crime if he or she lacks the mental capacity to have the required criminal intent. Likewise, a person who is insane cannot properly defend the suit, so insanity at the time of trial is also a defense.

The defense of insanity poses many difficult problems for courts and for juries. Many criminal acts are committed in fits of anger or passion. Others, by their very nature, are committed by persons whose mental state is other than normal. Therefore, a major difficulty exists in defining insanity. In the early criminal law, the usually accepted test of insanity was the "right-from-wrong" test. If the accused understood the nature and consequences of the act and had the ability to distinguish right from wrong at the time of the act involved, the accused was sane. If he or she did not know right from wrong or did not understand the consequences of the act, insanity was a defense.

Subsequently, the courts of some states, feeling that the right-and-wrong test did not go far enough, adopted a test known as "irresistible impulse." Under this test, it was not enough that the accused knew right from wrong. If the accused was possessed of an irresistible impulse to do what was wrong, and this impulse was so strong that it compelled him or her to do what was wrong, insanity was a defense.

As psychiatry and psychology began to play a greater role in the criminal law and in the rehabilitation of criminals, many courts became dissatisfied with both the right-and-wrong and irresistible-impulse tests of insanity. A new test, known as the Durham Rule, was developed. Under the Durham Rule, an accused is not criminally responsible if his or her act was the product of a mental disease or defect. This new test has not received universal acceptance. Perpetrators of some crimes almost always have some mental abnormality, and the Durham Rule makes their conduct not punishable. Sexual assault on a child is probably committed only by one with some mental depravity, but the Durham Rule makes prosecution of such cases more difficult and might result in freeing many who are guilty. Today there is a wide disparity among the states as to which test of insanity will be followed. All three tests have had significant acceptance. In the years ahead, additional developments in the law of insanity are likely.

INTOXICATION This defense is quite similar to insanity, but its application is much more restricted. Voluntarily becoming intoxicated is generally no defense to a crime. It is simply no excuse for wrongful conduct. However, if the crime charged is one of specific intent and the accused was so intoxicated that he or she could not form the specific intent required, then intoxication is a defense of sorts. It can be used to establish lack of the required specific intent. In a prosecution for an assault with intent to rape, intoxication sufficient to negate the intent would be a defense.

OTHER DEFENSES Return of property stolen, payment for damages caused, and forgiveness by the victim of a crime are not defenses. If a person shoplifts and is caught, it is no defense that the goods were returned or that the store owner has forgiven the wrongdoer. Since the wrong is against society as a whole, the attitude of the actual victim is technically immaterial. As a practical matter, however, many prosecutors do not prosecute cases that the victims are willing to abandon.

Ignorance of the law is not a defense to a criminal prosecution. Everyone is presumed to know the law and to follow it. No other system would be workable. The various constitutional protections and guarantees available to a defendant may prohibit or impede prosecution of a case. They may make it impossible for the prosecution to obtain a conviction. If evidence of the crime is illegally obtained, that evidence is inadmissible; and by preventing its admission, the accused may obtain an acquittal. These constitutional and procedural aspects of the criminal law are discussed in the following sections.

CONSTITUTIONAL PROTECTIONS

10. General Principles

The Constitution of the United States is a major source of the law as it relates to crimes. Constitutional protections and guarantees govern the procedural aspects of criminal cases. The Bill of Rights—especially the Fourth, Fifth, Sixth, and Eighth amendments—contains these constitutional guarantees. The Fourteenth Amendment "picks up" these constitutional protections and makes them applicable to the states.

As these constitutional guarantees are studied, three aspects of constitutional law should be kept in mind. First, constitutional guarantees are *not absolutes.* Every one of them is limited in its application. Just as freedom of speech under the First Amendment does not allow one to cry "Fire" in a crowded theater, the Fourth Amendment's constitutional protection against illegal search and seizure is not absolute. Both are limited protections.

Second, in determining the extent of limitations on constitutional guarantees, the courts are balancing constitutional protections against some other legitimate legal or social policy of society or other constitutional guarantees. A state enacted a so-called hit-and-run statute requiring the driver of a motor vehicle involved in an accident to stop at the scene and give his or her name and address. This action obviously may be self-incriminating, in that the person is admitting the identity of the driver of the vehicle involved. Thus, the law created a conflict between the state's demand for disclosures and the protection of the right against self-incrimination. The Supreme Court, in resolving this conflict, noted that the mere possibility of incrimination is insufficient to defeat the strong policies in favor of a disclosure; and it held that the law did not violate the Constitution. In criminal cases, courts are often required to balance the interest and rights of the accused with those of the victim of crime and of society as a whole.

Third, constitutional protections are variable. They change to meet the needs of modern society. The Constitution is often said to be interpreted relative to the times. The criminal law changes as the needs of society change.

11. The Fourth Amendment

Several procedural issues may arise as a result of the Fourth Amendment's protection against illegal search and seizure. Among the more common Fourth Amendment issues in criminal cases are (1) the validity of searches incident to an arrest without a warrant, (2) the validity of search warrants—the presence of probable cause, (3) the validity of consents to searches by persons other than the suspect, and (4) the extent of the protection afforded.

To illustrate the first issue, assume that a student is arrested for speeding. Is it a violation of the Fourth Amendment if the police officer searches the passenger area of the car without a search warrant and finds cocaine? The answer is no, and the student could be convicted of illegal possession of drugs because the evidence was constitutionally obtained. The Supreme Court grants police wide discretion in searching the interior of a vehicle as one means of the police ensuring their personal safety.

A search may be illegal even if it is conducted pursuant to a search warrant. The Constitution provides that a search warrant may be issued only if probable cause for its issue is presented to the court.

The validity of consent to search premises without a search warrant is frequently an issue in a criminal case. A parent may consent to a police search of a child's room in the family home. Is this a valid waiver of the constitutional protection of the Fourth Amendment? The decision depends on many factors, including the age of the child, the extent of emancipation, and the amount of control the parents have over the total premises. Similar issues are raised when a landlord consents to the search of premises leased to a tenant. As a general rule, such consents are not sufficient to eliminate the need for a search warrant.

Fourth Amendment issues frequently have an effect on civil law as well as criminal law. The protection has been extended to prohibit activities such as inspection of premises by a fire inspector without a search warrant. Criminal charges for violating building codes cannot be based on warrantless inspection of the premises if the owner objects to the inspection.

In recent years, the protection of the Fourth Amendment has been narrowed somewhat by court decisions and legislation. Electronic surveillance is possible pursuant to a search warrant, and the "bugs" may be installed by covert entry. Moreover, warrants may be issued based on information obtained by electronic means. The following case delves into the interplay between technology and the Fourth Amendment.

CASE

Danny Lee Kyllo v. United States

SUPREME COURT OF THE UNITED STATES

533 U.S. 27 (2001)

JUSTICE SCALIA DELIVERED THE OPINION OF THE COURT.

This case presents the question whether the use of a thermal-imaging device aimed at a private home from a public street to detect relative amounts of heat within the home constitutes a "search" within the meaning of the Fourth Amendment.

In 1991 Agent William Elliott of the United States Department of the Interior came to suspect that marijuana was being grown in the home belonging to petitioner Danny Kyllo, part of a triplex on Rhododendron Drive in Florence, Oregon. Indoor marijuana growth typically requires high-intensity lamps. In order to determine whether an amount of heat was emanating from petitioner's home consistent with the use of such lamps, at 3:20 a.m. on January 16, 1992, Agent Elliott and Dan Haas used an Agema Thermovision 210 thermal imager to scan the triplex. Thermal imagers detect infrared radiation, which virtually all objects emit but which is not visible to the naked eye. The imager converts radiation into images based on relative warmth—black is cool, white is hot, shades of gray connote relative differences; in that respect, it operates somewhat like a video camera showing heat images. The scan of Kyllo's home took only a few minutes and was performed from the passenger seat of Agent Elliott's vehicle across the street from the front of the house and also from the street in back of the house. The scan showed that the roof over the garage and a side wall of petitioner's home were relatively hot compared to the rest of the home and substantially warmer than neighboring homes in the triplex. Agent Elliott concluded that petitioner was using halide lights to grow marijuana in his house, which indeed he was. Based on tips from informants, utility bills, and the thermal imaging, a Federal Magistrate Judge issued a warrant authorizing a search of petitioner's home, and the agents found an indoor growing operation involving more than 100 plants. Petitioner was indicted on one count of manufacturing marijuana, in violation of 21 U.S.C. § 841(a)(1). He unsuccessfully moved to suppress the evidence seized from his home and then entered a conditional guilty plea.

It would be foolish to contend that the degree of privacy secured to citizens by the Fourth Amendment has been entirely unaffected by the advance of technology. For example, as the cases discussed above make clear, the technology enabling human flight has exposed to public view (and hence, we have said, to official observation) uncovered portions of the house and its curtilage that once were private. The question we confront today is what limits there are upon this power of technology to shrink the realm of guaranteed privacy.

We have said that the Fourth Amendment draws "a firm line at the entrance to the house." That line, we think, must be not only firm but also bright—which requires clear specification of those methods of surveillance that require a warrant. While it is certainly possible to conclude from the videotape of the thermal imaging that occurred in this case that no "significant" compromise of the homeowner's privacy has occurred, we must take the long view, from the original meaning of the Fourth Amendment forward.

"The Fourth Amendment is to be construed in the light of what was deemed an unreasonable search and seizure when it was adopted, and in a manner which will conserve public interests as well as the interests and rights of individual citizens."

Where, as here, the Government uses a device that is not in general public use, to explore details of the home that would previously have been unknowable without physical intrusion, the surveillance is a "search" and is presumptively unreasonable without a warrant.

Since we hold the Thermovision imaging to have been an unlawful search, it will remain for the District Court to determine whether, without the evidence it provided, the search warrant issued in this case was supported by probable cause—and if not, whether there is any other basis for supporting admission of the evidence that the search pursuant to the warrant produced.

■ *Reversed and remanded.*

CASE CONCEPTS REVIEW

1. According to the decision, the Fourth Amendment is to be interpreted in light of the situation existing at the time it was adopted, over two hundred years ago. Do you see any problems with this approach?
2. Why did the court find that the use of the thermal imaging device violated the Fourth Amendment?

The Supreme Court has held that administrative inspectors can inspect certain businesses without the inspectors having obtained a warrant. The Fourth Amendment does not protect businesses that have a reduced expectation of privacy because they are closely regulated. This exception to the statements made in the previous paragraphs further illustrates the trend to interpret the Fourth Amendment's application more narrowly.

One of the more controversial aspects of the Fourth Amendment is the so-called *exclusionary* rule. The exclusionary rule, which was created by the Supreme Court, is a rule of evidence. It provides that evidence illegally obtained by the police and all information flowing therefrom cannot be used to convict a person accused of crime. Thus, if evidence is obtained without a search warrant, or if the search warrant was not properly issued, then a defendant can ask the court to prevent the use of the evidence. This request is usually called a *motion to suppress evidence.*

As a result of the exclusionary rule, many persons who have in fact committed crimes are either not prosecuted or are found to be innocent because the evidence establishing their guilt is not admissible at the trial. In recent years, some courts have sought to modify the exclusionary rule and have argued that justice would be better served in certain cases if evidence were admissible, notwithstanding the fact that it was improperly or illegally obtained. For example, they argue that evidence illegally obtained by state and local police should, nevertheless, be admissible in a federal prosecution when the federal authorities were not a party to the illegal search and seizure of evidence.

The Supreme Court has created an exception to the exclusionary rule that permits the use of seized evidence in the trial as long as the police acted *in good faith* and believed that the warrant was properly valid. Therefore, even if the warrant is technically flawed, the evidence seized in good faith is not barred by the exclusionary rule.

12. The Fifth Amendment

Almost everyone understands that a person "pleading the Fifth Amendment" is exercising the right against compulsory self-incrimination. The Fifth Amendment also (1) contains a due process clause, which requires that all court procedures in criminal cases be fundamentally fair; (2) requires indictment by a grand jury for a capital offense or infamous crime; and (3) prohibits double jeopardy.

A grand jury decides if there is sufficient evidence of guilt to justify the accused's standing trial. It is contrasted with a petit or trial jury, which decides guilt or innocence. Grand juries are usually made up of twenty-three persons, and it takes a majority vote to indict a defendant. It takes less proof to indict a person and to require him or her to stand trial than it does to convict.

The grand-jury provision is limited to capital offenses and infamous crimes. *Infamous crimes* are those that involve moral turpitude. The term indicates that one convicted of such a crime will suffer infamy. Most felonies are infamous crimes.

The prohibition against *double jeopardy* means that a person cannot be tried twice for the same offense by the same governing body. A defendant who is acquitted in a criminal case cannot be retried in the same court system on the same offense by the same governing body. However, a defendant who, on appeal, obtains a reversal of a conviction may be tried again. The reversal, in effect, means that the defendant was not in jeopardy. If a crime is against the people of two or more states or in violation of the laws of both a state and the federal government, the defendant's protection against double jeopardy does not prevent multiple trials. As a practical matter, once a defendant is convicted and imprisoned, the other governing body usually does not prosecute.

Even considering these provisions of the Fifth Amendment, the protection against compulsory self-incrimination is still its most important constitutional protection. The prohibition against being compelled to be a witness against oneself extends to oral testimony of an accused before and during his or her trial, to documents, and to statements before grand juries, legislative investigation committees, and judicial bodies in civil and criminal proceedings.

Further, the Supreme Court has created procedural requirements, based on the Fourth, Fifth, and Sixth Amendments in particular. The famous + warnings, for example, provide that police officers must advise criminal suspects as they are being considered for arrest of their right against self-incrimination, right to counsel, and right to have a court-appointed attorney represent them.

The Supreme Court, through a series of cases, provides protection to the individual who possesses the business records of an organization. However, the organization's constitutional protection against self-incrimination is limited. For example, the contents of a proprietorship's documents are not protected, but the proprietor cannot be compelled to produce the documents. A corporation's records also are not protected, and the custodian of the records cannot refuse to produce them. The individual who works for a corporation has no Fifth Amendment protection against self-incrimination. The production of the corporate documents is deemed a representative act, not a personal one.

A statement or a document does not have to be a confession of crime to qualify under the privilege. Both are protected if they might serve as a "link in the chain of evidence" that could lead to prosecution. The protection of the Fifth Amendment is the right to remain silent and to suffer no penalty for silence.

To illustrate the extent of the protection provided by the Fifth Amendment, the Supreme Court has held that (1) a prosecutor may not comment on the failure of a defendant to explain evidence within his or her knowledge; (2) a court may not tell the jury that silence may be evidence of guilt; (3) an attorney may not be disbarred for claiming his or her privilege at a judicial inquiry into his or her activities, just as a police officer may not be fired for claiming the privilege before the grand jury; and (4) the privilege protects a state witness against incrimination under federal as well as state law, and a federal witness against incrimination under state law as well as federal law. To illustrate this latter concept, assume that a person is granted immunity from state prosecution to compel him or her to testify. This person cannot be compelled to testify if it is possible that his or her testimony will lead to a conviction under federal law. The granting of immunity must be complete.

Limitations on the protections afforded by the Fifth Amendment are also readily apparent. The drunk-driving laws that require a breath or blood test are one example. In a drunk-driving case the prosecution can use as evidence the analysis of a blood sample taken without consent of the accused, or a driver's license can be revoked if a person refuses to submit to a breath test. The evidence is admissible even though the accused objects to the extraction of blood or taking the breath test. The Fifth Amendment reaches an accused's communications, whatever form they might take, but compulsion that makes a suspect the source of "real or voice samples for evidence" does not violate the Fifth Amendment. In addition, the protection is personal and does not prevent the production of incriminating evidence by others. Thus an accountant in possession of a client's documents can be compelled to produce them.

13. The Sixth Amendment

The Sixth Amendment entitles a criminal defendant to a speedy trial, a trial by jury, a public trial, and the right to confront witnesses. Perhaps most important, the Sixth Amendment provides that the accused has the right to counsel. The Supreme Court has interpreted this provision to mean that if a criminal defendant does not have the assets to pay for an attorney, the court will appoint an attorney and the state will pay for services rendered. Further, an individual accused of a crime is entitled to attorney services that are effective; and if the services do not meet a standard of what a reasonable attorney would provide, the accused may be able to secure a new trial.

14. The Eighth Amendment

The Eighth Amendment provides that "excessive bail shall not be required, nor excessive fines imposed, nor cruel and unusual punishments inflicted." Bail is excessive if greater than necessary to guarantee the presence of the accused in court at the appointed time. Because of the presumption of innocence, the function of bail is not to restrict the freedom of the accused prior to trial. Most states today require that only a small percentage of the actual bail be posted. The law may require that ten percent of the total bail be deposited with the court. If the defendant fails to appear, the persons signing the bail bond then owe the other ninety percent.

At one time, the Eighth Amendment was used as the basis for declaring the death penalty to be unconstitutional; however, many legislative bodies reinstated the death penalty, and some of these laws were later held to be constitutional.

CHAPTER SUMMARY

BASIC CONCEPTS

Terminology

1. Criminal conduct is either wrongful per se (*malum per se*) or declared wrongful by a governing body (*malum prohibition*).
2. A criminal proceeding is called a prosecution.
3. A grand jury may declare that there is sufficient evidence to warrant a trial by *indicting* a defendant with a *true bill.* Otherwise, the grand jury returns a no *true bill,* and no trial will be held.
4. Some crimes (such as larceny, robbery, and burglary) have specific meaning associated with their names. Other crimes, known as *lesser included defenses,* are part of another crime.
5. The standard of proof that a prosecutor must meet for a criminal conviction is called *proof beyond a reasonable doubt.*

Classifications of Crimes

1. Crimes typically are classified as treason, felonies, and misdemeanors.
2. Some minor crimes are called petty offenses or public torts.

Administrative Crimes

1. Legislative bodies allow regulatory agencies to adopt rules, a violation of which may be punished as a crime.
2. Generally, agencies will not conduct trials. Exceptions for hearings do exist when the wrongful activity involves minor penalties being invoked.

White-Collar Crimes

1. White-collar crimes are the result of guile, deceit, or wrongful conduct, such as price fixing or insider trading.
2. The trend is toward harsher punishment for such crimes.

Damage Suits

1. Many statutes today authorize suits for triple damages by the victims of white-collar crime.

2. RICO cases are brought against many business specialists who have used the telephone or the mails to defraud others.

ESSENTIAL ELEMENTS

Act and Intent

1. A crime is a combination of act and intent.
2. Some crimes require a specific intent, while others require only a general intent.
3. In a few instances, conduct is criminal without intent, and doing the act is all that is required.

Capacity

1. Certain ages determine whether a person has the mental capacity to commit a crime.
2. The criminal law has special rules and procedures for handling crimes committed by juveniles. These cases are handled in special courts to rehabilitate and deter further criminal conduct by those under age.

Corporate Liability

1. Corporations may be held criminally liable for the acts of their directors, officers, and important managerial agents.
2. In addition to vicarious liability, corporations may be punished for strict liability crimes.

Defenses to Criminal Prosecutions

1. There are various defenses that may be used by one accused of crime to avoid liability.
2. Some of these defenses, such as insanity, are under challenge and are in the process of change.

CRIMINAL LAW AND THE CONSTITUTION

Fourth Amendment

1. The Fourth Amendment protects those accused of crime from having evidence illegally obtained.
2. If evidence is illegally obtained, the exclusionary rule prevents its use at trial.
3. Evidence may be illegally obtained even though a search warrant is used if the warrant was improperly issued.
4. In recent years the courts have narrowed the meaning of the Fourth Amendment. For example, evidence obtained by electronic surveillance is not an illegal search and seizure.
5. There is a good-faith exception to the exclusionary rule.

Fifth Amendment

1. The Fifth Amendment requires indictment by a grand jury for capital offenses and infamous crimes.
2. The Fifth Amendment provision on double jeopardy protects against a person's being tried twice for the same offense.
3. The Fifth Amendment protection against compulsory self-incrimination is personal to the accused. It does not prevent others from testifying or documents in the hands of others from being used as evidence.

Sixth Amendment

1. The Sixth Amendment provides a criminal defendant with the right to a speedy and public jury trial.
2. The Sixth Amendment also guarantees a criminal defendant the right to a competent attorney.

Eighth Amendment

1. The Eighth Amendment prohibits excessive bail and cruel and unusual punishment.

2. The death penalty may be imposed if subject to stringent safeguards by the courts.

REVIEW QUESTIONS AND PROBLEMS

1. Match each term in Column A with the appropriate statement in Column B.

A	B
(1) *Malum in se*	(a) The process by which the prosecution and defense, in effect, settle a criminal case
(2) True bill	(b) A defense in criminal cases when the criminal intent originated with the police
(3) Strict liability crime	(c) A group that has a responsibility to determine if there is probable cause sufficient to warrant a defendant's standing trial
(4) Entrapment	(d) An act that is historically a crime in any civilized society
(5) Irresistible impulse	(e) The decision of a grand jury that indicts an accused
(6) Exclusionary rule	(f) Something the police must give to inform a person of his or her rights
(7) Grand jury	(g) Criminal conduct that is not inherently wrongful but is declared so by legislative action
(8) *Miranda* warning	(h) An act that is criminal without proof of criminal intent
(9) Plea bargaining	(i) A test for insanity when the defendant knows right from wrong but is compelled to do what is wrong
(10) *Malum prohibitum*	(j) A rule of evidence that prevents the use of evidence obtained through illegal search and seizure

2. Compare and contrast the following terms:

   a. Indictment and information
   b. Grand jury and petit jury
   c. Felony and misdemeanor
   d. General intent and specific intent

3. For a crime to be committed, the prosecutor must be able to prove a criminal intent and an overt act to carry out that intent. Jack and Mary agreed to rob a series of banks. Prior to beginning their bank robbery spree, they were arrested and charged with criminal conspiracy. What act did Jack and Mary do that justifies a finding that they committed a crime? Explain.

4. When police entered her room without a warrant, Suzy swallowed two "uppers." Portions of the capsules were recovered by the police with the use of a stomach pump. What constitutional issue will be raised by her attorneys? Explain.
5. Dan was suspected by customs and immigration officers of having information concerning the smuggling of drugs into the United States. Acting undercover; a customs and immigration official went to Dan and suggested that he bring illegal drugs into this country. Dan refused, but at the official's insistence he later agreed. After the drugs entered this country, Dan was arrested. Does Dan have a valid defense to the charge of smuggling? Explain.
6. Devin was arrested and tried for embezzlement. After deliberating for three days, the jury informed the judge that it was hopelessly deadlocked and could not reach a verdict. The judge declared a mistrial and scheduled a new trial. Devin objected, contending that a second trial constituted double jeopardy. Is he correct? Explain.
7. Couch's financial records were kept with an accountant who prepared her tax returns. Pursuant to an IRS investigation, a summons was issued to the accountant demanding access to the records, which had been delivered to Couch's attorney by the accountant. Does the Fifth Amendment privilege against compulsory self-incrimination prevent the production of these business and tax records? Why or why not?
8. A policeman investigating a rape spotted Quarles, who matched the rapist's description. When Quarles saw the policeman, he began to run toward the back of a store. After a chase, the policeman cornered the suspect and noticed that he had an empty shoulder holster. The policeman asked where the gun was. Quarles pointed and said, "The gun is over there." The policeman retrieved the gun and then arrested Quarles. At this point, the *Miranda* warning was read to Quarles. Was the warning too late in violation of Quarles's constitutional rights? Why or why not?
9. A company was suspected of emitting smoke from its factory in violation of the environmental protection law. Police officers in helicopters collected air samples above the smokestack. They did so without a search warrant. The company moved to suppress the evidence, contending that the search violated the Fourth Amendment. Did the police violate the Fourth Amendment? Explain.
10. To what extent do sole proprietors differ from partners and corporate officials insofar as the Fifth Amendment is concerned? Explain.

Torts: Introduction and Intentional Torts | 7

CHAPTER OUTLINE

THEORIES OF TORT LIABILITY

1. Overview
2. Damages
3. Persons Liable

INTERNATIONAL TORTS

4. Introduction
5. Interference with Personal Freedom
6. Interference with Property Rights
7. Interference with Economic Relations
8. Wrongful Communications

CHAPTER PREVIEW

A *tort* is an omission (failure to act) or a wrongful act (other than a breach of contract) against a person or his or her property. The term is somewhat difficult to define, but the word *wrongful* in the definition means a violation of one person's legal duty to another. The victim of a tort may recover damages for the injuries received, usually because the other party was "at fault" in causing the injury.

Acts or omissions, to be tortious, need not involve moral turpitude or bad motive or maliciousness. Likewise, an act or an omission that does not invade another's rights is not tortious, even though the actor's motive is bad or malicious.

Torts as *private wrongs* must be contrasted with crimes, which are public wrongs. The purpose of the criminal law is to punish the wrongdoer, while the purpose of the law of torts is to compensate the victim of wrongful conduct. To deter intentional torts, however, the law may impose punitive, in addition to actual, damages.

The same act may be both a crime and a tort: An assault and battery is both a wrong against society and a wrong against the victim. Society may punish the guilty party, and the victim may sue in tort to recover damages. It must be recognized that the criminal action does not benefit the victim of the crime or compensate him or her for the injury. Such compensation is left to the civil law of torts.

The law of torts plays an important role in business activities in a number of ways. For instance, a business, through its employees, may interfere with other people's personal freedoms, their property, their economic opportunities, or their reputations. Businesses also may be liable for the careless actions of their employees when a third party is injured as the result of some unreasonable behavior.

This chapter explores the general arena of tort law. It also surveys the more specific subject of intentional torts, a critical area because of the potential for punitive damages. The next chapter, Chapter 8, covers the two remaining areas of tort law: negligence and strict liability.

BUSINESS MANAGEMENT DECISION

You are the general sales manager for a computer-manufacturing firm. To increase your firm's competitive advantage, you offer a competitor's district sales manager a similar position with a higher salary. This sales manager indicates that he can bring at least five of his salespeople with him.

Should you hire the sales manager and his salespeople?

THEORIES OF TORT LIABILITY

1. Overview

Tort

A wrongful act committed by one person against another person or his or her property—the breach of a legal duty imposed by law other than by contract.

Tort *liability* is predicated on two traditional premises: In a civilized society one person should not intentionally injure another or his or her property, and all persons should exercise reasonable care and caution in the conduct of their affairs. The first premise has resulted in a group of torts labeled *intentional torts.* This subject is presented later in the chapter. The second premise is the basis for the general field of tort liability known as **negligence** (covered in Chapter 8). Liability based on negligence requires fault, just as it is in an intentional tort. However, because the wrong in negligence is of a lesser degree than it is in intentional torts, the theory of damages in negligence cases does not

Negligence

Failure to do that which an ordinary, reasonable, prudent person would do, or the doing of some act that an ordinary, prudent person would not do

Strict liability

The doctrine under which a party may be required to respond in tort damages, without regard to that party's fault

include punishment. For simple negligence, a person is entitled to collect only actual damages from the wrongdoer, that is, enough money to make the injured party whole. The person is not entitled to collect punitive damages to discourage the wrongdoer from repeating his or her negligence.

A third theory of tort liability, called **strict liability** (addressed in Chapter 8), is not based on wrongful conduct in the usual sense, although the party committing the tort usually does something intentionally or negligently. Strict liability is based on peculiar factual situations and the relationship of the parties. To the extent that an activity by one party causes injury, there is liability because of the injury, not because the defendant was at fault in the traditional sense of wrongdoing. Although there is no fault in the sense of wrongdoing, there is fault in that actions caused the injuries. For example, strict liability is imposed when harm is caused by dangerous or trespassing animals, blasting operations, or the marketing of an unsafe product.

2. Damages

The purpose of tort litigation is to require a wrongdoer or the party at fault to compensate a victim for the injury incurred.

Compensatory damages

A sum of money the court imposes on a defendant as compensation for the plaintiff because the defendant has injured the plaintiff by breach of a legal duty

COMPENSATORY DAMAGES The theory of **compensatory damages**, is that the victim of a tort should receive a sum of money that will make him or her "whole." In other words, dollar damages are supposed to place the victim of the tort in as good a position as he or she would have been in had the tort not been committed. This, of course, is impossible because no amount of money can replace an arm, a leg, or an eye, let alone a life. Therefore, in very serious cases, especially those that involve substantial pain and suffering, any money damages are probably inadequate.

Compensatory damages in the typical tort case usually include medical expenses, lost income from earnings, property damage, and pain and suffering and loss of life or limb. Compensatory damages are often classified as either being economic or non-economic. *Economic damages* are easily calculated (eg., lost earnings). *Non-economic damages,* usually associated with pain and suffering, are not capable of being computed. Expert witnesses use life expectancy tables and present-value discount tables to help them testify so that a jury may determine the amount of damages to award. However, uncertainty about the life expectancy of injured plaintiffs and the impact of inflation make the use of these tables questionable. Also, awarding damages for pain and suffering may result from jury sympathy as much as for compensation for financial loss.

Punitive damages

Damages by way of punishment that are allowed by the court as the result of an injury caused by a wrong that is willful and malicious

PUNITIVE DAMAGES A plaintiff in a tort action also may be awarded **punitive damages**, which are awarded to punish defendants for committing intentional torts and, in some states, for negligent behavior considered "gross" or "willful and wanton." For an award of punitive damages the defendant's motive must be "malicious," "fraudulent," or "evil." Increasingly, punitive damages are also awarded for dangerously negligent conduct (gross negligence) that shows a conscious disregard for the interests of others. These damages are used to deter future wrongdoing. Because they make an example of the defendant, punitive damages are sometimes called *exemplary damages.* Punitive damages are a windfall to the injured plaintiff, who is also awarded compensatory damages.

To collect damages, most victims must hire an attorney, whose fee is usually contingent on the total amount collected. The contingent fee system means that the attorney is paid a percentage of the recovery, but nothing if the case is lost. Usual contingent fees are 33⅓ percent if a trial is held and 40 to 50 percent if the case is appealed. Contingent fees make the legal system and the best lawyers available to all, irrespective of ability to pay. However, if the injuries are very substantial and liability is easily established, the fees of the attorney may be viewed as unfair and unreasonable. Assume that a $15 million verdict is given for the loss of two legs. It is difficult to see how the attorney's $5 million fee could have been earned if the liability is clear.

3. Persons Liable

Every person legally responsible is liable for his or her own torts. It is no defense that the wrongdoer is working under the direction of another. That fact may create liability on the part of the other person, but it is no defense to the wrongdoer. The theory of liability by which one person is liable for the torts of another is known as *respondeat superior.* This theory imposes liability on principals or masters for the torts of their agents or servants if the agent or servant is acting within the scope of employment when the tort was committed. This subject is discussed more fully in Chapter 25.

Joint and several

Two or more persons have an obligation that binds them individually as well as jointly. The obligation can be enforced either by joint action against all of them or by separate actions against one or more.

If two or more persons jointly commit a tort, all may be held liable for the total injury. The liability is said to be **joint and several**. All are liable, and each is liable for the entire damage. This principle is often criticized, and there have been numerous efforts to change it by legislation. To illustrate the argument for abolishing the concept of joint and several liability, assume that defendant A is 99 percent at fault and defendant B is 1 percent at fault. If defendant A has no assets, defendant B must pay 100 percent of the judgment even though only 1 percent at fault. The concept of *joint and several liability* is examined in the following case.

CASE

Ansell Healthcare Products, Inc., and Becton Dickinson & Co., Inc. v. Owens & Minor, Inc. and Owens & Minor Medical, Inc.

COURT OF APPEALS OF TEXAS, SIXTH DISTRICT

189 S.W.3d 889 (2006)

Texas law allows an innocent seller to be indemnified by a manufacturer when the seller is sued in a products liability action. Based on that statute, the trial court granted the seller-distributor, Owens & Minor, Inc., and Owens & Minor Medical, Inc. (O&M), a judgment against two manufacturers of latex gloves, Ansell Healthcare Products, Inc., and Becton Dickinson & Company, Inc. (BD).

Janet McCabe found that the latex gloves she had been using in her occupation caused an allergic reaction. In January 2000, she sued more than ten manufacturers of latex gloves supplied to her employers as well as the seller-distributor, O&M. That case settled, and all of the defendants were released by McCabe. However, that was not the end of this lengthy and expensive litigation, but only the beginning.

O&M filed suit against five of the manufacturers, seeking indemnification for its attorney's fees and litigation costs. Claims against three of these were resolved, leaving O&M's claims against Ansell and BD. Texas law provides by statute that the manufacturer must indemnify a seller for the seller's losses, including attorney's fees, arising out of a products liability action. This requirement is imposed regardless of the manner in which the underlying action was concluded and is in addition to any other duty of indemnity established by law, contract, or otherwise.

Apparently, the suit to enforce the attorney's fees was more complicated than the underlying products liability case, as O&M now alleges it is entitled to collect from the two manufacturers not only the more than $73,000.00 incurred in the original suit, but an additional $310,000.00 for the trial of this case and another $65,000.00 for the appeal. After several summary judgment and other hearings, as well as a bench trial, the trial court found that each of the two manufacturers had an independent obligation for the damages and awarded all of the above to O&M against the two manufacturers as indemnity as authorized by law.

Ansell and BD argue that the trial court erred in finding them independently liable for O&M's entire damages, thereby assigning joint and several liability to the two defendant manufacturers. Ansell and BD point out that joint and several liability was recognized where the tortious acts of two or more wrongdoers were found to have joined and produced one indivisible injury. They argue that, since there was no finding of wrongdoing in this case, such analysis does not apply. The manufacturers further reason that joint and several liability is inappropriate because there is no mechanism to apportion any damage award among the manufacturers. Ansell and BD conclude that the Legislature never contemplated that one manufacturer would be held responsible for all costs and fees incurred by a distributor when multiple manufacturers are involved. It is argued that the proper allocation of these damages would be a pro rata distribution of the damages among all manufacturers named in the McCabe petition.

The manufacturers' argument has some logic and appeal. It is true that no party has been found to have caused the underlying damages to McCabe which prompted this action. The damages to O&M occurred in defending the McCabe lawsuit and are only recoverable by statutory authorization, as such recovery would not be authorized in common law. Common law indemnity was authorized when the wrongful conduct of one party subjected another party to liability and recovery could only be for expenditures made to discharge the liability. However, the Legislature's Act granted to seller-distributors remedies that were not previously available, i.e., it applies regardless of the outcome of the underlying case; it includes recovery of attorney's fees and costs.

We believe that Ansell and BD had a duty to indemnify O&M under the statute.

■ *Affirmed.*

CASE CONCEPTS REVIEW

1. Is it fair that the two manufacturers had to indemnify the supplier? Why?
2. Who benefits under joint and several liability? A plaintiff? Defendants? Why?

A child may have liability, depending on the age of the child, the nature of the tort involved, and whether the tort is intentional or based on a theory of negligence. In most states, a child under the age of 7 is conclusively presumed to be incapable of negligence; from ages 7 to 10, a child is still presumed to be incapable, but the presumption may be rebutted. A child older than 10 is treated as any other person insofar as tort liability is concerned. Some states use the age 14 instead of 10 for these rules. A minor above the minimum age is held to the same standard as an adult. A minor driving an automobile owes the same duty of due care that an adult owes.

Another area of substantial misunderstanding of the law is concerned with parents' liability for the torts of their children. As a general rule, a parent is not responsible for such torts. Parents are liable if the child is acting as an agent of the parent or if the parents are themselves at fault. In addition, some states have adopted the "family-purpose" doctrine, which provides that when a parent maintains an automobile for the pleasure and convenience of the family, any member of the family, including an infant, who uses it is presumed the owner's agent; and the owner is responsible for the negligence of the family member. The presumption may be rebutted, however. Other states have gone further and provided that anyone driving a car with the permission of the owner is the owner's agent, and the owner has vicarious liability to persons injured by the driver.

In recent years, courts have been faced with cases in which a person is injured by a product, but the person is unable to determine which company manufactured the product. Such cases are common when drugs cause injuries not only to the persons taking the drug but also to their children. While there are only a few cases to date, the trend is to hold all manufacturers liable and to allocate the loss based on some formula such as by the market share of each manufacturer. A manufacturer can avoid its share of liability only by proving that its products could not have been the cause of injury. Otherwise, all manufacturers may share responsibility for injuries.

INTENTIONAL TORTS

4. Introduction

Several intentional torts often involve the business community as either plaintiffs or defendants. The imposition of liability for these torts provides protection to basic individual interests of people and their property. The torts may involve (1) interference with the personal freedom of an individual, (2) interference with property rights, (3) interference with economic relations, and (4) wrongful communications. Table 7-1 briefly describes each.

TABLE 7-1 ■ Intentional Torts Common to Business

THEORY OF LIABILITY	DESCRIPTION
Interference with Personal Freedom	
Assault	Causing the apprehension of a harmful or offensive contact with a person's body
Battery	Intentional and unpermitted physical contact with a person's body
Assault and battery	A combination of assault and battery (some hits and some misses)
False imprisonment	A wrongful restraint of a person's freedom of movement
Mental distress	Wrongful interference with a person's peace of mind by insults, indignities, or outrageous conduct
Interference with Property Rights	
Trespass to land	Unauthorized entry upon the land of another
Trespass to chattels	Direct intentional interference with a chattel in possession of another person, such as taking it or damaging it
Conversion	Interference with a person's chattels to the extent that the wrongdoer ought to pay for the chattel
Nuisance	Intentional invasion or disturbance of a person's rights in land or the conduct of an abnormally dangerous activity
Interference with Economic Relations	
Disparagement	Injurious falsehoods about a person's business or property, damaging prospective advantage
Contracts	Inducing a party to a contract to breach it or interfering with its performance
Prospective advantage	Interfering with an expectancy such as employment or an opportunity to contract
Wrongful appropriation	Infringing goodwill, patents, trademarks, copyrights, and other business interests
Wrongful Communications	
Slander	Oral defamation; holding a person's name or reputation up to hatred, contempt, or ridicule, or causing others to shun him or her
Libel Written Defamation	
Invasion of privacy	Interfering with one's right to be let alone by (1) appropriating the name or picture of a person, (2) intruding on a person's physical solitude, (3) the public disclosure of private facts, and (4) publicity that places a person in a false light in the public eye
Fraud	An intentional misstatement of a material existing fact relied on by another, to his or her injury. Also a defense to formation of a contract, the concept of fraud is examined within Chapter 16.

5. Interference with Personal Freedom

ASSAULT, BATTERY, FALSE IMPRISONMENT *Assault, battery,* and *false imprisonment* involve business more commonly than they should. If an employee of a business engages in a fight with a customer, a lawsuit on the theory of battery is likely to follow. Battery is defined as harmful or offensive touching that is intentional in nature. For an assault to occur there need not be actual physical touching—apprehension by plaintiff of the touching is sufficient. Similarly, if an employee wrongfully, physically restrains a customer, there may be a tort action for false imprisonment. Assume that the plaintiff is suspected of shoplifting, and the defendant physically restrains him or her. If the defendant is wrong and the plaintiff is not a shoplifter, a tort has been committed.

MENTAL DISTRESS Inflicting *mental distress* is a tort very important to the business community. It is an invasion of a person's peace of mind by insults or other indignities or by outrageous conduct. If someone without a privilege to do so, by extreme and outrageous conduct, intentionally or recklessly causes another person severe emotional distress with bodily harm resulting from that distress, the offender is subject to liability for the other's emotional distress and bodily harm. Liability does not exist for every case of hurt feelings or bad manners—only where conduct is so outrageous in character and so extreme in degree that it goes beyond all possible bounds of decency. For liability, the conduct must be regarded as atrocious, utterly intolerable in a civilized community. Liability exists in cases in which the facts, if told to an average person, would lead this person to exclaim, "Outrageous!" High-pressure tactics of collection agencies, including violent cursing and accusations of dishonesty, have often been held to be outrageous. However, a person is not liable where he or she has done no more than to insist on his or her legal rights in a permissible way, even though that person is aware that such insistence is certain to cause emotional distress. Also, there is no liability for offensive conduct that is not extreme.

Consider carefully the following case dealing with the tort of intentional infliction of emotional distress.

CASE

Jeff Roach et al. v. Howard Stern et al.

SUPREME COURT OF NEW YORK, APPELLATE DIVISION, SECOND DEPARTMENT

675 N.Y.S.2d 133 (1998)

PRESIDING JUDGE OBRIEN DELIVERED THE OPINION.

The plaintiffs commenced this action against Stern, Infinity Broadcasting, Inc. (hereinafter Infinity), the owner of the radio station, and Hayden, in which they alleged, inter alia, that the defendants' conduct caused them severe emotional distress.

The transcript and videotape of the show, which were made available to the court, corroborate the allegations in the complaint that Stern at one point donned rubber gloves and held up certain bone fragments while he guessed whether they came from Tay's skull or ribs.

Stern and Infinity moved to dismiss the complaint on the ground that the allegations failed to state a cause of action. The Supreme Court granted the motion and dismissed the complaint.

The Supreme Court determined that, while the conduct complained of in the complaint was "vulgar and disrespectful", it did not rise to the level of outrageousness necessary to maintain a cause of action to recover damages for the intentional infliction of emotional distress. In order to impose liability for this intentional tort, the conduct complained of must be "so outrageous in character, and so extreme in degree, as to go beyond all possible bounds of decency, and to be regarded as atrocious, and utterly intolerable in a civilized community "The element of outrageous conduct is "rigorous, and difficult to satisfy, "and its purpose is to filter out trivial complaints and assure that the claim of severe emotional distress is genuine.

Upon our review of the allegations in the case at bar, we conclude that the Supreme Court erred in determining that the element of outrageous conduct was not satisfied as a matter of law. Although the defendants contend that the conduct at issue was not particularly shocking, in light of Stern's reputation for vulgar humor and Tay's actions during her guest appearances on his program, a jury might reasonably conclude that the manner in which Tay's remains were handled, for entertainment purposes and against the express wishes of her family, went beyond the bounds of decent behavior.

■ *Accordingly, the appellants' motion to dismiss the complaint is denied.*

CASE CONCEPTS REVIEW

1. Does the author of the opinion set too high of a standard for determining outrageous conduct? Why?
2. Does it make sense for the jury to consider the nature of the show in making the decision as to whether conduct is outrageous? Why?

An unauthorized entry to another person's land is called, trespass to land.

6. Interference with Property Rights

Trespass

An injury to the person, property, or rights of another person committed by actual force and violence or under such circumstances that the law will infer that the injury was caused by force or violence

TRESPASS The tort of **trespass** is a common one and is applied both to real and personal property. Trespass to land occurs when there is an unauthorized entry upon the land of another. The person in exclusive possession of land is entitled to enjoy the use of that land free from interference of others. Entry upon the land of another is a trespass even if the one who enters is under the mistaken belief that he or she is the owner or has a right, license, or privilege to enter.

Trespass to land may be *innocent* or *willful.* An innocent trespass would occur when one goes on another's land by mistake or under the impression that one has a right to be there. It is still an intentional wrong because persons intend the natural and probable consequences of their acts. A trespass is willful if the trespasser knowingly goes on another's land, aware that he or she has no right to do so. In a trespass case, if the trespass if willful, the plaintiff is entitled to exemplary or punitive damages, which may include attorney's fees. It should be kept in mind that except for tort cases involving punitive damages, every litigant pays his or her own attorney's fees in tort cases.

A trespass to personal property—goods and the like—is unlawful interference with the control and possession of the goods of another. One is entitled to have exclusive possession and control of one's personal property and may recover for any physical harm to one's goods by reason of the wrongful conduct of another. The intent need not be wrongful. If a person mistakenly interferes with the goods of another, a trespass has occurred. A trespass to goods may occur by theft of the goods or by damage to the goods. In such cases, the owner recovers the property and is entitled to be paid for the damage to the property and for its loss of use during the period that the owner lost possession of the property.

Chattel

A very broad term, derived from the word *cattle* and includes every kind of property that is not real property

CONVERSION The action of conversion is quite similar to trespass. It differs in that a suit for conversion of goods is used when the interference is so significant that the wrongdoer is compelled to pay the full value of the goods as damages. Conversion, in theory, is a judicial sale of the **chattel** to the wrongdoer. Using someone else's lumber for building purposes would be a conversion. Among the factors used to determine if the interference is relatively minor (trespass) or serious (conversion) are the extent and duration of the interference, the defendant's motives, the amount of actual damages to the goods, and the inconvenience and other harm suffered by the plaintiff. Conversion results from conduct intended to affect the chattel. The intent required is not conscious wrongdoing but intent to exercise control over the goods. For example, a purchaser of stolen goods is guilty of conversion even though he or she does not know the goods are stolen. An act of interference with the rights of the true owner establishes the conversion.

Conversion frequently occurs even though the defendant's original possession of the goods is lawful. It may result from several actions, such as a transfer of the goods to another person or to another location. A laundry that delivers shirts to the wrong person is guilt of a conversion. If the laundry refuses to deliver the shirts to the owner, a conversion has occurred. Destruction, alteration, or misuse of a chattel may also constitute a conversion. Conversion, as revealed in the following case, is a tort that while it has existed in United States and English law for centuries is equally applicable in the Internet environment.

CASE

Gary Kremen and Online Classified, Inc. v. Stephen Michael Cohen, Ocean Fund International, LTD. et al.

UNITED STATES COURT OF APPEALS FOR THE NINTH CIRCUIT

337 F.3d 1024 (2003)

KOZINSKI, CIRCUIT JUDGE

We decide whether Network Solutions may be liable for giving away a registrant's domain name on the basis of a forged letter.

"Sex on the Internet," they all said. "That'll never make any money." But computer-geek-turned-entrepreneur Gary Kremen knew an opportunity when he saw it. The year was 1994; domain names were free for the asking, and it would be several years yet before Henry Blodget and hordes of eager NASDAQ day traders would turn the Internet into the Dutch tulip craze of our times. With a quick e-mail to the domain name registrar Network Solutions, Kremen became the proud owner of sex.com. He registered the name to his business, Online Classifieds, and listed himself as the contact.

Con man Stephen Cohen, meanwhile, was doing time for impersonating a bankruptcy lawyer. He, too, saw the potential of the domain name. Kremen had gotten it first, but that was only a minor impediment for a man of Cohen's boundless resource and bounded integrity. Once out of prison, he sent Network Solutions what purported to be a letter he had received from Online Classifieds. It claimed the company had been "forced to dismiss Mr. Kremen," but "never got around to changing our administrative contact with the internet registration [sic] and now our Board of directors has decided to abandon the domain name sex.com." Why was this unusual letter being sent via Cohen rather than to Network Solutions directly? It explained: Because we do not have a direct connection to the internet, we request that you notify the internet registration on our behalf, to delete our domain name sex.com. Further, we have no objections to your use of the domain name sex.com and this letter shall serve as our authorization to the internet registration to transfer sex.com to your corporation.

Despite the letter's transparent claim that a company called "Online Classifieds" had no Internet connection, Network Solutions made no effort to contact Kremen. Instead, it accepted the letter at face value and transferred the domain name to Cohen. When Kremen contacted Network Solutions some time later, he was told it was too late to undo the transfer. Cohen went on to turn sex.com into a lucrative online porn empire.

And so began Kremen's quest to recover the domain name that was rightfully his. He sued Cohen and several affiliated companies in federal court, seeking return of the domain name and disgorgement of Cohen's profits. The district court found that the letter was indeed a forgery and ordered the domain name returned to Kremen. It also told Cohen to hand over his profits, invoking the constructive trust doctrine and California's "unfair competition" statute. It awarded $40 million in compensatory damages and another $25 million in punitive damages.

Kremen, unfortunately, has not had much luck collecting his judgment. The district court froze Cohen's assets, but Cohen ignored the order and wired large sums of money to offshore accounts. His real estate property, under the protection of a federal receiver, was stripped of all its fixtures—even cabinet doors and toilets—in violation of another order. The court commanded Cohen to appear and show cause why he shouldn't be held in contempt, but he ignored that order, too. The district judge finally took off the gloves—he declared Cohen a fugitive from justice, signed an arrest warrant and sent the U.S. Marshals after him.

Then things started getting really bizarre. Kremen put up a "wanted" poster on the sex.com site with a mug shot of Cohen, offering a $50,000 reward to anyone who brought him to justice. Cohen's lawyers responded with a motion to vacate the arrest warrant. They reported that Cohen was under house arrest in Mexico and that gunfights between Mexican authorities and would-be bounty hunters seeking Kremen's reward money posed a threat to human life. The district court rejected this story as "implausible" and denied the motion. Cohen, so far as the record shows, remains at large.

Given his limited success with the bounty hunter approach, it should come as no surprise that Kremen seeks to hold someone else responsible for his losses. That someone is Network Solutions, the exclusive domain name registrar at the time of Cohen's antics. Kremen sued it for mishandling his domain name. His theory is that he has a property right

continued

in the domain name sex.com, and Network Solutions committed the tort of conversion by giving it away to Cohen.

The district court granted summary judgment in favor of Network Solutions. The court agreed that sex.com was Kremen's property. It concluded, though, that it was intangible property to which the tort of conversion does not apply.

To establish that tort, a plaintiff must show "ownership or right to possession of property, wrongful disposition of the property right and damages." The preliminary question, then, is whether registrants have property rights in their domain names. Network Solutions all but concedes that they do.

Kremen, therefore, had an intangible property right in his domain name, and a jury could find that Network Solutions "wrongfully disposed of" that right to his detriment by handing the domain name over to Cohen. The district court, nevertheless, rejected Kremen's conversion claim. It held that domain names, although a form of property, are intangibles not subject to conversion. This rationale derives from a distinction tort law once drawn between tangible and intangible property. Conversion was originally a remedy for the wrongful taking of another's lost goods, so it applied only to tangible property.

Many courts today ignore or expressly reject that view. Indeed, the leading California Supreme Court case rejecting the tangibility requirement altogether is over one hundred years old. In *Payne* v. *Elliot*, 54 Cal. 339 (1880), the Court considered whether shares in a corporation (as opposed to the share certificates themselves) could be converted. It held that they could, reasoning: "The action no longer exists as it did at common law, but has been developed into a remedy for the conversion of *every species of personal property*." *Id.* at 341 (emphasis added). The Payne case recognized conversion of shares, not because share certificates customarily represent them, but because they are a species of personal property and, perforce, protected.

There is nothing unfair about holding a company responsible for giving away someone else's property even if it was not at fault. Cohen is obviously the guilty party here, and the one who should in all fairness pay for his theft. However, he's skipped the country, and his money is stashed in some offshore bank account. Unless Kremen's luck with his bounty hunters improves, Cohen is out of the picture. The question becomes whether Network Solutions should be open to liability for its decision to hand over Kremen's domain name. Negligent or not, it was Network Solutions that gave away Kremen's property. Kremen never did anything. It would not be unfair to hold Network Solutions responsible and force it to try to recoup its losses by chasing down Cohen. This, at any rate, is the logic of the common law, and we do not lightly discard it.

■ *Reversed and remanded. The evidence supported a claim for conversion, and the district court should not have rejected it.*

CASE CONCEPTS REVIEW

1. Should the tort of conversion apply to both tangible and intangible property? Why?
2. Did Network Solutions commit the tort of conversion? Why?

Nuisance

Generally, any continuous or continued conduct that causes annoyance, inconvenience, or damage to person or property (Nuisance usually applies to unreasonable, wrongful use of property, causing material discomfort, hurt, and damage to the person or property of another.)

NUISANCE Tort liability may also be predicated on the unreasonable use by a person of his or her own property. Any improper or indecent activity that causes harm to another person, to his or her property, or to the public generally is tortious. Such conduct is usually described as a **nuisance**, either private or public. A private nuisance disturbs only the interest of some private individual, whereas the public nuisance disturbs or interferes with the public in general. The legal theory supporting tort liability in these areas is that an owner of property, although conducting a lawful business thereon, is subject to reasonable limitations and must use the property in a way that will not unreasonably interfere with the health and comfort of neighbors or with their right to the enjoyment of their property. The ownership of land includes the right to reasonable comfort and convenience in its occupation. In addition to tort liability, the remedy of an injunction is used to abate a nuisance.

A nuisance may result from intentional conduct or from negligence. Although malice may not be involved, most nuisances are intentional in the sense that the party creating the nuisance did so with the knowledge that harm to the interests of others would follow. A nuisance requires a substantial and unreasonable interference with the rights of others and not a mere annoyance or inconvenience.

A nuisance may exist because of the type of business activity being conducted. Operation of a drag strip or a massage parlor has been held to constitute a private nuisance to the neighbors. Many nuisances result from the manner in which business is conducted. Pollution of the air or water by a business frequently results in tort liability based on the nuisance theory. Most tort litigation dealing with private nuisances is resolved by weighing the conflicting interests of adjoining landowners. If one party is seriously injuring the other, the activity may be enjoined and dollar damages awarded. Even if the courts are unwilling to enjoin an activity, dollar damages may still be awarded because of a nuisance.

7. Interference with Economic Relations

Interference with commercial or economic relations includes three business torts: disparagement, interference with contractual relations, and interference with prospective advantage.

DISPARAGEMENT *Disparagement* is a communication of an injurious falsehood about a person's property, quality of product, or character and conduct of business in general. Such false statements are regarded as "unfair" competition and are not privileged. The basis of the tort is the false communications that result in interference with the prospect of sale or some other advantageous business relation. The falsehood must be communicated to a third party and must result in specific pecuniary loss. The loss of specific customers, sales, or business transactions must be demonstrated. Although closely related, slander or personal defamation of one's reputation is another tort and is discussed in Section 8, on wrongful communications.

INTERFERENCE WITH CONTRACT *Interference with contractual relations* usually takes the form of inducing a breach of contract. To hold someone liable for interference with a contract, a direct causal relation and improper motive must be shown. Mere loss suffered from a broken contract is insufficient. Crucial to the question of liability is the balancing of the conflicting interests of the parties involved. For example, assume that a depositor tells the bank's president that she believes one of the cashiers is dishonest. She suggests that the cashier be discharged. Has the depositor committed a tort? The policy of protecting employees from wrongful interference with the employment contracts must be weighed against the desirability of ensuring that bank employees are honest. The trend of cases is to allow recovery for wrongful interferences with the rights of others. Any intentional invasion or interference with the property or contractual rights of others without just cause is a tort. The economic harm due to the breach of an existing contract is weighed against the motive and the reasonableness of the action. The courts tend to favor the sanctity of existing contracts over other interests, such as unrestricted competition.

INTERFERENCE WITH PROSPECTIVE ADVANTAGE *Interference with prospective or potential advantage* is considered a tort to protect the expectancies of future contractual relations, including the prospect of obtaining employment, employees, or customers. It is no tort to use fair business practices to beat a business rival to prospective customers; however, the competitor's motive and means of accomplishment determine liability. Fraud, violence, intimidation, and threats that drive away potential customers from one's market result in liability. As in suits for lost profits, obtaining sufficient proof that losses were actually suffered is sometimes difficult.

OTHER INFRINGEMENTS Another interference with economic relations tort is the wrongful appropriation of another's goodwill or business value. It is a tort to infringe on another's patent, copyright, or trademark. In addition, a trade name such as Holiday Inn or Coca-Cola is entitled to protection from theft or appropriation by another. Many cases involving the appropriation of another's business values involve words or actions that are deceptively similar to those of another. It is a tort to use a name or take an action that is deceptively similar to the protected interests of another. However, what degree of similarity may exist before a wrong is committed? In general, it can be said that whenever the causal observer, as distinct from the careful buyer, tends to be misled into purchasing the wrong article, an injunction as well as a tort action is available to the injured party.

The remedy of injunction is perhaps more important than the tort action where there is infringement of a patent, copyright, or trademark. The injunction that prohibits the continued appropriation protects not only the owner of the right but the consuming public as well.

Trade secrets also are protected by the law of torts and courts of equity. Information about one's trade, customers, processes, or manufacture is confidential; but if it is not patented or copyrighted, another firm may make the same discoveries fairly—through research, study, or observation—and may use them freely. "Reverse engineering" by which one party studies another's product to come up with a similar product is permissible. If the second firm bribes or hires an employee of the first company, however, to obtain secrets, the second firm may be enjoined from using them.

8. Wrongful Communications

Libel

The publication of a falsehood about a person by printing, writing, signs, or pictures for the purpose of injuring the reputation and good name of such person

Slander

An oral utterance of a false statement that injures the reputation of another

Defamation consists of the twin torts of libel and slander. **Libel** is generally written; **slander** is oral. A defamatory communication is one that holds a person up to hatred, contempt, or ridicule or causes a person to be shunned by others. Tort liability for defamation exists to protect a person's name and reputation.

Slander As a general rule, a charge of slander requires proof of actual damages; however, four categories of statements justify the awarding of damages without actual proof of damage: imputing the commission of a crime of moral turpitude; imputing the presence of a loathsome disease; imputing unfitness relating to the conduct of a business, trade, profession, or office; and accusing a female of being unchaste. All other slanders require proof of *special damage.*

Libel The law of libel is complicated by the written aspect of defamation. Freedom of the press, for example, is guaranteed by the First Amendment, to which the law must adhere. Furthermore, application of the law of libel depends on whether or not the person defamed is a public figure, subject to a set of standards different from those governing the rest of society. Celebrities must prove malice to collect damages. Businesses are not public figures, and they are not required to prove malice.

If a statement is libelous on its face, it is actionable without proof of special damages. If additional facts are necessary to establish that a writing is defamatory, the law for libel is the same as for slander; and unless the statement falls into one of the four categories previously noted, proof of actual damage is required.

General View While damage provisions are different for slander and libel, both torts are forms of defamation. Defamation requires proof that: (1) the defendant made a *false statement* (almost always that statement must be of a fact), (2) the statement was *published* (meaning only that it was passed on to a third party), (3) one's *reputation was harmed* by the statement, and (4) the *plaintiff was damaged* as a result of the statement. The intentional tort of fraudulent misrepresentation is the subject of more litigation than any other of the intentional torts. It is used not only as the basis of suits for dollar damages but also to avoid contract liability and as a basis to rescind or cancel otherwise valid contracts. (Note, too, that some states recognize, a tort of negligent misrepresentation where a defamatory statement was only made negligently.)

Exceptions Some defamatory statements are *absolutely privileged.* Statements made as a part of a judicial proceeding cannot constitute a tort because of the need for all witnesses to be able to testify freely, without fear of a subsequent lawsuit. Legislative proceedings and many executive communications are also absolutely privileged.

Some defamatory statements are subject to a *qualified or limited privilege.* For example, many communications to public officials are privileged to encourage citizens to report matters to officials. In addition, fair comment on matters of public concern cannot result in tort liability.

INVASION OF PRIVACY In recent years, the law has developed a tort known as *invasion of the right of privacy.* The right of privacy is the right to be let alone, but it may be invaded in four general ways:

(1) *Appropriation of a person's identity.* Using a person's photograph for commercial purposes, for example, is a common example of this type of tort.

(2) *Intrusion into one's privacy.* Many cases involve newspaper or magazine stories about one's private life. A detective magazine that publishes a picture of a family at the funeral of a loved one may be guilty of an invasion of privacy, but this tort must be distinguished from libel and slander.

(3) *Public disclosure of private facts.* A web site's disclosure of a private citizen's financial condition or sex life would qualify as such an invasion.

(4) *False light.* Information is posted in a blog that is false, but also highly objectionable, often attributing a belief or position that the person does not hold.

Invasion of privacy does not involve defamation. This type of invasion of privacy involves wrongful intrusion into one's private life in such a manner as to outrage or to cause mental suffering, shame, or humiliation to a person of ordinary sensibilities. The protection is for a mental condition, not a financial one. Invasion of privacy is the equivalent of a battery to one's integrity; actual damage need not be proved. Unjustified invasion of privacy entitles the victim to damages. Punitive damages may be collected if malice is shown. The tort is quite similar to inflicting mental distress by outrageous conduct. Many factual situations are given both labels.

CHAPTER SUMMARY

GENERAL PRINCIPLES

Damages

1. The theory of damages in tort liability is that the victim will be paid a sum of money that will put a person in as good a position as the person would have been in had the tort not occurred.
2. Compensatory damages include out-of-pocket losses plus pain and suffering, decreased life expectancy, and loss of life or limb.
3. Punitive damages are awarded in some cases to punish the wrongdoer and to deter wrongful conduct.

Persons Liable

1. Employers have liability for the torts of their employees if the employee is acting within the scope of employment.
2. If two or more persons commit a tort, they are jointly and severally liable.
3. A child may have tort liability after reaching a certain age.
4. Parents are generally not liable for the torts of their children unless the child is an agent or servant, or there is a special statute imposing liability.

INTENTIONAL TORTS

Interference with Personal Freedom

1. These torts include assault, battery, and false imprisonment.
2. The tort of inflicting mental distress is of growing importance. It is based on "outrageous" or "reckless" conduct.

Interference with Property Rights

1. Trespass may occur as to both real and personal property. A trespass may be innocent or willful.
2. When a conversion of personal property occurs, the wrongdoer has liability for the value of the goods.
3. A nuisance is the unreasonable use of one's property that causes injury to another. A nuisance may be enjoined or may result in dollar damages to the victim.

INTERFERENCE WITH ECONOMIC RELATIONS

1. Interference with commercial or economic relations includes four business torts: disparagement, interference with contractual relations, interference with prospective advantage, and wrongful appropriation of business interests.
2. Disparagement is a false communication about a product or business.
3. Interference with contractual relations usually takes the form of inducing a breach of contract.
4. Interference with prospective or potential advantage is considered a tort, to protect the expectancies of future contractual relations, including the prospect of obtaining employment, employees, or customers.
5. It is a tort to interfere with another's copyright, patent, trademark, or goodwill.

WRONGFUL COMMUNICATIONS

1. Defamation consists of the twin torts of libel and slander. Libel is generally written; slander is oral. Tort liability for defamation exists to protect a person's name and reputation.
2. The right of privacy is the right to be let alone. It involves wrongful intrusion into one's private life in such a manner as to outrage or to cause mental suffering, shame, or humiliation to a person of ordinary sensibilities.

REVIEW QUESTIONS AND PROBLEMS

1. Identify the terms in Column A by matching each with the appropriate statement in Column B.

A	B
(1) Contingent fee	(a) Unreasonable use of property
(2) Slander	(b) The right to be left alone
(3) Libel	(c) Property other than land
(4) Invasion of privacy	(d) Civil wrongful act
(5) Nuisance	(e) Written defamation
(6) Conversion	(f) Requires outrageous conduct
(7) Chattel	(g) Oral defamation
(8) Tort	(h) Liability without wrongful conduct
(9) Mental distress	(i) Major interference with goods
(10) Strict liability	(j) Assures equal access to the judicial system

2. Can an action result in both a crime and a tort? Why?
3. Describe the three types of tort liability and provide an example of each.
4. A child whose mother had taken the drug DES developed cancer. She sued all the manufacturers of DES and proved that through no fault of her own she was unable to determine which manufacturer caused the injury. Is she entitled to recover from all the manufacturers? Why?
5. Munley was divorced from her husband after they jointly incurred several debts. The divorce decree required the husband to pay the debts, but he failed to do so and they fell into default. The defendant loan company's agents then began contacting Munley regarding the debts and her husband's whereabouts. The agents visited her apartment on four or six different occasions, as well as asked her neighbors where she could be found and what type of furniture she owned. The agents indicated to the neighbor that Munley was in some sort of trouble. Did the actions of the defendant's agents constitute an intentional infliction of emotional distress or an invasion of privacy? Explain.
6. Mark is the manager of Mayhem Enterprises. Mark believes Angel, a twenty-year employee of Mayhem, is stealing from the business. Mark grabs Angel by the arm, starts screaming at her in front of other employees, puts Angel into his office, tells her to stay in the office until his return, and leaves the office. What tort or torts might Mark have committed? Why?
7. Marie was searching for a parking lot in downtown Baltimore that charged a reasonable fee. She found a lot surrounded by a high chain-link fence. The fence had a large open gate; inside was a "plain building" with an open door. There were some trucks on the lot but no cars. Unfortunately, she had not found a public parking lot but a truck garage facility. After she walked onto the lot, a guard dog, "Smokey," appeared, apparently unchained and "growling and snarling." Smokey knocked her to the ground, causing damage to her right knee and other injuries. Is she entitled to collect for her injuries? Why or why not?
8. Ninety-eight homeowners brought action seeking to enjoin as a nuisance the construction and operation of a ready-mix concrete plant on property adjacent to a residential area. Plaintiffs live southwest, west, and east across the highway from the plant. The plant is bounded immediately on the north and south by other business concerns. The trial court found for the plaintiffs. Did the defendant's operation of a concrete plant in an area zoned for light to general industrial use constitute a nuisance? Why?
9. A law firm sued several of its former associates for damages and to enjoin them from soliciting the firm's clients. These former associates actively encouraged the older firm's clients to terminate that relationship and become clients of the new firm. Was this new firm's conduct tortious? Why or why not?
10. Craig was identified in a newspaper as the father of an illegitimate child. The article dealt with teenage pregnancies, and most of it concerned the unmarried teenage mother. The reporter had talked to Craig but had not sought permission to identify him. Does Craig have a tort case against the newspaper? If so, on what theory? Explain.

Torts: Negligence and Strict Liability 8

CHAPTER OUTLINE

CHAPTER PREVIEW

This chapter presents the remaining two types of torts: negligence and strict liability. We are all careless at times. Through the law of negligence, society attributes responsibility for certain types of careless behavior. The essence of negligence is risk. In contrast to the law of intentional torts, which is based on someone or something meaning to harm, the law of negligence is focused on an actor creating a risk. As you will learn in the first portion of this chapter, in order to create legal liability, that risk must be one that is unreasonable.

Business practices, particularly the emergence of manufacturing during the latter part of the 19th century, prompted the growth of the law of negligence. Manufacturers created products that could injure the owner or others. If an intentional tort action were the sole method of seeking redress for injuries suffered, it would be very difficult to meet the required standard because these injuries were unintended. Courts found the need to embrace the notion of fault and the law of negligence. Today negligence is the most popular type of tort action brought. Also, the application of tort principles now has extended well beyond manufacturing. Service providers also must meet minimum standards of behavior. For example, accounting, medical, and other service providers can be sued for negligence when their behavior fails to meet accepted standards and injury to person or property results.

During the middle portion of the twentieth century, courts began to apply principles of strict liability, or liability without fault, to manufacturers of products. The doctrine of strict liability has been a part of the law for more than one hundred years, usually applied to those involved in abnormally dangerous activities. Early cases applied strict liability to trespass of dangerous animals or the manufacture of fireworks. As machines, tools, and other products became more complicated, plaintiffs were having an increasingly difficult time showing that a manufacturer was negligent. Courts, therefore, applied the doctrine of strict liability to products that are defective and cause harm—a process that does not require plaintiff to show fault. The subject strict liability, particularly as it is applied to manufacturers and those in the distribution chain, is covered in the latter portion of this chapter.

BUSINESS MANAGEMENT DECISION

The Iannelli family went to Burger King for lunch one Saturday. As they were eating their meal, a group of teenagers entered the restaurant and proceeded to yell, scream, and swear. Some in the group stated to the patrons of the Burger King that they were "hammered." Mr. Iannelli, Mrs. Iannelli, and their three small children became frightened. Mr. Iannelli approached the group and asked that they leave the restaurant. At that point, one of the teenagers stood and struck Mr. Iannelli, knocking him to the ground. The Iannelli family wishes to sue the Burger King. What tort or torts might be available to the Iannelli family?

NEGLIGENCE

1. Introduction

By most definitions, negligence has five basic elements: (1) a duty imposed on a person in favor of others, (2) an act or omission that constitutes a breach of this duty, (3) actual cause, (4) proximate cause, and (5) an injury or damage. Each of the five elements of this *prima facie* case must be established if the plaintiff is to be successful.

TABLE 8-1 ■ Elements of Prima Facie Case

Elements of Prima Facie Case of Negligence
1. Duty
2. Breach of duty
3. Breach of duty actually caused damage
4. Breach of duty was proximate cause of damage
5. Damage (or injury)

2. Duty

Duty
A legal obligation imposed by general law or voluntarily imposed by the creation of a binding promise

The concept of a legal **duty** means that a person must meet certain standards of conduct to protect others against unreasonable risks. These standards of conduct may vary, depending on the relationship of the parties. An owner of property would owe a higher duty to a business visitor than to a trespasser or a social guest. The duty owed to a trespasser is for the landowner not to entrap or willfully harm the trespasser. The landowner owes to a social guest the duty to warn that guest of known dangers. The duty to business visitors is to protect them against known dangers and dangers that, with reasonable care, the landowner might discover. The landowner's duty is to make the premises reasonably safe for business visitors.

Right
The phrase *legal right* is a correlative of the phrase *legal duty.* A person has a legal right if, upon the breach of the corresponding legal duty, that person can secure a remedy in a judicial proceeding.

Whenever the law imposes a duty on a person, another person has a **right**, and there exists a right-duty relationship. This relationship exists because the law recognizes it. Moral obligation does not impose a duty or create a right. The duty must be owed to the person claiming injury. An airline owes a duty to its passengers, and the passengers have the right to safe transportation. Assume that this duty is breached and the plane crashes, killing all on board. Assume also that one of the passengers was a key employee of a large company. The company has no claim or tort action against the airline because the right-duty relationship did not exist between the airline and the company.

3. Due Care

Negligence is sometimes defined as a failure to exercise *due care.* People are required to exercise due care and caution for the safety of others when the risk of injury to another is present. Failure to do so is negligence. In determining if a person has exercised due care and caution, the law recognizes that some injuries are caused by unavoidable accidents. There is no tort liability for injuries received in unavoidable accidents. It is only when a person is culpable of unreasonable conduct that tort liability is imposed. Some conduct is declared to be unreasonable by statute, while most conduct is judged by case law standards. The basic issue is whether or not the conduct alleged to be negligent was reasonable or unreasonable.

A person usually has no duty to avoid injuring others through lack of action. While there may be an ethical duty for a sunbather to warn a swimmer that sharks are in the water, there is no duty to speak or otherwise act to prevent the swimmer from becoming injured. A person or business may, because of a special relationship, possess an affirmative duty to speak or act in order to prevent injury. If a business located on the beach provides swimmers with masks and fins, they may possess an *affirmative duty* to warn if they knew sharks were in the water.

4. Reasonable-Person Test

Negligence presumes a uniform standard of behavior. This standard is that of a reasonable, prudent person using ordinary care and skill. The reasonable man or woman is a community ideal of reasonable behavior that varies from situation to situation. Therefore, the standard is applied by asking the question, "What would the reasonable person do under these circumstances?"

The reasonable person's physical characteristics are those of the defendant in the negligence case being tried. If a defendant is disabled, so is the reasonable person. On the other hand, the actual mental capacity of the defendant may be very different from that of a reasonable person. The law cannot allow a person who has bad judgment or a violent temper to injure others without liability simply because of these mental defects. While the mental capacity requited ignores temperament, intellect, and education, it does take age into account.

The *reasonable-person test* implies that everyone has a minimum level of knowledge. A reasonable person is presumed to know that gasoline will burn; that ice is slippery; and that the greater the speed of an automobile, the greater the danger of injury. In addition, if the person in question has knowledge superior to most people, the law requires that the person conduct himself or herself according to his or her actual skill and knowledge. A skilled orthopedic surgeon is held to a higher degree of care than a general practitioner of medicine.

Among the factors that affect the application of the reasonable-person standard are community customs, emergencies, and the conduct of others. If a person conducts himself or herself in the manner customary to the community, then such conduct probably is not negligent. If everyone does it, then it probably is not unreasonable behavior. Custom, however, does not as a matter of law establish due care because everybody may, in fact, be negligent. For example, it has been held that following generally accepted accounting principles may still constitute negligence.

The effect of emergencies is obvious. A person in an emergency situation is usually not held to as high a standard as a person who is not confronted with an emergency. The actual effect of the emergency is not to lower the standard, but to qualify it by asking, "Is this conduct reasonable under the circumstances?"

Negligence actions often involve the conduct of others. An operator of a business may be negligent in the selection of employees or in the failure to anticipate wrongful acts of others. The law requires that we take reasonable precautions to avoid injuries that are foreseeable. If a tavern employs a bartender with violent tendencies and he or she injures customers, liability based on a theory of negligence may be imposed. Likewise, entrusting an automobile to one incapable of driving would be a negligent act.

A central requirement associated with the reasonable-person test is that the duty to act in such a manner applies only to those who are foreseeable. The following case, perhaps the most famous of all tort cases and authored by one of the finest legal minds in the past century, addresses the issue of foreseeability.

5. Degrees of Negligence

Courts sometimes talk about degrees of negligence. These have been created for specific reasons, such as defining the extent of the risk involved. As a general rule, the greater the risk, the higher

CASE

Helen Palsgraf v. the Long Island Railroad Company

NEW YORK COURT OF APPEALS

248 N.Y. 339 (1928)

CARDOZO, CHIEF JUSTICE

Plaintiff was standing on a platform of defendant's railroad after buying a ticket to go to Rockaway Beach. A train stopped at the station, bound for another place. Two men ran forward to catch it. One of the men reached the platform of the car without mishap, though the train was already moving. The other man, carrying a package, jumped aboard the car, but seemed unsteady as if about to fall. A guard on the car, who had held the door open, reached forward to help him in, and another guard on the platform pushed him from behind. In this act, the package was dislodged, and fell upon the rails. It was a package of small size, about fifteen inches long, and was covered by a newspaper. In fact it contained fireworks, but there was nothing in its appearance to give notice of its contents. The fireworks, when they fell, exploded. The shock of the explosion threw down some scales at the other end of the platform, many feet away. The scales struck the plaintiff, causing injuries for which she sues.

The conduct of the defendant's guard, if a wrong in its relation to the holder of the package, was not a wrong in its relation to the plaintiff, standing far away. Relatively to her it was not negligence at all. Nothing in the situation gave notice that the falling package had in it the potency of peril to persons thus removed.

A different conclusion will involve us, and swiftly too, in a maze of contradictions. A guard stumbles over a package which has been left upon a platform. It seems to be a bundle of newspapers. It turns out to be a can of dynamite. To the eye of ordinary vigilance, the bundle is abandoned waste, which may be kicked or trod on with impunity. Is a passenger at the other end of the platform protected by the law against the unsuspected hazard concealed beneath the waste? If not, is the result to be any different, so far as the distant passenger is concerned, when the guard stumbles over a valise which a truckman or a porter has left upon the walk?

One who jostles one's neighbor in a crowd does not invade the rights of others standing at the outer fringe when the unintended contact casts a bomb upon the ground. The wrongdoer as to them is the man who carries the bomb, not the one who explodes it without suspicion of the danger. Life will have to be made over, and human nature transformed, before prevision so extravagant can be accepted as the norm of conduct, the customary standard to which behavior must conform.

The judgment of the Appellate Division and that of the Trial Term should be reversed, and the complaint dismissed, with costs in all courts.

■ *Reversed.*

CASE CONCEPTS REVIEW

1. Why did Palsgraf lose the case? What legal concept did the court focus on in the opinion?
2. How should a court make the determination of foreseeability?

the duty owed to others. In addition, the fact that a person is being paid to be careful usually increases the duty owed. A common carrier is an insurer of the goods carried and is liable except for acts of God and the public enemy if the goods are damaged. A common carrier is not an insurer of passengers, however. It owes the highest degree of care to them and will be liable to passengers for injuries resulting from even slight negligence. If a farmer is traveling on a train with hogs being delivered to market, the railroad is liable as an insurer for any injury to the hogs. It is liable to the farmer only if it is negligent.

The degrees of negligence are sometimes described as *slight negligence,* which is the failure to exercise great care; *ordinary negligence,* which is the failure to use ordinary care; and *gross negligence,* which is the failure to exercise even slight care. Such distinctions are of special importance when personal property is entrusted by one person to another. The duty owed depends on the legal relationship. If the duty is to exercise great care, there is liability for slight negligence; and if the duty is to exercise only slight care, there is liability only for gross negligence. Gross negligence is sometimes known as willful and wanton misconduct or a conscious disregard for the safety of others.

6. Negligence by Professional Persons: Malpractice

Among the more significant trends in the law of negligence is the substantial increase in malpractice suits by patients and clients against professional persons such as doctors or accountants. A malpractice suit may be predicated on a theory of breach of contract; but the usual theory is negligence, failure to exercise the degree of care and caution that the professional calling requires. Negligence by professional persons is not subject to the reasonable-person standard. Their standard is stated in terms of the knowledge, skill, and judgment usually possessed by members of the profession because a professional person holds himself or herself out to the public as having the degree of skill common to others in the same profession. However, professional persons do not guarantee infallibility. Although malpractice suits involve standards of professional conduct, the issue of negligence is submitted to a jury as a question of fact for a decision. Such cases usually require the testimony of experts to assist the jury in its findings of negligence. In many cases, juries find that liability exists, even though members of the profession contend and testify that the services performed were all that could reasonably be expected under the circumstances.

Malpractice suits against doctors and hospitals have multiplied so rapidly that they have significantly affected the practice of medicine and the cost of malpractice insurance. They have also been a significant cause of spiraling medical costs. Not only has the number of malpractice suits more than doubled in recent years, but the size of the verdicts has frequently reached astronomical proportions.

Many doctors and some hospitals have been unable to obtain adequate malpractice insurance coverage. More significantly, many doctors have been reluctant to attempt medical procedures that could result in a malpractice suit. Because of the trends in malpractice litigation, most doctors are practicing defensive medicine: prescribing tests that are probably not indicated, requiring longer hospital stays, and consulting with other doctors as a matter of routine. Defensive medicine obviously is more costly.

Malpractice cases against lawyers have also increased significantly; and although their impact on the cost of legal services is not as significant as it is in medical services, their importance is growing. Malpractice litigation against accountants is another area of great significance.

7. Special Doctrines that Show Negligence

Res ipsa loquitur

The thing speaks for itself, rebuttable presumption that a defendant was negligent.

RES IPSA LOQUITUR Liability for negligence is sometimes imposed on a defendant based on a presumption of negligence. This presumption is based on a doctrine known as **res ipsa loquitur**—the thing speaks for itself. It is used in cases where injury would not have occurred unless someone was negligent and the defendant is the only logical one that could have responsibility. This presumption of negligence is based on the defendant having exclusive control of the property causing the injury. The plaintiff's actions must not have contributed in any significant way to the injury.

For example, assume a customer in a department store steps into the elevator to go to another floor. Moments after the door closes, the elevator suddenly drops, resulting in the customer suffering back and neck injuries. This customer likely would satisfy the burden of proof that the department store was negligent by using the *res ipsa loquitur* doctrine.

Negligence per se

Negligence shown through the violation of a statute or ordinance

NEGLIGENCE PER SE Plaintiff may also be aided in proving the breach of a duty of care where defendant breaches a duty established by the legislative branch. Under the doctrine of **negligence per se**, a person is negligent, including situations where one acts or fails to act, where the actor violates a statute or ordinance that gives rise to the injury. A plaintiff, in order to draw on this potentially powerful legal tool, must establish that (1) the plaintiff is within the class of persons intended to be protected by the statute, (2) the plaintiff suffers the type of harm the statute was intended to prevent, and (3) the breach of the statute caused the injury.

Consider the common traffic accident. Brittany runs a red light and crashes into Donald. Brittany is cited for running the light and does not protest the citation. Donald can use the fact that Brittany was cited as strong evidence that Brittany was negligent in the civil action brought by Donald for negligence. Donald was a member of the group of individuals the statute was attempting to protect: drivers of automobiles. Also, the statute that requires individuals to stop at red lights was intended to prevent just the type of accident Donald experienced. Finally, Brittany's action of driving through the red light caused the accident.

8. Actual Cause

Actual cause is the element of the tort of negligence that requires plaintiff show a cause/effect relationship. The defendant's action must have caused plaintiff's injury. The essence of actual cause is phrased by courts in a variety of ways, including: "Did the defendant's conduct actually cause the plaintiff's harm?" "Was plaintiff injured because of an action of the defendant, or would plaintiff have been injured anyway?" "Was defendant's negligence a substantial factor in bringing about the injury or damage to plaintiff?" Courts ask juries to apply the "but for" test when making the determination as to whether defendant's action was the actual cause of the loss. That is, "but for" the negligent act by the defendant, would plaintiff have been injured?

Situations arise where two or more individuals or entities contribute to an injury to a plaintiff. For example, assume that two hunters negligently shot plaintiff, but only one bullet hit and injured the plaintiff. Both hunters fired at the same time at an object that later turned out to be plaintiff. The bullet was never found. In this situation, because both are negligent, principles of *joint and several liability* apply. As a result, each is responsible for the entire amount; plaintiff may recover the complete judgment from either. (If this occurs, the defendant who paid the entire sum may sue the defendant who did not pay at all for a sum equal to one-half of the entire judgment.)

9. Proximate Cause

Proximate cause

The negligent action that is close to the resulting injury or damage.

Proximate cause is the element of negligence perhaps most difficult to understand. Sometimes, the chain of events establishes that the injury is remote from the wrongful act. Proximate cause means that the act or the omission complained of must be close to injury or damage in order for the law to allow recovery for negligence. In other words, not all negligent actions where there is actual cause will result in recovery for the plaintiff. Policy limitations limit a defendant's responsibility to immediate, or foreseeable, harm. Problems in applying the rule of proximate cause arise because events sometimes *break the direct sequence* between an act and injury. Assume that a customer slips on the floor of a store and breaks a leg. While en route to the hospital in an ambulance, there is a collision in which the customer is killed. The store would not be liable for the wrongful death because its negligence was not the proximate cause of the death although it was one event in the chain of causation of death.

Difficult questions often arise over the issue of *superseding or intervening cause.* If liquor is sold to someone who is intoxicated and that person later causes an accident, is the chain of causation broken? Most modern courts would say no. Moreover, many courts also find that selling alcoholic beverages to a minor is an act of negligence that is one cause of subsequent auto accidents. Proximate cause is closely linked to foreseeability in these cases.

The issue of proximate cause must be decided on a case-by-case basis. Proximate cause requires that the injury be the natural and probable consequence of the wrong. Proximate cause means that the injury was *foreseeable* from the wrong. Issues of foreseeability are often quite difficult to resolve.

Assume that a plaintiff suffered a heart attack when informed that her daughter and granddaughter were killed in an auto accident. The plaintiff probably could not collect from the party at fault in the auto accident because her injury was not foreseeable and predictable. There was no proximate cause, even though actual cause was present.

The following case considers the issue of whether certain conduct might be an intervening case.

CASE

Kathleen Delaney v. John M. Reynolds

APPEALS COURT OF MASSACHUSETTS

825 N.E.2d 554 (2005)

PERRETTA, J.

After Kathleen Delaney shot and gravely injured herself with John M. Reynolds's gun, she brought this action against him. The action is grounded on allegations that although Reynolds knew that Delaney had serious emotional and mental problems, including thoughts of suicide, he nonetheless negligently kept his loaded gun in a place readily accessible to her. The judge granted Reynolds's motion for summary judgment on the ground that her independent act of shooting herself was a superseding cause of her injuries. We conclude that whether Delaney intended to commit suicide was one of several disputed material questions of fact and reverse the judgment.

We relate the facts as they appear in the materials submitted by the parties on Reynolds's motion for summary judgment. Sometime in July of 1998, Delaney and Reynolds, a police officer, began to live together at Reynolds's house. It was Reynolds's practice to store his handgun, loaded and unlocked, in his bedroom in a duffle bag or in a bureau drawer. The handgun was not equipped with a trigger lock. Reynolds was aware of the fact that Delaney knew where he kept his handgun. He was also aware of the fact that Delaney was receiving ongoing and active treatment for substance abuse and depression.

In the month leading up to May 8, 1999, the date of Delaney's self-inflicted injuries, Reynolds noticed that recent changes in her medication caused her to experience depression, feelings of isolation, and fatigue. Although Delaney claims to have informed Reynolds during this time that she previously had attempted to commit suicide by means of automobile exhaust inhalation, Reynolds denied having any knowledge of previous suicide attempts. On another occasion, Delaney claims and Reynolds denies, she told him that she had "had enough of this and [she] wanted to end [her] life." Reynolds's response was to hand Delaney his gun and instruct her to go outside so as not to make a mess in his house. Although Delaney took the gun and went outside, she did not shoot herself. When she went back into the house, Reynolds informed her that the gun was unloaded. Delaney also claimed that later that month she told Reynolds during a telephone conversation that she hated her life and wanted to die.

On the night of May 7, 1999, Delaney left Reynolds's residence to attend an Alcoholics Anonymous meeting. She purchased and smoked crack cocaine on the way to the meeting and stopped at a cocktail lounge where she drank two "White Russian" cocktails on her way back from the meeting. Upon arriving home, Delaney saw that Reynolds was asleep on the living room sofa. She then began doing light household chores while drinking vodka mixed with lemonade. When Reynolds awoke, he confronted Delaney about her substance abuse. An argument ensued, and Reynolds ordered Delaney to move out of the house. Delaney went to the second level of the house and to the master bedroom she shared with Reynolds in order to pack her belongings.

While packing, Delaney noticed Reynolds's duffle bag on the bedroom floor. She reached into the bag, removed his handgun, left the bedroom, and returned to the staircase. Reynolds was still on the sofa in the living room. Descending the stairs, Delaney aimed the gun at a window and pulled the trigger twice. The gun did not fire. Reynolds jumped from the sofa, and Delaney ran back up the stairs with him in pursuit. Delaney reached the master bedroom before Reynolds, put the gun beneath her chin, and pulled the trigger. This time the gun fired. A bullet entered her chin and exited from her right cheek. At the time of the medical treatment for her injury, Delaney tested positive for cocaine and had a blood alcohol level of .165.

Concluding that Delaney's injuries were deliberately self-inflicted, the judge treated the case as analogous to one involving liability in negligence for the suicide of another and ruled that her "voluntary act of using the gun to inflict harm upon herself was the intervening and superseding cause of [her injury]." Based on the events of May 8, Delaney argues that when she put Reynolds's gun beneath her chin and pulled the trigger, she intended neither to injure herself nor to commit suicide. Rather, she believed the gun to be unloaded.

Other jurisdictions have more recently gone beyond the traditional and often categorical basis for treating suicide as an intervening and superseding cause of injury and have considered various nontraditional circumstances as relevant to the issue of foreseeability. A review of these cases, as well as our more recent holdings, reveals that we have not limited our analysis of like cases to an ironclad rule that suicide or an intentionally self-inflicted injury constitutes an intervening and superseding cause as matter of law.

It is undisputed that when Delaney aimed at a window and twice pulled the trigger to Reynolds's gun, the weapon failed to discharge bullets and that only thereafter did she turn the gun on herself. She claims that she did so in the belief that the gun was not loaded. Based upon these facts and the inferences that can be drawn therefrom in favor of Delaney, we conclude that whether her act was intended to cause serious injury or death turns on the question of her intention at the time she pointed Reynolds's weapon to her chin and pulled the trigger.

The judge's conclusion, that Delaney's act was an intervening superseding cause of her injuries, made irrelevant any consideration of whether Reynolds might have been negligent in the first instance by leaving a loaded gun not equipped with a trigger lock accessible to Delaney, whom he knew or should have known to be suffering from substance abuse problems, depression, and thoughts of suicide.

Even were the jury to find that Delaney intended to commit suicide when she turned Reynolds's gun on herself with an intentional suicidal or self-injurious purpose, we think it should also be open to Delaney to show and the jury to find that the risk that she would handle or use Reynolds's gun in a manner so as to cause intentional injury to herself was foreseeable and that his failure to secure his gun was a proximate cause of her injury.

Further, and based upon whatever evidence might be presented at trial, a jury might find that although Delaney did not intend to kill or injure herself, her use of the gun in the manner that she did was far more negligent than any act on Reynolds's part.

■ *Reversed.*

CASE CONCEPTS REVIEW

1. Based on the facts of this case, why might a jury conclude that a superseding act was present?
2. In general, when does an event become superseding?

10. Defenses to Negligence

Two principal defenses to negligence exist. One is based on plaintiff's contribution to the injury or damage; the other is based on plaintiff accepting a known risk of harm. Both of these defenses are affirmative defenses, meaning that the defendant raises one of these defenses after the plaintiff has shown a *prima facie* case of negligence. As you consider these defenses, pay attention to whether the defense creates a complete bar that prohibits the plaintiff from recovering any damages or establishes a basis for reducing the amount of damages plaintiff may recover.

PLAINTIFF'S CONTRIBUTION The doctrine of *contributory negligence,* established, early in the development of negligence law, bars the plaintiff from recovering any damages if plaintiff's own fault contributed to the injury. Early cases favored businesses. If a business manufactured a horse buggy and the step on the buggy broke as the owner attempted to climb into the driver's seat, the manufacturer could assert the doctrine of contributory negligence if the driver acknowledged that he did not look at the step before placing his foot on the step. The slightest amount of negligence on the part of the plaintiff, under this view, would prevent any recovery for the injury.

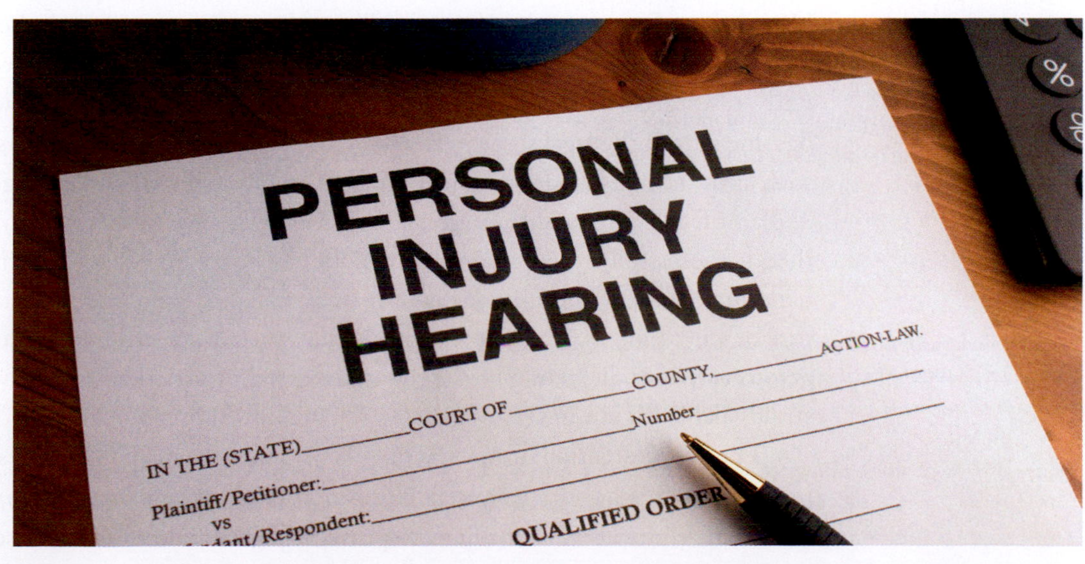

Proximate cause is an injury that occurs from the consequence of the wrong.

The harshness associated with this approach has caused almost all states to reject contributory negligence in favor of *comparative fault.* Under comparative fault, the plaintiff's contribution does not bar recovery. Instead, the fault of the plaintiff is compared with the fault of the defendant. Therefore, the plaintiff's award is reduced proportionately. This requires a jury verdict to assess the relative contribution of both parties. There are two types of comparative fault. Under a *modified comparative fault* system (sometimes termed the "50% Rule"), the plaintiff may recover diminished damages if the plaintiff's contribution is not greater than the defendant's. If a jury found plaintiff 25% responsible, the defendant is 75% responsible; the plaintiff could recover 75% of total damages suffered. In another situation, if the jury found plaintiff 55% responsible for a traffic accident, then under the modified system plaintiff would recover nothing. A large number of states have adopted another system: *pure comparative fault.* In negligence actions under this doctrine, plaintiff can recover damages even if plaintiff's negligence is greater than that of the defendant.

Assumption of the risk

Plaintiff voluntarily assumes a known risk of harm.

ASSUMPTION OF THE RISK Defendant may assert the defense of **assumption of the risk** when plaintiff is shown to have voluntarily assumed a known risk of harm. Under traditional negligence law, assumption of the risk is a complete bar to recover. Consider the following example. Julio goes to Fanny Mae's brake shop to have the brakes adjusted on his car. After Fanny Mae works on the brakes, Fanny Mae returns the car to Julio and states to him that he should not operate the vehicle if the brakes continue to make a screeching noise, as the noise is a signal the brakes may fail. Julio goes for a drive in the mountains. He hears the screeching noise for miles but fails to stop. The brakes fail, and Julio is injured. Julio was told of the potential danger but decided to ignore the warning. Julio voluntarily assumed the risk and will be prevented from recovering for his injuries. The assumption of the risk defense requires defendant to show: (1) plaintiff knew of the risk associated with a particular activity, and (2) voluntarily agreed to assume that risk.

The severe result under the traditional application of assumption of the risk has prompted many states to discard assumption of the risk as a complete bar to recover. In these states, plaintiff's decision to assume a known risk of harm simply becomes part of the calculation in determining the comparative fault of both parties.

STRICT LIABILITY

11. Theory

HISTORICAL PERSPECTIVE Strict liability creates a tort even though there is no intent or negligence. Therefore, a defendant is liable for harm caused without consideration of moral blame. Early cases dealt with dangerous animals and abnormally dangerous activities. Strict liability became part of the legal scene in the United States in cases where owners of dangerous animals, such as bears, lions, and alligators, were held strictly liable for any damage those animals caused. A plaintiff who suffered injury caused by a dangerous animal could, under the strict liability theory, successfully recover damages without having to show that the owner was negligent in the handling or care of the animal. Liability was created without fault because of the dangerous nature of wild animals. The law of strict liability then expanded into the area of abnormally dangerous activities, including holding manufacturers of fireworks, toxic chemicals, and explosives strictly liable for injuries resulting from the manufacturing process.

The latest extension of strict liability has been to the field of products liability. This development imposes liability wherever a defective product causes damage or injury. It is the logical result of the elimination of the need to prove negligence and of the demise of the privity requirement in breach-of-warranty actions. The lack of privity means that the injured party need not have purchased the product from a defendant. Under privity, the consumer had to sue the retailer who sold the defective product. Then the retailer would sue the wholesaler who sold the retailer the product. The wholesaler would then sue the manufacturer. By doing away with the privity requirement, the consumer can sue the manufacturer directly.

EARLY DIMENSIONS OF PRODUCT LIABILITY LAW Legal scholars, as a part of the *Restatement of the Law of Torts,* developed the theory of strict liability for harm caused by products. The American Law Institute (ALI) issued in 1964 Section 402A of the *Restatement (Second) of Torts,* which provides the following:

> 402A. Special Liability of Seller of Product for Physical Harm to User or Consumer.
>
> (1) One who sells any product in a defective condition unreasonably dangerous to the user or consumer, or to his property, is subject to liability for physical harm thereby caused to the ultimate user or consumer, or to his property if
> (a) the seller is engaged in the business of selling such a product, and
> (b) it is expected to and does reach the user or consumer without substantial change in the condition in which it is sold.
>
> (2) The rule stated in Subsection (1) applies although
> (a) the seller has exercised all possible care in the preparation and sale of his product, and
> (b) the user or consumer has not bought the product from or entered into any contractual relation with the seller.

The courts have relied heavily on these rules in developing the law of product liability. Under 402A, plaintiff in a product liability lawsuit need only to prove that (1) a product was defective, (2) this defect caused the product to be unreasonably dangerous, (3) the product has not been changed or modified by the plaintiff, and (4) the plaintiff suffered damages using the product. Not all states require all of these elements; and the law is progressing to a point where in some states there is no requirement that the plaintiff show the product was unreasonably dangerous.

Strict liability is imposed on manufacturers and designers, as well as on the seller of the goods. The theory of strict liability has been applied to leases of goods as well as to sales. The potential liability extends to all commercial suppliers of goods. While in many states it is not applicable to the sale of used goods, there is a trend toward applying it to used goods. In almost every state, the liability extends not only to users and consumers but also to bystanders such as pedestrians.

Strict liability has been applied both to personal injuries and to damage to the property of the user or consumer. Some courts have refused to extend it to property damage, and most courts have refused to extend it to economic loss.

Note significant shift in focus for assigning liability. Strict liability is oriented towards the product, while intentional and negligent liability is directed toward conduct.

12. Recent Trends in Product Liability

Since the 1960s, the law of product liability based on principles of strict liability has grown considerably. Unfortunately, aspects of Section 402A were unclear and courts, while attempting to follow the direction of 402A, developed varying interpretations of key principles of product liability law. As a result, the ALI issued the *Restatement (Third) of Torts: Products Liability* in 1997. This new pronouncement provides guidance to courts in three specific areas: manufacturing defects, design defects, and warning defects.

MANUFACTURING DEFECTS A manufacturing defect occurs when a product fails to conform to the manufacturer's design for the product. In a significant departure from Section 402A, the *Restatement (Third) of Torts: Products Liability* does *not* impose upon the plaintiff the requirement that it show that the product is unreasonably dangerous. This is the view California and a growing number of states had adopted in direct variance with the approach suggested in Section 402A ("unreasonably dangerous"). A chain on a new bicycle that was not correctly assembled and causes injury is an example of a manufacturing defect. Under this new view, it is immaterial that the manufacturer used all available means to ensure that the chain was manufactured according to plan. The social policy regarding the elimination of the "unreasonably dangerous" requirement regarding manufacturing defects is to encourage manufacturers to continue improving their quality control processes.

DESIGN DEFECTS The *Restatement (Third) of Torts: Products Liability* retains negligence principles, however, regarding defects in the design of a product. Under Section 2(b), a product is deemed to have a design defect "when the foreseeable risks of harm posed by the product could have been reduced or avoided by the adoption of a reasonable alternative design by the seller. ..." The use by the authors of the terms "foreseeable risks" and "reasonable alternative" certainly connotes reliance on principles of negligence not strict liability. Therefore, plaintiff in a design defect case must show that an alternative design was reasonable.

DEFECTS IN INSTRUCTIONS AND WARNINGS Negligence principles also are retained in *Restatement (Third) of Torts: Products Liability* provisions dealing with defects in instructions for use and product warnings. Manufacturers and those in the distribution chain are liable only for harm that is reasonably foreseeable.

The following case illustrates the importance of a manufacturer providing an adequate warning.

CASE

Leesa Bunch, a Minor, etc. v. Hoffinger Industries, Inc. and McMasker Enterprises, Inc.

COURT OF APPEAL OF CALIFORNIA, THIRD APPELLATE DISTRICT

123 Cal. App. 4th 1278 (2004)

RAYE, J.

One hot summer day, 11-year-old Leesa Bunch (Bunch) dove into a four-foot deep, aboveground swimming pool and changed her life forever. Rendered quadriplegic by the dive, Bunch eventually filed suit against, among others, defendants Hoffinger Industries, Inc., doing business as Doughboy Recreational Company, and Golden West Marketing, Inc. (collectively Hoffinger). Hoffinger manufactured the replacement pool liner used in the pool. Bunch also sued cross-complainant McMasker Enterprises, Inc. (McMasker), the seller of the liner. McMasker eventually settled with Bunch.

Warnings to children between the ages of seven and 12 must be concrete and spell out the dangers and consequences of actions in order to be effective. Buck found the labels supplied with the Hoffinger pool liner neither adequate nor effective. The labels failed to spell out any consequences of diving into shallow water. Buck reviewed the history of warning labels and claims of injury and found that the instances of injury decreased as the explicitness of the warnings increased.

A plaintiff's misuse of a product may be a cause of the plaintiff's injuries. However, if the product's manufacturer could foresee the misuse, the manufacturer remains liable unless it provides an adequate warning. A manufacturer is required to foresee some degree of misuse and abuse of a product and to take reasonable precautions to minimize the resulting harm.

Hoffinger concedes Bunch need not establish that its product was the only potential proximate cause of her injuries, but argues "any alleged deficiency falls far short of being a causal substantial factor in this incident." Instead, Hoffinger points to a variety of other causes of the tragedy: Mrs. Frank's decision to leave four young children unsupervised, Mr. Frank's decision not to affix the warning labels supplied with the replacement liner, and Bunch's decision to disregard any warnings and dive into the pool. Therefore, Hoffinger contends, the record "fails to establish or support an inference that more or different warnings would have prevented this accident: in other words, as a matter of law, there is no evidence of cause in fact or legal causation attributable to any alleged failure by [Hoffinger]." In effect, Hoffinger challenges the sufficiency of the evidence to support the jury's finding that its product was a substantial factor in bringing about Bunch's injuries.

At trial, Bunch testified she believed Mrs. Frank's admonition against diving was just "being a mom, and mom's [sic] say no all the time." Bunch believed the warning sticker showing a man doing a "pike" dive and stating "caution" meant do not do a pike dive. After being shown a 1989 Doughboy caution label depicting a man with lightning bolts coming out of his head and stating "crippling injury" and "danger," Bunch testified such a warning would have prevented her from diving the day of the accident. Bunch stated she did not know she could break her neck if she dove into four feet of water.

Dr. Buck, Bunch's expert, testified that a young diver standing at the edge of an aboveground pool cannot necessarily judge the depth of the pool. Warnings act as "brakes to stop dangerous behaviors." Warnings to children between the ages of seven and twelve must be concrete and spell out the dangers and consequences of actions in order to be effective. Buck found the labels supplied with the Hoffinger pool liner neither adequate nor effective. The labels failed to spell out any consequences of diving into shallow water. Buck reviewed the history of warning labels and claims of injury and found that the instances of injury decreased as the explicitness of the warnings increased.

Dr. Johnson, another of Bunch's experts testified that pool industry standards require manufacturers to prominently display permanent warnings on their pools. Johnson outlined several methods of installing adequate warnings during a pool's manufacture.

Given the testimony of Bunch and her two expert witnesses, we find sufficient evidence to support the conclusion that the lack of an adequate warning label was neither a negligible nor theoretical contribution to Bunch's injury. The evidence presented at trial revealed that the lack of a persuasive label outlining the consequences of diving into the pool was a substantial factor in causing the injury. As the Supreme Court points out, " 'a very minor force that does cause harm is a substantial factor.' " Here, at the very least, the lack of an effective warning was a minor force in bringing about the fateful dive.

■ *Affirmed.*

CASE CONCEPTS REVIEW

1. Why were the labels inadequate?
2. What do you believe would be adequate notice in this case?
3. Is the court articulating a different notice standard for adults and children? If so, why?

13. Defenses

Strict liability is not synonymous with *absolute liability.* There must be proof that some dangerous defect caused the injury, even though the product was being used in the manner reasonably anticipated by the seller or the manufacturer. In addition, there are defenses that may be asserted to limit liability.

COMPARATIVE FAULT While in the past courts have used principles of comparative negligence, assumption of the risk, and misuse of product as a complete bar to recovery, almost all states today simply examine plaintiff's actions and apply comparative fault principles. The apportionment of damages based on fault of the plaintiff brings negligence principles into the establishment of a defense to any of the three types of defects addressed in the *Restatement (Third) of Torts: Products and Liability.* For purposes of comparative fault, negligence of the plaintiff is not a defense when such negligence consists merely of a failure to discover the defect in the product or to guard against the possibility of its existence. A consumer's unobservant, inattentive, ignorant, or awkward failure to discover or guard against a defect is not a damage-reducing factor. The consumer or user is entitled to believe that the product will do the job for which it was built.

STATE OF THE ART A defense that is often asserted is called *state of the art.* This defense, simply stated, is that the product was manufactured according to the best and latest technology available. If a product is manufactured using the best technology but it nevertheless injures people, should the manufacturer still have liability? Most courts do not allow the state-of-the-art defense to defeat a claim based on strict liability. According to Section 402A(2)(a) of the Restatement (Second) of the Law of Torts, the rule of strict liability for a product defect can apply even when "the seller has exercised all possible care in the preparation and sale of his product." Therefore, in a strict liability claim, the sole subject of inquiry is the defective condition of the product, and not the manufacturer's knowledge, negligence, or fault.

In a negligence action, the inquiry focuses on the reasonableness of the maker's action in designing the product. However, in an action for strict liability, the focus is on the dangerous condition of the product as put into commerce. State-of-the-art evidence, or evidence of industry or federal government standards, concerns the manufacturer's standard of care, which relates to the reasonableness of the manufacturer's design choice, not the condition of the product. Therefore, this evidence is irrelevant in a strict liability case.

CHAPTER SUMMARY

NEGLIGENCE

Duty

1. The five basic elements of negligence are (1) a duty owed by one person to another and (2) a breach of that duty (3) that was the actual cause and (4) that was the proximate cause of (5) an injury.
2. The duty owed by one person to another varies depending on the relationship of the parties.

Due Care

1. Negligence is the failure to exercise due care. Due care is reasonable conduct under the circumstances.
2. The doctrine of *res ipsa loquitur* creates a presumption of negligence.

Reasonable-Person Test

1. The standard for judging whether or not a duty has been breached is to judge the conduct against the standards of the reasonable person.

Degrees of Negligence

1. The greater the risk, the higher the duty owed to others.
2. A common carrier is an insurer of goods and owes passengers the highest degree of care.
3. Slight negligence is the failure to use great care.
4. Ordinary negligence is the failure to use ordinary care.
5. Gross negligence is the failure to use slight care.

Malpractice

1. Malpractice by professional persons is the failure to exercise that degree of care and caution that the profession calls for. It is the failure to meet the standards of the profession.

Special Doctrines that Show Negligence

1. The doctrine of *res ipsa loquitur* creates a presumption of negligence.
2. *Negligence per se* occurs where a person violates a law or ordinance and damage results.

Actual Cause

1. Actual cause means that there is a connection between the breach of duty and injury.

Proximate Cause

1. Proximate cause is based on the foreseeability of the injury as a result of unreasonable behavior.

Defenses to Negligence

1. Plaintiff's contribution may be a total bar or simply used to proportionately reduce any damage award.
2. Assumption of the risk occurs where plaintiff voluntarily assumes a known risk of harm.

STRICT LIABILITY

Theory

1. In strict liability cases, the focus of attention is on the product.

2. A manufacturer selling a defective product in a defective condition that is unreasonably dangerous to the user or his or her property is liable for physical injuries caused by the defect.
3. The theory may apply to leases as well as sales.

Recent Trends in Product Liability

1. The *Restatement (Third)* does not impose upon the plaintiff the requirement to show that a manufacturing defect was unreasonably dangerous.

Defenses

1. Contributory negligence is not a defense to a suit based on the theory of strict tort liability.
2. Comparative fault is often used to reduce verdicts in strict products liability cases.
3. State-of-the-art defenses normally are rejected by courts.

Review Questions and Problems

1. Match each term in Column A with the appropriate statement in Column B.

A	B
(1) *Res ipsa loquitur*	(a) Negligence is shown through the violation of a law or ordinance.
(2) Actual cause	(b) General standard for behavior in negligence
(3) Assumption of the risk	(c) Failure to exercise even the slightest care
(4) Design defect	(d) Risk of harm could have been reduced or avoided by the adoption of a reasonable alternative plan for a product.
(5) Negligence	(e) A rebuttable presumption that defendant was negligent
(6) Proximate cause	(f) Liability without fault
(7) Negligence per se	(g) Failure to exercise due care
(8) Reasonable-person test	(h) Plaintiff assuming a known risk of harm
(9) Strict liability	(i) Defendant's action was close to plaintiff's harm.
(10) Gross negligence	(j) Defendant's action must have caused plaintiff's harm.

2. Helen toured a town house built by Thames. While inspecting the kitchen, she opened a cabinet; the cabinet door fell and struck her on the head. An examination revealed that no screws were affixed to the door to secure it to the cabinet. She filed suit against the cabinetmaker and offered proof of her injury relying on the doctrine of *res ipsa loquitur.* Should she recover? Explain.
3. A high school student teacher was injured during a donkey basketball game when the donkey she was riding put his head down and she fell *off.* She sued the Board of Education for damages. What will be the likely defense? Explain.
4. Plaintiff, while a patron in a restaurant, was shot by an armed robber. The robber was angry because the cashier had locked the cash register and fled. Is the defendant restaurant liable for negligence? Why?

5. Ann sued a grocery store for injuries. She had slipped on some accumulated rainwater as she stepped on a rubber mat just inside the door to the store. Prior to the fall, the bag boy had placed a "wet floor" sign approximately six feet directly in front of the door and had been instructed to mop the entrance area periodically in accordance with store procedure on rainy days. What defense will the store assert? Explain.
6. Plaintiff was injured in an automobile accident caused entirely by the defendant. Plaintiff was not wearing his seat belt. He was thrown from his Jeep and sustained a compression-type injury to the lower back when he landed on the pavement. The defendant offered evidence that had the plaintiff been wearing his seat belt, he would not have been thrown from the Jeep. If the doctrine of comparative fault is followed, will this fact reduce the damages to which the plaintiff is entitled? Explain.
7. A Montana tavern served beer to Michael, who was already intoxicated. He admitted that his speech was thick and that he was staggering when he ordered his last beer. Later he drove his car on the wrong side of a highway and killed the plaintiff. Suit was brought against the tavern operator for wrongful death. A Montana statute prohibited the sale of alcoholic beverages to intoxicated persons. Is the tavern liable? Why or why not?
8. Smith sued Ariens for injuries sustained while operating a snowmobile in a field. The snowmobile hit a rock that was partially covered by snow. On impact, the right side of Smith's face came down and hit a brake bracket on the left side of the snowmobile. The brake bracket had two sharp metal protrusions on the inside that were toward the plaintiffs face. What theory of recovery best supports the plaintiff's case? Explain. Should the plaintiff be awarded damages? Why?
9. The plaintiff bought a rotary power mower from the defendant. He had used similar mowers before and was thoroughly familiar with them. The rear of the housing of the plaintiff's mower is embossed with the warning, "Keep Hands & Feet From Under Mower." The instruction booklet twice advises the operator to mow slopes lengthwise, not up and down. While mowing up and down, the plaintiff fell and lifted the mower onto his feet. The plaintiff sues, using strict liability as his theory. Should the plaintiff recover? Explain.
10. Maude bought a plastic waste container; and when she got it home, she found the lid did not fit properly on the top of the container. In an attempt to make it fit, she hit the corner of the lid with her hand and suffered a deep gash in her hand. Will Maude successfully recover on a theory of strict liability against the manufacturer of the plastic waste container? Explain.

Internet Resources

For additional information regarding negligence, see: http://www.law.cornell.edu/wex/index.php/Tort

For additional information regarding product liability law, see: http://www.law.cornell.edu/wex/index.php/Products_liability

Property: Personal Property, Intellectual Property, and Wills 9

CHAPTER OUTLINE

continued

CHAPTER PREVIEW

While most people tend to think of property as a thing owned or possessed by someone, this is not the way the law thinks of and analyzes property. In the law, property is thought of as "a bundle of rights" that one or more persons may have with respect to a thing. These rights may include the right to physically control the thing (possession); the right to transfer the thing to another by sale, gift, or will; or even the right to destroy it. The bundle of rights concept means that property is a series of legal relationships in which some people have rights and all others have duties that are negative in character. For example, each of us has a duty not to interfere with another's use and enjoyment of his or her property. As you study this chapter and Chapter 10, keep in mind the bundle of rights concept.

The concept of property as a bundle of rights is meaningless unless it is associated with people or with legal entities that qualify as persons. Some of the terms frequently used in expressing this association are ownership, title, and possession. The word *owner* usually describes someone who possesses all the rights or interest associated with the thing involved. The word *title* often is thought to be synonymous with ownership. Title is also used to signify the method by which ownership is acquired, such as a transfer of title. It may also be used to indicate the evidence by which ownership is established—a written instrument called a title, such as a car title. Thus the word title has a variety of meanings, depending on the context.

The word *possession* is equally difficult to define accurately. Its meaning is also dependent somewhat on the context in which it is used. Possession implies the concept of physical control by a person over property and the personal and mental relationship to it. While it is physically possible to possess a watch or a ring, it is obviously physically impossible to possess 1,000 acres of land in the same manner; yet the word possession as a legal term is used in both instances. Possession describes not only physical control but also the power to obtain physical control by legal sanctions, if necessary. In general, the concepts of possession and title should be kept separate and distinct. In other words, having possession of property does not mean the possessor also has title. The reverse is also true—a person who has title to property does not always have possession of that property. For example, a landlord of an apartment building owns (has title to) each unit; the tenants have physical control (possession) of the premises.

This chapter presents first some introductory principles of property, including a discussion of the distinctions among categories of property and the property status of personal property added to land (called fixtures). The chapters then explores aspects of personal property, basic concepts of intellectual property, and elementary features associated with wills and intestate succession.

BUSINESS MANAGEMENT DECISION

You are a commercial loan officer at a local financial institution. You commit to loan $1,000,000 to an investor who plans to buy an apartment complex. In addition to having an interest in the land and the buildings, you want the heating and air-conditioning units, the carpeting, and the appliances to be part of your security.

What should you do to make certain you have the interests as security you desire?

CLASSIFICATIONS OF PROPERTY

1. Real versus Personal Property

Real property

The legal interests in land and things attached to or growing on land

Personal property

The rights, powers, and privileges a person has in things that are not real property

From the standpoint of its physical characteristics, property is classified as either **real property** or **personal property**. When describing property, the adjective real refers to land and things attached to the land. Therefore, land as part of the earth's surface, buildings, fences, and trees are examples of things classified as real property. Personal property consists of all other things that are not real property. By definition, all items of property are classified as either real or personal property, although lawyers sometimes refer to mixed property to describe such things as real estate leases.

2. Real Property

The legal terms real property and *real estate* are very similar and frequently confused. In fact, these terms are often used interchangeably. However, there is a technical distinction between real property and real estate. The term *real estate* refers to the physical aspects of land and its attachments. For example, the dirt on the land is real estate, as are any actual improvements, such as buildings, roads, fences, and landscaping. Also included in the definition of real estate are the spaces above and below the land's surface. Included in these spaces are mineral, water, and air rights. Historically, real estate included unlimited subsurface (mineral rights) and air rights. Today, these rights are limited to a reasonable distance. Despite this limitation, these rights still have great value to the landowner. Indeed, interference with mineral and air rights is treated similarly to trespass on the land's surface.

The term real property is used to describe the legal rights that a person can have in real estate. For instance, the ownership interest a person may have in land and its improvements is classified as a real property interest. Because the distinction between real property and real estate is a subtle one, the text and cases included in this book use the terms as synonyms.

The three most important areas of the law of real property concern (1) ownership interests, (2) methods of acquiring title, and (3) transactions. All of these areas are examined in Chapter 10.

Tangible

Describes property that is physical in character and capable of being moved

3. Personal Property

Personal property may be classified as tangible or intangible. The term **tangible** *personal property* includes objects such as goods. The term intangible personal property refers to things

Intangible

Something that represents value but has no physical nature

such as accounts receivable, goodwill, patents, and trademarks. **Intangible** *personal property* has value, as tangible property has; and each can be transferred.

The term *chattel* is used to describe personal property generally, but chattels may also be classified as chattels real and chattels personal. *Chattels real* describes an interest in land, such as a leasehold; *chattels personal* is applied to movable personal property. When the term *chattel* is used in connection with intangible personal property, the property is referred to as chattels personal in action. A *chattel personal in action*—or *chose in action,* as it is frequently called—is something to which one has a right to possession, but concerning which one may be required to bring some legal action ultimately to enjoy possession. A contract right may be said to be a chose in action because a lawsuit may be necessary to obtain the rights under the contract. A negotiable instrument such as a note or check is a common form of chose in action. Although the instrument itself may be said to be property, in reality it is simply evidence of a right to money; and it may be necessary to maintain an action to reduce the money to possession.

4. Reasons for Distinguishing between Real and Personal Property

The distinction between real and personal property appears to be obvious. However, this distinction may become difficult to make in a number of factual settings. Reasons why the law distinguishes between these broad categories of property are discussed in this section.

CONFLICT OF LAWS PRINCIPLES When property becomes involved in a multiple-state transaction, the law that governs the property rights may depend on whether that property is real or personal. Sorting out which state's laws are applicable may be determined by the conflict of laws principle. Chapter 1 may be reviewed for an overview of conflicts of laws problems.

Situs

"Place, situation", the place where a thing is located (The situs of land is the state or county where it is located.)

As a general rule, conflict of laws principles provide that the law of the **situs**—the law of the state where real property is located—determines all legal questions concerning real property. Legal issues concerning conflict of laws relating to personal property are not so easily resolved. Conflict of laws rules may refer to the law of the owner's domicile to resolve some questions and to the law of the state with the most significant contacts with the property to resolve others. The law of the situs of the personal property is also used to resolve some legal issues. Therefore, the description of property as real or personal has a significant impact on the determination of the body of substantive law used to decide legal issues concerning the property.

TRANSFER OF PROPERTY During the lifetime of the owner, the distinction between real and personal property is significant since the methods of transferring them are substantially different. Formal instruments such as deeds are required to transfer an interest in land, whereas few formalities are required in the case of personal property. A bill of sale may be used in selling personal property; but it is not generally required, and it does not, in any event, involve the technicalities of a deed. The transfer of personal property is, as a rule, quite simply accomplished (a motor vehicle transfer may require the delivery of a certificate of title), whereas formality is required to transfer real property.

When the owner of property dies, how the transfer of title is accomplished may depend on whether the owner had a will. If no will is found, ownership of real property typically passes to a court-appointed administrator who determines who is entitled to the real property under the terms of the state law. Title to personal property generally passes directly to the heirs of the deceased owner. A valid will can simplify this need to distinguish between real and personal property.

TAXES Systems for taxing real estate are different from those for taxing personal property in many states. Property taxes on real estate are significant in every state, while personal property taxes often are less significant. Typical of the issues that may arise are those relating to mobile homes. Is a mobile home that is placed on a foundation real estate and thus subject to real estate taxation, or is it personal property? Similar questions make it apparent that parties to various transactions and courts are frequently called on to label property as real or personal. If the issue is likely to arise, it should always be covered in agreements.

FIXTURES

5. What Is a Fixture?

Fixture

As an item of personal property that has become attached or annexed to real estate, a fixture generally is treated as part of the real estate.

The classification of property as real or personal may be very difficult at times, and it may change from time to time. For example, when a dishwasher is purchased at an appliance store, it is clearly personal property. However, what is its status if it is built into your kitchen cabinets? Does this dishwasher remain an item of personal property, or has it become a part of the real estate? The answers to these questions are determined by the law of fixtures. A **fixture** is personal property that has become a part of real estate.

In the following case the court is asked to determine whether a particular object is a fixture.

CASE

Prospect Hill Acquisition, LLC v. Tyco Electronics Corporation

UNITED STATES COURT OF APPEALS FOR THE FIRST CIRCUIT

414 F.3d 181 (2005)

GERTNER, U.S. DISTRICT JUDGE

Prospect Hill is a Delaware limited liability company. It was formed to own and operate a commercial building at 140 Fourth Avenue in Waltham, MA ("Premises"). Tyco is a Pennsylvania corporation that purchased the Premises in 1999 and sold it to Prospect Hill pursuant to a Purchase and Sale Agreement ("P&S") dated November 16, 2001. The closing for the sale of the Premises took place on November 30, 2001, the same day that Prospect Hill leased the Premises back to Tyco pursuant to a written Lease. The Lease term commenced on that date and expired on June 21, 2002.

The P&S provided for a "Due Diligence Period" prior to the closing, during which Prospect Hill was "to conduct [] surveys, reviews, analyses, and inspections of the environmental condition of the Premises." This provision is noteworthy because prior to the November 30, 2001 closing, Prospect Hill knew that metal plating operations—which involved the regular use of hazardous materials, including cyanide compounds—had been conducted on the Premises since 1975. On November 28, 2001, Prospect Hill's environmental consultant, Haley & Aldrich ("Haley"), provided an Oversight Expert Review of the Premises, in which it was advised that "metal plating and machining have constituted a majority of the site manufacturing operations since the 1970s"; that cyanide was among the "industrial waste streams" generated at the site; and that "manual plating is conducted in" an area of the building in which "recessed concrete floors are used to accommodate spilling from the plating operations." Tyco itself had conducted these operations on the Premises since 1999, and Prospect Hill plainly understood that Tyco would continue its metal plating operations into the Lease term.

The lease further provided that the tenant would: "remove from the Demised Premises any and all equipment, ducts, fixtures, materials or other property that are or might be contaminated, hazardous and/or subject to regulation by any Environmental Laws; and Tenant shall repair any damage to the Demised Premises caused by such removal (but excluding the replacement of any ducts or items of a similar nature removed as aforesaid) to the extent the aggregate cost of such repair is reasonably estimated by Landlord to exceed $10,000."

On May 20, 2002, Haley requested that Tyco test for the presence of cyanide in that concrete floor. Tyco agreed, even though it believed that it was not required to do so under the Lease. On June 18, 2002, Spaulding and Tyco representatives met to conduct a final inspection of the Premises. At that time, all Tyco personnel had vacated the area. All Tyco equipment and property had been removed and Tyco had completed the steam cleaning of the floors required by the Lease. While these tests revealed cyanide traces in some areas of the concrete, Tyco indicated that it was not aware of any regulatory requirement

continued

that would oblige Prospect Hill to remove the concrete floor. However, it noted that "if in the future [Prospect Hill] were to demolish the building, the concrete that has cyanide residues would have to be treated as hazardous waste and disposed of according to state and federal regulations."

On July 23, 2002, Prospect Hill made a written demand that Tyco remove the concrete floor from the Premises.

Prospect Hill argues that this construction of the contract's terms was in error. First, it contests the district court's reasoning that the phrase "equipment, ducts, fixtures, materials or other property" denotes moveable property. Fixtures are defined both by the Uniform Commercial Code and Black's Law Dictionary as immovable.

Tyco responds that the district court correctly interpreted the contract's terms. First, it contends that the surrender clause explicitly distinguishes between the materials or property to be removed at the expiration of the Lease on the one hand and the land and building on the other. The surrender clause requires Tyco to "remove from the Demised Premises any and all ... materials or other property. ..." (emphasis added). Art. I, § 1 defines the "Demised Premises" as the land "together with the building thereon . ..." Thus, the materials or other property to be removed are distinct from the land and building. Second, Tyco asserts that the phrase "equipment, ducts, fixtures, materials or other property" connotes moveable objects, as the district court found. As a practical matter, ducts and fixtures, like equipment and other moveable property and materials—but unlike floors and walls—can be removed without altering the basic structure of the Premises itself.

Tyco has the stronger argument. In context, the phrase "equipment, ducts, fixtures, materials or other property" denotes moveable objects, notwithstanding Prospect Hill's arguments about the definition of the term "fixture." While fixtures may include equipment or objects that are attached to the building, such as machinery installed in place, it is unreasonable to extend the term to cover components of the structure itself. Tyco's contention that the term "Demised Premises"—from which contaminated materials are to be removed—includes both the land and the building is especially persuasive. We agree with the district court that the phrase "equipment, ducts, fixtures, materials or other property" should not be construed so broadly as to include the concrete floor. Because Tyco had no obligation to remove the concrete floor under the surrender clause, it was not in breach of the Lease and did not become a holdover tenant when it failed to remove the concrete floor prior to the expiration of the Lease.

We likewise reject Prospect Hill's argument that the cyanide itself, as distinct from the concrete floor, was "material" that Tyco was obligated to remove. First, this interpretation of the surrender clause is contrary to Prospect Hill's own course of conduct. Prospect Hill conceded that Tyco had no obligation to remove asbestos and lead—both hazardous contaminants—that were embedded in various parts of the building. Second, Prospect Hill's argument is undermined by the plain language of the Lease. The surrender clause calls for the removal from the Demised Premises of any and all equipment, ducts, fixtures and "materials or other property that are or might be contaminated . ..." The Lease thus distinguishes between the materials to be removed and the contaminants embedded in them.

Accordingly, we find that Tyco was not obligated by the terms of the Lease to remove the concrete floor from the Premises.

■ *Affirmed.*

CASE CONCEPTS REVIEW

1. What was the argument Prospect Hill made in support of having Tyco remove the floor? What argument did Tyco advance that is had no duty to remove the floor?
2. Based on the court's opinion, what is the definition of a fixture?

6. Reasons for Determining Fixture Status

The question of whether or not an item is a fixture and thus part of the real estate arises in determining (1) the value of real estate for tax purposes; (2) whether or not a sale of the real estate includes the item of property in question; (3) whether or not the item of property is a part of the security given by a mortgagor of the real estate to a mortgagee; and (4) whether the item belongs to the owner of the building or to the tenant on termination of a lease.

If property is a fixture, (1) it is included in the value of real estate for tax purposes; (2) it is sold, and title passes with the real estate; (3) it is a part of the security covered by a mortgage; and (4) it belongs to the landlord owner, not to the tenant on termination of a lease.

Fixture issues also arise under Article 9 of the Uniform Commercial Code in disputes between secured creditors and persons with an interest in the land. The UCC provides that no security interest exists in goods incorporated into a structure in the manner of lumber, bricks, tile, cement, glass, metal work and the like. A party with a security interest in such goods loses it when the goods are incorporated into the real estate.

ACQUIRING TITLE TO PERSONAL PROPERTY

7. Methods of Transfer

As a general rule, a transferee of personal property receives the rights of the transferor, and a transferee takes no better title than the transferor had. If the transferor of the personal property did not have title to the property, the transferee would not have title either, even though the transferee believes that the transferor had a good title. Suppose Pastor Jones purchases a new stereo set for a church from parishioner Tithe. Unknown to Pastor Jones, Tithe had stolen the stereo from the Bulldog Music Store. The stereo set still belongs to Bulldog Music, and the church has no title to it. An innocent purchaser from a thief obtains no title to the property purchased, and no subsequent purchaser stands in any better position. Because the thief had no title or ownership, persons who acquired the property from or through the thief have no title or ownership.

What rights does a good-faith purchaser have in personal property? If the transferor of the property has a voidable title and sells property to an innocent purchaser, the transferee may obtain good title to the property. Assume that through fraudulent representations, Fred acquires title to Sam's property. Sam could avoid the transaction with Fred and obtain a return of his property. If Fred sells the property to Ann, and she does not know about his fraudulent representations, Sam cannot disaffirm against Ann. Ann has good title to the property since she is a good-faith purchaser for value.

Title to personal property may be transferred by *sale, gift, or will.* Since it is probably most relevant in business transactions, the law relating to transfer by sale is discussed in Chapters 21 and 22 dealing with Article 2 of the Uniform Commercial Code. Transfer of title by gift is discussed in the next section of this chapter. Finally, title to personal property also may be transferred at the owner's death through the provisions of a will or by intestate succession. This topic is discussed within the last portion of the chapter.

8. *Inter Vivos* Gift

The phrase *inter vivos* refers to gifts made voluntarily during the life of the party transferring title. A testamentary gift is one that is effective only at the owner's death. Generally, there are just two people required to accomplish an *inter vivos* gift. The *donor* is the party making the gift. The *donee* is the one receiving or acquiring title to the property. The law requires that three elements

If you buy a stereo that turns out to be stolen, the party it was stolen from retains the right to it.

be satisfied to have a valid *inter vivos* gift. These elements are (1) the donor's intent to make a gift, (2) delivery of possession by the donor, and (3) acceptance of the gift by the donee. From a legal standpoint, the element of *delivery* usually is most important. Unless a contrary intent is clear and obvious, the physical change of possession of personal property creates a presumption that both the donor and donee consent to a gift. However, in the event there is a dispute over the true ownership of personal property, all three elements must be established to have a valid gift.

The delivery can be actual or constructive or symbolic, as the situation demands. Thus, if the property is in storage, the donor could make a delivery by giving the donee the warehouse receipt. A donor may also accomplish delivery by giving the donee something that is a token representing the donee's dominion and control. A delivery of the keys to an automobile may be a valid symbolic delivery, although a symbolic or constructive delivery will not suffice if actual delivery is reasonably possible.

There are two general rules that you should keep in your mind concerning *inter vivos* gifts. First, an executory promise to make a gift is not enforceable since the donee typically has not given consideration to support the donor's promise. Second, an executed or completed gift cannot be rescinded by the donor. This latter general rule is subject to one important exception.

Gift *causa mortis*

A gift made in anticipation of death (If the donor survives, the gift is revocable.)

Gifts *causa mortis* constitute this exception to the general rule on the finality of completed gifts. A gift *causa mortis* is made in contemplation of death. This gift arises out of the situation in which a person is, or believes he or she is, facing death and makes a gift on the assumption that death is imminent. A person about to embark on a perilous trip or to undergo a serious operation or one who has an apparently incurable and fatal illness might make a gift and deliver the item to the donee on the assumption that he or she may soon die. If this donor returns safely or does not die, he or she is allowed to revoke the gift and recover the property from the donee.

9. Abandoned, Lost, and Mislaid Property

Property is said to be *abandoned* whenever it is discarded by the true owner who, at that time, has no intention of reclaiming it. The property belongs to the first individual again reducing it to possession.

Property is *lost* whenever, as a result of negligence, accident, or some other cause, it is found at some place other than that chosen by the owner. Title to lost property continues to rest with the true owner. However, until this owner has been ascertained, the finder may keep the property found. The finder's title is good against everyone except the true owner. The rights of the finder are superior to those of the person in charge of the property on which the lost article is found unless the finder is a trespasser. Occasionally, state statutes provide for newspaper publicity concerning articles that have been found. If the owner cannot be located, the found property or a portion of it reverts to the state or county if the property's value exceeds an established minimum. Otherwise, it goes to the finder.

Property is *mislaid* or *misplaced* if its owner has intentionally placed it at a certain spot, but the manner of placement indicates that he or she has forgotten to pick it up. The presumption is that the owner will eventually remember where he or she left it and return for it. The finder must turn it over to the owner of the premises, who may hold it until the owner is located. The distinctions between abandoned, lost, and mislaid property are subtle and frequently litigated.

BAILMENT OF PERSONAL PROPERTY

10. Required Elements

Possession of personal property is often temporarily surrendered by the owner to another person. The person to whom the goods are delivered may perform some service pertaining to the goods, such as a repair, after which the goods are returned to the owner; someone may, also, borrow or lease an article from its owner. Another temporary transfer of possession occurs when the owner causes the goods to he stored in a warehouse. In general, the provisions of the Uniform Commercial Code are applicable to these transactions involving the temporary transfer of possession of personal property.

Bailment

Delivery of personal property to another for a special purpose (Delivery is made under a contract, either expressed or implied, and upon the completion of the special purpose, the property shall be redelivered to the bailor or placed at his or her disposal.)

An agreement whereby possession of personal property is surrendered by the owner with provision for its return at a later time is known as a **bailment**. The owner of the goods is called the *bailor.* The one receiving possession is called the *bailee.* There are three distinct requirements for a bailment: retention of title by the bailor, possession and temporary control of the property by the bailee, and ultimate possession to revert to the bailor or to someone designated by the bailor.

11. Types of Bailments

Bailments can be categorized naturally into three classes: bailments for the benefit of the bailor, bailments for the benefit of the bailee, and bailments for the mutual benefit of bailor and bailee. Typical of the first group are those cases in which the bailor leaves goods in the safekeeping of the bailee without any provision for paying the bailee for caring for the article. Because the bailee is not to use the goods or to be paid in any manner, the bailment is for the exclusive benefit of the bailor.

A bailment for the benefit of the bailee is best illustrated by a loan of some article by the bailor to the bailee without any compensation to the bailor. Assume a student borrows a professor's automobile for a weekend date. The bailment is one for the sole benefit of the student, the bailee.

The most common type of bailment is the one in which both parties are to benefit. Contracts for repair, carriage, storage, or pledge of property fall within this class. The bailor receives the benefit of some service; the bailee benefits by the receipt of certain agreed compensation. Thus both parties benefit as a result of the bailment.

To constitute a bailment for mutual benefit, it is not essential that the bailee actually receive compensation in money or tangible property. If the bailment is an incident of the business in which the bailee makes a profit, or it was accepted because of benefits expected to accrue, it is a mutual benefit bailment.

12. Degree of Care Owed by Bailees

Provided that proper care has been exercised by the bailee, any loss or damage to the property bailed falls on the bailor. Each type of bailment requires a different degree of care by the bailee. In a bailment for the benefit of the bailor, the bailee is required to exercise only slight care. In a bailment for the benefit of the bailee, extraordinary care is required. A bailment for the mutual benefit of the parties demands ordinary care on the part of the bailee. *Ordinary care* is defined as care that the average individual usually exercises over his or her own property.

The amount of care demanded of a bailee varies with the nature and value of the article bailed. The care found to be sufficient in the case of a carpenter's tool chest would probably not be ample for a diamond ring worth $10,000. A higher standard of protection is required for valuable articles. Moreover, when damages are assessed against a bailee, they are based on retail replacement value, not the wholesale cost to a bailee. Table 9-1 depicts the degrees of care owed by the bailor and bailee depending on the type of bailment.

In addition to the duty to exercise due care, the bailee promises to return the property to the bailor undamaged upon termination of the bailment. This promise can be used to create a prima facie case of negligence. A bailor who proves that property delivered in good condition was returned from the bailee in bad condition establishes a presumption of negligence; that bailor is entitled to

TABLE 9-1 ■ Degrees of Care and Duties in Bailments

TYPE OF BAILMENT	BAILOR'S SPECIFIC DUTY	BAILOR'S STANDARD OF CARE	BAILEE'S NEGLIGENCE THAT BREACHES DUTY OF CARE
Sole benefit of bailor	Warn of known defects and those that should be known	Slight care	Extraordinary negligence
Mutual benefit	Warn of known defects and those that should be known	Ordinary care	Ordinary negligence
Sole benefit of bailee	Warn of known defects	Extraordinary care	Slight negligence

recover from the bailee unless the presumption is rebutted. If there is no other evidence, the bailor will win the suit. The bailee may rebut this prima facie case by introducing evidence to establish that there was no negligence on its part, but the bailee has the burden of proving that it has used reasonable care and caution after the prima facie case has been established. This prima facie case of negligence exists only if all elements of a bailment are present. If there is no bailment, there is no prima facie case upon nondelivery or damage to the goods.

13. Common Carriers as Bailees

Common carrier
One who is engaged in the business of transporting personal property from one place to another for compensation (Such person is bound to carry for all that tender their goods and the price for transportation. A common carrier operates as a public utility and is subject to state and federal regulations.)

The contract for carriage of goods constitutes a mutual benefit bailment, but the care required of the carrier greatly exceeds that of the ordinary bailee. A **common carrier** is an absolute insurer of the safe delivery of the goods to their destination. Proof of delivery to a carrier of a shipment in good condition and its arrival at the destination in a damaged condition creates a prima facie case against the carrier.

This absolute liability of a common carrier is subject to only five exceptions. Any loss or damage must fall on the shipper if it results from (1) an act of God, (2) action of an alien enemy, (3) order of public authority, (4) inherent nature of the goods, or (5) misconduct of the shipper. Thus, any loss that results from an accident or the willful misconduct of some third party must be borne by the carrier. A person who wanted to injure a certain railway company set fire to several boxcars loaded with freight. Losses due to damage to the goods fell on the carrier. On the other hand, if lightning, an act of God, had set fire to the cars, the loss would have fallen on the shipper. However, the defense of an act of God is narrowly construed to include only events that were not foreseeable.

14. Innkeepers as Bailees

Issues similar to those involved with common carriers frequently arise in suits against hotel and motel operators. Under common law, an innkeeper was an insurer of the safety of the goods of its guests. The law imposed liability as a matter of public policy because the innkeeper and his or her employees had easy access to the guests' rooms. Exceptions to this general rule relieved the innkeeper from liability for loss caused by an act of God, a public enemy, an act of public authority, the inherent nature of the property, or the fault of the guest.

Most states have enacted statutes pertaining to hotel or motel operators' liability. These statutes usually provide that if the operator appropriately notifies guests that a safe or lockbox is maintained for their use, there is no liability if guests' property is stolen from their rooms. Such laws usually cover property of "small compass," which includes money, negotiable instruments, jewelry, and precious stones. The requirement that notice of the availability of the safe be given with notice of the liability limitation is usually strictly enforced.

Some states also have laws that limit the maximum liability of hotel and motel operators to a stated amount, such as $500. Others have changed the liability from that of an insurer to that of a bailee of a mutual benefit bailment (ordinary care as the duty). In all states, the liability of the innkeeper is limited to the value of the property. There is no liability for consequential damages that may flow from the loss of the property.

DOCUMENTS OF TITLE

15. General Concepts and Definitions

A *document of title* is broadly defined under a provision of the Uniform Commercial Code as any "document which in the regular course of business or financing is treated as adequately evidencing that the person in possession of it is entitled to receive, hold and dispose of the document *and the* goods it *covers*" [1-201(15)]. Such a document must indicate that it was issued by a bailee or directed to a bailee and that it covers goods in the bailee's possession.

Documents of title are covered by Article 7 of the Uniform Commercial Code. Numerous other statutes, both state and federal, also regulate the business of carriers and warehousers. The federal Bills of Lading Act, for example, controls bills of lading covering foreign exports and interstate shipments of goods. The Code does not displace such statutes. Article 7 deals only with rights related to documents of title, not to the regulation of the services rendered by carriers or warehousers.

Documents of title can serve a dual function. They may serve as receipts for goods stored or shipped, and they may be representative of the goods. In the representative capacity, they are most useful in financing commercial transactions.

Some other common terms may be defined as follows:

- *Warehouse receipt:* An acknowledgement issued by a person engaged in the business of storing goods for hire [1-201(45)]
- *Bill of lading:* A document evidencing receipt of goods for shipment
- *Issuer:* A bailee who prepares the document of title
- *Consignor:* The person named in a bill of lading as the person from whom the goods have been received for shipment
- *Consignee:* The person named in a bill of lading as the one to whom delivery is to be made

Documents of title may be negotiable or nonnegotiable. The concept of negotiability for a document of title is similar to that of negotiability discussed in connection with commercial paper. The holder of a negotiable document is in a much more favorable position than he or she would be with a nonnegotiable document. The holder of a negotiable document obtains the direct obligation of the issuer to hold or deliver the goods free from most defenses and claims. In essence, the holder is so well protected that he or she can almost regard the document as the equivalent of the goods it represents.

16. Negotiation and Transfer

A warehouse receipt, bill of lading, or other document is negotiable if, by its terms, the goods are to be delivered to the bearer or to the "order *of*" a named person. A document not containing these "words of negotiability" is not negotiable. Thus, a bill of lading that states that goods are consigned to John Doe would not be negotiable.

Both negotiable and nonnegotiable documents can be transferred, but the method of transfer is different. A nonnegotiable document can be *assigned;* then the assignee acquires only the rights of the assignor and is subject to all defenses that are available against the assignor. The assignee is burdened with all defects in the assignor's title. *Negotiation* of a negotiable document places the transferee in a much more favorable position. If there is "due negotiation," the transferee is free from the defects of the transferor's title and the claims of third persons.

The method of negotiating a document of title depends on whether it is an order document or a bearer document. The *order* document is negotiated by endorsement and delivery; the *bearer* document, by delivery alone. The effects of blank and special endorsements are the same as those for commercial paper, and the last endorsement controls.

For the holder of a negotiable document of title to have the preferred status, there must have been a due negotiation. This means not only any necessary endorsement and delivery but also that the holder must satisfy certain requirements similar to those of a holder in due course of commercial paper. The holder must have purchased the document in good faith, without notice of a defense against it or claim to it on the part of any person. He or she must have paid value for it, and the negotiation must have been in the regular course of business or financing. One to whom a document is negotiated in satisfaction or payment of a prior debt has not paid value.

If there has been due negotiation, the holder acquires title to the document, title to the goods, and the direct obligation of the issuer to hold or deliver the goods according to the terms of the document. The holder's rights cannot be defeated by any stoppage of the goods or surrender of them by the bailee. His or her rights are not impaired even if the negotiation or any prior negotiation constituted a breach of duty; even if any person has been deprived of possession of the document by misrepresentation, fraud, accident, mistake, duress, loss, theft, or conversion; and even if a previous sale or other transfer of the goods or document has been made to a third person [7-502(2)].

LEASES OF PERSONAL PROPERTY

17. Basic Concepts

Historically, the lease of personal property has been a transaction that courts have analyzed as being similar to leases of real property, bailments of personal property, or even sales of goods. While these analogies are imperfect, the lack of volume of personal property leases kept the law from developing with such leases specifically in mind.

In recent years, the substitution of lease transactions for sales transactions has increased dramatically Perhaps this change in how business is conducted is best illustrated by the way people interact with automobile dealers today. To make increasingly expensive cars affordable, more and more lease opportunities are offered to the public. Because of this development in the number of lease transactions, the members of the National Conference of Commissioners on Uniform State Laws drafted a new part to the Uniform Commercial Code. This draft has become Article 2A.

18. Application of the UCC

A detailed discussion of Article 2A is beyond the scope of this book. Nevertheless, a brief explanation of why Article 2A is likely to be adopted widely is in order. Almost all states have adopted Article 2A.

Article 2A applies to all leases regardless of the form used [2A-102]. A *lease* is a transfer of the right of possession and use of goods for a term in return for consideration [2A-103(1)(j)]. In many respects, leases under Article 2A are treated in a manner similar to the way sales are treated under Article 2. Several observations about this definition can be made. First, a gratuitous bailment is not covered by Article 2A. Second, the word goods here basically has the same meaning as in Article 2: items of movable personal property and fixtures. Third, sales on approval and sales or return transactions are not covered; they remain subject to sections 2-326 and 2-327. Finally, the creation of a security interest in personal property is governed by Article 9 and is not to be confused with the Article 2A provisions on leases.

While the definition of a lease is broad enough to cover all types of personal property lease transactions, some of the Article 2A sections deal with two types of specific leases. A *consumer lease* occurs anytime the lessee is an individual who enters into the lease primarily for a personal, family, or household purpose [2A-103(1)(e)]. A *finance lease,* like those used in most automobile transactions, involves a lessor that does not select, manufacture, or supply the goods [2A-103(l)(g)].

In general, Article 2A provides aspects of the law that previously had to be borrowed from other areas. Specifically, the provisions in Part 2 of Article 2A include how the personal property is formed and how it should be interpreted. The effect of a lease of goods on the lessor, lessee, sublessee, lienholders, and creditors is discussed in Part 3. Issues related to performance of the lease agreement (Part 4) and questions that might arise upon the lessor's or lessee's default (Part 5) are also resolved.

It is anticipated that Article 2A's influence will increase as both consumer and commercial transactions continue to rely more heavily on the transfer of possession of property (leases) without a transfer of title (sales).

INTELLECTUAL PROPERTY

19. Creating Intellectual Property Rights

Intellectual property is defined as that type of intangible personal property created through the intellectual process. As we move toward a more technologically-based society, the law of intellectual property has increased in significance. While the notion of intellectual property has been recognized by the law for centuries, courts today continue to struggle with how to best protect and reward those that generate intellectual property and, at the same time, also allow society to take full advantage of the actual and potential benefits associated with intellectual property.

This section and the next address four types of intellectual property: patents, trademarks, copyrights, and trade secrets. This section presents the method of creating the property interest, while the next examines issues associated with infringement.

PATENTS Patents are mentioned in the United States Constitution, recognizing the long history and importance of patents to society. A *patent* is a grant from the government to an inventor that prohibits others from interfering in any manner with the inventor's right to manufacture and sell an invention for a period of twenty years.

A patent is granted by the United States Patent and Trademark Office (USPTO) after the inventor files an application containing *specifications* that describe the invention, *claims* that present the aspects of the invention that should be protected by the patent, *drawings* accurately depicting the invention, and a *declaration* that the invention is novel. The USPTO provides a web-accessed database that allows the public to search all U.S. patents granted since 1976. Thousands of patents are granted every year, with businesses (including International Business Machines (IBM), Motorola, and Genetech) and universities (e.g., the University of California) being granted hundreds of patents in a single year. In addition to legally recognizing the development of a product (e.g., sunglasses), patents are created to protect inventors of genes (the biotechnology field generates many patents each year), computer software programs, and business processes.

Under a number of treaties, United States patent protection extends internationally. Extreme care must be exercised, however, because the patent laws of other countries may differ considerably from patent law in the United States.

TRADEMARKS A *trademark* is defined, under the federal Lanham Act of 1947 and the Trademark Law Revision Act of 1988, as "any word, name, symbol, or device or any combination thereof adopted and used by a manufacturer or merchant to identify and distinguish his goods … and to indicate the source of the goods." Single words or names are often the subject of trademark protection, but a color scheme, slogan, or sound may also qualify as a trademark. While federal trademark law for many decades prevented the use of the same trademark on similar products or services only if the result would be confusion on the part of customers, the Federal Trademark Dilution Act of 1995 expanded trademark protection of "famous" trademarks even if there is no likelihood of confusion on the part of customers. A principal reason for trademark protection is to ensure the goodwill that is generated by the association of a particular name with high quality.

A trademark must be registered with a state or federal (USPTO) entity. In order to be registered, the product or service must be distinctive. Certain terms, like "a Kleenex issue" or a "Xerox copy," where the trademark is used as an adjective, are often necessary mechanisms manufacturers must employ when they have a product or service that has become a synonym for the product or service. Thus, use of the term "a Kleenex" or "a Xerox" causes the loss of the trademark protection. The trademark also must be used in commerce when the application for registration is made to the appropriate governmental entity; it cannot properly be registered as a trademark if it is a secret. Federal registration of a trademark lasts for 10 years and can be renewed for another 10 years.

Similar in many respects to a trademark, the term *trade dress* refers to the overall image of a product or service, including distinctive packaging. Also, a *service mark* provides similar protection to a service. Finally, the term *trade name* identifies a particular company or business.

How does the law of trademarks related to issues in cyberspace? In some respects application of traditional principles of trademark law do not fit well when facing the challenging digital world. However, Congress addressed one serious problem in 1999 by passing the Anticybersquatting Consumer Protection Act (ACPA), an amendment to the Lanham Act. Domain names on the Internet have considerable value. The ACPA allows an owner of a famous or distinctive name to sue an individual who, in bad faith, registers or uses a domain name that is identical to or confusingly similar to the famous or distinctive name. Damages under the ACPA are either actual damages (usually lost profits) or statutory damages from $1,000 to $100,000.

As with patents, trademark protection can be extended to other countries. Again, other countries may have approaches to trademark protection that are not identical to that offered in the United States.

COPYRIGHT A *copyright* is an intellectual property right granted under federal law to the originator of a literary work, musical work, dramatic work, or other creative efforts. Under federal copyright court decisions, an author may seek copyright protection even if the work is not registered under a statutory provision or being used by the author. The federal statute, the Copyright Act of 1976, provides originators of works protection for long periods of time. If the author is known, the term is the life of the author plus seventy years. For publishing houses and related entities, the copyright lasts the lesser of ninety-five years after the work is first published or one-hundred and twenty years from the date of creation. The Computer Software Copyright Act of 1980 includes computer programs as a type of work that will receive copyright protection. In addition, the Digital Millennium copyright Act of 1998 implemented the World Intellectual Property Organization copyright Treaty of 1996. Another problem associated with the use of the Internet is addressed in the following case.

CASE

Metro-Goldwyn-Mayer Studios, Inc. v. Grokster, Ltd.

SUPREME COURT OF THE UNITED STATES
545 U.S. 913 (2005)

JUSTICE SOUTER DELIVERED THE OPINION OF THE COURT.

The question is under what circumstances the distributor of a product capable of both lawful and unlawful use is liable for acts of copyright infringement by third parties using the product. We hold that one who distributes a device with the object of promoting its use to infringe copyright, as shown by clear expression or other affirmative steps taken to foster infringement, is liable for the resulting acts of infringement by third parties.

Respondents, Grokster, Ltd., and StreamCast Networks, Inc., defendants in the trial court, distribute free software products that allow computer users to share electronic files through peer-to-peer networks, so called because users' computers communicate directly with each other, not through central servers. The advantage of peer-to-peer networks over information networks of other types shows up in their substantial and growing popularity. Because they need no central computer server to mediate the exchange of information or files among users, the high-bandwidth communications capacity for a server may be dispensed with, and the need for costly server storage space is eliminated. Since copies of a file (particularly a popular one) are available on many users' computers, file requests and retrievals may be faster than on other types of networks, and since file exchanges do not travel through a server, communications can take place between any computers that remain connected to the network without risk that a glitch in the server will disable the network in its entirety. Given these benefits in security, cost, and efficiency, peer-to-peer networks are employed to store and distribute electronic files by universities, government agencies, corporations, and libraries, among others.

Other users of peer-to-peer networks include individual recipients of Grokster's and StreamCast's software, and although the networks that they enjoy through using the software can be used to share any type of digital file, they have prominently employed those networks in sharing copyrighted music and video files without authorization. A group of copyright holders (MGM for short, but including motion picture studios, recording companies, songwriters, and music publishers) sued Grokster and StreamCast for their users' copyright infringements, alleging that they knowingly and intentionally distributed their software to enable users to reproduce and distribute the copyrighted works in violation of the Copyright Act. MGM sought damages and an injunction.

MGM fault the Court of Appeals' holding for upsetting a sound balance between the respective values of supporting creative pursuits through copyright protection and promoting innovation in new communication technologies by limiting the incidence of liability for copyright infringement. The more artistic protection is favored, the more technological innovation may be discouraged; the administration of copyright law is an exercise in managing the tradeoff.

The tension between the two values is the subject of this case with its claim that digital distribution of copyrighted material threatens copyright holders as never before because every copy is identical to the original, copying is easy, and many people (especially the young) use file-sharing software to download copyrighted works.

The argument for imposing indirect liability in this case is, however, a powerful one, given the number of infringing downloads that occur every day using StreamCast's and Grokster's software. When a widely shared service or product is used to commit infringement, it may be impossible to enforce rights in the protected work effectively against all direct infringers, the only practical alternative being to go against the distributor of the copying device for secondary liability on a theory of contributory or vicarious infringement

One infringes contributorily by intentionally inducing or encouraging direct infringement and infringes vicariously by profiting from direct infringement while declining to exercise a right to stop or limit it. Although the Copyright Act does not expressly render anyone for infringement committed by another, these doctrines of secondary liability emerged from common law principles and are well established in the law.

The only apparent question about treating MGM's evidence as sufficient to withstand summary judgment under the theory of inducement goes to the need on MGM's part to adduce evidence that StreamCast and Grokster communicated an inducing message to their software users. The classic instance of inducement is by adver-

continued

tisement or solicitation that broadcasts a message designed to stimulate others to commit violations.

MGM claims that such a message is shown here. It is undisputed that StreamCast beamed onto the computer screens of users of Napster-compatible programs ads urging the adoption of its OpenNap program, which was designed, as its name implied, to invite the custom of patrons of Napster, then under attack in the courts for facilitating massive infringement. Those who accepted StreamCast's OpenNap program were offered software to perform the same services, which a fact finder could conclude would readily have been understood in the Napster market as the ability to download copyrighted music files. Grokster distributed an electronic newsletter containing links to articles promoting its software's ability to access popular copyrighted music. Anyone whose Napster or free file-sharing searches turned up a link to Grokster would have understood Grokster to be offering the same file-sharing ability as Napster, and to the same people who probably used Napster for infringing downloads; that would also have been the understanding of anyone offered Grokster's suggestively named Swaptor software, its version of OpenNap. Both companies communicated a clear message by responding affirmatively to requests for help in locating and playing copyrighted materials.

Here, evidence of the distributors' words and deeds going beyond distribution as such shows a purpose to cause and profit from third-party acts of copyright infringement. If liability for inducing infringement is ultimately found, it will not be on the basis of presuming or imputing fault, but from inferring a patently illegal objective from statements and actions showing what that objective was.

There is substantial evidence in MGM's favor on all elements of inducement, and summary judgment in favor of Grokster and StreamCast was error. On remand, reconsideration of MGM's motion for summary judgment will be in order. The judgment of the Court of Appeals is vacated, and the case is remanded for further proceedings consistent with this opinion.

■ *Vacated and remanded.*

CASE CONCEPTS REVIEW

1. How did StreamCast and Napster induce others to violate copyright law?
2. Is the inducement theory articulated by the court beneficial to society? Why?

Copyrights are formed to protect the *expressions* of ideas—not the *ideas* themselves. In this way an author can be guaranteed that his/her expression is protected while at the same time others are encouraged to build upon ideas included in any creative work. Also, copyright protection does not extend to the *application of an idea,* which would be covered by patent law.

The subject of considerable debate, federal law allows for the "fair use" of copyrighted materials. Therefore, those individuals engaged in literary criticism, education, news reporting, or scholarship may use copyrighted material without incurring liability. In determining whether the fair use doctrine applies, courts look at the nature of the work, the amount of that work used, the impact on the holder of the copyright, and the purpose of the use. As a result of provisions of the Berne Convention for the Protection of Literary and Artistic Works (1886), among other treaties, authors in the United States are provided the same level of protection in other countries as authors in those countries receive. It is very important, because differences exist in the level of protection, that originators in the United States understand the copyright protection available in other countries.

TRADE SECRETS As discussed above, in order to secure a patent one must register with the government. The mere filing of a patent application discloses to the public a great deal of information about the invention, a development many wish to avoid. Another method exists, however, for protecting innovative products. The law of *trade secrets,* in most states, is well developed and provides a nonpublic legal mechanism for securing intellectual property rights.

A trade secret is defined, under the Uniform Trade Secrets Act, as:

> Information, including a formula, pattern, compilation, program, device, method, technique, or process, that: (1) derives independent economic value, actual or potential, from not being generally known to, and not being readily ascertainable by, other persons who can obtain economic value from its disclosure or use, and (2) is the subject of efforts that are reasonable under the circumstances to maintain its secrecy.

Courts tend to focus on both of these components. They seek to determine whether the alleged trade secret has "independent value" and whether the owner treated the supposed trade secret in a manner to secure its secrecy (including methods of limiting who has access to the trade secret). Plans for a new product, cutting-edge software, private formula, and even marketing strategy plans and customer lists have been deemed trade secrets.

The most important attributes of various forms of intellectual property are presented in Table 9-2.

TABLE 9-2 ■ Characteristics Associated with Principal Types of Intellectual Property

FORM	DEFINITION	WHO CREATES?	DURATION
Patent	Government issued grant providing one with the exclusive right to an invention	**Federal government,** through the issuance of a patent	Making and selling: 20 years; design: 14 years
Trademark	Distinctive word or symbol that distinguishes its goods or services from those of another	**Owner by common law** and by **government**, through registration	Unlimited, as long as use continues—may have to renew registration
Copyright	Right of author to exclusive use for a period of time	**Author by common law**, once an expression is put in tangible form	Author: life plus 70 years; Publisher: either 95 or 120 years
Trade secret	Information of a business that gives it a competitive advantage	**Business—by common law,** as long as the information is secret and reasonable means are undertaken by the business to ensure secrecy	Unlimited

20. Enforcing Intellectual Property Rights

While the granting of intellectual property rights is an important step, once an individual or entity has the right they still must be able to protect themselves from others who wish infringe upon their rights in the property. This section explores infringement by examining the unique enforcement processes associated with each type of intellectual property.

PATENT INFRINGEMENT If a patent has been infringed upon, the holder of the patent may seek an injunction to prevent further infringement or damages for profits lost. In order to be successful, the holder of the patent must prove that they hold a valid patent and that the other party either directly (made or used the patented invention, even if there is only substantial similarity between the patented invention and that item, for example, that is said to violate the patent) or indirectly (Sam directly infringes on a patented toy for children held by Martha. If Alice provided the packaging for the toy manufactured by Sam, then Alice may be an infringer.).

TRADEMARK INFRINGEMENT Because there is a common law right of trademark infringement, a trademark does not have to be registered. The big advantage associated with registering the trademark is that it provides proof of the date that the holder began using the trademark. Infringement can be either intentional or unintentional and occurs if another uses the trademark in a manner where confusion on the part of purchasers might result. As with patent infringement, a court may grant the holder of a trademark relief in terms of an injunction or damages for lost profits against those that infringe upon either a common law or registered trademark.

COPYRIGHT INFRINGEMENT The copying, modification, or distribution of works without securing the approval of the holder of the copyright allows the holder to recover actual or statutory damages in addition to injunctive relief. Also, federal law provides criminal fines and prison sentences for infringers of copyrights.

Will

The formal instrument by which a person makes disposition of his or her property, to take effect on his or her death

TRADE SECRET INFRINGEMENT A successful lawsuit for violating a trade secret may be brought against an individual or entity that acquired a trade secret by improper means (e.g., spying) or through a breach of confidentiality (e.g., vice president of marketing, because she was not selected president, discloses a trade secret to a competitor). A trade secret that has been infringed upon is typically entitled to an injunction prohibiting the infringer from using the innovation or other type of trade secret. Also, monetary damages are appropriate, including punitive damages when the misappropriation was malicious.

ACQUIRING TITLE TO PERSONAL AND REAL PROPERTY: WILLS AND INTESTATE SUCCESSION

21. Terminology

Guardian

A person appointed by the court to look after the property rights and person of a minor

A **will** is a document that expresses a person's intention as to the disposition of his or her property on death. It also serves several additional functions. It designates the personal representative who is to be responsible for settling the affairs of the deceased. A will may make provision for the appointment of **guardians** of the person and the estate of a minor child. Indeed, for young parents who have not yet amassed much financial wealth, the appointment of a guardian for their minor children usually is the most important reason to have a will. Many wills also provide for payment of taxes that may be due on the death of the deceased and for matters such as whether or not the personal representative should be required to have sureties on the official bond.

A will directs the intention of disposition of a person's property upon a persons passing.

Testator
A person who has died leaving a will

Executor (of an estate)
The person whom the testator names or appoints to administer his or her estate on his or her death and to dispose of it according to the testator's intention

Administrator
A person to whom letters of administration have been issued by a probate court, giving such person authority to administer, manage, and close the estate of a person who died intestate

Testamentary capacity
Persons are said to have testamentary capacity when they understand the nature of their business and the value of their property, know those persons who are natural objects of their bounty, and comprehend the manner in which they have provided for the distribution of their property.

A person who dies leaving a valid will is said to die testate. This person, upon signing a will, generally is referred to as the **testator**. The personal representative of a testator is an **executor**. A person who dies without leaving a valid will dies intestate. The personal representative of a person who dies intestate is called an **administrator**. This personal representative (whether an executor or an administrator) is in charge of gathering the deceased's assets, paying the lawful debts, and distributing the assets to the appropriate persons. A *guardian* is the personal representative in charge of the well-being of a minor's person or property or both. A *conservator* may be appointed when the care of a mentally incompetent adult is involved. Some states use the term *guardian* as well.

A gift by will of real estate usually is called a *devise;* a gift of personal property other than money is called a *bequest;* and a gift of money is referred to as a legacy. Devises, bequests, and legacies are further classified as specific, general, or residuary. A *specific gift* (devise, bequest, or legacy) is a gift of particular property described to identify and distinguish it from all other parts of the deceased's property. If property described in a specific gift is not owned by the testator at death, the gift fails or is said to be *adeemed.* A *general gift* is one that does not describe any particular property, and it may be satisfied by delivery of any property of the general kind described. A gift of a specified sum of money is a general legacy. A *residuary gift* is one that includes all the property not included in the specific or general devises, bequests, or legacies. All of these terms are important in the payment and distribution of the shares of an estate and in determining which party actually receives a specific item of property.

22. Testamentary Capacity

Testamentary capacity does not require a perfect mind or average intelligence. Testamentary capacity does require a minimum age, such as eighteen years. Persons executing a will must have sufficient mental capacity to comprehend and remember who are the natural objects of their affection, to comprehend the kind and character of their property, and to understand that they are engaged in making a will. Less mental capacity is required to execute a will than is required to execute ordinary business transactions and contracts. Since many people at the time of making a will are in poor health, the law recognizes that many testators will not be of perfect mind. All that is required is a minimum capacity to understand the nature and extent of one's property and to formulate the plan involved in making the will.

The following case addresses the issue of testamentary capacity.

CASE

In the Matter of the Will of Marion L. Priddy, Deceased

COURT OF APPEALS OF NORTH CAROLINA

614 S.E.2d 454 (2005)

HUNTER, JUDGE

Vickie L. Dixon ("Caveator") appeals from summary judgment orders entered on 4 August 2004 and 24 August 2004 in favor of Susan L. Priddy ("Propounder").

On 8 June 2003, Marion L. Priddy ("Testator") died at the age of 71 years in Guilford County, North Carolina. At the time of his death, Testator was survived by his four children, including his daughter, Caveator, and his wife, Propounder. On 11 June 2003, Propounder presented to the clerk of superior court a paper-writing, purporting to be Testator's Last Will and Testament ("Will"). Rosemary Cummo ("Cummo") and Dorthea Tinnen ("Tinnen") each submitted an "Affidavit of Subscribing Witnesses for Probate of Will," stating that they had

continued

signed the paper-writing at the request and in the presence of Testator as an attesting witness. The clerk of court admitted the paper-writing to probate in common form.

On 21 August 2003, Caveator filed a Caveat, asserting that Testator did not possess the capacity to execute a will, and that the 2002 paper-writing was obtained through undue influence by his estranged wife, Propounder. Propounder filed a Motion for Summary Judgment in the caveat proceedings on 15 July 2004. The trial court, finding there were no genuine issues of material fact, granted Propounder's motions and the caveat proceedings were dismissed.

A testator has testamentary capacity if he comprehends the natural objects of his bounty, understands the kind, nature and extent of his property, knows the manner in which he desires his act to take effect, and realizes the effect his act will have upon his estate.

Here, the evidence tends to show that Testator devised his entire estate to his estranged wife, Propounder, and did not provide for any of his four surviving children. Additionally, Caveator's evidence shows that Testator and Propounder had separated in 1999, when Testator moved to North Carolina. Propounder remained in their home in Charleston, South Carolina. Testator and Propounder continued to live separate and apart until the time of Testator's death. Testator eventually came to live with his daughter, Caveator, where she cared for him until his death.

The evidence tends to show that Testator suffered from ischemic cardiomyopathy, kidney disease, and depression. There is evidence that Testator, who was 71, attempted to find work and shared concerns about his financial situation although he had considerable assets. Caveator has presented an affidavit from one of the attesting witnesses, Benjamin Butler ("Butler"), stating:

> Even though I signed the "will" as my friend requested, I did not then and I do not believe now that he was competent and aware enough to sign such a document. At the time, he was under considerable distress, stress, anxiety, and fear. I don't believe he was fully in touch with reality, nor was he acting under his own free, aware and conscious will.

Butler also noted that Testator was "showing increasingly erratic and irrational behavior" and "taking a considerable amount of medication." Additionally, an affidavit from Testator's friend, Fran Cuthbertson ("Cuthbertson"), stated that Testator had told Cuthbertson that Testator wished to leave everything to his daughter, Caveator.

Considering the evidence in the light most favorable to the non-moving party, Caveator, there are genuine issues of material fact as to whether Testator understood the effect of his actions. Because there are genuine issues of material fact as to whether Caveator has shown that an essential element of testamentary capacity did not exist, we hold that it was error for the trial court to grant Propounder's motion for summary judgment as to Testator's capacity to execute a will.

■ *Reversed.*

CASE CONCEPTS REVIEW

1. What is the standard for testamentary capacity?
2. What evidence indicates the testator in the above case lacked such capacity?

23. Formalities of Execution

In general, the testator must sign the will. In the alternative, since many people who are physically incapacitated may not be able to sign the will, it may be signed by someone else in the presence and at the direction of the testator. It will not be set aside simply by proving that the signature on it is not that of the deceased.

In most states, the testator need not sign in the presence of witnesses if acknowledging to them that the instrument is his or her own and that it bears his or her signature. The witnesses need not be informed that the document is a will, but only that it is the testator's instrument. The signature aspect of attestation is that the testator must watch the witnesses sign; and in most states it is essential that the witnesses testify that the testator watched them sign as attesting witnesses.

Credible witnesses are those who are competent to testify in support of the will. If the witnesses are interested parties because they take something under the will, such witnesses generally will not be allowed to receive any more property as a result of the will than they would have received had there been no will. In other words, witnesses to the will cannot profit or gain any property as a result of the will. They will be required to testify and will lose whatever the will gives them in excess of their intestate share of the deceased's estate.

The most important thing to remember about executing a will is that the number of credible witnesses and the formalities required vary from state to state. Consultation with a lawyer licensed in the state involved is always recommended.

24. Intestate Succession

Intestate succession
The transfer by operation of law of all rights and obligations of a deceased person to those who are entitled to them

As stated previously, a person who dies without leaving a valid will is said to die *intestate.* When a person dies intestate, the state law provides how the deceased's property will be distributed. In this sense, a state's **intestate succession** law acts as an alternative to a will. Although all of the states attempt to provide a scheme of distribution that a reasonable person likely would have intended, the statutes of intestacy do vary from state to state. To complicate matters, the intestate laws of two or more states may have to be used in settling the estate of a person who dies without a will. For example, when real estate is a part of the deceased's estate, the appropriate intestate statute is that of the state in which the land is located. When personal property is to be distributed, the law of the deceased's domicile generally controls.

The typical intestate succession statute provides that the deceased's assets are to be inherited by the deceased's closest living relatives. However, the intestate succession statute in one state may provide that a spouse of the deceased receives the entire estate if there are no surviving children. In another state, under similar circumstances the intestate statute may require that the property be divided between the deceased's spouse and parents. If a person is survived by a spouse and children, most states provide that the estate is divided among the spouse and children. Often this is an undesirable result because of the non-marketability of property owned by minors. This problem arises due to the fact that minors generally can void contractual transactions prior to reaching the age of majority.

Everyone over the legal age of testamentary capacity should be aware of his or her state's scheme of intestate succession. If that scheme contradicts a person's desires for distributing assets, that person should have a valid will prepared and executed. Indeed, as an alternative to a valid will that can be personalized to the testator's specific needs, the intestate succession scheme is considered inferior as an estate planning tool.

CHAPTER SUMMARY

INTRODUCTION

1. Ownership is synonymous with title.
2. Possession represents the physical control a person may exert over property.

CLASSIFICATIONS OF PROPERTY

Real versus Personal Property
1. Real property is defined as interests in land and things closely associated with land.
2. Personal property is defined as interests in property other than real property.

Real Property
1. Interests may include use and benefit of the land's surface, air space, and subsurface area.

Personal Property
1. Personal property includes tangible and intangible interests.

Reasons for Distinguishing between Real and Personal Property
1. Real and personal property may be treated differently when the owner dies.
2. Transactions involving real property, generally, are more formal than personal property transactions.

FIXTURES

What Is a Fixture?
1. A fixture is an item of personal property that has become part of the land.

Reasons for Determining Fixture Status	**1.** Fixtures increase the value of real estate. **2.** Fixtures usually remain as the landlord's property at the end of a lease, whereas personal property can often be taken by the tenant.

ACQUIRING TITLE TO PERSONAL PROPERTY

Methods of Transfer	**1.** Title of personal property may be acquired by sale, gift, or upon the death of the owner.
***Inter Vivos* Gifts**	**1.** An *inter vivos* gift is one made voluntarily during the life of the giver. **2.** There must be donative intent, delivery, and acceptance before a gift is valid.
Abandoned, Lost, and Mislaid Property	**1.** Abandoned property is discarded property. **2.** Lost property is found in a place other than that chosen by the owner. **3.** Mislaid property includes items that the owner has forgotten to pick-up.

BAILMENTS OF PERSONAL PROPERTY

Required Elements	**1.** A bailment involves the temporary transfer of possession of personal property with the understanding that possession must be returned. **2.** The bailor is the owner who grants temporary possession. The bailee receives temporary possession of personal property.
Types of Bailments	**1.** A bailment may be for the sole benefit of the bailor, for the sole benefit of the bailee, or for the mutual benefit of the parties.
Degree of Care Owed by Bailees	**1.** The degree of care owned by a bailee depends on the type of bailment.
Common Carriers as Bailees	**1.** As a bailee, a common carrier owes a duty of absolute assurance of the property's safe delivery.
Innkeepers as Bailees	**1.** Today, most states have statutes that limit the innkeeper's liability with respect to personal property owned by guests.

DOCUMENTS OF TITLE

General Concepts and Definitions	**1.** A document of title evidences the right to possess the personal property described in the document. **2.** Documents of title for personal property may be negotiable or nonnegotiable in form, with negotiable documents generally being preferable.
Negotiation and Transfer	**1.** Order documents are negotiated by proper endorsement and delivery. **2.** Bearer documents are negotiated by delivery alone.

LEASES OF PERSONAL PROPERTY

Basic Concepts	**1.** Leasing personal property is a business transaction that is becoming more frequent.
Application of the UCC	**1.** Provisions of the Uniform Commercial Code apply to personal property lease arrangements.

INTELLECTUAL PROPERTY

Methods of Creating	**1.** Intellectual property is a type of intangible personal property created through an intellectual process.

2. The law recognizes that individuals and entities can create legal rights in intellectual processes through the use of patent law, trademark law, copyright law, and trade secret law.

Enforcing

1. Infringement on a patent, trademark, copyright, and trade secret can result in civil liability.

WILLS AND INTESTATE SUCCESSION

Terminology

1. A person who dies leaving a valid will is called a *testator.*
2. An *executor* is the person who settles the estate of a person who dies with a will.

Testamentary Capacity

1. A testator must have reached a minimum age, often 18.
2. A testator must possess a required mental capacity.

Formalities of Execution

1. Generally, a will must be signed by the testator.
2. The signature of the testator on the will must be witnessed.

Intestate Succession

1. A person who dies without leaving a valid will is said to die intestate.
2. If a person dies without a will, distribution of the deceased person's property follows the requirements of state law.

REVIEW QUESTIONS AND PROBLEMS

1. Match each term in Column A with the appropriate statement in Column B.

A	B
(1) Abandoned property	(a) Grant of temporary possession of personal property
(2) Patent	(b) Held by the owner of the real estate on which it is found, subject to the true owner's claims
(3) Testator	(c) Right granted to one who creates a creative work, including a book
(4) Bailment	(d) Condition where a person dies without a valid will
(5) Chattel	(e) An item of personal property that has become attached to land and is treated as real property
(6) *Inter vivos* gift	(f) Right granted by the government to one who invents something
(7) Mislaid property	(g) Another name for personal property
(8) Intestate	(h) Discarded by the owner with no intent to reclaim it
(9) Fixture	(i) Gift made during life
(10) Copyright	(j) Person who dies with a valid will

2. The state of New Jersey sought to tax as real property cranes used in the loading and unloading of ships designed to carry freight in containers. These large cranes were mounted

and movable on tracks at the pier. Each crane weighed 1,000,000 pounds and required special concrete piles for the base of the piers. Each crane was 50 feet wide and stood 170 feet above the rail. The boom could be raised to 245 feet. Complex electrical systems were required for operation of the cranes. Were the cranes fixtures and thus taxable as part of the real estate? Explain.

3. Turner Company owned and operated a cable television business. The company owned more than 780 miles of feeder cable. The cable was annexed to telephone poles owned by BTT telephone company under a lease that required removal of the cable if BTT should need the space for is own service needs. Butte County assessed the Turner Company cable as real property because it is properly classified as a fixture. Is the county correct? Why?
4. Mary has a valuable painting in her living room. One day she told Penny that she would like Penny to have the painting. They arranged that Penny would pick-up the painting next week. Mary dies before any transfer is made. Does Penny have a right to the painting? Why?
5. Alice makes a deposit at her local bank. As she is filling-out the necessary forms, she discovers a $1,000 bill next to a deposit receipt near the teller's window. Alice asks the bank if anyone has lost the money. The bank investigates and cannot find who is missing the money. Is this lost or mislaid money? Does it make a difference? Why?
6. Jericho was on a business trip in December. He checked into a downtown hotel and parked his car in an unguarded parking lot under the hotel. The charge for parking was $12.00 per night. Jericho went gift shopping later in the day and put the gifts into the backseat of the car. Upon entering his car the next morning, he discovers that his gifts are gone. Is the hotel liable? Why?
7. Lucent Technologies, a very large business, registered as a trademark the word "Lucent." For years it sold telecommunications equipment under the name Lucent and was widely regarded as an excellent company producing high-quality goods. Russell registers the domain name "hotandheavylusent.com" and sells a variety of unsavory services. What advice would you give Lucent Technologies? Have they adequately protected their name? What claim(s) should Lucent bring against Russell? Why?
8. Ashley works for McKennel and Associates, a large business consulting firm. ABC Company has developed, according to industry sources, a new process of building low-emission, high mileage gas engines for automobiles. XYZ, a competitor of ABC, hires Ashley to write a report about the manufacturing process developed by ABC. Can Ashley photograph the ABC factory using a long lens? Can Ashley call the ABC plant manager and ask questions? What if the plant manager answered the questions in detail? Could Ashley simply ask for a tour of the plant without detailing why she wanted the tour? If Ashley were allowed to tour the plant, what conclusion might you reach? Discuss.
9. Josiah is ninety-eight years old who employed Fred, a certified care giver, twelve hours per day for one year. Josiah talks to Fred every day and even emails Fred at night. Fred is paid on an hourly basis by an insurance policy Josiah purchased years ago. Josiah and Fred have become good friends. Josiah makes oral statements heard by others and has written emails

to the effect that that he wants Fred to have one of his two prized horses when Josiah dies. When Josiah dies, a valid will provides that all property should be split between Josiah's two daughters. Does Fred have a good claim to the horse? Why?

10. Asta Charles is a single person with considerable wealth. His only living relative is a cousin, Dashiell; however, he has two close friends, Nick and Nora, who both are not very rich. He also believes strongly in the work of three charities. Should Asta have a will? Why? What will happen if Asta has no will upon his death? Discuss.

Internet Sources

Within the Patent and Trademark Office web address, a member of the public can search for issued patents and applications for patents. The specific address of this site is: http://www.uspto.gov/patft/index.html

Property: Real Property, Leases, and Mortgages | 10

CHAPTER OUTLINE

CHAPTER PREVIEW

In the preceding chapter, the law of property was introduced and various aspects of personal property law were covered. We also explored the basics of intellectual property and the law of wills. This chapter is devoted entirely to real property law. After introductory matters, the chapter is organized to address the topics of acquiring title, leases, and the use of real property as security. While the topic of acquiring title of real property generally requires the use of deeds between consenting parties, the manner of obtaining title of real property through adverse possession is also presented. Many individuals and businesses are in a landlord-tenant relationship. Until the past couple of decades the law favored the landlord, especially regarding residential tenancies. As discussed in the chapter, now that trend, in many respects, favors the tenant. Finally, because of the worth generally associated with real property, it is often advanced as security for a loan. The chapter concludes by examining important aspects of using real property as security.

BUSINESS MANAGEMENT DECISION

You are president of a company that owns several apartment complexes. Your company rents mainly to college students. Due to a number of news reports, you become concerned about your company's liability for excessive drinking and drug use by your tenants. You desire to have the opportunity to inspect the apartments from time to time.

What should you do to accomplish this goal?

REAL PROPERTY OWNERSHIP INTERESTS

1. Bundle of Rights

We have emphasized in the previous chapter that property interests are best defined as the bundle of rights a person has in a thing. Property is an object or a thing over which someone exercises legal rights.

Defining property interests as a bundle of rights enables courts and the law to develop a variety of such interests in property. A person may possess the entire bundle of rights in relation to a thing, in which case he or she is the only owner. On the other hand, the bundle of rights may be divided among several people, in which case there is multiple ownership of the rights. For example, the owner of a tract of land may authorize the local public utility companies to install power and telephone lines through the land. The utility companies are granted what is called an easement, which is a property right. As a result, the owner has less than the full bundle of rights, and the rights of others result in what is known as an **encumbrance**.

Encumbrance
A burden on the title to the land, such as a mortgage or other lien

Furthermore, this bundle-of-rights concept allows owners of real property to create a variety of ownership interests. In essence, the type of real property ownership interest is determined by the rights of an owner to possess, use, and transfer the land. To understand the possible variations of ownership interests, keep in mind that the complete bundle of rights must be accounted for at all times.

2. Ownership Interests

When used in connection with land, the legal term *estate* is synonymous with ownership interests. *Fee simple estates* are those interests classified as either absolute or qualified present interests. *Present interests* are those that allow the owner to possess the land now. In the alternative, the owner of a present interest may transfer the right of possession to another party.

Fee simple absolute

This is the most complete interest a person may have in land and includes the entire bundle of rights. Such an estate is not qualified by any other interest, and it passes upon the death of the owners to the heirs, free from any conditions.

FEE SIMPLE ABSOLUTE A **fee simple absolute** is the most complete ownership interest possible. It contains the largest bundle of rights of any estate in land. The fee simple absolute is the interest usually received by the grantee in a real estate sales transaction. The language used to create this unlimited interest does not contain words of limitation. A fee simple interest that may be defeated in the future by the occurrence or nonoccurrence of a stated event or condition is called a *qualified* or *conditional fee simple.* A gift of land "to my grandson as long as he remains married" is an example of a qualified or conditional fee simple interest.

The possible variations of these fee simple estates are complex and beyond the scope of this text. It is sufficient for you to keep two points in mind about qualified fee simple estates. First, these interests do not contain the complete bundle of rights that exists with every piece of land. Therefore, there is a future ownership interest that may become possessory, causing the holder of this future interest to gain superior title relative to the owner of the qualified fee simple interest. Second, these qualified interests usually are less valuable when compared with a fee simple absolute interest. Thus, you should always be aware of the ownership interest involved in a real estate transaction. Generally, you would not be willing to pay as much for a qualified fee simple as you would for a fee simple absolute interest.

LIFE ESTATE One of the most widely used ownership interests in estate planning is the *life estate.* When properly used, the life estate enables landowners to provide for those they desire while reducing both income and estate taxes. The life estate interest may be created either by will or by deed. A life estate may be for the *life of the grantee,* or it may be created for the duration of the *life of some other designated person.* It may be conditional upon the happening of an event, such as the marriage during the life of the tenant. A husband may convey property to his wife for life or until she remarries. Unless the instrument that creates the life estate places limitations on it, the interest can be sold or mortgaged like any other interest in real estate. The buyer or mortgagee must, of course, take into consideration the fact that the life estate may be terminated at any time by the death of the person for whose life it was created.

REMAINDERS AND REVERSIONS Because a life estate represents less than the complete bundle of rights, there must be a future interest accompanying every life estate. After the termination of a life estate, the remaining estate may be transferred to someone else or it may go back to the original owner or to his or her heirs. If the estate is to be given to someone else upon the termination of a life estate, it is called an *estate in remainder.* If it is to go back to the original owner, it is called a *reversion.* When a reversion exists and the original owner of that interest is dead, the property reverts to the heirs of that original owner. Regardless of whether a remainder or a reversion follows a life estate, these future interests may be sold, mortgaged, or otherwise transferred as if they were any other real property interest. This right to transfer these interests exists even before the life estate ends and the remainder or reversion becomes present possessory interests. Upon the death of the life tenant, the remainder or reversion generally converts into a fee simple absolute interest once again.

Waste

Damage to the real property, so its value is impaired

Since the owners of remainders and reversions have a valuable real property interest, they have the right to enforce the life tenant's duty not to **waste** the land's value. The timing for filing a suit to recover damages for or to enjoin waste depends on the type of waste occurring. For example, the holder of a life estate may actively destroy an improvement on the real estate or the destruction may only be passive—the neglect of an improvement—allowing it to deteriorate. In general, the statute of limitations for filing an action against waste begins to run when active waste occurs and when the life tenant dies if the passive type of waste has occurred.

3. Easements and Licenses

Easement

A right that one person has to some profit, benefit, or use in or over the land of another that is created by a deed, or acquired by prescription (the continued use of another's land for a statutory period) or by implication

License (privilege)

A mere personal privilege given by the owner to another to do designated acts on the land of the owner

An **easement** is a right granted for the use of real property. The grantor may convey to the grantee a right of way over his or her land, the right to erect a building that may shut off light or air, the right to lay drain tile under the land, or the right to extend utilities over the land. If these rights of easement are reserved in the deed conveying the property or granted by a separate deed, they pass along with the property to the next grantee and are burdens on the land. An easement made by special contract is binding only on the immediate parties to the agreement. If a right to use another's land is given orally, it is not an easement but a **license**. The owner of the land may revoke a license at any time unless it has become irrevocable by conduct constituting estoppel. An easement given by grant cannot be revoked except by deed since such a right of way is considered a right in real property; nor can it be modified without the consent of the owner of the easement.

An owner of land may create an easement for the benefit of another by deed. Usually, a party desiring an easement purchases it from the owner of the *servient land* (the land on which the easement exists). A seller of real estate may also reserve an easement in his or her favor when deeding the property to someone else. This situation will occur when a party sells only part of his or her land and the portion retained requires the easement. Assume that Farmer Brown sells half of his farm to a neighbor. Since the half that was sold borders on the only road touching the farm, Farmer Brown will need to reserve an easement for the entering and exiting of the land retained. This land retained is often called the *dominant land,* and the land transferred subject to an easement is called the *servient estate.*

Easements may be obtained through adverse use. Such easements are known as *easements by prescription.* These concepts of adverse use or possession are developed more fully in the next chapter. For now, suffice it to say that if a party uses an easement for a long period of time, the owner of the land may not deny the existence of the easement.

Easements may also be obtained through judicial proceedings in certain cases. Since the law takes the position that an owner of land should be entitled to access to that land, owners of land that would otherwise be landlocked may be entitled to an *easement by necessity.* Such an easement is, in effect, granted by the owner of the servient land to the owner of the other land by implication.

4. Types of Multiple-Party Ownership

Tenancy in common

This is the most usual method of two or more persons owning property at the same time. None of the formalities or unities required for other specialized forms of co-ownership is essential for this method.

In the preceding sections, there has been an assumption that each real property ownership interest is owned by only one person. In reality, these interests can be, and often are, owned by two or more parties. There are three distinct methods by which two or more people may own property at the same time: tenancy in common, joint tenancy, and tenancy by the entirety. The first two types of co-ownership are applicable to every kind of property, real or personal. However, *tenancy by the entirety* is a type of joint tenancy held by spouses in real estate only. Several states have modified the common-law characteristics of these forms of ownership, so it is essential that each state's law be consulted for the technicalities of these tenancies.

TENANCY IN COMMON Most states presume that the ownership interest in property held by two or more people is a **tenancy in common**. These co-owners, known as tenants in common, may acquire their interests at different times. Their percentage of ownership interests does not have to be equal. They may transfer their interests during their lifetime or upon their death to whomever they desire.

Tenants in common do have the right to possess the entire item of property subject to the co-owners' rights. However, the degree of control each owner has over the property and over who might become a future co-owner is limited when compared to that possessed by co-owners under the forms of multiple ownership.

JOINT TENANCY The basic distinction between a tenancy in common and a joint tenancy is that the latter involves the *right of survivorship.* In the event of the death of a tenant in common, his or her share in the property passes to the executor named in the will or to the administrator of the deceased's estate. If property is held in joint tenancy, the interest of a deceased owner automatically passes to the surviving joint owner. Such property is not subject to probate or to the debts of the deceased joint tenant. Thus, joint tenancy with the right of survivorship passes the title of the deceased by operation of law to the survivor or survivors, free of the claims of anyone else except for taxes that may be due. The case following demonstrates the impact of the death of a joint tenant on the beneficiaries named in that joint tenant's will.

When there is a question about which form of ownership exists in any specific case, the law usually favors tenancy in common and property passing by will or intestacy, rather than passing by right of survivorship. Courts do not find that property is held in joint tenancy with the right of survivorship unless there is a contract between the two co-owners clearly stating that such is the case and that the right of survivorship is to apply. Bank signature cards and stock certificates that use the term **joint tenancy** or "with the right of survivorship" create such a contract, as does the language "as joint tenants and not as tenants in common." In most states, the contract must be signed by both parties to be effective. Failure to use the proper language or have a properly executed contract results in a tenancy in common.

Joint tenancy

Two or more persons that own property in such manner that they have "one and the same interest, accruing by one and the same conveyance, commencing at one and the same time, and held by one and the same undivided possession" (Upon the death of one joint tenant, his or her property passes to the survivor or survivors.)

TENANCY BY THE ENTIRETY/COMMUNITY PROPERTY If the owners are related by marriage and the state law so provides (approximately half of the states do), a conveyance to a husband and wife creates a specialized joint tenancy, which is called *tenancy by the entireties.* A tenancy by the entirety in states that authorize such common ownership of real estate can exist only between husband and wife. A conveyance of real estate to a husband and wife in these states is automatically a tenancy by the entirety if all four of the aforementioned unities are present. Neither tenant can unilaterally sever or end the tenancy. It may be terminated only by divorce, a joint transfer to a third party, or a conveyance by one spouse to the other. The inability of either spouse to terminate the tenancy unilaterally is the primary difference between a joint tenancy and a tenancy by the entireties, as the basic characteristic of each is the right of survivorship.

In most states that authorize tenancy by the entireties, not only is there a prohibition on one tenant making a voluntary transfer of his or her share, but there are also severe restrictions on the rights of creditors to collect an individual debt from one tenant of the property. Suppose a husband and wife own their home as tenants by the entireties. A creditor has a judgment for $10,000 against the husband alone. In most states, the creditor could not cause a sale of the house to collect the debt. Of course, if the creditor had a judgment against both husband and wife, the creditor could collect from a judicial sale of the property.

Many western (e.g., California and Washington) and southern (e.g., Texas and Louisiana) states adopt *community property* as the method of allowing co-ownership of property by husband and wife. Community property is created at the time of marriage and continues to be amassed until either separation or death. Under community property principles, each spouse possesses an equal interest in the community property regardless of which spouse earned or acquired the property through their efforts. Note, though, that property brought into the marriage is assumed to be the *separate property* of the spouse, as is property that is acquired by gift or through inheritance during the marriage.

5. Restrictions on Ownership Interests

There can be no property rights without a government and a legal system to create and enforce them. Private property rights cannot exist without some method of keeping the bundle of rights for the true owner and for restoring these rights if he or she is deprived of them. It should also be recognized that no one person has a totally unrestricted bundle of rights. To some extent, the law always limits private property rights and the use of private property to protect the public's interest.

There are two basic methods of restricting ownership interests in land. First, governing bodies at the federal, state, and local levels may require an owner to sell land so it may be utilized for a public purpose. These governing bodies may also regulate the use of land through statutes and ordinances. For example, there are many environmental protection laws designed to control the use of land. Furthermore, zoning regulations are typical of the ordinances intended as land-use controls. Collectively, governmental regulations of an ownership interest are called *public restrictions.*

EMINENT DOMAIN One of the inherent rights the founders of our nation recognized was the right of individuals to own property. Indeed, the United States Constitution, in the Fifth Amendment, states that property shall not be taken from any person for a public use without just compensation. This language has been interpreted to be applicable to all levels of government. In essence, the Constitution not only protects the property owner, it also gives the governing body the power to buy private property when two conditions are satisfied. First, the property being acquired must be needed for the public's use and benefit. Second, the property owner must be justly compensated. This constitutional power is known as the power of **eminent domain**. In other words, the government may terminate an owner's interest by acquiring it for a public purpose upon payment of the fair market value.

Eminent domain

The right that resides in the United States, state, county, city, or other public body to take private property for public use upon payment of just compensation

Without question, the public-use requirement is satisfied when land is needed for the construction of a public highway, park, hospital, school, or airport. More recently there has been an expansion of the public-use doctrine to include the taking of private property, under a community economic development plan, that is then sold for private uses, perhaps a shopping center.

ZONING REGULATIONS The primary method local governments use to restrict a landowner's interest is the adoption of a *zoning ordinance.* These ordinances typically divide a community into zones and regulate the use of land within each zone. The type and intensity of the land's use in these zones can be classified as open space, residential, commercial, or industrial. Within each classification there can be several categories that further regulate the owner's use of the land. For example, property zoned R-1 might be reserved for single-family residences with lot sizes of not under one-half acre. R-5 could represent that zone wherein multiple-family residences (apartments or condominiums) are permitted.

A community's comprehensive zoning plan also restricts the use of land regarding the density of development allowed. Restrictions on building height and bulk are not uncommon. Height limitations usually restrict the maximum height of buildings in feet or stories. Bulk regulations control the percentage of the lot the building may occupy. Setback and lot size requirements are examples of typical bulk restrictions.

The overall purpose of zoning ordinances is to provide a more aesthetically pleasing environment for all citizens of the community. Few people want their residence located in or near the site of a major industrial facility. Although it is a restriction on ownership interests, properly designed and implemented zoning regulations can enhance property values. Despite these benefits, you should know that there are methods for changing zoning classifications when they become unreasonable. In other words, in most communities the local zoning ordinances are subject to a continuous review process.

CONDITIONS AND COVENANTS The second method of restricting ownership interests is referred to as *private restrictions.* By *private,* we mean that nongovernmental parties limit an owner's use and enjoyment of the land. Examples of private restrictions include easements, licenses, conditions, and covenants. Although these items may be considered to be interests in the hands of those that can enforce them, they are restrictions on the ownership interests on which they exist. They restrict the bundle of rights and create rights in others.

An ownership interest in land may be restricted by *conditions* or *covenants.* A qualified fee simple estate was discussed previously. In essence, these interests are conditioned on the occurrence of a stated event. For example, land may be conveyed by a grantee, Albert, on the condition that he marries before his twenty-fifth birthday. If Albert does not satisfy the condition of marriage, he loses all ownership interest in the property conveyed. In other words, a breach of a stated condition may result in termination of all interests previously held.

ACQUIRING TITLE TO REAL PROPERTY

6. Introduction

The primary methods to obtain title to real property are (1) by original entry, called title by occupancy; (2) by a deed from the owner; (3) by benefit of the period of the statue of limitations, called *adverse possession;* and (4) by will or descent under intestacy statues (discussed in Chapter 9).

7. Original Entry

Deed

A written instrument in a special form, signed, sealed, delivered, and used to pass the legal title of real property from one person to another

Original entry refers to a title obtained from the sovereign. Except in those portions of the United States where the original title to the land was derived from grants that were issued by the king of England and other sovereigns who took possession of the land by conquest, title to all the land in the United States was derived from the United States government. Private individuals who occupied land for the period of time prescribed by federal statue and met other conditions established by law acquired title by patent from the federal government.

8. Transfer by Deed

Grantor

A person who executes the deed, thereby transferring title

Grantee

A person to whom a grant is made; one named in a deed to receive title

A **deed** is the legal document that is issued to transfer the ownership interest in or title to land. Although there are other essential elements of deeds, one of the most important parts of any deed is the legal description of the land involved. By reference to the deed, people must be able to get the information that allows them to determine the exact location of the land described.

The statutes of the various states provide the necessary form, language, and execution requirements of deeds. For example, these statutes usually require that the parties involved be identified at the beginning of the deed. Often these parties are referred to as the **grantor** and **grantee**. All deeds must contain language that indicates the type of ownership interest being conveyed. Also, the deed must state clearly that this interest is being transferred to the grantee. A properly drafted deed needs to be signed by the grantor and, in some states, sealed, witnessed, or acknowledged in the presence of a **notary public**. Finally, the deed must be delivered.

Notary public
A public officer authorized to administer oaths

A deed is not effective until it is delivered—that is, placed entirely out of the control of the grantor. This delivery usually occurs by the handing of the instrument to the grantee or to some third party known as an **escrow agent**. The delivery by the grantor must occur during the lifetime of the grantor. It cannot be delivered by someone else after the grantor's death, even if the grantor has ordered the delivery.

Escrow agent
A third party other than the grantor and grantee who holds the signed deed until the buyer has paid the full purchase price

So that the owner of real estate may notify all persons of the change in title to the property, the statutes of the various states provide that deeds shall be *recorded* in the recording office of the county in which the land is located. Failure to record a deed by a new owner makes it possible for the former owner to convey and pass good title to the property to an innocent third party, although the former owner has no right to do so and would be liable to the first grantee in such a case.

Although the recording of a deed is necessary to give public notice of a change of ownership, the recording is not necessary to pass title as between the grantor and grantee. However, when a deed is recorded, there exists a very strong presumption that the deed was delivered by the grantor.

In addition to the essential requirements of all deeds, a deed may contain all, some, or none of the optional elements referred to as *covenants* or *warranties.* These covenants or warranties are promises or guarantees made by the grantor pertaining to the land and the grantor's bundle of rights with respect to it. These covenants may include a promise that (1) at the time of making the deed, the grantor has fee simple title and the right and power to convey it (*covenant of seizin*); (2) the property is free from all encumbrances except those noted in the deed (*covenant against encumbrances*); (3) the grantee and his successors will have the quiet and peaceful enjoyment of the property (*covenant of quiet enjoyment*); and (4) the grantor will defend the title of the grantee if anyone else should claim the property (*covenant of further assurances*).

9. Types of Deeds

Many different kinds of deeds are used throughout the United States, the statutes of each state providing for the various types. The common types are the *warranty deed,* the *grant deed,* the *bargain and sale deed,* and the *quitclaim deed.* There are also special types of deeds used when the grantor holds a special legal position at the time of conveyance. Special deeds are used by the executors and administrators of estates, by guardians, and by sheriffs or other court officials executing deeds in their official capacity. The major distinction among types of deeds relates to the covenants or warranties the grantor of the deed makes to the grantee. A deed may contain several warranties or none at all, depending on the type of deed and the language used.

WARRANTY DEED From the grantee's perspective, the *warranty* deed provides the broadest protection that the grantor is conveying clear title to the land described in the deed. This protection is provided because the warranty deed contains all four of the aforementioned covenants. Therefore, the warranty deed is the type of deed grantees usually insist on in traditional real estate sales transactions.

GRANT DEED In some states (California being one), a deed known as a grant deed is more commonly used than is the warranty deed. In a *grant deed,* the grantor covenants that no interest in the property has been conveyed to another party, that the property has not been encumbered except as noted, and that any title to the property the grantor might receive in the future will be transferred to the grantee. A grantor under a grant deed has liability only as a result of encumbrances or claims that arose while the property was owned by the grantor. A grant deed does not protect the grantee against encumbrances that existed prior to the grantor taking title. As a result, the grant deed is much narrower than the warranty deed in the promises made to the grantee.

BARGAIN AND SALE DEED A *bargain and sale deed* warrants that the grantor has title to the property and the right to convey, but it does not contain any express covenants as to the title's validity. This deed also is sometimes called a *warranty deed without covenants.* The bargain and sale deed simply states that the grantor "does hereby grant, bargain, sell, and convey" his or her interest in the real property to the grantee. In states that authorize a bargain and sale deed, a grantee who desires the covenants and warranties of a warranty deed must require that the sales contract state that a warranty deed will be delivered by the grantor. If the sales contract is silent about the type of deed, the grantor is obligated only to sign and deliver a bargain and sale deed.

QUICKCLAIM DEED A grantor who does not wish to make warranties with respect to the title may execute a *quitclaim deed,* merely transferring all the "right, title, and interest" of the grantor to the grantee. Whatever title the grantor has, the grantee receives; but the grantor makes no warranties. A quitclaim deed is used when the interest of the grantor is not clear, for example, where a deed will clear a defective title. It is also used to eliminate possible conflicting interests or when, in fact, there may be no interest in the grantor.

The grantee who takes property under a quitclaim deed must understand that he or she may be receiving nothing at all. A person could give a quitclaim deed to the Brooklyn Bridge to anyone willing to pay for it. The grantee obviously is not given anything at all by such a deed. The grantor simply conveyed all of his or her interest in the bridge, without assurances that any rights of ownership did, in fact, exist. To transfer all of a person's rights in someone else's property is to transfer nothing at all.

The amount of protection each deed gives to the grantee is the most important distinction to remember. The order in which these types of deeds are discussed is also the order of the amount of protection provided. The warranty deed contains the greatest protection for the grantee. The grant deed protects the grantee from encumbrances placed on the land's title by the grantor but not by others. The bargain and sale deed simply states that the grantor has the right to convey the title involved, but all other covenants and warranties are missing. Finally, the grantor who gives a quitclaim deed does not even promise that he or she has any rights in the land at all.

10. Title by Adverse Possession

Adverse possession

Acquisition of legal title to another's land by being in continuous possession during a period prescribed in the statute of limitations

Although the concepts of title and possession usually are treated as separate and distinct, physical control of land may result in the possessor's acquiring title under the principle known as **adverse possession**. A person who enters into actual possession of land and remains thereon openly and notoriously for the period of time prescribed in the statute of limitations, claiming title in denial of, and adversely to, the superior title of another, will at the end of the statutory period acquire legal title. In contrast to the discussion of voluntary transfers of title discussed in the previous section, this method of acquiring title is decidedly involuntary.

The owner's knowledge that his or her land is occupied adversely is not essential to the claim, but possession must be of a nature that would charge a reasonably diligent legal owner with knowledge of the adverse claim. In other words, the possessor must not try to hide his or her present use of the land. Indeed, any time the legal owner or anyone else asserts rights to the land, the possessor must deny that claim and be steadfast in his or her right to the property's use.

The legal doctrine of adverse possession is illustrated in the following case.

CASE

Neal W. Baker and Frances S. Baker v. Sidney Albert Quintal; Susan Martha Quintal; John Does 1–10; Jane Does 1-10; Doe Corporations 1-10; et al.

INTERMEDIATE COURT OF APPEALS OF HAWAII

2002 Haw. App. LEXIS 107 (2002)

The Bakers' Lot 57 and the Quintals' Lot 56 are both rectangular in shape and each is comprised of approximately 13 acres. The east side of Lot 57 adjoins the west side of Lot 56. The main fork of the Honopou Stream flows west to east across the middle of Lot 57 and then, at the boundary of Lots 57 and 56, it turns north (makai), joins a seasonal fork that flows east-northeast to west-southwest across the middle of Lot 56, turns back into Lot 57, and flows north (makai) out of Lot 57 and under the Hana Belt Road.

In 1960 Between Lots 56 and 57, a Historic Fence was built which starts at the boundary pin located at the north (makai) point of the common boundary between Lot 56 and Lot 57 and runs south (mauka) to a point near the EMI Ditch.

The Mauka Disputed Parcel was covered by tall grass, bushes, and trees. In 1973, the Bakers walked on the tall grass and cut away some of the vegetation on the Lot 57 side of the Historic Fence thereby creating a trail two to three feet wide along the Historic Fence. This trail was used by the Bakers to provide human access to the Historic Fence and to areas south (mauka) of Lot 57. Thereafter, the Bakers maintained and repaired the Historic Fence 4 to 5 times during the period from 1973 to 1986. Once or twice a month during the period from 1973 to 1997, the Bakers maintained the trail by walking on the vegetation, and by using a machete to cut shrubbery and bushes that were in the way. During those times when James Baker was on the Mauka Disputed Parcel and trespassers, such as hikers from Twin Falls, would come onto the Mauka Disputed Parcel, James Baker would "throw them out." The number of these "times" was not specified. When he was on the trail, James Baker also sought "to investigate the top and remote portions of the property to be sure there was no illegal agricultural activities ongoing." The Bakers did not put any "no trespassing" or similar signs on the Mauka Disputed Parcel.

The trial court concluded that "the BAKERS were in 'actual, open, and notorious possession' of the property. This is shown by the fact that the BAKERS cleared the property in question of overgrown vegetation and maintained the property from 1973 until 1997. They mowed, maintained, and improved it.

Actual, open, and notorious possession is established where a claimant shows use of the land to such an extent and in such a manner as to put the world on notice by means "so notorious as to attract the attention of every adverse claimant." Some use and occupancy is necessary. The limited activities by the Bakers regarding the Historic Fence and the crude trail on the Mauka Disputed Parcel along the Historic Fence did not show "'use of the land to such an extent and in such a manner as to put the world on notice by means so notorious as to attract the attention of every adverse claimant."

"The element of hostility is satisfied by showing possession for oneself under a claim of right. Such possession must import a denial of the owner's title." The activities by the Bakers on the trail on the Mauka Disputed Parcel along the Historic Fence have been noted above. The Bakers initially created and maintained the crude trail to maintain the Historic Fence so that it would keep cattle out and away from the Bakers' water supply. Commencing 1986 to 1987, after there were no cattle, the Bakers maintained the crude trail to get to the back of the property on hikes. During those times, the number of which was unspecified, when James Baker was on the crude trail and trespassers, such as hikers, would come onto the pathway, James Baker would tell them to leave because he did not want hikers in the area, and he was concerned about persons involved in illegal agricultural activities.

Nonuse is not use. Twice a month, the Bakers used and maintained a crude trail on the eastern boundary of the Mauka Disputed Parcel because the Historic Fence was useful to them. By the time the Historic Fence was not useful to them, they continued to use and maintain the crude trail along the Historic Fence merely because it was a way to go on hikes. During those times when James Baker was on the Mauka Disputed Parcel and trespassers, such as hikers, would come onto the walkway, he required their departure. There is no evidence of the number of these times. There is no evidence that the Bakers ever used the other part of the Mauka Disputed Parcel.

We conclude that the record lacks substantial evidence that the Bakers treated the Mauka Disputed Parcel as if it were their own, so as to satisfy the elements of "notorious" and "hostility" and "claim of right" necessary for the adverse possession claim. The activities of the Bakers did not show possession for the Bakers under a claim of right or import a denial of the Quintals' title.

■ *Reversed.*

CASE CONCEPTS REVIEW

1. What more would be necessary for the Bakers to show the element of "notorious"? Of "hostility"?
2. Do you believe that the law should favor claims associated with adverse possession? Why?

LEASES OF REAL PROPERTY

11. In General

A **lease** is a transfer of possession of real estate from a landlord (lessor) to a tenant (lessee) for a consideration called rent. A lease may be oral or written, expressed, or simply implied from the facts

Lease

A contract by which one person divests himself or herself of possession of land and grants such possession to another for a period of time

and circumstances. A lease differs from a mere *license,* which is a privilege granted by one person to another to use land for some particular purpose. A license is not an interest in the land. A license to the licensee is personal and not assignable.

A lease agreement is often needed between a landlord and tenant.

12. Classification of Leases

A lease may be a tenancy for a stated period, from period to period, at will, or at sufferance.

STATED PERIOD As its name implies, a *tenancy for a stated period* lasts for the specific time stated in the lease. The statute of frauds requires a written lease if the period exceeds one year. The lease for a stated period terminates without notice at the end of the period. It is not affected by the death of either party during the period. A lease of land for a stated period is not terminated by destruction of the improvements during the period unless the lease so provides. If a lease covers only the improvements on land, destruction of them creates impossibility of performance.

PERIOD TO PERIOD A *tenancy* from *period* to *period* may be created by the terms of the lease. A lease may run from January 1, 2007 to December 31, 2007, and from year to year thereafter unless terminated by the parties. Many leases from period to period arise when the tenant, with the consent of the landlord, holds over after the end of a lease for a stated period. When a *holdover* occurs, the landlord may object and evict the former tenant as a trespasser; or the landlord may continue to treat the tenant as a tenant, in which case the lease continues from period to period, with the period being identical to that of the original lease, not to exceed one year. The one-year limitation results from the language of the statute of frauds. The amount of rent is identical to that of the original lease.

Leases from year to year or from month to month can be terminated only upon giving proper notice. The length of the notice is usually prescribed by state statute—usually thirty days for a month-to-month lease and sixty to ninety days for one that is year to year. Statutes usually provide the time of the notice, such as on the day the rent is due. Farm leases usually have a special notice period so the tenant will have notice before planting the next year's crops.

AT WILL A tenancy at *will,* by definition, has no fixed period and can be terminated by either party at any time upon giving the prescribed statutory notice. A few states do not require notice; but if legal action is necessary to obtain possession for the lessor, a time lag will be automatically imposed.

AT SUFFERANCE A *tenancy at sufferance* occurs when a tenant holds over without the consent of the landlord. Until the landlord decides to evict the tenant or to allow him or her to stay, he or she is a tenant at sufferance.

13. Tenants: Rights and Duties

The rights and duties of the parties to the lease are determined by the lease itself and by the statutes of the state in which the real property is located. Several rights of tenants are frequently misunderstood. For example, the tenant is entitled to exclusive possession and control of the premises unless the lease provides to the contrary. The landlord has no right to go on the premises except to collect rent. This means that the owner of an apartment building cannot go into the leased apartments and inspect them unless the lease specifically reserves the right to do so. At the end of the lease, the landlord may retake possession of the premises and inspect for damage. A landlord may also retake possession for purposes of protecting the property if the tenant abandons the premises.

Unless the lease so provides, a tenant has no duty to make improvements or substantial repairs. A tenant is not obligated to replace a worn-out heating or air-conditioning system, but it is his or her duty to make minor repairs such as replacing a broken window. Because of the difficulty in classifying repairs, the lease should spell out the exact obligations of both parties. If the lease obligates the tenant to make repairs, the obligation includes significant items such as replacing a rotten floor or a defective furnace. The duty to repair usually does not extend to replacing the whole structure if it is destroyed.

An important right in many leases of commercial property is the tenant's right to remove *trade fixtures* that he or she has installed during the lease period. Remember the distinction between fixtures and trade fixtures. The former become a part of the real estate and belong to the owner of the land. The latter remain personalty and belong to the tenant. The right of removal terminates with the lease, and trade fixtures not removed become the property of the landlord.

Eviction

An action by a landlord to expel a tenant

Another important right of the tenant relates to his or her corresponding duty to pay rent. The duty to pay rent is subject to setoffs for violations of the provisions of the lease by the landlord. The duty to pay rent is released in the event of an **eviction**, actual or constructive. *Constructive eviction* occurs when the premises become not tenantable, not because of any fault of the tenant, or when some act of the landlord deprives the tenant of quiet enjoyment of the premises. (One example of such an act involves the landlord's breach of an implied warranty of habitability, which is discussed in Section 15.) Assume that Pablo Hernandez rents a basement apartment on campus. A spring rain floods the apartment and makes it uninhabitable. Pablo has been constructively evicted. He may move out, and his duty to pay rent is released. Failure to vacate the premises is a waiver of constructive eviction grounds, however. A tenant who continues in possession despite grounds for constructive eviction must continue to pay rent unless this duty is relieved by statute.

Some states and cities in recent years have enacted laws in an attempt to force landlords to maintain their property in a tenantable condition. These laws allow tenants to withhold rent where the premises are in such disrepair that the health and safety of the tenant is jeopardized. Such laws protect low-income tenants from slum landlords.

Unless prohibited by the lease, a tenant may assign the lease or sublet the premises without the consent of the landlord. In an *assignment,* the assignee becomes liable to the landlord for the rent (of course, the assignor remains liable also). In a *sublease,* the sub-lessee is liable to the tenant, and the tenant is liable to the landlord. An assignment transfers the original leasehold to the assignee. A sublease creates a new leasehold estate. Ordinarily, an assignment is for the balance of the original lease, whereas a sublease is only for part of the term.

If a lease prohibits assignment, it does not necessarily prevent a sublease; if a lease prohibits subleasing, it does not necessarily prevent assignment. If both assignment and sublease are to be prohibited, the lease should so provide. Most leases provide that any assignment or sublease must have the approval of the landlord. Whether the landlord can withhold consent arbitrarily is an issue that has frequently arisen. Historically, the landlord's consent to a proposed assignment or sublease could be withheld without any reason. However, the trend now is to require that the landlord's lack of consent be reasonable under the factual circumstances. This is based on the requirement of good faith and commercial reasonableness.

14. Landlords: Rights and Duties

Lien

The right of one person, usually a creditor, to keep possession or control of the property of another for the purpose of satisfying a debt

Distress for rent

The taking of personal property of a tenant in payment of rent

The landlord's foremost right is to collect payment for rent. In many states and by the express terms of many leases, the landlord has a **lien** for unpaid rent on the personal property of the tenant physically located on the premises. This lien right is exercised in a statutory proceeding known as **distress for rent**. By following the prescribed procedures, the landlord is able to physically hold personalty on the premises until the rent is paid. If not paid, the tenant's personal property may be sold pursuant to court order. The proceeds of the sale, after deducting court costs, are applied to the rent.

A second basic right belonging to the landlord is to have the tenant vacate the premises upon termination of the tenancy. If the tenancy is terminated lawfully, the landlord's right to possession is absolute. The tenant may not deny the landlord's title. Furthermore, tenants have a duty to redeliver physical control of the premises in the same condition as received, ordinary wear and tear excepted. The motive of the landlord in terminating the lease usually is immaterial. However, because of federal statutes, a landlord may not discriminate in leasing or terminating a lease on the basis of race, color, religion, sex, or national origin.

A landlord also is entitled to recover from either the tenant or third parties for injuries to or waste of property. Tenants may not make any material changes or improvements without the landlord's permission. They may not move walls, install new ones, or do anything else that would constitute a material change in the premises without permission.

It is common practice for a landlord to require that the tenant deposit a stated sum of money, such as one month's rent, as security for the lease. This security deposit covers nonpayment of rent and possible damage to the premises. Many landlords have been reluctant to return these security deposits, contending in most cases that damages, requiring repairs, were present. As a result, many tenants have refused to pay the last month's rent, demanding that the security deposit be applied. Such practices by landlords and tenants have created a great deal of animosity and litigation. To alleviate this problem, the legislatures of many states have passed laws governing lease security deposits. Such laws usually require that the landlord pay interest on the deposits and itemize the cost of any repairs that were made from the deposit. They further require the landlord to return the deposit promptly and prohibit the landlord from using it to repair conditions caused by normal wear and tear. In the event a tenant is required to sue the landlord to recover the deposit, the tenant is entitled to collect attorney's fees. Finally, under these statutes, the tenant usually is not allowed to set off the deposit against the last month's rent.

Tort liability is sometimes imposed on landlords for injuries to their tenants. Such liability only exists where there is a duty owed by the landlord to the tenant and the duty is breached. For example, the modern view is that the owner of a residential dwelling unit, who leases it to a tenant for residential purposes, has a duty to reasonably inspect the premises before allowing the tenant to take possession and to make the repairs necessary to transfer a reasonably safe dwelling unit to the tenant unless defects are waived by the tenant. This duty may be modified by agreement of the parties.

After the tenant takes possession, the landlord has a continuing duty to exercise reasonable care to repair dangerous defective conditions upon notice of their existence by the tenant, unless waived by the tenant. In most states, a landlord has no duty to maintain in a safe condition any part of the premises under the tenant's exclusive control. The landlord does, however, have a duty to use ordinary care to maintain in a reasonably safe condition any part of the leased premises that was reserved for the common use of all tenants. Further, if the landlord, after delivering possession of the premises to a tenant, enters to make repairs or improvements, the landlord must use reasonable care in making them.

15. Warranty of Habitability

In recent years, courts have been called on to decide if there is an implied *warranty of habitability* in a lease of residential property. Some courts have held that in all housing leases there is an implied warranty of habitability. One court held that the fact that a tenant knew of a substantial number of defects when he rented the premises and that rent was accordingly reduced did not remove the tenant from protection of the warranty. The court reasoned that permitting that type of bargaining would be contrary to public policy and the purpose of the doctrine of implied warranty of habitability. In determining the kinds of defects that will be deemed to constitute a breach of warranty of habitability, several factors are considered. Among the common factors are (1) the violation of any applicable housing code or building or sanitary regulations; (2) whether the nature of the deficiency affects a vital facility; (3) the potential or actual effect on safety and sanitation; and (4) whether the tenant was in any way responsible for the defect. A breach of this warranty may allow a tenant to terminate the lease. It may serve as a defense to a suit for rent and as a means to obtain a rent reduction.

Defects in vital portions of the premises that may affect health are more important than defects in extras such as swimming pools or recreational facilities, which are not likely to render the premises uninhabitable. It should be kept in mind that not all states recognize an implied warranty of habitability in residential leases. Also, most states have not extended implied warranties to commercial leases. In general, implied warranties of habitability are created either by courts on a case-by-case basis or by statutory enactment.

Minimum standards of habitability are increasingly shaped by housing codes. These municipal provisions may be used as a basis to negate the obligation to pay rent or, as illustrated in the following case, provide a means to sue under negligence theory.

CASE

Tiffany Childs, et al. v. Samuel B. Purll, Jr., et al.

DISTRICT OF COLUMBIA COURT OF APPEALS

882 A.2d 227 (2005)

Between December 1991 and October 1995, appellants Marcella Childs and her two minor children, Tiffany Childs and Robbie Davis, resided as tenants in an apartment at 1411 Ridge Place in Southeast Washington, D.C. The property was owned by appellees Samuel and Kathy Purll and managed by appellee Willoughby Real Estate Company ("Willoughby"). Appellants' lease agreements identified Willoughby as the landlord and lessor and listed each member of the Childs family by name as an occupant of the premises. It was stated in the leases that Tiffany and Robbie were one and three years old, respectively, at the start of the tenancy in 1991. In August 1993, mid-way through the tenancy, tests revealed that the two children had elevated levels of lead in their blood—in other words, they had lead poisoning.

Attributing her children's lead poisoning to their exposure to lead-based paint at 1411 Ridge Place, Marcella Childs filed suit against the Purlls, Willoughby, and the management company's three principals in February 2000. Her voluminous complaint charged each defendant with negligence in failing to eradicate a lead paint hazard that persisted on the walls and other surfaces throughout the premises, failing to prevent the paint from chipping, peeling and flaking, and failing to warn her of the resulting dangers - "thereby rendering the dwelling unsafe and dangerous, and unfit for human habitation, especially for children of tender years." The trial court granted defendant summary judgment on appellants' cause of action for negligence based on their claimed lack of notice of the lead paint hazard at the leased premises.

The Housing Regulations impose numerous duties on landlords and their agents to keep residential premises safe and habitable and not to rent habitations that are unsafe. Of particular pertinence to this case, during the time appellants resided at 1411 Ridge Place, Housing Regulations § 707.3 of Title 14 provided as follows:

> The owner of any residential premises in which there resides a child under the age of eight (8) years … shall maintain the interior and exterior surfaces of the residential premises free of lead or lead in its compounds in any quantity exceeding five-tenths (0.5) of one percent (1%) of the total weight of the material or more than seven-tenths of a milligram per square centimeter (0.7 mg/cm2), or in any quantity sufficient to constitute a hazard to the health of any resident of the residential premises or any regular visitor to the residential premises who spends a substantial portion of his or her time in the residential premises.

In § 707.3, we have before us a particular Housing Regulation that is designed to protect public safety and that requires landlords to be proactive when its specified preconditions are satisfied. Upon notification that the prospective tenants of 1411 Ridge Place would include children under eight years of age, § 707.3 imposed a specific, affirmative duty on the owners and their agents to provide those premises to the Childs' family in a lead-free condition or not at all. Although the Purlls and their management company may not have known there was lead paint in the premises, "actual knowledge [of the defect] is not required for liability; it is enough if, in the exercise of reasonable care, appellees should have known that the condition … violated the standards of the Housing Code." In effect, § 707.3 presumptively serves to put the landlord on constructive notice of any lead paint hazard in premises occupied by children under eight.

In sum, the requirement of constructive notice is satisfied in this case, given § 707.3 and the notice to the landlord that two young children would be residing in the leased premises. Further, it cannot be said as a matter of law that the owners and their agents in this case have demonstrated that the alleged violation of a regulation designed to promote public safety was "excusable under the circumstances or [that] other acts of due care negate the negligence implied by the statutory violation." In seeking summary judgment, the defendants have not presented evidence that they "did everything a reasonably prudent person would have done to comply with" § 707.3. We therefore are persuaded that the defendants were not entitled to summary judgment on appellants' cause of action for negligence based on their claimed lack of notice of the lead paint hazard at the leased premises. Accordingly, we reverse that portion of the trial court's judgment.

■ *Reversed and remanded.*

CASE CONCEPTS REVIEW

1. Under the code section, what duty is imposed on a landlord before renting property?
2. What is "constructive notice"? How does that doctrine apply in the case?

REAL PROPERTY AS SECURITY

16. Introduction

Mortgage
A conveyance of an interest in real property for the purpose of creating a security for a debt

A real estate **mortgage** is an interest in real property, an interest created for the purpose of securing the performance of an obligation, usually the payment of a debt. A mortgage is not a debt—only security for a debt. The owner of the land that is being used as security for the debt is called the *mortgagor* since that owner is granting a mortgage interest to the creditor. This party to whom the interest in the real estate is conveyed is called the mortgagee.

A mortgage is evidence of the interest a lender is receiving; it is not evidence of the loan being made. Therefore, typically there are two documents involved in the mortgage financing transaction.

The *promissory note* is the piece of paper that evidences the borrower's agreement to repay the amount of the loan. This note should include the principal borrowed, the interest rate charged, the term or the life of the loan, and the amount of the periodic payments.

In addition to the note, the *mortgage document* must be prepared. Since a mortgage is a

A mortgage is security for a debt.

contract, it must meet all the requirements of an enforceable agreement. A mortgage must be in writing and contain (1) the names of the mortgagor and mortgagee, (2) an accurate description of the mortgaged property, (3) the terms of the debt (incorporated from the note), and (4) the mortgagor's signature. This document must be executed with all the formalities of a deed.

So that the mortgagee may give notice to third parties that he or she has an interest in the real estate, it is necessary that the mortgage be recorded in the recording office of the county where the real estate is situated. Recording serves to notify subsequent parties of the lien or encumbrance of the mortgage.

17. Rights and Duties of the Parties

Payment of the mortgage debt terminates the mortgage. Upon payment, the mortgagor is entitled to a release or satisfaction of the mortgage. This release should be recorded to clear the title to the land; otherwise, the unreleased mortgage will remain a **cloud on the title**. If the mortgagee refuses to give a release, he or she can be compelled to do so in a court of equity.

Cloud on the title
A defect, encumbrance, or other interest that exists in the record title to land

The mortgagor is entitled to retain possession of the real estate during the period of the mortgage unless a different arrangement is provided for in the mortgage. The mortgagor may not use the property in a manner that will materially reduce its value. Mining ore, pumping oil, or cutting timber are operations that cannot be conducted by the mortgagor during the period of the mortgage unless the right to do so is reserved in the mortgage agreement. The rights will be implied when they are being conducted at the time the mortgage is created.

Any parcel of real estate may be subject to more than one mortgage. In addition, mortgaged land may be subject to a lien for property taxes. A mortgagee has a right to pay off any superior mortgage to protect his or her security and can charge the amount so paid to the mortgagor. Likewise, the mortgagee may pay taxes or special assessments that are a lien on the land and recover the sum expended. The mortgagor is under a duty to protect the security; but should he or she fail to do so, the mortgagee has the right to make any reasonable expenditure necessary to protect the security for a debt.

The rights and duties of the parties may change when the mortgaged property is transferred.

The mortgagor may sell, will, or give away the mortgaged property—subject, however, to the rights of the mortgagee. A transferee from a mortgagor has no greater rights or duties than the mortgagor. For example, a grantee of the mortgagor's interest may redeem the land by paying off the debt. A grantee of mortgaged property is not personally liable for the mortgage debt unless he or she impliedly or expressly assumes and agrees to pay the mortgage. An assumption of a debt secured by a mortgage must be established by dear and convincing evidence. A purchase "subject to" a mortgage is usually considered not to be a legally enforceable assumption. If the grantee assumes the mortgage, the grantee becomes personally liable for the debt, even when the land is worth less than the mortgage.

To illustrate, assume that Berg purchases real estate worth $88,000, which is subject to a mortgage of $60,000. Berg pays the former owner $28,000 cash. If she assumes and agrees to pay the mortgage, Berg becomes personally liable for the $60,000 debt. If the property is sold at a foreclosure sale, Berg is liable for any deficiency. However, if she merely purchased the property "subject to" the mortgage when she paid the $28,000, Berg would have no liability for any deficiency on foreclosure.

18. Alternative to the Mortgage: Deed of Trust

Deed of trust or trust deed

An instrument by which title to real property is conveyed to a trustee to hold as security for the holder of notes

A document known as a **deed of trust** or **trust deed** may be used as a substitute for a mortgage for the purpose of securing debts. Through this document, title to the real property is conveyed to a third party, who is the trustee, to be held for the benefit of the creditor. Whereas a mortgage involves two parties—the mortgagor (debtor) and the mortgagee (creditor)—the deed of trust involves three parties—the trustor (debtor), the trustee, and the beneficiary (creditor).

The trustee's title does not affect the debtor's use of the land as long as the loan is being repaid. If the debt is fully paid at the time required by the contract, the trustee reconveys the title to the debtor and releases the lien thereon. If there is a default, the trustee sells the property and applies the proceeds to the payment of the secured loan. Under this power of sale, the trustee transfers to the new purchaser all right, title, and interest that the debtor had at the time the deed trust was executed.

Deeds of trust are used instead of mortgages when the note is likely to be negotiated and when numerous notes are secured by the same property. The nature of the deed of trust is that the note secured by it can be freely transferred, separate and apart from the deed of trust. When the debtor pays the note, he or she surrenders it to the trustee under the trust deed, and the latter makes it a matter of record that the obligation has been satisfied.

19. Foreclosure

The issue of how the mortgage really protects the mortgagee is based on the assumption that the mortgagor has defaulted or will default prior to the loan being paid fully. If no default occurs, the mortgagee will recover that which it wants—repayment of the loan. However, upon a default, the real property described in the mortgage can be used as leverage to encourage the mortgagor to pay what is owed. If payment still is not forthcoming, **foreclosure** becomes the valuable, albeit last, means of collection.

Foreclosure

The forced sale of property, which is used as security, to satisfy the obligation of a defaulting debtor

The usual method of foreclosing a mortgage is a proceeding in a court of equity. If the mortgagor is in default, the court will authorize the sale of all the land at public auction. Following the sale, the purchaser receives a deed to the land. The funds received from the sale are used to pay court costs, the mortgage indebtedness, and inferior liens in the order of their priority. If any surplus remains, it is paid to the former owner of the property.

20. Priority to Proceeds

A mortgage that holds senior priority on a property and that will be paid first in the event of default and foreclosure is known as a *first mortgage.* The amount of money that can be raised through a first mortgage is often less than the borrower needs to complete a purchase. In such cases *junior mortgages*—that is, second, third, and fourth mortgages, which are subordinate to the first mortgage—are sometimes used. Such mortgages carry more risk than first mortgages and usually are issued for shorter periods of time and at higher interest rates.

The priority given to various mortgages on the same real estate normally is determined by which mortgagee is the first to record the mortgage document with the public records. However, order of recording does not always determine priority. One mortgagee whose mortgage is already on record may agree to subordinate its priority to another mortgagee. For example, a mortgagee that holds a security interest on a vacant land probably would agree to let a second mortgagee who has lent funds for a construction project have priority if the construction of an improvement will increase the land's value by more than the amount of the additional mortgage.

Junior mortgages also are commonly used to help in the financing of the sale of an existing home or income properties. For example, a homeowner may be able to get a higher price for his or her house if the purchaser can assume an existing mortgage at an interest rate lower than those currently charged by banks. The required down payment may be larger than the buyer can pay, however; and the seller may be willing to take a second mortgage for part of the purchase price. Furthermore, second mortgages commonly are used for home-improvement loans. A family that wants to add a room or make extensive repairs to its home can usually get the money to do so at a lower rate through a junior mortgage than by taking out a personal installment loan.

A mortgage that is recorded before other interests may not have priority if its recording is defective. The following case involves a first-in-time mortgage that loses its right to priority because of a defective legal description of the land involved.

Foreclosure of an inferior mortgage is made subject to all superior liens. In other words, the foreclosure of a second mortgage does not affect a first mortgage. The buyer at the foreclosure sale takes title, and the first mortgage remains a lien on the property. A foreclosure does cut off the enforceability of all inferior liens. For instance, the foreclosure of a first mortgage eliminates the rights of the second and subsequent mortgages. One right of the holder of a junior interest is examined in the following case.

CASE

Cynthia Young v. Kenneth Embley

SUPREME COURT OF ALASKA

143 P.3d 936 (2006)

This case concerns the disposition of property located at 2910 West 31st Avenue in the Spenard area of Anchorage. Cynthia Young and David Dang lived on and operated the property as a bed and breakfast called "The Alaska Wilderness Plantation." Dang held sole title to the property. Even so, Young held herself out as an "owner" of the property. She also used the name "Cynthia Dang" though she and Dang never married. Young and Dang have a daughter who was five years old in 2004.

On August 30, 2002, Dang executed a deed of trust on the property, using the property to secure a $40,000 loan made by Donald Joyner. Young was apparently unaware of the execution of this deed of trust. Dang subsequently defaulted on the deed of trust and Joyner had a notice of default recorded by Land Title Company of Alaska on November 21, 2002, and posted shortly thereafter. A foreclosure sale was scheduled for February 25, 2003. Joyner then sold the note and assigned his interest to appellee Kenneth Embley.

On March 12 and April 1, 2003, Young asked Embley not to hold the foreclosure sale, asserting that she had not been given the statutorily required notice. Young also asserted at that time that she had the right to cure Dang's default on the Embley/Joyner deed of trust. The sale was postponed until April 25, 2003. On that date Embley provided Young with a "Cure Figure Worksheet" and an "Offset Bid Figure Worksheet" enumerating the amounts for which Dang was in default. Young did not tender a cure at the time but objected to the foreclosure sale, though she did not seek to enjoin it. Embley purchased the property at the foreclosure sale for $165,201.04.

Young filed suit against Embley and Land Title in May 2003, seeking damages, a declaration voiding the foreclosure sale, and seeking a declaration that she was entitled to cure Dang's default.

While this appeal concerns the extent of a statutory right, we must begin with a brief detour into the history of mortgages. The mortgage was created by the early English court as a transfer of title from the mortgagor to the mortgagee, generally as security for a loan by the mortgagee to the mortgagor. Once the mortgagor repaid the loan proceeds, title to the property would return to him. If, however, the mortgagor failed to pay the mortgage by the due date, called the law day, he would forfeit all interest in the property. This deadline applied without exception, "even if the mortgagor could not find the mortgagee to pay him," or if "the borrower was robbed on his way to Law Day," and thus often resulted in injustice.

In response to these injustices, the Court of Chancery created the remedy of equitable redemption. Equitable redemption "allowed the borrower to come into court after default, and if he told a convincing story, he was allowed to force a reconveyance of the land." When mortgagors began to take advantage of this remedy, sometimes redeeming the property years after law day, the Court created the remedy of foreclosure "to end the period of equitable redemption so that the new owner could be sure that his title was secure and the previous owner could not redeem the land." Thus, a mortgage is said to carry with it an equity of redemption, "the right, until the foreclosure sale, to reimburse the mortgagee and cure the default." However, the mortagee's remedy of foreclosure limits this (mortagor's) remedy of equitable.

Alaska has partly codified the mortgagor's right of redemption: "The judgment debtor or a successor in interest may redeem the property before confirmation of sale on paying the amount of the purchase money, with interest" and any taxes due. Alaska has also enacted a procedure for redemption by the debtor within a year after confirmation of the foreclosure sale.

Further, we treat deeds of trust as identical to mortgages in almost all respects. This right of redemption for junior interest holders exists to protect their interests since a foreclosure cuts off all interests junior to the one foreclosed. Therefore, just as the junior lienholder has the right to redeem a mortgage, we determine that the junior lienholder also possesses the right to cure default on a deed of trust before the foreclosure sale.

The right of cure extends not only to the obligor on a deed of trust but also to holders of junior interests. Young presented enough evidence of an equitable lien on the property to withstand summary judgment. Accordingly, we REVERSE the judgment of the superior court on these matters.

■ *Reversed.*

CASE CONCEPTS REVIEW

1. Why should Young have a right to cure?
2. In this case, is there a proper balance between foreclosure and the right to cure? Why?

CHAPTER SUMMARY

REAL PROPERTY OWNERSHIP INTERESTS

Bundle of Rights

1. The rights described by the bundle of rights theory may be held by one person, or they may be divided among two or more people.
2. How these rights are divided determines the ownership interests that may be created. Regardless of how many interests are created, the entire bundle of rights must be accountable with respect to each piece of land.

Ownership Interests

1. A fee simple absolute represents the most complete bundle of rights possible.
2. A life estate must be followed by a future interest known as a remainder or reversion.

Easements and Licenses

1. An easement is the right of one person to use the land owned by another person. Usually an easement is thought of as a permanent restriction that passes from one owner to the next.
2. A license is a less permanent grant of use of land as compared with an easement.

Types of Multiple-Party Owners

1. Property may be owned by two or more persons as tenants in common, as joint tenants, or as tenants by the entireties.
2. Tenancy in common is the most common form of multiple ownership. It is presumed by the courts unless the co-owners clearly state otherwise.
3. Joint tenancy is a form of multiple ownership that is characterized by the right of survivorship.

Restrictions on Ownership Interests

1. Through its zoning regulations, a local community can restrict the use of land. Typically the zones include open space, residential, commercial, and industrial uses.
2. Restrictive covenants are commonly seen in subdivisions. Their purpose is to enhance the value of neighboring property by having all owners agree not to use their land in destructive or unpleasing ways.

ACQUIRING TITLE TO REAL PROPERTY

Introduction

1. The primary methods to obtain title to real property are (1) by original entry, called title by occupancy; (2) by a deed from the owner; and (3) by benefit of the period of the statue of limitations, called adverse possession.

Original Entry
1. Title is obtained from the government by a patent. It seldom occurs today.

Transfer by Deed
1. A deed is the legal document that represents title to land.
2. A valid deed must identify the parties involved, contain language transferring an ownership interest, be signed by the grantor, and be delivered to the grantee in the grantor's lifetime.

Types of Deeds
1. The common types are the warranty deed, the grant deed, the bargain and sale deed, and the quitclaim deed.

Title by Adverse Possession
1. The essential elements of adverse possession are satisfied if a person possesses land openly, notoriously, hostilely, and continuously for the statutory period under a claim of right.

LEASES OF REAL PROPERTY

In General
1. A lease is a contract where one person transfers the right to possess real property to another.

Classification of Leases
1. A tenancy for a stated period lasts for the time specified in the lease.
2. A tenancy from period to period may run from month to month or year to year. Such a lease often is created when a tenant holds over, with the landlord's consent, after a lease for a stated period.
3. A tenancy at will has no definite duration and can be terminated by either the landlord or tenant after proper notice is given.
4. A tenancy at sufferance occurs when a tenant holds over without the landlord's consent.

Tenants: Rights and Duties
1. In general, the tenant has the right to exclusive possession free from interference.
2. Tenant has the right to have the premises suitable for the intended use.
3. Unless the lease provides otherwise, the tenant is free to assign or sublease his or her interest to a third party. (Note that leases frequently require the landlord's approval prior to such transfer.)
4. The tenant's basic duty is to pay the rent and to return possession at the end of the lease term.

Landlords: Rights and Duties
1. The landlord has the right to expect the tenants to pay rent.
2. The landlord has legal remedies, such as distress for rent and eviction powers, to encourage the tenant's performance.
3. The landlord generally has the duty to maintain the premises. Although tenants may be liable for damages they caused, the landlord cannot unreasonably retain a security deposit.

Warranty of Habitability
1. Many courts have held that landlords implicitly warrant that residential property is habitable.
2. A breach of this warranty allows the tenant to reduce rental payments or to terminate the lease without further liability.

REAL PROPERTY AS SECURITY

Introduction
1. A *mortgage* is the document wherein a borrower grants to a lender a security interest in the borrower's real estate.
2. A mortgagor is the borrower who grants the security interest in real estate to the lender.
3. A mortgagee is the lender who receives a security interest in real estate.

4. The borrower in a mortgage transaction usually signs a promissory note, which is evidence of the borrower's personal obligation to repay.
5. The borrower also signs a mortgage, which is the document that grants the lender a security interest in described real estate.

Rights and Duties of the Parties

1. Payment of the mortgage debt terminates the mortgage.
2. Upon its termination, the mortgage must be marked satisfied in the public records.
3. Generally, the mortgagor retains possession of the real estate during the mortgage's term.
4. However, the mortgagor cannot use the real estate in a way that devalues it.
5. The mortgagee has the right to protect the value of the real estate by paying off other claimants and charging the amount paid to the mortgagor.

Alternative to the Mortgage: Deed of Trust

1. In many states, a three-party document, known as a deed of trust, is often used instead of a mortgage.
2. A deed, which is absolute on its face, may be treated as a mortgage if the parties' intent was for the deed to serve as security and not as an outright conveyance.

Foreclosure

1. A foreclosure is a forced sale of real property when it is used as security to satisfy the obligation of a defaulting debtor.

Priority to Proceeds

1. Mortgagees have priority to the proceeds of a sale in the same order in which their mortgages were recorded.
2. An exception to this order occurs if a mortgagee with a superior priority subordinates its claim to an inferior mortgagee.
3. Upon the foreclosure of a superior mortgage, all inferior mortgages are extinguished. However, the buyer at a foreclosure sale of an inferior mortgage takes subject to all superior mortgages.

REVIEW QUESTIONS AND PROBLEMS

1. Match each term in Column A with the appropriate statement in Column B.

A	B
(1) Joint tenancy	(a) Right granted to use real property
(2) Fee simple absolute	(b) Lease does not have fixed duration
(3) Quitclaim deed	(c) Right of government to take real property
(4) Mortgage	(d) Written document used to pass title
(5) Easement	(e) The most complete interest a person may have in land
(6) Tenancy at will	(f) Forced sale
(7) Encumbrance	(g) Passes all right to property of the grantor
(8) Deed	(h) Involves the right of survivorship
(9) Foreclosure	(i) Conveyance of an interest in real property for the purpose of creating a security for a debt.
(10) Eminent domain	(j) A burden on the title of land

2. Paula wishes to grant to her daughter, Sandy, the ability to live in a home Paula purchased years ago as an investment. However, Paula only wants the transfer to Sandy for Paula's life. Upon Paula's death, she wishes the home to go to her other daughter, Becky. Does the law provide a mechanism to transfer such an interest to Sandy? Discuss.
3. Red and Orange own a parcel of land as joint tenants. Red dies. Who owns Red's interest?
4. Jack and Joan are about to purchase their dream home. The home is located on a small hill with a view of the lake. One parcel, owned by Ray, exists between the lot owned by Jack and Joan and the lake. Jack and Joan are planning to build their home on the east side of their lot. Ray has not developed his lot. What advice do you have for Jack and Joan to secure a view of the lake? Discuss
5. Baker is about to sell forty-acres of land suitable for housing development to McKenzie. What type of deed will provide McKenzie with the least amount of protection? The greatest amount of protection? Why?
6. Milky Way Dairies purchased a 200-acre farm for raising cattle in 2006. An industrial park to the west, Mountain Estates, had in 1980 fenced off a 2-acre stretch of land that was properly within the 200-acre farm now owned by Milky Way Dairies. Mountain Estates has installed a well within the 2-acre parcel, constructed a road to the well, and built a storage shed next to the well. The well was used every day, the road once a day, and the shed one a week. Mountain Estates used the 2-acre parcel under the impression it was their property. Who do you believe owns the 2-acre parcel? Why?
7. Describe the basic types of leases based on duration. Provide an example of each type.
8. Cheri rents an apartment from Lake Properties. Cheri wishes to transfer, for six months, the right to live in the apartment to Charlie. Would you suggest a sublease or an assignment? Why?
9. Jamu rents an office in a twenty-suite complex on Main Street. Jamu is very upset that the condition of the office, the interior hallways, and the outside area is not very attractive … and perhaps even dangerous. Jamu complains to Rahma, the manager of the complex. Rahma does nothing. What advice would you provide Jamu? Would your advice be different if Jamu were renting a home instead of an office? Why?
10. Joy of Mountains Company owns land and a factory worth $450,000. Bank of New Orleans holds a $300,000 first mortgage on the parcel (land and factory). Charles Major holds a second mortgage ($200,000). Joy of Mountains discontinues payments to Bank of New Orleans and Major, who now foreclose. If the foreclosure sale brings $450,000, how much will Bank of New Orleans receive? How much will Major receive? Why?

Forms of Business Organizations | 11

CHAPTER OUTLINE

CHAPTER PREVIEW

Business organizations may operate under a variety of legal forms. The common ones are sole proprietorships, partnerships, limited partnerships, and corporations. There are also some specialized organizations, such as the subchapter S corporation and the professional service association, that are authorized by statute. These allow doctors, lawyers, dentists, and other professional persons to have many of the advantages of a corporation.

The form of organization is usually decided when the business is getting started. However, factors involved in the operation of a business may indicate that a change of organization is desirable. Therefore, the material contained in this chapter is important at the beginning and throughout a business's existence.

Businesses that are closely held (owned by relatively few parties) must decide which form, among many, is most appropriate. In contrast, businesses with a large number of owners are usually incorporated because the corporate organization provides the easiest method of transferring ownership interests without interfering with business operations.

The means of creation, the issues of control, the liability of the owners, and the taxation of income are among the most important factors to consider when choosing an organizational form.

BUSINESS MANAGEMENT DECISION

You and a business associate decide to make a movie concerning the role of women during World War II. This project will require $4,500,000 in capital, an amount that must be raised. You and your associate desire to maintain editorial and production control over this project.

What type of business organization should be created to achieve your objectives?

INTRODUCTION

1. Proprietorships

The simplest organizational form by which a business might operate is a *sole proprietorship*. The fundamental characteristic of this organization is that there is only one owner. Although the number of employees and the dollar volume of business may be quite large, a proprietorship has only one owner.

The creation of this organization simply involves a businessperson beginning business by obtaining the necessary local business licenses. The sole proprietor has complete control over the business decisions, but that person is 100% liable for the debts of the proprietorship. The proprietorship is not a taxable organization. Therefore, the sole proprietor incurs on a personal level the benefits and burdens of the organization's profits or losses.

Most business organizations involve two or more parties as co-owners. The proprietorship organization cannot be considered appropriate when there is more than one owner. Hence, for most businesses the organizations discussed throughout this chapter are viewed as more important when choosing an organizational form.

Partnership
A business organization consisting of two or more owners who agree to carry on a business and to share profits and losses

2. General Partnerships

A **partnership** is an association of two or more persons to carry on, as co-owners, a business for profit. It is the result of an agreement among the owners. While this agreement may be orally

A proprietorship is the simplest organizational form of business.

stated, it is always best to have it formally drafted into a document, frequently called *articles of partnership*. To facilitate the existence of co-owners, partnerships developed logically in the law. The common law of partnerships has been codified in the Uniform Partnership Act and in the Revised Uniform Partnership Act.

ADVANTAGES A partnership form of organization has many advantages:

1. Since it is a matter of contract between individuals, to which the state is not a party, it is easily formed.
2. Costs of formation are minimal.
3. It is not a taxable entity.
4. Each owner, as a general rule, has an equal voice in management.
5. It may operate in more than one state without being required to comply with many legal formalities.
6. Partnerships are generally subject to less regulations and less governmental supervision than corporations.

The fact that a partnership is not a taxable entity does not mean that partnership income is tax-free. A partnership files an information return allocating its income among the partners, and each partner reports for income tax purposes the portion allocated to him or her. The 2009 income tax rate for an individual who is a head of household begins at 10% of applicable income less than $11,950. The rate then rises to 15%, 25%, 28%, 33%, and then to 35%, depending on the amount of income. The application is depicted in Table 11-1.

Note, too, that losses within a partnership are passed through to the partners. Pauline is an employee of ABC Company and earns a salary, but she also has an interest in XY, a general partnership. If the partnership has a loss in one year, Pauline is able to use the loss against the income she made as an employee. The opportunity to use partnership losses, especially those that occur early the partnership's life, is a reason why some individuals and other types of entities enter into partnership agreements.

DISADVANTAGES Several aspects of partnerships may be considered disadvantageous. First, only a limited number of people may own such a business. Second, a partnership is dissolved every time a new member is added as a new partner or an old member ceases to be a partner either by withdrawal or by death. Although dissolution of partnerships is the subject of Chapter 28, it should be

TABLE 11-1 ■ Head of Household 2009 Federal Tax Rates

HEADS OF HOUSEHOLDS—2009

Taxable income:			Tax:	
Over	But not over	Tax	+%	On amount over
$ 0	$ 11,950	$ 0.00	10	$ 0
11,950	45,500	1,195.00	15	11,950
45,500	117,450	6,227.50	25	45,500
117,450	190,200	24,215.00	28	117,450
190,200	372,950	44,585.00	33	190,200
372,950	......	104,892.50	35	372,950

observed here that the perpetual existence of a corporation is often perceived as a distinct advantage for corporations, compared with partnerships that can more easily be dissolved.

Third, the liability of a partner is *unlimited*, contrasted with the limited liability of a shareholder. The unlimited liability of a partner is applicable both to contract and tort claims. Fourth, since a partner is taxed on his or her share of the profits of a partnership, whether distributed or not, a partner may be required to pay income tax on money that is not received. This burden is an important consideration in a new business that is reinvesting its profits for expansion. A partner in such a business would have to have an independent means of paying the taxes on such income.

The nature of a general partnership can be gleaned, in part, by examining the following case where the parties apparently created a "super partnership."

CASE

David G. Byker v. Thomas J. Mannes

SUPREME COURT OF MICHIGAN

641 N.W.2d 210 (2002)

This case arises out of an alleged partnership between plaintiff David Byker and defendant Tom Mannes. In 1985, plaintiff was doing accounting work for defendant. The two individuals talked about going into business together because they had complementary business skills—defendant could locate certain properties because of his real estate background and plaintiff could raise money for their property purchases. Indeed, the parties stipulated the following:

> *The Plaintiff ... and Defendant ... agreed to engage in an ongoing business enterprise, to furnish capital, labor and/or skill to such enterprise, to raise investment funds and to share equally in the profits, losses and expenses of such enterprise .... In order to facilitate investment of limited partners, Byker and Mannes created separate entities wherein they were general partners or shareholders for the purposes of operating each separate entity.*

Over a period of several years, the parties pursued various business enterprises. They have stipulated that the following business entities were created during this time:

a. A 100% general partner interest in M & B Properties Limited Partnership, a Michigan limited partnership, which limited partnership owns a 50% partnership interest in Hall Street Partners, a Michigan partnership.

b. A 100% general partner interest in M & B Properties Limited Partnership-II, a Michigan limited partnership, which limited partnership owns a 50% partnership interest in Breton Commercial Properties, a Michigan partnership.

c. A 66-2/3% of the issued and outstanding shares of the common stock of JTD Properties, Inc., a Michigan corporation, which is the general partner of JTD Properties Limited Partnership I, a Michigan limited partnership, and which is also the general partner of M & B Properties Limited Partnership-

III, a Michigan limited partnership. The interest was later increased to 100% when John Noel left the partnership.

d. A 66-2/3% of the issued and outstanding shares of the common stock of Pier 1000 Ltd., a Michigan corporation. The interest was later increased to 100% when John Noel left the partnership.

e. A 66-2/3% general partner interest in BMW Properties, a Michigan partnership.

With regard to these entities, the parties shared equally in the commissions, financing fees, and termination costs. The parties also personally guaranteed loans from several financial institutions.

The business relationship between the parties began to deteriorate after the creation of Pier 1000 Ltd., which was created to own and manage a marina. Shortly after the creation of Pier 1000 Ltd., the marina encountered serious financial difficulties. To address these difficulties, the parties placed their profits from M & B Limited Partnership II into Pier 1000 Ltd. and borrowed money from several financial institutions. Eventually, defendant refused to make any additional monetary contributions. Plaintiff, however, continued to make loan payments and incurred accounting fees on behalf of Pier 1000 Ltd., as well as on behalf of other business entities. Plaintiff also entered into several individual loans for the benefit of Pier 1000 Ltd. These business transactions were performed without defendant's knowledge. The marina was eventually returned to its previous owners in exchange for their assumption of plaintiff's and defendant's business obligations. At this point, the business ventures between plaintiff and defendant ceased.

Plaintiff then approached defendant with regard to equalizing payments as a result of the losses incurred from the various entities. Defendant testified that this was the first time that he had received notice from plaintiff concerning any outstanding payments, and that he was "absolutely dumfounded" by plaintiff's request for money.

After unsuccessfully seeking reimbursement from defendant, plaintiff filed suit for the recovery of the money on the basis that the parties had entered into a partnership. Specifically, plaintiff asserted that the obligations between him and defendant were not limited to their formal business relationships established by the individual partnerships and corporate entities, but that there was a "general" partnership underlying all their business affairs. In response, defendant asserted that he merely invested in separate business ventures with plaintiff and that there were no other understandings between them.

In 1917, the Michigan Legislature drafted the Michigan Uniform Partnership Act (UPA). In this act, a partnership was defined as "an association of two [2] or more persons to carry on as co-owners a business for profit . . . ." Over the years, the definition has remained essentially constant. At present, partnership is defined as "an association of 2 or more persons, which may consist of husband and wife, to carry on as co-owners a business for profit . . . ." This definition, as well as its predecessors, was modeled after the definition of partnership set forth in the 1914 UPA. In 1914, the UPA had defined a partnership as "an association of two or more persons to carry on as owners a business for profit." (Uniform Partnership Act of 1914, § 6.) In construing § 6, courts had "universally" determined that a partnership was formed by "the association of persons whose intent is to carry on as co-owners a business for profit, regardless of their subjective intention to be 'partners.'"

In 1994, however, the UPA definition of partnership was amended by the National Conference of Commissioners. The amended definition stated, "the association of two or more persons to carry on as co-owners a business for profit forms a partnership, *whether or not the persons intend to form a partnership.*" Although the commissioners were apparently satisfied with the existing judicial construction of the definition of partnership, the commissioners added the new language "whether or not the persons intend to form a partnership" in order to "codify the universal judicial construction of UPA Section 6(1) that a partnership is created by the association of persons whose intent is to carry on as co-owners a business for profit, regardless of their subjective intention to be 'partners.'" The commissioners emphasized that "no substantive change in the law" was intended by the amendment of § 6. To date, Michigan has not adopted the amended definition of partnership. However, we believe that our prior case law has properly examined the requirements of a legal partnership by focusing on whether the parties intentionally acted as co-owners of a business for profit, and not on whether they consciously intended to create the legal relationship of "partnership."

With the language of the statute as our focal point, we conclude that the intent to create a partnership is not required if the acts and conduct of the parties otherwise evidence that the parties carried on as co-owners of a business for profit. Thus, we believe that, to the extent that the Court of Appeals regarded the absence of subjective intent to create a partnership as dispositive regarding whether the parties carried on as co-owners a business for profit, it incorrectly interpreted the statutory (and the common) law of partnership in Michigan.

In ascertaining the existence of a partnership, the proper focus is on whether the parties intended to, and in fact did, "carry on as co-owners a business for profit" and not on whether the parties subjectively intended to form a partnership.

Accordingly, we remand this matter to the Court of Appeals for analysis under the proper test for determining the existence of a partnership under the Michigan Uniform Partnership Act.

■ *Reversed and remanded.*

CASE CONCEPTS REVIEW

1. Under the rationale of the court, do partners have to intend to form a partnership?
2. What practical consequences flow from this decision?

3. Joint Venture

A *joint venture,* or *joint adventure, occurs when two or more persons combine their efforts in a* particular business enterprise and agree to share the profits or losses jointly or in proportion to their contributions. It is distinguished from a partnership in that the joint venture is a less formal association and contemplates a single transaction or a limited activity, whereas a partnership contemplates the operation of a general business. A joint venture is a specific venture without the formation of a partnership or corporation.

A partnership in most states is a legal entity, apart from the partners; a joint venture is not. A joint venture cannot sue or be sued. A suit must be by, on behalf of, or against the joint ventures individually. Joint ventures file a partnership tax return and have many of the other legal aspects of partnerships.

4. Limited Partnership

Limited partnership

This is a partnership in which one or more individuals are general partners and one or more individuals are limited partners. The limited partners contribute assets to the partnership without taking part in the conduct of the business. They are liable for the debts of the partnership only to the extent of their contributions.

A **limited partnership**, like other partnerships, comes into existence by virtue of an agreement. Like a corporation, it is authorized by statute; and the liability of one or more, but not all, of the partners is limited to the amount of capital contributed at the time of the creation of the partnership. For liability purposes, a limited partnership is, in effect, a hybrid between the partnership and the corporation.

One or more *general partners* manage the business and are personally liable for its debts. One or more *limited partners* also contribute capital and share in profits and losses, but they take no part in running the business and incur no liability with respect to partnership obligations beyond their contribution to capital. The control of a limited partnership is in the hands of the general partners. Historically, limited partners who participated in the management of the partnership lost their limited liability benefits. Today, a limited partner who mistakenly or intentionally engages in managerial activities becomes liable as a general partner only if the third party seeking to recover against the partnership had knowledge of the expanded participation.While a limited partner has no right to participate in management, certain activities are within the rights of the limited partners, and the exercise of those rights does not result in that partner becoming personally liable as a general partner. For example, any change to a partnership agreement must be approved by the limited partners.

A limited partner's position is analogous to that of a corporate shareholder, whose role is that of an investor with limited liability. It is from the limited liability of the limited partners that the organization gets its name. Limited partnerships are governed in most states by the Revised Uniform Limited Partnership Act provisions. The purpose of a limited partnership enabling statute is to encourage trade by permitting persons to invest in a business and reap their share of the profits without becoming liable for debts or risking more than the capital contributed. This reduced risk is based on the investor's not being a general partner or participating actively in the conduct of the business.

Corporation

A collection of individuals created by statute as a legal person, vested with powers and capacity to contract, own, control, convey property, and transact business within the limits of the powers granted

The limited partnership as a tax shelter is of special value in many new businesses, especially real estate ventures such as shopping centers and apartment complexes. It gives the investor limited liability and the operators control of the venture. It allows the use of depreciation to provide a tax loss that can be deducted by the limited partner to the extent of risk in the investment. Offsetting this tax loss, usually, is a positive cash flow that gives a limited partner an income at the same time that he or she has a loss for tax purposes.

THE BUSINESS CORPORATION

5. Advantages and Disadvantages

A **corporation** is a legal entity that comes into existence when the state issues the corporate charter. Because a corporation is considered to be a legal person separate from its owners, it usually has a perpetual existence. In other words, the owners/shareholders are free to transfer their interests/shares of stocks without affecting the continuity of the business organization. Furthermore, due to the separateness of owners and organization, shareholders' liability generally is limited to their investment.

The following case illustrates a situation where a shareholder might be held personally liable.

CASE

Browning-Ferris Industries of Illinois, Inc. v. Richard Ter Maat

UNITED STATES COURT OF APPEALS FOR THE SEVENTH CIRCUIT

195 F.3d 953 (1999)

POSNER, CHIEF JUDGE

Browning-Ferris and several other companies have brought a suit for contribution under the Comprehensive Environmental Response, Compensation, and Liability Act (CERCLA—the Superfund statute). The suit is against Richard Ter Maat and two corporations of which he is (or was—one of the corporations has been sold) the president and principal shareholder; they are M.I.G. Investments, Inc. and AAA Disposal Systems, Inc.

Back in 1971 the owners of a landfill had leased it to a predecessor of Browning-Ferris, which operated it until the fall of 1975. Between then and 1988, M.I.G. and AAA operated it. In June of that year, after AAA was sold and Ter Maat moved to Florida, M.I.G. abandoned the landfill without covering it properly. For tax reasons, M.I.G. had been operated with very little capital, and it lacked funds for a proper cover. Two years after the abandonment, the EPA placed the site on the National Priorities List, the list of the toxic waste sites that the Superfund statute requires be cleaned up and shortly afterward Browning-Ferris and the other plaintiffs, which shared responsibility for some of the pollution at the site, agreed to clean it up.

Section 113(f)(1) of the Superfund law authorizes any person who incurs costs in cleaning up a toxic-waste site to "seek contribution from any other person who is liable or potentially liable under section 9607(a) of this title ... . In resolving contribution claims, the court may allocate response costs among liable parties using such equitable factors as the court determines are appropriate." Section 107(a)(1), a part of the statutory provision to which section 113(f)(1) refers, includes in the set of potentially liable persons anyone who owned or operated a landfill when a hazardous substance was deposited in it, and this set is conceded to include both M.I.G. and AAA.

The district judge held, however, that Ter Maat was not himself a potentially liable person because he had done nothing that would subject him to liability on a "piercing the corporate veil" theory for the actions of the two corporations.

Browning-Ferris and the other companies that have incurred clean-up costs at the site of the former landfill have appealed. All of them join in arguing that the corporate veil should be pierced to make Richard Ter Maat liable for the conduct of both "his" corporations, AAA and M.I.G.

The first issue is whether an individual can shield himself from liability for operating a hazardous-waste facility merely by being an officer or shareholder of a corporation that also operates the facility. The answer is no. The principle of limited liability shields a shareholder from liability for the debts (including debts arising from tortious conduct) of the corporation in which he owns shares (with the exception discussed later for "veil piercing" situations), but not for his personal debts, including debts arising from torts that he commits himself. In other words, the status of being a shareholder does not immunize a person for liability for his, as distinct from the corporation's, acts. There is no liability shield at all for an officer. If he commits an act that is outside the scope of his official duties, his employer may not be liable; but he is liable whether or not the act was within that scope. Which is not to say, however, that the officer is automatically liable for the acts of the corporation; there is no doctrine of "superiors' liability" comparable to the doctrine of respondeat superior, that is, the employer's strict liability for torts of the employee committed within the scope of his employment.

So if Ter Maat operated the landfill personally, rather than merely directing the business of the corporations of which he was the president and which either formally or jointly with him (as well as with each other) operated it, he is personally liable. The line between a personal act and an act that is purely an act of the corporation (or of some other employee) and so not imputed to the president or to other corporate officers is sometimes a fine one; however, often it is clear on which side of the line a particular act falls. If a negligently operated train hits an individual, the railroad is liable in tort to him, but the president of the railroad is not; or rather, not usually, had the president been driving the train when it hit the plaintiff or had been sitting beside the driver and ordered him to exceed the speed limit, the president would be jointly liable with the railroad. If Ter Maat did not merely direct the general operations of M.I.G. and AAA or specific operations unrelated to pollution, but supervised the day-to-day operations of the landfill. For example, if Ter Maat negotiated waste-dumping contracts with the owners of the wastes or directed where the wastes were to be dumped or designed or directed measures for preventing toxic substances in the wastes from leeching into the ground and thence into the groundwater—then he would be deemed the operator, jointly with his companies, of the site itself.

Unfortunately, the district court did not consider this possibility although it had been urged to do so by the plaintiffs, and so a remand is necessary to determine Ter Maat's status.

■ *Reversed and remanded.*

CASE CONCEPTS REVIEW

1. When can a shareholder be personally liable for a tort associated with a corporation?
2. Based on the opinion, how can a shareholder who is also closely associated with the corporation (e.g., the only shareholder) not be held liable for torts associated with a corporation?

A **corporation**, as a general rule, is a taxable entity paying a tax on its net profits. Dividends paid to stockholders are also taxable, giving rise to the frequent observation that corporate income is subject to double taxation. The accuracy of this observation is discussed in Section 10.

The advantages of the corporate form of organization may be summarized as follows:

1. It is the easiest method that will raise substantial capital from a large number of investors.
2. Tax laws have several provisions that are favorable to corporations.
3. Control can be vested in those with a minority of the investment by using techniques such as nonvoting or preferred stock.
4. Ownership may be divided into many separate and unequal shares.
5. Investors have limited liability.
6. The organization can have perpetual existence.
7. Certain laws, such as those relating to usury, are not applicable to corporations.
8. Investors, notwithstanding their status as owners, may also be employees entitled to benefits such as workers' compensation.

Among the frequently cited disadvantages of the corporate form of organization are these:

1. Cost of forming and maintaining the corporate form with its rather formal procedures
2. Expenditures such as license fees and franchise taxes that are assessed against corporations but not against partnerships
3. Double taxation of corporate income and the frequently higher rates
4. The requirement that it must be qualified to do business in all states where it is conducting intrastate business
5. Being subject to more regulations by government at all levels than are other forms

While individuals of whom not one is an attorney may form a corporation, it is usually wise to hire an attorney to not only create the corporation but also advise management and owners during the life of the entity. The role of the lawyer and his or her relationship to a business corporation is colorfully described by Roy A. Redfield in *Factors of Growth in a Law Practice:*

> When the business corporation is born, the lawyer is the midwife who brings it into existence; while it functions he is its philosopher, guide and friend; in trouble he is its champion, and when the end comes and the last sad rites must be performed, the lawyer becomes the undertaker who disincorporates it and makes final report to the Director of Internal Revenue.

6. Taxation of Corporate Income

The fact that taxation is listed as both an advantage and a disadvantage of the corporate form illustrates the importance of the tax factor in choosing this particular form of organization. Corporate tax law provisions change from time to time, depending on the economy and the effect of tax policy on employment, economic growth, and so on. The 2009 corporate (C corporation) income tax rates are included in Table 11-2.

Among the tax laws that favor corporations over partnerships are the following

1. Health insurance premiums are fully deductible and are not subject to the limitations applicable to individuals.
2. Deferred compensation plans may be adopted.

TABLE 11-2 ■ 2009 Federal Corporate Income Tax Rates

Between	and	The tax is
$ 0	$ 50,000	15%
50,000	75,000	$ 7,500 + 25%
75,000	100,000	13,750 + 34%
100,000	335,000	22,250 + 39%
335,000	10,000,000	113,900 + 34%
10,000,000	15,000,000	3,400,000 + 35%
15,000,000	18,333,333	5,150,000 + 38%
18,333,333		35%

3. Retained earnings are taxed at graduated rates that may be lower than the individual tax rates of the shareholders.
4. Income that is needed to be retained in the business is not taxed to persons who do not receive it, as does occur in a partnership.
5. The corporation may provide some life insurance for its employees as a deductible expense.
6. Medical expenses in excess of health insurance coverage may be paid on behalf of employees as a deductible expense.

The corporate form of organization also has some *major tax disadvantages.* First, corporate losses are not available as a deduction to shareholders, whereas partnership losses are immediately deductible on the individual returns of partners. Corporate losses can only be used to offset corporate profits during different taxable years.

Second, a major disadvantage to corporations occurs when a profit is made and the corporation pays a dividend to its shareholders. *The dividend will have been taxed at the corporate level and then taxed again to the shareholder.* The rate of the second tax depends on the personal tax rate of each shareholder receiving the dividend. This is known as the "*double tax*" on corporate income. (The next section explains why the "double tax" may not be as big a disadvantage as it first seems.)

Finally, some states impose a higher income tax on corporate income than on individual income. In addition, many other forms of taxes are imposed on corporations that are not imposed on individuals or on partnerships.

7. Avoidance of Double Taxation

Certain techniques may be used to legally avoid, in part, the double taxation of corporate income. First, reasonable salaries paid to corporate employees may be deducted in computing the taxable income of the business. Thus, in a closely held corporation in which all or most shareholders are officers or employees, this technique can be used to avoid double taxation of much of the corporate income. The Internal Revenue Code disallows a deduction for excessive or unreasonable compensation, and unreasonable payments to shareholder employees are taxable as dividends. Therefore the determination of the reasonableness of corporate salaries is an ever-present tax problem in the closely held corporation that employs shareholders.

Second, the capital structure of a corporation may include both common stock and interest-bearing loans from shareholders. Envision a company that needs $200,000 to begin business. If $200,000 of stock is purchased, there will be no expense to be deducted. Suppose, however, that $100,000 is loaned to the company at 10 percent interest. In this case, $10,000 of interest each year is deductible as an expense of the company and thus subject to only one tax as interest income to the owners. Just as in the case of salaries, the Internal Revenue Code contains a counteracting rule relating to corporations that are undercapitalized. If the corporation is undercapitalized, interest payments will be treated as dividends and disallowed as deductible expenses.

The third technique for avoiding double taxation—or to at least delay it—is simply not to pay dividends and to accumulate the earnings. Here again we have tax provisions designed to counteract the technique. There is a special income tax imposed on "excessive accumulated earnings" in addition to the normal tax rate.

Finally, a special provision in the Internal Revenue Code treats small, closely held business corporations and partnerships similarly for income tax purposes. These corporations are known as subchapter S corporations.

8. Subchapter S Corporations

The limited partnership is a hybrid between a corporation and a partnership in the area of liability. A similar hybrid known as a *tax-option* or subchapter *S corporation* exists in the tax area of the law. Such corporations have the advantages of the corporate form without the double taxation of income.

The tax-option corporation is one that elects to be taxed in a manner similar to that of partnerships—that is, to file an information return allocating income and losses among the shareholders for immediate reporting, regardless of dividend distributions, thus avoiding any tax on the corporation.

Subchapter S corporations cannot have more than thirty-five shareholders, each of whom must sign the election to be taxed in a manner similar to a partnership. There are many technical rules of law involved in subchapter S corporations; but as a rule of thumb, this method of taxation has distinct advantages for a business operating at a loss because the loss is shared and immediately deductible on the returns of shareholders active in the business. It is also advantageous for a business capable of paying out net profits as earned, thereby avoiding the corporate tax. If net profits must be retained in the business, subchapter S tax treatment is somewhat disadvantageous because income tax is paid by the shareholders on earnings not received.

9. Professional Service Associations

Traditionally, professional services—such as those of a doctor, lawyer, or dentist — could be performed only by an individual and could not be performed by a corporation because the relationship of doctor and patient or attorney and client was considered a highly personal one. The impersonal corporate entity could not render the personal services involved.

For many years there were significant tax advantages in corporate profit-sharing and pension plans that were not available to private persons and to partnerships to the same extent. An individual proprietor or partner was limited to a deduction of 15 percent of income or $15,000 under a *Keogh* pension plan provision. Professional persons, therefore, often incorporated or created professional associations to obtain the greater tax advantages of corporate pension and profit-sharing plans. To make this possible, every state enacted statutes authorizing *professional associations.* As legal entities similar to corporations, their payments to qualified pension and profit-sharing plans qualify for deductions equal to those of business corporations.

Doctors and lawyers are a part of professional service associations.

The tax laws have been changed in an attempt to equalize the tax treatment of Keogh plans and corporate pension and profit-sharing plans. While this has generally been achieved, there remain a few advantages to corporate plans. Most professional corporations that were created earlier remain in existence; and new ones are still being formed.

The law authorizing professional corporations does not authorize business corporations to practice a profession such as law or medicine. Professional corporations are special forms of business organizations that must meet strict statutory requirements. In addition, professional persons practicing a profession as a professional corporation do not obtain any limitation on their professional liability to third persons.

In some ways, the total liability of a professional association may be greater than if the profession were practiced as a partnership. For example, a professional association may have liability for discriminating against owner-employees because of age, whereas a partnership would not have liability to a partner because of age discrimination. Several laws that protect shareholder employees do not protect partners.

Today, there are thousands of professional corporations in all states. They can be identified by the letters *S.C.* (Service Corporation), *PC.* (Professional Corporation), *Inc.* (Incorporated), or by the word *company* in the name of the professional firm.

LIMITED LIABILITY COMPANIES

10. Nature of the Limited Liability Company

Traditionally, any business contemplating two or more owners would choose between a general partnership and a corporation. On the one hand, the partnership alternative allowed for all partners to participate, to the extent they desired, in the management of the business. Also, the partnership entity paid no federal income tax; all income was "passed through" to the partners. However, there was a negative associated with this form of conducting business: each partner in a general partnership assumed unlimited personal liability for the debts of the business.

On the other hand, the corporate form provided limited liability for all shareholders but had its own downside: profits from the business were taxed at the corporation level and, again, at the individual owner level, when distributions were made as dividends. Especially for the entrepreneur, neither of these traditional forms of conducting business was ideal.

In a strikingly-unique example of coordination between two government entities respecting the realities of modern business, the United States taxing authority (the Internal Revenue Service) and state legislatures from across the nation fashioned a new form of business that would provide both limited liability for owners *and* the ability for owners to be taxed on the profits from the business only once (similar to the tax treatment afforded partners in a general partnership). This new vehicle of conducting business is called a *limited liability company* (LLC). While LLC came into existence on the legal front in the United States only about thirty years ago, many small business owners are rejecting the general partnership, the limited partnership, and the corporation as the preferred vehicle for conducting business in favor of the LLC.

11. Advantages and Disadvantages

The advantages associated with the LLC form of conducting business are considerable. The LLC shields the owners of the LLC from all company debts, so the owners' contributions to capital are at risk. The only exception occurs if an owner agrees to be personally liable for a LLC obligation. Given the limited liability characteristic, it is common for creditors to request that individual owners personally guarantee an extension of credit. For income tax purposes, the LLC is now treated almost exactly as a general partnership: the income to the LLC is not subject to taxation, under the "pass through" concept.

The LLC is easier to form and operate than either a general corporation or Subchapter S corporation. Also, it has the additional benefit of acting as a conduit for all income to the entity, so that there is only one taxable incidence. Further, the LLC provides a mechanism for losses to flow directly to the owners, which can be a beneficial tax situation for owners. In a general corporation, all losses rest with the corporation and are not passed through to the owners.

There are two significant drawbacks to the LLC form. The law of general partnership and the law associated with the corporate form are quite developed. Every jurisdiction has numerous court decisions that provide guidance in the many difficult areas associated with both of these forms. However, because the LLC is such a new form of business, even though it is very popular, there are a very small number of court decisions dealing with the LLC choice of entity. Hence, it may be difficult to ascertain with any degree of certainty how a court will decide a case involving the formation, operation, and dissolution of an LLC.

Also, as with a general partnership, the LLC is based on the premise that those managing the entity will work well together. The following case reveals one method of ending a LLC.

Baskin Robins is an example of an LLC corporation

CASE

Peter A. Rapoza, M.D. v. Jonathan H. Talamo, M.D. et al.

SUPERIOR COURT OF MASSACHUSETTS, AT SUFFOLK

2006 Mass. Super. LEXIS 531 (2006)

Dr. Rapoza and the defendant Jonathan H. Talamo, M.D. ("Dr. Talamo") until at least November 2005, practiced together since 1995. They both are skilled ophthalmologists.

The joint practice was facilitated through three entities: Cornea Consultants, LLP ("Cornea"), of which Dr. Rapoza and Dr. Talamo are the sole partners; Laser Eye Specialists of Boston, LLC ("LESB"), of which Dr. Rapoza and Dr. Talamo are the sole members and managers; and Laser Eye Consultants of Boston, LLC ("LECB"), of which Dr. Rapoza and Dr. Talamo are also the sole members and managers.

Cornea is said to be a Massachusetts limited liability partnership; and LESB and LECB are each said to be Massachusetts limited liability companies. Cornea has operated on the basis of an oral agreement, there being no written partnership agreement; and LESB and LECB also have operated on the bases of oral agreements, there being no written operating agreements. Dr. Rapoza and Dr. Talamo ran their practices, and the three entities, from three offices, one in Boston, one in Waltham and one in Beverly.

At the time of a hearing on a request for preliminary injunctive relief, Dr. Rapoza contended that "[g]iven various serious disagreements that arose with respect to the operation of the [three entities], the parties agreed in November of 2005 to dissolve the [three entities] and have begun to wind-down."

Dr. Talamo filed an affidavit in which he contended that there was no agreement between him and Dr. Rapoza with respect to dissolution of the entities. Having said that, however, the Court observed that Dr. Talamo attached three exhibits (A, B and C) to his affidavit, the substance with which he neither challenges nor disagrees. His affidavit has neither been withdrawn nor corrected since its filing.

Exhibit A was an April 6, 2006, letter from Dr. Rapoza and Dr. Talamo—signed "Pete" and "Jonathan"—to their employees announcing that "we will be ending our business relationship, with the intent of continuing our individual practices of medicine in a seamless fashion." The letter went on to explain that "Dr. Talamo plans to maintain the Waltham office and establish a Boston office by July 1 [and] Dr. Rapoza plans to maintain the Beverly office and establish offices in Waltham and Boston as of July 1." This letter then added the following parenthetical: "(We will be closing our Boston office effective June 30, 2006 upon the expiration of our lease.)."

Exhibits B and C were undated form letters sent to Dr. Rapoza's and Dr. Talamo's patients and referring physicians in June 2006. Each letter advised the recipient that "[e]ffective July 1, 2006, we will be closing our Boston office ..." The letters went on to explain that Dr. Rapoza, and others, "will remain in our current Beverly office and will open a new Boston office at 50 Stamford Street and a new Waltham office at 40 Second Avenue" and that Dr. Talamo, and others, "will remain in our current Waltham office as well as open a new in-town office at 5 Cambridge Center, Kendall Square, Cambridge."

In its memorandum and order on the request for injunctive relief this Court observed that "[i]t appears that, for the most part, the patient end of the split up of the practices is being addressed, as it should be, by the two professionals involved. It is the economic and business end of the separation that has spurred some tasteless haggling, resulting in the request for injunctive relief."

The Court then urged the parties to make a conceited effort to reach an amicable accommodation of their remaining differences. Evidently they attempted to do so, but have failed in the effort.

Dr. Rapoza now presses his motion for a liquidating trustee.

In order to form a limited liability company, one or more authorized persons must execute a certificate of organization and file it with the Secretary of State. Included in that certificate must be whether the limited liability company is to have a specific date of dissolution and what that date is. Such a company is formed at the time of filing of the initial certificate of organization with the Secretary of State.

As with the Cornea limited liability partnership, this Court has not been shown any certificate of organization for LESB or LECB. It will act here, however, as if those limited liability companies were properly formed. At the same time, this Court will presume that neither certificate contains any specific date of dissolution. As noted above, Dr. Rapoza and Dr. Talamo are the sole two managers and the sole two members of LESB and LECB.

The dissolution of a limited liability company occurs upon the first of these events to occur: "(1) the time specified in the operating agreement; (2) the happening of an event as specified in the operating agreement; (3) the written consent of all members; ... or (5) the entry of a decree of judicial dissolution under section forty-four."

There being no written operating agreement for either LESB or LECB and no written consent of all members thereof, the Court must consider the question of a decree of judicial dissolution.

Under the law, "On application by or for a member or manager the superior court department of the trial court may decree dissolution of a limited liability company whenever it is not reasonably practicable to carry on its business in conformity with the certificate of organization or the operating agreement." Dr. Rapoza has made such an application.

For the reasons stated above with regard to Cornea, the partnership, this Court is of the belief, and so rules, that dissolution of the two limited liability companies—LESB and LECB—is warranted as they are not able to function in the manner intended and there is a clear and total deadlock between the sole two managers and members thereof. It clearly is not reasonably practicable to carry on the business in conformity with the presumed certificates of organization and there are no operating agreements.

Consequently, the two limited liability companies shall be decreed dissolved, and a single Liquidating Trustee shall be appointed to carry out the winding up of the affairs thereof.

■ *Motion granted.*

CASE CONCEPTS REVIEW

1. Why is it advisable to insert into a limited liability company operating agreement a provision detailing under what conditions should the entity be dissolved?
2. Should the petition of one owner be sufficient to end a limited liability company? Why?

MAKING THE DECISION

12. The Process

Earlier in this chapter, we listed advantages of incorporating a business with substantial capital. If the business is to be owned and operated by relatively few people, their choice of form of organization will be made with those factors in mind—especially taxation, liability, control, and legal capacity. *Legal capacity* is the power of the business, in its own name, to sue or be sued, own and dispose of property, and enter into contracts.

In evaluating the impact of taxation, an accountant or attorney will look at the projected profits or losses of the business, the ability to distribute earnings, and the tax brackets of the owners. An estimate of the tax burden under the various forms of organization will be made. The results will be considered along with other factors in making the decision on the form of business organization.

The generalization that partners have unlimited liability and shareholders limited liability must be qualified in the case of a closely held business. A small, closely held corporation with limited assets and capital will find it difficult to obtain credit on the strength of its own credit standing alone; and as a practical matter, the shareholders will usually be required to add their individual liability as security for the debts. If Tom, Dick, and Jane seek a loan for their corporation, they usually will be required to guarantee repayment of the loan. This is not to say that closely held corporations do not have some degree of limited liability. The investors in those types of businesses are protected with limited liability for contract-like obligations imposed as a matter of law (such as taxes) and for debts resulting from torts committed by company employees while engaged in company business. If the tax aspects dictate that a partnership and limited liability are desired by some investors, the limited partnership will be considered.

Issues of liability are not restricted to the investors in the business or to financial liability. Corporation law has developed several instances in which the directors and officers of a corporation will have liability to shareholders or the corporation for acts or omissions by those directors or officers in their official capacity. These matters are discussed more fully in Chapter 30.

The significance of the law relating to control will be apparent in the discussions on formation and operation of general partnerships (Chapter 28), corporations (Chapters 29 & 30), limited partnerships and limited liability companies (Chapter 31). The desire of one or more individuals to control the business is often a major factor in selecting the form.

CHAPTER SUMMARY

INTRODUCTION

Proprietorship

1. A sole proprietorship is the simplest form of a business organization.
2. This form is applicable if there is only one owner of the business.
3. The sole proprietor is in full control and is liable for all the debts of the proprietorship.
4. The proprietorship is not a taxable entity. All profits or losses flow to the proprietor personality.

General Partnerships

1. The partnership is easily formed by agreement, and the costs of formation are minimal.
2. The partnership is not a taxable entity, and losses are immediately deductible.
3. Income is taxed to a partner whether received or not.
4. As a general rule, each partner has an equal voice in management.

5. The partnership can operate in any state and is subject to less government regulation.
6. A partnership may involve only a limited number of people and is easily dissolved.
7. Partners have unlimited liability.

Joint Ventures

1. A joint venture is like a partnership, but for a single transaction.
2. A joint venture is not a legal entity but is treated as a partnership for tax purposes.

Limited Partnership

1. A limited partnership has at least one general partner with limited liability.
2. It is not a taxable entity, and any losses are immediately deductible.
3. The general partners manage the business.

LIMITED LIABILITY COMPANY

Nature of the Limited Liability Company

1. The Internal Revenue Service treats limited liability companies as general partnerships for income tax purposes.

Advantages and Disadvantages

1. The owners of a limited liability company do not assume personal responsibility for the debts of the firm.
2. Income to the limited liability company is "passed through" to the owners.
3. Because the limited liability company is a comparatively recent entry into the business world in the United States, many aspects of the law associated with the limited liability company has yet to be determined.

THE BUSINESS CORPORATION

Advantages & Disadvantages

1. Investors have limited liability, and the business may have perpetual existence.
2. This is a method by which even hundreds of thousands of persons can own a business together with varying percentages of ownership.
3. Several provisions in the tax law favor corporations.
4. As a separate entity, there are many laws covering only corporations.
5. There are significant costs in forming and maintaining a corporation.
6. Corporate income is taxed to the corporation, and dividends are taxed to the shareholder.

Taxation of Corporate Income

1. The Internal Revenue Code provides certain benefits to corporations.

Avoidance of Double Taxation

1. There are several techniques for avoiding double taxation of corporate income, such as the payment of salaries and expenses on behalf of the owners of the corporation.

Subchapter S Corporations

1. The subchapter S corporation is a corporation taxed in the same manner as a partnership.

Professional Service Associations

1. The professional service association gives some of the tax advantages of a corporation.

MAKING THE DECISION

The Process

1. Those responsible for deciding the form of organization must weigh the relative importance of a number of factors.

2. Among the most important factors used to help determine the best form of organization for a business are taxation, liability, and control.

REVIEW QUESTIONS AND PROBLEMS

1. Match each term in Column A with the appropriate statement in Column B.

A	B
(1) Partnership	(a) A business owned by one person who is personally liable for all losses
(2) Proprietorship	(b) An artificial being created by a state
(3) Limited partnership	(c) Two or more persons combine their efforts for a single transaction
(4) Corporation	(d) Created when shareholders elect to be treated as partners for tax purposes
(5) Legal capacity	(e) Created by an agreement between two or more persons who agree to share profits and losses
(6) Buy-and-sell agreement	(f) Provides for compensation to a deceased or withdrawing owner of a business in return for that owner's interest
(7) Subchapter S corporation	(g) The ability of an organization to sue or to own property
(8) Joint venture	(h) Exists when some partners are treated like shareholders for liability purposes
(9) Limited liability company	(i) Tax doctrine that allows income to be taxed at the owner level, not the organization level.
(10) "Pass through"	(j) Owners receive limited liability and tax treatment as if they were a partnership without filing as a corporation.

2. Jan and Dean desire to form a corporation. Both purchase a book on how to form a corporation, but do not seek the advice of an attorney. Jan and Dean forget to form a corporation and conduct business for three months before they realize they never formed the corporation. What form of business were they during that three months? Why?
3. Peter and Mary form a partnership. Does the partnership pay taxes on income to the organization? If not, who pays income taxes on the partnership's income?
4. A general partner agreed to provide a limited partner with a unilateral refund of his partnership contribution—if the limited partner became dissatisfied with the conduct of the business. The other partners did not consent to the modification of the partnership agreement. Is the agreement enforceable? Why or why not?

5. Lane and Louis were limited partners in a real estate venture. After the business was in financial difficulty, these limited partners had two meetings with the general partners to discuss the problems of the venture. In addition, Lane visited the construction site and "obnoxiously" complained about the work that was being conducted. Do these actions constitute taking part in the control of the business so that the limited partners become liable as general partners? Explain.
6. Paul, John, George, and Ringo properly form a corporation. Paul and Ringo are very wealthy individuals who simply purchase stock. John and George also purchase stock in the corporation; but, in addition, they work for the business as president and vice-president. Does the corporation pay income tax? Will the four shareholders have to pay income tax? Might John and George have an additional income tax burden? Why?
7. Same as number 6, but the corporation is formed as a subchapter S corporation. Would your answers to the questions in 6 change? Why?
8. What advantages and disadvantages are associated with the limited liability form?
9. Toby and Josh create a limited liability company. The two-person company provides consulting services for political candidates. In a fit of anger, Toby defames (commits the tort of defamation) a person running for a position currently held by an individual who is a client of the firm. Is Josh liable? If so, to what extent?
10. John Thompson and Richard Allenby wish to enter the camping equipment manufacturing business. If the following facts exist, which type of business organization would be most advantageous?

    a. Thompson is an expert in the field of camping gear production and sales but has no funds. Allenby knows nothing about such production but is willing to contribute all necessary capital.
    b. Camping gear production requires large amounts of capital, much more than Thompson and Allenby can raise personally or together; however, they wish to control the business.
    c. Some phases of production and sale are rather dangerous, and a relatively large number of tort judgments may be anticipated.
    d. Sales will be nationwide.
    e. Thompson and Allenby are both sixty-five years old. No profits are expected for at least five years, and interruption of the business before that time would make it a total loss.
    f. Several other persons wish to put funds into the business but are unwilling to assume personal liability.
    g. The anticipated earnings over cost, at least for the first few years, will be approximately $70,000. Thompson and Allenby wish to draw salaries of $25,000 each; they also want a hospitalization and retirement plan, all to be paid from these earnings.
    h. A loss is expected for the first three years, owing to the initial capital outlay and the difficulty in entering the market.

Legal Aspects of International Business | 12

CHAPTER OUTLINE

CHAPTER PREVIEW

The laws regulating international business transactions have a broad impact. As markets become increasingly globalized, businesses of all sizes become international. The transfer of goods, services, and human resources across national boundaries is no longer the exclusive domain of large multinational enterprises and transnational corporations. International business law can affect any business entity with a variety of relationships that transcend national boundaries.

For purposes of legal regulation, an *international business entity* (IBE) can be defined as any business entity with relationships that transcend national boundaries. The business entity could be a sole proprietorship, a partnership, or a corporation. A sole proprietor will need to get an export license to export certain types of goods in the same way that a large corporation would. A partnership should be aware of the restrictions of the Foreign Corrupt Practices Act—even if this partnership does not meet the Department of Commerce definition of a multinational enterprise. There is a legal significance in even the simplest relationship that transcends national boundaries. Merely providing product information to a customer in another country has legal consequences.

Regulation of an IBE takes place at several levels: home country regulation, host country regulation, regional regulation, and international regulation. *Home country regulation* refers to the laws of the country where the IBE has its principal place of business or is incorporated. For purposes of this chapter, we will assume that the IBE has its principal place of business in the United States or was incorporated in one of the states of the United States. In this case, home country control includes state and federal regulation of the IBE. Host *country regulation* refers to the legal system and laws of the foreign jurisdiction. For our purposes, this would refer to the laws of any country other than the United States. *Regional regulation* refers to the laws of groups of nations that have banded together for a particular purpose. The rules governing the European Union are of particular importance. Finally, *international regulation* of IBEs includes public international law, such as the various codes of conduct for multinational enterprises, as well as private international law, including the Convention on International Sale of Goods.

BUSINESS MANAGEMENT DECISION

Your company, located in California, manufactures fabric that changes color when exposed to heat. You have received an order for this fabric from a clothing manufacturer in a small Asian country, and you believe this will provide a lucrative market for your product.

What type of organization would you use to conduct this international business transaction? What are some of the clauses you would need in a contract covering this transaction?

INTERNATIONAL BUSINESS TRANSACTIONS

1. Comparative Legal Systems and International Law

Comparative law is the study of different legal systems. The United States and Great Britain, along with Israel, Nigeria, and India, have common-law legal systems. This refers to the source of law—where the law is found and how it is developed. The other major legal systems are referred to as civil law. These legal systems are based on codes, such as the Napoleonic codes or Roman codes. France, Germany, Brazil, Indonesia, and Egypt follow a civil law model.

Some of the major differences between a common-law system and a civil-law system include the use of precedents, or previous court decisions, and the purpose of judicial proceedings. In civil-law jurisdictions, the use of previous court decisions is very limited. Previous court decisions are not extensively reported, nor are they used to control the outcome of a similar case.

Judicial proceedings are also seen as having different purposes. A common-law trial could be considered a search for justice, while a civil-law trial is a search for the truth. Judges in a civil-law trial take an active role in questioning the witnesses, and the process is not adversarial.

International law

The body of rules, regulations, treaties, and conventions that govern the relationship between nations

International law refers to the body of rules and regulations, usually in the form of treaties and conventions, regulating relationships between nations. International law is sometimes referred to as "the law of war and peace." There are, however, areas of international law that have a direct impact on IBE activities. Furthermore, this impact appears to be increasing.

International law is a law of consent. International law is only binding on those who agree to be bound, and the entities that lay down the law are the entities that are governed by it. Many would argue that international law has no power because there is no mechanism for enforcement, such as a police force or an international army. In this sense, however, international law can be compared with domestic contract law. Contract law is also the law of consent in that a person is not bound by contract law unless he or she agrees to be bound. If one party to the contract breaches the contract, the remedy is usually monetary damages, not the possibility that the police will knock on the door with an arrest warrant for breaching the contract.

International law, however, rarely speaks clearly. It is not effective in areas where one nation is required to impair its vital interest. In other areas, such as setting standards for weights and measures, setting international standards for telecommunications, and regulating international aviation, as well as other matters dealing with health and safety, international treaties and international law have proved to be effective.

Private international law refers to the process of unification of law among nations, as well as the formation of substantive rules that affect private parties. Although treaties on private international law matters are entered into between nations, the impact is felt by individuals. For example, work is being done to develop an international will as well as a treaty to deal with the issues of custody of minor children.

2. Conflict-of-Laws Principles and International Litigation

If a dispute arises during an international business transaction, there may be some confusion as to which country's laws will apply in settling the dispute. Just as the laws may vary from state to state in the United States, the laws of different countries and legal systems may be in conflict. The body of law known as conflict-of-laws or choice-of-laws helps answer the question of which country's law will apply to the dispute.

As discussed in Section 4, the parties to a contract can specify in the contract that the law of a particular country will apply to a dispute arising from the contract. This is known as a choice-of-law clause. As a practical matter, however, the court of a particular country is best able to apply its own law to a case brought before it. If there is no choice-of-law clause in a contract, then the court will apply its own country's conflict-of-laws principles in deciding which law will apply. This can be a complicated process.

If a lawsuit is brought in a foreign country court, the judgment will be enforceable in that country. However, it is not always clear whether a foreign country judgment can be enforced in another country. Judgments of U.S. courts are generally not enforceable in other countries unless certain conditions are met. In the United States, foreign country judgments will generally be enforced unless there are strong public policy reasons against their enforcement. Further, the doctrine of sovereign immunity may exempt, for example, foreign nations from the jurisdiction of U.S. courts. In the following case the doctrine of sovereign immunity is examined within the context of the Foreign Sovereign Immunities Act of 1976, an act passed by Congress which embraces the notion of sovereign immunity but also establishes exceptions to the doctrine.

3. Methods of Conducting International Business

International business relationships take many forms. A business does not have to be a certain size or have several offices. Any one of the following methods can be used to facilitate the movement of information, goods, services, capital, or people across national boundaries.

INFORMATION/LIAISON OFFICE An information or liaison office is the simplest involvement in international business. This involves setting up an office in a foreign country for the sole pur-

CASE

Af-Cap Inc. v. Chevron Overseas (Congo) Limited, The Republic of Congo, et al.

UNITED STATES COURT OF APPEALS FOR THE NINTH CIRCUIT (2007)

475 F.3d 1080

RAWLINSON, JUDGE.

This case involves a garnishment action against the Congo's property in execution of a judgment for a defaulted $6.5 million loan made to the Congo by Af-Cap's predecessor, Equator Bank.

On December 18, 1984, pursuant to a loan agreement, Equator Bank loaned $6.5 million to the Congo for the construction of a highway. The Congo consented to "execution against any property whatsoever (irrespective of its use or intended use)," based on any action arising out of the 1984 Loan Agreement. The Congo also agreed to waive its "[sovereign] immunity from suit, execution, attachment ... or other legal process." In 1985, the Congo defaulted on the loan. Af-Cap, Equator Bank's successor in interest, possessed a judgment of a English court against Congo that Af-Cap had converted into a United States Bank in the state of New York.

Af-Cap now seeks to file liens against certain assets of the Congo, including prepayments, taxes, and other obligations to the Congo currently held by ChevronTexaco, among others. The district court dissolved and vacated garnishments and liens filed against the Congo, ChevronTexaco, subsidiaries of Chevron (both domestic and foreign).

Under the Foreign Sovereign Immunity Act (FSIA), "property in the United States of a foreign state shall be immune from attachment and execution." The FSIA provides, however, an exception if the "property in the United States of a foreign state is used for a commercial activity in the United States."

We adopt the test to determine whether property was "used for a commercial activity in the United States" as that term is used in the FSIA. We conclude that property is "used for a commercial activity in the United States" when the property in question is put into action, put into service, availed or employed *for* commercial activity—not *in connection* with a commercial activity or *in relation* to a commercial activity.

Af-Cap argues that all the obligations at issue were used for a commercial activity in the United States because the Congo pleaded the obligations as security for the loan agreement. However, that loan agreement was for the financing and construction of a highway in the Congo. None of the obligations associated with ChevronTexaco used for a commercial purpose were even in existence in 1984 when the loan agreement agreed upon.

The obligations identified by Af-Cap are not property of the Congo "used for commercial activity in the United States" under the FSIA and, therefore, are not subject to execution or collection under the FSIA. The judgments of the district court are affirmed.

■ *Affirmed.*

CASE CONCEPTS REVIEW

1. Why was the creditor unsuccessful in obtaining relief against the Congo?
2. Could the doctrine of sovereign immunity be abused? Was it in this case? Why or why not?

pose of conveying information or answering questions. An information/liaison office does not provide any services or sell any goods. The sole purpose of the office is to distribute pamphlets, brochures, and timetables or to report any questions or concerns that a customer might have. For example, airline companies set up these types of offices in countries where they have no landing rights and conduct no business. Manufacturers also find these types of offices useful in monitoring the market for their products.

The legal significance of an information/liaison office is that the office does not, as a general rule, constitute a "presence" in the foreign country. The foreign country has no jurisdiction over the IBE using such an office. To be sued in the foreign country, another basis of jurisdiction must be found. Host country regulations as to the rental of office space and employment of persons in that office will apply.

IMPORT/EXPORT In the most basic import or export operation, only the goods or the product crosses national boundaries. While orders can be taken and goods shipped without any person leaving the United States, these transactions are the subject of import regulations and quotas, customs duties, and export controls, as well as the laws governing product liability in both the home and the host country. In most circumstances, a simple import/export transaction does not constitute a presence as a basis of jurisdiction in the foreign country.

Goods that are shipped out of the country are subject to import regulations and export controls.

DISTRIBUTORSHIPS, SALES REPRESENTATIVES, AND SALES AGENTS A more complex export transaction involves the use of individuals or sales organizations to sell the product in the foreign country. The three basic types of sales relationships are distributorships, sales representatives, and sale agents. Although these entities may have different designations in different countries, the basic description and legal consequences are fairly consistent.

A distributorship relationship involves the sale of goods to an individual or sales organization that, in turn, resells the product in the foreign country. The relationship between the IBE and the distributor is governed by a contract typically known as a *distributorship agreement.* Ownership of the goods or title passes to the distributor, so this relationship does not constitute a presence as a basis of jurisdiction in the foreign country. Some host countries have laws that make it difficult to terminate distributorships without just cause.

A sales representative is a person who takes orders for the product and then transmits these orders to the manufacturer. A sales representative does not take title to the goods, cannot bind the manufacturer contractually, and is not an employee of the manufacturer. The sales representative receives a commission based on the value of the goods shipped.

A sales agent is an employee of the IBE in the foreign country. A sales agent can bind the IBE contractually and be sued in the foreign country on behalf of the IBE. A sales agent does constitute a presence in the foreign country, and the foreign country can exercise jurisdiction over the IBE through the sales agent. Some countries, such as Saudi Arabia, require that all business transactions involving foreign companies be done through an appointed sales agent.

Licensing A licensing relationship is based on a contract allowing a foreign individual, firm, or country to use the IBE's intellectual properties. The contract gives permission to use the IBE's patents, trademarks, and/or copyrights in that foreign country. In some instances, the contract allows the foreign firm to manufacture and sell the IBE's goods in that country for a royalty payment. Royalties are payments made in exchange for permission to use someone's intellectual properties. A licensing arrangement allows the IBE to enter a foreign market without a substantial investment and without creating a presence and a basis for jurisdiction. Some host countries, however, do not have the same protection for patents, copyrights, or trademarks as in the United States, and some countries even restrict the amount that can be paid to the IBE as royalties.

Direct Investment There are four types of direct investment: portfolio, branch, subsidiary, and joint venture.

1. *Portfolio investment:* Portfolio investment is simply the investment of money in the securities of a foreign country. Even though perhaps not technically considered an international business transaction, both home country and host country laws apply to the transaction. Of particular importance are the laws of the host country governing the investment of capital by people who are not nationals of that country. These regulations may include restricting the ability to repatriate profits or transfer currency into and out of that country.
2. *Branch:* A branch is an entity in the host country whose identity is not separate from the IBE. A branch is merely an arm of the IBE, completely owned by the IBE, and does not take on any special form in the foreign country. The branch may perform the same services, manufacture similar products, or sell the same goods as the company in the home country. By merely being an extension of the IBE, the branch functions as the IBE's presence in the foreign country. The branch can bind the IBE contractually in that if the branch enters into a contract, the contract is deemed to be with the IBE. Similarly, a lawsuit brought against the branch is deemed to be a lawsuit against the IBE.
3. *Subsidiary:* A subsidiary is an entity whose identity is separate from the IBE. A subsidiary takes the form of doing business specified by the laws of the foreign country. Usually, a subsidiary is a corporation incorporated under the laws of the foreign country. Typically, the IBE will own at least 51 percent of the subsidiary's stock. Under some regulations, however, a foreign entity will be deemed to be a subsidiary if the IBE has effective control over the subsidiary. *Effective control* may mean actually controlling the day-to-day operation of the subsidiary or providing the materials needed in manufacturing the product. A subsidiary may constitute the presence of the IBE in the foreign jurisdiction. A contract entered into by the subsidiary may not, however, be binding on the IBE.
4. *Joint venture:* A joint venture is usually considered to be a partnership between two corporations or a partnership between a corporation and a governmental entity. A joint venture is normally set up for a specific purpose or function and for a limited period of time. Some countries, such as China, strongly urge IBEs to make their investment in the form of a joint venture. Because a joint venture is an entity separate and apart from either of the participants, it may not constitute a presence of the IBE in all circumstances, nor will the IBE be bound by a contract entered into by the joint venture.

4. International Contracts

International business transactions often involve a variety of contracts. As previously mentioned, these might include contracts for the leasing of office space, employment contracts, licensing contracts, distributorship contracts, sales representative contracts, or agency contracts. Furthermore, contracts may be for the purchase of raw materials as well as the sale of finished products. Contracts may also include joint venture contracts or contracts for the purchase or sale of goods between a branch, a subsidiary, and the parent company.

As a general rule, parties to an international business contract must deal with many of the same considerations that they would with a domestic contract. However, because the parties are dealing with different legal systems, customs, and languages, additional terms must be negotiated. Some contract clauses to be considered in an international contract include (1) choice of language, (2) terms of payment, (3) force majeure, (4) government approval, (5) arbitration clause, (6) choice of forum, and (7) choice of law.

A *choice of language* clause will designate the official language that will be used for the contract document itself. It will also designate the language of interpretation if a dispute arises concerning the contract. If the contract is written in more than one language, problems can arise as to the meaning of the terms used. A contract might be translated into another language for convenience, but the meaning of the terms may also change with the translation. For convenience, the official language of the contract and the language of interpretation are usually the same.

A *term of payment clause* is not uncommon in any contract. In an international contract, however, this clause is important to designate the currency to be used in payment as well as the location of payment. It is possible to limit the risk of currency fluctuations through the purchase of futures contracts, but this can only be effective if the currency payment is designated. The location of payment is also important in that some currencies are not permitted to be repatriated. This means that some types of currencies cannot leave the particular foreign country. If payment is to be made in U.S. dollars, payable in the foreign country, the IBE must be careful to ensure that the dollars can be taken out of the country. Similarly, if payment is to be made in the local currency, the IBE must ensure that the local currency can be taken back to the home country.

A *force majeure clause* is often a part of international business contracts. The term *force majeure* refers to a superior power. Typically, this type of clause excuses nonperformance under specified circumstances. A force majeure clause may designate natural disasters such as floods, storms, earthquakes, or "acts of God" as an excuse for nonperformance. This type of clause may also designate political unrest—including war, riots, police action, or strikes—to excuse nonperformance. A force majeure clause may even include such occurrences as runaway inflation, dramatic currency devaluations, or stock market collapse as an excuse for nonperformance. In a force majeure clause, however, it is important to establish a standard such as the length of time or severity of the occurrence. It is also important to include a provision for recourse in the case of partial performance.

An international contract involves governmental regulation at several levels. As a result, it is important to include a *government approval clause.* Such a clause would specify which party is responsible for getting the necessary licenses, permits, or government permission for the transaction.

Arbitration clauses are becoming more familiar in domestic contracts, but they are also regularly used in international contracts. A mandatory arbitration clause specifies that arbitration is required as an attempt to resolve a contractual dispute before the filing of any lawsuit. A binding arbitration clause specifies that the parties will be bound to follow any arbitration decision. An arbitration clause could also specify which arbitration rules would apply and where the arbitration would take place. There are several bodies that deal with international arbitration. The American Arbitration Association has rules and facilities for international arbitration, as does the International Chamber of Commerce. The International Center for the Settlement of Investment Disputes has arbitration rules and facilities for certain kinds of arbitration, as does the United Nations Commission on International Trade Law, UNCITRAL.

Parties to an international contract have some flexibility in designating where a lawsuit will be brought in the case of a contract dispute. This is known as a *choice of forum clause.* The parties may choose a country for convenience, for familiarity with its legal process, or for the efficiency of its legal system. If the choice of forum has a rational relationship to the contract or to the contracting parties, these clauses are generally enforceable.

The parties to an international contract can also designate that a particular country's laws will apply to any dispute arising out of the contract. This is known as a *choice of law clause.* The choice of forum and choice of law clauses do not have to designate the same country. A contract can specify that any dispute arising out of the contract will be tried in the United States, but the law of another country will apply. In the United States, the laws of foreign countries are considered issues of fact, and evidence is introduced as to the law of that particular country. As a practical matter, however, courts are usually better equipped to apply the law of their own country to a contract dispute.

In negotiating these various contract clauses, the IBE must be sensitive to the laws and customs of the foreign country. As with all contracts, it is the relationship and not the document that is important. Many international contracts are simple documents consisting of only a few pages. While a contract does not have to include any of the foregoing provisions, an IBE must be aware of the issues raised in these types of clauses.

5. The Multinational Enterprise

Large IBEs with production capabilities in more than one country are often called *multinational corporations* or *multinational enterprises.* The United Nations limits the use of the term multinational corporation to those with a parent corporation that has more than one national identity. It refers to other corporations with international production capabilities as *transnational corporations.* These business entities have been the center of controversy and frequently face the criticism that they are international villains and exploiters.

Multinational enterprises face criticism in three areas. They are perceived as (1) having excessive market control, (2) having excessive political control, and (3) having a worldwide profit-maximizing point of view.

The perception that multinational enterprises exercise market control is really a restatement of the reasons why multinationals set up subsidiaries in foreign markets. Multinationals seek to take advantage of existing markets, whether for raw materials, labor, capital, or finished products. If, however, the multinational seeks to take full advantage of the markets it finds in the host country jurisdiction, then it may be faced with accusations of exploiting the foreign market.

The second area of criticism of multinationals is the political power they exercise. Much of this criticism stems from U.S. activity in Latin America during the 1970s and from disclosures linking U.S. covert actions with business organizations. It is also the case that governments of some less developed countries encourage multinational investment by offering corporate incentives. This may create a dependency between the government and the multinational to ensure that the business venture is successful and that the multinational remains in the country.

The third area of criticism is the worldwide profit-maximizing point of view of large multinationals. The common perception is that the multinational makes decisions based on a global perspective rather than on a country-by-country basis. An operation may be closed down in one country even if it is beneficial to the country if it does not fit into the multinational's overall goals. As a result, multinationals have gained a reputation for being more concerned with global profit than with local needs and benefits.

Multinational enterprises consider this criticism unfair. Multinationals provide employment and training, goods, and services to the host population and may assume investment risks that might not otherwise be undertaken. Furthermore, host countries do exercise control of multinationals in a variety of ways. The following regulations of international business do not always make it easy for them to operate.

REGULATING INTERNATIONAL BUSINESS

6. Introduction

An IBE is affected by laws and regulations from many sources, not just the laws of its home country or state. Of course, an IBE must comply with the laws of the city, county, state, and nation that is considered its home or principal place of doing business. An IBE must also comply with the laws and regulations of the host country or jurisdiction. If the host country is a member of a regional organizational structure, such as the European Community, these laws must also be observed. Finally, international regulations such as treaties or conventions may have an impact on the IBE and its business enterprise. The remainder of this chapter examines these different sources or levels of regulations.

7. International Controls

International agreements, treaties, and conventions are becoming increasingly important to IBEs. The scope of international conventions is no longer limited to relationships between governments.

Of particular interest to IBEs is the Convention on International Sale of Goods, to which the U.S. Senate gave its advice and consent in 1987. The Convention on International Sale of Goods is a type of international uniform commercial code. In fact, the Uniform Commercial Code was used as a model for the Convention. The Convention applies to sales transactions between two parties in different countries if each country has ratified the transaction. The Convention does not apply to the sale of goods to consumers. The two parties to the transaction can agree that the Convention will not apply to the transaction; but if they do not reach such an agreement, the Convention is applicable. The Convention deals with issues of contract formation as well as to obligations and remedies available to parties to the transaction.

A major international institution that affects international business is the World Trade Organization, formed in 1995 and charged with the responsibility of enforcing the General Agreement on Tariffs and Trade (GATT). The GATT was set up in 1947 as a means of liberalizing international trade policies. Specifically, the purpose of the GATT is to reduce or eliminate trade barriers, such as tariffs, quantity restrictions, and non-tariff barriers to trade. The process is one of multilateral tariff reduction negotiations. The primary principles of reciprocity and nondiscrimination are carried out through the use of most-favored-nation clauses.

Several other international bodies seek to control the activities of IBEs through the use of codes of conduct. It can be argued that these codes of conduct have no binding effect on the activities of IBEs; however, the negotiation process itself does lead to increased sensitivity of the issues involved on the part of all negotiating parties. The Tripartite Declaration of Principles Concerning Multi-National Enterprises and Social Policies was adopted by the International Labor Organization. This declaration deals with issues of labor relations, such as working conditions, training, and employment. It also deals with issues of social policy. The United Nations General assembly passed a resolution adopting the Restrictive Business Practices Code. The purpose of this code is to protect competition as well as social welfare and consumer interests. The code covers price fixing and refusals to deal, as well as mergers and trademark protection. The United Nations Conference on Trade and Development is working on an international code of conduct for the transfer of technology. One purpose of this code is to set up standards for technology transfer with respect to the interest of developing nations.

The Organization of Economic Cooperation and Development (OECD) has issued Guidelines for International Investment and Multinational Enterprises. The member governments of the OECD have adopted guidelines regarding the disclosure of information by IBEs, competition, employment and industrial relationship, financing, and taxation. These guidelines set standards for IBEs that include refraining from restrictive business activities and respecting the rights of employees to be represented by trade unions; and they, also, provide information regarding the IBE's activities and policies. Finally, the United National Commission on Trans-National Corporations created in 2003 a document entitled "Norms on the Responsibilities of Transnational Corporations and Other Business Enterprises with Regard to Human Rights." This is one of the broadest and most comprehensive codes of conduct dealing with the activities of IBEs. The code contains provisions regarding disclosing information, respecting human rights, and refraining from corrupt practices. It also sets guidelines for ownership and control, taxation, consumer protection, environmental protection, and transfer of technology.

8. Host Country Regulations

Host countries are the foreign countries in which the IBEs are doing business. Host countries have a variety of ways to regulate the conduct of IBEs. The following are types of regulations or controls an IBE may encounter in a host country. While specific regulations vary from country to country, these are the types of regulations that can affect the profitability of an international enterprise.

One of the ways of regulating is conditional entry. An IBE may be allowed to enter the foreign country, but only under certain conditions. These conditions might be that the IBE must do business as a joint venture or that a host country must own 50 percent of the business national or that within a certain number of years the firm will be turned over to the host country. The host country sets the conditions at the beginning.

The second method of regulating an IBE is by control over capital movements. This refers to the type of currency that can be brought into the host country and what currency can be removed. This raises several questions that the IBE must answer. Where is the IBE going to get the funding for the project? Must the capital come from a national or from a specific government-run or government-owned bank? Can the IBE take certain currencies out of the country? Is there repatriation of profits? Can the IBE convert the currency to the host country's dollars? Control over capital movements can have a big impact on the profitability of the enterprise.

A closely related type of regulation is tax legislation. Tax legislation can be very favorable (e.g., tax holidays, tax credits, and favorable tax rates). Tax legislation can start out favorably and then have an adverse impact on the business. For example, in Lebanon if you receive tax credits for five years, then you must continue to do business there for an additional five years. The regulation can be favorable tax terms as well as negative tax terms.

The fourth way of regulating is control through disclosure legislation. Reporting requirements to the host country might include who the IBEs hire, how much money they pay, what their future plans are, or what their secret processes might be. If an IBE has to disclose a certain amount of information, this will have an impact on how the IBE is going to conduct itself in the host country. In the United States, there are reporting requirements to the Securities and Exchange Commission and the Internal Revenue Service.

In the European Union, and in Germany in particular, specific disclosure requirements take the form of mandatory worker representation and participation on boards of directors. This may not appear to be a form of disclosure. However, if there are employees on the board of directors, the employees will know about the decisions of the board of directors. Knowledge of the decisions will affect the types of decisions the board makes.

Another form of control similar to our antitrust laws is merger legislation. This type of legislation may control what businesses the foreign firm can buy, what firms the foreign firm can take over, and whether or not the foreign firm can merge with an existing firm.

One of the major ways that host countries control the activities of international businesses is through nationalization. **Nationalization** is the taking of property by the host country government. There are two types of nationalizations. One type of nationalization is called expropriation. The second type of nationalization is called a confiscation.

Nationalization
The taking of property or control of a private enterprise by the government

Expropriation
Nationalization or taking of property by the government that is recognized as legal

Confiscation
Nationalization or taking of property by the government that is not recognized as legal under international law

Expropriation is defined as a legal taking of property. An unlawful taking is known as a **confiscation**. Who defines legal taking? This is a question of international law and also a question about which the United States and other countries do not agree. A legal taking, according to the U.S. standard, is a taking for a public purpose for which just compensation has been paid. Most countries agree with this. The problem is in defining just compensation.

The U.S. government defines *just compensation* as "prompt, effective and adequate compensation." Other countries apply what is known as the Calvo doctrine, which holds that a foreign firm should not be treated any differently than the nationals of the host country. For example, if the host country determines that no compensation will be paid for any nationalized property, then a U.S. IBE would not be entitled to any compensation.

A U.S. firm is entitled to file a complaint with the State Department if the firm has been nationalized or property has been taken. This is a political process, not a judicial proceeding. If the State Department decides not to pursue the claim, there is no appeal. If the State Department decides to pursue the claim, it will proceed on the firm's behalf. The State Department can freeze assets held in the United States by the nationalizing host country. If any compensation is recovered from the host country, the compensation goes through the Foreign Claims Settlement Commission. The firm must present evidence to the Foreign Claims Settlement Commission, and a determination will be made as to how much the firm is entitled.

The final way of controlling the activities of the international business entity is closely related to nationalization. It is known as *creeping expropriation,* and it occurs when the host country does not nationalize all of the holdings at one time. Instead, the host country makes it so difficult for the firm to operate that the host country may as well have taken it all. The host country can set up controls, laws, and restrictions so the firm must get government approval at every turn. The host country may also restrict where the IBE purchases its supplies, sells its product, or at what price. Creeping expropriation is not recognized under international law. The United States does recognize creeping expropriation and would like to establish some compensation for it, since it is the slow taking over of the assets of a firm.

The aforementioned regulations suggest what host countries can do to control the activities of international business entities. International business entities must be aware of these regulations when undertaking business ventures in foreign countries.

9. Regional Regulation—The European Community

The European Union is an example of regional regulation of IBEs. The European Union originally consisted of three separate communities—the European Coal and Steel Community (1951), the

The European Union unifies the internal markets of more than twenty-five democratic countries of Europe.

European Atomic Energy Community(1957), and the Treaty of Rome (1957)—that were combined in 1967 into the European Communities. The Single European Act was adopted in 1986, and this set the groundwork for achieving a unified internal market. In 1993, the Treaty on European Union (better known as the Maastricht Treaty) achieved this goal. More than twenty-five democratic countries of Europe now comprise the European Union. Under the Maastricht Treaty people, goods, technology, capital, and services can pass freely from one member country to another. Also, many of the members of the European Union have adopted a common currency (the euro). Moreover, the reach of the European Union has stretched beyond mere economic measures. Today, the European Union requires its members to comply with a host of social legislative directives, including workplace harassment and discrimination.

As the following case suggests, laws associated with the European Union are becoming very influential in solving disputes involving individuals living and working within the European Union.

CASE

Johann Gruber v. BayWa AG

COURT OF JUSTICE OF THE EUROPEAN COMMUNITIES

2004 ECJ CELEX LEXIS 626; 2005 ECR I-439 (2004)

OPINION OF MR. ADVOCATE GENERAL JACOBS DELIVERED ON 16 SEPTEMBER 2004

Mr. Gruber is a farmer in Austria, near the German border. His steading comprises a farmhouse, in part of which (stated to be 62% of the floor area) he lives with his family, the remainder being used as a pigsty and for storing fodder and separate outhouses including another pigsty, a room for machinery and a number of fodder silos. BayWa AG has a number of businesses in Germany. At an address in Pocking, not far from the Austrian border, it operates both a building materials centre and a DIY and garden centre. The DIY and garden centre publishes brochures, which are also distributed across the border in Austria.

Mr. Gruber became aware of BayWa through such brochures. Wishing to tile his farmhouse roof, he enquired by telephone about the available range of tiles and current prices, although there was no specific mention of tiles in the advertising material. He introduced himself by name and stated where he lived, but did not mention that he was a farmer. The employee he had spoken to later called him back with an oral offer. Mr. Gruber, however, wished to inspect the tiles, so he went to BayWa's premises.

There, he was handed a written offer. He stated that he was a farmer and wished to tile the roof of his farmhouse. He also mentioned that he had other buildings used principally for farming purposes, but not whether the building to be tiled was used predominantly for farming or private purposes. The following day, Mr. Gruber phoned BayWa from his home in Austria to accept the offer. BayWa faxed a confirmation of the contract to his bank.

On completion of the tiling, Mr. Gruber found significant colour variations in the tiles supplied, despite a warranty by BayWa that the colour would be uniform. He, therefore, brought proceedings against BayWa in the Austrian courts, on the basis of the warranty coupled with a claim for damages, seeking reimbursement of the price of the tiles and of the expense of removing them and retiling the roof, together with a declaration of liability for any future expenses.

Mr. Gruber relied on Article 13 et seq. of the Brussels Convention to found jurisdiction, but BayWa objected.

Brussels Convention concerned contracts requiring consumer protection in cross-border relationships. The operative provision applies to consumer contracts, establishing at the same time for future purposes that only final consumers acting in a private capacity should be given special protection and not those contracting in the course of their business ... . Under the section, a choice of law provision in a contract that would deprive a consumer of the protection afforded by the law of his country of residence is invalid.

The essential question is whether a 'mixed' contract of the kind that Mr. Gruber concluded with BayWa should be regarded as a consumer contract for the purposes of the Convention. There are three fundamental points to be borne in mind here. First, it is indeed the contract which has to be classified, not the customer. There is no personal status of consumer or non-consumer; what counts is the capacity in which the customer was acting in entering into the particular contract. Second, the contract must be classified as a whole and cannot be segmented. There is in fact, in this context, no such thing as a 'mixed contract'; there are only consumer contracts and other contracts. Third, and most importantly, the aim of the provision is to make it easier for a private consumer—who, in the context of a particular contract, is usually in a weaker position than his supplier, both in economic terms and in terms of business and legal experience and of resources—to bring proceedings against that supplier.

In the light of the above considerations, it seems likely that the contract between Mr. Gruber and BayWa cannot be classified as a consumer contract for the purposes of the Convention.

■ *Jurisdiction denied.*

CASE CONCEPTS REVIEW

1. Why do you believe the judge did not find the parties had entered into a consumer contract?
2. Is this a fair result to Mr. Gruber? To BayWa? Why or why not?

Has the formation of the European Union had an impact on U.S. business? The answer is clearly, yes. The laws that the European Union and its member nations have passed to implement the Maastricht Treaty have had a great impact on the nations that trade with members of the European Union. For example, International Business Entities must pay attention to the antitrust rules and regulations that have been enforced as Articles 85 and 86 of the Treaty of Rome. In some circumstances, the antitrust laws of the European Union are more restrictive than those of the United States. The freedom of movement of goods and workers between member states will also affect the way international business is conducted with the European Community, including allowing—with considerable ease—the creation of large European companies that can effectively compete with the largest U.S.corporations.

10. Import Controls

As the value of the dollar fluctuates with respect to foreign currencies, the cost of foreign products imported into the United States changes. As a result, U.S. manufacturers are experiencing increased competition both in the United States and in foreign markets. In some cases, however, the cost of imports is much less than would be justified by the exchange rate. Foreign manufacturers sometimes price their U.S. products to capture a large share of the market. When foreign goods are priced extremely low with the purpose of capturing a large market share, this is known as *dumping.* United States manufacturers are unable to compete against such extremely low-priced imports and, in many cases, are forced to go out of business. The danger exists that once the foreign manufacturer has captured a large enough market share, it will be able to raise the price of these products to an extremely high level, injuring the U.S. consumer. Although some relief from this type of activity can be found in the U.S. antitrust laws, such relief involves an extremely long and expensive process. Title VII of the United States Tariff Act provides some relief for U.S. manufacturers from this type of activity.

The Tariff Act provides for the imposition of *countervailing duties* or *antidumping duties* to counteract the effect of foreign goods being sold at below their fair value. A U.S. manufacturer must file a complaint with the U.S. Department of Commerce's International Trade Administration and with the International Trade Commission. The Department of Commerce makes a determination of whether or not the goods were sold at below fair value. This may mean that the goods are being sold in the United States at below cost of production or at below the price charged in the home market. The International Trade Commission then makes a determination as to whether or not this has resulted in material injury to the U.S. industry involved. If only one or two U.S. manufacturers are being injured by these import practices, relief will not be given. Industry-wide injury must be found.

If the Department of Commerce and the International Trade Commission determine that the goods are sold at an unfairly low price and that industry injury has occurred as a result of foreign government subsidies, they can make a determination to impose countervailing duties. These duties are designed to counteract the government subsidies. As this is an issue between two governments and may involve highly sensitive foreign policy questions, both the procedure and the determination are taken out of the hands of the complaining U.S. manufacturer. If the unfairly low price is not a result of government subsidies, then relief takes the form of antidumping duties. A determination to impose, or not to impose, antidumping duties can be appealed by the complaining party.

11. Export Controls

The U.S. government has a long history of controlling what goods are exported from the United States. It would not be too gross an exaggeration to say that nothing can be sent out of the United States without government permission. In reality, the permission takes the form of an export license. There are two types of export licenses. One is called a *general license,* which the exporter essentially issues to itself. The exporter must use the proper license designation for the type of good to be exported and the country of destination, but there is no special procedure for doing this. The other type of license, known as a *validated license,* is issued by the government and does require a special procedure.

Under the Export Administration Act of 1979, amended in 1984, the President has the power to control the export of goods and commodities for one of the following four reasons: (1) national security, (2) foreign policy, (3) commodities in short supply, and (4) nuclear nonproliferation. Technically, the EAA expired on August 20, 1994, but the president has continued the law by Executive Order.

Under this authority, several administrative agencies restrict the export of certain commodities through the use of validated licenses. Validated licenses are issued based on two criteria: (1) the type of product, and (2) the ultimate destination of the product. Certain types of products cannot be exported because of their high level of technology or their strategic or military purpose. There are some countries with only a few export restrictions, but there are other countries to which virtually nothing can be exported. The countries to which goods are exported are divided into seven categories. The country with the least restrictions is Canada, to which almost anything can be exported. The most restrictive countries include Cuba and North Korea.

One controversial aspect of these export controls is known as *end-user's certification.* In applying for a validated license, the exporter must certify who the ultimate end user of the product will be and the country of destination. If an exporter sells a product to a customer in Canada and the Canadian customer re-exports the product to an unauthorized end user or destination, the U.S. exporter could be charged with violating the Export Administration Act. Although the U.S. exporter may have no further control over the product, the exporter is still responsible for the ultimate destination of the product under this act. Criminal and civil penalties could apply to any violation. Although enforcement of this provision may seem difficult, it is not impossible. A violation may be reported by a disgruntled employee, a competitor, or even by the exporter.

12. Antitrust Laws

The United States has an extensive system of antitrust laws. Of course, these laws apply to an IBE's activities in the United States. They also apply, however, to an IBE's activities in a foreign country. United States antitrust laws can apply to an IBE's foreign activities—even if the foreign country's laws do not prohibit such conduct.

In 1995, the United States Department of Justice issued guidelines for antitrust enforcement for international business activities. Under these guidelines, the Department of Justice indicated that potential violations would be governed by the "rule of reason." This means that the Department of Justice will look at the particular conduct or activity in light of the entire business transaction, including any business justification or the availability of any less restrictive alternatives. Furthermore, the Department will investigate what impact the conduct has in the United States.

The purpose of this type of enforcement of U.S. antitrust laws is to protect two groups: (1) U.S. consumers, and (2) other U.S. exporters. If the conduct of the IBE in the foreign country has an adverse impact on foreign firms that import into the United States, U.S. consumers could be injured. United States consumers benefit from the low cost of imported goods; and if the foreign-conduct causes the foreign manufacturer to raise its prices, U.S. impact could be found. Similarly, other U.S. exporters may be trying to enter the foreign country market. If the actions of one U.S. exporter, the IBE, make it difficult or impossible for another U.S. exporter to enter the market, U.S. impact could be found.

The application of U.S. antitrust laws to activities of IBEs that take place in foreign countries is controversial. The application of U.S. law to activities that take place outside of the United States is known as *extra territoriality.* In enforcing antitrust laws, the United States bases jurisdiction on the citizenship of the IBE, as well as on the adverse impact within U.S. borders.

Affirmative responses to the following questions will result in the United States applying its antitrust laws in situations involving extraterritorial activities:

1. Does the alleged violation affect, or was it intended to affect, the foreign commerce of the United States?
2. Is the activity of the type and magnitude so as to be cognizable as a violation of the antitrust laws?
3. As a matter of international comity and fairness, should the extraterritorial jurisdiction of the United States be asserted to cover the alleged violation?

If any one of these questions is answered in the negative, the antitrust laws will not apply to activities in foreign countries. The following case from the United States Supreme Court examines the application of the Sherman Act to extraterritorial activities.

CASE

F. Hoffmann-La Roche Ltd, et al. v. Empagran S.A. et al.

SUPREME COURT OF THE UNITED STATES

542 U.S. 155 (2004)

JUSTICE BREYER DELIVERED THE OPINION OF THE COURT

The Foreign Trade Antitrust Improvements Act of 1982 (FTAIA) excludes from the Sherman Act's reach much anticompetitive conduct that causes only foreign injury. It does so by setting forth a general rule stating that the Sherman Act "shall not apply to conduct involving trade or commerce … with foreign nations." It then creates exceptions to the general rule, applicable where (roughly speaking) that conduct significantly harms imports, domestic commerce, or American exporters.

We, here, focus upon anticompetitive price-fixing activity that is in significant part foreign, that causes some domestic antitrust injury, and that independently causes separate foreign injury. We ask two questions about the price-fixing conduct and the foreign injury that it causes. First, does that conduct fall within the FTAIA's general rule excluding the Sherman Act's application? That is to say, does the price-fixing activity constitute "conduct involving trade or commerce … with foreign nations"? We conclude that it does.

Second, we ask whether the conduct nonetheless falls within a domestic-injury exception to the general rule, an exception that applies (and makes the Sherman Act nonetheless applicable) where the conduct (1) has a "direct, substantial, and reasonably foreseeable effect" on domestic commerce, and (2) "such effect gives rise to a [Sherman Act] claim." We conclude that the exception does not apply where the plaintiff's claim rests solely on the independent foreign harm.

To clarify: The issue before us concerns (1) significant foreign anticompetitive conduct with (2) an adverse domestic effect and (3) an independent foreign effect giving rise to the claim. In more concrete terms, this case involves vitamin sellers around the world that agreed to fix prices, leading to higher vitamin prices in the United States and independently leading to higher vitamin prices in other countries such as Ecuador. We conclude that, in this scenario, a purchaser in the United States could bring a Sherman Act claim under the FTAIA based on domestic injury, but a purchaser in Ecuador could not bring a Sherman Act claim based on foreign harm.

The FTAIA seeks to make clear to American exporters (and to firms doing business abroad) that the Sherman Act does not prevent them from entering into business arrangements (say, joint-selling arrangements), however anticompetitive, as long as those arrangements adversely affect only foreign markets. It does so by removing from the Sherman Act's reach (1) export activities and (2) other commercial activities taking place abroad, *unless* those activities adversely affect domestic commerce, imports to the United States, or exporting activities of one engaged in such activities within the United States.

This technical language initially lays down a general rule placing *all* non-import activity involving foreign commerce outside the Sherman Act's reach. It then brings such conduct back within the Sherman Act's reach *provided that* the conduct *both* (1) sufficiently affects American commerce, i.e., it has a "direct, substantial, and reasonably foreseeable effect" on American domestic, import, or (certain) export commerce, *and* (2) has an effect of a kind that antitrust law considers harmful, i.e., the "effect" must "giv[e] rise to a [Sherman Act] claim." We ask here how this language applies to price-fixing activity that is in significant part foreign, that has the requisite domestic effect, and that also has independent foreign effects giving rise to the plaintiff's claim.

Because the underlying antitrust action is complex, potentially raising questions not directly at issue here, we reemphasize that we base our decision upon the following: The price-fixing conduct significantly and adversely affects both customers outside the United States and customers within the United States, but the adverse foreign effect is independent of any adverse domestic effect. In these circumstances, we find that the FTAIA exception does not apply (and thus the Sherman Act does not apply).

This Court ordinarily construes ambiguous statutes to avoid unreasonable interference with the sovereign authority of other nations. This rule of statutory construction cautions courts to assume that legislators take account of the legitimate sovereign interests of other nations when they write American laws. It thereby helps the potentially conflicting laws of different nations work together in harmony—a harmony particularly needed in today's highly interdependent commercial world.

No one denies that America's antitrust laws, when applied to foreign conduct, can interfere with a foreign nation's ability independently to regulate its own commercial affairs. Our courts, however, have long held that application of our antitrust laws to foreign anticompetitive conduct is nonetheless reasonable and, hence, consistent with principles of prescriptive comity, insofar as they reflect a legislative effort to redress *domestic* antitrust injury that foreign anticompetitive conduct has caused.

Why is it reasonable to apply those laws to foreign conduct *insofar as that conduct causes independent foreign harm and that foreign harm alone gives rise to the plaintiff's claim?* We can find no good answer to the question.

Where foreign anticompetitive conduct plays a significant role and where foreign injury is independent of domestic effects, Congress might have hoped that America's antitrust laws, so fundamental a component of our own economic system, would commend themselves to other nations as well. If America's antitrust policies could not win their own way in the international marketplace for such ideas, Congress, we must assume, would not have tried to impose them in an act of legal imperialism through legislative fiat.

For these reasons, we conclude that petitioners' reading of the statute's language is correct. That reading furthers the statute's basic purposes, it properly reflects considerations of comity, and it is consistent with Sherman Act history.

For these reasons, the judgment of the Court of Appeals is vacated, and the case is remanded for further proceedings consistent with this opinion.

■ *Reversed and remanded.*

CASE CONCEPTS REVIEW

1. Does the approach taken in the opinion respect the antitrust laws of other nations or impose U.S. antitrust laws on other nations? Why?
2. When will Sherman Act provisions geared to combat antitrust activities beyond the borders of the United States apply?

13. Foreign Corrupt Practices Act

The Foreign Corrupt Practices Act of 1977 is an amendment to the Securities Exchange Act of 1934. There are two main sections of the Foreign Corrupt Practices Act, one dealing with bookkeeping and reporting requirements and the other dealing with conduct. Under the reporting requirements, any issuer of securities, as defined by the Securities Exchange Act of 1934, must keep its books and records in such a way that they accurately reflect the financial transactions of the issuer. Further, the issuer must establish internal accounting systems that will accurately reflect the assets of the issuer. The purpose behind the recording requirements of the Foreign Corrupt Practices Act is to make it more difficult for firms to hide questionable payments to foreign government officials. If such payments must be recorded, they are more likely to be discovered. Even firms that are not engaged in international transaction must comply with this section of the Foreign Corrupt Practices Act. A firm could violate the Foreign Corrupt Practices Act by failing to comply with this section, yet never actually make any questionable payments. This section of the foreign Corrupt Practices Act is enforced by the Securities and Exchange Commission.

The more controversial section of the Foreign Corrupt Practices Act is that addressing specific conduct. The Foreign Corrupt Practices Act prohibits giving anything of value to a foreign government official to influence a discretionary decision. The phrase *anything of value* includes money, gifts, or anything that would be deemed of value in that particular culture. The phrase *to a foreign government official* refers to individuals acting in their official capacity and to decisions they make that fall within their official functions. If, however, something is given to an individual, and there is a reasonable expectation that it will in turn to be given to a foreign official, this is also a violation of the law. The term *discretionary decision* refers to the making of a decision that will assist the firm in obtaining or retaining business.

One important exception to the Foreign Corrupt Practices Act is the "grease payment exception," which means that a firm is allowed to make a payment to expedite a function that does not require a discretionary decision. If a foreign government official, such as a clerk, has the job of stamping documents or processing paperwork, it is possible to make a payment that will expedite the matter. This is particularly true if delay would cause merchandise to be destroyed or damaged as a result of the delay.

The Foreign Corrupt Practices Act is controversial in that it seeks to regulate conduct that takes place outside the boundaries of the United States. Some experts complain that this act puts U.S. businesses at a competitive disadvantage. They further argue that the United States is regulating conduct that may be perfectly legal in the host country. On the other hand, it is argued that questionable payments put other U.S. firms at a competitive disadvantage. Firms that do not make these kinds of payments may be disadvantaged when they attempt to compete in the foreign market; or they may be disadvantaged in the United States if these questionable payments have made the competitor stronger. In either case, the result is injury to U.S. firms, and this injury occurs in the United States.

14. Anti-boycott Laws

The anti-boycott laws are found in provisions of the Export Administration Act of 1979 and the Internal Revenue Code. Although these provisions are not identical, they are similar enough to be discussed as a whole. Under the anti-boycott laws, any "U.S. person is prohibited from participating or cooperating in an international boycott. The exception to this rule, however, is for boycotts that have government approval. As a practical matter, these laws are applicable mainly to the Arab states' boycott of the State of Israel.

The second provision of the anti-boycott laws requires the reporting of any requests to participate in the boycott or requests to furnish information regarding the nationality or religious background of employees, suppliers, or customers.

Specifically, the anti-boycott laws prohibit a U.S. person from refusing to do business with anyone pursuant to a request from a boycotting country. This includes refusing to do business with the State of Israel, firms in the State of Israel, or firms that are on the "boycott black list." Further, a U.S. person may not furnish information regarding a blacklisted firm or person, or one's relationship with the boycotted country. If such a request to provide information is made, or a request to refrain from doing business is made, this must be reported to the Internal Revenue Service.

There are several broad exceptions to these laws that make it possible for a U.S. firm to do business with a boycotting country or firm. The law does allow a U.S. firm to comply with the laws of the boycotting country with respect to the firm's activities exclusively within that country, and the U.S. person can agree not to export goods into a boycotting country.

Some firms may fall into the trap of ignoring requests to furnish information (since that would violate the anti-boycott laws); but unless these requests are reported, the law is still violated. Reporting of any violations can come from a disgruntled employee or a competitor who has reported such requests.

The penalties for violating the anti-boycott laws include civil and criminal penalties, but the most significant is the potential loss of foreign tax credits on that transaction. It is no defense to the action that a controlled subsidiary participated in the boycott outside of the United States. Jurisdiction is based on the fact that the controlled subsidiary and the U.S. parent company transact business and the activity is "in U.S. commerce." In such a case, the U.S. parent can be held to violate the anti-boycott laws based on the boycott activities of its subsidiary.

CHAPTER SUMMARY

INTERNATIONAL BUSINESS TRANSACTIONS

International Business Entity	1. This is any business entity with relationships that transcend national boundaries. 2. An IBE is subject to home country, host country, and international regulation.
Comparative Legal Systems and International Law	1. Civil law legal systems are based on codes. 2. International law is consensual and binding only on those who agree to be bound. 3. Private international law refers to unification of law. 4. Conflict-of-laws rules determine which country's laws will apply to a dispute.
Methods of Conducting International Business	1. Import/export is the simplest form of business. 2. Distributorships, sale representatives, and sales agents sell the goods in the host country. 3. A license is the right to use another's intellectual property.
International Contracts	1. The parties to an international contract can specify contract clauses.

2. A *force majeure* clause excuses performance for specified circumstances beyond the party's control.
3. Arbitration clauses are enforced by U.S. courts.
4. A choice-of-law and choice-of-forum clause may add certainty to where a lawsuit must be brought and which country's law will apply.
5. The Convention on Contracts for the International Sale of goods provides certainty and rules of interpretation if there is no contract or the terms are unclear.

The Multinational Enterprise

1. The multinational enterprise faces criticism in three areas: market control, political control, and worldwide profit-maximizing perspective.
2. Multinational enterprises respond that they provide employment, goods, and services to the host population, and assume investment risks.

REGULATING INTERNATIONAL BUSINESS

International Controls

1. The Convention on Contracts for the International Sale of Goods is a type of international Uniform Commercial Code.
2. The WTO seeks to reduce or eliminate trade barriers.
3. Codes of conduct for IBEs have an impact on behavior through the process of negotiating these codes, rather than through direct enforcement.

Host Country Controls

1. Host countries can influence the activities of IBEs through restricting movements of capital, tax legislation, disclosure legislation, and merger restrictions.
2. Nationalization of IBE property can be either an expropriation, which is a legal taking, or a confiscation, for which just compensation has not been received.

Import Controls

1. Dumping is the practice of selling goods in the United States at unfairly low prices.
2. A manufacturer must prove that the goods are being sold at below production cost or below home market price, and must prove injury to the industry.
3. Countervailing duties are applied after a finding of unfair government subsidies.

Export Controls

1. A validated license is required for products at a certain level of technology or products that can be used for strategic or military purposes.
2. End-user certification is required for a validated license, and the exporter must certify the country of destination.

Antitrust Laws

1. U.S. antitrust laws can apply to an IBE's foreign activities, even if the foreign country's laws do not prohibit such conduct.
2. Extraterritoriality is the application of U.S. law beyond its borders.
3. There is a three-part test used by courts to determine if the antitrust laws should be enforced in any given case.

Foreign Corrupt Practices Act

1. The Foreign Corrupt Practices Act prohibits giving anything of value to a foreign government official to influence a discretionary decision.
2. The Foreign Corrupt Practices Act has reporting requirements that apply to any issuer of securities, even if it is not engaged in international business.

Anti-boycott Laws

1. Under the anti-boycott laws, any "U.S. person" is prohibited from participating or cooperating in an international boycott.

2. The anti-boycott laws require the reporting of any requests to participate in the boycott or requests to furnish information regarding the nationality or religious background of employees, suppliers, or customers.

REVIEW QUESTIONS AND PROBLEMS

1. Match the words in Column A with the definitions in Column B.

A	B
(1) IBE	(a) Giving something of value to expedite clerical function
(2) Sales agent	(b) International UCC
(3) Force majeure	(c) Presence in the host country; employee
(4) Dumping	(d) Selling below fair value, causing industry injury
(5) Grease payment	(e) Unification of laws among countries
(6) Validated license	(f) Superior force or power
(7) Expropriation	(g) Legal taking by government of the host country
(8) Private international law	(h) Any business entity with relationships that cross national boundaries
(9) Convention on the International Sale of Goods	(i) Association of nations creating political and economic union.
(10) European Union	(j) Permission from the government to export a particular product

2. Mr. Little manufactures paper clips and sells them to a distributor in Thailand. Would he be considered an international business entity? Explain.
3. Explain the significance of "presence" with respect to distributors, sales representatives, and sales agents.
4. XYZ Corp. is considering a contract to set up a manufacturing plant in Germany. What are some of the clauses they should consider including in such a contract?
5. Happy Days Motorcycle Co. is losing U.S. market share to Japanese Motorcycle Co. Happy Days believes this is because Japanese is dumping its motorcycles on the U.S. market. What steps can Happy Days take to get relief from these unfair import practices?
6. What standard is applied when enforcing U.S. antitrust laws to international business transactions?
7. How does the Foreign Corrupt Practices Act define bribery? Does the Act apply only to IBEs?
8. Do the anti-boycott laws require U.S. businesses to do business with the State of Israel?
9. List the types of regulations host countries may use to control the activities of IBEs. Which type of regulation has the most impact on IBEs?

10. A U.S. button manufacturer sells its product to a French garment producer. There was no written contract, and a dispute arises concerning delivery dates. What law will apply to this transaction?

Internet Resources

The United Nations Commission on International Trade Law web site is located at: http://www.uncitral.org/uncitral/en/index.html

The European Union provides an extensive web presence.
The entry point on the Internet for the European Union's site is: http://europa.eu/index_en.htm

PART III

CONTRACTUAL RELATIONSHIPS

Introduction to Contracts and Remedies | 13

CHAPTER OUTLINE

CHAPTER PREVIEW

Perhaps the everyday application of contract law best illustrates that we live in a legal environment. Ask yourself—when was the last time I entered into a contract or took part in contractual negotiations? If you are thinking about only a formally written contract, your answer may be "not very recently." However, when did you last buy gas at a self-service station, take clothes to a dry cleaner, order a meal at a restaurant, or stand in line to purchase something in a store? Each of these situations and hundreds more in our everyday lives involve the law of contracts.

In a similar vein, business simply could not be conducted without the law of contracts. Promises are a necessary part of any business venture. A manufacturing business relies on the promise of a customer to pay for the machine ordered. A teller relies on the promise of a bank to pay the teller for the hours worked. A legal framework is needed to deal effectively with promises made in the world of business. The law of contracts provides this essential aspect of business – necessary to the customer of an Internet-based music provider and necessary to a billion-dollar, multi national corporation contracting with the United States government. Because contracts play such an important role in our personal and business lives, we study this subject matter in some detail in Part III of this text.

In this first chapter on contracts, we introduce the subject by presenting basic terminology associated with the law of contracts. We also answer the important question: "So what?" That is, we can understand the supreme significance of the law of contracts to business transactions by studying early in our examination of the law of contracts what remedies exist when a party fails to perform under the terms of a contract. By examining basic terms and remedies, we will have a solid foundation for understanding the remainder of Part III, which details how contracts are formed (Chapters 14 through 17), documented (Chapter 18), performed (Chapter 19), and utilized by third parties (Chapter 20). This material also provides a gateway into Part IV, which deals largely with specialized principles appropriate for the law of sales.

BUSINESS MANAGEMENT DECISION

You have been authorized to negotiate a contract wherein your employer will lease a mainframe computer with periodic upgrades over a five-year period. As a part of these negotiations, you are concerned about the computer company providing adequate upgrades over the stated contractual term.

Should you insist on a clause specifying very significant damages if the computer company breaches the contract by failing to provide the agreed-upon upgrades?

BASIC CONCEPTS

Contract

A promise or promises enforceable in court

1. Contract Defined

In its simplest form, a contract involves a promise or several promises that are enforceable in court. As the result of these promises, the law recognizes a duty to perform. If this duty is breached, the law gives the aggrieved party a remedy. Realistically, a contract is a legal device to control the future through promises. By definition, a promise is a present commitment, however expressed, that something will or will not be done. Parties are allowed to create rights and duties between themselves, and the state will enforce them through legal systems.

When people make a contract, by their mutual assent they create the terms of their contract, which set up the bounds of their liability. It is important, then, that you keep *two points* in mind: (1) A contract contains a present undertaking or commitment concerning future conduct of the parties, and (2) the law enforces the commitment by providing a remedy if the commitment is not performed.

Note, though, that a set of promises does not always mean that a contract has been formed. That is, the very nature of a contract, as discussed in these chapters dealing with the law of contracts, demonstrates the precept that not all promises are enforceable in court. In essence, society has created the law of contracts to enforce only certain types of promises, particularly those related to business or, more generally, economic matters. It is therefore critical to understand what promises rise to the level of significance such that they are enforceable in court.

Finally, realize that the form of the contract is generally *unimportant.* Regardless of whether the contract is written, oral, or electronic, courts can find a contract. Certainly the existence of an oral contract may be more difficult; but if shown to exist, it has the same legal impact as any other form of contract.

2. Elements of a Contract

There are four basic elements to the formation of a contract:

1. *An agreement* that is a manifestation of the parties' mutual assent, as found in two legal concepts called offer and acceptance (Chapter 14)
2. *Bargained-for consideration* or other validation device, which the law uses to validate and make the mutual assent legally operative (Chapter 15)
3. Two or more parties who are legally competent; that is, they have the *legal capacity* to contract (are of legal age and sane) (Chapter 16)
4. A *legal purpose* consistent with law and sound public policy (Chapter 17)

These elements of a contract are considered in detail in the cited chapters. For the moment, the four elements are useful in giving us a way to think about contract law. Ask yourself the following progressive questions:

1. Has an offer been made? Why?
2. Has there been an acceptance? Why?
3. If there has been an offer and acceptance (mutual assent), is there a validation device, like consideration, to make the offer-acceptance legally operative? Why?
4. Assuming a valid contract has been formed, are there any legal defenses such as incapacity, illegality, fraud, mistake, or the statute of frauds that may nullify the contract? Why?
5. Assuming a valid contract with no defenses to its formation, how is the contract to be performed? (This question concerns performance problems under the general heading of the law of conditions.) Why?
6. Do third parties have rights or duties that may be legally recognized under the contract? Why?

At this introductory point, you are not expected to know the answers to these questions. However, when you have finished the chapters on contracts, come back and consider them. The law of contracts will then be in sharper focus.

3. Sources of Contract Law

The bulk of contract law is *judge-made* case law and is for the most part uncodified. The basic rules or principles of contract law are found in the written opinions of courts and not within statutes passed by state legislatures. Specialized areas of contract law such as employment law, consumer law, labor law and insurance law have been partially codified, but even in these areas the primary source of applicable legal principles is decided cases. A few states have codified their case law. The word *codified*, as used in this paragraph, means that a legislative body has enacted the law in a written statute.

As business became more sophisticated, courts in one state could create a contract rule that varied with a contract rule created by a court in another state. Businesses were having increased difficulty in knowing what their rights were under a contract because interpretations of contract principles varied from state to state. In order to remedy this gradually more vexing situation, during the 1940s the Commissioners of Uniform State Laws drafted the *Uniform Commercial Code* for consideration by the legislatures of the various states. The stated purpose of the Uniform Commercial Code was to collect in one body the law that "deals with all phases which may ordinarily arise in the handling of a commercial transaction from start to finish." The Code (or UCC, as it is often referred to) was initially enacted in Pennsylvania in 1952. Since then, every state has adopted the Code in whole or in part. In particular, as a result of the work of the Commissioners of Uniform State Laws and the adoption of Code provisions by state legislatures, there is generally a common law of contracts from state to state. That is, by and large, for those areas of contract law covered by the Code, the law from state to state is uniform. The detailed aspects of the Code constitute a significant portion of this text, and sections of the Code are referred to in brackets where appropriate. The references pertain to sections of this law, which are presented as an Appendix B at the end of this text.

As a result of the enactment of the *Uniform Commercial Code,* some contracts are subject to its provisions and some are not. It is essential that you keep in mind the limited applicability of the Code and that you recognize which contracts are covered by the general common law and which are covered by the Code. Most contracts (employment, construction, real property, general business, and the like) follow the common law rules as developed in cases. If a contract concerns the sale of goods (personal property), then it is governed by the Code. When the Code applies to a transaction, courts follow Code rules as adopted in a particular state through the legislative process and found in the statutes of that state.

FIGURE 13-1 ■ Source of Contract Law

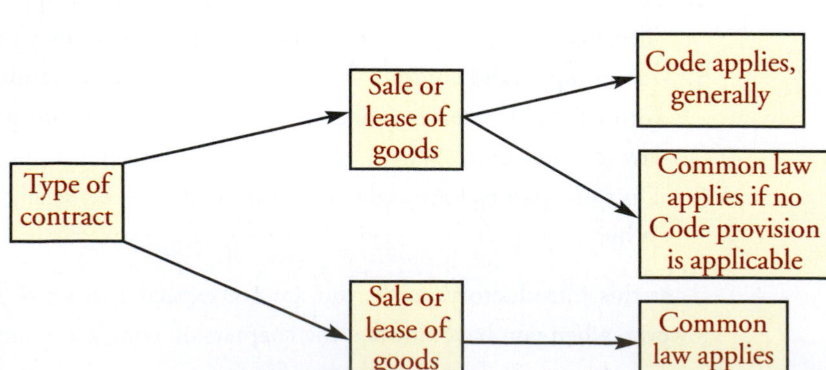

Our focus in Chapters 13 through 20 is on the common-law rules of contract. However, many rules concerning contracts are the same under the common law and under the Code. These rules are considered, whenever possible, at the same time. When the Code has special rules different from the common law, these will be set out in the text. Chapters 21-23 pertain exclusively to those aspects of contract law that are unique to the sale or lease of goods under the Code.

CONTRACT CLASSIFICATION AND TERMINOLOGY

4. Introduction

In the early common law, contracts were formal documents that included a seal. The seal was often a wax impression made by the ring of the contracting party. Today the requirement of using a seal to create a binding contract has been abolished.

As a general rule, contracts, either written or oral, are enforceable. However, a statute known as the *statute of frauds* does require that certain contracts be evidenced in writing to be enforceable. (This statute of frauds is discussed in depth in Chapter 18.)

In addition to being written or oral, contracts may be classified in a variety of ways. Among the more common classifications are the following:

1. *Form*: bilateral or unilateral
2. *Expression*: express, implied-in-fact or implied-in-law (quasi-contract)
3. *Enforcement*: valid, void, voidable, enforceable or unenforceable
4. *Performance*: executed or executory

The meaning and significance of these classifications are discussed in the following sections and throughout the other chapters on contracts.

5. Bilateral and Unilateral Contracts

Bilateral contract

An agreement containing mutual promises, with each party being both a promisor and a promisee

Contracts are either bilateral (a promise exchanged for another promise) or unilateral (a promise exchanged for an act of performance). Most contracts are bilateral, based on an *exchange of mutual promises*. A **bilateral contract** is formed when the promises are exchanged between the parties. It is immaterial that neither party has rendered any performance because the law recognizes that each party has a legal duty to perform its contractual duties. In Figure 13-2, note that there are *two promises, two duties, and two correlative rights*. This contract is bilateral (two sided).

EXAMPLE Mary promises to sell her truck to Dan for $5,000, and Dan promises to pay $5,000 for Mary's truck.

FIGURE 13-2 ■ Bilateral Contract

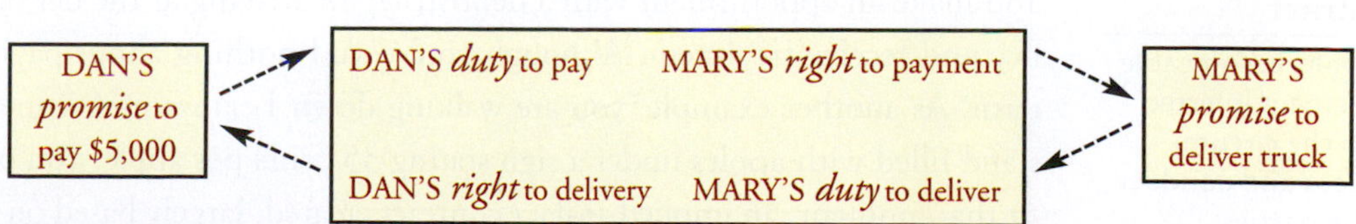

Unilateral contract

An agreement involving only one promise, which is exchanged for an act of performance

Whereas a bilateral contract is characterized by a promise for a promise, a **unilateral contract** is created once performance has occurred. The *offeror* (person who makes an offer) promises the *offeree* (person to whom the offer is addressed) a benefit *if* the offeree performs some act, such as building a house, mowing the grass, fixing a car, climbing a flagpole, or programming a computer. The offeror does not bargain for a promise, but for performance of an act. In Figure 13-3, note that there is only *one promise, one duty, and one right.* The contract is unilateral (one sided).

FIGURE 13-3 ■ Unilateral Contract

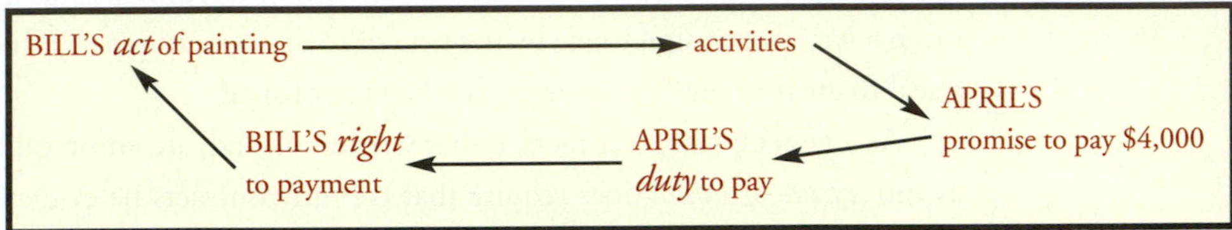

EXAMPLE April says to Bill, "Bill, I've had enough of your promises. If you paint my house by the end of the month, I promise to pay you $4,000." Bill paints April's house by the end of the month.

> *Step One:* Offer for a unilateral contract (April promises to pay $4,000 if Bill paints her house by the end of the month.)
>
> *Step Two:* Acceptance creates unilateral contract.

Performance of an act, such as fixing a car, is a part of a unilateral contract.

When April made her promise to pay $4,000, there was no unilateral contract, only an *offer* for a unilateral contract. When Bill did the act of performance bargained for (painting the house), a unilateral contract was created. This distinction is important in later chapters, especially concerning part performance of contracts. In the following case, consider closely whether all elements of a unilateral offer are present.

Express contract

An agreement that is either spoken or written by the parties

Implied-in-fact contract

A legally enforceable agreement inferred from the circumstances and conduct of the parties

6. Express and Implied-in-Fact Contracts

An **express contract** occurs when the parties state their agreement orally or in writing. When the parties manifest their agreement by conduct rather than by words, it is said to be **implied in fact**. You make an appointment with a dentist. Upon arriving at the dentist's office, you enter the office and receive treatment. Although you've said nothing about paying, it is an implied-in-fact term. As another example, you are walking down Lexington Avenue and come upon a grocery stand filled with apples under a sign stating 35 cents per apple. You pick one up and take a bite. At that moment, an implied-in-fact contract created, largely based on conduct..

CASE

Nebraska Beef, Lt.d v. Wells Fargo Business Credit, Inc.

UNITED STATES COURT OF APPEALS FOR THE EIGHTH CIRCUIT

470 F. 3d 1249 (2006)

SMITH, CIRCUIT JUDGE

Nebraska Beef, Ltd. ("Nebraska Beef") filed suit against Wells Fargo Business Credit, Inc., f/k/a Norwest Business Credit, Inc. ("Wells Fargo") claiming Wells Fargo wrongly assessed $211,000 in fees stemming from a 1997 loan. The district court entered summary judgment in favor of Wells Fargo. The court ruled the parties' unilateral contract provided for the additional fees in conjunction with additional extensions of credit. Nebraska Beef appeals. We affirm.

Nebraska Beef established a $30,000,000 line of credit with Wells Fargo, the terms of which were memorialized in a written credit agreement. The agreement detailed the maximum amount Nebraska Beef could borrow and established a mechanism whereby the company could receive an over-advance—a loan exceeding the established credit limit. The credit agreement required Nebraska Beef to pay an extra fee for each over-advance. During the next two years, Nebraska Beef sought three over-advances with each over-advance resulting in a formal written amendment to the original credit agreement. With each amendment, the amount of the over-advance fee increased.

In April 1997, Nebraska Beef began negotiations with Wells Fargo to establish the terms of an agreement covering a fourth over-advance in May. The parties concluded their negotiations with no definitive agreement regarding the terms of the May over-advance. Nebraska Beef maintains that Wells Fargo refused to approve additional over-advances on the same terms outlined in the third amendment. Instead, Nebraska Beef contends, Wells Fargo demanded a higher fee. Wells Fargo asserts it was willing to approve additional over-advances on the same terms outlined in the third amendment. Despite the lack of a formal written agreement, Nebraska Beef continued to take over-advances in early May and continued to do so throughout the month.

On May 23, 1997, Wells Fargo sent Nebraska Beef a letter informing Nebraska Beef that beginning May 27, the over-advance fees would climb to $2,000 per day per $150,000. The draft also stated that all over-advances before May 27 would be assessed at $1,500 per day per $150,000—the maximum amount charged in the third over-advance agreement. Nebraska Beef does not deny receiving the letter but maintains it never signed the accompanying fourth amendment. After receiving the letter, Nebraska Beef continued to withdraw funds through the over-advance provision.

By month's end, Wells Fargo reported that Nebraska Beef's May, 1997 over-advance fees totaled $211,000. Nebraska Beef sent Wells Fargo a letter challenging the $211,000 calculation. The letter acknowledged that Nebraska Beef had received funds through the over-advance but argued the May rates were unreasonable. Unable to resolve the dispute, Wells Fargo deducted the $211,000 amount from Nebraska Beef's account.

Nebraska Beef filed suit seeking to recover the $211,000 deducted from its account. The district court granted Wells Fargo's motion for summary judgment after finding, under Minnesota law, that Nebraska Beef had entered into a unilateral contract authorizing the increased over-advance fees.

Nebraska Beef argues the district court erred by granting summary judgment because no unilateral contract existed. Under Minnesota law, a unilateral contract requires: (1) an offer definite in form, (2) communication of offer, (3) acceptance and (4) consideration. Nebraska Beef argues that the first element, a definite offer, is lacking and therefore no unilateral contract was formed. Nebraska Beef contends that a genuine issue of material fact remains regarding the terms of Wells Fargo's offer, as evidenced by the parties' inability to agree about the amount of fees proposed at negotiations.

An offer must contain sufficiently definite terms to enable the fact-finder to interpret and apply them. An offer "may be inferred wholly or partly from words spoken or written or from the conduct of the parties or a combination thereof."

Viewing the evidence in a light most favorable to Nebraska Beef, we hold that the district court did not err in granting summary judgment to Wells Fargo. Wells Fargo offered to loan funds for the May 1997 over-advance, at a minimum, at the fee assessed under the third amendment to the original credit agreement. Further, Nebraska Beef acknowledges that it received the May 23 letter from Wells Fargo stating that over-advances after May 27 would be assessed an over-advance fee of "$1,500 per day through May 26, 1997, and $2,000 per day from and after May 27, 1997, … for each increment of $150,000 or portion thereof. …"

Therefore, it is undisputed that when Nebraska Beef began to withdraw funds through the May 1997 over-advance, it did so fully aware that an extension beyond the agreed line of credit would come at an additional cost. Wells Fargo's "offer" to permit continued over-advances at the stated terms constituted a unilateral contract offer that was accepted by Nebraska Beef's election to access the over-advance. These terms, as reflected in the third amended agreement and the May 23 letter, were sufficiently definite to establish a unilateral contract offer under Minnesota law.

Nebraska Beef emphasizes that it never agreed to the proposed fees stated in the May 23 Wells Fargo "Extension of Over-advance" letter. No express agreement is required to accept a unilateral contract. Under Minnesota Law, mere performance can constitute acceptance. The judgment of the district court is affirmed.

■ *Affirmed.*

CASE CONCEPTS REVIEW

1. How did the court determine that the offer was sufficiently definite?
2. How did Nebraska Beef indicate its acceptance?

Contracts implied in fact require that one party expects to be paid and that the other expects to pay. Conduct must establish both expectations.

An additional point should be noted. Businesses sometimes ship goods to persons who have not requested them. During the 1950s and 1960s in particular, this technique was used to sell items like neckties, tapes, kitchen-ware, and books. The business would then make a contract (implied-in-fact: based on consent of the customer) claim against an unsuspecting consumer alleging that the customer's decision to keep the item was tantamount to an acceptance. To stop this unfair method of selling goods, Congress enacted 39 U.S.C. §3009 (1970) of the U.S. Postal Services Act.This provision of federal allows the recipient of unsolicited goods to treat them as a gift and retain, use, discard, or dispose of the goods in any manner without obligation to pay for the item. It is important to note, though, that this law only applies to merchandise. For example, if a business provides through the mail an unsolicited policy of health insurance to a customer, the customer may not rely on the Postal Act section to claim that they have health insurance. Other consumer protection laws, either federal or state, may offer a remedy, including relieving the recipient of the obligation to pay in situations not covered by the Postal Act.

7. Implied-in-Law Contracts (Quasi-Contract)

Quasi-contract

A term used to describe a factual situation involving a duty that does not arise out of an actual contract and, in essence, is associated with a remedy designed to promote justice and fairness

Implied-in-law contracts, referred to as **quasi-contracts**, are *not true contracts*. Rather, they are legal fictions that courts use to prevent wrongdoing and the unjust enrichment of one person at the expense of another. So, *quasi-contracts are not based on the consent of two parties*. Rather, when one party confers a benefit on another in the absence of a contract, the party receiving the benefit may be unjustly enriched if he or she were not required to pay for the benefit received. In such situations, society imposes an obligation to pay the *reasonable value* of the benefit received.

Suppose that you mistakenly thought you owned a tract of land. You paid the taxes. Certainly, the true owner should legally have to reimburse you for the taxes. To avoid any unjust enrichment, courts permit the party who conferred the benefit to recover the reasonable value of that benefit. Under common law, this legal action was brought in the form of a contract action—hence the name quasi-contract. Nonetheless, there is no real promise, and none of the other elements of a true contract is present. If a contract exists, the remedy of quasi-contract cannot be used.

This legal fiction of quasi-contract does not rest on the intention of the parties, but rather on equitable principles. The two remedies most often associated with quasi-contract because of unjust enrichment are called restitution and *quantum meruit*. Restitution as a remedy is discussed further in Section 20 of this chapter.

Quantum meruit

The remedy used to avoid the unjust enrichment of one party at the expense of another, usually is in association with quasi-contract.

The Latin term ***quantum meruit*** means, "as much as he deserves." It is often used in cases involving the construction of a building and the repair of personal property. As an equitable doctrine, *quantum meruit* is based on the concept that no one who benefits by the labor and materials of another should be unjustly enriched thereby; under those circumstances, the law implies a promise to pay a reasonable amount for the labor and materials furnished, even absent a specific contract therefore.

The elements necessary to support a claim for relief based on *quantum meruit* are as follows:

1. Valuable services were rendered or materials furnished,
2. to the party to be charged for services rendered or materials furnished,
3. which services or materials were accepted, used, and enjoyed by that party,
4. under such circumstances, in rendering such services or furnishing such materials, it was reasonable that the party receiving the benefit of services or materials should pay, and
5. without such payment, the party who received the benefit would be *unjustly enriched*.

Quasi-contract, as an obligation based on equity and morality, exists to achieve justice. Not every benefit received by one party at the expense of another creates liability in quasi-contract. Suppose you answer the door to your home and a college student asks if you want your house painted. You indicate to the student that the entire house need not be painted, but you agree to have only the front of the house painted. The student indicates that she is only the salesperson and that a team of student-painters will perform the job in two days. You come home in two days to find the entire house has been painted. You call the student who made the sales call at your home, and she agrees that only the front of the home is to be painted. Have you been enriched? Yes, the entire home is painted. Was there "unjust" enrichment? No, because the painters made a mistake, the *quantum meruit* is inapplicable. You need only pay for the painting of the front of the house.

8. Enforcement Terminology

Contract terminology regarding enforcement involves the following terms: valid, void, voidable, enforceable, and unenforceable. A valid contract is one that is in all respects in accordance with the legal requirements for a contract (that is, offer, acceptance, consideration, legal capacity, and legal purpose).

Void

Having no legal effect (A contract that is void is a nullity and confers no rights or duties.)

Voidable

That which is valid until one party, who has the power of avoidance, exercises such power

A **void** contract is not a contract in the eyes of the law. For example, a contract for the sale of an illegal substance will not be enforceable in court. The term "void contract" is an unfortunate choice of words. As such, it lends to confusion for those attempting to understand contract law principles. Nonetheless, a "void contract" is a legal term that describes a situation where the parties make an agreement, but that agreement is not enforceable by either party.

A **voidable** contract is one in which one or more parties have the power to end the contract. A voidable contract will be enforced unless one of those parties elects to disaffirm it. For example, a contract entered into by a minor with an adult is voidable and can be disaffirmed (set aside) by the underage party. The adult, however, lacks the power to disaffirm.

When one party is entitled to a money judgment or to specific performance because the other party failed to keep a promise, the contract is *enforceable.* Although legally there may be a contract, a defense to that contract may deny any party any remedy under the contract. (Later chapters discuss these defenses to contract formation.) When such a defense exists, the contract is said to be *unenforceable.* For example, the law requires that a contract for the sale of land be in writing; if it is oral, then it is unenforceable.

9. Performance Terminology

Executed

The term used to mean that the performances of a contract have been completed

Executory contract

Until the performance required in a contract is completed, it is said to be executory as to that part not performed.

With respect to performance, contracts often are referred to as executed or executory. Yes, the two words are quite similar, but each represents vastly difference concepts. On the one hand, an **executed** contract is one that has been fully performed by the contracting parties. Both parties have fully performed their obligations under contract. Many courts also employ the term partially executed, meaning that only some of the promises have been performed. On the other hand, an **executory contract** is one that is yet to be performed. The traditional definition of contract, in terms of promises that are commitments regarding the future, stresses the executory nature of most contracts. For example, when Martha offers to sell Walter iced tea for $1, and Walter promises to buy, the contract is executory. If Martha (rather than promising) hands Walter the iced tea, and he simultaneously gives her $1, then the contract is executed. Although there is nothing to perform under an executed contract, modern definitions of contract include executed in addition to executory contracts. Note also that an agreement may be mixed; that is, executed by one party and executory on the part of the other. In such cases, this would be a partially executed contract.

LEGAL REMEDIES FOR BREACH OF CONTRACT

10. Introduction

When one of the parties to a contract fails to perform as promised, a *breach of contract* may have occurred. If such a breach exists, the nonbreaching party may seek a *remedy.* This remedy may be classified as legal or equitable. *Legal remedies (or remedies at law)* involve the recovery of money damages. *Equitable remedies,* in contrast to legal remedies, involve a request for something other than money. Equitable remedies available for a breach of contract are discussed in sections 17 through 20 of this chapter.

With respect to legal remedies, four types of money damages can be awarded by the courts: *nominal* damages, *compensatory* (or general) damages, *consequential* (or special) damages, and *punitive* (or exemplary) damages. Additionally, the parties may insert in their contract a provision that attempts to state the amount of money damages to be awarded for contract breach. This *liquidated damages clause,* if fair and not a penalty, will be adopted by the court. (See section 16 of this chapter.)

Nominal damages
A small sum assessed when no actual damages have been proven

Compensatory (general) damages
The amount of money awarded to the non-breaching party to provide that party with the benefit of the contractual bargain

11. Nominal Damages

For every legal wrong, there is a legal remedy. If there is a contract breach but the non-breaching party suffers no compensable loss, he or she can still recover **nominal damages**. The award (usually $1) symbolizes vindication of the wrong done by the mere breach of contract. Nominal damages thus recognize a technical injury and can be awarded even when the non-breaching party has not been harmed. Suppose that Bobby contracts to buy from Sammy 10,000 pounds of boiled peanuts at 50 cents per pound. Later, Sammy breaches and delivers nothing. If Bobby can buy boiled peanuts for 40 cents per pound on the open market, he can still recover nominal damages, even though he is not harmed by Sammy's breach.

12. Compensatory Damages: Theory

When the loss caused by the contract breach is more than nominal, the aggrieved party will sue for **compensatory (general) damages** designed to compensate for that party's loss of his or her

TABLE 13-1 ■ Types of Money Damages

Nominal	Damage is usually a small amount of money that recognizes one party has won a breach of contract suit, but with no proof of loss.
Compensatory	Purpose is to make the non-breaching party "whole," addressing the expectation interest and providing the benefit of the bargain along with costs and incidentals.
Consequential	Purpose is to cover unique but foreseeable losses flowing from the breach of contract and is based on evidence that the breaching party had that a special loss that would occur if that party breached.
Punitive	Rarely employed for contract breach, it is used in tort law to punish and deter wrongful behavior.

bargain. Compensatory damages are the primary damages sought in most contract actions. These damages must be a *direct, foreseeable* result of the breach of contract. They may include out-of-pocket losses as well as a sum of money required to give a party the benefit of the bargain.

The purpose and the theory of damages are to make the injured party whole. As a result of the payment of money, the injured party is in the same position he or she would have occupied had the breach of contract not occurred. Damages give just compensation for the losses that flowed from the breach. In other words, a person is entitled to the benefits of his or her bargain. If a purchaser receives less than what was bargained for, the difference between the actual value and the contract price constitutes the damages. Unusual and unexpected damages resulting from peculiar facts unknown to the breaching party at the time the agreement was entered into are, generally, not recoverable; nor is the injured party entitled to a profit from the breach of the contract. Recovery is limited to an amount that will place the injured party in the same position in which he or she would have been had the contract been carried out.

The amount of damages is usually one of fact and, therefore, presented to the jury. A jury may not speculate on the amount of damage. Damages that are uncertain, contingent, remote, or speculative cannot be awarded. Loss of profits may be included as an element of recoverable damages if they can be computed with reasonable certainty.

A party suing for breach of contract is not entitled to recover the amount expended for attorney's fees, unless the contract so provides or special legislation permits it. Litigation is expensive; and the party who wins the lawsuit is still "out of pocket" since attorney's fees will usually substantially reduce the net recovery. Court costs, which include witness fees and filing costs, are usually assessed against the losing party.

13. Compensatory Damages: Special Aspects

The injured party is duty bound to *mitigate* the damages—to take reasonable steps to reduce the actual loss to a minimum. The injured party cannot add to the loss or permit the damages to be enhanced when it is reasonably within his or her power to prevent such occurrence. An employee who has been wrongfully discharged cannot sit idly by and expect to draw his or her pay. A duty is imposed on the employee to seek other work of a substantially similar character in the same community. He or she is not required to accept employment of a different or an inferior kind.

When a contract is *willfully* and *substantially* breached after partial performance has occurred, there may be some benefit conferred on the non-breaching party. Furthermore, the benefit may be of such character that the non-breaching party cannot surrender it to the other. In construction contracts, the benefit received from partial performance cannot be returned. Under these circumstances, the law does not require the person entitled to performance to pay for the benefit conferred on him or her if the party conferring it is guilty of a substantial and willful breach. As a result, the party who has refused to complete the job is penalized because of his or her failure to perform. The remedy of quasi-contract is usually not available in such cases because of the existence of an express contract.

A different result occurs when the breach is unintentional, resulting from a mistake or a misunderstanding. In this situation, the party may be required to pay for the net benefit he or she has received. The court may award damages in the amount necessary to complete the performance, in which event the defaulting party is automatically credited for his or her partial performance.

In those contracts where partial performance confers benefits of such a nature that they can be returned, the recipient must return the benefits or pay for their reasonable value. This rule is applied to willful breaches as well as unintentional breaches.

14. Consequential Damages

Compensatory damages are general damages that arise directly and naturally from the contract breach. Everyone would expect (or foresee) these damages, yet special circumstances surrounding a contract might give rise to special damages that are not normally foreseeable. These damages are called **consequential damages**. Whereas compensatory damages are presumed and require no special proof, consequential damages are not presumed since they are caused by special circumstances beyond the contract itself. To recover these special damages, evidence must be submitted that the breaching party knew (or had reason to know) that special circumstances existed and would cause the other party to suffer additional losses if the contract were breached.

Consequential damages

Damages, beyond the compensatory damages, which arise from special circumstances causing special damages that are not clearly foreseeable. (However, before becoming liable for consequential damages, the breaching party must be aware of the special circumstances that may cause these damages.)

This requirement of actual knowledge (or reason to know) is only fair to prevent a windfall to the non-breaching party. This rule of a special knowledge of the "consequential" circumstances comes from the famous 1854 English case of *Hadley* v. *Baxendale*. Plaintiffs, owners of a mill, delivered a broken crankshaft (used in the mill operation) to the defendant, a common carrier, to be delivered to the factory for repair. Defendant delayed an unreasonable time in making the delivery. Since plaintiffs had no other crankshaft, they had to close the mill; and they lost considerable profits. At that time, it was customary (the usual situation) for large mills like theirs to have more than one crankshaft. The court limited the plaintiffs' damage recovery to compensatory damages since the consequential damages (lost profits) were not reasonably foreseeable. The defendant did not have knowledge of the special circumstances—that plaintiffs had only one shaft, which if broken would cause the entire mill to shut down.

Thus, in the usual case, a plaintiff is given compensation only for injuries that one would normally and naturally expect (that is, foresee) as a probable result of the breached contract. If the injury is beyond that naturally expected, then the plaintiff must prove that the defendant knew (or had reason to know) of these special facts, so that he or she could foresee the injury. Plaintiffs often fail to prove that the consequential damages they seek were in the contemplation of the parties. The following case is typical of those involving such a failure.

CASE

Lewis Jorge Construction Management, Inc. v. Pomona Unified School District

SUPREME COURT OF CALIFORNIA

34 Cal. 4th 960 (2004)

KENNARD, J.

A school district terminates a construction contract when the contractor, four and a half months after the promised due date, still has not finished the project. The contractor's bonding company then hires another firm to complete the project; but it suspends, and later reduces, the amount of bonding for the contractor. The latter successfully sues the school district for breach of contract, recovering in damages some $3 million for potentially lost profits, which the contractor claimed it would have earned on prospective construction contracts it never won because of its impaired bonding capacity. The Court of Appeal concluded that those potential profits were a proper item of general damages in this action for breach of contract. We disagree.

In 1994, the Pomona Unified School District (District) solicited bids for building improvements at Vejar Elementary School. The District awarded the contract to Lewis Jorge Construction Management, Inc. (Lewis Jorge), the low bidder at $6,029,000. Although the contract originally provided for completion in December of 1995, heavy rains delayed work, and the parties agreed to a revised completion date of January 22, 1996. That date came and went, but the project remained unfinished.

The District withheld payments to Lewis Jorge for work completed in April and May, 1996. On June 5, the District terminated the contract with Lewis Jorge and made a demand on the contractor's surety to finish the project under the performance bond the surety had provided for Lewis Jorge. The surety then hired another contractor to complete the school project for $164,000. That contractor completed the project between early July and mid-September, 1996.

Lewis Jorge sued the District, alleging it breached the contract by declaring Lewis Jorge in default and terminating it from the construction project. Lewis Jorge, in turn, was sued by a number of its subcontractors for nonpayment of their past due bills.

At trial, Lewis Jorge presented evidence from its bonding agent that in June 1996, it had a bonding limit of $10 million per project, with *an aggregate limit of $30 million for all work in progress. By mid-1997, the only sureties willing to provide Lewis Jorge with bonding imposed a limit of $5 million per project, with an aggregate limit of $15 million, a reduction of its bonding capacity to the level its surety had imposed in the early 1990's. Sometime in 1998, Lewis Jorge ceased bidding altogether and eventually closed down.*

Lewis Jorge sought to prove the extent of its lost future profits on unidentified construction projects, using as the relevant period the date of the District's breach to the date of trial, and relying on its profitability during the four years preceding the breach. Robert Knudsen, a financial analyst who specialized in calculating lost profits claims, projected that Lewis Jorge had lost $95 million in gross revenue for future contracts that, based on its past history, it would likely have been awarded. Historically, Lewis Jorge had realized a profit of about 6 percent of revenue. Knudsen calculated lost profits on unidentified projects at $4,500,000, which discounted to present value came to $3,148,107.

The jury returned special verdicts in favor of Lewis Jorge, finding the District liable for $362,671 owed on the school construction contract. It awarded $3,148,197 in profits Lewis Jorge did not realize "due to the loss or reduction of its bonding capacity

We granted the District's petition for review to resolve whether general damages for breach of a construction contract include potential profits lost on future contracts that a contractor does not win when, as a consequence of the property owner's breach, the contractor's surety reduces the contractor's bonding capacity. We later solicited and received briefing from the parties on the related issue of whether an award of lost potential profits would have been proper here as special damages.

Damages awarded to an injured party for breach of contract "seek to approximate the agreed-upon performance." The goal is to put the plaintiff "in as good a position as he or she would have occupied" if the defendant had not breached the contract. In other words, the plaintiff is entitled to damages that are equivalent to the benefit of the plaintiff's contractual bargain.

The injured party's damages cannot, however, exceed what it would have received if the contract had been fully performed on both sides. This limitation of damages for breach of a contract "serves to encourage contractual relations and commercial activity by enabling parties to estimate in advance the financial risks of their enterprise."

Contractual damages are of two types: general damages (sometimes called direct damages) and special damages (sometimes called consequential damages).

General damages are often characterized as those that flow directly and necessarily from a breach of contract or that are a natural result of a breach. Because general damages are a natural and necessary consequence of a contract breach, they are often said to be within the contemplation of the parties—meaning that because their occurrence is sufficiently predictable, the parties at the time of contracting are "deemed" to have contemplated them.

Unlike general damages, special damages are those losses that do not arise directly and inevitably from any similar breach of any similar agreement. Instead, they are secondary or derivative losses arising from circumstances that are particular to the contract or to the parties. Special damages are recoverable if the special or particular circumstances from which they arise were actually communicated to or known by the breaching party (a subjective test) or were matters of which the breaching party should have been aware at the time of contracting (an objective test). Special damages "will not be presumed from the mere breach" but represent loss that "occurred by reason of injuries following from" the breach. Special damages are among the losses that are foreseeable and proximately caused by the breach of a contract.

California follows the common law rule that an English court articulated some 150 years ago in Hadley v. Baxendale (1854).

Here, the Court of Appeal affirmed the jury's award to Lewis Jorge of $3,148,197 in general damages, based on profits Lewis Jorge did not earn on future unidentified contracts because its surety had reduced its bonding capacity after the District's termination of the construction contract. The Court of Appeal concluded that such potential profits were recoverable as general damages because they followed "from the breach in the ordinary course of events" and were a "natural and probable consequence." The Court of Appeal found it significant, as did the trial court, that the contract at issue, like much of Lewis Jorge's business, was a public contract that required bonding.

The Court of Appeal reasoned: When the contract was formed, the District knew of its own bond requirements; and it knew that public works contractors must provide bonds to secure their performance. Because impaired bonding capacity "has long been recognized as a direct consequence of an owner's breach of a construction contract," the Court of Appeal concluded that the District should have known that breaching the contract and resorting to the surety to complete the project could impair Lewis Jorge's ability to obtain bonds without which it could not bid on other public contracts. Accordingly, the Court of Appeal held that the potential profits Lewis Jorge lost on contracts it did not win after the District's termination of the school construction contract were general damages attributable to the District's breach.

The Court of Appeal, however, failed to consider a threshold inquiry. If the purpose of contractual damages is to give the nonbreaching party the benefit of its contractual bargain, then the first question is: What performance did the parties bargain for? General damages for breach of a contract "are based on the value of the performance itself, not on the value of some consequence that performance may produce."

We cannot say that the parties' bargain included Lewis Jorge's potential profits on future construction projects it had not bid on and been awarded. Full performance by the District would have provided Lewis Jorge with full payment of the contract price. Certainly, Lewis Jorge anticipated earning a profit on the school contract with the District, but that projected profit was limited by the contract price and Lewis Jorge's costs of performance. If Lewis Jorge's bid accurately predicted its costs, the benefit of its contractual bargain for profits was capped by whatever net profit it had assumed in setting its bid price.

The District's termination of the school contract did not directly or necessarily cause Lewis Jorge's loss of potential profits on future contracts. Such loss resulted from the decision of CNA, Lewis Jorge's surety at the time of the breach, to cease bonding Lewis Jorge.

Having here concluded that profits Lewis Jorge might have earned on future construction projects were improperly awarded as general damages, we now decide whether those lost potential profits were recoverable as special damages. Lost profits, if recoverable, are more commonly special rather than general damages and subject to various limitations.

At trial, Lewis Jorge presented evidence that its bonding capacity was reduced by its surety after the District's termination of the contract. Lewis Jorge did not, however, establish that when the contract was formed the District could have reasonably contemplated that its

continued

breach of the contract would probably lead to a reduction of Lewis Jorge's bonding capacity by its surety, which in turn would adversely affect Lewis Jorge's ability to obtain future contracts. As the evidence at trial disclosed, Lewis Jorge's bonding agent, who had obtained the construction bonds from CNA, anticipated that CNA's suspension of Lewis Jorge's bonding capacity would only be temporary.

Evidence at trial established that the owner's terminating a contract might or might not cause the contractor's surety to reduce its bonding capacity. As the District pointed out at oral argument, when it signed the contract it did not know what Lewis Jorge's balance sheet showed or what criteria Lewis Jorge's surety ordinarily used to evaluate a contractor's bonding limits. Absent such knowledge, the profits Lewis Jorge claimed it would have made on future, unawarded contracts were not actually foreseen or reasonably foreseeable. Hence, they are unavailable as special damages for the breach of this contract.

To summarize: It is indisputable that the District's termination of the school construction contract was the first event in a series of misfortunes that culminated in Lewis Jorge's closing down its construction business. Such disastrous consequences, however, are not the natural and necessary result of the breach of every construction contract involving bonding. Therefore, as we concluded earlier, lost profits are not general damages here. Nor were they actually foreseen or foreseeable as reasonably probable to result from the District's breach. Thus, they are not special damages in this case.

■ *Affirmed.*

CASE CONCEPTS REVIEW

1. What is the difference between general and special damages?
2. What is the test for awarding special damages?

15. Punitive Damages

Punitive (exemplary) damages

A sum (over and above the compensatory damages) assessed by the jury as punishment, to make an example of the wrongdoer and to deter like conduct by others (Injuries caused by willful, malicious, wanton, and reckless conduct will subject the wrongdoers to exemplary damages.)

The term **punitive damages,** or **exemplary damages,** refers to money damages awarded one party to *punish* the other's conduct, as well as to deter others from such conduct in the future. Since punitive damages seek to punish the wrongdoer, they bear no relationship to the actual (compensatory, consequential) damages. Although it is not the purpose of a civil action to punish a party who has committed wrongful conduct, punitive damages are frequently awarded in tort actions. Ordinarily, however, under common-law theory, punitive damages were not allowed in contracts cases since it was not "wrong" to breach a contract. That is, even someone who intentionally breaches a contract generally will not be subject to punitive damages.

However, today punitive damages can be awarded if the contract breach itself constitutes a separate tort. Therefore, the modern trend is to allow punitive damages when the contract breach is fraudulent, oppressive, malicious, or otherwise indicative of the breaching party's intent to harm the other's reasonable expectations under the contract. In those situations, tortuous behavior is intertwined with the breach of contract. Fraud is the most often used tort theory to justify punitive damages when a contract has been breached. These damages are in addition to actual damages. In some cases, juries award significant punitive damages as a way to regulate business conduct.

In court rooms such as pictured, punitive damages are sought to punish the wrongdoer.

In recent years, punitive damages have been assessed more readily, especially against insurance companies that act in bad faith. The law implies a covenant of good faith and fair dealing in every contract. When this covenant is breached, many courts allow juries to impose punitive damages.

At the same time, the amount of punitive damage awards has been very large in some cases. The issue of whether these large awards are constitutional is a subject that the United States Supreme Court has addressed in several cases. While the exact contours of the limitations on punitive damages are not set by the Supreme Court, they have recently offered guidance. The constitutional principle of due process generally will be honored if the ratio of punitive to compensatory does not exceed a single digit. If a jury awards punitive damages of $800,000 and compensatory damages of $100,000, the 8:1 ratio will likely pass the due process standard.

Liquidated damages

A fixed sum agreed on between the parties of a contract to be paid as ascertained damages by the party who breaches the contract (If the sum is excessive, the courts will declare it to be a penalty and unenforceable.)

16. Liquidated Damages Clause

The parties to a contract may state the money damages applicable when the contract is breached. The term **liquidated damages** describes this situation, and the provision in the contract is called a *liquidated damages clause.* These provisions will be enforced *unless the court considers the stipulation to be a penalty* for failure to perform, rather than compensation for damages. That is, should the court find that the term was inserted primarily to force actual performance and not to compensate for probable injury, it will be considered that the amount included in the contract as liquidated damages to be a penalty and will not be enforced. To be valid, the amount of recovery agreed on must bear a reasonable relation to the probable damage to be sustained by the breach. Note that recovery in the following case examines the question of whether liquidated damages are appropriate.

CASE

H&R Block Enterprises, Inc. v. Mary Short and AAA Tax Specialists, Inc.

2006 U.S. Dist. LEXIS 86926 (2006)

JUDGE JOAN N. ERICKSON

H&R Block Enterprises, Inc. (H&R Block), brought this action against Mary Short and AAA Tax Specialists, Inc., (collectively, Defendants) alleging breach of contract against Short and tortious interference with contractual relations and misappropriation of trade secrets against Defendants.

H&R Block provides tax preparation and related services to companies and individuals throughout the United States. Short was employed as a tax preparer for H&R Block in its St. Paul district for approximately twenty-four years. During her employment, Short executed a Premium Tax Service Tax Professional Employment Agreement (Employment Agreement). The Employment Agreement contains covenants restricting Short's ability to compete with H&R Block, solicit H&R Block clients, and solicit H&R Block employees after departure from H&R Block.

On December 31, 2004, Short resigned from H&R Block. Less than one month later, on January 26, 2005, she formed AAA Tax Specialists (AAA). Days or weeks after she left H&R Block, Short created a list of clients that she had serviced while working at H&R Block. From that list, Short created approximately 170 mailing labels. On or about February 9, 2005, she sent postcards to some of her former H&R Block clients. The postcards stated:

> *After being involved in your personal finances for these years, I wanted to let you know that I have ended my relationship with H&R Block.*
>
> *I am sorry for any inconvenience to you.*
>
> *I had too many problems with policies and pricing, as well as personal issues, which caused me to find employment elsewhere.*
>
> *If you have any questions or need help, please feel free to call me at 651-489-6939.*
>
> *Mary Short*

In 2005, at least 90 out of 127 tax returns prepared at AAA were for Short's former H&R Block clients. In 2006, over half of Short's clients were former H&R Block clients. After the Court issued an injunction, which restrained Short from soliciting or providing services to certain H&R Block clients, Short turned away approximately forty to forty-five former H&R Block clients. She referred these clients to another tax return preparer, not H&R Block.

continued

H&R Block brought this action against Mary Short and AAA Tax Specialists, Inc., (collectively, Defendants) alleging breach of contract against Short and tortious interference with contractual relations and misappropriation of trade secrets against Defendants. By Order dated March 2, 2006, the Court granted in part and denied in part H&R Block's motion for a preliminary injunction on its breach of contract claim. H&R Block now moves for summary judgment on its breach of contract claim. For the reasons set forth below, the Court grants in part and denies in part H&R Block's motion.

H&R Block argues that it is entitled to liquidated damages in the amount of $77,240.81 for Short's breach of sections 11 and 12 of the Employment Agreement and $5,000.00 for Short's breach of section 13 of the Employment Agreement. The Employment Agreement provides:

> *Associate acknowledges that damages for breach of Section ... 11, 12 and 13 are difficult if not impossible to establish and Associate therefore agrees to liquidated damages as set forth below as a fair and equitable measure of the Company's damages. ...*
>
> *(b) In the event Associate breaches Section 11 or 12 of this Agreement, Associate shall pay to Company an amount equal to two times the Average Fee charged by Associate during the term of this Agreement multiplied by the number of Non-Returning Company Clients multiplied by Associate's Baseline Client Retention Percentage. ...*
>
> *(c) In the event Associate breaches Section 13 through the solicitation of Company employees ... [and] the solicited employee is not a tax professional, Associate shall pay the Company ... $5,000 for each solicited non-management employee who leaves the Company.*

Under Missouri law, liquidated damages clauses are valid and enforceable, but penalty clauses are invalid. For a liquidated damages clause to be valid, the amount fixed as damages must be a reasonable forecast of the harm caused by the breach and the harm that is caused by the breach must be of a kind difficult to accurately estimate. The validity of a liquidated damages clause is viewed at the time the contract was executed.

The relevant provisions of the Employment Agreement provide that liquidated damages for a breach of the client covenants are calculated by multiplying the average fee charged by Short to her H&R Block customers in her final year at H&R Block by two and, then, multiplying that number by the number of Short's clients who did not return following her departure, as discounted by Short's expected retention percentage. Short argues that the formula is unreasonable and penal in nature because the amount sought exceeds her total income from H&R Block in 2004, as well as the total revenue for AAA in 2005 and 2006.

The Court concludes that the damages provided for violations of sections 11 and 12 represent a reasonable forecast of the harm caused by Short's breach and that the harm caused is of a kind difficult to accurately estimate. First, the formula is tied to the number of Short's clients who failed to return to H&R Block after her breach of the covenants, uses Short's average fee charged in 2003, discounts the total damages by Short's retention percentage, and accounts for two years of loss for each client. The Court concludes that this estimation of harm is reasonable. Second, the future damages associated with a breach of the covenants are difficult to calculate because the loss of H&R Block clients will have a recurring impact. While the formula accounts for the loss of clients for a period of two years, H&R Block has represented that some clients become long-term clients who stay with H&R Block for many years. There is no way to determine how long a particular client might have stayed with H&R Block and what each clients' future fees might have totaled absent Short's breach of the covenants. Moreover, there is no way to determine how many referrals H&R Block would have received from the lost clients. Thus, the Court concludes that H&R Block is entitled to $77,240.81 in liquidated damages.

H&R Block also seeks liquidated damages for Short's breach of the employee nonsolicitation clause in hiring Johnson. The Employment Agreement provides for $5,000 for each solicited non-management employee. H&R Block argues that $5,000 represents a reasonable calculation of damages caused by the loss of Johnson. The Court disagrees. H&R Block has made no showing that the damages associated with the loss of a receptionist are of a kind that are difficult to accurately calculate or that $5,000 is a reasonable forecast of any harm. Thus, the Court declines to award liquidated damages for Short's breach of section 13.

■ *Granted in part, Denied in part.*

CASE CONCEPTS REVIEW

1. From Short's perspective, why is the liquidated damages provision unreasonable?
2. At what point in time should "reasonableness" of the liquidated damages provision be made?
3. What test does the court apply to determine whether the liquidated damages provision is unreasonable?

EQUITABLE REMEDIES FOR BREACH OF CONTRACT

17. Introduction

As discussed previously, equitable remedies involve a request for some remedy other than money damages. These remedies generally will be allowed only if money does not provide adequate relief for the non-breaching party. Examples of equitable remedies for breach of contracts include spe-

TABLE 13-2 ■ Types of Equitable Remedies

Type	Use	Description
Specific Performance	Where object of contract is unique, usually employed in real estate and selected personal property sales contract settings—loss is not calculable in terms of money damages.	Party is instructed to perform under the terms of the contract.
Rescission	If contract was made based on mistake or fraud, a court in equity may grant rescission.	Parties are put back into the legal position they were in BEFORE the contract was created.
Restitution	After rescission, parties must return any benefit.	Benefit or item unjustly attained under contract is returned to the previous owner.

cific performance, rescission, and restitution. *Specific performance* is a remedy that requires the party in breach to do exactly what he or she agreed to do under the contract. *Rescission* disaffirms (annuls) the contract and returns the parties to the position each occupied before making the contract. *Restitution* (sometimes called quasi-contract) rectifies unjust enrichment by forcing the party who has been unjustly enriched to return the item unfairly gained or its value if the item cannot be returned. These remedies are discussed in more detail in the following sections.

18. Specific Performance

The legal remedy of dollar damages or the equitable remedy of rescission may not be adequate to provide a proper remedy to a party injured by a breach of contract. The only adequate remedy may be to require the breaching party to perform the contract. This remedy is called *specific performance.* It is used in contracts involving real estate and personal property; it is not available for contracts involving relationships and services.

Specific performance is granted in cases when the court in the exercise of its discretion determines that dollar damages would not be an adequate remedy. Specific performance is not a matter of right, but rests in the discretion of the court. To warrant specific performance, the contract must be clear, definite, complete, and free from any suspicion of fraud or unfairness. Dollar damages are considered inadequate and specific performance is the proper remedy when the subject matter of the contract is unique. Since each parcel of real estate differs from every other parcel of real estate, all land is unique; courts of equity will, therefore, specifically enforce contracts to sell real estate. Examples of unique personal property are antiques, racehorses, heirlooms, and the stock of a closely held corporation. Such stock is unique because each share has significance in the power to control the corporation. Items readily available in the marketplace are not unique.

The Uniform Commercial Code provides that specific performance may be decreed when the goods sold are *unique or in other proper circumstances* [2-716]. The Code retains the traditional requirement that the goods be unique and that there be no adequate remedy at law. However, the Code also allows this specific performance remedy "in other proper circumstances," which generally means that the goods cannot be bought elsewhere at a reasonable price. For example, peaches and oranges are not unique. If a severe frost destroys most of the peaches and oranges, however, drastically raising the price of the surviving crop, a court might award specific performance to a buyer in a contract for the purchase of peaches or oranges.

As indicated previously, specific performance is not appropriate in cases involving personal service contracts. Courts generally refuse to grant specific performance in situations where one party is under a duty to perform a service to another because if a court ordered someone to perform a service, it would be a type of involuntary servitude (or slavery) banned by the Thirteenth Amendment to the United States Constitution. In certain circumstances, courts have issued injunctions prohibiting a person from performing until he/she honors a particular contractual commitment. For example, a famous guitar player contracts to perform at Duke University on a particular night and then calls to cancel because there is an opportunity to play for a much larger audience for double the amount at Yale University. A court could not grant specific performance to Duke University. However, the court might prohibit the guitar player from performing at Yale or any other venue until the musician performs at Duke.

19. Rescission

Rescission involves one party seeking the court's assistance in undoing a contract previously made. In essence, this party desires to be returned to a precontractual position. This equitable remedy is available in a variety of circumstances. It may be granted by a court of equity when a transaction has been induced by fraud or mistake. Rescission will also be granted to a minor so the minor may exercise his or her privilege of withdrawing from a contract. It is also used as a remedy if one party's breach of a contract is so substantial that the other party should not be required to perform either.

A party who discovers facts that warrant rescission of a contract has a duty to act promptly. If the party elects to rescind, he or she must notify the other party within reasonable time so rescission may be accomplished when parties may still be restored, as nearly as possible, to their original positions. A party entitled to rescission may either avoid the contract or affirm it. Once the party makes the choice, he or she may not change it. Failure to rescind within a reasonable time is tantamount to affirming the contract. The party who seeks rescission must return what he or she has received in substantially as good condition as it was when he or she received it.

20. Restitution

In many cases, *restitution* follows rescission. As stated earlier, to rescind a contract both parties must make restitution to each other; that is, they must return any benefit received under the contract. Restitution thus prevents any party from being *unjustly enriched* when a contract has been legally annulled. The purpose of restitution is to place the parties in the position they were in prior to making the contract. Goods and property received must be returned if they exist and have not been consumed. Otherwise, each party must pay for the reasonable value of the goods consumed or of the services received so they will not be enriched unjustly.

Although restitution follows rescission, restitution alone can be a remedy. This occurs when a court imposes a contract (a quasi-contract) to prevent unjust enrichment. (Quasi-contracts were discussed earlier in this chapter.) Remember that a quasi-contract is not a true contract but is an implied-in-law contract to prevent unjust enrichment. Restitution is a flexible, equitable remedy that is used whenever a court finds that natural justice and equity require compensation for benefits received. Restitution may be ordered even though the parties did not intend compensation.

CHAPTER SUMMARY

BASIC CONCEPTS

Contract Defined
1. Contract is a promise or set of promises from which the law recognizes a duty to perform.
2. Failure of performance as promised gives rise to a remedy in favor of the aggrieved party.

Elements of a Contract
1. Offer and acceptance
2. Consideration
3. Legal capacity to contract
4. Legal purpose of contract

Sources of Contract Law
1. Common-law cases
2. The Uniform Commercial Code

CONTRACT CLASSIFICATIONS AND TERMINOLOGY

Bilateral and Unilateral
1. A *bilateral* contract is an exchange of a promise for a promise.
2. A promise exchanged for an act of performance creates a *unilateral* contract when the act is performed.

Express and Implied-in-Fact Contracts
1. A contract formed by words (oral, written, or a combination thereof) is an express contract.
2. A contract formed by parties' conduct, not by their words, is an implied-in-fact contract.

Implied-in-Law (Quasi-Contract)
1. This is not a true contract because there is no mutual consent.
2. This is a court-imposed remedy (a quasi-contract) to prevent unjust enrichment.
3. It cannot be used if there is a contract.

Enforcement Terminology
1. A contract is *valid* if it contains the requisite legal requirements of offer, acceptance, consideration, legal capacity, and legal purpose
2. When the term *void contract* is used, no contract legally exists (for example, illegal contract). The promises exchanged do not create legal obligations.
3. A contract one party has the option to avoid (set aside) or to enforce is a *voidable* contract.
4. An existing contract that cannot be legally enforced due to a legal defense is unenforceable.

Performance Terminology
1. A contract is executed when all duties are fully performed by all parties.
2. A contract is executory when duties remain to be performed by the parties.
3. A contract may be partially executed and partially executory.

LEGAL REMEDIES FOR BREACH OF CONTRACT

Nominal Damages
1. Nominal damages ($1) are an insignificant symbolic money award to acknowledge technical injury when no actual damage from the contract breach can be proved.

Compensatory Damages
1. Compensatory damages are a money award for injuries presumed in law to arise normally and naturally from the contract breach.

2. These damages are designed to place the non-breaching party in the same position as if the contract had been performed.

Consequential Damages

1. Consequential damages are a special money award in addition to the award of general compensatory damages.
2. The purpose of consequential damages is to compensate for indirect damage arising from special circumstances the breaching party could reasonably foresee would result from the contract breach.

Punitive Damages

1. Punitive damages are awarded to punish the breaching party and to deter others from such conduct in the future.
2. Punitive damages are generally not available in a contract action unless the contract breach itself constitutes an independent tort, such as fraud.

Liquidated Damages Clause

1. Liquidated damages are awarded in an amount agreed on by the parties in their contract (liquidated damages clause) to be reasonable compensation for future contract breach.
2. The agreed amount of liquidated damages cannot be a penalty; it must bear a reasonable relation to the actual damages that will probably occur if the contract is breached.

EQUITABLE REMEDIES FOR BREACH OF CONTRACT

Specific Performance

1. Specific performance is a remedy that requires the party in breach to perform the contract.
2. Specific performance is granted only when money damages are an inadequate remedy. Dollar damages are usually considered inadequate when the subject matter of the contract is unique.

Rescission

1. Rescission is a remedy that cancels the contract and restores the parties to the position they occupied before the contract was formed.
2. In many cases, to rescind a contract, the parties must make restitution.

Restitution

1. Restitution is a remedy to recapture a benefit conferred to prevent that party from being unjustly enriched.
2. In restitution, actual goods or property must be returned. But if the goods or property have been consumed, an equivalent amount of money must be given.

REVIEW QUESTIONS AND PROBLEMS

1. Match each type of contract in Column A with the appropriate statement in Column B.

A	B
(1) Express contract	(a) Contract duties completely performed
(2) Implied-in-fact contract	(b) Formed by parties' conduct
(3) Implied-in-law contract	(c) Contract exists but cannot be enforced in court
(4) Executed contract	(d) Formed either by oral or written words or both
(5) Executory contract	(e) Imposed by law to prevent unjust enrichment

(6) Void contract	(f) One party has option of avoiding or enforcing contract
(7) Voidable contract	(g) Contract duties have not been performed
(8) Unenforceable contract	(h) Illegal contract

2. Comfort Company assumed the operation of a hotel. The previous owner had a contract with Linen Supply. Linen Supply continued to furnish services after Comfort Company assumed ownership. Comfort Company argues that it does not have to pay for the linen services because it had no express contract with Linen Supply. Can Linen Supply recover based on breach of an express contract? Why or why not?
3. Virgil entered into a contract to sell Joe the OZ nightclub. The sale was conditioned on the successful transfer of the liquor license. Joe managed the club while the transfer application was pending, and it lost money. When the transfer was unsuccessful, Joe sued Virgil for the reasonable value of his services. Should he succeed? Why or why not?
4. A contractor was repairing a house damaged by a flood. During the course of the work the owner asked for some repairs not called for in the contract. Upon completion, the owner refused to pay for the extras. Is the contractor entitled to be paid for them? Why or why not?
5. Dewey, an employee of American Stair Glide, had a novel idea for a safety device for elevator chairs manufactured by American. Dewey on his own time made a drawing and model of his idea and showed it to officials of American. Later, American used the safety device, thereby saving money. American refused to pay Dewey anything, claiming it had no contract with Dewey. American also proved that Dewey was not employed by American to do any engineering or design concept work. Dewey claimed that American was unjustly enriched by his idea. Can Dewey recover using the theory of quasi-contract? Explain.
6. Plaintiff was engaged by defendant to act in a musical motion picture entitled *Bloomer Girl;* her compensation was to be $750,000. Prior to production, defendant notified plaintiff that *Bloomer Girl* had been canceled. She was offered a role in a western, to be titled *Big Country,* at the same compensation. Must plaintiff accept the new role? Why or why not?
7. McKibben, owner of a mining claim near Fairbanks, Alaska, signed a mining lease agreement with Mohawk Oil that provided that McKibben would receive 45 percent of the value of all ores and minerals mined. When the ore mined had a specified low value, however, McKibben would receive only 10 percent of the value of the ore mined. McKibben discovered that Mohawk Oil was diluting the ore and removing precious metals without reporting this to McKibben as required by the lease. McKibben sued, seeking both compensatory and punitive damages. Can punitive damages be recovered in this breach of contract action? Why or why not?
8. In December 1991, NSI contracted to provide laundry service for Secrist's nursing home for a three-year period. Secrist used the service until March 1993, when she unilaterally terminated the contract without NSI's consent. The written contract provided for liquidated damages in the event of an unlawful termination. The damages were 40 percent of the anticipated gross receipts under the contract for the unexpired term—30 percent for overhead and 10 percent for profits. NSI sued to collect the liquidated damages. The trial court found the liquidated damages provisions of the contract excessive because they included 30 percent recovery for overhead after fifteen months of contract period had been completed.

Was the trial court correct in rejecting the overhead portion of the liquidated damages clause as excessive? Explain.

9. Beckman signed a contract with Dillworth Lincoln-Mercury for the purchase of a Lincoln Continental automobile. Four weeks later, Beckman inquired about the car. The dealership said the purchase order agreement was lost, so no car was ordered. The dealership offered to order another Lincoln Continental but at a price higher than the price originally agreed on. Beckman sued the dealership for specific performance. Should specific performance be awarded? Why?
10. After buying a home and lot from Pyburn, Hutchison later discovered that the home site had not been approved by the health board because it lacked enough topsoil to sustain a septic tank and overflow field for sewage disposal. Hutchison charged that Pyburn knew of this condition and that there was no practical means of correcting it. If Hutchison's charge is true, is he entitled to rescission? Could punitive damages also be awarded?

The Agreement: Offer and Acceptance | 14

CHAPTER OUTLINE

continued

CHAPTER PREVIEW

This chapter is the first of four that discuss the essential elements necessary to create a valid contract. The first requirement of a valid contract is an *agreement* between the parties. An agreement is typically reached when one party (the *offeror*) makes an offer to another party (the offeree) who accepts the offer. *Offer* and *acceptance* are the acts by which the parties come to a meeting of the minds—a status that is captured in the term "agreement." They reach an accord on the terms of their agreement. This accord is referred to as a *manifestation of mutual assent.*

BUSINESS MANAGEMENT DECISION

As the manager of a garden/feed retail store, you order several items specifying that they are to be packaged in ten-pound plastic bags. Your supplier responds that the requested items will be shipped in twenty-pound cardboard boxes and that the items are sold free of any express or implied warranties. What should you do upon receiving your supplier's response?

BASIC CONCEPT

1. Objective Theory of Contracts

Mutual assent—resulting in the creation of an agreement—is the first ingredient of a contract. For many decades in the United States common-law rules required that the assent of both parties exactly match at the same point in time; that is, that there be a subjective meeting of the minds. Since nobody can actually know the inner thoughts of another, this requirement proved unworkable. Rather than dealing with subjective thoughts, modern contract law follows an objective theory based on the *manifestation of mutual assent.* Assent to the formation of a contract is legally operative only if it is objectively evident.

Unless there is an *objective* meeting of the minds of the parties on the subject matter and terms of the agreement, no contract is formed. To determine whether the minds have met, both offer and acceptance must be analyzed. The offeror may have had something in mind quite different from that of the offeree. The intention of the parties is determined not by what they think, but by their outward conduct—that is, by what each leads the other reasonably to believe.

One simple means for showing a manifestation of assent is to have both parties sign a written agreement. Each person possessing legal capacity to contract who signs a written document with the idea of entering into a contract is presumed to know the contents thereof. Where one who can read signs a contract without reading it, that party is bound by the terms thereof unless he or she is able to show (1) that an emergency existed at the time of signing that would excuse his or her failure to read it; (2) that the opposite party misled him or her by artifice or device, which prevented him or her from reading it; or (3) that a fiduciary or confidential relationship existed between parties on which he or she relied in not reading the contract. Because the act of signing indicates a person's intention to be bound by the terms contained in the writing, the person is in no position at a later date to contend effectively that he or she did not mean to enter into the particular agreement. All contracts should, therefore, be read carefully before they are signed.

Offers clearly made in jest or under the strain or stress of great excitement are usually not enforced because one is not reasonably justified in relying on them. Whether an offer is made in jest can be determined by applying the objective standard. If the jest is not apparent and a reasonable person hearing the statement would believe that the speaker was serious in making the statement, a contract is formed. The following case is typical of those that address the objective view of contracts.

CASE

Pamela Dalton v. Robert Jahn Corporation, and Opal Jahn, et al.

COURT OF APPEALS OF OREGON

146 P.3d 399 (2006)

BREITHAUPT, J. PRO TEMPORE

This case arises from a dispute between members of the Jahn family, primarily over control of the Robert Jahn Corporation. In 1980, Opal Jahn and her husband Robert Jahn formed a lumber company, the Robert Jahn Corporation (RJC), the corporate stock of which became owned by themselves and each of their children: Pamela Dalton, Teresa Gitomer, Linda Chertudi, and Chester Jahn. In 1992, Opal and Robert transferred their RJC shares to the Jahn Living Trust. The trust held those shares until Robert's death in 1996, at which point the trust was divided into two new trusts (the Opal Jahn Marital Trust and the Jahn Family Credit Shelter Trust), each of which held approximately half of the RJC shares previously held by the Jahn Living Trust. Under the terms of the new trusts, Opal, as trustee, exercised sole control over the RJC shares held by each trust. Through the trusts, Opal controlled a bare majority of RJC's stock. Opal also became the president, secretary, and sole director of RJC.

Subsequently, a dispute began over the future of RJC's assets and business. Particularly contentious was a proposed business deal known as the "Ten Mile" transaction, in which Chester apparently proposed to mortgage land or harvest and sell timber owned by RJC in order to buy property in southern Oregon; Chester's company, Superior Tree Stewards, Inc., was allegedly involved in the deal. Pamela thought the transaction would deplete RJC's assets and sought an injunction against it. Separately, Teresa brought suit regarding her 1995 sale of her RJC shares to RJC. She claimed that the sale should be rescinded or that it was subject to a right to repurchase, which she was prepared to exercise.

The trial court suggested that the parties attempt to reach a settlement and, when they agreed to do so, appointed William Richardson, a former Chief Judge and current Senior Judge of this court, to preside over the parties' settlement negotiations. Richardson conducted two settlement conferences in July and August 2000, during which a proposal developed to split RJC into several corporations. Whereas Pamela's attorney, Feibleman, favored a plan that would have ended in four corporations, each to be headed by one of the Jahn children, Opal's attorney, Brink, drafted documents that would split RJC into five corporations, one of which would still be headed by Opal. The Jahn family members had questions about the tax implications of both plans, so Feibleman asked a specialist in tax and business law, Jennings, to present a reorganization plan at a third settlement conference on September 12, 2000.

All of the Jahn family members—except Linda, who had no attorney, and Teresa, who participated via telephone but whose attorney was present—were present at the conference held on September 12, 2000. After the details of the settlement proposal had been discussed, Richardson met privately with Opal and her attorney, Brink, to ensure that Opal understood the proposal and to gauge her interest in signing an agreement. Richardson and Brink thoroughly explained the terms of the proposal to Opal. All apparently indicated orally that they agreed to terms.

To memorialize that oral agreement, Richardson went to the side room and drafted a document for the parties to sign. That document stated:

> *"Jahns Family*
>
> *"It is agreed between the undersigned Jahns family members that the division of property rights, corporate shareholder rights and asset distribution shall be in principle as described in the diagram attached as Exhibit A which shall be part of this agreement. A majority of the family members shall be sufficient to authorize finalization of the proposed distribution, as long as the majority includes Opal [Jahn].*
>
> *"The agreement in principle shall be finalized in writing and shall include dismissal of pending law suits [sic] and mutual releases of liability for all claims."*

On October 3, the parties met for the follow-up conference they had scheduled on September 12. That meeting did not last long because soon after the conference began, Brink announced that Opal would not proceed with the settlement agreement. On October 9, Brink informed Jennings that the settlement was off and that he would no longer serve as Opal's attorney.

Pamela and Teresa then brought an action for specific performance of the settlement agreement. The trial court found that the agreement was enforceable and entered a decree of specific performance, charging Senior Judge Richardson with the task of ensuring that the settlement was fully effectuated.

continued

Defendant Opal Jahn appeals a decree of specific performance granted by the circuit court, arguing that a settlement agreement signed by the parties is too indefinite to be enforced by that decree. Opal Jahn's daughter, Pamela Dalton, a plaintiff in this case, disagrees, claiming that the settlement agreement is sufficiently definite.

Opal makes several arguments as to why the September 12 settlement agreement is not enforceable. Opal's first argument entails several factors, each of which can be subsumed under the contention that no contract was formed because there was no meeting of the minds on September 12. Opal contends that she did not understand what she was signing when she signed the agreement and, more specifically, that she did not understand that the agreement would leave her without control over the RJC properties. Opal also argues that the agreement was incomprehensible to the average person, full of "laconic symbols and abbreviations."

Whether a contract existed is a question of law. At least as to a contract's essential terms, a valid contract exists only when there is a meeting of the minds and where all terms are either agreed upon or there is a method agreed upon by which open and disputed terms can be settled, such that nothing is left for future negotiation. Oregon subscribes to the objective theory of contracts. In determining whether a contract exists and what its terms are, we examine the parties' objective manifestations of intent, as evidenced by their communications and acts. Whether parties enter into a contract does not depend on their uncommunicated, subjective understanding; rather, it depends on whether the parties manifest assent to the same express terms.

The trial court made extensive findings regarding the process by which the September 12 agreement was reached and subsequent negotiations were handled. We find the trial court's findings well supported by the evidence in the record and adopt them as fact on *de novo* review. Opal's argument that she did not understand what she was signing is undermined by Richardson's and Brink's testimony that they carefully described to her the terms of Jennings's proposal, as well as her own statement that Chester would have to live with the consequences of the agreement. Opal cannot argue that her statements and actions at the September 12 settlement conference, viewed objectively, could be anything other than clear and unequivocal assent to the terms agreed on by the rest of the settling parties. There is nothing in the record to indicate that anyone knew or should have known that Opal believed anything different from what everyone else believed; the terms of the agreement were clear and comprehensible, even if complicated, and the testimony was unanimous. Everyone at the September 12 settlement conference knew, or had access to professional assistance to determine, what the agreement meant. To the degree that Opal did not understand the agreement, she never manifested that lack of understanding—but rather indicated the opposite, her knowing assent to all of the agreement's terms, through objective communications and acts.

We finally note the fact that when the parties were working on finalizing the agreement after September 12, no one proposed any modifications to the basic structure of the agreement or the fundamental economic terms or methods to which they had bound themselves. Instead, pursuant to an agreement to share legal costs by way of payment by RJC, they began working to effectuate the agreement and continued to do so until Opal unilaterally withdrew. The trial court did not err in entering a decree of specific performance in this case.

■ *Affirmed.*

CASE CONCEPTS REVIEW

1. In order to overcome the objective theory in this case, what should Opal have done?
2. Why is the objective theory beneficial to society? Why not a subjective theory? What are the costs (real and otherwise) to society associated with both theories?

OFFERS

2. Definition

Offer

A statement made by an offeror that he or she is prepared to be bound to a contractual position—the first essential element to the meeting of the minds of the contracting parties

An **offer** is a conditional promise made by the offeror to the offeree. It is conditional because the offeror will not be bound by his or her promise unless the offeree responds to it in the manner sought by the offeror. This may be that the offeree (1) *does something* (performs an act), (2) *refrains from doing something* (forbearance), or (3) *promises to do something or to refrain* from doing something. If the offeree complies with the terms of the offer within the proper time, there is an agreement.

The offeror's manifestation must create a reasonable expectation in the offeree that the offeror is willing to contract. This expectation arises when the offeror's promise demonstrates a *present commitment* in exchange for one of the aforementioned three responses by the offeree. The first task is to determine if an offer has been made.

3. Test of Offer's Existence

The test for determining when an offer is made is as follows. What would a reasonable person in the position of the offeree think the manifestation from the offeror means? In our legal system, the reasonable person is the jury; the test asks the jury to make that factual determination. The jury looks at all the surrounding circumstances to determine what the offeree ought to have understood. It makes no difference what the offeror actually intended because the test looks to the presumed intent of the offeror. In making the analysis of the offeror's presumed intent, juries weigh the answers to these three questions:

A mortgage contains promises from the offeror and the offeree.

1. Does the offeror's manifestation demonstrate a *present intention to contract* or *only* an intent to bargain? (Language of present commitment is necessary for an offer.)
2. How *definite* are the terms as communicated? (The more definite, the more likely it is an offer.)
3. To whom is the manifestation addressed? (If addressed to a specific person rather than the public generally, then it is probably an offer.)

4. Present Intention

To decide if an offer was made, the first step is to evaluate the language used. If there are no words of present commitment or undertaking, then probably the manifestation was only a preliminary negotiation or an invitation to the other party to make an offer. The following is preliminary negotiation language: "I am asking," "I would consider," "I am going to sell," etc. Such language is generally construed as inviting offers because there is no present commitment. Consider the following examples:

1. In reply to Patty's inquiry if Stuart would sell his car for $5,000, Stuart said, "It would not be possible for me to sell unless I got $6,000 in cash." There was no offer by Stuart. He only is saying that he would consider offers that were at least $6,000. Stuart made no commitment to sell.

FIGURE 14-1 ■ Requirements for an Offer

1. Present Intention to Contract
2. Definiteness
3. Proper Party

2. "I quote you $20 per hockey puck for immediate acceptance." This communication is an offer. In general, price quotations are not considered offers because there is no present commitment. Here there is promissory language "for immediate acceptance, which would lead a reasonable person in the offeree's position to think an offer is made.

5. Definiteness

Many transactions involve lengthy negotiations between the parties, often with an exchange of numerous letters, proposals, and conversations. It is frequently difficult to establish the point at which the parties have concluded the negotiation stage and have entered into a binding contract. The key question in such situations is whether a definite offer was made and accepted or whether the letters, communications, and proposals were simply part of continuing negotiations. The courts must examine the facts of each case, and to those facts they must apply the basic contract rules concerning the requirements of an offer. An offer must be definite and must be made under such circumstances that the person receiving it has reason to believe that the other party (offeror) is willing to deal on the terms indicated. As a general rule, courts require an offer be *reasonably definite.*

One of the reasons for the requirement of definiteness is that courts may have to determine at a later date whether or not the performance is in compliance with the terms. Consequently, if the terms are vague or impossible to measure with some precision or if major terms are absent, no contract results. Therefore, before a proposal can ripen into a contract, the offer must be sufficiently definite (when coupled with the acceptance) so a court can be reasonably certain regarding both the *nature* and *extent* of the assumed duties. Otherwise, a court has no basis for adjudicating liability. The more certain and definite the communications, the more reasonable it is to conclude that an offer is intended. However, the issue remains: How definite must an offer be?

If the parties have intended to make a contract, uncertainty concerning incidental or collateral matters is not fatal to the contract's existence. For example, assume that the parties agree that certain performances shall be mutually rendered by them "immediately" or "promptly" or as soon as possible" or "in about a month." Although these promises are indefinite, modern contract law would view them as sufficiently definite to form a contract. It should be noted, however, that the more terms the parties leave open, the less likely it is that they have intended to create a binding agreement.

In essence, the existence of a contract is determined by three rules: (1) The parties must intend (under the objective theory) to make a contract; (2) one or more material terms can be omitted from the agreement without the contract failing for indefiniteness; (3) a contract must have enough terms so a court can determine when the contract has been breached and then can fashion an appropriate remedy.

6. Gap Filling

Courts should be willing to fill gaps or missing terms under an agreement, especially if the parties intend to contract but are silent regarding some terms. The trend of the Code and modern case law is to supply reasonable terms—even material terms. *Time for performance* and the *price* to be paid, for example, are important terms and usually are included in the contract. If no time clause is included, a court in most contracts will supply a reasonable time for performances [2-309(1)]. If no price is specified, a court will rule that a reasonable price was intended [2-305]. Courts are willing, under the Code and under modern case law, to supply terms material to a contract under the impression that the parties have sufficiently indicated an intent to contract and, because they have not stated a particular, important term, the assumption is that a reasonable term is acceptable.

Gap filling the price term also applies when the parties have agreed that the price is to be fixed by a market or other standard and that standard fails. In a non-Code case, however, if the contract is totally executory (neither party has performed), the contract with an unspecified price term may not be enforced.

Distinguish omitted term from vague term: A court can gap-fill a missing term but cannot rewrite the contract. Courts follow the presumption that the parties intend reasonable terms; that presumption applies only to omitted terms. *If a term is vague, gap filling is not allowed.* Thus, when parties express their intention on a matter, the court cannot supply an external, reasonable term. To do so would be inconsistent with the express intention of the parties.

Although the Code allows material terms to be supplied by the court, the contract must contain sufficient terms so the court can fashion an appropriate remedy [2-204(3)]. Quite naturally, the question arises: What term or terms are absolutely necessary before a court can state a proper remedy? The one term that must be in every contract is the *quantity* term. Without it, a court has no basis to figure damages.

7. To Whom Addressed

In addition to the language used and the definiteness of the communication, another factor to consider is the *person addressed.* Since an offer creates in someone the power to accept, the communication must sufficiently identify the offeree or the class from whom the offeree may emerge. The usual rule is that if the addressee is an indefinite group, as in the case of advertisements, then there is no offer. Reward offers illustrate an exception to this rule. Although the offeree is unidentified and unknown at the time a reward offer is made, the performance of the act requested in the reward is an acceptance that also identifies the offeree.

In general, advertisements, estimates, quotes, catalogs, circulars, proposals, and the like are not offers, for several reasons. There is no quantity term or language of present commitment; the goods are seldom adequately described. Practically speaking, advertisers do not intend the communication to be an offer that can ripen into a contract on the basis of the terms expressed. While most ads do not constitute an offer, it is possible to have an ad be so specific as to the quantity available at a price that the ad is considered an offer open for the buyer's acceptance.

8. An Offer Must Be Communicated

An offer is not effective until it has been communicated to the offeree by the offeror. It can be effectively communicated only by the offeror, or duly authorized agent of the offeror. If the offeree learns of the offeror's intention to make an offer from some outside source, no offer results. Also, to be effective, the offer must be communicated through the medium or channel selected by the offeror. Thus, if Terry was in Margaret's office and noticed on the desk a letter directed to Terry and containing an offer, the offer would not have been communicated to Terry. Terry would not be in a position to accept the offer.

An offer to the public may be made through newspapers or posted notices. As far as a particular individual is concerned, it is not effective until he or she learns that the offer has been made. As a result, a person without actual knowledge cannot accept the offer. If a reward is offered for the arrest of a fugitive and a person makes the arrest without actual knowledge of the offer of the reward, there is no contract.

An offer is effective when received even though it is delayed in reaching the offeree. Because the delay normally results from the negligence of the offeror or the chosen means of communication (for example, an overnight private mail service), the offeror should bear the loss resulting from the delay. If the delay is apparent to the offeree, the acceptance will be effective only if it is communicated to the offeror within a reasonable time after the offer would normally have been received. If the offeree knows that there has been a delay in communicating the offer, he or she cannot take advantage of the delay.

It should be noted that printed material often found on the back of contract forms and occasionally on letterheads, unless embodied in the contract by reference to it, is not generally considered part of any contract set forth on the form or letterhead. It is not a part of the contract because it has not been communicated by the offeror to the offeree.

9. Auctions

With reserve

The right of the owner of an item sold at auction to withdraw the item prior to the sale being declared final

Without reserve

When the owner of an item sold at auction has no right to withdraw the item and the item must be sold to the highest bidder

Auctions are either with reserve or without reserve. An auction is considered to be with reserve unless it is specifically announced to be without reserve. In a **with reserve** auction, the bidders are the offerors, and the acceptance occurs with the fall of the hammer. Thus, the auctioneer may withdraw the property at any time and the owner, or owner's agents, may bid. In a **without reserve** auction, the auctioneer makes the offer, and each bid is an acceptance subject to there being no higher bid. In either auction, the bidder can withdraw the bid freely before the fall of the hammer.

The Code has a separate section that covers sales of goods by auction [2-328]. In an auction sale, the sale is completed when the auctioneer strikes the hammer. At the point when the hammer falls, the person making the highest bid is entitled to the article and must pay for it. It sometimes happens that while the auctioneer's hammer is falling, but before it has struck the table, another bid is made. In this case, the Code provides that the auctioneer can reopen the bidding or declare the goods sold under the bid on which the hammer was falling [2-328(2)].

One who is selling goods at auction cannot bid at his or her own sale unless notice has been given that this privilege is being retained. The Code provides that if the auctioneer knowingly receives a bid that has been made by the seller or on his or her behalf, and no notice has been given that the seller has the privilege of bidding at his or her own sale, the buyer has a choice of remedies. If the seller's wrongful bidding has bid up the price, the bidder can refuse to be bound by the sale. The bidder could demand that the goods be sold to him or her at the price of the last good-faith bid prior to the completion of the sale [2-328(4)]. The Code provisions are designed to protect people who bid at auction sales and to prevent them from being defrauded.

DURATION OF OFFERS

10. Introduction

Assuming that an offer has been made, you must consider the next legal issue—the duration of that offer; that is, how long does the offeree have the power to accept? The offeree has the power to accept until the offer is terminated. An offer that has been properly communicated continues in existence until it (1) lapses or expires, (2) is terminated by operation of law (illegality and incapacity), (3) is rejected by the offeree, or (4) is revoked (directly or indirectly) by the offeror.

11. Lapse of Time

Lapse

The termination of an offer's effectiveness due to the passage of time

An offer does not remain open indefinitely, even though the offeror fails to revoke it. If an offer does not stipulate the period during which it is to continue, it remains open for a *reasonable time*, a period that a reasonable person might conclude was intended. Whether an offer has **lapsed** because of the passage of time is usually a question of fact for the jury after it has given proper

FIGURE 14-2 ■ Methods of Terminating an Offer

1. **Lapse of time**
2. **Termination by operation of law**
3. **Rejection by offeree**
4. **Revocation by offeror**
5. **Counter-offer**

weight to all related circumstances, one of which is the nature of the property. An offer involving property that is constantly fluctuating in price remains open a relatively short time in comparison with property that has a more stable price. Other facts that should be considered are the circumstances under which the offer is made, the relation of the parties, and the means used in transmitting the offer. An offer made orally usually lapses when the conversation ends unless the offeror clearly indicates that the proposal may be considered further by the offeree.

If the offer stipulates the period during which it may be accepted, it automatically lapses at the end of that period. How do you measure the time period? Assume the offer is in a letter that states it will remain open for five days. The offer is dated May 1 and is received by the offeree on May 3. One might argue that the offer lapsed on May 5, since the letter is dated May 1. Since an offer is not an offer until communicated, however, and if there is no contrary intent, the time will be measured from the time the offeree *receives* the offer. The rationale is to protect the offeree unless he or she has some reason to know that time should be measured from some earlier date. The last day for acceptance would be May 7.

12. Termination by Operation of Law

Several events will terminate an offer as a *matter of law*. Notice of their occurrence need not be given or communicated to the offeree or the offeror, as the offer ends instantaneously upon the occurrence of the event. Such events include the death or adjudicated insanity of either party or the destruction of the subject matter of the offer or illegality that occurs after the offer is made. The occurrence of any one of these events eliminates one of the requisites for a contract, thereby destroying the effectiveness of the acceptance of the offer to create a contract. Thus, if the offeror dies before the acceptance is effective, the offer is terminated and there is no contract. The offer terminates at the moment of death or on the date a personal representative is appointed. Another event is the enactment of a statute making illegal the performance of any contract that would result from acceptance of the offer. Supervening illegality of the proposed contract legally terminates the offer.

If the delay in acting on an offer is unusually long, the issue of lapse may be a question of law for the court. In such cases, a jury is not allowed to reward the offeree for procrastination by finding that the offer had not terminated.

There is a distinct difference between the termination of an offer and the termination of a contract. It should be emphasized that death, for example, terminates an offer but not a contract. As a general rule, death of either party does not excuse performance of contracts although it would excuse performance in contracts for personal service. To illustrate the effect of the death of one of the parties to an offer, assume that Jeffrey offers to sell to Clint a computer for $5,000. After Jeffrey's death, Clint, without knowledge of the death, mails his acceptance to Jeffrey and immediately enters into a contract to resell the computer to West for $7,000. Jeffrey's estate has no duty to deliver the machine, even though West may have a claim against Clint for breach of contract if the latter failed to deliver the computer. Had Clint's acceptance become effective before Jeffrey's death, the executor of the estate would have been obligated to deliver the computer.

13. Rejection by Offeree

Rejection

The termination of an offer's effectiveness by the offeree's statement or conduct that is inconsistent with the offer's terms

An offeree's power of acceptance terminates if the *offeree rejects the offer*. An offeree who rejects cannot later bind the offeror by tendering an acceptance. A **rejection** terminates an offer even though the offeror had promised to keep the offer open for a specified time. Rejection of an offer is not effective in terminating the offer until the rejection has been received by the offeror or his or her authorized agent. Thus, a rejection that has been sent may be withdrawn at any time prior to delivery to the offeror. Such action does not bar a later acceptance.

It is often difficult to determine whether a communication by an offeree is a rejection or merely an expression of a desire to negotiate further on the terms of the agreement. Thus, it is possible to suggest a counterproposal in a way that clearly indicates the offer is still being considered and is not being rejected. The offeree wants a reaction from the offeror to the suggested changes. Also, the offeree, in accepting, may set forth terms not included in the offer, but only those that would be implied as normally included in such an agreement. The inclusion of such terms will not prevent formation of a contract. A request for further information by an offeree who indicates that the offer is still under consideration will not constitute a rejection of the offer. However, as discussed later in this chapter under the law of acceptances, a counteroffer usually is a rejection that terminates an offer.

14. Revocation by Offeror

Revocation

The termination of an offer's effectiveness by the offeror's statement that the offer is no longer available for acceptance

If the offer is not irrevocable, an offeror may **revoke** at any time before the offeree accept the offer. As stated, the *offeror may revoke* even though he or she has promised to hold the offer open for a definite period. As long as it remains a revocable offer, it can be legally withdrawn, although morally or ethically such action may be unjustified. However, the next three sections discuss ways the law may recognize that an offer is irrevocable.

The offeror, possessing the power to revoke, can terminate the offer by communicating the revocation to the offeree. This communication can be direct or indirect. A directly communicated revocation to the offeree is effective only when received. Merely sending a notice of revocation is insufficient. It must be received, regardless of how or by whom it is conveyed. Just as the offer is not an offer until received, a revocation is not effective until received.

Although most revocations are made directly, the law recognizes that the revocation can occur indirectly through some third party not associated with the offeror. Indirect revocation occurs when the offeree secures reliable information from a third party that the offeror has engaged in conduct that indicates to a reasonable person that the offeror no longer wishes to make the offer. An effective indirect revocation requires that (1) the third party give correct information, (2) the offeror's conduct would indicate to a reasonable person that the offeror no longer recognizes the offer, and (3) the third party is a reliable source.

IRREVOCABLE OFFERS

15. Options

The offeror, as master of the offer, retains the power to revoke his offer. Although most offers are thus revocable, the law acknowledges that an offer may be irrevocable. The power to revoke may be lost by (1) contract, (2) legislation, and (3) conduct of the offeree. All three ways are based on option contract principles.

The offeror can sell away his or her power to revoke. Recall that an offeror can revoke the offer despite saying that he or she will not or that the offer will remain open for a specified time. For a consideration, however, the offeror can sell away his or her power to revoke, thereby creating an option contract.

Option
A right secured by a contract to accept or reject an irrevocable offer, sometimes called a "paid-for offer", within a fixed period of time

An **option** is a contract based on some consideration, whereby the offeror binds himself or herself to hold an offer open for an agreed period of time. It gives the holder of the option the right to accept the continuing offer within the specified time. Quite often, the offeree pays or promises to pay money in order to have the option (the continuing offer) remain open. The consideration need not be money. It may be anything that the law recognizes as legal value. The significant fact is that the offer has been transformed into a contract of option because of consideration supplied by the offeree. The offer becomes irrevocable for the period of the option. Of course, the offeree in an option contract is under no obligation to accept the offer; he or she simply has the right to do so.

The option contract is a distinct contract. It effectively takes away the power of the offeror to revoke the offer and make an offer to another. An offeror is willing to wait because the offeror has received consideration in exchange for the promise to not make an offer to another. For example, suppose you wish to sell your laptop computer. You offer to sell the laptop to Alice for $400. Alice says she needs to think about buying the computer and offers you $50 if you agree to hold the offer open for her to accept for three days. You agree and receive the $50. An option contract is created. During the three day period, Alice may accept and pay the full price of $400 for the computer. After the three days have passed, you are free to sell the computer to anyone.

Frequently, an option is part of another contract. A lease may contain a clause that gives to the tenant the right to purchase the property within a given period at a stated price; a sale of merchandise may include a provision that obligates the seller to supply an additional amount at the same price if ordered by the purchaser within a specified time. Such options are enforceable because the initial promise to pay rent serves as consideration for both the lease and the right to buy. The original purchase price of goods serves as consideration for the goods purchased and the option to buy additional goods.

16. Firm Offers

Merchant
Under the UCC, a person who deals in goods of the kind under contract or who by occupation holds self out as having knowledge or skill peculiar to the goods involved

Firm offer
Under the UCC, an offer made by a merchant and accompanied by that offeror's promise not to revoke

States have statutes that make certain types of offers irrevocable. The most significant statute is based on a provision of the Code [2-205], which operates to make a merchant's offer irrevocable *without consideration.* A **merchant** is a businessperson dealing in goods [2-104(1)]. The requisites of this so-called **firm offer** under the Code are (1) assurance given in a signed writing that the offer will be held open, (2) the offeror is a merchant, and (3) the transaction involves the sale of goods. The offer is then irrevocable for the time stated in the offer (but no longer than three months) or for a reasonable time not to exceed three months if the offer has no stated time period. If the writing assuring the offer will remain open is on a form supplied by the offeree, it must be separately signed by the offeror. The offeree in a firm offer can rely on the continuing legal obligation of the offeror and make other commitments on the strength of it. In effect, the firm offer by a merchant is the equivalent of an option without consideration.

17. Conduct of the Offeree

The third type of irrevocable offer springs from a situation analogous to an option contract. When the offeree starts to perform or relies on the offer, the law protects the offeree by holding that the offeror has lost the power to revoke. Analytically, the offeree has done something that the law sees as legal value. This legal value buys away the offeror's power to revoke, just as actual consideration does in a true option contract. The legal value consists of either part performance in the unilateral contract situation or reliance (substantial change of position) by the offeree.

Suppose Lucy says to Shirley, "I will pay you $50 to sew the letter L on four of my sweaters." When Shirley finishes sewing the L's (the act requested), that is acceptance. At that moment, a contract springs into existence. It is a unilateral contract with only one duty—to pay $50; however, problems can arise prior to *complete* performance. After Shirley starts to perform, can Lucy revoke her offer for a unilateral contract? In the early common law, the offer could be revoked anytime prior to complete performance. The offeree who had partly performed was relegated to a quasi-contract action for the reasonable value of the services bestowed on the offeror. Since this action could cause unfair results, modern law favors the proposition that the offeree should be given a reasonable time to perform fully, once he or she starts to perform. The majority of courts hold that the offer is irrevocable for that reasonable time.

Sometimes it is difficult to decide if an offeree is partly performing or merely preparing to perform. Let's take the classic example. I offer to pay you $100 if you walk across the Brooklyn Bridge. You start to walk and get about halfway across the bridge, and I run up beside you and shout, "I revoke." You respond, "You cannot revoke, because my part performance has made your offer irrevocable, like an option contract." You are legally correct, but now decide if any of the following are part performances or merely preparing to perform: (1) You buy a pair of running shoes to use in crossing the bridge. (2) You start on a daily exercise routine to get in shape for the walk. (3) You catch a cab that delivers you to the Brooklyn Bridge. This is an offer to form a unilateral contact. These are only preparatory acts and do not make the offer irrevocable.

Reliance by an offeree on either a bilateral or unilateral offer can create an "option" contract. For example, assume that an offer is made that the offeror should reasonably expect will induce substantial reliance by the offeree and that such reliance happens. In such a case, the offer is binding to the extent necessary to avoid injustice, as if an option contract existed. Note that the reliance must be substantial as well as reasonably foreseeable by the offeror. In some instances, it is foreseeable that the offeree must incur substantial expense, or undertake substantial commitments, or forego alternatives, to put himself or herself in a position to accept by either a promise or performance. The offeree may have to borrow money, undertake special training, or refuse other offers before he or she can accept. In such cases, to avoid injustice the offer is irrevocable, like an option contract.

THE LAW OF ACCEPTANCE

18. Introduction

Acceptance
A statement by one party (called the offeree) that he or she is prepared to be bound to the contractual position stated in an offer, the second essential element to the meeting of the minds of the contracting parties

An agreement consists of an offer by one party (offeror) and its acceptance by the person (offeree) to whom the offer is made. An **acceptance** is an indication by the offeree of his or her willingness to be bound by the terms of the offer. Figuratively speaking, an offer hangs like a suspended question. The acceptance must be a positive answer to that question. For example, the offeror says, "I will sell you this article for $200. Will you buy it?" The offeree now has the legal power to accept this offer; and if he or she does so in proper fashion, a contract will result. A contract, therefore, results when the offeree answers the question in the affirmative.

Acceptance may, if the offer permits, take the form of an act (unilateral offer), a return promise communicated to the offeror (bilateral offer), or the signing and delivery of a written instrument (either by hard copy or electronically). The last-named method is the most common in transactions of considerable importance and in those that are more formal. Regardless of the manner of acceptance, there must be a clear indication of intent to accept. The following case examines this issue within the context of online arrangements between firms.

CASE

Register.com, Inc. v. Verio, Inc.

UNITED STATES COURT OF APPEALS FOR THE SECOND CIRCUIT

356 F.3d 393 (2004)

This plaintiff, Register, is one of over fifty companies serving as registrars for the issuance of domain names on the world wide web. As a registrar, Register issues domain names to persons and entities preparing to establish web sites on the Internet. Web sites are identified and accessed by reference to their domain names.

The Internet Corporation for Assigned Names and Numbers, known by the acronym "ICANN," Appointed Register a registrar of domain names. ICANN is a private, non-profit public benefit corporation that was established by agencies of the U.S. government to administer the Internet domain name system. To become a registrar of domain names, Register was required to enter into a standard form agreement with ICANN, designated as the ICANN Registrar Accreditation Agreement, November 1999 version (referred to herein as the "ICANN Agreement").

To register a domain name, applicants submit to the registrar contact information, including at a minimum, the applicant's name, postal address, telephone number, and electronic mail address. The ICANN Agreement, referring to this registrant contact information under the rubric "WHOIS information," requires the registrar, under terms discussed in greater detail below, to preserve it, update it daily, and provide for free public access to it through the Internet as well as through an independent access port, called port 43.

Section II.F.5 of the ICANN Agreement (which furnishes a major basis for the appellant Verio's contentions on this appeal) requires that the registrar "not impose terms and conditions" on the use made by others of its WHOIS data "except as permitted by ICANN -adopted policy." In specifying what restrictions may be imposed, the Agreement requires the registrar to permit use of its WHOIS data "for any lawful purposes except to: ... support the transmission of mass unsolicited, commercial advertising or solicitations via email (spam); [and other listed purposes not relevant to this appeal]." (emphasis added).

Another section of the ICANN Agreement (upon which appellee Register relies) provides as follows,

> *No Third-Party Beneficiaries: This Agreement shall not be construed to create any obligation by either ICANN or Registrar to any non-party to this Agreement . . . .*

ICANN Agreement § II.S.2. Third parties could nonetheless seek enforcement of a registrar's obligations set forth in the ICANN

- *Agreement by resort to a grievance process under ICANN's auspices.*
- *In compliance with § II.F.1 of the Agreement, Register updated the WHOIS information on a daily basis and established Internet and port 43 service, which allowed free public query of its WHOIS information. An entity making a WHOIS query through Register's Internet site or port 43 would receive a reply furnishing the requested WHOIS information, captioned by a legend devised by Register, which stated,*

> *By submitting a WHOIS query, you agree that you will use this data only for lawful purposes and that under no circumstances will you use this data to ... support the transmission of mass unsolicited, commercial advertising or solicitation via email.*

- *The terms of that legend tracked § II.F.5 of the Agreement in specifying the restrictions Register imposed on the use of its WHOIS data. Subsequently, as explained below, Register amended the terms of this legend to impose more stringent restrictions on the use of the information gathered through such queries*

In addition to performing the function of a registrar of domain names, Register also engages in the business of selling web-related services to entities that maintain web sites. These services cover various aspects of web site development. In order to solicit business for the services it offers, Register sends out marketing communications. Among the entities it solicits for the sale of such services are entities whose domain names it registered. However, during the registration process, Register offers registrants the opportunity to elect whether or not they will receive marketing communications from it.

The defendant Verio, against whom the preliminary injunction was issued, is engaged in the business of selling a variety of web site design, development and operation services. In the sale of such services, Verio competes with Register's web site development business. To facilitate its pursuit of customers, Verio undertook to obtain daily updates of the WHOIS information relating to newly registered domain names. To achieve this, Verio devised an automated software program, or robot, which each day would submit multiple successive WHOIS queries through the port 43 accesses of various registrars. Upon acquiring the WHOIS information of new registrants, Verio would send them marketing solicitations by email, telemarketing and direct mail. To the extent that Verio's solicitations were sent by email, the practice was inconsistent with the terms of the restrictive legend Register attached to its responses to Verio's queries.

Register wrote to Verio demanding that it cease using WHOIS information derived from Register not only for email marketing, but also for marketing by direct mail and telephone. Verio ceased using

continued

the information in email marketing, but refused to stop marketing by direct mail and telephone.

Register brought this suit and moved for a preliminary injunction.

Verio assumes that Register was legally authorized to demand that takers of WHOIS data from its systems refrain from using it for mass solicitation by mail and telephone, as well as by email. Verio contends that it, nonetheless, never became contractually bound to the conditions imposed by Register's restrictive legend because, in the case of each query Verio made, the legend did not appear until after Verio had submitted the query and received the WHOIS data. Accordingly, Verio contends that in no instance did it receive legally enforceable notice of the conditions Register intended to impose. Verio, therefore, argues it should not be deemed to have taken WHOIS data from Register's systems subject to Register's conditions.

Verio's argument might well be persuasive if its queries addressed to Register's computers had been sporadic and infrequent. If Verio had submitted only one query, or even if it had submitted only a few sporadic queries, that would give considerable force to its contention that it obtained the WHOIS data without being conscious that Register intended to impose conditions, and without being deemed to have accepted Register's conditions. Instead, Verio was daily submitting numerous queries, each of which resulted in its receiving notice of the terms Register exacted. Furthermore, Verio admits that it knew perfectly well what terms Register demanded. Verio's argument fails.

The situation might be compared to one in which plaintiff P maintains a roadside fruit stand displaying bins of apples. A visitor, defendant D, takes an apple and bites into it. As D turns to leave, D sees a sign, visible only as one turns to exit, which says "Apples—50 cents apiece." D does not pay for the apple. D believes he has no obligation to pay because he had no notice when he bit into the apple that 50 cents was expected in return. D's view is that he never agreed to pay for the apple. Thereafter, each day, several times a day, D revisits the stand, takes an apple, and eats it. D never leaves money.

P sues D in contract for the price of the apples taken. D defends on the ground that on no occasion did he see P's price notice until after he had bitten into the apples. D may well prevail as to the first apple taken. D had no reason to understand upon taking it that P was demanding the payment. In our view, however, D cannot continue on a daily basis to take apples for free, merely because the sign demanding payment is so placed that on each occasion D does not see it until he has bitten into the apple, because after the first day D saw the sign and knew full well that P is offering the apples only in exchange for 50 cents in compensation.

Verio's circumstance is effectively the same. Each day Verio repeatedly enters Register's computers and takes that day's new WHOIS data. Each day upon receiving the requested data, Verio receives Register's notice of the terms on which it makes the data available—that the data not be used for mass solicitation via direct mail, email, or telephone. Verio acknowledges that it continued drawing the data from Register's computers with full knowledge that Register offered access subject to these restrictions. Verio is no more free to take Register's data without being bound by the terms on which Register offers it, than D was free, in the example, once he became aware of the terms of P's offer, to take P's apples without obligation to pay the 50 cent price at which P offered them.

We find that the district court was within its discretion in concluding that Register showed likelihood of success on the merits of its contract claim. Therefore, that requirement associated with the issuance of a preliminary injunction is met.

■ *Affirmed.*

CASE CONCEPTS REVIEW

1. Why did the court conclude that Verio accepted the terms of the legend?
2. In another section of the opinion, the court stated that there was no reason why Verio be required to "click" acceptance of the terms? Based on the material presented above, why do you believe that the court did not impose a "click" requirement?

Only the person to whom the offer is made can accept the offer. Offers to the public may be accepted by any member of the public who is aware of the offer. In general, an offeree cannot assign the offer to a third party. For example, if goods are ordered from a firm that has discontinued business, that firm cannot transfer the order to another firm. If the goods are shipped by its successor, the offeror (the purchaser) is under no duty to accept the goods. If the offeror does accept them, knowing that they were shipped by the successor, then by implication he or she agrees to pay the new concern for the goods at the contract price. If the offeror does not know of the change of ownership when accepting the goods, he or she is not liable for the contract price. The offeror's only liability is in quasi-contract for the reasonable value of the goods. In the alternative, the purchaser could return them to the seller if he or she so elected.

Despite the general rule just discussed, option contracts may be transferred by the holder of the option to another person. Such a transfer is called an assignment. The reason an option is transferable is that the option is a completed contract, and its offer is not considered personal.

19. Accepting a Bilateral Offer

An offer for a bilateral contract is accepted by the offeree making a promise in response to the promise of the offeror. The offeree's promise is to perform in the manner required by the offer. The promise of the offeree (acceptance) must be communicated to the offeror or his or her agent and may consist of any conduct on the part of the offeree that clearly shows an intention to be bound by the conditions prescribed in the offer.

The acceptance may take the form of a signature to a written agreement or even a nod of the head or any other indication of a willingness to perform as required by the offer. No formal procedure is generally required. If the offer is made to two or more persons, the acceptance is not complete until each of the parties has indicated acceptance. Until all have responded and accepted, the offeror is at liberty to withdraw the offer.

When it is understood that the agreement will be set forth in a written instrument, the acceptance is effective only when the document has been signed and delivered (unless it was clearly the intention of the parties that the earlier verbal agreement be binding and that the writing act merely as a memorandum or evidence of the oral contract that was already effective and binding on the parties).

20. Counteroffers under the Mirror-Image Rule

Mirror-image (matching acceptance) rule
A common-law requirement that an acceptance could not vary from any term stated in the offer

In forming a bilateral contract, an attempted acceptance may have terms new or different from those stated in the offer. Under common law, this variance between the offer and acceptance violates the **mirror-image** or **matching acceptance rule**. Under this rule, to be effective, an acceptance must conform exactly to the terms of the offer. *Any* deviation from the terms of the offer and the acceptance will be held to be a counteroffer, which constitutes a rejection terminating the original offer. *Note:* Once a counteroffer is made (that is, the acceptance is not a mirror image of the offer), then the attempted acceptance becomes a *new* offer and the original offer terminates.

It may, at times, be difficult to decide if the acceptance is a counteroffer or merely a counter-inquiry. The original offer does not terminate if the offeree merely suggests or requests new or different terms or makes a counterinquiry. Monty offers to sell one antique cabinet to Brian for $3,500. Brian replies, "Will you take $3,000?" This is only a counter-inquiry. Suppose Brian wires, "Please send lowest cash price for cabinet." This is not a counteroffer but only a request for different terms; but in the usual case, Brian would say, "I'll pay only $2,500." This is a counteroffer under the mirror-image rule and a rejection.

21. Variance under the Code

The Code rejects the mirror-image rule. Under the Code, a definite expression of acceptance of a written confirmation operates as an acceptance. This is true even though the acceptance states terms additional to, or different from, those offered or agreed on, unless acceptance is made conditional on agreement to the additional or different terms [2-207(1)]. *This means that the additional or different terms do not prevent the formation of a contract unless they are expressed in the form of a counterproposal.*

Assuming that there is acceptance, what is the status of the additional or different terms? The different terms do not become part of the contract; they are eliminated. Regarding the additional terms, the impact of these terms depends on whether either party to the contract is a merchant. If at least one party is not a merchant, the additional terms become proposals for addition to the contract. Such proposals may be accepted or rejected by the offeror. However, if the contract is *between merchants,* the additional terms become part of the contract unless (a) the offer expressly limits acceptance to the terms of the offer; (b) the added terms materially alter the offer; or (c) notification of objection to them has already been given or is given within a reasonable time after notice of them is received.

The problem of variance arises in three similar situations: (1) An acceptance states terms additional to, or different from, those offered; (2) a written confirmation of an informal or oral agreement sets forth terms additional to, or different from, those previously agreed on; and (3) the printed forms used by the parties are in conflict, especially in the "fine print." The Code takes the position that in all three situations, "a proposed deal which in commercial understanding has in fact been closed is recognized as a contract" [2-207].

The following case is typical of those involving the Code change of the mirror-image rule.

CASE

Standard Bent Glass Corp. v. Glassrobots Oy, A Corporation Registered in Finland

UNITED STATES COURT OF APPEALS FOR THE THIRD CIRCUIT

333 F.3d 440 (2003)

On appeal is a motion to compel arbitration in a commercial dispute. At issue are principles of contract formation under the Uniform Commercial Code.

Standard Bent Glass, a Pennsylvania corporation, set out to purchase a machine for its factory that would produce cut glass, and in March 1998, commenced negotiations with representatives of Glassrobots Oy, a Finnish corporation. On March 19, 1998, Glassrobots tendered a written offer to sell Standard Bent Glass a glass fabricating system. The initial offer was rejected but negotiations continued and, in February 1999, reached a critical juncture. On February 1, Standard Bent Glass faxed an offer to purchase a glass fabricating system from Glassrobots. The offer sheet commenced, "Please find below our terms and conditions related to ORDER # DKH2199," and defined the items to be purchased, the quantity, the price of $1.1 million, the payment terms, and installation specifics, instructions, and warranties. The letter concluded, "Please sign this ORDER and fax to us if it is agreeable."

On February 2, Glassrobots responded with a cover letter, invoice, and standard sales agreement. The cover letter recited, in part: "Attached you'll find our standard sales agreement. Please read it through and let me know if there is anything you want to change. If not, I'll send you 2 originals, which will be signed." Glassrobots did not return, nor refer to, Standard Bent Glass's order.

Later that day, Standard Bent Glass faxed a return letter that began, "Please find our changes to the Sales Agreement," referring to Glassrobots's sales agreement. The letter apparently accepted Glassrobots's standard sales agreement as a template and requested five specific changes. The letter closed, "Please call me if the above is not agreeable. If it is we will start the wire today."

The five changes addressed using a wire transfer in lieu of a letter of credit, payment terms, late penalty for shipment delays, site visits, and technical specifications. All were straightforward modifications and spelled out in the Standard Bent Glass letter. On February 4, Standard Bent Glass wired the down payment to Glassrobots. On February 8, the wire transfer cleared Glassrobots's bank account.

No contract was ever signed by both parties. Nevertheless, the parties continued to perform. Glassrobots installed the glass fabricating system. On August 5, both parties signed the Acceptance Test Protocol, which stated: "We undersigners hereby certify the performance and acceptance test according to the Sales Agreement TSF II 200/320 between Standard Bent Glass Corp., USA and Glassrobots Oy has been carried out. All the equipment fulfill the conditions mentioned in the same Agreement, in quality an [sic] quantity." In November 1999, Standard Bent Glass made its final payment to Glassrobots.

Subsequently, Standard Bent Glass noticed defects in the equipment. The parties disputed the cause of the defects, and on November 8, 2000, Standard Bent Glass filed a complaint against Glassrobots in state court. After removal to federal court, Glassrobots filed a motion to compel arbitration under an appendix to the standard sales agreement that Standard Bent Glass claims it never received. The District Court granted Glassrobots's motion and Standard Bent Glass appealed.

Under UCC section 2-207(1), the offeree's expression of acceptance or transmission of a written confirmation generally results in the formation of a contract. This is true unless the offeree makes that expression or confirmation "expressly conditional" on the offeror's assent to the proposed additional or different terms.

UCC § 2-207 provides:

(1) A definite and seasonable expression of acceptance or a written confirmation which is sent within a reasonable time operates as an acceptance even though it states terms additional to or different from those offered or agreed upon, unless acceptance is expressly made conditional on assent to the additional or different terms.

(2) The additional terms are to be construed as proposals for addition to the contract. Between merchants such terms become part of the contract unless:

(a) the offer expressly limits acceptance to the terms of the offer;
(b) they materially alter it; or
(c) notification of objection to them has already been given or is given within a reasonable time after notice of them is received.

(3) Conduct by both parties which recognizes the existence of a contract is sufficient to establish a contract for sale although the writings of the parties do not otherwise establish a contract. In such case the terms of the particular contract consist of those terms on which the writings of the parties agree, together with any supplementary terms incorporated under any other provisions of this Title.

The flexibility permitted under section 2-207 allows parties to begin performance expediently rather than wait for all contract details to be resolved. This structure is well suited to the fast-paced environment of commercial dealings. Where parties perform but do not explicitly agree on a single uniform document, sections 2-207(2) and (3) govern proposed additional or different terms to the contract.

Here, Standard Bent Glass initiated written negotiations between the parties on February 1. This exchange represented an offer from Standard Bent Glass to purchase the glass fabricating machine from Glassrobots. The Standard Bent Glass offer contained a set of terms and conditions. On February 2, Glassrobots responded by enclosing its standard sales agreement, which contained a different set of terms and conditions. Later that day, Standard Bent Glass sent its own response, accepting the terms of the Glassrobots standard sales agreement and proposing five specific modifications. Referring to the Glassrobots agreement, the Standard Bent Glass letter began, "Please find our changes to the Sales Agreement."

This communication from Standard Bent Glass constituted either: (1) a definite and seasonable expression of acceptance under section 2-207(1); (2) a counteroffer; or (3) a rejection followed by conduct by both parties sufficient to recognize a valid contract under section 2-207(3). By using the Glassrobots standard sales agreement as a template and by authorizing a wire transfer of the down payment, Standard Bent Glass demonstrated its intent to perform under the essential terms of Glassrobots's standard sales agreement. Accordingly, its response was a definite and seasonable expression of acceptance of Glassrobots's offer.

Noteworthy was Standard Bent Glass's own immediate performance on the February 2 agreement. On February 4, Standard Bent Glass initiated a wire transfer to Glassrobots for the down payment. The following day, Glassrobots adopted most, but not all, of the proposed modifications and began to perform on the agreement. This was the last significant exchange of written documents between the parties. The parties continued to perform, with Glassrobots constructing and installing the desired equipment and Standard Bent Glass's timely paying for it.

In sum, Standard Bent Glass's conduct constituted a definite and seasonable expression of acceptance that evinced the formation of a contract rather than a counteroffer or rejection. For these reasons, there was a valid contract on the Glassrobots terms of February 2 that incorporated any non-material additions proposed by Standard Bent Glass.

■ *Affirmed.*

CASE CONCEPTS REVIEW

1. Why did the court find the response from Standard Bent Glass an acceptance instead of a counteroffer?
2. How does section 2-207 favor the formation of contracts? Does the traditional, common law "mirror-image" rule favor the formation of contracts to the same extent? Why?

22. Silence as Assent

As a general rule, the offeror cannot force the offeree to reply to the offer. In most cases, therefore, mere silence by the offeree does not amount to acceptance, even though the offeror in his or her offer may have stated that a failure to reply would constitute an acceptance. However, a previous course of dealing between the parties or the receipt of goods by the offeree under certain circumstances could impose a duty on the offeree to speak in order to avoid a contractual relationship. This duty to speak arises when the offeree has led the offeror to believe that silence or inaction is intended as a manifestation of intent to accept and the offeree believes that it is. In other words, silence where a duty exists to communicate either an acceptance or rejection is an acceptance.

Under the Code, a buyer has accepted goods when he or she fails to make an effective rejection or does any act inconsistent with the seller's ownership. However, failure to reject will not be construed as an acceptance unless the buyer has had a reasonable opportunity to examine the goods.

23. Communication of Acceptance

The offeror is the master of the offer. As such, the offeror has the power to control both the *manner* (promise or performance) and *mode* or *medium* of acceptance (phone, telegram, mail). If the offeror specifically seeks only a promise, then the offeree can accept only by promising (bilateral contract). Likewise, the offeror may authorize only one medium of acceptance, and that is the only medium the offeree can use in communicating the acceptance.

> EXAMPLE Tom mails a letter to Ralph stating the terms of a proposed contract. At the end Tom writes, "You can accept this offer only by signing on the dotted line below my signature and returning the contract by express mail." Ralph immediately sends a fax saying, "I accept your offer." There is no contract because a fax was not an authorized medium of acceptance.

In the early common law, unless the offeror stated otherwise, the only authorized medium of communication was the medium used by the offeror in communicating the offer. Assuming the offeree uses the authorized medium to accept, this question arises: When does the acceptance take effect? (1) Upon receipt by the offeror? (2) Or upon dispatch (such as mailing a letter) by the offeree?

Mailbox (deposited acceptance) rule

When the use of the mail is an appropriate way of communicating acceptance, such acceptance is effective when deposited in the mail.

The law generally adopted a rule that protects the offeree by making the acceptance effective at the time it is dispatched. This is known as the **mailbox** or **deposited acceptance rule**. If mail is the authorized medium, the acceptance letter is effective the moment it is mailed, even if the offeror never receives the letter of acceptance.

The deposited acceptance rule could be applied harshly, especially when the offeree accepted by a reasonable medium other than the one used by the offeror. In response, modern law recognizes that some offerors may be indifferent to how the offeree accepts. Some cases have held that an offer invites acceptance in any manner and by any medium reasonable under the circumstances. The Code has a provision that adopts this approach [2-206(1)(a)]. In cases under the Code, the offeror can insist on the manner and medium of acceptance; but if the offeror does not exercise his or her power to limit the manner or mode of acceptance, the offeree may accept in any *reasonable manner* and by any *reasonable medium.* Such acceptances are effective when deposited. What is reasonable depends on all the circumstances surrounding each situation. For example, an offer to sell certain stock is telephoned to you and nothing is said about the medium of acceptance. In a highly speculative market, a quicker medium than mail, such as fax or telephone may be the *reasonable* medium for acceptance.

The application of the mailbox rule can be avoided by the offeror simply stating in the offer that the acceptance is not effective until it is actually received. Any statement about the effective date of the acceptance should be clearly stated. Courts give enforcement to offers that prescribe an exclusive method of acceptance. However, offers that merely suggest a method of acceptance are interpreted as giving the offeree latitude in making and delivering an effective acceptance.

24. Accepting a Unilateral Offer

As indicated previously, an offer may be either unilateral or bilateral. Most offers are bilateral; when there is doubt as to whether they are unilateral or bilateral, the courts tend to construe them as bilateral. When an offer is unilateral, the offeror does not desire a promise of performance, but insists on substantial completion of the act or forbearance requested. As a general rule, substantial performance of the act requested constitutes an acceptance of a unilateral offer. If the offeree ceases performance short of substantial performance, there is no acceptance and no contract.

A difficult question arises when an offeror seeks to withdraw a unilateral offer during the course of the offeree's attempted performance of the act requested. As discussed in Section 17 of this chapter, the generally accepted view is that an offeror of a unilateral offer cannot withdraw during the performance by the offeree. The offeror becomes bound when performance is commenced or tendered, and the offeree has a duty to complete performance. It is part performance by the offeree that legally "buys away" the offeror's power to revoke.

The Code makes some changes in the law of acceptance of unilateral offers. Basically, the Code provides that an order for goods may be accepted either by a shipment of the goods or by a prompt promise to ship the goods [2-206(1)(b)]. For example, a merchant who desperately needs several items of merchandise mails a letter to a manufacturer asking for immediate shipment of the articles listed. This unilateral offer could be accepted by the act of shipment, even though the offeror (the buyer) had no actual knowledge of the acceptance. The buyer, however, could withdraw his or her offer at any time before the seller's delivery to the carrier. This revocation could harm a seller who has incurred expense by procuring, assembling, or packing the goods for shipment. Under the Code, such an offer may either be treated as a unilateral offer and accepted by shipment or be treated as a bilateral offer and accepted by a promise to ship. The seller, under the Code, is thus afforded an opportunity to bind the bargain prior to the time of shipment if he or she wants to do so.

CHAPTER SUMMARY

Objective Theory of Contracts

1. The formation of a contract requires a bargain in which there is a manifestation of mutual assent.
2. Manifestation of mutual assent to an exchange requires that each party either make a promise or begin to render a performance.

OFFERS

Definition

1. An offer is a promise to do or refrain from doing some specified thing in the future.

Tests for Offer

1. The language used must indicate a promise (present commitment) rather than bargaining language.
2. The language of an offer must be reasonably certain so a court can determine if a breach has occurred and fashion an appropriate remedy.
3. Assuming that an offer has been made, a court can gap-fill reasonable terms like time and place of performance, price, and the like.
4. An offer *must* contain a subject matter, a quantity term, and indicate the parties' intent to be contractually bound.
5. An offer must sufficiently identify the offeree or the class from whom the offeree may emerge.

Auctions

1. Auctions may be with or without reserve.
2. In auctions with reserve, the fall of the gavel is the acceptance, and all other bids may be rejected.
3. Sellers cannot bid at auctions under the Code unless notice of that fact is given.

DURATION OF OFFERS

Lapse of Time

1. If a time period for acceptance is stated in the offer, the offer lapses at the end of that time.
2. If no time period for acceptance is stated, the offer lapses at the end of a reasonable period of time.

Termination by Operation of Law

1. Death or insanity of either the offeror or offeree terminates an offer from that moment. Communication to the other party is not required.

2. Supervening illegality terminates an offer.
3. Destruction of the subject matter of the offer terminates the offer.

Rejection by Offeree

1. Rejection by the offeree terminates an offer.
2. Rejection requires words or conduct by the offeree that demonstrate a clear intent not to accept the offer. Inquiries or suggestions about the offer are not rejections.
3. A rejection is not effective until actually communicated to the offeror or his or her agent.
4. A counteroffer is both a rejection of the offer and a new offer.

Revocation by Offeror

1. Unless the offer is irrevocable, the offer can be revoked at any time without liability.
2. The revocation of an offer must be communicated, directly or indirectly, to be effective.
3. Indirect revocation occurs when a *reliable* source gives *reliable* information that would cause a *reasonable* person to think the offer had been revoked.

IRREVOCABLE OFFERS

Option Contracts

1. Offerors can always sell their power to revoke, which creates an option contract.
2. An option contract is based on consideration that binds the offeror to keep the offer open for a stated time period.
3. Option contracts must be strictly performed by the offeree.

Firm Offers

1. The UCC makes a merchant's written offer irrevocable without consideration. This is called a firm offer.
2. The *merchant's* offer to sell *goods* must be in *writing* and state that it will be firm. The firm offer is irrevocable for the time stated or a reasonable time, but in no event beyond three months.

Conduct of the Offeree

1. Part performance of the contract by the offeree makes the offer for a unilateral contract irrevocable.
2. Substantial reliance on the offer by the offeree that is foreseeable by the offeror makes the offer irrevocable, like an option contract.

THE LAW OF ACCEPTANCES

Introduction

1. Acceptance of an offer is a manifestation of assent to the proffered terms made by the offeree in a manner required or invited by the offeror.
2. Offers cannot be transferred unless they are part of an option contract.

Accepting of a Bilateral Offer

1. The offeree accepts a bilateral offer by making a promise.
2. The offeree's promise must be communicated to the offeror.
3. There are no formal procedures required for this communication. Written or verbal statements or conduct indicating a willingness to be bound may act as acceptance.

Counteroffers under the Mirror-Image Rule

1. Under the mirror-image rule at common law, the acceptance must be absolute, unconditional, and conform exactly to the terms of the offer. Otherwise it would be a counteroffer.

Variance under the Code

1. Under the Code, a variant acceptance operates as an acceptance even if it has terms *additional* to or *different from* the offer.
2. When one party is a nonmerchant, the additional terms are proposals for addition to the contract that may be accepted.

3. Between merchants, the additional terms become part of the contract unless (a) the offer limits acceptance to the terms of the offer, or (b) the new terms materially alter the contract, (c) the new terms are rejected by reasonable notice.

Silence as Assent

1. Silence in the absence of a duty to speak does not amount to an acceptance.
2. Under the Code, a buyer accepts goods if he or she fails to make an effective rejection.

Communication of Acceptances

1. In cases not under the Code, acceptance of an offer for a bilateral contract is effective at the time it is deposited in the offeror's medium of communication.
2. Under the Code, an acceptance is effective when deposited in the authorized medium or any other medium reasonable under the circumstances.
3. Modern cases adopt the Code approach for all contracts.

Accepting Unilateral Offers

1. A unilateral offer is accepted by substantial performance of the act requested.
2. Under the Code, an order for goods may be treated as either bilateral or unilateral.

REVIEW QUESTIONS AND PROBLEMS

1. Identify the terms in Column A by matching each with the appropriate statement in Column B.

A	B
(1) Irrevocable offer by offeree's conduct	(a) Written offer by merchant with a promise to keep it open for acceptance
(2) Offer terminated by operation of law	(b) Manifestation of mutual assent
(3) Counteroffer	(c) Reliable person gives reliable information that offer is revoked
(4) Offer terminated after reasonable time	(d) Applies only to acceptances
(5) Irrevocable firm offer	(e) Words or conduct by offeree that reasonably shows offer is not accepted
(6) Rejection	(f) Both a rejection and a new offer
(7) Option contract	(g) Death or insanity of offeror or supervening illegality
(8) Indirect revocation	(h) For consideration offeror sells power to revoke
(9) Meeting of the minds	(i) Offer without a time limit for acceptance
(10) Mailbox rule	(j) Part performance or reliance

2. Suppose that I invite you over next Saturday to a catfish and hush puppy dinner, and you agree to come. You arrive next Saturday, only to find I've left town.

    a. Do you have a contract action against me?
    b. Would it make any difference if we signed a contract stating, "We intend to make this a binding obligation"?
    c. Would it make any difference if you had to drive 325 miles to my house?

3. Seller wrote a general circular to ten buyers asking, "Do you want to buy 240 good 1,000-pound cattle at $8.25? Must be sold by Friday. Phone me at Wichita, Kans." One buyer faxes an immediate acceptance for all 240 cattle. Is there a contract? Why or why not?
4. The following ad appeared in our local newspaper: "1 black lapin stole, beautiful, worth $139.50. $1. FIRST COME, FIRST SERVED." You are the first to appear at the store and tender $1. Is a contract formed? Why or why not?
5. Seller and Buyer execute a contract for 500 jogging shoes. The contract has all the basic terms, except the parties "agree to agree" on the price per shoe at a later date.

   a. Is there a contract?
   b. If so, what happens if they later fail to agree?
   c. Would your answer change if Seller says, "I need at least $50 per set of shoes," and Buyer accepts? Explain.

6. Jimmy offers to sell Margaret a parcel of land for $5,000, stating that the offer will remain open for thirty days. Margaret replies, "Won't you take $4,700?" Jimmy answers, "No." Would an acceptance thereafter by Margaret within the thirty-day period be effective? Explain.
7. Seller offers to sell Buyer a boat for $500. Buyer replies, "I think I want the boat, but let me have a week to consider." Seller replies, "OK. I won't sell the boat to anyone until after one week from today." The next day, Seller sells the boat to Popeye for $600. The day after that, Seller says he has already sold the boat. Nevertheless, Buyer tenders $500.

   a. Is Seller contractually liable to Buyer?
   b. Would your answer change if Seller were a merchant and his promise not to sell for a week were in writing?

8. Plaintiff leased defendant's property for five years with an option to buy at "fair market value." Plaintiff sought to exercise its option by tendering to defendant $80,000. Defendant rejected this offer. Plaintiff sought specific performance of the option agreement, but defendant asserted that a price term of "fair market value" was too indefinite to create a binding contract. Was the defendant correct? Explain.
9. The Cowgers leased certain real property to Northwestern Bell for ten years. The contract granted an option to buy the property provided that the lessee gives sixty days' prior notice of its intention to purchase. Northwestern Bell gave the required sixty days' notice, but the Cowgers refused to sell because the buyer did not tender the purchase price at the time it gave notice. Northwestern Bell sued for specific performance. The Cowgers claimed that the option had not been properly exercised. Can Northwestern Bell accept the option without tendering the purchase price? Explain.
10. Dairy mails Grocery Store an offer to sell 200 quarts of milk at a stated price. Grocery Store immediately replies, "Please send immediately 200 quarts of milk in 1-quart plastic containers." Dairy ignores Grocery Store's reply. If the milk is not sent, has Dairy breached a contract? Explain.

Bargained-for Consideration | 15

CHAPTER OUTLINE

CHAPTER PREVIEW

To have a valid contract, the offer and acceptance must be validated by bargained-for consideration. Not every agreement will be legally enforced. In the validation process, promises that will be enforced are separated from those that will not. If an agreement is based on a bargain, then the promises are legally enforceable. Something is bargained for if it is sought by the promisor in exchange for his or her promise and is given by the promisee in exchange for that promise.

Consideration, then, is defined as a bargained-for exchange. The exchange can be a promise exchanged for a promise, a promise exchanged for an act of performance, or a promise exchanged for a forbearance to act. The doctrine of consideration requires that the promises or performance of both parties be legally valid. If mutuality of consideration is not present, there is no contract.

The doctrine of consideration is central to the idea of a contract.Often, the presence of consideration creates an otherwise unenforceable set of promises. However, care must be taken to analyze the area of consideration with caution. An individual can believe in good faith that they have made promises to another and further believe that the other party will perform. While ethical principles may suggest that the other individual will carry out his/her obligation, the law does not always treat promises made by another as statements of action that have the force of law. Therefore, one may make a promise and not be legally bound to carry out that promise. This chapter delves into the doctrine of consideration with a view toward presenting rules that will assist you in determining whether a set of promises is supported by consideration.

BUSINESS MANAGEMENT DECISION

As the sales manager for a manufacturing firm you contract to supply 500 steel filing cabinets to a customer. Due to unanticipated increased costs in raw materials and in the manufacturing process, you contact this customer and indicate that the price of the cabinets needs to be revised upwards $25 per unit. Your customer does not object to your statement.

Do you need to do anything else to make this price increase binding?

BARGAIN THEORY OF CONSIDERATION

1. Benefits and Detriments

To have consideration, both contracting parties typically will receive a *legal benefit* and incur a *legal detriment.* Legal benefit occurs when a party receives something that he or she had no prior legal right to receive. *Legal detriment* is a little more difficult to define. It is either (1) a promise to perform (or act of performance) that one had no prior legal obligation to perform, or (2) a promise not to do something (or actually refraining from doing something) that one could legally do and had no prior legal obligation not to do.

EXAMPLE Al promises to sell Mary his car for $2,000. Mary promises to pay Al $2,000 for his car. Al has incurred *legal detriment* (sold his car, which he had no prior obligation to do) and has received *legal benefit* (payment of $2,000, which he had no prior legal right to obtain). Mary likewise has incurred a *legal detriment* (must pay $2,000, which she had no prior legal obligation to do) and has received a *legal benefit* (legal right, which she did not previously have, to receive Al's car). Since both promises induced one another, a true bargain occurred. Therefore, this bilateral contract is validated by bargained-for consideration.

Consideration is the price paid for a promise. If nothing is paid for a promise, the courts will not enforce it because the element of consideration is missing. However, the surrender of any legal right is a detriment whether of substantial value or not. Following is perhaps the most famous case to illustrate this point.

CASE

Louisa W. Hamer v. Franklin Sidway, as Executor, etc.

COURT OF APPEALS OF NEW YORK

124 N.Y. 538; 27 N.E. 256 (1891)

OPINION BY: PARKER

*The question which provoked the most discussion by counsel on this appeal and which lies at the foundation of plaintiff's asserted right of recovery, is whether by virtue of a contract defendant's testator William E. Story became indebted to his nephew William E. Story, 2d, on his twenty-first birthday in the sum of five thousand dollars. The trial court found as a fact that "on the 20th day of March, 1869, * * * William E. Story agreed to and with William E. Story, 2d, that if he would refrain from drinking liquor, using tobacco, swearing, and playing cards or billiards for money until he should become 21 years of age then he, the said William E. Story, would at that time pay him, the said William E. Story, 2d, the sum of $5,000 for such refraining, to which the said William E. Story, 2d, agreed," and that he "in all things fully performed his part of said agreement."*

In further consideration of the questions presented, then, it must be deemed established for the purposes of this appeal, that on the 31st day of January, 1875, defendant's testator was indebted to William E. Story, 2d, in the sum of $5,000, and if this action were founded on that contract it would be barred by the Statute of Limitations which has been pleaded, but on that date the nephew wrote to his uncle as follows:

> *"Dear Uncle—I am now 21 years old today, and I am now my own boss, and I believe, according to agreement, that there is due me $5,000. I have lived up to the contract to the letter in every sense of the word."*

A few days later, and on February sixth, the uncle replied; and, so far as it is material to this controversy, the reply is as follows:

> *"Dear Nephew—Your letter of the 31st ult. came to hand all right saying that you had lived up to the promise made to me several years ago. I have no doubt but you have, for which you shall have $5,000 as I promised you. I had the money in the bank the day you was 21 years old that I intended for you, and you shall have the money certain. Now, Willie, I don't intend to interfere with this [***21] money in any way until I think you are capable of taking care of it, and the sooner that time comes the better it will please me. I would hate very much to have you start out in some adventure that you thought all right and lose this money in one year. * * * This money you have earned much easier than I did, besides acquiring good habits at the same time, and you are quite welcome to the money. Hope you will make good use of it. * * **
>
> *W. E. STORY.*
>
> *"P. S. — You can consider this money on interest."*

The trial court found as a fact that "said letter was received by said William E. Story, 2d, who thereafter consented that said money should remain with the said William E. Story in accordance with the terms and conditions of said letter." And further, "That afterwards, on the first day of March, 1877, with the knowledge and consent of his said uncle, he duly sold, transferred and assigned all his right, title and interest in and to said sum of $5,000 to his wife Libbie H. Story, who thereafter duly sold, transferred and assigned the same to the plaintiff in this action."

The defendant contends that the contract was without consideration to support it, and, therefore, invalid. He asserts that the promisee by refraining from the use of liquor and tobacco was not harmed but benefited, that that which he did was best for him to do independently of his uncle's promise, and insists that it follows that unless the promisor was benefited, the contract was without consideration. A contention, which if well founded, would seem to leave open for controversy in many cases whether that which the promisee did or omitted to do was, in fact, of such benefit to him as to leave no consideration to support the enforcement of the promisor's agreement. Such a rule could not be tolerated and is without foundation in the law. The Exchequer Chamber, in 1875, defined consideration as follows: "A valuable consideration in the

continued

sense of the law may consist either in some right, interest, profit or benefit accruing to the one party, or some forbearance, detriment, loss or responsibility given, suffered or undertaken by the other." Courts "will not ask whether the thing which forms the consideration does in fact benefit the promisee or a third party, or is of any substantial value to anyone. It is enough that something is promised, done, forborne or suffered by the party to whom the promise is made as consideration for the promise made to him."

Now, applying this rule to the facts before us, the promisee used tobacco, occasionally drank liquor, and he had a legal right to do so. That right he abandoned for a period of years upon the strength of the promise of the testator that for such forbearance he would give him $5,000. We need not speculate on the effort which may have been required to give up the use of those stimulants. It is sufficient that he restricted his lawful freedom of action within certain prescribed limits upon the faith of his uncle's agreement, and now having fully performed the conditions imposed, it is of no moment whether such performance actually proved a benefit to the promisor, and the court will not inquire into it, but were it a proper subject of inquiry, we see nothing in this record that would permit a determination that the uncle was not benefited in a legal sense.

■ *Affirmed.*

CASE CONCEPTS REVIEW

1. What did the nephew promise?
2. Why was the nephew's promise sufficient to qualify as consideration?

2. Elements of a Bargain

A bargain results when there is causation between the legal detriment and the legal benefit. For a promise to be supported by bargained-for consideration, the following three elements must be present:

1. The promisee must suffer *legal detriment.*
2. The promise in question must *induce* the legal detriment.
3. The legal detriment must *induce* the making of the promise.

As the previous case illustrated, legal detriment is not necessarily synonymous with real detriment or loss. For example, uncle tells niece that if she stops smoking for one month, then uncle will give her $500. If niece refrains from smoking for a month, she incurs legal detriment. Since quitting smoking may actually be a benefit, no real detriment may be present; but because she has a legal right to smoke, she incurs legal detriment by giving up that right.

The promisor must have made the promise, at least in part, to exchange it for the detriment incurred by the promisee. The detriment must be the price paid for the promise. Sometimes factual situations require one to decide if the detriment was merely a condition for a gift or was bargained for, in that it induced the promise. If the detriment is not a legal benefit to the promisor, it probably did not induce the promise. For example, suppose that you say to a homeless person, "If you go around the corner to the clothing store, you may purchase an overcoat on my credit." It is a detriment to the homeless person to make the walk, but the walk is not consideration because (on a reasonable construction) the walk was not requested as the price to be paid for the promise. It was merely a condition for a gratuitous promise. On the other hand, assume that Dotty writes to her sister-in-law: "If you will come down and take care of me, I promise you a place to raise your family." If the sister-in-law moves down to live with Dotty, then the sister-in-law has incurred legal detriment, which is a legal benefit to Dotty. The sister-in-law's move was thus bargained for as a trade for Dotty's promise.

3. Adequacy of Consideration

Historically, it has not been a function of law to make value judgments or economic judgments concerning contracts voluntarily entered into by the parties. As a general rule, courts have not attempted to weigh the consideration received by each party to determine if it is fair in the light of that which the other party gave. It has been sufficient in law if a party received something of legal value for which he or she bargained. The law is concerned only with the existence of consideration, not with its value. It does not inquire into the question of whether the bargain was a good one or bad one for either party. *In the absence of fraud, oppression, undue influence, illegality, or statutory limitation, parties have been free to make any contract they please.* The fact that it is onerous or burdensome for one or the other has been immaterial.

Today, this philosophy has changed somewhat. The Code provides that contracts that are so one-sided as to be unconscionable may be unenforceable [2-302]. Courts, as well as legislative bodies, have attempted to protect consumers by changing the historical view of one-sided contracts. These matters will be discussed further in subsequent chapters dealing with consumer protection and illegal contracts.

4. Recitals of Consideration

Many written contracts have a provision reciting that there is consideration. The contract may state, "For, and in consideration of, the mutual promises exchanged, the parties agree as follows." If the recital takes this form, "For, and in consideration of $l in hand paid," an issue may be raised related to the presence of consideration. Nominal consideration will generally validate a promise, especially if it is paid. However, *sham consideration* will not. The recital of $1, even if it is paid, may be a sham (pretense). A *sham* is a recital of fact contrary to fact. The recital of consideration may be a sham—not because $1 is economically inadequate but because it is not a material inducing factor.

There is an exception for option contracts because the business community customarily expects them to be valid. Consequently, the law does accept a recital of $1 if there is a signed writing in a business context involving either an option contract or a guarantee of credit. An exception also exists in many states regarding recitals of consideration in *deeds* conveying real estate.

MUTUALITY OF OBLIGATION

5. Introduction

Mutuality of consideration

The principle that requires both parties to contract to be bound to one another, or else neither party is bound

The doctrine of **mutuality of consideration** applies only to bilateral contracts. In a bilateral contract, each party must be bound, or neither party is bound. The problem of mutuality arises when one party tries to show that a promise is defective in that *it does not promise anything.* Since it is defective, it cannot provide consideration to support the other promise. When a promise is not supported by consideration, one party is not legally bound. Thus, since one party is not bound, no one is contractually bound. A promise will be held invalid if it falls under one of the following:

- The promise is *illusory* (sections 6 and 7).
- The promisor is already bound (*preexisting duty*) to do what he or she now promises to do (sections 8 through 12).
- The promise is to forbear from suing, but the promisor has an invalid claim—that is, no legal right to sue (section 13).

The following sections discuss these special problems of mutuality of obligation.

TABLE 15-1 ■ Categories of Invalid Promises

Type	Definition	Example
Illusory Promise	No promise exists because the promisor actually does not need to perform.	"If I decide to purchase an Ipod, I will buy yours."
Pre-existing Duty	One promises something the promisor is already under an obligation to perform.	"I agree to paint your house for $5,000 even though last week I agreed to paint it for $4,000."
Forbearance	Promise not to sue when a supposed claim is invalid	"Although I know the accident was entirely my fault, I agree not to sue you."
Past Considerations	A promise made for actions that already took place	Mike an attorney agrees to provide free legal services for his friend Jerry. Three months after performance of the services Jerry and Mike agree that Mike will receive $1,000. Jerry fails to pay and Mike sues. Mike will lose because Jerry's Promise is made for consideration in the past and cannot be enforced.

6. Illusory Promises

Illusory promise

A nonexisting or false commitment that is not consideration in support of a contractual obligation

An **illusory promise** is not a promise at all. What purports to be a promise is not one because the promisor need not perform it. There must be some restriction on the promisor's ability to avoid the promise; otherwise the promise cannot be construed as providing consideration. Courts require that there be a *possibility* that the promisor will incur legal detriment; otherwise the promisor's promise is illusory. In a typical illusory promise, the promisor's promise is conditional. The first step is to analyze the nature of the condition and determine if the condition is based on something beyond the promisor's control or within his or her control. An examination of many promises often reveals that there is in fact no promise at all.

When the promise is conditioned on a fortuitous event (something beyond either party's control), the promise is not illusory. For example, I promise to buy your car for $4,500 if it rains tomorrow or if I am hired by the TNT Corporation or if the Atlanta Braves win the next World Series. Since it is possible that it will rain or that I will get the job or Atlanta may win, there is a possibility that I will have to buy your car (legal detriment).

If the condition is within the total control of the promisor, then the promise may be illusory. For example, "If I decide to buy a car, I'll buy yours" or "I'll buy your car if I am fully satisfied with its performance" or "I'll buy your car, but I can cancel at any time." Since the condition in each example is within the promisor's control, the promise is illusory. Many promises are partially within the control of one party or the other. Such promises are not illusory if there are duties implied on the promisor or the condition is met.

If the condition is one of personal satisfaction, for instance, courts will usually restrict the promisor's free will by imposing a promise that any dissatisfaction must be in good faith. Thus, a promise to buy goods if satisfied is not illusory since the promisor cannot refuse the goods unless actually dissatisfied. Another example is the implied promise to use best efforts regarding the condition. If I promise to buy your car only if I get a bank loan, courts will imply that I promised to use reasonable diligence to get a loan. I must take affirmative action (detriment) to attempt to satisfy the condition.

Sometimes a person enters into a contract to be paid after the work has been performed. This is an example of past consideration that is insufficient to support a binding contract. For example, assume Frank sells his business to Harriet. Frank agrees, as part of the sales contract, to remain an advisor or consultant to Harriet. After Harriet makes money on several transactions that Frank assisted with, Frank presents Harriet with a contract that calls for Frank to receive $50,000 based on these recent successes. Even if Harriet signs the contract, she likely would not become obligated to pay Frank. This result occurs because Frank has not promised to do anything for the money. His detriment and Harriet's benefit are in the past. Frank's past performance is an illusion, and it is insufficient to support Harriet's promise to pay.

7. Requirement and Output Contracts

Requirement contracts ("I'll buy all the widgits I need from you this year") and output contracts ("I'll sell you all the widgits I manufacture") are not illusory. Courts find them enforceable because the seller of output or buyer of requirements has incurred legal detriment in that he or she has given up the right to sell to, or buy from, others. The Code explicitly enforces these contracts with a rule against unreasonably disproportionate quantities [2-306]. Both parties must act in good faith in their outputs or requirements. Moreover, the fact that a party to either contract might go out of business does not make the contract illusory. The Code provides protection by requiring 'that no quantity unreasonably disproportionate to any stated estimate or in the absence of a stated estimate to any normal or otherwise comparable prior output or requirements may be tendered or demanded" [2-306 (1)]. Therefore, the promisor must conduct his or her business in good faith and pursuant to commercially reasonable standards, so that his or her output or requirements will approximate a reasonably foreseeable figure.

8. Preexisting Duty

The preexisting duty rule is a second way in which a party may claim no mutuality of obligation. When one promises to do what one is already legally obligated to do or promises to refrain from what one legally cannot do, then the promisor incurs no legal detriment. Therefore, it is traditionally stated that a promise to perform or the performance of an existing duty is not consideration. The preexisting duty may be either a duty imposed by law or a contractual duty. Notice that in the following case the plaintiff was not a law enforcement official but was performing a contractual duty.

The problem of preexisting obligations has arisen in various circumstances. It is possible to categorize these cases under three headings: (1) modification of non-Code contracts, (2) modification of Code contracts, and (3) discharge of debts and forbearance.

9. Modification of Non-Code Contracts

Since an agreement to do that which one is already obliged to do does not constitute consideration, a subsequent agreement modifying an existing contract must be supported by new consideration independent of the consideration contained in the original agreement. Assume that one party to a contract refuses to continue performance unless and until the terms of the contract are modified. To ensure performance, the other party may assent to the demands and agree to terms that are more burdensome than those provided in the agreement. He or she may agree to pay more or accept less, but as a general rule the new promise is not supported by consideration. An employee may seek more money for the work he is already contractually bound to do, or a contractor may want more pay for the same work and materials specified in the original contract. In either case, the employee and contractor do not incur legal detriment to support the promise to modify.

Although some modifications are in bad faith or even extortionate, many are in good faith and should be validated. Assuming good-faith dealings, courts will find exceptions to the preexisting duty rule by using any of these rationales: (1) new or different duties, (2) unforeseeable difficulties, and (3) rescission.

CHANGES IN DUTY If the promisor agrees to assume a new duty, give something in addition, or vary the preexisting duty (e.g., accelerating performance), the promise supplies consideration to support the promised modification. Usually an owner who promises a contractor an additional sum to complete a job under contract is not legally bound to pay the additional sum. If, however, the promisee (contractor) agrees to do anything other than, or different from, that which the original contract required, consideration is provided. The contractor who agrees to complete his or her work at an earlier date or in a different manner may recover on a promise by the owner to pay an additional amount.

UNFORESEEN DIFFICULTIES The parties to a contract often make provisions for contingencies that may arise during the course of the performance of the contract. Wisely, they recognize that problems may arise which make performance more difficult. Frequently, however, contracting parties do not provide for any contingencies, or they make some that do not encompass all the difficulties that may render performance by either party more burdensome than anticipated. In the absence of an appropriate contract clause, two questions are raised when unanticipated difficulties arise during the course of performance: (1) Will the party whose performance is rendered

A contractor seeking more compensation for work already under contract would be seeking a modification of a non-code contract.

more difficult be required to complete performance without any adjustment in compensation? (2) Will a promise to pay an additional sum because of the difficulty be enforceable?

Excuses for breach of contract are discussed in Chapter 19. For purposes of this discussion, it must be recognized that additional hardship is not an excuse for breach of contract as a general rule. Thus, the answer to the first question is usually yes. Difficulties do not excuse performance.

The second question assumes that a promisor, although not required to do so, has promised to pay an additional sum because of the difficulty. Courts hold that where a truly unforeseen difficulty arises, and because of it a promise to pay an additional sum is made, the promise is legally valid and will be enforced. Unforeseen difficulties are those that seldom occur and are extraordinary in nature. Price changes, strikes, inclement weather, and shortage of material occur frequently and are not considered unforeseen. The following case illustrates the nature of the unforeseen difficulties doctrine.

CASE

Plante & Moran Cresa, LLC v. Kappa Enterprises, LLC, et al.

UNITED STATES DISTRICT COURT FOR THE EASTERN DISTRICT OF MICHIGAN, SOUTHERN DIVISION

2006 U.S. Dist. LEXIS 38135 (2006)

OPINION BY: JOHN CORBETT O'MEARA

Plaintiff, Plante & Moran Cresa, LLC, offers project management services to property owners to help them design and construct buildings; such services typically include overseeing the architect, land acquisition, contractor bidding, and construction. Plaintiff provided project management services to Defendant Kappa Enterprises, LLC, with respect to the development of a hotel in Southfield, Michigan. Plaintiff and Defendant Kappa entered into a contract on December 9, 1999, which stated that Plaintiff would provide project management services for the hotel design and construction in exchange for a lump sum payment of $189,000. Plaintiff apparently obtained the contract by convincing Kappa that its original choice intended to charge too much. Defendant Kappa paid Plaintiff in installments in accordance with the contract, beginning on January 15, 2000, and continuing until February 15, 2001. n1 The contract, which was drafted by Plaintiff, does not provide for a termination date or for any additional payment to Plaintiff should unforeseen delays occur. Kappa paid all of the contract price except for $5,000, which Plaintiff seeks to recover here, along with additional damages. The parties do not appear to dispute that Kappa owes Plaintiff $5,000.

According to Plaintiff, the hotel project took significantly longer than Plaintiff expected. One of Plaintiff's representatives, Paul Rivetto, testified that he expected the hotel to be designed and built within twelve months, with a completion date around the end of 2000. Plaintiff claims to have submitted a schedule to Defendant Kappa, but neither party has been able to produce it. The design and construction of the hotel was delayed for various reasons. The hotel was substantially complete in July 2002, when a sprinkler head burst and other water leaks caused flooding. The flooding damaged carpeting and drywall, which had to be ripped out and replaced. The flood remediation work took approximately 18 months and ended in January 2004.

Plaintiff contends that Kappa owes it an additional $105,000 for project management services it provided after the flood. According to Plaintiff, such services are outside the scope of the parties' fixed-fee agreement. Plaintiff further claims that Kappa agreed to pay the additional amount, but never followed through.

Defendant Kappa contends that the flood remediation work is within the scope of the parties' flat fee agreement and that it does not owe additional payments. Kappa denies that it agreed to pay any additional amount and argues that such an agreement is barred by the preexisting duty rule.

Essentially, Defendants argue that the alleged oral agreement to pay $105,000 above the contract price is invalid for lack of consideration. An essential element of a contract is legal consideration. Under the pre-existing duty rule, it is well settled that doing what one is legally bound to do is not consideration for a new promise. The pre-existing duty rule bars the modification of an existing contractual relationship when the purported consideration for the modification consists of the performance or promise to perform that which one party was already required to do under the terms of the existing agreement.

Plaintiff contends that the pre-existing duty rule does not apply here, due to the unforeseen circumstances of the flood.

The issue here is whether the project management services related to the flood remediation were within the scope of the parties' written agreement. Exhibit A to the agreement outlines the scope of services Plaintiff was to provide. These services included preliminary design and site selection, design and construction, contractor bidding, and project closeout. Specifically, Plaintiff agreed to "perform job observations as necessary to evaluate construction progress, adherence to project plans and specifications, and assist in resolving field problems and disputes in the most economical and expeditious manner possible." The parties clearly anticipated that problems would arise in the construction of the hotel and that Plaintiff would assist in resolving those problems. The work involved in providing project management services during the flood remediation phase was thus contemplated by the agreement and was within the scope of the services Plaintiff promised to provide.

continued

The court finds that the flood was not an "unforeseen difficulty" that would allow Plaintiff to seek additional payments beyond its fixed fee and defeat the application of the pre-existing duty rule. Plaintiff drafted this agreement, agreed to a fixed fee, and did not include any language regarding the anticipated time period for the project or what would constitute "extra work." Rather, Plaintiff specifically agreed to assist in resolving "field problems," which are presumably common in construction projects. Plaintiff assumed the risk that this project would take longer or involve more hours than it anticipated—that is the essence of a fixed-fee agreement. The court finds that the "additional work" performed by Plaintiff was covered by the parties' written agreement, and that any alleged modification of that agreement is barred by the pre-existing duty rule.

Therefore, IT IS HEREBY ORDERED that Defendant Kappa Enterprises LLC's March 30, 2006 Motion for Summary Judgment is GRANTED.

■ *Granted.*

CASE CONCEPTS REVIEW

1. Why doesn't the additional hardship associated with the flooding fit within the pre-existing duty exception?
2. What facts would have to change in order for the additional work to be considered "unforeseen"?

RESCISSION If the contract is rescinded, there is no longer a preexisting duty problem. The parties are now free to make a new contract on whatever terms they desire. Note that there are three contracts involved: (1) the original contract, (2) the rescission contract, and (3) the new contract. Further, note that rescission is generally not presumed, so the facts must show an actual rescission, such as tearing up the original contract.

10. Modification of Code Contracts

The Code has made substantial changes with respect to relaxing the requirement of the validation element of a contract. Especially regarding alteration or modification of contracts, the Code makes it easier for parties to bind one another by not requiring consideration to support the contractual changes.

NO CONSIDERATION Under the Code, parties to a binding contract for the sale of goods may change the terms; and if the change is mutually agreeable, no consideration is required to make it binding [2-209 (1)]. This means that if a buyer agrees with the seller to pay more than the contract price for goods purchased, he or she will be held to the higher price. For example, a car manufacturer entered into a contract with a tire dealer to purchase a certain number of tires at a stated price. Thereafter, the dealer told the manufacturer that because of higher production and labor costs, he would need to be paid $5 more per tire in order to carry on with the contract. If the automaker agrees to pay the additional sum, its promise to do so will be binding even though there is no consideration present for the new promise.

GOOD FAITH The Code section that sustains modifications of a contract without any additional consideration could, if not limited in some way, permit a party with a superior bargaining position to take advantage of the other party to a contract. Accordingly, the Code provides that the parties must act in good faith, and the exercise of bad faith to escape the duty to perform under the original terms is not permitted. The "extortion" of a modification without a legitimate reason therefore is ineffective because it violates the good-faith requirement.

To safeguard against false allegations that oral modifications have been made, it is permissible to include in the contract a provision that modifications are not effective unless they are set forth in a signed writing [2-209 (2)]. If a consumer enters into such a contract, in addition to signing the contract, the consumer must sign the restrictive provision to assure that he or she is aware of the limitation. Otherwise, it is not effective. If the restrictive provision is not signed, a consumer is entitled to rely on oral modifications. The provision is apparently designed to protect the unwary consumer against reliance on statements that certain provisions of the contract do not apply to him or her or that others are subject to oral change. The consumer is entitled to be forewarned not to rely on anything but the printed word; and it is expected that the double signing will bring this message to his or her attention.

The Code allows necessary and desirable modifications of sales contracts without regard to technicalities that hamper such adjustments under traditional contract law. The safeguards against improper and unfair use of this freedom are found in the requirements of good faith and the "observance of reasonable commercial standards of fair dealing in the trade." There is recognition of the fact that changes and adjustments in sales contracts are daily occurrences and that the parties do not cancel their old contract and execute an entirely new one each time a change or modification is required.

11. Discharge of Liquidated Debts and Claims

Liquidated debt

An obligation that has exact monetary value because it is not disputed

As previously noted, if the consideration on each side of an agreement involves money, the consideration must be equal. Because of this rule, a debtor and creditor cannot make an enforceable agreement to have a **liquidated debt** of a fixed amount discharged upon payment of less than the agreed upon owed amount. In other words, there is no consideration for the agreement to accept less than the full amount owed. In most states the unpaid portion is collectible even though the lesser sum has been paid. If there is no dispute as to the amount owed, a debtor who sends in a check for less than the amount of the indebtedness and marks on the check "paid in full" will still be liable for the balance due.

Payment of a lesser sum is only performance of an existing duty; it cannot serve as consideration for a release of the balance. However, if there is sufficient evidence that the creditor intended a gift of the balance to the debtor, then the creditor may not recover the balance. A paid-in-full receipt given to the debtor by the creditor is usually regarded as evidence (though not conclusive) that a gift was intended. Likewise, where the debt is evidenced by a note, the cancellation and return of the note upon receipt of part payment is evidence that a gift of the balance was intended.

Just as a promise to pay an additional sum for the completion of an existing contract is enforceable if the promisee does something other than, or in addition to, the required performance, a debtor may obtain a discharge of the debt by paying a lesser sum than the amount owing if he or she gives the creditor something in addition to the money. The settlement at the lower figure will then be binding on the creditor. Since the value of consideration is ordinarily unimportant, the added consideration may take any form. Payment in advance of the due date, payment at a place other than that agreed on, surrender of the privilege of bankruptcy, and substitution of a secured note for less than the face of the debt have all been found sufficient to discharge a larger amount than that paid. The mere giving of an unsecured note for a lesser sum than the entire debt will not release the debtor of his or her duty to pay the balance. The note is only a promise to pay; consequently, the promise to pay less than is due will not discharge the debt.

12. Discharge of Unliquidated Debts and Claims

Unliquidated debt

An obligation that is in dispute with respect to the dollar amount involved

Whereas a liquidated debt involves no question that the debt is due and payable, an **unliquidated debt** is a disputed debt. The dispute may involve the amount owed, the time or manner of payment, or related matters. An unliquidated debt may be subject to a compromise settlement. For example, when one party has a claim against another party and the amount due is disputed, a compromise settlement at a figure between the amount claimed or demanded and the amount admitted to be owing is binding on the parties. Payment of money that one party claims is not owed is consideration for the other party's loss of the right to litigate the dispute.

It does not matter whether the claim is one arising from a dispute that is contractual in nature, such as one involving damaged merchandise, or is tortious in character, such as one rising from an automobile accident. The compromise figure agreed to by both parties operates as a contract to discharge the claim. This kind of settlement contract is known legally as an accord and *satisfaction.*

An *accord and satisfaction* is a fully executed contract between a debtor and a creditor to settle a disputed claim. The accord consists of an agreement whereby one of the parties is to do something different by way of performance than that called for by the contract. This accord is satisfied when the substituted performance is completed and accepted by the other party. Both must be established. The cashing of a check marked "paid in full" when it is tendered to settle a *disputed* claim is a typical example of an accord and satisfaction. Keep in mind that the dispute must be in good faith.

The accord and satisfaction doctrine is illustrated by the following case. An accord may be either oral or written. For an accord and satisfaction to discharge a claim, the claim must be disputed between the parties. If the creditor is not aware of the dispute, the cashing of a check tendered in the usual course of business with a "full payment" notation will not operate as an accord and satisfaction. An accord, like any other agreement, requires a meeting of the minds. An accord will not be implied from ambiguous language. In other words, the intent to settle the dispute must be clear.

13. Forbearance

Forbearance

When done in good faith, the giving up of the right to enforce what one believes to be a valid claim is sufficient consideration to make another party's promise binding.

Consideration, which usually takes the form of a promise or an action, may take the opposite form: **forbearance** from acting or a promise to forbear from taking some action. The law also considers the waiver of a right or the forbearance to exercise a right to be sufficient consideration for a contract. The right that is waived or not exercised may be one that exists either at law or in equity. It may be a waiver of a right that one has against someone other than the promisor who bargains for such a waiver.

There are numerous other examples of forbearances that may constitute consideration. Relinquishment of alleged rights in an estate will furnish consideration to support a return promise to pay money. An agreement by the seller of a business not to compete with the person who has bought a business from him or her is another example of forbearance. Mutual promises to forbear are sufficient to support each other. They are commonly used as a part of a settlement of a dispute.

Although forbearances generally constitute consideration, a problem can arise when the forbearance is a promise not to bring a lawsuit. Clearly, a promise to forbear from suing is a legal detriment and, if bargained for, is valid consideration. The problem arises when the underlying claim is invalid. Arguably, a promise not to sue on an invalid claim really promises nothing since the promisor has no claim on which to sue. Older cases held that the promise regarding the invalid claim was not legal detriment. Modern courts hold that a promise to surrender or forbear from suing on an invalid claim is consideration, provided two matters are proved: the promisor

FIGURE 15-2 ■ Required Elements for Promissory Estoppel/Detrimental Reliance

1. A definite promise
2. Promisor should have expected that the promise would rely on the promise.
3. A reasonable person would have relied on the promise.
4. Promissee relied on the promise and it resulted in substantial detriment to the promissee.
5. Basic justice and fairness requires that the promise be honored and enforced.

CASE

Addison Express, LLC v. Medway Air Ambulance, Inc.

UNITED STATES DISTRICT COURT FOR THE NORTHERN DISTRICT OF TEXAS, DALLAS DIVISION

2006 U.S. Dist. LEXIS 31677 (2006)

This case presents an interaction of facts, contract theory, and statutory law worthy of the final exam of the most diabolical of contract professors. Each party to the contract at issue experienced financial loss and business interruption. In the main, each party conducted itself in the legitimate pursuit of its own business interests. The villain, if there is one, would appear to be a federal drug enforcement agency unaware of, or unconcerned with, the injury that indiscriminate governmental conduct can leave in its wake.

Plaintiff Addison Express, LLC, ["ADEX"] is an aircraft charter firm in Addison, Texas. Defendant Medway Air Ambulance, Inc., ["Medway"] operates an airborne medical transport and ambulance service from its principal place of business in Lawrenceville, Georgia. On September 5, 2003, ADEX and Medway entered into an agreement ["Lease"] under which Medway leased for a period of twenty-four months a 1976 Learjet 35, registration number N354LQ ["Lima Quebec"]. ADEX duly delivered Lima Quebec to Medway in October 2003, in full compliance with the Lease terms. Medway took possession of the aircraft in Addison, Texas, and began making timely lease payments of $19,000 per month. For approximately the first year, all was well.

The following summer, on or about August 18, 2004, the United States Drug Enforcement Administration ["DEA"] seized Lima Quebec with a warrant issued pursuant to the Patriot Act. At the time, the aircraft was undergoing regularly scheduled maintenance and inspection by Medway at the Lawrenceville facility. It had been partially disassembled—among other things, its landing gear had been removed for overhaul—and was not airworthy. The DEA instructed Medway to cease all activity with regard to Lima Quebec. Medway complied. Under the same warrant, the DEA seized Lima Quebec's flight logs and maintenance records, which were kept at ADEX's office in Addison.

This lawsuit was originally brought by ADEX on September 9, 2004, for specific performance of the Lease. By amendment, ADEX asks for damages for breach of contract in the amount of $580,129.72, including the remaining unpaid Lease payments and costs of restoring the aircraft to service. In addition, two 'side contracts' were entered into between the two parties, on which ADEX claims only partial payment was made. Medway has filed counterclaims, including breach of the Lease on ADEX's part.

In addition to the Lease, ADEX has sued for breach of two oral agreements between the parties. In about May 2004, ADEX and Medway made an oral agreement that ADEX would manage three of Medway's aircraft ["Management Agreement"]. Under that agreement, ADEX fully performed its obligation and invoiced Medway for a total of $9,223.81. Medway paid only $2,891.00.

In June or July 2004, ADEX and Medway made an oral agreement that ADEX would perform at Medway's expense certain maintenance on Lima Quebec identified when the aircraft's engines were removed for periodic maintenance in Houston, Texas ["Maintenance Agreement"]. ADEX fully performed its obligation and billed Medway $9,515.81. Medway paid only $4,895.56.

Because Medway made partial payments on the Management Agreement and the Maintenance Agreement, Medway contends that an accord and satisfaction occurred and that no further payment is due. Under the law of accord and satisfaction, parties may agree to discharge a legitimately disputed, existing obligation for an agreed amount. An "accord" is a bargain evidenced in a new contract, either express or implied, that replaces an old agreement. A good faith dispute as to liability on the underlying obligation furnishes sufficient consideration, and the satisfaction is the actual performance of the new agreement.

In this case, Medway establishes that a dispute existed with regard to payment of the full amount of ADEX's invoices for the Management Agreement and Maintenance Agreement. Medway tendered partial payment, and ADEX deposited that payment. The question is whether by accepting the partial payment, ADEX agreed that the invoice was satisfied in full.

Acceptance of a payment is binding if from the surrounding facts a party "obviously should understand that a check is tendered in full satisfaction." With regard to the Management Agreement, Medway's letter of August 13, 2004, lists disputed charges and informs ADEX: "I am enclosing a check for $2891, which I think is fair for what was done. … If you disagree with any of my reasoning please feel free to call me." The door was thus left open for continued negotiations and challenge. Seizure of Lima Quebec occurred shortly thereafter, and the parties may or may not have intended to resume squabbling over this bill. As a result, the Court cannot infer from this correspondence that ADEX accepted the tendered payment as full satisfaction of the debt.

With regard to the Maintenance Agreement, the Court reaches a similar result. Medway's letter of August 12, 2004, which accompanies partial payment of ADEX's invoice # 609, disputes certain charges and ends: 'Therefore I am enclosing a check for $4895.56 which represents what my cost would have been to perform these items. … I truly believe this invoice is out of line, and I feel I do not owe the full amount. I hope after your review you will agree that I am correct in my thinking." Again, the Court must conclude that negotiations were left open and that the amount tendered cannot be understood to be a full and final payment. This finding is supported by a copy of ADEX's invoice crediting the payment and showing a balance remaining due and payable.

Accordingly, Medway is liable to ADEX for the remaining amounts on the "side" contracts as follows: for the Management Agreement, $6,332.81 and for the Maintenance Agreement, $4,620.25.

■ *Judgment for ADEX..*

CASE CONCEPTS REVIEW

1. Did the court find that the parties had entered into an accord and satisfaction? Why?
2. What specific language included in Medway's two letters was pivotal in resolving this legal dispute?

thought the claim was valid (subjective honesty); and the claim had some reasonable basis in law and in fact (objective test). The general rule now is that surrender of or forbearance to assert an invalid claim is detriment if the claim is asserted in good faith and is not unreasonable.

CONTRACTS VALID WITHOUT CONSIDERATION

14. Promissory Estoppel

Promissory estoppel (detrimental reliance)
An equitable doctrine used as a substitute for consideration with respect to validating a contract-based promise—often called unbargained-for detriment

When bargained-for consideration is *not* present, a court may nonetheless validate a promise based on **promissory estoppel**. A good way to view promissory estoppel (sometimes called *detrimental reliance*) is to see it as an *unbargained-for* detriment. When a promisor's promise induces a promisee's detriment, this validation device prevents ("estops") the promisor from denying contractual duties because of a lack of consideration. Promissory estoppel forces the promisor to live up to his or her promise, even where there is no contract formed under the technical requirements of common law.

The doctrine of promissory estoppel is equitable in nature in that it compensates for harm that is caused by a promise when the harm is reasonably foreseeable by the promisor. Promissory estoppel involves a promise that the promisor should reasonably expect (foresee) to induce a detrimental change of position by the promisee. There is reliance on the promise and a change of position. The promise is binding if injustice can be avoided only by enforcement of the promise, and the remedy granted may be as limited as justice requires. A classic example demonstrates the main elements of promissory estoppel. Grandfather, knowing that his granddaughter is going to college, promises his granddaughter that he will give her $25,000 to buy a car on completion of her degree. Granddaughter goes to college and at the beginning of her last year borrows $20,000 to buy a car. When the granddaughter has nearly completed her degree, grandfather notifies her that he revokes his promise. Promissory estoppel makes grandfather's promise legally binding. First, grandfather should have reasonably expected the granddaughter to buy a car since the granddaughter knows that she will soon receive $25,000. Second, the granddaughter did in fact rely on the promise by borrowing $20,000 to buy a car. Third, justice under these facts requires the promise to be binding. Finally, the granddaughter should receive only $20,000 because the remedy should be limited to the change of position, as justice requires.

The doctrine of promissory estoppel is limited in its application and provides only a limited means of enforcing promises that fail to pass the test of consideration. Although the modern tendency is to apply the doctrine to a wide variety of situations, it has been used frequently in the following situations:

1. Bidding on construction projects: The cases hold that a subcontractor's bid is irrevocable if used by the general contractor in submitting his or her bid for the primary contract.
2. Promised pensions and other employee benefits: Notwithstanding the fact that the employee continues to work (preexisting duty and hence no consideration), courts validate employer promises of benefits by using promissory estoppel.
3. Promises of dealer franchises: The doctrine of promissory estoppel has been used to permit recovery when there has been justifiable reliance on preliminary negotiations, wherein a franchise was promised.

15. Moral Obligation

A promisor may from time to time make a promise based on his or her individual view of ethics and morality. The promisor feels some moral obligation to make a promise and to perform that promise. As a general rule, such promises are not supported by consideration, and an obligation arising out of ethics and morality alone is not enforceable.

Moral obligation is a concept used as a substitute for consideration with respect to validating a contract-based promise. This is often called unbargained-for benefit.

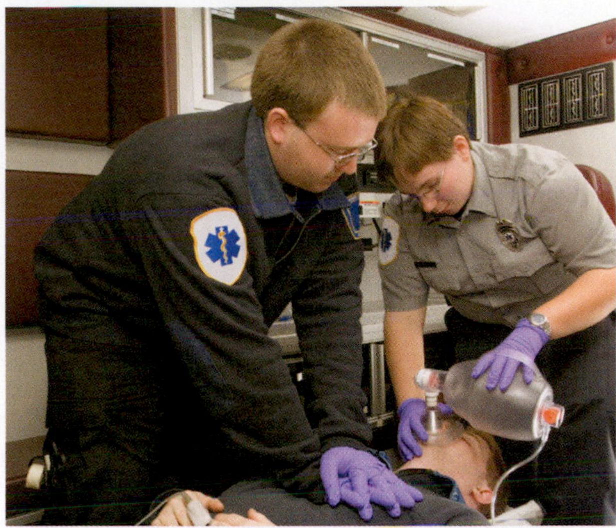

EMTs render medical services

Notwithstanding the general rule that bargained-for consideration must be present, moral obligation is sometimes used to validate a promise lacking consideration. Moral obligation in such cases may be seen as arising from an unbargained-for benefit. Some benefit previously received by the promisor is said to induce the later promise. The promise then becomes enforceable because of the moral obligation resulting from the benefit previously received. This theory is used to validate a subsequent promise only when the past benefit is a material one. Examples of such benefits conferred include the following: Someone rescues and repairs another's boat; medical services are rendered to an unconscious person; a person is injured in saving another's life. Then, there is a subsequent promise by the benefited party to pay the person who gave the benefit.

Obligations discharged by law may later be the subject matter of a new promise. Such promises also may be enforceable under the moral obligation theory. For example, a new promise to pay a debt may be enforceable without consideration even though it has been discharged in bankruptcy or barred by a statute of limitations (a statute that cuts off a claim if no suit is brought within a stated time period). Some courts state that the past debt, together with the moral obligation to pay, is sufficient to validate the new promise to pay the debt. A court can infer a new promise from part payment of a debt barred by the statute of limitations, but an express written promise is required for debts discharged in bankruptcy. There are some other special rules on reaffirming debts discharged in bankruptcy. These are covered by federal law and are discussed in Chapter 39.

16. Firm Offers and Renunciations

As noted in the preceding chapter, firm offers are irrevocable without consideration. More specifically, under the Code a written offer by a merchant to buy or sell goods is not revocable for lack of consideration during the time for it to remain open (but not to exceed three months). If no time is stated, it is irrevocable for a reasonable time, but again not to exceed three months.

Either party may voluntarily renounce or waive any right or claim arising out of a breach of contract. Such a renunciation or waiver is valid without consideration, provided it is in writing. A renunciation or waiver is recognized by both the Code and the common law.

CHAPTER SUMMARY

BARGAIN THEORY OF CONSIDERATION

Elements of 1. Promisee must suffer legal detriment.

Consideration (Bargain Requirement)

2. The promise must induce the detriment.
3. The detriment must induce the promise.

Adequacy of Consideration

1. Courts will not normally inquire into the adequacy of consideration.
2. Exception: Inadequacy may be evidence of fraud, duress, or undue influence.

Recitals of Consideration

1. Sham consideration: Failure to pay the recited amount renders the contract unenforceable.
2. Nominal consideration: The recited amount, even if nominal, is sufficient if bargained for.

MUTUALITY OF OBLIGATION

Illusory Promises

1. A promise is illusory if there is no restriction on a party's freedom of action.
2. A promise is not illusory if based on the occurrence of conditions.

Requirements and Output Contracts

1. Requirements and output contracts generally are not illusory and thus are enforceable.

Preexisting Duty

1. If a promisor is already legally bound to do the thing promised, there is no consideration present to support the promise made.

Past Consideration

1. If a promise or agreement is made in return for consideration in the past, the promise or agreement is unenforceable.

Modification of Non-Code Contracts

1. In general, non-Code modifications must be supported by consideration.
2. Non-Code modifications are valid if new duties are assumed, unforeseeable difficulties occur, or a rescission of the original contract occurs.

Modification of Code Contracts

1. In general, modifications of Code contracts are enforceable even though consideration is lacking.
2. Modifications of Code contracts are valid if the modifications are made in good faith (i.e., made for a legitimate commercial reason).

Discharge of Debts

1. The payment of a lesser sum than a liquidated debt or claim cannot serve as consideration for a release of the balance.
2. A promise to forbear from suing on an unliquidated debt or claim is sufficient consideration, and a binding compromise results.
3. An accord and satisfaction is one example of how unliquidated debts are discharged.

Forbearance

1. Refraining from doing something that a party has a right to do is called forbearance.
2. In general, forbearance is consideration to validate another's promise.
3. A promise not to sue on a valid claim is consideration.
4. A promise not to sue on an invalid claim is consideration if the promisor in good faith thinks the claim is valid and the claim is reasonable in law and fact.

CONTRACTS VALID WITHOUT CONSIDERATION

Promissory Estoppel

1. A promise induces a promisee to rely detrimentally on a promise.

2. Elements: (a) Definite promise (b) Promisor should expect promisee to rely; (c) a reasonable person would have relied on the promise; (d) promisee relies to his or her detriment; and (e) injustice can be avoided only by enforcing promise.

Moral Obligation

1. Moral obligation will validate a subsequent promise when the moral duty was previously a legal duty.
2. Moral obligation may validate a promise to pay for material benefits previously received.

Firm Offers and Renunciation under the Code

1. Firm offers are irrevocable even though they are not supported by consideration.
2. A renunciation is a written waiver of a right or claim arising under a contract.
3. A renunciation is enforceable without supporting consideration if it is in writing.

REVIEW QUESTIONS AND PROBLEMS

1. Match each term in Column A with the appropriate statement in Column B.

A	B
(1) Accord and satisfaction	(a) Renunciation
(2) Adequacy of consideration	(b) Validation device (unbargained-for benefit to promisor)
(3) Sham consideration	(c) No possibility promisor will incur legal detriment
(4) Written waiver of contract right	(d) Fully executed contract between debtor and creditor to settle disputed claim
(5) Illusory promise	(e) Promisor is already bound to do matter promised.
(6) Preexisting duty	(f) Courts will not inquire into this.
(7) Mutuality of obligation	(g) Failure to pay consideration recited
(8) Promissory estoppel	(h) Both parties are bound or nobody is bound.
(9) Moral obligation	(i) Promise valid if good-faith claim is reasonable in fact and law
(10) Promise not to sue on invalid claim	(j) Validation device (unbargained-for detriment to promisee)

2. Dickinson was employed by Auto Center under an oral contract terminable at will. His employer agreed to sell him part ownership of the business, but later refused to do so. When sued for breach of contract, Auto Center contended that there was no consideration for its promise to sell. Was it correct? Explain.
3. Brenner made a contract to enroll his son in the Little Red School House for the next school year and paid tuition of $1,080. Brenner's former wife had legal custody of his son, and she refused to enroll the boy. Brenner sought a refund. The school promised a refund, but later it refused to pay it. When Brenner sued for the promised refund, the school defended that

Brenner had incurred no legal detriment to support its promise to pay the tuition refund. Was there consideration for the school's promise to refund the tuition? Explain.

4. Humphrey pays Doug $250 for a sixty-day option to buy Doug's farm. Near the end of the option period, Humphrey asks for and gets a fifteen-day extension. No money was paid for the extension. After the original sixty-day period but within the fifteen-day extension, Doug withdraws the offer. Can Doug legally revoke the offer? Why or why not?
5. Burt pays $1 in return for a thirty-day option to purchase real estate from Reynold for $100,000. The next day Reynold tries to revoke the option. Can Reynold revoke? Why or why not?
6. Buyer agreed with seller that buyer would buy 1,500,000 gallons of a particular grade of oil. The agreement stated, "Seller may cancel any unshipped portion of this order if for any reason it should discontinue making this grade of oil." Was this a valid agreement? Why or why not?
7. Widgit, a manufacturer of widgits, agreed to supply Midgit all the widgits that Midgit needed in his gidgit business. For several years prior to this agreement, Midgit used between 2,500 and 3,000 Widgit widgits per month. In the sixth month of their agreement, Midgit ordered 10,000 widgits. Widgit said it would not honor the order. Is this a valid agreement? Is Widgit liable to Midgit for breach of contract? Why or why not?
8. Jack, a golf course architect, agrees with Sneed to direct a current construction project for a fixed fee of $5,000. During the course of the project, Jack, without excuse, takes away his plans and refuses to continue, and Sneed promises him an extra fee of $2,000 if Jack will resume work. Is Jack's resumption of work consideration for Sneed's promise of the extra fee? Explain.
9. Burgamy made a contract to furnish material and labor for plumbing modifications in Davis's house. A dispute developed over the amount that Davis owed Burgamy. Davis drafted a check on which he wrote "Payment of account IN FULL." When Burgamy received the check, he crossed out what Davis had written and wrote in "Paid on Account," and deposited it. Was there an accord and satisfaction? Explain.
10. Hoffman wanted to acquire a franchise from Red Owl Stores. Red Owl told Hoffman that if he would sell his bakery and buy a certain tract of land, he would be given a franchise. Hoffman did these things but was not given the promised franchise. Hoffman sued, and Red Owl defended on the ground that there is no consideration to support the contract. Who won? Why?

Contractual Capacity and Genuine Assent | 16

CHAPTER OUTLINE

CHAPTER PREVIEW

In Chapter 13, it was noted that a contract has four elements: (1) offer and acceptance (the agreement), (2) consideration, (3) legal capacity, and (4) legal purpose. The first two have been explained in the preceding two chapters. This chapter explores the third element.

A valid contract may be rendered inoperative through the equitable remedy of *rescission.* When a party has the right to disaffirm or rescind a contract, that contract is said to be voidable. All parties must have the legal capacity to give their consent. Some parties, such as minors, insane persons, and intoxicated persons, do not have the legal capacity to assent to contract terms, and they can undo (rescind) their contracts.

Even if a party has the legal ability to assent or consent, that consent may not be genuine. Genuine consent is not present when a contracting party promises because of a mistake, fraud, duress, or undue influence. Often one party creates an offer that is flawed, and the other party relies on the imperfect offer in the accepting. In such cases, the contract is avoidable by rescission because the consent given was not real or genuine.

BUSINESS MANAGEMENT DECISION

You are a sales manager for an automobile dealer. One of your salespeople wants to contract to sell a car to a sixteen-year-old who is going to make a $1,000 down payment and sign a promissory note in the amount of the remainder of the purchase price.

Should you approve this sale?

INCAPACITY TO CONTRACT

1. Types of Incapacity

Incapacity refers to the mental state of a party to a contract. Capacity-to-contract issues generally involve minors but, occasionally, pertain to mental incompetents, intoxicated persons, and drug addicts. Incapacity that makes a contract voidable may be permanent or temporary. Minors and insane persons are presumed to lack capacity to contract.

While the remaining materials under the heading of "Incapacity to Contract" primarily involve minors, it is appropriate to mention briefly those types of incapacity recognized by the law that are not the product of status as a minor. We first consider a person who has not been judged insane. A party without *mental capacity* to contract but who has not been adjudicated insane can avoid the contract or defend a suit for breach of contract on the grounds of lack of mental capacity. The contract is *voidable* only by the incapacitated party. In this situation, the party who lacks the capacity is in a unique position: he/she may allow the contract to be enforced or may have the contract voided. No other party may raise the issue. If an insane person disaffirms a contract, the general rule is that he or she must return all the consideration or benefit received, assuming the other party has treated him or her in good faith. However, if the contract is unconscionable or the other party has unfairly overreached, the incapacitated party can rescind by returning whatever he or she has left of the consideration received. A person who is insane, however, is responsible for the reasonable value of necessaries—a doctrine that is explored below in Section 5 dealing with minors.

However, if a court has judged a person insane, then the contract made by that person after being judged insane is *void,* not merely voidable. In this situation, a guardian is appointed and the insane person functions under the guardianship. The test of insanity for avoiding a contract is different from the test of insanity for matters involving criminal intent, making a will, commitment to a mental institution, or other purposes. In contract law, the test is whether the party was capable of understanding the nature, purpose, and consequences of his or her acts at the time of contract formation. A party is incompetent if unable to act in a reasonable manner in relation to the transaction, and the other party has reason to know of this condition.

2. Minors' Contracts

The age of majority and capacity to contract has been lowered to 18 in most states; however, the statutory law of each state must be examined to determine the age of majority for contract purposes. Just as there are several definitions of insanity, there are numerous laws that impose minimum age requirements.

A person below the age of capacity is called a minor. Minors have the right to avoid contracts. The law grants minors this right in order to promote justice and to protect them from their presumed immaturity, lack of judgment and experience, limited willpower, and imprudence. An adult deals with a minor at the adult's own peril. A contract between a minor and an adult is voidable only by the minor. The right to disaffirm exists, irrespective of the fairness of the contract and whether or not the adult knew he or she was dealing with a minor.

Legislation in many states has, in a limited way, altered the right of minors to avoid their contracts. Purchase of life insurance or contracts with colleges or universities entered into by a minor are binding, and some states take away the minor's right to avoid contracts after marriage. A few give the courts the right to approve contracts made by emancipated minors.

3. Avoiding Contracts by Minors

A minor has the right to *disaffirm* contracts; but until steps are taken to avoid the contract, the minor remains liable. A minor can disaffirm a purely executory contract by directly informing the adult of the disaffirmance or by any conduct that clearly indicates intent to disaffirm. If the contract has been fully or partially performed, the minor also can avoid it and obtain a return of his or her consideration. If the minor is in possession of consideration that is passed to him or her, it must be returned to the other party. The minor cannot disaffirm the contract and, at the same time, retain the benefits.

The courts of various states are in conflict about when a minor cannot return the property in the same condition in which it was purchased. The majority of the states hold that the minor may disaffirm the contract and demand the return of the consideration with which he or she has parted if the minor returns the property that remains. A few courts, however, hold that if the contract is advantageous to the minor and if the adult has been fair in every respect, the contract cannot be disaffirmed unless the minor returns all the consideration received.

TABLE 16-1 ■ Obligation of Minor to Disaffirm

Majority of States	Minor must return "remaining property" (if any) as a condition of disaffirming a contract.
Minority of States	Contract can be disaffirmed only if ALL property is returned.

The minor may avoid both executed and executory contracts at any time during the minority and for a reasonable period of time after majority. What constitutes a reasonable time depends on the nature of the property involved and the specific circumstances. Many states establish a maximum period, such as one or two years.

4. Ratification

Ratification means "to approve and sanction, to make valid, or to confirm." It applies to the approval of a voidable transaction by one who previously had the right to disaffirm. Applied to contracts entered into by minors, it refers to conduct of a former minor after majority, conduct that indicates approval of, or satisfaction with, a contract. It eliminates the right to disaffirm.

Generally, an executed contract is *ratified* if the consideration is retained for an unreasonable time *after majority*. Ratification also results from acceptance of the benefits incidental to ownership, such as rents, dividends, or interest. A sale of the property received or any other act that clearly indicates satisfaction with the bargain made will constitute ratification. In general, a contract that is fully executory is disaffirmed by continued silence or inaction after the minor reaches legal age, but ratification is presumed to occur when a reasonable time for disaffirmance passes after a minor joins the majority and continues to accept or utilize the benefits of the bargain. However, ratification is not possible until the minor reaches legal age because prior to that date the contract can always be avoided.

5. Liability for Necessaries

The law recognizes that certain transactions are clearly for the benefit of minors and hence are binding upon them. The term *necessaries* is used to describe the subject matter of such contracts. A minor is not liable in contract for necessaries; the liability is in quasi-contract. The fact that the liability is quasi-contractual has two significant features: (1) The liability is not for the contract price of necessaries furnished, but rather for the reasonable value of the necessaries. (2) There is no liability on executory contracts, but only for necessaries actually furnished.

What are necessaries? In general, the term includes whatever is needed for a minor's subsistence as measured by his or her age, station in life, and all his or her surrounding circumstances. Food and lodging, medical services, education, and clothing are the general classifications of *necessaries*. The question of whether emergency medical services are a necessary for a minor still living with his parents is addressed in the next case.

CASE

Yale Diagnostic Radiology v. Estate of Harun Fountain et al.

SUPREME COURT OF CONNECTICUT

267 Conn. 351; 838 A.2d 179 (2004)

BORDEN, J.

The sole issue in this appeal is whether a medical service provider that has provided emergency medical services to a minor may collect for those services from the minor when the minor's parents refuse or are unable to make payment. The defendants, the estate of Harun Fountain, an unemancipated minor, and Vernetta Turner-Tucker (Tucker), the fiduciary of Fountain's estate, appeal from the judgment of the Superior Court following an appeal from an order of the Probate Court for the district of Milford. The Probate Court had denied the motion of the plaintiff, Yale Diagnostic Radiology, for distribution of funds from the estate. The trial court ordered recovery of the funds sought by the plaintiff. The defendants claim that the trial court improperly determined that they are liable to the plaintiff for payment of Fountain's medical expenses. We affirm the judgment of the trial court.

The following facts and procedural history are undisputed. In March, 1996, Fountain was shot in the back of the head at point-blank range by a playmate. As a result of his injuries, including the loss of his right eye, Fountain required extensive lifesaving medical services from a variety of medical *services providers, including the plaintiff. The expense of the services rendered by the plaintiff to Fountain totaled $17,694. The plaintiff billed Tucker, who was Fountain's mother, but the bill went unpaid; and, in 1999, the plaintiff obtained a collection judgment against her. In January, 2001, however, all of Tucker's debts were discharged pursuant to an order of the Bankruptcy Court for the District of Connecticut. Among the discharged debts was the judgment in favor of the plaintiff against Tucker.*

During the time between the rendering of medical services and the bankruptcy filing, Tucker, as Fountain's next friend, initiated a tort action against the boy who had shot him. Among the damages claimed were "substantial sums of money [expended] on medical care and treatment. ..." A settlement was reached, and funds were placed in the estate established on Fountain's behalf under the supervision of the Probate Court. Tucker was designated the fiduciary of that estate. Neither Fountain nor his estate was involved in Tucker's subsequent bankruptcy proceeding.

Following the discharge of Tucker's debts, the plaintiff moved the Probate Court for payment of the $17,694 from the estate. The Probate Court denied the motion, reasoning that, pursuant to General Statutes § 46b-37 (b), parents are liable for medical services rendered to their minor children, and that a parent's refusal or inability to pay for those services does not render the minor child liable. The Probate Court further ruled that minor children are incapable of entering into a legally binding contract or consenting, in the absence of parental consent, to medical treatment. The Probate Court held, therefore, that the plaintiff was barred from seeking payment from the estate.

The plaintiff appealed from the decision of the Probate Court to the trial court. The trial court sustained the appeal and rendered judgment for the plaintiff, holding that, under Connecticut law, minors are liable for payment for their "necessaries," even though the provider of those necessaries "relies on the parents' credit for payment when [the] injured child lives with his parents. ..." The trial court reasoned that, although parents are primarily liable, pursuant to § 46b-37 (b) (2), for their child's medical bills, the parents' failure to pay renders the minor secondarily liable. Additionally, the trial court relied on the fact that Fountain had obtained money damages, based in part on the medical services rendered to him by the plaintiff. This appeal followed.

The defendants claim that the trial court improperly determined that a minor might be liable for payment for emergency medical services rendered to him. They further claim that the trial court, in reaching its decision, improperly considered the fact that Fountain had received a settlement, based in part on his medical expenses. We disagree with both of the defendants' claims.

Connecticut has long recognized the common-law rule that a minor child's contracts are voidable. Under this rule, a minor may, upon reaching majority, choose either to ratify or to avoid contractual obligations entered into during his minority. The traditional reasoning behind this rule is based on the well-established common-law principles that the law should protect children from the detrimental consequences of their youthful and improvident acts and that children should be able to emerge into adulthood unencumbered by financial obligations incurred during the course of their minority. The rule is further supported by a policy of protecting children from unscrupulous individuals seeking to profit from their youth and inexperience.

The rule that a minor's contracts are voidable, however, is not absolute. An exception to this rule, eponymously known as the doctrine of necessaries, is that a minor may not avoid a contract for goods or services necessary for his health and sustenance. Such contracts are binding even if entered into during minority; and a minor, upon reaching majority, may not, as a matter of law, disaffirm them.

Thus, when a medical service provider renders necessary medical care to an injured minor, two contracts arise: the primary contract between the provider and the minor's parents; and an implied in law contract between the provider and the minor himself. The primary contract between the provider and the parents is based on the parents' duty to pay for their children's necessary expenses, under both common law and statute. Such contracts, where not expressed, may be implied in fact and generally arise both from the parties' conduct and their reasonable expectations. The primacy of this contract means that the provider of necessaries must make all reasonable efforts to collect from the parents before resorting to the secondary, implied in law contract with the minor.

The secondary implied in law contract between the medical services provider and the minor arises from equitable considerations, including the law's disfavor of unjust enrichment. Therefore, where necessary medical services are rendered to a minor whose parents do not pay for them, equity and justice demand that a secondary implied in law contract arise between the medical services provider and the minor who has received the benefits of those services. These principles compel the conclusion that, in the circumstances of the present case, the defendants are liable to the plaintiff, under the common-law doctrine of necessaries, for the services rendered by the plaintiff to Fountain.

The present case illustrates the inequity that would arise if no implied in law contract arose between Fountain and the plaintiff. Fountain was shot in the head at close range and required emergency medical care. Under such circumstances, a medical services provider cannot stop to consider how the bills will be paid or by whom. Although the plaintiff undoubtedly presumed that Fountain's parent would pay for his care and was obligated to make reasonable efforts to collect from Tucker before seeking payment from Fountain, the direct benefit of the services, nonetheless, was conferred upon Fountain. Having received the benefit of necessary services, Fountain should be liable for payment for those necessaries in the event that his parents do not pay.

Furthermore, in the present case, we note, as did the trial court, that Fountain received through a settlement with the boy who caused his injuries funds that were calculated, at least in part, the costs of the medical services provided to him by the plaintiff in the wake of those injuries. Fountain, through Tucker, brought an action against the tortfeasor and, in his complaint, cited "substantial sums of money [expended] on medical care and treatment. ..." This fact further supports a determination of an implied in law contract under the circumstances of the case. The judgment is affirmed.

■ *Affirmed.*

CASE CONCEPTS REVIEW

1. Is the result in the case fair to the minor? Why?
2. Would the logic of the opinion expressed above apply to cases where emergency medical care was not involved? Why?

6. Third-Party Rights

Good-faith purchaser

A buyer who pays value honestly believing he or she has the legal right to acquire valid title to the item purchased

If a minor sells goods to an adult, the adult obtains only a voidable title to the goods. The minor can disaffirm and recover possession from the adult buyer. At common law, even a **good-faith purchaser** of property formerly belonging to a minor could not retain the property if the minor elected to rescind. This rule has been changed under the Code. It provides that a person with voidable title has power to transfer a good title to a good-faith purchaser for value [2-403]. The common-law rule, however, is still applicable to sales of real property by minors. If a minor sells his farm to an adult, who in turn sells the farm to a good-faith purchaser, the minor may avoid the original contract and regain the title to the farm against the good-faith purchaser. You may think that is unfair, but remember that the minor's name appears in the record books and is in the chain of title. The minor must return all remaining consideration to the adult. This adult, in turn, may be liable to the good-faith purchaser for failing to convey clear title.

MISTAKE

7. Definitions

Mistake

A state of mind that is inconsistent with reality

Mistake is some unintended act, omission, or error that arises from ignorance, surprise, imposition, or misplaced confidence. A variety of mistakes may occur in forming a contract. They may involve errors in arithmetic, errors in transmitting the offer or acceptance, errors in drafting the written contract, or errors about existing facts. A court may or may not grant relief because of a mistake. A court may grant relief if the mistake shows that there is no real or genuine assent. The mistake must be a *material* one. The relief granted may be *contract reformation* (court changes contract to correct a mistake) or *contract avoidance* (court allows any party adversely affected by the mistake to avoid his or her contract). As a general rule, courts may grant relief when there has been a *bilateral mistake of material fact* (both parties mistaken) as contrasted with a unilateral mistake (only one party mistaken).

The law will only provide the possibility of a defense to formation of a contract in those situations where mistake pertains to facts. Mistakes of judgment or value generally will not create a valid defense to enforcement of a contract because these are matters subjective in nature. Each party to a contract has their own set of criteria to apply as to whether a contract is "a good deal" or that the value of a product or service is worth a particular amount. As the following case reveals, sometimes the line between judgment and fact is blurred.

8. Bilateral Mistake

To have a bilateral or mutual mistake, all parties must have the same (identical) mistake. Before making a contract, a party usually evaluates the proposed bargain based on various assumptions regarding existing facts. Many of these assumptions are shared by the other party. A bilateral mistake occurs when both parties are mistaken as to the same assumption. Relief is appropriate where a mistake of both parties has a material effect on the agreed exchange of performances. Two examples may help illustrate when relief is appropriate:

1. Al contracts to sell and Bob agrees to buy a tract of land, the value of which has depended primarily on the timber on tract. Both Al and Bob believe the timber is on the land, but unknown to them a fire destroyed the timber the day before they contracted. The contract is voidable by Bob since he is adversely affected by the material bilateral mistake. Note that the court could not reform the contract to correct the mistake.

CASE

Bissell Inc., a Michigan corporation v. Orek Corporation, a Delaware corporation, and Oreck Manufacturing Company, a Delaware corporation.

UNITED STATES DISTRICT COURT FOR THE WESTERN DISTRICT OF MICHIGAN, SOUTHERN DIVISION

2000 U.S. Dist. LEXIS 3595 (2000)

As part of a bitter ending of a long-term business relationship, Bissell and Oreck sued each other in two different federal courts, shortly thereafter entering into the agreement at issue in settlement of both lawsuits. The apparent resolution of their differences proved to be an illusion, however, as each party now contends that the other has failed to fulfill obligations imposed by the settlement agreement.

The Settlement Agreement contained the following pertinent provisions:

> *In connection with Bissell's manufacture of Oreck vacuum cleaners in Ireland, the parties agree as follows:*
>
> > *Oreck will promptly purchase from Bissell at Bissell's cost all current, non-defective raw materials and parts on hand, or held by suppliers relating to Oreck vacuums, which materials and parts are estimated to total $230,000, payable no later than December 31, 1997. All costs of packing, shipping and transport for such raw materials and parts shall be borne by Oreck.*

Regarding the Bissell G.R. raw materials and parts, Bissell argues that the $230,000 amount stated in paragraph 7 of the Settlement Agreement is merely an estimate, and that to the extent that the actual amount is reasonably within the range of the estimate, Oreck is obligated to purchase all of the remaining current and nondefective Grand Rapids raw materials and parts on hand or held by suppliers relating to Oreck vacuums. In response, Oreck argues that any uncertainty in or significant deviation from that figure must be resolved against Bissell because Bissell supplied the estimated figure. The court concludes that Oreck is correct and that Bissell should be held to its estimate.

The law of unilateral mistake offers some guidance on this issue. Under this law, a contract will not be reformed because of a unilateral mistake in a bid or estimate unless the party making the mistake establishes that the error resulted from a clear cut mistake of fact. In contrast, an error based upon a mistake in judgment will not entitle the party to reformation of the contract. A mistake due solely to a poor estimate represents an error of judgment, for which relief is not available. Because Bissell was content to provide Oreck with an estimate rather than a more precise calculation of the amount of the inventory, it must be held to have assumed the risk that the estimate was materially wrong. The court concludes that it is reasonable to impose on Bissell the burden of its mistaken estimate.

■ *Injunction granted.*

CASE CONCEPTS REVIEW

1. Why would Bissell rely on an estimate in the settlement agreement instead of an actual amount?
2. Why would an error in judgment not qualify for reformation of the contract?

2. Al contracts to sell and Bob agrees to buy a tract of land for $500,000 that they believe contains 200 acres. In fact, the tract contains 205 acres. The contract is not voidable by either Al or Bob unless additional facts show that the effect on the agreed exchange is material.

In the transaction of business, it is customary in many situations to dispose of property about which the contracting parties willingly admit that all the facts are not known. In such instances, the property is sold without regard to its quality or characteristics. Such agreements may not be rescinded if later the property appears to have characteristics that neither of the parties had reason to suspect or if it otherwise differs from their

A contract is voidable if both parties are mistaken as to the same assumption and if one of the parties is adversely affected by the material mistake.

expectations. Under such conditions, the property forms the subject matter of the agreement, regardless of its nature. If shortly after a farm is sold oil is discovered on it, the agreement could not be rescinded by the seller on the grounds of bilateral mistake.

To illustrate and compare cases in which mutual mistake may be a ground for rescission, consider the two following examples:

EXAMPLE 1 A woman finds a yellow stone about the size of a bird's egg and thinks it might be a gem. She takes it to a jeweler, who honestly states that he is not sure what the stone is. Nonetheless, he offers her $15 for the stone, and she sells it. The stone is later discovered to be an uncut diamond worth $3,000. Result: No relief will be granted. There was no mistake of fact, only of value. Both parties bargained with the knowledge that they were consciously ignorant, both thereby assuming the risk that the stone might be worth nothing or might be a valuable gem. Rule: When the parties are uncertain or consciously ignorant of facts about the thing sold, there is no avoidance for mistake.

EXAMPLE 2 A buyer and a seller both mistakenly believed a cow of excellent breeding stock to be sterile. In fact, the cow could breed and was already pregnant. The cow was sold for beef at a price far below what she would otherwise have brought for breeding purposes. Result: When the mistake became apparent, the seller could rescind. The parties were not negligent in being mistaken, nor were they consciously ignorant. Both parties thought they knew what they were buying and selling; however, what they bought and sold was, in fact, not what they contemplated buying and selling. A sterile cow is substantially different from a breeding cow. There is as much difference between them as between a bull and a cow. Since there is no good basis to place the risk of the mistake on either party, the contract is voidable for mutual mistake. Rule: A mutual mistake regarding the quality of the item sold, a quality that goes to its very essence, is grounds for avoiding a contract.

9. Unilateral Mistake

When only one party is laboring under a mistake, it is said to be a unilateral (one-sided) mistake. Generally, a contract entered into because of some mistake or error by only one party affords no relief to that party. The majority of such mistakes results from carelessness or lack of diligence by the mistaken party and, therefore, should not affect the rights of the other party.

This general rule is subject to certain exceptions. An offeree who has reason to know of a unilateral mistake is not permitted to "snap up" such an offer and profit thereby. For example, if a mistake in a bid on a contract is clearly apparent to the offeree, it cannot be accepted by the offeree. Sometimes the mistake is discovered prior to the bid opening and the offeror seeks to withdraw the bid. Bids are often accompanied by bid bonds, which have the effect of making them irrevocable. Most courts will allow the bidder to withdraw the bid containing the error if (1) the bidder acted in good faith, (2) the bidder acted without gross negligence, (3) the bidder was reasonably prompt in giving notice of the error in the bid to the other party, (4) the bidder will suffer substantial detriment by forfeiture, and (5) the other party's status has not greatly changed and relief from forfeiture will work no substantial hardship on him or her. Courts clearly scrutinize the facts to make sure that all these requirements are met. It should be difficult for low bidders to claim an error in computation as the basis for escaping from a bid noticeably lower than the competition's. This is the "bad-faith" element of the aforementioned test.

FIGURE 16-1 ■ Bilateral and Unilateral Mistakes

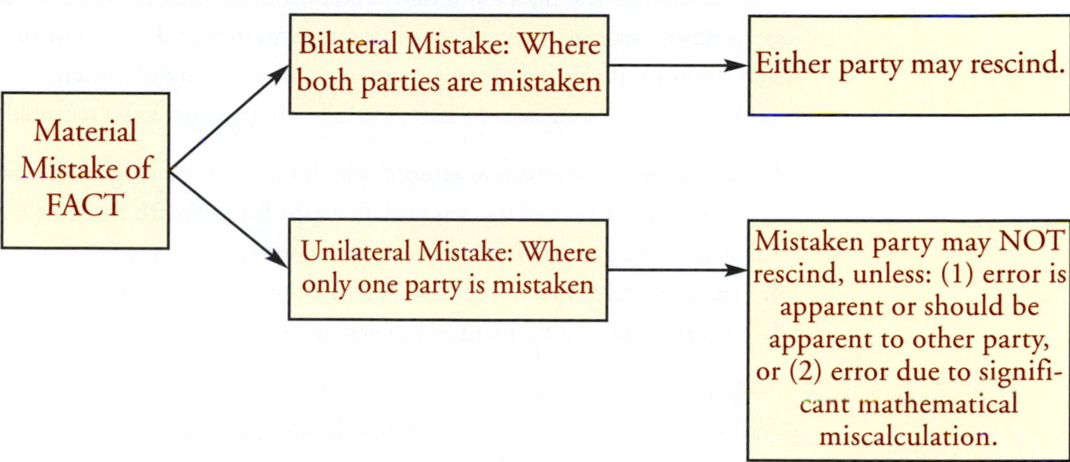

10. Reformation of Written Contracts

In most instances, a written contract is preceded by negotiations between the parties, who agree orally on the terms to be set forth in the final written contract. This is certainly the case when the parties contemplate a written statement signed by both as necessary to a binding agreement; that is, the oral agreement was not itself to have a binding effect. Of course, the parties could intend otherwise. They could regard the oral agreement as binding without any writing, or they could regard the writing as simply a subsequent memorial of their oral agreement.

Suppose the written agreement that is finally executed by the parties contains a mistake. The signed writing does not conform to what the parties agreed to orally. Frequently, the draftsperson or typist may make an error that is not discovered prior to the signing of the contract, and the party benefiting from the error seeks to hold the other party to the agreement as written. For such situations, courts of equity provide a remedy known as *reformation;* the court corrects (*reforms*) the contract.

The only remedy in cases of unilateral mistake apparent to the other party is rescission. Reformation is not an available remedy since it can be used only to correct the written contract to reflect the actual intentions of both parties. Reformation is available only for a case of mutual mistake.

If the facts do not support a finding of mutual mistake, the remedy of reformation is not available.

MISREPRESENTATION

11. Types of Misrepresentation

A contract is voidable if one party has been induced and injured by reliance on the other's misrepresentation of a material fact. The misrepresentation may be intentional, in which case the law considers the misrepresentation to be *fraudulent.* It may be based on a lack of due care, termed *negligent misrepresentation.* It may, also, be termed *innocent misrepresentation.* In all cases, the victim of the misrepresentation may rescind the contract.

In fraudulent misrepresentation, the victim is given the additional remedy of a suit for dollar damages, most often including punitive damages. Cases where negligent misrepresentation is shown will generally allow plaintiff to recover contract damages only. For innocent misrepresentation, no damages are allowed.

The focus of the discussion in this section is directed to fraud although references to the far less common actions for negligent misrepresentation and innocent misrepresentation are made when appropriate. While the elements of actionable fraud (intentional misrepresentation) are stated differently from state to state, the following are generally required:

Scienter
Knowledge or deliberate disregard of the falsity of a representation

1. ***Scienter***, or *intention to mislead*, which means knowledge of the falsity, or statements made with such utter recklessness and disregard for the truth that knowledge is inferred
2. A *false representation or the concealment* of a material fact
3. *Justifiable reliance* on the false statement or concealment
4. *Damages* as a consequence of the reliance

While fraud requires the proof on all four elements, negligent and innocent misrepresentation do not require proof of *scienter*, but do require proof of all the other elements of fraud. Negligent misrepresentation requires the additional element that the defendant failed to perform in a reasonable manner.

Rescission is permitted only in case the defrauded party acts with reasonable promptness after learning of the falsity of the representation. Undue delay on the defrauded's part waives his or her right to rescind, thus limiting the defrauded party to an action for recovery of damages. A victim of fraud loses the right to rescind if, after having acquired knowledge of the fraud, he or she indicates an intention to affirm the contract. These principles result from the fact that rescission is an equitable remedy.

12. *Scienter*

The requirement of intent to mislead is often referred to as *scienter*, a Latin word meaning "knowingly." *Scienter* may be present in circumstances other than the typical false statement made with actual intent to deceive. *Scienter* may be found when there has been a concealment of a material fact. Moreover, a statement that is partially or even literally true may be fraudulent in law if it is made to create a substantially false impression.

Intention to mislead may also be established by showing that a statement was made with *reckless disregard* for the truth. An accountant who certifies that financial statements accurately reflect the financial condition of a company may be guilty of fraud if he or she has no basis for the statement. Perhaps the accountant does not intend to mislead, but his or her statement is so reckless that the intention is inferred from the lack of actual knowledge.

Misrepresentation
The affirmative statement or affirmation of a fact that is not true

Fiduciary
A person who occupies a position of trust or confidence in relation to another person or his or her property

13. False Representation

To establish fraud, there must be an actual or implied ***misrepresentation*** *of a past or existing fact*. The misstatement of fact must be material or significant to the extent that it has a moving influence on a contracting party, but it need not be the sole inducing cause for entering into the contract.

False statements in *matters of opinion*, such as value of property, are not factual and usually are not considered actionable. For example, sales hype or puffery and promises about a sales item's future value generally do not constitute fraud. *However, statements of opinion may be considered misrepresentations of fact in certain situations.* An intentional misstatement even with regard to value may be fraudulent if the person making the statement has another opinion and knowingly states a false opinion. This concept is sometimes used when the person who is allegedly fraudulent is an expert, such as a physician, or when the parties stand in a **fiduciary** relationship (a position of trust) to each other. Assume that a doctor, after examining a patient for an insurance company physical, states that he is of the opinion that the person has no physical disability. If his actual opinion is that the patient has cancer, the doctor is guilty of fraud. He has misstated a fact (his professional opinion). The same is true if a partner sells property to the firm of which he or she is a member. The false statement of opinion concerning the value of the property will supply the misstatement-of-fact element. Each partner is a fiduciary toward fellow partners and the firm, and must give honest opinions.

A half-truth (or partial truth) that has the net effect of misleading may form the basis of fraud, just as if it were entirely false. A partial truth in response to a request for information becomes an untruth whenever it creates a false impression and is designed to do so. The following case is perhaps the most famous case dealing with this aspect of fraud to have been decided in the past fifty years.

CASE

Audrey E. Vokes v. Arthur Murray, Inc., A Corporation, J. P. Davenport, d/b/a Arthur Murray School of Dancing

COURT OF APPEALS OF FLORIDA, SECOND DISTRICT

212 So. 2d 906 (1968)

OPINION BY: PIERCE

This is an appeal by Audrey E. Vokes, plaintiff below, from a final order dismissing with prejudice, for failure to state a cause of action, her fourth amended complaint, hereinafter referred to as plaintiff's complaint.

Defendant Arthur Murray, Inc., a corporation, authorizes the operation throughout the nation of dancing schools under the name of "Arthur Murray School of Dancing" through local franchised operators, one of whom was defendant J. P. Davenport whose dancing establishment was in Clearwater.

Plaintiff Mrs. Audrey E. Vokes, a widow of 51 years and without family, had a yen to be "an accomplished dancer" with the hopes of finding "new interest in life". So, on February 10, 1961, a dubious fate, with the assist of a motivated acquaintance, procured her to attend a "dance party" at Davenport's "School of Dancing" where she whiled away the pleasant hours, sometimes in a private room, absorbing his accomplished sales technique, during which her grace and poise were elaborated upon and her rosy future as "an excellent dancer" was painted for her in vivid and glowing colors. As an incident to this interlude, he sold her eight 1/2-hour dance lessons to be utilized within one calendar month therefrom, for the sum of $14.50 cash in hand paid, obviously a baited "come-on".

Thus she embarked upon an almost endless pursuit of the terpsichorean art during which, over a period of less than sixteen months, she was sold fourteen"dance courses" totalling in the aggregate 2302 hours of dancing lessons for a total cash outlay of $31,090.45, all at Davenport's dance emporium. All of these fourteen courses were evidenced by execution of a written "Enrollment Agreement—Arthur Murray's School of Dancing" with the addendum in heavy black print, "No one will be informed that you are taking dancing lessons. Your relations with us are held in strict confidence", setting forth the number of "dancing lessons" and the "lessons in rhythm sessions" currently sold to her from time to time, and always of course accompanied by payment of cash of the realm.

These dance lesson contracts and the monetary consideration therefore of over $31,000 were procured from her by means and methods of Davenport and his associates which went beyond the unsavory, yet legally permissible, perimeter of "sales puffing" and intruded well into the forbidden area of undue influence, the suggestion of falsehood, the suppression of truth, and the free exercise of rational judgment, if what plaintiff alleged in her complaint was true. From the time of her first contact with the dancing school in February 1961, she was influenced unwittingly by a constant and continuous barrage of flattery, false praise, excessive compliments, and panegyric encomiums, to such extent that it would be not only inequitable, but unconscionable, for a Court exercising inherent chancery power to allow such contracts to stand.

She was incessantly subjected to over-reaching blandishment and cajolery. She was assured she had "grace and poise"; that she was "rapidly improving and developing in her dancing skill"; that the additional lessons would "make her a beautiful dancer, capable of dancing with the most accomplished dancers"; that she was "rapidly progressing in the development of her dancing skill and gracefulness", etc., etc. She was given "dance aptitude tests" for the ostensible purpose of "determining" the number of remaining hours instructions needed by her from time to time.

At one point she was sold 545 additional hours of dancing lessons to be entitled to award of the "Bronze Medal" signifying that she had reached "the Bronze Standard", a supposed designation of dance achievement by students of Arthur Murray, Inc.

Later she was sold an additional 926 hours in order to gain the "Silver Medal", indicating she had reached "the Silver Standard", at a cost of $12,501.35.

At one point, while she still had to her credit about 900 unused hours of instructions, she was induced to purchase an additional 24

continued

hours of lessons to participate in a trip to Miami at her own expense, where she would be "given the opportunity to dance with members of the Miami Studio."

She was induced at another point to purchase an additional 126 hours of lessons in order to be not only eligible for the Miami trip but also to become "a life member of the Arthur Murray Studio", carrying with it certain dubious emoluments, at a further cost of $1,752.30.

At another point, while she still had over 1,000 unused hours of instruction, she was induced to buy 151 additional hours at a cost of $2,049.00 to be eligible for a "Student Trip to Trinidad", at her own expense as she later learned.

Also, when she still had 1100 unused hours to her credit, she was prevailed upon to purchase an additional 347 hours at a cost of $4,235.74, to qualify her to receive a "Gold Medal" for achievement, indicating she had advanced to "the Gold Standard".

On another occasion, while she still had over 1200 unused hours, she was induced to buy an additional 175 hours of instruction at a cost of $2,472.75 to be eligible "to take a trip to Mexico".

Finally, sandwiched in between other lesser sales promotions, she was influenced to buy an additional 481 hours of instruction at a cost of $6,523.81 in order to "be classified as a Gold Bar Member, the ultimate achievement of the dancing studio".

All the foregoing sales promotions, illustrative of the entire fourteen separate contracts, were procured by defendant Davenport and Arthur Murray, Inc., by false representations to her that she was improving in her dancing ability, that she had excellent potential, that she was responding to instructions in dancing grace, and that they were developing her into a beautiful dancer, whereas in truth and in fact she did not develop in her dancing ability, she had no "dance aptitude," and in fact had difficulty in "hearing the musical beat." The complaint alleged that such representations to her "were in fact false and known by the defendant to be false and contrary to the plaintiff's true ability, the truth of plaintiff's ability being fully known to the defendants, but withheld from the plaintiff for the sole and specific intent to deceive and defraud the plaintiff and to induce her in the purchasing of additional hours of dance lessons." It was averred that the lessons were sold to her "in total disregard to the true physical, rhythm, and mental ability of the plaintiff." In other words, while she first exulted that she was entering the "spring of her life," she finally was awakened to the fact there was "spring" neither in her life nor in her feet.

The complaint prayed that the Court decree the dance contracts to be null and void and to be cancelled, that an accounting be had, and judgment entered against the defendants "for that portion of the $31,090.45 not charged against specific hours of instruction given to the plaintiff." The Court held the complaint not to state a cause of action and dismissed it with prejudice. We disagree and reverse.

The material allegations of the complaint must, of course, be accepted as true for the purpose of testing its legal sufficiency. Defendants contend that contracts can only be rescinded for fraud or misrepresentation when the alleged misrepresentation is as to a material fact, rather than an opinion, prediction or expectation, and that the statements and representations set forth at length in the complaint were in the category of "trade puffing", within its legal orbit.

It is true that "generally a misrepresentation, to be actionable, must be one of fact rather than of opinion," but this rule has significant qualifications, applicable here. It does not apply: where there is a fiduciary relationship between the parties, where there has been some artifice or trick employed by the representor, where the parties do not in general deal at "arm's length" as we understand the phrase, or where the representee does not have equal opportunity to become apprised of the truth or falsity of the fact represented. A statement of a party having superior knowledge may be regarded as a statement of fact although it would be considered as opinion if the parties were dealing on equal terms.

It could be reasonably supposed here that defendants had "superior knowledge" as to whether plaintiff had "dance potential" and as to whether she was noticeably improving in the art of terpsichore. It would, also, be a reasonable inference from the undenied averments of the complaint that the flowery eulogiums heaped upon her by defendants as a prelude to her contracting for 1944 additional hours of instruction in order to attain the rank of the Bronze Standard, thence to the bracket of the Silver Standard, thence to the class of the Gold Bar Standard, and finally to the crowning plateau of a Life Member of the Studio, proceeded as much or more from the urge to "ring the cash register" as from any honest or realistic appraisal of her dancing prowess or a factual representation of her progress.

Even in contractual situations where a party to a transaction owes no duty to disclose facts within his knowledge or to answer inquiries respecting such facts, the law is if he undertakes to do so he must disclose the whole truth. From the face of the complaint, it should have been reasonably apparent to defendants that her vast outlay of cash for the many hundreds of additional hours of instruction was not justified by her slow and awkward progress, which she would have been made well aware of if they had spoken the "whole truth".

We repeat that where parties are dealing on a contractual basis at arm's length with no inequities or inherently unfair practices employed, the Courts will in general "leave the parties where they find themselves". In this case, from the allegations of the unanswered complaint, we cannot say that enough of the accompanying ingredients, as mentioned in the foregoing authorities, were not present which otherwise would have barred the equitable arm of the Court to her. In our view, from the showing made in her complaint, plaintiff is entitled to her day in Court.

It accordingly follows that the order dismissing plaintiff's last amended complaint with prejudice should be and is reversed.

■ *Reversed.*

CASE CONCEPTS REVIEW

1. Should Vokes be protected by the law from her decisions to enter into numerous contracts for dance lessons? Why or why not?
2. When do actions of a businessperson move beyond legal puffing to unacceptable misrepresentation?
3. When does opinion become fact under the law of fraud?

An intentional misrepresentation of existing local or state law by someone other than an attorney affords no basis for rescission because it is not a statement of fact in the technical sense. Statements of law are traditionally seen as assertions of opinion; moreover, everyone is presumed to know the law, and therefore deception is not possible. However, a few courts in recent years have held such statements about the law by attorneys to be factual or the equivalent of professional opinions and thus fraudulent.

A misrepresentation may be made by conduct as well as by language. Any physical act that attempts to hide vital facts relating to property involved in the contract is, in effect, a misstatement. One who turns back the odometer on a car, fills a motor with heavy grease to keep it from knocking, or paints over an apparent defect asserts an untruth as effectively as if he or she were speaking. Such conduct, if it misleads the other party, amounts to fraud and makes rescission or an action for damages possible.

14. Silence as Fraud

Historically, the law of contracts has followed *caveat emptor* (let the buyer beware), especially in real estate transactions. The parties to a contract are required to exercise ordinary business sense in their dealings. As a result, the general rule is that silence in the absence of a duty to speak does not constitute fraud.

In at least three situations there is a duty to speak the truth, and failure to do so will constitute actionable fraud. First, there is a duty to speak when the parties stand in a *fiduciary* relationship (the trust that should exist among partners in a partnership, between a director and a corporation, or between an agent and a principal). Because such parties do not deal "at arm's length," there is the duty to speak and to make a full disclosure of all facts.

The second duty is based on justice, equity, and fair dealing. This duty typically arises when a material fact is known by one party but not by the other, who reasonably could not discover the fact; had the other party known the fact, there would have been no contract. For example, when there is a latent defect in property (such as termites in a home) that could not be reasonably discovered by a buyer, a seller who knows of the defect has a duty to inform the buyer. Failure to do so is fraudulent.

The third duty is that of a person who has misstated an important fact on some previous occasion and is obligated to correct the statement when negotiations are renewed or as soon as he or she learns about the misstatement. This is not a true exception to the silence rule because there is in fact a positive misstatement.

The gist of these exceptions is that one of the parties has the erroneous impression that certain things are true, whereas the other party is aware that they are not true and also knows of the misunderstanding. It, therefore, becomes the informed party's duty to disclose the truth. Unless he or she does so, most courts would hold that fraud exists. This does not mean that a potential seller or buyer has to disclose all the facts about the value of property he or she is selling or buying. The duty to speak arises only when the party knows that the other party to the agreement is harboring a misunderstanding on some vital matter.

15. Justifiable Reliance

Before a false statement can be considered a misrepresentation, the party to whom it has been made must *reasonably believe* it to be true and must act on it, to his or her damage. If the party investigates before acting on it, and the falsity is revealed, no action can be brought for fraud. Cases are in conflict concerning the need to investigate. Some courts have indicated that if all the information is readily available for ascertaining the truth of the statements, blind reliance on the misrepresentation is not justified. In such a case, the party is said to be negligent in not taking advantage of the facilities available for confirming the statement.

If a party inspects property or has an opportunity to do so, and if a reasonable investigation would have revealed that the property was not as it had been represented, the party cannot be considered misled. On the other hand, some courts deny that there is any need to investigate. They hold that one who has misrepresented facts cannot avoid the legal consequences by saying in effect, "You should not have believed me. You should have checked whether what I told you was true." Generally, reliance is justified when substantial effort or expense is required to determine the actual facts. The standard of justified reliance is not whether a reasonably prudent person would be justified in relying, but whether the particular individual involved had a right to rely. When the provisions of a written contract are involved, most people cannot be defrauded by its contents because the law charges the parties with actual knowledge of its contents.

16. Injury or Damage

To prevail, the party relying on the misstatement must offer proof of resulting damage. Normally, resulting damage is proved by evidence that the property in question would have been more valuable had the statements been true. Injury results when the party is not in as good a position as he or she would have been had the statements been true.

In an action for damages for fraud, the plaintiff may seek to recover damages on either of two theories. The plaintiff may use the "benefit of the bargain" theory and seek the difference between the actual market value of what he or she received and the value if he or she had received what was represented. A plaintiff may also use the "out-of-pocket" theory and collect the difference between the actual value of what was received and its purchase price.

Perhaps the most significant aspect of a suit for dollar damages is that the victim of fraud may be entitled to punitive damages in addition to compensatory damages. If the fraudulent representations are made maliciously, willfully, wantonly, or so recklessly that they imply a disregard of social obligations, punitive damages as determined by a jury may be awarded.

OTHER GROUNDS FOR RESCISSION

17. Undue Influence and Duress

Equity allows a party to rescind an agreement that was not entered into voluntarily. The lack of free will may take the form of undue influence or duress. A person who has obtained property under such circumstances should not in good conscience be allowed to keep it. A person may lose free will because of the subtle pressure of *undue influence,* whereby one person overpowers the will of another by use of moral, social, or domestic force as contrasted with physical or economic force. Cases of undue influence frequently arise in situations involving the elderly. In those cases where free will is lacking, some courts hold that the minds of the parties did not meet.

A party may also lose free will because of *duress*—some threat to his or her person, family, or property.

Elderly are often targets of undue influence

Under early common law, duress would not be present when a courageous person would have possessed a free will in spite of a threat, but modern courts do not require this standard of courage or firmness as a prerequisite for the equitable remedy. If the wrongful pressure applied in fact affected the individual involved to the extent that the contract was not voluntary, there is duress. If a person has a free choice, there is no duress even though some pressure may have been exerted on him or her. A threat of a lawsuit made in good faith is not duress that will allow rescission. Economic pressure may constitute duress if it is wrongful and oppressive.

CHAPTER SUMMARY

INCAPACITY TO CONTRACT

Types of Incapacity

1. A party is declared to lack capacity to contract if he or she is unable to understand the rights under the contract, the purpose of the agreement, or the legal effect of the contract.
2. Examples of parties who may be temporarily or permanently incapacitated include minors, mental incompetents, intoxicated persons, and drug addicts.
3. Contracts made before a person is adjudged incompetent are voidable. Contracts entered into after one of the parties is declared incompetent by a court generally are void.
4. If the competent party is unaware of the other party's incompetence, the incompetent party must make restitution before the contract is voidable.

Minors' Contracts

1. In most states, everyone below the age of 18 is considered to be a minor.
2. Minors' contracts generally may be disaffirmed by the minor, but not by the competent adult party.

Avoiding Contracts by Minors

1. To disaffirm, a minor must communicate his or her desire to avoid contractual liability.
2. This communication must be made to the competent adult party in writing, by spoken words, or by the minors' conduct.
3. To void a contract, the minor must return all the consideration received that he or she still has.

Ratification

1. Ratification of a contract occurs when the party who was incompetent becomes competent and affirms or approves of the contract.
2. Ratification can be by a manifestation of intent to be bound or by retaining the consideration for an unreasonable time after majority.
3. After reaching majority, a minor must disaffirm within a reasonable time or be held to have ratified the contract.

Liability for Necessaries

1. If a contract is for necessaries, the minor is bound to pay for the reasonable value of these items instead of the contract price. (Of course, in many situations, the contract price is a very good indication of the reasonable value of the items involved.)
2. What is a necessary often must be determined from the facts of each case.

Third-Party Rights

1. A minor cannot avoid a contract if the personal property involved has been transferred by the competent adult party to a good-faith purchaser for value.
2. This rule does not apply to real property. In other words, a minor can always rescind a contract involving land even when a third party is involved.

MISTAKE

Bilateral Mistake

1. Bilateral mistake occurs when all parties have the identical misconception of a material fact or of the contract terms.
2. Bilateral mistake negates the element of mutuality of contract and allows either party to rescind or reform the contract.

Unilateral Mistake

1. Unilateral mistake is not grounds for rescission unless the other party knew or should have known of the mistake.

Reformation of Written Contracts

1. Reformation occurs when courts correct a written contract to reflect the parties' actual intent.
2. Reformation is not an available remedy for unilateral mistake.

FRAUD AND MISREPRESENTATION

Elements of Fraud

1. *Scienter*
2. False material representation
3. Justifiable reliance on the representation
4. Injury caused by such reliance

Scienter

1. *Scienter* is the intent to mislead. It is supplied by proof of knowledge of the falsity.
2. *Scienter* is also established by proof that the statement was made with a reckless disregard for the truth.

False Misrepresentation

1. There must be a misstatement of a material existing fact,
2. Statements of opinion are not factual unless made by an expert or unless the actual opinion is not as stated.
3. Misstatements of applicable laws are not statements of fact.
4. Misstatements may be by conduct as well as language.

Silence as Fraud

1. In the absence of a duty to speak, silence is not fraud.
2. Duty to speak arises (a) from a fiduciary relationship or (b) when equity and justice so demand or (c) to correct a prior misrepresentation.

Justifiable Reliance

1. A party must reasonably believe the statement to be true and must act on it.
2. There is no duty to take extraordinary steps to investigate the accuracy of statements.

Injury or Damage

1. A plaintiff is entitled to the benefit of the bargain theory in some cases and to use the out-of-pocket theory in others.
2. Punitive damages may be awarded in addition to compensatory damages.

OTHER GROUNDS FOR RESCISSION

Undue Influence and Duress

1. One party exerts undue influence on another to compel a contract.
2. Undue influence normally occurs when a fiduciary or close family relationship exists.
3. Duress is compulsion or constraint that deprives another of the ability to exercise free will in making a contract.
4. Physical threats are generally required, but economic duress is recognized in a few states, especially when a party is responsible for the economic necessity of the other party.

REVIEW QUESTIONS AND PROBLEMS

1. Match each term in Column A with the appropriate statement in Column B.

A	B
(1) Ratification	(a) Minor must pay for their reasonable value
(2) *Scienter*	(b) Rescission not allowed unless other party has knowledge of it
(3) Concealment	(c) A fiduciary or someone in close family relationship exerts pressure
(4) Mutual mistake	(d) What minor may choose to do upon reaching majority
(5) Necessaries	(e) Upon reaching majority, minor keeps consideration and does nothing more
(6) Undue influence	(f) Rescission granted if a duty to speak is not performed
(7) Unilateral mistake	(g) Physical threats usually required
(8) Duress	(h) Misconception of material fact by all parties
(9) Disaffirmance	(i) Intent to defraud
(10) Reformation	(j) Court rewrites contract to make contract conform to parties' intent

2. Bill, under guardianship by reason of mental illness, buys an old car from Larry for $2,000, giving a promissory note for that amount. Subsequently, Bill abandons the car. Is Bill liable on the note? Would it make any difference if the car was a necessary? Explain your answers.
3. Youngblood, a minor, sold a wrecked Ford to Blakensopp, an adult, for $350. Blakensopp took possession of the car. Unknown to Blakensopp, Youngblood took the car back and sold it to another purchaser for $400. Youngblood was charged with theft. Was Youngblood guilty of stealing the car from Blakensopp? Explain.
4. Halbman (a minor) bought a used Oldsmobile from Lemke (an adult). About five weeks after the purchase and after Halbman had paid $3,100 of the $4,250 purchase price, the connecting rod in the engine broke. Halbman, while still a minor, disaffirmed the purchase contract and demanded all the money he had paid defendant. Is he entitled to a full refund even though the car is now damaged? Why or why not?
5. Leon, a minor, signed a contract with Step-Up Employment Agency, in which Leon promised to pay a fee if Step-Up secured him a job as a pianist. Step-Up did find suitable employment, but Leon refused to pay the $500 fee since he was a minor. Can Step-Up recover the fee? Why or why not?
6. Beachcomer, a coin dealer, sues to rescind a purchase by Boskett, who paid $50 for a dime both parties thought was minted in San Francisco. In fact, it was a very valuable dime minted in Denver. Beachcomer asserts a mutual mistake of fact regarding the genuineness of the coin as San Francisco-minted. Boskett contends that the mistake was as to value only. Explain who should win.

7. Brawner Contracting was the low bidder for construction of the Marine Service Building. After the award of the contract to Brawner, it discovered an arithmetical error of $10,000 in its bid based on a similar error of like amount in a quotation made to it by a subcontractor. Correction of the error would not have caused Brawner's contract price to equal or exceed that of the next lowest bidder. Is Brawner entitled to reformation of the contract? Why or why not?
8. After making a visual inspection, buyer bought property from seller and proceeded to build a home. When the possibility of soil slippage soon became apparent, construction was halted. Buyer sued seller to rescind the sale. Soil expert testified that the property was not suitable for the construction of a residence. Seller was unaware of the stability hazard of the soil when the sale was transacted. Could buyer rescind? Why or why not?
9. Janet Van Tassel met Charles Carver, president of McDonald Corporation, a subfranchisor of Baskin-Robbins Ice Cream Company. To induce her to become an ice-cream store operator in a Michigan mall, Carver told Van Tassel the following:

   a. The proposed location was a gold mine.
   b. It would not be long before she would be driving a big car and living in a big house, and she would do all right if she stuck by him.
   c. He would not steer her wrong because he liked her.
   d. This was the right store for her, and all she would be doing is playing golf and making bank deposits.
   e. She was not going to lose money, and this would be the best thing that would happen to her.

   Van Tassel invested in the franchise, but it failed to meet Carver's predictions of success. Van Tassel filed suit, seeking to reclaim her investment. Did the representations constitute fraud? Why or why not?

10. A representative for a data processing company bought a computer after the computer salesperson assured her that the machine would be adequate for her purposes. The data processing representative was aware of the specifications of the computer, but she later discovered that its printout was too slow for her company's needs. She seeks to rescind the contract on the basis of misrepresentation. Should she succeed? Explain.

Illegality and Public Policy | 17

CHAPTER OUTLINE

CHAPTER PREVIEW

A valid contract must have a lawful purpose or object. Contracts that do not have a lawful object are illegal and, therefore, unenforceable. It would seem preposterous for the law to embrace an agreement for the sale of cocaine, for example. A contract—or a specific provision within a contract—may be declared illegal in two situations: (1) if it is *prohibited by statute*, or (2) if it is *contrary to public policy*. It may be illegal in its subject matter, its formation, or its performance.

A variety of agreements have been held to be illegal: wagering agreements, agreements to affect the administration of justice (concealing evidence or suppressing a criminal investigation), agreements to influence legislation or executive action by bribery or undue influence, and agreements to interfere with public service. Other examples of illegal agreements are discussed throughout this chapter.

Cases involving public policy are often in conflict from jurisdiction to jurisdiction. One state may allow a contract while another state finds the contract illegal. For example, California law exempts lenders who cater to a "payday advance" from the general limit on interest rates common in consumer transactions. Other states, including Michigan and Texas, have established maximum interest rates for the same type of transaction. In a similar vein, some states embrace gambling (e.g., Nevada) while others remain generally opposed (e.g., Utah). Often the economic interests of a state may play a major role in the development of public policy. As the laws on illegal contracts are studied, care should be taken to ascertain the reason behind each rule or decision; and the major emphasis should be on indicated trends in the law.

BUSINESS MANAGEMENT DECISION

You are one of six accountants to enter into a partnership agreement. You recognize that one or more of your new partners may leave the firm at a future date.

What should you include in the partnership agreement to ensure that all the clients remain with the firm and do not use a withdrawing partner?

TABLE 17-1 ■ Types of Illegality

Type	Definition	Examples
Agreements in Violation of Statute	A specific statute prohibits a contract based on the activity or prohibits the activity.	▪ Usury ▪ Gambling ▪ Anti-trust
Agreements in Violation of Public Policy	Generally, a common law (judge-made) rule prohibits a contract based on the activity or prohibits the activity. The directed activity is contrary to a particular public policy. The common law rule may be adopted or modified by statute.	▪ Covenant not to compete ▪ Unconscionable contracts • Procedural Unconscionability • Substantive Unconscionability

STATUS OF ILLEGAL CONTRACTS

1. Litigation Disallowed

As a general rule, the status of an illegal contract is that a court will not allow litigation involving it. This means that if the illegal contract is executory, neither party may enforce performance by the other. If it is executed, the court will not order rescission—it will not allow recovery of what was given in performance. An illegal contract cannot be ratified by either party, and the parties can do nothing to make it enforceable. Stated simply, in an illegal contract situation, the court literally "leaves the parties where it finds them." *A party to an illegal contract cannot recover damages for breach of such contract. If one party has performed, he or she cannot generally recover either the value of his or her performance or any property or goods transferred to the other.* As a result of the rule, one wrongdoer may be enriched at the expense of the other wrongdoer, but the courts usually will not intercede to rectify this because the purpose is to deter illegal bargains.

The following case illustrates how courts typically handle contracts involving an illegal purpose.

CASE

Massoud Bassidji v. Simon Soul Sun Goe

UNITED STATES COURT OF APPEALS FOR THE NINTH CIRCUIT

413 F.3d 928 (2005)

BERZON, CIRCUIT JUDGE

Executive Order 13,059 (the "Executive Order" or "Order") (Aug. 21, 1997) prohibits United States citizens from investing in and trading with Iran. The question we face is whether an American citizen's guarantees of payments that furthered a trade agreement with an Iranian company are covered by the Executive Order and, if so, whether the guarantees are unenforceable as a result. We conclude that the guarantees were illegal under the Executive Order and, under the circumstances of this case, unenforceable.

"In or around" November 1999, an Iranian company, Seyd Sayyad Ltd. ("SSL"), and a Hong Kong company, Kingdom Enterprises Ltd. ("KEL"), entered into a business arrangement for the purpose of harvesting Artemia cysts (brine shrimp eggs) from a lake in Iran. The Iranian government required sizeable payments for licenses and other fees to authorize the shrimp egg harvesting project, and SSL undertook related "financial commitments." Karim Arshian, an Iranian citizen affiliated with SSL, "was required to execute several guarantee checks related to the proposed operations."

Simon Goe, a U.S. citizen affiliated with KEL, guaranteed repayment of Arshian's costs by executing two personal guarantees, one on November 12, 1999, and another on January 20, 2000. Each time, Goe promised to reimburse Arshian for any expenditures made in securing the "harvest license, customs clearance, office and living arrangement," up to $1,875,603. "Without the promised guarantees, [Arshian] would have been unwilling to execute the referenced guarantee checks."

Arshian subsequently paid more than $1,875,603 toward these expenses and requested repayment from Goe. Goe refused to honor the guarantees. He paid Arshian nothing. Because Goe did not reimburse Arshian as promised, Arshian could not make the required payments. Arshian was unable to pursue legal action on his own because he was imprisoned, and he sold his rights under the guarantees to Massoud Bassidji, who is identified in the complaint as "an individual residing in Toronto, Canada." The record does not show the terms of the assignment, including whether Arshian will receive any of the proceeds if the guarantees are enforced.

Bassidji filed a breach of contract claim in district court in California. Goe asked the court to dismiss the complaint, on the ground that the guarantees were illegal under Executive Order 12,959 (now superseded by Executive Order 13,059) and therefore unenforceable. The district court denied Goe's motion to dismiss.

The text of section 2(d) plainly prohibits Goe's conduct. The Artemia cysts were "goods … of Iranian origin," and the guarantee covered costs incurred in harvesting them. The transaction between Arshian and Goe was certainly "related to" the brine shrimp eggs; the only reason for the transaction was to facilitate their harvesting. Goe's "guaranteeing" of financial repayment is explicitly included as a type of "transaction or dealing" prohibited by section 2(d).

Similarly, although the transaction that Goe guaranteed was not directly related either to the import or to the export of goods between Iran and the United States, it furthered a result inconsistent with the purposes of the Executive Order. The transaction promoted the transfer of wealth to Iran, including, it appears, the payment of fees to the Iranian government. That the licenses pertained to a business deal—the export of brine shrimp eggs from Iran to Hong Kong, which is not illegal under the Executive Order—is irrelevant. While the Executive Order—does not, and could not, ban all trade between Hong Kong and Iran, see 50 U.S.C. § 1702(a)(1) (granting the President the authority under IEEPA to regulate trade only of persons "subject to the jurisdiction of the United States"), United States citizens are expressly prohibited from facilitating such trade by guaranteeing the payment of costs incurred by parties to the sale.

continued

Federal and California law would bar an American court from ordering Goe to pay Arshian pursuant to the illegal guarantees. Such a payment would violate the precise terms of the Executive Order, which prohibit "any transaction or dealing by a United States person … related to … goods or services of Iranian origin" and "any new investment by a United States person in Iran." A payment from Goe to Arshian would provide funds to the Iranian economy, paying for goods in Iran. As such, it would violate both the letter of the Executive Order and its fundamental purposes.

Thus, no damages remedy can be provided to Bassidji by an American court. The "shoes" in which he stands make his claim repugnant to the Executive Order. Goe could not be ordered to pay Arshian; therefore, a payment to Arshian's assignee is also prohibited. For the reasons stated, we reverse the district court's determination that, on the facts pled, the guarantees were not covered by the Executive Order. Moreover, Bassidji's complaint does not state a claim for which recovery can legally be ordered.

■ *Reversed.*

CASE CONCEPTS REVIEW

1. Is Goe benefiting unfairly by the court's decision? Why?
2. How does the court treat parties who enter into a contract that has an illegal purpose?

2. Exceptions

There are three basic exceptions to the rule that precludes the granting of any relief to a party to an illegal contract. First, if a person falls in the category of *those for whose protection the contract was made illegal,* that person may obtain restitution of what he or she has paid or parted with or may even obtain enforcement. For example, both federal and state statutes require that a corporation follow certain procedures before securities (stocks and bonds) may be offered for sale to the public. It is illegal to sell such securities without having complied with the legal requirements. Nevertheless, a purchaser is allowed to obtain a refund of the purchase price if he or she desires to do so. The act of one party (the seller) is more illegal than that of the other party (the buyer). Many statutes are designed to protect one party in an illegal transaction; and when this is the case, the protected party is allowed a legal remedy.

A second exception applies when a person is *induced by fraud or duress* to enter into an illegal agreement. In such cases, the courts do not regard the defrauded or coerced party as being an actual participant in the wrong and, therefore, will allow restitution of what he or she has rendered by way of performance. It has been suggested that the same result would occur if the party were induced by strong economic pressure to enter into an illegal agreement.

Third, there is a doctrine called *locus poenitentiae* that may provide the remedy of restitution to one who has become a party to an illegal contract. Literally, the phrase means "a place for repentance," by extension, "an opportunity for changing one's mind." As applied to an illegal contract, it means that within very strict limits, *a person who repents before actually having performed any illegal part of the contract* may rescind it and obtain restitution of his or her part performance. Thus wagers are illegal transactions except under certain circumstances. Suppose that A and B wager on the outcome of an election, and each places $100 with C, the stakeholder, who agrees to turn $200 over to the winner. Prior to the election, either A or B could recover $100 from C by legal action since the execution of the illegal agreement would not yet have occurred. Actually, the loser could obtain a judgment against C by giving notice of his or her demand prior to the time that the stake has been turned over to the winner.

Agreements in Violation of Statutes

3. Violations of License Requirements

Some contracts are void and unenforceable because they involve a purpose that violates a statute. Most personal service contracts do not involve an unlawful purpose. However, personal service agreements may be unenforceable if the party performing the service is not legally entitled to do so. For example, doctors, dentists, pharmacists, architects, lawyers, accountants, surveyors, real estate brokers, and others who perform professional services must be licensed by the appropriate body before they are allowed to contract with the general public.

As a general rule, if the service rendered requires a license, the party receiving the benefit of the service can successfully refuse to pay an unlicensed plaintiff on the ground that the contract is illegal. This is true even if the person is licensed in another jurisdiction but not the one in which the services were rendered. A real estate broker licensed in one state cannot perform services in another state. If the broker does so, he or she cannot collect for the services.

The practice of law by unauthorized persons is a significant problem. A person who practices law without a license is not only denied the right to a fee but also subject to criminal prosecution in many states; and such activity may also be enjoined. Since the practice of law primarily entails giving advice, difficult questions are presented when advice is given by business specialists such as certified public accountants, insurance brokers, bankers, and real estate brokers. Although the line between permissible and impermissible activities of these business specialists is often difficult to draw; some activities and services performed by various business specialists clearly constitute unauthorized practice of law. An accountant's handling of a complicated tax case has been held to constitute unauthorized practice of law, and a real estate broker's preparation of a real estate deed is illegal in most states. Business specialists should be aware that giving legal advice and preparing legal documents are illegal performances by one not licensed to practice law. A major danger in doing these things is the loss of the right to compensation for services that are otherwise legal.

However, there is a significant qualification to this rule. If the licensing requirement is designed more as a means to raise revenues than to protect the public, a failure to obtain the required license will not void a contract. In most communities, for example, a city provides a mechanism for a business to pay a fee and receive a license to operate a business. The following situation illustrates the point. Juan enters into a contract for a mechanic to fix his car. Juan does some investigation and discovers that the mechanic does not have a city business license. With that knowledge in mind, Juan believes the contract is illegal. If litigated, the court will probably side with the mechanic. Here, the primary purpose of the city business license regulation is to raise money for the municipality. In contrast, the requirement that a real estate broker be licensed is principally geared to protect the public, not raise money.

A real estate broker can only operate in the state he/she is licensed to operate

4. Usury

Usury

Requiring a payment of a rate of interest in excess of that permitted by statute

State statutes limit the amount of interest that may be charged on borrowed money. Any contract by which the lender is to receive more than the maximum interest allowed by the statute is usurious and illegal. In most states, the civil penalty for **usury** is that the lender is denied the right to collect any interest. In a few states, the lender is denied the right to collect both the interest and the principal. There are also criminal penalties for charging illegal interest.

Difficult issues often arise over what actually constitutes interest. Creditors develop ingenious schemes to charge more than the maximum legal rate of interest. For example, the calculation of interest on the basis of 360 days was held to be illegal if the computation produced in a single year more interest than would be produced by applying the maximum legal rate to a calendar year of 365 days.

The law against usury is generally not violated if the seller sets a cash price different from a credit price; but the seller cannot disguise interest by calling it something else, like a finder's fee or broker's fee. If the buyer is charged for making a loan, it is interest, regardless of the terminology used. As long as one lends the money of others, one may then charge a commission in addition to the maximum rate. A commission may not be legally charged when one is lending one's own funds, even though one has to borrow the money with which to make the loan and expects to sell the paper shortly thereafter.

The laws on usury are not violated by collection of the legal maximum interest in advance or by adding a service fee that is no larger than reasonably necessary to cover the incidental costs of making the loan (inspection, legal, and recording fees). A seller can also add a finance or carrying charge on long-term credit transactions. Some statutes allow special lenders such as pawnshops, small loan companies, or credit unions to charge in excess of the otherwise legal limit. In fact, the exceptions to the maximum interest rate in most states far exceed the situations in which the general rule is applicable. The laws relating to usury were designed to protect debtors from excessive interest. This goal has been thwarted by these exceptions, so only modest protection is actually available.

The purchase of a note at a discount greater than the maximum interest is not usurious unless the maker of the note is the person who is discounting it. A note is considered the same as any other personal property and may be sold for whatever it will bring on the market.

Today, in most states, there is no maximum legal rate of interest when the borrower is a business, whether or not it is incorporated. Some states limit this exception to loans over a fixed sum, such as $10,000, but little protection is afforded by such laws. Loans to corporations usually are exempt in most states, regardless of the amount of the loan.

5. Agreements and Activities in Restraint of Trade

Restraint of trade

Contracts that impede free competition

Laws commonly referred to as the antitrust laws serve to protect our economic system from monopolies, attempts to monopolize, and activities in **restraint of trade**. (Greater treatment of the subject of antitrust laws is included in Chapter 41.) In 1890, under its power to regulate interstate commerce, Congress passed the Sherman Antitrust Act, directed at these concerns. The law seeks to preserve competition by using three basic sanctions. First, violation of the Sherman Act is a federal felony punishable by fine or imprisonment or both. Second, the Sherman Act authorizes injunctions to prevent and restrain violations or continued violations of its provisions. Third, those who have been injured by violation of the act may collect treble (triple) damages plus court costs and reasonable attorney's fees. The treble-damage provision serves not only as a means of punishing the defendant for his or her wrongful act but also as a means of compensating the plaintiff for his or her injury.

SHERMAN ANTITRUST ACT AND CONTRACTS Section 1 of the Sherman Act prohibits contracts (express or implied), combinations, and conspiracies in restraint of trade. Activities that may constitute a contract, combination, or conspiracy in restraint of trade are limitless. However, these agreements and practices are illegal only if they are unreasonable. That is, they are illegal ONLY if they *unreasonably restrain trade.* In deciding if an agreement or practice is unreasonable, courts divide them into two types or categories. Some are said to be illegal **per se**. This means that they are conclusively presumed to be unreasonable and thus illegal. Such agreements are so plainly anticompetitive and lacking in any redeeming virtue that it is unnecessary to examine the effects of the activity. If an activity is illegal *per se,* proof of the activity is proof of a violation and proof that it is in restraint of trade. Proof of an anticompetitive effect is not required.

Per se

A contract clause may be inherently illegal—illegal *per se,* "by itself"

The second type or category includes activities that are illegal *only if the facts* establish that they are unreasonable. The standard here is called the "**rule of reason.**" On the one hand, an act is unreasonable if it suppresses or destroys competition. On the other hand, an act is reasonable if it promotes competition. In cases under this second category, courts analyze the facts to determine the significance of the activity or restraint on competition.. Under the rule of reason test, courts examine the scope of harm that may result, the reason for the agreement, and the history of any relationship.

Rule of reason

A contract will be held illegal if the facts indicate that the anticipated arrangement will result in an unreasonable restraint of trade.

PRICE-FIXING The most common type of Sherman Act violation is price-fixing, which is illegal per se. It is no defense that the prices fixed are fair or reasonable. It also is no defense that price-fixing is engaged in by small competitors to allow them to compete with larger competitors. It is just as illegal to fix a low price as it is to fix a high price. Today it is as illegal to fix the price of services as it is to fix the price of goods. Price-fixing in the service sector has been engaged in by professional persons as well as by service occupations such as automobile and TV repair workers, barbers, and refuse collectors. For many years it was contended that persons performing services were not engaged in trade or commerce, but the courts today reject such arguments.

Some professional groups have attempted to avoid the foregoing result through the use of ethical standards. Others have attempted to determine the price of services indirectly by the use of formulas and relative value scales. Some medical organizations have determined that a given medical procedure would be allocated a relative value on a scale of one to ten. Brain surgery might be labeled a nine and a face lift a four. All members of the profession would then use these values in determining professional fees. Such attempts have been uniformly held to be illegal as a form of price fixing.

Price-fixing may be *horizontal*—among competitors—or it may be thought of as *vertical. Vertical* price-fixing occurs when a manufacturer attempts to control the retail price of its product. Resale price maintenance attempts, other than simply announcing a price and refusing to deal with customers that do not follow the announced price, were for many years deemed illegal *per se.* Recently, the United States Supreme Court adopted the position that all forms of vertical price fixing are subject to rule of reason analysis. In part, this is because horizontal activities are generally more anticompetitive than vertical activities.

OTHER AGREEMENTS VIOLATING ANTITRUST LAWS There are other agreements that may violate the Sherman Act and its amendments. Although some of these are illegal per se, most are judged under the rule of reason. Typical of agreements subject to question under the Sherman Act are those granting exclusive rights to sell a product or to sell in exclusive territories. An agreement among competitors to divide territories is illegal *per se.* However, if a manufacturer gives an exclusive territory to a distributor, the agreement is illegal only if it has unreasonable anticompetitive effects. Since such territorial arrangements may in fact aid competition, they may be legal.

An agreement otherwise legal may be illegal under the antitrust laws because the price charged one customer is different from the price charged for the same product to another customer. Price discrimination is declared illegal under a federal law commonly referred to as the Robinson-Patman Act. It is illegal to discriminate in price among purchasers of commodities of like grade and quality if the price discrimination substantially lessens competition or tends to create a monopoly in any line of commerce or tends to injure competition. This law does not cover transactions with consumers, only sales by manufacturers and wholesalers to retailers.

The antitrust laws also prohibit agreements that seek to tie one product to another where the effect is to lessen competition. For example, it may be illegal to make an agreement to sell or lease a product only if the buyer or lessee purchases a different product or service. A strong argument can be crafted supporting the traditional view that a tying agreement should be governed by the per se rule. For example, a tying agreement is illegal *per se,* under this view, if the seller or lessor has strong economic power over the tying product and if a substantial amount of commerce is affected. Similarly, the tying of an unpatented product, for instance, to a patented product would be a *per se* violation of the antitrust laws. The contrary view, though, is increasingly popular. Under that approach, all tying arrangements should be judged under the rule of reason test because there has to be a determination, on a case-by-case basis, that a particular typing agreement "substantially" lessens competition or creates a monopoly.

In addition to tying products, exclusive arrangements and reciprocal dealing can be illegal. In an *exclusive* dealing agreement, the parties agree to deal solely with one another. In a *reciprocal* dealing arrangement, the parties deal with each other as both buyer and seller. Both of these agreements are illegal if they significantly restrain competition. However, some agreements that limit competition, such as those between a franchisor and its franchisees, are usually found to be legal. They are legal because their effect on competition is minimal compared with the interests of the franchisor in having similarity in all of its franchised operations. Thus, certain exclusive dealing contracts are legal.

AGREEMENTS IN VIOLATION OF PUBLIC POLICY

6. Introduction

A contract provision is contrary to public policy if it is injurious to the interests of the public, contravenes some established interest of society, violates the policy or purpose of some statute, or tends to interfere with the public health, safety, morals, or general welfare. Although all agreements are subject to the paramount power of the sovereign and to the judicial power to declare contracts illegal, contracts are not to be lightly set aside on the grounds of public policy; and doubts will usually be resolved in favor of legality.

The term *public policy* is vague and variable and changes as our social, economic, and policy climates change. As society becomes more complex, courts turn more and more to statutory enactments in search of current public policy. A court's own concept of right and wrong, as well as its total philosophy, will frequently come into play in answering complex questions of public policy.

The following sections present factual situations involving contracts that may be challenged as against public policy.

7. Agreements Not to Compete

A form of agreement that may be legal even though it is in partial restraint of trade is an agreement not to compete. An agreement by one person not to compete with another is frequently contained in a contract for the sale of a going business. The seller, by such a provision, agrees not to compete with the buyer. Agreements not to compete are also commonly found in contracts creating a business or a professional practice. Each partner or shareholder in the closely held corporation agrees not to compete with the firm or practice, should he or she leave the business or professional activity. In addition, as a part of their employment contract, many employees agree that they will not compete with their employer upon termination of their employment.

Such agreements will be enforced if they are reasonably necessary for the protection of a purchaser, the remaining members of a business, or an employer, provided the covenant (1) is reasonable in point of time, (2) is reasonable in the area of restraint, (3) is necessary to protect goodwill, (4) does not place an undue burden on the covenantor, and (5) does not violate the public interest. Each covenant is examined by the court to see if it is reasonable to both parties and to the general public. Factors such as uniqueness of product, patents, trade secrets, type of service, employee's contact with customers, and other goodwill factors are significant in determining the reasonableness issue. In the employment situation, whether or not the employee will become a burden on society and whether or not the public is being deprived of his or her skill are factors.

The law will look with more favor on these covenants if they involve the sale of a business interest rather than employment. In fact, an agreement not to compete is valid in the case of a sale of business and its goodwill as long as the restrictions are reasonable. Care must be exercised, though, that the seller must not thereafter directly or indirectly solicit business from former customers—although he or she may advertise generally. It is quite legal to advertise that the seller has opened a new business after the period of the restraint has ended; but it would be illegal for the seller to later solicit the customers or clients away from the purchaser of the business. Active solicitation could create tort liability for the seller.

Agreements between a buyer and seller of a business or between partners upon dissolution of a partnership are more likely to be held valid than are employer-employee contracts because there is more equality of bargaining power in the first two situations than in the last. A seller or a former partner could readily refuse to sign an agreement not to compete, whereas an employee seeking a job might feel obligated to sign almost anything to gain employment. In fact, a California statute provides that any attempt to interfere with an individual's right to earn a living is illegal. Most states do not go this far in favoring a former employee. Still, in the majority of jurisdictions, courts are mindful of restrictive covenants in the employment context. The following case illustrates these policy considerations.

CASE

Emerson Electric Co. v. Guy Rogers; Guy Rogers Sales, Inc.

UNITED STATES COURT OF APPEALS FOR THE EIGHTH CIRCUIT

418 F.3d 841 (2005)

MURPHY, CIRCUIT JUDGE

Guy Rogers worked as a manufacturer's representative for Emerson Electric Co. (Emerson), selling its ceiling fans to retailers in the southeast. When he left Emerson to begin selling the fans of a competitor, Minka Lighting Company, Emerson filed this lawsuit, alleging that Rogers misappropriated trade secrets and violated the covenant not to compete in their Sales Representation Agreement. The district court granted Emerson's motion for a preliminary injunction, and Rogers appealed We affirm.

Guyan T. Rogers has worked as a manufacturer's representative for various manufacturers since 1969. As a manufacturer's representative, Rogers markets and sells products to retailers who then market the products to the general public. He is currently the president and sole shareholder of Guy Rogers Sales, Inc., an incorporated entity that represents lighting and fan manufacturers to retailers in Georgia, Alabama, Tennessee, and Florida. The company pays three independent contractors to serve as representatives, and Rogers himself continues to visit and make sales calls to customers on a regular basis. He is presently 69 years old.

Rogers started selling Emerson's ceiling fans in 1988, and he began selling Minka lighting products in 1987. Minka became his largest account, generating approximately three million dollars annually in gross sales and $200,000 in annual commissions. When Minka started manufacturing fans in 1994, it attempted to persuade Rogers to sell its fans instead of Emerson's; Rogers declined. Before leaving Emerson in the fall of 2004, Rogers was selling approximately one million dollars annually of its ceiling fan products, generating approximately $50,000 in annual commissions.

Emerson first asked Rogers to sign a covenant not to compete in 1997 and then asked him to sign another copy of the covenant in 1999. In their standard Sales Representation Agreement, which contained the entire covenant, the parties acknowledged that "customer relationships can often be difficult to develop and require a significant investment of time and effort." Emerson agreed to engage and compensate Rogers based upon his promise "not to divert [its] customer contacts, loyalty and

continued

goodwill." If the parties were to end their relationship, Emerson "would need certain protections to prevent its competitors from gaining an unfair competitive advantage," loss of its goodwill, and misuse of proprietary information. By entering into the agreement, Rogers would be obliged not to sell competitive products for a period of one year after their relationship ended and during that period he would not:

(a) *in the Territory, enter the employment of, or act as a sales representative, manufacturer's representative or agent for, any person or entity which is engaged in the manufacture, supply or sale of ceiling fans and accessories ... which are competitive with those products manufactured, supplied or sold by Manufacturer ("Competitive Product"), or*

(b) *sell or provide any Competitive Product to any Customer with whom Sales Representative dealt, for which Sales Representative was responsible, or with respect to which Sales Representative was provided or had access to Confidential Information. ...*

In the fall of 2004, Rogers terminated his relationship with Emerson. He believed Minka was going to hire a new representative to represent its lighting products unless he agreed to discontinue his relationship with Emerson and begin to sell Minka's ceiling fans. On October 11, Rogers sent his resignation to Emerson to be effective November 1, 2004; the letter was dated October 1, 2004. Rogers also called his supervisor, Ed Springer, and informed him of his decision to leave Emerson and to begin selling Minka fans. Springer did not warn Rogers that he was contractually bound to wait one year before he began working for Minka nor did Springer remind Rogers of any other contractual obligations after he left Emerson.

Rogers took measures contrary to Emerson's interests almost immediately after he terminated his relationship with it. After giving Emerson his resignation, Rogers visited his contacts at Georgia Lighting. Georgia Lighting has been a valuable customer for both Rogers and Emerson; it has been one of Rogers' top two accounts and one of Emerson's top five national accounts. During this visit Rogers talked with Roxanne Todd and Mary Hardy, who influence the types and quantities of fan products purchased by Georgia Lighting. He told them that he was leaving Emerson and would be representing Minka's ceiling fan products and would like to continue doing business with them. Rogers did not return any of Emerson's materials until after its attorney sent him a "cease and desist" letter demanding immediate return of all Emerson materials. Even after he received the letter, Rogers did not return all of the materials; he claims he did not understand the breadth of materials which Emerson deemed confidential.

Under Missouri law, covenants not to compete may be enforced, for "an employer has a proprietary right in his stock of customers and their good will." Customer contacts may be protected under a restrictive covenant since sales personnel may "exert a special influence over [a] customer." "An express agreement not to compete may be enforced as to employees having substantial customer contacts. It is not necessary to show that there is a secret customer list."

Although Rogers represented the products of different manufacturers, his success as a representative shows that he has had special influence over Emerson's customers. Emerson's interest in protecting its relationships with customers to whom Rogers sold products prior to his relationship with it is now as important to Emerson as is its ability to sell to new customers. Emerson has a legitimate business interest in restraining Rogers from violating the terms of their agreement by unfairly using the relationships he developed or strengthened while working with it. During the course of Rogers' affiliation with Emerson, he has acquired knowledge regarding its sales practices, pricing strategies, and marketing mechanisms, and Emerson has a legitimate interest in restraining him from using that knowledge in the immediate future to lure away its customers. The district court did not abuse its discretion by finding that the agreement protected a recognizable interest.

Rogers also attempts to argue that he was unaware of the covenant not to compete and that Emerson has failed to enforce the covenant as to other employees and in other situations. The district court found that while Rogers claimed to be unaware of the covenant not to compete, his testimony was "not believable" because of correspondences between Emerson and Rogers in January 2003, that explicitly referenced the covenant. This finding is not clearly erroneous, and there is no dispute that Rogers voluntarily signed the agreement and that the covenant was clearly written in the main text of the agreement. While Emerson may not have exercised its rights under the covenant on every occasion, there is no credible evidence that Emerson's failure to do so rose to a waiver of its right to enforce the agreement as to Rogers or that its failure to enforce the agreement as to other employees makes it any less likely that Rogers could use information gained during his relationship with Emerson to unfairly compete against it.

Rogers also maintains that the covenant not to compete is unenforceable because it is unreasonably broad. "The question of reasonableness of a restraint requires a thorough consideration of surrounding circumstances, including the subject matter of the contract, the purpose to be served, the situation of the parties, the extent of the restraint, and the specialization of the business." The reasonableness of the covenant is determined in light of the specific circumstances present in the case.

The covenant and injunction only apply to the region in which Rogers worked for Emerson and only extend for one year from the time at which Rogers stopped selling Emerson's products. Thus, the restriction in the injunction runs only to November 1, 2005. Although it applies to potential as well as current Emerson customers, the district court heard evidence that Rogers attempted to solicit business from Emerson immediately after he resigned. Georgia Lighting's decision to go out of business illustrates the reasonableness of the restraint at issue. If Georgia Lighting's former employees were to start working for a new entity, the injunction would not protect Emerson from abuse of the relationship Rogers formed with its customers unless it extended to any customer in the region. The one year restriction will allow Emerson time to employ a new representative who can become acquainted with the territory and the customers before Rogers begins marketing Minka's fans. Since Rogers has a vast amount of knowledge about Emerson's products, sales methods, and pricing strategies, the district court did not abuse its discretion by finding it reasonable to keep Rogers from working for any of Emerson's competitors in any capacity for the limited period.

To show irreparable harm in Missouri an employer need only demonstrate that there is a threat of irreparable harm; the employer is not required to demonstrate that actual damage has occurred. If Rogers were to lure away Emerson's customers and retain them for Minka, it would be difficult to measure the amount of damages caused by the unfair competition and impossible to remedy fully because the consumers could not be forced to purchase Emerson's products.

Accordingly, we affirm the preliminary injunction issued by the district court and remand for further proceedings.

■ *Affirmed.*

CASE CONCEPTS REVIEW

1. What specific actions did Rogers undertake that violated the covenant not to compete?
2. According to the court, when is a covenant not to compete legal?

Many states by statute have limited the use of agreements not to compete. Some of these prohibit such agreements for certain professions or occupations. Other statutes set maximum limits for the area or time of the restraint. In states with statutes, such agreements tend to be more limited than in states that rely on the courts to decide legality simply on public policy.

Agreements not to compete must be a part of another contract to be enforceable. A bare agreement by one party not to compete with another is against public policy. If Lori threatens to open a business to compete with Elaine, and Elaine offers Lori $1,000 to agree not to do so, the contract is unenforceable since it is against public policy.

Comparable to the employee's agreement not to compete is a restrictive provision in a contract for the sale or lease of real property. The landowner may wish to prevent the use of his or her land for any purpose that would be competitive with his or her own business. In a lease, the landowner may provide that the lessee cannot operate an appliance store on the leased property. In that case, the landowner (who owns an appliance store) wants to avoid competition and does so by the restrictive provision. Although on its face the provision does restrict trade, it is binding because other property in the community can be used for competitive purposes.

8. Unconscionability

Unconscionable

In the law of contracts, provisions that are oppressive, overreaching, or shocking to the conscience

Freedom of contract is not a license for a party to insert into an agreement any provision that a party deems advantageous. A concept known as unconscionability allows a judge to strike any portion of a contract or even the entire contract to avoid any **unconscionable** result. Unconscionability is a question of law for the judge—not the jury. Although no precise meaning is given, its purpose is to prevent oppression and unfair surprise. There are basically two questions presented in such cases: (1) What is the relative bargaining power of the parties, their relative economic strength, and the alternative sources of supply—in a word, what are their options? (2) Is the challenged term substantively reasonable? The concept of unconscionability is an important part of the Code [2-302] and is applicable to transactions in goods.

For a contract to be conscionable, its material terms need to be conspicuous, to be understandable by an ordinary person, and to result from a true bargain. It is not a contract of bargain when one party imposes terms on another party. Thus a party must be able to *find* and to *understand* all material terms, as well as have the right to *bargain* over them. The contract cannot be oppressively imposed and must avoid unfair surprise. Many commentators divide cases dealing with unconscionability into two types.

In the first type, procedural unconscionability, the process of making the contract is scrutinized. Was the text of the contract in a font size large enough to be read? Did one party (usually the consumer) have an opportunity to read the entire contract? A major factor is whether the contract is one of adhesion (see next section). A finding of procedural unconscionability is almost always within the context of an adhesion contract.

The other type is substantive unconscionability. This is a powerful legal weapon. If a court finds the terms of the contract so one-sided that notions of justice would be insulted if the contract were enforced, then the court will find the contract illegal. If a business selling big screen televisions operates door-to-door in a very low income neighborhood with the promise of $100 down, $100 for month one, $100 for month two, and a balloon payment of $700 in month three, a court may deem the contract contrary to public policy. The chances are that the purchaser will have the television for three or so months, but then be forced to return the item because they cannot make the balloon payment. This, then, allows the business to re-sell the television. Substantive unconscionability will be shown if a purchaser demonstrates that the business plan is "oppressive."

Unconscionability has sometimes been found to exist when a seller seeks to disclaim warranties. For example, all sellers of seed were disclaiming warranties. Farmers had to buy seed from someone. The unequal bargaining power convinced a court that the disclaimer was unconscionable.

Another example of an unconscionable clause was found to exist in a contract for "Yellow Pages" that limited liability for mistakes to a refund of charges. It has also been applied in cases concerning real estate brokerage contracts, home improvement contracts, leases, contracts to open a checking account, construction contracts, and so on. In modern contract law, unconscionability may be applied to any contract of adhesion, to any contract oppressively imposed by a superior party, or to any contract term that causes unfair surprise to an inferior party. Additional examples are discussed in the following section on contracts of adhesion.

Since unconscionability involves questions of public policy, it is difficult to predict when a court will or will not find a particular contract or contract provision unconscionable. As noted earlier, a court's own concept of right and wrong as well as its total philosophy will often come into play in answering complex questions of public policy.

9. Contracts of Adhesion

An adhesion contract is a standardized contract entirely prepared by one party. As a result of the disparity or inequality of bargaining power between the drafter and the second party, the terms are submitted on a take-it-or-leave-it basis. The standardized provisions are such that they are merely "adhered to," with little choice as a practical matter on the part of the "adherer." If the terms are viewed as unsatisfactory, the party cannot obtain the desired service or product.

The term *contract of adhesion* was first used in the United States in 1919 in a case involving an insurance contract. For several decades it was almost exclusively applied to insurance contracts. However, many contracts today are standardized form contracts entered into by parties who are unequal in knowledge and unequal in bargaining power. The common law ignored this inequality and applied a doctrine of *caveat emptor*. In the 1960s, courts began to police contractual abuses by superior parties using contracts of adhesion. To do that, they used the equitable principle of unconscionability.

Contracts of adhesion are not illegal but are examined for fairness, and doubts about fairness are strictly construed against the drafting party. Courts review these contracts carefully to ensure that they are conscionable and will excise clauses that are oppressive or cause unfair surprise. Employment contracts, insurance policies, and leases are frequently held to be contracts of adhesion. The following case indicates the prevailing trend regarding arbitration agreements within the context of an employer-employee relationship.

10. Contracts Disclaiming Liability

Exculpatory clause

A provision in a contract whereby one of the parties attempts to relieve itself of tort liability

A party to a contract frequently includes a clause that provides that the party has no tort liability even if at fault. Such a clause is commonly called an **exculpatory clause**. These disclaimers of liability are not favored by the law and are strictly construed against the party relying on them. While some are valid, many disclaimers are frequently declared to be illegal by

CASE

Kenneth A. Batory v. Sears, Roebuck & Co., a New York corporation d/b/a "The Great Indoors"

UNITED STATES DISTRICT COURT FOR THE DISTRICT OF ARIZONA

456 F. Supp. 2d 1137, 2006 U.S. Dist. LEXIS 90161 (2006)

OPINION BY: JOHN W. SEDWICK

In March 2003 the court granted Sears' motion to refer this matter to arbitration and dismissed the case. Batory appealed that order to the Ninth Circuit, which in an unpublished decision reversed the finding that the Dispute Resolution Program and Agreement ("DRP") do not constitute an adhesion contract and remanded for an evidentiary hearing on unconscionability. Specifically, the Ninth Circuit directed this Court to consider whether the agreement and DRP are unconscionable because:

> *(1) there exists an "overall imbalance in the obligations and rights imposed by the bargain" in that, although Sears is obligated to arbitrate all "Covered Claims," these Covered Claims consist only of "claims against the Company" to the exclusion of claims that Sears may initiate against its employees, (2) although Sears "reserves the right to modify or terminate [the] DRP upon sixty (60) days notice," it affords no equivalent power to its employees, and (3) the fee provision, which requires employees to pay the lesser of $150 or the filing fee if the claim had been filed in court, does not provide for waiver in cases of indigence.*

Under Arizona law, "[t]o determine whether this contract of adhesion is enforceable, we look to two factors: the reasonable expectations of the adhering party and whether the contract is unconscionable." The *Broemmer* decision held that an adhesion agreement to arbitrate was unenforceable as beyond the reasonable expectations of the adhering party without reaching the issue of whether it was unconscionable.

In a later decision, the Maxwell decision made clear that "reasonable expectations and unconscionability are two distinct grounds for invalidating or limiting enforcement of a contract."

Taken together, *Broemmer* and *Maxwell* make clear that an adhesion agreement to arbitrate that is unconscionable is unenforceable under Arizona law.

For the reasons above, Sears' Motion for Reconsideration at docket is DENIED.

■ *Denied.*

CASE CONCEPTS REVIEW

1. What aspects of the arbitration agreement were suspect?
2. If an arbitration agreement in an employment contract were deemed unenforceable, would the employer or employee typically benefit more? Why?

courts as contrary to public policy. Some states have by statute declared these clauses, in certain types of contracts such as leases, to be illegal and void.

The reasoning behind these statutes and judicial decisions is clear. Absolute freedom of contract exists in a barter situation because of the equal bargaining position of the parties. At the other extreme are the contracts with public utilities, in which there is no equality of bargaining power between the parties because of the existence of a virtual monopoly. The law, therefore, denies freedom of contract in the monopoly situation.

The difficulty is that many contracts involve parties and circumstances that fall between these extremes. Many contracts are entered into between parties with substantially unequal bargaining power. When the subject matter of the contracts involves items of everyday necessity, courts frequently hold that one of the parties is a quasi-public institution and that such institutions are not entitled to complete freedom of contract because freedom of contract is not in the public interest. Thus, contracts or parts of the contracts of such institutions may be held illegal whenever the quasi-public institution has taken advantage of its superior bargaining power and drawn a contract, or included a provision in a contract, that in the eyes of the court excessively favors the quasi-public institution to the detriment of the other party and the public. This is especially true when the contract provision is an exculpatory clause or passes risks to a customer that a business should bear.

Not every exculpatory clause is unconscionable, just as not every printed contract is one of adhesion. Many businesses are allowed to contract away liability when the bargaining power is essentially equal and the contract is basically a fair one. This is especially true when the service is not essential, such as those provided to participants in hazardous recreational activities.

11. Tickets Disclaiming Liability

Tickets purchased for entrance into places of amusement, for evidence of a contract for transportation or for a service, often contain provisions that attempt to limit or to define the rights of the holder of the ticket. It is generally held that the printed matter on the ticket is a part of an offer that is accepted by the holder of the ticket if he or she is aware of the printed matter, even though he or she does not read it. Some cases hold that the purchaser is presumed to know about the printed matter, even though the purchaser's attention is not called to it at the time the ticket is delivered.

If a ticket is received merely as evidence of ownership and is to be presented later as a means of identification, the provisions on the ticket are not a part of the contract unless the recipient is aware of them or his or her attention is specifically directed to them. Tickets given at checkrooms or repair shops are usually received as a means of identifying the article to be returned, rather than as setting forth the terms of a contract. Thus the fine print on such tickets is usually not a part of the offer and acceptance unless communicated.

Many terms on tickets may be unconscionable and will not be enforced in any event. The terms are unconscionable when public policy, as previously noted, would declare such a provision in a formal contract to be unconscionable. The quality of the bargaining power of the parties and the nature of the product or service are major factors to be considered in determining unconscionability.

Printed matter on a ticket is generally not held as part of an offer that is accepted by the holder of the ticket

CHAPTER SUMMARY

STATUS OF ILLEGAL CONTRACTS

Litigation Disallowed

1. An illegal agreement is legally void, and courts will not provide a remedy for any party.

Exceptions

1. If a party is protected by statute, he or she can rescind and recover any consideration given.
2. If a party has been defrauded or unduly influenced, he or she can rescind and seek restitution.
3. Under the doctrine of *locus poenitentiae,* a person who repents before performing may rescind and seek restitution.

AGREEMENTS IN VIOLATION OF STATUTES

Violation of License Requirements

1. Unlicensed persons providing service that requires a license are not entitled to compensation.
2. Unlicensed persons practicing law cannot recover fees and may be subject to criminal prosecution.

Usury

1. Any contract by which a lender receives more interest than allowed by statute is usurious and illegal.
2. There are many exceptions to usury laws.

Agreements and Activities in Restraint of Trade

1. Antitrust laws protect our economy from monopolies, attempts to monopolize, and activities in restraint of trade.
2. Restraints of trade are either illegal per se or illegal only if they are unreasonable. A contract or activity is unreasonable if it suppresses or destroys competition.
3. Price-fixing, agreement among competitors to divide territories, and certain tying agreements (tying a unpatented to a patented product) are illegal per se.
4. Vertical price-fixing (resale price maintenance) is also illegal per se.
5. Price discrimination is illegal if purchasers of goods of like grade and quality are given a lower price than competitors, which substantially lessens competition or tends to create a monopoly or injures competition.
6. Exclusive dealing and reciprocal agreements, tying agreements, group boycotts, agreements among competitors to buy from one supplier, and an agreement of manufacturer to give dealer an exclusive territory are illegal if unreasonable.

AGREEMENTS IN VIOLATION OF PUBLIC POLICY

Agreements Not to Compete

1. Agreements not to compete that are unreasonable restraints of trade are illegal.
2. Reasonableness of covenants not to compete is determined by (1) length of time, (b) geographic area restrained, and (c) the need to protect goodwill.
3. To be legal, covenants not to compete must be part of another contract, such as the sale of a business or an employment contract.
4. In the sale of a business, an agreement not to operate a competing business is enforceable if reasonable.
5. In employment contracts, covenants not to compete are enforceable if reasonable in time and territorial effect, considering the business interest protected and the effect on the employee.

Unconscionability

1. Unconscionability is an equitable doctrine used by courts to prevent oppression and unfair surprise in contracts.
2. To be conscionable, material terms of a contract must be conspicuous, understandable, and the result of a true bargain.
3. The doctrine of unconscionability allows a judge to strike contract terms or eliminate the entire contract or limit the unconscionable effect of a term.

Contracts of Adhesion

1. A contract of adhesion is a form contract offered on a take-it-or-leave-it basis to one with little or no bargaining power.
2. These contracts may be enforceable, but they may be found to be unconscionable if they are oppressive.

Contracts Disclaiming Liability

1. An exculpatory clause is a provision that attempts to relieve a party of all tort liability.
2. An exculpatory clause may or may not be unconscionable depending on the bargaining power of the parties.

Tickets Disclaiming Liability

1. Provisions printed on tickets that disclaim liability are binding if the ticket is purchased as admission to a business establishment or for a service.
2. Similar disclaimer provisions are not part of the contract and thus not enforceable if the ticket is merely evidence of ownership.

REVIEW QUESTIONS AND PROBLEMS

1. Match each term in Column A with the appropriate statement in Column B.

A	B
(1) Usury	(a) Agreement in violation of statute or public policy
(2) Agreement in restraint	(b) Equitable doctrine to prevent unfair surprise and of trade oppression in contacts
(3) Covenant not to compete	(c) Must be reasonable in time and geographic scope to be legal
(4) Illegal agreement	(d) Contract terms imposed on adhering party
(5) *Locus poenitentiae*	(e) Clause that disclaims liability
(6) Contract of adhesion	(f) Lender receives more interest than allowed by statute
(7) Unconscionability	(g) Person who repents before performing can rescind and seek restitution
(8) Exculpatory clause	(h) Price-fixing or other agreement to limit
(9) Effect of illegality	competition
(10) Unlicensed practice of law	(i) Since agreement is legally void, no remedy is available.
	(j) Cannot recover fee for services and may violate criminal law

2. The Fourth of July Company agreed to ship a quantity of fireworks to Behan. After Behan pays in full, he learns that state law prohibits this type of sale. Before the fireworks are sent, Behan calls to cancel this contract and to demand his money back. May he recover his money in court? Why or why not?

3. Melvin, an attorney licensed in California, was hired by Jane, a resident of Alabama, to represent her in an automobile accident case. The accident occurred in Alabama. Melvin was not licensed in Alabama, so he hired a local attorney to assist. Is Melvin entitled to the fees called for in the contract? Why or why not?

4. Assume that you want to open a store in a shopping center that is being developed. How might you reduce competition by the terms of your lease with the shopping center? Explain.

5. Strickland, an insured under a Gulf Life disability policy, injured his right leg. Doctors worked unsuccessfully for 118 days to save his leg. The insurance policy provided that Gulf Life would pay disability benefits if an insured lost a leg through "dismemberment by severance" within ninety days after an accident. Gulf Life denied liability because severance of Strickland's leg was not within the ninety-day limitation. Strickland sued, claiming the ninety-day limitation was contrary to public policy. Should Strickland collect on the policy? Why or why not?

6. Rash signed a covenant not to compete contained in a medical partnership agreement. It prohibited a partner leaving the partnership from engaging in the practice of medicine or surgery within a 25-mile radius of the partnership office for a period of three years. Rash, in executing the covenant, expressly agreed that the covenant was reasonable and that breach of covenant would work harm to the partnership. Is the agreement enforceable? Why or why not?

7. Weniger's employment contract contained the following provision: "Weniger hereby agrees that throughout the two-year period commencing on the termination of his employment hereunder for whatever reason he will not, directly or indirectly, be or become engaged or financially interested in, or an officer or director employee, consultant or advisor of or to, any business, firm or corporation which is engaged anywhere in the United States or Canada in any business which competes in any way with Egnall." Is the provision enforceable? Why or why not?
8. Louis was hired by Kidder Corporation as a stockbroker. The employment contract provided that all disputes between the parties would be decided by arbitration. The employment agreement was a standardized form prepared by the corporation. Does Louis have a valid challenge to the legality of the contract? Explain.
9. Barbara employed Dwain and Robert to teach her to sky dive. Before her first jump, she signed an agreement releasing the instructors from all claims for personal injury resulting from parachuting and related activities. She made her first parachute jump with instructor Dwain and pilot Robert. During a difficult landing some distance from the target, Barbara suffered back, arm, and leg injuries. Barbara sued on a negligence theory, and the defendants argued that they were not liable because of the release. Does this release protect the defendants from liability? Explain.
10. A company made a deposit at its bank by using the night depository box. The company's account was not credited, and the bank denied any responsibility since the company's representative had signed an agreement providing that "the use of the night depository facilities shall be at the sole risk of the customer." Is this clause valid? Explain.

Form and Interpretation of Contracts | 18

CHAPTER OUTLINE

continued

CHAPTER PREVIEW

In Chapters 13 through 17, the elements of a valid, enforceable contract are explained (offer, acceptance, consideration, legal capacity, and legal purpose) Even if an *oral* contract has the required five elements, it may nonetheless be unenforceable because it is not evidenced by a writing.

As a general rule, an oral contract is just as valid and enforceable as a written contract; however, some oral contracts are unenforceable under a law known as the *statute of frauds.* The statute of frauds recognizes that some contracts are subject to fraudulent proofs and perjured testimony; therefore, it requires written proof of the contract for the contract to be enforceable. Numerous exceptions to the statute of frauds have been recognized by courts. This chapter considers those contracts within the statute of frauds, both common-law and Code exceptions to the statute, and the nature of the writing that will satisfy the statute.

The term *within the statute* is used throughout this chapter. If a contract is of a type that the law requires written proof, it is said to be "within the statute of frauds." If written proof is not required, the contract is deemed "outside the statute of frauds"—meaning that an oral contract will be valid.

When parties dispute the meaning of their contract, a court will be asked to decide what the contract terms mean. The process of discovering the meaning of a contract is called *interpretation.* For example, a court frequently must determine if a written contract is the sole evidence of the parties' agreement or if other evidence may be considered. Certain statements or promises that occur prior to the written contract may not be considered because of a rule of procedure called the *parol evidence rule.*

BUSINESS MANAGEMENT DECISION

As the general manager of a stereo store, you help a seventeen-year-old customer who wants to buy stereo equipment worth $2,750 on credit. When you object to this arrangement, the customer calls her father, who tells you over the phone, "If my daughter does not pay you, I will."

Are you willing to proceed with the sale?

STATUTE OF FRAUDS

1. The Approach

Of English origin, the statute of frauds was first enacted by Parliament in 1677. The statute of frauds is a legal doctrine designed to prevent fraud by excluding legal actions on certain important contracts unless there is written evidence of the contract signed by the defendant. Those contracts are said to be *unenforceable unless evidenced by a writing* signed by the party sought to be bound. There are numerous exceptions to the statute, and it is often narrowly construed.

Generally, the statute is a defense, even though there is no factual dispute over the existence of the contract or its terms. A contract may come into existence at the time of the oral agreement, but it is not enforceable until written evidence of the agreement is available. The agreement is valid in every respect except for the lack of proper evidence of its existence. The statute creates a defense in suits for the breach of executory oral contracts covered by its provisions.

Study of the statute of frauds involves three questions: Is the contract at issue within the statute? If the contract is within the statute, is there written evidence of the contract that satisfies the statute? If there is not sufficient written evidence, does an exception to the statute make the oral agreement legally enforceable?

FIGURE 18-1 ■ Application of the Statute of Frauds

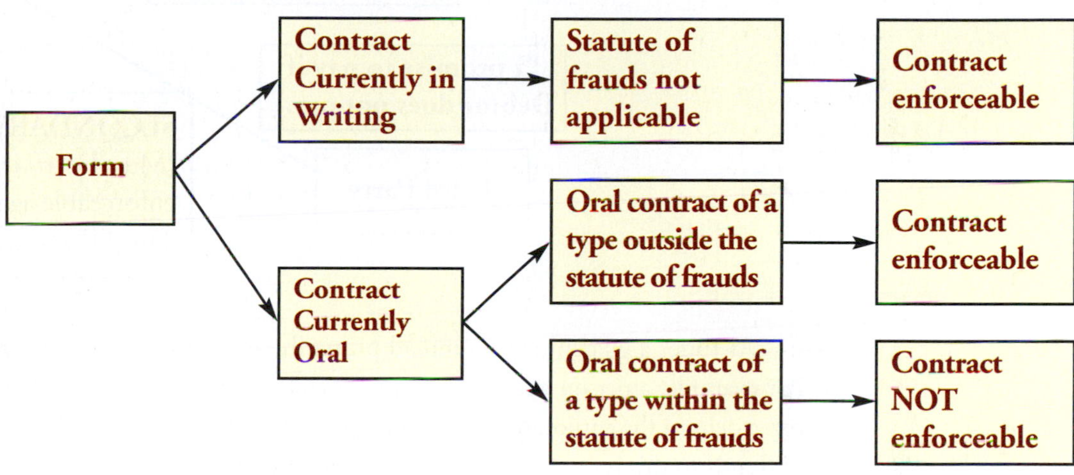

2. Contracts within the Statute

Under state law, the following contracts are *within the statute of frauds* and must have written evidence to be enforceable. They are discussed in the next five sections.

1. Special promise of a surety to *pay the debt of another*, commonly known as a guaranty contract
2. Agreements for the sale of land or an interest in land
3. Agreements that *cannot be performed within one year from the date of making*
4. Under the Code, contracts for the *sale of goods with a price of $500 or more*
5. Contracts for the sale of *certain personal property* other than goods

Guarantor

In general, a guarantor, a person who by contract undertakes to answer for the debt of another and agrees undertakes to pay if the principal debtor does not.

3. Guaranty Contracts

A person may seek to help another by guaranteeing the latter's debt. In such a case, the debtor is primarily liable and the **guarantor**, or surety, is secondarily liable. A guarantor is not liable to pay until it is shown that the debtor has not paid or cannot pay the debt. The statute of frauds requires only that the *guarantor's promise to be in writing*. An oral promise to be primarily liable is not within the statute. The statute "protects" only persons who assume a secondary liability—that is, a promise to pay another's debt only if the other person does not pay.

In some cases, it is difficult to determine whether a party has made a promise to be secondarily liable or has incurred a direct, primary obligation to pay. A person can make a direct obligation to pay for someone else. For example, father says to auto dealer, "Deliver the car to my son, and I'll pay for it." This primary direct promise is not within the statute of frauds. If, however, someone assumes a secondary obligation to pay, that promise is a guarantee and is within the statute. For example, father says to auto dealer, "Deliver the car to my son. If he does not pay for it, then I promise to pay." Father is secondarily liable, and his promise must be in writing to be enforceable.

FIGURE 18-2 ■ Guaranty Contracts

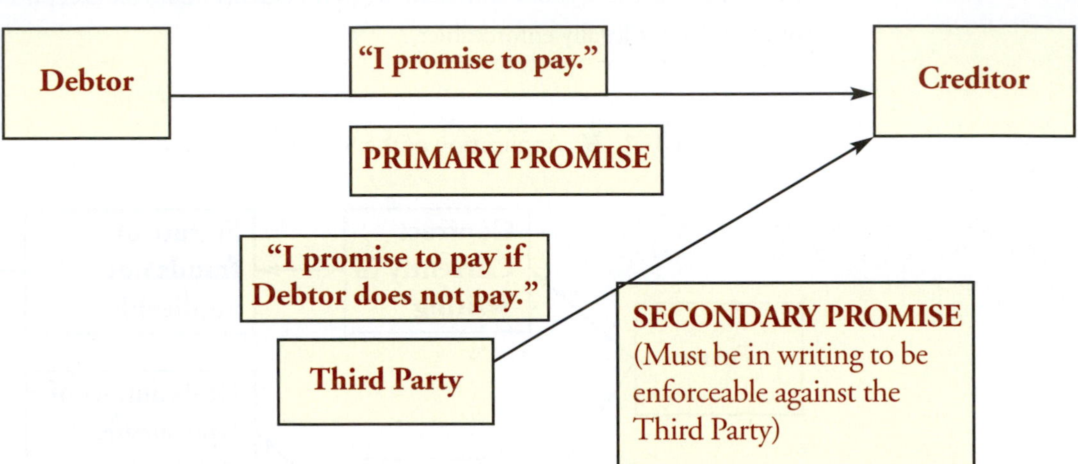

At times a guarantor may intend primarily to benefit himself or herself and not the debtor. For example, a person with a substantial financial interest in a corporation may promise orally to pay a debt of the corporation if it cannot pay. The law does not extend the protection of the statute of frauds to this type of guarantor. It analyzes the *main purpose* or *leading object* of the promisor in making the promise. When the leading object is to become a guarantor of another's debt primarily to benefit that other person, the promise is secondary and within the statute. When the leading object of the promisor is to serve some interest or purpose of his or her own, even though the promisor guarantees another's debt, the promise is direct and primary; it is not within the statute. Under the leading object rule, a court must determine whether the promisor intended primarily to benefit himself or herself or the debtor. The following case explores the question of whether the guarantor's promise was in proper form in order to satisfy the statute of frauds.

CASE

John Deere Company v. Haralson

SUPREME COURT OF GEORGIA

599 S.E.2d 164 (2004)

HINES, JUSTICE

This Court granted certiorari to determine whether the Court of Appeals correctly held that a promisor on a guaranty couldn't be sufficiently identified by his signature alone so that the guaranty is unenforceable under the statute of frauds. Finding that the Court of Appeals was incorrect, we reverse.

Tommy H. Haralson, Sr. ("Haralson") is the former owner of Farmers Supply Store, Inc. d/b/a Big Boys Equipment ("Farmers Supply") which sold equipment supplied by the John Deere Company ("John Deere"). In 1998, Haralson sold Farmers Supply to his daughter and son-in-law who continued to do business with John Deere until Farmers Supply went out of business in December 2000. At that time, Farmers Supply had an outstanding debt to John Deere.

John Deere alleges Haralson signed a "John Deere Dealer Guaranty" on April 30, 1996, making himself personally liable for Farmers Supply's debts to John Deere. The guaranty was directed to "JOHN DEERE COMPANY—A DIVISION OF DEERE & COMPANY OR JOHN DEERE INDUSTRIAL EQUIPMENT COMPANY." It identified the debt as John Deere's "past and/or future extension of credit" to the principal debtor, "FARMERS SUPPLY STORE, INC. DBA BIG BOYS EQUIPMENT of LAGRANGE, GA 30240." In the body of the guaranty, the guarantor is referred to as the "undersigned." Haralson's name is not typed anywhere on the guaranty; his allegedly illegible signature appears under the typed word "Guarantor(s)" and over the typed word "Name." His handwritten address follows.

After Haralson refused to pay Farmers Supply's debt, John Deere filed suit on the guaranty. Haralson filed an answer and a counterclaim, alleging that the guaranty was unenforceable under the statute of frauds and seeking damages for conversion. He also averred that he had no recollection of signing the personal guaranty. In response, John Deere presented the affidavit of its employee, Eric M. Thomas, stating that he had witnessed Haralson sign the guaranty. John Deere moved to dismiss Haralson's counterclaim, and both parties filed motions for summary judgment. The trial court denied Haralson's motion for summary judgment and partially granted John Deere's motion for summary judgment, rejecting Haralson's statute of frauds defense. Haralson appealed the grant of partial summary judgment to John Deere and the Court of Appeals reversed, holding that a signature alone does not sufficiently identify a guarantor so as to make a guaranty satisfy the statute of frauds.

The statute of frauds requires that a promise to answer for another's debt, to be binding on the promisor, "must be in writing and signed by the party to be charged therewith." This requirement has been interpreted to mandate further that a guaranty identify the debt, the principal debtor, the promisor, and the promisee.

Haralson argues that a signed guaranty is incomplete and invalid if the guarantor's name is not displayed separately on the guaranty, in addition to appearing by way of the signature.

However, there is no requirement that the writing must be of a certain type or form; even a completely handwritten guaranty is enforceable. See Cohen v. Capco Sportswear, Inc.,. In fact, it appears that the guaranty at issue in Cohen was not only handwritten, but that it, too, did not identify the guarantor except by signature. That opinion describes the guaranty as simply a signed, handwritten note on company letterhead that stated: "I am happy to personally guarantee our acct." Thus, in Cohen, the signature alone satisfies the element of guarantor identification. There is no requirement for the separate identification that Haralson asserts must be present.

■ *Reversed.*

CASE CONCEPTS REVIEW

1. Should it make any difference whether the printed name of the guarantor is on the agreement?
2. What is required for a promise to answer for the debt of another under the statute of frauds?

4. Contracts Involving Interests in Land

Since the law has always placed importance on contracts involving land, it is logical that the statute of frauds should require a writing for a contract *creating or transferring any interest in land.* In addition to contracts involving a sale of an entire interest, the statute is applicable to contracts involving interests for a person's lifetime (called life estates), to mortgages, to easements, and to leases for a period in excess of one year.

One problem under the statute is to determine what is real property. Generally, it is land and all things affixed to the land. What is the status of things such as standing timber or minerals? Is an oral contract to sell oil and gas a contract involving real estate? The general rule is that these items are real property if the title to them is to pass to the buyer before they are severed from the land; they are personal property if title to them passes subsequently. The Code provides that a contract to sell minerals, oil, and the like, or a contract for a structure or its materials to be removed from realty, is a contract for the sale of goods if they are to be severed by the seller. If the buyer is to sever them, the contract affects and involves land and is subject to the real estate provisions of the statute of frauds. The Code also provides that a contract for the sale of growing crops is a contract for the sale of goods, whether they are to be severed by the buyer or by the seller.

Note that one of the *exceptions to the statute* (discussed in more detail later) is the *doctrine of part performance.* This exception frequently applies to oral contracts granting an interest in land. For example, courts will enforce an oral contract for the sale of land if, with the seller's consent, the buyer takes possession of the land and makes a partial payment and valuable improvements on it.

5. Contracts that Cannot Be Performed within One Year

A contract is within the statute if, by its terms, it *cannot be performed within one year from the time it is made.* The period is measured from the time an oral contract is made to the time when the promised performance is to be completed. Thus an oral agreement to hire a person for two years or to form and carry on a partnership for ten years would not be enforceable.

The decisive factor in determining whether a long-term contract comes within the statute is whether performance is possible within a year from the date of making. If a contract, according to the intentions of the parties as shown by its terms, may be fully performed within a year from the time it is made, it is not within the statute of frauds, even though the time of its performance is uncertain and may extend—and, in fact, does extend—beyond the year. If one party has fully performed, the contract is then not within the statute of frauds.

Even though it is most unlikely that performance could be rendered within one year, the statute does not apply if there is even a remote possibility that it could. This rule is one of possibility and not probability. Thus, assuming all elements of a valid contract, a promise to pay $10,000 "when cars are no longer polluting the air" would be enforceable even though given orally. Moreover, if a contract, otherwise to continue for more than a year, is by its own terms subject to termination within a year, it is not within the prohibition of the statute of frauds.

Thus the question is not how long performance will *probably* run, but can the contract *possibly be performed* within one year from the making of the contract. To put the matter in sharper focus, the rule should be stated as follows: An oral contract that by its terms has no possibility of being performed within one year from the date of formation must be evidenced by a writing. If it is possible to perform it within one year from the date of making, it is not within the statute.

6. Contracts for the Sale of Goods

The Uniform Commercial Code contains several provisions regarding the statute of frauds. The provision applicable to the sale of goods stipulates that a contract for the *sale of goods for the price of $500 or more is not enforceable* unless there is some writing sufficient to indicate that a contract for sale has been made [2-201 (1)]. The writing must be signed by the defendant or his or her authorized agent or broker. The Code further states that a writing is not insufficient if it omits or incorrectly states a term agreed on, but the agreement will not be enforced beyond the quantity of goods mentioned in the writing.

The Code favors contract formation and performance. Given that philosophy, the Code has four exceptions to the statute of frauds provision. These exceptions are explained in sections 13 through 16 in this chapter.

7. Contracts for the Sale of Personal Property Other than Goods

The Code has several additional sections that require a writing. A contract for the sale of securities such as stocks and bonds is not enforceable unless (1) there is a signed writing setting forth a stated quantity of described securities at a defined or stated price, or (2) delivery of the security has been accepted or payment has been made, or (3) within a reasonable time a confirmation in writing of the sale or purchase has been sent and received and the party receiving it has failed to object to it within ten days after receipt, or (4) the party against whom enforcement is sought admits in court that such a contract was made. Note that this relates only to contracts for the sale of securities [8-319].

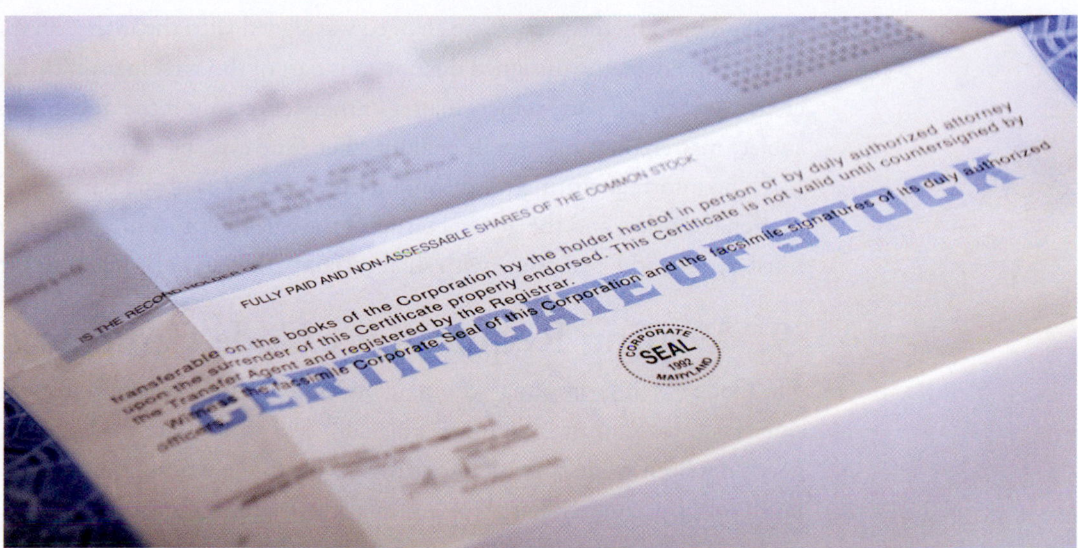

A stock certificate is an example of a contract for the sale of securities.

Another section concerns contracts for the sale of personal property other than goods or securities. For these contracts, which involve matters such as royalty rights, patent rights, and rights under a bilateral contract, a writing is required if the amount involved exceeds $5,000 [1-206].

As mentioned in our discussion of secured transactions (in Chapters 37 and 38), the Code usually requires a signed security agreement. Therefore, when a person borrows money and gives the lender an interest in property as security, the debtor (borrower) must sign a security agreement [9-203].

8. Writing Required by the Statute of Frauds

If a contract is within the statute of frauds, there must be a signed writing sufficient to satisfy the statute of frauds. Generally, the common law requires more terms to be in the writing than does the Code. The general common law is explained in this section, and the Code requirements are covered in the next section.

With regards to the writing required by the statute of frauds, two issues often arise. First, who must sign the writing for it to satisfy the statute of frauds requirement? Only the party (the defendant) charged with failing to comply with contract need sign the writing. This result is based on the theory that the contractual agreement is legal in all aspects, but proper evidence of such an agreement is lacking. This evidence is furnished when the party sought to be charged with the contract has signed the writing.

The rule that only the defendant needs to sign the writing to satisfy the statute of frauds means that it is possible that only one party be bound by an agreement. The other party is not bound since he or she has not signed the writing. Thus that party may still assert the statute of frauds as a defense.

The *signature of the party sought to be charged* may be quite informal and need not necessarily be placed at the close of the document. It may be in the body of the writing or elsewhere, as long as it identifies the writing with the signature of the person sought to be held.

The second issue regarding the statute of frauds writing requirements concerns the kind of writing needed to satisfy the statute of frauds. A formally drafted contract is not required. All that is required is a note or memorandum that provides written evidence of the agreement. Indeed, the note or memorandum may consist of several writings, even though the writing containing the requisite terms is unsigned. However, it must appear from an examination of all the writings that the writing signed by the party to be charged was signed with the intention that it refer to the unsigned writing. In effect, the unsigned document is part of the agreement if the documents by internal reference refer to the same subject matter or transaction; but if the documents do not refer to the same subject matter, they may not be read together. Oral evidence is not admissible to connect them.

The informal writing need contain only the names of the parties, a description of the subject matter, the price, and the general terms of the agreement. A memorandum of sale of real property must describe the real estate with such certainty that a court may order its conveyance.

9. Writing Required for Code Contracts

The Code has three minimal requirements for the writing to satisfy the Code statute of frauds provision. First, there must be some writing sufficient to indicate that a contract for the sale of certain goods has been made between the parties. Second, the writing must contain a quantity term, which need not be accurately stated, or a means for determining quantity, such as by outputs or requirements. If a contract states a quantity, it will not be enforced beyond the quantity term stated in the writing. Third, the writing must be signed by the party against whom the contract is being enforced. Thus a plaintiff who is seeking to enforce the contract is not required to have signed the writing. Beyond these three requirements, the writing need not contain the material terms of the contract.

COMMON-LAW EXCEPTIONS TO THE STATUTE OF FRAUDS

10. Introduction

The statute of frauds is not applicable to executed contracts. A party who has, for example, purchased or sold land under an oral contract cannot obtain a refund of his or her money or cannot obtain a return deed to his or her land. The statute of frauds does not allow rescission; it serves only as a defense to a suit for breach of an executory contract. Likewise, a contract that cannot be performed within one year that is fully executed cannot be rescinded.

If an agreement is within the statute of frauds and no written evidence of the contract exists, the contract will still be enforced and the defense ineffectual if one of the exceptions to the statute applies. Two exceptions are applicable to all types of contracts: part performance and promissory estoppel.

11. Part Performance

When a party has partly or fully performed his or her oral promise or has detrimentally relied on another's oral promise, it would be inequitable in most cases to deny that party relief because of the statute of frauds. Consequently, courts have made equitable exceptions to the statute. One exception is commonly called the **doctrine of part performance**. When one party to an oral contract partly or fully performs, then the other party is equitably estopped from using the statute as a defense. Another name for this doctrine is *equitable estoppel*. It is used primarily in oral contracts for the sale of real property because many oral contracts involving real estate became partially executed as a result of part payment by the buyer or surrender of possession to the buyer by the seller or both. Since the statute of frauds is a complete defense to an executory oral contract involving real estate and it is no defense to a fully executed contract, what is the status if the contract is partially performed?

Doctrine of part performance

A legal theory, drawn from the laws of equity, used to prevent a party to an oral contract that has been partially performed from asserting the defense of the statute of frauds

Performance to satisfy the statute of frauds has two aspects. First, the performance must establish and point unmistakably and exclusively to the existence of an oral contract. Performance eliminates the statute as a defense in such cases because it eliminates any doubt that a contract was made. Thus the reason for the defense of the statute does not exist.

Second, the performance must be substantial enough to warrant judicial relief, such as specific performance of the oral contract. In other words, it must be such that returning the parties to the status quo is unreasonable. To illustrate, assume that a buyer of real property under an oral contract has paid part of the purchase price. The money can be returned, and the statute of frauds would be a defense because there would be no equitable reason to enforce the oral agreement. However, when the seller under an oral contract also delivers possession to the buyer, the defense of the statute of frauds becomes more tenuous because returning the parties to the status quo becomes somewhat difficult. When improvements are made by one in possession, a return to the status quo becomes quite difficult, if not impossible.

It is clear that the transaction is taken out of the statute if the buyer has taken possession, paid all or part of the price, and made valuable improvements. Less part performance may also take the contract out of the statute if the buyer takes possession and pays part of the price, giving good evidence of a contract. If the buyer also pays taxes and mortgage payments while in possession, specific performance may be warranted. Payment of the price, standing alone, is not a basis for specific performance and will not satisfy the statute since the payment of money could be interpreted as rent for a lease rather than a sale.

Part performance issues are often difficult to apply in contracts that cannot be performed within one year of the date of making. There is almost always some part performance.

12. Promissory Estoppel

Chapter 15 explains *promissory estoppel* as a doctrine for validating contracts as an alternative to consideration. That same concept is sometimes used by courts to prevent a party to an oral contract from using the statute of frauds as a defense. When a party relies to his or her detriment on an oral promise, the oral promise may be enforceable, notwithstanding the statute of frauds. The reliance must be foreseeable by the promisor, and enforcement of the promise must be necessary to avoid injustice. The remedy may be limited as justice requires.

Like the part performance exception, courts may use promissory estoppel to achieve fairness and prevent an unfair result. Promissory estoppel is used whenever the plaintiff's equities are so great that any contrary decision would be inequitable. In many cases, parties will rely on oral promises. In such cases, to allow the statute of frauds to be used as a defense would itself constitute a type of fraud on the relying party. The trend of decisions is to use promissory estoppel to prevent an unfair use of the statute of frauds.

Code Exceptions to the Statute of Frauds

The Code has four exceptions to the requirement that contracts involving $500 or more must be in writing: confirmation between merchants, specially manufactured goods, judicial admissions, and part performance.

13. Written Confirmation between Merchants

This exception arises from the business practice of negotiating contracts orally, often by telephone. A merchant who contracts orally with another merchant can satisfy the statute of frauds requirement by sending a written confirmation to the other merchant [2-201 (2)]. This confirmation will satisfy the statute, even though it is not signed by the party to be charged, unless written notice of objection to its contents is given within ten days after it is received. This means that a merchant who has dealt orally with another merchant will have an enforceable contract unless the merchant receiving the writing objects within the ten-day period. As examined in the next case, courts must find an underlying oral contract in order to apply this provision of the Code.

CASE

Central Illinois Light Company v. Consolidation Coal Company

UNITED STATES COURT OF APPEALS FOR THE SEVENTH CIRCUIT

349 F.3d 488 (2003)

POSNER, CIRCUIT JUDGE

The district judge granted summary judgment for the defendant, Consolidation Coal Company, in this diversity breach of contract suit brought by Central Illinois Light Company (CILCO). The judge's ground was that CILCO had failed to comply with the Uniform Commercial Code's statute of frauds (codified in Illinois as 810 ILCS, ch. 5). Consolidation had been selling coal to CILCO for several years under one-year contracts. Between September 2000 and June 2001, the parties engaged in protracted negotiations for a contract to succeed their 2000 contract, which was due to expire on the last day of that year. CILCO contends that in December, in the course of the negotiations, it made an oral contract with Consolidation to buy from the latter 1.5 million tons of coal in 2001 and 2002, at a total price of $34 million.

The negotiations involved the exchange of many documents, but documents that merely evidence negotiations do not satisfy the statute of frauds. There has to be "some writing sufficient to indicate that a contract for sale has been made," provided it has been signed by the party (or the party's agent) against whom the contract is sought to be enforced. UCC § 2-201(1).

It is true that the contracting parties in this case are "merchants," defined as those "who deal in goods of the kind" involved in the transaction at issue or who hold themselves out "as having knowledge or skill peculiar to the practices or goods involved in the transaction." UCC § 2-104(1). In a contract between merchants, the requirement of a signature is relaxed; it is enough "if within a reasonable time" of the making of the alleged contract "a writing in confirmation of the contract and sufficient against the sender is received and the party receiving it has reason to know its contents," unless he objects in writing within ten days. UCC § 2-201(2). But signature, as we'll see, is not a serious issue in this case.

The principal document on which CILCO relies to show that an oral contract for the sale to it of 1.5 million tons of coal was indeed made in December of 2000 is an internal Consolidation document created that month entitled "Coal Sales Invoicing System Order Print." The document has the form of an invoice and contains most of the detail that an invoice for a two-year sale of 1.5 million tons of coal would be expected to contain, except the price for the second year's shipments.

The problem with the invoice is not that it wasn't signed by an agent, for it is obvious as we have said that Womack and Wilson were agents of Consolidation. The absence of a handwritten signature is not a problem either. However, all the invoice shows is that Consolidation prepared an invoice consistent with what it hoped would be a contract. The invoice was never sent, which—if anything—is evidence that there was no contract, at least no contract containing terms consistent with the invoice.

The invoice loses all possible significance, moreover, when placed in its documentary context. Beginning in September 2000, three months before the invoice was created, and continuing until the end of May of the following year, the parties exchanged at least eleven drafts of a possible contract, with many different terms, though the quantity remained at or close to 1.5 million tons over two years. Negotiations collapsed in June when Consolidation, having encountered production difficulties at its mine, told CILCO it would contract to sell it only 600,000 tons. (CILCO regards that statement as repudiation, and hence breach, of the oral contract made the previous December.)

Against this background it is apparent that the invoice was wishful thinking rather than evidence of an oral contract.

■ *Affirmed.*

CASE CONCEPTS REVIEW

1. Was there a contract is this case? Why?
2. Why should oral contracts, if confirmed in the manner provided by section 2-201(2), be valid?

14. Specially Manufactured Goods

This second exception to the writing requirement under the Code relates to conduct that clearly shows a contract has been made. The Code explicitly excludes from the statute transactions that involve goods to be specially manufactured. To fit within this exception, three requirements must be met [2-201 (3) (a)]:

1. The goods are to be specially manufactured for the particular buyer and are not suitable for sale to others.
2. The seller has made a substantial beginning to manufacture or commitments to obtain the goods.
3. The circumstances reasonably indicate that the goods are for the buyer.

15. Judicial Admissions

Another substitute for writing is based on recognition that the required writing is simply a formality and that a contract may very well exist. The oral contract is unenforceable without proof of its existence; but when proper proof is available, the contract becomes enforceable. If the party who is resisting the contract admits its existence in the proper circumstances and surroundings, such admission will substitute for a writing. Thus the Code provides that an oral contract for the sale of goods is enforceable if (when legal action is brought to enforce it) the defendant admits in the court proceedings that a contract for sale was made. It is quite possible that the admission will be made in the pleadings, during discovery, or as testimony during a trial. That judicial admission satisfies the Code statutory requirement of a writing [2-201 (3) (b)].

As a result of modern discovery techniques and liberal rules of evidence, this exception usually is available if a contract has in fact been entered into. There is usually no way to avoid the exception short of perjury.

Parol evidence

Legal proof based on oral statements or other evidence not in the written document

Parol evidence rule

A legal rule that forbids the introduction of prior statements—whether oral, written, or expressed in another manner—or statements made at the same time a written contract is formed that vary or contradict statements made in the written contract

16. Part Performance

The final exception is part performance. The Code excepts oral contracts for the sale of goods that have been paid for or received and accepted [2-201 (3) (c)]. In the sale of goods, the Code takes the contract out of the statute only to the extent of the part performance. In other words, these contracts are enforceable to the extent the buyer has made payment for goods or to the extent the seller has shipped goods that the buyer has accepted. Any unperformed part of the contract is still within the statute, and some writing is required unless one of the other exceptions is applicable.

Contracts are enforceable if the goods have either been shipped and accepted or payment has been made by the buyer.

PAROL EVIDENCE RULE

17. The Theory

Courts are often asked to interpret the meaning of a contract. If the contract is written, courts may face the question of whether or not they can consider oral, written, or other evidence that is not in the written document. This is called **parol evidence**. The law seeks to protect the sanctity of written contracts. Therefore, it is generally held that statements, promises, guarantees, and representations made by the parties prior to signing a written contract may not be considered if the written contract represents the entire agreement of the parties. This principle of law is called the **parol evidence rule**.

The parol evidence rule prevents the introduction of prior or contemporaneous oral or written statements that might vary or contradict the final written contract. When parties to a contract embody the terms of their agreement in a writing intended to be the final and exclusive expression of their agreement, the written contract cannot be contradicted, explained, varied, or supplemented. Everything that happens prior to or contemporaneously with the execution of the written contract is assumed to be integrated into it. The written contract is deemed the only permissible evidence of the agreement. All earlier negotiations, understandings, representations, and agreements are said to have merged in the written contract. Therefore *parol* (extrinsic) evidence is not admissible to supplement, subtract from, alter, vary, or contradict the agreement as written.

The following case is an example of how the parol evidence rule typically applies to a contractual transaction.

CASE

Charles Cagin v. The McFarland Clinic, P.C.

UNITED STATES COURT OF APPEALS FOR THE EIGHTH CIRCUIT

456 F.3d 903 (2006)

BOGUE, DISTRICT JUDGE

Dr. Charles Cagin ("Cagin") appeals the district court's adverse grant of summary judgment in his breach of contract action against The McFarland Clinic [the "Clinic"]. Cagin argues the district court erred in concluding that extrinsic evidence should not be admitted to aid in interpreting the employment. We affirm.

Cagin was an interventional cardiologist in solo practice in Des Moines, Iowa. The Clinic was a multi-specialty medical clinic located in Ames, Iowa. In 1999, Cagin began negotiating with Dale Anderson, Chief Executive Officer of the Clinic, regarding Cagin joining the Clinic as a cardiologist in an office the Clinic was opening in Des Moines. Cagin understood that as the first cardiologist hired, he would be the only physician in the Cardiology Department when he started. Cagin estimated he would be working as the only cardiologist in the department for six to eighteen months. Cagin was told that, if he joined the Clinic's Des Moines office, he would receive sufficient backup and call coverage from other cardiologists the Clinic would hire in the Des Moines area.

The parties entered a three-year employment agreement (the Agreement) on January 10, 2000, and Cagin soon began working for the Clinic.

Cagin resigned from the Clinic in August 2003. Cagin left the Clinic because he felt mistreated by the Clinic—because his 2003 income was well below his previous annual salaries, largely due to a new formula that changed the way overhead expenses were assigned; because he had worked "24/7" for three years without a vacation; and because the Clinic did not provide him with adequate backup and call coverage.

Cagin filed suit against the Clinic on February 5, 2004, alleging breach of the agreement.

Cagin also argues that the district court erred in concluding that extrinsic evidence would not be used to aid in the interpretation of the Agreement. Specifically, Cagin contends the court should have considered as extrinsic evidence the alleged representations made by Clinic administrators during contract negotiations leading up to the signing of the Agreement. The extrinsic evidence Cagin claims should have been considered relates to his understanding about which party (Cagin or the Clinic) would be responsible for backup and call coverage.

The Agreement contains an integration clause, which states that the Agreement constitutes the entire agreement of the parties and supercedes all previous negotiations and discussions on the subject matters contained in the Agreement. Under Iowa law, "[a]n agreement is fully integrated when the parties involved adopt a writing or writings as the final and complete expression of the agreement." "When an agreement is deemed fully integrated, the parol evidence rule prevents the receipt of any extrinsic evidence to contradict (or supplement) the terms of the written agreement." "Whether or not a written agreement is integrated is a question of fact to be determined by the totality of the evidence."

The Iowa Supreme Court has held the parol evidence rule applies to exclude such evidence when a "handcrafted contract contains an integration clause, where the parties were sophisticated business persons represented by counsel and of equal bargaining strength, and where terms of the alleged oral agreement reasonably would be expected to be included in the … agreement." This rule applies in the instant case. The Agreement was a handcrafted document, not a form document using boilerplate language. The Agreement contained a clear and unambiguous integration clause. The Clinic is a business and Cagin was a successful physician. Both parties were represented by counsel during lengthy negotiations on the Agreement. The parties negotiated at arm's length, as demonstrated by Cagin's ability to negotiate a higher annual salary and an additional year of guaranteed salary, neither of which were originally proposed by the Clinic.

Had Cagin desired provisions in the Agreement regarding backup and call coverage, he should have requested the same; but Cagin did not do so. Neither the Agreement nor the Manual contains any provision requiring backup and call coverage. The Agreement does, however, contain the integration clause, stating that it supercedes all negotiations preceding it. Cagin has not adduced any evidence to suggest the Agreement did not constitute the final expression of the parties' agreement. Accordingly, we conclude there are no facts in dispute which could lead a reasonable person to find the Agreement was not fully integrated. The parol evidence rule bars introduction of extrinsic evidence to modify the terms of the Agreement.

■ *For these reasons, we affirm the district court's order granting summary judgment to the Clinic.*

CASE CONCEPTS REVIEW

1. What is the significance of the Agreement in the case being "handcrafted"?
2. What evidence might be submitted to indicate that the Agreement was not the final expression?

18. Exceptions to the Parol Evidence Rule

Most legal rules have exceptions based on notions of equity, good conscience, and common sense. The parol evidence rule has several such exceptions. First, since the rule presumes all prior negotiations are merged into the written contract, it obviously cannot apply to agreements made after the written contract. Thus the rule does not prevent the use of oral evidence to establish modifications agreed on subsequent to the execution of the written contract. Likewise, the rule is inapplicable to evidence of a cancellation of the agreement. Other exceptions include evidence of fraudulent misrepresentations, lack of delivery of an instrument when delivery is required to give it effect, and errors in drafting or reducing the contract to writing. Moreover, oral evidence is always allowed to clarify the terms of an ambiguous contract.

Perhaps the most important exception is the *partial integration rule.* This exception requires the judge to determine if the written contract is totally or merely partially integrated. A total integration occurs when the parties intend the written contract to be the *final* and *complete* statement of their agreement. If they do, evidence of prior agreements is not permitted for any reason. A partial integration occurs when the parties intend the writing to be final on the terms as written but not necessarily complete on all terms of their agreement. Although the contract cannot be *contradicted* under the partial integration rule, it can be supplemented or explained by prior agreements between the parties.

Course of dealing

A sequence of previous conduct between the same parties to a particular transaction

Usage of trade

Any practice or method of dealing so regularly followed by businesspeople in a practice or trade that parties expect to follow the same practice or method of dealing

Course of performance

The expectation of the parties who have had a history of agreements that require repeated performances

19. Parol Evidence Rule and the Code

The Code recognizes that the parol evidence rule prevents the use of oral evidence to contradict or vary the terms of a written memorandum or of a contract that is intended to be the final expression of the parties. The impact of the rule is greatly reduced, however, by the Code's provision that a written contract may be explained or supplemented by a prior **course of dealing** between buyer and seller, by **usage of trade**, or by the **course of performance**. The Code also allows evidence of consistent additional terms to be introduced, based on the partial integration rule [2-202]. The provisions allowing such evidence are designed to ascertain the true understanding of the parties concerning the agreement and to place the agreement in its proper perspective. The assumption is that prior dealings between the parties and the usages of the trade were taken for granted when the contract was worded. Often a contract for sale involves repetitive performance by both parties over a period of time. The course of performance is indicative of the meaning that the parties, by practical construction, have given to their agreement. It is relevant to interpretation of the agreement and thus is admissible evidence.

When oral evidence of a course of dealing, trade usage, or course of performance is introduced under the Code's exceptions to the parol evidence rule, the law recognizes an order of preference in the event of inconsistencies. Express terms will prevail over an interpretation based on the course of performance, and the course of performance will prevail over an interpretation predicated on either the course of dealing or the usage of trade [2-208].

CONSTRUCTION AND INTERPRETATION OF CONTRACTS

20. Tools for Determining Intent of the Parties

Courts are often called on to construe or interpret contracts. Although there is a technical distinction between *construction* (courts construe a contract's legal effect) and *interpretation* (juries interpret the parties' intentions), these words are generally interchangeable. The basic purpose of construing a contract is to determine the intention of the parties. If the language is clear and unambiguous, construction is not required; and the intent expressed in the agreement will be followed. When the language of a contract is ambiguous or obscure, courts apply certain established rules of construction to ascertain the supposed intent of the parties. These rules will not be used to make a new contract for the parties or to rewrite the old one. They are applied by the court merely to resolve doubts and ambiguities within the framework of the agreement.

The general standard of interpretation is to use the meaning the contract language would convey to a *reasonably intelligent person* who is familiar with the circumstances in which the language was used. Thus language is judged objectively rather than subjectively and is given a reasonable meaning. What one party says he or she meant or thought he or she was saying or writing is immaterial since words are given effect in accordance with their meaning to a reasonable person in the circumstances of the parties. In determining the intention of the parties, it is the expressed intention that controls; and this will be given effect unless it conflicts with some rule of law, moral behavior, or public policy.

The language is judged with reference to the subject matter of the contract, its nature, objects, and purposes. Language is usually given its ordinary meaning, but technical words are given their technical meaning. Words with an established legal meaning are given that legal meaning. The law of the place where the contract was made is considered a part of the contract. Isolated words or clauses are not considered; instead, the contract is considered as a whole to ascertain the intent of the parties. If one party has prepared the agreement, an ambiguity in the contract language will be construed against that party since he or she had the chance to eliminate the ambiguity.

As an aid to the court in determining the intention of the parties, special provisions prevail over general provisions, handwritten provisions prevail over typewritten ones, and typewritten provisions prevail over printed ones. Furthermore, courts may consider business custom, usage, and prior dealings between the parties. The Uniform Commercial Code (UCC) encourages courts to supply contractual terms omitted by the parties. This gap-filling process is discussed in Chapter 21.

In the interpretation of contracts, the construction the parties have themselves placed on the agreement is often the most significant source of the intention of the parties. The parties themselves know best what they meant by their words of agreement; and their action under that agreement is the best indication of what that meaning was.

CHAPTER SUMMARY

STATUTE OF FRAUDS

The Approach

1. Contracts within the statute of frauds are unenforceable unless evidenced by a writing.
2. The statute of frauds results in an affirmative defense that must be pleaded.

Guaranty Contracts

1. A direct primary promise to pay another's debt is not within the statute.
2. A secondary promise to pay another's debt if the debtor does not pay is within the statute and must be evidenced by a writing.
3. If the promisor's leading object or main purpose is to serve his or her own interests, the promise is not within the statute.

Contracts Involving Interests in Land

1. Any contract that creates or transfers any interest in land must be evidenced by a writing and signed by the party to be charged.

2. Sale of realty, leases for one year or more, liens, mortgages, and easements are within the statute.
3. Promises to transfer timber, minerals, oil and gas, and structures are within the statute unless the seller is to sever them from the realty.
4. Growing crops are goods, not interests in land, and are not within the statute regardless of who severs them.

Contracts that Cannot Be Performed within One Year

1. Any contract that, by its terms, is impossible to perform within one year is within the statute.
2. If there is *any possibility* that a contract can be performed in one year, it is not within the statute.

Contracts for the Sale of Goods

1. Contracts for the sale of goods having a price of $500 or more are within the statute.

Contracts for the Sale of Personal Property Other than Goods

1. Contracts for the sale of securities, for the sale of more than $5,000 of other personal property, and for the creation of a security interest generally are within the statute and must be in writing.

Writing Required by the Statute of Frauds

1. A writing satisfies the statute if it states with *reasonable* certainty the identity of the parties, the subject matter, and the essential terms and conditions and is signed by the party to be charged.
2. If there is more than one writing and one writing is signed, the unsigned writing is part of the signed writing if the writings by internal reference refer to the same subject matter or transaction.

Writing Required for Code Contracts

1. A writing satisfies the statute if it: (a) indicates a sale of certain goods between the parties, (b) has a quantity term, and (c) is signed by the party to be charged.
2. Omission of any term other than quantity does not make writing insufficient. The quantity term may be supplied by any means, such as outputs and requirements.
3. The contract will not be enforced beyond the quantity stated in the writing.

COMMON-LAW EXCEPTIONS TO THE STATUTE OF FRAUDS

Part Performance

1. If an oral contract was fully performed by both parties, the statute is not applicable.
2. Performance must establish and point unmistakably and exclusively to the existence of an oral contract.
3. Performance must be so substantial that it would be inequitable not to grant judicial relief.
4. If it is reasonable to return the parties to the status quo, a court will rescind the transaction. A buyer who has only paid the price will have his or her money returned.
5. If a buyer has paid the price and taken other actions (such as making valuable improvements to land), courts will recognize an exception to the statute.
6. In contracts of long duration, full performance by one party makes the agreement enforceable.

Promissory Estoppel

1. If a party detrimentally relies on an oral promise, some courts will enforce the promise.
2. The reliance must be foreseeable by the promisor, enforcement of the promise is necessary to avoid injustice, and the remedy may be as limited as justice requires.

CODE EXCEPTIONS TO THE STATUTE OF FRAUDS

Written Confirmation between Merchants

1. The Code has four exceptions: written confirmation between merchants, specially manufactured goods, judicial admissions, and performance.
2. Between merchants, a signed confirmation of an oral contract sent within a reasonable time satisfies the statute if the merchant who actually receives it does not object by written notice within ten days.
3. At a minimum, the confirmation must be written, signed by the sender, evidence an actual contract between the parties, and contain a quantity term.

Specially Manufactured Goods

1. Contracts involving goods specially manufactured for the buyer are enforceable even though the contracts are not evidenced by signed writings.

Judicial Admissions

1. If the party to be charged admits in his or her pleadings, testimony, or otherwise in court that a contract of sale was made, the statute is satisfied.

Part Performance

1. Part or full payment or part or complete acceptance of goods satisfies the statute. The contract is enforced only to the extent of the part performance.

PAROL EVIDENCE RULE

The Theory

1. Evidence of prior or contemporaneous agreements (whether written or oral) is inadmissible to vary, contradict, or modify an unambiguous written contract.
2. Parol evidence will be excluded only if the court finds that the writing was intended as a final and complete agreement (totally integrated).
3. A merger or integration clause ("This is the final and complete agreement.") is generally given effect.

Exceptions to the Parol Evidence Rule

1. Parol evidence may be used to (a) show that writing was not the final and complete agreement, (b) show defects in formation, (c) show and explain ambiguity, and (d) show subsequent agreements.

Parol Evidence Rule and the Code

1. Under the Code, agreements may be explained by evidence of course of dealing, usage of trade, or course of performance.

CONSTRUCTION AND INTERPRETATION OF CONTRACTS

1. Words are given their plain and ordinary meanings.
2. Ambiguities are construed against the party who drafted or used the ambiguous language.
3. Writings are to be interpreted as a whole, and language is not to be taken out of context.
4. Specific provisions control general provisions.
5. Handwritten provisions prevail over typed provisions, and typed provisions prevail over printed provisions.
6. Courts may rely on business customs, usages of trade, and the parties' prior dealings to give meaning to a contract's language.
7. The Code supplies (gap-fills) terms omitted by the parties. Code-implied terms are applicable unless the parties provide otherwise in their agreement.

REVIEW QUESTIONS AND PROBLEMS

1. Match each term in Column A with the appropriate statement in Column B.

A	B
(1) Guarantor of another's debt primarily wants to benefit himself or her self	(a) Party detrimentally relies on oral promise
(2) Contract that cannot be performed within one year	(b) Indicates a contract between the parties, indicates quantity, and is signed by party to be charged
(3) Promissory estoppel exception	(c) A promise to pay another's debt, grant of an interest in land, a contract that cannot be performed in one year, and sale of goods of $500 or more
(4) Equitable estoppel exception	(d) Writing that satisfies statute but is not signed by the party to be charged
(5) Sufficient writing required by required by the Code	(e) Written contract is final but not the complete agreement
(6) Confirmation between merchants	(f) Confirmation between merchants, specially manufactured goods, judicial admissions, performance
(7) Parol evidence rule	(g) Leading object rule
(8) Partial integration	(h) Eliminates prior or contemporaneous evidence that varies, contradicts, or modifies a written contract
(9) Contracts granting interests in land	(i) Part or full performance by one party
(10) Merger or integration clause	(j) Two-year employment contract
(11) Code exceptions to the statute of frauds	(k) "This is the parties' entire agreement."
(12) Contracts within the statute of clause	(1) Easement, mortgage, lease for more than a year

2. A butcher sold hamburger meat on credit to the Good Eats Restaurant. When the restaurant was late in paying its bills, the butcher contacted Jim, who orally promised to pay any bill that the restaurant failed to pay. Is this oral promise enforceable in court? Why or why not? Would your answer change if Jim said, "The restaurant is on hard times. Send the bills to me, and I'll pay." Explain.

3. Livesay orally agreed to sell real estate to Drake. Before the closing, Livesay sold it to someone else and wrote Drake a letter apologizing for selling it at a higher price. The letter mentioned both prices and contained an adequate reference to the real estate. When Drake sues Livesay, will the statute of frauds be an adequate defense? Why or why not?

4. Hardin Associates, a developer of shopping centers, hired Brummet to head its development division. Brummet was hired on an oral contract of employment for an indefinite time. He was later discharged, and he sued for breach of contract. Hardin asserted the statute of frauds as a defense since the contract was to last an indefinite time. Is the defense valid? Explain.
5. On September 15, 2008, Builders orally agreed with K. Construction Company to work together on a project. Work was to begin January 1, 2009, and it was contemplated that the work would be completed by the end of 2009. Is the contract enforceable? Explain.
6. Seaman supplied fuel for ships and needed a long-term supply contract with a major oil company. In a letter dated October 11, Standard Oil offered Seaman a ten-year supply contract with three ten-year options for renewal. The letter made no mention of quantity requirements, price, particulars of performance, or other material terms. Seaman signed the letter indicating his acceptance of Standard's offer. When Standard later said it could not supply fuel, Seaman sued. Standard raised the defense of the statute of frauds. Is the October 11 letter a signed writing sufficient to satisfy the statute of frauds? Explain.
7. Chisholm had a written option to purchase 1.862 acres of land out of a 10-acre tract owned by the Cartwrights. The exact piece of property covered by the option was not specified. If Chisholm sues for specific performance of the option, will the statute of frauds be a valid defense? Explain.
8. Brown entered into an oral contract to purchase a farm from Burnside. Brown took possession of the farm, made several improvements, tore down an old farmhouse, paid taxes, and made payments on the purchase price. Burnside thereafter refused to deed the farm to Brown as orally agreed. Brown sought specific performance of the oral contract. Is the oral contract to sell real property enforceable under these circumstances? Why or why not?
9. Associated Lithographers made an oral contract to provide Stay Wood Products with special printed business cards, letterheads and envelopes, order forms, and an etching and rubber stamp with Stay Wood Products' name. When Stay Wood Products refused to pay, Associated Lithographers sued. Stay Wood raised the defense of the statute of frauds. Is the statute of frauds a defense? Explain.
10. Roper bought a triple-wide mobile home from Flamingo Home Sales. The written installment sale contract disclaimed any warranty obligation of the seller. Roper experienced several problems with the mobile home, which Flamingo refused to repair. Roper sued on Flamingo's oral promise that if problems did arise, Flamingo would "take care of them." Is this oral promise admissible in court? Explain why or why not.

Contract Performance, Nonperformance, and Discharge | 19

CHAPTER OUTLINE

CHAPTER PREVIEW

We have now encountered most of the basic issues in relating to contract formation. Let's take a moment and review. First, there must be an agreement consisting of offer and acceptance. Second, the agreement must be validated by bargained-for consideration. Third, the valid contract may be legally unenforceable because of defenses like incapacity, illegality, public policy, or form. Based on the assumption that a valid contract exists without any defense to its formation, the discussion here concerns performance of contracts.

This chapter focuses on the problems that may arise during the period of the *performance* of a contract. A major emphasis is on important provisions known as conditions. Questions arise as to the order of performance. Who must perform first in a bilateral contract? Usually, a default or breach of a contract will occur at or after the time when performance was due, but as noted in this chapter, a contract can be breached prior to the date for performance.

Two additional legal issues may arise during the performance of a contract. First, a party may be unable to perform because of circumstances beyond his or her control; or the party may contend that because of changed conditions, he or she should be excused from performing as agreed. These circumstances are known as excuses for non-performance.

Second, a contract must eventually come to an end. Most contracts end when they are fully performed; however, there are other events and legal principles that may result in the discharge or termination of a contract or contract liability. The discharge of contracts is discussed in the latter portion of this chapter.

BUSINESS MANAGEMENT DECISION

You are the low bidder on a construction project. The proposed contract, presented to you for signing, states that "time is of the essence in the performance of the agreement. This agreement also contains a completion date.

Should you agree to this contract?

CONDITIONS

1. Definition

Condition

A clause in a contract, either expressed or implied, that has the effect of investing or divesting the legal rights and duties of the parties to the contract

A **condition** is an act or event (other than the lapse of time) that, unless excused, must occur before performance under a contract becomes due. A condition is an act or event that limits or qualifies a promise. The condition must occur before the promisor has a present duty to perform. Assume that you promise to sell me your car for $3,000 and I promise to buy your car for $3,000 if I can obtain a loan of $2,000. I have no present duty to pay you $3,000. When and if I obtain a loan of $2,000, my promise to pay you is activated. My promise to pay is a conditional promise.

There is no exclusive or conclusive test to determine whether a particular contractual provision is a promise or a condition. Although no particular words are necessary for the existence of a condition, terms such as *if, provided that, on condition that,* and others that condition a party's performance usually connote an intent for a condition rather than a promise. In the absence of a clause expressly creating a condition, whether a certain contractual provision is a condition rather than a promise must be gathered from the contract as a whole and from the intent of the parties.

Conditions determine when a party has to perform. However, many promises are unconditional and absolute. The party who makes an unconditional promise has an immediate duty to perform, regardless of the other party's duties. The failure to perform such a promise is a breach of contract unless the duty is excused. Where a promise is conditional, the duty to perform it is dormant or inactivated until the condition occurs. A duty to perform is conditional if some event must occur before the duty becomes absolute.

2. Types of Conditions

Conditions may be classified by time—*when* the conditioning event must occur in relation to the promise. Under this classification, conditions are labeled *conditions precedent, conditions concurrent,* and *conditions subsequent.*

Conditions Precedent

A clause in a contract providing that immediate rights and duties shall vest only on the happening of some event

CONDITIONS PRECEDENT A **condition precedent** is an act or event that, unless excused, must exist or occur before a duty of immediate performance of a promise arises. It usually takes the form of performance by the other party. Contracts often expressly provide that one party must perform before there is a right to performance by the other party. The first party's performance is a condition precedent to the duty of the other party to perform. Since one party must perform before the other is under a duty to do so, the failure of the first party to perform permits the other to refuse to perform and to cancel the contract.

Not all the terms that impose a duty of performance on a person are of sufficient importance to constitute conditions precedent. As a general rule, if a provision is relatively insignificant, its performance is not required before recovery may be obtained from the other party. In such cases, the party who was to receive performance merely deducts the damages caused by the breach.

For example, a contractor substantially follows all the plans and specifications in building a house, but completes the work ten days late. Rescission is not justified. Such a breach is of minor importance. The purchaser would have been required to pay the contract price less any damages sustained because of the delay. It is often difficult to judge whether a breach of a particular provision is so material that it justifies rescission. If the damage caused by the breach can be readily measured in money, or if the other party receives basically what he or she was entitled to under the contract, the clause breached is not considered a condition precedent.

Conditions Concurrent

Mutually dependent conditions that must be performed at the same time by the parties to the contract–(Payment of money and delivery of goods in a cash sale are conditions concurrent.)

CONDITIONS CONCURRENT If parties are to exchange performances at the same time, their performances are **conditioned concurrently**. "I promise to sell you my stereo for $700 on April 1." Tender of $700 and tender of the stereo are concurrent conditions of exchange. Since a contract seldom states that performances are simultaneously conditioned on one another, courts will generally find concurrent conditions if both parties can perform simultaneously. Suppose, in the preceding example, no date for performance was set. In that case, neither party could demand that the other perform until he or she has performed or tendered performance. Each party conditions the other party's performance on concurrent performance

Conditions subsequent

A clause in a contract providing for the happening of an event that divests legal rights and duties

CONDITIONS SUBSEQUENT A **condition subsequent** stated in the contract is an event that *discharges a duty of performance* that has become absolute. In an insurance contract you might find the following example: "In the event of accident or loss, written notice containing all particulars shall be given by the insured to the Insurer within thirty days." The insurance company's duty to pay under the policy does not arise (become absolute) until the insured gives notice. The requirement of notice is an express condition subsequent to the insured's right to collect. Note that conditions subsequent are rare.

TABLE 19-1 ■ Conditions Classified Based on Time

Condition precedent	A condition must occur before a party's performance is required.
Condition concurrent	Each party's performance is dependent on the other party's performance.
Condition subsequent	A condition operates to end a party's promise to perform; the condition follows (or is subsequent to) the duty to perform.

3. Express Conditions

Conditions may also be classified according to the way they are created. This method of classification recognizes two types of conditions: *express conditions*, specifically set out in the contract, and *constructive conditions* that the parties did not consider but that the court imposes to achieve fundamental fairness between the parties. These two types of conditions are discussed in this section and the section that follows.

An *express condition* is included in a contract and designated as a condition that must be strictly performed before the other party's duty to perform arises. The penalty for failure to perform an express condition properly may be the loss of the right to receive payment or otherwise to obtain the return performance. The parties may stipulate that something is a condition precedent, even though it would not ordinarily be considered so. If that stipulation is made, failure to perform exactly as specified is ground for rescission unless the court construes the clause to be a penalty provision and, therefore, unenforceable.

A contract may provide that "time is of the essence of this agreement." This means that performance on or before the date specified is a condition precedent to the duty of the other party to pay or to perform.

4. Express Conditions of Personal Satisfaction

A common provision in many contracts expressly conditions a party's performance on *personal satisfaction* with the other party's performance. Suppose that Wyeth agrees to paint your portrait to your personal satisfaction for $20,000. When he is finished, you say that you are not satisfied with it and refuse to pay the $20,000. The condition precedent of your personal satisfaction, you argue, has not happened to activate your duty to pay. Would it make any difference if fifty art experts state that the portrait is a masterpiece? To answer that question and to avoid unfair forfeitures, the law has adopted rules involving two categories of satisfaction cases: situations involving *personal taste*, fancy, or judgment (*subjective dissatisfaction*) and situations involving *mechanical fitness*, utility, or marketability (*objective dissatisfaction*).

When the satisfaction condition concerns your individual taste or judgment, as in the case of Wyeth's painting, the law requires that you genuinely be dissatisfied. Your dissatisfaction must be honest and in *good faith*, which is a subjective fact question. If you are dissatisfied with the bargain (paying $20,000), however, then you are refusing to pay in bad faith.

The condition in that case is excused. The testimony of the art experts can, therefore, be used as circumstantial evidence of bad faith. This fact issue is given to the jury to determine.

When the satisfaction condition concerns something like construction or repair that can be *measured objectively*, the law requires *reasonable rather than personal satisfaction.* If the average person would be satisfied (reasonable, objective satisfaction), then you must pay—even though you personally might be dissatisfied. Thus performance that is objectively satisfactory must be paid for, notwithstanding personal (subjective) dissatisfaction. The following case, which includes both a majority and dissenting opinion, explores further the concept of personal satisfaction.

CASE

Michael Silvestri and Francisco Celestino v. Optus Software, Inc., A New Jersey Corp. and Joseph Avellino, Individually

SUPREME COURT OF NEW JERSEY

814 A.2d 602 (2003)

LAVECCHIA, J.

This is a breach of contract action. Defendant Optus Software, Inc. ("Optus" or "the company"), a small computer software company, hired plaintiff Michael Silvestri as its Director of Support Services, responsible for supervising the provision of technical support services to the company's customers. Silvestri's two-year employment contract contained a clause that reserved to the company the right to terminate his employment for failure to perform to the company's satisfaction (the "satisfaction clause").

Nine months into the contract, Silvestri was terminated under the satisfaction clause by the chief executive officer of Optus, Joseph Avellino. Silvestri filed this action, contending that the company's dissatisfaction was objectively unreasonable and that therefore his termination was a breach of the employment contract. The trial court granted summary judgment to the company. The Appellate Division reversed, however, holding that an employer must meet an objective standard for satisfaction in order to invoke a right to terminate pursuant to a satisfaction clause in an employment contract.

The question presented then is whether the employer's satisfaction is subject to an objective or subjective evaluation. We conclude that, absent language to the contrary, a subjective assessment of personal satisfaction applies and that the trial court's grant of summary judgment to the company was appropriate. We therefore reverse the contrary holding of the Appellate Division.

Optus hired Silvestri for a two-year period commencing January 4, 1999, at an annual salary of $70,000. According to the company's president and chief executive officer, defendant Avellino, Silvestri's duties as a manager in this small business encompassed all tasks assigned to him by the board of directors. Specifically, Silvestri was charged with supervision of the support services staff, responsibility for communication with resellers of the Optus computer software to end-users, and coordination of ongoing training for support staff and resellers of the company's products in order to maintain their proficiency in assisting end-users. The employment contract contained a clause allowing termination of Silvestri for "failure or refusal to perform faithfully, diligently or completely his duties ... to the satisfaction" of the company. Termination under that clause relieved the company of any further payment obligation to Silvestri.

The record indicates that Silvestri enjoyed the full support of Avellino during the first six months of his employment. Avellino's communications within and without the organization praised Silvestri's abilities and underscored his role as leader of the support services group. As late as July 16, 1999, Avellino sent an e-mail message to all members of the group, exhorting them to support their new supervisor. The e-mail referred to the problems Optus had been having in providing technical support to resellers and end-users, stressed that Optus had hired Silvestri to help alleviate those problems, and again asked the staff to support Silvestri.

Although Avellino repeatedly expressed his belief in Silvestri's ability and efforts during those early months, his attitude started to change during the summer months of 1999. In June, July, and August, several clients and resellers communicated to Avellino their disappointment with the performance and attitude of the support services staff generally, and several complaints targeted Silvestri specifically. Avellino informed Silvestri of those criticisms. As the criticisms mounted, Avellino's concerns and frustrations grew, as evidenced by his e-mail exchanges with Silvestri and others. Finally, on September 3, 1999, Avellino told Silvestri that they needed to have a "heart-to-heart" talk about his performance. On September 17, 1999, Silvestri was terminated.

Silvestri filed an action for breach of contract and tortious interference, naming Optus and Avellino as defendants. The complaint named another terminated support services employee as a co-plaintiff, but that employee's claim was dismissed and is not part of this appeal.

Both parties moved for summary judgment relying on copies of the numerous e-mail communications between them. Finding a triable issue of fact concerning the reasonableness of Avellino's dissatisfaction with Silvestri's performance, the court held that summary judgment was inappropriate, and reversed.

■ *We granted certification and now reverse the Appellate Division.*

Agreements containing a promise to perform in a manner satisfactory to another or to be bound to pay for satisfactory performance are a common form of an enforceable contract. Such "satisfaction" contracts are generally divided into two categories for purposes of

continued

review: (1) contracts that involve matters of personal taste, sensibility, judgment, or convenience; and (2) contracts that contain a requirement of satisfaction as to mechanical fitness, utility, or marketability. The standard for evaluating satisfaction depends on the type of contract. Satisfaction contracts of the first type are interpreted on a subjective basis, with satisfaction dependent on the personal, honest evaluation of the party to be satisfied. Absent language to the contrary, however, contracts of the second type—involving operative fitness or mechanical utility—are subject to an objective test of reasonableness because in those cases the extent and quality of performance can be measured by objective tests.

A subjective standard typically is applied to satisfaction clauses in employment contracts because "there is greater reason and a greater tendency to interpret [the contract] as involving personal satisfaction," rather than the satisfaction of a hypothetical "reasonable" person. In the employment context, "the party to be satisfied is far more likely to feel the need to exercise individual or even idiosyncratic judgment with respect to the retention of the employee ... and to act in accord with his or her sensibilities."

In the case of a high-level business manager, a subjective test is particularly appropriate to the flexibility needed by the owners and higher-level officers operating a competitive enterprise. When a manager has been hired to share responsibility for the success of a business entity, an employer is entitled to be highly personal and idiosyncratic in judging the employee's satisfactory performance in advancing the enterprise.

The subjective standard obliges the employer to act "honestly in accordance with his duty of good faith and fair dealing," but genuine dissatisfaction of the employer, honestly held, is sufficient for discharge.

We hold that a subjective test of performance governs the employer's resort to a satisfaction clause in an employment contract unless there is some language in the contract to suggest that the parties intended an objective standard. There is no such language here. Nothing in the text of the satisfaction clause suggests that dissatisfaction was to be measured by any standard other than the employer's good faith, unilateral judgment. We are, moreover, persuaded that in the circumstances before us, application of another's notion of satisfactory performance would undermine recognized and accepted notions of business judgment and individualized competitive strategy, as well as principles of freedom of contract. Idiosyncratic judgments as to what constitutes satisfactory performance are expected and should be permitted. The employer, not some hypothetical reasonable person, is best suited to determine if the employee's performance is satisfactory. Accordingly, notwithstanding the thoughtful dissent by our colleagues who favor application of an objective test, a subjective test shall apply generally to satisfaction employment contracts, unless the language of the contract signals otherwise.

Turning then to application of the subjective test in this setting, and granting Silvestri the benefit of all inferences in this motion record as we must, we conclude that the entry of summary judgment in favor of defendants was appropriate. The only issue available to Silvestri is whether the dissatisfaction with his performance was genuine, and he has failed to make a prima facie showing that it was not. Indeed, he does not even assert that it was not genuine, and he neither pleaded nor raised any issue of illegal or improper motivation for his dismissal. His moving papers attacked only the reasonableness of Avellino's dissatisfaction by contending that another more reasonable person would have otherwise viewed the merits of his performance. Consistent with that position, Silvestri sought to show that even when he did encounter difficulties with resellers and customers of Optus, the problems were not entirely his fault. Thus, applying the test of genuineness, and not reasonableness, we conclude based on the overwhelming evidence in this record that Silvestri has not demonstrated that a dispute exists requiring submission of the matter to jury trial.

The judgment of the Appellate Division is reversed and the matter remanded for entry of summary judgment in favor of defendants.

Chief Justice Poritz and Justices Coleman, Verniero, and Albin join in Justice LaVecchia's opinion. Justice Zazzali filed a separate dissenting opinion in which Justice Long joins.

DISSENT: ZAZZALI, J., DISSENTING

Because I believe the majority applies the wrong standard in evaluating Silvestri's satisfaction contract for employment, I respectfully dissent. In my opinion, application of an objective standard is appropriate based on both the subject matter and the language of the contract. Applying an objective standard helps to ensure that the employee is not exposed to the risk of forfeiture, properly places on the drafter of the employment agreement the burden of articulating effectively when a subjective standard should apply, and mitigates the problems of proof inherent in attempting to show an employer's bad faith.

I believe that the better rule is to extend a preference for the objective standard to satisfaction clauses in employment contracts whenever the subject matter or the language of the contract permits its application. By requiring an employer to be reasonable in its exercise of discretion under the satisfaction clause, an employee is better able to anticipate whether his or her performance will justify termination under the contract. Application of such a standard thereby reduces the risk of forfeiture by the employee. As Chief Judge Posner has noted, applying an objective standard in the satisfaction contract context indulges the sensible "presumption that the performing party would not have wanted to put himself at the mercy of the paying party's whim ..." Accordingly, that presumption should be overcome only "when the nature of the performance contracted for is such that there are no objective standards to guide the court."

An objective standard also is appropriate when, as in this case, preparation of the satisfaction contract is exclusively within the employer's control. A presumption that the objective standard applies properly places on the drafter of the employment agreement the burden of explicitly invoking application of a subjective standard.

■ *Reversed.*

CASE CONCEPTS REVIEW

1. How should subjective satisfaction be judged? Should good faith play a role? Why?
2. Is the majority's position reasonable given the concerns raised in the dissent? Why?

5. Constructive Conditions

A *constructive condition* is one not expressed by the parties but is read into the contract to serve justice (that is, an implied-in-law condition). In a bilateral contract, one party can perform, regardless of what the other party does. In most cases, however, it would be inequitable to require one party to perform without requiring the other to perform. In the interest of fairness, courts make performances of bilateral promises constructively conditional on one another. In an employment contract, for example, one must work before getting paid. Working is a constructive condition precedent, which must occur to activate the employer's duty to pay an employee.

When parties understand that one performance must occur before the other (or such is understood by custom), the former is a constructive condition precedent to the latter. When a contractor promises to build a house for an owner who will pay $200,000, a court will construe the builder's performance as a condition that must happen to activate the owner's duty to pay.

If both performances can be performed simultaneously, the promises are constructively concurrent. To activate the other's duty to perform, a party must tender his or her performances. Most contracts for the sale of goods under the Code are examples of constructive concurrent conditions of exchange.

Note: The express contract terms or custom, usage of trade, course of dealing, and the like can change the rule. A passenger, by custom, pays for an airline ticket before the airline's duty to provide transportation is activated.

PERFORMANCE OF CONDITIONS

6. Tender of Performance

Tender

Offer to do something

A **tender** in the law of contracts is an offer to perform. When a person makes a tender, it means that he or she is ready, willing, and able to perform. The tender is especially significant in contracts requiring both parties to perform at the same time. One party can place the other party in default by making a tender of performance without having actually rendered the performance.

The concept of tender is applied not only to concurrent condition situations but also to contract performance in general. In most contracts, one party or the other is required to tender payment. Such a tender requires that there be a bona fide, unconditional offer of payment of the amount of money due, coupled with an actual production of the money or its equivalent. A tender of payment by check is not a valid tender when an objection is made to this medium of payment. When a tender is refused for other reasons, one may not later complain about the use of a check as the medium of tender. A person to whom a tender is made must specify any objection to it or waive it, so that the debtor may know and comply with the creditor's demands.

Tenders of payment are often refused for one reason or another. A party may contend that the tender was too late. The creditor may refuse to accept the offer to pay because he or she believes that the amount tendered is less than the amount of the debt. If it turns out that the tender was proper, the valid tender will have three important legal effects:

1. It stops interest from accruing after the date of the tender.
2. In case the creditor later brings legal action recovering no more than the amount tendered, he or she must pay the court costs.
3. If the debt were secured by a security interest in property belonging to the debtor, this security interest would be extinguished.

Thus a tender of payment, although it does not discharge the debt, has important advantages to the person making it.

Article 2 of the Uniform Commercial Code, which deals with the sale of goods, has two sections relating to tender. Unless the buyer and the seller have otherwise agreed, *tender of payment* by the buyer is a condition to the seller's duty to deliver the goods sold [2-511 (1)]. Unless the seller demands payment in legal tender, the buyer is authorized to make payment by check [2-511 (2)]. The Code also provides for the manner of a seller's *tender of delivery* of the goods involved in the contract. The Code requires that the seller make the goods available to the buyer and that the seller give the buyer reasonable notification that the goods are available [2-503 (1)]. If the seller gives notice that the goods are available for the buyer and the buyer does not tender payment, then the buyer would be placed in default. Tender of delivery is a condition to the buyer's duty to accept the goods [2-507 (1)].

7. Substantial Performance

Express conditions must be strictly met, or there is a material breach of contract. Constructive conditions need be only significantly performed to avoid a material breach. Because constructive conditions are imposed in the interest of good faith and fair dealing, it naturally follows that **substantial performance** of a constructive condition satisfies the condition. Thus the other party's duty to perform is activated by substantial performance. Note that substantial performance is not complete performance; so there has been an immaterial breach, and dollar damages may be awarded. Although the non-breaching party can sue for damages for this immaterial breach, the suing party must still perform because the constructive condition precedent has been fulfilled. Thus an immaterial breach does not excuse the non-breaching party of the duty of performance under the contract.

Substantial performance

The only permissible omissions or derivations of substantial performance, performance of all the essential elements of a contract, are those that are trivial, inadvertent, and inconsequential.

The consequences of a material breach are more severe. Normally, a material breach gives the non-breaching party an option. He or she can opt to treat the contract as rescinded or can choose to continue under the contract by treating it as only a partial breach. A partial breach, in effect, continues the contract, and all parties must continue to perform. The non-breaching party can sue for damages that accrued from the breach, and the contract is not rescinded. If a total breach is elected, the contract is at an end; and there is an immediate right to all remedies for breach of the entire contract.

Issues of substantial performance often arise in construction contracts. Seldom is there total, complete, and perfect performance. Adjustments in the price are usually made for minor deviations. However, if a contractor fails to substantially perform as agreed, the other party may rescind the contract and the contractor is not entitled to collect anything even on the theory of quasi-contract. The following case, written by one of the most famous jurists in the 20th century, addresses the issue of substantial performance.

8. Divisibility: Installment Contracts

Whereas many contracts require a single performance by each party and are completely performed at one point of time, others require or permit performance by one or both parties in installments over a period of time. The rights and obligations of parties during the period when the contract is being performed frequently depend on whether the contract is "entire" or "divisible." A contract is said to be divisible if performance by each party is divided into two or more parts *and* performance of each part by one party is the agreed exchange for the corresponding part by the other party. It is to be noted that a contract is not divisible simply by virtue of the fact that it is to be performed in installments.

CASE

Jacob & Youngs, Inc., Respondent, v. George E. Kent, Appellant

COURT OF APPEALS OF NEW YORK

129 N.E. 889; 1921

OPINION BY: JUDGE CARDOZO

The plaintiff built a country residence for the defendant at a cost of upwards of $77,000, and now sues to recover a balance of $3,483.46, remaining unpaid. The work of construction ceased in June, 1914, and the defendant then began to occupy the dwelling. There was no complaint of defective performance until March, 1915. One of the specifications for the plumbing work provides that "all wrought iron pipe must be well galvanized, lap welded pipe of the grade known as 'standard pipe' of Reading manufacture."

The defendant learned in March, 1915, that some of the pipe, instead of being made in Reading, was the product of other factories. The plaintiff was accordingly directed by the architect to do the work anew. The plumbing was then encased within the walls except in a few places where it had to be exposed.

Obedience to the order meant more than the substitution of other pipe. It meant the demolition at great expense of substantial parts of the completed structure. The plaintiff left the work untouched and asked for a certificate that the final payment was due. Refusal of the certificate was followed by this suit.

The evidence sustains a finding that the omission of the prescribed brand of pipe was neither fraudulent nor willful. It was the result of the oversight and inattention of the plaintiff's subcontractor. Reading pipe is distinguished from Cohoes pipe and other brands only by the name of the manufacturer stamped upon it at intervals of between six and seven feet. Even the defendant's architect, though he inspected the pipe upon arrival, failed to notice the discrepancy. The plaintiff tried to show that the brands installed, though made by other manufacturers, were the same in quality, in appearance, in market value and in cost as the brand stated in the contract—that they were, indeed, the same thing, though manufactured in another place. The evidence was excluded, and a verdict directed for the defendant. The Appellate Division reversed, and granted a new trial.

We think the evidence, if admitted, would have supplied some basis for the inference that the defect was insignificant in its relation to the project.

Those who think more of symmetry and logic in the development of legal rules than of practical adaptation to the attainment of a just result will be troubled by a classification where the lines of division are so wavering and blurred. Something, doubtless, may be said on the score of consistency and certainty in favor of a stricter standard. The courts have balanced such considerations against those of equity and fairness, and found the latter to be the weightier. In the circumstances of this case, we think the measure of the allowance is not the cost of replacement, which would be great, but the difference in value, which would be either nominal or nothing. Some of the exposed sections might perhaps have been replaced at moderate expense.

It is true that in most cases the cost of replacement is the measure. The owner is entitled to the money which will permit him to complete, unless the cost of completion is grossly and unfairly out of proportion to the good to be attained. When that is true, the measure is the difference in value. Specifications call, let us say, for a foundation built of granite quarried in Vermont. On the completion of the building, the owner learns that through the blunder of a subcontractor part of the foundation has been built of granite of the same quality quarried in New Hampshire. The measure of allowance is not the cost of reconstruction. As an instrument of justice, the courts have developed the rule that gives a remedy in cases of substantial performance with compensation for defects of trivial or inappreciable importance.

The order should be affirmed, and judgment absolute directed in favor of the plaintiff upon the stipulation, with costs in all courts.

■ *Affirmed.*

CASE CONCEPTS REVIEW

1. Does the court provide a manner for determining when a defect is insignificant? Explain.
2. The decision of the court appears to allow those performing a contract to act in a manner different from what they promised? Is this true? Explain.

The parties may specify whether a contract is divisible or entire. Thus a contract may contain a clause stipulating that each delivery is a separate contract, or other language may be used to show the intention of the parties that their agreement is to be treated as if it were a series of contracts. Some contracts are obviously divisible. Assume Sam promises to sell and Dave promises to buy a car for $5,000 and a boat for $3,000. This contract is legally divisible into two parts, a sale of a car and a sale of a boat. If Sam tenders the car, he is entitled to $5,000 even though he has not performed the entire contract since he has not tendered the boat. Sam is liable for not tendering the boat, but he can still recover for the sale of the car.

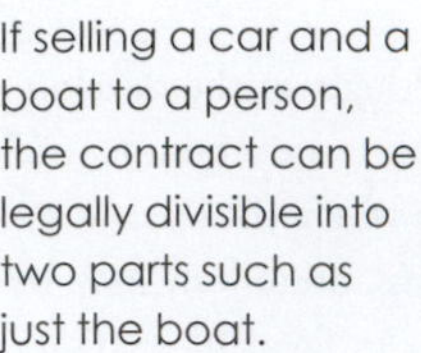
If selling a car and a boat to a person, the contract can be legally divisible into two parts such as just the boat.

The concept of divisibility is applicable to a variety of contracts, including insurance contracts, employment contracts, construction contracts, and sales contracts. As a general proposition, employment contracts are interpreted to be divisible, but construction contracts are usually deemed to be entire.

If a contract is divisible, the second party is under a duty to perform in part after the first party performs an installment. For example, the employer owes a duty to pay wages at the end of the pay period. A material breach of an installment justifies a rescission of the balance of the agreement. Assume that a party is to write five songs each month for a year. Only one song is written the first month. While the failure to deliver the other four would not be a substantial breach of the entire agreement, it would be a substantial breach of the installment. If the contract were treated as divisible, such a material breach would justify rescission of the contract. Likewise, if a party substantially performs an installment of a divisible contract, he or she may nevertheless recover the value of that installment, less damages, caused by any breach of the contract without rendering performance, of the balance of the agreement.

There have been numerous cases involving the question of whether or not a contract is divisible. No general test can be derived from these cases. Courts are called on to determine in any given case whether the parties intended that (1) each would accept part performance of the other in return for his or her own without regard to subsequent events or (2) the divisions of the contract were made merely for the purpose of requiring periodic payments as the work progresses. In any event, the party who breaches is liable for damages resulting from his or her breach.

Under the Code, unless the parties have otherwise agreed, a sales contract is entire; all the goods called for by the contract must be tendered in a single delivery, and payment in full is due upon such tender [2-307]. If the contract permits installment deliveries, the seller can demand a proportionate share of the price for each delivery as it is made, provided the price can be apportioned, as for goods sold at a certain price per item. If there is a substantial default on an installment (the goods tendered or delivered may not conform to the contract), the buyer may reject the installment [2-612 (2)]. When an installment breached indicates that the seller will not satisfactorily perform the balance of the contract or that such performance is unreliable, the buyer can rescind the entire contract [2-612 (3)]. Should the buyer accept a nonconforming installment without giving notice of cancellation or demanding that the seller deliver goods that conform, that buyer may not use the breach as a basis for rescission.

9. Anticipatory Repudiation

Before the time specified for performance, there can be no actual breach; however, there may be a breach by *anticipatory repudiation.* The expression means that repudiation occurs before performance is due. The repudiation may be express or implied. An express repudiation is a clear, positive, unequivocal refusal to perform. An implied repudiation results from conduct in which the promisor puts it out of his or her power to perform, making substantial performance of the promise impossible. In either case, the repudiation must be positive and unequivocal.

When a promisor repudiates the prospective duty to perform, the non-repudiating party has an election of remedies. On the one hand, this latter party can treat the repudiation as an *anticipatory breach* and immediately seek damages for breach of contract, rather than waiting until the time set for the repudiating party's performance. Thus the doctrine excuses any express or constructive condition to the repudiating party's duty and thereby permits an immediate lawsuit. On the other hand, rather than suing, the injured party can treat the repudiation as an empty threat, wait until the time for performance arrives, and exercise his or her remedies for actual breach if a breach does in fact occur. If the injured party disregards the repudiation and treats the contract as still in force, the repudiation is nullified; and the injured party is left with his or her remedies, if any, invocable at the time of performance.

The doctrine of anticipatory breach does not apply to promises to pay money on or before a specified date. If a promissory note matures on June 1, 1994, and in 1992 the maker states that he or she will not pay it when the maturity date arrives, that would not give rise to present cause of action by the holder.

The Code provides that after a breach including anticipatory repudiation, the buyer may "cover" by making in good faith and without unreasonable delay any reasonable purchase of, or contract to purchase, goods in substitution for those due from the seller [2-712]. The difference between the cost of cover and the contract price, together with any incidental or consequential damages, may be recovered by the buyer from the seller. Failure of the buyer to effect cover does not bar him or her from recovering damages for nondelivery, but damages will be limited to those that could not have been prevented by proper cover.

A party may retract his or her repudiation, provided he or she does so prior to any material change of position by the other party in reliance on it. The retraction would simply be a notice that performance of the contract will occur after all. The Code allows a retraction of anticipatory repudiation until the repudiating party's next performance is due, unless the aggrieved party has, since the repudiation, canceled or materially changed position or otherwise indicated that he or she considers the repudiation final [2-611]. Retraction may be by any method that clearly indicates to the aggrieved party that the repudiating party intends to perform; but it must include adequate assurance that in fact performance will occur if the other party demands it [2-609]. Retraction reinstates the repudiating party's rights under the contract, with due excuse and allowance to the aggrieved party for any delay occasioned by the repudiation.

EXCUSES FOR NONPERFORMANCE

10. Introduction

A party to a contract may be relieved from the duty to perform or from liability for breach if he or she is legally excused from contract performance. Moreover, a duty under a conditional promise may be activated not only by performance of the condition but also if the condition is excused. Actual failure of an express or a constructive condition may be legally excused in any of the following five ways: (1) hindrance, prevention, or noncooperation; (2) waiver; (3) impossibility; (4) frustration of purpose; and (5) commercial impracticability.

11. Hindrance, Prevention, or Noncooperation

In every contract there is an implied *duty of good faith and fair dealing* requiring each party not to prevent or substantially hinder the other party's performance. If a party whose promise is conditional wrongfully prevents the condition from occurring, then the condition is excused. Although the cases vary, the wrongful conduct can be characterized as hindrance, wrongful prevention, or noncooperation.

HINDRANCE When a party hinders another's performance of a promise, the first party makes it more difficult, but not impossible, for the second party to perform. To be an excuse for nonperformance, the hindrance must be *wrongful,* which usually means that no party reasonably contemplated or assumed the risk that occurred. For example, assume that seller agrees to sell buyer a product in short supply. Seller fails to deliver because buyer has been purchasing all available product from seller's only source of supply. A court held that although buyer did substantially hinder seller's performance, it was not wrongful. Seller assumed the risk of such market conditions when it unconditionally agreed to supply the product.

PREVENTION The wrongful prevention of performance by one party to a contract will excuse nonperformance by the other party. It is obvious that a person may not recover for nonperformance of a contract if he or she is responsible for the non-performance. If a party creates a situation that makes it impossible for the other party to perform, the other party is excused. For example, Barrow had leased a building to Calhoun for the operation of an ice cream store. The rent was to be a percentage of the gross income. Thereafter, Calhoun established another ice cream store a block away and did very little business in the building rented to her by Barrow. Calhoun has prevented the normal performance of the contract by carrying on another business that detracted from the profits. Barrow may cancel the lease without liability because Calhoun has prevented the anticipated performance of the contract.

TABLE 19-2 ■ Conditions Classified Based on Time

Type	Example
1. Excuse based on implied duty of good faith and fair dealing	Prevention
2. Excuse based on the passage of time	Waiver
3. Excuse based on fact that performance is not objectively possible	Performance becomes illegal
4. Excuse based on fact that essential purpose of the contract has been frustrated	Frustration of purpose
5. Excuse based on fact that performance has become impracticable	Commercial impracticability under 2-614

NONCOOPERATION As a part of the good-faith requirement, the law implies that the parties will reasonably cooperate with each other. If as the result of one party's failure to cooperate and to act in good faith the other party breaches the contract, then the noncooperating party is not entitled to the usual contract remedies. In fact, the other party may rescind the agreement because the implied condition of good faith has been breached.

A common example of noncooperation occurs in the landlord-tenant relationship. The written lease frequently contains a clause that states that the tenant may not assign or sublease rights and duties under the lease without the landlord's consent, A landlord who is unreasonable in refusing to consent to an assignment or a sublease fails to cooperate in the contract's performance. Upon such noncooperation, the tenant may be relieved of further liability.

12. Waiver

Waiver

The intentional relinquishment or giving up of a known right that may be done by express words or conduct that involves any acts inconsistent with an intention to claim the right

Waiver has been defined as the passing by of an occasion to enforce a legal right, whereby the legal right is lost. As applied to contract law, the essence of waivers is conduct by one party that indicates an intention not to enforce certain provisions of the agreement as against the other party. Generally, waiver occurs when there is either (1) a promise to forgo the benefit of a condition or (2) an election to continue under a contract after the other party has breached.

To illustrate the first situation, assume you had promised to purchase a new car only on the condition that you could get the car within two weeks. The dealer has not promised to make the delivery within the two-week period. If the seller notifies you that delivery will take four weeks, you might waive your right to the quicker delivery and promise to buy the car anyway.

The second situation when waiver typically occurs appears to be similar but is technically distinguishable. Assume that the car dealer promises to deliver the car within two weeks, and this promise is an essential part of the time of performance. The failure to make a timely delivery is a breach of the agreement. Rather than the failure of the delivery just excusing your performance (as in a condition not being satisfied), you now have a cause of action for damages since the dealer has breached the contract. Further assume that you decide not to make a claim against the dealer and agree to buy the car at the original price whenever it is delivered. You have waived your right to complain of the dealer's breach by agreeing to continue with the revised contract.

The waiver may be retracted unless it is supported by consideration or unless the promisee has made a substantial change of position in reliance on it. One who has waived the time for performance may withdraw the waiver if he or she gives the other party a reasonable opportunity to perform the condition waived.

The Uniform Commercial Code allows a party who has waived a provision of an executory contract to retract the waiver upon giving reasonable notice that he or she will require strict performance of the original contract, "unless the retraction would be unjust in view of a material change of position in reliance of the waiver" [2-209 (5)]. Under the Code, the retention or acceptance of defective goods may constitute a waiver of the defect. A buyer who fails to particularize defects in goods may in fact be waiving his or her objections based on these defects [2-605].

13. Impossibility of Performance

Actual impossibility of performance is a valid excuse for nonperformance and releases a party from the duty to perform. Impossibility is much more than mere "additional hardship." As a general rule, in the absence of an appropriate contract provision, circumstances that impose additional hardship on one party do not constitute an excuse for breach of contract. The fact that the promised performance of a contractual obligation may be more difficult than expected at the time the promise was made does not discharge the promisor from the duty to perform.

Therefore, most contracts provide that manufacturers, suppliers, or builders shall be relieved from performance in case of fire, strikes, difficulty in obtaining raw materials, or other incidents imposing hardship over which they have no control. Without such a provision, there would be no excuse, as the conditions do not constitute impossibility of performance.

In order to have the effect of releasing a party from the duty to perform, the impossibility must render performance "physically and objectively impossible." If objective impossibility is present, the discharge is mutual; that is, the promisor is discharged, and the promisee is also discharged from his or her corresponding obligation. Many cases state that for impossibility to exist, there must be a fortuitous or unavoidable occurrence that was not reasonably foreseeable. The fact that an act of God is involved does not necessarily create an excuse. If a house under construction is destroyed by fire caused by lightning, the contractor is not excused from the obligation to complete the house. Contractors take the risk of fire unless they protect themselves by expressly contracting that they shall not be held liable for such risks.

Likewise, if the situation is caused by the promisor or by developments that the promisor could have prevented, avoided, or remedied by corrective measures, there is no excuse. For this reason, the failure of a third party, such as a supplier, to make proper delivery does not create impossibility. Impossibility will not be allowed as a defense when the obstacle was created by the promisor or was within his or her power to eliminate. It must not exist merely because of the inability or incapacity of the promisor to do it; that is, subjective impossibility is no excuse.

14. Specific Cases of Impossibility

There are four basic situations in which impossibility of performance is frequently offered as an excuse for nonperformance.

PERFORMANCE BECOMES ILLEGAL In the first of these, performance becomes illegal because of the enactment of some law or governmental action. A manufacturer or supplier may be prevented from making delivery of merchandise because of government restrictions. However, government action that merely makes an agreement more burdensome than was anticipated does not afford a basis for relief.

DEATH OR INCAPACITATING ILLNESS The second situation is the death or incapacitating illness of one of the contracting parties. This is not deemed to be a form of impossibility unless the contract demands the personal services of the disabled or deceased person. Ordinary contracts of production, processing, and sale of property are unaffected by the death or illness of one or both of the parties. In the event of death, it is assumed that the contract will be carried out by the estate of the deceased. If a contract is for personal services or it clearly implies that the continued services of the contracting party are essential to performance, death or illness will excuse nonperformance. In contracts for personal services, the death of the employer also terminates the relationship. The estate of the employer in prematurely terminating the contract is not liable for damages to the employee.

CONTINUED EXISTENCE OF CERTAIN SUBJECT MATTER Many agreements involve the continued existence of certain subject matter essential to completion of the contract. The third rule is that destruction of any subject matter essential to the completion of the contract will operate to relieve the parties of the obligations assumed by their agreement. A different situation arises when material that only one of the parties expected to use in his or her performance is destroyed. For example, if a factory from which the owner expected to deliver certain material is destroyed by fire, performance is not excused. Performance is still possible, even though an undue hardship may result. The material needed to fill the order can be obtained from another source. However,

Performance is not excused if a factory is destroyed by fire

had the contract stipulated that the material were to be delivered from a particular factory, its destruction would have operated to excuse a failure to perform. In recent years, there has been a trend toward holding that when both parties understood that delivery was to be made from a certain source, even though it was not expressly agreed, destruction of the source of supply will relieve the obligor from performing.

LACK OF ESSENTIAL ELEMENT The last form of impossibility arises when there is an essential element lacking. This situation is difficult to define satisfactorily, but apparently the agreement may be rescinded when some element or property is lacking, although the parties assumed it existed or would exist. Some courts would hold that no contract, in fact, existed because of mutual mistake. This is said to be a form of impossibility at the time of making the contract, and courts have tended to act as if there had been no meeting of the minds. It must be definitely proved that performance is substantially impossible because of the missing element. For example, a builder contracts to build an office building at a certain location. Because of the nature of the soil, it is utterly impossible to build the type of building provided for in the agreement; the agreement must therefore be terminated. The missing element is the proper condition of the soil. In other words, from the very beginning, the contract terms could not possibly have been complied with; and in such cases the courts are prone to excuse the parties if nobody is at fault.

15. Commercial Frustration

Since the notion of requiring *absolute* impossibility may create harsh results in certain cases, courts may excuse performance using the *doctrine of commercial frustration.* The doctrine excuses performance when the essential purpose and value of the contract have been frustrated. Typically, something happens to prevent achievement of the object or purpose of the contract. If so, the courts may find an implied condition that the unforeseen development will excuse performance.

Commercial frustration arises whenever there is an intervening event or change of circumstances so fundamental it is entirely beyond that which was contemplated by the parties. Frustration is not impossibility, but it is more than mere hardship. It is an excuse created by law to eliminate liability when a fortuitous occurrence has defeated the reasonable expectations of the parties. It will not be used when the supervening event was foreseeable or assumed as a part of the agreement. This principle is illustrated in the following case.

CASE

PeopleSoft U.S.A., Inc. v. Softek, Inc.

UNITED STATES DISTRICT COURT FOR THE NORTHERN DISTRICT OF CALIFORNIA

227 F. Supp. 2d 1116 (2002)

OPINION BY: PHYLLIS J. HAMILTON

Plaintiff's motion for summary judgment came on for hearing on September 18, 2002, before this court, the Honorable Phyllis J. Hamilton presiding. Plaintiff appeared by its counsel Stuart C. Clark, and defendant appeared by its counsel Helene E. Swanson. Having read the parties' papers and carefully considered their arguments and the relevant legal authority, and good cause appearing, the court hereby GRANTS the motion for the following reasons.

This is a breach of contract case. Plaintiff PeopleSoft U.S.A., Inc. ("PeopleSoft"), which is based in California, designs and sells business software products. Defendant Softek, Inc. ("Softek"), which is based in Puerto Rico, provides software development services. In March 2000, the parties entered into a "Software License and Services Agreement." Pursuant to this agreement, PeopleSoft agreed to provide Softek with software, and Softek agreed to pay license and maintenance fees, which were noncancellable and nonrefundable, as well as installation and training fees. The agreement specified that the right to use PeopleSoft's software was exclusively for the purpose of facilitating the internal data processing operations of the Transportation Division of Softek's customer Policia de Puerto Rico ("Policia"—the Police Department of Puerto Rico).

After the agreement was signed, PeopleSoft had shipped the software and billed Softek. Unfortunately, Policia decided for some reason not to use the software. Softek advised PeopleSoft of the situation, and returned the software, unopened. Softek also told PeopleSoft that while it considered Policia's decision to be a contractual violation, it "preferred to avoid further controversies with the Policia and the Government of Puerto Rico" because they were important customers for Softek's future projects. Nonetheless,PeopleSoft demanded to be paid. Softek has apparently agreed to pay $87,931.63 of the amount in dispute, which represents charges for training expenses and airfares. However, Softek argues that it should not have to pay the $150,000 license fee for the software it returned to PeopleSoft.

PeopleSoft filed this action on July 23, 2001, alleging a single cause of action for breach of contract. Softek asserted 17 affirmative defenses, one of which was commercial frustration. PeopleSoft now seeks summary judgment, arguing that the facts are undisputed regarding the existence of the contract, PeopleSoft's performance thereunder, Softek's non-performance, and damages, and that there is no triable issue with regard to any of Softek's affirmative defenses.

Softek argues that even if performance is possible, it would be extremely impracticable because the purpose of the contract has been frustrated. In applying the frustration excuse, courts look first to see whether the fundamental reason of both parties for entering into the contract has been frustrated by an unanticipated supervening circumstance, which substantially destroys the value of the performance by the party standing on the contract.

Where, after a contract is made, a party's performance is made impracticable without his fault by the occurrence of an event the non-occurrence of which was a basic assumption on which the contract was made, his duty to render that performance is discharged, unless the language or the circumstances indicate the contrary.

The excuse of commercial frustration is a question of law to be determined by the court from the facts of the case. To excuse nonperformance of a contract on the ground of commercial frustration: 1) the basic purpose of the contract, which has been destroyed by the supervening event, must be recognized by both parties to the contract; 2) the event must be of a nature not reasonably to have been foreseen; 3) the frustration must be so severe that it is not fairly to be regarded as within the risks that were assumed under the contract; and 4) the value of counterperformance to the promisor seeking to be excused must be substantially or totally destroyed.

The purpose of the contract was the licensing of the software to Softek, so that it could be licensed to Policia, along with the provision of associated services. Softek did not seek to obtain software for its own use or the use of any entity other than Policia. PeopleSoft contends, however, that the parties expressly contracted with the awareness that Policia might not pay for the software and that Softek expressly assumed the risk of this eventuality by agreeing that "all payment obligations are noncancellable and nonrefundable" and by agreeing to "guarantee all payment to PeopleSoft on behalf of itself and ... Policia."

Softek maintains that it was not reasonably foreseeable that Policia would fail to implement the software nor that the Puerto Rican Treasury Department would reverse its prior position and decide that Policia could not use the PeopleSoft program to interface with the Treasury Department's existing software. Softek notes that the contract expressly states that the purpose of the agreement is to provide Policia with PeopleSoft's software, and it is not reasonable to interpret the language of the contract as meaning that Softek accepted the risk that Policia would decide not to implement the software.

"The question whether a risk was foreseeable is quite distinct from the question whether it was contemplated by the parties. ... When a risk has been contemplated and voluntarily assumed ... foreseeability is not an issue and the parties will be held to the bargain they made." The court finds that the language of the contract plainly assigns the risk of Policia's noncooperation to Softek.

Thus, Softek cannot avoid liability by means of the defenses of frustration.

CASE CONCEPTS REVIEW

1. What are the elements of a commercial frustration defense?
2. According to the court, what is the difference between whether something is foreseeable and whether something is contemplated by the parties?

16. Commercial Impracticability under the Code

The Code uses the term *commercial impracticability* to describe a defense similar to *commercial frustration.* The Code recognizes that without the fault of either party, unexpected developments or government action may cause the promised performance to become impracticable. In some cases, the Code authorizes substituted performance. If the loading or unloading facilities of the agreed-on carrier are unusable, a commercially reasonable substitute must be tendered and accepted if it is available [2-614].

The Code also provides that commercial impracticability is often an excuse for a seller who fails to deliver goods or is delayed in making the delivery. The excuse is limited to cases in which unforeseen supervening circumstances not within the contemplation of the parties arise [2-615(a)]. The law does not specify all the contingencies that may justify the application of the doctrine of commercial impracticability. Increased costs will not excuse the seller unless they are due to some unforeseen contingency that alters the basic nature of the contract. For example, currency fluctuations may significantly affect a contract between entities in different countries; but since those changes are foreseeable, the impracticability defense usually is not applicable.

Generally, a severe shortage of raw materials or of supplies due to a contingency such as war, an unforeseen shutdown of major sources of supply, or a local crop failure, which increases costs or prevents a seller from securing necessary supplies, does constitute commercial impracticability.

To use the excuse, the seller is required to notify customers seasonably of any delay or nondelivery. This notification is to allow the buyers to take prompt action to find another source of supply. The notice must include an estimate of the buyer's allocation when the seller is able to perform partially [2-615(c)] and is subject to the Code's allocation requirement [2-615(b)].

Upon receipt of a notice of a substantial or indefinite delay in delivery or of an allocation, the buyer has two alternative courses of action. The buyer may terminate the contract insofar as that delivery is concerned. He or she may also terminate and discharge the whole contract if the deficiency substantially impairs the value of the whole contract [2-616(1)]. The buyer may also modify the contract by agreeing to take his or her available quota in substitution. If the buyer fails to modify the contract within a reasonable time not exceeding thirty days, the contract lapses with respect to the deliveries covered by the seller's notice [2-616(2)].

DISCHARGE OF CONTRACTS

17. Methods

The rights and duties created by a contract continue in force until the contract is discharged. The term *discharge* is used to describe the cancellation of a contract and the acts by which the enforcement of its provisions are terminated. The usual and intended method of discharge is the complete performance by both parties of their obligations under the agreement. A valid excuse is a discharge in the sense that the excused party has no liability for failure to perform. The same may be said of grounds for rescission. A rescinded contract is, in effect, discharged.

Release

The voluntary relinquishing of a right, lien, or any other obligation

Although no particular form is required for an agreement to discharge a contract duty, the term **release** has traditionally been reserved for a formal written statement by one party that the other's duty is discharged. In chapter 15, the word *renunciation* was introduced; it is equivalent to a release. Either party may voluntarily renounce any right or claim arising under a contract. A renunciation is valid without consideration, provided it is in writing.

A cancellation of a written contract and the surrender of it by one party to the other will usually discharge the agreement. Such a discharge requires consideration or proof of a gift. If both parties have obligations, there is consideration on the mutual surrender of the rights to performance. If only one party has an obligation, the necessary intent to make a gift and delivery of it may be found in the delivery of the written cancelled contract. However, such evidence is not conclusive, and a jury may find that a gift was not in fact made.

The law makes a distinction between a writing that is merely the *evidence* of the obligation and one that is the obligation, such as a promissory note. There is no particular sanctity in the law to the physical evidence of an ordinary contract, and the destruction of this evidence does not destroy the contract. However, if the actual obligation such as a promissory note is surrendered or is intentionally destroyed by the holder of it, the obligation is discharged.

There are other methods of discharge, one of which is a novation. The term *novation* has two meanings. First, it is used to describe the situation in which the parties to a contract substitute a new debt or obligation for an existing one. The substitution of the new agreement operates to release or discharge the old one. Novation is also used to describe an agreement whereby an original party to a contract is replaced by a new party. The concept of novation is discussed further in Chapter 20.

The legal concept of *accord and satisfaction* allows discharge of a contract by a performance different from that agreed on in the agreement. Section 19 of this chapter discusses this concept.

Laws sometimes have the effect of discharging obligations by prohibiting lawsuits to enforce them. For example, passage of time without litigation to enforce one's rights will operate to discharge an obligation. This is further discussed in Section 20.

18. Payment

The obligation of one party to a contract is usually to pay the other for goods sold or services rendered. There are three especially significant issues about payment that affect the matter of discharge: What constitutes payment? What is good evidence that payment has been made and that the obligation has been discharged? When a debtor has several obligations to a creditor, how will a payment be applied?

WHAT CONSTITUTES PAYMENT? Certainly, the transfer of money constitutes payment; but this is not necessarily the case when the payment is by a negotiable instrument such as a check or a promissory note. Generally, payment by delivery of a negotiable instrument drawn or endorsed by the debtor to the creditor is a conditional payment and not an absolute discharge of the obligation. If the instrument is paid at maturity, the debt is discharged; if it is not so paid, the debt then exists as it did prior to the conditional payment. In the latter situation, the creditor can either bring an action to recover on the defaulted instrument or pursue his or her rights under the original agreement.

The parties may agree that payment by a negotiable instrument is an absolute discharge, in which event, if the instrument is not paid at maturity, the only recourse of the creditor is to bring action on the instrument—the original contract is discharged. A similar situation exists when accounts receivable are transferred by a debtor to his or her creditor. A transfer of accounts is a conditional payment only. If the accounts are not collected, the debtor is still obligated to pay his or her indebtedness. If the parties intend that the receipt of negotiable instruments or accounts receivable be treated as a discharge of the obligation, they must so specify.

WHAT IS GOOD EVIDENCE OF PAYMENT AND DISCHARGE? As to what constitutes acceptable evidence of payment and discharge, a receipt given by the creditor will usually suffice. Such receipt should clearly indicate the amount paid and specify the transaction to which it relates. However, the creditor may be able to rebut the receipt by evidence that it was in error or that it was given under mistake.

A cancelled check is also evidence of payment, but the evidence is more conclusive when the purpose for which it is given is stated on the check. The drawer of a check may specify on the instrument that the payee by endorsing or cashing it acknowledges full satisfaction of an obligation of the drawer.

Mutual debts do not extinguish each other. For one debt to constitute payment of another, in whole or in part, there must be agreement between the creditor and debtor that the one shall be applied in satisfaction of the other.

How is Payment Applied to Multiple Debts? Where a debtor owes several obligations to one creditor, the debtor may direct how any payment is to be applied. The creditor who receives such payment is obligated to follow the debtor's instructions. In the absence of any instructions, the creditor may apply the payment against any one of several obligations that are due. The creditor may, also, credit a portion of the payment against a claim that has been discharged by the statute of limitations, but this will not cause this claim to revive as to the unpaid balance.

If the source of a payment is someone other than the debtor and this fact is known to the creditor, the payment must be applied in such a manner as to protect the third party who makes the payment. Hence, if the money for the payment is supplied by a party who has guaranteed that a particular obligation will be paid by the debtor, and the creditor knows it, the creditor is bound to apply the payment on the obligation for which the guarantor is liable.

Finally, if the creditor fails to make a particular application, the payment will be applied by the courts to the obligation oldest in point of time. However, where the creditor holds both secured and unsecured obligations, the courts of most states are inclined to apply it on an unsecured obligation. Similarly, if both principal and interest are due, the court considers the interest to be paid first, with any balance being credited on the principal.

The application of these rules often has serious consequences. Debtors who are paying their own debts or whose debts are being paid by others should always direct that the payment be applied to the intended debt.

19. Accord and Satisfaction

An *accord* is an agreement whereby one of the parties undertakes to give or to perform something different from what was contracted for, and the other party agree to accept something different from what he or she is entitled to. An accord may arise from a disputed claim in either tort or contract. The term *satisfaction* means that the substituted performance is completed.

The doctrine of accord and satisfaction requires that there be a dispute or uncertainty as to amount due and that the parties enter into an agreement that debtor will pay, and the creditor will accept, a stated amount as a compromise of their differences and in satisfaction of the debt. It must clearly appear that the parties so understood and entered into a new and substitute contract. The surrender of the legal right to litigate the dispute or the settlement agreement often serves as consideration.

The usual accord and satisfaction case involves a debtor's sending a creditor a check for less than the amount claimed by the creditor to be due. This check is usually marked "Paid in full." The courts of a few states hold that the cashing of the check constitutes an accord and satisfaction without additional proof. Most states, however, require that the party asserting the accord and satisfaction also prove (1) that the debt or claim was in fact the subject of a bona fide dispute, (2) that the creditor was aware of the dispute, and (3) that the creditor was aware that the check was tendered as full payment.

Assuming that these three elements are present, if the creditor cashes the check, the creditor cannot change the language of the check, deposit it, or cash it and still contend that there was no accord and satisfaction. If the creditor cashes the check, this act constitutes the satisfaction of the accord and completes the discharge.

20. Statute of Limitations

The *statute of limitations* prescribes a time limit within which the lawsuit must be started after a cause of action arises. Failure to file suit within the time prescribed is an affirmative defense to the suit.

The purpose of a statute of limitations is to prevent actions from being brought long after evidence is lost or important witnesses have died or moved away. An action for breach of any contract for sale of personal property under the Code must be commenced within four years [2-725]. The Code further provides that the parties in their agreement may reduce the period of limitation to not less than one year but may not extend it. Contracts that are not controlled by the Code are covered by a variety of limitation periods. Some states distinguish between oral and written contracts, making the period longer for the latter.

Any voluntary part payment made on a money obligation by the debtor with intent to pay the balance tolls the statute, starting it to run anew. Similarly, any voluntary part payment, new promise, or clear acknowledgment of the indebtedness made after the claim has been discharged reinstates the obligation; and the statute commences to run again. A payment or part payment by a third person or a joint debtor does not operate to interrupt the running of the statute as to other debtors not participating in the payment. No new consideration is required to support the reinstatement promise. If the old obligation has been outlawed, a new promise may be either partial or conditional. Since there is no *duty* to pay the debt, the debtor may attach such conditions to the new promise as he or she sees fit or may promise to pay only part of the debt. A few states require the new promise or acknowledgment to be in writing. The Code does not alter the law on tolling of the statute of limitations [2-725 (4)].

A problem exists when a party is incapacitated by minority or insanity. Most jurisdictions hold that lack of capacity stops the running of the statute and extends the period of filing suit. A minor or an insane person usually has a specified time in which to bring an action—after the minor reaches his or her majority or the insane person regains capacity—although the full period set by statute has expired earlier.

CHAPTER SUMMARY

CONDITIONS

Definition

1. A condition is an act or event that limits or qualifies a promise.
2. A duty to perform is conditional if something other than the passage of time must occur before performance is due.
3. Conditions set the order of performance and prevent lawsuits by establishing defenses if conditions do not occur.
4. Failure of a promise gives rise to a remedy for breach; a failure of condition only excuses performance.

Types of Conditions

1. Conditions may be classified in terms of time (conditions precedent, concurrent, and subsequent) or manner of creation (express or constructive).
2. A condition precedent is an act or event that, unless excused, must occur before a duty to perform is activated.

3. Conditions concurrent require the parties to exchange performances at the same time.
4. A condition subsequent is an act or event that discharges a duty that had previously become absolute.

Express Conditions

1. An express condition is specifically stated by the parties' agreement as activating or discharging duties.
2. Express conditions must be strictly satisfied.

Express Conditions of Personal Satisfaction

1. If a condition involves personal taste or judgment, dissatisfaction is judged by a subjective standard. If good-faith dissatisfaction exists, the condition is not met.
2. If a condition involves mechanical fitness, utility, or marketability, an objective standard of dissatisfaction is used to decide if the condition has been met.

Constructive Conditions

1. A court-created condition is imposed to serve justice.
2. Substantial performance of constructive conditions will make the other party's duty to perform absolute.

PERFORMANCE OF CONDITIONS

Tender of Performance

1. Tender is an offer to perform. The party making the tender indicates that he or she is ready, willing, and able to perform.
2. Tender of payment by the buyer is a condition to the seller's duty to deliver the goods.
3. Tender by the seller occurs when the goods are available to the buyer. The seller must give reasonable notice that the goods are available.

Substantial Performance

1. Substantial performance of a constructive condition is required to make the other party's duty absolute.
2. Substantial performance is not full performance and is an immaterial breach.
3. Failure to perform at the proper time is not substantial performance if time was of the essence.

Divisibility: Installment Contracts

1. A party can recover for performance of divisible portions of a contract.
2. Breach of one part of a divisible contract does not allow the other party to refuse to pay for the part performed.

Anticipatory Repudiation

1. Before the time for performance, a party may expressly or implicitly repudiate his or her duty to perform. If the party does so, it is an anticipatory repudiation.
2. The repudiation is not favored and must be shown to be clear, positive, and unequivocal.
3. A repudiation may be withdrawn unless the other party relied on it.

EXCUSES FOR NONPERFORMANCE

Hindrance, Prevention, or Noncooperation

1. Wrongful conduct by a party that unduly hinders or prevents the other party's performance will excuse that performance.
2. Wrongful conduct is conduct that was not reasonably contemplated or the risk of which was not assumed by the nonperforming party.

Waiver

1. Waiver is a voluntary and intentional relinquishment of express or constructive conditions.
2. A waiver may be retracted unless it is supported by consideration or the other party has relied on the waiver.
3. A waiver may be made prior to or after a party has breached the agreement.

Impossibility of Performance

1. When an unforeseen event makes performance impossible, all duties to perform are excused.
2. Occurrence of reasonably foreseeable events will not excuse duties to perform.
3. Change in market price, strikes, accidents, unavailability of materials, and governmental regulations are normally foreseeable.
4. Acts of God, supervening illegalities, war, and death of a party or destruction of the contract's subject matter are normally unforeseeable.

Specific Cases of Impossibility

1. If the contractual performance becomes illegal, the performance is excused.
2. The death or incapacitating illness of a contracting party excuses his or her performance.
3. The destruction of the subject matter that is essential to the contract's performance excuses such performance.
4. When an essential element for contractual performance is lacking, such performance is excused.

Commercial Frustration

1. This is an intervening event or change of circumstances that was not foreseeable and that prevents achievement of the object or purpose of the contract.
2. The purpose or object frustrated must have been the basic purpose or object of the contract from the time the contract was made.

Commercial Impracticability under the Code

1. If the contract can be performed but performance is unduly burdensome, impracticability may excuse performance.
2. This is an excuse for unforeseeable events. However, events such as strikes, government regulation, increased costs, or unavailable material generally are viewed as being foreseeable.

DISCHARGE OF CONTRACTS

Methods

1. The term discharge describes the cancellation of a contract and the acts by which enforcement of its provisions is terminated.
2. The usual method of discharge is performance.
3. A contract may also be discharged as the result of excuses for nonperformance, a mutual release of terms, rescission either by agreement of the parties or operation of law, novation, accord and satisfaction, and the expiration of the period of the statute of limitations.
4. The intentional destruction of a negotiable instrument is a form of cancellation.

Payment

1. A check constitutes only conditional payment.
2. If a debtor owes several obligations, the debtor may specify which is being paid.
3. If the debtor fails to specify, the creditor may apply it to any debt.
4. If the payment is by a third party, it must be applied to the debt on which the third party is obligated.

Accord and Satisfaction

1. An accord is an agreement to change a contract, and the satisfaction is the performance of the accord.
2. If the parties agree to settle a dispute either in contract or tort, there is an accord and satisfaction. The consideration is the agreement not to litigate the dispute.

Statute of Limitations

1. The statute of limitations prescribes a time limit beyond which a suit cannot be brought on a claim.
2. There are various time periods for contracts and torts, and these vary from state to state.

3. The Code period is four years.
4. Various events may toll the running of the statute and commence the period over again. These include payment, part payment, and a new promise to pay.

REVIEW QUESTIONS AND PROBLEMS

1. Match each term in Column A with the appropriate statement in Column B.

A	B
(1) Condition precedent	(a) An unforeseen event that makes performance unattainable
(2) Discharge by operation of law	(b) Rescission, release, novation, accord and satisfaction
(3) Impossibility	(c) Condition that discharges a contract duty
(4) Waiver	(d) An act or event that limits or qualifies a contract duty
(5) Anticipatory repudiation	(e) Unforeseen intervening event that prevents fulfillment of contract's main purpose
(6) Condition	(f) Party clearly indicates nonperformance
(7) Commercial frustration	(g) Offer to perform
(8) Discharge by party's agreement	(h) Contract avoidance, bankruptcy, and statute of limitations
(9) Tender	(i) Condition that activates a contract duty
(10) Condition subsequent	(j) A voluntary, intentional relinquishment of a condition

2. Totten hired Lampenfeld to paint his house. Totten agreed to pay in installments as the painting progressed. While Totten was on vacation, Lampenfeld started painting the house. When Totten returned, he refused to pay for the partial painting. Since he was not paid as agreed, Lampenfeld refused to complete the painting. Lampenfeld sued Totten for the value of the painting he had done. Totten claimed that Lampenfeld had materially breached the contract by not finishing the job and thus should recover nothing. Was Totten's payment for the partial painting a condition precedent to Lampenfeld's duty to complete painting the house? Explain.
3. John contracts with Fay to install a heating system in Fay's factory for a price of $30,000 to be paid "on condition of satisfactory completion." John installs the heating system, but Fay states that she is not satisfied with it and refuses to pay the $30,000. Fay gives no reason except that she does not approve of the heating system. According to experts, the heating system as installed is entirely satisfactory. May John successfully recover $30,000 from Fay? Explain why or why not.
4. Harte contracted with Connolly to install a new roof on Connolly's house. It was agreed that the roofing shingles were to be "russet glow," a shade of brown. The roof was installed, and many of the shingles were discolored, showing streaks of yellow. Harte replaced some of the shingles, but the new shingles did not match the others. The overall appearance of

the roof is that it has been patched with nonblending colors. The roof is functional and is guaranteed to last fifteen years. Must Connolly pay? Why or why not? Would your answer change if Harte were building a house for Connolly and on the scheduled completion date had done everything required by the contract except grading and paving? Why or why not?

5. Rick agreed to buy two campers from McMahon and made a deposit of $1,000 as partial payment. Rick then wired McMahon not to ship the campers and explained his reasons for delaying shipment. Later, Rick decided not to buy the campers and demanded a return of his $1,000. Was Rick's instruction not to ship an anticipatory repudiation that will justify McMahon's retention of the $1,000? Explain.
6. Wells contracted with the state to erect a building according to the state's specifications and to lease it to the state. Time was made of the essence in the contract. Wells completed the building two months late. The state canceled the contract and leased space elsewhere. Wells sued and proved at trial that the delay was caused by the state's failure to indicate locations for electrical fixtures, outlets, and other details as required by the contract. Did Wells win? Why or why not?
7. A real estate broker contracted to sell a piece of land to Marilyn Curry. At her request, the contract states, "This contract is contingent upon the buyer obtaining a rezoning for a mobile home park and campground. This contract is to be void if the rezoning is not obtained within 120 days." After sixty-five days, Curry notifies the broker that she would buy the property, irrespective of a zoning change. The zoning change was not obtained during the 120-day period. The broker now refuses to convey, and Curry sues. Who wins? Why?
8. Pate, a contractor, agreed with the city of Kiteville to construct a golf course for the amount of $230,329.88. After Pate had completed all the clearing and dirt work, a torrential rainfall of 12.4 inches occurred in a ten-hour period. It will cost $60,000 to restore the golf course to its condition prior to the rain. Is Pate relieved from the contract by the doctrine of commercial frustration? Explain why or why not.
9. Draper agreed to sell a lot to Mohrland for $14,875. As a part of the agreement, Draper agreed to relocate a gas line that crossed the property. After signing the agreement, Draper found out that it would cost $10,050 to move the gas line. Should this fact excuse Draper's performance of the contract? Why or why not?
10. Barcomb Motor Sales agreed to purchase two bus bodies from School Lines, Inc., for the price of $46,464. School Lines required payment in full before delivery. Barcomb Motor delivered a check in the a mount of the purchase price to School Lines, and Barcomb Motors's agents picked up the bus bodies. Later, Barcomb Motor's president stopped payment on the check and issued a new check in the amount of $45,064.66, the difference representing various costs incurred by Barcomb Motor in connection with the transaction. The language "Payment in full for bus bodies Serial #'s B18550 and B18551" appeared on the back of Barcomb Motor's new check. School Lines cashed the check after indorsing it in the words, "Accepted as Partial Payment." School Lines sued Barcomb Motor for the balance of the agreed-on purchase price. Barcomb Motor claimed that School Lines' acceptance and cashing of the check effected an accord and satisfaction. Was the amount owed School Lines but withheld by Barcomb Motor the subject of a bona fide dispute so the doctrine of accord and satisfaction would apply? Explain.

Contract Rights of Third Parties | 20

CHAPTER OUTLINE

CHAPTER PREVIEW

The discussion of contracts up to this point has dealt with the law of contracts as applied to the contracting parties. However, frequently persons who are not original parties to the contracts may have rights and even duties under the contract. The rights and duties of third parties may come into play when there is (1) a *third-party beneficiary contract*—one party contracts with a second party for the purpose of conferring a benefit on a third party (beneficiary); (2) an assignment of the contract—an original party to a contract (assignor) transfers to a third party (assignee) the rights or duties under the contract; or (3) a *novation*—a new third party becomes a party to an existing contract as a substitute for one of the original parties.

BUSINESS MANAGEMENT DECISION

You are a loan officer at a local bank. You read in the newspaper that one of your delinquent borrowers has won a $250,000 verdict in a products liability suit. Upon contacting this borrower about payment, you arrange for an assignment to your bank of the borrower's rights against the negligent defendant.

What should your bank do as the assignee of this claim?

THIRD-PARTY BENEFICIARY CONTRACTS

1. Nature of Such Contracts

Contracts are often made for the express purpose of benefiting some third party. Such contracts, called *third-party beneficiary contracts,* are of two *types—donee-beneficiary* and *creditor-beneficiary.* Both types of third-party beneficiaries are entitled to enforce a contract made in their behalf because the original parties provide that the benefits shall go to the beneficiary.

Donee-beneficiary
A third party who receives a gift when a promisee secures a promise from a promisor for the purpose of making a gift to a third party

DONEE-BENEFICIARY If the promise of the promisor was contracted for by the promisee to make a gift to the third party, such third party is a **donee-beneficiary**. The most typical example of such an agreement is a contract for life insurance in which the beneficiary is someone other than the insured. The insured has made a contract with the life insurance company for the purpose of conferring a benefit on a third party, namely the beneficiary named in the policy.

Creditor-beneficiary
A third party who receives the benefits of a contract made between two contracting parties for the purpose of paying one original party's debt to the third party

CREDITOR-BENEFICIARY If the promisee has contracted for a promise to pay a debt that he or she owes to a third party, such third party is a **creditor-beneficiary**. In this situation, the debtor arranges to purchase the promise of the other contracting party to satisfy the obligation owed to the third party. The promisee obtains a benefit because his or her obligation to the creditor presumably will be satisfied.

A life insurance policy is an example of a third party contract

FIGURE 20-1 ■ Source of Contract Law

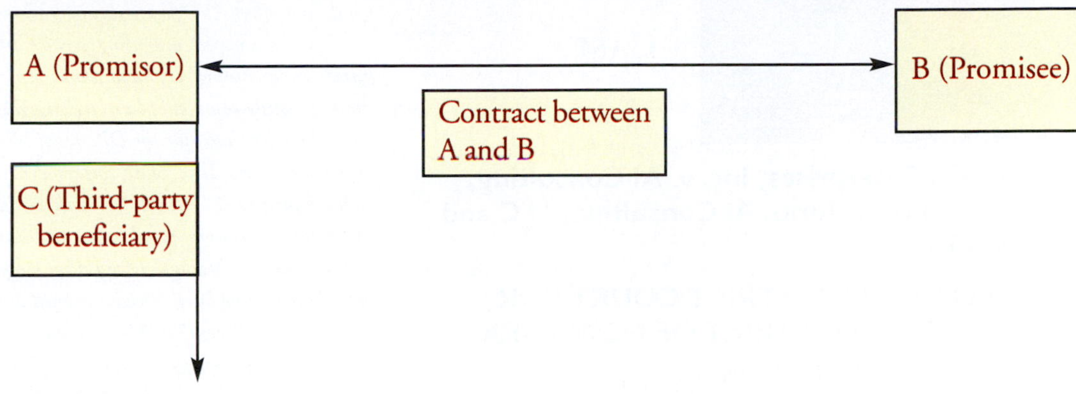

For example, A operates a department store. He sells his furniture, fixtures, and inventory to B, who, as part of the bargain, agrees to pay all of A's business debts. A's purpose for making this contract was to have his debts paid, and he obtained B's promise to pay them to confer a benefit on his creditors. A's creditors are creditor-beneficiaries and can enforce their claims directly against B. Of course, to the extent that B does not pay them, the creditors still have recourse against A.

2. Legal Requirements

A third-party beneficiary may enforce performance of a contractual promise, even though the third-party beneficiary was not a party that created the contract. However, the third-party beneficiary is not entitled to enforce such a contractual provision unless he or she can establish that the parties actually *intended* to benefit him (an "intended beneficiary"). This party must be something more than a mere **incidental beneficiary**. If the benefit to the third party is only incidental, the beneficiary cannot sue.

Incidental beneficiary

A third person who would only indirectly benefit from the performance of a contract and thus has no right to enforce the original contract

The intent to benefit the third party must clearly appear from the terms of the contract. The intent to benefit a third party is more easily inferred in creditor-beneficiary situations than in donee-beneficiary ones. The third party need not be named as an individual in the contract if he or she can show that he or she is a member of a group for whose direct benefit the contract was made. A third-party beneficiary need not have knowledge of the contract at the time it was made. The fact that the actual contracting party could also sue to enforce the agreement would not bar a suit by the beneficiary if he or she was intended to benefit directly from the contract. A third-party beneficiary need not be the exclusive beneficiary of the promise.

A contract made for the express purpose of benefiting a third party generally may not be rescinded without the consent of the beneficiary after its terms have been accepted by the beneficiary. The latter has a vested interest in the agreement from the moment it is made and accepted. For example, an insurance company has no right to change the named beneficiary in a life insurance policy without the consent of the beneficiary unless the contract gives the insured the right to make this change. Until the third-party beneficiary has either accepted or acted on provisions of a contract for his or her benefit, the parties to the contract may change the provisions and deny the beneficiary the benefits of the contract. Minors, however, are presumed to accept a favorable contract upon its execution, and such contract may not be changed to deprive the minor of its benefits.

The court in the following case examined whether a company was an intended or an incidental beneficiary.

CASE

@Wireless Enterprises, Inc. v. AI Consulting, LLC and Andrew Iorio, AI Consulting, LLC and Andrew Iorio

UNITED STATES DISTRICT COURT FOR THE WESTERN DISTRICT OF NEW YORK

2006 U.S. Dist. LEXIS 79874 (2006)

At all relevant times, Verizon was a wireless communications service provider, which sold cellular radio service and equipment through its own retail stores, as well as through agents. @Wireless sold cellular communications services. In August 2000, Verizon and @Wireless entered into an "Authorized Agency Agreement," in which Verizon appointed @Wireless as a "non-exclusive sales agent" for Verizon's cellular radio service. The agreement provided that @Wireless could delegate its obligations under the contract to "a subcontractor or sub-agent," by written contract, subject to the express written approval of Verizon. The agreement further stated: "Personnel employed by, or acting under the authority of, Agent shall not be or be deemed to be employees or agents of Verizon Wireless, and Agent assumes full responsibility for their acts and shall have sole responsibility for their supervision and control."

Exercising its right to hire sub-agents, @Wireless entered into a franchise agreement with third-party plaintiff AI Consulting ("AI") in March 2002, in exchange for a $145,000 franchise fee payment from AI to @Wireless. Subsequently, AI operated a retail outlet as an @Wireless franchisee in Southington, Connecticut. During the course of the business relationship between AI and @Wireless, AI dealt directly with third-party defendant Craig Jerabeck ("Jerabeck"), who was at all relevant times President of @Wireless. According to AI, Jerabeck told AI that he would "protect the interests of AI."

Unbeknownst to AI, between 2002 and 2004, @Wireless repeatedly breached the agreement with Verizon by, for example, selling products and services of Verizon's competitors. Although Verizon gave @Wireless numerous opportunities to cure the breaches, @Wireless continued to breach the agreement. AI contends that third-party defendant Linx, of which Jerabeck was the President and sole shareholder, and which was "affiliated" with @Wireless, also made unauthorized sales of Verizon's products on its website during this period. Verizon complained to Jerabeck about the actions of both @Wireless and 5Linx; and, according to AI, Jerabeck indicated that @Wireless and 5Linx would cease making unauthorized sales. AI contends, however, that Jerabeck lied, and that both @Wireless and 5Linx continued as before. Jerabeck did not inform AI of these unauthorized sales by @Wireless and 5Linx or of the resulting problems with Verizon. For example, Jerabeck did not inform AI that, in July 2004, Verizon had notified @Wireless that it was in breach of the agreement and that Verizon had decided to terminate the agreement. Instead, on or about September 10, 2004, Jerabeck sent an email to AI, informing it only that @Wireless was in the process of negotiating a new contract with Verizon, which would not affect AI's "day to day operations."

Verizon stopped providing service to @Wireless and @Wireless's franchises, including A1, on or about September 16, 2004. Verizon also simultaneously commenced an action against @Wireless in the United States District Court for the District of New Jersey. @Wireless then sued Verizon in New York State Supreme Court, Monroe County, on or about September 21, 2004. @Wireless and Verizon subsequently settled the lawsuits and terminated their agreement. As a result, @Wireless and its franchises, including A1, could no longer lawfully sell Verizon products. A short time later, Verizon opened a competing retail store "almost immediately adjacent" to AI's business.

As for the claims against Verizon, AI contends, on one hand, that Verizon's decision to terminate the agreement with @Wireless had "nothing to do" with AI. Nonetheless, AI seeks to hold Verizon liable for its business losses, since the termination of that agreement "killed off" AI's business. Finally, AI alleges that it was somehow improper for Verizon to open a competing shop near AI's store, after Verizon had terminated the agency agreement with @Wireless.

As for Verizon's motion, Verizon contends that AI's contractual claims must fail because there was no contract between them and because AI had no rights as a third-party beneficiary of the contract between Verizon and @Wireless.

AI alleges that 5Linx and Verizon are each liable for breach of contract and breach of the warranty of good faith and fair dealing.

As to the claims against Verizon, AI alleges that Verizon "caused the breach in the provisions of the interlocking contracts existing between" AI, @Wireless, and Verizon, and also "violated a number of affirmative or implied representations" to AI. However, despite AI's conclusory reference to "interlocking contracts," the complaint does not indicate any privity of contract between AI and Verizon.

AI is not a party to the contract between Verizon and @Wireless. Nor is AI a third-party beneficiary of that agreement. As to any third-party beneficiary claims,

> [a] party asserting rights as a third-party beneficiary must establish (1) the existence of a valid and binding contract between other parties, (2) that the contract was intended for his benefit and (3) that the benefit to him is sufficiently immediate, rather than incidental, to indicate the assumption by the contracting parties of a duty to compensate him if the benefit is lost.

It is well settled that sub-contractors and sub-agents are not third-party beneficiaries.

Here, there is no indication that the agreement between Verizon and @Wireless was for the benefit of AI. Rather, AI is merely a sub-agent or sub-contractor. Accordingly, the contract claims against Verizon are dismissed.

■ *Remanded.*

CASE CONCEPTS REVIEW

1. Why was there no intended beneficiary in the case?
2. What is the difference between a sub-agent and a third-party beneficiary?

ASSIGNMENTS

3. Terminology

Obligor
A debtor or promisor

Obligee
A creditor or promisee

Assignment
A transfer of the rights under a contract and it may include a delegation of the duties of the assignor

Assignor
One who makes an assignment

Assignee
One to whom an assignment is made

A bilateral contract creates rights for each party and imposes, on each, corresponding *duties.* Each party is an **obligor** (has an obligation to perform the duties), and each is an **obligee** (is entitled to receive the performance of the other). Either party may desire to transfer to another his or her rights o rights an duties. A party *assigns* rights and*delegates* duties.

The term **assignment** may mean a transfer of one's rights under a contract, or it may mean a transfer both of rights and duties. The phrase *assignment of the contract* is confusing because it does not specify whether rights or duties or both are being transferred. When the contracting parties use this ambiguous term, courts usually interpret it to mean that rights were assigned and duties were delegated. To further complicate our terminology, regardless of whether rights or duties are involved in a transfer, the person making the transfer is called the **assignor**; the one receiving the transfer is called the **assignee**.

4. General Principles

The next seven sections discuss the legal aspects of assignments in detail. By summarizing some of these principles, this section serves as an introduction to the more detailed discussion. In essence, five points about assignments should remain at the forefront of your understanding.

First, no particular formality is essential to an assignment. Consideration, although usually present, is not required. As a general proposition, an assignment may be either oral or written although it is, of course, desirable to have a written assignment. Some statutes require a writing in

FIGURE 20-2 ■ Assignments

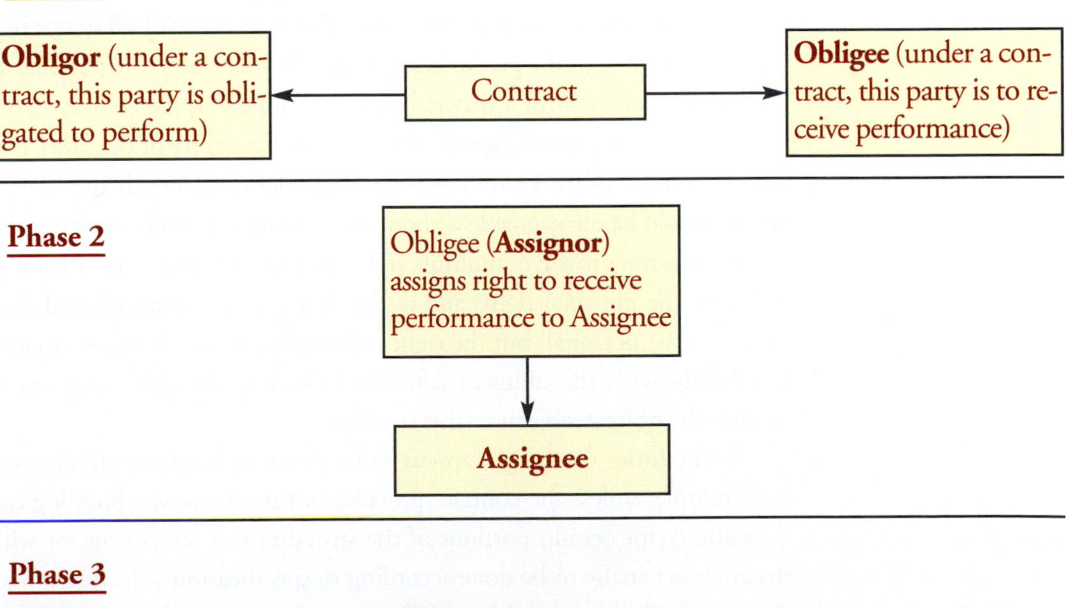

certain assignment situations. For example, an assignment of an interest in real property must be in writing, in most states.

Second, consent of the non-assigning party generally is not required when the assignor transfers rights or duties to the assignee. The next two sections describe a number of exceptions to this general rule.

Third, the rights and duties arising under an original contract usually are freely assignable. Contracting parties frequently include antiassignment clauses in their agreements. The impact of the clause is discussed in Section 7. The assignability of contracts involving the claims and payment of money is the subject matter of Section 8.

Fourth, an assignment is a completed transaction that simply involves another contract. The main feature of an assignment is a *present transfer* of a contract right. After the assignment, the assignor has no interest in the contract right. The assignor's right belongs exclusively to the assignee. The rights of the assignee are discussed in Section 9.

Fifth, a person who has duties under a contract cannot relieve himself or herself of those duties by transferring the contract or delegating the duties to another person. An obligor that delegates duties, as well as assigns rights, is not thereby relieved of liability for proper performance if the assignee fails to perform. In general, an assignor continues to be responsible for the ultimate performance. The continuing duty of the assignor and the obligations of the assignee, such as to give notice of the assignment, are the subject matter of Sections 10 and 11.

5. Consent Required

To understand when assignments may or may not be made without the consent of the non-assigning party, you must keep in mind that contracts involve both rights and duties of the parties.

As a general rule, contract *rights* may be assigned by one party without the consent of the other party. In most contracts, it is immaterial to the party performing who receives the performance. However, there are certain exceptions to this general rule.

Of the several classes of contracts that may not be transferred *without the consent* of the other party, the most important are contracts involving *personal rights or personal duties.* A personal right or duty is one in which personal trust and confidences are involved or one in which skill, knowledge, or experience of one of the parties is important. In such cases, the personal acts and qualities of one or both of the parties form a material and integral part of the contract. For example, a lease contract where the rent is a percentage of sales based on the ability of the lessee would be unassignable without the consent of the lessor. Likewise, a contract requiring the performance of service of a specific person would be unassignable without the consent of the other party to the original contract.

If a contract involves multiple rights and duties, those that are not personal may be assigned. It is only the personal rights and duties that my not be transferred. Frequently the duty to perform may be personal, but the right to payment is not. In these situations, the duty can be delegated only with the obligee's consent. However, the right to payment may be assigned even though the obligor objects to this transfer.

Some duties that might appear to be personal in nature are not considered so by the courts. For example, unless the contract provides to the contrary, a building contractor may delegate responsibility for certain portions of the structure to a subcontractor without consent. Since construction is usually to be done according to specifications, the duties are delegable. It is presumed that all contractors are able to follow specifications. Of course, the assignee must substantially complete the building according to the plans and specifications. The obligor will not be obligated to pay for it if it is not, and the assignor will be liable in event of default by the assignee.

Purchasing property on credit does not give you the right to assign that right to purchase to a third party

Another example of a contract that is unassignable without consent is one in which an assignment would place an *additional burden or risk on a party*—one not contemplated at the time of the agreement. Such appears to be true of an assignment of the right to purchase on credit. Most states hold that one who has agreed to purchase property on credit, and has been given the right to do so, may not assign his or her right to purchase the property to a third party (assignee) since the latter's credit may not be as good as that of the original contracting party—the assignor. This reasoning is questionable because the seller could hold both the assignor and the assignee responsible. However, the inconvenience to the seller in connection with collecting has influenced most courts to this result. However, in contracts where the seller has security for payment, such as retention of title to the property or a security interest in the property, the seller has such substantial protection that the courts have held that the right to purchase on credit is assignable.

Finally, it is important to note that the assignor is not relieved of the original liability under the contract just because the non-assigning party has consented to the delegation of duties. This general statement is equally applicable to those delegations that require the consent of the non-assigning party as to those that do not.

For example, assume that Ryder leases a truck to the Transportation Equipment Company. Later, Transportation Equipment, with the approval of Ryder, assigns the truck rental contract to Williams Transfer, which agrees to pay the rent. When Williams subsequently fails to pay the rent for the truck, Ryder could hold Transportation Equipment liable for the balance due on the truck lease.

6. Consent Required under the Code

The Code contains provisions that generally approve the assignment of rights and delegation of duties by buyers and sellers of goods. The duties of either party may be delegated *unless* the parties have agreed otherwise or the nondelegating party has "… a substantial interest in having his original promisor perform or control the acts required by the contract" [2-210(1)]. Accordingly, a seller can ordinarily delegate to someone else the duty to perform the seller's obligations under the contract. This would occur when no substantial reason exists why the delegated performance would be less satisfactory than the personal performance of the assignor.

The Code does provide that rights cannot be assigned here the assignment would materially change the duty of the other party, or increase materially the burden or risk imposed on him or her by the contract, or impair materially his or her chance of obtaining return performance [2-210(2)]. These Code provisions in effect incorporate the personal rights and duties exception previously discussed.

7. Antiassignment Clauses

Some contracts contain a clause stating that the contract cannot be assigned without the consent of the other party. Older cases often held these clauses to be against public policy and unenforceable as an unlawful restraint on alienation (right to sell one's property). Recognizing freedom of contract, modern courts usually uphold the clause prohibiting assignment and find it legally operative. Nonetheless, looking to the language of the clause in non-Code cases, courts have reached different results.

VARYING INTERPRETATIONS Some courts hold that if the clause *prohibits* assignment, this creates a promise (*duty* in the assignor) not to assign; but the assignor still has the power to assign. Thus the assignment is effective, but the obligor has a legal claim against the assignor for breach of his or her *promise* (duty) not to assign. Others hold that the clause *invalidates* the contract. The assignment is still effective, but the obligor has an option to avoid the contract for breach of the condition. Still others allow the parties to prohibit an assignment. Any purported assignment is void in these states, and the assignment itself is ineffective. Rather than merely creating a *duty* (promise) not to assign, this invalidation clause deprives any party of the power to assign.

The extent of an antiassignment clause is determined in the following case.

CASE

Phillip Traicoff, d/b/a Renegade Studios vs. Digital Media, Inc., and Staffing Tools, Inc., and Delbert Craig Hane, Graphic Computer Solutions Online University, Colorblind, Vantage Partners, LLC, Imaging Technologies, Inc., and Imaging Technologies Corp.

UNITED STATES DISTRICT COURT FOR THE SOUTHERN DISTRICT OF INDIANA

439 F. Supp. 2d 872 (2006)

JOHN DANIEL TINDER, JUDGE.

Plaintiff, Phillip Traicoff d/b/a Renegade Studios, brings this suit against Digital Media, Inc. ("Digital Media"), Staffing Tools, Inc ("Staffing Tools"), and Delbert Craig Hane (collectively, the "Defendants") claiming breach of contract, copyright infringement, and fraud. In addition, Graphic Computer Solutions Online University, Colorblind, Vantage Partners, LLC, Imaging Technologies, Inc., and Imaging Technologies Corporation remain named defendants in this case. Currently before the court are the Defendants' motions for summary judgment and the Plaintiff's cross-motion for summary judgment.

In the mid–1990s, three technologically savvy individuals, Michael Budd, lan Creighton, and Dan Hoover, formed Digital Media. Digital Media developed computer software programs to train computer users on how to use various other kinds of computer programs. The computer software programs contained a voice component in which the program would actually speak to the user of the teaching/learning software as part of the training.

From 1996 to 2001, the Plaintiff worked for Digital Media as a shipping clerk and salesperson. The Plaintiff also owned a recording studio. In 1998, the Plaintiff began to work with Digital Media's developers in order to help produce the voice component for the software. Although he worked as an employee for Digital Media in other roles, the Plaintiff performed his recording studio work solely as a subcontractor, not an employee, and received separate pay for his recording work. Typically, the Plaintiff received a script from Digital Media, hired a narrator to read the script in his recording studio, edited the script during the recording process, created a digital recording of the script, and turned the recording over to Digital Media to use as the voice component in the software programs.

On September 13, 2001, Michael Budd, Chief Executive Officer of Digital Media at the time, fired the Plaintiff from his employment position with Digital Media. In February 2002, Michael Budd resigned from his position with Digital Media and Delbert Craig Hane became the President of the company. On March 8, 2002, the Plaintiff entered into a written contract with Digital Media in which the Plaintiff agreed to grant Digital Media the right to use the Plaintiff's audio recordings in exchange for 50,000 shares of stock in Digital Media "[i]n lieu of fifty thousand dollars ($50,000.00)." The contract further stated that "this contract is not assignable by [Digital Media] and shall be binding upon the heirs, legal representatives, successor and assigns of the parties hereto." (Id.)

At some point previous to this time, around September 2001, Hane created a second entity, Staffing Tools, to continue selling the software at issue. In September 2001, Digital Media and Staffing Tools entered into a licensing agreement in which Digital Media granted Staffing Tools a non-exclusive license to sell its software training programs in exchange for five percent (5%) royalties on those sales. Around the same time, Digital Media lacked the financial resources to continue its operations and it ceased doing business. Digital Media had accrued tremendous debt to multiple creditors, including unpaid payroll taxes owed to the Internal Revenue Service. Its only income was the royalty stream it received from the licensing agreement with Staffing Tools and from a previously signed licensing agreement with a European company, Euro-Sync. Due to Digital Media's large amount of debt and little income, the Plaintiff's stock in Digital Media was worthless. However, Staffing Tools continued to sell the software at issue containing the audio recordings produced by the Plaintiff.

At the center of this case is the March 8, 2002 contract between the Plaintiff and Digital Media. The contract establishes a licensing agreement in which the Plaintiff granted Digital Media "the exclusive right, privilege and license" to use the audio recordings "and to make and/or use arrangements thereof, in the manufacture and sale of parts of voices serving to reproduce the Audio in the United States." In essence, the contract allows Digital Media to sell its computer training programs, which incorporated the Plaintiff's audio recordings, without violating the Plaintiff's copyright rights, if any, in the audio recordings. The contract also contains an anti-assignment provision, specifically stating that "[T]his contract is not assignable by [Digital Media] and shall be binding upon the heirs, legal representatives, successors and assigns of the parties hereto."

In a separate document, Digital Media granted Staffing Tools a non-exclusive license to sell Digital Media's computer training programs. In return, Staffing Tools agreed to pay Digital Media royalties in the amount of five percent (5%) on each sale of the training programs. Subsequently, Staffing Tools allegedly sold numerous copies of the training programs, including programs containing audio material extracted from the Plaintiff's audio recordings.

Accordingly, the Plaintiff claims that Digital Media breached the March 2002 contract, specifically the anti-assignment provision of the contract, by issuing the nonexclusive license to Staffing Tools and that Staffing Tools infringed on the Plaintiff's copyright interest in the audio recordings by selling the training programs without an appropriate license in the audio recordings. In response, the Defendants argue, among other things, that Digital Media did not breach the contract because the anti-assignment clause does not prohibit the assignment of rights under the contract, including the right to use the audio recordings. Likewise, because the anti-assignment clause does not prohibit the assignment of rights under the contract, the Defendants aver that Staffing Tools did not infringe on the Plaintiff's copyright interests in the audio recordings because it properly obtained Digital Media's right to use the audio recordings. The court, therefore, must determine whether the sublicensing agreement between Digital Media and Staffing Tools effectively passed along the right to use the audio recordings to Staffing Tools—in other words, that the sublicensing agreement is within the scope of the Copyright Act of 1976, 17 U.S.C. § 101 et seq. (the "1976 Act" or "Act") and that it does not violate the anti-assignment clause of the March 2002 contract.

At the center of the Plaintiff's arguments is the effect of the anti-assignment clause, included in the March 2002 contract, which states: "This contract is not assignable by [Digital Media] and shall be binding upon the heirs, legal representatives, successors and assigns of the parties hereto." The Plaintiff argues that the anti-assignment clause absolutely prevents Digital Media from sublicensing its rights under the contract to Staffing Tools. Thus, by sublicensing its rights, Digital Media breached its contract with the Plaintiff; and, in turn, Staffing Tools lacked legitimate rights to use the Plaintiff's audio recordings and infringed on the Plaintiff's copyright.

Normal rules of contract construction are generally applied in construing copyright agreements. Indiana common law recognizes the assignment of contractual rights. However, parties may include an anti-assignment provision in the contract, prohibiting (1) the assignment of rights, (2) the assignment of duties, or (3) both; but careful detail must be given to the language of such provision.

In the March 2002 contract, the anti-assignment provision merely prohibits the assignment of "the contract," but failed to detail whether the prohibition applies to the assignment of rights, duties, or both. The Restatement (Second) states that "[u]nless the circumstances indicate the contrary, a contract term prohibiting assignment of "the contract" bars only the delegation to an assignee of the performance by the assignor of a duty or condition."

The March 2002 contract fails to clearly state that the anti-assignment provision was intended to prohibit Digital Media's assignment of rights under the contract. The court, therefore, will apply the generally accepted rule stated above, interpreting the prohibition against the assignment of "the contract" to refer only to the delegation of contractual duties, not assignment of rights. Digital Media's sublicensing agreement with Staffing Tools assigns the latter certain nonexclusive rights, rights that Digital Media gained from the March 2002 contract. The contract's anti-assignment provision fails to preclude the assignment of rights. Consequently, the contract does not prevent Digital Media from assigning a portion of its rights to Staffing Tools in the subsequent sublicensing agreement.

Because the contract does not prevent the assignment of rights to Staffing Tools, Digital Media did not breach its contract. Likewise, the assignment of nonexclusive rights to Staffing Tools granted it the right to use the Plaintiff's audio recordings in the sale of the computer training programs. Therefore, Staffing Tools did not infringe on the Plaintiff's copyright. For these reasons, the court will GRANT summary judgment in favor of Digital Media on the Plaintiff's breach of contract claim, and in favor of Staffing Tools on his copyright infringement claim.

■ *Granted.*

CASE CONCEPTS REVIEW

1. Why did plaintiff's provision only apply to delegations?
2. Given the court's decision, what advice would you give to an entity that wished create an anti-assignment clause that includes both delegations and assignments?

CODE INTERPRETATION The Code has effected significant changes regarding anti-assignment clauses. First, in Article 2 it notes the progressive undermining of the original rule invalidating these clauses. The Code observes that the courts have already construed the heart out of antiassignment clauses. Second, in Article 9 it acknowledges the economic need of freedom of contract rights in modern commercial society. Thus an anti-assignment clause is ineffective to prohibit the assignment of an account or contract right [9-318(4)]. In a sale of business, typically both the rights are assigned and the duties are delegated. Lacking a release, the delegating party is still liable on the duties delegated. Consequently, Article 2 of the Code provides that in a sales situation, a clause prohibiting assignment should be construed as barring only the delegation of duties [2-210(3)]. Therefore, a generally phrased anti-assignment clause is to be read as allowing an assignment of rights but forbidding delegation of duties. Despite the use of the term *antiassignment*, the drafters of the Code took notice that in a sales situation the parties were usually more concerned with delegation than with assignment. Moreover, they saw great commercial need for free assignability of rights and struck the compromise of allowing assignment but prohibiting delegation when confronted with an anti-assignment clause.

8. Claims for Money

As a general rule, claims for money due or to become due under existing contracts may be assigned. An automobile dealer may assign to a bank the right to receive money due under contracts for the sale of automobiles on installment contracts. Although the law tends toward greatly reducing or eliminating the right of employees to assign wages, an employee may assign a portion of his or her pay to a creditor to obtain credit or to satisfy an obligation. However, the Uniform Consumer Credit Code (adopted in several states) provides that a seller cannot take an assignment of earnings for payment of a debt arising out of a consumer credit sale. Lenders also are not allowed to take an assignment of earnings for payment of a debt arising out of a consumer loan. The Consumer Credit Code is a part of the trend toward greater consumer and debtor protection.

When a claim for money is assigned, an issue that frequently arises is the liability of the assignor in case the assignee is unable to collect from the debtor-obligor. If the assignee takes the assignment merely as *security* for a debt owed to him or her by the assignor, it is clear that if the claim is not collected the assignor still has to pay the debt to the assignee. However, if someone *purchases* a claim against a third party, generally the purchaser has no recourse against the seller (assignor) if the third party (debtor-obligor) defaults. If the claim is *invalid* or sold expressly "with recourse," the assignor would be required to reimburse the assignee if the debtor-obligor did not pay.

In all cases, an assignor *warrants* that the claim he or she assigns is a valid, legal claim that the debtor-obligor is really obligated to pay and that there are no valid defenses to the assigned claim. If this *warranty* is breached (that is, if there are valid defenses or the claim is otherwise invalid), the assignee has recourse against the assignor.

9. Rights of the Assignee

An assignment is more than a mere authorization or request to pay or to perform for the assignee rather than the assignor. The obligor-debtor must pay or perform for the assignee, who now, in effect, owns the rights under the contract. If there is a valid assignment, the assignee owns the rights and is entitled to receive them. Performance for the original party will not discharge the contract. Unless the contract provides otherwise, the assignee receives the identical rights of the assignor.

Since the rights of the assignee are neither better nor worse than those of the assignor, any defense the third party (obligor) has against the assignor is available against the assignee. Part payment, fraud, duress, or incapacity can be used as a defense by the third party (obligor) if an action is brought against him or her by the assignee, just as the same defense could have been asserted against the assignor had the assignor been the plaintiff. A common expression defining the status of the assignee is that he or she "stands in the shoes" of the assignor.

Some contracts contain a provision to the effect that "if the seller assigns the contract to a finance company or bank, the buyer agrees that he will not assert against such assignee any defense that he has against the seller-assignor." This *waiver of defense* clause is an attempt to give the contract a quality usually described as *negotiability,* a concept discussed in Chapter 33. Negotiability is a rule that cuts off defenses by giving one party a protected status. If a negotiable instrument is properly negotiated to a party, that party may have a protected status called a **holder in due course**. Thus most defenses of the original party (the buyer) cannot be asserted against the holder in due course (the finance company or bank). The purpose of the concept of negotiability is to encourage the free flow of commercial paper. Adding a provision to a contract that gives it the same effect obviously places the assignee in a favored position and makes contracts with such clauses quite marketable.

Holder in due course

One who has acquired possession of a negotiable instrument through proper negotiation for value, in good faith, and without notice of any defenses to it and, as such is not subject to personal defenses that would otherwise defeat the obligation embodied in the instrument

As a part of the growing movement toward greater consumer protection, the Federal Trade Commission has ruled that such clauses cutting off defenses of consumer-debtors against delinquent sellers when a contract is assigned constitute an unfair method of competition. They are therefore illegal. The commission also has prohibited the use of the holder in due course concept against consumer-debtors. This concept is discussed further in Chapter 35.

10. Duties of the Parties

As previously noted, an assignor is not relieved of his other obligations by a delegation of them to the assignee. The assignor is still liable if the assignee fails to perform as agreed, in which case the assignor would have a cause of action against the assignee. If a party upon the transfer of a contract to a third person wishes to be released of liability, a legal arrangement known as a ***novation*** is required. The requirements for a valid novation are discussed later in this chapter.

Novation

The procedure of three parties agreeing to substitute a third party's obligation for that of one of the original contracting parties

The liability of the assignee to third persons is a much more complicated issue. The liability of the assignee is determined by a careful examination of the transactions to see whether it is an assignment of only the rights under the agreement or whether the duty has also been delegated. This is often difficult to determine when the language used refers only to an "assignment of the contract.

As a general rule, the *mere assignment* of a contract calling for the performance of affirmative duties by the assignor, with nothing more, does not impose those duties on the assignee. As a result, an assignee is not a guarantor of the products sold by the assignor.

Notwithstanding the foregoing situation, *there is a decided trend that holds that an assignment of an entire contract carries an implied assumption of the liabilities.* When the assignee undertakes and agrees to perform the duties as a condition precedent to enforcement of the rights or has assumed the obligation to perform as part of a contract of assignment, he or she has liability for failure to perform. For example, if a tenant assigns a lease, the assignee is not liable for future rents if the assignee vacates the property prior to expiration of the period of the lease, unless the assignee expressly assumes the burdens of the lease at the time of the assignment. The assignee is obligated simply to pay the rent for the period of his or her actual occupancy. To the extent that an assignee accepts the benefits of a contract, he or she becomes obligated to perform the duties that are related to such benefits.

If an "entire contract" has been assigned—that is, if duties have been delegated to the assignee as well as the assignment of the rights—a failure by the assignee to render the required performance gives rise to a cause of action in favor of the third party (obligee). The obligee can sue either the assignor or the assignee or both.

Under the Code, an assignment of "the contract" or of "all my rights under the contract" or an assignment in similar general terms is an assignment of rights; and unless the language or the circumstances (as in an assignment for security) indicate the contrary, it is also a delegation of performance of the duties of the assignor and an assumption of those duties by the assignee. Its acceptance by the assignee constitutes a promise by him or her to perform those duties. This promise is enforceable by either the assignor or the other party to the original contract [2-210(4)].

When the assignor delegates his or her duties, although the assignor remains liable, the obligee may feel insecure as to the ability of the assignee to perform the delegated duties. The obligee may demand that the assignor furnish adequate assurance that the assignee will in fact render proper performance [2-210(5)].

11. Notice of Assignment

Immediately after the assignment, the assignee should notify the obligor or debtor of the assignee's newly acquired right. This notification is essential for two reasons.

First, in the absence of any notice of the assignment, the debtor is at liberty to perform (pay the debt or do whatever else the contract demands) for the original contracting party, the assignor. In fact, the debtor would not know that anyone else had the right to require performance or payment. Thus, the right of the assignee to demand performance can be defeated by his or her failure to give this notice. The assignor who receives performance under such circumstances becomes a trustee of funds or property received from the obligor and can be compelled to turn them over to the assignee. Upon receipt of notice of assignment, the third party *must perform* for the assignee, and the third party's payment or performance to the assignor would not relieve him or her of the obligation to the assignee.

Second, the notice of assignment is also for the protection of innocent third parties. The assignor has the *power,* although not the *right,* to make a second assignment of the same subject matter. If notice of the assignment has been given to the obligor, it has much the same effect as the recording of a mortgage. It furnishes protection for a party who may later consider taking an assignment of the same right. A person considering an assignment should, therefore, always communicate with the debtor to confirm that the right has not previously been assigned. If the debtor has not been notified of a previous assignment and if the prospective assignee is aware of none, in many states the latter can feel free to take the assignment. That assignee should immediately give notice to the debtor. In other words, the first assignee to give notice to the debtor, provided such assignee has no knowledge of a prior assignment, will prevail over a prior assignee in most states.

In some states, it is held that the first party to receive an assignment has a prior claim, regardless of which assignee gave notice first. In these states, the courts act on the theory that the assignor has parted with all his or her interest by virtue of the original assignment and has nothing left to transfer to the second assignee. In all states, however, the party who is injured by reason of the second assignment has a cause of action against the assignor to recover the damages that assignee has sustained. The assignor has committed a wrongful and dishonest act by making a double assignment.

NOVATION

Novation

The procedure of three parties agreeing to substitute a third party's obligation for that of one of the original contracting parties

12. Meaning

Novation (*novo* = new) describes an agreement whereby one of the original parties to a contract is replaced by a new party. The word *novation* originated in Roman law to refer to the *substitution* of a new contract. Thus, when a *new* person becomes a party to a *new* contract by *substitution* to the same rights and duties of an original party, a ovation occurs and discharges the original contract. For example, Tommy, who is indebted to Nancy on an earlier contract, agrees with Nancy and Jesse that in consideration of Nancy's discharging Tommy, Jesse promises to do what Tommy was originally obligated to do. Jesse is thus substituted for Tommy, and a new contract exists between Nancy and Jesse.

13. Application

In this chapter, we have emphasized that an assignor generally is not relieved of the original obligation by delegating the duties to perform to an assignee. The novation in essence is an exception to this general rule. In a novation, *one party is dismissed completely from the contract as a third party is substituted.* In this situation, the dismissed party no longer has any liability under the original contract.

For a novation to be effective, *it must be agreed to by all the parties.* The remaining contracting party must agree to accept the new party and simultaneously specifically agree to release the withdrawing party. The latter must consent to withdraw and to permit the new party to take his or her place. The new party must agree to assume the burdens and duties of the retiring party. The agreement to release a former party and the agreement to assume the duties supplies bargained-for consideration to support the new or substituted contract. Note that a novation is never presumed. The burden of proving all the elements is on the party who claims a novation.

The following case illustrates the nature of a novation.

CASE

James William Burgess and Georgia Burgess v. Jim Walter Homes, Inc.; First Union National Bank

COURT OF APPEALS OF NORTH CAROLINA

588 S.E.2d 575 (2003)

TYSON, JUDGE

Jim Walter Homes, Inc. ("Jim Walter Homes") and First Union National Bank ("FUNB") appeal from the trial court's order denying their motion to stay action pending arbitration. We affirm.

On 27 October 1997, James William Burgess and Georgia Burgess ("plaintiffs") entered into a contract ("1997 contract") with Jim Walter Homes for construction of a house. While executing that contract, plaintiffs also signed a separate arbitration agreement which was incorporated by reference in paragraph nine. The arbitration agreement was attached as Exhibit D to the contract and stated, in part, "The parties agree that … any controversy or claim arising out of or relating to this contract … shall be settled by binding arbitration. … The parties agree and understand that they choose arbitration instead of litigation to resolve disputes." No work was performed by Jim Walter Homes pursuant to the terms of the 1997 contract.

The parties signed a second contract on 14 April 1999 ("1999 contract") for the construction of a house to be built at the same location but with different costs and specifications from those in the 1997 contract. Plaintiffs initialed paragraph nine, identical to paragraph nine signed in the 1997 contract, which states "BUYER ACKNOWLEDGES HAVING READ, UNDERSTOOD AND ACCEPTED THE ARBITRATION AGREEMENT SET FORTH IN EXHIBIT D ATTACHED HERETO AND INCORPORATED BY THIS REFERENCE." No Exhibit D was attached to the 1999 contract. The parties did not execute a separate arbitration agreement.

Subsequent to the signing of the 1999 contract, a controversy arose between the plaintiffs and Jim Walter Homes concerning Jim Walter Homes' performance of the 1999 contract terms. Discussions between the parties ultimately led to mediation. The parties did not reach a settlement.

Jim Walter Homes gave notice on 7 September 2001 that it was exercising its right, under the 1999 contract, to have the dispute arbitrated. A Notice of Commencement of Arbitration was forwarded to the parties on 14 September 2001. The parties held an administrative conference to discuss the procedures for the submission of claims and counterclaims, as well as the final selection of an arbitrator. Plaintiffs filed a complaint and moved for summary determination of the existence of an arbitration agreement, or in the alternative, to set aside any agreement to arbitrate. Jim Walter Homes and FUNB moved to stay action pending arbitration. The trial court determined that no arbitration agreement existed and denied Jim Walter Homes' and FUNB's motion to stay action pending arbitration. Jim Walter Homes and FUNB appeal.

continued

Jim Walter Homes and FUNB argue the trial court erred by concluding that the 1999 contract superseded the 1997 contract and was the only controlling contract.

If the parties do not say whether a new contract is being made, the courts will look to the words of the contracts and the surrounding circumstances, if the words do not make it clear, to determine whether the second contract supersedes the first. If the second contract deals with the subject matter of the first so comprehensively as to be complete within itself or if the two contracts are so inconsistent that the two cannot stand together, a novation occurs.

A novation requires the agreement of the parties that a new contract take the place of an existing obligation. The intention of the parties to effectuate a novation must be clear and definite, for novation is never to be presumed.

Here, the parties expressed their "clear and definite" intent to execute a new contract to supersede the 1997 contract. Paragraph eighteen in the 1999 contract reads "This Building Contract, promissory note, deed of trust and the contract documents executed herewith constitute the entire agreement between the parties hereto with respect to the transactions contemplated herein, and this Building Contract promissory note, deed of trust and the contract documents supersede all prior oral or written agreements, commitments or understandings with respect to the matters provided for herein." (Emphasis supplied).

We conclude that the 1999 contract supersedes the 1997 contract. The 1999 contract did not incorporate by reference the prior 1997 arbitration agreement. Without the execution of a new Exhibit D Arbitration Agreement, Jim Walter Homes and FUNB cannot prove the existence of an agreement to arbitrate all disputes arising out of the 1999 contract. This assignment of error is overruled.

■ *Affirmed.*

CASE CONCEPTS REVIEW

1. Why did the court find a clear intent on the part of both parties to create a novation?
2. What impact did the novation have on the rights of the parties in this dispute?

CHAPTER SUMMARY

THIRD-PARTY BENEFICIARY CONTRACTS

Nature of Third-Party Beneficiary Contracts

1. A noncontracting party may have enforceable contract rights if a party to the contract intended to confer a benefit on the third party.
2. Creditor-and donee-beneficiaries are intended beneficiaries.
3. If performance by the promisor will satisfy a duty owed to the beneficiary by the promisee, the beneficiary is a creditor-beneficiary.
4. If the promisee purchased a promise to make a gift to a third party, the party is a donee-beneficiary.

Legal Requirements

1. If a third party is not an intended beneficiary, he or she is an incidental beneficiary with no right to enforce the agreement.
2. Original parties can modify or rescind their contract until the third party's rights vest.
3. A third party's rights vest when he or she either relies on the contract to his or her detriment or manifests assent to the rights.
4. A third-party beneficiary is subject to all defenses arising out of the contract.

ASSIGNMENTS

Terminology

1. An assignment is a transfer of rights arising from an earlier contract.
2. A delegation is a transfer of duties arising from an earlier contract.
3. When A assigns his or her rights against B to C, A is the assignor, B is the promisor-obligor, and C is the assignee.
4. When A delegates his or her duties owed to B to C, A is the assignor (delegator), B is the promisee-obligee, and C is the assignee (delegatee).
5. "Assignment of the contract is usually held to be both an assignment and a delegation.

General Principles

1. There are no formal requirements for a valid assignment. Generally, neither consideration nor a writing is required.
2. No consent of the nonassigning party usually is required. Thus, contracts are said to be freely assignable.
3. The assignor must completely and irrevocably transfer rights to create an effective assignment.
4. An assignor is not relieved of his or her duties by delegating them to an assignee.

Consent Required

1. Most rights are assignable unless the assignment would (a)materially change the other party's duty, (b) materially increase the burden or risk imposed by the contract, or (c) materially impair the other party's chance of obtaining return performance.
2. The duties under contracts for personal services generally may not be delegated.
3. The right to purchase on credit cannot be assigned without consent in most states.

Consent Required under the Code

1. The Code generally approves the assignment of rights and the delegation of duties.
2. Unless the buyer has a substantial interest in having the seller perform, the seller may delegate the duty to deliver goods.

Antiassignment Clauses

1. Contractual limitations on assignments are strictly construed, in most cases, to prevent only a delegation of duties.
2. A breach of such a clause may be interpreted as (a) breaching the promise not to make an assignment, (b) invalidating the contract, or (c) voiding the assignment.

Claims for Money

1. As a general rule, claims for money may be assigned, but there are statutory exceptions.
2. If the assignment is as security for a debt, the assignor still owes the debt if it remains unpaid by the obligor.
3. If the assignor sells the debt, there is no recourse against the assignor if the obligor defaults.
4. An assignor warrants the genuineness of the money claims assigned.

Rights of the Assignee

1. The assignee may enforce all he rights of his or her assignor.
2. The obligor may raise all defenses against the assignee that the obligor had against the assignor prior to the assignment.
3. Failure of the assignor to fulfill his or her duties to the obligor will be a defense against the assignee.
4. Contract provisions cutting off defenses of consumer-debtors are illegal under a Federal Trade Commission rule.

Duties of the Parties

1. An assignor is not relieved of duties by a delegation of those duties.
2. The mere assignment of rights does not include the delegation of duties.
3. Under the Code, the assignment of the contract generally includes the assignment of rights and the delegation of duties.
4. If an assignor delegates duties to an assignee, the assignee thereby becomes primarily liable to perform for the obligee.

Notice of Assignment

1. Notice of the assignment must be given by the assignee to the obligor if the assignee is to receive performance.
2. In a case of multiple assignments, the first to give notice in good faith to the obligor has priority to receive performance in most states.

NOVATION

Meaning

1. A novation means a new contract. It involves the substitution with the express consent of all parties of a third party for one of the original parties.

Application

1. In essence, a novation works as an exception to the general rule that an assignor remains liable even after an effective delegation of duties.
2. A novation requires a prior valid contract, agreement for substitution of a third party, an express release of one party, and a new valid contract.

REVIEW QUESTIONS AND PROBLEMS

1. Match each term in Column A with the appropriate statement in Column B.

A	B
(1) Intended third-party beneficiary	(a) Performance will satisfy a duty the promisee owes the beneficiary
(2) Incidental third-party beneficiary	(b) A present transfer of rights arising from an earlier contract
(3) Creditor-beneficiary	(c) Transfer of rights would materially change the other party's duty, increase the risk imposed by the contract, or impair return performance
(4) Donee-beneficiary	(d) Third party who has no legally enforceable rights under a contract
(5) When beneficiary's rights vest	(e) Usually both an assignment and a delegation
6) Assignment	(f) Rights vest based on reliance or consent of third party.
(7) Delegation	(g) A new contract with the substitution of a third party for an original party
(8) Nonassignable rights	(h) Third party who has legally enforceable rights under a contract
(9) Nondelegable duties	(i) Duties of personal service or duties that may materially vary the performance given to the obligee
(10) Novation	(j) Transfer of duties arising from an earlier contract

2. Boyce contracts to build a house for Anne. Pursuant to the contract, Boyce and his surety, Travelers, execute a payment bond to Anne by which they promise Anne that all of Boyce's debts for labor and materials on the house will be paid. Boyce later employs Sam as a carpenter and buys lumber from Larry's Lumber Company. Are Sam and Larry's Lumber Company intended beneficiaries of Travelers' promise to Anne? Explain.
3. Wichita State University leased an airplane to fly its football team. The lease provided that the university would provide liability insurance to cover any deaths or injuries from the operation of the plane. No such insurance was bought. The plane later crashed, killing all on board. Can the estates of the deceased football players sue the university as intended third-party beneficiaries? Explain why or why not.

4. Hunt, an employee of the Marie Reading School, was injured when the elevator he was operating fell. The school had a contract with Shaft Elevator, Inc., whereby Shaft was to inspect and service the elevator on a regular basis. Hunt contended that Shaft had not properly inspected the elevator and that its omission caused the accident. Can Hunt maintain an action against Shaft? Why or why not?
5. Gaither entered into a contract with a nonprofit corporation whereby Gaither would receive $700 per month while in medical school, provided that he would return to his small hometown, Chester, to practice medicine for ten years after becoming a licensed physician. The residents of Chester voted approval of bonds to construct a medical clinic. Gaither practiced medicine in Chester for about five weeks but then left for Mt. Clement. Do the representatives of the medical clinic and the citizens of Chester have a right to sue Gaither? Explain.
6. Athens Lie Detector Company, for good consideration, gave Yarbrough an exclusive license to operate certain lie detector machines as part of the agreement. The company agreed to tell him how the manufacturing process works. Athens assigned its rights and delegated its duties under the contract to Travers. Are he rights assignable? Are the duties delegable? Explain.
7. Corey sold his property to Greer, who assigned the contract right to Bob. The original contract of sale provided for an extension of credit by Corey to Greer and did not require a total cash payment at the time of closing. Is a contract for the sale of real estate assignable by the buyer if it provides for credit from the seller to the buyer? Explain.
8. As part of his employment contract, an employee entered into a covenant not to compete with his corporate employer. The contract also contained a provision that stated: "This agreement is personal to each of the parties hereto, and neither party may assign or delegate any of the rights or obligations hereunder without first obtaining a written consent of the other party." Later the corporation was dissolved, and the assets were distributed to the shareholders who operated the business as a partnership. The employee filed suit to establish that the covenant not to compete was no longer enforceable. Can the partnership enforce the covenant not to compete? Explain.
9. Suppose that contract for the sale of goods contains this clause: "Under no circumstances may any rights under this contract be assigned." After the seller delivers goods to the buyer, may the seller assign the buyer's unpaid account to a third party? Explain.
10. Martin Stern sued for his architectural services rendered to Jacobson in Jacobson's development of a hotel and casino. In April, Jacobson contracted with Stern for the architect's services and the fee. On May 1, Jacobson acquired all the stock of A. L.W., Inc., a corporation that had previously operated a casino on the site of the new development. On May 9, A. L.W. began to operate the casino, but it filed bankruptcy. Stern did not file a claim in the bankruptcy proceeding but rather brought suit directly against Jacobson. When Stern was awarded $132,590.37 by the trial court, Jacobson appealed on the ground that his obligations were adopted by A. L.W., which constituted a novation. Has a valid novation occurred that would release Jacobson from his personal liability? Explain.

PART IV

SALES

Sales Contracts: Formation and Performance | 21

CHAPTER OUTLINE

ARTICLE 2 OF THE UCC

1. Summary of Common-Law Changes
2. Scope
3. Definitions
4. Abbreviations

THE SALES CONTRACT

5. Express Agreement
6. Documentary Transactions
7. Course of Dealing, Usage of Trade, Course of Performance
8. Gap Filling under the Code

TITLE

9. In General
10. Identification to the Contract
11. Transfer of Title to Goods
12. Good-Faith Purchasers

RISK OF LOSS

13. In Breach-of-Contract Cases
14. If No Breach Exists

CHAPTER PREVIEW

As we learned in Part III, the Uniform Commercial Code changes many older, classic contract rules to conform to business realities and the reasonable expectations of the contracting parties. In particular, Article 2 of the Code affects contracts involving the sale of movable objects of personal property. Article 2A governs the lease of goods. Because of the importance of Article 2 to business people, this chapter and the next one examine in detail key provisions of this Article.

Specifically, this chapter explores the formation of the sales contract, the transfer of title to goods, and the risk of loss when goods are destroyed, damaged, or stolen. Chapter 22 covers the topics of breach and remedies available to the parties when there is a breach of a sales contract. Chapter 23 concludes Part III with a discussion of warranties, guided almost entirely by Code provisions.

BUSINESS MANAGEMENT DECISION

You are the general manager of a wholesale mail-order distributor. The bulk of your customers are retailers who phone in their orders.

What policy should you develop for accepting these phone orders?

ARTICLE 2 OF THE UCC

1. Summary of Common-Law Changes

Many common-law contract rules also have been changed or modified by Article 2 of the Code to achieve a more commercially desirable result since some basic contract rules concerning employment, construction, and real property contracts are simply inappropriate in a sale-of-goods context. The important Code modifications or changes are summarized in Table 21-1. These Code rules have already been discussed in the chapters on contracts and will not be discussed further.

The rules and principles discussed in this chapter and the following two chapters are important ones contained in Article 2; they were not presented in the chapters on contracts (13-20).

2. Scope

A sales transaction can relate to real property, to goods, and to other forms of personal property. Within Part Four of this text, however, we limited ourselves to sales transactions in goods under Article 2 of the Uniform Commercial Code. Article 2 of the Code does not define the term *transaction.* Although a few sections are limited either explicitly or implicitly to the sale of goods [2-204, 2-314, 2-402, 2-703], courts have extended Article 2 to transactions such as leases (Article 2A) and even to bailments of goods in some cases.

When you lease a car or rent a golf cart, does Article 2 apply if problems arise? Historically, the answer has been unclear. Some courts have applied the Code to all commercial leases of goods. These courts emphasize that Article 2 governs "transactions" in goods, and a lease of goods is such a transaction. On the other hand, a few courts emphasize the word sales in the Code and will extend Article 2 only to transactions in goods that are analogous

TABLE 21-1 ■ Special Rules for Contracts for the Sale of Goods

UCC CODE SECTION 2	RULE
Offer and acceptance	
204	All terms need not be included in negotiations for a contract to result.
205	Firm written offers by merchants are irrevocable for a maximum of three months.
206 (1) (a)	Acceptance may be made by any reasonable means of communication and is effective when deposited.
206 (1) (b)	Unilateral offers may be accepted either by a promise to ship or by shipment.
206 (1) (b)	Failure to reject may constitute an acceptance.
206 (2)	Acceptance by performance requires notice within a reason able time, or the offer may be treated as lapsed
207	Variance in terms between offer and acceptance may not be a rejection and may be an acceptance.
305	The price need not be included in a contract.
311 (1)	Particulars of performance may be left open.
Consideration	
203	Adding a seal is of no effect.
209 (1)	Consideration is not required to support a modification of a contract for the sale of goods.
Voidable contracts	
403	A minor may not disaffirm against an innocent third party.
721	Rescission is not a bar to a suit for dollar damages.
Illegality	
302	Unconscionable bargains will not be enforced.
Form of the agreement	
201	Statute of frauds
	$500 price for goods
	Written confirmation between merchants
	Memorandum need not include all terms of agreement.
	Payment, acceptance, and receipt limited to quantity specified in writing.
	Specially manufactured goods
	Admission pleadings or court proceedings that a contract for sale was made
Rights of third parties	
210 (4)	An assignment of "the contract" or of "rights under the contract" includes a delegation of duties.
Performance of contracts	
209	Claims and rights may be waived without consideration.
307, 612	Rules on divisible contracts
511	Tender of payment is a condition precedent (rather than a condition concurrent) to a tender of delivery.
610, 611	Anticipatory breach may not be withdrawn if the other party gives notice that it is final.
614	Impracticability of performance in certain cases is an excuse for nonperformance.
Discharge	
725	The statute of limitations is four years, but parties can reduce it by mutual agreement to not less than one year.

to a sale of goods. Some leases, for example, contain an option to buy; and if exercised, it will cause the lease payments (rent) to be applied toward the purchase price. Cars, TV sets, musical instruments, and many other things are frequently leased with an option to buy. As a result of the need for clarification on the applicability of Article 2 concepts to leases of goods, the National Conference of Commissioners on Uniform State Laws drafted Article 2A. This suggested legislation has been adopted in most states.

Another question that arises is the application of Article 2 when a *sales transaction involves the rendering of services.* Article 2 will *not* apply if the subject matter of the contract is service; however, many contracts are "mixed" contracts in that they involve both sale of services and goods. You hire a painter to paint your house or a contractor to install a heating and air-conditioning system in an apartment complex, or a hairdresser to apply a special shampoo. In addition to providing services, these persons have also sold goods (the paint, heating and air unit, and shampoo). These contracts present borderline transactions, and courts must often make a decision regarding the applicability of Article 2. Most courts tend to apply Article 2 only if the goods aspect of the deal is predominant. Their approach is to ask which part of the transaction is the predominant feature—sale of goods or sale of services?

Some problem areas have definite answers. Article 2 applies to specially manufactured goods [2-105(1)] and to "the serving for value of food or drink to be consumed either on the premises or elsewhere" [2-314(1)]. By statue in many states, Article 2 is inapplicable to blood transfusions, bone transfers, or organ transplants. These are considered medical services.

The following case examines the question of whether Article 2 applies to water.

CASE

Leslie Adel and Joanne Adel v. Greensprings of Vermont, Inc., Dennis Glennnon, Thomas Cross, and Robert Rubin

UNITED STATES DISTRICT COURT FOR THE DISTRICT OF VERMONT

363 F. Supp. 2d 692 (2005)

WILLIAM K. SESSIONS III, CHIEF JUDGE

Plaintiffs Leslie and Joanne Adel are a married couple from Vineland, New Jersey. Defendant Greensprings of Vermont, Inc. ("Greensprings") is a Vermont corporation with its principle place of business in Vermont. Greensprings owns and operates the Greenspring at Mt. Snow resort in West Dover, Vermont. Defendant Dennis Glennon ("Glennon") is the president of Greensprings, and he fulfills duties similar to those of a general manager. Defendant Robert Rubin ("Rubin") was employed by defendant Greensprings from approximately 1992 through 2002. He remains a member of the Greensprings' board. During 1999, Rubin had primary responsibility for the water system at the Greensprings complex. Among other duties, Rubin was responsible for the maintenance and testing of the water supply. Defendant Thomas Cross is a self-employed management consultant. He appears to have had little involvement with events relevant to this lawsuit. The plaintiffs have agreed that all claims against Thomas Cross may be dismissed.

Together with their two children and eight friends, Leslie and Joanne Adel went on a ski vacation in southern Vermont from February 3 through February 7, 1999. The vacationers stayed in Unit 24 at Greenspring. Greenspring is a townhouse condominium owned by Thomas and Charlene Fallarco. The townhouse condominium is part of a larger complex developed by defendant Greensprings. Greensprings owns and maintains the water supply for the Greenspring condominiums. Greensprings also owns and maintains common areas of the complex such as a swimming pool and spa at the Greenspring recreation center. While he was in Vermont, Leslie Adel ("Adel") used the swimming pool and spa at the Greenspring recreation center as well as the bathrooms, showers, and a bathtub Jacuzzi in Unit 24.

On February 9, 1999, two days after he returned from his ski vacation, Adel began to experience flu-like symptoms. Unfortunately, his condition steadily worsened and he was transferred to the Hospital of the University of Pennsylvania on February 16.

On February 17, a physician took a sputum specimen from Adel's lungs. The hospital laboratory cultured Legionella pneumonphila from that specimen on February 23. As a result, Adel was diagnosed as suffering from Legionnaires' disease. Adel was hospitalized at the Hospital of the University of Pennsylvania for six weeks. His bout with Legionnaires' disease was serious and included 45 days in a coma. Adel claims to have suf-

fered permanent injuries as a result of contracting Legionnaires' disease. The primary means of transmission of Legionnaires' disease is the inhalation of aerosolized water droplets containing the Legionnella pneumonphila bacteria. The incubation period for Legionnaires' disease is usually between 2 and 14 days. Thus, Adel's Vermont vacation fell within the potential incubation period.

On February 24, 1999, the DOH sent sanitarian Alfred Burns ("Burns") to Greenspring to collect swabs and water samples. Burns collected 33 samples from locations at the Greensprings complex. These included seven samples from the spa in the recreation center and nine samples from inside unit 24. Of all the samples taken, two returned positive tests for Legionella pneumophila. The positive tests were from a jug of water collected from a bathroom on the lower floor of unit 24 and a jug of water collected in the upstairs master bathroom in Unit 24. Burns also inspected the spa in the recreation center. This inspection revealed many deficiencies.

Together with his wife Joanne, he brings this action alleging, in part, that Article 2's warranty of merchantability should apply. The defendants have moved for summary judgment.

A warranty of merchantability is implied only "if the seller is a merchant with respect to goods of that kind." The Vermont Supreme Court has not decided whether a water supplier is a "seller" of a "good" under Vermont's version of the UCC. This Court must, therefore, predict how the Vermont Supreme Court would rule if it were faced with this question. This is a difficult task as decisions from other state courts are divided. Nevertheless, the Court is persuaded by the reasoning of those decisions finding that water suppliers are sellers of goods under Article 2 of the UCC.

An item can be a "good" under the UCC even if the seller did not create or manufacture it. This is made clear under UCC 2-107 which provides that "[a] contract for the sale of minerals or the like (including oil and gas) ... to be removed from realty is a contract for the sale of goods within this article if they are to be severed by the seller." Thus, Mattoon is incorrect in so far as it suggests that water is not a good because it is captured rather than manufactured. Moreover, even if this were a relevant factor, the defendants alter the water when they treat it.

Mattoon also places undue emphasis on the fact that the cost of water reflects the cost of storage, treatment and distribution. The provision of goods always includes service elements such as storage and distribution. Thus, all sellers of goods will incur such costs and water providers are not unique in this regard.

Under the UCC, "'Goods' means all things (including specially manufactured goods) which are movable at the time of identification to the contract for sale." Water satisfies these requirements. As another court notes, "all who have paid bills for water can attest to its movability." In this case, the defendants extract water from an underground aquifer. Thus, their sale may also qualify as a sale of goods under Vt. Stat. Ann. tit. 9A § 2-107 which provides that the "the sale of minerals or the like (including oil and gas)" is a sale of goods within Article 2 of the UCC.

The defendants regularly provide water to the homeowners at the Greensprings complex. These homeowners pay for the water on a per-capita basis. As water is a good, the defendants are merchants with respect to water. Thus, a warranty of merchantability is implied in the defendants' sale of water. Consequently, the defendants are not entitled to summary judgment on Count II of the complaint.

■ *Granted.*

CASE CONCEPTS REVIEW

1. Why is water considered a "good" under the UCC?
2. If the warranty of merchantability applies to water, exactly what is being promised?

3. Definitions

Goods

Items of tangible personal property that are tangible

GOODS The precise meaning of the term *goods* is sometimes a problem for the courts. In general, the term **goods** encompasses things that are in existence, that is, items of personal property (chattels) that are of a tangible, physical nature [2-105(1)]. Although broadly interpreted to include even electricity, the definition of goods excludes investment securities (covered by Article 8 of the Code) and negotiable instruments (covered by Article 3 of the Code).

Being limited to goods, Article 2 necessarily excludes contracts for personal service, construction, intangible personal property, and the sale of real estate. Goods associated with real estate *may* be within Article 2 in sales of "structures," "minerals," and the "like" if severance is to be made by the seller. If severance is to be made by the buyer, the contract involves a sale of an interest in land [2-107(1)]. Growing crops, including timber, fall within Article 2, regardless of who severs them [2-107(2)].

Another term used in Article 2 is *future goods*—goods that are not in existence at the time of the agreement or that have not been designated as the specific goods that will be the subject matter of the sales transaction [2-105(2)].

Sales transaction

The transfer of title from a seller to a buyer in exchange for an agreed-upon price

SALE The **sales transaction** involves an exchange of title to the goods for a price [2-106(a)]. The basic obligation of the seller is to tender the goods, while that of the buyer is to accept the goods and pay the price [2-301]. In general, the parties to a sales contract can agree on any terms and conditions that are mutually acceptable.

Future goods like growing crops is covered in Article 2 of the Code.

Merchant

A person who deals in goods of the kind involved in a transaction or who otherwise, by occupation, holds himself or herself out as having knowledge or skill peculiar to the practices or goods involved

MERCHANT Special provisions of Article 2 relate to transactions involving a **merchant**, a professional businessperson who deals in the subject matter of the sales contract or who "holds himself out as having knowledge or skill peculiar to the practices or goods involved in the transaction" [2-104(1)]. This designation is of great importance and is recognition of a professional status for a businessperson, justifying standards of conduct different from those of "nonprofessionals." The courts of some states have held that farmers are merchants when selling grain and other items raised by them. Other courts have held that farmers are not merchants, so from state to state and case to case there is variation in whether or not Code provisions relating to merchants apply also to farmers.

Good faith

Honesty in fact in the conduct or transaction concerned or, for a merchant, the observance of reasonable commercial standards of fair dealing in the trade

GOOD FAITH The Code provisions on the sale of goods are based on two assumptions: (1) that the parties should be given the maximum latitude in fixing their own terms and (2) that the parties will act in "good faith." **Good faith** means honesty in fact in the conduct or transaction [1-201(19)]. In the case of a merchant, good faith also includes the observance of reasonable commercial standards of fair dealing in the trade [2-103(1)(b)].

RETURNED GOODS The buyer and seller may agree that the buyer has the privilege of returning the goods that have been delivered. If the goods are delivered primarily for use, as in a consumer purchase, the transaction is called a sale on approval. If the goods are delivered primarily for resale, it is called a *sale or return* [2-326(1)]. The distinction is an important one because goods delivered on approval are not subject to the claims of the buyer's creditors until the buyer has indicated acceptance of the goods; goods delivered on sale or return, however, are subject to the claims of the buyer's creditors while they are in the buyer's possession [2-326(2)]. Delivery of goods on consignment, such as a transaction in which a manufacturer or a wholesaler delivers goods to a retailer who has the privilege of returning any unsold goods, is a sale or return.

The distinction between sale on approval and sale or return also is important if the goods are lost, stolen, damaged, or destroyed. The issues arising in these factual situations are discussed in Section 14, along with other aspects of risk of loss.

4. Abbreviations

As a matter of convenience, a number of contract terms are generally expressed as abbreviations. *F.O.B.* (free on board) is the most commonly used. *F.O.B. the place of shipment* means that the seller is obligated to place the goods in possession of a carrier, so that they may be shipped to the buyer. *F.O.B. the place of destination* means that the seller is obligated to cause the goods to be delivered to the buyer [2-319(1)(b)]. Thus, if Athens, Georgia, is the seller's place of business, "F.O.B. Athens, Georgia," is a *shipment contract.* "F.O.B. Champaign, Illinois," Champaign being the place where the buyer is to receive the goods, is a *destination contract,* and the seller must provide transportation to that place at his or her own risk and expense.

If the terms of the contract also specify *F.O.B. vessel, car, or other vehicle,* the seller must at his or her own expense and risk load the goods on board. F.A.S. (free alongside) *vessel* at a named port requires the seller at his or her own expense and risk to drive the goods alongside the vessel in the manner usual in the port or on a dock designated and provided by the buyer [2-319(2)].

C.I.F. means that the price includes, in a lump sum, the cost of the goods and of the insurance and freight to the named destination [2-320]. The seller's obligation is to load the goods, to make provision for payment of the freight, and to obtain an insurance policy in favor of the buyer. Generally, C.I.F means that the parties will deal in terms of the documents that represent the goods. (Section 6 describes this documentary transaction more specifically.) Typically, the seller performs his or her obligation by tendering to the buyer the proper documents, including a negotiable bill of lading and an invoice of the goods. The buyer is required to make payment against the tender of the required documents [2-320(4)].

THE SALES CONTRACT

The terms of a sales contract are supplied by three sources: the express agreement of the parties; course of dealing, usage of trade, and course of performance; and the Code and other applicable statutes.

5. Express Agreement

The general rule in sales law is that the parties are free to make their own contract. The parties are privileged to contract expressly regarding most basic terms—quality, quantity, price, delivery, payment, and the like. In general, their agreement is sufficient to displace any otherwise applicable Code section. The principle of freedom of contract under the Code is not without exceptions, however. The parties cannot "disclaim" their Code obligations of good faith, diligence, and due care. Parties may provide a liquidated damages clause, but it cannot be a penalty [2-718(1)]. Consequential damages may be limited, but the limitations cannot be unconscionable [2-719(3)].

The buyer's duty in a sales contract is to pay for the goods. In the absence of a contrary agreement, payment is due at the time and place at which the buyer is to receive the goods [2-310(a)]. The basic obligations of the parties are concurrent conditions of exchange. Accordingly, a buyer who wants credit (to get the goods before paying in full) must specifically negotiate for it in the contract. Between merchants, most domestic sales transactions are handled on "open account" (the seller ships the goods on the buyer's simple promise to pay for them in thirty, sixty, or ninety days). The buyer is not required to sign a note evidencing obligation to pay or to grant the seller a security interest in the goods to cover the buyer's obligation.

Bill of lading
A document, issued by a person engaged in the business of providing transportation, evidencing receipt of goods for shipment

Warehouse receipt
A document, issued by a person providing space, evidencing that goods have been received for storage

6. Documentary Transactions

When the parties are separated by distance and the seller is unwilling to extend credit to the buyer, they may use a *documentary exchange.* As the procedure is sometimes called, the buyer is to pay "cash against documents." In this procedure, the seller uses documents of title to control the goods until he or she is paid. The document of title may be a **bill of lading** issued by a transportation company, a **warehouse receipt**, or any other document that is evidence that the person in possession of it is entitled to the goods it covers [1-201(15)]. Documents of title are multipurpose commercial instruments. They not only act as a receipt for the goods but also state the terms of the shipment or storage contract between the seller and the transit or warehouse company.

In a typical documentary exchange, the seller may ship the goods by air, rail, or truck to the buyer and receive from the airline, railroad, or trucking company a *negotiable* bill of lading made to the order of the seller. The carrier thereby obligates itself to deliver the goods to the holder of the bill of lading [7-403(4)]. At this point, the seller has shipped "under reservation." His or her procurement of the negotiable bill reserves a security interest in the goods for their price, which the buyer owes the seller [2-205]. The seller will endorse the bill of lading and send it to his or her bank. The seller will attach to it a sight draft or demand for immediate payment of the purchase price by the buyer. The seller's bank will forward the documents to a bank in the city of the buyer. It is the obligation of that bank to release the bill of lading to the buyer only after the buyer has paid the draft for the purchase price [4-503(a)]. Without the bill of lading, the buyer will not be able to get the goods from the carrier. Only when the buyer is in possession under a regular chain of endorsements is he or she the holder to whom the carrier is obligated to deliver.

This is only one common type of documentary transaction. There are many variations. Similar protections can be obtained if the seller ships under a nonnegotiable bill of lading, taking care to consign the goods to himself or herself or to an agent. The carrier is now obligated to deliver to the consignee or to the person specified by the seller's written instructions [7-403(4)]. The seller will withhold any instructions to deliver to the buyer until payment is received. Under this procedure, possession of the document of title is not required to take delivery from the carrier. Note, however, that the seller should not name the buyer as consignee in the bill of lading; if the seller does, control over the shipment is lost.

7. Course of Dealing, Usage of Trade, Course of Performance

Course of dealing

A sequence of previous conduct between the parties to a particular transaction

Usage of trade

Any practice or method of dealing so regularly observed in a place, vocation, or trade that observance may justly be expected in the transaction in question

Course of performance

A term used to give meaning to a contract based on the parties having had a history of dealings

The agreement of the parties includes in their bargain any previous course of dealing between the parties, general trade custom and usage, and any past course of performance on the present agreement. These three sources not only are relevant in interpreting express contract items but also may constitute contract terms.

A **course of dealing** is a sequence of prior conduct between the parties that gives a common basis of understanding for interpreting their communications and conduct between themselves [1-205(1)]. A **usage of trade** is a practice or custom in the particular trade, used so frequently that it justifies the expectation that it will be followed in the transaction in question [1-205(2)]. **Course of performance** concerns a contract that requires repeated performances. When the other party has accepted an earlier performance, that performance can be used to give meaning to the agreement regarding future performance [2-208(1)].

When any of these sources is conflicting, the Code [2-208(2)] adopts the following initial hierarchy of presumed probative values:

1. Express terms
2. Course of performance
3. Course of dealing
4. Usage of trade

However, the last three do more than interpret the first. They may supplement, cut down, and even subtract whole terms from the express agreement of the parties. More important, course of performance, course of dealing, and usage of trade may directly override express terms, so an express contract term like "one ton of ready-to-mix concrete" is changed to "1,800 pounds of ready-to-pour concrete. This is because courts are looking for the intent of the parties, and this intent may best be found in what the parties have done rather than in what they said.

The question of whether usage of trade existed was central to the resolution of the following case.

CASE

Todd Heller, Inc. v. Indiana Department of Transportation

COURT OF APPEALS OF INDIANA

819 N.E.2d 140 (2004)

RILEY, JUDGE

Appellant-Plaintiff, Todd Heller, Inc. (Heller Inc.), appeals a negative judgment in its breach of contract suit against Appellee-Defendant, Indiana Department of Transportation (INDOT).

In February of 2001, INDOT executed a Quantity Purchase Award agreement (the QPA with Heller Inc., according to which Heller Inc. was to manufacture, package, and deliver glass beads to INDOT districts throughout Indiana from March 1, 2001, to February 28, 2002. Glass beads are tiny spheres, approximately the size of table sugar, which are mixed into traffic paint to create a reflective property. Heller Inc., a Pennsylvania corporation, has been in the glass bead industry for approximately eight years.

AASHTO is an acronym for the American Association of State Highway Transportation Officials. ASHTO M 247 refers to a national standard specification for glass beads used in traffic paints. Both parties agree that the then-current AASHTO M 247 specification, to which INDOT's invitation to bid and the QPA were understood to refer, was M 247-81 (2000).

Heller Inc. conducted the AASHTO moisture resistance test according to what Todd Heller (Heller) calls the "customary practice in the industry." Specifically, Heller Inc. would tilt the beaker at an angle and slowly pour water down the side of the beaker, "Just as if you'd be trying to pour a beer without putting a head on it." The plant manager of Heller Inc.'s glass beads plant, Mike Muta (Muta), learned "how people in the industry introduced the water in the beaker" when he received AASHTO moisture resistance test training at a previous job.

During the time period from approximately March 15, 2001, to April 24, 2001, INDOT rejected several batches of Heller Inc.'s glass beads for moisture resistance failure. Pursuant to the QPA, Heller Inc. was required to dispatch a truck to retrieve the rejected batches. Upon the rejected beads' return, Heller Inc. would subject the beads to the AASHTO moisture resistance test; the rejected beads passed the AASHTO moisture resistance test as it was performed in Heller Inc.'s laboratory.

On April 24, 2001, Heller Inc. came to INDOT to discuss the moisture resistance failures. In INDOT's laboratory, INDOT's senior chemist, Todd Tracy (Tracy), performed the AASHTO moisture resistance test on a sample of Heller Inc.'s glass beads that had failed when tested previously by INDOT. Instead of tilting the beaker and slowly introducing water, Tracy "just dumped" water into the beaker such that "the weight of the water burrowed a hole through the beads so water got underneath the sample. ..." As Tracy began to pour the water off the beads, Heller objected because he observed that "water was still trapped underneath the sample." "Pockets of water trapped in the product ... can cause ... a clump in the product and cause a failure in the ... funnel." According to Heller, Tracy then took the time to carefully pour off the water from the beads, and the sample passed the moisture resistance test.

Next, Heller demonstrated for INDOT how Heller Inc. performs the AASHTO moisture resistance test by performing the test on samples of glass beads, both coated and uncoated, which Heller Inc. had brought to INDOT. In particular, Heller emphasized the practice of gently and carefully introducing water into the tilted beaker. Heller Inc. then requested that INDOT modify the way it performed the AASHTO moisture resistance test in order to perform it "the way the test should be done." To further illustrate the point, Heller Inc. subsequently produced a videotape of four variations on the AASHTO moisture resistance test. The first variation on the videotape was a demonstration of the proper method, according to Heller, while the last three variations incorporated the allegedly faulty testing methods employed by INDOT. Of the four variations depicted in the videotape, the glass beads passed only the first one.

By letter dated May 25, 2001, INDOT cancelled the QPA agreement with Heller Inc. due to the repeated failure of Heller Inc.'s beads to pass the AASHTO moisture resistance test. Before canceling the contract, however, Bowser called Penn DOT to inquire as to their method of performing the AASHTO moisture resistance test. Penn DOT's description of their method of performing the test was consistent with or similar to what Heller had described.

The trial court found that the contract does not require INDOT to adopt Penn DOT's method of moisture resistance testing under the AASHTO standard for glass beads, nor allow changing the test method during the contract period. Heller Inc. now appeals.

Heller Inc. argues that the trial court erred by concluding that there is no custom or usage of trade in the glass bead industry supplementing the QPA between Heller Inc. and INDOT. Specifically, Heller Inc. argues that its glass beads failed the AASHTO moisture resistance tests only because INDOT was not performing the test in accordance with this usage of trade. We agree.

continued

Because the QPA was for the delivery of "goods," the QPA is governed by the Uniform Commercial Code. As such, the terms of the QPA may be explained or supplemented by usage of trade. "Usage of trade" is explained in Indiana Code § 26-1-1-205(2):

> A usage of trade is any practice or method of dealing having such regularity of observance in a place, vocation or trade as to justify an expectation that it will be observed with respect to the transaction in question.

Heller Inc. contends that there is a glass bead industry usage of trade with respect to the proper method of performing the AASHTO moisture resistance test. Heller Inc. describes this usage of trade's method and rationale as follows: When performing the AASHTO moisture resistance test, it is a customary practice in the glass bead industry to tilt the beaker at an angle and to slowly add the water to the side of the beaker so as not to disturb the glass beads. It is important to not disturb the beads when adding the water to the beaker because water can become trapped under the beads, making it difficult or impossible to later pour all the water off as required by the AASHTO moisture resistance test.

INDOT argues and the trial court found that Heller Inc. failed to prove as a fact that the method it advocates as the proper way to perform the AASHTO moisture resistance test amounts to a usage of trade. INDOT argues further that because the AASHTO designation used in the Specifications section of the QPA was silent as to how exactly to perform the AASHTO moisture resistance test, INDOT had the discretion to decide whether to tilt the beaker, how to introduce the water into the beaker, and whether a thin coating of beads sticking to the inside of the beaker signals moisture resistance failure. Moreover, INDOT continues, the QPA specifies that Heller Inc. was required to be familiar with INDOT's testing methods. Finally, INDOT points to an in-court demonstration of the AASHTO moisture resistance test performed by INDOT's Tracy in which virtually no glass beads remained in the containers or beaker.

The record shows that INDOT offered no relevant evidence at trial to refute the uncontroverted evidence supporting the existence of a usage of trade in the glass beads industry. The uncontroverted evidence supporting the existence of a usage of trade includes, first, INDOT's survey of other states' Departments of Transportation, which revealed that the states performing the AASHTO moisture resistance test tilt the beaker and introduce the water slowly and gently, as it was done at Penn DOT. Second, INDOT's Bowser testified that this was the first year INDOT used the AASHTO moisture resistance test on glass beads, and Tracy admitted that he never received training in the AASHTO moisture resistance test and does not know its purpose. Third, INDOT modified its QPA after the Heller Inc. debacle, explicitly clarifying the method to be used when performing the AASHTO moisture resistance test, and the new method is consistent with the method that Heller Inc. was advocating.

Finally, there is the testimony of Heller, who has worked in the glass beads industry for eight years, and Muta, who has worked in the industry for eighteen years and received training in the AASHTO moisture resistance test at a previous job. Heller and Muta both testified that they are familiar with how people in the glass beads industry perform the AASHTO moisture resistance test and that there is a custom or usage of trade in the industry with respect to the method of introducing water into the beaker, in particular. The testimony of one individual has been found sufficient to establish a usage of trade.

We, therefore, conclude that the uncontroverted, relevant evidence and all reasonable inferences to be drawn therefrom point to the conclusion that there is a usage of trade in the glass beads industry that dictates how the AASHTO moisture resistance test is to be performed. Accordingly, we find that the trial court clearly erred in finding that Heller Inc. failed to prove by a preponderance of the evidence the existence of a usage of trade.

■ *Reversed and remanded.*

CASE CONCEPTS REVIEW

1. What evidence supported the conclusion that there was usage of trade in the industry with respect to the testing conducted in this case?
2. Why did the appellate court disagree with the trial court?

8. Gap Filling under the Code

Written contracts have gaps in them when the parties either intentionally or inadvertently leave out basic terms. Article 2 of the Code has a number of gap-filler provisions that, taken together, comprise a type of standardized statutory contract. The most important gap-filler provisions involve price, quantity, delivery, and time of performance.

PRICE The price term of the contract can be left open, with the price to be fixed by later agreement of the parties or by some agreed-on market standard [2-305]. It may even be agreed that the buyer or the seller shall fix the price, in which event there is an obligation to exercise good faith in doing so. If the contract is silent on price, or if for some reason the price is not set in accordance with the method agreed on, it will be determined as a reasonable price at the time of delivery. Thus, if it appears that it is their intention to do so, parties can bind themselves even though the exact price is not actually agreed on.

QUANTITY The Code also allows flexibility in the quantity term of a sales contract. There may be an agreement to purchase the entire output of the seller, or the quantity may be specified as all that is required by the buyer. To ensure fair dealing between the parties in "output" and "requirements" contracts, the Code provides that if parties estimate the quantity involved, no quantity that is unreasonably disproportionate to the estimate will be enforced [2-306]. If the parties have not agreed on an estimate, a quantity that is in keeping with normal or other comparable prior output or requirements is implied.

DELIVERY The term *delivery* signifies a transfer of possession of the goods from the seller to the buyer. A seller makes delivery when he or she physically transfers into the possession of the buyer the actual goods that conform to the requirements of the contract. A seller satisfies the requirement to "transfer and deliver" when he or she "tenders delivery" [2-507].

Tender of delivery

The requirement that the seller must put and hold conforming goods at the buyer's disposition and give the buyer any notification reasonably necessary to enable the buyer to take delivery

A proper **tender of delivery** requires the seller to make available conforming goods at the buyer's disposition and to give the buyer any notification reasonably necessary to take delivery [2-503(1)]. The seller's tender must be at a reasonable hour, and he or she must keep the goods available for a reasonable time to enable the buyer to take possession.

Unless the contract provides to the contrary, the place for delivery is the seller's place of business. If the seller has no place of business, it is the seller's residence [2-308(a)]. In a contract for the sale of identified goods that are known to both parties to be at some other place, that place is the place for their delivery [2-308(a)(b)].

Goods are frequently in the possession of a bailee, such as a warehouseperson. In this event, to make delivery, the seller is obligated to (1) tender a negotiable document of title (warehouse receipt) representing the goods or (2) procure acknowledgment by the bailee (warehouseperson) that the buyer is entitled to the goods [2-503(4)(a)].

Unless otherwise agreed, the seller is required to tender the goods in a single delivery rather than in installments over a period of time. The buyer's obligation to pay is not due until such a tender is made [2-307]. In some situations, the seller may not be able to deliver all the goods at once, or the buyer may not be able to receive the entire quantity at one time, in which event more than a single delivery is allowed.

TIME OF PERFORMANCE The time of delivery is often left out of contracts. Such contracts may nevertheless be generally enforceable. However, if the parties intended the written agreement to be complete and an exclusive statement of the contract and the time of performance is omitted, the contract is unenforceable. In the usual case, the time may be supplied by parol evidence if it was agreed on. If it was not agreed on, a reasonable time is presumed [2-309(1)].

Determining what is a reasonable time depends on what constitutes acceptable commercial conduct under all the circumstances, including the obligation of good faith and reasonable commercial standards of fair dealing in the trade. A definite time may be implied from a usage of the trade or course of dealing or performance or from the circumstances of the contract as previously noted.

Payment is due at the time when and place where the buyer is to receive the goods [2-310]. *Receipt of goods* means taking physical possession of them. The buyer is given the opportunity to inspect the goods before paying for them [2-513(1)]. However, when the shipment is C.O.D. (cash on delivery), the buyer is not entitled to inspect the goods before payment of the price [2-513(3)(a)]. This requirement of the buyer having to pay before the inspection is not equivalent to the buyer accepting the goods [2-512(2)]. A buyer who pays for a C.O.D. shipment and then discovers that the goods are defective has all the rights and remedies discussed in the next chapter.

TABLE 21-2 ■ Code Gap Fillers

Price	Reasonable price [2-305]
Quantity	"Output" and "Requirements" provisions: reasonable amount [2-306]
Delivery	Tender of delivery at seller's place of business [2-507; 2-308]
Time	Reasonable time for performance [2-309]

The parties may enter into an open-ended contract that calls for successive performances, such as delivery of 1,000 barrels of flour per week. If the contract does not state the duration, it will be valid for a reasonable time. Unless otherwise agreed, either party can terminate it at any time.

TITLE

9. In General

Title

The aggregate of legal relationships concerning the ownership of property

The concept of **title** to goods is somewhat nebulous, but it is generally equated with the bundle of rights that constitute ownership. Issues related to the passage of title are important in the field of taxation and in areas of the law such as wills, trusts, and estates. The Code has deemphasized the importance of title, and the location of title at any given time is usually not the controlling factor in determining the rights of the parties in a contract of sale. As a general rule, the rights, obligations, and remedies of the seller, the buyer, and the third parties are determined without regard to title [2-401]. However, the concept of title is still basic to the sales transaction since, by definition, a sale involves the passing of title from the seller to the buyer.

The parties can, with few restrictions, determine by their contract the manner in which title to goods passes from the seller to the buyer. They can specify any conditions that must be fulfilled for title to pass. However, since the parties seldom specify when title passes from seller to buyer, the Code contains specific provisions as *to* when title shall pass if the location of title becomes an issue. The most important concept related to the passage of title is the identification of the goods to the sales contract. This concept is discussed in the next section, and in Section 11 some Code rules on title transferring are presented.

10. Identification to the Contract

Title to goods cannot pass until the goods have been *identified* to the contract [2-401(1)]. Identification requires that the seller specify the particular goods involved in the transaction [2-501(1)]. Carson may contract with Boyd to purchase ten mahogany desks of a certain style. Boyd may have several hundred of these desks in the warehouse. Identification takes place when Carson or Boyd specifies the particular ten desks that will be sold to Carson. There could not, of course, be a present identification of future goods (those not yet in existence or not owned by the seller). However, there can be identification of goods that are not totally in a deliverable state. The fact that the seller must do something to the goods prior to delivery does not prevent identification and the vesting of rights in the buyer.

There are special provisions for agricultural items—crops and animals—because of their nature. When there is a sale of a crop to be grown, identification occurs when the crop is planted. If the sale is of the unborn young of animals, identification takes place when they are conceived [2-501(1)(c)].

When goods are identified to a contract, the buyer acquires a special property interest in the goods. This special interest is an insurable one, and it may be created before the passing of title or delivery of possession of the goods.

11. Transfer of Title to Goods

In general, the Code provides that title passes to the buyer at the time and place at which the seller completes his or her performance with reference to the physical delivery of the goods [2-401(2)]. The difficulty with this general rule is that it does not specify the numerous factual circumstances under which the seller must make delivery.

For example, assume that the buyer will pick up the goods at the seller's place of business. In other words, the goods are not in storage and the seller has no duty to ship. If the goods are identified to the contract, title passes to the buyer at the time and place the contract is made [2-401(3)(b)].

If the goods are in storage and the buyer has the responsibility to pick them up, title passes at the time when and the place where the seller delivers to the buyer the document (warehouse receipt) that entitles the buyer to get receipt of the goods [2-401(3)(a)].

Often a sales contract involves the shipment of goods from the seller to the buyer. If a contract requires the seller to send the goods but does not require the seller to deliver them to a destination, title passes to the buyer at the time and place of shipment [2-401(2)(a)]. If the sales contract requires the seller to make delivery at a specific destination, title passes only when the goods reach that destination [2-402(2)(b)].

If the buyer rejects the goods when tendered, title will be revested in the seller. Upon the buyer's refusal to receive or retain the goods, the title automatically returns to the seller, whether or not the buyer was justified in his or her action. The same result occurs if the buyer has accepted the goods but subsequently revokes his or her acceptance for a justifiable reason [2-401(4)].

As a means of assurance that the price will be paid before the buyer can obtain title to the goods, a seller may ship or deliver goods to the buyer and reserve title in the seller's name. Under the Code, such an attempted reservation of title does not prevent the title from passing to the buyer. It is limited to the reservation of a security interest in the goods [2-401(1)(2)]. To give protection to the seller, the security interest must be perfected under the provisions of Article 9. (This process is discussed in Chapters 37 and 38.) Accordingly, a seller who simply reserves a security interest will not have availed himself or herself of protection against the claims of third parties against the property sold unless the seller complies with the law relating to secured transactions.

12. Good-Faith Purchasers

A purchaser of goods acquires the title that his or her transferor has or had the power to transfer. If the seller has no title, the purchaser receives no title. A purchaser from a thief has no property interest in the goods because the thief had none. The original owner still has title and may recover the goods—even if a certificate of title has been issued by a governmental body.

A purchaser of a limited interest in goods has property rights only to the extent of the limited interest. If a person buys a one-half interest in a golf cart with his or her neighbor, that person's rights are limited to the one-half interest.

A purchaser of goods may acquire more rights and better title than the seller had. Such a purchaser must qualify as a good-faith purchaser for value. In addition, the seller's title must be at least voidable and not void [2-403].

The typical case in which a party has voidable title involves fraud in obtaining the title. Voidable title issues also arise when the same goods are sold to more than one buyer. For example, Franklin sells goods to Talmadge, who leaves them at Franklin's store with the intention of picking them up later. Before Talmadge takes possession, Franklin sells them to Bell, a good-faith purchaser. Bell has title to the goods because if possession of goods is entrusted to a merchant who deals in goods of that kind, the merchant has the power to transfer all rights of the entrusting owner to a buyer in the ordinary course of business [2-403(2)(3)]. A good-faith purchaser buying from a merchant in the ordinary course of business acquires good title. This rule is applicable to any delivery of possession to a merchant with the understanding that the merchant is to have possession. Thus the rule applies to consignments and bailments as well as to cash sale, but the facts of each case must be examined to ensure that the buyer qualified as a good-faith purchaser for value.

RISK OF LOSS

13. In Breach-of-Contract Cases

The Code sets forth a number of rules for determining which party to a sales contract must bear the risk of loss in the event of theft, destruction, or damage to the goods during the period of the performance of the contract. The approach is contractual rather than title oriented and covers two basic situations: no breach-of-contract cases and cases in which one of the parties is in breach. Of course, the provisions are applicable only if the contract has not allocated the risk of loss [2-303].

If the contract has been breached, the loss will be borne by the party who has breached [2-510(1)]. Thus, if the seller has tendered or delivered goods that are "nonconforming," the seller bears the risk of loss. The seller remains responsible until he or she rectifies the nonconformity or the buyer accepts the goods despite their defects.

A buyer has the privilege of revoking his or her acceptance of the goods under proper circumstances (discussed in Chapter 22). If the buyer rightfully revokes acceptance, the risk of loss is back on the seller to the extent that the buyer's insurance does not cover the loss. In this situation, the seller has the benefit of any insurance carried by the buyer (the party most likely to have applicable insurance), but any uninsured loss is on the breaching seller.

Loss may occur while goods are in the seller's control, before the risk of loss has passed to the buyer. If the buyer repudiates the sale (breaches the contract) at a time when the seller has identified proper goods to the contract, the seller can impose the risk of loss on the buyer for a reasonable time. The basic concept of the Code is that the burden of losses should be that of the party who has failed to perform as required by contract.

14. If No Breach Exists

Bailment

A transfer of possession of personal property with the expectation that possession will be returned, such as in a warehouse storage contract

Three situations may arise in no-breach risk-of-loss cases. When neither party is in breach, the contract may call for shipment of the goods, the goods may be the subject of a **bailment**, or the contract may be silent on shipment and no bailment exists.

SHIPMENT A shipment contract requires only that the seller make necessary arrangements for transport; a destination contract imposes on the seller the obligation to deliver at a destination. If a contract between buyer and seller provides for shipment by carrier under a shipment contract (F.O.B. shipping point), the risk of loss passes to the buyer when the goods are delivered to the carrier. If shipment is made under a destination contract (F.O.B. destination), risk of loss does not pass to the buyer until goods arrive at the destination and are available to the buyer for delivery [2-509(1)]. When the parties do not use symbols such as C.I.F., F.A.S., or F.O.B. or otherwise make provision for risk of loss, it is necessary to determine whether a contract does or does not require the seller to deliver to a destination. The presumption is that a contract is one of shipment, not destination, and that the buyer should bear the risk of loss until arrival unless the seller has either specifically agreed to do so or the circumstances indicate such an obligation.

The question of when risk of loss passes can create the potential for considerable controversy, as indicated in the following case.

CASE

Jacq Wilson et al. v. Brawn of California, Inc.

COURT OF APPEAL OF CALIFORNIA

132 Cal. App. 4th 549 (2005)

STEIN, J.

Brawn markets clothing through its catalogs and over the Internet. When a customer places an order, Brawn packages it and holds it at its warehouse where it is picked up by a common carrier and delivered to the customer, using an address provided by the customer. At all times relevant, the terms of Brawn's mail order form required the customer to pay the listed price for the goods purchased, plus a delivery fee and a $1.48 "insurance fee." As to the last, the form recited: "INSURANCE: Items Lost or Damaged in Transit Replaced Free." Brawn based the insurance fee on the costs to it of replacing any goods lost in transit; and Brawn did indeed replace, without further cost to the customer, any goods that had been lost in transit. Brawn rarely, if ever, sold its goods to a customer unwilling to pay the insurance fee.

On February 5, 2002, and again on February 7, 2002, plaintiff Jacq Wilson (plaintiff) purchased items from Brawn's catalogue, each time paying the insurance fee. On February 13, 2002, Wilson, acting on behalf of himself and all other similarly situated persons, brought suit against Brawn, contending that in charging the fee Brawn violated the unfair competition law, Business and Professions Code section 17200 et seq., prohibiting unfair competition, and Business and Professions Code section 17500 et seq., prohibiting false advertising.

Plaintiff's suit was premised on the theory that by charging customers an insurance fee, Brawn suggested to them that they were paying for and receiving a special benefit—insurance against loss in transit—when in fact, customers did not need insurance against loss in transit because Brawn already was required to pay for that loss as a matter of law. The trial court agreed, finding that irrespective of the insurance fee, Brawn bore the risk of loss of goods in transit, reasoning that the fee was an "illusory" benefit. The court found that Brawn's customers were likely to be deceived by the insurance fee and that Brawn, therefore, had engaged in a deceptive business practice, entitling its customers to restitution. The ruling presumed that Brawn, rather than its customers, bears the loss of risk in transit, so that its customers received nothing of value in return for paying the fee. The court also awarded plaintiff litigation expenses in the amount of $24,699.21 and attorney fees in the amount of $422,982.50.

Neither party has cited any significant source of law concerning mail order sales or the risk of loss in mail order consumer sales, resting their contentions on provisions of the California Uniform Commercial Code. As the California Uniform Commercial Code, and the cases cited there, typically involve arm's-length sales between fairly sophisticated parties, the fit is not perfect. Nonetheless, there appears to be little legislation or case law specifically concerned with mail order sales or risk of loss in consumer sales contracts, and we, too, turn to the California Uniform Commercial Code's provisions.

California Uniform Commercial Code section 2509 sets forth the general rules for determining which party bears the risk of loss of goods in transit when there has been no breach of contract. Subdivision (1) of section 2509 provides, as relevant: "(1) Where the contract requires or authorizes the seller to ship the goods by carrier (a) If it does not require him to deliver them at a particular destination, the risk of loss passes to the buyer when the goods are duly delivered to the carrier ... ; but (b) If it does require him to deliver them at a particular destination and the goods are there duly tendered while in the possession of the carrier, the risk of loss passes to the buyer when the goods are there duly so tendered as to enable the buyer to take delivery."

Official Code comment 5 to Uniform Commercial Code section 2-503, concerning the seller's manner of tendering delivery, explains: "[U]nder this Article the 'shipment' contract is regarded as the normal one and the 'destination' contract as the variant type. The seller is not obligated to deliver at a named destination and bear the concurrent risk of loss until arrival, unless he has specifically agreed so to deliver or the commercial understanding of the terms used by the parties contemplates such a delivery." (Official Comments on U. Com. Code, Deering's Ann. Cal. U. Com. Code (1999 ed.) foll. § 2503, p. 198.) Of course, a seller will have to provide the carrier with shipping

continued

instructions. It follows that a contract is not a destination contract simply because the seller places an address label on the package, or directs the carrier to "ship to" a particular destination. "Thus a 'ship to' term has no significance in determining whether a contract is a shipment or destination contract for risk of loss purposes."

It is not at all uncommon for a contract to shift the risk of loss to the buyer at the point at which the seller delivers the goods to a common carrier, while calling for the seller to pay for delivery and insurance. The California Uniform Commercial Code recognizes this type of contract in its provisions pertaining to the term "C.I.F." "The term C.I.F. means that the price includes in a lump sum the cost of the goods and the insurance and freight to the named destination." (Cal. U. Com. Code, § 2320, subd. (1).) Official comment 1 to the section explains that "[t]he C.I.F. contract is not a destination but a shipment contract with risk of subsequent loss or damage to the goods passing to the buyer upon shipment if the seller has properly performed all his obligations with respect to the goods. Delivery to the carrier is delivery to the buyer for purposes of risk and 'title.' " Official Code comment 5 to Uniform Code section 2-503, similarly, explains that a term requiring the seller to pay the freight or the cost of delivery is not to be interpreted as the equivalent of a term requiring the seller to deliver to the buyer or to an agreed destination. In a standard "C.I.F." contract, then, the buyer bears the risk of loss in transit even though the cost of insurance is rolled into the purchase price and is, in fact, paid by the seller. By breaking out the cost of insurance, and requiring the buyer to pay it, Brawn's mail order contracts even more clearly place the risk of loss in transit on the buyer.

Other evidence, while not determinative, is consistent with the conclusion that Brawn at least intended the contracts to be shipment contracts. Brawn's own insurance covers goods lost while in Brawn's possession but does not cover goods destroyed or lost after the goods left Brawn's physical possession. Brawn pays California use tax, rather than sales tax, on the theory that the goods were "sold" when they left Brawn's place of business, located outside of California. Brawn records the revenue for the goods sold at the point of shipment, and removes the goods from its inventory at the time of shipment.

In sum, nothing in Brawn's conduct, and nothing in the delivery or insurance terms of Brawn's mail order forms, suggests that it was offering anything other than a standard, C.I.F.-type shipment contract, which the customers agreed to when they used Brawn's mail order form to purchase goods.

The judgment is reversed. The order awarding litigation expenses and attorney fees is reversed. Brawn is awarded its costs on appeal.

■ *Reversed.*

CASE CONCEPTS REVIEW

1. Why did the court decide this was a shipment contract?
2. What impact does the question of who pays the insurance have determining who bears the risk of loss?

Bailee

A party who takes possession of property with the understanding that the property must be delivered to the owner or other designated person

BAILMENTS Often, the goods will be in the possession of a **bailee**, such as a warehouse, and the arrangement is for the buyer to take delivery at the warehouse. If the goods are represented by a negotiable document of title—a warehouse receipt, for instance—when the seller tenders the document to the buyer, the risk of loss passes to the buyer. Likewise, risk passes to the buyer upon acknowledgment by the bailee that the buyer is entitled to the goods [2-509(2)]. In this situation, it is proper that the buyer assume the risk, as the seller has done all that could be expected to make the goods available to the buyer. It should be noted that if a nonnegotiable document of title is tendered to the buyer, risk of loss does not pass until the buyer has had a reasonable time to present the document to the bailee [2-503(4)(b)]. A refusal by the bailee to honor the document defeats the tender, and the risk of loss remains with the seller.

OTHER CASES In cases other than shipment and bailments, the passage of risk of loss to the buyer depends on the status of the seller. If the seller is a merchant, risk of loss will not pass to the buyer until the goods are received [2-509(3)]. The risk of loss remains with the merchant seller even though the buyer has paid for the goods in full and has been notified that the goods are at his disposal. Continuation of the risk, in this case, is justified on the basis that the merchant would be likely to carry insurance on goods within his or her control, whereas a buyer would not likely do so until the goods are actually received.

A nonmerchant seller transfers the risk of loss by *tendering* the goods [2-509(3)]. *A tender of delivery* occurs when the seller makes conforming goods available to the buyer and gives reasonable notice, so that the buyer may take delivery. Both parties are in the same position insofar as the likelihood of insurance is concerned, so the risk of loss passes to the buyer in cases where it would not do so if the seller were a merchant.

Sales on approval and sales with the right to return the goods are often involved in risk-of-loss cases. A characteristic of the sale on approval is that risk of loss in the event of theft or destruction of the goods does not pass to the buyer until he or she accepts the goods [2-327(1)(a)]. The buyer's failure to give the seller notice of a decision to return the goods will be treated as an acceptance. After notification of election to return, the seller must pay the expenses of the return and bear the risk of loss. In contrast, the buyer in a sale-or-return transaction has the risk of loss in the event of theft or destruction of the goods. The risk of loss remains with the buyer in the sale-or-return situation, even during the return shipment to the seller [2-327(2)(b)].

CHAPTER SUMMARY

ARTICLE 2 OF THE UCC

Common-Law Contract Changes

1. See Table 21-1.

Scope

1. Article 2 covers the sale of goods. It does not cover the sale of real estate or service contracts.
2. In mixed contracts, the Code is applicable if the sale of goods is the predominant part of the transaction.

Definitions

1. The term *goods* encompasses things that are movable, that is, items of personal property (chattels) that are of a tangible, physical nature.
2. A *sale* consists of the passing of title to goods from the seller to the buyer for a price.
3. A *merchant* is a professional businessperson who "holds himself out as having knowledge or skill peculiar to the practices or goods involved in the transaction.
4. Good *faith* is honesty, in fact, in the transaction. In the case of a merchant, it also includes the observance of reasonable commercial standards of fair dealing in the trade.
5. A *sale on approval* gives the buyer a reasonable time to decide if the sale shall take place. It is used in consumer purchases.
6. A *sale or return* is a consignment of goods whereby the buyer may return the goods not sold.

Abbreviations

1. F.O.B.—free on board
2. F.A.S.—free along side
3. C.I.F.—cost, insurance, and freight
4. These abbreviations are used to distinguish between a shipment contract and a destination contract for the purposes of passage of title and the allocation of risk of loss.

THE SALES CONTRACT

Express Agreement

1. The general rule in sales law is that the parties are free to make their own contract.
2. Parties cannot disclaim their Code obligations of good faith, diligence, and care, and unconscionable provisions will not be enforced.

3. In the absence of a contrary agreement, payment is due at the time and place at which the buyer is to receive the goods. A buyer who wants credit must specifically negotiate it in the contract.

Documentary Transactions

1. If a seller is unwilling to extend credit to the buyer, the seller may use a documentary exchange or cash against documents.
2. The document of title usually involved in this transaction is either a bill of lading or a warehouse receipt.

Course of Dealing, Usage of Trade, Course of Performance

1. A *course of dealing* is a sequence of prior conduct between the parties that gives a firm basis for interpreting their communications and conduct between themselves.
2. A *usage of trade* is a practice or custom in the particular trade used so frequently that it justifies the expectation that it will be followed in the transaction in question.
3. *Course of performance* concerns a contract that requires repeated performances. When an earlier performance has been accepted by the other party, that performance can be used to give meaning to the agreement regarding future performance.

Gap Filling under the Code

1. The price term of the contract can be left open, with the price to be fixed by later agreement of the parties or by some agreed-on market standard.
2. If the contract is silent on price, it will be a reasonable one.
3. The Code also allows flexibility in the quantity term of a sales contract. There may be an agreement to purchase the entire output of the seller, or the quantity may be specified as all that is required by the buyer.
4. If no time of delivery is stated in the contract, it may be supplied by parol evidence of the agreement. If not agreed on, a reasonable time is assumed.
5. Unless the contract provides to the contrary, the place for delivery is the seller's place of business. If the seller has no place of business, it is his or her residence.
6. If the time for payment has not been agreed on by the parties, the time for payment is when the buyer is to receive the delivery of the goods. However, the buyer generally may inspect the goods prior to making payment.

TITLE

In General

1. The Code has deemphasized the importance of title, and the location of title at any given time is usually not the controlling factor in determining the rights of the parties in a contract of sale.
2. The parties can specify when title passes. If there is no provision, the Code provides a series of rules governing the passage of title.

Identification to the Contract

1. Title to goods cannot pass until the goods have been identified to the contract.
2. Identification requires that the seller specify the particular goods involved in the transaction.
3. Crops are identified when they are planted. Unborn animals are identified when they are conceived.

Transfer of Title to Goods

1. Identification occurs, and title passes insofar as the specific goods are concerned, when the seller completes his or her performance with respect to the physical delivery of the goods.
2. If the seller has no responsibility for delivering goods located at the seller's place of business, title passes at the time and place of contracting if the goods are identified to the contract.
3. If the goods are in storage and the buyer will pick them up, title transfers when the seller delivers to the buyer the necessary document that permits the buyer to receive the goods.
4. In a shipment contract, title passes at the time and place of shipment.
5. If the contract requires that the seller deliver at the destination, title will not pass until the seller has tendered the goods to the buyer at that location.

Good-Faith Purchasers

1. A purchaser of goods usually acquires at least as good a title as the seller possessed.
2. A good-faith purchaser for value may acquire a better title than the seller had if the seller's title was voidable.

RISK OF LOSS

In Breach-of-Contract Cases

1. If the contract has been breached, the loss will be borne by the party who has breached. Thus, if the seller has tendered or delivered goods that are "nonconforming," the seller bears the risk of loss.
2. If the buyer breaches the contract at a time when the seller has identified proper goods to the contract, the risk of loss is on the buyer for a reasonable time.

If No Breach Exists

1. If a contract between buyer and seller provides for shipment by carrier under a shipment contract (F.O.B. shipping point), the risk of loss passes to the buyer when the goods are delivered to the carrier.
2. If shipment is made under a destination contract (F.O.B. destination), risk of loss does not pass to the buyer until the goods arrive at the destination and are available to the buyer for delivery.
3. It is presumed that a contract is one of shipment, not destination, and that the buyer should bear the risk of loss until arrival unless the seller has specifically agreed to do so or the circumstances indicate such an obligation.
4. If the goods are represented by a negotiable document of title, risk of loss passes to the buyer when the document is tendered.
5. In all cases other than shipment and bailment contracts, the passage of risk of loss to the buyer depends on the status of the seller. If the seller is a merchant, risk of loss will not pass to the buyer until he or she receives the goods, which means "takes physical possession of them."
6. A nonmerchant seller transfers the risk of loss by tendering the goods.

REVIEW QUESTIONS AND PROBLEMS

1. Match each term in Column A with the appropriate statement in Column B.

A	B
(1) Merchant	(a) Sale on consignment
(2) C.I.F.	(b) A term used in shipment by merchant vessel
(3) Bill of lading	(c) Buyer has the risk of loss if the goods are destroyed.
(4) Sale or return	(d) A requirement for title to pass
(5) Shipment contract	(e) A farmer in many states
(6) F.A.S.	(f) The buyer pays the cost of insuring the goods.
(7) Sale on approval	(g) Contract of shipment by a common carrier
(8) Identification	(h) May acquire a better title than his or her transferor had
(9) Good-faith purchaser	(i) Not covered by Article 2 of the Code
(10) Organ transplant	(j) Buyer's creditors have no claim on the goods in this transaction.

2. Tom entered into a contract to sell Jerry twenty acres of sod for $1,000 per acre. Jerry was allowed to remove it any time during the next twelve-month period. Is the contract governed by the Uniform Commercial Code? Explain.
3. The Macon Whoopies, a newly formed hockey club, contracts to buy 150 hockey pucks from a wholesaler in Youngstown, Ohio. What are the wholesaler's delivery obligations if the agreement states

   a. F.O.B. Macon?
   b. F.O.B. Youngstown?
   c. C.I.F. Macon?
   d. Ship to Macon Whoopies, Macon, Georgia?
   Explain.

4. Landrum, a collector of automobiles, was interested in buying a limited edition Chevrolet Corvette from Devenport. Devenport agreed the price would be the sticker price, $24,000 to $28,000. The car arrived with a sticker price of $24,688.21, but as a result of the demand for the car, the market price was $32,000. Is Landrum entitled to buy it for the sticker price? Why or why not?
5. Royster agreed to buy at least 31,000 tons of phosphate for three years from Columbia. When market conditions changed, Royster ordered only a fraction of the minimum and sought to renegotiate the deal. Columbia refused and sued. At trial, Royster wanted to introduce two forms of proof: (a) A usage of trade that expresses that price and quantity terms

in such contracts were never considered in the trade as more than mere projections, to be adjusted according to market forces; (b) course of dealing over a six-year period, which showed repeated and substantial deviations from the stated quantities or prices in other written contracts between the parties. Is the evidence admissible? Explain.

6. On February 11, 2007, plaintiff entered into a written contract to buy three sprinkler systems from the defendant. The seller orally agreed to deliver by the middle of May 2007. The written contract contained no designated delivery date. The seller did not deliver by May 15, and plaintiff claimed a crop loss of $75,000 because of the late delivery. Is oral evidence admissible to show the agreed-on date of delivery? Explain. Is the contract enforceable without a delivery date? Why or why not?
7. The Big Knob Volunteer Fire Department agreed to purchase a fire truck from Custom Productions, Inc. The contract provided for a down payment and for title to pass upon full payment. Custom painted the buyer's name on the truck. The seller refused to deliver the truck, and the buyer filed suit for possession of the truck. Is the buyer entitled to the truck? Why or why not?
8. Don, engaged in the business of installing underground telephone lines, ordered three reels of underground cable from Pat to be delivered at Don's place of business. Pat delivered reels of aerial rather than underground cable. When informed of the mistake, Pat told Don to return the cable, but he was unable to do so because of a trucking strike. The cable was stolen from Don's regular storage space, where it had been delivered. Pat sued for the purchase price. Who has the risk of loss? Explain.
9. Amy delivered stereo tapes, compact discs, and stereo equipment to Tex, a service station operator, for resale. The invoice provided that the equipment would be picked up if not sold in ninety days. The service station was burglarized about two weeks later, and the stereo equipment was stolen. Who must bear the loss resulting from the burglary? Why?
10. How can a nonmerchant seller transfer the risk of loss to a buyer?

Sales Contracts: Breach and Remedies | 22

CHAPTER OUTLINE

CHAPTER PREVIEW

In the preceding chapter, several basic issues related to the sales contract were discussed. Throughout that discussion, we presumed that the contracting parties were willing to perform the promises made. This chapter discusses a variety of situations based on either the seller or the buyer failing to perform properly.

As a general rule, a seller is obligated to deliver or tender delivery of goods that measure up to the requirements of the contract and to do so at the proper time and at the proper place. The goods and other performance of the seller must conform to the contract. The seller is required to tender delivery as a condition to the buyer's duty to accept the goods and pay for them. Thus, the seller has performed when he or she has made the goods available to the buyer. The buyer, in turn, must render his or her performance, which means that the buyer must accept the goods and pay for them.

When one or both of these parties breach the sales contract, the Code provides for numerous remedies. These remedies are available unless, by the language in the sales contract, the buyer and seller have agreed to limit or modify the Code remedies.

BUSINESS MANAGEMENT DECISION

As the sales manager of a retail music store, you meet with a customer who has purchased a $3,500 set of drums. This customer complains that the bass drum is defective, and she wants her money back.

How would you respond to this customer?

OVERVIEW OF CODE REMEDIES

1. Checklist

Two sections of the Code [2-703, 2-711] list the remedies of the seller and the remedies of the buyer. Each section provides both parties with four remedies, which are exact counterparts. Table 22-1 shows their significant correlation.

The four remedies are listed in the Code not only as equivalent actions *but also as equivalent in order of importance*. The Code assumes that, upon a breach by the buyer, the seller will resell the goods and sue the buyer for any difference between the resale price and the original contract

TABLE 22-1 ■ Comparison of Code Remedies

Seller's Remedies [2-703]	Buyer's Remedies [2-711]
1. Resell the goods and recover damages [2-706].	1. Cover (buy same goods elsewhere) and recover damages [2-712].
2. Cancel the contract.	2. Reject the contract.
3. Recover damages for nonacceptance [2-708].	3. Recover damages for nondelivery [2-713].
4. Sue for the actual price of the goods [2-709].	4. Sue to get the goods (specific performance or replevy) [2-716].

price. When the seller breaches, the Code assumes that the buyer will cover by buying substitute goods and sue the seller for any difference between the cover price and the original contract price.

Obviously, before either party has one of the four remedies, the other party must have breached the contract. There are at least four possible situations in which either party may be in breach of contract:

1. *Anticipatory repudiation* by the buyer or by the seller
2. *Failure of performance* (buyer fails to pay or seller fails to deliver)
3. A rightful or wrongful *rejection* by the buyer
4. A rightful or wrongful *revocation of acceptance* by the buyer

Generally, the Code remedies are specified as either for the buyer's or seller's benefits. However, one remedy is available to both parties to a sales contract. This remedy, known as a request for adequate assurance of performance, is discussed in the next section.

2. Adequate Assurances

Under certain circumstances, either party may be concerned about the other's future performance. If a buyer is in arrears on other payments, the seller will naturally be concerned about making further deliveries. If the seller has been delivering faulty goods to other customers, the buyer will be fearful that the goods received may also be defective. The law recognizes that no one wants to buy a lawsuit and that merely having the right to sue for breach of contract is a somewhat hollow remedy. There is a need to protect the party whose reasonable expectation of due performance is jeopardized.

The Code grants this protection to seek adequate assurances by providing that the contract for sale imposes an obligation on each party that the other's expectation of receiving due performances will not be impaired [2-609]. A party who has reasonable grounds for insecurity about the other's performance can demand *in writing* that the other offer convincing proof that he or she will, in fact, perform. Having made the demand, the requesting party may then suspend performance until he or she receives assurance of the other party's commitment to perform. If no assurance is forthcoming within a reasonable time, not to exceed thirty days, the contract may be treated as repudiated [2-609(2)].

Two issues often arise: What are reasonable grounds for insecurity? What constitutes an adequate assurance of performance? The Code does not particularly answer these questions, but it does provide that between merchants commercial standards shall be applied to help provide the answers [2-609(2)]. In the event of a dispute, these are questions of fact for a jury.

BUYER'S RIGHTS AND REMEDIES

3. Summary

If the seller breaches the sales contract, the buyer has a number of options for action. First, the buyer is authorized to determine *whether a breach has occurred.* This right to inspect the goods being delivered is of paramount importance to the buyer as a method of avoiding complications. If the goods delivered by the seller are not in conformity with the contract, the buyer may reject them. Even a buyer who has accepted the goods may be able to revoke the acceptance and be in the same legal position as if the goods had been rejected initially.

If the seller fails to perform, the buyer may purchase (cover) his or her needs in the marketplace. This buyer may then sue the seller for the increased costs of the goods and the expenses related to the remedy of cover.

Finally, in a limited set of circumstances, the non-breaching buyer may be able to recover the actual goods described in the sales contract. This last remedy is an example of court-ordered specific performance.

These Code remedies available for the buyer's benefit are discussed in the next eight sections. While studying these remedies, remember that they are the exclusive basis for relief to a buyer in a commercial transaction.

4. Right to Inspect

The buyer has a right—before payment or acceptance—to *inspect* the goods at any reasonable time and place and in any reasonable manner [2-513(1)]. The place for the inspection is determined by the nature of the contract. If the seller is to send the goods to the buyer, the inspection may be postponed until after arrival of the goods. The buyer must pay the expenses of inspection but can recover his or her expenses from the seller if the inspection reveals that the goods are nonconforming and the buyer therefore rejects them [2-513(2)].

If the contract provides for delivery C.O.D., the buyer must pay prior to inspection. Likewise, payment must be made prior to inspection if the contract calls for payment against documents of title [2-513(3)]. When the buyer is required to make payment prior to inspection, the payment does not impair his or her right to pursue remedies if subsequent inspection reveals defects [2-512].

The buyer's right to inspect is tied to his or her right to reject the goods if they are defective or nonconforming to the contract. The following two sections discuss the buyer's responsibility with respect to the right of rejection.

5. Right to Reject

If the goods or the tender of delivery fails to conform to the contract, the buyer has the right to *reject* them. Several options are available. The buyer may reject the whole, or accept either the whole or any commercial unit or units and reject the rest [2-601]. A *commercial unit* is one that is generally regarded as a single whole for purposes of sale, one that would be impaired in value if divided [2-105(6)]. When accepting nonconforming goods, the buyer does not impair his or her right of recourse against the seller. Provided that the buyer notifies the seller of the breach

The buyer has the right to reject the goods if the contract is not adhered to.

within a reasonable time, the buyer may still pursue his or her remedy for damages for breach of contract, even though he or she accepts the goods.

6. Notice of Rejection

The right to reject defective or nonconforming goods is dependent on the buyer's taking action within a reasonable time after the goods are tendered or delivered. If rejecting, the buyer must **seasonably** notify the seller of this fact. Failing to do so would render the rejection ineffective and constitute an acceptance [2-602(1)]. If the buyer continues in possession of defective goods for an unreasonable time, he or she forfeits the right to reject them. However, a buyer who fails to reject defective goods still may sue for breach of contract.

Seasonably

An action is taken seasonably when it is taken at, or within, the time agreed; or if no time is agreed, at or within a reasonable time.

The requirement of seasonable notice of rejection is very important. Without such notice, the rejection is ineffective [2-602(1)]. As a general rule, a notice of rejection may simply state that the goods are not conforming, without particular specification of the defects relied on by the buyer. If, however, the defect could have been corrected by the seller had he or she been given particularized notice, then the failure to particularize will take away from the buyer the right to rely on that defect as a breach justifying a rejection [2-605(1)(a)]. Therefore, a buyer should always give detailed information relative to the reason for the rejection.

In transactions between merchants, the merchant seller is entitled to demand a full and final written statement of all the defects. If the statement is not forthcoming after a written request for it, the buyer may not rely on these defects to justify a rejection or to establish that a breach has occurred [2-605(1)(b)].

7. Rights and Duties on Rejection

A buyer who rejects the goods after taking physical possession of them is required to hold the goods with reasonable care long enough for the seller to remove them [2-602(2)(b)]. Somewhat greater obligations are imposed on a merchant buyer who rejects goods that have been delivered [2-603]. The merchant is under a duty to follow the seller's reasonable instructions as to the disposition of the goods. If the seller does not furnish instructions as to the disposition of the rejected goods, the merchant buyer must make reasonable efforts to sell them for the seller's account if they are perishable or if they threaten to decline in value speedily. If a sale is not mandatory for the reasons just stated, the buyer has three options. The buyer may store the rejected goods for the seller's account, reship them to the seller, or resell them for the seller's account [2-604].

Code Section 2-711(3) gives a buyer a security interest in the goods in his or her possession and the right to resell them. Thus a buyer of defective goods can reject and resell the goods, deduct all expenses regarding care, custody, resale, and other matters (such as the down payment), and then remit any money left over to the seller [2-604, 2-711(3)].

8. Right to Revoke Acceptance

ACCEPTANCE The buyer has *accepted* goods if (1) after a reasonable opportunity to inspect them, the buyer indicates to the seller that the goods are conforming or that he or she will take or retain them in spite of their nonconformity; (2) the buyer has failed to make an effective rejection of the goods; or (3) the buyer does any act inconsistent with the seller's ownership [2-606].

REVOCATION The buyer may revoke his or her acceptance under certain circumstances. In many instances, the buyer will have accepted nonconforming goods because the defect was not immediately discoverable or reasonably assumed that the seller would correct by substituting goods that did conform. In either case, the buyer has the privilege of "revoking" his or her acceptance by notifying the seller if, but only if, the nonconformity "substantially impairs the value to him" [2-608(1)].

Revocation must take place within a reasonable time after the buyer has discovered, or should have discovered, the reason for revocation [2-608(2)]. If a buyer revokes acceptance, he or she is then placed in the same position with reference to the goods as if he or she had rejected them in the first instance [2-608(3)]. The buyer has a security interest in the goods for the payments made and is entitled to damages as if no acceptance had occurred.

9. Right to Cover

Cover
A good-faith, prompt, reasonable purchase of, or contract to purchase, goods in substitution for those due from the seller

The buyer who has not received the goods bargained for may **cover**—that is, arrange to purchase the goods from some other source in substitution for those due from the seller [2-712]. This is a practical remedy, as the buyer must often proceed without delay to obtain goods needed for his or her own use or for resale. The buyer must act reasonably and in good faith in arranging for the cover [2-712(1)].

A buyer may collect from a seller the difference between what was paid for the substitute goods and the contract price [2-712(2)]. The buyer may also collect any incidental and consequential damages. *Incidental damages* are defined as those that are reasonably incurred in connection with handling rejected goods. These damages consist of "commercially reasonable charges, expenses or commissions in connection with effecting cover and any other reasonable expense incident to the delay or other breach" [2-715(1)]. *Consequential damages* include "any loss resulting from general or particular requirements and needs of which the seller at the time of contracting had reason to know and which could not reasonably be prevented by cover or otherwise" [2-715(2)]. The buyer is obligated to keep damages to a minimum by making an appropriate cover insofar as his or her right to any consequential damages is concerned.

The cover remedy provides certainty as to the amount of the buyer's damages. The difference between the contract price and the price paid by the buyer for substitute goods can be readily determined. Although the buyer must act reasonably and in good faith, the buyer need not prove that he or she obtained the goods at the cheapest price available.

10. Right to Damages for Nondelivery

The aggrieved buyer who did not receive any goods from the seller or who received nonconforming goods is not required to cover; instead, the buyer may bring an action for damages [2-712(3)]. The measure of damages for nondelivery or repudiation is the difference between the contract price and the market price when the buyer learned of the breach [2-713]. The buyer is also entitled to any incidental or consequential damages sustained. Damages to which a buyer is entitled consist of "the loss resulting in the ordinary course of events from the seller's breach as determined in any manner which is reasonable" [2-714(1)]. In a purchase for resale, it would be appropriate to measure the buyer's damage upon nondelivery as the difference between the contract price and the price at which the goods were to be resold. In other words, the damages equal the difference between the contract price and the fair market value of the goods.

Another recourse open to the buyer is the right to deduct damages from any part of the price still due under the same contract [2-717]. The buyer determines what his or her damages are and withholds this amount when paying the seller. The buyer is required to give notice to the seller of his or her intention to deduct damages. When the buyer's damages are established by the cover price, the amount is clear-cut. In other instances, the seller might question the amount of the deduction, and this dispute would have to be resolved between the parties or by a court.

Damages may be deducted only from the price due under the same contract. A buyer could not deduct damages for non-delivered goods under one contract from the price due under other contracts with the same seller.

Also, there are situations where the good are accepted but the buyer discovers a serious problem with the item. What are the appropriate damages for goods that are accepted but there is a breach of warranty? Consider the following case.

CASE

Jessica Mayberry v. Volkswagen of America, Inc.

SUPREME COURT OF WISCONSIN

692 N.W.2d 226 (2005)

JON P. WILCOX

On October 14, 2000, the plaintiff, Jessica Mayberry, purchased a new 2001 galactic blue Volkswagen Jetta GLS from Van Dyn Hoven Imports in Appleton, Wisconsin. The cash price of the vehicle was $17,800. After sales tax, registration, title, and other fees, the price of the vehicle came to $18,526. However, according to Mayberry, the total purchase price of the vehicle came to $22,548 after adding finance charges. As part of the vehicle purchase, the manufacturer, Volkswagen, issued a two-year or 24,000 mile limited warranty for the Jetta. Under the terms of the written warranty, Volkswagen agreed to repair any manufacturer's defect in material or workmanship and replace defective parts free of charge for the warranty period. However, the warranty did not give Mayberry the right to a refund or replacement of the vehicle if it was defective.

Shortly after taking possession of the Jetta, Mayberry began experiencing problems with the vehicle. Service records from Van Dyn Hoven indicate that Mayberry brought the vehicle in for service on a number of occasions for various problems. The problems consisted of a broken armrest, intermittent illumination of the "check engine" light, and burning and leaking oil. The engine problems culminated in the replacement of a piston ring in the engine on November 29, 2001. On all occasions, the vehicle was inspected or repaired free of charge under the warranty. Thereafter, Mayberry attempted to revoke acceptance of the vehicle in writing. Volkswagen refused the revocation.

On June 3, 2002, Mayberry filed suit against Volkswagen under the federal Magnuson-Moss Warranty Act, 15 U.S.C. § 2301 et seq. (2000), asserting three causes of action. First, Mayberry alleged that Volkswagen breached its written warranty for the vehicle. Second, Mayberry contended that Volkswagen breached its implied warranty of merchantability under 15 U.S.C. §§ 2301(7) & 2308. Finally, Mayberry claimed that she revoked her acceptance under 15 U.S.C. § 2310.

Subsequently, Mayberry traded in her Volkswagen for a 2003 Mazda Tribute at Mazda Knoxville. Mayberry received $15,100 as a trade-in allowance for the Jetta. The total purchase price of the Mazda Tribute was $24,149.32. At the time of the trade-in, the mileage on the Jetta was 32,737. On November 8, 2002, Mayberry amended her complaint to reflect the trade-in of the Jetta. As an affirmative defense to the amended complaint, Volkswagen alleged that Mayberry "suffered no damages as she received more than the full fair market value for the vehicle which is the subject of the action at the time of the trade in."

On May 28, 2003, the circuit court entered judgment in favor of Volkswagen, dismissing Mayberry's complaint in its entirety. The court of appeals reversed, concluding that the circuit court utilized an incorrect standard for measuring damages and that genuine issues of material fact concerning damages existed.

We begin by noting that we are not presented with any issue concerning whether Volkswagen actually breached any of its warranties in this case. Rather, the appeal concerns only the issue of what measure of damages is appropriate in this case. Thus, for purposes of this appeal, we will assume that Mayberry's allegations regarding Volkswagen's breach of warranties are true.

Wisconsin's Uniform Commercial Code governs the remedies available for transactions involving the sale of goods. Wisconsin Stat. § 402.714(2), governing a buyer's damages for breach of warranty, provides: "The measure of damages for breach of warranty is the difference at the time and place of acceptance between the value of the goods accepted and the value they would have had if they had been as warranted, unless special circumstances show proximate damages of a different amount."

The core of Volkswagen's argument is that special circumstances are present when an automobile purchaser uses the vehicle for an extended period of time, the manufacturer makes numerous repairs free of charge under its warranty, and the consumer later resells it for more than its fair market value. According to Volkswagen, under these circumstances, damages should be calculated based on the actual value and fair market value of the vehicle at the time of resale.

We have found no authority that stands for the proposition that the proper measure of damages under the Uniform Commercial Code is the difference between the market value and actual price of the defective product at the time and place of resale when the plaintiff alleges a breach of the manufacturer's written warranty and implied warranty of merchantability. Breach of contract remedies under the Uniform Commercial Code are designed to put the aggrieved party "in as good a position as if the other party had fully performed." Section 2-714 of the Uniform Commercial Code is designed to compensate "'damage flowing directly from insufficient product quality.'"

Mayberry has alleged that she suffered damages because her vehicle was defective when she accepted it and she did not receive a vehicle of the quality for which she paid. The fact that Mayberry later

continued

resold the vehicle for more than its fair market value does not totally negate the fact that she did not receive the benefit of her bargain. While the amount of profit realized on the resale may be relevant to the issue of mitigation, construing the "special circumstances" clause of § 402.714(2) to completely bar the plaintiff from maintaining a claim would defeat the manifest purpose of the remedies under the Uniform Commercial Code, which are to compensate the plaintiff for her direct economic loss and place her in as good a position as if the seller had fully performed.

Therefore, we hold that pursuant to Wis. Stat. § 402.714(2), the appropriate method for measuring damages, in this case, is the difference between the warranted value of the vehicle in question and its actual value at the time and place of acceptance. Further, we conclude that Mayberry has established a prima facie case of damages sufficient to survive summary judgment under this standard.

The decision of the court of appeals is affirmed.

■ *Affirmed.*

CASE CONCEPTS REVIEW

1. What was the appropriate method for determining damages in this case?
2. Did the consumer in this case receive a windfall in the amount of damages awarded? Is this appropriate?

11. Right to the Goods

Under proper circumstances, a buyer has rights in, and to, the actual goods purchased. The remedy of *specific performance* is available (1) when the goods are *unique* and (2) when other *circumstances make it equitable* that the seller renders the required performance [2-716(1)]. To obtain specific performance, the buyer must have been unable to cover. The Code does not define unique, but it is fair to assume that it would encompass output and requirement contracts in which the goods were not readily or practically available from other sources. Even if the goods are not unique, the Code provides that the buyer may recover them under "proper circumstances. When a buyer cannot practically buy the goods elsewhere, a proper circumstance for specific performance probably exists.

Replevin
A remedy by statute for the recovery of the possession of personal property

Another remedy that enables the buyer to reach the goods in the hands of the seller is the statutory remedy of replevin. **Replevin** is an action to recover the goods that one person wrongfully withholds from another. A buyer has the right to replevin goods from the seller if the goods have been *identified* to the contract and the buyer is unable to effect cover after making a reasonable effort to do so [2-716(3)].

A related remedy that also reaches the goods in the hands of the seller is the buyer's right to recover them if the seller becomes insolvent [2-502]. The right exists only if (1) the buyer has a "special property interest" in the goods (that is, existing goods have been identified to the contract) and (2) the seller becomes insolvent within ten days after receiving the first installment payment from the buyer. Without these circumstances, the buyer is relegated to the position of a general creditor of the seller. It is apparent that if the buyer can recover the goods, he or she is in a much better position than as a general creditor, particularly if the buyer had paid a substantial amount of the purchase price. To exercise this remedy, the buyer must make and maintain a tender of any unpaid portion of the price.

SELLER'S RIGHTS AND REMEDIES

12. Summary

The Code establishes certain rights and remedies for sellers, just as it does for buyers. A seller has several alternative courses of action when a buyer breaches the contract. One of the most significant rights is to *cure* a defective performance. The seller also may *cancel* the contract if the buyer's breach is material. Under certain circumstances, a seller may withhold delivery or stop delivery if the goods are in transit. A seller also has the right to *resell* the goods and recover damages or simply to recover damages for the buyer's failure to accept the goods. Finally, the seller may, under certain circumstances, file suit to *recover* the price of the goods. The remedies of the seller are cumulative and not exclusive. The technical aspects of "cure" and of these remedies are discussed in the following sections.

13. Right to Cure

Cure

An opportunity for the seller of defective goods to correct the defect and thereby not be held to have breached the sales contract

Upon inspecting the goods, if the buyer finds that they do not conform to the contract, he or she may reject them, provided that he or she acts fairly in doing so. If the rejection is for a relatively minor deviation from the contract requirements, the seller must be given an opportunity to correct the defective performance. This is called **cure**. The seller may accomplish this by notifying the buyer of his or her intention to cure and then tendering proper or conforming goods if the time for performance has not expired. If the time for performance has expired, the seller—if he or she has reasonable grounds to believe that the goods will be acceptable in spite of the nonconformity—will be granted further time to substitute goods that are in accordance with the contract. The main purpose of this rule allowing cure is to protect the seller from being forced into a breach by a surprise rejection at the last moment by the buyer.

14. Right to Reclaim Goods from an Insolvent Buyer

If a seller discovers that a buyer who has been extended credit is insolvent, the seller will want to withhold delivery before it is completed. An insolvent buyer is one "who either has ceased to pay his debts in the ordinary course of business or cannot pay his debts as they become due or is insolvent within the meaning of the federal bankruptcy law" [1-201(23)].

A seller, upon discovering that a buyer is insolvent, may refuse to make any further deliveries except for cash and may demand that payment be made for all goods previously delivered under the contract [2-702(1)]. If goods are en route to the buyer, they may be stopped in transit and recovered from the carrier [2-705]. If they are in a warehouse or other place of storage awaiting delivery to the buyer, the seller may stop delivery by the bailee. Thus the seller can protect his or her interests by retaining or reclaiming the goods prior to the time they come into the possession of the insolvent buyer.

This right to reclaim the goods on the buyer's insolvency includes situations in which the goods have come into the buyer's possession. If the buyer has received goods on credit while he or she is insolvent, the seller can reclaim the goods by making a demand for them within ten days after their receipt by the buyer [2-702(2)]. By receiving the goods, the buyer has, in effect, made a representation that he or she is solvent and able to pay for them. If the buyer has made a written misrepresentation of solvency within the three-month period before the goods were delivered, and the seller has justifiably relied on the writing, the ten-day limitation period during which the seller can reclaim the goods from the insolvent buyer is not applicable to the seller's right of reclamation [2-702(2)].

The importance to a seller of the privilege of reclaiming goods or stopping them in transit should be clear. If the insolvent buyer is adjudicated a bankrupt debtor, the goods will become a part of the debtor's estate and will be sold by the trustee in bankruptcy for the benefit of *all* the creditors of the buyer. If the seller is able to reclaim the goods, his or her loss will be kept to a minimum.

The following case details the efforts to reclaim goods and the application of Code principles to resolve a dispute.

CASE

In Re: Trico Steel Company, LLC, Inc., et al., Debtors. Trico Steel Company, LLC, Appellant, v. Cargill Inc., Appellee

UNITED STATES DISTRICT COURT FOR THE DISTRICT OF DELAWARE

302 B.R. 489 (2003)

By way of brief background, the Debtor (Trico Steel Company) arranged to purchase 35,000 metric tons of pig iron from Cargill at the price of $120.50 per ton "CIFFO New Orleans, Louisiana." To fill the Debtor's order, Cargill purchased iron from another company and arranged for carriers to ship and deliver the iron to New Orleans. Thereafter, the Debtor entered into an agreement with Celtic Marine Corporation ("Celtic") to arrange for barge transportation for a portion of the pig iron from New Orleans to the Debtor's facility in Decatur, Alabama. Celtic then arranged for the river carrier, Volunteer Barge & Transport, Inc. ("Volunteer"), to provide the actual barge transportation. When the pig iron arrived in New Orleans, the iron was loaded onto Volunteer's barges for transit to Decatur by stevedores hired by the Debtor. While the pig iron was in transit, Cargill learned that the Debtor was insolvent. Cargill then notified Celtic that it was exercising its right to stop the iron in transit due to the Debtor's insolvency. Shortly thereafter, Cargill filed an adversary action in the Bankruptcy Court seeking a declaration that it was entitled to immediate possession of the pig iron. Cross-motions for summary judgment were filed by the respective parties, and the Bankruptcy Court granted Cargill's motion for summary judgment and denied the Debtor's motion for summary judgment.

By their appeal, Appellants contend that the Debtor received the pig iron within the meaning of Article 2-705(2)(a) of the U.C.C., such that Cargill was precluded from exercising its rights under Article 2 to stop the goods in transit upon learning of the Debtor's insolvency. Appellants contend that the stevedores the Debtor hired were its agents and that they exercised constructive possession over the pig iron by unloading and reloading it pursuant to the Debtor's instructions. Appellants also maintain that the final destination of the pig iron was New Orleans, and therefore, the Debtor was in receipt of the pig iron when it arrived in New Orleans.

After reviewing the conclusions of the Bankruptcy Court under a plenary standard of review, the Court concludes that the Bankruptcy Court correctly concluded that the Debtor did not receive the pig iron within the meaning of Section 2-705(2)(a) of the U.C.C. The Bankruptcy Court correctly found that the stevedores hired by the Debtor were merely intermediaries or links in transit and not agents or employees of the Debtor who received the pig iron within the meaning of Section 2-705. The Bankruptcy Court also correctly concluded that New Orleans was not the final destination of the pig iron because the Debtor did not intend for the pig iron to remain in New Orleans. Thus, the Bankruptcy Court correctly concluded that the Debtor never came into possession of the pig iron. The Bankruptcy Court thoroughly analyzed all of the issues raised by the parties in this regard, and the Court agrees with and adopts the analysis of the Bankruptcy Court.

For the reasons discussed, the Court will affirm the Order of the Bankruptcy Court.

■ *Affirmed.*

CASE CONCEPTS REVIEW

1. Why did the court rule in favor of Cargill?
2. What would have happened if Cargill was unable to stop the goods in transit?

15. Right to Reclaim Goods from a Solvent Buyer

The *right to stop goods in transit or to withhold delivery* is not restricted to the insolvency situation. If the buyer has (1) wrongfully rejected a tender of goods, (2) revoked acceptance, (3) failed to make a payment due on or before delivery, or (4) repudiated with respect to either a part of the goods or the whole contract, the seller can also reclaim the goods. This right extends to any goods directly affected by the breach.

To stop delivery by a carrier, the seller must give proper and timely notice to the carrier so there is reasonable time to follow the instructions [2-705(3)]. Once the goods have been received by the buyer, or a bailee has acknowledged that he or she holds the goods for the buyer, the right of stoppage is at an end. Only in the case of insolvency [2-704(2)] can the seller reclaim the goods after they are in the buyer's possession.

The right to stop delivery to a solvent buyer is restricted to carload, truckload, planeload, or larger shipments. This restriction is designed to ease the burden on carriers that could develop if the right to stop for reasons other than insolvency applied to all small shipments. The seller who is shipping to a buyer of doubtful credit can always send the goods C.O.D. and thus preclude the

The right to stop delivery is restricted to certain shipments such as planeloads.

necessity for stopping the goods in transit. Of course, the seller must exercise care in availing himself or herself of this remedy, as improper stoppage is a breach by the seller and would subject him or her to an action for damages by the buyer.

16. Right to Resell Goods

The seller who is in possession of goods at the time of the buyer's breach has the *right to resell* the goods [2-706]. If part of the goods has been delivered, the seller can resell the undelivered portion. In this way the seller can quickly realize at least some of the amount due from the buyer. The seller also has a claim against the buyer for the difference between the resale price and the price that the buyer had agreed to pay. The resale remedy thus affords a practical method and course of action for the seller who has possession of goods that were intended for a breaching buyer. Any person in the position of a seller of goods has the right to resell the goods when a buyer defaults.

Frequently, a buyer will breach or repudiate the contract prior to the time that goods have been identified to the contract. This occurs when goods are in the process of manufacture. This does not defeat the seller's right to resell the goods. The seller may proceed to identify goods to the contract [2-704(1)(a)] and then use his or her remedy of resale. When the goods are unfinished, the seller may also use a remedy of resale if he or she can show that the unfinished goods were intended for the particular contract [2-704(1)(b)]. The seller may also resell the unfinished goods for scrap or salvage value or take any other reasonable action in connection with the goods [2-704(2)]. The only requirement is that the seller use reasonable commercial judgment in determining which course of action to take to mitigate the damages. Presumably the seller would rake into consideration factors such as the extent to which the manufacture had been completed and the resalability of the goods if he or she elected to complete the manufacture. Thus, the law allows the seller to proceed in a commercially reasonable manner to protect his or her interests.

When the seller elects to use his or her remedy of resale, the resale may be either a private sale or a public (auction) sale [2-706(2)]. The resale must be identified as one relating to the broken contract. If the resale is private, the seller must give the buyer reasonable notification of his or her intention to resell [2-706(3)]. If the resale is public, the seller must give the buyer reasonable notice of the time and place so the buyer can bid or can obtain the attendance of other bidders. With goods that are perishable or threaten to decline speedily in value, the notice is not required. The seller is permitted to buy at a public sale. The prime requirement is that the sale be conducted in a commercially reasonable manner [2-706(2)]. If the resale brings a higher price than that provided for in the contract, the seller is not accountable to the buyer for any profit [2-706(6)].

17. Right to Collect Damages

In many situations, a resale would not be an appropriate or sufficient remedy. The seller may elect to bring an *action for damages* if the buyer refuses to accept the goods or repudiates the contract [2-708]. The measure of damages is the difference between the market price at the place for tender and the unpaid contract price, plus incidental damages [2-708]. Incidental damages include expenses reasonably incurred as a result of the buyer's breach [2-710].

Usually, this measure of damages will not put the seller in as good a position as he or she would have had if the buyer had performed and the seller had not lost the sale. Under such circumstances, the measure of damages includes the profit the seller would have made from full performance by the buyer [2-708(2)] as well as incidental damages. In computing profit, the reasonable overhead of the seller may be taken into account. The measure of damages recognizes that a seller suffers a loss, even though the seller may ultimately resell for the same amount that he or she would have received from the buyer. The seller has lost a sale and the profit on that sale.

18. Right to Collect the Purchase Price

When the buyer fails to pay the price as it becomes due, the seller may sue for the *contract price* of the goods if the buyer has accepted the goods, the goods were destroyed after risk of loss passed to the buyer, or the resale remedy is not practicable. If goods are specially manufactured for a buyer and there is no market for the special goods, the seller may collect the purchase price since his or her right to resell is not available.

If the seller sues for the price, the goods are held by the seller on behalf of the buyer. In effect, the goods are to be treated as if they belong to the buyer. After the seller obtains a judgment against the buyer, the seller may still resell the goods at any time prior to collection of the judgment but must apply the proceeds toward satisfaction of the judgment. Payment of the balance due on the judgment entitles the buyer to any goods not resold [2-709(2)].

The following case illustrates the application of the "action for price" provision.

CASE

Oneida Ltd. v. RedTagBiz, Inc.

UNITED STATES DISTRICT COURT FOR THE NORTHERN DISTRICT OF NEW YORK

2002 U.S. Dist. LEXIS 22054 (2002)

JUDGE HOWARD G. MUNSON

In July of 2000, plaintiff Oneida Ltd. ("Oneida") entered into a written agreement with non-party CarLen Enterprises, Inc. ("CarLen") for the purchase of "closeout" goods from Oneida. CarLen was interested in selling the goods to its own customers, but it did not have the financial ability to pay Oneida in advance.

In October 2000, CarLen provided defendant RedTagBiz, Inc. ("RedTag") with the opportunity to purchase the goods from Oneida and re-sell them to CarLen's customers because RedTag had the ability to make advance payments to Oneida. RedTag accepted the opportunity and agreed with CarLen that CarLen would obtain orders from its customers and provide the orders to RedTag, who would forward them to Oneida. Then, RedTag would make the advance payment to Oneida, and RedTag and CarLen would split the profits from the sale equally.

On November 1, 2000, RedTag and Oneida entered into a two-page agreement ("Agreement"). After the Agreement was signed, RedTag made two payments of $250,000 each, and Oneida shipped a portion of *the goods that RedTag had ordered. The subsequent facts pertaining to the parties' actions pursuant to the Agreement are greatly disputed.*

On January 24, 2001, Oneida filed the present action in New York State Supreme Court, Madison County, primarily alleging breach of contract. The action was removed to this court on March 16, 2001. Currently before the court is RedTag's motion for partial summary judgment

RedTag claims that Oneida's failure to establish the elements of an "action for price" under § 2-709 warrants dismissal of the claim. Under § 2-709, if a buyer fails to pay the price for goods as it becomes due and a seller is unable to re-sell them at a reasonable price after a reasonable effort, then a seller may recover the price of accepted goods identified to the contract, plus incidental damages.

RedTag claims that Oneida's failure to allege and meet its burden under § 2-709(b) to prove that the goods identified to the Agreement cannot be re-sold warrants dismissal of the claim. Specifically, RedTag argues the validity of its claim for three reasons. First, RedTag argues that Oneida has failed to allege in its Complaint that the goods could not readily be re-sold. While this was originally the case, the court has subsequently granted Oneida's motion for leave to amend the Complaint and include specific allegations pertaining to the resale of goods. Therefore, RedTag's argument is without merit.

Secondly, RedTag argues that Oneida has failed to produce evidence of its inability to re-sell the goods at a reasonable price. This argument is also without merit. Oneida has alleged and offered evidence to support its claim that it was unable to sell all of the goods identified to the agreement.

Finally, RedTag argues that Oneida has failed to produce evidence that there is no market for the goods and, therefore, that it need not attempt to re-sell them. At this time, there is sufficient evidence to support a finding that Oneida did, in fact, undertake at least some reasonable efforts to re-sell the goods identified to the Agreement. Therefore, RedTag's argument that Oneida's failure to produce evidence that there is no market for the goods is irrelevant and without merit.

Because RedTag has failed to prove its claim that Oneida's failure to allege and meet its burden under § 2-709(b) to prove that the goods identified to the Agreement cannot be re-sold, its motion for summary judgment based on Oneida's alleged failure to establish the elements of an "action for price" under § 2-709(b) must be denied.

■ *Denied.*

CASE CONCEPTS REVIEW

1. What are the elements of an "action for price"?
2. What must the seller show to assert that the goods can be re-sold?

CHAPTER SUMMARY

OVERVIEW

Checklist

1. See Table 22-1.

Adequate Assurances

1. This is the one remedy that is available to both buyers and sellers.
2. The Code provides that either party may demand in writing that the other give assurance that performance will be forthcoming.
3. If assurance of performance is not given, the party who requested such assurance may treat the contract as breached.

BUYER'S RIGHTS AND REMEDIES

Right to Inspect

1. A buyer has a right before payment or acceptance to inspect the goods at any reasonable time and place.
2. If the contract is C.O.D. or calls for payment against documents, a buyer must pay before he or she can inspect. Payment, however, is not acceptance, and inspection still is permitted.

Right to Reject

1. If the goods fail in any respect to conform to the contract, a buyer can reject.
2. A buyer can reject the whole or accept any commercial unit and reject the rest.

Notice of Rejection

1. Rejection must be within a reasonable time, and notice of rejection must be timely. Failure to do either will result in an acceptance.

Rights and Duties on Rejection

1. After rejection, a buyer who takes possession of the goods must protect them and follow any reasonable instructions from the seller.
2. A buyer has a security interest in the goods and can resell them to recover his or her expenses in taking possession and caring for the goods.

Right to Revoke Acceptance

1. A buyer accepts if (1) after a reasonable opportunity to inspect, he or she indicates acceptance despite any nonconformity; (2) he or she fails to make an effective rejection; or (3) he or she does any act inconsistent with the seller's ownership.
2. A buyer can revoke acceptance of nonconforming goods if the nonconformity substantially impairs the value of the goods to the buyer.
3. This right might exist even if the buyer accepted the goods while thinking the seller would cure or if the nonconformity was very difficult to discover.
4. Revocation must be within a reasonable time, and the buyer has the same rights and duties as if he or she had rejected.

Right to Cover

1. A buyer covers when he or she buys the goods elsewhere, and cover is a buyer's primary remedy.
2. A buyer is not required to cover. If the buyer decides to cover, it must be in good faith.

Right to Damages for Nondelivery

1. After covering, a buyer can sue the seller for the difference between the cover price and the contract price, plus any incidental and consequential damages.
2. If a buyer does not cover, he or she can sue for the difference between the contract price and the market price, plus any incidental and consequential damages,

Right to the Goods

1. When the goods are unique, or in other proper circumstances, a buyer can get specific performance. The Code remedy is more flexible than the traditional remedy of specific performance in equity.
2. "Other proper circumstances" occur when the buyer simply cannot reasonably buy the goods elsewhere.

SELLER'S RIGHTS AND REMEDIES

Right to Cure

1. The right to cure exists for rejections that are for relatively minor deviations from the contract.
2. If the time for performance has not expired, a seller has an absolute right to cure (correct) his or her previous nonconforming tender of goods.
3. If the time for performance has expired, the seller can cure only if the seller had reasonable grounds to think his or her nonconforming tender would have been accepted by the buyer.

Right to Reclaim Goods from an Insolvent Buyer

1. When a seller discovers a buyer received goods while insolvent, the seller can reclaim them upon demand within ten days after receipt. If the buyer three months before delivery misrepresented his or her solvency in writing, the ten-day limitation does not apply.
2. The seller can also refuse to make further deliveries except for cash and can stop any goods en route to the buyer.

Right to Reclaim Goods from a Solvent Buyer

1. If the buyer has improperly rejected, wrongfully revoked acceptance, failed to pay, or repudiated the contract, the seller can reclaim the goods in transit.
2. The seller can stop goods in transit upon timely notice to the carrier. This right is limited to carload, truckload, or other large shipments.

Right to Resell Goods	**1.** Resale is the seller's primary remedy. **2.** A seller can resell the goods and sue for the difference between the resale price and the contract price, plus any incidental and consequential damages.
Right to Collect Damages	**1.** If the seller does not resell, he or she can sue for the difference between the market price at the place of tender and the contract price, plus any incidental and consequential damages.
Right to Collect the Purchase Price	**1.** A seller can collect the contract price if the buyer accepted the goods. **2.** A seller can collect the contract price if the goods were lost or damaged within a reasonable time after the risk of loss passed to the buyer. **3.** A seller can collect the contract price if the goods were identified to the contract and the seller cannot resell them, or the facts indicate that the goods cannot be resold.

REVIEW QUESTIONS AND PROBLEMS

1. Match each term in Column A with the appropriate statement in Column B.

A	B
(1) Seller can reclaim goods	(a) Buyer's remedy for undoing his or her acceptance
(2) Inspection	(b) Seller's primary remedy
(3) Rejection	(c) A remedy available to both parties
(4) Acceptance	(d) Buyer's right before he or she has to pay or accept
(5) Revocation of acceptance	(e) Seller's right to correct a nonconforming tender
(6) Cover	(f) Seller's right to collect the purchase price
(7) Buyer's specific performance	(g) Buyer fails to make an effective rejection.
(8) Cure	(h) Buyer's primary remedy
(9) Resale	(i) Buyer may do this if the tender of goods fails in any way to conform to the contract.
(10) Seller's specific performance	(j) Buyer's remedy if goods are unique or other proper circumstances

2. Amy orders three white slips from a department store. They arrive C.O.D. and Amy pays the delivery person. She opens the box and discovers that black slips were sent. If she does not want these slips, what are her rights? Explain.

3. Newman bought a mobile home from Moses. On February 9, Moses delivered the mobile home to Newman's rented lot, blocked and leveled it, and connected the sewer and water pipes. Later that day, Newman's fiancée cleaned the interior of the mobile home and moved some kitchen utensils and dishes into the mobile home. She noticed a broken window and water pipe. Newman called Moses and told him about these conditions, as well as his having no door keys. On February 10, a windstorm totally destroyed the mobile home. When Newman refused to pay the purchase price, Moses sued, claiming that Newman must bear the loss since Newman had accepted the mobile home. Newman contended that he had not accepted the mobile home since he had complained of specific defects. Did Newman accept the mobile home? Why or why not?

4. Casting and Made-Rite had an agreement under which Casting was to supply 1,600 barrel latches by January 27. Casting shipped 74 parts on January 21, 228 parts on February 27, 623 parts on March 9, 629 parts on April 8, and 70 parts on May 14. Made-Rite did not notify Casting of any intention to reject the barrel latches. Made-Rite inspected the latches in its possession in early April and sent back to Casting those latches found to be nonconforming, which Casting reworked and redelivered. Has Made-Rite accepted the castings? Why or why not?
5. ODA Nursery sold 985 spreading juniper plants to Garcia Tree and Lawn. The plants were delivered on March 14. They were planted in July and August, but in October many of them started to die. In November, an inspection revealed that the plants were root-bound, and the buyer notified the seller of the defect. Is the buyer entitled to recover the costs of the plants? Why or why not?
6. Slacks, Inc. sells tank tops to a fashionable boutique. Upon receipt, the store inspects them, discovers defects, and seasonably rejects them. Slacks instructs the store to sell the tank tops or return them. The boutique does neither. Is it liable for anything? Explain.
7. Sandra purchased a new Nissan from Rocky Mountain Nissan. During the first six months that she owned the car, it had to be towed to the dealer's shop for repairs on at least seven occasions. Sometimes the car would not start. On other occasions it would stop running and stall in traffic. Several of the dealer's mechanics told Sandra that they did not know what was wrong with the car but that it was a "lemon." She estimated that the car had been in the dealer's shop four out of the first six months that she owned it. Is she entitled to revoke her acceptance? Why or why not?
8. A country music festival promoter contracted to buy 2,000 kegs of beer at $50 per keg. When the beer that arrived was found to be flat, the promoter rejected it. He could not buy that brand from any other source in time for the festival, so he bought 2,000 kegs of another beer at $55 per keg. What are the promoter's Article 2 damages? Explain.
9. Plaintiff entered into a contract to purchase 4,000 tons of cryolite, a chemical used in the production of aluminum, from defendant. When the chemical was not delivered, plaintiff brought a suit for specific performance. He contended that cryolite was not readily available from any other source. Is plaintiff entitled to the remedy of specific performance? Why?
10. Defendant ordered from the plaintiff two lead-covered steel tanks to be constructed by the plaintiff according to specifications supplied by the defendant. The tanks were designed for the special purpose of testing X-ray tubes and were required to be radiation-proof within certain federal standards. The defendant inspected the goods and accepted them notwithstanding some defects. It then attempted to revoke the acceptance but did not do so properly. The seller retained possession of the tanks; and when the buyer failed to pay for them, suit was filed for the purchase price. Is the plaintiff entitled to the purchase price? Explain.

Warranties | 23

CHAPTER OUTLINE

CHAPTER PREVIEW

In the law of sales of goods, the word warranty describes the obligation of the seller with respect to goods that have been sold. As a general rule, a seller is responsible for transferring to the buyer good title to the goods and actual goods that are of the proper quality, free from defects. A seller may also be responsible for the proper functioning of the article sold and for its suitability to the needs of the buyer. Thus a warranty may extend not only to the present condition for goods but also to the performance that is to be expected of them.

A warranty made by a seller is an integral part of the contract. If the warranty is breached and the buyer notifies the seller of the breach within a reasonable time, the buyer may bring an action for damages caused by the breach of warranty. A breach of warranty may also result in injuries to the buyer or to third persons. Suits may be brought to recover damages for these injuries as well.

The law takes the position that if the goods are defective, the seller should be held responsible. Various tort and contract theories impose liability on manufacturers, packers, producers, and sellers for injuries caused by defective products. This chapter discusses the breach of warranty theories, based on contract theory. The tort theory of product liability is discussed extensively in Chapter 8. Keep in mind that the material in this chapter is also a part of the broader products liability legal arena.

The Uniform Commercial Code has several provisions relating to warranties. It draws a distinction between express warranties made by a seller and those implied as a matter of law from the transaction. If the seller guarantees the product directly through the use of words within a contract, it is an express warranty. If the warranty arises out of the transaction and its circumstances, then the warranty is imposed by society through out legal system and it is called an implied warranty. Further, when the seller is a merchant, special warranties often exist. All of these aspects of warranties are addressed in the following sections.

BUSINESS MANAGEMENT DECISION

You inherit a retail hardware store that you do not wish to operate. After being unsuccessful in selling the business, you decide to have a going-out-of-business sale. You want to sell all the merchandise on an as-is basis, but you realize that many customers rely on the expertise of your experienced sales staff and that many of your products can cause injury if used improperly.

What do you do to ensure that no express or implied warranties attach to the merchandise sold?

TYPES OF WARRANTIES

1. Express Warranties

An **express warranty** is one that is made as a part of the contract for sale and becomes a part of the basis of the bargain between the buyer and the seller [2-313(1)(a)]. An express warranty, as distinguished from an implied warranty, is part of the contract because it has been included as part of the individual bargain. To create an express warranty, the seller does not have to use formal words such as *warrant* or *guarantee,* nor must he or she have the specific intention to make a warranty [2-313(3)]. For example, the following statement by a seller of a used diesel engine was held to be an express warranty and not merely sales puffery: "All you have to do is take it home, put it in your

Express warranty

A positive representation concerning the nature, quality, character, use, and purpose of goods, which induces the buyer to buy and on which the seller intends the buyer to rely

truck, and it will go right to work. This engine is in good running condition." When the engine did not perform properly, the buyer was allowed to recover based on a breach of this express warranty.

A seller may make a variety of statements about the goods. It is necessary to evaluate these to determine which statements are warranties and which do not impose legal responsibility because they are merely sales talk. An express warranty may be any positive statement by a seller of the condition of personal property made during the negotiations for its sale. A label on a bag of insecticide stated that it was developed especially to control rootworms. This was an express warranty that the insecticide was effective to control the rootworm. The word guarantee is often used to give an express warranty. A contract of sale of automobile tires states that the tires were guaranteed for 36,000 miles against all road hazards, including blowouts. This constituted an express warranty that the tires would not blow out during the first 36,000 miles of use.

When the seller makes a *statement of fact or promise* about the goods to the buyer, an express warranty is created [2-313(1)(a)]. The express warranty is that the goods will conform to the statement of fact or promise. Any statement of fact or even of opinion, if it becomes a part of the basis of the bargain, is an express warranty. While an express warranty must become a part of the basis of the bargain, a plaintiff does not have to prove reliance on specific promises made by the seller. No particular reliance need be shown to weave an affirmation of fact into the fabric of the agreement.

Most *statements of opinion*, such as those concerning the value of the goods, *do not give rise to an express warranty*. As a general rule, a buyer is not justified in relying on mere opinions, and opinions are not usually a part of the basis of the bargain. However, the opinion of an expert, such as a jeweler with regard to the value of a gem, may justify the reliance of the buyer; and such an opinion becomes part of the basis of the bargain and a warranty. When a seller merely states his or her opinion or judgment on a matter of which the seller has no special knowledge, or on a matter of which the buyer may be expected to have an opinion or exercise judgment, the seller's statement does not constitute an express warranty.

An express warranty may be made in a variety of ways. The seller may specifically make a factual statement about the goods. These factual statements may be on labels or in a catalog or other sales promotion material. A direct promise may state, "This grass seed is free from weeds." Generally, words that are descriptive of the product are warranties that the goods will conform to the description [2-313(1)(b)]. Descriptions may also be in the form of diagrams, pictures, blueprints, and the like. Technical specifications of the product would constitute warranties if they were part of the basis for the bargain. An express warranty can also be based on the instructions of the seller regarding use of the product.

Just as the seller may describe the goods, he or she may also inform the buyer by showing to the buyer a model or a sample of what is being sold. Fabrics or clothing might be purchased on the basis of samples shown to the buyer, or a seller might display a working model of an engine. In either event, there would be an express warranty that the goods will conform to the sample or model if the parties have made this a part of their bargain [2-313(1)(c)].

2. Warranty of Title

A seller may expressly warrant the title to goods but usually does not do so. Therefore, the law imposes a *warranty of title* to protect buyers who may overlook this aspect of the sale and those who simply assume the seller has good title to the goods. The warranty of title is treated as a separate warranty under the Code.

A seller warrants that he or she is conveying good title to the buyer and has the right to sell the goods. The seller further warrants that there are no encumbrances or liens against the property sold and that no other person can claim a security interest in them [2-312]. In effect, the seller implicitly guarantees that the buyer will be able to enjoy the use of the goods free from the claims of any third party. Of course, property may be sold to a buyer who has full knowledge of liens or encumbrances, and he or she may buy the property subject to these claims. In this event, there would not be a breach of warranty of title. The purchase price would, however, reflect that the buyer was obtaining less than complete title.

In Chapter 21, it is noted that a good-faith purchaser from a seller with voidable title obtains good title. Is there a breach of the warranty of title in such a sale? While there are cases answering the question both ways, most courts would find a breach of warranty even if the buyer actually receives clear title. This results from Code language that requires that the conveyance of title be rightful and free from the difficulties of establishing clear title in such cases. The good-faith purchaser thus has a choice. He or she may claim the goods by use of the good-faith purchaser concept or may recover the purchase price or any payments made by electing to sue for breach of the implied warranty of title.

Warranty of title can be excluded or modified only by specific language or by circumstances making clear that the seller is not vouching for the title [2-312(2)].

Judicial sales and sales by executors of estates would not imply that the seller guarantees the title. Also, a seller could directly inform the buyer that he or she is selling only the interest and that the buyer takes it subject to all encumbrances.

A seller who is a merchant, regularly dealing in goods of the kind that are the subject of the sale, makes an additional warranty. This seller warrants that the goods are free of the rightful claim of any third person by way of infringement of the third person's interests—for example, that the goods sold do not infringe on a patent. However, a buyer may furnish to the seller specifications for the construction of an article, and this may result in the infringement of a patent. Not only does the seller not warrant against such infringement, but the buyer must also protect the seller from any claims arising out of such infringement [2-312(3)].

3. Implied Warranty of Merchantability

Implied warranties come into being as a matter of law, without any bargaining. As an integral part of the normal sales transaction, implied warranties are legally present unless clearly disclaimed or negated. Implied warranties exist even if a seller is unable to discover the defect involved or unable to cure it if it can be ascertained. Liability for breach of an implied warranty is not based on fault but, rather, on the public policy of protecting the buyer of goods.

A warranty that the goods shall be of merchantable quality is implied in a contract for sale if the seller is a merchant who deals in goods of the kind involved in the contract. It is not enough that the defendant sold the goods. The seller-defendant must have been a merchant dealing in the goods. A person making an isolated sale is not a merchant. For example, a bank selling a repossessed car is not a merchant, and there is no implied **warranty of merchantability** in such a sale.

Warranty of merchantability

A promise implied in a sale of goods by merchants that the goods are reasonably fit for the general purpose for which they are sold

If a bank is selling a repossessed car there is no implied warranty of merchantability because the bank is not a merchant.

The warranty extends to all sales of goods by merchants. It applies to new goods and to used goods, in most states, unless the warranty is excluded.

For a consumer to prevail in an action for damages for breach of an implied warranty of merchantability, he or she must demonstrate that the commodity was not reasonably suitable for the ordinary uses for which goods of that kind and description are sold, and that such defect or breach existed at the time of sale and proximately caused the damages complained of.

For goods to be merchantable, they must at least be the kind of goods that:

1. Pass without objection in the trade under the contract description
2. In the case of fungible goods, are of fair average quality within the description
3. Are fit for the ordinary purposes for which such goods are used
4. Run, within the variations permitted by the agreement, of even kind, quality, and quantity within each unit and among all units involved
5. Are adequately contained, packaged, and labeled as the agreement may require
6. Conform to the promises or affirmations of fact made on the container or label, if any [2-314]

Fungible goods

Goods of which any unit is, from its nature of mercantile usage, treated as the equivalent of any other unit, such as grain, wine, and similar items

These standards provide the basic acceptable standards of merchantability. **Fungible goods** (point 2) are those usually sold by weight or measure, such as grain or flour. The term *fair average quality* generally relates to agricultural bulk commodities and means that they are within the middle range of quality under the description. Fitness for ordinary purposes (point 3) is not limited to use by the immediate buyer. If a person is buying for resale, the buyer is entitled to protection, and the goods must be honestly resalable. They must be acceptable in the ordinary market without objection. Point 5 is applicable only if the nature of the goods and of the transaction requires a certain type of container, package, or label. Where there is a container or label and a representation thereon, the buyer is entitled to protection under point 6, so that he or she will not be in the position of reselling or using goods delivered under false representations appearing on the package or container. The buyer obtains this protection even though the contract did not require either the labeling or the representation.

The implied warranty of merchantability imposes a very broad responsibility on the merchant-seller to furnish goods that are at least of average quality. In any line of business, the word *merchantable* may have a meaning somewhat different from the Code definition, and the parties by their course of dealing may indicate a special meaning for the term.

One purpose of this warranty is to require sellers to provide goods that are reasonably safe for their ordinary intended use. Although the law does not require accident-proof products, it does require products that are reasonably safe for the purposes for which they were intended when they were placed in the stream of commerce. The mere fact that a product injures one person does not, in and of itself, establish that it is not fit for the ordinary purpose for which it was intended.

Liability for breach of the warranty of merchantability extends to direct economic loss as well as to personal injuries and to property damage. Direct economic loss includes damages based on insufficient product value. In other words, the buyer is entitled to collect the difference in value between what was received and what the product would have been if it had been of merchantable quality. Direct economic loss also includes the cost of replacements and the cost of repairs. These damages need not be established with mathematical certainty; however, reasonable degrees of certainty and accuracy are required so the damages are not based on speculation.

The following case explores the question of whether the implied warranty of merchantability applies.

CASE

Walker Gunning, an Infant, by His Mother and Natural Guardian, Deborah Gunning v. Small Feast Caterers, Inc., d/b/a Cucina, et al.

SUPREME COURT OF NEW YORK, KINGS COUNTY

777 N.Y.S.2d 268 (2004)

HON. HERBERT KRAMER, J.

A glass of water allegedly exploded in a patron's hand in one of our local Brooklyn restaurants. Can recovery be had against the restaurant as the "seller" of this glass under theory of implied warranty?

This appears to be a question of first impression in this state. Intriguingly, this court was unable to find any decisions in this state where a party had even complained about the food in one of our thousands of restaurants, let alone the utensils. This undoubtedly speaks well for our local restaurateurs, but requires us to go beyond our boarders for juridical guidance.

Defendants Small Feast Caterers, the restaurant at which the plaintiff dined, and Stoelzle-Oberglas, USA, an importer/distributor of items for restaurant tabletops including glasses, move for summary judgment to dismiss the complaint and cross claims.

The restaurant argues that it is not liable for the harm caused by the allegedly defective glass because it was not and is not in the "business of selling" the water or the water glasses it provides to its patrons.

With respect to implied warranty, the question is whether a "sale" occurred since the glass of water was provided free of charge; and the statute requires a service "for value" of food or drink.

Defendant was offering a complimentary drink to its patrons but was not doing so out of any sense of charity or hospitality. This glass of water was offered as an indispensable part of the meal that was sold to the patron. The defendant served water on a regular basis as part of its business. In fact, it would be difficult to imagine, except in times of severe drought, a restaurant that did not provide water to its patrons along with their meals. As to the question of value, even if we were to give this term a very restrictive meaning, it is reasonable to presume that the cost of providing this drink was built into the bill.

The second inquiry is whether the defendant gave an implied warranty to the glass as well as to the drink in it. The plaintiff was the ultimate consumer of the drink, but the glass remained the property of defendant. When the Uniform Commercial Code [2-314] states "the serving for value of food or drink to be consumed either on the premises or elsewhere is a sale" and that such food and drink must be "adequately contained, packaged and labeled as the agreement may require," it covers entirely the situation when a glass causes injury. The water and the container both must be fit for the ordinary purpose for which used.

This court holds that the defendant restaurant impliedly warranted that the water it served to the plaintiff was fit for consumption. If the container that held the water was defective, then the water was not fit for consumption; and consequently plaintiff's claim under the theory of implied warranty is viable.

In conclusion, the defendants' motion for summary judgment is denied.

■ *Denied.*

CASE CONCEPTS REVIEW

1. Is the "good" here the water, the glass, or both? Why?
2. Why did the court conclude that an implied warranty existed?

4. Implied Warranty of Fitness for a Particular Purpose

Under the warranty of merchantability, the goods must be fit for the ordinary purpose for which such goods are used. The warranty of merchantability is based on a purchaser's reasonable expectation that goods purchased from a merchant, with respect to goods of that kind, will be free of significant defects and will perform in the way goods of that kind should perform. It presupposes no special relationship of trust or reliance between the seller and buyer. On the other hand, the implied **warranty of fitness for a particular purpose** is narrower, more specific, and more precise. It is created if, at the time of contracting, the seller has reason to know any particular purpose for which the buyer requires the goods and is relying on the seller's skill or judgment to select or furnish suitable goods [2-315]. In these circumstances, the seller must select goods that will accomplish the purpose for which they are being purchased. It is based on a special reliance by the buyer on the seller to provide goods that will perform a specific use required and communicated by the buyer.

Warranty of fitness for a particular purpose

An implied promise by a seller of goods that arises when a buyer explains the special needs and relies on the seller's advice

The implied warranty of fitness applies both to merchants and non-merchants but normally pertains only to merchants since a non-merchant does not ordinarily possess the required skills or judgment on which buyers will rely. The buyer need not specifically state that he or she has a particular purpose in mind or is placing reliance on the seller's judgment if the circumstances are such that the seller has reason to realize the purpose intended or that the buyer is relying on the seller. For the warranty to apply, however, the buyer must actually rely on the seller's skill or judgment in selecting or furnishing suitable goods. If the buyer's knowledge or skill is equal to or greater than the seller's, there can be no justifiable reliance and no warranty. The existence of justifiable reliance, and hence a warranty, is a question of fact for a jury to answer.

The difference between the implied warranty of merchantability and the implied warranty of fitness for a particular purpose is very significant. While many cases allege a breach of both warranties, the decisions often only find a breach of one or the other, but not both. The implied warranty of fitness for a particular purpose does not exist nearly as often as the implied warranty of merchantability. Particular purpose involves a specific use by the buyer; ordinary use, as expressed in the concept of merchantability, means the customary function of the goods. Thus a household dishwasher would be of merchantable quality because it could ordinarily be used to wash dishes; but it might not be fit for a restaurant's particular purpose because it would not be suited for its dishwashing needs. Goods that are of merchantable quality may not fit for a particular purpose. Goods fit for a particular purpose will almost always be of merchantable quality. Goods that are not of merchantable quality usually will not be fit for a particular purpose.

Breach of the warranty of fitness for a particular purpose may result in disaffirmance of the contract. If the product causes an injury, including economic loss, it may also result in a suit for dollar damages.

TABLE 23-1 ■ Code Gap Fillers

Type	Relevant Code section
Title	2-312
Merchantability	2-314
Fitness for a Particular Purpose	2-315

LIMITATIONS

5. Express Warranties

A seller will often seek to avoid or restrict warranty liability. These attempts to limit liability may take the form of a disclaimer of warranties or a limitation of remedies. A *disclaimer of warranties* limits a seller's liability by reducing the number of circumstances in which the seller will be in breach of contract; it precludes the existence of a cause of action or greatly reduces it. A *limitation of remedies* clause restricts the remedies available to the buyer once a breach of warranty by the seller is established. The parties may also limit or alter the damages recoverable by limiting the buyer's remedy to repair or replace the nonconforming goods or parts.

The Code has provisions on exclusion or modification of warranties that are designed to protect the buyer from unexpected and unfair disclaimers of both express and implied warranties. Sometimes there are statements or conduct that create an express warranty and also statements or conduct that tend to negate or limit such warranties. To the extent that it is reasonable, the two different kinds of statements or conduct are construed as consistent with each other [2-316(1)]. However, negation of limitation of an express warranty is inoperative when such a construction is unreasonable. In other words, if the express warranty and the attempt to negate it cannot be construed as consistent, the warranty predominates. If a seller gives the buyer an express warranty and then includes in the contract a provision that purports to exclude "all warranties express or implied," that disclaimer will not be given effect. The express warranty is still enforceable.

6. Written Disclaimers of Implied Warranties

Implied warranties can be excluded if the seller makes it clear that the buyer is not to have the benefit of them. In general, to exclude or modify the implied warranty of merchantability, the word *merchantability* must be used [2-3l6(2)]. The warranty of merchantability may also be excluded by oral agreement or by the parties' course of performance. However, if the disclaimer is included in a written contract, it must be set forth in a conspicuous manner. The disclaimer clause of the contract should be in larger type or a different color ink or indented, so it will be brought to the buyer's attention. A disclaimer will not be effective if it is set forth in the same type and color as the rest of the contract.

To exclude or modify any implied warranty of fitness for a particular purpose, the exclusion must be conspicuously written. The statement "there are no warranties which extend beyond the description on the face hereof" is sufficient to exclude the implied warranty of fitness for a particular purpose [2-316(2)]. An exclusionary clause should be printed in type that will set it apart from the balance of the contract. The following case illustrates the type of writing required to disclaim implied warranties.

CASE

Sandra Wilson v. Royal Motor Sales, Inc.

COURT OF APPEALS OF INDIANA

812 N.E.2d 133 (2004)

MAY, JUDGE

The facts most favorable to Wilson, the non-moving party, follow. On May 26, 2001, Wilson purchased a 2000 Daewoo Nubria from Royal. The window sticker on the car did not indicate the car was being sold "As Is", rather it indicated it was being sold with a factory warranty. The purchase agreement contained a warranty disclaimer at the bottom of the page; however, Royal did not have Wilson sign the space indicating the car was being "SOLD WITH NO WARRANTY." Wilson's signature on the purchase agreement acknowledged that she had read the back of the purchase agreement, which included the following language: "THIS VEHICLE IS SOLD "AS IS"—NOT EXPRESSLY WARRANTED OR GUARANTEED" AND THE SELLER HEREBY DISCLAIMS ALL WARRANTIES, EITHER EXPRESS OR IMPLIED, INCLUDING ANY IMPLIED WARRANTY OF MERCHANTABILITY OR FITNESS FOR A PARTICULAR PURPOSE."

On June 14, 2001, Wilson began experiencing difficulties with the Nubria. Over the next year, the engine had an oil leak and the car had to be serviced more than once because the "check engine" light came on. The fuel tank, battery, and cam sensor all had to be replaced on separate occasions. The tires had to be rotated because they vibrated when driven at higher speeds. Water leaked into the car when it rained. The brakes made a grinding sound that required the front brake rotors to be machined and the brake pads to be replaced. Wilson also had concerns about the speedometer, fuse box, steering/suspension system, and starter. Wilson took the Nubria to Royal for repairs eight times between June 14, 2001, and October 21, 2002; however, the car continued to have problems. Wilson stopped driving the car in October 2002.

On October 24, 2002, Wilson notified Royal in writing she was revoking her acceptance of the Nubria. On November 12, 2002, Wilson filed a complaint alleging Royal breached its implied warranty of merchantability and she had a right to revoke her acceptance. Royal filed a motion for summary judgment. After a hearing at which Royal asserted it had disclaimed the implied warranty of merchantability, the trial court granted Royal's motion.

Indiana has adopted the Uniform Commercial Code ("UCC"). The back of the Buyer's Order contained the following relevant language:

8. FACTORY WARRANTY: ANY WARRANTY ON ANY NEW VEHICLE OR USED VEHICLE STILL SUBJECT TO A MANUFACTURER'S WARRANTY IS THAT MADE BY THE MANUFACTURER ONLY. THE SELLER HEREBY DISCLAIMS ALL WARRANTIES, EITHER EXPRESS OR IMPLIED, INCLUDING ANY IMPLIED WARRANTY OF MERCHANTABILITY OR FITNESS FOR A PARTICULAR PURPOSE.

USED VEHICLE WHETHER OR NOT SUBJECT TO MANUFACTURER'S WARRANTY: UNLESS A SEPARATE WRITTEN INSTRUMENT SHOWING THE TERMS OF ANY DEALER WARRANTY OR SERVICE CONTRACT IS FURNISHED BY DEALER TO BUYER, THE VEHICLE IS SOLD "AS IS—NOT EXPRESSLY WARRANTED OR GUARANTEED" AND THE SELLER HEREBY DISCLAIMS ALL WARRANTIES, EITHER EXPRESS OR IMPLIED, INCLUDING ANY IMPLIED WARRANTY OF MERCHANTABILITY OR FITNESS FOR A PARTICULAR PURPOSE.

In the context of the UCC, "conspicuous" means:

A term or clause is conspicuous when it is so written that a reasonable person against whom it is to operate ought to have noticed it. A printed heading in capitals (as: NONNEGOTIABLE BILL OF LADING) is conspicuous. Language in the body of a form is conspicuous if it is in larger or other contrasting type or color, but in a telegram any stated term is conspicuous. Whether a term or clause is conspicuous or not is for decision by the court. [1-201(10)].

The language on the back of that purchase agreement, which Wilson's signature acknowledged she had read and agreed to, was sufficiently conspicuous to be a valid disclaimer of any implied warranties.

Wilson claims the window sticker contradicts the language in the purchase agreement because Royal had not marked the box on the window sticker indicating the Nubria was being sold "As Is." The flaw in Wilson's reasoning is the purchase agreement also did not indicate the Nubria was being sold without any warranty. Rather, the purchase agreement indicated that if the car was being sold with a "factory warranty," that warranty was made by the manufacturer only and did not bind the dealer unless the parties signed an additional "dealer warranty or service contract" (capitalization removed). If no additional contract was signed, then the dealer disclaimed all express or implied warranties, including the implied warranty of merchantability. The language on the window sticker, while perhaps ineffective as a disclaimer of implied warranties if considered alone, did not contradict the language in the purchase agreement.

The trial court did not err when it granted Royal's motion for summary judgment.

■ *Affirmed.*

CASE CONCEPTS REVIEW

1. What factors led the court to conclude that the disclaimer was conspicuous?
2. Why was there no contradiction between the window sticker and the purchase agreement?

Disclaimers of implied warranties are greatly limited by federal law today. As a part of the law relating to consumer protection, the Magnuson-Moss warranty law was enacted in 1975. Under this law, Congress provides a federal right of action for consumers to enforce written or implied warranties where they claim to be damaged by the failure of a supplier, warrantor, or service contractor to comply with any obligation under that statute or under a written warranty, implied warranty, or service contract. The Act also limits the extent to which manufacturers who give express warranties may disclaim or modify implied warranties, but looks to state law as the source of any express or implied warranty. This law and the Federal Trade Commission rules adopted to carry out its purposes prohibit the disclaimer of implied warranties where an express warranty is given.

7. Other Exclusions of Implied Warranties

The Code also provides for other circumstances in which implied warranties may be wholly or partially excluded. The seller may inform the buyer that the goods are being sold "as is" or "with all faults." Other language also may call the buyer's attention to the exclusion and make it plain that the sale involves no implied warranty [2-316(3)(a)]. The Code does not guarantee every buyer a good deal. Buyers who purchase items marked "as is" (or other similar language) may acquire defective products without any rights against the seller.

The buyer's examination of the goods or a sample or a model is also significant in determining the existence of implied warranties. If, before entering into the contract, the buyer has examined the goods, sample, or model as fully as he or she desired, there is no implied warranty on defects that an examination ought to have revealed [2-316(3)(b)]. If the seller demands that the buyer examine the goods fully, but the buyer refuses to do so, there is no implied warranty on those defects that a careful examination would have revealed. By making the demand, the seller is giving notice to the buyer that the buyer is assuming the risk with regard to defects an examination ought to reveal. However, the seller will not be protected if a demand has not been made and the buyer fails to examine the goods [2-316(3)(a)].

If a buyer has examined the goods thoroughly then there is no implied warranty on defects

A course of dealing between the parties, course of performance, or usage of trade can also be the basis for exclusion or modification of implied warranties. These factors can be important in determining the nature and extent of implied warranties in any given transaction [2-316(3)(c)].

8. Remedies

As noted in Section 5, the Code also allows the parties to limit the remedies available in the event of a breach of warranty [2-719]. The agreement may provide for remedies in addition to, or in restriction *of*, those provided by the Code. The parties may also limit or alter the measure of damages. These provisions usually limit a buyer's damages to the repayment of the price on return of the goods. Contracts often allow a seller to repair defective goods or replace nonconforming parts, without further liability. These provisions in effect eliminate a seller's liability for consequential damages and allow a seller to cure a defect or cancel a transaction by refunding the purchase price, without further liability.

Clauses limiting the liability of a seller are subject to the Code requirement on unconscionability [2-719]. Limitations of consequential damages for personal injury related to consumer goods are prima facie unconscionable. Limitations of damages for commercial loss are presumed to be valid.

OTHER ASPECTS OF WARRANTIES

9. Notice

The Code requires a buyer to give *notice* of any alleged breach of express or implied warranties [2-607(3)(a)]. This notice must be given within a reasonable time after the facts constituting the breach are discovered or should have been discovered using reasonable care. Failure to give the required notice bars all remedies. The giving of notice within a reasonable time to a seller is a condition precedent to filing a suit for damages for breach of express or implied warranties.

POLICIES There are three policies behind the notice requirement. First, notice is required for the seller to exercise its right to cure. The seller should be given the opportunity to make adjustments to or replacement of defective products. Notice allows sellers to minimize their losses and the buyer's damages. For example, the purchaser of a computer with a defective part should not be allowed to wait several months and then sue for loss of use of the computer.

The second policy behind the notice requirement is to provide the seller an opportunity to arm itself for negotiation and litigation. The seller needs an opportunity to examine the product promptly so it can defend itself against possible false allegations of breach of warranty. If a delay operates to deprive the seller of a reasonable opportunity to discover facts that might provide a defense or lessen its liability, the notice probably has not been given within a reasonable time.

The third policy with respect to requiring the buyer to give notice of an alleged breach of warranty is to provide some psychological protection for sellers. They need to believe that their risk will end after a reasonable amount of time. The notice requirement is somewhat similar to a statute of limitations. Sellers know that after a time they can stop worrying about potential liability.

FORM The notice may be oral or in writing. Written notice is much more preferable because it serves as its own proof. The notice need not be a claim for damages or a threat to file suit. All that is required is that the buyer notifies the seller of the defect in the product. As a general rule, filing a lawsuit is not notice of breach of warranty, and lawsuits without prior notice are usually dismissed for failure to give the required notice. The notice of the breach of warranty requirement does not contemplate the buyer delivering a summons and complaint to the seller as notice. The Code provides no remedy for a breach of warranty until the buyer has given notice. Therefore, filing a suit cannot constitute notice.

TIME The requirement that notice be given within a reasonable time is interpreted flexibly. The comments to the Code encourage courts not to close the door too quickly on "retail consumers and especially those injured by defective products. The implication is that merchant-buyers are bound by a stricter notice requirement. A "reasonable time" for notification is to be judged by different standards so in cases involving consumers it will be extended. The rule of requiring notification is not designed to deprive a good-faith consumer of his or her remedy, especially a consumer who suffered personal injury. In such cases, the notice policies collide with a countervailing policy that unsophisticated consumers who suffer real and perhaps grievous injury at the hands of the defendant-seller ought to have an easy road to recovery. The rule of requiring notification is designed to defeat commercial bad faith, not to deprive a good-faith consumer of his or her remedy.

10. Third Parties

Privity of contract

The contractual connection that arises from a buyer-seller relationship

PRIVITY OF CONTRACT Historically, suits for breach of warranty required **privity of contract**, a contractual connection between the parties. Lack of privity of contract was a complete defense to a suit for breach of express warranty or for breach of the implied warranties. Two aspects of privity of contract requirements are sometimes described as horizontal and vertical. The *horizontal privity* issue is—To whom does the warranty extend? Does it run only in favor of the purchaser, or does it extend to others who may use or be affected by the product? The *vertical privity* issue is—Against whom can action be brought for breach of warranty? Can the party sue only the seller, or will direct action lie against wholesalers, manufacturers, producers, and growers?

When privity of contract is required, only the buyer can collect for breach of warranty and then can collect only from the seller. A seller who is liable may recover from the person who sold to him or her. Thus the requirement of privity of contract not only prevented many suits for breach of warranty where privity did not exist but also encouraged multiple lawsuits over the same product.

ABANDONMENT OF PRIVITY It is not surprising that the law has generally abandoned strict privity of contract requirements. It has done so by statute and in case law. The abandonment has occurred in cases involving express warranties, as well as in cases involving implied warranties. Both horizontal and vertical privity have generally been eliminated or significantly reduced.

The drafters of the Code prepared three alternative provisions that states could adopt on horizontal privity [2-318]. Alternative A has been adopted by approximately thirty jurisdictions. It provides that a warranty extends to any person in the family or household of the buyer or a guest in the home if it is reasonable to expect that such a person may consume, or be affected by, the goods and is injured by them.

Alternative B has been adopted in eight jurisdictions, and alternative C is the law in four states. The remaining states have either omitted the section entirely or have drafted their own version on the extent of the warranties. Alternatives B and C extend warranties to any natural person who may be reasonably expected to use, consume, or be affected by the goods and who is injured by them.

These Code provisions on horizontal privity do not attempt to deal with the vertical privity issue. The Code is neutral on it and leaves the development of the law to the courts, case by case. The courts of most states have abandoned the vertical privity of contract requirement, and persons injured by products are allowed to sue all businesses in the chain of distribution without regard to the presence of privity of contract. Some states have retained vertical privity in suits seeking damages for economic loss even though they have abandoned it in suits for personal injuries.

The following case illustrates the typical reasoning of a court deciding that vertical privity is not a requirement for asserting a claim asserting breach of the implied warrant of merchantability.

CASE

Hyundai Motor America, Inc. v. Sandra Goodin

SUPREME COURT OF INDIANA

822 N.E.2d 947 (2005)

BOEHM, JUSTICE

On November 18, 2000, Sandra Goodin test drove a Hyundai Sonata at AutoChoice Hyundai in Evansville, Indiana. The car was represented as new and showed nineteen miles on the odometer. Goodin testified that when she applied the brakes in the course of the test drive she experienced a "shimmy, shake, pulsating type feel." The AutoChoice salesperson told her that this was caused by flat spots on the tires from extended inactivity and offered to have the tires rotated and inspected. After this explanation, Goodin purchased the Sonata for $22,710.00.

The manufacturer, Hyundai, provided three limited warranties: 1 year/12,000 miles on "wear items;" 5 years/60,000 miles "bumper to bumper;" and 10 years/100,000 miles on the powertrain. Hyundai concedes that brake rotors, brake calipers, and brake caliper slides were subject to the 5 year/60,000 mile warranty covering "repair or replacement of any component originally manufactured or installed by [Hyundai] that is found to be defective in material or workmanship under normal use and maintenance." To claim under this warranty, a vehicle must be serviced by an authorized Hyundai dealer who is then reimbursed by Hyundai for any necessary parts or labor.

Three days after the car was purchased, Goodin's husband, Steven Hicks, took it back to AutoChoice for the promised tire work. Goodin testified that she continued to feel the shimmy but did nothing further for a month. On December 22, she took the car to a different Hyundai dealer, Bales Auto Mall, in Jeffersonville, Indiana, for an unrelated problem and also made an appointment six days later for Bales to inspect the brakes. Bales serviced the brake rotors for warping, but on May 1, 2001, Goodin returned to Bales complaining that the vehicle continued to vibrate when the brakes were applied. Goodin told Hawes that the brake problem had occurred about seventy percent of the time. On August 24, 2001, Goodin took her car back to her original dealer, AutoChoice, reporting that the brakes "squeak and grind when applied." Goodin left the car with AutoChoice where the left front rotor was machined and loose bolts on the front upper control arm were tightened. Goodin testified that after this five-day procedure the brakes began to make the same noises and vibrations even before she arrived home.

In October 2001, Goodin hired an attorney who faxed a letter to Hyundai Motor America giving notice of her complaint and requesting a refund of the purchase price. On November 13, 2001, Goodin filed a complaint against Hyundai Motor America, Inc. alleging claims under the Magnuson-Moss Warranty Act for breach of express warranty, breach of implied warranty, and revocation of acceptance.

At the conclusion of a two day trial, the jury was instructed on all claims. Over defendants' objection, the instructions on implied warranties made no reference to a privity requirement. The jury returned a verdict for Hyundai on Goodin's breach of express warranty claim, but found in favor of Goodin on her claim for breach of implied warranty of merchantability. Damages of $3,000.00 were assessed, and Goodin's counsel was later awarded attorneys' fees of $19,237.50 pursuant to the fee shifting provisions of the Magnuson-Moss Warranty Act.

Hyundai orally moved to set aside the verdict as contrary to law on the ground that Goodin purchased the car from AutoChoice and, therefore, did not enjoy vertical privity with Hyundai. The court initially denied that motion, but the following day set aside the verdict, holding lack of privity between Goodin and Hyundai precluded a cause of action for breach of implied warranty. Goodin then moved to reinstate the verdict; and, after briefing and oral argument, the trial court granted that motion on the ground that Hyundai was estopped from asserting lack of privity.

Indiana has adopted the Uniform Commercial Code, notably its provision that: "A warranty that the goods shall be merchantable is implied in a contract for their sale if the seller is a merchant with respect to goods of that kind. ..." 2-314(1) Hyundai asserts, and the Court of Appeals found, Indiana law requires vertical privity between manufacturer and consumer when economic damages are sought. Goodin argues that traditional privity of contract between the consumer and manufacturer is not required for a claim against a manufacturer for breach of the implied warranty of merchantability, especially if the manufacturer provides a Magnuson-Moss express warranty with the product.

Privity originated as a doctrine limiting tort relief for breach of warranties. The lack of privity defense was first recognized in Winterbottom v. Wright, 10 M. & W. 109, 152 Eng Rep 402 (Ex. 1842). In that case, the court sustained a demurrer to a suit by an injured coachman for breach of warranty by a third party who contracted with the owner to maintain the coach. In this century, however, MacPherson v. Buick Motor Co., 217 N.Y. 382, 111 N.E. 1050 (1916), and Henningsen v. Bloomfield Motors, Inc., 32 N.J. 358, 161 A.2d 69 (1960), established that lack of privity between an automobile manufacturer and a consumer would not preclude the consumer's action for personal injuries and property damage caused by the negligent manufacture of an automobile. "Vertical" privity typically becomes an issue when a purchaser files a breach of warranty action against a vendor in the purchaser's distribution chain who is not the purchaser's immediate seller. Simply put, vertical privity exists only between immediate links in a distribution chain. A buyer in the same chain who did not purchase directly from a seller is "remote" as to that seller. "Horizontal" privity, in contrast, refers to claims by non-purchasers, typically someone who did not purchase the product but who was injured while using it.

The basis for the privity requirement in a contract claim is essentially the idea that the parties to a sale of goods are free to bargain for themselves; and thus, allocation of risk of failure of a product is best left to the private sector. Otherwise stated, the law should not impose a contract the parties do not wish to make. Generally privity extends to the parties to the contract of sale. It relates to the bargained for expectations of the buyer and seller. Accordingly, when the cause of action arises out of economic loss related to the loss of the bargain or profits and consequential damages related thereto, the bargained for expectations of buyer and seller are relevant and privity between them is still required. Implied warranties of merchantability and fitness for a particular use, as they relate to economic loss from the bargain, cannot then ordinarily be sustained between the buyer and a remote manufacturer.

We think that this rationale has eroded to the point of invisibility as applied to many types of consumer goods in today's economy. The UCC recognizes an implied warranty of merchantability if "goods" are sold to "consumers" by one who ordinarily deals in this product. Warranties are often explicitly promoted as marketing tools, as was true in this case of the Hyundai warranties. Consumer expectations are framed by these legal developments to the point where technically advanced consumer goods are virtually always sold under express warranties, which, as a matter of federal law run to the consumer without regard to privity. Magnuson-Moss precludes a disclaimer of the implied warranty of merchantability as to consumer goods where an express warranty is given. Given this framework, we think ordinary consumers are entitled to, and do, expect that a consumer product sold under a warranty is merchantable, at least at the modest level of merchantability set by UCC section 2-314, where hazards common to the type of product do not render the product unfit for normal use.

Even if one party to the contract—the manufacturer—intends to extend an implied warranty only to the immediate purchaser, in a consumer setting, doing away with the privity requirement for a product subject to the Magnuson-Moss Warranty Act, rather than rewriting the deal, simply gives the consumer the contract the consumer expected. The manufacturer, on the other hand is encouraged to build quality into its products. To the extent that there is a cost of adding uniform or standard quality in all products, the risk of a lemon is passed to all buyers in the form of pricing and not randomly distributed among those unfortunate enough to have acquired one of the lemons. Moreover, elimination of privity requirement gives consumers, such as Goodin, the value of their expected bargain but will rarely do more than duplicate the Indiana Products Liability Act as to other consequential damages. The remedy for breach of implied warranty of merchantability is in most cases, including this one, the difference between "the value of the goods accepted and the value they would have had if they had been as warranted." This gives the buyer the benefit of the bargain. In most cases, however, if any additional damages are available under the UCC as the result of abolishing privity, Indiana law would award the same damages under the Products Liability Act as personal injury or damage to "other property" from a "defective" product.

For the reasons given above, we conclude that Indiana law does not require vertical privity between a consumer and a manufacturer as a condition to a claim by the consumer against the manufacturer for breach of the manufacturer's implied warranty of merchantability.

The judgment of the trial court is affirmed.

■ *Affirmed.*

CASE CONCEPTS REVIEW

1. Based on the courts review of the history of the privity requirement, why was privity thought to be a necessary component of an action for product liability?
2. Why did the court rule that no privity was required between a consumer and a manufacturer where the consumer is asserting a breach of the implied warranty of merchantability?

11. Comparison of Strict Liability and Warranty

Table 23-2 demonstrates a basic similarity between strict tort liability under the Restatement (Second) of Torts and the warranty of merchantability. For instance, "defective condition, unreasonably dangerous" and "fit for ordinary purposes" seem to be similar tests under the notion of "defect." Plaintiffs using strict liability, however, may have a lesser burden of proof. For example, in a breach-of-warranty case, the plaintiff may have to overcome contract defenses such as disclaimers of liability, the requirement of notice of breach, limitation of remedies, and lack of privity.

TABLE 23-2 ■ Comparison between Strict Liability and Warranty

	Warranty of Merchantability UCC 2-314	**Strict Tort Liability Restatement (Second) Torts 402A**
Condition of goods giving rise to liability	Not merchantable; that is, not fit for ordinary purpose [2-314(1), (2)(c)]	Defective condition, unreasonably dangerous [402A(1)]
Character of defendant	Must be seller who is a merchant with respect to goods of that kind [2-314(1), 2-104(1)]	Must be seller who is engaged in the business of selling such a product [402A(1) (a)]
Reliance	No explicit requirement such warranty "taken for granted," [2-314]; see, however, 2-316(3) (b)	No requirement of "any reliance on the part of the consumer upon the reputation, skill, or judgment of the seller" (402A Comment m)
Disclaimer	Limitation of consequential damages for injury to the person in the case of consumer goods is prima facie unconscionable [2-316(4), 2-719(3), 2-302].	Cause of action is not affected by any disclaimer or any other agreement (402A Comment m).
Notice	Buyer must within a reasonable time after he or she discovers, or should have discovered, any breach notify seller of breach or be barred from any remedy. Reason for rule: to defeat commercial base, not to deprive a good-faith consumer of his or her remedy [2-607(3) (a)].	Consumer is not required to give notice to seller of his or her injury within a reasonable time after it occurs (402A Comment m).
Causation	Buyer may recover consequential damages resulting from the seller's breach, including injury to person or property proximately resulting from any breach of warranty [2-714, 2-715(2)(b) 2-314; see 2-316(3)(b)].	Seller is subject to liability for physical harm caused [402A(1); see Comment n.] Contributory negligence is not a defense.
Protected persons	The third persons protected depend on the alternative of 2-318 adopted.	Ultimate user or consumer [402A(1), (2)b) and comment l]
Protected injuries	Injuries to person or his or her property (2-318)	Physical harm to ultimate user or consumer or to his or her property [402A(1)]
Statute of limitations	Four years form tender of delivery [2-725(1), (2)]	State law varies (from one to three years from injury).

Where there is only economic loss (no physical harm to person or property), most courts will not allow a recovery in strict liability. Warranty liability for economic loss, however, is available. Moreover, the UCC provides a longer statute of limitations in which to bring the warranty action. Practical considerations such as the availability or solvency of a particular defendant may also affect the choice of theory.

Finally, as discussed in Chapter 8, for those jurisdictions that have adopted provisions of the *Restatement (Third) of Torts: Products Liability* (as issued by the American Law Institute in 1997), the definition of a defect is revised significantly. For example, a "manufacturing defect" is simply an aberration from design specifications, regardless of whether the defect was unreasonably dangerous.

CHAPTER SUMMARY

TYPES OF WARRANTIES

Express Warranties

1. An express warranty is a statement of fact or promise that is made as a part of the contract for sale and becomes a part of the basis of the bargain between the buyer and the seller.
2. Most statements of opinion, such as those concerning the value of the goods, do not give rise to an express warranty.
3. Express warranties may be statements about the goods in sales material, or they may arise from a sale by sample or model.

Warranty of Title

1. A seller of goods makes a warranty that he or she has title to the goods and the right to sell them.
2. The warranty of title includes a warranty that there are no encumbrances and the buyer's use of the goods will be free from the claims of others.

Implied Warranty of Merchantability

1. A warranty that the goods shall be merchantable is implied in a contract for sale if the seller is a merchant who deals in goods of the kind involved in the contract.
2. For goods to be merchantable, they must at least be the kind of goods that are fit for the ordinary purposes for which such goods are used.
3. Liability for breach of the warranty of merchantability extends to direct economic loss, as well as to personal injuries and property damage.

Implied Warranty of Fitness for a Particular Purpose

1. An implied warranty of fitness for a particular purpose is created if, at the time of contracting, the seller has reason to know any particular purpose for which the buyer requires the goods and is relying on the seller's skill or judgment to select or furnish suitable goods.
2. The buyer need not specifically state that he or she has a particular purpose in mind or is placing reliance on the seller's judgment if the circumstances are such that the seller has reason to realize the purpose intended or that the buyer is relying on the seller.
3. Breach of the warranty of fitness for a particular purpose may result in disaffirmance of the contract. If the product causes an injury including economic loss, it may also result in a suit for dollar damages.

LIMITATIONS

Express Warranties

1. If there is an express warranty and an attempt to limit warranties, both will be given effect if possible.
2. If not, the express warranty will prevail, and the attempt to negate it will not be given effect.

Written Disclaimers of Implied Warranties

1. To exclude or modify the implied warranty of merchantability, the word *merchantability* must be used. If the disclaimer is included in a written contract, it must be set forth in a conspicuous manner.
2. To exclude or modify any implied warranty of fitness for a particular purpose, the exclusion must be conspicuously written.
3. Disclaimers of warranties are subject to the Magnuson-Moss warranty law.

Other Exclusions of Implied Warranties

1. The Code also provides for other circumstances in which implied warranties may be wholly or partially excluded. The seller may inform the buyer that the goods are being sold "as is", "with all faults." Other language may call the buyer's attention to the exclusion and make it plain that the sale involves no implied warranty.
2. If, before entering into the contract, the buyer has examined the goods, sample, or model, there is no implied warranty on defects that an examination ought to have revealed to him or her.

Remedies

1. Parties may agree to limit or alter the measure of damages.
2. Clauses limiting a seller's damages are subject to the Code rule on unconscionability.
3. Limiting consequential damages for personal injury is prima facie unconscionable.

OTHER ASPECTS OF WARRANTIES

Notice

1. A buyer must give notice of any breach of warranty within a reasonable time.
2. Failure to give notice prevents a suit for breach of warranty.
3. Filing suit is not notice.

Third Parties

1. The horizontal privity issue is—To whom does the warranty extend? In most states, it extends to any person in the family or household of the buyer or a guest in the home if it is reasonable to expect that such person may consume or be affected by the goods and is injured by them.
2. The vertical privity issue is—Against whom can action be brought for breach of warranty? The Code leaves the development of the law to the courts, case by case. The courts of most states have abandoned the vertical privity of contract requirement, and persons injured by products are allowed to sue all businesses in the chain of distribution without regard to the presence of privity of contract.

Comparison of Strict Liability and Warranty

1. Table 23-2 demonstrates a basic similarity between strict tort liability and the warranty of merchantability.

REVIEW QUESTIONS AND PROBLEMS

1. Identify the terms in Column A by matching each with the appropriate statement in Column B.

A	B
(1) Express warranty	(a) Made only by a merchant
(2) Warranty of merchantability	(b) Arises because of special skill of the seller
(3) Fungible goods	(c) To whom does the warranty extend
(4) Warranty of fitness for a particular purpose	(d) A guarantee

(5) Horizontal privity	(e) Limits available damages or other options upon breach
(6) Vertical privity	(f) Sold by weight or measure
(7) Notice	(g) Against whom can suit be brought
(8) Disclaimer of warranties	(h) Limits a cause of action that might otherwise create liability
(9) Disclaimer of remedies	(i) Guarantee
(10) Warranty	(j) A condition precedent to a suit for breach of warranty

2. A seller makes the following statements about goods to the buyer. Which are puffery and which are express warranties?

a. The jukebox is a good machine and will probably not get out of order.
b. October is not too late to plant this grass seed.
c. This car is supposed to last a lifetime. It's in perfect condition.
d. This dredge pipe has expandable ends that will seal upon the spill going through.
e. This feed additive will increase your milk production and will not harm your dairy herd.
f. These filter tanks should be able to remove iron and manganese from the water.
g. This used car has never been wrecked.

3. Plaintiff sued the manufacturer of a backyard driving range for personal injuries. Plaintiff was hit on the head by a golf ball following a practice swing with the golf-training device. The label on the shipping carton stated in bold type, "COMPLETELY SAFE—BALL WILL NOT HIT PLAYER." What theory did plaintiff use in this case? Explain.

4. A truck salesman told the buyer that the truck would be just right for plowing snow. In fact, the truck was incapable of pushing a snowplow. The buyer sued for breach of express warranty. Is there an express warranty? Explain.

5. Sumner, an Anchorage aircraft dealer, sold a Piper Navajo airplane to Fel-Air, Inc. for $105,000. The title to the airplane was actually in Century Aircraft, Inc., which had leased it to Sumner with an option to purchase. Fel-Air sued Sumner for breach of the warranty of title. Sumner denied liability on the ground that Fel-Air as a good-faith purchaser for value received good title. Is Sumner liable? Why or why not?

6. In which of the following circumstances was the implied warranty of merchantability breached?

a. In defendant's restaurant, plaintiff bought a martini with an unpitted olive. Plaintiff broke a tooth when he attempted to eat the olive.
b. Plaintiff is bitten by a spider concealed in a pair of blue jeans sold by defendant's store.
c. Seller sold cattle feed that contained the female hormone stilbestrol. It causes cattle to grow more rapidly than normal but also causes abortion in pregnant cows and sterility in bulls. The plaintiff farmer raises cattle for breeding rather than for slaughter, so he sues. The label on the cattle feed package did not mention that it contained stilbestrol.

- **d.** Plaintiff bought and used a power lawn mower. While the plaintiff was mowing, an unknown object was hurled out of the grass chute and penetrated the eye of plaintiff's five-year-old son.
- **e.** Plaintiff's Ford Pinto's gas tank exploded on impact.
- **f.** Plaintiff bought a cookbook from defendant retail book dealer. Four days later, while following a recipe in the book, plaintiff ate a small slice of one of the ingredients, a plant commonly known as elephant's ear, and became violently ill. Plaintiff sued for breach of the implied warranty of merchantability.
- **g.** Plaintiff bought a product that caused her to have an allergic reaction.

7. Stewart, a practicing dentist, sold his 42-foot Trojan yacht to Smith for $52,000. Three days after delivery of the boat, Smith notified Stewart that one of the boat's fuel tanks was leaking and requested that the condition be remedied at Stewart's expense. When Stewart refused, Smith sued Stewart for breach of the warranty of merchantability. Should Smith recover? Explain.

8. Pat, the buyer of a tractor and backhoe, sued the seller for breach of the implied warranty of merchantability. The sales contract contained the following:

> The equipment covered hereby is sold subject only to the applicable manufacturer's standard printed warranty, and no other warranties, express or implied, including the implied warranty of merchantability, shall apply.

The type size of the foregoing was slightly larger than the rest of the contract, but it was not boldface. Was the disclaimer effective to negate the implied warranty? Explain.

9. The purchase agreement for a mobile home stated Standard Manufacturer Warranty—OTHERWISE SOLD AS IS. The buyer subsequently discovered defects and sued for breach of the implied warranty of merchantability. He contended that the disclaimer was ineffective because it did not contain the word *merchantability* and was not conspicuous. Was the buyer correct? Why or why not?

10. Pam purchased a contaminated cheeseburger from a vending machine where she worked. She suffered acute food poisoning and sued the baking company that baked the bun for breach of the warranty of merchantability. The baking company moved to dismiss for lack of privity of contract. Is lack of privity of contract a defense? Explain.

PART V

AGENCY & EMPLOYMENT

Basic Principles of Agency | 24

CHAPTER OUTLINE

CHAPTER PREVIEW

This chapter serves as an introduction to Part V on agency and employment law. The term agency is used to describe the fiduciary relationship that exists when one person acts on behalf, and under the control, of another person. The principles of agency law are essential for the conduct of business transactions. A corporation and a limited liability company, as legal entities, can function only through agents. Most often, these agents are employees. The law of partnership comprises, to a large degree, agency principles specially applied to that particular form of business organization.

The person who acts for another is called an agent. The person for whom the agent acts, and who controls the agent, is called a principal. This chapter introduces the relationship between a principal and an agent. Traditionally, issues of agency law arise when the agent has attempted to enter into a contract on behalf of a principal. Similarly, the law of agency includes several aspects of the law of torts, in which case the principal usually is called a master and the agent is called a servant. The next chapter presents legal principles associated with agency law and the areas of contract and tort liability.

BUSINESS MANAGEMENT DECISION

As the sales manager of your company, you are responsible for a sales force of twenty-three people. You learn that two of your top salespeople are planning to go to work for a competitor. These salespeople have meetings scheduled with three of your recently hired salespeople. You suspect that the two might be trying to convince the three to leave with them.

What action should you take based on this information?

IN GENERAL

1. Introduction

Case law, as contrasted with statutory law, has developed most of the principles applicable to the law of agency. Agency issues are usually discussed within a framework of three parties: the principal (P), the agent (A), and the third party (T), with whom A contracts or against whom A commits a tort while in P's service. The following examples illustrate the problems and issues involved in the law of agency.

P v. A: Principal sues agent for a loss caused by A's breach of a fiduciary duty, such as to obey instructions.

P v. T: Principal sues third party for breach of a contract that A negotiated with T while A was acting on P's behalf.

A v. T: Agent sues third party for a loss suffered by A, such as the loss of a commission due to T's interference with contractual obligations.

T v. P: Third party sues principal for breach of a contract that A negotiated with T.

T v. A: Third party sues principal for damages caused by a tort committed by A.

2. Types of Principals

From the third party's perspective, an agent may act for one of three types of principals.

DISCLOSED An agent who reveals that he or she is working for another and who reveals the principal's identity is an agent of a *disclosed principal.* The existence of a disclosed principal will be found in most agency relationships, particularly employment situations.

UNDISCLOSED At the other extreme, a principal is *undisclosed* whenever a third party reasonably believes that the agent acts only on his or her own behalf. In essence, when an undisclosed principal is involved, the third party does not realize that any agency relationship exists. A well-known or wealthy principal may not want a third party to know he or she is interested in buying that third party's land, business, or merchandise. Therefore, the principal hires an agent to deal with the third party. This agent would be instructed by the principal to keep that principal's existence a secret from the third party.

PARTIALLY DISCLOSED A third situation falls between the disclosed and undisclosed principal's circumstances. A third party may know an agent represents a principal, but that third party may not know the identity of the principal. When a third party learns of the principal's existence but not his or her identity, a *partially disclosed principal* is present. For the most part, legal issues treat undisclosed and partially disclosed principals in a similar manner.

Broker

A person employed for a commission to make contracts with third persons on behalf of a principal

Factor

An agent for the sale of merchandise who may hold goods in his or her own name or in the name of a principal and who is authorized to sell and to receive payment for the goods

General agent

An agent authorized to do all the acts connected with carrying on a particular trade, business, or profession

Special agent

An agent with a limited amount of authority who usually has instructions to accomplish one specific task

3. Types of Agents

Agents serve a variety of functions on behalf of their principals. There are special terms used to describe these agents based on their responsibilities.

BROKERS AND FACTORS Some agents are known as **brokers** and others as factors. A broker is an agent with special, limited authority to procure a customer so the owner can affect a sale or exchange of property. A real estate broker has authority to find a buyer for another's real estate, but the real estate remains under the control of the owner. A **factor** is a person who has possession and control of another's personal property, such as goods, and is authorized to sell that property. A factor has a property interest and may sell the property in his or her own name, whereas a broker may not. Although the term is seldom used today, a retail merchant who has a manufacturer's goods on consignment is a factor.

GENERAL AND SPECIAL Agents are also classified as general or special agents. A **general agent** is one who has authority to transact all the business of the principal—of a particular kind or in a particular case. The powers of a general agent are coextensive with the business entrusted to the agent's care, authorizing him or her to act for the principal in all matters coming within the usual and ordinary scope and character of such business. A general agent has much broader authority than a special agent. Some cases define a general agent as one authorized to conduct a series of transactions involving a continuity of service, whereas a special agent conducts a single transaction or a series of transactions without continuity of service.

A **special agent** is authorized to act for the principal only in a particular transaction or in a particular way. Most agents usually are considered to be general agents of the employer as long as they stay within the scope of their employment. However, an athlete's agent assisting in contract negotiations likely would be a special agent and generally would not be authorized to make investments or purchase property.

Independent contractor

A person who exercises his or her independent judgment on the means used to accomplish the result

INDEPENDENT CONTRACTORS Some persons who perform services for others are known as **independent contractors**. When a person contracts for the services of another in a way that gives the employing party full and complete control over the details and manner in which the work will be conducted, a principal-agent relationship is established. On the other hand, when the employing party simply contracts for a certain end result and the employed party has full control over the manner and methods to be pursued in bringing about the result, the latter party is deemed an independent contractor. The person contracting with an independent contractor and receiving the benefit of his or her service is usually called a *proprietor.* A proprietor is generally not responsible to third parties for the independent contractor's actions, either in contract or in tort.

4. Capacity of Parties

It is generally stated that anyone who may act for himself or herself may act through an agent. For example, a minor may enter into a contract, and as long as the minor does not disaffirm it, the agreement is binding. Likewise, the majority of states have held that a contract of an agent on behalf of a minor principal is voidable. Therefore, such an agreement is subject to rescission or ratification by the minor, the same as if the minor personally had entered into the contract. To this general rule concerning an infant's capacity as a principal, some states recognize an exception. There is some authority to the effect that any appointment of an agent by an infant is void, not merely voidable. Under this view, any agreement entered into by an infant's agent would be ineffective, and an attempted disaffirmance by the principal would be unnecessary.

A minor may act as an agent for an adult. Any agreements the minor makes for a principal while acting within the authority of an agent are binding on the principal. Although the minor who acts as an agent has a right to terminate a contract of agency at will, so long as the minor continues employment, his or her acts within the scope of the authority conferred become those of the principal.

5. Formal Requirements

As a general rule, agency relationships are based on the consent of the parties involved. No particular formalities are required to create a principal-agent relationship. A principal may appoint an agent either in writing or orally. Further, the agency may be either expressed or implied.

Despite the general lack of formal requirements, some states require that the appointment of an agent be evidenced by a writing when the agent is to negotiate a contract required to be written by the statute of frauds. Recall from Chapter 18 that these written contracts include those involving title to real estate, guaranty contracts, performance that cannot be completed within one year of the date of making, and sales of goods for $500 or more.

Power of attorney

An instrument authorizing another to act as one's agent or attorney in fact

Attorney in fact

A person acting for another under a grant of special power created by an instrument in writing

When a formal instrument is used for conferring authority on an agent, it is known as a **power of attorney**. Generally, this written document is signed by the principal in the presence of a notary public. The agent named in a power of attorney is called an **attorney in fact**. The term distinguishes this formally appointed agent from an attorney at law, who is a licensed lawyer.

A power of attorney may be general, which gives the agent authority to act in all respects for the principal. Sometimes an elderly person signs a power of attorney appointing a general attorney in fact to handle all the necessary matters that may arise. Under other circumstances, a power of attorney, known as a special power of attorney, may be narrowly written. For example, a seller of land may need to be out of town on the date set to close the sales transaction. This seller can sign a special power of attorney appointing a special attorney in fact to act on the seller's behalf by signing the deed and other necessary papers required to complete the closing. Furthermore, a seller or buyer of real estate typically must appoint an agent via a special power of attorney for that agent to have authority to sign a binding contract.

Section 14 discusses real estate listing agreements. Although these documents are used to authorize a real estate agent to find a ready, willing, and able buyer, most states do not require these agreements to be in writing. Technically the agent cannot create a binding sales contract between the buyer and seller. In other words, the real estate agent is not authorized to sign a contract on the seller's behalf. That agent's responsibility is to bring the buyer and seller together so these parties may sign a contract. Despite oral listing agreements being enforceable, agents generally insist on a written one to ease the burden of proof required to establish when a commission is owed. Furthermore, a number of states do require that listing agreements be evidenced by a writing.

DUTIES OF AGENTS

6. Introduction

Fiduciary

A position of trust and confidence in relation to a person or his or her property

The nature and extent of the duties imposed on agents and servants are governed largely by the contract of employment. In addition to the duties expressly designated, certain others are implied by the **fiduciary** nature of the relationship and by the legal effects on the principal of actions or omissions by the agent. The essence of a fiduciary relationship is illustrated in the following case.

CASE

Lanna L. Lee, a/k/a Lanna Pai, and B. Lanna, Inc. v. Theodore Hasson, H. International Distribution, Inc. a/k/a Hasson International Distribution, Inc., and Diversified Financial Enterprises

COURT OF APPEALS OF TEXAS

2007 Tex. App. LEXIS 622 (2007)

GUZMAN

Lou Pai married Lee in 1976. They had a son, B.P., in September 1979, and a daughter, S.P., born in 1982. Pai has advanced degrees in economics, and at the time of these events he was an executive in various Enron companies; Lee was a college-educated homemaker. Through their children, the Pais met Theodore and Terry Hasson in 1993. Ted Hasson was a life insurance agent and securities dealer. The Hassons and the Pais became good friends and spent many vacations and holidays together. In 1995, Hasson sold the Pais a $5 million second-to-die life insurance policy and learned their personal medical information and some of their financial information. The Pais applied for a $6 million policy in June 1995, a $15 million policy in November 1996, and a $50 million policy in March 1998.

In January 1998, Lee discovered that Pai had been having an extra-marital affair and had another child outside of their marriage. She confided her discoveries to the Hassons. Pai moved out of the family home in 1999, and Lee interviewed various family law attorneys, including Lawrence Rothenberg. Lee's sister, who is also an attorney, accompanied Lee to some of these interviews.

On or about August 26, 1999, Lee sought Hasson's advice. Anticipating a divorce, Lee asked Hasson what actions she should take while she was still married. At Hasson's request, Lee forwarded financial statements from Pai's bank to Hasson. According to Hasson, he was "shocked" by the financial statements. Hasson discovered that the Pais' net worth was approximately two and half times the amount Hasson had believed it to be and that a large portion of their assets consisted of Enron stock and options.

Hasson contends he began working for Lee in October 1999 and reached an oral agreement with her regarding his compensation on January 18, 2000. Hasson claims that on May 3, 2000, Lee told him that she wanted to modify her oral agreement with him to eliminate the contemplated partnership and instead pay Hasson 10% of the value of her marital estate at the time of her divorce in exchange for services he had rendered in the past and was expected to render in the future.

Hasson sued Lee on July 10, 2000, alleging that Lee's share of the marital estate, including the New Power shares, totaled approximately $140 million, and that Lee owed him 10% of this amount in payment for his services under the terms of the May 3, 2000 modification of their oral agreement. At trial, Lee denied that she had an agreement with Hasson, and contended that he was instead a helpful friend.

In response to Question 16 of the charge, the jury found that a relationship of trust and confidence existed between Lee and Hasson at the time they entered into the oral agreement. The jury also answered Question 17 affirmatively, finding that Hasson had complied with his fiduciary duty to Lee.

In Lee's first issue, she contends that the trial court committed harmful error in disregarding the jury's finding that Hasson had a

continued

relationship of trust and confidence with her. Hasson's cross-point, in which he argues that the evidence is factually insufficient to support the jury's finding that Lee and Hasson had a relationship of trust and confidence, relates to the same jury question. This issue is important to both parties because the existence of such a relationship not only imposes on Hasson the elevated duty of a fiduciary but also places the burden on him to prove that he complied with that duty.

The term "fiduciary" refers to a person owing a duty of integrity and fidelity; and "it applies to any person who occupies a position of peculiar confidence towards another." In certain formal relationships, such as an attorney-client or trustee relationship, a fiduciary duty arises as a matter of law. Texas courts also have recognized that certain informal relationships may give rise to a fiduciary duty.

Mere subjective trust does not transform an arm's-length transaction into a fiduciary relationship. Rather, in order to establish the existence of an informal fiduciary relationship, the record must show that one of the parties relied on the other "for moral, financial, or personal support or guidance." The length of the relationship is another important factor in determining whether a fiduciary relationship should be recognized. Even a longstanding relationship of friendship or cordiality is insufficient, without more, to establish an informal fiduciary relationship.

The record reveals both legally and factually sufficient evidence that Hasson and Lee shared a long-standing business relationship and a close personal family relationship well beyond casual friendship and that Lee relied on Hasson for moral, financial, and personal guidance or support. Moreover, their relationship began in 1993 and, therefore, predated their agreements by approximately six years.

In sum, we conclude the evidence is legally sufficient to allow a jury of reasonable and fair-minded people to find that Lee and Hasson had a relationship of trust and confidence before entering into the agreement at issue. Moreover, because such a finding is not contrary to the overwhelming weight of the evidence, it is also factually sufficient.

We emphasize that fiduciary relationships are not lightly created. However, the extraordinary facts of this case present a rare example of the type of close personal relationship of trust and confidence that gives rise to a legally cognizable fiduciary duty. We therefore hold that the trial court erred in disregarding the jury's answer to Question 16.

■ *Reversed.*

CASE CONCEPTS REVIEW

1. What facts did the court use to fashion a fiduciary relationship in this case?
2. Were these facts truly "extraordinary"? Why?

The usual *implied duties* associated with being a fiduciary include the obligation (1) to be loyal to the principal, (2) to protect confidential information, (3) to obey all reasonable instructions, (4) to inform the principal of material facts that affect the relationship, (5) to refrain from being negligent, and (6) to account for all money or property received for the benefit of the principal. The following sections discuss how these implied duties are essential to the principal-agent relationship.

7. Duty of Loyalty

At the foundation of any fiduciary relationship is the *duty of loyalty* that each party owes to the other. Since an agent is in a position of trust and confidence, the agent owes an obligation of undivided loyalty to the principal. While employed, an agent should not undertake a business

TABLE 24-1 ■ Implied Fiduciary Duties

1.	Duty of loyalty
2.	Duty to protect confidential information
3.	Duty of obedience
4.	Duty to inform
5.	Duty of care
6.	Duty to account

venture that competes or interferes in any manner with the principal's business, nor should the agent make any contract for himself or herself that should have been made for the principal. A breach of this fundamental duty can result in the principal's enjoining the agent's new business or recovering money damages, or both.

This duty of loyalty also prevents an agent from entering into an agreement on the principal's behalf if the agent is the other contracting party. To create a binding agreement with the principal, the agent first must obtain the principal's approval. Since a contract between the agent and the principal is not a deal "at arm's length," the circumstances demand the utmost good faith from the agent. Indeed, an agent must disclose fully all facts that might materially influence the principal's decision-making process.

Likewise, an agent usually cannot represent two principals in the same transactions if the principals have differing interests. To act as dual agent often leads the agent to an unavoidable breach of the duty of loyalty to one, if not both, of the principals. To prevent the breach of this basic duty in this situation, the agent should inform both principals of all the facts in the transaction, including that the agent is working for both principals. If these principals agree to continue negotiations, the agent in effect becomes a "go-between" or messenger. The agent is acting on behalf of both principals while avoiding active negotiations. Due to the nature of their business, real estate agents particularly must be aware of the hazards of dual agencies.

Transactions violating the duty of loyalty may always be rescinded by the principal, even though the agent acted for the best interests of the principal and the contract was as favorable as could be obtained elsewhere. The general rule is applied without favor, so every possible motive or incentive for unfaithfulness may be removed.

In addition to the remedy of rescission, a principal is entitled to treat any profit realized by the agent in violation of this duty as belonging to the principal. Such profits may include rebates, bonuses, commissions, or divisions of profits received by an agent for dealing with a particular third party. Here again the contracts may have been favorable to the employer; but the result is the same because the agent should not be tempted to abuse the confidence placed in him or her. The principal may also collect from the agent a sum equal to any damages sustained as the result of the breach of the duty of loyalty.

8. Duty to Protect Confidential Information

The duty of loyalty demands that information of a confidential character acquired while in the service of the principal shall not be used by the agent to advance the agent's interests in opposition to those of the principal. In other words, an agent has a *duty to protect the principal's confidential information.* This confidential information is usually called a *trade secret.* Trade secrets include plans, processes, tools, mechanisms, compounds, and informational data used in business operations. They are known only to the owner of the business and to a limited number of other persons in whom it may be necessary to confide. An employer seeking to prevent the disclosure or use of trade secrets or information must demonstrate that he or she pursued an active course of conduct designed to inform employees that such secrets and information were to remain confidential. An issue to be determined in all cases involving trade secrets is whether the information sought to be protected is, in fact and in law, confidential. The result in each case depends on the conduct of the parties and the nature of the information.

An employee who learns of secret processes or formulas or comes into possession of lists of customers may not use this information to the detriment of his or her employer. Former employees may not use such information in a competing business, regardless of whether the

Employers need to inform employees that trade secrets are to remain confidential.

trade secrets were copied or memorized. The fact that a product is on the market does not amount to a divulgence or abandonment of the secrets connected with the product. The employer may obtain an injunction to prevent their use, as use is a form of unfair competition. The rule relating to trade secrets is applied with equal severity whether the agent acts before or after severing the connection with the principal.

Knowledge that is important, but not a trade secret, may be used although its use injures the agent's former employer. Information that by experience has become a part of a former employee's general knowledge should not and cannot be enjoined from further and different uses. For this reason, there usually is nothing to hinder a person who has made the acquaintance of his or her employer's customers from later contacting those whom he or she can remember. These acquaintances are part of the employee's acquired knowledge. The employer may protect himself or herself by a clause in the employment agreement to the effect that the employee will not compete with the employer or work for a competitor for a limited period of time after employment is terminated.

9. Duty to Obey Instructions

It is the duty of an agent to *obey all instructions* issued by his or her principal as long as they refer to duties contemplated by the contract of employment. Burdens not required by the agreement cannot be indiscriminately imposed by the employer, and any material change in an employee's duties may constitute a breach of the employment contract.

An instruction may not be regarded lightly merely because it departs from the usual procedure and seems fanciful and impractical to the agent. It is not the agent's business to question the procedure outlined by his or her superior. Any loss that results while the agent is pursuing any other course makes the agent absolutely liable to the principal for such resulting loss.

Furthermore, an instruction of the principal does not become improper merely because the motive is bad, unless it is illegal or immoral. The principal may be well aware of the agent's distaste for certain tasks; yet, if those tasks are called for under the employment agreement, it becomes the agent's duty to perform them. Failure to perform often results in proper grounds for discharge.

Closely allied to the duty to follow instructions is the duty to remain within the scope of the authority conferred. Because it often becomes possible for an agent to exceed his or her authority and still bind the principal, the agent has a duty not to exceed the authority granted. In case the agent does so, the employee or agent becomes responsible for any resulting loss.

Occasionally, circumstances arise that nullify instructions previously given. Because of the new conditions, the old instructions would, if followed, practically destroy the purpose of the agency. Whenever such an emergency arises, it becomes the duty of the agent, provided that the principal is not available, to exercise his or her best judgment in meeting the situation.

10. Duty to Inform

In Chapter 25, we will see that knowledge acquired by an agent within the scope of his or her authority binds the principal. More succinctly, the law states that an agent's knowledge is imputed as notice to the principal. Therefore, the law requires that the agent *inform* the principal of all facts that affect the subject matter of the agency that are obtained within the scope of the employment. The rule requiring full disclosure of all material facts that might affect the principal is equally applicable to gratuitous and to compensated agents.

This rule extends beyond the duty to inform the principal of conflicting interests of third parties or possible violations of the duty of loyalty in a particular transaction. It imposes on the agent a duty to give the principal all information that materially affects the interest of the principal. Knowledge of facts that may have greatly advanced the value of property placed with an agent for sale must be communicated before property is sold at a price previously established by the principal. Knowledge of financial problems of a buyer on credit must also be communicated to the principal.

This duty generally applies even if the agent is not currently working on behalf of the principle. Suppose an agent is at dinner with her family. The agent overhears two people talking at the next table. A portion of the conversation reveals information that would be relevant to a business venture involving the principal. The agent is under a duty to disclose the information to the principal.

11. Duty Not to Be Negligent

As is discussed more fully in Chapter 25, the doctrine of respondeat superior imposes liability on a principal or master for the torts of an agent or servant acting within the scope of his or her employment. The agent or servant is primarily liable, and the principal or master is vicariously or secondarily liable.

It is an implied condition of employment contracts, if not otherwise expressed, that the employee has a duty to act in good faith and to *exercise reasonable care* and diligence in performing tasks. Failure to do so is a breach of the employment contract. Therefore, if the employer has liability to third persons because of the employee's acts or negligent omissions, the employer may recover his or her loss from the employee. This right may be transferred by the doctrine of subrogation to the liability insurance carrier of the employer. For example, assume that a bakery company is held liable for damages to an injured child who was struck by a company delivery truck as the result of the employee-driver's negligence. After the company's insurance company pays the total coverage to the injured party, any unpaid damages can be collected from the company. The company, in turn can sue the employee for breach of the duty not to be negligent. In some states the insurance company could also collect from the employee. However, there are some reasons to keep liability from being passed ultimately to the careless employee. These reasons are discussed in Chapter 25 on agency and tort responsibility.

12. Duty to Account

Money or property entrusted to the agent must be accounted for to the principal. Because of this, the agent is required to *keep proper records* showing receipts and expenditures so a complete accounting may be rendered. Any money collected by an agent for a principal should not be mingled with funds of the agent. If they are deposited in a bank, they should be kept in a separate account. Otherwise, any loss resulting must be borne by the agent. Also, the duty to account can arise out of the agent's breach of any other fiduciary duty.

An agent who receives money from third parties for the benefit of the principal owes no duty to account to the third parties. The only duty to account is owed to the principal. On the other hand, money paid to an agent who has no authority to collect it and does not turn it over to the principal may be recovered from the agent in an action by the third party.

A different problem is presented when money is paid in error to an agent, as in the overpayment of an account. If the agent has passed the money on to the principal before the mistake is discovered, it is clear that only the principal is liable. Nevertheless, money that is still in the possession of the agent when he or she is notified of the error should be returned to the third party. The agent is not relieved of this burden by subsequently making payment to the principal.

Any payment made in error to an agent and caused by the agent's mistake or misconduct may always be recovered from him or her, even if the agent has surrendered it to the principal. Also, any overpayment may be recovered from the agent of an undisclosed principal because the party dealing with the agent was unaware of the existence of the principal.

The following case illustrates the duty to account.

CASE

Veronica Phillips v. Rupertha Andrews

UNITED STATES DISTRICT COURT FOR THE DISTRICT OF THE VIRGIN ISLANDS

332 F. Supp. 2d 797 (2004)

PER CURIAM

In 1995 Phillips, who at the time resided in New York, engaged real estate broker Rupertha Andrews ["Andrews"] to assist her in the purchase of a home on St. Croix. In May or June of 1995, Phillips entered into a contract for the purchase of a home at No. 230 Estate La Grange, Frederiksted. Phillips subsequently executed a special power of attorney authorizing Andrews to act on her behalf to complete the real estate closing. That power of attorney was executed on June 1, 1995 and was to be effective until closing. The real estate closing was scheduled for December 22, 1995. Prior to the scheduled closing, a hurricane struck St. Croix, causing damage to the La Grange home. Nonetheless, Phillips agreed to proceed with closing on December 22, 1995, with the condition that the seller turn over any insurance proceeds collected for necessary repairs. Following closing on December 22, 1995—which Phillips apparently attended on St. Croix—Phillips executed a second power of attorney on December 29, 1995, authorizing Andrews to receive the insurance proceeds on her behalf. Phillips asserts that was where Andrews' authority ended. However, Andrews maintained at trial that, around the same time period as the written power of attorney, Phillips gave her an additional oral grant of authority to expend the insurance proceeds for the purpose of securing repairs to Phillips' home. The only time reference appearing in the record for this purported oral grant of authority was sometime around "the ending of 1995" while Phillips was on St. Croix for the real estate closing.

Andrews testified that while Phillips was on St. Croix for that closing, Andrews introduced her brother, Wrigby Archibald ["Archibald"], to Phillips. Archibald, a contractor, testified Phillips asked him to take a look at the house to assess the damage, and he accompanied a bank officer and insurance adjuster to the house to aid in securing an insurance settlement. Thereafter, an insurance settlement amount of $14,081.75, which Archibald testified was still insufficient to do the needed repairs, was issued. Archibald further testified that Phillips asked him to repair the house and told him he would be paid by Andrews. He concedes he never prepared an estimate, never agreed on a price for the repairs, and never entered into an agreement with Phillips because he did not intend to do a "contract job" for her at a "fixed price." Rather, he said he merely intended "to go along with and help her with what she have to do(sic)."

Were we to uphold the court's determination that Andrews had authority to expend the insurance funds on Phillips' behalf, that would not end the inquiry where, as here, the principal disputes how those funds were used or whether she obtained the intended benefits. Rather, the relevant question becomes whether the agent exceeded the scope of her authority through the issuance of checks for undetermined or undocumented purposes and in her failure to obtain receipts or to provide a full accounting of those funds.

An agent who accepts the authority to disburse funds on behalf of the principal for a particular purpose necessarily assumes the duty to account for the purposes of such disbursements and to ensure the principal receives the intended benefit of those disbursements. Additionally, once it is proved an agent held funds for a principal, it is the agent's burden to prove those funds were properly put to their intended purpose.

Therefore, the agreement authorizes Andrews only to disburse funds for the limited purpose of securing repairs to Phillips' home. Given the duties of an agent imposed by law, mere proof that Andrews disbursed all of the insurance proceeds to the contractor is insufficient to satisfy the standards noted above. Rather, implicit in that limited grant of authority was a requirement that Andrews also maintain a record of the purposes of each disbursement by requiring, at minimum, the submission of receipts from the contractor evidencing services rendered and any other steps customarily taken in similar construction transactions. This duty also required Andrews to specifically inform Phillips of the purposes for which the payments were made.

This was not established at trial. The checks submitted on the record did not inform the inquiry whether the funds were spent for the intended purpose of the agency. Indeed, the record offers little to inform the principal of the benefits she received for the funds paid by her agent. Notably, some of those checks were written to the contractor and others merely to "Cash." Additionally, the notations on six of the seven checks issued indicated they were for the purpose of "Check Exchange(s)" and provided no clear indication that they were issued for Phillips' benefit. Some of those checks were also endorsed by Andrews' son and a staff member in her office; there was some testimony that Andrews' children often assisted the contractor with his banking. Archibald, however, did not testify regarding the checks written to "Cash", as the trial court did not permit him to be questioned regarding checks on which he was not listed as the payee.

While none of these facts, standing alone, may have independent significance, they become more so in the context of the other evidence at trial. Significantly, the agent offered no evidence of the amount of money actually expended for Phillips' benefit. Andrews also collected no receipts, despite remitting $14,000 plus dollars to a third party. There was never any cost estimate prepared to advise Phillips—or Andrews, for that matter—of the expected expenditures and no invoice was submitted to notify Phillips of any monies expended on her behalf and the benefits received. Indeed, Andrews could not even testify to the cost of repairs or the amount of funds actually spent for that purpose. Therefore, there was little to guide the determination that Andrews acted within the scope of her authority in applying the insurance funds to the specific purposes intended.

The court's judgment will be vacated and the matter remanded for further consideration.

■ *Vacated and remanded.*

CASE CONCEPTS REVIEW

1. What is the scope of the duty to account?
2. Consider this: "Archibald testified he never billed Phillips for any of the work done. Moreover, he asserted he did not know what the repairs actually cost and could produce no receipts evidencing the repairs made because, he said, his son had sold the truck in which those records were kept." Is it fair to put the burden on Andrews, given the lack of records provided by Archibald? Why?

DUTIES OF PRINCIPALS

13. Introduction

The principal-agent relationship is a fiduciary one. Like agents, principals also have fiduciary duties. The trust and confidence of a fiduciary relationship is a *two-way obligation.* Thus the law requires that the principal be loyal and honest in dealing with the agents. In addition, the agent is entitled to be compensated for his or her services in accordance with the terms of the contract of employment. If no definite compensation has been agreed on, there arises a duty to pay the reasonable value of such services—the customary rate in the community. Furthermore, the principal owes duties to reimburse agents for their reasonable expenses and to hold the agents harmless for liability that may be incurred while the agent is within the scope of employment. Finally, there is a duty not to discriminate in personnel decisions.

14. Duty to Compensate: In General

Many employment contracts include provisions for paying a percentage of profits to a key employee. If the employment contract does not include a detailed enumeration of the items to be considered in determining net income, it will be computed in accordance with generally accepted accounting principles, taking into consideration past custom and practice in the operation of the employer's business. It is assumed that the methods of determining net income will be consistent and that no substantial changes will be made in the methods of accounting without the mutual agreement of the parties. The employer cannot unilaterally change the accounting methods, nor can the employee require a change to affect an increase in his or her earnings.

The right of a real estate broker or agent to a commission is frequently the subject of litigation. In the absence of an express agreement, the real estate broker earns a commission (1) if he or she finds a purchaser who is ready, willing, and able to meet the terms outlined by the seller in the listing agreement or (2) if the owner contracts with the purchaser (whether or not the price is less than the listed price), even though it later develops that the purchaser is unable to meet the terms of the contract. The contract is conclusive evidence that the broker found a ready, willing, and able purchaser. If a prospective purchaser conditions the obligation to purchase on an approval of credit or approval of a loan, that purchaser is not ready, willing, and able to buy until such approval. If it is not forthcoming, the broker is not entitled to a commission.

Multiple listing is a method of listing property with several brokers simultaneously. These brokers belong to an organization, the members of which share listings and divide the commissions. A typical commission would be split 60 percent to the selling broker, 30 percent to the listing broker, and 10 percent to the organization for operating expenses. These multiple-listing groups give homeowners the advantage of increased exposure to potential buyers. In return for this advantage, most multiple-listing agreements are of the exclusive right to sell type.

15. Duty to Compensate: Sales Representatives

Sales representatives who sell merchandise on a commission basis are confronted by problems similar to those of the broker unless their employment contract is specific in its details. Let us assume that Low Cal Pies, Inc. appoints Albert, on a commission basis, as its exclusive sales representative in a certain territory. A grocery chain in the area involved sends a large order for pies directly to the home office of Low Cal Pies. Is Albert entitled to a commission on the sale? It is generally held that such a salesperson is entitled to a commission only on sales solicited and induced by him or her, unless the contract of employment gives the salesperson greater rights.

The sales representative usually earns a commission as soon as an order from a responsible buyer is obtained, unless the contract of employment makes payment contingent on delivery of the goods or collection of the sale's price. If payment is made dependent on performance by the purchaser, the employer cannot deny the sales representative's commission by terminating the agency prior to collection of the account. When the buyer ultimately pays for the goods, the seller is obligated to pay the commission.

An agent who receives a weekly or monthly advance against future commissions is not obligated to return the advance if commissions equal thereto are not earned. The advance, in the absence of a specific agreement, is considered by the courts as a minimum salary. For example, assume a salesperson works for six months on commission and is fired. If this person was granted a monthly draw of $1,500 and has earned only $6,000 in commissions, the general rule is that the $3,000 excess of draws over commissions does not have to be repaid.

16. Duty to Reimburse

An agent has a general right to *reimbursement* for money properly expended on behalf of his or her principal. It must appear that the money was reasonably spent and that its expenditure was not necessitated by the misconduct or negligence of the agent. Travel-related expenses—such as airfares, mileage, lodging, and meals—are typical examples of the items that a principal must reimburse an agent for unless those parties agree otherwise.

An agent also is entitled to be reimbursed for the costs of completing an agreement when the performance was intended to benefit the principal. This is an especially true statement when the agent has performed on behalf of an undisclosed principal. That principal must protect his or her agent by making funds available to perform the contract as agreed. Suppose that McDonald's is seeking prime locations for its franchises. Not wanting to pay an additional premium just because it is the buyer, McDonald's may hire a local real estate agent to purchase a site in its own name. McDonald's must reimburse this agent for any money that the agent may have used to complete performance of any contract signed.

17. Duty to Indemnify

Indemnify

Literally, "to save harmless"—thus one person agreeing to protect another against loss

Whereas to reimburse someone means to repay him or her for funds already spent, to **indemnify** means to hold a person harmless or free from liability. A servant is entitled to indemnity for certain tort losses. They are limited to factual situations in which the servant is not at fault and his or her liability results from following the instructions of the master. An agent or a servant is justified in presuming that a principal has a lawful right to give instructions and that performance resulting from the instructions will not injure third parties. When this is not the case, and the agent incurs a liability to some third party because of trespass or conversion, the principal must indemnify the agent against loss.

There will ordinarily be no indemnification for losses incurred in negligence actions because the servant's own conduct is involved. Any indemnification is usually of the master by the servant in tort situations. If the agent or servant is sued for actions within the course of employment in which he or she is not at fault, the agent or servant is entitled to be reimbursed for attorney's fees and court costs incurred if the principal or master does not furnish them in the first instance.

TERMINATION BY OPERATION OF LAW

18. In General

The occurrence of certain events is viewed as automatically terminating the agency. As a legal principle, any one of four happenings may end the principal-agent relationship: the death of either party, the insanity of either party, the bankruptcy of either party under specific conditions, and the destruction or illegality of the agency's subject matter.

19. Death

The *death* of an individual acting as a principal or agent immediately terminates the agency—even if the other party is unaware of the death. Once the time of death is established, there should not be any controversy about an agency ceasing to exist. The following case explains the existence of authority to act when a principal dies.

20. Insanity

Like death, *insanity* of either the principal or agent terminates their relationship. However, unlike death, insanity of a party does not always provide a distinctive time of termination. For example, if

CASE

In Re Estate of Eugene T. Capuzzi, M.D., Deceased, Michael Capuzzi and Eugene T. Capuzzi, Jr. v. Christina Fisher

SUPREME COURT OF MICHIGAN

684 N.W.2d 677 (2004)

CAVANAGH, J.

Decedent, Eugene T. Capuzzi, M.D., owned shares in a limited partnership. Dr. Capuzzi's will divided that interest equally among his three children: Michael, Eugene Jr., and Christina. A few days before his death, Dr. Capuzzi directed Michael to transfer the limited partnership shares to his sons, Michael and Eugene, Jr., petitioners in this case. Michael was acting as Dr. Capuzzi's agent pursuant to a durable power of attorney agreement. The agreement gave Michael "full power and authority to do and perform every act and thing whatsoever requisite and necessary to be done." The transfer would eliminate Christina's interest in the limited partnership shares; Christina is the respondent in this case.

Michael contacted the limited partnership on August 10, 1998; and again on August 11, 1998, and he directed that the shares be transferred pursuant to the power of attorney and Dr. Capuzzi's wishes. Dr. Capuzzi died on August 14, 1998. On August 19, 1998, the limited partnership sent Michael a letter stating that Dr. Capuzzi's death had revoked the power of attorney and, therefore, the transfer could not be completed. During probate proceedings, petitioners objected to the shares passing under the will. The probate court granted summary disposition for petitioners. The Court of Appeals reversed and remanded, holding that the transfer of the shares could not be completed because Dr. Capuzzi's death immediately revoked the power of attorney.

It is a longstanding legal principle that a duly authorized agent has the power to act and bind the principal to the same extent as if the principal acted. A power of attorney provides the agent with all the rights and responsibilities of the principal as outlined in the agreement. In effect, the agent stands in the shoes of the principal.

It is also well-settled that the death of the principal revokes the authority of the agent, unless the agency is coupled with an interest. Any act done by the agent after the principal dies cannot affect the estate. This is true even if an agent performed some of the acts necessary in a single transaction but not all of them. If an agent is in the midst of a transaction when the principal dies, the transaction cannot continue, regardless of the principal's previously stated wishes.

However, when an agent has completed all necessary actions and all that is left is for a third party to act to complete the transaction, we hold that the principal's death has no effect on the validity of the transaction and does not relieve the requirement on the third party to act. This is because the agent's actions were complete at the time of the principal's death.

When all necessary actions have been completed, just as the third party would be required to follow the directive of the principal, the third party is also required to follow the directive of the agent. Although the agent's authority to act terminates when the principal dies, actions completed before the termination no longer require the agent to exercise authority. Therefore, the principal's death does not revoke already completed actions by the agent.

In this case, in accord with Dr. Capuzzi's wishes and acting as Dr. Capuzzi's agent pursuant to a durable power of attorney, Michael contacted the third party and directed that the shares be transferred. Just as Dr. Capuzzi had the authority to compel the third party to transfer the shares, Michael, as Dr. Capuzzi's agent, possessed the same authority. Once he ordered the third party to transfer the shares, this concluded the agent's actions that were necessary to complete the transaction. All that remained was for the third party to act. Again, in this case, the agent did all that was required to transfer the shares. The failure to transfer the shares was solely the result of the third party's delay and had nothing to do with the third party's internal procedures or concerns that the agent did not have the proper authority.

Notably, the agent acted on behalf of the principal before the agent's authority was revoked by the principal's death; and, thus, there was nothing precluding the third party from relying on the agent's authority. Because there was nothing prohibiting the agent from ordering the transfer when he did, that is, while the principal was still alive, there was nothing prohibiting the third party from acting pursuant to the validly given order. The third party's authority to transfer the shares does not depend on the agent's authority to act on behalf of the principal at the time of the transfer of the shares; rather, it depends on the agent's authority to act at the time the agent ordered the shares to be transferred. Therefore, because the agent properly exercised his authority while the principal was still alive, the third party was not excused from acting on the agent's authority.

Accordingly, we reverse the decision of the Court of Appeals and affirm the decision of the trial court.

■ *Reversed.*

CASE CONCEPTS REVIEW

1. When did the agent's authority cease to exist?
2. Would the alternative, requiring that the death of the principal end the authority of the agent if the third party has not completed the transfer of limited partnership interests, be a better rule? Why?

the principal has not been adjudged insane publicly, courts often hold that an agent's contract with a third party is binding on the principal unless that third party was aware of the principal's mental illness. This ruling occurs especially when the contract is beneficial to the insane principal's estate.

21. Bankruptcy

The timing of the termination of an agency due to *bankruptcy* is not always clear. Bankruptcy has the effect of termination only when it affects the subject matter of the agency. Assume that a business organization files for reorganization under the bankruptcy laws. Since the court's order of relief will allow this organization to continue its business activity, its agency relationships will not be terminated. However, if the debtor's petition sought Chapter 7 liquidation, the organization's bankruptcy would terminate all its agencies. This result occurs because the organization will cease to exist as a viable principal. When a bankruptcy case will act to terminate an agency, its impact happens at the time the court grants an order of relief. At that time, a trustee typically is appointed to hold the debtor's assets. This substitution of the trustee for the debtor terminates that debtor's agency relationships. (See Chapter 39 for a thorough discussion of bankruptcy.)

22. Destruction or Illegality of Subject Matter

Events other than bankruptcy may destroy the agency's subject matter. For example, if the purpose of the agency relationship becomes illegal or impossible to perform, termination occurs automatically. Whereas it may be unlikely for the purpose of most business relationships to become illegal, the purpose may become impossible to perform whenever the agency's subject matter is destroyed. Suppose that an owner of real estate hires a real estate agent to find a ready, willing, and able buyer for his four-bedroom, two-bathroom house. If that house is destroyed by fire or wind or other causes, the agent's appointment would be terminated since the house could not now be sold in its former condition.

TERMINATION BY PARTIES' ACTIONS

23. Mutual Agreement

Termination of an agency may occur due to the terms of the principal-agent agreement. For example, an agency may be created to continue for a definite period of time. If so, it ceases, by virtue of the terms of the agreement, at the expiration of the stipulated period. If the parties consent to the continuation of the relationship beyond the period, the courts imply the formation of a new contract of employment. The new agreement contains the same terms as the old one and continues for a like period of time, except that no implied contract can run longer that one year because of the statute of frauds.

Another example is an agency created to accomplish a certain purpose, which ends automatically with the accomplishment of the purpose. Furthermore, when it is possible for one of several agents to perform the task, such as selling certain real estate, it is held that performance by the first party terminates the authority of the other agents without notice of termination being required.

An agency may always be terminated by the mutual agreement of the principal and agent. Even if their original agreement does not provide for a time period of duration, the parties may agree to cancel their relationship. Since the agency is, in essence, based on a consensual agreement, the principal and agent can agree to end their association.

24. Unilateral Action

In addition to the principal and agent's mutually agreeing to end their relationship, the law generally allows either one of these parties to act independently in terminating an agency unilaterally.

As a general rule, either party to an agency agreement has full *power* to terminate the agreement whenever desired, even though he or she possesses no *right* to do so. For example, if the Paulson Company agreed to employ Alicia for one year, an agency for a definite stated period has been created. That is, these parties have agreed to be principal and agent, respectively, for a one-year period. Despite this agreement, the courts are hesitant to force either an employer or employee to remain in an unhappy situation. Therefore, these parties generally do have the power to terminate this employment contract. A premature breach of the agreement is considered to be a wrongful termination, and the breaching party becomes liable for damages suffered by the other party. Of course, if an agent is discharged for cause, such as for failing to follow instructions, he or she may not recover damages from the employer.

CHAPTER SUMMARY

IN GENERAL

Types of Principals

1. A *disclosed principal* is one whose existence and identity are known by third parties.
2. A partially disclosed principal is one whose existence is known but whose identity is unknown by third parties.
3. An *undisclosed principal* is one whose identity and existence are unknown by third parties.

Types of Agents

1. A *broker* has limited authority to find a customer so that a sale of property may be completed.
2. A *factor* has possession and control of another person's property and is authorized to sell that property.
3. A *general agent* has broad authority to conduct a series of transactions with continuity of service.
4. A *special agent* has narrower authority and conducts a single transaction or lacks continuity of service.
5. An *independent contractor* retains control over the details of how work is to be accomplished. The person hiring an independent contractor contracts for a certain end result.

Capacity of Parties

1. In general, a minor may act as a principal. Actions by an adult agent on behalf of a minor principal generally are voidable by the minor.
2. In general, a minor may act as an agent. Actions by a minor agent on behalf of an adult principal generally are binding on the principal.

Formal Requirements

1. Usually, no particular requirements need to be followed to create an agency.
2. Agency may be expressed or implied. Expressed relationships may be created orally or in writing.
3. The appointment of an agent must be in writing when the agent is to negotiate a contract required to be in writing under the statute of frauds.
4. A power of attorney is the written document used to formally appoint an agent.
5. A power of attorney may be general or special in nature.

DUTIES OF AGENTS

Duty of Loyalty

1. This duty is the foundation of every agency relationship.

2. This duty is breached if the agent takes for himself or herself an opportunity intended to benefit the principal.
3. This duty is breached if the agent secretly contracts with the principal.
4. This duty is breached if the agent attempts to represent two principals in the same transaction. This is known as the dual agency situation.

Duty to Protect Confidential Information

1. The agent must protect the principal's trade secrets and not use them for personal profit.
2. Trade secrets might include plans, processes, tools, compounds, customer lists, and other information used in business operations.
3. Principals often have agents sign agreements not to compete to reinforce this duty.

Duty to Obey Instructions

1. An agent must follow all reasonable instructions given by the principal.
2. An agent must not exceed the authority granted by the principal.
3. If an emergency prevents the agent from obeying the instructions given, that agent must seek additional directions. If the principal is not available, the agent must use his or her best judgment.

Duty to Inform

1. Agents have the duty to give their principals all the information that materially affects the principals' interest.

Duty Not to Be Negligent

1. A principal (master) may be liable for the personal injuries caused by agents (servants) within the scope of their employment.
2. Because agents (servants) can create this liability by negligence, these parties have the legal duty to refrain from negligent acts.

Duty to Account

1. An agent always must account to the principal for any money the agent has received from or for the principal.
2. In general, an agent's duty to account is owed only to the principal, not to third parties.
3. However, an agent must account to third parties (a) if too much money is collected innocently and the agent still has the money, (b) if too much money is collected on purpose regardless of whether the agent has the money, and (c) if too much money is collected on behalf of an undisclosed principal.

DUTIES OF PRINCIPALS

Duty to Compensate: In General

1. Compensation of agents must be reasonable if an amount is not stated in an agreement.
2. A percentage of profits is calculated using generally accepted accounting principles.
3. Real estate agents are compensated in accordance with the type of listing agreement signed.

Duty to Compensate: Sales Representative

1. Unless their agreement states otherwise, a sales representative receives a commission only on sales solicited and induced directly.
2. The commission generally is earned as soon as an order is placed.
3. In general, an advance against commission is considered a minimum salary, and the sales representative does not have to return the excess advance.

Duty to Reimburse

1. A principal must reimburse agents who have expended reasonable amounts on behalf of the principal.
2. Expenses such as transportation costs, lodging, and meals are common reimbursable expenses.

Duty to Indemnify

1. To indemnify means to hold a person harmless or free from liability.

2. An agent is entitled to be indemnified when the agent becomes liable to third parties while that agent was following the principal's instructions.

TERMINATION BY OPERATION OF LAW

1. Death of either principal or agent ends the relationship.
2. Insanity of either principal or agent ends the relationship.
3. Bankruptcy of principal or agent may end the relationship if the subject matter of the relationship is affected.
4. Destruction or illegality of the agency's subject matter ends the relationship.

TERMINATION BY PARTIES' ACTIONS

Mutual Agreement

1. Due to their contractual nature, agency relationships can be terminated by the principal's and agent's consent at any time.
2. Such consent may be reflected in an original agreement that is to last for a stated time period.
3. Consent to terminate also occurs if the purpose of the relationship is accomplished or if the parties agree to end the relationship prior to the stated date of termination.

Unilateral Action

1. In general, even if the agency is to last for a stated time, either the principal or agent can end the relationship at any time.
2. The parties have the power of termination even if they lack the legal right.
3. If a party exercises the power of termination while lacking the right, that party is liable for money damages that the premature termination causes.

REVIEW QUESTIONS AND PROBLEMS

1. Match each term in Column A with the appropriate statement in Column B.

A	B
(1) Disclosed principal	(a) Principal whose identity and existence are unknown by third parties
(2) Undisclosed principal	(b) Agent must protect these and not use them for personal profit
(3) Broker	(c) Person who retains control over the details of how work is to be accomplished
(4) Independent contractor	(d) Type of agent who has limited authority to find a customer to complete a sale of property
(5) Power of attorney	(e) A principal whose existence and identity are known by third parties
(6) Duty of loyalty	(f) A duty generally owed only to principals but, in certain situations, also owed to third parties

(7) Trade secrets	(g) Means to hold a person harmless or free from liability—a duty owed by principals to agents
(8) Duty to account	(h) A method of terminating an agency relationship
(9) Indemnification	(i) The foundation of every agency relationship
(10) Consent	(j) The written document used to formally appoint an agent

2. The Pedestrian Shoe Company hired Angela, age sixteen, to work during the summer. Angela was to solicit orders from shoe stores in her hometown. She was to be paid $1 for each pair of shoes ordered. Angela was so successful that she hired Beth, age twenty-five, to help; and she promised to pay Beth 50 cents for each pair of shoes ordered. Can Angela properly be an agent for Pedestrian? Can Beth properly treat as void her appointment as an agent of Angela and submit her orders to Pedestrian for the larger compensation? Explain.
3. Jon Cady hired Telfair Realty to find a buyer for his house. On July 8, an offer to purchase was presented to Jon Cady. This offer was signed "Reta May Johnson by Jared Johnson, son" as purchaser. After studying the offer, Jon Cady accepted it; closing was scheduled for August 25. On that date, the purchaser did not appear. Reta May Johnson notified the seller and the real estate agent that she did not intend to complete the transaction. She requested that her earnest money be refunded since she was not bound to the sales contract. She argued that her son was not authorized in writing to bind her to a real estate sales agreement. Jon Cady and Telfair Realty sued to recover their respective damages resulting from this breach of contract. Was Mrs. Johnson liable for a breach of contract? Explain.
4. New World Fashions provides guidance to persons interested in entering the retail clothing business. Anderson was hired as a sales representative of New World. After several months of working for New World, Anderson decided to start a competing business. However, prior to resigning, Anderson encouraged one of New World's prospective clients to contract with Anderson personally. He then provided to this client services typically furnished by New World. Upon discovery of these facts, New World fired Anderson and sued him to recover lost profits. Must Anderson account to New World for the financial gain he obtained in this transaction? Explain.
5. Amos was sales manager of Plenty, a turkey-packing company. As a member of the management group, Amos was consulted on all phases of the business. He persuaded the company to enter into a contract to purchase 20,000 turkeys but concealed for some time the fact that he was the seller of the turkeys. Plenty Company did not carry out the contract, and Amos brought suit. Was the contract enforceable? Why?
6. Levinsky had an option to purchase a parcel of land and a right of first refusal on an adjacent parcel. Solomon, acting through a real estate agent, offered to purchase both tracts. The real estate agent knew of Levinsky's rights, but he did not tell Solomon. Is Solomon charged with notice of Levinsky's rights? Explain.
7. Peterson's Florist Company hired Alex to deliver floral arrangements. One day while on a delivery, Alex fell asleep and hit a telephone pole. The delivery van was damaged to the extent of $1,600. Can Peterson's Florist Company recover this amount from Alex? Explain.

8. Perry hired the Creditor's Collection Agency to collect overdue accounts. Perry informed the agency that Terry owed $500 for merchandise received. In fact, Terry owed only $400. However, the agency did collect $500 because Terry also was mistaken about the amount owed. Later, Terry discovered the overpayment. Under what circumstances does the agency owe an accounting to Terry? Explain.
9. Patricia listed her house for sale with Rex, a real estate broker, under a listing contract that gave Rex the exclusive right to sell this house for three months. During this time, Patricia sold her house to a friend who did not know Rex. Patricia refused to pay Rex any commission because Rex was not the procuring cause of the ready, willing, and able buyer. Is Rex entitled to a commission? Why?
10. Douglas, a newspaper reporter, sued his former employer, a newspaper publisher. Douglas sought to recover the attorney's fees and court costs incurred in his defense of a libel action. Douglas had been sued as the result of an article written for his employer's newspaper. Douglas had won the libel case. Is the employer obligated to indemnify Douglas for his legal expenses? Explain.

Agency Liability Concepts | 25

CHAPTER OUTLINE

CHAPTER PREVIEW

The law of agency is essentially concerned with issues of *contractual liability* and *tort liability*. Sections 1-8 address issues associated with agency and the law of contracts. Because corporations act only through agents, and because partners in a partnership are agents of the partnership, a substantial portion of all contracts entered into by businesses are entered into by agents on behalf of principals.

One ultimate goal of these transactions is to establish a relationship that binds the principal and third party contractually. In other words, although the agent negotiates with the third party, the principal is substituted for the agent in the contract with the third party. Despite this objective, whenever an agent enters into a contract, issues as to the liability of the various parties may arise. Is the agent personally liable on the contract? Is the principal bound? Can the principal enforce the agreement against the third party? This chapter discusses these issues and others that frequently arise out of contracts entered into by agents on behalf of principals.

Prior to addressing these questions, you must understand the fundamental legal concept of authority. Before an agent can create a binding contract between the principal and third party, that agent must have authority from the principal or the principal must have ratified the agent's unauthorized actions. As we will see, authority may actually be granted to the agent by the principal, or it may be apparent to the third party from the principal's actions or inactions.

Sections 9-18 present issues relating to agency and the law of torts. In the legal sense, the word tort means a noncontractual, noncriminal breach of a duty. Typically, the liability that arises from a tort involves a personal injury or property damage. An automobile accident is but one, albeit a classic, example of a factual situation that creates tort liability.

The agency relationship becomes involved with tort liability whenever an agent's actions produce injury or damage to a third party or that party's property. The terms *master (employer)* and *servant (employee)* are technically more accurate than the terms *principal* and *agent* in describing the parties when tort liability is discussed. Courts, nevertheless, frequently describe the parties as *principal* and *agent*. A principal, however, is liable for torts of only those agents who are subject to the kind of control that establishes the master-servant relationship. For the purpose of tort liability, an *employee* is a person who is employed with or without pay to perform personal services for another and who, in respect to the physical movements in the performance of such service, is subject to the master's right or power of control. A person who renders services for another but retains control over the manner of rendering such services is not an employee but, rather, an independent contractor. Generally, the party employing an independent contractor is not liable for the latter's torts.

In addition to the tort liability that may arise from an agency relationship, this chapter also discusses other aspects of the employer-employee relationship that are related to tort liability. Among the other aspects of employment are issues relating to workers' injuries and diseases and third parties' interference with the master-servant relationship.

The terms master/servant and employer/employee are synonymous with the words master and servant, common in older cases. Today, most commentators and judges use the more modern terms employer and employee.

BUSINESS MANAGEMENT DECISION

You are the president of a soft-drink bottling company. Drivers who own their trucks and who are paid on a commission basis deliver your products. These drivers work their own hours, and they pay their assistants. You consider these drivers to be independent contractors.

What risks are present, and what should you do to minimize them?

BASIC PRINCIPLES OF CONTRACT LIABILITY

1. Actual Authority

Express actual authority

A type of actual authority granted by a principal to an agent by written or spoken words

Implied (incidental) actual authority

A type of actual authority that is granted by a principal to an agent and incidental to express authority or arises from the position held by the agent

A principal may confer actual authority on the agent or may unintentionally, by want of ordinary care, allow the agent to believe himself or herself to possess it. Actual authority includes **express actual authority** and implied authority. The term express authority describes authority explicitly given to the agent through the principal's written or oral instructions. **Implied actual authority** is used to describe authority that is necessarily incidental to the express authority or that arises because of business custom and usage or prior practices of the parties. Implied actual authority is sometimes referred to as *incidental authority;* it is required or reasonably necessary to carry out the purpose for which the agency was created. Implied authority may be established by deductions or inferences from other facts and circumstances in the case, including prior habits or dealings of a similar nature between the parties.

Implied authority based on custom and usage varies from one locality to another and among different kinds of businesses. For example, Perfection Fashions, Inc., appoints Andrea as its agent to sell its casual wears to retail stores. As a part of this relationship, Andrea has express authority to enter into written contracts with the purchasers and to sign Perfection Fashions' name to such agreements. Whether Andrea has implied or incidental authority to consign the merchandise, thereby allowing the purchaser to return items not sold, may depend on local custom and past dealings. Likewise, whether Andrea may sell on credit instead of cash may be determined by similar standards. If it is customary for other agents of fashion companies in this locality to sell on consignment or on credit, Andrea and the purchasers with whom she deals may assume she possesses such authority. Custom, in effect, creates a presumption of authority. Of course, if the agent or third party has actual knowledge that contradicts customs or past dealings, such knowledge limits the existence of implied or incidental authority.

FIGURE 25-1 ■ Actual Authority

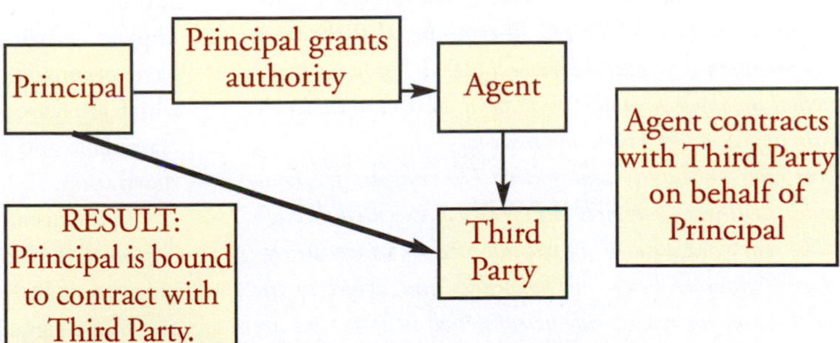

Implied authority cannot be derived from the words or conduct of the agent. A third person dealing with a known agent may not act negligently in regard to the extent of the agent's authority or blindly trust that agent's statements. The third party must use reasonable diligence and prudence in ascertaining whether the agent is acting within the scope of his or her authority. Similarly, if persons who deal with a purported agent desire to hold the principal liable on the contract, they must ascertain not only the fact of the agency but the nature and extent of the agent's authority. Should either the existence of the agency or the nature and extent of the authority be disputed, the burden of proof regarding these matters is on the third party.

All agents, even presidents of corporations, have limitations on their authority. Authority is not readily implied. Possession of goods by one not engaged in the business of selling such goods does not create the implication of authority to sell. Authority to sell does not necessarily include the authority to extend credit—although custom may create such authority. The officers of a corporation must have actual authority to enter into transactions that are not in the ordinary course of the business of the corporation. For this reason, persons purchasing real estate from a corporation usually require a resolution of the board of directors specifically authorizing the sale.

The following case delves into the areas of express and implied actual authority.

CASE

The Houston Exploration Company v. Halliburton Energy Services, Inc.

UNITED STATES COURT OF APPEALS FOR THE FIFTH CIRCUIT

359 F.3d 777 (2004)

This case arises from a 1997 natural gas explosion from a The Houston Exploration Company (THEC) well located in the Gulf of Mexico. THEC sued Halliburton in federal court, asserting that Halliburton's failure properly to perform drill stem testing operations led to the blowout. Halliburton argued that the party's indemnity provision precluded recovery. The case was tried before the district court in March 2000. The court awarded THEC approximately $7,000,000 in damages. In the first appeal, we reversed the district court's decision that Halliburton was grossly negligent in providing drill-testing services to THEC. On remand, the district court again found in favor of THEC, determining that the work order's indemnity provision was invalid because THEC's "company man" did not have actual or apparent authority to bind THEC to its terms. Halliburton again appealed. We reverse and remand.

The relevant facts are largely undisputed. The contract for Halliburton to provide drill-testing services to THEC was executed through a work order. The work order stated, in red ink directly above the signature line, that "Customer hereby acknowledges and agrees to the terms and conditions on the reverse side hereof which include, but are not limited to PAYMENT, RELEASE, INDEMNITY, and LIMITED WARRANTY provision." The reverse side of the work order contained the indemnity provision at issue.

Halliburton presented the work order to James Hileman, THEC's on-site company man and drilling supervisor. Hileman signed the work order in advance of the job, as was the customary practice between the parties. THEC does not dispute that Hileman had authority to sign the work orders to engage Halliburton's services. THEC asserts, instead, that he lacked the specific authority to negotiate or execute the indemnity provision on behalf of THEC.

The district court, applying Louisiana law, agreed with THEC and concluded that Hileman lacked "actual authority" because "no evidence was admitted at trial to demonstrate that THEC and Hileman agreed that Hileman could enter into an indemnity agreement with Halliburton on behalf of THEC."

The question here is one of actual agency by implication. "The essential test to be applied in determining whether an implied actual agency exists is whether the principal has the right to control the conduct of the agent, and whether the agent has the right and authority to represent or bind the principal." More specifically, implied actual agency is created when "the agent is deemed to have permission from the principal to undertake certain acts which are reasonably related to the agent's position and which are reasonable and necessary concomitants of the agent's express authorization."

In the instant case, THEC approved and paid hundreds of similar work orders without objection. Company men—including Hileman, who was THEC's "ultimate authority" for the well in question—signed many of these work orders. In fact, Hileman testified that he continued to sign similar work orders even after the blowout. The repeated approval of work orders manifests the scope of Hileman's authority. Furthermore, Halliburton refused to commence drill-testing unless THEC agreed each time to the terms of the work order. Without Hileman's consent to the indemnity provision, Halliburton would not have performed the service THEC readily admits Hileman was authorized to procure. Thus, Hileman's consent to the indemnity provision was "reasonably related to the agent's position" and was "a reasonable and necessary concomitant of the agent's express authorization."

Accordingly, we conclude that Hileman's express actual authority to enter into the work order agreements necessarily included the implied authority to consent to the release and indemnity provision.

■ *Reversed and remanded*

CASE CONCEPTS REVIEW

1. Why did the court find actual authority?
2. What is the difference between express authority and implied authority?

2. Apparent or Ostensible Authority

Apparent (ostensible) authority

The authority that a principal leads a third party to believe exists when there is no actual authority granted by the principal to the agent

Estoppel

When one is not allowed to deny the truth of the facts that one's acts, representations, or silence intentionally or through negligence induce another to believe certain facts exist, and then the other person acts to his or her detriment on the belief that such facts are true

To be distinguished from implied authority is **apparent or ostensible authority**, terms that are synonymous. These terms describe the authority a principal, intentionally or by want of ordinary care, causes or allow a third person to believe the agent possesses. Liability of the principal for the ostensible agent's acts rests on the doctrine of **estoppel**. The estoppel is created by some conduct of the principal that leads the third party to believe that a person is the principal's agent or that an actual agent possesses the requisite authority. The third party must know about this conduct and must be injured or damaged by his or her reliance on it. The injury or damage may be a change of position, and the facts relied on must be such that a reasonably prudent person would believe that the authority of the agency existed. Thus three usual essential elements of an estoppel—conduct, reliance, and injury—are required to create apparent authority.

The theory of apparent or ostensible authority is that if a principal's words or actions lead others to believe that he or she has conferred authority on an agent, the principal cannot deny his or her words or actions to third persons that have relied on them in good faith. The acts may include words, oral or written, or may be limited to conduct that reasonably interpreted by a third person causes that person to believe that the principal consents to have the act done on his or her behalf by the purported agent. Apparent authority requires more than the mere appearance of authority. The facts must be such that a person exercising ordinary prudence, acting in good faith, and conversant with business practices would be misled.

Apparent authority may be the basis for liability when the purported agent is, in fact, not an agent. It also may be the legal basis for finding that an actual agent possesses authority beyond that actually conferred. In other words, apparent authority may exist in one not an agent or it may expand the authority of an actual agent. However, an agent's apparent authority to do an act for a principal must be based on the *principal's words or conduct* and cannot be based on anything the agent has said or done. An agent cannot unilaterally create his or her own apparent authority.

An agency by estoppel or additional authority by estoppel may arise from the agent's dealings being constantly ratified by the principal, or it may result from a person's acting the part of an agent without any dissent from the purported principal.

Perhaps the most common situation in which apparent authority is found to exist occurs when the actual authority is terminated but notice of this fact is not given to those entitled to receive it. Cancellation of actual authority does not automatically terminate the apparent authority created by prior transactions. The ramification of apparent authority's surviving the termination of an agency relationship requires the principal to give notice of termination to third parties.

FIGURE 25-2 ■ Apparent Authority

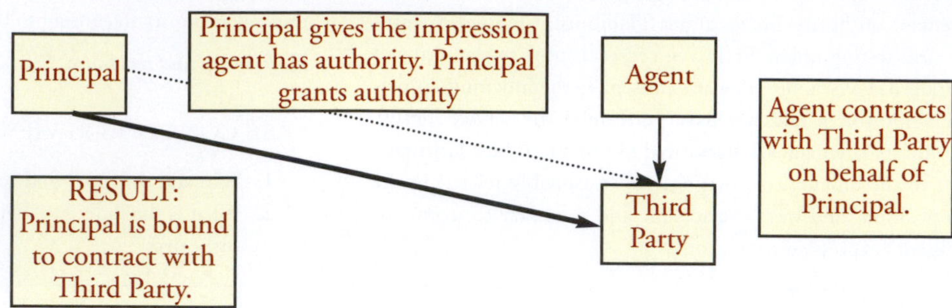

3. Ratification

As previously noted, a purported principal may become bound by ratifying an unauthorized contract. Having knowledge of all material matters, the principal may express or imply adoption or confirmation of a contract entered into on his or her behalf by someone who had no authority to do so. Ratification is implied by conduct of the principal, which is inconsistent with the intent to repudiate the agent's action. It is similar to ratification by an adult of a contract entered while a minor. Ratification relates back to, and is the equivalent of, authority at the commencement of the act or time of the contract. It is the affirmance of a contract already made. It cures the defect of lack of authority and creates the relation of principal and agent.

CAPACITY REQUIRED Various conditions must exist before ratification will be effective in bringing about a contractual relation between the principal and the third party. First, because ratification relates back to the time of the contract, ratification can be effective only when both the principal and the agent were capable of contracting at the time the contract was executed and are still capable at the time of ratification. For this reason, a corporation may not ratify contracts made by its promoters on the corporation's behalf before the corporation was formed. For the corporation to be bound by such agreements, a novation or an assumption of liability by the corporation must occur.

ACTING AS AGENT Second, an agent's act may be ratified only when the agent holds himself or herself out as acting for the one who is alleged to have approved the unauthorized agreement. In other words, the agent must have professed to act as an agent. A person who professes to act for himself or herself and who makes a contract in his or her own name does nothing that can be ratified, even though that person intends at the time to let another have the benefit of the agreement.

FULL KNOWLEDGE Third, as a general rule, ratification does not bind the principal unless he or she acts with full knowledge of all the material facts attending negotiation and execution of the contract. Of course, when there is express ratification and the principal acts without any apparent desire to know or to learn the facts, the principal may not later defend himself or herself on the ground that he or she was unaware of all the material facts. However, when ratification is to be implied from the conduct of the principal, he or she must act with knowledge of all important details.

Ratification

The confirmation of an act or act of another (e.g., a principal may ratify the previous unauthorized act of his or her agent.)

CONDUCT CONSTITUTING RATIFICATION **Ratification** may be either express or implied. Any conduct that definitely indicates an intention on the part of the principal to adopt the transaction will constitute ratification. It may take the form of words of approval to the agent, a promise to perform, or actual performance, such as delivery of the product called for in the agreement. Accepting the benefits of the contract or basing a suit on the validity of an agreement clearly amounts to ratification. Knowing what the agent has done, if the principal makes no objection for an unreasonable time, ratification results by operation of law. Generally, the question of what is an unreasonable time is for the jury to decide.

The issue of whether or not ratification has occurred is also a question to be decided by the jury. Among the facts to be considered by the jury are the relationships of the parties, prior conduct, circumstances pertaining to the transaction, and the action or inaction of the alleged principal upon learning of the contract. Inaction or silence by the principal creates difficulty in determining if ratification has occurred. Failure to speak may mislead the third party, and courts frequently find that a duty to speak exists where silence will mislead. Silence and inaction by the party to be charged as a principal, or failure to dissent and speak up when ordinary human conduct and fair play would normally call for some negative assertion within a reasonable time, tends to justify the inference that the principal acquiesced in the course of events and accepted the contract as his or her own. Acceptance and retention of the fruits of the contract with full knowledge of the material facts of the transaction is probably the most certain evidence of implied ratification. As soon as a principal learns of an unauthorized act by his or her agent, the principal should promptly repudiate it to avoid liability on the theory of ratification.

An unauthorized act may not be ratified in part and rejected in part. The principal cannot accept the benefits of the contract and refuse to assume its obligations. Because of this rule, a principal, by accepting the benefits of an authorized agreement, ratifies the means used in procuring the agreement, unless within a reasonable time after learning the actual facts the principal takes steps to return, as far as possible, the benefits received. Therefore, if an unauthorized agent commits fraud in procuring a contract, acceptance of the benefits ratifies not only the contract but the fraudulent acts as well; and the principal is then liable for the fraud.

CONTRACT LIABILITY OF PRINCIPLES

4. Introduction

With respect to contractual matters, a principal may become liable to its agents and third parties. The answers to when and why such liability is created depend in part on the type of principal involved. As mentioned in the previous chapter, there are three possible choices concerning the types of principals. From the third party's perspective, a principal may be *disclosed, partially disclosed,* or *undisclosed.* When studying the rest of this chapter, keep in mind the distinctions between these categories. For the most part, the law treats the disclosed principals differently from the other types of principals. In general, the law views the liability of partially disclosed and undisclosed principals as being the same. Therefore, in the following sections, any mention of an undisclosed principal's liability includes the liability of a partially disclosed principal, unless the text states otherwise.

5. Disclosed Principal's Liability to Agents

From a contractual perspective, a disclosed principal implicitly agrees to protect its agents from any liability as long as these agents act within the scope of authority granted. In other words, when a disclosed principal is involved, agency principles are applied in such a way that the third party must look to the principal for contractual performance if the agent acted within the authority given. If the third party seeks to hold the agent personally liable, that agent may insist that the disclosed principal hold him or her harmless for liability purposes. A similar result of the principal holding the agent harmless for contractual performance occurs if a disclosed principal ratifies an unauthorized agent's actions.

However, if an agent for a disclosed principal exceeds the authority granted, the principal is not liable to the agent and is not required to protect the agent from liability. In general, the agent who exceeds authority becomes personally liable to the third party and cannot rely on the principal as a substitute for liability or indemnification. The one exception to this general rule is when the disclosed principal ratifies the unauthorized actions of an agent. When ratification does occur, the liability of the parties is the same as if the agent's acts were authorized prior to their happening.

6. Disclosed Principal's Liability to Third Parties

Because of the concept of the principal holding the agent harmless, generally a disclosed principal becomes liable to third parties who negotiate and enter into contracts with authorized agents. With respect to transactions involving disclosed principals, the agent's authority may be either actual or apparent.

Furthermore, disclosed principals become liable to third parties if the unauthorized actions of an agent are ratified. With respect to such ratification, the laws of agency state that the act of ratification must occur before the third party withdraws from the contract. The reason for protecting the third party in this way is the constant legal concern with mutuality of obligations. One party should not be bound to a contract if the other party is not also bound. Therefore, the law recognizes that the third party may withdraw from an unauthorized contract entered into by an agent at any time before the principal ratifies it. If the third party were not allowed to withdraw, the unique situation in which one party is bound and the other is not would exist. Remember, though, that ratification does not require notice to the third party. As soon as the principal indulges in conduct constituting ratification, the third party loses the right to withdraw.

7. Undisclosed Principal's Liability to Agents

The fact that a principal's identity or even existence is hidden from third parties does not change the principal-agent relationship. Therefore, undisclosed principals may become liable for breach of a fiduciary duty owed to agents. Furthermore, undisclosed principals are liable to agents who negotiate and enter into contracts within their actual authority. Since a third party may hold an agent of an undisclosed principal personally liable, the authorized agent may recover the amount of its liability from the undisclosed principal.

The rule of law set forth in the previous sentence limits the undisclosed principal's liability only to contracts entered pursuant to the agent's actual authority. When a principal is undisclosed, neither apparent authority nor ratification can occur since these happenings arise as a result of the principal-third-party relationship. Of course, when the principal's identity or existence is unknown to the third party, there cannot be a principal–third-party relationship. In other words, an undisclosed principal has no liability to an agent who exceeds the actual authority granted by the principal.

8. Undisclosed Principal's Liability to Third Parties

The liability of undisclosed principals to third parties is limited by two important principles. First, undisclosed principals are liable to third parties only when the agent acted within the scope of actual authority. Remember, apparent authority and ratification cannot occur when the principal is undisclosed. However, an undisclosed principal who retains the benefits of a contract is liable to the third party in quasi-contract for the value of such benefits. To allow a principal to keep the benefits would be an unacceptable form of unjust enrichment at the third party's expense.

Second, the contract entered into by an actually authorized agent must be the type that can be assigned to the undisclosed principal. For example, an employment contract requiring the personal services of the agent would not bind the undisclosed principal and the third party. Suppose a group of young engineers form an architectural design firm. Wishing to be hired to design a new fifty-story building that will serve as Exxon's headquarters, these engineers decide to submit a bid. However, fearful that their lack of reputation will harm their chances of being employed, they hire Phillip Johnson, a renowned designer-architect, to present the bid. Mr. Johnson is instructed not to reveal the new firm's identity. In other words, the bid is to be submitted in Phillip Johnson's name alone. If Exxon awarded the design job to Mr. Johnson, it is very unlikely that the new firm and Exxon become contractually bound. This result would occur because of Exxon's belief that it was hiring the unique personal talents of Mr. Johnson. That is, the contract between the agent (Phillip Johnson) and the third party (Exxon) is not assignable to the undisclosed principal (young engineering firm) without the third party's consent. The vast majority of contracts negotiated by agents for undisclosed principals will not involve those agents' personal services. Thus most of these contracts will be freely assignable.

TORT LIABILITY PRINCIPLES

9. Introduction

The fundamental principles of tort liability in the law of agency, which are discussed in this chapter, can be summarized as follows:

1. Agents, employees, and independent contractors are personally liable for their own torts.
2. A employer is liable under a doctrine known as *respondeat superior* for the torts of an employee if the employee is acting within the scope of his or her employment.
3. A principal, proprietor, employer, or contractee (each of these terms is sometimes used) is not, as a general rule, liable for the torts of an independent contractor.

These three principles provide the focus for this chapter. Item 1 is discussed in the next section. Item 2 is the subject matter of Sections 11 through 15. The ramifications of principle 3 are examined in Sections 16 through 18.

Most contracts negotiated by agents on the behalf of undisclosed principals are freely assignable

10. Tort Liability of Agents, Employees, and Independent Contractors

Every person who commits a tort is personally liable to the individual whose body or property is injured or damaged by the wrongful act. An agent or officer of a corporation who commits or participates in the commission of a tort, whether or not acting on behalf of his or her corporation, is liable to third persons injured. One is not relieved of tort liability by establishing that the tortious act was committed under the direction of someone else or in the course of employment of another.

Joint and several liability

When two or more persons have an obligation that binds them individually as well as jointly (This obligation can be enforced either by joint action against all persons or by separate actions against one person or against any combination of these persons.)

The fact that the employer or principal may be held liable does not in any way relieve the employee or agent from liability. The agent's or employee's liability is **joint and several** with the liability of the principal or employer. Of course, the converse is not true. An agent, employee, or independent contractor is not liable for the torts of the principal, master, or employer.

Assume that an employer is liable as the result of a tort committed by an agent or employee. Is the employer upon paying the judgment entitled to recover from the agent or employee? The answer is technically yes because an employee is liable for his or her own misconduct either to others or to his or her employer.

Suits by employers against employees for indemnity are not common, for several reasons. First, the employees's financial condition frequently does not warrant suit. Second, the employer knows of the risk of negligence by employees and covers this risk with insurance. If indemnity were a common occurrence, the ultimate loss would almost always fall on employees or workers. If this situation developed, it would have an adverse effect on employee morale and would make labor-management relations much more difficult, Therefore, few employers seek to enforce the right to collect losses from employees.

Just as an employer may have a right to collect from the employee, under certain situations the employee may maintain a successful action for reimbursement and indemnity against the employer. Such a case would occur when the employee commits a tort by following the employer's instructions—if that employee did not know his or her conduct was tortious.

> EXAMPLE: Matthews, a retail appliance dealer, instructs Stewart to repossess a TV set from Trevor, who had purchased it on an installment contract. Matthews informs Stewart that Trevor is in arrears in his payments. Actually, Matthews had made a bookkeeping error, and Trevor is current in his payments. Despite Trevor's protests, Stewart repossesses the TV set pursuant to Matthew's instructions. Stewart has committed the torts of trespass and wrongful conversion. Matthews must indemnify Stewart and satisfy Trevor's claim if Trevor elects to collect tort damages from Stewart.

TORT LIABILITY OF EMPLOYERS

11. Respondeat Superior

Respondeat superior

The doctrine that places legal liability on an employer for an employee's torts committed within the scope of employment

An employer is liable to third persons for the torts committed by employees *within the scope of their employment* and in prosecution of the employer 's business. This concept, frequently known as **respondeat superior** (let the master respond), imposes vicarious liability on employers as a matter of public policy. Although negligence of the employee is the usual basis of liability, the doctrine of *respondeat superior* is also applicable to intentional torts, such as trespass, assault, libel, and fraud, which are committed by an employee acting within the scope of his or her employment. It is applicable even though the employer did not direct the willful act or assent to it.

This vicarious liability imposed on employers, which makes them pay for wrongs they have not actually committed, is not based on logic and reason but on business and social policy. The theory is that the employer is in a better position to pay for the wrong than is the employee. This concept is sometimes referred to as the "deep pocket" theory. The business policy theory is that injuries to persons and property are hazards of doing business, the cost of which the business should bear rather than have the loss borne by the innocent victim of the tort of society as a whole.

There is universal agreement that an employer is vicariously liable for the actual damages caused by an employee acting within the scope of employment. However, there is disagreement about when the employer is liable for punitive damages that may be awarded to punish the employee's wrong. One theory that has been widely adopted by courts in some states is called the *vicarious liability rule.* This rule states that the employer is always liable for punitive damages awarded against the employee if the wrong committed occurred within the scope of the employee's employment. The logic behind this rule involves the belief that making the employer liable for punitive damages will help deter reckless or intentional torts.

The more modern view of punitive damages that has been adopted by a growing number of states has been called the *complicity rule.* The advantage of this rule is that it allows for a determination of whether an employer actually is blameworthy before making that employer liable for punitive damages. In essence, under this second principle, to collect punitive damages from the employer, an injured third party must be able to prove that (1) the employer had authorized the employee to commit the tort, (2) the employer was reckless in employing or retaining the employee, (3) the employee was employed in a managerial position, or (4) the employer had ratified the employee's tortious conduct.

The application of the doctrine of *respondeat superior* usually involves the issue of whether the employee was *acting within the scope of his or her employment* at the time of the commission of the tort. The law imposes liability on the employer only if the tort occurs while the employee is carrying on the employer's business or if the employer authorizes or ratifies the employee's actions. The employer's liability does not arise when the employee steps aside from his or her employment to commit the tort or when the employee does a wrongful act to accomplish a personal purpose. This is discussed further in Section 13.

It is not possible to state a simple test to determine if the tort is committed within the scope of the employment. Factors to be considered include the nature of the employment, the right of control "not only as to the result to be accomplished but also as to the means to be used," the ownership of the instrumentality (such as an automobile), whether the instrumentality was furnished by the employer, whether the use was authorized, and the time of the occurrence. Most courts inquire into the intent of the employee and the extent of deviation from expected conduct involved in the tort.

As a general rule, the employer cannot avoid liability by showing that the employee was instructed not to do the particular act that is the focus of the complaint. When an employee disobeys the instructions of an employer, the fact of disobedience alone does not insulate the employer from liability. In addition, the employer is not released by evidence that the employee was not doing the work the employer had instructed him or her to do, when the employee had misunderstood the instruction. As long as the employee is attempting to further the employer's business, the employer is liable because the employee is acting within the scope of his or her employment. One of the most difficult situations to resolve is going to or coming from work. Generally, traveling from home to work and vice versa is not considered to be within the employee's employment.

However, the issue of whether an employee is acting within the scope of employment usually is one of fact. Therefore, a jury typically must resolve this issue. Seldom will a judge be able to make a ruling involving the doctrine of *respondeat superior* as a matter of law. The peculiar facts of each case are crucial in determining whether an employer is liable for the employee's acts.

12. Expanding Vicarious Liability

In recent years, the law has been expanding the concept of vicarious liability, even to acts of persons who are not employees. A person engaged in some endeavor gratuitously may still be an employee within the scope of the employer-employee doctrine. The two key elements for determination of whether a gratuitous undertaking is a part of the employer-employee relationship are (1) whether the actor has submitted to the directions and to the control of the one for whom the service is done, and (2) whether the primary purpose of the underlying act was to serve another. If so, the employer is liable for the torts of the unpaid "employee."

Most of the expansion of the application of *respondeat superior* and vicarious liability has been by statute. Liability for automobile accidents has been a major area of expansion. Some states have adopted what is known as the "family car doctrine." Under it, if the car is generally made available for family use, any member of the family is presumed to be an agent of the parent-owner when using the family car for his or her convenience or pleasure. The presumption may be rebutted, however. Other states have gone further and provided that anyone driving a car with the permission of the owner is the owner's agent, and the owner has vicarious liability to persons injured by the driver.

Under the "family car doctrine" any member of the family is considered to be an agent of the parent-owner of the vehicle if the vehicle is used for family use.

13. Exceptions: Frolics and Detours

Although it often is difficult to know with certainty whether an employee is or is not within the scope of employment, the law has recognized that the employer is *not* liable when the employee is on a frolic or when the employee has detoured in a substantial manner from the employer's instructions. A *frolic* exists whenever an employee pursues personal interests while neglecting the employer's business. For example, a route salesman who leaves or detours from his route to accomplish a personal errand is on a frolic. If an accident occurs while this salesman is on the frolic, his employer would not be liable for the third party's injuries. A very hard question to answer is this: When does a frolic or detour end so the employee is again within the scope of employment?

Not every deviation from the strict course of duty is a departure that will relieve an employer of liability for the acts of the employee. The fact that a employee, while performing a duty for the employer, incidentally does something for himself or herself or a third person does not automatically relieve the employer from liability for negligence that causes injury to another. To sever the employee from the scope of employment, the act complained of must be such a divergence from the employee's regular duties that its very character severs the relationship of employer and employee.

Another difficult situation is presented when the employee combines his or her own business with that of the employer. As a general rule, this dual purpose does not relieve the employer of liability. Furthermore, the doctrine of *respondeat superior* has been extended to create the employer's liability for the negligence of strangers while assisting an employee in carrying out the employer's business if the authority to obtain assistance is given or required, as in an emergency.

What follows is one of the more famous cases dealing with the concept of frolic.

CASE

Arthur F. Riley, an Infant, by Eleanor D. Riley, His Guardian Ad Litem v. The Standard Oil Company of New York

COURT OF APPEALS OF NEW YORK

132 N.E. 97 (1921)

JUDGE ANDREWS

Driving directly towards his master's mill; his master's truck loaded with his master's goods for which his master had sent him; his only purpose to deliver them as his master had commanded; with no independent object of his own in mind; Million, a chauffeur employed by the defendant, ran over the plaintiff, negligently, as the jury have said with some evidence to support their finding. Therefore, the complaint should not have been dismissed unless we can say as a matter of law that at the moment of the accident, this chauffeur was not engaged in the defendant's business. We reach no such conclusion.

There could be no debate on this subject were not the essential facts obscured or modified by other circumstances. It appears, however, that the chauffeur had been ordered to go from the mill to the freight yards of the Long Island railroad, about two and one-half miles away, obtain there some barrels of paint and return at once. After the truck was loaded, Million discovered some waste pieces of wood. He threw them on the truck and on leaving the yards turned, not towards the mill, but in the opposite direction. Four blocks away was the house of a sister, and there he left the wood. This errand served no purpose of the defendant nor did the defendant have knowledge of or consent to the act of the chauffeur. Million then started to return to the mill. His course would lead him back past the entrance to the yards. Before he reached this entrance and when he had gone but a short distance from his sister's house, the accident occurred.

An employer is liable for the result of an employee's negligence when the employee is acting in his business and when he still is engaged in the course of his employment. It is not the rule itself but its application that ever causes a doubt. The employee may be acting for himself. He may be engaged in an independent errand of his own. He may abandon his employer's service permanently or temporarily. While still doing his employer's work, he may be also serving a purpose of his own. He may be performing his employer's work but in a forbidden manner. Many other conditions may arise.

No formula can be stated that will enable us to solve the problem whether at a particular moment a particular employee is engaged in his employer's business. We recognize that the precise facts before the court will vary the result. We realize that differences of degree may produce unlike effects. However, whatever the facts, the answer depends upon a consideration of what the employee was doing, and why, when, where and how he was doing it.

An employee may be "going on a frolic of his own, without being at all on his employer's business." He may be so distant from the proper scene of his labor, or he may have left his work for such a length of time, as to evidence a relinquishment of his employment. The circumstances may, also, have a more doubtful meaning. That the employee is where he would not be had he obeyed his employer's orders is, in itself, immaterial except as it may tend to show a permanent or a temporary abandonment of his employer's service. Should there be such a temporary abandonment, the employer again becomes liable for the employee's acts when the latter once more begins to act in his business. Such a reentry is not affected merely by the mental attitude of the employee. There must be that attitude coupled with a reasonable connection in time and space with the work in which he should be engaged. No hard and fast rule on the subject either of space or time can be applied. It cannot be said of an employee in charge of his employer's vehicle who temporarily abandons his line of travel for a purpose of his own that he again becomes an employee only when he reaches a point on his route that he necessarily would have passed had he obeyed his orders. He may choose a different way back. Doubtless this circumstance may be considered in connection with the other facts involved. It is not controlling.

We are not called upon to decide whether the defendant might not have been responsible had this accident occurred while Million was on his way to his sister's house. That would depend on whether this trip is to be regarded as a new and independent journey on his own business, distinct from that of his employer or as a mere deviation from the general route from the mill and back. Considering the short distance and the little time involved, considering that the truck when it left the yards was loaded with the defendant's goods for delivery to its mill and that it was the general purpose of Million to return there, it is quite possible a question of fact would be presented to be decided by a jury. At least, however, with the wood delivered, with the journey back to the mill begun, at some point in the route Million again engaged in the defendant's business. That point, in view of all the circumstances, we think he had reached.

The judgment of the Appellate Division must be modified in so far as it directs the dismissal of the complaint and in so far as it fails to direct a new trial and as so modified affirmed, with costs to abide the event.

■ *Remanded.*

CASE CONCEPTS REVIEW

1. Why did the court find the employee was acting within the course of employment?
2. Is this a fair result for the employer? Discuss.

14. Intentional Torts

Intentional or willful torts are not as likely to occur within the scope of the employee's employment as are those predicated on a negligence theory. If the willful misconduct of the employee has nothing to do with the employer's business and is based entirely on hatred or a feeling of ill will toward the third party, the employer is not liable. Nor is the employer liable if the employee's act has no reasonable connection with his or her employment. However, the injured third party generally does not have to prove that the employer actually instructed the employee to commit the intentional tort. Once again, the key issue for determining the employer's liability is whether the employee was within the scope of employment. As revealed in the following case, sometimes these are not easy issues to resolve.

CASE

Kent Bodin v. Gregory S. Vagshenian, MD, et al.

UNITED STATES COURT OF APPEALS FOR THE FIFTH CIRCUIT

462 F.3d 481 (2006)

EMILIO M. GARZA, CIRCUIT JUDGE

Bodin was a psychiatric patient of Dr. Gregory Vagshenian at an outpatient facility in Austin operated by the Department of Veterans Affairs ("VA"). The plaintiff alleged and presented evidence that during regularly scheduled visits, Dr. Vagshenian performed illegal, inappropriate, and unnecessary physical examinations of his genitalia.

Applying Texas law, the district court found that Dr. Vagshenian was not acting within the scope of his employment when he committed the assaults. The district court reasoned that assaults on third persons fell outside the scope of authority granted to Dr. Vagshenian by the United States, particularly in light of the VA's "zero-tolerance policy" against the abuse of patients. The district court also found that Dr. Vagshenian assaulted Bodin for his own personal gratification, and not, in any way, for the purpose of carrying out the Clinic's treatment of patients. ... Dr. Vagshenian's assault of Bodin was an expression of Dr. Vagshenian's personal animosity. Thus, by assaulting Bodin, Dr. Vagshenian turned away from treating patients, and instead he pursued his own sexual pleasure.

Under Texas law, "an employee's conduct is considered to fall within the scope of his employment if his actions were (1) within the general authority given him, (2) in furtherance of the employer's business, and (3) for the accomplishment of the object for which the employee was employed.'"

Where an "intentional tort is committed in the accomplishment of a duty entrusted to the employee, rather than because of personal animosity, the employer may be liable." A principal is responsible for an unlawful act of his agent where the act is committed by the agent for the purpose of accomplishing the mission entrusted to him by his principal." "If the purpose of serving the employer's business actuates the employee to any appreciable extent his acts are within the scope of his employment." However, "when the employee turns aside, for however short a time, from the prosecution of the employer's work to engage in an affair wholly his own, he ceases to act for the employer, and the responsibility for that which he does in pursuing his own business or pleasure is upon him alone." "It is not ordinarily within the scope of an employee's authority to commit an assault on a third person." The plaintiff bears the burden of proving that the employee acted for reasons other than personal animus.

The district court in this case did not hold as a matter of law that all sexual assaults by a psychiatrist are outside the scope of their employment. Instead, based on the testimony of the plaintiffs' expert witness, the district court found as a matter of fact that Dr. Vagshenian's sexual assaults were 1) "not in furtherance of the VA's business"; 2) "for his own personal gratification, and not, in any way for the purpose of carrying out the Clinic's treatment of patients"; 3) "not for the accomplishment of the object for which he was hired"; and 4) "an expression of Dr. Vagshenian's personal animosity." Under Texas law, a finding that Dr. Vagshenian's conduct was solely motivated by his own personal gratification and not even in part by the Clinic's purpose forecloses the conclusion that he was acting within the scope of his employment.

The plaintiffs have, therefore, not demonstrated that the district court's finding that Dr. Vagshenian's tortious conduct was not motivated to an appreciable extent by the VA's purposes was clearly erroneous or that the court misapplied Texas law.

■ *Affirmed.*

CASE CONCEPTS REVIEW

1. The court used what standard to determine whether the employer was liable?
2. Is the result here fair to the plaintiff? To the employer? Why?

15. Tort Suits: Procedures

As previously noted, the law of torts in most states, unlike the law of contracts, allows joinder of the employer and employee as defendants in one cause of action or permits them to be sued separately. Although the plaintiff is limited to one recovery, the employer and employee are jointly and severally liable. The party may collect from either or both in any proportion until the judgment is paid in full. If the employee is sued first and a judgment is obtained that is not satisfied, the suit is not a bar to a subsequent suit against the employer; however, the amount of the judgment against the employee fixes the maximum limit of potential liability against the employer.

If the employee is found to be free of liability, either in a separate suit or as a codefendant with the employer, then the suit against the employer on the basis of respondeat superior will fail. As indicated in the following case, the employer's liability is predicated on the fault of the employee; if the employee is found to be free of fault, the employer has no liability as a matter of law.

INDEPENDENT CONTRACTORS' TORTS

16. Control over Independent Contractors

An *independent contractor* has power to control the details of the work he or she performs for an employer. Because the performance is within his or her control, an independent contractor is not an employee, and his or her only responsibility is to accomplish the result for which he/she is contracted. For example, Rush contracts to build a boat, according to certain specifications, for Ski-King at a cost of $40,000. It is clear that Rush is an independent contractor; the completed boat is the result. Had Ski-King engaged Rush by the day to assist in building the boat under Ski-King's supervision and direction, the employer-employee relationship would have resulted. Recall that an agent with authority to represent a principal contractually will, at the same time, is either an employee or an independent contractor for the purpose of tort liability.

The hallmark of an employer-employee relationship is that the employer not only controls the result of the work but also has the *right to direct the manner* in which the work will be accomplished. The distinguishing feature of a proprietor–independent-contractor relationship is that the person engaged to do the work has exclusive control of the manner of performing it, being responsible only to produce the desired result. Whether the relationship is employer-employee or proprietor–independent-contractor is usually a question of fact for the jury or for a fact finder if the issue arises in an administrative proceeding.

Without changing the relationship from that of proprietor and independent contractor or the duties arising from that relationship, an employer of an independent contractor may retain a broad general power of supervision of the work to ensure satisfactory performance of the contract. This employer may inspect, stop the work, make suggestions or recommendations about details of the work, or prescribe alterations or deviations.

17. General Rule: No Liability

The distinction between employees and independent contractors is important because, as a general rule, the doctrine of *respondeat superior* and the concept of vicarious liability in tort are not applicable to independent contractors. There is no tort liability, as a general rule, because the theories that justify liability of the employer for the employee's tort are not present when the person engaged to do the work is not an employee.

The application of the doctrine of *respondeat superior* and the tests for determining if the wrongdoer is an independent contractor are quite difficult to apply to professional and technically skilled personnel. It can be argued that a physician's profession requires such high skill and learning that others, especially laypeople, cannot as a matter of law be in control of the physician's activities. That argument, if accepted, would eliminate the liability of hospitals for acts of medical doctors.

Notwithstanding the logic of this argument, courts usually hold that *respondeat superior* may be applied to professional persons and that such persons may be employees. Of course, some professional and technical persons are independent contractors. Hospitals and others who render professional service through skilled employees have the same legal responsibilities as everyone else. If the person who commits a tort is an employee acting on the employer's behalf, the employer is liable, even though no one actually "controls" the employee in the performance of his or her skill. These concepts are applicable to doctors, chemists, airline pilots, lawyers, and other highly trained specialists.

Since it is generally understood that one is not liable for the torts of an independent contractor, contracts frequently provide that the relationship is that of proprietor–independent-contractor, not employer-employee. Such a provision is not binding on third parties, and the contract cannot be used to protect the contracting parties from the actual relationship as shown by the facts.

18. Exceptions: Liability Created

The rule of insulation from liability in the independent contractor situation is subject to several well-recognized exceptions. The most common of these is related to *work inherently dangerous* to the public, such as blasting dynamite. The basis of this exception is that it would be contrary to public policy to allow one engaged in such an activity to avoid liability by selecting an independent contractor rather than an employee to do the work.

Another exception to insulation from vicarious liability applies to *illegal work*. An employer cannot insulate himself or herself from liability by hiring an independent contractor to perform a task that is illegal. Still another common exception involves employees' duties considered to be duties that *cannot be delegated*. In discussing the law of contracts, we noted that personal rights and personal duties could not be transferred without consent of the other party. Many statutes impose strict duties on parties such as common carriers and innkeepers. If an attempt is made to delegate these duties to an independent contractor, it is clear that the employer on whom the duty is imposed has liability for the torts of the independent contractor. In a contract to perform a service or supply a product, liability for negligence cannot be avoided by engaging an independent contractor to perform the duty. Finally, an employer is liable for the torts of an independent contractor if the tort is *ratified*. If an independent contractor wrongfully repossesses an automobile, and the one hiring him or her refuses to return it on demand, the tort has been ratified; and both parties have liability.

Tort liability is also imposed on the employer who is at fault, as when the employer negligently selects the employee. This is true whether the party performing the work is an employee or an independent contractor.

CHAPTER SUMMARY

CONTRACT LIABILITY PRINCIPLES

Actual Authority

1. Actual authority is transmitted directly by the principal to the agent.
2. The principal may express such authority in either written or spoken form.

3. In the alternative, actual authority may be implied from the actions of the principal and agent or from the nature of either parry's position (such as a corporate officer).

Apparent or Ostensible Authority

1. When actual authority is missing, the doctrine of estoppel may create apparent authority.
2. The basis of apparent authority is the indication of an agency relationship by the principal to third parties. This authority is possible only with fully disclosed principals.
3. Apparent authority is most likely to exist when an agent is terminated and the principal fails to give notice to third parties of termination.

Ratification

1. If neither actual nor apparent authority can be found, ratification by the principal may still bind the principal and third party contractually.
2. Ratification of an unauthorized agent's acts can occur only when the principal is fully disclosed.
3. Furthermore, the principal must have full knowledge of all material facts and give a clear indication (expressed or implied) of ratification.

CONTRACT LIABILITY OF PRINCIPLES

Disclosed Principal's Liability to Agents

1. As long as agents act in an authorized manner, principals must indemnify agents.
2. When an agent exceeds the actual authority, the principal is not liable to the agent unless the unauthorized acts were ratified.

Disclosed Principal's Liability to Third Parties

1. If an agent negotiates a contract within either actual or apparent authority, the principal is legally bound to the third party.
2. If an agent exceeds authority, the principal is bound to the third party only if ratification occurs before the third party withdraws.

Undisclosed Principal's Liability to Agents

1. These rules apply to partially disclosed and undisclosed principals alike.
2. A principal is liable to hold an agent harmless if the agent acted within actual authority granted. (There is no apparent authority in these situations.)
3. A principal has no liability to an agent who exceeds actual authority. (Ratification is not possible.)

Undisclosed Principal's Liability to Third Parties

1. These rules apply to partially disclosed and undisclosed principals alike.
2. A principal is contractually bound to third parties if the agent acted within actual authority, and the contract can be assigned to the principal without the third parties' consent.

TORT LIABILITY PRINCIPLES

Introduction

1. Agents, employees, and independent contractors are personally liable for their own torts.
2. A employer is liable under the respondeat superior doctrine for the torts of an employee if the employee is acting within the scope of employment.
3. A principal, proprietor, employer, or contractee (each of these terms is sometimes used) is not, as a general rule, liable for the torts of an independent contractor.
4. Injured employees may have rights against their employer as well as against third parties who cause their injuries.

Tort Liability of Agents, Employees, and Independent Contractors

1. The person who commits a tort is liable for the harm done.
2. A wrongdoer is not relieved of personal liability by establishing that the tort was committed in the course of employment.

3. The employee and employer are jointly and severally liable for the torts of the employee committed within the scope of employment. Thus, the fact that an employer may be liable does not relieve the employee's personal liability.

TORT LIABILITY OF EMPLOYERS

Respondeat Superior

1. Literally, the term means "let the master respond."
2. This legal doctrine places liability, as a matter of public policy, on employers for the torts of their employees.
3. This doctrine allows injured persons to recover from the party with the "deeper pocket."
4. The basic issue is whether the employee was acting within the scope of employment at the time the tort occurred.
5. This issue is a factual one that usually must be decided by a jury.

Expanding Vicarious Liability

1. A person who is not paid may be a gratuitous "employee" and may make the "employer" liable.
2. The family car doctrine is an expansion of vicarious liability beyond the traditional employer-employee relationship.

Exceptions: Frolic and Detours

1. Typically, an employee is outside the scope of employment if the employee is on a frolic of his or her own or detours from assigned tasks.
2. A *frolic* exists when an employee pursues personal interests instead of the employer's business.
3. A *detour* may occur when an employee fails to follow the employer's instructions.

Intentional Torts

1. Intentional or willful torts are less likely to occur within the employee's scope of employment than are torts caused by negligence. Thus employers generally are not liable for harm intentionally caused by employees.

Tort Suits: Procedures

1. Employer and employees generally are jointly and severally liable for the employees' torts. If the employee is not liable, neither is the employer.
2. Although legal actions may be filed against both an employer and an employee, the third party is limited to only one recovery.

INDEPENDENT CONTRACTORS' TORTS

Control over Independent Contractors

1. If one has the power to control the details of the work, one is an independent contractor.
2. In the employer-employee relationship, the employer has the right to direct the manner of performing the work.

General Rule: No Liability

1. The doctrine of *respondeat superior* and the concept of vicarious liability are not applicable to torts caused by independent contractors.
2. Therefore, proprietors generally are not personally liable to third parties who are injured by independent contractors.

Exceptions: Liability Created Proprietors Are Liable under

1. The work of the independent contractor is inherently dangerous.
2. The independent contractor's work is illegal.
3. The work to be done by the independent contractor is non-delegable.
4. The proprietor ratifies the independent contractor's tort.

the Following: 5. The proprietor negligently selected the independent contractor.

REVIEW QUESTIONS AND PROBLEMS

1. Match each term in Column A with the appropriate statement in Column B.

A	B
(1) Actual authority	(a) Binds a principal and third party to a contract if the agent's actions are unauthorized
(2) Apparent authority	(b) Liability individually or together
(3) Ratification	(c) Example of expansion of vicarious liability by statute
(4) Disclosed principal	(d) Doctrine that makes employer liable for torts of employee
(5) Estoppel	(e) Employer not vicariously liable
(6) Joint and several liability	(f) Principal leads third party to believe agent has authority.
(7) *Respondeat superior*	(g) This type of authority may be conveyed by a principal to an agent by written or spoken words or by the parties' conduct.
(8) Family car doctrine	(h) Employee pursues personal interests
(9) Frolic	(i) Implicitly agrees to protect agents from any liability
(10) Illegal work	(j) Theory where one is not allowed to deny the existence of facts

2. Pat, the owner of a grocery store chain, hires Amy to manage one store. Pat tells Amy to stock the store. Pat also tells Amy, (a) "Be sure to buy soup"; (b) "Don't buy soup"; (c) nothing about soup. Amy then proceeds to buy forty cases of soup from Tom. In which situations, if any, is Pat liable to Tom? Explain.
3. Jim applied for health insurance coverage with Great American. An independent insurance agent who was not an agent of Great American took the application. The brochure stated that a policy would be issued after investigation. At the time, Jim was told that the insurance would be effective immediately upon payment of the premium. Later Great American denied coverage and returned Jim's check. Is it liable on the contract? Why or why not?
4. Kapp authorized Schlad to have an engine repaired at ABC Engine Repair Company. Kapp specified that he would not pay more than $3,000 in repair costs. Schlad spent $6,500 on the repairs. Is Kapp or Schlad liable for the additional $3,500? Explain.
5. Oxford operates a janitorial service and cleans commercial buildings. Oxford contracted with Gresham to clean several buildings on a regular basis, not knowing that Gresham was only an agent hired to manage these buildings. Gresham failed to make several payments

owed to Oxford. When Oxford sued Gresham for the money owed, Gresham argued that he was not liable since he was merely an agent. Is Gresham correct? Why or why not?

6. Which party, the employer or the employee, has the ultimate liability for torts that are the employee's rather than the employer's fault? How would your answer change if the tort by a employee was caused by the employer's improper instructions?
7. Mercury Motors Express employed Richard Welch as a truck driver. While driving in an intoxicated condition, Welch drove off the road and hit David Faircloth. As a result of this wreck, Faircloth died. The representative of Faircloth's estate sued Mercury Motors Express under the doctrine of *respondeat superior*. The trial jury awarded the plaintiff $400,000 in compensatory damages and $250,000 in punitive damages. Since it did not dispute the fact that its driver was under the influence of alcohol at the time of the wreck, Mercury paid the compensatory damages. However, Mercury appealed and argued it is not responsible to pay the punitive damages awarded. Is an employer liable in punitive damages for the willful and wanton misconduct of its employee acting within the scope of employment? Explain.
8. Greta employed Steve as a trainee photographer. Late one night after photographing a wedding, Steve was returning the camera equipment to the studio (he was not required to return the equipment that night) when his auto collided with Tim's auto; Tim was killed. Tim's estate sues Greta and Steve. Is Greta liable? Explain.
9. Sam was an employee of the Munchie Company. Sam's job was to drive an ice cream truck and sell ice cream from the truck. One day the truck stalled, and Sam asked Ted and his friends to push the truck. They agreed, and Sam gave each of them a can of whipped cream as compensation for their help. Ted's can exploded and injured his eye. When sued by Ted, Munchie Company argued that Sam was acting outside his scope of employment at the time he gave Ted the can of whipped cream. Is this a valid argument? Explain.
10. Joiner employed an independent contractor to spray pesticide on his crops. During the application process, the spray damaged a nearby fishing lake owned by Boroughs. When Boroughs sued, the trial court held that Joiner was not liable as a matter of law since an independent contractor inflicted the injury. Boroughs contends that Joiner is liable because the work done was inherently or intrinsically dangerous. On appeal, does Borough's argument have merit? Why or why not?

Employment and Labor Law | 26

CHAPTER OUTLINE

CHAPTER PREVIEW

Although the concept is difficult to imagine today, it was not that many years ago that the law hardly touched the employer-employee relationship. As a result, an employer could hire, fire, promote, demote, or alter any conditions of employment without worrying about violating the law. During that time, society believed that the market should control the employment relationship. Therefore, if a business treated applicants for a position or those who worked for the firm poorly, then the employer would have difficulty attracting and keeping good workers. Under such a market-driven system, government intervention was not necessary. Beginning eighty or so years ago, however, Congress, state legislatures, and the courts increasingly recognized that the traditional employment relationship favor too greatly the interests of employers. Therefore, two comparatively new areas of law have blossomed: employment and labor law.

This chapter and the next cover this critical area. Laws affecting the employment arrangement can be organized into four general categories. First, the concept of employment at-will and various exceptions to that doctrine are presented within this chapter. Also known as the law of wrongful discharge, this is an important topic for both employer and employee, as each wants to understand constraints the law asserts on employers who wish to terminate someone's employment. Where an employer violates one of the exceptions to at-will employment, the employer may be subject to legal liability for wrongful discharge. Next, this chapter explores various laws that shape the employment relationship. Statutes that impact an employee's pay and benefits greatly influence the conditions of employment within all types of employer-employee relations. This category also includes the important areas of worker safety and privacy. The third division of this chapter explores basic aspects of labor law, which is that area of jurisprudence devoted to controlling the union-management relationship.

The fourth category of laws impacting the workplace deals with discrimination, harassment, and related matters. This area is so expansive that it deserves a separate chapter (Chapter 27).

BUSINESS MANAGEMENT DECISION

Jakaya works for Wassira Enterprises in middle management as an accounts representative. Wassira Enterprises is an at-will employer. All individuals offered a job at Wassira Enterprises are told that the company embraces the employment at-will doctrine; language to that effect is included in the Wassira Enterprises' human resource management policy document that employees receive within one week of being hired. Jakaya has worked for Wassira Enterprises for six-years, nine-months. During that time, he received two promotions, five raises (for merit), exceeded all sales expectations assigned to him, and had been told by his supervisor, Benjamin, "You keep doing this type of work, and you can work for us as long as you wish." Last week Margareth, the president of Wassira Enterprises, wrote an email to Jakaya stating that Friday would be his last day at work. No explanation was given for the dismissal. Has Wassira Enterprises violated the law? If so, is Jakaya entitled to tort or contract damages?

WRONGFUL DISCHARGE

1. The Theory of Employment at-Will

The employer-employee relationship is based, for most purposes, on a contract. Yet this contract is somewhat unique because for more than one hundred years society has indicated that the theory of employment at-will is the foundation upon which the employment relationship is built. Drawing from the principle of reciprocity, this doctrine provides that the employee can quit at any time for any reason and that the employer can terminate the employee at any time for any reason. The common law doctrine of at-will employment is central to the employment relationship in the United States. However, this is not necessarily the law in other countries, where by either tradition or statute, there is a presumption of continued employment that can be overcome only if there is a reason for terminating the contract of employment. In other words, many countries adopt the doctrine that an individual can be terminated only for good cause.

The severe impact of the employment at-will doctrine on employees has been softened in recent years. For example, in almost all states today, employment at-will is simply a presumption; and this presumption can be overcome if the parties *expressly provide* in the contract that employment is only for a *set duration.* For example, Celine signs a contract to perform services as a singer in a specific concert hall for a period of two years. The contract provision indicating a specific duration of employment removes this arrangement from the presumption of at-will employment. A second method of overcoming the employment at-will presumption also exists. In a situation where the employer and employee expressly agree in a contract that continuing employment is dependent on the *existence or non-existence of certain conditions,* the employer no long has the unfettered discretion to terminate. In the marketing industry, for instance, it is common for a company to establish sales goals for their sales staff and provide in the contract of employment for each member of the staff a provision that states failure to meet the sales goals could result in dismissal.

2. Statutory and Judicial Exceptions to Employment at-Will

Employment at-will

A legal doctrine that allows an employee to quit at any time for any reason, or no reason, and that allows an employer to terminate employment for any reason or no reason

The **employment at-will** doctrine, in its purest form, allows the employer to terminate an employee for any reason, even a reason that is reprehensible and allows an employee to leave their employment at any time for any or no reason. During the past fifty years in particular, Congress and state legislators have created exceptions to at-will employment. In these situations, an exception to the employment at-will presumption is deemed necessary in order to further a particular interest. Roughly, these statutory exceptions can be categorized into two groups.

One set of laws might best be termed those statutes that *prevent discrimination* based on a protected trait or attribute. Under Title VII of the 1964 Civil Rights Act, for instance, an employer cannot terminate a person because of their gender. This statute, among others that erode employer prerogatives to terminate at will, is examined in Chapter 27. The second set of laws that protect an employee from being terminated for a "bad" reason encompasses situations where an employee is terminated for *exercising a legal right.* State workers compensation statutes generally prohibit an employer from firing an employee where that employee files a workers' compensation claim. In addition, federal and state "whistleblowing" statutes often provide protection from termination for an employee who reports alleged wrongdoing by an employer to a government agency.

The process of creating exceptions through the legislative process has, for many, been too slow. Therefore, given that employment at-will is a common law doctrine, many aggrieved employees or former employees during the past thirty years have sought to have the courts create exceptions to the strident impact of employment at-will on the employer/employee relationship.

These efforts have been surprisingly successful—with more than forty states recognizing two *judicially-created exceptions* to the doctrine of employment at will. Each of these judicial exceptions has significantly changed the legal landscape pertaining to the law of wrongful discharge. Exceptions to the employment at-will doctrine are presented in Table 26.1.

3. The Public Policy Exception

Public policy exception

An exception to at-will employment that occurs where an employee is terminated for refusing to perform an action that violates a public policy or for performing an act that advances a public policy

State courts have developed an exception to at-will employment where a termination violates a public policy. For an employer who violates the **public policy exception**, most states provide that an individual who is terminated may sue in *tort*. Therefore, in addition to recovering lost wages and benefits, a successful plaintiff may be entitled to damages for pain and suffering and, because the nature of the termination is generally egregious, punitive damages. As a result, it is very important that employers do not terminate an employee if that action violates an important public policy of the state. The public policy exception occurs where an employee is terminated for refusing to perform an action that violates a public policy or for performing an act that advances a public policy.

The following case exemplifies the narrow application of this tort action.

CASE

Steve Bastible, John Beyan, Douglas Rowan, Donald Payne, Larry Mullens, and Scott Darden v. Weyerhaeuser Company

UNITED STATES COURT OF APPEALS FOR THE TENTH CIRCUIT

437 F.3d 999 (2006)

ANDERSON, CIRCUIT JUDGE

Plaintiffs in these consolidated appeals are either former employees of defendant Weyerhaeuser Company ("Weyco") or former employees of contractors that supplied personnel for Weyco at its paper mill facility in Valliant, Oklahoma. Plaintiffs were terminated after a search by Weyco security personnel uncovered firearms in their vehicles parked in the employee parking lot at the mill, in violation of Weyco policies. They brought three separate actions in state court, which were subsequently removed to the federal district court on diversity grounds, alleging that their termination violated Oklahoma constitutional and statutory authority establishing their right to carry firearms. The district court granted summary judgment to Weyco in each action. We affirm.

Weyco's company policy provides the following: "the possession or carrying of firearms or other weapons, explicitly or concealed, by anyone within the work environment ..., including vehicles on company property, is STRICTLY PROHIBITED." "Work environment" explicitly encompasses "adjacent parking areas." Weyco's "contractor safety requirements" for the mill provide that "possession of firearms ... by any contractor employee subjects the contractor to potential termination of [the] contract and immediate removal from the site." They further state that "no firearms are allowed on the mill site including parking lots."

All Weyco employees found with contraband in their vehicles, including plaintiff Wyatt, were terminated. Weyco management told the supervisors for the various contractors with personnel at the mill, including KBR and Kenny Industrials, "that any contract personnel found with contraband would not be allowed to return to the Valliant Mill." Nebel Aff. KBR ultimately determined to terminate plaintiffs Bastible, Bryan, Rowan, Darden, Payne, and Mullens. Kenny Industrials terminated plaintiff Lewis.

The district court described this issue as "whether a public policy cause of action for wrongful discharge may be maintained by Plaintiffs based upon the right to keep arms espoused by the Oklahoma Constitution." As the district court acknowledged, Oklahoma law recognizes a public policy exception to the otherwise virtually unfettered ability of an employer to terminate an at-will employee. The circumstances which present an actionable tort claim under Oklahoma law is where an employee is discharged for refusing to act in violation of an established and well-defined public policy or for performing an act consistent with a clear and compelling public policy. The Oklahoma Supreme Court has, however, cautioned that this "unique tort" applies "to only a narrow class of cases and must be tightly circumscribed."

While the Oklahoma courts have not addressed the precise question of whether there is a clear and compelling public policy involving the right to bear arms, such that an at-will employee may not be terminated when he exercises that right, we are confident that those courts would not embrace that view. As indicated, both the Oklahoma Constitution and the Oklahoma courts recognize that the right to bear arms is not unlimited, and, indeed, may be regulated. We agree with the district court "given the finding by [the Oklahoma Supreme] Court that the right to keep arms is not unfettered, establishing a wrongful discharge tort for exercising a statutorily sanctioned restriction on the right would be counterintuitive."

■ *Affirmed.*

CASE CONCEPTS REVIEW

1. Does it make sense, generally, that there are exceptions to the constitutional right to bear arms? What exceptions should exist? Should an exception exist that would forbid an employer from have a rule that forbids employees from having a gun on the employer's land?
2. Why did the court refuse to extend the tort-based public policy exception to this situation?

TABLE 26-1 ■ Exceptions to the Employment at-Will Doctrine

Name of Exception	Nature	Who Creates	Type of Damages
Express Contract	Provision in a contract of employment that provides a set duration of employment or specific conditions for continued employment or dismissal	Employer and Employee	Contract
Statutory	Statutory provisions aimed at either preventing discrimination or ensuring the exercise of a legal right	Legislative branch	Statutory
Public Policy	Protects or encourages an important social objective	Judicial branch	Tort (often)
Good Cause	Through the actions of the employer, the presumption of at-will employment is changed to one of termination only if good cause exists	Judicial branch	Contract

Because the nature of this exception generally sounds in tort, as indicated by the decision presented above, courts are very reserved in applying this doctrine. Therefore, just because a termination is perceived as violating an employee's "rights" does not mean that the public policy exception to employment at will applies. As a general rule, the courts look at two factors. First, application of the *public* policy exception requires that the termination violate a public policy. That is, an employee must be asked to commit an illegal act, refuse to do so, and be terminated as a result. Or, the employee is told not to perform a legal act, which they indicate they will perform, and be terminated as a result. In both situations, there must be a benefit to the public associated with the employee's action in countering the wishes of the employer.

If the employee's position does not advance an interest of society in general, the "policy" is not a public one. For example, a bank employee believes that her newly hired boss is under investigation for embezzlement that is alleged to have occurred at the boss's previous place of employment. The employee discloses this belief to the president of the bank but is told to remain quiet. Instead, the employee continues to press her concern with the president. Ultimately, the employee is terminated. In a tort action for violating the public policy exception to at-will employment, the plaintiff's cause of action will fail because the disclosure was aimed at benefiting only her bank, not society. Instead, if the employee saw evidence that the boss was embezzling from her firm and told federal regulators or the police, courts would generally conclude that the interest was a public one. Therefore, a lawsuit against the bank for wrongful discharge may well succeed.

Also, the public policy exception applies only to protect *important* public policies. Usually, requiring that the public policy must be "tethered" to a constitutional provision, statute, or administrative regulation makes this determination. Examples include asking an employee to commit perjury, refusing to allow an employee to serve on a jury, or declining to take an illegal polygraph test. One of the most famous cases dealing with the public policy exception comes from the Arizona Supreme Court. In the case of *Wagenseller v. Scottsdale Memorial Hospital,* a nurse went on a camping trip with colleagues from the hospital that included a rafting trip down the Colorado River. While other employees staged a parody of the song *Moon River* during nightly campfire gatherings that included participants "mooning" their camping compatriots, the plaintiff in the case refused to bare her bottom. As a result, she was shunned on the trip and ostracized when she returned to duty at the hospital. Ultimately, she was terminated. The Arizona high court found that a public policy exception might well exist under these conditions because the plaintiff was asked to violate an indecent exposure criminal statute that the court believed existed to advance an important public policy.

4. The Good Cause Exception

As indicated above, the employer and employee can agree through their words that an employment relationship is not one based on employment at-will. Courts have, however, fashioned an exception to at-will employment where the parties, through their words and actions *after* an employment contract has been entered into, change the nature of the relationship from one that is at-will to one that provides an employee can be dismissed only for good cause. The *implied* **good cause exception** requires that the employer treat the employee in such a manner that the presumption of employment at-will is provided generally or the express language in an employment contract stating an at-will relationship is overcome. If the nature of the relationship has shifted to "good cause," then the employer must provide evidence that there was a good reason for terminating the employment relationship.

Good cause exception
An exception to at-will employment that occurs where the employer acts in such a manner that an implied contract to terminate only for good cause is formed

Courts will look at a variety of factors to decide whether the employer has created an environment where the employee can be terminated only for good cause. The human resource policy of the company is often a starting place for analysis. The policy manual may begin with a statement that all employees are at-will but then provide a detailed progressive discipline policy that indicates the various substantive and procedural steps the company should go through before a worker is terminated. A progressive discipline policy statement is evidence of a good cause relationship. Another major factor is the duration of employment. If someone has worked for a firm continuously for thirty years, then this is strong evidence of the creation of an implied contract to termination only for good cause. If someone has worked only three months, then the presumption of at-will will be much more difficult to overcome. Finally, courts will examine indications that the worker is being treated as if he/she were a "good cause" employee. Promotions, raises, statements from supervisors indicating continued employment, awards for performance, among many other factors, can be construed as evidence by a court that the employer has altered the employment relationship from at-will to good cause.

Note that good cause exception is based on contract law theory (implied contract), so only contract damages provide a viable monetary remedy for a former employee terminated in violation of this exception to at-will employment. Therefore, damages for pain and suffering, or punitive damages are not available. A number of courts are beginning to recognize a strategy that businesses might employ to keep at-will employment in the face of factors that might otherwise indicate an implied contract to terminate only for good cause. In a growing number of jurisdictions, businesses are having employees sign, on a yearly basis, a statement that provides they are an at-will employee; and courts are agreeing with employers that these statements, signed on a periodic basis, trump any other actions or statements of the employer that might indicate a good cause relationship.

5. Ancillary Torts

At-will employment and its recognized exceptions are concerned with why an employee might be or was terminated. Employers also have to be concerned about how they dismiss a worker. This section addresses two of the most popular ancillary torts associated with dismissals. An employer who terminates a single employee for having an affair with a married employee may be well within their rights if the employment relationship is based on at-will principles. However, naming the single employee and stating in a company-wide email the reason the employee was fired would violate the dismissed employee's right of privacy in many states. As a result, the employer might be liable for the tort of *invasion of privacy.*

Tort liability also arises where an employer terminates an individual and intentionally causes emotional distress. Calling a worker up in front of other workers during lunch, firing the employee, berating the employee, and then ceremoniously taking away a company clipboard, name badge, and electronic access card might well create liability for the company even if an at-will employment relationship does not require the employer to provide reasons for the dismissal. Where the tort of *intentional infliction of emotional distress* occurs in a termination scenario similar to that presented, an employer could be liable for punitive damages, along with damages for economic and non-economic (pain and suffering) harm.

Employers (management and supervisors) are advised to consider both why they are terminating and how they go about terminating an employee.

An employer who terminates someone intentionally to cause emotional distress can create a liability tort.

CONDITIONS OF EMPLOYMENT

6. Pay and Benefits

Recognizing the possibility that employers may take advantage of their superior bargaining position, Congress has been quite active in regulating the area of employee pay and benefits. Two of the areas addressed below, the Fair Labor Standards Act and the federal law creating unemployment compensation guidelines for the states to follow, were the product of Congress acting during the 1930s for the purpose of protecting aspects of pay. The statutory framework for granting and controlling benefits came along in the 1970s, 1980s, and 1990s.

Fair Labor Standards Act
A federal law that regulates child labor, minimum wage, and overtime

FAIR LABOR STANDARDS ACT In 1938, Congress passed a sweeping piece of legislation geared at nationalizing key aspects of the law regarding pay in the workplace. The **Fair Labor Standards Act** (FLSA) applies to almost all employers with two or more employees, as long as the company is engaged in interstate commerce. In essence, the FLSA applies in two areas. First, it regulates child labor. The FLSA forbids children under the age of 14 from working and regulates the activities of children from 14 to 18. Next, the act provides for a minimum wage (set by Congress) and a standard workweek (40 hours). Under the FLSA, an employee may work more than forty hours in a week may do so, but that person is entitled to one and one-half times the normal rate of pay for those hours worked in excess.

As the following case presents, at times it can be difficult to determine when work begins.

CASE

William E. Smith, III; Dennis L. Alcon; Eric Alcon; Paul Alcon; Sigfredo Alcon; Tony Alcon; Darrell Frederick; Chester Tiley; Carlos Montano v. Aztec Well Servicing Company

UNITED STATES COURT OF APPEALS FOR THE TENTH CIRCUIT

462 F.3d 1274 (2006)

MCCONNELL, CIRCUIT JUDGE

Aztec Well Servicing Company ("Aztec") is a natural gas and oil well drilling company located in Aztec, New Mexico. The plaintiffs are present or former Aztec employees who worked on drilling rigs in the San Juan basin. They brought suit under the Fair Labor Standards Act ("FLSA"), claiming that their employer should be required to pay them for the time they spend traveling from Aztec to the drill sites—some of them in remote locations hours away.

The 24-hour crews work in eight-hour shifts at the rig, commuting back and forth to the well site each day. The crewmembers typically live in the "tri-city area" of Farmington, Bloomfield, and Aztec, and the well sites can be anywhere from thirty minutes to a three-and-a-half-hour drive from those towns.

Because of their carpooling arrangement, the 24-hour crews would meet before each shift at a time and location designated by the driller. Usually this was at the Sundial convenience store in Aztec. The meeting time depended on which shift the crew was working and how far the well site was from the Sundial. When the 24-hour crew arrived at the Sundial before their shift, they would load their personal safety equipment, including hard hats, gloves, steel toed boots, and a type of coverall clothing they called "greasers," into whichever vehicle that they were driving out to the well site. One of the rig hands would fill a cooler with water, which the crew would use for drinking water at the well site. Some crew members would purchase food and drinks at the Sundial as well. The crew usually drove out in their driller's vehicle, and the driller usually did the driving. Sometimes one of the other rig hands would volunteer to drive, and a few of the crews rotated the driving among the four members. On rare occasion, drillers would be asked by a tool pusher to bring some paper work or equipment out to the well site, but it was always as a favor to the tool pusher rather than as a regular part of their job.

The FLSA typically requires employers to pay their employees for all time spent working on their behalf. Congress has never defined the term "work," however; and the courts are thus left to determine on a case-by-case basis whether an employee's activities are compensable under the FLSA. Early Supreme Court decisions on the issue defined "work" as "physical or mental exertion (whether burdensome or not) controlled or required by the employer and pursued necessarily and primarily for the benefit of the employer and his business." The Supreme Court has held that time spent by employees walking or riding to their workstation from the mine or factory entrance was compensable under the FLSA.

In 1947, one year after the Supreme Court's decision in Anderson, Congress passed the Portal-to-Portal Act which amended the FLSA to shield employers from "judicial interpretations of the FLSA [that] had superseded 'long-established customs, practices, and contracts between employers and employees, thereby creating wholly unexpected liabilities." The Portal-to-Portal Act provides that:

> no employer shall be subject to any liability or punishment under the Fair Labor Standards Act of 1938, as amended ..., on account of the failure of such employer to pay an employee minimum wages, or to pay an employee overtime compensation, for or on account of any of the following activities of such employee ...

(1) walking, riding, or traveling to and from the actual place of performance of the principal activity or activities which such employee is employed to perform, and

(2) activities which are preliminary to or postliminary to said principal activity or activities, which occur either prior to the time on any particular workday at which such employee commences, or subsequent to the time on any particular workday at which he ceases, such principal activity or activities.

Employers are, therefore, not required to compensate employees for time spent commuting between home and their workplace, or for any activities that are "preliminary to or postliminary to" their principal activities at work.

First, the plaintiffs argue that Aztec placed requirements on them during their travel—namely, that it required them to ride together with the other members of their crew—which made the Portal-to-Portal Act inapplicable to their travel-time claim. The plaintiffs were required to travel together for reasons related to the logistics of commuting rather than anything integral and indispensable to their principal activities. Additionally, the plaintiffs acknowledged that they would have traveled together even if their drillers did not require them to do so because it is more convenient than driving alone. Under these circumstances, even mandatory carpooling to and from the well sites is still "riding, or traveling" within the meaning of the Portal-to-Portal Act.

Next, the plaintiffs assert that their workday started at the Sundial because, after they arrived there, they were required to load their personal safety equipment—including their hard hats, gloves, steel-toed boots, and coverall clothing—into their driller's vehicle. It is simply a prerequisite for the job and is purely preliminary in nature." Consequently, the plaintiffs' travel to and from the well sites was not integral and indispensable to their principal activities merely because they were required to carry their personal safety equipment along with them.

Finally, the plaintiffs' third argument for why their travel was "work" within the meaning of the FLSA is that they were allegedly required to transport essential tools and paperwork while traveling to and from the well sites. While the plaintiffs occasionally carried equipment and paperwork on behalf of the tool pusher, this was a relatively rare occurrence; and the crews did it as a favor to the tool pusher rather than as an ordinary part of their job. Because they did not transport essential equipment or papers in the ordinary course of business, the few instances where they did transport such materials does not transform *all* of their travel time into an integral and indispensable part of their principal activities.

We therefore agree with the district court that the Plaintiffs failed to establish that the travel time in and of itself was work for which they must be compensated.

■ *Affirmed.*

CASE CONCEPTS REVIEW

1. Do you think the workers were treated appropriately, given the provisions of law applied?
2. How does an employer determine whether services are "integral and indispensable" an employee's principal activity?

Exempt employees
Selected categories of employees who are not subject to the overtime provisions of the Fair Labor Standards Act

Employee Retirement Income Security Act
Provides protection for pensions and, to a lesser degree, employer-sponsored health benefit plans

Workers in certain occupations are exempt from the wage and hour requirements, including agricultural workers and child actors. Perhaps even more important, selected categories of workers are deemed **exempt employees** who are not subject to these provisions of the FLSA (and, therefore, may not properly claim overtime). Executive, administrative, professional, and certain types of outside sales and computer workers are not subject to the overtime provisions of the FLSA.

PENSIONS AND HEALTH INSURANCE The **Employee Retirement Income Security Act** (ERISA), passed by Congress in 1974, regulates employer pension plans. This federal law establishes set standards for an employer who wishes to establish a pension plan, and it mandates that an employer disclose a great amount of information regarding the funding and related aspects of a pension program.

The provisions of ERISA also apply to employer-created medical, disability, and other types of welfare benefit plans. Here, in contrast to the considerable regulation ERISA provides those employers creating a pension plan, the law allows employers tremendous discretion to fashion benefit plans with little government oversight and to change those plans in almost any manner the employer wishes. It is important to recognize that federal law does not require that an employer provide either a pension or health insurance (among other benefits).

Further, for those workers whose jobs have been eliminated and are no longer eligible for the group health insurance plan offered by their former employer, the *Consolidated Omnibus*

Budget Reconciliation Act of 1985 (better known as COBRA) allows the former employee to continue with the employer's group plan. This can be a considerable advantage to the former employee, as group rates are generally far less than what the employee might find on the health insurance open market. Under COBRA, the right to continued eligibility extends for eighteen months. However, the former employee must pay the entire premium; the employer need not pay any part of the premium.

Family and Medical Leave Act

Act that provides a leave, subject to a variety of constraints, for an employee who cannot work in order to take care of family or medical responsibilities

Family and Medical Leave Act While a small number of states are providing a system that allows employees to be paid if they need to leave work for medical reasons or to care for a family member, the federal **Family and Medical Leave Act** (FMLA) only guarantees that the employee can retain their job. The FMLA, enacted by Congress in 1993, applies to employers with 50 or more employees. Under the law, an employee may receive the leave if they have worked for the employer for at least twelve months. If an employee qualifies, the FMLA entitles the employee to no more than twelve weeks of leave during a twelve-month period for family reasons (birth and care for a newborn, adoption of a child (or foster child)), or for medical reasons (employee's own serious health condition or the serious health condition of a spouse, child or parent). Determining a "serious health condition" has been the subject of considerable litigation, but generally the term refers to a situation that requires continued treatment by a health provider and includes three days of incapacitation.

Unemployment Insurance Every state provides an *unemployment compensation insurance program* that is covered by a tax paid by employers. In order to draw from the program, an employee must have worked for a specified period of time. Also, compensation is not provided if the employee quits without good cause or is fired for egregious behavior. Further, workers must be capable of work and actively looking for a job appropriate to their previous work history, skill set, education, and a host of additional factors. Benefits are a percentage of past earnings and are subject to asset duration.

7. Worker Safety

In general, laws dealing with worker safety are divided between the federal government and state government. The federal government provides a statutory and regulatory framework requiring employers to create a reasonably safe workplace. Individual states may also have laws that create additional mandates for employers, but the focus of this section is on federal law. In addition, when an employee is injured on the job, regardless of whether injury was a result of the employer's failure to provide a non-dangerous environment or caused by the employee's or a co-worker's actions, all states provide workers' compensation benefits. Each of these areas is examined below.

Occupational Safety and Health Act

Provides minimal standards for employee safety and health

Occupational Safety and Health Act In 1970, Congress passed the **Occupational Safety and Health Act** (OSH Act) in order to provide a minimum level of safety and health standards for employees across the country.

The OSH Act creates two obligations of an employer subject to provisions of the law. First, the act establishes a general duty on employers keep their workplaces reasonably safe. Under the *general duty clause* of the OSH Act, an employer must provide a place of employment free from recognized hazards that cause or are likely to cause death or serious physical injury. Also the legislation, under the *specific duty clause,* requires employers to comply with specific occupational safety and health regulations that are promulgated by the *Occupational Safety and Health Administration* (OSHA). These regulations are usually industry specific. For example, the construction industry is subject to regulations from the OSHA that require scaffolding used to

OSHA guidelines are created to help prevent workplace accidents

allow employees to work on roofs, ceilings, and walls to be constructed in a specific manner to prevent the structure's collapse while workers are on the scaffolding.

OSHA is the principal administrative agency in charge of creating regulations and enforcing federal occupational safety and health law (a separate entity, the Occupational Safety and Health Review Commission, performs the adjudicatory function). OSHA becomes aware of potential violations of the OSH Act and OSHA regulations primarily through one of three means. Employees may report violations directly to OSHA or through their employer who then reports to OSHA. Also, OSHA may conduct inspections of work sites and discover violations. Finally, if an injury on the job occurs, OSHA may conduct an investigation to determine if violations of federal laws contributed to the injury.

In most instances, violating the OSH Act or regulations created by OSHA results in the employer being cited and fined. It is possible, however, that criminal sanctions (including time in prison) can occur if a violation is willful.

WORKERS' COMPENSATION Every state has a set of laws that provide financial benefits to employees who are injured while at work or to families who suffer the death of an employee as a result of an illness or injury connected with work. This law, which creates a type of insurance system, is termed **workers' compensation**.

Workers' compensation

A set of laws that provide financial benefits to employees who are injured while at work or to families who suffer the death of an employee as a result of an illness or injury connected with work

It is critical to note that if an injury or death is subject to workers' compensation, this becomes the *exclusive remedy.* That means, for example, that an employee cannot sue an employer for injuries resulting from the employer's negligence that released harmful radiation into the employee's workspace. In essence, workers' compensation is *no-fault insurance.* There are two principal exceptions to the exclusive remedy doctrine. Workers' compensation does not cover *intentional actions* that result in harm, regardless of whether the employee purposefully injures herself (e.g., an employee drops an anvil on her foot in order to go home early) or the employer intentionally hurts the employee (e.g., a supervisor assaults a subordinate). Also, an employee is free to *sue the manufacturer of a defective product* used in the workplace that causes injury.

Certain types of workers are not within workers' compensation coverage. Independent contractors, along with agricultural workers and domestic workers, generally may not seek the benefits associated with workers compensation. For those covered, workers' compensation will provide compensation for the injury or death only if the harm *arose out of employment.* Courts generally require some connection in time and space with the workplace. However, the overriding purpose of the law is to provide benefits, so courts will liberally construe the language of a statute in order to cover a wide variety of work-related situations. For example, a number of jurisdictions will apply workers' compensation law where an employee, playing on the company softball team, injures his ankle while sliding into home base, especially if it is expected that employees will participate in sports teams sponsored by an employer. Benefits typically associated with workers' compensation include lost pay and benefits, medical costs, and expenses associated with rehabilitation.

8. Privacy

Perhaps there is no area of employment and labor law that is creating more need for creative solutions to workplace issues than those situations involving privacy. What is the proper balance between an employee's expectation of privacy and an employer's right to inquire into the actions and status of an employee? The issues associated with privacy are made all-the-more complicated with sophisticated technological developments.

SUBSTANCE AND MEDICAL TESTING A majority of large organizations and a sizeable percentage of smaller businesses require their employees to submit to *alcohol and drug testing* in order to ensure safety and reduce costs. While there is no comprehensive federal statute dealing with substance testing in the private sector workplace, states have been active in an attempt to balance interests of employers and employees. Generally, state statutes allow employers to conduct alcohol and drug testing, but they restrict when the test occurs and how it is conducted. The area is exceedingly complex as many of the tests are not terribly accurate, a test may detect off-site use (with a presence so small in the testing sample that the alcohol or drug presence would not impact performance at work), and the privacy expectations of employees continue to increase.

Medical testing, including the testing for acquired immune deficiency syndrome (AIDS), is generally monitored under provisions of the *Americans with Disabilities Act* (ADA)(examined more fully in Chapter 27). As a broad proposition, the ADA prohibits employers from testing an applicant for a job or an employee for any medical condition.

What about *genetic testing*? The ADA may or may not prohibit employers from conducting genetic testing—unless the employee has been exposed to radiation or a dangerous chemical and the testing is for the purpose of determining the level of exposure. Many states have moved to prohibit employers from conducting genetic tests on applicants or employees. Congress has followed the lead of those states in passing the *Genetic Information Nondiscrimination Act* (GINA) in 2008. GINA is aimed at prohibiting the improper use of genetic information in health insurance and employment. Specifically, GINA declares illegal any type of employment-related discrimination based on genetic information and forbids an employer from requesting, requiring or purchasing genetic information associated with an applicant, employee, or family member of an employee.

ELECTRONIC MONITORING One mid-western company has asked that a computer chip be imbedded in each employee's shoulder so that the employer could track the location of all of its employees during the workday. Is this action ethical? Is it legal? This is but one of a host of types of electronic means that employers are turning to as they seek to monitor their employees. Video recording of employee performance has been a method employed for decades. As we enter the twenty-first century, recording employee telephone conversations, reviewing employee emails, and tracking an employee's use of the Internet while at work are becoming more common forms of monitoring.

The general rule is that employees have *no expectation of privacy while at work.* Federal law, and the law of most states, allows employers to monitor employee the electronic communications of its employees, as long as those communications are not private in nature. However, it is possible for employees to waive the protection for private electronic communiqués where the employee consents in writing. Therefore, it is common practice today for businesses to require their employees to provide such consent. With a waiver in place, employers may monitor both public and private communications of their employees.

Note, however, that state causes of action for invasion of privacy may provide a remedy for an employee where employees have a reasonable expectation of privacy and the need for surveillance is insignificant. Numerous invasions of privacy suits have been successful where employers instituted, without notifying its employees, a video camera system for watching bathroom activities in the workplace in order to catch employees attempting to steal company tools.

LABOR LAW

9. Overview of Labor Law

Labor law impacts the working relationship of thousands upon thousands of employees within the United States. As you read this section, consider the role of government regarding union-management relations. Instead of mandating certain rights, the government has created an environment through a comprehensive set of laws wherein the worker, the union, and management can create a set of "internal laws," unique to that business, for the purpose of controlling the employment relationship and formulating a mechanism for resolving disputes (usually known as the grievance process). While the role of government is quite limited within a collective bargaining environment, labor laws provide the necessary framework that allows unions and management to function.

HISTORY The ever-changing functions of unions and the impact of labor laws in the United States for more than one hundred years provide strong evidence of the dynamic nature of law. With the growth of corporations during the Industrial Revolution (perhaps 1820-1870), the role of the worker also began to change. Instead of working in a small shop, many employees found themselves in a factory setting with hundreds or even thousands of fellow workers. If those workers were at odds with a decision of management, they might come together and function as a unit to influence their employer to take a more favorable position. In time, particularly after the Civil War, formal unions became more common. For example, the Knights of Labor union was formed in 1869, and the American Federation of Labor (AFL) was created in 1886. However, the political environment was often not supportive of union activity. Congress, state legislatures, and courts (federal and state) provided little protection for union activities and often sided with management in limiting the role of unions in society during the 19th century.

The early part of the 20th century, however, brought change to the political winds regarding the viability of the union movement. Congress passed the *Railway Act* in 1926, which provided protection for union activity within the railway industry. The *Norris-LaGuardia Act,* enacted in 1932, curtailed the role of the federal courts to enjoin strikes and picketing. These two acts of Congress laid the stage for the most important federal labor law statute: the **National Labor Relations Act of 1935** (NLRA). The NLRA (also known as the *Wagner Act)* provides employees with three important privileges: (1) the right to organize, (2) the right to collectively bargain, and (3) the right to strike. Also, Congress saw the need to create a federal administrative agency for the purpose of implementing the NLRA, so one provision of the NLRA establishes the *National*

National Labor Relations Act of 1935

The principal federal statute that governs union-management relations

Labor Relations Board (discussed below). In addition, the NLRA prohibits *employers* from entering into *unfair labor practices.* What types of activities are within the concept of an unfair labor practice under the NLRA? Examples include refusing to bargain with representatives of the employees, retaliating against employees who filed charges under the NLRA, discriminating against a member of a union because of their association with the union, interfering with the administration of a union, and discouraging employees from forming or joining a union. The NLRA was a significant boost to unions and union membership for several decades. In fact, during the mid-1950s, more than 30% of the private sector workforce carried a union card.

However, even before those years when the percentage of union membership was at its peak, forces were at work to change the direction of public policy once again. Some of these were legislative in nature. Congress amended the NLRA in 1947 to curtail certain union activities. This amendment, the *Labor Management Relations Act* (better known as the *Taft-Hartley Act*) made it illegal for a union to refuse to bargain with an employer, to engage in certain types of picketing, to discourage employees from joining a union, to encourage an employer to discriminate against an employee who is not a union member, to coordinate a secondary boycott (an action against a third party who deals with the employer but has no direct contact with the union), and to promote featherbedding (requiring an employer to hire more employees than necessary). The *Taft-Hartley Act* also created the Federal Mediation and Conciliation Service to aid unions and employers in settling disputes under a contract. Finally, this law articulated just how "union" a workforce could be under federal law. The legislation clearly prohibits a *closed shop*, where a business requires union membership before an individual is hired. Those arrangements where management requires that a person who is hired must join a union after a certain duration of employment, termed a *union shop,* are legal. Moreover, the *Taft-Harley Act* allows states to pass *right-to-work laws.* Today, almost one-half of all states have adopted this position, which makes it illegal for an employer to mandate union membership as a condition of employment.

Today, union membership is well below 10% of the private sector workforce. While some of the reasons for the decline of union strength are related to unfavorable legislation, a myriad of other factors have also contributed. Among those factors often mentioned include the well-publicized corruption of unions during the 1950s (prompting Congress to pass the *Landrum-Griffin Act i*n 1959 in an attempt to govern internal union activities), the shift away from a manufacturing to a service economy, population growth in the traditionally non-union regions in the western and southern parts of the United States, and the significant growth of a global economy.

COVERAGE The NLRA excludes certain groups of employers and individuals from coverage. For example, because other statutes govern the union relationship in the public sector, the NLRA does not apply to most divisions of the United States government, state government, or local government. What workers are excluded? Central to the idea of collective bargaining is the requirement that the worker be an employee. Therefore, the NLRA does not govern independent contractors. Also, individuals who are working for a member of their family are generally exempt. Perhaps the most important category of workers not subject to provisions of the NLRA is comprised of those employees who are supervisors.

THE NATIONAL LABOR RELATIONS BOARD The National Labor Relations Board (NLRB), comprised of five members appointed by the president, possesses powers normally associated with an administrative agency. The NLRB functions in a rulemaking capacity, generating in the form of regulations interpretations of the NLRA. Courts reviewing a NRLB action generally respect these regulations.

Most often, the public reads about the NLRB as it exercises its enforcement duties. This agency is charged with the responsibility of overseeing union elections. The law prescribes the method by which employees can determine, through an elective process, whether they wish to be represented by a union. The NLRB makes sure that the union and management campaign in a proper fashion. Also, if the union wins the election, then the NLRB will certify the union as the exclusive representative of the workers. In addition, the NLRB will investigate allegations of unfair labor practices by either union or management, whether the activity is alleged to have occurred during the election process or after a union is certified.

The adjudicatory function of the NLRB is entrusted primarily to administrative law judges. Under the statutory scheme of the NLRA, the NLRB's Office of General Counsel brings an action against individuals or entities that have engaged in illegal labor activities. These actions are heard before an administrative law judge. Appeals of a decision by an administrative law judge are decided by the NLRB.

10. Collective Bargaining

CREATING THE RELATIONSHIP As alluded to above, the NLRA provides the mechanism through which employees decide whether they wish to be represented by a union. Under section 9 of the NLRA, establishing a collective bargaining relationship occurs in two stages. First, before a representation election is held, the union must show that workers within a community of interest, or unit, are sufficiently interested in being represented. Having the union solicit employee signatures makes this showing. Under the NLRA and NLRB regulations, employers may limit the solicitation to non-work times (for example, lunch breaks) and non-work locations (an employee cafeteria is a common place).

If the union is able to secure the signatures on authorization cards of at least 30% of the company's employees within a particular unit, then the second stage occurs. Although the employer may choose to recognize the union as the bargaining agent once the signature solicitation process has registered the required percentage of employee interest, management will usually refuse to recognize the union. At this time, the union petitions the NRLB for a *representation election.* The NLRB usually will grant the petition as long as there is no collective bargaining agreement in place with another union or there has not been an election within the previous year.

During the campaign period (generally less than 50 days), both union and management may attempt to secure votes, but the process must be conducted under *laboratory conditions.* That is, a fair election can be held only if the conditions are so ideal, so free from undue influence by either union or management, that the uninhibited desires of those voting are expressed. If the NLRB rules that laboratory conditions were not attained because of undue pressure by either the union or the employer, then the results of the election may be set aside.

The following case examines behavior by the employer that might be construed as undue influence on the election process.

NEGOTIATING THE COLLECTIVE BARGAINING AGREEMENT If the union wins the election, then under section 7 of the NLRA the union becomes the *exclusive bargaining representative for the employees in a particular unit.* Therefore, an individual represented by a union cannot contract with the employer directly, for example, to achieve a higher hourly wage. The collective bargaining process into which a union and management enter creates a contract that determines the terms and conditions of employment. During this process, the employer and the union are under a *duty to bargain in good faith.*

CASE

National Labor Relations Board v. Curwood Inc.

UNITED STATES COURT OF APPEALS FOR THE SEVENTH CIRCUIT

397 F.3d 548 (2004)

WILLIAMS, CIRCUIT JUDGE

An employer who learns its employees are contemplating unionization need not remain silent. It must proceed with caution, however, lest it violate the National Labor Relations Act ("NLRA"). In this case, Curwood, Inc. attempted to counter a union campaign, in part, by promising improvements in pension benefits to employees in the voting unit. It also announced benefits to a small group of employees that were excluded from the unit. The National Labor Relations Board ("Board") ruled that these actions constituted several unfair labor practices; and the Board now seeks to enforce its order.

Curwood manufactures flexible film packaging for snack foods at three facilities in Oshkosh, Wisconsin, collectively known as the South Campus. It also has other plants throughout the United States. Historically, the company had provided two different pension benefit plans for its South Campus employees: the Bemis Hourly Retirement Plan ("BHRP") applied to hourly employees, while salaried employees were covered by the Bemis Retirement Plan ("BRP"). In most circumstances, the BRP provided more generous pension benefits than did the BHRP.

In September 1997, Curwood informed its hourly employees that BHRP benefits would increase by certain amounts on January 1 over the following three years, including January 1, 2000. Employees, though, remained concerned about their pension benefits. In February or March of 2000, the Graphic Communications Union ("Union") began an organizing drive at the South Campus, and pension benefits were an important issue in the campaign.

When Curwood learned in March that employees were distributing and signing union authorization cards, the company became concerned. On April 7, Curwood distributed a letter to its South Campus employees which began, "We are aware that union authorization cards are being circulated at the plants and at organizational meetings." The letter informed employees that the company had undertaken to "review and improve the current pension benefits effective January 2001"; and it anticipated that pension improvements would be announced in the spring or summer of 2000. The letter concluded by urging employees not to sign union authorization cards. Curwood distributed another memorandum to its South Campus employees on May 1. This letter stated the company had compared the BRP and BHRP and concluded that the BRP would be an "improvement" over the BHRP.

A week later, on May 8, the Union filed petitions seeking to represent South Campus production employees. Several weeks later, Curwood notified South Campus employees in a letter dated May 30 that it was "pleased to announce" that the (more generous) BRP would be "implemented effective January 1, 2001." On June 12, Curwood distributed a memorandum announcing that its plan to transfer production and maintenance employees to the BRP had a target implementation date of January 1, 2001. The letter also stated that any changes the company might make to the BHRP while the representation petition was pending might violate the law.

On June 20, the Regional Director issued a decision and direction of election which scheduled an election for July 20-21. Although Curwood had taken the position that maintenance employees should be included in the voting unit, the decision excluded the maintenance employees from the unit. On July 13, one week before the election, Curwood distributed a letter announcing an increase in BHRP benefits to the now-excluded maintenance employees. Production employees found copies of this letter taped to their work areas and on bulletin boards and desks.

The Union lost the election by a vote of 386 to 257. It then filed objections and alleged Curwood had committed unfair labor practices. After a hearing, the administrative law judge ("ALJ") issued a decision finding that Curwood violated the NLRA and that the election should be set aside. The Board affirmed the ALJ's decision that Curwood committed unfair labor practices by announcing and promising benefits to discourage union support on April 7, May 30, and June 12. The Board then brought this action to enforce its order.

Curwood challenges the finding that its letters to production employees on April 7, May 30, and June 12 improperly promised benefits with the intention of interfering with employees' Section 7 rights. Section 7 of the National Labor Relations Act provides employees with certain rights, including the right of self-organization and the right to form labor organizations. Section 8(a)(1) of the Act makes it an unfair labor practice for an employer "to interfere with, restrain, or coerce employees in the exercise" of their Section 7 rights.

The Supreme Court has interpreted Section 8(a)(1) to prohibit "conduct immediately favorable to employees which is undertaken with the express purpose of impinging upon their freedom of choice for or against unionization and is reasonably calculated to have that effect." In holding unlawful an employer's grant of benefits in response to a union campaign, the Court reasoned:

> the danger inherent in well-timed increases in benefits is the suggestion of a fist inside the velvet glove. Employees are not likely to miss the inference that the source of benefits now conferred is also the source from which future benefits must flow and which may dry up if it is not obliged.

We will briefly address why the Board was justified in finding that Curwood's purpose interfered with its employees' Section 7 rights. We first turn to the April 7 letter. In the very first sentence, Curwood said to its employees, "We are aware that union authorization cards are being circulated." It then declared, for the first time, that it anticipated pension improvements would be announced later in the spring or summer, and benefits would continue to be made without union intervention. This letter marked the first time that Curwood had announced a pension improvement since 1997. The text of the letter makes clear that Curwood promised these benefits precisely because the union was organizing, a point with which Curwood does not quarrel.

Curwood sent the May 30 and June 12 letters after the union filed its representation petition on May 8. Curwood reasoned that these letters merely reiterated the lawful (so it argued) pre-petition announcement of benefits contained in the April 7 letter. Because we agree that substantial evidence supports the finding that the promise of benefits contained in the April 7 letter violates Section 8(a)(1), Curwood's argument with respect to the May 30 and June 12 letters fails. Both the May 30 and June 12 letters further elaborate on the new pension benefit plan. The May 30 letter marked the first time Curwood announced to bargaining unit employees that they would be transferred into the BRP effective January 1, 2001, and the June 12 letter explicitly stated the new benefit was "clearly an improvement" to the employees' current retirement benefit. Moreover, Curwood did not argue to us that it had made a decision to implement these benefits before the union activity began or that it would have taken the same action in the absence of union activity for some other reason. We thus find that substantial evidence supports the Board's finding that the April 7, May 30, and June 12 letters constituted unfair labor practices.

■ *Petition for enforcement granted.*

CASE CONCEPTS REVIEW

1. What was indicated in the April 7 letter that was particularly hurtful to the case presented by the employer?
2. What should the employer have done in this case to ensure "laboratory conditions" as required under the National Labor Relations Act?

Negotiating in good faith involves, for example, the generation of information that is shared by both the union and management. Data such as the projected cost of providing medical insurance during the proposed contract period is typical of the type of information that management and union should possess before negotiating on the topic of this important employee benefit. Also, in order for good faith to be present, union and management must make a concerted effort to offer and compromise. Examples of an unfair labor practice pertaining to negotiation might include a situation where one side saying, "This is our only offer, take it or leave it." Another is where one party refuses to meet with the other.

11. Job Actions, Strikes, and Lockouts

If the union and management bargain in good faith but fail to reach a contract, or if management fails to fulfill an obligation under an existing contract, the workers may participate in either a job action or a strike against their employer. A union-sponsored activity by workers designed to put pressure on the employer without resorting to a strike is termed a *job action.* Examples include wearing T-shirts that have the union name, having selected individuals calling in sick, and refusing as a group to work voluntary overtime. The complete stoppage of work, or *strike,* is used in one of two situations. Where the strike is for economic purposes (e.g., higher wages or increased benefits), the NLRA allows the strike but also provides that the employer may hire replacement workers and is under no obligation to rehire those who participated in the strike. In a rare situation, the strike is to protest an unfair labor practice perpetrated by the employer. In this case, federal law allows the protesters to reclaim their jobs in most situations.

If the employer believes the union needs to be pressured, it may *lockout* the workers. Many times a lockout, just like a strike, is an acceptable strategy under the NLRA. For example, if the negotiation process is taking too long from the employer's perspective, it is legal for management to initiate a lockout as a means of encouraging greater activity on the part of the union. A lockout is not permissible and will be termed an unfair labor practice where, for example, the employer refuses to let employees come to work as a means of discouraging employees from joining a union.

CHAPTER SUMMARY

WRONGFUL DISCHARGE

The Theory of Employment at-Will

1. The common law doctrine of employment at-will underlies the employment relationship.
2. The presumption of at-will employment may be overcome by an express contractual provision indicating a specific duration of employment or conditions of employment.

Statutory and Judicial Exceptions to Employment at-Will

1. Federal and state legislation provides exceptions to at-will employment.
2. State courts have fashioned two primary exceptions to employment at-will.

The Public Policy Exception

1. Usually an action in tort, an individual who was terminated for exercising a legal right or not performing an illegal act requested by an employer may sue under the public policy exception.
2. The public policy exception requires that the plaintiff show that the policy furthered was public and important.

The Good Cause Exception

1. The good cause exception to at-will employment applies where the actions of the employer create an implied contract that the employee will not be terminated unless good cause exists.
2. Personnel policy manual provisions, duration of employment, and statements made by the employer to the employee are all factors courts weigh in determining if the employment relationship has shifted from at will to good cause.

Ancillary Torts

1. Employers should exercise care in how they terminate an employee in order to avoid tort liability for invasion of privacy and for intentional infliction of emotional distress.

CONDITIONS OF EMPLOYMENT

Pay and Benefits

1. The *Fair Labor Standards Act* regulates child labor, minimum wage, hours, and overtime.
2. The *Family and Medical Leave Act* provides employees with unpaid leave for a variety of situations associated with caring for a family and for medical purposes.

Worker Safety

1. The *Occupational Safety and Health Act* establishes minimum levels of safety for employees.
2. Workers' compensation insurance is provided by all states to financially assist workers who have been injured or contract an illness associated with employment.

Privacy

1. While employers are generally free to conduct alcohol and drug tests on applicants and employees, the *Americans with Disabilities Act* prohibits most forms of medical tests.
2. As a rule, employees have little expectation of privacy in the workplace. Therefore, employers have considerable discretion to monitor their employees.

LABOR LAW

Overview of Labor Law

1. The *National Labor Relations Act* provides the statutory framework for today's union-management relations.

2. The principal administrative agency charged with implementing provisions of federal law pertaining to union-management relations is the National Labor Relations Board.

Collective Bargaining

1. Often a union is recognized through a representation election.
2. If a union is recognized, it becomes the exclusive bargaining representative for the employees in a particular unit.
3. Both the union and management have the duty to bargain in good faith.

Job Actions, Strikes, and Lockouts

1. A union may institute a job action or strike, and management may conduct a lockout of their employees.

REVIEW QUESTIONS AND PROBLEMS

1. Match each term in Column A with the appropriate statement in Column B.

A	B
(1) National Labor Relations Board	(a) The generally legal process by which an employer keeps track of employees through the use of technology
(2) Family and Medical Leave Act	(b) Method for encouraging a union to bargain
(3) Public policy exception	(c) Tort that can occur when an employer terminates an employee in a manner where secret information is released by the employer
(4) Lockout	(d) Provides financial benefits to employees who are injured on the job
(5) Fair Labor Standards Act	(e) Obligation of both the union and management within the context of negotiating the collective bargaining agreement
(6) Employment at will	(f) An exception to at will employment where the termination violates an important public policy
(7) Duty to bargain in good faith	(g) Federal agency charged with implementing the provisions of federal law
(8) Electronic monitoring	(h) Establishes the rules for hiring minors, minimum wage, and overtime.
(9) Invasion of privacy	(i) Employer can terminate an employee for any reason or no reason.
(10) Workers' compensation	(j) Guarantees a position after a worker has left employment for a medical or family reason

2. Describe the benefits and detriments of employment at will from the standpoint of employers and employees.
3. Maurice is scheduled to go before a grand jury investigating a contractual relationship between Maurice's employer and the local school district. The president of the company instructs Maurice to make untrue statements to the grand jury. Maurice refuses and is terminated. Does the law provide relief to Maurice? If so, under what possible theory and what damages might be available?
4. Mabel has worked as a telephone answerer for ABC Company for forty years. She has received numerous pay raises and outstanding evaluations. Mabel works in a state where there is a presumption of at-will employment. Last week Mable received a notice from the company's human resources department indicating that she was being terminated. Does the law provide relief to Mable? If so, under what possible theory and what damages might be available?
5. Ruby, a five-year employee of Marvel Enterprises, comes to work one day and looks at the company announcements. The second announcement states that Ruby is fired because management has learned that she is living with her boyfriend. Assume Ruby is working in a state that has adopted the presumption of at-will employment, what legal recourse might Ruby have to attain damages connected to the termination?
6. Keith worked for Wal-Mart and took a leave under the *Family and Medical Leave Act.* Upon his return to work, the store refused to return him to his supervisory position and instead placed him in a subordinate position that paid him only two-thirds of the salary he had as a supervisor. Has the *Family and Medical Leave Act* been violated? Why?
7. Watson works as a "cleaner" for a chemical manufacturing corporation. In his capacity, Watson waits for the manufacturing process to cease and he is among the team members that clean pipes and other parts of the production assemblage. He works with dangerous chemicals in very confined spaces. Under the *Occupational Safety and Health Act*, what duties does his employer owe to Watson?
8. Sarah, the president of Lime Green Productions, is concerned that workers in the company's product development department may be using drugs in order to stay awake or to enhance their creative abilities. She wishes to institute random drug testing. Does the law allow random drug testing of employees? If so, under what conditions?
9. Bravo Enterprises has adopted a corporate strategy aimed at minimizing the possibility of their employees becoming unionized. The company recently instituted a rule that employees could not discuss unionizing or distribute union literature while on working time anywhere within the premises of Bravo Enterprises. Is this policy legal? Why?
10. The AFL-CIO wishes to organize a strike to protest the refusal of Metro Rail Company to boost its last wage offer. Does the law allow a strike for that purpose? If Metro Rail hires replacement workers, are they obligated to hire back the union workers at the end of the strike?

Internet Resources

The United States Bureau of Labor Statistics provides a treasure trove of information regarding employment in the United States, including materials dealing with demographics, pay, benefits, and safety. The starting place for reviewing Bureau of Labor Statistics on the web is at the bureau's home page, which is available at: http://www.bls.gov/

The home page for the Occupational Safety and Health Administration, a division of the federal Department of Labor, can be found at: http://www.osha.gov/

The web site for the National Labor Relations Board is available at: http://www.nlrb.gov/

Employment Discrimination | 27

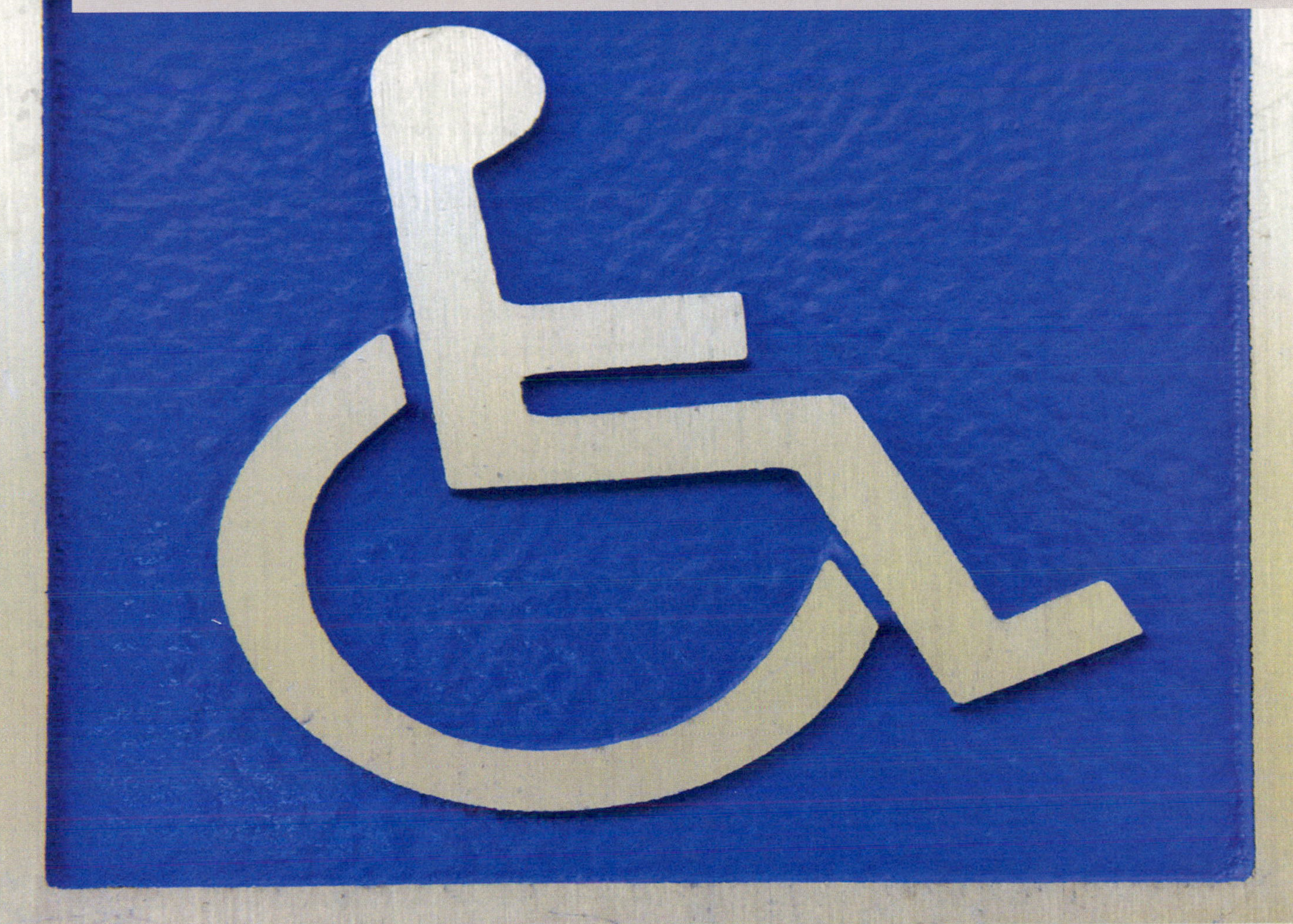

CHAPTER OUTLINE

CHAPTER PREVIEW

In the preceding chapter, at-will employment, non-discriminatory aspects of employment, and labor-management relations were addressed. The fourth leg of the employment law table pertains to the far-reaching subject of discrimination in the workplace. Both discrimination and the related area of harassment have captivated the attention of members of Congress and justices on the United States Supreme Court for decades. Considerable resources from organizations are devoted to creating workplaces free from illegal discrimination and harassment, yet instances of lawsuits based on alleged violations of civil rights relating to the workplace are commonplace.

This chapter addresses employment discrimination, delving into policy and practical aspects, and examining the subject from multiple perspectives (e.g., employee, employer). Title VII and related federal statutes prohibiting discrimination in the workplace are presented in considerable detail. Also, harassment, particularly sexual harassment, is examined with an eye toward addressing competing interests inherent within this subject.

BUSINESS MANAGEMENT DECISION

You are a senior-level executive. Annie, one of your employees, knocks on your door. As she enters, you see she is crying. Annie states she believes Steve, her immediate supervisor, is sexually harassing her. Annie states that Steve just asked her out on a date.

What additional information would you need to clarify whether sexual harassment has occurred?

1. Laws Prohibiting Employment Discrimination

Two significant events in American history have focused the nation's attention on *discrimination:* the abolition of slavery resulting from the Civil War and the civil rights movement of the 1960s. Because discrimination against individuals pursuing economic interests is a central aspect of any public policy agenda aimed at eradicating unsavory types of discrimination, Congress responded to both events with laws that have been used to prohibit discrimination in the workplace. A portion of the *Civil Rights Act of 1866* continues to be a viable legal cause of action for employees who wish to claim discrimination because of race. More prominent today, Title VII of the *Civil Rights Act of 1964* prohibits discrimination based on race, color, religion, national origin, and gender. Of course, a statutory scheme that restricts an employer's ability to discriminate on the basis of these categories necessarily erodes the doctrine of employment at-will discussed in the previous chapter.

Congress also has expanded protection to job applicants and employees in situations where discrimination is based on factors other than those addressed in Title VII, including age (the *Age Discrimination in Employment Act of 1967*), disability (the *Americans with Disabilities Act of 1990*), and genetic information (the *Genetic Information Nondiscrimination Act of 2008*). Some states have gone further. California, for example, prohibits discrimination based on economic factors, family relationships, and sexual preference. Florida provides protection based on marital status. The major federal acts addressing discrimination matters are presented below.

TABLE 27-1 ■ Important Federal Employment Discrimination Laws

Type of Discrimination	Act of Congress
Race	Civil Rights Act of 1866 Title VII of the Civil Rights Act of 1964
Color	Title VII of the Civil Rights Act of 1964
Religion	Title VII of the Civil Rights Act of 1964
National Origin	Title VII of the Civil Rights Act of 1964 Immigration Reform and Control Act of 1986
Sex	Equal Pay Act of 1963, Title VII of the Civil Rights Act of 1964 Pregnancy Discrimination Act of 1978
Age	Age Discrimination in Employment Act of 1967
Disability	Americans with Disabilities Act of 1990
Genes	Genetic Information Nondiscrimination Act of 2008

Moreover, the judiciary has been exceedingly active in the arena of prohibiting employment discrimination *and* providing defenses to employers sued for discrimination. The United States Supreme Court in particular has provided employers and employees with considerable guidance in interpreting anti-discrimination laws relating to the workplace. Numerous lower federal courts and many state courts rule on matters of employment discrimination every year.

Perhaps even more surprising is the general reticence of Congress to legislate in the areas pertaining to discrimination. For example, Congress has never passed a major piece of legislation specifically forbidding *harassment* in the private sector workplace. The federal law that dictates the rights and duties associated with harassment in the workplace, while having its genesis in Title VII, is entirely the product of the Supreme Court and the lower federal courts. This type of case-by-case development of harassment law explains why the area is quite complicated. Also, Congress and most states have yet to address the subject of workplace bullying, a behavior that is expressly prohibited, for example, in certain European countries.

TITLE VII

2. Scope of Title VII

COVERAGE Title VII applies to employers engaged in interstate commerce with fifteen (15) or more employees. Employers subject to the provisions of this statute include sole proprietorships, partnerships, and corporations on the private sector side, and state and local governments on the public sector side. Also, Title VII and most state equal opportunity laws similar to Title VII apply only to individuals who are "employees." Therefore, the provisions of Title VII do not protect a true independent contractor. The anti-discrimination provisions of Title VII do, however, apply to employees of United States firms who are working in another country, as long as compliance with Title VII would not force the organization into violating the law of the host country.

Procedure The *Equal Employment Opportunity Commission* (EEOC) was created by Congress to administer the provisions of Title VII. Specifically, the EEOC is authorized to conduct investigations of discrimination in the workplace and sue to enforce the provisions of Title VII. If, as is often the case, an individual wishes to pursue a claim against a covered employer for violating Title VII, the prospective plaintiff must still use an EEOC procedure before being able to sue. While the procedure is not overly cumbersome, it does slow the process for some in pursuing a legal cause of action. Any individual who believes they have been discriminated against on the basis of Title VII must first file a *charge* with the EEOC or the appropriate state agency. The EEOC or the state agency will then usually investigate the claim and, if there is sufficient proof of discrimination revealed after the investigation, an attempt will be made to reach a voluntary settlement. Because of the volume of claims, the EEOC does not investigate many allegations. In those instances where no investigation occurs or where a voluntary settlement is not achieved, the EEOC or state agency may issue a "right-to-sue" letter that allows the individual to privately sue the employer.

Remedies Title VII provides several types of remedies. Courts are given the discretion of awarding a successful plaintiff *equitable relief.* For example, courts might impose an injunction (e.g., prohibiting an employer from discriminating against ethnic minorities in hiring) or issue an *order* (e.g., requiring female candidates be awarded additional points on an entrance examination).

More prominent in successful Title VII actions is the award of *money damages.* Title VII provides compensation to a current employee for lost salary and benefits for up to two years prior to the filing of the charge, "front pay" equal to what the former employee would have earned if not discharged, and attorney's fees. For the plaintiff who is successful with an intentional (disparate treatment) cause of action, federal law provides the potential for full *compensatory damages* (including damages for emotional pain and suffering) and *punitive damages* (to punish the defendant for acting in an egregious manner). While state law may provide that these damages are unlimited, Title VII limits (or caps) the amount of compensatory and punitive damages a plaintiff may recover against an employer who intentionally discriminates. The limitation is based on the size of the employer. For organizations with 100 or fewer employees, the cap is $50,000. The range then proceeds in a graduated fashion up to employers with more than 500 employees who are subject to a $300,000 limit.

3. Proving Discrimination under Title VII

The central thrust of Title VII is directed at prohibiting an employer from discriminating against an applicant for a job or a current employee (e.g., in the case of promotion, assignment, or termination) "because of" membership in a protected classification. Any legal action brought by the government or by an impacted individual, therefore, must require that a plaintiff prove the reason for the adverse employment action was the product of discrimination.

In the situation where a corporation posts a sign in front of its headquarters, includes a disclosure on its application form, and creates a banner on the corporation's Internet home page with each indicating that the firm will not hire a person from a certain protected class, it is easy for plaintiff to provide evidence of the discriminatory rationale for a decision not to hire. Unfortunately, few of these simplistic cases exist. Instead, the courts have crafted two methods of showing discrimination under Title VII: disparate treatment and disparate impact.

Disparate treatment

A type of discrimination that requires plaintiff to show the presence of intentional discrimination

Intentional Discrimination Courts will find a Title VII violation where an employer intentionally discriminates against an applicant or employee. This type of discrimination is also known as **disparate treatment**. Usually intent is difficult to prove, unless it is of the obvious type illustrated previously. Therefore, the courts have fashioned a scheme that provides guidance in determining whether an adverse action by an employer was based on an individual difference in a person's race,

FIGURE 27-1 ■ Burdens in Proving Intentional Discrimination

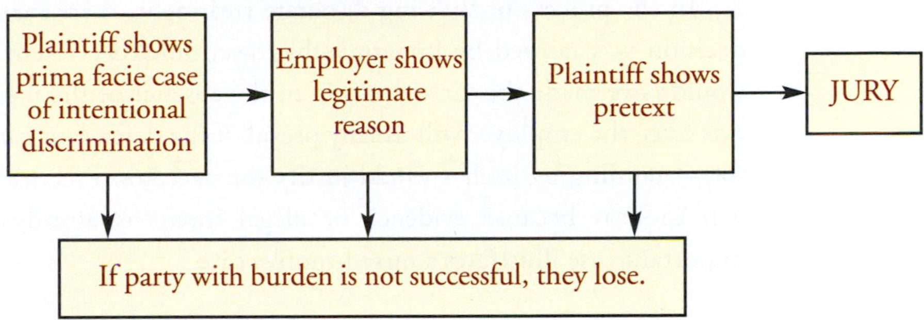

color, religion, national origin, or gender. In disparate treatment cases, the plaintiff first shows a *prima facie* case consisting of four elements: (1) membership in a protected class, (2) adequate qualifications, (3) rejection, and (4) the benefit applied for remains open (or went to another individual).

Meeting these four elements of the prima *facie case* is relatively easy. Assume a woman with many years experience in sales within the software industry applies for a position with a software-manufacturing firm but was denied the job. The applicant has probably met the requirements of the *prima facie* case for intentional discrimination.

The plaintiff does *not* immediately win the case with the showing of a prima facie case. Instead, the burden now shifts to the defendant (employer) to show that the challenged employment action (e.g., refusal to hire) was taken because of a *legitimate, nondiscriminatory reason*. If the defendant cannot offer proof of a legitimate reason, then plaintiff prevails. Usually, an employer is able to show a satisfactory, legal reason for denying plaintiff an employment-related benefit. An employer might provide evidence that the female applicant for the sales position at the software firm lacked the minimum qualifications posted for the job, or another person (even if male) possessed superior qualifications.

With sufficient evidence of a legitimate reason, the burden then shifts back to the plaintiff to show that the employer's offered reason is mere *pretext*. That is, the supposedly legitimate reason is not the true reason, that discriminatory intent motivated the employer to deny the benefit. The female applicant for the position at the software firm would win a case based on

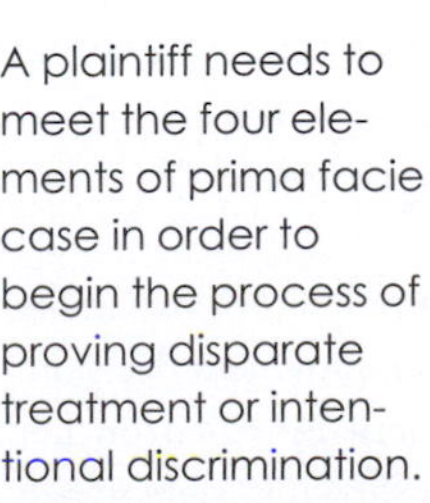
A plaintiff needs to meet the four elements of prima facie case in order to begin the process of proving disparate treatment or intentional discrimination.

disparate treatment if she could show that the president of the company, in an email, directed the human resources department not to hire any more women for sales positions.

In the process of showing disparate treatment, there may be proof that the employer's decision was tainted by impermissible discriminatory intent and proof that the employer would have made the same decision in the absence of the illegal intent. In these *mixed-motive cases,* the employer will usually prevail if the defendant can show that the legitimate reason—standing by itself—would justify the decision. Practically, this can be a difficult burden to bear because evidence of illegal intent is already present. The following very important case illustrates a mixed-motive case.

CASE

Price Waterhouse v. Hopkins

SUPREME COURT OF THE UNITED STATES

490 U.S. 228 (1989)

JUSTICE BRENNAN DELIVERED THE OPINION OF THE COURT

Ann Hopkins was a senior manager in an office of Price Waterhouse when she was proposed for partnership in 1982. She was neither offered nor denied admission to the partnership; instead, her candidacy was held for reconsideration the following year. When the partners in her office later refused to propose her for partnership, she sued Price Waterhouse under Title VII of the Civil Rights Act of 1964, charging that the firm had discriminated against her on the basis of sex in its decisions regarding partnership.

At Price Waterhouse, a nationwide professional accounting partnership, a senior manager becomes a candidate for partnership when the partners in her local office submit her name as a candidate. All of the other partners in the firm are then invited to submit written comments on each candidate—either on a "long" or a "short" form, depending on the partner's degree of exposure to the candidate. Not every partner in the firm submits comments on every candidate. After reviewing the comments and interviewing the partners who submitted them, the firm's Admissions Committee makes a recommendation to the Policy Board. This recommendation will be either the firm accept the candidate for partnership, put her application on "hold," or deny her the promotion outright. The Policy Board then decides whether to submit the candidate's name to the entire partnership for a vote, to "hold" her candidacy, or to reject her. The recommendation of the Admissions Committee and the decision of the Policy Board are not controlled by fixed guidelines: a certain number of positive comments from partners will not guarantee a candidate's admission to the partnership, nor will a specific quantity of negative comments necessarily defeat her application. Price Waterhouse places no limit on the number of persons whom it will admit to the partnership in any given year.

Ann Hopkins had worked at Price Waterhouse's Office of Government Services in Washington, D. C., for five years when the partners in that office proposed her as a candidate for partnership. Of the 662 partners at the firm at that time, 7 were women. Of the 88 persons proposed for partnership that year, only 1—Hopkins—was a woman. Forty-seven of these candidates were admitted to the partnership, 21 were rejected, and 20—including Hopkins—were "held" for reconsideration the following year. Thirteen of the 32 partners who had submitted comments on Hopkins supported her bid for partnership. Three partners recommended that her candidacy be placed on hold, eight stated that they did not have an informed opinion about her, and eight recommended that she be denied partnership.

In a jointly prepared statement supporting her candidacy, the partners in Hopkins' office showcased her successful 2-year effort to secure a $25 million contract with the Department of State, labeling it "an outstanding performance" and one that Hopkins carried out "virtually at the partner level." The partners in Hopkins' office praised her character as well as her accomplishments, describing her in their joint statement as "an outstanding professional" who had a "deft touch," a "strong character, independence and integrity."

On too many occasions, however, Hopkins' aggressiveness apparently spilled over into abrasiveness. Staff members seem to have borne the brunt of Hopkins' brusqueness. Long before her bid for partnership, partners evaluating her work had counseled her to improve her relations with staff members. There were clear signs, though, that some of the partners reacted negatively to Hopkins' personality because she was a woman. One partner described her as "macho"; another suggested that she "overcompensated for being a woman"; a third advised her to take "a course at charm school". Several partners criticized her use of profanity; in response, one partner suggested that those partners objected to her swearing only "because it's a lady using foul language." [I]n order to improve her chances for partnership, Thomas Beyer advised, Hopkins should "walk more femininely, talk more femininely, dress more femininely, wear make-up, have her hair styled, and wear jewelry."

Remarks at work that are based on sex stereotypes do not inevitably prove that gender played a part in a particular employment decision. The plaintiff must show that the employer actually relied on her gender in making its decision. In making this showing, stereotyped remarks can certainly be evidence that gender played a part. In any event, the stereotyping in this case did not simply consist of stray remarks. On the contrary, Hopkins proved that Price Waterhouse invited partners to submit comments; that some of the comments stemmed from sex stereotypes; that an important part of the Policy Board's decision on Hopkins was an assessment of the submitted comments; and that Price Waterhouse in no way disclaimed reliance on the sex-linked evaluations. This is not, as Price Waterhouse suggests, "discrimination in the air"; rather, it is, as Hopkins puts it, "discrimination brought to ground and visited upon" an employee.

As to the employer's proof, in most cases, the employer should be able to present some objective evidence as to its probable decision in the absence of an impermissible motive. An employer may not, in other words, prevail in a mixed-motives case by offering a legitimate and sufficient reason for its decision if that reason did not motivate it at the time of the decision. Finally, an employer may not meet its burden in such a case by merely showing that at the time of the decision it was motivated only in part by a legitimate reason. The very premise of a mixed-motives case is that a legitimate reason was present; and indeed, in this case, Price Waterhouse already has made this showing by convincing Judge Gesell that Hopkins' interpersonal problems were a legitimate concern. The employer instead must show that its legitimate reason, standing alone, would have induced it to make the same decision.

■ *Reversed and remanded.*

CASE CONCEPTS REVIEW

1. Why is this termed a "mixed-motive" case?
2. What remedy is appropriate for a plaintiff in Hopkins' position? Is reinstatement appropriate? Are damages appropriate? If so, when?

Disparate impact

A type of discrimination that occurs where an employer uses an employment practice that, while neutral on its face, has an adverse impact on members of a protected group

UNINTENTIONAL DISCRIMINATION Early in the development of anti-discrimination law under Title VII, the United States Supreme Court endorsed the position that Title VII can be violated by employer conduct that is intentional and by conduct that is unintentional. This later type of discrimination is called **disparate impact** (or adverse impact). While disparate treatment is most common when an individual sues under Title VII, disparate impact is the type of analysis used when the alleged discrimination is oriented more broadly to a group.

The idea behind disparate impact is that an employer uses an *employment practice* that has a disproportionately adverse effect on one of the groups protected under Title VII. A high school graduation requirement for hiring, a passing grade on an aptitude test for promotion, completing a web-based training program for a raise are examples of common employment practices that may have an unintended impact on members of a protected class. Note that these practices are *neutral on their face*; the concern is that *as applied, they discriminate illegally*.

The *prima facie* case for disparate impact requires that the complaining party show statistically the discriminatory effect of a specific employment practice. The EEOC has created the "four-fifths rule," or the "80% rule," as a mechanism that assists in determining whether an employment practice is unlawful. Under this rule, if the selection rate for members in a protected class is less than four-fifths the selection rate for those in the majority, there is evidence of disparate impact. Suppose that fifty minority applicants take an entrance examination and five pass. The passage rate is ten percent. Two hundred members of a majority class take the same examination, with one hundred passing. The resulting fifty percent passage rate is then compared to the ten percent rate. Because the ten percent rate is less than four-fifths (80%) of the fifty percent pass rate, the plaintiff could use this disparity to show a *prima facie* case of disparate impact.

From another perspective, the nature of disparate impact requires comparing the impact of an employment practice (or policy) on various groups. Usually the statistical comparison is between the racial, religious, or gender-based composition of the group that currently holds a position and the racial, religious, or gender-based composition of qualified individuals in the labor pool. If the position requires only the most basic of skills, then all members of the labor pool (usually based on a geographic area) might well be considered. If, however, a particular degree, certification, license, or skill is required, then the relevant labor pool will include that attribute or ability.

With plaintiff having established a *prima facie* case, the employer will lose a disparate impact case unless it presents evidence that the employment practice under scrutiny is *job-related and consistent with business necessity.* Courts increasingly scrutinize employers attempting to indicate a particular employment practice is necessary. If a business sets minimum height or weight requirements that could have a negative impact on female applicants or those from selected racial groups, the employer must show that physical size is a necessary in order to perform duties associated with the job. In those instances where the employer is able to show an employment practice is necessary, the burden shifts to the plaintiff.

At this point in the case, plaintiff will win if the party comes forward with proof that the challenged employment practice is merely *pretext* for discrimination or that there is *another employment practice* equivalent in the information it provides the employer that could be substituted for the offending practice. In the instance of height and weight requirements, plaintiff could offer a lifting test that would not have the discriminatory impact.

FIGURE 27-2 ■ Burdens in Proving Unintentional Discrimination

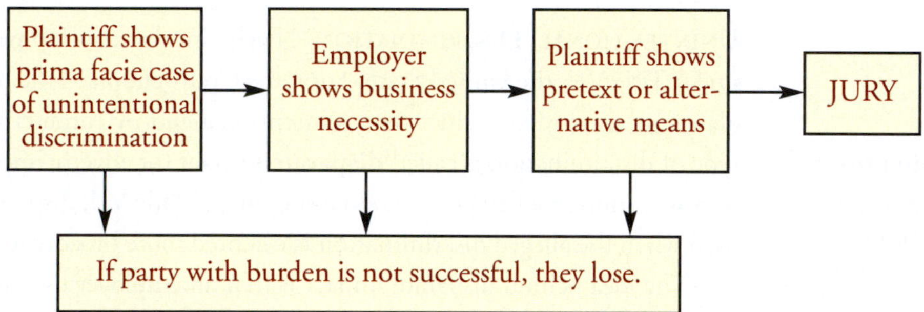

4. Constructive Discharge and Retaliation

CONSTRUCTIVE DISCHARGE Actual discharge occurs when an employee is fired. If the cause of the firing is based upon a classification protected by Title VII, then the former employee may have a good cause of action. If an employee quits, then there is no action of the employer that could be termed a discharge. A growing number of jurisdictions are embracing, however, the notion that **constructive discharge** can serve as an adverse employment action that deserves protection under Title VII. In those situations where an employer creates a workplace that is so intolerable that a reasonable person in the shoes of an employee would feel compelled to quit, then the employee can seek protection under Title VII.

Constructive discharge
Where the employer creates a work environment that is so uncomfortable that a reasonable employee would quit

RETALIATION Although not a popular cause of action for many years, plaintiffs are increasingly using the provision of Title VII that prohibits an employer from taking adverse actions that "discriminate against" an applicant or employee where an employee has "opposed" a practice illegal under Title VII. A complaint to a company official or the EEOC is often the basis for a supervisor or co-employee acting in **retaliation** against an employee. The United States Supreme Court has ruled that any retaliation need not even be work related as long as the action by the employer would dissuade a reasonable employee from complaining about discrimination. As a result of plaintiffs receiving favorable rulings in recent years from prominent courts, the retaliation cause of action is increasingly common.

Retaliation
Employer penalizes an employee when the employee reports an illegal employment practice

Moreover, employers have to be quite cognizant of retaliation claims as they administer human resource policies within their organizations. Suppose an employee is about to receive a poor evaluation. He knows that the evaluation may lead to his dismissal, so he goes to the human resource management office and claims that he is working in a hostile work environment under sexual harassment laws. This puts the organization is a potential bind: issue the negative review and risk a retaliation action (the employee alleging that the negative review is "retaliation" for the claim of sexual harassment) or not issue the negative review and risk a further degradation in the quality of work generated from this employee.

5. Categories of Discrimination

RACE, COLOR, AND NATIONAL ORIGIN Title VII's provisions barring discrimination based on *race* and *color* are designed to protect against employers taking adverse employment actions against blacks, other racial minorities, Eskimos, and American Indians. Title VII also prohibits discrimination against whites. It is acceptable under Title VII, however, for a private employer to voluntarily create a minority racial preference plan if (1) the plan is geared to open traditionally segregated job categories to minorities, (2) does not unnecessarily trammel the employment rights of whites, and (3) is only temporary. The following scenario illustrates discrimination based on color. Dark-skinned blacks dominate the management ranks at a particular factory. The dark-skinned supervisors discriminate against light-skinned black subordinates. This behavior would violate Title VII's color provision.

With an increasingly global workforce, instances of discrimination based on *national origin* are common. The prohibition certainly applies to situations where an employer discriminates against a worker who was born in another country. The Title VII ban also extends, however, to protect discrimination based on an individual's ancestor's country of origin and an individual's physical, cultural, or linguistic characteristics that are identified by people of a certain national origin. For example, English-only rules in the workplace would violate the national origin provision of Title VII unless the employer can show a business necessity for the rule (e.g., job safety). The *Immigration Reform and Control Act of 1986* also prohibits discrimination on the basis of national origin or citizenship.

GENDER Title VII forbids an employer from discriminating against an individual on the basis of *gender.* While women claim the protections of Title VII in the vast majority of cases, men are also protected. An advertisement in a newspaper asking for women only to apply for a waitress position at a restaurant would provide strong evidence that the employer was violating Title VII. Because the provision of Title VII prohibiting "sex" discrimination has been interpreted to pertain only to gender-based discrimination, adverse employment actions based on sexual orientation or transsexuality are not covered by this federal law.

Two acts of Congress are closely associated with the Title VII provision that prohibits gender discrimination. The *Pregnancy Discrimination Act* amends Title VII to made illegal discrimination based on pregnancy, childbirth, or related conditions. A principal component of this provision requires that pregnancy and related conditions must be treated like other medical conditions that similarly affect an employee's status.

Equal Pay Act

The statute that prohibits an employer from paying employees of one gender less than employees of another gender for doing substantially equal work

Also, in 1963, just one year before they passed Title VII, Congress enacted the **Equal Pay Act** (EPA). The focus of this provision is narrow: it forbids sex discrimination regarding *pay only.* An employer has violated the EPA if a woman receives lower pay than a man for performing substantially equal work. Plaintiff in an EPA action must show that the woman's job and the higher-paid man's job involve (1) equal effort, (2) equal skill, (3) equal responsibility, and (4) similar working conditions. If this is proven, the employer prevails only if it is able to show the disparity in pay relates to (1) seniority, (2) merit, (3) quality or quantity of work product, or (4) a factor other than sex.

Religion Title VII prohibits an employer from discriminating based on an individual's *religious beliefs, practices, and observances.* The notion of *belief* is broadly interpreted, covering Catholics to the same degree as atheists. In fact, at least according to the EEOC, religious belief includes almost all moral or ethical beliefs that are sincerely held in a manner similar to those beliefs associated with followers of traditional religions. As the following case presents, however, there are limits to the concept of religious belief for Title VII purposes.

Protections associated with religion extend beyond belief to *religious practices and observances.* Requiring an employee to work on the Sabbath, for example, may violate Title VII.

There is an important difference associated with the religion provision in contrast with other protected classification schemes under Title VII. Congress also requires employers to *"reasonably accommodate"* the religious practices of its employees, unless that accommodation would create an *"undue hardship"* on the employer. Therefore, if other employees could and would work on the Sabbath, then a shift change is probably a reasonable accommodation that would not create an undue hardship. The failure to provide such an accommodation would result in strong evidence of discrimination on the basis of religion. The courts have interpreted the accommodation provision quite narrowly, so employers today have considerable discretion to discriminate if an accommodation will create anything more than a *minimal disruption to the workplace.*

6. Defenses to Discrimination

Seniority and Merit While considered more an exception than an affirmative defense, Title VII provides that as long as *seniority* and *merit-based* systems utilized in the organization are not the product of intentional discrimination, Title VII is not violated.

Bona Fide Occupational Qualification While *not* applicable to discrimination based on *race or color*, Title VII does provide that an employer may discriminate on the basis of *national*

Case

Brown v. Pena

UNITED STATES DISTRICT COURT

441 F. Supp. 1382 (1977)

James Lawrence King, District Judge.

The plaintiff brought suit against the Director of the Equal Employment Opportunity Commission as a result of the dismissal of two employment discrimination charges filed with the Miami District Office. The charges claimed that the plaintiff had been discriminated against because of his religion. An E.E.O.C. affidavit executed by the plaintiff and filed with this court as an exhibit reveals that the charges were based upon the plaintiff's "personal religious creed" that "Kozy Kitten People/Cat Food ... is contributing significantly to [his] state of well being ... [and therefore] to [his] overall work performance" by increasing his energy. These charges were dismissed by the Miami District Office on July 14, 1976, as not falling under the jurisdiction of Title VII because plaintiff failed to establish a religious belief generally accepted as a religion.

The Fifth Circuit has identified three major factors that enter into a determination of whether a belief is religious. The "religious" nature of a belief depends on whether the belief is (1) based on a theory of "man's nature or his place in the Universe," (2) not merely a personal preference but has an institutional quality about it, and (3) sincere.

Plaintiff's "personal religious creed" concerning Kozy Kitten Cat Food can only be described as such a mere personal preference and, therefore, is beyond the parameters of the concept of religion as protected by the constitution or, by logical extension and relevant within this context, Title VII.

Since plaintiff's belief in pet food does not qualify legally as a religion, the Equal Employment Opportunity Commission acted correctly in declining to pursue his charges of employment discrimination on religious grounds.

■ *Denied.*

CASE CONCEPTS REVIEW

1. Does the definition of a religious belief make sense? Why?
2. Is it possible that a personal religious creed could qualify as a religious belief? If so, how?

origin, religion, or gender if such action is necessary to the operation of the business. For example, a theater company hiring an actor to play a female role may assert this defense successfully in limiting those auditioning for the part to women. The defense only applies in cases of disparate treatment. Perhaps it is not surprising that the **bona fide occupational qualification** (BFOQ) defense is narrowly construed.

AGE AND DISABILITY DISCRIMINATION

7. Age Discrimination

Bona fide occupational qualification
An attribute or trait of an employee associated with national origin, religion or gender that is necessary to the employer's particular business

Age Discrimination in Employment Act
Prohibits an employer from discriminating against applicants and employees who are at least 40 years of age

In 1967, Congress passed the **Age Discrimination in Employment Act** (ADEA) to protect discrimination against applicants and employees who are *at least forty (40) years of age*. The ADEA covers employers with twenty (20) or more employees who are engaged in interstate commerce. In terms of operation, the processes associated with ADEA are very similar to those employed under Title VII. For example, before an individual asserting a violation of the ADEA can sue, a claim must be filed with the EEOC or appropriate state agency. Also, both disparate treatment and disparate impact theories apply to ADEA actions.

The ADEA does recognize, for purposes of statute of limitations, remedies that violate may be willful or nonwillful. Note, also, that it is not a violation of the ADEA for an employer to favor older employees over younger employees, even if those younger employees are in the 40 and over age group.

The ADEA has a bona fide occupational qualification (BFOQ) defense and also a "reasonable factor other than age" defense.

8. Disability Discrimination

The *Americans with Disabilities Act* (ADA), enacted in 1990, is a comprehensive piece of civil rights legislation relating, in part, to discrimination in the workplace that draws heavily on aspects of Title VII yet also incorporating new approaches to dealing with discrimination.

BASIC PROVISIONS The ADA is similar to Title VII in that it provides for both administrative action under EEOC and a private right of action. Compensatory and punitive damages are

The *Age Discrimination in Employment Act* (ADEA) was implemented to protect older workers against discrimination.

available, subject to the limitations (or caps) applicable under Title VII. In addition, as with Title VII, this federal law applies to employers with fifteen (15) or more employees and those employers who are engaged in interstate commerce.

DEFINITION OF A DISABILITY Congress crafted an exceedingly broad definition of the term "disability." Under the ADA, a *disability* is a person: (1) with a physical or mental impairment that substantially limits one or more of an individual's life activities, (2) with a record of such an impairment, or (3) who is regarded as having such an impairment. The first category, at least on a cursory level, is straightforward. The second category covers an individual who had an impairment in the past but no longer is so situated. A person who had a bad heart value that was surgically replaced would fall into this category. As for the third type of disability covered by the ADA, if employees believe rumors that co-employee Monroe is HIV-positive, then he is regarded as being disabled even though Monroe is not HIV-positive. The statute provides a list of exclusions from the definition of disability, including homosexuality, compulsive gambling, behavior flowing from the illegal use of drugs, and use of alcohol in the workplace that violates company policy.

Note that the definition includes both *physical and mental impairments.* Also, the protection afforded by the ADA extends only to those *impairments that substantially limit one or more of an individual's life activities.* The United States Supreme Court during the 1990s and 2000s has favored a narrow reading of this aspect of the ADA. For example, in one case severely nearsighted twin sisters were denied jobs as airline pilots even though their eyesight was 20/20 with corrective lenses. The Court ruled that corrective measures must be taken into account in determining whether a particular impairment is a disability. In another case, the Court found that carpel tunnel syndrome was not a disability because, while the plaintiff could not perform certain manual tasks associated with her specific job, she was still able perform other manual tasks.

> In an attempt to expand the scope of ADA protections along the lines of what Congress intended in the original act, Congress adopted the *ADA Amendments Act of 2008.* The major change that comes from the *ADA Amendments Act of 2008* is an expansion of employees who will qualify for coverage under the Act because of the broader interpretation of what is considered a covered disability. The *ADA Amendments Act of 2008* still uses the ADA's basic definition of "disability" as an impairment that substantially limits one or more major life activities, a record of such an impairment, or being regarded as having such an impairment. However, it changes the way these terms are interpreted so that employees are not inadvertently omitted from coverage under the ADA because they do not meet the previously narrow court interpretations of what is considered a covered disability. The definition of "major life activities" is expanded by including two example lists: one for major life activities (caring for oneself, performing manual tasks, seeing, hearing, eating, sleeping, walking, standing, lifting, bending, speaking, breathing, learning, reading, concentrating, thinking, communicating and working) and another for major bodily functions (functions of the immune system, normal cell growth, digestive, bowel, bladder, neurological, brain, respiratory, circulatory, endocrine and reproductive functions). Also, the amendment states that employers may *not* consider mitigating measures other than "ordinary eyeglasses or contact lenses" in assessing whether an individual has a disability. This means that even if an employee's condition is correctable, either through therapy or medication, it may still be considered a covered disability. In general, this new legislation requires the term "disability" be interpreted broadly.

REASONABLE ACCOMMODATION AND UNDUE HARDSHIP Borrowing language from the religion provisions of Title VII, the ADA requires employers to make *reasonable accommodations* to a job applicant's or an employee's disability, so long as making the accommodation does not create an undue hardship for the employer. While the statutory language is quite similar, it is clear that Congress intended greater accommodations under the ADA than those found under Title VII dealing with religious accommodation. The courts have followed the wishes of Congress and created a fairly significant obligation on employers to accommodate. The ADA protects two types of individuals: (1) those who can perform essential functions associated with their position despite their disability, and (2) those who can perform duties if the employer provides a reasonable accommodation. Because each disability and the situation surrounding the person claiming a disability are unique, employers should give considerable weight to the employee's accommodation preferences.

There is a constraint on the employer's duty to accommodate. Contrary to the minimum level of accommodation necessary under the religion provision of Title VII, the ADA mandates that an *undue hardship* will occur only if the financial or other type of burden is *substantial.* The nature and cost of the accommodation, the overall financial resources of the employer, and the number of employees are factors that are considered in determining whether an undue hardship exists. Therefore, a court could find an undue hardship exists in a call-center operation with thirty employees but not make a similar finding in a manufacturing firm with five hundred employees. The following diagram provides the processes associated with an ADA claim.

HARASSMENT

9. Theoretical Aspects of Harassment

While Title VII was initially directed at situations where an individual was deprived of a benefit associated with employment, this concept of discrimination was insufficient to adequately protect job applicants and employees in view of members of the judiciary. Courts in the 1970s and 1980s expanded the reach of Title VII to cover situations where an employee was harassed. While it is possible that *harassment* can be associated with any of the groups protected by Title VII, by far the most common version is harassment based on sex. Sexual harassment includes unwelcome sexual advances, requests for sexual favors, and other verbal, physical, visual (including the use of a computer) conduct of a sexual nature.

Quid pro quo sexual harassment

Occurs where sexual favors are exchanged for a benefit connected to employment.

Hostile environment sexual harassment

Occurs where the workplace is permeated with unwelcome sexual conduct that creates an offensive work environment

TYPE The courts have determined that sexual harassment, broadly speaking, can take one of two forms. The first is called **quid pro quo sexual harassment**. In this form, a benefit relating to employment is offered to an employee in exchange for sexual favors. *Quid pro quo* sexual harassment will arise when, because an employee refuses to submit to the request for sexual favors, the individual suffers a *tangible job detriment.* Thus, if a male supervisor fails to promote a female subordinate because she refuses to date him, *quid pro quo* sexual harassment has occurred. Note that there is no requirement that the supervisor state explicitly that the penalty for refusing the advance is failure to advance. Because *quid pro quo* sexual harassment involves the potential granting of an economic benefit relating to employment, this type of sexual harassment is committed only by supervisory employees.

The other type of sexual harassment is far more frequent. **Hostile environment sexual harassment** occurs when, according to the United States Supreme Court, "the workplace is permeated with discriminatory intimidation, ridicule, and insult that is sufficiently severe or pervasive to alter the conditions of the victim's employment and create an abusive working

FIGURE 27-3 ■ Decision Tree for the ADA

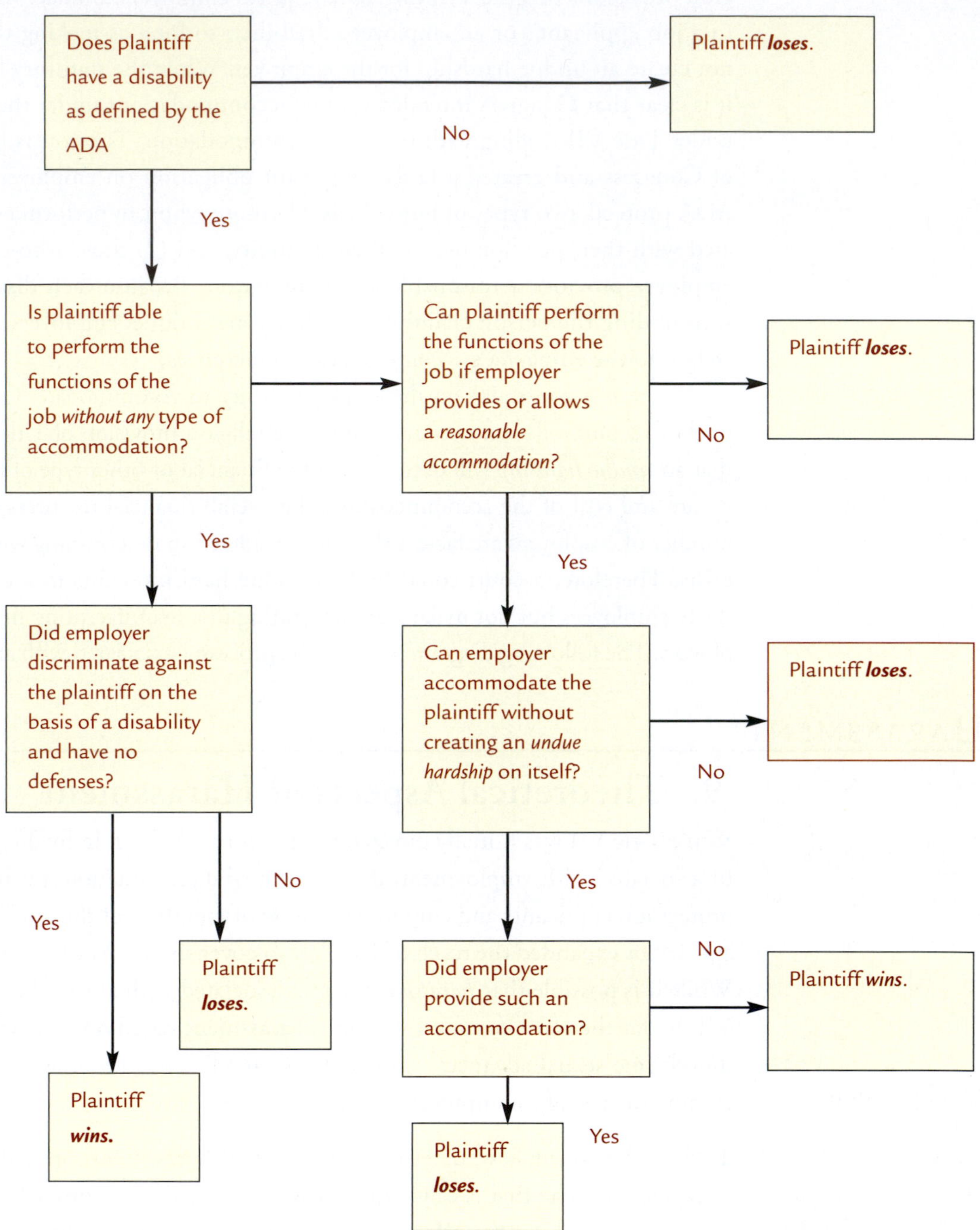

environment." *No tangible economic impact* on the workplace is necessary to establish a violation of Title VII if a claim is brought under hostile environment theory. Specific aspects of hostile environment sexual harassment are addressed in the next section.

SAME-GENDER HARASSMENT Recall that Title VII prohibits sex discrimination only where the actions are based on gender differences, so the statute does not cover incidents of homosexual or transgender discrimination. However, the United States Supreme Court has extended the reach of harassment law to cover instances in which the individual harassing and the victim are of the same gender. As with male-female harassment, there is no need for a plaintiff to show that the creation of a hostile environment was motivated by sexual desire when the harassment is male-male or female-female.

SEXUAL FAVORITISM Does an employee have a valid cause of action under the *quid pro quo* theory of harassment law where another employee has submitted to sexual harassment or voluntarily entered into a romantic or sexual relationship and receives tangible employment benefits as a result? Manuel is supervising both Anita and Bonita, but also dating Bonita. Manuel is allowed to promote either of these two, and Bonita is selected even though Anita is more deserving. In another consideration, what if the situation is one where there is no tangible job benefit, but the working environment is tainted. Manuel is spending time in Bonita's office, bringing her coffee, taking her to lunch … all in front of Anita and others. Does Anita have a valid hostile environment claim? At this point, the courts are split as to whether sexual favoritism violates Title VII.

10. Hostile Environment Sexual Harassment

In order for a plaintiff to be successful in a sexual harassment suit based on the hostile environment theory, two requirements must be shown. First, the sexual conduct must be *unwelcome.* The following case, where the United States Supreme Court first acknowledged that discrimination law allowed for protection against certain forms of harassment, addresses this issue.

CASE

Meritor Savings Bank v. Vinson

SUPREME COURT OF THE UNITED STATES

477 U.S. 57 (1986)

JUSTICE REHNQUIST DELIVERED THE OPINION OF THE COURT

This case presents important questions concerning claims of workplace "sexual harassment" brought under Title VII of the Civil Rights Act of 1964, 78 Stat. 253, as amended, 42 U. S. C. § 2000e et seq.

In 1974, respondent Mechelle Vinson met Sidney Taylor, a vice president of what is now petitioner Meritor Savings Bank (bank) and manager of one of its branch offices. When respondent asked whether she might obtain employment at the bank, Taylor gave her an application, which she completed and returned the next day; later that same day Taylor called her to say that she had been hired. With Taylor as her supervisor, respondent started as a teller-trainee and, thereafter, was promoted to teller, head teller, and assistant branch manager. She worked at the same branch for four years, and it is undisputed that her advancement there was based on merit alone. In September 1978, respondent notified Taylor that she was taking sick leave for an indefinite period. On November 1, 1978, the bank discharged her for excessive use of that leave.

Respondent brought this action against Taylor and the bank, claiming that during her four years at the bank she had "constantly been subjected to sexual harassment" by Taylor in violation of Title VII. She sought injunctive relief, compensatory and punitive damages against Taylor and the bank, and attorney's fees.

At the 11-day bench trial, the parties presented conflicting testimony about Taylor's behavior during respondent's employment. Respondent testified that during her probationary period as a teller-trainee, Taylor treated her in a fatherly way and made no sexual advances. Shortly thereafter, however, he invited her out to dinner and, during the course of the meal, suggested that they go to a motel to have sexual relations. At first she refused, but out of what she described as fear of losing her job she eventually agreed. According to respondent, Taylor thereafter made repeated demands upon her for sexual favors, usually at the branch, both during and after business hours; she estimated that over the next several years she had intercourse with him some 40 or 50 times. In addition, respondent testified that Taylor fondled her in front of other employees, followed her into the women's restroom when she went there alone, exposed himself to her, and even forcibly raped her on several occasions. These activities ceased after 1977, respondent stated, when she started going with a steady boyfriend.

The question remains, however, whether the District Court's ultimate finding that respondent "was not the victim of sexual harassment," effectively disposed of respondent's claim. The Court of Appeals recognized, we think correctly, that this ultimate finding was likely based on one or both of two erroneous views of the law. First, the District Court apparently believed that a claim for sexual harassment will not lie absent an economic effect on the complainant's employment. Since it appears that the District Court made its findings without ever considering the "hostile environment" theory of sexual harassment, the Court of Appeals' decision to remand was correct.

Second, the District Court's conclusion that no actionable harassment occurred might have rested on its earlier "finding" that "[if] [respondent] and Taylor did engage in an intimate or sexual relationship …, that relationship was a voluntary one." But the fact that sex-related conduct was "voluntary," in the sense that the complainant was not forced to participate against her will, is not a defense to a sexual harassment suit brought under Title VII. The gravamen of any sexual harassment claim is that the alleged sexual advances were "unwelcome."

continued

While the question whether particular conduct was indeed unwelcome presents difficult problems of proof and turns largely on credibility determinations committed to the trier of fact, the District Court in this case erroneously focused on the "voluntariness" of respondent's participation in the claimed sexual episodes. The correct inquiry is whether respondent by her conduct indicated that the alleged sexual advances were unwelcome, not whether her actual participation in sexual intercourse was voluntary.

■ *Affirmed and remanded.*

CASE CONCEPTS REVIEW

1. Why does the court not equate "voluntary" with "welcome"?
2. What does the court identify as indicators of whether behavior is welcome?

The requirement that the alleged victim of the harassment consider the actions as unwelcome is, practically, somewhat difficult to assess. If a female employee participates in making jokes of a sexual nature, can she claim a hostile environment if males offer similar types of attempts at humor? Moreover, how do individuals in the workplace, whether they are superiors, co-workers, subordinates, or customers, know that an individual finds behavior to be unwelcome? Does an individual who finds offense necessarily have to express objection? These are some of the tough questions that must be addressed in determining whether conduct is unwelcome.

The second requirement requires that plaintiff show that the offending behavior is *so severe or pervasive* that it creates an *intimidating, hostile, or offensive working environment.* Certainly one particularly serious incident, for example, an attempted rape, would be sufficient to create a hostile environment; but isolated statements of teasing or offhand remarks are simply not going to be sufficient to change the conditions of employment. Therefore, as the courts have held, there is sufficient leeway in the law such that employers should not fear having to enforce a general civility code. The United States Supreme Court has further indicated that "common sense" should prevail in making these determinations, which means that cultural and economic matters can be considered. Therefore, stevedores working the docks in Houston are going to be given a bit more leeway in their actions than corporate executives in New York City. In a similar vein, a football coach patting the bottom of a player as they enter the stadium will not create a hostile environment, but a male executive touching the bottom of a female clerk certainly might. Still, there are large areas of grey in making this determination. In one case, a court failed to find the creation of a hostile working environment when a male coworker touched a female co-employee's breast while she was working. The fact that the incident occurred only once, others did not see the touching, and there was no physical injury compelled the court to rule against the plaintiff. It is clear that other courts would reach a different decision.

11. Employer Liability for Harassment

The employer is not liable for all harassment that occurs in the workplace. Under the doctrine of *respondeat superior,* discussed in Chapter 25, employers are vicariously liable only for those torts conducted by employees acting within the scope of employment. In those instances when a supervisor harasses, it is appropriate that aspects of agency law apply. If there is harassment by a coworker or a non-employee, agency principles are not applicable. Still the employer may be liable, based on negligence. The remaining portion of this section discusses in greater detail important legal principles associated with employer liability for harassment conducted by a supervisor and for harassment conducted by someone other than a supervisor.

HARASSMENT BY SUPERVISOR Sexual harassment conducted by a supervisor with immediate or higher authority over the employee creates liability for the organization based on principles of vicarious liability. The current state of law regarding employer liability is roughly based on agency principles. Two principal factors shape the doctrine: (1) whether the victim suffered a tangible job loss, and (2) the degree to which the employer has created an anti-harassment atmosphere.

In those situations where tangible job action is taken against the victim, the employer is liable because the supervisor is drawing on the power of the employer to harass. All *quid pro quo* harassment cases and those hostile environment cases involving a tangible job action (such as termination or demotion) require, under federal judicial decisions, that the employer is strictly liable. For hostile environment cases not involving a tangible job loss, however, the United States Supreme Court has crafted a *defense* for employers. To establish the defense, the employer must show (1) it exercised reasonable care to prevent (e.g., establishing an adequate sexual harassment policy, conducting reasonable investigations) and correct promptly any sexually harassing behavior (e.g., dealing appropriately with instances of harassment), and (2) the employee unreasonably failed to take advantage of any preventive or corrective opportunities provided by the by the employer (e.g., waited a long time to report the harassment) or to otherwise avoid harm.

HARASSMENT BY CO-WORKER AND NON-EMPLOYEE Because sexual harassment by a co-worker or non-employee does not entail the harasser using the power of the employer to harass, the doctrine of respondeat superior is inapplicable. The employer, however, may be *negligent* regarding sexual harassment if (1) it knew or should have known of the sexual harassment, and (2) failed to take immediate action to stop the offending behavior. For those organizations that possess a sexual harassment policy, implement means for employees to report alleged instances of harassment and corrective action taken after a reasonable investigation, liability for sexual harassment is limited. The underlying policy is quite simple: while the employer should be responsible for creating a workplace free of harassment, an employer should have notice and an opportunity to correct before being liable. The same rule and policy applies when the harasser is not a co-worker but is a client or customer. A male bank customer who repeatedly harasses female tellers by attempting to kiss them or hold their hands creates notice for the employer given the public nature of the behavior. If the bank fails take steps to prevent the harassment, then the employer is liable.

CHAPTER SUMMARY

Laws Prohibiting Employment Discrimination

1. The *Civil Rights Act of 1866* provides protection against discrimination in employment on the basis of race.
2. The *Civil Rights Act of 1964* bans discrimination in employment based on race, color, religion, national origin, and sex.
3. Harassment law is largely the product of the courts.

TITLE VII

Scope

1. Title VII of the *Civil Rights Act of 1964* applies to employers with 15 or more employees.
2. Only employees, not independent contractors, are subject to the provisions of Title VII.

Procedures

1. The Equal Employment Opportunity Commission (EEOC) was created to administer the provisions of Title VII.

2. An individual who is the victim of discrimination must pursue a claim with EEOC before suing in a court.

Remedies

1. Equitable relief and money damages are available under Title VII.
2. Federal law caps the amount of damages for intentional discrimination.

Proving Discrimination under Title VII

1. Disparate treatment requires a plaintiff to show intentional discrimination.
2. Intentional discrimination requires plaintiff to show that he or she was discriminated against on the basis of a category protected under Title VII.
3. Unintentional discrimination occurs where an employment practice that is neutral on its face has a negative affect on members of a protected class.

Constructive Discharge and Retaliation

1. Constructive discharge occurs where an employer creates an employment relationship that is so intolerable that a reasonable person would quit.
2. Retaliation against an employee who reports an illegal act is covered under Title VII.

Categories of Discrimination

1. Race, color, and national origin discrimination are prohibited under Title VII.
2. Gender discrimination is prohibited under both Title VII and the Equal Pay Act.
3. Religious discrimination principles under Title VII require an employer to make a reasonable accommodation for the religious practices of an employee.

Defenses to Discrimination

1. A bona fide occupational qualification is an attribute or trait of an employee associated with national origin, religion or gender that is necessary to the employer's particular business.

AGE AND DISABILITY DISCRIMINATION

Age Discrimination

1. The *Age Discrimination in Employment Act* (ADEA) prohibits discrimination against employees who are at least forty years of age.
2. EEOC administers provisions of the ADEA.

Disability Discrimination

1. The *Americans with Disabilities Act* (ADA) covers those with an impairment, those with a record of impairment, and those who are thought to have an impairment.
2. The ADA covers both physical and mental impairments.
3. The ADA requires an employer to make a reasonable accommodation to those with a disability, limited only by the requirement that the accommodation does not create an undue hardship on the employer.

HARASSMENT

Theoretical Aspects

1. Quid pro quo sexual harassment occurs where sexual favors are exchanged for benefits associated with employment.
2. Hostile environment sexual harassment exists where unwelcome sexual conduct creates an offensive work environment.

Hostile Environment Sexual Harassment

1. Requires that conduct be unwelcome
2. The conduct must be so severe or pervasive that it creates an offensive work environment.

Employer Liability for Harassment

1. The organization is always responsible for quid pro quo harassment.
2. The organization may be liable for hostile work environment harassment, but a defense does exist that would prohibit liability where the employer acts reasonably and the victim of the harassment acts unreasonably.

REVIEW QUESTIONS AND PROBLEMS

1. Match each term in Column A with the appropriate statement in Column B.

A	B
(1) Equal Employment Opportunity Commission	(a) Unintentional discrimination
(2) Disparate treatment	(b) Employer penalizes an employee when the employee reports an illegal employment practice.
(3) Disparate impact	(c) An attribute or trait of an employee associated with national origin, religion or gender that is necessary to the employer's particular business
(4) Constructive discharge	(d) The administrative agency charged with investigating and enforcing the provisions of Title VII
(5) Retaliation	(e) Prohibits an employer from discriminating against applicants and employees who are at least 40 years of age
(6) Equal Pay Act	(f) Employer creates a work environment so uncomfortable that a reasonable person would quit.
(7) Bona fide occupational qualification	(g) Occurs where the workplace is permeated with unwelcome sexual conduct that creates an offensive work environment
(8) Age Discrimination in Employment Act	(h) Statute that prohibits an employer from paying employees of one gender less than employees of another gender for doing substantially equal work
(9) Quid pro quo sexual harassment	(i) Occurs where benefit of employment is exchanged for sexual favor
(10) Hostile environment sexual harassment	(j) Intentional discrimination

2. Slalom Ski Co. is alleged to have discriminated against certain employees on the basis of race. What federal legislation could be used by the employees to sue Slalom?

3. Beatrice owns a health club in Arizona. She has incorporated her business and employs twenty-five individuals. One former employee is suing the health club for national origin discrimination under Title VII. Does Title VII apply?

4. Molly believes she has been discriminated against on the basis of gender. She was denied a promotion, and the job went to a male. Molly is quite angry. She calls the first attorney she finds in the telephone book, ordering the attorney to immediately file a lawsuit in federal court for a violation of Title VII. Can the attorney file a lawsuit at this time?

5. Rasheed, who was terminated five months ago from his job at ABC, Corp., believes he was intentionally discriminated against because of his religion when the company terminated him. If Rasheed should win, what remedies might he secure under Title VII?
6. Harry and Sally work side-by side on a production line. Both do exactly the same job. Harry received fifty cents more per hour. What laws might be violated? What defenses might the employer offer?
7. Annie, an Asian woman, applied for a security guard job with Steel Protective Services (SPS), a private security firm. SPS provides businesses with guards, especially on weekends and at night. Applicants for the guard position must be at least 5 foot, 9 inches tall and be able to lift a sixty-pound weight over their head. Annie is 5 foot, 2 inches and cannot lift the required weight. If Annie sues SPS for violating Title VII, what process will be employed? What are the burdens on each party?
8. Nesser worked as a customer service agent with Fly 'Em High Airlines. He became ill with Crohn's disease, a chronic intestinal ailment, which caused him to miss work for a large number of days each month. He asked for an accommodation: working from home. The airline refused to allow him to work at home. Nesser files a lawsuit against the Fly 'Em High. Who should win and why?
9. Samson was the supervisor of Susie. Susie has filed a sexual harassment suit against Samson and her employer. Susie alleges that Samson "looked her up, looker her down" every day for five weeks, grabbed her wrist and attempted to dance with her in the hallway at work a dozen times during the same period, and constantly tried to give Susie a neck massage. Does Susie have a case? Why?
10. Johnson & Johnson Company's senior vice president was found by a court last week to have sexually harassed a subordinate. Might Johnson & Johnson have a defense? If so, what are the elements of the defense?

Internet Source:

EEOC Web Site: http://www.eeoc.gov

PART VI

BUSINESS ORGANIZATIONS

Partnerships | 28

CHAPTER OUTLINE

continued

CHAPTER PREVIEW

A *partnership* is defined as an association of two or more persons to carry on as co-owners of a business for profit. It is the result of an agreement between competent parties to place their money, property, or labor in a business and to divide the profits and losses. The existence of a partnership is more dependent on what the facts reveal than on what the parties state is their intent. If the parties' conduct indicates there is an agreement to carry on a business and to share profit and losses, there is a partnership even though the parties may not call themselves partners.

To overcome possible confusion about a partnership's existence, the parties should enter into a formally drafted *partnership agreement*. The contents of such an agreement are of critical importance to the parties involved.

In addition to issues that arise between the partners, questions about the relationship of partners to third parties also arise. The rights and duties of third parties and of partners related to the formation of a partnership are discussed in this chapter.

The provisions of the partnership agreement and the applicable statutory law, which in most states is based on the *Revised Uniform Partnership Act* (RUPA), governs the operation of a partnership. The RUPA is a model partnership statute created by the National Commissioners on Uniform State Laws—a group of distinguished judges, law professors, attorneys who work to establish the same provisions of statutory law from state to state. Most states have adopted the RUPA.

Thus the rights, duties, and powers of partners are both expressed (those in the agreement) and implied (those created by state law). Throughout this discussion, remember that a partner is essentially an agent for the other partners and that the general principles of the law of agency are applicable. The rights, duties, and powers of partners and the operation of the partnership are discussed in this chapter.

What happens when the partnership ceases to exist? The last portion of this chapter discusses how a dissolution of partnership occur, the impact of such an event, and how the partnership assets are distributed when the business of the organization is terminated.

BUSINESS MANAGEMENT DECISION

You and two friends agree to practice public accounting together as partners. Each of you agrees to pay $50,000 in capital to begin the practice

What should be your major concerns at the outset of this relationship?

WHEN DOES A PARTNERSHIP EXIST?

1. Introduction

Between the parties, the intention to create a partnership may be expressed or implied from their conduct. The basic question is whether the parties intend a relationship that includes the essential elements of a partnership, not whether they intend to be partners. In fact, under certain circumstances, a corporation may be held to be a partnership at least between the owners of the business.

In essence, then, the parties doing business are partners if they satisfy three requirements. First, are there *two or more parties* involved? Second, is there a *common interest* to conduct business activities? Third, is there an *understanding to share profits and losses*?

The following case illustrates the ease with which a partnership is formed and the consequences of being a partner.

CASE

Ted Norris, et al. v. Stafford P. Fontenot, et al.

COURT OF APPEAL OF LOUISIANA

867 So. 2d 179 (2004)

AMY, JUDGE

Ted Norris, plaintiff herein, designed and built a "mobile kitchen" for use at festivals by installing cooking equipment—such as stoves, burners, and coolers—in an empty eighteen-wheeler trailer. Mr. Norris estimated the value of the completed kitchen to be $50,000.

Stafford Fontenot, defendant herein, testified at trial that, approximately six or seven months before the 1996 Summer Olympics, he and some friends—Steve Turner, Mike Montelaro, Joe Sokol, and Doug Brinsmade—discussed going to Atlanta, Georgia, the site of the Games, to sell seafood and other Cajun dishes. However, they did not have the cooking equipment needed for the endeavor. Mr. Fontenot testified that Mr. Turner and Mr. Montelaro learned of Mr. Norris's "mobile kitchen" and entered into preliminary negotiations with him for its purchase.

The act of sale was executed on June 12, 1996, at the office of William Bennett, Mr. Norris's attorney. The record reflects that at this time, Mr. Brinsmade gave Mr. Norris a down payment of $8,000, in the form of a check drawn on an account titled, "Prairie Cajun Seafood Catering of LA." Mr. Bennett then presented Mr. Fontenot with two promissory notes representing the balance of the purchase price of the kitchen: one for $12,000, and the other for $20,000.

Mr. Fontenot testified that the results of the group's catering endeavor in Atlanta were "disastrous" and that what little money they made "went back through [the group's] checking account." He stated that the group has not engaged in business since the Olympics.

On June 9, 1998, Mr. Norris filed suit against Mr. Fontenot, d/b/a Prairie Cajun Seafood Catering of Louisiana, in the district court for Avoyelles Parish, the parish of his—Mr. Norris's—domicile. In his petition, he asserted that no payments had been made on either of the two promissory notes. On December 10, 1998, Mr. Norris filed a supplemental and amending petition, in which he named as defendants Mr. Brinsmade, Mr. Montelaro, and Mr. Turner, noting that they were "principals in the business Prairie Cajun Seafood Catering of Louisiana." However, Mr. Norris voluntarily dismissed Messrs. Brinsmade, Montelaro, and Turner in open court on May 7, 2001; and on May 29, 2002, in a second supplemental and amending petition, he requested that references to these gentlemen be "deleted" from his petition. On May 24, 2002, Mr. Fontenot filed an exception of failure to join an indispensable party—viz., the partnership, Prairie Cajun Seafood Catering of Louisiana.

The trial court awarded a judgment in favor of Plaintiffs and against the partnership, Prairie Cajun Seafood Catering of Louisiana in the sum of thirty-two thousand dollars plus interest and 25% attorney fees.

Mr. Norris appeals this judgment, claiming in his sole assignment of error that the trial judge incorrectly determined that Mr. Fontenot was not personally liable on the notes.

Louisiana courts have established criteria whereby a business association may be categorized as a partnership. In determining whether a partnership has been established, courts generally employ the following three-part test: (1) the parties must have mutually consented to form a partnership and to participate in the profits which may accrue from property, skill, or industry, furnished to the business in determined proportions by them; (2) all parties must share in the losses as well as the profits of the venture; and (3) the property or stock of the enterprise must form a community.

The first identifying characteristic of a partnership is that the parties involved must have consented to the formation of a

continued

partnership and must have agreed to participate in the profits derived from the partnership business and to contribute property, skill, or industry to the partnership in agreed-upon proportions. In the instant matter, Mr. Fontenot testified that six or seven months before the 1996 Summer Olympics, he and his friends had come to an understanding that they would sell Cajun food in Atlanta together. They had begun making preparations to this effect. The record reflects that these preparations did not contemplate that Mr. Fontenot would be the sole proprietor of the business with the other gentlemen as his employees. In addition, the record indicates that the first instance of the group calling themselves by the name "Prairie Cajun Seafood Catering of Louisiana" was on a Special Food Services application dated May 19, 1996, that was submitted to the Fulton County Department of Public Health-Environmental Health Services. This application stated that all five gentlemen named above were partners.

Our review of the law of partnership does not indicate that members of an alleged partnership must be able to point to a specific date upon which the partnership began. Although the record reflects that the partnership agreement was not signed until July 31, 1996, it is apparent from the evidence that Mr. Fontenot and his friends had an oral agreement to form an association and to work together toward a common goal before they purchased the mobile kitchen on June 12, 1996.

The second feature of a partnership is that all parties involved must share in the business's profits as well as losses. In the partnership agreement dated July 31, 1996, the parties indicated that profits and losses would be allocated according to the following percentages: Stafford Fontenot, 24%; Doug Brinsmade, 19%; Joe Sokol, 19%; Mike Montelaro, 19%; and Steve Turner, 19%.

The record reflects that the above-named gentlemen intended to share in the profits and losses of the partnership and also intended to contribute personal resources toward the accomplishment of the group's objectives.

The third characteristic of a partnership is that "the property or stock of the enterprise must form a community of goods in which each party has a proprietary interest." The record indicates that Mr. Fontenot did not consider the "mobile kitchen" to be his personal property; instead, he thought that it belonged to the partnership. He testified at trial that its title was still in the name of Stafford Fontenot, d/b/a Prairie Cajun Seafood Catering of Louisiana. Furthermore, the various receipts for services that were among the business records introduced into evidence at trial are all in the name of Prairie Cajun Seafood Catering. The bank account at Nations Bank of Atlanta was established on May 31, 1996, in the name of "Prairie Cajun Seafood Catering of LA and Associates." No receipts or documents were in any one party's name. This indicates that the parties intended to do business through Prairie Cajun Seafood Catering as a separate entity, with the result that any property acquired for the business was the property of the partnership, not of any one particular party.

Furthermore, Mr. Fontenot testified that he and Mr. Montelaro, Mr. Brinsmade, and Mr. Turner were present when the act of sale was passed; and he introduced these gentlemen as his partners.

Our review of the record does not indicate that the trial judge was manifestly erroneous or clearly wrong in determining that the elements necessary for formation of a partnership were present and that the partnership, as an entity, coalesced before the sale of the "mobile kitchen."

For the foregoing reasons, the judgment of the trial court is affirmed.

■ *Affirmed.*

CASE CONCEPTS REVIEW

1. What are the requirements for a partnership?
2. What is the role of intent in forming a partnership? Is there evidence that Mr. Montelaro, Mr. Brinsmade, and Mr. Turner showed intent to become partners with Mr. Fontenot?

To simplify the question of whether a partnership exists, the parties could sign a formally drafted partnership agreement. The signatures are one indication that an *express partnership* exists. If an expression has not been made by the parties, an *implied partnership* may be found from the parties' conduct.

These two types of partnerships are discussed next, followed by a section on partnerships by estoppel, which is an argument made by third parties when an express or implied partnership does not exist.

2. Express Partnerships

Any oral or written statement by the parties that they have agreed to be partners carries substantial weight in concluding that a partnership exists. Such an agreement justifies the finding that an express partnership exists.

While an oral agreement is binding with respect to the parties to the agreement, proof of the contents of such agreement is difficult. Often courts must accept one party's word over that of another party regarding what their agreement really stated. To avoid such conflicts, partners should reduce their agreement to the form of articles of partnership and sign the document. The typical provisions that should be included in a formal written agreement are discussed in Sections 5 through 11.

3. Implied Partnerships

Even though no oral or written partnership agreement can be proven, courts still may find that a partnership exists. Such a finding is based on the conduct of the parties. When this conduct satisfies the three essential elements of a partnership, an *implied partnership* is said to exist.

If the essential elements of a partnership are present, the mere fact that the parties do not think they are becoming partners is immaterial. If the parties agree on an arrangement that is a partnership in fact, it is immaterial whether they call it something else or even declare in writing that they are not partners! On the other hand, the mere fact that the parties themselves call the relation a partnership will not make it so if they have not, by their conduct, agreed on an agreement that by the law is a partnership in fact.

The essential attributes of a partnership are a common interest in the business and management and an agreement to share in the profits and losses. This common interest may be established by a holding of property and a sharing of the profits and losses related to the property. If there is a sharing of profits, a partnership may be found to exist even though there is no sharing of losses.

The presence of a common interest in property and management is not enough to establish a partnership by implication; nor, of itself, does an agreement to share the gross returns of a business, sometimes called gross profits, prove an intention to form a partnership. If a person receives a share of net profits in a business, that is *prima facie* (but not conclusive) evidence of partnership. It may be overcome by evidence that the share in the profits is received for some other purpose, such as payment of a debt by installments, wages, rent, annuity to a widow of a deceased partner, interest on a loan, or payment of goodwill by installments. Bonuses are frequently paid as a percent of profit, but they do not make the employee a partner. Likewise, many leases provide for rent based on profits, but such an arrangement is generally not a partnership.

4. Partnership by Estoppel

Estoppel

To prevent a party from denying the legal consequences of that party's conduct

Insofar as third persons are concerned, *partnership liability*, like the apparent authority of an agent, may be predicated on the legal theory of **estoppel**. If a person by words spoken or written or by conduct represents himself or herself or consents to another's representing him or her as a partner in an existing partnership, that person is not a partner but is liable to any party to whom such representation has been made. If the representation is made in a public manner either personally or with consent of the apparent partner, the apparent partner is liable if credit is extended to the partnership, even if the creditor did not actually know of the representation. This is an exception to the usual estoppel requirement of actual reliance.

The courts are not in accord as to whether a person must affirmatively disclaim a reputed partnership that he or she did not consent to or claim. Some court cases hold that if a person is held out as a partner and knows it, that person should be chargeable as a partner unless he or she takes reasonable steps to give notice that he or she is not, in fact, a partner. These courts impose a duty on a person to deny that he or she is a partner, once that person knows that third persons are relying on representations that he or she is a partner. Other cases indicate that there is no duty to deny false representations of partnership if the apparent partner did not participate in making the misrepresentation.

THE PARTNERSHIP AGREEMENT

5. Introduction

The content of a partnership agreement may vary from business to business. Among the subjects usually contained in such agreements are the following: the names of the partners and of the partnership, its purpose and duration, the capital contributions of each partner, the method of sharing profits and losses, the effect of advances, the salaries (if any) to be paid the partners, the method of accounting and the fiscal year, the rights and liabilities of the parties upon the death or withdrawal of a partner, and the procedures to be followed upon dissolution.

The following sections discuss some of the more important provisions of the partnership agreement and indicate the effect of the RUPA on the agreement.

6. Firm Name Provision

Because a partnership is created by the agreement of the parties, they select the name to be used. This right of selection is subject to two limitations by statute in many states. First, a partnership may not use the word *company* or other language that would imply the existence of a corporation. Second, if the name is other than that of the partners, they must comply with assumed name statutes that require the giving of public notice as to the actual identity of the partners (e.g., fictitious business name statement). Failure to comply with this assumed name statute may result in the partnership's being denied access to the courts to sue its debtors, or it may result in criminal actions being brought against those operating under the assumed name.

The firm name is an asset of the firm; and as such it may also be sold, assigned, or disposed of in any manner on which the parties agree. At common law, a partnership was not a legal entity that could sue and be sued in the firm name. All actions had to be brought in behalf of, or against, all the partners as individuals. Today, statutes in most states have changed the common law and allow partnerships to sue or be sued in the firm name. Most states also consider the partnership a legal entity for purposes of litigation—even in the absence of a statute.

7. Capital Provision

Partnership *capital* consists of the total credits to the capital accounts of the various partners, provided the credits are for permanent investments in the business. Such capital represents the amount that the partnership's obligated to return to the partners at the time of dissolution; and it can be done only with the consent of all the partners. Undivided profits that only some of the partners permit to accumulate in the business do not become part of the capital. They, like temporary advances by firm members, are subject to withdrawal at any time unless the agreement provides to the contrary.

The amount that each partner is to contribute to the firm, as well as the credit he or she is to receive for assets contributed, is entirely dependent on the partnership agreement. A person may become a partner without a capital contribution. For example, a partner may contribute services to balance the capital investment of the other partners. Such a partner, however, has no capital to be returned at the time of liquidation. Only those who receive credit for capital investments—which may include goodwill, patent rights, and so forth, if agreed on—are entitled to the return of capital when dissolution occurs. Business experience is not a contribution to capital.

8. Property Provision

In conducting its business, a partnership may use its own property, the property of the individual partners, or the property of some third person. It frequently becomes important, especially on dissolution and where claims of firm creditors are involved, to ascertain exactly what property constitutes partnership property in order to ascertain the rights of partners and firm creditors in specific property.

As a general rule, the agreement of the parties will determine what property is properly classified as partnership property. In the absence of an express agreement, what constitutes partnership property is ascertained from the conduct of the parties and from the purpose for, and the way in which, property is used in the pursuit of the business.

The RUPA provides that all property specifically brought into partnership or acquired by it is partnership property. Therefore, unless a contrary intention appears, property acquired with partnership funds is partnership property. In other words, there is a presumption that property acquired with partnership funds is partnership property, but this presumption is rebuttable.

Property acquired by a partner individually is often transferred to the partnership as a part of a partner's contribution to capital. If this contribution is in a form other than money, the property no longer belongs to the contributing partner. The contributing partner has vested the firm with title and has no greater equity in the property than has any other party. At dissolution, this partner recovers only the amount allowed to him or her for the property invested. If this property is purchased by the partner on credit, the creditor has no claim against the partnership, even though the property can be traced to it. A personal loan made to a partner does not become a partnership debt unless it is expressly assumed by the partnership.

Because a partnership has the right to acquire, own, and dispose of personal property in the firm name, legal documents affecting the title to partnership personal property may be executed in the firm name by any partner. The RUPA also treats a partnership as a legal entity for the purposes of title to real estate that may be held in the firm name. Title so acquired can be conveyed in the partnership name.

9. Profit-and-Loss Provision

Unless the agreement is to the contrary, *each partner has a right to share equally in the profits of the enterprise, and each partner is under a duty to contribute equally to the losses.* Capital contributed to the firm is a liability owed by the firm to the contributing partners. If, on dissolution, there are not sufficient assets to repay each partner his capital, the amount is considered as a loss; and like any other loss of the partnership, it must be met.

> EXAMPLE A partnership is composed of A, B, and C. A contributed $20,000, B contributed $10,000, and C contributed $4,000. The firm is dissolved, and upon the payment of debts only $10,000 of firm assets remain. Because the total contribution to capital was $34,000, the operating loss is $24,000. If these partners have not agreed otherwise, this loss must be borne equally by A, B, and C, so the loss for each is $8,000. This means that A is entitled to be reimbursed to the extent of her $20,000 contribution less $8,000, her share of the loss, or net of $12,000. B is entitled to $10,000, less $8,000, or $2,000. Because C has contributed only $4,000, he must now contribute to the firm an additional $4,000, so his loss will equal $8,000. The additional $4,000 contributed by C, plus the $10,000 remaining, will now be distributed so A will receive $12,000 and B $2,000.

Occasionally, articles of partnership specify the manner in which profits are to be divided, but they neglect to mention possible losses. In such cases, the losses are borne in the same proportion that profits are to be shared. In the event that losses occur when one of the partners is insolvent and his or her share of the loss exceeds the amount owed him or her for advances and capital, the excess must be shared by the other partners. They share this unusual loss in the same ratio that they share profits. Thus, in the preceding example, if C were insolvent, A and B would each bear an additional $2,000 loss.

In addition to the right to be repaid for contributions, whether by way of capital or advances to the partnership property, the partnership must indemnify every partner for payments made and personal liabilities reasonably incurred in the ordinary and proper conduct of its business or for the preservation of its business or property.

10. Goodwill Provision

Goodwill, which is usually transferred with the name, is based on the justifiable expectation that a firm's good reputation, satisfied customers, established location, and past advertising will result in continued patronage of old customers and the probable patronage of new customers. Goodwill is usually considered in an evaluation of the assets of the business, and it is capable of being sold and transferred. Upon dissolution caused by the death of one of the partners, the surviving partner must account for the goodwill to the legal representative of the deceased partner, unless otherwise agreed on in the buy-and-sell agreement.

When goodwill and the firm name are sold, an agreement not to compete is usually part of the sales agreement. Such an agreement may be implied but should be a part of the buy-and-sell provision.

11. Buy-and-Sell Provision

Either as part of the partnership agreement or by separate contract, the partners should provide for the contingency of death or withdrawal of a partner. This contingency is covered by a *buy-and-sell agreement,* and it is imperative that the terms of the buy-and-sell provision be agreed on before either party knows whether he or she is a buyer or a seller. After the status of the parties becomes known, agreement is extremely difficult, if not impossible. If such agreement is lacking, many additional problems will arise upon the death or withdrawal of a partner, and there are many possibilities of litigation and economic loss to all concerned.

A buy-and-sell agreement avoids these types of problems by providing a method whereby the surviving partner or partners can purchase the interest of the deceased partner, or the remaining partner or partners can purchase the interest of the withdrawing partner. A method of determining the price to be paid for such interest is provided. The time and method of payment are usually stipulated. The buy-and-sell agreement should specify whether a partner has an option to purchase the interest of a dying or withdrawing partner or whether he or she has a duty to do so.

It is common for partners to provide for life insurance on each other's lives as a means of funding the buy-and-sell provision. In the event of a partner's death, proceeds of the insurance are used to purchase the deceased partner's interest. Premiums on such life insurance are not deductible for tax purposes but are usually treated as an expense for accounting purposes. There are a variety of methods for holding title to the insurance. It may be individually owned or business owned. The provisions of the policy should be carefully integrated into the partnership agreement; each partner's estate plan should also properly consider the ramifications of this insurance and of the buy-and-sell agreement.

THE RIGHTS OF PARTNERS

12. Terminology

Silent partner

A partner who has no voice in the management of the partnership

Secret partner

A partner whose existence is not known to the public

Dormant partner

A partner who is both secret and silent

Before examining the rights, duties, and powers of partners, certain terminology must be understood. A **silent partner** in a general partnership is one who does not participate in management. If the silent partner is to have limited liability, the provisions of the *Revised Uniform Limited Partnership Act* must be followed. So, unless a limited partnership is formed, a silent partner is treated as a general partner. A **secret partner** is unknown to third parties and may advise management and participate in decisions, but his or her interest is not known to third parties. A **dormant partner** is both secret and silent.

These terms are used in this chapter in explaining the role of these types of partners in the operation of their partnership. Other terms defined elsewhere in this chapter are *accounting, charging order, tenancy in partnership, trading partnership,* and *nontrading partnership.*

13. To Participate in Management

All partners have equal rights in the management and conduct of the firm's business. These rights are not necessarily determined by the capital that each partner has invested in the business. The partners may, however, agree to place the management within the control of one or more partners.

The majority of the partners decides ordinary matters arising in the conduct of the partnership business. The right to participate in management, as a partner, does not mean that partners owe each other a duty to agree. If a partner refuses to agree to a demand by another, it is usually not a breach of the fiduciary duties owed by one partner to another.

If the firm consists of only two persons who are unable to agree, and the articles of partnership make no provision for the settlement of disputes, dissolution is the only remedy. Whenever the possibility of a deadlock is present, the partnership agreement should provide for some form of arbitration of deadlocks between partners. Such provisions avoid dissolution and should always be used when there is an even number of partners.

The majority cannot, however, without the consent of the minority, change the essential nature of the business by altering the partnership agreement or by reducing or increasing the capital of the partners. It cannot embark on a new business or admit new members to the firm. In a limited partnership, the agreement cannot be modified without the unanimous consent of all partners.

Certain acts other than those enumerated previously require the unanimous consent of the partners to bind the firm, namely (1) assigning the firm property to a trustee for the benefit of creditors; (2) confessing a judgment; (3) disposing of the goodwill of the business; (4) submitting a partnership agreement to arbitration; and (5) doing any act that would make impossible the conduct of the partnership business.

14. To Be Compensated for Services

It is the duty of each partner, in the absence of an agreement to the contrary, to give his or her entire time, skill, and energy to the pursuit of the partnership affairs. *No partner is entitled to payment for services rendered in the conduct of the partnership business unless an agreement to that effect has been expressed or may be implied from the conduct of the partners.*

An agreement to compensate may be implied from the practice of actually paying a salary. If an agreement or practice contemplates a salary to one or more partners but no amount is specified, it may be presumed that the payment of reasonable compensation is intended. This often occurs when one partner is actually engaged in the business and others are not. Often, one of the partners does not desire to participate in the management of the business. The partnership agreement in such case usually provides that the active partners receive a salary for their services in addition to their share in the profits.

15. To Interest

Contributions to capital are not entitled to draw interest unless they are not repaid when the repayment should be made. The partner's share in the profits constitutes the earnings on his or her capital investment. In the absence of an expressed provision for the payment of interest, it is presumed that interest will be paid only on advances above the amount originally contributed as capital. Advances in excess of the prescribed capital, even though credited to the capital account of the contributing partners, are entitled to draw interest from the date of the advance.

Profits remaining in the firm, in lieu of being withdrawn, are not entitled to draw interest. They are not considered advances or loans merely because they are left with the firm although custom, usage, and circumstances may show an intention to treat them as loans.

16. To Information and to Inspection of Books

All partners are entitled to secure and inspect the books concerning the conduct of the business.

Every partner is entitled to full and complete information concerning the conduct of the business and to inspect the books to secure that information. The partnership agreement usually contains provisions relative to the records that the business will maintain. Each partner is under a duty to give the person responsible for keeping the records whatever information is necessary to carry on the business efficiently and effectively. It is the duty of the person keeping the records to allow each partner access to them, but no partner has a right to remove the records from the agreed-on location without the consent of the other partners. Each partner is entitled to make copies of the records, provided he or she does not make the inspection for fraudulent purposes.

Each partner has implied authority to receive notices and information for all other partners concerning matters within the pursuit of the partnership business. Knowledge held by any partner in his or her mind but not revealed to the other partners is nevertheless notice to the partnership. Knowledge of one partner is legally knowledge of all partners, provided that the facts became known or were knowledge obtained within the scope of the partnership business. A partner has a duty to communicate known facts to the other partners and to add them to the records of the partnership. Failure to do so is fraud on the partnership by the partner possessing the knowledge. This failure to inform is also a breach of the duty to assist in the maintenance of accurate records.

Accounting
The financial condition of an organization at a specific point in time

17. To an Accounting

The partners' proportionate share of the partnership assets or profits, when not determined by a voluntary settlement of the parties, may be ascertained in a suit for an **accounting**. Such suits are equitable in nature; and in states that still distinguish between suits at law and suits in equity, these actions must be filed in the court of equity.

As a general rule, a partner cannot maintain an *action at law* against other members of the firm on the partnership agreement because until there is an accounting and all partnership affairs are settled, the indebtedness among the firm members is undetermined. This general rule is subject to a few common sense exceptions. For example, if the partnership is formed for the carrying out of a single venture or transaction, or the action involves a segregated or single unadjusted item of account, or a personal covenant or transaction entirely independent of the partnership affairs, a suit at law may be filed. Since the affairs of a partnership usually involve multiple and complicated transactions, the requirement of an accounting before a suit for damages is usually applied.

Because partners ordinarily have equal access to the partnership records, there is usually no need for formal accountings to determine partnership interests. A suit for an accounting is not permitted for settling incidental matters or disputes between the partners. If a dispute is of such grievous nature that the continued existence of the partnership is impossible, a suit for an accounting in equity is allowed.

In all cases, a partner is entitled to an accounting upon the dissolution of the firm. Without dissolution of the firm, a partner has a right to a formal accounting in the following situations:

1. There is an agreement for an accounting at a definite date.
2. One partner has withheld profits arising from secret transactions.
3. There has been an execution levied against the interest of one of the partners.
4. One partner does not have access to the books.
5. The partnership is approaching insolvency, and all parties are not available.

Upon an agreement between themselves, the partners may make a complete accounting and settle their claims without resort to a court of equity.

18. To Partnership Property and Interest in the Partnership

It is critical to distinguish a partner's rights associated with partnership property and the interest the partner has in the partnership. As to the former, a partner is a co-owner with his or her partners of *partnership property*. Subject to any agreement among partners, a partner has an equal right among partners to possess partnership property for partnership purposes. He or she has no right to possess partnership property for other purposes without the consent of the partners. (This interest is often termed a *tenancy in partnership*, a term further defined within Section 22, below.)

Partnership property must be used in the pursuit of the partnership business and to pay firm creditors. Since a *partner does not own any specific item of the partnership property*, he or she has no right in specific partnership property that is transferable. A partner has no right to use the firm property in satisfaction of personal debts; conversely, his or her personal creditors cannot make a levy on specific partnership property.

When a partner dies, his or her interest in specific partnership property passes to the surviving partner or partners, who have the duty of winding up the affairs of the partnership in accordance with the partnership agreement and the applicable laws. Note the nature of this type of property: the business is favored over heirs. That is, if A, B, and C are partners and each share equally, and if A dies, the interest in specific partnership property is split between the remaining partners, B and C. In this scenario, the heirs of A have no claim to specific partnership property.

A partner's *interest in the firm* consists of his or her rights to share in the profits that are earned and, after dissolution and liquidation, to the return of his or her capital and undistributed profits. This assumes, of course, that the partner's capital has not been absorbed or impaired by losses.

When the winding-up process is complete, the estate of the deceased partner will be paid whatever sum to which the estate is entitled, according to law and the partnership agreement, based on the value of the partner's interest in the partnership. The surviving partner may sell the property, real and personal, of the partnership in connection with winding up the business to obtain the cash to pay the estate of the deceased partner.

A partner may assign his or her interest, or right to share, in the profits of the partnership. Such an assignment will not of itself work dissolution of the firm. The assignee is not entitled to participate in the management of the business. The only right of the assignee is to receive the profits to which the assignor would otherwise have been entitled and, in the event of dissolution, to receive his or her assignor's interest.

Charging order
An order by a court that a creditor is entitled to receive a debtor-partner's interest in a partnership as a means of satisfying an obligation owed to the creditor

A partner's interest in the partnership cannot be levied on by his or her separate creditors and sold at public sale. A judgment creditor of a partner must proceed by obtaining a **charging order** from the court. This order charges the interest of the debtor partner with the unsatisfied amount of the judgment debt. The court will ordinarily appoint a receiver, who will receive the partner's share of the profits and any other money due or to fall due to him or her in respect of the partnership and apply that money upon the judgment. Likewise, the court may order that the interest charged be sold. Such a sale is not a sale of the partnership assets or property. Neither the charging order nor the sale of the interest will cause dissolution of the firm unless the partnership is one that is terminable at will.

If there is more than one judgment creditor seeking a charging order, the first one to seek it is usually paid in full before others are paid anything. There is no pro rata distribution unless the partnership is dissolved.

TABLE 28-1 ■ Types of Money Damages

Type	Definition	Ability to use as collateral for a personal loan	Ability to transfer to another during partner's life	Status upon death of partner
Partnership property	Ownership with other partner's specific property of the partnership	No	No	Under the theory of tenancy in partnership, the deceased partner's portion of partnership property is transferred to remaining partners.
Interest in the partnership	(1) Right to receive profits (2) Right to receive distributions upon end of business	Yes	Yes	Transferred to heirs of the deceased partner

DUTIES AND POWERS OF PARTNERS

19. Duties

A partnership is a *fiduciary relationship*. Perhaps the most famous judicial expression of fiduciary duties is Justice Cardozo's lines from *Meinhard v. Salmon,* a 1928 case from New York.

> Joint adventurers, like copartners, owe to one another, while the enterprise continues, the duty of the finest loyalty. Many forms of conduct permissible in a workaday world for those acting at arm's length are forbidden to those bound by fiduciary ties. A trustee is held to something stricter than the morals of the market place. Not honesty alone, but the punctilio of an honor the most sensitive, is then the standard of behavior. As to this there has developed a tradition that is unbending and inveterate. Uncompromising rigidity has been the attitude of courts of equity when petitioned to undermine the rule of undivided loyalty by the "disintegrating erosion" of particular exceptions (citation omitted). Only thus has the level of conduct for fiduciaries been kept at a level higher than that trodden by the crowd.

As a fiduciary, *each partner owes the duty of undivided loyalty to the other.* Therefore, every partner must account to the partnership for any benefit and hold as a trustee for benefit of the partnership's any profits gained by him or her without consent of the other partners. This duty also rests on representatives of deceased partners engaged in the liquidation of the affairs of the partnership.

The partnership relation is a personal one, obligating each partner to exercise good faith and to consider the mutual welfare of all the partners in the conduct of the business. If one partner attempts to secure an advantage over the others, he or she thereby breaches the partnership relation and must account for all benefits that he or she obtains. This includes transactions with partners and with others. It also includes transactions connected with winding up the business. The duty continues, even though the partnership is dissolved, if the partnership opportunity arose prior to dissolution.

20. Power to Contract

A partner is an agent of the partnership for the purpose of its business, and the general rules of agency are applicable to all partnerships. *Each partner has authority to bind the partnership with contractual liability whenever he or she is apparently carrying on the business of the partnership in the usual way.* If it is apparent that a partner is not carrying on business of the partnership in the usual way, his or her act does not bind the partnership unless it is authorized by the other partners.

The rules of agency relating to authority, ratification, and secret limitations on the authority of a partner are applicable to partnerships; however, the extent of implied authority is generally greater for partners than for ordinary agents. Each partner has implied power to do all acts necessary for carrying on the business of the partnership. Admissions or representations pertaining to the conduct of the partnership business and made by a partner may be used as evidence against the partnership.

The nature and scope of the business and what is usual in the particular business determine the extent of the implied powers. Among the common implied powers are the following: to compromise, adjust, and settle claims or debts owed by or to the partnership; to sell goods in the regular course of business and to make warranties; to buy property within the scope of the business for cash or on credit; to buy insurance; to hire employees; to make admissions against interest; to enter into contracts within the scope of the firm; and to receive notices. In a trading partnership, a partner has the implied authority to borrow funds and to pledge the assets of the firm. Some of these implied powers are discussed more fully in the following sections.

21. Power to Impose Tort Liability

A partner has the power to impose tort liability on the partnership through the doctrine of respondeat superior. Because a partnership is the principal of all the partners acting as agents, the law imposes tort liability on a partnership for all wrongful acts or omissions of any partner acting in the ordinary course of the partnership and for its benefit. *In addition to the partnership's liability, each partner is liable for the torts of fellow partners.* This result occurs because partners are jointly and severally liable for the partnership's liability and because each partner, in essence, is a principal with respect to the fellow partners acting as agents.

If a partnership or partner has liability because of a tort of a partner, the firm may have the right to collect its losses from the partner at fault. In effect, a partnership or partner that is liable in tort to a third person has a right of indemnity against the partner at fault. Likewise, if the injured third party collects directly from the partner at fault, the partner cannot seek contribution from his or her copartners.

When a partner is negligent within the course of business, the partnership is not entitled to indemnity from the negligent partner, as illustrated in the following case.

CASE

Martin Moren, as Parent and Guardian of Remington Moren, a Minor v. Jax Restaurant, John Doe, et al. and Jax Restaurant

COURT OF APPEALS OF MINNESOTA

679 N.W.2d 165 (2004)

CRIPPEN, JUDGE

Jax Restaurant, the partnership, operates its business in Foley, Minnesota. One afternoon in October 2000, Nicole Moren, one of the Jax partners, completed her day shift at Jax at 4:00 p.m. and left to pick up her two-year-old son Remington from day care. At about 5:30, Moren returned to the restaurant with Remington after learning that her sister and partner, Amy Benedetti, needed help. Moren called her husband who told her that he would pick Remington up in about 20 minutes.

Because Nicole Moren did not want Remington running around the restaurant, she brought him into the kitchen with her, set him on top of the counter, and began rolling out pizza dough using the dough-pressing machine. As she was making pizzas, Remington reached his hand into the dough press. His hand was crushed, and he sustained permanent injuries.

Through his father, Remington commenced a negligence action against the partnership. The partnership served a third-party complaint on Nicole Moren, arguing that, in the event it was obligated to compensate Remington, the partnership was entitled to indemnity or contribution from Moren for her negligence. The district court's summary judgment was premised on a legal conclusion that Moren has no obligation to indemnify Jax Restaurant so long as the injury occurred while she was engaged in ordinary business conduct. The district court rejected the partnership's argument that its obligation to compensate Remington is diminished in proportion to the predominating negligence of Moren as a mother—although it is responsible for her conduct as a business owner. This appeal followed.

Under Minnesota's *Uniform Partnership Act of 1994* (UPA), a partnership is an entity distinct from its partners, and as such, a partnership may sue and be sued in the name of the partnership. "A partnership is liable for loss or injury caused to a person ... as a result of a wrongful act or omission, or other actionable conduct, of a partner acting in the ordinary course of business of the partnership or with authority of the partnership." Accordingly, a "partnership shall ... indemnify a partner for liabilities incurred by the partner in the ordinary course of the business of the partnership. ..." Stated conversely, an "act of a partner which is not apparently for carrying on in the ordinary course the partnership business or business of the kind carried on by the partnership binds the partnership only if the act was authorized by the other partners." Thus, under the plain language of the UPA, a partner has a right to indemnity from the partnership, but the partnership's claim of indemnity from a partner is not authorized or required.

The district court correctly concluded that Nicole Moren's conduct was in the ordinary course of business of the partnership; and, as a result, indemnity by the partner to the partnership was inappropriate. It is undisputed that one of the cooks scheduled to work that evening did not come in and that Moren's partner asked her to help in the kitchen. It also is undisputed that Moren was making pizzas for the partnership when her son was injured. Because her conduct at the time of the injury was in the ordinary course of business of the partnership under the UPA, her conduct bound the partnership and it owes indemnity to her for her negligence.

Because Minnesota law requires a partnership to indemnify its partners for the result of their negligence, the district court properly granted summary judgment to respondent Nicole Moren. In addition, we conclude that the conduct of a partner may be partly motivated by personal reasons and still occur in the ordinary course of business of the partnership.

■ *Affirmed.*

CASE CONCEPTS REVIEW

1. Why did the partnership owe to indemnity to the negligent partner?
2. Is this a fair result to other partners? To the negligent partner? To the injured plaintiff? Why or why not?

22. Powers over Property

Each partner has implied authority to sell to good-faith purchasers personal property that is held for the purpose of resale and to execute any documents necessary to effect a transfer of title. Of course, if the partner's authority in this connection has been limited, and that is known to the purchaser, the transfer of title will be ineffective or voidable. A partner has no power to sell the fixtures and equipment used in the business unless he or she has been duly authorized. This partner's acts are not a regular feature of the business; and a prospective purchaser should make certain that the particular partner has been given authority to sell. The power to sell, where it is present, also gives the power to make warranties that normally accompany similar sales.

The right to sell a firm's real property is to be inferred only if the firm is engaged in the real estate business. In other cases, there is no right to sell and convey realty unless it has been authorized by a partnership agreement. In most states, a deed by one partner without authority is not binding on the firm, but it does convey the individual interest of the parties executing and delivering the deed. This conveyance, however, is subject to the rights of creditors of the partnership.

Under the RUPA, title to real property may be taken in the firm name as a *tenancy in partnership,* and any member of the firm has the power to execute a deed thereto by signing the firm name. If that happens, what is the effect of a wrongful transfer of real estate that has been acquired for use in the business and not for resale? The conveyance may be set aside by the other partners because the purchaser should have known that one partner has no power to sell real estate without the approval of the others. However, if the first purchaser has resold and conveyed the property to an innocent third party, the latter takes good title.

If the title to real estate is held in the firm name, a conveyance by the partners as individuals is not effective to convey title to the real estate. The conveyance must be in the firm name. This is true even if the conveyance is to a partner as part of a settlement agreement between the partners.

If the title to firm property is not held in the firm name but, rather, is held in the names of one or more of the partners, a conveyance by those in whose names the title is held passes good title, unless the purchaser knows or should know that title was held for the firm. There is nothing in the record title in such a situation to call the buyer's attention to the fact that the firm has an interest in the property.

23. Financial Powers

To determine the limit of a partner's financial powers, partnerships are divided into two general classes—trading and nontrading partnerships. A *trading partnership* is one that has for its primary purpose the buying and selling of merchandise. In such a trading firm, each partner has an implied power to borrow money and to extend the credit of the firm, in the usual course of business, by signing negotiable paper.

A *nontrading partnership* is one that does not buy and sell commodities but has for its primary purpose the production of commodities or is organized for the purpose of selling services—for example, professional partnerships in law, medicine, or accounting. In such partnerships, a partner's powers are more limited, and a partner does not have implied power to borrow money. However, if the partner's act is within the scope of partnership business, a member of a nontrading partnership may bind the firm by the exercise of implied authority, just as a partner in trading partnership may.

The power to mortgage or pledge a firm's property is primarily dependent on the power to borrow money and bind the firm. A partner with authority to borrow may, as an incident to that power, give the security normally demanded for similar loans. Because no single partner without the consent of the others has the power to commit an act that will destroy or terminate the business, the power to give a mortgage on the entire stock of merchandise and fixtures of a business is usually denied. Such a mortgage would make it possible, upon default, to liquidate the firm's assets and thus destroy its business. Subject to this limitation, the power to borrow carries the power to pledge or mortgage.

METHODS OF DISSOLUTION

24. Terminology

Three steps are necessary to end a partnership: dissolution, winding up, and termination. **Dissolution**, the legal destruction of the partnership relation, occurs whenever any partner ceases to be a member of the firm or whenever a new partner is admitted. It is the change in the relation of the partners caused by any partner's ceasing to be associated in carrying on—as distinguished from winding up—the business. Dissolution alone does not terminate the partnership, but it designates the time when partners cease to carry on business together.

Dissolution
Occurs any time there is a change in the partners, either by adding a new partner or by having a preexisting partner die, retire, or otherwise leave

Winding up involves the process of reducing the assets to cash, paying off the creditors, and distributing the balance to the partners. A winding up may be partial or complete. A partial winding up becomes necessary when a partnership lacks sufficient cash and borrowing power to pay its debts, such as those owed to one or more partners who have caused a dissolution by withdrawing from the partnership.

Winding up
The process of liquidating a business organization

When a partnership engages in a total winding up, the completion of this process is called the **termination** of the partnership as an organization and as a viable business. Prior to the actual moment of termination, the partnership still has an existence and is able to function.

Termination
Occurs when the winding up or liquidation is completed and is the end of the organization and its business

25. By Acts of Partners

Dissolutions will occur without violation of the partnership agreement (1) at the end of the stipulated term or particular undertaking specified in the agreement, (2) by the express will of any partner when no definite term or particular undertaking is specified, (3) by the agreement of all the partners, or (4) by the expulsion—in good faith—of any partner from the business, in accordance with power conferred by the partnership agreement. Dissolution also may occur even though such action by a partner is a breach of the partnership agreement.

When parties agree to be partners for a specific time period or for a stated purpose, the conclusion of the period or the accomplishment of the purpose marks the dissolution of the partnership. More frequently, however, partners enter into agreement that does not have a stated duration. When a definite term of duration is not stated, a *partnership at will* exists.

In a partnership at will, any partner may, without liability, legally dissolve it at any time. Dissolution may be accomplished by giving notice to the other parties. No particular form of notice is required; it will be implied from circumstances inconsistent with the continuation of the partnership. When a partner whose services are essential leaves the organization, his or her departure is an act and notice of dissolution.

Even when the partnership agreement specifies a duration period, partners may mutually agree to dissolve their relationship. Since a partnership, in its essential form, is a contract, the partners to the contract may mutually agree to a shorter period for the life of the partnership.

Expulsion in good faith is a method of dissolution limited to the terms of the partnership agreement. Expulsion of a partner is a breach of the partnership agreement unless the agreement confers the power of the expulsion on a majority of the partners. Assume that A, B, and C are partners. Partners A and B cannot expel C unless that power is specifically granted in the agreement. Without the power to expel, partners may seek judicial dissolution if one partner is guilty of violating the partnership agreement (see Section 4). If C was not devoting his time to the business, as he was required to do in the partnership agreement, A and B could seek a dissolution on these grounds although they could not expel C.

Dissolution may also occur in violation of the partnership agreement. Although the agreement stipulates the length of time the partnership is to last, dissolution is always possible because the relationship is a personal one that courts are hesitant to enforce. Like most agency relationships, each partner has the *power,* though not the *right,* to revoke the relationship. In the event of wrongful dissolution, the wrongdoer is liable for the damages.

However, subject to a few exceptions, a breach of a partnership agreement does not mean that the breaching partner loses his or her interest in the partnership. The law does not favor such forfeitures. Nevertheless, where the partnership agreement provides for the forfeiture of the breaching partner's interest in the firm property, such a provision will be enforced.

Breaches of the partnership agreement, whether or not committed in bad faith, do not cause a partner to lose his or her rights to share in the profits; but a partner who refuses to contribute funds essential to the operation of a partnership business may be excluded from participation in any profit. Additionally, if one of the partners abandons the business, that partner may forfeit some or all of his or her share of the profits as damages.

26. By Operation of Law

If, during the period of the partnership, events make it impossible or illegal for the partnership to continue, it will be dissolved by operation of law. Such events or conditions are the death or bankruptcy of one of the partners or a change in the law that makes the continuance of the business illegal. Of course, a partnership may also be illegal at its inception. In such a case, the courts will leave the partners where it finds them and will not grant relief to a partner in a suit against the other partner or partners.

Since a partnership is a personal relationship existing by reason of contract, when one of the partners dies, the partnership is dissolved. It is not terminated on dissolution, but it continues for the purpose of winding up the partnership's affairs. The process of winding up is, in most states, the exclusive obligation and right of the surviving partner or partners. The executor or administrator of the deceased partner has no right to participate in, or interfere with, the winding-up processes unless, of course, the deceased was the last surviving partner. The only right of the personal representative of a deceased partner is to demand an accounting upon completion of the winding up of the partnership's affairs. As a general rule, the estate of the deceased partner is not bound on contracts entered into by the surviving partners if the contracts are unconnected with the winding up of the affairs of the partnership. This is discussed more fully later in this chapter.

The bankruptcy of a partner will dissolve the partnership because the control of that partner's property passes to the trustee in bankruptcy for the benefit of the creditors. The mere insolvency of a partner will not be sufficient to justify dissolution. The bankruptcy of the firm itself is a cause for dissolution, as is a valid assignment of all the firm's assets for the benefit of creditors.

27. By Court Decree

When a partnership by its agreement is to be continued for a term of years, circumstances sometimes make continued existence of the firm impossible and unprofitable. Upon application of one of the partners to a court of equity, the partnership may be dissolved. Under the following circumstances and situations, a court of equity may order dissolution:

1. Total incapacity of a partner to conduct business and to perform the duties required under the contract of partnership
2. A declaration by judicial process that a partner is insane
3. Willful and persistent commitment of a breach of the partnership agreement, misappropriation of funds, or commitment of fraudulent acts
4. An innocent party's application for dissolution because the partnership was entered into as a result of fraud
5. Gross misconduct and neglect or breach of duty by a partner to such an extent that it is impossible to carry out the purposes of the partnership agreement
6. In some states, any grounds that make dissolution equitable or in the best interests of the partners

Courts will not interfere and grant a decree of dissolution for mere discourtesy, temporary inconvenience, minor differences of opinion, or errors in judgment. The misconduct must be of such gross nature that the continued operation of the business would be unprofitable. In those states that have incorporated item 6 of the preceding list into their law, courts of equity will order dissolution if there is serious disharmony among the partners.

In cases arising out of the dissolution of a partnership, a court of equity may appoint a receiver to liquidate the partnership, obtain an accounting of the proceeds, and distribute the assets. A receiver may be appointed when the evidence indicates that it is necessary to preserve the property and to protect the rights of the parties. For example, a receiver may be appointed where the remaining parties are delaying the winding-up process or are breaching any of the fiduciary duties of partners.

THE EFFECT OF DISSOLUTION

28. On Powers of Partners

The process of winding up, except when the agreement provides for continuation by purchase of former partners' shares, involves liquidation of the partnership assets so cash may be available to pay creditors and to make a distribution to the partners. When the agreement provides for continuation and purchase of a deceased partner's interest, the technical dissolution is followed by valuation and payment, and the new firm immediately commences business.

As a general rule, dissolution terminates the actual authority of any partner to act for the partnership except when such authority is necessary to wind up partnership affairs, to liquidate the assets of the firm in an orderly manner, or to complete transactions begun but not finished. Insofar as third persons who had dealings with the firm are concerned, apparent authority still exists until notice of termination is given.

This apparent authority means that one partner of a dissolved partnership binds the firm on contracts unconnected with winding up the firm's affairs. When a partner enters such contracts, issues arise as to whether or not the new obligations may be met with partnership funds or whether the contracting partner is entitled to contribution toward payment of the debt or obligation from the other partners.

The resolution of these issues depends on the cause of the dissolution. If the dissolution is caused by (1) the act of a partner, (2) bankruptcy of the partnership, or (3) the death of a partner, each partner is liable for his or her share of any liability incurred on behalf of the firm after dissolution, just as if there had been no dissolution, unless the partner incurring the liability had knowledge of the dissolution. Of course, such knowledge is usually present. In these situations, if knowledge of the dissolution is present, the partner incurring the liability is solely responsible and cannot require the other partners to share the burden of an unauthorized act. If the dissolution is not caused by the act, bankruptcy, or death of a partner but by some event such as a court decree, no partner has authority to act and therefore has no right to contribution from other partners for liabilities incurred after dissolution.

When dissolution results from the death of a partner, title to partnership property remains in the surviving partner or partners for purposes of winding up and liquidation. Thus, both real and personal property are, through the survivors, made available to a firm's creditors. All realty is treated as though it were personal property. It is sold, and the surviving partners finally account, usually in cash, to the personal representative of the deceased partner for the latter's share in the proceeds of liquidation.

29. On Rights of Partners

Upon dissolution, a withdrawing partner who has not breached the partnership agreement has certain options with regard to his or her interest in the dissolved partnership. This partner may require the partnership to be wound up and terminated. The partnership will be liquidated and the assets distributed among the partners. The alternative is to allow the business to continue, or accept that it has continued.

If the withdrawing partner allows the business to continue, the value of his or her interest in the partnership as of the date of dissolution is ascertained. The withdrawing partner then has the right to receive, at his or her option after an accounting, either the value of this interest in the partnership with interest or, in lieu of interest, the profits attributable to the use of his or her rights in the property of the dissolved partnership. The portion of profits to which a withdrawing partner is entitled because of the use of property will usually be less than his or her portion prior to dissolution. This is true because a portion of the profit is usually attributable to services of the continuing partners, and most courts allow for compensation to be paid to the continuing partners.

When dissolution is caused in any way other than breach of the partnership agreement, each partner has a right to insist that all the partnership assets be used first to pay firm debts. After firm obligations are paid, remaining assets are used to return capital contributions and then to provide for a distribution of profits. All the partners except those who have caused a wrongful dissolution of the firm have the right to participate in the winding up of the business.

The majority selects the method and procedures to be followed in the liquidation. The assets are turned into cash unless all agree to distribute them in kind.

If a partnership that is to continue for a fixed period is dissolved by the wrongful withdrawal of one partner, the remaining members may continue as partners under the same firm name for the balance of the agreed term of the partnership. They are required to settle with the withdrawing partner for his or her interest in the partnership and to compensate that partner, but the remaining partners are allowed to subtract from the amount due in cash the damages caused by the withdrawing partner's wrongful withdrawal. In the calculation of that partner's share, the goodwill of the business is not taken into consideration. The fact that a partner breached the agreement does not take away that partner's right to an accounting and to receive his or her share of the partnership after deducting any damages caused by the breach of the agreement.

Upon dissolution, it is the duty of the remaining partner or partners to wind up the affairs. If they fail to do so and instead continue the business, they have liability to the withdrawing partner or his or her assignee or personal representative for use of partnership assets. The liability may include interest, if the value of the former partner's portion of the partnership can be ascertained, or it may include liability for a share of post-dissolution profits. This liability arises because the business is continuing to use the assets of all the former partners, and the continuing partners have failed to wind up the business and terminate it.

Is a partner entitled to be paid for services rendered during the winding-up process? If the dissolution is caused by the death of a partner, the answer is yes. This exception to the general rule that partners are not compensated for their services rendered to the partnership makes sense because the deceased partner obviously is unavailable to assist the surviving partners.

If the dissolution is caused by any act or occurrence other than a partner's death, the general rule of no compensation for the partners still applies. It is presumed, unless the partners agree otherwise, that all partners are contributing to the winding-up process. The partnership's income during the winding up is allocated to former and continuing partners in accordance with their shares stated in the partnership agreement.

It is often difficult to value accurately the interest of a withdrawing or deceased partner when the business continues. The buy-and-sell provisions will control the method for establishing the value of the interest as of the date of dissolution. If there are no buy-and-sell provisions and the parties cannot agree, a judicial decision on the value may be required. This decision may sometimes involve which of the parties is to continue the business, as well as the amount to be paid the withdrawing partner; but it cannot be made with mathematical certainty.

30. On New Partners

A person admitted as a new partner into an existing partnership is liable only to the extent of his or her capital contribution for all obligations incurred before admission. This new partner is not personally liable for such obligations, and the creditors of the old firm can look only to the firm's assets and to the partners of the old firm. With respect to obligations that arise after the new partner joins the partnership, the liability is personal and unlimited as though he or she has been a partner.

Prior debts sometimes become new debts (for example, upon the renewal of a note). In the following case, if the note had not been renewed, the liability of the new partner would have been limited to $100,000—his capital contribution. As a result of the renewal, the liability was over $300,000, even though the new partner was not involved in the renewal of the note. This case demonstrates the risk of unlimited liability in a partnership.

CASE

Moseley v. Commercial State Bank

SUPREME COURT OF ALABAMA

457 So.2d 967 (1984)

FAULKNER, J

Commercial State Bank of Donaldsonville, Georgia, brought this action against Southern Distilleries, a partnership, and against the partners of Southern Distilleries for money due on several promissory notes executed by Southern Distilleries. One of the partners, Julius Moseley, appeals from a judgment against him for $303,241.52.

On September 17, 1980, five individuals formed a partnership named Southern Distilleries in order to engage in the business of producing fuel grade alcohol (gasahol). The partners signed an agreement providing that any three partners having an aggregate interest in the partnership of at least 60% were authorized to borrow money and execute promissory notes on behalf of the partnership.

On December 19, 1980, three partners, Adams, Fitch and Moulthrop, executed two promissory notes on behalf of Southern Distilleries to Commercial State Bank. Both notes came due on March 19, 1981. Southern Distilleries failed to satisfy either note when they came due.

On April 2,1981, an amended partnership agreement was executed by the five original partners and by three other individuals, including the appellant, Moseley. The purpose of the amendment was to "change the percentage interests of the partners and to admit new partners." The document indicates that Moseley contributed $100,000.00 to the capital account of the partnership and acquired a "profit and loss interest in the partnership" slightly in excess of 6%. The amended agreement provides that the provisions of the prior agreement were to remain in full force and effect.

On July 21, 1981, Southern Distilleries paid the interest due on the outstanding notes and Adams, Fitch, and Moulthrop executed a new note on behalf of Southern Distilleries to the bank. The bank marked the notes dated December 19 "paid" and returned them to Southern Distilleries.

Southern Distilleries failed to satisfy the July 21 note when it matured, and the bank brought this action to enforce payment. In support of his contention that the trial court improperly granted the bank's motion for a summary judgment, Moseley argues: that Moseley is not personally liable for the debt because it pre-existed his becoming a partner in Southern Distilleries.

Clearly, Adams, Fitch, and Moulthrop bound the partners of Southern Distilleries by executing a note on its behalf to the bank. Execution of an instrument in the partnership's name for the purpose of carrying on the usual business of the partnership binds the partners, unless the partner executing the instrument has no authority to act and the person with whom he is dealing has knowledge that he has no authority to act. A person admitted as a partner into an existing partnership is liable for partnership obligations arising before his admission into the partnership. His liability for pre-existing obligations can be satisfied only out of partnership property, however. The bank's judgment is against Moseley personally. The dispositive issue of this case, therefore, is whether the obligation sued on arose before Moseley's admission into the partnership. In support of Moseley's contention that the debt pre-existed his admission into the partnership, Moseley argues that the new note was merely a renewal of a pre-existing obligation.

There is no dispute in this case as to the material facts. Moseley entered into a general partnership agreement with other individuals doing business under the name Southern Distilleries. The partners who executed the note sued on were expressly authorized to bind the other partners. Although the defendant chooses to categorize the debt created by the note sued on as the renewal of a pre-existing debt, it is clear that the obligation created by the old note terminated when the bank accepted the new note. Prior to the execution of the new note the bank could have brought an action to collect the debt. After it accepted the new note and satisfied the old one, there was no obligation which was due and payable to the bank until the new note matured. In agreeing to the forbearance of its rights to collect the money owed it by Southern Distilleries, the bank relied on the representations of the partnership agreement that the new note would bind the partners, including Moseley. Since the contract sued on was entered into by a partnership which included Moseley, and since there was valid consideration for the contract sued on, the plaintiff is entitled to enforce the contract against the defendant.

We understand that Moseley had no knowledge of the day-to-day operations of the partnership and that he did not find out about the note until the bank brought this action. While Moseley apparently considered his interest in the firm to be that of merely an investor, he signed an agreement granting him all the rights of a general partner in the firm and authorizing the other partners to obligate him as a general partner, which they did. The parties are competent business men dealing at arm's length, who presumably have ample access to counsel. If Moseley had wished to limit his exposure to liability he should have taken steps to do so when he chose to become involved in the enterprise.

■ *Affirmed.*

CASE CONCEPTS REVIEW

1. When did Southern Distilleries originally borrow money from the Commercial State Bank?
2. When did Moseley become a partner in Southern Distilleries? What was the amount of his capital contribution?
3. When did Southern Distilleries "pay off the original loan" and obtain a new loan with Commercial State Bank?
4. What was the extent of Moseley's increased liability as a result of the new loans being obtained?

31. On Third Parties

Dissolution of a partnership terminates the authority of the partners to create liability, but it does not discharge any existing liability of any partner. An agreement between the partners themselves that one or more of the partners will assume the partnership liabilities and that a withdrawing partner will not have any liability does not bind the firm's creditors.

If a business is continued without liquidation of the partnership affairs, creditors of the first, or dissolved, partnership are also creditors of the partnership continuing the business. Likewise, if the partners assign all their interest to a former partner or a third person who continues the business without liquidation of the partnership affairs, creditors of the dissolved partnership are also creditors of the person continuing the business.

If a partner wishes to be discharged from an existing liability, he or she must get the creditor and the continuing partners to agree to this discharge. Such an arrangement in essence is a *novation.* This three-party agreement is discussed in detail in Chapter 20.

After dissolution, two categories of parties are entitled to notice of the dissolution. First, the firm's creditors, including all former creditors, are entitled to actual notice of the dissolution. Notice of the dissolution is required, whether the dissolution is caused by an act of the parties or by operation of law, unless a partner becomes bankrupt or the continuation of the business becomes illegal. Therefore, upon death of a partner, the personal representative should give immediate notice of the death and dissolution to avoid further liability.

Transactions entered into after dissolution without such notice continue to bind withdrawing partners and the estate of deceased partners. If proper notice is given, former partners are not liable for contracts unconnected with winding up the partnership's affairs. Notice eliminates the apparent authority to bind the former firm and its partners. Failure to give notice and the continuation of apparent authority in effect creates a partnership by estoppel. As between the partners, the original partnership is dissolved; but as to third parties, a partner carrying on the business of the former partnership binds the partners if notice of dissolution is not given properly.

The second category of parties entitled to notice of dissolution consists of persons who knew about the partnership but who were not creditors. Unlike creditors, who are entitled to actual notice of dissolution, these third parties receive sufficient notice to absolve the partners of further liability when such notice is of a public nature. Notice by publication in a newspaper in the community where the business has been transacted is sufficient public notice. Because the bankruptcy of a partner, the illegality of the partnership's activities, and court decrees are part of the public record, the requirement to give public notice to non-creditors applies only when the partnership is dissolved by the acts of the partners.

Assume a partner has not actively engaged in the conduct of the partnership business. If the third parties have not learned that he or she was a partner and have dealt with the partnership without placing their faith in this partner, there is no duty to give notice to either of the groups (creditors/non-creditors) on his or her withdrawal.

Distributions on Termination

32. Solvent Partnerships

Upon dissolution of a solvent partnership and winding up of its business, an accounting is made to determine its assets and liabilities. At termination, all firm creditors other than partners are entitled to be paid before the partners are entitled to participate in any of the assets. After firm creditors are paid, the assets of the partnership are distributed among the partners as follows:

1. Each partner who has made advances to the firm or has incurred liability for or on behalf of the firm is entitled to be reimbursed.
2. Each partner is then entitled to the return of the capital that he or she has contributed to the firm.
3. Any balance is distributed as profits in accordance with the partnership agreement.

In many partnerships, one partner contributes capital and the other contributes labor; and so the partner contributing labor has nothing to be returned in step 2. Of course, the original agreement could place a value on such labor; but unless it does, only the partner who contributes cash or other property will be repaid in step 2.

In the absence of agreement to the contrary, goodwill is a partnership asset that should be accounted for on termination of a partnership. Goodwill is usually defined as "the advantage or benefit, which is acquired by an establishment, beyond the mere value of the capital, stock, funds, or property employed therein, in consequence of the general public patronage and encouragement, which it receives from constant or habitual customers, on account of its local position, or common celebrity, or reputation for skill or affluence, or punctuality, or from other accidental circumstances or necessities, or even from ancient partialities or prejudices." A much narrower definition has been stated as the probability that the old customers will resort to the old place.

Most partnerships build goodwill as an asset. Difficult ethical questions arise, however, in professional partnerships. Traditionally, the prevailing rule relative to professional partnerships was that goodwill did not exist at dissolution, as the reputation of the business entity was dependent on the individual skills of each member.

There appears, however, to be a growing trend throughout the country that recognizes that a professional service partnership possesses goodwill. An ever-increasing number of jurisdictions have held that goodwill may lawfully exist in a professional partnership and that the actual existence of this asset in a particular partnership is a question of fact. The rationale for many of these cases is that the reputation for skill and learning in a particular profession often creates an intangible but valuable asset by gaining the confidence of clients who will speak well of the practice.

If one partner appropriates the goodwill or retains it for his or her own use, he or she must account for it to the other partner unless the other partner is in breach of the agreement.

33. Insolvent Partnerships

When the firm is insolvent and a court of equity is responsible for making the distribution of the assets of the partnership, the assets are distributed in accordance with a rule known as **marshaling of assets**. Persons entering into a partnership agreement implicitly agree that the partnership assets will be used for the payment of the firm debts before the payment of any individual debts of the partners. Consequently, a court of equity, in distributing the assets, will give them to the firm's creditors before awarding them to separate creditors or individual partners. The court will give separate assets of the partners to their private creditors before awarding these assets to the firm's creditors. Neither class of creditors is permitted to use the funds belonging to the other until the claims of the other have been satisfied.

Marshaling of assets

A principle in equity for a fair distribution of a debtor's assets among creditors

The firm's creditors have available two funds out of which to seek payment: assets of the firm and the individual assets of the partners. Individual creditors of the partners have only one fund: the personal assets of the partners. Because of this difference, equity compels the firm's creditors to exhaust the firm's assets before having recourse to the partners' individual assets.

The doctrine of marshaling of assets does not apply if a partner conceals his or her existence and permits the other members of the firm to deal with the public as the owners of the business. Under these circumstances, the secret partner's conduct has led the creditors of the active partner to rely on the firm's assets as the separate property of the active partner; and by reason of his or her conduct, the secret partner is estopped from demanding an application of the equity rule that the firm's assets shall be used to pay the firm's creditors first and individual assets used to pay individual creditors. Thus, the firm's assets must be shared equally with its creditors and the individual creditors of the active partner. In such a case, because the firm's assets may not be sufficient to pay all its debts when depleted by payments to individual creditors, there may be unpaid firm creditors; and secret partners will be personally liable.

Just as the individual creditors are limited to individual assets, firm creditors are limited to firm assets. Therefore, firm creditors are not entitled to payment out of the individual assets of the partners until the individual creditors have been paid. This rule applies even though the firm creditors may at the same time be individual creditors of a member of the firm. There are two main exceptions to this general rule: (1) The limit of firm creditors to firm assets applies only where there are firm assets. If no firm assets or no living solvent partner exists, the firm creditors may share equally with the individual creditors in the distribution of the individual estates of the partners. (2) If a partner has fraudulently converted the firm assets to his or her own use, the firm's creditors will be entitled to share equally with individual creditors in the guilty partner's individual assets.

The doctrine of marshaling of assets is not applicable to tort claims under the RUPA. Partners are individually liable in tort for the acts of the firm, its agent, and servants. The liability is joint and several. Thus, the injured party may sue the partners individually or as a partnership. The firm assets need not be first used to collect a judgment, and direct action may be taken against individual assets.

CHAPTER SUMMARY

WHEN DOES A PARTNERSHIP EXIST?

Express Partnerships

1. A partnership may be created by express agreement or may be implied from conduct. In either case it is a question of the intent of the parties.

Implied Partnerships

1. The essential elements of a partnership are a common interest in the business and a share in the profits and losses.
2. The receipt of a share of the profits is prima facie evidence of a partnership, but this presumption may be overcome by evidence that the share of profits is for some other purpose.

Partnership by Estoppel

1. While parties may not be partners as between themselves, a partnership may exist insofar as third parties are concerned.
2. A partnership by estoppel is created if a person by words or conduct represents himself or herself or consents to another's representing him or her as a partner.

THE PARTNERSHIP AGREEMENT

Firm Name Provision

1. The partnership may not use words indicating that it is a corporation.
2. When the partnership's name is other than the names of the partners, it must comply with the assumed name statute.

3. The firm name is an asset and may be treated as such.
4. A partnership can sue and be sued in its firm name.

Capital Provision
1. Partnership capital is the amount contributed by a partner and the amount that is to be returned on dissolution.
2. Undivided profits are not a part of capital.
3. A party may become a partner without a capital contribution.

Property Provision
1. All property brought into the partnership or acquired by it is partnership property.
2. Property contributed as part of a capital contribution is partnership property.
3. Partnership property may be acquired and disposed of in the partnership name.
4. Services to the partnership are not capital.

Profit-and-Loss Provision
1. Unless there is an agreement to the contrary, profits and losses are shared equally.
2. If the agreement does not cover losses, they are shared in the same manner as profits.

Goodwill Provision
1. Goodwill is an asset that may be transferred to others and that must be accounted for upon the death of a partner.

Buy-and-Sell Provision
1. The partnership agreement must provide for the contingency of the death, withdrawal, or expulsion of a partner.
2. Such agreements are usually funded with life insurance as an expense of the partnership.

RIGHTS OF PARTNERS

Terminology
1. A silent partner has no voice in the management of the partnership.
2. A secret partner's existence is not known to the public.
3. A dormant partner is both silent and secret

To Participate in Management
1. Unless the agreement provides to the contrary, each partner has an equal right to manage and to conduct the firm's business.
2. The majority of partners can make final decisions concerning normal operations.
3. Certain actions require unanimous consent to bind the firm.

To Be Compensated for Services
1. Partners are not generally compensated other than with a share of the profits, unless their agreement provides otherwise.
2. Unless the agreement is to the contrary, partners have a duty to devote all of their time, skill, and energy to partnership affairs.

To Interest
1. Capital contributions do not earn interest.
2. Interest is paid on advances above capital contributions.
3. Interest is not paid on unwithdrawn profits.

To Information and Inspection of Books
1. Each partner is entitled to all information concerning the business and to inspect the books and records of the partnership.
2. Partners have a duty to furnish information necessary to operate the business.
3. Partners have a right to make copies of partnership records.

To an Accounting
1. In the event of a dispute as to the rights of the parties to assets or income, the equity action of an accounting is available to determine the rights of the partners.
2. As a general rule, partners are not allowed to sue each other in courts of law for dollar damages.
3. The suit for an accounting cannot be brought for minor disputes.

4. The suit for an accounting is usually a part of the dissolution process.

To Partnership Property and Interest in the Partnership

1. Each partner has an equal right to possess partnership property for partnership purposes.
2. A partner has no right in specific partnership property and no right to use partnership property for personal purposes.
3. Upon the death of a partner, the property belongs to the surviving partners, who have a duty to wind up the affairs. These surviving partners must pay the deceased partner's estate the sum to which the deceased partner was entitled.
4. A partner's interest cannot be levied on by his or her separate creditors. Creditors are entitled to obtain a charging order and to collect the partner's share of profits to satisfy the judgment.

DUTIES AND POWERS OF PARTNERS

Duties

1. A partnership is a fiduciary relationship, and each partner must act only on behalf of the partnership.
2. A partner cannot take for himself or herself an opportunity of the partnership, and any gains that should have belonged to the partnership must be paid to it.
3. All acts of partners are subject to the good-faith standard.
4. Since knowledge of any partner is charged to all partners, there is a duty on one partner to inform all other partners of all facts affecting the partnership business.

Power to Contract

1. A partner is an agent of the partnership business, and the general rules of agency are applicable.
2. The implied authority of a partnership is greater than that of an ordinary agent. A partner has the implied power to do all acts necessary to carry on the business.

Power to Impose Tort Liability

1. The doctrine of *respondeat superior* is applicable to the partnership relationship.
2. If the partnership incurs liability because of the tort of a partner, it has the right to collect the loss from the partner.

Powers over Property

1. Partners have authority to sell personal property held by the partnership for resale in the ordinary course of business.
2. A partner has no right to sell firm real estate unless it is engaged in the business of selling real estate.
3. Real property held in the partnership name can be conveyed only with the agreement of all partners.

Financial Powers

1. In a trading partnership, each partner has the implied power to borrow money to extend the credit of the firm in the usual course of business.
2. In a nontrading partnership, a partner does not have the implied power to borrow money.
3. The power to mortgage property or to pledge assets is narrowly granted. However, if a partner has the power to borrow money, the power to mortgage or pledge assets is assumed.

METHODS OF DISSOLUTION

Terminology

1. Dissolution occurs whenever there is a change (deletion or addition) in the partners as members of a partnership.

2. Winding up involves the process of reducing the assets to cash, paying creditors, returning capital contributions, and distributing the balance to the partners.
3. Termination of a partnership occurs when the winding-up process is completed

By Acts of Partners

1. In a partnership at will, any partner may dissolve the partnership at any time without liability.
2. Expulsion of a partner is a breach of the partnership agreement unless it provides for such expulsion.
3. Dissolution may occur in violation of the partnership agreement, in which case there is liability for wrongful dissolution.

By Operation of Law

1. Any event that makes it impossible or illegal to continue the partnership operates as a dissolution.
2. Death or bankruptcy of a partner or the partnership operates as a dissolution.
3. Insolvency of a partner is not a basis for dissolution.

By Court Decree

1. A court of equity may order dissolution if a partner is incapacitated or is in willful and persistent breach of the partnership agreement.
2. Other grounds, such as gross misconduct, may also justify a court in ordering dissolution.

THE EFFECT OF DISSOLUTION

On Powers of Partners

1. Dissolution terminates the authority of a partner to act except to wind up partnership affairs.
2. The winding-up process includes liquidating the assets, completing transactions, paying debts, and distributing the balance.
3. Partners possess apparent authority to bind the dissolved partnership unless persons dealing with the partners have actual or constructive notice of the dissolution.
4. On the death of a partner, title to partnership property remains with the surviving partners for the purpose of winding up the partnership.

On Rights of Partners

1. A withdrawing partner has the right to be paid the value of his or her interest in the partnership as of the date of dissolution.
2. A partner has the right to have partnership property used to pay firm debts.
3. If a partnership is wrongfully dissolved, the remaining partners may continue for the agreed term of the partnership. They must settle with the withdrawing partner but may deduct damages caused by the wrongful dissolution.
4. If the partnership is terminated, the former partner is entitled to a share of the net profits earned during the winding-up process.
5. If the partnership is continued, the former partner is entitled to either interest on the value of his or her share of the partnership or a share of the profits until he or she is paid off in the final accounting.
6. The winding-up parties are not entitled to be paid for services in completing unfinished business except in the case of dissolution caused by the death of a partner.

On New Partners

1. A new partner joining an existing partnership is liable for the preexisting debts of the firm only to the extent of the capital contributed.
2. This new partner is personally liable to an unlimited extent for all firm debts that arise after becoming a partner.

On Third Parties

1. An agreement between partners that a withdrawing partner will have no liability is not binding on firm creditors.
2. A withdrawing partner or the estate of a deceased partner has liability for firm debts in the event that firm assets are insufficient to discharge them.
3. Notice of dissolution must be given to third parties to abolish the partners' apparent authority to act on behalf of the firm.
4. This notice may be actual (personal) or constructive (public).
5. All creditors (past and present) must receive actual notice of dissolution if the dissolution is caused by the acts of partners or by a partner's death or incompetence.
6. All other third parties can be informed by constructive notice.
7. No notice needs to be given any third party if the dissolution was caused by bankruptcy, illegality, or court decree.

DISTRIBUTIONS ON TERMINATION

Solvent Partners

1. After firm creditors are paid, the assets are distributed in the following order: (1) partnership advances, (2) partnership capital, and (3) undistributed profits.
2. Goodwill is a partnership asset that must be accounted for if either partner retains it.

Insolvent Partners

1. If the partnership is unable to pay all of its debts, the doctrine of marshaling of assets will be followed.
2. Firm assets are paid to firm creditors. Individual assets are used to pay individual creditors. Each class must be paid in full before assets can be used to pay the other class.
3. If a firm has no assets, the firm creditors may share in the individual assets. The same is true if a partner has fraudulently converted firm assets to his or her own use.
4. The doctrine of marshaling of assets is not applicable to tort claims.

REVIEW QUESTIONS AND PROBLEMS

1. Match each term in Column A with the appropriate statement in Column B.

A	B
(1) Partnership by estoppel	(a) A court procedure for collecting an undivided debt of a partner from the partnership
(2) Implied partnership	(b) The contribution of partners to the partnership
(3) Tenancy in partnership	(c) A partnership created by conduct
(4) Articles of partnership	(d) The legal destruction of the partnership relationship that occurs whenever any partner ceases to be a member
(5) Partnership capital	(e) Partnership liability that is imposed on one who has held himself or herself out to be a partner when in fact he or she is not a partner
(6) Charging orders	(f) The completion of the winding-up process

(7) Dissolution	(g) The agreement creating a partnership
(8) Winding up	(h) A method for allocating property among the firm creditors and the individual creditors of the partner
(9) Termination	(i) The process of reducing assets to cash, paying creditors, returning capital contributions, and distributing the balance to the partners
(10) Marshaling of assets	(j) Describes the title to property held in the partnership name

2. Les and Turner entered into a written agreement whereby Turner was to farm Les's land in exchange for one-third of the crop as rental. The contract also provided that Les was to advance financing and Turner was to furnish the equipment. It was also agreed that after delivery of the one-third of the crops, all net proceeds and losses were to be shared equally. The contract specifically stated that Les and Turner were not partners, but landlord and tenant. Are Les and Turner partners? Why or why not?
3. David was employed by Walter to sell and service boilers. He was paid 50 percent of the net profit of each sale. Are David and Walter partners? Why or why not?
4. Pursuant to an oral agreement, Andy and Jeff formed a partnership to do kitchen remodeling. It was agreed that Andy was to invest $10,000 and manage the business affairs. Jeff, who would invest $1,000, was to work as job superintendent and manage the work. Profits were to be split fifty-fifty, but possible losses were not discussed. The business proved unprofitable, and Andy brought action against Jeff for one-half of the losses. To what extent is Jeff liable? Explain
5. The partners in a partnership composed of seven members have differing views on several partnership issues. If the partnership agreement makes no provision for the number of partners required to decide particular issues, how many votes does it take

    a. To discharge a clerk accused of stealing?
    b. To cause the dissolution of the partnership?
    c. To require the change of the partnership business from a wholesale to a retail operation?
    d. To require the submission of a partnership claim for arbitration?
    e. To submit to a confession of judgment on behalf of the partnership?

6. Bedford and Eckhart formed a partnership and built a shopping center. Three years later, Bedford, the managing partner, informed Eckhart that the business was in deep financial trouble and that he had tried to sell the complex but had failed. Bedford said that the best thing to do would he for one to buy the other out, and that their equity in the business was not worth more than $3 million. Eckhart sold his half interest in the partnership to Bedford for $1.5 million. Later he discovered that their equity in the business amounted to over $10 million and that Bedford had received several offers to purchase the business. Eckhart brought suit to rescind the sale, to have the partnership dissolved, and for accounting. Should Eckhart succeed? Why or why not?

7. Defendants Smith and Brook were partners in the automobile business under the name of Greenwood Sales and Service. Defendant Brook borrowed $6,000 from plaintiff and gave a partnership note in return. Is Smith liable on the note? Why or why not?
8. Mark and Stacy, brother and sister, were partners who had irreconcilable differences. In a suit to dissolve the partnership, a referee was appointed. The referee, to dispose of the assets, asked each partner to submit a bid. The brother submitted a bid for $65,000, but the sister did not bid. She now objects to the sale to her brother. The parties had stipulated that one of them could continue the business. On dissolution, is it permissible for the court to order a sale of partnership property to one of the partners for the purpose of continuing the business? Explain.
9. Carson, Crocket, and Kitt were partners in the importing business. They needed additional capital to expand. They located an investor named White, who agreed to purchase a one-fourth interest in the partnership by contributing $50,000 in capital. At the time White became a partner, there were several large creditors who had previously lent money to the partnership. The partnership subsequently failed, and the creditors are attempting to assert personal liability against White. Is he liable for these debts? Explain.
10. A partnership consists of three partners, Monroe, Adams, and Madison, who share profits equally. The partnership agreement is silent on the sharing of losses. Monroe loaned the partnership $10,000 and made a capital contribution of $20,000; Adams made a $10,000 capital contribution; Madison made no capital contribution. The partnership now has assets of $80,000 and owes outside creditors $55,000. The partners have decided to dissolve the firm. How much is each partner entitled to receive on dissolution? Explain.

Nature of Corporations | 29

CHAPTER OUTLINE

CHAPTER PREVIEW

The corporate form of doing business is a legal fiction. In that the organization is created by compliance with state law …, it cannot exist unless the originators comply with state law and the state approves the existence of the entity. This form of organizing a business is predicated on the theory that government has allowed an entity to be created that is separate and apart from its owners. The nature of this form of entity—the product laws of a state allowing its creation—deserves special attention.

This chapter is devoted to exploring the essence of the corporate form. When owners of a business decide that a corporate organization is best suited for their purposes, issues relating to how corporations are formed are among the first questions these owners face. In addition to issues associated with formation, this chapter examines the termination or death of the corporation. The automatic dissolution of a corporation does not occur frequently because most charters provide for the corporation's perpetual existence. Therefore, formal action is usually necessary to end the corporation's life. Finally, the subject of combinations of corporations, through merger or consolidation, is presented. By studying the formation, termination, and combination of the corporate form, one obtains a strong sense of the nature of the corporation.

The next chapter, Chapter 30, covers two areas of corporate law in greater detail. First, financial aspects of the corporation are examined. Also, operational features are presented, with particular attention paid to the roles of shareholder and director.

Because corporations are the product of a state, the law of corporations is determined for the most part by state courts and state legislative bodies. Although there is some degree of uniformity, the law of corporations does vary from state to state. Therefore, the laws of the particular states involved in the corporation's existence must be examined carefully.

BUSINESS MANAGEMENT DECISION

You are a promoter for a corporation to be formed. Among other activities, you hire an attorney to draft the incorporation papers, you rent office space, and you contract for printing services.

What should you do to avoid becoming personally liable on these transactions?

1. Corporation Defined

A *corporation* is an artificial, intangible person or being, created through a process provided by state law. Incorporating is a method by which individual persons are united into a new legal entity. For this new legal entity, they select a common name and the purposes that the entity is to accomplish. As a legal entity separate and apart from the persons or entities that had it created, the corporate existence is not affected by the death, incapacity, or bankruptcy of any of the persons involved in its creation or in its operation. Its owners do not have personal liability on its contracts, and the corporation has no liability for the obligations of its shareholders. As a legal entity, a corporation is able to own property and to sue or be sued in its own name in the same manner as a natural person. It has rights and duties separate and apart from its shareholders, and the law recognizes this separation in a variety of situations.

A corporation is also a person for purposes of both tort and criminal law. As an impersonal entity, it can act only through agents and servants; but the corporation is subject to the doctrine of *respondeat superior* and may be punished for certain criminal acts of its agents or servants.

Although a corporation is considered a person under most statutes, there are a few situations, such as those allowing the appointment of "suitable persons" as parole officers, in which it is *not* a "person." A corporation is a person for purpose of the due process clause of the Fifth and Fourteenth Amendments to the United States Constitution. For purposes of the privilege against compulsory self-incrimination, it is not a person.

Corporations may be classified in a variety of ways: public or private, for profit (business corporations) or not-for-profit. Each state classifies corporations doing business within the state as foreign or domestic, to denote the state where incorporation took place. Moreover, each state has a variety of statutes relating to specialized corporations such as cooperatives, church and religious corporations, and fraternal organizations. Although all classifications of corporations have significant importance, in this chapter and the following two we are primarily concerned with private, for-profit (business) corporations.

The following case explores the distinct nature of the corporate form and how individual owners might be treated.

CASE

J&J Sports Productions, Inc., Plaintiff v. Coach's, Inc. d/b/a Jock's Sports Bar & Grill, Gilbert Duncan and Carol Ann Malone, Defendants

UNITED STATES DISTRICT COURT FOR THE WESTERN DISTRICT OF KENTUCKY

2007 U.S. Dist. LEXIS 7897 (2007)

JOHN G. HEYBURN II

Plaintiff, J&J Sports Productions, owned the distribution rights to the prize fight in question. Apparently, without entering into the appropriate agreements, an unauthorized showing of the pay-per-view fight occurred on the premises of Jock's Sports Bar. This occurrence provides the foundation for Plaintiff's charges that Coach's and the Individual Defendants violated the Communications Act of 1934 ("the Act"), 47 U.S.C. § 553 and 47 U.S.C. § 605. Apparently, Plaintiff is suing the Individual Defendants on a derivative cause of action for personal liability for actions taken in violation of the Act. Plaintiff would need to show that the Individual Defendants personally participated in or aided with the statutory violation.

Kentucky law states that, "[u]nless otherwise provided in the articles of incorporation, a shareholder of a corporation shall not be personally liable for the acts or debts of the corporation except that he may become personally liable by reason of his own acts or conduct." Thus, if the Individual Defendants are absentee shareholders, they cannot be personally liable for the acts of the corporation performed by other agents or employees of Coach's.

The Individual Defendants can be liable under the Act for their individual actions, even on behalf of the corporation. The Court has nothing upon which it can base its decision other than the complaint. The Individual Defendants have not presented an affidavit and no one has conducted even limited discovery. It could very well be true that the Individual Defendants are absentee shareholders who engaged in no unlawful activity themselves, but the Court cannot make that determination without discovery.

A motion to dismiss for failure to state a claim should not be granted "unless it appears beyond doubt that the plaintiff can prove no set of facts in support of his claim which would entitle him to relief." Thus, it would be premature to dismiss the Individual Defendants at this stage of the litigation.

■ *Denied.*

CASE CONCEPTS REVIEW

1. When can individual shareholders be liable for acts associated with a corporation?
2. Why was this litigation against the individual shareholders allowed to continue?

PROCEDURE FOR INCORPORATION

2. The Application for a Charter

Charter

The document issued by a state that creates the corporation

Articles of incorporation

The basic governing document of a corporation

The law prescribes the steps to be taken for the creation of the corporation. Most state corporate laws provide that a specified number of adult persons, usually not less than three, may file an application for a **charter**. The application contains the names and addresses of the incorporators, the name of the proposed corporation, the object for which it is to be formed, its proposed duration, the location of its registered office, the name of its registered agent, and information about the stock of the corporation. In most states the information in the application is prepared in a format called the **articles of incorporation**.

Many of these items contained in the articles of incorporation are self-explanatory or are discussed in subsequent sections. Perhaps the least clear items are the registered office and registered agent. The *registered office* is the location where notices, such as a summons or other legal documents, may be delivered. The *registered agent* is the person designated to receive such notices for the corporation. A registered agent of a corporation need not simultaneously serve as an officer or director of such corporation, but an officer usually serves as registered agent. If a corporation fails to maintain a registered agent at its registered office, then the secretary of state becomes the agent of the corporation to receive service of process.

The information supplied in the articles of incorporation about the corporate stock usually includes (1) whether there will be preferred stock or only common stock, (2) the stated or par value of the stock (if the stock has no stated value, then it is called no-par stock), (3) the number of shares of stock that will be authorized, and (4) the number of shares of stock that will actually be issued.

Some states also require the names and addresses of the subscribers to the stock and the amount subscribed and paid in by each. Most applications usually indicate whether the stock is to be paid for in cash or in property.

The application, signed by all the incorporators, is forwarded to a state official, usually the secretary of state. If the application is in order, the official then issues a charter. If the application is not in proper form or if the corporation is being formed for an illegal purpose, the secretary of state will refuse to create the corporation and deny it a charter.

Upon return of the charter properly signed by the secretary of state, it is filed by the incorporators in the proper recording office. The receipt of the charter and its filing are the operative facts that bring the corporation into existence and give it authority and power to do business. It is not necessary that stock be issued or bylaws be adopted for the corporation to exist as a legal entity.

After the charter has been received and filed, the incorporators and all others who have agreed to purchase stock meet and elect a board of directors. They may also approve the bylaws of the corporation if the applicable law so provides. In most instances, the bylaws are approved by the board, not by the shareholders. The board of directors that has been elected then meets, approves the bylaws, elects the officers, calls for the payment of the subscription price for the stock, and makes whatever decisions are necessary to commence business.

3. Corporate Name

One of the provisions in the application for a corporate charter is the proposed name of the corporation. So that persons dealing with a business will know that it is a corporation and that the investors, therefore, have limited liability, the law requires that the corporate name include one of the following words or end with an abbreviation of them: *corporation, company, incorporated,* or *limited.* A corporate name must not be the same as, or deceptively similar to, the name of any domestic corporation or a foreign corporation authorized to do business in the state in which the application is made.

The law requires that a corporate name include an abbreviation of either corporation, company, incorporated, or limited. For example, the corporate name for Starbucks is Starbucks Corp.

Most states have procedures for reserving a corporate name for a limited period. Inquiry is usually made concerning the availability of a name; if it available, it is reserved while the articles of incorporation are being prepared. The name may be changed by charter amendment at any time without affecting corporate contracts or title to corporate property in any way.

4. Corporate Powers

The application for a charter includes a statement of the powers desired by the corporation. These are usually stated in quite broad language. A corporation has only such powers as are conferred on it by the state that creates it. The charter, together with the statute under which it is issued, sets forth the express powers of the corporation. All powers reasonably necessary to carry out the expressed powers are implied.

The following general powers are ordinarily granted to the corporation by statute: (1) to have perpetual existence; (2) to sue and be sued; (3) to have a corporate name and corporate seal; (4) to own, use, convey, and deal in both real and personal property; (5) to borrow and lend money other than to officers and directors; (6) to purchase, own, and dispose of securities; (7) to enter into contracts of every kind; (8) to make charitable contributions; (9) to pay pensions and establish pension plans,; and (10) to have all powers necessary or convenient to effect any of the other purposes.

Ultra vires

The acts of a corporation that are "beyond power" or authority of the corporation as granted by the state in its charter

Any acts of a corporation that are beyond the authority, express or implied, given to it by the state in the charter are said to be ***ultra vires*** acts—"beyond the authority." If a corporation performs acts or enters into contracts to perform acts that are *ultra vires,* the state creating such a corporation may forfeit its charter for misuse of its corporate authority. The extent of the misuse is controlling in determining whether the state will take away its franchise or merely enjoin the corporation from further *ultra vires* conduct.

Although third parties have no right to object to the *ultra vires* acts of a corporation, a stockholder may bring court action to enjoin a corporation from performing an *ultra vires* contract. If the corporation sustains losses or damages because of the *ultra vires* venture, the corporation may recover from the directors who approved the contracts. When the directors exceed corporate powers, they may become personally liable for resulting losses.

At common law, a corporation had no liability on contracts beyond its corporate powers because the corporation had capacity to do only those things expressly authorized within its charter or incidental thereto. Most modern statutes, including the *Model Business Corporation Act*, provide that all *ultra vires* contracts are enforceable. Neither party to such a contract may use *ultra vires* as a defense. The state or any shareholder may enjoin *ultra vires* conduct on the part of the corporation; but otherwise, contracts previously made are binding whether they are wholly executory, partially executed, or fully performed.

5. Bylaws

Bylaws

Rules for operating a corporation or other organization

A **bylaw** is a rule governing and managing the affairs of the corporation. It is binding on all shareholders but not third parties, unless the third parties have knowledge of it. The bylaws contain provisions establishing the corporate seal and the form of the stock certificate, the number of officers and directors, the method of electing them and removing them from office, as well as the enumeration of their duties. Bylaws specify the time and place of the meetings of the directors and the shareholders. Together with the articles of incorporation and the applicable statute, the bylaws provide rules for operating the corporation. The bylaws are subservient to the articles of incorporation and the statute but are of greater authority than, for instance, a single resolution of the board. Failure to follow the bylaws constitutes a breach of the fiduciary duties of a director or officer.

Bylaws are valid if they are reasonable and are consistent with the corporate charter and the applicable statutes. Bylaws may be illegal and void, however. For example, a bylaw of a corporation gave the president the power to manage the corporation's affairs. Such a bylaw is void because the law provides that the affairs of corporations shall be managed by a board of directors.

The power to alter, amend, or revoke the bylaws is vested in the board of directors unless reserved to the shareholders by statute or by the articles of incorporation. The board cannot, however, repeal, amend, or add to the bylaws if the change will affect the vested rights of a shareholder.

6. Domestic and Foreign Corporations

To a state or country, corporations organized under its laws are domestic corporations; those organized under the laws of another state or country are *foreign* corporations.

Domestic corporations become qualified to do business upon receipt and recording of their charter. Foreign corporations with significant intrastate activities must also "qualify" to do business by obtaining a certificate of authority and by paying the license fees and taxes levied on local businesses. A foreign corporation engaged wholly in *interstate* commerce through a state need not qualify in that state.

Most state statutes require foreign corporations to qualify to do business by filing a copy of their articles of incorporation with the secretary of state. They are also required to appoint an agent upon whom process may be served and to maintain an office in the state. Failure to comply results in a denial of the right of access to the courts as a plaintiff. Some states allow a plaintiff that has failed to obtain a certificate of authority a continuance in the case for a short time to obtain the certificate.

Of course, a corporation that cannot be a plaintiff because of lack of a certificate could be sued in a state if it had sufficient minimum contacts to satisfy due process. Generally, subjecting a foreign corporation to a state's qualification statutes requires more activity within a state than for service of process or for taxation of its income and property. Qualification is essential if there are local activities that constitute transacting business.

In a real sense, this denial of access to the courts as a plaintiff prevents a corporation from conducting business because its contracts are not enforceable by suit; debtors would thus be able to avoid payment to the corporation. Transacting business within the state without complying with the statute also subjects the corporation and its officers to statutory penalties, such as fines.

The term *doing business* is not reducible to an exact and certain definition. The Model Business Corporation Act defines the term by saying that a foreign corporation is doing business when "some part of its business substantial and continuous in character and not merely casual or occasional" is transacted within a state. A corporation is not *doing business* in a state merely because it is involved in litigation or maintains a bank account or an office within a state for the transfer of its stock. The Act also states that a foreign corporation is not required to obtain a license to do business by reason of the facts that (1) it is in the mail-order business and receives orders from a state that are accepted and filled by shipment from without the state, and (2) it uses salespeople within a state to obtain orders that are accepted outside the state. If the orders are accepted or filled within the state, or if any sale, repair, or replacement is made from stock physically present within the state in which the order is obtained, a foreign corporation is required to obtain a license.

7. Promoters

A *promoter,* as the name implies, promotes the corporation and assists in bringing it into existence. One or more promoters may be involved in making application for the charter, holding the first meeting of shareholders, entering into pre-incorporation subscription agreements, and engaging in other activities necessary to bring the corporation into existence. Promoters are responsible for compliance with the applicable federal securities laws and **blue-sky laws** (state statutes relating to the sale of securities), including the preparation of a prospectus if required.

Blue-sky laws

Popular name for state acts providing for the regulation and supervision of investment securities

LIABILITY Many of these activities involve the incurring of contractual obligations or debts. Preparation of the application for a charter usually requires the assistance of a lawyer, and it must be accompanied by the required filing fee. Legal questions about who has liability for these obligations and debts frequently arise. Is the promoter liable? Is the corporation after formation liable? Are both liable?

Certain general principles of contract and agency law prevent simple answers to these questions. First, a promoter is not an agent prior to incorporation because there is no principal. A party who purports to act as an agent for a nonexistent principal is generally liable as a principal. Thus, a promoter is liable on pre-incorporation contracts unless the other party is aware that the corporation has not been formed and agrees that the promoter is not to be bound by the contract personally. Second, the corporation technically cannot ratify the contracts of promoters because ratification requires capacity to contract both at the time of the contract and at the time of the ratification.

NO LIABILITY To avoid the difficulties caused by these legal theories, the law has used certain fictions to create an obligation on the part of the corporation—once it comes into existence—and to provide a means to eliminate liability on the part of the promoters. One fiction is that a novation occurs. This theory proceeds on the premise that when the corporation assents to the contract, the third party agrees to discharge the promoter and to look only to the corporation.

THEORIES OF CORPORATE LIABILITY Another theory that is used to determine liability on preincorporation obligations may be described as the *offer and acceptance theory.* Under this theory, a contract made by a promoter for the benefit of the corporation is an offer that may be accepted by the corporation after it comes into existence. Acceptance of the benefits of the contract constitutes a formal ratification of it. If the corporation does not accept the offer, it is not liable. The promoter may or may not be liable, depending on the degree of disclosure.

Corporations have also been held liable on promoters' contracts on theories that may be called the *consideration theory* and the *quasi-contract theory.* After incorporation, directors may promise to pay for expenses and services of promoters. Under the consideration theory, their promise will be binding and supported by sufficient consideration, on the theory of services previously rendered.

The quasi-contract theory holds that corporations are liable by implication for the necessary expenses and services incurred by the promoters in bringing them into existence because such expenses and services accrue or inure to the benefit of the corporation. The corporation would be unjustly enriched if liability did not exist.

Finally, some states have abandoned trying to justify corporate liability with a legal theory and have simply provided by statute that corporations are liable for the reasonable expenses incurred by promoters.

AVOIDANCE OF LIABILITY The parties frequently do not intend the promoter to be liable on a pre-incorporation contract. A promoter may avoid personal liability by informing the other party that he or she does not intend to be liable and is acting in the name of, and solely on the credit of, a corporation that has yet to be formed. However, if the promoter represents that there is an existing corporation when there is none, the promoter is liable. A promoter should make sure that contracts entered into on behalf of the proposed corporation are worded to relieve him or her of personal liability, if that is the intent.

Promoters occupy a *fiduciary relationship* toward the prospective corporation. Their position does not give them the right to secure any benefit or advantage over the corporation itself or over other shareholders. Promoters cannot purchase property and then sell it to the corporation at a profit; nor do they have a right to receive a commission from a third party for the sale of property to the corporation. In general, however, they may sell property acquired prior to the time they started promoting the corporation, provided that they sell it to an unbiased board of directors after full disclosure of all pertinent facts.

Courts looks at a variety of facts to determine whether individuals are promoters, as illustrated in the following case.

CASE

P.I.M.L., Inc., a Florida Corp. v. Chain Link Graphix, LLC, Edwin W. Davidson, Christopher J. Hilburn, and John D. McKelvey

UNITED STATES DISTRICT COURT FOR THE DISTRICT OF MINNESOTA

2006 U.S. Dist. LEXIS 88600 (2006)

The jury found that Defendants Edwin W. Davidson (Davidson), Christopher J. Hilburn (Hilburn), and John D. McKelvey (McKelvey) were pre-incorporation promoters of a business to be called Fashion Links. The jury found that at least one of these Defendants entered into a contract on behalf of Fashion Links with Plaintiff P.I.M.L. (PIML). The jury found that the contract was breached by nonpayment of commissions due Plaintiff on two separate accounts, namely Maurice's and Target.

On the Maurice's account, the jury found that Plaintiff was due commissions for sales made in the amount of $170,415.95. Based upon the stipulated sales volume to Maurice's, this amounted to a commission rate of 5%. On the Target account, the jury found that Plaintiff was due commissions for goods shipped to and accepted by Target in the amount of $29,000.00. The jury also found that there were unpaid commissions for goods delivered to and accepted by Maurice's due on the last day Plaintiff worked for any of the promoters in the amount of $122,514.66 and for goods delivered to and accepted by Target in the amount of $29,000.00. After the verdict, the parties submitted briefs on the issue of the statutory penalty due.

On October 26, 2006, the Court adopted the verdicts of the jury in both phases and ordered judgment in favor of Plaintiff PIML and against the Defendants Davidson, Hilburn, and McKelvey, jointly and *severally in the sum of $350,930.61. Included in the judgment was a penalty due under Minnesota law in the sum of $151,514.66. The action is now before the Court on the renewed motions of all Defendants for judgment as a matter of law as to all of Plaintiff's claims.*

Each individual Defendant contends that no reasonable juror could have found that he was engaged as a pre-incorporation promoter of the business to be called Fashion Links. The Court does not agree.

During trial, evidence was presented that before Fashion Links was incorporated, each Defendant had his own business card that contained his respective name and title in a company called Fashion Links. Moreover, Defendant Hilburn testified that he signed a document on behalf of Fashion Links and as a "partner" of Fashion Links. A copy of this document revealed Defendant Hilburn's signature and printed notation that he was a partner of Fashion Links at the time he signed the document. Defendant Davidson testified that he designed the Fashion Links business cards. There was evidence that Defendant McKelvey sent emails discussing business strategies for both the Target and Maurice's accounts. There was also testimony that Plaintiff met with the individual Defendants for an interview with a company called Fashion Links, even though Fashion Links had not been incorporated yet.

The Court instructed the jury that a promoter of a corporation is one who actually participates in taking preliminary steps in the organization of a new business or company and associates himself with others for the purpose of organizing the company and promoting its business. Viewing the evidence in the light most favorable to the non-moving Plaintiff, which the Court must do, the Court finds that reasonable jurors could differ as to whether the evidence showed that each of the individual Defendants was actively participating in the promotion of Fashion Links by taking preliminary steps in its formation prior to its incorporation. The Court is satisfied that the jury's findings as to each individual Defendant being a pre-incorporation promoter is amply supported by the evidence.

■ *Denied.*

CASE CONCEPTS REVIEW

1. Why did the court find that the three individual defendants were promoters?
2. What might the promoters have done to eliminate the possibility that they would be held liable?

DISREGARDING THE CORPORATE ENTITY

8. Piercing the Corporate Veil

One of the basic advantages of the corporate form of business organization is the limitation of shareholder liability. Corporations are formed for the express purpose of limiting one's risk to the amount of one's investment in the stock. Sometimes suits are brought to hold the shareholders personally liable for an obligation of a corporation or to hold a parent corporation liable for debts of a subsidiary.

Such suits attempt to "pierce the corporate veil." They ask the court to look behind the corporate entity and take action as though no entity existed separating it from the owners. Plaintiffs in these suits may not ask that the corporate entity be disregarded simply because all the stock is owned by the members of a family or by one person or by another corporation.

The lending of money to a corporation one controls or guaranteeing its debts is not enough to justify piercing the corporate veil. It would frustrate the purposes of corporate law to expose directors, officers, and shareholders to personal liability for the debts of the corporation when they contribute funds to, or on behalf of, a corporation for the purpose of assisting the corporation to meet its financial obligations. The loan or guarantee may assist the corporate efforts to survive, thus benefiting the creditors. If such acts were grounds to eliminate the separate corporate entity, such loans and guarantees usually would not be forthcoming.

9. Alter Ego Theory

Notwithstanding the foregoing general principles, courts today frequently disregard the separate corporate entity and pierce the corporate veil. They do so to hold parent corporations liable for the debts of a subsidiary and to hold individual shareholders liable for corporate obligations. Many cases use a theory known as the *alter ego theory.*

The alter ego theory disregards the separate corporate existence when one corporation is organized, controlled, and conducted to make it a mere instrumentality of another corporation or when individual shareholders conduct themselves in disregard of the separate entity. If the corporate entity is disregarded by the shareholders themselves, so there is such a unity of ownership and interest that separateness of the corporation has ceased to exist, the alter ego doctrine will be followed.

Some of the factors considered significant in justifying a disregard of the corporate entity using the alter ego theory are (1) undercapitalization of a corporation, (2) failure to observe corporate formalities such as annual meetings, (3) nonpayment of dividends, (4) siphoning of corporate funds by the dominant stockholders, (5) nonfunctioning of other officers or directors, (6) absence of corporate records, and (7) use of the corporation as a facade for operations of the dominant stockholders.

10. Promotion of Justice Theory

In addition to the alter ego theory, courts will pierce the corporate veil if the ends of justice require it. Justice will require the disregarding of the corporate entity if the liability-causing activity did not occur only for the benefit of the corporation, if the liable corporation has been gutted and left without funds by those controlling it to avoid actual or potential liability, or if the corporation has been used to defraud or otherwise promote injustice, such as the violation of a statute.

For example, assume that A and B sold a business and agreed not to compete with the buyer for a given number of years. In violation of the contract, A and B organized a corporation in which they became the principal stockholders and managers; the buyer may enjoin the corporation from competing with him, and he may do so effectively—as he could have enjoined A and B from establishing a competing business. Similarly, assume that a state law provides that a person may not hold more than one liquor license at a time. This law cannot be circumvented by forming multiple corporations. The attempt to evade the statute would justify piercing the corporate veil.

VOLUNTARY DISSOLUTIONS

11. Procedures

A corporation that has obtained its charter but has not commenced business may be dissolved by its incorporators. The incorporators file articles of dissolution with the state; and a certificate of dissolution is issued if all fees are paid and the articles are in order.

A corporation that has commenced business may be voluntarily dissolved either by the written consent of *all* its shareholders or by corporate action instituted by its board of directors and approved by the requisite percentage (usually two-thirds) of the shareholders. The board action, usually in the form of a recommendation, directs that the issue be submitted to the shareholders. A meeting of shareholders is called to consider the dissolution issue; and if the vote is in favor of it to the degree required by statute, the officers follow the statutory procedures for dissolution.

These procedures require the corporate officers to file a statement of intent to dissolve. The statement is filed with the state of incorporation, and it includes either the consent of all shareholders or the resolutions instituted by the board of directors. Upon filing the statement of intent to dissolve, the corporation must cease to carry on its business, except for winding up its affairs, even though corporate existence continues until a certificate of dissolution is issued by the state.

The filing of a statement of intent to dissolve is revocable. If the shareholders change their minds before the articles of dissolution are issued, the decision may be revoked by filing a statement of revocation of voluntary dissolution proceedings. When such a statement is filed, the corporation may resume its business.

12. Notice to Creditors

In winding up its affairs, the corporation must give notice to all known creditors of the corporation. If notice is not given, the corporation remains liable on the debts. Statutes of limitation, which eventually wipe out claims against corporations and their shareholders, do not start to run until notice of dissolution is given. More importantly, directors become personally liable for any debt of which notice is not given. These debts include tort claims as well as contract claims.

Consider the following case where the sole shareholder of a corporation that was dissolved is asking the court to reinstate the corporation.

CASE

Joseph and Beverly Butcher v. Keith Hebert Carpentry/Vinyl Siding, Inc.

COURT OF APPEAL OF LOUISIANA

945 So. 2d 914 (2006)

THIBODEAUX, CHIEF JUDGE

On February 25, 2000, Joseph and Beverly Butcher sued the Corporation for damages arising out of the construction of their home. The Corporation responded by filing a reconventional demand against the Butchers, alleging breach of contract. Although the litigation had not yet been resolved, on March 13, 2001, Hebert dissolved the Corporation by affidavit.

On December 13, 2005, four years after the dissolution, the Butchers amended their suit and added Hebert, individually, as a defendant in the pending litigation. Shortly thereafter, on January 2, 2006, the Corporation—and later, Hebert—filed a motion to have the Corporation reinstated. He claimed that the reinstatement was needed so that the Corporation could maintain its pending lawsuit in its name. He further explained that the act of voluntarily dissolving the Corporation prior to resolution of the litigation was an "inadvertent" act carried out due to "the ill advice of the Corporation's CPA." After a contradictory hearing on the motion, the trial court denied the motion, finding that Hebert was impermissibly seeking the reinstatement of the Corporation to avoid the potential for personal liability in the pending action.

We consider this application for supervisory review to address the issue of whether the trial court erred in failing to recognize that the Corporation's desire to maintain its litigation, which was filed before the dissolution occurred, is a lawful and valid business purpose that warrants the reinstatement of the Corporation to active status.

The Louisiana Business Corporation Law provides for the voluntary or involuntary dissolution of corporations. This case involves the voluntary dissolution of a corporation. State law allows for dissolution by affidavit. This is the simplest dissolution procedure, requiring only an attestation in the form of an affidavit by the shareholders or incorporator that states the corporation is no longer doing business, owes no debts, and requests that the corporation be dissolved.

The statute clearly imposes personal liability on a shareholder or incorporator for the pending claims of corporation once dissolution by affidavit has occurred. The statute also clearly states that the court may order reinstatement of a corporation after dissolution. However, the legislature has failed to offer any guidance to the courts as to what evidence is necessary or sufficient for a court to order the reinstatement and has not provided any language addressing the subsequent effects, if any, of corporate reinstatement on the automatic imposition of personal liability.

Here, we find that because the request for reinstatement was for the purpose of resolving pending litigation instituted before dissolution, the purpose for seeking reinstatement was valid and the trial court erred in denying the reinstatement of corporate status in this case. However, we also find that the Louisiana Business Corporation Law does not absolve a shareholder or incorporator, who has voluntarily dissolved a corporation by affidavit, of the personal liability for subsequent debts arising out of those claims brought against the entity, or which could have been brought against it, prior to its dissolution. Therefore, although we find that Hebert's request for reinstatement of the corporate status should have been granted, we do not find that the reinstatement will absolve him of any personal liability that may ultimately be imposed on the Corporation.

For the foregoing reasons, this writ is granted and the ruling of the trial court is reversed.

■ *Reversed.*

CASE CONCEPTS REVIEW

1. Why do you believe Herbert wanted reinstatement of the corporation?
2. Why did the court grant reinstatement?

13. Distributions

In dissolution proceedings, corporate assets are first used to pay debts. After all debts are paid, the remainder is distributed proportionately among the shareholders. If there are insufficient assets to pay all debts, a receiver will be appointed by a court, and the proceedings will be similar to those of involuntary dissolutions, discussed later.

When all funds are distributed, the corporation will prepare duplicate articles of dissolution and forward them to the state for approval. When signed by the appropriate state official, usually the secretary of state, one copy is filed with state records and one copy is returned to the corporation to be kept with the corporate records.

If the assets of a dissolved corporation are not used to pay the organization's debts, the directors and shareholders who approved the improper distribution of assets may be personally liable to the unpaid creditors.

INVOLUNTARY DISSOLUTIONS

14. Commenced by the State

Quo warranto

A proceeding in court by which a governmental body tests or inquires into the authority or legality of a corporation's existence

The state, having created the corporation, has the right to institute proceedings to cancel the charter. Suits by a state to cancel or forfeit a charter are known as ***quo warranto*** proceedings. They are filed by the attorney general, usually at the request of the secretary of state. Statutes often allow charters to be canceled by executive action also.

Charters may be canceled by suit or executive action if a corporation (1) did not file its annual report, (2) neglected to pay its franchise tax and license fees, (3) procured its charter by fraud, (4) abused and misused its authority, (5) failed to appoint and maintain a registered agent for the service of notices and process or had not informed the state of the name and address of its registered agent, or (6) ceased to perform its corporate functions for a long period of time. By proper proceedings and without charter forfeiture, the attorney general may also enjoin a corporation from engaging in a business not authorized by its charter. If a corporation is dissolved for any of the foregoing reasons, it may not continue its business. Its officers and directors may wind up the business, but any other contract is null and void.

By statute in most states, the officers and directors do not have personal liability for debts incurred on behalf of the corporation when its charter is suspended for failure to comply with state laws. Such statutes only suspend the right of a corporation to transact business while the corporation is delinquent for failure to file its annual report or pay its annual fees to the state. They do not expose the corporation's officers or directors to personal liability for debts incurred during the period of delinquency.

15. Commenced by Shareholders

DEADLOCKS Involuntary dissolution may be ordered by a court of equity at the request of a shareholder when the directors are deadlocked in the management of corporate affairs or the shareholders are deadlocked and unable to elect a board of directors. Deadlocks require proof that irreparable injury is likely and that the deadlock cannot be broken. A mere deadlock in voting to elect directors is not sufficient in itself, in most states, to cause a court to order dissolution.

Since the proceedings are in a court of equity, the issue is whether dissolution will be beneficial to the shareholders and not injurious to the public. The power to order dissolution is discretionary. In exercising its discretion, the court considers the seriousness of the deadlock and whether the corporation is able to conduct business profitably despite the deadlock. It also may consider such factors as the length of time the company has been in business, the stated purpose of the business, the original incorporators, whether one shareholder has shown a clear design to take over the business and is in a financial posture to do so to the detriment of other shareholders who may be injured financially by tax consequences, what the market for sale and purchase is at the instant time, whether the shareholders are in a relatively equal bargaining position, and whether it is in the best interests of all the shareholders to leave them to find their own solutions by one party buying out the others in a fair market value situation rather than by a forced sale.

ILLEGAL, FRAUDULENT, OR OPPRESSIVE CONDUCT The general rule throughout the United States is that a minority shareholder or group of shareholders of a going and solvent corporation cannot, without statutory authority, maintain a suit to have the corporation dissolved. Most states have statutes that authorize courts of equity to liquidate a corporation at the request of a shareholder when it is proved that those in control of the corporation are acting illegally, fraudulently, or oppressively. It is so difficult to define oppressive conduct that each case must be decided on its own facts.

Today, conduct that is not illegal or fraudulent may be held to be oppressive. Although controlling shareholders in a closely held corporation are not fiduciaries in the strict sense of the word, the general concepts of fiduciary duties are useful in deciding if conduct is oppressive. The law imposes equitable limitations on dominant shareholders. They are under a duty to refrain from using their control to profit for themselves at the expense of the minority. Repeated violations of these duties will serve as a ground for dissolution. Even though it takes substantially less evidence to justify dissolution of a partnership than of a closely held corporation, the trend is to treat the issues as similar; *oppressive conduct* may be summarized as conduct that is burdensome, harsh, and wrongful. It is a substantial deviation from fair dealing and a violation of fair play. It is a violation of the fiduciary duty of good faith in those states that recognize such a duty.

PROTECTION OF MINORITY SHAREHOLDERS Actions by majority shareholders intended to squeeze out or freeze out minority shareholders may provide grounds for dissolution or other equitable relief. Minority shareholders have been granted relief when the majority has refused to declare dividends but have paid out all profits to themselves in the form of salaries and bonuses. Relief was also granted in a recent case where the majority shareholders of a corporation that was not in need of funds sold additional stock to dilute the percentage of control of the minority, who the majority knew were unable financially to exercise their preemptive right. Such conduct is a breach of the fiduciary relationship.

All states allow minority shareholders to obtain dissolution when it is established that corporate assets are being wasted or looted or the corporation is unable to carry out its purposes. Some states have, by statute, broadened the grounds for court-ordered dissolution. These states allow courts to order dissolution when it is reasonably necessary for the protection of the rights or interests of minority shareholders. Even in these states, a corporation will not be dissolved by a court for errors of judgment of the board of directors (who are controlled by the majority of shareholders) or because the court confronted with a question of policy would decide it differently than would the directors. Dissolutions by decree at the request of a shareholder are rare; but as previously noted, the trend is to give greater protection to the minority shareholders.

16. Commenced by Creditors

A corporation is in the same position as a natural person insofar as its creditors are concerned. A suit may be brought against it; and when a judgment is obtained, an execution may be levied against its property, which may then be sold. Corporate assets may, also, be attached. If the corporation has no property subject to execution, its assets may be traced by order of a court of equity.

The creditors have no right, because they are creditors, to interfere with the management of the business. A creditor who has an unsatisfied judgment against a corporation may seek, as a matter of equitable relief, to set aside conveyances and transfers of corporate property that have been fraudulently transferred for the purpose of delaying and hindering creditors. Creditors may also, under the aforementioned circumstances, ask for a **receiver** to take over the assets of the corporation and to apply them to the payment of debts.

Receiver
An officer of the court appointed on behalf of all parties to the litigation to take possession of, hold, and control the property involved in the suit, for the benefit of the party who will be determined to be entitled thereto

When there is an unsatisfied execution and it is established that the corporation is insolvent, a court may order dissolution. The same is true if the corporation admits its insolvency. Dissolution in such cases proceeds in the same manner as if instituted by the state or by voluntary proceedings when the corporation is insolvent. These procedures are discussed in the next section.

17. Procedures

In liquidating a corporation, courts have the full range of judicial powers at their disposal. They may issue injunctions, appoint receivers, and take whatever steps are necessary to preserve the corporate assets for the protection of creditors and shareholders. The receiver will usually collect the assets, including any amount owed to the corporation for shares. The receiver will then sell the assets, pay the debts and expenses of liquidation, and if any funds are left, divide them proportionately among the shareholders. Courts usually require creditors to prove their claims in court in a manner similar to that in bankruptcy proceedings. When all funds in the hands of a receiver are paid out, the court issues a decree of dissolution that is filed with the secretary of state. Funds due persons who cannot be located are deposited with the state treasurer and held for a specified number of years. If not claimed by the creditor or shareholder within the declared period, the funds belong to the state.

18. Liability of Shareholders

As a general rule, shareholders are *not personally liable* for the debts of the corporation; but a shareholder who has not fully paid the corporation for the original issue of stock is liable to the receiver or to a creditor for the unpaid balance. In addition, statutes in most states allow creditors to reach assets of the former corporation that are in the hands of shareholders. The assets of a corporation are a trust fund for the payment of creditors, and the directors must manage this fund for their benefit. The liability of shareholders to creditors of the corporation is predicated on the theory that the transfer of corporate assets on dissolution is in fraud of creditors, and a shareholder knowingly receiving such assets ought to have liability.

Claims that existed before dissolution may be enforced afterward by statute in most states. For a specified period after dissolution, remedies survive against a corporation, its directors, officers, and shareholders. Suits against the corporation may be prosecuted or defended in the corporate name even though the corporate existence has

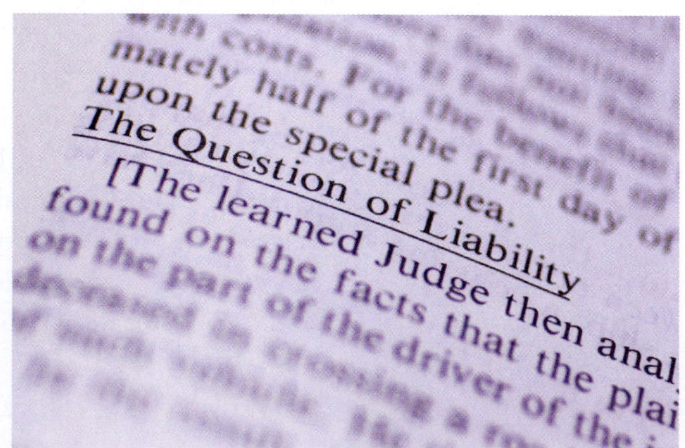

Debts of a corporation are not the personal responsibility of the shareholders.

technically ended. A judgment on such a claim may be collected from the corporation if it has property or from any former insurance carrier of the corporation. A claim may also be collected from property distributed to shareholders on dissolution, or the creditor may proceed directly against the shareholder receiving property. As previously noted, failure to give notice to creditors of intent to dissolve stops the time period from running.

Consolidation
The combination of two corporations when these two entities are dissolved and a new corporation is created

The time period to sue after dissolution was created to protect creditors from losses that could easily result from the "death" of the corporate debtor. However, this protection is limited to whatever period is specified by the law of the state of incorporation; liability does not continue indefinitely. In addition, there is no liability for post-dissolution causes of action unless a statute imposes it.

CONSOLIDATIONS, MERGERS, AND ACQUISITIONS

19. Definitions

A business may acquire other businesses in a variety of ways. It may singly *purchase the assets* of the other firm. Such purchases include the plant, equipment, and even the goodwill of the other business. In such cases, the selling business retains its liabilities and its corporate structure.

Merger
A combination of two corporations when one absorbs the other and the acquiring corporation continues to exist, but the target corporation is dissolved

Businesses may also consolidate or merge. **Consolidation** is the uniting of two or more corporations. A new corporation is created, and the old entities are dissolved. The new corporation takes title to all the property, rights, powers, and privileges of the old corporations, subject to the liabilities and obligations of the old corporations. In a **merger**, one of the corporations continues its existence but absorbs the other corporation, which ceases to have an independent existence. The continuing corporation may expressly or impliedly assume and agree to pay the debts and liabilities of the absorbed corporation, whose creditors become third-party creditor beneficiaries. By statute in most states, the surviving corporation is deemed to have assumed all the liabilities and obligations of the absorbed corporation.

FIGURE 29-1 ■ Consolidations and Mergers

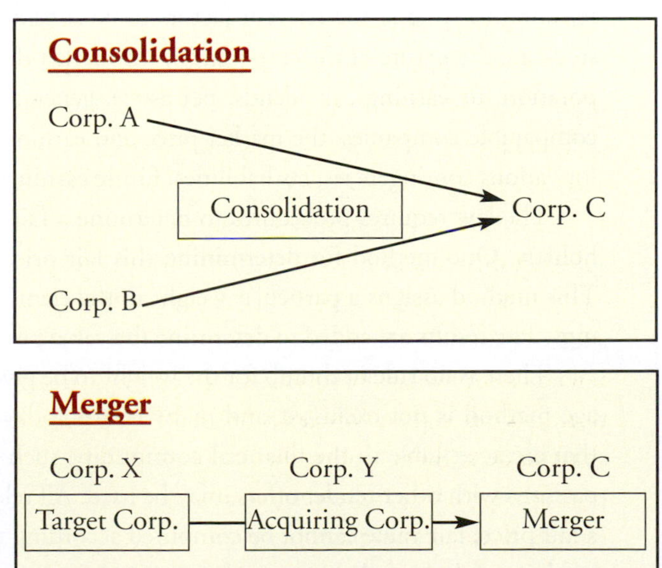

20. Procedures

The procedures for consolidations and mergers are statutory. Usually, the board of directors gives its approval by resolution that sets forth in detail all facts of the planned merger or consolidation. The plan is submitted to the shareholders for approval. Notice of the meeting typically includes the resolution passed by the directors. If proxies are submitted for the vote, proxy material must disclose all material facts required for an intelligent decision by the shareholders. In most states, the shareholders must approve the plan by a two-thirds vote of all shares and two-thirds of each class if more than one class of stock is voting. If the consolidation or merger is approved by the shareholders of both corporations, articles of consolidation or articles of merger will be prepared and filed with the state. If the papers are in order and all fees are paid, a certificate of consolidation or a certificate of merger will be issued.

21. Rights of Dissenting Shareholders

Statutes of the appropriate state may be strictly complied with, yet the courts may block a merger or acquisition. A merger may not be effected for the purpose of freezing out or squeezing out minority shareholders. If a merger has no valid business purpose other than the elimination of minority shareholders, courts will enjoin the merger or consolidation. Even if the minority shareholders receive the investment value of their interest in the merged corporation, the policy favoring corporate flexibility is not furthered by permitting the elimination of minority interests for the benefit of the majority, when no benefit thereby accrues to the corporation. Moreover, the majority shareholders owe the minority shareholders a fiduciary obligation in dealing with corporate assets. This duty includes the protection of corporate interests and restraint from doing anything that would injure the corporation or deprive it of profits or the ability to exercise its powers. Since dissolution may cause these effects, the majority may not dissolve when the only purpose is to get rid of the minority.

A shareholder who dissents from a consolidation or merger, and who makes the dissent a matter of record prior to the decision by serving a written demand that the corporation purchase his or her stock, is entitled to be paid the fair value of the stock on the day preceding the vote on the corporate action. Procedures are established for ascertaining the fair value and for a judicial decision of that issue if necessary. Once committed to the procedure, a shareholder cannot change his or her mind and keep the stock. This stops a party from finding out the price and then accepting or rejecting it. Among the relevant factors to be considered in evaluating a dissenting shareholder's stock are the nature of the corporation, the market demand for the stock, the business of the corporation, its earnings, dividends, net assets, general economic conditions, the market prices of comparable companies, the market price and earnings ratio, management and policies, revenues for various contingencies, tax liabilities, future earnings, and the permanency of the business.

The law requires procedures to determine a fair price for the stock of the dissenting shareholders. One method for determining this fair price is known as the *weighted average method.* This method assigns a particular weight to the elements of value: assets, market price, and earnings. The results are added to determine the value per share.

There is no rule of thumb for the weight to be given any factor. Moreover, the weighted average method is not exclusive, and many courts today believe it is outmoded. Other techniques that are acceptable in the financial community, such as discounted cash flow analysis and comparisons with other tender offers, may be used. All relevant factors are considered in determining a fair price; fair value cannot be computed according to any precise mathematical formula. If the stock is regularly traded in an exchange, market value may be the dominant factor.

The laws relating to dissenting shareholders petitioning for appraisal and the right to be paid the fair values of their stock apply to a cash-for-stock merger as well as a stock-for-stock merger. Also, a shareholder who dissents from a sale or exchange of all or substantially all the assets or property of the corporation, other than in the usual course of business, has the same right to be paid for his or her stock. When the statutory procedures are followed, the dissenting shareholder ceases to be a shareholder when notice is given; he or she then becomes a creditor.

Tender offers create problems in valuing the stock of dissenting shareholders. Such offers usually include a premium to overcome objections of many shareholders; however, dissenting shareholders who refuse a tender offer and insist on a judicial determination of the fair value of shares are not entitled to receive the tender offer premium. A premerger tender offer price does not establish a floor on the amount that the court may fix as the value of shares in an appraisal proceeding, but it does have some evidentiary significance.

22. Liability of Successors

In the case of a merger or a consolidation of corporations, the changed entity ordinarily remains liable for prior debts; a business cannot shrug off personal liability to its creditors simply by merging, consolidating, switching from the partnership to the corporate form or vice versa, or changing its name. By statute in most states, the surviving corporation is deemed to have assumed all the liabilities and obligations of the absorbed corporation or of the former corporations. These liabilities may even include punitive damages.

To avoid assuming the debts and liabilities of corporations that are being acquired, the acquiring businesses often purchase the assets of a corporation without assuming the liabilities and without any change of organization. The buyer does not become involved with the seller, and there is no merger or consolidation. As a general rule, if one corporation acquires only the assets of another corporation, the acquiring corporation is not liable for the debts and liabilities of the transferor. An exception exists if the transfer is an attempt to defraud creditors.

This general rule is subject to attack today. Under what circumstances should an acquiring corporation have liability for the debts and the obligations of the business whose assets it acquired? This becomes a difficult question when the assets acquired include the firm name and its product line. The contract of acquisition usually provides for no assumption of liabilities, but should such a provision bind third parties when the selling corporation dissolves as soon as the sale is complete? This issue arises quite frequently in product liability cases. It is not surprising that the courts of different states have answered the liability issue differently in product liability cases. The majority view is to find no liability, but many states take the opposite view. Therefore, an examination of each state's laws and court decisions is essential prior to knowing the answer to the question posed above.

Horizontal merger

Merger of corporations that were competitors prior to the merger

Vertical merger

A merger of corporations, one corporation being the supplier of the other

Conglomerate merger

Merging of companies that have neither the relationship of competitors nor that of supplier and customer

23. Antitrust Considerations

Mergers and acquisitions are usually classified as horizontal, market extension, vertical, or conglomerate. A **horizontal merger** combines two businesses in the same field or industry, reducing the number of competitors. A market extension merger is an acquisition in which the acquiring company extends its markets. This market extension may be either in new products (product extension) or in new areas (geographical extension). A **vertical merger** brings together two companies, one being the customer of the other. Such a combination usually removes the customer from the market as far as other suppliers are concerned. It may remove a source of supply, also, if the acquiring company is a customer of the acquired one. A **conglomerate merger** is one in which the businesses involved are neither competitors nor related as customer and supplier in any given line of commerce.

Society has been concerned for decades about the concentration of power that can occur if a corporation becomes too large in its market. Antitrust laws at both the federal and state levels attempt to provide consumers and competitors with certain protections against a single corporation or a group of corporations controlling unfairly a particular market. In general, the nature of horizontal mergers creates the greatest concern; therefore, most antitrust activity is aimed at horizontal mergers. Vertical mergers are of less concern. Conglomerate mergers have little trouble passing muster under antitrust laws because their anticompetitive impact is slight.

The subject of antitrust law is treated extensively in Chapter 41.

CHAPTER SUMMARY

Corporation Defined

1. A corporation is an artificial, intangible entity created by state law.
2. This organization, generally ,is considered a person for both contract and tort law purposes.
3. A corporation is a person under the due process clause but not under the Fifth Amendment's protection against self-incrimination.
4. The classifications of public versus private, profit versus nonprofit, and domestic versus foreign are commonly applied to corporations.

PROCEDURE FOR INCORPORATION

The Application for a Charter

1. The incorporators prepare an application for a charter that includes basic information such as the purpose of the corporation, the location of its office and registered agent, and information about its stock.
2. The application will indicate the value of authorized stock and the amount to be issued.
3. When the application is approved, it is returned as a charter, which is filed in the proper recording office.

Corporate Name

1. The name of a corporation must include words such as *corporation, company, incorporated, or limited, which provides notice of the limited liability of the shareholders.*
2. A corporate name must not be deceptively similar to names of other corporations.

Corporate Powers

1. A corporation has all the powers granted in its charter and those set forth in the statutes of the state of incorporation.
2. The usual powers include the power to sue and be sued, to own, convey, and deal in property, to enter into contracts, and to purchase and dispose of securities.
3. An *ultra vires* act is one beyond the authority of the corporation.
4. Neither the corporation nor parties dealing with it may avoid liability on the ground of *ultra vires.*
5. *Ultra vires* conduct on the part of the corporation may be enjoined at the request of the shareholders or may be the basis of a revocation of the charter by the state.

Bylaws

1. After filing the charter, the incorporators meet with all stock subscribers and elect a board of directors. The board, in turn, meets and adopts bylaws.
2. The bylaws provide the rules for managing the corporation. They cover such activities as the corporate seal, stock certificates, the number and manner of election of officers, and the time and place of meetings of shareholders as well as the board of directors.

Domestic and Foreign Corporations

1. A corporation organized under a state's laws is a *domestic* corporation in that state; a corporation incorporated in one state is a *foreign* corporation in all other states.
2. Foreign corporations transacting local business in a state must qualify to do business in that state. If they fail to do so, they are denied access to the courts as well as being subject to other sanctions.
3. If a business is only engaged in interstate commerce and is not conducting intrastate activities, it is not required to obtain a license to do business.

Promoters

1. A promoter is usually an incorporator and is active in obtaining pre-incorporation agreements. Promoters are responsible for compliance with all applicable laws.
2. A promoter may be personally liable to contracts prior to incorporation, but this liability may be avoided.
3. A corporation after it is formed may have liability on pre-incorporation agreements under a variety of theories.
4. Promoters stand in a fiduciary relationship to the corporation and cannot secure benefits at the expense of other shareholders or the corporation.

DISREGARDING THE CORPORATE ENTITY

Piercing the Corporate Veil

1. Creditors may seek to look through the corporation to the shareholders and seek to impose liability as if the corporate entity did not exist.
2. The corporate entity is not disregarded simply because all of the stock is owned by one person.

Alter Ego Theory

1. The alter ego theory is used to pierce the corporate veil where a corporation is actually nothing more than the alter ego of another corporation or of an individual.
2. This theory is used where the business is actually operated as if the separate corporate entity did not exist.

Promotion of Justice Theory

1. Courts will pierce the corporate veil to avoid fraud, to prevent the violation of a statute, and to promote the ends of justice.

VOLUNTARY DISSOLUTIONS

Procedures

1. A corporation with a charter that has not commenced business may be dissolved by its incorporators filing articles of dissolution.
2. A corporation that has commenced business may be dissolved by all of its shareholders.
3. A corporation that has commenced business may be dissolved by its board of directors with the approval of two-thirds of the shareholders.

Notice to Creditors

1. A corporation must give notice to all creditors of its intent to dissolve. The directors are personally liable to creditors to whom notice is not given.

Distributions

1. Corporate assets are first used to pay debts. Any remaining assets are distributed proportionately among the shareholders.
2. If there are insufficient assets to pay debts, a receiver will be appointed, and the dissolution will proceed as if it were involuntary.

INVOLUNTARY DISSOLUTIONS

Commenced by the State

1. The state may file a quo *warranto* proceeding to cancel a corporate charter.
2. Such proceedings are brought by failure of the corporation to comply with the law in such areas as annual reports, franchise taxes, and registered agents.

Commenced by the Shareholders

1. Shareholders may petition a court of equity to dissolve a corporation if there is a deadlock in management and irreparable injury is likely.
2. Shareholders may obtain dissolution if the directors are acting illegally, fraudulently, or oppressively.
3. Modern statutes do not allow the majority to freeze out minority shareholders, and dissolution is an appropriate remedy in such cases.
4. Shareholders in closely held corporations have duties similar to partners in a partnership.

Commenced by the Creditors

1. Creditors have no right to interfere with the management of a corporation.
2. Creditors may ask for a receiver to be appointed when they have an unsatisfied judgment. If insolvency is established, dissolution is possible.

Procedures

1. Courts of equity have the full range of procedures to protect corporate assets, the creditors, and shareholders.
2. Creditors are required to prove their claims before they share in assets.

Liability of Shareholders

1. Shareholders have no personal liability to creditors unless the stock is not paid for in full or assets have been transferred to them in default of creditors.
2. Claims against the corporation exist for a specified time after dissolution and may be enforced against shareholders receiving corporate assets.

CONSOLIDATIONS, MERGERS AND ACQUISITIONS

Definitions

1. A consolidation is the uniting of two or more corporations into a newly created one.
2. A merger occurs when one corporation absorbs another, with the latter one being dissolved.

Procedures

1. There are statutory procedures that must be followed. These usually require submission to the shareholders for approval.
2. Each class of shareholders must approve the plan and usually by a two-thirds vote.

Rights of Dissenting Shareholders

1. Minority shareholders who dissent to a merger or consolidation are entitled to be paid the fair value of their stock immediately prior to the change in the corporation. Various methods are in use for determining fair market value.
2. A tender offer does not establish fair market value, but it is evidence of the value.

Liability of Successors

1. In a merger or consolidation, the new corporation is liable for the debts of the old corporation.
2. When one corporation acquires the assets of another, there may be liability in some states if the facts warrant it.

Antitrust Considerations

1. The law covers mergers between competitors that are known as horizontal mergers, mergers between buyer and seller that are known as vertical mergers, and mergers where there is no connection between the parties that are called conglomerate mergers.

REVIEW QUESTIONS AND PROBLEMS

1. Match each term in Column A with the appropriate statement in Column B.

A	B
(1) Incorporator	(a) A theory used to pierce the corporate veil
(2) Bylaw	(b) Merger of competitors
(3) Foreign corporation	(c) Tests corporation's existence
(4) Promoter	(d) One who signs an application for a corporate charter
(5) *Ultra vires*	(e) One who assists in organizing a corporation
(6) Alter ego	(f) A corporation operating in a state other than the state that issues its charter
(7) *Quo warranto*	(g) Merger of supplier with buyer
(8) Consolidation	(h) A rule for governing a corporation
(9) Vertical merger	(i) A contract defense that is unavailable to the parties to a contract today
(10) Horizontal merger	(j) Uniting of two or more corporations into a new one

2. LST Company was the parent company, and BAG Company was a subsidiary. LST Company extended credit to BAG Company. The latter became insolvent, and the other creditors objected to LST's sharing equally in the assets. Is LST entitled to its pro rata share of BAG's assets? Why or why not?
3. The plaintiffs entered into a series of contracts involving coal excavations with Doral Coal Company and Dean Coal Company. Robert W. William, defendant, was president of both coal companies. When royalty payments owed were not made by the corporations as agreed, plaintiffs canceled the agreements and filed suit against the defendant individually. They contended that the defendant was personally liable because he was the sole shareholder of each corporation. Is the defendant liable? Why or why not?
4. The XYZ Corporation was to be formed by Peter, a promoter. To operate the corporation after incorporation, it was necessary for Peter to lease certain facilities. Peter executed a lease in the corporate name for office space without revealing to the lessor that the corporation had not yet been organized. The corporation subsequently came into existence, and the board declined to accept the lease of office space that Peter had executed in the corporate name.

   a. Can the corporation validly decline the lease of office space? Explain.
   b. Does Peter have any liability on any of the leases he made? Explain.

5. Plaintiff corporation, engaged in the sale of plastics, entered into a pre-incorporation contract that was initiated and concluded by two persons who later became officers of the corporation. It formed the basis for the subsequent sale to defendant of over $1 million in

goods. Suit was brought to recover balance due on goods sold. The defendant denied liability because the plaintiff was not incorporated at the time of the contract. Should the plaintiff be allowed to recover? Explain.

6. David formed a corporation for tax purposes. No directors' meetings were held. David retained total control of the corporation's operations, and he took money from the corporate account for personal purchases. Creditors sought to pierce the corporate veil. Should they succeed? Explain.
7. What persons must approve a voluntary dissolution of a corporation if business has not been commenced? What persons must approve a voluntary dissolution if the corporation has commenced business activities?
8. Adams—the owner of all capital stock of the Gazette Corporation, a newspaper business—sold all his shares to Burr and promised to serve as adviser to the newspaper for a period of five years in return for an annual salary of $50,000. After three years, Burr petitioned for dissolution, which was obtained. Does Adams have a right to collect the balance of the salary from the corporation? Explain.
9. David was president of Music, Inc. He owned 53 percent of the common stock. David received a salary of $10,000 per year and bonuses of $7,000 per year. The corporation had a net worth of $100,000 and sales of $245,000. The net profit of the company had been under $2,000 each year, and dividends were either small or nonexistent. Minority shareholders brought suit to compel dissolution of the corporation on the ground of waste, alleging that the waste occurred in the payment of bonuses to David. Should the company be dissolved? Why or why not?
10. The shareholders of a corporation met to vote on a proposed merger. After the vote was taken and the meeting adjourned, a minority shareholder gave written notice of objection to the proposed merger. Are the minority shareholders entitled to obtain the fair cash value for their shares? Why or why not?

Financial and Operational Features of Corporations | 30

CHAPTER OUTLINE

CHAPTER PREVIEW

The preceding chapter discussed the nature of the corporate form as an entity created under state law that is separate and distinct from its owners. This chapter explores financial and operational aspects of a corporation. Attention is paid first to stock and those that hold stock, the *shareholders* of the corporation. The role of shareholders that own an equity interest in the entity is distinguished from holders of a bond, for example, who are creditors of the corporation. Further, a preferred shareholder has superior rights to those owners who hold common stock. However, common stockholders generally have the right to vote.

The shareholders are the owners of the corporation, but typically shareholders are not involved in setting policy or overseeing the operation of this form of conducting business. Responsibilities associated with controlling the corporation fall to the *directors* and, to a lesser extent, the *officers*. The rights, responsibilities, and liabilities associated with those serving on the *board of directors* also are examined within this chapter. It is the responsibility of the officers to carry out the policies established by the directors. The duties and powers of the shareholders, the board of directors, and the various officers are regulated by statute, by the bylaws of the corporation, and by corporate resolutions passed by the board of directors.

Within the context of discussing financial and operational features of the corporate form, this chapter presents information regarding the type of corporation known as the *closely held corporation*. This type of corporation has a small number of shareholders, typically less than thirty-five. As a result, many of the technical aspects of law dealing with internal matters are liberalized to recognize the fact that ownership and control are not separated in the same manner as they are in a larger corporation.

BUSINESS MANAGEMENT DECISION

You serve as an outside director on the board of the All-at-Once Corporation. During a board meeting, the president of All-at-Once makes a fifteen-minute presentation on the benefits and detriments of merging All-at-Once with Take-Your-Time, Inc. After this presentation, the president asks for a vote of the directors approving the merger.

Should you have any concerns about casting your vote?

CORPORATE STOCK

1. Stock Basics

A *stock certificate* is written evidence of the ownership of a certain number of *shares of stock* of a corporation. The certificate recognizes a certain person as being a *shareholder* with rights in the corporation—primarily, the right to share in profits and to receive a portion of the assets at time of dissolution. Shareholders also may have the right to elect directors, but shareholders do not take an active role in the daily management of the business.

STOCKS VERSUS BONDS Stock must be distinguished from a bond. A bond is an obligation of the corporation to pay a certain sum of money in the future at a specified rate of interest. It is comparable to a corporation's promissory note. A *bondholder* is a *creditor* of the corporation, whereas a shareholder is an owner of the corporation. A shareholder has a right to receive dividends if they are declared by the board of directors and to participate in the assets of the corporation after all

TABLE 30-1 ■ Stock vs. Bonds

	Creates	Payment Type	Due Date	Priority
Stock	Corporation/Shareholder Relationship	Dividend, if declared	Unlimited	Last, subject to rights of debt holders
Bond	Creditor/Debtor Relationship	Interest	Set	Superior to rights of debtors

creditors have been paid. A bondholder has no right to vote or to participate in the management and control of a corporation.

A stock certificate is written evidence proving ownership of stocks.

COMMON AND PREFERRED STOCK Common stock is the simplest type of corporate stock. It generally entitles the owner to share in the control, profits, and assets of the corporation in proportion to the amount of common stock held. Such a shareholder has no advantage, priority, or preference over any other class of shareholders unless otherwise specified.

Preferred stock has priority over other classes of stock in claiming dividends or assets on dissolution. The most important right given to a preferred shareholder is the right to receive a certain specified dividend, even though the earnings are not sufficient to pay like dividends to common shareholders.

Preferred stock may be cumulative or noncumulative. If *cumulative,* any dividends that are not paid because of lack of earnings accrue and are paid when earnings are available. If *noncumulative,* only the current year's preferred dividend is paid out of current earnings. If nothing is stated about the payment of the dividends, the preferred stock is cumulative; and preferred dividends and all arrears thereon must be paid before a dividend is declared on common stock.

Preferred stock also may be classified as participating or nonparticipating. Owners of *participating* preferred stock are entitled to the preferred dividend and to any dividends declared after the common shareholders have been paid an amount equal to the preferred dividend. When the only amount of dividend a preferred shareholder is entitled to receive is the preference, the preferred stock is *nonparticipating.* In this latter situation, the common shareholders receive as dividends whatever amount the company can pay after paying the preferred dividends. The common shareholders may earn an amount of dividends equal to, less than, or greater than that received by the preferred shareholders. When the preferred stock is not explicitly described in the articles of incorporation, it is presumed to be nonparticipating.

Stock warrant

A certificate that gives the holder the right to subscribe for and purchase, at a stated price, a given number of shares of stock in a corporation

STOCK WARRANT A **stock warrant** is a certificate that gives its holder the right to subscribe for and purchase a given number of shares of stock in a corporation at a stated price. It is usually issued in connection with the sale of other shares of stock or of bonds although the law of some states permits the issuance of stock warrants entirely separate and apart from the sale of other securities. Warrants are transferable. The option to purchase contained in the warrant may or may not be limited as to time or otherwise conditioned. Warrants have value and can readily be sold on the market in the same fashion as other securities.

PAR VALUE STOCK Each share of stock traditionally is designated by the incorporators as having a stated par value. This par value notation is not necessarily related to the fair market value of the stock. In essence, the par value is the dollar amount that the corporation must receive and enter into its stated capital account for each share of stock sold.

NO-PAR STOCK The statutes of most states provide that a corporation may issue stock with *no par value.* The value of no-par stock is determined by its sale price in the open market or by the price set by the directors as a "stated value." Shareholders, creditors of the corporation, and the public are not misled or prejudiced by this type of stock because there is no holding out that the stock has any particular face value. All persons dealing in no-par stock are put on notice that they should investigate the corporation's assets and its financial condition.

Watered stock

Corporate stock issued by a corporation for property at an overvaluation, or stock issued for which the corporation receives nothing in payment

WATERED STOCK **Watered stock** is stock that has been issued as fully paid, when in fact its full *par value* has not been paid in money, property, or services. The original owner of watered stock has liability for the unpaid portion of its stated value. If Catherine exchanges property worth $200 for 1,000 shares of $1 par value stock, she owes the corporation $800. If the corporation becomes insolvent, a creditor may require that the balance due be paid by Catherine.

The liability for watered stock arises because the stated capital account of a corporation represents the total par value of all the shares of the corporation. The public, including corporate creditors, has a right to assume that the stock issued has been paid for in full. The corporation in effect represents that assets have been received in payment equal in amount to the corporation's stated capital account. If stock is issued and the actual assets in money value received by the corporation are less than the par value, there is watered stock.

While the watering of par value stock is easy to envision, the watering of no par value is less obvious. Nevertheless, because the board of directors designates a stated value for even no-par-value stock, watering of this stock does occur when the corporation receives less than the designated value for the no-par-value shares.

Treasury stock

Stock of a corporation that has been issued by the corporation for value but is later returned to the corporation by way of gift or purchase

TREASURY STOCK **Treasury stock** has been issued by the corporation for value and returned to the corporation by gift or purchase. It may be sold at any price, including below par, and the proceeds returned to the treasury of the corporation for working capital. It differs from stock originally issued below par in that the purchaser is not liable for the difference between par and the sale price. It may be sold at any price the company sees fit to charge.

A corporation is restricted in its power to purchase treasury stock because the purchase might effect a reduction of its capital, to the detriment of creditors. In most states a corporation is permitted to purchase treasury stock only out of accumulated profits or surplus. This restriction retains stockholders' investment, equivalent to the original capital, as a protective cushion for creditors in case subsequent losses develop.

A corporation may redeem its preferred stock if there is no injury to, or objection by, creditors. Here again, many of the states require the preferred stock to be redeemed out of surplus, or they demand that authority to reduce the capital stock be obtained from the state.

2. Stock Subscriptions

A *preincorporation* stock *subscription* is an agreement to purchase stock in a corporation. It is a binding agreement (a subscriber cannot revoke a subscription) created among the subscribers for stock in a corporation to be formed. The subscription is usually drafted in a manner that creates a contract. By statute some states have provided that a preincorporation subscription constitutes a binding, irrevocable offer to the corporation, by reason of the mutual promises of the parties. The offer is usually limited to a specified period of time, such as six months.

Certain conditions are inherent in the preincorporation subscription contract. The subscriber will not be liable unless the corporation is completely organized; the full amount of the capital stock is subscribed; and the purpose, articles, and bylaws of the corporation are as originally stated and relied on by the subscriber. Conditions, expressed or implied, are often waived by the subscriber if, with knowledge of the nonperformance, he or she participates in stockholders' meetings, pays part or all of his or her subscription, or acts as an officer or director of the corporation.

A subscription to stock of a corporation already in existence is a contract between the subscriber and the corporation. Such a contract may come into existence by reason of an offer either made by the corporation and accepted by the subscriber or made by the subscriber and accepted by the corporation. If the corporation opens subscription books and advertises its stock, it is seeking for an offer to be made by the subscriber. The corporation may, however, make a general offer to the public, which may be accepted by the subscriber in accordance with the terms of the general offer.

3. Right to Transfer Stock

A share of stock is personal property, and the owner has the right to transfer it just as he or she may transfer any other personal property. The right to transfer freely one's share in the corporation is one of the features of corporate life that distinguishes it from a partnership. A share of stock is generally transferred by an indorsement and the delivery of the certificate of stock and by surrender of the certificate to the stock transfer agent for reissue.

Shareholders of close corporations usually attempt to restrict the transfer of stock. Such attempts may be part of a contract, or they may be included in the bylaws. These restrictions may be a simple right of first refusal to the corporation, the other shareholder, or both, or there may be a binding buy-and-sell agreement among the shareholders. By these restrictions there may be a sale of the stock upon the occurrence of a specified event, even if the owner or the estate of the owner does not desire to sell.

A corporate bylaw that makes shares of stock transferable only to the corporation or to those approved by the board of directors is unenforceable. It places too severe a restraint on the alienation of property. Society is best protected when property may be transferred freely, but an agreement or bylaw approved by all shareholders to the effect that no transfer of stock shall be made until it has first been offered to the other shareholders or to the corporation is generally enforced. Notice of the bylaw or agreement should be set forth in the stock certificate because an innocent purchaser without notice of the restriction on alienation receives ownership free from the restriction.

In a closely held corporation, sometimes the buy-and-sell agreements between shareholders provide for matters such as salary continuation in the event of death or disability and the amount of dividends to be paid in the future. Some agreements even commit the shareholders to vote for certain persons in the election of directors. *Such agreements are valid in closely held corporations,* providing the duration of the agreement is not so long that it becomes contrary to public policy and providing the agreement does not adversely affect minority interests in the corporation. These agreements are used by the majority owners to ensure the election of the desired board of directors. Corporations are governed by the republican principle that the whole is bound by lawful acts of the majority. It is not against public policy or dishonest for shareholders to contract for the purpose of control.

The importance of shareholder buy-and-sell provisions must not be overlooked. It is just as important to have a means of getting a shareholder out of a closely held corporation as it is to have a means of getting a partner out of a partnership.

Shareholder buy-and-sell provisions should be worked out before any shareholder knows whether he or she is a buyer or a seller. Although withdrawal from active participation will not affect dissolution, it can have the serious effect of precipitating a lawsuit; or a shareholder may continue to participate in management when he or she does not desire to do so. Frequently, a withdrawing shareholder will be forced to sell stock for less than it is worth because a buy-and-sell agreement was not worked out in advance.

4. Mechanics of Transfer

A share may be transferred or assigned by a bill of sale or by any other method that will pass title to intangible property. Whenever a share of stock is sold and a new stock certificate issued, the name of the new owner is entered on the stock records of the corporation. In a small corporation, the secretary of the corporation usually handles all transfers of stock and also the canceling of old certificates and the issuing of new. Large corporations, in which there are hundreds and even thousands of transactions, employ transfer agents. The transfer agents transfer stock, cancel old certificates, issue new ones, keep an up-to-date list of the names of shareholders of the corporation, distribute dividends, mail out shareholders' notices, and perform many functions to assist the corporation secretary. Stock exchange rules provide that corporations listing stock for sale must maintain a transfer agency and registry, operated and maintained under exchange regulations. The registrar of stock is an agent of the corporation whose duty is to see that no stock certificates are issued in excess of the authorized capitalization of the corporation.

Article 8 of the Uniform Commercial Code (UCC) deals with investment securities. The general approach of Article 8 is that securities are negotiable instruments and that bona fide purchasers have greater rights than they would have "if the things bought were chattels or simple contracts." The particular rules of Article 3 that relate to the establishment of preferred status for commercial paper are applied to securities. Defenses of the issuer are generally not effective against a purchaser for value who has received the securities without being given notice of the particular defense raised.

A bona fide purchaser is one who purchases in good faith and without notice of any adverse claim. This purchaser is the equivalent of a holder in due course of a negotiable instrument, which is discussed in Chapter 35. A bona fide purchaser is not subject to "adverse claims," which include a claim that a transfer was wrongful or that some other person is the owner of, or has an interest in, the security.

SHAREHOLDERS

5. Rights in General

A shareholder has the following rights, usually created by statute and reiterated in the bylaws: (1) the right to inspect the books and papers of the corporation, (2) the right to attend shareholders' meetings and to vote for directors and on certain other matters such as dissolution or merger, (3) the preemptive right, (4) the right to bring a shareholder's derivative suit, and (5) the right to share in the profits when a dividend is declared. In some states a shareholder has the additional right to cumulative voting.

The right to inspect the books and papers is limited to good-faith inspections for proper and honest purposes at the proper time and the proper place. The general rule applied by the courts reviewing inspection statutes has been that the primary purpose of the inspection must not be one that is adverse to the best interests of the corporation. A *proper purpose* is one that seeks to protect the interests of the corporation as well as the interests of the shareholder seeking the information. To protect his or her interests, a shareholder is legitimately entitled to know anything and everything that the records, books, and papers of the company would show. A shareholder must have an honest motive and not proceed for vexatious or speculative reasons. A shareholder must seek something more than satisfaction of curiosity and must not be conducting a general fishing expedition. A shareholder's desire to learn the reasons for lack of dividends or low dividends, and suspicion of mismanagement arising from such dividend policy, will constitute a proper purpose. Most courts consider an attempt to oust present management to be a proper purpose.

In general, the burden of proof rests on the corporation to prove the shareholder's purpose for inspecting corporate documents is improper. However, courts in other states have held that the burden of proving good faith and proper purpose for a shareholder's examination of corporate records rests on the shareholder. Proof of actual mismanagement or wrongdoing is not necessary, and good-faith fears of mismanagement are sufficient to justify the shareholder's inspection.

The business hours of the corporation are the reasonable and proper hours in which stockholders are entitled to inspect the books. They also have the right to the assistance of accountants and attorneys in that inspection. The assistance of qualified professionals is often required to understand the books and records and to know what to ask for.

In some states, a shareholder who is refused access to the books and records is entitled to damages as provided by statute. A typical statute provides that a shareholder who is denied the right to inspect books and records is entitled to damages equal to 10 percent of the value of the stock owned. This right to inspect includes contracts and correspondence as well as books and records. The right extends even to confidential records.

The shareholders' other rights, in addition to the right of inspection, are discussed in the following sections.

6. Meetings

Action by the shareholders normally binds the corporation only when taken in a regular or properly called special meeting after notice required by the bylaws or statute has been given. It is generally conceded, however—and most states so provide by statute—that action approved informally by *all* shareholders will bind the corporation. If there is less than unanimous approval, informal action is not possible.

NOTICE Notice of a special meeting must include a statement concerning matters to be acted on at the meeting; any action taken on other matters will be ineffective. If unusual action, such as a sale of corporate assets, is to be taken at the regular annual meeting, notice of the meeting must call specific attention to that fact; but otherwise, any business may be transacted at the annual meeting.

Failure to give proper notice of a meeting generally invalidates the action taken at the meeting. A stockholder who has not received notice but attends and participates in a meeting waives the lack of notice by his or her presence.

Proxy

Authority to act for another, used by absent stockholders to have their votes cast by others

QUORUM A quorum of shareholders must be present to transact business. Shareholders may be present at a meeting either in person or by **proxy**. When a shareholder cannot attend the meeting, that shareholder may grant another the right to vote by signing a proxy statement. In essence, a proxy is an appointment by the shareholder of an agent to serve as a representative during the shareholder's absence. If shareholders leave during the meeting, they can no longer be counted as present.

A *quorum* is usually a majority of the voting shares outstanding unless some statute or the bylaws provide for a larger or smaller percentage. Affirmative action is approved by majority vote of the shares represented at a meeting, provided a quorum exists. Under common law, certain unusual matters such as a merger or sale of all corporate assets require a unanimous vote. Today, statutes usually provide that such actions can be taken by a vote of two-thirds or three-fourths of the shareholders. Many of these statutes also provide that the dissenting shareholders have the right to surrender their shares and receive their fair value if they disapprove of the action taken.

PURPOSES In large, publicly held corporations, the annual meeting of shareholders serves a variety of purposes. Management has usually solicited enough proxies in advance to control any vote that is taken, so the outcome is usually a certainty. Nevertheless, many shareholders attend meetings to question management on a variety of issues and to lobby for certain policies. Management uses the annual meeting of shareholders of large corporations as a public relations opportunity to educate the shareholders on company accomplishments as well as its problems.

7. Voting

Statutes of the states and the charters issued under their authority prescribe the matters on which shareholders are entitled to vote. Usually, they vote on the *election of directors*; on *major policy issues* such as mergers, consolidations, and dissolution; and, in some instances, on a *change in the bylaws.*

Some state laws allow a corporation to deny some shareholders the vote on certain issues, such as the election of directors. This denial allows a minority of shareholders to obtain control. Since public policy supports the right of an investor to vote, however, the status of stock as nonvoting must be communicated to the investor, or the stock purchase may be rescinded.

As a general rule, every shareholder of common stock is entitled to as many votes as he or she owns shares of stock. The shareholder whose name appears in the corporate records is usually designated by the bylaws as the person entitled to vote. Owners of preferred stock, depending on their contract with the corporation, may or may not be entitled to vote.

Straight voting
In voting for directors, when each shareholder may cast votes for each director position equal to the number of shares owned

Directors are elected through either a straight voting or cumulative voting process. Many states adopt **straight voting** (e.g., Delaware), where a shareholder may cast as many votes for a nominee for a director position as the shareholder has shares. In this manner, the holder of a majority of shares can dominate the voting of the board. In fact, the majority shareholder could elect ALL of the directors; therefore, minority shareholders could end up with no representation on the board.

Cumulative voting
In voting for directors, when stockholders may cast as many votes as they have shares of stock multiplied by the number to be elected and their votes may be cast as all for one candidate or distributed among as many candidates as there are positions to be filled.

Some states, including California, provide for **cumulative voting** in the election of directors. In cumulative voting, a shareholder may cast as many votes for one board candidate as there are board members to be filled, multiplied by the number of shares of stock owned. Alternatively, this shareholder may distribute the votes among the candidates as he or she sees fit. A shareholder owning 100 shares of stock has 300 votes if three directors are to be elected. He or she may case all 300 for one candidate, or they may be spread among the candidates. In this manner of voting, it is possible for a minority shareholder to elect a member to the board.

A shareholder is entitled to vote only by virtue of his or her ownership of stock but may specifically authorize another to vote this stock. Authorization is made by power of attorney and must specifically state that the agent of the shareholder has power to vote the principal's stock. This voting by proxy is a personal relationship that the shareholder may revoke before the authority is exercised. Laws pertaining to principal and agent control this relationship.

A shareholder, unlike a director, is permitted to vote on a matter in which he or she has a personal interest. Although in certain respects shareholders represent the corporate welfare in their voting, in most respects they vote to serve their interests. A majority of shareholders is not permitted to take action that is clearly detrimental to the corporate and minority interest.

8. Preemptive Rights

The original application for a charter specifies the amount of stock that will be issued without further notice to the state. The amount of authorized stock and the amount of issued stock are used to compute the license fees and franchise taxes due to the state of incorporation. These limitations on stocks cannot be increased or exceeded without the authority of the state.

Shareholders may authorize an increase in the authorized capital stock, but such action may not be taken by the directors. An increase in the authorized capital stock is an amendment to the corporate charter, which requires state approval.

The board of directors may sell unissued capital stock when the amount previously issued is less than that authorized. This sale does not require an amendment to the charter. All that is required is that the state be informed of the additional issue of the stock so the correct taxes may be collected.

When an increase in the capital stock has been properly authorized, *the existing shareholders have a prior right over third parties to subscribe to the increased capital stock.* This right is called the shareholders' *preemptive rights.* It is based on the shareholders' right to protect and maintain their proportionate control and interest in the corporation. The preemptive rights may be limited or waived by contract and by provisions in the charter or bylaws of the corporation in most states.

The issue of whether a corporate charter allowed the board to issue stock with preemptive rights is central to the following case.

CASE

Benihana of Tokyo, Inc., Individually and on Behalf of Benihana, Inc. v. Benihana, Inc., John E. Abdo, Norman Becker, Darwin Dornbush, Max Pine, Yoshihiro Sano, Joel Schwartz, Robert B. Sturges, Takanori Yoshimoto, and BFC Financial Corp.

SUPREME COURT OF DELAWARE

906 A.2d 114 (2006)

Rocky Aoki founded Benihana of Tokyo, Inc. (BOT), and its subsidiary, Benihana, which own and operate Benihana restaurants in the United States and other countries. Aoki owned 100% of BOT until 1998, when he pled guilty to insider trading charges. In order to avoid licensing problems created by his status as a convicted felon, Aoki transferred his stock to the Benihana Protective Trust. The trustees of the Trust were Aoki's three children (Kana Aoki Nootenboom, Kyle Aoki and Kevin Aoki) and Darwin Dornbush (who was then the family's attorney, a Benihana director, and, effectively, the company's general counsel).

Benihana, a Delaware corporation, has two classes of common stock. There are approximately 6 million shares of Class A common stock outstanding. Each share has 1/10 vote, and the holders of Class A common are entitled to elect 25% of the directors. There are approximately 3 million shares of Common stock outstanding. Each share of Common has one vote, and the holders of Common stock are entitled to elect the remaining 75% of Benihana's directors. Before the transaction at issue, BOT owned 50.9% of the Common stock and 2% of the Class A stock. The nine-member board of directors is classified, and the directors serve three-year terms.

In 2003, shortly after Aoki married Keiko Aoki, conflicts arose between Aoki and his children. In August, the children were upset to learn that Aoki had changed his will to give Keiko control over BOT. Joel Schwartz, Benihana's president and chief executive officer, also was concerned about this change in control. He discussed the situation with Dornbush, and they briefly considered various options, including the issuance of sufficient Class A stock to trigger a provision in the certificate of incorporation that would allow the Common and Class A to vote together for 75% of the directors.

The Aoki family's turmoil came at a time when Benihana also was facing challenges. Many of its restaurants were old and outmoded. Benihana hired WD Partners to evaluate its facilities and to plan and design appropriate renovations. The resulting Construction and Renovation Plan anticipated that the project would take at least five years and cost $56 million or more. Wachovia offered to provide Benihana a $60 million line of credit for the Construction and Renovation Plan; but the restrictions Wachovia imposed made it unlikely that Benihana would be able to borrow the full amount. Because the Wachovia line of credit did not assure that Benihana would have the capital it needed, the company retained Morgan Joseph & Co. to develop other financing options.

Joseph explained in a report that the preferred stock would provide the funds needed for the Construction and Renovation Plan and also put the company in a better negotiating position if it sought additional financing

continued

from Wachovia. Joseph gave the directors a board book, marked "Confidential," containing an analysis of the proposed stock issuance (the Transaction). The book included, among others, the following anticipated terms: (i) issuance of $20,000,000 of preferred stock, convertible into Common stock; (ii) dividend of 6% +/- 0.5%; (iii) conversion premium of 20% +/- 2.5%; (iv) buyer's approval required for material corporate transactions; and (v) one to two board seats to the buyer. At trial, Joseph testified that the terms had been chosen by looking at comparable stock issuances and analyzing the Morgan Joseph proposal under a theoretical model.

The board met again on February 17, 2004, to review the terms of the Transaction. Shortly after the February meeting, Abdo contacted Joseph and told him that BFC Financial Corporation was interested in buying the new convertible stock. In April 2005, Joseph sent BFC a private placement memorandum. Abdo negotiated with Joseph for several weeks. They agreed to the Transaction on the following basic terms: (i) $20 million issuance in two tranches of $10 million each, with the second tranche to be issued one to three years after the first; (ii) BFC obtained one seat on the board, and one additional seat if Benihana failed to pay dividends for two consecutive quarters; (iii) ***BFC obtained preemptive rights on any new voting securities;*** *(iv) 5% dividend; (v) 15% conversion premium; (vi) BFC had the right to force Benihana to redeem the preferred stock in full after ten years; and (vii) the stock would have immediate "as if converted" voting rights. Joseph testified that he was satisfied with the negotiations, as he had obtained what he wanted with respect to the most important points.*

On April 22, 2004, Abdo sent a memorandum to Dornbush, Schwartz and Joseph, listing the agreed terms of the Transaction. He did not send the memorandum to any other members of the Benihana board. Schwartz did tell Becker, Sturges, Sano, and possibly Pine that BFC was the potential buyer. At its next meeting, held on May 6, 2004, the entire board was officially informed of BFC's involvement in the Transaction. Abdo made a presentation on behalf of BFC and then left the meeting. Joseph distributed an updated board book, which explained that Abdo had approached Morgan Joseph on behalf of BFC, and included the negotiated terms. The trial court found that the board was not informed that Abdo had negotiated the deal on behalf of BFC, but the board did know that Abdo was a principal of BFC. After discussion, the board reviewed and approved the Transaction, subject to the receipt of a fairness opinion.

On May 18, 2004, after he learned that Morgan Joseph was providing a fairness opinion, Schwartz publicly announced the stock issuance. Two days later, Aoki's counsel sent a letter asking the board to abandon the Transaction and pursue other, more favorable, financing alternatives. The letter expressed concern about the directors' conflicts, the dilutive effect of the stock issuance, and its "questionable legality."

On June 8, 2004, Benihana and BFC executed the Stock Purchase Agreement. On June 11, 2004, the board met and approved resolutions ratifying the execution of the Stock Purchase Agreement and authorizing the stock issuance.

On July 2, 2004, BOT filed this action against all of Benihana's directors, except Kevin Aoki, alleging breaches of fiduciary duties, and against BFC, alleging that it aided and abetted the fiduciary violations. The Court of Chancery held a four-day trial in November 2004. In December 2005, after post-trial briefing and argument, the trial court issued an opinion holding that Benihana was authorized to issue the preferred stock with preemptive rights and that the board's approval of the Transaction was a valid exercise of business judgment. This appeal followed.

We must decide whether Benihana's certificate of incorporation authorized the board to issue preferred stock with preemptive rights. Article 4, P2 of the certificate provides that, "[n]o stockholder shall have any preemptive right to subscribe to or purchase any issue of stock ... of the corporation. ..."

Article 4 (b) authorizes the board to issue "Preferred Stock of any series and to state in the resolution or resolutions providing for the issuance of shares of any series the voting powers, if any, designations, preferences and relative, participating, optional or other special rights, and the qualifications, limitations or restrictions of such series to the full extent now or hereafter permitted by the law of the State of Delaware..."

BOT contends that Article 4, P2 clearly and unambiguously prohibits preemptive rights. BOT acknowledges that Article 4(b) gives the board so-called "blank check" authority to designate the rights and preferences of Benihana's preferred stock. Reading the two provisions together, BOT argues that they give the board blank check authority to designate rights and preferences as to all enumerated matters except preemptive rights.

The trial court reviewed the history of 8 Del. C. § 102, and decided that the boilerplate language in Article 4, P2 merely confirms that no stockholder has preemptive rights under common law. As a result, the seemingly absolute language in P2 has no bearing on the availability of contractually created preemptive rights. The trial court explained:

Before the 1967 amendments, § 102(b)(3) provided that a certificate of incorporation may contain provisions "limiting or denying to the stockholders the preemptive rights to subscribe to any or all additional issues of stock of the corporation." As a result, a common law rule developed that shareholders possess preemptive rights unless the certificate of incorporation provided otherwise. In 1967, the Delaware Legislature reversed this presumption. Section 102(b)(3) was amended to provide in relevant part: "No stockholder shall have any preemptive right ... unless, and except to the extent that, such right is expressly granted to him in the certificate of incorporation."

Thereafter, companies began including boilerplate language in their charters to clarify that no shareholder possessed preemptive rights under common law.

The blank check provision in Benihana's Certificate of Incorporation suggests that the certificate was never intended to limit Benihana's ability to issue preemptive rights by contract to purchasers of preferred stock. Therefore, I do not read Article 4 of the charter as doing anything more than confirming that the common law presumption does not apply and that the Certificate of Incorporation itself does not grant any preemptive rights.

It is settled law that certificates of incorporation are contracts, subject to the general rules of contract and statutory construction. Thus, if the charter language is clear and unambiguous, it must be given its plain meaning. If there is ambiguity, however, the language must be construed in a manner that will harmonize the apparent conflicts and give effect to the intent of the drafters. The Court of Chancery properly applied these principles, and we agree with its conclusion that the Benihana certificate does not prohibit the issuance of preferred stock with preemptive rights.

■ *Affirmed.*

CASE CONCEPTS REVIEW

1. Why was the granting of preemptive rights important to those involved in this litigation?
2. Why did the court find articles of incorporation allowed the board to issue stock with preemptive rights?

The preemptive rights are applicable to new authorizations of stock. They are generally not applicable to new issues of stock previously authorized. If the new issue of an original authorization takes place a long time after the original issue, many states provide that the preemptive rights exist. Most states approve the issuance of stock to employees under stock option plans without regard to the preemptive rights.

9. Derivative Suits

A shareholder cannot maintain an action *at law* for injuries to the corporation because the corporation is a legal entity and by law has a right to bring a suit in its own name. Any cause of action based on conduct injurious to the corporation accrues in the first instance to the corporation. Nor can a shareholder bring a suit against the directors or other officers of the corporation for negligence, waste, and mismanagement in the conduct of the corporate business. The right to sue for injuries to the corporation rests strictly with the corporation itself, unless modified by statute.

A shareholder may, however, bring a suit in equity known as a shareholder's *derivative suit* to enjoin the officers of a corporation from entering into ultra *vires* contracts or from doing anything that would impair the corporate assets. Likewise, the shareholder has a right to bring suit for dollar damages on behalf of the corporation if the officers are acting outside the scope of their authority, are guilty of negligent conduct, or are engaging in fraudulent transactions that are injurious to the corporation itself. Any judgment received in such an action is paid to the corporation. The shareholder who initiates the action is permitted to recover the expenses involved in the suit.

The purpose of a derivative action is twofold. First, it is the equivalent of a suit by the shareholders to compel the corporation to sue; and second, it is a suit by the corporation, asserted by the shareholders on its behalf, against those liable to it.

As a general rule, the shareholder bringing the derivative suit must have been a shareholder at the time of the action complained of and at the time the suit was filed. Individuals are not allowed to acquire stock for the purpose of filing a derivative action or to reacquire it.

Before shareholders may bring a derivative suit, they must show that they have done everything possible to secure action by the managing officers and directors, who have refused to act. Shareholders must first seek to persuade the officers and directors to take action. Shareholders upset at a corporate failure to bring a lawsuit may not initiate a derivative suit without first demanding it of the directors. If the directors refuse and the derivative action challenges that refusal, courts normally accept the business judgment of the directors. The directors' decision will hold unless bad faith is proved. The corporate decision not to file a lawsuit against directors or others will rarely be set aside by a court if it is made on the basis of a recommendation by outside directors or disinterested investigators. This deference to objective board decisions is based on the *business judgment rule,* which is discussed in Section 16.

However, the futility of a stockholder's demand on a board of directors will excuse the demand. Futility of a stockholder's demand on a board of directors to redress an alleged wrong to the corporation is gauged by circumstances existing at the commencement of the derivative suit. For example, if the officers and directors are under an influence that sterilizes their discretion, they cannot be considered proper persons to conduct litigation on behalf of the corporation. Thus, if there is a conflict of interests in the directors' decision not to sue because the directors themselves have profited from the transaction underlying the litigation, no demand need be made and the shareholders can proceed directly with the derivative suit. In such cases, the business judgment rule does not come into play. The United States Supreme Court has held that whether a demand on the corporate directors is essential or whether a demand is futile and thus excused is to be resolved by applying the appropriate state law, not federal law.

Mere dissatisfaction with the management of the corporation will not justify a derivative suit. In the law of corporations, it is fundamental that the majority shareholders control the policies and decisions of the corporation. Every shareholder implicitly agrees that he or she will be bound by the acts and decisions of a majority of the shareholders or by the agents of the corporation they choose. Courts will not undertake to control the business of a corporation although it may be seen that better decisions might be made and the business might be more successful if other methods were pursued. If a majority of disinterested directors acting in good faith and with reasonable business judgment adopt a course of action, it will not be overturned by a derivative suit.

In essence, to be the plaintiffs in a proper derivative suit, the shareholders first must have a claim that is for the corporation's benefit and not the shareholders personally. Second, the plaintiffs must be able to represent the interests of similarly situated shareholders.

10. Dividends

Dividend

A stockholder's pro rata share in the distributed profits of a corporation

Although a shareholder has a right to share in **dividends** when declared, whether or not a dividend is declared is within the discretion of the board of directors. *Shareholders are not entitled to the payment of a dividend simply because earned surplus exists.* The board of directors may see fit to continue the profits in the business for the purpose of expansion, but it must act reasonably and in good faith. Where fraud or a gross abuse of discretion is shown and there are profits out of which dividends may be declared, the shareholders may compel the board of directors to declare dividends. Before there is a right to interfere by asking a court to order the payment of dividends, however, it must be clear that the board of directors has illegally, wantonly, and without justification refused to declare a dividend.

The following famous case illustrates the rare exception when a court will order the board of directors to grant a dividend.

CASE

Dodge v. Ford Motor Co.

SUPREME COURT OF MICHIGAN

170 N.W. 668 (1919)

OSTRANDER, J.

The parties in the first instance associating, who signed the articles, included Henry Ford, whose subscription was for 255 shares, John F. Dodge, Horace E. Dodge, the plaintiffs, Horace H. Rackham and James Couzens, who each subscribed for 50 shares, and several other persons. The company began business in June 1903. In the year 1908, its articles were amended, and the capital stock increased from $150,000 to $2,000,000, the number of shares being increased to 20,000; and the number increased again as the company prospered.

When plaintiffs made their complaint and demand for further dividends the Ford Motor Company had concluded its most prosperous year of business. The demand for its cars at the price of the preceding year continued. It could make and could market in the year beginning August 1, 1916, more than 500,000 cars. Sales of parts and repairs would necessarily increase. The cost of materials was likely to advance and, perhaps, the price of labor, but it reasonably might have expected a profit for the year of upwards of $60,000,000. It had assets of more than $132,000,000, a surplus of almost $112,000,000, and its cash on hand and municipal bonds were nearly $54,000,000. Its total liabilities, including capital stock, were a little over $20,000,000. It had declared no special dividend during the business year except the October 1915, dividend. It had been the practice, under similar circumstances, to declare larger dividends. Considering only these facts, a refusal to declare and pay further dividends appears to be not an exercise of discretion on the part of the directors but, rather, an arbitrary refusal to do what the circumstances required to be done. These facts and others call upon the directors to justify their action, or failure or refusal to act.

Mr. Henry Ford is the dominant force in the business of the Ford Motor Company. No plan of operations could be adopted unless he consented; and no board of directors can be elected whom he does not favor. One of the directors of the company has no stock. One share was assigned to him to qualify him for the position, but it is not claimed that he owns it. A business, one of the largest in the world, and one of the most profitable, has been built up. It employs many men, at good pay.

"My ambition," said Mr. Ford, "is to employ still more men, to spread the benefits of this industrial system to the greatest possible number, to help them build up their lives and their homes. To do this we are putting the greatest share of our profits back in the business." "With regard to dividends, the company paid 60 per cent on its capitalization of two million dollars, or $1,200,000, leaving $58,000,000 to reinvest for the growth of the company. This is Mr. Ford's policy at present, and it is understood that the other stockholders cheerfully accede to this plan." He had made up his mind in the summer of 1916 that no dividends other than the regular dividends should be paid, "for the present."

*Bill by John F. Dodge and another against the Ford Motor Company and others to compel the declaration of dividends. From the decree rendered, defendants appeal. Affirmed as to dividends.*The record, and especially the testimony of Mr. Ford, convinces that he has, to some extent, the attitude towards shareholders of one who has dispensed and distributed to them large gains and that they should be content to take what he chooses to give. His testimony creates the impression, also, that he thinks the Ford Motor Company has made too much money, has had profits that are too large, and that although large profits might be still earned, a sharing of them with the public, by reducing the price of the output of the company, ought to be undertaken. We have no doubt that certain sentiments, philanthropic and altruistic, creditable to Mr. Ford, had large influence in determining the policy to be pursued by the Ford Motor Company.

Assuming the general plan and policy of expansion and the details of it to have been sufficiently and formally approved at the October and November 1917, meetings of directors, and assuming further that the plan and policy and the details agreed upon were for the best ultimate interest of the company and, therefore, of its shareholders, what does it amount to in justification of a refusal to declare and pay a special dividend or dividends?

Defendants say, and it is true, that a considerable cash balance must be at all times carried by such a concern; but, as has been stated, there was a large daily, weekly, monthly, receipt of cash. The output was practically continuous and was continuously, and within a few days, turned into cash. Moreover, the contemplated expenditures were not to be immediately made. So that, without going further, it would appear that, accepting and approving the plan of the directors, it was their duty to distribute on or near the first of August, 1916, a very large sum of money to stockholders.

In reaching this conclusion, we do not ignore, but rather recognize, the validity of the proposition that plaintiffs have from the beginning profited by—if they have not lately, officially, participated in—the general policy of expansion pursued by this corporation. We do not lose sight of the fact that it had been, upon an occasion, agreeable to the plaintiffs to increase the capital stock to $100,000,000 by a stock dividend of $98,000,000. These things go only to answer other contentions now made by plaintiffs and do not and cannot operate to estop them to demand proper dividends upon the stock they own. It is obvious that an annual dividend of sixty per cent upon $2,000,000, or $1 - $200,000, is the equivalent of a very small dividend upon $100,000,000, or more.

The decree of the court below, fixing and determining the specific amount to be distributed to stockholders, is affirmed. In other respects, except as to the allowance of costs, the said decree is reversed. Plaintiffs will recover interest at 5 per cent per annum upon their proportional share of said dividend from the date of the decree of the lower court. Appellants will tax the costs of their appeal, and two-thirds of the amount thereof will be paid by plaintiffs. No other costs are allowed.

■ *Affirmed in part, reversed in part.*

CASE CONCEPTS REVIEW

1. Why was Mr. Ford not inclined to encourage the board of directors to grant a dividend?
2. Why did the appellate court support the trial court's decision to order dividends be granted?

Stock dividend

New shares of its own stock issued as a dividend by a corporation to its shareholders, to transfer retained earnings to capital stock

Stock split

A readjustment of the financial plan of a corporation, whereby each existing share of stock is split into new shares, usually with a lowering of par value

A *cash dividend,* when declared, becomes a debt of the corporation. Once the declaration of a dividend has been made public, it may not be rescinded. A declaration of dividends is proper as long as it does not impair the corporation's capital stock. Any dividend that reduces the net assets of the corporation below its stated capital account is illegal. Directors are personally liable to creditors for dividends improperly declared. In addition to the directors' personal liability, shareholders who receive illegal dividends generally may be compelled to return them.

The cash dividend will be paid to the person whose name appears on the corporate stock records as the owner of the share on the record date the dividend is payable. This is known as the ex-dividend date. The fact that it is paid to this person does not necessarily mean that the payee is entitled to keep it. If the stock has been sold prior to the dividend date but not transferred on the books of the corporation, the buyer is entitled to the dividend. On the other hand, if there is only a contract to sell the stock, the seller is entitled to any dividend paid prior to the delivery of the stock.

A **stock dividend** involves a transfer of retained earnings to the capital account. This dividend is used when the earnings are required for growth of the business. Stock dividends of the issuing company are not taxable income to shareholders. A **stock split** differs from a stock dividend in that with the stock split there is no transfer of earnings to capital but only a reduction in par value and an increase in the number of shares.

11. Fiduciary Aspects

The law as it relates to shareholders' relationships in closely held corporations is somewhat different from the law as it relates to them in publicly held corporations. Publicly held corporations have many shareholders, none of whom owns a majority of the stock. As a general rule, there is no fiduciary relationship between shareholders in publicly held corporations. One owner of stock listed on the New York Stock Exchange, for example, owes no duty to other owners of the same stock unless, of course, the shareholder is also an insider subject to regulation by the Securities and Exchange Commission.

A *closely held corporation* is one in which management and ownership are substantially identical, to the extent that it is unrealistic to believe that the judgment of the directors will be independent of that of the shareholders. The shareholders in a closely held corporation owe one another substantially the same fiduciary duty that partners owe one another. They must discharge their management and shareholder responsibilities in conformity with the strict good-faith standard, and they may not act out of avarice, expediency, or self-interest in derogation of their loyalty to other shareholders and to the corporation. A shareholder in a closely held corporation may not permit his or her private interests to clash with those of the corporation and other shareholders.

Some courts have called closely held corporations "incorporated partnerships." They are corporations for liability, perpetual existence, and taxation, but the shareholders expect to act and to be treated as partners in their dealings among themselves. The practical realities dictate that the relationship be considered a fiduciary one, demanding fairness, honesty, and fall disclosure of all functions.

Suits alleging a breach of fiduciary duty often involve the purchase of stock by a majority shareholder or director from a minority shareholder. Such purchases usually involve the use of inside information. A seller under these circumstances should be aware that the buyer has superior knowledge. In deciding such cases, there are three different views among the various states. The majority view is that a director does not stand in a fiduciary relationship to a shareholder in the acquisition of stock and, therefore, has no duty to disclose inside information. The minority view is that a director is under a duty to disclose all material information. The third view is that although a director ordinarily owes no fiduciary duty to shareholders when acquiring stock, under special circumstances a fiduciary relationship arises. The special facts creating the fiduciary relationship may include the familial relationship of the parties, the forthcoming sale of corporate assets, the director's initiation of the sale, and/or the relative ages and experience in financial affairs of the directors and the selling shareholder.

There are limits to the duties owed to minority shareholders. For example, in the absence of a valid buy-and-sell agreement, the majority shareholders or the corporation has no duty to redeem the stock upon the death of a minority shareholder.

DIRECTORS

12. Powers

Directors of a corporation are elected by the shareholders. They ordinarily attend board of director meetings, exercise judgment on propositions brought before the board, and direct management although they need not be involved actively in the day-to-day operation of the business. A director has no power to issue orders to any officer or employee, to institute policies by himself or herself, or command or veto any other action by the board.

It is not essential that directors hold stock in the corporation. Because they are to supervise the business activities, select key employees, and plan for the future development of the enterprise, they are presumably selected for their business ability.

At one time, most directors of major publicly held corporations were insiders—officials of the corporation. Today, insider-dominated corporate boards seem to be on the way out. Outside directors now constitute the majority on almost nine out of ten boards of directors. These outside directors provide greater independence, more minority representation, and greater diversification in the backgrounds of the directors. Moreover, many people feel that such boards accept more corporate social responsibility and greater accountability for their actions. They also demand higher standards of performance by corporate officers.

Directors have power to take action necessary or proper to conduct the ordinary business activities of the company. However, they may not amend the charter, approve a merger, or bring about a consolidation with another corporation without the approval of the shareholders.

13. Meetings

The bylaws usually provide for the number of directors. Historically, at least three directors were required; but in recent years, many corporate statutes have authorized two directors—and in some cases—one director. This development is especially prevalent in professional associations or corporations, which frequently have only one shareholder and thus only one director.

Since the board of directors must act as a unit, it is traditional that it assembles at board meetings. The bylaws provide for the method of calling directors' meetings and for the time and the place of the meetings. A record is usually kept of the activities of the board of directors, and the evidence of the exercise of its powers is stated in resolutions kept in the corporate minute book. A majority of the members of the board of directors is necessary to constitute a quorum, unless a bylaw provides to the contrary. Special meetings are proper only when all directors are notified or are present at the meetings. Directors may not vote by proxy, having been selected as agents because of their personal qualifications.

Modern statutes make it possible for a board to take informal action (usually by telephone), provided the action is subsequently reduced to writing and signed by all of the directors. This gives a board the flexibility and capability to make decisions without delay. Failure to have unanimous approval of such informal action or to give proper notice is fatal to actions attempted by the board of directors.

Traditionally, directors were forbidden to vote on any matter in which they had a personal interest. Even though their vote was not necessary to carry the proposition considered, many courts would regard any action voidable if it was taken as a result of that vote. Some courts went so far as to hold that if a director was present at the meeting, favorable action was not binding. Most courts held that if a director's presence was required to make a quorum, no transaction in which he or she was interested could be acted on. These rather severe rules were developed so directors would not be tempted to use their position to profit at the expense of the corporation.

Today, many states have somewhat relaxed traditional rules on directors' voting and participation. The trend of the law is to allow interested directors to be present and to be counted as a part of the quorum. Actions taken with interested directors are valid if the participating director's interest is fully and completely disclosed, provided the action is approved by a majority of disinterested directors. Even in states that have changed the earlier common-law view, a director with a personal interest in a subject is not allowed to vote on the matter. The problem of acting in good faith is discussed later in this chapter.

14. Compensation

The charter, bylaws, or a resolution by the shareholders usually stipulates payment of directors' fees. If not, service as a director is uncompensated. Directors who are appointed as officers of the corporation should have their salaries fixed at a meeting of the shareholders or in the bylaws. Because directors are not supposed to vote on any matter in which they have a personal interest, director officers of small corporations usually vote on salaries for each other but not their own; in addition, the action to determine salaries should be ratified by the shareholders to ensure the validity of the employment contracts.

Some states by statute allow a majority of directors to fix all salaries irrespective of financial interest. In these states, courts are often called on to review the reasonableness of approved salaries.

LIABILITY OF OFFICERS AND DIRECTORS

15. In General

The officers and directors of a corporation may have personal liability both in tort and in contract. The principles of the law of agency are applicable; liability is usually to the corporation although it may extend to shareholders and third parties as well.

The liability of corporate officers and directors for tortious conduct is predicated on basic common-law principles. Those who personally participate in a tort have personal liability to the third party on the usual common-law tort theories, as does any other agent or servant. This liability is based on the participation theory.

Several statutes impose liability on directors and officers. Officers and directors who have responsibility for federal withholding and social security taxes may be liable to the federal government for failure to collect and transfer these taxes for their employees.

There are numerous other statutes that impose liability on officers and directors of corporations. For example, they are subject to third-party liability for aiding a corporation in such acts as patent, copyright, or trademark infringements, unfair competition, antitrust violations, violation of the laws relating to discrimination, or violations of the securities laws. They are also personally liable when they issue stock as fully paid when it is not paid in full, or when dividends are declared or treasury stock is purchased without the requisite retained earnings.

The relationship between the officers and directors and a corporation is a fiduciary one. The existence and exercise of the statutory power of directors, rather than shareholders, to manage the business and the affairs of a corporation carries with it certain fundamental fiduciary obligations to the corporation and its shareholders. These fiduciary duties of corporate directors require that they act in the best interests of the corporation's shareholders; and this extends to protecting the corporation and its owners from perceived harm whether a threat originates from third parties or other shareholders. Liability is often imposed for violation of these fiduciary duties owed to the corporation. When liability is sought, the usual defense is the business judgment rule discussed in the next section. The fiduciary relationship requires that directors act in good faith and with due care. It prohibits conflicts of interest and imposes a duty of undivided loyalty on officers and directors. This rule is discussed further in the following sections.

16. The Business Judgment Rule

The *business judgment rule* means that courts honoring principles of corporate self-government will not inquire into the good-faith decisions involving business judgment. Directors are not liable for breach of fiduciary duties because of mere mistakes of judgment. The rule protects directors from personal liability in damages. It applies to cases of transactional justification where an injunction is sought against board action or against its decision. It puts the focus on the decision of the board as contrasted with any possible liability of the board of directors. The rule arises from the fiduciary duties of directors. It creates a presumption that places the burden of demonstrating bad faith on the party attacking an action of a board of directors. The presumption is that the directors of corporations act on an informed basis in good faith and in the honest belief that the action taken was in the best interests of the company. Thus, they are presumed not to be personally liable.

The following case illustrates the reach of the good faith commitment.

CASE

Gerald Madvig, Derivatively on Behalf of Nominal Defendant Ingles Markets, Inc. v. Charles L. Gaither, Jr., et al.

UNITED STATES DISTRICT COURT FOR THE WESTERN DISTRICT OF NORTH CAROLINA

461 F. Supp. 2d 398 (2006)

DENNIS L. HOWELL

This is a shareholder's derivative action, whereby plaintiff seeks on behalf of the shareholders to have the company sue its directors for what plaintiff contends is malfeasance or misfeasance that resulted in loss to the corporation.

Plaintiff is a shareholder of nominal defendant Ingles Markets, Inc. ("Ingles"). Ingles is a North Carolina corporation that owns and operates supermarket stores in Alabama, Georgia, North Carolina, South Carolina, Tennessee, and Virginia. The individual defendants are all directors and/or officers, former directors and/or officers, or now deceased former directors/officers of Ingles.

On February 11, 2005, a demand letter by plaintiff's counsel was sent to the Chairman of the Board of Directors of Ingles, defendant Robert P. Ingle, II. Such letter was sent in accordance with Chapter 55-7-42 of the North Carolina General Statutes, which requires that an aggrieved party first send a written demand to take suitable action to the corporation prior to filing a shareholder derivative action. In the letter, it was alleged that misconduct had occurred in the form of accounting errors, which was in turn based on a December 6, 2004, disclosure by Ingles that the Securities and Exchange Commission ("SEC") had initiated an informal inquiry into Ingles' accounting for a vendor contract.

In the demand letter, plaintiff contended that defendants as directors and officers of Ingles bore the responsibility for the consequences of the restatement of earnings by knowing approval of or gross negligence in failing to prevent and correct Ingles' improper financial reporting and accounting practices. Based on such contentions, plaintiff urged Ingles to pursue legal action against the defendants.

In accordance with North Carolina law, when a company receives a demand letter requesting that a derivative action be filed, the Board of Directors is authorized to establish a special committee of independent directors to determine through majority vote, and after conducting a reasonable inquiry, whether maintenance of a derivative proceeding is in a company's best interests. In accordance with that provision, the Board of Directors of Ingles established the Special Committee and appointed Defendants Pollard, Russell, and Wingate to serve thereon. Defendant Wingate died in August 2005, after resigning from the Special Committee.

While the report itself is undated, it was received by this court on October 10, 2005. In the fifty one page report, the Special Committee concluded and determined that: "It is not in the best interests of Ingles to continue the prosecution of the claims asserted in the Derivative Action, or to assert claims against other directors or officers regarding the mistakes that occurred with respect to accounting for certain operating leases and vendor allowances." The Special Committee based such determination on findings, among others, that there was no evidence to support plaintiffs' claims because defendants acted in good faith. The inquiry of a court reviewing the corporation's decision not to pursue the proposed litigation is limited to determining whether the decision was made in good faith.

"Good faith" in the corporate setting is defined as a decision that is made "honestly, conscientiously, fairly, and with undivided loyalty to the corporation." Further, such good faith requirement is the foundation of the business judgment rule, which has full force and effect in North Carolina. The business judgment rule, first, an initial evidentiary presumption that in making a decision the directors acted with due care (i.e., on an informed basis) and in good faith in the honest belief that their action was in the best interest of the corporation, and second, absent rebuttal of the initial presumption, a

continued

powerful substantive presumption that a decision by a loyal and informed board will not be overturned by a court unless it cannot be attributed to any rational business purpose.

North Carolina courts have consistently held that "the business judgment rule protects corporate directors from being judicially second-guessed when they exercise reasonable care and business judgment." On the other hand, in a shareholder derivative action, directors on a Special Committee act in bad faith where the committee's investigation was "so restricted in scope, so shallow in execution, or otherwise so *pro forma* or halfhearted as to constitute a pretext or sham."

Beyond the presumption that arises under North Carolina law that the actions of the Special Committee were taken in good faith, the overwhelming evidence before this court is the extensive report that documents the Special Committee's investigation as well as its findings. Such report documents that the Special Committee interviewed witnesses it considered relevant to the allegations, secured written statements from others, closely reviewed the transactions that caused the restatement of earnings, and went beyond plaintiff's allegations to investigate additional claims. Such an investigation is, on its face, a thorough consideration of the potential causes of action Ingles might have had against defendants.

In addition, the directors on the Special Committee submitted sworn affidavits—placing their own liberty interests on the line—that they would act in the best interests of the company. The Special Committee employed and actively used independent, experienced counsel, which also weighs in favor of a finding of good faith.

Plaintiff challenges the "good faith" of the Special Committee by arguing that Russell and Pollard are (1) defendants in this action and (2) were members of the audit committee. These claims are wholly without merit in showing a lack of "good faith."

As discussed above, plaintiff named all member of the Ingles' Board of Directors as defendants in this action. The Special Committee is, necessarily comprised of defendants, a fact which is solely attributable to plaintiff's pleading. Again, plaintiff's argument flatly ignores North Carolina law that holds that the status of a director as a defendant in the action does not undermine his eligibility to serve on the Special Committee.

As to being members of the Audit Committee, such fact has absolutely zero impact on whether a person can act, serve, and render an opinion in "good faith" as a member of a special committee composed to investigate a derivative action. Indeed, the only evidence on point is the deposition testimony of Pollard, who when asked if his roles on the Audit Committee conflicted with his work on the Special Committee answered, "No." When asked to explain, Pollard stated, "I felt I could be objective about it."

Defendants' Motion to Dismiss is GRANTED, and plaintiff's Complaint is DISMISSED WITH PREJUDICE.

■ *Dismissed.*

CASE CONCEPTS REVIEW

1. Based on the opinion, how would you define "good faith"?
2. What factors influenced the court to conclude that the directors who served on the special committee acted in good faith?

The presumption is also based on the belief that directors are better equipped than courts to make business judgments and that directors act independently, without self-dealing or personal interest, and exercise reasonable diligence. There are exceptions to the business judgment rule. The business judgment rule can only sustain corporate decision making or transactions that are within the power or authority of the board of directors. If the directors are guilty of fraud, bad faith, gross overreaching, an abuse of discretion, or gross negligence—in all such cases, the business judgment rule does not prevent a court from imposing personal liability on directors or from changing a board decision. If corporate directors are not entitled to protection of the business judgment rule, the courts scrutinize directors' decisions as to their intrinsic fairness to the corporation and to its minority shareholders.

The business judgment rule is asserted in a variety of cases. As was previously indicated, many cases involve derivative suits and a board decision to sue on behalf of the corporation. In recent years, corporate takeover issues have frequently been litigated. For example, boards of directors have amended corporate bylaws to change the rights of shareholders and have restructured corporations to avoid takeovers. Boards have granted officers of corporations "golden parachutes" to protect them should a takeover occur. Preferred stock has been issued to avoid proxy fights. In cases such as these, the corporation usually defends its action by using the business judgment rule. In doing so, the directors must show that they had reasonable grounds for believing that a danger to corporate policy and effectiveness existed that required the action taken. The proof in takeover cases that a defense is reasonable in relation to the defenses posed is materially enhanced where a majority of the board favoring the proposal consisted of outside independent directors who have acted on an informed basis, in good faith, and in the honest belief that the action taken was in the best interests of the company. This also applies to a decision of disinterested directors, made in good faith and in the exercise of honest judgment, not to litigate a claim of the corporation.

17. Loyalty

A director occupies a position of trust and confidence with respect to the corporation and cannot, by reason of his or her position, directly or indirectly derive any personal benefits that are not enjoyed by the corporation or the shareholders. This duty of loyalty prohibits directors from acting with a conflict of interest. The most common violation of this duty occurs when a director enters into a contract with, or personally deals with, the corporation. A conflict of interest also arises in transactions between the director's corporation and another entity in which he or she may be a director, employee, investor, or one who is otherwise interested. In all circumstances, the director or officer must fully disclose a conflict of interest to the corporation. If the director fails to do so, the contract may be rescinded.

Under common law, a contract between a corporation and one of its directors was voidable unless it was shown to be approved by a disinterested board *and* "fair" to the corporation, in that its terms were as favorable as those available from any other person. Under some modern statutes, the transaction is valid if it is approved, with knowledge of the material facts, by a vote of disinterested directors or shareholders or if the director can show it to be "fair."

Issues of loyalty frequently arise when a corporation is in financial difficulty. For example, the loyalty of a director or officer is an issue when such a person is attempting to collect a personal loan to the corporation. Directors and officers may make loans to their corporations, and they may use the same methods as other creditors to collect bona fide corporation debts owed to them, but only as long as the corporation is solvent. When a corporation is insolvent or on the verge of insolvency, its directors and officers become fiduciaries of corporate assets for the benefit of creditors. As fiduciaries, directors and officers cannot by reason of their special position give themselves preference over the other creditors in collecting bona fide business debts.

Many cases involve the *corporate opportunity doctrine.* This doctrine precludes corporate fiduciaries from diverting to themselves business opportunities in which the corporation has an expectancy, property interest, or right, or which in fairness should otherwise belong to the corporation. The doctrine follows from a corporate fiduciary's duty of undivided loyalty to the corporation. The loyalty requirement is lacking when a director or officer takes for himself or herself an opportunity that the corporation should have had.

A director must present all possible corporate opportunities to the corporation first. Only after disinterested, informed directors have determined that the corporation should not pursue such opportunities can a director pursue them for his or her own benefits. If a corporate director acquires property for himself or herself, knowing the corporation desires it, the director breaches his or her fiduciary relation to the corporation, and it may obtain the property.

Persons charged with violating the corporate opportunity doctrine sometimes seek to avoid liability by claiming that the corporation was not in a financial position to take advantage of the opportunity. In most states, if the corporation is solvent, financial inability to undertake an opportunity does not absolve a corporate fiduciary from liability for diverting what is otherwise a corporate opportunity. Financial insolvency will, however, excuse corporate fiduciaries from liability in most states. The fiduciary has the burden of proving insolvency; mere financial difficulty is not enough.

To allow a corporate fiduciary to take advantage of a business opportunity when the fiduciary determines the corporation to be unable to avail itself of it would create the worst sort of temptation for the fiduciary. He or she could rationalize an inaccurate and self-serving assessment of the corporation's financial ability and thereby compromise the duty of loyalty to the corporation. If a corporate fiduciary's duty of loyalty conflicts with personal interest, the latter must give way.

The appropriate method to determine whether or not a corporate opportunity exists is to let the corporation decide at the time the opportunity is presented. If a fiduciary is uncertain whether a given opportunity is corporate or not, or whether the corporation has the financial ability to pursue it, this fiduciary needs merely to disclose the existence of the opportunity to the directors and let them decide. Disclosure is a fundamental fiduciary duty. It cannot be burdensome, and it resolves the issue for all parties concerned and eliminates the necessity for a judicial determination after the fact.

A corporate officer or director does not become free to appropriate a business opportunity of the corporation by resigning his or her office. The duty continues after the resignation.

18. Due Care

In addition to the duty of loyalty, directors must exercise due care. In its simplest terms, the duty to exercise *due care* is synonymous with a duty not to be negligent. As a general rule, directors owe that degree of care that a businessperson of ordinary prudence would exercise in the management of his or her own affairs. The nature and extent of reasonable care depend on the type of corporation, its size, and its financial resources. A bank director is held to stricter accountability than the director of an ordinary business. In large corporations many duties must be delegated, so directors' intimate knowledge of details is not possible. In corporations invested with a public interest—such as insurance companies, banks, and public utilities—rigid supervision and specific obligations are imposed on directors. If a director fails to exercise the requisite degree of care and skill, the corporation will have a right of action against him or her for any resulting losses.

As a general rule, a director should acquire at least a rudimentary understanding of the business of the corporation and should be familiar with the fundamentals of that business. Since directors are bound to exercise ordinary care, they cannot set up as a defense to a suit against them lack of knowledge needed to exercise the requisite degree of care. If one has not had sufficient business experience to perform the duties of a director, one should either acquire the knowledge by inquiry or refuse to serve.

Directors must keep informed about the activities of the corporation. Otherwise, they may not be able to participate in the overall management of corporate affairs. Directors may not shut their eyes to corporate misconduct and then claim that because they did not see the misconduct, they did not have a duty to look. They have a duty to protect the corporation. This does not require a detailed inspection of day-to-day activities but a general monitoring of corporate affairs and policies. Accordingly, a director should attend board meetings regularly. Indeed, a director who is absent from a board meeting is presumed to concur in action taken on a corporate matter, unless a dissent is filed with the secretary of the corporation within a reasonable time after learning of such action.

Although directors are not required to audit corporate books, they should be familiar with the financial affairs of the corporation through a regular review of its financial statements. In some circumstances, directors may be charged with ensuring that bookkeeping methods conform to industry custom and usage. The extent of review, as well as the nature and frequency of financial statements, depends not only on the customs of the industry but also on the nature of the corporation and the business in which it is engaged. Financial statements of some small corporations may be prepared internally and only on an annual basis; in a large, publicly held corporation, the statements may be produced monthly or at some other regular interval. Adequate financial review normally would be more informal in a private corporation than in a publicly held corporation.

Generally, directors are immune from liability if, in good faith, they rely on the opinion of counsel for the corporation or on written reports prepared by a certified public accountant or on financial statements, books of account, or reports of the corporation represented to them to be correct by the president, the officer of the corporation having charge of its books of account, or the person presiding at a meeting of the board. The review of financial statements, however, may give rise to a duty to inquire further into matters revealed by those statements. Upon discovery of an illegal course of action, a director has a duty to object, and if the corporation does not correct the conduct, to resign.

In certain circumstances, the fulfillment of the duty of a director may call for more than mere objection and resignation; sometimes a director may be required to seek the advice of legal counsel. A director may require legal advice concerning the propriety of his or her own conduct, the conduct of other officers and directors, or the conduct of the corporation. A director should consult with corporate counsel or his or her own legal adviser whenever there is doubt regarding a proposed action. Sometimes the duty of a director may require more than consulting with outside counsel. A director may have a duty to take reasonable means to prevent illegal conduct by co-directors, including the threat of suit.

A director is not an ornament, but an essential component of corporate governance. Consequently, a director cannot protect himself or herself behind a paper shield bearing the motto "dummy director." A director may incur liability by failing to do more than passively rubber-stamp the decisions of the active managers. Directors must use their best business judgment. As previously discussed, they have no liability for honest mistakes. Directors are liable to the corporation for negligence in management. As a general rule, since no duty extends to third-party creditors, there is no liability to them or to the shareholders individually.

19. Indemnification and Insurance

In recent years, dissenting shareholders, public interest groups, and government regulators have caused a dramatic increase in the number of lawsuits filed against directors and officers of publicly held corporations. Many of the lawsuits result from the failure of directors to prevent activities such as bribery of foreign officials and illegal political contributions. Most large corporations carry liability insurance for directors, and costs for this insurance are soaring because of the increased number of suits.

To reimburse directors and officers for the expenses of defending lawsuits if the insurance is nonexistent or inadequate, most states provide by statute for indemnification by the corporation. The *Model Business Corporation Act* provides that the standard for indemnification is that the director must have "acted in good faith and in a manner he reasonably believed to be in or not opposed to the best interests of the corporation" and, if a criminal action, "had no reasonable cause to believe his conduct was unlawful." The indemnification is automatic if the director has been successful in the defense of any action.

CHAPTER SUMMARY

CORPORATE STOCK

Stock Basics

1. Some stock is preferred over others in either dividends, distributions on dissolution, or both.
2. Unless stated otherwise, preferred stock is both cumulative and nonparticipating.
3. A stock warrant gives a person a right to subscribe and to purchase corporate stock at a stated price. Such warrants are transferable.
4. Stock may be issued without par value, in which case the directors provide a stated value for stated capital account purposes.
5. Watered stock is stock that is issued as fully paid when in fact an equivalent value has not been paid to the corporation.
6. Treasury stock is stock of the corporation that has been purchased by or returned to the corporation.
7. Treasury stock may only be purchased out of accumulated earnings. Otherwise, the purchase could constitute a reduction of capital.

Stock Subscriptions

1. A preincorporation stock subscription is binding and irrevocable for a stated period of time after its execution.
2. Preincorporation subscriptions are usually conditioned on such things as final organization of the corporation and subscription to all the stock.
3. Stock may also be subscribed after incorporation, and such contracts are subject to the same rules as other contracts.

Right to Transfer Stock

1. In a closely held corporation, the bylaws may grant a right of first refusal to the corporation or to other shareholders.
2. A buy-and-sell agreement may require the purchase of stock on death or withdrawal of a shareholder.

Mechanics of Transfer

1. Stock is transferred on the records of the corporation by surrender of the stock certificate and issuing a new one. Large corporations retain stock transfer agents to perform this task.
2. Article 8 of the Uniform Commercial Code deals with investment securities. If its provisions are complied with, a party purchasing stock has greater rights than the seller.

SHAREHOLDERS

Rights in General

1. Shareholders have rights created by statute. These usually include the right to inspect the books and papers of the corporation, the right to attend meetings and to vote, and the right to dividends.
2. The right to inspect the books and papers is limited to good-faith inspections for proper and honest purposes at the proper time and the proper place.
3. An attempt to oust present management is a proper purpose for inspection.
4. Shareholders have the right to the assistance of accountants and attorneys in that inspection.

Meetings

1. Shareholders are entitled to notice of the annual meeting and of special meetings as well. The notice must include the matters to be acted on at special meetings and all unusual matters that are on the agenda of the annual meeting.
2. Informal action by all shareholders may be taken without an actual meeting.

3. A quorum is usually a majority of the voting stock.

Voting

1. Shareholders usually vote to elect directors and on issues such as dissolution.
2. Election of directors by cumulative voting is possible in some states.
3. Shareholders may vote by proxy.
4. Shareholders may vote on matters in which they have a personal interest.

Preemptive Rights

1. Shareholders also may have preemptive rights, which are the rights to buy a proportionate share of new stock.
2. These rights usually are associated with newly authorized stock and not with previously authorized, but unissued, stock.

Derivative Suits

1. A shareholder has the right to bring a suit on behalf of the corporation when the directors fail to do so. Before filing such a suit, shareholders usually must demand that the directors take action.
2. The minority shareholders of a corporation agree tacitly to be bound by the acts of the majority. The majority controls the business unless acting illegally, oppressively, or fraudulently.

Dividends

1. A shareholder has a right to dividends declared but has no right to have dividends declared.
2. It is generally up to the board of directors to declare a dividend.
3. A stock dividend is a transfer of retained earnings to capital.
4. A stock split is the reduction of par value and the increase in the number of shares outstanding. It in effect gives the shareholder nothing of additional value.

Fiduciary Aspects

1. In a publicly held corporation, the shareholders do not stand in a fiduciary relationship with each other.
2. In a closely held corporation, the shareholders do stand in a fiduciary relationship to the enterprise and to each other.
3. Shareholders in a closely held corporation must act in good faith. In many states, this includes the duty to disclose relevant information.

DIRECTORS

Powers

1. The directors determine policy in the ordinary course of business and elect the officers.
2. Directors need not be shareholders.

Meetings

1. The bylaws provide the procedures for calling and conducting directors' meetings, and minutes of them are maintained.
2. The majority of the directors constitute a quorum, and action is usually by a majority.
3. Directors may not vote by proxy, but informal action that is unanimous is allowed in most states.
4. Directors may not vote on matters in which they have a personal interest, although their presence may be used to constitute a quorum.

Compensation

1. Directors are compensated as provided in the bylaws.
2. Directors fix the salary of officers, but generally they cannot vote on their own salary.

LIABILITY OF OFFICERS AND DIRECTORS

In General

1. Directors and officers may have personal liability both in tort and in contract. This liability may be to the corporation or to third parties.

2. Directors are liable to the corporation for breach of their fiduciary duties or of duties imposed by statute.

The Business Judgment Rule

1. Directors are not liable for breach of fiduciary duties because of mere mistakes of judgment.
2. The presumption is that the directors of corporations act on an informed basis in good faith and in the honest belief that the action taken was in the best interests of the company.
3. The presumption is based on the belief that directors are better equipped than courts to make business judgments.
4. If the directors are guilty of fraud, bad faith, gross overreaching, an abuse of discretion, or gross negligence, then the business judgment rule does not prevent a court from imposing personal liability on directors or from changing a board decision.

Loyalty

1. The duty of loyalty creates liability if there is a conflict of interest.
2. The *corporate opportunity doctrine* precludes corporate fiduciaries from diverting to themselves business opportunities in which the corporation has an expectancy, property interest, or right, or which in fairness should otherwise belong to the corporation.

Due Care

1. As a general rule, directors owe that degree of care that a businessperson of ordinary prudence would exercise in the management of his or her own affairs.
2. Directors may rely on experts such as accountants or attorneys in exercising their responsibilities.
3. Directors are not liable to third parties for negligence in management.

Indemnification and Insurance

1. Corporations usually carry liability insurance to protect directors.

REVIEW QUESTIONS AND PROBLEMS

1. Match each term in Column A with the appropriate statement in Column B.

A	B
(1) Watered stock	(a) A lawsuit filed on behalf of a corporation by a shareholder as a result of the failure of the officers and directors to file the suit
(2) Treasury stock	(b) Stock issued for property overvalued
(3) Cumulative voting	(c) The record date on which a dividend is payable
(4) Preemptive right	(d) A reduction in par value and an increase in the number of shares outstanding
(5) Derivative suit	(e) Stock returned to the corporation
(6) Quorum	(f) A shareholder is entitled to the number of votes in electing directors that is the product of number of shares times number of directors to be elected. All the shareholders' votes may be cast for one director.

(7) Proxy	(g) The right to vote someone else's stock
(8) Ex-dividend date	(h) The right of a shareholder to purchase additional stock of subsequent stock issues so he or she may maintain the overall percentage of total stock outstanding
(9) Stock split	(i) Court's deference to officers and directors
(10) Business judgment rule	(j) A majority of the shares of a corporation

2. A corporation decided to repurchase stock of a shareholder who recently died. The corporation was in existence for three years and had lost $50,000 during this period. The original shareholders had invested $25,000 in the business, of which the deceased had invested $5,000. How much may the corporation pay for the stock of the deceased? Explain.
3. Albert sold Betty some stock representing ownership of the Cobra Corporation. Albert delivered the stock certificate to Betty, but he failed to indorse it. Albert died, and the executor of his estate claims that the stock certificate should be returned since it was not indorsed. Betty contends she is entitled to have the certificate indorsed by Albert's representative. Who is correct? Explain.
4. Miles, a bank shareholder, requested an unlimited inspection of the bank's books and records. He said that he wanted to ascertain whether any action had been taken contrary to the best interests of the stockholders, such as misuses of corporate funds; abuse of corporate office; diversion of corporate assets to the personal benefit of any officer, director, employee, or stockholder; misapplication of corporate assets; or favoring of certain customers of the bank because of personal connections with officers or directors of the bank. He also wanted to determine whether the directors had lived up to their fiduciary obligation to the stockholders. Must the bank honor his request? Explain.
5. All stockholders were present at the annual stockholders' meeting of a corporation whose bylaws required only a majority of shareholders to constitute a quorum. During the meeting, two stockholders who owned a majority of the stock withdrew from the meeting while it was in progress. Following their withdrawal, the remaining stockholders elected five members to the board of directors. Should the election of the directors be invalidated? Why or why not?
6. A corporation board authorized a director, Wilson, to negotiate the purchase of some land. Instead, Wilson secretly bought the land himself and sold it to the corporation at a profit. After learning of the deceit, the corporation failed to act. Do the minority shareholders have any remedy? Explain.
7. Abner owned a majority of the stock of Lum Company, and he ran the corporation by himself. The balance of the stock was owned by Abner's brother and sister, who agreed to sell all their stock to him. At the time of the purchase, Abner was negotiating a sale of the company, but he did not reveal this fact to his brother and sister. The sale of the company resulted in a great profit to Abner. The brother and sister brought suit to recover the difference. Should the brother and sister succeed? Why?
8. Wilkes and three other individuals formed a corporation to operate a nursing home many years ago. The four corporate shareholders were also elected directors, and they served as employees of the close corporation. Plaintiff had a quarrel with one of the other directors

after years of successful operation. As a result, the other board members canceled plaintiff's salary, refused to reelect him as director, and stopped paving dividends in an attempt to freeze him out. He sued for damages on the ground that the majority had breached the fiduciary duty owed to him. Is the plaintiff's argument correct? Why?

9. Andrews, a director of Omega Corporation, learned of a very valuable mineral discovery on certain land that could be acquired at a bargain price. Without revealing this information to Omega, Andrews, acting through his brother-in-law, acquired the mineral rights for the property and resold them to Omega at a large profit. Did Andrews incur any liability to Omega as a result of these transactions? Explain.

10. Plaintiffs sued the president, vice president, and secretary of the corporation that built them new houses. They alleged that due to faulty planning, their homes were built in an area that was often flooded by the drainage of the other areas of the development. Do the officers have personal liability? Why or why not?

Limited Liability Companies and Related Forms

31

CHAPTER OUTLINE

LIMITED LIABILITY COMPANIES

1. Background
2. Comparing Forms
3. Formation
4. Management

RELATED FORMS

5. Limited Partnerships
6. Limited Liability Partnerships

CHAPTER PREVIEW

Venturing beyond the sole proprietorship, any business contemplating two or more owners traditionally would choose between a general partnership and a corporation. On the one hand, the partnership alternative required all owners to undertake a considerable obligation: unlimited personal liability for the debts of the business. On the other hand, the corporate form provided limited liability for all shareholders, but it had its own downside: profits from the business were taxed at the corporation level and, again, at the individual owner level when distributions were made as dividends. Especially for the entrepreneur, neither of these traditional forms of conducting business was ideal.

In a strikingly-unique example of coordination between two government entities respecting the realities of modern business, the United States taxing authority (the Internal Revenue Service) and state legislatures from across the nation fashioned a new form of business that would provide limited liability for owners and the ability for owners to be taxed on the profits from the business only once (similar to the tax treatment afforded partners in a general partnership). This new vehicle of conducting business is called a limited liability company (LLC). As a result of its significant benefits, today it is a very popular form of business.

In addition to focusing on the LLC, this chapter also addresses other forms of conducting business that, while not as popular today as the LLC, still may be worth considering as members of the business community select a proper legal structure for their commercial enterprise.

BUSINESS MANAGEMENT DECISION

Ashley White and Jared Black formed "Blanco and Negro Pedicab Company, LLC" as a limited liability company. The business plan provided a detailed explanation of the need for an environmentally friendly transportation service for a specific university community. It also indicated that with several large cycling organizations in the area, finding individuals to pedal the pedicabs would be easy. No LLC operating agreement exists. Ashley and Jared agreed that Ashley would provide capital to purchase the pedicabs, secure necessary permits, acquire insurance, buy advertising, and create a small office for the company. Jared would hire drivers, provide mechanics, and serve as the overall manager of the operation. Although business was sparse and the company was failing to make any money, Jared entered into a contract to purchase ten new pedicabs. Blanco and Negro Pedicab was incapable of making payments on the contract of sale, and the firm was sued. Ashley asserts that Jared, on his own, entered into the contract and thus should be solely responsible for the debt. Is Jared responsible? Is Ashley? Is the limited liability company responsible?

LIMITED LIABILITY COMPANY

1. Background

For decades business owners were forced to choose between a general partnership and a corporation as their method of conducting business. Limited partnerships (discussed below) and close corporations (mentioned in the previous chapter) are alternatives that allow owners to avoid negative aspects of the general partnership and corporate forms; but, for the most part, both of these options remain appropriate only for narrowly tailored situations.

Limited liability company
A form of business that guarantees owners limited liability for the debts of the business and "pass through" income tax treatment

In 1977, the state of Wyoming adopted legislation that would allow all members of an entity to enjoy limited liability for business debts. This form of doing business was termed a **limited liability company** (LLC). In stark contrast to the general partnership form where all partners have unlimited liability and in partial contrast to the limited partnership form where only limited partners are protected from personal liability for business debts, the type of business envisioned by the legislature in Wyoming would protect every owner from unlimited liability. While this form of business was new to the United States, numerous countries in other continents recognized the LLC. However, in the United States there was a significant problem associated with the LLC.

"Pass through" concept
Idea that income from a business entity not be treated as a taxable incident but simply passed through to the owners

Under then-existing Internal Revenue Service (IRS) regulations, a LLC was to be treated as a corporation for income tax purposes. The tax law for corporations provided for one incident of taxation at the corporate level (profits from operations) and another incident of taxation at the shareholder level (dividends). Business owners and state officials began a lobbying effort with the IRS to treat the LLC as a partnership for tax purposes. If this method of taxation was adopted, under the **"pass through" concept** income from the business entity is not treated as a taxable incident and is simply passed through to the owners.

As more states followed the lead of Wyoming in creating statutes that allowed for the formation of LLCs, efforts intensified to have the IRS recognize the LLC as a partnership for tax purposes. Somewhat begrudgingly, in 1988 the IRS ruled that LLCs could be taxed as a partnership although the rules imposed by the IRS were quite onerous.

As a result of this IRS ruling, the growth LLCs grew in popularity. The National Conference of Commissioners on Uniform State Laws ("the Commissioners") issued the *Uniform Limited Liability Company Act* in 1996, but it has been adopted in less than one-half of the states. However, by 1996 all states and the District of Columbia had adopted LLC statutory provisions of one type or another. In a surprise to many in the business community, in 1997 the IRS issued new regulations that actually favored the adoption of the LLC form by declaring that any unincorporated entity will be treated as a partnership (regardless of whether the owners benefit from limited liability) unless the owners choose to be taxed as a corporation. At this point, the floodgates opened for LLCs. From the standpoint of many entrepreneurial-minded business owners, the LLC offers the best of both worlds: limited liability (from the law of corporations) and favorable tax treatment (that is, only one taxable incidence, as is the case under IRS rules for a general partnership).

The Commissioners recently revised selected portions of the 1996 document and have published the *Revised Uniform Limited Liability Company of 2006* for state lawmakers to consider. This newer template for legislation contains fewer mandates and leaves greater discretion to LLC members in determining the nature of a particular LLC.

2. Comparing Forms

In a *general partnership,* all partners are jointly and severally liable for the debts of the business whether those debts are generated through contract breach or tort liability. It is also assumed that all partners will participate in management—although by agreement this presumption can be altered. From a tax standpoint, the income and losses of the partnership flow through directly to the partners. In other words, the partnership acts only as a conduit for purposes of income taxation. Therefore, since a partnership is not a taxable entity under IRS rules, the general partnership files only an information return but no tax return with the IRS. The LLC, however, shields the owners of the LLC from all company debts. The only exception occurs if an owner agrees to be personally liable for a LLC obligation. For income tax purposes, the LLC is now treated almost exactly as a general partnership: the income to the LLC is not subject to taxation under the "pass through" concept.

In a *limited partnership,* taxation is roughly similar to how the IRS treats a general partnership. Liability for many owners can be reduced through this form of business, but limited partnerships by definition must have at least one general partner. This general partner is personally liable for limited partnership debts. Also, a limited partner can lose their limited liability protection if the limited partner becomes too active in the operation of the limited partnership. The LLC provides a cleaner mechanism to assure limited liability to those who are inactive in the business along with those who are active in the management of the enterprise. Of course, the LLC is treated as a partnership for income tax purposes.

The *general corporate* form provides limited liability for all owners. But because the corporation is recognized as a distinct entity from its owners for most purposes, the law has created a fairly sophisticated mechanism within which the corporation must function—from creation, through operation, and even including termination. Also, income to the corporation is taxed unless the corporation is formed under Subchapter S. As indicated above, income to a general corporation (non-Subchapter S) that is passed on to shareholders as dividends is taxed a second time. There are avenues that shareholders can pursue to minimize the impact of double taxation, but the possibilities are generally fraught with complexities requiring advice from members of both the accounting and legal professions. The LLC is easier to form and operate than either a general corporation or Subchapter S corporation; and it has the additional benefit of acting as a conduit for all income to the entity, so that there is only one taxable incidence. Further, the LLC provides a mechanism for losses to flow directly to the owners, which can be a beneficial tax situation for owners. In a general corporation, all losses rest with the corporation and are not passed through to the owners.

There is a significant drawback to the LLC form. The law of general partnership and the law associated with the corporate form are quite developed. Every jurisdiction has numerous

TABLE 31-1 ■ Selected Comparison of LLC with General Partnership and Corporation Forms

	Liability	**Created by Enabling Statute of State**	**Entity Taxed**	**Legal Principles Developed**
General Partnership	Owners personally liable	No	No	Yes
Corporation	No personal liability of owners beyond capital contribution	Yes	Yes	Yes
LLC	No personal liability of owners beyond capital contribution	Yes	No	No

court decisions that provide guidance in the many difficult areas associated with both of these forms. However, because the LLC is such a new form of business, even though it is very popular, there are a very small number of court decisions dealing with the LLC choice of entity. Hence, it may be difficult to ascertain with any degree of certainty how a court will decide a case involving the formation, operation, and dissolution of an LLC.

3. Formation

The LLC is a creature of state law. That is, as is true with a general corporation, there must be state enabling legislation that provides for the formation of an LLC. Filing a document similar to the articles of incorporation used to create a corporation forms the entity. The LLC document submitted to the secretary of state's office is called the **articles of organization**.

Submitting a document to the secretary of state's office begins the process of creating an LLC.

Articles of organization
Document filed with the secretary of state's office that creates a limited liability company

This filing process also ensures that the name chosen is not already in use by another business. Under the law of all states, the name of the business must include the term "Limited Liability Company" or "LLC." In the majority of states, an LLC can be formed with only one owner.

While not required by state law, it is an excellent idea for the owners, generally termed *"members,"* of the LLC to create an *operating agreement.* This is a document that does not have to be filed with the secretary of state's office. The operating agreement should approach the same topics as are common in a partnership agreement: contributions to capital, internal operations (including meetings), roles of the members, distributions of profits and losses, how the company can be dissolved, along with a number of additional topics. If there is no operating agreement or the operating agreement does not cover a particular subject, then the members are governed by appropriate provisions of the LLC law that exists in the state in which the LLC is formed. Given the many similarities between the general partnership and the LLC law, it should not be surprising that the statutory scheme for LLCs is quite similar to partnership law. For instance, unless the operating agreement states the apportionment of voting rights, most state law dealing with the LLC provides that voting rights are apportioned according to the capital contribution made by each member.

State LLC laws avoid many of the formalities associated with creating and operating a corporation. For example, ownership interest certificates need not be created and distributed. There are, however, certain aspects of operating a LLC that are identical to those that choose to function under partnership or corporate law. Perhaps one of the most important subjects that must be addressed is to establish clearly the nature of capital contributions. The following case examines this important concept within the ambit of an LLC.

4. Management

Under state LLC law, the articles of organization filed with the secretary of state's office must include under which one of two methods of management the LLC will function. A *member-managed*

CASE

Carrie Burkle v. Ronald Burkle

COURT OF APPEAL OF CALIFORNIA, SECOND APPELLATE DISTRICT, DIVISION EIGHT

141 Cal. App. 4th 1029 (2006)

Carrie Burkle is Ronald Burkle's adult daughter. In 1995, when Carrie was 19, her father formed Yucaipa Monterey, LLC, a Delaware limited liability company that was formed to purchase art and owns an unspecified number of paintings. Carrie has had a 1 percent interest in Yucaipa Monterey since its formation. Carrie's father owns 99 percent of the company and provided the funds for Carrie's 1 percent interest.

In November 2003, several months after her mother, Janet Burkle, filed a petition for dissolution of her marriage to Carrie's father, Carrie filed a lawsuit naming her father and her mother as defendants. Carrie's mother is paying Carrie's legal fees for the lawsuit. The lawsuit alleged that Carrie's parents made various investments for her benefit, during her minority and thereafter, and asserted numerous causes of action for breach of fiduciary duty and constructive fraud, fraudulent suppression of fact, unjust enrichment and constructive trust, declaratory relief, an accounting, and for the return of personal property. Among the investments identified was Ronald's acquisition for Carrie of her 1 percent interest in Yucaipa Monterey. As to the Yucaipa Monterey investment, Carrie alleged causes of action for declaratory relief and an accounting. Specifically, Carrie's first amended complaint alleged that she learned of her 1 percent ownership interest on approximately September 23, 2003, and that her father claimed she owed him $14,783 allegedly lent to her to acquire her 1 percent interest. Carrie asserted the value of Yucaipa Monterey was $8.5 million and sought declaratory relief, requesting the court to "determine the rights and obligations of the parties arising from [Carrie's] claims regarding her interest in [Yucaipa Monterey] and Ronald's claims that [Carrie] owes him money," and to "determine the value of [Carrie's] 1% interest . . . and that her interest be liquidated and the funds paid to [Carrie]."

The question on appeal is whether a triable issue of fact exists as to Carrie's claim that Ronald misappropriated her investment in Yucaipa Monterey by taking $107,017 from her capital account. This question turns on whether the funds invested for Carrie were a gift or a loan.

Ronald contends that the undisputed facts—consisting of his own declaration that he intended a loan, not a gift—show he lent Carrie the funds for her capital contribution to the company and was entitled to repayment of the loan with interest. According to Ronald, Carrie failed to present sufficient evidence demonstrating a triable issue of fact that the monies he advanced were a gift. Carrie contends otherwise, asserting that Ronald did not establish his right to appropriate the funds in her capital account as a matter of law, and poses the factual dispute this way: "Carrie's Declaration created an evident factual dispute which went to the heart of Ronald's motion for summary judgment. He claimed the existence of a loan agreement in 1995; she denied the existence of any such agreement and denied that the subject ever even came up or was discussed."

We agree with Carrie. The question whether a transfer of funds was a gift or a loan often presents questions of fact, and this case is no different. The question depends principally upon Ronald's intent at the time he advanced the funds to acquire Carrie's 1 percent interest.

In short, on this record we cannot say that Ronald has met his burden of establishing no triable issue of fact exists as to whether his advance of funds was a gift or a loan. A fact finder could reasonably infer—from the absence of any evidence of the terms of a loan, from Ronald's failure to tell Carrie he was lending her funds she would be obligated to repay with interest, and from the lack of any agreement to loan terms—that Ronald intended a gift at the time he made the investment for Carrie. The only evidence of a loan is Ronald's declaration that he made the capital contributions for Carrie "in the form of a loan. ..." A trier of fact, however, might disbelieve Ronald's testimony.

In sum, the evidence presented in the summary judgment proceeding does not compel the conclusion that Ronald lent, rather than gave, Carrie the funds for her 1 percent investment in Yucaipa Monterey. That question is for the trier of fact, and the trial court therefore erred in granting summary judgment to Ronald.

■ *Reversed and remanded.*

CASE CONCEPTS REVIEW

1. Why does the court disagree with the trial court regarding the question of whether the daughter's interest may not be a loan?
2. After reading this case, what concerns do you have about going into business with a family member within the LLC structure? Is there a way to reduce the possibility of internal problems of members, regardless of whether they are related to one another?

LLC functions like a general partnership. For example, each member of the LLC has the power to bind the LLC to a contract, and all members must approve by majority vote the hiring of a new employee. This type of management construct is quite appropriate in family LLCs or those where members are also employees of the LLC.

In a *manager-managed* LLC, a single person or a select group has the power to manage the LLC. The manager or managers may be nonmembers. In some respects, this approach is similar to the corporate form where individuals function as officers of the corporation. Depending on the provisions dealing with management within an operating agreement, even in a manager-managed LLC members may have the ability to approve specified decisions. This structure tends to work better in larger LLCs where it is impractical to have a high degree of member participation in management.

In the next case, the issue of when a LLC manager is personally liable for actions undertaken in furtherance of an LLC interest is addressed.

CASE

The People of the State of California v. Pacific Landmark, LLC, et al.

COURT OF APPEAL OF CALIFORNIA, SECOND APPELLATE DISTRICT, DIVISION THREE

129 Cal. App. 4th 1203 (2005)

ALDRICH, J.

The City of Los Angeles and the People of the State of California (collectively, the City) brought a red light abatement action (Pen. Code, § 11225) against the operators of a business and the owners of the strip mall where the business was located. The action alleged that the business was a front for prostitution and an illegal massage parlor. In July 2001, Pacific leased the premises to Melikyan for three years with an option for a five-year extension. Mavaddat signed the lease on behalf of Pacific. Thereunder, the tenant was to obtain Pacific's written approval for all signs. Pacific retained the right to enter the premises to inspect its condition and the tenant's compliance with laws, ordinances, permit requirements, and the lease. The permitted use was "Medical Therapy Offices." The premises were to be used for the business known as Victoria's Health Care.

Victoria's Health Care has a well-established reputation as a location where illicit activity, notably prostitution, occurs on an open and systematic basis. Defendant Spencer, whose chiropractic license was displayed on the wall in the reception area, was "known to the law enforcement community as a chiropractor engaged in several illegal massage parlor and prostitution operations in the City. ..." The trial court issued a preliminary injunction prohibiting the operation of a massage parlor or a house of prostitution. Pacific Landmark, LLC (Pacific), a limited liability company and owner of the property, and Ron Mavaddat, Pacific's manager (collectively, appellants), appeal contends, as manager of Pacific, that he is exempt from personal liability for any order or judgment against Pacific.

The Legislature enacted the Beverly-Killea Limited Liability Company Act (the Act) in 1994. (Corp. Code, § 17000 et seq.) "A limited liability company is a hybrid business entity formed under the Corporations Code ... [which] provides members with limited liability to the same extent enjoyed by corporate shareholders [citation] ...," while maintaining the attributes of a partnership for federal income tax purposes.

While generally *members* of a limited liability company are not personally liable for judgments, debts, obligations, or liabilities of the company "solely by reason of being a member" (Corp. Code, § 17101, subd. (a)), they are subject to liability under the same circumstances and to the same extent as corporate shareholders under common law principles governing alter ego liability and are *personally* liable under the same circumstances and extent as corporate shareholders. Also, the Act "do[es] not relieve a member from liability arising from (1) the member's tortious conduct, or (2) the terms of a member's written guarantee or contractual obligation." By contrast, the Act does not contain a similar provision specifically exposing managers to personal liability.

Mavaddat focuses on Corporations Code section 17158, subdivision (a) to contend that the trial court erred in issuing the nuisance abatement injunction against him because that section exempts him from personal liability for any judgments against or obligations of the limited liability company he manages. Corporations Code section 17158 reads, "No person who is a manager or officer or both a manager and officer of a limited liability company shall be personally liable under any judgment of a court, or in any other manner, for any debt, obligation, or liability of the limited liability company, whether that liability or obligation arises in contract, tort, or otherwise, *solely by reason of being a manager* or officer or both a manager and officer of the limited liability company." A manager may agree to become personally responsible for the limited liability company's debts and liabilities by written contract, or if the operating agreement or articles so specify.

Although research has revealed no California case to address this issue, we hold that whereas managers of limited liability companies may not be held liable for the wrongful conduct of the companies *merely* because of the managers' status, they may nonetheless be held accountable under Corporations Code section 17158, subdivision (a) for their personal participation in tortious or criminal conduct, even when performing their duties as manager.

The plain language of Corporations Code section 17158, subdivision (a), above quoted, expresses a circumscribed protection from liability. The phrase declaring managers exempt from liability is qualified by the phrase "solely by reason of being a manager ..." Reading the language of section 17158, subdivision (a) as a whole, it is clear that managers were not intended to be held liable for the wrongs their companies commit simply because of their status as managers. The qualifying clause, however, does not preclude personal liability for a manager's own conduct.

continued

By way of analogy, it has long been the law elsewhere that although officers cannot be held liable solely by virtue of their corporate title, they can and are held personally liable for actively participating in criminal and tortious conduct.

Turning to Mavaddat, the preliminary injunction was not imposed on him solely because of his *status* as manager of Pacific, but also because of his personal involvement in allowing the nuisance to persist. By his own admission, Mavaddat occupied a prominent and influential position at Pacific. Mavaddat declared he had extensive knowledge and control over Pacific's affairs, and was "thoroughly familiar with all of its operations and business ..." He selected and authorized counsel to appear at the meeting with the City's attorney. Mavaddat had full responsibility for and authority over the property where the nuisance occurred. He leased the premises to Melikyan, and his name appears on the lease as the agent of Pacific. He retained the right under the lease to inspect the premises to determine its compliance with the lease and all laws and ordinances. It was Mavaddat who served the notice to perform covenant and yet failed, thereafter, to inspect the premises to ascertain whether defendants had complied with the notice. Mavaddat served the notice to quit, arranged to have the locks changed and signs removed after defendants moved out, and intended to arrange for another tenant to lease the premises. Yet the sign for Victoria's Health Care remained on the strip mall's main pylon sign in September 2003. Mavaddat had the knowledge and the responsibility to prevent the nuisance. He is not insulated from liability by virtue of Corporations Code section 17158, subdivision (a) for his personal involvement in aiding and abetting the nuisance and for failing to abate it, which thereby forced the City to bring this Red Light Abatement action.

■ *Affirmed.*

CASE CONCEPTS REVIEW

1. Do you believe Mavaddat knew that the tenants were conducting illegal behavior? Why?
2. According to the opinion, when can a manager of an LLC be held personally responsible for a nuisance associated with an LLC? Why?

Regardless of the type of management structure adopted, LLC law provides members with certain rights that cannot be changed by the operating agreement. Those rights that are guaranteed to members by statute include: right to dissolve the LLC, right to approve a merger, and the right of access to LLC books and records. Further, unless the operating agreement provides to the contrary, LLC law provides that an operating agreement can only be amended by unanimous consent of the members.

Another area that should be addressed in an LLC operating agreement is the transfer of LLC interests. Some LLC operating agreements give a "right of first refusal" to members, providing that a member who wishes to sell their interest must offer to the remaining members before contacting individuals or entities outside of the membership of the LLC. Note, as is the case with a partnership, an economic interest in the LLC might be freely transferable while the operating agreement may prohibit full voting rights in the LLC unless all members approve. The operating agreement, also, will generally set forth the events that will cause the dissolution of the LLC. Common situations that will trigger dissolution include the death of a member and the personal bankruptcy of a manager or a member.

RELATED FORMS

5. Limited Partnerships

Limited partnership

A form of business consisting of at least one general partner and one limited partner

The **limited partnership** form of conducting business has been a staple of many European countries for more than one hundred years, yet it is a comparatively recent phenomenon in the United States. It realized its heyday during the 1960s, 70s, and 80s as many shopping mall operations, real estate developments, and movie productions adopted this mode of conducting business.

Most states and the District of Columbia have adopted the *Revised Uniform Limited Partnership Act (*RULPA), which was finalized in 1976. However, in light of changes in business and legal arenas during the past few decades, the National Conference of Commissioners on Uniform State Laws adopted a new version of the RULPA, now termed the *Uniform Limited Partnership Act of 2001.*

In the 1960s, 70s, and 80s many shopping mall operations used limited partnerships

Creation of a limited partnership requires that the state have an enabling statute. The founders must create and submit to the secretary of state's office a *certificate of limited partnership* that is signed by all general partners and contains all information required under the enabling statute. Any limited partnership must include in its title the term "limited partnership" or the letters "LP." Note that if the major provisions of a limited partnership enabling statute are not met (for example, a certificate of limited partnership is never filed), most courts will treat the business as a general partnership. If that determination is made, those owners that believed they were limited partners become personally liable for business debts because they are considered general partners.

While not required by state law, it is generally recommended that the complicated nature of most limited partnerships requires that those interested in adopting this form of conducting business execute a *limited partnership agreement.* This document, which is not submitted to the secretary of state's office, typically states the capital contributions of all partners, each partner's share of profits and losses, and the procedure that will be followed upon the death of a partner.

All general partners owe a *fiduciary duty,* a duty of trust and confidence, to all limited partners. The following case discusses the ability of the limited partnership to alter the specific duties owed.

CASE

Gotham Partners, LP, v. Hallwood Realty Partners, LP, Hallwood Realty Corp., the Hallwood Group Inc., Anthony J. Gumbiner and Wialliam L. Guzzetti

SUPREME COURT OF DELAWARE

817 A.2d 160 (2002)

VEASEY, CHIEF JUSTICE

In this appeal, we hold that a limited partnership agreement may provide for contractually created fiduciary duties substantially mirroring traditional fiduciary duties that apply in the corporation law. The Court of Chancery held that the limited partnership agreement here provided for such fiduciary duties by requiring the general partner and its controlling

continued

entity to treat the limited partners in accordance with the entire fairness standard. We agree with this holding and also agree with the trial court that the defendants are jointly and severally liable because the challenged transaction breached the entire fairness provisions of the partnership agreement.

Hallwood Realty Partners, L.P. ("the Partnership") is a Delaware limited partnership that owns commercial office buildings and industrial parks in several locations in the United States and lists its partnership units on the American Stock Exchange. Gotham Partners, L.P. ("Gotham") is a hedge fund, the investments of which include real estate. It is the largest independent limited partner in the Partnership with approximately 14.8 percent of the outstanding partnership units. Hallwood Realty Corporation ("the General Partner") is the sole general partner and is a wholly-owned subsidiary of Hallwood Group Incorporated ("HGI"), which owned 5.1 percent of the outstanding partnership units before the transactions challenged in this case. Anthony Gumbiner and William Guzzetti were members of the board of directors of the General Partner. They were also officers of HGI at the time of the challenged transaction.

In 1994, the Partnership's units were trading at a low price because of the ongoing economic recession in real estate. On October 12, 1994, Guzzetti proposed to the Partnership's board of directors that it approve a reverse split [A reverse split reduces the number of outstanding units and consequently increases the per unit value of each unit; reverse splits usually create odd lots.], a unit option plan [In this case, the option plan would sell post-reverse split units to officers and employees of the General Partner, including Gumbiner and Guzzetti.],and an odd lot tender offer [An odd lot offer is a tender offer by the issuer for blocks of fewer than one hundred outstanding units or shares. Such "odd lots" are considered small and thus create inefficient administrative costs for issuers and may be difficult to sell at an attractive price. Odd lot offers are designed to provide liquidity to small holders and to reduce issuer costs.] subject to HGI's willingness to finance the transactions by buying any fractional units generated by a reverse split and any units purchased by the Partnership in an odd lot tender offer. At the time, more than half of the Partnership's units were held in odd lots and could be resold to HGI. Guzzetti told the board that HGI was the only source of financing available and that the transactions would, among other things, raise the trading price of the Partnership's units, reduce the Partnership's administrative costs, and give odd lot holders the chance to sell at market price without incurring brokerage fees. The Partnership's board approved the transactions, citing Guzzetti's reasons.

From June 9 to July 25, 1995, when the Odd Lot Offer closed, the Partnership purchased 293,539 units from odd lot holders and placed them in a holding account. The Partnership then resold the units to HGI at the same price the Partnership paid for them, approximately $4.1 million. The Odd Lot Resale resulted in HGI purchasing approximately 23.4 percent of the Partnership's outstanding units. Thus, HGI increased its stake in the outstanding Partnership units from 11.4 percent to 29.7 percent and solidified its control over the Partnership. The Partnership Agreement requires the written consent or affirmative vote by at least 66 and 1/3 percent of the limited partners to remove a general partner.

Gotham began purchasing Partnership units in 1994 and owned 14.8 percent of the outstanding units as of September 1996. Gotham was aware of the Odd Lot Offer and Resale but did not complain to the Partnership until January 1997 when it requested access to the Partnership's books and records. The Partnership denied the request.

We refer to one aspect of the Vice Chancellor's discussion of the Delaware Revised Uniform Limited Partnership Act ("DRULPA") in his summary judgment opinion in this case. As the Vice Chancellor noted at summary judgment, a general partner owes the traditional fiduciary duties of loyalty and care to the limited partnership and its partners, but DRULPA § 17-1101(d)(2) "expressly authorizes the ... modification, or enhancement of these fiduciary duties in the written agreement governing the limited partnership." Indeed, we have recognized that, by statute, the parties to a Delaware limited partnership have the power and discretion to form and operate a limited partnership "in an environment of private ordering" according to the provisions in the limited partnership agreement. We have noted that DRULPA embodies "the policy of freedom of contract" and "maximum flexibility." DRULPA's "basic approach is to permit partners to have the broadest possible discretion in drafting their partnership agreements and to furnish answers only in situations where the partners have not expressly made provisions in their partnership agreement" or "where the agreement is inconsistent with mandatory statutory provisions." In those situations, a court will "look for guidance from the statutory default rules, traditional notions of fiduciary duties, or other extrinsic evidence." However, if the limited partnership agreement unambiguously provides for fiduciary duties, any claim of a breach of a fiduciary duty must be analyzed generally in terms of the partnership agreement.

The Vice Chancellor found, and the parties do not contest, that Partnership Agreement Sections 7.05 and 7.10(a) set forth fiduciary duties of entire fairness owed by the General Partner to its partners generally in self-dealing transactions, such as the Odd Lot Resale. Section 7.05 expressly permits the Partnership to enter into self-dealing transactions with the General Partner or its affiliate "provided that the terms of any such transaction are substantially equivalent to terms obtainable by the Partnership from a comparable unaffiliated third party." Section 7.10(a) requires the General Partner to form an independent Audit Committee that shall review and approve self-dealing transactions between the Partnership and the General Partner and any of its affiliates. The Vice Chancellor found, and the parties do not contest, that Sections 7.05 and 7.10(a) "operate together as a contractual statement of the traditional entire fairness standard [of fair price and fair dealing], with § 7.05 reflecting the substantive aspect of that standard and reflecting the procedural aspect of that standard."

Because the Partnership Agreement provided for fiduciary duties, the Vice Chancellor properly held that the Partnership Agreement, as a contract, provides the standard for determining whether the General Partner breached its duty to the Partnership through its execution of the Odd Lot Resale. As the Vice Chancellor stated, the Partnership Agreement "leaves no room for the application of common law fiduciary duty principles to measure the General Partner's conduct" because the Partnership Agreement "supplanted fiduciary duty and became the sole source of protection for the public unit holders of the Partnership." Thus, "the General Partner was subject, by contract, to a fairness standard akin to the common law one applicable to self-dealing transactions by fiduciaries."

The General Partner is liable for breaching the contractually created fiduciary duties of entire fairness provided by Sections 7.05 and 7.10(a) of the Partnership Agreement.

■ *Affirmed.*

CASE CONCEPTS REVIEW

1. Was the General Partner acting to improve the financial outlook of all partners in the firm?
2. Why is it advisable for the limited partnership agreement to specify the extent of fiduciary duties?

Under the law of all states, a limited partnership must have at least one general partner and one limited partner. Conceptually, the general partner operates the business and the limited partners contribute capital. As a general partner in a limited partnership, the general partner has unlimited liability for all partnership debts. The limited partner is prohibited from participating in management of the firm; and because the limited partner is not active in management, the limited partner is not liable personally for partnership debts. Of course, any capital contribution made by a limited partner may be sacrificed to a creditor of the limited partnership.

While limited partners have the right to access limited partnership records (among other privileges), any limited partner that actively participates in the management of the business forfeits the limited liability shield with regard to any transaction that the limited partner participates in that furthers the business of the limited partnership. Determining the degree of behavior that triggers the loss of limited liability protection is an oft-litigated question because limited partners often are wealthy and can provide a creditor with a source of resources if the general partner fails to have sufficient wealth to pay a limited liability partnership's debt.

6. Limited Liability Partnerships

Limited liability partnership

A partnership, usually formed by professional service firms, that grants owners limited liability

While not as popular as a limited liability company, all states have adopted **limited liability partnership** (LLP) laws that allow an organization that is truly a partnership to continue to function as a partnership but provide the partners with limited liability. The states of California and New York limit this form of entity to professional service firms. Even in those states without an express restriction of this type, the LLP is generally appropriate for accounting, legal, and other professional organizations along with family businesses.

The LLP provides the same attractive characteristics as the LLC: limited liability and pass-through treatment for tax purposes. The limited liability advantage is particularly important for accounting and law firms where the principals of the business act as partners. Under general partnership law, if an attorney in a law partnership commits malpractice, then any amount not covered by insurance falls on the partner that committed the mistake and, then, on the other partners. The LLP grants limited liability to the other partners. In most states, any partner not involved in the contract or tort that generated the liability is totally exempt from liability.

CHAPTER SUMMARY

LIMITED LIABILITY COMPANIES

Background

1. The limited liability company is a comparably recent form of conducting a business.

Comparing Forms

1. Like a general partnership, in a limited liability company all income of the business is passed through to the members for federal income tax purposes.
2. Like a corporation, all members of a limited liability company are liable for debts of the enterprise to the extent of their capital contribution.

Formation

1. Each state has an enabling law under which a business can form a limited liability company.
2. In order to create a limited liability company, the organization must file articles of organization with the secretary of state's office.

Management

1. A limited liability company may be established as a member-managed organization or a manager-managed organization.

RELATED FORMS

Limited Partnerships

1. All limited partnerships must have at least one general partner, who has unlimited liability for the debts of the business.
2. Limited partners may forfeit their shield from unlimited liability for partnership debts if they become too involved in the management of the firm.

Limited Liability Partnerships

1. A limited liability partnership, often employed as a vehicle for conducting a family business or as a professional firm, offers limited liability for the partners and partnership income tax treatment.

REVIEW QUESTIONS AND PROBLEMS

1. Match each term in Column A with the appropriate statement in Column B.

A	B
(1) Limited liability partnership	(a) Income from a business entity that is not treated as a taxable incident and is simply passed through to the owners
(2) Certificate of limited partnership	(b) A form of doing business that consists of at least one general partner and one limited partner
(3) Fiduciary duty	(c) LLC managed by individuals who are directed by the membership to manage the firm
(4) Limited liability company	(d) A form of business, often used in professional partnerships, that provides limited liability for its owners
(5) Member-managed LLC	(e) Document filed at the secretary of state's office that forms a limited liability company
(6) "Pass through" concept	(f) A duty of trust and confidence
(7) Right of first refusal	(g) A form of business that guarantees owners limited liability for the debts of the business and "pass through" income tax treatment
(8) Limited partnership	(h) Document filed with the secretary of state's office that forms a limited partnership
(9) Manager-managed LLC	(i) LLC managed by the membership
(10) Articles of organization	(j) Guarantees current owners the opportunity to purchase an interest in an entity from a member who wishes to sell their interest before it is made available to those outside prospective buyers

2. Compare and contrast the limited liability company with a general partnership. Perform the same analysis regarding the limited liability company and a corporation.
3. Sam, Jan, and Pam are interested in forming a limited liability company. What advice would you give them regarding the process that must be followed to form a limited liability company?
4. Dino and Giada purchased a book that explained the process of creating a limited liability company in the state in which they hope to conduct business. After several meetings, they both have established a business plan and performed all functions so that they can open their doors on Monday. Their first week was very successful. Upon reflecting on the bright future ahead for their business, Giada asks Dino about the status of the limited liability company filing. With a quizzical on his face, Dino states that he thought she was going to make the filing with the secretary of state's office. Since no limited liability company was formed, what form of business are they?
5. Kamsui, Hotaka, and Moriko desire to form a limited liability company. Kamsui possesses years of experiencing managing a business. Hotaka is a brilliant software engineer. Moriko is wealthy. Would you advise that the three owners adopt a member-managed or a manager-managed limited liability company? Why?
6. Jonathan, Mary, Bonnie, and Melvin are the members of a limited liability company that has functioned well for three years. Unfortunately, Jonathan, Mary, and Bonnie are less and less happy with Melvin's judgment. The three sit down one afternoon and amend the operating agreement without securing Melvin's consent. Is their amendment legal? Why?
7. Zach, Jordan, and Jared form a limited partnership. They choose not to create a limited partnership agreement. Zach is the general partner, with Jordan and Jared serving as limited partners. Jordan and Jared have lots of energy and great ideas for making the business run smoother. What concerns would you have with Jordan and Jared taking an active role in the limited partnership?
8. Greta and Hansel form a limited partnership under which Greta is the general partner and Hansel is the limited partner. The business purchases an apartment complex. Greta manages the business, but one day learns that Hansel has purchased twelve new water heaters for the complex. What advice would you give Greta and Hansel?
9. Torts R Us is a law firm formed by limited liability partnership law. The owners, all attorneys, have decided to have a manager-managed organization with Tanya Nordstrom chosen to be the manager. One of the partners, Simon, just purchased a $20,000 software package to assist the firm with their information technology needs without telling Tanya or getting her permission. Tanya has already chosen another software package and entered into a contract for the purchase of that software on behalf of Torts R Us. Who is responsible for paying for the software Simon purchases?
10. Chip, Robbie, and Mike were accounting students at a local university. Upon graduation and becoming certified public accountants, the three formed a limited liability partnership. One of their clients, Maxim Enterprises, worked primarily with Chip. Unfortunately, Chip provided tax advice to Maxim that proved wrong and cost Maxim thousands of dollars. Who is liable and to what extent?

Internet Resources

The text of and explanatory provisions relating to the Revised Uniform Limited Liability Company Act (2006), a product of the National Conference of Commissioners on Uniform State Laws, is available at: http://www.law.upenn.edu/bll/ulc/ullca/2006act_final.htm

Securities Regulation | 32

CHAPTER OUTLINE

1. Introduction
2. Securities Regulation Landscape
3. Securities and Exchange Commission

INITIAL SALES OF SECURITIES: THE SECURITIES ACT OF 1933

4. Purpose of the 1933 Act
5. Definition of a Security
6. Registration Statement and Prospectus
7. Exempt Securities
8. Exempt Transactions: Background
9. Exempt Transactions: Categories
10. Integration and Resale
11. Liability and Due Diligence Defense

SECONDARY SECURITIES TRANSFERS: THE SECURITIES AND EXCHANGE ACT OF 1934

12. Purpose of the 1934 Act
13. Registration and Reporting Requirements
14. Proxy Solicitation
15. Insider Trading—Fraud: Basics
16. Insider Trading—Fraud: Elements
17. Insider Trading—Short-Swing Profits

CHAPTER PREVIEW

Information! Any purchaser wants information regarding the product, service, technology, or idea they are thinking about buying. The information provided must be accurate, relevant, freely available, and sufficient enough so that the purchaser can make an informed decision. For example, if a person is about to purchase a bicycle, there are a number of pieces of information the potential buyer will wish to know before proceeding with the purchase.

In a similar vein, a person or entity wishing to invest in corporate securities desires information that has all the same qualities mentioned previously. However, it is critical that the market for securities be regulated by the government because of the large degree of separation that typically exists between management of the corporation (those that possess relevant information) and potential investors (those desiring the information). Protection of the investing public (current and prospective investors) is a paramount concern for the government in two general arenas. One is where a corporation sells its securities to the investing public for the purpose of raising capital. The government acts in this situation to make sure that the corporation is supplying appropriate information to potential purchasers. The other circumstance occurs where those who already own securities wish to transfer their interest in the corporation to others. Here the government is concerned that those with inside knowledge regarding the corporation may use that information to their advantage and to the disadvantage of those without such knowledge.

As you read this chapter, reflect on why the government seeks to protect the investing public through the laws associated with securities regulation. Also consider whether current statutes and regulations provide corporations and individuals involved in the management of corporations with sufficient leeway to meet the capital needs of corporations in a highly-competitive business environment and allow individuals closely associated with the corporation to reap the financial rewards that should be available to those who excel in business.

BUSINESS MANAGEMENT DECISION

Mary works the night shift at a high-end print shop. Much of the work Mary manages involves making copies of materials for law firms, accounting practices, banks, and, on occasion, general corporations. Some of the material is confidential, but most is not. At the beginning of a shift, Mary sees a press release from WowUm Company, an Internet computer game manufacturer. Mary reads the release, which indicates that WowUm is a company whose stock is sold on a national exchange and who is about to announce a new game that will allow multiple users to interface in a virtual world. The release goes on to say that the company has mastered a technique that allows the interactive game to be projected, in three dimensions, into the space of a room. The release ends by indicating that the WowUm game will change the world of computer gaming. The press release indicates that the information is confidential until its planned release on the next day, at noon.

Mary immediately contacts her stockbroker's office and finds that her broker is still working at the office. Mary instructs the broker to purchase 1,000 shares of WowUm, but she does not reveal anything stated in the press release to the broker. The broker is able to purchase WowUm stock for Mary the next morning, and by mid-afternoon the stock has doubled in value. Has Mary violated the law? Has the broker?

1. Introduction

The corporate form of organization is a marvelous mechanism for conducting business. Management is allowed the potential to generate large amounts of capital, investors are generally "passive" and simply wait for a return on their investment, and society reaps the benefits associated with a form of business that has few limits in terms of size. Yet there are serious hazards associated with the corporate form, particularly when the size of a company requires that management (and others closely involved in the business) are not known to those members of the public who choose to invest in the organization.

Protection of public investors in securities became a matter of national concern after the stock market crash of 1929 propelled the United States into the Great Depression. Laws were then enacted to protect potential and actual investors in the corporate form for two reasons. First, the sale of securities directly from the corporation to the investing public (termed *primary sales*) is inherently fraught with the potential that the corporation or those selling an interest in the corporation might commit fraud or otherwise mislead an individual seeking to purchase stock (becoming a holder of an equitable interest in the corporation) or a person wishing to purchase a bond (creating a debtor/creditor relationship).

The annals of business are replete with instances where individuals have invested their monies in a corporate form that either does not exist or was formed with no intention of actually conducting business. The principal act of Congress aiming to protect investors at the time of an initial sale of securities s called the *Securities Act of 1933* (1933 Act).

Also, there is the matter of trading securities, termed *secondary sales.* Most of us are familiar with the operation of a national stock exchange. In this venue, among others including face-to-face and over-the-counter sales, securities are trade after the initial sale of securities by the corporation has occurred. Secondary sales deserve the attention of public policy makers because there exists the potential that individuals within a corporation know information that is not available to the public and trade on that information by buying shares (if the news is good) or selling shares (if the news is bad). In order to create a level playing field for the purchase and sale of securities, society must place certain burdens on the corporation and on those who purchase and sell in the secondary market. The main act of Congress that regulates secondary trading of securities is the *Securities Exchange Act f 1934* (1934 Act).

2. Securities Regulation Landscape

The federal government began regulating securities with the 1933 At and the 1934 Act, but congressional attention has continued to be directed for succeeding decades toward developing a regulatory environment that is fair for investors while also encouraging economic growth. For example, Congress has passed the *Trust Indenture Act of 1939* (regulating the sale of debt securities), the *Investment Advisors Act of 1940* (controlling the behavior of investment advisors), the *Williams Act of 1968* (targeting the area of hostile takeovers of one corporation over another), the *Foreign Corrupt Practices Act of 1977* (as amended in 1988, prohibits certain bribes to foreign government officials), the *Insider Trading Sanctions Act of 1984* (increasing punishment for those involved in trading on insider information), and the *Private Securities Litigation Reform Act of 1995* (aimed at eliminating spurious lawsuits against corporations). Finally, a number of provisions of the *Sarbanes-Oxley Act of 2002*, the primary congressional response to Enron and other corporate scandals occurring during the turn of the century, make adjustments to the 1934 Act.

Blue Sky Laws
State laws that regulate securities

State laws regulating securities are often referred to as **blue sky laws**. The term refers to the hope that the laws will prevent individuals from purchasing nothing more than an interest in blue sky. Kansas was the first state to experiment (in 1911) with regulating securities. In order to attempt to standardize state regulation, many states have adopted the *Uniform Securities Act*. The National Conference of Commissioners on Uniform State Laws has drafted various editions of the Uniform Securities Act, and now more than 35 states have adopted all or significant parts of one version or another. Some states, including California and New York, have crafted their own rather distinct statutory scheme for regulating securities. An issuer must comply with both federal and state laws.

3. Securities and Exchange Commission

Securities and Exchange Commission (SEC)

The federal administrative agency whose primary duty is to regulate securities

Congress created and empowered the **Securities and Exchange Commission** (SEC) to provide federal regulation in the area of corporate securities. The SEC is specifically charged with administering both the 1933 Act and the 1934 Act, but also has responsibilities for a number of other federal laws pertaining to the issuance and trading of corporate securities.

As with most administrative agencies, the SEC functions in three realms. First, it possesses rulemaking power. The SEC promulgates regulations and interpretative rules in all areas of securities regulation, from initial sale f securities through periodic disclosure to insider trading. Over the years, the SEC also has built an enviable reputation as an independent and fair administrative agency. Therefore, today the SEC is often invited by Congress to propose legislation in areas pertaining to its scope of expertise.

Next, the SEC possesses considerable enforcement abilities. While some investigations of corporate practices or the conduct of buyers and sellers of securities are triggered by complaints of the investing public, often the SEC begins investigating whether a law or regulation has been violated as a result of the SEC's sophisticated process of studying the markets' behavior and monitoring securities trading activities. The SEC has the power to interview witnesses, review trading records, and evaluate information regarding securities transaction.

Finally, the SEC possesses adjudicatory capacities. At one level, the SEC may proceed against a firm or individual through the administrative hearing process. An administrative law judge (ALJ), who is an expert in securities laws and regulations, hears the accusations and listens to responses from those accused. The ALJ possesses the power to revoke a securities broker's license, order civil money penalties, or require *disgorgement* (the return of moneys obtained illegally). At another level, the SEC may sue in federal court for civil penalties, an injunction, or other appropriate remedies. At still another level, the SEC refers to the Department of Justice serious violations of securities laws and regulations. These may bring criminal actions against entities and individuals.

While the SEC actively enforces securities laws in the United States, many prominent aspects of securities regulations also can be enforced through civil actions brought by members of the public. The United States is fairly unique in the world in that it allows private parties to sue in civil court for damages resulting from the breach of securities laws. These suits are an effective mechanism to bring corporations and others into compliance. Thus, the investing public, along with the government, enforces many aspects of securities regulation in this country. In most other nations that have sophisticated securities regulations, only the government enforces thee laws.

INITIAL SALES OF SECURITIES: THE SECURITIES ACT OF 1933

4. Purpose of the 1933 Act

The 1933 Act regulates the sale of securities from a corporation to members of the public, whether they are individuals or institutions, sophisticated in the ways of investing in securities or novices, investing $100 or $100,000. The principle purpose of the 1933 Act is to require any corporation that wishes to sell its securities make adequate *disclosures of information.* In general a corporation desiring to issue its securities to the public must generate sufficient disclosures of information t meet the expectations of a prudent investor about to purchase an interest in an entity.

Because many corporations provided little or false information about critical financial information, thousands lost millions of dollars. Soon after the country would experience the Great Depression.

During the 1920s, many corporations and those individuals selling interests in corporations either provided little information or provided false information regarding critical financial and managerial aspects of the business. Not only did thousands of well-meaning individuals during the "Roaring 20s" lose millions of dollars because they believed the claims of corporations and those that were selling interests in businesses of questionable worth, but, also, the public's confidence in the securities industry was badly shaken. The 1933 Act has largely remedied the problems associated with lack of disclosure by corporations seeking to sell their securities to the investing public.

Underwriting

Primary process by which a corporation sells a new security

An integral part of the issuing process is called **underwriting**, the primary mechanism by which the corporation distributes a new security. Investment banking firms or broker-dealer companies often assume the role of an underwriter. The underwriter works with the corporation to either purchase the entire issue of securities itself or to assist the corporation in selling the securities to others. Because of the intimate relationship the underwriter has with the offering corporation, the underwriter assumes major responsibilities to ensure that the corporation, under the 1933 Act, makes proper disclosures of information.

5. Definition of a Security

The 1933 Act applies only to those entities selling a *security.* It is commonly understood that a security includes *stocks* (equity) and *bonds* (debt) issued by a corporation. This view is entirely correct. However, Congress and the courts have adopted very expansive definitions of the term, an area that is worth our consideration as we understand the significant reach of the 1933 Act into the world of corporate finance.

The term "security" under the 1933 Act also includes those activities that qualify as an *investment contact.* In 1946, the United States Supreme Court, in the *Securities and Exchange Commission vs. Howey Co.* case, defined n investment contract as:

> [A] contract, transaction or scheme whereby a person invests his money in a common enterprise and is led to expect profits solely from the efforts of the promoter or a third party, it being immaterial whether the shares in the enterprise are evidenced

> by formal certificates or by nominal interests in the physical assets employed in the enterprise. It embodies a flexible rather than a static principle, one that is capable of adaptation to meet the countless and variable schemes devised by those who seek the use of the money of others on the promise of profits.

This definition incorporates four elements: (1) an investment of money, (2) in a common enterprise or scheme, (3) from which the investor expects a profit, (4) that is derived from the efforts of others.

Courts have found a security for purposes of the 1933 Act in a number of situations that only remotely resemble a stock or bond. For example, courts have found that the 1933 Act was applicable to the sale of an interest in a limited partnership, farm animals and related animal care agreements, and in a repurchase agreement covering casks of whiskey. Therefore, members of the business community should exercise extreme care anytime an individual is making a purchase of an interest in a business or a business-related effort to make sure the purchase does not fall within the 1933 Act definition of a security.

6. Registration Statement and Prospectus

How is the disclosure mandate of the 1933 Act met? While there are numerous exemptions (the most popular are addressed below), as a general proposition the 1933 Act requires any corporation that wishes to proceed with issuing securities must provide the SEC with a *registration statement* and must make a *prospectus* available to potential investors.

Registration statement

Information from an issuing corporation regarding a contemplated sale of securities that must be filed with the SEC

REGISTRATION STATEMENT A **registration statement** is a set of documents that must be submitted to the SEC.

The SEC requires an issuer of securities to provide it with information in the registration statement regarding the:

- *Management of the corporation* (the names and backgrounds of the executive leadership of the corporation, payments in salaries, benefits, and other types of remuneration paid to management, interests that management possesses in the issuer, and usually multiple years of information relating to management's discussions and analysis),
- *Financial condition of the corporation* (usually multiple years of audited financial statements, an analysis of any pending lawsuits), and
- *Proposed security* (description of the proposed security, planned use of the moneys raised from the sale of the security, list of risks associated with the sale).

The registration statement becomes effective automatically after a 20-day waiting period, unless the SEC changes the date.

Prospectus

Information from an issuing corporation regarding a contemplated sale of securities that must be provided to the investing public

PROSPECTUS Broadly defined, a **prospectus** is a communication to the public from a corporation that offers a security for sale.

The SEC is very concerned about when information regarding the issuance of stock is released to the public and what type of information is communicated. As a result, a three-stage process is adopted for the sale of a security under the 1933 Act, consisting of a quite period, a waiting period, and an effective period.

- *Quite Period.* During the *pre-filing period*, no detailed information regarding the issuance may be released. For this reason, the pre-filing period is known as the *quiet period.* This is the time prior to filing the registration statement with the SEC, perhaps three to eight months before the filing, that the corporation makes decisions regarding the issuance and drafts the registration statement and the prospectus.

- *Waiting Period.* Once the registration statement is filed, then the 20-day *waiting period* begins. The SEC critiques the registration statement and allows the issuer to respond. Oral offers to purchase the security may be entertained. Only two types of written advertising are allowed during the waiting period. One is the preliminary prospectus, also known as a *red herring.* (The SEC requires that this type of prospectus contain a statement, in red print, that the registration has been filed but is not yet effective, hence the name "red herring.") The red herring prospectus simply notifies prospective investors of the potential sale; it may not include the offering price. The red herring only may be used during the waiting period. The other type of advertising is called a *tombstone ad,* so named because its design resembles a tombstone. Only the most basic information is allowed on a tombstone ad; but unlike a red herring prospectus, the tombstone ad may include the price of the offering. It is interesting to note that the SEC has allowed the use of the Internet during the waiting period, as long as the same information available by non-digital means is also available to those through the Internet. Therefore, under SEC rules a corporation may post a red herring prospectus and a tombstone ad on the issuer's web site.
- *Effective Period.* Once the waiting period ends, the issuer may begin selling the securities. At his point, the issuer must distribute a *final prospectus,* which contains a similar amount of detail, as does the registration statement. This last communiqué from the corporation should provide sufficient information for a prospective purchaser to make an informed decision. During the effective period, tombstone ads may be downloaded from the Internet, as well as copies of the final prospectus. Again, the use of the Internet does not violate the language or the spirit of the 1933 Act to create an environment of full disclosure.

7. Exempt Securities

Given the broad definition of a security included in the 1933 Act, Congress created a host of *exempt securities* to reflect the realization that detailed disclosure is not required when certain types of securities are sold. Issuers of these securities need *not* comply with the registration and prospectus requirements. Among the most prominent examples of exempt securities are:

- Securities issued by the government or by a charitable institution
- Commercial paper, as long as the maturity date does not exceed nine months
- Securities issued by railroads and trucking companies regulated by the Interstate Commerce Commission
- Securities issued by banking institutions
- Securities issued in exchange (e.g., stock dividends)
- Securities issued as part of reorganization within the laws of bankruptcy

8. Exempt Transactions: Background

Costs associated with complying with the registration and prospectus requirements of the 1933 Act are considerable, often exceeding one million dollars. Also, as indicated earlier, it may take many months to move through the registration process to a place where the investing public can be contacted. Of course, during that period there is always the possibility that disclosures are made of the corporation's intent to issue securities. Therefore, many firms attempt to structure their efforts sell securities in such a manner so that a specific transaction fits within one of a host of statutory or regulatory transaction exemptions.

Many decades ago, the "safe harbors" were exceedingly difficult to determine, largely because they were created by courts. The following case illustrates the problem.

In the *Ralston Purina* case, the United States Supreme Court held that the company's offer of stock to its employees was not exempt from registration required under the 1933 Act. However, this decision and many other judicial interpretations of the exemption provisions of the 1933 Act during the 1950s, 1960s and 1970s did little to elucidate boundaries associated with exemptions

CASE

SEC v. Ralston Purina Company

SUPREME COURT OF THE UNITED STATES

346 U.S. 119 (1953)

MR. JUSTICE CLARK DELIVERED THE OPINION OF THE COURT

Section 4 (1) of the Securities Act of 1933 exempts "transactions by an issuer not involving any public offering" from the registration requirements of § 5. We must decide whether Ralston Purina's offerings of treasury stock to its "key employees" are within this exemption. On a complaint brought by the Commission under § 20 (b) of the Act seeking to enjoin respondent's unregistered offerings, the District Court held the exemption applicable and dismissed the suit. The Court of Appeals affirmed. The question has arisen many times since the Act was passed; an apparent need to define the scope of the private offering exemption prompted certiorari.

Ralston Purina manufactures and distributes various feed and cereal products. Its processing and distribution facilities are scattered throughout the United States and Canada, staffed by some 7,000 employees. At least since 1911 the company has had a policy of encouraging stock ownership among its employees; more particularly, since 1942 it has made authorized but unissued common shares available to some of them. Between 1947 and 1951, the period covered by the record in this case, Ralston Purina sold nearly $2,000,000 of stock to employees without registration and, in so doing, made use of the mails.

In each of these years, a corporate resolution authorized the sale of common stock "to employees . . . who shall, without any solicitation by the Company or its officers or employees, inquire of any of them as to how to purchase common stock of Ralston Purina Company." A memorandum sent to branch and store managers after the resolution was adopted advised that "The only employees to whom this stock will be available will be those who take the initiative and are interested in buying stock at present market prices." Among those responding to these offers were employees with the duties of artist, bakeshop foreman, chow loading foreman, clerical assistant, copywriter, electrician, stock clerk, mill office clerk, order credit trainee, production trainee, stenographer, and veterinarian.

The company bottoms its exemption claim on the classification of all offerees as "key employees" in its organization. Its position on trial was that "A key employee . . . is not confined to an organization chart. It would include an individual who is eligible for promotion, an individual who especially influences others or who advises others, a person whom the employees look to in some special way, an individual, of course, who carries some special responsibility, who is sympathetic to management and who is ambitious and who the management feels is likely to be promoted to a greater responsibility." That an offering to all of its employees would be public is conceded.

The Securities Act nowhere defines the scope of § 4 (1)'s private offering exemption nor is the legislative history of much help in staking out its boundaries.

Exemption from the registration requirements of the Securities Act is the question. The design of the statute is to protect investors by promoting full disclosure of information thought necessary to informed investment decisions. The natural way to interpret the private offering exemption is in light of the statutory purpose. Since exempt transactions are those to which "there is no practical need for [the bill's] application," the applicability of § 4 (1) should turn on whether the particular class of persons affected needs the protection of the Act. An offering to those who are shown to be able to fend for themselves is a transaction "not involving any public offering."

Keeping in mind the broadly remedial purposes of federal securities legislation, imposition of the burden of proof on an issuer who would plead the exemption seems to us fair and reasonable. Agreeing, the court below thought the burden met primarily because of the respondent's purpose in singling out its key employees for stock offerings. However, once it is seen that the exemption question turns on the knowledge of the offerees, the issuer's motives, laudable though they may be, fade into irrelevance. The focus of inquiry should be on the need of the offerees for the protections afforded by registration. The employees here were not shown to have access to the kind of information which registration would disclose. The obvious opportunities for pressure and imposition make it advisable that they be entitled to compliance with the registration provisions of § 5.

■ *Reversed.*

CASE CONCEPT REVIEW

1. Do you agree with the company's broad definition of who is a "key employee"? Why? Is it reasonable?
2. What is purpose is served by an exemption to the registration requirement under the 1933 Act? What class of person should not fall within an exemption, per the court's decision?
3. Is a case-by-case determination by the courts of when an exemption should apply the best approach to interpreting the intent of Congress? Would an administrative agency do a better job? Why?

for participants in an increasingly complex corporate finance environment. Fortunately, in the 1980s and 1990s, the SEC became more active in promulgating regulations that now guide well a corporation in qualifying for exemption under the 1933 Act.

9. Exempt Transactions: Categories

The most popular exempt transactions are presented within this section. As you examine these exemptions, keep in mind the overall purpose of the 1933 Act is to force corporations to disclose information regarding an impending sale of securities. Consider, specifically, if the attributes associated with each of these categories trump the need for disclosure as required under general provisions of the 1933 Act.

INTRASTATE OFFERING EXEMPTION The concept of federalism requires that state governments regulate those activities that fall within the boundaries of a state and the federal government should regulate those actions that involve more than one state. Investors should be protected sufficiently under state securities laws in those situations where activity associated with the issuance of securities occurs primarily within a state. SEC *Rule 147* honors this concept y creating a safe harbor for *intrastate offerings.* In order to qualify, the following general conditions must exist: (1) the issuer must be *domiciled and doing business* within the state of domicile; (2) the issuer must offer and sell securities only to residents of the state where the corporation is incorporated; (3) *no reselling* of the securities may be made to an out-of-state investor for nine months (in fact, each security that qualifies under Rule 147 must contain a legend indicating the restriction on reselling the security); and (4) the issuer must be *doing business primarily within the state* where the corporation is domiciled. This last element is satisfied under Rule 147 where at least 80 percent of the company's gross revenues are generated within the domicile state, at least 80 percent of its assets are located in the state, and at least 80 percent of the issued security's proceeds are expended within the state.

PRIVATE PLACEMENT EXEMPTION The 1933 Act specifically provides that the registration and prospectus requirements are not applicable if there is no offering to the public, a safe harbor called the *private placement exemption.* That is, if the theory of the 1933 Act is to protect the investing *public,* where the offering is made to *private* individuals or entities that are not in need of the protections offered by the 1933 Act, then the corporation can proceed without complying with the disclosure provisions.

The SEC issued Regulation D, in part, to cover private placement exemptions. A particular aspect of Regulation D, *Rule 506,* creates a *private placement exemption.* Under Rule 506, a company may offer an unlimited amount of securities for sale. However, the offering must be made to only two groups of potential buyers. First, the corporation may offer to an *unlimited number of accredited investors.* Accredited investors typically include wealthy individuals who have the financial wherewithal to undertake a risk of this type (e.g., an individual whose net worth exceeds $1 million), executives within the issuing firm, and institutional investors (for instance, banks, insurance companies, investment firms). It is assumed by the SEC that these types of individuals and entities are so sophisticated with regard to the world of corporate finance (or are advised by experts from that field) that the disclosure protections are not needed. Also, under Rule 506, no more than *thirty-five unaccredited investors* may participate, provided that the issuer *believes that each of the unaccredited investors possesses sufficient knowledge in financial matters to properly evaluate the offering.* Individuals who fall within this category under Rule 506 are known as *sophisticated investors.*

While Rule 506 does not require that any information from the issuer be reported if all investors are accredited, the presence of unaccredited investors triggers a requirement that all investors receive material information about the securities and the firm. Also, a notice to the SEC that this exemption is being invoked mst be filed within 15 days of the first sale.

SMALL OFFERING EXEMPTIONS Congress and the SEC contemplated the plight faced by an issuer that wishes to raise smaller amounts of capital and responded by crafting specific "safe harbor" provisions based on a combination of the amount the corporation hopes to generate and the sophistication of those who will purchase the issue.

One popular exemption is provided under *Rule 504.* This provision, part of Regulation D, provides that a company may offer exempt securities of up to $1 million within a twelve-month period. This exemption is used primarily for small businesses because it is not available to corporations registered under the 1934 Act and may not be used by investment companies (companies, like a mutual fund, whose primary business is the purchase and sale of securities). Usually, the company that invokes Rule 504 has a specific business plan and ha matriculated to the point where a potential investor has a good idea of the nature of the business and of the risks associated with the issuance. For businesses that are still at the development stage (usually without a business plan), the Rule 504-A provides a more qualified exemption for these types of businesses, generally known as *blank check companies.* Rule 504-A sets the limit for this type of exemption at $500,000.

Another often-used small offering exemption under Regulation D is provided by *Rule 505.* Similar to Rule 506, this exemption is available to an unlimited number of accredited investors and no more than 35 unaccredited investors. *Note, though, that under Rule 506 the issuer must believe that each unaccredited investor has sufficient business acumen to qualify as a sophisticated investor, while under Rule 505 the issuer is not required to make such a showing.* Also, unlike Rule 506, Rule 505 sets an issuance limit ($5 million). As with Rule 506, if unaccredited investors are involved in the purchase of these securities, there is a disclosure requirement.

Finally, under *Section 4(6)* of the 1933 Act,securities may be sold entirely to accredited investors as long as the total amount is less tan $5 million. There is no limit on the number of accredited investors under the Section 4(6) transaction exemption.

Table 32-1 (below) provides a summary of the principal transaction exemptions allowed under the 1933 Act.

TABLE 32-1 ■ Transaction Exemptions Under the 1933 Act

Category	Designation	Amount	Number of Purchasers	Qualifications of Purchasers
Interstate	Rule 147	Unlimited	Unlimited	Resident of State of Domicile
Private	Rule 506	Unlimited	35	Unaccredited (with belief requirement)
			and Unlimited	Accredited
Small	Rule 504	$1 million	Unlimited	None
Small	Rule 505	$5 million	35	Unaccredited (with NO belief requirement
			and Unlimited	Accredited
Small	Section 4(6)	$5 million	Unlimited	Accredited

10. Integration and Resale

Suppose Huron Corporation is interested in raising $30 million through the issuance of securities. The executive officers of Huron, after consulting with legal experts, find that they cannot fit within any of the transaction exemptions and are faced with the prospect of complying with the costly and time-consuming process of complying with the registration and prospectus requirements under the 1933 Act. What if, though, Huron took the $30 million offering and broke it into smaller parts that would fit within one or more of the exemptions discussed above?

What if Erie Corporation issued securities under the Rule 506 exemption, but unaccredited investors then turned around and sold those securities to other unaccredited investors within a few weeks of the initial sale by the corporation? If that situation was allowed—secondary sales of exempt securities within a short time after issuance—would not the protections inherent in the exemption under Rule 506 disappear and those purchasing the securities would not have an investment that was subject to either the main provisions of the 1933Act or provisions of an exemption?

These two situations, where either the issuer or a purchaser of the issue attempt to avoid the public policy protections of the 1933 Act, are examined in this section.

Integration

Process used by the issuing corporation to combine several supposedly separate exempt transaction offerings

INTEGRATION **Integration** is the process used by the issuer to combine several supposedly separate exempt transaction offerings. The SEC examines the closeness of the offerings and the purposes associated with each of the issuances to determine if a corporation is attempting to abuse the exemptions provided under the 1933 Act. If a firm attempts to split what the SEC determines is truly a single issuance of securities, then the multiple issuances is treated as a single one and the appropriate exemption must apply or the issuer is in violation of the 1933 Act. Rule 502, however, provides that offers and sales of a Regulation D offering made more than six months before the start of an offering or more than six months after its completion will not be considered part of that offering.

RESALE *Restricted securities* are those securities that are supposed to be held by the purchaser from an issuer for a period of one year. Securities that fall within the provisions of Rule 505, Rule 506, and sometimes withinRule 504 are restricted securities. By restricting initial purchasers from immediately reselling their securities, the disclosure provisions of the 1933 Act are respected. The restriction put on these types of Regulation D securities discourage issuers from selling securities to a private individual within a transactio exemption that they know will soon turn around and sell the security to a member of the public who may not be protected and who may be willing to pay a premium for the securities. Usually the fact that securities are restricted is represented on the paperwork (e.g., stock certificate) associated with this type of transaction.

11. Liability and Due Diligence Defense

The 1933 Act provides that the SEC may impose civil sanctions and the Department of Justice may pursue criminal actions (with penalties including fines and time in prison) against those who willfully violate the disclosure provisions of this congressional edict. Further, those individuals or entities that purchase securities during an initial public offering and were harmed because a material statement was false o omitted from the registration statement or the prospectus may sue for civil damages. Note there is no requirement that the plaintiff in such a case show that the defendant was negligent or intended to defraud. Liability for damages extends beyond those who signed the registration statement, for example, and may include experts such as investment bankers, accountants, attorneys, or others who provided information to the issuer.

Due diligence defense

A defense available to non-issuers under the 1933 Act

All parties involved in the registration and prospectus process (except the issuer) may assert the **due diligence defense.** This defense is premised on the fact that a party was not negligent and it acted in good faith in believing the statements made in the documents were true. In most circumstances, a defendant (particularly an expert who advised the corporation) is able to escape liability under the due diligence defense only if they conducted a reasonable investigation. For example, Jerry is a certified public accountant who was hired by Prime Timers Software Associates to audit financial statements of the firm. Jerry was told that the statements would be part of registration and prospectus materials. Jerry conducted the audit according to generally accepted accounting standards, but critical financial information included in the registration statement and prospectus was false. Jerry was sued under the 1933 Act by investors who were harmed. In order to properly assert the due diligence defense, Jerry will have to show that he acted as a reasonable professional in his field would have acted. Here, because Jerry followed his profession's standards, his actions would meet the reasonable investigation criterion; and he would not be liable under the 1933 Act.

SECONDARY SECURITIES TRANSFERS: THE SECURITIES AND EXCHANGE ACT OF 1934

12. Purpose of the 1934 Act

Like the 1933 Act, the purpose of the 1934 Act is to require corporations to disclose of material information to the investing public. The timing, nature, and types of disclosures under the 1934 Act, however, differ from those associated with the 1933 Act. The 1934 Act is geared to provide *periodic disclosures* instead of the one-time disclosure requirement under the 1933 Act. Why? Because the nature of secondary securities transfers is directed to a continuing market for securities, society should impose an on-going obligation by corporations and those individuals involved in management to provide the investing public (current investors and potential investors alike) with information sufficient so that informed decisions can be made. Therefore, while regular disclosures of general information about the history, current health, and possible future of a corporation who has public investors is helpful, it would also be wise to require a corporation to provide information that might impact the price of securities immediately, should the need arise. In addition to addressing the issue of disclosures in a very thorough manner, the 1934 Act also creates additional duties for those who are assumed to have inside information and wish to participate in trading their own firm's securities. Registration under the 1934 Act is separate from that done under the 1933 Act.

13. Registration and Reporting Requirements

The 1934 Act requires certain types of issuers register with the SEC. Registration is necessary so that the SEC can monitor the corporation's compliance with various provisions of the law and SEC regulations. A major obligation under the 1934 Act, as noted in the previous section, is to report periodically and, perhaps, to disclose information if an event occurs that could impact the price of the securities. Each of these aspects of the 1934 Act is examined in this section.

REGISTRATION An issuer is required to register securities under the 1934 Act if either (1) *a company has **securities** (equity and debt) that are **registered on a national securities exchange*** (e.g., the New York Stock Exchange), or (2) *a company whose **assets total more than $10 million** has a class of **equity** securities held by **500 or more shareholders.*** In many respects, the registration statement required under he 1934 Act is similar to that mandated by the 1933 Act.

REPORTING As discussed earlier in the chapter, under the 1933 Act an issuer is required to make only one report. The rationale for the single report is quite simple: only one sale is contemplated. That is, the 1933 Act is geared to control the sale from the issuer corporation to a purchaser. The 1934 Act, however, contemplates continuing sales and opportunities to purchase securities. Therefore, the issuer is obligated to make multiple reports to the SEC and the public because of the nature of a secondary securities market.

As a general proposition, issuers registered under the 1934 Act are required to file three types of reports. An *annual report* (Form 10-K) must be filed with the SEC and distributed to all holders of securities. Materials to be included within an annual report include audited financial statements, management discussion and analysis (MD&A), and other information relevant to the conduct of the business and the treatment of management (e.g., executive compensation). Next, a *quarterly report* (Form 10-Q) contains unaudited quarterly reports and related information. Finally, a current report (Form 8-K) is filed and distributed when extraordinary and material events occur. For example, bankruptcy, resignation of directors over disagreements in policy, acquisition of significant assets, or any other "materially important event" would trigger the filing of a current report under the 1934 Act.

The SEC sponsors a sophisticated electronic processing and access system that provides members of the public with the ability to read on-line all SEC financial filings, including 1934 registration statements and reporting forms.

14. Proxy Solicitation

One important area regulated by the 1934 Act is *proxy solicitation.* Corporations are theoretically based on democratic principles with shareholders (assuming they have the appropriate right) able to vote on important matters associated with the corporation. The theory of a vibrant democracy controlling a corporation's operation is challenged to some degree because of the impossibility that many holders of a voting interest in the corporation can attend an annual or special meeting of the shareholders or be well-versed on matters associated with the corporation. The law allows those who cannot attend a shareholder meeting or do not believe they are conversant enough with financial and managerial aspects of the corporation to transfer their power to vote to another. The process to accomplish this result is through voting by **proxy.** A proxy is an instrument that transfers the right to vote from one who cannot or will not attend to one who will attend the shareholder meeting.

Proxy

An instrument that transfers the right to vote from one who cannot or will not attend to one who will attend the shareholder meeting

Government regulation is necessary in the proxy solicitation process because of the possibility that proxy solicitors who are management or those who oppose management (called dissidents) could commit fraud or otherwise interfere with creating a well-informed electorate and a fair election. Needless-to-say, proxy soliciting is often a high-stakes endeavor. It involves convincing shareholders to vote for particular board candidates (perhaps those currently serving which generally favors current management or other individuals, which might indicate those serving in management are not doing a good job at operating the corporation) or to either support or turn down a particular proposal that requires shareholder approval.

A *proxy statement,* which can be used by either management or dissidents, must be filed with the SEC before it is distributed to all exchanges trading the voting securities and to all those individuals and entities that hold the power to vote. The proxy statement includes the identity o the proxy solicitor, information regarding the election of directors and the content of shareholder proposals; and it states the source of the moneys used to pay for the proxy solicitation. Management must also include in its proxy solicitation additional information, required by the SEC, pertaining to executive compensation, shareholder return, and the return on investment for an industry index or other comparable index.

Historically, because dissidents must pay their own proxy solicitation expenses, battles for corporate control between management and dissidents (along with their independent proxy solicitors) have been infrequent. As a result of the ease and inexpensive means available today to transmit information, however, *proxy contests* are increasingly common. Many also become quite public. Therefore, during the past decade or so, the SEC has played a significant role in ensuring that misleading or outright fraudulent statements are not included in proxy materials, regardless of whether the source is management or a dissident group. Further, the SEC recently has made the proxy solicitation process even more democratic. The SEC allows issuers to distribute via the Internet materials relating to board elections or other significant matters affecting shareholders, along with actual proxies. That same rule allows dissident shareholders to have electronic access to shareholder information, thus making contact with shareholders much easier and significantly less expensive than what has occurred in the past.

15. Insider Trading—Fraud Liability: Basics

Insider trading

A person with confidential information about an issuer not available to the investing public that uses such information when they trade with unaware traders

A second area regulated by the 1934 Act and SEC regulations deals with **insider trading**. Insider trading is truly a species of fraud. Insider trading occurs when a person with confidential information about an issuer not available to the investing public uses that information when they trade with unaware traders.

While state common law notions of insider trading tracked fairly close to the traditional structures associated with the tort of fraud, Congress, the SEC, and the courts have broadened liability considerably.

The single most prominent antifraud provision under securities law is SEC Rule 10b-5. This regulation covers *anyone having inside information.* Therefore, the obligations associated with *Rule 10b-5* stretch beyond those who may be a corporate officer or director to mid- and low-level employees who possess information not available to the public. Also, Rule 10b-5 applies to *securities trading regardless of whether the issuer is registered* under the 1993 Act or the 1934 Act.

Trading on inside information may include either purchasing or selling securities based on inside information. Consider the following scenario. Marsha is a research chemist with a biotechnology firm.As part of her employment, Marsha has worked on a vaccine that, if approved by the Food and Drug Administration, would potentially cause the value of the company's stock to rise precipitously. Assume that Marsha owns 100 shares of stock in the company. She finds out that the company will receive government approval for the vaccine and quickly purchases 200 more shares before the corporation makes a public announcement. After the public release of the vaccine's approval, the price of the stock doubles. Marsha violated Rule 10b-5 in the *purchase* of the 200 shares.

Instead, assume that the vaccine is not going to be approved. Marsha again knows of the decision before any public disclosure occurs. She sells her 100 shares, and then a press release from the corporation details the fact that the vaccine was not approved. The price of the shares of stock falls by one-half. Marsha violated Rule 10b-5 in the *sale* of the 100 shares.

Many positions in a company can, like mentioned in the text, create an opportunity for insider trading temptations.

It is critical to understand what Rule 10b-5 allows and what it does not allow. In sum, 10b-5 mandates one either to *disclose information or abstain from trading.* Reflecting back on the purpose of Rule 10b-5, the notion underlying the regulation is to prevent insider trading. If an individual possesses material information regarding a corporation that is not available to the public, then the SEC regulation simply forbids that person from trading on the information until it is made public. Of course, the "insider" can always simply wait until the release of pertinent data concerning the corporation and then trade—which places the insider on the same level as those not privy to the information prior to a public release. The application of the disclose or abstain requirement of Rule 10b-5 is seen in the following case, *SEC v. Texas Gulf Sulphur Co.,* which is probably the most famous of all cases dealing with securities regulation.

CASE

SEC v. Texas Gulf Sulphur Co.

UNITED STATES COURT OF APPEALS FOR THE SECOND CIRCUIT

401 F.2d 833 (1968)

This action was commenced in the United States District Court for the Southern District of New York by the Securities and Exchange Commission (the SEC) pursuant to Sec. 21(e) of the Securities Exchange Act of 1934 (the Act), against Texas Gulf Sulphur Company (TGS) and several of its officers, directors and employees, to enjoin certain conduct by TGS and the individual defendants said to violate Section 10(b) of the Act and Rule 10b-5.

This action derives from the exploratory activities of TGS begun in 1957 on the Canadian Shield in eastern Canada. In March 1959, aerial geophysical a group conducted surveys over more than 15,000 square miles of this area led by defendant Mollison, a mining engineer and a Vice President of TGS. The group included defendant Holyk, TGS's chief geologist, defendant Clayton, an electrical engineer and geophysicist, and defendant Darke, a geologist. These operations resulted in the detection of numerous anomalies, i.e., extraordinary variations in the conductivity of rocks, one of which was on the Kidd 55 segment of land located near Timmins, Ontario.

During this period, from November 12, 1963 when K-55-1 was completed, to March 31, 1964 when drilling was resumed, certain of the individual defendants and persons said to have received "tips" from them, purchased TGS stock or calls thereon. Prior to these transactions these persons had owned 1135 shares of TGS stock and possessed no calls; thereafter they owned a total of 8235 shares and possessed 12,300 calls.

Meanwhile, rumors that a major ore strike was in the making had been circulating throughout Canada. With the aid of one Carroll, a public relations consultant, Fogarty drafted a press release designed to quell the rumors, which release, after having been channeled through Stephens and Huntington, a TGS attorney, was issued at 3:00 P.M. on Sunday, April 12, and which appeared in the morning newspapers of general circulation on Monday, April 13.

The evidence as to the effect of this release on the investing public was equivocal and less than abundant. On April 13 the New York Herald Tribune in an article head-noted "Copper Rumor Deflated" quoted from the TGS release of April 12 and backtracked from its original April 11 report of a major strike but nevertheless inferred from the TGS release that "recent mineral exploratory activity near Timmins, Ontario, has provided preliminary favorable results, sufficient at least to require a step-up in drilling operations." Some witnesses who testified at the hearing stated that they found the release encouraging.

A statement relative to the extent of the discovery, in substantial part drafted by Mollison, was given to the Ontario Minister of Mines for release to the Canadian media. Mollison and Holyk expected it to be released over the airways at 11 P.M. on April 15th, but, for undisclosed reasons, it was not released until 9:40 A.M. on the 16th. An official detailed statement, announcing a strike of at least 25 million tons of ore, based on the drilling data set forth above, was read to representatives of American financial media from 10:00 A.M. to 10:10 or 10:15 A.M. on April 16, and appeared over Merrill Lynch's private wire at 10:29 A.M. and, somewhat later than expected, over the Dow Jones ticker tape at 10:54 A.M.

During the period of drilling in Timmins, the market price of TGS stock fluctuated but steadily gained overall. On Friday, November 8, when the drilling began, the stock closed at 17 3/8; on Friday, November 15, after K-55-1 had been completed, it closed at 18. On April 13, the day on which the April 12 release was disseminated, TGS opened at 30 1/8, rose immediately to a high of 32 and gradually tapered off to close at 30 7/8. It closed at 30 1/4 the next day, and at 29 3/8 on April 15. On April 16, the day of the official announcement of the Timmins discovery, the price climbed to a high of 37 and closed at 36 3/8. By May 15, TGS stock was selling at 58 1/4.

Rule 10b-5, on which this action is predicated, provides:

> It shall be unlawful for any person, directly or indirectly, by the use of any means or instrumentality of interstate commerce, or of the mails, or of any facility of any national securities exchange,
>
> (1) to employ any device, scheme, or artifice to defraud,
>
> (2) to make any untrue statement of a material fact or to omit to state a material fact necessary in order to make the

continued

statements made, in the light of the circumstances under which they were made, not misleading, or

(3) to engage in any act, practice, or course of business which operates or would operate as a fraud or deceit upon any person, in connection with the purchase or sale of any security.

Rule 10b-5 was promulgated pursuant to the grant of authority given the SEC by Congress in Section 10(b) of the Securities Exchange Act of 1934. By that Act Congress purposed to prevent inequitable and unfair practices and to insure fairness in securities transactions generally, whether conducted face-to-face, over the counter, or on exchanges.

Thus, anyone in possession of material inside information must either disclose it to the investing public, or if he is disabled from disclosing it in order to protect a corporate confidence or he chooses not to do so, must abstain from trading in or recommending the securities concerned while such inside information remains undisclosed. So, it is here, no justification for insider activity—that disclosure was forbidden by the legitimate corporate objective of acquiring options to purchase the land surrounding the exploration site—if the information was, as the SEC contends, material its possessors should have kept out of the market until disclosure was accomplished.

In each case, then, whether facts are material within Rule 10b-5 when the facts relate to a particular event and are undisclosed by those persons who are knowledgeable thereof will depend at any given time upon a balancing of both the indicated probability that the event will occur and the anticipated magnitude of the event in light of the totality of the company activity.

Our survey of the facts found below conclusively establishes that knowledge of the results of the discovery hole, K-55-1, would have been important to a reasonable investor and might have affected the price of the stock. On April 16, *The Northern Miner*, a trade publication in wide circulation among mining stock specialists, called K-55-1, the discovery hole, "one of the most impressive drill holes completed in modern times."

The core of Rule 10b-5 is the implementation of the Congressional purpose that all investors should have equal access to the rewards of participation in securities transactions. It was the intent of Congress that all members of the investing public should be subject to identical market risks, which include, of course, the risk that one's evaluative capacity or one's capital available to put at risk may exceed another's capacity or capital. The insiders here were not trading on an equal footing with the outside investors. They alone were in a position to evaluate the probability and magnitude of what seemed from the outset to be a major ore strike. They alone could invest safely, secure in the expectation that the price of TGS stock would rise substantially in the event such a major strike should materialize, but would decline little, if at all, in the event of failure; for the public, ignorant at the outset of the favorable probabilities would likewise be unaware of the unproductive exploration, and the additional exploration costs would not significantly affect TGS market prices. Such inequities based upon unequal access to knowledge should not be shrugged off as inevitable in our way of life, or, in view of the congressional concern in the area, remain uncorrected.

We hold, therefore, that all transactions in TGS stock or calls by individuals apprised of the drilling results of K-55-1 were made in violation of Rule 10b-5.

As it is our holding that the information acquired after the drilling of K-55-1 was material, we, on the basis of the findings of direct and circumstantial evidence on the issue that the trial court has already expressed, hold that Darke violated Rule 10b-5 (3) and Section 10(b) by "tipping" and we remand, pursuant to the agreement of the parties, for a determination of the appropriate remedy. As Darke's "tippees" are not defendants in this action, we need not decide whether, if they acted with actual or constructive knowledge that the material information was undisclosed, their conduct is as equally violative of the Rule as the conduct of their insider source, though we note that it certainly could be equally reprehensible.

Appellant Crawford, who ordered the purchase of TGS stock shortly before the TGS April 16 official announcement, and defendant Coates, who placed orders with and communicated the news to his broker immediately after the official announcement was read at the TGS-called press conference, concede that they were in possession of material information. They contend, however, that their purchases were not proscribed purchases for the news had already been effectively disclosed. We disagree.

Crawford telephoned his orders to his Chicago broker about midnight on April 15 and again at 8:30 in the morning of the 16th, with instructions to buy at the opening of the Midwest Stock Exchange that morning. The trial court's finding that "he sought to, and did, 'beat the news,'" is well documented by the record. The rumors of a major ore strike which had been circulated in Canada and, to a lesser extent, in New York, had been disclaimed by the TGS press release of April 12, which significantly promised the public an official detailed announcement when possibilities had ripened into actualities. The abbreviated announcement to the Canadian press at 9:40 A.M. on the 16th by the Ontario Minister of Mines and the report carried by *The Northern Miner*, parts of which had sporadically reached New York on the morning of the 16th through reports from Canadian affiliates to a few New York investment firms, are assuredly not the equivalent of the official 10-15 minute announcement which was not released to the American financial press until after 10:00 A.M. Crawford's orders had been placed before that. Before insiders may act upon material information, such information must have been effectively disclosed in a manner sufficient to insure its availability to the investing public. Particularly here, where a formal announcement to the entire financial news media had been promised in a prior official release known to the media, all insider activity must await dissemination of the promised official announcement.

■ *Affirmed in part, reversed in part.*

CASE CONCEPT REVIEW

1. Were the employees of the company under a legal duty to disclose the discovery to the public?
2. What factors influence whether a fact is "material"?
3. How much of a "public release" is necessary to meet the requirement of a legal release under the opinion of the court?

Insider

Any person who is trusted with confidential information of a material nature about a corporation by that corporation

INSIDER In contrast to the small group of individuals subject to the provisions of the short-swing profit prohibition associated with Section 16 of the 1934 Act (discussed below), Rule 10b-5 of the 1934 Act imposes potential liability to a broad array of individuals who generally are categorized in one of two groups. An **insider** is any person *who is trusted with confidential information of a material nature about a corporation by that corporation.* Certainly corporate officers, members of the board of directors, and those employees high within the management ranks could be considered an insider.

As illustrated in the *SEC v. Texas Gulf Sulphur Co.* case (above), employees at fairly low levels within the hierarchy of a corporation also can qualify as an insider, and those who are not employees can fall within the definition of an insider. For example, non-employee lawyers, accountants, and consultants hired by the corporation can be deemed insiders, as could government employees and television reporters. This type of insider designation is attached where a non-employee is entrusted with inside information as part of their position (some call these individuals t*emporary insiders).* Again, the sweeping reach of the definition of an insider under Rule 10b-5 encompasses anyone (employee or not) who is given custody of inside information regarding a corporation by that entity within the normal course of business.

OUTSIDER A second group of individuals also falls within the ambit of Rule 10b-5. An individual from this group is an *outsider* who has acquired inside information. Courts predicate outsider liability under Rule 10b-5 on the basis of either a fiduciary theory or a misrepresentation theory. In the 1983 case of *Dirks v. SEC,* the United States Supreme Court established the parameters of the *fiduciary theory* of liability for *tippees,* individuals who receive a tip from an insider. A tippee may be a relative or a close friend of an insider. If the tippee receives confidential information as a result of the *insider breaching a fiduciary duty* owed to the corporation and the tippee *knew or should have known* of the breach of duty, then the tippee may well have violated Rule 10b-5. Note that the tippee does not breach any fiduciary duty; only the insider has violated confidences entrusted in him or her.

If a tippee trades on inside information provided by an insider, Rule 10b-5 may or may not be violated. It is the manner in which the tippee receives the information that is critical for determining whether the purchase or sale of securities is illegal. That is, merely possessing inside information as a result of one's meticulous research, for example, is not illegal. Often, especially with the volume of information available through the Internet, an individual can come across confidential information (i.e., data yet to be released to the public) through a variety of mechanisms commonly used by market analysts. Securing information in this manner is acceptable. However, where the tippee receives information as a result of an insider violating a fiduciary duty, then Rule 10b-5 is violated.

The 1997 Supreme Court case of *U.S. v. Hogan* significantly broadened an outsider's liability for insider trading under Rule 10b-5. Again, how the tippee received the information is the central focus of the theory. Under the *misappropriation theory,* an individual who wrongly takes corporate inside information and trades on that information has violated Rule 10b-5. Therefore, if someone in a restaurant overhears two individuals discussing inside information and the listener trades on that information, there is no liability because the listener has *taken* nothing from the company. Liability would be found under the misappropriate theory, though, if an employee, who does not have access to confidential information of the corporation through that person's normal responsibilities, steals an access code, reads confidential memoranda of the company, and trades on information contained in the company files. In that situation, the "outsider" has misappropriated the information.

LIABILITY Rule 10b-5 provides that those who are harmed under provisions of the regulation are entitled to sue those who violated Rule 10b-5 for either their out-of-pocket loss (usually if there is a loss on the sale) or to have the transaction rescinded (thus allowing them back the securities that they traded away). The government may also pursue civil and criminal actions, assuming that scienter proved Criminal penalties for violating Rule 10b-5 are severe, with an individual facing a fine of up to $5 million and/or imprisonment for up to twenty years. An entity could be fined for up to $25 million.

16. Insider Trading—Fraud Liability: Elements

A plaintiff in a Rule10-5 action must show the following elements: (1) defendant issued a statement that included *false information or omitted information* from a statement, (2) the information was *material,* (3) *scienter* was present, and (4) plaintiff's *reliance* on the defendant's action (or inaction) resulted in the plaintiff suffering a loss connected with the purchase of sale of a security. Each of these requirements is addressed in greater detail below.

MISSTATEMENT OR OMISSION Under common law, fraud generally requires an affirmative misrepresentation. Rule 10b-5 extends the reach of the "fraud" notion to include half-truths and omissions. Therefore, both an outright lie and an omission left out of a company's communiqué that misleads a reader of the company's message are both the types of behavior Rule 10b-5 aims to curtail. Certain comments from a corporation that attempt to predict the future (e.g., "our new toy will be a quite popular") would not be determined to be a misstatement because of the predictive nature of the statement; however, if the company has no reasonable basis for making such a statement, it may be deemed a misstatement.

MATERIAL FACT Whether a particular fact is material, either in its misstatement or in its omission, is determined by looking at two factors. First, materiality is determined based on the time of the misstatement or omission. The entire context of the situation is examined to determine whether the timing of the misstatement or omission creates a material fact. Also, as the United States Supreme Court has determined on numerous occasions, materiality is judged by the reasonableness standard. Therefore, materiality is based on whether there is a substantial likelihood that a reasonable shareholder would consider the fact (misstated or omitted) important in determining whether to purchase or sell.

Scienter
Intent to deceive

SCIENTER Rule 10b-5 requires that the misstatement or omission of a material fact be made with **scienter**, which is generally defined as an intent to deceive.

Again, Rule 10b-5 has strong roots to the common law action for fraud, so it is not surprising that the SEC would require scienter. Mere negligence in terms of writing a corporate press release, such as including misstatements of material facts, does not qualify as a violation.

RELIANCE A successful plaintiff under Rule 10b-5 must prove that he/she relied on the misrepresentation or omission in making (or not making) an investment decision. In the case of a misrepresentation, the investor may show reliance by proof of having read a statement from the issuer. For example, a shareholder reads a report from the issuer stating facts that would indicate a positive development is forthcoming and then purchases additional shares. However, the assertion of fact in the report is false. The price of the stock falls, resulting in a loss for the shareholder. Reading the report is sufficient to show reliance. In the case of an omission, the United States Supreme Court has created a presumption of reliance, one that is capable of being rebutted.

Short-swing transaction
Purchase and sale of the issuer's equity securities within a six-month period

17. Insider Trading—Short-Swing Profit Liability

Section 16(b) of the 1934 Act prohibits short-swing profits, which is the third area covered by the 1934 Act. The term **short-swing transaction** refers to the *purchase and sale* (or in the rare case, sale and purchase) of the issuer's *equity securities within a six-month period.* Only *officers, directors, and shareholders owning 10% or more* of an issue are subject to this provision.

The rationale is quite simple: any individual who has or could have access to confidential information and trades within a brief period of time is presumed to have traded on inside information. Interestingly, the remedy for a Section 16(b) violation, whether the action is brought by the corporation or by a shareholder, is that all profits made on the purchase and sale must be disgorged to the corporation.

Section 16(b) may appear unfair because it imposes *strict liability.* However, Congress recognized the importance of having those in high levels of management or those who have considerable control over management give up certain rights to trade on the securities of the issuing corporation. The following case suggests just how severely the courts interpret Section 16(b) in favor of protecting the investing public.

CASE

Charles D. Winston v. Federal Express Corp.

UNITED STATES COURT OF APPEALS FOR THE SIXTH CIRCUIT

853 F.2d 455(1988)

BOYCE F. MARTIN, JR., CIRCUIT JUDGE

Charles D. Winston appeals the district court's decision to grant summary judgment in favor of the Federal Express Corporation. Winston contends that the court erroneously concluded that he was an "officer" within the meaning of section 16(b) of the Securities Exchange Act of 1934 such that the profits realized from his short-swing purchase and sale of stock in Federal Express must be surrendered. We affirm.

In September 1981, Winston was hired by Federal Express to be Vice President of Network Systems. About two years later, he was promoted to Senior Vice President of Electronic Products. In that capacity, Winston was responsible for the development and implementation of the company's electronic products and systems, such as the company's overnight package delivery service and the company's same-day document delivery service. Winston reported directly to the chief operating officer, and he had substantial supervisory responsibilities.

On August 27, 1985, Winston resigned from Federal Express. Although his resignation was not to become effective until September 30, 1985, Winston ceased performing any duties for Federal Express as of August 27, and he was replaced almost immediately. Until September 30, however, Winston remained on the Federal Express payroll. Moreover, until the date of his resignation became effective, Winston was available to discuss transition matters with his successor although he was never actually consulted by the company after August 27.

In fact, Winston's only contact with Federal Express after he resigned occurred on September 30 when he visited the company's offices in order to exercise options to purchase 8,298 shares of Federal Express stock. According to Winston, the sole reason that the effective date of his resignation was postponed was that the option to purchase 2,000 of those shares did not vest until September 26, 1985.

On March 26, 1986, Winston sold the shares he had purchased on September 30 for a profit in excess of $176,000. The stock was sold through a brokerage house which erroneously advised him that the "settlement date," as opposed to the "trade date," determined the date of the transaction for both tax and securities law purposes. Section 16 of the Exchange Act, which was designed to prevent insiders from taking advantage of their access to non-public information, provides that any profit realized by a beneficial owner, officer ,or director of an issuer of stock from the purchase and sale of that issuer's stock within any six-month period shall be retained by the issuer. If the brokerage house's advice had been accurate, the transaction would have fallen outside the six-month short-swing profit period. When Winston informed Federal Express of the transaction, however, the company explained to him that the trade date was determinative. Therefore, Winston had technically engaged in a short-swing transaction under section 16(b), and Federal Express was entitled to recoup the profits from the sale.

Winston brought suit in federal court to recover those profits. In his complaint, Winston alleged that, because he did not actively participate in the duties of his office after August 27, he was not an officer of the company for the purposes of section 16(b) when he bought the stock at issue here on September 30. The district court, however, granted Federal Express' motion for summary judgment, finding that Winston was an officer within the meaning of section 16(b). We agree.

Section 16(b) was intended to protect the investing public from the "evils of insider trading" by enacting "a flat rule taking the profits out of a class of transactions in which the possibility of abuse was believed to be intolerably great." "It does not matter whether the insider actually received the information, or utilized it; his mere status makes him

continued

liable." A strict-liability "approach maximize[s] the ability of the rule to eradicate speculative abuses by reducing difficulties in proof." Because Congress intended section 16(b) to be a "relatively arbitrary rule capable of easy administration," id., courts generally interpret the statute so as to preserve its "mechanical quality." In deciding whether an individual is an officer for purposes of section 16(b), therefore, courts tend to look solely at the title the individual holds.

An exception exists, however, "where the title is essentially honorary or ceremonial," or where the "title was purely 'titular' and not real." In such cases, the individual's transactions are not subject to section 16(b) restrictions because the person does not actually perform executive functions that put him or her in a position of being able to acquire the kind of confidential information about the company's affairs that provides an advantage in dealing in the company's securities.

Here, however, we are presented with a rather unusual case. Winston concedes that, up until he tendered his resignation, he exercised substantial executive responsibilities and that he did have access to confidential information. He contends, though, that he ceased performing such duties after August 27 and that, therefore, the stock he purchased on September 30 is not subject to the short-swing profit rule. In such a circumstance, however, the presumption that the officer continues to have access to confidential information during the interim period is a strong one, and the officer must produce substantial evidence to overcome this presumption.

We believe the evidence adduced by Winston is clearly insufficient to rebut the presumption that he continued to have access to confidential information until September 30. Winston testified that, after he tendered his resignation on August 27, he only returned to the company's office once, on September 30, to exercise his stock options. He also testified that, although he was available to help his successor during the interim period, he was never actually consulted. This testimony is incontrovertible. It is also inconsequential, however, because Winston failed to produce any evidence that, had he requested access to the kind of confidential information which routinely crossed his desk prior to his resignation, such access would have been denied by the company. Winston also failed to offer any evidence that other officers and management personnel were expressly instructed that they were not to provide him confidential information. In short, although he was an officer in title only during the interim period, Winston offered no evidence that the company had constructed a kind of "Chinese wall" around him, shielding him from potential access to current confidential information.

The relatively short period of time between his tendered resignation and the date it became effective is also a factor here. Here, the interim period was only one month.

Such a brief period is insufficient evidence, standing alone, to rebut the presumption that Winston continued to have potential access to confidential information until September 30.

We recognize that the result in this case may appear harsh. There have been no allegations that Winston exploited confidential information, and he sold the stock only four days before the expiration of the six-month short-swing profit period on the basis of erroneous "expert" advice. Moreover, had he waited those few days, his profit would have been even greater because the price of Federal Express continued to rise after he sold his shares. Unfortunately for Mr. Winston, however, such seemingly unjust results are an inevitable consequence of a strict-liability rule which is necessarily arbitrary. The statutory scheme "place[s] responsibility for meticulous observance of the provision upon the shoulders of the insider . . . . [and he or she] must bear the risks of any inadvertent miscalculation."

In sum, we hold that an officer who previously exercised executive responsibilities can escape section 16(b) liability prior to the effective date of his or her resignation if there is substantial evidence to rebut the presumption that he or she continued to have access to confidential information during the interim period. The burden is on the officer seeking to avoid section 16(b) forfeiture to prove that there was no potential access to current information; it is not enough to show that he or she did not actually gain access to such information. We conclude that Winston failed to produce the evidence needed to overcome this strong presumption.

Accordingly, the judgment of the district court in favor of Federal Express is hereby affirmed.

■ *Affirmed.*

CASE CONCEPT REVIEW

1. Should the date that the senior vice president resigned or the date that he no longer had access to information control the application of the short-swing law? Why?
2. What could the former employee have done to prevent application of section 16(b)?

In addition, Section 16(a) requires those subject to the short-swing profit prohibition also must *disclose* to the SEC and to all exchanges on which the securities are traded whenever they purchase or sell subject securities. These disclosures are quickly made public. There is n short-swing requirement. For example, a member of the board of directors who holds on to shares for ten years and then sells must disclose the sale under Section 16(a) but does not fall within the short-swing provision of Section 16(b).

CHAPTER SUMMARY

Introduction

1. An initial public offering (IPO) occurs where a corporation originally sells an issuance of securities to the investing public.
2. The *Securities Act of 1933* (the 1933 Act) is aimed at controlling the initial sale of securities from a corporation.
3. The *Securities Exchange Act of 1934* (the 1934 Act) regulates secondary trading of securities.

Securities Regulation Landscape

1. Sine the passage of the 1933 Act and the 1934 Act, Congress has passed additional laws dealing with Securities regulation.
2. States also regulate securities, under acts termed blue sky laws.

Securities and Exchange Commission

1. The Securities and Exchange Commission (SEC) is the primary federal administrative agency charged with the responsibility of regulating securities transactions.
2. The SEC performs rule-making, enforcement, and adjudicatory functions.

INITIAL SALES OF SECURITIES: THE SECURITIES ACT OF 1933

Purpose of the 1933 Act

1. The general purpose of the 1934 Act is to require corporations make adequate disclosures before offering securities to the public.
2. Underwriting is the primary method, used within the process of issuing securities, of selling the offering.

Definition of a Security

1. The definition of a security under the 1933 is extremely broad.

Registration Statement and Prospectus

1. A registration statement is a set of documents containing information about the offering and the corporation making the offering that must be submitted to the SEC prior to selling any securities.
2. A prospectus is a set of documents, similar to a registration statement, which is made available to the investing public.

Exempt Securities

1. Certain types of securities are exempt from the registration and prospectus requirements of the 1933 Act.

Exempt Transactions: Background

1. Certain types of transactions involving the issuance of securities may not need the protections associated with the 1933 Act and, therefore, are exempt from the registration and prospectus provisions of that law.

Exempt Transactions: Categories

1. Under SEC regulations, certain types of intrastate, private, and small issuances of securities may be exempt.

Integration and Resale

1. Integration is the process used by the issuer to combine several supposedly separate exempt transaction offerings.
2. In order to protect the integrity of the protection afforded under the 1933 Act, sales of certain types of securities may be restricted.

Liability and Due Diligence Defense

1. Violating the provisions of the 1933 act may result in civil and criminal sanctions, along with private lawsuits filed by those injured as a consequence of the violation.

2. The due diligence defense is available to non-issuer defendants.

SECONDARY SECURITIES TRANSFERS: THE SECURITIES AND EXCHANGE ACT OF 1934

Purpose of the 1934 Act

1. The purpose of the 1934 Act is to provide the investing public with a continuous flow of information regarding the activities of corporations who have registered securities.

Registration and Reporting Requirement

1. Certain types of corporations are required to register their securities under the 1934 Act.
2. Registered corporations are subject to reporting requirements.

Proxy Solicitation

1. A proxy is the right to vote for another.
2. The 1934 Act regulates proxy solicitations.

Insider Trading—Fraud: Basics

1. Insider trading occurs when a person with confidential information about an issuer not available to the investing public trades on that information.
2. Rule 10b-5 liability extends to securities trading regardless of whether the securities are registered under either the 1933 Act or the 1934 Act.
3. Rule 10b-5 mandates that the ether a corporation discloses or individuals abstain from trading.

Insider Trading—Fraud: Elements

1. Rule 10b-5 applies to affirmative misrepresentations, half-truths, and omissions.
2. In order to be actionable, a statement or omission must concern a material fact.
3. Scienter, or the intent to deceive, is required under Rule 10b-5.
4. Plaintiff must show that it relied on the misstatement or omission.

Insider Trading—Short-Swing Profits

1. Under Section 16(b), certain insiders must disgorge to the corporation any profits made on the purchase and sale of the issuer's equity securities within a six-month period.
2. Officers, directors, and shareholders with more than 10% of an issue are subject to this provision of securities law.

REVIEW QUESTIONS AND PROBLEMS

1. Match each term in Column A with the appropriate statement in Column B.

A	B
(1) 1933 Act	(a) A person with confidential information uses that information to trade
(2) Scienter	(b) An intent to deceive
(3) Proxy	(c) Law that applies to the initial sale of securities by the corporation
(4) Prospectus	(d) State securities laws
(5) Disgorgement	(e) Law that applies to secondary sales of securities
(6) Insider trading	(f) Purchase and sale of the issuer's equity securities within a six-month period
(7) Initial public offering	(g) Instrument that grants to another the right to vote

(8) 1934 Act	(h) Return of profits made by an individual on a securities trade to the corporation
(9) Short-swing transaction	(i) Sale of securities from the issuing corporation
(10) Blue sky laws	(j) Communication from a corporation that is offering a security for sale

2. Based on materials dealing with the 1933 Act, create a definition of a security.
3. Kamal and his brother Tamal own Resort Management Company in San Diego, California. They are proposing to create an IPO to sell $600,000 of stock in their company. The company limits its business to the management of resorts in California, and they want to restrict purchasers of the issue to California residents. Does this offering need to be registered? Why?
4. Alaska Enterprises made a private offering of one issue of their stock on January 1, another of the same issue on April 1, and a final offering on July 1. What concerns would you have regarding this method of raising capital?
5. Jouet, Inc. hired an underwriter, a law firm, and an accounting firm to guide it through an IPO. Under the pressure to meet deadlines for the IPO set by Jouet, the outside entities failed to include information in the registration statement and prospectus that two of the Jouet directors owned a business that was supplying large amounts of critical materials to Jouet at a price slightly above market. The price of the Jouet issue of securities has fallen 20% since that date the securities were made public, and those who participated in the IPO now are quite upset. Have the outside entities violated securities laws? If so, what law or laws Do they have a defense? Why?
6. Javier, vice president of labor relations at AT&T, tells his good friend Francine to read the business section of the New York Times and then call him back. Within one-half hour Francine calls Javier and indicates that the Times had published an article reporting the possible merger of AT&T with NCR, another large corporation. Javier replies, "Yes, I read that article, too; and I believe the rumors to be true." Francine then immediately makes a series of purchases of NCR stock. Seven days after the conversation between Javier and Francine, AT& T and NCR announce the merger. Did Javier violate federal securities laws? If so, what law and why?
7. Same facts as in 6. Did Francine violate federal securities laws? If so, what law, why, and under what theory?
8. Spyropoulos and Courtois worked for two different New York investment-banking firms, in both the respective mergers and acquisitions departments of both firms. Newman was a close friend of both Spyropoulos and Courtois and received numerous tips of impending mergers and acquisitions from the two investment banking employees. Newman not only traded on the tips but also passed along the tips to two more of his friends, Antoniu and Carniol. Newman, Antoniu, and Carniol have made money based on the tips. Are all three tippees liable? Why?
9 Janice needed psychological counseling and hired Dr. Harrold Rovus, a board-certified psychiatrist, to assist her. During a counseling session, Janice indicated that there was a great deal of stress in her life and the life of her husband at the present time because the company for which her husband served as the chief executive officer was contemplating a merger with another company. Janice provided sufficient information for Rovus to

reasonably conclude that the merger was going to occur. Rovus trades on the information and makes a large profit. Has Rovus violated securities law? Why?

10. Miranda is the chief executive officer of Mirrormax, Inc., a firm with shares traded on a national exchange. On January 15, Miranda purchases 3,000 shares of Mirrormax, intending to keep the shares for many years. In late spring, however, Miranda decides she wishes to build a pool at her home. On May 1, Miranda sells 2,000 of the 3,000 shares she had bought earlier in the year. Has Miranda violated federal securities law? Why?

Internet Resources

Access to the SEC's Electronic Data Gathering Analysis and Retrieval (EDGAR) system, which allows one to review SEC filings, is available at: www.sec.gov/edgar.shtml

A fascinating and thorough site that provides background information on myriad subjects relating to securities regulation is available at: http://www.seclaw.com/centers/lawcent.shtml

PART VII

NEGOTIABLE INSTRUMENTS

Introduction to Negotiable Instruments | 33

CHAPTER OUTLINE

CHAPTER PREVIEW

This chapter covers contract obligations that are in the form of *negotiable instruments.* These principles are primarily found in Articles 3 and 4 of the Uniform Commercial Code, with Article 3 creating a general legal framework for all negotiable instruments and Article 4 aimed specifically at banking and banking-related activities. Negotiable instruments, often referred to as *commercial paper,* are commercial obligations created to move freely in financial transactions as a substitute for money or to represent a credit transaction. For example, checks are negotiable instruments used instead of cash to pay for goods and services. When a person borrows money or purchases goods on credit, the usual practice is for that person to sign a promissory note payable to the lender or seller.

Chapters 34 through 36 cover the law as it relates to negotiable instruments and the rights and liabilities of the various parties to a commercial paper transaction. This chapter serves as an introduction to the relevant terminology and to the role of banks in these transactions involving commercial paper.

BUSINESS MANAGEMENT DECISION

As treasurer of a large company, you are charged with overseeing all your company's relationships with financial institutions.

What procedures should you adopt with respect to the company checking account and bank statements?

CONCEPT OF NEGOTIABILITY

Negotiable instruments

Paper that serves as a substitute for money or as a credit transaction

Negotiable instruments developed because of the commercial need for something that would be readily acceptable in lieu of money and would accordingly be readily transferable in trade or commerce. Substantial protection and assurance of payment must be given to any person to whom the paper might be transferred. To accomplish this protection, it is necessary to insulate the transferee from most of the defenses that a primary party, such as the maker of a note, might have against the payee. The purpose of the negotiability trait is to prevent the parties to an underlying contract from asserting defenses against the person to whom the paper is transferred.

To accomplish the foregoing, Article 3 of the Code provides that a person to whom negotiable paper is negotiated takes it free of personal defenses arising out of the agreement from which the negotiable paper was created.

This basic theory of negotiability can be further explained by noting the difference between the *assignment* of a contract and the *negotiation* of a negotiable instrument. Assume that a dealer owes a manufacturer $1,000 but has a counterclaim against the manufacturer because the product was defective. If a third party, such as a bank, purchased the manufacturer's contract right to collect the $1,000 from the dealer, it would be subject to the dealer's defense of failure of consideration. The bank, as assignee, would secure no better right against the dealer than the original right held by the manufacturer, the assignor. The bank, therefore, could not collect the full $1,000 from the dealer.

In this example, if the evidence of the debt is not a simple contract for money but, rather, a negotiable promissory note given by the dealer to the manufacturer, and if it is properly negotiated, the bank is in a position superior to that which it occupied when it was an assignee. Assuming that it is a "holder in due course," the bank has a better title because it is free of the personal defenses that are available against the manufacturer, the original party to the paper. The dealer, therefore, cannot use the defense of failure of consideration, and the bank can collect the $1,000.

Transfer of the instrument free of personal defenses is the very essence of negotiability. Three requirements must be met before a transferee is free from personal defenses. First, the instrument must be negotiable; that is, it must comply with the statutory formalities and language requirements. An instrument that does not qualify is nonnegotiable, and any transfer is an assignment subject to all defenses. Second, the instrument must be properly *negotiated* to the transferee. If the instrument is not properly negotiated, the transfer is an assignment subject to all defenses. Third, the party to whom negotiable commercial paper is negotiated must be a *holder in due course* or have the rights of a holder in due course. Each of these concepts is discussed in detail in the following chapters.

The defenses that cannot be asserted against a holder in due course are called *personal defenses. Real defenses,* on the other hand, may be asserted against anyone, including a holder in due course. Real defenses are matters that go to the very existence of the instruments. Personal defenses, such as failure of consideration, involve less serious matters and usually relate to the transaction out of which the negotiable instrument arose or events such as payment of the note.

KINDS OF COMMERCIAL PAPER

1. Terminology

Article 3 of the Code, Commercial Paper, is restricted in its coverage to the negotiable note, certificate of deposit, draft, and check. A note is two-party paper, as is a certificate of deposit. The parties to a note are the *maker,* who promises to pay, and the *payee,* to whom the promise is made. The draft and the check are three-party instruments. A draft presupposes a debtor-creditor relationship between the *drawer* and the *drawee* or some other obligation on the part of the drawee in favor of the drawer. The drawee is the debtor; the drawer is the creditor. The drawer-creditor orders the drawee-debtor to pay money to a third party, who is the payee. The mere execution of the draft does not obligate the drawee on the paper. The drawee's liability on the paper arises when it formally *accepts* the obligation to pay in writing on the draft itself. By accepting, the drawee becomes primarily liable on the paper [3-413]. Thereafter, the drawee is called an *acceptor,* and its liability is similar to the liability of the maker of a promissory note.

2. Notes

Bearer

The person in possession of an instrument

A *note* initially is a two-party instrument in which the issuer (the *maker*) promises to pay to the order of a *payee* or to **bearer**. A note is used to evidence an obligation to pay in the future and is typically employed in loan and secured sales transactions. Figure 33-1 is a sample of a simple note payable to the order of a specific payee.

3. Certificates of Deposit

A *certificate of deposit* (commonly called a CD) is a two-party, usually short-term, species of note in which a bank is the maker [3-104(j)]. A CD is a bank's written acknowledgment of money on deposit that the bank promises to pay to the depositor, to his or her order, or to some third person. The promise to repay distinguishes the CD from a deposit slip. A CD basically is a promissory note issued by a bank as a means of investment. People buy CDs to earn the interest CDs bear. The bank may pay higher rates of interest than on a savings account

FIGURE 33-1 ■ A Simple Note Payable to a Specific Payee

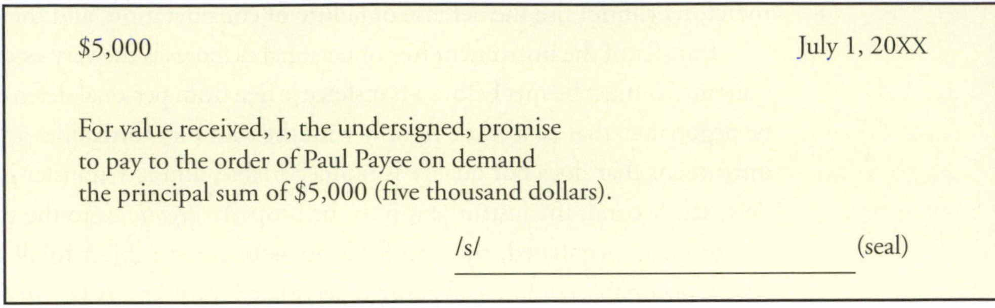

$5,000 July 1, 20XX

For value received, I, the undersigned, promise to pay to the order of Paul Payee on demand the principal sum of $5,000 (five thousand dollars).

/s/ (seal)

since a CD may not be redeemed until the date specified without significant penalties. Figure 33-2 is an example of a negotiable CD.

FIGURE 33-2 ■ A Negotiable CD

CERTIFICATE OF DEPOSIT
First Athens Bank
Athens, GA

Has received on deposit and on May 1, 1996 will pay to the order of Darlene Depositer $20,000.00 (twenty thousand dollars) with interest at a rate of ten percent (10%) payable upon return of this certificate properly indorsed. No payment before maturity. No interest after maturity.

First Athens Bank

May 1, 1993 (date of issue) /s/ (authorized signature)

4. Drafts

A *draft* (sometimes called a bill of exchange) is a simple order to pay money [3-104e]. It is addressed by one person (the *drawer*) to another person (the *payor* or *drawee*), requiring that payor or drawee to pay on demand or at a fixed future time a definite amount to the order of a named person (the *payee* or *holder*) or to the bearer. A seller of goods or services may draw a draft on the buyer for purchase price of the goods, making the instrument payable to himself or herself. In this case, the seller is both the drawer and the payee, while the buyer is the drawee of the draft. In drawing this draft, the seller implicitly promises to pay its amount to any holder if it is not paid by the drawee [3-413]. By putting the demand for payment in the stylized form of a draft, the seller thereby facilitates the transfer of his or her right to receive payment from the buyer.

Drafts may be payable on demand or at a fixed or determinable time. Usually demand drafts are presented to the drawee for payment and are said to be payable *on sight.* Time drafts may be presented to the drawee for payment or *acceptance.* They are said to be payable at a fixed time after sight.

5. Checks

A *check* is a demand draft drawn on a bank. A check drawn by a bank on itself is a *cashier's check*. *Travelers' checks* are like cashier's checks in that the financial institution issuing them is both the drawer and the drawee. Travelers' checks are negotiable when they have been completed by the identifying signature. A *bank draft* is a banker's check; that is, it is a check drawn by one bank on another bank, payable on demand.

A *certified check* is one that has been accepted by the drawee bank. Either the drawer or the holder of a check may present it to the drawee bank for certification. The bank will stamp "certified" on the check, and an official of the bank will sign it and date it. By certifying, the bank assumes responsibility for payment and sets aside funds from its customer's account to cover the check.

Certification may or may not change the legal liability of the parties on the instrument. When the *drawer* has a check certified, such a certification merely acts as additional security and does not relieve the drawer of any liability. On the other hand, when the *holder* of a check secures certification by the drawee bank, the holder thereby accepts the bank as the only party liable thereon. Such an act discharges the drawer and all prior endorsers from any liability [3-411(a)]. The effect of such certification is similar to a payment by the bank and redeposit by the holder.

The refusal of a bank to certify a check at the request of a holder is not a dishonor of the instrument. The bank owes the depositor a duty to pay but not necessarily the duty to certify checks that are drawn on it, unless there is a previous agreement to certify [3-411(b)]. A drawer cannot stop payment on a check after the bank has certified it.

BANK DEPOSITS AND COLLECTIONS

6. Terminology

Article 4 of the Code, Bank Deposits and Collections, provides uniform rules to govern the collection of checks and other instruments for the payment of money. These rules govern the relationship of banks with one another and with depositors in the collection and payment of items.

The following terminology of Section 4-105 of the Code is significant with regard to the designation of the various banks in the collection process for checks:

1. *Depositary bank* means the first bank to which an item is transferred for collection even though it is also the payor bank.
2. *Payor bank* means a bank by which an item is payable as drawn or accepted.
3. *Intermediary bank* means any bank to which an item is transferred in course of collection except the depositary or payor bank.

There are various designations for the different banks involved in the collection process for a check.

4. *Collecting bank* means any bank handling the item for collection, except the payor bank.
5. *Presenting bank* means any bank presenting an item to a payor bank.

A bank may occupy more than one status in the collection process. For example, a bank that receives a customer's deposit drawn on another bank is both a depositary and a collecting bank. A bank accepting a deposit of a check drawn by another customer is both a depositary and a payor bank.

Timing is important in the check collection process. Many of the technical rules of law refer to a *banking day*, which is defined as "that part of any day on which a bank is open to the public for carrying on substantially all of its banking functions" [4-104(a)(3)]. A bank is permitted to establish a cutoff hour of 2 P.M. or later, so the bank may have an opportunity to process items, prove balances, and make the necessary entries to determine its position for the day. If an item is received after the cutoff hour or after the close of the banking day, it may be treated as having been received at the opening of the next banking day. The term *midnight deadline* with respect to a bank means midnight on its banking day following the banking day on which it receives a check or a notice regarding the check [4-104(a)(10)].

The relationship between banks and parties to a transaction has a long history. In the following case, decided by an English court more than one-hundred years ago, the bank attempted to take back money that it had paid on a check cashed by the plaintiff.

CASE

Chambers v. Miller and Others

COURT OF COMMON BENCH

[1861-1873] All ER Rep 2277 (1862)

Erle CJ

This was an action of trespass brought by the plaintiff, who had been imprisoned by the defendants under a claim by the bank, that certain moneys in the pocket of the plaintiff were the property of the defendants and that they had a right to hold him and take it from him. Now, the point that is reserved for us, on which the court is to act as judge as well as jury, is whether the money in the pocket of the plaintiff was his property; it had been the property of the defendants, and had passed to the plaintiff. Now, property will pass from the transferor to the transferee according to the intention of the parties. Sometimes it is by a sale of property, and then the word "done" will fix the bargain, and the property will pass from the seller to the buyer. It may be matter of gift; then, the property passes according to our law if accompanied by actual delivery. So in the various transactions of life, those conversant with the passing of property have fixed on a time when the transferor no longer has the property and when the transferee has the property in him.

Now, with respect to cheques presented at the counter of a banker—when the cheque is presented to him as his authority on the part of the customer to pay on his behalf, he is the owner of the money in his own till; and when the cheque has been presented, he is to be considered to pass the property in the money and take the property in the cheque. The cheque was presented to him; the banker went through the process, resolved to pay it, took the money and put it on the counter. The value in money had passed; he delivered over the property, and the party to whom he so intended to pay it was then bound to accept the property. There was no choice on his part whether the property passed or no. He was counting it out; if there had been a mistake, or there was an additional note, as an honest man he would have given it back if there was a note too much. The instrument had passed when the property was out of the pocket of the customer.

The banker soon finds there is a mistake in the management of the business, not between him and the plaintiff who was then claiming to have the property passed to him, to whom the banker intended to pass it, namely, the bearer of the cheque presented at the bank; but there was a mistake between him and the customer. Then he claims to revoke that which was irrevocable; and then, without any further act to be done, he claims to revoke against the party holding the cheque and who had hold of the money. He claims to revoke the passing of the property and revest it in him. I am of opinion that that cannot be done.

The money was put down on the counter; the banker has passed the property to the holder of the cheque, who took it. I am clear that was a question of fact; if there was no more in the matter than that, the owner of that property had transferred and passed the property to the opposite party. Upon that ground, therefore, I am clearly of opinion the plaintiff was right and was not bound to give it back. It was a payment as between the banker and the holder of the cheque, and he had a legitimate right to hold it. The option is in the owner. "I am owner of that cheque; you choose to pay it. Then, as the owner of the cheque, I put my hand upon the money. It is irrecoverably gone from you. If you take it back by force you are liable to an action of trespass."

■ *Judgment for plaintiff.*

CASE CONCEPTS REVIEW

1. Why do you believe the bank wanted the money back?
2. Do you believe the result would be the same today? Why?

7. The Bank Collection Process

If a check is deposited in a bank other than the bank on which it is drawn, it must be sent to the payor bank for payment. This collection process may involve routing the item through a number of banks that typically credit or debit accounts they maintain with one another. In particular, the regional Federal Reserve banks, with which most banks have accounts, play a major role in this process. An example may help you understand the collection process.

Suppose that Carson in Athens, Georgia, mails his check drawn on the First Athens Bank to Exxon in Houston, Texas, in payment of an obligation. Exxon deposits the check in the First National Bank of Houston, which forwards it to the Federal Reserve Bank of Houston, which sends it to the Federal Reserve Bank of Atlanta, which presents it to the First Athens Bank for payment. The relationship of these parties is depicted in Figure 33-3.

FIGURE 33-3 ■ Process of Collecting Transit Item

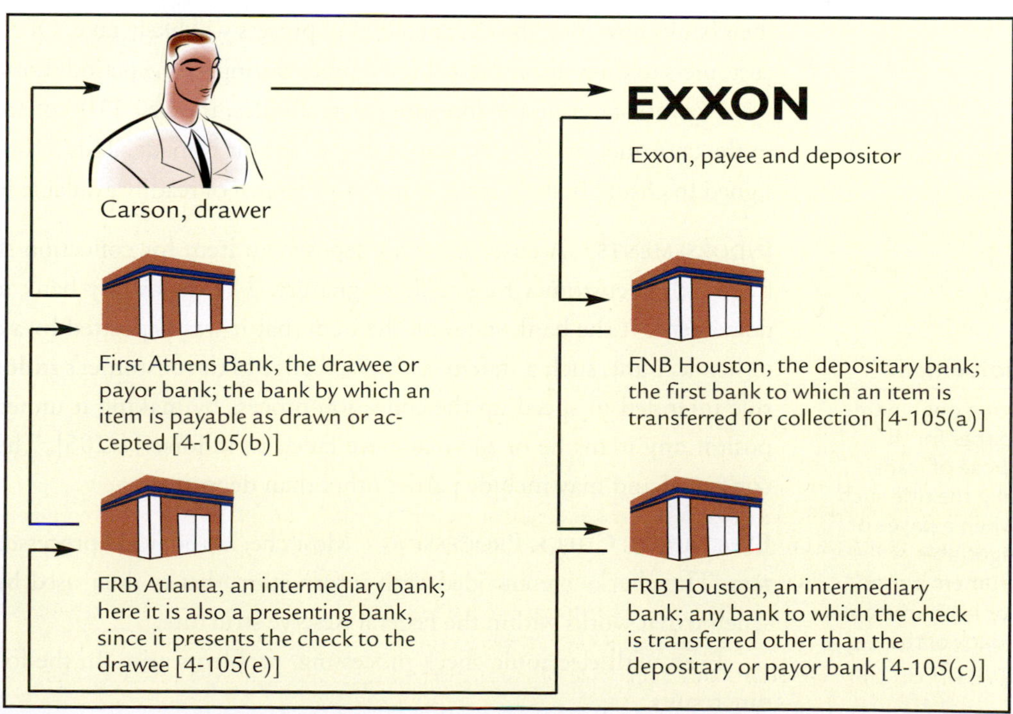

As Figure 33-3 indicates, the collection process begins when the customer (Exxon) deposits a check to its account. The account is provisionally credited by the bank. The check then passes through the collecting banks, each of which provisionally credits the account of the prior bank. When the check finally reaches the payor-drawee bank (First Athens Bank), that bank debits the drawer's (Carson's) account.

Clearinghouse
An association of banks or other payors regularly clearing items

Honor
To pay or to accept the instrument

Dishonor
Acceptance or payment that is refused or cannot be obtained

Customer
A person having an account with a bank or for whom a bank has agreed to collect items

The payor bank then credits the account of the presenting bank, remits to it, or, if both belong to the same **clearinghouse**, includes the check in its balance there. If the payor bank **honors** the check, the settlement is final. Transactions prior to this final settlement by the payor bank are called "provisional settlements" because it is not known until final settlement whether the check is "good." If the payor bank **dishonors** the check, as in the case of an "N.S.F" (not sufficient funds) check, the presenting bank will revoke its provisional settlement and charge the item back to the account of the prior collecting bank. Likewise, other banks in the chain of collection will charge back. The final step is a chargeback to the **customer's** account by the depositary bank and the return of the check to the customer. Each of the collecting banks must return the item or send notification of the facts by its midnight deadline. The right to charge back by the depositary bank is not affected by the fact that the depositor may have drawn against the provisional credit.

A depositor does not have the right to draw against uncollected funds. Accordingly, a depositor is not entitled to draw against an item payable by another bank until the provisional settlement his or her depositary bank has received becomes final [4-213].

AVAILABILITY OF FUNDS Funds from cashier's checks, certified checks, government checks, and electronic deposits must be available to the customer on the next business day after deposit. Funds from local checks (those written on financial institutions within the same Federal Reserve check-processing region as the depositary bank) must be made available within two business days after deposit. Finally, funds represented by out-of-town checks must be made available within five business days after deposit.

These time periods on making funds available do not apply to new accounts (those less than thirty days old), to automated teller machines (ATMs) not owned by the bank receiving a deposit, or to checks written for more than $5,000. Customers under these circumstances must inquire of their banks how long the check collection process will likely take. Of course, banks may allow their customers to draw against uncollected funds during a time period shorter than that just discussed.

Notwithstanding the foregoing general rules, the first $100 of any deposit must be available to the customer on the next day after the deposit is made. This $100 tomorrow exception is designed to ensure that a customer has some source of readily available funds.

INDORSEMENTS A customer who deposits an item for collection should indorse it, but quite frequently a customer forgets that signature. The depositary bank may supply the missing indorsement. If the bank states on the item that it was deposited by a customer or credited to his or her account, such a statement is as effective as the customer's **indorsement**. This is a practical rule intended to speed up the collection process by making it unnecessary to return to the depositor any items he or she may have failed to indorse [4-205]. The term customer is broadly construed and may include parties other than depositors.

Indorsement
Writing one's name on paper for the purpose of transferring the title such as when a payee of a negotiable instrument writes his or her name on the back of the instrument

ELECTRONIC CHECK PROCESSING Most checks today are processed through an electronic system. The checks are encoded with information that is then used by a sophisticated computer scheme that works within the Federal Reserve structure.

Even with electronic check processing, problems arise. In the following case, the errors had dire results.

CASE

Douglas Companies, Inc. v. Commercial National Bank of Texarkana

UNITED STATES COURT OF APPEALS FOR THE EIGHTH CIRCUIT

419 F.3d 812 (2005)

BYE, CIRCUIT JUDGE

Douglas is a wholesale grocery, beverage and tobacco supplier which serviced several convenience stores in Arkansas and Texas owned by USA Express (USA). On April 28, 2000, USA issued Douglas a check for $240,000 to pay for merchandise, and Douglas deposited the check into its account at CNB. CNB's proof operator mistakenly encoded the check for $24,000 and sent it on to USA's bank—Wells Fargo. Wells Fargo failed to notice the encoding error and debited USA's account for $24,000. As a result, Douglas's account was credited with only $24,000 or $216,000 less than the payment from USA.

Douglas received its bank statement showing the deposit error within days of the transaction. Douglas's controller, however, had quit in late 1999, and Douglas was unable to find an immediate replacement. By the time a new controller was hired, there was a three-month backlog. Additionally, the new controller became ill during the spring of 2000, adding to the backlog. Consequently, Douglas did not reconcile its April 2000 bank statement until November 2, 2000. On November 2, when Douglas's controller discovered the mistake, she immediately called CNB. CNB reviewed its records, discovered the encoding error and advised the controller the mistake would be corrected. Relying on CNB's assurances, the controller did not tell Steven Douglas, Douglas's president, about the discrepancy.

On November 3, 2000, CNB credited Douglas's account with $216,000 and sent an adjustment request for $216,000 to Wells Fargo through the Federal Reserve System. The Federal Reserve, however, does not process adjustment requests over 180 days old. CNB's employee testified she sent the request through the Federal Reserve hoping it would not notice it was untimely. She also testified the Federal Reserve had processed stale requests in the past. This time, the Federal Reserve rejected the adjustment request and on, November 6, 2000, returned it to CNB. On November 7, 2000, CNB mailed an adjustment request directly to the Wells Fargo branch bank in Houston, Texas. CNB's employee testified she did not make any inquiries to verify where the adjustment request should be mailed. Instead, she consulted her "big bank book" and looked up the address for Wells Fargo, Houston. She further testified she chose not to telephone or fax the request. CNB's president testified the information should have been verified.

The adjustment request was received by Wells Fargo, Houston, sometime after November 7 but before November 14. Individual Wells Fargo banks, however, because of the large volume of such requests, do not process adjustment requests. Instead, adjustment requests are handled by regional adjustment centers. Thus, when the request was received in Houston, it was forwarded to Wells Fargo's Southwestern Adjustment Center (SAC) in Phoenix, Arizona. SAC logged the request in on November 14, 2000, and generated an automatic notice to CNB indicating the request had been received and would be processed in the normal course of business. A Wells Fargo's employee worked on the adjustment request on November 17 and 20, but because she looked in the wrong database, could not find any record of the USA check. On November 28, having found no record of the check, Wells Fargo closed out the request without notice to CNB of its findings. The parties agree that between November 7 and November 14, there were occasions when USA's Wells Fargo account had sufficient funds to cover the discrepancy, e.g., on November 14, 2000 the account held a balance of $240,566.70. On November 15, 2000, however, the funds were transferred out of the account, and there were no longer any funds to pay the adjustment request.

As these events were unfolding, USA was sliding into insolvency. By the summer of 2000, USA had defaulted on a loan from its bank, Credit Suisse First Boston (CSFB). In September 2000, USA agreed to sign over its assets to CSFB in lieu of foreclosure. CSFB, in turn, in hopes of minimizing its losses on the defaulted loan, formed Houston Convenience (Houston) to continue operating the convenience stores. In order to ensure Douglas would continue supplying the convenience stores, Houston contacted Douglas and advised it would bring all of USA's accounts with Douglas up to date. Between October 25, 2000, and November 13, 2000, Houston paid Douglas $719,000. On November 15, 2000, Houston closed USA's account at Wells Fargo and transferred the funds into its account.

At the time Houston agreed to pay USA's indebtedness to Douglas, Steven Douglas remained unaware of the problem with USA's earlier payment dating back to April 2000. The controller, relying on CNB's assurances, had never mentioned the matter because the $216,000 had been deposited into Douglas's account. The parties agree Houston would have paid the additional $216,000 had it been advised of the problem.

In January 2001, CNB, having heard nothing from Wells Fargo's adjustment center, followed up on its adjustment request. SAC reviewed its file and after conducting further investigations located USA's April check and confirmed the $216,000 encoding error. Unfortunately, the account had been closed on November 15, 2000, when Houston transferred the money to its account. SAC notified CNB there were no funds in the account and denied the adjustment request. CNB advised Douglas of these developments and reversed the $216,000 credit previously issued to Douglas. Steven Douglas met with CNB officials, and it was agreed CNB would re-credit his account pending further investigations. CNB then wrote Houston asking it to pay Douglas in accordance with its agreement to take care of USA's indebtedness to Douglas. Houston, however, refused and on March 5, 2001, filed for bankruptcy. Thereafter, CNB again debited Douglas's account for $216,000.

On January 14, 2002, Douglas sued CNB for negligence and breach of contract. Douglas contended CNB owed a duty to use reasonable care and breached the duty when it improperly encoded USA's check. Douglas also contended it had an implied contract with CNB requiring CNB to properly credit its account, and it breached the contract by erroneously encoding the check.

The case was tried, and the jury found for Douglas and awarded $216,000. The jury rejected CNB's third-party claims against Wells Fargo, and judgment was entered accordingly. In post-trial motions, the

continued

district court denied CNB's motions for JAML and a new trial, awarding attorney's fees to Douglas and Wells Fargo. CNB now appeals the denial of its post-trial motions and the award of attorney's fees.

CNB argues encoding errors are part and parcel of the banking industry; and therefore, the encoding error was not evidence of negligence. CNB concedes banks are required to use ordinary care when processing checks, but it argues compliance with Federal Reserve regulations and operating circulars presumptively establishes ordinary care. CNB contends, without identifying any particular regulation or circular, its procedures for encoding checks complied with said regulations; and, therefore, it was not negligent. We find little merit in this argument. Assuming CNB's encoding procedures complied with Federal Reserve regulations, an error nonetheless occurred within the process. Encoding errors, just like motor vehicle accidents, do not escape the scrutiny of a jury simply because they are known to occur. Thus, we conclude the district court was correct in holding the issue of CNB's negligence was for a jury to decide.

Arkansas law imposes an encoding warranty on banks. The law also imposes a concomitant duty on payor banks to mitigate damages once they become aware of encoding errors. When carrying out these obligations, banks are required to exercise ordinary care. The district court concluded it could not determine as a matter of law whether CNB or Wells Fargo had been negligent. Thus, it could not determine which UCC provision, if any, had been breached. Because the evidence of negligence was disputed, it was necessary to submit the question to a jury for resolution. Here, the jury heard the evidence and determined CNB was negligent. We conclude the evidence was sufficient to support the verdict.

■ *Affirmed.*

CASE CONCEPTS REVIEW

1. Should Douglas have shared responsibility? Why?
2. What should the bank have done to avoid liability for the loss?

8. Collecting Banks

When a bank has received a check for collection, it has the duty to use ordinary care in performing its collection operations. These operations include presenting the check to the drawee or forwarding it for **presentment**, sending notice of nonpayment if it occurs and returning the check after learning that it has not been paid, and **settling** for the check when it receives final payment. Failure of the collecting bank to use ordinary care in handling a check subjects the bank to liability to the depositor for any loss or damage sustained.

Presentment
A demand for acceptance or payment made on the maker, acceptor, drawee, or other payor by, or on behalf of, the holder

Settle
To pay in cash, by clearinghouse settlement, or by remittance or otherwise as instructed (A settlement may be either provisional or final.)

To act seasonably, a bank is generally required to take proper action before the midnight deadline following the receipt of a check, a notice, or a payment. Thus, if a collecting bank receives a check on Monday and presents it or forwards it to the next collecting bank anytime prior to midnight Tuesday, it has acted seasonably. If it fails to do so, it has liability unless it is excused by matters beyond its control.

9. Payor Banks

An item is finally paid by a payor bank when the bank (1) pays the item in cash, (2) settles for the item without reserving the right to revoke the settlement, (3) completes the process of posting the item, or (4) makes a provisional settlement and fails to revoke it within the time prescribed [4-213]. Upon final payment, the payor bank is accountable for the item, and it has substituted its own obligation for that of the drawer. Final payment usually occurs whenever the payor bank makes a provisional settlement for the item (a credit) and then fails to revoke its credit within its midnight deadline after receipt of the item.

A payor bank that is not also the depositary bank must make a provisional settlement for an item on the banking day it is received. However, that bank has until final payment of the check—but not later than its midnight deadline—to decide whether or not the item is good [4-302(a)]. Within this time, the bank may revoke the settlement and return the item or, if this is not possible, send written notice of nonpayment. This enables the bank to defer posting until the next day.

When a check drawn by one customer of a bank is deposited by another customer of the same bank for credit on its books, the bank may return the item and revoke any credit given at any time prior to its midnight deadline [4-302(b)]. The deposit of an item on which the depositary bank is itself the payor bank becomes available for withdrawal on the opening of the second banking day following receipt of the item.

Failure of the payor-drawee bank to take action within the prescribed time limits may make it accountable to the person who deposited the check if the check is not paid. This liability is imposed if the bank (1) retains a check presented to it by another bank without settling for it by midnight of the banking day of receipt or (2) does not pay or return the check or send notice of dishonor within the period of its midnight deadline [4-302].

Another problem relates to the *order of payment of checks.* There is no priority among checks drawn on a particular account and presented to a bank on any particular day. The checks and other items may be accepted, paid, certified, or charged to the indicated account of its customer in any order convenient to the bank [4-303(b)].

An item does not always proceed through the clearinghouse. It may be presented directly to the payor bank by a customer of that bank for payment over the counter. If the payor bank pays the item in cash, it may not later collect back the payments if its customer had insufficient funds on deposit [4-213].

BANKS AND THEIR CUSTOMERS

10. The Debtor-Creditor Relationship

The legal relationship between a bank and its depositors is that of debtor and creditor. If the depositor is a borrower of the bank, the reverse relationship (creditor-debtor) also exists between the bank and its customers. The dual relationship provides the bank with a prompt and easy method of protecting itself in the event of a depositor's default or pending insolvency. A bank can "seize" bank deposits under its right of **setoff** if such action becomes necessary to protect its account receivable.

Setoff

The right of a creditor, such as a bank, to seize money from the account of a customer who is the debtor

A bank is under a duty to honor properly payable checks drawn by its customer when there are sufficient funds in his or her account to cover the checks. A check is not properly payable if it has been altered or if it contains a forgery. If a bank pays a check that is not properly payable, the customer may insist on the account being recredited.

If there are insufficient funds, the bank may honor the properly payable checks, even though this action creates an overdraft. The customer is indebted to the bank for the overdraft and implicitly promises to reimburse the bank [4-401(a)]. While most overdrafts are dishonored, they are sometimes paid and the customer owes the bank for the check.

If a bank in good faith pays an altered check, it can charge the account of its customer only according to the original tenor of the check. Thus, if a check is raised, the bank can charge its customer's account only with the original amount of the check [4-401(b)]. If a person signs his or her name to an incomplete check and it is thereafter completed and presented to the drawee bank that pays it, the bank can charge the customer's account for the full amount if it pays in good faith and does not know that the completion was improper [4-401(d)]. The improperly completed check is not an altered check.

11. Wrongful Dishonor

If a bank wrongfully dishonors a check, it is liable to its customer for damages proximately caused by the wrongful dishonor. When the dishonor occurs by mistake, or by a malicious or willful dishonor, liability includes *actual damages proved* [4-402]. These damages may include *consequential damages* proximately caused by the wrongful dishonor, damages such as for arrest or prosecution of the customer [4-402]. State law may provide additional damages. For example, if the wrongful dishonor is willful, punitive damages in addition to actual damages may be awarded.

The Code rejects early common-law decisions holding that, if the dishonored item were drawn by a merchant, the merchant was defamed in business because of the reflection on the merchant's credit. Therefore, today a merchant cannot recover damages on the basis of defamation because of wrongful dishonor of a check.

12. Stop Payment Orders

A customer has the right to stop payment on checks drawn on his or her account. Only the drawer has this right; it does not extend to holders—payees or indorsers. To be effective, a stop payment order must be received at a time and in a manner that will afford the bank a reasonable opportunity to stop payment before it has taken other action on the item [4-403]. For example, if a check has been certified, the depositor cannot stop payment, whether the depositor or the payee procured the certification.

A bank must act reasonably in complying with a valid stop payment order. It cannot avoid liability by asserting immaterial differences between the check and the stop payment order. An oral stop order is binding on the bank for only fourteen days unless confirmed in writing within that period. Unless renewed in writing, a written stop order is effective for only six months [4-404].

A bank that honors a check on which payment has been stopped is liable to the drawer of the check for any loss the drawer suffers because of the bank's failure to obey the stop order. The burden is on the customer to establish the amount of the loss. Thus, if the drawer did not have a valid reason to stop payment, he or she cannot collect from a bank that fails to obey the stop payment order. Because of the concept of negotiability previously noted, a stop order on a check gives the drawer only limited protection. If the check is negotiated by the payee to a holder in due course, that holder can require payment of the amount by the drawer of the check, notwithstanding the stop order.

The bank cannot by agreement disclaim its responsibility for its failure to obey stop payment orders [4-303]. Thus a form signed by a customer agreeing not to hold the bank responsible for failure to stop payment could not be enforced.

13. Banks' Rights and Duties

A bank is entitled, but not *obligated,* to pay a check that is over six months old, and it may charge the check to the customer's account [4-404]. Certified checks do not fall within the six-month rule; they are the primary obligation of the certifying bank, and the obligation runs directly to the holder of the check.

In paying *stale checks,* the bank must act in good faith and exercise ordinary care. It must ask questions; and if a reasonable person would be put on notice that something is wrong, it should contact the drawer for authority to pay the stale item.

As a general proposition, the death or incompetence of a person terminates the authority of others to act on that person's behalf. If this principle were applied to banks, a tremendous burden would be imposed on them to verify the continued life and competence of drawers. A bank's authority to pay checks, therefore, continues until it knows that a customer has died or has been judged incompetent and the bank has had a reasonable opportunity to act [4-405].

What role does the bank play when a personal representative of the deceased transfers funds out of the decedent's account and into her own? That is the issue presented in the following case.

CASE

Estate of Eugene Christian Freitag v. Frontier Bank

COURT OF APPEALS OF WASHINGTON

75 P.3d 596 (2003)

COX, A.C.J.

The rights and duties of parties relating to "payment orders" are governed by Article 4A of the Uniform Commercial Code ("Funds Transfers"), not Article 3 ("Negotiable Instruments"). The primary issue in this case is whether Frontier Bank (Bank) or the estate of its deceased customer, Eugene Freitag (Estate), should bear the loss arising from certain payment orders to the Bank that Estate contends were not authorized. Patricia Olson, the original personal representative of the estate (PR), made the payment orders and later absconded with the funds that were the subjects of these orders.

Eugene Freitag died on June 5, 1998. On June 15, 1998, his will was admitted to probate and letters testamentary were issued that designated Olson, Freitag's niece, as the personal representative with nonintervention powers under the terms of the Freitag will. On June 29, 1998, Olson presented to the Bank a certified copy of Freitag's death certificate, the letters testamentary issued by the court designating her as the PR, and personal identification proving she was the PR named in the letters testamentary. She directed the Bank to close both a CD account and a checking account in Freitag's name, and to transfer a total of approximately $120,000 in proceeds from these sources into two accounts that she established at the Bank as individual, not fiduciary, accounts. The Bank executed this payment order.

Thereafter, Olson wrote checks on her individual accounts at the Bank to pay what were later determined to be her personal debts from the funds originating from the Estate. She later directed the Bank to wire transfer the remaining funds from her individual accounts, just over $100,000, to her bank in Montana. The Bank executed this second payment order.

John Blackburn was appointed successor PR following discovery of Olson's thefts. He commenced this action against the Bank on behalf of the Estate. Following cross motions for summary judgment the trial court granted the Bank's motion, denying relief to the Estate.

The Estate appeals.

As the parties recognize, the transaction at issue here is a "funds transfer" that is exclusively governed by Article 4A of the Uniform Commercial Code. The official comments to RCW 62A.4A-102, which defines the subject matter of the article, explain that it was drafted to create a comprehensive body of law to define funds transfers and the rights and obligations associated with payment orders. The drafters made a deliberate decision "to treat a funds transfer as a unique method of payment to be governed by unique rules that address the particular issues raised by this method of payment." The rules embodied in Article 4A are the "exclusive means of determining the rights, duties and liabilities of the affected parties in any situation covered by particular provisions of the Article."

The key question is whether the payment order initiated by Olson on behalf of the Estate was authorized under RCW 62A.4A-202(1). This controlling statute states, "A payment order received by the receiving bank is the authorized order of the person identified as sender if that person authorized the order or is otherwise bound by it under the law of agency."

Simply stated, the question is whether Olson, as PR with nonintervention powers under Freitag's will, had actual or apparent authority to cause the payment order to be issued in the name of the Estate. We conclude that she did.

The Estate essentially argues that it was not reasonable for the Bank to believe that Olson's payment order was authorized because it directed transfer of Estate funds to individual rather than fiduciary accounts only two weeks after she was appointed PR with nonintervention powers. Specifically, the Estate maintains that the Bank was put on inquiry notice that the order was not authorized because Olson transferred the funds before the conclusion of the four-month period for claims of creditors. Also, Olson "commingled" the money with her own by placing it in an individual account. Finally, Estate contends Olson could not possibly have earned over $120,000 in PR fees in two weeks. None of these arguments is persuasive.

In assessing whether the Bank's execution of the payment order was reasonable, we first consider the extent of the Bank's knowledge of Olson's authority to direct transfer of the Estate's funds. What did the Bank know and when did it know it? At the time of the payment order in question, the Bank knew that Olson was the PR under Freitag's will. This was evidenced by the letters testamentary that she presented to the Bank. The record is not clear precisely when the Bank became aware that Olson was a PR with nonintervention powers, but the Estate does not challenge that the Bank had such knowledge at the time of the payment order. In any event, such information was available to the Bank at that time—had it asked Olson. Nothing in the record indicates that the Bank knew at the time of the payment order that Olson would later divert the Estate's funds to her own use.

Based on this knowledge, the Estate claims that the Bank was on inquiry notice that something was awry by virtue of Olson's directive

continued

to place funds in her individual accounts so soon after qualifying as the PR.

The Estate argues, without citation to any relevant authority, that the Bank was on inquiry notice by virtue of Olson's directive to move the funds to her individual accounts. But assuming without deciding that the Bank was on such notice, it is unclear what information relevant to Olson's authority to issue the payment order on behalf of the Estate would have been obtained. Again, we have not been directed to any authority that makes the undesirable practice of commingling funds an illegal one. In short, the Bank's decision to honor the payment order as one authorized by the Estate was reasonable.

To summarize, Olson's payment order was authorized. The Bank did not breach its duty under RCW 62A.4A-202, and there was no duty of further inquiry under either RCW 62A.4A-202 or 11.68 RCW. The Estate, not the Bank, must bear the loss. We affirm the summary judgment order.

■ *Affirmed.*

CASE CONCEPTS REVIEW

1. What obligation should the bank have in the above case?
2. Should the transfer of funds from the estate into the personal account of Olson been a "red flag" to the bank?

14. Depositors' Rights and Duties

Banks make available to their customers a statement of account and canceled checks. Within a reasonable time after they are received, the customer must examine them for forgeries and for alterations. The bank does not have the right to charge an account with forged or altered checks; but the customer's failure to examine the statement and to notify the bank will prevent the customer from asserting the forgery (or alteration) against the bank if the bank can establish that it suffered a loss because of this failure. The bank may be able to prove that prompt notification would have enabled it to recover from the forger [4-406(d)].

The Code does not specify the period of time within which the customer must report forgeries or alterations. It does specify that if the same wrongdoer commits successive forgeries or alterations, the customer must examine and notify the bank within thirty days after the first item and statement were available to him or her. Otherwise, the customer cannot assert the same person's forgeries or alterations paid in good faith by the bank. This rule is intended to prevent the wrongdoer from having the opportunity to repeat these misdeeds.

If the customer can establish that the bank itself was negligent in paying a forged or altered item, the bank cannot avail itself of a defense based on the customer's tardiness in examining and reporting. Instead, the loss is allocated between the customer (who failed to examine the statement) and the bank [4-406(e)].

15. Funds Transfers

The occurrence of paperless transactions between banks and their customers has increased greatly during the past decade. Congress has passed the *Electronic Fund Transfer Act* to regulate the use of wire transfers in point-of-sale transactions and other consumer payments, such as automatic deposits and withdrawals from accounts. Aspects of this law, and Federal Reserve Board Regulation E that implements parts of the law, are examined in Chapter 42.

CHAPTER SUMMARY

CONCEPT OF NEGOTIABILITY

1. An assignee of a contract takes it subject to any defense the obligor may have against the assignor.
2. The goal of negotiability is to insulate a transferee from personal defenses that a primary party, such as a maker of a note, might have against the transferor.

3. For a holder to take an instrument free of personal defenses, the instrument must be negotiable, must be properly negotiated, and the holder must be a holder in due course.

KINDS OF COMMERCIAL PAPER

Notes

1. A promissory note is a two-party instrument in which the maker promises to pay a stated amount to the payee.

Certificates of Deposit

1. A certificate of deposit is a two-party instrument in which a financial institution, such as a bank, promises to repay a stated sum with interest on a certain date.

Drafts

1. A draft is a bill of exchange in which a drawer orders a drawee to pay a stated amount to a payee.

Checks

1. A check is a demand draft drawn on a bank.
2. A check drawn by a bank on itself is a cashier's check. Travelers' checks are cashier's checks in which the financial institution is both the drawer and the drawee.
3. A certified check is one that has been accepted by the drawee bank, and by the acceptance it assumes the obligation of the drawer. Certification at the request of a holder releases the drawer from any further liability. A bank has no duty to certify a check.

BANK DEPOSITS AND COLLECTIONS

Terminology

1. Depositary bank is the first bank to which an item is transferred for collection.
2. Payor bank is the bank by which an item is payable as drawn or accepted.
3. Intermediary bank is any bank to which an item is transferred in the course of collection, except the depositary or payor bank,
4. Collecting bank is any bank handling the item for collection, except the payor bank.
5. Presenting bank is any bank presenting an item to a payor bank.
6. A banking day is that part of the day in which a bank is open and which usually ends at 2:00 P.M. so the bank may process items before it closes. Items received after 2:00 P.M., are generally posted the following day.
7. A midnight deadline is midnight on the banking day following the banking day the item or notice is received by the bank.

The Bank Collection Process

1. A check deposited in the account is a provisional settlement until the check is honored by the payor bank.
2. If the payor bank dishonors a check, provisional settlements are revoked. This must occur for each bank by its midnight deadline.
3. Depositors do not have the right to draw against provisional settlements although many banks allow them to do so.
4. Items deposited for collection without indorsement may be indorsed by the depositary bank on behalf of its customer. The indorsement indicates that it was deposited to the account of the customer.
5. Depositary banks may not supply indorsements of persons who are not customers.

Collecting Banks

1. Banks have a duty to use ordinary care in the collection process. Failure to do so creates liability for losses sustained.
2. Banks must take action before the midnight deadline on checks, notices from other banks, and making payments.

Payor Banks

1. An item is paid by a payor bank when it actually pays the item, settles for it without reserving the right to revoke the settlement, completes the posting of the item, or makes a provisional settlement and does not revoke it within the time allowed.
2. A provisional settlement may be revoked until the midnight deadline.
3. If a check is drawn on the payor bank by a customer of the same bank, the bank may revoke the credit any time until the close of business the next day.
4. There is no priority in the order of paying checks presented on the same day.

BANKS AND THEIR CUSTOMERS

The Debtor-Creditor Relationship

1. The relationship between a bank and its depositors is that of debtor and creditor. If the depositor borrows money from the bank, the opposite relationship also exists.
2. A bank can seize deposits and set them off against debts to the bank.
3. A bank has a duty to honor checks when there are sufficient funds on deposit. It may also pay other checks and collect the amounts from its depositors.
4. A bank can charge a customer's account for an altered check only to the extent of the original amount of the check.
5. If an incomplete check is signed by a depositor and it is completed improperly, a bank can, in good faith, charge the account with the completed amount.

Wrongful Dishonor

1. A bank is liable for all damages caused by wrongful dishonor.
2. If the dishonor is willfully wrong, punitive damages may be collected.
3. Wrongful dishonor is not defamation of a merchant.

Stop Payment Orders

1. A customer has the right to stop payment on checks drawn on his or her account.
2. The stop order must be received in a time and manner that will allow the bank a reasonable opportunity to stop payment.
3. Oral stop orders expire in fourteen days unless confirmed in writing.
4. Written stop orders are effective for only six months but may be renewed in writing.
5. A bank that fails to stop payment upon proper notice is liable to the drawer of the check for any proven losses.
6. A bank may not contractually disclaim liability for failure to obey a stop order.

Banks' Rights and Duties

1. A bank may pay a check more than six months old but need not do so.
2. The death or incompetence of a customer terminates the bank's authority to honor checks written on the customer's account.
3. Notice of these events must be given to the bank.

Depositors' Rights and Duties

1. Upon receipt of the statement of account and canceled checks, the depositor has a duty o examine them within a reasonable time for forged, unauthorized, or altered checks.

2. Although the bank does not initially have the right to charge the customer's account for forged, unauthorized, or altered checks, the customer's failure to examine and notify may prevent him or her from asserting the improper charge to his or her account.
3. If both the customer and the bank are at fault in allowing the forged, altered, or unauthorized check to be paid, the bank is liable.
4. The customer cannot assert a forged, altered, or unauthorized check after one year from the time the canceled check or the statement of account was available for examination.
5. Forged indorsements must be reported within three years.

REVIEW QUESTIONS AND PROBLEMS

1. Match each term in Column A with the appropriate statement in Column B.

A	B
(1) Depositary bank	(a) Period after which a forged indorsement may no longer be asserted
(2) Personal defense	(b) Period after which written stop payment order expires
(3) Midnight deadline	(c) Period after which a forged check may no longer be asserted by depositor
(4) Six months	(d) The first bank to which an item is transferred for collection
(5) Fourteen days	(e) Part of next banking day
(6) Certification	(f) Period after which an oral stop payment order expires
(7) Real defense	(g) Precludes a bank from honoring a stop order
(8) One year	(h) May not be asserted against a holder in due course
(9) Three years	(i) May be asserted against a holder in due course
(10) Presenting bank	(j) Any bank presenting an item except a payor bank

2. Give the name of each of the following three forms and parties to the form.

John E. Murray, Jr.
School of Law
Pittsburgh, PA

NO. 157

8-26
430

January 4, 20 XX

PAY TO THE ORDER OF George Harlin $ 70.00

Seventy and no/100 DOLLARS

Pleasant Hills Office
MELLON BANK

John E. Murray Jr.

:0430-0026: 243--7716: 0157 :0000000007000:

(a)

FIRST CITY BANK OF NEW YORK
New York, New York

No. 4762 May 1, 20XX

THIS CERTIFIES THAT THERE HAS BEEN DEPOSITED with the undersigned the sum of $400,000.00

four hundred thousand DOLLARS

Payable to the order of Sierra Oil Company on July 27, 1993 with interest only to maturity at the rate of TWELVE per cent (12%) per annum upon surrender of this certificate properly indorsed.

FIRST CITY BANK OF NEW YORK BY:
M. Hopkins, Vice President
Authorized Signature

(b)

Moscow, Idaho June 7, 20 XX

One year from date pay to the order of Betty Stein

Four thousand Dollars

Andre Pellier

To: Robert Shaw
47 Peachtree Street
Atlanta, Georgia 30303

(c)

3. A check was issued payable to Chuck. Sam indorsed the check and deposited it in his account with National Bank. Chuck did not indorse the check, but is a customer of National Bank. National Bank supplied Chuck's missing indorsement and forwarded the check to the drawee bank. Chuck sued National Bank for cashing the check without his indorsement. May the bank supply the missing indorsement of a joint payee who is not a customer-depositor with the bank? Explain.
4. Pearl is the holder of a check drawn by Sharpe on Washington State Bank. Pearl also maintains an account at Washington State Bank. The check is deposited at the bank on Monday. On that same day, Sharpe's account is overdrawn; but she promises to make a substantial deposit, so the bank holds the check until Thursday. Sharpe does not make the deposit, and the bank, on Friday, returns the check to Pearl marked "Insufficient Funds." Can Pearl require the bank to make good on the check? Why or why not?
5. Equipment Company bought equipment from Wells and paid him with a check drawn on Citizens Bank. When the equipment was not delivered the next day, Equipment Company stopped payment on the check. Wells cashed the check at his own bank, Fargo Bank. When the check was presented to Citizens Bank, it refused to honor the check because of the stop order. Can Fargo Bank successfully collect from Wells? Why or why not?

6. Fitting issued a check for $800. After writing the check, she had second thoughts and contacted the bank about the possibility of stopping payment. A bank employee advised Fitting to deliberately create an overdraft situation by withdrawing enough money so there would remain insufficient funds to cover the check in question. The bank employee indicated that in those circumstances the bank would not pay the check. Fitting proceeded to withdraw money from the account, leaving enough money to cover other checks she had written. The bank nevertheless paid the $800 check in question. Is Fitting liable for the overdraft? Why or why not?
7. On January 29, Edwards, a wholesale grocer, made a large deposit in cash to his account at Cattlemen's Bank. In error, Edwards's deposit was posted to the account of Edmunds, another depositor. On the following day, Nevins, a local producer jobber, deposited a check to his account at Watermill bank drawn on Cattlemen's Bank to Nevins's order by Edwards. When the check was presented for payment, Cattlemen's Bank refused to honor it and stamped it "Insufficient Funds." The check was promptly returned to Nevins by Watermill Bank. If Edwards's deposit on January 29 had been properly posted, his bank account balance would have been substantially greater than the amount of his check to Nevins. Edwards sues the Cattlemen's Bank for damages. What should this recovery be? Why? Should Edwards recover?
8. The facts are as in Problem 7. Assume that Edwards's check had been given to Nevins in payment for a carload of produce that Edwards had arranged to resell at a large profit, that the bank was aware of this, that on dishonor of the check Nevins stopped the goods in transit, and that Edwards as a result lost his profit on the resale of the goods. May Edwards recover such lost profits from the bank? Explain.
9. Franklin, a depositor of the Milltown Bank, orally ordered the cashier of the bank to stop payment on a check he had issued. The check was issued in payment for goods that were not received. Franklin learned that the seller was a notorious confidence man. The cashier in turn notified the tellers that an oral stop order had been given. Ten days later one of the tellers, who was not paying much attention to his business, paid the seller's wife, who had been sent to the bank to cash the check for the seller. Franklin, while examining his canceled check5 at the end of the month, discovered the error and promptly demanded that his account be credited for the amount of the check. Is he entitled to the credit? Why?
10. Men's Wear drew a check payable to Zino & Co. When Zino did not receive it in the mail, Men's Wear placed a stop payment order in writing with the Drawee Bank. Approximately one year later, Drawee Bank paid on the check to a collecting bank and charged Men's Wear's account. Men's Wear had not renewed its stop payment order. Is Drawee Bank liable to Men's Wear for failing to honor the stop payment order? Why or why not?

Creation and Negotiation 34

CHAPTER OUTLINE

GENERAL REQUIREMENTS

1. Writing Signed by a Maker or Drawer
2. Necessity of a Promise or Order
3. Unconditional Promise or Order
4. The Particular Fund Concept
5. Sum Certain in Money
6. Certain Time of Payment
7. Acceleration and Extension Clauses

THE MAGIC WORDS OF NEGOTIABILITY

8. Introduction
9. Order Paper
10. Bearer Paper

OTHER FACTORS AFFECTING NEGOTIABILITY

11. Terms and Omissions Not Affecting Negotiability
12. Incomplete Instruments
13. Ambiguous Terms and Rules of Construction

TRANSFER OF COMMERCIAL PAPER

14. Introduction
15. Transfer by Negotiation
16. Types of Indorsements
17. Blank Indorsements
18. Special Indorsements
19. Restrictive Indorsements

CHAPTER PREVIEW

The preceding chapter introduced the four requirements that must be satisfied if a third party is to take commercial paper free of the defenses that arise from underlying contractual transactions. These four requirements may be stated so an affirmative response to each of the following questions must be given:

1. Does the paper meet the prerequisites of a negotiable instrument?
2. Has the negotiable instrument been properly negotiated?
3. Is the holder of the instrument in due course?
4. Are the defenses personal as opposed to real?

This chapter analyzes the first two of these four questions: The requirements of a negotiable instrument and its proper negotiation. Chapter 35 addresses the last two questions.

BUSINESS MANAGEMENT DECISION

One of your responsibilities as an officer of a financial institution is to decide whether or not to purchase (at a discount) the promissory notes that are payable to your customers.

What criteria should you use in making your decision to purchase these notes?

GENERAL REQUIREMENTS

The negotiability of an instrument is determined by the terms written on the face of the instrument. To be negotiable, an instrument must satisfy four basic requirements: (1) be signed by the maker or drawer, (2) contain an unconditional promise or order to pay a sum certain in money, (3) be payable on demand or at a definite time, and (4) be payable to the order of bearer or to cash [3-104].

1. Writing Signed by a Maker or Drawer

The first requirement is simply that there be a writing signed by the maker or drawer [3-104(a)(1)]. It is not required that any particular type or kind of writing be used, nor is it necessary that the signature be at any particular place on the instrument. The instrument may be in any form that includes printing, typewriting, or any other intentional reduction to tangible form. A symbol is a sufficient signature if "executed or adopted by a party with present intention to authenticate a writing" [1-201(39)]. The use of the word *authenticate* in the definition of *signed* makes it clear that a complete signature is not required. The authentication may be printed or written and may be placed on the instrument by stamp.

For purposes of internal control, many businesses and other organizations require that instruments be signed by at least two persons or that they be counter-signed. When the agreement requires two signatures, the drawee may not pay on only one signature, even if the one signing is authorized. The authority is limited or divided; both must sign.

2. Necessity of a Promise or Order

A negotiable note must contain a *promise* to pay. Although the word *promise* is used in almost all notes, a word or words expressing an undertaking to pay may be substituted. The promise must be derived from the language of the instrument, not from the fact that a debt exists. A mere acknowledgment of a debt in writing (an IOU) does not contain a promise. Even though an IOU is a valid enforceable instrument on which recovery may be had, it is not negotiable.

Order
A direction to pay that must be more than an authorization or request and must identify with reasonable certainty, the person to pay

A draft must contain an **order** to pay. The purpose of the instrument is to order the drawee to pay money to the payee or his or her order. The drawer must use plain language to show an intention to make an order and to signify more than an authorization or request. It must be a direction to pay. Thus an instrument in the following form would not be negotiable: "To John Doe. I wish you would pay $1,000 to the order of Richard Roe. [Signed] Robert Lee." This would, nevertheless, be a valid authorization for John Doe to make payment to Richard Roe. The correct method to create an order to pay would be, "To John Doe. Pay $1,000 to the order of Richard Roe. [Signed] Robert Lee."

3. Unconditional Promise or Order

Negotiable instruments serve as a substitute for money and as a basis for short-term credit. If these purposes are to be served, it is essential that the instruments be readily received in lieu of money and freely transferable. Conditional promises or orders would defeat these purposes, for it would be necessary that every person determine whether or not the condition had been performed prior to taking the instrument. The instruments would not freely circulate. In recognition of these facts, the law requires that the promise or order be *unconditional*.

The question of whether or not the promise or order is conditional arises when the instrument contains language in addition to the promise or order to pay money. The promise or order is conditional if the language of the instrument provides that payment is controlled by, or is subject to, the terms of some other agreement [3-104(a)(3)]. Clearly, a promise or order is conditional if reference to some other agreement is *required* and if payment is *subject* to the terms of another contract. Such a reference imposes the terms of the other writing.

However, a mere reference to some other contract or document does not condition the promise or order and does not impair negotiability. Such reference simply gives information about the transaction that gave rise to the instrument. Thus the words *subject to contract* condition the promise or order, but the words *as per contract* do not render the promise or order conditional. The latter is informative rather than restrictive.

Statements of the consideration for which the instrument was given and statements of the transaction out of which the instrument arose are simply informative. A draft may have been drawn under a letter of credit, and a reference to this fact does not impose a condition. Notes frequently contain a statement that some sort of security has been given, such as a mortgage on property, or that title to goods has been retained as security for the payment of the note. In either case, the purpose is to make clear to the holder that the promise to pay is secured by something in addition to the general credit of the maker; and as a consequence, a mere reference to the security does not destroy negotiability.

Normally implied or constructive conditions in an agreement that underlies the instrument do not make the instrument conditional. For example, a promise that payment will be made when the contract is performed does not make the promise to pay conditional. However, express conditions stated in the instrument itself can make the promise to pay conditional.

Whether a promise to pay is conditional is an issue addressed in the following case.

CASE

In Re: Apponline.com, Inc. Island Mortgage Network, Inc., et al., Debtors, Broward Title Company v. Matrix Capital Bank and HSA Residential Mortgage Services of Texas, Inc.

UNITED STATES DISTRICT COURT FOR THE EASTERN DISTRICT OF NEW YORK

321 B.R. 614; 2003 U.S. Dist. LEXIS 26258 (2003)

Pending before this Court is an appeal arising from a bankruptcy action filed in the United States Bankruptcy Court for the Eastern District of New York by Debtors AppOnline.com, Inc. ("AppOnline") and Island Mortgage Network, Inc. ("Island Mortgage") (collectively, "Debtors"). Appellant Broward Title Company ("Broward") appeals from the Order of the Honorable Dorothy Eisenberg, U.S.B.J., dated December 4, 2002, which held that Appellees Matrix Capital Bank ("Matrix") and HSA Residential Mortgage Services of Texas, Inc. ("RMST") were the holders in due course of the underlying notes and mortgages in question, thus defeating any equitable claims Broward may have had to the notes and mortgages.

Alan M. Jacobs is the Court appointed Chapter 11 Trustee of AppOnline and Island Mortgage.

On June 19, 2000, AppOnline and Island Mortgage filed voluntary petitions for relief under Chapter 11 of the Bankruptcy Code. Prior to the commencement of the bankruptcy proceedings, Island Mortgage was a mortgage banker and broker that originated and sold mortgages. Island Mortgage originated the mortgage loans at issue in the present case. The *loans at issue were made to Gilbert and Susan Amarante ("Amarante Loan") and Simaye Ciceron and Shirley Brown ("Ciceron Loan"). The Amarante Loan and the Ciceron Loan have since been sold by the trustee, Alan M. Jacobs, who was appointed by the bankruptcy court.*

On or about January 12, 2000, Matrix entered into a Mortgage Purchase/Repurchase Agreement with Island Mortgage for the sale of residential mortgage loans to Matrix ("Matrix Purchase Agreement"). Matrix subsequently sold the Amarante Loan to Island Mortgage in accordance with the Matrix Purchase Agreement. On May 30, 2000, Matrix wired funds for the mortgage to Action Abstract, in accordance with Island Mortgage's instructions, prior to the scheduled closing of the Amarante Loan.

Broward expected the loan proceeds for the Amarante Mortgage to be wired to it on May 31, 2000. However, the closing was postponed to June 1, 2000, and as of the time of the rescheduled closing, Broward received a check from National Settlement in the sum of $115,117.61 representing the net proceeds of the loan, rather than a wire transfer. The Amarantes executed the mortgage and note in favor of Island Mortgage at the closing on June 1, 2000.

Broward paid off the pre-existing mortgage and paid the sellers their net proceeds from the sale with the money from its escrow account. These checks were each dated May 31, 2000. By deposit slip dated June 2, 2000, Broward deposited a check from Island Mortgage into Broward's bank account. On June 6, 2000, the check from Island Mortgage, drawn on a National Settlement account, which represented the proceeds from the Amarante Loan, was dishonored due to a stop payment order issued against the check. A replacement check was sent to Broward on June 6, 2000, at its request, which was also dishonored.

Broward transmitted the original Amarante Note and related documents to Matrix. At all relevant times after the Amarante closing, Matrix remained in possession of the Amarante Note. The Chapter 11 Trustee sold the Amarante mortgage loan to Empire Mortgage IX.

The facts surrounding the Ciceron Loan are substantially similar to those surrounding the Amarante Loan.

Both the Amarante Note and the Ciceron Note are identical except for the amount of the monthly principal and interest payments to be made by the borrowers. They provide, in relevant part:

> *In return for a loan ... Borrower promises to pay ... plus interest. ... Interest will be charged on unpaid principal, from the date of disbursement of the loan proceeds by Lender, at the rate of nine percent (9.000%) per year until the full amount of the principal has been paid. ... Borrower shall make payment of principal and interest to Lender on the first day of each month beginning on [specified date]. ... Payment shall be made at ... Melville, New York. ... Each monthly payment of principal and interest will be in the amount of $663.01. This amount will be part of a larger monthly payment required by the Security Instrument [defined in P 3 as the mortgage], that shall be applied to principal, interest and other items in the order described in the Security Instrument. ... If Lender has not received the full monthly payment required by the Security Instrument ... by the end of fifteen calendar days after the payment is due, the Lender may collect a late charge in the amount of FOUR percent (4.0000%) of the overdue amount of each payment.*

Both the Amarante Mortgage and the Ciceron Mortgage include the following clause:

"This Security Instrument secures to Lender: (a) the repayment of the debt evidenced by the Note, with interest, and all renewals, extensions and modifications; (b) the payment of all other sums, with interest, advanced under paragraph 6 to protect the security of this Security Instrument; and (c) the performance of Borrower's covenants and agreements under this Security Instrument and Note."

In order for an instrument to be negotiable, it must "(a) be signed by the maker or drawer; and (b) contain an unconditional promise or order to pay a sum certain in money and no other promise, order, obligation or power given by the maker or drawer except as authorized by [N.Y. UCC Article 3]; and (c) be payable on demand or at a definite time; and (d) be payable to [the payee's] order or to [the instrument's] bearer."

Broward admits that the notes in question meet the requirements under sections (a), (c) and (d) to determine whether an instrument is negotiable. However, they assert that the notes fail under section (b) because they do not contain an unconditional promise or order to pay a sum certain in money and no other promise. A promise or order is not unconditional if the instrument states that it is subject to or governed by any other agreement. Broward must demonstrate that the notes in question are subject to or governed by another agreement in order to establish that the promise was not unconditional.

Both the Amarante Note and the Ciceron Note contain unconditional promises to pay. Appellant argues that the promises in each of these notes are not unconditional because they are governed by another agreement, namely the mortgage. However, neither note contains any language that the notes are "subject to" or "governed by" the mortgages, as required to eradicate negotiability under UCC § 3-105. Nor can it be said that the language in the notes, fairly construed, requires one to look at the mortgages in order to determine the terms of repayment.

Appellant relies on a provision in the notes stating that amounts to be paid under the notes "shall be applied to principal, interest and other items in the order described in the Security Instrument." However, as stated in the Official Commentary to UCC § 3-105, mere recitals of the existence of the separate agreement or references to it for information, such as this provision, do not affect negotiability. Official Comment 1 to UCC § 3-119 states that the separate agreement referred to in this section is "most commonly an agreement creating or providing for a security interest such as a mortgage, chattel mortgage, conditional sale or pledge." Although both notes do provide for a security interest in the mortgages, and references same, their negotiability is not destroyed by the existence and mere reference to the Security Instrument.

Here, the references to the mortgages in the Amarante and Ciceron Notes do not affect the unconditional nature of the promises or the terms of repayment; their sole purpose is to provide the lenders with additional security.

In addition, the terms of repayment can be determined from the face of the notes. With respect to the Amarante Note, there is an unconditional promise to pay $119,900, at a fixed interest rate, over a 30-year period, in monthly installments of $964.75, and no other promises except as authorized under the UCC. With respect to the Ciceron Note, there is an unconditional promise to pay $82,400, at a fixed interest rate, over a 30-year period, in monthly installments of $663.01, and no other promises except as authorized. Clearly, one does not have to look at the respective mortgages in order to determine the terms of repayment. Therefore, the promises to pay in the Amarante and Ciceron Notes are unconditional.

For all the reasons set forth herein, the Order of the Bankruptcy Court is AFFIRMED, in its entirety; and Broward's appeal is DISMISSED.

■ *Affirmed.*

CASE CONCEPTS REVIEW

1. What is the essence of Broward's argument?
2. Why did the court find that the promises were unconditional?

4. The Particular Fund Concept

A maker or drawer must engage or pledge his or her general credit, or the promise or order is conditional. A statement that an instrument is to be paid only out of a particular fund imposes a condition [3-106(b)]. Such an instrument does not carry the general personal credit of the maker or drawer. It is contingent on the sufficiency of the fund on which it is drawn. For example, if a note states, "I promise to pay to the order of John only out of my corn profits," the note is conditioned on having corn profits. The promise is conditional, and the instrument is non-negotiable. This result is due to the *particular fund concept.*

There are three exceptions to this concept. First, an instrument is not considered conditional merely because it makes reference to a particular source or fund from which payment is expected but not required. For example, although a check indicates it will be paid out of a particular account, it still may be negotiable. This conclusion with respect to checks is based on the fact that if the payor bank does not honor the check, the drawer remains personally liable for its payment. Thus, the reference to the checking account as the source of payment does not limit the payment to the resources of that particular fund or account.

The second exception involves an instrument that is issued by a government or governmental unit and is limited to payment out of a particular fund. The third exception is when an unincorporated association, such as a partnership, trust, or an estate, limits its obligation to pay the instrument only from the assets of the organization and eliminates liability of the individual members, such as partners. The instrument may still be negotiable. For purposes of negotiability, the Code recognizes partnerships and other unincorporated associations as "commercial entities" that may execute negotiable instruments as an entity.

5. Sum Certain in Money

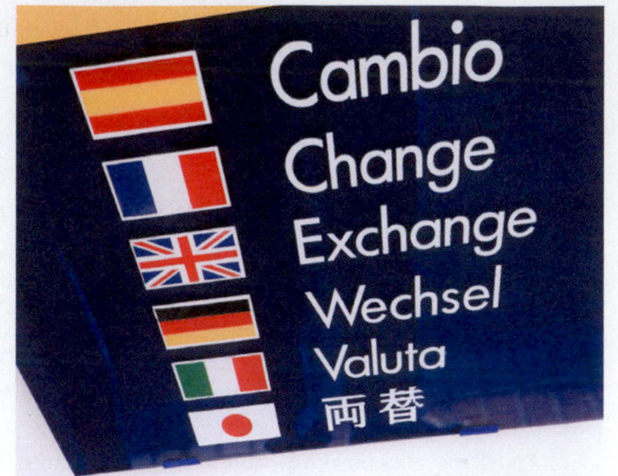

Instruments must be payable in money, be it foreign or domestic.

To be negotiable, an instrument must be payable in money. Instruments payable in chattels such as wheat or platinum are not payable in money. *Money* means a medium of exchange that is authorized or adopted by a domestic or foreign government as a part of its currency [1-201(24)]. The amount payable may be stated in foreign as well as domestic money. If the sum payable is stated in foreign currency, payment may be made in the dollar equivalent unless it is specified in the instrument that the foreign currency is the only medium of payment.

The language used in creating commercial paper must be certain with respect to the amount of money promised or ordered to be paid. Otherwise, its value at any period could not be definitely determined. If the principal sum to be paid is definite, negotiability is not affected by the fact that it is to be paid with interest, in installments, with exchange at a fixed or current rate, or with cost of collection and attorney's fees in case payment is not made at maturity.

If at any time during the term of the paper its full value can be ascertained, the requirement that the sum must be certain is satisfied. The obligation to pay costs and attorney's fees is part of the security contract, separate and distinct from the primary promise to pay money; therefore, it does not affect the required sum certain. The certainty of amount is not affected if the instrument specifies different rates of interest before and after default; nor is the certainty affected by a provision for a stated discount for early payment or an additional charge if payment is made after the date fixed. The principal amount to be paid, however, must be certain for the note to be negotiable.

6. Certain Time of Payment

As a substitute for money, negotiable instruments would be of little value if the holder were unable to determine when he or she could demand payment. A negotiable instrument, therefore, must be payable on demand or at a definite time [3-108].

An instrument is payable on *demand* when it so states, when payable at sight or on presentation, or when no time of payment is stated [3-108]. In general, the words *payable on demand* are used in notes, and the words at *sight* in drafts. If nothing is said about the due date, the instrument is demand paper. A check is a good illustration of such an instrument. The characteristic of demand paper is that its holder can require payment at any time by making a demand on the person who is obligated on the paper.

Not every instrument that indicates no time of payment is a demand instrument. If the instrument provides for periodic payment of interest or contains an acceleration clause without specifying the actual due date, such instruments are nonnegotiable. The interest clauses and acceleration clauses clearly indicate an intent that it not be payable on demand.

The requirement of a definite time is in keeping with the necessity for certainty in instruments. It is important that the value of an instrument can always be determined. This value will be dependent on the ultimate maturity date of the instrument. If an instrument is payable only upon an act or event, the time of its occurrence being uncertain, the instrument is not payable at a definite time even though the act or event has occurred. Thus, an instrument payable "thirty days after my father's death" would not be negotiable.

The requirement of certainty as to the time of payment is satisfied if it is payable on or before a specified date. Thus an instrument payable "on or before" June 1, 2006 is negotiable. The obligor on the instrument has the privilege of making payment prior to June 1, 2006 but is not required to pay until the specified date. An instrument payable at a fixed period after a stated date, or at a fixed period after sight, is payable at a definite time. The expressions "one year after date" or "sixty days after sight" are definite as to time.

7. Acceleration and Extension Clauses

Two types of provisions appearing on the face of instruments may affect the definite time requirement. One, an *acceleration clause,* hastens or accelerates the maturity date of an instrument. Accelerating provisions may be of many different kinds. A typical one provides that in case of default in payment, the entire note shall become due and payable. Another kind gives the holder an option to declare the instrument due and payable when he or she feels insecure about ultimate payment. An instrument payable at a definite time subject to any acceleration is negotiable [3-108(b)]. If, however, the acceleration provision permits the holder to declare the instrument due when he or she feels insecure, the holder must act in good faith in the honest belief that the likelihood of payment is impaired. The presumption is that the holder has acted in good faith, placing the burden on the obligor-payor to show that such act was not in good faith.

The second type of provision affecting time is an *extension clause,* the converse of the acceleration provision. It lengthens the time for payment beyond that specified in the instrument. A note payable in two years might provide that the maker has the right to extend the time of payment six months. An instrument is payable "at a definite time subject to extension at the option of the holder, or to extension to a further definite time at the option of the maker or acceptor" [3-108(b)]. If an extension is at the option of the holder, no time limit is required. The holder always has a right to refrain from undertaking collection. An extension at the option of the maker or acceptor, however, must specify a definite time for ultimate payment or negotiability is destroyed.

THE MAGIC WORDS OF NEGOTIABILITY

8. Introduction

The *words of negotiability* express the intention to create negotiable paper. The usual words of negotiability are *order* and *bearer* [3-109]. When these words are used, the maker or drawer has in effect stated that the instrument may be negotiated to another party. When the word *bearer* is used, it means that payment will be made to anyone who *bears or* possesses it. When the word *order* is used, it means that it will be paid to the designated payee or anyone to whom the payee orders it to be paid.

Other words of equivalent meaning may be used, but to ensure negotiability it is preferable to use the conventional words. If the instrument is not payable to order or to bearer, it is not negotiable, and all defenses are available in suits on the instrument. The following case illustrates how easy it is to overlook the magic words.

CASE

First Investment Co. v. Andersen

621 P.2d 683 (Utah 1980)

MAUGHAN, J.

Andersen gave promissory notes to Great Lakes in return for Great Lakes' promise to deliver 65,000 trees for Andersen's nursery business. The notes recited,

For value received, Robert Andersen of Nephi, Utah, promises to pay to Great Lakes Nursery Corp. at Waukesha, Wisconsin, six thousand four hundred twelve dollars payable as follows: $100 per month beginning Oct. 1, 1965 for 24 months and then $111.30 per month for 36 months including interest computed at 7% per annum added to the principal amount of $4,750.00.

In return for a loan, Great Lakes transferred the notes to First Investment. When Great Lakes failed to deliver the trees, Andersen refused to pay First Investment. First Investment sued Andersen claiming that it was not subject to Andersen's defense of failure of consideration because the notes were negotiable. The trial court found for the defendant.

Defendants prevailed before the trial court on the ground the notes were not negotiable, and failure of consideration was a defense against any person not a holder in due course.

The primary issue is whether the two promissory notes were negotiable. A negotiable promissory note is an unconditional promise in writing made by one person to another, signed by the maker, engaging to pay on demand, or at a fixed or determinable future time, a sum certain in money, to order or to bearer.

An instrument to be negotiable must be payable to the order or to bearer. An instrument is payable to order where it is drawn payable to the order of a specified person, or to him or his order.

Under the U.C.C. 70A-3-104(1) (d), one of the requirements to qualify a writing as a negotiable instrument is that it contain the time-honored "words of negotiability," such as "pay to the order" or "pay to the bearer." The mere promise to pay, absent the magic words "payable to order or to bearer" renders the note non-negotiable, and the liability is determined as a matter of simple contract law.

In the instant case, the notes were payable simply to the payee, and were not payable to the order of the payee or to the payee or its order and were thus not negotiable instruments. Since the notes were not negotiable, the transfer by the Nursery to plaintiff must be deemed an assignment, and the assignee (plaintiff) stood in the shoes of the assignor and took subject to existing equities and defenses.

■ *Affirmed.*

CASE CONCEPTS REVIEW

1. What was the reason Andersen signed promissory notes in favor of Great Lakes Nursery?
2. What did Great Lakes do with these notes?
3. Why does the court allow Andersen to assert the defense of Great Lakes' nonperformance when First Investment sued to collect the note?
4. What words are missing from these notes that would have changed the result of this case?

9. Order Paper

If the terms of an instrument provide that it is payable to the order or assigns of a person who is specified with reasonable certainty, the instrument is payable to order [3-109(b), 3-110]. The expressions "Pay to the order of John Doe" or "Pay to John Doe or order" or "Pay to John Doe or assigns" create order paper (see Figure 34-1).

An instrument may be payable to the order of two or more payees together, such as A and B, or in the alternative, A or B. An instrument payable to the order of A and B must be indorsed by both. One payable to the order of A or B may be indorsed and negotiated by either.

An instrument may be payable to the order of an estate, a trust, or a fund. Such instruments are payable to the order of the representative of the estate, trust, or fund [3-110(c)(2)]. An instrument payable to the order of a partnership or an unincorporated association, such as a labor union, is payable to such partnership or association. It may be indorsed by any person authorized by the partnership or association.

Article 3 addresses the proper treatment of the situation where two names deemed payees, as the following case illustrates.

FIGURE 34-1 ■ **Order Paper Payable to the Order of John Doe (It requires John Doe's indorsement if it is to be negotiated.)**

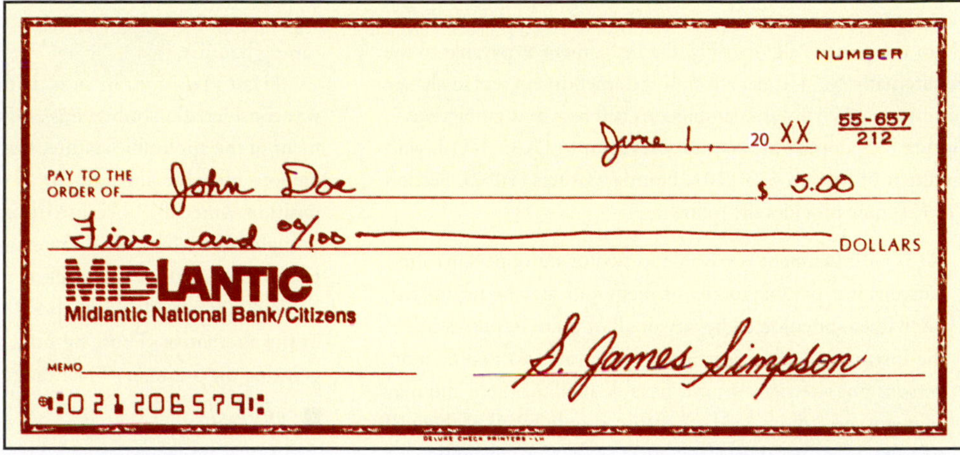

CASE

The Hyatt Corp. v. Palm Beach National Bank, et al.

COURT OF APPEAL OF FLORIDA

840 So. 2d 300 (2003)

LEVY, JUDGE

J&D Financial Corporation is a factoring company. Skyscraper Building Maintenance, LLC, had a contract with Hyatt to perform maintenance work for various Hyatt hotels in South Florida. Skyscraper entered into a factoring agreement with J&D. As part of the factoring agreement, J&D requested Hyatt to make checks payable for maintenance services to Skyscraper and J&D. Of the many checks issued by Hyatt to Skyscraper and J&D, two were negotiated by the bank but endorsed only by Skyscraper. They were made payable as follows:

1. *Check No. 1-78671 for $22,531 payable to:*
   J&D Financial Corp.
   Skyscraper Building Maint
   P.O. Box 610250
   North Miami, Florida 33261-0250

2. *Check No. 1-75723 for $21,107 payable to:*
   Skyscraper Building Maint
   J&D Financial Corp.
   P.O. Box 610250
   North Miami, Florida 33261-0250

Only one of the payees, Skyscraper, endorsed these two checks. The bank cashed the checks. According to J&D, it did not receive the benefit of these two payments.

J&D filed a complaint against Skyscraper and its principals on the guarantee, Hyatt and the bank. J&D sought damages against Skyscraper under the factoring agreement and separately against Hyatt and the bank for negotiation of the two checks. Hyatt answered and raised the bank's "fault" as an affirmative defense. The bank answered and raised Section 673.1101(4), Florida Statutes (1993) as an affirmative defense. The bank, Hyatt and J&D then moved for summary judgment on the issue of whether the bank properly negotiated the checks. It was uncontested that the bank had a duty to negotiate the checks only on proper endorsement; and if it did not, it would be liable.

The bank argued that the checks were payable to J&D and Skyscraper alternatively, and thus the bank could properly negotiate the checks based upon the endorsement of either of the two payees. The bank further argued that the checks were drafted ambiguously as to whether they were payable alternatively or jointly, and thus under Section 673.1101(4), Florida Statutes, the checks would be construed as a matter of law to be payable alternatively.

Hyatt's position was that the checks were not ambiguous, were payable jointly and not alternatively, and thus under Section 673.1101, the checks could only be negotiated by endorsement of both of the payees. J&D similarly argued that the checks were payable jointly. The trial court granted Summary Judgment in favor of the bank, finding that Section 673.1101(4) precluded the bank's liability. Hyatt appealed. J&D filed a cross-appeal.

The issue on appeal is whether or not a check payable to:

J&D Financial Corporation
Skyscraper Building Maintenance

(stacked payees) is payable jointly to both payees requiring the endorsement of both, or whether it is ambiguous regarding whether the check was drafted payable alternatively, so that the bank could negotiate the check when it was endorsed by only one of the two payees.

continued

In 1990, Article 3 of the UCC was revised, and the language of UCC Section 3-116 was added to UCC section 3-110 and became subsection (d). Revised UCC Section 3-110(d), which added language to follow former 3-116(a) and (b), states, "If an instrument payable to two or more persons is ambiguous as to whether it is payable to the persons alternatively, the instrument is payable to the persons alternatively." The net effect of the amendment was to change the presumption. What was unambiguous before is now ambiguous.

Florida has adopted the statutory revision to UCC 3-110, with its enactment of Section 673.1101, Florida Statutes (1992). Section 673.1101(4) now provides the following:

> (4) If an instrument is payable to two or more persons alternatively, it is payable to any of them and may be negotiated, discharged, or enforced by any or all of them in possession of the instrument. If an instrument is payable to two or more persons not alternatively, it is payable to all of them and may be negotiated, discharged, or enforced only by all of them. If an instrument payable to two or more persons is ambiguous as to whether it is payable to the persons alternatively, the instrument is payable to the persons alternatively.

We conclude that based on the 1990 amendment to the Uniform Commercial Code, when a check lists two payees without the use of the word "and" or "or", the nature of the payee is ambiguous as to whether they are alternative payees or joint payees. Therefore, the UCC amendment prevails; and they are to be treated as alternative payees, thus requiring only one of the payees' signatures. Consequently, the bank could negotiate the check when it was endorsed by only one of the two payees, thereby escaping liability.

Hyatt's position, in sum, is that if a stacked payee designation was considered unambiguous and payable jointly before the amendment of the applicable statute, that same payee designation is unambiguous after the amendment of the statute. However, we find this position untenable because it ignores the shift in presumption brought about by the UCC revision. With the statutory presumption removed, the same stacked payee designation that was unambiguous and payable jointly pre-1992 is now ambiguous and payable in the alternative. Thus, we hold that the trial court was correct in granting the Summary Final Judgment.

■ *Affirmed.*

CASE CONCEPTS REVIEW

1. Who are "stacked payees"? Why would such a situation occur?
2. Is the 1990 revision a better position? Is paying in the alternative a better alternative? Why?

10. Bearer Paper

The basic characteristic of bearer paper (see Figure 34-2) as distinguished from order paper is that it is payable to bearer when created if it is payable (1) to bearer, (2) to the order of bearer (as distinguished from the order of a specified person or bearer), (3) to a specified person or bearer (notice that it is not to *the order of* a specified person or bearer), or (4) to "cash" or "the order of cash," or any other indication that does not purport to designate any specific payee [3-109]. An instrument will be considered bearer paper only after it is determined that it cannot be order paper.

OTHER FACTORS AFFECTING NEGOTIABILITY

11. Terms and Omissions Not Affecting Negotiability

Some additional terms, usually for the benefit of the payee or other holder, may be included in commercial paper without impairing negotiability. Many instruments contain statements indicating that collateral has been given. These statements, including provisions relating to the rights of the payee or holder in the collateral, do not affect negotiability [3-104(a)].

The drawer of a check or draft may include a provision that the payee, by indorsing or cashing it, acknowledges full satisfaction of an obligation of the drawer. The provision will not affect negotiability. Checks or drafts drawn by insurance companies in settlement of claims usually contain such a provision.

Often, the consideration for which an instrument was given is set forth in the instrument, and it is common to include words such as "for value received" or 'in payment for services ren-

FIGURE 34-2 ■ Bearer Paper (Its negotiation is effective without an indorsement.)

dered." The omission of words stating the consideration for which an instrument was given will not affect its negotiability. Nor is the negotiable character of an instrument otherwise negotiable impaired by omission of a statement of the place where the instrument is drawn or payable.

Whether there is no date, a wrong date, an antedate, or a postdate is not important from the standpoint of negotiability [3-113]. Any date that does appear on the instrument is presumed correct until evidence is introduced to establish a contrary date [3-113]. Any fraud or illegality connected with the date of the instrument does not affect its negotiability but merely gives a defense.

12. Incomplete Instruments

A person may sign an instrument that is incomplete in that it lacks one or more of the necessary elements of a complete instrument. Thus a paper signed by the maker or drawer, in which the payee's name or the amount is omitted, is incomplete.

An incomplete instrument cannot be enforced until it is completed [3-115(a)]. If the blanks are subsequently filled in by any person in accordance with the authority or instructions given by the party who signed the incomplete instrument, it is then effective as completed. A person might leave blank, signed checks with an employee who must pay for goods to be delivered. When the employee fills in the amounts and names of the payees, the checks are perfectly valid.

A date is not required for an instrument to be negotiable; however, if a date is necessary to ascertain maturity ("payable sixty days from date"), an undated instrument is an incomplete instrument. The date may be inserted by the holder. If an instrument is payable on demand or at a fixed period after date, the date that is put on the instrument controls, even though it is antedated or postdated.

13. Ambiguous Terms and Rules of Construction

In view of the millions of negotiable instruments that are made and drawn daily, it is to be expected that a certain number of them will be ambiguously worded. Accordingly, the code provides a number of rules to be applied in interpreting negotiable instruments.

Some instruments are drawn in such a manner that it is doubtful whether the instrument is a draft or a note. It may be directed to a third person but contain a promise to pay, rather than an order to pay. The holder may treat it as either a draft or a note and present it for payment to either the person who signed it or the apparent drawee. Where a draft is drawn on the drawer, it is treated as a note.

An instrument may contain handwritten terms, typewritten terms, or printed terms. Where there are discrepancies in the instrument, handwritten terms control typewritten and printed terms, and typewritten terms control printed terms [3-114]. Thus a printed note form may state that it is payable on demand, but there may be typed or written on the note "payable thirty days from date." Such an instrument would be payable in thirty days.

There may also be a conflict between the words and the figures on an instrument. Thus a check may have the words "fifty dollars" and the figures "$5000." The words control, and the check would be for $50. If the words are ambiguous, the figures will control [3-114]. In a check with the words "Five seventy-five dollars" and figures $5.75," the figures will control. In some cases, the ambiguity may arise from the context of the words.

If an instrument provides for the payment of interest but does not state the rate, the rate will be at the judgment rate at the place of payment. An unsatisfied money judgment bears interest at a rate specified by statute, and whatever this judgment rate is in a particular state will thus be applicable in this situation. Interest will run from the date of the instrument or, if it is undated, from the date of issue [3-112(a)].

If two or more persons sign an instrument as maker, acceptor, drawer, or indorser as part of the same transaction, they are jointly and severally liable unless the instrument specifies otherwise. This means that the full amount of the obligation could be collected from any one of them or that all of them might be joined in a single action. Joint and several liability is imposed even though the instrument contains such words as "I promise to pay" [3-116].

Transfer of Commercial Paper

14. Introduction

The general rule governing the transfer of almost all types of property is that a person can transfer no greater interest than he or she owns. *Assignments* follow that general rule. The general law of assignments is discussed in Chapter 20. When one attempts to transfer rights by assignment, it is generally stated that the assignee steps into the shoes of the assignor. Thus, the transfer of an instrument by assignment vests in the assignee only those rights the assignor had.

When transferring property, one can only transfer what he or she owns.

By contrast, the key feature of negotiability is that a *negotiation* might confer on a transferee greater rights than were held by the transferor. If the transfer is by negotiation, the transferee becomes a *holder* [3-201(a)]. A holder has, for example, the legal power to transfer the instrument by assignment or negotiation; the holder can usually enforce it in his or her own name;

he or she can discharge the liability of any party in several ways (as we shall later explain); and he or she enjoys several procedural advantages. Moreover, the holder has the opportunity to become a *holder in due course* with rights not granted by the instrument.

Thus, in an *assignment,* only the rights of the transferor are passed to the transferee, but in a *negotiation,* there is the possibility of granting greater rights. Any contract can be assigned; only a negotiable instrument can be negotiated.

15. Transfer by Negotiation

Two methods of negotiating an instrument make the transferee a holder. If the instrument is payable to bearer, it may be negotiated by delivery alone; if it is order paper, indorsement and delivery are required [3-201(b)]. Although bearer paper can be negotiated without indorsement, the person to whom it is transferred will often require an indorsement. The reason for this is that an indorser has a greater liability than one who negotiates without indorsement. Also, if the instrument is dishonored, identification of the person who negotiated the paper becomes easier with an indorsement.

The indorsement must be placed on the instrument itself or on a paper so firmly affixed to it that it becomes a part thereof. The indorsement paper that is annexed is called an *allonge.* The holder or by someone who has the authority to do so on behalf of the holder must make the indorsement. If the payee is a corporation, an officer will indorse on its behalf. The indorsement should include the corporate name, but this is not actually required.

The indorsement, to be effective as a negotiation, must convey the entire instrument or any unpaid balance due on the instrument. If it purports to indorse less than the entire instrument, it will be effective only as a partial assignment [3-203(d)]. An indorsement reading "Pay to A one-half of this instrument" would not be a negotiation, and A's position would be that of an assignee.

The indorser may add to the indorsement words of assignment, condition, waiver, guarantee, or limitation or disclaimer of liability, and the like. The indorsement is, nevertheless, effective to negotiate the instrument. Thus if A, the payee of a negotiable instrument, signs his name on the reverse side with the words "1 hereby assign this instrument to B," he has effectively indorsed the instrument and upon delivery to B, B is a holder.

If the name of the payee is misspelled, the payee may negotiate by indorsing either the name appearing on the instrument or in his or her true name, or both. A person who pays the instrument or gives value for it may require that both names be indorsed. The desirable practice is to indorse in both names when the name of the payee is misspelled.

All parties to negotiate the instrument must indorse instruments payable to multiple parties. If authorized, one party may sign for the other. A bank may supply missing indorsements for its depositors. If there is a joint account, it may add the indorsement of either party or both in the event an item is payable to both.

16. Types of Indorsements

Revised Article 3 provides a definition for the term *indorsement.* An indorsement is defined from the perspective of its purpose in the negotiation process. An indorsement is a signature, other than that of the maker, drawer, or acceptor, which is made to (1) negotiate the instrument, (2) restrict payment of the instrument, or (3) incur the indorser's liability on the instrument [3-204(a)].

The ordinary indorsements used in negotiating paper are either special or blank. If added terms condition the indorsement, it is also a restrictive indorsement, which limits the indorsee's use of the paper. Also, the indorser may *limit* or *qualify* his or her liability as an indorser by adding words such as "without recourse." This qualified indorsement has the effect of relieving the indorser of contractual liability as an indorser—that he or she will pay if the primary obligor refuses to do so. A qualified indorsement will also be a blank or a special indorsement. These indorsements are discussed in the following sections.

17. Blank Indorsements

A blank indorsement consists of the indorser's name written on the instrument. If an instrument drawn payable to order is indorsed in blank (see Figure 34-3), it becomes payable to bearer [3-205(b)]. After the blank indorsement, if it is indorsed specially, it reverts to its status as order paper, and an indorsement is required for further negotiation. If a check, on its face payable to the order of Henry Smith, is indorsed "Henry Smith," it becomes bearer payable and can be negotiated by mere delivery. A thief or finder could pass title to the instrument.

FIGURE 34-3 ■ Order Paper, Payable to the Order of Henry Smith (With his blank indorsement, shown at right, the order paper becomes bearer paper, negotiable by mere delivery.)

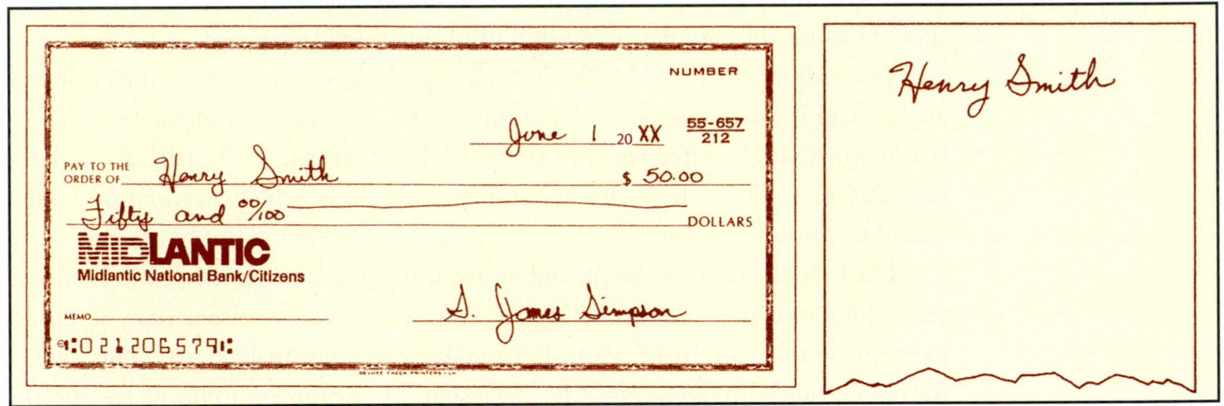

18. Special Indorsements

A special indorsement specifies the person to whom or to whose order it makes the instrument payable (see Figure 34-4). When an instrument is specially indorsed, it becomes payable to the *order of* the special indorsee and requires his or her indorsement for further negotiation. Thus an indorsement "Pay to John Jones" or "Pay to the order of John Jones" is a special indorsement and requires the further indorsement by John Jones for negotiation. If a bearer instrument is indorsed specially, it requires further indorsement by the indorsee. This is true if the instrument was originally bearer paper or if it became bearer paper as the result of a blank indorsement. In other words, the last indorsement determines whether the instrument is order paper or bearer paper [3-205].

The holder of an instrument may convert a blank indorsement into a special indorsement by writing above the blank indorser's signature any contract consistent with the character of the indorsement [3-205 (c)]. Thus Richard Roe, to whom an instrument has been indorsed in blank by John Doe, could write above Doe's signature, "Pay to Richard Roe." The paper would require Roe's indorsement for further negotiation.

FIGURE 34-4 ■ A Special Indorsement by Henry Smith (For negotiation, it requires further indorsement by John Jones.)

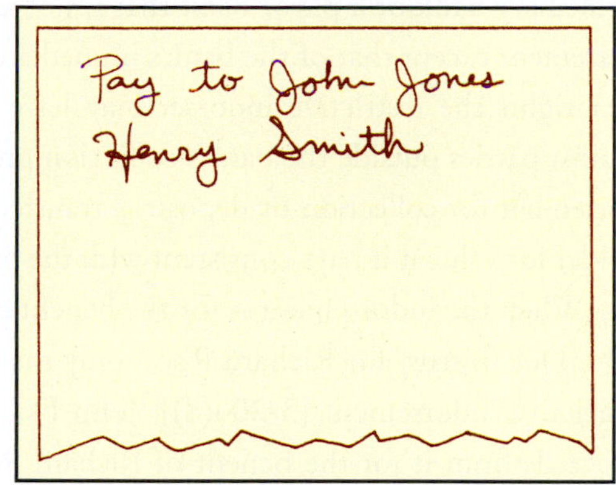

19. Restrictive Indorsements

A person who indorses an instrument may impose certain restrictions on the indorsement; that is, the indorser may protect or preserve certain rights in the paper and limit the rights of the indorsee [3-206]. Of the four types of restrictive indorsement, one is conditional (for example, "Pay John Doe if Generator XK-711 arrives by June 1, 2007"); or the indorsement may purport to prohibit further transfer of the instrument, such as "Pay to John Doe only." When a check is deposited in a bank and will be processed through bank collection, the indorsements "For collection," "For deposit only," and "Pay any bank" are restrictive. In the fourth type, the indorser stipulates that it is for the benefit or use of the indorser or some other person, such as "Pay John Doe in trust for Richard Roe."

A restrictive indorsement does not prevent further transfer or negotiation of the instrument. Thus, an instrument indorsed "Pay to John Doe only" could be negotiated by John Doe in the same manner as if it had been indorsed "Pay to John Doe."

The most common restrictive indorsement is "For deposit only" (see Figure 34-5). It is a common practice for payees of checks to use such an indorsement to safeguard checks. Once a check is

FIGURE 34-5 ■ A Restrictive Indorsement by Henry Smith (Subsequent holders should be only the banks in the collection process.)

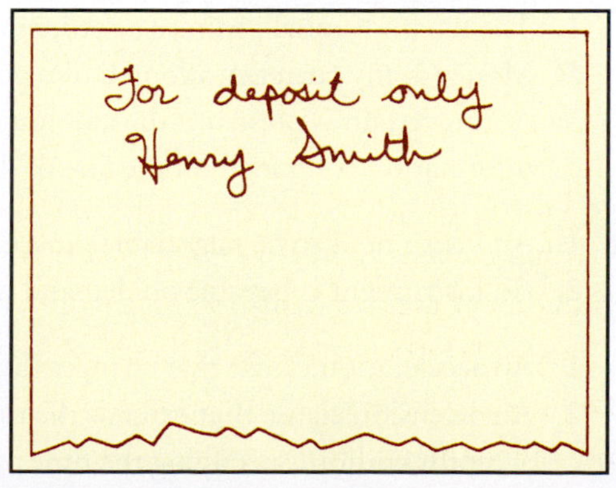

stamped "For deposit only," a thief or finder of the check cannot cash it. The only action the bank can take is to deposit it into the indorser's account. If it fails to do so, it has liability to the indorser.

The effect of restrictive indorsements is substantially limited when applied to banks. An intermediary bank or a payor bank that is not a depositary bank can disregard any restrictive indorsement except that of the bank's immediate transferor. This limitation does not affect whatever rights the restrictive indorser may have against the bank of deposit or his or her right against parties outside the bank's collection process. Under a conditional indorsement or an indorsement for collection or deposit, a transferee (other than an intermediary bank) becomes a holder for value if it pays consistent with the indorsement.

When the indorsement is for the benefit of the indorser or another person, such as "Pay to John Doe in trust for Richard Roe," only the first taker is required to act consistently with the restrictive indorsement [3-206(d)]. John Doe has the obligation to use the instrument or the proceeds from it for the benefit of Richard Roe. John Doe could negotiate the instrument to John Smith, who could qualify as a holder and ignore the restriction.

CHAPTER SUMMARY

GENERAL REQUIREMENTS

Signed Writing

1. The negotiable instrument must be signed by the maker or drawer.
2. The signature can be anything intended to authenticate the instrument, and it can be applied by mechanical means.

Promise or Order

1. A note must contain a promise, and a draft must contain an order.

Unconditional Promise or Order

1. The promise or order must be unconditional. A promise is conditional if reference to some other document is required or the instrument is subject to the terms of another document.
2. A recital of consideration does not destroy negotiability.

Particular Fund Concept

1. A promise that is limited to a particular fund is conditional, and the instrument is not negotiable.
2. Exceptions to the particular fund concept involve instruments specifying an account to be debited and instruments issued by governmental units, partnerships, or unincorporated associations.

Sum Certain in Money

1. The unconditional promise or order must involve a sum certain in money.
2. Money is any currency adopted by a government.
3. A sum certain is present if the amount of money involved can be calculated from the information contained on the face of the instrument.

Certain Time of Payment

1. An instrument to be negotiable must be payable on demand or at a definite time.
2. An instrument is payable on demand when no time of payment is stated.

Acceleration and Extension Clauses

1. An acceleration clause that changes the maturity date does not destroy negotiability.
2. An extension clause that extends the time of payment at the option of the maker or acceptor without specifying the time of ultimate payment destroys negotiability.

3. An extension clause exercised by the holder does not destroy negotiability.

THE MAGIC WORDS OF NEGOTIABILITY

Order Paper

1. To be negotiable, a note must be payable to the order of some person or to bearer. A note or check that is simply payable to a specified person is nonnegotiable.
2. An instrument payable to the order of two people must be indorsed by both.
3. An instrument payable to an estate, trust, or fund may be indorsed by the appropriate representative.

Bearer Paper

1. Bearer paper may be negotiated without indorsement by delivery.
2. An instrument is bearer paper if it specifies that it is payable to bearer or to cash.
3. Bearer paper may be negotiated by a finder or thief, and anyone in possession of it is entitled to collect.

OTHER FACTORS AFFECTING NEGOTIABILITY

Terms and Omissions Not Affecting Negotiability

1. Many terms do not affect negotiation. For example, a statement acknowledging satisfaction of an obligation on a check does not destroy negotiability.
2. An undated instrument is nevertheless negotiable as is a postdated instrument.

Incomplete Instruments

1. An incomplete instrument cannot be enforced until it is completed.
2. Instruments may be completed as authorized or unauthorized. Unauthorized completion is a personal defense that cannot be asserted against a holder in due course.

Ambiguous Terms and Rules of Construction

1. Handwritten terms prevail over typewritten terms or printed terms, and typewritten terms control printed terms.
2. If there is a conflict between words and figures, the words control.
3. If an instrument provides for interest without stating the rate, the rate on judgments will be followed.

TRANSFER OF COMMERCIAL PAPER

Negotiation

1. The term *negotiation* is used to describe the method of transferring a negotiable instrument in a manner that makes the transferee a holder.
2. A transfer that is not a proper negotiation is an assignment, and the assignee has the same rights as the assignor.
3. For proper negotiation, the whole instrument must be negotiated.
4. Bearer paper is negotiated by delivery. Order paper requires indorsement and delivery.

Blank Indorsements

1. A blank indorsement consists of the indorser's name, usually written on the back of the instrument.
2. A blank indorsement converts order paper to bearer paper.

Special Indorsements

1. Special indorsements indicate the person to whom the instrument is payable. Special indorsements require the indorsement of such person for further negotiation.

Restrictive Indorsements

1. Restrictive indorsements allow the indorser to preserve rights and limit the options of the indorsee.
2. The most common restrictive indorsement is "for deposit only." This means that the bank may not cash the check but must deposit the proceeds into the account of the indorser.

3. A restrictive indorsement when applied to banks does not prevent further negotiation and is applicable only to the immediate indorsee.

REVIEW QUESTIONS AND PROBLEMS

1. Match each term in Column A with the appropriate statement in Column B.

A	B
(1) IOU	(a) Varying exchange rates have no impact
(2) Particular fund concept	(b) A statement of the transaction out of which the instrument arose
(3) Sum certain in money	(c) Requires good faith in its execution
(4) Restrictive indorsement	(d) Without recourse
(5) Negotiability unaffected	(e) Not a promise
(6) Acceleration clause	(f) Does not destroy negotiability if a governmental unit is the maker or drawer
(7) Extension clause	(g) May or may not destroy negotiability
(8) Blank indorsement	(h) For deposit only
(9) Qualified indorsement	(i) Pay to John Jones./s/Paul Pringle
(10) Special indorsement	(j) A signature

2. Comment briefly on the provisions described in these instruments as to their bearing on negotiability. In each instance, the other portions of the instrument are in proper form.

   a. A bill of exchange drawn by Y on Z directs Z to pay $1,000 to the order of A and charge this amount to Y's "Book Fund."
   b. The XYZ Company (a partnership) signed a note promising to pay $1,000 and bearing the notation "limited to payment out of the entire assets of the maker."
   c. X signed a note promising to pay $5,000 or deliver 100 barrels of oil at the option of the holder.
   d. One of the notes is payable "five days after the death of the maker."
   e. A note containing the following notation: "with interest at bank rates.

3. Mary executed a note and a purchase money mortgage to Al. Al negotiated the note to Tiger Bank. The note contained the following stipulation: "This note with interest is secured by a mortgage on real estate, of even date herewith, made by the maker hereof in favor of the said payee. The terms of said mortgage are by this reference made a part hereof." Is the note negotiable? Explain.
4. Skyblast Freight executed a note that contained the following provisions: "This note is payable only from the proceeds of the sale of the Skyblast Freight Building." Is the note negotiable? Why or why not?

5. Employer gave Pension Fund and Company a note stating that Employer promises to pay Pension Fund Company "all current contributions as they become due under the collective bargaining agreement in addition to the sum of $15,606.44 with interest." Is this note negotiable? Why or why not?
6. Horace Brace has in his possession the following instrument:

   November 1,2006

   I, Walter Forgel, hereby promise to pay Charles Smidlap ONE THOUSAND DOLLARS ($1,000.00) one year after date. This instrument was given for the purchase of FIVE HUNDRED (500) shares of Beefstake Mining Corporation. Interest at 10 percent.

   Walter Forgel (Signature)

   Horace Brace purchased the instrument from Charles Smidlap at a substantial discount. Smidlap specializes in the sale of counterfeit mining stock. Walter Forgel is one of his innocent victims. What are the rights of Brace against Forgel on the instrument? Explain.
7. Roberts was a holder in due course of a properly drawn check payable to "Bearer." He indorsed the check as follows:

   Pay to the order of Wilson Hall without recourse.
   /s/Peter Roberts

   What type of indorsement did Roberts make? If Hall wishes to negotiate the instrument, what is required? Explain.
8. Casey held a negotiable instrument payable to his order. He transferred the instrument to Dale for value. At the time of transfer, Casey failed to indorse his name on the back of the instrument, and Dale accepted the instrument as given to him. What rights does Dale have on the instrument? Explain.
9. Quincy signed a promissory note payable to the order of Unger, who indorsed the note in blank over to Pritchard. Pritchard then transferred the note to Truax by delivery. Is Truax a holder of the instrument? Why or why not?
10. Bob issued a check payable to the order of Gary, who lost it without indorsing it. Can a finder of the check negotiate it? Why or why not?

Holders in Due Course and Defenses | 35

CHAPTER OUTLINE

CHAPTER PREVIEW

The questions introduced in Chapter 34, which summarize the requirements to create negotiable instruments free of the defenses that arise from an underlying contract, are worthy of being repeated:

1. Does the paper meet the prerequisites of a negotiable instrument?
2. Has the negotiable instrument been properly negotiated?
3. Is the holder of the instrument in due course?
4. Are the defenses personal as opposed to real?

In the preceding chapter, the first two questions were examined and answered. This chapter considers questions 3 and 4 regarding holders in due course and types of defenses.

BUSINESS MANAGEMENT DECISION

You are the senior loan officer of your bank. Among your many customers is a mobile home dealer, whose inventory your bank finances. This dealer typically takes promissory notes from its customers. The dealer then indorses these notes to your bank as partial payment for its debt. A dissatisfied customer of the dealer refuses to pay your bank until the defects with the mobile home are corrected.

Can you successfully sue this dissatisfied customer of the mobile home dealer to collect on the note? What should you do?

STATUS OF THIRD PARTIES

The original party to whom an instrument is issued or drawn has the right to transfer the instrument to someone else. The party to whom it is transferred may be an *assignee*, a *holder*, or a *holder in due course.*

Assignee
A third party who receives the right to have a contract performed and is viewed as "standing in the shoes" of the assignor and not free from the defenses that could be asserted against the assignor's claim of performance

ASSIGNEE A third party becomes an **assignee** of an instrument in one of two situations. First, if the instrument being transferred does not satisfy the elements of being negotiable, the third party receiving the instrument is an assignee. Second, if the instrument being transferred is negotiable but is not properly negotiated, the third party receiving the instrument is once again an assignee. As an assignee, the third party is subject to all the defenses that could have been asserted against the assignor had that party sought collection of the instrument.

Holder
The party to whom a negotiable instrument is issued or properly negotiated and technically satisfied irrespective of that party's actions or knowledge.

HOLDER If a negotiable instrument is properly negotiated, the party receiving it is a **holder**. If certain requirements are met, the holder may qualify as a **holder in due course** and have a special status [3-302]. If a holder does not qualify as a holder in due course, his or her position is equivalent to that of an assignee; and any defenses available to the original parties may be asserted against the holder.

Either the original payee or a third party may qualify as a holder of an instrument and may transfer or negotiate it. A holder may legally discharge the instrument or enforce payment in his or her own name [3-301]. A thief or finder may qualify as a holder of a bearer instrument. As we will see later, a thief or finder cannot qualify as a holder in due course because he or she gave no value for the instrument.

Holder in due course

A holder of a negotiable instrument who takes it for value, in good faith, and without notice of defenses—free from the personal defenses on the contract that give rise to the commercial paper

The following case provides a further explanation of this status as a holder. Note in this case that the payees of a note are considered as the holders of the note, the parties who can discharge the makers' liability.

HOLDER IN DUE COURSE If there is no claim or defense to the instrument, it is immaterial whether the party seeking to enforce it is a holder or a holder in due course. The Code makes all holders the functional equivalent of holders in due course until a defense is claimed. The burden of proving a defense is on the party asserting it. When the defense is proved, the holder has the burden of proving that he or she is a holder in due course. If the holder can prove that, he or she can enforce payment, notwithstanding the presence of a personal defense to the instrument. (Later

CASE

Edwards v. Mesch

763 P.2d 1169 (N.M. 1988)

SCARBOROUGH, C. J.

Defendants-appellants, Robert J. and Florence M. Mesch (Mesches), executed a promissory note in favor of plaintiffs-appellees, John E. and Jean M. Edwards (Edwards), as payees on March 14, 1986. The promissory note for the amount of $6,000.00 with interest at the rate of 10% per annum on the balance was for money the Edwards had loaned to the Mesches. The Mesches subsequently defaulted on the note after making a single payment, and the Edwards brought suit to collect all unpaid principal and accrued interest. After a trial on the merits on November 11, 1987, the district court entered judgment for the Edwards in the sum of $6,751.10, with interest on the principal balance accruing at the rate of 10% per annum, and awarded attorney's fees and costs to the Edwards.

On appeal, the Mesches argue that the Edwards have no enforceable rights in the note and were not the real party in interest at the time of the trial. During the trial the Edwards did not deny assigning their interests in the note to the Tres Santos Corp., a closely held corporation, 100% of whose shares are owned by plaintiff-appellee, John E. Edwards. The Mesches argued at trial, and again on appeal, that since the Edwards assigned their interests in the note to the Tres Santos Corp., it became the real party in interest, and thus an indispensable party to the lawsuit. This argument finds no support in legal authority.

The promissory note that the Mesches executed to the Edwards is a negotiable instrument and, as such, is governed by the Uniform Commercial Code (UCC). According to the UCC, a "holder" of a negotiable instrument is "a person who is in possession of an instrument drawn, issued or indorsed to him or to his order or to bearer or in blank." Before a person can become a "holder", two conditions must be satisfied: (1) the obligation evidenced by the instrument must run to him and (2) he must have possession of the instrument. A negotiable instrument payee (the Edwards) is always a holder if the payee has the instrument in his possession because the payee is the person to whom the instrument was issued. "It is inherent in the character of negotiable paper that any person in possession of an instrument which by its terms runs to him is a holder, and that anyone may deal with him as a holder."

The Edwards were payees and holders of the note and could enforce payment of the note after they had assigned it to the Tres Santos Corp. According to New Mexico law, "The holder of an instrument whether or not he is the owner may enforce payment in his own name." The Mesches' argument on appeal that the district court ruling exposes them to double liability is without merit. "The liability of any party is discharged to the extent of his payment or satisfaction to the holder even though it is made with knowledge of a claim of another person to the instrument."

Rule 1-017 of Civil Procedure for the District Courts requires that "[e]very action shall be prosecuted in the name of the real party in interest. The capacity of an individual to sue or be sued shall be determined by the law of this state." This court has held that the test for determining who is the real party in interest is whether one is the owner of the right being enforced and is in a position to discharge the defendant from the liability being asserted in the suit. The Edwards, in the instant case, were the holders and payees on the promissory note and properly asserted their rights as plaintiffs at trial. Furthermore, the Edwards were in a position at trial to discharge the Mesches from all liabilities to any third party from the promissory note. Therefore, the arguments that the Tres Santos Corp. was the real party in interest and an indispensable party at trial are without merit.

A review of the record below reveals the district judge expended commendable effort to explain the governing principles of law and his rulings in the instant case to the Mesches. We uphold the decision of the district court, and further hold that since the promissory note provides for costs and attorney's fees to payees for collection and enforcement of the note, the Edwards are entitled to recover reasonable attorney's fees on appeal.

■ *Affirmed.*

CASE CONCEPTS REVIEW

1. Who are the makers of the promissory note? Who are the payees?
2. What procedural defense did the Mesches assert when the Edwards sued to collect payment?
3. How does the court describe the transfer of the note by Edwards to Tres Santos Corp.?
4. Should this case have been decided differently if the Edwards had negotiated the note to Tres Santos Corp. rather than merely having assigned their interest in the note?

in this chapter we discuss both types of defenses: personal and real.) A holder in due course will not be able to enforce the instrument in the event that a real defense is proven. The preferred status of a holder in due course exists only where the defense to the instrument is a personal defense.

Issues as to whether or not a party is a holder in due course usually arise when the party seeks to collect on the instrument; but occasionally a party is sued on a negligence theory for losses incurred in transactions involving an instrument. To avoid liability, the defendant must establish that he or she is or was a holder in due course. Thus a holder in due course is free of claims and is not subject to personal defenses.

CONTRACT PROVISIONS Contract provisions frequently attempt to give a status equivalent to a holder in due course to an assignee of contract. These provisions purport to waive defenses if the contract is assigned. Some states have declared such provisions to be illegal, as against public policy, if the drawer or maker is a consumer. Other states have enforced waiver of defense clauses provided the assignee meets the requirements to qualify as a holder in due course and the defense waived is a personal defense. Thus the material in this chapter is significant for many non-negotiable contracts as well as negotiable instruments.

HOLDER IN DUE COURSE

1. Requirements

To qualify as a holder in due course, a holder must meet three basic requirements. He or she must take the instrument (1) for value, (2) in good faith, and (3) without notice that it is overdue, that it has been dishonored, or that any other person has a claim to it or defense against it [3-302(b)].

A payee may be a holder in due course if all the requirements are met. Most payees deal with the maker or drawer. However, a payee may be a holder in due course when the instrument is not delivered to the payee by the maker but is delivered by an intermediary or agent of the maker. A payee that participates in the transaction out of which the instrument arises cannot be a holder in due course.

When an instrument is acquired in a manner other than through the usual channels of negotiation or transfer, the holder will not be a holder in due course. Thus, if an instrument is obtained by an executor in taking over an estate, is purchased at a judicial sale, is obtained through legal process by an attaching creditor, or is acquired as a transaction not in the regular course of business, the party acquiring it is not a holder in due course [3-302(c)].

2. Value

A holder must have given value for an instrument to qualify as a holder in due course. A person to whom an instrument was transferred as a gift would not qualify as a holder in due course. In the law of contracts, *value* does not have the same meaning as *consideration.* A mere promise can be consideration, but it is not necessarily value. As long as a promise is executory, the value requirement to be a holder in due course has not been met [3-303].

Whereas the original Article 3 states that an executory promise is not generally viewed as value, revisions to Article 3 now permit the holder to enjoy a freedom from defenses to the extent of the value of the performance that is rendered [3-303(b)]. For example, assume Debra issues a check for $250 to Pauline in return for Pauline having typed four term papers of equal length. Pauline negotiates this check to Terry in payment for Terry's promise to fix Pauline's printer next week. If Debra discovers that Pauline's typing is unacceptable (perhaps due to a printing problem), Debra has a defense that can be asserted against Terry since Terry did not give value for the check. Now suppose

Terry performed $150 worth of labor on Pauline's printer before Debra discovers the defense of Pauline's defective performance. Terry can recover up to $150 against Debra, but Debra can assert the defense to defeat Terry's claim for the additional $100.

While a mere promise is not value, if the promise to pay is negotiable in form, it does constitute value [3-303 (b)]. A drawer who issues a check in payment for a negotiable note that he or she is purchasing from the holder becomes a holder for value even before the check is cashed.

A holder who takes an instrument in payment of an existing debt is a holder for value. Thus, if Ada owed Brenda $500 on a past-due account and transferred a negotiable instrument to Brenda in payment of such account, Brenda would qualify as a holder for value. The same holds true if the instrument is received as collateral for an existing debt, whether the debt is due or not.

A purchaser of a limited interest in paper can be a holder in due course only to the extent of the interest purchased. If a negotiable instrument is transferred as collateral for a loan, the transferee may be a holder in due course, but only to the extent of the debt that is secured by the pledge of the instrument. For example, George loans Gerry $2,500. To secure the loan, Gerry negotiates Ron's note in the amount of $4,000 to George. George is a holder in due course only to the extent of $2,500.

A person who purchases an instrument for less than its *face value* can be a holder in due course to the full amount of the instrument. Cora is the payee of a note for $1,000. She may discount the note and indorse it to Wick for $800. Wick has nevertheless paid value and is entitled to collect the full $1,000.

3. Good Faith

A holder must take the instrument in good faith to qualify as a holder in due course [3-302(a)(2)]. *Good faith* is defined as "honesty in fact in the conduct or transaction concerned" [1-201(19)]. If a person takes an instrument under circumstances that clearly establish that there is a defense to the instrument, this person does not take it in good faith. Failure to follow accepted business practices or to act reasonably by commercial standards, however, does not establish lack of good faith. Good faith is a subjective rather than an objective determination. Honesty, rather than diligence or negligence, is the issue.

Taking a note on large discount does not in and of itself establish lack of good faith. A large discount may result from factors other than the existence of a defense to the instrument. The burden is on the party seeking to deny the holder-in-due-course status to prove lack of good faith. Good faith is presumed in the absence of facts to show bad faith.

4. Without Notice

Notice

Evidence of a fact that occurs when a person (a) has actual knowledge of it, (b) has received notification of it, or (c) has reason to know that it exists based on all the facts and circumstances known at the time in question

Closely related to good faith is the requirement that the transferee must not have **notice** of the following: (1) instrument is overdue, (2) instrument has been dishonored, (3) instrument is part of a series and there is an uncured defect with respect to payment of another instrument, (4) instrument contains an unauthorized signature, (5) instrument has been altered, (6) instrument is subject to defenses, (7) instrument is subject to any claim to the instrument, and (8) instrument is subject to any claim in recoupment [3-302(a)(2)].

A person has notice of a fact if he or she has actual knowledge of it, has received notification of it, or (from the facts and circumstances known to him or her) has "reason to know" that it exists [1-201 (25)]. The law generally provides that a person has reason to know a fact if his or her information would indicate its existence to a person of ordinary intelligence (or of the intelligence of the person involved, if that is above the ordinary). A person also has reason to know the facts if they are so highly probable that a person exercising reasonable care will assume their existence.

If there is visible evidence of forgery or alteration, a purchaser is put on notice of a claim or defense [3-302(a)(1)]. Certain irregularities on the face of an instrument also put a purchaser on notice that there may be a claim or defense to the instrument. Many are obvious, such as a signature that is obviously affixed by someone else.

If an instrument is incomplete in some important respect at the time it is purchased, notice is imparted [3-302(a)(3)]. Blanks in an instrument that do not relate to material terms do not give notice of a claim or defense; but if the purchaser has notice that the completion was improper, he or she is not a holder in due course.

Knowledge that a defense exists or that the instrument has been dishonored prohibits the status of a holder in due course. In some situations, knowledge of certain facts does not, of itself, give the purchaser notice of a defense or claim. Awareness that an instrument is antedated or postdated does not prevent a holder from taking in due course. Knowledge of a separate contract is not notice. Although a defense will arise if the contract is not performed, such knowledge does not prevent one from becoming a holder in due course. Of course, if the purchaser is aware that the contract has been breached or repudiated, he or she will not qualify as a holder in due course.

Actual notice to prevent a party from being holder in due course must be received at a time and in a way that will give a reasonable opportunity to act on it [3-302(f)]. A notice received by the president of a bank one minute before the bank's teller cashes a check is not effective in preventing the bank from becoming a holder in due course.

In the following case, the court was asked to dismiss a complaint filed in the United States District Court in favor of filing the same action in a Philippines court. To make this decision, the court analyzed the similarity of United States law and Philippine law in the application of the holder in due course doctrine, along with the proof necessary to establish notice.

CASE

Carl W. Henderson, Jr., Administrator of the Estate of David M. Henderson, Francisco Solis, Trustee of Messenger Trust One, and Michael S. Henderson, Successor Trustee of Messenger Trust One v. Metropolitan Bank & Trust Company

UNITED STATES DISTRICT COURT FOR THE SOUTHERN DISTRICT OF NEW YORK

470 F. Supp. 2d 294 (2006)

SHIRA A. SCHEINDLIN

On February 9, 2006, Carl W. Henderson, Jr., of Tennessee, Administrator of the Estate of David M. Henderson; Francisco Solis, of California, Trustee of Messenger Trust One ("the Trust"); and Michael S. Henderson, of New Mexico, Successor Trustee of the Trust (collectively "Plaintiffs"), filed suit against Metropolitan Bank and Trust Co. ("Metrobank"), a corporation headquartered in Makati City, Philippines, n1 seeking to enforce a "Manager's Check" allegedly issued by Metrobank, with a face value of twelve billion pesos. Plaintiffs also seek damages of $75 million, representing interest accrued since the instrument was issued.

A manager's check is a negotiable instrument akin to a cashier's check, which is "drawn by the cashier of a bank upon the bank itself." The Manager's Check in dispute here was issued as interest payments on accounts at Metrobank "established by confidential benefactors for humanitarian and sociopolitical purposes in the Philippines." Although the accounts in question were held at Metrobank, the "assets which gave rise to the Manager's Check" originated as cash transfers from Citibank in New York. Jocelyn C. Duran was an "arranged signatory" on the Metrobank accounts, one of which was Account No. 00701-5500691-8. The Manager's Check was issued on this account to Duran as payee, on March 21, 2000.

At some point subsequent to the check's issuance, Duran "attempted to convert the instrument into cash funds" at Metrobank, and it was dishonored. Duran "sought the assistance of a high-placed government official," and "[t]hereafter, [Metrobank], through its President and Director, Antonio S. Abacon, Jr., offered to convert the instrument into cash equivalent to one-half its [face] value … if [Duran] would execute a release of any and all claims against accounts held in her name, at that time, in Metrobank." Duran refused this offer. Plaintiffs allege that as a result, Duran "experienced threats to the physical safety of herself and her family." Duran thereupon "transferred her authority to negotiate the Manager's Check … via a

Special Power of Attorney ... to Janito C. Perez." The Complaint does not state whether Duran ever endorsed or negotiated the check to Perez.

Perez met with Metrobank representatives in October, 2002, and Metrobank once again refused to honor the check. In order to safeguard the instrument, and to facilitate "further efforts to resolve any issues that were preventing the check from being honored," Perez arranged for another transfer of the instrument. Perez delivered the check to David M. Henderson, and executed "a formal assignment [of the check] and Special Power of Attorney, individually and as Trustee of Messenger Trust One." The Trust was formed "under the laws of Nevada" on August 7, 2002, shortly before Perez' meeting with Metrobank representatives. Plaintiffs allege that the check was endorsed to the Trust sometime thereafter, but do not state who endorsed it or when.

On April 2, 2003, David Henderson brought the Manager's Check into the United States. He died on September 11, 2003. David Henderson's "interest in the check is now an asset of his estate, administered by his brother ... Carl W. Henderson." Henderson's son, Michael Henderson, is identified as successor trustee to the Trust.

Neither party disputes that Plaintiff's right to enforce the instrument will be determined to a great extent by *The Negotiable Instruments Law of the Philippines* ("Act 2031"). Act 2031 has much in common with Articles three and four of the Uniform Commercial Code ("U.C.C."), including use of the concepts of negotiation, holder, and holder in due course. Under Philippine law, a holder in due course holds the instrument "free from defenses available to prior parties among themselves, and may enforce the payment of the instrument thereon." However, "in the hands of any holder other than a holder in due course, a negotiable instrument is subject to the same defenses as if it were non-negotiable." A holder is one who possesses an instrument payable to bearer, or is the named payee or endorsee of an instrument and is in possession of that instrument. A holder in due course is one who:

> has taken the instrument under the following conditions: (a) That it is complete and regular on its face; (b) That he became the holder before it was overdue, and without notice that it has previously been dishonored, if such was the fact; (c) That he took it in good faith and for value; and (d) That at the time it was negotiated to him, he had no notice of any infirmity in the instrument or defect in the title of the person negotiating it.

Metrobank has moved to dismiss the complaint on the ground that the action should be heard in the Philippines.

The degree to which Plaintiffs may be able to step into the shoes of Duran, the payee, and insist on payment, will be determined by the manner in which the instrument passed from Duran, to Perez, to David Henderson and the Trust, and finally to Michael Henderson and the Trust. Plaintiffs contend that they are holders in due course of the Manager's Check, and there is a rebuttable presumption under Philippine law that any holder is a holder in due course. However, the Complaint suggests that Perez took the instrument from Duran with notice that it had been dishonored, and that David Henderson also had notice that the check had been dishonored. Under Philippine law, a person who takes an instrument with notice that it has been dishonored is not a holder in due course. Thus, it may be that Perez, David Henderson, or Plaintiffs are not or were not holders in due course. Indeed, it is unclear whether Duran ever endorsed or negotiated the check to Perez. Plaintiffs' right to enforce the instrument, if any, will almost certainly require testimony concerning the transfer of the instrument from Duran to Perez, and then to David Henderson.

The testimony of Perez and Duran, both of whom are presumed to be in the Philippines, will be necessary to resolve these questions. Plaintiffs listed both as witnesses. Plaintiffs also list three witnesses from the Philippines who "are or were Metrobank employees," including Rafael Ayuste and two others, and state that these individuals attended the October 2002 meeting between Metrobank officials and Perez. Plaintiffs list three other individuals with knowledge of this meeting. One of these, Lilia C. Pastoral, is a trustee of the Trust and a Philippine resident. The other two, Arturo Balbastro and Dr. Ambu Moraka, worked with Plaintiffs or their predecessors to resolve issues relating to the check and are residents of the Philippines and India, respectively. What occurred at this meeting is relevant to determining Plaintiffs' right to enforce the instrument. Metrobank also lists Ayuste in its initial disclosures as a person possessing information concerning the dishonor of the check at the October 2002 meeting.

Because Plaintiffs may not be holders in due course of the instrument, Metrobank may be able to assert defenses arising from the underlying obligation. Metrobank discloses one witness, Jovencio R. Capulong, Jr., a Metrobank employee whose knowledge of the cash transfers from Citibank would be relevant to such defenses. Capulong is a Philippine resident. Plaintiffs list three managers and executives of Metrobank's headquarters in Makati City and unnamed managers of Citibank's offices in Makati City, whom they claim have information relevant to the transactions. Plaintiffs also intend to seek testimony from unnamed managers at Citibank's New York offices.

Plaintiffs disclose that they may testify although the subject matter of their testimony is not specified. It appears, however, that the only matters of which Plaintiffs have direct knowledge relate to the existence and management of the Trust. These issues are incidental to the outcome of the case, especially by comparison to the far more critical questions discussed above.

Finally, both sides intend to offer documentary evidence. Metrobank specifies six documents or categories of documents that relate to the issue of the authenticity of the Manager's Check, and one data compilation relating to the transactions underlying the check's issuance. All of these documents are located in the Philippines. Plaintiffs intend to offer documents relating to the underlying transaction and the issuance of the check. They further intend to offer correspondence of David Henderson and a deposition of Henderson taken by Plaintiffs' attorney before Henderson's death. Although the location of these documents is not specified, it is presumably in the United States. Finally, Plaintiffs will offer the Manager's Check itself, which is in a safe deposit box at a PNC bank branch in Louisville, Kentucky. It is apparent that the Negotiable Instruments Law of the Philippines, like the U.C.C., is a legal framework whose integrity is of vital importance to the Philippine economy. In contrast, to the extent that United States law is implicated here, the issues are minor. Thus, the Philippines' interest in adjudicating this dispute is much greater than that of the United States.

■ *Motion to dismiss granted.*

CASE CONCEPTS REVIEW

1. Briefly, what evidence supports plaintiffs' view that they are a holder in due course?
2. What evidence supports the view that Metrobank has a defense?

5. Before Overdue

To be a holder in due course, a purchaser of an instrument must take it without notice that it is overdue [3-304(a)]. A purchaser of overdue paper is charged with knowledge that some defense may exist. A purchaser has notice that an instrument is overdue if he or she has reason to know that any part of the principal amount is overdue. Past-due interest does not impart notice to the holder. The instrument itself will usually indicate if it is past due.

With respect to the holder having notice that the instrument is overdue, demand paper poses a special problem. This type of instrument does not have a fixed date of maturity. Purchasers of demand paper cannot be holders in due course if they have reason to know that they are taking it after a demand has been made, or if they take it more than a reasonable length of time after its issue. What is a reasonable or an unreasonable time is determined on the basis of a number of factors—the kind of instrument, the customs and usages of the trade or business, and the particular facts and circumstances involved. In the case of a check, a reasonable time is presumed to be ninety days [3-304(a)(2)].

6. Holder from a Holder in Due Course

A transferee may have the rights of a holder in due course, even though he or she personally does not meet all the requirements. Because a transferee obtains all the rights that the transferor had, a person who derives title through a holder in due course also has those rights. Code Section 3-203(b) states this principle, the shelter provision, which advances the marketability of commercial paper.

The main significance of the shelter provision is that it permits one who is not a holder in due course to share the shelter from claims and defenses enjoyed by the holder in due course from whom he or she got the instrument.

> Example Paul fraudulently induces Mary to execute and deliver a note to him. Paul then negotiates the note to Tom, who qualifies as a holder in due course. Tom makes a gift of the note to Al, who sells it to Bob, a friend of Paul's, who knew of Paul's fraud. Bob sells it to Carl after maturity. Is Carl a holder in due course? No. Were Bob and Al holders in due course when they owned the instrument? No. Is Carl

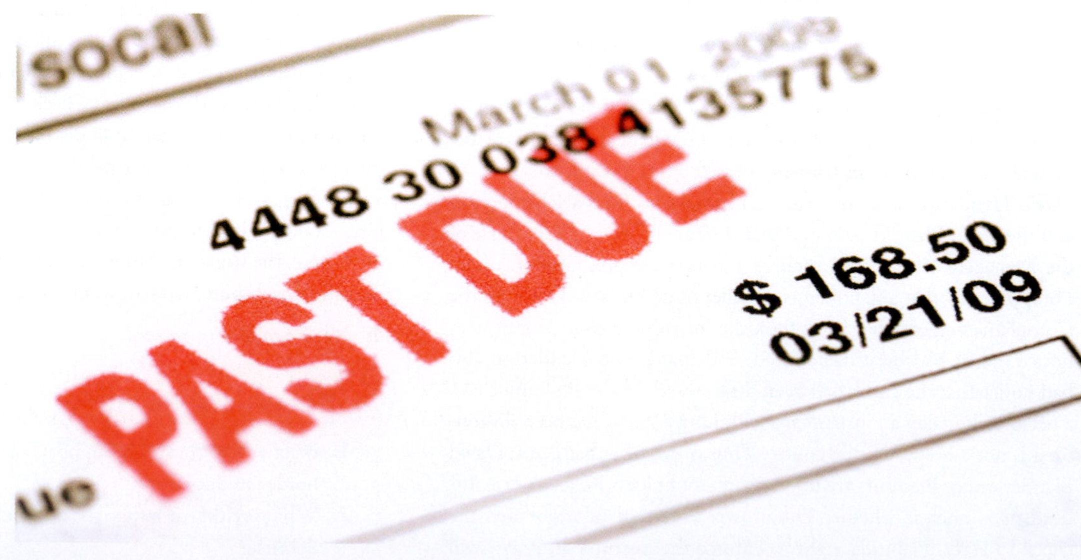

Notification is given when an instrument of purchase is overdue.

subject to Mary's defense? No. While Al, Bob, and Carl are not and were not holders in due course, they have the rights of a holder in due course. They have Tom's rights and are free of the personal defense. Mary's defense was cut off by Tom's status as a holder in due course. (See Figure 35-1.)

The shelter provision is subject to a limitation. A person who formerly held the paper cannot improve his or her position by later reacquiring it from a holder in due course. If a former holder was a party to any fraud or illegality affecting the instrument, or had notice of a defense or claim against it as a prior holder, he or she cannot claim the rights of a holder in due course by taking from a later holder in due course.

FIGURE 35-1 ■ Example for Shelter Provision

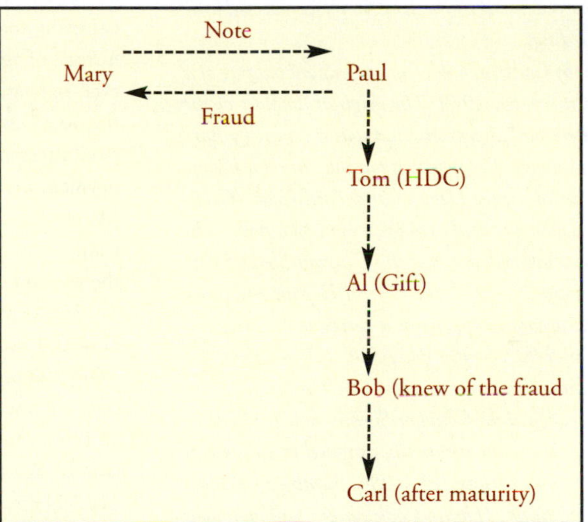

DEFENSES

7. Classifications

As discussed above, the status of being a holder or a holder in due course has a significant impact on the rights of the parties. Defenses can be successfully asserted that prevents collection from a party that could otherwise be responsible for payment.

A holder in due course takes commercial paper free from the *personal defenses* of the parties to the paper [3-305]. One who is not a holder in due course or who does not have the rights of one under the shelter provision is subject to such defenses. All transferees, including holders in due course, are subject to what are referred to as *real defenses.*

In general, real defenses relate to the existence of any obligation on the part of the person who asserts them. The most obvious real defense is forgery of the signature of the maker of a note or the drawer of a check. The person whose signature was forged has not entered into any contract, and he or she has an absolute defense even against a holder in due course. The following case presents a situation where a defense to payment is asserted.

Case

The Cadle Company v. Barbara E. Shearer and Barbara J. Couvion

COURT OF APPEALS OF MISSOURI

69 S.W. 3d 122 (2002)

Opinion by: Harold L. Lowenstein

Appellant, The Cadle Company (Cadle), the holder of a note, appeals from the grant of a directed verdict in a court-tried case in favor of the makers of the note, Barbara Shearer and Barbara Couvion. Because this court finds that Cadle made a prima facie case, the trial court's grant of a directed verdict to the defendants after plaintiff's case was against the weight of the evidence. The judgment of the trial court is reversed and remanded for further proceedings.

This case involves a suit by Cadle, as holder, on an unpaid balance of a promissory note dated September 13, 1979. The original amount of the note was $22,500, with interest at 11 percent, and was executed by Barbara Shearer and Barbara Couvion. The note was payable, in monthly installments of $232.25, to Edgar House (House) and Paul Cook (Cook) (Couvion-Shearer note). The note was used to secure a loan on a home. On September 20, 1979, House and Cook assigned the Couvion-Shearer note to Southside Bank. On January 30, 1997, the Federal Deposit Insurance Corporation (FDIC), in its corporate capacity as a successor in interest to Republic Bank of Kansas City F/K/A South Side Bank, assigned the Couvion-Shearer note to Midstates Resources Corporation (Midstates). On March 16, 2000, Midstates assigned the Couvion-Shearer note to Cadle.

Another promissory note that was eventually assigned to Cadle was executed by House and Cook on February 23, 1984, payable to Republic Bank (formerly Southside Bank) (House-Cook note). This note was secured by the Couvion-Shearer note, which had already been assigned to Southside bank in September of 1979. The FDIC also assigned the House-Cook note to Midstates, and Midstates assigned the note to Cadle. This note is mentioned because the respondents made reference to it in their brief to cast doubt upon Cadle's evidence concerning how it arrived at a balance due on the Couvion-Shearer note.

In July 2000, Cadle filed a petition seeking payment on the Couvion-Shearer note. Cadle claimed that despite its demands for payment, payments were not made in accordance with the terms of the note and that the note was considered in default. Cadle prayed for judgment in the amount of $12,716.05 with accrued interest at the rate of 11 percent. Couvion and Shearer alleged in their answer that they had made timely payments on the note and that Cadle and previous holders of the note failed and refused to timely and accurately apply the payments to the reduction of principal and interest due on the note. In fact, their answer states that the note, "is either paid in full and satisfied or very close to being paid in full and satisfied."

After Cadle presented its case, Couvion's and Shearer's counsel moved for a directed verdict, which was granted. No timely motion was made for findings or conclusions. Cadle appeals.

Cadle argues in its sole point on appeal that the trial court erred in granting defendant's motion for directed verdict at the close of Cadle's evidence because Cadle had established that it was entitled to payment on the note. Cadle claims that it made a prima facie case—in that the note, the signatures of the makers, and the balance due on the note were received in evidence.

In a suit on a promissory note, the holder makes a prima facie case by producing a note admittedly signed by the maker and showing the balance due. "Where signatures are admitted or established, production of the note entitles the holder of the note to recover on it unless the defendant establishes a defense."

In this case, the Couvion-Shearer note was received in evidence. Couvion's and Shearer's signatures appeared on the note as makers; and both parties admitted in their answer that they executed the note on September 13, 1979, and promised to pay $22,500, at 11 percent interest. All of the subsequent assignments of the note were also admitted in evidence.

Jeffrey Joseph (Joseph), an account officer for Cadle, testified that he was responsible for verifying the information that Cadle received regarding the Couvion-Shearer note and was also responsible for collection of payment. Joseph obtained from Midstates (the company that assigned the note to Cadle) a recap of their payment history of the Couvion-Shearer note. The Midstates' recap, however, indicated that the starting principal balance when it acquired the note was $13,509.46, the interest rate was 12 percent; the unpaid interest was $6,736.41 as of May 18, 1992, and the monthly payment was $232.25. The principal balance due on the note on March 16, 2000, the date it was transferred from Midstates to Cadle, was $12,716.05. Joseph prepared a summary for Cadle of the amount due on the note.

While preparing the summary, Joseph reviewed the file and the note and noticed that Midstates had been making its calculations using a 12 percent interest rate. Because the note reflected an 11 percent interest rate, Joseph recalculated the Midstates payments using an 11 percent interest rate. Joseph testified that based on his recalculations, as of trial, the amount of principal due on the note was $12,594.17, the accrued interest was $2,708.92, and the late fees were $870.75. Joseph testified that the total amount owed on the note at the time of trial was $16,173.85. The transcript of Cadle's evidence was brief. However, there seems to be no dispute that the note was held by Cadle and there was a default by the makers. The amount of the note balance was arrived at with difficulty, but the evidence did show that the note had not been paid in full. Difficulty in determining the exact amount of Cadle's damages should not have resulted in a directed verdict in favor of the makers.

Based upon the foregoing evidence, this court finds that Cadle made a prima facie case and therefore, the trial court's grant of a directed verdict was against the weight of the evidence. The trial court should have overruled the defendants' motion for directed verdict at the close of their case and requested the defendants put on their evidence. The judgment of the trial court is reversed and the cause remanded to the trial court for further proceedings.

■ *Reversed and remanded.*

CASE CONCEPTS REVIEW

1. Why does Cadle make a convincing argument?
2. What impact do the different means of calculating the amount due have on the decision? Why?

The Code generally specifies which defenses are real and which are personal. A few defenses—infancy being one—are real in some states and personal in others. Table 35-1 groups defenses according to their usual status. The basic aspects of most personal defenses are discussed in the materials on contracts in Chapters 13 through 20.

TABLE 35-1 ■ Commercial Paper: Typical Defenses

PERSONAL DEFENSES	REAL DEFENSES
Lack or failure of consideration	Unauthorized signature
Nonperformance of a condition precedent	Material alteration
Nondelivery, conditional delivery, or delivery for a special purpose	Infancy, if it is a defense to a simple contract
Payment	Lack of capacity
Slight duress	Illegality
Fraud in the inducement	Extreme duress
Theft by the holder or one through whom the holder has taken	Fraud in the execution
Violation of a restrictive indorsement	Discharge in bankruptcy
Unauthorized completion	Discharge of which the holder has notice
Other defenses to a simple contract	
Any real defense where the parry was negligent	

8. Personal Defenses

A distinction exists between *fraud in the inducement* and *fraud in the execution.* Inducement pertains to the consideration for which an instrument is given. The primary party intended to create an instrument but was fraudulently induced to do so. Such a *defense is personal* and is not available against a holder in due course. Fraud in the execution exists where a negotiable instrument is procured from a party when circumstances are such that the party does not know that he or she is giving a negotiable instrument. Fraud in the execution is a real defense [3-305(a)]. The theory is that since the party primarily to be bound has no intention of creating an instrument, none is created. Such fraud is rare because persons are usually charged with knowledge of what they sign.

Another personal defense, acquisition of title by or through a thief, is easily preventable. Conversion of bearer paper to order paper precludes its negotiation by a thief or finder.

A holder in due course is not subject to the defense of unauthorized completion of an instrument. The defense is personal. The person who left the blank space must bear the risk of wrongful completion.

Negligence of a party, frequently present in situations of fraud and material alteration, will reduce a real defense to a personal defense. A check written with a wide, blank space preceding the amount offers a wrongdoer an easy place to raise that amount. The negligent check writer reduces the defense of material alteration to a personal one. This negligence by the drawer typically means that the payor bank (drawee) does not have to recredit the drawer's account for the amount of the alteration. This bank, as a holder in due course, is free from the personal defense that resulted from the drawer's negligence.

9. Real Defenses

The *real defense* of unauthorized signature includes signatures by agents without authority and forgeries [3-401, 3-403]. It applies to indorsements as well as to the signature creating the instrument.

The most common example of a material alteration is the "raising" of a check [3-407]. A check drawn in the amount of $50 might be raised by alteration to $500. This creates a real defense to the extent of the alteration. A subsequent holder in due course could enforce the check only in the amount of its original $50.

The defense of lack of capacity is a real defense if the state law so provides. If it is a defense to a simple contract, it is a real defense [3-305]. The same is true for all forms of illegality. If a contract is merely voidable, the defense is personal; if the contract is void or unenforceable, the defense is a real one. If state law provides that usurious contracts are null and void, usury is a real defense.

EXCEPTIONS TO HOLDER-IN-DUE-COURSE STATUS

10. Introduction

The holder in due course concept was predicated on the need for commercial paper to move quickly, freely, and as "a courier without luggage" in the financial community. Negotiable instruments were intended to be the equivalent of money. Use of commercial paper was encouraged by freeing it of personal defenses if its holder is a holder in due course. Today, consumer advocates argue that protection of the consumer in credit transactions is more important than the reasons for the holder-in-due-course concept, and that all defenses should always be available to the consumer-debtor. They feel that the best protection for a consumer is the right to withhold payment if goods are defective or not delivered. The logic of this argument also has been extended to commercial credit transactions when there is a close business relationship between an original contracting party and the transferee that receives the negotiable instrument.

A number of states have enacted statutes prohibiting the use or enforcement of clauses that cut off defenses in contracts such as leases. Courts in many states have held that a holder was not a holder in due course when the finance company was closely connected with the seller. Courts have also strictly construed the application of the holder-in-due-course rule. Doubts about the negotiability of instruments have been resolved against negotiability. Several states have achieved this result by the enactment of the Uniform Consumer Credit Code, whose provisions are applicable to instruments other than checks. This code offers two alternative approaches to the problem. A state legislature can select the one it considers best suited to the needs of the state.

One alternative simply gives maximum protection to the consumer by allowing him or her to assert all claims and defenses against the assignee of any paper that he or she signed. The other alternative provides that the assignee can give written notice of the assignment to the debtor. The consumer is then given the right to assert defenses for three months. After the three-month period, the assignee is free of any defense, and the debtor's only remedy is against the seller.

11. FTC Rule

Since states were not universal in formulating exceptions to Holder-In-Due-Course status, the Federal Trade Commission (FTC), acting under its authority to prohibit unfair or deceptive methods of competition, adopted a rule that prohibits the use of the holder-in-due-course concept against consumers in credit transactions. It also provides that a clause purporting to cut off defenses is an unfair method of competition and illegal.

The FTC rule is designed to eliminate substantial abuses often inflicted on the purchaser of consumer goods. For example, assume that Carter purchases stereo equipment on credit from The Stereo Company. Carter intends to use this equipment in a personal, noncommercial manner. Carter signs a negotiable promissory note promising to pay the purchase price over a thirty-six month period. The Stereo Company then sells this note to the First National Bank. The note is properly negotiated to the Bank. Now, what would happen if the equipment did not perform as Carter expected and The Stereo Company refuses or is unable to fix the equipment? Carter likely would refuse to make further payments on the note. The First National Bank might assert its right to payment against Carter. When Carter explains that the equipment is defective, the Bank argues that it is free from this personal defense since it is holder in due course. The impact of the Bank's status is that Carter would be liable to pay for merchandise that is defective. Carter's only recourse is against The Stereo Company, which already has indicated its willingness to correct the defective equipment. Carter, the consumer debtor, is caught between the uncooperative seller and the protected holder in due course.

The FTC rule is applicable to any sale or lease of goods or services to consumers in commerce. In such a transaction, it is an unfair or deceptive act or practice for a seller to receive a credit contract that does not contain the following provision in at least 10-point bold type:

NOTICE
ANY HOLDER OF THIS CONSUMER CREDIT CONTRACT
IS SUBJECT TO ALL CLAIMS AND DEFENSES
WHICH THE DEBTOR COULD ASSERT AGAINST THE SELLER
OF GOODS OR SERVICES OBTAINED PURSUANT HERETO
OR WITH THE PROCEEDS HEREOF.

Thus the holder could not be a holder in due course because the holder agrees to be subject to all defenses.

To prevent sellers from sending buyers directly to the lender and thus circumventing the law, the rule has a special provision relating to lending institutions. It declares that it is an unfair or deceptive practice for a seller to accept in payment the proceeds of a purchase-money loan unless a similar notice is included in the loan agreement in 10-point bold type.

For the purpose of the foregoing rule, a purchase-money loan exists if the seller refers the consumer to the creditor or is affiliated with the creditor by common control, contract, or business arrangement. This means that if the lending institution regularly does business with the seller or has an understanding that its customers may obtain financing, the provision must be included in the loan contract. Again, it provides that all defenses are available to the consumer.

As a result of the FTC rule, if a consumer-purchaser has any defense against the seller, it may assert that defense against the bank or other financial institution that seeks to collect the debt. Thus, banks and other financial institutions must make sure that the seller stands behind the products sold. In addition, they must deal only with responsible parties on a recourse basis if losses are to be avoided.

12. Close Connectedness Doctrine

While the FTC rule applies only to consumer credit transactions, many arguments have been made that a similar result should occur in some commercial credit transactions. Continuing the preceding example, suppose that Carter purchased the stereo equipment for use in the reception area of a business. Are there situations when Carter, as a commercial debtor, should be free from the claims of the bank as a holder in due course?

Under a doctrine known as *close connectedness,* a transferee does not take an instrument in good faith when the transferee is so closely connected with the transferor that the transferee may be charged with knowledge of an infirmity in the underlying transaction. The rationale for the close connectedness doctrine is the basic philosophy of the holder-in-due-course concept: to encourage free negotiability of commercial paper by removing certain anxieties from one who takes the paper as an innocent purchaser, knowing no reason why the paper is not sound as its face would indicate. Therefore, the more the holder knows about the underlying transaction, and particularly the more he or she controls or participates or becomes involved in it, the less he or she fits the role of a good-faith purchaser for value. The closer the holder's relationship to the underlying agreement that is the source of the note, the less need there is for giving him or her the tension-free rights.

Among the factors that tend to establish the close connection are (1) drafting by the transferee of forms for the transferor; (2) approval of the transferor's procedures by the transferee (e.g., setting the interest rate); (3) an independent check by the transferee on the credit of the debtor; (4) heavy reliance by the transferor on the transferee (e.g., transfer by the transferor of all or substantial part of his or her paper to the transferee); and (5) common or connected ownership or management of the transferor and transferee.

Close connectedness exists also (1) when the transferee or assignee has substantial voice in, or control of, a vested interest in the underlying transaction, or (2) if the transferee has knowledge of the particular transaction or of the way the seller does business, so he or she knows of claims the buyer has against the seller. The basic question is whether the holder of the instrument is actually a party to the transaction.

As a result of the close connectedness doctrine, many courts have held that a transferee of a negotiable note does not take in "good faith" and is not a holder in due course of a note given in the sale of goods where the transferee is a finance company involved with the seller of the goods and has a pervasive knowledge of factors relating to the terms of the sale.

CHAPTER SUMMARY

STATUS OF THIRD PARTIES

Status Possibilities

1. A transferee of commercial paper may be an assignee, a holder, or a holder in due course.
2. An assignee is a transferee of a simple contract, or one to whom a negotiable instrument has not been properly negotiated.
3. A holder has a negotiable instrument that has been properly negotiated.
4. A holder that meets certain requirements is a holder in due course and takes instruments free of personal defenses.

Contract Provisions

1. Contracts often contain clauses that waive defenses in the event the contract is assigned.
2. Such clauses are illegal in some states and legal in others.
3. If legal, most states require that the assignee meet the same requirements as a holder in due course, and these states waive only personal defenses.

HOLDER IN DUE COURSE

Value

1. A holder in due course must take the instrument for value and not as a gift. A mere promise is not value, but a preexisting debt is value.

Good Faith

1. A holder in due course must take in good faith. Good faith is honesty in fact. If the holder knows that there is a defense, he or she is not a good-faith taker.

Without Notice

1. A holder in due course must take without notice that it is overdue, has been dishonored, or that there is a claim or defense to the instrument. A person has notice if he or she has actual knowledge or reason to know the fact.

Before Overdue

1. An instrument is overdue if it is demand paper and more than a reasonable length of time has passed. In the case of a check, this time period is thirty days.

Holder from a Holder in Due Course

1. A transferee from a holder in due course has the rights of a holder in due course and thus is free of personal defenses. A person may take by gift, with knowledge of a defense, or after maturity and still be able to collect on an instrument if it has passed through the hands of a holder in due course.
2. The shelter provision is not applicable to who reaquires the paper from a holder in due course.

DEFENSES

Personal Defenses

1. A personal defense is one that arises out of the transaction that created the instrument. It is generally based on the law of contracts.
2. Payment is a very important personal defense.
3. Negligence reduces a real defense to a personal defense.

Real Defenses

1. A real defense may be asserted against any party, including a holder in due course.
2. Real defenses go to the essence of the instrument. The most important real defense is forgery.

EXCEPTIONS TO HOLDER-IN-DUE-COURSE STATUS

FTC Rule

1. The FTC rule prevents the use of the holder-in-due-course concept in a consumer credit transaction.
2. In such transactions involving consumers, the contract must contain a notice in 10-point bold type informing all holders that any defense available against the seller of goods can be asserted against the holder.
3. The same notice must be contained in purchase-money loan documents.

Close Connectedness Doctrine

1. To provide nonconsumer debtors similar protection to that given to consumers under the FTC rule, some courts conclude that a transferee lacks good faith if it is closely connected to the transferor.
2. Lacking good faith, this transferee cannot qualify as a holder in due course and thus is subject to the defenses the debtor has against the original seller-transferor.

REVIEW QUESTIONS AND PROBLEMS

1. Match each term in Column A with the appropriate statement in Column B.

A	B
(1) Shelter provision	(a) May be a real defense or a personal one depending on state law
(2) Value	(b) Prohibits consumers from holder-in-due-course status
(3) Good faith	(c) Always a real defense
(4) Holder	(d) Eliminates real defenses
(5) FTC rule	(e) Allows a transferee to have the rights of a holder in due course
(6) Fraud in the execution	(f) A mere promise does not qualify as this
(7) Infancy	(g) Has possession of a negotiable instrument that has been properly negotiated
(8) Negligence	(h) Honesty in fact
(9) Assignee	(i) Holder who takes for value, in good faith and without notice of defenses
(10) Holder in due course	(j) A third person who receives the right to have a contract performed

2. Siegman, a diamond merchant, issued a note for diamonds purchased. The seller indorsed the note to a bank "as collateral for his pre-existing obligations to the banks and as collateral for the diamonds shipped to defendants." Did the bank give value so as to qualify as a holder in due course? Explain.
3. A bank received a check to deposit in Seve's account. Seve subsequently wrote checks withdrawing most of the proceeds of the deposited check. The bank paid these checks before receiving notice that the deposited check was dishonored. Does the bank qualify as a holder in due course? Explain.
4. Andrews owed Martin, his accountant, a fee for services rendered. Andrews drew a check on his bank payable to "Cash" and signed it. He left the amount blank because he was not sure of the exact amount owed. On his way to Martin's office, Andrews lost the check. Oliver found the check, filled it in for $500, and handed it to Ernest to satisfy a $500 debt that Oliver owed to Ernest. Ernest accepted the check in good faith as payment for the debt and immediately presented it to the drawee bank. The drawee bank refused to cash it because of a stop payment order. Is Andrews liable to Ernest for the $500? Why?
5. C&S Bank sued Johnson to collect a $50,000 note. Johnson had signed the note payable to Peek. Peek had transferred the note to the bank as security for a $20,000 loan. Johnson seeks to assert a defense of fraud and lack of consideration. Is the bank a holder in due course? Why or why not?

6. Nevers executed a note payable to the order of Young due on January 1, 2006. On March 1, 2006, Young negotiated the note to Glassen. Will Glassen be subject to the personal defenses of Nevers? Why?
7. Wells issued a check on its account at First National Bank payable to the order of Tayman in the amount of $4,200. Wells stopped payment on the check early the next banking day. Later that day, Tayman attempted to cash the check at First National, and when payment was refused, he took the check to his own bank, Second National, which cashed it. Is Second National a holder in due course? Why or why not?
8. Arthur purchased securities from William, giving William his check payable to William's order and drawn on Produce Bank in payment. William immediately indorsed the check to the order of Robert, and it was accepted by Robert in payment of a debt owed him by William. Robert indorsed the check in blank and delivered it to his son, Charles, as a birthday gift. Arthur has discovered that the securities sold him by William are worthless and has directed Produce Bank to stop payment. When Produce Bank refuses to pay Charles on the check and Charles sues Arthur, may Arthur assert the defense of failure of consideration against Charles? Explain.
9. Hilda executed a note payable to Home Improvements, Inc., for various improvements to her house. The company negotiated the note to a bank, which sued Hilda. If the bank is a holder in due course, can Hilda raise the defense that Home Improvements made several material misrepresentations in inducing her to sign the note? Explain.
10. Smith delivered to Janett his check drawn on National Bank payable to Janett. Janett had the check certified and delivered it to Cook as payment on account. The certification was stamped on the face of the check. It said "Certified payable as originally drawn." The original check was for $1,000. Janett had raised the amount to $4,000 prior to the certification. No one but an expert would have realized that the check had been raised. How much can Cook collect on the check? How much can the bank charge to Smith's account? Explain.

Liability of Parties to Negotiable Instruments | 36

CHAPTER OUTLINE

CHAPTER PREVIEW

The discussion in the previous two chapters is premised on the notion that one party has a valid defense to excuse nonperformance of the contract that gives rise to the commercial paper transaction. In this chapter, we examine the parties' liability for payment of the commercial paper itself. We assume there is no defense with respect to the underlying contract.

In this chapter, you will learn that a person must sign the commercial paper to be held liable for its payment. You will study the various types of liability the law imposes based on how a party signs the paper. Aspects of conditional liability and unconditional liability are discussed. One way to help simplify what may seem like complex material is to ask a series of questions: What party is expected to pay on the instrument? If that party does not pay, who else can you expect to pay? If the expected party does pay but later discovers it paid by mistake, can this party recover from any other party?

These questions are answered through the presentation of material in this chapter.

BUSINESS MANAGEMENT DECISION

You are the president of a closely held corporation that runs a retail clothing store. Your business has grown to the point where your store needs expanding and remodeling. This will cost $150,000, an amount you wish to borrow on behalf of the corporation.

How should you sign a promissory note on behalf of the corporation to avoid becoming personally liable?

LIABILITY BASED ON SIGNATURES

1. In General

A person's liability on commercial paper results from his or her signature on the instrument. The signature may be affixed as a maker, drawer, or acceptor on the face of the instrument, or it may be an indorsement on the back. Liability varies, based on the capacity of the signer. However, the signature generally must be genuine or signed by an authorized agent to impose liability on the signer. As with almost every general rule, this one is also subject to exceptions, which are discussed in Section 4.

2. Capacity of the Signature

The liability of makers of notes is different from the liability of drawers of drafts and checks, which is different from that of indorsers of commercial paper. The liability of these parties varies because of the different capacities in which they sign commercial paper. A person signing commercial paper may do so to assist or accommodate someone else. This signer may enjoy a special status insofar as liability is concerned. These various liabilities are described throughout this chapter.

Where a person signs usually indicates his/her capacity or status. Makers and drawers usually sign in the lower right-hand corner of an instrument, and indorsers sign on the back of an instrument. A drawee normally places his or her signature of acceptance on the face of the instrument, but signing the back would clearly indicate that the drawee was signing as an acceptor unless he or she could establish otherwise. When the signature does not reveal the obligation of the party who signs, the signature is an indorsement [3-402].

3. Agency Principles

The general principles of the law of agency are applicable to commercial paper. A principal is bound when a duly authorized agent signs the principal's name on commercial paper. If the agent is not authorized to sign, the principal is not bound unless the principal (1) ratifies the signature or (2) is estopped from asserting lack of authority. An agent who fails to bind his or her principal because of lack of authority will usually be personally liable to third parties.

With respect to agency principles, current Article 3 provisions make it easier for agents, regardless of how they sign an instrument, to establish that their principal should be the liable party. For example, principals that are undisclosed to the payee and subsequent holders are liable for their instruments once their existence and identity are disclosed. This liability continues regardless of how the agent signed the instrument [3-402(a)]. In another situation designed to protect the agent, Article 3 allows a person who signs in an ambiguous manner to prove, with oral testimony or other evidence, that the original party to the instrument did not intend to hold this agent liable [3-402(b)(ii)]. This opportunity for the agent to prove the lack of personal responsibility does not apply when a holder in due course takes the instrument. Finally, an agent may sign a check written on the principal's account without indicating a representative capacity. If this check contains the principal's name, the agent is not liable [3-402(c)]. This rule seems logical since the preprinted form of the check gives the payee and holders notice that an agency relationship must exist.

The general trend toward protecting agents from personal liability is illustrated in the following case.

CASE

Helmer, et al. v. Rumarson Technologies, Inc.

COURT OF APPEALS OF GEORGIA

538 S.E.2d 504 (2000)

BLACKBURN, PRESIDING JUDGE

Robert E. Helmer a/k/a Bob Helmer and Percy Helmer, Jr. appeal the trial court's orders in which it granted plaintiff Rumarson Technologies, Inc.'s (RTI) motion for summary judgment, denied the Helmers' motion for summary judgment, and awarded damages to plaintiff on the underlying suit on an account and for bad check charges. The issue presented on appeal is whether an authorized signatory on a corporate account can be held personally liable for corporate checks returned for insufficient funds. Because this issue is controlled adversely to RTI by our decision in Peterson v. Holtrachem, Inc., we reverse.

The relevant facts are not in dispute. The Helmers, as authorized signatories on the corporate account of Event Marketing, Inc., signed a check drawn on Event Marketing's account issued to RTI in the amount of $24,965. The check was dated August 14, 1998, although there was evidence presented that the check was actually signed on or around July 13, 1998. The check was dishonored at the bank due to insufficient funds. Thereafter, RTI filed the underlying complaint to collect the amount owed from the Helmers personally.

The trial court relied upon Kolodkin v. Cohen, in granting RTI's motion for summary judgment which held the Helmers personally liable on Event Marketing's check. In Kolodkin, this Court construed an earlier version of O.C.G.A. § 11-3-403. Therein, the Court found that, in 1995, an individual signing a check drawn on a business account could be personally liable if the check was not honored by the bank. However, the present case is controlled by our recent decision in Peterson, supra, which construed the 1996 amendments to the Commercial Code:

> The revised statute [O.C.G.A. § 11-3-402 (c)] has the exact opposite effect of the previous statute in that it codifies the rule that an authorized representative is not personally liable when he or she signs a negotiable instrument on behalf of the represented entity, even if the instrument does not indicate on its face that it is being signed in a representative capacity.

RTI asserts that Peterson is inapplicable because it was decided after the check was written and dishonored, and after the trial court's order. The statute, however, was amended in 1996, and it is applicable to the present case as the check was written in 1998. Furthermore, we must apply the law as it exists at the time of our judgment, not as it existed at the time of the trial court's determination. Therefore, not only does Peterson apply, it controls the outcome of this case.

The trial court erred in granting summary judgment to RTI and in denying the Helmers' motion for summary judgment.

■ *Reversed.*

CASE CONCEPTS REVIEW

1. Who is favored by the 1996 amendment?
2. Are there ways to secure personal liability for a representative of a corporation without relying on section 3-402? What avenues are available?

4. Exceptions: Impostors and Fictitious Payees

An exception to the requirement that signatures be genuine arises when an instrument is made payable to an imposter or to a fictitious person. The drawer's signature is genuine, but the instrument is indorsed in the name of the person who is being impersonated or in the fictitious name.

In the imposter situation, one person poses as someone else and induces the drawer to issue a check payable to the order of the person being impersonated. In the fictitious payee case, the person who induces the issuance of the instrument simply provides the name of the payee while never intending for this payee to have any interest in the instrument. In both cases the instrument is then indorsed in the name of the person being impersonated or the name of the fictitious payee. The indorsement in the name of the payee is effective because it was made by the person that the drawer intended to indorse, and the named payee was not intended to have an interest in the check. The loss falls on the drawer rather than on the person who took the check or the bank that honored it. Revisions to Article 3 broaden the imposter rule and holds the drawer, rather than the drawee, liable even when the check is written to a purported principal of the imposter. Thus, the imposter who is posing as an agent may provide an effective indorsement even though it is unauthorized [3-404(a)]. If the check is intended for the party named but is diverted and forged by an employee, the indorsement is not effective because the instrument is not indorsed by the party intended by the drawer. This covers two factual situations. First, the imposter rule placing liability on the drawer does not apply if the imposter acts as an agent and has the check made payable to the principal. Second, the fictitious payee rule does not apply if the drawer's employee steals the check after it has been intended for the payee's benefit. In both of these situations, the liability would initially be on the drawee who accepted the forged indorsement.

A typical fictitious payee case involves a dishonest employee authorized to sign his employer's name to checks, or one who draws checks that he presents to his employer for the latter's signature. Thus, the employee may draw payroll checks or checks payable to persons with whom the employer would be expected to do business. He either signs the checks or obtains his employer's signature and then cashes the checks, indorsing the name of the payee. If he is in charge of the company's books, he is able to manipulate the books when the canceled checks are returned and may thus avoid detection. The Code imposes this loss on the employer; the dishonest employee can effectively indorse in the payee's name. Under the revised fictitious payee rule, the indorsement needs to be substantially similar to the name of the payee on the instrument [3-405 (c)]. The original Article 3 requires an indorsement that exactly matches the payee's name. A second change with the fictitious payee rule concerns an expansion of the rule to cover a broader range of activities by a fraudulent employee. For example, an employee of the drawer who steals a check that the drawer actually intended for the named payee can provide an indorsement, effectively shifting the loss to the employer/drawer and away from the drawee [3-405(a) and (b)].

5. Classification of Parties

For the purposes of liability, the Code divides the parties to commercial paper into two groups—primary parties and secondary parties. The classification of the parties is based on how they signed the paper. The capacity in which the party signed determines how that party is classified. The **primary parties** are the makers of notes and acceptors of drafts. These parties have incurred a definite obligation to pay and are the parties who, in the normal course of events, will actually pay the instrument. The acceptor of a draft normally is the drawee. Thus, the payor banks of checks are primary parties.

Primary party
The one that all other parties expect to pay the maker of a note and the acceptor of a draft

Secondary party
Drawers of drafts and endorsers, persons who expect the primary party to pay but become liable if the primary party does not pay and certain conditions are met

The **secondary parties** are drawers of drafts, drawers of checks, and indorsers of any instrument. These parties do not expect to pay the instrument but assume, rather, that the primary parties will fulfill their obligations. The drawer and indorsers expect that the acceptor will pay the draft. The indorsers of a note expect that the maker will pay when the note matures. Drawers and indorsers have a responsibility to pay if the primary parties do not, *provided* that certain conditions precedent are satisfied. The drawer and the indorser are, in effect, saying that they will pay if the primary party (acceptor or maker) does not, but only if the party entitled to payment has made proper demand on the primary party and due notice of the primary party's dishonor of the instrument has then been given to the secondary parties [3-413(2), 3-414(1)]. These conditions are described in detail in Sections 7 through 12. A more thorough discussion of the liability of secondary parties is presented in Sections 15 through 20.

6. Liability of Primary Parties

A primary party engages that he or she will pay the instrument according to its terms. The maker thus assumes an obligation to pay the note as it was worded at the time he or she executed it. The acceptor assumes responsibility for the draft as it was worded when he or she gave acceptance [3-413(1)].

If a maker signs an incomplete note, when the note is completed—even though the completion is unauthorized—it can be enforced against the maker by a holder in due course. On the other hand, if an instrument is materially altered after it is made, the maker has a real defense in the absence of negligence. The maker confirms to all subsequent parties the existence of the payee and the payee's capacity to indorse [3-413(3)].

Acceptance
The written commitment that an instrument will be paid upon the holder's request for payment

The drawee of a check or draft is not liable on the instrument until **acceptance**. Upon acceptance, the acceptor is primarily liable. An acceptance must be in writing on the draft and signed by the drawee-acceptor [3-410(1)]. Acceptance is usually made by the drawee's writing or stamping the word accepted, with the name and the date, across the face of the instrument. The usual means for accepting a check is to have it certified.

A party presenting a draft for acceptance is entitled to an unqualified acceptance by the drawee. Thus, when the drawee offers an acceptance that in any manner varies or changes the direct order to pay or accept, the holder may refuse the acceptance [3-412(1)]. The paper is dishonored; and upon notice of dishonor or protest, the holder may hold responsible all prior parties on the paper—back to, and including, the drawer.

You should understand that most checks are paid directly rather than be accepted first. Typically, the collection process results in the payor bank making final payment. Sometimes the payee or other holder of a check might not want payment but does want an assurance that payment will be made later. Sellers in transactions involving large dollar amounts may request acceptance, rather than payments, before completing a delivery to the buyers.

CONDITIONAL LIABILITY

7. Introduction

The term *conditional liability* is used to describe the secondary liability that results from the status of parties as drawers or indorsers. The adjective *conditional* refers to the fact that certain conditions precedent must be fulfilled to establish liability. The conditions precedents are *presentment, dishonor, notice of dishonor,* and in some instances *protest.* The importance of exact compliance with the conditions precedent cannot be overemphasized. Failure to comply may result in the discharge of the secondary parties.

8. Presentment: In General

Presentment
The demand for payment or acceptance made on the primary party by a holder of an instrument

Presentment is a demand made on a maker or drawee [3-501(a)]. In relation to a note, it is a demand for payment made by the holder on the maker. In the case of a draft, it may be either a demand for acceptance or a demand for payment.

The drawee of a draft is not bound on the instrument as a primary party until acceptance. The holder will usually wait until maturity and present the draft to the drawee for payment, but the holder may present it to the drawee for acceptance before maturity to give credit to the instrument during the period of its term. The drawee is under no legal duty to the holder to accept. If the acceptance is refused, the draft must be presented for payment. If dishonor occurs, liability may be passed to the indorsers and the drawer upon proper notice of dishonor.

In most instances, it is not necessary to present an instrument for acceptance. Presentment for payment alone is usually sufficient, but presentment for acceptance must be made to charge the drawer and indorsers of some drafts. For example, if the date of payment depends on presentment, as in the case of a draft payable after sight, presentment for acceptance is required to fix the maturity date of the instrument.

9. Presentment: How and Where

Presentment may be made by personally contacting the primary party and making a demand for acceptance or payment. Presentment may be made by mail or through a clearinghouse [3-501(a)]. Presentment by mail or by electronic means is effective when received [3-501(b)(1)]. If the instrument specifies the place of acceptance or payment, presentment is made there. If no place is specified, presentment may be made at the place of business of the party to accept or to pay. Presentment is excused if neither the party to accept or pay nor anyone authorized to act for him or her is present or accessible at such place. A draft accepted or a note made payable at a bank in the United States must be presented at that bank. Presentment of a check to the data processing center of the payor bank is effective if the records are maintained at the center. This is important when a bank has several branches.

To balance the liberal attitude regarding what will suffice as a presentment, Section 3-505(b)(2) empowers the party on whom presentment is made to require:

1. Exhibition of the instrument
2. Reasonable identification of the person making presentment
3. Evidence of authority if presentment is made for another
4. Production of the instrument at a place specified in it or (if none is specified) at any reasonable place
5. A signed receipt on the instrument for any partial or full payment and its surrender upon full payment

If the primary party does not avail himself or herself of these rights, the presentment is perfectly valid, no matter how or where the presentment is made. If the primary party does require proper presentment, a failure to comply invalidates the presentment, but the instrument is not dishonored. The requirement of identification of the presenting party applies to bearer paper as well as order paper [3-501].

In the interesting case that follows the court is asked to consider the propriety of a bank requiring a thumbprint as a means of identification.

CASE

Jeff E. Messing v. Bank of America, N.A.

COURT OF APPEALS OF MARYLAND

821 A.2d 22 (2003)

This arises from Petitioner's irritation with the Bank of America's Thumbprint Signature Program. Under the Thumbprint Signature Program, a bank requests non-customer presenters of checks over the counter to place an "inkless" thumbprint or fingerprint on the face of the check as part of the identification process.

At some point in time prior to 3 August 2000, Petitioner, as a holder, came into possession of a check in the amount of Nine Hundred Seventy-Six Dollars ($976.00) from Toyson J. Burruss, the drawer, doing business as Prestige Auto Detail Center. Instead of depositing the check into his account at his own bank, Petitioner elected to present the check for payment at a branch of Mr. Burruss' bank, Bank of America, the drawee. On 3 August 2000, Petitioner approached a teller at Bank of America's 10 Light Street Banking Center in Baltimore City and asked to cash the check. The teller, by use of a computer, confirmed the availability of funds on deposit, and placed the check into the computer's printer slot. The computer stamped certain data on the back of the check, including the time, date, amount of the check, account number, and teller number. The computer also effected a hold on the amount of $976.00 in the customer's account. The teller gave the check back to the Petitioner, who endorsed it. The teller then asked for Petitioner's identification. Petitioner presented his driver's license and a major credit card. The teller took the endorsed check from Petitioner and manually inscribed the driver's license information and certain credit card information on the back of the check.

At some point during the transaction, the teller counted out $976.00 in cash from her drawer in anticipation of completing the transaction. She asked if the Petitioner was a customer of Bank of America. The Petitioner stated that he was not. The teller returned the check to Petitioner and requested, consistent with bank policy when cashing checks for non-customers, that Petitioner place his thumbprint on the check. Petitioner refused and the teller informed him that she would be unable to complete the transaction without his thumbprint.

Petitioner requested, and was referred to, the branch manager. Petitioner presented the check to the branch manager and demanded that the check be cashed notwithstanding Petitioner's refusal to place his thumbprint on the check. The branch manager examined the check and returned it to the Petitioner, informing him that, because Petitioner was a non-customer, Bank of America would not cash the check without Petitioner's thumbprint on the instrument. After some additional exchanges, Petitioner left the bank with the check in his possession. The branch manager advised the teller that Petitioner had left the bank with his check. In response, the teller released the hold on the customer's funds, voided the transaction in the computer, and placed the cash back in her teller drawer.

On 15 November 2000, the Bank filed a Motion to Dismiss or, in the alternative, for Summary Judgment. Petitioner opposed the Bank's Motion and filed a "cross" Motion for Summary Judgment. After the Circuit Court heard oral arguments on the pending motions, it denied Petitioner's request for injunctive relief and entered summary judgment in favor of the Bank, dismissing the Complaint with prejudice. Petitioner appealed on 17 January 2001. The Court of Special Appeals concluded that the Circuit Court's decision in favor of the Bank was legally correct.

We now turn to the issue of whether the Bank's refusal to accept the check as presented constituted dishonor under § 3-501 and § 3-502 as Petitioner contends. The reason that § 3-502(b)(2) potentially is relevant to the case is because of § 3-501(b)(2) and (3), which state:

> (2) Upon demand of the person to whom presentment is made, the person making presentment must (i) exhibit the instrument, (ii) give reasonable identification and, if presentment is made on behalf of another person reasonable evidence of authority to do so, and (iii) sign a receipt on the instrument for any payment made or surrender the instrument if full payment is made.
>
> (3) Without dishonoring the instrument, the party to whom presentment is made may (i) return the instrument for lack of a necessary indorsement, or (ii) refuse payment or acceptance for failure of the presentment to comply with the terms of the instrument, an agreement of the parties, or other applicable law or rule.

The question is whether requiring a thumbprint constitutes a request for "reasonable identification" under § 3-501(b)(2)(ii). If it is "reasonable," then under § 3-501(b)(3)(ii) the refusal of the Bank to accept the check from Petitioner did not constitute dishonor. If, however, requiring a thumbprint is not "reasonable" under § 3-501(b)(2)(ii), then the refusal to accept the check may constitute dishonor under § 3-502(b)(2). The issue of dishonor is arguably relevant because Petitioner has no cause of action against any party, including the drawer, until the check is dishonored.

Nowhere does the language of C.L. § 3-501(b)(2) suggest that "reasonable identification" is limited to information [Respondent] can authenticate at the time presentment is made. Rather, all that is required is that the "person making presentment must ... give reasonable identification." C.L. § 3-501(b)(2). While providing a thumbprint signature does not necessarily confirm identification of the checkholder at

continued

presentment—unless of course the drawee bank has a duplicate thumbprint signature on file—it does assist in the identification of the checkholder should the check later prove to be bad. It therefore serves as a powerful deterrent to those who might otherwise attempt to pass a bad check. That one method provides identification at the time of presentment and the other identification after the check may have been honored, does not prevent the latter from being "reasonable identification" for purposes of C.L. § 3-501(b)(2).

In short, when a bank cashes a check over the counter, it assumes the risk that it may suffer losses for counterfeit documents, forged endorsements, or forged or altered checks. Nothing in the Commercial Law Article forces a bank to assume such risks. To the extent that banks are willing to cash checks over the counter, with reasonable identification, such willingness expands and facilitates the commercial activities within the State.

Because the reduction of risk promotes the expansion of commercial practices, we believe that the direction of § 1-102(2)(b) requires that we conclude that a bank's requirement of a thumbprint placed upon a check presented over the counter by a non-customer is reasonable. As the intermediate appellate court well documented, the Thumbprint Program is part of an industry wide response to the growing threat of check fraud. Prohibiting banks from taking reasonable steps to protect themselves from losses could result in banks refusing to cash checks of non-customers presented over the counter at all, a result which would be counter to the direction of § 1-102(2)(b).

As a result of this conclusion, Bank of America in the present case did not dishonor the check when it refused to accept it over the counter. Under § 3-501 (b)(3)(ii), Bank of America "refused payment or acceptance for failure of the presentment to comply with ... other applicable law or rule." The rule not complied with by the Petitioner-presenter was § 3-502(b)(2)(ii), in that he refused to give what we have determined to be reasonable identification. Therefore, there was no dishonor of the check by Bank of America's refusal to accept it.

■ *Affirmed.*

CASE CONCEPTS REVIEW

1. Do you agree that requiring a thumbprint is a reasonable manner of identification?
2. Why did the court find that the bank did not dishonor the check?

10. Presentment: When

There is no explicit provision requiring presentment to be made with a stated time period. However, with respect to discharging the indorser's contract, a reference to presentment within thirty days is discussed later. The timing for a bank to give an effective notice of dishonor continues to be within the applicable midnight deadline [3-503(c)(i)]. However, non-banking entities have thirty days to give notice of dishonor rather than the original three business days [3-503(c)(ii)].

Dishonor

The primary party's refusal to make payment or grant acceptance within the allocated time after presentment is properly made by a holder

11. Dishonor

The party who presents an instrument is entitled to have the instrument paid or accepted. If the party to whom the instrument is presented refuses to pay or accept, the instrument is **dishonored**

Presentment has no explicit provision requiring it to be made with a stated time period.

[3-502]. The timing of the primary party's response to a presentment becomes crucial in determining whether dishonor occurs.

When a draft is presented to the drawee for *acceptance,* the drawee may wish to ascertain some facts from the drawer before assuming the obligation of an acceptor. As a result, the law allows the drawee to defer acceptance until the close of the next business day following presentment [3-502(b)]. If the drawee needs more time within which to obtain information, the holder can give the drawee one additional business day within which to accept. The secondary parties are not discharged by the one-day postponement. The holder who presents the draft for *acceptance* is seeking the drawee's obligation on the paper and will not receive payment until a later date. For this reason, the Code permits a longer period of time within which to accept a draft than is allowed when the draft is presented for payment.

When an instrument is presented for *payment,* the party to whom presentment is made is allowed a reasonable time to examine the instrument, to determine whether the instrument is properly payable; but payment must be made in any event on the same day that it is presented and before the close of business on that day. With respect to checks, the use of the word payment on the day of the presentment must include a provisional payment or settlement that can be revoked within the payor bank's midnight deadline [4-302(a)]. If this provisional payment is not made by the payor bank on the day of presentment or if the bank revokes such a payment within its midnight deadline, a dishonor of the check occurs.

12. Notice of Dishonor

When an instrument has been dishonored on proper presentment, the holder must give prompt **notice of the dishonor** to have a right of recourse against secondary parties [3-503].

Notice of dishonor

Notification that the primary party has dishonored the instrument by refusing payment or acceptance, whichever one was requested upon presentment

The timing for the delivery of an effective notice of dishonor is of the utmost importance. Except for banks, notice must be given within thirty days after dishonor [3-503(c)].

Banks must give any necessary notice before the bank's "midnight deadline"—before midnight of the next banking day following the day on which a bank receives the notice of dishonor [3-503(c)]. Notice may be given in any reasonable manner, including oral notice, notice by telephone, notice by mail, and notice by e-mail.

13. Protest

Protest is a certificate stating the following: An instrument was presented for payment or acceptance; it was dishonored; and the reasons, if any, given for refusal to accept or pay [3-505(b)]. It is a formal method for satisfying the conditions precedent and is required only for drafts that are drawn or payable outside the United States. The protest requirement is in conformity with foreign law in this respect. In other cases, protest is optional with the holder. Protest serves as evidence that presentment was made, dishonor occurred, and notice of dishonor was given. It creates a presumption that the conditions precedent was satisfied.

LIABILITY OF SECONDARY PARTIES

14. Introduction

So far in this chapter, we have studied which parties are classified as having secondary liability, and we have examined the conditions that generally must be satisfied to hold these secondary parties liable. In the following six sections, we will refine our understanding of the liability of the parties on commercial paper. After reading these sections, you should feel comfortable determining which parties are liable if the primary party does not pay the instrument and which parties are liable if the primary party pays by mistake.

15. Accommodation Parties

One who signs an instrument for the purpose of lending his or her name and credit to another party to an instrument is an *accommodated party* [3-419]. He or she may sign as an indorser, maker, or acceptor or as a co-maker or co-acceptor. The accommodation party is liable in the capacity in which he or she signed. As an indorser, the accommodation party does not indorse for the purpose of transferring the paper, but rather to lend security to it.

Since any party, including a co-maker, may be an accommodation party, and accommodation parties are treated somewhat differently from other parties, issues as to the status of a party frequently arise. The intention of parties is the significant element in determining whether one who signs a note is an accommodation party or a principal maker. The primary factors to be considered in determining the intent of the parties are (1) whether or not the proceeds of the instrument are received by the party, and (2) whether the signature was required as a condition of the loan. If the party did not receive the proceeds but the creditor demanded the signature as a condition for the loan, the party signing is an accommodation party. Whether the signature is as a co-maker or indorser, it should be recognized that the liability of an accommodation party is supported by the consideration that flows from the creditor to the principal debtor; the fact that no consideration flowed directly to the accommodation party is no defense. Lack of benefit to a party does tend to show the status of the party, however.

Suretyship

The legal relationship whereby one person becomes a surety for the benefit of the creditor and debtor

Surety

A person who agrees to become liable to the creditor for the debtor's obligation in the event the debtor fails to perform as promised

The significance of being an accommodation party is found in the law of **suretyship**. An accommodation party is a **surety**. In some situations a surety is entitled to a discharge from liability where other parties are not. The right to discharge may be asserted against one who is not a holder in due course. Sureties have a right of contribution from co-sureties. Sureties are not liable to the party accommodated. If a surety is required to pay, he or she can obtain reimbursement from the accommodated party.

16. Guarantors

The liability of an accommodation party arises without express words. A guarantor's liability is based on words of guaranty. If the words *payment guaranteed* or their equivalent are added to a signature, the signer engages that if the instrument is not paid when due, he or she will pay it without previous resort by the holder to other parties on the paper. If the words *collection guaranteed* are added to a signature, the signer becomes liable only after the holder has reduced a claim against the maker or acceptor to judgment, and execution has been returned unsatisfied, or after the maker or acceptor has become insolvent or it is otherwise apparent that it is useless to proceed against him or her.

A guarantor differs from other types of secondary parties in that the guarantor's liability is based on the primary party's failure to pay alone. The conditions precedent of presentment and notice of dishonor being given within reasonable times do not have to be satisfied to hold the guarantor liable on the guaranty.

17. Drawers

While drawers are secondary parties in the sense that they expect their drawees to pay, it is accurate to state that generally a drawer is going to be liable to pay if the drawee refuses to pay a properly drawn draft. There are two reasons that support this conclusion. First, most drawers are parties to the underlying contract that gives rise to the commercial paper. For example, if a buyer writes a check in payment for the goods or services received and the check is dishonored, that buyer remains liable to pay since such payment is the performance due under the sales or service contract.

A second reason that drawers generally are liable when their drafts are dishonored concerns the application of the UCC provisions. Under Article 3, anytime a person signs a negotiable draft (such as a check) as a drawer, that party implicitly makes a promise. This promise is known as the **drawer's contract**. By his or her signature, the drawer has committed to pay the draft if presentment is properly made, dishonor occurs, and notice of dishonor is timely given [3-414]. A certificate of protest can substitute for proof that these conditions have occurred.

Drawer's contract

The implicit promise that is made when the drawer signs a negotiable draft and states that the drawer generally will pay the amount of the instrument if the drawee dishonors it

For the purposes of this drawer's contract, presentment must be made within thirty days of the draft's issuance. The notice of dishonor is timely if it is delivered by a bank within its midnight deadline or by any other party before midnight of the third business day after dishonor occurred or that party received the notice of dishonor [3-503(c)]. These timely requirements make it appear that the drawer is discharged of liability under the drawer's contract if either presentment or notice of dishonor is delayed beyond these reasonable periods. However, this discharge occurs only if the delay in presentment or in delivery of notice of dishonor causes the drawer to lose money due to the drawee's insolvency. Since payor banks seldom become insolvent and federal insurance protects the bank's customers in the event of such insolvency, a drawer of a check is likely to remain liable on the check even if there is an unreasonable delay in presentment or notice of dishonor being given. Therefore, while the UCC classifies the drawer as a secondary party, in reality the drawer's liability for checks is very similar to that of a primary party.

18. Indorsers

CONDITIONAL LIABILITY An indorser of a note, certificate of deposit, draft, or check implicitly creates a contract of liability by the indorsement. Like that of the drawer, this **indorser's contract** is based on the conditional liability of the indorser as a secondary party. In essence, by indorsing a negotiable instrument, the indorser is saying, "I will pay if this instrument is properly presented, dishonored, and notice of dishonor is timely given" [3-414(a)].

Indorser's contract

The implicit promise that an indorser makes to pay the instrument if certain conditions are satisfied

The relevant time period for presentment (or furtherance of the collection process) is within a reasonable time after the indorsement. The time period allowed for a proper delivery of notice of dishonor is the same as provided in the drawer's contract (midnight deadline for banks; thirty days for other parties). In contrast with the drawer, if either the presentment or notice of dishonor is unreasonably delayed, the indorser is relieved of all liability on the instrument.

> EXAMPLE David signs a $50 check payable to Paula. This check is in payment for Paula letting David use her car during the past weekend. Paula indorses the check to Terry in payment for Terry giving Paula a ride to an out-of-town concert. Terry keeps the check for two months before depositing it. When this check is presented, through the collection process, to David's bank, it is dishonored because David's account has insufficient funds. If notice of dishonor is appropriately given to all the banks in the collection process and if Terry's depositary bank gives Terry timely notice of dishonor, can Terry collect from Paula on her indorser's contract? The answer is no. Terry's unreasonable delay in making presentment or in initiating the collection process by depositing the check discharges Paula, as an indorser, from further liability on the check. Note: Terry can collect from David because the delay in presentment (and possible delay in

delivering notice of dishonor) does not relieve David of liability. The payor bank was not insolvent in this example; hence, David has not lost any money due to Terry's delays.

Suppose that, in this preceding example, there had been a number of indorsers. In essence, because the collection process may involve several banks, there probably are numerous indorsers. Indorsers are liable in the order of their indorsements. An indorser who is required to pay the instrument will seek recovery from the preceding indorser. One indorser in the chain of negotiation may fail to deliver notice of dishonor to the preceding indorser within a reasonable time period. This indorser may still recover if he can show that notice of dishonor was received by the preceding indorser from another source. Proper notice operates for the benefit of all parties who have rights on the instrument against the party notified [3-503(b)]. Thus, it is necessary to notify a party only once for his or her liability to be fixed. Assume that A, B, C, and D are indorsers in that order.

- Holder gives notice to A and C only.
- C will not be required to give additional notice to A.
- If C is compelled to pay, C would have recourse against A.
- B and D are discharged if they are not notified by the holder or one of the indorsers.

WITHOUT RECOURSE The conditional liability of indorsers can be disclaimed if they indorse the negotiable instrument with the words *without recourse* [3-414(e)]. These words are interpreted to mean that even if the instrument is dishonored upon proper presentment and timely notice of dishonor is delivered, the indorser cannot be held liable to pay the instrument. The holder of the unpaid instrument then can attempt to hold another secondary party liable. Such a party might be an indorser who did not sign *without recourse* or the drawer.

Perhaps you are asking yourself, as a potential holder of the instrument, what good is it to have an indorsement which is qualified by the phrase *without recourse?* The answer is presented in the next subsection.

UNCONDITIONAL LIABILITY In addition to having conditional liability, all indorsers become unconditionally liable to pay the indorsed instrument under certain circumstances. This unconditional nature of the indorser's liability is designed to assist in allocating losses when a primary party pays an instrument by mistake. The following situations are covered by the indorser's unconditional liability:

1. A primary party pays an instrument that contains a forged indorsement.
2. A primary party pays an instrument that contains a forged maker's or drawer's signature.
3. A primary party pays an instrument that has been materially altered.

By indorsing the instrument, the indorser makes certain warranties. The existence of specific warranties depends on whether the party receiving the instrument is the primary party or simply another holder who is assisting in the collection process. The five warranties made to a transferee who is not the payor are called "Transfer Warranties" [3-416]. The three warranties made to obtain presentment of the instrument for payment are known as "Presentment Warranties" [3-417]. Similar sets of warranties are a part of Article 4 [4-207 and 4-208].

The reason for distinguishing between these two sets of warranties, depending on the status of the recipient, can best be explained by examining which parties to the commercial paper should be liable if the instrument contains a forgery. A discussion of situations 1 and 2 in the preceding list is presented in detail in Sections 20 and 21. Prior to turning to that material, some additional points about these warranties need to be addressed.

In addition to separating the warranties based on to whom they are made, Article 3 also provides three general rules regarding these warranties. First, the three *presentment warranties* (rights to enforce the instrument, no alteration, and no knowledge of the drawer's signature being forged) are made only to the drawee of an unaccepted draft. If a holder is seeking payment from (1) an indorser or the drawer of a dishonored draft or (2) a maker of a note, that holder warrants only that he or she has the right to enforce the instrument [3-417(d)]. The warranties of no alteration and no knowledge of the drawer's or maker's signature being forged are viewed as unnecessary to protect these paying parties. They should have as much, if not more, knowledge and ability to detect alterations and forged signatures as the holder seeking payment.

Second, any party (whether a transferee or a payor) asserting a claim for breach of warranty must have provided notice of such a claim within thirty days of learning of the breach [3-416(c) and 3-417(e)].

Third, the qualified indorsement made with the phrase *without recourse* has no impact whatsoever on the warranties made by the indorser of a check [3-416(c) and 3-417(e)]. The removal of this type of indorsement having any impact on the warranties allows banks in the collection process to rely on these warranties in passing liability to the wrongdoer or at least to the party who dealt with the wrongdoer.

19. Transferors without Indorsement

In the preceding subsection, our discussion was limited to warranties made by indorsers. In fact, these warranties arise whenever there is a transfer of an instrument. Even when bearer paper is negotiated by delivery alone, warranties are given by the transferor to the transferee. They are the same warranties an unqualified indorser makes, except that the warranties run only to the immediate transferee whereas the indorser's warranties extend to all subsequent holders.

20. Forgeries

Now we return to two situations in which the primary party has paid an instrument by mistake. When the mistake is based on the unauthorized signature of the drawer or of an indorser, the primary party once again looks to the warranties discussed in the preceding two sections.

Forgery

False writing or alteration of an instrument with the fraudulent intent of deceiving and injuring another, writing another's name on a check without consent

Banks have a special problem in connection with **forgeries**. Checks presented to payor banks for payment may bear forged signatures of drawers or forged indorsements. If the drawer's signature is forged, the bank that honors the check has not followed the order of the drawer and cannot charge the account. If charged, it must be recredited. Likewise, the bank will have to make restitution to the party whose name was forged on the check as an indorsement. In either case, the loss initially is that of the bank that pays the instrument bearing the forgery.

In the case of a *forged drawer's signature*, the payor bank as a general rule cannot collect payment from the party who received the payment. This party simply warranted that he or she had no knowledge of the drawer's signature being forged. Assuming this party had no actual knowledge of the forgery, there is no breach of the warranty. The bank has the signature of the drawer on file and is charged with knowledge of the forgers. This general rule is subject to the exception that if the party receiving payment is the forger or dealt with the forger and was negligent in doing so, the payor may recover the payment. Thus, if a collecting bank was negligent, the payor bank that paid on a forged drawer's signature could recover from the collecting bank.

A payor bank that pays on a *forged indorsement* has greater rights in seeking to recover the payment than does the payor who pays on a forged drawer's signature. In the case of a forged indorsement, the payor has no way of knowing about the forgery, and thus it can collect from the person to whom payment was made, who in turn can collect from all prior parties back to the forger. The following case illustrates how banks utilize the warranties made within the collection process in the event that the instrument contains a forgery.

CASE

E.S.P., Inc. v. Midway National Bank

447 N.W.2d 882 (Minn. 1989)

KELLEY, J.

Barr and Nelson, Inc. maintained a checking account with Midway. On February 3, 1981, Barr and Nelson, Inc. issued a check for $30,000 payable to Mechanical Constructors and E.S.P. Heating as joint payees. That same day Mechanical Constructors deposited the check into its First Bank account. At the time of deposit, E.S.P., Inc.'s endorsement had apparently been forged on the back of the check. E.S.P., Inc.'s share of the $30,000 check was $17,600. On February 6, 1981, First Bank received payment of the $30,000 from Midway. E.S.P., Inc. claims it never received its portion of the proceeds.

More than four years later, on February 25, 1985, E.S.P., Inc. sent to Midway an affidavit of forgery. Upon receipt, Midway notified First Bank of the forgers claim and requested that First Bank remit to Midway the $17,600 claimed by E.S.P., Inc. First Bank disclaimed responsibility and failed to remit.

Nearly six years after Midway paid the check, on January 30, 1987, E.S.P., Inc. commenced this action against Midway. Its claim is based upon conversion under Minn. Stat. § 336.3-419(1)(c)(1988). Under Minnesota law, E.S.P., Inc. is prevented from suing First Bank directly even though First Bank was that bank which collected the check without verifying the endorsements. Minn. Stat. §336.3-419(3)(1988) provides a depositary or collecting bank with defenses in a direct suit by a payee; it does, however, permit a payee, such as E.S.P., Inc., to sue the payor bank for conversion because it converted the check when it paid on a forged endorsement.

Although Midway, as payor bank, may be liable for conversion, it, in turn, may look to First Bank, the collecting and depositary bank, for restitution. The warranty of good title automatically arises as part of the interbank collection process. All banks in the collection chain are liable if that warranty is breached, but only the initial collecting or depositary bank has a duty to check endorsements. The purpose underlying the rule is to place the loss upon the party who last dealt with the wrongdoer. This party is best able to prevent the conversion by carefully checking endorsements. Therefore, First Bank, as the result of the warranty of title arising under Minn. Stat. § 336.4-207(1)(a), ultimately would be liable to Midway, the payor bank.

Because the Uniform Commercial Code places that ultimate responsibility for E.S.P., Inc.'s loss on First Bank, Midway served upon First Bank this third-party action. In reply, First Bank argues that Midway's action is barred by the statute of limitations because it was commenced more than six years after the statutory warranty was breached.

The question in this case is when the six-year limitation period commences to run. First Bank argues that Midway's claim is for a breach of warranty and, therefore, the statute commenced to run at the time of the breach (February 6, 1981). In contrast, Midway argues that its action is for indemnity for the loss it may sustain as the result of First Bank's breach of statutory warranty of title. Because limitation statutes generally commence to run on indemnity claims at the time the indemnitee sustained a loss, and since Midway sustains no loss until it is compelled to pay E.S.P., Inc., the statute has not yet commenced to run. Accordingly, Midway asserts, its third party action is timely.

Both the trial court, when it granted First Bank summary judgment, and the court of appeals, when it affirmed that judgment, rejected Midway's argument. Both courts concluded that Midway's third-party action was premised on the breach of warranty, which, if it occurred at all, took place six years and six days before institution of this third-party action against First Bank.

The court of appeals opined that Midway received from E.S.P., Inc. in 1985 an affidavit of forgery and was put on notice of the potential claim, after which it could have commenced a declaratory judgment action against First Bank. Because it did not do so, the majority implied that Midway cannot now complain if the six-year statute is now applied to bar its claim. To require a payor bank, such as Midway, to commence suit before it has suffered a loss each time it receives an affidavit of forgery, although suit ultimately may never be brought against the bank for conversion, would create an intolerable burden on banks. Not only would such a requirement be burdensome on payor banks, but also other banks as well in the collection chain that have not at the time of receiving the notice sustained a loss, or who may never sustain one as a result of the forged endorsement. It is likewise burdensome on the judicial system itself by imposing on it the processing of "litigation" which may never ripen into a case or controversy capable of judicial resolution. To employ a colloquialism, a rule requiring banks in the collection chain to take such precipitate action would be somewhat akin to "putting the cart before the horse." This we decline to do.

We hold that the payor bank who seeks indemnity from the collecting and depositary bank is not barred by the statute of limitations because the statute on that claim does not commence running until the payor bank has sustained loss.

In doing so, however, we emphasize the narrow application of today's holding. It is limited to actions by payor banks, or other banks in the collection chain, for indemnity arising from the breach of the warranty of title under the Uniform Commercial Code, and is specifically designed to further a major purpose of that code—the development of consistent and commercially reasonable rules of law to govern commercial transactions.

■ *Reversed and remanded.*

CASE CONCEPTS REVIEW

1. Which party was the customer-depositor of Midway National Bank?
2. To whom did Barr and Nelson, Inc. write a $30,000 check?
3. Whose indorsement on this check is allegedly forged?
4. What bank is the depositary bank that assisted in the collection of this check with the forged indorsement?
5. Why does E.S.P., Inc sue the Midway Bank, as the payor bank, instead of the depositary bank?

21. Double Forgeries

Assume that a drawer's signature is forged and that there is no indorsement by the payee or that the payee's indorsement is also forged. Which party bears the loss if the check is paid by the drawee bank? If the rule applicable to forged drawer's signature is followed, the drawee bears the loss because of the prescription that it is familiar with the drawer's signature. If the loss allocation scheme for a check with a forged indorsement is followed, the loss would be on the party who dealt with the forger because that party was in the best position to notice the flaw in the indorsement and to verify the identity of the person forging the indorsement.

The courts that have faced this conflict have resolved it in favor of placing the loss on the drawee bank. A check bearing a double forgery is treated like a check bearing only a forged drawer's signature. This rationale is that in a double forgery situation, no true payee can make a legitimate claim to the check, so any loss suffered by the drawer is attributable to the forged drawer's signature rather than the forged indorsement. The fictitious payee rule is not applicable to cases of double forgeries because the forged indorsement does not cause the drawer's loss. The drawer did not intend payment to any payee, so no payee can appear and demand payment. It is irrelevant whether the payee is real or fictitious and whether the indorsement is forged, missing, or otherwise defective.

ADDITIONAL ASPECTS OF LIABILITY

22. Excuses for Failure to Perform Conditions Precedent

An unexcused delay in making any *necessary* presentment or in giving notice of dishonor discharges parties who are entitled to performance of the conditions precedent. Indorsers are completely discharged by such delay; and drawers, makers of notes payable at a bank, and acceptors of drafts payable at a bank are discharged to the extent of any loss caused by the delay. Delay in making presentment, in giving notice of dishonor, or in making protest is excused when the holder has acted with reasonable diligence and the delay is not due to any fault of the holder. The holder must, however, comply with these conditions or attempt to do so as soon as the cause of the delay ceases to exist [3-504].

The performance of the conditions precedent is entirely excused if the party to be charged has waived the condition. When such waiver is stated on the face of the instrument, it is binding on all parties; when it is written above the signature of the indorser, it binds only the indorser. Most promissory notes contain such a waiver.

The performance of the conditions precedent is also excused if the party to be charged has dishonored the instrument or has countermanded payment or otherwise has no reason to expect or right to require that the instrument be accepted or paid. If a drawer of a check has stopped payment on the check, the drawer is not in a position to complain about slow presentment or any lack of notice of dishonor.

23. Discharge of Liability

The liability of various parties maybe discharged in a variety of ways, many of them previously noted [3-601]. Certification of a check at the request of a holder discharges all prior parties. Any ground for discharging a simple contract also discharges commercial paper [3-601(a)].

Payment usually discharges a party's liability. This is true even if the payor has knowledge of the claim of another person. Payment does not operate to discharge liability if the payor acts in bad faith and pays one who acquired the instrument by theft. Payment is also no defense if paid in violation of a restrictive indorsement.

A holder may discharge any party by intentionally canceling the instrument or by striking out or otherwise eliminating a party's signature. The surrender of the instrument to a party will also discharge that party.

If a holder agrees not to sue one party or agrees to release *collateral*, then all parties with rights against such party or against the collateral are discharged from liability. This assumes that there is no express reservation of rights by the holder and that the party claiming discharge did not consent to the holder's actions.

When an instrument is reacquired by a prior party, this party may cancel all intervening indorsements. In this event, all indorsements are canceled and the indorsers are discharged.

Fraudulent and material alteration of an instrument discharges any party whose liability is affected by the alteration. Of course, this is not true if the alteration is agreed to or if the party seeking to impose liability is a holder in due course. In fact, no discharge is effective against a holder in due course unless he or she has notice of the discharge when taking the instrument.

CHAPTER SUMMARY

LIABILITY BASED ON SIGNATURES

In General

1. Signatures of makers, drawers, and acceptors are affixed to the front of an instrument. Indorsements, generally, are on the back of the paper.
2. All signatures, generally, must be genuine to hold the signer liable.

Capacity of the Signature

1. Liability of the signer varies, depending on whether the signature is that of a maker, acceptor, drawer, or indorser.
2. The signature also may indicate the accommodation nature of the signer.
3. The capacity of the signature usually is reflected by its location.
4. When the signature is not clear as to the capacity, the signature is an indorsement.

Agency Principles

1. No person is liable on an instrument unless his or her signature is on the instrument, but it may be affixed by an agent.
2. A principal is bound by acts of his or her agent. If the agent is not authorized to sign, the principal is not bound unless he or she ratifies it or is estopped from asserting lack of authority.
3. An agent is personally liable if he or she fails to show representative capacity or fails to bind the principal.

Exceptions: Impostors and Fictitious Payees

1. If a check is payable to an imposter or fictitious payee and indorsed by the impostor or by the person supplying the name of the fictitious person, the indorsement is effective as a negotiation. In such a case, the loss falls on the drawer and not the bank.
2. These situations usually are a part of an embezzlement scheme, and the loss is placed on the employer who was in a position to prevent it from occurring.

Classification of Parties

1. Parties to commercial paper are either primarily or secondarily liable.
2. Primary parties include makers of notes, drawees of drafts, and acceptors.
3. Secondary parties include accommodation parties, guarantors, drawers of drafts, and indorsers.

Liability of Primary Parties

1. These parties agree to pay the instruments in accordance with their terms.
2. The secondary parties and holders expect the primary party to make payment or grant acceptance, whichever is requested.

CONDITIONAL LIABILITY

Presentment

1. Presentment is a demand on a maker or drawee for payment or acceptance. Failure to make a proper presentment results in complete discharge of indorsers.
2. Presentment by mail or through a clearinghouse is effective. It may also be made at the place of business of the party to accept or pay. The party on whom presentment is made has the power to require exhibition of the instrument.
3. Presentment must be made on the day of maturity, or if payable on demand, it must be presented or negotiated within a reasonable time after such secondary party became liable.
4. Drawer of a check is liable for thirty days after date or issue, whichever is later. An indorser is liable for seven days after indorsement. Presentment beyond these time periods releases indorsers, but the drawer may remain liable.

Dishonor

1. If an instrument is presented and not paid or accepted, it is dishonored.
2. If presentment is for acceptance, the drawee has one additional day to act.
3. If presentment is for payment, the drawee must act on the presentment that day.

Notice of Dishonor

1. When an instrument is dishonored, the presenting party has recourse against indorsers or other secondary parties, provided that he or she gives notice of dishonor.
2. Notice of dishonor requires the holder to be prompt in order to have a right of recourse against unqualified indorsers. Except for a bank, the notice must be given before midnight of the third business day.
3. Banks must give notice of dishonor before the bank's midnight deadline.
4. Notice may be by any reasonable manner. It may be written, oral, or by phone.

Protest

1. Protest is a certificate stating the instrument was presented for payment, it was dishonored, and the reasons for refusal to accept or pay. It is used primarily in foreign transactions.

LIABILITY OF SECONDARY PARTIES

Accommodation Parties

1. An accommodation party is a surety. Such a party may sign as a maker, acceptor, or indorser.
2. The nature of this party's signature determines whether the classification of primary or secondary party is more appropriate.
3. As an indorser, this party does not indorse to negotiate but to lend credit to the instrument.
4. An accommodation party may collect from co-makers and is not liable to the party accommodated.

Guarantors

1. These parties are identified by the nature of the language accompanying their signatures.
2. These parties are classified as either payment guarantors or collection guarantors.

Drawers

1. Through the drawer's contract, these secondarily liable parties promise to pay the instrument if presentment is made, dishonor occurs, and notice of dishonor is given.
2. Even when there is an unreasonable delay in satisfying these conditions, drawers generally remain liable to pay the instrument.
3. In addition to their liability as parties on the commercial paper, drawers usually are liable as parties to the underlying contract.

Indorsers

1. Through the indorser's contract, these secondarily liable parties promise to pay the instrument if presentment is made, dishonor occurs, and notice of dishonor is given.

2. If there is an unreasonable delay in presentment being made or in notice of dishonor being delivered, the indorsers are discharged from liability.
3. Indorsers may disclaim the conditional nature of their liability by indorsing "without recourse.
4. By their indorsements, these parties promise to the primary party that the indorsers have good title to the instrument and no knowledge of the maker's or drawer's signature being forged, and that the instrument is not materially altered.
5. Indorsers warrant to holders other than the primary party that the indorsers have good title to the instrument, all signatures are genuine, the instrument is not materially altered, there are no good defenses, and there is no knowledge of insolvency proceedings involving the primary parties.

Transferors without Indorsement

1. Transferors who do not indorse, but who simply deliver the bearer paper, still make the unconditional warranties.
2. These warranties bind the transferor only to the immediate transferee and not to subsequent holders.

Forgeries

1. A bank that pays on a forged signature of the drawer cannot charge the drawer's account.
2. A bank paying on the forged signature of an indorser must return the instrument to the party whose name was forged.
3. In the event of the forged signature of a drawer, the bank cannot collect from the party receiving payment unless that party is the forger or the party dealt with the forger negligently.
4. A payor bank that pays on a forged indorsement can collect from the person to whom payment was made.

Double Forgeries

1. If both the drawer's signature and an indorsement are forged, the loss falls on the drawee.
2. If the drawer's signature is forged, it is irrelevant whether the payee is real or fictitious and whether the indorsement is forged, missing, or otherwise defective.

ADDITIONAL ASPECTS OF LIABILITY

Excuses for Failure to Perform Conditions Precedent

1. Conditions precedent of notice of dishonor, presentment, or protest may be waived by the party to be charged. Such waivers are contained in most notes.

Discharge of Liability

1. Discharge of a party's liability may be accomplished by payment, cancellation of the instrument, surrender of the instrument, or fraudulent and material alteration of an instrument.

REVIEW QUESTIONS AND PROBLEMS

1. Match each term in Column A with the appropriate statement in Column B.

A	B
(1) Presentment	(a) One who signs an instrument for the purpose of lending his or her name and credit to another party

(2) Dishonor	(b) The secondary liability that results from the status of parties as drawers or unqualified indorsers
(3) Notice of dishonor	(c) A person who agrees to pay an instrument according to its terms
(4) Accommodation party	(d) Person who signs
(5) Protest	(e) The liability of one who negotiates by use of a qualified indorsement
(6) Primary party	(f) A refusal to pay or to accept
(7) Acceptor	(g) A requirement for conditional liability
(8) Unconditional liability	(h) A formal method of satisfying conditions precedent
(9) Conditional liability	(i) A demand made on a maker or drawee
(10) Indorser	(j) A person who is primarily liable on a draft

2. Security Bank sued a corporate borrower, Fastwich, Inc., and certain guarantors of the note. The note was signed as follows:

[typed] FASTWICH, INC.
[/s/] John J. Smith II [/s/] Carolyn Smith
[/s/] Gary D. Smith [/s/] Cheryl J. Smith

Is the corporation bound on the note? Why or why not?

3. Lee executed and delivered a promissory note due November 1, 2007, to the plaintiff bank. The note was a consolidation of previous loans made to Village Homes, Inc., which were in default. The note was signed by Lee personally. "Village Homes, Inc." does not appear anywhere on the note. Is Lee personally liable on the note? Why or why not?

4. John Madera signed a promissory note payable to A. Duda & Sons, Inc., in the amount of $47,872. The note began "for value received, we promise to pay A. Duda & Sons, Inc. …" Madera signed the note beneath the name and address of Tomatoes, Inc., as follows:

TOMATOES, INC.
3118 Produce Row
Houston, Texas 77023
/s/ John Madera

When the note was not paid, Duda & Sons filed suit against Tomatoes and against Madera individually, alleging that the two defendants were jointly and severally liable for the balance due on the note. Is Madera liable on the note in an individual capacity? Explain.

5. Alex was employed by a brokerage company. He devised a scheme to defraud his employer by issuing fraudulent orders to sell customers' securities. When the brokerage firm issued a check to the customer whose stock had been sold, Alex would obtain the check, forge the customer's indorsement, and pocket the money. When the fraud was discovered, the brokerage company sought to recover its losses from the bank on whom the checks were drawn. Is the bank liable for honoring the checks on a forged indorsement? Explain.

6. Anne loaned Donna's son David money to start a business, which later failed. David offered to sign a promissory note for the debt to prevent Anne from instituting legal proceedings against the remaining assets of the failed business. Anne agreed, but would only accept a note cosigned or indorsed by Donna. Donna signed the back of her son's note. Anne sued Donna to collect the note when David could not be located. Is Donna liable? Why?
7. A check in settlement of a lawsuit was made payable jointly to the client and to the attorney. The attorney indorsed it in blank and delivered it to the client. When the check was dishonored, the client sued the attorney to collect the face of the check. Is the attorney liable as an indorser? Why or why not?
8. The defendant received a check drawn on plaintiffs bank. The defendant indorsed the check and received payment from his bank. That bank sent the check for collection to the plaintiff bank, and the check was honored. Several days later, the bank discovered that the drawer of the check did not have an account and that it had mistakenly charged the check to another of its customers. Plaintiff then sought to recover from defendant as an indorser. He contended that the check had not been dishonored within the time allowed by law. Is he liable as an indorser? Why or why not?
9. Mark delivers a negotiable promissory note to Peter. Peter specially indorses it and delivers it to Art. Art adds his signature and delivers it to Bill. Bill, without signing it, delivers it to Carl. Carl indorses without recourse and delivers it to Dick. Dick presents the instrument to Mark, who replies, "I'm sorry, but I have no money." From whom can Dick collect the note? What must he do to collect? Explain.
10. Drawer issues a check "to the order of Payee" for $5,000. Forger steals the check from payee, forges payee's name on the check and sells the check to Jane, who deposits it in her account with Depositary Bank. The check proceeds through the bank collection process, where it is ultimately paid by drawee. Because the check was stolen, payee was not paid.

    a. Will Depositary Bank now be able to recover from Jane? Why?
    b. Can Jane now recover from forger? Why?

PART VIII

CREDITORS AND DEBTORS

Secured Transactions | 37

CHAPTER OUTLINE

1. Unsecured Creditors
2. Secured Creditors

SCOPE OF ARTICLE 9

3. In General
4. Classifications of Collateral
5. Tangible Goods
6. Documentary Collateral
7. Intangible Collateral

CREATION OF A SECURITY INTEREST

8. Introduction
9. The Security Agreement
10. Debtor's Rights in Collateral
11. Creditor's Value

PERFECTION OF A SECURITY INTEREST

12. Introduction
13. Perfection by Filing
14. Perfection by Possession
15. Perfection by Attachment

FLOATING LIENS

16. In General
17. After-Acquired Property
18. Future Advances

continued

CHAPTER PREVIEW

With this chapter, we begin an in-depth examination of the *creditor-debtor* relationship. The creation of this relationship is one of the most common examples of contracts in our society today. The extension of credit occurs at every level of business as well as in our personal lives. For example, manufacturers finance raw materials and equipment; wholesalers and retailers finance inventory; and consumers finance their purchases. The common denominator in all these financial transactions is that the creditor wants to be paid.

Creditors often might feel uncomfortable relying only on the debtor's promise to repay a debt. Particularly when the dollar amount involved is large, creditors often insist on a second source of repayment in addition to the debtor's personal promise to repay. The second source may take several forms. Very often, if the debtor owns any real estate, it is mortgaged to secure a debt. The use of real estate as security as a critical aspect of the law of property is discussed in Chapter 10. Another source of repayment is a second person's commitment to pay the debt. This source creates a *suretyship,* which is discussed in Chapter 38. A third source is the use of the debtor's personal property as collateral. It is this use of personal property that is the subject matter of this chapter.

Article 9 of the Uniform Commercial Code (UCC) provides for a *secured transaction.* This transaction involves a *security interest* in personal property or fixtures granted by a debtor to a creditor, which the creditor can use to obtain satisfaction of the debt in the event of nonpayment. A *fixture* is an item of personal property that has become attached to real estate. Items of personal property and fixtures used as security are called *collateral* [9-102(a)(12)]. A creditor who is protected by a valid Article 9 security interest is known as a *secured creditor.* A creditor obtains a security interest by entering into a *security agreement* with the debtor. To be secured as to third parties, the creditor must *perfect* the security interest.

This chapter discusses the scope of Article 9, the creation of a security interest, and the perfection of such an interest. In addition, this chapter presents two areas of Article 9 that arise once an interest is created and secured. First, does a perfected secured creditor have priority over other parties claiming an interest in the personal property that is the collateral? By the word *priority,* we mean the party that is first in line to have its claim paid from the proceeds made from the sale of the collateral. Also, what are the rights and duties of the secured creditor and the debtor when the debtor defaults?

BUSINESS MANAGEMENT DECISION

As president of a large bank, you are contacted by the president of your community's largest department store. This store seeks an open line of credit of $10 million to finance its inventory worth an estimated $15 million.

If you grant the line of credit, what should you require of the store?

1. Unsecured Creditors

Most debtors voluntarily repay their obligations, and most creditors depend only on the debtor's personal promise to pay. Such creditors are said to be *unsecured*. An unsecured creditor does not have any source other than the debtor from which to collect the debt. A credit sales transaction wherein the seller is unsecured is often called a sale on *open account* or *open credit*.

The danger facing unsecured creditors is illustrated by the steps an unsecured creditor must take if the debtor fails to repay voluntarily. The unsecured creditor must first sue the debtor and obtain a judgment. Then, as a *judgment creditor*, it may pursue the enforcement procedures available to a judgment creditor. These post-judgment procedures include obtaining a writ of execution—having a legal, enforceable official levy on the debtor's property and having the property sold at a public auction. The process of litigation and enforcement of the judgment are costly in terms of both time and money. More importantly, the debtor may not have any property that can be sold to pay the judgment, in which case the creditor will be unable to collect the debt. Many unsecured debts become simply uncollectible.

2. Secured Debt

As stated in the introductory paragraphs to this chapter, an Article 9 secured creditor has an interest in one or more items of the debtor's personal property. When these secured creditors perfect their security interests, they are in a much more favorable position than unsecured creditors. For example, the secured creditor, upon the debtor's default, can seize the collateral and have the collateral applied to the payment of the debt. These rights of a secured creditor upon the debtor's default are explained toward the end of the chapter.

Secured creditors enjoy an advantage when a debtor becomes insolvent or files for bankruptcy. The secured creditor has personal property from which repayment may be obtained. By having a security interest in the debtor's personal property, a secured creditor, in effect, is given priority over unsecured creditors.

However, a perfected secured party is not assured that the debt will be repaid. As discussed later in the chapter, secured creditors may lose their claim to the property under a number of circumstances. Furthermore, the value of the debtor's personal property may be insufficient to satisfy the entire debt. It is the secured creditor's responsibility always to keep informed of the debtor's business practices and personal obligations.

SCOPE OF ARTICLE 9

3. In General

To gain an appreciation for how an Article 9 secured transaction protects creditors, our study is divided into five parts:

1. The scope of Article 9
2. The creation of a security interest
3. The perfection of a security interest
4. The priorities to the collateral
5. The creditor's rights and duties when a debtor defaults

Although Article 9 deals primarily with secured transactions, it also covers outright sales of certain types of property, such as accounts receivable. Thus, a sale of the accounts receivable of a business must comply with the Code requirements as if the accounts were security for a loan.

Except for sales such as those of accounts receivable, the main test to be applied in determining whether a given transaction falls within the purview of Article 9 is whether it was intended to have effect as security. Every transaction with such intent is covered by Article 9. A lease with option to buy may be considered a security transaction rather than a lease if the necessary intent is present.

Certain credit transactions are expressly excluded from Article 9 coverage. In general, these exclusions involve transactions that are not of a commercial nature. Examples of common exclusions include a landlord's lien, an assignment of wages, and a transfer of an insurance policy. Another important exclusion is the lien created by state law in favor of those who service or repair personal property, such as automobiles. This lien, known as an *artisan's lien,* is discussed in more detail in Chapter 38.

4. Classifications of Collateral

Collateral

An item of value placed with a creditor to assure the performance of the debtor

The broad application of Article 9 can best be seen by examining the various types of **collateral** covered by it. There is not an item of personal property that cannot be used as collateral in a secured transaction. The only limitation to what is acceptable as collateral is the creditor's willingness to accept an interest in a particular item of personal property.

Collateral may be classified according to its physical makeup into three types: (1) tangible, physical property or goods; (2) documentary property that has physical existence, such as a negotiable instrument, but is simply representative of a contractual obligation; and (3) purely intangible property, such as an account receivable. Each type of collateral presents its own peculiar problems, and the framework of Article 9 is structured on the peculiarities of each type. Table 37-1 summarizes the various classifications of personal property that may be the collateral that is the subject of a security interest. The following three sections also discuss each of these three classifications.

As demonstrated in the following case, care must be taken by a creditor to make certain that an individual or entity does indeed have an interest in the property being offered as collateral.

A field of wheat could be classified as collateral under physical property or goods.

TABLE 37-1 ■ Collateral Subject to a Security Interest

TANGIBLE PROPERTY (GOODS)	DOCUMENTARY COLLATERAL	INTANGIBLE PROPERTY
Any personal property that is movable at the time the security interest attaches or that is a fixture. A fixture is a special type of Article 9 collateral. Goods are classified as one of the following: Consumer goods Equipment Farm products Inventory	Involves some indispensable piece of paper and has both tangible and intangible aspects. Documentary collateral is classified into one of the following: Chattel paper Documents Instruments	This property is not evidenced by an indispensable writing, which distinguishes it from documentary collateral. Intangible property consists of one of the following: Account General intangibles

CASE

Jerke Construction, Inc. v. Home Federal Savings Bank and Matt Peck and Tank Testing, Inc.

SUPREME COURT OF SOUTH DAKOTA

693 N.W.2d 590 (2005)

TICE, CIRCUIT JUDGE

Home Federal Savings Bank, Inc. (Bank) appeals from an order entered against it in a declaratory judgment action initiated by Jerke Construction Corporation (Jerke). Jerke sought to establish its ownership of a bulldozer it had placed in the possession of Justin Peck (Peck), who in turn had offered the machine as collateral to Bank as security for a loan. Having concluded that no security interest attached to the machinery and that Jerke owned the bulldozer, the trial court ordered that Jerke was entitled to possession of the equipment. We affirm that order.

On December 4, 1995, Peck entered into a written agreement with Sweetman Corporation (Sweetman) to purchase a D-9 Caterpiller bulldozer (D-9) from Sweetman for $20,000. On December 12, 1995, Jerke provided a $6,000 check to Sweetman as a down payment on the D-9. On February 22, 1996, Jerke paid Diesel Machinery, Inc. $12,238.17 to fix the transmission on the D-9. On March 13, 1996, Jerke issued a check to Sweetman in the amount of $14,000 as the final payment on the D-9. Sweetman thereupon issued a bill of sale to Jerke for the D-9. In the spring of 1996, the D-9 was delivered to Peck. The D-9 remained in his possession from the time of the repair of the transmission until March 17, 1999, when Jerke physically took possession of the D-9.

Peck testified that the monies paid by Jerke were a loan to him in order that he might purchase the D-9. He further testified that it was agreed that he would reimburse Jerke by using the D-9 on Jerke jobs. This was referred to by Peck as a bartering agreement. Though Peck testified that he had completely reimbursed Jerke for the cost of the D-9, the records indicate that, at most, credit could be given by Jerke for somewhere between $14,000 and $18,000 for the work done by Peck. This was testified to by Peck.

Bank produced no evidence that Peck submitted billings or documents to Jerke indicating that his work with the D-9 was done to offset a financial obligation he owed to Jerke. The total amount paid out by Jerke for the D-9 and its repairs prior to delivery to Peck was $32,238.17. There was no written financing agreement in existence, nor was there any evidence presented as to what the terms of such an agreement might have been. No evidence at the trial established interest rates, methods of repayment, or a timeline for repayment of the alleged loan. No records suggested that Peck had an ownership interest in the D-9 other than the original purchase agreement between Peck and Sweetman.

On March 9, 1999, Peck obtained a $400,000 loan from Bank secured by his assets. His list of assets included the D-9. At the time of the agreement with Bank, the D-9 was on Peck's property. The only time the D-9 was observed by anyone connected with Bank was in December 1998. Bank never sought to obtain any evidence of ownership, such as a bill of sale, other than accepting the listing submitted by Peck at the time of the issuance of the loan. There was no evidence that Bank had any knowledge whatsoever of the original purchase of the D-9, nor of the use of the D-9 at any time. Bank did a UCC search of Peck's property which was referred to at some points as a title search. In the course of the UCC search, no liens against the D-9 were found that named Peck as the owner. The only evidence Bank had of the D-9's existence was the one observation in December 1998 and Peck's listing of it in his application for the loan obtained on March 9, 1999. On March 17, 1999, Jerke's employees serviced the D-9 on Peck's property and then proceeded to remove it to Jerke's property without Peck's permission.

continued

This case first requires us to examine the trial court's determination of whether Peck possessed rights in the collateral to which Bank could attach a security interest. To claim a valid, perfected security interest in collateral, the security interest must attach to the collateral. A security interest attaches when (1) there is an agreement that it attach; (2) value has been given by the secured party; and (3) the debtor has rights in the collateral." The phrase "rights in the collateral" describes the range of transferable interests that a debtor may possess in property. For example, such rights may be as comprehensive as full ownership of property with legal title or as limited as a license. Formal title is not required for a debtor to have rights in collateral. An equitable interest can suffice. On the other hand, mere naked possession does not create "rights in the collateral."

Against this background, this Court first addresses a key finding of fact, namely that Peck only had naked possession of the D-9. As already mentioned, naked possession cannot support a finding of rights in collateral. Hence, if the trial court's finding on this question is correct, its conclusion that no security interest could attach to the D-9 must be upheld.

The record supports the finding that Peck only had naked possession of the D-9. As between Jerke and Peck, Peck's conduct consistently established intent not to claim direct ownership of the D-9. Though he maintained possession of it from the effective date of purchase until removal after the security agreement was entered into, he did nothing else to establish or indicate a belief that he was the owner of the D-9. He never sought to have Jerke provide him with a bill of sale or other indicia of ownership, he never sought to confirm a financing agreement of any kind with Jerke, and he never claimed depreciation on the D-9 for income tax purposes. In addition, he never came close to paying the entire cost of the original acquisition of the D-9. Though he did on occasion use it for his personal interest, it appears to have been used more substantially for Jerke's benefit. Also, Peck never provided notice of any kind to Jerke of the set-off he claimed for the work he performed with the D-9 until a document for the purpose of this case was prepared in January 1999.

In addition to these facts, Bank failed to prove that Peck possessed a contractual right to the D-9. Despite the existence of the document identifying Sweetman and Peck as the parties to the agreement for Peck's purchase of the machine, Jerke subsequently wrote the check, received the bill of sale and claimed depreciation expenses on the equipment. This provided a prima facie showing that, notwithstanding the preliminary contractual document, Jerke became the owner of the D-9. Once that showing was made, the burden shifted to Bank to show that, by means of a financing agreement or otherwise, Peck possessed rights in the collateral. Bank failed to meet the burden of showing that Peck had rights in the collateral.

Based upon the foregoing, the trial court did not err in concluding that no security interest attached to the D-9 as Peck had only naked possession and nothing more.

■ *Affirmed.*

CASE CONCEPTS REVIEW

1. Are there facts that indicate Peck held rights greater than "mere possession"?
2. Why is mere possession not sufficient to satisfy the "rights in collateral" requirement?

5. Tangible Goods

In secured transactions under Article 9, four categories of tangible goods are established. These categories include the following:

1. Consumer goods
2. Equipment
3. Farm products
4. Inventory

Consumer goods
Goods that are used or bought for use primarily for personal, family, or household purposes

Equipment
Goods that are used or bought for use primarily in business or by a debtor that is a nonprofit organization or a governmental subdivision or agency

In determining the classification of any particular item of goods, it is necessary to take into account not only the physical attributes of the collateral but also the status of the debtor who is buying the property or using it as security for a loan and the use the debtor will make of the goods. *Keep in mind that the classification will determine the place of filing to perfect the security interest against third parties.* It may also affect the rights of the debtor on default.

CONSUMER GOODS Goods fall into the **consumer goods** classification if they are used or bought primarily for personal, family, or household purposes [9-102(a)(23)].

EQUIPMENT Goods that are used or bought for use primarily in a business, in farming, in a profession, or by a nonprofit organization or governmental agency fall within the **equipment** category [9-102(a)(33)]. The category is something of a catchall, embracing goods that otherwise defy classification. Since equipment often is attached to realty and becomes a fixture, the discussion of fixtures later is especially significant for the equipment classification.

Farm products

Crops or livestock used or produced in farming operations

FARM PRODUCTS The **farm products** category includes crops and livestock, supplies used or produced in farming operations, and the products of crops or livestock in their unmanufactured state (ginned cotton, wool, milk, and eggs), provided that the items are in the possession of a debtor who is engaged in farming operations [9-102(a)(34)]. Farm products are *not* equipment or inventory. Note that goods cease to be farm products and must therefore be reclassified when (1) they are no longer in the farmer's possession or (2) they have been subjected to a manufacturing process. Thus, when the farmer delivers his or her farm products to a marketing agency for sale or to a frozen-food processor as raw materials, the products in the hands of the other party are inventory. Likewise, if the farmer maintained a canning operation, the canned product would be inventory, even though it remained in the farmer's possession.

Inventory

Goods that a person holds for sale or lease or goods that are raw materials, work in process, or materials used or consumed in a business

INVENTORY **Inventory** consists of goods that are held by a person for sale or lease or are to be furnished under a contract of service. They may be raw materials, work in process, completed goods, or material used or consumed in a business [9-102(a)(48)]. The basic test to be applied in determining whether goods are inventory is whether they are held for immediate or ultimate sale or lease. The reason for the inclusion of materials used or consumed in a business (e.g., supplies of fuel, boxes, and other containers for packaging the goods) is that they will soon be used in making an end product for sale.

The proper classification of goods is determined on the basis of their nature and intended use by a debtor. For example, a television set in a dealer's warehouse is inventory to the dealer. When the set is sold and delivered to a consumer customer, it becomes a consumer good. If an identical set were sold on the same terms to the owner of a tavern, to be used for entertaining customers, the set would be equipment in the hands of the tavern owner. The secured party, generally, cannot rely on the classification furnished by the debtor. The secured party must analyze all facts to ensure proper classification of the collateral and proper perfection of the security interest.

6. Documentary Collateral

In secured transactions, three types of paper are considered to represent such valuable property interests that they are included as potential collateral. These items of paper property include chattel paper, documents of title, and instruments. These items comprise various categories of paper frequently used in commerce. These papers may be negotiable or nonnegotiable. Each of these items of potential collateral is evidenced by a writing, and each represents rights and duties of the parties who signed the writing.

Chattel paper

A writing that evidences both a monetary obligation and a security interest in, or a lease of, specific goods

CHATTEL PAPER **Chattel paper** refers to a writing or writings that evidence both (1) an obligation to pay money and (2) a security interest in, or a lease of, specific goods [9-102(a)(11)]. The chattel paper is *itself* a security agreement. A security agreement in the form of a conditional sales contract, for example, is often executed in connection with a negotiable note or a series of notes. The group of writings (the contract plus the note) taken together as a composite constitutes *chattel paper.*

A typical situation involving chattel paper as collateral is one in which a secured party who has obtained it in a transaction with a customer may wish to borrow against it in his or her own financing. For example, a dealer sells an electric generator to a customer in a conditional sales contract, and the customer signs a negotiable installment note. At this point, the contract is the security agreement; the dealer is the secured party; the customer is the debtor; and the generator is the collateral (equipment). The dealer, needing funds for working capital, transfers the contract and the note to a financing agency as security for a loan. In the transaction between dealer and finance company, the contract and note are the collateral (chattel paper), the finance company is the secured party, the dealer is the debtor, and the customer is now designated as the **account debtor**.

Account debtor

The person who is obligated on an account, chattel paper, contract right, or general intangible

Document of title
Includes bill of lading, dock warrant, dock receipt, warehouse receipt, or order for the delivery of goods

Bill of lading
A document evidencing the receipt of goods for shipment, issued by a person engaged in the business of transporting or forwarding goods

Warehouse receipt
Issued by a person engaged in the business of storing goods for hire

Instrument
A writing that evidences an obligation to pay money, a negotiable instrument, or an investment security

Account
A right to payment that is not evidenced by a writing

General intangibles
Any personal property (including things in action) other than goods, chattel paper, documents, instruments, and accounts

DOCUMENTS OF TITLE Included under the heading of **documents of title** are **bills of lading**, **warehouse receipts**, and any other document that in the regular course of business or financing is treated as sufficient evidence that the person in possession of it is entitled to receive, hold, and dispose of the document and the goods it covers [1-201(15)].

INSTRUMENTS As distinguished from chattel paper, an **instrument** means (1) negotiable instrument, (2) an investment security such as stocks and bonds, or (3) any other writing that evidences a right to the payment of money and is not itself a security agreement or lease [9-102(a)(47)]. To qualify as an instrument, the other writing must also be one that is, in the ordinary course of business, transferred by indorsement or assignment. Thus the classification includes, in addition to negotiable instruments, those that are recognized as having some negotiable attributes. Instruments are frequently used as collateral, and they present certain problems in this connection because of their negotiable character. These problems are discussed further in the part of this chapter concerning perfection. Due to the readily transferable nature of negotiable instruments, priority issues also are complicated when this type of collateral is used in a secured transaction. These complications are explained in the next chapter.

7. Intangible Collateral

In the law of secured transactions, there is a third basic classification of collateral called *intangibles.* This classification includes the following categories: (1) accounts and (2) general intangibles. These categories are distinguished from documentary collateral by virtue of the fact that they are not represented by a writing. In other words, these categories of potential collateral are truly lacking any physical characteristics.

ACCOUNTS An **account** is any right to payment arising out of a contract for the sale of goods or services if that right is not evidenced by a writing [9-102(a)(2)]. An account receivable, which arose from a sale on open credit, is a typical example of an account. These rights of payments may be a valuable business asset that a creditor is willing to take a security interest in as collateral for the business' debt.

GENERAL INTANGIBLES The **general intangibles** category is a catchall that includes miscellaneous intangible personal property that may be used as commercial security, but does not fall within any of the preceding classifications of collateral. Examples of general intangibles include goodwill, literary rights, patents, and copyrights [9-102(a)(42)].

CREATION OF A SECURITY INTEREST

8. Introduction

Attachment
A four-step process of creating an enforceable security interest

The ultimate goal of the secured party is to have an enforceable, attached, and perfected security interest. The remainder of this chapter is devoted to these three concepts: *enforceability, attachment,* and *perfection.* Completing the steps as outlined in Section 9-203 causes a security interest to spring into existence. This moment of *creation* is called **attachment**. At the time of attachment, the security interest is also enforceable against the debtor and third parties [9-203(a), 9-201]. However, third parties may defeat the security interest if it is not perfected. Perfection is discussed later in this chapter.

The following steps are required of creditors to create a security interest:

1. Make a security agreement with the debtor.
2. Make sure the debtor has "rights in the collateral."
3. Give value.
4. Make the security interest enforceable either by putting the security agreement in writing, which the debtor signs, or by taking possession of the collateral pursuant to the agreement.

The four steps can occur in any order. A security agreement may be executed and the secured party may give value (such as a loan) before the debtor acquires rights in the collateral. Assume that Sewall, a small manufacturing company, is seeking a loan of $5,000 from a bank. Sewall intends to buy a Model 711 Reaper sewing machine, which will be the collateral. Assume that the following progressive steps occur:

1. A security agreement is signed by Sewall, but not by the bank. Sewall has yet to deal with Reaper. Only the debtor is required to sign this document.
2. *Now Sewall contracts with Reaper to buy the Model 711 machine.* According to Article 2, a buyer does not have any rights in the goods until the goods are identified to the contract.
3. *Reaper removes a Model 711 machine from its inventory and marks it for delivery to Sewall.* Now the goods are identified to the contract. Therefore the debtor, Sewall, has rights in the collateral.
4. *The bank, for the first time, makes a binding commitment to lend Sewall the $5,000.* The requirement that the secured party give value is met. Agreeing to lend money, as well as actually making a loan, is the giving of value.

Not until step 4 is completed does an Article 9 security interest exist. Only after these four steps are completed has a security interest attached to the collateral (sewing machine). After step 4, we find a written security agreement signed by the debtor; the debtor has rights in the collateral; and the secured party has given value. Thus an attached and enforceable security interest comes into existence. The following three sections describe a few more rules about the elements of creating a valid security interest.

9. The Security Agreement

The basic instrument in a secured transaction is the security agreement [9-105(a)(73)]. It must be *written or authenticated* unless the security arrangement is a possessory one and the secured party is in possession of the collateral. Allowing the creditor to possess the collateral is not always feasible. Indeed, most circumstances require that the debtor have possession of the collateral. In these situations, the security agreement must be in writing, and it must be signed by the debtor. Regardless of whether the security agreement is in oral or written form, this agreement must describe the collateral in a manner sufficient so it can be reasonably identified [9-108].

When it is a written form, the security agreement usually will contain many other provisions in addition to the names of the parties, a grant of a security interest, and an identification of the collateral. The forms, in general, use include a statement of the amount of the obligation and the terms of repayment; the debtor's duties in respect to the collateral, such as insuring it; and the rights of the secured party on default. In general, the parties can include such terms and provisions as they may deem appropriate to their particular transactions.

10. Debtor's Rights in Collateral

Another requirement for attachment (or creation of a valid security interest) is that the debtor must have *rights in the collateral.* It is clear that the debtor-buyer gets rights in the collateral against the seller upon delivery of the goods. A number of recent cases have held that the buyer can acquire rights prior to shipment, the earliest time being when the seller identifies the goods to the contract. The rights acquired by the buyer are subject to the seller's right of reclamation if the buyer fails to pay or if the buyer's check bounces. If a security interest created by the buyer attaches to the goods prior to the seller exercising a right to reclaim, the secured party generally prevails over the unpaid seller holding the bounced check.

There are many situations in which a debtor grants a creditor an interest in collateral that the debtor is not acquiring under a contract. Typically, in these situations a debtor has rights in the collateral if the debtor has possession of the property. However, when does a commercial fisher have rights in the fish as inventory? When does a farmer have rights in the crops to be grown or in the unborn offspring of livestock? The best answers to these questions seem to be that the fisher has rights in the fish when they are caught and the farmer has rights in the crops when they are planted and in the offspring of livestock when they are conceived.

While the debtor's possession of the collateral is an important factor in considering the debtor's rights in the collateral, such possession cannot be viewed as conclusive.

11. Creditor's Value

For purposes of attachment, *value* means that a secured party has furnished to the debtor any consideration sufficient to support a simple contract. When a creditor loans money, value is clearly given. Even when the creditor agrees to loan money in the future, perhaps by establishing a line of credit for the debtor, value is given. The executory nature of the creditor's promise to loan money in the future does not destroy the existence of value being given. Furthermore, value also is present when a creditor takes a security interest to secure a preexisting claim against the debtor.

PERFECTION OF A SECURITY INTEREST

12. Introduction

Perfection

A process that may occur by filing a financing statement, by possession, by attachment, or by noting the security interest on a certificate of title and is essential to inform the public that a creditor has an interest in the debtor's personal property.

Between the debtor and secured party, the security agreement protects the secured party's security interest; however, the secured party also wants protection against third parties, who may later make claims against the secured collateral. **Perfection** of the security interest will give this desired protection to the secured party. *Perfection is designed to give notice to third parties that financing is occurring on the basis of collateral described.* In general, an unperfected secured party's claim is subordinate to the claims of others who acquire an interest in the collateral without knowledge of the unperfected security interest.

Article 9 provides numerous ways in which a security interest can be perfected. The methods of perfection include the following: (1) filing a financing statement, (2) taking possession of the collateral, or (3) simply creating a security interest (automatic perfection). Several factors must be taken into account in determining which of the three methods is appropriate in any given transaction: (1) the kind of collateral in which security interest was created, (2) the use the debtor intends to make of the collateral, and (3) the status of the debtor in relation to the secured party.

13. Perfection by Filing

The most common method of perfecting a security interest that arises out of a business-related loan transaction occurs when the creditor files in the appropriate public office. Several issues arise related to this type of filing: (1) What must be filed? (2) Where is the appropriate public office for the filing? (3) When should the filing occur?

Financing statement

The legal documentation that must be properly filed by the creditor to be perfected by filing includes the names and addresses of the parties, an identification of the collateral, and the debtor's signature

WHAT MUST BE FILED The document that creditors file to perfect a security interest is known as a **financing statement**. This document includes the names and addresses of the creditor and debtor. It also contains a statement that identifies the collateral. If the collateral includes crops, timber, minerals, or fixtures, the financing statement needs to include a description of the real estate involved. This financing statement must indicate that the debtor and creditor have entered into a security agreement. Finally, the financing statement must be signed by the debtor. Simple forms, often referred to as a UCC-1 form, are available for use as a financing statement. These forms have spaces for additional provisions as agreed on by the parties. However, the basic information, as stated in this paragraph, is all that is necessary to have a valid financing statement.

The purpose of filing a financing statement is to give notice that the secured party has a security interest in the described collateral. *Potential creditors are charged with the task of going to public office to see if the proposed collateral is already encumbered.* A person searching the records finds only minimal information and may seek more from the parties listed in the financing statement. The addresses of the creditor and debtor are available so interested third parties know the sources of the additional information.

At times, the issue of whether a financing statement can substitute for a security agreement, or vice versa, arises. Generally, a financing statement is not a substitute for a security agreement. A security agreement may be filed as a financing statement if it contains the required information and is signed by the debtor. However, a financing statement usually will not qualify as a security agreement. Most businesspeople use a separate financing statement, because filing a security agreement would make public some information the parties might prefer to keep confidential.

WHERE SHOULD IT BE FILED The Code allows the states to require that the financing statement be filed in a central filing system, a local filing system, or a combination [9-301]. A central filing system means that all filing is in the state capital except for fixtures, which are filed locally. Local filing means that filing is at the county level. Most states have enacted dual filing systems. The usual system requires local filing for fixtures, local filing for farm-related collateral and consumer goods, and central filing for other business-related collateral, such as inventory and equipment. If the appropriate office for filing is unclear, the secured party should file the financing statement in every office that might be considered proper.

The three proposed alternatives for a filing system create problems when the secured transaction involves parties and collateral in several states. Because the states' filing systems are not uniform, where a creditor should file becomes an important question. Suppose that the Nationwide Construction Company is headquartered in Chicago, Illinois and that it has a major construction project underway in Atlanta, Georgia. If Nationwide borrows money from Bank of America in San Francisco and grants this creditor a security interest in the equipment located on the Atlanta construction site, where would Bank of America file its financing statement? The proper location for filing is determined by the debtor's residence or principal place of business [9-307]. Therefore, Bank of America would look to the filing system established by the state of Illinois. Any other party with a potential interest in the construction equipment located in Atlanta would also look to the filing system in the state of Illinois to learn whether conflicting interests exist.

WHEN SHOULD IT BE FILED A secured party can file a financing statement before the security interest attaches to the collateral. In fact, since the filing serves as notice to third parties, it is wise for the secured party to file at the earliest possible moment. Nevertheless, the filing of a financing statement does not perfect a security interest until such interest is in existence by attachment.

The financing statement may provide a maturity or expiration date, but more often it is silent on this point. In the absence of such data, the filing is effective for a period of five years, subject to being renewed by the filing of a continuation statement signed by the secured party [9-515(a)]. To be effective, a continuation statement must be filed within six months of the financing statement's termination. If it is properly renewed, the original financing statement continues to be valid for another five years [9-515(b)].

The presence in the records of a financing statement constitutes a burden on the debtor since it reveals to all persons with whom the debtor may be dealing that his or her property is or may be subject to the claims of others. The Code, therefore, provides for the filing of a *termination statement* to clear the record when the secured party is no longer entitled to a security interest. Failure of the secured party to send a termination statement within one month of the final payment or twenty days after written demand by the debtor, whichever is earlier, subjects the secured party to a $500 penalty and makes him or her liable for any loss suffered by the debtor [9-925(e), (f))].

CERTIFICATES OF TITLE Under certain circumstances, the filing of a financing statement does not perfect the creditor's security interest. The Code makes special provisions for goods such as motor vehicles that have a certificate of title. The filing requirements of the Code do not apply, and the usual method of indicating a security interest is to have it noted on the certificate of title. If the security interest is properly perfected on the certificate of title, the security interest is valid even though a substitute certificate of title fails to disclose the interest of the secured party. In most states, taking title in the name of the secured party is not a valid means of perfection.

14. Perfection by Possession

Pledge

Personal property, as security for a debt or other obligation, deposited or placed with a person called a pledgee

The simplest way to give notice of a security interest is for the secured party to take possession *of* the collateral [9-313]. This transfer of the collateral's possession from the debtor to the secured party is called a **pledge**. Since a secured party's possession of the collateral gives notice of his or her security interest, no public filing is required. As noted previously, the possessory security interest is very easy to accomplish because a written security agreement is not required. However, the use of possession as perfection is quite limited because most debtors either need or want possession of the collateral.

Possession is the required method of perfection of a security interest in instruments. Filing a financing statement is deemed inappropriate since instruments are created to be freely transferable in commercial transactions. Because a third party accepting an instrument as security or as payment would not think to check for the existence of a financing statement, the Code limits the method of perfection in instruments to possession.

Possession is an optional method of perfection if the collateral consists of goods, negotiable documents of title, and chattel paper. Since intangible collateral lacks a physical existence, it cannot be possessed. Therefore, the filing of a financing statement is essential for perfection if the collateral is an account or a general intangible.

Although it usually is considered an alternative to filing, possession of the collateral is the only method whereby complete protection in documents and chattel paper can be obtained. The reason possession of documents is necessary for absolute perfection is that the rights of good-faith holders to whom a document has been negotiated by the debtor will prevail over the secured party, even though there has been a filing. Possession of chattel paper is necessary to prevent buyers who purchase chattel paper in the ordinary course of their business from obtaining a superior claim in the paper. These situations involving issues of priority to the collateral are discussed in more detail later in the chapter.

15. Perfection by Attachment

Another method of perfection simply involves the attachment of the security interest to the collateral. In other words, *in some situations, the creation of the security interest, which is attachment, is also perfection.* In these situations, the secured party is *automatically perfected* by attachment. Two examples of when and why the Code permits perfection by attachment are discussed next. A third situation involving this type of perfection is presented in Section 19.

PMSI IN CONSUMER GOODS Probably the most common example of perfection by attachment occurs when a creditor receives a purchase-money security interest in consumer goods as collateral. To understand why perfection by attachment is necessary in these situations, you must first appreciate what a purchase-money security interest is.

Purchase-money security interest

A security interest that is taken or retained by the seller of the collateral to secure all or part of its price; or taken by a person who, by making a loan, gives value to enable the debtor to acquire rights in, or the use of, collateral

There are two types of **purchase-money security interests** (often referred to as PMSI) [9-309)]. The first one is called the seller's PMSI. This occurs when a seller of goods finances the purchase price and retains a security interest in the goods sold as collateral. The second example of a PMSI involves the lender's PMSI. This situation arises when a lender advances money to enable a debtor to acquire the collateral, and the money is, in fact, used to buy the collateral [9-107(1)(b)].

Perfection by attachment is possible when a PMSI is created in any item of consumer goods. Creditors are allowed to be automatically perfected when they have taken a PMSI in consumer goods because it would be very burdensome to have to file a financing statement after every consumer credit sales transaction. Furthermore, this perfection by attachment prevents the official record keepers from being overworked with a multitude of filings.

TEMPORARY PERFECTION BY ATTACHMENT For a variety of commercial reasons, it may be necessary or desirable that the secured party with a security interest perfected by possession not have this possession for a short period of time. For example, a debtor granting a new security interest in instruments or negotiable documents may not have these papers to hand to the creditor at the time the loan-related papers, such as the note and security agreement, are signed. The Code provides the secured party twenty-one days at the outset of this transaction to get possession of the instruments or negotiable documents used as collateral. During this initial twenty-one days, the secured party is automatically perfected by attachment [9-315(d)]. If the secured party fails to obtain possession of this collateral within this twenty-one days, that creditor is no longer perfected.

Even after obtaining possession of the collateral, a second party may find it necessary to release possession of the collateral to the debtor. Since the release is of short duration, it would be cumbersome to require a filing. The Code therefore provides that a security interest *remains perfected* for a period of twenty-one days without filing when a secured party having a perfected security interest releases the collateral to the debtor. This grace period applies only to (1) instruments, (2) negotiable documents, and (3) goods in the hands of a bailee not covered by a negotiable document of title.

If an *instrument* is temporarily released to the debtor, the purpose must be to enable the debtor to make a presentation of it, collect it, renew it, obtain registration of a transfer, or make an ultimate sale or exchange. The risks associated with such a release involve the debtor's improper or unauthorized negotiation of the instrument, or the debtor's sale of the instrument to a bona fide purchaser. If the debtor has possession of the instruments, these risks always are present.

The purposes for which *goods* or *documents* may be released to the debtor are limited. The release to the debtor of these items of collateral must be for the purpose of (1) ultimate sale or exchange or (2) loading, unloading, storing, shipping, transshipping, manufacturing, processing, or otherwise dealing with them in a manner preliminary to their sale or exchange.

FLOATING LIENS

16. In General

Often a creditor may create a security interest in collateral that is likely to be sold by the debtor. This event is very common when the *collateral is inventory.* To remain secured, the creditor will want to create a *floating lien.* A floating lien is created when the security agreement describes the collateral as including property acquired in the future by the debtor. The security agreement may also provide that future advances made to the debtor will be covered. The secured party can also have a security interest in the proceeds of the sale of collateral in the debtor's ordinary course of business.

The secured party's floating lien is protected against the claims of third parties by virtue of the public notice that such a financing arrangement has been made. The amount of the debt and the actual collateral can be constantly changing if the security agreement is worded to include after-acquired property, future advances of money, and the proceeds of any sale. This sort of arrangement allows the secured party to tie up most of the assets of a debtor, a possibility considered acceptable in business financing but restricted toward consumers, as the next section indicates.

17. After-Acquired Property

The security agreement may provide that property acquired by the debtor at any later time shall also secure some or the debtor's entire obligation under the security agreement. Many security agreements contain an *after-acquired property clause* such as the following:

> The security interest of the secured party under this security agreement extends to all collateral of the type that is the subject of this agreement and is acquired by the debtor at any time during the continuation of this agreement.

Under this clause, as soon as the debtor acquires rights in new property, a security interest in the new property vests in favor of the secured party [9-204(a)].

This clause obviously binds a debtor severely. The Code limits the effect of after-acquired property clauses in relation to consumer goods since the clauses seem best suited to commercial transactions and might work undue hardship on a consumer. Unless a consumer obtains goods within ten days after the secured party gives value, a security interest usually cannot attach under an after-acquired property clause in consumer goods contracts [9-204(b)].

18. Future Advances

A creditor may include in a security agreement that the collateral protects him or her with respect to future advances in addition to the original loan[9-204(c)]. Such a provision is usually referred to as a *dragnet clause.* Dragnet clauses are also used to pick up existing debts. A *future advance* occurs when the secured party makes another loan to the debtor. This additional loan is a future advance covered by a properly worded security agreement even if the secured party was not obligated to make the second loan. A problem that arises with future advances occurs in this context: SP-1 lends money, files a financing statement, and has perfected his security interest. SP-2 later lends money, files, and perfects his interest in the same collateral. SP-l generally would have priority since he was the first to file. What happens, however, when SP-1 lends additional money after SP-2 has filed and perfected? SP-1 still has priority.

If the future advance is made while a security interest is perfected, the secured party with priority to the original collateral has the same priority with respect to the future advance. Likewise, if a perfected secured party makes a commitment to lend money later, that party has the same priority regarding the future advance as he or she has with respect to the original collateral. These rules are justified by the necessity of protecting the filing system. In other words, a secured party that is perfected by filing remains perfected when future advances are made without having to check for filings made later than his or her financing statement.

19. Proceeds

Proceeds

Whatever is received when collateral is sold, exchanged, collected, or otherwise disposed of

The passing of the security interest from goods to the **proceeds** of the sale is an important part of the floating lien concept. A debtor may sell or otherwise dispose of the collateral, but the secured party may have an interest in the identifiable proceeds [9-315(c)]. These proceeds may take the form of cash or non-cash proceeds. Examples of non-cash proceeds include accounts receivable, instruments, chattel paper, documents of title, or any form of goods. Insurance payments also clearly are proceeds.

Two different factual situations concerning proceeds may arise. A debtor may have the authority to dispose of the collateral, as in a sale of inventory; or the debtor may dispose of the collateral without authority to do so. In either situation, the secured party has an interest in the proceeds. In the former, the debtor loses security interest in the collateral that is sold in the ordinary course of business but retains an interest in the proceeds. If the debtor sells the collateral without authority, the secured party retains a security interest in the original collateral, and the secured party gains an interest in the proceeds.

An interest in the proceeds from the sale of collateral may remain perfected even if the original financing statement does not specifically mention proceeds. This continuous perfection occurs if the original financing statement's description of collateral includes the type of collateral that covers the proceeds. For example, suppose that the original financing statement describes the collateral as inventory and accounts. If an item of inventory is sold on account, the proceeds are an account receivable. The secured party is perfected with respect to this account by the original financing statement. However, suppose that the item of inventory is sold and the buyer signs a promissory note. This note, as an instrument, is not covered by the original financing statement. Indeed, to be perfected, the secured party must take possession of this note. In this situation, the Code provides that the secured party is automatically perfected for twenty days with regard to the proceeds not covered by the original financing statement. To remain perfected, the secured party must perfect the interest in these proceeds by some acceptable method during this twenty-day period.

Special provisions relate to the secured party's interest in proceeds if the debtor becomes involved in bankruptcy or other insolvency proceedings. In general, the secured party is entitled to reclaim from the trustee in bankruptcy proceeds that can be identified as relating to the original collateral. If the proceeds are no longer identifiable because they have been commingled or deposited in an account, the secured party nonetheless has a perfected security interest in an amount up to the proceeds received by the debtor within ten days prior to the commencement of the bankruptcy proceedings.

The following case illustrates the reach of Article 9 protection to proceeds.

CASE

In Re: Jim Lee Wiersma and Patricia Darlene Wiersma, Debtors. Jim Lee Wiersma; Patricia Darlene Wiersma, Appellants and Cross-Appellees, V.O.H. Kruse Grain and Milling, NKA Ferndale Grain, et al.

UNITED STATES BANKRUPTCY APPELLATE PANEL FOR THE NINTH CIRCUIT

324 B.R. 92 (2005)

MARLAR, BANKRUPTCY JUDGE

Idaho dairy farmers Jim and Patricia Wiersma ("Debtors") filed a chapter 11 petition and proposed a plan to relocate their failed dairy business to Georgia. Debtors' cows had been subjected to electrical shocks from faulty wiring and had been culled until the herd was completely liquidated. Debtors sued the electrical contractor and, upon settlement of the state court lawsuit for $2.5 million cash ("Settlement Proceeds"), Debtors proposed to use the Settlement Proceeds to purchase cows and begin anew in Georgia. They proposed to give their major secured creditor, United California Bank, nka Bank of the West ("Bank"), a replacement lien in the new cows, but Bank objected. The bankruptcy court had already determined that Bank and another creditor, O.H. Kruse Grain and Milling, nka Ferndale Grain ("Ferndale") had secured interests in the Settlement Proceeds. At plan confirmation, the bankruptcy court held that new cows were not the "indubitable equivalent" of cash and dismissed the bankruptcy case.

Debtors owned and operated an Idaho dairy consisting of two facilities with 2,000 cows. They filed a chapter 11 petition on October 1, 2001. Debtors' financial problems stemmed from faulty electrical work performed in an expansion of their dairy by Geitzen Electric, Inc. ("Geitzen"). As a result, Debtors' dairy cows were subjected to varying degrees of electrical shocks which caused the cows to produce less milk, become sick or die. The entire herd was eventually lost.

Debtors initiated a lawsuit against Geitzen ("Geitzen Lawsuit") in which they sought $6 million in damages. The Geitzen Lawsuit was brought under both tort and breach of contract theories. Bank was Debtors' largest secured creditor. Following liquidation of the cows, its claim was approximately $2.2 million. Bank held a valid and perfected security interest in Debtors' dairy herd and, among other things, in all of Debtors' "Inventory ... Accounts and Contract Rights ... General Intangibles ... Livestock ... Milk Products Quota ... [and] Monies, Deposits or Accounts in Possession." In addition, Bank had a security interest in after-acquired property, and in "all proceeds and products of the collateral including, but not limited to, the proceeds of any insurance thereon."

Debtors also owed about $550,000 to Ferndale for livestock feed. This debt was evidenced by a promissory note and an assignment for security ("Assignment") of Debtors' right, title, and interest in any proceeds from the Geitzen Lawsuit. Ferndale perfected its security interest by filing a UCC-1 Financing Statement as to "any and all proceeds received by Debtors from the lawsuit. ..." Additionally, Debtors owed approximately $125,000 in priority taxes and $1.2 million in unsecured claims. The dairies were eventually foreclosed and their dairy operation was terminated.

In 2002, Debtors and their Special Counsel reached a settlement with Geitzen and its insurer to pay Debtors $2.5 million. The estate stood to receive approximately $1.6 million of the Settlement Proceeds upon bankruptcy court approval of the settlement. However, Bank claimed the entire estate's interest as its cash collateral, and Ferndale also claimed against the Settlement Proceeds pursuant to its security agreement and Assignment.

Revised Article 9 created a new subcategory of "general intangible" called a "payment intangible," which is defined as "a general intangible under which the account debtor's principal obligation is a monetary obligation." The authorities hold that it is irrelevant whether the payment intangible is based on a contract or a tort lawsuit because the collateral does not consist of the claim but, rather, the contractual right to payment evident in any settlement involving destruction of collateral.

In other words, revised Article 9 considers payment intangibles of either consumer or commercial tort actions to be general intangibles. Once the payment intangible comes into existence, in this case as an after-acquired settlement fund general intangible, it is automatically within the scope of Article 9 as part of the secured creditor's collateral.

The purpose and effect of these revisions are to enhance certainty so that lenders will be willing to provide more credit on the basis of these types of personal property when they are provided as collateral. It makes sense that the settlement fund should be within the scope of Article 9 because streams of payment from structured settlements are assigned outright or pledged as collateral in zillions of transactions around the country.

In summary, Debtors' argument that the Settlement Proceeds are excluded from Bank's security interest is based on pre-revision case law. The plain language of the current statutes provides that Bank has a security interest in the Settlement Proceeds characterized as after-acquired collateral. We therefore affirm the bankruptcy court's conclusion.

■ *Affirmed.*

CASE CONCEPTS REVIEW

1. What do you believe is the difference between a "claim" and "right to payment"?
2. Why was this provision revised? Does the revision favor debtors or creditors?

PRIORITY ISSUES IN GENERAL

Collateral is frequently the subject of conflicting claims. Two or more persons may claim a security interest in the same collateral, or a person may claim that he or she has a better right to the collateral than does the secured party. Interests that may compete with the secured party's claim of priority fall into the following two basic categories: (1) those who purchase the collateral from the debtor and (2) those who are creditors of the debtor. These creditors may be further subdivided into those who have a conflicting security interest in the same collateral and those who have some other lien on the collateral. Among the many ways in which conflicting claims to collateral may arise, the following are some of the more important situations:

1. A debtor sells the collateral to a good-faith purchaser who may or may not know of the security interest.
2. A debtor gives more than one security interest in the same collateral.
3. Collateral becomes attached to real property, so it is a fixture.
4. Collateral becomes attached to personal property that belongs to another or in which another has security interest.
5. Collateral has been processed (such as raw material, in which there is a security interest, being converted into a finished product).
6. The government or some other creditor claims a lien on the property.
7. Collateral has been repaired or improved by the services or materials of another.
8. A trustee in bankruptcy claims the collateral in connection with a bankruptcy case involving the debtor.

In all these situations, as well as in many others, it is necessary to sort out the conflicting interests and determine the priority among them. Keep in mind that the priority of a secured party's claim often is determined by whether or not the secured party has perfected his or her security interest. If it is not properly perfected, there is no priority. The general rule of Article 9 of the Uniform Commercial Code regarding priority is that after proper perfection, the secured party has priority over (1) those who purchase the collateral from the debtor, (2) those who are also creditors of the debtor, and (3) those who represent creditors in insolvency proceedings instituted by, or against, the debtor.

The bulk of the following material involves exceptions to this general rule. In addition to these exceptions, a secured party that has priority to collateral may agree, explicitly or implicitly, to subordinate its claim in preference to the rights of a third party. We assume in these discussions that this has not occurred.

SECURED PARTY VERSUS BUYERS OF COLLATERAL

20. General Rule

We now turn our attention to the secured party's priority when the collateral is sold or transferred to a third party. In general, the secured party's security interest continues in any collateral sold or transferred unless the security agreement authorizes such a sale or transfer free of the security interest. This general rule makes sense, since the secured party and the debtor are free to make any legal agreement they wish and a secured party may voluntarily give up the security interest. A more likely issue arises when the debtor sells the collateral without the secured party's approval. If the debtor makes an unauthorized sale or transfer, the security interest usually continues in the collateral in the hands of the buyer.

There are two principal situations in which the buyers take priority over the secured party, even though the sale was unauthorized. These situations are considered in the next two sections.

21. Buyers in the Ordinary Course of Business

Buyer in ordinary course of business

A person who, in good faith and without knowledge that the sale is in violation of the ownership rights or security interest of a third party in the goods, buys in ordinary course from a person in the business of selling goods of that kind

A **buyer in the ordinary course of business** takes free of a security interest created by his seller even though the security interest is perfected and even though the buyer knows of its existence [9-320(a)]. A buyer in the ordinary course of business is a buyer who buys goods from a seller who is in the business of selling goods of that kind [1-201(9)]. When you buy goods at the grocery store, department store, and gas station, you are a buyer in the ordinary course of business. In general, a transaction in the ordinary course of business involves the sale of a seller's inventory.

The reason for giving priority to a buyer in the ordinary course of business is obvious. When you buy goods from a professional seller, you expect to get clear title to the goods and would never think that they might be subject to a security interest. This rule, then, simply codifies the customary expectations of buyers in our society. It has been applied to buyers of new cars from a dealership and to a dealer buyer who buys from another dealer. Generally, this rule would not apply if you bought a used car from a car repair garage since the garage is not in the business of selling cars on a daily basis. In other words, the garage does not sell cars in the ordinary course of its business.

The buyer-in-ordinary-course-of-business rule does not apply to a person buying farm products from a person engaged in farming operations. Typically, farmers or ranchers get loans and grant security interest in their crops or cattle. This rule allows the secured party to follow its security interest into the hands of a cattle buyer or a grain elevator or food processor. To understand the reason for this exception, you should recognize that most farmers borrow money to plant and raise their crops. These loans are repaid when the crops are sold. If the law did not grant priority to creditors of farmers, these farmers would not be able to function. Creditors of farmers and those who do business with farmers must keep this exception to the buyer-in-ordinary-course-of-business rule clearly in mind.

22. Buyers of Consumer Goods

The rule of continuing priority for the secured party does not apply when a consumer-buyer purchases consumer goods from a consumer-debtor. The consumer-debtor, by definition, cannot sell his or her property in the ordinary course of business. This is because, as a consumer, the seller is not engaged in a business activity. Previously, we discuss that a secured party with a purchase-money security interest (PMSI) in consumer goods is automatically perfected when the security interest is created. In other words, a PMSI in consumer goods is perfected by attachment. Nevertheless, a secured party who relies on this automatic perfection may lose priority. As the next paragraph explains, a secured party with a PMSI in consumer goods has to file a financing statement to be assured of priority over a consumer-buyer of the collateral.

Section 9-302(b) allows a consumer-buyer of consumer goods from a consumer-debtor to take free of the PMSI unless prior to the purchase the secured party has filed a financing statement covering such goods. Suppose that Smith buys a sofa from Furniture Company and gives it a PMSI in the sofa for the unpaid purchase price. Furniture Company does not file a financing statement. A few months later, Smith sells the sofa to her next-door neighbor, Jones, who uses the sofa in his home. Although Furniture Company has an automatically perfected security interest in the sofa, the sale is free of that PMSI if Jones paid value, did not know of the PMSI, and uses the sofa for consumer purposes. If Furniture Company had filed a financing statement, Jones's purchase would be subject to the PMSI. In the alternative, if Jones had purchased this sofa from Smith for a resale in his used-furniture store, Jones's purchase would be subject to the Furniture Company's security interest even if the Furniture Company had not filed a financing statement. This result is because Jones would not be a consumer-buyer in this latter example.

The next case illustrates the application of the buyer of consumer goods provision.

CASE

John Meskell v. John Bertone, et al.

SUPERIOR COURT OF MASSACHUSETTS

18 Mass. L. Rep. 423; 2004 Mass. Super. LEXIS 494 (2004)

JUSTICE JOHN C. CRATSLEY

This case arises from a dispute over ownership rights to a sixty-six-foot 2001 Chapparral boat ("the boat"). The controversy is governed by Article 9 of the Uniform Commercial Code as adopted by the Commonwealth of Massachusetts ("Article 9").

On September 28, 2001, Meskell borrowed $31,601.75 from the Bank to finance his purchase of the boat. That day Meskell also executed a "Note, Security Agreement, and Disclosure Statement" in connection with a loan he received from the Bank. The security agreement lists the boat as collateral for the loan. The note terms prohibit Meskell from transferring ownership or possession of the boat by sale, lease, or other means without first obtaining the Bank's written permission.

In late 2002, Meskell advertised the boat for sale in the Boston Globe. Kimberly Friedman contacted Meskell in response to the advertisement. Kimberly Friedman stated that her husband, Dale Friedman of Sea Dog, would be willing to procure a buyer for Meskell for a commission of ten percent of the purchase price. Meskell agreed to enlist Friedman as his sales agent and in February of 2003 Meskell towed the boat to Sea Dog's yard in Salisbury, Massachusetts. Friedman then placed a "For Sale" sign displaying Sea Dog's logo on the boat and marked the asking price as $49,000.00. Meskell and Friedman did not sign a written agency agreement.

In the spring of 2003, John Bertone was researching boats for sale. He discovered Sea Dog's website and later met with Friedman to discuss purchasing a boat from Sea Dog. Friedman informed John Bertone that he was the owner of Sea Dog and represented all sellers. John Bertone later made a $44,000.00 offer on the boat to Friedman. Friedman told Bertone that the seller must approve the offer before Friedman could accept it. Friedman contacted Meskell, who accepted John Bertone's offer. Friedman then informed John Bertone that the seller had accepted the offer.

On January 23, 2004, John Meskell ("Meskell") commenced this lawsuit by filing a complaint against John and Linda Bertone ("the Bertones") for return of a boat that the Bertones purchased from Meskell's agent, Dale Friedman ("Friedman") of Sea Dog Yacht Sales ("Sea Dog"). Based on allegations that the Bertones converted the boat from him, Meskell seeks a permanent injunction barring the Bertones from further depriving him of possession of the boat.

On June 21, 2004, Key Bank ("the Bank") filed an amended complaint, naming Meskell and the Bertones as defendants. In Count I, the Bank sets forth a breach of contract claim against Meskell. On September 28, 2001, Meskell granted a security interest in the boat to the Bank to secure purchase money funds the Bank furnished to him. The Bank alleges that Meskell's purported sale of the boat to the Bertones breached the security agreement. Consequently, the Bank seeks payment of the full amount due on the underlying promissory note. In Count II, the Bank asserts a claim for equitable relief against the Bertones. The Bank alleges that it is the rightful owner of the boat, and seeks to enjoin the Bertones from preventing the boat's repossession. In addition, the Bank requests a judgment awarding it interest, attorneys fees, and costs.

Article 9 guides the resolution of the competing ownership claims presented in these two cases. A sweeping revision of Article 9 became effective in Massachusetts on July 1, 2001, but many historical secured transactions principles remain relevant to the resolution of this dispute.

The Bank seeks replevin of the boat from the Bertones, claiming that under Article 9 it is the rightful possessor of the boat. By placing the boat for sale without the Bank's express written permission, Meskell breached the security agreement and the promissory note. Consequently, the Bank was entitled to immediate possession of the collateral, unless the Bertones took free of the Bank's security interest in the boat.

The security agreement and note executed by Meskell and the Bank gave the Bank a security interest in the boat. A security interest is "effective according to its terms between the parties, against purchasers of the collateral and against creditors" unless the secured party is required to file a financing statement in order to perfect the interest. The secured party must file a financing statement to perfect the security interest in all cases except, among others, that of a purchase money security interest ("PMSI"). Therefore, the Bank was required to file a financing statement to perfect its interest in the boat unless the interest constituted a PMSI. Article 9 defines a PMSI as follows: "a security interest in goods is a [PMSI] ... to the extent that the goods are purchase-money collateral with respect to that security interest."

Meskell borrowed funds from the Bank to finance the sale of the boat and, in turn, granted the Bank a security interest in the boat to secure the purchase price. Therefore, the Bank's security interest in the boat constituted a PMSI and the Bank was not required to file a financing statement to perfect its security interest in the collateral.

A PMSI is automatically perfected upon attachment. The Bank's security interest attached when the events occurred as follows:

continued

(1) Meskell signed the security agreement describing the boat as collateral, (2) the Bank gave Meskell value in the form of a loan, and (3) Meskell used the loan funds to obtain rights in the boat. The Bank's interest is, therefore, enforceable according to its terms between the parties, any purchasers of the collateral, and any creditors, subject to the buyer of consumer goods exception set forth in G.L.c. 106, § 9-320(b). G.L.c. 106, § 9-201(a). The Bank's interest in the boat takes priority over the Bertones' interest unless the Bertones demonstrate that they meet the requirements of the buyer of consumer goods exception as described below.

The buyer of consumer goods exception in revised Article 9 mirrors the historical notion of buyer in ordinary course. The aim of both provisions may be summarized as follows: "One who buys consumer goods *from another consumer* for his own personal use without knowledge of a perfected security interest takes the goods free of such interest unless the secured party has previously filed."

To invoke the protection of 9-320(b), both the buyer and seller of the goods must be consumers. Although negotiated by Meskell's agent, the Final P&S and Bill of Sale evidenced an agreement between the Bertones and Meskell for the sale of consumer goods. I am therefore persuaded by a preponderance of the evidence that the transaction in question falls within the buyer of consumer goods exception.

Because the Bertones purchased the boat for value from another consumer, intended to use the boat for household purposes, and did not have knowledge of the Bank's security interest, their ownership rights are superior to those of the Bank. Article 9 imposes the burden on the party most able to insulate itself from risk. Here, the Bank had the option of filing a financing statement to ensure its priority in this factual situation, even though it was not required to file to perfect its PMSI. G.L.c. 106, § 9-320(b)(4). The Bank chose not to avail itself of the additional protection afforded by filing a financing statement. In addition, Meskell enlisted Friedman as his agent to represent him in the boat sale and accepted the benefits of that transaction. Therefore, Meskell bears the loss resulting from Friedman's apparent malfeasance.

■ *Dismissed.*

CASE CONCEPTS REVIEW

1. Why did the buyer of consumer goods exception apply?
2. In light of this opinion, what actions should the bank have undertaken?

SECURED PARTY VERSUS SECURED PARTY

23. General Rule

Two or more creditors may obtain security interests covering the same collateral. If the value of the collateral is less than the total of the claims it secures, upon the debtor's default it will be necessary to determine the priority of competing security interests.

Section 9-322 governs most secured party versus secured party priority contests. It contains special rules to be applied when the conflicting security interests are regular or when at least one of the interests is a purchase-money security interest.

This section basically provides a *first-in-time rule.* In other words, the first creditor to file or to perfect, if filing is not required, will have priority. This rule emphasizes the special status of filing a financing statement. Remember, filing can occur at any time, even prior to attachment. The Code adopts a pure race type statute: The first to file or perfect wins. Knowledge is unimportant. The benefit of a race statute is that it provides for certainty and predictability. Whichever party wins the race has priority.

This first-in-time rule also makes it advantageous to be perfected by attachment. Suppose a retail merchant sold a refrigerator to Smith to be used in Smith's home. Assume the merchant sold this refrigerator to Smith on credit, and the merchant had Smith sign a security agreement. This merchant is automatically perfected by attachment since he has a PMSI in consumer goods. If Smith then granted a security interest in this refrigerator to a bank in return for a loan, the bank must file a financing statement to be perfected. If Smith defaults on his payments to both the merchant and the bank, which party has priority to the refrigerator? The merchant has priority, since he was perfected before the bank filed. Section 9-322(a)(1) states that the creditor who files or perfects first has priority.

There are a number of exceptions to this general rule, and each is designed to meet the needs of a specific commercial situation. The next two sections examine the most prominent of these exceptions. For example, a secured party with a PMSI enjoys a preferred status in some situations.

24. PMSI in Inventory Collateral

To be really protected, a secured party with a security interest in inventory usually will insist on having the security agreement contain an after-acquired inventory clause. If that security interest is perfected by filing, the general rule is that this secured party will have priority over a later secured party, since he or she was first in time. However, what happens if the debtor wants to finance a new line of inventory? This general rule effectively stops the debtor unless the secured party is willing to make a future advance. For the purpose of allowing the debtor more control over his or her inventory, Section 9-324(b) creates an exception to this general rule.

For example, a bank lends to a store money secured by all the store's inventory now owned or hereafter acquired. The bank properly files a financing statement. A year later, a loan company advances money to allow the store to acquire a new line of appliances. Before the new appliances arrive, the loan company properly files a financing statement covering the appliances. The loan company then notifies the bank that the loan company intends to finance the new appliances for the store on a PMSI. The loan company now has priority over the bank, but only in relation to the new appliances.

The requirements of Section 9-324(b) are rather simple. First, the PMSI secured party must perfect its PMSI and give the other secured party written notice that it has (or expects to have) a PMSI in certain described inventory. Perfection and notice must occur prior to the debtor's receiving the inventory. The purpose of the notice is to protect the first secured party so he or she will not make new loans based on the after-acquired inventory or otherwise rely on the new inventory as collateral.

It is not important whether the perfection of the PMSI or the notification to the preexisting secured party occurs first. What is important is that these steps must occur before the debtor takes possession of the new inventory. Proof of the time that each of the steps was accomplished is essential if the PMSI creditor is to have priority.

25. PMSI in Non-inventory Collateral

For collateral other than inventory, a purchase-money security interest is superior to conflicting security interests in the same collateral, provided the purchase-money security interest is perfected at the time the debtor receives the collateral or within twenty days thereafter [9-324(a)]. Thus, prior notice to other secured parties is not required in cases of equipment if the security interest is perfected within twenty days after the debtor receives the equipment. The prior notice requirement is limited to a PMSI in new inventory.

Why is prior notice required for inventory but not other classifications of collateral? The answer is that secured parties are likely to rely on the debtor's inventory more than on other types of collateral as a primary source of repayment. In other words, the sale of inventory is much more likely to produce regular income from which debts can be paid. Therefore, the secured parties need to be informed more readily about the fact that they cannot rely on new inventory. The lack of prior notice about new equipment being purchased on credit, for example, does not create a problem for the preexisting secured parties, since their reliance on that equipment should be minimal.

A secured party with a purchase-money security interest in non-inventory collateral is given a special status for twenty days after the debtor receives the property. The protection during this period is limited. It gives priority over the rights of only (1) transferees in bulk (buyers of all or a substantial portion of a business) from the debtor and (2) lien creditors to the extent that such rights arise between the time the purchase-money security interest attaches and the time of filing. The purchase-money secured party is not protected against (1) a sale by the debtor to another party or (2) a secured transaction in which the collateral is given as security for a loan during the period prior to filing. Of course, to remain continuously perfected, the secured party must file a financing statement or otherwise perfect during this twenty-day period.

SECURED PARTY VERSUS LIEN CREDITORS

In addition to other secured parties and buyers of the collateral, a secured party's security interest can conflict with parties holding liens arising from operation of law. Four types of liens created by law may come into conflict with an Article 9 security interest: (1) federal tax lien; (2) laborer's, artisan's, or material person's lien; (3) judgment creditor's lien; and (4) the bankruptcy trustee's lien. In general, the rule determining priority between a secured party and a lien holder is the first-in-time rule. In other words, the party that is first to indicate its interest on the public record has priority.

For example, failure to pay federal taxes allows the Internal Revenue Service to file a notice of a tax lien on any property of the delinquent taxpayer. The property described in a federal tax lien may also be subject to an Article 9 security interest. The secured party has a priority claim to this property if the notice of the tax lien is filed after the security interest is perfected. If the notice of the tax lien is filed before the security interest is perfected, the Internal Revenue Service has priority.

RIGHTS AND DUTIES ON DEBTOR'S DEFAULT

26. Introduction

A debtor's default is the event that illustrates the real benefits of being an Article 9 secured party. Article 9 defines the rights and duties of both secured parties and debtors in default situations. The provisions of Part 6 of Article 9 permit the secured party to take possession of the collateral and dispose of it to satisfy the claim. This secured party may obtain the collateral by self-help (if this procedure does not breach the peace) or by court action [9-609(b)]. Once the collateral is in hand, the secured party has two alternatives [9-620]. The first one is to conduct a *foreclosure sale* with the proceeds to be applied to the unpaid debt. The second option is *strict foreclosure,* which occurs when the secured creditor retains the collateral in satisfaction of the debt. At any time before either alternative regarding disposition of the collateral becomes final, the debtor has the right to *redeem* his or her interest in the collateral by paying off the debt.

The first event that a secured party must establish is a *default* by the debtor. The security agreement will set forth the debtor's obligations, which, if breached, will constitute a default. A default may occur even though payments on the debt are current. For example, a note may require that the debtor insure the collateral. Failure to maintain proper insurance coverage may justify the creditor's repossessing the collateral and selling it according to the procedures described in the sections that follow.

27. Rights and Duties of Secured Party in Possession

The secured party has certain rights against the debtor who has defaulted. First, any reasonable expenses incurred in connection with the collateral are chargeable to the debtor and are secured by the collateral [9-607]. Second, the risk of accidental loss or damage to the collateral is on the debtor to the extent that the loss is not covered by insurance. Finally, the secured party is entitled to hold as additional security any increase in or profits received from the collateral, unless the increase or profit is money.

Once the secured party has obtained possession of the collateral, that party must decide what to do with the collateral. The secured party may sell the collateral and apply the sale proceeds to satisfy the debt, or the secured party may decide to keep the collateral in satisfaction of the debt. Because of the potential harshness of strict foreclosure, there are situations when a debtor or other interested party can force the secured party to sell the collateral.

The Code imposes certain duties on a secured party in possession of the collateral. The most important is to exercise reasonable care in the custody and preservation of the collateral. If the collateral is chattel paper or instruments, reasonable care includes taking steps to preserve rights against prior parties unless otherwise agreed.

> EXAMPLE Debtor pledged its stock in ABC Corporation to creditor to secure a loan. While creditor was in possession, ABC issued rights to current stockholders to buy additional shares, which rights would expire if not exercised by a stated date. Knowing of this right, creditor failed to notify debtor about it before the expiration date. Creditor thus failed to exercise due care and would be liable to debtor for any loss caused by the failure to notify.

28. Foreclosure Sale

Foreclosure

The forced sale of a defaulting debtor's property at the insistence of the creditor

After default, a secured party may sell, lease, or otherwise dispose of the collateral [9-610(a)]. The usual disposition is by public or private **foreclosure** sale. The primary goal is to get the best possible price on the resale, since that benefits both the debtor and the secured party. For example, the higher the foreclosure sale price, the greater the likelihood of a surplus for the debtor. Also, the likelihood of a deficiency is diminished.

The foreclosure sale can be public or private, and it can be by one or more contracts [9-610(b)]. A *public sale* is a sale by auction open to the general public. A public sale often occurs on the courthouse steps. A *private sale* is a sale through commercial channels to a buyer arranged by the secured party. Such a buyer could be a dealer who regularly buys and sells goods like the collateral.

Although the Code provides flexible rules for the foreclosure sale, it does not leave the debtor unprotected and at the secured party's mercy. Indeed, the Code imposes definite restrictions on the secured party, who must adhere to these restrictions or risk losing the remedies provided by the Code. Of these restrictions, three are the most important: (1) *reasonable notification* of the foreclosure sale given to the debtor by the secured party, (2) *reasonable timing* of the foreclosure sale, and (3) *commercial reasonableness* of every aspect of the foreclosure sale.

Sham sale

A sales transaction arranged by the seller to benefit a buyer who pays an unreasonably low price for the item sold

The Code allows the secured party to buy the collateral at any public sale, but the right to buy at a private sale is restricted. Only if the collateral is of a type normally sold in a recognized market or is subject to universal price quotations can the secured party buy at a private sale. This prohibition against the creditor's buying at a private sale acknowledges that creditors can overreach the debtor's rights by conducting a sham sale. A **sham sale** occurs if the collateral is purchased by the creditor at an unreasonably low price that allows the creditor to make the debtor liable for a substantial deficiency. Obviously, this type of resale is commercially unreasonable.

A resale is recognized as commercially reasonable if the secured party (1) sells the collateral in the customary manner in a recognized market or (2) sells at a price current in such market at the time of resale or (3) sells in conformity with reasonable commercial practices among dealers in the type of property sold.

29. Rights of Parties after Foreclosure

The buyer of the collateral at a foreclosure sale receives it free of the security interest under which the sale was held. This buyer also is free of any inferior security interest. Thus the good-faith purchaser at a disposition sale receives substantial assurance that he or she will be protected in purchase.

After the sale has been made, the proceeds of the sale will be distributed and applied as follows. First, the expenses the secured party incurred in taking repossession and conducting the foreclosure sale will be paid. After these expenses are paid, the sale's proceeds are used to satisfy the debt owed to the secured party. Third, any indebtedness owed to persons who have inferior security interest in the collateral will be paid. Fourth and finally, any surplus remaining after all these debts are satisfied will be returned to the debtor. If the foreclosure sale is commercially reasonable in all respects but does not produce enough to satisfy all these charges, the debtor is liable for any deficiency.

30. Strict Foreclosure

The secured party who intends to keep the collateral in satisfaction of the debt rather than conduct a foreclosure sale must send written notice to the debtor indicating this intent [9-620(a)]. Like with the notice of resale, this notice is not required if the debtor has signed, after default, a statement modifying or renouncing the right to this notice. If the collateral is consumer goods, only the debtor needs to be given notice of the proposed **strict foreclosure**. Notice to other interested parties is not necessary when consumer goods are involved since most of the secured parties claiming a conflicting interest will have PMSI and will be relying on perfection by attachment. Thus, the secured party proposing a strict foreclosure will not even know of conflicting interests.

Strict foreclosure

The agreement by the creditor and debtor to allow the creditor to retain possession of the debtor's property in satisfaction of the creditor's claim

When collateral other than consumer goods is involved, written notice proposing strict foreclosure must be sent to all persons who have filed a financing statement covering the collateral or who are known to have a security interest in it. Within the time period (discussed in the next subsection), the debtor or any interested party may object in writing to the proposed strict foreclosure. If no objections are received, the secured party can retain the collateral in satisfaction of the debt.

Strict foreclosure is disallowed in two situations. First, special provisions relate to consumer transactions. Disposition of consumer goods may be *compulsory,* and, if so, a sale must be made within ninety days after possession is taken by the secured party. This resale of the collateral is mandatory when there exists either (1) a purchase-money security interest in consumer goods and 60 percent of the purchase price has been paid or (2) an interest in consumer goods to secure a non-purchase money loan and 60 percent of the loan has been repaid [9-620(e) & (f)]. As stated previously, these rules exist because there is a presumption that the resale will result in surplus proceeds. The resale within ninety days ensures that the consumer debtor will not be deprived of this surplus. Of course, it is possible that even though a large percentage of the purchase price or loan amount has been paid, the resale of the collateral clearly will not produce a surplus. Thus the consumer debtor is allowed to waive the right of mandatory resale. This waiver must be in writing and must be signed by the debtor after default.

The second situation when strict foreclosure may be prevented involves an objection to the secured party keeping the collateral. As noted above, the debtor and all other interested parties must be sent written notice that a strict foreclosure is proposed. Any of these parties may object to this proposal. This objection must be made in writing, and it must be received by the secured party's proposing the strict foreclosure within twenty days of the original notice's being sent. If these requirements for objecting to a strict foreclosure are met, the collateral must be sold [9-620(a)].

31. Debtor's General Remedies

Except for the ninety-day period for consumer goods, the secured party is not required to make disposition of the repossessed goods within any time limit. The debtor has the right to *redeem* or reinstate his or her interest in the collateral until (1) that property has been sold or contracted to be sold, or (2) the obligation has been satisfied by the retention of the property [9-623]. The debtor must, as a condition of **redemption**, tender the full amount of the obligation secured by the collateral plus expenses incurred by the secured party in connection with the collateral and (if so provided in the security agreement) attorneys' fees and legal expenses.

Redemption

When a debtor redeems, buys back, his or her mortgaged property in paying the debt

CHAPTER SUMMARY

INTRODUCTION

Unsecured Creditors

1. An unsecured creditor has only the debtor to look to for payment of a debt or performance of a contractual promise.
2. If the debtor fails to perform, the unsecured creditor must file suit and try to collect.
3. An unsecured creditor who has obtained a judgment is a judgment creditor. This creditor must obtain a writ of execution, have the writ levied on the debtor's property, and have the property, if any, sold at public auction.

Secured Creditors

1. To avoid the time and expenses of seeking a judgment and having the debtor's property sold, creditors often seek an interest in collateral.
2. Collateral may take many forms. However, Article 9 is limited to the debtor's personal property and fixtures.
3. Secured creditors have many advantages in collecting unpaid debts over unsecured creditors.

SCOPE OF ARTICLE 9

In General

1. Article 9 includes any commercial transaction wherein the purpose is to use the debtor's personal property or fixtures as collateral.
2. Article 9 also covers transactions involving the outright sale of accounts receivable.

3. Article 9 does not govern transactions involving security interests that are not commercial in nature.
4. Such excluded transactions are the creation of a landlord's lien, an assignment of wages, and a transfer of an insurance policy.

Classifications of Collateral

1. Collateral is classified on the basis of its physical characteristics and on the basis of the debtor's use of the collateral.
2. Article 9 collateral can be classified as tangible goods, documentary collateral, or intangible collateral.
3. Tangible goods can be categorized as consumer goods, equipment, farm products, and inventory.
4. Documentary collateral can be subdivided into documents of title, chattel paper, and instruments.
5. Intangible collateral consists of accounts and general intangibles.

CREATION OF A SECURITY INTEREST

Introduction

1. To create a valid Article 9 security interest, the interest must attach to the collateral and become enforceable.
2. This process is achieved by (a) the existence of a security agreement, (b) the debtor having rights in the collateral, (c) the creditor granting value, and (d) the debtor signing the agreement or the creditor taking possession of the collateral.
3. These steps of attachment may occur in any order as long as all have occurred.

The Security Agreement

1. The agreement is the grant of a security interest by the debtor to the creditor.
2. The agreement must name the parties and describe the collateral involved.
3. The agreement may be oral if the creditor takes possession of the collateral. If possession remains with the debtor, this agreement must be in writing and signed by the debtor.

Debtor's Rights in Collateral

1. In general, a debtor has rights in the collateral when it is identified to a sales contract.
2. Normally, the debtor has rights in the collateral when the debtor has possession. However, a debtor-lessee may not have sufficient rights in items possessed to create a security interest in these items.

Creditor's Value

1. Value is defined as consideration sufficient to support a contract.
2. A creditor's executory promise to lend money is value.

PERFECTION OF A SECURITY INTEREST

Introduction

1. Perfection is the step that notifies the public that a creditor has an interest in the described collateral.
2. Perfection generally gives a secured creditor priority to collateral over the claims of third parties.

Perfection by Filing

1. The most common method of perfection is filing a financing statement.

2. The financing statement is a separate document from a security agreement. The debtor must sign a written financing statement.
3. A financing statement is effective for five years unless a shorter time period is clearly stated or unless a continuation statement is filed to extend the statement's duration.
4. To be valid, a financing statement must be filed in the appropriate office, as required by state law.

Perfection by Possession

1. Notice of the creditor's interest in collateral clearly is given if the creditor has possession of the collateral.
2. Possession is an optional method of perfection if the collateral is tangible goods, negotiable documents, or chattel paper.
3. Possession is mandatory if the collateral is instruments.
4. An interest in intangible collateral cannot be perfected by possession. A financing statement must be filed when the collateral is intangible in form.

Perfection by Attachment

1. In some situations, the creation (or attachment) of a security interest automatically perfects the secured creditor.
2. The most common example of perfection by attachment involves the secured party's PMSI in consumer goods.
3. The twenty-one-day exceptions to the creditor's having possession of instruments, negotiable documents, or goods held by a bailee that are not under a negotiable document are other examples of perfection by attachment.

FLOATING LIENS

In General

1. A floating lien is created when a creditor's security interest covers after-acquired collateral, future advances, and proceeds.
2. This concept avoids the necessity of the secured party having to create a new security interest and file a new financing statement every time the debtor acquires additional property or borrows additional money.

After-Acquired Property

1. A clause granting the creditor an interest in new property acquired by the debtor may be included in the security agreement.
2. This clause's application is limited to a ten-day period if the property is consumer goods.

Future Advances

1. A security agreement may state that the security interest covers future loans made by the creditor.
2. In general, priority with respect to future advances made is determined by the date of original perfection.

Proceeds

1. A secured party's floating lien also gives that party's interest in the proceeds of a sale of collateral.
2. These proceeds may be in the form of cash or noncash collateral.
3. An interest in proceeds continues as perfected if the original financing statement included a description of the type of collateral that covers the proceeds. Otherwise, the secured party is perfected by attachment for a ten-day period.

SECURED PARTY VERSUS BUYERS OF COLLATERAL

General Rule

1. Secured parties who are perfected generally have priority over buyers of collateral. However, there are at least two exceptions.

Buyers in the Ordinary Course of Business

1. Such a buyer takes free from a perfected secured party's interest.
2. A buyer in the ordinary course of business is a buyer who buys goods from a seller who is in the business of selling goods of that kind from inventory.
3. This rule of priority does not apply when the collateral is farm products.

Buyers of Consumer Goods

1. A buyer of consumer goods from a consumer cannot make this purchase in the ordinary course of business, since the consumer is not in business.
2. A buyer of consumer goods from a consumer has priority over a secured party who has relied on perfection by attachment of a purchase-money security interest if the buyer has no knowledge of the security interest and if the buyer uses the goods as consumer goods.
3. A secured party can be assured of priority with respect to consumer goods if a financing statement is properly filed.

SECURED PARTY VERSUS SECURED PARTY

General Rule

1. The secured party who is first to file or perfect has priority to the described collateral. When PMSIs are involved, exceptions do exist.

PMSI in Inventory Collateral

1. A second-in-time secured party who has a PMSI in inventory may have priority over a preexisting secured party.
2. This purchase-money secured party must notify the preexisting secured party in writing and must file a financing statement before the debtor gets possession of the collateral.

PMSI in Non-inventory Collateral

1. A second-in-time secured party who has a PMSI in non-inventory collateral may have priority over a preexisting secured party.
2. This purchase-money secured party does not have to give notice of its PMSI. However, this party must file a financing statement before or within ten days after the debtor takes possession of the collateral.

SECURED PARTY VERSUS LIEN CREDITORS

1. Whichever party, the secured party or the lien creditor who is on record first in time, has priority.
2. Federal tax liens follow this general rule. A tax lien is considered to be on record when the notice of the lien is filed.

RIGHTS AND DUTIES ON DEBTOR'S DEFAULT

Rights and Duties of Secured Party in Possession

1. The secured party can recover the cost of repossession from the debtor.
2. Any increase in the collateral is additional security protecting the secured party.
3. Once the secured party has possession of the collateral, that party must decide to conduct a foreclosure sale or to keep the collateral in satisfaction of the debt, which is called strict foreclosure.

4. In general, the secured party must handle the collateral with reasonable care.

Foreclosure Sale

1. A foreclosure sale may be public or private. A public sale is open to the general public and usually is an auction.
2. A private sale is arranged by the secured party who locates one or more buyers of the collateral.
3. The secured party always must give the debtor notice of the foreclosure sale. This notice must include the time and place of a public sale. The notice need only inform the debtor of the time after which a private sale may occur.
4. If the collateral is consumer goods, notice of resale needs to be given only to the debtor. If other types of collateral are involved, notice also must be given to the other secured parties who have notified the secured party arranging the sale of their interest.
5. This type of notice is not required if the collateral is perishable, threatens to decline in value rapidly, or is sold on a recognized market.
6. In general, there is no time limit within which a foreclosure sale must occur.
7. The applicable standard is that the sale must occur within a reasonable time.
8. All aspects of a foreclosure sale must be handled in a commercially reasonable manner.
9. This standard has been and continues to be developed by case law, since the Code does not provide a definition of commercial reasonableness.

Rights of Parties after Foreclosure

1. A buyer at a commercially reasonable foreclosure sale takes the property free from the security interest of the seller and all inferior security interests.
2. The proceeds of a resale of collateral will be distributed to the secured party to pay for the expenses of repossession and resale and for the debt. Any remaining proceeds will be paid to other parties secured by the same collateral. Any surplus is paid to the debtor. Any deficiency is owed by the debtor.

Strict Foreclosure

1. A secured party who proposes to keep the collateral in satisfaction of the debt must send the debtor written notice of this proposal unless the debtor has waived after default the right to such notice.
2. If the collateral is not consumer goods, written notice of strict foreclosure also must be sent to all other known interested parties.
3. If the collateral is consumer goods and 60 percent of the purchase price or loan amount has been paid, the consumer goods must be sold within ninety days of the secured party's possession of them.
4. Any debtor or interested party may object to the strict foreclosure and force a foreclosure sale. This objection must be given in writing within twenty days of the secured party's notice of strict foreclosure being sent.

Debtor's General Remedies

1. The debtor has a right to redeem his or her interest in the collateral anytime prior to final action being taken by the secured party.
2. To redeem interests in default, the debtor must pay all amounts owed to the secured party.
3. If the secured party fails to comply with any Code provision, the debtor can sue for actual damages plus any applicable Code remedy.

REVIEW QUESTIONS AND PROBLEMS

1. Match each term in Column A with the appropriate statement in Column B.

A	B
(1) Unsecured creditor	(a) Created when a creditor's security interest covers after-acquired collateral or future advances or both
(2) Redemption	(b) Exists when either a seller or lender, as a secured party, lends the money that enables the debtor to buy the collateral
(3) Strict foreclosure	(c) Debtor may buy back
(4) Chattel paper	(d) The document that must be filed to perfect a security interest
(5) Foreclosure	(e) Occurs when collateral is sold or disposed of
(6) Floating lien	(f) A party whose only collateral is the debtor's promise to repay
(7) Security agreement	(g) Forced sale
(8) Financing statement	(h) Creditor retains possession in satisfaction of claim
(9) Proceeds	(i) A writing that evidences both an obligation to pay money and a security interest or lease
(10) Purchase-money security interest	(j) An essential document that must be signed by the debtor if he or she retains possession of the collateral if a security interest is to be created

2. Classification of collateral is not always easy. Classify the following collateral:

a. Burns Rentals leases and sells TV sets and cars. Burns obtains financing from City Bank, enabling him to buy twenty-five cars and 100 new TV sets.

b. Burns has fifty cars on his lot for lease.

c. Burns sells a truck to Boyce and retains a security interest in the truck. Boyce uses the truck exclusively for weekend camping and fishing trips.

d. Burns assigns Boyce's promissory note and security agreement to City Bank as collateral for a loan.

e. Burns Rentals buys 300 new Philco TV sets for his annual summer sale. Classify the TV sets in the hands of Philco; in Burns's possession. Virgil, owner of Virgil's Truck City and Bar buys a TV set during the sale. The set is delivered to Virgil in its original carton and put in the back of his sixteen-wheeler. What type of goods did Virgil buy?

f. When Philco sells TV sets to Burns, it packages them in special shipping cartons, using packaging materials such as Styrofoam and excelsior. Philco maintains a large supply of these materials.

g. Burns has a large supply of diesel fuel and oil for his fleet of trucks.

3. Jim Gibbs purchased a used truck and delivered it to Vernie King for needed repairs. After one month, Gibbs was notified that the truck was repaired. The total cost of the repairs was more than Gibbs could afford. King agreed to lend Gibbs $1,250 as a partial payment for the repairs. Gibbs orally agreed to give King a security interest in the truck in return for the loan. However no written security agreement was prepared or signed. Gibbs took possession of the truck and later defaulted on his repayment of the $1,250. King sought to repossess the truck as a secured creditor. Gibbs argued that King did not have a security interest in this truck. Can a creditor be secured on the basis of an oral security agreement if the debtor has possession of the collateral? Explain.
4. Paula, an accountant, lent money to a company that was already indebted to her for services rendered. As security for the loan and to secure payment for the services, the company assigned to Paula a portion of its expected recovery of a pending lawsuit. Paula did not file a financing statement with regard to the assignment. Subsequently, Debra was awarded a judgment against the company in another lawsuit. Debra, without knowledge of the assignment to Paula, had the sheriff levy against the company's property. At the sheriff's execution sale, all of the company's rights in the pending lawsuit were sold to Debra. When the lawsuit was settled, Paula claimed rights to the proceeds. Is Paula entitled to the proceeds of the lawsuit pursuant to her security interest? Explain.
5. Tom and Marie Shafer purchased a household washing machine and dishwasher on credit from the Georgia Power Company (GPC). GPC took purchase money security interests in each of these appliances that were perfected by attachment. Later, the Shafers granted security interests in these same appliances to Personal Thrift as collateral for a loan. Personal Thrift perfected its interests by filing a proper financing statement. The Shafers defaulted on all these loans, and Personal Thrift took possession of the appliances. GPC sued Personal Thrift, seeking to recover the two appliances. Personal Thrift argued that GPC's automatic perfection is not effective. Discuss.
6. By answering the following, check your knowledge of the business decisions involved in secured transactions:

    a. Assume that you are a retailer with a large amount of outstanding accounts receivable and you are in need of cash to pay expenses. How might you raise the necessary cash? Explain.
    b. Assume that you are considering lending to Fred Tauber of Tauber & Sons and taking a security interest in certain property of Tauber & Sons. What should you do prior to lending the money? Explain.
    c. Assume that you are arranging to finance another's business. It will be a secured financing plan that works on a continuing basis. What provisions should you require for inclusion in the security agreement and in the financing statement? Explain.
    d. Assume that you are a secured party and are in doubt about whether you have to file and, if so, where to file. What do you do? Explain.

7. Assume that the following events occur. Answer each part based on these and any additional facts given.

    The First National Bank agrees to lend $500,000 to Custom Sound Stereo and Television Company. To secure its position, the bank takes a security interest in Custom Sound's inventory, equipment, accounts, and chattel paper and in its after-acquired inventory, equipment, accounts, and chattel paper. A security agreement and financing statement is filed in the proper location to give the bank a perfected security interest.

a. Corliss purchases a TV set for her personal use. If Custom Sound defaults on its loan payments, who has priority between the bank and Corliss? Explain.
b. Deborah, a doctor, purchases a stereo for her office waiting room. If Custom Sound defaults on its loan payments, does the bank or Deborah have priority to the stereo? Explain.
c. Suppose Deborah purchased her stereo on credit. She signed a promissory note, but not a security agreement. Does the bank have any interest in this note? If so, how is this interest perfected? Explain.

8. A furniture manufacturer, secured by a security agreement, sold furniture to Daniel on credit. When Daniel did not pay as agreed, the creditor repossessed the furniture. This creditor approached one possible buyer for the items but failed to sell them. The creditor then bought the collateral at a private sale and sued Daniel for a deficiency of $7,000. Daniel contends that he is entitled to credit for the full value of the repossessed goods because the private sale was improper. Is Daniel correct? Why or why not?

9. McIlroy Bank lent money to Seven Day Builders (SDB) to enable SDB to purchase some equipment. This equipment was used as collateral to secure the bank that repayment would be made. When SDB defaulted, the bank took possession of the equipment. Although it never notified SDB of its intentions, the bank planned to retain possession of this equipment in satisfaction of the debt. SDB argued that the bank could not keep the collateral and that the bank was liable for damages caused to SDB. Did the bank fail to follow proper procedures such that it is liable to the debtor? Explain.

10. The secured party repossessed Crosby's personal pickup truck after Crosby had paid over 60 percent of the cash price. The secured patty failed to sell the truck within the ninety days required by the Code. Discuss rights of all parties fully.

Additional Creditor Rights, Responsibilities, and Remedies 38

CHAPTER OUTLINE

CHAPTER PREVIEW

This chapter presents a set of additional rights and responsibilities primarily associated with creditors in the business-to-business realm. (Debtor rights, particularly created by statutes to protect *consumer debtors*, are examined in Chapter 42.) Also, the material in this chapter is organized according to whether property is personal property or real property, an approach that is typical in considering issues associated with property in general.

Most of the material presented in this chapter deals with personal property interests. The topics of artisan's liens, where one party performs work or adds value to another party's personal property, and suretyships, where a third party commits to a creditor that the debtor will perform as promised or the third party will become liable—both relate to personal property. These aspects of the debtor-creditor relationship complement the area of secured transactions presented in the previous chapter.

Basic aspects of mechanic's lien law are examined later in the chapter. This lien against the real property is analogous to artisan's liens against personal property. At the end of the chapter, the topic of enforcement of a judicial judgment or decree is considered, as the use of litigation is often the last resort of creditors attempting to secure payment of a debt.

BUSINESS MANAGEMENT DECISION

As a commercial loan officer for the First Bank, you are responsible for the bank's relationship with its business debtors. The Hi-Fashion Clothing Store Inc. is one of your best customers, and it currently owes the bank $1.5 million. The repayment of this loan is guaranteed by Paul Dress, the founder and former chairman of Hi-Fashion. Mr. Dress is retired and is no longer actively involved in the day-to-day operations of Hi-Fashion.

The current chief financial officer of Hi-Fashion has asked you to arrange extending the term of this loan from five to eight years. This extension would allow Hi-Fashion to reduce its current monthly payment. The bank is inclined to approve this request, upon your recommendation.

What must you do to ensure that Mr. Dress continues to be liable?

ARTISAN'S LIENS

Artisan's lien

The claim against an item of personal property that arises when one has expended labor on, or added to, the property with the result that the person is entitled to possession of the property as security until paid for the value of his or her labor or material

An **artisan's lien** is a security interest in personal property in favor of one who has performed services on the personal property. Such services often take the form of a repair. From a very early date, the common law permitted one who expended labor or materials on the personal property of another to retain possession of the property as security for compensation. This right to possession creates a lien against the owner's personal property when the task is completed. By court decisions, such a lien typically has been interpreted to exist in favor of public warehouse people and common carriers of goods entrusted to their care. Today, in almost every state, the artisan's lien has been extended by statute to cover all cases of storage or repair. However, the artisan's lien, generally, is considered to be personal to the party who performs the services. The lien is not assignable.

Because the artisan's lien is perfected by possession, voluntary surrender of the property, generally, terminates the lien. If the artisan parts with possession, reacquisition of the goods involved will not re-create the lien. As exceptions to the general rule that the lienholder must maintain possession to have perfection of the artisan's lien, two points are emphasized. First, a lienholder may temporarily surrender possession with an agreement that the lien will continue. However, if rights of a third party arise while the lienholder is not in possession of the property, the lien is inferior to the third party's rights. Also, surrender of possession of part of the goods will not affect the lien on the remaining goods.

Second, the release of possession will not terminate the lien if a notice of lien is recorded in accordance with state lien and recording statutes prior to surrender of possession of the goods. Notice of an artisan's lien in the public records serves as an adequate substitute for possession. The concept of a filing in the public records has been adopted by some states as an essential step in perfecting an artisan's lien.

Under common law, the lienholder had to retain the property until a judgment was obtained; then he or she levied execution on the property. Modern statutes permit the lienholder to have the property sold to satisfy the claim. These statutes usually require notice to the owner prior to the sale. With respect to the proceeds of a forced sale, the artisan generally has a superior claim when compared with a preexisting Article 9 secured party. The lienholder has priority because the law presumes that the work of improvement done on the personal property has increased that property's value at least in an amount equal to the lienholder's claim. Therefore, the secured creditor has not been damaged by having inferior status. Any surplus proceeds left after all claims against the property are satisfied are paid to the owner of the property.

SURETYSHIP IN GENERAL

1. Introduction

Suretyship

The relationship created between the debtor, creditor, and third party when that third party promises the creditor that the debtor will perform the promises made or, in the alternative, the third party will perform

Suretyship provides security for a creditor without involving an interest in property. In suretyship, the security for the creditor is provided by a third person's promise to be responsible for the debtor's obligation.

Suretyship may have commenced with the beginning of civilization. Although there is evidence of surety contracts as far back as 2750 B.C., and in the Code of Hammurabi, about 2250 B.C., the earliest written contract of suretyship that has been found dates to 670 B.C. By A.D. 150, the Romans had developed a highly technical law of suretyship. The concept of a corporate surety did not evolve until the Industrial Revolution. Today, suretyship plays a major role in many business transactions, especially construction contracts. Suretyship also is involved in a substantial percentage of loan transactions.

2. Terminology

A *principal* or *principal debtor* or *obligor* is the party who borrows money or assumes direct responsibility to perform a contractual obligation. The party entitled to receive payment or performance is called the *creditor* or *obligee*. Any party who promises the creditor to be liable for a principal's payment of performance is either a surety or *guarantor*. The word *party* includes individuals as well as all types of business organizations.

What is the difference of a surety or a guarantor? Historically, the distinction has involved the difference between a third party being primarily and secondarily liable. Also involved is the distinction between assuring a creditor that the principal will perform a noncredit contractual promise and that the principal will repay money borrowed.

SURETY A surety's promise to be liable for a principal's obligation is created as a part of and dependent on the principal's agreement to perform. In a narrow sense, a surety is considered primarily liable for the principal's performance. In other words, a creditor could demand performance from the surety rather than the principal. From this concept came the general rule that no notice of the principal's default had to be given for the creditor to hold the surety liable. This notice requirement and its ramifications are discussed in Section 7.

Since a surety's promise is part of the creditor-debtor relationship, a creditor may sue the surety simultaneously when action is taken against the principal. Finally, a surety's obligation can be summarized as being a promise to do what the principal agreed to do.

GUARANTOR On the other hand, a guarantor's promise to be liable for a principal's obligation is created separate from and independent of the principal's agreement to perform. In other words, a guarantor's promise is only related to, but not an essential part of, the principal's obligation. A guarantor will become liable to the creditor only when the principal has defaulted. Therefore, the principal is primarily liable and the guarantor is secondarily liable. Historically, this concept has required the creditor to give the guarantor notice of the debtor's default before action could be commenced against the guarantor. Furthermore, a creditor, if necessary, must bring two legal actions—first against the principal and, second and separately, against the guarantor. To summarize—a guarantor promises that the principal will do what the principal promised to do.

GUARANTY AGREEMENTS There are two types of guaranty agreements: general and special. A *general guarantor* is a party whose promise is not limited to a single transaction or to a single creditor. For example, a principal may have an open line of credit and may borrow from the creditor many times within the overall credit limitation. A guarantor who promises to be liable upon the principal's default regardless of the number of transactions within the credit line is called a general guarantor. The general guarantor has significant potential liability.

A *special guarantor* is a party who limits the promise made to a single transaction or to a single creditor or both. A special guarantor's obligation would not protect a creditor to the full extent of an open line of credit if the initial loan transaction was for a lesser amount. In addition, a creditor cannot assign the special guarantor's promise to a new creditor, as the following case discusses. This case also provides an example of the language of a guaranty agreement.

CASE

Flying J, Inc. v. Booth

SUPREME COURT OF WYOMING

773 P.2d 144 (1989)

URBIGKIT, J.

Elvin and Jacqueline Booth owned one-half of the shares of Booth Livestock, Inc. (BL). The other half of BL's stock was owned by Paul and Joan Gillett. BL ran a truck stop under the name Husky Super Stop. Husky Oil Company (Husky) sold diesel fuel and other products necessary for the operation of the truck stop. BL sought to purchase these products from Husky on credit. Before beginning to extend credit to BL in 1974, Husky required the Booths to sign a guaranty, which stated in part:

> *THE UNDERSIGNED, jointly and severally (herein called Guarantor...), do hereby guarantee and agree to pay any and all indebtedness of any nature whatsoever incurred by BOOTH LIVESTOCK, INC. (herein called Debtor) a corporation ... unto HUSKY OIL COMPANY OF DELAWARE (herein called Husky).*
>
> *The guaranty herein is given in consideration of future extension of credit to Debtor by Husky. This guaranty covers any indebtedness incurred by Debtor prior to or subsequent to the date hereof. Guarantor covenants and agrees that this guaranty is absolute,*

unconditional, and unlimited as to such indebtedness and any charges or interest thereon, and any costs of collection, including attorneys fees and court costs. ...

For nearly ten years, Husky supplied merchandise to BL. In 1983, the Booths sold their interest in BL to the Gilletts. Husky continued to sell items to BL on credit. In 1984, Husky sold its business to a subsidiary of Flying J, Inc., which continued to do business with BL. Thereafter, BL defaulted on its obligation. Flying J, Inc. sued the Booths to recover under the guaranty agreement signed in 1974. The Gilletts were not sued because Paul had died and Joan had filed bankruptcy

The Booths, appellees, moved for a summary judgment on the grounds that they had signed a special guaranty that could not be assigned by Husky to Flying J, Inc. The trial court granted this motion, and Flying J, Inc. appealed.

... Appellant launches a two-pronged attack with initial contention that summary judgment was improperly granted against it because the district court erred in holding this instrument to be an unassignable special guaranty. Alternatively, appellant then argues that even if we agree that this is a special guaranty, we should follow the states that allow a modification of the common law to permit assignment and enforcement of any special guaranty where there has been no material change in the obligation to the guarantor. We disagree with appellant on both bases.

A general guaranty is drawn to address all potential creditors in general such as "to whom it may concern," and effectively promises all those creditors that the principal's obligations will be performed. By limitation, a special guaranty is drawn with reference to only one creditor such as a particular person, firm, or corporation. The appellees' guaranty in the instant case specifically refers to only one creditor, Husky. Therefore, the district court did not err in finding a special guaranty intent by the parties.

Our second inquiry is assignability. At common law, a general guaranty is assignable or transferable, but a special guaranty is not.... The rationale supporting the common law rule is that when a written instrument names only a specific creditor, there is no demonstration of an intent to make the instrument enforceable by someone not named within it. ...

Essentially, appellant argues that appellees' guaranty is ambiguous with respect to assignability because the instrument purports to be "absolute, unconditional, and unlimited," and contains no provision which expressly forbids assignments. ...

There is nothing ambiguous about the guaranty executed by appellees. The guaranty was drafted and given "in consideration of future extension of credit to Debtor by Husky," the sole and specific obligee. That language expressly and clearly indicates that the relationship and intent of these parties was rooted in appellees' reliance on Husky's ability and willingness to perform its contract with BL. A guaranty expressly given in consideration of the extension of future credit by a specific individual is generally held to be nontransferable. This is expressly the situation here where future sales were anticipated. Even where obligee sells his business and his successors continue to extend credit, the guarantor is liable only for debts resulting which accrued prior to the transfer of the original obligee's assets but not after. Unquestionably, in the instant case, all the disputed debts occurred after appellees transferred BL wholly to the Gilletts and discontinued their participation. ...

Appellant asks us to join those courts which permit the assignment of special guaranties in the absence of actual prejudice to the guarantor. While some courts may have modified the common law approach, we decline to follow them. ... Appellant provides no compelling reason for us to abandon a position that has existed unchanged in nearly eighty-seven years in Wyoming jurisprudence. Consequently, we determine that lacking any genuine issue of material fact or error of law, the district court did not err in granting summary judgment.

■ *Affirmed.*

CASE CONCEPTS REVIEW

1. Which party is the original debtor? Which is the original creditor? Who are the original guarantors?
2. How does the Flying J, Inc. become involved in this litigation?
3. What are the two arguments made by Flying J, Inc. as to why it should be allowed to enforce the guaranty agreement?
4. Why does the court reject both these arguments?

Guaranty agreements also are classified as absolute or conditional. Under an *absolute guaranty,* a creditor can go directly to the guarantor to collect. In a *conditional guaranty,* the creditor must have made reasonable, but unsuccessful, attempts to collect from the principal before the guarantor can be held liable.

LEGAL SIGNIFICANCE BETWEEN SURETY AND GUARANTOR Fortunately, today the distinction between a surety and a guaranty has very little significance. This result is due in large part to the *Restatement of Security,* a legal treatise on the subject of suretyship. Although the *Restatement* is not the law, its influence on the law is quite substantial. Those scholars who prepared the *Restatement of Security* considered *surety* to be interchangeable with *guarantor.* Therefore, unless stated otherwise, the general principles presented next are applicable to sureties as well as guarantors. Keep in mind that the statute of frauds applies only to guaranty contracts involving secondary promises and not to contracts involving a primary promise.

FIGURE 38-1 ■ Surety/Guarantor Status

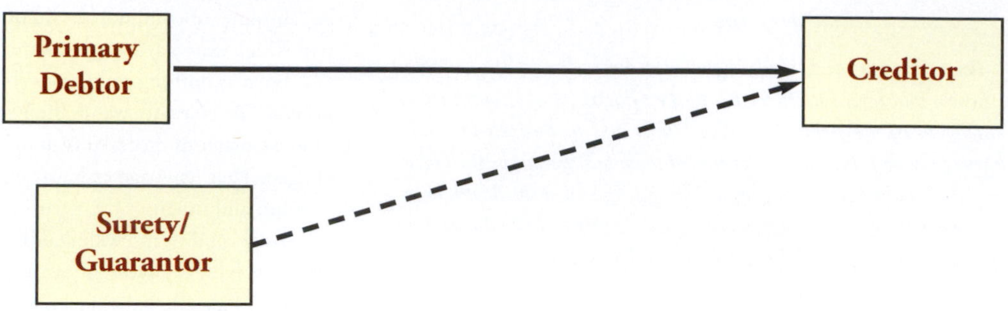

3. Suretyship versus Indemnity

A contract of suretyship should be distinguished from a contract of *indemnity.* Both contracts ultimately provide protection that what has been promised will be performed. However, the approach to accomplishing this purpose is vitally different. A surety makes a promise to a person (creditor) who is *to receive* the performance of an act or payment of a debt by another (principal). In a contract of indemnity, the assurance of performance is made to the party (principal) who is promising *to do* an act or *to pay* a debt. Whereas suretyship provides security to creditors, indemnity provides security to principal debtors. In other words, indemnity is a promise to the debtor, or obligor, to hold that debtor harmless from any loss incurred as a result of nonpayment of a debt or nonperformance of a promise. Most insurance contracts are examples of indemnification agreements between the insurer and the insured.

4. Creation of Suretyship Contracts

Two basic situations exist when a surety's promise would benefit the creditor: (1) when the creditor is concerned about the principal's ability to repay a loan and (2) when the creditor is concerned about the principal's completion of a contractual promise other than repayment.

Typically, a surety's promise to the creditor to pay the principal's loan is made gratuitously. The consideration (or money) given to the principal is sufficient consideration to make the surety's promise enforceable. Such sureties are generally known as *uncompensated sureties,* and their liabilities may be limited by law.

Performance bonds and fidelity bonds are also examples of suretyship. A *performance bond* provides protection against losses that may result from the failure of a contracting party to perform the contract as agreed. The surety (bonding company) promises the party entitled to performance to pay losses caused by nonperformance by the principal in an amount not to exceed the face of the bond. *Fidelity bonds* give protection against the dishonest acts of a person. In other words, such a

Performance and fidelity bonds provide protection against losses or dishonest acts.

bonding company promises to repay the employer any loss, not to exceed a stated amount, caused by the covered employees' embezzlement. Bonding companies are sureties in the sense that the term *surety* includes security either for the payment of money or for the faithful performance of some other duty. Bonding companies usually are *compensated sureties*.

Whereas uncompensated sureties are given special protection as favorites of the law, compensated sureties are perceived as being able to take care of themselves. This difference is illustrated in the interpretation of the contract. Ambiguous provisions of surety agreements are construed in favor of the unpaid surety and against the creditor. Ambiguous provisions of surety agreements involving compensated sureties are resolved against the surety. This distinction results from the fact that ambiguous language is generally construed against the party writing it. In the case of unpaid sureties, the language is usually framed by the creditor and signed by the surety. In the case of compensated sureties, the contract is usually prepared by the surety.

The question of whether a surety was gratuitous or compensated is examined in the following case.

CASE

WRS, Inc., d/b/a WRS Motion Picture Laboratories, a Corp., v. Plaza Entertainment, Inc., A Corp., Eric Parkinson, Charles von Bernuth and John Herklotz

UNITED STATES DISTRICT COURT FOR THE WESTERN DISTRICT OF PENNSYLVANIA

2006 U.S. Dist. LEXIS 49890 (2006)

JUDGE ARTHUR J. SCHWAB

Plaza Entertainment was formed in 1996 to engage in the commercial exploitation of film and video titles through licenses, assignments or other transfers of rights by the producers or other owners of the copyrights in the film and video titles. Defendant Eric Parkinson ("Parkinson"), defendant Charles von Bernuth ("von Bernuth") and Herklotz were shareholders, owners and/or principals of Plaza Entertainment.

At all relevant times, WRS was engaged in the business of film and video duplication and fulfillment services, as well as the administration of funds generated by distribution of the duplicated films and videos, for film and video distributors. WRS and Plaza Entertainment began a business relationship in 1996. By April 1998, WRS had performed a significant amount of duplication and fulfillment services for Plaza Entertainment for which it had not been fully paid.

On April 29, 1998, Plaza Entertainment submitted an order to WRS for duplication of a video entitled "The Giant of Thunder Mountain," requesting the duplication services on a credit basis. WRS allegedly was unwilling to extend additional credit to Plaza Entertainment unless Plaza Entertainment paid its past due balance or updated its credit application, provided additional collateral as security, and provided a guaranty from Herklotz.

On May 5, 1998, Parkinson or von Bernuth, or both, told Herklotz that Wal-Mart had placed an order with Plaza Entertainment for a large number of The Giant of Thunder Mountain video, and that WRS required his execution of a guaranty to duplicate The Giant of Thunder Mountain videos.

As a result, on May 6, 1998, Herklotz executed a surety agreement.

As of August 31, 1998, WRS was carrying a significant receivable amount on Plaza Entertainment's account. In order to induce WRS to continue providing duplication and fulfillment services for Plaza Entertainment, despite Plaza Entertainment's failure to make timely payments to WRS, Parkinson and von Bernuth executed a Services Agreement on October 12, 1998, pursuant to which WRS agreed to provide administrative services to Plaza Entertainment (including generation of sales invoices, collection of accounts receivable, performance of general accounting and record keeping functions and inventory monitoring and maintenance), in addition to duplication and fulfillment services.

The Services Agreement provided for a lockbox arrangement for the receipt of payments on Plaza Entertainment's accounts receivable to be distributed by WRS as set forth in the agreement. To compensate WRS for the provision of administrative services, the Services Agreement provided for a monthly payment of $5,000 by Plaza Entertainment, as well as reimbursement by Plaza Entertainment for all out of pocket expenses incurred by WRS to perform the administrative services. Finally, the Services Agreement provided WRS with a security interest in certain collateral of Plaza Entertainment and the personal guaranties of Plaza Entertainment's obligations to WRS by Parkinson and von Bernuth.

Plaza Entertainment never cured the delinquency in its account with WRS as contemplated by the Services Agreement. As a result, on October 13, 2000, WRS filed this civil action seeking damages from Plaza Entertainment for breach of contract based on Plaza Entertainment's failure to pay WRS for duplication, fulfillment and administrative services (Count I), and damages from Parkinson, von Bernuth and Herklotz for breach of contract based on their personal guaranties of Plaza Entertainment's

continued

obligations to WRS (Count II), as well as foreclosure of a security interest (Count III), injunctive relief (Count IV), declaratory relief (Count V) and an accounting (Count VI). Defaults have been entered against Plaza Entertainment, Parkinson and von Bernuth for failure to defend. Thus, Herklotz is the only defendant whose liability remains at issue.

Customarily, a suretyship arrangement arises when a creditor refuses to extend credit to a debtor unless a third party (the surety) agrees to provide additional security for repayment of the debt by undertaking the debtor's obligation to the creditor if the debtor fails to perform. In general terms, a suretyship represents a three-party association wherein a creditor is entitled to performance of a contractual duty by the principal debtor or alternatively, if the debtor defaults, by the debtor's surety.

Usually, suretyship problems arise because the three-party structure of a suretyship becomes dynamic rather than remaining static. After the signing of a suretyship contract, the creditor and the principal debtor may renegotiate the terms of the debtor's obligation to the creditor without obtaining the surety's assent to the changed obligation. When the debtor defaults, the creditor then seeks to have the surety perform the debtor's renegotiated obligation. Commonly, the surety asserts as a defense that he does not have a duty to perform the renegotiated obligation of the principal debtor since he did not consent to be liable for that new obligation.

Cognizant of the problems posed by the three-party composition of suretyships, Pennsylvania courts have uniformly recognized that where the creditor and the debtor materially modify the terms of their relationship without obtaining the surety's assent thereto, the surety's liability may be affected. A material modification in the creditor-debtor relationship consists of a significant change in the principal debtor's obligation to the creditor that in essence substitutes an agreement substantially different from the original agreement on which the surety accepted liability. Where, without the surety's consent, there has been a material modification in the creditor-debtor relationship, a gratuitous (uncompensated) surety is completely discharged. A compensated surety is discharged only if, without the surety's consent, there has been a material modification in the creditor-debtor relationship and said modification has substantially increased the surety's risk.

Turning first to Herklotz's surety status, Herklotz maintains that he was a "gratuitous" surety. Therefore, according to Herklotz, his obligation to WRS was completely discharged because the October 12, 1998 Services Agreement between WRS and Plaza Entertainment, which was executed by Parkinson and von Bernuth without his consent, materially changed the creditor-debtor relationship between WRS and Plaza Entertainment. On the other hand, WRS maintains that Herklotz was a "compensated" surety; that the October 12, 1998 Services Agreement did not materially modify the creditor-debtor relationship between WRS and Plaza Entertainment; that, even if the October 12, 1998 Services Agreement did materially modify the creditor-debtor relationship between WRS and Plaza Entertainment, Herklotz consented to such modification in the May 6, 1998 surety agreement; and that, in any event, the October 12, 1998 Services Agreement did not substantially increase Herklotz's risk as surety for Plaza Entertainment's debt to WRS. Thus, WRS contends that Herklotz is liable as surety for the debt of Plaza Entertainment to WRS.

Based on the undisputed facts, the Court concludes that Herklotz was a compensated surety. There is no evidence that Herklotz executed the May 6, 1998 surety agreement "for reasons involving familial or neighborly affection" or that his execution of the May 6, 1998 surety agreement "was motivated by selfless generosity."

Rather, as a principal of Plaza Entertainment and the producer of *The Giant of Thunder Mountain* video, Herklotz had a personal interest in signing the May 6, 1998, surety agreement: that is, to ensure that WRS continued to provide duplication and fulfillment services to Plaza Entertainment.

Based on Herklotz's status as a compensated surety, he is discharged from his obligation to WRS for Plaza Entertainment's debt only if the October 12, 1998 Services Agreement constituted a material modification in the creditor-debtor relationship between WRS and Plaza Entertainment and the modification substantially increased his risk. After consideration, the Court concludes that neither prong is satisfied in this case. Therefore, Herklotz is liable as surety for the debt of Plaza Entertainment to WRS.

As to the issue of whether the October 12, 1998 Services Agreement materially modified the creditor-debtor relationship between WRS and Plaza Entertainment, the Court agrees with WRS that the agreement "simply transferred the billing and collection function from Plaza [Entertainment] to WRS", due to Plaza Entertainment's recognition that it was "not doing a good job of collections." In all other respects, the manner in which WRS and Plaza Entertainment conducted business remained the same. Under the circumstances, the October 12, 1998 Services Agreement cannot be construed as "an agreement substantially different from the original agreement on which the surety accepted liability."

Moreover, even if the October 12, 1998 Services Agreement could be construed as a material modification of the creditor-debtor relationship between WRS and Plaza Entertainment, the agreement did not substantially increase Herklotz's risk. In fact, as noted by WRS, the October 12, 1998 Services Agreement decreased Herklotz's risk as surety for Plaza Entertainment's debt to WRS by providing (1) additional collateral as security, (2) personal guaranties of Plaza Entertainment's obligations to WRS by Parkinson and von Bernuth, and (3) procedures to ensure that Plaza Entertainment's accounts receivable would be applied to its debt to WRS.

Based on the foregoing, WRS's motion for summary judgment as to Herklotz's liability will be granted, and Herklotz's cross-motion for summary judgment as to liability will be denied.

■ *Motion of WRS granted.*

CASE CONCEPTS REVIEW

1. Why was it important to determine whether the surety was gratuitous or compensated?
2. Why did the court not find a material alteration or a substantial increase in risk?

Suretyship agreements are usually express written contracts, whereby the surety assumes responsibility for the principal's performance for the creditor. The surety agrees to pay or to perform in case the principal defaults.

Contracts of suretyship also may result by operation of law. Assume that Jones sells his retail lumber business to Smith, who assumes and agrees to pay, as part of the purchase price, all of Jones's outstanding liabilities. Between Smith and Jones, Smith has now become the primary debtor. Jones is a surety and secondarily liable.

As soon as the creditors are notified of the sale, they are obligated to respect the new relationship by attempting to recover from Smith before looking to Jones for payment.

5. Liability of the Parties in General

The surety's liability is dependent on the many factors that exist in a three-party relationship. Therefore the following discussion is divided into three parts, each based on the following relationships:

1. Creditor-surety (Sections 6 through 8)
2. Creditor-principal (Sections 9 through 13)
3. Principal-surety (Sections 14 through 16)

CREDITOR-SURETY RELATIONSHIP

6. Fiduciary Aspects

The suretyship relationship has some fiduciary aspects. It requires good faith and fair dealing. For this reason, a creditor possessing information affecting the risk must communicate such information to the surety before the contract is made. This duty applies only to information that is *significant* to the risk. It does not cover all matters that might affect the risk. If some facts make the risk a materially greater one than the surety intends to assume, and if the creditor knows this, the creditor has a duty to disclose those facts to the surety. The duty to disclose exists only if the creditor has reason to believe that the surety does not know the facts and the creditor has a reasonable opportunity to communicate them to the surety.

When we concentrate on a typical loan transaction, the surety generally will have as much, if not more, knowledge about the principal than will the creditor. Therefore, the fiduciary duty of disclosure will seldom arise if the surety is a relative of or otherwise related in a business sense to the principal. However, in keeping with conservative lending practices—when in doubt about its appropriateness—the creditor should disclose what it knows about the principal when the surety inquires.

Since the contract is between the surety and the creditor, any misconduct of the principal that induces a party to become a surety does not allow that surety to avoid the contract. At the time of the contract, however, a creditor who is aware of the principal's misrepresentation is obligated to inform the surety of the misrepresentation. This duty to inform probably occurs most frequently when a creditor learns that a principal has misrepresented its financial condition to a prospective surety. Particularly when the surety does not have access to the principal's records and books, the creditor is obligated to warn the surety of the increased risk. In this situation, a creditor's failure to warn the surety will release that surety from liability.

Perhaps the most common application of these fiduciary duties occurs when a financial institution is bonding its employees. An employer who knows of an employee's past financial transgressions (such as embezzlement) must inform the bonding company of this fact at the time a bond is sought. Furthermore, an employer who discovers that a bonded employee has been guilty of misappropriation of funds should immediately discharge the employee unless the surety assents to his or her continued employment. To allow the employee to continue subjects the surety to a risk not contemplated. Rehabilitation of the employee by giving him or her a second chance can be undertaken only with the consent of the surety. If the surety does not consent, and if the employee is guilty of misappropriation a second time, the surety is not liable on the surety bond.

7. Principal's Default: Notice

By the nature of the agreement, a surety has no obligation to the creditor unless the principal fails to perform. Although no performance is owed prior to that time, a surety is liable to the creditor *as soon as* the principal defaults. This simple-sounding rule means that the creditor usually does not have to exhaust his or her remedies against the principal before seeking to recover from the surety. Additionally, a creditor may take action against the surety without having to give notice to the surety that the principal has defaulted. The action will provide the notice. The rule that notice need not be given the surety is subject to the following three exceptions:

1. The contract may require notice to the surety.
2. A surety who is a drawer or indorser of commercial paper is entitled to notice unless waived in the paper.
3. A surety who only guarantees collection is entitled to notice.

SURETY-CREDITOR AGREEMENT A surety may insist on including a clause in the contract with the creditor requiring the notice of the principal's default be given within a specified time. Whenever such a clause is included, courts will enforce it. If such a clause is binding on the parties, the creditor's failure to notify the surety of the principal's default discharges the surety from liability. However, the notice requirement must be reasonably, and not strictly, interpreted.

SURETY AS DRAWER OR INDORSER OF COMMERCIAL PAPER Any drawer of a draft (check) and any indorser of a note, draft, or certificate of deposit becomes liable on the instrument signed if (1) presentment for payment or acceptance was made within a reasonable time, (2) dishonor occurred, and (3) notice of dishonor was given within the time allowed. Since this notice of dishonor must be given, parties who become a surety through their status as an accommodating drawer or indorser or both are entitled to be notified of the principal's (primary party's) default (dishonor). Chapter 36, on the liability of parties to commercial paper, gives further details of the notice requirement in this exception.

SURETY AS COLLECTION GUARANTOR Chapter 36 also explains that a collection guarantor under the terms of the Uniform Commercial Code assures the creditor that collection can be obtained from the guarantor if all efforts to collect from the principal prove unsuccessful. Due to the nature of this assurance, equity requires that the guarantor's potential liability not be unresolved indefinitely while the creditor pursues its claim against the principal.

To the extent that a collection guarantor suffers from a lack of notice, that guarantor is discharged. For example, assume that a creditor attempts to collect a debt owed by the principal for two years without notifying that collection guarantor of any such actions. Then the creditor seeks to collect from the guarantor. Also assume that the guarantor can prove that two years before, the guarantor could have recovered 75 percent of the obligation owed from the principal, but now the guarantor can recover nothing. The creditor's lack of notice relieves the guarantor of 75 percent of the original obligation.

The collection guarantor is not damaged by a lack of notice if that guarantor is aware of what actions the creditor is taking to collect from the principal. In the preceding example, if the guarantor knew of the creditor's efforts despite no notice being received, that guarantor has not been prejudiced in any way. In other words, the guarantor could have satisfied its potential obligation at any time and pursued its rights against the principal. Therefore, in this situation, the collection guarantor remains liable for 100 percent of the obligation.

8. Surety's Performance and Subrogation Rights

In general, when a principal defaults, the surety immediately becomes liable to the creditor. The surety can satisfy its obligation to the creditor by performing as promised or by showing that it has a valid excuse for not performing. The following sections present several situations in which the surety is relieved of liability. However, for the time being, assume that upon the principal's default, the surety does perform as promised. When performance has been completed, the surety's most important right involves the concept of **subrogation**.

Subrogation

The substitution of one person in another's place, whether as a creditor or as the possessor of any lawful right, so the substituted person may succeed to the rights, remedies, or proceeds of the claim

The term *subrogation* literally means the substitution of one person in the place of another. The surety who fully performs the obligation of the principal is subrogated to the creditor's rights against the principal. The surety who pays the principal's debt becomes entitled to any security interest the principal has granted to the creditor regarding the debt paid. Furthermore, whenever the creditor obtains a judgment against the principal, the surety receives the benefit of this judgment when the surety satisfies the principal's debts.

Because of the right of subrogation, a creditor in possession of collateral given to him or her by the principal is not at liberty to return it without the consent of the surety. Any surrender of security releases the surety to the extent of its value, with the loss of subrogation damaging the surety to that extent. Failure of the creditor to make use of the security, however, does not release the surety since the latter is free to pay the indebtedness and to obtain the security for his or her own protection. If the creditor loses the benefit of collateral by inactivity—failure to record a mortgage or notify an indorser—the surety is released to the extent that he or she is injured. In general, if the person who is entitled to protection under the contract of suretyship does anything that will materially prejudice the rights of the surety, the surety will, to that extent at least, be discharged.

The right of subrogation protects the creditor as well as the surety. In other words, a creditor has the right to step into the shoes of the surety and to enforce the surety's rights against the principal. Assume that the principal delivered corporate stock to the surety to protect the surety in the event of the principal's default. The creditor, to the extent of the claim, may substitute his or her position for that of the surety with reference to the stock. In the event of the return of the stock by the surety to the principal, the creditor is entitled to follow the stock into the hands of the debtor and subject it to a lien. The creditor may also secure an injunction against return of the stock to the principal, thus having it impounded by the court until the principal debt falls due, at which time the stock may be sold for the benefit of the creditor.

Creditor-Principal Relationship

9. Introduction

As has been stated previously, a surety generally becomes liable only when the principal defaults. Therefore, if the principal does not default, the surety never becomes liable to the creditor; no default occurs if the principal performs as promised. However, there may be other situations in which the principal has not defaulted because he or she has a valid excuse for nonperformance. These situations may involve a defense the principal can assert against the creditor, a release of the principal by the creditor, or a modification of the creditor-principal relationship. Any of these possible situations may have an impact on the surety's liability.

10. Principal's Defenses

In general, any defense the principal can use to reduce liability to the creditor may also be used by a surety to reduce liability. This idea of making the principal's defenses available to the surety is not conditioned on the principal's utilizing the defense first. The surety is protected by the defense regardless of whether or not the principal is relieved of liability.

One important defense is that of lack of a primary obligation. In other words, the surety is not bound if the principal is not bound. This may occur when the principal fails to sign a contract, although expected to do so. Other common examples of defenses that may be available to the principal and surety include mutual mistake, fraud, duress, undue influence, illegality, impossibility, and lack or failure of consideration.

Setoffs and counterclaims of both the principal and the surety may be used as a defense by the surety under certain circumstances. The surety can set off any claim it has against the creditor and use the setoff to reduce or eliminate the liability. If the principal is insolvent, if the principal and surety are sued jointly, or if the surety has taken an assignment of the claim of the principal, the surety is entitled to use as a defense any setoff that could be used by the principal debtor in a suit by the creditor.

There are three important exceptions to the general rule that defenses available to the principal may be used by the surety to avoid liability to the surety: (1) the principal's lack of capacity, (2) the principal's discharge in bankruptcy, and (3) the principal's performance excused due to the statute of limitations having run.

LACK OF CAPACITY AND DISCHARGE IN BANKRUPTCY Lack of capacity and discharge in bankruptcy are not available to the surety as defenses because the surety promised in the first instance to protect the creditor against the principal's inability to perform. Most creditors, particularly those in loan transactions, anticipate the principal's lack of capacity or discharge in bankruptcy. A creditor is likely to protect against the consequences of these possible events by insisting that a surety becomes involved.

When a principal who lacks capacity avoids a contract and fails to return the consideration that was received from the creditor, the surety is required to make up any deficiency between the value of whatever the principal has performed and the complete performance. If, on the other hand, the principal returns all or some of the consideration received from the creditor, the surety's liability is reduced by the value of the consideration returned.

STATUTE OF LIMITATION The principal's defense that the statute of limitations prevents collection by the creditor may not be used by the surety. The principal and the surety have separate time periods for which they remain liable to the creditor, and that period may be longer for the surety. For example, the principal may be liable only on the basis of an oral promise (two-year statute of limitations, for instance). The surety's obligation may be based on a written agreement subject to a six-year statute of limitations. Obviously, the creditor who waits for three years after the principal's default cannot recover from the principal. Nevertheless, in this situation, the surety remains liable.

11. Releases

In general, a creditor who voluntarily releases the principal from liability also releases the surety. The logic of this general rule is based on the fact that the surety becomes liable only upon the principal's default. If the principal never defaults since the creditor relinquishes its claim against the principal, the surety never becomes liable either. Any conclusion to the contrary would mean the creditor could indirectly require the principal's performance even after a release. If a creditor could hold the surety liable, the surety could seek reimbursement from the principal. Therefore, the creditor would indirectly be requiring the principal's performance.

As always, we must consider some exceptions to this general rule. The following three are discussed here: (1) A surety that consents to a principal's release is not released; (2) a creditor that reserves rights against a surety does not release that surety; and (3) a release obtained by that principal's fraud does not release the surety if the creditor rescinds the release prior to the surety's reliance on the release.

THE SURETY'S CONSENT It is hard to imagine why any commercial surety would voluntarily consent to remain liable when a principal is released from liability. Indeed, most situations involving a surety's consent to remain personally liable probably will involve a friendship or kinship between the surety and the principal. For example, a surety may wish to help a friend or relative by improving that principal's financial record. To achieve this result, the surety may actually seek the principal's release by consenting to remain liable.

Furthermore, a surety may be secured by the principal in return for acting as a surety. We could assume that a business, as principal, granted its president, as surety, a security interest in all its accounts and general intangibles. A creditor may be willing to take the surety's security interest in full satisfaction of the performance owed. The creditor might agree to release the principal from further personal liability if the surety consents to the creditor's having the right to pursue its claim against the accounts and general intangibles. The basis for this conclusion is the creditor's right of subrogation, discussed in section 8.

RESERVATION OF RIGHTS Even a non-consenting surety is not released when a principal is released if the creditor reserves rights against the surety. In essence, the creditor's reservation of rights is interpreted to be a promise by the creditor that the principal will not be sued. The creditor can still hold the surety liable, and the surety can seek reimbursement from the principal upon the surety's performance. Therefore, in essence, the principal ultimately remains liable despite the prior release. The creditor really has promised only that the creditor will not sue the principal. To protect the surety's potential claim against the principal, the surety may perform for the creditor any time after that creditor has released the principal and has reserved rights against the surety. Due to its vital importance and its impact on the surety's liability, notice of the reservation of rights against a surety should be given in writing to both the surety and the principal.

PRINCIPAL'S FRAUD With the use of false financial statements, the principal may induce a creditor to accept less than full performance from the principal or no performance at all in return for the creditor's release. Once that creditor learns of this fraudulent scheme by the principal, the creditor may rescind its release agreement. What impact these events have on a surety's liability depends on the factual situation. Normally, a surety (that has not consented and has not had rights reserved against it) is released when the principal is released. However, if the release is obtained by fraud by the principal, the creditor would be greatly disadvantaged if the surety is released altogether. Therefore, if the surety had no knowledge of the fraud, that surety is released only to the extent it has relied on the release and the changed legal position as a result of the release. If the surety had knowledge of the principal's wrongful acts, the surety is not justified in relying on the release. In this latter situation, the creditor still may hold the surety liable for the principal's uncompleted performance.

12. Extensions of Time for Payment

Before discussing the rules regarding the surety's liability, we need to have a clear understanding of what is meant by an extension of time for performance. To affect the surety's liability, the extension agreement must be a binding, enforceable contract. As such, it must be for a definite time and supported by consideration. In other words, the principal must induce the creditor to extend the time originally involved by promising something in addition to what the principal is already obligated to do. A principal's consideration for an extension may take the form of a refinancing agreement or an advance payment of interest. Merely promising to pay the original debt at a future date will not supply the consideration because performance of a preexisting obligation is not consideration.

The creditor's gratuitous indulgence or passive permission to the principal to take more time than the contract provides has no impact on the surety's liability. Such conduct by the creditor does not injure the surety in any way. Upon the principal's default, the surety is free to perform at any time and pursue all available remedies.

If there is a formalized agreement between creditor and principal whereby the time for performance is extended to a definite time, a non-consenting, uncompensated surety is discharged from liability. This rule is necessary since the extension of time delays any potential default by the principal. Such a delay could adversely affect the surety's ability to recover from the principal if the surety has to perform. During the extension, the principal's financial condition could worsen, which could increase the surety's ultimate risk of loss.

As with releases, this general rule of releasing the surety upon the creditor granting a formal extension of time does not apply if the surety consents to the extension. Furthermore, a surety is not discharged by a formal extension of time if the creditor expressly reserves rights against the surety. This reservation of rights must be a part of the extension agreement. The creditor's stipulation that rights are reserved against the surety does not bind the surety to the extension agreement. Thus, the surety may proceed to satisfy the creditor's claim and sue the principal for reimbursement at any time. The principal, therefore, is not really protected by an extension agreement that includes the creditor's reservation of rights against the surety. This type of extension agreement simply is a limited promise by the creditor not to sue the principal during the extension period.

Finally, a formalized extension of the time for performance discharges a compensated surety only to the extent that surety is injured by the extension. Of course, this rule assumes that the surety does not consent to the extension agreement. A compensated surety is perceived as being capable of protecting itself by anticipating possible extension agreements and charging a premium in accordance with expectations.

13. Other Modifications

In addition to an extension of the time for payment, any other modification of the creditor-principal agreement generally discharges the surety. The logic behind this general rule is that a surety should not be liable for the performance of some agreement made after the surety's commitment to the creditor. A modification agreed to by creditor and principal is a novation that relieves the surety from its obligation. In general, evidence of a renewed obligation is not considered to be a modification that relieves the surety of liability. However, if the renewal note increases the principal's obligation, the surety is relieved of further liability unless the surety consents to the renewal agreement.

An examination of the exceptions or qualifications to this general rule may make the philosophy behind it clearer. These exceptions include the following: (1) A surety that consents to the modification is not discharged; (2) an uncompensated but non-consenting surety is not discharged to the extent that the modification benefits the surety; and (3) a compensated surety is not discharged if the modification does not materially increase the surety's risk.

SURETY'S CONSENT As in other areas of suretyship, the parties can override the application of the general rule on modification by this agreement. A surety who consents to remain liable is not discharged by a modification to the creditor-principal agreement. This exception is applicable regardless of when the surety consents. Whether consent to modifications occurs before, at the time of, or after the modification, the consenting surety remains liable to the creditor.

If the surety's consent is not a part of the original agreement signed by the surety, the creditor has the responsibility to notify the surety of the modification and to obtain the surety's consent. Failure to obtain this consent upon full notice of the modification automatically discharges the surety.

UNCOMPENSATED SURETIES The surety who is not paid is a favorite of the law. In fact, the uncompensated surety is so protected in some states that any modification to the principal's obligation results in an absolute discharge of this surety, assuming no consent.

Courts in some states have disliked the harshness of the rule that discharges an uncompensated surety whenever any modification is made without that surety's consent. Therefore, there are decisions that hold that an uncompensated (and non-consenting) surety should not be discharged if the creditor-principal modification benefits the surety. This benefit must be so obvious that there is no way to doubt its beneficial nature. Typically, such a modification occurs only when the creditor agrees to reduce the amount due or the rate of interest. In some states, a change in interest rates (up or down) does not discharge a continuing surety. Since interest rates are expected to change in today's economy, that change should not discharge the continuing surety.

COMPENSATED SURETIES Sureties that receive consideration (separate from that received by the principal) in return for their promises are *not* protected by the law to the same extent as uncompensated sureties. Thus, with respect to the impact of creditor-principal modifications, a compensated surety is discharged altogether only if that surety's risk has materially increased. If the increased risk to the surety cannot be readily determined, it is immaterial. To the extent that a compensated surety's risk is increased only slightly by the modification, that surety is discharged only to the extent of the increased risk. And if the compensated surety's risk is not affected by the modification, the surety remains liable as promised.

Why is an extension of time for payment treated differently from other modifications? This distinction in treatment basically is due to the creditor's ability to reserve rights against the surety upon an extension of the time of performance. In this discussion of modification, there has been no mention of reservation of rights. A creditor cannot reserve rights against a surety when a general modification of the principal's agreement is made.

PRINCIPAL-SURETY RELATIONSHIP

14. Surety's Duty to Account

Not only does the principal owe a duty to perform to the creditor, but the principal also owes that same duty to the surety. This duty arises by express agreement or by implication. Whenever a surety is present, the principal owes the duty to protect that surety from liability regardless of whether the surety has a contract with that principal or with the creditor. The only exception to this general rule is when the principal is relieved of liability due to a defense assertable against the creditor's claim. It is this general duty the principal owes the surety that justifies the surety's right to be reimbursed by the principal after the surety has satisfied the creditor's claim.

The surety owes a duty to account to the principal for any profits obtained after the surety performs. For example, suppose a principal gave a creditor a security interest in some equipment, and assume that a surety personally paid $100,000 to satisfy the principal's delinquent obligation. As noted previously, the surety has the right to the security interest via subrogation. If the surety sold the equipment for $175,000, that surety would have to return $75,000 to the principal. This surety's duty to account emphasizes that the surety is liable for the principal's performance of an obligation. In essence, the surety should be liable for no more than, and should not benefit from, the commitment made.

15. Surety's Right to Reimbursement

Generally, after the surety has performed, the surety is entitled to be reimbursed by the principal. As you have come to expect, this general rule on the surety's right to be reimbursed is subject to at least two exceptions. First, a principal may inform a surety of a valid defense that a principal can assert to deny the creditor's claim. If the surety fails to use this defense as a means of reducing liability, the surety is not entitled to be reimbursed by the principal. Basically, the law requires the principal to bear the burden of informing the surety of available defenses. However, this requirement to inform does not apply when the principal's defense cannot be asserted by the surety. For example, the surety cannot assert the principal's defenses of (1) lack of capacity, (2) discharge in bankruptcy, and/or (3) expiration of the statute of limitations. Regardless of whether a surety knows of these defenses, that surety cannot force the principal to reimburse expenses after the surety has satisfied the creditor's claim. In other words, these defenses extinguish the principal's liability altogether.

A second exception to the principal's duty to reimburse occurs when a surety has performed for a creditor after a principal has been released. A surety that performs is not entitled to be reimbursed by the principal if the principal has been released by the creditor's agreement. This rule makes logical sense, since it would be fraudulent for a creditor of a discharged or released principal to seek performance from a surety. If a surety does perform under the circumstances, the surety has a right to have the value of performance returned from the creditor.

This rule relieving the principal of the duty to reimburse the surety is not applicable when the creditor releasing the principal reserves rights against the surety. As discussed in sections 11 and 12, a surety remains liable to perform the principal's obligations if the creditor reserves rights against the surety. If the surety must perform for the creditor, it is only fair that the surety be reimbursed by the principal. The use of the concept of reservation of rights is allowed when a principal is released by a creditor or when time for payment is extended formally. In both cases, the principal debtor remains liable to the surety.

16. Liability of Co-Sureties

Throughout this chapter, there has been an implicit assumption that only one surety was involved in protecting the creditor This assumption is too simplistic to reflect the actual situation in the marketplace. In any contract, a creditor may insist on or otherwise be benefited by the existence of two or more sureties. Generally, these sureties may exist as co-sureties or as subsureties. *Co-sureties* are jointly and severally liable to the creditor. The term *joint and several* means the creditor may sue the co-sureties jointly for the performance promised or may sue each surety separately for the entire performance due. A *subsurety* promises to be liable only in the event that the surety refuses to perform and thereby defaults. A subsurety is a surety's surety. Unless the sureties involved in a transaction agree otherwise, they are considered co-sureties. A subsuretyship normally must be created by the agreement of the parties, whereas a co-suretyship may be created by implication.

Numerous legal principles govern the rights of all the parties involved in a transaction with two or more sureties. In general, all the basic rules and exceptions discussed in this chapter remain applicable. For example, a release of the principal is a release of the surety if the surety does not consent to the release and if the creditor does not reserve rights against the surety. When a creditor releases one surety but not the other sureties, the general rule is that the remaining sureties are released to the extent that they cannot seek contribution against the released surety. Once again, this rule is not applicable if the remaining sureties consent or if the creditor reserves rights against the remaining sureties.

In addition to the applicability of the aforementioned legal principles, there are rules that govern the liability of co-sureties one to another. Similar to the surety's right to be reimbursed by the principal, the fundamental rule among co-sureties is their right of contribution. This right is how co-sureties work out among themselves their fair share of the performance completed for the creditor. Whereas a creditor can hold one surety liable for the principal's entire obligation, that surety is liable for only a pro rata share (among the co-sureties) of the performance rendered. The right of contribution works to allocate the liability 50–50 among two co-sureties, 33 1/3–3 1/3–33 1/3 among three co-sureties, and so forth. Before one co-surety can collect from another, proof of payment of the obligation is required. In general, any recovery does not include attorneys' fees, although interest calculated at the statutory rate may be recovered.

MECHANIC'S LIENS

17. Introduction

Mechanic's lien

A lien for the value of material and labor expended in the construction of buildings and other improvements

Mechanic's lien laws provide for the filing of liens on real estate that has been improved. An improvement is any addition to the land. While the term *improvement* does not always mean that the land's value has been increased, most improvements usually do increase the real estate's value. The purpose of a mechanic's lien is to protect contractors, suppliers, and laborers in the event of nonpayment of their accounts. This purpose is accomplished by state laws that grant to the unpaid party a lien against real estate.

To gain an understanding of how mechanic's liens generally are used to secure payment for one who contributed to an improvement, the following sections discuss potential lienholders, the perfection and enforcement of liens, priority issues, and protection against liens.

Keep in mind that the mechanic's lien law is quite complicated and, as illustrated in the following case, very technical in nature.

18. Potential Lienholders

The persons usually entitled to a lien include those who (1) deliver material, fixtures, apparatus, machinery, or forms to be used in repairing, altering, or constructing a building on the premises; (2) fill, sod, or do landscape work in connection with the premises; (3) act as architect, engineer, or superintendent during the construction of a building; or (4) furnish labor for repairing, altering, or constructing a building.

CASE

Wesco Distribution, Inc. v. Westport Group, Inc.

COURT OF APPEALS OF TEXAS

150 S.W.3d 553 (2004)

JUSTICE DAVID PURYEAR

Westport, a general contractor, agreed to build a dental office for E&M Properties and hired J&D Electric as its electrical subcontractor for the project. J&D Electric agreed to provide all the labor and materials necessary to perform the subcontract work. J&D Electric purchased some of the materials used in the dental office from Wesco, but failed to fully pay Wesco for these materials. On July 11, 2001, Wesco attempted to send notice by mail to Westport of J&D Electric's outstanding bill for materials purchased between March 2001 and June 25, 2001, in order to notify Westport of Wesco's claim for a mechanic's lien on the property. The post office returned this notice to Wesco because Wesco failed to attach sufficient postage. Wesco added postage and again mailed its notice to Westport on July 25, 2001. On July 19, Westport, having received no notice of lien, made a payment to J&D Electric. Although it is unclear when notice was actually received, it is clear that no payments were made by Westport after receipt of notice. By the time it received notice, Westport had paid J&D Electric almost everything it was owed. Wesco filed an affidavit claiming a lien on September 13, 2001.

Westport filed suit to remove Wesco's claimed lien, and Wesco filed suit for damages and foreclosure of its lien. The two lawsuits were consolidated. Westport filed a summary motion "to remove invalid or unenforceable lien" and Wesco opposed the motion. The trial court initially denied Westport's summary motion, but when the parties filed cross-motions for summary judgment, the trial court granted Westport's request for summary judgment made on the same grounds as its earlier motion. Wesco then brought this appeal.

Wesco's argues that the trial court mistakenly interpreted the notice provisions contained in the mechanic's lien statute by finding that Wesco did not comply with its terms. The statute sets out deadlines for giving notice of unpaid balances owed by subcontractors to material-men, to the original contractor, and to the property owner and requires timely notice as a prerequisite for a valid lien claim. For Wesco's lien claim to be valid, Wesco must have effectively notified Westport by July 15 of any unpaid balance for materials delivered in May. Because it attempted to send a notice on July 11, before the deadline, Wesco argues that it timely notified Westport under the statute. When that notice was returned to Wesco for insufficient postage, and the notice was re-sent on July 25, 2001, Westport argued that there was no timely notice of lien for nonpayment for supplies delivered to J&D Electric prior to the end of May.

Wesco contends that its deposit of the notice with insufficient postage substantially complies with the statutory requirements of section 53.003 of the property code because Westport eventually received a notice. Despite the insufficient postage, it argues, Wesco deposited the notice within the statutory time period; the statute requires nothing more. Westport responds that notice mailed with insufficient postage does not comply with statutory requirements because "sending" notice by mail necessarily includes attaching sufficient postage. Because Wesco failed to timely notify Westport of its lien claim, Westport argues, the lien it claims is invalid. We agree.

Construing the statute to not require postage at all would produce absurd results. Here, the first attempt at notice would have been effective; there would be no need for Wesco to re-send the returned correspondence because the statute's requirements for constructive notice would have already been met. According to that construction, "notice" that would never and could never arrive would nonetheless be considered effective against Westport.

In an attempt to temper this extreme result, Wesco asserts that its interpretation would indeed require some kind of notice. Because the statute should be liberally interpreted for the benefit of material men, Wesco argues, its timely but postage-deficient notice should, combined with its postage-prepaid but untimely notice, qualify as substantial compliance with the statute. Wesco characterizes the return of its notice for insufficient postage as a delay in delivery by the Postal Service and argues that it substantially complied with the requirement that it mail its notice within the statutory time period because the initial mailing occurred on July 11, and the general purpose of the statute's notice provision was achieved.

The liberal construction for which Wesco argues does not excuse failure to comply with the statutory requirement that the materialman provide "timely written notice."

The notice requirement, unlike the technical defects excused by substantial compliance, plays a critical role in achieving the purposes of this statute. The mechanic's lien statute is designed to protect contractors, subcontractors, and owners. The purposes of notice are; (1) to give those parties entitled to notice an opportunity to protect their interests, and (2) to prevent surprise.

The district court's decision that Wesco's lien is invalid because its attempt to timely notify Westport failed for lack of sufficient postage is consistent with the statute. The effort Wesco made did not satisfy the notice requirements mandated by the mechanic's lien statute. We affirm.

.■ *Affirmed.*

CASE CONCEPTS REVIEW

1. According to the court, when was notice received?
2. Why do you believe the court was not willing to overlook the lack of postage and deem this to be a "technical defect excused by substantial compliance"?

Persons who contract with the owner, whether they furnish labor or material or agree to construct the building, are known as *contractors.* Thus, virtually any contract between the owner and another that has for its purpose the improvement of real estate gives rise to a lien on the premises in favor of those responsible for the improvement.

In addition to contractors, anyone to whom a distinct part of the contract has been sublet has a right to a lien. These parties are customarily referred to as *subcontractors.* Their rights differ slightly from those of contractors, and some of these differences are considered in later sections.

Those parties who furnish materials to a contractor or subcontractor and those who do the physical work, also, may have the right to mechanic's liens. These parties are known as suppliers and *laborers,* respectively.

19. Perfection and Enforcement

In some states, a contractor has a lien as soon as the contract to repair or to improve the real estate is entered into. In others, the lien attaches as soon as the work is commenced. A supplier of materials usually has a lien as soon as the materials are furnished. A laborer has a lien when the work is performed. The statutes relating to mechanic's liens provide for the method of perfecting these mechanic's liens and for the time period during which they may be perfected. The time period begins when the work is substantially completed.

The usual procedure is that the party seeking to perfect a mechanic's lien files or records a notice of lien in the office of the county in which deeds to real estate are recorded. Some statutes provide for filing in the county of residence of the owner. A copy of the notice is sent to the owner of record and to the party contracting for the repair or improvement. This notice must be filed within the prescribed statutory period. The law then requires a suit to foreclose the lien and specifies that it be commenced within an additionally prescribed period, such as one year. Anything less than strict observance of the filing requirements eliminates the mechanic's lien, but not the debt.

Most mechanic's lien laws provide a relatively long period, such as one year, during which a contractor may file a mechanic's lien and proceed to enforce it against the property interest of the party with whom he or she contracted. This time period is relatively long because the obligation is known to the owner, and he or she is in no way prejudiced if the lien is not promptly filed.

A much shorter time period is set for subcontractors, suppliers, and laborers to file a mechanic's lien. The owner of the premises may not know the source of materials and may not know the names of all persons performing services on the premises. To this extent, the liens of subcontractors, suppliers, and laborers may be secret, and the owner may pay the wrong person. Therefore, the time period in which the statutory procedures must be followed is relatively short, such as sixty to ninety days.

If the property is sold or mortgaged, the existence of any mechanic's lien often would be unknown to the purchaser or mortgagee. For this reason the statutes on mechanic's liens usually specify the same short period of time for the perfection of the mechanic's lien—whether by a contractor, subcontractor, supplier, or laborer—if it is to be effective against good-faith purchasers of the property or subsequent mortgagees. Under these statutory provisions, a mechanic's lien that could be enforced against the property interest of the original contracting owner cannot be enforced against the property interest of the new owner or mortgagee after the expiration of the prescribed statutory period. Thus, during the relatively short statutory period, a mechanic's lien is good against innocent third parties even though it has not been properly perfected. Consequently, a purchaser of real estate should always ascertain if any repairs or improvements have been made to the premises within the time period for filing mechanic's liens. If it is determined that repairs or improvements have been made, the procedures outlined in the next section should be followed.

If a contractor, subcontractor, supplier of material, or laborer fails to file notice of the lien within the appropriate prescribed time period, or fails to commence suit within the additional period, the lien is lost.

Since a person entitled to a mechanic's lien has a prescribed period within which to file the lien, the date on which this time period starts to run is frequently quite important. Most statutes provide that in the case of a supplier, the time period starts to run from the date the materials are delivered; and in the case of a contractor or subcontractor performing services, the time for filing starts to run from the completion of the work. This latter concept requires further clarification, however.

Should a contractor or subcontractor be able to postpone the time for filing by performing additional services at a later date? Assume that a contractor has allowed the time for filing his lien to elapse. Should the time period start all over if he makes a minor repair, such as adjusting a doorknob or touching up a paint job? Common sense would say no, and most statutes provide that a contractor or subcontractor cannot extend the statutory period of time by performing minor, trifling repairs after the work has been substantially completed. In other words, trivial work done or materials furnished after the contract has been substantially completed will not extend the time in which a lien claim can be filed.

20. Priorities

Two basic situations create issues of priorities concerning mechanic's liens. The first concerns priority among similar mechanic's liens. The second situation involves the priority of a mechanic's lienholder compared with the rights of a mortgagee to the proceeds from the forced sale of the real estate.

AMONG MECHANIC'S LIENHOLDERS If there are several mechanic's liens filed as the result of the same improvement project, the liens are entitled to priority on the basis of when the lienholder began work on the project. If several liens are considered equal in priority and there are insufficient funds to satisfy all these claims, the lienholders must share the proceeds on a pro rata basis. Each lienholder is entitled to that portion of the proceeds that his or her work represented of the entire improvement.

BETWEEN MECHANIC'S LIENHOLDER AND MORTGAGEE When determining the priority of a mechanic's lien and a mortgage on the same property, the date of attachment is crucial. Nearly all states provide that a mortgage attaches when it is properly recorded. If the state where the land is located is one of the few providing that a mechanic's lien attaches when a notice of lien is filed, then priority is given to the creditor who is first to file.

The majority of states' laws on mechanic's liens say that these liens attach when work first begins or when supplies are first delivered. In these states a mortgage may be filed before a notice of lien is filed, and yet the lien has priority. A mortgagee must, therefore, make sure there are no potential mechanic's liens or obtain an agreement from contractors, laborers, and suppliers that their liens are subordinated to the mortgage. Without these actions, a mortgagee may lose all or at least part of the foreclosure proceeds to a mechanic's lienholder.

Still other states give priority to mechanic's liens over a previously recorded mortgage because the lienholder has increased the value of the real property. This added value should be evident in the greater proceeds obtained at the foreclosure sale. After the lienholder is paid, the mortgagee still has the remaining proceeds, which should be the same as if no improvement had been made. This priority given to the mechanic's lien may not apply if the items added to the real estate become inseparable from the entire improvement.

Some states by statute give priority to a construction mortgage over mechanic's liens. This preference is given because all the parties intend that the contractors and suppliers will be paid out of the proceeds of the construction loan. This priority is usually limited to the amounts that the construction mortgagee is obligated to advance. If the funds do not have to be advanced by the mortgagee, an unpaid perfected mechanic's lien will have priority over the prior mortgage.

21. Protection against Liens

Mechanic's lien statutes usually provide that an owner is not liable for more than the contract price if he or she follows the procedures outlined in the law. These usually require that the owner, prior to payment, obtain from the contractor a sworn statement setting forth all the creditors and the amounts due, or to become due, to each of them. It is then the duty of the owner to retain sufficient funds at all times to pay the amounts indicated by the sworn statements. In addition, if any liens have been filed by the subcontractors, it is the owner's duty to retain sufficient money to pay them. The owner is at liberty to pay any balance to the contractor.

An owner has a right to rely on the truthfulness of the sworn statement of the contractor. If the contractor misstates the facts and obtains a sum greater than that to which he or she is entitled, the loss falls on the subcontractors who dealt with the contractor rather than on the owner. Under such circumstances, the subcontractors may look only to the contractor for payment. Payments made by the owner, without first obtaining a sworn statement, may not be used to defeat the claims of subcontractors, suppliers, and laborers. Before making any payment, the owner has the duty to require the sworn statement and to withhold the amount necessary to pay the claims indicated.

The owner may also protect himself or herself by obtaining waivers of the contractor's lien and of the liens of subcontractors, suppliers, and laborers. A *waiver* is the voluntary relinquishment of the right to a lien before a notice of lien is filed. In a few states, a waiver of the lien by the contractor is also a waiver of the lien of the subcontractors, as they derive their rights through those of the contractor. However, in most states, lien waivers are effective only against those who agree not to claim a mechanic's lien and who execute a waiver.

Even after a notice of lien is filed, lienholders may extinguish their right to enforce the lien. This post-filing process is known as a *release* of the lien. Very often, the concept of waivers and that of releases is confused. A waiver occurs before a notice of lien is filed, whereas a release is used after there is a public filing. A mechanic's lien commonly is released when the landowner pays the lienholder after a notice of lien has been filed.

ENFORCEMENT OF JUDGMENTS AND DECREES

A decision of a court becomes final when the time provided for a review of the decision has expired. In the trial court, a decision is final at the expiration of time for appeal. In a reviewing court, it is expiration of the time to request a rehearing or to request a further review of the case. After the decision has become final, judicial action may be required to enforce the decision. In most cases the losing party will voluntarily comply with the decision and satisfy the judgment or otherwise do what the decree requires, but the assistance of the court is sometimes required to enforce its final decision.

Execution
The process by which the court, through the sheriff, enforces the payment of the judgment and seizes the unsuccessful party's property and sells it to pay the judgment creditor

WRIT OF EXECUTION If a judgment for dollar damages is not paid, the judgment creditor may apply for a writ of **execution**. This writ directs the sheriff to seize personal property of the judgment debtor and to sell enough thereof to satisfy the judgment and to cover the costs and expenses of the sale. The writ authorizes the sheriff to seize both tangible and intangible personal property, such as bank accounts. If the judgment debtor's personal property seized and sold by the sheriff does not produce sufficient funds to pay the judgment, the writ of execution is returned to the court with a statement of the extent to which the judgment is unsatisfied. If an execution is returned unsatisfied in whole or in part, the judgment becomes a lien on any real estate owned by the debtor if it is within the jurisdiction of the court that issued the writ of execution. An unpaid judgment creditor is entitled to have the real estate sold at a judicial sale and to have the net proceeds of the sale applied on the judgment. A judgment creditor with an unsatisfied writ of execution has not only a lien on real property owned by the judgment debtor at the time the judgment becomes final, but also a judicial lien on any real property acquired by the judgment debtor during the life of the judgment.

Garnishment
A proceeding by which a plaintiff seeks to reach the assets of the defendant that are in the hands of a third party, the garnishee

GARNISHMENT **Garnishment** is another important method used by judgment creditors to collect a judgment. Judgment creditors can "garnish" the wages of judgment debtors or their bank accounts or any other obligations owing to them from third parties. In the process of garnishment, the person owing the money to a judgment debtor—the employer, bank of deposit, third party—will be directed to pay the money into court rather than to the judgment debtor; and such money will be applied against the judgment debt.

In connection with writs of execution and garnishment proceedings, it is extremely significant that the laws of the various states have statutory provisions that exempt certain property from writs of execution and garnishment. The state laws limit the amount of wages that can be garnished and usually provide for both real property and personal property exemptions. This is discussed in detail in Chapter 42.

CITATION PROCEEDING In recent years, many states have adopted a citation proceeding, which greatly assists the creditor in collecting a judgment. The citation procedure begins with the service of a "citation" on the judgment debtor to appear in court at a stated time for examination under oath about his or her financial affairs. It also prohibits the judgment debtor from making any transfer of property until after the examination in court. At the hearing, the judgment creditor or representing attorney questions the judgment debtor about his or her income, property, and affairs. Any nonexempt property that is discovered during the questioning may be ordered sold by the judge, with the proceeds applied to the judgment. The court may also order that weekly or monthly payments be made by the judgment debtor. In states that have adopted the citation proceeding, the difficulties in collecting a judgment have been substantially reduced.

Attachment
A legal proceeding accompanying an action in court by which a plaintiff may acquire a lien on a defendant's property as a security for the payment of any judgment that the plaintiff may recover

ATTACHMENT One important method of collecting a judgment is also relevant to the procedures that may be used to commence a lawsuit. The procedure with these dual purposes is known as **attachment**. Attachment is a method of acquiring in *rem* jurisdiction of a nonresident defendant who is not subject to the service of process. The court may "attach" property of the nonresident defendant; and in so doing, the court acquires jurisdiction over the defendant to the extent of the value of the property attached. Attachment as a means of obtaining in *rem* jurisdiction is used in cases involving the status of a person, such as divorce, or the status of property, such as in eminent domain (acquisition of private property for public use) proceedings.

A plaintiff who fears that the defendant will dispose of his or her property before the court is able to enter a final decision uses attachment as a method of ensuring collection of a judgment. The plaintiff has the property of the defendant seized, pending the outcome of the lawsuit. A risk of vital importance to the success of the attachment is that the creditor proves that the property being attached is either owed to the debtor or is some of the debtor's property.

Attachment and the procedures controlling its use are governed by statutes that vary among the states. The attaching plaintiff-creditor must put up a bond with the court for the protection of the defendant, and the statutes provide methods whereby the attachment may be set aside by the defendant. If the plaintiff receives a judgment against the defendant, the attached property will be sold to satisfy the judgment.

IS IT WORTH IT? In spite of the remedies the creditor may use, it frequently develops that the judgment is of little value because of the lack of assets that can be reached or because of other judgments. It must be remembered that a judgment standing alone has little value. In many cases, the debtor may file a voluntary petition in bankruptcy, discussed in the next chapter, which may extinguish the judgment debt.

In other cases, the creditor recognizes the futility of attempting to use additional legal process to collect; and the matter simply lies dormant until it dies a natural death by the expiration of the time allowed to collect the claim or judgment. Everyone should be aware that some people are judgment-proof and that in such cases the law has no means of collecting a judgment. Debtors are not sent to prison simply because of their inability to pay debts or judgments.

CHAPTER SUMMARY

ARTISAN'S LIENS

1. Artisan's liens are the right to possess, for leverage in the collection process, personal property that one has serviced or repaired.
2. The "improved" personal property must be possessed at all times.
3. If possession is surrendered voluntarily, the lien is lost unless a claim of lien is filed in the public records.
4. Artisan's liens are personal and cannot generally be assigned.
5. The property is sold and the proceeds are used to satisfy the lienholder's claim.
6. In general, a lienholder of an artisan has priority to the sale proceeds.

SURETYSHIP IN GENERAL

Terminology

1. A principal is a debtor or one who is obligated to perform a contractual promise.
2. A creditor is the party to whom money is owed or who is entitled to some other contractual performance.
3. A surety is a party who assures the creditor that the principal will perform as promised.
4. The term surety should be compared and contrasted with guarantor and indemnitor.

Creation of Suretyship Contracts

1. These contracts usually arise in relationship to the principal's obligation to repay a debt or to complete some other promised performance.
2. These contracts may be created as expressed written agreements or by operation of law.

CREDITOR-SURETY RELATIONSHIP

Fiduciary Aspects

1. A suretyship is based on trust and confidence.
2. Both creditor and surety must share any information that may adversely affect that party's potential liability.

Principal's Default: Notice

1. A surety becomes liable to the creditor when the principal defaults.
2. In general, the creditor does not have to give notice of default to hold the surety liable.
3. However, notice of default is required if the creditor-surety agreement requires it, if the surety is a drawer or indorser of commercial paper, or if the surety is a collection guarantor.

Surety's Performance and Subrogation Rights

1. A surety satisfies its obligation upon performance.
2. Having performed, the surety is entitled to any rights of the creditor.
3. Likewise, the creditor is entitled to be protected by any rights held by the surety.

CREDITOR-PRINCIPAL RELATIONSHIP

Principal's Defense

1. Sureties generally can utilize any defense a principal has against the creditor to reduce liability.
2. The surety cannot assert the principal's defenses of lack of capacity, discharge in bankruptcy, and expiration of the statute of limitations.

Releases

1. In general, a creditor who releases a principal from liability also releases any surety.
2. The principal's release does not relieve the surety of liability if the surety consents to the release, if the creditor reserves rights against the surety, or if the release is obtained by the principal's fraud.

Extensions of Time for Payment

1. An extension must be a valid agreement supported by consideration if it is to have an impact on the surety's liability.
2. A formal extension does discharge the surety's liability unless the surety consents, unless the creditor reserves rights against the surety, or unless the surety is compensated and not injured by the extension.

Other Modifications

1. In general, any modification of the creditor-principal relationship discharges the surety.
2. Exceptions to this general rule include the surety's consent to the modification, the uncompensated surety to the extent of any benefit, and the compensated surety as long as the modification does not materially increase that surety's risk.

PRINCIPAL-SURETY RELATIONSHIP

Surety's Duty to Account

1. The surety must account to the principal for any benefits the surety receives from performance.

Surety's Right to Reimbursement

1. In general, after performance a surety is entitled to be reimbursed by the principal. This right of the surety is based on the principal's obligation not to default.
2. The surety's right to reimbursement does not apply if the principal has informed the surety of a valid defense that would defeat the creditor's claim of performance.

3. The right to reimbursement is also lacking if the surety performs after the principal has been discharged or released by the creditor, unless the creditor reserves rights against the surety.

Liability of Co-Sureties

1. In general, the liability of co-sureties is based on the same principles as the liability of one surety.
2. Co-sureties are jointly and severally liable. Generally, the right of contribution assures that co-sureties share liability on a pro rata basis.

MECHANIC'S LIENS

Introduction

1. A mechanic's lien gives security to any party who has contributed to an improvement of real estate.
2. An improvement does not necessarily increase the value of real estate.

Potential Lienholders

1. Those parties who contract directly or indirectly with an owner for an improvement are potential lienholders. Typically, these parties include general contractors and subcontractors.
2. Suppliers of materials and laborers who provide work also are potential lienholders.

Perfection and Enforcement

1. Since mechanic's liens are created by state law, each state's requirements for a valid lien vary to some degree.
2. In general, a lienholder must file a notice of a lien within a statutory time period after work is completed.
3. In addition to the notice of lien, a lawsuit must be filed within the time provided.
4. As a result of the lawsuit, a court may order that the improved real estate be sold to satisfy the lienholder's claim for payment.

Priorities

1. Among mechanic's lienholders, the beginning of that lienholder's work or delivery of materials usually determines priority.
2. If lienholders are equal in priority, they share the proceeds on a pro rata basis. Each should receive the same percentage of the proceeds that his or her work contributed to the whole improvement.
3. The priority between mechanic's liens and mortgages depends on the state's law and the time each claim attached to the real estate.

Protection against Liens

1. A real estate owner who is improving his or her land should obtain a sworn statement from the contractor prior to making any payment. This statement should explain who are potential lienholders. The owner can then take steps to satisfy these parties' claims.
2. An owner generally can prevent claims by making payment to the lienholders or by having these lienholders waive or release their rights to a mechanic's lien.

ENFORCEMENT OF JUDGMENTS AND DECREES

1. It is not enough for a party to obtain a judgment against another. If the losing party does not voluntarily satisfy the judgment, then further legal proceedings may be required.
2. These may include judicial sales of property, garnishment of wages, and court orders requiring parties to take certain actions.

REVIEW QUESTIONS AND PROBLEMS

1. Match each term in Column A with the appropriate statement in Column B.

A	B
(1) Artisan's lien	(a) Literally means, "to stand in the place of another"
(2) Garnishment	(b) A method by which a creditor can continue to hold a surety liable
(3) Indemnity	(c) A surety's right against a principal
(4) Subrogation	(d) Created when a repairperson agrees to do work on personal property
(5) Uncompensated surety	(e) The right that exists between co-sureties
(6) Reservation of rights	(f) In modern law, another term for a guarantor
(7) Reimbursement	(g) A promise to hold someone harmless
(8) Contribution	(h) Viewed as a favorite of law
(9) Surety	(i) Process where sheriff seizes property
(10) Execution	(j) Process where wages are taken to pay a judgment

2. Mary took her car to the local Chevrolet dealer for service and necessary repairs. After the dealer performed the desired work, Mary paid the bill in full. However, the dealer refused to relinquish possession of her car since Mary had not paid for repairs previously made on the same car. Does the dealer have a lien on her car so Mary cannot regain possession of it? Why or why not?

3. Plaintiff, known as 660 Syndicate, owned an airplane that had been leased to Wyoming Airlines. The Wyoming Airlines had Rocky Mountain Turbines (R.M.T.) service and repair the airplane. Although it had not been paid, R.M.T. returned the airplane to Wyoming Airlines. After it could not collect the money it was owed, R.M.T. reacquired possession of the repaired airplane. R.M.T. planned to enforce its lien by selling the airplane. Plaintiff filed suit claiming that it was entitled to possession of the airplane. Plaintiff argued that R.M.T.'s lien was unenforceable. Was R.M.T.'s lien on the plane made valid by the subsequent acquisition of the plane? Explain.

4. Sam wrote a letter of guaranty to Carl on behalf of Rex, a retailer. The letter stated that Sam "does guarantee payment of any credit granted by you not to exceed ten thousand dollars ($10,000)." Rex was involved in a series of individual transactions with Carl, of which none exceeded $10,000. Rex failed to pay, but Sam contends that his total liability is limited to one transaction. Is Sam correct? Why or why not?

5. Lee signed as guarantor of a promissory note signed by Akins and payable to Vaughn. Lee expressly inserted a provision into the note that if the principal debtor defaulted, Lee must be notified promptly if he was to be liable. After the maker defaulted, no notice was given of that fact by Vaughn to Lee. When Vaughn sued Lee for payment, Lee contended that the lack of notice discharged this liability. When a surety contract expressly requires notice of the default, is the surety liable on the note if the payee does not promptly notify the surety? Why or why not?

6. Owens hired Terry, a general contractor, to build a house. Terry, in turn, hired Paint-It-All, a subcontractor, to paint the house. Being concerned about Paint-It-All's reputation, Terry required that a performance bond be obtained. Paint-It-All paid the Aetna Insurance Company to assure its performance. Paint-It-All failed to do the job, and Terry brought an action against Aetna alone. May he do so? Explain.
7. A newspaper entered into a contract with Alan by the terms of which Alan was to purchase newspapers at wholesale and deliver them to residential buyers. Alan's father agreed to serve as accommodation surety. Although the contract called for weekly payments by Alan, the newspaper allowed him to pay monthly. Did this allowance relieve Alan's father from any liability as surety? Why or why not?
8. The Graffs, plaintiffs, brought this action to invalidate a mechanic's lien claimed against their property by Boise Cascade on the grounds that the notice of lien was invalid because it did not set forth the name of the person who requested the materials. The defendant, Boise Cascade Corporation, argued that the omissions were inconsequential and that the notice of the lien complied with the statutory requirements. Is the statutory requirement that the notice of lien contain the name of the person to whom the material was furnished a condition precedent to the creation and existence of a lien? Explain.
9. List and explain three methods used to enforce a judgment.
10. Do the legal principles presented in this chapter favor creditors or debtors? Explain.

Bankruptcy | 39

CHAPTER OUTLINE

continued

CHAPTER PREVIEW

The law of bankruptcy provides possible solutions to problems that arise when a person, partnership, limited liability company, corporation, farmer, or municipality is unable, or finds it difficult, to satisfy obligations to creditors. Bankruptcy has its roots in the law of the Roman Empire and has been a part of English jurisprudence since 1542. Article I, Section 8 of the United States Constitutions empowers Congress with the responsibility to create a bankruptcy system at the federal level. The bankruptcy laws in the United States have been amended periodically. Today's bankruptcy law is based on the Bankruptcy Reform Act of 1978 (1978 Bankruptcy Act). While this act has been amended several times, the most significant revision to bankruptcy law occurred with the Bankruptcy Abuse Prevention and Consumer Protection Act of 2005 (BAPCPA). The BAPCPA was enacted primarily in response to the fact that personal bankruptcy filings were increasing each year at an alarming rate. The provisions of the BAPCPA, which are so new that few courts have ruled on major aspects of the legislation, generally make it more difficult for individuals to declare bankruptcy (and thus have their debts to business eliminated). Congress observed that bankruptcies were declared in many instances where consumers should be able to pay-off their debts. Also, the BAPCPA mandates that an individual may not be deemed a debtor under any provision of federal bankruptcy law unless the debtor received appropriate credit counseling within 180 days of filing.

The basic concept underlying bankruptcy is to allow a debtor who is in a difficult financial situation a fresh financial start. In other words, the bankruptcy laws permit a deserving debtor the opportunity to come out from under overwhelming financial burdens and to begin life anew. For the large majority of personal bankruptcies, seeking protection under bankruptcy law comes after a catastrophic event has occurred that is beyond the control of the individuals filing for bankruptcy (e.g., death of the principal wage-earner, devastating illness of a family member, or natural disaster).

However, this "fresh start" is not granted without the debtor's paying something for the opportunity. In essence, the bankruptcy laws have always attempted to balance the rights of the debtor with the rights of the creditors. To protect the creditors, the debtor must turn over his or her assets to court supervision in the form of a trust. Loss of every asset would deprive the debtor of the opportunity for a fresh financial start. Therefore, the debtor may exempt certain items from the bankruptcy estate and retain them as the basis for a new beginning.

As you study this chapter, keep in mind that the bankruptcy laws provide an acceptable alternative for debtors in financial difficulty. Filing for bankruptcy is no longer socially unacceptable or an admission of failure. More than ever before, bankruptcy has become an acceptable solution to the financial distress individuals or businesses could not otherwise overcome.

This chapter discusses the types of bankruptcy proceedings, some procedural aspects of a bankruptcy case, and rights and duties of the parties involved in a bankruptcy case.

BUSINESS MANAGEMENT DECISION

Your company, which is self-insured, faces thousands of products liability suits. The potential liability could reach hundreds of millions of dollars. Other than these suits, your company is financially sound and profitable.

Should your company consider filing for bankruptcy protection?

TERMINOLOGY

Debtor
The party who files a bankruptcy petition or against whom such a petition is filed

Claim
A creditor's right to payment in a bankruptcy case

At the outset of your study of this chapter, you should be familiar with some of the more common terms used in bankruptcy proceedings. A **debtor** is the individual, business organization, municipality, or farmer that a bankruptcy proceeding involves. A **claim** is a right to payment from the debtor. Claims are held and asserted by creditors. An **order of relief** is entered by the bankruptcy judge when he or she finds that the debtor is entitled to the protection of the bankruptcy law. A **discharge** is an order by the bankruptcy judge that a debtor is relieved of paying specific debts. Finally, the **trustee** is the person responsible for managing the debtor's assets and for satisfying the creditor's claim to the extent possible.

TYPES OF PROCEEDINGS

Order of relief
The ruling by a bankruptcy judge that a particular case is properly before the bankruptcy court

Discharge
An order by a bankruptcy court that a debt is no longer valid—in essence, the debtor's forgiven obligation

Trustee
The person named to handle the assets and obligations of the debtor during the bankruptcy proceeding

Liquidation
The process of winding up the affairs of a corporation or firm for the purpose of paying its debts and disposing of its assets

1. In General

The federal bankruptcy laws have two distinct approaches to the problems of debtors. One approach is to liquidate debts. The liquidation approach recognizes that misfortune and poor judgment often create a situation in which debtors will never be able to pay their debts by their own efforts, or at least it will be very difficult to do so.

The second approach is to postpone the time of payment of debts or to reduce some of them to levels that make repayment possible. This approach is found in the reorganization sections for businesses and in the adjustment of debts provisions for municipalities, farmers, and individuals with regular incomes. The reorganization and adjustment provisions are aimed at rehabilitation of debtors. These procedures, if utilized, prevent harassment of debtors and spare them undue hardship while enabling most creditors eventually to obtain some repayment.

There are three types of bankruptcy proceedings relevant to business, each identified by a chapter of the statute: Chapter 7, Liquidation; Chapter 11, Reorganization; Chapter 13, Adjustment of Debts of an Individual with Regular Income. For the year ending June 30, 2008, there were 967,831 bankruptcy filings, according to the United States Bankruptcy Court. Of those, 63% (615,748) of all bankruptcies filed were for Chapter 7 (liquidation), 36% (344,421) were for Chapter 13 (wage earner), and less than 1% (7,607) were for other chapters. (While not covered in this text, Adjustment of Debts of a Family Farmer under Chapter 12 is treated in a manner somewhat similar to those that file under Chapter 13.)

2. Liquidation Proceedings under Chapter 7

Liquidation proceedings are used to eliminate most of the debts of a debtor. In exchange for having the debts declared uncollectible, the debtor must allow many, if not most, of his or her assets to be used to satisfy creditors' claims. Cases under Chapter 7 of the statute may involve individuals, partnerships, limited liability companies, or corporations, but only individuals may receive a *discharge* from the court. A discharge voids any judgment against the debtor to the extent that it creates a personal liability. A discharge covers all scheduled debts that arose before the date of the order for relief. It is irrelevant whether or not a claim was filed or allowed. A discharge also operates as an *injunction* against all attempts to collect the debt—by judicial proceedings, telephone calls, letters, personal contacts, or other efforts. *Under all types of proceedings, once they are commenced, creditors are prohibited from attempting to collect their debts.*

The debts of partnerships, limited liability companies, and corporations that go through liquidation proceedings are not discharged. These businesses are still technically liable for their debts; however, the lack of discharge is immaterial unless the partnership, limited liability company, or corporation acquires assets later. This lack of discharge stops people from using "shell" businesses after bankruptcy for other purposes.

Certain businesses are denied the right to liquidation proceedings. Railroads, insurance companies, banks, savings and loan associations, homestead associations, and credit unions may not be debtors under Chapter 7 of the Bankruptcy Act. These organizations are subject to the jurisdiction of administrative agencies that handle all aspects of such organizations, including problems related to insolvency. Under this arrangement, there are alternative legal provisions for their liquidation.

Also, under the BAPCPA, Congress instituted a mechanism to reduce the abuse of Chapter 7 filings that was being experienced in the 1990s. The new law grants to a bankruptcy judge the power to dismiss a petition of bankruptcy for "substantial abuse" where the debtor's income fails to meet the "means test." Substantial abuse will be presumed where the debtor's family income is greater than that of the median income of a family in the debtor's state. (Section 707 of the BAPCPA provides a detailed explanation of the means test, including allowed expenses and exceptions)

Chapter 7 has special provisions relating to liquidation proceedings involving stockbrokers and commodity brokers. These special provisions are necessary to protect their customers, because bankruptcies of this kind usually involve large indebtedness and substantial assets. Stockbrokers and commodity brokers are subject only to Chapter 7. Chapter 11 and Chapter 13 proceedings are not available to them.

3. Reorganization Proceedings under Chapter 11

Reorganization proceedings are utilized when debtors wish to restructure their finances and attempt to pay creditors over an extended period, as required by a court-approved plan. Such cases almost always involve a business as the debtor. Chapter 11 of the 1978 Bankruptcy Act contains detailed provisions on all aspects of the plan of reorganization and its execution. In addition, the BAPCPA creates a special group of "small business debtors" (with less than $2 million in debt) that are allowed to function under special rules that expedite the process.

As soon as practicable after the order for relief, a committee of creditors holding unsecured claims is formed. The committee ordinarily consists of persons with the largest claims, and it may employ attorneys, accountants, or other agents to assist it. Working with the trustee and the debtor concerning the administration of the case, it represents the interests of the creditors. It may investigate the financial condition of the debtor and will assist in the formulation of the reorganization plan.

The court in reorganization cases will usually appoint a trustee before approval of the plan of reorganization. If the court does not appoint a trustee, it will appoint an examiner who conducts an investigation into the affairs of the debtor, including any mismanagement or irregularities.

After the trustee or the examiner conducts the investigation of the acts, conduct, assets, liabilities, financial conditions, and other relevant aspects of the debtor, a written report of this investigation is filed with the court. The trustee may file a plan of reorganization if the debtor does not; or it may recommend conversion of the case to liquidation proceedings. The trustee will also file tax returns for the debtor, file reports with the court, and may even operate the debtor's business unless the court orders otherwise. The debtor may file a *plan of reorganization* with the voluntary petition or later in an attempt to extricate the business from its financial difficulties and help it to survive. The plan will classify claims, and all claims within a class will be treated the same. All unsecured claims for less than a specified amount may be classified together. The plan will designate those classes of claims that are unimpaired under the plan and will specify the treatment to be given claims that are impaired.

The plan must provide a means for its execution. It may provide that the debtor will retain all or part of the property of the estate. It may also propose that property be sold or transferred to creditors or other entities. Mergers and consolidations may be proposed. In short, the plan will deal with all aspects of the organization of the debtor, its property, and its debts. Some debts will be paid in full; some will be partially paid over an extended period of time; and others may not be paid at all. The only limitation is that all claimants must receive as much as they would receive in liquidation proceedings.

Holders of claims or interests in the debtor's property are allowed to vote and to accept or reject the proposed plan of reorganization. A class of claims has accepted a plan if at least two-thirds in amount and more than half in number of claims vote yes. Acceptance by a class of interests, such as equity holders, requires a two-thirds "yes" vote.

A hearing is held on the confirmation of a plan to determine if it is fair and equitable. The statute specifies several conditions, such as good faith, which must be met before the plan is approved. Also before approval, it must be established that each holder of a claim or interest has either accepted the plan or will receive as much under the reorganization plan as would be received in liquidation proceedings. For secured creditors, this means that they will receive the value of their security either by payment or by delivery of the property. Confirmation of the plan makes it binding on the debtor, equity security holders, and creditors. Confirmation vests the property of the estate in the debtor and releases the debtor from any payment not specified in the reorganization plan.

As a general rule, any debtor subject to liquidation under the statute (Chapter 7) is also subject to reorganization (Chapter 11).

4. Adjustment of Individuals' Debts under Chapter 13

Chapter 13 proceedings are used to adjust the debts of individuals with regular income whose debts are small enough and whose income is significant enough that substantial repayment is feasible. Such persons often seek to avoid the stigma of bankruptcy. Moreover, under the BAPCPA, many Chapter 7 liquidations provisions will be turned into Chapter 13 repayments plans. Unsecured debts of individuals utilizing Chapter 13 proceedings cannot exceed $336,900, and the secured debts cannot exceed $1,010,650. Persons utilizing Chapter 13 are usually employees earning a salary, but persons engaged in business also qualify. Self-employed persons who incur trade debts are considered to be engaged in business.

The debtor files a plan that provides for the use of all or a portion of future earnings or income for the payment of debts. The income is under the supervision and control of the trustee. Except as provided in the plan, the debtor keeps possession of his or her property. If the debtor is engaged in business, the debtor continues to operate the business. The plan must provide for the full payment of all claims entitled to priority unless the creditors with priority agree to a different treatment. If a plan divides unsecured claims into classes, all claims within a class must be given the same treatment.

Unsecured claims not entitled to priority may be repaid in full or reduced to a level not lower than the amount that would be paid upon liquidation. Since this amount is usually zero, any payment to unsecured creditors will satisfy the law. The secured creditors may be protected by allowing them to retain their lien, by payment of the secured claim in full, or by the surrender of the property to the secured claimant. Under provisions of the BAPCPA, the debtor's median income determines whether the length of the plan is three or five years. A typical plan allocates one-fourth of a person's take-home pay to repay debts.

The plan may modify the rights of holders of secured and unsecured claims, except that the rights of holders or real estate mortgages may not be modified. Claims arising after the filing of the petition may be included in the plan. This is a realistic approach because all the debts of the debtor must be taken into account if the plan is to accomplish its objectives.

When the court conducts a hearing on the confirmation of the plan, if it is satisfied that the debtor will be able to make all payments to comply with it, the plan will be approved. Of course, the plan must be proposed in good faith, be in compliance with the law, and be in the best interest of the creditors.

As soon as the debtor completes all payments under the plan, the court grants the debtor a discharge of all debts unless the debtor waives the discharge or the debts are not legally dischargeable (see Sections 7 and 8).

After a hearing, courts may also grant a discharge, even though all payments have not been made, if the debtor's failure to complete the payments is due to circumstances for which the debtor should not justly be held accountable. In such cases, the payments under the plan must be not less than those that would have been paid on liquidation, and modification must not be practicable.

TABLE 39-1 ■ Type of Bankruptcy

Chapter	Type	Debtor	Who may file	Impact
Chapter 7	Liquidation	Individuals, partnerships, corporations, and other business entities	Debtor or creditors	Most or all debts are discharged, economic activity ceases, and debtor may start anew.
Chapter 11	Reorganization	Individuals, partnerships, corporations, and other business entities	Debtor or creditors	Debtor remains in business and debts are liquidated through approved plan
Chapter 13	Adjustment of Debts	Individual	Debtor only	Debt repayment plan is executed.

GENERAL PRINCIPLES

5. Property of the Estate

The *bankruptcy estate* consists of all legal or equitable interests of the debtor in property, wherever located. The property may be tangible or intangible and includes causes of action. To begin, all property is included in the estate, but the debtor may exempt portions entitled to exemption, as discussed in the next section.

The estate includes property that the trustee recovers by using his or her power to avoid prior transactions. It also includes property inherited by the debtor or received as a beneficiary of life insurance within 180 days of the petition. Proceeds, products, offspring, rents, and profits generated by, or coming from, property in the estate are also part of the estate.

In general, property acquired by the debtor after commencement of the case—including earnings from employment—belongs to the debtors. Property held in trust for the benefit of the debtor under a *spendthrift trust* does not become a part of the estate. In essence, the trustee in bankruptcy acquires the same interest with the same restrictions as the debtor had at the time the bankruptcy petition was filed. However, the trustee can require creditors to turn over possession of assets that were held by the creditors at the time the petition was filed. In return, the trustee must provide adequate protection for these creditors' claims. These concepts apply to the IRS and other government agencies.

6. Exemptions

Technically, all property of the debtor becomes property of the bankruptcy estate, but an individual debtor is then permitted to claim some of it as exempt from the proceedings. That property is then returned to the debtor. Exemptions Federal, state, and local laws grant exemptions.

FEDERAL EXEMPTIONS Federal bankruptcy law provides for exemptions, adjusted every three years based on the Consumer Price Index, including the following based on April 1, 2007, adjustments:

1. Real property used as a residence, up to $20,200 in equity
2. The debtor's interest, not to exceed $3,225, in one motor vehicle
3. The debtor's interest, not to exceed $525 in any particular item or $10,775 in aggregate value, in household furnishings, wearing apparel, appliances, books, animals, crops, or musical instruments that are held primarily for the personal family or household use of the debtor and his dependents
4. The debtor's interest in jewelry, not to exceed $1,350
5. The debtor's interest in other property, not to exceed $1,075, plus up to $10,125 of any unused real property exemption
6. The debtor's interest, not to exceed $2,025, in any implements, professional books, or tools of the trade of the debtor, or the trade of his or her dependents
7. Unmatured life insurance contracts
8. The cash value of life insurance, not to exceed $10,775
9. Professionally prescribed health aids
10. The debtor's right to receive benefits such as social security, unemployment compensation, public assistance, disability benefits, alimony, child support and separate maintenance reasonably necessary, and current payments of pension, profit sharing, annuity, or similar plans

11. The debtor's right to receive payment traceable to the wrongful death of an individual on whom the debtor was dependent or to life insurance on the life of such a person or to payments for personal injury, not to exceed $20,200
12. Retirement funds and pensions up to $1,000,000, along with education savings accounts, which are exempt from taxation under the Internal Revenue Code.

STATE EXEMPTIONS Every state has enacted statutes granting exemptions to debtors domiciled there, but these exemptions vary greatly from state to state. For example, some state exemptions exceed those provided by the federal bankruptcy laws. Other state exemptions are too small to give a debtor a real chance at a fresh financial start. To encourage some states to raise their exemptions, the 1978 Act provides that the federal exemptions will be available to debtors unless the state specifically passes a law denying its residents the federal exemptions. Debtors may claim the larger exemptions offered by their state if it is to their advantage to do so. Over half the states have adopted laws denying debtors the use of the federal exemptions; however, these states have substantially increased their own exemptions.

One of the most popular exemptions provided by state law is the *homestead exemption.* In prior years, some states allowed debtors to shield an unlimited amount of equity in their homes though the use of the homestead exemption. However, the BAPCPA now restricts the maximum equity exempted to no more than $136,875 and provides other restrictions to those who wish to use a state homestead exemption.

STATUS OF EXEMPT PROPERTY As a general rule, exempt property is not subject to any debts that arise before the commencement of the case. Exceptions to the general rule apply to tax claims, alimony, child support, and separate maintenance. Exempt property can be used to collect such debts after the proceeding. The discharge in bankruptcy does not prevent enforcement of valid liens against exempt property; however, judicial liens and non-possessory, non-purchase money, security interests in household goods, wearing apparel, professional books, tools, and professionally prescribed health aids may be avoided. A debtor may redeem such tangible personal property from a lien securing a dischargeable consumer debt by paying the lienholder the amount of the secured claim. Exempt property is free of such liens after the proceedings. Waivers of exemptions are unenforceable, to prevent creditors from attempting to deny debtors the necessary property to gain a fresh start.

7. Debts that Are Not Discharged

A debt is a liability on a claim. A claim may be based on the right to payment that could be enforced in a proceeding at law, or it may be based on the right to an equitable remedy for breach of performance if the breach gives a right to payment. Claims based on equitable remedies may be dischargeable the same as those based on legal remedies.

Not all debts are discharged in Chapter 7 cases. A discharge in bankruptcy does not discharge an individual debtor from the following debts:

1. Certain taxes and customs duties accruing within two years of bankruptcy
2. Debts for obtaining money, property, services, or credit by false pretenses, false representations, or actual fraud
3. Consumer debts over $500 for luxury goods and services incurred within ninety days of the order of relief

4. Cash advances over $750 that are extensions of consumer credit under an open-end credit plan within seventy days of the order of relief
5. Unscheduled debts
6. Debts for fraud or defalcation while acting in a fiduciary capacity and debts created by embezzlement or larceny
7. Alimony, child support, and separate maintenance
8. Liability for willful and malicious torts
9. Tax penalties if the tax is not dischargeable
10. Student loans less than five years old, unless payment creates an undue hardship.
11. Debts incurred as a result of an accident caused by driving while intoxicated
12. Debts owed before a previous bankruptcy
13. Fines and penalties payable to and for the benefit of governmental units that are not compensation for actual pecuniary losses

The taxes that are not discharged are the same ones that receive priority under the second, third, and seventh categories discussed in Section 23 of this chapter. If debtors fail to file a return, file it beyond its last due date, or file a fraudulent return, those taxes are not discharged. One of the most common tax liabilities not discharged in bankruptcy is for unpaid withholding and social security taxes.

Items 3 and 4, which were added by the 1984 amendments, now prevent the debtor from going on a spending spree or "loading up" at creditors' expense just before filing a bankruptcy petition. The phrase "luxury goods and services" is defined as not including goods or services acquired for the support or maintenance of the debtor or his or her dependents.

The denial of a discharge of debts that are not properly scheduled on the bankruptcy petition means that the claim of any creditor who is not listed or who does not learn of the proceedings in time to file a claim continues to be valid. The debtor, under such circumstances, remains liable to pay the creditor unless the debtor can prove that the creditor did have knowledge of the proceeding in time to file a claim. Proof of actual knowledge is required; and although such knowledge often exists, care should be taken to list all creditors so all claims are subject to being discharged.

Typically, for a debt to be denied discharge because of fraud, the creditor must have placed reasonable reliance on a false written statement. One issue involving the use of fraud to deny a discharge of the underlying debt has concerned the creditor's burden of proof in establishing that the fraud exists.

Tort liability claims based on negligence are discharged. Tort liability claims arising from willful and malicious acts are not discharged. A judgment arising out of an assault and battery is not discharged. Item 11 was added by the 1984 amendments. The logic behind making this tort liability nondischargeable indicates support in the battle to discourage drunk driving. A 1990 amendment made it clear that this policy of nondischargeability extends to injuries arising out of the operation of a motor vehicle under the influence of alcohol, drugs, or other substances.

The provision generally denying discharge to student loans was added in the 1978 revision. It seeks to give creditors and the government five years to collect student loans. There is an exception if the debtor is able to convince the court that undue hardship will result on him or her and dependents if the student loan debt is not discharged. If the debtor fails to prove the undue hardship caused by the student loan, a general discharge will not relieve the debtor of the obligation to pay that student loan. Student loans are not discharged automatically. A person seeking a discharge of them must prove undue hardship in the bankruptcy court. Application of this provision is illustrated in the following case.

CASE

In the matter of Jonathon R. Gerhardt, Debtor: United States Department of Education, Appellee v. Jonathon R. Gerhardt, Appellant

UNITED STATES COURT OF APPEALS FOR THE FIFTH CIRCUIT

348 F.3d 89 (2003)

EDITH H. JONES, CIRCUIT JUDGE

Over a period of years, Jonathon Gerhardt obtained over $77,000 in government-insured student loans to finance his education at the University of Southern California, the Eastman School of Music, the University of Rochester, and the New England Conservatory of Music. Gerhardt is a professional cellist. He subsequently defaulted on each loan owed to the United States Government.

In 1999, Gerhardt filed for Chapter 7 bankruptcy and, thereafter, filed an adversary proceeding seeking discharge of his student loans. The bankruptcy court discharged Gerhardt's student loans as causing undue hardship. On appeal, the district court reversed, holding that it would not be an undue hardship for Gerhardt to repay his student loans. Finding no error, we affirm the district court's judgment.

This circuit has not explicitly articulated the appropriate test with which to evaluate the undue hardship determination. The Second Circuit in *Brunner* crafted the most widely-adopted test. To justify discharging the debtor's student loans, the *Brunner* test requires a three-part showing: (1) that the debtor cannot maintain, based on current income and expenses, a "minimal" standard of living for [himself] and [his] dependents if forced to repay the loans; (2) that additional circumstances exist indicating that this state of affairs is likely to persist for a significant portion of the repayment period of the student loans; and (3) that the debtor has made good faith efforts to repay the loans. Because the Second Circuit presented a workable approach to evaluating the "undue hardship" determination, this court expressly adopts the Brunner test.

Under the first prong of the *Brunner* test, the bankruptcy court determined that Gerhardt could not maintain a minimal standard of living if forced to repay his student loans. Evidence was produced at trial that Gerhardt earned $1,680.47 per month as the principal cellist for the Louisiana Philharmonic Orchestra ("LPO"), including a small amount of supplemental income earned as a cello teacher for Tulane University. His monthly expenses, which included a health club membership and Internet access, averaged $1,829.39. The bankruptcy court's factual findings are not clearly erroneous. Consequently, we agree with the bankruptcy court's conclusion of law that flows from these factual findings. Given that Gerhardt's monthly expenses exceed his monthly income, he has no ability at the present time to maintain a minimal standard of living if forced to repay his loans.

The second prong of the *Brunner* test asks if "additional circumstances exist indicating that this state of affairs is likely to persist [for a significant period of time]." "Additional circumstances" encompass "circumstances that impacted on the debtor's future earning potential but which [were] either not present when the debtor] applied for the loans or [have] since been exacerbated." This second aspect of the test is meant to be "a demanding requirement." Thus, proving that the debtor is "currently in financial straits" is not enough. Instead, the debtor must specifically prove "a total incapacity ... in the future to pay [his] debts for reasons not within [his] control." Some examples of "additional circumstances" include "psychiatric problems, lack of usable job skills, and severely limited education."

Under the second prong of the test, the district court correctly concluded that Gerhardt has not established persistent undue hardship entitling him to discharge his student loans. Gerhardt holds a masters degree in music from the New England Conservatory of Music. He is about 43 years old, healthy, well-educated, and has no dependents; yet he has repaid only $755 of his over $77,000 debt. During the LPO's off-seasons, Gerhardt has collected unemployment, but he has somehow managed to attend the Colorado Music Festival. Although trial testimony tended to show that Gerhardt would likely not obtain a position at a higher-paying orchestra, he could obtain additional steady employment in a number of different arenas. For instance, he could attempt to teach full-time, obtain night-school teaching jobs, or even work as a music store clerk. Thus, no reasons out of Gerhardt's control exist that perpetuate his inability to repay his student loans.

Our analysis of the second *Brunner* prong inevitably overlaps, to some degree, with the third prong, which asks if the debtor has made a good faith effort to repay the loan. However, because we resolve this case under the second prong, it is unnecessary to explore the third prong in depth.

In addition, nothing in the Bankruptcy Code suggests that a debtor may choose to work only in the field in which he was trained, obtain a low-paying job, and then claim that it would be an undue hardship to repay his student loans. Under the facts presented by Gerhardt, it is difficult to imagine a professional orchestra musician who would not qualify for an undue hardship discharge. Accordingly, Gerhardt "has failed to demonstrate the type of exceptional circumstances that are necessary in order to meet [his] burden under the second prong" of *Brunner*. Finding no error, the judgment of the district court is AFFIRMED.

■ *Affirmed.*

CASE CONCEPTS REVIEW

1. Did it surprise you that the debtor had repaid only $755 of his over $77,000 debt? Do you believe this fact might have influenced the decision of the judges on appeal? Why?
2. What are the provisions of the test used to determine undue hardship?

As a result of item 13, criminals will not be able to use the bankruptcy laws to avoid fines that have been levied. The Supreme Court has extended this nondischargeable debt to include restitution obligations imposed on debtors in state criminal proceedings. Great deference is given to state criminal proceedings, and amounts owed to accomplish the penal goals of a state, such as the deterrence of crime, are not dischargeable.

8. Grounds for Denying Discharge

A discharge in bankruptcy is a privilege, not a right. Therefore, in addition to providing that certain debts are not discharged, the 1978 Bankruptcy Act specifies the following grounds for denying an individual debtor a discharge:

1. Fraudulent transfers
2. Inadequate records
3. Commission of a bankruptcy crime
4. Failure to explain a loss of assets or deficiency of assets
5. Refusing to testify in the proceedings or to obey a court order
6. Any of the above within one year in connection with another bankruptcy case of an insider
7. Another discharge within eight years (under the 1978 Bankruptcy Act, the time between discharges was six years, but the BAPCPA extended this duration)
8. Approval by the court of a waiver of discharge
9. Failure to complete the required consumer credit education course, as mandated under the BAPCPA.The first three grounds for denying discharge are predicated on wrongful conduct by the debtor in connection with the case. Fraudulent transfers involve such acts as removing, destroying, or concealing property with the intent to hinder, delay, or defraud creditors or the trustee. The conduct must occur within one year preceding the case, or it may occur after the case is commenced.

A debtor is also denied a discharge if he or she has concealed, destroyed, mutilated, falsified, or failed to keep or preserve any books and records relating to his or her financial condition. A debtor is required to keep records from which his or her financial condition may be ascertained, unless the failure is justified.

Bankruptcy crimes are generally related to the proceedings. They include a false oath, the use or presentation of a false claim, or bribery in connection with the proceedings and with the withholding of records.

The six-year rule, which allows a discharge only if another discharge has not been ordered within six years, extends to Chapter 11 and Chapter 13 proceedings, as well as to those under Chapter 7. Confirmation of a plan under Chapter 11 or 13 does not have the effect of denying a discharge within six years if all the unsecured claims were paid in full, or if 70 percent of them were paid and the debtor has used his or her best efforts to pay the debts.

Either a creditor or the trustee may object to the discharge. The court may order the trustee to examine the facts to see if grounds for the denial of the discharge exist. Courts are also granted the authority to revoke a discharge within one year if it was obtained by fraud on the court.

PROCEDURAL STEPS

9. Introduction

Chapter 3 of the 1978 Bankruptcy Reform Act is concerned with procedural aspects and administration of all types of bankruptcy cases, regardless of the chapter under which the case is filed. The provisions of Chapter 3 give guidance in how to and who can file a case, in how the automatic stay prohibits any action against the debtor, and in how creditors are informed of the debtor's status. These provisions are discussed in the next five sections. The most technical portion of Chapter 3 is entitled "administrative powers." These provisions grant the bankruptcy court and the trustee a wide range of powers to accomplish the purposes of the bankruptcy law. Sections 15 through 19 present a more detailed examination of these powers and duties.

10. Voluntary Commencement

A debtor may voluntarily instigate a bankruptcy case under any appropriate chapter by filing a *petition* with the bankruptcy court. In recognition of the fact that husbands and wives often owe the same debts, a joint case may be filed. A *joint case* is a voluntary one concerning a husband and wife, and it requires only one petition. Both spouses must sign the petition since one spouse cannot take the other into bankruptcy without the other's consent. Insolvency is not a condition precedent to any form of voluntary bankruptcy action.

As of June 2009, all petitioners must pay a filing fee, in installments if they prefer, of $299 for Chapter 7, $1,039 for Chapter 11, and $274 for Chapter 13 . Only one filing fee is required in a joint case. A petition filed by a partnership as a firm is not a petition on behalf of the partners as individuals. If they intend to obtain individual discharges, separate petitions are required.

The petition contains lists of secured and unsecured creditors, all property owned by the debtor, property claimed by the debtor to be exempt, and a statement of affairs of the debtor. This statement includes current income and expenses, so the judge can dismiss a case if he or she believes that a substantial abuse of the bankruptcy code has occurred. This is an important consideration when a debtor's liabilities do not exceed assets and the filing is based on some fact other than that the debtor cannot pay debts as they come due. The statement of affairs of a debtor engaged in business is much more detailed than the one filed by a debtor not in business.

In general, the filing of a voluntary petition constitutes an order of relief indicating that the debtor is entitled to the bankruptcy court's protection. Further, the filing of the petition (either voluntary or involuntary) triggers an *automatic stay* that has the effect of suspending almost all actions by creditors against the debtor or the debtor's assets. This powerful doctrine is discussed below in Section 13.

11. Involuntary Commencement

Involuntary cases are commenced by one or more creditors filing a petition. If there are twelve or more creditors, the petition must be signed by at least three creditors whose unsecured claims are not contingent and aggregate at least $13,475. If there are fewer than twelve creditors, only one need sign the petition, but the $13,475 amount must still be met. Employees, insiders, and transferees of voidable transfers are not counted in determining the number of creditors. "Insiders" are persons such as relatives, partners of the debtor, and directors and officers of the corporation involved. The subject of voidable transfers is discussed later in this chapter.

Creditors may commence involuntary proceedings to harass the debtor. To protect the debtor, the court may require the petitioning creditors to file a bond to indemnify the debtor. This bond will cover the amounts for which the petitioning creditors may have liability to the debtor. The liability may include court costs, attorney's fees, and damages caused by taking the debtor's property.

Until the court enters an order for relief in an involuntary case, the debtor may continue to operate his or her business and to use, acquire, and dispose of property. However, the court may order an interim trustee appointed to take possession of the property and to operate the business. If the case is a liquidation proceeding, the appointment of the interim trustee is mandatory unless the debtor posts a bond guaranteeing the value of the property in his or her estate.

Since some debtors against whom involuntary proceedings are commenced are, in fact, not bankrupt, the debtor has a right to file an answer to the petition of the creditors and to deny the allegations of the petition. If the debtor does not file an answer, the court orders relief against the debtor. If an answer is filed, the court conducts a trial on the issues raised by the petition and the answer. A court will order relief in an involuntary proceeding against the debtor only if it finds that the debtor is generally not paying debts as they become due. Insolvency in the balance sheet sense (liabilities exceeding assets) is not required. Relief may also be ordered if, within 120 days before the filing of the petition, a custodian, receiver, or agent has taken possession of property of the debtor for the purpose of enforcing a lien against the debtor.

Creditors also are prohibited from forcing any debtor into a Chapter 13 proceeding. The reason for this rule is that a Chapter 13 debtor is required to pay off his or her debts pursuant to an approved plan. To force an individual debtor to work to pay debts is equivalent to involuntary servitude, which violates the Thirteenth Amendment of the Constitution. Moreover, federal bankruptcy law provides penalties against creditors who file frivolous petitions and allow a debtor to receive damages, including punitive damages, against such creditors.

12. Conversion of Cases

Because a case may be filed voluntarily or involuntarily under the various chapters, the issue arises as to whether the debtor or the creditors can convert a filing to another type of proceeding. If the original filing is under Chapter 7, the debtor can request a conversion to a Chapter 11 or 13 proceeding. Creditors can have a Chapter 7 case converted to Chapter 11, but not to Chapter 13. If the case was filed voluntarily as a Chapter 11 reorganization proceeding, the debtor may request that the case be converted to a Chapter 7 or 13 proceeding. However, if the Chapter 11 proceeding was begun involuntarily, the creditors must consent to a conversion to Chapter 7. Creditors may seek to convert a Chapter 11 proceeding to Chapter 7 as long as the debtor is neither a farmer nor a nonprofit corporation. Creditors cannot convert a case from Chapter 11 to Chapter 13 without the debtor's consent.

In general, a debtor may convert a Chapter 13 proceeding to Chapter 7 or 11, whichever is more appropriate. Creditors also may ask the court to convert a case filed under Chapter 13 to Chapter 7 or 11 unless the debtor is a farmer. If the debtor is a farmer, any conversion must be agreed to by that farmer before that conversion will occur.

The following United States Supreme Court case discusses a variety of issues concerning the conversion of cases. Principally involved is the question of whether an individual debtor may convert a Chapter 7 case into a Chapter 11 case.

CASE

Toibb v. Radloff

SUPREME COURT OF THE UNITED STATES

501 U.S. 157 (1991)

BLACKMUN, J.

In this case we must decide whether an individual debtor not engaged in business is eligible to reorganize under Chapter 11 of the Bankruptcy Code.

From March 1983 until April 1985, petitioner Sheldon Baruch Toibb, a former staff attorney with the Federal Energy Regulatory Commission, was employed as a consultant by Independence Electric Corporation (IEC), a company he and two others organized to produce and market electric power. Petitioner owns 24 percent of the company's shares. After IEC terminated his employment, petitioner was unable to find work as a consultant in the energy field; he has been largely supported by his family and friends since that time.

On November 18, 1986, petitioner filed a voluntary petition for relief under Chapter 7 of the Code in the United States Bankruptcy Court. The Schedule of Assets and Liabilities accompanying petitioner's filing disclosed unsecured debts of $170,605. Petitioner listed as nonexempt assets his IEC shares and a possible claim against his former business associates. He stated that the market value of each of these assets was unknown.

On August 6, 1987, the Chapter 7 Trustee notified the creditors that the Board of Directors of IEC had offered to purchase petitioner's IEC shares for $25,000. When petitioner became aware that this stock had such value, he decided to avoid its liquidation by moving to convert his Chapter 7 case to one under the reorganization provisions of Chapter 11.

The Bankruptcy Court granted petitioner's conversion motion, and on February 1, 1988, petitioner filed a plan of reorganization. Under the plan, petitioner proposed to pay his unsecured creditors $25,000 less administrative expenses and priority tax claims, a proposal that would result in a payment of approximately 11 cents on the dollar. He further proposed to pay the unsecured creditors, for a period of six years, 50 percent of any dividends from IEC or of any proceeds from the sale of the IEC stock, up to full payment of the debts.

On March 8, 1988, the Bankruptcy Court on its own motion ordered petitioner to show cause why his petition should not be dismissed because petitioner was not engaged in business and, therefore, did not qualify as a Chapter 11 debtor. Petitioner argued that Chapter 11 should be available to an individual debtor not engaged in an ongoing business. On August 1, the Bankruptcy Court ruled that petitioner failed to qualify for relief under Chapter 11.

The District Court upheld the Bankruptcy Court's dismissal of petitioner's Chapter 11 case. The Court of Appeals affirmed. We granted certiorari.

In our view, the plain language of the Bankruptcy Code disposes of the question before us. Section 109 defines who may be a debtor under the various chapters of the Code. Section 109(d) provides: "Only a person that may be a debtor under Chapter 7 of this title, except a stockbroker or a commodity broker, and a railroad may be a debtor under Chapter 11 of this title." The Code defines "person" as used in Title 11 to "include [an] individual." Under the express terms of the Code, therefore, petitioner is "a person who may be a debtor under Chapter 7" and satisfies the statutory requirements for a Chapter 11 debtor.

The Code contains no ongoing business requirement for reorganization under Chapter 11, and we are loath to infer the exclusion of certain classes of debtors from the protections of Chapter 11 because Congress took care in § 109 to specify who qualifies—and who does not qualify—as a debtor under the various chapters of the Code. Congress knew how to restrict recourse to the avenues of bankruptcy relief; it did not place Chapter 11 reorganization beyond the reach of a nonbusiness individual debtor.

We are not persuaded by the contention that Chapter 11 is unavailable to a debtor without an ongoing business because many of the Chapter's provisions do not apply to a nonbusiness debtor. There is no doubt that Congress intended that a business debtor be among those who might use Chapter 11. Code provisions certainly are designed to aid in the rehabilitation of a business. It does not follow, however, that a debtor whose affairs do not warrant recourse to these provisions is ineligible for Chapter 11 relief. Instead, these provisions reflect an understandable expectation that Chapter 11 would be used primarily by debtors with ongoing businesses; they do not constitute an additional prerequisite for Chapter 11 eligibility beyond those established in § 109(d).

Although the foregoing analysis is dispositive of the question presented, we deal briefly with policy considerations inferring a congressional intent to preclude a nonbusiness debtor from reorganizing under Chapter 11. Petitioner suggests, and we agree, that Chapter 11 embodies the general Code policy of maximizing the value of the bankruptcy estate. Under certain circumstances a consumer debtor's estate will be worth more if reorganized under Chapter 11 than if liquidated under Chapter 7. Allowing such a debtor to proceed under Chapter 11 serves the congressional purpose of deriving as much value as possible from the debtor's estate.

Section 1129 (a) (7) provides that a reorganization plan may not be confirmed unless all the debtor's creditors accept the plan or will receive not less than they would receive under a Chapter 7 liquidation. Because creditors cannot be expected to approve a plan in which they would receive less than they would from an immediate liquidation of the debtor's assets, it follows that a Chapter 11 reorganization plan usually will be confirmed only when creditors will receive at least as much as if the debtor were to file under Chapter 7. Absent some showing of harm to the creditors of a nonbusiness debtor allowed to reorganize under Chapter 11, we see nothing in the allocation of "burdens" and "benefits" of Chapter 11 that warrants an inference that Congress intended to exclude a consumer debtor from its coverage.

The plain language of the Bankruptcy Code permits individual debtors not engaged in business to file for relief under Chapter 11. Although the structure and legislative history of Chapter 11 indicate that this Chapter was intended primarily for the use of business debtors, the Code contains no "ongoing business" requirement for Chapter 11 reorganization, and we find no basis for imposing one. Accordingly, the judgment of the Court of Appeals is reversed.

■ *Reversed.*

CASE CONCEPTS REVIEW

1. What type of bankruptcy proceeding was utilized initially by the debtor?
2. What motivated the debtor to convert the initial case to a Chapter 11 proceeding?
3. The lower courts all agreed on the proper outcome of this case. What was that judgment?
4. Why does the Supreme Court reverse these judgments? Discuss at least three reasons for this conclusion.

13. Automatic Stay

Stay

The order of relief. that prevents all creditors from taking any action to collect debts owed by the protected debtor

Bankruptcy cases operate to **stay** other judicial or administrative proceedings against the debtor. These stays of proceedings may operate to the detriment of a creditor or third party. For example, a stay would prevent a utility company from shutting off service. Despite this potential harm to creditors, the stay automatically becomes applicable immediately upon the bankruptcy petition being filed.

The stay provision often works to the disadvantage of secured creditors, especially in reorganization cases under Chapter 11. If the value of the property securing the debt does not cover the full debt, the creditor will lose because he or she cannot sell the property during the period of the stay. Creditors whose collateral is worth less than the loan amount are not entitled to compensation for the period of the stay in the bankruptcy court.

When the trustee continues to operate the debtor's business, it is frequently necessary to use, sell, or lease property of the debtor. To prevent irreparable harm to creditors and other third parties as a result of stays, a trustee may be required to provide "adequate protection" to third parties. In some cases, adequate protection requires that the trustee make periodic cash payments to creditors. In others, the trustee may be required to provide a lien to the creditor. When the sale, lease, or rental of the debtor's property may decrease the value of an entity's interest in property held by the trustee, a creditor may be entitled to a lien on the proceeds of any sale, lease, or rental. The court is empowered to determine if the trustee has furnished adequate protection; and when the issue is raised, the burden of proof is on the trustee.

The automatic stay is designed to protect both debtor and creditor. The stay provides the debtor time and freedom from financial pressures to attempt repayment or to develop a plan of reorganization. The stay protects creditors since it forces them to comply with the orderly administration of the debtor's estate. In other words, the stay prevents some creditors from grabbing all the debtor's assets while other creditors receive nothing. It also allows for orderly trials of claims such as those for personal injury or wrongful death. Such claims are tried in the federal district courts and not in the bankruptcy courts.

Despite these advantages of staying all proceedings against the debtor who files a bankruptcy petition, there are exceptions to the application of the automatic stay. These exceptions apply to proceedings that are not directly related to the debtor's financial situation. Proceedings that are not automatically stayed when a bankruptcy petition is made include (1) criminal actions against the debtor; (2) the collection of alimony, maintenance, or support from property that is not part of the estate; and (3) the commencement or continuation of an action by a governmental unit to enforce that governmental unit's police power. Although these actions are not stayed automatically by the filing of a bankruptcy petition, the trustee may seek to enjoin these actions if they harm the debtor's estate.

The significance of the automatic stay can be appreciated as the court in the following case determines the proper recourse for debtors who filed, but had not completed, the statutory credit counseling.

CASE

Diana Adams, Acting United States Trustee—against—Diana M. Finlay, et al.

UNITED STATES DISTRICT COURT FOR THE SOUTHERN DISTRICT OF NEW YORK

2006 U.S. Dist. LEXIS 81591 (2006)

Debtor Lena Elmendorf filed a voluntary Chapter 7 Petition on November 29, 2005, with the aid of a retained attorney. It was her first bankruptcy filing. Ms. Elmendorf did not file with her Bankruptcy Petition a Credit-Counseling Certificate. On February 1, 2006, the United States Trustee filed a Motion to Dismiss. A hearing on the Motion was held May 16, 2006, at which time the Bankruptcy Court reserved decision.

Ms. Diana Finlay filed a Chapter 13 case on April 3, 2006, acting pro se. Ms. Finlay also did not file a Credit Counseling Certificate but did seek an extension of time to file such a certificate. The Court denied the request for an extension because Ms. Finlay had failed to state that she attempted to obtain the counseling within five days of her filing. This was Ms. Finlay's third bankruptcy filing in the past year. On May 9, 2006, the Bankruptcy Judge issued an Order at the request of Ameriquest Mortgage Company to the affect that due to the prior two filings, no automatic stay came into effect upon the filing of this Petition.

Mrs. Shayna A. Zarnel, also acting pro se, filed a Chapter 13 case on March 13, 2006. This was her first filing. However, her husband, Alfred R. Zarnel, had filed five bankruptcy petitions in this District since January, 2004. Mrs. Zarnel did not file a Credit Counseling Certificate. She did seek from the Bankruptcy Court an extension of time to do so, but the request was denied because she had failed to set forth exigent circumstances in support of the extension, as required by BAPCPA. On April 3, 2006, she did file a Credit Counseling Certificate, which stated that on March 21, 2006, she received credit counseling. The Trustee moved to dismiss Mrs. Zarnel's Petition for literal Non-Compliance with respect to credit counseling.

In all three cases now on appeal by the United States Trustee, the Bankruptcy Court by a decision in writing on July 18, 2006, "struck the petitions" of the would-be debtors, concluding that striking the petition was the proper remedy for a debtor's failure to obtain counseling prior to filing the petition because: 1) no case was "commenced" by such filing, and 2) Congress didn't intend for debtor's protections under the BAPCPA to be limited in respect to a future bankruptcy filing "where the debtor's failure to comply with § 109(h) was obviously done out of ignorance of the gate-keeping requirement." The Court noted that the vast majority of debtors who fail to obtain credit counseling before filing a petition are pro se petitioners, but acknowledged that, in some cases, such failure combined with other circumstances revealing a larger scheme of delay or hindrance could merit some other sort of relief with prejudice

The consolidated structure of BAPCPA is such that no rational pro se litigant or attorney would intentionally fail to satisfy § 109(h). Although modern courts generally act to relieve pro se litigants (and also careless lawyers) from inadvertent defaults or procedural failures, Congress has, by its terms, so constructed § 109(b) that it is impossible to relieve non-compliance even in the most compelling situation where no credit counseling has been obtained or certified to have been timely sought and not obtained within five days of a request for same. This is so even where credit counseling would be an empty charade, for example, where sudden illness, loss of employment, divorce, incarceration of the breadwinner or any number of causes not related to fiscal irresponsibility, compel a person to seek refuge in the bankruptcy court.

The draconian consequences of a dismissal could include a resultant limited applicability of the fundamental protection of the automatic stay under § 362(c), in subsequent filings, merely for an initial failure to comply properly with the credit counseling requirement. This Court is loathe to believe that those drafting this "reform" legislation, in this nation whose westward expansion was largely facilitated by those fleeing debtor's prison, intended such a consequence.

The United States Trustee argues that when an individual is ineligible for debt relief for failure to seek credit counseling before filing, dismissal of the case pursuant to 11 U.S.C. § 707(a), and not striking the petition, is the only proper response of the Court.

The Bankruptcy Court concluded that when read together, Sections 109(h), 301, and 362(a) establish that no automatic stay can exist for debtors who fail to obtain the required credit counseling or qualify for a "waiver" or extension of time to do so.

This Court agrees.

The filing of a petition is not synonymous with the commencement of a case, and only petitions filed by those eligible to be debtors can commence a case; and if no case is commenced, there is no case to dismiss. Thus, striking is the appropriate way to conclude the matter.

The appeals are dismissed for want of standing to appeal. Alternatively, the Orders appealed from are affirmed in all respects because they are within the power of the Bankruptcy Court.

■ *Affirmed.*

CASE CONCEPTS REVIEW

1. Are there exceptions to the credit-counseling requirement? Explain.
2. Why might the debtors be pleased with the decision of the court?

14. Meeting of Creditors

In a voluntary case, the debtor has filed the required schedules with the petition. In an involuntary case, if the court orders relief, the debtor will be required to complete the same schedules as the debtor in a voluntary proceeding. From this point, the proceedings are identical. All parties are given notice of the order for relief. If the debtor owns real property, notice is usually filed in the public records of the county where the land is situated. The notice to creditors will include the date by which all claims are to be filed and the date of a meeting of the creditors with the debtor. This meeting of creditors must be within a reasonable time after the order for relief. The debtor appears at the meeting with the creditors, and the creditors are allowed to question the debtor under oath. The court may also order a meeting of any equity security holders of the debtor.

At the meeting of creditors, the debtor may be examined by the creditors to ascertain if property has been omitted from the list of assets, if property has been conveyed in defraud of creditors, and other matters that may affect the right of the debtor to have his or her obligations discharged.

In liquidation cases, the first meeting of creditors includes the important step of electing a *permanent trustee.* This trustee will replace the interim trustee appointed by the court at the time the order for relief was entered. The unsecured creditors who are not insiders elect this permanent trustee. To have a valid election, creditors representing at least 20 percent of the amount of unsecured claims held against the debtor must vote. The election is then determined by a majority of the unsecured creditors voting.

TRUSTEE AND CASE ADMINISTRATION

15. Trustee and the Estate

The trustee may be an individual or a corporation that has the capacity to perform the duties of a trustee. In a case under Chapter 7 or 13 of the Act, an individual trustee must reside or have an office and the corporate trustee must have an office in the judicial district in which the case is pending or in an adjacent district. Prior to becoming a trustee in a particular case, the trustee must file with the court a bond in favor of the United States. This bond may be used as a source of collection if the trustee should fail to faithfully perform his or her duties.

The trustee is the representative of the *estate* and has the capacity to sue and to be sued. Trustees are authorized to employ professional persons such as attorneys, accountants, appraisers, and auctioneers and to deposit or invest the money of the estate during the proceedings. In making deposits or investments, the trustee must seek the maximum reasonable net return, taking into account the safety of the deposit or investment.

The statute has detailed provisions on the responsibilities of the trustee under the tax laws. As a general rule, the trustee has responsibility for filing tax returns for the estate. After the order for relief, income received by the estate is taxable to it and not to an individual debtor. The estate of a partnership or a corporation debtor is not a separate entity for tax purposes. While the technical requirements of the tax laws are beyond the scope of this text, it should be remembered that the bankruptcy laws contain detailed rules complementary to the Internal Revenue Code in bankruptcy cases; the trustee must follow both.

16. General Duties and Powers

The statutory duties of the trustees in liquidation proceedings are to (1) collect and reduce to money the property of the estate; (2) account for all property received; (3) investigate the financial affairs of the debtor; (4) examine proofs of claims and object to the allowance of any claim that is improper; (5) oppose the discharge of the debtor, if advisable; (6) furnish information required by a party in interest; (7) file appropriate reports with the court and the taxing authorities, if a business is operated; and (8) make a final report and account and file it with the court.

A trustee that is authorized to operate the business of the debtor is authorized to obtain unsecured credit and to incur debts in the ordinary course of business. These debts are paid as administrative expenses.

A trustee in bankruptcy has several rights and powers with respect to the property of the debtor. First, the trustee has a judicial lien on the property, just as if the trustee were a creditor. Second, the trustee has the rights and powers of a judgment creditor who obtained a judgment against the debtor on the date of the adjudication of bankruptcy and who had an execution issued that was returned unsatisfied.

Third, the trustee has the rights of a bona fide purchaser of the real property of the debtor as of the date of the petition. Finally, the trustee has the rights of an actual unsecured creditor to avoid any transfer of the debtor's property and to avoid any obligation incurred by the debtor that is voidable under any federal or state law. As a result of these rights, the trustee is able to set aside transfers of property and to eliminate the interests of other parties where creditors or the debtor could do so.

The trustee also has the power to avoid certain liens of others on the property of the debtor. Liens that first become effective on the bankruptcy or insolvency of the debtor are voidable. As a general rule, liens that are not perfected or enforceable against a bona fide purchaser of the property are also voidable. Assume that a seller or creditor has an unperfected lien on goods in the hands of the debtor on the date the petition is filed. The lien is perfected later. That lien is voidable if it could not be asserted against a good-faith purchaser of the goods. Liens for rent and for distress for rent are also voidable.

The law imposes certain limitations on all these rights and powers of the trustee. A purchase-money security interest under Article 9 of the Code may be perfected after the petition is filed if it is perfected within ten days of delivery of the property. Such a security interest cannot be avoided by the trustee if properly perfected.

The rights and powers of the trustee are subject to those of a seller of goods in the ordinary course of business that has the right to reclaim goods if the debtor was insolvent when the debtor received them. The seller must demand the goods back within ten days, and the right to reclaim is subject to any superior rights of secured creditors. Courts may deny reclamation and protect the seller by giving his or her claim priority as an administrative expense.

17. Executory Contracts and Unexpired Leases

Debtors are frequently parties to contracts that have not been performed. Also, there are often lessees of real property, and the leases usually cover long periods of time. As a general rule, the trustee is authorized, subject to court approval, to assume or to reject an executory contract or unexpired lease. If the contract or lease is rejected, the other party has a claim subject to some statutory limitations. A rejection by the trustee creates a pre-petition claim for the rejected contract or lease debt subject to these limitations.

If the contract or lease is assumed, the trustee will perform the contract or assign it to someone else, and the estate will presumably receive the benefits. If the trustee assumes a contract or lease, he or she must cure any default by the debtor and provide adequate assurance of future performance. In shopping-center leases, adequate assurance includes protection against declines in percentage rents and preservation of the tenant mix, among other things.

A trustee may not assume an executory contract that requires the other party to make a loan, deliver equipment, or issue a security to the debtor. A party to a contract based on the financial strength of the debtor is not required to extend new credit to a debtor in bankruptcy.

Contracts and leases often have clauses prohibiting assignment. The law also prohibits the assignment of certain contract rights, such as those that are personal in nature. The trustee in bankruptcy is allowed to assume contracts, notwithstanding a clause prohibiting the assumption or assignment of the contract or lease. The trustee is not allowed to assume a contract if applicable nonbankruptcy law excuses the other party from performance to someone other than the debtor, unless the other party consents to the assumption.

The statute invalidates contract clauses that automatically terminate contracts or leases upon filing of a petition in bankruptcy or upon the assignment of the lease or contract. The law also invalidates contract clauses that give a party other than the debtor the right to terminate the contract upon assumption by the trustee or assignment by the debtor. Such clauses hamper rehabilitation efforts and are against public policy. They are not needed because the court can require the trustee to provide adequate protection and can ensure that the other party receives the benefit of its bargain.

If the trustee assigns a contract to a third party and the third party later breaches the contract, the trustee has no liability. This is a change of the common law in which an assignor is not relieved of liability by an assignment. An assignment by a trustee in bankruptcy is, in effect, a novation if the assignment is valid.

18. Voidable Preferences

One of the goals of bankruptcy proceedings is to provide an equitable distribution of a debtor's property among creditors. To achieve this goal, the trustee in bankruptcy is allowed to recover transfers that constitute a **preference** of one creditor over another. As one judge said, "A creditor who dips his hand in a pot which he knows will not go round must return what he receives, so that all may share." To constitute a recoverable preference, the transfer must (1) have been made by an insolvent debtor; (2) have been made to a creditor for, or on account of, an antecedent debt owed by the debtor before the transfer; (3) have been made within ninety days of the filing of the bankruptcy petition; and (4) enable the creditor to receive a greater percentage of the claim than he or she would receive under a distribution from the bankruptcy estate in a liquidation proceeding.

Preference

If an insolvent debtor pays some creditors a greater percentage of the debts than other creditors in the same class, and if the payments are made within ninety days prior to filing a bankruptcy petition; illegal and voidable payments to one creditor over another

Insofar as the time period is concerned, there is an exception when the transfer is to an insider. In this case, the trustee may avoid the transfer if it occurred within one year of the date of filing the petition, provided the insider had reasonable cause to believe the debtor was insolvent at the time of the transfer.

A debtor is presumed to be insolvent during the ninety-day period prior to the filing of the petition. Any person contending that the debtor was solvent has the burden of coming forward with evidence to prove solvency. Once credible evidence is introduced, the party with the benefit of the presumption of insolvency has the burden of persuasion on the issue.

Recoverable preferences include not only payments of money but also the transfer of property as payment of, or as security for, a prior indebtedness. Since the law is limited to debts, payments by the debtor of tax liabilities are exempt from the preference provision and are not recoverable. A mortgage or pledge may be set aside as readily as direct payments. A pledge or mortgage can be avoided if received within the immediate ninety-day period prior to the filing of the petition in bankruptcy, provided it was obtained as security for a previous debt. The effective date of a transfer or a mortgage of real property may be questioned if the date the legal documents are signed is different from the date these documents are recorded. A logical solution to this potential problem seems to be to rely on the date the document is recorded in the public records.

Payment of a fully secured claim does not constitute a preference and, therefore, may not be recovered. Transfers of property for a contemporaneous consideration may not be set aside, because there is a corresponding asset for the new liability. A mortgage given to secure a contemporaneous loan is valid even when the mortgagee took the security with knowledge of the debtor's insolvency. An insolvent debtor has a right to attempt to extricate himself or herself, as far as possible, from financial difficulty. If the new security is personal property, it must be perfected within ten days after the security interest attaches. The law also creates an exception for transfers in the ordinary course of business or in the ordinary financial affairs of persons not in business. The payment of such debts is not recoverable by the trustee. This exception covers ordinary debt payments such as utility bills. The law on preferences is directed at unusual transfers and payments, not those occurring promptly in the ordinary course of the debtor's affairs.

19. Fraudulent Transfers

A transfer of property by a debtor may be fraudulent under federal or state law. The trustee may proceed under either to set aside a fraudulent conveyance. Under federal law, a *fraudulent conveyance* is a transfer within two years of the filing of the petition, with the intent to hinder, delay, or defraud creditors. Under state law, the period may be longer and is usually within the range of two to five years.

Fraudulent intent may be inferred from the fact that the consideration is unfair, inadequate, or nonexistent. Solvency or insolvency at the time of the transfer is significant, but it is not controlling. Fraudulent intent exists when the transfer makes it impossible for the creditors to be paid in full or for the creditors to use legal remedies that would otherwise be available.

The intent to hinder, delay, or defraud creditors may also be implied. Such is the case when the debtor is insolvent and makes a transfer for less than a full and adequate value. Fraudulent intent is present if the debtor was insolvent on the date of the transfer or if the debtor becomes insolvent as a result of the transfer.

If the debtor is engaged in business or is about to become so, the fraudulent intent will be implied when the transfer leaves the businessperson with an unreasonably small amount of capital. The businessperson may be solvent; nevertheless, he or she has made a fraudulent transfer if the net result of the transfer leaves him or her with an unreasonably small amount of capital, provided the transfer was without fair consideration. Whether or not the remaining capital is unreasonably small is a question of fact.

The trustee may also avoid a transfer made in contemplation of incurring obligations beyond the debtor's ability to repay as they mature. Assume that a woman is about to enter business and that she plans to incur debts in the business. Because of her concern that she may be unable to meet these potential obligations, she transfers all her property to her husband, without consideration. Such a transfer may be set aside as fraudulent. The requisite intent is supplied by the factual situation at the time of the transfer and the state of mind of the transferor. The actual financial condition of the debtor in such a case is not controlling, but it does shed some light on the intent factor and state of mind of the debtor.

The trustee of a partnership debtor may avoid transfers of partnership property to partners if the debtor was or thereby became insolvent. This rule was made to prevent a partnership's preferring partners who are also creditors over other partners. Such transfers may be avoided if they occurred within one year of the date of filing the petition.

If a transferee is liable to the trustee only because the transfer was to defraud creditors, the law limits the transferee's liability. To the extent that the transferee does give value in good faith, the transferee has a lien on the property. For the purpose of defining value in the fraudulent transfer situation, the term includes property or the satisfaction or securing of a present or existing debt. It does not include an unperformed promise to support the debtor or a relative of a debtor.

CREDITORS

20. Creditors and Claims

Creditors are required to file proof of their claims if they are to share in the debtor's estate. Filed claims are allowed unless a party in interest objects. If an objection is filed, the court conducts a hearing to determine the validity of the claim. A claim may be disallowed if it is (1) unenforceable because of usury, unconscionability, or failure of consideration, (2) for unmatured interest, (3) an insider's or attorney's claim and exceeds the reasonable value of the services rendered, (4) for unmatured alimony or child support, (5) for rent, and (6) for breach of an employment contract. These latter two claims may be disallowed to the extent that they exceed the statutory limitations for such claims.

Illegality can be raised because any defense available to the debtor is available to the trustee. Post-petition interest is not collectible because interest stops accruing at the date of filing the petition. Bankruptcy operates as an acceleration of the principal due. From the date of filing, the amount of the claim is the total principal plus interest to that date.

Unreasonable attorney's fees and claims of insiders are disallowed because they encourage concealing assets or returning them to the debtor. Since alimony claims are not dischargeable in bankruptcy, there is no reason to allow a claim for post-petition alimony and child support.

Claims are sometimes contingent or otherwise unliquidated and uncertain. Personal injury and wrongful death claims against a debtor that cannot be settled are tried in federal district courts and not in bankruptcy courts. The law authorizes the bankruptcy court to estimate and to fix the amount of such claims, if necessary, to avoid undue delay in closing the estate or approving of a plan of reorganization. The same is true of equitable remedies such as specific performance. Courts will convert such remedies to dollar amounts and proceed to close the estate or approve the plan.

If a secured claim is undersecured—that is, if the debt exceeds the value of the collateral—the claim is divided into two parts. The claim is secured to the extent of the value of the collateral. It is an unsecured claim for the balance.

FIGURE 39-1 ■ General Distribution Process

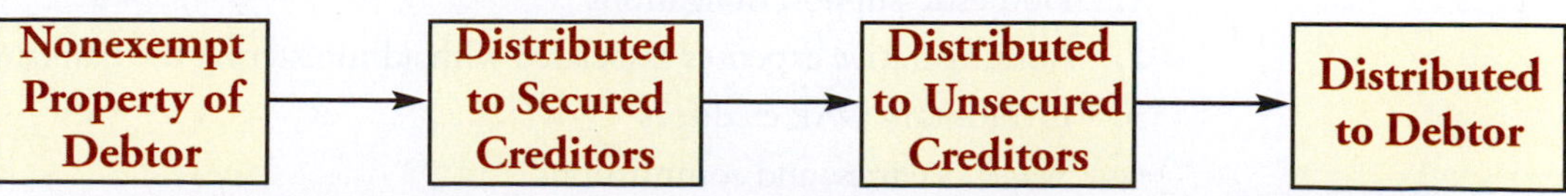

21. Right of Setoff

Any creditor who also owes the debtor money may have a right of *setoff.* In essence, this creditor is allowed to cancel out these obligations. For example, suppose that a bank lends a debtor $2,000 and that this debtor has $1,500 on deposit at the bank. If the debtor fails to make payment on the $2,000 loan, the bank can use the deposit to reduce the amount of the debtor's loan.

If a debtor files a bankruptcy petition and the creditor exercises the right of setoff, the issue of a preference arises. In our example, the bank becomes a preferred creditor to the extent of the $1,500 setoff; but the bank, generally, is legally entitled to this preference if the amount of the deposit has not increased during the ninety days preceding the filing of the petition in bankruptcy. However, this preference would be nullified if the deposit was made or increased just before the bankruptcy petition was filed for the purpose of preferring the bank over other creditors. In that case, the deposit becomes a part of the debtor's estate, and the setoff is disallowed.

Since the filing of the petition in bankruptcy operates as a stay of all proceedings, the right of setoff operates at the time of final distribution of the estate. Since the law allows the trustee, with court approval, to use the funds of the debtor, parties who wish to exercise the right of setoff should seek "adequate protection."

The right to setoff will usually be exercised by a creditor against a deposit that has been made within ninety days of the filing of a petition in bankruptcy. Quite frequently, there are several such deposits, and there may also have been several payments on the debt during the ninety-day period. As a result of these variables, the application of setoff principles is sometimes difficult.

The law seeks to prohibit a creditor from improving his or her position during the ninety-day period. It does so by allowing the trustee to recover that portion of the setoff that would be considered a preference. This amount recoverable by the trustee is the insufficiency between the amount owed and the amount on deposit on the first day of the ninety-day period preceding the filing of a bankruptcy petition that a deficiency occurred—to the extent that this insufficiency is greater than the insufficiency existing on the day the petition is filed. If the deposit on the first day of the preceding ninety-day period exceeds the creditor's claim, look for the first insufficiency during the ninety-day period and calculate the setoff based on the first insufficiency.

Assume that a bankruptcy petition was filed on September 2. Throughout the ninety days prior to this filing, the debtor owes $2,000 to the creditor. On June 4, the debtor has $1,500 on deposit with the creditor. On July 15, the amount on deposit is reduced to $700. On September 1, the debtor's balance is increased to $1,800. At the time of the filing, the creditor seeks to use the entire $1,800 on deposit to set off its claim against the debtor. The trustee would be able to recover $300 of this attempted setoff since there was a greater insufficiency of that amount on the first day of the ninety-day period prior to the petition's being filed. In other words, the creditor's setoff would be limited to $1,500.

22. Priorities

The bankruptcy law establishes certain priorities in the payment of claims. After *secured* creditors have had the opportunity to benefit from a security interest in collateral, the general order of priority for *unsecured debts* is as follows (from first priority to last):

1. Domestic-support obligations
2. Administrative expenses associated with administering the bankruptcy estate
3. Involuntary GAP creditors
4. Wages, salaries, and commissions

5. Contributions to employee benefit plans
6. Suppliers of grain to a grain storage facility or of fish to a fish produce storage or processing facility
7. Consumer deposits
8. Governmental units for certain taxes
9. Certain claims for death or personal injury
10. Claims of general creditors

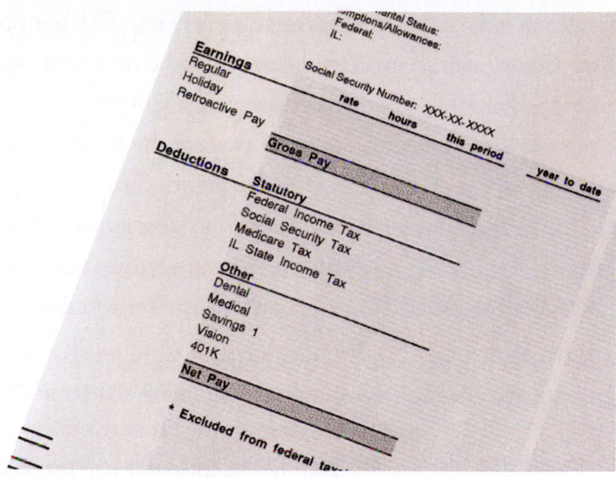

Wages are one of the priorities considered in discharging debt in a bankruptcy filing.

Alimony and child support are the most prominent examples of domestic-support obligations. Administrative expenses include all costs of administering the debtor's estate, including taxes incurred by the estate. Typical costs include attorney's fees, appraiser's fees, and wages paid to persons employed to help preserve the estate.

The term *involuntary GAP creditor* describes a person who extends credit to the estate after the filing of an involuntary petition under Chapter 11 and before a trustee is appointed or before the order for relief is entered. Such claims include taxes incurred as the result of the conduct of business in this period.

The fourth class of priority is limited to amounts earned by an individual within 180 days of the filing of the petition or the cessation of the debtor's business, whichever occurred first. The priority is limited to $10,950 for each individual, but it includes vacation, severance, and sick leave pay as well as regular earnings. The employee's share of employment taxes is included in this fourth category, provided the wages and the employee's share of taxes have been paid in full. The category does not include fees paid to independent contractors.

The fifth priority recognizes that fringe benefits are an important part of many employment contracts. The priority is limited to claims for contributions to employee benefit plans, arising from services rendered within 180 days before commencement of the case or cessation of the debtor's business, whichever occurs first. The priority is limited to $10,950 multiplied by the number of employees less the amount paid under priority 4. The net effect is to limit the total priority for wages and employee benefits to $10,950 per employee.

The sixth priority is designed to protect the farmer who raises grain and the fisherman if their grain or fish are held by the owner of a production or storage facility. If the farmers or fishermen have not been paid for the grain or fish transferred, they have a priority claim to the extent of $5,400 per creditor.

The seventh priority is an additional method of consumer protection. It protects consumers who have deposited money in connection with the purchase, lease, or rental of property or the purchase of services for personal, family, or household use that were not delivered or provided. The priority is limited to $2,245 per consumer.

The eighth priority is for certain taxes. Priority is given to income taxes for a taxable year that ended on or before the date of filing the petition. The last due date of the return must have occurred not more than three years before the filing. Employment taxes and transfer taxes such as gift, estate, sale, and excise taxes are also given seventh-class priority. Again the transaction or event that gave rise to the tax must precede the petition date, and the return must have been due within three years. The bankruptcy laws have several very technical aspects relating to taxation, and they must be reviewed carefully for tax returns filed by the trustee and claims for taxes.

The ninth priority is for claims of death or serious injury resulting from an automobile accident caused by the unlawful use of alcohol or drugs.

In liquidation cases, the property available is first distributed among the priority claimants in the order just discussed. Then, the property is distributed to *general unsecured creditors* who file their claims on time. Next, payment is made to unsecured creditors who tardily file their claims. Thereafter distribution is made to holders of penalty, forfeiture, or punitive damage claims. Punitive penalties, including tax penalties, are subordinated to the first three classes of claims, as a matter of policy. Regular creditors should be paid before windfalls to persons and entities collecting penalties. Finally, post-petition interest on pre-petition claims is paid if any property is available to do so. After the interest is paid, any surplus goes to the debtor. Claims within a particular class are paid pro rata if the trustee is unable to pay them in full.

CHAPTER SUMMARY

1. Of major importance today is the *Bankruptcy Reform Act of 1978* as it has been amended in 1984, 1986, 1988, 1990, and substantially with the BAPCPA in 2005.
2. The basic purpose of the bankruptcy law is to give a debtor in financial difficulty an opportunity to overcome this problem.
3. Terms to remember include *debtor, claim, order of relief, discharge,* and *trustee.*

TYPES OF PROCEEDINGS

In General

1. The bankruptcy law has two basic approaches to resolving a debtor's financial problems: one is liquidation, and the other is reorganization.

Liquidation Proceedings

1. This proceeding is governed by Chapter 7 of the statute.
2. In general, a debtor surrenders all assets from which creditors are paid as much as possible.
3. Individual debtors generally have all unpaid debts discharged or forgiven. Technically, a business organization's debts are not discharged.

Reorganization Proceedings

1. This proceeding is governed by Chapter 11 of the statute.
2. In essence, the debtor attempts to restructure the financial situation so creditors can be substantially paid over time.
3. The key to a successful reorganization is the court's approval of a reasonable confirmation plan.

Adjustment of Individuals' Debts

1. This proceeding is governed by Chapter 13 of the statute.
2. The debtor must be an individual who has regular income and who has unsecured debts not exceeding $307,675, and the secured debts cannot exceed $922,975.
3. Again, a plan of repayment must be approved. The unsecured creditors must receive at least as much as they would under a Chapter 7 liquidation proceeding.

GENERAL PRINCIPLES

Property of the Estate

1. All the property interests of a debtor are used to create an estate.

2. The trustee, in essence, has whatever interests a debtor had at the time a bankruptcy petition was filed.

Exemptions

1. To enhance the debtor's fresh start, the debtor may exempt certain property from the estate.
2. These exemptions are governed by either federal or state law, whichever the state law provides.

Debts that Are Not Discharged

1. Certain debts are not discharged; therefore, they survive the bankruptcy case and remain payable to the creditor.

Grounds for Denying Discharge

1. There also are grounds for denying a discharge.
2. Basically, in its balancing process, the drafters of the law decided that debts created in certain situations should not be forgiven.

PROCEDURAL STEPS

Voluntary Commencement

1. Any proceeding may be started by a debtor filing a petition in bankruptcy.
2. The voluntary filing acts as an order of relief unless the bankruptcy judge decides that a consumer debtor is not entitled to Chapter 7 protection.

Involuntary Commencement

1. In general, cases may also be started by creditors with at least $12,300 in claims filing a petition. This creditor-commenced action is known as an *involuntary case.*
2. In an involuntary case, the bankruptcy judge must decide whether an order of relief is appropriate.
3. An involuntary case cannot be filed under Chapter 13 of the statute regardless of who the debtor is. An involuntary case under Chapters 7 and 11 cannot be filed when the debtor is a farmer or a nonprofit corporation.

Automatic Stay

1. The filing of a bankruptcy petition protects the debtor against any action taken by creditors.
2. This stay is automatic even before the creditors learn of the petition's being filed.
3. The stay remains in effect until the bankruptcy judge permits actions by creditors.

Meeting of Creditors

1. After the order of relief is entered, a meeting of the creditors will be scheduled. At this meeting, creditors can question the debtor and examine documents.
2. Also at this meeting, unsecured creditors will elect a permanent trustee.

TRUSTEE AND CASE ADMINISTRATION

Trustee and the Estate

1. The trustee must satisfy statutory prerequisites before he, she, or it is qualified.
2. The trustee has the responsibility for preserving the estate for the benefit of all creditors.
3. The trustee must fulfill the administrative duties with regard to taxes and similar matters.
4. In general, the trustee is a fiduciary of the estate.

General Duties and Powers

1. The trustee may employ professionals in representing the estate. The trustee also may sue and be sued in a representative capacity.
2. The trustee has several statutory duties designed to ensure the proper workings of the bankruptcy law.

3. The trustee may operate the business of the debtor and may incur expenses associated with such an operation.
4. The trustee may assume the position of a lienholder or a good-faith purchaser if such positions enhance the estate.
5. The trustee also may avoid certain liens on the debtor's property.

Executory Contracts and Unexpired Leases

1. The trustee has the general power to perform or avoid executory contracts and unexpired leases, regardless of what the agreement may state about the debtor's right to assign.
2. The trustee's power to avoid or modify a collective bargaining contract has been limited, but not removed, by the 1984 amendments.
3. The 1988 amendment added a mechanism whereby the obligation to pay insurance benefits to retired employees might be modified.

Voidable Preferences

1. To keep all creditors on an equal basis, the trustee can avoid any transfer or payment to a creditor if such was made within ninety days of the petition being filed, if such was made to satisfy all or part of antecedent debts, if such was made while the debtor was insolvent, and if such was indeed a preference.
2. The debtor is presumed to be insolvent during the ninety days prior to the petition's being filed.
3. If the preferred creditor is an insider, the time period of concern is one year, not ninety days, before the petition was filed.

Fraudulent Transfers

1. A transfer of property may be fraudulent under either federal or state law.
2. In general, any transfer within a statutory time period prior to the filing of a bankruptcy petition is fraudulent if the debtor intended to hinder, delay, or defraud creditors.
3. The trustee has the power to declare these transfers invalid to protect the estate for the creditors' benefit.

CREDITORS

Creditors and Claims

1. Creditors must be able to prove their claims to be paid from the debtor's estate.
2. There are numerous reasons why a claim may be disallowed altogether or otherwise limited.

Right of Setoff

1. Because the debtor may have a claim against the creditor, that creditor can set off the amount owed to the debtor against the claims the creditor makes on the debtor's estate.
2. This setoff must not give an unreasonable preference to the creditor. The trustee will examine all events during the ninety days prior to the filing of the bankruptcy to determine the proper amount of the setoff.

Priorities

1. The creditors' claims are subject to payment according to the priority established by the bankruptcy law.
2. Seven categories of priority claims must be paid before the first general unsecured creditor's claim is paid.

REVIEW QUESTIONS AND PROBLEMS

1. Match each term in Column A with the appropriate statement in Column B.

A	B
(1) Liquidation	(a) A creditor's right to payment
(2) Reorganization	(b) Entered by bankruptcy judge whenever debtor is entitled to the court's protection
(3) Claim	(c) The creditor's right to reduce the amount of its claim by the amount it owes the debtor
(4) Discharge	(d) The type of proceeding pursued under Chapter 7
(5) Order of relief	(e) A transfer that gives a creditor an unfair advantage over other creditors
(6) Meeting of creditors	(f) The legal forgiveness of a debt
(7) Voidable preference	(g) The type of proceeding pursued under Chapter 11
(8) Right of setoff	(h) The event when, among other things, a permanent trustee is elected
(9) Debtor	(i) Person who handles the assets and obligations during bankruptcy
(10) Trustee	(j) Person or entity who files for bankruptcy or has a petition filed against them

2. The bankruptcy court approved a repayment plan proposed by debtors, Eddie and Angela Freeman, pursuant to Chapter 13. Under the plan, the Freemans agreed to pay their secured creditors in full, but their unsecured creditors were to receive nothing. Public Finance is an unsecured creditor and appeals the affirmation of the plan, arguing that a plan that proposes no payment to unsecured creditors fails to meet the good-faith requirement of the bankruptcy law. Does "good faith" exist only when the debtor proposes payment to unsecured creditors? Explain.

3. Pauline lives in a state that exempts $800 for an automobile owned by a debtor in a bankruptcy proceeding. Pauline's car was worth more than $800, so she sought to recover $800 of the sales price when the court sold the car to satisfy her debts. Her creditors contend that she is not entitled to any exemption for a car worth more than $800. Who is correct? Explain.

4. A state court awarded a wife $100,000 in alimony. The ex-husband did not pay it and later filed a petition under Chapter 7 of the bankruptcy law. He proved that his ex-wife did not need the money, as she was now gainfully employed and was in fact quite wealthy. Is this debt dischargeable? Explain.

5. Taylor borrowed money pursuant to the Guaranteed Student Loan Program. Three years later he filed a petition in voluntary bankruptcy and included his student loans on his list of debts. Taylor was given a general discharge in bankruptcy. Is he still liable for his student loans? Why or why not?
6. Robinson pleaded guilty to larceny in the second degree. The charge was based on her wrongful receipt of $9,932.95 in welfare benefits from the state of Connecticut. As a part of her sentence, Robinson was required to make restitution at the rate of $100 per month during her probationary period. Robinson filed a Chapter 7 bankruptcy petition. She sought to have her obligation to make restitution discharged. Although they received notice of the Chapter 7 petition, the staff members of the Connecticut Department of Income Maintenance and of the Probation Office did not respond. Robinson's obligation to make restitution was discharged. Later the Probation Office objected when the restitution payments ceased. Robinson filed this action to have the discharge affirmed. Were the restitution payments, as required as a condition of Robinson's probation, dischargeable in a Chapter 7 bankruptcy proceeding? Why?
7. The Chocolate Cookie Company entered into a twenty-year lease at an annual rental of $4,000 a year. This lease contained a clause that the lease was not assignable without the lessor's consent. Eighteen months after the lease was signed, the Chocolate Cookie Company commenced voluntary liquidation proceedings. The trustee sought to enforce the lease, despite the non-assignability clause. May the trustee enforce the lease as written? Why?
8. With the facts as in problem 7, how much could the lessor claim in the bankruptcy proceeding if the trustee terminated the lease six months after the petition was filed (after two years of the lease term had passed)? Explain.
9. Despite financial difficulties, Barney bought two suits for $500. When he received a bill for the suits, two weeks later, he was insolvent; however, he fully paid this bill in cash. One month later he filed a petition in bankruptcy. The appointed trustee sued to recover the $500 paid, contending that the payment was a preferential transfer. Was the trustee correct? Why?
10. After filing for Chapter 11 reorganization, an employer continued to pay wages to its employees and to withhold the required amounts of FICA and income taxes from their paychecks. However, it did not pay the withheld amount to the IRS. Subsequently, the bankruptcy court appointed a trustee to supervise the liquidation of the estate. The government filed a claim for the taxes due from the reorganization period. Which priority claim does the government have? Explain.

Internet Sources

The United States government provides general information bankruptcy at:

http://www.uscourts.gov/bankruptcycourts/bankruptcybasics.html

PART IX

GOVERNMENT REGULATIONS

Administrative Law | 40

CHAPTER OUTLINE

CHAPTER PREVIEW

Central to the constitutional form of government in the United States is the principle of separation of powers. As discussed in Chapter 5, the members of the Constitutional Convention were highly suspect of government in general and believed that in those situations where government was necessary, the powers of government should be dispersed among three branches. The notion of having separate legislative, executive, and judicial branches was intended to keep one branch of government from assuming a preeminent position over the other branches. Those framers of the Constitution probably never envisioned a day when legislative, executive, and judicial functions are brought under one tent. Yet in the day-to-day operation of business in the 21st century, the regulatory environment of business is shaped primarily by a form of government that does not operate under the theory of separation of powers. The form of government possessing this characteristic is called an *administrative agency.* As a result of the increasing prominence administrative agencies play in government, they are often referred to as the "fourth branch" of government.

What circumstance would necessitate violating the principle of separation of powers? The escalating complexity of social interactions, particularly regarding commerce, necessitated a new approach to governing. Certain government entities must be able to assemble all components of government in order to adequately address a specific social problem. In this manner, the public should be better served because individuals and entities that possess specific expertise relating to a single domain wield government power. Therefore, in order to achieve worthwhile goals of society within a more complicated setting, this type of government unit must be able to ignore—in their specific area of proficiency—the doctrine of separation of powers.

The law associated with administrative agencies is called *administrative law.* This chapter begins by examining the nature and role of administrative agencies. It then addresses the three principal functions associated with an administrative agency: rulemaking, enforcement, and adjudication. Next, the process by which courts review administrative agency actions is discussed. The chapter concludes with a presentation of the major means that administrative agencies are accountable to the public.

BUSINESS MANAGEMENT DECISION

Fluffy Toy Company manufactures toy animals suitable for children from ages 2-10. The Consumer Product Safety Commission, a federal administrative agency, has received an increasing number of complaints that children are chewing on the firm plastic parts of stuffed toys and the pieces of plastic are injuring the mouths of the children. The Commission is considering a rule that would prohibit the sale of soft toys containing any hard plastic parts. Fluffy Toy Company is quite concerned about such a regulation because most of their animal toys contain noses and eyes made from hard plastic. Fluffy Toy Company is a member of the Toy Manufacturing Association. What avenues are open to Fluffy Toy Company to stop the proposed rule from becoming a regulation?

NATURE OF ADMINISTRATIVE AGENCIES

1. Role of Administrative Agencies

Administrative agencies exist today at all levels of government. The Federal Trade Commission is an administrative agency. So, too, a state fair employment department is deemed, properly, an administrative agency. County, city, and town boards, bureaus, and commissions—all might well be termed administrative agencies. With the prominence of administrative agencies, it is easy to understand the significant impact administrative agencies have on our lives as customers, consumers, and shareholders, among a host of other categories relevant to each of us. Of equal magnitude, administrative agencies shape the environment within which business functions, regardless of whether the commercial entity is a small grocery store operated as a sole proprietorship or global consulting firm organized as a publicly traded corporation. In fact, administrative agencies may well impact the business community to a greater extent than economic, political, or judicial factors.

2. Purposes of Administrative Agencies

Administrative agencies are needed to afford business and the general public with a more focused, and hopefully more effective and efficient, response to recognized problems of society. Benefits associated with administrative agencies may be couched in four general categories. First, administrative agencies act to *guard* the consuming public against the actions of overzealous members of the business community. Because of the complexity of products and services offered for sale and the great distances that now may exist between merchant and consumer, opportunities for business (especially large businesses) to take advantage of individuals and other types of entities are considerable. Gone are the days where one walks to town to purchase horseshoes from the neighborhood shoemaker. Today, buying a laptop computer necessarily anticipates that the consumer has no idea how the computer operates; and, indeed, such a purchase may involve a commercial transaction spanning thousands of miles. Administrative agencies exist to provide protection to the public in general, to consumers, to employees, to shareholders … and a host of other groups within society. Ethical and moral principles have proven insufficient to appropriately control the highly competitive world of business. For example, while most citizens would want to keep our oceans, lakes, rivers, and streams clean, decisions by some members of the manufacturing community to dump pollutants into our waterways led Congress to charge the Environmental Protection Agency with the responsibility of holding polluters responsible and instituting regulatory process aimed at keeping our waterways clean. Another example applies to consumers. The Consumer Product Safety Commission investigates complaints of manufactured goods that

The EPA was created to help minimize industrial pollution of the environment.

cause harm to people and then acts, if appropriate, to mandate the recall of a dangerous product or curtail its production.

Next, administrative agencies possess *proficiency.* Administrative agencies are the government's experts in a relevant area of social concern. The administrative agency is able to develop a level of proficiency far beyond what members of the legislative, executive, or judicial branches could hope to achieve. Because agency employees are devoted to one area of the regulatory environment of business, they can be more aware of economic, scientific, and other aspects of their area of specialty as they work to create rules and regulations affecting business. While this approach to regulation necessarily infuses in administrative agencies considerable power to craft government edicts that may impact greatly individual businesses or entire industries, the theory of administrative agency regulation presumes that those who possess proficiency in one subject can best apply the broad provisions of a statute to a specific area in need of regulation through the appropriate formation of administrative rules. The detailed nature of administrative rules demands that enforcement is conducted by individuals well-versed in those rules. Asking a city police officer to enforce edicts created by the Environmental Protection Agency regarding air pollution standards is not an effective use of the officer's time and is not the best means of accomplishing the goal of agency rule enforcement. Enforcement of administrative rules is best left to agency employees who possess a solid understanding of science, production processes, and a number of other areas germane to the issue of air pollution. Finally, courts and quasi-judicial dispute resolution systems are ill equipped to address the huge number of disputes arising out of the government's regulation of business. Administrative agencies provide mechanisms where those disputes can be effectively handled—at least at the first level—without having to burden our court system.

The structure of the Occupational Safety and Health Agency (OSHA) illustrates the how all three functions operate. OSHA is charged with taking the broad edicts from Congress mandating that the workplace be reasonably safe and creating rules capable of giving practical meaning to the intent of Congress. OSHA has done so, generating thousands of workplace safety rules tailored to specific business settings (e.g., manufacturing, construction). The division of OSHA responsible for rulemaking is devoted to solicit advice, conduct hearings, and write draft language, among a host of other activities that will produce specific rules regarding workplace safety. In addition to promulgating rules, OSHA also will cite employers for violating the rules. OSHA possesses a staff of individuals charged with the responsibility of conducting investigations into allegations that a specific workplace has violated an OSHA rule. The investigators are highly trained. Sometimes a business is investigated after an accident, sometimes based on a whistle-blower statement, and sometimes (depending on the situation) as a result of a random inspection. Finally, OSHA provides a quasi-judicial process for hearing disputes regarding whether a particular OSHA rule has been violated, with each "judge" at the possessing considerable knowledge of OSHA rules.

Third, administrative agencies provide greater *certainty.* The complex and rapidly changing nature of certain problems facing society demands an approach not suited to legislative law making. Congress and state legislatures cannot provide sufficient detail in statutes to cover all aspects of a given difficulty. Therefore, for example, it is sensible for Congress to delegate to the Internal Revenue Service the authority to create rules and regulations capable of effectively implementing the broad statutory directions provided by Congress. Administrative agency rules and regulations, because they are more specific than legislation, may reduce greatly the uncertainty associated with government regulation. As a result, the business community benefits because administrative agencies can provide a better view, than the traditional three-branch system, of what behavior of business Congress or a state legislature has deemed illegal.

Finally, administrative agencies supply *information* to the business community and the general public. Guidance is provided to business on a large number of fronts. Human resource management officials can access the Department of Labor's Office of Compliance Assistance Policy materials on the web, for example, if they are struggling to comply with the complicated laws and regulations associated with overtime pay. In the past decade, administrative agencies have attempted to provide business with explanations of regulations in common language, allowing readers to understand better the intent of the agency in promulgating regulations. Most major administrative agencies also will provide "opinion letters" that allow businesses to pose a factual scenario to the agency and then have the agency provide a response. In addition, administrative agencies gear their information to members of the public. An illustration comes from Massachusetts. That state's Securities Division will review securities offering documents, check the status of persons offering or selling securities, verify the status of persons giving investment advice within the state, make available copies of public records on securities offerings, and provide free investor education materials. Given the complexity of modern commercial transactions, the information offered by administrative agencies closes a critical gap in the relationship between business and members of the public.

3. Conceptual Framework for Administrative Agencies

HISTORICAL AND CONSTITUTIONAL DIMENSIONS Considering the important role administrative agencies play in business operations and the fact that the separation of powers doctrine is largely inapplicable to agencies, the historical development of administrative agencies, along with the formation of basic precepts of administrative law, deserves significant attention. As the agrarian sector diminished in significance during the late 19th century, the dominance of manufacturing created a number of new challenges to society. Technology allows sophisticated products to be manufactured. Unfortunately, the complex nature of goods meant that products could more easily harm customers. Also, technology spawned larger and larger organizations. Huge organizations could be formed and sustained, sometimes without considering the hardships created on employees, competitors, and others. While the legislative, executive, and judicial branches could address successfully selected aspects of this sea-change in the manner in which business operated, it was clear to Congress that the tripartite structure of the United States government lacked the ability to adequately address more and more prevalent concerns raised by individuals and groups.

Congress first responded to the challenges brought about by new and powerful economic forces in 1887 with the passage of the *Interstate Commerce Act*. The statute created the first major administrative agency at the federal level: the Interstate Commerce Commission. This early agency was charged with regulating the transportation industry ratemaking process. Since that time, federal and state administrative agencies have flourished, usually in response to a new societal problem (e.g., discrimination in the workplace, which was the reason why the Equal Employment Opportunity Commission was created) or to a new technology (e.g., the Nuclear Regulatory Commission).

In creating administrative agencies at the federal level, Congress recognized that this novel form of government must be able to focus on its area of expertise. While deep concerns associated with concentrations of government power necessitated the separation of powers we see in the structure of the government under the Constitution, Congress further understood that the ability for an agency to adequate perform its assigned tasks would be severely stymied if the separation of powers doctrine was applied to administrative agencies. Therefore, administrative agencies are given considerable power to achieve their regulatory objectives.

Agency Creation: The Enabling Statute The enactment by Congress of a statute creating a federal administrative agency is called *enabling legislation.* This statute will determine the purpose and scope of activity within which the agency will function. Enabling legislation not only establishes the agency, but also delegates to the agency the power to regulate in a specific area. Some enabling legislation is quite general, leaving tremendous discretion to the agency the extent of its power. In such circumstances, litigation often results and the judicial system is called upon to establish the reach of an administrative agency. Enabling legislation usually provides that the president or another member of the executive branch appoint the leadership of the agency.

Administrative Procedures Act Recognizing the potentially unwieldy nature of administrative agencies within the federal government, Congress passed the *Administrative Procedures Act* (APA) in 1946 for the purpose of guaranteeing uniformity and fairness to all who are called to deal with federal administrative agencies. The APA is a very comprehensive and very complicated statute that controls all aspects of agency activity. For example, the APA provides the mechanisms by which agencies can create rules, and it establishes the processes under which courts can review administrative agency actions. Congress mandates, through the APA, that federal agencies must comply with provisions of the APA, unless a particular agency's enabling legislation or other statute specifically exempts the agency from following APA edicts. All states have adopted the APA, or large portions thereof, for the regulation a particular state's own administrative agency.

4. Agency Types and Functions

Types While administrative agencies are created by the legislative branch, they are deemed to be a part of the executive branch because their primary purpose is to *implement* the will of Congress or a state legislature. At the federal level, two types of administrative agencies are recognized. An *executive agency* functions within an established cabinet department. For example, the Food and Drug Administration is positioned within the Department of Health and Human Services, the U.S. Patent and Trademark Office is within the Department of Commerce, and the Internal Revenue Service is within the Department of the Treasury. An entity deemed to be an *independent agency* functions within the executive branch of the federal government, but it is not directly connected to an executive department. A number of well-known agencies are of this type, including the Federal Trade Commission, the Environmental Protection Agency, the Securities and Exchange Commission, and the National Labor Relations Board.

Theoretically, the president has greater power over an executive agency than an independent agency. Practically, however, there is little difference between the two types of federal agencies. The president has considerable power over those who possess leadership positions in both types, and the agenda for each type of agency is generally shaped, in large part, by the president.

Functions Administrative agencies carry out their purpose of regulating a particular area of society through the exercise of power in three functional areas. These three are a mirror of the three branches of government. First, administrative agencies are engaged in *rulemaking.* This is a quasi-legislative function. Next, agencies are involved in *enforce-*

Administrative agencies implement the will of Congress or state legislature.

ment—a quasi-executive function. Finally, agencies are charged with *adjudicatory* responsibilities. This is a quasi-judicial function. The exact nature of the function dictates the rights a business or industry possess to influence the administrative process as it is occurring or challenge the process in court at a later time.

The following diagram presents the three functions of administrative agencies.

FIGURE 40-1 ■ Functions of Administrative Agencies

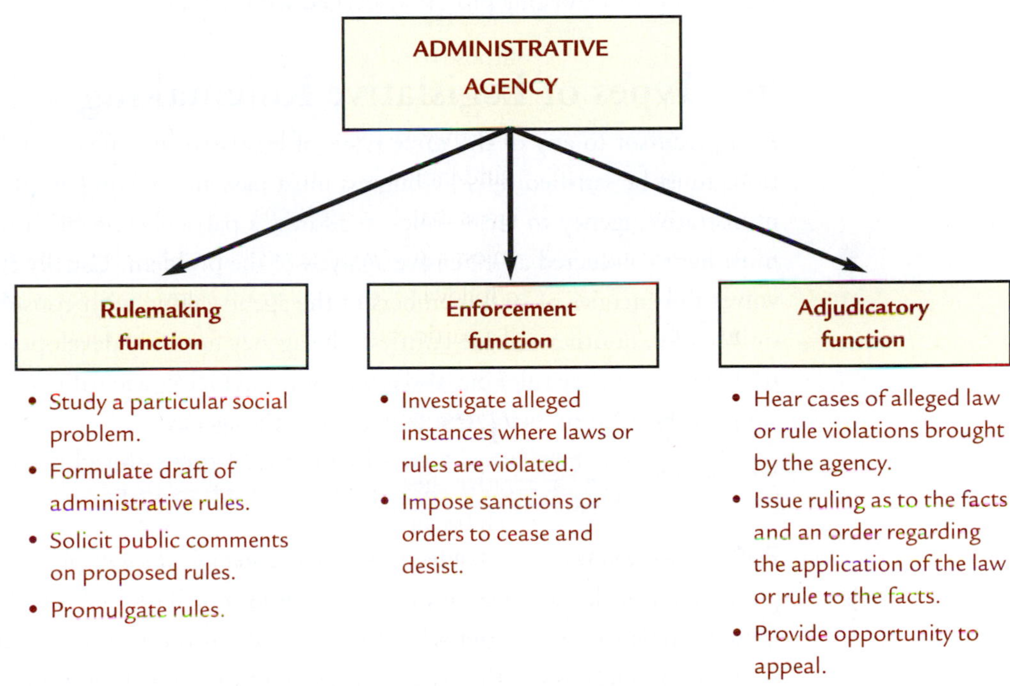

RULEMAKING

5. Types of Rules

Enabling legislation dictates the types of rules an administrative agency may create. Typically, administrative rules are characterized as internal, procedural, interpretative, or legislative. *Internal rules* are those policies and procedures an administrative agency adopts for its in-house operation. Knowing how an administrative agency operates is extremely important to the business community that must deal with a particular agency. For example, internal rules of the Environmental Protection Agency (EPA) provide a listing of the locations of the regional offices of the agency. The starting place for a business to formulate a relationship with members of the EPA staff is to contact a regional office. *Procedural rules* provide the public with the processes associated with various agency functions and, most critically, those opportunities for interchange with individuals and commercial enterprises. Under the rules of the EPA, for instance, there is a set procedure for reporting pollution emission inventory requirements. *Interpretive rules* are guidelines—informed suggestions—from an administrative agency to those members of society regulated by the agency. For example, the EPA has issued guidelines directed at communities to assist them in managing urban storm water. This type of rule does not possess the force of law; the administrative agency is not legally held to its statements in such guidelines. Administrative law judges and the judicial system, however, will provide considerable weight to interpretive rules. Interpretive rules issued by an agency are strong evidence as to how the agency views a particular issue, so members of the business community pay considerable attention to these edicts. *Legislative rules,* if formed in the proper manner, are a direct extension of the legislative act an agency is created to administer and, therefore, have the force and effect of law. The nature of legislative rules, in contrast to the other three types of administrative agency rules, require that they be created with greater formality and with considerable participation from the sector of the public that will be regulated. The APA applies to the creation and operation of these types of rules, and the following section provides information regarding the rulemaking process associated with legislative rules.

6. Types of Legislative Rulemaking

As a precursor to any of the three types of legislative rulemaking examined below, two conditions must be satisfied. First, Congress must pass an enabling act that empowers a specific administrative agency to create rules to address a particular problem in society. Also, the agency must have conducted an extensive analysis of the problem. Usually the examination process involves the energies of staff members of the agency along with consultants hired from business, universities, or other outside entities. The agency not only develops a regulatory solution to the problem (an agency rule) but also assembles convincing scientific or other types of evidence that support the solution being contemplated by the agency.

The agency then moves forward with one of three procedures for making legislative rules: formal rulemaking, informal rulemaking, or hybrid rulemaking.

FORMAL RULEMAKING There are four basic steps in *formal rulemaking.* First, members of the public are provided are given *notice of the proposed rule.* The established manner for giving notice is quite narrow: the agency publishes the draft administrative rule in a daily edition of the *Federal Register,* a publication of the executive branch of the federal government. Most agencies also post the proposed rule on their agency's web site. The notice provides the complete text of the draft rule, a schedule of when and where hearings regarding the proposal will be held, and the manner that members of the public can contribute to the discussion as to whether the rule is necessary, whether as drafted it will accomplish its desired result, and whether more study is needed. The second step in the formal rulemaking process is a *mandatory hearing.* This type of hearing may span weeks or months. It requires the agency to make formal presentations and allow others to cross-examine those individuals testifying on behalf of the proposed rule. Industry members opposing the proffered rule are allowed the opportunity to make their own presentations at the hearing. Upon conclusion of the mandatory hearing, a detailed *report* is prepared by the agency, with extensive coverage of all findings developed as a result of the evidence presented. At this stage, the agency decides whether it wants to stop the process, conduct more studies, rewrite the language of the proposal, or proceed with the current draft. If the agency continues with the formal rulemaking process, the last stage is *publishing the final rule,* once again in the *Federal Register.* At this point, unless a court finds that the agency's action was unsupported by *substantial evidence,* the administrative rule is legal. Under the APA, the formal rulemaking process is required only in those instances where Congress expressly requires it in the relevant enabling act.

INFORMAL RULEMAKING While formal rulemaking provides a significant stage to debate the propriety of a suggested rule, it also is an expensive process for the government and for those entities opposing the draft. That process also allows opposing forces to delay the rulemaking function through unnecessary cross-examinations of agency witnesses and the presentation of evidence that is not germane to the language included in the proposed rule. As a result, *informal rulemaking* is increasingly popular. This rulemaking is also known as *notice and comment rulemaking*. The first step in this process is for the agency to provide *notice of the proposed rule*. This step is identical to that followed in formal rulemaking. The next step, however, is quite different. The agency invites interested parties to participate in a *comment period* during which written submissions may be presented to the agency. While a hearing may be a part of the comment period, it is not mandatory. All comments become part of the official record. The last step is the publication of the final rule in the *Federal Register*. As required under the APA, the rule cannot become effective until at least 30 days after the publication of the rule and the agency's statement of purpose and basis.

There are three significant advantages from the agency's standpoint to the informal rulemaking process. Informal rulemaking is usually swift, in contrast to the time generally devoted to formal rulemaking. The mandatory hearing requirement is eliminated, allowing a less adversarial and time-consuming period for soliciting comments. Also, this second type of rulemaking is efficient. Because the second stage is abbreviated, government and those factions opposing the proposed rule generally spend far less time and money on informal rulemaking than formal rulemaking. Finally, courts adopt the least rigorous test for determining whether an agency acted properly in promulgating a rule under the informal rulemaking process. The *arbitrary and capricious test* requires a court to overturn a newly crafted agency rule only where there is a showing of no factual basis for the rule. Thus courts give considerable deference to the agency's rule if it is a product of informal rulemaking.

The following case provides an illustration as to when the notice requirement under informal rulemaking is required.

CASE

National Tour Brokers Association v. United States of America and the Interstate Commerce Commission, Respondents

UNITED STATES COURT OF APPEALS, DISTRICT OF COLUMBIA CIRCUIT

591 F.2d 896 (1978)

OPINION BY JUDGE WILKEY

Petitioner seeks review of an order of the Interstate Commerce Commission (Commission or ICC) which prescribes new rules, and adopts new procedures, for the licensing of tour brokers. Since we find that the Commission failed to comply with the procedural requirements of the Administrative Procedure Act, we vacate the order and rules prescribed thereunder, and remand to the Commission.

On 22 September 1975 the Commission had published in the Federal Register a Notice and Order which provided, in pertinent part, as follows:

ENTRY CONTROL OF BROKERS

Notice of Proceeding

Purpose: The Interstate Commerce Commission has always endeavored to review the current extent of its jurisdiction over the surface transportation industry and to propose to the Congress appropriate legislation which would alter that jurisdiction, pursuant to the provisions of the Interstate Commerce Act. The purpose of this document is to institute a proceeding to investigate the need for continued regulation of brokers of property and passengers, operating in interstate or foreign commerce, and to consider what, if any, legislative amendments of Section 211 of the Act ought to be recommended to the Congress.

It is ordered, That based on the reasons set forth in the attached notice, a proceeding be, and it is hereby, instituted (1) for the purposes of investigating the present licensing requirements for brokers of property and passengers, operating in interstate or foreign commerce, And (2) for the possible formulation of legislation which would amend Section 211 of the Interstate Commerce Act for subsequent recommendation to the Congress.

On July 7, 1975, the Interstate Commerce Commission announced the results of an internal staff study of the Agency's

continued

> *operations. The unprecedented "Blue Ribbon Staff Study Panel" made four reports to the Commission, including over 60 recommendations for internal, procedural, and substantive reform. Among these was the recommendation that Section 211 of the Interstate Commerce Act be amended so as to eliminate entry control requirements for broker licenses.*
>
> *(In) light of the study panel's recommendation and our continuing interest in scrutinizing the scope of this Commission's regulatory jurisdiction, we deem it in the public interest to institute this proceeding to consider (1) the need for and effectiveness of Section 211 of the Interstate Commerce Act in its present form, And (2) any possible legislative amendments to that section which should be proposed to the Congress.*
>
> *This Commission, however, would appreciate the views, comments, and suggestions of any interested parties relating to the above inquiries and to any possible, pertinent, and constructive legislation we may propose to the Congress in this area.*

A period of comment followed, during which written statements were received. The Commission then closed the record but, upon request from National Tour Brokers Association (NTBA), reopened the proceeding to hear oral argument on 9 August 1976.

In April of the following year, rather than proposing legislative changes to Congress, the Commission issued final rules involving both substantive and procedural changes with regard to the licensing of tour brokers.

On 8 July 1977 NTBA filed a "Petition to Reconsider and Vacate Report and Order and for Further Relief" (Petition for Reconsideration). This petition alleged six specifications of error, the first of which was:

> *(A) That the purported Notice initiating the proceeding, later characterized by the Commission as a notice of proposed rulemaking, failed to comply with the Administrative Procedure Act and the requirements of constitutional due process; ...*

By order served 26 August 1977, the Commission denied the Petition for Reconsideration, disagreeing with each specification of error. NTBA is now before this court seeking review of the Commission's action.

We hold that in this case the ICC failed to comply with the notice requirements of the Administrative Procedure Act. Section 4(a) of the Act (5 U.S.C. § 553(b)) provides:

> General notice of proposed rule making shall be published in the Federal Register, unless persons subject thereto are named and either personally served or otherwise have actual notice thereof in accordance with law. The notice shall include
>
> (1) a statement of the time, place, and nature of public rule making proceedings;
>
> (2) reference to the legal authority under which the rule is proposed; and
>
> (3) either the terms or substance of the proposed rule or a description of the subjects and issues involved.

The first clause of § 553(b) provides for constructive notice: "General notice of proposed rule making shall be published in the *Federal Register*." We are unable to find that the Commission satisfied this requirement. It is true that the Commission published a general notice in the *Federal Register*, but it was not a notice of proposed rulemaking. A fair reading of that item clearly indicates that it was one looking toward the formulation of possible legislative amendments which might be proposed to Congress, not administrative rulemaking. It seems that the Commission changed its mind halfway through this proceeding and is now attempting to correct its procedural deficiencies by characterizing the proceeding ex post facto as informal rulemaking. If this court were to countenance such procedure in this case, it is difficult to see where the line would ultimately be drawn. The constructive notice requirement of § 553(b) would be gutted of virtually all its meaning. Agencies could in the future publish vague, ambiguous notices in the *Federal Register*, adverting obliquely to certain issues or proceedings, and then, months or years later, promulgate final rules and claim that constructive notice had been given. This cannot be the objective of the APA notice requirement.

The purpose of this requirement is clear—to put interested parties on notice that Administrative rulemaking in certain areas is about to take place. We hold that the Commission failed to meet this requirement in this case.

In conclusion, since we find that the Commission failed to comply with the relevant requirements of the APA, the order and rules at issue in this case are vacated and this case is remanded to the Commission for further proceedings not inconsistent with this opinion.

■ *So ordered.*

CASE CONCEPT REVIEW

1. A notice was published in the *Federal Register*. Why did the court find that the initial notice failed to meet the requirements of the APA?
2. Is the remedy for the Commission's failure to follow the notice requirement (vacating the rules) too severe? Might other remedies be less burdensome on the administrative agency? What are the advantages of the remedy invoked in the case?

HYBRID RULEMAKING Formal rulemaking provides considerable opportunity for public comment regarding a proposed administrative agency rule, but it also allows those opposing the rule to stop or slow considerably the rulemaking process. Informal rulemaking allows the agency to generate rules quickly, but limits access for those wishing to comment. As a compromise, administrative agencies will occasionally blend the two processes, called *hybrid rulemaking.* The typical format requires notice and a hearing, but the hearing is not as extensive as that provided under formal rulemaking. Cross-examination of witnesses is eliminated. The Courts reviewing agency rules generated through this process apply the *substantial evidence test.* With growing concerns associated with both formal and informal rulemaking, the hybrid rulemaking process may become more popular.

ENFORCEMENT FUNCTION

7. Investigative Power

Administrative agencies perform powers associated with the executive branch of government to enforce administrative rules. Contrary to investigations conducted by police into possible criminal behavior, administrative agencies do not need to have probable cause before commencing enforcement procedures. While agencies may begin an enforcement action based on a tip provided by a whistleblower (perhaps a current employee reporting an alleged violation of an administrative rule), agencies also are free to investigate simply to ascertain the extent to which the rules are being followed. The information gathering process occurs primarily through two mechanisms: inspections and subpoenas.

INSPECTIONS Agencies employ inspections of businesses for two purposes. First, to determine if statutes or administrative rules have been violated, agencies are given the power to inspect business premises. Also, valuable information can be obtained through inspections that will cause the agency to propose new rules, alter existing rules, or make other adjustments to the regulatory environment. As explained in the next section, the Fourth Amendment may provide an individual or business with protection from unreasonable searches and seizures.

SUBPOENAS Agencies can obtain valuable information through the use of subpoenas. A personal subpoena, known as a *subpoena ad testificandum,* is an order from the agency to compel an unwilling witness to testify under oath at an administrative agency hearing. The other popular type of subpoena, a *subpoena duces tecum,* is used to force an individual or entity to produce documents or other physical evidence that might be germane to an investigation.

With the power to subpoena people and physical evidence as part of an investigation comes the risk that an agency will trample privacy and other rights of those individuals and entities that are the focus of an investigation. Therefore, the courts require an administrative agency to show a number of factors before a subpoena will be deemed a legal exercise of administrative agency power. Included are the requirements that the agency:

- Establish that the purpose of the investigation in legitimate.
- Possesses the power to conduct an investigation of the type specified.
- Describe the information being sought.
- Explain the relationship between the purpose of the investigation and the information being sought.
- Show that the information being demanded does not create an unreasonable burden on the individual or entity possessing such information.

8. Constitutional Protections

With administrative agencies being an arm of the government, perhaps the full force of constitutional protections afforded citizens (including corporations) should be in effect. Or, because violating an administrative agency rule is not a true crime, perhaps those constitutional protections limiting the investigatory processes conducted by an agency or constitutional rights associated with the adjudicatory process are not applicable. As a general rule, individuals and members of the business community are afforded little constitutional protections today where an administrative agency conducts an investigation.

RIGHT TO A JURY The United States Supreme Court has interpreted the Seventh Amendment right to a jury trial applies only to governmental actions existing in the common law at the time the Constitution came into existence. What this means is that only adjudications involving an individual or business being accused of a crime may be entitled to a trial by jury. Because administrative agency adjudications arose well after the Constitution came into being, there is no right to a jury trial even if the penalty for violating an administrative rule includes prison time.

SEARCH WARRANTS Under the Fourth Amendment to the Constitution, the government is prohibited from conducting unreasonable searches and seizures that could produce evidence relating to a violation of a criminal law. The prime component of the Fourth Amendment is the requirement that the government secure a search warrant from a judge that instructs law enforcement personnel to search a particular area for specific items. Technically, though, an administrative rule is not a criminal provision and administrative enforcement personnel are not law enforcement officers.

While administrative agencies may well desire to be free of the warrant requirement because of the unique nature of administrative agency functions, the courts have generally held that because there government action can be taken if there is a violation (although not as potentially onerous as a violation of a criminal statute) and those executing the search are not police officers, a *modified warrant* is required. The following case created the basic parameters of this position still in effect today.

CASE

Marshall, Secretary of Labor, et al. v. Barlow's, Inc.

SUPREME COURT OF THE UNITED STATES

436 U.S. 307 (1978)

MR. JUSTICE WHITE DELIVERED THE OPINION OF THE COURT

Section 8 (a) of the Occupational Safety and Health Act of 1970 (OSHA or Act) empowers agents of the Secretary of Labor (Secretary) to search the work area of any employment facility within the Act's jurisdiction. The purpose of the search is to inspect for safety hazards and violations of OSHA regulations. No search warrant or other process is expressly required under the Act.

On the morning of September 11, 1975, an OSHA inspector entered the customer service area of Barlow's, Inc., an electrical and plumbing installation business located in Pocatello, Idaho. The president and general manager, Ferrol G. "Bill" Barlow, was on hand; and the OSHA inspector, after showing his credentials, informed Mr. Barlow that he wished to conduct a search of the working areas of the business. Mr. Barlow inquired whether any complaint had been received about his company. The inspector answered no, but that Barlow's, Inc., had simply turned up in the agency's selection process. The inspector again asked to enter the nonpublic area of the business; Mr. Barlow's response was to inquire whether the inspector had a search warrant. The inspector had none. Thereupon, Mr. Barlow refused the inspector admission to the employee area of his business. He said he was relying on his rights as guaranteed by the Fourth Amendment of the United States Constitution.

The Secretary urges that warrantless inspections to enforce OSHA are reasonable within the meaning of the Fourth Amendment. Among other things, he relies on § 8 (a) of the Act, 29 U. S. C. § 657 (a), which authorizes inspection of business premises without a warrant and which the Secretary urges represents a congressional construction of the Fourth Amendment that the courts should not reject. Regrettably, we are unable to agree.

The Warrant Clause of the Fourth Amendment protects commercial buildings as well as private homes. To hold otherwise would belie the origin of that Amendment, and the American colonial experience. An important forerunner of the first ten Amendments to the United States Constitution, the Virginia Bill of Rights, specifically opposed "general warrants, whereby an officer or messenger may be commanded to search suspected places without evidence of a fact committed." The general warrant was a recurring point of contention in the Colonies immediately preceding the Revolution. The particular offensiveness it engendered was acutely felt by the merchants and businessmen whose premises and products were inspected for compliance with the several parliamentary revenue measures that most irritated the colonists. "[The] Fourth Amendment's commands grew in large measure out of the colonists' experience with the writs of assistance ... [that] granted sweeping power to customs officials and other agents of the King to search at large for smuggled goods." Against this background, it is untenable that the ban on warrantless searches was not intended to shield places of business as well as of residence.

This Court has already held that warrantless searches are generally unreasonable, and that this rule applies to commercial premises as well as homes. In *Camara v. Municipal Court,* we held:

> "[Except] in certain carefully defined classes of cases, a search of private property without proper consent is 'unreasonable' unless it has been authorized by a valid search warrant."

On the same day, we also ruled:

> "As we explained in *Camara,* a search of private houses is presumptively unreasonable if conducted without a warrant. The businessman, like the occupant of a residence, has a constitutional right to go about his business free from unreasonable official entries upon his private commercial property. The businessman, too, has that right placed in jeopardy if the decision to enter and inspect for violation of regulatory laws can be made and enforced by the inspector in the field without official authority evidenced by a warrant." *See v. Seattle.*

These same cases also held that the Fourth Amendment prohibition against unreasonable searches protects against warrantless intrusions during civil as well as criminal investigations. The reason is found in the "basic purpose of this Amendment ... [which] is to safeguard the privacy and security of individuals against arbitrary invasions by governmental officials." If the government intrudes on a person's property, the privacy interest suffers whether the government's motivation is to investigate violations of criminal laws or breaches of other statutory or regulatory standards. It therefore appears that unless some recognized exception to the warrant requirement applies, *See v. Seattle* would require a warrant to conduct the inspection sought in this case.

The Secretary urges that an exception from the search warrant requirement has been recognized for "pervasively regulated [businesses]," and for "closely regulated" industries "long subject to close supervision and inspection." These cases are indeed exceptions, but they represent responses to relatively unique circumstances. Certain industries have such a history of government oversight that no reasonable expectation of privacy could exist for a proprietor over the stock of such an enterprise. Liquor and firearms are industries of this type; when an entrepreneur embarks upon such a business, he has voluntarily chosen to subject himself to a full arsenal of governmental regulation.

The clear import of our cases is that the closely regulated industry of the type involved is the exception. The Secretary would make it the rule. The Secretary attempts to support a conclusion that all businesses involved in interstate commerce have long been subjected to close supervision of employee safety and health conditions. The degree of federal involvement in employee working circumstances, however, has never been of the order of specificity and pervasiveness that OSHA mandates. It is quite unconvincing to argue that the imposition of minimum wages and maximum hours on employers who contracted with the Government under the *Walsh-Healey Act* prepared the entirety of American interstate commerce for regulation of working conditions to the minutest detail. Nor can any but the most fictional sense of voluntary consent to later searches be found in the single fact that one conducts a business affecting interstate commerce; under current practice and law, few businesses can be conducted without having some effect on interstate commerce.

Whether the Secretary proceeds to secure a warrant or other process, with or without prior notice, his entitlement to inspect will not depend on his demonstrating probable cause to believe that conditions in violation of OSHA exist on the premises. Probable cause in the criminal law sense is not required. For purposes of an administrative search such as this, probable cause justifying the issuance of a warrant may be based not only on specific evidence of an existing violation but also on a showing that "reasonable legislative or administrative standards for conducting an ... inspection are satisfied with respect to a particular [establishment]." A warrant showing that a specific business has been chosen for an OSHA search on the basis of a general administrative plan for the enforcement of the Act derived from neutral sources such as, for example, dispersion of employees in various types of industries across a given area, and the desired frequency of searches in any of the lesser divisions of the area, would protect an employer's Fourth Amendment rights. We doubt that the consumption of enforcement energies in the obtaining of such warrants will exceed manageable proportions.

We hold that Barlow's was entitled to a declaratory judgment that the Act is unconstitutional insofar as it purports to authorize inspections without warrant or its equivalent and to an injunction enjoining the Act's enforcement to that extent. The judgment of the District Court is therefore affirmed.

■ *Affirmed.*

CASE CONCEPT REVIEW

1. Why should businesses be afforded Fourth Amendment protection? Is there historical evidence that supports your view?
2. What are the requirements of the modified warrant requirement articulated in the case?
3. Why should administrative agencies be able to conduct warrantless searches of certain types of businesses?

As a result of a line of cases, including *Marshall v. Barlow's Inc.,* administrative agencies may conduct *warrantless* searches only if a business is a member of a highly regulated industry or in an emergency. Otherwise, the *modified warrant* requirement applies.

SELF-INCRIMINATION The Fifth Amendment protects against self-incrimination. This may be oral, or it may result from records kept in writing or in digital form. However, in regard to administrative agency functions, this right is severely curtailed. First, the right against self-incrimination does not extend to corporations. Further, as to businesses created in a non-corporate form, the Fifth Amendment protections are inapplicable to records kept for a purely regulatory or customary reason. Therefore, the Fifth Amendment provides modest protection during an administrative agency investigation.

ADJUDICATORY FUNCTION

9. Elementary Aspects of Adjudication

Administrative agency adjudication is the principal mechanism agencies employ to enforce their actions. The process is a trial-like proceeding. It is also adversarial in nature. Yet the nature of administrative agency adjudication necessarily lends itself to varying levels of formality, depending on the process (e.g. granting of a permit) and the nature of the area regulated (e.g., nuclear product manufacturing). The United States Constitutional provisions, particularly the due process clause, apply in a flexible fashion commensurate with the nature of the agency adjudication. It is common for adjudication to be quite informal. Where informal adjudication occurs (e.g., termination of welfare benefits), agencies tend to include only selected aspects of trial proceedings. These agencies wish to incorporate elements that will assist with the decision-making process but avoid the time and expense associated with formal adjudication.

10. Formal Adjudication

In most respects, *formal adjudication* is like a trial. The administrative agency begins the process with the filing of a complaint. The party against whom the complaint is filed is called the *respondent,* who is afforded the right to respond to the complaint in writing. At this point, both parties usually conduct extensive discovery. Depositions and other methods, including subpoena power, are at the disposal of the agency and the respondent for the purpose of ascertaining the facts. The discovery process has the potential for being expensive and taking a great amount of time to complete. A hearing occurs next. While no jury exists for agency adjudicatory hearings, the respondent is entitled to an attorney. An individual called an *administrative law judge* (ALJ) presides over the hearing. The usual burden of proof when an ALS hears cases is the civil preponderance of the evidence standard. Various aspects of formal adjudication are controlled by the *Administrative Procedures Act,* which lends integrity to a process where the accusing body and the adjudicatory body are both aspects of a single administrative agency.

The hearing concludes with the ALJ preparing findings of facts and conclusions of law. This written report also includes the ALJ's determination as to what penalty is appropriate. If neither party challenges the ALJ's decision, it becomes final. Often, however, one party will seek to pursue the matter further. The appeal is usually to the administrative agency's governing body. They may then either accept the ALJ's factual record or conduct a hearing *de novo* (from the beginning).

JUDICIAL REVIEW OF AGENCY ACTIONS

11. Basic Requirements

The APA provides for judicial review of almost all administrative agency decisions. The notion of abandoning the separation of powers idea and concentrating governmental authority in one type of entity allows the agency to function well in its area of expertise. However, evaluation by the judicial system of administrative actions provides the principal mechanism by which the powers of an agency can be held in check. Before an individual or entity can use the court system to review administrative actions, two requirements must be satisfied: administrative remedies must be exhausted and a party challenging the action must have standing.

EXHAUSTION OF ADMINISTRATIVE REMEDIES As explored in the previous section, administrative agencies provide a method of adjudicating disputes within an agency. The requirement that a party challenging an administrative action *exhaust administrative remedies* provides a degree of respect to the administrative adjudicatory processes, particularly regarding the appeal from an initial determination. A major advantage to this process is that a paper trail is created within the adjudicatory process that can be used by the agency, the party objecting, and the court once a dispute moves from the administrative agency to the judicial system.

STANDING Judicial review of administrative agency actions will be afforded only to individuals or entities that have a personal stake in the outcome of the controversy. *Standing* generally requires that the individual wishing to employ the powers of the judiciary must show an injury. The real or potential injury does not have to be to them personally; but it must be occur to those who are to be the beneficiaries of agency action. This allows environmentalists to show an injury under the standing doctrine when they claim that an agency has improperly reallocated wilderness land for commercial development.

12. Legal Foundations for Judicial Review

Courts honor the place administrative agencies possess in modern law by giving agencies significant discretion to regulate in their area of expertise. Through the years, courts have recognized only selected reasons for questioning the decision of an agency. Those include:

- *Authority exceeded.* A challenge to an agency action may be upheld by a court where the plaintiff is successful in showing that the agency's action exceeded the authority granted to in the enabling statute.
- *Incorrect statutory interpretation.* A challenge may succeed where an agency did not properly interpret statutory law.
- *Procedural errors.* The agency failed to follow the procedural requirements, usually found in the APA.
- *Constitutional impediments.* Agency action will be struck if constitutional rights were infringed upon or other aspects of the Constitution were not followed.
- Arbitrary and capricious decision. While discretion will be granted to the agency, the agency's decision will be invalid if the factual or legal determinations appear to be groundless.

The following case illustrates a situation where the agency exceeded its statutory authority.

13. Scope of Review

Courts generally allow administrative agencies significant discretion to make decisions, whether the decision pertains to rulemaking, enforcement, or adjudication. Several reasons exist for this extension

CASE

Food and Drug Administration, et al. v. Brown & Williamson Tobacco Corp., et. al.

SUPREME COURT OF THE UNITED STATES

529 U.S. 120 (2000)

JUSTICE O'CONNOR DELIVERED THE OPINION OF THE COURT

This case involves one of the most troubling public health problems facing our Nation today: the thousands of premature deaths that occur each year because of tobacco use. In 1996, the Food and Drug Administration (FDA), after having expressly disavowed any such authority since its inception, asserted jurisdiction to regulate tobacco products. The FDA concluded that nicotine is a "drug" within the meaning of the Food, Drug, and Cosmetic Act (FDCA or Act), 52 Stat. 1040, as amended, 21 U.S.C. § 301 et seq., and that cigarettes and smokeless tobacco are "combination products" that deliver nicotine to the body. Pursuant to this authority, it promulgated regulations intended to reduce tobacco consumption among children and adolescents. The agency believed that, because most tobacco consumers begin their use before reaching the age of 18, curbing tobacco use by minors could substantially reduce the prevalence of addiction in future generations and thus the incidence of tobacco-related death and disease.

On August 11, 1995, the FDA published a proposed rule concerning the sale of cigarettes and smokeless tobacco to children and adolescents. The rule, which included several restrictions on the sale, distribution, and advertisement of tobacco products, was designed to reduce the availability and attractiveness of tobacco products to young people. A public comment period followed, during which the FDA received over 700,000 submissions, more than "at any other time in its history on any other subject."

On August 28, 1996, the FDA issued a final rule entitled "Regulations Restricting the Sale and Distribution of Cigarettes and Smokeless Tobacco to Protect Children and Adolescents." The FDA determined that nicotine is a "drug" and that cigarettes and smokeless tobacco are "drug delivery devices"; and, therefore, it had jurisdiction under the FDCA to regulate tobacco products as customarily marketed—that is, without manufacturer claims of therapeutic benefit. First, the FDA found that tobacco products "'affect the structure or any function of the body'" because nicotine "has significant pharmacological effects." Specifically, nicotine "exerts psychoactive, or mood-altering, effects on the brain" that cause and sustain addiction, have both tranquilizing and stimulating effects, and control weight. Second, the FDA determined that these effects were "intended" under the FDCA because they "are so widely known and foreseeable that [they] may be deemed to have been intended by the manufacturers, "consumers use tobacco products "predominantly or nearly exclusively" to obtain these effects; and the statements, research, and actions of manufacturers revealed that they "have 'designed' cigarettes to provide pharmacologically active doses of nicotine to consumers." Finally, the agency concluded that cigarettes and smokeless tobacco are "combination products" because, in addition to containing nicotine, they include device components that deliver a controlled amount of nicotine to the body.

Respondents, a group of tobacco manufacturers, retailers, and advertisers, filed suit in United States District Court for the Middle District of North Carolina challenging the regulations.

A threshold issue is the appropriate framework for analyzing the FDA's assertion of authority to regulate tobacco products. Because this case involves an administrative agency's construction of a statute that it administers, a reviewing court must first ask, "whether Congress has directly spoken to the precise question at issue." If Congress has done so, the inquiry is at an end; the court "must give effect to the unambiguously expressed intent of Congress." However, if Congress has not specifically addressed the question, a reviewing court must respect the agency's construction of the statute so long as it is permissible. Such deference is justified because "the responsibilities for assessing the wisdom of such policy choices and resolving the struggle between competing views of the public interest are not judicial ones," and because of the agency's greater familiarity with the ever-changing facts and circumstances surrounding the subjects regulated.

In determining whether Congress has specifically addressed the question at issue, a reviewing court should not confine itself to examining a particular statutory provision in isolation. The meaning—or ambiguity—of certain words or phrases may only become evident when placed in context.

With these principles in mind, we find that Congress has directly spoken to the issue here and precluded the FDA's jurisdiction to regulate tobacco product.

Considering the FDCA as a whole, it is clear that Congress intended to exclude tobacco products from the FDA's jurisdiction. A fundamental precept of the FDCA is that any product regulated by the FDA—but not banned—must be safe for its intended use. Various provisions of the Act make clear that this refers to the safety of using the product to obtain its intended effects, not the public health ramifications of alternative administrative actions by the FDA. That is, the FDA must determine that there is a reasonable assurance that the product's therapeutic benefits outweigh the risk of harm to the consumer. According to this standard, the FDA has concluded that, although tobacco products might be effective in delivering certain pharmacological effects, they are "unsafe" and "dangerous" when used for these purposes. Consequently, if tobacco products were within the FDA's jurisdiction, the Act would require the FDA to remove them from the market entirely; but a ban would contradict Congress' clear intent as expressed in its more recent, tobacco-specific legislation. The inescapable conclusion is that there is no room for tobacco products within the FDCA's regulatory scheme. If they cannot be used safely for any therapeutic purpose, and yet they cannot be banned, they simply do not fit.

In determining whether Congress has spoken directly to the FDA's authority to regulate tobacco, we must also consider in greater detail the tobacco-specific legislation that Congress has enacted over the past 35 years. At the time a statute is enacted, it may have a range of plausible meanings. Over time, however, subsequent acts can shape or focus those meanings. The "classic judicial task of reconciling many laws enacted over time, and getting them to 'make sense' in combination, necessarily assumes that the implications of a statute may be altered by the implications of a later statute." This is particularly so where the scope of the earlier statute is broad but the subsequent statutes more specifically address the topic at hand. As we recognized recently in *United States v. Estate of Romani,* "a specific policy embodied in a later federal statute should control our construction of the [earlier] statute, even though it has not been expressly amended."

Congress has enacted six separate pieces of legislation since 1965 addressing the problem of tobacco use and human health. Those statutes, among other things, require that health warnings appear on all packaging and in all print and outdoor advertisements; prohibit the advertisement of tobacco products through "any medium of electronic communication" subject to regulation by the Federal Communications Commission (FCC); require the Secretary of Health and Human Services (HHS) to report every three years to Congress on research findings concerning "the addictive property of tobacco"; and make States' receipt of certain federal block grants contingent on their making it unlawful "for any manufacturer, retailer, or distributor of tobacco products to sell or distribute any such product to any individual under the age of 18."

In adopting each statute, Congress has acted against the backdrop of the FDA's consistent and repeated statements that it lacked authority under the FDCA to regulate tobacco absent claims of therapeutic benefit by the manufacturer. In fact, on several occasions over this period, and after the health consequences of tobacco use and nicotine's pharmacological effects had become well known, Congress considered and rejected bills that would have granted the FDA such jurisdiction. Under these circumstances, it is evident that Congress' tobacco-specific statutes have effectively ratified the FDA's long-held position that it lacks jurisdiction under the FDCA to regulate tobacco products. Congress has created a distinct regulatory scheme to address the problem of tobacco and health, and that scheme, as presently constructed, precludes any role for the FDA.

Under these circumstances, it is clear that Congress' tobacco-specific legislation has effectively ratified the FDA's previous position that it lacks jurisdiction to regulate tobacco.

By no means do we question the seriousness of the problem that the FDA has sought to address. The agency has amply demonstrated that tobacco use, particularly among children and adolescents, poses perhaps the single most significant threat to public health in the United States. Nonetheless, no matter how "important, conspicuous, and controversial" the issue, and regardless of how likely the public is to hold the Executive Branch politically accountable, an administrative agency's power to regulate in the public interest must always be grounded in a valid grant of authority from Congress. And "'in our anxiety to effectuate the congressional purpose of protecting the public, we must take care not to extend the scope of the statute beyond the point where Congress indicated it would stop. Reading the FDCA as a whole, as well as in conjunction with Congress' subsequent tobacco-specific legislation, it is plain that Congress has not given the FDA the authority that it seeks to exercise here.

■ *Affirmed.*

CASE CONCEPT REVIEW

1. Did Congress expressly limit the authority of the FDA to regulate tobacco?
2. Why did the FDA believe it had the authority to regulate tobacco?

of discretion. First, courts recognize that administrative agencies are designed to be the experts in their field, so the court system should respect the expertise agencies possess. Also, if courts could examine closely each decision of an agency, affected businesses, individuals, and others would be provided a tool by which they could slow or even stop agencies from functioning.

Today, the courts recognize three types of tests that set the scope of review: de novo, substantial evidence, and arbitrary and capricious. The enabling legislation establishes which test applies; and if the legislature is silent, the APA provides the type of review. The *de novo test* is employed sparingly. Under this test, the courts give no deference to the administrative agency decision and make an independent determination of the facts after performing a new hearing. The *de novo test* is used only when an administrative agency makes a decision without providing a sufficient factual record. The courts use the *substantial evidence test* in two settings: to review formal rulemaking and to review a formal adjudication. This test gives considerable deference to the agency because it has provided a well-developed record of facts. An agency decision is overturned under this test only if the court finds that the decision is unsupported by substantial evidence. For informal rulemaking and informal adjudications, the *arbitrary and capricious test* is employed. This test gives the greatest deference to the administrative agency. Under this standard of review, an administrative agency decision is upheld as long as it is not irrational—arbitrary and capricious. Practically, there is not a great amount of difference between the substantial evidence test and the arbitrary and capricious test.

PUBLIC ACCESS TO AGENCY INFORMATION

14. Improving Public Accountability

The nature of administrative agencies—with their expertise, resources, and concentrated government power—cause many to believe that they operate without sufficient accountability or transparency. As federal administrative agencies have proliferated, Congress has responded on numerous occasions to concerns regarding the lack of openness exhibited by agencies. Most states have similar provisions to those adopted by Congress. The principal federal legislative responses are examined below.

FREEDOM OF INFORMATION ACT In 1966 Congress passed the *Freedom of Information Act* (FIOA), which empowers private citizens with the tools to request information from the federal government. The process is quite simple. A person or business sends a letter to the director or management of an agency and requests information regarding a particular topic. The agency then has 10 days to respond. It may state its intention to release the information and then do so. If the agency fails to respond or denies the request, the person or business making the request may either appeal the decision within the agency or sue in federal court for the information.

Not all information is subject to disclosure. FOIA exemptions include (1) national security and foreign policy, (2) trade secrets and financial information, (3) inter-agency documents detailing internal deliberations or agency personnel practices, (4) unwarranted invasions of personal privacy, and (5) law enforcement information. Beyond the FOIA exemptions, agencies are compelled to disclose. It is important that managers understand the potential impact of releasing information to an agency. Many members of the business community assume that in responding to an administrative rule or other type of agency request for information, the disclosed information will be kept confidential by the agency. Unless an exemption applies, however, the agency must disclose if a FIOA request is filed. Often the media or trade groups will request information under the FOIA, and that information will be made public. Also, competitors can request information from administrative agencies regarding a business and use that information to their advantage.

PRIVACY ACT OF 1974 The *Privacy Act of 1974* protects the confidentiality of private information collected by federal government agencies and provides a mechanism for citizens to correct information that was submitted to an agency. The Privacy Act also limits the information that can be gathered about individuals. Generally, records and other information of an individual may be disclosed only upon the written permission of that person. A host of exceptions exist, including for law enforcement.

SUNSHINE ACT The *Government in the Sunshine Act of 1976* recognizes the appearance of impropriety that may accompany the decision of government to act in secrecy. This act requires, with exemptions, that meetings of administrative agencies must be open to the public. Note, however, that this legislation does not require that the public have a right to speak at the meetings or otherwise participate, only that it may attend.

CHAPTER SUMMARY

THE NATURE OF ADMINISTRATIVE AGENCIES

Role of Administrative Agencies	1. Administrative agencies exist at the local, state, and federal levels. 2. Administrative agencies have a significant impact on the regulatory environment within which business functions.

Purposes of Administrative Agencies

1. Administrative agencies exist to guard against overzealous members of the business community, offer proficiency in needed areas of government regulation, provide certainty to the public and to those regulated, and supply information.

Conceptual Framework for Administrative Agencies

1. Administrative agencies became part of the government's structure as a result of the change from an agrarian to a manufacturing economy and the increasingly important role technology is playing in the economy.
2. Administrative agencies are not guided by the separation of powers doctrine, allowing them greater expertise in a specific field of regulation.
3. An enabling statute creates an administrative agency.
4. The Administrative Procedures Act attempts to guarantee uniformity and fairness.

Agency Types and Functions

1. Agencies at the federal level are either executive agencies or independent agencies.
2. Administrative agencies possess three functional powers: rulemaking, enforcement, and adjudication.

RULEMAKING FUNCTION

Types of Rules

1. Administrative rules are typically characterized as internal, procedural, interpretative, or legislative.
2. Legislative rules generally have the force of law.

Types of Legislative Rulemaking

1. Formal rulemaking requires—in addition to notice—a report, a hearing, and a publication of the final rule.
2. Informal rulemaking does not require a hearing.
3. Hybrid rulemaking requires a hearing, but it is a less prescribed than what is mandated under formal rulemaking.

ENFORCEMENT FUNCTION

Investigative Power

1. Inspections are a valuable enforcement tool since they provide evidence as to whether a person or entity has violated an administrative rule and evidence regarding whether changes in the relevant set of administrative rules are needed.
2. Administrative agencies generally have the power to subpoena individuals to testify and to supply information.

Constitutional Protections

1. Depending on the circumstances and the type of business being regulated, administrative agencies may have to obtain a modified warrant in order to conduct proper search under the Fourth Amendment.
2. The Fifth Amendment protection against self-incrimination provides modest protection during an administrative agency investigation.

ADJUDICATORY FUNCTION

Elementary Aspects of Adjudication

1. Administrative agencies performing the adjudicatory function tend to adopt a trial-like format for conducting a hearing.

Formal Adjudication

1. Formal adjudication normally includes extensive investigation of facts.
2. An administrative law judge presides over formal hearings.

JUDICIAL REVIEW OF AGENCY ACTIONS

Basic Requirements

1. Before a court can review a decision by an administrative agency, the complaining party must exhaust all administrative remedies and have standing to pursue the action.

Legal Foundations for Judicial Review

1. Because of the tremendous discretion given to administrative agencies so that they may perform functions necessary for regulation of complex entities and processes, courts will review agency decisions only for selected infirmities.

Scope of Review

1. A *de novo* review occurs when a court decides it will disregard the agency's determination and take a fresh look at the decision.
2. Under the *substantial evidence* scope of review, an agency decision will be overturned only if the court finds that the decision is unsupported by substantial evidence.
3. The greatest amount of deference to an administrative agency is granted under the *arbitrary and capricious* test where a court will overrule a judge only if the decision by the agency is irrational.

PUBLIC ACCESS TO AGENCY INFORMATION

Improving Public Accountability

1. Congress has attempted to improve public accountability of administrative agencies through the Freedom of Information Act, the Privacy Act of 1974, and the Government in the Sunshine Act of 1976.

REVIEW QUESTIONS AND PROBLEMS

1. Match each term in Column A with the appropriate statement in Column B.

A	B
(1) Subpoena	(a) Requirement that all administrative adjudicatory measures must be exercised before filing a lawsuit against an administrative agency
(2) Administrative Procedure Act	(b) Act by a legislative body that creates an administrative agency
(3) Informal rulemaking	(c) Federal law that allows a person or entity to request information from the federal government
(4) Government in the Sunshine Act	(d) Agency rulemaking process that requires a hearing
(5) Administrative agency	(e) Federal law that requires most meetings of federal agencies be held in public
(6) Standing	(f) Often referred to as the "fourth branch" of government
(7) Freedom of Information Act	(g) Order by a court for an individual or entity to testify or provide information
(8) Enabling statue	(h) Requirement that a person who wishes to sue must show injury

(9) Exhaustion of administrative remedies	(i) Act by Congress that controls major aspects of all federal administrative agencies
(10) Formal rulemaking	(j) Agency rulemaking process that does not require a hearing

2. What purposes do administrative agencies serve?
3. The Occupational Safety and Health Act provides that an employer "shall furnish to each of his employees employment and a place of employment which are free from recognized hazards." The Occupational Safety and Health Agency (OSHA) is studying the possibility of issuing a rule stating that all OSHA rules apply to areas of the home if an employee works at home. In reading the selected portion of the enabling statute, do you believe OSHA can regulate areas of the home? Why?
4. Describe the three functions of an administrative agency. How do these compare with the three branches of government?
5. The Securities and Exchange Commission (SEC) is contemplating issuing a set of rules dealing with the back dating of securities for sale. Would the SEC prefer to proceed through formal or informal rulemaking? Why?
6. The Consumer Product Safety Commission has received complaints that swimming pool slides cause death and serious injury. Many individuals have asked the Commission to establish rules regarding swimming pool slides in order to reduce the risks associated with the slides. If you were a member of the Commission, what information might you wish to have presented that would assist you in making a decision to regulate in this area? Why?
7. Describe the extent of constitutional protections a business is afforded when it is being investigated by an administrative agency of the federal government.
8. Prison inmates in four states were sentenced to death by legal injection. The inmates initially petitioned the Food and Drug Administration (FDA) claiming that the use of the drugs for the purpose of capital punishment violated federal law. The FDA failed to act. The inmates then sued the FDA and claimed judicial review of the agency action under the Administrative Procedure Act. Do the inmates have standing? Why?
9. The federal *Clean Water Act* charges the Environmental Protection Agency (EPA) with the power to create a permit system that will allow pollution to be discharged into a navigable body of water and to grant those permits. The EPA granted a discharge permit to ABC Concrete Company. The permit listed a set of conditions, all of which are the product of formal rulemaking by the EPA, that must be satisfied before ABC Concrete can discharge. ABC wishes to challenge the EPA's determination of conditions in federal court. What standard of review should the court follow?
10. The Federal Bureau of Investigation (FBI) is investigating Mary Magillicutty. The FBI has contacted Mary's bank, the First Bank of Desilu, requesting that the bank turn over Mary's bank records. The bank disclosed the information to the FBI. Mary sues the Bank, claiming that the *Privacy Act of 1974* applies. Does the *Privacy Act* apply to the bank?

Internet Resources

The text of the APA, along with related material, is available at: http://www.thecre.com/fedlaw/legal1/libapa.htm

For access to the Federal Register, see: http://www.gpoaccess.gov/fr/index.html

Antitrust Law | 41

CHAPTER OUTLINE

BACKGROUND
1. History
2. Schools of Thought
3. Basic Principles
4. Enforcement

MONOPOLIZATION
5. Nature of a Monopoly
6. Monopoly Power
7. Relevant Market
8. Intent
9. Attempting to Monopolize

RESTRAINTS OF TRADE—BASIC PROVISIONS
10. Concerted Action
11. Per Se and Rule of Reason Violations
12. Horizontal Restraints under the Sherman Act
13. Vertical Restraints under the Sherman Act

RESTRAINTS OF TRADE—ADVANCED PROVISIONS
14. Exclusionary Contracts under the Clayton Act
15. Mergers under the Clayton Act
16. Price Discrimination Fundamentals
17. Price Discrimination Defenses

INTERNATIONAL CONSIDERATIONS
18. Reach of United States Laws
19. Reach of Foreign Laws

CHAPTER PREVIEW

The owner of a business wishes to make a profit. How? At the risk of oversimplifying the task, the owner will want to consider the costs of doing business, the price charged, and the amount of sales made. If the costs of doing business among competitors are roughly equal, then the owner focuses on price and market. Under the free market system prevalent in the United States, if an owner reduces the price, consumers tend to purchase the product or service and the owner's market share increases. Of course, a lower price means less profit on each sale. In theory, competition unbridled by government regulation should result in the best product or service offered to the consuming public at the lowest price.

Should government regulate the competitive world of business? Unfortunately, the natural consequence of increasing market share within a free market economy may well freeze out competitors, stifle innovation, create unneeded barriers to entry into the marketplace, and, ultimately, create a monopoly. In a monopoly, the market is no longer setting the price or controlling other relevant aspects of the product or service; rather, it is the single business that has the power to mandate all factors. Anti-competitive forces can and do enter into the United States world of commerce, and they require a regulatory response. Therefore, for more than one hundred years, laws have existed in the United States aimed at controlling the "game" of business. These rules aimed at moderating the impact of competition are termed antitrust laws.

After introducing the topic of antitrust, this chapter examines the two principal thrusts of modern anti-trust law. First, the area of monopolization is discussed, emphasizing the elements of market share and intent. Then, the topic of restraints of trade, which generally require two or more businesses acting in concert to impact the free flow of goods or services, is presented. The final section surveys international aspects of antitrust law.

BUSINESS MANAGEMENT DECISION

Ashley began a business six years ago bottling and selling water under the name "Natural Hy." She believed strongly that individuals in society were not adequately hydrating their bodies and that providing bottled water to the largest number of people possible was one way that she could help folks stay healthy. The "Natural Hy" business was a terrific success, with marketing survey data indicating that Ashley's business had 95% of the bottled water business in her town, 85% of the business within a fifty-mile radius, and 75% within a one-hundred mile radius. She now finds her competitors are beginning to discuss litigation against her for violating anti-trust laws. Should Ashley be concerned? Why?

BACKGROUND

1. History

Free enterprise is the theory that frames the United States business model. It has provided the overall conceptual framework for our world of commerce for decades. This theory of conducting commerce provides the ultimate freedom for businesses to compete in the belief that free enterprise principles will generate operating efficiencies and favorable consumer responses. However, this model assumes no government regulation. Unfortunately, unethical behavior by individuals and firms can undermine the free market model, resulting in, for example, higher than needed prices and unnecessary barriers to entry. Therefore, it is necessary for the government to create a system of *antitrust laws* that provide the "rules" by which businesses may complete.

As the Industrial Revolution took hold in the United States after the Civil War, power became concentrated in the hands of a few extremely wealth individuals in selected industries with those business titans taking advantage of the free enterprise system. In order to further maximize the control they had over particular industries, certain industrialists would transfer their stock of competing corporations into a single *trust.* The trustees of a trust then set the price of products, mandated exclusive geographic regions in which individual corporations could conduct business, instigated outright industrial espionage, and directed a host of other less-than-savory business activities. As a result, smaller businesses that were not part of the trust were driven to bankruptcy, new competitors were prevented from entering the market, and prices for consumers rose.

Sherman Act
The first major federal antitrust law aimed at restraints of trade and monopolization

Clayton Act
An antitrust law focusing on exclusive dealing contracts and mergers

Federal Trade Commission Act
Established the Federal Trade Commission, the principal administrative agency charged with enforcing antitrust laws

Robinson-Patman Act
An antitrust law focusing on price discrimination

Traditional School
Believes the primary goal of antitrust laws should be to protect competitors

Chicago School
Believes the primary goal of antitrust laws should be to promote competition.

The abuses associated with these trusts generated a strong negative reaction from the consuming public and among many members of the business community. While states attempted to reign in powerful trust mechanisms, these efforts tended to fail because of the interstate nature of the problem. Therefore, Congress entered the fray in 1890 with the passage of the first of several anti-trust laws. This law, the **Sherman Act**, was structured to address collaborative activities (i.e., involving two or more parties) that were anticompetitive (under Section 1) and monopolization (usually requiring the action of only one entity under Section 2 of the Act).

While the Sherman Act was created to address the most egregious of anti-competitive behaviors, Congress passed the **Clayton Act**, in 1914 (with major amendments in 1936 and 1950) to supplement the Sherman Act. The Clayton Act was designed to curb a number of anti-competitive business practices, including exclusive dealing contracts and mergers. In the same year, the **Federal Trade Commission Act** was passed. This legislation created the Federal Trade Commission, a powerful administrative agency charged specifically with protecting consumers against deceptive practices (e.g., false advertising) and enforcing antitrust laws. The final major antitrust law, aimed primarily at price discrimination, was the **Robinson-Patman Act** passed by Congress in 1936.

2. Schools of Thought

In applying antitrust law, the courts today are influenced by two somewhat different schools of thought dealing with antitrust. The proponents of the **Traditional School** believe that while economic efficiency is an important goal of antitrust theory, other important social and political interests should also enter into the matrix. Followers of this school believe that concentrated economic power is almost always undesirable. Therefore, antitrust laws should exist to encourage the largest number of competitors in an industry, even if doing so results in certain losses in economic efficiency (e.g., higher prices for consumers). This theory is very supportive of small business, recognizing that an industry comprised of only a few large businesses is generally not in the best interests of society. In general, those that follow the Traditional School of antitrust theory believe the general public is best served where the overriding objective of antitrust law is to *protect competitors.*

Scholars from the University of Chicago first advanced, in a comprehensive manner, an alternative view of antitrust theory. Followers of the **Chicago School** tend to believe the crucial goal of antitrust law is to *promote competition.* Under this view, considerable attention is paid to the impact of any regulatory action on the consumer. Advocates of the Chicago School do not automatically pounce on instances where economic power is concentrated or a particular entity is large. In some instances, these conditions may actually benefit the consumer, as long as there is some competition and economic efficiencies are maximized. Political or other non-economic considerations matter far less to those who follow this approach. Therefore, proponents of the Chicago School tend to find fewer behaviors to be in violation of antitrust laws and favor more selected enforcement of antitrust laws.

Why are these two schools relevant to our study of antitrust laws? For one important reason: the justices on the United States Supreme Court tend to embrace either the Traditional School or the Chicago School as they set the course of antitrust law for the country. For a great number of decades, the Supreme Court followed theories associated with the Traditional School as they applied antitrust statutes. However, in the past twenty-five or so years, appointees to the Supreme Court often embrace in their opinions or doctrines associated with the Chicago School as they have interpreted antitrust laws. In fact, the Supreme Court recently has reversed antitrust cases decided decades ago that tended to disfavor large businesses. For example, for many years the Supreme Court found many types of vertical restraints (agreements down the chain of distribution) to be illegal, believing that they were patently anticompetitive. In a surprise to many, the Supreme Court has ruled that the previous decisions were in error. As a result, a number of instances of vertical agreements are no longer conclusively presumed to be illegal (e.g., price-fixing between a manufacturer and a wholesaler).

3. Basic Principles

JURISDICTION Congress has the power to create antitrust laws under Article I of the United States Constitution that allows Congress to regulate interstate commerce. As discussed in Chapter 5, this power extends to business activities conducted within a single state but have a significant impact on commerce among the states. Therefore, federal antitrust laws extend to a wide range of business activities. (Of course, even in those situations where the federal government does not have jurisdiction, state antitrust provisions likely would apply.) Also, as discussed in Sections 18 & 19, there is an international dimension to the topic.

EXEMPTIONS Congress or the courts, for assorted reasons, have granted certain activities and industries an exemption from federal antitrust laws. Some of the exemptions were created because of the nature of the supposedly anticompetitive activity, while others exist because a particular industry is subject to extensive regulation. The most prominent exemptions include:

- **Professional Baseball** The United States Supreme Court ruled in 1922 that professional baseball did not affect "interstate commerce" and was, therefore, exempt from federal antitrust law. No other sport has achieved this exempt status. However, Congress enacted a law in 1988 that has lessened the impact of the Supreme Court decision by allowing players to sue owners for anticompetitive activities.
- **Labor Unions** Section 6 of the Clayton Act allows labor unions to organize, bargain, and strike without the activity being considered an illegal group boycott.
- **Traditionally Regulated Industries** The insurance, airline, utility, transportation, securities, and banking industries are exempt from federal antitrust laws largely because they are heavily regulated by other federal or state laws.
- **Agricultural and Fishing Cooperatives** A narrowly construed exemption allows agricultural and fishing cooperatives to participate in marketing activities as long as those seeking the exemption are actually producing the product. Courts have held that retailers or wholesalers associated with the product are not within the purview of the exemption.

- **Joint Export Activities** Congress allows United States exporters to engage in cooperative activities so that they may compete effectively with trade associations existing in other countries.
- **The Noerr-Pennigton Doctrine** Two Supreme Court cases decided in the 1960s established a doctrine providing an exemption from antitrust law for individuals who desire to work together to persuade a legislative, executive, or judicial entity to take an action that would have an anti-competitive impact. For example, competitors in an industry might gather to lobby Congress to change a law, even if that change would favor established businesses by inserting a barrier to entry.
- **State Action** In the 1943 case of *Parker v. Brown,* the Supreme Court found the regulatory actions of a state, even if those actions are anti-competitive, are exempt from federal antitrust laws.

4. Enforcement

Depending on the statute, a violation of a federal antitrust provision may be a criminal offense. While the government may pursue various methods to enforce antitrust laws, private businesses that have been injured as a result of anti-competitive practices may sue for damages.

CRIMINAL The United States Department of Justice may initiate criminal prosecutions of violations of the Sherman Act as felonies. If convicted, an individual may face a fine of up to $1 million per violation and 10 years in prison. A corporation may be fined as much as $100 million per violation. The following chart from the Department of Justice indicates the increased success this branch of government is having during the recent past in securing criminal fines.

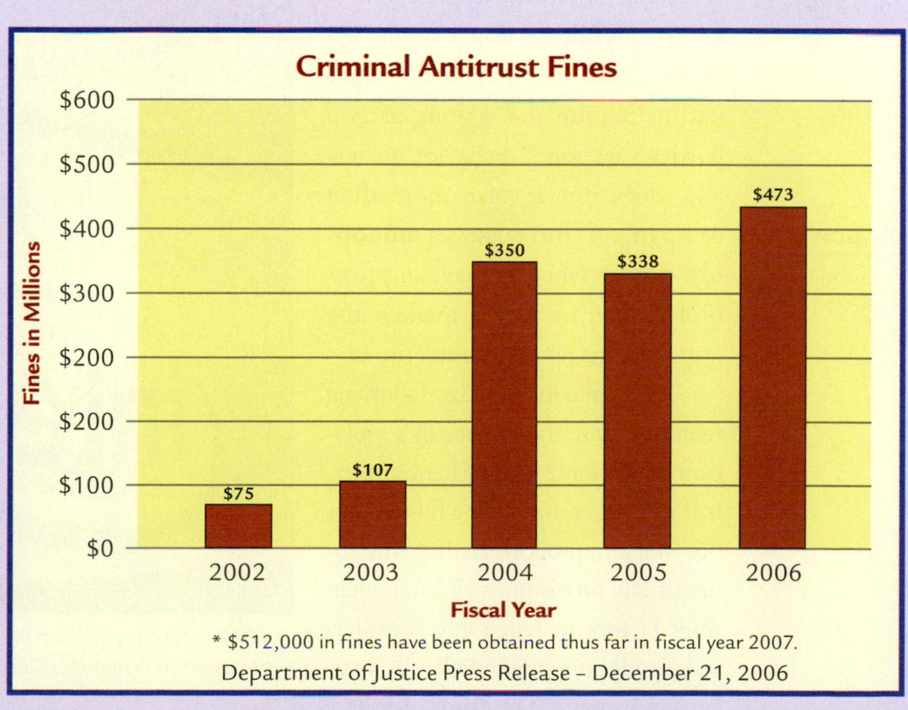

CIVIL SANCTIONS Both the Department of Justice and the Federal Trade Commission may pursue civil remedies under the Sherman Act, Clayton Act, or other federal antitrust laws. These remedies include (1) an *injunction* (a court order prohibiting the business from committing any further violations), (2) a *consent decree* (agreement, approved by a court, in which a party does not admit wrongdoing but agrees to change their behavior), and (3) a *divesture order* (requiring a company to sell an interest in an acquired company).

PRIVATE ACTIONS Under what is termed a "private attorney general" approach to enforcing laws, businesses injured as a result of a firm violating federal antitrust laws are allowed to pursue civil actions against the violator. A major incentive for this activity is provided by a provision of the Clayton Act. This provision allows a successful party suing under either the Sherman Act or the Clayton Act to recover *treble damages* and their *attorney's fees.* Together, these remedies encourage civil actions by any member of the business community who is able to show that specific anticompetitive behaviors *directly resulted in a tangible injury.* Although proving an activity of one business directly impacted in a tangible manner another business is difficult, the ability to recover three times the amount of harm and to have the violator pay a significant amount of the costs of engaging in the litigation provides considerable inducements for plaintiffs in antitrust cases. Perhaps not surprisingly, the extent of potential damages also is mentioned as a significant factor of why many businesses do not engage in questionable business practices.

MONOPOLIZATION

5. Nature of a Monopoly

Section 2 of the Sherman Act provides: "Every person who shall monopolize, or attempt to monopolize … any part of trade or commerce … shall be deemed guilty of a felony." While Section 1 is directed at concerted activities that by their nature require the actions of two parties, Section 2 behavior, generally, does not involve more than one party. A firm possesses **monopoly power** when it may fix prices unilaterally; in such a market, the one firm has no true competitors.

Monopoly power

The ability for one firm to fix prices unilaterally

In 2009, Intel Corporation was fined for monopoly abuse and was asked to halt their sales tactics.

As you consider the following material, note the essence of a violation of Section 2 of the Sherman Act. It is not necessarily unlawful to be or become a monopoly. Rather, this antitrust law provision is violated when three factors are taken into consideration: relevant power, relevant market, and intent. The law is directed, in part, at considering whether a firm has monopoly power, which is the ability for the business (and not the market) to effect the price of the firm's products or services in the market (usually the power of a firm within the relevant market … the first two factors listed previously), and in part on how the business attained (or uses) monopoly power (what is commonly referred to as intent).

6. Monopoly Power

When does a single entity have the power to control an entire market? Certainly if the entity is the only firm in the market, 100 percent market share would indicate monopoly power. What is the magic number below 100 percent when a firm has such power? The courts have not indicated a specific number. However, as a general rule, a firm is deemed to have monopoly power if its share of the relevant market is 70 percent or greater.

A monopoly occasionally may be found if the share is between 51 to 69 percent. Within this range, courts will consider factors in addition to market share. Other factors used to determine whether a firm possesses monopoly power include the structure of the industry (e.g., number of competitors), market concentration, degree of difficulty for new firms to enter the industry, and the nature of the industry. For example, in Scenario A, Firm X has 55 percent of the market share. There are twenty other competitors of note, with the largest having 12 percent of the market. Substantial costs in production machinery are required in order to enter this market. Technological innovation is slow. In Scenario B, Firm X also has 55 percent market share. There are two competitors, one with twenty-five percent and one with twenty percent of the market. Barriers to entry are low, and the technology required for adequate participation in this industry changes rapidly. A court may well find Firm X in Scenario A to have monopoly power but not in Scenario B. There is no monopoly power where market share is 50% or less.

7. Relevant Market

The determination of monopoly power based on a calculation of market share, however, is not quite as easy as it may appear. In Sherman Act Section 2 cases, courts are thrust into a difficult task in establishing the appropriate market. Two terms are necessary in order to determine the relevant market: appropriate product (or service) and appropriate geographic area.

PRODUCT (OR SERVICE) The first element in ascertaining the relevant market is to determine what goods or services are interchangeable in the minds of the market. Economists term this "substitutability" or "functional interchangeability." The ability to substitute one product for another is often determined by considering cross-elasticity of demand, which is where economists measure the effect that a change in price on one good or service has on the relationship between the demand for that good or service and another. This can be a daunting task and one where, ultimately, there is considerable discretion left to the judge to determine the appropriate product or service for determining the relevant market.

Consider the situation associated with Coca-Cola. Coca-Cola competes directly with Pepsi in the market of dark, carbonated soft drinks. If Coca-Cola Company should raise their prices, customers devoted to Coca-Cola may well switch to Pepsi. However, do we have the correct articulation of the product for determining market share? Might folks switch to 7-Up? If so, then our "product" becomes simply carbonated soft drinks. Might customers turn to sweetened iced tea? If so, then our market broadens even more. Note that the business accused of having monopoly power will attempt to convince the court to cast the widest possible net to determine the appropriate product or service. Those accusing a firm of having monopoly power will paint a much more exclusive picture of the appropriate product or service to determine market share.

GEOGRAPHIC AREA Determining the market power of a firm also necessarily entails establishing the appropriate geographic area within which the company competes. Again, this tends to be a subjective judgment on the part of a judge. A family farm located on the slopes of Mauna Loa on the Big Island of Hawaii that grows and produces Kona coffee may have monopoly power in that their Kona coffee is the only one served in the three coffee houses located in the town located one mile away from their farm. Is that the appropriate geographic area, however? Perhaps it should be the entire island? Or does the entire Hawaiian island chain best capture the area? Perhaps the appropriate area is the entire United States? In general, the geographic market area is identified as that area in which a business can increase its price without attracting new competitors and without losing sales to competitors located beyond the boundaries of the area.

8. Intent

As indicated previously, simply having monopoly power is never enough to violate Section 2. Courts examine how that power was attained and how that power is used. In some instances, the power is "thrust upon" a particular firm. For example, in an industry having tremendous difficulty, all other competitors may have simply given up and gone out of business. The lone company is certainly a monopoly, but their position was the product of firms abandoning a dying industry. The intent requirement is not present.

The intent to acquire or use monopoly power is often established by examining the conduct of a firm. A firm that actively purchases small competitors in order to increase its market share is providing evidence of intent to monopolize. Similarly, a company engaging in below-cost pricing, often termed "predatory pricing," certainly demonstrates the requisite intent.

The following case illustrates the difficulty a plaintiff will have in showing predatory intent.

Case

Weyerhaeuser Company v. Ross-Simmons Hardwood Lumber Company, Inc.

SUPREME COURT OF THE UNITED STATES

127 S. Ct. 1069; 2007 U.S. LEXIS 1333 (2007)

Thomas, J., delivered the opinion for a unanimous Court.

This antitrust case concerns the acquisition of red alder sawlogs by the mills that process those logs in the Pacific Northwest. These hardwood-lumber mills usually acquire logs in one of three ways. Some logs are purchased on the open bidding market. Some come to the mill through standing short- and long-term agreements with timberland owners. Others are harvested from timberland owned by the sawmills themselves. The allegations relevant to our decision in this case relate to the bidding market.

Ross-Simmons began operating a hardwood-lumber sawmill in Longview, Washington, in 1962. Weyerhaeuser entered the Northwestern hardwood-lumber market in 1980 by acquiring an existing lumber company. Weyerhaeuser gradually increased the scope of its hardwood-lumber operation, and it now owns six hardwood sawmills in the region. By 2001, Weyerhaeuser's mills were acquiring approximately 65 percent of the alder logs available for sale in the region.

From 1990 to 2000, Weyerhaeuser made more than $75 million in capital investments in its hardwood mills in the Pacific Northwest. During this period, production increased at every Northwestern hardwood mill that Weyerhaeuser owned. In addition to increasing production, Weyerhaeuser used "state-of-the-art technology," including sawing equipment, to increase the amount of lumber recovered from every log. By contrast, Ross-Simmons appears to have engaged in little efficiency-enhancing investment.

Logs represent up to 75 percent of a sawmill's total costs; and from 1998 to 2001, the price of alder sawlogs increased while prices for finished hardwood lumber fell. These divergent trends in input and output prices cut into the mills' profit margins, and Ross-Simmons suffered heavy losses during this time. Saddled with several million dollars in debt, Ross-Simmons shut down its mill completely in May 2001.

Ross-Simmons blamed Weyerhaeuser for driving it out of business by bidding up input costs, and it filed an antitrust suit against Weyerhaeuser for monopolization and attempted monopolization under § 2 of the Sherman Act. Proceeding in part on this "predatory-bidding" theory, Ross-Simmons argued that Weyerhaeuser had overpaid for alder sawlogs to cause sawlog prices to rise to artificially high levels as part of a plan to drive Ross-Simmons out of business. As proof that this practice had occurred, Ross-Simmons pointed to Weyerhaeuser's large share of the alder purchasing market, rising alder sawlog prices during the alleged predation period, and Weyerhaeuser's declining profits during that same period.

Finding that Ross-Simmons had proved its claim for monopolization, the jury returned a $26 million verdict against Weyerhaeuser. The verdict was trebled to approximately $79 million. The Ninth Circuit affirmed the verdict against Weyerhaeuser.

In our 1993 case of *Brooke Group Ltd.* v. *Brown & Williamson Tobacco Corp.*, we considered what a plaintiff must show in order to succeed on a claim of predatory pricing under § 2 of the Sherman Act. In a typical predatory-pricing scheme, the predator reduces the sale price of its product (its output) to below cost, hoping to drive competitors out of business. Then, with competition vanquished, the predator raises output prices to a supracompetitive level. For the scheme to make economic sense, the losses suffered from pricing goods below cost must be recouped (with interest) during the supracompetitive-pricing stage of the scheme. Recognizing this economic reality, we established in *Brooke Group* two prerequisites to recovery on claims of predatory pricing. "First, a plaintiff seeking to establish competitive injury resulting from a rival's low prices must prove that the prices complained of are below an appropriate measure of its rival's costs." Second, a plaintiff must demonstrate that "the competitor had ... a dangerous probability of recouping its investment in below-cost prices."

Predatory bidding, which Ross-Simmons alleges in this case, involves the exercise of market power on the buy side or input side of a market. In a predatory-bidding scheme, a purchaser of inputs "bids up the market price of a critical input to such high levels that rival buyers cannot survive (or compete as vigorously); and, as a result, the predating buyer acquires (or maintains or increases its) monopsony power." Monopsony power is market power on the buy side of the market. As such, a monopsony is to the buy side of the market what a monopoly is to the sell side and is sometimes colloquially called a "buyer's monopoly."

A predatory bidder ultimately aims to exercise the monopsony power gained from bidding up input prices. To that end, once the predatory bidder has caused competing buyers to exit the market for purchasing inputs, it will seek to "restrict its input purchases below the competitive level," thus "reducing the unit price for the remaining inputs it purchases." The reduction in input prices will lead to "a significant cost saving that more than offsets the profits that would have been earned on the output." If all goes as planned, the predatory bidder will reap monopsonistic profits that will offset any losses suffered in bidding up input prices. (In this case, the plaintiff was the defendant's competitor in the input-purchasing market. Thus, this case does not present a situation of suppliers suing a monopsonist buyer under § 2 of the Sherman Act, nor does it present a risk of significantly increased concentration in the market in which the monopsonist sells, *i.e.*, the market for finished lumber.)

Predatory-pricing and predatory-bidding claims are analytically similar. Tracking the economic similarity between monopoly and monopsony, predatory-pricing plaintiffs and predatory-bidding plaintiffs make strikingly similar allegations. A predatory-pricing plaintiff alleges that a predator cut prices to drive the plaintiff out of business and, thereby, to reap monopoly profits from the output market. In parallel fashion, a predatory-bidding plaintiff alleges that a predator raised prices for a key input to drive the plaintiff out of business and, thereby, to reap monopsony profits in the input market. Both claims involve the deliberate use of unilateral pricing measures for anticompetitive purposes; and both claims logically require firms to incur short-term losses on the chance that they might reap supracompetitive profits in the future.

More importantly, predatory bidding mirrors predatory pricing in respects that we deemed significant to our analysis in *Brooke Group*. In *Brooke Group*, we noted that "'predatory pricing schemes are rarely tried, and even more rarely successful.'" Predatory pricing requires a firm to suffer certain losses in the short term on the chance of reaping supracompetitive profits in the future. A rational business will rarely make this sacrifice. The same reasoning applies to predatory bidding. A predatory bidding scheme requires a buyer of inputs to suffer losses today on the chance that it will reap supracompetitive profits in the future. For this reason, "successful monopsony predation is probably as unlikely as successful monopoly predation."

Like the predatory conduct alleged in *Brooke Group*, actions taken in a predatory bidding scheme are often "the very essence of competition." Just as sellers use output prices to compete for purchasers, buyers use bid prices to compete for scarce inputs. There are a myriad of legitimate reasons—ranging from benign to affirmatively procompetitive—why a buyer might bid up input prices. A firm might bid up inputs as a result of miscalculation of its input needs or as a response to increased consumer demand for its outputs. A more efficient firm might bid up input prices to acquire more inputs as a part of a procompetitive strategy to gain market share in the output market. A firm that has adopted an input-intensive production process might bid up inputs to acquire the inputs necessary for its process. A firm might, also, bid up input prices to acquire excess inputs as a hedge against the risk of future rises in input costs or future input shortages. There is nothing illicit about these bidding decisions. Indeed, this sort of high bidding is essential to competition and innovation on the buy side of the market.

The general, theoretical similarities of monopoly and monopsony combined with the theoretical and practical similarities of predatory pricing and predatory bidding convince us that our two-pronged *Brooke Group* test should apply to predatory bidding claims.

The first prong of *Brooke Group's* test requires little adaptation for the predatory bidding context. A plaintiff must prove that the alleged predatory bidding led to below-cost pricing of the predator's outputs. That is, the predator's bidding on the buy side must have caused the cost of the relevant output to rise above the revenues generated in the sale of those outputs. As with predatory pricing, the exclusionary effect of higher bidding that does not result in below-cost output pricing "is beyond the practical ability of a judicial tribunal to control without courting intolerable risks of chilling legitimate" procompetitive conduct. Given the multitude of procompetitive ends served by higher bidding for inputs, the risk of chilling procompetitive behavior with too lax a liability standard is as serious here as it was in *Brooke Group*. Consequently, only higher bidding that leads to below-cost pricing in the relevant output market will suffice as a basis for liability for predatory bidding.

A predatory bidding plaintiff also must prove that the defendant has a dangerous probability of recouping the losses incurred in bidding up input prices through the exercise of monopsony power. Absent proof of likely recoupment, a strategy of predatory bidding makes no economic sense because it would involve short-term losses with no likelihood of offsetting long-term gains. As with predatory pricing, making a showing on the recoupment prong will require "a close analysis of both the scheme alleged by the plaintiff and the structure and conditions of the relevant market."

Ross-Simmons has conceded that it has not satisfied the *Brooke Group* standard. Therefore, its predatory bidding theory of liability cannot support the jury's verdict.

For these reasons, we vacate the judgment of the Court of Appeals and remand the case for further proceedings consistent with this opinion. It is so ordered.

■ *Vacated and remanded.*

CASE CONCEPTS REVIEW

1. What is the difference between monopoly power and monopsony power?
2. Why are predatory pricing and predatory bidding "rarely tried, and even more rarely successful"?
3. Why does the Court find that predatory bidding is often the "essence of competition?"

9. Attempting to Monopolize

Section 2 reaches beyond simply monopolizing. The provision expressly makes illegal *attempting* to monopolize. The United States Supreme Court has determined that an attempt to monopolize requires (1) predatory or anticompetitive conduct, (2) a specific intent to control prices or destroy competition, and (3) a "dangerous probability" of success. The type of conduct in successful cases is often predatory pricing or establishing barriers that prohibit firms from entering the industry. In establishing a case of monopolization under Section 2, the courts only require the showing of a general intent. However, for attempt cases, plaintiff must show a specific intent to control prices or exclude competitors. Finally, the dangerous probability of success element generally means that defendant's market share is already higher than 50 percent.

RESTRAINTS OF TRADE—BASIC PROVISIONS

10. Concerted Action

Section 1 of the Sherman Act addresses the topic of illegal restraints of trade. The section, in pertinent part, provides that "[e]very contract, combination in the form of trust or otherwise, or conspiracy, in restraint of trade or commerce among the several states, or with foreign nations is declared illegal." The "3Cs" of contract, combination, or conspiracy all require the involvement of more than one party, thus the nature of a section 1 violation is *concerted* action.

What type of involvement triggers liability under Section 1? Certainly if there is an express or implied agreement to restrain trade, Section 1 may well be violated, but what about companies in a market following what other competitors are doing? Courts generally find that *conscious parallelism*—identical or similar conduct in the market by competitors—is insufficient to create an inference of a contract, combination, or conspiracy.

11. Per Se and Rule of Reason Violations

It is perfectly legal—and quite expected—that business will make competitive decisions that may, in a sense, restrain trade. Tyree owns a tire store. He is purchasing tires for the month of April and has three potential suppliers of tires. Each supplier carries a line of tires from different manufacturers. Supplier A, Supplier B, and Supplier C each submit information to Tyree about their products. Tyree chooses to purchase tires for the month of April from Supplier B. Once Tyree enters into a contract with Supplier B, trade is technically restrained; and a literal interpretation of the Section 1 provision would find that Tyree and Supplier B have violated the Sherman Act. The United States Supreme Court has declared (first in 1911) that not every contract, combination, or conspiracy is illegal; rather, the statute is violated only when the restraint of trade is *unreasonable.*

The United States Supreme Court has decided during past decades numerous antitrust cases, many dealing with whether particular behavior is an unreasonable restraint on trade. As a result of these decisions, the Supreme Court has created two methods of analyzing whether conduct is unreasonable under antitrust law provisions.

PER SE VIOLATIONS Certain business practices are on their face unreasonable. These are called *per se violations.* Under the per se rule, specific anticompetitive behavior is *conclusively presumed* to be unreasonable. A defendant cannot rebut the presumption; also, there is no defense to a per se violation (perhaps showing that the activity is of benefit to the consumer). If a plaintiff is able to show a violation within one of the per se categories, then there is no need to prove that the behavior unreasonably restrained trade. Once a concerted activity is shown to fall within a per se category, plaintiff simply moves to prove damages.

RULE OF REASON VIOLATIONS Those types of restraints of trade not termed per se unreasonable are judged under the *rule of reason* test. Under this approach, courts make the determination that specific behavior is an unreasonable restraint on trade on a case-by-case basis. This test allows a court to examine the impact of the contract, combination, or conspiracy. Therefore, some concerted activity is legal. Other factors enter into the rule of reason test, including the purpose of the restraint, the intent of the parties to the restraint, the social benefits associated with the restraint (e.g., increased efficiency), the number of competitors in an industry, the sizes of the various participants, and the type of industry. Defendants in rule of reason situations may present information aimed at countering plaintiff's allegation that a restraint of tread is unreasonable. Needless to say, this type of analysis is fact-specific and takes a great deal of time in court.

COMPARING THE TWO APPROACHES The worst, most anticompetitive types of restraints of trade are deemed per se violations. Businesses should be most sensitive to behavior that may be deemed to fall into one of the per se categories because of the conclusive presumption of unreasonableness that is attached to such behavior. Within the area of antitrust law enforcement, if either the government or a private party proves a per se violation, then the defendant usually wishes to settle and avoid a trial. Note, however, that the United States Supreme Court during the past twenty or so years, often following the thinking of the Chicago School, have moved behaviors that were once well-established as per se violations into the rule of reason category.

The rule of reason approach provides an opportunity for a court to analyze each case to determine whether specific behavior in a particular setting is an unreasonable restraint on trade. This approach is based on common law doctrines associated with agreements not to compete and other types of trade restraints outside of statutory antitrust laws and developed well before the Sherman Act was passed. The reasonableness standard recognizes the truism that sometimes contracts among those in the business community may have little negative impact on competition and may, on occasion, actually further competition and ultimately benefit consumers.

Table 41-1 lists prominent examples of behaviors associated with restraining trade that fall into one of the two categories.

Horizontal agreement
Agreement between firms that directly compete with one another

As suggested by Table 41.1, whether an agreement is horizontal or vertical may determine whether the behavior is judged under the per se or rule of reason test. **Horizontal agreements** are contracts between firms that directly compete with one another. Automakers are in direct

TABLE 41-1 ■ Per Se and Rule of Reason Violations under Sherman Act and Clayton Act

Per Se	Rule of Reason
Horizontal price-fixing (Sherman Act)	Vertical price-fixing (Sherman Act)*
Horizontal division of the markets (Sherman Act)*	Vertical division of the markets (Sherman Act)
Horizontal group boycotts (Sherman Act) *	Vertical boycotts (Sherman Act)
	Tying arrangements (Sherman Act & Clayton Act)
	Reciprocal dealing arrangements (Sherman Act)
	Exclusive dealing arrangements (Sherman Act & Clayton Act)

* Indicating the general trend, this is possible for the alternative characterization to apply in selected situations.

Vertical agreement

Agreement between firms at different places along the distribution chain

competition with one another, so a contract between Ford and Toyota would be a horizontal agreement. The horizontal agreements are treated more severely than **vertical agreements** because these agreements almost always reduce *interbrand competition.* That is, they compete in a market where the competitors are producing the same type of product or offering the same type of service.

Courts are more favorably disposed regarding vertical agreements. In these situations, the firms are at different places along the distribution chain. For example, Proctor-Gamble entering into a contract with a grocery wholesaler to distribute its hair shampoos. Because vertical agreements only reduce intrabrand competition, where regional wholesalers are purchasing and selling Proctor-Gamble products, they generally have less impact on consumers.

12. Horizontal Restraints under the Sherman Act

HORIZONTAL PRICE-FIXING *Horizontal price-fixing* is concerted action where competitors establish the price instead of the market. This type of breach of Section 1 of the Sherman Act is a classic example of a per se violation. This category also includes anticompetitive behavior that affects price. Therefore, an agreement among competitors limiting the amount of goods the competitors will produce, sell, or buy also violates Section 1. It would also include an agreement among competitors to set the terms of credit for contracts entered into by buyers or sellers. While simply exchanging price information will not by itself be sufficient concerted activity, any additional concerted actions will probably reach a level of activity prohibited by the Sherman Act.

HORIZONTAL DIVISION OF THE MARKET Another per se violation of Section 1 of the Sherman Act occurs where competitors at the same level enter into an agreement creating a *horizontal division of the market.* In order to save costs of sales staff, Company X (who sells copy machines to businesses within California) enters into an agreement with Company Y (who sells a different brand of copy machine also within California). Company X is based in San Francisco, Company Y in San Diego. The two agree that Company X will sell its products north of Santa Barbara; conversely, Company Y promises to sell their product only to businesses located in or south of Santa Barbara. This division of the market violates Section 1. Note in this scenario how a horizontal division of the market reduces interbrand competition.

Lower courts have suggested in recent years that an "ancillary" horizontal divisions of the market agreement that is part of a larger agreement among competitors may be judged under the rule of reason test if the larger agreement actually furthers competition. The Supreme Court has yet to provide contemporary guidance on this point, but many leading antitrust scholars embrace this view.

HORIZONTAL GROUP BOYCOTTS While a single firm may decide not to enter into a contract with a particular business, if two or more competitors agree to refuse to purchase products from a specific business or sell to a specific business, then a per se violation of Section 1 of the Sherman Act has occurred. This is called a *horizontal group boycott.* However, the Supreme Court has ruled, in selected horizontal group boycott cases decided in the past few decades, that the rule of reason test is appropriate for selected instances of horizontal group boycotts. While the Supreme Court has not extended the rule of reason test to all horizontal group boycotts, it is possible in the future that this type of violation will no longer be treated as a per se violation.

13. Vertical Restraints under the Sherman Act

VERTICAL PRICE-FIXING *Vertical price-fixing* occurs when, for example, a manufacturer and its distributor agree on the price the distributor will offer the product to the next level of the distribution chain. As part of a business plan, the manufacturer may wish require that the distributor sell the product at a *minimum* price in order to enforce an image of high quality. Despite some commentary to the contrary, the Supreme Court appears to embrace the notion that such an arrangement should be judged under the rule of reason.

Court interpretations of this aspect of Section 1 of the Sherman Act do allow a manufacturer to *suggest* the price (i.e., "suggested manufacturer's price") that the produce will be sold and refuse to deal with those who do not follow the wishes of the manufacturer in this regard, under what is known as the *Colgate* doctrine. As long as there is no agreement indicating that the distributor agreed to sell at the "suggested" price, the arrangement is legal because a manufacturer has the freedom to unilaterally determine whom it wishes to contract with and the conditions of such an agreement.

While vertical price-fixing involving vertical *maximum* pricing was for many years considered a per se violation, the Supreme Court in 1997 ruled that these types of cases should be reviewed on a case-by-case basis to determine whether the price-fixing arrangement was unreasonable. This decision, along with others, indicates that the Court is following Chicago School arguments supporting the idea that economic efficiencies are often present in vertical price-fixing arrangements; and, therefore, the rule of reason test is appropriate, regardless of whether the case deals with minimum or maximum pricing.

VERTICAL DIVISION OF THE MARKETS *Vertical divisions of the market* are arrangements, for example, between a manufacturer and its wholesalers that limit their ability to market the product. One type of vertical division of the markets is the exclusive distributorship where the manufacturer grants to a single distributor a given territory within which it may distribute the product. Under the rule of reason test, used today in all vertical division of the markets cases, such an arrangement will be legal as long as the manufacturer does not have dominant power in the market. Another type is a territorial restrictive agreement where the distributor is prevented from selling outside of a particular geographic area.

In the following famous United States Supreme Court case, the Court decided whether the per se or rule of reason test should apply to vertical division of the market cases. This case also illustrates the influence of the Chicago School approach to antitrust issues.

CASE

Continental T.V., Inc., et al. v. GTE Sylvania Inc.

SUPREME COURT OF THE UNITED STATES

433 U.S. 36 (1977)

MR. JUSTICE POWELL DELIVERED THE OPINION OF THE COURT

Franchise agreements between manufacturers and retailers frequently include provisions barring the retailers from selling franchised products from locations other than those specified in the agreements. This case presents important questions concerning the appropriate antitrust analysis of these restrictions under § 1 of the Sherman Act and the Court's decision in United States v. Arnold, Schwinn & Co. (1967).

Respondent GTE Sylvania Inc. (Sylvania) manufactures and sells television sets through its Home Entertainment Products Division. Prior to 1962, like most other television manufacturers, Sylvania sold its televisions to independent or company-owned distributors who in turn resold to a large and diverse group of retailers. RCA at that time was the dominant firm with as much as 60% to 70% of national television sales in an industry with more than 100 manufacturers. Prompted by a decline in its market share to a relatively insignificant 1% to 2% of national television sales, Sylvania conducted an intensive reassessment of its marketing strategy and, in 1962, adopted the franchise plan challenged here. Sylvania phased out its wholesale distributors and began to sell its televisions directly to a smaller and more select group of franchised retailers. An acknowledged purpose of the change was to decrease the number of competing Sylvania retailers in the hope of attracting the more aggressive and competent retailers thought necessary to the improvement of the company's market position. To this end, Sylvania limited the number of franchises granted for any given area and required each franchisee to sell his Sylvania products only from the location or locations at which he was franchised. Sylvania imposed no restrictions on the right of the franchisee to sell the products of competing

continued

manufacturers. A franchise did not constitute an exclusive territory, and Sylvania retained sole discretion to increase the number of retailers in an area in light of the success or failure of existing retailers in developing their market. The revised marketing strategy appears to have been successful during the period at issue here, for by 1965 Sylvania's share of national television sales had increased to approximately 5%, and the company ranked as the Nation's eighth largest manufacturer of color television sets.

This suit is the result of the rupture of a franchiser-franchisee relationship that had previously prospered under the revised Sylvania plan. Dissatisfied with its sales in the city of San Francisco, Sylvania decided in the spring of 1965 to franchise Young Brothers, an established San Francisco retailer of televisions, as an additional San Francisco retailer. The proposed location of the new franchise was approximately a mile from a retail outlet operated by petitioner Continental T. V., Inc. (Continental), one of the most successful Sylvania franchisees. Continental protested that the location of the new franchise violated Sylvania's marketing policy, but Sylvania persisted in its plans. Continental then canceled a large Sylvania order and placed a large order with Phillips, one of Sylvania's competitors. Sylvania then terminated Continental's franchises

At trial, the jury found that Sylvania had violated Section 1 of the Sherman Act and awarded: damages at $591,505, which was trebled to produce an award of $1,774,515. On appeal, the Court of Appeals for the Ninth Circuit reversed.

We turn to Continental's contention that Sylvania's restriction on retail locations is a per se violation of § 1 of the Sherman Act as interpreted in *Schwinn.* The Court in *Schwinn* articulated the following "bright line" per se rule of illegality for vertical restrictions: "Under the Sherman Act, it is unreasonable without more for a manufacturer to seek to restrict and confine areas or persons with whom an article may be traded after the manufacturer has parted with dominion over it."

We are convinced that the need for clarification of the law in this area justifies reconsideration. *Schwinn* itself was an abrupt and largely unexplained departure from White Motor Co. v. United States (1963), where only four years earlier the Court had refused to endorse a per se rule for vertical restrictions. Since its announcement, *Schwinn* has been the subject of continuing controversy and confusion, both in the scholarly journals and in the federal courts.

The traditional framework of analysis under § 1 of the Sherman Act is familiar and does not require extended discussion. Section 1 prohibits "[e]ery contract, combination..., or conspiracy, in restraint of trade or commerce." Since the early years of this century a judicial gloss on this statutory language has established the "rule of reason" as the prevailing standard of analysis. Standard Oil Co. v. United States (1911). Under this rule, the fact-finding weighs all of the circumstances of a case in deciding whether a restrictive practice should be prohibited as imposing an unreasonable restraint on competition. Per se rules of illegality are appropriate only when they relate to conduct that is manifestly anticompetitive.

The market impact of vertical restrictions is complex because of their potential for a simultaneous reduction of intrabrand competition and stimulation of interbrand competition. Interbrand competition is the competition among the manufacturers of the same generic product—television sets in this case—and is the primary concern of antitrust law. The extreme example of a deficiency of interbrand competition is monopoly, where there is only one manufacturer. In contrast, intrabrand competition is the competition between the distributors—wholesale or retail—of the product of a particular manufacturer. Significantly, the Court in *Schwinn* did not distinguish among the challenged restrictions on the basis of their individual potential for intrabrand harm or interbrand benefit. Restrictions that completely eliminated intrabrand competition among Schwinn distributors were analyzed no differently from those that merely moderated intrabrand competition among retailers. The pivotal factor was the passage of title. All restrictions were held to be per se illegal where title had passed, and all were evaluated and sustained under the rule of reason where it had not. The location restriction at issue here would be subject to the same pattern of analysis under *Schwinn.*

Vertical restrictions reduce intrabrand competition by limiting the number of sellers of a particular product competing for the business of a given group of buyers. Location restrictions have this effect because of practical constraints on the effective marketing area of retail outlets. Although intrabrand competition may be reduced, the ability of retailers to exploit the resulting market may be limited both by the ability of consumers to travel to other franchised locations and, perhaps more importantly, to purchase the competing products of other manufacturers. None of these key variables, however, is affected by the form of the transaction by which a manufacturer conveys his products to the retailers.

Vertical restrictions promote interbrand competition by allowing the manufacturer to achieve certain efficiencies in the distribution of his products. These "redeeming virtues" are implicit in every decision sustaining vertical restrictions under the rule of reason. Economists have identified a number of ways in which manufacturers can use such restrictions to compete more effectively against other manufacturers. For example, new manufacturers and manufacturers entering new markets can use the restrictions in order to induce competent and aggressive retailers to make the kind of investment of capital and labor that is often required in the distribution of products unknown to the consumer. Established manufacturers can use them to induce retailers to engage in promotional activities or to provide service and repair facilities necessary to the efficient marketing of their products. Service and repair are vital for many products, such as automobiles and major household appliances. The availability and quality of such services affect a manufacturer's goodwill and the competitiveness of his product. Because of market imperfections, such as the so-called "free rider" effect, these services might not be provided by retailers in a purely competitive situation, despite the fact that each retailer's benefit would be greater if all provided the services than if none did.

Certainly, there has been no showing in this case, either generally or with respect to Sylvania's agreements, that vertical restrictions have or are likely to have a "pernicious effect on competition" or that they "lack... any redeeming virtue." Accordingly, we conclude that the per se rule stated in *Schwinn* must be overruled.

In sum, we conclude that the appropriate decision is to return to the rule of reason that governed vertical restrictions prior to *Schwinn.* When anticompetitive effects are shown to result from particular vertical restrictions they can be adequately policed under the rule of reason, the standard traditionally applied for the majority of anticompetitive practices challenged under § 1 of the Act. Accordingly, the decision of the Court of Appeals is

■ *Remanded.*

CASE CONCEPTS REVIEW

1. What is the difference between interbrand and intrabrand competition?
2. Why did the court reverse the Schwinn decision?
3. What impact does the case have on business? Regarding the business community, is the decision more restrictive or more liberal? Why?

VERTICAL GROUP BOYCOTTS *Vertical group boycotts* are judged under the rule of reason test. These situations occur where one business agrees with another firm at a different place on the distribution chain not to deal with a third business that is in direct competition with either of the businesses engaged in the concerted activity. If one supplier conspired with one retailer such that the supplier would not sell to another retailer, a vertical group boycott would result. The rule of reason test is sensible because in the normal course of business such behavior is typical. However, if the intent of the contract is to forbid the non-conspiring business from succeeding, perhaps by offering the product at below-cost, then the boycott might be declared illegal.

RESTRAINTS OF TRADE—ADVANCED PROVISIONS

14. Exclusionary Contracts under the Clayton Act

The Clayton Act supplements Sections 1 and 2 of the Sherman Act by addressing two major areas: exclusionary contracts and mergers. Section 3 of the Clayton Act restricts businesses from selling or leasing products on the condition that the purchaser or lessee shall not use or deal in the goods of a competitor of the seller. The two types of vertical agreements most commonly associated with Section 3 are tying arrangements and exclusive dealing arrangements. Both are subject to the rule of reason test. Each is covered in the remainder of this section. Section 15 of the chapter examines the second principal subject covered by the Clayton Act—mergers.

Tying arrangement

Situation where a buyer is not permitted to purchase one item without also purchasing another.

TYING ARRANGEMENTS A **tying arrangement** occurs when a buyer is not permitted to purchase one item without also purchasing another. This is a common occurrence in the grocery industry. For example, one wishes to purchase toothpaste, but the tube of toothpaste comes with a toothbrush. From a seller's perspective, tying arrangements allow the seller to wed a popular item to one that is less desirable. An employer can also use this approach to introduce a new product that is complementary to an existing one. From a buyer's viewpoint, the free choice a purchaser would have to buy a popular product without being tied into purchasing the second product is curtailed. In effect, free market principles associated with the second product are hampered.

Under the rule of reason analysis, courts will find a violation of Section 3 of the Clayton Act if (1) the agreement involves two distinct products (not closely associated component parts or integral parts of a whole), (2) a significant amount of commerce is impacted, and (3) the seller has sufficient economic power in the typing product to enforce the tie-in. In one case, McDonald's required their franchisees to lease their stores directly from McDonald's. McDonald's conducts considerable demographic research to determine the appropriate type and size of a store. McDonald's then uses this information to determine the best possible site and build the shell of the store. It is at this point that McDonald's selects an operator. While plaintiff sued McDonald's asserting that the franchise and the lease were tied "products," the court disagreed stating that the franchise and lease were "integral components of the business method being franchised."

Exclusive dealing agreement

Agreement where buyer agrees to purchase all of its requirements from a single seller or a seller agrees to sell all of its output to a single buyer.

EXCLUSIVE DEALING AGREEMENTS An **exclusive dealing arrangement** exists when a buyer agrees to purchase all of its requirements from a single seller or a seller agrees to sell all of its output to a single buyer. Sherman Act Section 1 and Clayton Act Section 3 both apply to exclusive dealing arrangements, and the rule of reason is used to judge whether an arrangement is an unreasonable restraint on trade. The Sherman Act provision applies to both goods and services. Section 3 of the Clayton Act, while applicable to goods only, casts a wider net, making an exclusive dealing contract illegal if its effect will *substantially lessen* competition or tend to create a monopoly. Courts will examine the extent of exclusive dealing arrangements in a particular industry, the degree of disparity in bargaining strength between the buyer and seller, and the area of effective competition, in addition to a host of other factors, in determining whether an exclusive dealing agreement is illegal.

15. Mergers under the Clayton Act

A *merger* occurs when one company acquires another. Mergers may be through a friendly agreement or by a hostile takeover. Regardless of the motivation for the merger, Section 7 of the Clayton Act was designed to prohibit a merger when the merger may substantially lessen competition or tend to create a monopoly. Also, a merger may be horizontal, vertical, or conglomerate. Each of these types is described below. In analyzing an impending merger, a court under Section 7 will examine three elements: (1) the relevant market, (2) the pre-merger profile, and (3) the post-merger profile.

The relevant market is determined by examining the relevant product (applying the concept of substitutability) and geographic area. The pre-merger profile requires the determination of the type of merger (see below), the size of the companies, and the concentration of the industry. The final step is to prepare, using the same factors, a post-merger profile. At this point the court determines whether the merger will substantially lessen competition or tend to create a monopoly. Section 7 of the Clayton Act is written, and has been interpreted by the courts, to bar mergers that *may* have an anticompetitive impact.

HORIZONTAL MERGER Of the three types of mergers, the *horizontal merger,* where competitors on the same level of the distribution chain merge, are under the greatest scrutiny. Why? Because competition is immediately impeded in a horizontal merger where firms that were once competing against one another are now combined into one firm. A court will determine whether Section 7 of the Clayton Act is violated by examining: (1) whether the post-merger entity will have a significant market share, (2) the concentration of the relevant market, (3) the history of competition within the specific market, and (4) the intent of the parties to the merger. Merger guidelines promulgated by the United States Department of Justice and the Federal Trade Commission are employed by those agencies to determine whether a proposed merger will receive approval.

VERTICAL MERGER A *vertical merger* occurs when two businesses at different places on the distribution chain merge. A manufacturer of sportswear may decide to purchase the retail outlets that sell its products. Courts will examine market concentration, barriers to entry and the potential that competitors will be eliminated, among other factors, to determine the legality of a vertical merger. Because a vertical merger may result in efficiencies of distribution, they often are found legal because such mergers generally have little anti-competitive effect.

CONGLOMERATE MERGER The types of mergers that generate the least amount of concern are *conglomerate mergers.* A merger of two firms that deal in totally unrelated products or services is termed a conglomerate merger. The merger of Time Warner and AOL in 2001 is considered a conglomerate merger. The courts are involved infrequently in conglomerate mergers.

16. Price Discrimination Fundamentals

The Robinson-Patman Act, which extended the price discrimination provisions of Section 2 of the Clayton Act, is the primary antitrust law dealing with price discrimination. As you consider this material, keep in mind that the types of price discrimination forbidden by the Robinson-Patman Act often reduce the prices customers ultimately pay. Some commentators, observing that the legislation protects competitors instead of promoting competition, argue the other provisions of antitrust law can deal with situations where competitors offer lower prices in an attempt to secure and use monopoly power. Therefore, the United States government tends not to enforce Robinson-Patman Act violations, leaving to private parties the obligation to pursue the goals of the act through private suits.

TYPES OF PRICE DISCRIMINATION The provisions of the Robinson-Patman Act prohibit three types of price discrimination. *First line price discrimination* occurs where a seller offers a price to one buyer and a higher price to another buyer. The lower price is offered to buyers where the seller is functioning in a highly competitive marketplace; but where there is little or no competition for the product offered by the seller, the buyer in that area must pay the higher price. From the seller's standpoint, this strategy allows it to finance its low prices by charging high prices in a less competitive marketplace. A likely consequence of first line price discrimination is that a national supplier can drive out smaller, locally owned suppliers from the market. That is, injury occurs to *competitors of the seller* who is engaging in price discrimination.

First line price discrimination was the focus of the original Clayton Act provision, but with the explosion of large chain stores in the 1920s and 30s, *second line price discrimination* became a common business practice. The Robinson-Patman Act's primary purpose is to address second line price discrimination. This type of price discrimination involves another step in the distribution chain. Because of the size of the large chains, they were able to use their market power to command lower prices from their suppliers. The suppliers to the chain stores offered discounts, promotional materials, and other advantages to those purchasers that were not offered to independent, smaller buyers. As a result, the chain stores were able to offer their products at a lower price. In such situations, the injury occurs to competitors of a *customer of the seller* who reaps the benefits of the discrimination.

The final form of anti-competitive behavior dealt with by the Robinson-Patman Act is *third line price discrimination.* Here, a *customer of a customer of the seller* is benefited by the actions of the seller. For example, a large clothing wholesaler receives discounts from a clothing manufacturer and passes those savings along to a retailer, who in turn reduces prices for consumers. The retailers receive the benefit of the price discrimination.

ELEMENTS A violation of the Robinson-Patman Act occurs where the following elements are met: (1) a price difference occurs, (2) involving the sale of goods, (3) of like grade and quality, and (4) probable anticompetitive effect. Regarding the last element, first line price discrimination claims require a plaintiff to show the greatest probability of adverse impact to competition. Generally, the competitive harm resulting from the price discrimination in first line price discrimination cases must be fairly significant actual or potential injury to competition. In cases of second line and third line price discrimination, a plaintiff need only show substantial price discrimination between competitors over a period of time; the existence of injury is inferred from that activity.

17. Price Discrimination Defenses

The Robinson-Patman Act provides two defenses to price discrimination. Under Section 2, *cost justification* is a defense. If a defendant is able to show that price differences extended to customers result from differences in the cost of manufacture, sale, or delivery, then no violation occurs. A seller may offer a lower price to purchasers who buy large quantities of the good. In such a case, the seller has the burden of showing the difference in price results from savings in transporting the item, in inventory expenses, or other benefits accrued directly because of a cost savings.

The second type of defense is based on the notion of *meeting competition.* Where a seller discriminates in its pricing policy in good faith to meet an equally low price of a competitor, the price discrimination is legal. The center of this defense is the "good faith" requirement. The test is whether, depending on the market conditions, a reasonable person would conclude that the seller lowered the price in order to meet the price being offered by a competitor. This defense is illustrated in the following case.

CASE

Water Craft Management LLC, Douglas Wayne Glascock, Nick A. Martrain v. Mercury Marine, a Division of Brunswick Corp., et al.

UNITED STATES COURT OF APPEALS FOR THE FIFTH CIRCUIT

457 F.3d 484 (2006)

GARWOOD, CIRCUIT JUDGE

Appellants, Water Craft Management LLC, d/b/a LA Boating Centre (Water Craft) was a Mercury Marine retail dealership selling Mercury Marine outboard motors in Baton Rouge, Louisiana. It was founded on November 25, 1996, by its two members, Nick Martrain and Douglas Glascock, and went out of business roughly two years later on December 7, 1998.

Water Craft Water Craft then filed this suit against one of its suppliers, Mercury Marine, for secondary-line price discrimination in violation of sections 2(a) and 4 of the Clayton Act, as amended by the Robinson-Patman Act.

In price discrimination cases, courts analyze the competitive injury component at three basic levels: (1) primary-line effects, i.e. injury to other sellers; (2) secondary-line effects, i.e. injury to purchasers of a certain seller; and (3) tertiary-line effects, i.e. injury to the customers of those purchasers. A secondary-line violation occurs when a large purchaser uses its purchasing power to obtain lower prices from a manufacturer, allowing it to undersell its competitors.

Water Craft alleges that Mercury Marine discriminated in favor of Water Craft's largest competitor, Travis Boating Center ("Travis"), by offering Travis discounts on motors that far exceeded the discounts available to Water Craft or other Mercury retail dealerships in the Baton Rouge market. Mercury does not dispute the fact that Travis got a better deal on motors than Water Craft, but Mercury explains that it was forced to offer these lower prices to Travis in order to compete with the Outboard Marine Corporation ("OMC"), one of Mercury's principal competitors. At the time, OMC manufactured Johnson and Evinrude outboard motors.

Before Mercury began selling motors to Travis, Mercury was losing market share to OMC in the gulf coast region because the Travis chain, which until October 1998 had a sales agreement with OMC but not with Mercury, was rapidly expanding, sometimes buying out Mercury dealerships and converting them to Travis retail stores which did not sell Mercury products. During his testimony at trial, Jeffery Behan, a marketing research director at Mercury, explained that Mercury approached Travis several times in an effort to sign them up, but was rebuffed because their prices were not competitive with OMC's.

With this explanation for its price discrimination, Mercury invoked the "meeting competition defense," an affirmative defense provided under section 2(b) of the Robinson-Patman Act that permits a seller to rebut a prima facie case of discrimination by "showing that his lower price ... was made in good faith to meet an equally low price of a competitor. ..."

Following a bench trial, the district court entered judgment in favor of Mercury on their Robinson-Patman Act claim believing that Mercury had established the "meeting competition defense" to the Robinson-Patman claim.

We find Water Craft's argument unpersuasive and hold that the district court did not clearly err in finding that Mercury's lower pricing to Travis was made in a good faith attempt to meet OMC's prices. The Robinson-Patman Act was passed in response to the rapid growth of chain stores, which, by exploiting the efficiencies of centralization, were able to threaten the existence of small, independent retailers. However, Congress did not seek by the Robinson-Patman Act either to abolish competition or so radically to curtail it that a seller would have no substantial right of self-defense against a price raid by a competitor. To this end, as noted above, it is an absolute defense to liability under the Robinson-Patman act that the price discrimination is the result of price concessions made "in good faith *for the purpose* of meeting the competitor's price."

Our focus, then, is on Mercury's motivation for discriminating since a good-faith belief, rather than absolute certainty, that a price concession is being offered to meet an equally low price offered by a competitor is sufficient to satisfy the defense. Furthermore, the Court has emphasized that the concept of good faith, which is at the heart of the meeting competition defense, is "flexible and pragmatic, not technical or doctrinaire." Indeed, rigid rules and inflexible absolutes are especially inappropriate in dealing with the defense; the facts and circumstances of the particular case, not abstract theories or remote conjectures, should govern its interpretation and application.

Some guidelines, however, do emerge from Supreme Court opinions. For example, the Court sustained a meeting competition defense, holding that although "casual reliance on uncorroborated reports of buyers or sales representatives without further investigation may not ... be sufficient to make the requisite showing of good faith," the defense "can be satisfied by efforts falling short of interseller verification

. . . ." The Court then identified certain indicia of good faith that are relevant to determining whether the meeting competition defense should apply. Among these are (1) whether the seller "had received reports of similar discounts from other customers"; (2) whether the seller "was threatened with a termination of purchases if the discount were not met"; (3) whether the seller made "[e]fforts to corroborate the reported discount by seeking documentary evidence or by appraising its reasonableness in terms of available market data"; and (4) whether the seller had "past experience with the particular buyer in question."

Under the circumstances of this case, Mercury has shown the existence of facts, particularly those facts that the Court has listed as indicia of good faith, "which would lead a reasonable and prudent person to believe that the granting of a lower price would in fact meet the equally low price of a competitor." First, Mercury relied on several different sources for their approximation of OMC's discounts, including Ron Spradling and Mark Walton, both of whom had personal knowledge of the competing bid and neither of whose credibility had been questioned. Then, as a Mercury Marketing director explained at trial, Mercury attempted to corroborate their information. "[W]e kind of looked at what the boat pricing was out in the marketplace, and some people started to do some math there, and we listened to what you heard at boat shows and other people that tended to talk about what they thought they knew, a lot of that information triangulated pretty closely."

We agree with the district court's finding that such information forms a sufficient basis on which Mercury could have acted in good faith. Indeed, its is doubtful that Mercury could have investigated any further without exposing themselves to risk of liability under Section 1 of the Sherman Act.

■ *The judgment of the district court is AFFIRMED.*

CASE CONCEPTS REVIEW

1. What is needed in order to establish the meeting competition defense?
2. What factors influenced the court to agree with the trial court that the defense was established?

INTERNATIONAL CONSIDERATIONS

18. Reach of United States Laws

Section 1 of the Sherman Act provided that its provisions cover restraints of trade "among the several states, or with foreign nations." Congress intended in 1890 that United States antitrust law would have substantial extraterritorial effect. Congress later, with the adoption of the Foreign Trade Antitrust Improvement Act (FRAIA) in 1982, fine-tuned the reach of United States antitrust provisions to conduct outside of the United States that has a "direct, substantial, and reasonably foreseeable effect on United States commerce or on the business of a person engaged in exporting goods from the united States to foreign nations." The primary goal of the act was to exempt certain *export trade* from the reach of the Sherman Act by requiring such commerce have considerable impact within the United States.

Regarding *import trade,* the FRAIA does not apply. Under the latest Supreme Court decision dealing with import trade, the Sherman Act applies to "foreign conduct that was meant to produce and did in fact produce some substantial effect in the United States."Under this broad provision, it is possible that a Pakistani clothing company doing business in France could sue a French clothing company in the United States for alleged anticompetitive behavior in France because the French company's behavior would prevent the Pakistani company from exporting its clothing to the United States. Note, as in this scenario, the anticompetitive conduct can occur outside of the United States … yet United States antitrust law still applies.

The largest criminal antitrust fines are detailed in the chart in Table 41-2.

19. Reach of Foreign Laws

The antitrust laws of most countries are far more restrained in their reach than those of the United States. However, there is mounting evidence that individual countries and groups of countries are

TABLE 41-2 ■ Major Antitrust Fines

ANTITRUST DIVISION Sherman Act Violations Yielding a Corporate Fine of $200 Million or More				
Defendant (FY)	**Product**	**Fine in Millions**	**Geographic Scope**	**Country**
F. Hoffmann-La Roche, Ltd. (1999)	Vitamins	$500	International	Switzerland
LG Display Co., Ltd. and LG Display America (2009)	Liquid Crystal Display (LCD) Panels	$400	International	Korea
Société Air France and Koninklijke Luchtvaart Maatschappij, N.V. (2008)	Air Transportation (Cargo)	$350	International	France (Société Air France) The Netherlands (KLM)
Korean Air Lines Co., Ltd. (2007)	Air Transportation (Cargo & Passenger)	$300	International	Korea
British Airways PLC (2007)	Air Transportation (Cargo & Passenger)	$300	International	UK
Samsung Electronics Company, Ltd. Samsung Semiconductor, Inc. (2006)	DRAM	$300	International	Korea
BASF AG (1999)	Vitamins	$225	International	Germany

As of 2/19/2009, per Department of Justice < http://www.usdoj.gov/atr/public/criminal.htm>

increasingly asserting their influence into antitrust matters on the global stage. For example, individual countries in Europe for decades however, would rarely extend their antitrust laws beyond their national boundaries. Within the past decade, the European Union (EU), with its twenty-five member nations, has taken vigorous stands in asserting EU antitrust laws. For example, in 2001, the EU blocked the proposed merger of General Electric and Honeywell International, both com-

The merger of GE and Honeywell was blocked by the EU even though it was approved in the United States.

panies based in the United States that did considerable business in Europe—even though United States officials had approved the merger. Also, Microsoft was recently ordered by the EU regulators to change its Windows operating system and fined more than $500 million for violating EU antitrust provisions.

Further, the underlying purpose of antitrust laws can vary among governmental entities. Again turning to the EU, Article 82 of the Economic Community Treaty prohibits willfully acquiring or maintaining monopoly power. This provision is similar to Section 2 of the Sherman Act. Article 81 of the Economic Community Treaty prohibits mergers and other concerted practices that restrain trade, a provision comparable to Section 1 of the Sherman Act. Yet the interpretations of the provisions vary considerably between the EU and the United States. On the one hand, the EU follows the Traditional School in believing the aim of antitrust laws is to protecting competitors as they interpret and apply EU antitrust laws. On the other hand, the United States, drawing on principles espoused by the Chicago School, applies antitrust law provisions with the overriding purpose of promoting competition. As in the General Electric-Honeywell situation, conflicts can arise between the United States and foreign entities as a result of the reach of foreign antitrust provisions. Hopefully, in the future there will be greater consultation and coordination as we function more and more in a global economy.

CHAPTER SUMMARY

BACKGROUND

History 1. The United States, since 1890, has recognized the need for antitrust laws to moderate competition in the business world.

2. While the Sherman Act addresses the most egregious forms of anticompetitive behavior, Congress also has passed the Clayton Act, the Federal Trade Commission Act, and the Robinson-Patman Act to address less critical anti-competitive problems.

Schools of Thought

1. Followers of the Traditional School believe the primary goal of antitrust laws should be to protect competitors.
2. Followers of the Chicago School believe the primary goal of antitrust laws should be to promote competition.

Basic Principles

1. Congress is able to legislate in the antitrust arena through the provision of the United States Constitution empowering Congress to regulate commerce.
2. Congress and the courts have granted certain industries and entities an exemption from antitrust laws.

Enforcement

1. Violating certain antitrust laws is a crime.
2. Businesses harmed by firms that violate antitrust laws may be entitled to treble damages and the payment of attorney's fees.

MONOPOLIZATION

Nature of a Monopoly

1. Monopoly power is the ability for one firm to fix prices unilaterally.

Monopoly Power

1. Monopoly power exists if a business has more than 70 percent of the market share, may exist if the share is between 51 to 69 percent, and does not exist if the share is 50 percent or less.

Relevant Market

1. Relevant market is determined by examining the appropriate product or service and the appropriate geographic area.

Intent

1. Possessing monopoly power does not trigger antitrust liability; if a business also has the intent to monopolize, then there is a violation.

Attempting to Monopolize

1. Section 2 of the Sherman Act also is violated if a firm is attempting to monopolize.

RESTRAINTS OF TRADE—BASIC PROVISIONS

Concerted Action

1. Section 1 of the Sherman Act addresses concerted activities. That is, a contract, combination, or conspiracy to restrain trade.
2. Conscious parallelism, simply following the lead of a competitor, is acceptable practice.

Per Se and Rule of Reason Violations

1. In determining whether a restraint of trade is unreasonable, certain anticompetitive behavior is determined to always be a violation of Section 1. These situations are per se violations.
2. Other anticompetitive behavior is judged under the rule of reason, where the number of competitors in the industry, market concentration, and other factors are considered by a court in deciding whether an anticompetitive behavior is unreasonable.

Horizontal Restraints under the Sherman Act

1. Horizontal price-fixing is concerted action where competitors establish the price instead of the market.
2. If competitors at the same level enter into an agreement to only work is specific areas, a horizontal division of the market occurs.
3. A horizontal group boycott occurs where two or more competitors agree to refuse to purchase products from a specific business or sell to a specific business.

Vertical Restraints under the Sherman Act

1. Vertical price-fixing occurs when, for example, a manufacturer and its distributor agree on the price for which the distributor will offer the product to the next level of the distribution chain.
2. Vertical divisions of the market are arrangements, for example, between a manufacturer and its wholesalers that limit their ability to market the product.
3. Vertical group boycotts occur where one business agrees with another firm at a different place on the distribution chain not to deal with a third business that is in direct competition with either of the businesses engaged in the concerted activity.

RESTRAINTS OF TRADE—ADVANCED PROVISIONS

Exclusionary Contracts under the Clayton Act

1. A tying arrangement occurs when a buyer is not permitted to purchase one item without also purchasing another.
2. An exclusive dealing arrangement occurs where a buyer agrees to purchase all of its requirements from a single seller or a seller agrees to sell all of its output to a single buyer.

Mergers under the Clayton Act

1. Mergers are characterized as horizontal, vertical, or conglomerate.

Price Discrimination Fundamentals

1. Price discrimination cases are classified as first line, second line, and third line.
2. A violation of the Robinson-Patman Act occurs where the following elements are met: (1) a price difference occurs, (2) involving the sale of goods, (3) of like grade and quality, and (4) probable anticompetitive effect.

Price Discrimination Defenses

1. Two defenses exist: cost justification and meeting competition.

INTERNATIONAL CONSIDERATIONS

Reach of United States Laws

1. United States antitrust law reaches to anticompetitive behaviors that may occur in another country by impact commerce in the United States.

Reach of Foreign Laws

1. While traditionally the antitrust laws of other countries had little impact on the business conducted by United States firms, that trend is changing. For example, European Union antitrust provisions are increasingly shaping the manner in which United States businesses operate.

REVIEW QUESTIONS AND PROBLEMS

1. Match each term in Column A with the appropriate statement in Column B.

A	B
(1) Sherman Act	(a) An antitrust law focusing on price discrimination
(2) Clayton Act	(b) The rule of reason generally applies to this type of price fixing
(3) Robinson-Patman Act	(c) Followers believe the primary goal of antitrust laws should be to promote competition
(4) Traditional School	(d) May or may not be an unreasonable restraint on trade
(5) Chicago School	(e) Antitrust statute aimed at restraints of trade and monopolization
(6) Monopoly power	(f) Always an unreasonable restraint on trade
(7) Vertical price fixing	(g) Antitrust law focusing on exclusive dealing contracts and mergers
(8) Per se rule	(h) The per se rule is applied to this type of price fixing
(9) Rule of reason	(i) The ability for one firm to fix prices unilaterally
(10) Horizontal price fixing	(j) Followers believe the primary goal of antitrust laws should be to protect competitors

2. Is the Traditional School or the Chicago School approach best? Why?
3. Lilly works for Sam Software for twelve years and resigns to start her own firm, Lilly Likeware. Sam Software and Lilly Likeware compete directly for the same customers. According to recent data, Sam Software's market share has dropped from 50 percent to 30 percent. During the same time, Lilly Likeware's market share has risen from 0 to 20 percent. Within the past weeks, however, Lilly believes Sam Software is participating in below cost pricing. What is below cost pricing? How can it be shown? What antitrust law or laws might apply to this situation?
4. Best View Theatres (BVT) and Prime Time Entertainment (PTE) both were talent booking entities located in Las Vegas, Nevada. Each firm aggressively pursued possible acts, and each worked hard to secure venues for their performers. At a trade convention, the president of BVT and the president of PTE met for dinner. Each decided to direct their respective employees to quit calling on the same acts and the same venues. The two presidents, on a napkin, outlined a "working relationship" that would allow each business to make a nice profit without having to enter into costly "wars" with the other. Is such an arrangement legal? Why?

5. Microsoft Corporation includes its Internet-browsing software (Internet Explorer) as part of the Windows operating system at no extra cost. In order to sell the operating system, original equipment manufacturers were prohibited from disassembling the package. Is this arrangement legal? Why?
6. The National Collegiate Athletic Association (NCAA) limits the number of basketball coaches an institution may have to four (one head, two assistants, and one entry-level). Moreover, the NCAA limits the salary of the entry-level coach to $32,000. A group of entry-level coaches challenge the compensation limit as a violation of Section 1 of the Sherman Act. The NCAA states that some horizontal restraints are necessary in order to promote competition among their membership. Is the restriction legal? Why?
7. Fall City Brewery sells its beer to a variety of distributors located throughout the mid-western portion of the United States. Fall City prices its beer based on each state, recognizing that competitors in the market change from state to state. An Indiana distributor who sells in Evansville must pay a higher price than a Kentucky distributor who sells beer in the town of Dawson. What defense might Fall City raise? Why?
8. Gerber (65 percent market share), Heinz (17 percent), and Beech-Nut (15 percent) are the three firms that dominate the baby food market. However, Heinz was the largest producer of baby food in the world. Across the United States, approximately 90 percent of supermarkets carry Gerber products. Heinz, products appeared in 40 percent of the stores, generally in the Northeast, South, and Mid-West. Beech-Nut also appears in 40 percent of the stores, mostly in New York, New Jersey, California, and Florida. Heinz and Beech-Nut wish to merge. Discuss.
9. Von's Grocery Company is the third largest grocery chain in the Los Angeles market with 4.7 percent of sales. It wishes to merge with the sixth largest firm, which has 2.8 percent of sales. Is this legal? Why?
10. Nippon Paper Industries Company (NPIC), a Japanese company, manufactured facsimile (fax) paper. Officials of that company met with other competitors in the market in Japan for the purpose of fixing the price of thermal fax paper throughout the United States. Would United States antitrust law apply? Why?

Internet Sources

The Federal Trade Commission has prepared a primer on antitrust laws, available at: http://www.ftc.gov/bc/compguide/index.html

More detailed information regarding Federal Trade Commission enforcement is available at: http://www.ftc.gov/ftc/antitrust.htm

The Antitrust Division of the Department of Justice provides a considerable amount of information on the Internet, beginning at: http://www.usdoj.gov/atr/

Consumer Law | 42

CHAPTER OUTLINE

CHAPTER PREVIEW

Although it is becoming increasingly rare, instances of being able to purchase an item directly from the individual who made the product still occur. For example, one may live a few blocks away from a small, family-owned and operated sandal store. The same individuals who inspect the raw materials necessary for creating the sandals, in turn, make them. Further, the sandal-makers are also the individuals who sell the product. If you desire to purchase sandals, you may enter the storefront and hold the product, inspect the stitching, pull on the straps, and ask the maker questions regarding the integrity of the sandals. The close proximity of buyer and seller to one another (same neighborhood) and the simplicity of the product (a sandal) create a setting well suited to traditional application of contract law where breach of the contract was easy to show and recovering damages presented few significant obstacles. In addition, rules associated with the marketplace supported a proper bargain. For example, should a sandal maker generate shoddy product, the reputation of the business will soon suffer; and the sandal maker will have considerable difficulty staying in business. In an unsophisticated business relationship where the product is simple and the buyer and seller are close to one another, there was no need for a greater presence of government in regulating the consumer-merchant relationship.

However, if the consumer and the seller are hundreds (or thousands) of miles apart, if the seller is not necessarily the manufacturer of the product but rather the last of many entities in the distribution chain, and if the product is complicated in its design, manufacture, and operation (e.g., an automobile), then opportunities for a business to take advantage of a remote consumer increase significantly. In an attempt to remedy the inequality of the buyer/seller relationship in modern life, Congress has enacted various acts aimed at curbing behaviors of members of the business community who, in their fervor to sell, exceed societal standards of propriety. This chapter first presents pertinent aspects of these laws, primarily focusing on the advertising and sales functions.

There is a second, equally important, aspect of the consumerism age that also deserves legal treatment. What happens if the sale is not for cash, but based on credit? Government's interest in regulating members of the business community increases if consumer credit is involved. Debtor/creditor relations are worthy of significant government scrutiny because the

BUSINESS MANAGEMENT DECISION

Pablo is a respected customer of Citibank. Upon examining his monthly statement, Pablo discovers that an unauthorized person has withdrawn $400 from his account, using an automated teller machine (ATM). Pablo remembers that a "nice-looking person" was standing next to Pablo operating a second ATM machine while Pablo was operating withdrawing $20. That person said that he was having troubles with his machine and wondered if Pablo would put his card into the second machine to see if it worked. Pablo accommodated the unknown person's request. Then that person asked Pablo to again insert his card into the first machine to make sure it was still working. Pablo did not understand that when he left the ATMs, both machines were activated with his account. Further, the Citibank manager believes that unknown person probably saw Pablo enter his four-digit number and then used Pablo's number to withdraw the maximum amount allowed ($200) from each machine. The bank refuses to repay Pablo the $400. What law may assist Pablo? Do you think he can successfully sue the bank?

extension of credit creates the possibility that a business or a credit granting entity may not have sufficiently disclosed necessary information regarding the debtor/creditor relationship or that the creditor undertakes unsavory actions in an attempt to recover moneys owed. Congress has enacted a number of laws aimed at protecting prospective and current consumer debtors. These restrictions on business are generally aimed at requiring businesses that grant credit to make certain disclosures and controlling numerous creditor practices (from soliciting credit applications through collecting the debt). The second portion of the chapter addresses the vast statutory landscape Congress has created for the purpose of protecting the consumer debtor.

PROTECTING THE PURCHASER

Federal laws aimed at regulating the purchasing decision must balance the needs of business to communicate with potential buyers with the needs of consumers to be treated fairly in an ever-more complex marketplace. Laws protecting the purchaser tend to fit into three broad categories of regulation. One set of federal laws and administrative agency regulatory activities are directed to the arena of labeling and packaging. It is in this category that Congress has been most active. Beginning in significant fashion in the 1930s, federal statutory laws have altered businesses ability to label and package goods in a narrow manner (for example, the Wool Products Labeling Act applies to wool and other types of fabrics) and more broadly (for example, the Fair Packaging and Labeling Act mandates basic information be included in the labeling and packaging of most products). In the second arena, advertising, the Federal Trade Commission, under authority granted to it by the Trade Commission Act, is primarily charged with eliminating advertising that is deemed deceptive. Lastly, actual sales transactions are controlled in significant part by Federal Trade Commission regulations. Each of these three arenas of federal law is examined below.

FIGURE 42-1 ■ Major Federal Efforts Aimed at Protecting the Purchaser

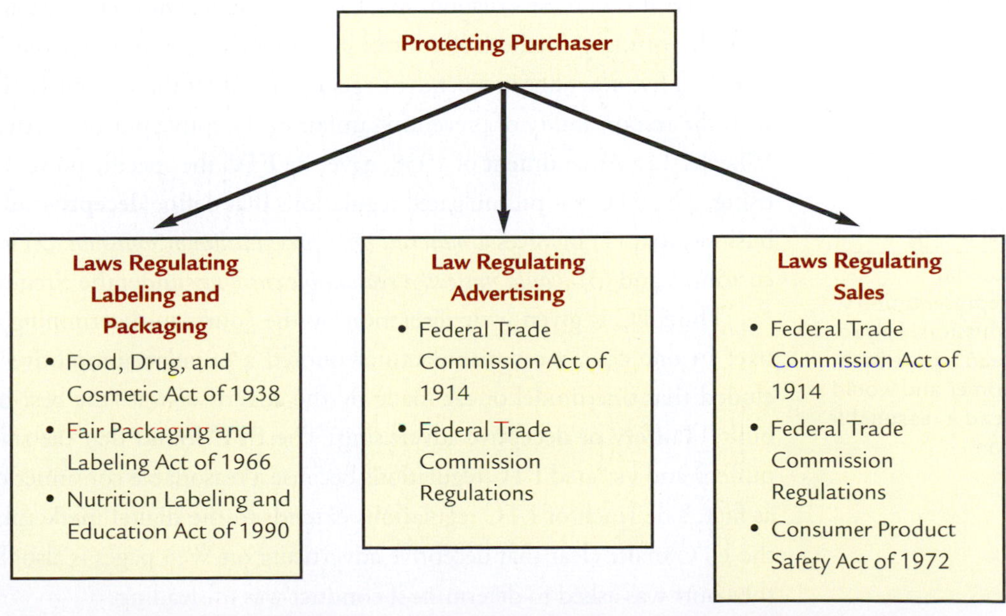

1. Labeling and Packaging

Information included on labels and packaging influences the purchase decision. Such information allows a consumer to understand the contents of a container or package, and it provides a means to compare similar products or the same product being sold by different sellers. Congress has been active in generating laws aimed at labeling and packaging.

Much of federal legislation addresses products that are potentially dangerous. The Federal Food, Drug, and Cosmetic Act of 1938 (requires truth in labeling of food, drugs, and cosmetics), the Flammable Fabrics Act of 1953, the Hazardous Substance Act of 1960 (mandates warning labels on dangerous products used in the home), the Cigarette Labeling Act of 1966, and the Poison Prevention Packaging Act of 1970 (demands childproof caps on certain products) are examples of these types of legislation.

Other acts of Congress are aimed at particular products. Laws of this type include the Wool Products Labeling Act of 1939, the Fur Products Labeling Act of 1951, and the Textile Fiber Products identification Act of 1958 (dealing with the labeling of man-made fibers). A third category of legislation is directed primarily at educating the public generally. Examples include the Fair Packaging and Labeling Act of 1966 and the Nutrition Labeling and Education Act of 1990

2. Advertising

Underlying all commercial transactions is the principle that the parties will be honest with one another. Of course, honesty is often treated as a subjective value, one that varies depending on whom is involved in a transaction, along with a variety of other factors. Further, in the process of desiring to make a deal, members of the business community may push further than society desires in articulating, generally through advertisements, attributes of the subject of the contract.

Attempting to delineate the exact line of what advertising and other statements by a merchant should be illegal is difficult. It is well accepted that businesses should be able to advertise through all-to-common sweeping statements and exaggerations, what is known as **puffery**.

Puffery

Promotional statements made by business about a product or service that are not intended to be taken literally

It is also quite clear that false statements associated with an important characteristic should be illegal and, under both contract and tort law, should allow the consumer who is harmed recovery. However, there are vast areas of pre-purchase activities that are not governed by common law principles. For example, does an advertisement that includes a "half truth" exceed society's standard of propriety? It is in these situations that Congress, along with state legislatures, has acted.

The primary method of controlling advertising is through the Federal Trade Commission (FTC), a five-member independent agency tasked by the Federal Trade Commission Act of 1914 with the responsibility of preventing unfair or deceptive practices. An amendment to this act, the Wheeler-Lea Amendment of 1938, gave the FTC the specific power to prohibit deceptive advertising. The FTC has promulgated regulations that define **deceptive advertising** as an activity by a business that (1) involves a *material misrepresentation or omission,* (2) is *likely to mislead* a potential customer, and (3) *would mislead a reasonable customer* under the circumstances.

Deceptive advertising

A material misrepresentation or omission likely to mislead a potential customer and would mislead a reasonable customer

The FTC is given wide discretion by the courts in determining when advertising is deceptive. In one case, a car manufacturer quoted a popular automotive magazine article that concluded that one model of car made by the advertiser was "the best-handling passenger car ever built." Puffery or deceptive advertising? The FTC found that the statement went beyond mere puffery and violated FTC regulations because a reasonable consumer might believe the statement as fact. The reach of FTC regulations extends to the digital marketplace, also. Regulations from the FTC make clear that deceptive advertising on Web pages is also illegal. In the following case the court was asked to determine if conduct was misleading.

CASE

Federal Trade Commission v. QT, Inc., Q-Ray Company, Bio-Metal, Inc., Quete Park, a.k.a. Andrew Q. Park, and Jung Joo Park

UNITED STATES DISTRICT COURT FOR THE NORTHERN DISTRICT OF ILLINOIS, EASTERN DIVISION

448 F. Supp. 2d 908 (2006)

MAGISTRATE JUDGE MORTON DENLOW DELIVERED THE MEMORANDUM OPINION AND ORDER.

"The pain just went away."

"Within seconds the pain was gone."

"You don't have to live with pain."

The Q-Ray(R) Ionized Bracelet(R) ("Q-Ray bracelet") achieved tremendous commercial success through a series of 30-minute infomercials. The Federal Trade Commission ("FTC") brings this action claiming Defendants marketed the Q-Ray bracelet in a deceptive and misleading manner by representing that the bracelet provides immediate, significant or complete pain relief and scientific tests prove their pain-relief claims. Defendants deny their advertising was false or misleading. They contend adequate substantiation exists for the advertising claims made in connection with the promotion and sale of the Q-Ray bracelet.

Defendant QT, Inc. ("QT") is an Illinois corporation with its principal place of business at 500 W. Algonquin Road, Mt. Prospect, Illinois. Since at least 1996, QT has advertised, marketed, and sold the Q-Ray bracelet via U.S. media outlets and identical Internet sites, www.qray.com, www.q-ray.com, and www.bio-ray.com.

Defendant Q-Ray Company ("QRC") is an Illinois corporation performing the fulfillment operations of QT, including shipping the Q-Ray bracelet to consumers and receiving returned products from consumers since mid-2002.

Defendant Bio-Metal, Inc. ("Bio-Metal"), which was formerly known as Bio-Ray International, Inc., is an Illinois corporation with its principal place of business at 500 W. Algonquin Road, Mt. Prospect, Illinois.

At all relevant times, defendant Que Te Park, also known as Andrew Q. Park ("Que Te Park"), was and is the President of QT, QRC, and Bio-Metal. He resides and/or transacts business in the Northern District of Illinois. Que Te Park has been the Chief Executive Officer of QT and QRC since at least 2001. Que Te Park is the sole shareholder of QT and QRC.

The Q-Ray bracelet is a C-shaped bracelet with screw caps that is manufactured in Spain by Bio-Ray S.A. The bracelet comes in four sizes: x-small, small, medium and large. The bracelet is made in six styles at different price points: Natural Titan Finish, Standard Silver Plated, Standard Gold Plated, Deluxe Silver Finish, Deluxe Combo and Deluxe Gold Plated.

Que Te Park first saw the bracelet in the Barcelona, Spain airport in 1994. It was being sold by Bio-Ray, S.A. as the Bio-Ray bracelet. He purchased the bracelet and he believes it helped relieve his lower back pain. He also purchased one for his wife to relieve her migraines.

Beginning in 1996, QT began selling the bracelet on a mostly wholesale basis in the United States under the Q-Ray name. QT began selling directly to consumers by means of infomercials in 2000.

None of the experts analyzed the composition of the Q-Ray bracelet. Que Te Park represented to the Mayo Clinic that the bracelet is 85% copper and 15% zinc. Although the bracelet is composed of more than 50% copper, Que Te Park acknowledged that the infomercials say the Q-Ray bracelet is not copper. Que Te Park testified that all of the different compositions of the bracelet and different metal plating used in the various styles do not affect the performance of the Q-Ray bracelet in any way. Each bracelet works the same through ionization.

According to Que Te Park, the Q-Ray bracelet is unique because of the ionization. Que Te Park does not know how much electric charge is delivered to the Q-Ray bracelet. Although he has seen a figure of 150,000 volts put out on a technical information sheet by the factory, he does not believe that figure because if it were a secret, the factory would not disclose it. Que Te Park testified during the trial, however, that he picked the term 'ionized' because "ionized is very simple, very easy to remember."

QT does not confirm through independent testing that each bracelet it receives from Bio-Ray S.A., the manufacturer in Spain, is actually ionized. QT does not have any tests or studies to prove that the Q-Ray bracelet actually discharges ions.

Que Te Park testified that "ionization" has no scientific meaning. He has no idea what the phrase "ionization performance," which appears in his consumer brochures, means. His testimony on ionization was contradictory and full of obfuscation. He was lacking in credibility. He is a clever marketer but a poor witness.

Que Te Park made up the theory that the bracelet works like acupuncture or Eastern medicine. He has no testing or studies to support his theory. He testified that anyone can find the theory on Google.

There was no scientific evidence presented that the Q-Ray bracelet actually receives, retains, or emits an electrical charge or has any properties different from any other bracelet made from the same metals. The Q-Ray bracelet was marketed as an "ionized bracelet" as part of a scheme devised by Que Te Park and the corporate defendants (hereafter collectively referred to as "Defendants") to defraud consumers out of millions of dollars by preying on their desire to find a simple solution to alleviate their physical pain.

Since at least September 2000, QT, QRC, and/or Bio-Metal advertised, promoted, offered for sale, sold, and distributed the Q-Ray bracelet to the public nationally, using advertisements in print media, the Internet, and on cable television stations such as the Golf Channel, the Learning Channel, USA Network, and the Discovery Channel.

QT also has dealers, which are mostly stores, and Internet distributors. The company does not give its dealers advertisements, but asks them to refer to QT's website. QT monitors its distributors' claims.

To induce consumers to purchase Q-Ray bracelets, QT, QRC, and/or Bio-Metal have disseminated or caused to be disseminated at least four different television infomercials, Internet advertisements on www.qray.com, www.q-ray.com and www.bio-ray.com, and a product brochure.

Infomercials for the Q-Ray bracelet aired 42,213 times between April 14, 2001 and June 29, 2003. Short spot television advertisements

continued

for the Q-Ray bracelet aired approximately 10,147 times between March 11, 2002 and September 8, 2003.

The retail price of the Q-Ray bracelet sold by QT ranges from $49.95 to $249.95. QT's wholesale cost for the Q-Ray bracelet ranges between $7.50 and $28 depending on the style. Defendants thus marked up the bracelet over 650 percent in setting the retail price to consumers.

QT's gross sales of the Q-Ray bracelet from January 1, 1996 through June 30, 2003 were $137,172,907. There was a substantial jump in sales of the Q-Ray bracelet after the infomercials started airing in 2000 and that significant increase in sales continued as the infomercials kept airing. QT's net profit for the years 1996 through September 2003 was approximately $22,600,000. QT's net profit for 2000 was approximately $440,000. QT's net profit for 2001 was approximately $860,000. QT's net profit for 2002 was approximately $9,100,000. QT's net profit for 2003 was approximately $12,100,000.

The websites, brochures, packaging, and four infomercials aired by Defendants between 2000 and 2003 convey an overall, net impression that the Q-Ray bracelet provides immediate, significant, or complete relief from various types of pain. The claim conveyed in these advertisements was either expressed or, if considered an implied claim, it was "so conspicuous as to be virtually synonymous with express claims." The Court required no testimony from an expert in consumer psychology or consumer behavior to discern the claim set forth in these advertisements. Nor did the Court need the assistance of a consumer market survey to extrapolate the net impression of the advertisements. The claim was obvious and apparent from viewing the infomercials. Considering the overall, net impression made by Defendants' advertisements, the Court finds that in their advertising Defendants conveyed the claim that the Q-Ray bracelet provides immediate, significant, or complete pain relief from various types of pain.

Having established that Defendants made the claim that the Q-Ray bracelet provides immediate, significant, or complete relief from various types of pain, the FTC must show that this claim was misleading. The FTC may use two theories to prove Defendants' claim was misleading: (1) the falsity theory and (2) the reasonable basis theory. Relying on the latter theory, the Court finds that Defendants lacked a reasonable basis to advertise that the Q-Ray bracelet provides immediate, significant, or complete relief from various types of pain.

As of the date of the FTC's complaint and at the present time, Que Te Park was and is the President of QT, QRC, and Bio-Metal. He has been the Chief Executive Officer of QT and QRC since at least 2001. Que Te Park is the sole shareholder of QT and QRC. In his capacity as President of QT and QRC, he is the signatory on all ten of QT's bank accounts. Que Te Park and Ciprian were responsible for generating, collecting, reviewing, or evaluating substantiation for claims regarding the Q-Ray bracelet. Ciprian was responsible for collecting studies about the Q-Ray bracelet and for identifying researchers to conduct studies on the Q-Ray bracelet; she reported to Que Te Park regarding proposed studies and consulted him for approval of the proposed studies.

Clearly, Que Te Park possessed the authority to control the corporate Defendants' deceptive acts or practices, and he participated directly in them. Next, the evidence shows that Que Te Park should have known about the deceptive practices, and, in fact, did know about them. Que Te Park was intimately involved with the business of the corporate Defendants and possessed more control and authority than any other employee. The Court finds Que Te Park individually liable for the violations.

In the instant case, the Court orders the disgorgement of Defendants' $22,500,000 in profits made during the period of the four infomercials plus interest. The Court also orders that every Q-Ray bracelet purchaser during the period of the four infomercials is entitled to rescission and restitution in the form of a full refund. However, the total amount of restitution must not exceed $87,019,840, which is the amount of Defendants' net sales to consumers from January 1, 2000, through June 30, 2003. Therefore, Defendants will be required to disgorge not less than $22,500,000 or more than $87,019,840 in equitable relief. Thus, for example, if only $10,000,000 is paid out in refunds, Defendants will pay a total of $22,500,000. If $40,000,000 is paid out in refunds, Defendants will pay a total of $40,000,000; and if $95,000,000 is claimed in refunds, Defendants will pay a total of $87,019,840.

■ *So ordered.*

CASE CONCEPT REVIEW

1. Upon what basis did the FTC find the defendants had practiced deceptive advertising?
2. Should the president of the corporations described above be held personally liable? Why?
3. Is the action brought by the FTC the best way to control deceptive advertising? Are there better ways?

In recent years, Congress has directed the FTC to act in specific areas as a result of the ability of businesses to use electronic means to advertise their products and services. Abuses associated with automatic telephone dialing systems and prerecorded messages prompted Congress in 1991 to pass the Telephone Consumer Protection Act. Under this act, businesses are prohibited from soliciting through the use of an automated telephone system and faxing advertisements without obtaining the permission of the recipient. In 1994, Congress passed the Telemarketing and Consumer Fraud and Abuse Prevention Act, which required the FTC to draft regulations aimed at prohibiting deceptive telemarketing practices. This legislation is also the basis for the FTC's decision to create, in 2003, the "Do Not Call Registry." If a consumer places their name in the registry, telemarketers may not contact that individual.

3. Sales

The FTC has enacted a number of regulations for the purpose of protecting consumers at the point of sale and after the sale. Regarding *door-to-door sales,* regulations mandate that consumers must be told that they have three days within which to cancel any door-to-door sale (commonly referred to as a "cooling off period"). In the areas of *telephone and mail order sales,* regulations provide that orders must be shipped within the time frame established and that if the merchant cannot meet the stated date of shipping, the customer must be so notified. For *online sales,* specific rules address fraud and other deceptive practices perpetrated over the Internet. In addition, specific industries are under particular scrutiny by the FTC—including funeral homes, correspondence schools, and home insulation providers; and specific sales practices also have drawn the attention of the FTC (for example, pyramid sales schemes.)

Although labeling and packaging laws are effective, to some degree, the complicated nature of many products prompted Congress to adopt the Consumer Product Safety Act (CPSA) in 1972 for the purpose of providing a mechanism for establishing safety standards for consumer products and for banning certain types of products that were deemed too dangerous for the consuming public. The CPSA created the Consumer Product Safety Commission (CPSC) to conduct research on the safety of consumer products, establish regulations dealing with ensuring products that reach consumers are safe for the intended use and other reasonable uses, forbid the sale of objectionable products, and recall products already in the hands of consumers.

In 2008, Congress passed major amendments to the CPSA. One major focus of the amendments was aimed at providing greater protection to children playing with toys, particularly those imported to the United States. Congress expressed concern over stories of children being hurt and dying from contact with toys containing dangerous chemicals. Another area addressed by the 2008 amendments dealt with greater control over three-wheeled and four-wheeled all-terrain vehicles.

For telephone and mail order sales, regulations stipulate that orders must be shipped within the given timeframe.

PROTECTING THE DEBTOR

This second portion of the chapter provides coverage of the primary federal laws that protect a debtor (the person or entity who owes money) from various activities that a creditor (the individual or entity who is owed money) might undertake. Centuries ago, creditors could use the legal process to place individuals who owed them money in debtor's prisons. The days of incarcerating an individual for nonpayment of a debt are long gone, yet the area of debtor-creditor relations remains a crucial area of concern for the law.

Credit (or debt) is a necessary part of the financial picture for businesses and individuals alike. For consumers, there are two general types of debtor-creditor relationships. In a *closed-end* credit transaction, the amount of the loan is set. Typical examples include the loan of money from a bank to purchase a car. In *open-end* credit transactions, as is provided under a credit card contract, the amount is left open and the extension of credit is repeated. Regardless of whether the transaction is closed-end or open-end, Congress has adopted legislation impacting the granting of credit, the reporting of credit, electronic funds transfers, identity theft, and collecting the debt. Figure 42-2 provides an overview of the general area in which the legislation pertains and the principal federal actions that protect the consumer debtor.

4. Attaining Credit

The process of granting credit is controlled by two acts of Congress. The first is the Truth in Lending Act. This legislation imposes duties on creditors who wish to extend credit, primarily in the area

FIGURE 42-2 ■ Major Federal Statutes that Protect the Debtor

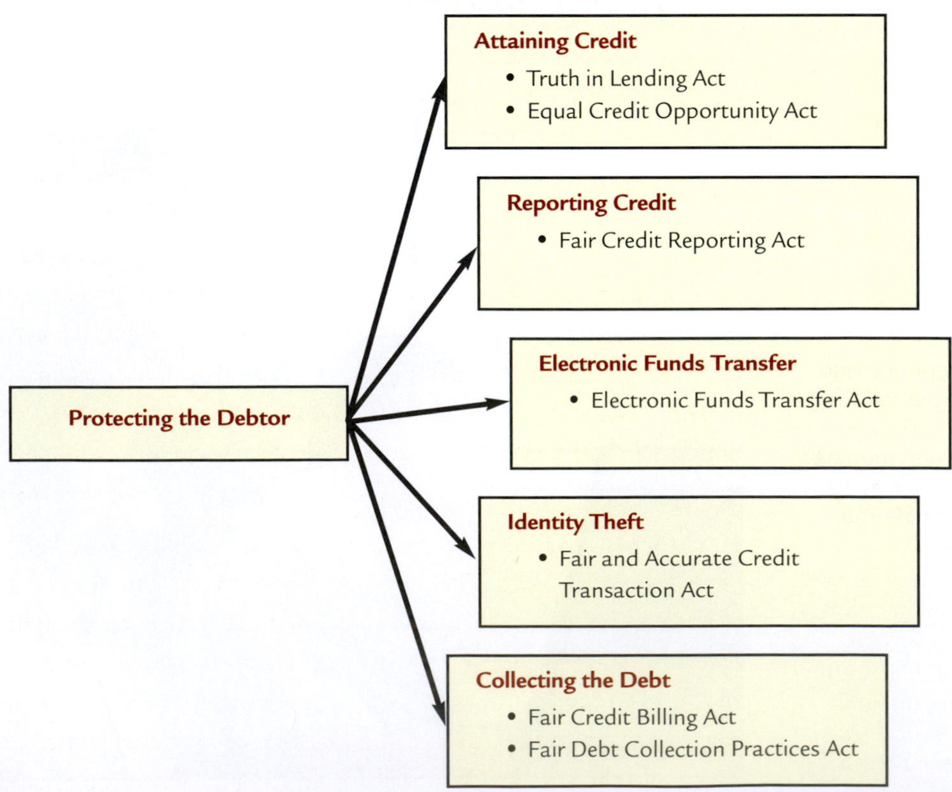

of making disclosures to potential debtors. The second act is called the Equal Credit Opportunity Act. The purpose of this legislation is to forbid creditors from discriminating against individuals applying for credit based on certain criteria that are deemed unconnected to the granting of credit.

Truth in Lending Act

Act of Congress that requires issuers of consumer credit to make certain disclosures to individuals interested in securing credit

TRUTH IN LENDING ACT For the individual applying for credit, the information provided by potential creditors, whether a bank, credit union, or department store, can be confusing. In an effort to assist the consumer in comparing the various credit terms available, Congress originally enacted the **Truth in Lending Act** (TILA) in 1968 as part of the Consumer Protection Act. The law was simplified and improved as part of the Depository Institutions Deregulations and Monetary Control Act of 1980

The TILA applies only to consumer credit transactions and consumer leasing; the provisions of the act do not extend to commercial credit. Further, disclosure provisions apply only to certain types of creditors and only to specific types of credit arrangements. A creditor under the TILA is an individual or institution that regularly grants credit. If Juan loans money to Maria, a family friend, does Juan need to comply with the disclosure provisions of the TILA? Unless Juan was in the business of granting loans or credit, Juan is not deemed to be a creditor subject to the TILA. The act applies to all real estate transactions, but it only applies to other consumers when the amount of the credit extended is $25,000 or less. Finally, the TILA affects credit extensions where either a finance charge will be assessed or the loan is repayable in more than four installments.

The TILA empowers the Federal Reserve Board to enact regulations for the purpose of implementing the act. By far the most important aspect associated with the TILA is *Regulation Z.* Regulation Z mandates that certain disclosures be made for both open-end and close-end credit arrangements. For open-end credit, the provisions of the plan being offered by a creditor must be disclosed before the transaction is consummated and periodically thereafter on each billing statement. For close-end arrangements, the potential customer is provided all necessary disclosures before entering into the contract for credit. All disclosures must be "clear and conspicuous."

Regulation Z also mandates that the finance charge needs to make to any potential debtor. The *finance charge* includes the interest charges, service charges, and credit reporting charges. In addition to disclosing the finance charge, Regulation Z requires disclosure of the annual percentage rate (APR). The APR is a uniform method of calculating the interest rate. Because all creditors must compute the interest rate in the same manner, the debtor can easily compare rates. The APR is calculated based on the amount financed, the finance charge, and the rate of repayment.

The TILA, also, regulates credit card usage. Under provisions of the act, a credit card company may not issue a credit card unless it has been requested; and a credit cardholder's liability is limited to $50 for any charges incurred as a result of unauthorized use, including the situation where the card is lost or stolen. While little change in the regulation of credit cards had occurred for several decades, major legislation aimed at curbing some perceived abuses of credit card companies passed Congress and was signed by the president in 2009. The Credit Card Accountability, Responsibility and Disclosure Act contains a number of provisions, including one that prohibits card companies from raising interest rates on existing balances unless the borrower pays at least 60 days late.

Equal Credit Opportunity Act

Act of Congress that forbids creditors from discriminating against potential debtors on the basis of selected attributes

EQUAL CREDIT OPPORTUNITY ACT Passed by Congress in 1975, the **Equal Credit Opportunity Act** (ECOA) prohibits creditors from discriminating against credit applicants on the basis of sex, marital status, race, color, age, national origin, and religion. In addition, the act forbids creditors from discriminating against an individual because they are on public assistance. The idea behind the ECOA is to require creditors to consider those attributes of a potential debtor that pertain to creditworthiness rather than one's status or attributes associated with one's status that could then be used as a basis for denying the extension of credit.

While little changes in the regulation of credit cards had occurred for several decades, major legislation aimed at curbing some perceived abuses of credit card companies passed Congress and was signed by the president in 2009. The Credit Card Accountability, Responsibility and Disclosure Act contains a number of provisions, including one that prohibits card companies from raising interest rates on existing balances unless the borrower pays at least 60 days late.

While the focus of ECOA is directed to those persons or entities that extend credit to consumers (for personal or family purposes), this legislation also affects many types of commercial credit relationships. In addition, the reach of the ECOA is extremely broad in terms of its substantive provisions. The use of any information relating to the categories addressed above is clearly prohibited. Creditors are forbidden from making statements to applicants that would discourage them from applying for credit. Regulations promulgated under the ECOA provide creditors with considerable guidance regarding what questions may not be asked. For example, the following inquires are illegal:

- What are your birth control practices?
- What capacities do you possess or lack regarding the ability to raise children?
- Does income stated on the application come from alimony or child support?
- Are you married?

With some exceptions, the ECOA requires a creditor to notify an applicant with the creditor within thirty days (30) as to whether credit is going to be extended. If credit is not extended, the creditor must provide a statement of the specific reasons for the adverse decision. For example, Jared applies for a credit card through American Express. Within the stated time for making a decision, American Express sends Jared a letter indicating only that he was "deemed noncreditworthy." A general rationale of this type fails to meet the mandate of regulations emanating from the ECOA; American Express must provide, based on the information supplied by Jared and the investigation conducted by American Express, the specific reasons for denying Jared the credit card.

5. Reporting Credit Information

Once an individual or business has requested credit, the decision to extend credit will be based on information provided by the potential debtor and by consumer credit reporting entities (primarily credit bureaus and investigative reporting companies). Information from such organizations also may be provided to employers as decisions are made regarding whether to hire a particular person. Society has an interest in making sure that the information provided by consumer credit reporting entities is accurate and complete. Congress passed the Fair Credit Reporting Act in 1970 for the purpose of regulating the gathering, preservation, and reporting of credit-related information.

Fair Credit Reporting Act

Act of Congress that controls the gathering, preservation, and reporting of credit-related information

GENERAL PROVISIONS **The Fair Credit Reporting Act** (FCRA) is a comprehensive act aimed at consumer information only; the provisions of this act do not impact the process of granting credit to business organizations. Consumer credit reporting entities are generally divided into two types. A *credit bureau* maintains and distributes to potential creditors information regarding the credit worthiness of potential debtors. *Investigative reporting companies* actively solicit information by questioning acquaintances of the person under review.

Under the FCRA, the reports generated by consumer credit reporting agencies may be furnished to any entity that possesses a legitimate need for the information, including credit card companies, banks, insurance companies, and employers. In this regard, before information is released, the FCRA requires the agency to ascertain the identity of the entity making the request and verify its use.

NOTICE It is important to realize that the FCRA, in general, does not require that the target of the inquiry consent to the disclosure of the credit information. Moreover, consumers are usually not entitled to a copy of the report generated by the consumer credit reporting agency unless they make a specific request (discussed below). There are several situations under the act where the agency may have to be proactive in notifying the consumer-debtor. One situation exits when a consumer credit reporting entity furnishes *a report for employment purposes* that is based on public information and that information may include facts that could have a negative effect on the individual's ability to obtain a job. The consumer is entitled, in most circumstances, to know that public information is being reported by the agency to a prospective employer and to know the name of the prospective employer. Another situation when notice is required occurs if a consumer is *denied credit, insurance, or employment* because of information included in the report provided by a consumer credit reporting agency. In this circumstance, the user of the report (e.g., employer) is charged under the FCRA with notifying the consumer with the name and address of the agency that supplied the report. The final requirement that triggers notice to the consumer occurs when *an investigative report is requested.* The entity asking for the preparation of an investigative report is required by the FCRA to inform the subject of the investigation in writing that an investigation will occur. Further, the consumer must be informed that the report will contain information regarding the consumer's character, personal attributes, and living arrangements, among a host of other private information. As part of the notice, the business requesting the investigative report must inform the consumer of their right to a written disclosure that includes the nature and scope of the investigation.

INFORMATION The FCRA imposes on agencies the affirmative obligation to purge their files of *obsolete information,* generally once information is seven years old. Exceptions to this purging requirement exist. For example, information about bankruptcies may remain for 10 years. In the case of investigative reports, the FCRA mandates that information older than three months must be reverified before it can be used again.

The FCRA allows a consumer the opportunity to *dispute information* included in a credit report. When a consumer objects to such information, the consumer credit reporting agency may be required to reinvestigate and confirm information included in the report. If erroneous information is found by the agency after conducting a review, such information must be deleted. In those situations where the consumer continues to object to the report after reinvestigation, provisions of the FCRA allow the consumer to have a statement placed in the file that reflects the consumer's objections. Also, the consumer may request that notice of alleged inaccuracies be sent to all prior users of the report.

While reporting agencies must follow reasonable procedures to ensure accurate information is included, no specific requirements are required by the FCRA. The following case presents an instance where the court is asked, in part, to determine whether the requirements of reasonable compliance were met.

CASE

Wood v. Holiday Inns, Inc., et al.

UNITED STATES COURT OF APPEALS FOR THE FIFTH CIRCUIT

508 F.2d 167 (1975)

LEWIS R. MORGAN, CIRCUIT JUDGE

Glen Wood, an executive vice president of SAR Manufacturing Company, checked into the Holiday Inn facility at Phenix City, Alabama, during the late afternoon of February 1, 1972. When Wood checked in, he tendered payment for his room by using his Gulf Oil Company credit card. An imprint was made of his card, and it was returned to him, as was the normal practice.

After Gulf issues a card it continues to evaluate a customer account; and, if it concludes from available information that a customer cannot afford to pay, it cancels credit to that customer. In order to facilitate this process, Gulf furnishes to National Data Corporation a list of all credit

continued

cancellations. Under the system established by Gulf, Holiday Inns are authorized to contact National Data, which disperses undetailed credit information concerning Gulf credit cards upon inquiry by telephone from properly identified parties authorized to extend credit to Gulf card holders. The information is generally brief and consists of either an authorization or denial of credit.

Gulf maintained a file on Wood. In compiling its information, Gulf had received a credit report on the plaintiff from a credit bureau in Tupelo, Mississippi. The report was incomplete in that it did not contain the plaintiff's annual income; in all other respects the credit report was favorable to the plaintiff.

The credit manager of Gulf testified that on January 17, 1972, sixteen days preceding the incident in question, he reviewed the credit file of Wood. Although the file was current at the time he reviewed it, he expressed concern about the increasing amounts which were being charged on the card in relation to Wood's monthly income and made the determination that Wood's card should be placed in the "derog" file. Apparently, Wood had not informed Gulf that the credit card was used for business as well as personal expenses. Wood was not notified, but Gulf directed National Data to give the following reply to anyone seeking credit approval on Wood:

> *Pick up travel card. Do not extend further credit. Send card to billing office for reward.*

Sometime during the early morning of February 2, 1972, Jessie Goynes, the "night auditor" of the Phenix City Holiday Inn, called National Data in Atlanta on a toll-free number provided by Gulf in order to confirm the plaintiff's credit card number and receive an authorization to extend credit on the basis of the card. He received a communication from National Data advising him: "Do not honor this sale. Pick up the credit card and send it in for reward."

Wood testified that Goynes awakened him about 5:00 a.m. and told Wood that he, Goynes, needed the credit card for the purpose of making another imprint since the imprint at the time of the registration was indistinct. Goynes then came to appellant's room and took his card for the avowed purpose of securing the imprint and with the promise to return it in a few minutes. After 30 minutes Wood became concerned because his card had not been returned and was fearful that someone had taken it under a scheme to fraudulently secure it. Wood then dressed and went to the front desk of the motel where he was told by Goynes that the card was "seized upon the authority of National Data" and that cash payment was required. Goynes refused to call Gulf Oil at appellant's request. Wood then paid in cash and left the motel. Upon returning home Wood called Gulf and explained that he used the card for business purposes. He complained that his account was current and his credit was immediately reinstated.

Goynes, however, stated that after getting the directive from National Data, he telephoned the plaintiff's room at 7:00 a.m., and advised him that he was unable to obtain credit authorization and requested plaintiff to surrender the card. Goynes said that Wood voluntarily complied.

At any rate, Wood's anger and frustration continued to build. Three days later, while he was relating the incident to a friend, he had a heart attack, precipitated apparently by the stress of the incidents surrounding the revocation of credit.

Wood sued the Gulf Oil Corporation, Holiday Inns, Inc., Interstate Inns, Inc. (the owner of the Phenix City Holiday Inn) and Jessie Goynes. Interstate and Goynes denied any negligence or wrongful conduct and asserted by way of cross-claim that they were acting under the direction of Gulf and were, therefore, entitled to indemnification by Gulf.

After trial, the jury returned a verdict in favor of Wood but apportioned damages in the amounts of $25,000 compensatory damages against Gulf, $25,000 punitive damages against Interstate and Goynes, and $10,000 punitive damages against Holiday Inns. The court then granted the motions of Gulf and Holiday Inns, Inc., for judgments notwithstanding the verdict and granted the motion of Interstate and Goynes for a new trial.

Wood appeals. Interstate and Goynes also appeal the district court's action in overturning the jury's verdict on the cross-claim in their favor through the granting of Gulf's motion for judgment notwithstanding the verdict.

Wood's primary claim against Gulf is based upon the Fair Credit Reporting Act. The Act charges "consumer reporting agencies" and users of "consumer credit reports" with various responsibilities. Failure to discharge these duties appropriately may give rise to civil liability.

Wood alleged that Gulf negligently failed to comply with the provisions of the Fair Credit Reporting Act as both a consumer reporting agency and a user of a consumer report. Gulf argues that it was not a consumer-reporting agency as defined in 15 U.S.C. § 1681a(f), and the district court so held, apparently as a matter of law.

The Act defines a consumer-reporting agency as:

> Any person which, for monetary fees, dues, or on a cooperative nonprofit basis, regularly engages in whole or in part in the practice of assembling or evaluating consumer credit information or other information on consumers for the purpose of furnishing consumer reports to third parties ... 15 U.S.C. § 1681a(f).

Gulf vigorously asserts that it falls outside the purview of this statute because no third party was furnished a report. In essence, Gulf contends, and the district court held, that the credit in this case was to be extended only by Gulf, not by Interstate. Hence, while Gulf did terminate Wood's credit vis-a-vis Gulf, it did not make a report advising Interstate as to whether to extend its own credit.

Much of the confusion in this case stems from the multifaceted position of the Phenix City facility, the recipient of Gulf's communication. The Phenix City Holiday Inn accepted the Gulf credit card and was therefore Gulf's representative in facilitating the extension of Gulf's credit. The Phenix City facility also honored a number of major credit cards; and, in fact, nothing prevented the Phenix City Inn from extending credit on its own account.

The communication by Gulf to the Phenix City Inn was made to a separate business entity. However, the credit to be extended was Gulf's, and the Phenix City facility was merely acting as Gulf's representative in extending the credit. Hence, the communication was not "for the purpose of furnishing consumer reports to third parties." It was merely directed from Gulf to its local representative, made for the purpose of protecting Gulf rather than for the purpose of influencing the Phenix City Inn's own credit decision.

Hence, we feel that the district judge properly dismissed the cause of action under the Fair Credit Reporting Act.

■ *Affirmed but remanded on other grounds.*

CASE CONCEPT REVIEW

1. What actions of the hotel were proper? What actions were improper?
2. Why was Gulf not a "user" under the Fair Credit Reporting Act?

6. Electronic Funds Transfers

The phenomenal growth in the use of technology as the means of transferring funds has brought with it significant concerns relating to the potential for unauthorized use of funds, among other situations that may adversely impact a consumer's account. Congress responded in 1978 to these concerns by enacting the **Electronic Funds Transfer Act** (EFTA).

Electronic Funds Transfer Act

Act of Congress aimed at controlling processes of banks and other institutions relating to the electronic transfer of funds within a consumer's account

SUBSTANTIVE PROVISIONS The EFTA controls the flow of funds for accounts that were established primarily for consumers. The act covers a variety of types of transactions, including direct deposits and withdrawals, dealings with automated teller machines, and point-of-sale transactions with merchants. Three areas of electronic funds transfers are impacted by the EFTA. First, Congress has mandated in provisions of the EFTA that banking institutions investigate quickly claims that an error was made by a bank. If the institution determines an error occurred, it must correct the error within one business day from the date that the determination was made. If an investigation reveals no error, the customer must be notified within three business days. Also, the EFTA requires institutions to make certain disclosures regarding the terms of the contract creating electronic funds transferring services. Finally, the act establishes requirements for the types of documentation the banking institution must provide at the time a transfer is made and on regular intervals for each account so that the customer can check to see if errors were made.

LIABILITY A consumer's liability for unauthorized transfers under the EFTA is limited to $50 or the amount obtained in the transfer, whichever is less, for those transactions that were made before the customer notified the bank that unauthorized use had occurred. There is no liability for transactions that occur after the bank is notified. However, if the consumer fails to notify the bank of the loss within two business days from the time that the customer learns of the loss, the maximum amount that the customer is responsible for increases to $500.

A financial institution is liable if it fails to properly make an electronic funds transfer or fails to honor a customer's request to stop payment on a preauthorized transfer. Liability does not attach if there are insufficient funds in the customer's account, if the transfer would exceed a credit limit, or if an ATM fails to have sufficient cash to complete the transaction.

7. Identity Theft

Identity theft is an increasingly serious concern for both consumers and members of the business community. The Federal Trade Commission has estimated that more than 10 million individuals annually are the objects of identity theft, sometimes on a reoccurring basis. With greater reliance on Social Security, credit card, and bank account numbers to facilitate transactions, all of us are at risk that someone will steal those numbers and commit fraud in the purchase of goods and services in the name of another. In 2003, Congress amended the Fair Credit Reporting Act with the **Fair and Accurate Credit Transaction Act** (FACT Act).

Fair and Accurate Credit Transaction Act

Act of Congress that creates attempts to reduce the impact on individuals who are the target of identity theft schemes

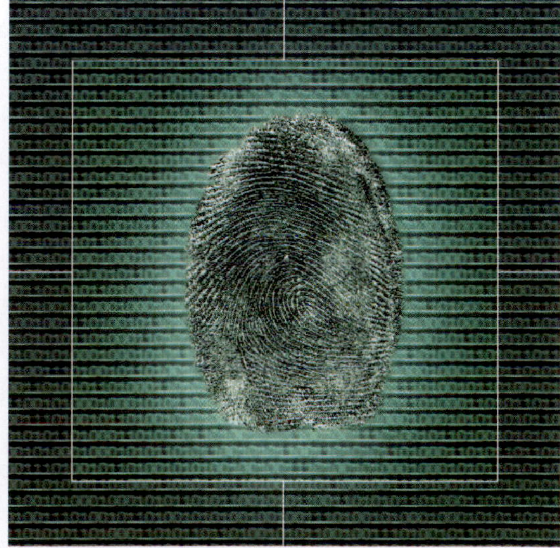

Victims of identity theft may take advantage of a national fraud alert system

One provision of the legislation creates a national fraud alert system that allows the victims of identity theft to file a fraud alert with consumer credit reporting companies and have the alert posed as part of the consumer's credit report. When a business discovers the fraud alert on a credit report, they must verify the identity of the individual desiring to secure credit before issuing credit. The FACT Act also includes mechanisms aimed at assisting victims of identity theft to rebuild their credit reputations.

8. Collecting the Debt

Creditors have the option of using the judicial process as a means of securing a judgment from a court and then pursuing payment of the judgment (usually through an examination of a judgment debtor, execution (forced sale of property), or garnishment of wages or bank account). The judicial option, however, can be time-consuming and expensive. Therefore, creditors have adopted a host of other methods aimed at encouraging consumers to pay their debts, particularly if the debtor is in arrears. Unfortunately, the nature of the debt-collecting process affords creditors many opportunities to exceed the boundaries of propriety as they attempt to recover sums owed to them. Congress has acted on two main fronts to prevent creditors from acting in an unconscionable fashion as they attempt, without the assistance of the court system, to collect a debt. One law, the Fair Credit Billing Act, is addressed at credit cards and charge cards. The other, the Fair Debt Collection Practices Act, covers all types of consumer credit transactions.

Fair Credit Billing Act

An Act of Congress that provides a mechanism for consumers to remedy errors received on credit card bills.

FAIR CREDIT BILLING ACT Just as Congress was concerned about the impact of errors regarding electronic funds transfers when the EFTA was passed, the increased use of computers by creditors in the credit billing process was a major reason Congress passed the **Fair Credit Billing Act** (FCBA), an amendment to the Truth in Lending Act, in 1974. The FCBA provides a mechanism for consumers who use a credit card and then discover errors on their bill. This act provides that a creditor must make certain disclosures to any prospective debtor and requires that certain disclosures be repeated in the periodic statements presented to the debtor. This act also allows consumers to dispute billing errors by notifying the creditor of a dispute within sixty days of the time when the error was detected. After receiving notice, the creditor has ninety days to investigate the claim and either correct the account or explain why no error exists.

Another provision of the FCBA prohibits banks from using money in a debtor's checking or savings account to pay a delinquent credit card account with the same bank. Finally, the FCBA allows a customer to sue the credit company, instead of the merchant, if there is a dispute regarding the quality of goods or services provided. The amount of a claim under this provision, however, cannot exceed the amount of charges on the account for the goods or services.

Fair Debt Collection Practices Act

An Act of Congress that controls the behavior of debt collectors

FAIR DEBT COLLECTION PRACTICES ACT With individual states providing a patchwork of protection to consumer debtors, in 1978 Congress amended the Consumer Credit Protection Act with the **Fair Debt Collection Practices Act** (FDCRA) to establish a uniform set of guidelines to control debt collectors. The act specifies that its provisions apply to the activities of third-party debt collectors (e.g., collection agencies), not to actions of the original creditor. Some states, however, have statutory provisions that also regulate the practices of those businesses that collect their own debts.

Substantive provisions of the FDCRA prohibit debt collectors from participating in "abusive and deceptive" behaviors, and it does so in rather specific ways. For example, the FDCRA:

- mandates that debt collectors may not contact consumer debtors by telephone from 9:00 p.m. to 8:00 a.m.

- prohibits the use of obscene language, threats of arrest, false or misleading statements (including false statements such as, "I am an attorney," or "I am an agent with the government)"
- prevents a debtor collector from publishing on the Internet or in a newspaper the consumer's name and address on a "bad debt" list
- forbids debt collectors from communicating with the debtor's friends, neighbors, employers, and most family members (e.g., a spouse may be contacted)
- requires debt collectors to identify themselves as a third-party debt collector
- empowers a debtor with the ability to cause all communications between the debtor and the debt collector to stop if the debtor so states in writing
- provides that a debt collector must give to the debtor the name and address of the original creditor, if asked

Consider the following case where language in a demand letter threatens legal action.

CASE

Elizabeth Brown, on Behalf of Herself and All Others Similarly Situated, f/k/a Elizabeth Schenck, Appellant v. Card Service Center; Cardholder Management Services

UNITED STATES COURT OF APPEALS FOR THE THIRD CIRCUIT

464 F.3d 450 (2006)

FUENTES, CIRCUIT JUDGE

Seeking to recover what it considered a bad debt, Card Service Center sent Elizabeth Brown a collection letter telling her that unless she made arrangements to pay within five days, the matter "could" result in referral of the account to an attorney and "could" result in "a legal suit being filed." Brown sued, claiming that because Card Service Center had no intention of referring her account to an attorney and no intention of filing a law suit, the letter violates the Fair Debt Collection Practices Act's ban on false, misleading or deceptive communications. The District Court dismissed Brown's suit, concluding that because "[t]he letter neither states nor implies that legal action is imminent, only that it is possible," Brown had failed to state a claim upon which relief could be granted. We disagree, and for the reasons that follow we vacate the District Court's judgment and remand for further proceedings.

Card Service Center and Cardholder Management Services (collectively, "CSC") are debt-collection firms. In February 2004, CSC sent Brown a collection letter (the "CSC Letter") demanding payment of a delinquent credit card balance of $1,874, which it stated was due. The letter threatened referral of Brown's account to CSC's attorney if payment was not made within five days. In relevant part, the letter reads:

> *You are requested to contact the Recovery Unit of the Card Service Center ... to discuss your account.*
>
> *Refusal to cooperate could result in a legal suit being filed for collection of the account.*
>
> *You now have five (5) days to make arrangements for payment of this account. Failure on your part to cooperate could result in our forwarding this account to our attorney with directions to continue collection efforts.*

Though Brown did not make arrangements for payment on her delinquent account within five days, CSC did not institute a suit or otherwise enlist an attorney to assist with its collection efforts. Rather, Brown's decision not to comply with CSC's request resulted only in her receiving additional debt-collection letters from CSC.

In February 2005, Brown filed suit against CSC in the United States District Court for the Eastern District of Pennsylvania on behalf of herself and all other similarly situated Pennsylvania consumers. In her complaint Brown alleged that the CSC Letter contained "false and misleading" statements "designed to coerce and intimidate the consumer ... by false threat" and that the complaint suggested a deadline for debtor action that was "false and overstated." In support of this claim, Brown alleged that the 5-day deadline was illusory because CSC never intended to bring suit against her or to refer her debt-or that of the members of her putative class-to an attorney.

In response to the complaint, CSC filed a motion to dismiss the complaint for failure to state a claim under the Fair Debt Collection Practices Act (the "FDCPA" or the "Act"). The District Court granted the motion without prejudice in June 2005. The District Court's order dismissing the complaint, which was amended by a second order in August 2005, granted Brown through the end of September to conduct further investigation so that she might amend her complaint, with the caveat that if she failed to do so, the June dismissal would automatically

continued

become a dismissal with prejudice. Brown opted not to amend her complaint, and the dismissal became final. This appeal followed.

Brown maintains that the CSC Letter ran afoul of § 1692e of the FDCPA, which reads in relevant part:

> A debt collector may not use any false, deceptive, or misleading representation or means in connection with the collection of any debt. Without limiting the general application of the foregoing, the following conduct is a violation of this section: …
>
> (5) The threat to take any action that cannot legally be taken or that is not intended to be taken.

Because CSC qualifies as a "debt collector" under the Act, to the extent the CSC Letter is "false, deceptive, or misleading" or constitutes a "threat to take any action … not intended to be taken," it violates § 1692e.

A significant purpose of the Act is not only to eliminate abusive practices by debt collectors, but also "to insure that those debt collectors who refrain from using abusive debt collection practices are not competitively disadvantaged." Accordingly, the Act provides consumers with a private cause of action against debt collectors who fail to comply with the Act. A prevailing plaintiff under the Act is entitled to an award of damages, costs of suit, and reasonable attorneys' fees.

Because the FDCPA is a remedial statute, we construe its language broadly, so as to affect its purpose. Accordingly, in considering claims under another provision of the FDCPA, we have held that certain communications from lenders to debtors should be analyzed from the perspective of the "least sophisticated debtor."

The least sophisticated debtor standard requires more than "simply examining whether particular language would deceive or mislead a reasonable debtor" because a communication that would not deceive or mislead a reasonable debtor might still deceive or mislead the least sophisticated debtor. This lower standard comports with a basic purpose of the FDCPA: as previously stated, to protect "all consumers, the gullible as well as the shrewd," "the trusting as well as the suspicious," from abusive debt collection practices. However, while the least sophisticated debtor standard protects naive consumers, it also prevents liability for bizarre or idiosyncratic interpretations of collection notices by preserving a quotient of reasonableness and presuming a basic level of understanding and willingness to read with care.

In its thorough analysis, the District Court determined that, even accepting all of Brown's factual allegations as true and drawing all reasonable inferences in her favor, no reasonable reading of her complaint could entitle her to relief. In reaching this conclusion, the District Court emphasized that the CSC Letter employed the conditional term "could" as opposed to the affirmative term "will." The District Court observed that the CSC Letter "neither states nor implies that legal action is imminent, only that it is possible."

We disagree with the District Court because we conclude that it would be deceptive under the FDCPA for CSC to assert that it could take an action that it had no intention of taking and has never or very rarely taken before. The CSC Letter highlights two possible outcomes for debtors failing to respond within five days: the commencement of a lawsuit or the referral of the debt to CSC's attorney. In her complaint, Brown alleges that CSC never intended to file a suit against her for collection, never had any intention of referring her case to its attorney, and that as a matter of course, CSC does not "refer class member's [sic] alleged debts to their attorney for prosecution, but only refer[s] the alleged debt(s) to another collection agency." In light of these allegations, Brown has stated a claim under § 1692e upon which relief can be granted.

Upon reading the CSC Letter, the least sophisticated debtor might get the impression that litigation or referral to a CSC lawyer would be imminent if he or she did not respond within five days. If Brown can prove, after discovery that CSC seldom litigated or referred debts such as Brown's and those of the putative class members to an attorney, a jury could conclude that the CSC Letter was deceptive or misleading vis-à-vis the least sophisticated debtor.

We therefore vacate the judgment of the District Court and remand for further proceedings consistent with this opinion.

■ *Vacated and remanded.*

CASE CONCEPT REVIEW

1. Is the intent of the creditor to pursue promised actions pivotal in determining whether the FDCPA is violated?
2. What is the "least sophisticated debtor" standard?
3. Why did the court side with the debtor?

Under the FDCPA, a debt collector must notify a debtor with 30 days that the debtor has the right to dispute all or part of the debt. At that point, the collection activities must stop and the debt collector must investigate the allegation. Once the debt collector provides evidence that the claim is verified, it may continue the collection process.

CHAPTER SUMMARY

PROTECTING THE PURCHASER

Labeling and Packaging

1. Federal legislation aimed at controlling the content of wording used on labels and packaging can be categorized as addressing concerns associated with all products, certain types of products, or dangerous products.

Advertising
1. Puffery is a category of promotional statements made by business about a product or service that are not intended to be taken literally.
2. Deceptive advertising, according to the Federal Trade Commission (FTC), includes any material misrepresentation or omission likely to mislead a potential customer and would likely mislead a reasonable customer.

Sales
1. The FTC promulgates and enforces regulations dealing with door-to-door sales, telephone and mail-order sales, and on-line sales.

PROTECTING THE DEBTOR

Attaining Credit
1. The Truth in Lending Act requires that entities desiring to extend credit make certain disclosures to the consuming public.
2. The Equal Credit Opportunity Act forbids creditors from discriminating against potential debtors on the basis of selected attributes.

Reporting Credit Information
1. The Fair Credit Reporting Act controls the gathering, preservation, and reporting of credit-related information.

Electronic Funds Transfers
1. The Electronic Funds Transfer Act regulates the processes banks and other institutions use to transfer consumer funds through electronic means.

Identity Theft
1. The Fair and Accurate Credit Transaction Act attempts to reduce the impact on individuals who are the target of identity theft schemes.

Collecting the Debt
1. The Fair Credit Billing Act provides a mechanism for consumers to remedy errors received on credit card bills.
2. The Fair Debt Collection Practices Act controls the behavior of debt collectors.

REVIEW QUESTIONS AND PROBLEMS

1. Match each term in Column A with the appropriate statement in Column B.

A	B
(1) Puffery	(a) Forbids creditors from discriminating in the granting of credit based on selected attributes
(2) Deceptive advertising	(b) Legislation controlling the actions of debt collection agencies
(3) Consumer Product Safety Commission	(c) Provides a mechanism for consumers who use a credit card to dispute billing errors
(4) Truth in Lending Act	(d) Statements made about a product or service that violate FTC rules
(5) Equal Credit Opportunity Act	(e) Mandates that a creditor make disclosures
(6) Fair Credit Reporting Act	(f) Legislation aimed at identity theft
(7) Electronic Funds Transfer Act	(g) Regulates ATM transfers

continues

(8) Fair and Accurate Credit Transaction Act	(h) Allows a consumer the opportunity to dispute information included in a credit report
(9) Fair Credit Billing Act	(i) Promotional statements made by business about a product or service
(10) Fair Debt Collection Practices Act	(j) Federal agency charged with making sure products are not dangerous

2. Create a one-line statement about a common product that is mere puffery. Then, fashion another one-line statement about a product that qualifies as deceptive advertising.
3. What are the elements of deceptive advertising according to the FTC?
4. Miranda's Auto Sales sells previously owned cars. Some sales are made on a cash basis, but most are sales based on an installment payment contract. The company provides a cash price and a "deferred payment price." However, they are the same price. Miranda's Auto Sales discloses the finance charge as zero and the annual percentage rate as zero. Is the company violating the Truth in Lending Act? Why?
5. Blanche and Thomas, husband and wife, apply for a $300,000 loan to purchase a home. The loan is approved; but they are told that because of their credit record, the lending institution had to raise the interest rate by 2% over what was originally contemplated in the application documents. What law may be violated? Why?
6. Machelle applied for an oil company credit card. The company uses a computerized system to evaluate credit applications. One factor is ZIP codes. A low rating is assigned for applicants who live in selected ZIP code areas. Machelle, a white woman, lives in a predominately Hispanic neighborhood that was assigned a low rating because of its ZIP code. What law may be violated? Why?
7. Pluto was convicted of stealing government property, but the conviction was set aside under the Youth Corrections Act. Pluto was hired as an insurance agent, but a credit report stated that Pluto, as a youth, had been convicted and that the conviction had been set aside. In other words, the credit report was accurate. Pluto then lost his job. Pluto sued to obtain an order to prohibit the credit agency from reporting the conviction and to set aside information under the Fair Credit Reporting Act. Will Pluto be successful? Why?
8. Freddy had his wallet stolen while he was eating at a local restaurant. On the next day, Freddy reported to his credit card company that his wallet containing the card was stolen. On the day of the theft, Freddy had a $600 unauthorized charge. The day after Freddy reported the theft, Freddy had a $900 charge. What law applies? What is Freddy's liability?
9. Golden and his family run a family farm in Iowa. The farm had severe financial problems, and Golden was forced to assign a large portion of their income to creditors for several years. Golden's brother and father both died from cancer, and Golden agreed to pay medical expenses for each. The Mayo Clinic was owed $1,000 by Golden for medical treatments for his brother and father. Mayo has a long-standing policy of not charging interest on debts owed. Mayo authorized ABC Collections to pursue payment of the principal amount only. ABC representatives called Golden's home numerous times during a day for several weeks. Some of the conversations became heated, with ABC Collections representatives threatening Golden and calling him a "deadbeat." ABC finally sued for both the principal and interest. What act may be violated? Why?

10. Benny owed a debt to ABC Stores. ABC Stores turned Benny's debt over to A-1 Collection Agency. A-1 sent a letter to Benny that included this language: "Final Notice. Next step is to notify attorney. You have five days." Has A-1 violated the Fair Debt Collection Practices Act? Why?

Internet Resources

The federal government provides a site that captures a wide array of consumer protection web sites at: http://www.consumer.gov

The Federal Trade Commission offers specific information that deals with debtor protection through various Internet sites. For example:

Information dealing with Identity Theft is available at: http://www.ftc.gov/bcp/edu/microsites/idtheft/

The latest annual report to Congress regarding FDCPA enforcement activities, including the number of consumer complaints, is provided at: http://www.ftc.gov/os/2008/03/P084802fdcpareport.pdf

Environmental Regulation | 43

CHAPTER OUTLINE

1. Business, Law, and the Environment: An Overview

GOVERNMENT REGULATION OF THE ENVIRONMENT

2. The National Environmental Policy Act
3. Regulatory Agencies

AIR POLLUTION

4. Air Pollution Regulatory Principles
5. Enforcement of the Clean Air Act
6. Current Issues in Air Pollution Control

WATER POLLUTION

7. Water Pollution Regulatory Principles
8. Enforcement of the Clean Water Act

WATER POLLUTION

9. Solid Waste
10. Hazardous and Toxic Waste

TOXIC SUBSTANCES

11. The Toxic Substances Control Act

CHAPTER PREVIEW

Government action aimed at regulating the impact of business on the physical environment is a very recent area of law. Many also recognize this area of government regulation as overly burdensome on business, and all parties agree it is becoming increasingly complex. Little doubt exists today, however, that protection of the environment deserves the attention of law makers. Our physical environment, of course, creates pollutants. However, Nature incorporates mechanisms to clean the pollutants. A volcano spews forth highly toxic gases, but in time those gases are diluted and absorbed. Similarly, hot ash from a volcano falling on a forest may level all vegetation, but in years the foliage returns.

Unfortunately, a number of factors—human factors—have arisen in recent decades causing members of society to wonder whether we are overburdening Nature's ability to process waste products generated from human sources. With business being responsible for a large share of these additional substances, government regulation aimed at protecting the environment necessarily impacts manufacturers and other members of the business community. We also increasingly recognize that the byproducts of production can be extremely harmful to humans and the environment. Based on this possibility of considerable harm and greater scientific knowledge, both federal and state governments have become quite active in regulating business for the purpose of securing a cleaner environment. This chapter organizes the area of environmental regulation into four subjects: (1) air pollution, (2) water pollution, (3) waste management, and (4) toxic substances.

BUSINESS MANAGEMENT DECISION

Your company operates a successful manufacturing plant in Ohio. The president of the firm wants to establish a second plant. You are charged with the responsibility of finding another location in the United States. What legal factors would you consider in reviewing possible sites and making a recommendation to the president?

1. Business, Law, and the Environment: An Overview

An individual's right to sue another for harm caused to the air, ground, and water around them dates back centuries. The early common law of England includes cases where one property owner sues another to recover for harm done to property. For example, if a dam located on one farmer's land breaks as a result of poor upkeep of the dam, affected land owners down stream could sue for *negligence* under common law principles. Another cause of action that could be employed by a private party who has suffered a loss of their right to use or enjoy their property is the tort of *nuisance.* This tort is used where the interference is non-trespassory in nature. Consider the following scenario. Sandeep started a poultry farm three years ago. Marcus has lived in his home, one-quarter mile away from the poultry farm, for fifty years. The odor from the poultry farm is overpowering, and the flies generated from the business are a constant bother. Marcus would probably be successful in bringing a private nuisance action. In contrast with the law of negligence where the defendant's fault is an issue, the focus of a private nuisance suit is on the harm created.

What can the government do, however, in the public sector to protect the environment and control the impact of the commercial activities associated with agriculture and commerce, particularly manufacturing? As we experience population growth, limitations on natural resources, and the recognition of greater risks to our health and safety from business activities, the government

Public nuisance

Action brought by the government, usually to stop or prevent pollution, where there is an actual or potential loss of a right to use or enjoy property

is well suited to act. One possibility is through the common law. **Public nuisance** actions are a conventional legal action government entities use, usually to stop or reduce pollution. Public officials can employ nuisance actions to secure an injunction from a court that will prohibit a company from continuing to discharge waste contaminates into a stream or into the air.

Unfortunately, common law remedies (including nuisance) are a cumbersome and complicated method of addressing the issue. Damage must have already occurred, and suits are brought on an individual basis. Moreover, a topic as far-reaching as environmental protection deserves a public stage for the purpose of debating the views of competing interests as society struggles with defining what activities that adversely impact our environment will be deemed illegal. With the failure of common law remedies to address environmental protection as production methods became more complex and instances of pollution increased, beginning in the 1950s, Congress enacted a number of important statutes aimed at abating pollution and protecting our physical environment.

Congressional action aimed at addressing environmental issues allows all interested parties to provide information regarding the advantages and disadvantages of various approaches to address a specific environmental concern. Also, because of the complexity of the subject, administrative agencies are heavily involved in the process of regulating business. Finally, as with any regulatory process, the courts are available to hear disputes regarding the propriety of applying laws or regulations in specific instances. While the focus of this chapter is on environmental regulation within the United States, it is important to note that every country addresses this topic in its own manner—weighing various public policy factors in crafting an appropriate response. With a global economy, however, there is increasing interest in coordinating the responses of individual governments to environmental issues.

GOVERNMENTAL REGULATION OF THE ENVIRONMENT

2. The National Environmental Policy Act

The National Environmental Policy Act (NEPA) was passed by Congress in 1969. The act accomplishes two goals. First, it states clearly that as a matter of national policy, the federal government is entrusted with the responsibility of ensuring that successive generations can enjoy the environment. Specifically, NEPA provides the following:

Congress recognized that the natural environment should be protected for future generations. NEPA was thus created.

> The Congress, recognizing the profound impact of man's activity on the interrelations of all components of the natural environment, particularly the profound influences of population growth, high-density urbanization, industrial expansion, resource exploitation, and new and expanding technological advances and recognizing further the critical importance of restoring and maintaining environmental quality to the overall welfare and development of man, declares that it is the continuing policy of the Federal Government, in cooperation with State and local governments, and other concerned public and private organizations, to use all practicable means and measures, including financial and technical assistance, in a manner calculated to foster and promote the general welfare, to create and maintain conditions under which man and nature can exist in productive harmony, and fulfill the social, economic, and other requirements of present and future generations of Americans.

While land use regulation is primarily the responsibility of state and local government, NEPA expressly requires that the federal government will have a significant role in protecting the physical environment.

Environmental impact statement
Prepared by the federal government, the document that addresses those actions associated with a proposed federal project that might affect the environment

Also, NEPA requires that the federal government prepare an **environmental impact statement** (EIS) for every major federal action that significantly affects the quality of the environment. An EIS must be prepared by the federal government, for example, if it wishes to construct a dam as part of a federal flood control project. The EIS must (1) describe the environmental impact of the proposed action, (2) present adverse effects on the environment that might result from the action, (3) discuss alternative actions to the proposed action that could be taken, (4) provide short- and long-term impacts, and (5) list any irreversible impacts on the environment resulting from the proposed action.

In preparing the EIS, the federal agency proposing the project must solicit opinions from other regulatory entities (federal, state, and local) and interested private parties (perhaps members of the business community or the environmental community). Should an agency decide that a particular project does not warrant the preparation of an EIS, members of the local community, environmental groups, and others may challenge that decision in court. The required scope of an EIS is addressed in the following case.

CASE

Metropolitan Edison Company v. People Against Nuclear Energy

SUPREME COURT OF THE UNITED STATES

460 U.S. 766 (1983)

JUSTICE REHNQUIST DELIVERED THE OPINION OF THE COURT

The issue in these cases is whether petitioner Nuclear Regulatory Commission (NRC) complied with the National Environmental Policy Act of 1969 (NEPA) when it considered whether to permit petitioner Metropolitan Edison Co. to resume operation of the Three Mile Island Unit 1 nuclear powerplant (TMI-1). The Court of Appeals for the District of Columbia Circuit held that the NRC improperly failed to consider whether the risk of an accident at TMI-1 might cause harm to the psychological health and community well-being of residents of the surrounding area. We reverse.

Metropolitan owns two nuclear powerplants at Three Mile Island near Harrisburg, Pa. Both of these plants were licensed by the NRC after extensive proceedings, which included preparation of Environmental Impact Statements (EIS's). On March 28, 1979, TMI-1 was not operating; it had been shut down for refueling. TMI-2 was operating, and it suffered a serious accident that damaged the reactor. Although, as it turned out, no dangerous radiation was released, the accident caused widespread concern. The Governor of Pennsylvania recommended an evacuation of all pregnant women and small children, and many area residents did leave their homes for several days.

Respondent People Against Nuclear Energy (PANE) intervened and responded to this invitation. PANE is an association of residents of the Harrisburg area who are opposed to further operation of either TMI reactor. PANE contended that restarting TMI-1 would cause both severe psychological health damage to persons living in the vicinity, and serious damage to the stability, cohesiveness, and well-being of the neighboring communities.

Our understanding of the congressional concerns that led to the enactment of NEPA suggests that the terms "environmental effect" and "environmental impact" in § 102 be read to include a requirement of a reasonably close causal relationship between a change in the physical environment and the effect at issue. This requirement is like the familiar doctrine of proximate cause from tort law.

PANE argues that the psychological health damage it alleges "will flow directly from the risk of [a nuclear] accident," but a risk of an accident is not an effect on the physical environment. A risk is, by definition, unrealized in the physical world. In a causal chain from renewed operation of TMI-1 to psychological health damage, the element of risk and its perception by PANE's members are necessary middle links. We believe that the element of risk lengthens the causal chain beyond the reach of NEPA.

Risk is a pervasive element of modern life; to say more would belabor the obvious. Many of the risks we face are generated by modern technology, which brings both the possibility of major accidents and opportunities for tremendous achievements. Medical experts apparently agree that risk can generate stress in human beings that, in turn, may rise to the level of serious health damage. For this reason, among many others, the question of whether the gains from any technological advance are worth its attendant risks may be an important public policy issue. Nonetheless, it is quite different from the question whether the same gains are worth a given level of alteration of our physical environment or depletion of our natural resources. The latter question, rather than the former, is the central concern of NEPA.

Time and resources are simply too limited for us to believe that Congress intended to extend NEPA as far as the Court of Appeals has taken it. If contentions of psychological health damage caused by risk were cognizable under NEPA, agencies would, at the very least, be obliged to expend considerable resources developing psychiatric expertise that is not otherwise relevant to their congressionally assigned functions. The available resources may be spread so thin that agencies are unable adequately to pursue protection of the physical environment and natural resources.

■ *Reversed and remanded.*

CASE CONCEPT REVIEW

1. Why does the Supreme Court of the United States rule that potential psychological harm is not within the realm of NEPA?
2. If PANE were to prevail, how would psychological harm be shown?

Because business organizations usually are intimately involved in working on a federal project, commercial enterprises that contract to provide materials, services, or other types of expertise to the federal government also may be impacted greatly by an EIS. An EIS is required when there is "federal action," a term that might well include the granting of permits to private organizations. The Federal Bureau of Land Management's decision to grant a permit for a group of investors to build a ski resort on federal land or for a rancher to graze cattle on federal land might well invoke the requirements of NEPA.

3. Regulatory Agencies

Environmental Protection Agency (EPA)

The primary federal administrative agency in charge of coordinating all of the federal government's efforts relating to environmental protection

The **Environmental Protection Agency (EPA)** was created in 1970 for the purpose of coordinating all of the federal government's responsibilities relating to environmental protection. The EPA administers federal law and implements federal policy regarding the pollution of air and water, disposal of solid waste and toxic substances, and use of pesticides and radiation. Among the responsibilities of the EPA is to provide an assessment of the quality of the environment, particularly regarding the impact of industrial and other types of pollutants. This aspect of EPA's charge is becoming ever-more complicated. Pollution of a bay along the Gulf Coast in the EPA's early days could be seen, smelled, or tasted. As governmental efforts were focused on these easily discernable forms of pollution, many of the most egregious geographic areas have shown marked improvement in environmental quality.

These early successes have allowed the EPA to shift their focus to less visible forms of pollution. However, gaining public support for these efforts is often more difficult because the nature of the pollution is not easily discernable to members of the public and requires greater reliance on scientific analysis. Also, the aim of federal environmental laws and regulation is not to create air that is *entirely* free of smoke, for example. Inherent in the regulatory scheme is a balancing of the degree of risk of the proposed action with other factors, including economic impact. Where the risks are not visible, a federal agency may have a more difficult time making the case for regulation.

While the EPA is the most well known regulatory agency devoted to environmental protection, other federal agencies also regulate in the area. The Nuclear Regulatory Commission, for instance, has broad authority to administer laws and regulations relating to nuclear power. In addition, state and local regulatory agencies play a significant role in shaping the restrictions government imposes on businesses in order to protect the environment. In addition to creating state and local edicts aimed at protecting the environment (e.g., zoning laws), the federal government often tasks state and local agencies with the responsibility of enforcing federal environmental mandates.

AIR POLLUTION

4. Air Pollution Regulatory Principles

Individuals might identify automobile emissions as a significant source of air pollution, and they would be correct. Nevertheless, there are other forms of air pollution that are more closely associated with business, primarily the manufacturing process. Manufacturing involves fuel combustion, solid waste generation, and industrial production—all of which contribute to air pollution. The Clean Air Act—passed in 1963 and amended significantly in 1965, 1967, 1970, and 1990—provides a comprehensive statutory approach to controlling air pollution. The Clear Air Act mandates that the EPA set **national ambient air quality standards** for the major pollutants capable of causing harm to humans. These standards set the maximum amount of pollutants in outdoor air that are compatible with reasonable public health.

National ambient air quality standards
The maximum allowable amount of exposure to major pollutants in outdoor air as mandated by the Clean Air Act

State implementation plan
A plan, required under the Clean Air Act, that each state creates and implements for the purpose of meeting the national standards

At present, standards have been set for the following: (1) lead, (2) carbon monoxide, (3) ozone, (4) nitrogen dioxide, (5) sulfur dioxide, and (6) particulate matter.

While the federal government has established the maximum amount of certain pollutants that can be in the air through national ambient air quality standards, the Clear Air Act requires each state to create a **state implementation plan** for meeting the national standards. Therefore, state—not federal—government agencies are mandated to investigate sources of air pollution and require industrial emitters to reduce their omissions so that the federal standards are met.

In 1990, Congress amended the Clean Air Act to address *toxic pollutants*. The six traditional air pollutants addressed in the original Clean Air Act will harm one's health if there is sufficient exposure over an extended time. In contrast, the 1990 amendments address toxic pollutants—substances where exposure to low concentrations is sufficient to cause serious harm. Toxic substances currently recognized include asbestos, benzene, mercury, arsenic, and vinyl chloride.

5. Enforcement of the Clean Air Act

Violating the Clean Air Act has significant consequences for both the entity that is polluting and for individuals who are managing that entity. The EPA can assess penalties reaching $25,000 per day for polluters who fail to meet emission limits. Even failing to keep adequate records can result in penalties of up to $5,000 per day. Private citizens can sue, typically asking the court for an injunction that prohibits the business from continuing to violate provisions of the Clean Air Act.

TABLE 43-1 ■ Clean Air Act Recognized Pollutants

Pollutant	Description	Source	Harm
Lead	Harmful gas	Burning of leaded gasoline and processing of metals	Damage to neurological system and kidneys
Carbon Monoxide	Harmful gas	Incomplete burning of fuels	Impact on brain's ability to focus
Ozone	Harmful gas	Formed when nitrogen oxide combines with sunshine and oxygen	Damage to eyes and nasal passages
Nitrogen Oxide	Harmful gas	Motor vehicle and industrial emissions	Smog, depletion of the ozone layer, damage to lungs and other parts of the respiratory system
Sulfur Dioxide	Harmful gas	Burning of fossil fuels containing sulfur	Damage to lungs and other parts of the respiratory system, contributes to acid rain
Particulates	Liquid or solid materials	Emissions from industrial plants, dust from construction sites	Varies depending on nature of the substance

For those who are shown to have *knowingly* violated the Clean Air Act, fines may be assessed up to $1,000,000 and corporate officers (among others) can be imprisoned for up to two years.

6. Current Issues in Air Pollution Control

ADMINISTRATIVE Implementation of the provisions of the Clean Air Act, as amended, is a daunting task for the EPA, state agencies, industry, and others. The Clean Air Act provides that standards applied in areas where the air is clean can be different from those standards applied in regions where the air quality is poor. Also, while state implementation plans apply to non-mobile sources of air pollution existing prior to 1970, for those plants built more recently, the EPA established performance standards based on the *best available control technology* capable of restraining the extent of pollution that emanates into the air. This approach forces new plants and those that are modified to employ a system of emissions reduction that is the most effective on the market.

Also, air pollution rights in certain circumstances can be traded. In the area of sulfur dioxide, for example, the Clean Air Act allows a polluter who removes more sulfur from the atmosphere than is required to earn a *credit* that can then be sold to another air polluter, one who would not be able to meet the standard without the credit. The notion of a credit system has met with considerable resistance by members of the environmental community. Finally, costs that business must bear in order to comply with air quality standards are considerable, in part because of the complicated nature of the administrative scheme. There is little doubt that Congress and others will continue to search for means of administering the EPA in a manner that achieves the twin goals of effectiveness and efficiency.

Greenhouse effect

Theory suggesting that chemical changes in the atmosphere brought about by pollutants cause a rise in atmospheric temperatures

Acid rain

Pollutants in the atmosphere that fall to Earth as an acid

ENVIRONMENTAL International discussions in recent years have focused attention on three issues. The **greenhouse effect** refers to increased temperatures at lower levels of the atmosphere. resulting is *global warming*. Many in the scientific community postulate that an increase in carbon dioxide, among other gases, in the atmosphere causes temperatures to rise because energy from the sun is retained in the atmosphere near the ground. In other words, more than a normal amount of heat radiating from the ground is caught in the lower atmosphere.

Acid rain has been linked to the destruction of forests and other habitats for both animals and aquatic life. The principal source of the sulfur dioxide and nitrogen oxide comes from coal-burning power plants. These pollutants rise into the upper atmosphere, combine with water, and fall to Earth as a form of acid. The worst effects of acid rain occur in Europe, southern Canada, and the eastern portion of the United States, as these areas have concentrations of smelters and electric utility operations that rely on coal. However, the Midwest and other areas are impacted as well because air currents can move the pollutants hundreds of miles away from the source.

WATER POLLUTION

7. Water Pollution Regulatory Principles

Federal protection of water dates back to the River and Harbor Act of 1886, which was recodified in 1899. Later, the Public Health Service Act of 1912 addressed, in part, discharges into waterways that affected public health, and the Oil Pollution Act of 1924 prohibited the discharge of oil into coastal waters. While Congress again entered the field of regulating water pollution in 1948 with the passage of the Federal Water Pollution Control Act, it was not until amendments to that act passed in 1972 that the federal government asserted a leadership role in the area of cleaning the nation's water. This later congressional action is known as the *Clean Water Act.*

The Clean Water Act, in some way modeled after the 1970 Clean Air Act, was enacted to (1) make water clean enough for swimming and other recreational uses, (2) protect fish and wildlife from water pollutants, and (3) eliminate the discharge of pollutants into the water. It is critical to understand the provisions of the Clean Water Act impact only *navigable waters.* While the term is expansive, including lakes and rivers, along with coastal and freshwater wetlands, the history of federal involvement in addressing water pollution is respected; coverage continues to be limited to those waterways that are navigable. In other words, non-navigable waters, for example an aquifer located beneath a city or a seasonal pond, are *not* subject to the provisions of the Clean Water Act. Water pollution policy as stated in the Clean Water Act is implemented by the states.

Discharge permit

A government permit that allows an industrial polluter to discharge limited amounts of certain pollutants into navigable waters

The principal method of executing the provisions of the Clean Water Act is through a permitting process. Factories that discharge pollutants, among others, are required to obtain a **discharge permit** before releasing waste products from a *point source* (such as a pipe) into a navigable waterway. Issued by the EPA or the appropriate state agency in response to an application from a business, the discharge permit usually provides a listing of the pollutants (including amount and concentration) that can be discharged and mandates that the business monitor those discharges. The permitting process may also require an entity to treat wastewater before it is released.

As with the Clean Air Act, new sources of pollution (for example, a recently-constructed factory) under the Clean Water Act are subject to more rigorous limits than long-existing sources. *Non-point source pollution* does not fall within the purview of the Clean Water Act. Therefore, runoffs from agricultural fertilizers or discharges directly into the ground are not subject to the Clean Water Act permit requirements. The following case examines the definitions of navigable waters and point source.

CASE

Colvin v. United States

U. S. DISTRICT COURT (Central District of California)

181 F. Supp. 2d 1050 (2001)

ROBERT J. TIMLIN, DISTRICT JUDGE

Between approximately July 1996 and February 1997, Colvin arranged for 5.4 million pounds of screw press rejects ("waste") to be dumped on the Lady Lu Ranch ("Lady Lu"). Lady Lu is located on the northern shoreline of the Salton Sea. Once deposited on Lady Lu, the waste was spread by Colvin, using a bulldozer, throughout Lady Lu. Some of the waste ended up in the Salton Sea. On September 9, 1997, Colvin was charged in a one-count indictment with discharging pollutants into navigable waters of the United States without a permit, in violation of the Clean Water Act (CWA). Elements the prosecution must show are: First, the defendant knowingly discharged a pollutant, Second, the pollutant was discharged from a point source, Third, the pollutant entered waters of the United States; and Fourth, the discharge was unpermitted.

Colvin was convicted but moved to dismiss.

Colvin argues the Salton Sea is not a "navigable water" under the CWA, and a bulldozer is not a "point source" under the CWA. First, it is irrelevant whether Colvin dumped the waste into the middle of the Sea or placed the waste in contact with the Sea at the shoreline, knowing that the tides would transport the waste out to sea. The trial record reflects that the Salton Sea is a popular destination for out-of-state and foreign tourists, who fish and recreate in and on its waters and shoreline. Some tourists visit the Salton Sea for medicinal purposes, believing its water is good for their skin. Other international and domestic visitors frequent the Salton Sea to water ski, fish, hunt ducks, and race boats and jet skis on the Sea. Many Canadian tourists frequent the Sea in the winter, while many others use it in the summer. The record further shows that the Sea ebbs and flows with the tide. The Ninth Circuit defines waters of the United States broadly, indicating waters of the United States include at least some waters that are not navigable in the classical sense, such as non-navigable tributaries and streams. Under most any meaning of the term, the Salton Sea is a body of "navigable water" and "water of the United States."

[I]t is well established that bulldozers and similar vehicles may be "point sources" under the CWA when they are, as here, utilized to spread waste.

■ *Motion to dismiss is denied.*

CASE CONCEPT REVIEW

1. What factor associated with the Salton Sea most influenced the court to find that the Salton Sea is a body of "navigable water" under provisions of the Clean Water Act?
2. Why do you believe the court found it irrelevant that the defendant dumped the waste on the ground?

8. Enforcement of the Clean Water Act

The Clean Water Act provides for both civil and criminal sanctions. Furthermore, either the government or a private party can sue under this federal legislation, usually seeking an injunction prohibiting an entity from discharging pollutants. A violation of the Clean Water Act may result in a monetary award to cover damages, the costs of cleaning the illegal pollution, along with civil penalties. Criminal penalties are significant. Even a *negligent violation* of the permitting scheme established under the Clean Water Act can result in fines of at least $2,500 to a maximum of $25,000 per day or one year in prison, or both. A *knowing violation* may result in a maximum penalty of $50,000 per day or imprisonment of three years, or both. State agencies and the EPA may act to enforce provisions of this federal law.

WASTE MANAGEMENT

9. Solid Waste

For decades, federal and state governments let local governments deal with solid waste, including household and industrial garbage. Population was not as concentrated as it is today, and the basic composition of the waste produced created few problems. The agriculture community, which generated a large proportion of the waste in most local geographic areas, found ways to dispose of their waste without impacting residential or business communities.

During the past forty years, however, we have shifted away from an agrarian economy. Rampant consumerism in recent decades also contributed to significant solid waste problems that threaten the public health of communities across the nation. For many years, issues associated with proper disposal of waste generated from complex manufacturing processes were too often ignored by local officials. While solid waste disposal in open dumps and landfills was an appropriate approach for more than one-hundred years, in the 1960s members of Congress and state legislators agreed that a more comprehensive approach was needed.

The *Solid Waste Disposal Act,* passed by Congress in 1965 and amended in 1970 with the Resourse Recovery Act, propelled the solid waste problem to the national stage. Both acts dealt primarily with nontoxic waste management. Unfortunately, other than providing general research and technical assistance, the Solid Waste Disposal Act does little more than acknowledge the issue and charge regional, state, and local agencies with the responsibility for addressing the issue. Through state legislation and agency actions, non-federal entities across the nation have sought to (1) encourage recycling at the consumer and business levels, (2) mandate that landfills be sanitized to reduce odors and disease, and (3) create regulations regarding the proper manner of collecting, transporting, and disposing of solid waste.

10. Hazardous and Toxic Waste

The 1970s brought renewed attention to the issue of waste, but in a far different light. Love Canal, for example, caught the attention of the public. Located in Buffalo, New York, this waterway was found to be a dumping area for chemicals from industrial sites, with the pollution threatening the health of scores of families living in the area. These chemicals were highly toxic, capable of negatively impacting the lives of humans even though the concentrations were slight and exposure was limited.

THE RESOURCE CONSERVATION AND RECOVERY ACT Congress was quick to begin addressing issues associated with hazardous and toxic waste. The *Resource Conservation and Recovery Act* (RCRA) was passed by Congress in 1976 (and markedly amended in 1984). The RCRA authorizes the EPA to create a list of hazardous wastes, develop standards for those entities that are generating hazardous wastes, establish procedures that organizations that transport and store hazardous wastes must follow, and provide guidelines for the construction and maintenance of facilities devoted to the treatment and disposal of such substances. The RCRA states that hazardous waste occurs where (1) the waste causes an increase in the death rate or serious irreversible illness or (2) the waste possesses a substantial hazard to human health or the environment if not properly managed. Enforcement of the RCRA is taken seriously. Secret dumping of hazardous waste, for example, becomes a federal crime under the RCRA with fines up to $250,000 and a maximum prison term of fifteen (15) years for a violation that endangers human life. Further, significant civil penalties may be assessed by the EPA for violations of the RCRA that do not involve a "knowing" violation.

Perhaps most important, the RCRA mandates *"cradle-to-grave" responsibility* on entities that generate hazardous waste. Consider the case of Chavez, Inc. This organization creates waste that, under the RCRA, is considered hazardous. The manufacturing process may result in waste that is hazardous as its usefulness to the operation ceases. In addition, the material may be hazardous not only when it becomes waste, but also when the substance is incinerated at the factory in an effort to destroy the waste because the heat used to incinerate the substance might release toxic gases in the substance. The RCRA system casts a wide net aimed at addressing all aspects of hazardous and toxic wastes. The central focus of the RCRA-mandated program is a **manifest system**: Any entity, like Chavez, Inc., that generates hazardous waste must secure from the EPA an identification number and a manifest (permit) that accompanies the waste from the time of its creation until its disposal. In this manner, the EPA can track the entire life of the waste. While the chemical industry is the largest group of businesses required to follow this RCRA mandate,

RCRA Manifest

Permit issued to those entities that produce hazardous waste for the purpose of assisting the EPA in tracking the waste from "cradle-to-grave" the provisions of the act apply to any producer of hazardous wastes. The RCRA also addresses related aspects of effectively dealing with hazardous wastes. For example, companies affected by the act must maintain adequate liability insurance coverage and provide evidence that they have sufficient financial resources to remedy any hazardous waste issue even after a facility is closed.

FEDERAL SUPERFUND LAW In addition to the RCRA, Congress continues to address critical health issues associated with hazardous waste. In 1980, Congress passed the Comprehensive Environmental Response, Compensation, and Liability Act (CERCLA), and then amended that act with the Superfund Amendments and Reauthorization Act (Superfund) of 1986. CERCLA and Superfund legislation focuses on individuals and businesses that currently own or have owned land considered by the EPA to be a toxic waste dump—even if they have no knowledge that hazardous waste exists on the property. The approach of Congress in this legislation is two-fold: (1) create a fund that is used to clean up these sites (it is not uncommon for expenses associated with this process to exceed $10 million or even $100 million per site), and (2) impose strict *liability* on owners of property containing toxic and hazardous substances.

Owners (current and past) are liable under CERCLA and Superfund laws for the costs of remediation, which largely includes the costs of restoring the affected land to its natural state free of toxic and hazardous wastes. These acts provide for joint and several liability, meaning that any one entity (e.g., the current owner) can be liable for the entire cost of cleaning up the site even though the polluter and subsequent owners knew of the waste and hid it from the current owner. In the normal course, the owner shoulders the costs of clean up finds that other responsible parties are incapable of contributing to the effort.

Innocent landowner defense

A defense to liability for clean-up costs available to a landowner who did not know and should not have known of the presence of toxic waste on land

A narrow defense does exist under federal law. In the rare case where an owner did not know of the toxic and hazardous wastes existing on the land and executed due diligence in ascertaining whether such wastes were dumped on the land, the law provides an **innocent landowner defense**. As a result of the difficulty and expense associated with providing due diligence, individuals and entities wishing to purchase land today are exceedingly cautious. The application of this defense is illustrated in the following case.

CASE

United States of America v. Timmons Corporation, Donald w. Stone Sr., and Real Property Located at 191 Watervliet Shaker Road, Colonie, Albany County, New York

UNITED STATES DISTRICT COURT (Northern District of New York)

2006 U.S. Dist. LEXIS 7642 (2006)

RANDOLPH F. TREECE, MAGISTRATE JUDGE

Plaintiff, the United States of America ("USA"), brings suit alleging violations of the Comprehensive Environmental Response, Compensation and Liability Act of 1980 ("CERCLA"). On March 15, 1989, Timmons purchased the Real Property from the bankruptcy estate of the Adirondack Steel Casting Company, Inc., along with a larger parcel of land consisting of approximately one hundred and sixty-three (163) acres. The Real Property contains a vacant building, formerly used as a steel foundry, consisting of electrical transformers used to "power electric arc furnaces," as well as several other buildings leased to commercial tenants. When the Real Property was purchased by Timmons, the electrical transformers were already on the property. In September 1988, the Real Property was assessed by civil engineers with a recommendation that the transformers be removed and disposed of. In March 1989, prior to Timmons' purchase of the Real Property, an environmental assessment report (the Goldberg-Zoino Report) was given to Timmons stating that fluid in the transformers contained polychlorinated biphenyls ("PCBs"). Timmons, consistent with good practice, examined both reports prior to purchase.

continued

Most transformers located in the northern substation contained PCB labels. PCBs are classified as a hazardous substance under CERCLA. In March 1989 and August 1992, there was noticeable staining on the lower portions of the transformers as well as on the ground; the March 1989 assessment described the area around the transformers as a "hot spot"; and prior to July 6, 1992, large quantities of fluid from the transformers were released into the environment. On July 6, 1992, the New York State Department of Environmental Conservation ("NYSDEC") identified areas on the Real Property that were contaminated with the PCB laden fluid. Concrete pads supporting the transformers had been soaked with the fluid that ultimately spilled into the nearby soil.

On July 6, 1992, NYSDEC requested that the EPA begin a removal action pursuant to CERCLA on the Real Property. The removal process commenced in 1992 and concluded, seven years later, in December 1999. During the removal process, particularly in 1993, it was confirmed that the soil surrounding the northern transformers was stained with PCBs. In February 1993, the EPA contacted Timmons to negotiate the removal action. Negotiations failed and on September 30, 1994, the EPA effectuated an Administrative Order obligating Timmons to remove the PCBs from the Real Property. Although Timmons performed some of the removal, the Defendant failed to fully comply with the Administrative Order. The EPA, therefore, conducted the remainder of the removal activities, consistent with the National Contingency Plan ("NCP"), and completed the action on December 4, 1999. Direct costs by the EPA total $771,680.52 and indirect costs total $210,073.24 for a combined total of $981,753.76. The costs incurred by the Department of Justice Environment and Natural Resources Division total $191,346.52. In addition to the costs, interest beginning on October 31, 2001 to June 30, 2005 total $73,299.71. The sum for all expenses including interest is $1,246,399.99.

Additionally, the Real Property is surrounded by residential areas, a school, and nearly 9,500 people live within a mile of the Real Property. Many people, including children and dirt-bike riders, were exposed to the contaminated property.

The USA claims that Timmons is liable under CERCLA for costs associated with the removal action. Plaintiff seeks all costs associated with the removal action plus prejudgement interest. The Defendants claim that they were not the owners or operators of a facility when hazardous substances were disposed of and as a counterpoint they assert that the USA is a potentially responsible party as they "sold this [Real Property] after World War II" without testing for contamination of PCBs in the 1940's and therefore cannot recover damages. Defendants further allege that the transformers were used by the prior owner, the Adirondack Steel Casting Company, Inc. Although they were never used by Timmons, the transformers were not abandoned by Timmons and remain available for use by proposed tenants. Plaintiff moves for a Summary Judgment.

[T]he defendant may assert an "innocent landowner" defense. In order to plead this defense, the owners of the property must show, "by a preponderance of the evidence, that the disposal of the hazardous substances occurred before they purchased the property, and that at the time of acquisition they 'did not know and had no reason to know' that the substances had been disposed at the facility." The "innocent landowner" can qualify for this defense if they undertook "'all appropriate inquiry' into the previous ownership and uses of the property, consistent with 'good commercial or customary' practice at the time of transfer." The "good commercial or customary" practice, though not defined by statute, has been interpreted to mean, "'a reasonable inquiry must have been made in all circumstances, in light of best business and land transfer principles.'" To determine if the landowner complied with the practice, the court considers specialized knowledge attained by the defendant on the subject, "whether the purchase price indicated awareness of the presence of a risk of contamination, commonly known or reasonable information about the property," any obvious contamination on the property, and "the ability to detect such contamination by appropriate inspection."

Defendants cannot prove by a preponderance of the evidence that they are entitled to the "innocent landowner" defense. To the extent that the Defendants assert the "innocent landowner" defense, the Defendants would have to show that the disposal of hazardous substances occurred before purchase and at the time of purchase they had no knowledge of the substances that had been disposed of upon the property. Defendants could also have had to make an appropriate inquiry into the prior ownership of the property in light of good commercial practice. At the time of purchase, the Defendants examined the Goldberg-Zoino Report that showed the existence of PCBs and stated that the area around the transformers was a PCB "hot spot." Because it may be said that an appropriate inquiry was made by Defendants that was consistent with a good commercial practice, considering they viewed these two reports prior to purchase, the Defendants cannot claim they were "innocent" as they had knowledge of the existence of PCBs at the facility at the time of purchase.

■ *Motion for a summary judgment is granted.*

CASE CONCEPT REVIEW

1. In order to assert successfully the innocent landowner defense, what must be proven?
2. Why was the defendant unable to use the innocent landowner defense?

TOXIC SUBSTANCES

11. The Toxic Substances Control Act

With the Clean Air Act, the Clean Water Act, and the Solid Waste Disposal Act working to reduce pollutants in many venues, there are special problems associated with toxic substances. Under the *Toxic Substances Control Act* (TSCA) of 1976, the EPA is charged with the responsibility of identifying those substances that are considered toxic. The EPA participates in this balancing of interests, as they may consider the economic, social, health, and environmental impacts of any decision in this

There is a need for a balance between the use of chemicals for the creation of goods and the environment.

regard. The balancing of interests is complicated; business must be able to create and use chemicals in order to produce goods, but this must be done in manners that do not allow for exposure to members of the public and others toxic substances with toxic effects. Toxics are generally defined as substances known to be poisonous to humans. For example, a substance that causes cancer or birth defects would most likely be classified as toxic. Note that some acts of Congress (e.g., the Clean Air Act) do not require the EPA consider the economic impact of a proposed pollution standard.

The TSCA and its implementation have both weathered considerable criticism. On the one hand, environmental groups are critical with the lack of progress the EPA has made in regulating toxic substances. Very few chemicals are classified as toxic; some of the better known include PCBs and chlorofluorocarbons. Proponents of changing the TSCA complain that under current law, the EPA has the burden of showing that a particular substance is toxic. However, the principal method of making that proof relies on members of the chemical industry to provide information that they are reticent to deliver. On the other hand, industry points to the considerable expense associated with compliance and the possible loss of trade secrets if disclosure is mandated. They also observe that many of their global competitors are not burdened by the requirements of TSCA.

CHAPTER SUMMARY

Business, Law, and the Environment: An Overview

1. The common law torts of negligence and nuisance are available to landowners and others who suffer a loss for harm done to their property or for loss of the right to enjoy their property.
2. The government may sue a land owner under the doctrine of public nuisance where there is an actual or potential loss of a right to use or enjoy property.

GOVERNMENT REGULATION OF THE ENVIRONMENT

The National Environmental Policy Act

1. The National Environmental Policy Act (NEPA) expressly states that it is the responsibility of the federal government to ensure that successive generations can enjoy the environment.
2. NEPA requires the federal government to file an environmental impact statement for every major federal action that significantly affects the quality of the environment.

Regulatory Agencies

1. The principal federal agency charged with administering federal policy aimed at reducing and eliminating environmental pollution is the Environmental Protection Agency (EPA).

AIR POLLUTION

Air Pollution Regulatory Principles

1. The Clean Air Act, as amended, mandates that the EPA set national ambient air quality standards for major pollutants.

2. States are required under the Clean Air Act to create a strategy, called the state implementation plan, which indicates how the state will meet the national ambient air quality standards.

Enforcement of the Clean Air Act

1. Penalties may reach $25,000 per day for polluters who fail to meet emission standards.

Current Issues in Air Pollution Control

1. Administrative costs on businesses who must comply with provisions of the Clean Air Act can be considerable.
2. The greenhouse effect theory suggests that chemical changes in the atmosphere brought about by pollutants cause a rise in atmospheric temperatures.
3. Acid rain is the process by which pollutants in the atmosphere combine with water and fall to Earth as a form of acid.

WATER POLLUTION

Water Pollution Regulatory Principles

1. The Clean Water Act applies to navigable waters and where waste products are released from a point source.
2. Under the Clean Water Act, the government may require polluters to secure a discharge permit that limits the type and amount of pollutants that can be discharged.
3. The Clean Water Act imposes more stringent requirements on new sources of pollution than those emanating from older sources.

Enforcement of the Clean Water Act

1. Both negligent and knowing violations of the Clean Water Act can result in civil and criminal sanctions.

WASTE MANAGEMENT

Solid Waste

1. For many years, solid wastes were disposed of in landfills and open dumps.
2. The Solid Waste Disposal Act encourages recycling of solid wastes, mandates that landfills be sanitized, and creates regulations regarding the proper manner of collecting, transporting, and disposing of solid waste.

Hazardous and Toxic Waste

1. The Resource Conservation and Recovery Act (RCRA) mandates “cradle-to-grave” responsibility on entities that generate hazardous waste.
2. A manifest system is created under RCRA to track the entire life of toxic waste.
3. The federal Superfund law (CERCLA) imposes strict liability on owners of property containing toxic and hazardous waste.
4. Under CERCLA, a past property owner may not be responsible for costs of clean-up under the innocent landowner defense.

TOXIC SUBSTANCES

The Toxic Substances Control Act

1. Under the Toxic Substances control Act, the EPA is charge with the responsibility of identifying those substances that are considered toxic.

REVIEW QUESTIONS AND PROBLEMS

1. Match each term in Column A with the appropriate statement in Column B.

A	B
(1) Resource Conservation and Recovery Act	(a) Mandates that landfills are sanitized
(2) Solid Waste Disposal Act	(b) Coordinates the federal government's activities relating to environmental protection
(3) National ambient air quality standards	(c) Prepared by the federal government for every major federal action that significantly affects the quality of the environment
(4) Public nuisance	(d) Result of pollutants that rise into the upper atmosphere, combine with water, and fall to Earth as a form of acid
(5) The greenhouse effect	(e) Mandated by the Clean Air Act, the standards that set the maximum amount of pollutant in outdoor air that are compatible with reasonable public health
(6) Environmental Impact Statement	(f) Action brought by the government to stop or prevent pollution
(7) Environmental Protection Agency	(g) Mandates "cradle-to-grave" responsibility on entities that generate hazardous waste
(8) Federal Superfund Law	(h) Theory suggesting that chemical changes in the atmosphere brought about by pollutants cause a rise in atmospheric temperatures
(9) Acid rain	(i) Only applies to navigable waters
(10) The Clean Water Act	(j) Imposes strict liability on owners and former owners of land that contains toxic wastes

2. Jaime owns a hill located above property owned by Marguerite. Every winter the rains bring landslides from the hill onto Marguerite's property. What legal action(s) are available to Marguerite?

3. Every fall the winds shift for a few weeks in the Monroe Valley. The City of Monroe usually enjoys clean air, but during those weeks in the fall the valley fills with smoke from a large lumber processing plan located at the end of the valley. What legal action(s) are available to the City of Monroe?
4. The federal government, in partnership with a private business, is planning to create a field of windmills that will be used for generating electrical energy. Would the government be required to file an environmental impact statement? Why?
5. Narragansett operates an asphalt concrete plant. New source performance standards apply to any facility that "constructed" a new source or "modified" an old source. Narragansett wants to replace the existing fabric filter dust collector with one that uses an electrostatic precipitator. Both processes will emit the same level of pollutants. "New source performance standards" require the use of the best available control technology. The electrostatic precipitator does not fall within that category of technology. Does the replacement planned by Narragansett trigger the new source performance standard? Why?
6. An individual with severe mental problems opened a valve on a railroad's tank car while the car was parked in a railroad lot, releasing hundreds of gallons of a toxic liquid. The spill flowed into a nearby creek and then into a navigable river. Would provisions of the Clean Water Act apply? Why?
7. Friendly Farms operates a thousand acres of fruit trees. Runoff from fertilizers and other chemicals used by the farming operation drain into an aquifer that is used by the residents of a community five miles away from Friendly Farms. Would provisions of the Clear Water Act Apply? Why?
8. Lemon Company manufactures a hazardous chemical. The chemical is transported to various industrial plants by Melon Transportation Services. One of the plants, owned by Nectarine Enterprises, stores the chemicals on site for use in their production process. What process for accessing responsibility for the dangerous chemical is required under RCRA?
9. Able Company, in 1950, manufactured dyes for use in the clothing industry in a St. Louis, Missouri plant. Beta Company bought the plant in 1960 and continued to make dyes. In 1970, Cammy Company purchased the plant from Beta. Cammy Company operated the facility for twenty years until it was sold in 1990 to Dobney Company. Dobney spent $35 million to clean the grounds of the factory and now seeks reimbursement for a portion of the expenses from the three previous owners under CERCLA. Would any of the owners be successful in asserting the innocent landowner defense? Why?
10. The EPA is considering whether XYZ solution should be placed on the list of toxic chemicals. XYZ is used in hospital surgical wards to clean surgical instruments, equipment, and furniture. The substance is very effective and is the least expensive substance of its kind on the market. Humans who have prolonged exposure to XYZ may contract forms of cancer, although no study on the subject has been termed definitive. Under the Toxic Substances Control Act, what factors should the EPA consider in making this determination?

Internet Contact:

United States Environmental Protection Agency at http://www.epa.gov

Superfund information at http://www.epa.gov/superfund/

The Constitution of the United States

Appendix A

PREAMBLE

We the People of the United States, in Order to form a more perfect Union, establish Justice, insure domestic Tranquility, provide for the common defense, promote the general Welfare, and secure the Blessings of Liberty to ourselves and our Posterity, do ordain and establish this Constitution for the United States of America.

Article I

Section 1 All legislative Powers herein granted shall be vested in a Congress of the United States, which shall consist of a Senate and House of Representatives.

Section 2 The House of Representatives shall be composed of Members chosen every second Year by the People of the several States, and the Electors in each State shall have the Qualifications requisite for Electors of the most numerous Branch of the State Legislature.

No Person shall be a Representative who shall not have attained to the age of twenty five Years, and been seven Years a Citizen of the United States, and who shall not, when elected, be an Inhabitant of that State in which he shall be chosen.

Representatives and direct Taxes shall be apportioned among the several States which may be included within this Union, according to their respective Numbers, which shall be determined by adding to the whole Number of free Persons, including those bound to Service for a Term of Years, and excluding Indians not taxed, three fifths of all other Persons. The actual Enumeration shall be made within three Years after the first Meeting of the Congress of the United States, and within every subsequent Term of ten Years, in such Manner as they shall by Law direct. The Number of Representatives shall not exceed one for every thirty Thousand, but each State shall have at Least one Representative; and until such enumeration shall be made, the State of New Hampshire shall be entitled to choose three, Massachusetts eight, Rhode-Island and Providence Plantations one, Connecticut five, New-York six, New Jersey four, Pennsylvania eight, Delaware one, Maryland six, Virginia ten, North Carolina five, South Carolina five, and Georgia three.

When vacancies happen in the Representation from any State, the Executive Authority thereof shall issue Writs of Election to fill such Vacancies.

The House of Representatives shall choose their Speaker and other Officers; and shall have the sole Power of Impeachment.

Section 3 The Senate of the United States shall be composed of two Senators from each State, chosen by the Legislature thereof, for six Years; and each Senator shall have one Vote.

Immediately after they shall be assembled in Consequence of the first Election, they shall be divided as equally as may be into three Classes. The Seats of the Senators of the first Class shall be vacated at the Expiration of the second Year, of the second Class at the Expiration of the fourth Year, and of the third Class at the Expiration of the sixth Year, so that one third may be chosen every second Year; and if Vacancies happen by Resignation, or otherwise, during the Recess of the Legislature of any State, the Executive thereof may make temporary Appointments until the next Meeting of the Legislature, which shall then fill such Vacancies.

No Person shall be a Senator who shall not have attained to the Age of thirty Years, and been nine Years a Citizen of the United States, and who shall not, when elected, be an Inhabitant of that State for which he shall be chosen.

The Vice President of the United States shall be President of the Senate but shall have no Vote, unless they be equally divided.

The Senate shall choose their other Officers, and also a President pro tempore, in the Absence of the Vice President, or when he shall exercise the Office of President of the United States.

The Senate shall have the sole Power to try all Impeachments. When sitting for that Purpose, they shall be on Oath or Affirmation. When the President of the United States is tried the Chief Justice shall preside: And no Person shall be convicted without the Concurrence of two thirds of the Members present.

Judgment in Cases of Impeachment shall not extend further than to removal from Office, and disqualification to hold and enjoy any Office of honor, Trust or Profit under the United States: but the Party convicted shall nevertheless be liable and subject to Indictment, Trial, Judgment and Punishment, according to Law.

Section 4 The Times, Places and Manner of holding Elections for Senators and Representatives, shall be prescribed in each State by the Legislature thereof; but the Congress may at any time by Law make or alter such Regulations, except as to the Places of choosing Senators.

The Congress shall assemble at least once in every Year, and such Meeting shall be on the first Monday in December, unless they shall by Law appoint a different Day.

Section 5 Each House shall be the Judge of the Elections, Returns and Qualifications of its own Members, and a Majority of each shall constitute a Quorum to do Business; but a smaller Number may adjourn from day to day, and may be authorized to compel the Attendance of absent Members, in such Manner, and under such Penalties as each House may provide.

Each House may determine the Rules of its Proceedings, punish its Members for disorderly Behaviour, and, with the Concurrence of two thirds, expel a Member.

Each House shall keep a Journal of its Proceedings, and from time to time publish the same, excepting such Parts as may in their Judgment require Secrecy; and the Yeas and Nays of the Members of either House on any question shall, at the Desire of one fifth of those Present, be entered on the Journal.

Neither House, during the Session of Congress, shall, without the Consent of the other, adjourn for more than three days, nor to any other Place than that in which the two Houses shall be sitting.

Section 6 The Senators and Representatives shall receive a Compensation for their Services, to be ascertained by Law, and paid out of the Treasury of the United States. They shall in all Cases, except Treason, Felony and Breach of the Peace, be privileged from Arrest during their Attendance at the Session of their respective Houses, and in going to and returning from the same; and for any Speech or Debate in either House, they shall not be questioned in any other Place.

No Senator or Representative shall, during the Time for which he was elected, be appointed to any civil Office under the Authority of the United States, which shall have been created, or the Emoluments whereof shall have been increased during such time; and no Person holding any Office under the United States, shall be a Member of either House during his Continuance in Office.

Section 7 All Bills for raising Revenue shall originate in the House of Representatives; but the Senate may propose or concur with amendments as on other Bills.

Every Bill which shall have passed the House of Representatives and the Senate, shall, before it become a law, be presented to the President of the United States: If he approve he shall sign it, but if not he shall return it, with his Objections to that House in which it shall have originated, who shall enter the Objections at large on their Journal, and proceed to reconsider it. If after such Reconsideration two thirds of that House shall agree to pass the Bill, it shall be sent, together with the Objections, to the other House, by which it shall likewise be reconsidered, and if approved by two thirds of that House, it shall become a Law. But in all such Cases the Votes of both Houses shall be determined by Yeas and Nays, and the Names of the Persons voting for and against the Bill shall be entered on the Journal of each House respectively. If any Bill shall not be returned by the President within ten Days (Sundays excepted) after it shall have been presented to him, the Same shall be a Law, in like Manner as if he had signed it, unless the Congress by their Adjournment prevent its Return, in which Case it shall not be a Law

Every Order, Resolution, or Vote to which the Concurrence of the Senate and House of Representatives may be necessary (except on a question of Adjournment) shall be presented to the President of the United States; and before the Same shall take Effect, shall be approved by him, or being disapproved by him, shall be repassed by two thirds of the Senate and House of Representatives, according to the Rules and Limitations prescribed in the Case of a Bill.

Section 8 The Congress shall have Power To lay and collect Taxes, Duties, Imposts and Excises, to pay the Debts and provide for the common Defence and general Welfare of the United States; but all Duties, Imposts and Excises shall be uniform throughout the United States;

To borrow Money on the credit of the United States;

To regulate Commerce with foreign Nations, and among the several States, and with the Indian Tribes;

To establish an uniform Rule of Naturalization, and uniform Laws on the subject of Bankruptcies throughout the United States;

To coin Money, regulate the Value thereof, and of foreign Coin, and fix the Standard of Weights and Measures;

To provide for the Punishment of counterfeiting the Securities and current Coin of the United States;

To establish Post Offices and post Roads;

To promote the Progress of Science and useful Arts, by securing for limited Times to Authors and Inventors the exclusive Right to their respective Writings and Discoveries;

To constitute Tribunals inferior to the supreme Court;

To define and punish Piracies and Felonies committed on the high Seas, and Offences against the Law of Nations;

To declare War, grant Letters of Marque and Reprisal, and make Rules concerning Captures on Land and Water;

To raise and support Armies, but no Appropriation of Money to that Use shall be for a longer Term than two Years;

To provide and maintain a Navy;

To make Rules for the Government and Regulation of the land and naval Forces;

To provide for calling forth the Militia to execute the Laws of the Union, suppress Insurrections and repeal Invasions;

To provide for organizing, arming, and disciplining, the Militia, and for governing such Part of them as may be employed in the Service of the United States, reserving to the States respectively, the Appointment of the Officers, and the Authority of training the Militia according to the discipline prescribed by Congress;

To exercise exclusive Legislation in all Cases whatsoever, over such District (not exceeding ten Miles square) as may, by Cession of Particular States, and the Acceptance of Congress, become the Seat of the Government of the United States, and to exercise like Authority over all Places purchased by the Consent of the Legislature of the State in which the Same shall be, for the Erection of Forts, Magazines, Arsenals, dock-Yards and other needful Buildings; — And

To make all Laws which shall be necessary and proper for carrying into Execution the foregoing Powers and all other Powers vested by this Constitution in the Government of the United States, or in any Department or Officer thereof.

Section 9 The Migration or Importation of such Persons as any of the States now existing shall think proper to admit, shall not be prohibited by the Congress prior to the Year one thousand eight hundred and eight, but a Tax or duty may be imposed on such Importation, not exceeding ten dollars for each Person.

The Privilege of the Writ of Habeas Corpus shall not be suspended, unless when in Cases or Rebellion or Invasion the public Safety may require it.

No Bill of Attainder or ex post facto Law shall be passed.

No Capitation, or other direct, Tax shall be laid, unless in Proportion to the Census of Enumeration herein before directed to be taken.

No Tax or Duty shall be laid on Articles exported from any State.

No Preference shall be given by any Regulation of Commerce or Revenue to the Ports of one State over those of another: nor shall Vessels bound to, or from, one State, be obliged to enter, clear or pay Duties in another.

No Money shall be drawn from the Treasury, but in Consequence of Appropriations made by Law; and a regular Statement and Account of the Receipts and Expenditures of all public Money shall be published from time to time.

No Title of Nobility shall be granted by the United States: And no Person holding any Office of Profit or Trust under them, shall, without the Consent of the Congress, accept of any present, Emolument, Office, or Title, of any kind whatever, from any King, Prince or foreign State.

Section 10 No State shall enter into any Treaty, Alliance, or Confederation; grant Letters of Marque and Reprisal; coin Money; emit Bills of Credit; make any Thing but gold and silver Coin a Tender in Payment of Debts; pass any Bill of Attainder, ex post facto Law, or Law impairing the Obligation of Contracts, or grant any Title of Nobility.

No State shall, without the Consent of the Congress, lay any Imposts or Duties on Imports or Exports, except what may be absolutely necessary for executing it's inspection Laws: and the net Produce of all Duties and Imposts, laid by any State on Imports or Exports, shall be for the Use of the Treasury of the United States; and all such Laws shall be subject to the Revision and Control of the Congress.

No State shall, without the Consent of Congress, lay any Duty of Tonnage, keep Troops, or Ships of War in time of Peace, enter into any Agreement or Compact with another State, or with a foreign Power, or engage in War, unless actually invaded, or in such imminent Danger as will not admit of delay.

Article II

Section 1 The executive Power shall be vested in a President of the United States of America. He shall hold his Office during the Term of four Years, and, together with the Vice President, chosen for the same Term, be elected, as follows:

Each State shall appoint, in such Manner as the Legislature thereof may direct, a Number of Electors, equal to the whole Number of Senators and Representatives to which the State may be entitled in the Congress: but no Senator or Representative, or Person holding an Office of Trust or Profit under the United States, shall be appointed an Elector.

The Electors shall meet in their respective States, and vote by Ballot for two Persons, of whom one at least shall not be an Inhabitant of the same State with themselves. And they shall make a List of all the Persons voted for, and of the Number of Votes for each; which List they shall sign and certify, and transmit sealed to the Seat of the Government of the United States, directed to the President of the Senate. The President of the Senate shall, in the Presence of the Senate and House of Representatives, open all the Certificates, and the Votes shall then be counted. The Person having the greatest Number of Votes shall be the President, if such Number be a Majority of the whole Number of Electors appointed; and if there be more than one who have such Majority, and have an equal Number of Votes, then the House of Representatives shall immediately choose by Ballot one of them for President; and if no Person have a Majority, then from the five highest on the List the said House shall in like Manner choose the President. But in choosing the President, the Votes shall be taken by States, the Representatives from each State having one Vote; a quorum for this Purpose shall consist of a Member or Members from two thirds of the States, and a Majority of all the States shall be necessary to a Choice. In every Case, after the Choice of the President, the Person having the greatest Number of Votes of the Electors shall be the Vice President. But if there should remain two or more who have equal Votes, the Senate shall choose from them by Ballot the Vice President.

The Congress may determine the Time of choosing the Electors, and the Day on which they shall give their Votes; which Day shall be the same throughout the United States.

No Person except a natural born Citizen, or a Citizen of the United States, at the time of the Adoption of this Constitution, shall be eligible to the Office of President; neither shall any person be eligible to that Office who shall not have attained to the Age of thirty five Years, and been fourteen Years a Resident within the United States.

In Case of the Removal of the President from Office, or of his Death, Resignation, or Inability to discharge the Powers and Duties of the said Office, the Same shall devolve on the Vice President, and the Congress may by Law provide for the Case of Removal, Death, Resignation or Inability, both of the President and Vice President, declaring what Officer shall then act as President, and such Officer shall act accordingly, until the Disability be removed, or a President shall be elected.

The President shall, at stated Times, receive for his Services, a Compensation, which shall neither be increased nor diminished during the Period for which he shall have been elected, and he shall not receive within that Period any other Emolument from the United States, or any of them.

Before he enter on the Execution of his Office, he shall take the following Oath or Affirmation:--"I do solemnly swear (or affirm) that I will faithfully execute the Office of President of the United States, and will to the best of my Ability, preserve, protect and defend the Constitution of the United States."

Section 2 The President shall be Commander in Chief of the Army and Navy of the United States, and of the Militia of the several States, when called into the actual Service of the United States; he may require the Opinion, in writing, of the principal Officer in each of the executive Departments, upon any Subject relating to the Duties of their respective Offices, and he shall have Power to Grant Reprieves and Pardons for Offences against the United States, except in Cases of Impeachment.

He shall have Power, by and with the Advice and Consent of the Senate, to make Treaties, provided two thirds of the Senators present concur; and he shall nominate, and by and with the Advice and Consent of the Senate, shall appoint Ambassadors, other public Ministers and Consuls, Judges of the supreme Court, and all other Officers of the United States, whose Appointments are not herein otherwise provided for, and which shall be established by Law: but the Congress may by Law vest the Appointment of such inferior Officers, as they think proper, in the President alone, in the Courts of Law, or in the Heads of Departments.

The President shall have Power to fill up all Vacancies that may happen during the Recess of the Senate, by granting Commissions which shall expire at the End of their next Session.

Section 3 He shall from time to time give to the Congress Information on the State of the Union, and recommend to their Consideration such Measures as he shall judge necessary and expedient; he may, on extraordinary Occasions, convene both Houses, or either of them, and in Case of Disagreement between them, with Respect to the Time of Adjournment, he may adjourn them to such Time as he shall think proper; he shall receive Ambassadors and other public Ministers; he shall take Care that the Laws be faithfully executed, and shall Commission all the Officers of the United States.

Section 4 The President, Vice President and all Civil Officers of the United States, shall be removed from Office on Impeachment for and Conviction of, Treason, Bribery, or other high Crimes and Misdemeanors.

Article III

Section 1 The judicial Power of the United States, shall be vested in one supreme Court, and in such inferior Courts as the Congress may from time to time ordain and establish. The Judges, both of the supreme and inferior Courts, shall hold their Offices during good Behaviour, and shall, at stated Times, receive for their Services, a Compensation, which shall not be diminished during their Continuance in Office.

Section 2 The judicial Power shall extend to all Cases, in Law and Equity, arising under this Constitution, the Laws of the United States, and Treaties made, or which shall be made, under their Authority;--to all Cases affecting Ambassadors, other public ministers and Consuls;--to all Cases of admiralty and maritime Jurisdiction;--to Controversies to which the United States shall be a Party;--to Controversies between two or more States;--between a State and Citizens of another State; — between Citizens of different States; — between Citizens of the same State claiming Lands under Grants of different States, and between a State, or the Citizens thereof, and foreign States, Citizens or Subjects.

In all Cases affecting Ambassadors, other public Ministers and Consuls, and those in which a State shall be Party, the supreme Court shall have original Jurisdiction. In all the other Cases before mentioned, the supreme Court shall have appellate Jurisdiction, both as to Law and Fact, with such Exceptions, and under such Regulations as the Congress shall make.

The Trial of all Crimes, except in Cases of Impeachment, shall be by Jury; and such Trial shall be held in the State where the said Crimes shall have been committed; but when not committed within any State, the Trial shall be at such Place or Places as the Congress may by Law have directed.

Section 3 Treason against the United States, shall consist only in levying War against them, or in adhering to their Enemies, giving them Aid and Comfort. No Person shall be convicted of Treason unless on the Testimony of two Witnesses to the same overt Act, or on Confession in open Court.

The Congress shall have Power to declare the Punishment of Treason, but no Attainder of Treason shall work Corruption of Blood, or Forfeiture except during the Life of the Person attainted.

Article IV

Section 1 Full Faith and Credit shall be given in each State to the public Acts, Records, and judicial Proceedings of every other State. And the Congress may by general Laws prescribe the Manner in which such Acts, Records and Proceedings shall be proved, and the Effect thereof.

Section 2 The Citizens of each State shall be entitled to all Privileges and Immunities of Citizens in the several States.

A Person charged in any State with Treason, Felony, or other Crime, who shall flee from Justice, and be found in another State, shall on Demand of the executive Authority of the State from which he fled, be delivered up, to be removed to the State having Jurisdiction of the Crime.

No Person held to Service or Labour in one State, under the Laws thereof, escaping into another, shall, in Consequence of any Law or Regulation therein, be discharged from such Service or Labour, but shall be delivered up on Claim of the Party to whom such Service or Labour may be due.

Section 3 New States may be admitted by the Congress into this Union; but no new State shall be formed or erected within the Jurisdiction of any other State; nor any State be formed by the Junction of two or more States, or Parts of States, without the Consent of the Legislatures of the States concerned as well as of the Congress.

The Congress shall have Power to dispose of and make all needful Rules and Regulations respecting the Territory or other Property belonging to the United States; and nothing in this Constitution shall be so construed as to Prejudice any Claims of the United States, or of any particular State.

Section 4 The United States shall guarantee to every State in this Union a Republican Form of Government, and shall protect each of them against Invasion; and on Application of the Legislature, or of the Executive (when the Legislature cannot be convened) against domestic Violence.

Article V

The Congress, whenever two thirds of both Houses shall deem it necessary, shall propose Amendments to this Constitution, or, on the Application of the Legislatures of two thirds of the several States, shall call a Convention for proposing Amendments, which, in either Case, shall be valid to all Intents and Purposes, as Part of this Constitution, when ratified by the Legislatures of three fourths of the several States, or by Conventions in three fourths thereof, as the one or the other Mode of Ratification may be proposed by the Congress; Provided that no Amendment which may be made prior to the Year One thousand eight hundred and eight shall in any Manner affect the first and fourth Clauses in the Ninth Section of the first Article; and that no State, without its Consent, shall be deprived of its equal Suffrage in the Senate.

Article VI

All Debts contracted and Engagements entered into, before the Adoption of this Constitution, shall be as valid against the United States under this Constitution, as under the Confederation.

This Constitution, and the Laws of the United States which shall be made in Pursuance thereof; and all Treaties made, or which shall be made, under the Authority of the United States, shall be the supreme Law of the Land; and the Judges in every State shall be bound thereby, any Thing in the Constitution or Laws of any state to the Contrary notwithstanding.

The Senators and Representatives before mentioned, and the Members of the several State Legislatures, and all executive and judicial Officers, both of the United States and of the several States, shall be bound by Oath or Affirmation, to support this Constitution; but no religious Test shall ever be required as a Qualification to any Office or public Trust under the United States.

Article VII

The Ratification of the Conventions of nine States, shall be sufficient for the Establishment of this Constitution between the States so ratifying the same.

AMENDMENTS TO THE CONSTITUTION OF THE UNITED STATES OF AMERICA

Articles in addition to, and amendment of, the Constitution of the United States of America, proposed by Congress, and ratified by the several states, pursuant to the Fifth Article of the original Constitution

Amendment I

Congress shall make no law respecting an establishment of religion, or prohibiting the free exercise thereof; or abridging the freedom of speech, or of the press; or the right of the people peaceably to assemble, and to petition the Government for a redress of grievances.

Amendment II

A well regulated Militia, being necessary to the security of a free State, the right of the people to keep and bear Arms, shall not be infringed.

Amendment III

No Soldier shall, in time of peace be quartered in any house, without the consent of the Owner, nor in time of war, but in a manner to be prescribed by law.

Amendment IV

The right of the people to be secure in their persons, houses, papers, and effects, against unreasonable searches and seizures, shall not be violated, and no Warrants shall issue, but upon probable cause, supported by Oath or affirmation, and particularly describing the place to be searched, and the persons or things to be seized.

Amendment V

No person shall be held to answer for a capital, or otherwise infamous crime, unless on a presentment or indictment of a Grand Jury, except in cases arising in the land or naval forces, or in the Militia, when in actual service in time of War or public danger; nor shall any person be subject for the same offence to be twice put in jeopardy of life or limb; nor shall be compelled in any criminal case to be a witness against himself, nor be deprived of life, liberty, or property, without due process of law; nor shall private property be taken for public use, without just compensation.

Amendment VI

In all criminal prosecutions, the accused shall enjoy the right to a speedy and public trial, by an impartial jury of the State and district wherein the crime shall have been committed, which district shall have been previously ascertained by law, and to be informed of the nature and cause of the accusation; to be confronted with the witnesses against him; to have compulsory process for obtaining witnesses in his favor, and to have the Assistance of Counsel for his defence.

Amendment VII

In Suits at common law, where the value in controversy shall exceed twenty dollars, the right of trial by jury shall be preserved, and no fact tried by a jury, shall be otherwise re-examined in any Court of the United States, than according to the rules of the common law.

Amendment VIII

Excessive bail shall not be required, nor excessive fines imposed, nor cruel and unusual punishments inflicted.

Amendment IX

The enumeration in the Constitution, of certain rights, shall not be construed to deny or disparage others retained by the people.

Amendment X

The powers not delegated to the United States by the Constitution, nor prohibited by it to the States, are reserved to the States respectively, or to the people.

Amendment XI

The Judicial power of the United States shall not be construed to extend to any suit in law or equity, commenced or prosecuted against one of the United States by Citizens of another State, or by Citizens or Subjects of any Foreign State.

Amendment XII

The Electors shall meet in their respective states and vote by ballot for President and Vice-President, one of whom, at least, shall not be an inhabitant of the same state with themselves; they shall name in their ballots the person voted for as President, and in distinct ballots the person voted for as Vice-President, and they shall make distinct lists of all persons voted for as President, and of all persons voted for as Vice-President, and of the number of votes for each, which lists they shall sign and certify, and transmit sealed to the seat of the government of the United States, directed to the President of the Senate; — The President of the Senate shall, in the presence of the Senate and House of Representatives, open all the certificates and the votes shall then be counted; — The person having the greatest Number of votes for President, shall be the President, if such number be a majority of the whole number of Electors appointed; and if no person have such majority, then from the persons having the highest numbers not exceeding three on the list of those voted for as President, the House of Representatives shall choose immediately, by ballot, the President. But in choosing the President, the votes shall be taken by states, the representation from each state having one vote; a quorum for this purpose shall consist of a member or members from two-thirds of the states, and a majority of all the states shall be necessary to a choice. And if the House of Representatives shall not choose a President whenever the right of choice shall devolve upon them, before the fourth day of March next following, then the Vice- President shall act as President, as in the case of the death or other constitutional disability of the President — The person having the greatest number of votes as Vice-President, shall be the Vice-President, if such number be a majority of the whole number of Electors appointed, and if no person have a majority, then from the two highest numbers on the list, the Senate shall choose the Vice-President; a quorum for the purpose shall consist of two-thirds of the whole number of Senators, and a majority of the whole number shall be necessary to a choice. But no person constitutionally ineligible to the office of President shall be eligible to that of Vice-President of the United States.

Amendment XIII

Section 1 Neither slavery nor involuntary servitude, except as a punishment for crime whereof the party shall have been duly convicted, shall exist within the United States, or any place subject to their jurisdiction.

Section 2 Congress shall have power to enforce this article by appropriate legislation.

Amendment XIV

Section 1 All persons born or naturalized in the United States and subject to the jurisdiction thereof, are citizens of the United States and of the State wherein they reside. No State shall make or enforce any law which shall abridge the privileges or immunities of citizens of the United States; nor shall any State deprive any person of life, liberty, or property, without due process of law; nor deny to any person within its jurisdiction the equal protection of the laws.

Section 2 Representatives shall be apportioned among the several States according to their respective numbers, counting the whole number of persons in each State, excluding Indians not taxed. But when the right to vote at any election for the choice of electors for President and Vice President of the United States, Representatives in Congress, the Executive and Judicial officers of a State, or the members of the Legislature thereof, is denied to any of the male inhabitants of such State, being twenty-one years of age, and citizens of the United States, or in any way abridged, except for participation in rebellion, or other crime, the basis of representation therein shall be reduced in the proportion which the number of such male citizens shall bear to the whole number of male citizens twenty-one years of age in such State.

Section 3 No person shall be a Senator or Representative in Congress, or elector of President and Vice President, or hold any office, civil or military, under the United States, or under any State, who, having previously taken an oath, as a member of Congress, or as an officer of the United States, or as a member of any State legislature, or as an executive or judicial officer of any State, to support the Constitution of the United States, shall have engaged in insurrection or rebellion against the same, or given aid or comfort to the enemies thereof. But Congress may by a vote of two-thirds of each House, remove such disability.

Section 4 The validity of the public debt of the United States, authorized by law, including debts incurred for payment of pensions and bounties for services in suppressing insurrection or rebellion, shall not be questioned. But neither the United States nor any State shall assume or pay any debt or obligation incurred in aid of insurrection or rebellion against the United States, or any claim for the loss or emancipation of any slave; but all such debts, obligations and claims shall be held illegal and void.

Section 5 The Congress shall have power to enforce, by appropriate legislation, the provisions of this article.

Amendment XV

Section 1 The right of citizens of the United States to vote shall not be denied or abridged by the United States or by any State on account of race, color, or previous condition of servitude.

Section 2 The Congress shall have power to enforce this article by appropriate legislation.

Amendment XVI

The Congress shall have power to lay and collect taxes on incomes, from whatever source derived, without apportionment among the several States, and without regard to any census or enumeration.

Amendment XVII

The Senate of the United States shall be composed of two Senators from each State, elected by the people thereof, for six years; and each Senator shall have one vote. The electors in each State shall have the qualifications requisite for electors of the most numerous branch of the State legislatures.

When vacancies happen in the representation of any State in the Senate, the executive authority of such State shall issue writs of election to fill such vacancies: Provided, That the legislature of any State may empower the executive thereof to make temporary appointments until the people fill the vacancies by election as the legislature may direct.

This amendment shall not be so construed as to affect the election or term of any Senator chosen before it becomes valid as part of the Constitution.

Amendment XVIII

Section 1 After one year from the ratification of this article the manufacture, sale, or transportation of intoxicating liquors within, the importation thereof into, or the exportation thereof from the United States and all territory subject to the jurisdiction thereof for beverage purposes is hereby prohibited.

Section 2 The Congress and the several States shall have concurrent power to enforce this article by appropriate legislation.

Section 3 This article shall be inoperative unless it shall have been ratified as an amendment to the Constitution by the legislatures of the several States, as provided in the Constitution, within seven years from the date of the submission hereof to the States by the Congress.

Amendment XIX

The right of citizens of the United States to vote shall not be denied or abridged by the United States or by any State on account of sex. Congress shall have power to enforce this article by appropriate legislation.

Amendment XX

Section 1 The terms of the President and Vice President shall end at noon on the 20th day of January, and the terms of Senators and Representatives at noon on the 3d day of January, of the years in which such terms would have ended if this article had not been ratified; and the terms of their successors shall then begin.

Section 2 The Congress shall assemble at least once in every year, and such meeting shall begin at noon on the 3d day of January, unless they shall by law appoint a different day.

Section 3 If, at the time fixed for the beginning of the term of the President, the President elect shall have died, the Vice President elect shall become President. If a President shall not have been chosen before the time fixed for the beginning of his term, or if the President elect shall have failed to qualify, then the Vice President elect shall act as President until a President shall have qualified; and the Congress may by law provide for the case wherein neither a President elect nor a Vice President elect shall have qualified, declaring who shall then act as President, or the manner in which one who is to act shall be selected, and such person shall act accordingly until a President or Vice President shall have qualified.

Section 4 The Congress may by law provide for the case of the death of any of the persons from whom the House of Representatives may choose a President whenever the right of choice shall have devolved upon them, and for the case of the death of any of the persons from whom the Senate may choose a Vice President whenever the right of choice shall have devolved upon them.

Section 5 Sections 1 and 2 shall take effect on the 15th day of October following the ratification of this article.

Section 6 This article shall be inoperative unless it shall have been ratified as an amendment to the Constitution by the legislatures of three-fourths of the several States within seven years from the date of its submission.

Amendment XXI

Section 1 The eighteenth article of amendment to the Constitution of the United States is hereby repealed.

Section 2 The transportation or importation into any State, Territory, or possession of the United States for delivery or use therein of intoxicating liquors, in violation of the laws thereof, is hereby prohibited.

Section 3 This article shall be inoperative unless it shall have been ratified as an amendment to the Constitution by conventions in the several States, as provided in the Constitution, within seven years from the date of the submission hereof to the States by the Congress.

Amendment XXII

Section 1 No person shall be elected to the office of the President more than twice, and no person who has held the office of President, or acted as President, for more than two years of a term to which some other person was elected President shall be elected to the office of the President more than once. But this Article shall not apply to any person holding the office of President, when this Article was proposed by the Congress, and shall not prevent any person who may be holding the office of President, or acting as President, during the term within which this Article becomes operative from holding the office of President or acting as President during the remainder of such term.

Section 2 This article shall be inoperative unless it shall have been ratified as an amendment to the Constitution by the legislatures of three-fourths of the several States within seven years from the date of its submission to the States by the Congress.

Amendment XXIII

Section 1 The District constituting the seat of Government of the United States shall appoint in such manner as the Congress may direct: A number of electors of President and Vice President equal to the whole number of Senators and Representatives in Congress to which the District would be entitled if it were a State, but in no event more than the least populous State; they shall be in addition to those appointed by the States, but they shall be considered, for the purposes of the election of President and Vice President, to be electors appointed by a State; and they shall meet in the District and perform such duties as provided by the twelfth article of amendment.

Section 2 The Congress shall have power to enforce this article by appropriate legislation.

Amendment XXIV

Section 1 The right of citizens of the United States to vote in any primary or other election for President or Vice President, for electors for President or Vice President, or for Senator or Representative in Congress, shall not be denied or abridged by the United States or any State by reason of failure to pay any poll tax or other tax.

Section 2 The Congress shall have power to enforce this article by appropriate legislation.

Amendment XXV

Section 1 In case of the removal of the President from office or of his death or resignation, the Vice President shall become President.

Section 2 Whenever there is a vacancy in the office of the Vice President, the President shall nominate a Vice President who shall take office upon confirmation by a majority vote of both Houses of Congress.

Section 3 Whenever the President transmits to the President pro tempore of the Senate and the Speaker of the House of Representatives has written declaration that he is unable to discharge the powers and duties of his office, and until he transmits to them a written declaration to the contrary, such powers and duties shall be discharged by the Vice President as Acting President.

Section 4 Whenever the Vice President and a majority of either the principal officers of the executive departments or of such other body as Congress may by law provide, transmit to the President pro tempore of the Senate and the Speaker of the House of Representatives their written declaration that the President is unable to discharge the powers and duties of his office, the Vice President shall immediately assume the powers and duties of the office as Acting President.

Thereafter, when the President transmits to the President pro tempore of the Senate and the Speaker of the House of Representatives has written declaration that no inability exists, he shall resume the powers and duties of his office unless the Vice President and a majority of either the principal officers of the executive department or of such other body as Congress may by law provide, transmit within four days to the President pro tempore of the Senate and the Speaker of the House of Representatives their written declaration that the President is unable to discharge the powers and duties of his office. Thereupon Congress shall decide the issue, assembling within forty-eight hours for that purpose if not in session. If the Congress, within twenty-one days after receipt of the latter written declaration, or, if Congress is not in session, within twenty-one days after Congress is required to assemble, determines by two-thirds vote of both Houses that the President is unable to discharge the powers and duties of his office, the Vice President shall continue to discharge the same as Acting President; otherwise, the President shall resume the powers and duties of his office.

Amendment XXVI

Section 1 The right of citizens of the United States, who are eighteen years of age or older, to vote shall not be denied or abridged by the United States or by any State on account of age.

Section 2 The Congress shall have power to enforce this article by appropriate legislation.

Amendment XXVII

No law varying the compensation for the services of the Senators and Representatives shall take effect, until an election of Representatives shall have intervened.

The Ratification of the Conventions of nine States, shall be sufficient for the Establishment of this Constitution between the States so ratifying the same.

The Uniform Commercial Code

Appendix B

AUTHORS' NOTE: The Uniform Commercial Code (UCC) is a document promulgated to all states and other types of jurisdictions by the Uniform Law Commissioners (ULC) under the auspices of the National Conference of Commissioners on Uniform State Laws and the American Law Institute. Each jurisdiction (state, District of Columbia, and Virgin Islands) has the option of adopting one or more of the eleven (11) articles included in the UCC, with each article covering a different area of commercial law. Moreover, those jurisdictions that adopt a particular article also may change a provision of the UCC, although changes to the UCC by legislative entities are surprisingly infrequent. It is the hope of the ULC that all jurisdictions adopt all eleven articles of the UCC and that they adopt the proposed text of each Article as written by the ULC, thereby creating a uniform set of laws throughout the United States. Today, the UCC has been adopted, usually as proposed by the ULC, by almost all states and jurisdictions. As a result, the commercial law of the United States is quite uniform from state to state.

However, in order to meet the needs of an ever-changing business community, the ULC updates each Article on an irregular basis. These updates are known as "revisions." Appendix B is structured to provide t*he most appropriate version* of a particular article, whether it is the established version or the revised version, given the material provided in the text and the popularity of a version of a specific article of the UCC. Therefore, Appendix B provides all eleven articles.

For reference purposes, Appendix C includes four articles that have been revised. These four revised articles are either too new to have been adopted by a significant number of jurisdictions or, while they have been available for adoption for a number of years, the particular revision has not found a significant audience of legislatures who wish to adopt the specific revision. Using the information included within the two web sites provided below, one can determine whether a revision has been adopted by a particular jurisdiction.

A brief description of each version of UCC articles follows, with directions as to whether the version is included in Appendix B or Appendix C.

Article I — General Provisions

Appendix B: Article 1 (established) – This established version is currently the law in 21 states and the District of Columbia. While Article 1 was revised in 2001 and adopted by 29 states and the Virgin Islands, the established version is included in Appendix B because almost all cases referencing Article 1 reference this version.

Appendix C: Article 1 (Revised) – The 2001 revision of Article 1 has been adopted by 29 states and the Virgin Islands as of 2007. The text of Article 1 (Revised) is provided in Appendix B.

Article 2 — Sales

Appendix B: Article 2 has been adopted by all states (except Louisiana), the District of Columbia, and the Virgin Islands. While the ULC proposed a revision in 2003 to reflect developments in business practices and to accommodate electronic commerce, as of 2007 no jurisdiction has adopted the Article 2 (Revised). Therefore, this edition of the text does not reference Article 2 (Revised) and the revision is not included in the appendices.

Article 2A — Leases

Appendix B: Article 2A has been adopted by all states (except Connecticut and Louisiana), the District of Columbia, and the Virgin Islands.

Article 3 — Negotiable Instruments

Appendix B: Article 3 (established) – This version has been adopted in all jurisdictions, except Article 3 (Revised) recently has been accepted as a substitute for Article 3 (established) in Arkansas, Kentucky, Minnesota, Nevada, and Texas.

Appendix C: Article 3 (Revised) was promulgated by the ULC in 2002 and has recently been accepted (as of 2007) as a substitute for Article 3 (established) in Arkansas, Kentucky, Minnesota, Nevada, and Texas.

Article 4 — Bank Deposits

Appendix B: Article 4 (established) – This version has been adopted in all jurisdictions, except Article 4 (Revised) recently has been accepted as a substitute for Article 4 (established) in Arkansas, Kentucky, Minnesota, Nevada, and Texas as of 2007.

Appendix C: Article 4 (Revised) – This version was promulgated by the ULC in 2002 and as of 2007 has been accepted as a substitute for Article 4 (established) in Arkansas, Kentucky, Minnesota, Nevada, and Texas.

Article 4A — Funds Transfers

Appendix B: Article 4A has been adopted by all states, the District of Columbia, and the Virgin Islands.

Article 5 — Letters of Credit

Appendix B: Article 5, last revised in 1995, has been adopted by all states, the District of Columbia, and the Virgin Islands.

Article 6 – Bulk Transfers and Bulk Sales

Appendix B: Article 6, last revised in 1989, has been adopted by all states, the District of Columbia, and the Virgin Islands.

[The nature of the 1989 revisions is worthy of further comment. The original Article 6 was established decades ago to provide buyers who purchased a "bulk sale" to provide notice to the seller's creditors that a sale was contemplated. The notification was geared to curb the practice whereby a merchant would acquire merchandise on credit from suppliers, then sell the entire inventory ("in bulk") to a buyer (usually of the entire business) and then flee with the proceeds, leaving creditors of the seller unpaid.

Changes to the credit environment occurring during the past thirty years, coupled with the widespread adoption of the Uniform Fraudulent Transfer Act and provisions of Article 9 of the UCC, have reduced the need for the protection provided under the old version of Article 6. The 1989 revision, however, provides states an option. Article 6, as proposed today, allows jurisdictions to repeal all provisions of the old Article 6 without providing any substitutions. In this manner, a jurisdiction effectively removes bulk sale protection. Almost all states have adopted this option. California, Virginia, and the District of Columbia adopted the alternative option provided under Article 6. These jurisdictions continue to embrace bulk sales protection, but under a revised statutory scheme that better reflect the realities associated with the sale of certain types of businesses.]

Article 7 – Warehouse Receipts, Bills of Lading and Other Documents of Title

Appendix B: Article 7 (established) – This version of Article 7 is currently the law in 22 states, the District of Columbia, and the Virgin Islands.

Appendix C: Article 7 (Revised) – This version of Article 7 was promulgated by the ULC in 2003 and has since been adopted by 28 states.

Article 8

Appendix B: Article 8, last revised in 1994, has been adopted by all states, the District of Columbia, and the Virgin Islands.

Article 9

Appendix B: Article 9, last revised in 1998, has been adopted by all states, the District of Columbia, and the Virgin Islands (with 2001 clarifying amendments included in strike/score format).

Internet Reference: To determine the version a particular state or jurisdiction has adopted, please refer to the following web sites:

http://www.law.cornell.edu/uniform/ucc.html and

http://www.nccusl.org/Update/DesktopDefault.aspx?tabindex=2&tabid=60

ARTICLE 1 / General Provisions

PART 1 General Provisions

§ 1-101. Short Titles.

(a) This [Act] may be cited as the Uniform Commercial Code.

(b) This article may be cited as Uniform Commercial Code — General Provisions.

§ 1-102. Scope of Article. This article applies to a transaction to the extent that it is governed by another article of [the Uniform Commercial Code].

(1) This Act shall be liberally construed and applied to promote its underlying purposes and policies.

(2) Underlying purposes and policies of this Act are

(a) to simplify, clarify and modernize the law governing commercial transactions;

(b) to permit the continued expansion of commercial practices through custom, usage and agreement of the parties;

(c) to make uniform the law among the various jurisdictions.

(3) The effect of provisions of this Act may be varied by agreement, except as otherwise provided in this Act and except that the obligations of good faith, diligence, reasonableness and care prescribed by this Act may not be disclaimed by agreement but the parties may by agreement determine the standards by which the performance of such obligations is to be measured if such standards are not manifestly unreasonable.

(4) The presence in certain provisions of this Act of the words "unless otherwise agreed" or words of similar import does not imply that the effect of other provisions may not be varied by agreement under subsection (3).

(5) In this Act unless the context otherwise requires

(a) words in the singular number include the plural, and in the plural include the singular;

(b) words of the masculine gender include the feminine and the neuter, and when the sense so indicates words of the neuter gender may refer to any gender.

§ 1-103. Supplementary General Principles of Law Applicable. Unless displaced by the particular provisions of this Act, the principles of law and equity, including the law merchant and the law relative to capacity to contract, principal and agent, estoppel, fraud, misrepresentation, duress, coercion, mistake, bankruptcy, or other validating or invalidating cause shall supplement its provisions.

§ 1-104. Construction Against Implicit Repeal. This Act being a general act intended as a unified coverage of its subject matter, no part of it shall be deemed to be impliedly repealed by subsequent legislation if such construction can reasonably be avoided.

§ 1-105. Territorial Application of the Act; Parties' Power to Choose Applicable Law.

(1) Except as provided hereafter in this section, when a transaction bears a reasonable relation to this state and also to another state or nation the parties may agree that the law either of this state or of such other state or nation shall govern their rights and duties. Failing such agreement this Act applies to transactions bearing an appropriate relation to this state.

(2) Where one of the following provisions of this Act specifies the applicable law, that provision governs and a contrary agreement is effective only to the extent permitted by the law (including the conflict of laws rules) so specified:

Rights of creditors against sold goods. Section 2-402.

Applicability of the Article on Leases. Sections 2A-105 and 2A-106.

Applicability of the Article on Bank Deposits and Collections. Section 4-102.

Governing law in the Article on Funds Transfers. Section 4A-507.

Bulk sales subject to the Article on Bulk Sales. Section 6-103.

Applicability of the Article on Investment Securities. Section 8-106.

Perfection provisions of the Article on Secured Transactions. Section 9-103.

As amended in 1972,1987,1988 and 1989.

§ 1-106. Remedies to Be Liberally Administered.

(1) The remedies provided by this Act shall be liberally administered to the end that the aggrieved party may be put in as good a position as if the other party had fully performed but neither consequential or special nor penal damages may be had except as specifically provided in this Act or by other rule of law.

(2) Any right or obligation declared by this Act is enforceable by action unless the provision declaring it specifies a different and limited effect.

§ 1-107. Waiver or Renunciation of Claim or Right After Breach. Any claim or right arising out of an alleged breach can be discharged in whole or in part without consideration by a written waiver or renunciation signed and delivered by the aggrieved party.

§ 1-108. Severability. If any provision or clause of this Act or application thereof to any person or circumstances is held invalid, such invalidity shall not affect other provisions or applications of the Act which can be given effect without the invalid provision or application, and to this end the provisions of this Act are declared to be severable.

§ 1-109. Section Captions. Section captions are parts of this Act.

PART 2 General Definitions and Principles of Interpretation

§ 1-201. General Definitions. Subject to additional definitions contained in the subsequent Articles of this Act which are applicable to specific Articles or Parts thereof, and unless the context otherwise requires, in this Act:

(1) "Action" in the sense of a judicial proceeding includes recoupment, counterclaim, set-off, suit in equity and any other proceedings in which rights are determined.

(2) "Aggrieved party" means a party entitled to resort to a remedy.

(3) "Agreement" means the bargain of the parties in fact as found in their language or by implication from other circumstances including course of dealing or usage of trade or course of performance as provided in this Act (Sections 1-205 and 2-208). Whether an agreement has legal consequences is determined by the provisions of this Act, if applicable; otherwise by the law of contracts (Section 1-103). (Compare "Contract".)

(4) "Bank" means any person engaged in the business of banking.

(5) "Bearer" means the person in possession of an instrument, document of title, or certificated security payable to bearer or indorsed in blank.

(6) "Bill of lading" means a document evidencing the receipt of goods for shipment issued by a person engaged in the business of transporting or forwarding goods, and includes an airbill. "Airbill" means a document serving for air transportation as a bill of lading does for marine or rail transportation, and includes an air consignment note or air waybill.

(7) "Branch" includes a separately incorporated foreign branch of a bank.

(8) "Burden of establishing" a fact means the burden of persuading the triers of fact that the existence of the fact is more probable than its non-existence.

(9) "Buyer in ordinary course of business" means a person who in good faith and without knowledge that the sale to him is in violation of the ownership rights or security interest of a third party in the goods buys in ordinary course from a person in the business of selling goods of that kind but does not include a pawnbroker. All persons who sell minerals or the like (including oil and gas) at wellhead or minehead shall be deemed to be persons in the business of selling goods of that kind. "Buying" may be for cash or by exchange of other property or on secured or unsecured credit and includes receiving goods or documents of title under a pre-existing contract for sale but does not include a transfer in bulk or as security for or in total or partial satisfaction of a money debt.

(10) "Conspicuous": A term of clause is conspicuous when it is so written that a reasonable person against whom it is to operate ought to have noticed it. A printed heading in capitals (as: NON-NEGOTIABLE BILL OF LADING) is conspicuous. Language in the body of a form is "conspicuous" if it is in larger or other contrasting type or color. But in a telegram any stated term is "conspicuous". Whether a term or clause is "conspicuous" or not is for decision by the court.

(11) "Contract" means the total legal obligation which results from the parties' agreement as affected by this Act and any other applicable rules of law. (Compare "Agreement".)

(12) "Creditor" includes a general creditor, a secured creditor, a lien creditor and any representative of creditors, including an assignee for the benefit of creditors, a trustee in bankruptcy a receiver in equity and an executor or administrator of an insolvent debtor's or assignor's estate.
(13) "Defendant" includes a person in the position of defendant in a cross-action or counterclaim.
(14) "Delivery" with respect to instruments, documents of title, chattel paper, or certificated securities means voluntary transfer of possession.
(15) "Document of title" includes bill of lading, dock warrant, dock receipt, warehouse receipt or order for the delivery of goods, and also any other document which in the regular course of business or financing is treated as adequately evidencing that the person in possession of it is entitled to receive, hold and dispose of the document and the goods it covers. To be a document of title a document must purport to be issued by or addressed to a bailee and purport to cover goods in the bailee's possession which are either identified or are fungible portions of an identified mass.
(16) "Fault" means wrongful act, omission or breach.
(17) "Fungible" with respect to goods or securities means goods or securities of which any unit is, by nature or usage of trade, the equivalent of any other like unit. Goods which are not fungible shall be deemed fungible for the purposes of this Act to the extent that under a particular agreement or document unlike units are treated as equivalents.
(18) "Genuine" means free of forgery or counterfeiting.
(19) "Good faith" means honesty in fact in the conduct or transaction concerned.
(20) "Holder," with respect to a negotiable instrument means the person in possession if the instrument is payable to bearer or, in the case of an instrument payable to an identified person, if the identified person is in possession. "Holder" with respect to a document of title means the person in possession if the goods are deliverable to bearer or to the order of the person in possession.
(21) To "honor" is to pay or to accept and pay, or where a credit so engages to purchase or discount a draft complying with the terms of the credit.
(22) "Insolvency proceedings" includes any assignment for the benefit of creditors or other proceedings intended to liquidate or rehabilitate the estate of the person involved.
(23) A person is "insolvent" who either has ceased to pay his debts in the ordinary course of business or cannot pay his debts as they become due or is insolvent within the meaning of the federal bankruptcy law.
(24) "Money" means a medium of exchange authorized or adopted by a domestic or foreign government and includes a monetary unit of account established by an intergovernmental organization or by agreement between two or more nations.
(25) A person has "notice" of a fact when

- (a) he has actual knowledge of it; or
- (b) he has received a notice or notification of it; or
- (c) from all the facts and circumstances known to him at the time in question he has reason to know that it exists.

A person "knows" or has "knowledge" of a fact when he has actual knowledge of it. "Discover" or "learn" or a word or phrase of similar import refers to knowledge rather than to reason to know. The time and circumstances under which a notice or notification may cease to be effective are not determined by this Act.
(26) A person "notifies" or "gives" a notice or notification to another by taking such steps as may be reasonably required to inform the other in ordinary course whether or not such other actually comes to know of it. A person "receives" a notice or notification when

- (a) it comes to his attention; or
- (b) it is duly delivered at the place of business through which the contract was made or at any other place held out by him as the place for receipt of such communications.

(27) Notice, knowledge or a notice or notification received by an organization is effective for a particular transaction from the time when it is brought to the attention of the individual conducting that transaction, and in any event from the time when it would have been brought to his attention if the organization had exercised due diligence. An organization exercises due diligence if it maintains reasonable routines for communicating significant information to the person conducting the transaction and there is reasonable compliance with the routines. Due diligence does not require an individual acting for the organization to communicate information unless such communication is part of his regular duties or unless he has reason to know of the transaction and that the transaction would be materially affected by the information.
(28) "Organization" includes a corporation, government or governmental subdivision or agency, business trust, estate, trust, partnership or association, two or more persons having a joint or common interest, or any other legal or commercial entity.
(29) "Party", as distinct from "third party", means a person who has engaged in a transaction or made an agreement within this Act.
(30) "Person" includes an individual or an organization (See Section 1-102).
(31) "Presumption" or "presumed" means that the trier of fact must find the existence of the fact presumed unless and until evidence is introduced which would support a finding of its nonexistence.
(32) "Purchase" includes taking by sale, discount, negotiation, mortgage, pledge, lien, issue or re-issue, gift or any other voluntary transaction creating an interest in property.
(33) "Purchaser" means a person who takes by purchase.
(34) "Remedy" means any remedial right to which an aggrieved party is entitled with or without resort to a tribunal.
(35) "Representative" includes an agent, an officer of a corporation or association, and a trustee, executor or administrator of an estate, or any other person empowered to act for another.
(36) "Rights" includes remedies.
(37) "Security interest" means an interest in personal property or fixtures which secures payment or performance of an obligation. The retention or reservation of title by a seller of goods notwithstanding shipment or delivery to the buyer (Section 2-401) is limited in effect to a reservation of a "security interest". The term also includes any interest of a buyer of accounts or chattel paper which is subject to Article 9. The special property interest of a buyer of goods on identification of those goods to a contract for sale under Section 2-401 is not a "security interest", but a buyer

may also acquire a "security interest" by complying with Article 9. Unless a consignment is intended as security, reservation of title thereunder is not a "security interest", but a consignment in any event is subject to the provisions on consignment sales (Section 2-326).

Whether a transaction creates a lease or security interest is determined by the facts of each case; however, a transaction creates a security interest if the consideration the lessee is to pay the lessor for the right to possession and use of the goods is an obligation for the term of the lease not subject to termination by the lessee, and

(a) the original term of the lease is equal to or greater than the remaining economic life of the goods,

(b) the lessee is bound to renew the lease for the remaining economic life of the goods or is bound to become the owner of the goods,

(c) the lessee has an option to renew the lease for the remaining economic life of the goods for no additional consideration or nominal additional consideration upon compliance with the lease agreement, or

(d) the lessee has an option to become the owner of the goods for no additional consideration or nominal additional consideration upon compliance with the lease agreement.

A transaction does not create a security interest merely because it provides that

(a) the present value of the consideration the lessee is obligated to pay the lessor for the right to possession and use of the goods is substantially equal to or is greater than the fair market value of the goods at the time the lease is entered into,

(b) the lessee assumes risk of loss of the goods, or agrees to pay taxes, insurance, filing, recording, or registration fees, or service or maintenance costs with respect to the goods,

(c) the lessee has an option to renew the lease or to become the owner of the goods,

(d) the lessee has an option to renew the lease for a fixed rent that is equal to or greater than the reasonably predictable fair market rent for the use of the goods for the term of the renewal at the time the option is to be performed, or

(e) the lessee has an option to become the owner of the goods for a fixed price that is equal to or greater than the reasonably predictable fair market value of the goods at the time the option is to be performed.

For purposes of this subsection (37):

(x) Additional consideration is not nominal if (i) when the option to renew the lease is granted to the lessee the rent is stated to be the fair market rent for the use of the goods for the term of the renewal determined at the time the option is to be performed, or (ii) when the option to become the owner of the goods is granted to the lessee the price is stated to be the fair market value of the goods determined at the time the option is to be performed. Additional consideration is nominal if it is less than the lessee's reasonably predictable cost of performing under the lease agreement if the option is not exercised;

(y) "Reasonably predictable" and "remaining economic life of the goods" are to be determined with reference to the facts and circumstances at the time the transaction is entered into; and

(z) "Present value" means the amount as of a date certain of one or more sums payable in the future, discounted to the date certain. The discount is determined by the interest rate specified by the parties if the rate is not manifestly unreasonable at the time the transaction is entered into; otherwise, the discount is determined by a commercially reasonable rate that takes into account the facts and circumstances of each case at the time the transaction was entered into.

(38) "Send" in connection with any writing or notice means to deposit in the mail or deliver for transmission by any other usual means of communication with postage or cost of transmission provided for and properly addressed and in the case of an instrument to an address specified thereon or otherwise agreed, or if there be none to any address reasonable under the circumstances. The receipt of any writing or notice within the time at which it would have arrived if properly sent has the effect of a proper sending.

(39) "Signed" includes any symbol executed or adopted by a party with present intention to authenticate a writing.

(40) "Surety" includes guarantor.

(41) "Telegram" includes a message transmitted by radio, teletype, cable, any mechanical method of transmission, or the like.

(42) "Term" means that portion of an agreement which relates to a particular matter.

(43) "Unauthorized" signature means one made without actual, implied, or apparent authority and includes a forgery.

(44) "Value". Except as otherwise provided with respect to negotiable instruments and bank collections (Sections 3-303, 4-208 and 4-209) a person gives "value" for rights if he acquires them

(a) in return for a binding commitment to extend credit or for the extension of immediately available credit whether or not drawn upon and whether or not a charge-back is provided for in the event of difficulties in collection; or

(b) as security for or in total or partial satisfaction of a pre-existing claim; or

(c) by accepting delivery pursuant to a pre-existing contract for purchase; or

(d) generally, in return for any consideration sufficient to support a simple contract.

(45) "Warehouse receipt" means a receipt issued by a person engaged in the business of storing goods for hire.

(46) "Written" or "writing" includes printing, typewriting or any other intentional reduction to tangible form.

As amended in 1962, 1972, 1977, 1987 and 1990.

§ 1-202. Prima Facie Evidence by Third Party Documents. A document in due form purporting to be a bill of lading, policy or certificate of insurance, official weigher's or inspector's certificate, consular invoice, or any other document authorized or required by the contract to be issued by a third party shall be prima facie evidence of its own authenticity and genuineness and of the facts stated in the document by the third party.

§ 1-203. Obligation of Good Faith. Every contract or duty within this Act imposes an obligation of good faith in its performance or enforcement.

§ 1-204. Time; Reasonable Time; "Seasonably".
(1) Whenever this Act requires any action to be taken within a reasonable time, any time which is not manifestly unreasonable may be fixed by agreement.
(2) What is a reasonable time for taking any action depends on the nature, purpose and circumstances of such action.
(3) An action is taken "seasonably" when it is taken at or within the time agreed or if no time is agreed at or within a reasonable time.

§ 1-205. Course of Dealing and Usage of Trade.
(1) A course of dealing is a sequence of previous conduct between the parties to a particular transaction which is fairly to be regarded as establishing a common basis of understanding for interpreting their expressions and other conduct.
(2) A usage of trade is any practice or method of dealing having such regularity of observance in a place, vocation or trade as to justify an expectation that it will be observed with respect to the transaction in question. The existence and scope of such a usage are to be proved as facts. If it is established that such a usage is embodied in a written trade code or similar writing the interpretation of the writing is for the court.
(3) A course of dealing between parties and any usage of trade in the vocation or trade in the vocation or trade in which they are engaged or of which they are or should be aware give particular meaning to and supplement or qualify terms of an agreement.
(4) The express terms of an agreement and an applicable course of dealing or usage of trade shall be construed wherever reasonable as consistent with each other, but when such construction is unreasonable express terms control both course of dealing and usage of trade and course of dealing controls usage of trade.
(5) An applicable usage of trade in the place where any part of performance is to occur shall be used in interpreting the agreement as to that part of the performance.
(6) Evidence of a relevant usage of trade offered by one party is not admissible unless and until he has given the other party such notice as the court finds sufficient to prevent unfair surprise to the latter.

§ 1-206. Statute of Frauds for Kinds of Personal Property Not Otherwise Covered.
(1) Except in the cases described in subsection (2) of this section a contract for the sale of personal property is not enforceable by way of action or defense beyond five thousand dollars in amount or value of remedy unless there is some writing which indicates that a contract for sale has been made between the parties at a defined or stated price, reasonably identifies the subject matter, and is signed by the party against whom enforcement is sought or by his authorized agent.
(2) Subsection (1) of this section does not apply to contracts for the sale of goods (Section 2-201) nor of securities (Section 8-319) nor to security agreements (Section 9-203).

§ 1-207. Performance or Acceptance Under Reservation of Rights.
(1) A party who, with explicit reservation of rights performs or promises performance or assents to performance in a manner demanded or offered by the other party does not thereby prejudice the rights reserved. Such words as "without prejudice", "under protest" or the like are sufficient.
(2) Subsection (1) does not apply to an accord and satisfaction.
As amended in 1990.

§ 1-208. Option to Accelerate at Will. A term providing that one party or his successor in interest may accelerate payment or performance or require collateral or additional collateral "at will" or "when he deems himself insecure or in words of similar import shall be construed to mean that he shall have power to do so only if he in good faith believes that the prospect of payment or performance is impaired. The burden of establishing lack of good faith is on the party against whom the power has been exercised.

§ 1-209. Subordinated Obligations. An obligation may be issued as subordinated to payment of another obligation of the person obligated, or a creditor may subordinate his right to payment of an obligation by agreement with either the person obligated or another creditor of the person obligated. Such a subordination does not create a security interest as against either the common debtor or a subordinated creditor. This section shall be construed as declaring the law as it existed prior to the enactment of this section and not as modifying it. Added 1966.

Note: *This new section is proposed as an optional provision to make it clear that a subordination agreement does not create a security interest unless so intended*

ARTICLE 2 / Sales

PART 1 Short Title, General Construction and Subject Matter

§ 2-101. Short Title. This Article shall be known and may be cited as Uniform Commercial Code—Sales.

§ 2-102. Scope; Certain Security and Other Transactions Excluded From This Article. Unless the context otherwise requires, this Article applies to transactions in goods; it does not apply to any transaction which although in the form of an unconditional contract to sell or present sale is intended to operate only as a security transaction nor does this Article impair or repeal any statute regulating sales to consumers, farmers or other specified classes of buyers.

§ 2-103. Definitions and Index of Definitions.
(1) In this Article unless the context otherwise requires
(a) "Buyer" means a person who buys or contracts to buy goods.
(b) "Good faith" in the case of a merchant means honesty in fact and the observance of reasonable commercial standards of fair dealing in the trade.

(c) "Receipt" of goods means taking physical possession of them.

(d) "Seller" means a person who sells or contracts to sell goods.

(2) Other definitions applying to this Article or to specified Parts thereof, and the sections in which they appear are:

"Acceptance". Section 2-606.
"Banker's credit". Section 2-325.
"Between merchants". Section 2-104.
"Cancellation". Section 2-106(4).
"Commercial unit". Section 2-105.
"Confirmed credit". Section 2-325.
"Conforming to contract". Section 2-106.
"Contract for sale". Section 2-106.
"Cover". Section 2-712.
"Entrusting". Section 2-403.
"Financing agency". Section 2-104.
"Future goods". Section 2-105.
"Goods". Section 2-105.
"Identification". Section 2-501.
"Installment contract". Section 2-612.
"Letter of Credit". Section 2-325.
"Lot". Section 2-105.
"Merchant". Section 2-104.
"Overseas". Section 2-323.
"Person in position of seller". Section 2-707.
"Present sale". Section 2-106.
"Sale". Section 2-106.
"Sale on approval". Section 2-326.
"Sale or return". Section 2-326.
"Termination". Section 2-106.

(3) The following definitions in other Articles apply to this Article:

"Check". Section 3-104.
"Consignee". Section 7-102.
"Consignor". Section 7-102.
"Consumer goods". Section 9-109.
"Dishonor". Section 3-507.
"Draft". Section 3-104.

(4) In addition Article 1 contains general definitions and principles of construction and interpretation applicable throughout this Article.

§ 2-104. Definitions: "Merchant"; "Between Merchants"; "Financing Agency".

(1) "Merchant" means a person who deal in goods of the kind or otherwise by his occupation holds himself out as having knowledge or skill peculiar to the practices or goods involved in the transaction or to whom such knowledge or skill may be attributed by his employment of an agent or broker or other intermediary who by his occupation holds himself out as having such knowledge or skill.

(2) "Financing agency" means a bank, finance company or other person who in the ordinary course of business makes advances against goods or documents of title or who by arrangement with either the seller or the buyer intervenes in ordinary course to make or collect payment due or claimed under the contract for sale, as by purchasing or paying the seller's draft or making advances against it or by merely taking it for collection whether or not documents of title accompany the draft. "Financing agency" includes also a bank or other person who similarly intervenes between persons who are in the position of seller and buyer in respect to the goods (Section 2-707).

(3) "Between merchants" means in any transaction with respect to which both parties are chargeable with the knowledge or skill of merchants.

§ 2-105. Definitions: Transferability; "Goods"; "Future" Goods; "Lot"; "Commercial Unit".

(1) "Goods" means all things (including specially manufactured goods) which are movable at the time of identification to the contract for sale other than the money in which the price is to be paid, investment securities (Article 8) and things in action. "Goods" also includes the unborn young of animals and growing crops and other identified things attached to realty as described in the section on goods to be severed from realty (Section 2-107).

(2) Goods must be both existing and identified before any interest in them can pass. Goods which are not both existing and identified are "future" goods. A purported present sale of future goods or of any interest therein operates as a contract to sell.

(3) There may be a sale of a part interest in existing identified goods.

(4) An undivided share in an identified bulk of fungible goods is sufficiently identified to be sold although the quantity of the bulk is not determined. Any agreed proportion of such a bulk or any quantity thereof agreed upon by number, weight or other measure may to the extent of the seller's interest in the bulk be sold to the buyer who then becomes an owner in common.

(5) "Lot" means a parcel or a single article which is the subject matter of a separate sale or delivery, whether or not it is sufficient to perform the contract.

(6) "Commercial unit" means such a unit of goods as by commercial usage is a single whole for purposes of sale and division of which materially impairs its character or value on the market or in use. A commercial unit may be a single article (as a machine) or a set of articles (as a suite of furniture or an assortment of sizes) or a quantity (as a bale, gross, or carload) or any other unit treated in use or in the relevant market as a single whole.

§ 2-106. Definitions: "Contract"; "Agreement"; "Contract for Sale"; "Sale"; "Present Sale"; "Conforming" to Contract; "Termination"; "Cancellation".

(1) In this Article unless the context otherwise requires "contract" and "agreement" are limited to those relating to the present or future sale of goods. "Contract for sale" includes both a present sale of goods and a contract to sell goods at a future time. A "sale" consists in the passing of title from the seller to the buyer for a price (Section 2-401). A "present sale" means a sale which is accomplished by the making of the contract.

(2) Goods or conduct including any part of a performance are "conforming" or conform to the contract when they are in accordance with the obligations under the contract.

(3) "Termination" occurs when either party pursuant to a power created by agreement or law puts an end to the contract otherwise than for its breach. On "termination" all obligations which are still executory on both sides are discharged but any right based on prior breach or performance survives.
(4) "Cancellation" occurs when either party puts an end to the contract for breach by the other and its effect is the same as that of "termination" except that the cancelling party also retains any remedy for breach of the whole contract or any unperformed balance.

§ 2-107. Goods to Be Severed From Realty: Recording.
(1) A contract for the sale of minerals or the like (including oil and gas) or a structure or its materials to be removed from realty is a contract for the sale of goods within this Article if they are to be severed by the seller but until severance a purported present sale thereof which is not effective as a transfer of an interest in land is effective only as a contract to sell.
(2) A contract for the sale apart from the land of growing crops or other things attached to realty and capable of severance without material harm thereto but not described in subsection (1) or of timber to be cut is a contract for the sale of goods within this Article whether the subject matter is to be severed by the buyer or by the seller even though it forms part of the realty at the time of contracting, and the parties can by identification effect a present sale before severance.
(3) The provisions of this section are subject to any third party rights provided by the law relating to realty records, and the contract for sale may be executed and recorded as a document transferring an interest in land and shall then constitute notice to third parties of the buyer's rights under the contract for sale.

As amended in 1972.

PART 2 Form, Formation and Readjustment of Contract

§ 2-201. Formal Requirements; Statute of Frauds.
(1) Except as otherwise provided in this section a contract for the sale of goods for the price of 500 or more is not enforceable by way of action or defer unless there is some writing sufficient to indicate that a contract for sale has been made between the parties and signed by the party against whom enforcement is sought or by his authorized agent or broker. A writing is not insufficient because it omits or incorrectly states a term agreed upon but the contract is not enforceable under this paragraph beyond the quantity of goods shown in such writing.
(2) Between merchants if within a reasonable time a writing in confirmation of the contract and sufficient against the sender is received and the party receiving it has reason to know its contents, it satisfies the requirements of subsection (1) against such party unless written notice of objection to its contents is given within 10 days after it is received.
(3) A contract which does not satisfy the requirements of subsection (1) but which is valid in other respects is enforceable

(a) if the goods are to be specially manufactured for the buyer and are not suitable for sale to others in the ordinary course of the seller's business and the seller, before notice of repudiation is received and under circumstances which reasonably indicate that the goods are for the buyer, has made either a substantial beginning of their manufacture or commitments for their procurement; or
(b) if the party against whom enforcement is sought admits in his pleading, testimony or otherwise in court that a contract for sale was made, but the contract is not enforceable under this provision beyond the quantity of goods admitted; or
(c) with respect to goods for which payment has been made and accepted or which have been received and accepted (Sec. 2-606).

§ 2-202. Final Written Expression: Parol or Extrinsic Evidence. Terms with respect to which the confirmatory memoranda of the parties agree or which are otherwise set forth in a writing intended by the parties as a final expression of their agreement with respect to such terms as are included therein may not be contradicted by evidence of any prior agreement or of a contemporaneous oral agreement but may be explained or supplemented
(a) by course of dealing or usage of trade (Section 1-205) or by course of performance (Section 2-208); and
(b) by evidence of consistent additional terms unless the court finds the writing to have been intended also as a complete and exclusive statement of the terms of the agreement.

§ 2-203. Seals Inoperative. The affixing of a seal to a writing evidencing a contract for sale or an offer to buy or sell goods does not constitute the writing a sealed instrument and the law with respect to sealed instruments does not apply to such a contract or offer.

§ 2-204. Formation in General.
(1) A contract for sale of goods may be made in any manner sufficient to show agreement, including conduct by both parties which recognizes the existence of such a contract.
(2) An agreement sufficient to constitute a contract for sale may be found even though the moment of its making is undetermined.
(3) Even though one or more terms are left open a contract for sale does not fail for indefiniteness if the parties have intended to make a contract and there is a reasonably certain basis for giving an appropriate remedy.

§ 2-205. Firm Offers. An offer by a merchant to buy or sell goods in a signed writing which by its terms gives assurance that it will be held open is not revocable, for lack of consideration, during the time stated or if no time is stated for a reasonable time, but in no event may such period of irrevocability exceed three months; but any such term of assurance on a form supplied by the offeree must be separately signed by the offeror.

§ 2-206. Offer and Acceptance in Formation of Contract.
(1) Unless otherwise unambiguously indicated by the language or circumstances

(a) an offer to make a contract shall be construed as inviting acceptance in any manner and by any medium reasonable in the circumstances;

(b) an order or other offer to buy goods for prompt or current shipment shall be construed as inviting acceptance either by a prompt promise to ship or by the prompt or current shipment of conforming or non-conforming goods, but such a shipment of non-conforming goods does not constitute an acceptance if the seller seasonably notifies the buyer that the shipment is offered only as an accommodation to the buyer.

(2) Where the beginning of a requested performance is a reasonable mode of acceptance an offeror who is not notified of acceptance within a reasonable time may treat the offer as having lapsed before acceptance.

§ 2-207. Additional Terms in Acceptance or Confirmation.

(1) A definite and seasonable expression of acceptance or a written confirmation which is sent within a reasonable time operates as an acceptance even though it states terms additional to or different from those offered or agreed upon, unless acceptance is expressly made conditional on assent to the additional or different terms.

(2) The additional terms are to be construed as proposals for addition to the contract. Between merchants such terms become part of the contract unless:

(a) the offer expressly limits acceptance to the terms of the offer;

(b) they materially alter it; or

(c) notification of objection to them has already been given or is given within a reasonable time after notice of them is received.

(3) Conduct by both parties which recognizes the existence of a contract is sufficient to establish a contract for sale although the writings of the parties do not otherwise establish a contract. In such case the terms of the particular contract consist of those terms on which the writings of the parties agree, together with any supplementary terms incorporated under any other provisions of this Act.

§ 2-208. Course of Performance or Practical Construction.

(1) Where the contract for sale involves repeated occasions for performance by either party with knowledge of the nature of the performance and opportunity for objection to it by the other, any course of performance accepted or acquiesced in without objection shall be relevant to determine the meaning of the agreement.

(2) The express terms of the agreement and any such course of performance, as well as any course of dealing and usage of trade, shall be construed whenever reasonable as consistent with each other, but when such construction is unreasonable, express terms shall control course of performance and course of performance shall control both course of dealing and usage of trade (Section 1-205).

(3) Subject to the provisions of the next section on modification and waiver, such course of performance shall be relevant to show a waiver or modification of any term inconsistent with such course of performance.

§ 2-209. Modification, Rescission and Waiver.

(1) An agreement modifying a contract within this Article needs no consideration to be binding.

(2) A signed agreement which excludes modification or rescission except by a signed writing cannot be otherwise modified or rescinded, but except as between merchants such a requirement on a form supplied by the merchant must be separately signed by the other party.

(3) The requirements of the statute of frauds section of this Article (Section 2-201) must be satisfied if the contract as modified is within its provisions.

(4) Although an attempt at modification or rescission does not satisfy the requirements of subsection (2) or (3) it can operate as a waiver.

(5) A party who has made a waiver affecting an executory portion of the contract may retract the waiver by reasonable notification received by the other party that strict performance will be required of any term waived, unless the retraction would be unjust in view of a material change of position in reliance on the waiver.

§ 2-210. Delegation of Performance; Assignment of Rights.

(1) A party may perform his duty through a delegate unless otherwise agreed or unless the other party has a substantial interest in having his original promisor perform or control the acts required by the contract. No delegation of performance relieves the party delegating of any duty to perform or any liability for breach.

(2) Unless otherwise agreed all rights of either seller or buyer can be assigned except where the assignment would materially change the duty of the other party, or increase materially the burden or risk imposed on him by his contract, or impair materially his chance of obtaining return performance. A right to damages for breach of the whole contract or a right arising out of the assignor's due performance of his entire obligation can be assigned despite agreement otherwise.

(3) Unless the circumstances indicate the contrary a prohibition of assignment of "the contract" is to be construed as barring only the delegation to the assignee of the assignor's performance.

(4) An assignment of "the contract" or of "all my rights under the contract" or an assignment in similar general terms is an assignment of rights and unless the language or the circumstances (as in an assignment for security) indicate the contrary, it is a delegation of performance of the duties of the assignor and its acceptance by the assignee constitutes a promise by him to perform those duties. This promise is enforceable by either the assignor or the other party to the original contract.

(5) The other party may treat any assignment which delegates performance as creating reasonable grounds for insecurity and may without prejudice to his rights against the assignor demand assurances from the assignee (Section 2-609).

PART 3 General Obligation and Construction of Contract

§ 2-301. General Obligations of Parties. The obligation of the seller is to transfer and deliver and that of the buyer is to accept and pay in accordance with the contract.

§ 2-302. Unconscionable Contract or Clause.

(1) If the court as a matter of law finds the contract or any clause of the contract to have been unconscionable at the time it

was made the court may refuse to enforce the contract, or it may enforce the remainder of the contract without the unconscionable clause, or it may so limit the application of any unconscionable clause as to avoid any unconscionable result.
(2) When it is claimed or appears to the court that the contract or any clause thereof may be unconscionable the parties shall be afforded a reasonable opportunity to present evidence as to its commercial setting, purpose and effect to aid the court in making the determination.

§ 2-303. Allocation or Division of Risks. Where this Article allocates a risk or a burden as between the parties "unless otherwise agreed", the agreement may not only shift the allocation but may also divide the risk or burden.

§ 2-304. Price Payable in Money, Goods, Realty, or Otherwise.
(1) The price can be made payable in money or otherwise. If it is payable in whole or in part in goods each party is a seller of the goods which he is to transfer.
(2) Even though all or part of the price is payable in an interest in realty the transfer of the goods and the seller's obligations with reference to them are subject to this Article, but not the transfer of the interest in realty or the transferor's obligations in connection therewith.

§ 2-305. Open Price Term.
(1) The parties if they so intend can conclude a contract for sale even though the price is not settled. In such a case the price is a reasonable price at the time for delivery if
(a) nothing is said as to price; or
(b) the price is left to be agreed by the parties and they fail to agree; or
(c) the price is to be fixed in terms of some agreed market or other standard as set or recorded by a third person or agency and it is not so set or recorded.
(2) A price to be fixed by the seller or by the buyer means a price for him to fix in good faith.
(3) When a price left to be fixed otherwise than by agreement of the parties fails to be fixed through fault of one party the other may at his option treat the contract as cancelled or himself fix a reasonable price.
(4) Where, however, the parties intend not to be bound unless the price be fixed or agreed and it is not fixed or agreed there is no contract. In such a case the buyer must return any goods already received or if unable so to do must pay their reasonable value at the time of delivery and the seller must return any portion of the price paid on account.

§ 2-306. Output, Requirements and Exclusive Dealings.
(1) A term which measures the quantity by the output of the seller or the requirements of the buyer means such actual output or requirements as may occur in good faith, except that no quantity unreasonably disproportionate to any stated estimate or in the absence of a stated estimate to any normal or otherwise comparable prior output or requirements may be tendered or demanded.
(2) A lawful agreement by either the seller or the buyer for exclusive dealing in the kind of goods concerned imposes unless otherwise agreed an obligation by the seller to use best efforts to supply the goods and by the buyer to use best efforts to promote their sale.

§ 2-307. Delivery in Single Lot or Several Lots. Unless otherwise agreed all goods called for by a contract for sale must be tendered in a single delivery and payment is due only on such tender but where the circumstances give either party the right to make or demand delivery in lots the price if it can be apportioned may be demanded for each lot.

§ 2-308. Absence of Specified Place for Delivery. Unless otherwise agreed
(a) the place for delivery of goods is the seller's place of business or if he has none his residence; but
(b) in a contract for sale of identified goods which to the knowledge of the parties at the time of contracting are in some other place, that place is the place for their delivery; and
(c) documents of title may be delivered through customary banking channels.

§ 2-309. Absence of Specific Time Provisions; Notice of Termination.
(1) The time for shipment or delivery or any other action under a contract if not provided in this Article or agreed upon shall be a reasonable time.
(2) Where the contract provides for successive performances but is indefinite in duration it is valid for a reasonable time but unless otherwise agreed may be terminated at any time by either party.
(3) Termination of a contract by one party except on the happening of an agreed event requires that reasonable notification be received by the other party and an agreement dispensing with notification is invalid if its operation would be unconscionable.

§ 2-310. Open Time for Payment or Running of Credit; Authority to Ship Under Reservation. Unless otherwise agreed
(a) payment is due at the time and place at which the buyer is to receive the goods even though the place of shipment is the place of delivery; and
(b) if the seller is authorized to send the goods he may ship them under reservation, and may tender the documents of title, but the buyer may inspect the goods after their arrival before payment is due unless such inspection is inconsistent with the terms of the contract (Section 2-513); and
(c) if delivery is authorized and made by way of documents of title otherwise than by subsection (b) then payment is due at the time and place at which the buyer is to receive the documents regardless of where the goods are to be received; and
(d) where the seller is required or authorized to ship the goods on credit the credit period runs from the time of shipment but post-dating the invoice or delaying its dispatch will correspondingly delay the starting of the credit period.

§ 2-311. Options and Cooperation Respecting Performance.

(1) An agreement for sale which is otherwise sufficiently definite (subsection (3) of Section 2-204) to be a contract is not made invalid by the fact that it leaves particulars of performance to be specified by one of the parties. Any such specification must be made in good faith and within limits set by commercial reasonableness.
(2) Unless otherwise agreed specifications relating to assortment of the goods are at the buyer's option and except as otherwise provided in subsections (1) (c) and (3) of Section 2-319 specifications or arrangements relating to shipment are at the seller's option.
(3) Where such specification would materially affect the other party's performance but is not seasonably made or where one party's cooperation is necessary to the agreed performance of the other but is not seasonably forthcoming, the other party in addition to all other remedies

(a) is excused for any resulting delay in his own performance; and

(b) may also either proceed to perform in any reasonable manner or after the time for a material part of his own performance treat the failure to specify or to cooperate as a breach by failure to deliver or accept the goods.

§ 2-312. Warranty of Title and Against Infringement; Buyer's Obligation Against Infringement.

(1) Subject to subsection (2) there is in a contract for sale a warranty by the seller that

(a) the title conveyed shall be good, and its transfer rightful; and

(b) the goods shall be delivered free from any security interest or other lien or encumbrance of which the buyer at the time of contracting has no knowledge.

(2) A warranty under subsection (1) will be excluded or modified only by specific language or by circumstances which give the buyer reason to know that the person selling does not claim title in himself or that he is purporting to sell only such right or title as he or a third person may have.
(3) Unless otherwise agreed a seller who is a merchant regularly dealing in goods of the kind warrants that the goods shall be delivered free of the rightful claim of any third person by way of infringement or the like but a buyer who furnishes specifications to the seller must hold the seller harmless against any such claim which arises out of compliance with the specifications.

§ 2-313. Express Warranties by Affirmation, Promise, Description, Sample.

(1) Express warranties by the seller are created as follows:

(a) Any affirmation of fact or promise made by the seller to the buyer which relates to the goods and becomes part of the basis of the bargain creates an express warranty that the goods shall conform to the affirmation or promise.

(b) Any description of the goods which is made part of the basis of the bargain creates an express warranty that the goods shall conform to the description.

(c) Any sample or model which is made part of the basis of the bargain creates an express warranty that the whole of the goods shall conform to the sample or model.

(2) It is not necessary to the creation of an express warranty that the seller use formal words such as "warrant" or "guarantee" or that he have a specific intention to make a warranty, but an affirmation merely of the value of the goods or a statement purporting to be merely the seller's opinion or commendation of the goods does not create a warranty.

§ 2-314. Implied Warranty: Merchantability; Usage of Trade.

(1) Unless excluded or modified (Section 2-316), a warranty that the goods shall be merchantable is implied in a contract for their sale if the seller is a merchant with respect to goods of that kind. Under this section the serving for value of food or drink to be consumed either on the premises or elsewhere is a sale.
(2) Goods to be merchantable must be at least such as

(a) pass without objection in the trade under the contract description; and

(b) in the case of fungible goods, are of fair average quality within the description; and

(c) are fit for the ordinary purposes for which such goods are used; and

(d) run, within the variations permitted by the agreement, of even kind, quality and quantity within each unit and among all units involved; and

(e) are adequately contained, packaged, and labeled as the agreement may require; and

(f) conform to the promise or affirmations of fact made on the container or label if any.

(3) Unless excluded or modified (Section 2-316) other implied warranties may arise from course of dealing or usage of trade.

§ 2-315. Implied Warranty: Fitness for Particular Purpose.

Where the seller at the time of contracting has reason to know any particular purpose for which the goods are required and that the buyer is relying on the seller's skill or judgment to select or furnish suitable goods, there is unless excluded or modified under the next section an implied warranty that the goods shall be fit for such purpose.

§ 2-316. Exclusion or Modification of Warranties.

(1) Words or conduct relevant to the creation of an express warranty and words or conduct tending to negate or limit warranty shall be construed wherever reasonable as consistent with each other, but subject to the provisions of this Article on parol or extrinsic evidence (Section 2-202) negation or limitation is inoperative to the extent that such construction is unreasonable.
(2) Subject to subsection (3), to exclude or modify the implied warranty of merchantability or any part of it the language must mention merchantability and in case of a writing must be conspicuous, and to exclude or modify any implied warranty of fitness the exclusion must be by a writing and conspicuous. Language to exclude all implied warranties of fitness is sufficient if it states, for example, that "There are no warranties which extend beyond the description on the face hereof."
(3) Notwithstanding subsection (2)

(a) unless the circumstances indicate otherwise, all implied warranties are excluded by expressions like "as is", "with all faults" or other language which in common understanding calls the buyer's attention to the exclusion of warranties and makes plain that there is no implied warranty; and

(b) when the buyer before entering into the contract has examined the goods or the sample or model as fully as he desired or has refused to examine the goods there is no implied warranty with regard to defects which an examination ought in the circumstances to have revealed to him; and

(c) an implied warranty can also be excluded or modified by course of dealing or course of performance or usage of trade.

(4) Remedies for breach of warranty can be limited in accordance with the provisions of this Article on liquidation or limitation of damages and on contractual modification of remedy (Sections 2-718 and 2-719).

§ 2-317. Cumulation and Conflict of Warranties Express or Implied. Warranties whether express or implied shall be construed as consistent with each other and as cumulative, but if such construction is unreasonable the intention of the parties shall determine which warranty is dominant. In ascertaining that intention the following rules apply:

(a) Exact or technical specifications displace an inconsistent sample or model or general language of description.

(b) A sample from an existing bulk displaces inconsistent general language of description.

(c) Express warranties displace inconsistent implied warranties other than an implied warranty of fitness for a particular purpose.

§ 2-318. Third Party Beneficiaries of Warranties Express or Implied.

Note: *If this Act is introduced in the Congress of the United States this section should be omitted. (States to select one alternative.)*

Alternative A

A seller's warranty whether express or implied extends to any natural person who is in the family or household of his buyer or who is a guest in his home if it is reasonable to expect that such person may use, consume or be affected by the goods and who is injured in person by breach of the warranty. A seller may not exclude or limit the operation of this section.

Alternative B

A seller's warranty whether express or implied extends to any natural person who may reasonably be expected to use, consume or be affected by the goods and who is injured in person by breach of the warranty. A seller may not exclude or limit the operation of this section.

Alternative C

A seller's warranty whether express or implied extends to any person who may reasonably be expected to use, consume or be affected by the goods and who is injured by breach of the warranty. A seller may not exclude or limit the operation of this section with respect to injury to the person of an individual to whom the warranty extends.

As amended in 1966.

§ 2-319. F.O.B. and F.A.S. Terms.

(1) Unless otherwise agreed the term F.O.B. (which means "free on board") at a named place, even though used only in connection with the stated price, is a delivery term under which

(a) when the term is F.O.B. the place of shipment, the seller must at that place ship the goods in the manner provided in this Article (Section 2-504) and bear the expense and risk of putting them into the possession of the carrier; or

(b) when the term is F. O. B. the place of destination, the seller must at his own expense and risk transport the goods to that place and there tender delivery of them in the manner provided in this Article (Section 2-503);

(c) when under either (a) or (b) the term is also E. O. B. vessel, car or other vehicle, the seller must in addition at his own expense and risk load the goods on board. If the term is F. O. B. vessel the buyer must name the vessel and in an appropriate case the seller must comply with the provisions of this Article on the form of bill of lading (Section 2-323).

(2) Unless otherwise agreed the term F.A.S. vessel (which means "free alongside") at a named port, even though used only in connection with the stated price, is a delivery term under which the seller must

(a) at his own expense and risk deliver the goods alongside the vessel in the manner usual in that port or on a dock designated and provided by the buyer; and

(b) obtain and tender a receipt for the goods in exchange for which the carrier is under a duty to issue a bill of lading.

(3) Unless otherwise agreed in any case falling within subsection (1) (a) or (c) or subsection (2) the buyer must seasonably give any needed instructions for making delivery, including when the term is F.A.S. or F.O.B. the loading berth of the vessel and in an appropriate case its name and sailing date. The seller may treat the failure of needed instructions as a failure of cooperation under this Article (Section 2-311). He may also at his option move the goods in any reasonable manner preparatory to delivery or shipment.

(4) Under the term F.O.B. vessel or F.A.S. unless otherwise agreed the buyer must make payment against tender of the required documents and the seller may not tender nor the buyer demand delivery of the goods in substitution for the documents.

§ 2-320. C.I.F. and C. & F. Terms.

(1) The term C.I.F. means that the price includes in a lump sum the cost of the goods and the insurance and freight to the named destination. The term C. & F. or C.F. means that the price so includes cost and freight to the named destination.

(2) Unless otherwise agreed and even though used only in connection with the stated price and destination, the term C.I.F. destination or its equivalent requires the seller at his own expense and risk to

(a) put the goods into the possession of a carrier at the port for shipment and obtain a negotiable bill or bills of lading covering the entire transportation to the named destination; and

(b) load the goods and obtain a receipt from the carrier (which may be contained in the bill of lading) showing that the freight has been paid or provided for; and

(c) obtain a policy or certificate of insurance, including any war risk insurance, of a kind and on terms then current at the port of shipment in the usual amount, in the currency of the contract, shown to cover the same goods covered by the bill of lading and providing for payment of loss to the order of the buyer or for the account of whom it may concern; but the seller may add to the price the amount of the premium for any such war risk insurance; and

(d) prepare an invoice of the goods and procure any other documents required to effect shipment or to comply with the contract; and

(e) forward and tender with commercial promptness all the documents in due form and with any indorsement necessary to perfect the buyer's rights.

(3) Unless otherwise agreed the term C. & F. or its equivalent has the same effect and imposes upon the seller the same obligations and risks as a C.I.F. term except the obligation as to insurance.

(4) Under the term C.I.F. or C. & F. unless otherwise agreed the buyer must make payment against tender of the required documents and the seller may not tender nor the buyer demand delivery of the goods in substitution for the documents.

§ 2-321. C.I.F. or C. & F.: "Net Landed Weights"; "Payment on Arrival"; Warranty of Condition on Arrival. Under a contract containing a term C.I.F. or C. & F.

(1) Where the price is based on or is to be adjusted according to "net landed weights", "delivered weights", "out turn" quantity or quality or the like, unless otherwise agreed the seller must reasonably estimate the price. The payment due on tender of the documents called for by the contract is the amount so estimated, but after final adjustment of the price a settlement must be made with commercial promptness.

(2) An agreement described in subsection (1) or any warranty of quality or condition of the goods on arrival places upon the seller the risk of ordinary deterioration, shrinkage and the like in transportation but has no effect on the place or time of identification to the contract for sale or delivery or on the passing of the risk of loss.

(3) Unless otherwise agreed where the contract provides for payment on or after arrival of the goods the seller must before payment allow such preliminary inspection as is feasible; but if the goods are lost delivery of the documents and payment are due when the goods should have arrived.

§ 2-322. Delivery "Ex-Ship".

(1) Unless otherwise agreed a term for delivery of goods "ex-ship" (which means from the carrying vessel) or in equivalent language is not restricted to a particular ship and requires delivery from a ship which has reached a place at the named port of destination where goods of the kind are usually discharged.

(2) Under such a term unless otherwise agreed

(a) the seller must discharge all liens arising Out of the carriage and furnish the buyer with a direction which puts the carrier under a duty to deliver the goods; and

(b) the risk of loss does not pass to the buyer until the goods leave the ship's tackle or are otherwise properly unloaded.

§ 2-323. Form of Bill of Lading Required in Overseas Shipment; "Overseas".

(1) Where the contract contemplates overseas shipment and contains a term C.I.F. or C. & F. or F.O.B. vessel, the seller unless otherwise agreed must obtain a negotiable bill of lading stating that the goods have been loaded in board or, in the case of a term C.I.F. or C. & F., received for shipment.

(2) Where in a case within subsection (1) a bill of lading has been issued in a set of parts, unless otherwise agreed if the documents are not to be sent from abroad the buyer may demand tender of the full set; otherwise only one part of the bill of lading need be tendered. Even if the agreement expressly requires a full set

(a) due tender of a single part is acceptable within the provisions of this Article on cure of improper delivery (subsection (1) of Section 2-508); and

(b) even though the full set is demanded, if the documents are sent from abroad the person tendering an incomplete set may nevertheless require payment upon furnishing an indemnity which the buyer in good faith deems adequate.

(3) A shipment by water or by air or a contract contemplating such shipment is "overseas" insofar as by usage of trade or agreement it is subject to the commercial, financing or shipping practices characteristic of international deep water commerce.

§ 2-324. "No Arrival, No Sale" Term. Under a term "no arrival, no sale" or terms of like meaning, unless otherwise agreed,

(a) The seller must properly ship conforming goods and if they arrive by any means he must tender them on arrival but he assumes no obligation that the goods will arrive unless he has caused the non-arrival; and

(b) where without fault of the seller the goods are in part lost or have so deteriorated as no longer to conform to the contract or arrive after the contract time, the buyer may proceed as if there had been casualty to identified goods (Section 2-613).

§ 2-325. "Letter of Credit" Term; "Confirmed Credit".

(1) Failure of the buyer seasonably to furnish an agreed letter of credit is a breach of the contract for sale.

(2) The delivery to seller of a proper letter of credit suspends the buyer's obligation to pay. If the letter of credit is dishonored, the seller may on seasonable notification to the buyer require payment directly from him.

(3) Unless otherwise agreed the term "letter of credit" or "banker's credit" in a contract for sale means an irrevocable credit issued by a financing agency of good repute and, where the shipment is overseas, of good international repute. The term "confirmed credit" means that the credit must also carry

the direct obligation of such an agency which does business in the seller's financial market.

§ 2-326. Sale on Approval and Sale or Return; Consignment Sales and Rights of Creditors.

(1) Unless otherwise agreed, if delivered goods may be returned by the buyer even though they conform to the contract, the transaction is

(a) a "sale on approval" if the goods are delivered primarily for use, and

(b) a "sale or return" if the goods are delivered primarily for resale.

(2) Except as provided in subsection (3), goods held on approval are not subject to the claims of the buyer's creditors until acceptance; goods held on sale or return are subject to such claims while in the buyer's possession.

(3) Where goods are delivered to a person for sale and such person maintains a place of business at which he deals in goods of the kind involved, under a name other than the name of the person making delivery, then with respect to claims of creditors of the person conducting the business the goods ate deemed to be on sale or return. The provisions of this subsection are applicable even though an agreement purports to reserve title to the person making delivery until payment or resale or uses such words as on consignment or on memorandum". However, this subsection is not applicable if the person making delivery

(a) complies with an applicable law providing for a consignor's interest or the like to be evidenced by a sign, or

(b) establishes that the person conducting the business is generally known by his creditors to be substantially engaged in selling the goods of others, or

(c) complies with the filing provisions of the Article on Secured Transactions (Article 9).

(4) Any "or return" term of a contract for sale is to be treated as a separate contract for sale within the statute of frauds section of this Article (Section 2-201) and as contradicting the sale aspect of the contract within the provisions of this Article on parol or extrinsic evidence (Section 2-202).

§ 2-327. Special Incidents of Sale on Approval and Sale or Return.

(1) Under a sale on approval unless otherwise agreed

(a) although the goods are identified to the contract the risk of loss and the title do not pass to the buyer until acceptance; and

(b) use of the goods consistent with the purpose of trial is not acceptance but failure seasonably to notify the seller of election to return the goods is acceptance, and if the goods conform to the contract acceptance of any part is acceptance of the whole; and

(c) after due notification of election to return, the return is at the seller's risk and expense but a merchant buyer must follow any reasonable instructions.

(2) Under a sale or return unless otherwise agreed

(a) the option to return extends to the whole or any commercial unit of the goods while in substantially their original condition, but must be exercised seasonably; and

(b) the return is at the buyer's risk and expense.

§ 2-328. Sale by Auction.

(1) In a sale by auction if goods are put up in lots each lot is the subject of a separate sale.

(2) A sale by auction is complete when the auctioneer so announces by the fall of the hammer or in other customary manner. Where a bid is made while the hammer is falling in acceptance of a prior bid the auctioneer may in his discretion reopen the bidding or declare the goods sold under the bid on which the hammer was falling.

(3) Such a sale is with reserve unless the goods are in explicit terms put up without reserve. In an auction with reserve the auctioneer may withdraw the goods at any time until he announces completion of the sale. In an auction without reserve, after the auctioneer calls for bids on an article or lot, that article or lot cannot be withdrawn unless no bid is made within a reasonable time. In either case a bidder may retract his bid until the auctioneer's announcement of completion of the sale, but a bidder's retraction does not revive any previous bid.

(4) If the auctioneer knowingly receives a bid on the seller's behalf or the seller makes or procures such a bid, and notice has not been given that liberty for such bidding is reserved, the buyer may at his option avoid the sale or take the goods at the price of the last good faith bid prior to the completion of the sale. This subsection shall not apply to any bid at a forced sale.

PART 4 Title, Creditors and Good Faith Purchasers

§ 2-401. Passing of Title; Reservation for Security; Limited Application of This Section. Each provision of this Article with regard to the rights, obligations and remedies of the seller, the buyer, purchasers or other third parties applies irrespective of title to the goods except where the provisions refers to such title. Insofar as situations are not covered by the other provisions of this Article and matters concerning title become material the following rules apply:

(1) Title to goods cannot pass under a contract for sale prior to their identification to the contract (Section 2-501), and unless otherwise explicitly agreed the buyer acquires by their identification a special property as limited by this Act. Any retention or reservation by the seller of the title (property) in goods shipped or delivered to the buyer is limited in effect to a reservation of a security interest. Subject to these provisions and to the provisions of the Article on Secured Transactions (Article 9), title to goods passes from the seller to the buyer in any manner and on any conditions explicitly agreed on by the parties.

(2) Unless otherwise explicitly agreed title passes to the buyer at the time and place at which the seller completes his performance with reference to the physical delivery of the goods, despite any reservation of a security interest and even though a document of title is to be delivered at a different time or place; and in particular and despite any reservation of a security interest by the bill of lading

(a) if the contract requires or authorizes the seller to send the goods to the buyer but does not require him to deliver them at destination, title passes to the buyer at the time and place of shipment; but

(b) if the contract requires delivery at destination, title passes on tender there.

(3) Unless otherwise explicitly agreed where delivery is to be made without moving the goods,

(a) if the seller is to deliver a document of title, title passes at the time when and the place where he delivers such documents; or

(b) if the goods are at the time of contracting already identified and no documents are to be delivered, title passes at the time and place of contracting.

(4) A rejection or other refusal by the buyer to receive or retain the goods, whether or not justified, or a justified revocation of acceptance revests title to the goods in the seller. Such revesting occurs by operation of law and is not a "sale".

§ 2-402. Rights of Seller's Creditors Against Sold Goods.

(1) Except as provided in subsections (2) and (3), rights of unsecured creditors of the seller with respect to goods which have been identified to a contract for sale are subject to the buyer's rights to recover the goods under this Article (Sections 2-502 and 2-716).

(2) A creditor of the seller may treat a sale or an identification of goods to a contract for sale as void if as against him a retention of possession by the seller is fraudulent under any rule of law of the state where the goods are situated, except that retention of possession in good faith and current course of trade by a merchant-seller for a commercially reasonable time after a sale or identification is not fraudulent.

(3) Nothing in this Article shall be deemed to impair the rights of creditors of the seller

(a) under the provisions of the Article on Secured Transactions (Article 9); or

(b) Where identification to the contract or delivery is made not in current course of trade but in satisfaction of or as security for a pre-existing claim for money security or the like and is made under circumstances which under any rule of law of the state where the goods are situated would apart from this Article constitute the transaction a fraudulent transfer or voidable preference.

§ 2-403. Power to Transfer; Good Faith Purchase of Goods; "Entrusting".

(1) A purchaser of goods acquires all title which his transferor had or had power to transfer except that a purchaser of a limited interest acquires rights only to the extent of the interest purchased. A person with voidable title has power to transfer a good title to a good faith purchaser for value. When goods have been delivered under a transaction of purchase the purchaser has such power even though

(a) the transferor was deceived as to the identity of the purchaser, or

(b) the delivery was in exchange for a check which is later dishonored, or

(c) it was agreed that the transaction was to be a "cash sale", or

(d) the delivery was procured through fraud punishable as larcenous under the criminal law.

(2) Any entrusting of possession of goods to a merchant who deals in goods of that kind gives him power to transfer all rights of the entruster to a buyer in ordinary course of business.

(3) "Entrusting" includes any delivery and any acquiescence in retention of possession regardless of any condition expressed between the parties to the delivery or acquiescence and regardless of whether the procurement of the entrusting or the possessor's disposition of the goods have been such as to be larcenous under the criminal law.

Note: *If a state adopts the repealer of Article 6—Bulk Transfers (Alternative A), subsection (4) should read as follows:*

(4) The rights of other purchasers of goods and of lien creditors are governed by the Articles on Secured Transactions (Article-9) and Documents of Title (Article 7).

Note: *If a state adopts Revised Article 6—Bulk Sales (Alternative B), subsection (4) should read as follows:*

(4) The rights of other purchasers of goods and of lien creditors are governed by the Articles on Secured Transactions (Article 9), Bulk Sales (Article 6) and Documents of Title (Article 7).

As amended in 1988.

PART 5 Performance

§ 2-501. Insurable Interest in Goods; Manner of Identification of Goods.

(1) The buyer obtains a special property and an insurable interest in goods by identification of existing goods as goods to which the contract refers even though the goods so identified are nonconforming and he has an option to return or reject them. Such identification can be made at any time and in any manner explicitly agreed to by the parties. In the absence of explicit agreement identification occurs

(a) when the contract is made if it is for the sale of goods already existing and identified;

(b) if the contract is for the sale of future goods other than those described in paragraph (c), when goods are shipped, marked or otherwise designated by the seller as goods to which the contract refers;

(c) when the crops are planted or otherwise become growing crops or the young are conceived if the contract is for the sale of unborn young to be born within twelve months after contracting or for the sale of crops to be harvested within twelve months or the next normal harvest season after contracting whichever is longer.

(2) The seller retains an insurable interest in goods so long as title to or any security interest in the goods remains in him and where the identification is by the seller alone he may until default or insolvency or notification to the buyer that the identification is final substitute other goods for those identified.

(3) Nothing in this section impairs any insurable interest recognized under any other statute or rule of law.

§ 2-502. Buyer's Right to Goods on Seller's Insolvency.

(1) Subject to subsection (2) and even though the goods have not been shipped a buyer who has paid a part or all of the price of goods in which he has a special property under the provisions of the immediately preceding section may on making and keeping good a tender of any unpaid portion of their price recover them from the seller if the seller becomes insolvent within ten days after receipt of the first installment on their price.

(2) If the identification creating his special property has been made by the buyer he acquires the right to recover the goods only if they conform to the contract for sale.

§ 2-503. Manner of Seller's Tender of Delivery.

(1) Tender of delivery requires that the seller put and hold conforming goods at the buyer's disposition and give the buyer any notification reasonably necessary to enable him to take delivery. The manner, time and place for tender are determined by the agreement and this Article, and in particular

(a) tender must be at a reasonable hour, and if it is of goods they must be kept available for the period reasonably necessary to enable the buyer to take possession; but

(b) unless otherwise agreed the buyer must furnish facilities reasonably suited to the receipt of the goods.

(2) Where the case is within the next section respecting shipment tender requires that the seller comply with its provisions.

(3) Where the seller is required to deliver at a particular destination tender requires that he comply with subsection (1) and also in any appropriate case tender documents as described in subsections (4) and (5) of this section.

(4) Where goods are in the possession of a bailee and are to be delivered without being moved

(a) tender requires that the seller either tender a negotiable document of title covering such goods or procure acknowledgement by the bailee of the buyer's right to possession of the goods; but

(b) tender to the buyer of a non-negotiable document of title or of a written direction to the bailee to deliver is sufficient tender unless the buyer seasonably objects, and receipt by the bailee of notification of the buyer's rights fixes those rights as against the bailee and all third persons; but risk of loss of the goods and of any failure by the bailee to honor the non-negotiable document of title or to obey the direction remains on the seller until the buyer has had a reasonable time to present the document or direction, and a refusal by the bailee to honor the document or to obey the direction defeats the tender.

(5) Where the contract requires the seller to deliver documents

(a) he must tender all such documents in correct form, except as provided in this Article with respect to bills of lading in a set (subsection (2) of Section 2-323); and

(b) tender through customary banking channels is sufficient and dishonor of a draft accompanying the documents constitutes non-acceptance or rejection.

§ 2-504. Shipment by Seller. Where the seller is required or authorized to send the goods to the buyer and the contract does not require him to deliver them at a particular destination, then unless otherwise agreed he must

(a) put the goods in the possession of such a carrier and make such a contract for their transportation as may be reasonable having regard to the nature of the goods and other circumstances of the case; and

(b) obtain and promptly deliver or tender in due form any document necessary to enable the buyer to obtain possession of the goods or otherwise required by the agreement or by usage of trade; and

(c) promptly notify the buyer of the shipment.

Failure to notify the buyer under paragraph (c) or to make a proper contract under paragraph (a) is a ground for rejection only if material delay or loss ensues.

§ 2-505. Seller's Shipment Under Reservation.

(1) Where the seller has identified goods to the contract by or before shipment:

(a) his procurement of a negotiable bill of lading to his own order or otherwise reserves in him a security interest in the goods. His procurement of the bill to the order of a financing agency or of the buyer indicates in addition only the seller's expectation of transferring that interest to the person named.

(b) a non-negotiable bill of lading to himself or his nominee reserves possession of the goods as security but except in a case of conditional delivery (subsection (2) of Section 2-507) a non-negotiable bill of lading naming the buyer as consignee reserves no security interest even though the seller retains possession of the bill of lading.

(2) When shipment by the seller with reservation of a security interest is in violation of the contract for sale it constitutes an improper contract for transportation within the preceding section but impairs neither the rights given to the buyer by shipment and identification of the goods to the contract nor the seller's powers as a holder of a negotiable document.

§ 2-506. Rights of Financing Agency.

(1) A financing agency by paying or purchasing for value a draft which relates to a shipment of goods acquires to the extent of the payment or purchase and in addition to its own rights under the draft and any document Of title securing it any rights of the shipper in the goods including the right to stop delivery and the shipper's right to have the draft honored by the buyer.

(2) The right to reimbursement of a financing agency which has in good faith honored or purchased the draft under commitment to or authority from the buyer is not impaired by subsequent discovery of defects with reference to any relevant document which was apparently regular on its face.

§ 2-507. Effect of Seller's Tender; Delivery on Condition.

(1) Tender of delivery is a condition to the buyer's duty to accept the goods and, unless otherwise agreed, to his duty to pay for them. Tender entitles the seller to acceptance of the goods and to payment according to the contract.

(2) Where payment is due and demanded on the delivery to the buyer of goods or documents of title, his right as against the seller to retain or dispose of them is conditional upon his making the payment due.

§ 2-508. Cure by Seller of Improper Tender or Delivery; Replacement.

(1) Where any tender or delivery by the seller is rejected because non-conforming and the time for performance has not yet expired, the seller may seasonably notify the buyer of his intention to cure and may then within the contract time make a conforming delivery.

(2) Where the buyer rejects a non-conforming tender which the seller had reasonable grounds to believe would be acceptable with or without money allowance the seller may if he seasonably notifies the buyer have a further reasonable time to substitute a conforming tender.

§ 2-509. Risk of Less in the Absence of Breach.

(1) Where the contract requires or authorizes the seller to ship the goods by carrier

(a) if it does not require him to deliver them at a particular destination, the risk of loss passes to the buyer when the goods are duly delivered to the carrier even though the shipment is under reservation (Section 2-505); but

(b) if it does require him to deliver them at a particular destination and the goods are there duly tendered while in the possession of the carrier, the risk of loss passes to the buyer when the goods are there duly so tendered as to enable the buyer to take delivery.

(2) Where the goods are held by a bailee to be delivered without being moved, the risk of loss passes to the buyer

(a) on his receipt of a negotiable document of title covering the goods; or

(b) on acknowledgment by the bailee of the buyer's right to possession of the goods; or

(c) after his receipt of a non-negotiable document of title or other written direction to deliver, as provided in subsection (4) (b) of Section 2-503.

(3) In any case not within subsection (1) or (2), the risk of loss passes to the buyer on his receipt of the goods if the seller is a merchant; otherwise the risk passes to the buyer on tender of delivery.

(4) The provisions of this section are subject to contrary agreement of the parties and to the provisions of this Article on sale on approval (Section 2-327) and on effect of breach on risk of loss (Section 2-510).

§ 2-510. Effect of Breach on Risk of Loss.

(1) Where a tender or delivery of goods so fails to conform to the contract as to give a right of rejection the risk of their loss remains on the seller until cure or acceptance.

(2) Where the buyer rightfully revokes acceptance he may to the extent of any deficiency in his effective insurance coverage treat the risk of loss as having rested on the seller from the beginning.

(3) Where the buyer as to conforming goods already identified to the contract for sale repudiates or is otherwise in breach before risk of their loss has passed to him, the seller may to the extent of any deficiency in his effective insurance coverage treat the risk of loss as resting on the buyer for a commercially reasonable time.

§ 2-511. Tender of Payment by Buyer; Payment by Check.

(1) Unless otherwise agreed tender of payment is a condition to the seller's duty to tender and complete any delivery.

(2) Tender of payment is sufficient when made by any means or in any manner current in the ordinary course of business unless the seller demands payment in legal tender and gives any extension of time reasonably necessary to procure it.

(3) Subject to the provisions of this Act on the effect of an instrument on an obligation (Section 3-310), payment by check is conditional and is defeated as between the parties by dishonor of the check on due presentment.

§ 2-512. Payment by Buyer Before Inspection.

(1) Where the contract requires payment before inspection nonconformity of the goods does not excuse the buyer from so making payment unless

(a) the non-conformity appears without inspection; or

(b) despite tender of the required documents the circumstances would justify injunction against honor under the provisions of this Act (Section 5-114).

(2) Payment pursuant to subsection (1) does not constitute an acceptance of goods or impair the buyer's right to inspect or any of his remedies.

§ 2-513. Buyer's Right to Inspection of Goods.

(1) Unless otherwise agreed and subject to subsection (3), where goods are tendered or delivered or identified to the contract for sale, the buyer has a right before payment or acceptance to inspect them at any reasonable place and time and in any reasonable manner. When the seller is required or authorized to send the goods to the buyer, the inspection may be after their arrival.

(2) Expenses of inspection must be borne by the buyer but may be recovered from the seller if the goods do not conform and are rejected.

(3) Unless otherwise agreed and subject to the provisions of this Article on C.I.F. contracts (subsection (3) of Section 2-321), the buyer is not entitled to inspect the goods before payment of the price when the contract provides

(a) for delivery "C.O.D." or on other like terms; or

(b) for payment against documents of title, except where such payment is due only after the goods are to become available for inspection.

(4) A place or method of inspection fixed by the parties is presumed to be exclusive but unless otherwise expressly agreed it does not postpone identification or shift the place for delivery or for passing the risk of loss. If compliance becomes impossible, inspection shall be as provided in this section unless the place or method fixed was clearly intended as an indispensable condition failure of which avoids the contract.

§ 2-514. When Documents Deliverable on Acceptance; When on Payment. Unless otherwise agreed documents against which a draft is drawn are to be delivered to the drawee on acceptance of the draft if it is payable more than three days after presentment; otherwise, only on payment.

§ 2-515. Preserving Evidence of Goods in Dispute. In furtherance of the adjustment of any claim or dispute

(a) either party on reasonable notification to the other and for the purpose of ascertaining the facts and preserving evidence has the right to inspect, test and sample the goods including such of them as may be in the possession or control of the other; and
(b) the parties may agree to a third party inspection or survey to determine the conformity or condition of the goods and may agree that the findings shall be binding upon them in any subsequent litigation or adjustment.

PART 6 Breach, Repudiation and Excuse

§ 2-601. Buyer's Rights on Improper Delivery. Subject to the provisions of this Article on breach in installment contracts (Section 2-612) and unless otherwise agreed under the sections on contractual limitations of remedy (Sections 2-718 and 2-719), if the goods or the tender of delivery fail in any respect to conform to the contract, the buyer may
(a) reject the whole; or
(b) accept the whole; pr
(c) accept any commercial unit or units and reject the rest.

§ 2-602. Manner and Effect of Rightful Rejection.
(1) Rejection of goods must be within a reasonable time after their delivery or tender. It is ineffective unless the buyer seasonably notifies the seller.
(2) Subject to the provisions of the two following sections on rejected goods (Sections 2-603 and 2-604),
(a) after rejection any exercise of ownership by the buyer with respect to any commercial unit is wrongful as against the seller; and
(b) if the buyer has before rejection taken physical possession of goods in which he does not have a security interest under the provisions of this Article (subsection (3) of Section 2-711), he is under a duty after rejection to hold them with reasonable care at the seller's disposition for a time sufficient to permit the seller to remove them; but
(c) the buyer has no further obligations with regard to goods rightfully rejected.
(3) The seller's rights with respect to goods wrongfully rejected are governed by the provisions of this Article on Seller's remedies in general (Section 2-703).

§ 2-603. Merchant Buyer's Duties as to Rightfully Rejected Goods.
(1) Subject to any security interest in the buyer (subsection (3) of Section 2-711), when the seller has no agent or place of business at the market of rejection a merchant buyer is under a duty after rejection of goods in his possession or control to follow any reasonable instructions received from the seller with respect to the goods and in the absence of such instructions to make reasonable efforts to sell them for the seller's account if they are perishable or threaten to decline in value speedily. Instructions are not reasonable if on demand indemnity for expenses is not forthcoming.
(2) When the buyer sells goods under subsection (1), he is entitled to reimbursement from the seller or out of the proceeds for reasonable expenses of caring for and selling them, and if the expenses include no selling commission then to such commission as is usual in the trade or if there is none to a reasonable sum not exceeding ten per cent on the gross proceeds.
(3) In complying with this section the buyer is held only to good faith and good faith conduct hereunder is neither acceptance nor conversion nor the basis of an action for damages.

§ 2-604. Buyer's Options as to Salvage of Rightfully Rejected Goods. Subject to the provisions of the immediately preceding section on perishables if the seller gives no instructions within a reasonable time after notification of rejection the buyer may store the rejected goods for the seller's account or reship them to him or resell them for the seller's account with reimbursement as provided in the preceding section. Such action is not acceptance or conversion.

§ 2-605. Waiver of Buyer's Objections by Failure to Particularize.
(1) The buyer's failure to state in connection with rejection a particular defect which is ascertainable by reasonable inspection precludes him from relying on the unstated defect to justify rejection or to establish breach
(a) where the seller could have cured it if stated seasonably; or
(b) between merchants when the seller has after rejection made a request in writing for a full and final written statement of all defects on which the buyer proposes to rely.
(2) Payment against documents made without reservation of rights precludes recovery of the payment for defects apparent on the face of the documents.

§ 2-606. What Constitutes Acceptance of Goods.
(1) Acceptance of goods occurs when the buyer
(a) after a reasonable opportunity to inspect the goods signifies to the seller that the goods are conforming or that he will take or retain them in spite of their nonconformity; or
(b) fails to make an effective rejection (subsection (1) of Section 2-602), but such acceptance does not occur until the buyer has had a reasonable opportunity to inspect them; or
(c) does any act inconsistent with the seller's ownership; but if such act is wrongful as against the seller it is an acceptance only if ratified by him.
(2) Acceptance of a part of any commercial unit is acceptance of that entire unit.

§ 2-607. Effect of Acceptance; Notice of Breach; Burden of Establishing Breach After Acceptance; Notice of Claim or Litigation to Person Answerable Over.
(1) The buyer must pay at the contract rate for any goods accepted.
(2) Acceptance of goods by the buyer precludes rejection of the goods accepted and if made with knowledge of a nonconformity cannot be revoked because of it unless the acceptance was on the reasonable assumption that the nonconformity would be seasonably cured but acceptance does not of itself impair any other remedy provided by this Article for non-conformity.
(3) Where a tender has been accepted

(a) the buyer must within a reasonable time after he discovers or should have discovered any breach notify the seller of breach or be barred from any remedy; and

(b) if the claim is one for infringement or the like (subsection (3) of Section 2-312) and the buyer is sued as a result of such a breach he must so notify the seller within a reasonable time after he receives notice of the litigation or be barred from any remedy over for liability established by the litigation.

(4) The burden is on the buyer to establish any breach with respect to the goods accepted.

(5) Where the buyer is sued for breach of a warranty or other obligation for which his seller is answerable over

(a) he may give his seller written notice of the litigation. If the notice states that the seller may come in and defend and that if the seller does not do so he will be bound in any action against him by his buyer by any determination of fact common to the two litigations, then unless the seller after seasonable receipt of the notice does come in and defend he is so bound.

(b) if the claim is one for infringement or the like (subsection (3) of Section 2-312) the original seller may demand in writing that his buyer turn over to him control of the litigation including settlement or else be barred from any remedy over and if he also agrees to bear all expense and to satisfy any adverse judgment, then unless the buyer after seasonable receipt of the demand does turn over control the buyer is so barred.

(6) The provisions of subsections (3), (4) and (5) apply to any obligation of a buyer to hold the seller harmless against infringement or the like (subsection (3) of Section 2-312).

§ 2.608. Revocation of Acceptance in Whole or in Part.

(1) The buyer may revoke his acceptance of a lot or commercial unit whose non-conformity substantially impairs its value to him if he has accepted it

(a) on the reasonable assumption that its nonconformity would be cured and it has not been seasonably cured; or

(b) without discovery of such non-conformity if his acceptance was reasonably induced either by the difficulty of discovery before acceptance or by the seller's assurances.

(2) Revocation of acceptance must occur within a reasonable time after the buyer discovers or should have discovered the ground for it and before any substantial change in condition of the goods which is not caused by their own defects. It is not effective until the buyer notifies the seller of it.

(3) A buyer who so revokes has the same rights and duties with regard to the goods involved as if he had rejected them.

§ 2-609. Right to Adequate Assurance of Performance.

(1) A contract for sale imposes an obligation on each party that the other's expectation of receiving due performance will not be impaired. When reasonable grounds for insecurity arise with respect to the performance of either party the other may in writing demand adequate assurance of due performance and until he receives such assurance may if commercially reasonable suspend any performance for which he has not already received the agreed return.

(2) Between merchants the reasonableness of grounds for insecurity and the adequacy of any assurance offered shall be determined according to commercial standards.

(3) Acceptance of any improper delivery or payment does not prejudice the aggrieved party's right to demand adequate assurance of future performance.

(4) After receipt of a justified demand failure to provide within a reasonable time not exceeding thirty days such assurance of due performance as is adequate under the circumstances of the particular case is a repudiation of the contract.

§ 2-610. Anticipatory Repudiation.

When either party repudiates the contract with respect to a performance not yet due the loss of which will substantially impair the value of the contract to the other, the aggrieved party may

(a) for a commercially reasonable time await performance by the repudiating party; or

(b) resort to any remedy for breach (Section 2-703 or Section 2-711), even though he has notified the repudiating party that he would await the latter's performance and has urged retraction; and

(c) in either case suspend his own performance or proceed in accordance with the provisions of this Article on the seller's right to identify goods to the contract notwithstanding breach or to salvage unfinished goods (Section 2-704).

§ 2-611. Retraction of Anticipatory Repudiation.

(1) Until the repudiating party's next performance is due he can retract his repudiation unless the aggrieved party has since the repudiation cancelled or materially changed his position or otherwise indicated that he considers the repudiation final.

(2) Retraction may be by any method which clearly indicates to the aggrieved party that the repudiating party intends to perform, but must include any assurance justifiably demanded under the provisions of this Article (Section 2-609).

(3) Retraction reinstates the repudiating party's rights under the contract with due excuse and allowance to the aggrieved party for any delay occasioned by the repudiation.

§ 2-612. "Installment Contract"; Breach.

(1) An "installment contract" is one which requires or authorizes the delivery of goods in separate lots to be separately accepted, even though the contract contains a clause "each delivery is a separate contract" or its equivalent.

(2) The buyer may reject any installment which is nonconforming if the non-conformity substantially impairs the value of that installment and cannot be cured or if the nonconformity is a defect in the required documents; but if the non-conformity does not fall within subsection (3) and the seller gives adequate assurance of its cure the buyer must accept that installment.

(3) Whenever non-conformity or default with respect to one or more installments substantially impairs the value of the whole contract there is a breach of the whole. But the aggrieved party reinstates the contract if he accepts a nonconforming installment without seasonably notifying of cancellation or if he brings an action with respect only to past

installments or demands performance as to future installments.

§ 2-613. Casualty to Identified Goods. Where the contract requires for its performance goods identified when the contract is made, and the goods suffer casualty without fault of either party before the risk of loss passes to the buyer, or in a proper case under a "no arrival, no sale" term (Section 2-324) then

(a) if the loss is total the contract is avoided; and

(b) if the loss is partial or the goods have so deteriorated as no longer to conform to the contract the buyer may nevertheless demand inspection and at his option either treat the contract as avoided or accept the goods with due allowance from the contract price for the deterioration or the deficiency in quantity but without further right against the seller.

§ 2-614. Substituted Performance.

(1) Where without fault of either party the agreed berthing, loading, or unloading facilities fail or an agreed type of carrier becomes unavailable or the agreed manner of delivery otherwise becomes commercially impracticable but a commercially reasonable substitute is available, such substitute performance must be tendered and accepted.

(2) If the agreed means or manner of payment fails because of domestic or foreign governmental regulation, the seller may withhold or stop delivery unless the buyer provides a means or manner of payment which is commercially a substantial equivalent. If delivery has already been taken, payment by the means or in the manner provided by the regulation discharges the buyer's obligation unless the regulation is discriminatory, oppressive or predatory.

§ 2-615. Excuse by Failure of Presupposed Conditions. Except so far as a seller may have assumed a greater obligation and subject to the preceding section on substituted performance:

(a) Delay in delivery or non-delivery in whole or in part by a seller who complies with paragraphs (b) and (c) is not a breach of his duty under a contract for sale if performance as agreed has been made impracticable by the occurrence of a contingency the non-occurrence of which was a basic assumption on which the contract was made or by compliance in good faith with any applicable foreign or domestic governmental regulation or order whether or not it later proves to be invalid.

(b) Where the causes mentioned in paragraph (a) affect only a part of the seller's capacity to perform, he must allocate production and deliveries among his customers but may at his option include regular customers not then under contract as well as his own requirements for further manufacture. He may so allocate in any manner which is fair and reasonable.

(c) The seller must notify the buyer seasonably that there will be delay or non-delivery and, when allocation is required under paragraph (b), of the estimated quota thus made available for the buyer.

§ 2-616. Procedure on Notice Claiming Excuse.

(1) Where the buyer receives notification of a material or indefinite delay or an allocation justified under the preceding section he may by written notification to the seller as to any delivery concerned, and where the prospective deficiency substantially impairs the value of the whole contract under the provisions of this Article relating to breach of installment contracts (Section 2-612), then also as to the whole,

(a) terminate and thereby discharge any unexecuted portion of the contract; or

(b) modify the contract by agreeing to take his available quota in substitution.

(2) If after receipt of such notification from the seller the buyer fails so to modify the contract within a reasonable time not exceeding thirty days the contract lapses with respect to any deliveries affected.

(3) The provisions of this section may not be negated by agreement except in so far as the seller has assumed a greater obligation under the preceding section.

PART 7 Remedies

§ 2-701. Remedies for Breach of Collateral Contracts Not Impaired. Remedies for breach of any obligation or promise collateral or ancillary to a contract for sale are not impaired by the provisions of this Article.

§ 2-702. Seller's Remedies on Discovery of Buyer's Insolvency.

(1) Where the seller discovers the buyer to be insolvent he may refuse delivery except for cash including payment for all goods theretofore delivered under the contract, and stop delivery under this Article (Section 2-705).

(2) Where the seller discovers that the buyer has received goods on credit while insolvent he may reclaim the goods upon demand made within ten days after the receipt, but if misrepresentation of solvency has been made to the particular seller in writing within three months before delivery the ten day limitation does not apply. Except as provided in this subsection the seller may not base a right to reclaim goods on the buyer's fraudulent or innocent misrepresentation of solvency or of intent to pay.

(3) The seller's right to reclaim under subsection (2) is subject to the rights of a buyer in ordinary course or other good faith purchaser under this Article (Section 2-403). Successful reclamation of goods excludes all other remedies with respect to them.

As amended in 1966.

§ 2-703. Seller's Remedies in General. Where the buyer wrongfully rejects or revokes acceptance of goods or fails to make a payment due on or before delivery or repudiates with respect to a part or the whole, then with respect to any goods directly affected and, if the breach is of the whole contract (Section 2-612), then also with respect to the whole undelivered balance, the aggrieved seller may

(a) withhold delivery of such goods;

(b) stop delivery by any bailee as hereafter provided (Section 2-705);

(c) proceed under the next section respecting goods still unidentified to the contract;

(d) resell and recover damages as hereafter provided (Section 2-706);

(e) recover damages for non-acceptance (Section 2-708) or in a proper case the price (Section 2-709);

(f) cancel.

§ 2-704. Seller's Right to Identity Goods to the Contract Notwithstanding Breach or to Salvage Unfinished Goods.

(1) An aggrieved seller under the preceding section may

(a) identify to the contract conforming goods not already identified if at the time he learned of the breach they are in his possession or control;

(b) treat as the subject of resale goods which have demonstrably been intended for the particular contract even though those goods are unfinished.

(2) Where the goods are unfinished an aggrieved seller may in the exercise of reasonable commercial judgment for the purposes of avoiding loss and of effective realization either complete the manufacture and wholly identify the goods to the contract or cease manufacture and resell for scrap or salvage value or proceed in any other reasonable manner.

§ 2-705. Seller's Stoppage of Delivery in Transit or Otherwise.

(1) The seller may stop delivery of goods in the possession of a carrier or other bailee when he discovers the buyer to be insolvent (Section 2-702) and may stop delivery of carload, truckload, planeload or larger shipment& of express or freight when the buyer repudiates or fails to make a payment due before delivery or if for any other reason the seller has a right to withhold or reclaim the goods.

(2) As against such buyer the seller may stop delivery until

(a) receipt of the goods by the buyer; or

(b) acknowledgment to the buyer by any bailee of the goods except a carrier that the bailee holds the goods for the buyer; or

(c) such acknowledgment to the buyer by a carrier by reshipment or as warehouseman; or

(d) negotiation to the buyer of any negotiable document of title covering the goods.

(3) (a) To stop delivery the seller must so notify as to enable the bailee by reasonable diligence to prevent delivery of the goods.

(b) After such notification the bailee must hold and deliver the goods according to the directions of the seller but the seller is liable to the bailee for any ensuing charges or damages.

(c) If a negotiable document of title has been issued for goods the bailee is not obliged to obey a notification to stop until surrender of the document.

(d) A carrier who has issued a non-negotiable bill of lading is not obliged to obey a notification to stop received from a person other than the consignor.

§ 2-706. Seller's Resale Including Contract for Resale.

(1) Under the conditions stated in Section 2-703 on seller's remedies, the seller may resell the goods concerned or the undelivered balance thereof. Where the resale is made in good faith and in a commercially reasonable manner the seller may recover the difference between the resale price and the contract price together with any incidental damages allowed under the provisions of this Article (Section 2-710), but less expenses saved in consequence of the buyer's breach.

(2) Except as otherwise provided in subsection (3) or unless otherwise agreed resale may be at public or private sale including sale by way of one or more contracts to sell or of identification to an existing contract of the seller. Sale may be as a unit or in parcels and at any time and place and on any terms but every aspect of the sale including the method, manner, time, place and terms must be commercially reasonable. The resale must be reasonably identified as referring to the broken contract, but it is not necessary that the goods be in existence or that any or all of them have been identified to the contract before the breach.

(3) Where the resale is at private sale the seller must give the buyer reasonable notification of his intention to resell.

(4) Where the resale is at public sale

(a) only identified goods can be sold except where there is a recognized market for a public sale of futures in goods of the kind; and

(b) it must be made at a usual place or market for public sale if one is reasonably available and except in the case of goods which are perishable or threaten to decline in value speedily the seller must give the buyer reasonable notice of the time and place of the resale; and

(c) if the goods are not to be within the view of those attending the sale the notification of sale must state the place where the goods are located and provide for their reasonable inspection by prospective bidders; and

(d) the seller may buy.

(5) A purchaser who buys in good faith at a resale takes the goods free of any rights of the original buyer even though the seller fails to comply with one or more of the requirements of this section.

(6) The seller is not accountable to the buyer for any profit made on any resale. A person in the position of a seller (Section 2-707) or a buyer who has rightfully rejected or justifiably revoked acceptance must account for any excess over the amount of his security interest, as hereinafter defined (subsection (3) of Section 2-711).

§ 2-707. "Person in the Position of a Seller".

(1) A "person in the position of a seller" includes as against a principal an agent who has paid or become responsible for the price of goods of his principal or anyone who otherwise holds a security interest or other right in goods similar to that of a seller.

(2) A person in the position of a seller may as provided in this Article withhold or stop delivery (Section 2-705) and resell (Section 2-706) and recover incidental damages (Section 2-710).

§ 2-708. Seller's Damages for Non-acceptance or Repudiation.

(1) Subject to subsection (2) and to the provisions of this Article with respect to proof of market price (Section 2-723), the measure of damages for non-acceptance or repudiation by the buyer is the difference between the market price at the time and place for tender and the unpaid contract price together with any incidental damages provided in this Article (Section 2-710), but less expenses saved in consequence of the buyer's breach.

(2) If the measure of damages provided in subsection (1) is inadequate to put the seller in as good a position as performance would have done then the measure of damages is the profit (including reasonable overhead) which the seller would have made from full performance by the buyer, together with any incidental damages provided in this Article (Section 2-710), due allowance for costs reasonably incurred and due credit for payments or proceeds of resale.

§ 2-709. Action for the Price.
(1) When the buyer fails to pay the price as it becomes due the seller may recover, together with any incidental damages under the next section, the price

(a) of goods accepted or of conforming goods lost or damaged within a commercially reasonable time after risk of their loss has passed to the buyer; and

(b) of goods identified to the contract if the seller is unable after reasonable effort to resell them at a reasonable price or the circumstances reasonably indicate that such effort will be unavailing.

(2) Where the seller sues for the price he must hold for the buyer any goods which have been identified to the contract and are still in his control except that if resale becomes possible he may resell them at any time prior to the collection of the judgment. The net proceeds of any such resale must be credited to the buyer and payment of the judgment entitles him to any goods not resold.

(3) After the buyer has wrongfully rejected or revoked acceptance of the goods or has failed to make a payment due or has repudiated (Section 2-610), a seller who is held not entitled to the price under this section shall nevertheless be awarded damages for non-acceptance under the preceding section.

§ 2-710. Seller's Incidental Damages. Incidental damages to an aggrieved seller include any commercially reasonable charges, expenses or commissions incurred in stopping delivery, in the transportation, care and custody of goods after the buyer's breach, in connection with return or resale of the goods or otherwise resulting from the breach.

§ 2-711. Buyer's Remedies in General; Buyer's Security Interest in Rejected Goods.
(1) Where the seller fails to make delivery or repudiates or the buyer rightfully rejects or justifiably revokes acceptance then with respect to any goods involved, and with respect to the whole if the breach goes to the whole contract (Section 2-612), the buyer may cancel and whether or not he has done so may in addition to recovering so much of the price as has been paid

(a) "cover" and have damages under the next section as to all the goods affected whether or not they have been identified to the contract; or

(b) recover damages for non-delivery as provided in this Article (Section 2-713).

(2) Where the seller fails to deliver or repudiates the buyer may also

(a) if the goods have been identified recover them as provided in this Article (Section 2-502); or

(b) in a proper case obtain specific performance or replevy the goods as provided in this Article (Section 2-716).

(3) On rightful rejection or justifiable revocation of acceptance a buyer has a security interest in goods in his possession or control for any payments made on their price and any expenses reasonably incurred in their inspection, receipt, transportation, care and custody and may hold such goods and resell them in like manner as an aggrieved seller (Section 2-706).

§ 2-712. "Cover"; Buyer's Procurement of Substitute Goods.
(1) After a breach within the preceding section the buyer may "cover" by making in good faith and without unreasonable delay any reasonable purchase of or contract to purchase goods in substitution for those due from the seller.

(2) The buyer may recover from the seller as damages the difference between the cost of cover and the contract price together with any incidental or consequential damages as hereinafter defined (Section 2-715), but less expenses saved in consequence of the seller's breach.

(3) Failure of the buyer to effect cover within this section does not bar him from any other remedy.

§ 2-713. Buyer's Damages for Non-delivery or Repudiation.
(1) Subject to the provisions of this Article with respect to proof of market price (Section 2-723), the measure of damages for non-delivery or repudiation by the seller is the difference between the market price at the time when the buyer learned of the breach and the contract price together with any incidental and consequential damages provided in this Article (Section 2-715), but less expenses saved in consequence of the seller's breach.

(2) Market price is to be determined as of the place for tender or, in cases of rejection after arrival or revocation of acceptance, as of the place of arrival.

§ 2-714. Buyer's Damages for Breach in Regard to Accepted Goods.
(1) Where the buyer has accepted goods and given notification (subsection (3) of Section 2-607) he may recover as damages for any non-conformity of tender the loss resulting in the ordinary course of events from the seller's breach as determined in any manner which is reasonable.

(2) The measure of damages for breach of warranty is the difference at the time and place of acceptance between the value of the goods accepted and the value they would have had if they had been as warranted, unless special circumstances show proximate damages of a different amount.

(3) In a proper case any incidental and consequential damages under the next section may also be recovered.

§ 2-715. Buyer's Incidental and Consequential Damages.
(1) Incidental damages resulting from the seller's breach include expenses reasonably incurred in inspection, receipt, transportation and care and custody of goods rightfully rejected, any commercially reasonable charges, expenses or commissions in connection with effecting cover and any other reasonable expense incident to the delay or other breach.

(2) Consequential damages resulting from the seller's breach include

(a) any loss resulting from general or particular requirements and needs of which the seller at the time of contracting had reason to know and which could not reasonably be prevented by cover or otherwise; and

(b) injury to person or property proximately resulting from any breach of warranty.

§ 2-716. Buyer's Right to Specific Performance or Replevin.

(1) Specific performance may be decreed where the goods are unique or in other proper circumstances.

(2) The decree for specific performance may include such terms and conditions as to payment of the price, damages, or other relief as the court may deem just.

(3) The buyer has a right of replevin for goods identified to the contract if after reasonable effort he is unable to effect cover for such goods or the circumstances reasonably indicate that such effort will be unavailing or if the goods have been shipped under reservation and satisfaction of the security interest in them has been made or tendered.

§ 2-717. Deduction of Damages From the Price. The buyer on notifying the seller of his intention to do so may deduct all or any part of the damages resulting from any breach of the contract from any part of the price still due under the same contract.

§ 2-718. Liquidation or Limitation of Damages; Deposits.

(1) Damages for breach by either party may be liquidated in the agreement but only at an amount which is reasonable in the light of the anticipated or actual harm caused by the breach, the difficulties of proof of loss, and the inconvenience or nonfeasibility of otherwise obtaining an adequate remedy. A term fixing unreasonably large liquidated damages is void as a penalty.

(2) Where the seller justifiably withholds delivery of goods because of the buyer's breach, the buyer is entitled to restitution of any amount by which the sum of his payments exceeds

(a) the amount to which the seller is entitled by virtue of terms liquidating the seller's damages in accordance with subsection (1), or

(b) in the absence of such terms, twenty per cent of the value of the total performance for which the buyer is obligated under the contract or $500, whichever is smaller.

(3) The buyer's right to restitution under subsection (2) is subject to offset to the extent that the seller establishes

(a) a right to recover damages under the provisions of this Article other than subsection (1), and

(b) the amount or value of any benefits received by the buyer directly or indirectly by reason of the contract.

(4) Where a seller has received payment in goods their reasonable value or the proceeds of their resale shall be treated as payments for the purposes of subsection (2); but if the seller has notice of the buyer's breach before reselling goods received in part performance, his resale is subject to the conditions laid down in this Article on resale by an aggrieved seller (Section 2-706).

§ 2-719. Contractual Modification or Limitation of Remedy.

(1) Subject to the provisions of subsections (2) and (3) of this section and of the preceding section on liquidation and limitation of damages,

(a) the agreement may provide for remedies in addition to or in substitution for those provided in this Article and may limit or alter the measure of damages recoverable under this Article, as by limiting the buyer's remedies to return of the goods and repayment of the price or to repair and replacement of nonconforming goods or parts; and

(b) resort to a remedy as provided is optional unless the remedy is expressly agreed to be exclusive, in which case it is the sole remedy.

(2) Where circumstances cause an exclusive or limited remedy to fail of its essential purpose, remedy may be had as provided in this Act.

(3) Consequential damages may be limited or excluded unless the limitation or exclusion is unconscionable. Limitation of consequential damages for injury to the person in the case of consumer goods is prima facie unconscionable but limitation of damages where the loss is commercial is not.

§ 2-720. Effect of "Cancellation" or "Rescission" on Claims for Antecedent Breach. Unless the contrary intention clearly appears, expressions of "cancellation" or "rescission" of the contract or the like shall not be construed as a renunciation or discharge of any claim in damages for an antecedent breach.

§ 2-721. Remedies for Fraud. Remedies for material misrepresentation or fraud include all remedies available under this Article for non-fraudulent breach. Neither rescission or a claim for rescission of the contract for sale nor rejection or return of the goods shall bar or be deemed inconsistent with a claim for damages or other remedy.

§ 2-722. Who Can Sue Third Parties for Injury to Goods.

Where a third party so deals with goods which have been identified to a contract for sale as to cause actionable injury to a party to that contract

(a) a right of action against the third party is in either party to the contract for sale who has title to or a security interest or a special property or an insurable interest in the goods; and if the goods have been destroyed or converted a right of action is also in the party who either bore the risk of loss under the contract for sale or has since the injury assumed that risk as against the other;

(b) if at the time of the injury the party plaintiff did not bear the risk of loss as against the other party to the contract for sale and there is no arrangement between them for disposition of the recovery, his suit or settlement is, subject to his own interest, as a fiduciary for the other party to the contract; (c) either party may with the consent of the other sue for the benefit of whom it may concern.

§ 2-723. Proof of Market Price: Time and Place.

(1) If an action based on anticipatory repudiation comes to trial before the time for performance with respect to some or all of the goods, any damages based on market price (Section 2-708

or Section 2-713) shall be determined according to the price of such goods prevailing at the time when the aggrieved party learned of the repudiation.

(2) If evidence of a price prevailing at the times or places described in this Article is not readily available the price prevailing within any reasonable time before or after the time described or at any other place which in commercial judgment or under usage of trade would serve as a reasonable substitute for the one described may be used, making any proper allowance for the cost of transporting the goods to or from such other place.

(3) Evidence of a relevant price prevailing at a time or place other than the one described in this Article offered by one party is not admissible unless and until he has given the other party such notice as the court finds sufficient to prevent unfair surprise.

§ 2-724. Admissibility of Market Quotations. Whenever the prevailing price or value of any goods regularly bought and sold in any established commodity market is in issue, reports in official publications or trade journals or in newspapers or periodicals of general circulation published as the reports of such market shall be admissible in evidence. The circumstances of the preparation of such a report may be shown to affect its weight but not its admissibility.

§ 2-725. Statute of Limitations in Contracts for Sale.

(1) An action for breach of any contract for sale must be commenced within four years after the cause of action has accrued. By the original agreement the parties may reduce the period of limitation to not less than one year but may not extend it.

(2) A cause of action accrues when the breach occurs, regardless of the aggrieved party's lack of knowledge of the breach. A breach of warranty occurs when tender of delivery is made, except that where a warranty explicitly extends to future performance of the goods and discovery of the breach must await the time of such performance the cause of action accrues when the breach is or should have been discovered.

(3) Where an action commenced within the time limited by subsection (1) is so terminated as to leave available a remedy by another action for the same breach such other action may be commenced after the expiration of the time limited and within six months after the termination of the first action unless the termination resulted from voluntary discontinuance or from dismissal for failure or neglect to prosecute.

(4) This section does not alter the law on tolling of the statute of limitations nor does it apply to cause of action which have accrued before this Act becomes effective.

ARTICLE 2A / Leases

PART 1 General Provisions

§ 2A-101. Short Title.

This Article shall be known and may be cited as the Uniform Commercial Code—Leases.

§ 2A-102. Scope.

This Article applies to any transaction, regardless of form, that creates a lease.

§ 2A-103. Definitions and Index of Definitions.

(1) In this Article unless the context otherwise requires:

(a) "Buyer in ordinary course of business" means a person who in good faith and without knowledge that the sale to him lot hen is in violation of the ownership rights or security interest or leasehold interest of a third party in the goods buys in ordinary course from a person in the business of selling goods of that kind but does not include a pawnbroker. "Buying" may be for cash or by exchange of other property or on secured or unsecured credit and includes receiving goods or documents of title under a preexisting contract for sale but does not include a transfer in bulk or as security for or in total or partial satisfaction of a money debt.

(b) "Cancellation" occurs when either party puts an end to the lease contract for default by the other party.

(c) "Commercial unit" means such a unit of goods as by commercial usage is a single whole for purposes of lease and division of which materially impairs its character or value on the market or in use A commercial unit may be a single article, as a machine, or a set of articles, as a suite of furniture or a line of machinery, or a quantity, as a gross or carload, or any other unit treated in use or in the relevant market as a single whole.

(d) "Conforming" goods or performance under a lease contract means goods or performance that are in accordance with the obligations under the lease contract.

(e) "Consumer lease" means a lease that a lessor regularly engaged in the business of leasing or selling makes to alessee who is an individual and who takes under the lease primarily for a personal, family, or household purpose [, if the total payments to be made under the lease contract, excluding payments for options to renew or buy, do not exceed $_______].

(f) "Fault" means wrongful act, omission, breach, or default.

(g) "Finance lease" means a lease with respect to which:

(i) the lessor does not select, manufacture, or supply the goods;

(ii) the lessor acquires the goods or the right to possession and use of the goods in connection with the lease; and

(iii) one of the following occurs:

(A) the lessee receives a copy of the contract by which the lessor acquired the goods or the right to possession and use of the goods before signing the lease contract;

(B) the lessee's approval of the contract by which the lessor acquired the goods or the right to possession and use of the goods is a condition to effectiveness of the lease contract;

(C) the lessee, before signing the lease contract, receives an accurate and complete statement designating the promises and warranties, and any disclaimers of warranties, limitations or modifications of remedies, or liquidated damages, including those of a third party, such as the manufacturer of the goods, provided to the lessor by the person supplying the goods in connection with or as part of the contract by which the lessor acquired the goods or the right to possession and use of the goods; or

(D) if the lease is not a consumer lease, the lessor, before the lessee signs the lease contract, informs the lessee in writing (a) of the identity of the person supplying the goods to the lessor, unless the lessee has selected that person and directed the lessor to acquire the goods or the right to possession and use of the goods from that person, (b) that the lessee is entitled under this Article to the promises and warranties, including those of any third party, provided to the lessor by the person supplying the goods in connection with or as part of the contract by which the lessor acquired the goods or the right to possession and use of the goods, and (c) that the lessee may communicate with the person supplying the goods to the lessor and receive an accurate and complete statement of those promises and warranties, including any disclaimers and limitations of them or of remedies.

(h) "Goods" means all things that are movable at the time of identification to the lease contract, or are fixtures (Section 2A-309), but the term does not include money, documents, instruments, accounts, chattel paper, general intangibles, or minerals or the like, including oil and gas, before extraction. The term also includes the unborn young of animals.

(i) "Installment lease contract" means a lease contract that authorizes or requires the delivery of goods in separate lots to be separately accepted, even though the lease contract contains a clause "each delivery is a separate lease" or its equivalent.

(j) "Lease" means a transfer of the right to possession and use of goods for a term in return for consideration, but a sale, including a sale on approval or a sale or return, or retention or creation of a security interest is not a lease. Unless the context clearly indicates otherwise, the term includes a sublease.

(k) "Lease agreement" means the bargain, with respect to the lease, of the lessor and the lessee in fact as found in their language or by implication from other circumstances including course of dealing or usage of trade or course of performance as provided in this Article. Unless the context clearly indicates otherwise, the term includes a sublease agreement.

(l) "Lease contract" means the total legal obligation that results from the lease agreement as affected by this Article and any other applicable rules of law. Unless the context clearly indicates otherwise, the term includes a sublease contract.

(m) "Leasehold interest" means the interest of the lessor or the lessee under a lease contract.

(n) "Lessee" means a person who acquires the right to possession and use of goods under a lease. Unless the context clearly indicates otherwise, the term includes a sublessee.

(o) "Lessee in ordinary course of business" means a person who in good faith and without knowledge that the lease to him [or her] is in violation of the ownership rights or security interest or leasehold interest of a third party in the goods, leases in ordinary course from a person in the business of selling or leasing goods of that kind but does not include a pawnbroker. "Leasing" may be for cash or by exchange of other property or on secured or unsecured credit and includes receiving goods or documents of title under a pre-existing lease contract but does not include a transfer in bulk or as security for or in total or partial satisfaction of a money debt.

(p) "Lessor" means a person who transfers the right to possession and use of goods under a lease. Unless the context clearly indicates otherwise, the term includes a sublessor.

(q) "Lessor's residual interest" means the lessor's interest in the goods after expiration, termination, or cancellation of the lease contract.

(r) "Lien" means a charge against or interest in goods to secure payment of a debt or performance of an obligation, but the term does not include a security interest.

(s) "Lot" means a parcel or a single article that is the subject matter of a separate lease or delivery, whether or not it is sufficient to perform the lease contract.

(t) "Merchant lessee" means a lessee that is a merchant with respect to goods of the kind subject to the lease.

(u) "Present value" means the amount as of a date certain of one or more sums payable in the future, discounted to the date certain. The discount is determined by the interest rate specified by the parties if the rate was not manifestly unreasonable at the time the transaction was entered into; otherwise, the discount is determined by a commercially reasonable rate that takes into account the facts and circumstances of each case at the time the transaction was entered into.

(v) "Purchase" includes taking by sale, lease, mortgage, security interest, pledge, gift, or any other voluntary transaction creating an interest in goods.

(w) "Sublease" means a lease of goods the right to possession and use of which was acquired by the lessor as a lessee under an existing lease.

(x) "Supplier" means a person from whom a lessor buys or leases goods to be leased under a finance lease.

(y) "Supply contract" means a contract under which a lessor buys or leases goods to be leased.

(z) "Termination" occurs when either party pursuant to a power created by agreement or law puts an end to the lease contract otherwise than for default.

(2) Other definitions applying to this Article and the sections in which they appear are:

"Accessions". Section 2A-310(1).

"Construction mortgage". Section 2A-309(1) (d).

"Encumbrance". Section 2A-309(1) (e).

"Fixtures". Section 2A-309(1) (a).

"Fixture filing". Section 2A-309(1) (b).

"Purchase money lease". Section 2A-309 (1) (c).

(3) The following definitions in other Articles apply to this Article:

"Account". Section 9-106.

"Between merchants". Section 2-104(3).

"Buyer". Section 2-103(1) (a).

"Chattel paper". Section 9-105(1) (b).

"Consumer goods". Section 9-109(1).

"Document". Section 9-105(1) (f).

"Entrusting". Section 2-403(3).

"General intangibles". Section 9-106.

"Good faith" Section 2-103(1) (b).

"Instrument". Section 9-105(1) (i).

"Merchant". Section 2-104(1).

"Mortgage". Section 9-105(1) (j).

"Pursuant to commitment". Section 9-105(1)(k).

"Receipt". Section 2-103(1) (c).

"Sale". Section 2-106(1).

"Sale on approval". Section 2-326.

"Sale or return . Section 2-326.

"Seller". Section 2-103(1) (d).

(4) In addition Article 1 contains general definitions and principles of construction and interpretation applicable throughout this Article.

§ 2A-104 Leases Subject to Other Law.

(1) A lease, although subject to this Article, is also subject to any applicable:

(a) certificate of title statute of this State: (list any certificate of title statutes covering automobiles, trailers, mobile homes, boats, farm tractors, and the like);

(b) certificate of title statute of another jurisdiction (Section 2A-105); or

(c) consumer protection statute of this State, or final consumer protection decision of a court of this State existing on the effective date of this Article.

(2) In case of conflict between this Article, other than Sections 2A-105, 2A-304(3), and 2A-305(3), and a statute or decision referred to in subsection (1), the statute or decision controls.

(3) Failure to comply with an applicable law has only the effect specified therein.

§ 2A-105. Territorial Application of Article to Goods Covered by Certificate of Title.

Subject to the provisions of Sections 2A-304 (3) and 2A-305(3), with respect to goods covered by a certificate of title issued under a statute of this State or of another jurisdiction, compliance and the effect of compliance or noncompliance with a certificate of title statute are governed by the law (including the conflict of laws rules) of the jurisdiction issuing the certificate until the earlier of (a) surrender of the certificate, or (b) four months after the goods are removed from that jurisdiction and thereafter until a new certificate of title is issued by another jurisdiction.

§ 2A-106. Limitation on Power of Parties to Consumer Lease to Choose Applicable Law and Judicial Forum.

(1) If the law chosen by the parties to a consumer lease is that of a jurisdiction other than a jurisdiction in which the lessee resides at the time the lease agreement becomes enforceable or within 30 days thereafter or in which the goods are to be used, the choice is not enforceable.

(2) If the judicial forum chosen by the parties to a consumer lease is a forum that would not otherwise have jurisdiction over the lessee, the choice is not enforceable.

§ 2A-107. Waiver or Renunciation of Claim or Right After Default.

Any claim or right arising out of an alleged default or breach of warranty may be discharged in whole or in part without consideration by a written waiver or renunciation signed and delivered by the aggrieved party.

§ 2A-108. Unconscionability.

(1) If the court as a matter of law finds a lease contract or any clause of a lease contract to have been unconscionable at the time it was made the court may refuse to enforce the lease contract, or it may enforce the remainder of the lease contract without the unconscionable clause, or it may so limit the application of any unconscionable clause as to avoid any unconscionable result.

(2) With respect to a consumer lease, if the court as a matter of law finds that a lease contract or any clause of a lease contract has been induced by unconscionable conduct or that unconscionable conduct has occurred in the collection of a claim arising from a lease contract, the court may grant appropriate relief.

(3) Before making a finding of unconscionability under subsection (1) or (2), the court, on its own motion or that of a party, shall afford the parties a reasonable opportunity to present evidence as to the setting, purpose, and effect of the lease contract or clause thereof, or of the conduct.

(4) In an action in which the lessee claims unconscionability with respect to a consumer lease:

(a) If the court finds unconscionability under subsection (1) or (2), the court shall award reasonable attorney's fees to the lessee.

(b) If the court does not find unconscionability and the lessee claiming unconscionability has brought or maintained an action he [or she] knew to be groundless, the court shall award reasonable attorney's fees to the party against whom the claim is made.

(c) In determining attorney's fees, the amount of the recovery on behalf of the claimant under subsections (1) and (2) is not controlling.

§ 2A-109. Option to Accelerate at Will.

(1) A term providing that one party or his [or her] successor in interest may accelerate payment or performance or require collateral or additional collateral "at will" or "when he [or she] deems himself [or herself] insecure" or in words of similar import must be construed to mean that he [or she] has power to do so only if he [or she] in good faith believes that the prospect of payment or performance is impaired.

(2) With respect to a consumer lease, the burden of establishing good faith under subsection (1) is on the party who exercised

the power, otherwise the burden of establishing lack of good faith is on the party against whom the power has been exercised.

PART 2 Formation and Construction of Lease Contract

§ 2A-201. Statute of Frauds.

(1) A lease contract is not enforceable by way of action or defense unless:

(a) the total payments to be made under the lease contract, excluding payments for options to renew or buy, are less than $1,000; or

(b) there is a writing, signed by the party against whom enforcement is sought or by that party's authorized agent, sufficient to indicate that a lease contract has been made between the parties and to describe the goods leased and the lease term.

(2) Any description of leased goods or of the lease term is sufficient and satisfies subsection (1) (b), whether or not it is specific, if it reasonably identifies what is described.

(3) A writing is not insufficient because it omits or incorrectly states a term agreed upon, but the lease contract is not enforceable under subsection (1) (b) beyond the lease term and the quantity of goods shown in the writing.

(4) A lease contract that does not satisfy the requirements of subsection (1), but which is valid in other respects, is enforceable:

(a) if the goods are to be specially manufactured or obtained for the lessee and are not suitable for lease or sale to others in the ordinary course of the lessor's business, and the lessor, before notice of repudiation is received and under circumstances that reasonably indicate that the goods are for the lessee, has made either a substantial beginning of their manufacture or commitments for their procurement;

(b) if the party against whom enforcement is sought admits in that party's pleading, testimony or otherwise in court that a lease contract was made, but the lease contract is not enforceable under this provision beyond the quantity of goods admitted; or

(c) with respect to goods that have been received and accepted by the lessee.

(5) The lease term under a lease contract referred to in subsection (4) is:

(a) if there is a writing signed by the party against whom enforcement is sought or by that party's authorized agent specifying the lease term, the term so specified;

(b) if the party against whom enforcement is sought admits in that party's pleading, testimony, or otherwise in court a lease term, the term so admitted; or

(c) a reasonable lease term.

§ 2A-202. Final Written Expression: Parol or Extrinsic Evidence.

Terms with respect to which the confirmatory memoranda of the parties agree or which are otherwise set forth in a writing intended by the parties as a final expression of their agreement with respect to such terms as are included therein may not be contradicted by evidence of any prior agreement or of a contemporaneous oral agreement but may be explained or supplemented:

(a) by course of dealing or usage of trade or by course of performance; and

(b) by evidence of consistent additional terms unless the court finds the writing to have been intended also as a complete and exclusive statement of the terms of the agreement.

§ 2A-203. Seals Inoperative.

The affixing of a seal to a writing evidencing a lease contract or an offer to enter into a lease contract does not render the writing a sealed instrument and the law with respect to sealed instruments does not apply to the lease contract or offer.

§ 2A-204. Formation in General.

(1) A lease contract may be made in any manner sufficient to show agreement, including conduct by both parties which recognizes the existence of a lease contract.

(2) An agreement sufficient to constitute a lease contract may be found although the moment of its making is undetermined.

(3) Although one or more terms are left open, a lease contract does not fail for indefiniteness if the parties have intended to make a lease contract and there is a reasonably certain basis for giving an appropriate remedy.

§ 2A-205. Firm Offers.

An offer by a merchant to lease goods to or from another person in a signed writing that by its terms gives assurance it will be held open is not revocable, for lack of consideration, during the time stated or, if no time is stated, for a reasonable time, but in no event may the period of irrevocability exceed 3 months. Any such term of assurance on a form supplied by the offeree must be separately signed by the offeror.

§ 2A-206. Offer and Acceptance in Formation of Lease Contract.

(1) Unless otherwise unambiguously indicated by the language or circumstances, an offer to make a lease contract must be construed as inviting acceptance in any manner and by any medium reasonable in the circumstances.

(2) If the beginning of a requested performance is a reasonable mode of acceptance, an offeror who is not notified of acceptance within a reasonable time may treat the offer as having lapsed before acceptance.

§ 2A-207. Course of Performance or Practical Construction.

(1) If a lease contract involves repeated occasions for performance by either party with knowledge of the nature of the performance and opportunity for objection to it by the other, any course of performance accepted or acquiesced in without objection is relevant to determine the meaning of the lease agreement.

(2) The express terms of a lease agreement and any course of performance, as well as any course of dealing and usage of trade, must be construed whenever reasonable as consistent with each other, but if that construction is unreasonable, express terms control course of performance, course of performance controls both course of dealing and usage of trade, and course of dealing controls usage of trade.

(3) Subject to the provisions of Section 2A-208 on modification and waiver, course of performance is relevant to show a waiver or modification of any term inconsistent with the course of performance.

§ 2A-208. Modification, Rescission and Waiver.

(1) An agreement modifying a lease contract needs no consideration to be binding.

(2) A signed lease agreement that excludes modification or rescission except by a signed writing may not be otherwise modified or rescinded, but, except as between merchants, such a requirement on a form supplied by a merchant must be separately signed by the other party.

(3) Although an attempt at modification or rescission does not satisfy the requirements of subsection (2), it may operate as a waiver

(4) A party who has made a waiver affecting an executory portion of a lease contract may retract the waiver by reasonable notification received by the other party that strict performance will be required of any term waived, unless the retraction would be unjust in view of a material change of position in reliance on the waiver.

§ 2A-209. Lessee Under Finance Lease as Beneficiary of Supply Contract.

(1) The benefit of a supplier's promises to the lessor under the supply contract and of all warranties, whether express or implied, including those of any third party provided in connection with or as part of the supply contract, extends to the lessee to the extent of the lessee's leasehold interest under a finance lease related to the supply contract, but is subject to the terms of the warranty and of the supply contract and all defenses or claims arising therefrom.

(2) The extension of the benefit of a supplier's promises and of warranties to the lessee (Section 2A-209(l)) does not: (i) modify the rights and obligations of the parties to the supply contract, whether arising therefrom or otherwise, or (ii) impose any duty or liability under the supply contract on the lessee.

(3) Any modification or rescission of the supply contract by the supplier and the lessor is effective between the supplier and the lessee unless, before the modification or rescission the supplier has received notice that the lessee has entered into a finance lease related to the supply contract. If the modification or rescission is effective between the supplier and the lessee, the lessor is deemed to have assumed, in addition to the obligations of the lessor to the lessee under the lease contract, promises of the supplier to the lessor and warranties that were so modified or rescinded as they existed and were available to the lessee before modification or rescission.

(4) In addition to the extension of the benefit of the supplier's promises and of warranties to the lessee under subsection (1), the lessee retains all rights that the lessee may have against the supplier which arise from an agreement between the lessee and the supplier or under other law.

§ 2A-210. Express Warranties.

(1) Express warranties by the lessor are created as follows:

(a) Any affirmation of fact or promise made by the lessor to the lessee which relates to the goods and becomes part of the basis of the bargain creates an express warranty that the goods will conform to the affirmation or promise.

(b) Any description of the goods which is made part of the basis of the bargain creates an express warranty that the goods will conform to the description.

(c) Any sample or model that is made part of the basis of the bargain creates an express warranty that the whole of the goods will conform to the sample or model.

(2) It is not necessary to the creation of an express warranty that the lessor use formal words, such as "warrant" or "guarantee," or that the lessor have a specific intention to make a warranty, but an affirmation merely of the value of the goods or a statement purporting to be merely the lessor's opinion or commendation of the goods does not create a warranty.

§ 2A-211. Warranties Against Interference and Against Infringement; Lessee's Obligation Against Infringement.

(1) There is in a lease contract a warranty that for the lease term no person holds a claim to or interest in the goods that arose from an act or omission of the lessor, other than a claim by way of infringement or the like, which will interfere with the lessee's enjoyment of its leasehold interest.

(2) Except in a finance lease there is in a lease contract by a lessor who is a merchant regularly dealing in goods of the kind a warranty that the goods are delivered free of the rightful claim of any person by way of infringement or the like.

(3) A lessee who furnishes specifications to a lessor or a supplier shall hold the lessor and the supplier harmless against any claim by way of infringement or the like that arises out of compliance with the specifications.

§ 2A-212. Implied Warranty of Merchantability.

(1) Except in a finance lease, a warranty that the goods will be merchantable is implied in a lease contract if the lessor is a merchant with respect to goods of that kind.

(2) Goods to be merchantable must be at least such as

(a) pass without objection in the trade under the description in the lease agreement;

(b) in the case of fungible goods, are of fair average quality within the description;

(c) are fit for the ordinary purposes for which goods of that type are used;

(d) run, within the variation permitted by the lease agreement, of even kind, quality, and quantity within each unit and among all units involved;

(e) are adequately contained, packaged, and labeled as the lease agreement may require; and

(f) conform to any promises or affirmations of fact made on the container or label.

(3) Other implied warranties may arise from course of dealing or usage of trade.

§ 2A-213. Implied Warranty of Fitness for Particular Purpose.

Except in a finance lease, if the lessor at the time the lease contract is made has reason to know of any particular purpose for which the goods are required and that the lessee is relying on the lessor's skill or judgment to select or furnish suitable goods, there is in the lease contract an implied warranty that the goods will be fit for that purpose.

§ 2A-214. Exclusion or Modification of Warranties.

(1) Words or conduct relevant to the creation of an express warranty and words or conduct tending to negate or limit a warranty must be construed wherever reasonable as consistent with each other, but, subject to the provisions of Section 2A-202 on parol or extrinsic evidence, negation or limitation is inoperative to the extent that the construction is unreasonable.

(2) Subject to subsection (3), to exclude or modify the implied warranty of merchantability or any part of it the language must mention "merchantability", be by a writing, and be conspicuous. Subject to subsection (3), to exclude or modify any implied warranty of fitness the exclusion must be by a writing and be conspicuous. Language to exclude all implied warranties of fitness is sufficient if it is in writing, is conspicuous and states, for example, "There is no warranty that the goods will be fit for a particular purpose

(3) Notwithstanding subsection (2), but subject to subsection (4),

(a) unless the circumstances indicate otherwise, all implied warranties are excluded by expressions like "as is," or "with all faults," or by other language that in common understanding calls the lessee's attention to the exclusion of warranties and makes plain that there is no implied warranty, if in writing and conspicuous;

(b) if the lessee before entering into the lease contract has examined the goods or the sample or model as fully as desired or has refused to examine the goods, there is no implied warranty with regard to defects that an examination ought in the circumstances to have revealed; and

(c) an implied warranty may also be excluded or modified by course of dealing, course of performance, or usage of trade.

(4) To exclude or modify a warranty against interference or against infringement (Section 2A-211) or any part of it, the language must be specific, be by a writing, and be conspicuous, unless the circumstances, including course of performance, course of dealing, or usage of trade, give the lessee reason to know that the goods are being leased subject to a claim or interest of any person.

§ 2A-215. Cumulation and Conflict of Warranties Express or Implied.

Warranties, whether express or implied, must be construed as consistent with each other and as cumulative, but if that construction is unreasonable, the intention of the parties determines which warranty is dominant. In ascertaining that intention the following rules apply:

(a) Exact or technical specifications displace an inconsistent sample or model or general language of description.

(b) A sample from an existing bulk displaces inconsistent general language of description.

(c) Express warranties displace inconsistent implied warranties other than an implied warranty of fitness for a particular purpose.

§ 2A-216. Third-Party Beneficiaries of Express and Implied Warranties.

Alternative A

A warranty to or for the benefit of a lessee under this Article, whether express or implied, extends to any natural person who is in the family or household of the lessee or who is a guest in the lessee's home if it is reasonable to expect that such person may use, consume, or be affected by the goods and who is injured in person by breach of the warranty. This section does not displace principles of law and equity that extend a warranty to or for the benefit of a lessee to other persons. The operation of this section may not be excluded, modified, or limited, but an exclusion, modification, or limitation of the warranty, including any with respect to rights and remedies, effective against the lessee is also effective against any beneficiary designated under this section.

Alternative B

A warranty to or for the benefit of a lessee under this Article, whether express or implied, extends to any natural person who may reasonably be expected to use, consume, or be affected by the goods and who is injured in person by breach of the warranty. This section does not displace principles of law and equity that extend a warranty to or for the benefit of a lessee to other persons. The operation of this section may not be excluded, modified, or limited, but an exclusion, modification, or limitation of the warranty, including any with respect to rights and remedies, effective against the lessee is also effective against the beneficiary designated under this section.

Alternative C

A warranty to or for the benefit of a lessee under this Article, whether express or implied, extends to any person who may reasonably be expected to use, consume, or be affected by the goods and who is injured by breach of the warranty. The operation of this section may not be excluded, modified, or limited with respect to injury to the person of an individual to whom the warranty extends, but an exclusion, modification, or limitation of the warranty, including any with respect to rights and remedies, effective against the lessee is also effective against the beneficiary designated under this section.

§ 2A-217. Identification.

Identification of goods as goods to which a lease contract refers may be made at any time and in any manner explicitly agreed to by the parties. In the absence of explicit agreement, identification occurs:

(a) when the lease contract is made if the lease contract is for a lease of goods that are existing and identified;

(b) when the goods are shipped, marked, or otherwise designated by the lessor as goods to which the lease contract refers, if the lease contract is for a lease of goods that are not existing and identified; or

(c) when the young are conceived, if the lease contract is for a lease of unborn young of animals.

§ 2A-218. Insurance and Proceeds.

(1) A lessee obtains an insurable interest when existing goods are identified to the lease contract even though the

goods identified are nonconforming and the lessee has an option to reject them.
(2) If a lessee has an insurable interest only by reason of the lessor's identification of the goods, the lessor, until default or insolvency or notification to the lessee that identification is final, may substitute other goods for those identified.
(3) Notwithstanding a lessee's insurable interest under subsections (1) and (2), the lessor retains an insurable interest until an option to buy has been exercised by the lessee and risk of loss has passed to the lessee.
(4) Nothing in this section impairs any insurable interest recognized under any other statute or rule of law.
(5) The parties by agreement may determine that one or more parties have an obligation to obtain and pay for insurance covering the goods and by agreement may determine the beneficiary of the proceeds of the insurance.

§ 2A-219. Risk of Loss.

(1) Except in the case of a finance lease, risk of loss is retained by the lessor and does not pass to the lessee. In the case of a finance lease, risk of loss passes to the lessee.
(2) Subject to the provisions of this Article on the effect of default on risk of loss (Section 2A-220), if risk of loss is to pass to the lessee and the time of passage is not stated, the following rules apply:

(a) If the lease contract requires or authorizes the goods to be shipped by carrier
(i) and it does not require delivery at a particular destination, the risk of loss passes to the lessee when the goods are duly delivered to the carrier; but
(ii) if it does require delivery at a particular destination and the goods are there duly tendered while in the possession of the carrier, the risk of loss passes to the lessee when the goods are there duly so tendered as to enable the lessee to take delivery.

(b) If the goods are held by a bailee to be delivered without being moved, the risk of loss passes to the lessee on acknowledgment by the bailee of the lessee's right to possession of the goods.
(c) In any case not within subsection (a) or (b), the risk of loss passes to the lessee on the lessee's receipt of the goods if the lessor, or, in the case of a finance lease, the supplier, is a merchant; otherwise the risk passes to the lessee on tender of delivery.

§ 2A-220. Effect of Default on Risk of Loss.

(1) Where risk of loss is to pass to the lessee and the time of passage is not stated:

(a) If a tender or delivery of goods so fails to conform to the lease contract as to give a right of rejection, the risk of their loss remains with the lessor, or, in the case of a finance lease, the supplier, until cure or acceptance.
(b) If the lessee rightfully revokes acceptance, he [or she], to the extent of any deficiency in his [or her] effective insurance coverage, may treat the risk of loss as having remained with the lessor from the beginning.

(2) Whether or not risk of loss is to pass to the lessee, if the lessee as to conforming goods already identified to a lease contract repudiates or is otherwise in default under the lease contract, the lessor, or, in the case of a finance lease, the supplier, to the extent of any deficiency in his [or her] effective insurance coverage may treat the risk of loss as resting on the lessee for a commercially reasonable time.

§ 2A-221. Casualty to Identified Goods.

If a lease contract requires goods identified when the lease contract is made, and the goods suffer casualty without fault of the lessee, the lessor or the supplier before delivery, or the goods suffer casualty before risk of loss passes to the lessee pursuant to the lease agreement or Section 2A-219, then:

(a) if the loss is total, the lease contract is avoided; and
(b) if the loss is partial or the goods have so deteriorated as to no longer conform to the lease contract, the lessee may nevertheless demand inspection and at his [or her] option either treat the lease contract as avoided or, except in a finance lease that is not a consumer lease, accept the goods with due allowance from the rent payable for the balance of the lease term for the deterioration or the deficiency in quantity but without further right against the lessor.

PART 3 Effect of Lease Contract

§ 2A-301. Enforceability of Lease Contract.

Except as otherwise provided in this Article, a lease contract is effective and enforceable according to its terms between the parties, against purchasers of the goods and against creditors of the parties.

§ 2A-302. Title to and Possession of Goods.

Except as otherwise provided in this Article, each provision of this Article applies whether the lessor or a third party has title to the goods, and whether the lessor, the lessee, or a third party has possession of the goods, notwithstanding any statute or rule of law that possession or the absence of possession is fraudulent.

§ 2A-303. Alienability of Party's Interest Under Lease Contract or of Lessor's Residual Interest in Goods; Delegation of Performance; Transfer of Rights.

(1) As used in this section, "creation of a security interest includes the sale of a lease contract that is subject to Article 9, Secured Transactions, by reason of Section 9-102(1) (b).
(2) Except as provided in subsections (3) and (4), a provision in a lease agreement which (i) prohibits the voluntary or involuntary transfer, including a transfer by sale, sublease, creation or enforcement of a security interest, or attachment, levy, or other judicial process, of an interest of a party under the lease contract or of the lessor's residual interest in the goods, or (ii) makes such a transfer an event of default, gives rise to the rights and remedies provided in subsection (5), but a transfer that is prohibited or is an event of default under the lease agreement is otherwise effective.
(3) A provision in a lease agreement which (i) prohibits the creation or enforcement of a security interest in an interest of a party under the lease contract or in the lessor's residual interest in the goods, or (ii) makes such a transfer an event of default, is not enforceable unless, and then only to the extent that, there is an actual transfer by the lessee of the lessee's right of possession or use of the goods in violation of

the provision or an actual delegation of a material performance of either party to the lease contract in violation of the provision. Neither the granting nor the enforcement of a security interest in (1) the lessor's interest under the lease contract or (ii) the lessor's residual interest in the goods is a transfer that materially impairs the prospect of obtaining return performance by, materially changes the duty of, or materially increases the burden or risk imposed on, the lessee within the purview of subsection (5) unless, and then only to the extent that, there is an actual delegation of a material performance of the lessor.

(4) A provision in a lease agreement which (i) prohibits a transfer of a right to damages for default with respect to the whole lease contract or of a right to payment arising out of the transferor's due performance of the transferor's entire obligation, or (ii) makes such a transfer an event of default, is not enforceable, and such a transfer is not a transfer that materially impairs the prospect of obtaining return performance by, materially changes the duty of, or materially increases the burden or risk imposed on, the other party to the lease contract within the purview of subsection (5).

(5) Subject to subsections (3) and (4):

(a) if a transfer is made which is made an event of default under a lease agreement, the party to the lease contract not making the transfer, unless that party waives the default or otherwise agrees, has the rights and remedies described in Section 2A-50l (2);

(b) if paragraph (a) is not applicable and if a transfer is made that (i) is prohibited under a lease agreement or (ii) materially impairs the prospect of obtaining return performance by, materially changes the duty of, or materially increases the burden or risk imposed on, the other party to the lease contract, unless the party not making the transfer agrees at any time to the transfer in the lease contract or otherwise, then, except as limited by contract, (i) the transferor is liable to the party not making the transfer for damages caused by the transfer to the extent that the damages could not reasonably be prevented by the party not making the transfer and (ii) a court having jurisdiction may grant other appropriate relief, including cancellation of the lease contract or an injunction against the transfer.

(6) A transfer of "the lease" or of "all my rights under the lease", or a transfer in similar general terms, is a transfer of rights and, unless the language or the circumstances, as in a transfer for security, indicate the contrary, the transfer is a delegation of duties by the transferor to the transferee. Acceptance by the transferee constitutes a promise by the transferee to perform those duties. The promise is enforceable by either the transferor or the other party to the lease contract.

(7) Unless otherwise agreed by the lessor and the lessee, a delegation of performance does not relieve the transferor as against the other party of any duty to perform or of any liability for default.

(8) In a consumer lease, to prohibit the transfer of an interest of a party under the lease contract or to make a transfer an event of default, the language must be specific, by a writing, and conspicuous.

§ 2A-304. Subsequent Lease of Goods by Lessor.

(1) Subject to Section 2A-303, a subsequent lessee from a lessor of goods under an existing lease contract obtains, to the extent of the leasehold interest transferred, the leasehold interest in the goods that the lessor had or had power to transfer, and except as provided in subsection (2) and Section 2A-527 (4), takes subject to the existing lease contract. A lessor with voidable title has power to transfer a good leasehold interest to a good faith subsequent lessee for value, but only to the extent set forth in the preceding sentence. If goods have been delivered under a transaction of purchase, the lessor has that power even though:

(a) the lessor's transferor was deceived as to the identity of the lessor;

(b) the delivery was in exchange for a check which is later dishonored;

(c) it was agreed that the transaction was to be a "cash sale"; or

(d) the delivery was procured through fraud punishable as larcenous under the criminal law.

(2) A subsequent lessee in the ordinary course of business from a lessor who is a merchant dealing in goods of that kind to whom the goods were entrusted by the existing lessee of that lessor before the interest of the subsequent lessee became enforceable against that lessor obtains, to the extent of the leasehold interest transferred, all of that lessor's and the existing lessee's rights to the goods, and takes free of the existing lease contract.

(3) A subsequent lessee from the lessor of goods that are subject to an existing lease contract and are covered by a certificate of title issued under a statute of this State or of another jurisdiction takes no greater rights than those provided both by this section and by the certificate of title statute.

§ 2A-305. Sale or Sublease of Goods by Lessee.

(1) Subject to the provisions of Section 2A-303, a buyer or sublessee from the lessee of goods under an existing lease contract obtains, to the extent of the interest transferred, the leasehold interest in the goods that the lessee had or had power to transfer, and except as provided in subsection (2) and Section 2A-511(4), takes subject to the existing lease contract. A lessee with a voidable leasehold interest has power to transfer a good leasehold interest to a good faith buyer for value or a good faith sublessee for value, but only to the extent set forth in the preceding sentence. When goods have been delivered under a transaction of lease the lessee has that power even though:

(a) the lessor was deceived as to the identity of the lessee;

(b) the delivery was in exchange for a check which is later dishonored; or

(c) the delivery was procured through fraud punishable as larcenous under the criminal law.

(2) A buyer in the ordinary course of business or a sublessee in the ordinary course of business from a lessee who is a merchant dealing in goods of that kind to whom the goods were entrusted by the lessor obtains, to the extent of the interest transferred, all of the lessor's and lessee's rights to the goods, and takes free of the existing lease contract.

(3) A buyer or sublessee from the lessee of goods that are subject to an existing lease contract and are covered by a certificate of

title issued under a statute of this State or of another jurisdiction takes no greater rights than those provided both by this section and by the certificate of title statute.

§ 2A-306. Priority of Certain Liens Arising by Operation of Law.

If a person in the ordinary course of his [or her] business furnishes services or materials with respect to goods subject to a lease contract, a lien upon those goods in the possession of that person given by statute or rule of law for those materials or services takes priority over any interest of the lessor or lessee under the lease contract or this Article unless the lien is created by statute and the statute provides otherwise or unless the lien is created by rule of law and the rule of law provides otherwise.

§ 2A-307. Priority of Liens Arising by Attachment or Levy on, Security Interests in, and Other Claims to Goods.

(1) Except as otherwise provided in Section 2A-306, a creditor of a lessee takes subject to the lease contract.

(2) Except as otherwise provided in subsections (3) and (4) and in Sections 2A-306 and 2A-308, a creditor of a lessor takes subject to the lease contract unless:

(a) the creditor holds a lien that attached to the goods before the lease contract became enforceable,

(b) the creditor holds a security interest in the goods and the lessee did not give value and receive delivery of the goods without knowledge of the security interest; or

(c) the creditor holds a security interest in the goods which was perfected (Section 9-303) before the lease contract became enforceable.

(3) A lessee in the ordinary course of business takes the leasehold interest free of a security interest in the goods created by the lessor even though the security interest is perfected (Section 9-303) and the lessee knows of its existence.

(4) A lessee other than a lessee in the ordinary course of business takes the leasehold interest free of a security interest to the extent that it secures future advances made after the secured party acquires knowledge of the lease or more than 45 days after the lease contract becomes enforceable, whichever first occurs, unless the future advances are made pursuant to a commitment entered into without knowledge of the lease and before the expiration of the 45-day period.

§ 2A-308. Special Rights of Creditors.

(1) A creditor of a lessor in possession of goods subject to a lease contract may treat the lease contract as void if as against the creditor retention of possession by the lessor is fraudulent under any statute or rule of law, but retention of possession in good faith and current course of trade by the lessor for a commercially reasonable time after the lease contract becomes enforceable is not fraudulent.

(2) Nothing in this Article impairs the rights of creditors of a lessor if the lease contract (a) becomes enforceable, not in current course of trade but in satisfaction of or as security for a pre-existing claim for money, security, or the like, and (b) is made under circumstances which under any statute or rule of law apart from this Article would constitute the transaction a fraudulent transfer or voidable preference.

(3) A creditor of a seller may treat a sale or an identification of goods to a contract for sale as void if as against the creditor retention of possession by the seller is fraudulent under any statute or rule of law, but retention of possession of the goods pursuant to a lease contract entered into by the seller as lessee and the buyer as lessor in connection with the sale or identification of the goods is not fraudulent if the buyer bought for value and in good faith.

§ 2A-309. Lessor's and Lessee's Rights When Goods Become Fixtures.

(1) In this section:

(a) goods are "fixtures" when they become so related to particular real estate that an interest in them arises under real estate law;

(b) a "fixture filing" is the filing, in the office where a mortgage on the real estate would be filed or recorded, of a financing statement covering goods that are or are to become fixtures and conforming to the requirements of Section 9-402(5);

(c) a lease is a "purchase money lease" unless the lessee has possession or use of the goods or the right to possession or use of the goods before the lease agreement is enforceable;

(d) a mortgage is a "construction mortgage" to the extent it secures an obligation incurred for the construction of an improvement on land including the acquisition cost of the land, if the recorded writing so indicates; and

(e) "encumbrance" includes real estate mortgages and other liens on real estate and all other rights in real estate that are not ownership interests.

(2) Under this Article a lease may be of goods that are fixtures or may continue in goods that become fixtures, but no lease exists under this Article of ordinary building materials incorporated into an improvement on land.

(3) This Article does not prevent creation of a lease of fixtures pursuant to real estate law.

(4) The perfected interest of a lessor of fixtures has priority over a conflicting interest of an encumbrancer or owner of the real estate if:

(a) the lease is a purchase money lease, the conflicting interest of the encumbrancer or owner arises before the goods become fixtures, the interest of the lessor is perfected by a fixture filing before the goods become fixtures or within ten days thereafter, and the lessee has an interest of record in the real estate or is in possession of the real estate; or

(b) the interest of the lessor is perfected by a fixture filing before the interest of the encumbrancer or owner is of record, the lessor's interest has priority over any conflicting interest of a predecessor in title of the encumbrancer or owner, and the lessee has an interest of record in the real estate or is in possession of the real estate.

(5) The interest of a lessor of fixtures, whether or not perfected, has priority over the conflicting interest of an encumbrancer or owner of the real estate if:

(a) the fixtures are readily removable factory or office machines, readily removable equipment that is not primarily used or leased for use in the operation of the real estate, or readily removable replacements of domestic appliances that are goods subject to a consumer lease, and before the goods become fixtures the lease contract is enforceable; or

(b) the conflicting interest is a lien on the real estate obtained by legal or equitable proceedings after the lease contract is enforceable; or

(c) the encumbrancer or owner has consented in writing to the lease or has disclaimed an interest in the goods as fixtures; or

(d) the lessee has a right to remove the goods as against the encumbrancer or owner. If the lessee's right to remove terminates, the priority of the interest of the lessor continues for a reasonable time.

(6) Notwithstanding subsection (4) (a) but otherwise subject to subsections (4) and (5), the interest of a lessor of fixtures, including the lessor's residual interest, is subordinate to the conflicting interest of an encumbrancer of the real estate under a construction mortgage recorded before the goods become fixtures if the goods become fixtures before the completion of the construction. To the extent given to refinance a construction mortgage, the conflicting interest of an encumbrancer of the real estate under a mortgage has this priority to the same extent as the encumbrancer of the real estate under the construction mortgage.

(7) In cases not within the preceding subsections, priority between the interest of a lessor of fixtures, including the lessor's residual interest, and the conflicting interest of an encumbrancer or owner of the real estate who is not the lessee is determined by the priority rules governing conflicting interests in real estate.

(8) If the interest of a lessor of fixtures, including the lessor's residual interest, has priority over all conflicting interests of all owners and encumbrancers of the real estate, the lessor or the lessee may (i) on default, expiration, termination, or cancellation of the lease agreement but subject to the agreement and this Article, or (ii) if necessary to enforce other rights and remedies of the lessor or lessee under this Article, remove the goods from the real estate, free and clear of all conflicting interests of all owners and encumbrancers of the real estate, but the lessor or lessee must reimburse any encumbrancer or owner of the real estate who is not the lessee and who has not otherwise agreed for the cost of repair of any physical injury, but not for any diminution in value of the real estate caused by the absence of the goods removed or by any necessity of replacing them. A person entitled to reimbursement may refuse permission to remove until the party seeking removal gives adequate security for the performance of this obligation.

(9) Even though the lease agreement does not create a security interest, the interest of a lessor of fixtures, including the lessor's residual interest, is perfected by filing a financing statement as a fixture filing for leased goods that are or are to become fixtures in accordance with the relevant provisions of the Article on Secured Transactions (Article 9).

§ 2A-310. Lessor's and Lessee's Rights When Goods Become Accessions.

(1) Goods are accessions" when they are installed in or affixed to other goods.

(2) The interest of a lessor or a lessee under a lease contract entered into before the goods became accessions is superior to all interests in the whole except as stated in subsection (4).

(3) The interest of a lessor or a lessee under a lease contract entered into at the time or after the goods became accessions is superior to all subsequently acquired interests in the whole except as stated in subsection (4) but is subordinate to interests in the whole existing at the time the lease contract was made unless the holders of such interests in the whole have in writing consented to the lease or disclaimed an interest in the goods as part of the whole.

(4) The interest of a lessor or a lessee under a lease contract described in subsection (2) or (3) is subordinate to the interest of

(a) a buyer in the ordinary course of business or a lessee in the ordinary course of business of any interest in the whole acquired after the goods became accessions; or

(b) a creditor with a security interest in the whole perfected before the lease contract was made to the extent that the creditor makes subsequent advances without knowledge of the lease contract.

(5) When under subsections (2) or (3) and (4) a lessor or a lessee of accessions holds an interest that is superior to all interests in the whole, the lessor or the lessee may (a) on default, expiration, termination, or cancellation of the lease contract by the other party but subject to the provisions of the lease contract and this Article, or (b) if necessary to enforce his [or her] other rights and remedies under this Article, remove the goods from the whole, free and clear of all interests in the whole, but he [or she] must reimburse any holder of an interest in the whole who is not the lessee and who has not otherwise agreed for the cost of repair of any physical injury but not for any diminution in value of the whole caused by the absence of the goods removed or by any necessity for replacing them. A person entitled to reimbursement may refuse permission to remove until the party seeking removal gives adequate security for the performance of this obligation.

§ 2A-311. Priority Subject to Subordination.

Nothing in this Article prevents subordination by agreement by any person entitled to priority.

PART 4 Performance of Lease Contract: Repudiated, Substituted and Excused

§ 2A-401. Insecurity: Adequate Assurance of Performance.

(1) A lease contract imposes an obligation on each party that the other's expectation of receiving due performance will not be impaired.

(2) If reasonable grounds for insecurity arise with respect to the performance of either party, the insecure party may demand in writing adequate assurance of due performance. Until the insecure party receives that assurance, if commercially reasonable the insecure party may suspend any performance for which he [or she] has not already received the agreed return.

(3) A repudiation of the lease contract occurs if assurance of due performance adequate under the circumstances of the particular case is not provided to the insecure party within a reasonable time, not to exceed 30 days after receipt of a demand by the other party.

(4) Between merchants, the reasonableness of grounds for insecurity and the adequacy of any assurance offered must be determined according to commercial standards.

(5) Acceptance of any nonconforming delivery or payment does not prejudice the aggrieved party's right to demand adequate assurance of future performance.

§ 2A-402. Anticipatory Repudiation.

If either party repudiates a lease contract with respect to a performance not yet due under the lease contract, the loss of which performance will substantially impair the value of the lease contract to the other, the aggrieved party may:

(a) for a commercially reasonable time, await retraction of repudiation and performance by the repudiating party;

(b) make demand pursuant to Section 2A-40 1 and await assurance of future performance adequate under the circumstances of the particular case; or

(c) resort to any right or remedy upon default under the lease contract or this Article, even though the aggrieved party has notified the repudiating party that the aggrieved party would await the repudiating party's performance and assurance and has urged retraction. In addition, whether or not the aggrieved party is pursuing one of the foregoing remedies, the aggrieved party may suspend performance or, if the aggrieved party is the lessor, proceed in accordance with the provisions of this Article on the lessor's right to identify goods to the lease contract notwithstanding default or to salvage unfinished goods (Section 2A-524).

§ 2A-403. Retraction of Anticipatory Repudiation.

(1) Until the repudiating party's next performance is due, the repudiating party can retract the repudiation unless, since the repudiation, the aggrieved party has cancelled the lease contract or materially changed the aggrieved party's position or otherwise indicated that the aggrieved party considers the repudiation final.

(2) Retraction may be by any method that clearly indicates to the aggrieved party that the repudiating party intends to perform under the lease contract and includes any assurance demanded under Section 2A-401.

(3) Retraction reinstates a repudiating party's rights under a lease contract with due excuse and allowance to the aggrieved party for any delay occasioned by the repudiation.

§ 2A-404. Substituted Performance.

(1) If without fault of the lessee, the lessor and the supplier, the agreed berthing, loading, or unloading facilities fail or the agreed type of carrier becomes unavailable or the agreed manner of delivery otherwise becomes commercially impracticable, but a commercially reasonable substitute is available, the substitute performance must be tendered and accepted.

(2) If the agreed means or manner of payment fails because of domestic or foreign governmental regulation:

(a) the lessor may withhold or stop delivery or cause the supplier to withhold or stop delivery unless the lessee provides a means or manner of payment that is commercially a substantial equivalent; and

(b) if delivery has already been taken, payment by the means or in the manner provided by the regulation discharges the lessee's obligation unless the regulation is discriminatory, oppressive, or predatory.

§ 2A-405. Excused Performance.

Subject to Section 2A-404 on substituted performance, the following rules apply:

(a) Delay in delivery or nondelivery in whole or in part by a lessor or a supplier who complies with paragraphs (b) and (c) is not a default under the lease contract if performance as agreed has been made impracticable by the occurrence of a contingency the nonoccurrence of which was a basic assumption on which the lease contract was made or by compliance in good faith with any applicable foreign or domestic governmental regulation or order, whether or not the regulation or order later proves to be invalid.

(b) If the causes mentioned in paragraph (a) affect only part of the lessor's or the supplier's capacity to perform, he [or she] shall allocate production and deliveries among his [or her] customers but at his [or her] option may include regular customers not then under contract for sale or lease as well as his [or her] own requirements for further manufacture. He [or she] may so allocate in any manner that is fair and reasonable.

(c) The lessor seasonably shall notify the lessee and in the case of a finance lease the supplier seasonably shall notify the lessor and the lessee, if known, that there will be delay or nondelivery and, if allocation is required under paragraph (b), of the estimated quota thus made available for the lessee.

§ 2A-406. Procedure on Excused Performance.

(1) If the lessee receives notification of a material or indefinite delay or an allocation justified under Section 2A-405, the lessee may by written notification to the lessor as to any goods involved, and with respect to all of the goods if under an installment lease contract the value of the whole lease contract is substantially impaired (Section 2A-510):

(a) terminate the lease contract (Section 2A-505 (2)); or

(b) except in a finance lease that is not a consumer lease, modify the lease contract by accepting the available quota in substitution, with due allowance from the tent payable for the balance of the lease term for the deficiency but without further right against the lessor.

(2) If, after receipt of a notification from the lessor under Section 2A-405, the lessee fails so to modify the lease agreement within a reasonable time not exceeding 30 days, the lease contract lapses with respect to any deliveries affected.

§ 2A-407. Irrevocable Promises: Finance Leases.

(1) In the case of a finance lease that is not a consumer lease the lessee's promises under the lease contract become irrevocable and independent upon the lessee's acceptance of the goods.

(2) A promise that has become irrevocable and independent under subsection (1):

(a) is effective and enforceable between the parties, and by or against third parties including assignees of the parties; and

(b) is not subject to cancellation; termination, modification, repudiation, excuse, or substitution without the consent of the party to whom the promise runs.

(3) This section does not affect the validity under any other law of a covenant in any lease contract making the lessee's promises irrevocable and independent upon the lessee's acceptance of the goods.

PART 5 Default

A. In General

§ 2A-501. Default: Procedure.

(1) Whether the lessor or the lessee is in default under a lease contract is determined by the lease agreement and this Article.

(2) If the lessor or the lessee is in default under the lease contract, the party seeking enforcement has rights and remedies as provided in this Article and, except as limited by this Article, as provided in the lease agreement.

(3) If the lessor or the lessee is in default under the lease contract, the party seeking enforcement may reduce the party's claim to judgment, or otherwise enforce the lease contract by self-help or any available judicial procedure or nonjudicial procedure, including administrative proceeding, arbitration, or the like, in accordance with this Article.

(4) Except as otherwise provided in Section 1-106(1) or this Article or the lease agreement, the rights and remedies referred to in subsections (2) and (3) are cumulative.

(5) If the lease agreement covers both real property and goods, the party seeking enforcement may proceed under this Part as to the goods, or under other applicable law as to both the real property and the goods in accordance with that party's rights and remedies in respect of the real property, in which case this Part does not apply.

§ 2A-502. Notice After Default.

Except as otherwise provided in this Article or the lease agreement, the lessor or lessee in default under the lease contract is not entitled to notice of default or notice of enforcement from the other party to the lease agreement.

§ 2A-503. Modification or Impairment of Rights and Remedies.

(1) Except as otherwise provided in this Article, the lease agreement may include rights and remedies for default in addition to or in substitution for those provided in this Article and may limit or alter the measure of damages recoverable under this Article.

(2) Resort to a remedy provided under this Article or in the lease agreement is optional unless the remedy is expressly agreed to be exclusive. If circumstances cause an exclusive or limited remedy to fail of its essential purpose, or provision for an exclusive remedy is unconscionable, remedy may be had as provided in this Article.

(3) Consequential damages may be liquidated under Section 2A-504, or may otherwise be limited, altered, or excluded unless the limitation, alteration, or exclusion is unconscionable. Limitation, alteration, or exclusion of consequential damages for injury to the person in the case of consumer goods is prima facie unconscionable but limitation, alteration, or exclusion of damages where the loss is commercial is not prima facie unconscionable.

(4) Rights and remedies on default by the lessor or the lessee with respect to any obligation or promise collateral or ancillary to the lease contract are not impaired by this Article.

§ 2A-504. Liquidation of Damages.

(1) Damages payable by either party for default, or any other act or omission, including indemnity for loss or diminution of anticipated tax benefits or loss or damage to lessor's residual interest, may be liquidated in the lease agreement but only at an amount or by a formula that is reasonable in light of the then anticipated harm caused by the default or other act or omission.

(2) If the lease agreement provides for liquidation of damages, and such provision does not comply with subsection (1), or such provision is an exclusive or limited remedy that circumstances cause to fail of its essential purpose, remedy may be had as provided in this Article.

(3) If the lessor justifiably withholds or stops delivery of goods because of the lessee's default or insolvency (Section 2A-525 or 2A-526), the lessee is entitled to restitution of any amount by which the sum of his [or her] payments exceeds:

(a) the amount to which the lessor is entitled by virtue of terms liquidating the lessor's damages in accordance with subsection (1); or

(b) in the absence of those terms, 20 percent of the then present value of the total rent the lessee was obligated to pay for the balance of the lease term, or, in the case of a consumer lease, the lesser of such amount or $500.

(4) A lessee's right to restitution under subsection (3) is subject to offset to the extent the lessor establishes:

(a) a right to recover damages under the provisions of this Article other than subsection (1); and

(b) the amount or value of any benefits received by the lessee directly or indirectly by reason of the lease contract.

§ 2A-505. Cancellation and Termination and Effect of Cancellation, Termination, Rescission, or Fraud on Rights and Remedies.

(1) On cancellation of the lease contract, all obligations that ate still executory on both sides are discharged, but any right based on prior default or performance survives, and the cancelling party also retains any remedy for default of the whole lease contract or any unperformed balance.

(2) On termination of the lease contract, all obligations that are still executory on both sides are discharged but any right based on prior default or performance survives.

(3) Unless the contrary intention clearly appears, expressions of "cancellation,' rescission," or the like of the lease contract may not be construed as a renunciation or discharge of any claim in damages for an antecedent default.

(4) Rights and remedies for material misrepresentation or fraud include all rights and remedies available under this Article for default.

(5) Neither rescission nor a claim for rescission of the lease contract nor rejection or return of the goods may bar or be deemed inconsistent with a claim for damages or other right or remedy.

§ 2A-506. Statute of Limitations.

(1) An action for default under a lease contract, including breach of warranty or indemnity, must be commenced within 4 years after the cause of action accrued. By the original lease contract the parties may reduce the period of limitation to not less than one year.

(2) A cause of action for default accrues when the act or omission on which the default or breach of warranty is based is or should have been discovered by the aggrieved patty, or when the default occurs, whichever is later. A cause of action for indemnity accrues when the act or omission on which the claim for indemnity is based is or should have been discovered by the indemnified party, whichever is later.

(3) If an action commenced within the time limited by subsection (1) is so terminated as to leave available a remedy by another action for the same default or breach of warranty or indemnity, the other action may be commenced after the expiration of the time limited and within 6 months after the termination of the first action unless the termination resulted from voluntary discontinuance or from dismissal for failure or neglect to prosecute.

(4) This section does not alter the law on tolling of the statute of limitations nor does it apply to causes of action that have accrued before this Article becomes effective.

§ 2A-507. Proof of Market Rent: Time and Place.

(1) Damages based on market rent (Section 2A-519 or 2A-528) are determined according to the tent for the use of the goods concerned for a lease term identical to the remaining lease term of the original lease agreement and prevailing at the times specified in Sections 2A-519 and 2A-528.

(2) If evidence of rent for the use of the goods concerned for a lease term identical to the remaining lease term of the original lease agreement and prevailing at the times or places described in this Article is not readily available, the tent prevailing within any reasonable time before or after the time described or at any other place or for a different lease term which in commercial judgment or under usage of trade would serve as a reasonable substitute for the one described may be used, making any proper allowance for the difference, including the cost of transporting the goods to or from the other place.

(3) Evidence of a relevant rent prevailing at a time or place or for a lease term other than the one described in this Article offered by one party is not admissible unless and until he [or she] has given the other party notice the court finds sufficient to prevent unfair surprise.

(4) If the prevailing rent or value of any goods regularly leased in any established market is in issue, reports in official publications or trade journals or in newspapers or periodicals of general circulation published as the reports of that market are admissible in evidence. The circumstances of the preparation of the report may be shown to affect its weight but not its admissibility.

B. Default by Lessor

§ 2A-508. Lessee's Remedies.

(1) If a lessor fails to deliver the goods in conformity to the lease contract (Section 2A-509) or repudiates the lease contract (Section 2A-402), or a lessee rightfully rejects the goods (Section 2A-509) or justifiably revokes acceptance of the goods (Section 2A-517), then with respect to any goods involved, and with respect to all of the goods if under an installment lease contract the value of the whole lease contract is substantially impaired (Section 2A-510), the lessor is in default under the lease contract and the lessee may:

(a) cancel the lease contract (Section 2A-505 (1));

(b) recover so much of the rent and security as has been paid and is just under the circumstances;

(c) cover and recover damages as to all goods affected whether or not they have been identified to the lease contract (Sections 2A-518 and 2A-520), or recover damages for nondelivery (Sections 2A-519 and 2A-520);

(d) exercise any other rights or pursue any other remedies provided in the lease contract.

(2) If a lessor fails to deliver the goods in conformity to the lease contract or repudiates the lease contract, the lessee may also:

(a) if the goods have been identified, recover them (Section 2A-522); or

(b) in a proper case, obtain specific performance or replevy the goods (Section 2A-521).

(3) If a lessor is otherwise in default under a lease contract, the lessee may exercise the rights and pursue the remedies provided in the lease contract, which may include a right to cancel the lease, and in Section 2A-519(3).

(4) If a lessor has breached a warranty, whether express or implied, the lessee may recover damages (Section 2A-519(4)).

(5) On rightful rejection or justifiable revocation of acceptance, a lessee has a security interest in goods in the lessee's possession or control for any rent and security that has been paid and any expenses reasonably incurred in their inspection, receipt, transportation, and care and custody and may hold those goods and dispose of them in good faith and in a commercially reasonable manner' subject to Section 2A-527(5).

(6) Subject to the provisions of Section 2A-407, a lessee, on notifying the lessor of the lessee's intention to do so, may deduct all or any part of the damages resulting from any default under the lease contract from any part of the rent still due under the same lease contract.

§ 2A-509. Lessee's Rights on Improper Delivery; Rightful Rejection.

(1) Subject to the provisions of Section 2A-510 on default in installment lease contracts, if the goods or the tender or delivery fail in any respect to conform to the lease contract, the lessee may reject or accept the goods or accept any commercial unit or units and reject the rest of the goods.

(2) Rejection of goods is ineffective unless it is within a reasonable time after tender or delivery of the goods and the lessee seasonably notifies the lessor.

§ 2A-510. Installment Lease Contracts: Rejection and Default.

(1) Under an installment lease contract a lessee may reject any delivery that is nonconforming if the nonconformity substantially impairs the value of that delivery and cannot be cured or the

nonconformity is a defect in the required documents; but if the nonconformity does not fall within subsection (2) and the lessor or the supplier gives adequate assurance of its cure, the lessee must accept that delivery.

(2) Whenever nonconformity or default with respect to one or more deliveries substantially impairs the value of the installment lease contract as a whole there is a default with respect to the whole. But, the aggrieved party reinstates the installment lease contract as a whole if the aggrieved party accepts a nonconforming delivery without seasonably notifying of cancellation or brings an action with respect only to past deliveries or demands performance as to future deliveries.

§ 2A-511. Merchant Lessee's Duties as to Rightfully Rejected Goods.

(1) Subject to any security interest of a lessee (Section 2A-508(5)), if a lessor or a supplier has no agent or place of business at the market of rejection, a merchant lessee, after rejection of goods in his [or] her possession or control, shall follow any reasonable instructions received from the lessor or the supplier with respect to the goods. In the absence of those instructions, a merchant lessee shall make reasonable efforts to sell, lease, or otherwise dispose of the goods for the lessor's account if they threaten to decline in value speedily. Instructions are not reasonable if on demand indemnity for expenses is not forthcoming.

(2) If a merchant lessee (subsection (1)) or any other lessee (Section 2A-512) disposes of goods, he [or she] is entitled to reimbursement either from the lessor or the supplier or out of the proceeds for reasonable expenses of caring for and disposing of the goods and, if the expenses include no disposition commission, to such commission as is usual in the trade, or if there is none, to a reasonable sum not exceeding 10 percent of the gross proceeds.

(3) In complying with this section or Section 2A-512, the lessee is held only to good faith. Good faith conduct hereunder is neither acceptance or conversion nor the basis of an action for damages.

(4) A purchaser who purchases in good faith from a lessee pursuant to this section or Section 2A-512 takes the goods free of any rights of the lessor and the supplier even though the lessee fails to comply with one or more of the requirements of this Article.

§ 2A-512. Lessee's Duties as to Rightfully Rejected Goods.

(1) Except as otherwise provided with respect to goods that threaten to decline in value speedily (Section 2A-511) and subject to any security interest of a lessee (Section 2A-508(5)):

(a) the lessee, after rejection of goods in the lessee's possession, shall hold them with reasonable care at the lessor's or the supplier's disposition for a reasonable time after the lessee's seasonable notification of rejection;

(b) if the lessor or the supplier gives no instructions within a reasonable time after notification of rejection, the lessee may store the rejected goods for the lessor's or the supplier's account or ship them to the lessor or the supplier or dispose of them for the lessor's or the supplier's account with reimbursement in the manner provided in Section 2A-511; but

(c) the lessee has no further obligations with regard to goods rightfully rejected.

(2) Action by the lessee pursuant to subsection (1) is not acceptance or conversion.

§ 2A-513. Cure by Lessor of Improper Tender or Delivery; Replacement.

(1) If any tender or delivery by the lessor or the supplier is rejected because nonconforming and the time for performance has not yet expired, the lessor or the supplier may seasonably notify the lessee of the lessor's or the supplier's intention to cure and may then make a conforming delivery within the time provided in the lease contract.

(2) If the lessee rejects a nonconforming tender that the lessor or the supplier had reasonable grounds to believe would be acceptable with or without money allowance, the lessor or the supplier may have a further reasonable time to substitute a conforming tender if he [or she] seasonably notifies the lessee.

§ 2A-514. Waiver of Lessee's Objections.

(1) In rejecting goods, a lessee's failure to state a particular defect that is ascertainable by reasonable inspection precludes the lessee from relying on the defect to justify rejection or to establish default:

(a) if, stated seasonably, the lessor or the supplier could have cured it (Section 2A-513); or

(b) between merchants if the lessor or the supplier after rejection has made a request in writing for a full and final written statement of all defects on which the lessee proposes to rely.

(2) A lessee's failure to reserve rights when paying rent or other consideration against documents precludes recovery of the payment for defects apparent on the face of the documents.

§ 2A-515. Acceptance of Goods.

(1) Acceptance of goods occurs after the lessee has had a reasonable opportunity to inspect the goods and

(a) the lessee signifies or acts with respect to the goods in a manner that signifies to the lessor or the supplier that the goods are conforming or that the lessee will take or retain them in spite of their nonconformity; or

(b) the lessee fails to make an effective rejection of the goods (Section 2A-509(2)).

(2) Acceptance of a part of any commercial unit is acceptance of that entire unit.

§ 2A-516. Effect of Acceptance of Goods; Notice of Default; Burden of Establishing Default After Acceptance; Notice of Claim or Litigation to Person Answerable Over.

(1) A lessee must pay rent for any goods accepted in accordance with the lease contract, with due allowance for goods rightfully rejected or not delivered.

(2) A lessee's acceptance of goods precludes rejection of the goods accepted. In the case of a finance lease, if made with knowledge of a nonconformity, acceptance cannot be revoked because of it. In any other case, if made with knowledge of a nonconformity, acceptance cannot be revoked because of it unless the acceptance was on the reasonable assumption that the noncon-

formity would be seasonably cured. Acceptance does not of itself impair any other remedy provided by this Article or the lease agreement for nonconformity.

(3) If a tender has been accepted:

(a) within a reasonable time after the lessee discovers or should have discovered any default, the lessee shall notify the lessor and the supplier, if any, or be barred from any remedy against the party not notified;

(b) except in the case of a consumer lease, within a reasonable time after the lessee receives notice of litigation for infringement or the like (Section 2A-211) the lessee shall notify the lessor or be barred from any remedy over for liability established by the litigation; and

(c) the burden is on the lessee to establish any default.

(4) If a lessee is sued for breach of a warranty or other obligation for which a lessor or a supplier is answerable over the following apply:

(a) The lessee may give the lessor or the supplier' or both, written notice of the litigation. If the notice states that the person notified may come in and defend and that if the person notified does not do so that person will be bound in any action against that person by the lessee by any determination of fact common to the two litigations, then unless the person notified after seasonable receipt of the notice does come in and defend that person is so bound.

(b) The lessor or the supplier may demand in writing that the lessee turn over control of the litigation including settlement if the claim is one for infringement or the like (Section 2A-211) or else be barred from any remedy over. If the demand states that the lessor or the supplier agrees to bear all expense and to satisfy any adverse judgment, then unless the lessee after seasonable receipt of the demand does turn over control the lessee is so barred.

(5) Subsections (3) and (4) apply to any obligation of a lessee to hold the lessor or the supplier harmless against infringement or the like (Section 2A-211).

§ 2A-517. Revocation of Acceptance of Goods.

(1) A lessee may revoke acceptance of a lot or commercial unit whose nonconformity substantially impairs its value to the lessee if the lessee has accepted it:

(a) except in the case of a finance lease, on the reasonable assumption that its nonconformity would be cured and it has not been seasonably cured; or

(b) without discovery of the nonconformity if the lessee's acceptance was reasonably induced either by the lessor's assurances or, except in the case of a finance lease, by the difficulty of discovery before acceptance.

(2) Except in the case of a finance lease that is not a consumer lease, a lessee may revoke acceptance of a lot or commercial unit if the lessor defaults under the lease contract and the default substantially impairs the value of that lot or commercial unit to the lessee.

(3) If the lease agreement so provides, the lessee may revoke acceptance of a lot or commercial unit because of other defaults by the lessor.

(4) Revocation of acceptance must occur within a reasonable time after the lessee discovers or should have discovered the ground for it and before any substantial change in condition of the goods which is not caused by the nonconformity. Revocation is not effective until the lessee notifies the lessor.

(5) A lessee who so revokes has the same rights and duties with regard to the goods involved as if the lessee had rejected them.

§ 2A-518. Cover; Substitute Goods.

(1) After a default by a lessor under the lease contract of the type described in Section 2A-508 (1), or, if agreed, after other default by the lessor, the lessee may cover by making any purchase or lease of or contract to purchase or lease goods in substitution for those due from the lessor.

(2) Except as otherwise provided with respect to damages liquidated in the lease agreement (Section 2A-504) or otherwise determined pursuant to agreement of the parties (Sections 1-102(3) and 2A-503), if a lessee's cover is by a lease agreement substantially similar to the original lease agreement and the new lease agreement is made in good faith and in a commercially reasonable manner' the lessee may recover from the lessor as damages (i) the present value, as of the date of the commencement of the term of the new lease agreement, of the rent under the new lease agreement applicable to that period of the new lease term which is comparable to the then remaining term of the original lease agreement minus the present value as of the same date of the total rent for the then remaining lease term of the original lease agreement, and (ii) any incidental or consequential damages, less expenses saved in consequence of the lessor's default.

(3) If a lessee's cover is by lease agreement that for any reason does not qualify for treatment under subsection (2), or is by purchase or otherwise, the lessee may recover from the lessor as if the lessee had elected not to cover and Section 2A-519 governs.

§ 2A-519. Lessee's Damages for Non-delivery, Repudiation, Default, and Breach of Warranty in Regard to Accepted Goods.

(1) Except as otherwise provided with respect to damages liquidated in the lease agreement (Section 2A-504) or otherwise determined pursuant to agreement of the parties (Sections 1-102(3) and 2A-503), if a lessee elects not to cover or a lessee elects to cover and the cover is by lease agreement that for any reason does not qualify for treatment under Section 2A-518(2), or is by purchase or otherwise, the measure of damages for non-delivery or repudiation by the lessor or for rejection or revocation of acceptance by the lessee is the present value, as of the date of the default, of the then market rent minus the present value as of the same date of the original rent, computed for the remaining lease term of the original lease agreement, together with incidental and consequential damages, less expenses saved in consequence of the lessor's default.

(2) Market rent is to be determined as of the place for tender or, in cases of rejection after arrival or revocation of acceptance, as of the place of arrival.

(3) Except as otherwise agreed, if the lessee has accepted goods and given notification (Section 2A-516(3)), the measure of damages for nonconforming tender or delivery or other default by a lessor is the loss resulting in the ordinary course of events from the lessor's default as determined in any manner that is reasonable

together with incidental and consequential damages, less expenses saved in consequence of the lessor's default.

(4) Except as otherwise agreed, the measure of damages for breach of warranty is the present value at the time and place of acceptance of the difference between the value of the use of the goods accepted and the value if they had been as warranted for the lease term, unless special circumstances show proximate damages of a different amount, together with incidental and consequential damages, less expenses saved in consequence of the lessor's default or breach of warranty.

§ 2A-520. Lessee's Incidental and Consequential Damages.

(1) Incidental damages resulting from a lessor's default include expenses reasonably incurred in inspection, receipt, transportation, and care and custody of goods rightfully rejected or goods the acceptance of which is justifiably revoked, any commercially reasonable charges, expenses or commissions in connection with effecting cover' and any other reasonable expense incident to the default.

(2) Consequential damages resulting from a lessor's default include:

(a) any loss resulting from general or particular requirements and needs of which the lessor at the time of contracting had reason to know and which could not reasonably be prevented by cover or otherwise; and

(b) injury to person or property proximately resulting from any breach of warranty.

2A-521. Lessee's Right to Specific Performance or Replevin.

(1) Specific performance may be decreed if the goods are unique or in other proper circumstances.

(2) A decree for specific performance may include any terms and conditions as to payment of the rent, damages, or other relief that the court deems just.

(3) A lessee has a right of replevin, detinue, sequestration, claim and delivery, or the like for goods identified to the lease contract if after reasonable effort the lessee is unable to effect cover for those goods or the circumstances reasonably indicate that the effort will be unavailing.

§ 2A-522. Lessee's Right to Goods on Lessor's Insolvency.

(1) Subject to subsection (2) and even though the goods have not been shipped, a lessee who has paid a part or all of the rent and security for goods identified to a lease contract (Section 2A-217) on making and keeping good a tender of any unpaid portion of the rent and security due under the lease contract may recover the goods identified from the lessor if the lessor becomes insolvent within 10 days after receipt of the first installment of rent and security.

(2) A lessee acquires the right to recover goods identified to a lease contract only if they conform to the lease contract.

C. Default by Lessee

§ 2A-523. Lessor's Remedies.

(1) If a lessee wrongfully rejects or revokes acceptance of goods or fails to make a payment when due or repudiates with respect to a part or the whole, then, with respect to any goods involved, and with respect to all of the goods if under an installment lease contract the value of the whole lease contract is substantially impaired (Section 2A-510), the lessee is in default under the lease contract and the lessor may:

(a) cancel the lease contract (Section 2A-505 (1));

(b) proceed respecting goods not identified to the lease contract (Section 2A-524);

(c) withhold delivery of the goods and take possession of goods previously delivered (Section 2A-525);

(d) stop delivery of the goods by any bailee (Section 2A-526);

(e) dispose of the goods and recover damages (Section 2A-527), or retain the goods and recover damages (Section 2A-528), or in a proper case recover rent (Section 2A-529).

(f) exercise any other rights or pursue any other remedies provided in the lease contract.

(2) If a lessor does not fully exercise a right or obtain a remedy to which the lessor is entitled under subsection (1), the lessor may recover the loss resulting in the ordinary course of events from the lessee's default as determined in any reasonable manner, together with incidental damages, less expenses saved in consequence of the lessee's default.

(3) If a lessee is otherwise in default under a lease contract, the lessor may exercise the rights and pursue the remedies provided in the lease contract, which may include a right to cancel the lease. In addition, unless otherwise provided in the lease contract:

(a) if the default substantially impairs the value of the lease contract to the lessor, the lessor may exercise the rights and pursue the remedies provided in subsections (1) or (2); or

(b) if the default does not substantially impair the value of the lease contract to the lessor, the lessor may recover as provided in subsection (2).

§ 2A-524. Lessor's Right to Identify Goods to Lease Contract.

(1) After default by the lessee under the lease contract of the type described in Section 2A-523 (1) or 2A-523 (3) (a) or, if agreed, after other default by the lessee, the lessor may:

(a) identify to the lease contract conforming goods not already identified if at the time the lessor learned of the default they were in the lessor's or the supplier's possession or control; and

(b) dispose of goods (Section 2A-527 (1)) that demonstrably have been intended for the particular lease contract even though those goods are unfinished.

(2) If the goods are unfinished, in the exercise of reasonable commercial judgment for the purposes of avoiding loss and of effective realization, an aggrieved lessor or the supplier may either complete manufacture and wholly identify the goods to the lease contract or cease manufacture and lease, sell, or otherwise dispose of the goods for scrap or salvage value or proceed in any other reasonable manner.

§ 2A-525. Lessor's Right to Possession of Goods.

(1) If a lessor discovers the lessee to be insolvent, the lessor may refuse to deliver the goods.

(2) After a default by the lessee under the lease contract of the type described in Section 2A-523 (1) or 2A-523 (3) (a) or, if agreed, after other default by the lessee, the lessor has the right to

take possession of the goods. If the lease contract so provides, the lessor may require the lessee to assemble the goods and make them available to the lessor at a place to be designated by the lessor which is reasonably convenient to both parties. Without removal, the lessor may render unusable any goods employed in trade or business, and may dispose of goods on the lessee's premises (Section 2A-527).

(3) The lessor may proceed under subsection (2) without judicial process if it can be done without breach of the peace or the lessor may proceed by action.

§ 2A-526. Lessor's Stoppage of Delivery in Transit or Otherwise.

(1) A lessor may stop delivery of goods in the possession of a carrier or other bailee if the lessor discovers the lessee to be insolvent and may stop delivery of carload, truckload, planeload, or larger shipments of express or freight if the lessee repudiates or fails to make a payment due before delivery, whether for rent, security or otherwise under the lease contract, or for any other reason the lessor has a right to withhold or take possession of the goods.

(2) In pursuing its remedies under subsection (1), the lessor may stop delivery until

(a) receipt of the goods by the lessee;

(b) acknowledgment to the lessee by any bailee of the goods, except a carrier' that the bailee holds the goods for the lessee; or

(c) such an acknowledgment to the lessee by a carrier via reshipment or as warehouseman.

(3) (a) To stop delivery, a lessor shall so notify as to enable the bailee by reasonable diligence to prevent delivery of the goods.

(b) After notification, the bailee shall hold and deliver the goods according to the directions of the lessor, but the lessor is liable to the bailee for any ensuing charges or damages.

(c) A carrier who has issued a nonnegotiable bill of lading is not obliged to obey a notification to stop received from a person other than the consignor.

§ 2A-527. Lessor's Rights to Dispose of Goods.

(1) After a default by a lessee under the lease contract of the type described in Section 2A-523(1) or 2A-523(3) (a) or after the lessor refuses to deliver or takes possession of goods (Section 2A-525 or 2A-526), or, if agreed, after other default by a lessee, the lessor may dispose of the goods concerned or the undelivered balance thereof by lease, sale, or otherwise.

(2) Except as otherwise provided with respect to damages liquidated in the lease agreement (Section 2A-504) or otherwise determined pursuant to agreement of the parties (Sections 1-102(3) and 2A-503), if the disposition is by lease agreement substantially similar to the original lease agreement and the new lease agreement is made in good faith and in a commercially reasonable manner' the lessor may recover from the lessee as damages (i) accrued and unpaid rent as of the date of the commencement of the term of the new lease agreement, (ii) the present value, as of the same date, of the total rent for the then remaining lease term of the original lease agreement minus the present value, as of the same date, of the rent under the new lease agreement applicable to that period of the new lease term which is comparable to the then remaining term of the original lease agreement, and (iii) any incidental damages allowed under Section 2A-530, less expenses saved in consequence of the lessee's default.

(3) If the lessor's disposition is by lease agreement that for any reason does not qualify for treatment under subsection (2), or is by sale or otherwise, the lessor may recover from the lessee as if the lessor had elected not to dispose of the goods and Section 2A-528 governs.

(4) A subsequent buyer or lessee who buys or leases from the lessor in good faith for value as a result of a disposition under this section takes the goods free of the original lease contract and any rights of the original lessee even though the lessor fails to comply with one or more of the requirements of this Article.

(5) The lessor is not accountable to the lessee for any profit made on any disposition. A lessee who has rightfully rejected or justifiably revoked acceptance shall account to the lessor for any excess over the amount of the lessee's security interest (Section 2A-508 (5)).

§ 2A-528. Lessor's Damages for Non-acceptance, Failure to Pay, Repudiation, or Other Default.

(1) Except as otherwise provided with respect to damages liquidated in the lease agreement (Section 2A-504) or otherwise determined pursuant to agreement of the parties (Sections 1-102(3) and 2A-503), if a lessor elects to retain the goods or a lessor elects to dispose of the goods and the disposition is by lease agreement that for any reason does not qualify for treatment under Section 2A-527(2), or is by sale or otherwise, the lessor may recover from the lessee as damages for a default of the type described in Section 2A-523 (1) or 2A-523 (3) (a), or, if agreed, for other default of the lessee, (i) accrued and unpaid rent as of the date of default if the lessee has never taken possession of the goods, or, if the lessee has taken possession of the goods, as of the date the lessor repossesses the goods or an earlier date on which the lessee makes a tender of the goods to the lessor, (ii) the present value as of the date determined under clause (i) of the total rent for the then remaining lease term of the original lease agreement minus the present value as of the same date of the market rent at the place where the goods are located computed for the same lease term, and (iii) any incidental damages allowed under Section 2A-530, less expenses saved in consequence of the lessee's default.

(2) If the measure of damages provided in subsection (1) is inadequate to put a lessor in as good a position as performance would have, the measure of damages is the present value of the profit, including reasonable overhead, the lessor would have made from full performance by the lessee, together with any incidental damages allowed under Section 2A-530, due allowance for costs reasonably incurred and due credit for payments or proceeds of disposition.

§ 2A-529. Lessor's Action for the Rent.

(1) After default by the lessee under the lease contract of the type described in Section 2A-523(1) or 2A-523(3) (a) or, if agreed, after other default by the lessee, if the lessor complies with subsection (2), the lessor may recover from the lessee as damages:

(a) for goods accepted by the lessee and not repossessed by or tendered to the lessor, and for conforming goods lost or damaged within a commercially reasonable time after risk of loss passes to the lessee (Section 2A-219), (i) accrued and unpaid rent as of the date of entry of judgment in favor of the lessor, (ii) the present value as of the same date of the rent for the then remaining lease term of the lease agreement, and (iii) any incidental damages allowed under Section 2A-530, less expenses saved in consequence of the lessee's default; and

(b) for goods identified to the lease contract if the lessor is unable after reasonable effort to dispose of them at a reasonable price or the circumstances reasonably indicate that effort will be unavailing, (i) accrued and unpaid rent as of the date of entry of judgment in favor of the lessor, (ii) the present value as of the same date of the rent for the then remaining lease term of the lease agreement, and (iii) any incidental damages allowed under Section 2A-530, less expenses saved in consequence of the lessee's default.

(2) Except as provided in subsection (3), the lessor shall hold for the lessee for the remaining lease term of the lease agreement any goods that have been identified to the lease contract and are in the lessor's control.

(3) The lessor may dispose of the goods at any time before collection of the judgment for damages obtained pursuant to subsection (1). If the disposition is before the end of the remaining lease term of the lease agreement, the lessor's recovery against the lessee for damages is governed by Section 2A-527 or Section 2A-528, and the lessor will cause an appropriate credit to be provided against a judgment for damages to the extent that the amount of the judgment exceeds the recovery available pursuant to Section 2A-527 or 2A-528.

(4) Payment of the judgment for damages obtained pursuant to subsection (1) entitles the lessee to the use and possession of the goods not then disposed of for the remaining lease term of and in accordance with the lease agreement.

(5) After default by the lessee under the lease contract of the type described in Section 2A-523 (1) or Section 2A-523 (3) (a) or, if agreed, after other default by the lessee, a lessor who is held not entitled to rent under this section must nevertheless be awarded damages for non-acceptance under Section 2A-527 or Section 2A-528.

§ 2A-530. Lessor's Incidental Damages.

Incidental damages to an aggrieved lessor include any commercially reasonable charges, expenses, or commissions incurred in stopping delivery, in the transportation, care and custody of goods after the lessee's default, in connection with return or disposition of the goods, or otherwise resulting from the default.

§ 2A-531. Standing to Sue Third Parties for Injury to Goods.

(1) If a third party so deals with goods that have been identified to a lease contract as to cause actionable injury to a party to the lease contract (a) the lessor has a right of action against the third party, and (b) the lessee also has a right of action against the third party if the lessee:

(i) has a security interest in the goods;

(ii) has an insurable interest in the goods; or

(iii) bears the risk of loss under the lease contract or has since the injury assumed that risk as against the lessor and the goods have been converted or destroyed.

(2) If at the time of the injury the party plaintiff did not bear the risk of loss as against the other party to the lease contract and there is no arrangement between them for disposition of the recovery, his [or her] suit or settlement, subject to his [or her] own interest, is as a fiduciary for the other party to the lease contract.

(3) Either party with the consent of the other may sue for the benefit of whom it may concern.

§ 2A-532. Lessor's Rights to Residual Interest.

In addition to any other recovery permitted by this Article or other law, the lessor may recover from the lessee an amount that will fully compensate the lessor for any loss of or damage to the lessor's residual interest in the goods caused by the default of the lessee.

ARTICLE 3 / Commercial Paper

PART 1 Short Title, Form and Interpretation

§ 3-101. Short Title. This article shall be known and may be cited as Uniform Commercial Code—Commercial Paper.

§ 3-102. Definitions and Index of Definitions.

(1) In this Article unless the context otherwise requires

(a) "Issue" means the first delivery of an instrument to a holder or a remitter.

(b) An "order" is a direction to pay and must be more than an authorization or request. It must identify the person to pay with reasonable certainty. It may be addressed to one or more such persons jointly or in the alternative but not in succession.

(c) A "promise" is an undertaking to pay and must be more than an acknowledgment of an obligation.

(d) "Secondary party" means a drawer or endorser.

(e) "Instrument" means a negotiable instrument.

(2) Other definitions applying to this Article and the sections in which they appear are:

"Acceptance." Section 3-410.
"Accommodation party. Section 3-415.
"Alteration." Section 3-407.
"Certificate of deposit." Section 3-104.
"Certification." Section 3-411.
"Check." Section 3-104.
"Definite time." Section 3-109.
"Dishonor." Section 3-507.
"Draft." Section 3-104.
"Holder in due course." Section 3-302.
"Negotiation." Section 3-202.
"Note." Section 3-104.
"Notice of dishonor." Section 3-508.

"On demand." Section 3-108.
"Presentment." Section 3-504.
"Protest." Section 3-509.
"Restrictive Indorsement." Section 3-205.
"Signature." Section 3-401.

(3) The following definitions in other Articles apply to this Article:

"Account." Section 4-104.
"Banking Day." Section 4-104.
"Clearing house." Section 4-104.
"Collecting bank." Section 4-105.
"Customer." Section 4-104.
"Depository Bank." Section 4-105.
"Documentary Draft." Section 4-104.
"Intermediary Bank." Section 4-105.
"Item." Section 4-104.
"Midnight deadline." Section 4-104.
"Payor bank." Section 4-105.

(4) In addition Article 1 contains general definitions and principles of construction and interpretation applicable throughout this Article.

§ 3-103. Limitations on Scope of Article.

(1) This Article does not apply to money, documents of title or investment securities.

(2) The provisions of this Article are subject to the provisions of the Article on Bank Deposits and Collections (Article 4) and Secured Transactions (Article 9).

§ 3-104. Form of Negotiable Instruments: "Draft"; "Check"; "Certificate of Deposit"; "Note."

(1) Any writing to be a negotiable instrument within this Article must

(a) be signed by the maker or drawer; and

(b) contain an unconditional promise or order to pay a sum certain in money and no other promise, order, obligation or power given by the maker or drawer except as authorized by this Article; and

(c) be payable on demand or at a definite time; and

(d) be payable to order or to bearer.

(2) A writing which complies with the requirements of this section is

(a) a "draft" ("bill of exchange") if it is an order;

(b) a "check" if it is a draft drawn on a bank and payable on demand;

(c) a "certificate of deposit" if it is an acknowledgment by a bank of receipt of money with an engagement to repay it;

(d) a "note" if it is a promise other than a certificate of deposit.

(3) As used in other Articles of this Act, and as the context may require, the terms "draft," "check," "certificate of deposit" and "note" may refer to instruments which are not negotiable within this Article as well as to instruments which are so negotiable.

§ 3-105. When Promise or Order Unconditional.

(1) A promise or order otherwise unconditional is not made conditional by the fact that the instrument

(a) is subject to implied or constructive conditions; or

(b) states its consideration, whether performed or promised, or the transaction which gave rise to the instrument, or that the promise or order is made or the instrument matures in accordance with or "as per" such transaction; or

(c) refers to or states that it arises out of a separate agreement or refers to a separate agreement for rights as to prepayment or acceleration; or

(d) states that it is drawn under a letter of credit; or

(e) states that it is secured, whether by mortgage, reservation of title or otherwise; or

(f) indicates a particular account to be debited or any other fund or source from which reimbursement is expected; or

(g) is limited to payment out of a particular fund or the proceeds of a particular source, if the instrument is issued by a government or governmental agency or unit; or

(h) is limited to payment out of the entire assets of a partnership, unincorporated association, trust or estate by or on behalf of which the instrument is issued.

(2) A promise or order is not unconditional if the instrument

(a) states that it is subject to or governed by any other agreement; or

(b) states that it is to be paid only out of a particular fund or source except as provided in this section.

§ 3-106. Sum Certain.

(1) The sum payable is a sum certain even though it is to be paid

(a) with stated interest or by stated installments; or

(b) with stated different rates of interest before and after default or a specified date; or

(c) with a stated discount or addition if paid before or after the date fixed for payment; or

(d) with exchange or less exchange, whether at a fixed rate or at the current rate; or

(e) with costs of collection or an attorney's fee or both upon default.

(2) Nothing in this section shall validate any term which is otherwise illegal.

§ 3-107. Money.

(1) An instrument is payable in money if the medium of exchange in which it is payable is money at the time the instrument is made. An instrument payable in "currency" or "current funds" is payable in money.

(2) A promise or order to pay a sum stated in a foreign currency is for a sum certain in money and, unless a different medium of payment is specified in the instrument, may be satisfied by payment of that number of dollars which the stated foreign currency will purchase at the buying sight rate for that currency on the day on which the instrument is payable or, if payable on demand, on the day of demand. If such an instrument specifies a foreign currency as the medium of payment the instrument is payable in that currency.

§ 3-108. Payable on Demand.

Instruments payable on demand include those payable at sight or on presentation and those in which no time for payment is stated.

§ 3-109. Definite Time.
(1) An instrument is payable at a definite time if by its terms it is payable

(a) on or before a stated date or at a fixed period after a stated date; or
(b) at a fixed period after sight; or
(c) at a definite time subject to any acceleration; or
(d) at a definite time subject to extension at the option of the holder, or to extension to a further definite time at the option of the maker or acceptor or automatically upon or after a specified act or event.

(2) An instrument which by its terms is otherwise payable only upon an act or event uncertain as to time of occurrence is not payable at a definite time even though the act or event has occurred.

§ 3-110. Payable to Order.
(1) An instrument is payable to order when by its terms it is payable to the order or assigns of any person therein specified with reasonable certainty, or to him or his order, or when it is conspicuously designated on its face as "exchange" or the like and names a payee. It may be payable to the order of

(a) the maker or drawer; or
(b) the drawee; or
(c) a payee who is not maker, drawer or drawee; or
(d) two or more payees together or in the alternative; or
(e) an estate, trust or fund, in which case it is payable to the order of the representative of each estate, trust or fund or his successors; or
(f) an office, or an officer by his title as such in which case it is payable to the principal but the incumbent of the office or his successors may act as if he or they were the holder; or
(g) a partnership or unincorporated association, in which case it is payable to the partnership or association and may be indorsed or transferred by any person thereto authorized.

(2) An instrument not payable to order is not made so payable by such words as "payable upon return of this instrument properly indorsed."
(3) an instrument made payable both to order and to bearer is payable to order unless the bearer words are handwritten or typewritten.

§ 3-111. Payable to Bearer. An instrument is payable to bearer when by its terms it is payable to

(a) bearer or the order of bearer; or
(b) a specified person or bearer; or
(c) "cash" or the order of "cash," or any other indication which does not purport to designate a specific payee.

§ 3-112. Terms and Omissions Not Affecting Negotiability.
(1) The negotiability of an instrument is not affected by

(a) the omission of a statement of any consideration or of the place where the instrument is drawn or payable; or
(b) a statement that collateral has been given to secure obligations either on the instrument or otherwise of an obligor on the instrument or that in case of default on those obligations the holder may realize on or dispose of the collateral; or
(c) a promise or power to maintain or protect collateral or to give additional collateral; or
(d) a term authorizing a confession of judgment on the instrument if it is not paid when due; or
(e) a term purporting to waive the benefit of any law intended for the advantage or protection of any obligor; or
(f) a term in a draft providing that the payee by indorsing or cashing it acknowledges full satisfaction of an obligation of the drawer; or
(g) a statement in a draft drawn in a set of parts (Section 3-801) to the effect that the order is effective only if no other part has been honored.

(2) Nothing in this section shall validate any term which is otherwise illegal.

§ 3-113. Seal. An instrument otherwise negotiable is within this Article even though it is under a seal.

§ 3-114. Date, Antedating, Postdating.
(1) The negotiability of an instrument is not affected by the fact that it is undated, antedated or postdated.
(2) Where an instrument is antedated or postdated the time when it is payable is determined by the stated date if the instrument is payable on demand or at a fixed period after date.
(3) Where the instrument or any signature thereon is dated, the date is presumed to be correct.

§ 3-115. Incomplete Instruments.
(1) When a paper whose contents at the time of signing show that it is intended to become an instrument is signed while still incomplete in any necessary respect it cannot be enforced until completed.
(2) If the completion is unauthorized the rules as to material alteration apply (Section 3-407), even though the paper was not delivered by the maker or drawer, but the burden of establishing that any completion is unauthorized is on the party so asserting.

§ 3-116. Instruments Payable to Two or More Persons.
An instrument payable to the order of two or more persons

(a) if in the alternative is payable to any one of them and may be negotiated, discharged or enforced by any of them who has possession of it;
(b) if not in the alter name is payable to all of them and may be negotiated, discharged or enforced only by all of them.

§ 3-117. Instruments Payable with Words of Description.
An instrument made payable to a named person with the addition of words describing him

(a) as agent or officer of a specified person is payable to his principal but the agent or officer may act as if he were the holder;
(b) as any other fiduciary for a specified person or purpose is payable to the payee and may be negotiated, discharged or enforced by him;

(c) in any other manner is payable to the payee unconditionally and the additional words are without effect on subsequent parties.

§ 3-118. Ambiguous Terms and Rules of Construction.

The following rules apply to every instrument:

(a) Where there is doubt whether the instrument is a draft or a note the holder may treat it as either. A draft drawn on the drawer is effective as a note.

(b) Handwritten terms control typewritten and printed terms, and typewritten control printed.

(c) Words control figures except that if the words are ambiguous figures control.

(d) Unless otherwise specified a provision for interest means interest at the judgment rate at the place of payment from the date of the instrument, or if it is undated from the date of issue.

(e) Unless the instrument otherwise specifies two or more persons who sign as maker, acceptor or drawer or indorser and as a part of the same transaction are jointly and severally liable even though the instrument contains such words as "I promise to pay.

(f) Unless otherwise specified consent to extension authorizes a single extension for not longer than the original period. A consent to extension, expressed in the instrument, is binding on secondary parties and accommodation makers. A holder may not exercise his option to extend an instrument over the objection of a maker or acceptor or other party who in accordance with Section 3-604 tenders full payment when the instrument is due.

§ 3-119. Other Writings Affecting Instrument.

(1) As between the obligor and his immediate obligee or any transferee the terms of an instrument may be modified or affected by any other written agreement executed as a part of the same transaction, except that a holder in due course is not affected by any limitation of his rights arising out of the separate written agreement if he had no notice of the limitation when he took the instrument.

(2) A separate agreement does not affect the negotiability of an instrument.

§ 3-120. Instruments "Payable Through" Bank. An instrument which states that it is "payable through" a bank or the like designates that bank as a collecting bank to make presentment but does not of itself authorize the bank to pay the instrument.

§ 3-121. Instruments Payable at Bank.

Note: *If this Act is introduced in the Congress of the United States this section should he omitted. (States to select either alternative)*

Alternative A

A note or acceptance which states that it is payable at a bank is the equivalent of a draft drawn on the bank payable when it falls due out of any funds of the maker or acceptor in current account or otherwise available for such payment.

Alternative B

A note or acceptance which states that it is payable at a bank is not of itself an order or authorization to the bank to pay it.

§ 3-122. Accrual of Cause of Action.

(1) A cause of action against a maker or an acceptor accrues

(a) in the case of a time instrument on the day after maturity;

(b) in the case of a demand instrument upon its date or, if no date is stated, on the date of issue.

(2) A cause of action against the obligor of a demand or time certificate of deposit accrues upon demand, but demand on a time certificate may not be made until on or after the date of maturity.

(3) A cause of action against a drawer of a draft or an indorser of any instrument accrues upon demand following dishonor of the instrument. Notice of dishonor is a demand.

(4) Unless an instrument provides otherwise, interest runs at the rate provided by law for a judgment

(a) in the case of a maker, acceptor or other primary obligor of a demand instrument, from the date of demand;

(b) in all other cases from the date of accrual of the cause of action.

PART 2 Transfer and Negotiation

§ 3-201. Transfer: Right to Indorsement.

(1) Transfer of an instrument vests in the transferee such rights as the transferor has therein, except that a transferee who has himself been a party to any fraud or illegality affecting the instrument or who as a prior holder had notice of a defense or claim against it cannot improve his position by taking from a later holder in due course.

(2) A transfer of a security interest in an instrument vests the foregoing rights in the transferee to the extent of the interest transferred.

(3) Unless otherwise agreed any transfer for value of an instrument not then payable to bearer gives the transferee the specifically enforceable right to have the unqualified indorsement of the transferor. Negotiation takes effect only when the indorsement is made and until that time there is no presumption that the transferee is the owner.

§ 3-202. Negotiation.

(1) Negotiation is the transfer of an instrument in such form that the transferee becomes a holder. If the instrument is payable to order it is negotiated by delivery with any necessary indorsement; if payable to bearer it is negotiated by delivery.

(2) An indorsement must be written by or on behalf of the holder and on the instrument or on a paper so firmly affixed thereto as to become a part thereof.

(3) An indorsement is effective for negotiation only when it conveys the entire instrument or any unpaid residue. If it purports to be of less it operates only as a partial assignment.

(4) Words of assignment, condition, waiver, guaranty, limitation or disclaimer of liability and the like accompanying an indorsement do not affect its character as an indorsement.

§ 3-203. Wrong or Misspelled Name.
Where an instrument is made payable to a person under a misspelled name or one other than his own he may indorse in that name or his own or both; but signature in both names may be required by a person paying or giving value for the instrument.

§ 3-204. Special Indorsement; Blank Indorsement.
(1) A special indorsement specifies the person to whom or to whose order it makes the instrument payable. Any instrument specially indorsed becomes payable to the order of the special indorsee and may be further negotiated only by his indorsement.
(2) An indorsement in blank specifies no particular indorsee and may consist of a mere signature. An instrument payable to order and indorsed in blank becomes payable to bearer and may be negotiated by delivery alone until specially indorsed.
(3) The holder may convert a blank indorsement into a special indorsement by writing over the signature of the indorser in blank any contract consistent with the character of the indorsement.

§ 3-205. Restrictive Indorsements. An indorsement is restrictive which either

(a) is conditional; or

(b) purports to prohibit further transfer of the instrument; or

(c) includes the words "for collection," "for deposit, pay any bank" or like terms signifying a purpose of deposit or collection; or

(d) otherwise states that it is for the benefit or use of the indorser or of another person.

§ 3-206. Effect of Restrictive Indorsement.
(1) No restrictive indorsement prevents further transfer or negotiation of the instrument.
(2) An intermediary bank, or a payor bank which is not the Depository bank, is neither given notice nor otherwise affected by a restrictive indorsement of any person except the bank's immediate transferor or the person presenting for payment.
(3) Except for an intermediary bank, any transferee under an indorsement which is conditional or includes the words "for collection," "for deposit, "pay any bank," or like terms (subparagraphs (a) and (c) of Section 3-205) must pay or apply any value given by him for or on the security of the instrument consistently with the indorsement and to the extent that he does so he becomes a holder for value. In addition such transferee is a holder in due course if he otherwise complies with the requirements of Section 3-302 on what constitutes a holder in due course.
(4) The first taker under an indorsement for the benefit of the indorser of another person (subparagraph (d) of Section 3-205) must pay or apply any value given by him for or on the security of the instrument consistently with the indorsement and to the extent that he does so he becomes a holder for value. In addition such taker is a holder in due course if he otherwise complies with the requirements of Section 3-302 on what constitutes a holder in due course. A later holder for value is neither given notice nor otherwise affected by such restrictive indorsement unless he has knowledge that a fiduciary or other person has negotiated the instrument in any transaction for his own benefit or otherwise in breach of duty (subsection (2) of Section 3-304).

§ 3-207. Negotiation Effective Although It May Be Rescinded.
(1) Negotiation is effective to transfer the instrument although the negotiation is

(a) made by an infant, a corporation exceeding its power, or any other person without capacity; or

(b) obtained by fraud, duress or mistake of any kind; or

(c) part of an illegal transaction; or

(d) made in breach of duty.

(2) Except as against a subsequent holder in due course such negotiation is in an appropriate case subject to rescission, the declaration of a constructive trust or any other remedy permitted by law.

§ 3-208. Reacquisition. Where an instrument is returned to or reacquired by a prior party he may cancel any indorsement which is not necessary to his title and reissue or further negotiate the instrument, but any intervening party is discharged as against the reacquiring party and subsequent holders not in due course and if his indorsement has been cancelled is discharged as against subsequent holders in due course as well.

PART 3 Rights of a Holder

§ 3-301. Rights of a Holder.
The holder of an instrument whether or not he is the owner may transfer or negotiate it and, except as otherwise provided in Section 3-603 on payment or satisfaction, discharge it or enforce payment in his own name.

§ 3-302. Holder in Due Course.
(1) A holder in due course is a holder who takes the instrument

(a) for value; and

(b) in good faith; and

(c) without notice that it is overdue or has been dishonored or of any defense against or claim to it on the part of any person.

(2) A payee may be a holder in due course.
(3) A holder does not become a holder in due course of an instrument:

(a) by purchase of it at judicial sale or by taking it under legal process; or

(b) by acquiring it in taking over an estate; or

(c) by purchasing it as part of a bulk transaction not in regular course of business of the transferor.

(4) A purchaser of a limited interest can be a holder in due course only to the extent of the interest purchased.

§ 3-303. Taking for Value. A holder takes the instrument for value

(a) to the extent that the agreed consideration has been performed or that he acquires a security interest in or a lien on the instrument otherwise than by legal process; or
(b) when he takes the instrument in payment of or as security for an antecedent claim against any person whether or not the claim is due; or
(c) when he gives a negotiable instrument for it or makes an irrevocable commitment to a third person.

§ 3-304. Notice to Purchaser.

(1) The purchaser has notice of a claim or defense if
(a) the instrument is so incomplete, bears such visible evidence of forgery or alteration, or is otherwise so irregular as to call into question its validity, terms or ownership or to create an ambiguity as the party to pay; or
(b) the purchaser has notice that the obligation of any party is voidable in whole or in part, or that all parties have been discharged.

(2) The purchaser has notice of a claim against the instrument when he has knowledge that a fiduciary has negotiated the instrument in payment of or as security for his own debt or in any transaction for his own benefit or otherwise in breach of duty.

(3) The purchaser has notice that an instrument is overdue if he has reason to know
(a) that any part of the principal amount is overdue or that there is an uncured default in payment of another instrument of the same series; or
(b) that acceleration of the instrument has been made; or
(c) that he is taking a demand instrument after demand has been made or more than a reasonable length of time after its issue. A reasonable time for a check drawn and payable within the states and territories of the United States and the District of Columbia is presumed to be thirty days.

(4) Knowledge of the following facts does not of itself give the purchaser notice of a defense of claim
(a) that the instrument is antedated or postdated;
(b) that it was issued or negotiated in return for an executory promise or accompanied by a separate agreement, unless the purchaser has notice that a defense or claim has arisen from the terms thereof;
(c) that any party has signed for accommodation;
(d) that an incomplete instrument has been completed, unless the purchaser has notice of any improper completion;
(e) that any person negotiating the instrument is or was a fiduciary;
(f) that there has been default in payment of interest on the instrument or in payment of any other instrument, except one of the same series.

(5) The filing or recording of a document does not of itself constitute notice within the provisions of this Article to a person who would otherwise be a holder in due course.

(6) To be effective notice must be received at such time and in such manner as to give a reasonable opportunity to act on it.

§ 3-305. Rights of a Holder in Due Course. To the extent that a holder is a holder in due course he takes the instrument free from

(1) all claims to it on the part of any person; and

(2) all defenses of any party to the instrument with whom the holder has not dealt except
(a) infancy, to the extent that it is a defense to a simple contract; and
(b) such other incapacity, or duress, or illegality of the transaction, as renders the obligation of the party a nullity; and
(c) such misrepresentation as has induced the party to sign the instrument with neither knowledge nor reasonable opportunity to obtain knowledge of its character or its essential terms; and
(d) discharge in insolvency proceedings; and
(e) any other discharge of which the holder has notice when he takes the instrument.

§ 3-306. Rights of One Not Holder in Due Course. Unless he has the rights of a holder in due course any person takes the instrument subject to
(a) all valid claims to it on the part of any person; and (b) all defenses of any party which would be available in an action on a simple contract; and
(c) the defenses of want or failure of consideration, nonperformance of any condition precedent, non-delivery, or delivery for a special purpose (Section 3-408); and
(d) the defense that he or a person through whom he holds the instrument acquired it by theft, or that payment or satisfaction to such holder would be inconsistent with the terms of a restrictive indorsement. The claim of any third person to the instrument is not otherwise available as a defense to any party liable thereon unless the third person himself defends the action for such party.

§ 3-307. Burden of Establishing Signatures, Defenses and Due Course.

(1) Unless specifically denied in the pleadings each signature on an instrument is admitted. When the effectiveness of a signature is put in issue
(a) the burden of establishing it is on the party claiming under the signature; but
(b) the signature is presumed to be genuine or authorized except where the action is to enforce the obligation of a purported signer who has died or become incompetent before proof is required.

(2) When signatures are admitted or established, production of the instrument entitles a holder to recover on it unless the defendant establishes a defense.

(3) After it is shown that a defense exists a person claiming the rights of a holder in due course has the burden of establishing that he or some person under whom he claims is in all respects a holder in due course.

PART 4 Liability of Parties

§ 3-401. Signature.

(1) No person is liable on an instrument unless his signature appears thereon.

(2) A signature is made by use of any name, including any trade or assumed name, upon an instrument, or by any word or mark used in lieu of a written signature.

§ 3-402. Signature in Ambiguous Capacity. Unless the instrument clearly indicates that a signature is made in some other capacity it is an indorsement.

§ 3-403. Signature of Authorized Representative.
(1) A signature may be made by an agent or other representative, and his authority to make it may be established as in other cases of representation. No particular form of appointment is necessary to establish such authority.
(2) An authorized representative who signs his own name to an instrument

(a) is personally obligated if the instrument neither names the person represented nor shows that the representative signed in a representative capacity;

(b) except as otherwise established between the immediate parties, is personally obligated if the instrument names the person represented but does not show that the representative signed in a representative capacity, or if the instrument does not name the person represented but does show that the representative signed in a representative capacity.

(3) Except as otherwise established the name of an organization preceded or followed by the name and office of an authorized individual is a signature made in a representative capacity.

§ 3-404. Unauthorized Signatures.
(1) Any unauthorized signature is wholly inoperative as that of the person whose name is signed unless he ratifies it or is precluded from denying it; but it operates as the signature of the unauthorized signer in favor of any person who in good faith pays the instrument or takes it for value.
(2) Any unauthorized signature may be ratified for all purposes of this Article. Such ratification does not of itself affect any rights of the person ratifying against the actual signer.

§ 3-405. Impostors; Signature in Name of Payee.
(1) An indorsement by any person in the name of a named payee is effective if

(a) an impostor by use of the mails or otherwise has induced the maker or drawer to issue the instrument to him or his confederate in the name of the payee; or

(b) a person signing as or on behalf of a maker or drawer intends the payee to have no interest in the instrument; or

(c) an agent or employee of the maker or drawer has supplied him with the name of the payee intending the latter to have no such interest.

(2) Nothing in this section shall affect the criminal or civil liability of the person so indorsing.

§ 3-406. Negligence Contributing to Alteration or Unauthorized Signature. Any person who by his negligence substantially contributes to a material alteration of the instrument or to the making of an unauthorized signature is precluded from asserting the alteration or lack of authority against a holder in due course or against a drawee or other payor who pays the instrument in good faith and in accordance with the reasonable commercial standards of the drawee's or payor's business.

§ 3-407. Alteration.
(1) Any alteration of an instrument is material which changes the contract of any party thereto in any respect, including any such change in

(a) the number or relations of the parties; or

(b) an incomplete instrument, by completing it otherwise than as authorized; or

(c) the writing as signed, by adding to it or by removing any part of it.

(2) As against any person other than a subsequent holder in due course

(a) alteration by the holder which is both fraudulent and material discharges any party whose contract is thereby changed unless that party assents or is precluded from asserting the defense;

(b) no other alteration discharges any party and the instrument may be enforced according to its original tenor, or as to incomplete instruments according to the authority given.

(3) A subsequent holder in due course may in all cases enforce the instrument according to its original tenor, and when an incomplete instrument has been completed, he may enforce it as completed.

§ 3-408. Consideration. Want or failure of consideration is a defense as against any person not having the rights of a holder in due course (Section 3-305), except that no consideration is necessary for an instrument or obligation thereon given in payment of or as security for an antecedent obligation of any kind. Nothing in this section shall be taken to displace any statute outside this Act under which a promise is enforceable notwithstanding lack or failure of consideration. Partial failure of consideration is a defense pro tanto whether or not the failure is in an ascertained or liquidated amount.

§ 3-409. Draft Not an Assignment.
(1) A check or other draft does not of itself operate as an assignment of any funds in the hands of the drawee available for its payment, and the drawee is not liable on the instrument until he accepts it.
(2) Nothing in this section shall affect any liability in contract, tort or otherwise arising from any letter of credit or other obligation or representation which is not an acceptance.

§ 3-410. Definition and Operation of Acceptance.
(1) Acceptance is the drawee's signed engagement to honor the draft as presented. It must be written on the draft, and may consist of his signature alone. It becomes operative when completed by delivery or notification.
(2) A draft may be accepted although it has not been signed by the drawer or is otherwise incomplete or is overdue or has been dishonored.
(3) Where the draft is payable at a fixed period after sight and the acceptor fails to date his acceptance the holder may complete it by supplying a date in good faith.

§ 3-411. Certificate of a Check.
(1) Certification of a check is acceptance. Where a holder procures certification the drawer and all prior indorsers are discharged.
(2) Unless otherwise agreed a bank has no obligation to certify a check.
(3) A bank may certify a check before returning it for lack of proper indorsement. If it does so the drawer is discharged.

§ 3-412. Acceptance Varying Draft.
(1) Where the drawee's proffered acceptance in any manner varies the draft as presented the holder may refuse the acceptance and treat the draft as dishonored in which case the drawee is entitled to have his acceptance cancelled.
(2) The terms of the draft are not varied by an acceptance to pay at any particular bank or place in the United States, unless the acceptance states that the draft is to be paid only at such bank or place.
(3) Where the holder assents to an acceptance varying the terms of the draft each drawer and indorser who does not affirmatively assent is discharged.

§ 3-413. Contract of Maker, Drawer and Acceptor.
(1) The maker or acceptor engages that he will pay the instrument according to its tenor at the time of his engagement or as completed pursuant to Section 3-115 on incomplete instruments.
(2) The drawer engages that upon dishonor of the draft and any necessary notice of dishonor or protest he will pay the amount of the draft to the holder or to any indorser who takes it up. The drawer may disclaim this liability by drawing without recourse.
(3) By making, drawing or accepting the party admits as against all subsequent parties including the drawee the existence of the payee and his then capacity to indorse.

§ 3-414. Contract of Indorser; Order of Liability.
(1) Unless the indorsement otherwise specifies (as by such words as "without recourse") every indorser engages that upon dishonor and any necessary notice of dishonor and protest he will pay the instrument according to its tenor at the time of his indorsement to the holder or to any subsequent indorser who takes it up, even though the indorser who takes it up was not obligated to do so.
(2) Unless they otherwise agree indorsers are liable to one another in the order in which they indorse, which is presumed to be the order in which their signatures appear on the instrument.

§ 3-415. Contract of Accommodation Party.
(1) An accommodation party is one who signs the instrument in any capacity for the purpose of lending his name to another party to it.
(2) When the instrument has been taken for value before it is due the accommodation party is liable in the capacity in which he has signed even though the taker knows of the accommodation.
(3) As against a holder in due course and without notice of the accommodation oral proof of the accommodation is not admissible to give the accommodation party the benefit of discharges dependent on his character as such. In other cases the accommodation character may be shown by oral proof.
(4) An indorsement which shows that it is not in the chain of title is notice of its accommodation character.
(5) An accommodation party is not liable to the party accommodated, and if he pays the instrument has a right of recourse on the instrument against such party.

§ 3-416. Contract of Guarantor.
(1) "Payment guaranteed" or equivalent words added to a signature means that the signer engages that if the instrument is not paid when due he will pay it according to its tenor without resort by the holder to any other party.
(2) "Collection guaranteed" or equivalent words added to a signature mean that the signer engages that if the instrument is not paid when due he will pay it according to its tenor, but only after the holder has reduced his claim against the maker or acceptor to judgment and execution has been returned unsatisfied, or after the maker or acceptor has become insolvent or it is otherwise apparent that it is useless to proceed against him.
(3) Words of guaranty which do not otherwise specify guarantee payment.
(4) No words of guaranty added to the signature of a sole maker or acceptor affect his liability on the instrument. Such words added to the signature of one of two or more makers or acceptors create a presumption that the signature is for the accommodation of the others.
(5) When words of guaranty are used presentment, notice of dishonor and protest are not necessary to charge the user.
(6) Any guaranty written on the instrument is enforcible notwithstanding any statute of frauds.

§ 3-417. Warranties on Presentment and Transfer.
(1) Any person who obtains payment or acceptance and any prior transferor warrants to a person who in good faith pays or accepts that

(a) he has a good title to the instrument or is authorized to obtain payment or acceptance on behalf of one who has a good title; and

(b) he has no knowledge that the signature of the maker or drawer is unauthorized, except that this warranty is not given by a holder in due course acting in good faith

(i) to a maker with respect to the maker's own signature; or

(ii) to a drawer with respect to the drawer's own signature, whether or not the drawer is also the drawee; or

(iii) to an acceptor of a draft if the holder in due course took the draft after the acceptance or obtained the acceptance without knowledge that the drawer's signature was unauthorized; and

(c) the instrument has not been materially altered, except that this warranty is not given by a holder in due course acting in good faith

(i) to the maker of a note; or

(ii) to the drawer of a draft whether or not the drawer is also the drawee; or

(iii) to the acceptor of a draft with respect to alteration made prior to the acceptance, even though the acceptance provided "payable as originally drawn" or equivalent terms; or

(iv) to the acceptor of a draft with respect to an alteration made after the acceptance.

(2) Any person who transfers an instrument and receives consideration warrants to his transferee and if the transfer is by indorsement to any subsequent holder who takes the instrument in good faith that

(a) he has a good title to the instrument or is authorized to obtain payment or acceptance on behalf of one who has a good title and the transfer is otherwise rightful; and

(b) all signatures are genuine or authorized; and

(c) the instrument has not been materially altered; and

(d) no defense of any party is good against him; and

(e) he has no knowledge of any insolvency proceeding instituted with respect to the maker or acceptor or the drawer of an unaccepted instrument.

(3) By transferring "without recourse" the transferor limits the obligation stated in subsection (2) (d) to a warranty that he has no knowledge of such a defense.

(4) A selling agent or broker who does not disclose the fact that he is acting only as such gives the warranties provided in this section, but if he makes such disclosure warrants only his good faith and authority.

§ 3-418. Finality of Payment or Acceptance. Except for recovery of bank payments as provided in the Article on Bank Deposits and Collections (Article 4) and except for liability for breach of warranty on presentment under the preceding section, payment or acceptance of any instrument is final in favor of a holder in due course, or a person who has in good faith changed his position in reliance on the payment.

§ 3-419. Conversion of Instrument; Innocent Representative.

(1) An instrument is converted when

(a) a drawee to whom it is delivered for acceptance refuses to return it on demand; or

(b) any person to whom it is delivered for payment refuses on demand either to pay or to return it; or

(c) it is paid on a forged indorsement.

(2) In an action against a drawee under subsection (1) the measure of the drawee's liability is the face amount of the instrument. In any other action under subsection (1) the measure of liability is presumed to be the face amount of the instrument.

(3) Subject to the provisions of this Act concerning restrictive indorsements a representative, including a Depository or collecting bank, who has in good faith and in accordance with the reasonable commercial standards applicable to the business of such representative dealt with an instrument or its proceeds on behalf of one who was not the true owner is not liable in conversion or otherwise to the true owner beyond the amount of any proceeds remaining in his hands.

(4) An intermediary bank or payor bank which is not a Depository bank is not liable in conversion solely by reason of the fact that proceeds of an item indorsed restrictively (Sections 3-205 and 3-206) are not paid or applied consistently with the restrictive indorsement of an indorser other than its immediate transferor.

PART 5 Presentment, Notice of Dishonor and Protest

§ 3.501. When Presentment, Notice of Dishonor, and Protest Necessary or Permissible

(1) Unless excused (Section 3-511) presentment is necessary to charge secondary parties as follows:

(a) presentment for acceptance is necessary to charge the drawer and indorsers of a draft where the draft so provides, or is payable elsewhere than at the residence or place of business of the drawee, or its date of payment depends upon such presentment. The holder may at his option present for acceptance any other draft payable at a stated date;

(b) presentment for payment is necessary to charge any indorser;

(c) in the case of any drawer, the acceptor of a draft payable at a bank or the maker of a note payable at a bank, presentment for payment is necessary, but failure to make presentment discharges such drawer, acceptor or maker only as stated in Section 3-502(1) (b).

(2) Unless excused (Section 3-511)

(a) notice of any dishonor is necessary to charge any indorser;

(b) in the case of any drawer, the acceptor of a draft payable at a bank or the maker of a note payable at a bank, notice of any dishonor is necessary, but failure to give such notice discharges such drawer, acceptor or maker only as stated in Section 3-502(1) (b).

(3) Unless excused (Section 3-511) protest of any dishonor is necessary to charge the drawer and indorsers of any draft which on its face appears to be drawn or payable outside of the states and territories of the United States and the District of Columbia. The holder may at his option make protest of any dishonor of any other instrument and in the case of a foreign draft may on insolvency of the acceptor before maturity make protest for a better security.

(4) Notwithstanding any provision of this section, neither presentment nor notice of dishonor nor protest is necessary to charge an indorser who has indorsed an instrument after maturity.

§ 3-502. Unexcused Delay; Discharge.

(1) Where without excuse any necessary presentment or notice of dishonor is delayed beyond the time when it is due

(a) any indorser is discharged; and

(b) any drawer or the acceptor of a draft payable at a bank or the maker of a note payable at a bank who because the drawee or payor bank becomes insolvent during the delay is deprived of funds maintained with the drawee or payor bank to cover the instrument may discharge his liability by written assignment to the holder of his rights against the drawee or payor bank in respect of such funds, but such drawer, acceptor or maker is not otherwise discharged.

(2) Where without excuse a necessary protest is delayed beyond the time when it is due any drawer or indorser is discharged.

§ 3-503. Time of Presentment.

(1) Unless a different time is expressed in the instrument the time for any presentment is determined as follows:

(a) where an instrument is payable at or a fixed period after a stated date any presentment for acceptance must be made on or before the date it is payable;

(b) where an instrument is payable after sight it must either be presented for acceptance or negotiated within a reasonable time after date or issue whichever is later;

(c) where an instrument shows the date on which it is payable presentment for payment is due on that date;

(d) where an instrument is accelerated presentment for payment is due within a reasonable time after the acceleration;

(e) with respect to the liability of any secondary party presentment for acceptance or payment of any other instrument is due within a reasonable time after such party becomes liable thereon.

(2) A reasonable time for presentment is determined by the nature of the instrument, any usage of banking or trade and the facts of the particular case. In the case of an uncertified check which is drawn and payable within the United States and which is not a draft drawn by a bank the following are presumed to be reasonable periods within which to present for payment or to initiate bank collection:

(a) with respect to the liability of the drawer, thirty days after date or issue whichever is later and

(b) with respect to the liability of an indorser, seven days after his indorsement.

(3) Where any presentment is due on a day which is not a full business day for either the person making presentment or the party to pay or accept, presentment is due on the next following day which is a full business day for both parties.

(4) Presentment to be sufficient must be made at a reasonable hour, and if at a bank during its banking day.

§ 3-504. How Presentment Made.

(1) Presentment is a demand for acceptance or payment made upon the maker, acceptor, drawee or other payor by or on behalf of the holder.

(2) Presentment may be made

(a) by mail, in which even the time of presentment is determined by the time or receipt of the mail; or

(b) through a clearing house; or

(c) at the place of acceptance or payment specified in the instrument or if there be none at the place of business or residence of the party to accept or pay. If neither the party to accept or pay nor anyone authorized to act for him is present or accessible at such place presentment is excused.

(3) It may be made

(a) to any one of two or more makers, acceptors, drawees or other payors; or

(b) to any person who has authority to make or refuse the acceptance or payment.

(4) A draft accepted or a note made payable at a bank in the United States must be presented at such bank.

(5) In the cases described in Section 4-210 presentment may be made in the manner and with the result stated in that section.

§ 3-505. Rights of Party to Whom Presentment Is Made.

(1) The party to whom presentment is made may without dishonor require

(a) exhibition of the instrument; and

(b) reasonable identification of the person making presentment and evidence of his authority to make it if made for another; and

(c) that the instrument be produced for acceptance or payment at a place specified in it, or if there be none at any place reasonable in the circumstances; and

(d) a signed receipt on the instrument for any partial or full payment and its surrender upon full payment.

(2) Failure to comply with any such requirement invalidates the presentment but the person presenting has a reasonable time in which to comply and the time for acceptance or payment runs from the time of compliance.

§ 3-506. Time Allowed for Acceptance or Payment.

(1) Acceptance may be deferred without dishonor until the close of the next business day following presentment. The holder may also in good faith effort to obtain acceptance and without either dishonor of the instrument or discharge of secondary parties allow postponement of acceptance for an additional business day.

(2) Except as a longer time is allowed in the case of documentary drafts drawn under a letter of credit, and unless an earlier time is agreed to by the party to pay, payment of an instrument may be deferred without dishonor pending reasonable examination t6 determine whether it is properly payable, but payment must be made in any event before the close of business on the day of presentment.

§ 3-507. Dishonor; Holder's Right of Recourse; Term Allowing Representment.

(1) An instrument is dishonored when

(a) a necessary or optional presentment is duly made and due acceptance or payment is refused or cannot be obtained within the prescribed time or in case of bank collections the instrument is seasonably returned by the midnight deadline (Section 4-301); or

(b) presentment is excused and the instrument is not duly accepted or paid.

(2) Subject to any necessary notice of dishonor and protest, the holder has upon dishonor an immediate right of recourse against the drawers and indorsers.

(3) Return of an instrument for lack of proper indorsement is not dishonor.

(4) A term in a draft or an indorsement thereof allowing a stated time for representment in the event of any dishonor of the draft by nonacceptance if a time draft or by nonpayment if a sight draft gives the holder as against any secondary party bound by the term an option to waive the dishonor without affecting the liability of the secondary party and he may present again up to the end of the stated time.

§ 3-508. Notice of Dishonor.

(1) Notice of dishonor may be given to any person who may be liable on the instrument by or on behalf of the holder or any party who has himself received notice, or any other party who

can be compelled to pay the instrument. In addition an agent or bank in whose hands the instrument is dishonored may give notice to his principal or customer or to another agent or bank from which the instrument was received.
(2) Any necessary notice must be given by a bank before its midnight deadline and by any other person before midnight of the third business day after dishonor or receipt of notice of dishonor.
(3) Notice may be given in any reasonable manner. It may be oral or written and in any terms which identify the instrument and state that it has been dishonored. A misdescription which does not mislead the party notified does not vitiate the notice. Sending the instrument bearing a stamp, ticket or writing stating that acceptance or payment has been refused or sending a notice of debit with respect to the instrument is sufficient.
(4) Written notice is given when sent although it is not received.
(5) Notice to one partner is notice to each although the firm has been dissolved.
(6) When any party is in insolvency proceedings instituted after the issue of the instrument notice may be given either to the party or to the representative of his estate.
(7) When any party is dead or incompetent notice may be sent to his last known address or given to his personal representative.
(8) Notice operates for the benefit of all parties who have rights on the instrument against the party notified.

§ 3-509. Protest; Noting for Protest.
(1) A protest is a certificate of dishonor made under the hand and seal of a United States consul or vice consul or a notary public or other person authorized to certify dishonor by the law of the place where dishonor occurs. It may be made upon information satisfactory to such person.
(2) The protest must identify the instrument and certify either that due presentment has been made or the reason why it is excused and that the instrument has been dishonored by a nonacceptance or nonpayment.
(3) The protest may also certify that notice of dishonor has been given to all parties or to specified parties.
(4) Subject to subsection (5) any necessary protest is due by the time that notice of dishonor is due.
(5) If, before protest is due, an instrument has been noted for protest by the officer to make protest, the protest may be made at any time thereafter as of the date of the noting.

§ 3-510. Evidence of Dishonor and Notice of Dishonor.
The following are admissible as evidence and create a presumption of dishonor and of any notice or dishonor therein shown:
(a) a document regular in form as provided in the preceding section which purports to be a protest;
(b) the purported stamp or writing of the drawee, payor bank or presenting bank on the instrument or accompanying it stating that acceptance or payment has been refused for reasons consistent with dishonor;
(c) any book or record of the drawee, payor bank, or any collecting bank kept in the usual course of business which shows dishonor, even though there is no evidence of who made the entry.

§ 3-511. Waived or Excused Presentment, Protest or Notice of Dishonor or Delay Therein.
(1) Delay in presentment, protest or notice of dishonor is excused when the party is without notice that it is due or when the delay is caused by circumstances beyond his control and he exercises reasonable diligence after the cause of the delay ceases to operate.
(2) Presentment or notice or protest as the case may be is entirely excused when
(a) the party to be charged has waived it expressly or by implication either before or after it is due; or
(b) such party has himself dishonored the instrument or has countermanded payment or otherwise has no reason to expect or right to require that the instrument be accepted or paid; or
(c) by reasonable diligence the presentment or protest cannot be made or the notice given.
(3) Presentment is also entirely excused when
(a) the maker, acceptor or drawee of any instrument except a documentary draft is dead or in insolvency proceedings instituted after the issue of the instrument; or
(b) acceptance or payment is refused but not for want of proper presentment.
(4) Where a draft has been dishonored by nonacceptance a later presentment for payment and any notice of dishonor and protest for nonpayment are excused unless in the meantime the instrument has been accepted.
(5) A waiver of protest is also a waiver of presentment and of notice of dishonor even though protest is not required.
(6) Where a waiver of presentment or notice or protest is embodied in the instrument itself it is binding upon all parties; but where it is written above the signature of an indorser it binds him only.

PART 6 Discharge

§ 3-601. Discharge of Parties.
(1) The extent of the discharge of any party from liability on an instrument is governed by the section on
(a) payment or satisfaction (Section 3-603; or
(b) tender of payment (Section 3-604); or
(c) cancellation or renunciation (Section 3-605); or
(d) impairment of right of recourse or of collateral (Section 3-606); or
(e) reacquisition of the instrument by a prior party (Section 3-208); or
(f) fraudulent and material alteration (Section 3-407); or
(g) certification of a check (Section 3-411); or
(h) acceptance varying a draft (Section 3-412); or
(i) unexcused delay in presentment or notice of dishonor or protest (Section 3-502).
(2) Any party is also discharged from his liability on an instrument to another party by any other act or agreement with such party which would discharge his simple contract for the payment of money.

(3) The liability of all parties is discharged when any party who has himself no right of action or recourse on the instrument

(a) reacquires the instrument in his own right; or

(b) is discharged under any provision of this Article, except as otherwise provided with respect to discharge for impairment of recourse or of collateral (Section 3-606).

§ 3-602. Effect of Discharge Against Holder in Due Course. No discharge of any party provided by this Article is effective against a subsequent holder in due course unless he has notice thereof when he takes the instrument.

§ 3-603. Payment or Satisfaction.

(1) The liability of any party is discharged to the extent of his payment or satisfaction to the holder even though it is made with knowledge of a claim of another person to the instrument unless prior to such payment or satisfaction the person making the claim either supplies indemnity deemed adequate by the party seeking the discharge or enjoins payment or satisfaction by order of a court of competent jurisdiction in an action in which the adverse claimant and the holder are parties. This subsection does not, however, result in the discharge of the liability

(a) of a party who in bad faith pays or satisfies a holder who acquired the instrument, by theft or who (unless having the rights of a holder in due course) holds through one who so acquired it; or

(b) of a party (other than an intermediary bank or a payor bank which is not a Depository bank) who pays or satisfies the holder of an instrument which has been restrictively indorsed in a manner not consistent with the terms of such restrictive indorsement.

(2) Payment or satisfaction may be made with the consent of the holder by any person including a stranger to the instrument. Surrender of the instrument to such a person gives him the rights of a transferee (Section 3-201).

§ 3-604. Tender of Payment.

(1) Any party making tender of full payment to a holder when or after it is due is discharged to the extent of all subsequent liability for interest, costs and attorney's fees.

(2) The holder's refusal of such tender wholly discharges any party who has a right or recourse against the party making the render.

(3) Where the maker or acceptor of an instrument payable otherwise than on demand is able and ready to pay at every place of payment specified in the instrument when it is due, it is equivalent to tender.

§ 3-605. Cancellation and Renunciation.

(1) The holder of an instrument may even without consideration discharge any party

(a) in any manner apparent on the face of the instrument or the indorsement, as by intentionally cancelling the instrument or the party's signature by destruction or mutilation, or by striking out the party's signature; or

(b) by renouncing his rights by a writing signed and delivered or by surrender of the instrument to the party to be discharged.

(2) Neither cancellation nor renunciation without surrender of the instrument affects the title thereto.

§ 3-606. Impairment of Recourse or of Collateral.

(1) The holder discharges any party to the instrument to the extent that without such party's consent the holder

(a) without express reservation of rights releases or agrees not to sue any person against whom the party has to the knowledge of the holder a right of recourse or agrees to suspend the right to enforce against such person the instrument or collateral or otherwise discharges such person, except that failure or delay in effecting any required presentment, protest or notice of dishonor with respect to any such person does not discharge any party as to whom presentment, protest or notice of dishonor is effective or unnecessary; or

(b) unjustifiably impairs any collateral for the instrument given by or on behalf of the party or any person against whom he has a right of recourse.

(2) By express reservation of rights against a party with a right of recourse the holder preserves

(a) all his rights against such party as of the time when the instrument was originally due; and

(b) the right of the party to pay the instrument as of that time; and

(c) all rights of such party to recourse against others.

PART 7 Advice of International Sight Draft

§ 3-701. Letter of Advice of International Sight Draft.

(1) A "letter of advice" is a drawer's communication to the drawee that a described draft has been drawn.

(2) Unless otherwise agreed when a bank receives from another bank a letter of advice of an international sight draft the drawee bank may immediately debit the drawer's account and stop the running of interest pro tanto. Such a debit and any resulting credit to any account covering outstanding drafts leaves in the drawer full power to stop payment or otherwise dispose of the amount and creates no trust or interest in favor of the holder.

(3) Unless otherwise agreed and except where a draft is drawn under a credit issued by the drawee, the drawee of an international sight draft owes the drawer no duty to pay an unadvised draft but if it does so and the draft is genuine, may appropriately debit the drawer's account.

PART 8 Miscellaneous

§ 3-801. Drafts in a Set.

(1) Where a draft is drawn in a set of parts, each of which is numbered and expressed to be an order only if no other part has been honored, the whole of the parts constitutes one draft but a taker of any part may become a holder in due course of the draft.

(2) Any person who negotiates, indorses or accepts a single part of a draft drawn in a set thereby becomes liable to any holder in due course of that part as if it were the whole set, but as between different holders in due course to whom different parts have been negotiated the holder whose title first accrues has all rights to the draft and its proceeds.

(3) As against the drawee the first presented part of a draft drawn in a set is the part entitled to payment, or if a time draft to

acceptance and payment. Acceptance of any subsequently presented part renders the drawee liable thereon under subsection (2). With respect both to a holder and to the drawer payment of a subsequently presented part of a draft payable at sight has the same effect as payment of a check notwithstanding an effective stop order (Section 4-407).
(4) Except as otherwise provided in this section, where any part of a draft in a set is discharged by payment or otherwise the whole draft is discharged.

§ 3-802. Effect of Instrument on Obligation for Which It Is Given.
(1) Unless otherwise agreed where an instrument is taken for an underlying obligation

(a) the obligation is pro tanto discharged if a bank is drawer, maker or acceptor of the instrument and there is no recourse on the instrument against the underlying obligor; and

(b) in any other case the obligation is suspended pro tanto until the instrument is due or if it is payable on demand until its presentment. If the instrument is dishonored action may be maintained on either the instrument or the obligation; discharge of the underlying obligor on the instrument also discharges him on the obligation.

(2) The taking in good faith of a check which is not postdated does not of itself so extend the time on the original obligation as to discharge a surety.

§ 3-803. Notice to Third Party.
Where a defendant is sued for breach of an obligation for which a third person is answerable over under this Article he may give the third person written notice of the litigation, and the person notified may then give similar notice to any other person who is answerable over to him under this Article. If the notice states that the person notified may come in and defend and that if the person notified does not do so he will in any action against him by the person giving the notice be bound by any determination of fact common to the two litigations, then unless after seasonable receipt of the notice the person notified does come in and defend he is so bound.

§ 3-804. Lost, Destroyed or Stolen Instruments. The owner of an instrument which is lost, whether by destruction, theft or otherwise, may maintain an action in his own name and recover from any party liable thereon upon due proof of his ownership, the facts which prevent his production of the instrument and its terms. The court may require security indemnifying the defendant against loss by reason of further claims on the instrument.

§ 3-805. Instruments Not Payable to Order or to Bearer. This Article applies to any instrument whose terms do not preclude transfer and which is otherwise negotiable within this Article but which is not payable to order to bearer, except that there can be no holder in due course of such an instrument.

ARTICLE 4 / Bank Deposits and Collections

PART 1 General Provisions and Definitions

§ 4-101. Short Title. This Article shall be known and may be cited as Uniform Commercial Code—Bank Deposits and Collections.

§ 4-102. Applicability.
(1) To the extent that items within this Article are also within the scope of Articles 3 and 8, they are subject to the provisions of those Articles. In the event of conflict the provisions of this Article govern those of Article 3 but the provisions of Article 8 govern those of this Article.
(2) The liability of a bank for action or non-action with respect to any item handled by it for purposes of presentment, payment or collection is governed by the law of the place where the bank is located. In the case of action or non-action by or at a branch or separate office of a bank, its liability is governed by the law of the place where the branch or separate office is located.

§ 4-103. Variation by Agreement; Measure of Damages; Certain Action Constituting Ordinary Care.
(1) The effect of the provisions of this Article may be varied by agreement except that no agreement can disclaim a bank's responsibility for its own lack of good faith or failure to exercise ordinary care or can limit the measure of damages for such lack or failure; but the parties may by agreement determine the standards by which such responsibility is to be measured if such standards are not manifestly unreasonable.
(2) Federal Reserve regulations and operating letters, clearing house rules, and the like, have the effect of agreements under subsection (1), whether or not specifically assented to by all parties interested in items handled.
(3) Action or non-action approved by this Article or pursuant to Federal Reserve regulations or operating letters constitutes the exercise of ordinary care and, in the absence of special instructions, action or non-action consistent with clearing house rules and the like or with a general banking usage not disapproved by this Article, prima facie constitutes the exercise of ordinary care.
(4) The specification or approval of certain procedures by this Article does not constitute disapproval of other procedures which may be reasonable under the circumstances.
(5) The measure of damages for failure to exercise ordinary care in handling an item is the amount of the item reduced by an amount which could not have been realized by the use of ordinary care, and where there is bad faith it includes other damages, if any, suffered by the party as a proximate consequence.

§ 4-104. Definitions and Index of Definitions.
(1) In this Article unless the context otherwise requires

(a) "Account" means any account with a bank and includes a checking, time, interest or savings account;

(b) "Afternoon" means the period of a day between noon and midnight;

(c) "Banking day" means that part of any day on which a bank is open to the public for carrying on substantially all of its banking functions;

(d) "Clearing house" means any association of banks or other payors regularly clearing items;

(e) "Customer" means any person having an account with a bank or for whom a bank has agreed to collect items and includes a bank carrying an account with another bank;

(f) "Documentary draft" means any negotiable or non-negotiable draft with accompanying documents, securities or other papers to be delivered against honor of the draft;
(g) "Item" means any instrument for the payment of money even though it is not negotiable but does not include money;
(h) "Midnight deadline" with respect to a bank is midnight on its next banking day following the banking day on which it receives the relevant item or notice or from which the time for taking action commences to run, whichever is later;
(i) "Properly payable" includes the availability of funds for payment at the time of decision to pay or dishonor;
(j) "Settle" means to pay in cash, by clearing house settlement, in a charge or credit or by remittance, or otherwise as instructed. A settlement may be either provisional or final;
(k) "Suspends payments" with respect to a bank means that it has been closed by order of the supervisory authorities, that a public officer has been appointed to take it over or that it ceases or refuses to make payments in the ordinary course of business.

(2) Other definitions applying to this Article and the sections in which they appear are:

"Collecting bank." Section 4-105.
"Depository bank." Section 4-105.
"Intermediary bank." Section 4-105.
"Payor bank." Section 4-105.
"Presenting bank." Section 4-105.
"Remitting bank." Section 4-105.

(3) The following definitions in other Articles apply to this Article:

"Acceptance." Section 3-410.
"Certificate of deposit." Section 3-104.
"Certification." Section 3-411.
"Check." Section 3-104.
"Draft." Section 3-104.
"Holder in due course." Section 3-302.
"Notice of dishonor." Section 3-508.
"Presentment." Section 3-504.
"Protest." Section 3-509.
"Secondary party." Section 3-102.

(4) In addition Article 1 contains general definitions and principles of construction and interpretation applicable throughout this Article.

§ 4-105. "Depository Bank"; "Intermediary Bank"; "Collecting Bank"; "Payor Bank"; "Presenting Bank"; "Remitting Bank."

In this Article unless the context otherwise requires

(a) "Depository bank" means the first bank to which an item is transferred for collection even though it is also the payor bank;
(b) "Payor bank" means a bank by which an item is payable as drawn or accepted;
(c) "Intermediary bank" means any bank to which an item is transferred in course of collection except the Depository or payor bank;
(d) "Collecting bank" means any bank handling the item for collection except the payor bank;
(e) "Presenting bank" means any bank presenting an item except a payor bank;
(f) "Remitting bank" means any payor or intermediary bank remitting for an item.

§ 4-106. Separate Office of a Bank. A branch or separate office of a bank [maintaining its own deposit ledgers] is a separate bank for the purpose of computing the time within which and determining the place at or to which action may be taken or notices or orders shall be given under this Article and under Article 3.

Note. **The words in Brackets are optional.**

§ 4-107. Time of Receipt of Items.

(1) For the purpose of allowing time to process items, prove balances and make the necessary entries on its books to determine its position for the day, a bank may fix an afternoon hour of two P.M. or later as a cut-off hour for the handling of money and items and the making of entries on its books.
(2) Any item or deposit of money received on any day after a cut-off hour so fixed or after the close of the banking day may be treated as being received at the opening of the next banking day.

§ 4-108. Delays.

(1) Unless otherwise instructed, a collecting bank in a good faith effort to secure payment may, in the case of specific items and with or without the approval of any person involved, waive, modify or extend time limits imposed or permitted by this Act for a period not in excess of an additional banking day without discharge of secondary parties and without liability to its transferor or any prior party.
(2) Delay by a collecting bank or payor bank beyond time limits prescribed or permitted by this Act or by instructions is excused if caused by interruption of communication facilities, suspension of payments by another bank, war, emergency conditions or other circumstances beyond the control of the bank provided it exercises such diligence as the circumstances require.

§ 4-109. Process of Posting. The "process of posting" means the usual procedure followed by a payor bank in determining to pay an item and in recording the payment including one or more of the following or other steps as determined by the bank:

(a) verification of any signature;
(b) ascertaining that sufficient funds are available;
(c) affixing a "paid" or other stamp;
(d) entering a charge or entry to a customer's account;
(e) correcting or reversing an entry or erroneous action with respect to the item.

PART 2 Collection of Items: Depository and Collecting Banks

§ 4-201. Presumption and Duration of Agency Status of Collecting Banks and Provisional Status of Credits; Applicability of Article; Item Indorsed "Pay any Bank."

(1) Unless a contrary intent clearly appears and prior to the time that a settlement given by a collecting bank for an item is or becomes final (subsection (3) of Section 4-211 and Sections

4-212 and 4-213) the bank is an agent or sub-agent of the owner of the item and any settlement given for the item is provisional. This provision applies regardless of the form of indorsement or lack of indorsement and even though credit given for the item is subject to immediate withdrawal as of right or is in fact withdrawn; but the continuance of ownership of an item by its owner and any rights of the owner to proceeds of the item are subject to rights of a collecting bank such as those resulting from outstanding advances on the item and valid rights of setoff. When an item is handled by banks for purposes of presentment, payment and collection, the relevant provisions of this Article apply even though action of parties clearly establishes that a particular bank has purchased the item and is the owner of it.

(2) After an item has been indorsed with the words "pay any bank" or the like, only a bank may acquire the rights of a holder

(a) until the item has been returned to the customer initiating collection; or

(b) until the item has been specially indorsed by a bank to a person who is not a bank.

§ 4-202. Responsibility for Collection; When Action Seasonable.

(1) A collecting bank must use ordinary care in

(a) presenting an item or sending it for presentment; and

(b) sending notice of dishonor or nonpayment or returning an item other than a documentary draft to the bank's transferor [or directly to the Depository bank under subsection (2) of Section 4-212] (see note to Section 4-212) after learning that the item has not been paid or accepted, as the case may be; and

(c) settling for an item when the bank receives final settlement; and

(d) making or providing for any necessary protest; and

(e) notifying its transferor of any loss or delay in transit within a reasonable time after discovery thereof.

(2) A collecting bank taking proper action before its midnight deadline following receipt of an item, notice or payment acts seasonably; taking proper action within a reasonably longer time may be seasonable but the bank has the burden of so establishing.

(3) Subject to subsection (1) (a), a bank is not liable for the insolvency, neglect, misconduct, mistake or default of another bank or person or for loss or destruction of an item in transit or in the possession of others.

§ 4-203. Effect of Instructions. Subject to the provisions of Article 3 concerning conversion of instruments (Section 3-429) and the provisions of both Article 3 and this Article concerning restrictive indorsements only a collecting bank's transferor can give instructions which affect the bank or constitute notice to it and a collecting bank is not liable to prior parties for any action taken pursuant to such instructions or in accordance with any agreement with its transferor.

§ 4-204. Methods of Sending and Presenting; Sending Direct to Payor Bank.

(1) A collecting bank must send items by reasonably prompt method taking into consideration any relevant instructions, the nature of the item, the number of such items on hand, and the cost of collection involved and the method generally used by it or others to present such items.

(2) A collecting bank may send

(a) any item direct to the payor bank;

(b) any item to any non-bank payor if authorized by its transferor; and

(c) any item other than documentary drafts to any non-bank payor, if authorized by Federal Reserve regulation or operating letter, clearing house rule or the like.

(3) Presenting may be made by a presenting bank at a place where the payor bank has requested that presentment be made.

§ 4-205. Supplying Missing Indorsement; No Notice from Prior Indorsement.

(1) A Depository bank which has taken an item for collection may supply any indorsement of the customer which is necessary to title unless the item contains the words "payee's indorsement required" or the like. In the absence of such a requirement a statement placed on the item by the Depository bank to the effect that the item was deposited by a customer or credited to his account is effective as the customer's indorsement.

(2) An intermediary bank, or payor bank which is not a Depository bank, is neither given notice nor otherwise affected by a restrictive indorsement of any person except the bank's immediate transferor.

§ 4-206. Transfer Between Banks. Any agreed method which identifies the transferor bank is sufficient for the item's further transfer to another bank.

§ 4-207. Warranties or Customer and Collecting Bank on Transfer or Presentment of Items; Time for Claims.

(1) Each customer or collecting bank who obtains payment or acceptance of an item and each prior customer and collecting bank warrants to the payor bank or other payor who in good faith pays or accepts the item that

(a) he has a good title to the item or is authorized to obtain payment of acceptance on behalf of one who has a good title and the transfer is otherwise rightful; and

(b) he has no knowledge that the signature of the maker or drawer is unauthorized, except that this warranty is not given by any customer or collecting bank that is a holder in due course and acts in good faith

(i) to a maker with respect to the maker's own signature; or

(ii) to a drawer with respect to the drawer's own signature, whether or not the drawer is also the drawee; or

(iii) to an acceptor of an item if the holder in due course took the item after the acceptance or obtained the acceptance without knowledge that the drawer's signature was unauthorized; and

(c) the time has not been materially altered, except that this warranty is not given by any customer or collecting bank that is a holder in due course and acts in good faith

(i) to the maker of a note; or

(ii) to the drawer of a draft whether or not the drawer is also the drawee; or

(iii) to the acceptor of an item with respect to an alteration made prior to the acceptance if the holder in due course took the item after the acceptance provided "payable as originally drawn or equivalent terms; or

(iv) to the acceptor of an item with respect to an alteration made after the acceptance.

(2) Each customer and collecting bank who transfers an item and receives a settlement or other consideration for it warrants to his transferee and to any subsequent collecting bank who takes the item in good faith that

(a) he has a good title to the item or is authorized to obtain payment or acceptance on behalf of one who has a good title and the transfer is otherwise rightful; and

(b) all signatures are genuine or authorized; and

(c) the item has not been materially altered; and

(d) no defense of any party is good against him; and

(e) he has no knowledge of any insolvency proceeding instituted with respect to the maker or acceptor or the drawer of an unaccepted item.

In addition each customer and collecting bank so transferring an item and receiving a settlement or other consideration engages that upon dishonor and any necessary notice of dishonor and protest he will take up the item.

(3) The warranties and the engagement to honor set forth in the two preceding subsections arise notwithstanding the absence of indorsement or words of guaranty or warranty in the transfer or presentment and a collecting bank remains liable for their breach despite remittance to its transferor. Damages for breach of such warranties or engagement to honor shall not exceed the consideration received by the customer or collecting bank responsible plus finance charges and expenses related to the item, if any.

(4) Unless a claim for breach of warranty under this section is made within a reasonable time after the person claiming learns of the breach, the person liable is discharged to the extent of any loss caused by the delay in making claim.

§ 4-208. Security Interest of Collecting Bank in Items, Accompanying Documents and Proceeds.

(1) A bank has a security interest in an item and any accompanying documents or the proceeds of either

(a) in case of an item deposited in an account to the extent to which credit given for the item has been withdrawn or applied;

(b) in case of an item for which it has given credit available for withdrawal as of right, to the extent of the credit given whether or not the credit is drawn upon and whether or not there is a right of charge-back; or

(c) if it makes an advance on or against the item.

(2) When credit which has been given for several items received at one time or pursuant to a single agreement is withdrawn or applied in part the security interest remains upon all the items, any accompanying documents or the proceeds of either. For the purpose of this section, credits first given are first withdrawn.

(3) Receipt by a collecting bank of a final settlement for an item is a realization on its security interest in the item, accompanying documents and proceeds. To the extent and so long as the bank does not receive final settlement for the item or give up possession of the item or accompanying documents for purposes other than collection, the security interest continues and is subject to the provisions of Article 9 except that

(a) no security agreement is necessary to make the security interest enforceable (subsection (1) (b) of Section 9-203); and

(b) no filing is required to perfect the security interest; and

(c) the security interest has priority over conflicting perfected security interests in the item, accompanying documents or proceeds.

§ 4-209. When Bank Gives Value for Purposes of Holder in Due Course. For purposes of determining its status as a holder in due course, the bank has given value to the extent that it has a security interest in an item provided that the bank otherwise complies with the requirements of Section 3-302 on what constitutes a holder in due course.

§ 4-210. Presentment by Notice of Item Not Payable by, through or at a Bank; Liability of Secondary Parties.

(1) Unless otherwise instructed, a collecting bank may present an item not payable by, through or at a bank by sending to the party to accept or pay a written notice that the bank holds the item for acceptance or payment. The notice must be sent in time to be received on or before the day when presentment is due and the bank must meet any requirement of the party to accept or pay under Section 3-505 by the close of the bank's next banking day after it knows of the requirement.

(2) Where presentment is made by notice and neither honor nor request for compliance with a requirement under Section 3-505 is received by the close of business on the day after maturity or in the case of demand items by the close of business on the third banking day after notice was sent, the presenting bank may treat the item as dishonored and charge any secondary party by sending him notice of the facts.

§ 4-211. Media or Remittance; Provisional and Final Settlement in Remittance Cases.

(1) A collecting bank may take in settlement of an item

(a) a check of the remitting bank or of another bank on any bank except the remitting bank; or

(b) a cashier's check or similar primary obligation of a remitting bank which is a member of or clears through a member of the same clearing house or group as the collecting bank; or

(c) appropriate authority to charge an account of the remitting bank or of another bank with the collecting bank; or

(d) if the item is drawn upon or payable by a person other than a bank, a cashier's check, certified check or other bank check or obligation.

(2) If before its midnight deadline the collecting bank properly dishonors a remittance check or authorization to charge on itself or presents or forwards for collection a remittance instrument of

or on another bank which is of a kind approved by subsection (1) or has not been authorized by it, the collecting bank is not liable to prior parties in the event of the dishonor of such check, instrument or authorization.

(3) A settlement for an item by means of a remittance instrument or authorization to charge is or becomes a final settlement as to both the person making and the person receiving the settlement

(a) if the remittance instrument or authorization to charge is of a kind approved by subsection (1) or has not been authorized by the person receiving the settlement and in either case the person receiving the settlement acts seasonably before its midnight deadline in presenting, forwarding for collection or paying the instrument or authorization is finally paid by the payor by which it is payable;

(b) if the person receiving the settlement has authorized remittance by a non-bank check or obligation or by a cashier's check or similar primary obligation of or a check upon the payor or other remitting bank which is not of a kind approved by subsection (1) (b),—at the time of the receipt of such remittance check or obligation; or

(c) if in case not covered by sub paragraphs (a) or (b) the person receiving the settlement fails to seasonably present, forward for collection, pay or return a remittance instrument of authorization to it to charge before its midnight deadline,—at such midnight deadline.

§ 4-212. Right of Charge-Back or Refund.

(1) If a collecting bank has made provisional settlement with its customer for an item and itself fails by reason of dishonor, suspension of payments by a bank or otherwise to receive a settlement for the item which is or becomes final, the bank may revoke the settlement given by it, charge back the amount of any credit given for the item to its customer whether or not it is able to return the items if by its midnight deadline or within a longer reasonable time after it learns the facts it returns the item or sends notification of the facts. These rights to revoke, charge-back and obtain refund terminate if and when a settlement for the item received by the bank is or becomes final (subsection (3) of Section 4-211 and subsections (2) and (3) of Section 4-213).

[(2) Within the time and manner prescribed by this section and Section 4-301, an intermediary or payor bank, as the case may be, may return an unpaid item directly to the Depository bank and may send for collection a draft on the Depository bank and obtain reimbursement. In such case, if the Depository bank has received provisional settlement for the item, it must reimburse the bank drawing the draft and any provisional credits for the item between banks shall become and remain final.]

Note: *Direct returns is recognized as an innovation that is not yet established bank practice, and therefore, Paragraph 2 has been bracketed. Some lawyers have doubted whether it should be included in legislation or left to development by agreement.*

(3) A Depository bank which is also the payor may charge-back the amount of an item to its customer's account or obtain refund in accordance with the section governing return of an item received by a payor bank for credit on its books (Section 4-301).

(4) The right to charge-back is not affected by

(a) prior use of the credit given for the item; or

(b) failure by any bank to exercise ordinary care with respect to the item but any bank so failing remains liable.

(5) A failure to charge-back or claim refund does not affect other rights of the bank against the customer or any other party.

(6) If credit is given in dollars as the equivalent of the value of an item payable in a foreign currency the dollar amount of any charge-back or refund shall be calculated on the basis of the buying site rate for the foreign currency prevailing on the day when the person entitled to the charge-back or refund learns that it will not receive payment in ordinary course.

§ 4-213. Final Payment of Item by Payor Bank; When Provisional Debits and Credits Become Final; When Certaiti Credits Become Available for Withdrawal.

(1) An item is finally paid by a payor bank when the bank has done any of the following whichever happens first:

(a) paid the item in cash; or

(b) settled for the item without reserving a right to revoke the settlement and without having such right under statute, clearing house rule or agreement; or

(c) completed the process of posting the item to the indicated account of the drawer, maker or other person to be charged therewith; or

(d) made a provisional settlement for the item and failed to revoke the settlement in the time and manner permitted by statute, clearing house rule or agreement.

Upon a final payment under subparagraphs (b), (c) or (d) the payor bank shall be accountable for the amount of the item.

(2) If provisional settlement for an item between the presenting and payor banks is made through a clearing house or by debits or credits in an account between them, then to the extent that provisional debits or credits for the item are entered in accounts between the presenting and payor banks or between the presenting and successive prior collecting banks seriatim, they become final upon final payment of the item by the payor bank.

(3) If a collecting bank receives a settlement for an item which is or becomes final (subsection (3) of Section 4-211, subsection (2) of Section 4-213) the bank is accountable to its customer for the amount of the item and any provisional credit given for the item in an account with its customer becomes final.

(4) Subject to any right of the bank to apply the credit to an obligation of the customer, credit given by a bank for an item in an account with its customer becomes available for withdrawal as of right

(a) in any case where the bank has received a provisional settlement for the item,—when such settlement becomes final and the bank has had a reasonable time to learn that the settlement is final;

(b) in any case where the bank is both a Depository bank and a payor bank and the item is finally paid,-at the opening of the bank's second banking day following receipt of the item.

(5) A deposit of money in a bank is final when made but, subject to any right of the bank to apply the deposit to an obligation of the customer, the deposit becomes available for withdrawal as

of right at the opening of the bank's next banking day following receipt of the deposit.

§ 4-214. Insolvency and Preference.

(1) Any item in or coming into the possession of a payor or collecting bank which suspends payment and which item is not finally paid shall be returned by the receiver, trustee or agent in charge of the closed bank to the presenting bank or the closed bank's customer.

(2) If a payor bank finally pays an item and suspends payments without making a settlement for the item with its customer or the presenting bank which settlement is or becomes final, the owner of the item has a preferred claim against the payor bank.

(3) If a payor bank gives or a collecting bank gives or receives a provisional settlement for an item and thereafter suspends payments, the suspension does not prevent or interfere with the settlement becoming final if such finality occurs automatically upon the lapse of certain time or the happening of certain events (subsection (3) of Section 4-211, subsections (l)(d), (2) and (3) of Section 4-213).

(4) If a collecting bank receives from subsequent parties settlement for an item which settlement is or becomes final and suspends payments without making a settlement for the item with its customer which is or becomes final, the owner of the item has a preferred claim against such collecting bank.

PART 3 Collection of Items: Payor Banks

§ 4-301. Deferred Posting; Recovery of Payment by Return of Items; Time of Dishonor.

(1) Where an authorized settlement for a demand item (other than a documentary draft) received by a payor bank otherwise than for immediate payment over the counter has been made before midnight of the banking day of receipt the payor bank may revoke the settlement and recover any payment if before it has made final payment (subsection (1) of Section 4-213) and before its midnight deadline it

(a) returns the item; or

(b) sends written notice of dishonor or nonpayment if the item is held for protest or is otherwise unavailable for return.

(2) If a demand item is received by a payor bank for credit on its books it may return such item or send notice of dishonor and may revoke any credit given or recover the amount thereof withdrawn by its customer, if it acts within the time limit and in the manner specified in the preceding subsection.

(3) Unless previous notice of dishonor has been sent an item is dishonored at the time when for purposes of dishonor it is returned or notice sent in accordance with this section.

(4) An item is returned:

(a) as to an item received through a clearing house, when it is delivered to the presenting or last collecting bank or to the clearing house or is sent or delivered in accordance with its rules; or

(b) in all other cases, when it is sent or delivered to the bank's customer or transferor or pursuant to his instructions.

§ 4-302. Payor Bank's Responsibility for Late Return of Item. In the absence of a valid defense such as breach of a presentment warranty (subsection (1) of Section 4-207), settlement effected or the like, if an item is presented on and received by a payor bank the bank is accountable for the amount of

(a) a demand item other than a documentary draft whether properly payable or not if the bank, in any case where it is not also the Depository bank, retains the item beyond midnight of the banking day of receipt without settling for it or, regardless of whether it is also the Depository bank, does not pay or return the item or send notice of dishonor until after its midnight deadline; or

(b) any other properly payable item unless within the time allowed for acceptance or payment of that item the bank either accepts or pays the item or returns it and accompanying documents.

§ 4-303. When Items Subject to Notice, Stop-Order, Legal Process or Setoff; Order in which Items May Be Charged or Certified.

(1) Any knowledge, notice or stop-order received by, legal process served upon or setoff exercised by a payor bank, whether or not effective under other rules of law to terminate, suspend or modify the bank's right or duty to pay an item or to charge its customer's account for the item, comes too late to so terminate, suspend or modify such right or duty if the knowledge, notice, stop-order or legal process is received or served and a reasonable time for the bank to act thereon expires or the setoff is exercised after the bank has done any of the following:

(a) accepted or certified the item;

(b) paid the item in cash;

(c) settled for the item without reserving the right to revoke the settlement and without having such right under statute, clearing house rule or agreement;

(d) completed the process of posting the item to the indicated account of the drawer, maker or other person to be charged therewith or otherwise has evidenced by examination of such indicated account and by action its decision to pay the item; or

(e) become accountable for the amount of the item under subsection (1) (d) of Section 4-213 and Section 4-302 dealing with the payor bank's responsibility for late return of items.

(2) Subject to the provisions of subsection (1) items may be accepted, paid, certified or charged to the indicated account of its customer in any order convenient to the bank.

PART 4 Relationship Between Payor Bank and Its Customer

§ 4-401. When Bank May Charge Customer's Account.

(1) As against its customer, a bank may charge against his account any item which is otherwise properly payable from that account even though the charge creates an overdraft.

(2) A bank which in good faith makes payment to a holder may charge the indicated account of its customer according to

(a) the original tenor of his altered item; or

(b) the tenor of his completed item, even though the bank knows the item has been completed unless the bank has notice that the completion was improper.

§ 4-402. Bank's Liability to Customer for Wrongful Dishonor. A payor bank is liable to its customer for damages proximately caused by the wrongful dishonor of an item. When the dishonor occurs through mistake liability is limited to actual damages proved. If so proximately caused and proved damages may include damages for an arrest or prosecution of the customer or other consequential damages. Whether any consequential damages are proximately caused by the wrongful dishonor is a question of fact to be determined in each case.

§ 4-403. Customer's Right to Stop Payment; Burden of Proof of Loss.

(1) A customer may by order to his bank stop payment of any item payable for his account but the order must be received at such time and in such manner as to afford the bank a reasonable opportunity to act on it prior to any action by the bank with respect to the item described in Section 4-303.

(2) An oral order is binding upon the bank only for fourteen calendar days unless confirmed in writing within that period. A written order is effective for only six months unless renewed in writing.

(3) The burden of establishing the fact and amount of loss resulting from the payment of an item contrary to a binding stop payment order is on the customer.

§ 4-404. Bank Not Obligated to Pay Check More Than Six Months Old. A bank is under no obligation to a customer having a checking account to pay a check, other than a certified check, which is presented more than six months after its date, but it may charge its customer's account for a payment made thereafter in good faith.

§ 4-405. Death or Incompetence of Customer.

(1) A payor or collecting bank's authority to accept, pay or collect an item or to account for proceeds of its collection if otherwise effective is not rendered ineffective by incompetence of a customer of either bank existing at the time the item is issued or its collection is undertaken if the bank does not know of an adjudication of incompetence. Neither death nor incompetence of a customer revokes such authority to accept, pay, collect or account until the bank knows of the fact of death or of an adjudication of incompetence and has reasonable opportunity to act on it.

(2) Even with knowledge a bank may for ten days after the date of death pay or certify checks drawn on or prior to that date unless ordered to stop payment by a person claiming an interest in the account.

§ 4-406. Customer's Duty to Discover and Report Unauthorized Signature or Alteration.

(1) When a bank sends to its customer a statement of account accompanied by items paid in good faith in support of the debit entries or holds the statement and items pursuant to a request or instructions of its customer or otherwise in a reasonable manner makes the statement and items available to the customer, the customer must exercise reasonable care and promptness to examine the statement and items to discover his unauthorized signature or any alteration on an item and must notify the bank promptly after discovery thereof.

(2) If the bank establishes that the customer failed with respect to an item to comply with the duties imposed on the customer by subsection (1) the customer is precluded from asserting against the bank

(a) his unauthorized signature or any alteration on the item if the bank also establishes that it suffered a loss by reason of such failure; and

(b) an unauthorized signature or alteration by the same wrongdoer on any other item paid in good faith by the bank after the first item and statement was available to the customer for a reasonable period not exceeding fourteen calendar days and before the bank receives notification from the customer of any such unauthorized signature or alteration.

(3) The preclusion under subsection (2) does not apply if the customer establishes lack of ordinary care on the part of the bank in paying the item(s).

(4) Without regard to care or lack of care of either the customer or the bank a customer who does not within one year from the time the statement and items are made available to the customer (subsection (1)) discover and report his unauthorized signature or any alteration on the face or back of the item or does not within three years from that time discover and report any unauthorized indorsement is precluded from asserting against the bank such unauthorized signature or indorsement or such alteration.

(5) If under this section a payor bank has a valid defense against a claim of a customer upon or resulting from payment of an item and waives or fails upon request to assert the defense the bank may not assert against any collecting bank or other prior party presenting or transferring the item a claim based upon the unauthorized signature or alteration giving rise to the customer's claim.

§ 4-407. Payor Bank's Right to Subrogation on Improper Payment. If a payor bank has paid an item over the stop payment order of the drawer or maker, or otherwise under circumstances giving a basis for objection by the drawer or maker, to present unjust enrichment and only to the extent necessary to prevent loss to the bank by reason of its payment of the item, the payor bank shall be subrogated to the rights

(a) of any holder in due course on the item against the drawer or maker; and

(b) of the payee or any other holder of the item against the drawer or maker either on the item or under the transaction out of which the item arose; and

(c) of the drawer or maker against the payee or any other holder of the item with respect to the transaction out of which the item arose.

PART 5 Collection of Documentary Drafts

§ 4-501. Handling of Documentary Drafts; Duty to Send for Presentment and to Notify Customer of Dishonor. A bank which takes a documentary draft for collection must present or send the draft and accompanying documents for presentment and upon learning that the draft has not been paid or accepted in due course must seasonably notify its customer of such fact even though it may have discounted or bought the draft or extended credit available for withdrawal as if right.

§ 4-502. Presentment of "On Arrival" Drafts. When a draft or the relevant instructions require presentment "on arrival," "when goods arrive" or the like, the collecting bank need not present until in its judgment a reasonable time for arrival of the goods has expired. Refusal to pay or accept because the goods have not arrived is not dishonor, the bank must notify its transferor of such refusal but need not present the draft again until it is instructed to do so or learns of the arrival of the goods.

§ 4-503. Responsibility of Presenting Bank for Documents and Goods; Report or Reasons for Dishonor; Referee in Case of Need. Unless otherwise instructed and except as provided in Article 5 a bank presenting a documentary draft

(a) must deliver the documents to the drawee on acceptance of the draft if it is payable more than three days after presentment; otherwise, only on payment; and

(b) upon dishonor, either in the case of presentment for acceptance or presentment for payment, may seek and follow instructions from any referee in case of need designated in the draft or if the presenting bank does not choose to utilize his services it must use diligence and good faith to ascertain the reason for dishonor, must notify its transferor of the dishonor and of the results of its effort to ascertain the reasons therefor and must request instructions.

But the presenting bank is under no obligation with respect to goods represented by the documents except to follow any reasonable instructions seasonably received; it has a right to reimbursement for any expense incurred in following instructions and to prepayment of or indemnity for such expenses.

§ 4-504. Privilege of Presenting Bank to Deal with Goods, Security Interest for Expenses.

(1) A presenting bank which, following the dishonor of a documentary draft, has seasonably requested instructions but does not receive them within a reasonable time may store, sell, or otherwise deal with the goods in any reasonable manner.

(2) For its reasonable expenses incurred by action under subsection (1) the presenting bank has a lien upon the goods or their proceeds, which may be foreclosed in the same manner as an unpaid seller's lien.

ARTICLE 4A / Funds Transfers

PART 1 Subject Matter and Definitions

§ 4A-101. Short Title.

This Article may be cited as Uniform Commercial Code—Funds Transfers.

§ 4A-102. Subject Matter.

Except as otherwise provided in Section 4A-108, this Article applies to funds transfers defined in Section 4A-l04.

§ 4A-103. Payment Order—Definitions.

(a) In this Article:

(1) "Payment order means an instruction of a sender to a receiving bank, transmitted orally, electronically, or in writing, to pay, or to cause another bank to pay, a fixed or determinable amount of money to a beneficiary if:

(i) the instruction does not state a condition to payment to the beneficiary other than time of payment,

(ii) the receiving bank is to be reimbursed by debiting an account of, or otherwise receiving payment from, the sender; and

(iii) the instruction is transmitted by the sender directly to the receiving bank or to an agent, funds-transfer system, or communication system for transmittal to the receiving bank.

(2) "Beneficiary" means the person to be paid by the beneficiary's bank.

(3) "Beneficiary's bank" means the bank identified in a payment order in which an account of the beneficiary is to be credited pursuant to the order or which otherwise is to make payment to the beneficiary if the order does not provide for payment to an account.

(4) "Receiving bank" means the bank to which the sender's instruction is addressed.

(5) "Sender" means the person giving the instruction to the receiving bank.

(b) If an instruction complying with subsection (a) (1) is to make more than one payment to a beneficiary, the instruction is a separate payment order with respect to each payment.

(c) A payment order is issued when it is sent to the receiving bank.

§ 4A-104. Funds Transfer-Definitions.

In this Article:

(a) "Funds transfer" means the series of transactions, beginning with the originator's payment order, made for the purpose of making payment to the beneficiary of the order. The term includes any payment order issued by the originator's bank or an intermediary bank intended to carry out the originator's payment order. A funds transfer is completed by acceptance by the beneficiary's bank of a payment order for the benefit of the beneficiary of the originator's payment order.

(b) "Intermediary bank" means a receiving bank other than the originator's bank or the beneficiary's bank.

(c) "Originator" means the sender of the first payment order in a funds transfer.

(d) "Originator's bank" means (i) the receiving bank to which the payment order of the originator is issued if the originator is not a bank, or (ii) the originator if the originator is a bank.

§ 4A-105. Other Definitions.

(a) In this Article:

(1) "Authorized account" means a deposit account of a customer in a bank designated by the customer as a source of payment of payment orders issued by the customer to the bank. If a customer does not so designate an account, any account of the customer is an authorized account if payment of a payment order from that account is not inconsistent with a restriction on the use of that account.

(2) "Bank" means a person engaged in the business of banking and includes a savings bank, savings and loan association, credit union, and trust company. A branch or separate office of a bank is a separate bank for purposes of this Article.

(3) "Customer" means a person, including a bank, having an account with a bank or from whom a bank has agreed to receive payment orders.

(4) "Funds-transfer business day" of a receiving bank means the part of a day during which the receiving bank is open for the receipt, processing, and transmittal of payment orders and cancellations and amendments of payment orders.

(5) "Funds-transfer system" means a wire transfer network, automated clearing house, or other communication system of a clearing house or other association of banks through which a payment order by a bank may be transmitted to the bank to which the order is addressed.

(6) "Good faith" means honesty in fact and the observance of reasonable commercial standards of fair dealing.

(7) "Prove" with respect to a fact means to meet the burden of establishing the fact (Section l-20l(8)).

(b) Other definitions applying to this Article and the sections in which they appear are:

"Acceptance" Section 4A-209

"Beneficiary" Section 4A-103

"Beneficiary's bank" Section 4A-103

"Executed" Section 4A-301

"Execution date" Section 4A-301

"Funds transfer" Section 4A-104

"Funds-transfer system rule" Section 4A-501

"Intermediary bank" Section 4A-104

"Originator" Section 4A-104

"Originator's bank" Section 4A-104

"Payment by beneficiary's bank to beneficiary" Section 4A-405

"Payment by originator to beneficiary" Section 4A-406

"Payment by sender to receiving bank" Section 4A-403

"Payment date" Section 4A-40 1

"Payment order" Section 4A-103

"Receiving bank" Section 4A-103

"Security procedure" Section 4A-201

"Sender" Section 4A-103

(c) The following definitions in Article 4 apply to this Article:

"Clearing house" Section 4-104

"Item" Section 4-104

"Suspends payments" Section 4-104

(d) In addition Article 1 contains general definitions and principles of construction and interpretation applicable throughout this Article.

§ 4A-106. Time Payment Order Is Received.

(a) The time of receipt of a payment order or communication cancelling or amending a payment order is determined by the rules applicable to receipt of a notice stated in Section 1-201(27). A receiving bank may fix a cut-off time or times on a funds-transfer business day for the receipt and processing of payment orders and communications cancelling or amending payment orders. Different cut-off times may apply to payment orders, cancellations, or amendments, or to different categories of payment orders, cancellations, or amendments. A cut-off time may apply to senders generally or different cut-off times may apply to different senders or categories of payment orders. If a payment order or communication cancelling or amending a payment order is received after the close of a funds-transfer business day or after the appropriate cut-off time on a funds-transfer business day, the receiving bank may treat the payment order or communication as received at the opening of the next funds-transfer business day.

(b) If this Article refers to an execution date or payment date or states a day on which a receiving bank is required to take action, and the date or day does not fall on a funds-transfer business day, the next day that is a funds-transfer business day is treated as the date or day stated, unless the contrary is stated in this Article.

§ 4A-107. Federal Reserve Regulations and Operating Circulars.

Regulations of the Board of Governors of the Federal Reserve System and operating circulars of the Federal Reserve Banks supersede any inconsistent provision of this Article to the extent of the inconsistency.

§ 4A-108. Exclusion of Consumer Transactions Governed by Federal Law

This Article does not apply to a funds transfer any part of which is governed by the Electronic Fund Transfer Act of 1978 (Title XX, Public Law 95-630, 92 Stat. 3728,15 U.S.C. § 1693 et seq.) as amended from time to time.

Part 2 Issue and Acceptance of Payment Order

§ 4A-201. Security Procedure.

"Security procedure" means a procedure established by agreement of a customer and a receiving bank for the purpose of (i) verifying that a payment order or communication amending or cancelling a payment order is that of the customer, or (ii) detecting error in the transmission or the content of the payment order or communication. A security procedure may require the use of algorithms or other codes, identifying words or numbers, encryption, callback procedures, or similar security devices. Comparison of a signature on a payment order or communication with an authorized specimen signature of the customer is not by itself a security procedure.

§ 4A-202. Authorized and Verified Payment Orders.

(a) A payment order received by the receiving bank is the authorized order of the person identified as sender if that person authorized the order or is otherwise bound by it under the law of agency.

(b) If a bank and its customer have agreed that the authenticity of payment orders issued to the bank in the name of the customer as sender will be verified pursuant to a security procedure, a payment order received by the receiving bank is effective as the order of the customer, whether or not authorized, if (i) the security procedure is a commercially reasonable method of providing security against unauthorized payment orders, and (ii) the bank proves that it accepted the payment order in good faith and in compliance with the security procedure and any written agreement or instruction of the customer restricting acceptance of payment orders issued in the name of the customer. The bank is not required to follow an instruction that violates a written agreement with the customer or notice of which is not received at a time and in a manner affording the bank a reasonable opportunity to act on it before the payment order is accepted.

(c) Commercial reasonableness of a security procedure is a question of law to be determined by considering the wishes of the customer expressed to the bank, the circumstances of the customer known to the bank, including the size, type, and frequency of payment orders normally issued by the customer to the bank, alternative security procedures offered to the customer, and security procedures in general use by customers and receiving banks similarly situated. A security procedure is deemed to be commercially reasonable if (i) the security procedure was chosen by the customer after the bank offered, and the customer refused, a security procedure that was commercially reasonable for that customer, and (ii) the customer expressly agreed in writing to be bound by any payment order, whether or not authorized, issued in its name and accepted by the bank in compliance with the security procedure chosen by the customer.

(d) The term "sender" in this Article includes the customer in whose name a payment order is issued if the order is the authorized order of the customer under subsection (a), or it is effective as the order of the customer under subsection (b).

(e) This section applies to amendments and cancellations of payment orders to the same extent it applies to payment orders.

(f) Except as provided in this section and in Section 4A-203(a)(1), rights and obligations arising under this section or Section 4A-203 may not be varied by agreement.

§ 4A-203. Unenforceability of Certain Verified Payment Orders.

(a) If an accepted payment order is not, under Section 4A-202(a), an authorized order of a customer identified as sender, but is effective as an order of the customer pursuant to Section 4A-202 (b), the following rules apply:

(1) By express written agreement, the receiving bank may limit the extent to which it is entitled to enforce or retain payment of the payment order.

(2) The receiving bank is not entitled to enforce or retain payment of the payment order if the customer proves that the order was not caused, directly or indirectly, by a person (i) entrusted at any time with duties to act for the customer with respect to payment orders or the security procedure, or (ii) who obtained access to transmitting facilities of the customer or who obtained, from a source controlled by the customer and without authority of the receiving bank, information facilitating breach of the security procedure, regardless of how the information was obtained or whether the customer was at fault. Information includes any access device, computer software, or the like.

(b) This section applies to amendments of payment orders to the same extent it applies to payment orders.

§ 4A-204. Refund of Payment and Duty of Customer to Report With Respect to Unauthorized Payment Order.

(a) If a receiving bank accepts a payment order issued in the name of its customer as sender which is (1) not authorized and not effective as the order of the customer under Section 4A-202, or (ii) not enforceable, in whole or in part, against the customer under Section 4A-203, the bank shall refund any payment of the payment order received from the customer to the extent the bank is not entitled to enforce payment and shall pay interest on the refundable amount calculated from the date the bank received payment to the date of the refund. However, the customer is not entitled to interest from the bank on the amount to be refunded if the customer fails to exercise ordinary care to determine that the order was not authorized by the customer and to notify the bank of the relevant facts within a reasonable time not exceeding 90 days after the date the customer received notification from the bank that the order was accepted or that the customer's account was debited with respect to the order. The bank is not entitled to any recovery from the customer on account of a failure by the customer to give notification as stated in this section.

(b) Reasonable time under subsection (a) may be fixed by agreement as stated in Section 1-204(1), but the obligation of a receiving bank to refund payment as stated in subsection (a) may not otherwise be varied by agreement.

§ 4A-205. Erroneous Payment Orders.

(a) If an accepted payment order was transmitted pursuant to a security procedure for the detection of error and the payment order (1) erroneously instructed payment to a beneficiary not intended by the sender, (ii) erroneously instructed payment in an amount greater than the amount intended by the sender, or (iii) was an erroneously transmitted duplicate of a payment order previously sent by the sender, the following rules apply:

(1) If the sender proves that the sender or a person acting on behalf of the sender pursuant to Section 4A-206 complied with the security procedure and that the error would have been detected if the receiving bank had also complied, the sender is not obliged to pay the order to the extent stated in paragraphs (2) and (3).

(2) If the funds transfer is completed on the basis of an erroneous payment order described in clause (i) or (iii) of subsection (a), the sender is not obliged to pay the order and the receiving bank is entitled to recover from the beneficiary any amount paid to the beneficiary to the extent allowed by the law governing mistake and restitution.

(3) If the funds transfer is completed on the basis of a payment order described in clause (ii) of subsection (a), the sender is not obliged to pay the order to the extent the amount received by the beneficiary is greater than the amount intended by the sender In that case, the receiving bank is entitled to recover from the beneficiary the excess

amount received to the extent allowed by the law governing mistake and restitution.

(b) If (1) the sender of an erroneous payment order described in subsection (a) is not obliged to pay all or part of the order, and (ii) the sender receives notification from the receiving bank that the order was accepted by the bank or that the sender's account was debited with respect to the order, the sender has a duty to exercise ordinary care, on the basis of information available to the sender, to discover the error with respect to the order and to advise the bank of the relevant facts within a reasonable time, not exceeding 90 days, after the bank's notification was received by the sender. If the bank proves that the sender failed to perform that duty, the sender is liable to the bank for the loss the bank proves it incurred as a result of the failure, but the liability of the sender may not exceed the amount of the sender's order.

(c) This section applies to amendments to payment orders to the same extent it applies to payment orders.

§ 4A-206. Transmission of Payment Order Through Funds-Transfer or Other Communication System.

(a) If a payment order addressed to a receiving bank is transmitted to a funds-transfer system or other third-party communication system for transmittal to the bank, the system is deemed to be an agent of the sender for the purpose of transmitting the payment order to the bank. If there is a discrepancy between the terms of the payment order transmitted to the system and the terms of the payment order transmitted by the system to the bank, the terms of the payment order of the sender are those transmitted by the system. This section does not apply to a funds-transfer system of the Federal Reserve Banks.

(b) This section applies to cancellations and amendments of payment orders to the same extent it applies to payment orders.

§ 4A-207. Misdescription of Beneficiary.

(a) Subject to subsection (b), if, in a payment order received by the beneficiary's bank, the name, bank account number, or other identification of the beneficiary refers to a nonexistent or unidentifiable person or account, no person has rights as a beneficiary of the order and acceptance of the order cannot occur.

(b) If a payment order received by the beneficiary's bank identifies the beneficiary both by name and by an identifying or bank account number and the name and number identify different persons, the following rules apply:

(1) Except as otherwise provided in subsection (c),if the beneficiary's bank does not know that the name and number refer to different persons, it may rely on the number as the proper identification of the beneficiary of the order. The beneficiary's bank need not determine whether the name and number refer to the same person.

(2) If the beneficiary's bank pays the person identified by name or knows that the name and number identify different persons, no person has rights as beneficiary except the person paid by the beneficiary's bank if that person was entitled to receive payment from the originator of the funds transfer. If no person has rights as beneficiary, acceptance of the order cannot occur.

(c) If (i) a payment order described in subsection (b) is accepted, (ii) the originator's payment order described the beneficiary inconsistently by name and number, and (iii) the beneficiary's bank pays the person identified by number as permitted by subsection (b) (1), the following rules apply:

(1) If the originator is a bank, the originator is obliged to pay its order.

(2) If the originator is not a bank and proves that the person identified by number was not entitled to receive payment from the originator, the originator is not obliged to pay its order unless the originator's bank proves that the originator, before acceptance of the originator's order, had notice that payment of a payment order issued by the originator might be made by the beneficiary's bank on the basis of an identifying or bank account number even if it identifies a person different from the named beneficiary. Proof of notice may be made by any admissible evidence. The originator's bank satisfies the burden of proof if it proves that the originator, before the payment order was accepted, signed a writing stating the information to which the notice relates.

(d) In a case governed by subsection (b) (1), if the beneficiary's bank rightfully pays the person identified by number and that person was not entitled to receive payment from the originator, the amount paid may be recovered from that person to the extent allowed by the law governing mistake and restitution as follows:

(1) If the originator is obliged to pay its payment order as stated in subsection (c), the originator has the right to recover.

(2) If the originator is not a bank and is not obliged to pay its payment order, the originator's bank has the right to recover.

§ 4A-208. Misdescription of Intermediary Bank or Beneficiary's Bank.

(a) This subsection applies to a payment order identifying an intermediary bank or the beneficiary's bank only by an identifying number.

(1) The receiving bank may rely on the number as the proper identification of the intermediary or beneficiary's bank and need not determine whether the number identifies a bank.

(2) The sender is obliged to compensate the receiving bank for any loss and expenses incurred by the receiving bank as a result of its reliance on the number in executing or attempting to execute the order.

(b) This subsection applies to a payment order identifying an intermediary bank or the beneficiary's bank both by name and an identifying number if the name and number identify different persons.

(1) If the sender is a bank, the receiving bank may rely on the number as the proper identification of the intermediary or beneficiary's bank if the receiving bank, when it executes the sender's order, does not know that the name and number identify different persons. The receiving bank need not determine whether the name and number refer to the same person or whether the number refers to a bank. The sender is obliged to compensate the receiving bank for any loss and

expenses incurred by the receiving bank as a result of its reliance on the number in executing or attempting to execute the order.

(2) If the sender is not a bank and the receiving bank proves that the sender, before the payment order was accepted, had notice that the receiving bank might rely on the number as the proper identification of the intermediary or beneficiary's bank even if it identifies a person different from the bank identified by name, the rights and obligations of the sender and the receiving bank are governed by subsection (b) (1), as though the sender were a bank. Proof of notice may be made by any admissible evidence. The receiving bank satisfies the burden of proof if it proves that the sender, before the payment order was accepted, signed a writing stating the information to which the notice relates.

(3) Regardless of whether the sender is a bank, the receiving bank may rely on the name as the proper identification of the intermediary or beneficiary's bank if the receiving bank, at the time it executes the sender's order, does not know that the name and number identify different persons. The receiving bank need not determine whether the name and number refer to the same person.

(4) If the receiving bank knows that the name and number identify different persons, reliance on either the name or the number in executing the sender's payment order is a breach of the obligation stated in Section 4A-302 (a) (1).

§ 4A-209. Acceptance of Payment Order.

(a) Subject to subsection (d), a receiving bank other than the beneficiary's bank accepts a payment order when it executes the order.

(b) Subject to subsections (c) and (d), a beneficiary's bank accepts a payment order at the earliest of the following times:

(1) when the bank (i) pays the beneficiary as stated in Section 4A-405 (a) or 4A-405 (b), or (ii) notifies the beneficiary of receipt of the order or that the account of the beneficiary has been credited with respect to the order unless the notice indicates that the bank is rejecting the order or that funds with respect to the order may not be withdrawn or used until receipt of payment from the sender of the order;

(2) when the bank receives payment of the entire amount of the sender's order pursuant to Section 4A-403 (a) (l) or 4A-403 (a) (2); or

(3) the opening of the next funds-transfer business day of the bank following the payment date of the order if, at that time, the amount of the sender's order is fully covered by a withdrawable credit balance in an authorized account of the sender or the bank has otherwise received full payment from the sender, unless the order was rejected before that time or is rejected within (i) one hour after that time, or (ii) one hour after the opening of the next business day of the sender following the payment date if that time is later. If notice of rejection is received by the sender after the payment date and the authorized account of the sender does not bear interest, the bank is obliged to pay interest to the sender on the amount of the order for the number of days elapsing after the payment date to the day the sender receives notice or learns that the order was not accepted, counting that day as an elapsed day. If the withdrawable credit balance during that period falls below the amount of the order, the amount of interest payable is reduced accordingly.

(c) Acceptance of a payment order cannot occur before the order is received by the receiving bank. Acceptance does not occur under subsection (b) (2) or (b) (3) if the beneficiary of the payment order does not have an account with the receiving bank, the account has been closed, or the receiving bank is not permitted by law to receive credits for the beneficiary's account.

(d) A payment order issued to the originator's bank cannot be accepted until the payment date if the bank is the beneficiary's bank, or the execution date if the bank is not the beneficiary's bank. If the originator's bank executes the originator's payment order before the execution date or pays the beneficiary of the originator's payment order before the payment date and the payment order is subsequently canceled pursuant to Section 4A-211(b), the bank may recover from the beneficiary any payment received to the extent allowed by the law governing mistake and restitution.

§ 4A-210. Rejection of Payment Order.

(a) A payment order is rejected by the receiving bank by a notice of rejection transmitted to the sender orally, electronically, or in writing. A notice of rejection need not use any particular words and is sufficient if it indicates that the receiving bank is rejecting the order or will not execute or pay the order. Rejection is effective when the notice is given if transmission is by a means that is reasonable in the circumstances. If notice of rejection is given by a means that is not reasonable, rejection is effective when the notice is received. If an agreement of the sender and receiving bank establishes the means to be used to reject a payment order, (1) any means complying with the agreement is reasonable and (ii) any means not complying is not reasonable unless no significant delay in receipt of the notice resulted from the use of the noncomplying means.

(b) This subsection applies if a receiving bank other than the beneficiary's bank fails to execute a payment order despite the existence on the execution date of a withdrawable credit balance in an authorized account of the sender sufficient to cover the order. If the sender does not receive notice of rejection of the order on the execution date and the authorized account of the sender does not bear interest, the bank is obliged to pay interest to the sender on the amount of the order for the number of days elapsing after the execution date to the earlier of the day the order is canceled pursuant to Section 4A-211(d) or the day the sender receives notice or learns that the order was not executed, counting the final day of the period as an elapsed day. If the withdrawable credit balance during that period falls below the amount of the order, the amount of interest is reduced accordingly.

(c) If a receiving bank suspends payments, all unaccepted payment orders issued to it are deemed rejected at the time the bank suspends payments.

(d) Acceptance of a payment order precludes a later rejection of the order. Rejection of a payment order precludes a later acceptance of the order.

§ 4A-211. Cancellation and Amendment of Payment Order.

(a) A communication of the sender of a payment order cancelling or amending the order may be transmitted to the receiving bank orally, electronically, or in writing. If a security procedure is in effect between the sender and the receiving bank, the communication is not effective to cancel or amend the order unless the communication is verified pursuant to the security procedure or the bank agrees to the cancellation or amendment.

(b) Subject to subsection (a), a communication by the sender cancelling or amending a payment order is effective to cancel or amend the order if notice of the communication is received at a time and in a manner affording the receiving bank a reasonable opportunity to act on the communication before the bank accepts the payment order.

(c) After a payment order has been accepted, cancellation or amendment of the order is not effective unless the receiving bank agrees or a funds-transfer system rule allows cancellation or amendment without agreement of the bank.

(1) With respect to a payment order accepted by a receiving bank other than the beneficiary's bank, cancellation or amendment is not effective unless a conforming cancellation or amendment of the payment order issued by the receiving bank is also made.

(2) With respect to a payment order accepted by the beneficiary's bank, cancellation or amendment is not effective unless the order was issued in execution of an unauthorized payment order, or because of a mistake by a sender in the funds transfer which resulted in the issuance of a payment order (i) that is a duplicate of a payment order previously issued by the sender, (ii) that orders payment to a beneficiary not entitled to receive payment from the originator, or (iii) that orders payment in an amount greater than the amount the beneficiary was entitled to receive from the originator. If the payment order is canceled or amended, the beneficiary's bank is entitled to recover from the beneficiary any amount paid to the beneficiary to the extent allowed by the law governing mistake and restitution.

(d) An unaccepted payment order is canceled by operation of law at the close of the fifth funds-transfer business day of the receiving bank after the execution date or payment date of the order.

(e) A canceled payment order cannot be accepted. If an accepted payment order is canceled, the acceptance is nullified and no person has any right or obligation based on the acceptance. Amendment of a payment order is deemed to be cancellation of the original order at the time of amendment and issue of a new payment order in the amended form at the same time.

(f) Unless otherwise provided in an agreement of the parties or in a funds-transfer system rule, if the receiving bank, after accepting a payment order, agrees to cancellation or amendment of the order by the sender or is bound by a funds-transfer system rule allowing cancellation or amendment without the bank's agreement, the sender, whether or not cancellation or amendment is effective, is liable to the bank for any loss and expenses, including reasonable attorney's fees, incurred by the bank as a result of the cancellation or amendment or attempted cancellation or amendment.

(g) A payment order is not revoked by the death or legal incapacity of the sender unless the receiving bank knows of the death or of an adjudication of incapacity by a court of competent jurisdiction and has reasonable opportunity to act before acceptance of the order.

(h) A funds-transfer system rule is not effective to the extent it conflicts with subsection (c) (2).

§ 4A-212. Liability and Duty of Receiving Bank Regarding Unaccepted Payment Order.

If a receiving bank fails to accept a payment order that it is obliged by express agreement to accept, the bank is liable for breach of the agreement to the extent provided in the agreement or in this Article, but does not otherwise have any duty to accept a payment order or, before acceptance, to take any action, or refrain from taking action, with respect to the order except as provided in this Article or by express agreement. Liability based on acceptance arises only when acceptance occurs as stated in Section 4A-209, and liability is limited to that provided in this Article. A receiving bank is not the agent of the sender or beneficiary of the payment order it accepts, or of any other party to the funds transfer, and the bank owes no duty to any party to the funds transfer except as provided in this Article or by express agreement.

PART 3 Execution of Sender's Payment Order by Receiving Bank

§ 4A-301. Execution and Execution Date.

(a) A payment order is "executed" by the receiving bank when it issues a payment order intended to carry out the payment order received by the bank. A payment order received by the beneficiary's bank can be accepted but cannot be executed.

(b) "Execution date" of a payment order means the day on which the receiving bank may properly issue a payment order in execution of the sender's order. The execution date may be determined by instruction of the sender but cannot be earlier than the day the order is received and, unless otherwise determined, is the day the order is received. If the sender's instruction states a payment date, the execution date is the payment date or an earlier date on which execution is reasonably necessary to allow payment to the beneficiary on the payment date.

§ 4A-302. Obligations of Receiving Bank in Execution of Payment Order.

(a) Except as provided in subsections (b) through (d),if the receiving bank accepts a payment order pursuant to Section 4A-209 (a), the bank has the following obligations in executing the order:

(1) The receiving bank is obliged to issue, on the execution date, a payment order complying with the sender's order and to follow the sender's instructions concerning (1) any intermediary bank or funds-transfer system to be used in carrying out the funds transfer, or (ii) the means by which payment orders are to be transmitted in the funds

transfer. If the originator's bank issues a payment order to an intermediary bank, the originator's bank is obliged to instruct the intermediary bank according to the instruction of the originator. An intermediary bank in the funds transfer is similarly bound by an instruction given to it by the sender of the payment order it accepts.

(2) If the sender's instruction states that the funds transfer is to be carried out telephonically or by wire transfer or otherwise indicates that the funds transfer is to be carried out by the most expeditious means, the receiving bank is obliged to transmit its payment order by the most expeditious available means, and to instruct any intermediary bank accordingly. If a sender's instruction states a payment date, the receiving bank is obliged to transmit its payment order at a time and by means reasonably necessary to allow payment to the beneficiary on the payment date or as soon thereafter as is feasible.

(b) Unless otherwise instructed, a receiving bank executing a payment order may (1) use any funds-transfer system if use of that system is reasonable in the circumstances, and (ii) issue a payment order to the beneficiary's bank or to an intermediary bank through which a payment order conforming to the sender's order can expeditiously be issued to the beneficiary's bank if the receiving bank exercises ordinary care in the selection of the intermediary bank. A receiving bank is not required to follow an instruction of the sender designating a funds-transfer system to be used in carrying out the funds transfer if the receiving bank, in good faith, determines that it is not feasible to follow the instruction or that following the instruction would unduly delay completion of the funds transfer.

(c) Unless subsection (a) (2) applies or the receiving bank is otherwise instructed, the bank may execute a payment order by transmitting its payment order by first class mail or by any means reasonable in the circumstances. If the receiving bank is instructed to execute the sender's order by transmitting its payment order by a particular means, the receiving bank may issue its payment order by the means stated or by any means as expeditious as the means stated.

(d) Unless instructed by the sender, (1) the receiving bank may not obtain payment of its charges for services and expenses in connection with the execution of the sender's order by issuing a payment order in an amount equal to the amount of the sender's order less the amount of the charges, and (ii) may not instruct a subsequent receiving bank to obtain payment of its charges in the same manner.

§ 4A-303. Erroneous Execution of Payment Order.

(a) A receiving bank that (1) executes the payment order of the sender by issuing a payment order in an amount greater than the amount of the sender's order, or (ii) issues a payment order in execution of the sender's order and then issues a duplicate order, is entitled to payment of the amount of the sender's order under Section 4A-402 (c) if that subsection is otherwise satisfied. The bank is entitled to recover from the beneficiary of the erroneous order the excess payment received to the extent allowed by the law governing mistake and restitution.

(b) A receiving bank that executes the payment order of the sender by issuing a payment order in an amount less than the amount of the sender's order is entitled to payment of the amount of the sender's order under Section 4A-402 (c) if (1) that subsection is otherwise satisfied and (ii) the bank corrects its mistake by issuing an additional payment order for the benefit of the beneficiary of the sender's order. If the error is not corrected, the issuer of the erroneous order is entitled to receive or retain payment from the sender of the order it accepted only to the extent of the amount of the erroneous order. This subsection does not apply if the receiving bank executes the sender's payment order by issuing a payment order in an amount less than the amount of the sender's order for the purpose of obtaining payment of its charges for services and expenses pursuant to instruction of the sender.

(c) If a receiving bank executes the payment order of the sender by issuing a payment order to a beneficiary different from the beneficiary of the sender's order and the funds transfer is completed on the basis of that error, the sender of the payment order that was erroneously executed and all previous senders in the funds transfer are not obliged to pay the payment orders they issued. The issuer of the erroneous order is entitled to recover from the beneficiary of the order the payment received to the extent allowed by the law governing mistake and restitution.

§ 4A-304. Duty of Sender to Report Erroneously Executed Payment Order.

If the sender of a payment order that is erroneously executed as stated in Section 4A-303 receives notification from the receiving bank that the order was executed or that the sender's account was debited with respect to the order, the sender has a duty to exercise ordinary care to determine, on the basis of information available to the sender, that the order was erroneously executed and to notify the bank of the relevant facts within a reasonable time not exceeding 90 days after the notification from the bank was received by the sender. If the sender fails to perform that duty, the bank is not obliged to pay interest on any amount refundable to the sender under Section 4A-402 (d) for the period before the bank learns of the execution error. The bank is not entitled to any recovery from the sender on account of a failure by the sender to perform the duty stated in this section.

§ 4A-305. Liability for Late or Improper Execution or Failure to Execute Payment Order.

(a) If a funds transfer is completed but execution of a payment order by the receiving bank in breach of Section 4A-302 results in delay in payment to the beneficiary, the bank is obliged to pay interest to either the originator or the beneficiary of the funds transfer for the period of delay caused by the improper execution. Except as provided in subsection (c), additional damages are not recoverable.

(b) If execution of a payment order by a receiving bank in breach of Section 4A-302 results in (i) noncompletion of the funds transfer, (ii) failure to use an intermediary bank designated by the originator, or (iii) issuance of a payment order that does not comply with the terms of the payment order of the originator, the bank is liable to the originator for its expenses in the funds transfer and for incidental expenses and interest losses, to the extent not covered by subsection (a), resulting from the improper execution. Except as provided in subsection (c), additional damages are not recoverable.

(c) In addition to the amounts payable under subsections (a) and (b), damages, including consequential damages, are recoverable to the extent provided in an express written agreement of the receiving bank.

(d) If a receiving bank fails to execute a payment order it was obliged by express agreement to execute, the receiving bank is liable to the sender for its expenses in the transaction and for incidental expenses and interest losses resulting from the failure to execute. Additional damages, including consequential damages, are recoverable to the extent provided in an express written agreement of the receiving bank, but are not otherwise recoverable.

(e) Reasonable attorney's fees are recoverable if demand for compensation under subsection (a) or (b) is made and refused before an action is brought on the claim. If a claim is made for breach of an agreement under subsection (d) and the agreement does not provide for damages, reasonable attorney's fees are recoverable if demand for compensation under subsection (d) is made and refused before an action is brought on the claim.

(f) Except as stated in this section, the liability of a receiving bank under subsections (a) and (b) may not be varied by agreement.

PART 4 Payment

§ 4A-401. Payment Date.

"Payment date" of a payment order means the day on which the amount of the order is payable to the beneficiary by the beneficiary's bank. The payment date may be determined by instruction of the sender but cannot be earlier than the day the order is received by the beneficiary's bank and, unless otherwise determined, is the day the order is received by the beneficiary's bank.

§ 4A-402. Obligation of Sender to Pay Receiving Bank.

(a) This section is subject to Sections 4A-205 and 4A-207.

(b) With respect to a payment order issued to the beneficiary's bank, acceptance of the order by the bank obliges the sender to pay the bank the amount of the order, but payment is not due until the payment date of the order.

(c) This subsection is subject to subsection (e) and to Section 4A-303. With respect to a payment order issued to a receiving bank other than the beneficiary's bank, acceptance of the order by the receiving bank obliges the sender to pay the bank the amount of the sender's order. Payment by the sender is not due until the execution date of the sender's order. The obligation of that sender to pay its payment order is excused if the funds transfer is not completed by acceptance by the beneficiary's bank of a payment order instructing payment to the beneficiary of that sender's payment order.

(d) If the sender of a payment order pays the order and was not obliged to pay all or part of the amount paid, the bank receiving payment is obliged to refund payment to the extent the sender was not obliged to pay. Except as provided in Sections 4A-204 and 4A-304, interest is payable on the refundable amount from the date of payment.

(e) If a funds transfer is not completed as stated in subsection (c) and an intermediary bank is obliged to refund payment as stated in subsection (d) but is unable to do so because not permitted by applicable law or because the bank suspends payments, a sender in the funds transfer that executed a payment order in compliance with an instruction, as stated in Section 4A-302 (a) (1), to route the funds transfer through that intermediary bank is entitled to receive or retain payment from the sender of the payment order that it accepted. The first sender in the funds transfer that issued an instruction requiring routing through that intermediary bank is subrogated to the right of the bank that paid the intermediary bank to refund as stated in subsection (d).

(f) The right of the sender of a payment order to be excused from the obligation to pay the order as stated in subsection (c) or to receive refund under subsection (d) may not be varied by agreement.

§ 4A-403. Payment by Sender to Receiving Bank.

(a) Payment of the sender's obligation under Section 4A-402 to pay the receiving bank occurs as follows:

> (1) If the sender is a bank, payment occurs when the receiving bank receives final settlement of the obligation through a Federal Reserve Bank or through a funds-transfer system.
>
> (2) If the sender is a bank and the sender (i) credited an account of the receiving bank with the sender, or (ii) caused an account of the receiving bank in another bank to be credited, payment occurs when the credit is withdrawn or, if not withdrawn, at midnight of the day on which the credit is withdrawable and the receiving bank learns of that fact.
>
> (3) If the receiving bank debits an account of the sender with the receiving bank, payment occurs when the debit is made to the extent the debit is covered by a withdrawable credit balance in the account.

(b) If the sender and receiving bank are members of a funds-transfer system that nets obligations multilaterally among participants, the receiving bank receives final settlement when settlement is complete in accordance with the rules of the system. The obligation of the sender to pay the amount of a payment order transmitted through the funds-transfer system may be satisfied, to the extent permitted by the rules of the system, by setting off and applying against the sender's obligation the right of the sender to receive payment from the receiving bank of the amount of any other payment order transmitted to the sender by the receiving bank through the funds-transfer system. The aggregate balance of obligations owed by each sender to each receiving bank in the funds-transfer system may be satisfied, to the extent permitted by the rules of the system, by setting off and applying against that balance the aggregate balance of obligations owed to the sender by other members of the system. The aggregate balance is determined after the right of setoff stated in the second sentence of this subsection has been exercised.

(c) If two banks transmit payment orders to each other under an agreement that settlement of the obligations of each bank to the other under Section 4A-402 will be made at the end of the day or other period, the total amount owed with respect to all orders transmitted by one bank shall be set off against the total amount owed with respect to all orders transmitted by the other bank. To the extent of the setoff, each bank has made payment to the other.

(d) In a case not covered by subsection (a), the time when payment of the sender's obligation under Section 4A-402 (b) or 4A-402 (c) occurs is governed by applicable principles of law that determine when an obligation is satisfied.

§ 4A-404. Obligation of Beneficiary's Bank to Pay and Give Notice to Beneficiary.

(a) Subject to Sections 4A-211(e), 4A-405 (d), and 4A-405(e), if a beneficiary's bank accepts a payment order, the bank is obliged to pay the amount of the order to the beneficiary of the order. Payment is due on the payment date of the order, but if acceptance occurs on the payment date after the close of the funds-transfer business day of the bank, payment is due on the next funds-transfer business day. If the bank refuses to pay after demand by the beneficiary and receipt of notice of particular circumstances that will give rise to consequential damages as a result of nonpayment, the beneficiary may recover damages resulting from the refusal to pay to the extent the bank had notice of the damages, unless the bank proves that it did not pay because of a reasonable doubt concerning the right of the beneficiary to payment.

(b) If a payment order accepted by the beneficiary's bank instructs payment to an account of the beneficiary, the bank is obliged to notify the beneficiary of receipt of the order before midnight of the next funds-transfer business day following the payment date. If the payment order does not instruct payment to an account of the beneficiary, the bank is required to notify the beneficiary only if notice is required by the order. Notice may be given by first class mail or any other means reasonable in the circumstances. If the bank fails to give the required notice, the bank is obliged to pay interest to the beneficiary on the amount of the payment order from the day notice should have been given until the day the beneficiary learned of receipt of the payment order by the bank. No other damages are recoverable. Reasonable attorney's fees are also recoverable if demand for interest is made and refused before an action is brought on the claim.

(c) The right of a beneficiary to receive payment and damages as stated in subsection (a) may not be varied by agreement or a funds-transfer system rule. The right of a beneficiary to be notified as stated in subsection (b) may be varied by agreement of the beneficiary or by a funds-transfer system rule if the beneficiary is notified of the rule before initiation of the funds transfer.

§ 4A-405. Payment by Beneficiary's Bank to Beneficiary.

(a) If the beneficiary's bank credits an account of the beneficiary of a payment order, payment of the bank's obligation under Section 4A-404 (a) occurs when and to the extent (i) the beneficiary is notified of the right to withdraw the credit, (ii) the bank lawfully applies the credit to a debt of the beneficiary, or (iii) funds with respect to the order are otherwise made available to the beneficiary by the bank.

(b) If the beneficiary's bank does not credit an account of the beneficiary of a payment order, the time when payment of the bank's obligation under Section 4A-404(a) occurs is governed by principles of law that determine when an obligation is satisfied.

(c) Except as stated in subsections (d) and (e), if the beneficiary's bank pays the beneficiary of a payment order under a condition to payment or agreement of the beneficiary giving the bank the right to recover payment from the beneficiary if the bank does not receive payment of the order, the condition to payment or agreement is not enforceable.

(d) A funds-transfer system rule may provide that payments made to beneficiaries of funds transfers made through the system are provisional until receipt of payment by the beneficiary's bank of the payment order it accepted. A beneficiary's bank that makes a payment that is provisional under the rule is entitled to refund from the beneficiary if (i) the rule requires that both the beneficiary and the originator be given notice of the provisional nature of the payment before the funds transfer is initiated, (ii) the beneficiary, the beneficiary's bank and the originator's bank agreed to be bound by the rule, and (iii) the beneficiary's bank did not receive payment of the payment order that it accepted. If the beneficiary is obliged to refund payment to the beneficiary's bank, acceptance of the payment order by the beneficiary's bank is nullified and no payment by the originator of the funds transfer to the beneficiary occurs under Section4A-406.

(e) This subsection applies to a funds transfer that includes a payment order transmitted over a funds-transfer system that (i) nets obligations multilaterally among participants, and (ii) has in effect a loss-sharing agreement among participants for the purpose of providing funds necessary to complete settlement of the obligations of one or more participants that do not meet their settlement obligations. If the beneficiary's bank in the funds transfer accepts a payment order and the system fails to complete settlement pursuant to its rules with respect to any payment order in the funds transfer, (i) the acceptance by the beneficiary's bank is nullified and no person has any right or obligation based on the acceptance, (ii) the beneficiary's bank is entitled to recover payment from the beneficiary, (iii) no payment by the originator to the beneficiary occurs under Section 4A-406, and (iv) subject to Section 4A-402 (e), each sender in the funds transfer is excused from its obligation to pay its payment order under Section 4A-402(c) because the funds transfer has not been completed.

§ 4A-406. Payment by Originator to Beneficiary; Discharge of Underlying Obligation.

(a) Subject to Sections 4A-211(e), 4A-405 (d), and 4A-405(e), the originator of a funds transfer pays the beneficiary of the originator's payment order (1) at the time a payment order for the benefit of the beneficiary is accepted by the beneficiary's bank in the funds transfer and (ii) in an amount equal to the amount of the order accepted by the beneficiary's bank, but not more than the amount of the originator's order.

(b) If payment under subsection (a) is made to satisfy an obligation, the obligation is discharged to the same extent discharge would result from payment to the beneficiary of the same amount in money, unless (1) the payment under subsection (a) was made by a means prohibited by the contract of the beneficiary with respect to the obligation, (ii) the beneficiary, within a reasonable time after receiving notice of receipt of the order by the beneficiary's bank, notified the originator of the beneficiary's refusal of the payment, (iii) funds with respect to the order were not withdrawn by the beneficiary or applied to a debt of the beneficiary, and (iv) the beneficiary would suffer a loss that could reasonably have been avoided if payment had been made by a means complying with the contract. If payment by the originator does not result in discharge under this section, the originator is subrogated to the rights of the beneficiary to receive payment from the beneficiary's bank under Section 4A-404 (a)

(c) For the purpose of determining whether discharge of an obligation occurs under subsection (b), if the beneficiary's bank accepts a payment order in an amount equal to the amount of the originator's payment order less charges of one or more receiving banks in the funds transfer, payment to the beneficiary is deemed to be in the amount of the originator's order unless upon demand by the beneficiary the originator does not pay the beneficiary the amount of the deducted charges.

(d) Rights of the originator or of the beneficiary of a funds transfer under this section may be varied only by agreement of the originator and the beneficiary.

PART 5 Miscellaneous Provisions

§ 4A-501. Variation by Agreement and Effect of Funds-Transfer System Rule.

(a) Except as otherwise provided in this Article, the rights and obligations of a party to a funds transfer may be varied by agreement of the affected party.

(b) "Funds-transfer system rule" means a rule of an association of banks (i) governing transmission of payment orders by means of a funds-transfer system of the association or rights and obligations with respect to those orders, or (ii) to the extent the rule governs rights and obligations between banks that are parties to a funds transfer in which a Federal Reserve Bank, acting as an intermediary bank, sends a payment order to the beneficiary's bank. Except as otherwise provided in this Article, a funds-transfer system rule governing rights and obligations between participating banks using the system may be effective even if the rule conflicts with this Article and indirectly affects another party to the funds transfer who does not consent to the rule. A funds-transfer system rule may also govern rights and obligations of parties other than participating banks using the system to the extent stated in Sections 4A-404 (c), 4A-405 (d), and 4A-507 (c).

§ 4A-502. Creditor Process Served on Receiving Bank; Setoff by Beneficiary's Bank.

(a) As used in this section, "creditor process" means levy, attachment, garnishment, notice of lien, sequestration, or similar process issued by or on behalf of a creditor or other claimant with respect to an account.

(b) This subsection applies to creditor process with respect to an authorized account of the sender of a payment order if the creditor process is served on the receiving bank. For the purpose of determining rights with respect to the creditor process, if the receiving bank accepts the payment order the balance in the authorized account is deemed to be reduced by the amount of the payment order to the extent the bank did not otherwise receive payment of the order, unless the creditor process is served at a time and in a manner affording the bank a reasonable opportunity to act on it before the bank accepts the payment order.

(c) If a beneficiary's bank has received a payment order for payment to the beneficiary's account in the bank, the following rules apply:

(1) The bank may credit the beneficiary's account. The amount credited may be set off against an obligation owed by the beneficiary to the bank or may be applied to satisfy creditor process served on the bank with respect to the account.

(2) The bank may credit the beneficiary's account and allow withdrawal of the amount credited unless creditor process with respect to the account is served at a time and in a manner affording the bank a reasonable opportunity to act to prevent withdrawal.

(3) If creditor process with respect to the beneficiary's account has been served and the bank has had a reasonable opportunity to act on it, the bank may not reject the payment order except for a reason unrelated to the service of process.

(d) Creditor process with respect to a payment by the originator to the beneficiary pursuant to a funds transfer may be served only on the beneficiary's bank with respect to the debt owed by that bank to the beneficiary. Any other bank served with the creditor process is not obliged to act with respect to the process.

§ 4A-503. Injunction or Restraining Order With Respect to Funds Transfer.

For proper cause and in compliance with applicable law, a court may restrain (i) a person from issuing a payment order to initiate a funds transfer, (ii) an originator's bank from executing the payment order of the originator, or (iii) the beneficiary's bank from releasing funds to the beneficiary or the beneficiary from withdrawing the funds. A court may not otherwise restrain a person from issuing a payment order, paying or receiving payment of a payment order, or otherwise acting with respect to a funds transfer.

§ 4A-504. Order in Which Items and Payment Orders May Be Charged to Account; Order of Withdrawals From Account.

(a) If a receiving bank has received more than one payment order of the sender or one or more payment orders and other items that are payable from the sender's account, the bank may charge the sender's account with respect to the various orders and items in any sequence.

(b) In determining whether a credit to an account has been withdrawn by the holder of the account or applied to a debt of the holder of the account, credits first made to the account are first withdrawn or applied.

§ 4A-505. Preclusion of Objection to Debit of Customer's Account.

If a receiving bank has received payment from its customer with respect to a payment order issued in the name of the customer as sender and accepted by the bank, and the customer received notification reasonably identifying the order, the customer is precluded from asserting that the bank is not entitled to retain the payment unless the customer notifies the bank of the customer's objection to the payment within one year after the notification was received by the customer.

§ 4A-506. Rate of Interest.
(a) If, under this Article, a receiving bank is obliged to pay interest with respect to a payment order issued to the bank, the amount payable may be determined (i) by agreement of the sender and receiving bank, or (ii) by a funds-transfer system rule if the payment order is transmitted through a funds-transfer system.
(b) If the amount of interest is not determined by an agreement or rule as stated in subsection (a), the amount is calculated by multiplying the applicable Federal Funds rate by the amount on which interest is payable, and then multiplying the product by the number of days for which interest is payable. The applicable Federal Funds rate is the average of the Federal Funds rates published by the Federal Reserve Bank of New York for each of the days for which interest is payable divided by 360. The Federal Funds rate for any day on which a published rate is not available is the same as the published rate for the next preceding day for which there is a published rate. If a receiving bank that accepted a payment order is required to refund payment to the sender of the order because the funds transfer was not completed, but the failure to complete was not due to any fault by the bank, the interest payable is reduced by a percentage equal to the reserve requirement on deposits of the receiving bank.

§ 4A-507. Choice of Law.
(a) The following rules apply unless the affected parties otherwise agree or subsection (c) applies:

(1) The rights and obligations between the sender of a payment order and the receiving bank are governed by the law of the jurisdiction in which the receiving bank is located.

(2) The rights and obligations between the beneficiary's bank and the beneficiary are governed by the law of the jurisdiction in which the beneficiary's bank is located.

(3) The issue of when payment is made pursuant to a funds transfer by the originator to the beneficiary is governed by the law of the jurisdiction in which the beneficiary's bank is located.

(b) If the parties described in each paragraph of subsection (a) have made an agreement selecting the law of a particular jurisdiction to govern rights and obligations between each other, the law of that jurisdiction governs those rights and obligations, whether or not the payment order or the funds transfer bears a reasonable relation to that jurisdiction.
(c) A funds-transfer system rule may select the law of a particular jurisdiction to govern (i) rights and obligations between participating banks with respect to payment orders transmitted or processed through the system, or (ii) the rights and obligations of some or all parties to a funds transfer any part of which is carried out by means of the system. A choice of law made pursuant to clause (i) is binding on participating banks. A choice of law made pursuant to clause (ii) is binding on the originator, other sender, or a receiving bank having notice that the funds-transfer system might be used in the funds transfer and of the choice of law by the system when the originator, other sender, or receiving bank issued or accepted a payment order. The beneficiary of a funds transfer is bound by the choice of law if, when the funds transfer is initiated, the beneficiary has notice that the funds-transfer system might be used in the funds transfer and of the choice of law by the system. The law of a jurisdiction selected pursuant to this subsection may govern, whether or not that law bears a reasonable relation to the matter in issue.
(d) In the event of inconsistency between an agreement under subsection (b) and a choice-of-law rule under subsection (c), the agreement under subsection (b) prevails.
(e) If a funds transfer is made by use of more than one funds-transfer system and there is inconsistency between choice-of-law rules of the systems, the matter in issue is governed by the law of the selected jurisdiction that has the most significant relationship to the matter in issue.

ARTICLE 5 / Letters of Credit

§ 5-101. Short Title. This article may be cited as Uniform Commercial Code Letters of Credit.

§ 5-102. Definitions.
(a) In this article:

(1) "Adviser" means a person who, at the request of the issuer, a confirmer, or another adviser, notifies or requests another adviser to notify the beneficiary that a letter of credit has been issued, confirmed, or amended.

(2) "Applicant" means a person at whose request or for whose account a letter of credit is issued. The term includes a person who requests an issuer to issue a letter of credit on behalf of another if the person making the request undertakes an obligation to reimburse the issuer.

(3) "Beneficiary" means a person who under the terms of a letter of credit is entitled to have its complying presentation honored. The term includes a person to whom drawing rights have been transferred under a transferable letter of credit.

(4) "Confirmer" means a nominated person who undertakes, at the request or with the consent of the issuer, to honor a presentation under a letter of credit issued by another.

(5) "Dishonor" of a letter of credit means failure timely to honor or to take an interim action, such as acceptance of a draft, that may be required by the letter of credit.

(6) "Document" means a draft or other demand, document of title, investment security, certificate, invoice, or other record, statement, or representation of fact, law, right, or opinion (i) which is presented in a written or other medium permitted by the letter of credit or, unless prohibited by the letter of credit, by the standard practice referred to in Section 5-108(e) and (ii) which is capable of being examined for compliance with the terms and conditions of the letter of credit. A document may not be oral.

(7) "Good faith" means honesty in fact in the conduct or transaction concerned.
(8) "Honor" of a letter of credit means performance of the issuer's undertaking in the letter of credit to pay or deliver an item of value. Unless the letter of credit otherwise provides, "honor" occurs

(i) upon payment,
(ii) if the letter of credit provides for acceptance, upon acceptance of a draft and, at maturity, its payment, or
(iii) if the letter of credit provides for incurring a deferred obligation, upon incurring the obligation and, at maturity, its performance.

(9) "Issuer" means a bank or other person that issues a letter of credit, but does not include an individual who makes an engagement for personal, family, or household purposes.
(10) "Letter of credit" means a definite undertaking that satisfies the requirements of Section 5-104 by an issuer to a beneficiary at the request or for the account of an applicant or, in the case of a financial institution, to itself or for its own account, to honor a documentary presentation by payment or delivery of an item of value.
(11) "Nominated person" means a person whom the issuer (i) designates or authorizes to pay, accept, negotiate, or otherwise give value under a letter of credit and (ii) undertakes by agreement or custom and practice to reimburse.
(12) "Presentation" means delivery of a document to an issuer or nominated person for honor or giving of value under a letter of credit.
(13) "Presenter" means a person making a presentation as or on behalf of a beneficiary or nominated person.
(14) "Record" means information that is inscribed on a tangible medium, or that is stored in an electronic or other medium and is retrievable in perceivable form.
(15) "Successor of a beneficiary" means a person who succeeds to substantially all of the rights of a beneficiary by operation of law, including a corporation with or into which the beneficiary has been merged or consolidated, an administrator, executor, personal representative, trustee in bankruptcy, debtor in possession, liquidator, and receiver.

(b) Definitions in other Articles applying to this article and the sections in which they appear are:

"Accept" or "Acceptance"Section 3-409

"Value" Sections 3-303, 4-211

(c) Article 1 contains certain additional general definitions and principles of construction and interpretation applicable throughout this article.

§ 5-103. Scope.

(a) This article applies to letters of credit and to certain rights and obligations arising out of transactions involving letters of credit.
(b) The statement of a rule in this article does not by itself require, imply, or negate application of the same or a different rule to a situation not provided for, or to a person not specified, in this article.
(c) With the exception of this subsection, subsections (a) and (d), Sections 5-102(a)(9) and (10), 5-106(d), and 5-114(d), and except to the extent prohibited in Sections 1-102(3) and 5-117(d), the effect of this article may be varied by agreement or by a provision stated or incorporated by reference in an undertaking. A term in an agreement or undertaking generally excusing liability or generally limiting remedies for failure to perform obligations is not sufficient to vary obligations prescribed by this article.
(d) Rights and obligations of an issuer to a beneficiary or a nominated person under a letter of credit are independent of the existence, performance, or nonperformance of a contract or arrangement out of which the letter of credit arises or which underlies it, including contracts or arrangements between the issuer and the applicant and between the applicant and the beneficiary.

§ 5-104. Formal Requirements. A letter of credit, confirmation, advice, transfer, amendment, or cancellation may be issued in any form that is a record and is authenticated (i) by a signature or (ii) in accordance with the agreement of the parties or the standard practice referred to in Section 5-108(e).

§ 5-105. Consideration. Consideration is not required to issue, amend, transfer, or cancel a letter of credit, advice, or confirmation.

§ 5-106. Issuance, Amendment, Cancellation, and Duration.

(a) A letter of credit is issued and becomes enforceable according to its terms against the issuer when the issuer sends or otherwise transmits it to the person requested to advise or to the beneficiary. A letter of credit is revocable only if it so provides.
(b) After a letter of credit is issued, rights and obligations of a beneficiary, applicant, confirmer, and issuer are not affected by an amendment or cancellation to which that person has not consented except to the extent the letter of credit provides that it is revocable or that the issuer may amend or cancel the letter of credit without that consent.
(c) If there is no stated expiration date or other provision that determines its duration, a letter of credit expires one year after its stated date of issuance or, if none is stated, after the date on which it is issued.
(d) A letter of credit that states that it is perpetual expires five years after its stated date of issuance, or if none is stated, after the date on which it is issued.

§ 5-107. Confirmer, Nominated Person, and Adviser.

(a) A confirmer is directly obligated on a letter of credit and has the rights and obligations of an issuer to the extent of its confirmation. The confirmer also has rights against and obligations to the issuer as if the issuer were an applicant and the confirmer had issued the letter of credit at the request and for the account of the issuer.
(b) A nominated person who is not a confirmer is not obligated to honor or otherwise give value for a presentation.
(c) A person requested to advise may decline to act as an adviser. An adviser that is not a confirmer is not obligated to honor or give value for a presentation. An adviser undertakes

to the issuer and to the beneficiary accurately to advise the terms of the letter of credit, confirmation, amendment, or advice received by that person and undertakes to the beneficiary to check the apparent authenticity of the request to advise. Even if the advice is inaccurate, the letter of credit, confirmation, or amendment is enforceable as issued.

(d) A person who notifies a transferee beneficiary of the terms of a letter of credit, confirmation, amendment, or advice has the rights and obligations of an adviser under subsection (c). The terms in the notice to the transferee beneficiary may differ from the terms in any notice to the transferor beneficiary to the extent permitted by the letter of credit, confirmation, amendment, or advice received by the person who so notifies.

§ 5-108. Issuer's Rights and Obligations.

(a) Except as otherwise provided in Section 5-109, an issuer shall honor a presentation that, as determined by the standard practice referred to in subsection (e), appears on its face strictly to comply with the terms and conditions of the letter of credit. Except as otherwise provided in Section 5-113 and unless otherwise agreed with the applicant, an issuer shall dishonor a presentation that does not appear so to comply.

(b) An issuer has a reasonable time after presentation, but not beyond the end of the seventh business day of the issuer after the day of its receipt of documents:

(1) to honor,

(2) if the letter of credit provides for honor to be completed more than seven business days after presentation, to accept a draft or incur a deferred obligation, or

(3) to give notice to the presenter of discrepancies in the presentation.

(c) Except as otherwise provided in subsection (d), an issuer is precluded from asserting as a basis for dishonor any discrepancy if timely notice is not given, or any discrepancy not stated in the notice if timely notice is given.

(d) Failure to give the notice specified in subsection (b) or to mention fraud, forgery, or expiration in the notice does not preclude the issuer from asserting as a basis for dishonor fraud or forgery as described in Section 5-109(a) or expiration of the letter of credit before presentation.

(e) An issuer shall observe standard practice of financial institutions that regularly issue letters of credit. Determination of the issuer's observance of the standard practice is a matter of interpretation for the court. The court shall offer the parties a reasonable opportunity to present evidence of the standard practice.

(f) An issuer is not responsible for:

(1) the performance or nonperformance of the underlying contract, arrangement, or transaction,

(2) an act or omission of others, or

(3) observance or knowledge of the usage of a particular trade other than the standard practice referred to in subsection (e).

(g) If an undertaking constituting a letter of credit under Section 5-102(a)(10) contains nondocumentary conditions, an issuer shall disregard the nondocumentary conditions and treat them as if they were not stated.

(h) An issuer that has dishonored a presentation shall return the documents or hold them at the disposal of, and send advice to that effect to, the presenter.

(i) An issuer that has honored a presentation as permitted or required by this article:

(1) is entitled to be reimbursed by the applicant in immediately available funds not later than the date of its payment of funds;

(2) takes the documents free of claims of the beneficiary or presenter;

(3) is precluded from asserting a right of recourse on a draft under Sections 3-414 and 3-415;

(4) except as otherwise provided in Sections 5-110 and 5-117, is precluded from restitution of money paid or other value given by mistake to the extent the mistake concerns discrepancies in the documents or tender which are apparent on the face of the presentation; and

(5) is discharged to the extent of its performance under the letter of credit unless the issuer honored a presentation in which a required signature of a beneficiary was forged.

§ 5-109. Fraud and Forgery.

(a) If a presentation is made that appears on its face strictly to comply with the terms and conditions of the letter of credit, but a required document is forged or materially fraudulent, or honor of the presentation would facilitate a material fraud by the beneficiary on the issuer or applicant:

(1) the issuer shall honor the presentation, if honor is demanded by (i) a nominated person who has given value in good faith and without notice of forgery or material fraud, (ii) a confirmer who has honored its confirmation in good faith, (iii) a holder in due course of a draft drawn under the letter of credit which was taken after acceptance by the issuer or nominated person, or (iv) an assignee of the issuer's or nominated person's deferred obligation that was taken for value and without notice of forgery or material fraud after the obligation was incurred by the issuer or nominated person; and

(2) the issuer, acting in good faith, may honor or dishonor the presentation in any other case.

(b) If an applicant claims that a required document is forged or materially fraudulent or that honor of the presentation would facilitate a material fraud by the beneficiary on the issuer or applicant, a court of competent jurisdiction may temporarily or permanently enjoin the issuer from honoring a presentation or grant similar relief against the issuer or other persons only if the court finds that:

(1) the relief is not prohibited under the law applicable to an accepted draft or deferred obligation incurred by the issuer;

(2) a beneficiary, issuer, or nominated person who may be adversely affected is adequately protected against loss that it may suffer because the relief is granted;

(3) all of the conditions to entitle a person to the relief under the law of this State have been met; and

(4) on the basis of the information submitted to the court, the applicant is more likely than not to succeed under its

claim of forgery or material fraud and the person demanding honor does not qualify for protection under subsection (a)(1).

§ 5-110. Warranties.

(a) If its presentation is honored, the beneficiary warrants:

(1) to the issuer, any other person to whom presentation is made, and the applicant that there is no fraud or forgery of the kind described in Section 5-109(a); and

(2) to the applicant that the drawing does not violate any agreement between the applicant and beneficiary or any other agreement intended by them to be augmented by the letter of credit.

(b) The warranties in subsection (a) are in addition to warranties arising under Article 3, 4, 7, and 8 because of the presentation or transfer of documents covered by any of those articles.

§ 5-111. Remedies.

(a) If an issuer wrongfully dishonors or repudiates its obligation to pay money under a letter of credit before presentation, the beneficiary, successor, or nominated person presenting on its own behalf may recover from the issuer the amount that is the subject of the dishonor or repudiation. If the issuer's obligation under the letter of credit is not for the payment of money, the claimant may obtain specific performance or, at the claimant's election, recover an amount equal to the value of performance from the issuer. In either case, the claimant may also recover incidental but not consequential damages. The claimant is not obligated to take action to avoid damages that might be due from the issuer under this subsection. If, although not obligated to do so, the claimant avoids damages, the claimant's recovery from the issuer must be reduced by the amount of damages avoided. The issuer has the burden of proving the amount of damages avoided. In the case of repudiation the claimant need not present any document.

(b) If an issuer wrongfully dishonors a draft or demand presented under a letter of credit or honors a draft or demand in breach of its obligation to the applicant, the applicant may recover damages resulting from the breach, including incidental but not consequential damages, less any amount saved as a result of the breach.

(c) If an adviser or nominated person other than a confirmer breaches an obligation under this article or an issuer breaches an obligation not covered in subsection (a) or (b), a person to whom the obligation is owed may recover damages resulting from the breach, including incidental but not consequential damages, less any amount saved as a result of the breach. To the extent of the confirmation, a confirmer has the liability of an issuer specified in this subsection and subsections (a) and (b).

(d) An issuer, nominated person, or adviser who is found liable under subsection (a), (b), or (c) shall pay interest on the amount owed thereunder from the date of wrongful dishonor or other appropriate date.

(e) Reasonable attorney's fees and other expenses of litigation must be awarded to the prevailing party in an action in which a remedy is sought under this article.

(f) Damages that would otherwise be payable by a party for breach of an obligation under this article may be liquidated by agreement or undertaking, but only in an amount or by a formula that is reasonable in light of the harm anticipated.

§ 5-112. Transfer of Letter or Credit.

(a) Except as otherwise provided in Section 5-113, unless a letter of credit provides that it is transferable, the right of a beneficiary to draw or otherwise demand performance under a letter of credit may not be transferred.

(b) Even if a letter of credit provides that it is transferable, the issuer may refuse to recognize or carry out a transfer if:

(1) the transfer would violate applicable law; or

(2) the transferor or transferee has failed to comply with any requirement stated in the letter of credit or any other requirement relating to transfer imposed by the issuer which is within the standard practice referred to in Section 5-108(e) or is otherwise reasonable under the circumstances.

§ 5-113. Transfer by Operation of Law.

(a) A successor of a beneficiary may consent to amendments, sign and present documents, and receive payment or other items of value in the name of the beneficiary without disclosing its status as a successor.

(b) A successor of a beneficiary may consent to amendments, sign and present documents, and receive payment or other items of value in its own name as the disclosed successor of the beneficiary. Except as otherwise provided in subsection (e), an issuer shall recognize a disclosed successor of a beneficiary as beneficiary in full substitution for its predecessor upon compliance with the requirements for recognition by the issuer of a transfer of drawing rights by operation of law under the standard practice referred to in Section 5-108(e) or, in the absence of such a practice, compliance with other reasonable procedures sufficient to protect the issuer.

(c) An issuer is not obliged to determine whether a purported successor is a successor of a beneficiary or whether the signature of a purported successor is genuine or authorized.

(d) Honor of a purported successor's apparently complying presentation under subsection (a) or (b) has the consequences specified in Section 5-108(i) even if the purported successor is not the successor of a beneficiary. Documents signed in the name of the beneficiary or of a disclosed successor by a person who is neither the beneficiary nor the successor of the beneficiary are forged documents for the purposes of Section 5-109.

(e) An issuer whose rights of reimbursement are not covered by subsection (d) or substantially similar law and any confirmer or nominated person may decline to recognize a presentation under subsection (b).

(f) A beneficiary whose name is changed after the issuance of a letter of credit has the same rights and obligations as a successor of a beneficiary under this section.

§ 5-114. Assignment of Proceeds.

(a) In this section, "proceeds of a letter of credit" means the cash, check, accepted draft, or other item of value paid or delivered upon honor or giving of value by the issuer or any nominated person under the letter of credit. The term does not include a beneficiary's drawing rights or documents presented by the beneficiary.

(b) A beneficiary may assign its right to part or all of the proceeds of a letter of credit. The beneficiary may do so before presentation as a present assignment of its right to receive proceeds contingent upon its compliance with the terms and conditions of the letter of credit.

(c) An issuer or nominated person need not recognize an assignment of proceeds of a letter of credit until it consents to the assignment.

(d) An issuer or nominated person has no obligation to give or withhold its consent to an assignment of proceeds of a letter of credit, but consent may not be unreasonably withheld if the assignee possesses and exhibits the letter of credit and presentation of the letter of credit is a condition to honor.

(e) Rights of a transferee beneficiary or nominated person are independent of the beneficiary's assignment of the proceeds of a letter of credit and are superior to the assignee's right to the proceeds.

(f) Neither the rights recognized by this section between an assignee and an issuer, transferee beneficiary, or nominated person nor the issuer's or nominated person's payment of proceeds to an assignee or a third person affect the rights between the assignee and any person other than the issuer, transferee beneficiary, or nominated person. The mode of creating and perfecting a security interest in or granting an assignment of a beneficiary's rights to proceeds is governed by Article 9 or other law. Against persons other than the issuer, transferee beneficiary, or nominated person, the rights and obligations arising upon the creation of a security interest or other assignment of a beneficiary's right to proceeds and its perfection are governed by Article 9 or other law.

§ 5-115. Statute of Limitations. An action to enforce a right or obligation arising under this article must be commenced within one year after the expiration date of the relevant letter of credit or one year after the [claim for relief] [cause of action] accrues, whichever occurs later. A [claim for relief] [cause of action] accrues when the breach occurs, regardless of the aggrieved party's lack of knowledge of the breach.

§ 5-116. Choice of Law and Forum.

(a) The liability of an issuer, nominated person, or adviser for action or omission is governed by the law of the jurisdiction chosen by an agreement in the form of a record signed or otherwise authenticated by the affected parties in the manner provided in Section 5-104 or by a provision in the person's letter of credit, confirmation, or other undertaking. The jurisdiction whose law is chosen need not bear any relation to the transaction.

(b) Unless subsection (a) applies, the liability of an issuer, nominated person, or adviser for action or omission is governed by the law of the jurisdiction in which the person is located. The person is considered to be located at the address indicated in the person's undertaking. If more than one address is indicated, the person is considered to be located at the address from which the person's undertaking was issued. For the purpose of jurisdiction, choice of law, and recognition of interbranch letters of credit, but not enforcement of a judgment, all branches of a bank are considered separate juridical entities and a bank is considered to be located at the place where its relevant branch is considered to be located under this subsection.

(c) Except as otherwise provided in this subsection, the liability of an issuer, nominated person, or adviser is governed by any rules of custom or practice, such as the Uniform Customs and Practice for Documentary Credits, to which the letter of credit, confirmation, or other undertaking is expressly made subject. If (i) this article would govern the liability of an issuer, nominated person, or adviser under subsection (a) or (b), (ii) the relevant undertaking incorporates rules of custom or practice, and (iii) there is conflict between this article and those rules as applied to that undertaking, those rules govern except to the extent of any conflict with the nonvariable provisions specified in Section 5-103(c).

(d) If there is conflict between this article and Article 3, 4, 4A, or 9, this article governs.

(e) The forum for settling disputes arising out of an undertaking within this article may be chosen in the manner and with the binding effect that governing law may be chosen in accordance with subsection (a).

§ 5-117. Subrogation of Issuer, Applicant, and Nominated Person.

(a) An issuer that honors a beneficiary's presentation is subrogated to the rights of the beneficiary to the same extent as if the issuer were a secondary obligor of the underlying obligation owed to the beneficiary and of the applicant to the same extent as if the issuer were the secondary obligor of the underlying obligation owed to the applicant.

(b) An applicant that reimburses an issuer is subrogated to the rights of the issuer against any beneficiary, presenter, or nominated person to the same extent as if the applicant were the secondary obligor of the obligations owed to the issuer and has the rights of subrogation of the issuer to the rights of the beneficiary stated in subsection (a).

(c) A nominated person who pays or gives value against a draft or demand presented under a letter of credit is subrogated to the rights of:

(1) the issuer against the applicant to the same extent as if the nominated person were a secondary obligor of the obligation owed to the issuer by the applicant;

(2) the beneficiary to the same extent as if the nominated person were a secondary obligor of the underlying obligation owed to the beneficiary; and

(3) the applicant to same extent as if the nominated person were a secondary obligor of the underlying obligation owed to the applicant.

(d) Notwithstanding any agreement or term to the contrary, the rights of subrogation stated in subsections (a) and (b) do not arise until the issuer honors the letter of credit or otherwise pays and the rights in subsection (c) do not arise until the nominated person pays or otherwise gives value. Until then, the issuer, nominated person, and the applicant do not derive under this section present or prospective rights forming the basis of a claim, defense, or excuse.

REPEALER OF ARTICLE 6 / Bulk Transfers and Revised Article 6 Bulk Sales (States to Select One Alternative)

Alternative A

§ 1. Repeal. Article 6 and Section 9-111 of the Uniform Commercial Code are hereby repealed, effective ________.

§ 2. Amendment. Section 1-105(2) of the Uniform Commercial Code is hereby amended to read as follows:

(2) Where one of the following provisions of this Act specifies the applicable law, that provision governs and a contrary agreement is effective only to the extent permitted by the law (including the conflict of laws rules) so specified:

Rights of creditors against sold goods. Section 2-402.

Applicability of the Article on Leases. Sections 2A- 105 and 2A-106.

Applicability of the Article on Bank Deposits and Collections. Section 4-102.

Applicability of the Article on Investment Securities. Section 8-106.

Perfection provisions of the Article on Secured Transactions. Section 9-103.

§ 3. Amendment. Section 2-403(4) of the Uniform Commercial Code is hereby amended to read as follows:

(4) The rights of other purchasers of goods and of lien creditors are governed by the Articles on Secured Transactions (Article 9), and Documents of Title (Article 7).

§ 4. Savings Clause. Rights and obligations that arose under Article 6 and Section 9-111 of the Uniform Commercial Code before their repeal remain valid and may be enforced as though those statutes had not been repealed.]

[End Of Alternative A]

Alternative B

§ 6-101. Short Title.

This Article shall be known and may be cited as Uniform Commercial Code—Bulk Sales.

§ 6-102. Definitions and Index of Definitions.

(1) In this Article, unless the context otherwise requires:

(a) "Assets" means the inventory that is the subject of a bulk sale and any tangible and intangible personal property used or held for use primarily in, or arising from, the seller's business and sold in connection with that inventory, but the term does not include:

(i) fixtures (Section 9-313(1) (a)) other than readily removable factory and office machines;

(ii) the lessee's interest in a lease of real property; or

(iii) property to the extent it is generally exempt from creditor process under nonbankruptcy law.

(b) "Auctioneer" means a person whom the seller engages to direct, conduct, control, or be responsible for a sale by auction.

(c) "Bulk sale" means:

(i) in the case of a sale by auction or a sale or series of sales conducted by a liquidator on the seller's behalf, a sale or series of sales not in the ordinary course of the seller's business of more than half of the seller's inventory, as measured by value on the date of the bulk-sale agreement, if on that date the auctioneer or liquidator has notice, or after reasonable inquiry would have had notice, that the seller will not continue to operate the same or a similar kind of business after the sale or series of sales; and

(ii) in all other cases, a sale not in the ordinary course of the seller's business of more than half the seller's inventory, as measured by value on the date of the bulk-sale agreement, if on that date the buyer has notice, or after reasonable inquiry would have had notice, that the seller will not continue to operate the same or a similar kind of business after the sale.

(d) "Claim" means a right to payment from the seller, whether or not the right is reduced to judgment, liquidated, fixed, matured, disputed, secured, legal, or equitable. The term includes costs of collection and attorney's fees only to the extent that the laws of this state permit the holder of the claim to recover them in an action against the obligor.

(e) "Claimant" means a person holding a claim incurred in the seller's business other than:

(i) an unsecured and unmatured claim for employment compensation and benefits, including commissions and vacation, severance, and sick-leave pay;

(ii) a claim for injury to an individual or to property, or for breach of warranty, unless:

(A) a right of action for the claim has accrued;

(B) the claim has been asserted against the seller; and

(C) the seller knows the identity of the person asserting the claim and the basis upon which the person has asserted it; and

(States to Select One Alternative)

Alternative A

[(iii) a claim for taxes owing to a governmental unit.]

Alternative B

[(iii) a claim for taxes owing to a governmental unit, if:

(A) a statute governing the enforcement of the claim permits or requires notice of the bulk sale to be given to the governmental unit in a manner other than by compliance with the requirements of this Article; and

(B) notice is given in accordance with the statute.]

(f) "Creditor" means a claimant or other person holding a claim.

(g) (i) "Date of the bulk sale" means:

(A) if the sale is by auction or is conducted by a liquidator on the seller's behalf, the date on which more than ten percent of the net proceeds is paid to or for the benefit of the seller; and

(B) in all other cases, the later of the date on which:

(I) more than ten percent of the net contract price is paid to or for the benefit of the seller; or

(II) more than ten percent of the assets, as measured by value, are transferred to the buyer.

(ii) For purposes of this subsection:

(A) Delivery of a negotiable instrument (Section 3-104(1)) to or for the benefit of the seller in exchange for assets constitutes payment of the contract price pro tanto;

(B) To the extent that the contract price is deposited in an escrow, the contract price is paid to or for the benefit of the seller when the seller acquires the unconditional right to receive the deposit or when the deposit is delivered to the seller or for the benefit of the seller, whichever is earlier; and

(C) An asset is transferred when a person holding an unsecured claim can no longer obtain through judicial proceedings rights to the asset that are superior to those of the buyer arising as a result of the bulk sale. A person holding an unsecured claim can obtain those superior rights to a tangible asset at least until the buyer has an unconditional right, under the bulk-sale agreement, to possess the asset, and a person holding an unsecured claim can obtain those superior rights to an intangible asset at least until the buyer has an unconditional right, under the bulk-sale agreement, to use the asset.

(h) "Date of the bulk-sale agreement" means:

(i) in the case of a sale by auction or conducted by a liquidator (subsection (c) (i)), the date on which the seller engages the auctioneer or liquidator; and

(ii) in all other cases, the date on which a bulk-sale agreement becomes enforceable between the buyer and the seller.

(i) "Debt" means liability on a claim.

(j) "Liquidator" means a person who is regularly engaged in the business of disposing of assets for businesses contemplating liquidation or dissolution.

(k) "Net contract price" means the new consideration the buyer is obligated to pay for the assets less:

(i) the amount of any proceeds of the sale of an asset, to the extent the proceeds are applied in partial or total satisfaction of a debt secured by the asset; and

(ii) the amount of any debt to the extent it is secured by a security interest or lien that is enforceable against the asset before and after it has been sold to a buyer. If a debt is secured by an asset and other property of the seller, the amount of the debt secured by a security interest or lien that is enforceable against the asset is determined by multiplying the debt by a fraction, the numerator of which is the value of the new consideration for the asset on the date of the bulk sale and the denominator of which is the value of all property securing the debt on the date of the bulk sale.

(l) "Net proceeds" means the new consideration received for assets sold at a sale by auction or a sale conducted by a liquidator on the seller's behalf less:

(i) commissions and reasonable expenses of the sale;

(ii) the amount of any proceeds of the sale of an asset, to the extent the proceeds are applied in partial or total satisfaction of a debt secured by the asset; and

(iii) the amount of any debt to the extent it is secured by a security interest or lien that is enforceable against the asset before and after it has been sold to a buyer. If a debt is secured by an asset and other property of the seller, the amount of the debt secured by a security interest or lien that is enforceable against the asset is determined by multiplying the debt by a fraction, the numerator of which is the value of the new consideration for the asset on the date of the bulk sale and the denominator of which is the value of all property securing the debt on the date of the bulk sale.

(m) A sale is "in the ordinary course of the seller's business" if the sale comports with usual or customary practices in the kind of business in which the seller is engaged or with the seller's own usual or customary practices.

(n) "United States" includes its territories and possessions and the Commonwealth of Puerto Rico.

(o) "Value" means fair market value.

(p) "Verified" means signed and sworn to or affirmed.

(2) The following definitions in other Articles apply to this Article:

(a) "Buyer." Section 2-103(1) (a).

(b) "Equipment." Section 9-109(2).

(c) "Inventory." Section 9-109(4).

(d) "Sale." Section 2-106(1).

(e) "Seller." Section 2-103(1) (d).

(3) In addition, Article 1 contains general definitions and principles of construction and interpretation applicable throughout this Article.

§ 6-103. Applicability of Article

(1) Except as otherwise provided in subsection (3), this Article applies to a bulk sale if:

(a) the seller's principal business is the sale of inventory from stock; and

(b) on the date of the bulk-sale agreement the seller is located in this state or, if the seller is located in a jurisdiction that is not a part of the United States, the seller's major executive office in the United States is in this state.

(2) A seller is deemed to be located at his [or her] place of business. If a seller has more than one place of business, the seller is deemed located at his [or her] chief executive office.

(3) This Article does not apply to:

(a) a transfer made to secure payment or performance of an obligation;

(b) a transfer of collateral to a secured party pursuant to Section 9-503;

(c) a sale of collateral pursuant to Section 9-504;

(d) retention of collateral pursuant to Section 9-505;

(e) a sale of an asset encumbered by a security interest or lien if (i) all the proceeds of the sale are applied in partial or total satisfaction of the debt secured by the security interest or lien or (ii) the security interest or lien is enforceable against the asset after it has been sold to the buyer and the net contract price is zero;

(f) a general assignment for the benefit of creditors or to a subsequent transfer by the assignee;

(g) a sale by an executor, administrator, receiver, trustee in bankruptcy, or any public officer under judicial process;

(h) a sale made in the course of judicial or administrative proceedings for the dissolution or reorganization of an organization;

(i) a sale to a buyer whose principal place of business is in the United States and who:

(i) not earlier than 21 days before the date of the bulk sale, (A) obtains from the seller a verified and dated list of claimants of whom the seller has notice three days before the seller sends or delivers the list to the buyer or (B) conducts a reasonable inquiry to discover the claimants;

(ii) assumes in full the debts owed to claimants of whom the buyer has knowledge on the date the buyer receives the list of claimants from the seller or on the date the buyer completes the reasonable inquiry, as the case may be;

(iii) is not insolvent after the assumption; and

(iv) gives written notice of the assumption not later than 30 days after the date of the bulk sale by sending or delivering a notice to the claimants identified in subparagraph (ii) or by filing a notice in the office of the [Secretary of State];

(j) a sale to a buyer whose principal place of business is in the United States and who:

(i) assumes in full the debts that were incurred in the seller's business before the date of the bulk sale;

(ii) is not insolvent after the assumption; and

(iii) gives written notice of the assumption not later than 30 days after the date of the bulk sale by sending or delivering a notice to each creditor whose debt is assumed or by filing a notice in the office of the [Secretary of State];

(k) a sale to a new organization that is organized to take over and continue the business of the seller and that has its principal place of business in the United States if:

(i) the buyer assumes in full the debts that were incurred in the seller's business before the date of the bulk sale;

(ii) the seller receives nothing from the sale except an interest in the new organization that is subordinate to the claims against the organization arising from the assumption; and

(iii) the buyer gives written notice of the assumption not later than 30 days after the date of the bulk sale by sending or delivering a notice to each creditor whose debt is assumed or by filing a notice in the office of the [Secretary of State];

(l) a sale of assets having:

(i) a value, net of liens and security interests, of less than $10,000. If a debt is secured by assets and other property of the seller, the net value of the assets is determined by subtracting from their value an amount equal to the product of the debt multiplied by a fraction, the numerator of which is the value of the assets on the date of the bulk sale and the denominator of which is the value of all property securing the debt on the date of the bulk sale; or

(ii) a value of more than $25,000,000 on the date of the bulk-sale agreement; or

(m) a sale required by, and made pursuant to, statute.

(4) The notice under subsection (3) (i) (iv) must state: (i) that a sale that may constitute a bulk sale has been or will be made; (ii) the date or prospective date of the bulk sale; (iii) the individual, partnership, or corporate names and the addresses of the seller and buyer; (iv) the address to which inquiries about the sale may be made, if different from the seller's address; and (v) that the buyer has assumed or will assume in full the debts owed to claimants of whom the buyer has knowledge on the date the buyer receives the list of claimants from the seller or completes a reasonable inquiry to discover the claimants.

(5) The notice under subsections (3) (j) (iii) and (3) (k) (iii) must state: (i) that a sale that may constitute a bulk sale has been or will be made; (ii) the date or prospective date of the bulk sale; (iii) the individual, partnership, or corporate names and the addresses of the seller and buyer; (iv) the address to which inquiries about the sale may be made, if different from the seller's address; and (v) that the buyer has assumed or will assume the debts that were incurred in the seller's business before the date of the bulk sale.

(6) For purposes of subsection (3) (l), the value of assets is presumed to be equal to the price the buyer agrees to pay for the assets. However, in a sale by auction or a sale conducted by a liquidator on the seller's behalf, the value of assets is presumed to be the amount the auctioneer or liquidator reasonably estimates the assets will bring at auction or upon liquidation.

§ 6-104. Obligations of Buyer.

(1) In a bulk sale as defined in Section 6-102(1) (c) (ii) the buyer shall:

(a) obtain from the seller a list of all business names and addresses used by the seller within three years before the date the list is sent or delivered to the buyer;

(b) unless excused under subsection (2), obtain from the seller a verified and dated list of claimants of whom the seller has notice three days before the seller sends or delivers the list to the buyer and including, to the extent known by the seller, the address of and the amount claimed by each claimant;

(c) obtain from the seller or prepare a schedule of distribution (Section 6-106(1));

(d) give notice of the bulk sale in accordance with Section 6-105;

(e) unless excused under Section 6-106(4), distribute the net contract price in accordance with the undertakings of the buyer in the schedule of distribution; and

(f) unless excused under subsection (2), make available the list of claimants (subsection (1) (b)) by:

(i) promptly sending or delivering a copy of the list without charge to any claimant whose written request is received by the buyer no later than six months after the date of the bulk sale;

(ii) permitting any claimant to inspect and copy the list at any reasonable hour upon request received by the buyer no later than six months after the date of the bulk sale; or

(iii) filing a copy of the list in the office of the [Secretary of State] no later than the time for giving a notice of the bulk sale (Section 6-105(5)). A list filed in accordance with this subparagraph must state the individual, partnership, or corporate name and a mailing address of the seller.

(2) A buyer who gives notice in accordance with Section 6-105(2) is excused from complying with the requirements of subsections (1) (b) and (1) (f).

§ 6-105. Notice to Claimants.

(1) Except as otherwise provided in subsection (2), to comply with Section 6-104(1) (d), the buyer shall send or deliver a written notice of the bulk sale to each claimant on the list of claimants (Section 6-104(1) (b)) and to any other claimant of whom the buyer has knowledge at the time the notice of the bulk sale is sent or delivered.

(2) A buyer may comply with Section 6-104(1) (d) by filing a written notice of the bulk sale in the office of the [Secretary of State] if:

(a) on the date of the bulk-sale agreement the seller has 200 or more claimants, exclusive of claimants holding secured or matured claims for employment compensation and benefits, including commissions and vacation, severance, and sick-leave pay; or

(b) the buyer has received a verified statement from the seller stating that, as of the date of the bulk-sale agreement, the number of claimants, exclusive of claimants holding secured or matured claims for employment compensation and benefits, including commissions and vacation, severance, and sick-leave pay, is 200 or more.

(3) The written notice of the bulk sale must be accompanied by a copy of the schedule of distribution (Section 6-106(1)) and state at least:

(a) that the seller and buyer have entered into an agreement for a sale that may constitute a bulk sale under the laws of the State of_______;

(b) the date of the agreement;

(c) the date on or after which more than ten percent of the assets were or will be transferred;

(d) the date on or after which more than ten percent of the net contract price was or will be paid, if the date is not stated in the schedule of distribution;

(e) the name and a mailing address of the seller;

(f) any other business name and address listed by the seller pursuant to Section 6-104(1) (a);

(g) the name of the buyer and an address of the buyer from which information concerning the sale can be obtained;

(h) a statement indicating the type of assets or describing the assets item by item;

(i) the manner in which the buyer will make available the list of claimants (Section 6-104(1) (f)), if applicable; and

(j) if the sale is in total or partial satisfaction of an antecedent debt owed by the seller, the amount of the debt to be satisfied and the name of the person to whom it is owed.

(4) For purposes of subsections (3) (e) and (3) (g), the name of a person is the person's individual, partnership, or corporate name.

(5) The buyer shall give notice of the bulk sale not less than 45 days before the date of the bulk sale and, if the buyer gives notice in accordance with subsection (1), not more than 30 days after obtaining the list of claimants.

(6) A written notice substantially complying with the requirements of subsection (3) is effective even though it contains minor errors that are not seriously misleading.

(7) A form substantially as follows is sufficient to comply with subsection (3):

Notice of Sale

(1) _______, whose address is _______, is described in this notice as the "seller."

(2) _______, whose address is _______, is described in this notice as the "buyer."

(3) The seller has disclosed to the buyer that within the past three years the seller has used other business names, operated at other addresses, or both, as follows: __________________.

(4) The seller and the buyer have entered into an agreement dated _______, for a sale that may constitute a bulk sale under the laws of the state of

(5) The date on or after which more than ten percent of the assets that are the subject of the sale were or will be transferred is _______, and [if not stated in the schedule of distribution] the date on or after which more than ten percent of the net contract price was or will be paid is _______.

(6) The following assets are the subject of the sale: _______.

(7) [If applicable] The buyer will make available to claimants of the seller a list of the seller's claimants in the following manner: ______________.

(8) [If applicable] The sale is to satisfy $__________ of an antecedent debt owed by the seller to

(9) A copy of the schedule of distribution of the net contract price accompanies this notice.

[End of Notice]

§ 6-106. Schedule of Distribution.

(1) The seller and buyer shall agree on how the net contract price is to be distributed and set forth their agreement in a written schedule of distribution.

(2) The schedule of distribution may provide for distribution to any person at any time, including distribution of the entire net contract price to the seller.

(3) The buyer's undertakings in the schedule of distribution run only to the seller. However, a buyer who fails to distribute the net contract price in accordance with the buyer's undertakings in the schedule of distribution is liable to a creditor only as provided in Section 6-107(1).

(4) If the buyer undertakes in the schedule of distribution to distribute any part of the net contract price to a person other than the seller, and, after the buyer has given notice in accordance with Section 6-105, some or all of the anticipated net contract price is or becomes unavailable for distribution as a consequence of the buyer's or seller's having complied with an order of court, legal process, statute, or rule of law, the buyer is excused from any obli-

gation arising under this Article or under any contract with the seller to distribute the net contract price in accordance with the buyer's undertakings in the schedule if the buyer:

(a) distributes the net contract price remaining available in accordance with any priorities for payment stated in the schedule of distribution and, to the extent that the price is insufficient to pay all the debts having a given priority, distributes the price pro rata among those debts shown in the schedule as having the same priority;

(b) distributes the net contract price remaining available in accordance with an order of court;

(c) commences a proceeding for interpleader in a court of competent jurisdiction and is discharged from the proceeding; or

(d) reaches a new agreement with the seller for the distribution of the net contract price remaining available, sets forth the new agreement in an amended schedule of distribution, gives notice of the amended schedule, and distributes the net contract price remaining available in accordance with the buyer's undertakings in the amended schedule.

(5) The notice under subsection (4) (d) must identify the buyer and the seller, state the filing number, if any, of the original notice, set forth the amended schedule, and be given in accordance with subsection (1) or (2) of Section 6-105, whichever is applicable, at least 14 days before the buyer distributes any part of the net contract price remaining available.

(6) If the seller undertakes in the schedule of distribution to distribute any part of the net contract price, and, after the buyer has given notice in accordance with Section 6-105, some or all of the anticipated net contract price is or becomes unavailable for distribution as a consequence of the buyer's or seller's having complied with an order of court, legal process, statute, or rule of law, the seller and any person in control of the seller are excused from any obligation arising under this Article or under any agreement with the buyer to distribute the net contract price in accordance with the seller's undertakings in the schedule if the seller:

(a) distributes the net contract price remaining available in accordance with any priorities for payment stated in the schedule of distribution and, to the extent that the price is insufficient to pay all the debts having a given priority, distributes the price pro rata among those debts shown in the schedule as having the same priority;

(b) distributes the net contract price remaining available in accordance with an order of court;

(c) commences a proceeding for interpleader in a court of competent jurisdiction and is discharged from the proceeding; or

(d) prepares a written amended schedule of distribution of the net contract price remaining available for distribution, gives notice of the amended schedule, and distributes the net contract price remaining available in accordance with the amended schedule.

(7) The notice under subsection (6) (d) must identify the buyer and the seller, state the filing number, if any, of the original notice, set forth the amended schedule, and be given in accordance with subsection (1) or (2) of Section 6-105, whichever is applicable, at least 14 days before the seller distributes any part of the net contract price remaining available.

§ 6-107. Liability for Noncompliance.

(1) Except as provided in subsection (3), and subject to the limitation in subsection (4):

(a) a buyer who fails to comply with the requirements of Section 6-104(1) (e) with respect to a creditor is liable to the creditor for damages in the amount of the claim, reduced by any amount that the creditor would not have realized if the buyer had complied; and

(b) a buyer who fails to comply with the requirements of any other subsection of Section 6-104 with respect to a claimant is liable to the claimant for damages in the amount of the claim, reduced by any amount that the claimant would not have realized if the buyer had complied.

(2) In an action under subsection (1), the creditor has the burden of establishing the validity and amount of the claim, and the buyer has the burden of establishing the amount that the creditor would not have realized if the buyer had complied.

(3) A buyer who:

(a) made a good faith and commercially reasonable effort to comply with the requirements of Section 6-104(1) or to exclude the sale from the application of this Article under Section 6-103(3); or

(b) on or after the date of the bulk-sale agreement, but before the date of the bulk sale, held a good faith and commercially reasonable belief that this Article does not apply to the particular sale is not liable to creditors for failure to comply with the requirements of Section 6-104. The buyer has the burden of establishing the good faith and commercial reasonableness of the effort or belief.

(4) In a single bulk sale the cumulative liability of the buyer for failure to comply with the requirements of Section 6-104(1) may not exceed an amount equal to:

(a) if the assets consist only of inventory and equipment, twice the net contract price, less the amount of any part of the net contract price paid to or applied for the benefit of the seller or a creditor; or

(b) if the assets include property other than inventory and equipment, twice the net value of the inventory and equipment less the amount of the portion of any part of the net contract price paid to or applied for the benefit of the seller or a creditor which is allocable to the inventory and equipment.

(5) For the purposes of subsection (4) (b), the "net value" of an asset is the value of the asset less (i) the amount of any proceeds of the sale of an asset, to the extent the proceeds are applied in partial or total satisfaction of a debt secured by the asset and (ii) the amount of any debt to the extent it is secured by a security interest or lien that is enforceable against the asset before and after it has been sold to a buyer. If a debt is secured by an asset and other property of the seller, the amount of the debt secured by a security interest or lien that is enforceable against the asset is determined by multiplying the debt by a fraction, the numerator of which is the value of the asset on the

date of the bulk sale and the denominator of which is the value of all property securing the debt on the date of the bulk sale. The portion of a part of the net contract price paid to or applied for the benefit of the seller or a creditor that is "allocable to the inventory and equipment" is the portion that bears the same ratio to that part of the net contract price as the net value of the inventory and equipment bears to the net value of all of the assets.

(6) A payment made by the buyer to a person to whom the buyer is, or believes he [or she] is, liable under subsection (1) reduces pro tanto the buyer's cumulative liability under subsection (4).

(7) No action may be brought under subsection (1) (b) by or on behalf of a claimant whose claim is unliquidated or contingent.

(8) A buyer's failure to comply with the requirements of Section 6-104(1) does not (i) impair the buyer's rights in or title to the assets, (ii) render the sale ineffective, void, or voidable, (iii) entitle a creditor to more than a single satisfaction of his [or her] claim, or (iv) create liability other than as provided in this Article.

(9) Payment of the buyer's liability under subsection (1) discharges pro tanto the seller's debt to the creditor.

(10) Unless otherwise agreed, a buyer has an immediate right of reimbursement from the seller for any amount paid to a creditor in partial or total satisfaction of the buyer's liability under subsection (1).

(11) If the seller is an organization, a person who is in direct or indirect control of the seller, and who knowingly, intentionally, and without legal justification fails, or causes the seller to fail, to distribute the net contract price in accordance with the schedule of distribution is liable to any creditor to whom the seller undertook to make payment under the schedule for damages caused by the failure.

§ 6-108. Bulk Sales by Auction; Bulk Sales Conducted by Liquidator.

(1) Sections 6-104, 6-105, 6-106, and 6-107 apply to a bulk sale by auction and a bulk sale conducted by a liquidator on the seller's behalf with the following modifications:

(a) "buyer" refers to auctioneer or liquidator, as the case may be;

(b) "net contract price" refers to net proceeds of the auction or net proceeds of the sale, as the case may be;

(c) the written notice required under Section 6-105 (3) must be accompanied by a copy of the schedule of distribution (Section 6-106(1)) and state at least:

(i) that the seller and the auctioneer or liquidator have entered into an agreement for auction or liquidation services that may constitute an agreement to make a bulk sale under the laws of the State of _______.

(ii) the date of the agreement;

(iii) the date on or after which the auction began or will begin or the date on or after which the liquidator began or will begin to sell assets on the seller's behalf;

(iv) the date on or after which more than ten percent of the net proceeds of the sale were or will be paid, if the date is not stated in the schedule of distribution;

(v) the name and a mailing address of the seller;

(vi) any other business name and address listed by the seller pursuant to Section 6-104(1) (a);

(vii) the name of the auctioneer or liquidator and an address of the auctioneer or liquidator from which information concerning the sale can be obtained;

(viii) a statement indicating the type of assets or describing the assets item by item;

(ix) the manner in which the auctioneer or liquidator will make available the list of claimants (Section 6-104(1) (f), if applicable; and

(x) if the sale is in total or partial satisfaction of an antecedent debt owed by the seller, the amount of the debt to be satisfied and the name of the person to whom it is owed; and

(d) in a single bulk sale the cumulative liability of the auctioneer or liquidator for failure to comply with the requirements of this section may not exceed the amount of the net proceeds of the sale allocable to inventory and equipment sold less the amount of the portion of any part of the net proceeds paid to or applied for the benefit of a creditor which is allocable to the inventory and equipment.

(2) A payment made by the auctioneer or liquidator to a person to whom the auctioneer or liquidator is, or believes he [or she] is, liable under this section reduces pro tanto the auctioneer's or liquidator's cumulative liability under subsection (1) (d).

(3) A form substantially as follows is sufficient to comply with subsection (l)(c):

Notice of Sale

(1) _______, whose address is _______, is described in this notice as the "seller."

(2) _______, whose address is _______, is described in this notice as the "auctioneer" or "liquidator."

(3) The seller has disclosed to the auctioneer or liquidator that within the past three years the seller has used other business names, operated at other addresses, or both, as follows: _______.

(4) The seller and the auctioneer or liquidator have entered into an agreement dated _________ for auction or liquidation services that may constitute an agreement to make a bulk sale under the laws of the State of

(5) The date on or after which the auction began or will begin or the date on or after which the liquidator began or will begin to sell assets on the seller's behalf is _______, and [if not stated in the schedule of distribution] the date on or after which more than ten percent of the net proceeds of the sale were or will be paid is ________.

(6) The following assets are the subject of the sale: ________.

(7) [If applicable] The auctioneer or liquidator will make available to claimants of the seller a list of the seller's claimants in the following manner: ________.

(8) [If applicable] The sale is to satisfy $______ of an antecedent debt owed by the seller to ________.

(9) A copy of the schedule of distribution of the net proceeds accompanies this notice.

[End of Notice]

(4) A person who buys at a bulk sale by auction or conducted by a liquidator need not comply with the requirements of Section 6-104(1) and is not liable for the failure of an auctioneer or liquidator to comply with the requirements of this section.

§ 6-109. What Constitutes Filing; Duties of Filing Officer; Information From Filing Officer.

(1) Presentation of a notice or list of claimants for filing and tender of the filing fee or acceptance of the notice or list by the filing officer constitutes filing under this Article.

(2) The filing officer shall:

(a) mark each notice or list with a file number and with the date and hour of filing;

(b) hold the notice or list or a copy for public inspection;

(c) index the notice or list according to each name given for the seller and for the buyer; and

(d) note in the index the file number and the addresses of the seller and buyer given in the notice or list.

(3) If the person filing a notice or list furnishes the filing officer with a copy, the filing officer upon request shall note upon the copy the file number and date and hour of the filing of the original and send or deliver the copy to the person.

(4) The fee for filing and indexing and for stamping a copy furnished by the person filing to show the date and place of filing is $________ for the first page and $________ for each additional page. The fee for indexing each name more than two is $_______.

(5) Upon request of any person, the filing officer shall issue a certificate showing whether any notice or list with respect to a particular seller or buyer is on file on the date and hour stated in the certificate. If a notice or list is on file, the certificate must give the date and hour of filing of each notice or list and the name and address of each seller, buyer, auctioneer, or liquidator. The fee for the certificate is $_________ if the request for the certificate is in the standard form prescribed by the [Secretary of State] and otherwise is $_______. Upon request of any person, the filing officer shall furnish a copy of any filed notice or list for a fee of $_______.

(6) The filing officer shall keep each notice or list for two years after it is filed.

§ 6-110. Limitation of Actions.

(1) Except as provided in subsection (2), an action under this Article against a buyer, auctioneer, or liquidator must be commenced within one year after the date of the bulk sale.

(2) If the buyer, auctioneer, or liquidator conceals the fact that the sale has occurred, the limitation is tolled and an action under this Article may be commenced within the earlier of (i) one year after the person bringing the action discovers that the sale has occurred or (ii) one year after the person bringing the action should have discovered that the sale has occurred, but no later than two years after the date of the bulk sale. Complete noncompliance with the requirements of this Article does not of itself constitute concealment.

(3) An action under Section 6-107(11) must be commenced within one year after the alleged violation occurs.]

ARTICLE 7 / Warehouse Receipts, Bills of Lading and Other Documents of Title

PART 1 General

§ 7-101. Short Title. This Article shall be known and may be cited as Uniform Commercial Code—Documents of Title.

§ 7-102. Definitions and Index of Definitions.

(1) In this Article, unless the context otherwise requires:

(a) "Bailee" means the person who by a warehouse receipt, bill of lading or other document of title acknowledges possession of goods and contracts to deliver them.

(b) "Consignee" means the person named in a bill to whom or to whose order the bill promises delivery.

(c) "Consignor" means the person named in a bill as the person from whom the goods have been received for shipment.

(d) "Delivery order" means a written order to deliver goods directed to a warehouseman, carrier or other person who in the ordinary course of business issues warehouse receipts or bills of lading.

(e) "Document" means document of title as defined in the general definitions in Article 1 (Section 1-201).

(f) "Goods" means all things which are treated as movable for the purposes of a contract of storage or transportation.

(g) "Issuer" means a bailee who issues a document except that in relation to an unaccepted delivery order it means the person who orders the possessor of goods to deliver. Issuer includes any person for whom an agent or employee purports to act in issuing a document if the agent or employee has real or apparent authority to issue documents, notwithstanding that the issuer received no goods or that the goods were misdescribed or that in any other respect the agent or employee violated his instructions.

(h) "Warehouseman" is a person engaged in the business of storing goods for hire.

(2) Other definitions applying to this Article or to specified Parts thereof, and the sections in which they appear are:

"Duly negotiate". Section 7-501.

"Person entitled under the document." Section 7-403(4).

(3) Definitions in other Articles applying to this Article and the sections in which they appear are:

"Contract for sale". Section 2-106.

"Overseas". Section 2-323.

"Receipt" of goods. Section 2-103.

(4) In addition Article 1 contains general definitions and principles of construction and interpretation applicable throughout this Article.

§ 7-103. Relation of Article to Treaty, Statute, Tariff, Classification or Regulation. To the extent that any treaty or statute of the United States, regulatory statute of this State or tariff, classification or regulation filed or issued pursuant thereto is applicable, the provisions of this Article are subject thereto.

§ 7-104. Negotiable and Non-negotiable Warehouse Receipt, Bill of Lading or Other Document of Title.

(1) A warehouse receipt, bill of lading or other document of title is negotiable

(a) if by its terms the goods are to be delivered to bearer or to the order of a named person; or

(b) where recognized in overseas trade, if it runs to a named person or assigns.

(2) Any other document is non-negotiable. A bill of lading in which it is stated that the goods are consigned to a named person is not made negotiable by a provision that the goods are to be delivered only against a written order signed by the same or another named person.

§ 7-105. Construction Against Negative Implication. The omission from either Part 2 or Part 3 of this Article of a provision corresponding to a provision made in the other Part does not imply that a corresponding rule of law is not applicable.

PART 2 Warehouse Receipts: Special Provisions

§ 7-201. Who May Issue a Warehouse Receipt; Storage Under Government Bond.

(1) A warehouse receipt may be issued by any warehouseman.

(2) Where goods including distilled spirits and agricultural commodities are stored under a statute requiring a bond against withdrawal or a license for the issuance of receipts in the nature of warehouse receipts, a receipt issued for the goods has like effect as a warehouse receipt even though issued by a person who is the owner of the goods and is not a warehouseman.

§ 7-202. Form of Warehouse Receipt; Essential Terms; Optional Terms.

(1) A warehouse receipt need not be in any particular form.

(2) Unless a warehouse receipt embodies within its written or printed terms each of the following, the warehouseman is liable for damages caused by the omission to a person injured thereby:

(a) the location of the warehouse where the goods are stored;

(b) the date of issue of the receipt;

(c) the consecutive number of the receipt;

(d) a statement whether the goods received will be delivered to the bearer, to a specified person, or to a specified person or his order;

(e) the rate of storage and handling charges, except that where goods are stored under a field warehousing arrangement a statement of that fact is sufficient on a non-negotiable receipt;

(f) a description of the goods or of the packages containing them;

(g) the signature of the warehouseman, which may be made by his authorized agent;

(h) if the receipt is issued for goods of which the warehouseman is owner, either solely or jointly or in common with others, the fact of such ownership; and

(i) a statement of the amount of advances made and of liabilities incurred for which the warehouseman claims a lien or security interest (Section 7-209). If the precise amount of such advances made or of such liabilities incurred is, at the time of the issue of the receipt, unknown to the warehouseman or to his agent who issues it, a statement of the fact that advances have been made or liabilities incurred and the purpose thereof is sufficient.

(3) A warehouseman may insert in his receipt any other terms which are not contrary to the provisions of this Act and do not impair his obligation of delivery (Section 7-403) or his duty of care (Section 7-204). Any contrary provisions shall be ineffective.

§ 7-203. Liability for Non-receipt or Misdescription. A party to or purchaser for value in good faith of a document of title other than a bill of lading relying in either case upon the description therein of the goods may recover from the issuer damages caused by the non-receipt or misdescription of the goods, except to the extent that the document conspicuously indicates that the issuer does not know whether any part or all of the goods in fact were received or conform to the description, as where the description is in terms of marks or labels or kind, quantity or condition, or the receipt or description is qualified by "contents, condition and quality unknown", "said to contain" or the like, if such indication be true, or the party or purchaser otherwise has notice.

§ 7-204. Duty of Care; Contractual Limitation of Warehouseman's Liability.

(1) A warehouseman is liable for damages for loss of or injury to the goods caused by his failure to exercise such care in regard to them as a reasonably careful man would exercise under like circumstances but unless otherwise agreed he is not liable for damages which could not have been avoided by the exercise of such care.

(2) Damages may be limited by a term in the warehouse receipt or storage agreement limiting the amount of liability in case of loss or damage, and setting forth a specific liability per article or item, or value per unit of weight, beyond which the warehouseman shall not be liable; provided, however, that such liability may on written request of the bailor at the time of signing such storage agreement or within a reasonable time after receipt of the warehouse receipt be increased on part or all of the goods thereunder, in which event increased rates may be charged based on such increased valuation, but that no such increase shall be permitted contrary to a lawful limitation of liability contained in the warehouseman's tariff, if any. No such limitation is effective with respect to the warehouseman's liability for conversion to his own use.

(3) Reasonable provisions as to the time and manner of presenting claims and instituting actions based on the bailment may be included in the warehouse receipt or tariff.

(4) This section does not impair or repeal ...

Note: *Insert in subsection (4) a reference to any statute which imposes a higher responsibility upon the warehouseman or invalidates contractual limitations which would be permissible under this Article.*

§ 7-205. Title Under Warehouse Receipt Defeated in Certain Cases. A buyer in the ordinary course of business of fungible goods sold and delivered by a warehouseman who is also in the business of buying and selling such goods takes free of any claim under a warehouse receipt even though it has been duly negotiated.

§ 7-206. Termination of Storage at Warehouseman's Option.

(1) A warehouseman may on notifying the person on whose account the goods are held and any other person known to claim

an interest in the goods require payment of any charges and removal of the goods from the warehouse at the termination of the period of storage fixed by the document, or, if no period is fixed, within a stated period not less than thirty days after the notification. If the goods are not removed before the date specified in the notification, the warehouseman may sell them in accordance with the provisions of the section on enforcement of a warehouseman's lien (Section 7-210).

(2) If a warehouseman in good faith believes that the goods are about to deteriorate or decline in value to less than the amount of his lien within the time prescribed in subsection (1) for notification, advertisement and sale, the warehouseman may specify in the notification any reasonable shorter time for removal of the goods and in case the goods are nor removed, may sell them at public sale held not less than one week after a single advertisement or posting.

(3) If as a result of a quality or condition of the goods of which the warehouseman had no notice at the time of deposit the goods are a hazard to other property or to the warehouse or to persons, the warehouseman may sell the goods at public or private sale without advertisement on reasonable notification to all persons known to claim an interest in the goods. If the warehouseman after a reasonable effort is unable to sell the goods he may dispose of them in any lawful manner and shall incur no liability by reason of such disposition.

(4) The warehouseman must deliver the goods to any person entitled to them under this Article upon due demand made at any time prior to sale or other disposition under this section.

(5) The warehouseman may satisfy his lien from the proceeds of any sale or disposition under this section but must hold the balance for delivery on the demand of any person to whom he would have been bound to deliver the goods.

§ 7-207. Goods Must Be Kept Separate; Fungible Goods.

(1) Unless the warehouse receipt otherwise provides, a warehouseman must keep separate the goods covered by each receipt so as to permit at all times identification and delivery of those goods except that different lots of fungible goods may be commingled.

(2) Fungible goods so commingled are owned in common by the persons entitled thereto and the warehouseman is severally liable to each owner for that owner's share. Where because of overissue a mass of fungible goods is insufficient to meet all the receipts which the warehouseman has issued against it, the persons entitled include all holders to whom overissued receipts have been duly negotiated.

§ 7-208. Altered Warehouse Receipts. Where a blank in a negotiable warehouse receipt has been filled in without authority, a purchaser for value and without notice of the want of authority may treat the insertion as authorized. Any other unauthorized alteration leaves any receipt enforceable against the issuer according to its original tenor.

§ 7-209. Lien of Warehouseman.

(1) A warehouseman has a lien against the bailor on the goods covered by a warehouse receipt or on the proceeds thereof in his possession for charges for storage or transportation (including demurrage and terminal charges), insurance, labor, or charges present or future in relation to the goods, and for expenses necessary for preservation of the goods or reasonably incurred in their sale pursuant to law. If the person on whose account the goods are held is liable for like charges or expenses in relation to other goods whenever deposited and it is stated in the receipt that a lien is claimed for charges and expenses in relation to other goods, the warehouseman also has a lien against him for such charges and expenses whether or not the other goods have been delivered by the warehouseman. But against a person to whom a negotiable warehouse receipt is duly negotiated a warehouseman's lien is limited to charges in an amount or at a rate specified on the receipt or if no charges are so specified then to a reasonable charge for storage of the goods covered by the receipt subsequent to the date of the receipt.

(2) The warehouseman may also reserve a security interest against the bailor for a maximum amount specified on the receipt for charges other than those specified in subsection (1), such as for money advanced and interest. Such a security interest is governed by the Article on Secured Transactions (Article 9).

(3)

(a) A warehouseman's lien for charges and expenses under subsection (1) or a security interest under subsection (2) is also effective against any person who so entrusted the bailor with possession of the goods that a pledge of them by him to a good faith purchaser for value would have been valid but is not effective against a person as to whom the document confers no right in the goods covered by it under Section 7-503.

(b) A warehouseman's lien on household goods for charges and expenses in relation to the goods under subsection (1) is also effective against all persons if the depositor was the legal possessor of the goods at the time of deposit. "Household goods" means furniture, furnishings and personal effects used by the depositor in a dwelling.

(4) A warehouseman loses his lien on any goods which he voluntarily delivers or which he unjustifiably refuses to deliver.

As amended in 1966.

§ 7-210. Enforcement of Warehouseman's Lien.

(1) Except as provided in subsection (2), a warehouseman's lien may be enforced by public or private sale of the goods in block or in parcels, at any time or place and on any terms which are commercially reasonable, after notifying all persons known to claim an interest in the goods. Such notification must include a statement of the amount due, the nature of the proposed sale and the time and place of any public sale. The fact that a better price could have been obtained by a sale at a different time or in a different method from that selected by the warehouseman is not of itself sufficient to establish that the sale was not made in a commercially reasonable manner. If the warehouseman either sells the goods in the usual manner in any recognized market therefore, or if he sells at the price current in such market at the time of his sale, or if he has otherwise sold in conformity with commercially reasonable practices among dealers in the type of goods sold, he has sold in a commercially reasonable manner. A sale of more goods than

apparently necessary to be offered to insure satisfaction of the obligation is not commercially reasonable except in cases covered by the preceding sentence.

(2) A warehouseman's lien on goods other than goods stored by a merchant in the course of his business may be enforced only as follows:

(a) All persons known to claim an interest in the goods must be notified.

(b) The notification must be delivered in person or sent by registered or certified letter to the last known address of any person to be notified.

(c) The notification must include an itemized statement of the claim, a description of the goods subject to the lien, a demand for payment within a specified time not less than ten days after receipt of the notification, and a conspicuous statement that unless the claim is paid within that time the goods will be advertised for sale and sold by auction at a specified time and place.

(d) The sale must conform to the terms of the notification.

(e) The sale must be held at the nearest suitable place to that where the goods are held or stored.

(f) After the expiration of the time given in the notification, an advertisement of the sale must be published once a week for two weeks consecutively in a newspaper of general circulation where the sale is to be held. The advertisement must include a description of the goods, the name of the person on whose account they are being held, and the time and place of the sale. The sale must take place at least fifteen days after the first publication. If there is no newspaper of general circulation where the sale is to be held, the advertisement must be posted at least ten days before the sale in not less than six conspicuous places in the neighborhood of the proposed sale.

(3) Before any sale pursuant to this section any person claiming a right in the goods may pay the amount necessary to satisfy the lien and the reasonable expenses incurred under this section. In that event the goods must not be sold, but must be retained by the warehouse man subject to the terms of the receipt and this Article.

(4) The warehouseman may buy at any public sale pursuant to this section.

(5) A purchaser in good faith of goods sold to enforce a warehouseman's lien takes the goods free of any rights of persons against whom the lien was valid, despite noncompliance by the warehouseman with the requirements of this section.

(6) The warehouseman may satisfy his lien from the proceeds of any sale pursuant to this section but must hold the balance, if any, for delivery on demand to any person to whom he would have been bound to deliver the goods.

(7) The rights provided by this section shall be in addition to all other rights allowed by law to a creditor against his debtor.

(8) Where a lien is on goods stored by a merchant in the course of his business the lien may be enforced in accordance with either subsection (1) or (2).

(9) The warehouseman is liable for damages caused by failure to comply with the requirements for sale under this section and in case of willful violation is liable for conversion.

As amended in 1962.

PART 3 Bills of Lading: Special Provisions

§ 7-301. Liability for Non-receipt or Misdescription; "Said to Contain"; "Shipper's Load and Count"; Improper Handling.

(1) A consignee of a non-negotiable bill who has given value in good faith or a holder to whom a negotiable bill has been duly negotiated relying in either case upon the description therein of the goods, or upon the date therein shown, may recover from the issuer damages caused by the misdating of the bill or the non-receipt or misdescription of the goods, except to the extent that the document indicates that the issuer does not know whether any part or all of the goods in fact were received or conform to the description, as where the description is in terms of marks or labels or kind, quantity, or condition or the receipt or description is qualified by "contents or condition of contents of packages unknown", "said to contain", "shipper's weight, load and count" or the like, if such indication be true.

(2) When goods are loaded by an issuer who is a common carrier, the issuer must count the packages of goods if package freight and ascertain the kind and quantity if bulk freight. In such cases "shipper's weight, load and count" or other words indicating that the description was made by the shipper are ineffective except as to freight concealed by packages.

(3) When bulk freight is loaded by a shipper who makes available to the issuer adequate facilities for weighing such freight, an issuer who is a common carrier must ascertain the kind and quantity within a reasonable time after receiving the written request of the shipper to do so. In such cases "shipper's weight" or other words of like purport are ineffective.

(4) The issuer may be inserting in the bill the words "shipper's weight, load and count" or other words of like purport indicate that the goods were loaded by the shipper, and if such statement be true the issuer shall not be liable for damages caused by the improper loading. But their omission does not imply liability for such damages.

(5) The shipper shall be deemed to have guaranteed to the issuer the accuracy at the time of shipment of the description, marks, labels, number, kind, quantity, condition and weight, as furnished by him; and the shipper shall indemnify the issuer against damage caused by inaccuracies in such particulars. The right of the issuer to such indemnity shall in no way limit his responsibility and liability under the contract of carriage to any person other than the shipper.

§ 7-302. Through Bills of Lading and Similar Documents.

(1) The issuer of a through bill of lading or other document embodying an undertaking to be performed in part by persons acting as its agents or by connecting carriers is liable to anyone entitled to recover on the document for any breach by such other persons or by a connecting carrier of its obligation under the document but to the extent that the bill covers an undertaking to be performed overseas or in territory not contiguous to the continental United States or an undertaking including matters other than transportation this liability may be varied by agreement of the parties.

(2) Where goods covered by a through bill of lading or other document embodying an undertaking to be performed in part by persons other than the issuer are received by any such person, he is subject with respect to his own performance while the goods are in his possession to the obligation of the issuer. His obligation is discharged by delivery of the goods to another such person pursuant to the document, and does not include liability for breach by any other such persons or by the issuer.
(3) The issuer of such through bill of lading or other document shall be entitled to recover from the connecting carrier or such other person in possession of the goods when the breach of the obligation under the document occurred, the amount it may be required to pay to anyone entitled to recover on the document therefor, as may be evidenced by any receipt, judgment, or transcript thereof, and the amount of any expense reasonably incurred by it in defending any action brought by anyone entitled to recover on the document therefore.

§ 7-303. Diversion; Reconsignment; Change of Instructions.
(1) Unless the bill of lading otherwise provides, the carrier may deliver the goods to a person or destination other than that stated in the bill or may otherwise dispose of the goods on instructions from

(a) the holder of a negotiable bill; or
(b) the consignor on a non-negotiable bill notwithstanding contrary instructions from the consignee; or
(c) the consignee on a non-negotiable bill in the absence of contrary instructions from the consignor; if the goods have arrived at the billed destination or if the consignee is in possession of the bill; or
(d) the consignee on a non-negotiable bill if he is entitled as against the consignor to dispose of them.

(2) Unless such instructions are noted on a negotiable bill of lading, a person to whom the bill is duly negotiated can hold the bailee according to the original terms.

§ 7-304. Bills of Lading in a Set.
(1) Except where customary in overseas transportation, a bill of lading must not be issued in a set of parts. The issuer is liable for damages caused by violation of this subsection.
(2) Where a bill of lading is lawfully drawn in a set of parts, each of which is numbered and expressed to be valid only if the goods have not been delivered against any other part, the whole of the parts constitute one bill.
(3) Where a bill of lading is lawfully issued in a set of parts and different parts are negotiated to different persons, the title of the holder to whom the first due negotiation is made prevails as to both the document and the goods even though any later holder may have received the goods from the carrier in good faith and discharged the carrier's obligation by surrender of his part.
(4) Any person who negotiates or transfers a single part of a bill of lading drawn in a set is liable to holders of that part as if it were the whole set.
(5) The bailee is obliged to deliver in accordance with Part 4 of this Article against the first presented part of a bill of lading lawfully drawn in a set. Such delivery discharges the bailee's obligation on the whole bill.

§ 7-305. Destination Bills.
(1) Instead of issuing a bill of lading to the consignor at the place of shipment a carrier may at the request of the consignor procure the bill to be issued at destination or at any other place designated in the request.
(2) Upon request of anyone entitled as against the carrier to control the goods while in transit and on surrender of any outstanding bill of lading or other receipt covering such goods, the issuer may procure a substitute bill to be issued at any place designated in the request.

§ 7-306. Altered Bills of Lading. An unauthorized alteration or filling in of a blank in a bill of lading leaves the bill enforceable according to its original tenor.

§ 7-307. Lien of Carrier.
(1) A carrier has a lien on the goods covered by a bill of lading for charges subsequent to the date of its receipt of the goods for storage or transportation (including demurrage and terminal charges) and for expenses necessary for preservation of the goods incident to their transportation or reasonably incurred in their sale pursuant to law. But against a purchaser for value of a negotiable bill of lading a carrier's lien is limited to charges stated in the bill or the applicable tariffs, or if no charges are stated then to a reasonable charge.
(2) A lien for charges and expenses under subsection (1) on goods which the carrier was required by law to receive for transportation is effective against the consignor or any person entitled to the goods unless the carrier had notice that the consignor lacked authority to subject the goods to such charges and expenses. Any other lien under subsection (1) is effective against the consignor and in any person who permitted the bailor to have control or possession of the goods unless the carrier had notice that the bailor lacked such authority.
(3) A carrier loses his lien on any goods which he voluntarily delivers or which he unjustifiably refuses to deliver.

§ 7-308. Enforcement of Carrier's Lien.
(1) A carrier's lien may be enforced by public or private sale of the goods, in block or in parcels, at any time or place and on any terms which are commercially reasonable, after notifying all persons known to claim an interest in the goods. Such notification must include a statement of the amount due, the nature of the proposed sale and the time and place of any public sale. The fact that a better price could have been obtained by a sale at a different time or in a different method from that selected by the carrier is not of itself sufficient to establish that the sale was not made in a commercially reasonable manner. If the carrier either sells the goods in the usual manner in any recognized market therefor or if he sells at the price current in such market at the time 6f his sale or if he has otherwise sold in conformity with commercially reasonable practices among dealers in the type of goods sold he has sold in a commercially reasonable manner. A sale of more goods than apparently necessary to be offered to ensure satisfaction of the obligation is not commercially reasonable except in cases covered by the preceding sentence.
(2) Before any sale pursuant to this section any person claiming a right in the goods may pay the amount necessary to satisfy the

lien and the reasonable expenses incurred under this section. In that event the goods must not be sold, but must be retained by the carrier subject to the terms of the bill and this Article.

(3) The carrier may buy at any public sale pursuant to this section.

(4) A purchaser in good faith of goods sold to enforce a carrier's lien takes the goods free of any rights of persons against whom the lien was valid, despite noncompliance by the carrier with the requirements of this section.

(5) The carrier may satisfy his lien from the proceeds of any sale pursuant to this section but must hold the balance, if any; for delivery on demand to any person to whom he would have been bound to deliver the goods.

(6) The rights provided by this section shall be in addition to all other rights allowed by law to a creditor against his debtor.

(7) A carrier's lien may be enforced in accordance with either subsection (1) or the procedure set forth in subsection (2) of Section 7-210.

(8) The carrier is liable for damages caused by failure to comply with the requirements for sale under this section and in case of willful violation is liable for conversion.

§ 7-309. Duty of Care; Contractual Limitation of Carrier's Liability.

(1) A carrier who issues a bill of lading whether negotiable or non-negotiable must exercise the degree of care in relation to the goods which a reasonably careful man would exercise under like circumstances. This subsection does not repeal or change any law or rule of law which imposes liability upon a common carrier for damages not caused by its negligence.

(2) Damages may be limited by a provision that the carrier's liability shall not exceed a value stated in the document if the carrier's rates are dependent upon value and the consignor by the carrier's tariff is afforded an opportunity to declare a higher value or a value as lawfully provided in the tariff, or where no tariff is filed he is otherwise advised of such opportunity; but no such limitation is effective with respect to the carrier's liability for conversion to its own use.

(3) Reasonable provisions as to the time and manner of presenting claims and instituting actions based on the shipment may be included in a bill of lading or tariff.

PART 4 Warehouse Receipts and Bills of Lading: General Obligations

§ 7-401. Irregularities in Issue of Receipt or Bill or Conduct of Issuer. The obligations imposed by this Article on an issuer apply to a document of title regardless of the fact that

(a) the document may not comply with the requirements of this Article or of any other law or regulation regarding its issue, form or content; or

(b) the issuer may have violated laws regulating the conduct of his business; or

(c) the goods covered by the document were owned by the bailee at the time the document was issued; or

(d) the person issuing the document does not come within the definition of warehouseman if it purports to be a warehouse receipt

§ 7-402. Duplicate Receipt or Bill; Overissue. Neither a duplicate nor any other document of the title purporting to cover goods already represented by an outstanding document of the same issuer confers any right in the goods, except as provided in the case of bills in a set, overissue of documents for fungible goods and substitutes for lost, stolen or destroyed documents. But the issuer is liable for damages caused by his overissue or failure to identify a duplicate document as such by conspicuous notation on its face.

§ 7-403. Obligation of Warehouseman or Carrier to Deliver; Excuse.

(1) The bailee must deliver the goods to a person entitled under the document who complies with subsections (2) and (3), unless and to the extent that the bailee establishes any of the following:

(a) delivery of the goods to a person whose receipt was rightful as against the claimant;

(b) damage to or delay, loss or destruction of the goods for which the bailee is not liable [, but the burden of establishing negligence in such cases is on the person entitled under the document];

Note: *The brackets in (1) (b) indicate that State enactments may differ on this point without serious damage to the principle of uniformity.*

(c) previous sale or other disposition of the goods in lawful enforcement of a lien or on warehouseman's lawful termination of storage;

(d) the exercise by a seller of his right to stop delivery pursuant to the provisions of the Article on Sales (Section 2-705);

(e) a diversion, reconsignment or other disposition pursuant to the provisions of this Article (Section 7-303) or tariff regulating such right;

(f) release, satisfaction or any other fact affording a personal defense against the claimant;

(g) any other lawful excuse.

(2) A person claiming goods covered by a document of title must satisfy the bailee's lien where the bailee so requests or where the bailee is prohibited by law from delivering the goods until the charges are paid.

(3) Unless the person claiming is one against whom the document confers no right under Sec. 7-503(1), he must surrender for cancellation or notation of partial deliveries any outstanding negotiable document covering the goods, and the bailee must cancel the document or conspicuously note the partial delivery thereon or be liable to any person to whom the document is duly negotiated.

(4) "Person entitled under the document" means holder in the case of a negotiable document, or the person to whom delivery is to be made by the terms of or pursuant to written instructions under a non-negotiable document.

§ 7-404. No Liability for Good Faith Delivery Pursuant to Receipt or Bill. A bailee who in good faith including observance of reasonable commercial standards has received goods and delivered or otherwise disposed of them according to the terms of the document of title or pursuant to this Article is not liable therefor. This rule applies even though the person from whom he received the goods had no authority to procure the document or to dispose of the goods and even though the person to whom he delivered the goods had no authority to receive them.

PART 5 Warehouse Receipts and Bills of Lading: Negotiation and Transfer

§ 7-501. Form of Negotiation and Requirements of "Due Negotiation".

(1) A negotiable document of title running to the order of a named person is negotiated by his indorsement and delivery. After his indorsement in blank or to bearer any person can negotiate it by delivery alone.

(2)

(a) A negotiable document of title is also negotiated by delivery alone when by its original terms it runs to bearer.

(b) When a document running to the order of a named person is delivered to him the effect is the same as if the document had been negotiated.

(3) Negotiation of a negotiable document of title after it has been indorsed to a specified person requires indorsement by the special indorsee as well as delivery.

(4) A negotiable document of title is "duly negotiated" when it is negotiated in the manner stated in this section to a holder who purchases it in good faith without notice of any defense against or claim to it on the part of any person and for value, unless it is established that the negotiation is not in the regular course of business or financing or involves receiving the document in settlement or payment of a money obligation.

(5) Indorsement of a non-negotiable document neither makes it negotiable nor adds to the transferee's rights.

(6) The naming in a negotiable bill of a person to be notified of the arrival of the goods does not limit the negotiability of the bill nor constitute notice to a purchaser thereof of any interest of such person in the goods.

§ 7-502. Rights Acquired by Due Negotiation.

(1) Subject to the following section and to the provisions of Section 7-205 on fungible goods, a holder to whom a negotiable document of title has been duly negotiated acquires thereby:

(a) title to the document;

(b) title to the goods;

(c) all rights accruing under the law of agency or estoppel, including rights to goods delivered to the bailee after the document was issued; and

(d) the direct obligation of the issuer to hold or deliver the goods according to the terms of the document free of any defense or claim by him except those arising under the terms of the document or under this Article In the case of a delivery order the bailee's obligation accrues only up acceptance and the obligation acquired by the holder is that the issuer and any indorser will procure the acceptance of the bailee.

(2) Subject to the following section, title and rights so acquired are not defeated by any stoppage of the goods represented by the document or by surrender of such goods by the bailee, and are not impaired even though the negotiation or any prior negotiation or any prior negotiation constituted a breach of duty or even though any person has been deprived of possession of the document by misrepresentation, fraud, accident, mistake, duress, loss, theft or conversion, or even though a previous sale or other transfer of the goods or document has been made to a third person.

§ 7-503. Document of Tide to Goods Defeated in Certain Cases.

(1) A document of title confers no right in goods against a person who before issuance of the document had a legal interest or a perfected security interest in them and who neither

(a) delivered or entrusted them or any document of title covering them to the bailor or his nominee with actual or apparent authority to ship, store or sell or with power to obtain delivery under this Article (Section 7-403) or with power of disposition under this Act (Sections 2-403 and 9-307) or other statute or rule of law; nor

(b) acquiesced in the procurement by the bailor or his nominee of any document of title.

(2) Title to goods based upon an unaccepted delivery order is subject to the rights of anyone to whom a negotiable warehouse receipt or bill of lading covering the goods has been duly negotiated. Such a title may be defeated under the next section to the same extent as the rights of the issuer or a transferee from the issuer.

(3) Title to goods based upon a bill of lading issued to a freight forwarder is subject to the rights of anyone to whom a bill issued by the freight forwarder is duly negotiated; but delivery by the carrier in accordance with Part 4 of this Article pursuant to its own bill of lading discharges the carrier's obligation to deliver.

§ 7-504. Rights Acquired in the Absence of Due Negotiation; Effect of Diversion; Seller's Stoppage of Delivery.

(1) A transferee of a document, whether negotiable or non-negotiable, to whom the document has been delivered but not duly negotiated, acquires the title and rights which his transferor had or had actual authority to convey.

(2) In the case of a non-negotiable document, until but not after the bailee receives notification of the transfer, the rights of the transferee may be defeated

(a) by those creditors of the transferor who could treat the sale as void under Section 2-402; or

(b) by a buyer from the transferor in ordinary course of business if the bailee has delivered the goods to the buyer or received notification of his rights; or

(c) as against the bailee by good faith dealings of the bailee with the transferor.

(3) A diversion or other change of shipping instructions by the consignor in a non-negotiable bill of lading which causes the bailee not to deliver to the consignee defeats the consignee's title to the goods if they have been delivered to a buyer in ordinary course of business and in any event defeats the consignee's rights against the bailee.

(4) Delivery pursuant to a non-negotiable document may be stopped by a seller under Section 2-705, and subject to the requirement of due notification there provided. A bailee honoring

the seller's instructions is entitled to be indemnified by the seller against any resulting loss or expense.

§ 7-505. Indorser Not a Guarantor for Other Parties. The indorsement of a document of title issued by a bailee does not make the indorser liable for any default by the bailee or by previous indorsers.

§ 7-506. Delivery Without Indorsement: Right to Compel Indorsement. The transferee of a negotiable document of title has a specifically enforceable right to have his transferor supply any necessary indorsement but the transfer becomes a negotiation only as of the time the indorsement is supplied.

§ 7-507. Warranties on Negotiation or Transfer of Receipt or Bill. Where a person negotiates or transfers a document of title for value otherwise than as a mere intermediary under the next following section, then unless otherwise agreed he warrants to his immediate purchaser only in addition to any warranty made in selling the goods

(a) that the document is genuine; and

(b) that he has no knowledge of any fact which would impair its validity or worth; and

(c) that his negotiation or transfer is rightful and fully effective with respect to the title to the document and the goods it represents.

§ 7-508. Warranties of Collecting Bank as to Documents. A collecting bank or other intermediary known to be entrusted with documents on behalf of another or with collection of a draft or other claim against delivery of documents warrants by such delivery of the documents only its own good faith and authority. This rule applies even though the intermediary has purchased or made advances against the claim or draft to be collected.

§ 7-509. Receipt or Bill: When Adequate Compliance With Commercial Contract. The question whether a document is adequate to fulfill the obligations of a contract for sale or the conditions of a credit is governed by the Articles on Sales (Article 2) and on Letters of Credit (Article 5).

PART 6 Warehouse Receipts and Bills of Lading: Miscellaneous Provisions

§ 7-601. Lost and Missing Documents.

(1) If a document has been lost, stolen or destroyed, a court may order delivery of the goods or issuance of a substitute document and the bailee may without liability to any person comply with such order. If the document was negotiable the claimant must post security approved by the Court to indemnify any person who may suffer loss as a result of nonsurrender of the document. If the document was not negotiable, such security may be required at the discretion of the court. The court may also in its discretion order payment of the bailee's reasonable costs and counsel fees.

(2) A bailee who without court order delivers goods to a person claiming under a missing negotiable document is liable to any person injured thereby, and if the delivery is not in good faith becomes liable for conversion. Delivery in good faith is not conversion if made in accordance with a filed classification or tariff or, where no classification or tariff is filed, if the claimant posts security with the bailee in an amount at least double the value of the goods at the rime of posting to indemnify any person injured by the delivery who files a notice of claim within one year after the delivery.

§ 7-602. Attachment of Goods Covered by a Negotiable Document. Except where the document was originally issued upon delivery of the goods by a person who had no power to dispose of them, no lien attaches by virtue of any judicial process to goods in the possession of a bailee for which a negotiable document of title is outstanding unless the document be first surrendered to the bailee or its negotiation enjoined, and the bailee shall nor be compelled to deliver the goods pursuant to process until the document is surrendered to him or impounded by the court. One who purchases the document for value without notice of the process or injunction takes free of the lien imposed by judicial process.

§ 7-603. Conflicting Claims; Interpleader. If more than one person claims title or possession of the goods, the bailee is excused from delivery until he has had a reasonable time to ascertain the validity of the adverse claims or to bring an action to compel all claimants to interplead and may compel such interpleader, either in defending an action for non-delivery of the goods, or by original action, whichever is appropriate.

REVISION (1994) OF ARTICLE 8 / Investment Securities

PART 1 Short Title and General Matters

§ 8-101. Short Title. This Article may be cited as Uniform Commercial Code Investment Securities.

§ 8-102. Definitions.

(a) In this Article:

(1) "Adverse claim" means a claim that a claimant has a property interest in a financial asset and that it is a violation of the rights of the claimant for another person to hold, transfer, or deal with the financial asset.

(2) "Bearer form," as applied to a certificated security, means a form in which the security is payable to the bearer of the security certificate according to its terms but not by reason of an indorsement.

(3) "Broker" means a person defined as a broker or dealer under the federal securities laws, but without excluding a bank acting in that capacity.

(4) "Certificated security" means a security that is represented by a certificate.

(5) "Clearing corporation" means:

(i) a person that is registered as a "clearing agency" under the federal securities laws;

(ii) a federal reserve bank; or

(iii) any other person that provides clearance or settlement services with respect to financial assets that would require it to register as a clearing agency under the federal securities laws but for an exclusion or exemption from the registration requirement, if its activities as a clearing corporation, including promulgation of rules, are subject to regulation by a federal or state governmental authority.

(6) "Communicate" means to:

(i) send a signed writing; or

(ii) transmit information by any mechanism agreed upon by the persons transmitting and receiving the information.

(7) "Entitlement holder" means a person identified in the records of a securities intermediary as the person having a security entitlement against the securities intermediary. If a person acquires a security entitlement by virtue of Section 8-501(b)(2) or (3), that person is the entitlement holder.

(8) "Entitlement order" means a notification communicated to a securities intermediary directing transfer or redemption of a financial asset to which the entitlement holder has a security entitlement.

(9) "Financial asset," except as otherwise provided in Section 8-103, means:

(i) a security;

(ii) an obligation of a person or a share, participation, or other interest in a person or in property or an enterprise of a person, which is, or is of a type, dealt in or traded on financial markets, or which is recognized in any area in which it is issued or dealt in as a medium for investment; or

(iii) any property that is held by a securities intermediary for another person in a securities account if the securities intermediary has expressly agreed with the other person that the property is to be treated as a financial asset under this Article.

As context requires, the term means either the interest itself or the means by which a person's claim to it is evidenced, including a certificated or uncertificated security, a security certificate, or a security entitlement.

(10) "Good faith," for purposes of the obligation of good faith in the performance or enforcement of contracts or duties within this Article, means honesty in fact and the observance of reasonable commercial standards of fair dealing.

(11) "Indorsement" means a signature that alone or accompanied by other words is made on a security certificate in registered form or on a separate document for the purpose of assigning, transferring, or redeeming the security or granting a power to assign, transfer, or redeem it.

(12) "Instruction" means a notification communicated to the issuer of an uncertificated security which directs that the transfer of the security be registered or that the security be redeemed.

(13) "Registered form," as applied to a certificated security, means a form in which:

(i) the security certificate specifies a person entitled to the security; and

(ii) a transfer of the security may be registered upon books maintained for that purpose by or on behalf of the issuer, or the security certificate so states.

(14) "Securities intermediary" means:

(i) a clearing corporation; or

(ii) a person, including a bank or broker, that in the ordinary course of its business maintains securities accounts for others and is acting in that capacity.

(15) "Security," except as otherwise provided in Section 8-103, means an obligation of an issuer or a share, participation, or other interest in an issuer or in property or an enterprise of an issuer:

(i) which is represented by a security certificate in bearer or registered form, or the transfer of which may be registered upon books maintained for that purpose by or on behalf of the issuer;

(ii) which is one of a class or series or by its terms is divisible into a class or series of shares, participations, interests, or obligations; and

(iii) which:

(A) is, or is of a type, dealt in or traded on securities exchanges or securities markets; or

(B) is a medium for investment and by its terms expressly provides that it is a security governed by this Article.

(16) "Security certificate" means a certificate representing a security.

(17) "Security entitlement" means the rights and property interest of an entitlement holder with respect to a financial asset specified in Part 5.

(18) "Uncertificated security" means a security that is not represented by a certificate.

(b) Other definitions applying to this Article and the sections in which they appear are:

Appropriate person Section 8-107

Control Section 8-106

Delivery Section 8-301

Investment company security Section 8-103

Issuer Section 8-201

Overissue Section 8-210

Protected purchaser Section 8-303

Securities account Section 8-501

(c) In addition, Article 1 contains general definitions and principles of construction and interpretation applicable throughout this Article.

(d) The characterization of a person, business, or transaction for purposes of this Article does not determine the characterization of the person, business, or transaction for purposes of any other law, regulation, or rule.

§ 8-103. Rules for Determining Whether Certain Obligations and Interests are Securities or Financial Assets.

(a) A share or similar equity interest issued by a corporation, business trust, joint stock company, or similar entity is a security.

(b) An "investment company security" is a security. "Investment company security" means a share or similar equity interest issued by an entity that is registered as an investment company under the federal investment company laws, an interest in a unit investment trust that is so registered, or a face-amount certificate issued by a face-amount certificate company that is so registered. Investment company security does not include an insurance policy or endowment policy or annuity contract issued by an insurance company.

(c) An interest in a partnership or limited liability company is not a security unless it is dealt in or traded on securities exchanges or in securities markets, its terms expressly provide that it is a security governed by this Article, or it is an investment company security. However, an interest in a partnership or limited liability company is a financial asset if it is held in a securities account.

(d) A writing that is a security certificate is governed by this Article and not by Article 3, even though it also meets the requirements of that Article. However, a negotiable instrument governed by Article 3 is a financial asset if it is held in a securities account.

(e) An option or similar obligation issued by a clearing corporation to its participants is not a security, but is a financial asset.

(f) A commodity contract, as defined in Section 9-115, is not a security or a financial asset.

§ 8-104. Acquisition of Security or Financial Asset or Interest Therein.

(a) A person acquires a security or an interest therein, under this Article, if:

(1) the person is a purchaser to whom a security is delivered pursuant to Section 8-301; or

(2) the person acquires a security entitlement to the security pursuant to Section 8-501.

(b) A person acquires a financial asset, other than a security, or an interest therein, under this Article, if the person acquires a security entitlement to the financial asset.

(c) A person who acquires a security entitlement to a security or other financial asset has the rights specified in Part 5, but is a purchaser of any security, security entitlement, or other financial asset held by the securities intermediary only to the extent provided in Section 8-503.

(d) Unless the context shows that a different meaning is intended, a person who is required by other law, regulation, rule, or agreement to transfer, deliver, present, surrender, exchange, or otherwise put in the possession of another person a security or financial asset satisfies that requirement by causing the other person to acquire an interest in the security or financial asset pursuant to subsection (a) or (b).

§ 8-105. Notice of Adverse Claim.

(a) A person has notice of an adverse claim if:

(1) the person knows of the adverse claim;

(2) the person is aware of facts sufficient to indicate that there is a significant probability that the adverse claim exists and deliberately avoids information that would establish the existence of the adverse claim; or

(3) the person has a duty, imposed by statute or regulation, to investigate whether an adverse claim exists, and the investigation so required would establish the existence of the adverse claim.

(b) Having knowledge that a financial asset or interest therein is or has been transferred by a representative imposes no duty of inquiry into the rightfulness of a transaction and is not notice of an adverse claim. However, a person who knows that a representative has transferred a financial asset or interest therein in a transaction that is, or whose proceeds are being used, for the individual benefit of the representative or otherwise in breach of duty has notice of an adverse claim.

(c) An act or event that creates a right to immediate performance of the principal obligation represented by a security certificate or sets a date on or after which the certificate is to be presented or surrendered for redemption or exchange does not itself constitute notice of an adverse claim except in the case of a transfer more than:

(1) one year after a date set for presentment or surrender for redemption or exchange; or

(2) six months after a date set for payment of money against presentation or surrender of the certificate, if money was available for payment on that date.

(d) A purchaser of a certificated security has notice of an adverse claim if the security certificate:

(1) whether in bearer or registered form, has been indorsed "for collection" or "for surrender" or for some other purpose not involving transfer; or

(2) is in bearer form and has on it an unambiguous statement that it is the property of a person other than the transferor, but the mere writing of a name on the certificate is not such a statement.

(e) Filing of a financing statement under Article 9 is not notice of an adverse claim to a financial asset.

§ 8-106. Control.

(a) A purchaser has "control" of a certificated security in bearer form if the certificated security is delivered to the purchaser.

(b) A purchaser has "control" of a certificated security in registered form if the certificated security is delivered to the purchaser, and:

(1) the certificate is indorsed to the purchaser or in blank by an effective indorsement; or

(2) the certificate is registered in the name of the purchaser, upon original issue or registration of transfer by the issuer.

(c) A purchaser has "control" of an uncertificated security if:

(1) the uncertificated security is delivered to the purchaser; or

(2) the issuer has agreed that it will comply with instructions originated by the purchaser without further consent by the registered owner.

(d) A purchaser has "control" of a security entitlement if:

(1) the purchaser becomes the entitlement holder; or

(2) the securities intermediary has agreed that it will comply with entitlement orders originated by the purchaser without further consent by the entitlement holder.

(e) If an interest in a security entitlement is granted by the entitlement holder to the entitlement holder's own securities intermediary, the securities intermediary has control.

(f) A purchaser who has satisfied the requirements of subsection (c)(2) or (d)(2) has control even if the registered owner in the case of subsection (c)(2) or the entitlement holder in the case of subsection (d)(2) retains the right to make substitutions for the uncertificated security or security entitlement, to originate instructions or entitlement orders to the issuer or securities intermediary, or otherwise to deal with the uncertificated security or security entitlement.

(g) An issuer or a securities intermediary may not enter into an agreement of the kind described in subsection (c)(2) or (d)(2) without the consent of the registered owner or entitlement holder, but an issuer or a securities intermediary is not required to enter into such an agreement even though the registered owner or entitlement holder so directs. An issuer or securities intermediary that has entered into such an agreement is not required to confirm the existence of the agreement to another party unless requested to do so by the registered owner or entitlement holder.

§ 8-107. Whether Indorsement, Instruction, or Entitlement Order is Effective.

(a) "Appropriate person" means:

(1) with respect to an indorsement, the person specified by a security certificate or by an effective special indorsement to be entitled to the security;

(2) with respect to an instruction, the registered owner of an uncertificated security;

(3) with respect to an entitlement order, the entitlement holder;

(4) if the person designated in paragraph (1), (2), or (3) is deceased, the designated person's successor taking under other law or the designated person's personal representative acting for the estate of the decedent; or

(5) if the person designated in paragraph (1), (2), or (3) lacks capacity, the designated person's guardian, conservator, or other similar representative who has power under other law to transfer the security or financial asset.

(b) An indorsement, instruction, or entitlement order is effective if:

(1) it is made by the appropriate person;

(2) it is made by a person who has power under the law of agency to transfer the security or financial asset on behalf of the appropriate person, including, in the case of an instruction or entitlement order, a person who has control under Section 8-106(c)(2) or (d)(2); or

(3) the appropriate person has ratified it or is otherwise precluded from asserting its ineffectiveness.

(c) An indorsement, instruction, or entitlement order made by a representative is effective even if:

(1) the representative has failed to comply with a controlling instrument or with the law of the State having jurisdiction of the representative relationship, including any law requiring the representative to obtain court approval of the transaction; or

(2) the representative's action in making the indorsement, instruction, or entitlement order or using the proceeds of the transaction is otherwise a breach of duty.

(d) If a security is registered in the name of or specially indorsed to a person described as a representative, or if a securities account is maintained in the name of a person described as a representative, an indorsement, instruction, or entitlement order made by the person is effective even though the person is no longer serving in the described capacity.

(e) Effectiveness of an indorsement, instruction, or entitlement order is determined as of the date the indorsement, instruction, or entitlement order is made, and an indorsement, instruction, or entitlement order does not become ineffective by reason of any later change of circumstances.

§ 8-108. Warranties in Direct Holding.

(a) A person who transfers a certificated security to a purchaser for value warrants to the purchaser, and an indorser, if the transfer is by indorsement, warrants to any subsequent purchaser, that:

(1) the certificate is genuine and has not been materially altered;

(2) the transferor or indorser does not know of any fact that might impair the validity of the security;

(3) there is no adverse claim to the security;

(4) the transfer does not violate any restriction on transfer;

(5) if the transfer is by indorsement, the indorsement is made by an appropriate person, or if the indorsement is by an agent, the agent has actual authority to act on behalf of the appropriate person; and

(6) the transfer is otherwise effective and rightful.

(b) A person who originates an instruction for registration of transfer of an uncertificated security to a purchaser for value warrants to the purchaser that:

(1) the instruction is made by an appropriate person, or if the instruction is by an agent, the agent has actual authority to act on behalf of the appropriate person;

(2) the security is valid;

(3) there is no adverse claim to the security; and

(4) at the time the instruction is presented to the issuer:

(i) the purchaser will be entitled to the registration of transfer;

(ii) the transfer will be registered by the issuer free from all liens, security interests, restrictions, and claims other than those specified in the instruction;

(iii) the transfer will not violate any restriction on transfer; and

(iv) the requested transfer will otherwise be effective and rightful.

(c) A person who transfers an uncertificated security to a purchaser for value and does not originate an instruction in connection with the transfer warrants that:

(1) the uncertificated security is valid;

(2) there is no adverse claim to the security;

(3) the transfer does not violate any restriction on transfer; and

(4) the transfer is otherwise effective and rightful.

(d) A person who indorses a security certificate warrants to the issuer that:

(1) there is no adverse claim to the security; and

(2) the indorsement is effective.

(e) A person who originates an instruction for registration of transfer of an uncertificated security warrants to the issuer that:

(1) the instruction is effective; and

(2) at the time the instruction is presented to the issuer the purchaser will be entitled to the registration of transfer.

(f) A person who presents a certificated security for registration of transfer or for payment or exchange warrants to the issuer that the person is entitled to the registration, payment, or exchange, but a purchaser for value and without notice of adverse claims to whom transfer is registered warrants only that the person has no knowledge of any unauthorized signature in a necessary indorsement.

(g) If a person acts as agent of another in delivering a certificated security to a purchaser, the identity of the principal was known to the person to whom the certificate was delivered, and the certificate delivered by the agent was received by the agent from the principal or received by the agent from another person at the direction of the principal, the person delivering the security certificate warrants only that the delivering person has authority to act for the principal and does not know of any adverse claim to the certificated security.

(h) A secured party who redelivers a security certificate received, or after payment and on order of the debtor delivers the security certificate to another person, makes only the warranties of an agent under subsection (g).

(i) Except as otherwise provided in subsection (g), a broker acting for a customer makes to the issuer and a purchaser the warranties provided in subsections (a) through (f). A broker that delivers a security certificate to its customer, or causes its customer to be registered as the owner of an uncertificated security, makes to the customer the warranties provided in subsection (a) or (b), and has the rights and privileges of a purchaser under this section. The warranties of and in favor of the broker acting as an agent are in addition to applicable warranties given by and in favor of the customer.

§ 8-109. Warranties in Indirect Holding.

(a) A person who originates an entitlement order to a securities intermediary warrants to the securities intermediary that:

(1) the entitlement order is made by an appropriate person, or if the entitlement order is by an agent, the agent has actual authority to act on behalf of the appropriate person; and

(2) there is no adverse claim to the security entitlement.

(b) A person who delivers a security certificate to a securities intermediary for credit to a securities account or originates an instruction with respect to an uncertificated security directing that the uncertificated security be credited to a securities account makes to the securities intermediary the warranties specified in Section 8-108(a) or (b).

(c) If a securities intermediary delivers a security certificate to its entitlement holder or causes its entitlement holder to be registered as the owner of an uncertificated security, the securities intermediary makes to the entitlement holder the warranties specified in Section 8-108(a) or (b).

§ 8-110. Applicability; Choice of Law.

(a) The local law of the issuer's jurisdiction, as specified in subsection (d), governs:

(1) the validity of a security;

(2) the rights and duties of the issuer with respect to registration of transfer;

(3) the effectiveness of registration of transfer by the issuer;

(4) whether the issuer owes any duties to an adverse claimant to a security; and

(5) whether an adverse claim can be asserted against a person to whom transfer of a certificated or uncertificated security is registered or a person who obtains control of an uncertificated security.

(b) The local law of the securities intermediary's jurisdiction, as specified in subsection (e), governs:

(1) acquisition of a security entitlement from the securities intermediary;

(2) the rights and duties of the securities intermediary and entitlement holder arising out of a security entitlement;

(3) whether the securities intermediary owes any duties to an adverse claimant to a security entitlement; and

(4) whether an adverse claim can be asserted against a person who acquires a security entitlement from the securities intermediary or a person who purchases a security entitlement or interest therein from an entitlement holder.

(c) The local law of the jurisdiction in which a security certificate is located at the time of delivery governs whether an adverse claim can be asserted against a person to whom the security certificate is delivered.

(d) "Issuer's jurisdiction" means the jurisdiction under which the issuer of the security is organized or, if permitted by the law of that jurisdiction, the law of another jurisdiction specified by the issuer. An issuer organized under the law of this State may specify the law of another jurisdiction as the law governing the matters specified in subsection (a)(2) through (5).

(e) The following rules determine a "securities intermediary's jurisdiction" for purposes of this section:

(1) If an agreement between the securities intermediary and its entitlement holder specifies that it is governed by the law of a particular jurisdiction, that jurisdiction is the securities intermediary's jurisdiction.

(2) If an agreement between the securities intermediary and its entitlement holder does not specify the governing law as provided in paragraph (1), but expressly specifies that the securities account is maintained at an office in a particular jurisdiction, that jurisdiction is the securities intermediary's jurisdiction.

(3) If an agreement between the securities intermediary and its entitlement holder does not specify a jurisdiction as provided in paragraph (1) or (2), the securities intermediary's jurisdiction is the jurisdiction in which is located the office identified in an account statement as the office serving the entitlement holder's account.

(4) If an agreement between the securities intermediary and its entitlement holder does not specify a jurisdiction as provided in paragraph (1) or (2) and an account statement does not identify an office serving the entitlement holder's account as provided in paragraph (3), the securities intermediary's jurisdiction is the jurisdiction in

which is located the chief executive office of the securities intermediary.

(f) A securities intermediary's jurisdiction is not determined by the physical location of certificates representing financial assets, or by the jurisdiction in which is organized the issuer of the financial asset with respect to which an entitlement holder has a security entitlement, or by the location of facilities for data processing or other record keeping concerning the account.

§ 8-111. Clearing Corporation Rules. A rule adopted by a clearing corporation governing rights and obligations among the clearing corporation and its participants in the clearing corporation is effective even if the rule conflicts with this [Act] and affects another party who does not consent to the rule.

§ 8-112. Creditor's Legal Process.

(a) The interest of a debtor in a certificated security may be reached by a creditor only by actual seizure of the security certificate by the officer making the attachment or levy, except as otherwise provided in subsection (d). However, a certificated security for which the certificate has been surrendered to the issuer may be reached by a creditor by legal process upon the issuer.

(b) The interest of a debtor in an uncertificated security may be reached by a creditor only by legal process upon the issuer at its chief executive office in the United States, except as otherwise provided in subsection (d).

(c) The interest of a debtor in a security entitlement may be reached by a creditor only by legal process upon the securities intermediary with whom the debtor's securities account is maintained, except as otherwise provided in subsection (d).

(d) The interest of a debtor in a certificated security for which the certificate is in the possession of a secured party, or in an uncertificated security registered in the name of a secured party, or a security entitlement maintained in the name of a secured party, may be reached by a creditor by legal process upon the secured party.

(e) A creditor whose debtor is the owner of a certificated security, uncertificated security, or security entitlement is entitled to aid from a court of competent jurisdiction, by injunction or otherwise, in reaching the certificated security, uncertificated security, or security entitlement or in satisfying the claim by means allowed at law or in equity in regard to property that cannot readily be reached by other legal process.

§ 8-113. Statute of Frauds Inapplicable. A contract or modification of a contract for the sale or purchase of a security is enforceable whether or not there is a writing signed or record authenticated by a party against whom enforcement is sought, even if the contract or modification is not capable of performance within one year of its making.

§ 8-114. Evidentiary Rules Concerning Certificated Securities.

The following rules apply in an action on a certificated security against the issuer:

(1) Unless specifically denied in the pleadings, each signature on a security certificate or in a necessary indorsement is admitted.

(2) If the effectiveness of a signature is put in issue, the burden of establishing effectiveness is on the party claiming under the signature, but the signature is presumed to be genuine or authorized.

(3) If signatures on a security certificate are admitted or established, production of the certificate entitles a holder to recover on it unless the defendant establishes a defense or a defect going to the validity of the security.

(4) If it is shown that a defense or defect exists, the plaintiff has the burden of establishing that the plaintiff or some person under whom the plaintiff claims is a person against whom the defense or defect cannot be asserted.

§ 8-115. Securities Intermediary and Others Not Liable to Adverse Claimant. A securities intermediary that has transferred a financial asset pursuant to an effective entitlement order, or a broker or other agent or bailee that has dealt with a financial asset at the direction of its customer or principal, is not liable to a person having an adverse claim to the financial asset, unless the securities intermediary, or broker or other agent or bailee:

(1) took the action after it had been served with an injunction, restraining order, or other legal process enjoining it from doing so, issued by a court of competent jurisdiction, and had a reasonable opportunity to act on the injunction, restraining order, or other legal process; or

(2) acted in collusion with the wrongdoer in violating the rights of the adverse claimant; or

(3) in the case of a security certificate that has been stolen, acted with notice of the adverse claim.

§ 8-116. Securities Intermediary as Purchaser for Value. A securities intermediary that receives a financial asset and establishes a security entitlement to the financial asset in favor of an entitlement holder is a purchaser for value of the financial asset. A securities intermediary that acquires a security entitlement to a financial asset from another securities intermediary acquires the security entitlement for value if the securities intermediary acquiring the security entitlement establishes a security entitlement to the financial asset in favor of an entitlement holder.

PART 2 Issue and Issuer

§ 8-201. Issuer.

(a) With respect to an obligation on or a defense to a security, an "issuer" includes a person that:

(1) places or authorizes the placing of its name on a security certificate, other than as authenticating trustee, registrar, transfer agent, or the like, to evidence a share, participation, or other interest in its property or in an enterprise, or to evidence its duty to perform an obligation represented by the certificate;

(2) creates a share, participation, or other interest in its property or in an enterprise, or undertakes an obligation, that is an uncertificated security;

(3) directly or indirectly creates a fractional interest in its rights or property, if the fractional interest is represented by a security certificate; or

(4) becomes responsible for, or in place of, another person described as an issuer in this section.

(b) With respect to an obligation on or defense to a security, a guarantor is an issuer to the extent of its guaranty, whether or not its obligation is noted on a security certificate.
(c) With respect to a registration of a transfer, issuer means a person on whose behalf transfer books are maintained.

§ 8-202. Issuer's Responsibility and Defenses; Notice of Defect or Defense.
(a) Even against a purchaser for value and without notice, the terms of a certificated security include terms stated on the certificate and terms made part of the security by reference on the certificate to another instrument, indenture, or document or to a constitution, statute, ordinance, rule, regulation, order, or the like, to the extent the terms referred to do not conflict with terms stated on the certificate. A reference under this subsection does not of itself charge a purchaser for value with notice of a defect going to the validity of the security, even if the certificate expressly states that a person accepting it admits notice. The terms of an uncertificated security include those stated in any instrument, indenture, or document or in a constitution, statute, ordinance, rule, regulation, order, or the like, pursuant to which the security is issued.
(b) The following rules apply if an issuer asserts that a security is not valid:

(1) A security other than one issued by a government or governmental subdivision, agency, or instrumentality, even though issued with a defect going to its validity, is valid in the hands of a purchaser for value and without notice of the particular defect unless the defect involves a violation of a constitutional provision. In that case, the security is valid in the hands of a purchaser for value and without notice of the defect, other than one who takes by original issue.

(2) Paragraph (1) applies to an issuer that is a government or governmental subdivision, agency, or instrumentality only if there has been substantial compliance with the legal requirements governing the issue or the issuer has received a substantial consideration for the issue as a whole or for the particular security and a stated purpose of the issue is one for which the issuer has power to borrow money or issue the security.

(c) Except as otherwise provided in Section 8-205, lack of genuineness of a certificated security is a complete defense, even against a purchaser for value and without notice.
(d) All other defenses of the issuer of a security, including nondelivery and conditional delivery of a certificated security, are ineffective against a purchaser for value who has taken the certificated security without notice of the particular defense.
(e) This section does not affect the right of a party to cancel a contract for a security "when, as and if issued" or "when distributed" in the event of a material change in the character of the security that is the subject of the contract or in the plan or arrangement pursuant to which the security is to be issued or distributed.
(f) If a security is held by a securities intermediary against whom an entitlement holder has a security entitlement with respect to the security, the issuer may not assert any defense that the issuer could not assert if the entitlement holder held the security directly.

§ 8-203. Staleness As Notice of Defect or Defense.
After an act or event, other than a call that has been revoked, creating a right to immediate performance of the principal obligation represented by a certificated security or setting a date on or after which the security is to be presented or surrendered for redemption or exchange, a purchaser is charged with notice of any defect in its issue or defense of the issuer, if the act or event:
(1) requires the payment of money, the delivery of a certificated security, the registration of transfer of an uncertificated security, or any of them on presentation or surrender of the security certificate, the money or security is available on the date set for payment or exchange, and the purchaser takes the security more than one year after that date; or
(2) is not covered by paragraph (1) and the purchaser takes the security more than two years after the date set for surrender or presentation or the date on which performance became due.

§ 8-204. Effect of Issuer's Restriction on Transfer. A restriction on transfer of a security imposed by the issuer, even if otherwise lawful, is ineffective against a person without knowledge of the restriction unless:
(1) the security is certificated and the restriction is noted conspicuously on the security certificate; or
(2) the security is uncertificated and the registered owner has been notified of the restriction.

§ 8-205. Effect of Unauthorized Signature on Security Certificate. An unauthorized signature placed on a security certificate before or in the course of issue is ineffective, but the signature is effective in favor of a purchaser for value of the certificated security if the purchaser is without notice of the lack of authority and the signing has been done by:
(1) an authenticating trustee, registrar, transfer agent, or other person entrusted by the issuer with the signing of the security certificate or of similar security certificates, or the immediate preparation for signing of any of them; or
(2) an employee of the issuer, or of any of the persons listed in paragraph (1), entrusted with responsible handling of the security certificate.

§ 8-206. Completion or Alteration of Security Certificate.
(a) If a security certificate contains the signatures necessary to its issue or transfer but is incomplete in any other respect:

(1) any person may complete it by filling in the blanks as authorized; and

(2) even if the blanks are incorrectly filled in, the security certificate as completed is enforceable by a purchaser who took it for value and without notice of the incorrectness.

(b) A complete security certificate that has been improperly altered, even if fraudulently, remains enforceable, but only according to its original terms.

§ 8-207. Rights and Duties of Issuer with Respect to Registered Owners.
(a) Before due presentment for registration of transfer of a certificated security in registered form or of an instruction requesting registration of transfer of an uncertificated security, the issuer or indenture trustee may treat the registered

owner as the person exclusively entitled to vote, receive notifications, and otherwise exercise all the rights and powers of an owner.
(b) This Article does not affect the liability of the registered owner of a security for a call, assessment, or the like.

§ 8-208. Effect of Signature of Authenticating Trustee, Registrar, or Transfer Agent.
(a) A person signing a security certificate as authenticating trustee, registrar, transfer agent, or the like, warrants to a purchaser for value of the certificated security, if the purchaser is without notice of a particular defect, that:

(1) the certificate is genuine;

(2) the person's own participation in the issue of the security is within the person's capacity and within the scope of the authority received by the person from the issuer; and

(3) the person has reasonable grounds to believe that the certificated security is in the form and within the amount the issuer is authorized to issue.
(b) Unless otherwise agreed, a person signing under subsection (a) does not assume responsibility for the validity of the security in other respects.

§ 8-209. Issuer's Lien. A lien in favor of an issuer upon a certificated security is valid against a purchaser only if the right of the issuer to the lien is noted conspicuously on the security certificate.

§ 8-210. Overissue.
(a) In this section, "overissue" means the issue of securities in excess of the amount the issuer has corporate power to issue, but an overissue does not occur if appropriate action has cured the overissue.
(b) Except as otherwise provided in subsections (c) and (d), the provisions of this Article which validate a security or compel its issue or reissue do not apply to the extent that validation, issue, or reissue would result in overissue.
(c) If an identical security not constituting an overissue is reasonably available for purchase, a person entitled to issue or validation may compel the issuer to purchase the security and deliver it if certificated or register its transfer if uncertificated, against surrender of any security certificate the person holds.
(d) If a security is not reasonably available for purchase, a person entitled to issue or validation may recover from the issuer the price the person or the last purchaser for value paid for it with interest from the date of the person's demand.

PART 3 Transfer of Certificated and Uncertificated Securities

§ 8-301. Delivery.
(a) Delivery of a certificated security to a purchaser occurs when:

(1) the purchaser acquires possession of the security certificate;

(2) another person, other than a securities intermediary, either acquires possession of the security certificate on behalf of the purchaser or, having previously acquired possession of the certificate, acknowledges that it holds for the purchaser; or

(3) a securities intermediary acting on behalf of the purchaser acquires possession of the security certificate, only if the certificate is in registered form and has been specially indorsed to the purchaser by an effective indorsement.

(b) Delivery of an uncertificated security to a purchaser occurs when:

(1) the issuer registers the purchaser as the registered owner, upon original issue or registration of transfer; or

(2) another person, other than a securities intermediary, either becomes the registered owner of the uncertificated security on behalf of the purchaser or, having previously become the registered owner, acknowledges that it holds for the purchaser.

§ 8-302. Rights of Purchaser.
(a) Except as otherwise provided in subsections (b) and (c), upon delivery of a certificated or uncertificated security to a purchaser, the purchaser acquires all rights in the security that the transferor had or had power to transfer.
(b) A purchaser of a limited interest acquires rights only to the extent of the interest purchased.
(c) A purchaser of a certificated security who as a previous holder had notice of an adverse claim does not improve its position by taking from a protected purchaser.

§ 8-303. Protected Purchaser.
(a) "Protected purchaser" means a purchaser of a certificated or uncertificated security, or of an interest therein, who:

(1) gives value;

(2) does not have notice of any adverse claim to the security; and

(3) obtains control of the certificated or uncertificated security.

(b) In addition to acquiring the rights of a purchaser, a protected purchaser also acquires its interest in the security free of any adverse claim.

§ 8-304. Indorsement.
(a) An indorsement may be in blank or special. An indorsement in blank includes an indorsement to bearer. A special indorsement specifies to whom a security is to be transferred or who has power to transfer it. A holder may convert a blank indorsement to a special indorsement.
(b) An indorsement purporting to be only of part of a security certificate representing units intended by the issuer to be separately transferable is effective to the extent of the indorsement.
(c) An indorsement, whether special or in blank, does not constitute a transfer until delivery of the certificate on which it appears or, if the indorsement is on a separate document, until delivery of both the document and the certificate.
(d) If a security certificate in registered form has been delivered to a purchaser without a necessary indorsement, the purchaser may become a protected purchaser only when the indorsement is supplied. However, against a transferor, a transfer is complete upon delivery and the purchaser has a specifically enforceable right to have any necessary indorsement supplied.

(e) An indorsement of a security certificate in bearer form may give notice of an adverse claim to the certificate, but it does not otherwise affect a right to registration that the holder possesses.
(f) Unless otherwise agreed, a person making an indorsement assumes only the obligations provided in Section 8-108 and not an obligation that the security will be honored by the issuer.

§ 8-305. Instruction.
(a) If an instruction has been originated by an appropriate person but is incomplete in any other respect, any person may complete it as authorized and the issuer may rely on it as completed, even though it has been completed incorrectly.
(b) Unless otherwise agreed, a person initiating an instruction assumes only the obligations imposed by Section 8-108 and not an obligation that the security will be honored by the issuer.

§ 8-306. Effect of Guaranteeing Signature, Indorsement, or Instruction.
(a) A person who guarantees a signature of an indorser of a security certificate warrants that at the time of signing:

(1) the signature was genuine;
(2) the signer was an appropriate person to indorse, or if the signature is by an agent, the agent had actual authority to act on behalf of the appropriate person; and
(3) the signer had legal capacity to sign.

(b) A person who guarantees a signature of the originator of an instruction warrants that at the time of signing:

(1) the signature was genuine;
(2) the signer was an appropriate person to originate the instruction, or if the signature is by an agent, the agent had actual authority to act on behalf of the appropriate person, if the person specified in the instruction as the registered owner was, in fact, the registered owner, as to which fact the signature guarantor does not make a warranty; and
(3) the signer had legal capacity to sign.

(c) A person who specially guarantees the signature of an originator of an instruction makes the warranties of a signature guarantor under subsection (b) and also warrants that at the time the instruction is presented to the issuer:

(1) the person specified in the instruction as the registered owner of the uncertificated security will be the registered owner; and
(2) the transfer of the uncertificated security requested in the instruction will be registered by the issuer free from all liens, security interests, restrictions, and claims other than those specified in the instruction.

(d) A guarantor under subsections (a) and (b) or a special guarantor under subsection (c) does not otherwise warrant the rightfulness of the transfer.
(e) A person who guarantees an indorsement of a security certificate makes the warranties of a signature guarantor under subsection (a) and also warrants the rightfulness of the transfer in all respects.
(f) A person who guarantees an instruction requesting the transfer of an uncertificated security makes the warranties of a special signature guarantor under subsection (c) and also warrants the rightfulness of the transfer in all respects.
(g) An issuer may not require a special guaranty of signature, a guaranty of indorsement, or a guaranty of instruction as a condition to registration of transfer.
(h) The warranties under this section are made to a person taking or dealing with the security in reliance on the guaranty, and the guarantor is liable to the person for loss resulting from their breach. An indorser or originator of an instruction whose signature, indorsement, or instruction has been guaranteed is liable to a guarantor for any loss suffered by the guarantor as a result of breach of the warranties of the guarantor.

§ 8-307. Purchaser's Right to Requisites for Registration of Transfer. Unless otherwise agreed, the transferor of a security on due demand shall supply the purchaser with proof of authority to transfer or with any other requisite necessary to obtain registration of the transfer of the security, but if the transfer is not for value, a transferor need not comply unless the purchaser pays the necessary expenses. If the transferor fails within a reasonable time to comply with the demand, the purchaser may reject or rescind the transfer.

PART 4 Registration

§ 8-401. Duty of Issuer to Register Transfer.
(a) If a certificated security in registered form is presented to an issuer with a request to register transfer or an instruction is presented to an issuer with a request to register transfer of an uncertificated security, the issuer shall register the transfer as requested if:

(1) under the terms of the security the person seeking registration of transfer is eligible to have the security registered in its name;
(2) the indorsement or instruction is made by the appropriate person or by an agent who has actual authority to act on behalf of the appropriate person;
(3) reasonable assurance is given that the indorsement or instruction is genuine and authorized (Section 8-402);
(4) any applicable law relating to the collection of taxes has been complied with;
(5) the transfer does not violate any restriction on transfer imposed by the issuer in accordance with Section 8-204;
(6) a demand that the issuer not register transfer has not become effective under Section 8-403, or the issuer has complied with Section 8-403(b) but no legal process or indemnity bond is obtained as provided in Section 8-403(d); and
(7) the transfer is in fact rightful or is to a protected purchaser.

(b) If an issuer is under a duty to register a transfer of a security, the issuer is liable to a person presenting a certificated security or an instruction for registration or to the person's principal for loss resulting from unreasonable delay in registration or failure or refusal to register the transfer.

§ 8-402. Assurance that Indorsement or Instruction is Effective.
(a) An issuer may require the following assurance that each necessary indorsement or each instruction is genuine and authorized:

(1) in all cases, a guaranty of the signature of the person making an indorsement or originating an instruction including, in the case of an instruction, reasonable assurance of identity;

(2) if the indorsement is made or the instruction is originated by an agent, appropriate assurance of actual authority to sign;

(3) if the indorsement is made or the instruction is originated by a fiduciary pursuant to Section 8-107(a)(4) or (a)(5), appropriate evidence of appointment or incumbency;

(4) if there is more than one fiduciary, reasonable assurance that all who are required to sign have done so; and

(5) if the indorsement is made or the instruction is originated by a person not covered by another provision of this subsection, assurance appropriate to the case corresponding as nearly as may be to the provisions of this subsection.

(b) An issuer may elect to require reasonable assurance beyond that specified in this section.

(c) In this section:

(1) "Guaranty of the signature" means a guaranty signed by or on behalf of a person reasonably believed by the issuer to be responsible. An issuer may adopt standards with respect to responsibility if they are not manifestly unreasonable.

(2) "Appropriate evidence of appointment or incumbency" means:

(i) in the case of a fiduciary appointed or qualified by a court, a certificate issued by or under the direction or supervision of the court or an officer thereof and dated within 60 days before the date of presentation for transfer; or

(ii) in any other case, a copy of a document showing the appointment or a certificate issued by or on behalf of a person reasonably believed by an issuer to be responsible or, in the absence of that document or certificate, other evidence the issuer reasonably considers appropriate.

§ 8-403. Demand That Issuer Not Register Transfer.

(a) A person who is an appropriate person to make an indorsement or originate an instruction may demand that the issuer not register transfer of a security by communicating to the issuer a notification that identifies the registered owner and the issue of which the security is a part and provides an address for communications directed to the person making the demand. The demand is effective only if it is received by the issuer at a time and in a manner affording the issuer reasonable opportunity to act on it.

(b) If a certificated security in registered form is presented to an issuer with a request to register transfer or an instruction is presented to an issuer with a request to register transfer of an uncertificated security after a demand that the issuer not register transfer has become effective, the issuer shall promptly communicate to (i) the person who initiated the demand at the address provided in the demand and (ii) the person who presented the security for registration of transfer or initiated the instruction requesting registration of transfer a notification stating that:

(1) the certificated security has been presented for registration of transfer or the instruction for registration of transfer of the uncertificated security has been received;

(2) a demand that the issuer not register transfer had previously been received; and

(3) the issuer will withhold registration of transfer for a period of time stated in the notification in order to provide the person who initiated the demand an opportunity to obtain legal process or an indemnity bond.

(c) The period described in subsection (b)(3) may not exceed 30 days after the date of communication of the notification. A shorter period may be specified by the issuer if it is not manifestly unreasonable.

(d) An issuer is not liable to a person who initiated a demand that the issuer not register transfer for any loss the person suffers as a result of registration of a transfer pursuant to an effective indorsement or instruction if the person who initiated the demand does not, within the time stated in the issuer's communication, either:

(1) obtain an appropriate restraining order, injunction, or other process from a court of competent jurisdiction enjoining the issuer from registering the transfer; or

(2) file with the issuer an indemnity bond, sufficient in the issuer's judgment to protect the issuer and any transfer agent, registrar, or other agent of the issuer involved from any loss it or they may suffer by refusing to register the transfer.

(e) This section does not relieve an issuer from liability for registering transfer pursuant to an indorsement or instruction that was not effective.

§ 8-404. Wrongful Registration.

(a) Except as otherwise provided in Section 8-406, an issuer is liable for wrongful registration of transfer if the issuer has registered a transfer of a security to a person not entitled to it, and the transfer was registered:

(1) pursuant to an ineffective indorsement or instruction;

(2) after a demand that the issuer not register transfer became effective under Section 8-403(a) and the issuer did not comply with Section 8-403(b);

(3) after the issuer had been served with an injunction, restraining order, or other legal process enjoining it from registering the transfer, issued by a court of competent jurisdiction, and the issuer had a reasonable opportunity to act on the injunction, restraining order, or other legal process; or

(4) by an issuer acting in collusion with the wrongdoer.

(b) An issuer that is liable for wrongful registration of transfer under subsection (a) on demand shall provide the person entitled to the security with a like certificated or uncertificated security, and any payments or distributions that the person did not receive as a result of the wrongful registration. If an overissue would result, the issuer's liability to provide the person with a like security is governed by Section 8-210.

(c) Except as otherwise provided in subsection (a) or in a law relating to the collection of taxes, an issuer is not liable to an owner or other person suffering loss as a result of the registration of a transfer of a security if registration was made pursuant to an effective indorsement or instruction.

§ 8-405. Replacement of Lost, Destroyed, or Wrongfully Taken Security Certificate.

(a) If an owner of a certificated security, whether in registered or bearer form, claims that the certificate has been lost, destroyed, or wrongfully taken, the issuer shall issue a new certificate if the owner:

(1) so requests before the issuer has notice that the certificate has been acquired by a protected purchaser;

(2) files with the issuer a sufficient indemnity bond; and

(3) satisfies other reasonable requirements imposed by the issuer.

(b) If, after the issue of a new security certificate, a protected purchaser of the original certificate presents it for registration of transfer, the issuer shall register the transfer unless an overissue would result. In that case, the issuer's liability is governed by Section 8-210. In addition to any rights on the indemnity bond, an issuer may recover the new certificate from a person to whom it was issued or any person taking under that person, except a protected purchaser.

§ 8-406. Obligation To Notify Issuer of Lost, Destroyed, or Wrongfully Taken Security Certificate. If a security certificate has been lost, apparently destroyed, or wrongfully taken, and the owner fails to notify the issuer of that fact within a reasonable time after the owner has notice of it and the issuer registers a transfer of the security before receiving notification, the owner may not assert against the issuer a claim for registering the transfer under Section 8-404 or a claim to a new security certificate under Section 8-405.

§ 8-407. Authenticating Trustee, Transfer Agent, and Registrar. A person acting as authenticating trustee, transfer agent, registrar, or other agent for an issuer in the registration of a transfer of its securities, in the issue of new security certificates or uncertificated securities, or in the cancellation of surrendered security certificates has the same obligation to the holder or owner of a certificated or uncertificated security with regard to the particular functions performed as the issuer has in regard to those functions.

PART 5 Security Entitlements

§ 8-501. Securities Account; Acquisition of Security Entitlement from Securities Intermediary.

(a) "Securities account" means an account to which a financial asset is or may be credited in accordance with an agreement under which the person maintaining the account undertakes to treat the person for whom the account is maintained as entitled to exercise the rights that comprise the financial asset.

(b) Except as otherwise provided in subsections (d) and (e), a person acquires a security entitlement if a securities intermediary:

(1) indicates by book entry that a financial asset has been credited to the person's securities account;

(2) receives a financial asset from the person or acquires a financial asset for the person and, in either case, accepts it for credit to the person's securities account; or

(3) becomes obligated under other law, regulation, or rule to credit a financial asset to the person's securities account.

(c) If a condition of subsection (b) has been met, a person has a security entitlement even though the securities intermediary does not itself hold the financial asset.

(d) If a securities intermediary holds a financial asset for another person, and the financial asset is registered in the name of, payable to the order of, or specially indorsed to the other person, and has not been indorsed to the securities intermediary or in blank, the other person is treated as holding the financial asset directly rather than as having a security entitlement with respect to the financial asset.

(e) Issuance of a security is not establishment of a security entitlement.

§ 8-502. Assertion of Adverse Claim Against Entitlement Holder. An action based on an adverse claim to a financial asset, whether framed in conversion, replevin, constructive trust, equitable lien, or other theory, may not be asserted against a person who acquires a security entitlement under Section 8-501 for value and without notice of the adverse claim.

§ 8-503. Property Interest of Entitlement Holder in Financial Asset Held by Securities Intermediary.

(a) To the extent necessary for a securities intermediary to satisfy all security entitlements with respect to a particular financial asset, all interests in that financial asset held by the securities intermediary are held by the securities intermediary for the entitlement holders, are not property of the securities intermediary, and are not subject to claims of creditors of the securities intermediary, except as otherwise provided in Section 8-511.

(b) An entitlement holder's property interest with respect to a particular financial asset under subsection (a) is a pro rata property interest in all interests in that financial asset held by the securities intermediary, without regard to the time the entitlement holder acquired the security entitlement or the time the securities intermediary acquired the interest in that financial asset.

(c) An entitlement holder's property interest with respect to a particular financial asset under subsection (a) may be enforced against the securities intermediary only by exercise of the entitlement holder's rights under Sections 8-505 through 8-508.

(d) An entitlement holder's property interest with respect to a particular financial asset under subsection (a) may be enforced against a purchaser of the financial asset or interest therein only if:

(1) insolvency proceedings have been initiated by or against the securities intermediary;

(2) the securities intermediary does not have sufficient interests in the financial asset to satisfy the security entitlements of all of its entitlement holders to that financial asset;

(3) the securities intermediary violated its obligations under Section 8-504 by transferring the financial asset or interest therein to the purchaser; and

(4) the purchaser is not protected under subsection (e).

The trustee or other liquidator, acting on behalf of all entitlement holders having security entitlements with respect to a particular financial asset, may recover the financial asset, or interest therein, from the purchaser. If the trustee or other liquidator elects not to pursue that right, an entitlement holder whose security entitlement remains unsatisfied has the right to recover its interest in the financial asset from the purchaser.

(e) An action based on the entitlement holder's property interest with respect to a particular financial asset under subsection (a), whether framed in conversion, replevin, constructive trust, equitable lien, or other theory, may not be asserted against any purchaser of a financial asset or interest therein who gives value, obtains control, and does not act in collusion with the securities intermediary in violating the securities intermediary's obligations under Section 8-504.

§ 8-504. Duty of Securities Intermediary to Maintain Financial Asset.
(a) A securities intermediary shall promptly obtain and thereafter maintain a financial asset in a quantity corresponding to the aggregate of all security entitlements it has established in favor of its entitlement holders with respect to that financial asset. The securities intermediary may maintain those financial assets directly or through one or more other securities intermediaries.
(b) Except to the extent otherwise agreed by its entitlement holder, a securities intermediary may not grant any security interests in a financial asset it is obligated to maintain pursuant to subsection (a).
(c) A securities intermediary satisfies the duty in subsection (a) if:

(1) the securities intermediary acts with respect to the duty as agreed upon by the entitlement holder and the securities intermediary; or

(2) in the absence of agreement, the securities intermediary exercises due care in accordance with reasonable commercial standards to obtain and maintain the financial asset.

(d) This section does not apply to a clearing corporation that is itself the obligor of an option or similar obligation to which its entitlement holders have security entitlements.

§ 8-505. Duty of Securities Intermediary with Respect to Payments and Distributions.
(a) A securities intermediary shall take action to obtain a payment or distribution made by the issuer of a financial asset. A securities intermediary satisfies the duty if:

(1) the securities intermediary acts with respect to the duty as agreed upon by the entitlement holder and the securities intermediary; or

(2) in the absence of agreement, the securities intermediary exercises due care in accordance with reasonable commercial standards to attempt to obtain the payment or distribution.

(b) A securities intermediary is obligated to its entitlement holder for a payment or distribution made by the issuer of a financial asset if the payment or distribution is received by the securities intermediary.

§ 8-506. Duty of Securities Intermediary to Exercise Rights as Directed by Entitlement Holder. A securities intermediary shall exercise rights with respect to a financial asset if directed to do so by an entitlement holder. A securities intermediary satisfies the duty if:
(1) the securities intermediary acts with respect to the duty as agreed upon by the entitlement holder and the securities intermediary; or
(2) in the absence of agreement, the securities intermediary either places the entitlement holder in a position to exercise the rights directly or exercises due care in accordance with reasonable commercial standards to follow the direction of the entitlement holder.

§ 8-507. Duty of Securities Intermediary to Comply with Entitlement Order.
(a) A securities intermediary shall comply with an entitlement order if the entitlement order is originated by the appropriate person, the securities intermediary has had reasonable opportunity to assure itself that the entitlement order is genuine and authorized, and the securities intermediary has had reasonable opportunity to comply with the entitlement order. A securities intermediary satisfies the duty if:

(1) the securities intermediary acts with respect to the duty as agreed upon by the entitlement holder and the securities intermediary; or

(2) in the absence of agreement, the securities intermediary exercises due care in accordance with reasonable commercial standards to comply with the entitlement order.

(b) If a securities intermediary transfers a financial asset pursuant to an ineffective entitlement order, the securities intermediary shall reestablish a security entitlement in favor of the person entitled to it, and pay or credit any payments or distributions that the person did not receive as a result of the wrongful transfer. If the securities intermediary does not reestablish a security entitlement, the securities intermediary is liable to the entitlement holder for damages.

§ 8-508. Duty of Securities Intermediary to Change Entitlement Holder's Position to Other Form of Security Holding. A securities intermediary shall act at the direction of an entitlement holder to change a security entitlement into another available form of holding for which the entitlement holder is eligible, or to cause the financial asset to be transferred to a securities account of the entitlement holder with another securities intermediary. A securities intermediary satisfies the duty if:
(1) the securities intermediary acts as agreed upon by the entitlement holder and the securities intermediary; or
(2) in the absence of agreement, the securities intermediary exercises due care in accordance with reasonable commercial standards to follow the direction of the entitlement holder.

§ 8-509. Specification of Duties of Securities Intermediary by Other Statute or Regulation; Manner of Performance of Duties of Securities Intermediary and Exercise of Rights of Entitlement Holder.
(a) If the substance of a duty imposed upon a securities intermediary by Sections 8-504 through 8-508 is the subject of other statute, regulation, or rule, compliance with that statute, regulation, or rule satisfies the duty.
(b) To the extent that specific standards for the performance of the duties of a securities intermediary or the exercise of the rights

of an entitlement holder are not specified by other statute, regulation, or rule or by agreement between the securities intermediary and entitlement holder, the securities intermediary shall perform its duties and the entitlement holder shall exercise its rights in a commercially reasonable manner.
(c) The obligation of a securities intermediary to perform the duties imposed by Sections 8-504 through 8-508 is subject to:
(1) rights of the securities intermediary arising out of a security interest under a security agreement with the entitlement holder or otherwise; and
(2) rights of the securities intermediary under other law, regulation, rule, or agreement to withhold performance of its duties as a result of unfulfilled obligations of the entitlement holder to the securities intermediary.
(d) Sections 8-504 through 8-508 do not require a securities intermediary to take any action that is prohibited by other statute, regulation, or rule.

§ 8-510. Rights of Purchaser of Security Entitlement from Entitlement Holder.
(a) An action based on an adverse claim to a financial asset or security entitlement, whether framed in conversion, replevin, constructive trust, equitable lien, or other theory, may not be asserted against a person who purchases a security entitlement, or an interest therein, from an entitlement holder if the purchaser gives value, does not have notice of the adverse claim, and obtains control.
(b) If an adverse claim could not have been asserted against an entitlement holder under Section 8-502, the adverse claim cannot be asserted against a person who purchases a security entitlement, or an interest therein, from the entitlement holder.
(c) In a case not covered by the priority rules in Article 9, a purchaser for value of a security entitlement, or an interest therein, who obtains control has priority over a purchaser of a security entitlement, or an interest therein, who does not obtain control. Purchasers who have control rank equally, except that a securities intermediary as purchaser has priority over a conflicting purchaser who has control unless otherwise agreed by the securities intermediary.

§ 8-511. Priority Among Security Interests and Entitlement Holders.
(a) Except as otherwise provided in subsections (b) and (c), if a securities intermediary does not have sufficient interests in a particular financial asset to satisfy both its obligations to entitlement holders who have security entitlements to that financial asset and its obligation to a creditor of the securities intermediary who has a security interest in that financial asset, the claims of entitlement holders, other than the creditor, have priority over the claim of the creditor.
(b) A claim of a creditor of a securities intermediary who has a security interest in a financial asset held by a securities intermediary has priority over claims of the securities intermediary's entitlement holders who have security entitlements with respect to that financial asset if the creditor has control over the financial asset.
(c) If a clearing corporation does not have sufficient financial assets to satisfy both its obligations to entitlement holders who have security entitlements with respect to a financial asset and its obligation to a creditor of the clearing corporation who has a security interest in that financial asset, the claim of the creditor has priority over the claims of entitlement holders.

PART 6 Transition Provisions for Revised Article 8

§ 8-601. Effective Date. This [Act] takes effect ... .

§ 8-602. Repeals. This [Act] repeals ... .

§ 8-603. Savings Clause.
(a) This [Act] does not affect an action or proceeding commenced before this [Act] takes effect.
(b) If a security interest in a security is perfected at the date this [Act] takes effect, and the action by which the security interest was perfected would suffice to perfect a security interest under this [Act], no further action is required to continue perfection. If a security interest in a security is perfected at the date this [Act] takes effect but the action by which the security interest was perfected would not suffice to perfect a security interest under this [Act], the security interest remains perfected for a period of four months after the effective date and continues perfected thereafter if appropriate action to perfect under this [Act] is taken within that period. If a security interest is perfected at the date this [Act] takes effect and the security interest can be perfected by filing under this [Act], a financing statement signed by the secured party instead of the debtor may be filed within that period to continue perfection or thereafter to perfect.

REVISION (1998) OF ARTICLE 9 / Secured Transactions (with 2001 Amendments in Stike/Score)

PART 1 General Provisions

[Subpart 1. Short Title, Definitions, and General Concepts]

§ 9-101. Short Title. This article may be cited as Uniform Commercial Code–Secured Transactions.

§ 9-102. Definitions and Index of Definitions.
(a) [Article 9 definitions.] In this article:
(1) "Accession" means goods that are physically united with other goods in such a manner that the identity of the original goods is not lost.
(2) "Account", except as used in "account for", means a right to payment of a monetary obligation, whether or not earned by performance, (i) for property that has been or is to be sold, leased, licensed, assigned, or otherwise disposed of, (ii) for services rendered or to be rendered, (iii) for a policy of insurance issued or to be issued, (iv) for a secondary obligation incurred or to be incurred, (v) for energy provided or to be provided, (vi) for the use or hire of a vessel under a charter or other contract, (vii) arising out of the use of a credit or charge card or information contained on or for use with the card, or (viii) as winnings

in a lottery or other game of chance operated or sponsored by a State, governmental unit of a State, or person licensed or authorized to operate the game by a State or governmental unit of a State. The term includes health-care-insurance receivables. The term does not include (i) rights to payment evidenced by chattel paper or an instrument, (ii) commercial tort claims, (iii) deposit accounts, (iv) investment property, (v) letter-of-credit rights or letters of credit, or (vi) rights to payment for money or funds advanced or sold, other than rights arising out of the use of a credit or charge card or information contained on or for use with the card.

(3) "Account debtor" means a person obligated on an account, chattel paper, or general intangible. The term does not include persons obligated to pay a negotiable instrument, even if the instrument constitutes part of chattel paper.

(4) "Accounting", except as used in "accounting for", means a record:

(A) authenticated by a secured party;

(B) indicating the aggregate unpaid secured obligations as of a date not more than 35 days earlier or 35 days later than the date of the record; and

(C) identifying the components of the obligations in reasonable detail.

(5) "Agricultural lien" means an interest, other than a security interest, in farm products:

(A) which secures payment or performance of an obligation for:

(i) goods or services furnished in connection with a debtor's farming operation; or

(ii) rent on real property leased by a debtor in connection with its farming operation;

(B) which is created by statute in favor of a person that:

(i) in the ordinary course of its business furnished goods or services to a debtor in connection with a debtor's farming operation; or

(ii) leased real property to a debtor in connection with the debtor's farming operation; and

(C) whose effectiveness does not depend on the person's possession of the personal property.

(6) "As-extracted collateral" means:

(A) oil, gas, or other minerals that are subject to a security interest that:

(i) is created by a debtor having an interest in the minerals before extraction; and

(ii) attaches to the minerals as extracted; or

(B) accounts arising out of the sale at the wellhead or minehead of oil, gas, or other minerals in which the debtor had an interest before extraction.

(7) "Authenticate" means:

(A) to sign; or

(B) to execute or otherwise adopt a symbol, or encrypt or similarly process a record in whole or in part, with the present intent of the authenticating person to identify the person and adopt or accept a record.

(8) "Bank" means an organization that is engaged in the business of banking. The term includes savings banks, savings and loan associations, credit unions, and trust companies.

(9) "Cash proceeds" means proceeds that are money, checks, deposit accounts, or the like.

(10) "Certificate of title" means a certificate of title with respect to which a statute provides for the security interest in question to be indicated on the certificate as a condition or result of the security interest's obtaining priority over the rights of a lien creditor with respect to the collateral.

(11) "Chattel paper" means a record or records that evidence both a monetary obligation and a security interest in specific goods, a security interest in specific goods and software used in the goods, a security interest in specific goods and license of software used in the goods, a lease of specific goods, or a lease of specific goods and license of software used in the goods. In this paragraph, "monetary obligation" means a monetary obligation secured by the goods or owed under a lease of the goods and includes a monetary obligation with respect to software used in the goods. The term does not include (i) charters or other contracts involving the use or hire of a vessel or (ii) records that evidence a right to payment arising out of the use of a credit or charge card or information contained on or for use with the card. If a transaction is evidenced by records that include an instrument or series of instruments, the group of records taken together constitutes chattel paper.

(12) "Collateral" means the property subject to a security interest or agricultural lien. The term includes:

(A) proceeds to which a security interest attaches;

(B) accounts, chattel paper, payment intangibles, and promissory notes that have been sold; and

(C) goods that are the subject of a consignment.

(13) "Commercial tort claim" means a claim arising in tort with respect to which:

(A) the claimant is an organization; or

(B) the claimant is an individual and the claim:

(i) arose in the course of the claimant's business or profession; and

(ii) does not include damages arising out of personal injury to or the death of an individual.

(14) "Commodity account" means an account maintained by a commodity intermediary in which a commodity contract is carried for a commodity customer.

(15) "Commodity contract" means a commodity futures contract, an option on a commodity futures contract, a commodity option, or another contract if the contract or option is:

(A) traded on or subject to the rules of a board of trade that has been designated as a contract market for such a contract pursuant to federal commodities laws; or

(B) traded on a foreign commodity board of trade, exchange, or market, and is carried on the books of a commodity intermediary for a commodity customer.

(16) "Commodity customer" means a person for which a commodity intermediary carries a commodity contract on its books.

(17) "Commodity intermediary" means a person that:

(A) is registered as a futures commission merchant under federal commodities law; or

(B) in the ordinary course of its business provides clearance or settlement services for a board of trade that has been designated as a contract market pursuant to federal commodities law.

(18) "Communicate" means:

(A) to send a written or other tangible record;

(B) to transmit a record by any means agreed upon by the persons sending and receiving the record; or

(C) in the case of transmission of a record to or by a filing office, to transmit a record by any means prescribed by filing-office rule.

(19) "Consignee" means a merchant to which goods are delivered in a consignment.

(20) "Consignment" means a transaction, regardless of its form, in which a person delivers goods to a merchant for the purpose of sale and:

(A) the merchant:

(i) deals in goods of that kind under a name other than the name of the person making delivery;

(ii) is not an auctioneer; and

(iii) is not generally known by its creditors to be substantially engaged in selling the goods of others;

(B) with respect to each delivery, the aggregate value of the goods is $1,000 or more at the time of delivery;

(C) the goods are not consumer goods immediately before delivery; and

(D) the transaction does not create a security interest that secures an obligation.

(21) "Consignor" means a person that delivers goods to a consignee in a consignment.

(22) "Consumer debtor" means a debtor in a consumer transaction.

(23) "Consumer goods" means goods that are used or bought for use primarily for personal, family, or household purposes.

(24) "Consumer-goods transaction" means a consumer transaction in which:

(A) an individual incurs an obligation primarily for personal, family, or household purposes; and

(B) a security interest in consumer goods secures the obligation.

(25) "Consumer obligor" means an obligor who is an individual and who incurred the obligation as part of a transaction entered into primarily for personal, family, or household purposes.

(26) "Consumer transaction" means a transaction in which (i) an individual incurs an obligation primarily for personal, family, or household purposes, (ii) a security interest secures the obligation, and (iii) the collateral is held or acquired primarily for personal, family, or household purposes. The term includes consumer-goods transactions.

(27) "Continuation statement" means an amendment of a financing statement which:

(A) identifies, by its file number, the initial financing statement to which it relates; and

(B) indicates that it is a continuation statement for, or that it is filed to continue the effectiveness of, the identified financing statement.

(28) "Debtor" means:

(A) a person having an interest, other than a security interest or other lien, in the collateral, whether or not the person is an obligor;

(B) a seller of accounts, chattel paper, payment intangibles, or promissory notes; or

(C) a consignee.

(29) "Deposit account" means a demand, time, savings, passbook, or similar account maintained with a bank. The term does not include investment property or accounts evidenced by an instrument.

(30) "Document" means a document of title or a receipt of the type described in Section 7-201(2).

(31) "Electronic chattel paper" means chattel paper evidenced by a record or records consisting of information stored in an electronic medium.

(32) "Encumbrance" means a right, other than an ownership interest, in real property. The term includes mortgages and other liens on real property.

(33) "Equipment" means goods other than inventory, farm products, or consumer goods.

(34) "Farm products" means goods, other than standing timber, with respect to which the debtor is engaged in a farming operation and which are:

(A) crops grown, growing, or to be grown, including:

(i) crops produced on trees, vines, and bushes; and

(ii) aquatic goods produced in aquacultural operations;

(B) livestock, born or unborn, including aquatic goods produced in aquacultural operations;

(C) supplies used or produced in a farming operation; or

(D) products of crops or livestock in their unmanufactured states.

(35) "Farming operation" means raising, cultivating, propagating, fattening, grazing, or any other farming, livestock, or aquacultural operation.

(36) "File number" means the number assigned to an initial financing statement pursuant to Section 9-519(a).

(37) "Filing office" means an office designated in Section 9-501 as the place to file a financing statement.

(38) "Filing-office rule" means a rule adopted pursuant to Section 9-526.

(39) "Financing statement" means a record or records composed of an initial financing statement and any filed record relating to the initial financing statement.

(40) "Fixture filing" means the filing of a financing statement covering goods that are or are to become fixtures and satisfying Section 9-502(a) and (b). The term includes the

filing of a financing statement covering goods of a transmitting utility which are or are to become fixtures.

(41) "Fixtures" means goods that have become so related to particular real property that an interest in them arises under real property law.

(42) "General intangible" means any personal property, including things in action, other than accounts, chattel paper, commercial tort claims, deposit accounts, documents, goods, instruments, investment property, letter-of-credit rights, letters of credit, money, and oil, gas, or other minerals before extraction. The term includes payment intangibles and software.

(43) "Good faith" means honesty in fact and the observance of reasonable commercial standards of fair dealing.

(44) "Goods" means all things that are movable when a security interest attaches. The term includes (i) fixtures, (ii) standing timber that is to be cut and removed under a conveyance or contract for sale, (iii) the unborn young of animals, (iv) crops grown, growing, or to be grown, even if the crops are produced on trees, vines, or bushes, and (v) manufactured homes. The term also includes a computer program embedded in goods and any supporting information provided in connection with a transaction relating to the program if (i) the program is associated with the goods in such a manner that it customarily is considered part of the goods, or (ii) by becoming the owner of the goods, a person acquires a right to use the program in connection with the goods. The term does not include a computer program embedded in goods that consist solely of the medium in which the program is embedded. The term also does not include accounts, chattel paper, commercial tort claims, deposit accounts, documents, general intangibles, instruments, investment property, letter-of-credit rights, letters of credit, money, or oil, gas, or other minerals before extraction.

(45) "Governmental unit" means a subdivision, agency, department, county, parish, municipality, or other unit of the government of the United States, a State, or a foreign country. The term includes an organization having a separate corporate existence if the organization is eligible to issue debt on which interest is exempt from income taxation under the laws of the United States.

(46) "Health-care-insurance receivable" means an interest in or claim under a policy of insurance which is a right to payment of a monetary obligation for health-care goods or services provided or to be provided.

(47) "Instrument" means a negotiable instrument or any other writing that evidences a right to the payment of a monetary obligation, is not itself a security agreement or lease, and is of a type that in ordinary course of business is transferred by delivery with any necessary indorsement or assignment. The term does not include (i) investment property, (ii) letters of credit, or (iii) writings that evidence a right to payment arising out of the use of a credit or charge card or information contained on or for use with the card.

(48) "Inventory" means goods, other than farm products, which:

(A) are leased by a person as lessor;

(B) are held by a person for sale or lease or to be furnished under a contract of service;

(C) are furnished by a person under a contract of service; or

(D) consist of raw materials, work in process, or materials used or consumed in a business.

(49) "Investment property" means a security, whether certificated or uncertificated, security entitlement, securities account, commodity contract, or commodity account.

(50) "Jurisdiction of organization", with respect to a registered organization, means the jurisdiction under whose law the organization is organized.

(51) "Letter-of-credit right" means a right to payment or performance under a letter of credit, whether or not the beneficiary has demanded or is at the time entitled to demand payment or performance. The term does not include the right of a beneficiary to demand payment or performance under a letter of credit.

(52) "Lien creditor" means:

(A) a creditor that has acquired a lien on the property involved by attachment, levy, or the like;

(B) an assignee for benefit of creditors from the time of assignment;

(C) a trustee in bankruptcy from the date of the filing of the petition; or

(D) a receiver in equity from the time of appointment.

(53) "Manufactured home" means a structure, transportable in one or more sections, which, in the traveling mode, is eight body feet or more in width or 40 body feet or more in length, or, when erected on site, is 320 or more square feet, and which is built on a permanent chassis and designed to be used as a dwelling with or without a permanent foundation when connected to the required utilities, and includes the plumbing, heating, air-conditioning, and electrical systems contained therein. The term includes any structure that meets all of the requirements of this paragraph except the size requirements and with respect to which the manufacturer voluntarily files a certification required by the United States Secretary of Housing and Urban Development and complies with the standards established under Title 42 of the United States Code.

(54) "Manufactured-home transaction" means a secured transaction:

(A) that creates a purchase-money security interest in a manufactured home, other than a manufactured home held as inventory; or

(B) in which a manufactured home, other than a manufactured home held as inventory, is the primary collateral.

(55) "Mortgage" means a consensual interest in real property, including fixtures, which secures payment or performance of an obligation.

(56) "New debtor" means a person that becomes bound as debtor under Section 9-203(d) by a security agreement previously entered into by another person.

(57) "New value" means (i) money, (ii) money's worth in property, services, or new credit, or (iii) release by a transferee of an interest in property previously transferred to the transferee. The term does not include an obligation substituted for another obligation.

(58) "Noncash proceeds" means proceeds other than cash proceeds.

(59) "Obligor" means a person that, with respect to an obligation secured by a security interest in or an agricultural lien on the collateral, (i) owes payment or other performance of the obligation, (ii) has provided property other than the collateral to secure payment or other performance of the obligation, or (iii) is otherwise accountable in whole or in part for payment or other performance of the obligation. The term does not include issuers or nominated persons under a letter of credit.

(60) "Original debtor", except as used in Section 9-310(c), means a person that, as debtor, entered into a security agreement to which a new debtor has become bound under Section 9-203(d).

(61) "Payment intangible" means a general intangible under which the account debtor's principal obligation is a monetary obligation.

(62) "Person related to", with respect to an individual, means:

(A) the spouse of the individual;

(B) a brother, brother-in-law, sister, or sister-in-law of the individual;

(C) an ancestor or lineal descendant of the individual or the individual's spouse; or

(D) any other relative, by blood or marriage, of the individual or the individual's spouse who shares the same home with the individual.

(63) "Person related to", with respect to an organization, means:

(A) a person directly or indirectly controlling, controlled by, or under common control with the organization;

(B) an officer or director of, or a person performing similar functions with respect to, the organization;

(C) an officer or director of, or a person performing similar functions with respect to, a person described in subparagraph (A);

(D) the spouse of an individual described in subparagraph (A), (B), or (C); or

(E) an individual who is related by blood or marriage to an individual described in subparagraph (A), (B), (C), or (D) and shares the same home with the individual.

(64) "Proceeds", except as used in Section 9-609(b), means the following property:

(A) whatever is acquired upon the sale, lease, license, exchange, or other disposition of collateral;

(B) whatever is collected on, or distributed on account of, collateral;

(C) rights arising out of collateral;

(D) to the extent of the value of collateral, claims arising out of the loss, nonconformity, or interference with the use of, defects or infringement of rights in, or damage to, the collateral; or

(E) to the extent of the value of collateral and to the extent payable to the debtor or the secured party, insurance payable by reason of the loss or nonconformity of, defects or infringement of rights in, or damage to, the collateral.

(65) "Promissory note" means an instrument that evidences a promise to pay a monetary obligation, does not evidence an order to pay, and does not contain an acknowledgment by a bank that the bank has received for deposit a sum of money or funds.

(66) "Proposal" means a record authenticated by a secured party which includes the terms on which the secured party is willing to accept collateral in full or partial satisfaction of the obligation it secures pursuant to Sections 9-620, 9-621, and 9-622.

(67) "Public-finance transaction" means a secured transaction in connection with which:

(A) debt securities are issued;

(B) all or a portion of the securities issued have an initial stated maturity of at least 20 years; and

(C) the debtor, obligor, secured party, account debtor or other person obligated on collateral, assignor or assignee of a secured obligation, or assignor or assignee of a security interest is a State or a governmental unit of a State.

(68) "Pursuant to commitment", with respect to an advance made or other value given by a secured party, means pursuant to the secured party's obligation, whether or not a subsequent event of default or other event not within the secured party's control has relieved or may relieve the secured party from its obligation.

(69) "Record", except as used in "for record", "of record", "record or legal title", and "record owner", means information that is inscribed on a tangible medium or which is stored in an electronic or other medium and is retrievable in perceivable form.

(70) "Registered organization" means an organization organized solely under the law of a single State or the United States and as to which the State or the United States must maintain a public record showing the organization to have been organized.

(71) "Secondary obligor" means an obligor to the extent that:

(A) the obligor's obligation is secondary; or

(B) the obligor has a right of recourse with respect to an obligation secured by collateral against the debtor, another obligor, or property of either.

(72) "Secured party" means:

(A) a person in whose favor a security interest is created or provided for under a security agreement, whether or not any obligation to be secured is outstanding;

(B) a person that holds an agricultural lien;

(C) a consignor;

(D) a person to which accounts, chattel paper, payment intangibles, or promissory notes have been sold;

(E) a trustee, indenture trustee, agent, collateral agent, or other representative in whose favor a security interest or agricultural lien is created or provided for; or

(F) a person that holds a security interest arising under Section 2-401, 2-505, 2-711(3), 2A-508(5), 4-210, or 5-118.

(73) "Security agreement" means an agreement that creates or provides for a security interest.

(74) "Send", in connection with a record or notification, means:

(A) to deposit in the mail, deliver for transmission, or transmit by any other usual means of communication, with postage or cost of transmission provided for, addressed to any address reasonable under the circumstances; or

(B) to cause the record or notification to be received within the time that it would have been received if properly sent under subparagraph (A).

(75) "Software" means a computer program and any supporting information provided in connection with a transaction relating to the program. The term does not include a computer program that is included in the definition of goods.

(76) "State" means a State of the United States, the District of Columbia, Puerto Rico, the United States Virgin Islands, or any territory or insular possession subject to the jurisdiction of the United States.

(77) "Supporting obligation" means a letter-of-credit right or secondary obligation that supports the payment or performance of an account, chattel paper, a document, a general intangible, an instrument, or investment property.

(78) "Tangible chattel paper" means chattel paper evidenced by a record or records consisting of information that is inscribed on a tangible medium.

(79) "Termination statement" means an amendment of a financing statement which:

(A) identifies, by its file number, the initial financing statement to which it relates; and

(B) indicates either that it is a termination statement or that the identified financing statement is no longer effective.

(80) "Transmitting utility" means a person primarily engaged in the business of:

(A) operating a railroad, subway, street railway, or trolley bus;

(B) transmitting communications electrically, electromagnetically, or by light;

(C) transmitting goods by pipeline or sewer; or

(D) transmitting or producing and transmitting electricity, steam, gas, or water.

(b) [Definitions in other articles.] The following definitions in other articles apply to this article:

"Applicant" Section 5-102.
"Beneficiary" Section 5-102.
"Broker" Section 8-102.
"Certificated security" Section 8-102.
"Check" Section 3-104.
"Clearing corporation" Section 8-102.
"Contract for sale" Section 2-106.
"Customer" Section 4-104.
"Entitlement holder" Section 8-102.
"Financial asset" Section 8-102.
"Holder in due course" Section 3-302.
"Issuer" (with respect to a letter of credit or letter-of-credit right) Section 5-102.
"Issuer" (with respect to a security) Section 8-201.
"Lease" Section 2A-103.
"Lease agreement" Section 2A-103.
"Lease contract" Section 2A-103.
"Leasehold interest" Section 2A-103.
"Lessee" Section 2A-103.
"Lessee in ordinary course of business" Section 2A-103.
"Lessor" Section 2A-103.
"Lessor's residual interest" Section 2A-103.
"Letter of credit" Section 5-102.
"Merchant" Section 2-104.
"Negotiable instrument" Section 3-104.
"Nominated person" Section 5-102.
"Note" Section 3-104.
"Proceeds of a letter of credit" Section 5-114.
"Prove" Section 3-103.
"Sale" Section 2-106.
"Securities account" Section 8-501.
"Securities intermediary" Section 8-102.
"Security" Section 8-102.
"Security certificate" Section 8-102.
"Security entitlement" Section 8-102.
"Uncertificated security" Section 8-102.

(c) [Article 1 definitions and principles.] Article 1 contains general definitions and principles of construction and interpretation applicable throughout this article.

§ 9-103. Purchase-Money Security Interest; Application of Payments; Burden of Establishing.

(a) [Definitions.] In this section:

(1) "purchase-money collateral" means goods or software that secures a purchase-money obligation incurred with respect to that collateral; and

(2) "purchase-money obligation" means an obligation of an obligor incurred as all or part of the price of the collateral or for value given to enable the debtor to acquire rights in or the use of the collateral if the value is in fact so used.

(b) [Purchase-money security interest in goods.] A security interest in goods is a purchase-money security interest:

(1) to the extent that the goods are purchase-money collateral with respect to that security interest;

(2) if the security interest is in inventory that is or was purchase-money collateral, also to the extent that the security interest secures a purchase-money obligation incurred with respect to other inventory in which the secured party holds or held a purchase-money security interest; and

(3) also to the extent that the security interest secures a purchase-money obligation incurred with respect to software in which the secured party holds or held a purchase-money security interest.

(c) [Purchase-money security interest in software.] A security interest in software is a purchase-money security interest to the extent that the security interest also secures a purchase-money obligation incurred with respect to goods in which the secured party holds or held a purchase-money security interest if:

(1) the debtor acquired its interest in the software in an integrated transaction in which it acquired an interest in the goods; and

(2) the debtor acquired its interest in the software for the principal purpose of using the software in the goods.

(d) [Consignor's inventory purchase-money security interest.] The security interest of a consignor in goods that are the subject of a consignment is a purchase-money security interest in inventory.

(e) [Application of payment in non-consumer-goods transaction.] In a transaction other than a consumer-goods transaction, if the extent to which a security interest is a purchase-money security interest depends on the application of a payment to a particular obligation, the payment must be applied:

(1) in accordance with any reasonable method of application to which the parties agree;

(2) in the absence of the parties' agreement to a reasonable method, in accordance with any intention of the obligor manifested at or before the time of payment; or

(3) in the absence of an agreement to a reasonable method and a timely manifestation of the obligor's intention, in the following order:

(A) to obligations that are not secured; and

(B) if more than one obligation is secured, to obligations secured by purchase-money security interests in the order in which those obligations were incurred.

(f) [No loss of status of purchase-money security interest in non-consumer-goods transaction.] In a transaction other than a consumer-goods transaction, a purchase-money security interest does not lose its status as such, even if:

(1) the purchase-money collateral also secures an obligation that is not a purchase-money obligation;

(2) collateral that is not purchase-money collateral also secures the purchase-money obligation; or

(3) the purchase-money obligation has been renewed, refinanced, consolidated, or restructured.

(g) [Burden of proof in non-consumer-goods transaction.] In a transaction other than a consumer-goods transaction, a secured party claiming a purchase-money security interest has the burden of establishing the extent to which the security interest is a purchase-money security interest.

(h) [Non-consumer-goods transactions; no inference.] The limitation of the rules in subsections (e), (f), and (g) to transactions other than consumer-goods transactions is intended to leave to the court the determination of the proper rules in consumer-goods transactions. The court may not infer from that limitation the nature of the proper rule in consumer-goods transactions and may continue to apply established approaches.

§ 9 104. Control of Deposit Account.

(a) [Requirements for control.] A secured party has control of a deposit account if:

(1) the secured party is the bank with which the deposit account is maintained;

(2) the debtor, secured party, and bank have agreed in an authenticated record that the bank will comply with instructions originated by the secured party directing disposition of the funds in the deposit account without further consent by the debtor; or

(3) the secured party becomes the bank's customer with respect to the deposit account.

(b) [Debtor's right to direct disposition.] A secured party that has satisfied subsection (a) has control, even if the debtor retains the right to direct the disposition of funds from the deposit account.

§ 9-105. Control of Electronic Chattel Paper. A secured party has control of electronic chattel paper if the record or records comprising the chattel paper are created, stored, and assigned in such a manner that:

(1) a single authoritative copy of the record or records exists which is unique, identifiable and, except as otherwise provided in paragraphs (4), (5), and (6), unalterable;

(2) the authoritative copy identifies the secured party as the assignee of the record or records;

(3) the authoritative copy is communicated to and maintained by the secured party or its designated custodian;

(4) copies or revisions that add or change an identified assignee of the authoritative copy can be made only with the participation of the secured party;

(5) each copy of the authoritative copy and any copy of a copy is readily identifiable as a copy that is not the authoritative copy; and

(6) any revision of the authoritative copy is readily identifiable as an authorized or unauthorized revision.

§ 9-106. Control of Investment Property.

(a) [Control under Section 8-106.] A person has control of a certificated security, uncertificated security, or security entitlement as provided in Section 8-106.

(b) [Control of commodity contract.] A secured party has control of a commodity contract if:

(1) the secured party is the commodity intermediary with which the commodity contract is carried; or

(2) the commodity customer, secured party, and commodity intermediary have agreed that the commodity in-

termediary will apply any value distributed on account of the commodity contract as directed by the secured party without further consent by the commodity customer.

(c) [Effect of control of securities account or commodity account.] A secured party having control of all security entitlements or commodity contracts carried in a securities account or commodity account has control over the securities account or commodity account.

§ 9-107. Control of Letter-of-Credit Right. A secured party has control of a letter-of-credit right to the extent of any right to payment or performance by the issuer or any nominated person if the issuer or nominated person has consented to an assignment of proceeds of the letter of credit under Section 5-114(c) or otherwise applicable law or practice.

§ 9-108. Sufficiency of Description.

(a) [Sufficiency of description.] Except as otherwise provided in subsections (c), (d), and (e), a description of personal or real property is sufficient, whether or not it is specific, if it reasonably identifies what is described.

(b) [Examples of reasonable identification.] Except as otherwise provided in subsection (d), a description of collateral reasonably identifies the collateral if it identifies the collateral by:

(1) specific listing;

(2) category;

(3) except as otherwise provided in subsection (e), a type of collateral defined in [the Uniform Commercial Code];

(4) quantity;

(5) computational or allocational formula or procedure; or

(6) except as otherwise provided in subsection (c), any other method, if the identity of the collateral is objectively determinable.

(c) [Supergeneric description not sufficient.] A description of collateral as "all the debtor's assets" or "all the debtor's personal property" or using words of similar import does not reasonably identify the collateral.

(d) [Investment property.] Except as otherwise provided in subsection (e), a description of a security entitlement, securities account, or commodity account is sufficient if it describes:

(1) the collateral by those terms or as investment property; or

(2) the underlying financial asset or commodity contract.

(e) [When description by type insufficient.] A description only by type of collateral defined in [the Uniform Commercial Code] is an insufficient description of:

(1) a commercial tort claim; or

(2) in a consumer transaction, consumer goods, a security entitlement, a securities account, or a commodity account.

[Subpart 2. Applicability of Article]

§ 9-109. Scope.

(a) [General scope of article.] Except as otherwise provided in subsections (c) and (d), this article applies to:

(1) a transaction, regardless of its form, that creates a security interest in personal property or fixtures by contract;

(2) an agricultural lien;

(3) a sale of accounts, chattel paper, payment intangibles, or promissory notes;

(4) a consignment;

(5) a security interest arising under Section 2-401, 2-505, 2-711(3), or 2A-508(5), as provided in Section 9-110; and

(6) a security interest arising under Section 4-210 or 5-118.

(b) [Security interest in secured obligation.] The application of this article to a security interest in a secured obligation is not affected by the fact that the obligation is itself secured by a transaction or interest to which this article does not apply.

(c) [Extent to which article does not apply.] This article does not apply to the extent that:

(1) a statute, regulation, or treaty of the United States preempts this article;

(2) another statute of this State expressly governs the creation, perfection, priority, or enforcement of a security interest created by this State or a governmental unit of this State;

(3) a statute of another State, a foreign country, or a governmental unit of another State or a foreign country, other than a statute generally applicable to security interests, expressly governs creation, perfection, priority, or enforcement of a security interest created by the State, country, or governmental unit; or

(4) the rights of a transferee beneficiary or nominated person under a letter of credit are independent and superior under Section 5-114.

(d) [Inapplicability of article.] This article does not apply to:

(1) a landlord's lien, other than an agricultural lien;

(2) a lien, other than an agricultural lien, given by statute or other rule of law for services or materials, but Section 9-333 applies with respect to priority of the lien;

(3) an assignment of a claim for wages, salary, or other compensation of an employee;

(4) a sale of accounts, chattel paper, payment intangibles, or promissory notes as part of a sale of the business out of which they arose;

(5) an assignment of accounts, chattel paper, payment intangibles, or promissory notes which is for the purpose of collection only;

(6) an assignment of a right to payment under a contract to an assignee that is also obligated to perform under the contract;

(7) an assignment of a single account, payment intangible, or promissory note to an assignee in full or partial satisfaction of a preexisting indebtedness;

(8) a transfer of an interest in or an assignment of a claim under a policy of insurance, other than an assignment by or to a health-care provider of a health-care-insurance receivable and any subsequent assignment of the right to payment, but Sections 9-315 and 9-322 apply with respect to proceeds and priorities in proceeds;

(9) an assignment of a right represented by a judgment, other than a judgment taken on a right to payment that was collateral;

(10) a right of recoupment or set-off, but:
(A) Section 9-340 applies with respect to the effectiveness of rights of recoupment or set-off against deposit accounts; and
(B) Section 9-404 applies with respect to defenses or claims of an account debtor;
(11) the creation or transfer of an interest in or lien on real property, including a lease or rents thereunder, except to the extent that provision is made for:
(A) liens on real property in Sections 9-203 and 9-308;
(B) fixtures in Section 9-334;
(C) fixture filings in Sections 9-501, 9-502, 9-512, 9-516, and 9-519; and
(D) security agreements covering personal and real property in Section 9-604;
(12) an assignment of a claim arising in tort, other than a commercial tort claim, but Sections 9-315 and 9-322 apply with respect to proceeds and priorities in proceeds; or
(13) an assignment of a deposit account in a consumer transaction, but Sections 9-315 and 9-322 apply with respect to proceeds and priorities in proceeds.

§ 9-110. Security Interests Arising Under Article 2 or 2A. A security interest arising under Section 2-401, 2-505, 2-711(3), or 2A-508(5) is subject to this article. However, until the debtor obtains possession of the goods:
(1) the security interest is enforceable, even if Section 9-203(b)(3) has not been satisfied;
(2) filing is not required to perfect the security interest;
(3) the rights of the secured party after default by the debtor are governed by Article 2 or 2A; and
(4) the security interest has priority over a conflicting security interest created by the debtor.

PART 2 Effectiveness of Security Agreement; Attachment of Security Interest; Rights of Parties to Security Agreement

[Subpart 1. Effectiveness and Attachment]

§ 9-201. General Effectiveness of Security Agreement.
(a) [General effectiveness.] Except as otherwise provided in [the Uniform Commercial Code], a security agreement is effective according to its terms between the parties, against purchasers of the collateral, and against creditors.
(b) [Applicable consumer laws and other law.] A transaction subject to this article is subject to any applicable rule of law which establishes a different rule for consumers and [insert reference to (i) any other statute or regulation that regulates the rates, charges, agreements, and practices for loans, credit sales, or other extensions of credit and (ii) any consumer-protection statute or regulation].
(c) [Other applicable law controls.] In case of conflict between this article and a rule of law, statute, or regulation described in subsection (b), the rule of law, statute, or regulation controls. Failure to comply with a statute or regulation described in subsection (b) has only the effect the statute or regulation specifies.
(d) [Further deference to other applicable law.] This article does not:
(1) validate any rate, charge, agreement, or practice that violates a rule of law, statute, or regulation described in subsection (b); or
(2) extend the application of the rule of law, statute, or regulation to a transaction not otherwise subject to it.

§ 9-202. Title to Collateral Immaterial. Except as otherwise provided with respect to consignments or sales of accounts, chattel paper, payment intangibles, or promissory notes, the provisions of this article with regard to rights and obligations apply whether title to collateral is in the secured party or the debtor.

§ 9-203. Attachment and Enforceability of Security Interest; Proceeds; Supporting Obligations; Formal Requisites.
(a) [Attachment.] A security interest attaches to collateral when it becomes enforceable against the debtor with respect to the collateral, unless an agreement expressly postpones the time of attachment.
(b) [Enforceability.] Except as otherwise provided in subsections (c) through (i), a security interest is enforceable against the debtor and third parties with respect to the collateral only if:
(1) value has been given;
(2) the debtor has rights in the collateral or the power to transfer rights in the collateral to a secured party; and
(3) one of the following conditions is met:
(A) the debtor has authenticated a security agreement that provides a description of the collateral and, if the security interest covers timber to be cut, a description of the land concerned;
(B) the collateral is not a certificated security and is in the possession of the secured party under Section 9-313 pursuant to the debtor's security agreement;
(C) the collateral is a certificated security in registered form and the security certificate has been delivered to the secured party under Section 8-301 pursuant to the debtor's security agreement; or
(D) the collateral is deposit accounts, electronic chattel paper, investment property, or letter-of-credit rights, and the secured party has control under Section 9-104, 9 105, 9 106, or 9 107 pursuant to the debtor's security agreement.
(c) [Other UCC provisions.] Subsection (b) is subject to Section 4 210 on the security interest of a collecting bank, Section 5-118 on the security interest of a letter-of-credit issuer or nominated person, Section 9-110 on a security interest arising under Article 2 or 2A, and Section 9-206 on security interests in investment property.
(d) [When person becomes bound by another person's security agreement.] A person becomes bound as debtor by a security agreement entered into by another person if, by operation of law other than this article or by contract:
(1) the security agreement becomes effective to create a security interest in the person's property; or
(2) the person becomes generally obligated for the obligations of the other person, including the obligation secured under the security agreement, and acquires or succeeds to all or substantially all of the assets of the other person.

(e) [Effect of new debtor becoming bound.] If a new debtor becomes bound as debtor by a security agreement entered into by another person:

(1) the agreement satisfies subsection (b)(3) with respect to existing or after-acquired property of the new debtor to the extent the property is described in the agreement; and

(2) another agreement is not necessary to make a security interest in the property enforceable.

(f) [Proceeds and supporting obligations.] The attachment of a security interest in collateral gives the secured party the rights to proceeds provided by Section 9-315 and is also attachment of a security interest in a supporting obligation for the collateral.

(g) [Lien securing right to payment.] The attachment of a security interest in a right to payment or performance secured by a security interest or other lien on personal or real property is also attachment of a security interest in the security interest, mortgage, or other lien.

(h) [Security entitlement carried in securities account.] The attachment of a security interest in a securities account is also attachment of a security interest in the security entitlements carried in the securities account.

(i) [Commodity contracts carried in commodity account.] The attachment of a security interest in a commodity account is also attachment of a security interest in the commodity contracts carried in the commodity account.

§ 9-204. After-Acquired Property; Future Advances.

(a) [After-acquired collateral.] Except as otherwise provided in subsection (b), a security agreement may create or provide for a security interest in after-acquired collateral.

(b) [When after-acquired property clause not effective.] A security interest does not attach under a term constituting an after acquired property clause to:

(1) consumer goods, other than an accession when given as additional security, unless the debtor acquires rights in them within 10 days after the secured party gives value; or

(2) a commercial tort claim.

(c) [Future advances and other value.] A security agreement may provide that collateral secures, or that accounts, chattel paper, payment intangibles, or promissory notes are sold in connection with, future advances or other value, whether or not the advances or value are given pursuant to commitment.

§ 9-205. Use or Disposition of Collateral Permissible.

(a) [When security interest not invalid or fraudulent.] A security interest is not invalid or fraudulent against creditors solely because:

(1) the debtor has the right or ability to:

(A) use, commingle, or dispose of all or part of the collateral, including returned or repossessed goods;

(B) collect, compromise, enforce, or otherwise deal with collateral;

(C) accept the return of collateral or make repossessions; or

(D) use, commingle, or dispose of proceeds; or

(2) the secured party fails to require the debtor to account for proceeds or replace collateral.

(b) [Requirements of possession not relaxed.] This section does not relax the requirements of possession if attachment, perfection, or enforcement of a security interest depends upon possession of the collateral by the secured party.

§ 9-206. Security Interest Arising in Purchase or Delivery of Financial Asset.

(a) [Security interest when person buys through securities intermediary.] A security interest in favor of a securities intermediary attaches to a person's security entitlement if:

(1) the person buys a financial asset through the securities intermediary in a transaction in which the person is obligated to pay the purchase price to the securities intermediary at the time of the purchase; and

(2) the securities intermediary credits the financial asset to the buyer's securities account before the buyer pays the securities intermediary.

(b) [Security interest secures obligation to pay for financial asset.] The security interest described in subsection (a) secures the person's obligation to pay for the financial asset.

(c) [Security interest in payment against delivery transaction.] A security interest in favor of a person that delivers a certificated security or other financial asset represented by a writing attaches to the security or other financial asset if:

(1) the security or other financial asset:

(A) in the ordinary course of business is transferred by delivery with any necessary indorsement or assignment; and

(B) is delivered under an agreement between persons in the business of dealing with such securities or financial assets; and

(2) the agreement calls for delivery against payment.

(d) [Security interest secures obligation to pay for delivery.] The security interest described in subsection (c) secures the obligation to make payment for the delivery.

[Subpart 2. Rights and Duties]

§ 9-207. Rights and Duties of Secured Party Having Possession or Control of Collateral.

(a) [Duty of care when secured party in possession.] Except as otherwise provided in subsection (d), a secured party shall use reasonable care in the custody and preservation of collateral in the secured party's possession. In the case of chattel paper or an instrument, reasonable care includes taking necessary steps to preserve rights against prior parties unless otherwise agreed.

(b) [Expenses, risks, duties, and rights when secured party in possession.] Except as otherwise provided in subsection (d), if a secured party has possession of collateral:

(1) reasonable expenses, including the cost of insurance and payment of taxes or other charges, incurred in the custody, preservation, use, or operation of the collateral are chargeable to the debtor and are secured by the collateral;

(2) the risk of accidental loss or damage is on the debtor to the extent of a deficiency in any effective insurance coverage;

(3) the secured party shall keep the collateral identifiable, but fungible collateral may be commingled; and

(4) the secured party may use or operate the collateral:

(A) for the purpose of preserving the collateral or its value;

(B) as permitted by an order of a court having competent jurisdiction; or

(C) except in the case of consumer goods, in the manner and to the extent agreed by the debtor.

(c) [Duties and rights when secured party in possession or control.] Except as otherwise provided in subsection (d), a secured party having possession of collateral or control of collateral under Section 9-104, 9 105, 9 106, or 9 107:

(1) may hold as additional security any proceeds, except money or funds, received from the collateral;

(2) shall apply money or funds received from the collateral to reduce the secured obligation, unless remitted to the debtor; and

(3) may create a security interest in the collateral.

(d) [Buyer of certain rights to payment.] If the secured party is a buyer of accounts, chattel paper, payment intangibles, or promissory notes or a consignor:

(1) subsection (a) does not apply unless the secured party is entitled under an agreement:

(A) to charge back uncollected collateral; or

(B) otherwise to full or limited recourse against the debtor or a secondary obligor based on the nonpayment or other default of an account debtor or other obligor on the collateral; and

(2) subsections (b) and (c) do not apply.

§ 9-208. Additional Duties of Secured Party Having Control of Collateral.

(a) [Applicability of section.] This section applies to cases in which there is no outstanding secured obligation and the secured party is not committed to make advances, incur obligations, or otherwise give value.

(b) [Duties of secured party after receiving demand from debtor.] Within 10 days after receiving an authenticated demand by the debtor:

(1) a secured party having control of a deposit account under Section 9-104(a)(2) shall send to the bank with which the deposit account is maintained an authenticated statement that releases the bank from any further obligation to comply with instructions originated by the secured party;

(2) a secured party having control of a deposit account under Section 9-104(a)(3) shall:

(A) pay the debtor the balance on deposit in the deposit account; or

(B) transfer the balance on deposit into a deposit account in the debtor's name;

(3) a secured party, other than a buyer, having control of electronic chattel paper under Section 9-105 shall:

(A) communicate the authoritative copy of the electronic chattel paper to the debtor or its designated custodian;

(B) if the debtor designates a custodian that is the designated custodian with which the authoritative copy of the electronic chattel paper is maintained for the secured party, communicate to the custodian an authenticated record releasing the designated custodian from any further obligation to comply with instructions originated by the secured party and instructing the custodian to comply with instructions originated by the debtor; and

(C) take appropriate action to enable the debtor or its designated custodian to make copies of or revisions to the authoritative copy which add or change an identified assignee of the authoritative copy without the consent of the secured party;

(4) a secured party having control of investment property under Section 8-106(d)(2) or 9 106(b) shall send to the securities intermediary or commodity intermediary with which the security entitlement or commodity contract is maintained an authenticated record that releases the securities intermediary or commodity intermediary from any further obligation to comply with entitlement orders or directions originated by the secured party; and

(5) a secured party having control of a letter-of-credit right under Section 9-107 shall send to each person having an unfulfilled obligation to pay or deliver proceeds of the letter of credit to the secured party an authenticated release from any further obligation to pay or deliver proceeds of the letter of credit to the secured party.

§ 9-209. Duties of Secured Party if Account Debtor Has Been Notified of Assignment.

(a) [Applicability of section.] Except as otherwise provided in subsection (c), this section applies if:

(1) there is no outstanding secured obligation; and

(2) the secured party is not committed to make advances, incur obligations, or otherwise give value.

(b) [Duties of secured party after receiving demand from debtor.] Within 10 days after receiving an authenticated demand by the debtor, a secured party shall send to an account debtor that has received notification of an assignment to the secured party as assignee under Section 9-406(a) an authenticated record that releases the account debtor from any further obligation to the secured party.

(c) [Inapplicability to sales.] This section does not apply to an assignment constituting the sale of an account, chattel paper, or payment intangible.

§ 9-210. Request for Accounting; Request Regarding List of Collateral or Statement of Account.

(a) [Definitions.] In this section:

(1) "Request" means a record of a type described in paragraph (2), (3), or (4).

(2) "Request for an accounting" means a record authenticated by a debtor requesting that the recipient provide an accounting of the unpaid obligations secured by collateral and reasonably identifying the transaction or relationship that is the subject of the request.

(3) "Request regarding a list of collateral" means a record authenticated by a debtor requesting that the recipient approve or correct a list of what the debtor believes to be the collateral securing an obligation and reasonably identifying the transaction or relationship that is the subject of the request.

(4) "Request regarding a statement of account" means a record authenticated by a debtor requesting that the recipient approve or correct a statement indicating what the debtor believes to be the aggregate amount of unpaid obligations secured by collateral as of a specified date and reasonably identifying the transaction or relationship that is the subject of the request.

(b) [Duty to respond to requests.] Subject to subsections (c), (d), (e), and (f), a secured party, other than a buyer of accounts, chattel paper, payment intangibles, or promissory notes or a consignor, shall comply with a request within 14 days after receipt:

(1) in the case of a request for an accounting, by authenticating and sending to the debtor an accounting; and

(2) in the case of a request regarding a list of collateral or a request regarding a statement of account, by authenticating and sending to the debtor an approval or correction.

(c) [Request regarding list of collateral; statement concerning type of collateral.] A secured party that claims a security interest in all of a particular type of collateral owned by the debtor may comply with a request regarding a list of collateral by sending to the debtor an authenticated record including a statement to that effect within 14 days after receipt.

(d) [Request regarding list of collateral; no interest claimed.] A person that receives a request regarding a list of collateral, claims no interest in the collateral when it receives the request, and claimed an interest in the collateral at an earlier time shall comply with the request within 14 days after receipt by sending to the debtor an authenticated record:

(1) disclaiming any interest in the collateral; and

(2) if known to the recipient, providing the name and mailing address of any assignee of or successor to the recipient's interest in the collateral.

(e) [Request for accounting or regarding statement of account; no interest in obligation claimed.] A person that receives a request for an accounting or a request regarding a statement of account, claims no interest in the obligations when it receives the request, and claimed an interest in the obligations at an earlier time shall comply with the request within 14 days after receipt by sending to the debtor an authenticated record:

(1) disclaiming any interest in the obligations; and

(2) if known to the recipient, providing the name and mailing address of any assignee of or successor to the recipient's interest in the obligations.

(f) [Charges for responses.] A debtor is entitled without charge to one response to a request under this section during any six-month period. The secured party may require payment of a charge not exceeding $25 for each additional response.

PART 3 Perfection and Priority

[Subpart 1. Law Governing Perfection and Priority]

§ 9-301. Law Governing Perfection and Priority of Security Interests. Except as otherwise provided in Sections 9-303 through 9-306, the following rules determine the law governing perfection, the effect of perfection or nonperfection, and the priority of a security interest in collateral:

(1) Except as otherwise provided in this section, while a debtor is located in a jurisdiction, the local law of that jurisdiction governs perfection, the effect of perfection or nonperfection, and the priority of a security interest in collateral.

(2) While collateral is located in a jurisdiction, the local law of that jurisdiction governs perfection, the effect of perfection or nonperfection, and the priority of a possessory security interest in that collateral.

(3) Except as otherwise provided in paragraph (4), while negotiable documents, goods, instruments, money, or tangible chattel paper is located in a jurisdiction, the local law of that jurisdiction governs:

(A) perfection of a security interest in the goods by filing a fixture filing;

(B) perfection of a security interest in timber to be cut; and

(C) the effect of perfection or nonperfection and the priority of a nonpossessory security interest in the collateral.

(4) The local law of the jurisdiction in which the wellhead or minehead is located governs perfection, the effect of perfection or nonperfection, and the priority of a security interest in as-extracted collateral.

§ 9-302. Law Governing Perfection and Priority of Agricultural Liens. While farm products are located in a jurisdiction, the local law of that jurisdiction governs perfection, the effect of perfection or nonperfection, and the priority of an agricultural lien on the farm products.

§ 9-303. Law Governing Perfection and Priority of Security Interests in Goods Covered by a Certificate of Title.

(a) [Applicability of section.] This section applies to goods covered by a certificate of title, even if there is no other relationship between the jurisdiction under whose certificate of title the goods are covered and the goods or the debtor.

(b) [When goods covered by certificate of title.] Goods become covered by a certificate of title when a valid application for the certificate of title and the applicable fee are delivered to the appropriate authority. Goods cease to be covered by a certificate of title at the earlier of the time the certificate of title ceases to be effective under the law of the issuing jurisdiction or the time the goods become covered subsequently by a certificate of title issued by another jurisdiction.

(c) [Applicable law.] The local law of the jurisdiction under whose certificate of title the goods are covered governs perfection, the effect of perfection or nonperfection, and the priority of a security interest in goods covered by a certificate of title from the time the goods become covered by the certificate of title until the goods cease to be covered by the certificate of title.

§ 9-304. Law Governing Perfection and Priority of Security Interests in Deposit Accounts.

(a) [Law of bank's jurisdiction governs.] The local law of a bank's jurisdiction governs perfection, the effect of perfection or nonperfection, and the priority of a security interest in a deposit account maintained with that bank.
(b) [Bank's jurisdiction.] The following rules determine a bank's jurisdiction for purposes of this part:

(1) If an agreement between the bank and the debtor its customer governing the deposit account expressly provides that a particular jurisdiction is the bank's jurisdiction for purposes of this part, this article, or [the Uniform Commercial Code], that jurisdiction is the bank's jurisdiction.

(2) If paragraph (1) does not apply and an agreement between the bank and its customer governing the deposit account expressly provides that the agreement is governed by the law of a particular jurisdiction, that jurisdiction is the bank's jurisdiction.

(3) If neither paragraph (1) nor paragraph (2) applies and an agreement between the bank and its customer governing the deposit account expressly provides that the deposit account is maintained at an office in a particular jurisdiction, that jurisdiction is the bank's jurisdiction.

(4) If none of the preceding paragraphs applies, the bank's jurisdiction is the jurisdiction in which the office identified in an account statement as the office serving the customer's account is located.

(5) If none of the preceding paragraphs applies, the bank's jurisdiction is the jurisdiction in which the chief executive office of the bank is located.

§ 9-305. Law Governing Perfection and Priority of Security Interests in Investment Property.

(a) [Governing law: general rules.] Except as otherwise provided in subsection (c), the following rules apply:

(1) While a security certificate is located in a jurisdiction, the local law of that jurisdiction governs perfection, the effect of perfection or nonperfection, and the priority of a security interest in the certificated security represented thereby.

(2) The local law of the issuer's jurisdiction as specified in Section 8-110(d) governs perfection, the effect of perfection or nonperfection, and the priority of a security interest in an uncertificated security.

(3) The local law of the securities intermediary's jurisdiction as specified in Section 8-110(e) governs perfection, the effect of perfection or nonperfection, and the priority of a security interest in a security entitlement or securities account.

(4) The local law of the commodity intermediary's jurisdiction governs perfection, the effect of perfection or nonperfection, and the priority of a security interest in a commodity contract or commodity account.

(b) [Commodity intermediary's jurisdiction.] The following rules determine a commodity intermediary's jurisdiction for purposes of this part:

(1) If an agreement between the commodity intermediary and commodity customer governing the commodity account expressly provides that a particular jurisdiction is the commodity intermediary's jurisdiction for purposes of this part, this article, or [the Uniform Commercial Code], that jurisdiction is the commodity intermediary's jurisdiction.

(2) If paragraph (1) does not apply and an agreement between the commodity intermediary and commodity customer governing the commodity account expressly provides that the agreement is governed by the law of a particular jurisdiction, that jurisdiction is the commodity intermediary's jurisdiction.

(3) If neither paragraph (1) nor paragraph (2) applies and an agreement between the commodity intermediary and commodity customer governing the commodity account expressly provides that the commodity account is maintained at an office in a particular jurisdiction, that jurisdiction is the commodity intermediary's jurisdiction.

(4) If none of the preceding paragraphs applies, the commodity intermediary's jurisdiction is the jurisdiction in which the office identified in an account statement as the office serving the commodity customer's account is located.

(5) If none of the preceding paragraphs applies, the commodity intermediary's jurisdiction is the jurisdiction in which the chief executive office of the commodity intermediary is located.

(c) [When perfection governed by law of jurisdiction where debtor located.] The local law of the jurisdiction in which the debtor is located governs:

(1) perfection of a security interest in investment property by filing;

(2) automatic perfection of a security interest in investment property created by a broker or securities intermediary; and

(3) automatic perfection of a security interest in a commodity contract or commodity account created by a commodity intermediary.

§ 9-306. Law Governing Perfection and Priority of Security Interests in Letter-of-Credit Rights.

(a) [Governing law: issuer's or nominated person's jurisdiction.] Subject to subsection (c), the local law of the issuer's jurisdiction or a nominated person's jurisdiction governs perfection, the effect of perfection or nonperfection, and the priority of a security interest in a letter-of-credit right if the issuer's jurisdiction or nominated person's jurisdiction is a State.
(b) [Issuer's or nominated person's jurisdiction.] For purposes of this part, an issuer's jurisdiction or nominated person's jurisdiction is the jurisdiction whose law governs the liability of the issuer or nominated person with respect to the letter-of-credit right as provided in Section 5-116.
(c) [When section not applicable.] This section does not apply to a security interest that is perfected only under Section 9-308(d).

§ 9-307. Location of Debtor.

(a) ["Place of business."] In this section, "place of business" means a place where a debtor conducts its affairs.
(b) [Debtor's location: general rules.] Except as otherwise provided in this section, the following rules determine a debtor's location:

(1) A debtor who is an individual is located at the individual's principal residence.

(2) A debtor that is an organization and has only one place of business is located at its place of business.

(3) A debtor that is an organization and has more than one place of business is located at its chief executive office.

(c) [Limitation of applicability of subsection (b).] Subsection (b) applies only if a debtor's residence, place of business, or chief executive office, as applicable, is located in a jurisdiction whose law generally requires information concerning the existence of a nonpossessory security interest to be made generally available in a filing, recording, or registration system as a condition or result of the security interest's obtaining priority over the rights of a lien creditor with respect to the collateral. If subsection (b) does not apply, the debtor is located in the District of Columbia.

(d) [Continuation of location: cessation of existence, etc.] A person that ceases to exist, have a residence, or have a place of business continues to be located in the jurisdiction specified by subsections (b) and (c).

(e) [Location of registered organization organized under State law.] A registered organization that is organized under the law of a State is located in that State.

(f) [Location of registered organization organized under federal law; bank branches and agencies.] Except as otherwise provided in subsection (i), a registered organization that is organized under the law of the United States and a branch or agency of a bank that is not organized under the law of the United States or a State are located:

(1) in the State that the law of the United States designates, if the law designates a State of location;

(2) in the State that the registered organization, branch, or agency designates, if the law of the United States authorizes the registered organization, branch, or agency to designate its State of location; or

(3) in the District of Columbia, if neither paragraph (1) nor paragraph (2) applies.

(g) [Continuation of location: change in status of registered organization.] A registered organization continues to be located in the jurisdiction specified by subsection (e) or (f) notwithstanding:

(1) the suspension, revocation, forfeiture, or lapse of the registered organization's status as such in its jurisdiction of organization; or

(2) the dissolution, winding up, or cancellation of the existence of the registered organization.

(h) [Location of United States.] The United States is located in the District of Columbia.

(i) [Location of foreign bank branch or agency if licensed in only one state.] A branch or agency of a bank that is not organized under the law of the United States or a State is located in the State in which the branch or agency is licensed, if all branches and agencies of the bank are licensed in only one State.

(j) [Location of foreign air carrier.] A foreign air carrier under the Federal Aviation Act of 1958, as amended, is located at the designated office of the agent upon which service of process may be made on behalf of the carrier.

(k) [Section applies only to this part.] This section applies only for purposes of this part.

[Subpart 2. Perfection]

§ 9-308. When Security Interest or Agricultural Lien is Perfected; Continuity of Perfection.

(a) [Perfection of security interest.] Except as otherwise provided in this section and Section 9-309, a security interest is perfected if it has attached and all of the applicable requirements for perfection in Sections 9-310 through 9-316 have been satisfied. A security interest is perfected when it attaches if the applicable requirements are satisfied before the security interest attaches.

(b) [Perfection of agricultural lien.] An agricultural lien is perfected if it has become effective and all of the applicable requirements for perfection in Section 9-310 have been satisfied. An agricultural lien is perfected when it becomes effective if the applicable requirements are satisfied before the agricultural lien becomes effective.

(c) [Continuous perfection; perfection by different methods.] A security interest or agricultural lien is perfected continuously if it is originally perfected by one method under this article and is later perfected by another method under this article, without an intermediate period when it was unperfected.

(d) [Supporting obligation.] Perfection of a security interest in collateral also perfects a security interest in a supporting obligation for the collateral.

(e) [Lien securing right to payment.] Perfection of a security interest in a right to payment or performance also perfects a security interest in a security interest, mortgage, or other lien on personal or real property securing the right.

(f) [Security entitlement carried in securities account.] Perfection of a security interest in a securities account also perfects a security interest in the security entitlements carried in the securities account.

(g) [Commodity contract carried in commodity account.] Perfection of a security interest in a commodity account also perfects a security interest in the commodity contracts carried in the commodity account.

Legislative Note: *Any statute conflicting with subsection (e) must be made expressly subject to that subsection.*

§ 9-309. Security Interest Perfected Upon Attachment.

The following security interests are perfected when they attach:

(1) a purchase-money security interest in consumer goods, except as otherwise provided in Section 9-311(b) with respect to consumer goods that are subject to a statute or treaty described in Section 9-311(a);

(2) an assignment of accounts or payment intangibles which does not by itself or in conjunction with other assignments to the same assignee transfer a significant part of the assignor's outstanding accounts or payment intangibles;

(3) a sale of a payment intangible;

(4) a sale of a promissory note;

(5) a security interest created by the assignment of a health-care-insurance receivable to the provider of the health-care goods or services;

(6) a security interest arising under Section 2-401, 2-505, 2-711(3), or 2A-508(5), until the debtor obtains possession of the collateral;
(7) a security interest of a collecting bank arising under Section 4-210;
(8) a security interest of an issuer or nominated person arising under Section 5-118;
(9) a security interest arising in the delivery of a financial asset under Section 9-206(c);
(10) a security interest in investment property created by a broker or securities intermediary;
(11) a security interest in a commodity contract or a commodity account created by a commodity intermediary;
(12) an assignment for the benefit of all creditors of the transferor and subsequent transfers by the assignee thereunder; and
(13) a security interest created by an assignment of a beneficial interest in a decedent's estate.; and
(14) a sale by an individual of an account that is a right to payment of winnings in a lottery or other game of chance.

§ 9-310. When Filing Required To Perfect Security Interest or Agricultural Lien; Security Interests and Agricultural Liens to Which Filing Provisions Do Not Apply.

(a) [General rule: perfection by filing.] Except as otherwise provided in subsection (b) and Section 9-312(b), a financing statement must be filed to perfect all security interests and agricultural liens.

(b) [Exceptions: filing not necessary.] The filing of a financing statement is not necessary to perfect a security interest:

(1) that is perfected under Section 9-308(d), (e), (f), or (g);
(2) that is perfected under Section 9-309 when it attaches;
(3) in property subject to a statute, regulation, or treaty described in Section 9-311(a);
(4) in goods in possession of a bailee which is perfected under Section 9-312(d)(1) or (2);
(5) in certificated securities, documents, goods, or instruments which is perfected without filing or possession under Section 9-312(e), (f), or (g);
(6) in collateral in the secured party's possession under Section 9-313;
(7) in a certificated security which is perfected by delivery of the security certificate to the secured party under Section 9-313;
(8) in deposit accounts, electronic chattel paper, investment property, or letter-of-credit rights which is perfected by control under Section 9-314;
(9) in proceeds which is perfected under Section 9-315; or
(10) that is perfected under Section 9-316.

(c) [Assignment of perfected security interest.] If a secured party assigns a perfected security interest or agricultural lien, a filing under this article is not required to continue the perfected status of the security interest against creditors of and transferees from the original debtor.

§ 9-311. Perfection of Security Interests in Property Subject to Certain Statutes, Regulations, and Treaties.

(a) [Security interest subject to other law.] Except as otherwise provided in subsection (d), the filing of a financing statement is not necessary or effective to perfect a security interest in property subject to:

(1) a statute, regulation, or treaty of the United States whose requirements for a security interest's obtaining priority over the rights of a lien creditor with respect to the property preempt Section 9-310(a);
(2) [list any certificate-of-title statute covering automobiles, trailers, mobile homes, boats, farm tractors, or the like, which provides for a security interest to be indicated on the certificate as a condition or result of perfection, and any non-Uniform Commercial Code central filing statute]; or
(3) a certificate-of-title statute of another jurisdiction which provides for a security interest to be indicated on the certificate as a condition or result of the security interest's obtaining priority over the rights of a lien creditor with respect to the property.

(b) [Compliance with other law.] Compliance with the requirements of a statute, regulation, or treaty described in subsection (a) for obtaining priority over the rights of a lien creditor is equivalent to the filing of a financing statement under this article. Except as otherwise provided in subsection (d) and Sections 9-313 and 9-316(d) and (e) for goods covered by a certificate of title, a security interest in property subject to a statute, regulation, or treaty described in subsection (a) may be perfected only by compliance with those requirements, and a security interest so perfected remains perfected notwithstanding a change in the use or transfer of possession of the collateral.

(c) [Duration and renewal of perfection.] Except as otherwise provided in subsection (d) and Section 9-316(d) and (e), duration and renewal of perfection of a security interest perfected by compliance with the requirements prescribed by a statute, regulation, or treaty described in subsection (a) are governed by the statute, regulation, or treaty. In other respects, the security interest is subject to this article.

(d) [Inapplicability to certain inventory.] During any period in which collateral subject to a statute specified in subsection (a)(2) is inventory held for sale or lease by a person or leased by that person as lessor and that person is in the business of selling goods of that kind, this section does not apply to a security interest in that collateral created by that person.

Legislative Note: *This Article contemplates that perfection of a security interest in goods covered by a certificate of title occurs upon receipt by appropriate State officials of a properly tendered application for a certificate of title on which the security interest is to be indicated, without a relation back to an earlier time. States whose certificate-of-title statutes provide for perfection at a different time or contain a relation-back provision should amend the statutes accordingly.*

§ 9-312. Perfection of Security Interests in Chattel Paper, Deposit Accounts, Documents, Goods Covered by Documents, Instruments, Investment Property, Letter-of-Credit Rights, and Money; Perfection by Permissive Filing; Temporary Perfection without Filing or Transfer of Possession.

(a) [Perfection by filing permitted.] A security interest in chattel paper, negotiable documents, instruments, or investment property may be perfected by filing.
(b) [Control or possession of certain collateral.] Except as otherwise provided in Section 9-315(c) and (d) for proceeds:

(1) a security interest in a deposit account may be perfected only by control under Section 9-314;
(2) and except as otherwise provided in Section 9-308(d), a security interest in a letter-of-credit right may be perfected only by control under Section 9-314; and
(3) a security interest in money may be perfected only by the secured party's taking possession under Section 9-313.

(c) [Goods covered by negotiable document.] While goods are in the possession of a bailee that has issued a negotiable document covering the goods:

(1) a security interest in the goods may be perfected by perfecting a security interest in the document; and
(2) a security interest perfected in the document has priority over any security interest that becomes perfected in the goods by another method during that time.

(d) [Goods covered by nonnegotiable document.] While goods are in the possession of a bailee that has issued a nonnegotiable document covering the goods, a security interest in the goods may be perfected by:

(1) issuance of a document in the name of the secured party;
(2) the bailee's receipt of notification of the secured party's interest; or
(3) filing as to the goods.

(e) [Temporary perfection: new value.] A security interest in certificated securities, negotiable documents, or instruments is perfected without filing or the taking of possession for a period of 20 days from the time it attaches to the extent that it arises for new value given under an authenticated security agreement.
(f) [Temporary perfection: goods or documents made available to debtor.] A perfected security interest in a negotiable document or goods in possession of a bailee, other than one that has issued a negotiable document for the goods, remains perfected for 20 days without filing if the secured party makes available to the debtor the goods or documents representing the goods for the purpose of:

(1) ultimate sale or exchange; or
(2) loading, unloading, storing, shipping, transshipping, manufacturing, processing, or otherwise dealing with them in a manner preliminary to their sale or exchange.

(g) [Temporary perfection: delivery of security certificate or instrument to debtor.] A perfected security interest in a certificated security or instrument remains perfected for 20 days without filing if the secured party delivers the security certificate or instrument to the debtor for the purpose of:

(1) ultimate sale or exchange; or
(2) presentation, collection, enforcement, renewal, or registration of transfer.

(h) [Expiration of temporary perfection.] After the 20 day period specified in subsection (e), (f), or (g) expires, perfection depends upon compliance with this article.

§ 9-313. When Possession by or Delivery to Secured Party Perfects Security Interest without Filing.

(a) [Perfection by possession or delivery.] Except as otherwise provided in subsection (b), a secured party may perfect a security interest in negotiable documents, goods, instruments, money, or tangible chattel paper by taking possession of the collateral. A secured party may perfect a security interest in certificated securities by taking delivery of the certificated securities under Section 8-301.
(b) [Goods covered by certificate of title.] With respect to goods covered by a certificate of title issued by this State, a secured party may perfect a security interest in the goods by taking possession of the goods only in the circumstances described in Section 9-316(d).
(c) [Collateral in possession of person other than debtor.] With respect to collateral other than certificated securities and goods covered by a document, a secured party takes possession of collateral in the possession of a person other than the debtor, the secured party, or a lessee of the collateral from the debtor in the ordinary course of the debtor's business, when:

(1) the person in possession authenticates a record acknowledging that it holds possession of the collateral for the secured party's benefit; or
(2) the person takes possession of the collateral after having authenticated a record acknowledging that it will hold possession of collateral for the secured party's benefit.

(d) [Time of perfection by possession; continuation of perfection.] If perfection of a security interest depends upon possession of the collateral by a secured party, perfection occurs no earlier than the time the secured party takes possession and continues only while the secured party retains possession.
(e) [Time of perfection by delivery; continuation of perfection.] A security interest in a certificated security in registered form is perfected by delivery when delivery of the certificated security occurs under Section 8-301 and remains perfected by delivery until the debtor obtains possession of the security certificate.
(f) [Acknowledgment not required.] A person in possession of collateral is not required to acknowledge that it holds possession for a secured party's benefit.
(g) [Effectiveness of acknowledgment; no duties or confirmation.] If a person acknowledges that it holds possession for the secured party's benefit:

(1) the acknowledgment is effective under subsection (c) or Section 8-301(a), even if the acknowledgment violates the rights of a debtor; and
(2) unless the person otherwise agrees or law other than this article otherwise provides, the person does not owe any duty to the secured party and is not required to confirm the acknowledgment to another person.

(h) [Secured party's delivery to person other than debtor.] A secured party having possession of collateral does not relinquish possession by delivering the collateral to a person other than the debtor or a lessee of the collateral from the debtor in the ordinary course of the debtor's business if the person was instructed before the delivery or is instructed contemporaneously with the delivery:

(1) to hold possession of the collateral for the secured party's benefit; or
(2) to redeliver the collateral to the secured party.

(i) [Effect of delivery under subsection (h); no duties or confirmation.] A secured party does not relinquish possession, even if a delivery under subsection (h) violates the rights of a debtor. A person to which collateral is delivered under subsection (h) does not owe any duty to the secured party and is not required to confirm the delivery to another person unless the person otherwise agrees or law other than this article otherwise provides.

§ 9-314. Perfection by Control.

(a) [Perfection by control.] A security interest in investment property, deposit accounts, letter-of-credit rights, or electronic chattel paper may be perfected by control of the collateral under Section 9-104, 9 105, 9 106, or 9 107.

(b) [Specified collateral: time of perfection by control; continuation of perfection.] A security interest in deposit accounts, electronic chattel paper, or letter-of-credit rights is perfected by control under Section 9-104, 9 105, or 9 107 when the secured party obtains control and remains perfected by control only while the secured party retains control.

(c) [Investment property: time of perfection by control; continuation of perfection.] A security interest in investment property is perfected by control under Section 9-106 from the time the secured party obtains control and remains perfected by control until:

(1) the secured party does not have control; and

(2) one of the following occurs:

(A) if the collateral is a certificated security, the debtor has or acquires possession of the security certificate;

(B) if the collateral is an uncertificated security, the issuer has registered or registers the debtor as the registered owner; or

(C) if the collateral is a security entitlement, the debtor is or becomes the entitlement holder.

§ 9-315. Secured Party's Rights on Disposition of Collateral and Proceeds.

(a) [Disposition of collateral: continuation of security interest or agricultural lien; proceeds.] Except as otherwise provided in this article and in Section 2-403(2):

(1) a security interest or agricultural lien continues in collateral notwithstanding sale, lease, license, exchange, or other disposition thereof unless the secured party authorized the disposition free of the security interest or agricultural lien; and

(2) a security interest attaches to any identifiable proceeds of collateral.

(b) [When commingled proceeds identifiable.] Proceeds that are commingled with other property are identifiable proceeds:

(1) if the proceeds are goods, to the extent provided by Section 9-336; and

(2) if the proceeds are not goods, to the extent that the secured party identifies the proceeds by a method of tracing, including application of equitable principles, that is permitted under law other than this article with respect to commingled property of the type involved.

(c) [Perfection of security interest in proceeds.] A security interest in proceeds is a perfected security interest if the security interest in the original collateral was perfected.

(d) [Continuation of perfection.] A perfected security interest in proceeds becomes unperfected on the 21st day after the security interest attaches to the proceeds unless:

(1) the following conditions are satisfied:

(A) a filed financing statement covers the original collateral;

(B) the proceeds are collateral in which a security interest may be perfected by filing in the office in which the financing statement has been filed; and

(C) the proceeds are not acquired with cash proceeds;

(2) the proceeds are identifiable cash proceeds; or

(3) the security interest in the proceeds is perfected other than under subsection (c) when the security interest attaches to the proceeds or within 20 days thereafter.

(e) [When perfected security interest in proceeds becomes unperfected.] If a filed financing statement covers the original collateral, a security interest in proceeds which remains perfected under subsection (d)(1) becomes unperfected at the later of:

(1) when the effectiveness of the filed financing statement lapses under Section 9-515 or is terminated under Section 9-513; or

(2) the 21st day after the security interest attaches to the proceeds.

§ 9-316. Continued Perfection of Security Interest Following Change in Governing Law.

(a) [General rule: effect on perfection of change in governing law.] A security interest perfected pursuant to the law of the jurisdiction designated in Section 9-301(1) or 9 305(c) remains perfected until the earliest of:

(1) the time perfection would have ceased under the law of that jurisdiction;

(2) the expiration of four months after a change of the debtor's location to another jurisdiction; or

(3) the expiration of one year after a transfer of collateral to a person that thereby becomes a debtor and is located in another jurisdiction.

(b) [Security interest perfected or unperfected under law of new jurisdiction.] If a security interest described in subsection (a) becomes perfected under the law of the other jurisdiction before the earliest time or event described in that subsection, it remains perfected thereafter. If the security interest does not become perfected under the law of the other jurisdiction before the earliest time or event, it becomes unperfected and is deemed never to have been perfected as against a purchaser of the collateral for value.

(c) [Possessory security interest in collateral moved to new jurisdiction.] A possessory security interest in collateral, other than goods covered by a certificate of title and as-extracted collateral consisting of goods, remains continuously perfected if:

(1) the collateral is located in one jurisdiction and subject to a security interest perfected under the law of that jurisdiction;

(2) thereafter the collateral is brought into another jurisdiction; and

(3) upon entry into the other jurisdiction, the security interest is perfected under the law of the other jurisdiction.

(d) [Goods covered by certificate of title from this state.] Except as otherwise provided in subsection (e), a security interest in goods covered by a certificate of title which is perfected by any method under the law of another jurisdiction when the goods become covered by a certificate of title from this State remains perfected until the security interest would have become unperfected under the law of the other jurisdiction had the goods not become so covered.

(e) [When subsection (d) security interest becomes unperfected against purchasers.] A security interest described in subsection (d) becomes unperfected as against a purchaser of the goods for value and is deemed never to have been perfected as against a purchaser of the goods for value if the applicable requirements for perfection under Section 9-311(b) or 9 313 are not satisfied before the earlier of:

(1) the time the security interest would have become unperfected under the law of the other jurisdiction had the goods not become covered by a certificate of title from this State; or

(2) the expiration of four months after the goods had become so covered.

(f) [Change in jurisdiction of bank, issuer, nominated person, securities intermediary, or commodity intermediary.] A security interest in deposit accounts, letter-of-credit rights, or investment property which is perfected under the law of the bank's jurisdiction, the issuer's jurisdiction, a nominated person's jurisdiction, the securities intermediary's jurisdiction, or the commodity intermediary's jurisdiction, as applicable, remains perfected until the earlier of:

(1) the time the security interest would have become unperfected under the law of that jurisdiction; or

(2) the expiration of four months after a change of the applicable jurisdiction to another jurisdiction.

(g) [Subsection (f) security interest perfected or unperfected under law of new jurisdiction.] If a security interest described in subsection (f) becomes perfected under the law of the other jurisdiction before the earlier of the time or the end of the period described in that subsection, it remains perfected thereafter. If the security interest does not become perfected under the law of the other jurisdiction before the earlier of that time or the end of that period, it becomes unperfected and is deemed never to have been perfected as against a purchaser of the collateral for value.

[Subpart 3. Priority]

§ 9-317. Interests That Take Priority Over or Take Free of Security Interest or Agricultural Lien.

(a) [Conflicting security interests and rights of lien creditors.] A security interest or agricultural lien is subordinate to the rights of:

(1) a person entitled to priority under Section 9-322; and

(2) except as otherwise provided in subsection (e), a person that becomes a lien creditor before the earlier of the time:

(A) the security interest or agricultural lien is perfected; or

(B) one of the conditions specified in Section 9-203(b)(3) is met and a financing statement covering the collateral is filed.

(b) [Buyers that receive delivery.] Except as otherwise provided in subsection (e), a buyer, other than a secured party, of tangible chattel paper, documents, goods, instruments, or a security certificate takes free of a security interest or agricultural lien if the buyer gives value and receives delivery of the collateral without knowledge of the security interest or agricultural lien and before it is perfected.

(c) [Lessees that receive delivery.] Except as otherwise provided in subsection (e), a lessee of goods takes free of a security interest or agricultural lien if the lessee gives value and receives delivery of the collateral without knowledge of the security interest or agricultural lien and before it is perfected.

(d) [Licensees and buyers of certain collateral.] A licensee of a general intangible or a buyer, other than a secured party, of accounts, electronic chattel paper, general intangibles, or investment property other than a certificated security takes free of a security interest if the licensee or buyer gives value without knowledge of the security interest and before it is perfected.

(e) [Purchase-money security interest.] Except as otherwise provided in Sections 9-320 and 9-321, if a person files a financing statement with respect to a purchase-money security interest before or within 20 days after the debtor receives delivery of the collateral, the security interest takes priority over the rights of a buyer, lessee, or lien creditor which arise between the time the security interest attaches and the time of filing.

§ 9-318. No Interest Retained in Right to Payment That Is Sold; Rights and Title of Seller of Account or Chattel Paper with Respect to Creditors and Purchasers.

(a) [Seller retains no interest.] A debtor that has sold an account, chattel paper, payment intangible, or promissory note does not retain a legal or equitable interest in the collateral sold.

(b) [Deemed rights of debtor if buyer's security interest unperfected.] For purposes of determining the rights of creditors of, and purchasers for value of an account or chattel paper from, a debtor that has sold an account or chattel paper, while the buyer's security interest is unperfected, the debtor is deemed to have rights and title to the account or chattel paper identical to those the debtor sold.

§ 9-319. Rights and Title of Consignee with Respect to Creditors and Purchasers.

(a) [Consignee has consignor's rights.] Except as otherwise provided in subsection (b), for purposes of determining the rights of creditors of, and purchasers for value of goods from, a consignee, while the goods are in the possession of the consignee, the consignee is deemed to have rights and title to the goods identical to those the consignor had or had power to transfer.

(b) [Applicability of other law.] For purposes of determining the rights of a creditor of a consignee, law other than this article determines the rights and title of a consignee while goods are in the consignee's possession if, under this part, a perfected security interest held by the consignor would have priority over the rights of the creditor.

§ 9-320. Buyer of Goods.

(a) [Buyer in ordinary course of business.] Except as otherwise provided in subsection (e), a buyer in ordinary course of business, other than a person buying farm products from a person engaged in farming operations, takes free of a security interest created by the buyer's seller, even if the security interest is perfected and the buyer knows of its existence.

(b) [Buyer of consumer goods.] Except as otherwise provided in subsection (e), a buyer of goods from a person who used or bought the goods for use primarily for personal, family, or household purposes takes free of a security interest, even if perfected, if the buyer buys:

(1) without knowledge of the security interest;

(2) for value;

(3) primarily for the buyer's personal, family, or household purposes; and

(4) before the filing of a financing statement covering the goods.

(c) [Effectiveness of filing for subsection (b).] To the extent that it affects the priority of a security interest over a buyer of goods under subsection (b), the period of effectiveness of a filing made in the jurisdiction in which the seller is located is governed by Section 9-316(a) and (b).

(d) [Buyer in ordinary course of business at wellhead or minehead.] A buyer in ordinary course of business buying oil, gas, or other minerals at the wellhead or minehead or after extraction takes free of an interest arising out of an encumbrance.

(e) [Possessory security interest not affected.] Subsections (a) and (b) do not affect a security interest in goods in the possession of the secured party under Section 9-313.

§ 9-321. Licensee of General Intangible and Lessee of Goods in Ordinary Course of Business.

(a) ["Licensee in ordinary course of business."] In this section, "licensee in ordinary course of business" means a person that becomes a licensee of a general intangible in good faith, without knowledge that the license violates the rights of another person in the general intangible, and in the ordinary course from a person in the business of licensing general intangibles of that kind. A person becomes a licensee in the ordinary course if the license to the person comports with the usual or customary practices in the kind of business in which the licensor is engaged or with the licensor's own usual or customary practices.

(b) [Rights of licensee in ordinary course of business.] A licensee in ordinary course of business takes its rights under a nonexclusive license free of a security interest in the general intangible created by the licensor, even if the security interest is perfected and the licensee knows of its existence.

(c) [Rights of lessee in ordinary course of business.] A lessee in ordinary course of business takes its leasehold interest free of a security interest in the goods created by the lessor, even if the security interest is perfected and the lessee knows of its existence.

§ 9-322. Priorities Among Conflicting Security Interests in and Agricultural Liens on Same Collateral.

(a) [General priority rules.] Except as otherwise provided in this section, priority among conflicting security interests and agricultural liens in the same collateral is determined according to the following rules:

(1) Conflicting perfected security interests and agricultural liens rank according to priority in time of filing or perfection. Priority dates from the earlier of the time a filing covering the collateral is first made or the security interest or agricultural lien is first perfected, if there is no period thereafter when there is neither filing nor perfection.

(2) A perfected security interest or agricultural lien has priority over a conflicting unperfected security interest or agricultural lien.

(3) The first security interest or agricultural lien to attach or become effective has priority if conflicting security interests and agricultural liens are unperfected.

(b) [Time of perfection: proceeds and supporting obligations.] For the purposes of subsection (a)(1):

(1) the time of filing or perfection as to a security interest in collateral is also the time of filing or perfection as to a security interest in proceeds; and

(2) the time of filing or perfection as to a security interest in collateral supported by a supporting obligation is also the time of filing or perfection as to a security interest in the supporting obligation.

(c) [Special priority rules: proceeds and supporting obligations.] Except as otherwise provided in subsection (f), a security interest in collateral which qualifies for priority over a conflicting security interest under Section 9-327, 9 328, 9 329, 9 330, or 9 331 also has priority over a conflicting security interest in:

(1) any supporting obligation for the collateral; and

(2) proceeds of the collateral if:

(A) the security interest in proceeds is perfected;

(B) the proceeds are cash proceeds or of the same type as the collateral; and

(C) in the case of proceeds that are proceeds of proceeds, all intervening proceeds are cash proceeds, proceeds of the same type as the collateral, or an account relating to the collateral.

(d) [First-to-file priority rule for certain collateral.] Subject to subsection (e) and except as otherwise provided in subsection (f), if a security interest in chattel paper, deposit accounts, negotiable documents, instruments, investment property, or letter-of-credit rights is perfected by a method other than filing, conflicting perfected security interests in proceeds of the collateral rank according to priority in time of filing.

(e) [Applicability of subsection (d).] Subsection (d) applies only if the proceeds of the collateral are not cash proceeds, chattel paper, negotiable documents, instruments, investment property, or letter-of-credit rights.

(f) [Limitations on subsections (a) through (e).] Subsections (a) through (e) are subject to:

(1) subsection (g) and the other provisions of this part;

(2) Section 4-210 with respect to a security interest of a collecting bank;

(3) Section 5-118 with respect to a security interest of an issuer or nominated person; and

(4) Section 9-110 with respect to a security interest arising under Article 2 or 2A.

(g) [Priority under agricultural lien statute.] A perfected agricultural lien on collateral has priority over a conflicting security interest in or agricultural lien on the same collateral if the statute creating the agricultural lien so provides.

§ 9-323. Future Advances.

(a) [When priority based on time of advance.] Except as otherwise provided in subsection (c), for purposes of determining the priority of a perfected security interest under Section 9-322(a)(1), perfection of the security interest dates from the time an advance is made to the extent that the security interest secures an advance that:

(1) is made while the security interest is perfected only:

(A) under Section 9-309 when it attaches; or

(B) temporarily under Section 9-312(e), (f), or (g); and

(2) is not made pursuant to a commitment entered into before or while the security interest is perfected by a method other than under Section 9-309 or 9 312(e), (f), or (g).

(b) [Lien creditor.] Except as otherwise provided in subsection (c), a security interest is subordinate to the rights of a person that becomes a lien creditor to the extent that the security interest secures an advance made more than 45 days after the person becomes a lien creditor unless the advance is made:

(1) without knowledge of the lien; or

(2) pursuant to a commitment entered into without knowledge of the lien.

(c) [Buyer of receivables.] Subsections (a) and (b) do not apply to a security interest held by a secured party that is a buyer of accounts, chattel paper, payment intangibles, or promissory notes or a consignor.

(d) [Buyer of goods.] Except as otherwise provided in subsection (e), a buyer of goods other than a buyer in ordinary course of business takes free of a security interest to the extent that it secures advances made after the earlier of:

(1) the time the secured party acquires knowledge of the buyer's purchase; or

(2) 45 days after the purchase.

(e) [Advances made pursuant to commitment: priority of buyer of goods.] Subsection (d) does not apply if the advance is made pursuant to a commitment entered into without knowledge of the buyer's purchase and before the expiration of the 45 day period.

(f) [Lessee of goods.] Except as otherwise provided in subsection (g), a lessee of goods, other than a lessee in ordinary course of business, takes the leasehold interest free of a security interest to the extent that it secures advances made after the earlier of:

(1) the time the secured party acquires knowledge of the lease; or

(2) 45 days after the lease contract becomes enforceable.

(g) [Advances made pursuant to commitment: priority of lessee of goods.] Subsection (f) does not apply if the advance is made pursuant to a commitment entered into without knowledge of the lease and before the expiration of the 45 day period.

§ 9-324. Priority of Purchase-Money Security Interests.

(a) [General rule: purchase-money priority.] Except as otherwise provided in subsection (g), a perfected purchase-money security interest in goods other than inventory or livestock has priority over a conflicting security interest in the same goods, and, except as otherwise provided in Section 9-327, a perfected security interest in its identifiable proceeds also has priority, if the purchase-money security interest is perfected when the debtor receives possession of the collateral or within 20 days thereafter.

(b) [Inventory purchase-money priority.] Subject to subsection (c) and except as otherwise provided in subsection (g), a perfected purchase-money security interest in inventory has priority over a conflicting security interest in the same inventory, has priority over a conflicting security interest in chattel paper or an instrument constituting proceeds of the inventory and in proceeds of the chattel paper, if so provided in Section 9-330, and, except as otherwise provided in Section 9-327, also has priority in identifiable cash proceeds of the inventory to the extent the identifiable cash proceeds are received on or before the delivery of the inventory to a buyer, if:

(1) the purchase-money security interest is perfected when the debtor receives possession of the inventory;

(2) the purchase-money secured party sends an authenticated notification to the holder of the conflicting security interest;

(3) the holder of the conflicting security interest receives the notification within five years before the debtor receives possession of the inventory; and

(4) the notification states that the person sending the notification has or expects to acquire a purchase-money security interest in inventory of the debtor and describes the inventory.

(c) [Holders of conflicting inventory security interests to be notified.] Subsections (b)(2) through (4) apply only if the holder of the conflicting security interest had filed a financing statement covering the same types of inventory:

(1) if the purchase-money security interest is perfected by filing, before the date of the filing; or

(2) if the purchase-money security interest is temporarily perfected without filing or possession under Section 9-312(f), before the beginning of the 20 day period thereunder.

(d) [Livestock purchase-money priority.] Subject to subsection (e) and except as otherwise provided in subsection (g), a perfected purchase-money security interest in livestock that are farm products has priority over a conflicting security interest in the same livestock, and, except as otherwise provided in Section 9-327, a perfected security interest in their identifiable proceeds and identifiable products in their unmanufactured states also has priority, if:

(1) the purchase-money security interest is perfected when the debtor receives possession of the livestock;

(2) the purchase-money secured party sends an authenticated notification to the holder of the conflicting security interest;

(3) the holder of the conflicting security interest receives the notification within six months before the debtor receives possession of the livestock; and

(4) the notification states that the person sending the notification has or expects to acquire a purchase-money security interest in livestock of the debtor and describes the livestock.

(e) [Holders of conflicting livestock security interests to be notified.] Subsections (d)(2) through (4) apply only if the holder of the conflicting security interest had filed a financing statement covering the same types of livestock:

(1) if the purchase-money security interest is perfected by filing, before the date of the filing; or

(2) if the purchase-money security interest is temporarily perfected without filing or possession under Section 9-312(f), before the beginning of the 20 day period thereunder.

(f) [Software purchase-money priority.] Except as otherwise provided in subsection (g), a perfected purchase-money security interest in software has priority over a conflicting security interest in the same collateral, and, except as otherwise provided in Section 9-327, a perfected security interest in its identifiable proceeds also has priority, to the extent that the purchase-money security interest in the goods in which the software was acquired for use has priority in the goods and proceeds of the goods under this section.

(g) [Conflicting purchase-money security interests.] If more than one security interest qualifies for priority in the same collateral under subsection (a), (b), (d), or (f):

(1) a security interest securing an obligation incurred as all or part of the price of the collateral has priority over a security interest securing an obligation incurred for value given to enable the debtor to acquire rights in or the use of collateral; and

(2) in all other cases, Section 9-322(a) applies to the qualifying security interests.

§ 9-325. Priority of Security Interests in Transferred Collateral.

(a) [Subordination of security interest in transferred collateral.] Except as otherwise provided in subsection (b), a security interest created by a debtor is subordinate to a security interest in the same collateral created by another person if:

(1) the debtor acquired the collateral subject to the security interest created by the other person;

(2) the security interest created by the other person was perfected when the debtor acquired the collateral; and

(3) there is no period thereafter when the security interest is unperfected.

(b) [Limitation of subsection (a) subordination.] Subsection (a) subordinates a security interest only if the security interest:

(1) otherwise would have priority solely under Section 9-322(a) or 9-324; or

(2) arose solely under Section 2-711(3) or 2A-508(5).

§ 9-326. Priority of Security Interests Created by New Debtor.

(a) [Subordination of security interest created by new debtor.] Subject to subsection (b), a security interest created by a new debtor which is perfected by a filed financing statement that is effective solely under Section 9-508 in collateral in which a new debtor has or acquires rights is subordinate to a security interest in the same collateral which is perfected other than by a filed financing statement that is effective solely under Section 9-508.

(b) [Priority under other provisions; multiple original debtors.] The other provisions of this part determine the priority among conflicting security interests in the same collateral perfected by filed financing statements that are effective solely under Section 9-508. However, if the security agreements to which a new debtor became bound as debtor were not entered into by the same original debtor, the conflicting security interests rank according to priority in time of the new debtor's having become bound.

§ 9-327. Priority of Security Interests in Deposit Account.

The following rules govern priority among conflicting security interests in the same deposit account:

(1) A security interest held by a secured party having control of the deposit account under Section 9-104 has priority over a conflicting security interest held by a secured party that does not have control.

(2) Except as otherwise provided in paragraphs (3) and (4), security interests perfected by control under Section 9-314 rank according to priority in time of obtaining control.

(3) Except as otherwise provided in paragraph (4), a security interest held by the bank with which the deposit account is maintained has priority over a conflicting security interest held by another secured party.

(4) A security interest perfected by control under Section 9-104(a)(3) has priority over a security interest held by the bank with which the deposit account is maintained.

§ 9-328. Priority of Security Interests in Investment Property.

The following rules govern priority among conflicting security interests in the same investment property:

(1) A security interest held by a secured party having control of investment property under Section 9-106 has priority over a security interest held by a secured party that does not have control of the investment property.

(2) Except as otherwise provided in paragraphs (3) and (4), conflicting security interests held by secured parties each of which has control under Section 9-106 rank according to priority in time of:

(A) if the collateral is a security, obtaining control;

(B) if the collateral is a security entitlement carried in a securities account and:

(i) if the secured party obtained control under Section 8-106(d)(1), the secured party's becoming the person for which the securities account is maintained;

(ii) if the secured party obtained control under Section 8-106(d)(2), the securities intermediary's agreement to comply with the secured party's entitlement orders with respect to security entitlements carried or to be carried in the securities account; or

(iii) if the secured party obtained control through another person under Section 8-106(d)(3), the time on which priority would be based under this paragraph if the other person were the secured party; or

(C) if the collateral is a commodity contract carried with a commodity intermediary, the satisfaction of the requirement for control specified in Section 9-106(b)(2) with respect to commodity contracts carried or to be carried with the commodity intermediary.

(3) A security interest held by a securities intermediary in a security entitlement or a securities account maintained with the securities intermediary has priority over a conflicting security interest held by another secured party.

(4) A security interest held by a commodity intermediary in a commodity contract or a commodity account maintained with the commodity intermediary has priority over a conflicting security interest held by another secured party.

(5) A security interest in a certificated security in registered form which is perfected by taking delivery under Section 9-313(a) and not by control under Section 9-314 has priority over a conflicting security interest perfected by a method other than control.

(6) Conflicting security interests created by a broker, securities intermediary, or commodity intermediary which are perfected without control under Section 9-106 rank equally.

(7) In all other cases, priority among conflicting security interests in investment property is governed by Sections 9-322 and 9-323.

§ 9-329. Priority of Security Interests in Letter-of-Credit Right. The following rules govern priority among conflicting security interests in the same letter-of-credit right:

(1) A security interest held by a secured party having control of the letter-of-credit right under Section 9-107 has priority to the extent of its control over a conflicting security interest held by a secured party that does not have control.

(2) Security interests perfected by control under Section 9-314 rank according to priority in time of obtaining control.

§ 9-330. Priority of Purchaser of Chattel Paper or Instrument.

(a) [Purchaser's priority: security interest claimed merely as proceeds.] A purchaser of chattel paper has priority over a security interest in the chattel paper which is claimed merely as proceeds of inventory subject to a security interest if:

(1) in good faith and in the ordinary course of the purchaser's business, the purchaser gives new value and takes possession of the chattel paper or obtains control of the chattel paper under Section 9-105; and

(2) the chattel paper does not indicate that it has been assigned to an identified assignee other than the purchaser.

(b) [Purchaser's priority: other security interests.] A purchaser of chattel paper has priority over a security interest in the chattel paper which is claimed other than merely as proceeds of inventory subject to a security interest if the purchaser gives new value and takes possession of the chattel paper or obtains control of the chattel paper under Section 9-105 in good faith, in the ordinary course of the purchaser's business, and without knowledge that the purchase violates the rights of the secured party.

(c) [Chattel paper purchaser's priority in proceeds.] Except as otherwise provided in Section 9-327, a purchaser having priority in chattel paper under subsection (a) or (b) also has priority in proceeds of the chattel paper to the extent that:

(1) Section 9-322 provides for priority in the proceeds; or

(2) the proceeds consist of the specific goods covered by the chattel paper or cash proceeds of the specific goods, even if the purchaser's security interest in the proceeds is unperfected.

(d) [Instrument purchaser's priority.] Except as otherwise provided in Section 9-331(a), a purchaser of an instrument has priority over a security interest in the instrument perfected by a method other than possession if the purchaser gives value and takes possession of the instrument in good faith and without knowledge that the purchase violates the rights of the secured party.

(e) [Holder of purchase-money security interest gives new value.] For purposes of subsections (a) and (b), the holder of a purchase-money security interest in inventory gives new value for chattel paper constituting proceeds of the inventory.

(f) [Indication of assignment gives knowledge.] For purposes of subsections (b) and (d), if chattel paper or an instrument indicates that it has been assigned to an identified secured party other than the purchaser, a purchaser of the chattel paper or instrument has knowledge that the purchase violates the rights of the secured party.

§ 9-331. Priority of Rights of Purchasers of Instruments, Documents, and Securities Under Other Articles; Priority of Interests in Financial Assets and Security Entitlements Under Article 8.

(a) [Rights under Articles 3, 7, and 8 not limited.] This article does not limit the rights of a holder in due course of a negotiable instrument, a holder to which a negotiable document of title has been duly negotiated, or a protected purchaser of a security. These holders or purchasers take priority over an earlier security interest, even if perfected, to the extent provided in Articles 3, 7, and 8.

(b) [Protection under Article 8.] This article does not limit the rights of or impose liability on a person to the extent that the person is protected against the assertion of a claim under Article 8.

(c) [Filing not notice.] Filing under this article does not constitute notice of a claim or defense to the holders, or purchasers, or persons described in subsections (a) and (b).

§ 9-332. Transfer of Money; Transfer of Funds from Deposit Account.

(a) [Transferee of money.] A transferee of money takes the money free of a security interest unless the transferee acts in collusion with the debtor in violating the rights of the secured party.

(b) [Transferee of funds from deposit account.] A transferee of funds from a deposit account takes the funds free of a security interest in the deposit account unless the transferee acts in collusion with the debtor in violating the rights of the secured party.

§ 9-333. Priority of Certain Liens Arising by Operation of Law.

(a) ["Possessory lien."] In this section, "possessory lien" means an interest, other than a security interest or an agricultural lien:

(1) which secures payment or performance of an obligation for services or materials furnished with respect to goods by a person in the ordinary course of the person's business;

(2) which is created by statute or rule of law in favor of the person; and

(3) whose effectiveness depends on the person's possession of the goods.

(b) [Priority of possessory lien.] A possessory lien on goods has priority over a security interest in the goods unless the lien is created by a statute that expressly provides otherwise.

§ 9-334. Priority of Security Interests in Fixtures and Crops.

(a) [Security interest in fixtures under this article.] A security interest under this article may be created in goods that are fixtures or may continue in goods that become fixtures. A security interest does not exist under this article in ordinary building materials incorporated into an improvement on land.

(b) [Security interest in fixtures under real-property law.] This article does not prevent creation of an encumbrance upon fixtures under real property law.

(c) [General rule: subordination of security interest in fixtures.] In cases not governed by subsections (d) through (h), a security interest in fixtures is subordinate to a conflicting interest of an encumbrancer or owner of the related real property other than the debtor.

(d) [Fixtures purchase-money priority.] Except as otherwise provided in subsection (h), a perfected security interest in fixtures has priority over a conflicting interest of an encumbrancer or owner of the real property if the debtor has an interest of record in or is in possession of the real property and:

(1) the security interest is a purchase-money security interest;

(2) the interest of the encumbrancer or owner arises before the goods become fixtures; and

(3) the security interest is perfected by a fixture filing before the goods become fixtures or within 20 days thereafter.

(e) [Priority of security interest in fixtures over interests in real property.] A perfected security interest in fixtures has priority over a conflicting interest of an encumbrancer or owner of the real property if:

(1) the debtor has an interest of record in the real property or is in possession of the real property and the security interest:

(A) is perfected by a fixture filing before the interest of the encumbrancer or owner is of record; and

(B) has priority over any conflicting interest of a predecessor in title of the encumbrancer or owner;

(2) before the goods become fixtures, the security interest is perfected by any method permitted by this article and the fixtures are readily removable:

(A) factory or office machines;

(B) equipment that is not primarily used or leased for use in the operation of the real property; or

(C) replacements of domestic appliances that are consumer goods;

(3) the conflicting interest is a lien on the real property obtained by legal or equitable proceedings after the security interest was perfected by any method permitted by this article; or

(4) the security interest is:

(A) created in a manufactured home in a manufactured-home transaction; and

(B) perfected pursuant to a statute described in Section 9-311(a)(2).

(f) [Priority based on consent, disclaimer, or right to remove.] A security interest in fixtures, whether or not perfected, has priority over a conflicting interest of an encumbrancer or owner of the real property if:

(1) the encumbrancer or owner has, in an authenticated record, consented to the security interest or disclaimed an interest in the goods as fixtures; or

(2) the debtor has a right to remove the goods as against the encumbrancer or owner.

(g) [Continuation of paragraph (f)(2) priority.] The priority of the security interest under paragraph (f)(2) continues for a reasonable time if the debtor's right to remove the goods as against the encumbrancer or owner terminates.

(h) [Priority of construction mortgage.] A mortgage is a construction mortgage to the extent that it secures an obligation incurred for the construction of an improvement on land, including the acquisition cost of the land, if a recorded record of the mortgage so indicates. Except as otherwise provided in subsections (e) and (f), a security interest in fixtures is subordinate to a construction mortgage if a record of the mortgage is recorded before the goods become fixtures and the goods become fixtures before the completion of the construction. A mortgage has this priority to the same extent as a construction mortgage to the extent that it is given to refinance a construction mortgage.

(i) [Priority of security interest in crops.] A perfected security interest in crops growing on real property has priority over a conflicting interest of an encumbrancer or owner of the real property if the debtor has an interest of record in or is in possession of the real property.

(j) [Subsection (i) prevails.] Subsection (i) prevails over any inconsistent provisions of the following statutes:

[List here any statutes containing provisions inconsistent with subsection (i).]

Legislative Note: *States that amend statutes to remove provisions inconsistent with subsection (i) need not enact subsection (j).*

§ 9-335. Accessions.

(a) [Creation of security interest in accession.] A security interest may be created in an accession and continues in collateral that becomes an accession.

(b) [Perfection of security interest.] If a security interest is perfected when the collateral becomes an accession, the security interest remains perfected in the collateral.

(c) [Priority of security interest.] Except as otherwise provided in subsection (d), the other provisions of this part determine the priority of a security interest in an accession.

(d) [Compliance with certificate-of-title statute.] A security interest in an accession is subordinate to a security interest in the whole which is perfected by compliance with the requirements of a certificate-of-title statute under Section 9-311(b).

(e) [Removal of accession after default.] After default, subject to Part 6, a secured party may remove an accession from other goods if the security interest in the accession has priority over the claims of every person having an interest in the whole.

(f) [Reimbursement following removal.] A secured party that removes an accession from other goods under subsection (e) shall promptly reimburse any holder of a security interest or other lien on, or owner of, the whole or of the other goods, other than the debtor, for the cost of repair of any physical injury to the whole or the other goods. The secured party need not reimburse the holder or owner for any diminution in value of the whole or the other goods caused by the absence of the accession removed or by any necessity for replacing it. A person entitled to reimbursement may refuse permission to remove until the secured party gives adequate assurance for the performance of the obligation to reimburse.

§ 9-336. Commingled Goods.

(a) ["Commingled goods."] In this section, "commingled goods" means goods that are physically united with other goods in such a manner that their identity is lost in a product or mass.

(b) [No security interest in commingled goods as such.] A security interest does not exist in commingled goods as such. However, a security interest may attach to a product or mass that results when goods become commingled goods.

(c) [Attachment of security interest to product or mass.] If collateral becomes commingled goods, a security interest attaches to the product or mass.

(d) [Perfection of security interest.] If a security interest in collateral is perfected before the collateral becomes commingled goods, the security interest that attaches to the product or mass under subsection (c) is perfected.

(e) [Priority of security interest.] Except as otherwise provided in subsection (f), the other provisions of this part determine the priority of a security interest that attaches to the product or mass under subsection (c).

(f) [Conflicting security interests in product or mass] If more than one security interest attaches to the product or mass under subsection (c), the following rules determine priority:

(1) A security interest that is perfected under subsection (d) has priority over a security interest that is unperfected at the time the collateral becomes commingled goods.

(2) If more than one security interest is perfected under subsection (d), the security interests rank equally in proportion to the value of the collateral at the time it became commingled goods.

§ 9-337. Priority of Security Interests in Goods Covered by Certificate of Title. If, while a security interest in goods is perfected by any method under the law of another jurisdiction, this State issues a certificate of title that does not show that the goods are subject to the security interest or contain a statement that they may be subject to security interests not shown on the certificate:

(1) a buyer of the goods, other than a person in the business of selling goods of that kind, takes free of the security interest if the buyer gives value and receives delivery of the goods after issuance of the certificate and without knowledge of the security interest; and

(2) the security interest is subordinate to a conflicting security interest in the goods that attaches, and is perfected under Section 9-311(b), after issuance of the certificate and without the conflicting secured party's knowledge of the security interest.

§ 9-338. Priority of Security Interest or Agricultural Lien Perfected by Filed Financing Statement Providing Certain Incorrect Information. If a security interest or agricultural lien is perfected by a filed financing statement providing information described in Section 9-516(b)(5) which is incorrect at the time the financing statement is filed:

(1) the security interest or agricultural lien is subordinate to a conflicting perfected security interest in the collateral to the extent that the holder of the conflicting security interest gives value in reasonable reliance upon the incorrect information; and

(2) a purchaser, other than a secured party, of the collateral takes free of the security interest or agricultural lien to the extent that, in reasonable reliance upon the incorrect information, the purchaser gives value and, in the case of chattel paper, documents, goods, instruments, or a security certificate, receives delivery of the collateral.

§ 9-339. Priority Subject to Subordination. This article does not preclude subordination by agreement by a person entitled to priority.

[Subpart 4. Rights of Bank]

§ 9-340. Effectiveness of Right of Recoupment or Set-off Against Deposit Account.

(a) [Exercise of recoupment or set-off.] Except as otherwise provided in subsection (c), a bank with which a deposit account is maintained may exercise any right of recoupment or set-off against a secured party that holds a security interest in the deposit account.

(b) [Recoupment or set-off not affected by security interest.] Except as otherwise provided in subsection (c), the application of this article to a security interest in a deposit account does not affect a right of recoupment or set-off of the secured party as to a deposit account maintained with the secured party.

(c) [When set-off ineffective.] The exercise by a bank of a set-off against a deposit account is ineffective against a secured party that holds a security interest in the deposit account which is perfected by control under Section 9-104(a)(3), if the set-off is based on a claim against the debtor.

§ 9-341. Bank's Rights and Duties with Respect to Deposit Account. Except as otherwise provided in Section 9-340(c), and unless the bank otherwise agrees in an authenticated record, a bank's rights and duties with respect to a deposit account maintained with the bank are not terminated, suspended, or modified by:

(1) the creation, attachment, or perfection of a security interest in the deposit account;

(2) the bank's knowledge of the security interest; or

(3) the bank's receipt of instructions from the secured party.

§ 9-342. Bank's Right To Refuse To Enter into or Disclose Existence of Control Agreement. This article does not require a bank to enter into an agreement of the kind described in Section 9-104(a)(2), even if its customer so requests or directs. A bank that has entered into such an agreement is not required to confirm the existence of the agreement to another person unless requested to do so by its customer.

PART 4 Rights of Third Parties

§ 9-401. Alienability of Debtor's Rights.
(a) [Other law governs alienability; exceptions.] Except as otherwise provided in subsection (b) and Sections 9-406, 9-407, 9-408, and 9-409, whether a debtor's rights in collateral may be voluntarily or involuntarily transferred is governed by law other than this article.
(b) [Agreement does not prevent transfer.] An agreement between the debtor and secured party which prohibits a transfer of the debtor's rights in collateral or makes the transfer a default does not prevent the transfer from taking effect.

§ 9-402. Secured Party Not Obligated on Contract of Debtor in Tort. The existence of a security interest, agricultural lien, or authority given to a debtor to dispose of or use collateral, without more, does not subject a secured party to liability in contract or tort for the debtor's acts or omissions.

§ 9-403. Agreement Not To Assert Defenses Against Assignee.
(a) ["Value."] In this section, "value" has the meaning provided in Section 3-303(a).
(b) [Agreement not to assert claim or defense.] Except as otherwise provided in this section, an agreement between an account debtor and an assignor not to assert against an assignee any claim or defense that the account debtor may have against the assignor is enforceable by an assignee that takes an assignment:
(1) for value;
(2) in good faith;
(3) without notice of a claim of a property or possessory right to the property assigned; and
(4) without notice of a defense or claim in recoupment of the type that may be asserted against a person entitled to enforce a negotiable instrument under Section 3-305(a).
(c) [When subsection (b) not applicable.] Subsection (b) does not apply to defenses of a type that may be asserted against a holder in due course of a negotiable instrument under Section 3-305(b).
(d) [Omission of required statement in consumer transaction.] In a consumer transaction, if a record evidences the account debtor's obligation, law other than this article requires that the record include a statement to the effect that the rights of an assignee are subject to claims or defenses that the account debtor could assert against the original obligee, and the record does not include such a statement:
(1) the record has the same effect as if the record included such a statement; and
(2) the account debtor may assert against an assignee those claims and defenses that would have been available if the record included such a statement.
(e) [Rule for individual under other law.] This section is subject to law other than this article which establishes a different rule for an account debtor who is an individual and who incurred the obligation primarily for personal, family, or household purposes.
(f) [Other law not displaced.] Except as otherwise provided in subsection (d), this section does not displace law other than this article which gives effect to an agreement by an account debtor not to assert a claim or defense against an assignee.

§ 9-404. Rights Acquired by Assignee; Claims and Defenses Against Assignee.
(a) [Assignee's rights subject to terms, claims, and defenses; exceptions.] Unless an account debtor has made an enforceable agreement not to assert defenses or claims, and subject to subsections (b) through (e), the rights of an assignee are subject to:
(1) all terms of the agreement between the account debtor and assignor and any defense or claim in recoupment arising from the transaction that gave rise to the contract; and
(2) any other defense or claim of the account debtor against the assignor which accrues before the account debtor receives a notification of the assignment authenticated by the assignor or the assignee.
(b) [Account debtor's claim reduces amount owed to assignee.] Subject to subsection (c) and except as otherwise provided in subsection (d), the claim of an account debtor against an assignor may be asserted against an assignee under subsection (a) only to reduce the amount the account debtor owes.
(c) [Rule for individual under other law.] This section is subject to law other than this article which establishes a different rule for an account debtor who is an individual and who incurred the obligation primarily for personal, family, or household purposes.
(d) [Omission of required statement in consumer transaction.] In a consumer transaction, if a record evidences the account debtor's obligation, law other than this article requires that the record include a statement to the effect that the account debtor's recovery against an assignee with respect to claims and defenses against the assignor may not exceed amounts paid by the account debtor under the record, and the record does not include such a statement, the extent to which a claim of an account debtor against the assignor may be asserted against an assignee is determined as if the record included such a statement.
(e) [Inapplicability to health-care-insurance receivable.] This section does not apply to an assignment of a health-care-insurance receivable.

§ 9-405. Modification of Assigned Contract.
(a) [Effect of modification on assignee.] A modification of or substitution for an assigned contract is effective against an assignee if made in good faith. The assignee acquires corresponding rights under the modified or substituted contract. The assignment may provide that the modification or substitution is a breach of contract by the assignor. This subsection is subject to subsections (b) through (d).
(b) [Applicability of subsection (a).] Subsection (a) applies to the extent that:
(1) the right to payment or a part thereof under an assigned contract has not been fully earned by performance; or

(2) the right to payment or a part thereof has been fully earned by performance and the account debtor has not received notification of the assignment under Section 9-406(a).

(c) [Rule for individual under other law.] This section is subject to law other than this article which establishes a different rule for an account debtor who is an individual and who incurred the obligation primarily for personal, family, or household purposes.

(d) [Inapplicability to health-care-insurance receivable.] This section does not apply to an assignment of a health-care-insurance receivable.

§ 9-406. Discharge of Account Debtor; Notification of Assignment; Identification and Proof of Assignment; Restrictions on Assignment of Accounts, Chattel Paper, Payment Intangibles, and Promissory Notes Ineffective.

(a) [Discharge of account debtor; effect of notification.] Subject to subsections (b) through (i), an account debtor on an account, chattel paper, or a payment intangible may discharge its obligation by paying the assignor until, but not after, the account debtor receives a notification, authenticated by the assignor or the assignee, that the amount due or to become due has been assigned and that payment is to be made to the assignee. After receipt of the notification, the account debtor may discharge its obligation by paying the assignee and may not discharge the obligation by paying the assignor.

(b) [When notification ineffective.] Subject to subsection (h), notification is ineffective under subsection (a):

(1) if it does not reasonably identify the rights assigned;

(2) to the extent that an agreement between an account debtor and a seller of a payment intangible limits the account debtor's duty to pay a person other than the seller and the limitation is effective under law other than this article; or

(3) at the option of an account debtor, if the notification notifies the account debtor to make less than the full amount of any installment or other periodic payment to the assignee, even if:

(A) only a portion of the account, chattel paper, or payment intangible has been assigned to that assignee;

(B) a portion has been assigned to another assignee; or

(C) the account debtor knows that the assignment to that assignee is limited.

(c) [Proof of assignment.] Subject to subsection (h), if requested by the account debtor, an assignee shall seasonably furnish reasonable proof that the assignment has been made. Unless the assignee complies, the account debtor may discharge its obligation by paying the assignor, even if the account debtor has received a notification under subsection (a).

(d) [Term restricting assignment generally ineffective.] Except as otherwise provided in subsection (e) and Sections 2A 303 and 9 407, and subject to subsection (h), a term in an agreement between an account debtor and an assignor or in a promissory note is ineffective to the extent that it:

(1) prohibits, restricts, or requires the consent of the account debtor or person obligated on the promissory note to the assignment or transfer of, or the creation, attachment, perfection, or enforcement of a security interest in, the account, chattel paper, payment intangible, or promissory note; or

(2) provides that the assignment or transfer or the creation, attachment, perfection, or enforcement of the security interest may give rise to a default, breach, right of recoupment, claim, defense, termination, right of termination, or remedy under the account, chattel paper, payment intangible, or promissory note.

(e) [Inapplicability of subsection (d) to certain sales.] Subsection (d) does not apply to the sale of a payment intangible or promissory note.

(f) [Legal restrictions on assignment generally ineffective.] Except as otherwise provided in Sections 2A-303 and 9-407 and subject to subsections (h) and (i), a rule of law, statute, or regulation that prohibits, restricts, or requires the consent of a government, governmental body or official, or account debtor to the assignment or transfer of, or creation of a security interest in, an account or chattel paper is ineffective to the extent that the rule of law, statute, or regulation:

(1) prohibits, restricts, or requires the consent of the government, governmental body or official, or account debtor to the assignment or transfer of, or the creation, attachment, perfection, or enforcement of a security interest in the account or chattel paper; or

(2) provides that the assignment or transfer or the creation, attachment, perfection, or enforcement of the security interest may give rise to a default, breach, right of recoupment, claim, defense, termination, right of termination, or remedy under the account or chattel paper.

(g) [Subsection (b)(3) not waivable.] Subject to subsection (h), an account debtor may not waive or vary its option under subsection (b)(3).

(h) [Rule for individual under other law.] This section is subject to law other than this article which establishes a different rule for an account debtor who is an individual and who incurred the obligation primarily for personal, family, or household purposes.

(i) [Inapplicability to health-care-insurance receivable.] This section does not apply to an assignment of a health-care-insurance receivable.

(j) [Section prevails over specified inconsistent law.] This section prevails over any inconsistent provisions of the following statutes, rules, and regulations:

[List here any statutes, rules, and regulations containing provisions inconsistent with this section.]

Legislative Note: *States that amend statutes, rules, and regulations to remove provisions inconsistent with this section need not enact subsection (j)*

§ 9-407. Restrictions on Creation or Enforcement of Security Interest in Leasehold Interest or in Lessor's Residual Interest.

(a) [Term restricting assignment generally ineffective.] Except as otherwise provided in subsection (b), a term in a lease agreement is ineffective to the extent that it:

(1) prohibits, restricts, or requires the consent of a party to the lease to the assignment or transfer of, or the creation, attachment, perfection, or enforcement of a security interest in, an interest of a party under the lease contract or in the lessor's residual interest in the goods; or

(2) provides that the assignment or transfer or the creation, attachment, perfection, or enforcement of the security interest may give rise to a default, breach, right of recoupment, claim, defense, termination, right of termination, or remedy under the lease.

(b) [Effectiveness of certain terms.] Except as otherwise provided in Section 2A-303(7), a term described in subsection (a)(2) is effective to the extent that there is:

(1) a transfer by the lessee of the lessee's right of possession or use of the goods in violation of the term; or

(2) a delegation of a material performance of either party to the lease contract in violation of the term.

(c) [Security interest not material impairment.] The creation, attachment, perfection, or enforcement of a security interest in the lessor's interest under the lease contract or the lessor's residual interest in the goods is not a transfer that materially impairs the lessee's prospect of obtaining return performance or materially changes the duty of or materially increases the burden or risk imposed on the lessee within the purview of Section 2A-303(4) unless, and then only to the extent that, enforcement actually results in a delegation of material performance of the lessor.

§ 9-408. Restrictions on Assignment of Promissory Notes, Health-Care-Insurance Receivables, and Certain General Intangibles Ineffective.

(a) [Term restricting assignment generally ineffective.] Except as otherwise provided in subsection (b), a term in a promissory note or in an agreement between an account debtor and a debtor which relates to a health-care-insurance receivable or a general intangible, including a contract, permit, license, or franchise, and which term prohibits, restricts, or requires the consent of the person obligated on the promissory note or the account debtor to, the assignment or transfer of, or creation, attachment, or perfection of a security interest in, the promissory note, health-care-insurance receivable, or general intangible, is ineffective to the extent that the term:

(1) would impair the creation, attachment, or perfection of a security interest; or

(2) provides that the assignment or transfer or the creation, attachment, or perfection of the security interest may give rise to a default, breach, right of recoupment, claim, defense, termination, right of termination, or remedy under the promissory note, health-care-insurance receivable, or general intangible.

(b) [Applicability of subsection (a) to sales of certain rights to payment.] Subsection (a) applies to a security interest in a payment intangible or promissory note only if the security interest arises out of a sale of the payment intangible or promissory note.

(c) [Legal restrictions on assignment generally ineffective.] A rule of law, statute, or regulation that prohibits, restricts, or requires the consent of a government, governmental body or official, person obligated on a promissory note, or account debtor to the assignment or transfer of, or creation of a security interest in, a promissory note, health-care-insurance receivable, or general intangible, including a contract, permit, license, or franchise between an account debtor and a debtor, is ineffective to the extent that the rule of law, statute, or regulation:

(1) would impair the creation, attachment, or perfection of a security interest; or

(2) provides that the assignment or transfer or the creation, attachment, or perfection of the security interest may give rise to a default, breach, right of recoupment, claim, defense, termination, right of termination, or remedy under the promissory note, health-care-insurance receivable, or general intangible.

(d) [Limitation on ineffectiveness under subsections (a) and (c).] To the extent that a term in a promissory note or in an agreement between an account debtor and a debtor which relates to a health-care-insurance receivable or general intangible or a rule of law, statute, or regulation described in subsection (c) would be effective under law other than this article but is ineffective under subsection (a) or (c), the creation, attachment, or perfection of a security interest in the promissory note, health-care-insurance receivable, or general intangible:

(1) is not enforceable against the person obligated on the promissory note or the account debtor;

(2) does not impose a duty or obligation on the person obligated on the promissory note or the account debtor;

(3) does not require the person obligated on the promissory note or the account debtor to recognize the security interest, pay or render performance to the secured party, or accept payment or performance from the secured party;

(4) does not entitle the secured party to use or assign the debtor's rights under the promissory note, health-care-insurance receivable, or general intangible, including any related information or materials furnished to the debtor in the transaction giving rise to the promissory note, health-care-insurance receivable, or general intangible;

(5) does not entitle the secured party to use, assign, possess, or have access to any trade secrets or confidential information of the person obligated on the promissory note or the account debtor; and

(6) does not entitle the secured party to enforce the security interest in the promissory note, health-care-insurance receivable, or general intangible.

(e) [Section prevails over specified inconsistent law.] This section prevails over any inconsistent provisions of the following statutes, rules, and regulations:

[List here any statutes, rules, and regulations containing provisions inconsistent with this section.]

Legislative Note: *States that amend statutes, rules, and regulations to remove provisions inconsistent with this section need not enact subsection (e).*

§ 9-409. Restrictions on Assignment of Letter-of-Credit Rights Ineffective.

(a) [Term or law restricting assignment generally ineffective.] A term in a letter of credit or a rule of law, statute, regulation, custom, or practice applicable to the letter of credit which prohibits, restricts, or requires the consent of an applicant, issuer, or nominated person to a beneficiary's assignment of or creation of a security interest in a letter-of-credit right is ineffective to the extent that the term or rule of law, statute, regulation, custom, or practice:

(1) would impair the creation, attachment, or perfection of a security interest in the letter-of-credit right; or

(2) provides that the assignment or the creation, attachment, or perfection of the security interest may give rise to a default, breach, right of recoupment, claim, defense, termination, right of termination, or remedy under the letter-of-credit right.

(b) [Limitation on ineffectiveness under subsection (a).] To the extent that a term in a letter of credit is ineffective under subsection (a) but would be effective under law other than this article or a custom or practice applicable to the letter of credit, to the transfer of a right to draw or otherwise demand performance under the letter of credit, or to the assignment of a right to proceeds of the letter of credit, the creation, attachment, or perfection of a security interest in the letter-of-credit right:

(1) is not enforceable against the applicant, issuer, nominated person, or transferee beneficiary;

(2) imposes no duties or obligations on the applicant, issuer, nominated person, or transferee beneficiary; and

(3) does not require the applicant, issuer, nominated person, or transferee beneficiary to recognize the security interest, pay or render performance to the secured party, or accept payment or other performance from the secured party.

PART 5 Filing

[Subpart 1. Filing Office; Contents and Effectiveness of Financing Statement]

§ 9-501. Filling Office.

(a) [Filing offices.] Except as otherwise provided in subsection (b), if the local law of this State governs perfection of a security interest or agricultural lien, the office in which to file a financing statement to perfect the security interest or agricultural lien is:

(1) the office designated for the filing or recording of a record of a mortgage on the related real property, if:

(A) the collateral is as-extracted collateral or timber to be cut; or

(B) the financing statement is filed as a fixture filing and the collateral is goods that are or are to become fixtures; or

(2) the office of [ ] [or any office duly authorized by [ ]], in all other cases, including a case in which the collateral is goods that are or are to become fixtures and the financing statement is not filed as a fixture filing.

(b) [Filing office for transmitting utilities.] The office in which to file a financing statement to perfect a security interest in collateral, including fixtures, of a transmitting utility is the office of [ ]. The financing statement also constitutes a fixture filing as to the collateral indicated in the financing statement which is or is to become fixtures.

Legislative Note: *The State should designate the filing office where the brackets appear. The filing office may be that of a governmental official (e.g., the Secretary of State) or a private party that maintains the State's filing system.*

§ 9-502. Contents of Financing Statement; Record of Mortgage as Financing Statement; Tine of Filing Financing Statement.

(a) [Sufficiency of financing statement.] Subject to subsection (b) a financing statement is sufficient only if it:

(1) provides the name of the debtor;

(2) provides the name of the secured party or a representative of the secured party; and

(3) indicates the collateral covered by the financing statement.

(b) [Real-property-related financing statements.] Except as otherwise provided in Section 9-501(b), to be sufficient, a financing statement that covers as-extracted collateral or timber to be cut, or which is filed as a fixture filing and covers goods that are or are to become fixtures, must satisfy subsection (a) and also:

(1) indicate that it covers this type of collateral;

(2) indicate that it is to be filed [for record] in the real property records;

(3) provide a description of the real property to which the collateral is related [sufficient to give constructive notice of a mortgage under the law of this State if the description were contained in a record of the mortgage of the real property]; and

(4) if the debtor does not have an interest of record in the real property, provide the name of a record owner.

(c) [Record of mortgage as financing statement.] A record of a mortgage is effective, from the date of recording, as a financing statement filed as a fixture filing or as a financing statement covering as-extracted collateral or timber to be cut only if:

(1) the record indicates the goods or accounts that it covers;

(2) the goods are or are to become fixtures related to the real property described in the record or the collateral is related to the real property described in the record and is as-extracted collateral or timber to be cut;

(3) the record satisfies the requirements for a financing statement in this section other than an indication that it is to be filed in the real property records; and

(4) the record is [duly] recorded.

(d) [Filing before security agreement or attachment.] A financing statement may be filed before a security agreement is made or a security interest otherwise attaches.

Legislative Note: *Language in brackets is optional. Where the State has any special recording system for real property other than the usual grantor grantee index (as, for instance, a tract system or a title registration or Torrens system) local adaptations of subsection (b)* *and Section 9-519(d) and (e) may be necessary. See, e.g., Mass. Gen. Laws Chapter 106, Section 9-410.*

§ 9-503. Name of Debtor and Secured Party.
(a) [Sufficiency of debtor's name.] A financing statement sufficiently provides the name of the debtor:

(1) if the debtor is a registered organization, only if the financing statement provides the name of the debtor indicated on the public record of the debtor's jurisdiction of organization which shows the debtor to have been organized;

(2) if the debtor is a decedent's estate, only if the financing statement provides the name of the decedent and indicates that the debtor is an estate;

(3) if the debtor is a trust or a trustee acting with respect to property held in trust, only if the financing statement:

(A) provides the name specified for the trust in its organic documents or, if no name is specified, provides the name of the settlor and additional information sufficient to distinguish the debtor from other trusts having one or more of the same settlors; and

(B) indicates, in the debtor's name or otherwise, that the debtor is a trust or is a trustee acting with respect to property held in trust; and

(4) in other cases:

(A) if the debtor has a name, only if it provides the individual or organizational name of the debtor; and

(B) if the debtor does not have a name, only if it provides the names of the partners, members, associates, or other persons comprising the debtor.

(b) [Additional debtor-related information.] A financing statement that provides the name of the debtor in accordance with subsection (a) is not rendered ineffective by the absence of:

(1) a trade name or other name of the debtor; or

(2) unless required under subsection (a)(4)(B), names of partners, members, associates, or other persons comprising the debtor.

(c) [Debtor's trade name insufficient.] A financing statement that provides only the debtor's trade name does not sufficiently provide the name of the debtor.

(d) [Representative capacity.] Failure to indicate the representative capacity of a secured party or representative of a secured party does not affect the sufficiency of a financing statement.

(e) [Multiple debtors and secured parties.] A financing statement may provide the name of more than one debtor and the name of more than one secured party.

§ 9-504. Indication of Collateral. A financing statement sufficiently indicates the collateral that it covers if the financing statement provides:
(1) a description of the collateral pursuant to Section 9-108; or
(2) an indication that the financing statement covers all assets or all personal property.

§ 9-505. Filing and Compliance with Other Statutes and Treaties for Consignments, Leases, Other Bailments, and Other Transactions.
(a) [Use of terms other than "debtor" and "secured party."] A consignor, lessor, or other bailor of goods, a licensor, or a buyer of a payment intangible or promissory note may file a financing statement, or may comply with a statute or treaty described in Section 9-311(a), using the terms "consignor", "consignee", "lessor", "lessee", "bailor", "bailee", "licensor", "licensee", "owner", "registered owner", "buyer", "seller", or words of similar import, instead of the terms "secured party" and "debtor".

(b) [Effect of financing statement under subsection (a).] This part applies to the filing of a financing statement under subsection (a) and, as appropriate, to compliance that is equivalent to filing a financing statement under Section 9-311(b), but the filing or compliance is not of itself a factor in determining whether the collateral secures an obligation. If it is determined for another reason that the collateral secures an obligation, a security interest held by the consignor, lessor, bailor, licensor, owner, or buyer which attaches to the collateral is perfected by the filing or compliance.

§ 9-506. Effect of Errors or Omissions.
(a) [Minor errors and omissions.] A financing statement substantially satisfying the requirements of this part is effective, even if it has minor errors or omissions, unless the errors or omissions make the financing statement seriously misleading.

(b) [Financing statement seriously misleading.] Except as otherwise provided in subsection (c), a financing statement that fails sufficiently to provide the name of the debtor in accordance with Section 9-503(a) is seriously misleading.

(c) [Financing statement not seriously misleading.] If a search of the records of the filing office under the debtor's correct name, using the filing office's standard search logic, if any, would disclose a financing statement that fails sufficiently to provide the name of the debtor in accordance with Section 9-503(a), the name provided does not make the financing statement seriously misleading.

(d) ["Debtor's correct name."] For purposes of Section 9-508(b), the "debtor's correct name" in subsection (c) means the correct name of the new debtor.

§ 9-507. Effect of Certain Events on Effectiveness of Financing Statement.
(a) [Disposition.] A filed financing statement remains effective with respect to collateral that is sold, exchanged, leased, licensed, or otherwise disposed of and in which a security interest or agricultural lien continues, even if the secured party knows of or consents to the disposition.

(b) [Information becoming seriously misleading.] Except as otherwise provided in subsection (c) and Section 9-508, a financing statement is not rendered ineffective if, after the financing statement is filed, the information provided in the financing statement becomes seriously misleading under Section 9-506.

(c) [Change in debtor's name.] If a debtor so changes its name that a filed financing statement becomes seriously misleading under Section 9-506:

(1) the financing statement is effective to perfect a security interest in collateral acquired by the debtor before, or within four months after, the change; and

(2) the financing statement is not effective to perfect a security interest in collateral acquired by the debtor more than four months after the change, unless an amendment to the financing statement which renders the financing statement not seriously misleading is filed within four months after the change.

§ 9-508. Effectiveness of Financing Statement if New Debtor Becomes Bound by Security Agreement.

(a) [Financing statement naming original debtor.] Except as otherwise provided in this section, a filed financing statement naming an original debtor is effective to perfect a security interest in collateral in which a new debtor has or acquires rights to the extent that the financing statement would have been effective had the original debtor acquired rights in the collateral.

(b) [Financing statement becoming seriously misleading.] If the difference between the name of the original debtor and that of the new debtor causes a filed financing statement that is effective under subsection (a) to be seriously misleading under Section 9-506:

(1) the financing statement is effective to perfect a security interest in collateral acquired by the new debtor before, and within four months after, the new debtor becomes bound under Section 9-203(d); and

(2) the financing statement is not effective to perfect a security interest in collateral acquired by the new debtor more than four months after the new debtor becomes bound under Section 9-203(d) unless an initial financing statement providing the name of the new debtor is filed before the expiration of that time.

(c) [When section not applicable.] This section does not apply to collateral as to which a filed financing statement remains effective against the new debtor under Section 9-507(a).

§ 9-509. Persons Entitles to File a Record.

(a) [Person entitled to file record.] A person may file an initial financing statement, amendment that adds collateral covered by a financing statement, or amendment that adds a debtor to a financing statement only if:

(1) the debtor authorizes the filing in an authenticated record or pursuant to subsection (b) or (c); or

(2) the person holds an agricultural lien that has become effective at the time of filing and the financing statement covers only collateral in which the person holds an agricultural lien.

(b) [Security agreement as authorization.] By authenticating or becoming bound as debtor by a security agreement, a debtor or new debtor authorizes the filing of an initial financing statement, and an amendment, covering:

(1) the collateral described in the security agreement; and

(2) property that becomes collateral under Section 9-315(a)(2), whether or not the security agreement expressly covers proceeds.

(c) [Acquisition of collateral as authorization.] By acquiring collateral in which a security interest or agricultural lien continues under Section 9-315(a)(1), a debtor authorizes the filing of an initial financing statement, and an amendment, covering the collateral and property that becomes collateral under Section 9-315(a)(2).

(d) [Person entitled to file certain amendments.] A person may file an amendment other than an amendment that adds collateral covered by a financing statement or an amendment that adds a debtor to a financing statement only if:

(1) the secured party of record authorizes the filing; or

(2) the amendment is a termination statement for a financing statement as to which the secured party of record has failed to file or send a termination statement as required by Section 9-513(a) or (c), the debtor authorizes the filing, and the termination statement indicates that the debtor authorized it to be filed.

(e) [Multiple secured parties of record.] If there is more than one secured party of record for a financing statement, each secured party of record may authorize the filing of an amendment under subsection (d).

§ 9-510. Effectiveness of File Record.

(a) [Filed record effective if authorized.] A filed record is effective only to the extent that it was filed by a person that may file it under Section 9-509.

(b) [Authorization by one secured party of record.] A record authorized by one secured party of record does not affect the financing statement with respect to another secured party of record.

(c) [Continuation statement not timely filed.] A continuation statement that is not filed within the six-month period prescribed by Section 9-515(d) is ineffective.

§ 9-511. Secured Party of Record.

(a) [Secured party of record.] A secured party of record with respect to a financing statement is a person whose name is provided as the name of the secured party or a representative of the secured party in an initial financing statement that has been filed. If an initial financing statement is filed under Section 9-514(a), the assignee named in the initial financing statement is the secured party of record with respect to the financing statement.

(b) [Amendment naming secured party of record.] If an amendment of a financing statement which provides the name of a person as a secured party or a representative of a secured party is filed, the person named in the amendment is a secured party of record. If an amendment is filed under Section 9-514(b), the assignee named in the amendment is a secured party of record.

(c) [Amendment deleting secured party of record.] A person remains a secured party of record until the filing of an amendment of the financing statement which deletes the person.

§ 9-512. Amendment of Financing Statement.

[Alternative A]

(a) [Amendment of information in financing statement.] Subject to Section 9-509, a person may add or delete collateral covered by, continue or terminate the effectiveness of, or, subject to subsection (e), otherwise amend the information provided in, a financing statement by filing an amendment that:

(1) identifies, by its file number, the initial financing statement to which the amendment relates; and

(2) if the amendment relates to an initial financing statement filed [or recorded] in a filing office described in Section 9-501(a)(1), provides the information specified in Section 9-502(b).

[Alternative B]

(a) [Amendment of information in financing statement.] Subject to Section 9-509, a person may add or delete collateral covered by, continue or terminate the effectiveness of, or, subject to subsection (e), otherwise amend the information provided in, a financing statement by filing an amendment that:

(1) identifies, by its file number, the initial financing statement to which the amendment relates; and

(2) if the amendment relates to an initial financing statement filed [or recorded] in a filing office described in Section 9-501(a)(1), provides the date [and time] that the initial financing statement was filed [or recorded] and the information specified in Section 9-502(b).

[End of Alternatives]

(b) [Period of effectiveness not affected.] Except as otherwise provided in Section 9-515, the filing of an amendment does not extend the period of effectiveness of the financing statement.

(c) [Effectiveness of amendment adding collateral.] A financing statement that is amended by an amendment that adds collateral is effective as to the added collateral only from the date of the filing of the amendment.

(d) [Effectiveness of amendment adding debtor.] A financing statement that is amended by an amendment that adds a debtor is effective as to the added debtor only from the date of the filing of the amendment.

(e) [Certain amendments ineffective.] An amendment is ineffective to the extent it:

(1) purports to delete all debtors and fails to provide the name of a debtor to be covered by the financing statement; or

(2) purports to delete all secured parties of record and fails to provide the name of a new secured party of record.

Legislative Note: *States whose real-estate filing offices require additional information in amendments and cannot search their records by both the name of the debtor and the file number should enact Alternative B to Sections 9-512(a), 9-518(b), 9-519(f) and 9-522(a).*

§ 9-513. Termination Statement.

(a) [Consumer goods.] A secured party shall cause the secured party of record for a financing statement to file a termination statement for the financing statement if the financing statement covers consumer goods and:

(1) there is no obligation secured by the collateral covered by the financing statement and no commitment to make an advance, incur an obligation, or otherwise give value; or

(2) the debtor did not authorize the filing of the initial financing statement.

(b) [Time for compliance with subsection (a).] To comply with subsection (a), a secured party shall cause the secured party of record to file the termination statement:

(1) within one month after there is no obligation secured by the collateral covered by the financing statement and no commitment to make an advance, incur an obligation, or otherwise give value; or

(2) if earlier, within 20 days after the secured party receives an authenticated demand from a debtor.

(c) [Other collateral.] In cases not governed by subsection (a), within 20 days after a secured party receives an authenticated demand from a debtor, the secured party shall cause the secured party of record for a financing statement to send to the debtor a termination statement for the financing statement or file the termination statement in the filing office if:

(1) except in the case of a financing statement covering accounts or chattel paper that has been sold or goods that are the subject of a consignment, there is no obligation secured by the collateral covered by the financing statement and no commitment to make an advance, incur an obligation, or otherwise give value;

(2) the financing statement covers accounts or chattel paper that has been sold but as to which the account debtor or other person obligated has discharged its obligation;

(3) the financing statement covers goods that were the subject of a consignment to the debtor but are not in the debtor's possession; or

(4) the debtor did not authorize the filing of the initial financing statement.

(d) [Effect of filing termination statement.] Except as otherwise provided in Section 9-510, upon the filing of a termination statement with the filing office, the financing statement to which the termination statement relates ceases to be effective. Except as otherwise provided in Section 9-510, for purposes of Sections 9-519(g), 9-522(a), and 9-523(c), the filing with the filing office of a termination statement relating to a financing statement that indicates that the debtor is a transmitting utility also causes the effectiveness of the financing statement to lapse.

§ 9-514. Assignment of Powers of Secured Party of Record.

(a) [Assignment reflected on initial financing statement.] Except as otherwise provided in subsection (c), an initial financing statement may reflect an assignment of all of the secured party's power to authorize an amendment to the financing statement by providing the name and mailing address of the assignee as the name and address of the secured party.

(b) [Assignment of filed financing statement.] Except as otherwise provided in subsection (c), a secured party of record may assign of record all or part of its power to authorize an amendment to a financing statement by filing in the filing office an amendment of the financing statement which:

(1) identifies, by its file number, the initial financing statement to which it relates;

(2) provides the name of the assignor; and

(3) provides the name and mailing address of the assignee.

(c) [Assignment of record of mortgage.] An assignment of record of a security interest in a fixture covered by a record of a mortgage which is effective as a financing statement filed as a fixture filing under Section 9-502(c) may be made only by an assignment of record of the mortgage in the manner provided by law of this State other than [the Uniform Commercial Code].

§ 9-515. Duration and Effectiveness of Financing Statement; Effect of Lapsed Financing Statement.

(a) [Five-year effectiveness.] Except as otherwise provided in subsections (b), (e), (f), and (g), a filed financing statement is effective for a period of five years after the date of filing.

(b) [Public-finance or manufactured-home transaction.] Except as otherwise provided in subsections (e), (f), and (g), an initial financing statement filed in connection with a public-finance transaction or manufactured-home transaction is effective for a period of 30 years after the date of filing if it indicates that it is filed in connection with a public-finance transaction or manufactured-home transaction.

(c) [Lapse and continuation of financing statement.] The effectiveness of a filed financing statement lapses on the expiration of the period of its effectiveness unless before the lapse a continuation statement is filed pursuant to subsection (d). Upon lapse, a financing statement ceases to be effective and any security interest or agricultural lien that was perfected by the financing statement becomes unperfected, unless the security interest is perfected otherwise. If the security interest or agricultural lien becomes unperfected upon lapse, it is deemed never to have been perfected as against a purchaser of the collateral for value.

(d) [When continuation statement may be filed.] A continuation statement may be filed only within six months before the expiration of the five-year period specified in subsection (a) or the 30-year period specified in subsection (b), whichever is applicable.

(e) [Effect of filing continuation statement.] Except as otherwise provided in Section 9-510, upon timely filing of a continuation statement, the effectiveness of the initial financing statement continues for a period of five years commencing on the day on which the financing statement would have become ineffective in the absence of the filing. Upon the expiration of the five-year period, the financing statement lapses in the same manner as provided in subsection (c), unless, before the lapse, another continuation statement is filed pursuant to subsection (d). Succeeding continuation statements may be filed in the same manner to continue the effectiveness of the initial financing statement.

(f) [Transmitting utility financing statement.] If a debtor is a transmitting utility and a filed financing statement so indicates, the financing statement is effective until a termination statement is filed.

(g) [Record of mortgage as financing statement.] A record of a mortgage that is effective as a financing statement filed as a fixture filing under Section 9-502(c) remains effective as a financing statement filed as a fixture filing until the mortgage is released or satisfied of record or its effectiveness otherwise terminates as to the real property.

§ 9-516. What Constitutes Filing; Effectiveness of Filing.

(a) [What constitutes filing.] Except as otherwise provided in subsection (b), communication of a record to a filing office and tender of the filing fee or acceptance of the record by the filing office constitutes filing.

(b) [Refusal to accept record; filing does not occur.] Filing does not occur with respect to a record that a filing office refuses to accept because:

(1) the record is not communicated by a method or medium of communication authorized by the filing office;

(2) an amount equal to or greater than the applicable filing fee is not tendered;

(3) the filing office is unable to index the record because:

(A) in the case of an initial financing statement, the record does not provide a name for the debtor;

(B) in the case of an amendment or correction statement, the record:

(i) does not identify the initial financing statement as required by Section 9-512 or 9 518, as applicable; or

(ii) identifies an initial financing statement whose effectiveness has lapsed under Section 9-515;

(C) in the case of an initial financing statement that provides the name of a debtor identified as an individual or an amendment that provides a name of a debtor identified as an individual which was not previously provided in the financing statement to which the record relates, the record does not identify the debtor's last name; or

(D) in the case of a record filed [or recorded] in the filing office described in Section 9-501(a)(1), the record does not provide a sufficient description of the real property to which it relates;

(4) in the case of an initial financing statement or an amendment that adds a secured party of record, the record does not provide a name and mailing address for the secured party of record;

(5) in the case of an initial financing statement or an amendment that provides a name of a debtor which was not previously provided in the financing statement to which the amendment relates, the record does not:

(A) provide a mailing address for the debtor;

(B) indicate whether the debtor is an individual or an organization; or

(C) if the financing statement indicates that the debtor is an organization, provide:

(i) a type of organization for the debtor;

(ii) a jurisdiction of organization for the debtor; or

(iii) an organizational identification number for the debtor or indicate that the debtor has none;

(6) in the case of an assignment reflected in an initial financing statement under Section 9-514(a) or an amendment filed under Section 9-514(b), the record does not provide a name and mailing address for the assignee; or

(7) in the case of a continuation statement, the record is not filed within the six-month period prescribed by Section 9-515(d).

(c) [Rules applicable to subsection (b).] For purposes of subsection (b):

(1) a record does not provide information if the filing office is unable to read or decipher the information; and

(2) a record that does not indicate that it is an amendment or identify an initial financing statement to which it relates, as required by Section 9-512, 9 514, or 9 518, is an initial financing statement.

(d) [Refusal to accept record; record effective as filed record.] A record that is communicated to the filing office with tender of the filing fee, but which the filing office refuses to accept for a reason other than one set forth in subsection (b), is effective as a filed record except as against a purchaser of the collateral which gives value in reasonable reliance upon the absence of the record from the files.

§ 9-517. Effect of Indexing Errors. The failure of the filing office to index a record correctly does not affect the effectiveness of the filed record.

§ 9-518. Claim Concerning Inaccurate or Wrongfully Filed Record.
(a) [Correction statement.] A person may file in the filing office a correction statement with respect to a record indexed there under the person's name if the person believes that the record is inaccurate or was wrongfully filed.

[Alternative A]
(b) [Sufficiency of correction statement.] A correction statement must:

(1) identify the record to which it relates by the file number assigned to the initial financing statement to which the record relates;
(2) indicate that it is a correction statement; and
(3) provide the basis for the person's belief that the record is inaccurate and indicate the manner in which the person believes the record should be amended to cure any inaccuracy or provide the basis for the person's belief that the record was wrongfully filed.

[Alternative B]
(b) [Sufficiency of correction statement.] A correction statement must:

(1) identify the record to which it relates by:
(A) the file number assigned to the initial financing statement to which the record relates; and
(B) if the correction statement relates to a record filed [or recorded] in a filing office described in Section 9-501(a)(1), the date [and time] that the initial financing statement was filed [or recorded] and the information specified in Section 9-502(b);
(2) indicate that it is a correction statement; and
(3) provide the basis for the person's belief that the record is inaccurate and indicate the manner in which the person believes the record should be amended to cure any inaccuracy or provide the basis for the person's belief that the record was wrongfully filed.

[End of Alternatives]

(c) [Record not affected by correction statement.] The filing of a correction statement does not affect the effectiveness of an initial financing statement or other filed record.

Legislative Note: *States whose real-estate filing offices require additional information in amendments and cannot search their records by both the name of the debtor and the file number should enact Alternative B to Sections 9-512(a), 9-518(b), 9-519(f) and 9-522(a).*

[Subpart 2. Duties and Operation of Filing Office]

§ 9-519. Numbering, Maintaining, and Indexing Records; Communicating Information Provided in Records.
(a) [Filing office duties.] For each record filed in a filing office, the filing office shall:

(1) assign a unique number to the filed record;
(2) create a record that bears the number assigned to the filed record and the date and time of filing;
(3) maintain the filed record for public inspection; and
(4) index the filed record in accordance with subsections (c), (d), and (e).

(b) [File number.] A file number [assigned after January 1, 2002,] must include a digit that:

(1) is mathematically derived from or related to the other digits of the file number; and
(2) aids the filing office in determining whether a number communicated as the file number includes a single-digit or transpositional error.

(c) [Indexing: general.] Except as otherwise provided in subsections (d) and (e), the filing office shall:

(1) index an initial financing statement according to the name of the debtor and index all filed records relating to the initial financing statement in a manner that associates with one another an initial financing statement and all filed records relating to the initial financing statement; and
(2) index a record that provides a name of a debtor which was not previously provided in the financing statement to which the record relates also according to the name that was not previously provided.

(d) [Indexing: real-property-related financing statement.] If a financing statement is filed as a fixture filing or covers as-extracted collateral or timber to be cut, [it must be filed for record and] the filing office shall index it:

(1) under the names of the debtor and of each owner of record shown on the financing statement as if they were the mortgagors under a mortgage of the real property described; and
(2) to the extent that the law of this State provides for indexing of records of mortgages under the name of the mortgagee, under the name of the secured party as if the secured party were the mortgagee thereunder, or, if indexing is by description, as if the financing statement were a record of a mortgage of the real property described.

(e) [Indexing: real-property-related assignment.] If a financing statement is filed as a fixture filing or covers as-extracted collateral or timber to be cut, the filing office shall index an assignment filed under Section 9-514(a) or an amendment filed under Section 9-514(b):

(1) under the name of the assignor as grantor; and
(2) to the extent that the law of this State provides for indexing a record of the assignment of a mortgage under the name of the assignee, under the name of the assignee.

[Alternative A]
(f) [Retrieval and association capability.] The filing office shall maintain a capability:

(1) to retrieve a record by the name of the debtor and by the file number assigned to the initial financing statement to which the record relates; and
(2) to associate and retrieve with one another an initial financing statement and each filed record relating to the initial financing statement.

[Alternative B]
(f) [Retrieval and association capability.] The filing office shall maintain a capability:
(1) to retrieve a record by the name of the debtor and:
(A) if the filing office is described in Section 9-501(a)(1), by the file number assigned to the initial financing statement to which the record relates and the date [and time] that the record was filed [or recorded]; or
(B) if the filing office is described in Section 9-501(a)(2), by the file number assigned to the initial financing statement to which the record relates; and
(2) to associate and retrieve with one another an initial financing statement and each filed record relating to the initial financing statement.

[End of Alternatives]

(g) [Removal of debtor's name.] The filing office may not remove a debtor's name from the index until one year after the effectiveness of a financing statement naming the debtor lapses under Section 9-515 with respect to all secured parties of record.
(h) [Timeliness of filing office performance.] The filing office shall perform the acts required by subsections (a) through (e) at the time and in the manner prescribed by filing-office rule, but not later than two business days after the filing office receives the record in question.

[(i) [Inapplicability to real-property-related filing office.] Subsection[s] [(b)] [and] [(h)] do[es] not apply to a filing office described in Section 9-501(a)(1).]

Legislative Notes:
1. States whose filing offices currently assign file numbers that include a verification number, commonly known as a "check digit," or can implement this requirement before the effective date of this Article should omit the bracketed language in subsection (b).
2. In States in which writings will not appear in the real property records and indices unless actually recorded the bracketed language in subsection (d) should be used.
3. States whose real-estate filing offices require additional information in amendments and cannot search their records by both the name of the debtor and the file number should enact Alternative B to Sections 9-512(a), 9-518(b), 9-519(f) and 9-522(a).
4. A State that elects not to require real-estate filing offices to comply with either or both of subsections (b) and (h) may adopt an applicable variation of subsection (i) and add "Except as otherwise provided in subsection (i)," to the appropriate subsection or subsections.

§ 9-520. Acceptance and Refusal To Accept Record.

(a) [Mandatory refusal to accept record.] A filing office shall refuse to accept a record for filing for a reason set forth in Section 9-516(b) and may refuse to accept a record for filing only for a reason set forth in Section 9-516(b).
(b) [Communication concerning refusal.] If a filing office refuses to accept a record for filing, it shall communicate to the person that presented the record the fact of and reason for the refusal and the date and time the record would have been filed had the filing office accepted it. The communication must be made at the time and in the manner prescribed by filing-office rule but [, in the case of a filing office described in Section 9-501(a)(2),] in no event more than two business days after the filing office receives the record.
(c) [When filed financing statement effective.] A filed financing statement satisfying Section 9-502(a) and (b) is effective, even if the filing office is required to refuse to accept it for filing under subsection (a). However, Section 9-338 applies to a filed financing statement providing information described in Section 9-516(b)(5) which is incorrect at the time the financing statement is filed.
(d) [Separate application to multiple debtors.] If a record communicated to a filing office provides information that relates to more than one debtor, this part applies as to each debtor separately.
Legislative Note: *A State that elects not to require real-property filing offices to comply with subsection (b) should include the bracketed language.*

§ 9-521. Uniform Form of Written Financing Statement and Amendment.

(a) [Initial financing statement form.] A filing office that accepts written records may not refuse to accept a written initial financing statement in the following form and format except for a reason set forth in Section 9-516(b):
(b) [Amendment form.] A filing office that accepts written records may not refuse to accept a written record in the following form and format except for a reason set forth in Section 9-516(b):

§ 9-522. Maintenance and Destruction of Records.

[Alternative A]
(a) [Post-lapse maintenance and retrieval of information.] The filing office shall maintain a record of the information provided in a filed financing statement for at least one year after the effectiveness of the financing statement has lapsed under Section 9-515 with respect to all secured parties of record. The record must be retrievable by using the name of the debtor and by using the file number assigned to the initial financing statement to which the record relates.

[Alternative B]
(a) [Post-lapse maintenance and retrieval of information.] The filing office shall maintain a record of the information provided in a filed financing statement for at least one year after the effectiveness of the financing statement has lapsed under Section 9-515 with respect to all secured parties of record. The record must be retrievable by using the name of the debtor and:

(1) if the record was filed [or recorded] in the filing office described in Section 9-501(a)(1), by using the file number assigned to the initial financing statement to which the record relates and the date [and time] that the record was filed [or recorded]; or

(2) if the record was filed in the filing office described in Section 9-501(a)(2), by using the file number assigned to the initial financing statement to which the record relates.

[End of Alternatives]

(b) [Destruction of written records.] Except to the extent that a statute governing disposition of public records provides otherwise, the filing office immediately may destroy any written record evidencing a financing statement. However, if the filing office destroys a written record, it shall maintain another record of the financing statement which complies with subsection (a).

Legislative Note: *States whose real-estate filing offices require additional information in amendments and cannot search their records by both the name of the debtor and the file number should enact Alternative B to Sections 9-512(a), 9-518(b), 9-519(f) and 9-522(a).*

§ 9-523. Information from Filing Office; Sale or License of Records.

(a) [Acknowledgment of filing written record.] If a person that files a written record requests an acknowledgment of the filing, the filing office shall send to the person an image of the record showing the number assigned to the record pursuant to Section 9-519(a)(1) and the date and time of the filing of the record. However, if the person furnishes a copy of the record to the filing office, the filing office may instead:

(1) note upon the copy the number assigned to the record pursuant to Section 9-519(a)(1) and the date and time of the filing of the record; and

(2) send the copy to the person.

(b) [Acknowledgment of filing other record.] If a person files a record other than a written record, the filing office shall communicate to the person an acknowledgment that provides:

(1) the information in the record;

(2) the number assigned to the record pursuant to Section 9-519(a)(1); and

(3) the date and time of the filing of the record.

(c) [Communication of requested information.] The filing office shall communicate or otherwise make available in a record the following information to any person that requests it:

(1) whether there is on file on a date and time specified by the filing office, but not a date earlier than three business days before the filing office receives the request, any financing statement that:

(A) designates a particular debtor [or, if the request so states, designates a particular debtor at the address specified in the request];

(B) has not lapsed under Section 9-515 with respect to all secured parties of record; and

(C) if the request so states, has lapsed under Section 9-515 and a record of which is maintained by the filing office under Section 9-522(a);

(2) the date and time of filing of each financing statement; and

(3) the information provided in each financing statement.

(d) [Medium for communicating information.] In complying with its duty under subsection (c), the filing office may communicate information in any medium. However, if requested, the filing office shall communicate information by issuing [its written certificate] [a record that can be admitted into evidence in the courts of this State without extrinsic evidence of its authenticity].

(e) [Timeliness of filing office performance.] The filing office shall perform the acts required by subsections (a) through (d) at the time and in the manner prescribed by filing-office rule, but not later than two business days after the filing office receives the request.

(f) [Public availability of records.] At least weekly, the [insert appropriate official or governmental agency] [filing office] shall offer to sell or license to the public on a nonexclusive basis, in bulk, copies of all records filed in it under this part, in every medium from time to time available to the filing office.

Legislative Notes:

1. States whose filing office does not offer the additional service of responding to search requests limited to a particular address should omit the bracketed language in subsection (c)(1)(A).

2. A State that elects not to require real-estate filing offices to comply with either or both of subsections (e) and (f) should specify in the appropriate subsection(s) only the filing office described in Section 9-501(a)(2).

§ 9-524. Delay by Filing Office.

Delay by the filing office beyond a time limit prescribed by this part is excused if:

(1) the delay is caused by interruption of communication or computer facilities, war, emergency conditions, failure of equipment, or other circumstances beyond control of the filing office; and

(2) the filing office exercises reasonable diligence under the circumstances.

§ 9-525. Fees.

(a) [Initial financing statement or other record: general rule.] Except as otherwise provided in subsection (e), the fee for filing and indexing a record under this part, other than an initial financing statement of the kind described in subsection (b), is [the amount specified in subsection (c), if applicable, plus]:

(1) $ __[X]______ if the record is communicated in writing and consists of one or two pages;

(2) $ __[2X]______ if the record is communicated in writing and consists of more than two pages; and

(3) $ __[1/2X]___ if the record is communicated by another medium authorized by filing-office rule.

(b) [Initial financing statement: public-finance and manufactured-housing transactions.] Except as otherwise provided in subsection (e), the fee for filing and indexing an initial financing statement of the following kind is [the amount specified in subsection (c), if applicable, plus]:

(1) $ _____ if the financing statement indicates that it is filed in connection with a public-finance transaction;

(2) $ _____ if the financing statement indicates that it is filed in connection with a manufactured-home transaction.

[Alternative A]

(c) [Number of names.] The number of names required to be indexed does not affect the amount of the fee in subsections (a) and (b).

[Alternative B]

(c) [Number of names.] Except as otherwise provided in subsection (e), if a record is communicated in writing, the fee for each name more than two required to be indexed is $ _______.

[End of Alternatives]

(d) [Response to information request.] The fee for responding to a request for information from the filing office, including for [issuing a certificate showing] [communicating] whether there is on file any financing statement naming a particular debtor, is:

(1) $ ____ if the request is communicated in writing; and

(2) $ ____ if the request is communicated by another medium authorized by filing-office rule.

(e) [Record of mortgage.] This section does not require a fee with respect to a record of a mortgage which is effective as a financing statement filed as a fixture filing or as a financing statement covering as-extracted collateral or timber to be cut under Section 9-502(c). However, the recording and satisfaction fees that otherwise would be applicable to the record of the mortgage apply.

Legislative Notes:

1. To preserve uniformity, a State that places the provisions of this section together with statutes setting fees for other services should do so without modification.

2. A State should enact subsection (c), Alternative A, and omit the bracketed language in subsections (a) and (b) unless its indexing system entails a substantial additional cost when indexing additional names.

§ 9-526. Filing-Office Rules.

(a) [Adoption of filing-office rules.] The [insert appropriate governmental official or agency] shall adopt and publish rules to implement this article. The filing-office rules must be[:

(1)] consistent with this article[; and

(2) adopted and published in accordance with the [insert any applicable state administrative procedure act]].

(b) [Harmonization of rules.] To keep the filing-office rules and practices of the filing office in harmony with the rules and practices of filing offices in other jurisdictions that enact substantially this part, and to keep the technology used by the filing office compatible with the technology used by filing offices in other jurisdictions that enact substantially this part, the [insert appropriate governmental official or agency], so far as is consistent with the purposes, policies, and provisions of this article, in adopting, amending, and repealing filing-office rules, shall:

(1) consult with filing offices in other jurisdictions that enact substantially this part; and

(2) consult the most recent version of the Model Rules promulgated by the International Association of Corporate Administrators or any successor organization; and

(3) take into consideration the rules and practices of, and the technology used by, filing offices in other jurisdictions that enact substantially this part.

§ 9-527. Duty To Report. The [insert appropriate governmental official or agency] shall report [annually on or before ________] to the [Governor and Legislature] on the operation of the filing office. The report must contain a statement of the extent to which:

(1) the filing-office rules are not in harmony with the rules of filing offices in other jurisdictions that enact substantially this part and the reasons for these variations; and

(2) the filing-office rules are not in harmony with the most recent version of the Model Rules promulgated by the International Association of Corporate Administrators, or any successor organization, and the reasons for these variations.

PART 6 Default

[Subpart 1. Default and Enforcement of Security Interest]

§ 9-601. Rights after Default; Judicial Enforcement; Consignor or Buyer of Accounts, Chattel Paper, Payment Intangibles, or Promissory Notes.

(a) [Rights of secured party after default.] After default, a secured party has the rights provided in this part and, except as otherwise provided in Section 9-602, those provided by agreement of the parties. A secured party:

(1) may reduce a claim to judgment, foreclose, or otherwise enforce the claim, security interest, or agricultural lien by any available judicial procedure; and

(2) if the collateral is documents, may proceed either as to the documents or as to the goods they cover.

(b) [Rights and duties of secured party in possession or control.] A secured party in possession of collateral or control of collateral under Section 9-104, 9 105, 9 106, or 9 107 has the rights and duties provided in Section 9-207.

(c) [Rights cumulative; simultaneous exercise.] The rights under subsections (a) and (b) are cumulative and may be exercised simultaneously.

(d) [Rights of debtor and obligor.] Except as otherwise provided in subsection (g) and Section 9-605, after default, a debtor and an obligor have the rights provided in this part and by agreement of the parties.

(e) [Lien of levy after judgment.] If a secured party has reduced its claim to judgment, the lien of any levy that may be made upon the collateral by virtue of an execution based upon the judgment relates back to the earliest of:

(1) the date of perfection of the security interest or agricultural lien in the collateral;

(2) the date of filing a financing statement covering the collateral; or

(3) any date specified in a statute under which the agricultural lien was created.

(f) [Execution sale.] A sale pursuant to an execution is a foreclosure of the security interest or agricultural lien by judicial procedure within the meaning of this section. A secured party may purchase at the sale and thereafter hold the collateral free of any other requirements of this article.

(g) [Consignor or buyer of certain rights to payment.] Except as otherwise provided in Section 9-607(c), this part imposes no duties upon a secured party that is a consignor or is a buyer of accounts, chattel paper, payment intangibles, or promissory notes.

§ 9-602. Waiver and Variance of Rights and Duties. Except as otherwise provided in Section 9-624, to the extent that they give rights to a debtor or obligor and impose duties on a secured party, the debtor or obligor may not waive or vary the rules stated in the following listed sections:
(1) Section 9-207(b)(4)(C), which deals with use and operation of the collateral by the secured party;
(2) Section 9-210, which deals with requests for an accounting and requests concerning a list of collateral and statement of account;
(3) Section 9-607(c), which deals with collection and enforcement of collateral;
(4) Sections 9-608(a) and 9-615(c) to the extent that they deal with application or payment of noncash proceeds of collection, enforcement, or disposition;
(5) Sections 9-608(a) and 9-615(d) to the extent that they require accounting for or payment of surplus proceeds of collateral;
(6) Section 9-609 to the extent that it imposes upon a secured party that takes possession of collateral without judicial process the duty to do so without breach of the peace;
(7) Sections 9-610(b), 9-611, 9-613, and 9-614, which deal with disposition of collateral;
(8) Section 9-615(f), which deals with calculation of a deficiency or surplus when a disposition is made to the secured party, a person related to the secured party, or a secondary obligor;
(9) Section 9-616, which deals with explanation of the calculation of a surplus or deficiency;
(10) Sections 9-20, 9-621, and 9-622, which deal with acceptance of collateral in satisfaction of obligation;
(11) Section 9-623, which deals with redemption of collateral;
(12) Section 9-624, which deals with permissible waivers; and
(13) Sections 9-625 and 9-626, which deal with the secured party's liability for failure to comply with this article.

§ 9-603. Agreement on Standards Concerning Rights and Duties.
(a) [Agreed standards.] The parties may determine by agreement the standards measuring the fulfillment of the rights of a debtor or obligor and the duties of a secured party under a rule stated in Section 9-602 if the standards are not manifestly unreasonable.
(b) [Agreed standards inapplicable to breach of peace.] Subsection (a) does not apply to the duty under Section 9-609 to refrain from breaching the peace.

§ 9-604. Procedure if Security Agreement Covers Real Property or Fixtures.
(a) [Enforcement: personal and real property.] If a security agreement covers both personal and real property, a secured party may proceed:
(1) under this part as to the personal property without prejudicing any rights with respect to the real property; or
(2) as to both the personal property and the real property in accordance with the rights with respect to the real property, in which case the other provisions of this part do not apply.
(b) [Enforcement: fixtures.] Subject to subsection (c), if a security agreement covers goods that are or become fixtures, a secured party may proceed:
(1) under this part; or
(2) in accordance with the rights with respect to real property, in which case the other provisions of this part do not apply.
(c) [Removal of fixtures.] Subject to the other provisions of this part, if a secured party holding a security interest in fixtures has priority over all owners and encumbrancers of the real property, the secured party, after default, may remove the collateral from the real property.
(d) [Injury caused by removal.] A secured party that removes collateral shall promptly reimburse any encumbrancer or owner of the real property, other than the debtor, for the cost of repair of any physical injury caused by the removal. The secured party need not reimburse the encumbrancer or owner for any diminution in value of the real property caused by the absence of the goods removed or by any necessity of replacing them. A person entitled to reimbursement may refuse permission to remove until the secured party gives adequate assurance for the performance of the obligation to reimburse.

§ 9-605. Unknown Debtor or Secondary Obligor. A secured party does not owe a duty based on its status as secured party:
(1) to a person that is a debtor or obligor, unless the secured party knows:
(A) that the person is a debtor or obligor;
(B) the identity of the person; and
(C) how to communicate with the person; or
(2) to a secured party or lienholder that has filed a financing statement against a person, unless the secured party knows:
(A) that the person is a debtor; and
(B) the identity of the person.

§ 9-606. Time of Default for Agricultural Lien. For purposes of this part, a default occurs in connection with an agricultural lien at the time the secured party becomes entitled to enforce the lien in accordance with the statute under which it was created.

§ 9-607. Collection and Enforcement by Secured Party.
(a) [Collection and enforcement generally.] If so agreed, and in any event after default, a secured party:
(1) may notify an account debtor or other person obligated on collateral to make payment or otherwise render performance to or for the benefit of the secured party;
(2) may take any proceeds to which the secured party is entitled under Section 9-315;
(3) may enforce the obligations of an account debtor or other person obligated on collateral and exercise the rights of the debtor with respect to the obligation of the account debtor or other person obligated on collateral to make payment or otherwise render performance to the debtor, and with respect to any property that secures the obligations of the account debtor or other person obligated on the collateral;
(4) if it holds a security interest in a deposit account perfected by control under Section 9-104(a)(1), may apply the balance of the deposit account to the obligation secured by the deposit account; and

(5) if it holds a security interest in a deposit account perfected by control under Section 9-104(a)(2) or (3), may instruct the bank to pay the balance of the deposit account to or for the benefit of the secured party.

(b) [Nonjudicial enforcement of mortgage.] If necessary to enable a secured party to exercise under subsection (a)(3) the right of a debtor to enforce a mortgage nonjudicially, the secured party may record in the office in which a record of the mortgage is recorded:

(1) a copy of the security agreement that creates or provides for a security interest in the obligation secured by the mortgage; and

(2) the secured party's sworn affidavit in recordable form stating that:

(A) a default has occurred; and

(B) the secured party is entitled to enforce the mortgage nonjudicially.

(c) [Commercially reasonable collection and enforcement.] A secured party shall proceed in a commercially reasonable manner if the secured party:

(1) undertakes to collect from or enforce an obligation of an account debtor or other person obligated on collateral; and

(2) is entitled to charge back uncollected collateral or otherwise to full or limited recourse against the debtor or a secondary obligor.

(d) [Expenses of collection and enforcement.] A secured party may deduct from the collections made pursuant to subsection (c) reasonable expenses of collection and enforcement, including reasonable attorney's fees and legal expenses incurred by the secured party.

(e) [Duties to secured party not affected.] This section does not determine whether an account debtor, bank, or other person obligated on collateral owes a duty to a secured party.

§ 9-608. Application of Proceeds of Collection or Enforcement; Liability for Deficiency and Right to Surplus.

(a) [Application of proceeds, surplus, and deficiency if obligation secured.] If a security interest or agricultural lien secures payment or performance of an obligation, the following rules apply:

(1) A secured party shall apply or pay over for application the cash proceeds of collection or enforcement under Section 9-607 in the following order to:

(A) the reasonable expenses of collection and enforcement and, to the extent provided for by agreement and not prohibited by law, reasonable attorney's fees and legal expenses incurred by the secured party;

(B) the satisfaction of obligations secured by the security interest or agricultural lien under which the collection or enforcement is made; and

(C) the satisfaction of obligations secured by any subordinate security interest in or other lien on the collateral subject to the security interest or agricultural lien under which the collection or enforcement is made if the secured party receives an authenticated demand for proceeds before distribution of the proceeds is completed.

(2) If requested by a secured party, a holder of a subordinate security interest or other lien shall furnish reasonable proof of the interest or lien within a reasonable time. Unless the holder complies, the secured party need not comply with the holder's demand under paragraph (1)(C).

(3) A secured party need not apply or pay over for application noncash proceeds of collection and enforcement under Section 9-607 unless the failure to do so would be commercially unreasonable. A secured party that applies or pays over for application noncash proceeds shall do so in a commercially reasonable manner.

(4) A secured party shall account to and pay a debtor for any surplus, and the obligor is liable for any deficiency.

(b) [No surplus or deficiency in sales of certain rights to payment.] If the underlying transaction is a sale of accounts, chattel paper, payment intangibles, or promissory notes, the debtor is not entitled to any surplus, and the obligor is not liable for any deficiency.

§ 9-609. Secured Party's Right To Take Possession after Default.

(a) [Possession; rendering equipment unusable; disposition on debtor's premises.] After default, a secured party:

(1) may take possession of the collateral; and

(2) without removal, may render equipment unusable and dispose of collateral on a debtor's premises under Section 9-610.

(b) [Judicial and nonjudicial process.] A secured party may proceed under subsection (a):

(1) pursuant to judicial process; or

(2) without judicial process, if it proceeds without breach of the peace.

(c) [Assembly of collateral.] If so agreed, and in any event after default, a secured party may require the debtor to assemble the collateral and make it available to the secured party at a place to be designated by the secured party which is reasonably convenient to both parties.

§ 9-610. Disposition of Collateral after Default.

(a) [Disposition after default.] After default, a secured party may sell, lease, license, or otherwise dispose of any or all of the collateral in its present condition or following any commercially reasonable preparation or processing.

(b) [Commercially reasonable disposition.] Every aspect of a disposition of collateral, including the method, manner, time, place, and other terms, must be commercially reasonable. If commercially reasonable, a secured party may dispose of collateral by public or private proceedings, by one or more contracts, as a unit or in parcels, and at any time and place and on any terms.

(c) [Purchase by secured party.] A secured party may purchase collateral:

(1) at a public disposition; or

(2) at a private disposition only if the collateral is of a kind that is customarily sold on a recognized market or the subject of widely distributed standard price quotations.

(d) [Warranties on disposition.] A contract for sale, lease, license, or other disposition includes the warranties relating to title, possession, quiet enjoyment, and the like which by operation of law accompany a voluntary disposition of property of the kind subject to the contract.

(e) [Disclaimer of warranties.] A secured party may disclaim or modify warranties under subsection (d):

(1) in a manner that would be effective to disclaim or modify the warranties in a voluntary disposition of property of the kind subject to the contract of disposition; or

(2) by communicating to the purchaser a record evidencing the contract for disposition and including an express disclaimer or modification of the warranties.

(f) [Record sufficient to disclaim warranties.] A record is sufficient to disclaim warranties under subsection (e) if it indicates "There is no warranty relating to title, possession, quiet enjoyment, or the like in this disposition" or uses words of similar import.

§ 9-611. Notification before Disposition of Collateral.

(a) ["Notification date."] In this section, "notification date" means the earlier of the date on which:

(1) a secured party sends to the debtor and any secondary obligor an authenticated notification of disposition; or

(2) the debtor and any secondary obligor waive the right to notification.

(b) [Notification of disposition required.] Except as otherwise provided in subsection (d), a secured party that disposes of collateral under Section 9-610 shall send to the persons specified in subsection (c) a reasonable authenticated notification of disposition.

(c) [Persons to be notified.] To comply with subsection (b), the secured party shall send an authenticated notification of disposition to:

(1) the debtor;

(2) any secondary obligor; and

(3) if the collateral is other than consumer goods:

(A) any other person from which the secured party has received, before the notification date, an authenticated notification of a claim of an interest in the collateral;

(B) any other secured party or lienholder that, 10 days before the notification date, held a security interest in or other lien on the collateral perfected by the filing of a financing statement that:

(i) identified the collateral;

(ii) was indexed under the debtor's name as of that date; and

(iii) was filed in the office in which to file a financing statement against the debtor covering the collateral as of that date; and

(C) any other secured party that, 10 days before the notification date, held a security interest in the collateral perfected by compliance with a statute, regulation, or treaty described in Section 9-311(a).

(d) [Subsection (b) inapplicable: perishable collateral; recognized market.] Subsection (b) does not apply if the collateral is perishable or threatens to decline speedily in value or is of a type customarily sold on a recognized market.

(e) [Compliance with subsection (c)(3)(B).] A secured party complies with the requirement for notification prescribed by subsection (c)(3)(B) if:

(1) not later than 20 days or earlier than 30 days before the notification date, the secured party requests, in a commercially reasonable manner, information concerning financing statements indexed under the debtor's name in the office indicated in subsection (c)(3)(B); and

(2) before the notification date, the secured party:

(A) did not receive a response to the request for information; or

(B) received a response to the request for information and sent an authenticated notification of disposition to each secured party or other lienholder named in that response whose financing statement covered the collateral.

§ 9-612. Timeliness of Notification before Disposition of Collateral.

(a) [Reasonable time is question of fact.] Except as otherwise provided in subsection (b), whether a notification is sent within a reasonable time is a question of fact.

(b) [10-day period sufficient in non-consumer transaction.] In a transaction other than a consumer transaction, a notification of disposition sent after default and 10 days or more before the earliest time of disposition set forth in the notification is sent within a reasonable time before the disposition.

§ 9-613. Contents and Form of Notification before Disposition of Collateral: General.

Except in a consumer-goods transaction, the following rules apply:

(1) The contents of a notification of disposition are sufficient if the notification:

(A) describes the debtor and the secured party;

(B) describes the collateral that is the subject of the intended disposition;

(C) states the method of intended disposition;

(D) states that the debtor is entitled to an accounting of the unpaid indebtedness and states the charge, if any, for an accounting; and

(E) states the time and place of a public disposition or the time after which any other disposition is to be made.

(2) Whether the contents of a notification that lacks any of the information specified in paragraph (1) are nevertheless sufficient is a question of fact.

(3) The contents of a notification providing substantially the information specified in paragraph (1) are sufficient, even if the notification includes:

(A) information not specified by that paragraph; or

(B) minor errors that are not seriously misleading.

(4) A particular phrasing of the notification is not required.

(5) The following form of notification and the form appearing in Section 9-614(3), when completed, each provides sufficient information:

NOTIFICATION OF DISPOSITION OF COLLATERAL

To: [Name of debtor, obligor, or other person to which the notification is sent]

From: [Name, address, and telephone number of secured party]

Name of Debtor(s): [Include only if debtor(s) are not an addressee]

[For a public disposition:]

We will sell [or lease or license, as applicable] the [describe collateral] [to the highest qualified bidder] in public as follows:

Day and Date:

Time:

Place:

[For a private disposition:]

We will sell [or lease or license, as applicable] the [describe collateral] privately sometime after [day and date].

You are entitled to an accounting of the unpaid indebtedness secured by the property that we intend to sell [or lease or license, as applicable] [for a charge of $]. You may request an accounting by calling us at [telephone number]

[End of Form]

§ 9-614. Contents and Form of Notification before Disposition of Collateral: Consumer-Goods Transaction. In a consumer-goods transaction, the following rules apply:

(1) A notification of disposition must provide the following information:

(A) the information specified in Section 9-613(1);

(B) a description of any liability for a deficiency of the person to which the notification is sent;

(C) a telephone number from which the amount that must be paid to the secured party to redeem the collateral under Section 9-623 is available; and

(D) a telephone number or mailing address from which additional information concerning the disposition and the obligation secured is available.

(2) A particular phrasing of the notification is not required.

(3) The following form of notification, when completed, provides sufficient information:

[Name and address of secured party]

[Date]

NOTICE OF OUR PLAN TO SELL PROPERTY

[Name and address of any obligor who is also a debtor]

Subject: [Identification of Transaction]

We have your [describe collateral], because you broke promises in our agreement.

[For a public disposition:]

We will sell [describe collateral] at public sale. A sale could include a lease or license. The sale will be held as follows:

Date:

Time:

Place:

You may attend the sale and bring bidders if you want.

[For a private disposition:]

We will sell [describe collateral] at private sale sometime after [date]. A sale could include a lease or license.

The money that we get from the sale (after paying our costs) will reduce the amount you owe. If we get less money than you owe, you [will or will not, as applicable] still owe us the difference. If we get more money than you owe, you will get the extra money, unless we must pay it to someone else.

You can get the property back at any time before we sell it by paying us the full amount you owe (not just the past due payments), including our expenses. To learn the exact amount you must pay, call us at [telephone number] .

If you want us to explain to you in writing how we have figured the amount that you owe us, you may call us at [telephone number] [or write us at [secured party's address]] and request a written explanation. [We will charge you $ for the explanation if we sent you another written explanation of the amount you owe us within the last six months.]

If you need more information about the sale call us at [telephone number]] [or write us at [secured party's address]].

We are sending this notice to the following other people who have an interest in [describe collateral] or who owe money under your agreement:

[Names of all other debtors and obligors, if any]

[End of Form]

(4) A notification in the form of paragraph (3) is sufficient, even if additional information appears at the end of the form.

(5) A notification in the form of paragraph (3) is sufficient, even if it includes errors in information not required by paragraph (1), unless the error is misleading with respect to rights arising under this article.

(6) If a notification under this section is not in the form of paragraph (3), law other than this article determines the effect of including information not required by paragraph (1).

§ 9-615. Application of Proceeds of Disposition; Liability for Deficiency and Right to Surplus.

(a) [Application of proceeds.] A secured party shall apply or pay over for application the cash proceeds of disposition under Section 9-610 in the following order to:

(1) the reasonable expenses of retaking, holding, preparing for disposition, processing, and disposing, and, to the extent provided for by agreement and not prohibited by law, reasonable attorney's fees and legal expenses incurred by the secured party;

(2) the satisfaction of obligations secured by the security interest or agricultural lien under which the disposition is made;

(3) the satisfaction of obligations secured by any subordinate security interest in or other subordinate lien on the collateral if:

(A) the secured party receives from the holder of the subordinate security interest or other lien an authenticated demand for proceeds before distribution of the proceeds is completed; and

(B) in a case in which a consignor has an interest in the collateral, the subordinate security interest or other lien is senior to the interest of the consignor; and

(4) a secured party that is a consignor of the collateral if the secured party receives from the consignor an authenticated demand for proceeds before distribution of the proceeds is completed.

(b) [Proof of subordinate interest.] If requested by a secured party, a holder of a subordinate security interest or other lien shall furnish reasonable proof of the interest or lien within a reasonable time. Unless the holder does so, the secured party need not comply with the holder's demand under subsection (a)(3).

(c) [Application of noncash proceeds.] A secured party need not apply or pay over for application noncash proceeds of disposition under Section 9-610 unless the failure to do so would be commercially unreasonable. A secured party that applies or pays over for application noncash proceeds shall do so in a commercially reasonable manner.

(d) [Surplus or deficiency if obligation secured.] If the security interest under which a disposition is made secures payment or performance of an obligation, after making the payments and applications required by subsection (a) and permitted by subsection (c):

(1) unless subsection (a)(4) requires the secured party to apply or pay over cash proceeds to a consignor, the secured party shall account to and pay a debtor for any surplus; and

(2) the obligor is liable for any deficiency.

(e) [No surplus or deficiency in sales of certain rights to payment.] If the underlying transaction is a sale of accounts, chattel paper, payment intangibles, or promissory notes:

(1) the debtor is not entitled to any surplus; and

(2) the obligor is not liable for any deficiency.

(f) [Calculation of surplus or deficiency in disposition to person related to secured party.] The surplus or deficiency following a disposition is calculated based on the amount of proceeds that would have been realized in a disposition complying with this part to a transferee other than the secured party, a person related to the secured party, or a secondary obligor if:

(1) the transferee in the disposition is the secured party, a person related to the secured party, or a secondary obligor; and

(2) the amount of proceeds of the disposition is significantly below the range of proceeds that a complying disposition to a person other than the secured party, a person related to the secured party, or a secondary obligor would have brought.

(g) [Cash proceeds received by junior secured party.] A secured party that receives cash proceeds of a disposition in good faith and without knowledge that the receipt violates the rights of the holder of a security interest or other lien that is not subordinate to the security interest or agricultural lien under which the disposition is made:

(1) takes the cash proceeds free of the security interest or other lien;

(2) is not obligated to apply the proceeds of the disposition to the satisfaction of obligations secured by the security interest or other lien; and

(3) is not obligated to account to or pay the holder of the security interest or other lien for any surplus.

§ 9-616. Explanation of Calculation of Surplus or Deficiency.

(a) [Definitions.] In this section:

(1) "Explanation" means a writing that:

(A) states the amount of the surplus or deficiency;

(B) provides an explanation in accordance with subsection (c) of how the secured party calculated the surplus or deficiency;

(C) states, if applicable, that future debits, credits, charges, including additional credit service charges or interest, rebates, and expenses may affect the amount of the surplus or deficiency; and

(D) provides a telephone number or mailing address from which additional information concerning the transaction is available.

(2) "Request" means a record:

(A) authenticated by a debtor or consumer obligor;

(B) requesting that the recipient provide an explanation; and

(C) sent after disposition of the collateral under Section 9-610.

(b) [Explanation of calculation.] In a consumer-goods transaction in which the debtor is entitled to a surplus or a consumer obligor is liable for a deficiency under Section 9-615, the secured party shall:

(1) send an explanation to the debtor or consumer obligor, as applicable, after the disposition and:

(A) before or when the secured party accounts to the debtor and pays any surplus or first makes written demand on the consumer obligor after the disposition for payment of the deficiency; and

(B) within 14 days after receipt of a request; or

(2) in the case of a consumer obligor who is liable for a deficiency, within 14 days after receipt of a request, send to the consumer obligor a record waiving the secured party's right to a deficiency.

(c) [Required information.] To comply with subsection (a)(1)(B), a writing must provide the following information in the following order:

(1) the aggregate amount of obligations secured by the security interest under which the disposition was made, and, if the amount reflects a rebate of unearned interest or credit service charge, an indication of that fact, calculated as of a specified date:

(A) if the secured party takes or receives possession of the collateral after default, not more than 35 days before the secured party takes or receives possession; or

(B) if the secured party takes or receives possession of the collateral before default or does not take possession of the collateral, not more than 35 days before the disposition;

(2) the amount of proceeds of the disposition;

(3) the aggregate amount of the obligations after deducting the amount of proceeds;

(4) the amount, in the aggregate or by type, and types of expenses, including expenses of retaking, holding, preparing for disposition, processing, and disposing of the collateral, and attorney's fees secured by the collateral which are known to the secured party and relate to the current disposition;

(5) the amount, in the aggregate or by type, and types of credits, including rebates of interest or credit service charges, to which the obligor is known to be entitled and which are not reflected in the amount in paragraph (1); and

(6) the amount of the surplus or deficiency.

(d) [Substantial compliance.] A particular phrasing of the explanation is not required. An explanation complying substantially with the requirements of subsection (a) is sufficient, even if it includes minor errors that are not seriously misleading.

(e) [Charges for responses.] A debtor or consumer obligor is entitled without charge to one response to a request under this section during any six-month period in which the secured party did not send to the debtor or consumer obligor an explanation pursuant to subsection (b)(1). The secured party may require payment of a charge not exceeding $25 for each additional response.

§ 9-617. Rights of Transferee of Collateral.

(a) [Effects of disposition.] A secured party's disposition of collateral after default:

(1) transfers to a transferee for value all of the debtor's rights in the collateral;

(2) discharges the security interest under which the disposition is made; and

(3) discharges any subordinate security interest or other subordinate lien [other than liens created under [cite acts or statutes providing for liens, if any, that are not to be discharged]].

(b) [Rights of good-faith transferee.] A transferee that acts in good faith takes free of the rights and interests described in subsection (a), even if the secured party fails to comply with this article or the requirements of any judicial proceeding.

(c) [Rights of other transferee.] If a transferee does not take free of the rights and interests described in subsection (a), the transferee takes the collateral subject to:

(1) the debtor's rights in the collateral;

(2) the security interest or agricultural lien under which the disposition is made; and

(3) any other security interest or other lien.

§ 9-618. Rights and Duties of Certain Secondary Obligors.

(a) [Rights and duties of secondary obligor.] A secondary obligor acquires the rights and becomes obligated to perform the duties of the secured party after the secondary obligor:

(1) receives an assignment of a secured obligation from the secured party;

(2) receives a transfer of collateral from the secured party and agrees to accept the rights and assume the duties of the secured party; or

(3) is subrogated to the rights of a secured party with respect to collateral.

(b) [Effect of assignment, transfer, or subrogation.] An assignment, transfer, or subrogation described in subsection (a):

(1) is not a disposition of collateral under Section 9-610; and

(2) relieves the secured party of further duties under this article.

§ 9-619. Transfer of Record or Legal Title.

(a) ["Transfer statement."] In this section, "transfer statement" means a record authenticated by a secured party stating:

(1) that the debtor has defaulted in connection with an obligation secured by specified collateral;

(2) that the secured party has exercised its post-default remedies with respect to the collateral;

(3) that, by reason of the exercise, a transferee has acquired the rights of the debtor in the collateral; and

(4) the name and mailing address of the secured party, debtor, and transferee.

(b) [Effect of transfer statement.] A transfer statement entitles the transferee to the transfer of record of all rights of the debtor in the collateral specified in the statement in any official filing, recording, registration, or certificate-of-title system covering the collateral. If a transfer statement is presented with the applicable fee and request form to the official or office responsible for maintaining the system, the official or office shall:

(1) accept the transfer statement;

(2) promptly amend its records to reflect the transfer; and

(3) if applicable, issue a new appropriate certificate of title in the name of the transferee.

(c) [Transfer not a disposition; no relief of secured party's duties.] A transfer of the record or legal title to collateral to a secured party under subsection (b) or otherwise is not of itself a disposition of collateral under this article and does not of itself relieve the secured party of its duties under this article.

§ 9-620. Acceptance of Collateral in Full or Partial Satisfaction of Obligation; Compulsory Disposition of Collateral.

(a) [Conditions to acceptance in satisfaction.] Except as otherwise provided in subsection (g), a secured party may accept collateral in full or partial satisfaction of the obligation it secures only if:

(1) the debtor consents to the acceptance under subsection (c);

(2) the secured party does not receive, within the time set forth in subsection (d), a notification of objection to the proposal authenticated by:

(A) a person to which the secured party was required to send a proposal under Section 9-621; or

(B) any other person, other than the debtor, holding an interest in the collateral subordinate to the security interest that is the subject of the proposal;

(3) if the collateral is consumer goods, the collateral is not in the possession of the debtor when the debtor consents to the acceptance; and

(4) subsection (e) does not require the secured party to dispose of the collateral or the debtor waives the requirement pursuant to Section 9-624.

(b) [Purported acceptance ineffective.] A purported or apparent acceptance of collateral under this section is ineffective unless:

(1) the secured party consents to the acceptance in an authenticated record or sends a proposal to the debtor; and

(2) the conditions of subsection (a) are met.

(c) [Debtor's consent.] For purposes of this section:

(1) a debtor consents to an acceptance of collateral in partial satisfaction of the obligation it secures only if the debtor agrees to the terms of the acceptance in a record authenticated after default; and

(2) a debtor consents to an acceptance of collateral in full satisfaction of the obligation it secures only if the debtor agrees to the terms of the acceptance in a record authenticated after default or the secured party:

(A) sends to the debtor after default a proposal that is unconditional or subject only to a condition that collateral not in the possession of the secured party be preserved or maintained;

(B) in the proposal, proposes to accept collateral in full satisfaction of the obligation it secures; and

(C) does not receive a notification of objection authenticated by the debtor within 20 days after the proposal is sent.

(d) [Effectiveness of notification.] To be effective under subsection (a)(2), a notification of objection must be received by the secured party:

(1) in the case of a person to which the proposal was sent pursuant to Section 9-621, within 20 days after notification was sent to that person; and

(2) in other cases:

(A) within 20 days after the last notification was sent pursuant to Section 9-621; or

(B) if a notification was not sent, before the debtor consents to the acceptance under subsection (c).

(e) [Mandatory disposition of consumer goods.] A secured party that has taken possession of collateral shall dispose of the collateral pursuant to Section 9-610 within the time specified in subsection (f) if:

(1) 60 percent of the cash price has been paid in the case of a purchase-money security interest in consumer goods; or

(2) 60 percent of the principal amount of the obligation secured has been paid in the case of a non-purchase-money security interest in consumer goods.

(f) [Compliance with mandatory disposition requirement.] To comply with subsection (e), the secured party shall dispose of the collateral:

(1) within 90 days after taking possession; or

(2) within any longer period to which the debtor and all secondary obligors have agreed in an agreement to that effect entered into and authenticated after default.

(g) [No partial satisfaction in consumer transaction.] In a consumer transaction, a secured party may not accept collateral in partial satisfaction of the obligation it secures.

§ 9-621. Notification of Proposal To Accept Collateral.

(a) [Persons to which proposal to be sent.] A secured party that desires to accept collateral in full or partial satisfaction of the obligation it secures shall send its proposal to:

(1) any person from which the secured party has received, before the debtor consented to the acceptance, an authenticated notification of a claim of an interest in the collateral;

(2) any other secured party or lienholder that, 10 days before the debtor consented to the acceptance, held a security interest in or other lien on the collateral perfected by the filing of a financing statement that:

(A) identified the collateral;

(B) was indexed under the debtor's name as of that date; and

(C) was filed in the office or offices in which to file a financing statement against the debtor covering the collateral as of that date; and

(3) any other secured party that, 10 days before the debtor consented to the acceptance, held a security interest in the collateral perfected by compliance with a statute, regulation, or treaty described in Section 9-311(a).

(b) [Proposal to be sent to secondary obligor in partial satisfaction.] A secured party that desires to accept collateral in partial satisfaction of the obligation it secures shall send its proposal to any secondary obligor in addition to the persons described in subsection (a).

§ 9-622. Effect of Acceptance of Collateral.

(a) [Effect of acceptance.] A secured party's acceptance of collateral in full or partial satisfaction of the obligation it secures:

(1) discharges the obligation to the extent consented to by the debtor;

(2) transfers to the secured party all of a debtor's rights in the collateral;

(3) discharges the security interest or agricultural lien that is the subject of the debtor's consent and any subordinate security interest or other subordinate lien; and

(4) terminates any other subordinate interest.

(b) [Discharge of subordinate interest notwithstanding noncompliance.] A subordinate interest is discharged or terminated under subsection (a), even if the secured party fails to comply with this article.

§ 9-623. Right To Redeem Collateral.

(a) [Persons that may redeem.] A debtor, any secondary obligor, or any other secured party or lienholder may redeem collateral.

(b) [Requirements for redemption.] To redeem collateral, a person shall tender:

(1) fulfillment of all obligations secured by the collateral; and

(2) the reasonable expenses and attorney's fees described in Section 9-615(a)(1).

(c) [When redemption may occur.] A redemption may occur at any time before a secured party:

(1) has collected collateral under Section 9-607;

(2) has disposed of collateral or entered into a contract for its disposition under Section 9-610; or

(3) has accepted collateral in full or partial satisfaction of the obligation it secures under Section 9-622.

§ 9-624. Waiver.

(a) [Waiver of disposition notification.] A debtor or secondary obligor may waive the right to notification of disposition of collateral under Section 9-611 only by an agreement to that effect entered into and authenticated after default.

(b) [Waiver of mandatory disposition.] A debtor may waive the right to require disposition of collateral under Section 9-620(e) only by an agreement to that effect entered into and authenticated after default.

(c) [Waiver of redemption right.] Except in a consumer-goods transaction, a debtor or secondary obligor may waive the right to redeem collateral under Section 9-623 only by an agreement to that effect entered into and authenticated after default.

[Subpart 2. Noncompliance with Article]

§ 9-625. Remedies for Secured Party's Failure To Comply with Article.

(a) [Judicial orders concerning noncompliance.] If it is established that a secured party is not proceeding in accordance with this article, a court may order or restrain collection, enforcement, or disposition of collateral on appropriate terms and conditions.

(b) [Damages for noncompliance.] Subject to subsections (c), (d), and (f), a person is liable for damages in the amount of any loss caused by a failure to comply with this article. Loss caused by a failure to comply may include loss resulting from the debtor's inability to obtain, or increased costs of, alternative financing.

(c) [Persons entitled to recover damages; statutory damages in consumer-goods transaction.] Except as otherwise provided in Section 9-628:

(1) a person that, at the time of the failure, was a debtor, was an obligor, or held a security interest in or other lien on the collateral may recover damages under subsection (b) for its loss; and

(2) if the collateral is consumer goods, a person that was a debtor or a secondary obligor at the time a secured party failed to comply with this part may recover for that failure in any event an amount not less than the credit service charge plus 10 percent of the principal amount of the obligation or the time-price differential plus 10 percent of the cash price.

(d) [Recovery when deficiency eliminated or reduced.] A debtor whose deficiency is eliminated under Section 9-626 may recover damages for the loss of any surplus. However, a debtor or secondary obligor whose deficiency is eliminated or reduced under Section 9-626 may not otherwise recover under subsection (b) for noncompliance with the provisions of this part relating to collection, enforcement, disposition, or acceptance.

(e) [Statutory damages: noncompliance with specified provisions.] In addition to any damages recoverable under subsection (b), the debtor, consumer obligor, or person named as a debtor in a filed record, as applicable, may recover $500 in each case from a person that:

(1) fails to comply with Section 9-208;

(2) fails to comply with Section 9-209;

(3) files a record that the person is not entitled to file under Section 9-509(a);

(4) fails to cause the secured party of record to file or send a termination statement as required by Section 9-513(a) or (c);

(5) fails to comply with Section 9-616(b)(1) and whose failure is part of a pattern, or consistent with a practice, of noncompliance; or

(6) fails to comply with Section 9-616(b)(2).

(f) [Statutory damages: noncompliance with Section 9-210.] A debtor or consumer obligor may recover damages under subsection (b) and, in addition, $500 in each case from a person that, without reasonable cause, fails to comply with a request under Section 9-210. A recipient of a request under Section 9-210 which never claimed an interest in the collateral or obligations that are the subject of a request under that section has a reasonable excuse for failure to comply with the request within the meaning of this subsection.

(g) [Limitation of security interest: noncompliance with Section 9-210.] If a secured party fails to comply with a request regarding a list of collateral or a statement of account under Section 9-210, the secured party may claim a security interest only as shown in the list or statement included in the request as against a person that is reasonably misled by the failure.

§ 9-626. Action in which Deficiency or Surplus Is in Issue.

(a) [Applicable rules if amount of deficiency or surplus in issue.] In an action arising from a transaction, other than a consumer transaction, in which the amount of a deficiency or surplus is in issue, the following rules apply:

(1) A secured party need not prove compliance with the provisions of this part relating to collection, enforcement, disposition, or acceptance unless the debtor or a secondary obligor places the secured party's compliance in issue.

(2) If the secured party's compliance is placed in issue, the secured party has the burden of establishing that the collection, enforcement, disposition, or acceptance was conducted in accordance with this part.

(3) Except as otherwise provided in Section 9-628, if a secured party fails to prove that the collection, enforcement, disposition, or acceptance was conducted in accordance with the provisions of this part relating to collection, enforcement, disposition, or acceptance, the liability of a debtor or a secondary obligor for a deficiency is limited to an amount by which the sum of the secured obligation, expenses, and attorney's fees exceeds the greater of:

(A) the proceeds of the collection, enforcement, disposition, or acceptance; or

(B) the amount of proceeds that would have been realized had the noncomplying secured party proceeded in accordance with the provisions of this part relating to collection, enforcement, disposition, or acceptance.

(4) For purposes of paragraph (3)(B), the amount of proceeds that would have been realized is equal to the sum of the secured obligation, expenses, and attorney's fees unless the secured party proves that the amount is less than that sum.

(5) If a deficiency or surplus is calculated under Section 9-615(f), the debtor or obligor has the burden of establishing that the amount of proceeds of the disposition is significantly below the range of prices that a complying disposition to a person other than the secured party, a person related to the secured party, or a secondary obligor would have brought.

(b) [Non-consumer transactions; no inference.] The limitation of the rules in subsection (a) to transactions other than consumer transactions is intended to leave to the court the determination of the proper rules in consumer transactions. The court may not infer from that limitation the nature of the proper rule in consumer transactions and may continue to apply established approaches.

§ 9-627. Determination of Whether Conduct Was Commercially Reasonable.

(a) [Greater amount obtainable under other circumstances; no preclusion of commercial reasonableness.] The fact that a greater amount could have been obtained by a collection, enforcement, disposition, or acceptance at a different time or in a different method from that selected by the secured party is not of itself sufficient to preclude the secured party from establishing that the collection, enforcement, disposition, or acceptance was made in a commercially reasonable manner.

(b) [Dispositions that are commercially reasonable.] A disposition of collateral is made in a commercially reasonable manner if the disposition is made:

(1) in the usual manner on any recognized market;

(2) at the price current in any recognized market at the time of the disposition; or

(3) otherwise in conformity with reasonable commercial practices among dealers in the type of property that was the subject of the disposition.

(c) [Approval by court or on behalf of creditors.] A collection, enforcement, disposition, or acceptance is commercially reasonable if it has been approved:

(1) in a judicial proceeding;

(2) by a bona fide creditors' committee;

(3) by a representative of creditors; or

(4) by an assignee for the benefit of creditors.

(d) [Approval under subsection (c) not necessary; absence of approval has no effect.] Approval under subsection (c) need not be obtained, and lack of approval does not mean that the collection, enforcement, disposition, or acceptance is not commercially reasonable.

§ 9-628. Nonliability and Limitation on Liability of Secured Party; Liability of Secondary Obligor.

(a) [Limitation of liability of secured party for noncompliance with article.] Unless a secured party knows that a person is a debtor or obligor, knows the identity of the person, and knows how to communicate with the person:

(1) the secured party is not liable to the person, or to a secured party or lienholder that has filed a financing statement against the person, for failure to comply with this article; and

(2) the secured party's failure to comply with this article does not affect the liability of the person for a deficiency.

(b) [Limitation of liability based on status as secured party.] A secured party is not liable because of its status as secured party:

(1) to a person that is a debtor or obligor, unless the secured party knows:

(A) that the person is a debtor or obligor;

(B) the identity of the person; and

(C) how to communicate with the person; or

(2) to a secured party or lienholder that has filed a financing statement against a person, unless the secured party knows:

(A) that the person is a debtor; and

(B) the identity of the person.

(c) [Limitation of liability if reasonable belief that transaction not a consumer-goods transaction or consumer transaction.] A secured party is not liable to any person, and a person's liability for a deficiency is not affected, because of any act or omission arising out of the secured party's reasonable belief that a transaction is not a consumer-goods transaction or a consumer transaction or that goods are not consumer goods, if the secured party's belief is based on its reasonable reliance on:

(1) a debtor's representation concerning the purpose for which collateral was to be used, acquired, or held; or

(2) an obligor's representation concerning the purpose for which a secured obligation was incurred.

(d) [Limitation of liability for statutory damages.] A secured party is not liable to any person under Section 9-625(c)(2) for its failure to comply with Section 9-616.

(e) [Limitation of multiple liability for statutory damages.] A secured party is not liable under Section 9-625(c)(2) more than once with respect to any one secured obligation.

PART 7 Transition

§ 9-701. Effective Date. This [Act] takes effect on July 1, 2001.

§ 9-702. Savings Clause.

(a) [Pre-effective-date transactions or liens.] Except as otherwise provided in this part, this [Act] applies to a transaction or lien within its scope, even if the transaction or lien was entered into or created before this [Act] takes effect.

(b) [Continuing validity.] Except as otherwise provided in subsection (c) and Sections 9-703 through 9-709:

(1) transactions and liens that were not governed by [former Article 9], were validly entered into or created before this [Act] takes effect, and would be subject to this [Act] if they had been entered into or created after this [Act] takes effect, and the rights, duties, and interests flowing from those transactions and liens remain valid after this [Act] takes effect; and

(2) the transactions and liens may be terminated, completed, consummated, and enforced as required or permit-

ted by this [Act] or by the law that otherwise would apply if this [Act] had not taken effect.

(c) [Pre-effective-date proceedings.] This [Act] does not affect an action, case, or proceeding commenced before this [Act] takes effect.

§ 9-703. Security Interest Perfected before Effective Date.

(a) [Continuing priority over lien creditor: perfection requirements satisfied.] A security interest that is enforceable immediately before this [Act] takes effect and would have priority over the rights of a person that becomes a lien creditor at that time is a perfected security interest under this [Act] if, when this [Act] takes effect, the applicable requirements for enforceability and perfection under this [Act] are satisfied without further action.

(b) [Continuing priority over lien creditor: perfection requirements not satisfied.] Except as otherwise provided in Section 9-705, if, immediately before this [Act] takes effect, a security interest is enforceable and would have priority over the rights of a person that becomes a lien creditor at that time, but the applicable requirements for enforceability or perfection under this [Act] are not satisfied when this [Act] takes effect, the security interest:

(1) is a perfected security interest for one year after this [Act] takes effect;

(2) remains enforceable thereafter only if the security interest becomes enforceable under Section 9-203 before the year expires; and

(3) remains perfected thereafter only if the applicable requirements for perfection under this [Act] are satisfied before the year expires.

§ 9-704. Security Interest Unperfected before Effective Date. A security interest that is enforceable immediately before this [Act] takes effect but which would be subordinate to the rights of a person that becomes a lien creditor at that time:

(1) remains an enforceable security interest for one year after this [Act] takes effect;

(2) remains enforceable thereafter if the security interest becomes enforceable under Section 9-203 when this [Act] takes effect or within one year thereafter; and

(3) becomes perfected:

(A) without further action, when this [Act] takes effect if the applicable requirements for perfection under this [Act] are satisfied before or at that time; or

(B) when the applicable requirements for perfection are satisfied if the requirements are satisfied after that time.

§ 9-705. Effectiveness of Action Taken before Effective Date.

(a) [Pre-effective-date action; one-year perfection period unless reperfected.] If action, other than the filing of a financing statement, is taken before this [Act] takes effect and the action would have resulted in priority of a security interest over the rights of a person that becomes a lien creditor had the security interest become enforceable before this [Act] takes effect, the action is effective to perfect a security interest that attaches under this [Act] within one year after this [Act] takes effect. An attached security interest becomes unperfected one year after this [Act] takes effect unless the security interest becomes a perfected security interest under this [Act] before the expiration of that period.

(b) [Pre-effective-date filing.] The filing of a financing statement before this [Act] takes effect is effective to perfect a security interest to the extent the filing would satisfy the applicable requirements for perfection under this [Act].

(c) [Pre-effective-date filing in jurisdiction formerly governing perfection.] This [Act] does not render ineffective an effective financing statement that, before this [Act] takes effect, is filed and satisfies the applicable requirements for perfection under the law of the jurisdiction governing perfection as provided in [former Section 9-103]. However, except as otherwise provided in subsections (d) and (e) and Section 9-706, the financing statement ceases to be effective at the earlier of:

(1) the time the financing statement would have ceased to be effective under the law of the jurisdiction in which it is filed; or

(2) June 30, 2006.

(d) [Continuation statement.] The filing of a continuation statement after this [Act] takes effect does not continue the effectiveness of the financing statement filed before this [Act] takes effect. However, upon the timely filing of a continuation statement after this [Act] takes effect and in accordance with the law of the jurisdiction governing perfection as provided in Part 3, the effectiveness of a financing statement filed in the same office in that jurisdiction before this [Act] takes effect continues for the period provided by the law of that jurisdiction.

(e) [Application of subsection (c)(2) to transmitting utility financing statement.] Subsection (c)(2) applies to a financing statement that, before this [Act] takes effect, is filed against a transmitting utility and satisfies the applicable requirements for perfection under the law of the jurisdiction governing perfection as provided in [former Section 9-103] only to the extent that Part 3 provides that the law of a jurisdiction other than the jurisdiction in which the financing statement is filed governs perfection of a security interest in collateral covered by the financing statement.

(f) [Application of Part 5.] A financing statement that includes a financing statement filed before this [Act] takes effect and a continuation statement filed after this [Act] takes effect is effective only to the extent that it satisfies the requirements of Part 5 for an initial financing statement.

§ 9-706. When Initial Financing Statement Suffices To Continue Effectiveness of Financing Statement.

(a) [Initial financing statement in lieu of continuation statement.] The filing of an initial financing statement in the office specified in Section 9-501 continues the effectiveness of a financing statement filed before this [Act] takes effect if:

(1) the filing of an initial financing statement in that office would be effective to perfect a security interest under this [Act];

(2) the pre-effective-date financing statement was filed in an office in another State or another office in this State; and

(3) the initial financing statement satisfies subsection (c).

(b) [Period of continued effectiveness.] The filing of an initial financing statement under subsection (a) continues the effectiveness of the pre-effective-date financing statement:

(1) if the initial financing statement is filed before this [Act] takes effect, for the period provided in [former Section 9-403] with respect to a financing statement; and

(2) if the initial financing statement is filed after this [Act] takes effect, for the period provided in Section 9-515 with respect to an initial financing statement.

(c) [Requirements for initial financing statement under subsection (a).] To be effective for purposes of subsection (a), an initial financing statement must:

(1) satisfy the requirements of Part 5 for an initial financing statement;

(2) identify the pre-effective-date financing statement by indicating the office in which the financing statement was filed and providing the dates of filing and file numbers, if any, of the financing statement and of the most recent continuation statement filed with respect to the financing statement; and

(3) indicate that the pre-effective-date financing statement remains effective.

§ 9-707. Amendment of Pre-Effective-Date Financing Statement.

(a) ["Pre-effective-date financing statement".] In this section, "pre-effective-date financing statement" means a financing statement filed before this [Act] takes effect.

(b) [Applicable law.] After this [Act] takes effect, a person may add or delete collateral covered by, continue or terminate the effectiveness of, or otherwise amend the information provided in, a pre-effective-date financing statement only in accordance with the law of the jurisdiction governing perfection as provided in Part 3. However, the effectiveness of a pre-effective-date financing statement also may be terminated in accordance with the law of the jurisdiction in which the financing statement is filed.

(c) [Method of amending: general rule.] Except as otherwise provided in subsection (d), if the law of this State governs perfection of a security interest, the information in a pre-effective-date financing statement may be amended after this [Act] takes effect only if:

(1) the pre-effective-date financing statement and an amendment are filed in the office specified in Section 9-501;

(2) an amendment is filed in the office specified in Section 9-501 concurrently with, or after the filing in that office of, an initial financing statement that satisfies Section 9-706(c); or

(3) an initial financing statement that provides the information as amended and satisfies Section 9-706(c) is filed in the office specified in Section 9-501.

(d) [Method of amending: continuation.] If the law of this State governs perfection of a security interest, the effectiveness of a pre-effective-date financing statement may be continued only under Section 9-705(d) and (f) or 9-706.

(e) [Method of amending: additional termination rule.] Whether or not the law of this State governs perfection of a security interest, the effectiveness of a pre-effective-date financing statement filed in this State may be terminated after this [Act] takes effect by filing a termination statement in the office in which the pre-effective-date financing statement is filed, unless an initial financing statement that satisfies Section 9-706(c) has been filed in the office specified by the law of the jurisdiction governing perfection as provided in Part 3 as the office in which to file a financing statement.

§ 9-708. Persons Entitled To File Initial Financing Statement or Continuation Statement. A person may file an initial financing statement or a continuation statement under this part if:

(1) the secured party of record authorizes the filing; and

(2) the filing is necessary under this part:

(A) to continue the effectiveness of a financing statement filed before this [Act] takes effect; or

(B) to perfect or continue the perfection of a security interest.

§ 9-709. Priority.

(a) [Law governing priority.] This [Act] determines the priority of conflicting claims to collateral. However, if the relative priorities of the claims were established before this [Act] takes effect, [former Article 9] determines priority.

(b) [Priority if security interest becomes enforceable under Section 9-203.] For purposes of Section 9-322(a), the priority of a security interest that becomes enforceable under Section 9-203 of this [Act] dates from the time this [Act] takes effect if the security interest is perfected under this [Act] by the filing of a financing statement before this [Act] takes effect which would not have been effective to perfect the security interest under [former Article 9]. This subsection does not apply to conflicting security interests each of which is perfected by the filing of such a financing statement.

Selected Revisions to the Uniform Commercial Code

Appendix C

REVISION (2001) OF ARTICLE 1 / General Provisions

§ 1-101. Short Titles.
(a) This [Act] may be cited as the Uniform Commercial Code.
(b) This article may be cited as Uniform Commercial Code – General Provisions.

Source: Former Section 1-101.

§ 1-102. Scope of Article. This article applies to a transaction to the extent that it is governed by another article of [the Uniform Commercial Code].

Source: New.

§ 1-103. Construction of [Uniform Commercial Code] To Promote Its Purposes and Policies; Applicability of Supplemental Principles of Law.
(a) [The Uniform Commercial Code] must be liberally construed and applied to promote its underlying purposes and policies, which are:

(1) to simplify, clarify, and modernize the law governing commercial transactions;
(2) to permit the continued expansion of commercial practices through custom, usage, and agreement of the parties; and
(3) to make uniform the law among the various jurisdictions.

(b) Unless displaced by the particular provisions of [the Uniform Commercial Code], the principles of law and equity, including the law merchant and the law relative to capacity to contract, principal and agent, estoppel, fraud, misrepresentation, duress, coercion, mistake, bankruptcy, and other validating or invalidating cause supplement its provisions.

Source: Former Section 1-102 (1)-(2); Former Section 1-103.

§ 1-104. Construction Against Implied Repeal. [The Uniform Commercial Code] being a general act intended as a unified coverage of its subject matter, no part of it shall be deemed to be impliedly repealed by subsequent legislation if such construction can reasonably be avoided.

Source: Former Section 1-104.

§ 1-105. Severability. If any provision or clause of [the Uniform Commercial Code] or its application to any person or circumstance is held invalid, the invalidity does not affect other provisions or applications of [the Uniform Commercial Code] which can be given effect without the invalid provision or application, and to this end the provisions of [the Uniform Commercial Code] are severable.

Source: Former Section 1-108.

§ 1-106. Use of Singular and Plural; Gender. In [the Uniform Commercial Code], unless the statutory context otherwise requires:
(1) words in the singular number include the plural, and those in the plural include the singular; and
(2) words of any gender also refer to any other gender.

Source: Former Section 1-102(5). See also 1 U.S.C. Section 1.

§ 1-107. Section Caption. Section captions are part of [the Uniform Commercial Code].

Source: Former Section 1-109.

§ 1-108. Relation to Electronic Signatures in Global and National Commerce Act. This [Act] modifies, limits, and supersedes the federal Electronic Signatures in Global and National Commerce Act, (15 U.S.C. Section 7001, et. seq.) but does not modify, limit, or supersede Section 101(c) of that act (15 U.S.C. Section 7001(c)) or authorize electronic delivery of any of the notices described in Section 103(b) of that act (15 U.S.C. Section 103(b)).

Source: New

PART 2 General Definitions and Principles of Interpretation

§ 1-201. General Definitions.
(a) Unless the context otherwise requires, words or phrases defined in this section, or in the additional definitions contained in other articles of [the Uniform Commercial Code] that apply to particular articles or parts thereof, have the meanings stated.
(b) Subject to definitions contained in other articles of [the Uniform Commercial Code] that apply to particular articles or parts thereof:

(1) "Action", in the sense of a judicial proceeding, includes recoupment, counterclaim, set-off, suit in equity, and any other proceeding in which rights are determined.
(2) "Aggrieved party" means a party entitled to pursue a remedy.

(3) "Agreement", as distinguished from "contract", means the bargain of the parties in fact, as found in their language or inferred from other circumstances, including course of performance, course of dealing, or usage of trade as provided in Section 1_303.

(4) "Bank" means a person engaged in the business of banking and includes a savings bank, savings and loan association, credit union, and trust company.

(5) "Bearer" means a person in possession of a negotiable instrument, document of title, or certificated security that is payable to bearer or indorsed in blank.

(6) "Bill of lading" means a document evidencing the receipt of goods for shipment issued by a person engaged in the business of transporting or forwarding goods.

(7) "Branch" includes a separately incorporated foreign branch of a bank.

(8) "Burden of establishing" a fact means the burden of persuading the trier of fact that the existence of the fact is more probable than its nonexistence.

(9) "Buyer in ordinary course of business" means a person that buys goods in good faith, without knowledge that the sale violates the rights of another person in the goods, and in the ordinary course from a person, other than a pawnbroker, in the business of selling goods of that kind. A person buys goods in the ordinary course if the sale to the person comports with the usual or customary practices in the kind of business in which the seller is engaged or with the seller's own usual or customary practices. A person that sells oil, gas, or other minerals at the wellhead or minehead is a person in the business of selling goods of that kind. A buyer in ordinary course of business may buy for cash, by exchange of other property, or on secured or unsecured credit, and may acquire goods or documents of title under a preexisting contract for sale. Only a buyer that takes possession of the goods or has a right to recover the goods from the seller under Article 2 may be a buyer in ordinary course of business. "Buyer in ordinary course of business" does not include a person that acquires goods in a transfer in bulk or as security for or in total or partial satisfaction of a money debt.

(10) "Conspicuous", with reference to a term, means so written, displayed, or presented that a reasonable person against which it is to operate ought to have noticed it. Whether a term is "conspicuous" or not is a decision for the court. Conspicuous terms include the following:

(A) a heading in capitals equal to or greater in size than the surrounding text, or in contrasting type, font, or color to the surrounding text of the same or lesser size; and

(B) language in the body of a record or display in larger type than the surrounding text, or in contrasting type, font, or color to the surrounding text of the same size, or set off from surrounding text of the same size by symbols or other marks that call attention to the language.

(11) "Consumer" means an individual who enters into a transaction primarily for personal, family, or household purposes

(12) "Contract", as distinguished from "agreement", means the total legal obligation that results from the parties' agreement as determined by [the Uniform Commercial Code] as supplemented by any other applicable laws.

(13) "Creditor" includes a general creditor, a secured creditor, a lien creditor, and any representative of creditors, including an assignee for the benefit of creditors, a trustee in bankruptcy, a receiver in equity, and an executor or administrator of an insolvent debtor's or assignor's estate.

(14) "Defendant" includes a person in the position of defendant in a counterclaim, cross-claim, or third-party claim.

(15) "Delivery", with respect to an instrument, document of title, or chattel paper, means voluntary transfer of possession.

(16) "Document of title" includes bill of lading, dock warrant, dock receipt, warehouse receipt or order for the delivery of goods, and also any other document which in the regular course of business or financing is treated as adequately evidencing that the person in possession of it is entitled to receive, hold, and dispose of the document and the goods it covers. To be a document of title, a document must purport to be issued by or addressed to a bailee and purport to cover goods in the bailee's possession which are either identified or are fungible portions of an identified mass.

(17) "Fault" means a default, breach, or wrongful act or omission.

(18) "Fungible goods" means:

(A) goods of which any unit, by nature or usage of trade, is the equivalent of any other like unit; or

(B) goods that by agreement are treated as equivalent.

(19) "Genuine" means free of forgery or counterfeiting.

(20) "Good faith," except as otherwise provided in Article 5, means honesty in fact and the observance of reasonable commercial standards of fair dealing.

(21) "Holder" means:

(A) the person in possession of a negotiable instrument that is payable either to bearer or to an identified person that is the person in possession; or

(B) the person in possession of a document of title if the goods are deliverable either to bearer or to the order of the person in possession.

(22) "Insolvency proceeding" includes an assignment for the benefit of creditors or other proceeding intended to liquidate or rehabilitate the estate of the person involved.

(23) "Insolvent" means:

(A) having generally ceased to pay debts in the ordinary course of business other than as a result of bona fide dispute;

(B) being unable to pay debts as they become due; or

(C) being insolvent within the meaning of federal bankruptcy law.

(24) "Money" means a medium of exchange currently authorized or adopted by a domestic or foreign government. The term includes a monetary unit of account established by an intergovernmental organization or by agreement between two or more countries.

(25) "Organization" means a person other than an individual.

(26) "Party", as distinguished from "third party", means a person that has engaged in a transaction or made an agreement subject to [the Uniform Commercial Code].

(27) "Person" means an individual, corporation, business trust, estate, trust, partnership, limited liability company, association, joint venture, government, governmental subdivision, agency, or instrumentality, public corporation, or any other legal or commercial entity.

(28) "Present value" means the amount as of a date certain of one or more sums payable in the future, discounted to the date certain by use of either an interest rate specified by the parties if that rate is not manifestly unreasonable at the time the transaction is entered into or, if an interest rate is not so specified, a commercially reasonable rate that takes into account the facts and circumstances at the time the transaction is entered into.

(29) "Purchase" means taking by sale, lease, discount, negotiation, mortgage, pledge, lien, security interest, issue or reissue, gift, or any other voluntary transaction creating an interest in property.

(30) "Purchaser" means a person that takes by purchase.

(31) "Record" means information that is inscribed on a tangible medium or that is stored in an electronic or other medium and is retrievable in perceivable form.

(32) "Remedy" means any remedial right to which an aggrieved party is entitled with or without resort to a tribunal.

(33) "Representative" means a person empowered to act for another, including an agent, an officer of a corporation or association, and a trustee, executor, or administrator of an estate.

(34) "Right" includes remedy.

(35) "Security interest" means an interest in personal property or fixtures which secures payment or performance of an obligation. "Security interest" includes any interest of a consignor and a buyer of accounts, chattel paper, a payment intangible, or a promissory note in a transaction that is subject to Article 9. "Security interest" does not include the special property interest of a buyer of goods on identification of those goods to a contract for sale under Section 2- 401, but a buyer may also acquire a "security interest" by complying with Article 9. Except as otherwise provided in Section 2-505, the right of a seller or lessor of goods under Article 2 or 2A to retain or acquire possession of the goods is not a "security interest", but a seller or lessor may also acquire a "security interest" by complying with Article 9. The retention or reservation of title by a seller of goods notwithstanding shipment or delivery to the buyer under Section 2-401 is limited in effect to a reservation of a "security interest." Whether a transaction in the form of a lease creates a "security interest" is determined pursuant to Section 1-203.

(36) "Send" in connection with a writing, record, or notice means:

(A) to deposit in the mail or deliver for transmission by any other usual means of communication with postage or cost of transmission provided for and properly addressed and, in the case of an instrument, to an address specified thereon or otherwise agreed, or if there be none to any address reasonable under the circumstances; or

(B) in any other way to cause to be received any record or notice within the time it would have arrived if properly sent.

(37) "Signed" includes using any symbol executed or adopted with present intention to adopt or accept a writing.

(38) "State" means a State of the United States, the District of Columbia, Puerto Rico, the United States Virgin Islands, or any territory or insular possession subject to the jurisdiction of the United States.

(39) "Surety" includes a guarantor or other secondary obligor.

(40) "Term" means a portion of an agreement that relates to a particular matter.

(41) "Unauthorized signature" means a signature made without actual, implied, or apparent authority. The term includes a forgery.

(42) "Warehouse receipt" means a receipt issued by a person engaged in the business of storing goods for hire.

(43) "Writing" includes printing, typewriting, or any other intentional reduction to tangible form. "Written" has a corresponding meaning.

Source: Former Section 1-201.

§ 1-202. Notice; Knowledge.

(a) Subject to subsection (f), a person has "notice" of a fact if the person:

(1) has actual knowledge of it;

(2) has received a notice or notification of it; or

(3) from all the facts and circumstances known to the person at the time in question, has reason to know that it exists.

(b) "Knowledge" means actual knowledge. "Knows" has a corresponding meaning.
(c) "Discover", "learn", or words of similar import refer to knowledge rather than to reason to know.
(d) A person "notifies" or "gives" a notice or notification to another person by taking such steps as may be reasonably required to inform the other person in ordinary course, whether or not the other person actually comes to know of it.
(e) Subject to subsection (f), a person "receives" a notice or notification when:

(1) it comes to that person's attention; or
(2) it is duly delivered in a form reasonable under the circumstances at the place of business through which the contract was made or at another location held out by that person as the place for receipt of such communications.

(f) Notice, knowledge, or a notice or notification received by an organization is effective for a particular transaction from the time it is brought to the attention of the individual conducting that transaction and, in any event, from the time it would have been brought to the individual's attention if the organization had exercised due diligence. An organization exercises due diligence if it maintains reasonable routines for communicating significant information to the person conducting the transaction and there is reasonable compliance with the routines. Due diligence does not require an individual acting for the organization to communicate information unless the communication is part of the individual's regular duties or the individual has reason to know of the transaction and that the transaction would be materially affected by the information.

Source: Derived from former Section 1-201(25)-(27).

§ 1-203. Lease Distinguished from Security Interest.
(a) Whether a transaction in the form of a lease creates a lease or security interest is determined by the facts of each case.
(b) A transaction in the form of a lease creates a security interest if the consideration that the lessee is to pay the lessor for the right to possession and use of the goods is an obligation for the term of the lease and is not subject to termination by the lessee, and:

(1) the original term of the lease is equal to or greater than the remaining economic life of the goods;
(2) the lessee is bound to renew the lease for the remaining economic life of the goods or is bound to become the owner of the goods;
(3) the lessee has an option to renew the lease for the remaining economic life of the goods for no additional consideration or for nominal additional consideration upon compliance with the lease agreement; or
(4) the lessee has an option to become the owner of the goods for no additional consideration or for nominal additional consideration upon compliance with the lease agreement.

(c) A transaction in the form of a lease does not create a security interest merely because:

(1) the present value of the consideration the lessee is obligated to pay the lessor for the right to possession and use of the goods is substantially equal to or is greater than the fair market value of the goods at the time the lease is entered into;
(2) the lessee assumes risk of loss of the goods;
(3) the lessee agrees to pay, with respect to the goods, taxes, insurance, filing, recording, or registration fees, or service or maintenance costs;
(4) the lessee has an option to renew the lease or to become the owner of the goods;
(5) the lessee has an option to renew the lease for a fixed rent that is equal to or greater than the reasonably predictable fair market rent for the use of the goods for the term of the renewal at the time the option is to be performed; or
(6) the lessee has an option to become the owner of the goods for a fixed price that is equal to or greater than the reasonably predictable fair market value of the goods at the time the option is to be performed.

(d) Additional consideration is nominal if it is less than the lessee's reasonably predictable cost of performing under the lease agreement if the option is not exercised. Additional consideration is not nominal if:

(1) when the option to renew the lease is granted to the lessee, the rent is stated to be the fair market rent for the use of the goods for the term of the renewal determined at the time the option is to be performed; or
(2) when the option to become the owner of the goods is granted to the lessee, the price is stated to be the fair market value of the goods determined at the time the option is to be performed.

(e) The "remaining economic life of the goods" and "reasonably predictable" fair market rent, fair market value, or cost of performing under the lease agreement must be determined with reference to the facts and circumstances at the time the transaction is entered into.

Source: Former Section 1-201(37).

§ 1-204. Value. Except as otherwise provided in Articles 3, 4, [and] 5, [and 6], a person gives value for rights if the person acquires them:
(1) in return for a binding commitment to extend credit or for the extension of immediately available credit, whether or not drawn upon and whether or not a charge-back is provided for in the event of difficulties in collection;
(2) as security for, or in total or partial satisfaction of, a preexisting claim;
(3) by accepting delivery under a preexisting contract for purchase; or
(4) in return for any consideration sufficient to support a simple contract.

Source: Former Section 1-201(44).

§ 1-205. Reasonable Time; Seasonableness.

(a) Whether a time for taking an action required by [the Uniform Commercial Code] is reasonable depends on the nature, purpose, and circumstances of the action.

(b) An action is taken seasonably if it is taken at or within the time agreed or, if no time is agreed, at or within a reasonable time.

Source: Former Section 1-204(2)-(3).

§ 1-206. Presumptions. Whenever [the Uniform Commercial Code] creates a "presumption" with respect to a fact, or provides that a fact is "presumed," the trier of fact must find the existence of the fact unless and until evidence is introduced that supports a finding of its nonexistence.

Legislative Note: Former Section 1-206, a Statute of Frauds for sales of "kinds of personal property not otherwise covered," has been deleted. The other articles of the Uniform Commercial Code make individual determinations as to requirements for memorializing transactions within their scope, so that the primary effect of former Section 1_206 was to impose a writing requirement on sales transactions not otherwise governed by the UCC. Deletion of former Section 1-206 does not constitute a recommendation to legislatures as to whether such sales transactions should be covered by a Statute of Frauds; rather, it reflects a determination that there is no need for uniform commercial law to resolve that issue.

Source: Former Section 1-201(31).

PART 3 Territorial Applicability and General Rules

§ 1-301. Territorial Applicability; Parties' Power To Choose Applicable Law.

(a) In this section:

(1) "Domestic transaction" means a transaction other than an international transaction.

(2) "International transaction" means a transaction that bears a reasonable relation to a country other than the United States.

(b) This section applies to a transaction to the extent that it is governed by another article of the [Uniform Commercial Code].

(c) Except as otherwise provided in this section

(1) an agreement by parties to a domestic transaction that any or all of their rights and obligations are to be determined by the law of this State or of another State is effective, whether or not the transaction bears a relation to the State designated; and

(2) an agreement by parties to an international transaction that any or all of their rights and obligations are to be determined by the law of this State or of another State or country is effective, whether or not the transaction bears a relation to the State or country designated.

(d) In the absence of an agreement effective under subsection (c), and except as provided in subsections (e) and (g), the rights and obligations of the parties are determined by the law that would be selected by application of this State's conflict of laws principles.

(e) If one of the parties to a transaction is a consumer, the following rules apply:

(1) An agreement referred to in subsection (c) is not effective unless the transaction bears a reasonable relation to the State or country designated.

(2) Application of the law of the State or country determined pursuant to subsection (c) or (d) may not deprive the consumer of the protection of any rule of law governing a matter within the scope of this section, which both is protective of consumers and may not be varied by agreement:

(A) of the State or country in which the consumer principally resides, unless subparagraph (B) applies; or

(B) if the transaction is a sale of goods, of the State or country in which the consumer both makes the contract and takes delivery of those goods, if such State or country is not the State or country in which the consumer principally resides.

(f) An agreement otherwise effective under subsection (c) is not effective to the extent that application of the law of the State or country designated would be contrary to a fundamental policy of the State or country whose law would govern in the absence of agreement under subsection (d).

(g) To the extent that [the Uniform Commercial Code] governs a transaction, if one of the following provisions of [the Uniform Commercial Code] specifies the applicable law, that provision governs and a contrary agreement is effective only to the extent permitted by the law so specified:

(1) Section 2-402;

(2) Sections 2A-105 and 2A-106;

(3) Section 4-102;

(4) Section 4A-507;

(5) Section 5-116;

(6) Section 6-103;

(7) Section 8-110;

(8) Sections 9-301 through 9-307.

Source: Former Section 1-105.

§ 1-302. Variation by Agreement.

(a) Except as otherwise provided in subsection (b) or elsewhere in [the Uniform Commercial Code], the effect of provisions of [the Uniform Commercial Code] may be varied by agreement.

(b) The obligations of good faith, diligence, reasonableness, and care prescribed by [the Uniform Commercial Code] may not be disclaimed by agreement. The parties, by agreement, may determine the standards by which the performance of those obligations is to be measured if those standards are not manifestly unreasonable. Whenever [the Uniform Commercial Code] requires an action to be taken within a reasonable time, a time that is not manifestly unreasonable may be fixed by agreement.

(c) The presence in certain provisions of [the Uniform Commercial Code] of the phrase "unless otherwise agreed", or words of similar import, does not imply that the effect of other provisions may not be varied by agreement under this section.

Source: Former Sections 1-102(3)-(4) and 1-204(1).

§ 1-303. Course of Performance, Course of Dealing, and Usage of Trade.

(a) A "course of performance" is a sequence of conduct between the parties to a particular transaction that exists if:

(1) the agreement of the parties with respect to the transaction involves repeated occasions for performance by a party; and

(2) the other party, with knowledge of the nature of the performance and opportunity for objection to it, accepts the performance or acquiesces in it without objection.

(b) A "course of dealing" is a sequence of conduct concerning previous transactions between the parties to a particular transaction that is fairly to be regarded as establishing a common basis of understanding for interpreting their expressions and other conduct.

(c) A "usage of trade" is any practice or method of dealing having such regularity of observance in a place, vocation, or trade as to justify an expectation that it will be observed with respect to the transaction in question. The existence and scope of such a usage must be proved as facts. If it is established that such a usage is embodied in a trade code or similar record, the interpretation of the record is a question of law.

(d) A course of performance or course of dealing between the parties or usage of trade in the vocation or trade in which they are engaged or of which they are or should be aware is relevant in ascertaining the meaning of the parties' agreement, may give particular meaning to specific terms of the agreement, and may supplement or qualify the terms of the agreement. A usage of trade applicable in the place in which part of the performance under the agreement is to occur may be so utilized as to that part of the performance.

(e) Except as otherwise provided in subsection (f), the express terms of an agreement and any applicable course of performance, course of dealing, or usage of trade must be construed whenever reasonable as consistent with each other. If such a construction is unreasonable:

(1) express terms prevail over course of performance, course of dealing, and usage of trade;

(2) course of performance prevails over course of dealing and usage of trade; and

(3) course of dealing prevails over usage of trade.

(f) Subject to Section 2_209, a course of performance is relevant to show a waiver or modification of any term inconsistent with the course of performance.

(g) Evidence of a relevant usage of trade offered by one party is not admissible unless that party has given the other party notice that the court finds sufficient to prevent unfair surprise to the other party.

Source: Former Sections 1-205, 2-208, and Section 2A-207.

§ 1-304. Obligation of Good Faith. Every contract or duty within [the Uniform Commercial Code] imposes an obligation of good faith in its performance and enforcement.

Source: Former Section 1-203.

§ 1-305. Remedies To Be Liberally Administered.

(a) The remedies provided by [the Uniform Commercial Code] must be liberally administered to the end that the aggrieved party may be put in as good a position as if the other party had fully performed but neither consequential or special damages nor penal damages may be had except as specifically provided in [the Uniform Commercial Code] or by other rule of law.

(b) Any right or obligation declared by [the Uniform Commercial Code] is enforceable by action unless the provision declaring it specifies a different and limited effect.

Source: Former Section 1-106.

§ 1-306. Waiver or Renunciation of Claim or Right after Breach. A claim or right arising out of an alleged breach may be discharged in whole or in part without consideration by agreement of the aggrieved party in an authenticated record.

Source: Former Section 1-107.

§ 1-307. Prima Faciie Evidence by Third-Party Documents. A document in due form purporting to be a bill of lading, policy or certificate of insurance, official weigher's or inspector's certificate, consular invoice, or any other document authorized or required by the contract to be issued by a third party is prima facie evidence of its own authenticity and genuineness and of the facts stated in the document by the third party.

Source: Former Section 1-202.

§ 1-308. Performance or Acceptance under Reservation of Rights.

(a) A party that with explicit reservation of rights performs or promises performance or assents to performance in a manner demanded or offered by the other party does not thereby prejudice the rights reserved. Such words as "without prejudice," "under protest," or the like are sufficient.

(b) Subsection (a) does not apply to an accord and satisfaction.

Source: Former Section 1-207.

§ 1-309. Option To Accelerate at Will. A term providing that one party or that party's successor in interest may accelerate payment or performance or require collateral or additional collateral "at will" or when the party "deems itself insecure," or words of similar import, means that the party has power to do so only if that party in good faith believes that the prospect of payment or performance is impaired. The burden of establishing lack of good faith is on the party against which the power has been exercised.

Source: Former Section 1-208.

§ 1-310. Subordinated Obligations. An obligation may be issued as subordinated to performance of another obligation of the person obligated, or a creditor may subordinate its right to performance of an obligation by agreement with either the person obligated or another creditor of the person obligated. Subordination does not create a security interest as against either the common debtor or a subordinated creditor.

Source: Former Section 1-209.

REVISION (2002) OF ARTICLE 3 / Negotiable Instruments

PART 1 General Provisions and Definitions

§ 3-101. Short Title. This Article may be cited as Uniform Commercial Code—Negotiable Instruments.

§ 3-102. Subject Matter.
(a) This Article applies to negotiable instruments. It does not apply to money, to payment orders governed by Article 4A, or to securities governed by Article 8.
(b) If there is conflict between this Article and Article 4 or 9, Articles 4 and 9 govern.
(c) Regulations of the Board of Governors of the Federal Reserve System and operating circulars of the Federal Reserve Banks supersede any inconsistent provision of this Article to the extent of the inconsistency.

§ 3-103. Definitions.
(a) In this Article:
(1) "Acceptor" means a drawee who has accepted a draft.
(2) "Drawee" means a person ordered in a draft to make payment.
(3) "Drawer" means a person who signs or is identified in a draft as a person ordering payment.
(4) "Good faith" means honesty in fact and the observance of reasonable commercial standards of fair dealing.
(5) "Maker" means a person who signs or is identified in a note as a person undertaking to pay.
(6) "Order" means a written instruction to pay money signed by the person giving the instruction. The instruction may be addressed to any person, including the person giving the instruction, or to one or more persons jointly or in the alternative but not in succession. An authorization to pay is not an order unless the person authorized to pay is also instructed to pay.
(7) "Ordinary care" in the case of a person engaged in business means observance of reasonable commercial standards, prevailing in the area in which the person is located, with respect to the business in which the person is engaged. In the case of a bank that takes an instrument for processing for collection or payment by automated means, reasonable commercial standards do not require the bank to examine the instrument if the failure to examine does not violate the bank's prescribed procedures and the bank's procedures do not vary unreasonably from general banking usage not disapproved by this Article or Article 4.
(8) "Party" means a party to an instrument.
(9) "Promise" means a written undertaking to pay money signed by the person undertaking to pay. An acknowledgment of an obligation by the obligor is not a promise unless the obligor also undertakes to pay the obligation.
(10) "Prove" with respect to a fact means to meet the burden of establishing the fact (Section 1-201(8)).
(11) "Remitter" means a person who purchases an instrument from its issuer if the instrument is payable to an identified person other than the purchaser.
(b) Other definitions applying to this Article and the sections in which they appear are:

"Acceptance" Section 3-409
"Accommodated party" Section 3-419
"Accommodation party" Section 3-419
"Alteration" Section 3-407
"Anomalous indorsement" Section 3-205
"Blank indorsement" Section 3-205
"Cashier's check" Section 3-104
"Certificate of deposit" Section 3-104
"Certified check" Section 3-409
"Check" Section 3-104
"Consideration" Section 3-303
"Draft" Section 3-104
"Holder in due course" Section 3-302
"Incomplete instrument" Section 3-115
"Indorsement" Section 3-204
"Indorser" Section 3-204
"Instrument" Section 3-104
"Issue" Section 3-105
"Issuer" Section 3-105
"Negotiable instrument" Section 3-104
"Negotiation" Section 3-201
"Note" Section 3-104
"Payable at a definite time" Section 3-108
"Payable on demand" Section 3-108

"Payable to bearer" Section 3-109
"Payable to order" Section 3-109
"Payment" Section 3-602
"Person entitled to enforce" Section 3-301
"Presentment Section 3-501
"Reacquisition" Section 3-207
"Special indorsement" Section 3-205
"Teller's check" Section 3-104
"Transfer of instrument" Section 3-203
"Traveler's check" Section 3-104
"Value" Section 3-303

(c) The following definitions in other Articles apply to this Article:

"Bank" Section 4-105
"Banking day" Section 4-104
"Clearing house" Section 4-104
"Collecting bank" Section 4-105
"Depositary bank" Section 4-105
"Documentary draft" Section 4-104
"Intermediary bank" Section 4-105
"Item" Section 4-104
"Payor bank" Section 4-105
"Suspends payments" Section 4-104

(d) In addition, Article 1 contains general definitions and principles of construction and interpretation applicable throughout this Article.

§ 3-104. Negotiable Instrument.

(a) Except as provided in subsections (c) and (d), "negotiable instrument" means an unconditional promise or order to pay a fixed amount of money, with or without interest or other charges described in the promise or order' if it:

(1) is payable to bearer or to order at the time it is issued or first comes into possession of a holder'

(2) is payable on demand or at a definite time; and

(3) does not state any other undertaking or instruction by the person promising or ordering payment to do any act in addition to the payment of money, but the promise or order may contain (i) an undertaking or power to give, maintain, or protect collateral to secure payment, (ii) an authorization or power to the holder to confess judgment or realize on or dispose of collateral, or (iii) a waiver of the benefit of any law intended for the advantage or protection of an obligor.

(b) "Instrument" means a negotiable instrument.

(c) An order that meets all of the requirements of subsection (a), except paragraph (1), and otherwise falls within the definition of "check" in subsection (f) is a negotiable instrument and a check.

(d) A promise or order other than a check is not an instrument if' at the time it is issued or first comes into possession of a holder, it contains a conspicuous statement, however expressed, to the effect that the promise or order is not negotiable or is not an instrument governed by this Article.

(e) An instrument is a "note" if it is a promise and is a "draft" if it is an order. If an instrument falls within the definition of both "note" and "draft," a person entitled to enforce the instrument may treat it as either.

(f) "Check" means (i) a draft, other than a documentary draft, payable on demand and drawn on a bank or (ii) a cashier's check or teller's check. An instrument may be a check even though it is described on its face by another term, such as "money order."

(g) "Cashier's check" means a draft with respect to which the drawer and drawee are the same bank or branches of the same bank.

(h) "Teller's check" means a draft drawn by a bank (i) on another bank, or (ii) payable at or through a bank.

(i) "Traveler's check" means an instrument that (i) is payable on demand, (ii) is drawn on or payable at or through a bank, (iii) is designated by the term "traveler's check" or by a substantially similar term, and (iv) requires, as a condition to payment, a countersignature by a person whose specimen signature appears on the instrument.

(j) "Certificate of deposit" means an instrument containing an acknowledgment by a bank that a sum of money has been received by the bank and a promise by the bank to repay the sum of money. A certificate of deposit is a note of the bank.

§ 3-105. Issue of Instrument.

(a) "Issue" means the first delivery of an instrument by the maker or drawer' whether to a holder or nonholder, for the purpose of giving rights on the instrument to any person.

(b) An unissued instrument, or an unissued incomplete instrument that is completed, is binding on the maker or drawer, but nonissuance is a defense. An instrument that is conditionally issued or is issued for a special purpose is binding on the maker or drawer' but failure of the condition or special purpose to be fulfilled is a defense.

(c) "Issuer" applies to issued and unissued instruments and means a maker or drawer of an instrument.

§ 3-106. Unconditional Promise or Order.

(a) Except as provided in this section, for the purposes of Section 3-104(a), a promise or order is unconditional unless it states (i) an express condition to payment, (ii) that the promise or order is subject to or governed by another writing, or (iii) that rights or obligations with respect to the promise or order are stated in another writing. A reference to another writing does not of itself make the promise or order conditional.

(b) A promise or order is not made conditional (i) by a reference to another writing for a statement of rights with respect to collateral, prepayment, or acceleration, or (ii) because payment is limited to resort to a particular fund or source.

(c) If a promise or order requires, as a condition to payment, a countersignature by a person whose specimen signature appears on the promise or order' the condition does not make the promise or order conditional for the purposes of Section 3 - 104(a). If the person whose specimen signature appears on an instrument fails to countersign the instrument, the failure to countersign is a defense to the obligation of the issuer, but the failure does not prevent a transferee of the instrument from becoming a holder of the instrument.

(d) If a promise or order at the time it is issued or first comes into possession of a holder contains a statement, required by applicable statutory or administrative law, to the effect that the rights of a holder or transferee are subject to claims or defenses that the issuer could assert against the original payee, the promise or order is not thereby made conditional for the purposes of Section 3-104(a); but if the promise or order is an instrument, there cannot be a holder in due course of the instrument.

§ 3-107. Instrument Payable in Foreign Money.

Unless the instrument otherwise provides, an instrument that states the amount payable in foreign money may be paid in the foreign money or in an equivalent amount in dollars calculated by using the current bank-offered spot rate at the place of payment for the purchase of dollars on the day on which the instrument is paid.

§ 3-108. Payable on Demand or at Definite Time.

(a) A promise or order is "payable on demand" if it (i) states that it is payable on demand or at sight, or otherwise indicates that it is payable at the will of the holder, or (ii) does not state any time of payment.

(b) A promise or order is "payable at a definite time" if it is payable on elapse of a definite period of time after sight or acceptance or at a fixed date or dates or at a time or times readily ascertainable at the time the promise or order is issued, subject to rights of (i) prepayment, (ii) acceleration, (iii) extension at the option of the holder, or (iv) extension to a further definite time at the option of the maker or acceptor or automatically upon or after a specified act or event.

(c) If an instrument, payable at a fixed date, is also payable upon demand made before the fixed date, the instrument is payable on demand until the fixed date and, if demand for payment is not made before that date, becomes payable at a definite time on the fixed date.

§ 3-109 Payable to Bearer or to Order.

(a) A promise or order is payable to bearer if it:

(1) states that it is payable to bearer or to the order of bearer or otherwise indicates that the person in possession of the promise or order is entitled to payment;

(2) does not state a payee; or

(3) states that it is payable to or to the order of cash or otherwise indicates that it is not payable to an identified person.

(b) A promise or order that is not payable to bearer is payable to order if it is payable (i) to the order of an identified person or (ii) to an identified person or order. A promise or order that is payable to order is payable to the identified person.

(c) An instrument payable to bearer may become payable to an identified person if it is specially indorsed pursuant to Section 3-205 (a). An instrument payable to an identified person may become payable to bearer if it is indorsed in blank pursuant to Section 3-205(b).

§ 3-110. Identification of Person to Whom Instrument Is Payable.

(a) The person to whom an instrument is initially payable is determined by the intent of the person, whether or not authorized, signing as, or in the name or behalf of, the issuer of the instrument. The instrument is payable to the person intended by the signer even if that person is identified in the instrument by a name or other identification that is not that of the intended person. If more than one person signs in the name or behalf of the issuer of an instrument and all the signers do not intend the same person as payee, the instrument is payable to any person intended by one or more of the signers.

(b) If the signature of the issuer of an instrument is made by automated means, such as a check-writing machine, the payee of the instrument is determined by the intent of the person who supplied the name or identification of the payee, whether or not authorized to do so.

(c) A person to whom an instrument is payable may be identified in any way, including by name, identifying number' office, or account number. For the purpose of determining the holder of an instrument, the following rules apply:

(1) If an instrument is payable to an account and the account is identified only by number' the instrument is payable to the person to whom the account is payable. If an instrument is payable to an account identified by number and by the name of a person, the instrument is payable to the named person, whether or not that person is the owner of the account identified by number.

(2) If an instrument is payable to:

(i) a trust, an estate, or a person described as trustee or representative of a trust or estate, the instrument is payable to the trustee, the representative, or a successor of either' whether or not the beneficiary or estate is also named;

(ii) a person described as agent or similar representative of a named or identified person, the instrument is payable to the represented person, the representative, or a successor of the representative;

(iii) a fund or organization that is not a legal entity, the instrument is payable to a representative of the members of the fund or organization; or

(iv) an office or to a person described as holding an office, the instrument is payable to the named person, the incumbent of the office, or a successor to the incumbent.

(d) If an instrument is payable to two or more persons alternatively, it is payable to any of them and may be negotiated, discharged, or enforced by any or all of them in possession of the instrument. If an instrument is payable to two or more persons not alternatively, it is payable to all of them and may be negotiated, discharged, or enforced only by all of them. If an instrument payable to two or more persons is ambiguous as to whether it is payable to the persons alternatively, the instrument is payable to the persons alternatively.

§ 3-111. Place of Payment.

Except as otherwise provided for items in Article 4, an instrument is payable at the place of payment stated in the instrument. If no place of payment is stated, an instrument is payable at the address of the drawee or maker stated in the instrument. If no address is stated, the place of payment is the place of business of the drawee or maker. If a drawee or maker has more than one place of business, the place of payment is any place of business of the drawee or maker chosen by the person entitled to enforce the instrument. If the drawee or maker has no place of business, the place of payment is the residence of the drawee or maker.

§ 3-112. Interest.

(a) Unless otherwise provided in the instrument, (i) an instrument is not payable with interest, and (ii) interest on an interest-bearing instrument is payable from the date of the instrument.

(b) Interest may be stated in an instrument as a fixed or variable amount of money or it may be expressed as a fixed or variable rate or rates. The amount or rate of interest may be stated or described in the instrument in any manner and may require reference to information not contained in the instrument. If an instrument provides for interest, but the amount of interest payable cannot be ascertained from the description, interest is payable at the judgment rate in effect at the place of payment of the instrument and at the time interest first accrues.

§ 3-113. Date of Instrument.

(a) An instrument may be antedated or postdated. The date stated determines the time of payment if the instrument is payable at a fixed period after date. Except as provided in Section 4-401(c), an instrument payable on demand is not payable before the date of the instrument.

(b) If an instrument is undated, its date is the date of its issue or, in the case of an unissued instrument, the date it first comes into possession of a holder.

§ 3-114. Contradictory Terms of Instrument.

If an instrument contains contradictory terms, typewritten terms prevail over printed terms, handwritten terms prevail over both, and words prevail over numbers.

§ 3-115. Incomplete Instrument.

(a) "Incomplete instrument" means a signed writing, whether or not issued by the signer, the contents of which show at the time of signing that it is incomplete but that the signer intended it to be completed by the addition of words or numbers.

(b) Subject to subsection (c), if an incomplete instrument is an instrument under Section 3-104, it may be enforced according to its terms if it is not completed, or according to its terms as augmented by completion. If an incomplete instrument is not an instrument under Section 3-104, but, after completion, the requirements of Section 3-104 are met, the instrument may be enforced according to its terms as augmented by completion.

(c) If words or numbers are added to an incomplete instrument without authority of the signer, there is an alteration of the incomplete instrument under Section 3-407.

(d) The burden of establishing that words or numbers were added to an incomplete instrument without authority of the signer is on the person asserting the lack of authority.

§ 3-116. Joint and Several Liability; Contribution.

(a) Except as otherwise provided in the instrument, two or more persons who have the same liability on an instrument as makers, drawers, acceptors, indorsers who indorse as joint payees, or anomalous indorsers are jointly and severally liable in the capacity in which they sign.

(b) Except as provided in Section 3-419(e) or by agreement of the affected parties, a party having joint and several liability who pays the instrument is entitled to receive from any party having the same joint and several liability contribution in accordance with applicable law.

(c) Discharge of one party having joint and several liability by a person entitled to enforce the instrument does not affect the right under subsection (b) of a party having the same joint and several liability to receive contribution from the party discharged.

§ 3-117. Other Agreements Affecting Instrument.

Subject to applicable law regarding exclusion of proof of contemporaneous or previous agreements, the obligation of a party to an instrument to pay the instrument may be modified, supplemented, or nullified by a separate agreement of the obligor and a person entitled to enforce the instrument, if the instrument is issued or the obligation is incurred in reliance on the agreement or as part of the same transaction giving rise to the agreement. To the extent an obligation is modified, supplemented, or nullified by an agreement under this section, the agreement is a defense to the obligation.

§ 3-118. Statute of Limitations.

(a) Except as provided in subsection (e), an action to enforce the obligation of a party to pay a note payable at a definite time must be commenced within six years after the due date or dates stated in the note or, if a due date is accelerated, within six years after the accelerated due date.

(b) Except as provided in subsection (d) or (e), if demand for payment is made to the maker of a note payable on demand, an action to enforce the obligation of a party to pay the note must be commenced within six years after the demand. If no demand for payment is made to the maker, an action to enforce the note is barred if neither principal nor interest on the note has been paid for a continuous period of 10 years.

(c) Except as provided in subsection (d), an action to enforce the obligation of a party to an unaccepted draft to pay the draft must be commenced within three years after dishonor of the draft or 10 years after the date of the draft, whichever period expires first.
(d) An action to enforce the obligation of the acceptor of a certified check or the issuer of a teller's check, cashier's check, or traveler's check must be commenced within three years after demand for payment is made to the acceptor or issuer, as the case may be.
(e) An action to enforce the obligation of a party to a certificate of deposit to pay the instrument must be commenced within six years after demand for payment is made to the maker' but if the instrument states a due date and the maker is not required to pay before that date, the six-year period begins when a demand for payment is in effect and the due date has passed.
(f) An action to enforce the obligation of a party to pay an accepted draft, other than a certified check, must be commenced (i) within six years after the due date or dates stated in the draft or acceptance if the obligation of the acceptor is payable at a definite time, or (ii) within six years after the date of the acceptance if the obligation of the acceptor is payable on demand.
(g) Unless governed by other law regarding claims for indemnity or contribution, an action (i) for conversion of an instrument, for money had and received, or like action based on conversion, (ii) for breach of warranty, or (iii) to enforce an obligation, duty, or right arising under this Article and not governed by this section must be commenced within three years after the [cause of action] accrues.

§ 3-119. Notice of Right to Defend Action.

In an action for breach of an obligation for which a third person is answerable over pursuant to this Article or Article 4, the defendant may give the third person written notice of the litigation, and the person notified may then give similar notice to any other person who is answerable over. If the notice states (i) that the person notified may come in and defend and (ii) that failure to do so will bind the person notified in an action later brought by the person giving the notice as to any determination of fact common to the two litigations, the person notified is so bound unless after seasonable receipt of the notice the person notified does come in and defend.

PART 2 Negotiation, Transfer, and Indorsement

§ 3-201. Negotiation.

(a) "Negotiation" means a transfer of possession, whether voluntary or involuntary, of an instrument by a person other than the issuer to a person who thereby becomes its holder.
(b) Except for negotiation by a remitter, if an instrument is payable to an identified person, negotiation requires transfer of possession of the instrument and its indorsement by the holder. If an instrument is payable to bearer, it may be negotiated by transfer of possession alone.

§ 3-202. Negotiation Subject to Rescission.

(a) Negotiation is effective even if obtained (i) from an infant, a corporation exceeding its powers, or a person without capacity, (ii) by fraud, duress, or mistake, or (iii) in breach of duty or as part of an illegal transaction.
(b) To the extent permitted by other law, negotiation may be rescinded or may be subject to other remedies, but those remedies may not be asserted against a subsequent holder in due course or a person paying the instrument in good faith and without knowledge of facts that are a basis for rescission or other remedy.

§ 3-203. Transfer of Instrument; Rights Acquired by Transfer.

(a) An instrument is transferred when it is delivered by a person other than its issuer for the purpose of giving to the person receiving delivery the right to enforce the instrument.
(b) Transfer of an instrument, whether or not the transfer is a negotiation, vests in the transferee any right of the transferor to enforce the instrument, including any right as a holder in due course, but the transferee cannot acquire rights of a holder in due course by a transfer, directly or indirectly, from a holder in due course if the transferee engaged in fraud or illegality affecting the instrument.
(c) Unless otherwise agreed, if an instrument is transferred for value and the transferee does not become a holder because of lack of indorsement by the transferor, the transferee has a specifically enforceable right to the unqualified indorsement of the transferor, but negotiation of the instrument does not occur until the indorsement is made.
(d) If a transferor purports to transfer less than the entire instrument, negotiation of the instrument does not occur. The transferee obtains no rights under this Article and has only the rights of a partial assignee.

§ 3-204. Indorsement.

(a) "Indorsement" means a signature, other than that of a signer as maker, drawer, or acceptor, that alone or accompanied by other words is made on an instrument for the purpose of (i) negotiating the instrument, (ii) restricting payment of the instrument, or (iii) incurring indorser's liability on the instrument, but regardless of the intent of the signer, a signature and its accompanying words is an indorsement unless the accompanying words, terms of the instrument, place of the signature, or other circumstances unambiguously indicate that the signature was made for a purpose other than indorsement. For the purpose of determining whether a signature is made on an instrument, a paper affixed to the instrument is a part of the instrument.
(b) "Indorser" means a person who makes an indorsement.
(c) For the purpose of determining whether the transferee of an instrument is a holder, an indorsement that transfers a security interest in the instrument is effective as an unqualified indorsement of the instrument.
(d) If an instrument is payable to a holder under a name that is not the name of the holder, indorsement may be made by the holder in the name stated in the instrument or in the holder's

name or both, but signature in both names may be required by a person paying or taking the instrument for value or collection.

§ 3-205. Special Indorsement; Blank Indorsement; Anomalous Indorsement.

(a) If an indorsement is made by the holder of an instrument, whether payable to an identified person or payable to bearer, and the indorsement identifies a person to whom it makes the instrument payable, it is a "special indorsement." When specially indorsed, an instrument becomes payable to the identified person and may be negotiated only by the indorsement of that person. The principles stated in Section 3-110 apply to special indorsements.

(b) If an indorsement is made by the holder of an instrument and it is not a special indorsement, it is a "blank indorsement." When indorsed in blank, an instrument becomes payable to bearer and may be negotiated by transfer of possession alone until specially indorsed.

(c) The holder may convert a blank indorsement that consists only of a signature into a special indorsement by writing, above the signature of the indorser, words identifying the person to whom the instrument is made payable.

(d) "Anomalous indorsement" means an indorsement made by a person who is not the holder of the instrument. An anomalous indorsement does not affect the manner in which the instrument may be negotiated.

§ 3-206. Restrictive Indorsement.

(a) An indorsement limiting payment to a particular person or otherwise prohibiting further transfer or negotiation of the instrument is not effective to prevent further transfer or negotiation of the instrument.

(b) An indorsement stating a condition to the right of the indorsee to receive payment does not affect the right of the indorsee to enforce the instrument. A person paying the instrument or taking it for value or collection may disregard the condition, and the rights and liabilities of that person are not affected by whether the condition has been fulfilled.

(c) If an instrument bears an indorsement (i) described in Section 4-201(b), or (ii) in blank or to a particular bank using the words "for deposit," "for collection," or other words indicating a purpose of having the instrument collected by a bank for the indorser or for a particular account, the following rules apply:

(1) A person, other than a bank, who purchases the instrument when so indorsed converts the instrument unless the amount paid for the instrument is received by the indorser or applied consistently with the indorsement.

(2) A depositary bank that purchases the instrument or takes it for collection when so indorsed converts the instrument unless the amount paid by the bank with respect to the instrument is received by the indorser or applied consistently with the indorsement.

(3) A payor bank that is also the depositary bank or that takes the instrument for immediate payment over the counter from a person other than a collecting bank converts the instrument unless the proceeds of the instrument are received by the indorser or applied consistently with the indorsement.

(4) Except as otherwise provided in paragraph (3), a payor bank or intermediary bank may disregard the indorsement and is not liable if the proceeds of the instrument are not received by the indorser or applied consistently with the indorsement.

(d) Except for an indorsement covered by subsection (c), if an instrument bears an indorsement using words to the effect that payment is to be made to the indorsee as agent, trustee, or other fiduciary for the benefit of the indorser or another person, the following rules apply:

(1) Unless there is notice of breach of fiduciary duty as provided in Section 3-307, a person who purchases the instrument from the indorsee or takes the instrument from the indorsee for collection or payment may pay the proceeds of payment or the value given for the instrument to the indorsee without regard to whether the indorsee violates a fiduciary duty to the indorser.

(2) A subsequent transferee of the instrument or person who pays the instrument is neither given notice nor otherwise affected by the restriction in the indorsement unless the transferee or payor knows that the fiduciary dealt with the instrument or its proceeds in breach of fiduciary duty.

(e) The presence on an instrument of an indorsement to which this section applies does not prevent a purchaser of the instrument from becoming a holder in due course of the instrument unless the purchaser is a converter under subsection (c) or has notice or knowledge of breach of fiduciary duty as stated in subsection (d).

(f) In an action to enforce the obligation of a party to pay the instrument, the obligor has a defense if payment would violate an indorsement to which this section applies and the payment is not permitted by this section.

§ 3-207. Reacquisition.

Reacquisition of an instrument occurs if it is transferred to a former holder, by negotiation or otherwise. A former holder who reacquires the instrument may cancel indorsements made after the reacquirer first became a holder of the instrument. If the cancellation causes the instrument to be payable to the reacquirer or to bearer, the reacquirer may negotiate the instrument. An indorser whose indorsement is canceled is discharged, and the discharge is effective against any subsequent holder.

PART 3 Enforcement of Instruments

§ 3-301. Person Entitled to Enforce Instrument.

"Person entitled to enforce" an instrument means (i) the holder of the instrument, (ii) a nonholder in possession of the instrument who has the rights of a holder, or (iii) a person not in possession of the instrument who is entitled to enforce the instrument pursuant to Section 3-309 or 3-418(d). A person may be a person entitled to enforce the instrument even though the person is not the owner of the instrument or is in wrongful possession of the instrument.

§ 3-302. Holder in Due Course.

(a) Subject to subsection (c) and Section 3-106(d), "holder in due course" means the holder of an instrument if:

(1) the instrument when issued or negotiated to the holder does not bear such apparent evidence of forgery or alteration or is not otherwise so irregular or incomplete as to call into question its authenticity; and

(2) the holder took the instrument (i) for value, (ii) in good faith, (iii) without notice that the instrument is overdue or has been dishonored or that there is an uncured default with respect to payment of another instrument issued as part of the same series, (iv) without notice that the instrument contains an unauthorized signature or has been altered, (v) without notice of any claim to the instrument described in Section 3-306, and (vi) without notice that any party has a defense or claim in recoupment described in Section 3-305(a).

(b) Notice of discharge of a party, other than discharge in an insolvency proceeding, is not notice of a defense under subsection (a), but discharge is effective against a person who became a holder in due course with notice of the discharge. Public filing or recording of a document does not of itself constitute notice of a defense, claim in recoupment, or claim to the instrument.

(c) Except to the extent a transferor or predecessor in interest has rights as a holder in due course, a person does not acquire rights of a holder in due course of an instrument taken (i) by legal process or by purchase in an execution, bankruptcy, or creditor's sale or similar proceeding, (ii) by purchase as part of a bulk transaction not in ordinary course of business of the transferor, or (iii) as the successor in interest to an estate or other organization.

(d) If, under Section 3-303 (a) (1), the promise of performance that is the consideration for an instrument has been partially performed, the holder may assert rights as a holder in due course of the instrument only to the fraction of the amount payable under the instrument equal to the value of the partial performance divided by the value of the promised performance.

(e) If (i) the person entitled to enforce an instrument has only a security interest in the instrument and (ii) the person obliged to pay the instrument has a defense, claim in recoupment, or claim to the instrument that may be asserted against the person who granted the security interest, the person entitled to enforce the instrument may assert rights as a holder in due course only to an amount payable under the instrument which, at the time of enforcement of the instrument, does not exceed the amount of the unpaid obligation secured.

(f) To be effective, notice must be received at a time and in a manner that gives a reasonable opportunity to act on it.

(g) This section is subject to any law limiting status as a holder in due course in particular classes of transactions.

§ 3-303. Value and Consideration.

(a) An instrument is issued or transferred for value if:

(1) the instrument is issued or transferred for a promise of performance, to the extent the promise has been performed;

(2) the transferee acquires a security interest or other lien in the instrument other than a lien obtained by judicial proceeding;

(3) the instrument is issued or transferred as payment of, or as security for, an antecedent claim against any person, whether or not the claim is due;

(4) the instrument is issued or transferred in exchange for a negotiable instrument; or

(5) the instrument is issued or transferred in exchange for the incurring of an irrevocable obligation to a third party by the person taking the instrument.

(b) "Consideration" means any consideration sufficient to support a simple contract. The drawer or maker of an instrument has a defense if the instrument is issued without consideration. If an instrument is issued for a promise of performance, the issuer has a defense to the extent performance of the promise is due and the promise has not been performed. If an instrument is issued for value as stated in subsection (a), the instrument is also issued for consideration.

§ 3-304. Overdue Instrument.

(a) An instrument payable on demand becomes overdue at the earliest of the following times:

(1) on the day after the day demand for payment is duly made;

(2) if the instrument is a check, 90 days after its date; or

(3) if the instrument is not a check, when the instrument has been outstanding for a period of time after its date which is unreasonably long under the circumstances of the particular case in light of the nature of the instrument and usage of the trade.

(b) With respect to an instrument payable at a definite time the following rules apply:

(1) If the principal is payable in installments and a due date has not been accelerated, the instrument becomes overdue upon default under the instrument for nonpayment of an installment, and the instrument remains overdue until the default is cured.

(2) If the principal is not payable in installments and the due date has not been accelerated, the instrument becomes overdue on the day after the due date.

(3) If a due date with respect to principal has been accelerated, the instrument becomes overdue on the day after the accelerated due date.

(c) Unless the due date of principal has been accelerated, an instrument does not become overdue if there is default in payment of interest but no default in payment of principal.

§ 3-305. Defenses and Claims in Recoupment.

(a) Except as stated in subsection (b), the right to enforce the obligation of a party to pay an instrument is subject to the following:

(1) a defense of the obligor based on (i) infancy of the obligor to the extent it is a defense to a simple contract, (ii) duress, lack of legal capacity, or illegality of the transaction which, under other law; nullifies the obligation of the obligor, (iii) fraud that induced the obligor to sign the instrument with neither knowledge nor reasonable opportunity to learn of its character or its essential terms, or (iv) discharge of the obligor in insolvency proceedings;

(2) a defense of the obligor stated in another section of this Article or a defense of the obligor that would be available if the person entitled to enforce the instrument were enforcing a right to payment under a simple contract; and

(3) a claim in recoupment of the obligor against the original payee of the instrument if the claim arose from the transaction that gave rise to the instrument; but the claim of the obligor may be asserted against a transferee of the instrument only to reduce the amount owing on the instrument at the time the action is brought.

(b) The right of a holder in due course to enforce the obligation of a party to pay the instrument is subject to defenses of the obligor stated in subsection (a) (1), but is not subject to defenses of the obligor stated in subsection (a) (2) or claims in recoupment stated in subsection (a) (3) against a person other than the holder.

(c) Except as stated in subsection (d), in an action to enforce the obligation of a party to pay the instrument, the obligor may not assert against the person entitled to enforce the instrument a defense, claim in recoupment, or claim to the instrument (Section 3-306) of another person, but the other person's claim to the instrument may be asserted by the obligor if the other person is joined in the action and personally asserts the claim against the person entitled to enforce the instrument. An obligor is not obliged to pay the instrument if the person seeking enforcement of the instrument does not have rights of a holder in due course and the obligor proves that the instrument is a lost or stolen instrument.

(d) In an action to enforce the obligation of an accommodation party to pay an instrument, the accommodation party may assert against the person entitled to enforce the instrument any defense or claim in recoupment under subsection (a) that the accommodated party could assert against the person entitled to enforce the instrument, except the defenses of discharge in insolvency proceedings, infancy, and lack of legal capacity.

§ 3-306. Claims to an Instrument.

A person taking an instrument, other than a person having rights of a holder in due course, is subject to a claim of a property or possessory right in the instrument or its proceeds, including a claim to rescind a negotiation and to recover the instrument or its proceeds. A person having rights of a holder in due course takes free of the claim to the instrument.

§ 3-307. Notice of Breach of Fiduciary Duty.

(a) In this section:

(1) "Fiduciary" means an agent, trustee, partner, corporate officer or director, or other representative owing a fiduciary duty with respect to an instrument.

(2) "Represented person" means the principal, beneficiary, partnership, corporation, or other person to whom the duty stated in paragraph (1) is owed.

(b) If (i) an instrument is taken from a fiduciary for payment or collection or for value, (ii) the taker has knowledge of the fiduciary status of the fiduciary, and (iii) the represented person makes a claim to the instrument or its proceeds on the basis that the transaction of the fiduciary is a breach of fiduciary duty, the following rules apply:

(1) Notice of breach of fiduciary duty by the fiduciary is notice of the claim of the represented person.

(2) In the case of an instrument payable to the represented person or the fiduciary as such, the taker has notice of the breach of fiduciary duty if the instrument is (i) taken in payment of or as security for a debt known by the taker to be the personal debt of the fiduciary, (ii) taken in a transaction known by the taker to be for the personal benefit of the fiduciary, or (iii) deposited to an account other than an account of the fiduciary, as such, or an account of the represented person.

(3) If an instrument is issued by the represented person or the fiduciary as such, and made payable to the fiduciary personally, the taker does not have notice of the breach of fiduciary duty unless the taker knows of the breach of fiduciary duty.

(4) If an instrument is issued by the represented person or the fiduciary as such, to the taker as payee, the taker has notice of the breach of fiduciary duty if the instrument is (i) taken in payment of or as security for a debt known by the taker to be the personal debt of the fiduciary, (ii) taken in a transaction known by the taker to be for the personal benefit of the fiduciary, or (iii) deposited to an account other than an account of the fiduciary, as such, or an account of the represented person.

§ 3-308. Proof of Signatures and Status as Holder in Due Course.

(a) In an action with respect to an instrument, the authenticity of, and authority to make, each signature on the instrument is admitted unless specifically denied in the pleadings. If the validity of a signature is denied in the pleadings, the burden of establishing validity is on the person claiming validity, but the signature is presumed to be authentic and authorized unless the action is to enforce the liability of the purported signer and the signer is dead or incompetent at the time of trial of the issue of validity of the signature. If an action to enforce the instrument is brought against a person as the undisclosed principal of a person who signed the instrument as a party to the instrument, the plaintiff has the burden of establishing that the defendant is liable on the instrument as a represented person under Section 3-402 (a).

(b) If the validity of signatures is admitted or proved and there is compliance with subsection (a), a plaintiff producing the instrument is entitled to payment if the plaintiff proves entitlement to enforce the instrument under Section 3-301, unless the defendant proves a defense or claim in recoupment. If a defense or claim in recoupment is proved, the right to payment of the plaintiff is subject to the defense or claim, except to the extent the plaintiff proves that the plaintiff has rights of a holder in due course which are not subject to the defense or claim.

§ 3-309. Enforcement of Lost, Destroyed, or Stolen Instrument.

(a) A person not in possession of an instrument is entitled to enforce the instrument if (i) the person was in possession of the instrument and entitled to enforce it when loss of possession occurred, (ii) the loss of possession was not the result of a transfer by the person or a lawful seizure, and (iii) the person cannot reasonably obtain possession of the instrument because the instrument was destroyed, its whereabouts cannot be determined, or it is in the wrongful possession of an unknown person or a person that cannot be found or is not amenable to service of process.

(b) A person seeking enforcement of an instrument under subsection (a) must prove the terms of the instrument and the person's right to enforce the instrument. If that proof is made, Section 3-308 applies to the case as if the person seeking enforcement had produced the instrument. The court may not enter judgment in favor of the person seeking enforcement unless it finds that the person required to pay the instrument is adequately protected against loss that might occur by reason of a claim by another person to enforce the instrument. Adequate protection may be provided by any reasonable means.

§ 3-310. Effect of Instrument on Obligation for Which Taken.

(a) Unless otherwise agreed, if a certified check, cashier's check, or teller's check is taken for an obligation, the obligation is discharged to the same extent discharge would result if an amount of money equal to the amount of the instrument were taken in payment of the obligation. Discharge of the obligation does not affect any liability that the obligor may have as an indorser of the instrument.

(b) Unless otherwise agreed and except as provided in subsection (a),if a note or an uncertified check is taken for an obligation, the obligation is suspended to the same extent the obligation would be discharged if an amount of money equal to the amount of the instrument were taken, and the following rules apply:

(1) In the case of an uncertified check, suspension of the obligation continues until dishonor of the check or until it is paid or certified. Payment or certification of the check results in discharge of the obligation to the extent of the amount of the check.

(2) In the case of a note, suspension of the obligation continues until dishonor of the note or until it is paid. Payment of the note results in discharge of the obligation to the extent of the payment.

(3) Except as provided in paragraph (4), if the check or note is dishonored and the obligee of the obligation for which the instrument was taken is the person entitled to enforce the instrument, the obligee may enforce either the instrument or the obligation. In the case of an instrument of a third person which is negotiated to the obligee by the obligor, discharge of the obligor on the instrument also discharges the obligation.

(4) If the person entitled to enforce the instrument taken for an obligation is a person other than the obligee, the obligee may not enforce the obligation to the extent the obligation is suspended. If the obligee is the person entitled to enforce the instrument but no longer has possession of it because it was lost, stolen, or destroyed, the obligation may not be enforced to the extent of the amount payable on the instrument, and to that extent the obligee's rights against the obligor are limited to enforcement of the instrument.

(c) If an instrument other than one described in subsection (a) or (b) is taken for an obligation, the effect is (i) that stated in subsection (a) if the instrument is one on which a bank is liable as maker or acceptor; or (ii) that stated in subsection (b) in any other case.

§ 3-311. Accord and Satisfaction by Use of Instrument.

(a) If a person against whom a claim is asserted proves that (i) that person in good faith tendered an instrument to the claimant as full satisfaction of the claim, (ii) the amount of the claim was unliquidated or subject to a bona fide dispute, and (iii) the claimant obtained payment of the instrument, the following subsections apply.

(b) Unless subsection (c) applies, the claim is discharged if the person against whom the claim is asserted proves that the instrument or an accompanying written communication contained a conspicuous statement to the effect that the instrument was tendered as full satisfaction of the claim.

(c) Subject to subsection (d), a claim is not discharged under subsection (b) if either of the following applies:

(1) The claimant, if an organization, proves that (i) within a reasonable time before the tender, the claimant sent a conspicuous statement to the person against whom the claim is asserted that communications concerning disputed debts, including an instrument tendered as full satisfaction of a debt, are to be sent to a designated person, office, or place, and (ii) the instrument or accompanying communication was not received by that designated person, office, or place.

(2) The claimant, whether or not an organization, proves that within 90 days after payment of the instrument, the claimant tendered repayment of the amount of the instrument to the person against whom the claim is asserted. This paragraph does not apply if the claimant is an organization that sent a statement complying with paragraph (1)(i).

(d) A claim is discharged if the person against whom the claim is asserted proves that within a reasonable time before collection of the instrument was initiated, the claimant, or an agent of the claimant having direct responsibility with respect to the disputed obligation, knew that the instrument was tendered in full satisfaction of the claim.

§ 3-312. Lost, Destroyed, or Stolen Cashier's Check, Teller's Check, or Certified Check.

(a) In this section:

(1) "Check" means a cashier's check, teller's check, or certified check.

(2) "Claimant" means a person who claims the right to receive the amount of a cashier's check, teller's check, or certified check that was lost, destroyed, or stolen.

(3) "Declaration of loss" means a written statement, made under penalty of perjury, to the effect that (i) the declarer lost possession of a check, (ii) the declarer is the drawer or payee of the check, in the case of a certified check, or the remitter or payee of the check, in the case of a cashier's check or teller's check, (iii) the loss of possession was not the result of a transfer by the declarer or a lawful seizure, and (iv) the declarer cannot reasonably obtain possession of the check because the check was destroyed, its whereabouts cannot be determined, or it is in the wrongful possession of an unknown person or a person that cannot be found or is not amenable to service of process.

(4) "Obligated bank" means the issuer of a cashier's check or teller's check or the acceptor of a certified check.

(b) A claimant may assert a claim to the amount of a check by a communication to the obligated bank describing the check with reasonable certainty and requesting payment of the amount of the check, if (i) the claimant is the drawer or payee of a certified check or the remitter or payee of a cashier's check or teller's check, (ii) the communication contains or is accompanied by a declaration of loss of the claimant with respect to the check, (iii) the communication is received at a time and in a manner affording the bank a reasonable time to act on it before the check is paid, and (iv) the claimant provides reasonable identification if requested by the obligated bank. Delivery of a declaration of loss is a warranty of the truth of the statements made in the declaration. The warranty is made to the obligated bank and any person entitled to enforce the check. If a claim is asserted in compliance with this subsection, the following rules apply:

(1) The claim becomes enforceable at the later of (i) the time the claim is asserted, or (ii) the 90th day following the date of the check, in the case of a cashier's check or teller's check, or the 90th day following the date of the acceptance, in the case of a certified check.

(2) Until the claim becomes enforceable, it has no legal effect and the obligated bank may pay the check or, in the case of a teller's check, may permit the drawee to pay the check. Payment to a person entitled to enforce the check discharges all liability of the obligated bank with respect to the check.

(3) If the claim becomes enforceable before the check is presented for payment, the obligated bank is not obligated to pay the check.

(4) When the claim becomes enforceable, the obligated bank becomes obliged to pay the amount of the check to the claimant if payment of the check has not been made to a person entitled to enforce the check. Subject to Section 4-302 (a) (1), payment to the claimant discharges all liability of the obligated bank with respect to the check.

(c) If the obligated bank pays the amount of a check to a claimant under subsection (b) (4) and, after the claim became enforceable, the check is presented for payment by a person having rights of a holder in due course, the claimant is obliged to (i) refund the payment to the obligated bank if the check is paid, or (ii) pay the amount of the check to the person having rights of a holder in due course if the check is dishonored.

(d) If a claimant has the right to assert a claim under subsection (b) and is also a person entitled to enforce a cashier's check, teller's check, or certified check which is lost, destroyed, or stolen, the claimant may assert rights with respect to the check either under this section or Section 3-309.

Part 4 Liability of Parties

§ 3-401. Signature.

(a) A person is not liable on an instrument unless (i) the person signed the instrument, or (ii) the person is represented by an agent or representative who signed the instrument and the signature is binding on the represented person under Section 3-402.

(b) A signature may be made (i) manually or by means of a device or machine, and (ii) by the use of any name, including a trade or assumed name, or by a word, mark, or symbol executed or adopted by a person with present intention to authenticate a writing.

§ 3-402. Signature by Representative.

(a) If a person acting, or purporting to act, as a representative signs an instrument by signing either the name of the represented person or the name of the signer, the represented person is bound by the signature to the same extent the represented person would be bound if the signature were on a simple contract. If the represented person is bound, the signature of the representative is the "authorized signature of the represented person" and the represented person is liable on the instrument, whether or not identified in the instrument.

(b) If a representative signs the name of the representative to an instrument and the signature is an authorized signature of the represented person, the following rules apply:

(1) If the form of the signature shows unambiguously that the signature is made on behalf of the represented person who is identified in the instrument, the representative is not liable on the instrument.

(2) Subject to subsection (c), if (i) the form of the signature does not show unambiguously that the signa-

ture is made in a representative capacity or (ii) the represented person is not identified in the instrument, the representative is liable on the instrument to a holder in due course that took the instrument without notice that the representative was not intended to be liable on the instrument. With respect to any other person, the representative is liable on the instrument unless the representative proves that the original parties did not intend the representative to be liable on the instrument.

(c) If a representative signs the name of the representative as drawer of a check without indication of the representative status and the check is payable from an account of the represented person who is identified on the check, the signer is not liable on the check if the signature is an authorized signature of the represented person.

§ 3-403. Unauthorized Signature.

(a) Unless otherwise provided in this Article or Article 4, an unauthorized signature is ineffective except as the signature of the unauthorized signer in favor of a person who in good faith pays the instrument or takes it for value. An unauthorized signature may be ratified for all purposes of this Article.

(b) If the signature of more than one person is required to constitute the authorized signature of an organization, the signature of the organization is unauthorized if one of the required signatures is lacking.

(c) The civil or criminal liability of a person who makes an unauthorized signature is not affected by any provision of this Article which makes the unauthorized signature effective for the purposes of this Article.

§ 3-404. Impostors; Fictitious Payees.

(a) If an impostor, by use of the mails or otherwise, induces the issuer of an instrument to issue the instrument to the impostor, or to a person acting in concert with the impostor, by impersonating the payee of the instrument or a person authorized to act for the payee, an indorsement of the instrument by any person in the name of the payee is effective as the indorsement of the payee in favor of a person who, in good faith, pays the instrument or takes it for value or for collection.

(b) If (i) a person whose intent determines to whom an instrument is payable (Section 3-110(a) or (b)) does not intend the person identified as payee to have any interest in the instrument, or (ii) the person identified as payee of an instrument is a fictitious person, the following rules apply until the instrument is negotiated by special indorsement:

(1) Any person in possession of the instrument is its holder.

(2) An indorsement by any person in the name of the payee stated in the instrument is effective as the indorsement of the payee in favor of a person who, in good faith, pays the instrument or takes it for value or for collection.

(c) Under subsection (a) or (b), an indorsement is made in the name of a payee if (i) it is made in a name substantially similar to that of the payee or (ii) the instrument, whether or not indorsed, is deposited in a depositary bank to an account in a name substantially similar to that of the payee.

(d) With respect to an instrument to which subsection (a) or (b) applies, if a person paying the instrument or taking it for value or for collection fails to exercise ordinary care in paying or taking the instrument and that failure substantially contributes to loss resulting from payment of the instrument, the person bearing the loss may recover from the person failing to exercise ordinary care to the extent the failure to exercise ordinary care contributed to the loss.

§ 3-405. Employer's Responsibility for Fraudulent Indorsement by Employee.

(a) In this section:

(1) "Employee" includes an independent contractor and employee of an independent contractor retained by the employer.

(2) "Fraudulent indorsement" means (i) in the case of an instrument payable to the employer, a forged indorsement purporting to be that of the employer; or (ii) in the case of an instrument with respect to which the employer is the issuer, a forged indorsement purporting to be that of the person identified as payee.

(3) "Responsibility" with respect to instruments means authority (i) to sign or indorse instruments on behalf of the employer, (ii) to process instruments received by the employer for bookkeeping purposes, for deposit to an account, or for other disposition, (iii) to prepare or process instruments for issue in the name of the employer, (iv) to supply information determining the names or addresses of payees of instruments to be issued in the name of the employer, (v) to control the disposition of instruments to be issued in the name of the employer, or (vi) to act otherwise with respect to instruments in a responsible capacity. "Responsibility" does not include authority that merely allows an employee to have access to instruments or blank or incomplete instrument forms that are being stored or transported or are part of incoming or outgoing mail, or similar access.

(b) For the purpose of determining the rights and liabilities of a person who, in good faith, pays an instrument or takes it for value or for collection, if an employer entrusted an employee with responsibility with respect to the instrument and the employee or a person acting in concert with the employee makes a fraudulent indorsement of the instrument, the indorsement is effective as the indorsement of the person to whom the instrument is payable if it is made in the name of that person. If the person paying the instrument or taking it for value or for collection fails to exercise ordinary care in paying or taking the instrument and that failure substantially contributes to loss resulting from the fraud, the person bearing the loss may recover from the person failing to exercise ordinary care to the extent the failure to exercise ordinary care contributed to the loss.

(c) Under subsection (b), an indorsement is made in the name of the person to whom an instrument is payable if (i) it is made in a name substantially similar to the name of that person or (ii) the instrument, whether or not indorsed, is deposited in a depositary bank to an account in a name substantially similar to the name of that person.

§ 3-406. Negligence Contributing to Forged Signature or Alteration of Instrument.

(a) A person whose failure to exercise ordinary care substantially contributes to an alteration of an instrument or to the making of a forged signature on an instrument is precluded from asserting the alteration or the forgery against a person who, in good faith, pays the instrument or takes it for value or for collection.

(b) Under subsection (a), if the person asserting the preclusion fails to exercise ordinary care in paying or taking the instrument and that failure substantially contributes to loss, the loss is allocated between the person precluded and the person asserting the preclusion according to the extent to which the failure of each to exercise ordinary care contributed to the loss.

(c) Under subsection (a), the burden of proving failure to exercise ordinary care is on the person asserting the preclusion. Under subsection (b), the burden of proving failure to exercise ordinary care is on the person precluded.

§ 3-407. Alteration.

(a) "Alteration" means (i) an unauthorized change in an instrument that purports to modify in any respect the obligation of a party, or (ii) an unauthorized addition of words or numbers 6r other change to an incomplete instrument relating to the obligation of a party.

(b) Except as provided in subsection (c), an alteration fraudulently made discharges a party whose obligation is affected by the alteration unless that party assents or is precluded from asserting the alteration. No other alteration discharges a party, and the instrument may be enforced according to its original terms.

(c) A payor bank or drawee paying a fraudulently altered instrument or a person taking it for value, in good faith and without notice of the alteration, may enforce rights with respect to the instrument (i) according to its original terms, or (ii) in the case of an incomplete instrument altered by unauthorized completion, according to its terms as completed.

§ 3-408. Drawee Not Liable on Unaccepted Draft.

A check or other draft does not of itself operate as an assignment of funds in the hands of the drawee available for its payment, and the drawee is not liable on the instrument until the drawee accepts it.

§ 3-409. Acceptance of Draft; Certified Check.

(a) "Acceptance" means the drawee's signed agreement to pay a draft as presented. It must be written on the draft and may consist of the drawee's signature alone. Acceptance may be made at any time and becomes effective when notification pursuant to instructions is given or the accepted draft is delivered for the purpose of giving rights on the acceptance to any person.

(b) A draft may be accepted although it has not been signed by the drawer, is otherwise incomplete, is overdue, or has been dishonored.

(c) If a draft is payable at a fixed period after sight and the acceptor fails to date the acceptance, the holder may complete the acceptance by supplying a date in good faith.

(d) "Certified check" means a check accepted by the bank on which it is drawn. Acceptance may be made as stated in subsection (a) or by a writing on the check which indicates that the check is certified. The drawee of a check has no obligation to certify the check, and refusal to certify is not dishonor of the check.

§ 3-410. Acceptance Varying Draft.

(a) If the terms of a drawee's acceptance vary from the terms of the draft as presented, the holder may refuse the acceptance and treat the draft as dishonored. In that case, the drawee may cancel the acceptance.

(b) The terms of a draft are not varied by an acceptance to pay at a particular bank or place in the United States, unless the acceptance states that the draft is to be paid only at that bank or place.

(c) If the holder assents to an acceptance varying the terms of a draft, the obligation of each drawer and indorser that does not expressly assent to the acceptance is discharged.

§ 3-411. Refusal to Pay Cashier's Checks, Teller's Checks, and Certified Checks.

(a) In this section, "obligated bank" means the acceptor of a certified check or the issuer of a cashier's check or teller's check bought from the issuer.

(b) If the obligated bank wrongfully (i) refuses to pay a cashier's check or certified check, (ii) stops payment of a teller's check, or (iii) refuses to pay a dishonored teller's check, the person asserting the right to enforce the check is entitled to compensation for expenses and loss of interest resulting from the nonpayment and may recover consequential damages if the obligated bank refuses to pay after receiving notice of particular circumstances giving rise to the damages.

(c) Expenses or consequential damages under subsection (b) are not recoverable if the refusal of the obligated bank to pay occurs because (i) the bank suspends payments, (ii) the obligated bank asserts a claim or defense of the bank that it has reasonable grounds to believe is available against the per-son entitled to enforce the instrument, (iii) the obligated bank has a reasonable doubt whether the person demanding payment is the person entitled to enforce the instrument, or (iv) payment is prohibited by law.

§ 3-412. Obligation of Issuer of Note or Cashier's Check.

The issuer of a note or cashier's check or other draft drawn on the drawer is obliged to pay the instrument (i) according to its terms at the time it was issued or, if not issued, at the time it first came into possession of a holder, or (ii) if the issuer signed an incomplete instrument, according to its terms when completed, to the extent stated in Sections 3-115 and 3-407. The obligation is owed to a person entitled to enforce the instrument or to an indorser who paid the instrument under Section 3-415.

§ 3-413. Obligation of Acceptor.

(a) The acceptor of a draft is obliged to pay the draft (i) according to its terms at the time it was accepted, even though the acceptance states that the draft is payable "as originally drawn" or equivalent terms, (ii) if the acceptance varies the terms of the draft, according to the terms of the draft as varied, or (iii) if the acceptance is of a draft that is an incomplete instrument, according to its terms when completed, to the extent stated in Sections 3-115 and 3-407. The obligation is owed to a person entitled to enforce the draft or to the drawer or an indorser who paid the draft under Section 3-414 or 3-415.

(b) If the certification of a check or other acceptance of a draft states the amount certified or accepted, the obligation of the acceptor is that amount. If (i) the certification or acceptance does not state an amount, (ii) the amount of the instrument is subsequently raised, and (iii) the instrument is then negotiated to a holder in due course, the obligation of the acceptor is the amount of the instrument at the time it was taken by the holder in due course.

§ 3-414. Obligation of Drawer.

(a) This section does not apply to cashier's checks or other drafts drawn on the drawer.

(b) If an unaccepted draft is dishonored, the drawer is obliged to pay the draft (i) according to its terms at the time it was issued or, if not issued, at the time it first came into possession of a holder, or (ii) if the drawer signed an incomplete instrument, according to its terms when completed, to the extent stated in Sections 3-115 and 3-407. The obligation is owed to a person entitled to enforce the draft or to an indorser who paid the draft under Section 3-415.

(c) If a draft is accepted by a bank, the drawer is discharged, regardless of when or by whom acceptance was obtained.

(d) If a draft is accepted and the acceptor is not a bank, the obligation of the drawer to pay the draft if the draft is dishonored by the acceptor is the same as the obligation of an indorser under Section 3-415(a) and (c).

(e) If a draft states that it is drawn "without recourse" or otherwise disclaims liability of the drawer to pay the draft, the drawer is not liable under subsection (b) to pay the draft if the draft is not a check. A disclaimer of the liability stated in subsection (b) is not effective if the draft is a check.

(f) If (i) a check is not presented for payment or given to a depositary bank for collection within 30 days after its date, (ii) the drawee suspends payments after expiration of the 30-day period without paying the check, and (iii) because of the suspension of payments, the drawer is deprived of funds maintained with the drawee to cover payment of the check, the drawer to the extent deprived of funds may discharge its obligation to pay the check by assigning to the person entitled to enforce the check the rights of the drawer against the drawee with respect to the funds.

§ 3-415. Obligation of Indorser.

(a) Subject to subsections (b), (c), and (d) and to Section 3-419(d), if an instrument is dishonored, an indorser is obliged to pay the amount due on the instrument (i) according to the terms of the instrument at the time it was indorsed, or (ii) if the indorser indorsed an incomplete instrument, according to its terms when completed, to the extent stated in Sections 3-115 and 3-407. The obligation of the indorser is owed to a person entitled to enforce the instrument or to a subsequent indorser who paid the instrument under this section.

(b) If an indorsement states that it is made "without recourse" or otherwise disclaims liability of the indorser, the indorser is not liable under subsection (a) to pay the instrument.

(c) If notice of dishonor of an instrument is required by Section 3-503 and notice of dishonor complying with that section is not given to an indorser, the liability of the indorser under subsection (a) is discharged.

(d) If a draft is accepted by a bank after an indorsement is made, the liability of the indorser under subsection (a) is discharged.

(e) If an indorser of a check is liable under subsection (a) and the check is not presented for payment, or given to a depositary bank for collection, within 30 days after the day the indorsement was made, the liability of the indorser under subsection (a) is discharged.

§ 3-416. Transfer Warranties.

(a) A person who transfers an instrument for consideration warrants to the transferee and, if the transfer is by indorsement, to any subsequent transferee that:

(1) the warrantor is a person entitled to enforce the instrument;

(2) all signatures on the instrument are authentic and authorized;

(3) the instrument has not been altered;

(4) the instrument is not subject to a defense or claim in recoupment of any party which can be asserted against the warrantor; and

(5) the warrantor has no knowledge of any insolvency proceeding commenced with respect to the maker or acceptor or, in the case of an unaccepted draft, the drawer.

(b) A person to whom the warranties under subsection (a) are made and who took the instrument in good faith may recover from the warrantor as damages for breach of warranty an amount equal to the loss suffered as a result of the breach, but not more than the amount of the instrument plus expenses and loss of interest incurred as a result of the breach.

(c) The warranties stated in subsection (a) cannot be disclaimed with respect to checks. Unless notice of a claim for breach of warranty is given to the warrantor within 30 days after the claimant has reason to know of the breach and the identity of the warrantor, the liability of the warrantor under subsection (b) is discharged to the extent of any loss caused by the delay in giving notice of the claim.

(d) A [cause of action] for breach of warranty under this section accrues when the claimant has reason to know of the breach.

§ 3-417. Presentment Warranties.

(a) If an unaccepted draft is presented to the drawee for payment or acceptance and the drawee pays or accepts the draft, (i) the person obtaining payment or acceptance, at the time of presentment, and (ii) a previous transferor of the draft, at the time of transfer, warrant to the drawee making payment or accepting the draft in good faith that:

(1) the warrantor is, or was, at the time the warrantor transferred the draft, a person entitled to enforce the draft or authorized to obtain payment or acceptance of the draft on behalf of a person entitled to enforce the draft;

(2) the draft has not been altered; and

(3) the warrantor has no knowledge that the signature of the drawer of the draft is unauthorized.

(b) A drawee making payment may recover from any warrantor damages for breach of warranty equal to the amount paid by the drawee less the amount the drawee received or is entitled to receive from the drawer because of the payment. In addition, the drawee is entitled to compensation for expenses and loss of interest resulting from the breach. The right of the drawee to recover damages under this subsection is not affected by any failure of the drawee to exercise ordinary care in making payment. If the drawee accepts the draft, breach of warranty is a defense to the obligation of the acceptor. If the acceptor makes payment with respect to the draft, the acceptor is entitled to recover from any warrantor for breach of warranty the amounts stated in this subsection.

(c) If a drawee asserts a claim for breach of warranty under subsection (a) based on an unauthorized indorsement of the draft or an alteration of the draft, the warrantor may defend by proving that the indorsement is effective under Section 3-404 or 3-405 or the drawer is precluded under Section 3-406 or 4-406 from asserting against the drawee the unauthorized indorsement or alteration.

(d) If (i) a dishonored draft is presented for payment to the drawer or an indorser or (ii) any other instrument is presented for payment to a party obliged to pay the instrument, and (iii) payment is received, the following rules apply:

(1) The person obtaining payment and a prior transferor of the instrument warrant to the person making payment in good faith that the warrantor is, or was, at the time the warrantor transferred the instrument, a person entitled to enforce the instrument or authorized to obtain payment on behalf of a person entitled to enforce the instrument.

(2) The person making payment may recover from any warrantor for breach of warranty an amount equal to the amount paid plus expenses and loss of interest resulting from the breach.

(e) The warranties stated in subsections (a) and (d) cannot be disclaimed with respect to checks. Unless notice of a claim for breach of warranty is given to the warrantor within 30 days after the claimant has reason to know of the breach and the identity of the warrantor, the liability of the warrantor under subsection (b) or (d) is discharged to the extent of any loss caused by the delay in giving notice of the claim.

(f) A [cause of action] for breach of warranty under this section accrues when the claimant has reason to know of the breach.

§ 3-418. Payment or Acceptance by Mistake.

(a) Except as provided in subsection (c), if the drawee of a draft pays or accepts the draft and the drawee acted on the mistaken belief that (i) payment of the draft had not been stopped pursuant to Section 4-403 or (ii) the signature of the drawer of the draft was authorized, the drawee may recover the amount of the draft from the person to whom or for whose benefit payment was made or, in the case of acceptance, may revoke the acceptance. Rights of the drawee under this subsection are not affected by failure of the drawee to exercise ordinary care in paying or accepting the draft.

(b) Except as provided in subsection (c), if an instrument has been paid or accepted by mistake and the case is not covered by subsection (a), the person paying or accepting may, to the extent permitted by the law governing mistake and restitution, (i) recover the payment from the person to whom or for whose benefit payment was made or (ii) in the case of acceptance, may revoke the acceptance.

(c) The remedies provided by subsection (a) or (b) may not be asserted against a person who took the instrument in good faith and for value or who in good faith changed position in reliance on the payment or acceptance. This subsection does not limit remedies provided by Section 3-417 or 4-407.

(d) Notwithstanding Section 4-215, if an instrument is paid or accepted by mistake and the payor or acceptor recovers payment or revokes acceptance under subsection (a) or (b), the instrument is deemed not to have been paid or accepted and is treated as dishonored, and the person from whom payment is recovered has rights as a person entitled to enforce the dishonored instrument.

§ 3-419. Instruments Signed for Accommodation.

(a) If an instrument is issued for value given for the benefit of a party to the instrument ("accommodated party") and another party to the instrument ("accommodation party") signs the instrument for the purpose of incurring liability on the instrument without being a direct beneficiary of the value given for the instrument, the instrument is signed by the accommodation party "for accommodation."

(b) An accommodation party may sign the instrument as maker, drawer, acceptor, or indorser and, subject to subsection (d), is obliged to pay the instrument in the capacity in which the accommodation party signs. The obligation of an accommodation party may be enforced notwithstanding any statute of frauds and whether or not the accommodation party receives consideration for the accommodation.

(c) A person signing an instrument is presumed to be an accommodation party and there is notice that the instrument is signed for accommodation if the signature is an anomalous indorsement or is accompanied by words indicating that the signer is acting as surety or guarantor with respect to the obligation of another party to the instrument. Except as provided in Section 3-605, the obligation of an accommodation party to pay the instrument is not affected by the fact that the person enforcing the obligation had notice when the instrument was taken by that person that the accommodation party signed the instrument for accommodation.

(d) If the signature of a party to an instrument is accompanied by words indicating unambiguously that the party is guaranteeing collection rather than payment of the obligation of another party to the instrument, the signer is obliged to pay the amount due on the instrument to a person entitled to enforce the instrument only if (i) execution of judgment against the other party has been returned unsatisfied, (ii) the other party is insolvent or in an insolvency proceeding, (iii) the other party cannot be served with process, or (iv) it is otherwise apparent that payment cannot be obtained from the other party.

(e) An accommodation party who pays the instrument is entitled to reimbursement from the accommodated party and is entitled to enforce the instrument against the accommodated party. An accommodated party who pays the instrument has no right of recourse against, and is not entitled to contribution from, an accommodation party.

§ 3-420. Conversion of Instrument.

(a) The law applicable to conversion of personal property applies to instruments. An instrument is also converted if it is taken by transfer, other than a negotiation, from a person not entitled to enforce the instrument or a bank makes or obtains payment with respect to the instrument for a person not entitled to enforce the instrument or receive payment. An action for conversion of an instrument may not be brought by (i) the issuer or acceptor of the instrument or (ii) a payee or indorsee who did not receive delivery of the instrument either directly or through delivery to an agent or a co-payee.

(b) In an action under subsection (a), the measure of liability is presumed to be the amount payable on the instrument, but recovery may not exceed the amount of the plaintiff's interest in the instrument.

(c) A representative, other than a depositary bank, who has in good faith dealt with an instrument or its proceeds on behalf of one who was not the person entitled to enforce the instrument is not liable in conversion to that person beyond the amount of any proceeds that it has not paid out.

PART 5 Dishonor

§ 3-501. Presentment.

(a) "Presentment" means a demand made by or on behalf of a person entitled to enforce an instrument (i) to pay the instrument made to the drawee or a party obliged to pay the instrument or, in the case of a note or accepted draft payable at a bank, to the bank, or (ii) to accept a draft made to the drawee.

(b) The following rules are subject to Article 4, agreement of the parties, and clearing-house rules and the like:

(1) Presentment may be made at the place of payment of the instrument and must be made at the place of payment if the instrument is payable at a bank in the United States; may be made by any commercially reasonable means, including an oral, written, or electronic communication; is effective when the demand for payment or acceptance is received by the person to whom presentment is made; and is effective if made to any one of two or more makers, acceptors, drawees, or other payors.

(2) Upon demand of the person to whom presentment is made, the person making presentment must (i) exhibit the instrument, (ii) give reasonable identification and, if presentment is made on behalf of another person, reasonable evidence of authority to do so, and (...) sign a receipt on the instrument for any payment made or surrender the instrument if full payment is made.

(3) Without dishonoring the instrument, the party to whom presentment is made may (i) return the instrument for lack of a necessary indorsement, or (ii) refuse payment or acceptance for failure of the presentment to comply with the terms of the instrument, an agreement of the parties, or other applicable law or rule.

(4) The party to whom presentment is made may treat presentment as occurring on the next business day after the day of presentment if the party to whom presentment is made has established a cut-off hour not earlier than 2 p.m. for the receipt and processing of instruments presented for payment or acceptance and presentment is made after the cut-off hour.

§ 3-502. Dishonor.

(a) Dishonor of a note is governed by the following rules:

(1) If the note is payable on demand, the note is dishonored if presentment is duly made to the maker and the note is not paid on the day of presentment.

(2) If the note is not payable on demand and is payable at or through a bank or the terms of the note require presentment, the note is dishonored if presentment is duly made and the note is not paid on the day it becomes payable or the day of presentment, whichever is later.

(3) If the note is not payable on demand and paragraph (2) does not apply, the note is dishonored if it is not paid on the day it becomes payable.

(b) Dishonor of an unaccepted draft other than a documentary draft is governed by the following rules:

(1) If a check is duly presented for payment to the payor bank otherwise than for immediate payment over the counter, the check is dishonored if the payor bank makes timely return of the check or sends timely notice of dishonor or nonpayment under Section 4-301 or 4-302, or becomes accountable for the amount of the check under Section 4-302.

(2) If a draft is payable on demand and paragraph (1) does not apply, the draft is dishonored if presentment for payment is duly made to the drawee and the draft is not paid on the day of presentment.

(3) If a draft is payable on a date stated in the draft, the draft is dishonored if (i) presentment for payment is duly

made to the drawee and payment is not made on the day the draft becomes payable or the day of presentment, whichever is later; or (ii) presentment for acceptance is duly made before the day the draft becomes payable and the draft is not accepted on the day of presentment.

(4) If a draft is payable on elapse of a period of time after sight or acceptance, the draft is dishonored if presentment for acceptance is duly made and the draft is not accepted on the day of presentment.

(c) Dishonor of an unaccepted documentary draft occurs according to the rules stated in subsection (b) (2), (3), and (4), except that payment or acceptance may be delayed without dishonor until no later than the close of the third business day of the drawee following the day on which payment or acceptance is required by those paragraphs.

(d) Dishonor of an accepted draft is governed by the following rules:

(1) If the draft is payable on demand, the draft is dishonored if presentment for payment is duly made to the acceptor and the draft is not paid on the day of presentment.

(2) If the draft is not payable on demand, the draft is dishonored if presentment for payment is duly made to the acceptor and payment is not made on the day it becomes payable or the day of presentment, whichever is later.

(e) In any case in which presentment is otherwise required for dishonor under this section and presentment is excused under Section 3-504, dishonor occurs without presentment if the instrument is not duly accepted or paid.

(f) If a draft is dishonored because timely acceptance of the draft was not made and the person entitled to demand acceptance consents to a late acceptance, from the time of acceptance the draft is treated as never having been dishonored.

§ 3-503. Notice of Dishonor.

(a) The obligation of an indorser stated in Section 3-415(a) and the obligation of a drawer stated in Section 3-414(d) may not be enforced unless (i) the indorser or drawer is given notice of dishonor of the instrument complying with this section or (ii) notice of dishonor is excused under Section 3-504(b).

(b) Notice of dishonor may be given by any person; may be given by any commercially reasonable means, including an oral, written, or electronic communication; and is sufficient if it reasonably identifies the instrument and indicates that the instrument has been dishonored or has not been paid or accepted. Return of an instrument given to a bank for collection is sufficient notice of dishonor.

(c) Subject to Section 3-504(c), with respect to an instrument taken for collection by a collecting bank, notice of dishonor must be given (i) by the bank before midnight of the next banking day following the banking day on which the bank receives notice of dishonor of the instrument, or (ii) by any other person within 30 days following the day on which the person receives notice of dishonor. With respect to any other instrument, notice of dishonor must be given within 30 days following the day on which dishonor occurs.

§ 3-504. Excused Presentment and Notice of Dishonor.

(a) Presentment for payment or acceptance of an instrument is excused if (i) the person entitled to present the instrument cannot with reasonable diligence make presentment, (ii) the maker or acceptor has repudiated an obligation to pay the instrument or is dead or in insolvency proceedings, (iii) by the terms of the instrument presentment is not necessary to enforce the obligation of indorsers or the drawer, (iv) the drawer or indorser whose obligation is being enforced has waived presentment or otherwise has no reason to expect or right to require that the instrument be paid or accepted, or (v) the drawer instructed the drawee not to pay or accept the draft or the drawee was not obligated to the drawer to pay the draft.

(b) Notice of dishonor is excused if (i) by the terms of the instrument notice of dishonor is not necessary to enforce the obligation of a party to pay the instrument, or (ii) the party whose obligation is being enforced waived notice of dishonor. A waiver of presentment is also a waiver of notice of dishonor.

(c) Delay in giving notice of dishonor is excused if the delay was caused by circumstances beyond the control of the person giving the notice and the person giving the notice exercised reasonable diligence after the cause of the delay ceased to operate.

§ 3-505. Evidence of Dishonor.

(a) The following are admissible as evidence and create a presumption of dishonor and of any notice of dishonor stated:

(1) a document regular in form as provided in subsection (b) which purports to be a protest;

(2) a purported stamp or writing of the drawee, payor bank, or presenting bank on or accompanying the instrument stating that acceptance or payment has been refused unless reasons for the refusal are stated and the reasons are not consistent with dishonor;

(3) a book or record of the drawee, payor bank, or collecting bank, kept in the usual course of business which shows dishonor, even if there is no evidence of who made the entry.

(b) A protest is a certificate of dishonor made by a United States consul or vice consul, or a notary public or other person authorized to administer oaths by the law of the place where dishonor occurs. It may be made upon information satisfactory to that person. The protest must identify the instrument and certify either that presentment has been made or, if not made, the reason why it was not made, and that the instrument has been dishonored by nonacceptance or nonpayment. The protest may also certify that notice of dishonor has been given to some or all parties.

Part 6 Discharge and Payment

§ 3-601. Discharge and Effect of Discharge.

(a) The obligation of a party to pay the instrument is discharged as stated in this Article or by an act or agreement with the party which would discharge an obligation to pay money under a simple contract.

(b) Discharge of the obligation of a party is not effective against a person acquiring rights of a holder in due course of the instrument without notice of the discharge.

§ 3-602. Payment.

(a) Subject to subsection (b), an instrument is paid to the extent payment is made (i) by or on behalf of a party obliged to pay the instrument, and (ii) to a person entitled to enforce the instrument. To the extent of the payment, the obligation of the party obliged to pay the instrument is discharged even though payment is made with knowledge of a claim to the instrument under Section 3-306 by another person.

(b) The obligation of a party to pay the instrument is not discharged under subsection (a) if:

(1) a claim to the instrument under Section 3-306 is enforceable against the party receiving payment and (i) payment is made with knowledge by the payor that payment is prohibited by injunction or similar process of a court of competent jurisdiction, or (ii) in the case of an instrument other than a cashier's check, teller's check, or certified check, the party making payment accepted, from the person having a claim to the instrument, indemnity against loss resulting from refusal to pay the person entitled to enforce the instrument; or

(2) the person making payment knows that the instrument is a stolen instrument and pays a person it knows is in wrongful possession of the instrument.

§ 3-603. Tender of Payment.

(a) If tender of payment of an obligation to pay an instrument is made to a person entitled to enforce the instrument,the effect of tender is governed by principles of law applicable to tender of payment under a simple contract.

(b) If tender of payment of an obligation to pay an instrument is made to a person entitled to enforce the instrument and the tender is refused, there is discharge, to the extent of the amount of the tender, of the obligation of an indorser or accommodation party having a right of recourse with respect to the obligation to which the tender relates.

(c) If tender of payment of an amount due on an instrument is made to a person entitled to enforce the instrument, the obligation of the obligor to pay interest after the due date on the amount tendered is discharged. If presentment is required with respect to an instrument and the obligor is able and ready to pay on the due date at every place of payment stated in the instrument, the obligor is deemed to have made tender of payment on the due date to the person entitled to enforce the instrument.

§ 3-604. Discharge by Cancellation or Renunciation.

(a) A person entitled to enforce an instrument, with or without consideration, may discharge the obligation of a party to pay the instrument (i) by an intentional voluntary act, such as surrender of the instrument to the party, destruction, mutilation, or cancellation of the instrument, cancellation or striking out of the party's signature, or the addition of words to the instrument indicating discharge, or (ii) by agreeing not to sue or otherwise renouncing rights against the party by a signed writing.

(b) Cancellation or striking out of an indorsement pursuant to subsection (a) does not affect the status and tights of a party derived from the indorsement.

§ 3-605. Discharge of Indorsers and Accommodation Parties.

(a) In this section, the term "indorser" includes a drawer having the obligation described in Section 3-414(d).

(b) Discharge, under Section 3-604, of the obligation of a party to pay an instrument does not discharge the obligation of an indorser or accommodation party having a right of recourse against the discharged party.

(c) If a person entitled to enforce an instrument agrees, with or without consideration, to an extension of the due date of the obligation of a party to pay the instrument, the extension discharges an indorser or accommodation party having a right of recourse against the party whose obligation is extended to the extent the indorser or accommodation party proves that the extension caused loss to the indorser or accommodation party with respect to the right of recourse.

(d) If a person entitled to enforce an instrument agrees, with or without consideration, to a material modification of the obligation of a party other than an extension of the due date, the modification discharges the obligation of an indorser or accommodation party having a right of recourse against the person whose obligation is modified to the extent the modification causes loss to the indorser or accommodation party with respect to the right of recourse. The loss suffered by the indorser or accommodation party as a result of the modification is equal to the amount of the right of recourse unless the person enforcing the instrument proves that no loss was caused by the modification or that the loss caused by the modification was an amount less than the amount of the right of recourse.

(e) If the obligation of a party to pay an instrument is secured by an interest in collateral and a person entitled to enforce the instrument impairs the value of the interest in collateral, the obligation of an indorser or accommodation party having a right of recourse against the obligor is discharged to the extent of the impairment. The value of an interest in collateral is impaired to the extent (i) the value of the interest is reduced to an amount less than the amount of the right of recourse of the party asserting discharge, or (ii) the reduction in value of the interest causes an increase in the amount by which the amount of the right of recourse exceeds the value of the interest. The burden of proving impairment is on the party asserting discharge.

(f) If the obligation of a party is secured by an interest in collateral not provided by an accommodation party and a person entitled to enforce the instrument impairs the value of the interest in collateral, the obligation of any party who is jointly and severally liable with respect to the secured obligation is discharged to the extent the impairment causes the party asserting discharge to pay more than that party would have been obliged to pay, taking into

account rights of contribution, if impairment had not occurred. If the party asserting discharge is an accommodation party not entitled to discharge under subsection (e), the party is deemed to have a right to contribution based on joint and several liability rather than a right to reimbursement. The burden of proving impairment is on the party asserting discharge.
(g) Under subsection (e) or (f), impairing value of an interest in collateral includes (i) failure to obtain or maintain perfection or recordation of the interest in collateral, (ii) release of collateral without substitution of collateral of equal value, (iii) failure to perform a duty to preserve the value of collateral owed, under Article 9 or other law, to a debtor or surety or other person secondarily liable, or (iv) failure to comply with applicable law in disposing of collateral.
(h) An accommodation party is not discharged under subsection (c), (d), or (e) unless the person entitled to enforce the instrument knows of the accommodation or has notice under Section 3-419(c) that the instrument was signed for accommodation.
(i) A party is not discharged under this section if (i) the party asserting discharge consents to the event or conduct that is the basis of the discharge, or (ii) the instrument or a separate agreement of the party provides for waiver of discharge under this section either specifically or by general language indicating that parties waive defenses based on suretyship or impairment of collateral.

REVISION (2002) OF ARTICLE 4 / Bank Deposits and Collections

Part 1 General Provisions and Definitions

§ 4-101. Short Title. This Article may be cited as Uniform Commercial Code—Bank Deposits and Collections.

§ 4-102. Applicability.
(a) To the extent that items within this Article are also within Articles 3 and 8, they are subject to those Articles. If there is conflict, this Article governs Article 3, but Article 8 governs this Article.
(b) The liability of a bank for action or non-action with respect to an item handled by it for purposes of presentment, payment, or collection is governed by the law of the place where the bank is located. In the case of action or non-action by or at a branch or separate office of a bank, its liability is governed by the law of the place where the branch or separate office is located.

§ 4-103. Variation by Agreement; Measure of Dam-ages; Action Constituting Ordinary Care.
(a) The effect of the provisions of this Article may be varied by agreement, but the parties to the agreement cannot disclaim a bank's responsibility for its lack of good faith or failure to exercise ordinary care or limit the measure of damages for the lack or failure. However, the parties may determine by agreement the standards by which the bank's responsibility is to be measured if those standards are not manifestly unreasonable.
(b) Federal Reserve regulations and operating circulars, clearing-house rules, and the like have the effect of agreements under subsection (a), whether or not specifically assented to by all parties interested in items handled.
(c) Action or non-action approved by this Article or pursuant to Federal Reserve regulations or operating circulars is the exercise of ordinary care and, in the absence of special instructions, action or non-action consistent with clearinghouse rules and the like or with a general banking usage not disapproved by this Article, is prima facie the exercise of ordinary care.
(d) The specification or approval of certain procedures by this Article is not disapproval of other procedures that may be reasonable under the circumstances.
(e) The measure of damages for failure to exercise ordinary care in handling an item is the amount of the item reduced by an amount that could not have been realized by the exercise of ordinary care. If there is also bad faith it includes any other damages the party suffered as a proximate consequence.

§ 4-104. Definitions and Index of Definitions.
(a) In this Article, unless the context otherwise requires:
(1) "Account" means any deposit or credit account with a bank, including a demand, time, savings, passbook, share draft, or like account, other than an account evidenced by a certificate of deposit;
(2) "Afternoon" means the period of a day between noon and midnight;
(3) "Banking day" means the part of a day on which a bank is open to the public for carrying on substantially all of its banking functions;
(4) "Clearing house" means an association of banks or other payors regularly clearing items;
(5) "Customer" means a person having an account with a bank or for whom a bank has agreed to collect items, including a bank that maintains an account at another bank;
(6) "Documentary draft" means a draft to be presented for acceptance or payment if specified documents, certificated securities (Section 8-102) or instructions for uncertificated securities (Section 8-308), or other certificates, statements, or the like are to be received by the drawee or other payor before acceptance or payment of the draft;
(7) "Draft" means a draft as defined in Section 3-104 or an item, other than an instrument, that is an order;
(8) "Drawee" means a person ordered in a draft to make payment;
(9) "Item" means an instrument or a promise or order to pay money handled by a bank for collection or payment, The term does not include a payment order governed by Article 4A or a credit or debit card slip;
(10) "Midnight deadline" with respect to a bank is midnight on its next banking day following the banking day on which it receives the relevant item or notice or from which the time for taking action commences to run, whichever is later;

(11) "Settle" means to pay in cash, by clearing-house settlement, in a charge or credit or by remittance, or otherwise as agreed. A settlement may be either provisional or final'

(12) "Suspends payments" with respect to a bank means that it has been closed by order of the supervisory authorities, that a public officer has been appointed to take it over, or that it ceases or refuses to make payments in the ordinary course of business.

(b) Other definitions applying to this Article and the sections in which they appear are:

"Agreement for electronic presentment" Section 4-110.

"Bank" Section 4-105.

"Collecting bank" Section 4-105.

"Depositary bank" Section 4-105.

"Intermediary bank" Section 4-105.

"Payor bank" Section 4-105.

"Presenting bank" Section 4-105.

"Presentment notice" Section 4-110.

(c) The following definitions in other Articles apply to this Article:

"Acceptance" Section 3-409.

"Alteration" Section 3-407.

"Cashier's check" Section 3-104.

"Certificate of deposit" Section 3-104.

"Certified check" Section 3-409.

"Check" Section 3-104.

"Good faith" Section 3-103.

"Holder in due course" Section 3-302.

"Instrument" Section 3-104.

"Notice of dishonor" Section 3-503.

"Order" Section 3-103.

"Ordinary care Section 3-103.

"Person entitled to enforce" Section 3-301.

"Presentment" Section 3-501.

"Promise" Section 3-103.

"Prove" Section 3-103.

"Teller's check" Section 3-104.

"Unauthorized signature" Section 3-403.

(d) In addition, Article 1 contains general definitions and principles of construction and interpretation applicable throughout this Article.

§ 4-105. "Bank"; "Depositary Bank"; "Payor Bank"; "Intermediary Bank"; "Collecting Bank"; "Presenting Bank". In this Article:

(1) "Bank" means a person engaged in the business of banking, including a savings bank, savings and loan association, credit union, or trust company;

(2) "Depositary bank" means the first bank to take an item even though it is also the payor bank, unless the item is presented for immediate payment over the counter;

(3) "Payor bank" means a bank that is the drawee of a draft;

(4) "Intermediary bank" means a bank to which an item is transferred in course of collection except the depositary or payor bank;

(5) "Collecting bank" means a bank handling an item for collection except the payor bank;

(6) "Presenting bank" means a bank presenting an item except a payor bank.

§ 4-106. Payable Through or Payable at Bank: Collecting Bank.

(a) If an item states that it is "payable through" a bank identified in the item, (i) the item designates the bank as a collecting bank and does not by itself authorize the bank to pay the item, and (ii) the item may be presented for payment only by or through the bank.

(b) If an item states that it is "payable at" a bank identified in the item, the item is equivalent to a draft drawn on the bank.

Alternative B

(b) If an item states that it is "payable at" a bank identified in the item, (i) the item designates the bank as a collecting bank and does not by itself authorize the bank to pay the item, and (ii) the item may be presented for payment only by or through the bank.

(c) If a draft names a nonbank drawee and it is unclear whether a bank named in the draft is a co-drawee or a collecting bank, the bank is a collecting bank.

§ 4-107. Separate Office of Bank.

A branch or separate office of a bank is a separate bank for the purpose of computing the time within which and determining the place at or to which action may be taken or notices or orders shall be given under this Article and under Article 3.

§ 4-108. Time of Receipt of Items.

(a) For the purpose of allowing time to process items, prove balances, and make the necessary entries on its books to determine its position for the day, a bank may fix an afternoon hour of 2 P.M. or later as a cutoff hour for the handling of money and items and the making of entries on its books.

(b) An item or deposit of money received on any day after a cutoff hour so fixed or after the close of the banking day may be treated as being received at the opening of the next banking day.

§ 4-109. Delays.

(a) Unless otherwise instructed, a collecting bank in a good faith effort to secure payment of a specific item drawn on a payor other than a bank, and with or without the approval of any person involved, may waive, modify, or extend time limits imposed or permitted by this [Act] for a period not exceeding two additional banking days without discharge of drawers or indorsers or liability to its transferor or a prior party.

(b) Delay by a collecting bank or payor bank beyond time limits prescribed or permitted by this [Act] or by instructions is excused if (i) the delay is caused by interruption of communication or computer facilities, suspension of payments by another bank, war, emergency conditions, failure of equipment, or other circumstances beyond the control of the bank, and (ii) the bank exercises such diligence as the circumstances require.

§ 4-110. Electronic Presentment.

(a) "Agreement for electronic presentment" means an agreement, clearing-house rule, or Federal Reserve regulation or operating circular, providing that presentment of an item may be made by transmission of an image of an item or information describing the item ("presentment notice") rather than delivery of the item itself. The agreement may provide for procedures governing retention, presentment, payment, dishonor, and other matters concerning items subject to the agreement.

(b) Presentment of an item pursuant to an agreement for presentment is made when the presentment notice is received.

(c) If presentment is made by presentment notice, a reference to "item" or "check" in this Article means the presentment notice unless the context otherwise indicates.

§ 4-111. Statute of Limitations.

An action to enforce an obligation, duty, or right arising under this Article must be commenced within three years after the [cause of action] accrues.

Part 2 Collection of Items: Depositary and Collecting Banks

§ 4-201. Status of Collecting Bank as Agent and Provisional Status of Credits; Applicability of Article; Item Indorsed "Pay Any Bank".

(a) Unless a contrary intent clearly appears and before the time that a settlement given by a collecting bank for an item is or becomes final, the bank, with respect to an item, is an agent or subagent of the owner of the item and any settlement given for the item is provisional. This provision applies regardless of the form of indorsement or lack of indorsement and even though credit given for the item is subject to immediate withdrawal as of right or is in fact withdrawn; but the continuance of ownership of an item by its owner and any rights of the owner to proceeds of the item are subject to rights of a collecting bank, such as those resulting from outstanding advances on the item and rights of recoupment or setoff. If an item is handled by banks for purposes of presentment, payment, collection, or return, the relevant provisions of this Article apply even though action of the parties clearly establishes that a particular bank has purchased the item and is the owner of it

(b) After an item has been indorsed with the words "pay any bank" or the like, only a bank may acquire the rights of a holder until the item has been:

(1) returned to the customer initiating collection; or

(2) specially indorsed by a bank to a person who is not a bank.

§ 4-202. Responsibility for Collection or Return; When Action Timely.

(a) A collecting bank must exercise ordinary care in:

(1) presenting an item or sending it for presentment;

(2) sending notice of dishonor or nonpayment or returning an item other than a documentary draft to the bank's transferor after learning that the item has not been paid or accepted, as the case may be;

(3) settling for an item when the bank receives final settlement; and

(4) notifying its transferor of any loss or delay in transit within a reasonable time after discovery thereof.

(b) A collecting bank exercises ordinary care under subsection (a) by taking proper action before its midnight deadline following receipt of an item, notice, or settlement. Taking proper action within a reasonably longer time may constitute the exercise of ordinary care, but the bank has the burden of establishing timeliness.

(c) Subject to subsection (a) (1), a bank is not liable for the insolvency, neglect, misconduct, mistake, or default of another bank or person or for loss or destruction of an item in the possession of others or in transit.

§ 4-203. Effect of Instructions. Subject to Article 3 concerning conversion of instruments (Section 3-420) and restrictive indorsements (Section 3-206), only a collecting bank's transferor can give instructions that affect the bank or constitute notice to it, and a collecting bank is not liable to prior parties for any action taken pursuant to the instructions or in accordance with any agreement with its transferor.

§ 4-204. Methods of Sending and Presenting; Sending Directly to Payor Bank.

(a) A collecting bank shall send items by a reasonably prompt method, taking into consideration relevant instructions, the nature of the item, the number of those items on hand, the cost of collection involved, and the method generally used by it or others to present those items.

(b) A collecting bank may send:

(1) an item directly to the payor bank;

(2) an item to a nonbank payor if authorized by its transferor; and

(3) an item other than documentary drafts to a nonbank payor, if authorized by Federal Reserve regulation or operating circular, clearing-house rule, or the like.

(c) Presentment may be made by a presenting bank at a place where the payor bank or other payor has requested that presentment be made. As amended in 1962 and 1990.

§ 4-205. Depositary Bank Holder of Unindorsed Item. If a customer delivers an item to a depositary bank for collection:

(1) the depositary bank becomes a holder of the item at the time it receives the item for collection if the customer at the time of delivery was a holder of the item, whether or not the customer

indorses the item, and, if the bank satisfies the other requirements of Section 3-302, it is a holder in due course; and

(2) the depositary bank warrants to collecting banks, the payor bank or other payor, and the drawer that the amount of the item was paid to the customer or deposited to the customer's account.

§ 4-206. Transfer Between Banks. Any agreed method that identifies the transferor bank is sufficient for the item's further transfer to another bank.

§ 4-207. Transfer Warranties.

(a) A customer or collecting bank that transfers an item and receives a settlement or other consideration warrants to the transferee and to any subsequent collecting bank that:

(1) the warrantor is a person entitled to enforce the item

(2) all signatures on the item are authentic and authorized;

(3) the item has not been altered;

(4) the item is not subject to a defense or claim in recoupment (Section 3-305(a)) of any party that can be asserted against the warrantor; and

(5) the warrantor has no knowledge of any insolvency proceeding commenced with respect to the maker or acceptor or, in the case of an unaccepted draft, the drawer.

(b) If an item is dishonored, a customer or collecting bank transferring the item and receiving settlement or other consideration is obliged to pay the amount due on the item (1) according to the terms of the item at the time it was transferred, or (ii) if the transfer was of an incomplete item, according to its terms when completed as stated in Sections 3-115 and 3-407. The obligation of a transferor is owed to the transferee and to any subsequent collecting bank that takes the item in good faith. A transferor cannot disclaim its obligation under this subsection by an indorsement stating that it is made 'without recourse" or otherwise disclaiming liability.

(c) A person to whom the warranties under subsection (a) are made and who took the item in good faith may recover from the warrantor as damages for breach of warranty an amount equal to the loss suffered as a result of the breach, but not more than the amount of the item plus expenses and loss of interest incurred as a result of the breach.

(d) The warranties stated in subsection (a) cannot be disclaimed with respect to checks. Unless notice of a claim for breach of warranty is given to the warrantor within 30 days after the claimant has reason to know of the breach and the identity of the warrantor, the warrantor is discharged to the extent of any loss caused by the delay in giving notice of the claim.

(e) A cause of action for breach of warranty under this section accrues when the claimant has reason to know of the breach.

§ 4-208. Presentment Warranties.

(a) If an unaccepted draft is presented to the drawee for payment or acceptance and the drawee pays or accepts the draft, (i) the person obtaining payment or acceptance, at the time of presentment, and (ii) a previous transferor of the draft, at the time of transfer, warrant to the drawee that pays or accepts the draft in good faith that:

(1) the warrantor is, or was, at the time the warrantor transferred the draft, a person entitled to enforce the draft or authorized to obtain payment or acceptance of the draft on behalf of a person entitled to enforce the draft;

(2) the draft has not been altered; and

(3) the warrantor has no knowledge that the signature of the purported drawer of the draft is unauthorized.

(b) A drawee making payment may recover from a warrantor damages for breach of warranty equal to the amount paid by the drawee less the amount the drawee received or is entitled to receive from the drawer because of the payment. In addition, the drawee is entitled to compensation for expenses and loss of interest resulting from the breach. The right of the drawee to recover damages under this subsection is not affected by any failure of the drawee to exercise ordinary care in making payment. If the drawee accepts the draft (i) breach of warranty is a defense to the obligation of the acceptor, and (ii) if the acceptor makes payment with respect to the draft, the acceptor is entitled to recover from a warrantor for breach of warranty the amounts stated in this subsection.

(c) If a drawee asserts a claim for breach of warranty under subsection (a) based on an unauthorized indorsement of the draft or an alteration of the draft, the warrantor may defend by proving that the indorsement is effective under Section 3-404 or 3-405 or the drawer is precluded under Section 3-406 or 4-406 from asserting against the drawee the unauthorized indorsement or alteration.

(d) If (i) a dishonored draft is presented for payment to the drawer or an indorser or (ii) any other item is presented for payment to a party obliged to pay the item, and the item is paid, the person obtaining payment and a prior transferor of the item warrant to the person making payment in good faith that the warrantor is, or was, at the time the warrantor transferred the item, a person entitled to enforce the item or authorized to obtain payment on behalf of a person entitled to enforce the item. The person making payment may recover from any warrantor for breach of warranty an amount equal to the amount paid plus expenses and loss of interest resulting from the breach.

(e) The warranties stated in subsections (a) and (d) cannot be disclaimed with respect to checks. Unless notice of a claim for breach of warranty is given to the warrantor within 30 days after the claimant has reason to know of the breach and the identity of the warrantor, the warrantor is discharged to the extent of any loss caused by the delay in giving notice of the claim.

(f) A cause of action for breach of warranty under this section accrues when the claimant has reason to know of the breach.

§ 4-209. Encoding and Retention Warranties.

(a) A person who encodes information on or with respect to an item after issue warrants to any subsequent collecting bank and to the payor bank or other payor that the information is correctly encoded. If the customer of a depositary bank encodes, that bank also makes the warranty.

(b) A person who undertakes to retain an item pursuant to an agreement for electronic presentment warrants to any subsequent collecting bank and to the payor bank or other payor that retention and presentment of the item comply with the agreement. If a customer of a depositary bank undertakes to retain an item, that bank also makes this warranty.

(c) A person to whom warranties are made under this section and who took the item in good faith may recover from the warrantor as damages for breach of warranty an amount equal to the loss suffered as a result of the breach, plus expenses and loss of interest incurred as a result of the breach.

§ 4-210. Security Interest of Collecting Bank in Items, Accompanying Documents and Proceeds.

(a) A collecting bank has a security interest in an item and any accompanying documents or the proceeds of either:

(1) in case of an item deposited in an account, to the extent to which credit given for the item has been withdrawn or applied;

(2) in case of an item for which it has given credit available for withdrawal as of right, to the extent of the credit given, whether or not the credit is drawn upon or there is a right of chargeback; or

(3) if it makes an advance on or against the item.

(b) If credit given for several items received at one time or pursuant to a single agreement is withdrawn or applied in part, the security interest remains upon all the items, any accompanying documents or the proceeds of either. For the purpose of this section, credits first given are first withdrawn.

(c) Receipt by a collecting bank of a final settlement for an item is a realization on its security interest in the item, accompanying documents, and proceeds. So long as the bank does not receive final settlement for the item or give up possession of the item or accompanying documents for purposes other than collection, the security interest continues to that extent and is subject to Article 9, but:

(1) no security agreement is necessary to make the security interest enforceable (Section 9-203(1) (a));

(2) no filing is required to perfect the security interest; and

(3) the security interest has priority over conflicting perfected security interests in the item, accompanying documents, or proceeds.

§ 4-211. When Bank Gives Value for Purposes of Holder in Due Course. For purposes of determining its status as a holder in due course, a bank has given value to the extent it has a security interest in an item, if the bank otherwise complies with the requirements of Section 3-302 on what constitutes a holder in due course.

§ 4-212. Presentment by Notice of Item Not Payable by, Through, or at Bank; Liability of Drawer or Indorser.

(a) Unless otherwise instructed, a collecting bank may present an item not payable by, through, or at a bank by sending to the party to accept or pay a written notice that the bank holds the item for acceptance or payment. The notice must be sent in time to be received on or before the day when presentment is due and the bank must meet any requirement of the party to acceptor pay under Section 3-501 by the close of the bank's next banking day after it knows of the requirement.

(b) If presentment is made by notice and payment, acceptance, or request for compliance with a requirement under Section 3-501 is not received by the close of business on the day after maturity or, in the case of demand items, by the close of business on the third banking day after notice was sent, the presenting bank may treat the item as dishonored and charge any drawer or indorser by sending it notice of the facts.

As amended in 1990.

§ 4-213. Medium and Time of Settlement by Bank.

(a) With respect to settlement by a bank, the medium and time of settlement may be prescribed by Federal Reserve regulations or circulars, clearing-house rules, and the like, or agreement. In the absence of such prescription:

(1) the medium of settlement is cash or credit to an account in a Federal Reserve bank of or specified by the person to receive settlement; and

(2) the time of settlement, is:

(i) with respect to tender of settlement by cash, a cashier's check, or teller's check, when the cash or check is sent or delivered;

(ii) with respect to tender of settlement by credit in an account in a Federal Reserve Bank, when the credit is made;

(iii) with respect to tender of settlement by a credit or debit to an account in a bank, when the credit or debit is made or, in the case of tender of settlement by authority to charge an account, when the authority is sent or delivered; or

(iv) with respect to tender of settlement by a funds transfer, when payment is made pursuant to Section 4A-406 (a) to the person receiving settlement.

(b) If the tender of settlement is not by a medium authorized by subsection (a) or the time of settlement is not fixed by subsection (a), no settlement occurs until the tender of settlement is accepted by the person receiving settlement.

(c) If settlement for an item is made by cashier's check or teller's check and the person receiving settlement, before its midnight deadline:

(1) presents or forwards the check for collection, settlement is final when the check is finally paid; or

(2) fails to present or forward the check for collection, settlement is final at the midnight deadline of the person receiving settlement.

(d) If settlement for an item is made by giving authority to charge the account of the bank giving settlement in the bank receiving settlement, settlement is final when the charge is made by the bank receiving settlement if there are funds available in the account for the amount of the item.

§ 4-214. Right of Charge-Back or Refund; Liability of Collecting Bank: Return of Item.

(a) If a collecting bank has made provisional settlement with its customer for an item and fails by reason of dishonor, suspension of payments by a bank, or otherwise to receive settlement for the item which is or becomes final, the bank may revoke the settlement given by it, charge back the amount of any credit given for the item to its customer's account, or obtain refund from its customer, whether or not it is able to return the item, if by its midnight deadline or within a longer reasonable time after it learns the facts it returns the item or sends notification of the facts. If the return or notice is delayed beyond the bank's midnight deadline or a longer reasonable time after it learns the facts, the bank may revoke the settlement, charge back the credit, or obtain refund from its customer, but it is liable for any loss resulting from the delay. These rights to revoke, charge back, and obtain refund terminate if and when a settlement for the item received by the bank is or becomes final.

(b) A collecting bank returns an item when it is sent or delivered to the bank's customer or transferor or pursuant to its instructions.

(c) A depositary bank that is also the payor may charge back the amount of an item to its customer's account or obtain refund in accordance with the section governing return of an item received by a payor bank for credit on its books (Section 4-301).

(d) The right to charge back is not affected by:

(1) previous use of a credit given for the item; or

(2) failure by any bank to exercise ordinary care with respect to the item, but a bank so failing remains liable.

(e) A failure to charge back or claim refund does not affect other rights of the bank against the customer or any other party.

(f) If credit is given in dollars as the equivalent of the value of an item payable in foreign money, the dollar amount of any charge-back or refund must be calculated on the basis of the bank-offered spot rate for the foreign money prevailing on the day when the person entitled to the charge-back or refund learns that it will not receive payment in ordinary course.

§ 4-215. Final Payment of Item by Payor Bank; When Provisional Debits and Credits Become Final; When Certain Credits Become Available for Withdrawal.

(a) An item is finally paid by a payor bank when the bank has first done any of the following:

(1) paid the item in cash;

(2) settled for the item without having a right to revoke the settlement under statute, clearing-house rule, or agreement; or

(3) made a provisional settlement for the item and failed to revoke the settlement in the time and manner permitted by statute, clearing-house rule, or agreement.

(b) If provisional settlement for an item does not become final, the item is not finally paid.

(c) If provisional settlement for an item between the presenting and payor banks is made through a clearing house or by debits or credits in an account between them, then to the extent that provisional debits or credits for the item are entered in accounts between the presenting and payor banks or between the presenting and successive prior collecting banks seriatim, they become final upon final payment of the item by the payor bank.

(d) If a collecting bank receives a settlement for an item which is or becomes final, the bank is accountable to its customer for the amount of the item and any provisional credit given for the item in an account with its customer becomes final.

(e) Subject to (i) applicable law stating a time for availability of funds and (ii) any right of the bank to apply the credit to an obligation of the customer, credit given by a bank for an item in a customer's account becomes available for withdrawal as of right:

(1) if the bank has received a provisional settlement for the item, when the settlement becomes final and the bank has had a reasonable time to receive return of the item and the item has not been received within that time;

(2) if the bank is both the depositary bank and the payor bank, and the item is finally paid, at the opening of the bank's second banking day following receipt of the item.

(f) Subject to applicable law stating a time for availability of funds and any right of a bank to apply a deposit to an obligation of the depositor, a deposit of money becomes available for withdrawal as of right at the opening of the bank's next banking day after receipt of the deposit.

§ 4-216. Insolvency and Preference.

(a) If an item is in or comes into the possession of a payor or collecting bank that suspends payment and the item has not been finally paid, the item must be returned by the receiver, trustee, or agent in charge of the closed bank to the presenting bank or the closed bank's customer.

(b) If a payor bank finally pays an item and suspends payments without making a settlement for the item with its customer or the presenting bank which settlement is or becomes final, the owner of the item has a preferred claim against the payor bank.

(c) If a payor bank gives or a collecting bank gives or receives a provisional settlement for an item and thereafter suspends payments, the suspension does not prevent or interfere with the settlement's becoming final if the finality occurs automatically upon the lapse of certain time or the happening of certain events.

(d) If a collecting bank receives from subsequent parties settlement for an item, which settlement is or becomes final and the bank suspends payments without making a settlement for the item with its customer which settlement is or becomes final, the owner of the item has a preferred claim against the collecting bank.

Part 3 Collection of Items: Payor Banks

§ 4-301. Deferred Posting; Recovery of Payment by Re-turn of Items; Time of Dishonor; Return of Items by Payor Bank.

(a) If a payor bank settles for a demand item other than a documentary draft presented otherwise than for immediate payment over the counter before midnight of the banking day of receipt, the payor bank may revoke the settlement and recover the settlement if, before it has made final payment and before its midnight deadline, it

(1) returns the item; or

(2) sends written notice of dishonor or nonpayment if the item is unavailable for return.

(b) If a demand item is received by a payor bank for credit on its books, it may return the item or send notice of dishonor and may revoke any credit given or recover the amount thereof withdrawn by its customer, if it acts within the time limit and in the manner specified in subsection (a)

(c) Unless previous notice of dishonor has been sent, an item is dishonored at the time when for purposes of dishonor it is returned or notice sent in accordance with this section.

(d) An item is returned:

(1) as to an item presented through a clearing house, when it is delivered to the presenting or last collecting bank or to the clearing house or is sent or delivered in accordance with clearing-house rules; or

(2) in all other cases, when it is sent or delivered to the bank's customer or transferor or pursuant to instructions.

§ 4-302. Payor Bank's Responsibility for Late Return of Item.

(a) If an item is presented to and received by a payor bank, the bank is accountable for the amount of:

(1) a demand item, other than a documentary draft, whether properly payable or not, if the bank, in any case in which it is not also the depositary bank, retains the item beyond midnight of the banking day of receipt without settling for it or, whether or not it is also the depositary bank, does not pay or return the item or send notice of dishonor until after its midnight deadline; or

(2) any other properly payable item unless, within the time allowed for acceptance or payment of that item, the bank either accepts or pays the item or returns it and accompanying documents.

(b) The liability of a payor bank to pay an item pursuant to subsection (a) is subject to defenses based on breach of a presentment warranty (Section 4-208) or proof that the person seeking enforcement of the liability presented or transferred the item for the purpose of defrauding the payor bank.

§ 4-303. When Items Subject to Notice, Stop-Payment Order, Legal Process, or Setoff; Order in Which Items May Be Charged or Certified.

(a) Any knowledge, notice, or stop-payment order received by, legal process served upon, or setoff exercised by a payor bank comes too late to terminate, suspend, or modify the bank's right or duty to pay an item or to charge its customer's account for the item if the knowledge, notice, stop-payment order, or legal process is received or served and a reasonable time for the bank to act thereon expires or the setoff is exercised after the earliest of the following:

(1) the bank accepts or certifies the item;

(2) the bank pays the item in cash;

(3) the bank settles for the item without having a right to revoke the settlement under statute, clearing-house rule, or agreement;

(4) the bank becomes accountable for the amount of the item under Section 4-302 dealing with the payor bank's responsibility for late return of items; or

(5) with respect to checks, a cutoff hour no earlier than one hour after the opening of the next banking day after the banking day on which the bank received the check and no later than the close of that next banking day or, if no cutoff hour is fixed, the close of the next banking day after the banking day on which the bank received the check.

(b) Subject to subsection (a), items may be accepted, paid, certified, or charged to the indicated account of its customer in any order.

Part 4 Relationship Between Payor Bank and its Customer

§ 4-401. When Bank May Charge Customer's Account.

(a) A bank may charge against the account of a customer an item that is properly payable from the account even though the charge creates an overdraft. An item is properly payable if it is authorized by the customer and is in accordance with any agreement between the customer and bank.

(b) A customer is not liable for the amount of an overdraft if the customer neither signed the item nor benefited from the proceeds of the item.

(c) A bank may charge against the account of a customer a check that is otherwise properly payable from the account, even though payment was made before the date of the check, unless the customer has given notice to the bank of the postdating describing the check with reasonable certainty. The notice is effective for the period stated in Section 4-403 (b) for stop-payment orders, and must be received at such time and in such manner as to afford the bank a reasonable opportunity to act on it before the bank takes any action with respect to the check described in Section 4-303. If a bank charges against the account of a customer a check before the date stared in the notice of postdating, the bank is liable for damages for the loss resulting from its act. The loss may include damages for dishonor of subsequent items under Section 4-402.

(d) A bank that in good faith makes payment to a holder may charge the indicated account of its customer according to:

(1) the original terms of the altered item; or

(2) the terms of the completed item, even though the bank knows the item has been completed unless the bank has notice that the completion was improper.

§ 4-402. Bank's Liability to Customer for Wrongful Dishonor; Time of Determining Insufficiency of Account.

(a) Except as otherwise provided in this Article, a payor bank wrongfully dishonors an item if it dishonors an item that is properly payable, but a bank may dishonor an item that would create an overdraft unless it has agreed to pay the overdraft.

(b) A payor bank is liable to its customer for damages proximately caused by the wrongful dishonor of an item. Liability is limited to actual damages proved and may include damages for an arrest or prosecution of the customer or other consequential damages. Whether any consequential damages are proximately caused by the wrongful dishonor is a question of fact to be determined in each case.

(c) A payor bank's determination of the customer's account balance on which a decision to dishonor for insufficiency of available funds is based may be made at any time between the time the item is received by the payor bank and the time that the payor bank returns the item or gives notice in lieu of return, and no more than one determination need be made. If, at the election of the payor bank, a subsequent balance determination is made for the purpose of reevaluating the bank's decision to dishonor the item, the account balance at that time is determinative of whether a dishonor for insufficiency of available funds is wrongful.

§ 4-403. Customer's Right to Stop Payment; Burden of Proof of Loss.

(a) A customer or any person authorized to draw on the account if there is more than one person may stop payment of any item drawn on the customer's account or close the account by an order to the bank describing the item or account with reasonable certainty received at a time and in a manner that affords the bank a reasonable opportunity to act on it before any action by the bank with respect to the item described in Section 4-303. If the signature of more than one person is required to draw on an account, any of these persons may stop payment or close the account.

(b) A stop-payment order is effective for six months, but it lapses after 14 calendar days if the original order was oral and was not confirmed in writing within that period. A stop-payment order may be renewed for additional six-month periods by a writing given to the bank within a period during which the stop-payment order is effective.

(c) The burden of establishing the fact and amount of loss resulting from the payment of an item contrary to a stop-payment order or order to close an account is on the customer. The loss from payment of an item contrary to a stop-payment order may include damages for dishonor of subsequent items under Section 4-402.

§ 4-404. Bank Not Obliged to Pay Check More Than Six Months Old. A bank is under no obligation to a customer having a checking account to pay a check, other than a certified check, which is presented more than six months after its date, but it may charge its customer's account for a payment made thereafter in good faith.

§ 4-405. Death or Incompetence of Customer.

(a) A payor or collecting bank's authority to accept, pay, or collect an item or to account for proceeds of its collection, if otherwise effective, is not rendered ineffective by incompetence of a customer of either bank existing at the time the item is issued or its collection is undertaken if the bank does not know of an adjudication of incompetence. Neither death nor incompetence of a customer revokes the authority to accept, pay, collect, or account until the bank knows of the fact of death or of an adjudication of incompetence and has reasonable opportunity to act on it.

(b) Even with knowledge, a bank may for 10 days after the date of death pay or certify checks drawn on or before that date unless ordered to stop payment by a person claiming an interest in the account.

§ 4-406. Customer's Duty to Discover and Report Unauthorized Signature or Alteration.

(a) A bank that sends or makes available to a customer a statement of account showing payment of items for the account shall either return or make available to the customer the items paid or provide information in the statement of account sufficient to allow the customer reasonably to identify the items paid. The statement of account provides sufficient information if the item is described by item number, amount, and date of payment.

(b) If the items are not returned to the customer, the person retaining the items shall either retain the items or, if the items are destroyed, maintain the capacity to furnish legible copies of the items until the expiration of seven years after receipt of the items. A customer may request an item from the bank that paid the item, and that bank must provide in a reasonable time either the item or, if the item has been destroyed or is not otherwise obtainable, a legible copy of the item.

(c) If a bank sends or makes available a statement of account or items pursuant to subsection (a), the customer must exercise reasonable promptness in examining the statement or the items to determine whether any payment was not authorized because of an alteration of an item or because a purported signature by or on behalf of the customer was not authorized. If, based on the statement or items provided, the customer should reasonably have discovered the unauthorized payment, the customer must promptly notify the bank of the relevant facts.

(d) If the bank proves that the customer failed, with respect to an item, to comply with the duties imposed on the customer by subsection (c), the customer is precluded from asserting against the bank:

(1) the customer's unauthorized signature or any alteration on the item, if the bank also proves that it suffered a loss by reason of the failure; and

(2) the customer's unauthorized signature or alteration by the same wrongdoer on any other item paid in good faith by the bank if the payment was made before the bank received notice from the customer of the unauthorized signature or alteration and after the customer had been afforded a reasonable period of time, not exceeding 30 days, in which to examine the item or statement of account and notify the bank.

(e) If subsection (d) applies and the customer proves that the bank failed to exercise ordinary care in paying the item and that the failure substantially contributed to loss, the loss is allocated between the customer precluded and the bank asserting the preclusion according to the extent to which the failure of the customer to comply with subsection (c) and the failure of the bank to exercise ordinary care contributed to the loss. If the customer proves that the bank did not pay the item in good faith, the preclusion under subsection (d) does not apply.

(f) Without regard to care or lack of care of either the customer or the bank, a customer who does not within one year after the statement or items are made available to the customer (subsection (a)) discover and report the customer's unauthorized signature on or any alteration on the item is precluded from asserting against the bank the unauthorized signature or alteration. If there is a preclusion under this subsection, the payor bank may not recover for breach or warranty under Section 4-208 with respect to the unauthorized signature or alteration to which the preclusion applies.

§ 4-407. Payor Bank's Right to Subrogation on Improper Payment. If a payor bank has paid an item over the order of the drawer or maker to stop payment, or after an account has been closed, or otherwise under circumstances giving a basis for objection by the drawer or maker, to prevent unjust enrichment and only to the extent necessary to prevent loss to the bank by reason of its payment of the item, the payor bank is subrogated to the rights

(1) of any holder in due course on the item against the drawer or maker;

(2) of the payee or any other holder of the item against the drawer or maker either on the item or under the transaction out of which the item arose; and

(3) of the drawer or maker against the payee or any other holder of the item with respect to the transaction out of which the item arose.

Part 5 Collection of Documentary Drafts

§ 4-501. Handling of Documentary Drafts; Duty to Send for Presentment and to Notify Customer of Dishonor. A bank that takes a documentary draft for collection shall present or send the draft and accompanying documents for presentment and, upon learning that the draft has not been paid or accepted in due course, shall seasonably notify its customer of the fact even though it may have discounted or bought the draft or extended credit available for withdrawal as of right.

§ 4-502. Presentment of "On Arrival" Drafts. If a draft or the relevant instructions require presentment on arrival", "when goods arrive" or the like, the collecting bank need not present until in its judgment a reasonable time for arrival of the goods has expired. Refusal to pay or accept because the goods have not arrived is not dishonor, the bank must notify its transferor of the refusal but need not present the draft again until it is instructed to do so or learns of the arrival of the goods.

§ 4-503. Responsibility of Presenting Bank for Documents and Goods; Report of Reasons for Dishonor; Referee in Case of Need. Unless otherwise instructed and except as provided in Article 5, a bank presenting a documentary draft:

(1) must deliver the documents to the drawee on acceptance of the draft if it is payable more than three days after presentment; otherwise, only on payment; and

(2) upon dishonor, either in the case of presentment for acceptance of presentment for payment, may seek and follow instructions from any referee in case of need designated in the draft or, if the presenting bank does not choose to utilize the referee's services, it must use diligence and good faith to ascertain the reason for dishonor, must notify its transferor of the dishonor and of the results of its effort to ascertain the reasons therefor, and must request instructions.

However, the presenting bank is under no obligation with respect to goods represented by the documents except to follow any reasonable instructions seasonably received; it has a right to reimbursement for any expense incurred in following instructions and to prepayment of or indemnity for those expenses.

§ 4-504. Privilege of Presenting Bank to Deal With Goods; Security Interest for Expenses.

(a) A presenting bank that, following the dishonor of a documentary draft, has seasonably requested instructions but does not receive them within a reasonable time may store, sell, or otherwise deal with the goods in any reasonable manner.

(b) For its reasonable expenses incurred by action under subsection (a) the presenting bank has a lien upon the goods or their proceeds, which may be foreclosed in the same manner as an unpaid seller's lien.

REVISION (2003) OF ARTICLE 7 / Documents of Title

PART 1. General

§ 7-101. Short Title. This article may be cited as Uniform Commercial Code Documents of Title.

§ 7-102. Definitions and Index of Definitions.

(a) In this article, unless the context otherwise requires:

(1) "Bailee" means a person that by a warehouse receipt, bill of lading, or other document of title acknowledges possession of goods and contracts to deliver them.

(2) "Carrier" means a person that issues a bill of lading.

(3) "Consignee" means a person named in a bill of lading to which or to whose order the bill promises delivery.

(4) "Consignor" means a person named in a bill of lading as the person from which the goods have been received for shipment.

(5) "Delivery order" means a record that contains an order to deliver goods directed to a warehouse, carrier, or other person that in the ordinary course of business issues warehouse receipts or bills of lading.

(6) "Good faith" means honesty in fact and the observance of reasonable commercial standards of fair dealing.

(7) "Goods" means all things that are treated as movable for the purposes of a contract for storage or transportation.

(8) "Issuer" means a bailee that issues a document of title or, in the case of an unaccepted delivery order, the person that orders the possessor of goods to deliver. The term includes a person for which an agent or employee purports to act in issuing a document if the agent or employee has real or apparent authority to issue documents, even if the issuer did not receive any goods, the goods were misdescribed, or in any other respect the agent or employee violated the issuer's instructions.

(9) "Person entitled under the document" means the holder, in the case of a negotiable document of title, or the person to which delivery of the goods is to be made by the terms of, or pursuant to instructions in a record under, a nonnegotiable document of title.

(10) "Record" means information that is inscribed on a tangible medium or that is stored in an electronic or other medium and is retrievable in perceivable form.

(11) "Sign" means, with present intent to authenticate or adopt a record:

(A) to execute or adopt a tangible symbol; or

(B) to attach to or logically associate with the record an electronic sound, symbol, or process.

(12) "Shipper" means a person that enters into a contract of transportation with a carrier.

(13) "Warehouse" means a person engaged in the business of storing goods for hire.

(b) Definitions in other articles applying to this article and the sections in which they appear are:

(1) "Contract for sale", Section 2 106.

(2) "Lessee in the ordinary course of business", Section 2A-103.

(3) "Receipt" of goods, Section 2 103.

(c) In addition, Article 1 contains general definitions and principles of construction and interpretation applicable throughout this article.

Legislative Note: If the state has enacted Revised Article 1, the definitions of "good faith" in subsection (a)(6) and "record" in (a)(10) need not be enacted in this section as they are contained in Article 1, Section 1-201. These subsections should be marked as "reserved" in order to provide for uniform numbering of subsections.

§ 7-103. Relation of Article to Treaty or Statute.

(a) This article is subject to any treaty or statute of the United States or regulatory statute of this state to the extent the treaty, statute, or regulatory statute is applicable.

(b) This article does not modify or repeal any law prescribing the form or content of a document of title or the services or facilities to be afforded by a bailee, or otherwise regulating a bailee's business in respects not specifically treated in this article. However, violation of such a law does not affect the status of a document of title that otherwise is within the definition of a document of title.

(c) This [act] modifies, limits, and supersedes the federal Electronic Signatures in Global and National Commerce Act (15 U.S.C. Section 7001, et. seq.) but does not modify, limit, or supersede Section 101(c) of that act (15 U.S.C. Section 7001(c)) or authorize electronic delivery of any of the notices described in Section 103(b) of that act (15 U.S.C. Section 7003(b)).

(d) To the extent there is a conflict between [the Uniform Electronic Transactions Act] and this article, this article governs.

Legislative Note: In states that have not enacted the Uniform Electronic Transactions Act in some form, states should consider their own state laws to determine whether there is a conflict between the provisions of this article and those laws particularly as those other laws may affect electronic documents of title.

§ 7-104. Negotiable and Nonnegotiable Document of Title.

(a) Except as otherwise provided in subsection (c), a document of title is negotiable if by its terms the goods are to be delivered to bearer or to the order of a named person.

(b) A document of title other than one described in subsection (a) is nonnegotiable. A bill of lading that states that the goods are consigned to a named person is not made negotiable by a provision that the goods are to be delivered only against an order in a record signed by the same or another named person.

(c) A document of title is nonnegotiable if, at the time it is issued, the document has a conspicuous legend, however expressed, that it is nonnegotiable.

§ 7-105. Reissuance in Alternative Medium.

(a) Upon request of a person entitled under an electronic document of title, the issuer of the electronic document may issue a tangible document of title as a substitute for the electronic document if:

(1) the person entitled under the electronic document surrenders control of the document to the issuer; and

(2) the tangible document when issued contains a statement that it is issued in substitution for the electronic document.

(b) Upon issuance of a tangible document of title in substitution for an electronic document of title in accordance with subsection (a):

(1) the electronic document ceases to have any effect or validity; and

(2) the person that procured issuance of the tangible document warrants to all subsequent persons entitled under the tangible document that the warrantor was a person entitled under the electronic document when the warrantor surrendered control of the electronic document to the issuer.

(c) Upon request of a person entitled under a tangible document of title, the issuer of the tangible document may issue an electronic document of title as a substitute for the tangible document if:

(1) the person entitled under the tangible document surrenders possession of the document to the issuer; and

(2) the electronic document when issued contains a statement that it is issued in substitution for the tangible document.

(d) Upon issuance of an electronic document of title in substitution for a tangible document of title in accordance with subsection (c):

(1) the tangible document ceases to have any effect or validity; and

(2) the person that procured issuance of the electronic document warrants to all subsequent persons entitled under the electronic document that the warrantor was a person entitled under the tangible document when the warrantor surrendered possession of the tangible document to the issuer.

§ 7-106. Control of Electronic Document of Title.

(a) A person has control of an electronic document of title if a system employed for evidencing the transfer of interests in the electronic document reliably establishes that person as the person to which the electronic document was issued or transferred.

(b) A system satisfies subsection (a), and a person is deemed to have control of an electronic document of title, if the document is created, stored, and assigned in such a manner that:

(1) a single authoritative copy of the document exists which is unique, identifiable, and, except as otherwise provided in paragraphs (4), (5), and (6), unalterable;

(2) the authoritative copy identifies the person asserting control as:

(A) the person to which the document was issued; or

(B) if the authoritative copy indicates that the document has been transferred, the person to which the document was most recently transferred;

(3) **the authoritative copy is communicated to and maintained by the person asserting control or its designated custodian;**

(4) copies or amendments that add or change an identified assignee of the authoritative copy can be made only with the consent of the person asserting control;

(5) each copy of the authoritative copy and any copy of a copy is readily identifiable as a copy that is not the authoritative copy; and

(6) any amendment of the authoritative copy is readily identifiable as authorized or unauthorized.

PART 2. Warehouse Receipts: Special Provisions

§ 7-201. Person That May Issue a Warehouse Receipt; Storage under Bond.

(a) A warehouse receipt may be issued by any warehouse.

(b) If goods, including distilled spirits and agricultural commodities, are stored under a statute requiring a bond against withdrawal or a license for the issuance of receipts in the nature of warehouse receipts, a receipt issued for the goods is deemed to be a warehouse receipt even if issued by a person that is the owner of the goods and is not a warehouse.

§ 7-202. Form of Warehouse Receipt; Effect of Omission.

(a) A warehouse receipt need not be in any particular form.

(b) Unless a warehouse receipt provides for each of the following, the warehouse is liable for damages caused to a person injured by its omission:

(1) a statement of the location of the warehouse facility where the goods are stored;

(2) the date of issue of the receipt;

(3) the unique identification code of the receipt;

(4) a statement whether the goods received will be delivered to the bearer, to a named person, or to a named person or its order;

(5) the rate of storage and handling charges, unless goods are stored under a field warehousing arrangement, in which case a statement of that fact is sufficient on a nonnegotiable receipt;

(6) a description of the goods or the packages containing them;

(7) the signature of the warehouse or its agent;

(8) if the receipt is issued for goods that the warehouse owns, either solely, jointly, or in common with others, a statement of the fact of that ownership; and

(9) a statement of the amount of advances made and of liabilities incurred for which the warehouse claims a lien or security interest, unless the precise amount of advances made or liabilities incurred, at the time of the issue of the receipt, is unknown to the warehouse or to its agent that issued the receipt, in which case a statement of the fact that advances have been made or liabilities incurred and the purpose of the advances or liabilities is sufficient.

(c) A warehouse may insert in its receipt any terms that are not contrary to [the Uniform Commercial Code] and do not impair its obligation of delivery under Section 7-403 or its duty of care under Section 7-204. Any contrary provision is ineffective.

§ 7-203. Liability for Nonreceipt or Misdescription. A party to or purchaser for value in good faith of a document of title, other than a bill of lading, that relies upon the description of the goods in the document may recover from the issuer damages caused by the nonreceipt or misdescription of the goods, except to the extent that:

(1) the document conspicuously indicates that the issuer does not know whether all or part of the goods in fact were received or conform to the description, such as a case in which the description is in terms of marks or labels or kind, quantity, or condition, or the receipt or description is qualified by "contents, condition, and quality unknown", "said to contain", or words of similar import, if the indication is true; or

(2) the party or purchaser otherwise has notice of the nonreceipt or misdescription.

§ 7-204. Duty of Care; Contractual Limitation of Contractual Limitation of Warehouse's Liability.
(a) A warehouse is liable for damages for loss of or injury to the goods caused by its failure to exercise care with regard to the goods that a reasonably careful person would exercise under similar circumstances. Unless otherwise agreed, the warehouse is not liable for damages that could not have been avoided by the exercise of that care.
(b) Damages may be limited by a term in the warehouse receipt or storage agreement limiting the amount of liability in case of loss or damage beyond which the warehouse is not liable. Such a limitation is not effective with respect to the warehouse's liability for conversion to its own use. On request of the bailor in a record at the time of signing the storage agreement or within a reasonable time after receipt of the warehouse receipt, the warehouse's liability may be increased on part or all of the goods covered by the storage agreement or the warehouse receipt. In this event, increased rates may be charged based on an increased valuation of the goods.
(c) Reasonable provisions as to the time and manner of presenting claims and commencing actions based on the bailment may be included in the warehouse receipt or storage agreement.
(d) This section does not modify or repeal [Insert reference to any statute that imposes a higher responsibility upon the warehouse or invalidates a contractual limitation that would be permissible under this Article].

Legislative Note: Insert in subsection (d) a reference to any statute which imposes a higher responsibility upon the warehouse or invalidates a contractual limitation that would be permissible under this Article. If no such statutes exist, this section should be deleted.

§ 7-205. Title under Warehouse Receipt Defeated in Certain Cases. A buyer in ordinary course of business of fungible goods sold and delivered by a warehouse that is also in the business of buying and selling such goods takes the goods free of any claim under a warehouse receipt even if the receipt is negotiable and has been duly negotiated.

§ 7-206. Termination of Storage at Warehoues's Option.
(a) A warehouse, by giving notice to the person on whose account the goods are held and any other person known to claim an interest in the goods, may require payment of any charges and removal of the goods from the warehouse at the termination of the period of storage fixed by the document of title or, if a period is not fixed, within a stated period not less than 30 days after the warehouse gives notice. If the goods are not removed before the date specified in the notice, the warehouse may sell them pursuant to Section 7-210.
(b) If a warehouse in good faith believes that goods are about to deteriorate or decline in value to less than the amount of its lien within the time provided in subsection (a) and Section 7-210, the warehouse may specify in the notice given under subsection (a) any reasonable shorter time for removal of the goods and, if the goods are not removed, may sell them at public sale held not less than one week after a single advertisement or posting.
(c) If, as a result of a quality or condition of the goods of which the warehouse did not have notice at the time of deposit, the goods are a hazard to other property, the warehouse facilities, or other persons, the warehouse may sell the goods at public or private sale without advertisement or posting on reasonable notification to all persons known to claim an interest in the goods. If the warehouse, after a reasonable effort, is unable to sell the goods, it may dispose of them in any lawful manner and does not incur liability by reason of that disposition.
(d) A warehouse shall deliver the goods to any person entitled to them under this article upon due demand made at any time before sale or other disposition under this section.
(e) A warehouse may satisfy its lien from the proceeds of any sale or disposition under this section but shall hold the balance for delivery on the demand of any person to which the warehouse would have been bound to deliver the goods.

§ 7-207. Goods Must Be Kept Separate; Fungible Goods.
(a) Unless the warehouse receipt provides otherwise, a warehouse shall keep separate the goods covered by each receipt so as to permit at all times identification and delivery of those goods. However, different lots of fungible goods may be commingled.
(b) If different lots of fungible goods are commingled, the goods are owned in common by the persons entitled thereto and the warehouse is severally liable to each owner for that owner's share. If, because of overissue, a mass of fungible goods is insufficient to meet all the receipts the warehouse has issued against it, the persons entitled include all holders to which overissued receipts have been duly negotiated.

§ 7-208. Altered Warehouse Receipts. If a blank in a negotiable tangible warehouse receipt has been filled in without authority, a good-faith purchaser for value and without notice of the lack of authority may treat the insertion as authorized. Any other unauthorized alteration leaves any tangible or electronic warehouse receipt enforceable against the issuer according to its original tenor.

§ 7-209. Lien of Warehouse.
(a) A warehouse has a lien against the bailor on the goods covered by a warehouse receipt or storage agreement or on the proceeds thereof in its possession for charges for storage or transportation, including demurrage and terminal charges, insurance, labor, or other charges, present or future, in relation to the goods, and for expenses necessary for preservation of the goods or reasonably incurred in their sale pursuant to law. If the person on whose account the goods are held is liable for similar charges or expenses in relation to other goods whenever deposited and it is stated in the warehouse receipt or storage agreement that a lien is claimed for charges and expenses in relation to other goods, the warehouse also has a lien against the goods covered by the ware-

house receipt or storage agreement or on the proceeds thereof in its possession for those charges and expenses, whether or not the other goods have been delivered by the warehouse. However, as against a person to which a negotiable warehouse receipt is duly negotiated, a warehouse's lien is limited to charges in an amount or at a rate specified in the warehouse receipt or, if no charges are so specified, to a reasonable charge for storage of the specific goods covered by the receipt subsequent to the date of the receipt.

(b) A warehouse may also reserve a security interest against the bailor for the maximum amount specified on the receipt for charges other than those specified in subsection (a), such as for money advanced and interest. The security interest is governed by Article 9.

(c) A warehouse's lien for charges and expenses under subsection (a) or a security interest under subsection (b) is also effective against any person that so entrusted the bailor with possession of the goods that a pledge of them by the bailor to a good-faith purchaser for value would have been valid. However, the lien or security interest is not effective against a person that before issuance of a document of title had a legal interest or a perfected security interest in the goods and that did not:

(1) deliver or entrust the goods or any document of title covering the goods to the bailor or the bailor's nominee with:

(A) actual or apparent authority to ship, store, or sell;

(B) power to obtain delivery under Section 7-403; or

(C) power of disposition under Sections 2-403, 2A-304(2), 2A-305(2), 9-320, or 9-321(c) or other statute or rule of law; or

(2) acquiesce in the procurement by the bailor or its nominee of any document.

(d) A warehouse's lien on household goods for charges and expenses in relation to the goods under subsection (a) is also effective against all persons if the depositor was the legal possessor of the goods at the time of deposit. In this subsection, "household goods" means furniture, furnishings, or personal effects used by the depositor in a dwelling.

(e) A warehouse loses its lien on any goods that it voluntarily delivers or unjustifiably refuses to deliver.

§ 7-210. Enforcement of Warehouse's Lien.

(a) Except as otherwise provided in subsection (b), a warehouse's lien may be enforced by public or private sale of the goods, in bulk or in packages, at any time or place and on any terms that are commercially reasonable, after notifying all persons known to claim an interest in the goods. The notification must include a statement of the amount due, the nature of the proposed sale, and the time and place of any public sale. The fact that a better price could have been obtained by a sale at a different time or in a method different from that selected by the warehouse is not of itself sufficient to establish that the sale was not made in a commercially reasonable manner. The warehouse sells in a commercially reasonable manner if the warehouse sells the goods in the usual manner in any recognized market therefor, sells at the price current in that market at the time of the sale, or otherwise sells in conformity with commercially reasonable practices among dealers in the type of goods sold. A sale of more goods than apparently necessary to be offered to ensure satisfaction of the obligation is not commercially reasonable, except in cases covered by the preceding sentence.

(b) A warehouse may enforce its lien on goods, other than goods stored by a merchant in the course of its business, only if the following requirements are satisfied:

(1) All persons known to claim an interest in the goods must be notified.

(2) The notification must include an itemized statement of the claim, a description of the goods subject to the lien, a demand for payment within a specified time not less than 10 days after receipt of the notification, and a conspicuous statement that unless the claim is paid within that time the goods will be advertised for sale and sold by auction at a specified time and place.

(3) The sale must conform to the terms of the notification.

(4) The sale must be held at the nearest suitable place to where the goods are held or stored.

(5) After the expiration of the time given in the notification, an advertisement of the sale must be published once a week for two weeks consecutively in a newspaper of general circulation where the sale is to be held. The advertisement must include a description of the goods, the name of the person on whose account the goods are being held, and the time and place of the sale. The sale must take place at least 15 days after the first publication. If there is no newspaper of general circulation where the sale is to be held, the advertisement must be posted at least 10 days before the sale in not fewer than six conspicuous places in the neighborhood of the proposed sale.

(c) Before any sale pursuant to this section, any person claiming a right in the goods may pay the amount necessary to satisfy the lien and the reasonable expenses incurred in complying with this section. In that event, the goods may not be sold but must be retained by the warehouse subject to the terms of the receipt and this article.

(d) A warehouse may buy at any public sale held pursuant to this section.

(e) A purchaser in good faith of goods sold to enforce a warehouse's lien takes the goods free of any rights of persons against which the lien was valid, despite the warehouse's noncompliance with this section.

(f) A warehouse may satisfy its lien from the proceeds of any sale pursuant to this section but shall hold the balance, if any, for delivery on demand to any person to which the warehouse would have been bound to deliver the goods.

(g) The rights provided by this section are in addition to all other rights allowed by law to a creditor against a debtor.

(h) If a lien is on goods stored by a merchant in the course of its business, the lien may be enforced in accordance with subsection (a) or (b).

(i) A warehouse is liable for damages caused by failure to comply with the requirements for sale under this section and, in case of willful violation, is liable for conversion.

PART 3. Bills of Lading: Special Provisions

§ 7-301. Liability for Nonreceipt or Misdescription; "Said to Contain"; "Shipper's Weight, Load, and Count"; Improper Handling.

(a) A consignee of a nonnegotiable bill of lading which has given value in good faith, or a holder to which a negotiable bill has been duly negotiated, relying upon the description of the goods in the bill or upon the date shown in the bill, may recover from the issuer damages caused by the misdating of the bill or the nonreceipt or misdescription of the goods, except to the extent that the bill indicates that the issuer does not know whether any part or all of the goods in fact were received or conform to the description, such as in a case in which the description is in terms of marks or labels or kind, quantity, or condition or the receipt or description is qualified by "contents or condition of contents of packages unknown", "said to contain", "shipper's weight, load, and count," or words of similar import, if that indication is true.

(b) If goods are loaded by the issuer of a bill of lading;

(1) the issuer shall count the packages of goods if shipped in packages and ascertain the kind and quantity if shipped in bulk; and

(2) words such as "shipper's weight, load, and count," or words of similar import indicating that the description was made by the shipper are ineffective except as to goods concealed in packages.

(c) If bulk goods are loaded by a shipper that makes available to the issuer of a bill of lading adequate facilities for weighing those goods, the issuer shall ascertain the kind and quantity within a reasonable time after receiving the shipper's request in a record to do so. In that case, "shipper's weight" or words of similar import are ineffective.

(d) The issuer of a bill of lading, by including in the bill the words "shipper's weight, load, and count," or words of similar import, may indicate that the goods were loaded by the shipper, and, if that statement is true, the issuer is not liable for damages caused by the improper loading. However, omission of such words does not imply liability for damages caused by improper loading.

(e) A shipper guarantees to an issuer the accuracy at the time of shipment of the description, marks, labels, number, kind, quantity, condition, and weight, as furnished by the shipper, and the shipper shall indemnify the issuer against damage caused by inaccuracies in those particulars. This right of indemnity does not limit the issuer's responsibility or liability under the contract of carriage to any person other than the shipper.

§ 7-302. Through Bills of Lading and Similar Documents of Title.

(a) The issuer of a through bill of lading, or other document of title embodying an undertaking to be performed in part by a person acting as its agent or by a performing carrier, is liable to any person entitled to recover on the bill or other document for any breach by the other person or the performing carrier of its obligation under the bill or other document. However, to the extent that the bill or other document covers an undertaking to be performed overseas or in territory not contiguous to the continental United States or an undertaking including matters other than transportation, this liability for breach by the other person or the performing carrier may be varied by agreement of the parties.

(b) If goods covered by a through bill of lading or other document of title embodying an undertaking to be performed in part by a person other than the issuer are received by that person, the person is subject, with respect to its own performance while the goods are in its possession, to the obligation of the issuer. The person's obligation is discharged by delivery of the goods to another person pursuant to the bill or other document and does not include liability for breach by any other person or by the issuer.

(c) The issuer of a through bill of lading or other document of title described in subsection (a) is entitled to recover from the performing carrier, or other person in possession of the goods when the breach of the obligation under the bill or other document occurred:

(1) the amount it may be required to pay to any person entitled to recover on the bill or other document for the breach, as may be evidenced by any receipt, judgment, or transcript of judgment; and

(2) the amount of any expense reasonably incurred by the issuer in defending any action commenced by any person entitled to recover on the bill or other document for the breach.

§ 7-303. Diversion; Reconsignment; Change of Instructions.

(a) Unless the bill of lading otherwise provides, a carrier may deliver the goods to a person or destination other than that stated in the bill or may otherwise dispose of the goods, without liability for misdelivery, on instructions from:

(1) the holder of a negotiable bill;

(2) the consignor on a nonnegotiable bill, even if the consignee has given contrary instructions;

(3) the consignee on a nonnegotiable bill in the absence of contrary instructions from the consignor, if the goods have arrived at the billed destination or if the consignee is in possession of the tangible bill or in control of the electronic bill; or

(4) the consignee on a nonnegotiable bill, if the consignee is entitled as against the consignor to dispose of the goods.

(b) Unless instructions described in subsection (a) are included in a negotiable bill of lading, a person to which the bill is duly negotiated may hold the bailee according to the original terms.

§ 7-304. Tangible Bills of Lading in a Set.

(a) Except as customary in international transportation, a tangible bill of lading may not be issued in a set of parts. The issuer is liable for damages caused by violation of this subsection.
(b) If a tangible bill of lading is lawfully issued in a set of parts, each of which contains an identification code and is expressed to be valid only if the goods have not been delivered against any other part, the whole of the parts constitutes one bill.
(c) If a tangible negotiable bill of lading is lawfully issued in a set of parts and different parts are negotiated to different persons, the title of the holder to which the first due negotiation is made prevails as to both the document of title and the goods even if any later holder may have received the goods from the carrier in good faith and discharged the carrier's obligation by surrendering its part.
(d) A person that negotiates or transfers a single part of a tangible bill of lading issued in a set is liable to holders of that part as if it were the whole set.
(e) The bailee shall deliver in accordance with Part 4 against the first presented part of a tangible bill of lading lawfully issued in a set. Delivery in this manner discharges the bailee's obligation on the whole bill.

§ 7-305. Destination Bills.
(a) Instead of issuing a bill of lading to the consignor at the place of shipment, a carrier, at the request of the consignor, may procure the bill to be issued at destination or at any other place designated in the request.
(b) Upon request of any person entitled as against a carrier to control the goods while in transit and on surrender of possession or control of any outstanding bill of lading or other receipt covering the goods, the issuer, subject to Section 7-105, may procure a substitute bill to be issued at any place designated in the request.

§ 7-306. Altered Bills of Lading. An unauthorized alteration or filling in of a blank in a bill of lading leaves the bill enforceable according to its original tenor.

§ 7-307. Lien of Carrier.
(a) A carrier has a lien on the goods covered by a bill of lading or on the proceeds thereof in its possession for charges after the date of the carrier's receipt of the goods for storage or transportation, including demurrage and terminal charges, and for expenses necessary for preservation of the goods incident to their transportation or reasonably incurred in their sale pursuant to law. However, against a purchaser for value of a negotiable bill of lading, a carrier's lien is limited to charges stated in the bill or the applicable tariffs or, if no charges are stated, a reasonable charge.
(b) A lien for charges and expenses under subsection (a) on goods that the carrier was required by law to receive for transportation is effective against the consignor or any person entitled to the goods unless the carrier had notice that the consignor lacked authority to subject the goods to those charges and expenses. Any other lien under subsection (a) is effective against the consignor and any person that permitted the bailor to have control or possession of the goods unless the carrier had notice that the bailor lacked authority.
(c) A carrier loses its lien on any goods that it voluntarily delivers or unjustifiably refuses to deliver.

§ 7-308. Enforcement of Carrier's Lien.
(a) A carrier's lien on goods may be enforced by public or private sale of the goods, in bulk or in packages, at any time or place and on any terms that are commercially reasonable, after notifying all persons known to claim an interest in the goods. The notification must include a statement of the amount due, the nature of the proposed sale, and the time and place of any public sale. The fact that a better price could have been obtained by a sale at a different time or in a method different from that selected by the carrier is not of itself sufficient to establish that the sale was not made in a commercially reasonable manner. The carrier sells goods in a commercially reasonable manner if the carrier sells the goods in the usual manner in any recognized market therefor, sells at the price current in that market at the time of the sale, or otherwise sells in conformity with commercially reasonable practices among dealers in the type of goods sold. A sale of more goods than apparently necessary to be offered to ensure satisfaction of the obligation is not commercially reasonable, except in cases covered by the preceding sentence.
(b) Before any sale pursuant to this section, any person claiming a right in the goods may pay the amount necessary to satisfy the lien and the reasonable expenses incurred in complying with this section. In that event, the goods may not be sold but must be retained by the carrier, subject to the terms of the bill of lading and this article.
(c) A carrier may buy at any public sale pursuant to this section.
(d) A purchaser in good faith of goods sold to enforce a carrier's lien takes the goods free of any rights of persons against which the lien was valid, despite the carrier's noncompliance with this section.
(e) A carrier may satisfy its lien from the proceeds of any sale pursuant to this section but shall hold the balance, if any, for delivery on demand to any person to which the carrier would have been bound to deliver the goods.
(f) The rights provided by this section are in addition to all other rights allowed by law to a creditor against a debtor.
(g) A carrier's lien may be enforced pursuant to either subsection (a) or the procedure set forth in Section 7 210(b).
(h) A carrier is liable for damages caused by failure to comply with the requirements for sale under this section and, in case of willful violation, is liable for conversion.

§ 7-309. Duty of Care; Contractual Limitation of Carrier's Liability.
(a) A carrier that issues a bill of lading, whether negotiable or nonnegotiable, shall exercise the degree of care in relation to the goods which a reasonably careful person would exercise under similar circumstances. This subsection does not affect any statute,

regulation, or rule of law that imposes liability upon a common carrier for damages not caused by its negligence.

(b) Damages may be limited by a term in the bill of lading or in a transportation agreement that the carrier's liability may not exceed a value stated in the bill or transportation agreement if the carrier's rates are dependent upon value and the consignor is afforded an opportunity to declare a higher value and the consignor is advised of the opportunity. However, such a limitation is not effective with respect to the carrier's liability for conversion to its own use.

(c) Reasonable provisions as to the time and manner of presenting claims and commencing actions based on the shipment may be included in a bill of lading or a transportation agreement.

PART 4. Warehouse Receipts and Bills of Lading: General Obligations

§ 7-401. Irregularities in Issue of Receipt or Bill or Conduct of Issuer. The obligations imposed by this article on an issuer apply to a document of title even if:

(1) the document does not comply with the requirements of this article or of any other statute, rule, or regulation regarding its issuance, form, or content;

(2) the issuer violated laws regulating the conduct of its business;

(3) the goods covered by the document were owned by the bailee when the document was issued; or

(4) the person issuing the document is not a warehouse but the document purports to be a warehouse receipt.

§ 7-402. Duplicate Document of Title; Overissue. A duplicate or any other document of title purporting to cover goods already represented by an outstanding document of the same issuer does not confer any right in the goods, except as provided in the case of tangible bills of lading in a set of parts, overissue of documents for fungible goods, substitutes for lost, stolen, or destroyed documents, or substitute documents issued pursuant to Section 7-105. The issuer is liable for damages caused by its overissue or failure to identify a duplicate document by a conspicuous notation.

§ 7-403. Obligation of Bailee To Deliver; Excuse.

(a) A bailee shall deliver the goods to a person entitled under a document of title if the person complies with subsections (b) and (c), unless and to the extent that the bailee establishes any of the following:

(1) delivery of the goods to a person whose receipt was rightful as against the claimant;

(2) damage to or delay, loss, or destruction of the goods for which the bailee is not liable;

(3) previous sale or other disposition of the goods in lawful enforcement of a lien or on a warehouse's lawful termination of storage;

(4) the exercise by a seller of its right to stop delivery pursuant to Section 2 705 or by a lessor of its right to stop delivery pursuant to Section 2A-526;

(5) a diversion, reconsignment, or other disposition pursuant to Section 7 303;

(6) release, satisfaction, or any other personal defense against the claimant; or

(7) any other lawful excuse.

(b) A person claiming goods covered by a document of title shall satisfy the bailee's lien if the bailee so requests or if the bailee is prohibited by law from delivering the goods until the charges are paid.

(c) Unless a person claiming the goods is a person against which the document of title does not confer a right under Section 7 503(a):

(1) the person claiming under a document shall surrender possession or control of any outstanding negotiable document covering the goods for cancellation or indication of partial deliveries; and

(2) the bailee shall cancel the document or conspicuously indicate in the document the partial delivery or the bailee is liable to any person to which the document is duly negotiated.

§ 7-404. No Liability for Good-faith Deliver Pursuant to Document of Title. A bailee that in good faith has received goods and delivered or otherwise disposed of the goods according to the terms of a document of title or pursuant to this article is not liable for the goods even if:

(1) the person from which the bailee received the goods did not have authority to procure the document or to dispose of the goods; or

(2) the person to which the bailee delivered the goods did not have authority to receive the goods.

PART 5. Warehouse Receipts and Bills of Lading: Negotiation and Transfer

§ 7-501. Form of Negotiation and Requirement of Due Negotiation.

(a) The following rules apply to a negotiable tangible document of title:

(1) If the document's original terms run to the order of a named person, the document is negotiated by the named person's indorsement and delivery. After the named person's indorsement in blank or to bearer, any person may negotiate the document by delivery alone.

(2) If the document's original terms run to bearer, it is negotiated by delivery alone.

(3) If the document's original terms run to the order of a named person and it is delivered to the named person, the effect is the same as if the document had been negotiated.

(4) Negotiation of the document after it has been indorsed to a named person requires indorsement by the named person and delivery.

(5) A document is duly negotiated if it is negotiated in the manner stated in this subsection to a holder that purchases it in good faith, without notice of any defense against or claim

to it on the part of any person, and for value, unless it is established that the negotiation is not in the regular course of business or financing or involves receiving the document in settlement or payment of a monetary obligation.

(b) The following rules apply to a negotiable electronic document of title:

(1) If the document's original terms run to the order of a named person or to bearer, the document is negotiated by delivery of the document to another person. Indorsement by the named person is not required to negotiate the document.

(2) If the document's original terms run to the order of a named person and the named person has control of the document, the effect is the same as if the document had been negotiated.

(3) A document is duly negotiated if it is negotiated in the manner stated in this subsection to a holder that purchases it in good faith, without notice of any defense against or claim to it on the part of any person, and for value, unless it is established that the negotiation is not in the regular course of business or financing or involves taking delivery of the document in settlement or payment of a monetary obligation.

(c) Indorsement of a nonnegotiable document of title neither makes it negotiable nor adds to the transferee's rights.

(d) The naming in a negotiable bill of lading of a person to be notified of the arrival of the goods does not limit the negotiability of the bill or constitute notice to a purchaser of the bill of any interest of that person in the goods.

§ 7-502. Rights Acquired by Due Negotiation.

(a) Subject to Sections 7 205 and 7-503, a holder to which a negotiable document of title has been duly negotiated acquires thereby:

(1) title to the document;

(2) title to the goods;

(3) all rights accruing under the law of agency or estoppel, including rights to goods delivered to the bailee after the document was issued; and

(4) the direct obligation of the issuer to hold or deliver the goods according to the terms of the document free of any defense or claim by the issuer except those arising under the terms of the document or under this article, but in the case of a delivery order, the bailee's obligation accrues only upon the bailee's acceptance of the delivery order and the obligation acquired by the holder is that the issuer and any indorser will procure the acceptance of the bailee.

(b) Subject to Section 7-503, title and rights acquired by due negotiation are not defeated by any stoppage of the goods represented by the document of title or by surrender of the goods by the bailee and are not impaired even if:

(1) the due negotiation or any prior due negotiation constituted a breach of duty;

(2) any person has been deprived of possession of a negotiable tangible document or control of a negotiable electronic document by misrepresentation, fraud, accident, mistake, duress, loss, theft, or conversion; or

(3) a previous sale or other transfer of the goods or document has been made to a third person.

§ 7-503. Document of Title to Goods Defeated in Certain Cases.

(a) A document of title confers no right in goods against a person that before issuance of the document had a legal interest or a perfected security interest in the goods and that did not:

(1) deliver or entrust the goods or any document of title covering the goods to the bailor or the bailor's nominee with:

(A) actual or apparent authority to ship, store, or sell;

(B) power to obtain delivery under Section 7 403; or

(C) power of disposition under Section 2 403, 2A-304(2), 2A-305(2), 9 320, or 9-321(c) or other statute or rule of law; or

(2) acquiesce in the procurement by the bailor or its nominee of any document.

(b) Title to goods based upon an unaccepted delivery order is subject to the rights of any person to which a negotiable warehouse receipt or bill of lading covering the goods has been duly negotiated. That title may be defeated under Section 7-504 to the same extent as the rights of the issuer or a transferee from the issuer.

(c) Title to goods based upon a bill of lading issued to a freight forwarder is subject to the rights of any person to which a bill issued by the freight forwarder is duly negotiated. However, delivery by the carrier in accordance with Part 4 pursuant to its own bill of lading discharges the carrier's obligation to deliver.

§ 7-504. Rights Acquired in Absence of Due Negotiation; Effect of Diversion; Stoppage of Delivery.

(a) A transferee of a document of title, whether negotiable or nonnegotiable, to which the document has been delivered but not duly negotiated, acquires the title and rights that its transferor had or had actual authority to convey.

(b) In the case of a transfer of a nonnegotiable document of title, until but not after the bailee receives notice of the transfer, the rights of the transferee may be defeated:

(1) by those creditors of the transferor which could treat the transfer as void under Section 2 402 or 2A-308 ;

(2) by a buyer from the transferor in ordinary course of business if the bailee has delivered the goods to the buyer or received notification of the buyer's rights;

(3) by a lessee from the transferor in ordinary course of business if the bailee has delivered the goods to the lessee or received notification of the lessee's rights; or

(4) as against the bailee, by good-faith dealings of the bailee with the transferor.

(c) A diversion or other change of shipping instructions by the consignor in a nonnegotiable bill of lading which causes the bailee not to deliver the goods to the consignee defeats the consignee's title to the goods if the goods have been delivered to a buyer in ordinary course of business or a lessee in ordinary course of business and, in any event, defeats the consignee's rights against the bailee.

(d) Delivery of the goods pursuant to a nonnegotiable document of title may be stopped by a seller under Section 2 705 or a lessor under Section 2A-526, subject to the requirements of due notification in those sections. A bailee that honors the seller's or lessor's instructions is entitled to be indemnified by the seller or lessor against any resulting loss or expense.

§ 7-505. Indorser Not Guaranto for Other Parties. The indorsement of a tangible document of title issued by a bailee does not make the indorser liable for any default by the bailee or previous indorsers.

§ 7-506. Delivery without Indorsement: Right To Compel Indorsement. The transferee of a negotiable tangible document of title has a specifically enforceable right to have its transferor supply any necessary indorsement, but the transfer becomes a negotiation only as of the time the indorsement is supplied.

§ 7-507. Warranties on Negotiation or Delivery of Document of Title. If a person negotiates or delivers a document of title for value, otherwise than as a mere intermediary under Section 7-508, unless otherwise agreed, the transferor, in addition to any warranty made in selling or leasing the goods, warrants to its immediate purchaser only that:

(1) the document is genuine;

(2) the transferor does not have knowledge of any fact that would impair the document's validity or worth; and

(3) the negotiation or delivery is rightful and fully effective with respect to the title to the document and the goods it represents.

§ 7-508. Warranties of Collecting Bank As to Documents of Title. A collecting bank or other intermediary known to be entrusted with documents of title on behalf of another or with collection of a draft or other claim against delivery of documents warrants by the delivery of the documents only its own good faith and authority even if the collecting bank or other intermediary has purchased or made advances against the claim or draft to be collected.

§ 7-509. Adequate Compliance with Commercial Contract. Whether a document of title is adequate to fulfill the obligations of a contract for sale, a contract for lease, or the conditions of a letter of credit is determined by Article 2, 2A, or 5.

PART 6. Warehouse Receipts and Bills of Lading: Miscellaneous Provisions

§ 7-601. Lost, Stolen, or Destroyed Documents of Title.

(a) If a document of title is lost, stolen, or destroyed, a court may order delivery of the goods or issuance of a substitute document and the bailee may without liability to any person comply with the order. If the document was negotiable, a court may not order delivery of the goods or issuance of a substitute document without the claimant's posting security unless it finds that any person that may suffer loss as a result of nonsurrender of possession or control of the document is adequately protected against the loss. If the document was nonnegotiable, the court may require security. The court may also order payment of the bailee's reasonable costs and attorney's fees in any action under this subsection.

(b) A bailee that, without a court order, delivers goods to a person claiming under a missing negotiable document of title is liable to any person injured thereby. If the delivery is not in good faith, the bailee is liable for conversion. Delivery in good faith is not conversion if the claimant posts security with the bailee in an amount at least double the value of the goods at the time of posting to indemnify any person injured by the delivery which files a notice of claim within one year after the delivery.

§ 7-602. Judicial Process against Goods Covered by Negotiable Document of Title. Unless a document of title was originally issued upon delivery of the goods by a person that did not have power to dispose of them, a lien does not attach by virtue of any judicial process to goods in the possession of a bailee for which a negotiable document of title is outstanding unless possession or control of the document is first surrendered to the bailee or the document's negotiation is enjoined. The bailee may not be compelled to deliver the goods pursuant to process until possession or control of the document is surrendered to the bailee or to the court. A purchaser of the document for value without notice of the process or injunction takes free of the lien imposed by judicial process.

§ 7-603. Conflicting Claims; Interpleader. If more than one person claims title to or possession of the goods, the bailee is excused from delivery until the bailee has a reasonable time to ascertain the validity of the adverse claims or to commence an action for interpleader. The bailee may assert an interpleader either in defending an action for nondelivery of the goods or by original action.

PART 7. Miscellaneous Provisions

§ 7-701. Effective Date. This [Act] takes effect on [ ].

§ 7-702. Repeals. [Existing Article 7] and [Section 10-104 of the Uniform Commercial Code] are repealed.

§ 7-703. Applicability. This [Act] applies to a document of title that is issued or a bailment that arises on or after the effective date of this [Act]. This [Act] does not apply to a document of title that is issued or a bailment that arises before the effective date of this [Act] even if the document of title or bailment would be subject to this [Act] if the document of title had been issued or bailment had arisen on or after the effective date of this

[Act]. This [Act] does not apply to a right of action that has accrued before the effective date of this [Act].

§ 7-704. Savings Clause. A document of title issued or a bailment that arises before the effective date of this [Act] and the rights, obligations, and interests flowing from that document or bailment are governed by any statute or other rule amended or repealed by this [Act] as if amendment or repeal had not occurred and may be terminated, completed, consummated, or enforced under that statute or other rule.

Glossary

Abandonment Applies to many situations Abandonment of property is giving up dominion and control over it, with intention to relinquish all claims to it. Losing property is an involuntary act; abandonment is voluntary. When used with duty, the word *abandonment* is synonymous with *repudiation.*

Abatement of a nuisance An action to end any act detrimental to the public; e.g., suit to enjoin a plant from permitting the escape of noxious vapors.

Acceptance A statement by one party (called the offeree) that he is prepared to be bound to the contractual position stated in an offer. The acceptance is a second essential element to the meeting of the minds of the contracting parties. Offer.

Acceptance* Under Article 3—Commercial Paper, this is the drawee's signed engagement to honor a draft as presented. It must be written on the draft and may consist of drawee's signature alone. It becomes operative when completed by delivery or notification.

Accessions Items of personal property that become incorporated into other items of personal property.

Accommodation party* In the law of commercial paper, any person who signs an instrument for the purpose of lending his name and his credit.

Accord and satisfaction An agreement between two persons—one of whom has a right of action against the other—that the latter should do or give, and the former accept, something in satisfaction of the right of action—something different from, and usually less than, what might legally be enforced.

Account* Any right to payment for goods sold or leased or for services rendered but not evidenced by an instrument or chattel paper. Under Article 4—Bank Deposits and Collections, account is any account with a bank and includes a checking, time, interest, or savings account.

*Terms followed by an asterisk are defined in the Uniform Commercial Code and have significance in connection with Code materials. They are often given a particular meaning in relation to the Code, and their definitions do not necessarily conform with meanings Outside the framework of the Code.

Account debtor The person who is obligated on an account, chattel paper, contract right, or general intangible.

Accretion Gradual, imperceptible accumulation of land by natural causes, usually next to a stream or river.

Action ex contractu An action at law to recover damages for the breach of a duty arising out of contract. There are two types of causes of action: those arising out of contract, ex contractu, and those arising out of tort, ex delicto.

Action ex delicto An action at law to recover damages for the breach of a duty existing by reason of a general law. An action to recover damages for an injury caused by the negligent use of an automobile is an ex delicto action. Tort or wrong is the basis of the action. *See* Action ex contractu.

Adjudicate The exercise of judicial power by hearing, trying, and determining the claims of litigants before the court.

Administrative law The branch of public law dealing with the operation of the various agency boards and commissions of government.

Administrator A person to whom letters of administration have been issued by a probate court, giving such person authority to administer, manage, and close the estate of a deceased person.

Adverse possession Acquisition of legal title to another's land by being in continuous possession during a period prescribed in the statute. Possession must be actual, visible, known to the world, and with intent to claim title as owner, against the rights of the true owner. Claimant usually must pay taxes and liens lawfully charged against the property. Cutting timber or grass from time to time on the land of another is not the kind of adverse possession that will confer title.

Advising bank* A bank that gives notification of the issuance of a credit by another bank.

Affidavit A voluntary statement of facts formally reduced to writing, sworn to, or affirmed before, some officer authorized to administer oaths. The officer is usually a notary public.

Affirmative action program Active recruitment and advancement of minority workers.

Affirmative defense A matter that constitutes opposition to the allegations of a complaint, which are assumed to be true.

A fortiori Latin words meaning "by a stronger reason." Often used in judicial opinions to say that since specific, proven facts lead to a certain conclusion, there are for this reason other facts that logically follow and strengthen the argument for the conclusion.

Agency coupled with an interest When an agent has possession or control over the property of his principal and has a right of action against interference by third parties, an agency with an interest has been created. An agent who advances freight for goods sent him by his principal has an interest in the goods.

Agency coupled with an obligation When an agent is owed money by his principal and the agency relationship is created to facilitate the agent collecting this money from a third party, an agency coupled with an obligation is created. This type of agency cannot be terminated by the actions of the principal, but it may be terminated by operation of law.

Agent A person authorized to act for another (principal). The term may apply to a person in the service of another; but in the strict sense, an agent is one who stands in place of his principal. A works for B as a gardener and is thus a servant, but he may be an agent. If A sells goods for B, he becomes more than a servant. He acts in the place of B.

Agreement* The bargain of the parties in fact as found in their language or by implication from other circumstances, including course of dealing or usage of trade or course of performance as provided in the Uniform Commercial Code.

Amicus curiae A friend of the court who participates in litigation, usually on appeal, though not a party to the lawsuit.

Annuity A sum of money paid yearly to a person during his lifetime. The sum arises out of a contract by which the recipient or another had previously deposited sums in whole or in part with the grantor—the grantor to return a designated portion of the principal and interest in periodic payments when the beneficiary attains a designated age.

Appellant The party who takes an appeal from one court or jurisdiction to another.

Appellee The party in a cause against whom an appeal is taken.

A priori A generalization resting on presuppositions, not upon proven facts.

Arbitration The submission for determination of disputed matter to private, unofficial persons selected in a manner provided by law or agreement.

Architect's certificate A formal statement signed by an architect that a contractor has performed under his contract and is entitled to be paid. The construction contract provides when and how such certificates shall be issued.

Artisan's lien One who has expended labor upon, or added to, another's property is entitled to possession of the property as security until reimbursed for the value of labor or material. A repairs B's watch. A may keep the watch in his possession until B pays for the repairs.

Assignee An assign or assignee is one to whom an assignment has been made.

Assignment The transfer by one person to another of a right that usually arises out of a contract. Such rights are called *choses in action.* A sells and assigns to C his contract right to purchase B's house. A is an assignor. C is an assignee. The transfer is an assignment.

Assignment* A transfer of the "contract" or of "all my rights under the contract or an assignment in similar general terms is an assignment of rights. Unless the language or the circumstances (as in an assignment for security) indicate the contrary, it is a delegation of performance by the duties of the assignor, and its acceptance by the assignee constitutes a promise by him to perform those duties. This promise is enforceable by either the assignor or the other party to the original contract.

Assignment for the benefit of creditors A, a debtor, has many creditors. An assignment of his property to X, a third party, with directions to make distribution of his property to his creditors, is called an assignment for the benefit of creditors. *See* Composition of creditors.

Assignor One who makes an assignment.

Assumption of the risk Negligence doctrine that bars the recovery of damages by an injured party on the ground that such party acted with actual or constructive knowledge of the hazard causing the injury.

Attachment A legal proceeding accompanying an action in court by which a plaintiff may acquire a lien on a defendant's property as a security for the payment of any judgment that the plaintiff may recover. It is provisional and independent of the court action and is usually provided for by statute. A sues B. Before judgment, A attaches B's automobile, in order to make sure of the payment of any judgment that A may secure.

Attorney at law A person to whom the state grants a license to practice law.

Attorney in fact A person acting for another under a grant of special power created by an instrument in writing. B, in writing, grants special power A to execute and deliver for B a conveyance of B's land to X.

Bad faith "Actual intent" to mislead or deceive another. It does not mean misleading by an honest, inadvertent, or careless misstatement.

Bali (verb) To set at liberty an arrested or imprisoned person after that person or at least two others have given security to the state that the accused will appear at the proper time and place for trial.

Bailee A person into whose possession personal property is delivered.

Bailee* The person who, by a warehouse receipt, bill of lading, or other document of title, acknowledges possession of goods and contracts to deliver it.

Bailment Delivery of personal property to another for a special purpose. Delivery is made under a contract, either expressed or implied, that upon the completion of the special purpose, the property shall be redelivered to the bailor or placed at his disposal. A loans B his truck. A places his watch with B for repair. A places his furniture in B's warehouse. A places his securities in B's bank safety deposit vault. In each case, A is a bailor and B is a bailee.

Bailor One who delivers personal property into the possession of another.

Banking day* Under Article 4—Bank Deposits and Collections, this is the part of any day on which a bank is open to the public for carrying on substantially all of its banking functions.

Bankruptcy The law which provides a process for protecting creditors and debtors when a debtor is unable to pay his obligations.

Bearer* The person in possession of an instrument, document of title, or security payable to bearer or indorsed in blank.

Bearer form* A security is in bearer form when it runs to bearer according to its terms and not by reason of any indorsement.

Beneficiary A person (not a promisee) for whose benefit a trust, an insurance policy, a will, or a contract promise is made.

Beneficiary* A person who is entitled under a letter of credit to draw or demand payment.

Bequest In a will, a gift of personal property.

Bid An offering of money in exchange for property placed for sale. At an ordinary auction sale, a bid is an offer to purchase. It may be withdrawn before acceptance is indicated by the fall of the hammer.

Bilateral contract One containing mutual promises, with each party being both a promisor and a promisee.

Bilateral mistake A situation in which parties to a contract reach a bargain on the basis of an incorrect assumption common to each party.

Bill of lading* A document evidencing the receipt of goods for shipment, issued by a person engaged in the business of transporting or forwarding goods. Includes an airbill, a document that serves air transportation as a bill of lading serves marine or rail transportation. It includes an air consignment note or air waybill.

Bill of particulars In legal practice, a written statement that one party to a lawsuit gives to another, describing in detail the elements upon which the claim of the first party is based.

Bill of sale Written evidence that the title to personal property has been transferred from one person to another. It must contain words of transfer and be more than a receipt.

Blue-sky laws Popular name for acts providing for the regulation and supervision of investment securities.

Bona fide purchaser* A purchaser of a security for value, in good faith, and without notice of any adverse claim, who takes delivery of a security in bearer form or in registered form issued to him or indorsed to him or in blank.

Bond A promise under seal to pay money. The term generally designates the promise made by a corporation, either public or private, to pay money to bearer; e.g., U.S. government bonds or Illinois Central Railroad bonds. Also, an obligation by which one person promises to answer for the debt or default of another—a surety bond.

Breach of the peace* In the law of secured transactions, this occurrence invalidates the creditor's legal right to take possession of the collateral without the assistance of a court. This event occurs whenever the possession by the creditor is accompanied by violence, deception, or an objection by the debtor.

Broker A person employed to make contracts with third persons on behalf of his principal. The contracts involve trade, commerce, buying and selling for a fee (called brokerage or commission).

Broker* A person engaged full or part time in the business of buying and selling securities, who in the transaction concerned acts for, or buys a security from, or sells a security to, a customer.

Bulk transfer* Transfer made outside the ordinary course of the transferor's business but involving a major part of the materials, supplies, merchandise, or other inventory of an enterprise subject to Article 6.

Burden of proof This term has two distinctive meanings. One meaning is used to identify the party that has the burden of coming forward with evidence of a particular fact. The second meaning is used to identify the party with the burden of persuasion. This second meaning is used in litigation to determine whether one party or another wins regarding an issue in dispute.

Business judgment rule A legal doctrine requiring the officers and directors of corporations to act in good faith as if they were dealing with their own property interests.

Buyer* A person who buys or contracts to buy goods.

Buyer in ordinary course of business* A person who, in good faith and without knowledge that the sale to him is in violation of the ownership rights or security interest of a third party in the goods, buys in ordinary course from a person in the business of selling goods of that kind. Does not include a pawnbroker. "Buying" may be for cash or by exchange of other property or on secured or unsecured credit. Includes receiving goods or documents of title under a preexisting contract for sale but does not include a transfer in bulk or as security for, or in total or partial satisfaction of, a money debt.

Bylaws Rules for government of a corporation or other organization. Adopted by members or the board of directors, these rules must not be contrary to the law of the land. They affect the rights and duties of the members of the corporation or organization, only, not third persons.

Call An assessment upon a subscriber for partial or full payment on shares of unpaid stock of a corporation. Also, the power of a corporation to make an assessment, notice of an assessment, or the time when the assessment is to be paid.

Cancellation* Either party puts an end to the contract because of breach by the other. Its effect is the same as that of "termination," except that the canceling party also retains any remedy for breach of the whole contract or any unperformed balance.

Capital The net assets of an individual enterprise, partnership, joint stock company, corporation, or business institution, including not only the original investment but also all gains and profits realized from the continued conduct of the business.

Carrier A natural person or a corporation who receives goods under a contract to transport for a consideration from one place to another. A railroad, truckline, busline, airline.

Cashier's check A bill of exchange drawn by the cashier of a bank, for the bank, upon the bank. After the check is delivered or issued to the payee or holder, the drawer bank cannot put a "stop order" against itself. By delivery of the check, the drawer bank has accepted and thus becomes the primary obligor.

Cause of action When one's legal rights have been invaded either by a breach of a contract or by a breach of a legal duty toward one's person or property, a cause of action has been created.

Caveat Literally, "let him beware." It is used generally to mean a warning.

Caveat emptor An old idea at common law—"let the buyer beware." When a vendor sells goods without an express warranty as to their quality and capacity for a particular use and purpose, the buyer must take the risk of loss due to all defects in the goods.

Caveat venditor "Let the seller beware." Unless the seller, by express language, disclaims any responsibility, he shall be liable to the buyer if the goods delivered are different in kind, quality, use, and purpose from those described in the contract of sale.

Cease and desist order An administrative agency order directing a party to refrain from doing a specified act.

Certiorari An order issuing out of an appellate court to a lower court, at the request of an appellant, directing that the record of a case pending in the lower court be transmitted to the upper court for review.

Cestui que trust A person who is the real or beneficial owner of property held in trust. The trustee holds the legal title to the property for the benefit of the cestui que trust.

Chancery Court of equity.

Charter Referring to a private corporation, charter includes the contract between the created corporation and the state, the act creating the corporation, and the articles of association granted to the corporation by authority of the legislative act. Referring to municipal corporations, charter does not mean a contract between the legislature and the city created. A city charter is a delegation of powers by a state legislature to the governing body of the city. The term includes the creative act, the powers enumerated, and the organization authorized.

Chattel A very broad term derived from the word cattle. Includes every kind of property that is not real property. Movable properties, such as horses, automobiles, choses in action, stock certificates, bills of lading, and all "good wares, and merchandise" are chattels personal. Chattels real concern real property such as a lease for years, in which case the lessee owns a chattel real.

Chattel paper* A writing or writings that evidence both a monetary obligation and a security interest in, or a lease of, specific goods. When a transaction is evidenced both by such a security agreement or a lease and by an instrument or a series of instruments, the group of writings taken together constitutes chattel paper.

Chose in action The "right" one person has to recover money or property from another by a judicial proceeding. The right arises out of contract, claims for money, debts, and rights against property. Notes, drafts, stock certificates, bills of lading, warehouse receipts, and insurance policies are illustrations of choses in action. They are called tangible choses. Book accounts, simple debts, and obligations not evidenced by formal writing are called intangible choses. Choses in action are transferred by assignment.

Circumstantial evidence If, from certain facts and circumstances, according to the experience of mankind, an ordinary, intelligent person may infer that other connected facts and circumstances must necessarily exist, the latter facts and circumstances are considered proven by circumstantial evidence. Proof of fact A from which fact B may be inferred is proof of fact B by circumstantial evidence.

Civil action A proceeding in a law court or a suit in equity by one person against another for the enforcement or protection of a private right or the prevention of a wrong. It includes actions on contract, ex delicto, and all suits in equity. Civil action is in contradistinction to criminal action, in which the state prosecutes a person for breach of a duty.

Civil law The area of law dealing with rights and duties of private parties as individual entities. To be distinguished from criminal law. Sometimes the phrase refers to the European system of codified law.

Claim A creditor's right to payment in a bankruptcy case.

Class-action suit A legal proceeding whereby one or more persons represent in litigation a larger group of people who might have a claim similar to the representative(s).

Clearinghouse* Under Article 4—Bank Deposits and Collections, clearinghouse is any association of banks or other payors regularly clearing items.

Cloud on title Some evidence of record that shows a third person has some prima facie interest in another's property.

Code A collection or compilation of the statutes passed by the legislative body of a state. Often annotated with citations of cases decided by the state supreme courts. These decisions construe the statutes. Examples: Oregon Compiled Laws Annotated, United States Code Annotated.

Codicil An addition to, or a change in, an executed last will and testament. It is a part of the original will and must be executed with the same formality as the original will.

Coinsurer A term in a fire insurance policy that requires the insured to bear a certain portion of the loss when he fails to carry complete coverage. For example, unless the insured carries insurance that totals 80 percent of the value of the property, the insurer shall be liable for only that portion of the loss that the total insurance carried bears to 80 percent of the value of the property.

Collateral With reference to debts or other obligations, *collateral* means security placed with a creditor to assure the performance of the obligator. If the obligator performs, the collateral is returned by the creditor. A owes B $1,000. To secure the payment, A places with B a $500 certificate of stock in X company. The $500 certificate is called collateral security.

Collateral* The property subject to a security interest. Includes accounts, contract rights, and chattel paper that have been sold.

Collecting bank* Under Article 4—Bank Deposits and Collections, any bank handling the item for collateral except the payor bank.

Collective bargaining The process of good-faith negotiation between employer's and employees' representatives, concerning issues of mutual interest.

Commerce clause Article I, Section 8, Clause 3 of the Constitution of the United States, granting Congress the authority to regulate commerce with foreign nations and among the states.

Commercial unit* A unit of goods that, by commercial usage, is a single whole for purposes of sale. Its division would materially impair its character or value on the market or in use. A commercial unit may be a single article (as a machine) or a set of articles (as a suite of furniture or an assortment of sizes) or a quantity (as a bale, gross, or carload) or any other unit treated in use or in the relevant market as a single whole.

Commission The sum of money, interest, brokerage, compensation, or allowance given to a factor or broker for carrying on the business of his principal.

Commission merchant An agent or factor employed to sell "goods, wares, and merchandise" consigned or delivered to him by his principal.

Common carrier One who is engaged in the business of transporting personal property from one place to another for compensation. Such person is bound to carry for all who tender their goods and the price for transportation. A common carrier operates as a public utility and is subject to state and federal regulations.

Common law That body of law deriving from judicial decisions, as opposed to legislatively enacted statutes and administrative regulations.

Common stock In the law of corporations, the type of ownership interest that must exist.

Community property All property acquired after marriage by husband and wife, other than separate property acquired by devise, bequest, or from the proceeds of noncommunity property. Community property is a concept of property ownership by husband and wife inherited from the civil law. The husband and wife are somewhat like partners in their ownership of property acquired during marriage.

Comparative negligence A modification to the defense of contributory negligence. Under this doctrine, a plaintiff's negligence is compared to that of a defendant. The plaintiffs right to recover against the defendant is reduced by the percentage of the plaintiff's negligence. *See* Contributory negligence.

Compensatory damages *See* Damages.

Complaint The first paper a plaintiff files in a court in a lawsuit. It is called a pleading. It is a statement of the facts upon which the plaintiff rests his cause of action.

Composition of creditors An agreement among creditors and their debtors by which the creditors will take a lesser amount in complete satisfaction of the total debt. A owes B and C $500 each. A agrees to pay B and C $250 each in complete satisfaction of the $500 due each. B and C agree to take $250 in satisfaction.

Compromise An agreement between two or more persons, usually opposing parties in a lawsuit, to settle the matters of the controversy without further resort to hostile litigation. An adjustment of issues in dispute by mutual concessions before resorting to a lawsuit.

Condemnation proceedings An action or proceeding in court authorized by legislation (federal or state) for the purpose of taking private property for public use. It is the exercise by the judiciary of the sovereign power of eminent domain.

Condition A clause in a contract, either expressed or implied, that has the effect of investing or divesting the legal rights and duties of the parties to the contract. In a deed, a condition is a qualification or restriction providing for the happening or nonhappening of events that, on occurrence, will destroy, commence, or enlarge an estate. "A grants Blackacre to B, so long as said land shall be used for church purposes." If it ceases to be used for church purposes, the title to Blackacre will revert to the grantor.

Condition precedent A clause in a contract providing that immediate rights and duties shall vest only upon the happening of some event. Securing an architect's certificate by a contractor before the contractor is entitled to payment is a condition precedent. A condition is not a promise; hence, its breach will not give rise to a cause of action for damages. A breach of a condition is the basis for a defense. If the contractor sues the owner without securing the architect's certificate, the owner has a defense.

Conditions concurrent Conditions concurrent are mutually dependent and must be performed at the same time by the parties to the contract. Payment of money and delivery of goods in a cash sale are conditions concurrent. Failure to perform by one party permits a cause of action upon tender by the other party. If S refuses to deliver goods in a cash sale, B, upon tender but not delivery of the money, places S in default and thus may sue S. B does not part with his money without getting the goods. If S sued B, B would have a defense.

Condition subsequent A clause in a contract providing for the happening of an event that divests legal rights and duties. A clause in a fire insurance policy providing that the policy shall be null and void if combustible material is stored within 10 feet of the building is a condition subsequent. If a fire occurs and combustible material was within 10 feet of the building, the insurance company is excused from its duty to pay for the loss.

Confirming bank A bank that engages either that it will itself honor a credit already issued by another bank or that such a credit will be honored by the issuer or a third bank.

Conforming* Goods or conduct, including any part of a performance, are "conforming" or conform to the contract when they are in accordance with the obligations under contract.

Conglomerate merger Merging of companies that have neither the relationship of competitors nor that of supplier and customer.

Consequential damages Those damages, beyond the compensatory damages, which arise from special circumstances causing special damages that are not clearly foreseeable. However, before becoming liable for these damages, the breaching party must be aware of the special circumstances that may cause consequential damages.

Consideration An essential element in the creation of contract obligation. A detriment to the promisee and a benefit to the promisor. One promise is consideration for another promise. They create a bilateral contract. An act is consideration for a promise. This creates a unilateral contract. Performance of the act asked for by the promisee is a legal detriment to the promisee and a benefit to the promisor.

Consignee A person to whom a shipper usually directs a carrier to deliver goods; generally the buyer of goods and called a consignee on a bill of lading.

Consignee* The person named in a bill to whom or to whose order the bill promises delivery.

Consignment The delivery, sending, or transferring of property, "goods, wares, and merchandise" into the possession of another, usually for the purpose of sale. Consignment may be a bailment or an agency for sale.

Consignor The shipper who delivers freight to a carrier for shipment and who directs the bill of lading to be executed by the carrier. May be the consignor-consignee if the bill of lading is made to his own order.

Consignor* The person named in a bill as the person from whom the goods have been received for shipment.

Consolidation Two corporations are consolidated when both corporations are dissolved and a new one created, the new one taking over the assets of the dissolved corporations.

Conspicuous* A term or clause is conspicuous when it is written so that a reasonable person against whom it is to operate ought to have noticed it. A printed heading in capitals (as NON-NEGOTIABLE BILL OF LADING) is conspicuous. Language in the body of a form is "conspicuous" if it is in larger or other contrasting type or color. But in a telegram, any stated term is "conspicuous." Whether a term or clause is "conspicuous" or not is for decision by the court.

Conspiracy A combination or agreement between two or more persons for the commission of a criminal act.

Constructive delivery Although physical delivery of personal property has not occurred, the conduct of the parties may imply that possession and title has passed between them. S sells large and bulky goods to B. Title and possession may pass by the act and conduct of the parties.

Consumer A person who does not intend to resell an item of property but rather intends to use it for a personal, noncommercial purpose.

Consumer goods* Goods that are used or bought for use primarily for personal, family, or household purposes.

Contingent fee An arrangement whereby an attorney is compensated for services in a lawsuit according to an agreed percentage of the amount of money recovered.

Contract An agreement involving one or more promises that courts will enforce or for the breach of which courts provide a remedy.

Contract right* Under a contract, any right to payment not yet earned by performance and not evidenced by an instrument or chattel paper.

Contributory negligence In a negligence suit, failure of the plaintiff to use reasonable care.

Conversion A legal theory used to create a "sale" of property to a person who interferes with the owner's use of the property to the extent that damages must be paid to compensate the owner for the loss of property.

Conversion* Under Article 3—Commercial Paper, an instrument is converted when a drawee to whom it is delivered for acceptance refuses to return it on demand; or any person to whom it is delivered for payment refuses on demand either to pay or to return it; or it is paid on a forged indorsement.

Conveyance A formal written instrument, usually called a deed, by which the title or other interests in land (real property) are transferred from one person to another. The word expresses also the fact that the title to real property has been transferred from one person to another.

Corporation A collection of individuals created by statute as a legal person, vested with powers and capacity to contract, own, control, convey property, and transact business within the limits of the powers granted.

Corporation de facto If persons have attempted in good faith to organize a corporation under a valid law (statute) and have failed in some minor particular but have thereafter exercised corporate powers, they are a corporation de facto. Failure to notarize incorporators' signatures on applications for charter is an illustration of non-compliance with statutory requirements.

Corporation de jure A corporation that has been formed by complying with the mandatory requirements of the law authorizing such a corporation.

Corporeal Physical; perceptible by the senses. Automobiles, grain, fruit, and horses are corporeal and tangible and are called chattels. Corporeal is used in contradistinction to incorporeal or intangible. A chose in action (such as a check) is corporeal and tangible, or a chose in action may be a simple debt, incorporeal and intangible.

Costs In litigation, an allowance authorized by statute to a party for expenses incurred in prosecuting or defending a lawsuit. The word costs, unless specifically designated by statute or contract, does not include attorney's fees.

Counterclaims By cross-action, the defendant claims that he is entitled to recover from the plaintiff. Claim must arise out of the same transaction set forth in the plaintiff's complaint and be connected with the same subject matter. S sues B for the purchase price. B counterclaims that the goods were defective and that he thereby suffered damages.

Course of dealing A sequence of previous conduct between the parties to a particular transaction. The conduct is fairly to be regarded as establishing a common basis of understanding for interpreting their expressions and other conduct.

Course of performance A term used to give meaning to a contract based on the parties having had a history of dealings or an agreement that requires repeated performances.

Covenant A promise in writing under seal. It is often used as a substitute for the word *contract.* There are covenants (promises) in deeds, leases, mortgages, and other instruments under seal. The word is used sometimes to name promises in unsealed instruments such as insurance policies.

Cover* After a breach by a seller, the buyer may cover' by making in good faith and without unreasonable delay any reasonable purchase of' or contract to purchase, goods in substitution for those due from the seller.

Credit* ("Letter of credit") An engagement by a bank or other person made at the request of a customer and of a kind within the scope of Article 5—Letters of Credit, that the issuer will honor drafts or other demands for payment upon compliance with the conditions specified in the credit. A credit may be either revocable or irrevocable. The engagement may be either an agreement to honor or a statement that the bank or other person is authorized to honor.

Creditor* Includes a general creditor, a secured creditor, a lien creditor, and any representative of creditors, including an assignee for the benefit of creditors, a trustee in bankruptcy, a receiver in equity, and an executor or administrator of an insolvent debtor's or assignor's estate.

Creditor-beneficiary One who, for a consideration, promises to discharge another's duty to a third party. A owes C $100. B, for a consideration, promises A to pay A's debt to C. B is a creditor beneficiary.

Cumulative voting In voting for directors, a stockholder may cast as many votes as he has shares of stock multiplied by the number to be elected. His votes may be all for one candidate or distributed among as many candidates as there are offices to be filled.

Cure* An opportunity for the seller of defective goods to correct the defect and thereby not be held to have breached the sales contract.

Custodian bank* A bank or trust company that acts as custodian for a clearing corporation. It must be supervised and examined by the appropriate state or federal authority.

Custody (personal property) The words custody and possession are not synonymous. Custody means in charge of, to keep and care for under the direction of the true owner, without any interest therein adverse to the true owner. A servant is in custody of his master's goods. *See* Possession.

Customer* Under Article 4—Bank Deposits and Collections, a customer is any person having an account with a bank or for whom a bank has agreed to collect items. It includes a bank carrying an account with another bank. As used in Letters of Credit, a customer is a buyer or other person who causes an issuer to issue a credit. The term also includes a bank that procures insurance or confirmation on behalf of that bank's customer.

Damages A sum of money the court imposes upon a defendant as compensation for the plaintiff because the defendant has injured the plaintiff by breach of a legal duty.

d.b.a. "Doing business as." A person who conducts his business under an assumed name is designated "John Doe d.b.a. Excelsior Co."

Debenture A corporate obligation sold as an investment. Similar to a corporate bond but not secured by a trust deed. It is not like corporate stock.

Debtor* The person who owes payment or other performance of the obligation secured, whether or not he owns, or has rights in, the collateral. Includes the seller of accounts, contract rights, or chattel paper. When the debtor and the owner of the collateral are not the same person, debtor means the owner of the collateral in any provision of the Article dealing with the obligation and may include both if the context so requires.

Deceit Conduct in a business transaction by which one person, through fraudulent representations, misleads another who has a right to rely on such representations as the truth or who, by reason of an unequal station in life, has no means of detecting such fraud.

Declaratory judgment A determination by a court on a question of law, the court simply declaring the rights of the parties but not ordering anything to be done.

Decree The judgment of the chancellor (judge) in a suit in equity. Like a judgment at law, it is the determination of the rights between the parties and is in the form of an order that requires the decree to be carried out. An order that a contract be specifically enforced is an example of a decree.

Deed A written instrument in a special form, signed, sealed, delivered, and used to pass the legal title of real property from one person to another. (*See* Conveyance.) In order that the public may know about the title to real property, deeds are recorded in the Deed Record office of the county where the land is situated.

Deed of trust An instrument by which title to real property is conveyed to a trustee to hold as security for the holder of notes or bonds. It is like a mortgage, except the security title is held by a person other than the mortgagee-creditor. Most corporate bonds are secured by a deed of trust.

De facto Arising out of, or founded upon, fact, although merely apparent or colorable. A de facto officer is one who assumes to be an officer under some color of right, acts as an officer, but in point of law is not a real officer. *See* Corporation de facto.

Defendant A person who has been sued in a court of law; the person who answers the plaintiff's complaint. The word is applied to the defending party in civil actions. In criminal actions, the defending party is referred to as the accused.

Deficiency judgment If, upon the foreclosure of a mortgage, the mortgaged property does not sell for an amount sufficient to pay the mortgage indebtedness, the difference is called a deficiency and is chargeable to the mortgagor or to any person who has purchased the property and assumed and agreed to pay the mortgage. M borrows $10,000 from B and as security gives a mortgage on Blackacre. At maturity, M does not pay the debt. B forecloses, and at public sale Blackacre sells for $8,000. There is a deficiency of $2,000, chargeable against M. If M had sold Blackacre to C and C had assumed and agreed to pay the mortgage, he would also be liable for the deficiency.

Defraud To deprive one of some right by deceitful means. To cheat; to withhold wrongfully that which belongs to another. Conveying one's property for the purpose of avoiding payment of debts is a transfer to "hinder, delay, or defraud creditors."

Del credere agency When an agent, factor, or broker guarantees to his principal the payment of a debt due from a buyer of goods, that agent, factor, or broker is operating under a del credere commission or agency.

Delivery A voluntary transfer of the possession of property, actual or constructive, from one person to another, with the intention that title vests in the transferee. In the law of sales, delivery contemplates the absolute giving up of control and dominion over the property by the vendor, and the assumption of the same by the vendee.

Delivery* With respect to instruments, documents of title, chattel paper, or securities, delivery means voluntary transfer of possession.

Delivery order* A written order to deliver goods directed to a warehouseman, carrier, or other person who, in the ordinary course of business, issues warehouse receipts or bills of lading.

Demand A request by a party entitled, under a claim of right, to the performance of a particular act. In order to bind an indorser on a negotiable instrument, the holder must first make a demand on the primary party, who must dishonor the instrument. Demand notes mean "due when demanded." The word demand is also used to mean a claim or legal obligation.

Demurrage Demurrage is a sum provided for in a contract of shipment, to be paid for the delay or detention of vessels or railroad cars beyond the time agreed upon for loading or unloading.

Demurrer A common law procedural method by which the defendant admits all the facts alleged in the plaintiff's complaint but denies that such facts state a cause of action. It raises a question of law on the facts, which must be decided by the court.

Dependentcovenants (promises) In contracts, covenants are either concurrent or mutual, dependent or independent. Dependent covenants mean the performance of one promise must occur before the performance of the other promise. In a cash sale, the buyer must pay the money before the seller is under a duty to deliver the goods.

Depositary bank* Under Article 4—Bank Deposits and Collections, this means the first bank to which an item is transferred for collection, even though it is also the payor bank.

Descent The transfer of the title of property to the heirs upon the death of the ancestor; heredity succession. If a person dies without making a will, his property will "descend" according to the Statute of Descent of the state wherein the property is located.

Devise A gift, usually of real property, by a last will and testament.

Devisee The person who receives title to real property by will.

Dictum (dicta—plural) The written opinion of a judge, expressing an idea, argument, or rule that is not essential for the determination of the issues. It lacks the force of a decision in a judgment.

Directed verdict If it is apparent to reasonable men and the court that the plaintiff, by his evidence, has not made out his case, the court may instruct the jury to bring in a verdict for the defendant. If, however, different inferences may be drawn from the evidence by reasonable men, then the court cannot direct a verdict.

Discharge The word has many meanings. An employee, upon being released from employment, is discharged. A guardian or trustee, upon termination of his trust, is discharged by the court. A debtor released from his debts is discharged in bankruptcy. A person who is released from any legal obligation is discharged.

Discovery The disclosure by one party of facts, titles, documents, and other things in his knowledge of possession and necessary to the party seeking the discovery as a part of a cause of action pending.

Dishonor A negotiable instrument is dishonored when it is presented for acceptance or payment but acceptance or payment is refused or cannot be obtained.

Dissolution In the law of partnerships, this event occurs any time there is a change in the partners, either by adding a new partner or by having a preexisting partner die, retire, or otherwise leave.

Distress for rent The taking of personal property of a tenant in payment of rent on real estate.

Divestiture The antitrust remedy that forces a company to get rid of assets acquired through illegal mergers or monopolistic practices.

Dividend A stockholder's pro rata share in the profits of a corporation. Dividends are declared by the board of directors of a corporation. They are paid in cash, script, property, and stock.

Docket A book containing a brief summary of all acts done in court in the conduct of each case.

Documentary collateral* In the law of secured transactions, this category of collateral consists of documents of title, chattel paper, and instruments.

Documentary draft* Under Article 4—Bank Deposits and Collections, this means any negotiable or nonnegotiable draft with accompanying documents, securities, or other papers to be delivered against honor of the draft. Also called a "documentary demand for payment (Article 5—Letters of Credit). Honoring is conditioned upon the presentation of a document or documents. "Document" means any paper, including document of title, security, invoice, certificate, notice of default, and the like.

Document of title* Includes bill of lading, dock warrant, dock receipt, warehouse receipt, or order for the delivery of goods, and any other document that in the regular course of business or financing is treated as adequately evidencing that the person in possession of it is entitled to receive, hold, and dispose of the document and the goods it covers. To be a document of title, a document must purport to be issued by, or addressed to, a bailee and purport to cover goods in the bailee's possession that are either identified or are fungible portions of an identified mass.

Domicile The place a person intends as his fixed and permanent home and establishment and to which, if he is absent, he intends to return. A person can have but one domicile. The old one continues until the acquisition of a new one. One can have more than one residence at a time, but only one domicile. The word is not synonymous with residence.

Dominion Applied to the delivery of property by one person to another, *dominion* means all control over the possession and ownership of the property being separated from the transferor or donor and endowed upon the transferee or donee. *See* Gift.

Donee Recipient of a gift.

Donee-beneficiary If a promisee is under no duty to a third party, but for a consideration secures a promise from a promisor for the purpose of making a gift to a third party, then the third party is a donee-beneficiary. A, promisee for a premium paid, secures a promise from the insurance company, the promisor, to pay A's wife $10,000 upon A's death. A's wife is a donee-beneficiary.

Donor One that gives, donates, or presents.

Dormant partner A partner who is not known to third persons but is entitled to share in the profits and is subject to the losses. Since credit is not extended upon the strength of the dormant partner's name, he may withdraw without notice and not be subject to debts contracted after his withdrawal.

Double jeopardy A constitutional doctrine that prohibits an individual from being prosecuted twice in the same tribunal for the same criminal offense.

Due process Fundamental fairness. Applied to judicial proceedings, it includes adequate notice of a hearing and an opportunity to appear and defend in an orderly tribunal.

Duress (of person) A threat of bodily injury, criminal prosecution, or imprisonment of a contracting party or his near relative to such extent that the threatened party is unable to exercise free will at the time of entering into or discharging a legal obligation.

Duress (of property) Seizing by force or withholding goods by one not entitled, and such person's demanding something as a condition for the release of the goods.

Duty (in law) A legal obligation imposed by general law or voluntarily imposed by the creation of a binding promise. For every legal duty there is a corresponding legal right. By general law, A is under a legal duty not to injure B's person or property. B has a right that A not injure his person or property. X may voluntarily create a duty in himself to Y by a promise to sell Y a horse for $100. If Y accepts, X is under a legal duty to perform his promise. *See* Right.

Earnest money A term used to describe money that one contracting party gives to another at the time of entering into the contract in order to "bind the bargain" and which will be forfeited by the donor if he fails to carry out the contract. Generally, in real estate contracts such money is used as part payment of the purchase price.

Easement An easement is an interest in land—a right that one person has to some profit, benefit, or use in or over the land of another. Such right is created by a deed, or it may be acquired by prescription (the continued use of another's land for a statutory period).

Ejectment An action to recover the possession of real property. It is now generally defined by statute and is a statutory action. *See* Forcible entry and detainer.

Ejusdem generis "Of the same class." General words taking their meaning from specific words which precede the general words. General words have the same meaning as specific words mentioned.

Election A concept applicable in agency relationships when the principal is undisclosed. The third party may elect to hold either the agent or the previously undisclosed principal liable. By electing to hold one party liable, the third party has chosen not to seek a recovery against the other party.

Embezzlement The fraudulent appropriation by one person, acting in a fiduciary capacity, of the money or property of another. *See* Conversion.

Eminent domain The right that resides in the United States, state, county, city, school, or other public body to take private property for public use upon payment of just compensation.

Employment-at-will A doctrine stating that an employee who has no specific agreement as to the length of his employment may be discharged at any time without any reason being given by the employer. This doctrine has been modified in many states in recent years.

Encumbrance A burden on either the title to land or thing or upon the land or thing itself. A mortgage or other lien is an encumbrance upon the title. A right-of-way over the land is an encumbrance upon the land and affects its physical condition.

Enjoin To requite performance or abstention from some act through issuance of an injunction.

Entity "In being" or "existing." The artificial person created when a corporation is organized is "in being" or "existing" for legal purposes, thus an entity. It is separate from the stockholders. The estate of a deceased person while in administration is an entity. A partnership for many legal purposes is an entity.

Equal protection A principle of the Fifth and Fourteenth Amendments to the Constitution, ensuring that individuals under like circumstances shall be accorded the same benefits and burdens under the law of the sovereign.

Equipment* Goods that are used or bought for use primarily in business (including farming or a profession) or by a debtor who is a nonprofit organization or a governmental subdivision or agency; or goods not included in the definitions of inventory, farm products, or consumer goods.

Equitable action In Anglo-American law, there have developed two types of courts and procedures for the administration of justice: law courts and equity courts. Law courts give as a remedy money damages only, whereas equity courts give the plaintiff what he bargains for. A suit for specific performance of a contract is an equitable action. In many states these two courts are now merged.

Equitable conversion An equitable principle that, for certain purposes, permits real property to be converted into personalty. Thus, real property owned by a partnership is, for the purpose of the partnership, personal property because to ascertain a partner's interest, the real property must be reduced to cash. This is an application of the equitable maxim, "Equity considers that done which ought to be done."

Equitable estoppel A legal theory used to prevent a party to an oral contract that has been partially performed from asserting the defense of the statute of frauds. *See* Part performance.

Equitable mortgage A written agreement to make certain property security for a debt, and upon the faith of which the parties have acted in making advances, loans, and thus creating a debt. Example: an improperly executed mortgage, one without seal where a seal is required. An absolute deed made to the mortgagee and intended for security only is an equitable mortgage.

Equity Because the law courts in early English law did not always give an adequate remedy, an aggrieved party sought redress from the king. Since this appeal was to the king's conscience, he referred the case to his spiritual adviser, the chancellor. The chancellor decided the case according to rules of fairness, honesty, right, and natural justice. From this there developed the rules in equity. The laws of trust, divorce, rescission of contracts for fraud, injunction, and specific performance are enforced in courts of equity.

Equity of redemption The right a mortgagor has to redeem or get back his property after it has been forfeited for nonpayment of the debt it secured. By statute, within a certain time before final foreclosure decree, a mortgagor has the privilege of redeeming his property by paying the amount of the debt, interest, and costs.

Escrow An agreement under which a grantor, promisor, or obligor places the instrument upon which he is bound with a third person called escrow holder, until the performance of a condition or the happening of an event stated in the agreement permits the escrow holder to make delivery or performance to the grantee, promisee, or obligee. A (grantor) places a deed to C (grantee) accompanied by the contract of conveyance with B bank, conditioned upon B bank delivering the deed to C (grantee) when C pays all moneys due under contract. The contract and deed have been placed in escrow.

Estate All the property of a living, deceased, bankrupt, or insane person. Also applied to the property of a ward. In the law of taxation, wills, and inheritance, estate has a broad meaning. Historically, the word was limited to an interest in land: i.e., estate in fee simple, estate for years, estate for life, and so forth.

Estoppel When one ought to speak the truth but does not, and by one's acts, representations, or silence intentionally or through negligence induces another to believe certain facts exists, and the other person acts to his detriment on the belief that such facts are true, the first person is estopped to deny the truth of the facts. B, knowingly having kept and used defective goods delivered by S under a contract of sale, is estopped to deny the goods are defective. X holds out Y as his agent. X is estopped to deny that Y is his agent. Persons are estopped to deny the legal effect of written instruments such as deeds, contracts, bills and notes, court records, and judgments. A man's own acts speak louder than his words.

Et al. "And other persons." Used in pleadings and cases to indicate that persons other than those specifically named are parties to a lawsuit,

Ethics Conduct based on a commitment of what is right. This conduct often is at a level above that required by legal standards.

Eviction An action to expel a tenant from the estate of the landlord. Interfering with the tenant's right of possession or enjoyment amounts to an eviction. Eviction may be actual or constructive. Premises made uninhabitable because the landlord maintains a nuisance is constructive eviction.

Evidence In law, *evidence* has two meanings. (1) Testimony of witnesses and facts presented to the court and jury by way of writings and exhibits, which impress the minds of the court and jury, to the extent that an allegation has been proven. *Testimony* and *evidence* are not synonymous. Testimony is a broader word and includes all the witness says. *Proof* is distinguished from *evidence,* in that proof is the legal consequence of evidence. (2) The rules of law, called the law of evidence, that determine what evidence shall be introduced at a trial and what shall not; also, what importance shall be placed upon the evidence.

Exclusive dealing contract A contract under which a buyer agrees to purchase a certain product exclusively from the seller or in which the seller agrees to sell all his product production to the buyer.

Ex contractu *See* Action ex contractu.

Exculpatory clause A provision in a contract whereby one of the parties attempts to relieve itself of liability for breach of a legal duty.

Ex delicto *See* Action ex delicto.

Executed Applied to contracts or other written instruments, *executed* means signed, sealed, and delivered. Effective legal obligations have thus been created. The term is also used to mean that the performances of a contract have been completed. The contract is then at an end. All is done that is to be done.

Execution Execution of a judgment is the process by which the court, through the sheriff, enforces the payment of the judgment received by the successful party. The sheriff, by a "writ," levies upon the unsuccessful party's property and sells it to pay the judgment creditor.

Executor (of an estate) The person whom the testator (the one who makes the will) names or appoints to administer his estate upon his death and to dispose of it according to his intention. The terms *executor* and *administrator* are not synonyms. A person who makes a will appoints an executor to administer his estate. A court appoints an administrator to administer the estate of a person who dies without having made a will. *See* Intestate.

Executory contract Until the performance required in a contract is completed, it is said to be executory as to that part not executed. *See* Executed.

Exemplary damages A sum assessed by the jury in a tort action (over and above the compensatory damages) as punishment, in order to make an example of the wrongdoer and to deter like conduct by others. Injuries caused by willful, malicious, wanton, and reckless conduct will subject the wrongdoers to exemplary damages.

Exemption The condition of a person who is free or excused from a duty imposed by some rule of law, statutory or otherwise.

Express contract An agreement which is either spoken or written by the parties. *See* Contract.

Express warranty When a seller makes some positive representation concerning the nature, quality, character, use, and purpose of goods, which induces the buyer to buy, and the seller intends the buyer to rely thereon, the seller has made an express warranty.

Factor An agent for the sale of merchandise. He may hold possession of the goods in his own name or in the name of his principal. He is authorized to sell and to receive payment for the goods. *See* Agent.

Factor's lien A factor's right to keep goods consigned to him if he may reimburse himself for advances previously made to the consignor.

Farm products* Crops or livestock or supplies used or produced in farming operations; products of crops or livestock in their unmanufactured states (such as ginned cotton, wool-clip, maple syrup, milk, and eggs); and goods in the possession of a debtor engaged in raising, fattening, grazing, or other farming operations. If goods are farm products, they are neither equipment or inventory.

Featherbedding In labor relations, a demand for the payment of wages for a service not actually rendered.

Fee simple absolute The total interest a person may have in land. Such an estate is not qualified by any other interest, and it passes upon the death of the owners to the heirs, free from any conditions.

Fellow-servant doctrine Precludes an injured employee from recovering damages from his employer when the injury resulted from the negligent act of another employee.

Felony All criminal offenses that are punishable by death or imprisonment in a penitentiary.

Fiduciary In general, a person is a fiduciary when he occupies a position of trust or confidence in relation to another person or his property. Trustees, guardians, and executors occupy fiduciary positions.

Final decree *See* Decree.

Financing agency* A bank, finance company, or person who, in the ordinary course of business, makes advances against goods or documents of title; or who, by arrangement with either the seller or the buyer, intervenes in ordinary course to make a collect payment due or claimed under the contract for sale, as by purchasing or paying the seller's draft or making advances against it or by merely taking it for collection, whether or not documents of title accompany the draft. "Financing agency" includes a bank or person who similarly intervenes between persons who are in the position of seller and buyer in respect to the goods.

Fine A sum of money collected by a court from a person guilty of some criminal offense. The amount may be fixed by statute or left to the discretion of the court.

Firm offer* An offer by a merchant to buy or sell goods in a signed writing that, by its terms, gives assurance it will be held open.

Fixture An item of personal property that has become attached or annexed to real estate. Fixtures generally are treated as part of the real estate.

Floating lien* In the law of secured transactions, this concept allows a creditor to become secured with regards to future advances and to collateral acquired by the debtor after the perfection occurs.

Forbearance Giving up the right to enforce what one honestly believes to be a valid claim, in return for a promise. It is sufficient "consideration" to make a promise binding.

Forcible entry and detainer A remedy given to a land owner to evict persons unlawfully in possession of his land. A landlord may use such remedy to evict a tenant in default.

Foreclosure The forced sale of a defaulting debtor's property at the insistence of the creditor.

Forfeiture Money or property taken as compensation and punishment for injury or damage to the person or property of another or to the state. One may forfeit interest earnings for charging a usurious rate.

Forgery False writing or alteration of an instrument with the fraudulent intent of deceiving and injuring another. Writing another's name upon a check, without his consent, to secure money.

Franchise A right conferred or granted by a legislative body. It is a contract right and cannot be revoked without cause. A franchise is more than a license. A license is only a privilege and may be revoked. A corporation exists by virtue of a "franchise." A corporation secures a franchise from the city council to operate a waterworks within the city. *See* License.

Franchise tax A tax on the right of a corporation to do business under its corporate name.

Fraud An intentional misrepresentation of the truth for the purpose of deceiving another person. The elements of fraud are (1) intentionally false representation of fact, not opinion, (2) intent that the deceived person act thereon, (3) knowledge that such statements would naturally deceive, and (4) that the deceived person acted to his injury.

Fraudulent conveyance A conveyance of property by a debtor for the intent and purpose of defrauding his creditors. It is of no effect, and such property may be reached by the creditors through appropriate legal proceedings.

Freehold An estate in fee or for life. A freeholder is usually a person who has a property right in the title to real estate amounting to an estate of inheritance (in fee), or one who has title for life or an indeterminate period.

Full-line forcing An arrangement in which a manufacturer refuses to supply any portion of the product line unless the retailer agrees to accept the entire line.

Fungible* Goods and securities of which any unit is, by nature or usage of trade, the equivalent of any other like unit.

Fungible goods Fungible goods are those "of which any unit is from its nature of mercantile usage treated as the equivalent of any other unit." Grain, wine, and similar items are examples.

Future goods* Goods that are not both existing and identified.

Futures Contracts for the sale and delivery of commodities in the future, made with the intention that no commodity be delivered or received immediately.

Garnishee A person upon whom a garnishment is served. He is a debtor of a defendant and has money or property that the plaintiff is trying to reach in order to satisfy a debt due from the defendant. Also used as a verb: "to garnishee wages or property.

Garnishment A proceeding by which a plaintiff seeks to reach the credits of the defendant that are in the hands of a third party, the garnishee. A garnishment is distinguished from an attachment in that by an attachment, an officer of the court takes actual possession of property by virtue of his writ. In a garnishment, the property or money is left with the garnishee until final adjudication.

General agent An agent authorized to do all the acts connected with carrying on a particular trade, business, or profession.

General intangibles* Any personal property (including things in action) other than goods, accounts, contract rights, chattel paper, documents, and instruments.

General verdict *See* Verdict *in contrast to* Special verdict.

Gift A gift is made when a donor delivers the subject matter of the gift into the donee's hands or places in the donee the means of obtaining possession of the subject matter, accompanied by such acts that show clearly the donor's intentions to divest himself of all dominion and control over the property.

Gift *causa mortis* A gift made in anticipation of death. The donor must have been in sickness and have died as expected, otherwise no effective gift has been made. If the donor survives, the gift is revocable.

Gift *inter vivos* An effective gift made during the life of the donor. By a gift inter vivos, property vests immediately in the donee at the time of delivery, whereas a gift causa mortis is made in contemplation of death and is effective only upon the donor's death.

Good faith* Honesty in fact is the conduct or transaction concerned. Referring to a merchant, good faith means honesty in fact and the observance of reasonable commercial standards of fair dealing in the trade.

Goods* All things that are movable at the time of identification to the contract for sale, including specially manufactured goods but not money in which the price is to be paid, investment securities, and things in action. Includes unborn young animals, growing crops, and other identified things attached to realty as described in the section on goods to be severed from realty.

Goodwill The value, beyond its assets, of a business organization created by its customers.

Grant A term used in deeds for the transfer of the title to real property. The words *convey, transfer,* and *grant,* as operative words in a deed to pass title, are equivalent. The words *grant, bargain,* and *sell* in a deed, in absence of statute, mean the grantor promises he has good title to transfer free from incumbrances and warrants it to be such.

Grantee A person to whom a grant is made; one named in a deed to receive title.

Grantor A person who makes a grant. The grantor executes the deed by which he divests himself of title.

Gross negligence The lack of even slight or ordinary care.

Guarantor One who by contract undertakes "to answer for the debt, default, and miscarriage of another." In general, a guarantor undertakes to pay if the principal debtor does not; a surety, on the other hand, joins in the contract of the principal and becomes an original party with the principal.

Guardian A person appointed by the court to look after the property rights and person of minors, the insane, and other incompetents or legally incapacitated persons.

Guardian ad litem A special guardian appointed for the sole purpose of carrying on litigation and preserving the interests of a ward. He exercises no control or power over property.

Habeas corpus A writ issued to a sheriff, warden, or other official having allegedly unlawful custody of a person, directing the official to bring the person before a court, in order to determine the legality of the imprisonment.

Hearsay evidence Evidence that is learned from someone else. It does not derive its value from the credit of the witness testifying but rests upon the veracity of another person. It is not good evidence, because there is no opportunity to cross-examine the person who is the source of the testimony.

Hedging contract A contract of purchase or sale of an equal amount of commodities in the future, by which brokers, dealers, or manufacturers protect themselves against the fluctuations of the market. It is a type of insurance against changing prices. A grain dealer, to protect himself, may contract to sell for future delivery the same amount of grain he has purchased in the present market.

Heirs Persons upon whom the statute of descent casts the title to real property upon the death of the ancestor. Consult Statute of Descent for the appropriate state. *See* Descent.

Holder* A person who is in possession of a document of title or an instrument or an investment security drawn, issued, or indorsed to him or to his order or to bearer or in blank.

Holder in due course One who has acquired possession of a negotiable instrument through proper negotiation for value, in good faith, and without notice of any defenses to it. Such a holder is not subject to personal defenses that would otherwise defeat the obligation embodied in the instrument.

Holding company A corporation organized for the purpose of owning and holding the stock of other corporations. Shareholders of underlying corporations receive in exchange for their stock, upon an agreed value, the shares in the holding corporation.

Homestead A parcel of land upon which a family dwells or resides, and which to them is home. The statute of the state or federal governments should be consulted to determine the meaning of the term as applied to debtor's exemptions, federal land grants, and so forth.

Honor* To pay or to accept and pay or, where a creditor so engages, to purchase or discount a draft complying with the terms of the instrument.

Horizontal merger Merger of corporations that were competitors prior to the merger.

Hot-cargo contract An agreement between employer and union, whereby an employer agrees to refrain from handling, using, selling, transporting, or otherwise dealing in the products of another employer or agrees to cease doing business with some other person.

Illegal Contrary to public policy and the fundamental principles of law. Illegal conduct includes not only violations of criminal statutes but also the creation of agreements that are prohibited by statute and the common law.

Illusory That which has a false appearance. If that which appears to be a promise is not a promise, it is said to be illusory. "I promise to buy your lunch if I decide to." This equivocal statement would not justify reliance, so it is not a promise.

Immunity Freedom from the legal duties and penalties imposed upon others. The "privileges and immunities" clause of the United States Constitution means no state can deny to the citizens of another state the same rights granted to its own citizens. This does not apply to office holding. *See* Exemption.

Implied The finding of a legal right or duty by inference from facts or circumstances. *See* Warranty.

Implied-in-fact contract A legally enforceable agreement inferred from the circumstances and conduct of the parties.

Imputed negligence Negligence that is not directly attributable to the person himself but is the negligence of a person who is in privity with him and with whose fault he is chargeable.

Incidental beneficiary If the performance of a promise would indirectly benefit a person not a party to a contract, such person is an incidental beneficiary. A promises B, for a consideration, to plant a valuable nut orchard on B's land. Such improvement would increase the value of the adjacent land. C, the owner of the adjacent land, is an incidental beneficiary. He has no remedy if A breaches his promise with B.

Indemnify Literally, "to save harmless." Thus, one person agrees to protect another against loss.

Indenture A deed executed by both parties, as distinguished from a deed poll that is executed only by the grantor.

Independent contractor The following elements are essential to establish the relation of independent contractor, in contradistinction to principal and agent. An independent contractor must (1) exercise his independent judgment on the means used to accomplish the result; (2) be free from control or orders from any other person; (3) be responsible only under his contract for the result obtained.

Indictment A finding by a grand jury that it has reason to believe the accused is guilty as charged. It informs the accused of the offense with which he is charged, so that he may prepare its defense. It is a pleading in a criminal action.

Indorsement Writing one's name upon paper for the purpose of transferring the title. When a payee of a negotiable instrument writes his name on the back of the instrument, his writing is an indorsement.

Infringement Infringement of a patent on a machine is the manufacturing of a machine that produces the same result by the same means and operation as the patented machine. Infringement of a trademark consists in reproduction of a registered trademark and its use upon goods in order to mislead the public to believe that the goods are the genuine, original product.

Inherit The word is used in contradistinction to acquiring property by will. *See* Descent.

Inheritance An estate that descends to heirs. *See* Descent.

Injunction A writ of judicial process issued by a court of equity, by which a party is required to do a particular thing or to refrain from doing a particular thing.

In personam A legal proceeding, the judgment of which binds the defeated party to a personal liability.

In rem A legal proceeding, the judgment of which binds, affects, or determines the status of property.

Insolvent* Refers to a person who either has ceased to pay his debts in the ordinary course of business or cannot pay his debts as they become due or is insolvent within the meaning of the federal bankruptcy law.

Installment contract* One which requires or authorizes the delivery of goods in separate lots to be separately accepted, even though the contract contains a clause "each delivery is a separate contract or its equivalent.

Instrument* A negotiable instrument or a security or any other writing that evidences a right to the payment of money and is not itself a security agreement or lease and is of a type that is in ordinary course of business transferred by delivery with any necessary indorsement or assignment.

Insurable interest A person has an insurable interest in a person or property if he will be directly and financially affected by the death of the person or the loss of the property.

Insurance By an insurance contract, one party, for an agreed premium, binds himself to another, called the insured, to pay the insured a sum of money conditioned upon the loss of life or property of the insured.

Intangible Something which represents value but has no intrinsic value of its own, such as a note or bond.

Intent A state of mind that exists prior to, or contemporaneous with, an act. A purpose or design to do or forbear to do an act. It cannot be directly proven but is inferred from known facts.

Interlocutory decree A decree of a court of equity that does not settle the complete issue but settles only some intervening part, awaiting a final decree.

Intermediary bank* Under Article 4—Bank Deposits and Collections, it is any bank—except the depositary or payor bank—to which an item is transferred in course of collection.

Interpleader A procedure whereby a person who has an obligation, e.g., to pay money, but does not know which of two or more claimants are entitled to performance, can bring a suit that requires the contesting parties to litigate between themselves.

Interrogatory A written question from one party to another in a lawsuit; a type of discovery procedure.

Intestate The intestate laws are the laws of descent or distribution of the estate of a deceased person. A person who has not made a will dies intestate.

Inventory* Goods that a person holds for sale or lease or to be—or which have been—furnished under contracts of service, or goods that are raw materials, work in process or materials used or consumed in a business. Inventory of a person is not to be classified as his equipment.

Irreparable damage or injury Irreparable does not mean injury beyond the possibility of repair, but it does mean that it is so constant and frequent in occurrence that no fair or reasonable redress can be had in a court of law. Thus, the plaintiff must seek a remedy in equity by way of an injunction.

Issue* Under Article 3—Commercial Paper, issue means the first delivery of an instrument to a holder or a remitter.

Issuer* A bailee who issues a document; but in relation to an unaccepted delivery order, the issuer is the person who orders the possessor of goods to deliver. Issuer includes any person for whom an agent or employee purports to act in issuing a document if the agent or employee has real or apparent authority to issue documents, notwithstanding that the issuer received no goods or that the goods were misdescribed or that in any other respect the agent or employee violated the issuer's instructions.

Item* Under Article 4—Bank Deposits and Collections, *item* means any instrument for the payment of money, even though it is not negotiable, but does not include money.

Jeopardy A person is in jeopardy when he is regularly charged with a crime before a court properly organized and competent to try him. If acquitted, he cannot be tried again for the same offense.

Joint and several Two or more persons have an obligation that binds them individually as well as jointly. The obligation can be enforced either by joint action against all of them or by separate actions against one or more.

Joint ownership The interest that two or more parties have in property.

Joint tenancy Two or more persons to whom land is deeded in such manner that they have "one and the same interest, accruing by one and the same conveyance, commencing at one and the same time, and held by one and the same undivided possession." Upon the death of one joint tenant, his property passes to the survivor or survivors.

Joint tortfeasors When two persons commit an injury with a common intent, they are joint tortfeasors.

Judgment (in law) The decision, pronouncement, or sentence rendered by a court upon an issue in which it has jurisdiction.

Judgment *in personam* A judgment against a person, directing the defendant to do or not to do something. *See In personam.*

Judgment *in rem* A judgment against a thing, as distinguished from a judgment against a person. *See In rem.*

Judicial restraint A judicial philosophy. Those following it believe that the power of judicial review should be exercised with great restraint.

Judicial review The power of courts to declare laws and executive actions unconstitutional.

Judicial sale A sale authorized by a court that has jurisdiction to grant such authority. Such sales are conducted by an officer of the court.

Jurisdiction The authority to try causes and determine cases. Conferred upon a court by the Constitution.

Jury A group of persons, usually twelve, sworn to declare the facts of a case as they are proved from the evidence presented to them and, upon instructions from the court, to find a verdict in the cause before them.

Juvenile court A court with jurisdiction to hear matters pertaining to those persons under a certain age (usually 16 or 18). This court will hear cases involving delinquent behavior.

Laches A term used in equity to name conduct that neglects to assert one's rights or to do what, by the law, a person should have done. Failure on the part of one to assert a right will give an equitable defense to another party.

Latent defect A defect in materials not discernible by examination. Used in contradistinction to patent defect, which is discernible.

Lease A contract by which one person divests himself of possession of lands or chattels and grants such possession to another for a period of time. The relationship in which land is involved is called landlord and tenant.

Leasehold The land held by a tenant under a lease.

Legacy Personal property disposed of by a will. Sometimes the term is synonymous with bequest. The word devise is used in connection with real property distributed by will. *See* Bequest; Devise.

Legal benefit An analysis used to determine if contractual consideration exists. As an inducement for a party to make a promise, that party (promisor) must receive a legal benefit, or the other party (promisee) must suffer a legal detriment, or both. *See* Consideration; Legal Detriment.

Legal detriment An analysis used to determine if contractual consideration exists. Parties suffer legal detriment when they promise to perform an act that they have no obligation to perform or promise to refrain from taking action that they have the right to take. *See* Consideration; Legal benefit.

Legatee A person to whom a legacy is given by will.

Liability In its broadest legal sense, *liability* means any obligation one may be under by reason of some rule of law. It includes debt, duty, and responsibility.

Libel Malicious publication of a defamation of a person by printing, writing, signs, or pictures, for the purposes of injuring the reputation and good name of such person. "The exposing of a person to public hatred, contempt, or ridicule."

License (governmental regulation) A license is a privilege granted by a state or city upon the payment of a fee. It confers authority upon the licensee to do some act or series of acts, which otherwise would be illegal. A license is not a contract and may be revoked for cause. It is a method of governmental regulation exercised under the police power.

License (privilege) A mere personal privilege given by the owner to another to do designated acts upon the land of the owner. It is revocable at will and creates no estate in the land. The licensee is not in pos session. "It is a mere excuse for what otherwise would be a trespass.

Lien The right of one person, usually a creditor, to keep possession of, or control, the property of another for the purpose of satisfying a debt. There are many kinds of liens: judgment lien, attorney's lien, innkeeper's lien, logger's lien, vendor's lien. Consult statute of state for type of lien. *See* Judgment.

Lien creditor* A creditor who has acquired a lien on property involved by attachment, levy, or the like. Includes an assignee for benefit of creditors from the time of assignment and a trustee in bankruptcy from the date of the filing of the petition or a receiver in equity from the time of appointment. Unless all the creditors represented had knowledge of the security interest, such a representative of creditors is a lien creditor without knowledge even though he personally has knowledge of the security interest.

Life estate An interest in real property that lasts only as long as a designated person lives.

Limited partnership A partnership in which one or more individuals are general partners and one or more individuals are limited partners. The limited partners contribute assets to the partnership without taking part in the conduct of the business. They are liable for the debts of the partnership only to the extent of their contributions.

Liquidated A claim is liquidated when it has been made fixed and certain by the parties concerned.

Liquidated damages A fixed sum agreed upon between the parties to a contract, to be paid as ascertained damages by the party who breaches the contract. If the sum is excessive, the courts will declare it to be a penalty and unenforceable.

Liquidation The process of winding up the affairs of a corporation or firm for the purpose of paying its debts and disposing of its assets. May be done voluntarily or under the orders of a court.

Lis pendens "Pending the suit nothing should be changed." The court, having control of the property involved in the suit, issues notice lis pendens, that persons dealing with the defendant regarding the subject matter of the suit do so subject to final determination of the action.

Long-arm statute A law which allows courts in the state court systems to extend their personal jurisdiction beyond the state boundaries to nonresident defendants if such defendants have had sufficient minimal contacts with the state to justify the exercise of personal jurisdiction.

Lot* A parcel or a single article that is the subject matter of a separate sale or delivery, whether or not it is sufficient to perform the contract.

Magistrate A public officer, usually a judge, "who has power to issue a warrant for the arrest of a person charged with a public offense." The word has wide application and includes justices of the peace, notaries public, recorders, and other public officers who have power to issue executive orders.

Malice Describes a wrongful act done intentionally without excuse. It does not necessarily mean ill will, but it indicates a state of mind that is reckless concerning the law and the rights of others. Malice is distinguished from *negligence.* With *malice* there is always a purpose to injure, whereas such is not true of the word *negligence.*

Malicious prosecution The prosecution of another at law with malice and without probable cause to believe that such legal action will be successful.

Mandamus A writ issued by a court of law, in the name of the state. Writs of mandamus are directed to inferior courts, officers, corporations, or persons, commanding them to do particular things that appertain to their offices or duties.

Mandatory injunction An injunctive order issued by a court of equity that compels affirmative action by the defendant.

Market extension merger A combination of two business organizations allowing one to extend its business to new products or geographical areas. *See* Product extension merger.

Marketable title A title of such character that no apprehension as to its validity would occur to the mind of a reasonable and intelligent person. The title to goods is not marketable if it is in litigation, subject to incumbrances, in doubt as to a third party's right, or subject to lien.

Marshaling of assets A principle in equity for a fair distribution of a debtor's assets among his creditors. For example, a creditor of A, by reason of prior right, has two funds, X and Y, belonging to A, out of which he may satisfy his debt. But another creditor of A also has a right to X fund. The first creditor will be compelled to exhaust Y fund before he will be permitted to participate in X fund.

Master In agency relationships involving torts, this party is in a position similar to that of a principal.

Master in chancery An officer appointed by the court to assist the court of equity in taking testimony, computing interest, auditing accounts, estimating damages, ascertaining liens, and doing other tasks incidental to a suit, as the court requires. The power of a master is merely advisory, and his tasks are largely fact finding.

Maxim A proposition of law that because of its universal approval needs no proof or argument; the mere statement of which gives it authority. Example: "A principal is bound by the acts of his agent when the agent is acting within the scope of his authority."

Mechanic's lien Created by statute to assist suppliers and laborers in collecting their accounts and wages. Its purpose is to subject the land of an owner to a lien for material and labor expended in the construction of buildings and other improvements.

Mediation The process by which a third party attempts to help the parties in dispute find a resolution. The mediator has no authority to bind the parties to any particular resolution.

Merchant A person who deals in goods of the kind involved in a transaction; or one who otherwise, by his occupation, holds himself out as having knowledge or skill peculiar to the practices or goods involved; or one to whom such knowledge or skill may be attributed because he employs an agent or broker or other intermediary who, by his occupation, holds himself out as having such knowledge or skill.

Merger Two corporations are merged when one corporation continues in existence and the other loses its identity by its absorption into the first. *Merger* must be distinguished from *consolidation.* In *consolidation,* both corporations are dissolved, and a new one is created, the new one taking over the assets of the dissolved corporations.

Metes and bounds The description of the boundaries of real property.

Midnight deadline* Under Article 4—Bank Deposits and Collections, this is midnight on the next banking day following the banking day on which a bank receives the relevant item or notice, or from which the time for taking action commences to run, whichever is later.

Ministerial duty A prescribed duty that requires little judgment or discretion. A sheriff performs ministerial duties.

Minutes The record of a court or the written transactions of the members or board of directors of a corporation. Under the certificate of the clerk of a court or the secretary of a corporation, the minutes are the official evidence of court or corporate action.

Misdemeanor A criminal offense, less than a felony, that is not punishable by death or imprisonment. Consult the local statute.

Misrepresentation The affirmative statement or affirmation of a fact that is not true; the term does not include concealment of true facts or nondisclosure or the mere expression of opinion.

Mistake (of fact) The unconscious ignorance or forgetfulness of the existence or nonexistence of a fact, past or present, which is material and important to the creation of a legal obligation.

Mistake (of law) An erroneous conclusion of the legal effect of known facts.

Mitigation of damages A plaintiff is entitled to recover damages caused by the defendant's breach, but the plaintiff is also under a duty to avoid increasing or enhancing such damages. This duty is called a duty to *mitigate the damages.* If a seller fails to deliver the proper goods on time, the buyer, where possible, must buy other goods, thus mitigating damages.

Monopoly Exclusive control of the supply and price of a commodity. May be acquired by a franchise or patent from the government; or the ownership of the source of a commodity or the control of its distribution.

Mortgage A conveyance or transfer of an interest in property for the purpose of creating a security for a debt. The mortgage becomes void upon payment of the debt, although the recording of a release is necessary to clear the title of the mortgaged property.

Municipal court Another name for a police court. *See* Police court.

Mutual assent In every contract, each party must agree to the same thing. Each must know what the other intends; they must mutually assent or be in agreement.

Mutual mistake *See* Bilateral mistake.

Mutuality The binding of both parties in every contract. Each party to the contract must be bound to the other party to do something by virtue of the legal duty created.

Negligence Failure to do that which an ordinary, reasonable, prudent man would do, or the doing of some act that an ordinary, prudent man would not do. Reference must always be made to the situation, the circumstances, and the knowledge of the parties.

Negotiation* Under Article 3—Commercial Paper, this is the transfer of an instrument in such form that the transferee becomes a holder. If the instrument is payable to order, it is negotiated by delivery with any necessary indorsement; if payable to bearer, it is negotiated by delivery.

Net assets Property or effects of a firm, corporation, institution, or estate, remaining after all its obligations have been paid.

Nexus Connection, tie, or link used in the law of taxation to establish a connection between a tax and the activity or person being taxed.

NLRB National Labor Relations Board

No-fault laws Laws barring tort actions by injured persons against third-party tortfeasors and requiring injured persons to obtain recovery from their own insurers.

Nolo contendere A plea by an accused in a criminal action. It does not admit guilt of the offense charged but does equal a plea of guilty for purpose of sentencing.

Nominal damages A small sum assessed as sufficient to award the case and cover the costs when no actual damages have been proven.

Nonsuit A judgment given against the plaintiff when he is unable to prove his case or fails to proceed with the trial after the case is at issue.

Noscitur a sociis The meaning of a word is or may be known from the accompanying words.

Notary public A public officer authorized to administer oaths by way of affidavits and depositions. Attests deeds and other formal papers, in order that they may be used as evidence and be qualified for recording.

Notice* A person has "notice" of a fact when (a) he has actual knowledge of it; or (b) he has received a notice or notification of it; or (c) from all the facts and circumstances known to him at the time in question, he has reason to know that it exists. A person "knows" or has "knowledge" of a fact when he has actual knowledge of it. "Discover" or "learn" or a word or phrase of similar import refers to knowledge rather than to reason to know.

Novation The substitution of one obligation for another. When debtor A is substituted for debtor B, and by agreement with the creditor C, debtor B is discharged, a novation has occurred.

Nudum pactum A naked promise—one for which no consideration has been given.

Nuisance Generally, any continuous or continued conduct that causes annoyance, inconvenience, or damage to person or property. Nuisance usually applies to unreasonable, wrongful use of property, causing material discomfort, hurt, and damage to the person or property of another. Example: fumes from a factory.

Obligee A creditor or promisee.

Obligor A debtor or promisor.

Offer A statement by one party (called the offeror) that he is prepared to be bound to a contractual position. The offer is the first essential element to the meeting of the minds of the contracting parties. *See* Acceptance.

Oligopoly Control of a commodity or service in a given market by a small number of companies or suppliers.

Option A right secured by a contract to accept or reject an offer to purchase property at a fixed price within a fixed time. It is an irrevocable offer sometimes called a "paid-for offer."

Order* Under Article 3—Commercial Paper, order is a direction to pay and must be more than an authorization or request. It must, with reasonable certainty, identify the person to pay. It may be addressed to one or more such persons jointly or in the alternative but not in succession.

Order of relief The ruling by a bankruptcy judge that a particular case is properly before the bankruptcy court.

Ordinance Generally speaking, the legislative act of a municipality. A city council is a legislative body, and it passes ordinances that are the laws of the city.

Ordinary care Care that a prudent man would take under the circumstances of the particular case.

Par value "Face value." The par value of stocks and bonds on the date of issuance is the principal. At a later date, the par value is the principal plus interest.

Pari delicto The fault or blame is shared equally.

Pari materia "Related to the same matter or subject." Statutes and covenants concerning the same subject matter are in pan materia and as a general rule, for the purpose of ascertaining their meaning, are construed together.

Parol evidence Legal proof based on oral statements; with regard to a document, any evidence extrinsic to the document itself.

Part performance A legal doctrine created as an exception to the requirement that contracts be in written form pursuant to the statute of frauds. If the contracting parties have partially performed an oral contract to the extent that a judge is comfortable in ruling that the contract exists, this doctrine is used to enforce the contract. *See* Equitable estoppel.

Partition Court proceedings brought by an interested party's request that the court divide real property among respective owners as their interests appear. If the property cannot be divided in kind, then it is to be sold and the money divided as each interest appears.

Partnership A business organization consisting of two or more owners who agree to carry on a business and to share profits and losses.

Party* A person who has engaged in a transaction or made an agreement within the Uniform Commercial Code.

Patent ambiguity An obvious uncertainty in a written instrument.

Payor bank* Under Article 4—Bank Deposits and Collections, a bank by which an item is payable as drawn or accepted.

Penal bond A bond given by an accused, or by another person in his behalf, for the payment of money if the accused fails to appear in court on a certain day.

Pendente lite "Pending during the progress of a suit at law."

Per curiam A decision by the full court without indicating the author of the decision.

Peremptory challenge An objection raised by a party to a lawsuit who rejects a person serving as a juror. No reason need be given.

Perfection* In the law of secured transactions, this process is essential to inform the public that a creditor has an interest in the debtor's personal property. Perfection may occur by attachment, by filing a financing statement, by possession, and by noting the security interest on a certificate of title.

Perjury False swearing upon an oath properly administered in some judicial proceedings.

Per se "By itself." Thus, a contract clause may be inherently unconscionable—unconscionable *per se.*

Personal property The rights, powers, and privileges a person has in movable things, such as chattels and choses in actions. Personal property is used in contradistinction to real property.

Personal representative The administrator or executor of a deceased person or the guardian of a child or the conservator of an incompetent.

Personal service The sheriff personally delivers a service of process to the defendant.

Petitioner The party who files a claim in a court of equity. Also the party who petitions the Supreme Court for a writ of certiorari.

Plaintiff In an action at law, the complaining party or the one who commences the action. The person who seeks a remedy in court.

Pleading Process by which the parties in a lawsuit arrive at an issue.

Pledge Personal property, as security for a debt or other obligation, deposited or placed with a person called a pledgee. The pledgee has the implied power to sell the property if the debt is not paid. If the debt is paid, the right to possession returns to the pledgor.

Police court A court with jurisdiction to hear cases involving violations of local ordinances which are punishable as misdemeanors.

Polling jury Calling the name of each juror to inquire what his verdict is before it is made a matter of record.

Possession The method recognized by law and used by one's self or by another to hold, detain, or control either personal or real property, thereby excluding others from holding, detaining, or controlling such property.

Power of attorney An instrument authorizing another to act as one's agent or attorney in fact.

Precedent A previously decided case that can serve as an authority to help decide a present controversy. Use of such case is called the doctrine of *stare decisis,* which means to adhere to decided cases and settled principles. Literally, "to stand as decided."

Preference The term is used most generally in bankruptcy law. If an insolvent debtor pays some creditors a greater percentage of the debts than he pays other creditors in the same class, and if the payments are made within ninety days prior to his filing a bankruptcy petition, those payments constitute illegal and voidable preference. An intention to prefer such creditors must be shown.

Preferred stock Stock that entitles the holder to dividends from earnings before the owners of common stock can receive a dividend.

Preponderance Preponderance of the evidence means that evidence, in the judgment of the jurors, is entitled to the greatest weight, appears to be more credible, has greater force, and overcomes not only the opposing presumptions but also the opposing evidence.

Presenting bank* Under Article 4—Bank Deposits and Collections, this is any bank presenting an item except a payor bank.

Presentment* Under Article 3—Commercial Paper, presentment is a demand for acceptance or payment made upon the maker, acceptor, drawee, or other payor by or on behalf of, the holder.

Presumption (presumed)* The trier of fact must find the existence of the fact presumed unless and until evidence is introduced that would support a finding of its nonexistence.

Prima facie Literally, "at first view." Thus, that which first appears seems to be true. A prima facie case is one that stands until contrary evidence is produced.

Primary party* In the law of commercial paper, this person is the one all other parties expect to pay. The maker of a note and the drawee of a draft are the primary party to those instruments.

Principal In agency relationships, this party employs the services of an agent to accomplish those goals that he cannot accomplish on his own.

Privilege A legal idea or concept of lesser significance than a right. An invitee has only a privilege to walk on another's land, because such privilege may be revoked at will; whereas a person who has an easement to go on another's land has a right created by a grant, which is an interest in land and cannot be revoked at will. To be exempt from jury service is a privilege.

Privity Mutual and successive relationship to the same interest. Offeror and offeree, assignor and assignee, grantor and grantee are in privity. Privity of estate means that one takes title from another. In contract law, privity denotes parties in mutual legal relationship to each other by virtue of being promisees and promisors. At early common law, third-party beneficiaries and assignees were said to be not in "privity."

Probate court Handles the settlement of estates.

Procedural law The laws which establish the process by which a lawsuit is filed, a trial is conducted, an appeal is perfected, and a judgment is enforced. In essence, these laws can be called the rules of litigation.

Proceeds* Whatever is received when collateral or proceeds are sold, exchanged, collected, or otherwise disposed of. Includes the account arising when the right to payment is earned under a contract right. Money, checks, and the like are "cash proceeds." All other proceeds are "noncash proceeds."

Process In a court proceeding, before or during the progress of the trial, an instrument issued by the court in the name of the state and under the seal of the court, directing an officer of the court to do, act, or cause some act to be done incidental to the trial.

Product extension merger A merger that extends the products of the acquiring company into a similar or related product but one which is not directly in competition with existing products.

Promise* Under Article 3—Commercial Paper, it is an undertaking to pay, and it must be more than an acknowledgment of an obligation.

Promissory note The legal writing that evidences a debtor's promise to repay an amount of money borrowed.

Property All rights, powers, privileges, and immunities that one has concerning tangibles and intangibles. The term includes everything of value subject to ownership.

Protest* In the law of commercial paper, this event signifies that a proper presentment has been made', that dishonor has occurred, and that notice of dishonor was given in a timely fashion. Protest is required in international commercial paper transactions, but it is optional in domestic transactions.

Proximate cause The cause that sets other causes in operation. The responsible cause of an injury.

Proxy Authority to act for another, used by absent stockholders or members of legislative bodies to have their votes cast by others.

Punitive damages Damages by way of punishment. Allowed for an injury caused by a wrong that is willful and malicious.

Purchase* Includes taking by sale, discount, negotiation, mortgage, pledge, lien, issue or re-issue, gift, or any other voluntary transaction creating an interest in property.

Purchase-money security interest* A security interest that is taken or retained by the seller of the collateral to secure all or part of its price; or taken by a person who, by making advances or incurring an obligation, gives value to enable the debtor to acquire rights in, or the use of, collateral if such value is in fact so used.

Quantum meruit "As much as he deserves." This remedy is used to avoid the unjust enrichment of one party at the expenses of another. This remedy usually is in association with quasi-contracts.

Quasi-contract A situation in which there arises a legal duty that does not rest upon a promise but does involve the payment of money. In order to do justice by a legal fiction, the court enforces the duty as if a promise in fact exists. Thus, if A gives B money by mistake, A can compel B to return the money by an action in quasi-contract.

Quasi-judicial Administrative actions involving factual determinations and the discretionary application of rules and regulations.

Quasi-legislative The function of administrative agencies whereby rules and regulations are promulgated. This authority permits agencies to make enforceable "laws."

Quid pro quo The exchange of one thing of value for another.

Quiet title A suit brought by the owner of real property for the purpose of bringing into court any person who claims an adverse interest in the property, requiring him either to establish his claim or be barred from asserting it thereafter. It may be said that the purpose is to remove "clouds" from the title.

Quitclaim A deed that releases a right or interest in land but does not include any covenants of warranty. The grantor transfers only that which he has.

Quo warranto A proceeding in court by which a governmental body tests or inquires into the authority or legality of the claim of any person to a public office, franchise, or privilege.

Ratification The confirmation of one's own previous act or act of another: e.g., a principal may ratify the previous unauthorized act of his agent. B's agent, without authority, buys goods. B, by keeping the goods and receiving the benefits of the agent's act, ratifies the agency.

Ratio decidendi Logical basis of judicial decision.

Real property Land with all its buildings, appurtenances, equitable and legal interests therein. In contradistinction to personal property, which refers to movables or chattels.

Reasonable care The care that prudent persons would exercise under the same circumstances.

Receiver An officer of the court appointed on behalf of all parties to the litigation to take possession of, hold, and control the property involved in the suit, for the benefit of the party who will be determined to be entitled thereto.

Recoupment "A cutting back." A right to deduct from the plaintiff's claim any payment or loss that the defendant has suffered by reason of the plaintiffs wrongful act.

Redemption To buy back. A debtor buys back or redeems his mortgaged property when he pays the debt.

Referee A person to whom a cause pending in a court is referred by the court, to take testimony, hear the parties, and report thereon to the court.

Registered form* A security is in registered form when it specifies a person entitled to the security or to the rights it evidences and when its transfer may be registered upon books maintained for that purpose by, or on behalf of, an issuer, as security states.

Reinsurance In a contract of reinsurance, one insurance company agrees to indemnify another insurance company in whole or in part against risks that the first company has assumed. The original contract of insurance and the reinsurance contract are distinct contracts. There is no privity between the original insured and the reinsurer.

Release The voluntary relinquishing of a right, lien, or any other obligation. A release need not be under seal, nor does it necessarily require consideration. The words *release, remise,* and *discharge* are often used together to mean the same thing.

Remand To send back a case from the appellate court to the lower court, in order that the lower court may comply with the instructions of the appellate court. Also to return a prisoner to jail.

Remedy The word is used to signify the judicial means or court procedures by which legal and equitable rights are enforced.

Remitting bank* Under Article 4—Bank Deposits and Collections, any payor or intermediary bank remitting for an item.

Replevin A remedy given by statute for the recovery of the possession of a chattel. Only the right to possession can be tried in such action.

Res "Thing."

Res judicata A controversy once having been decided or adjudged upon its merits is forever settled so far as the particular parties involved are concerned. Such a doctrine avoids vexatious lawsuits.

Rescind To cancel or annul a contract and return the parties to their original positions.

Rescission An apparently valid act may conceal a defect that will make it null and void if any of the parties demand that it be rescinded.

Respondeat superior "The master is liable for the acts of his agent.

Respondent One who answers another's bill or pleading, particularly in an equity case. Quite similar, in many instances, to a defendant in a law case.

Responsible bidder In the phrase "lowest responsible bidder," responsible, as used by most statutes concerning public works, means that such bidder has the requisite skill, judgment, and integrity necessary to perform the contract involved and has the financial resources and ability to carry the task to completion.

Restitution When a contract is rescinded, all parties must return that which they have received. This remedy attempts to place the parties in the same positions they were in prior to making the contract.

Restraining order Issued by a court of equity in aid of a suit, to hold matters in abeyance until parties may be heard. A temporary injunction.

Restraint of trade Monopolies, combinations, and contracts that impede free competition.

Right The phrase "legal right" is a correlative of the phrase "legal duty." One has a legal right if, upon the breach of the correlative legal duty, he can secure a remedy in a court of law.

Right of action Synonymous with *cause of action:* a right to enforce a claim in a court.

Right-to-work law A state statute that outlaws a union shop contract; one by which an employer agrees to require membership in the union sometime after an employee has been hired, as a condition of continued employment.

Riparian A person is a riparian owner if his land is situated beside a stream of water, either flowing over or along the border of the land.

Sale* The agreement to exchange title to goods for a price.

Satisfaction In legal phraseology, the release and discharge of a legal obligation. Satisfaction may be partial or full performance of the obligation. The word is used with accord, a promise to give a substituted performance for a contract obligation; *satisfaction* means the acceptance by the obligee of such performance.

Scienter Knowledge by a defrauding party of the falsity of a representation. In a tort action of deceit, knowledge that a representation is false must be proved.

Seal A seal shows that an instrument was executed in a formal manner. At early common law, sealing legal documents was of great legal significance. A promise under seal was binding by virtue of the seal. Today under most statutes, any stamp, wafer, mark, scroll, or impression made, adopted and affixed, is adequate. The printed word *seal* or the letters L.S. (*locus sigilli,* "the place of the seal") are sufficient.

Seasonably* An action is taken "seasonably" when it is taken at, or within, the time agreed; or if no time is agreed, at or within a reasonable time.

Secondary boycott Conspiracy or combination to cause the customers or suppliers of an employer to cease doing business with that employer.

Secondary party* Under Article 3—Commercial Paper, a drawer or indorser.

Secret partner A partner whose existence is not known to the public.

Secured party* A lender, seller, or other person in whose favor there is a security interest, including a person to whom accounts, contract rights, or chattel paper have been sold. When the holders of obligations issued under an indenture of trust, equipment trust agreement, or the like are represented by a trustee or other person, the representative is the secured party.

Security May be bonds, stocks, and other property that a debtor places with a creditor, who may sell them if the debt is not paid. The plural, securities, is used broadly to mean tangible choses in action, such as promissory notes, bonds, stocks, and other vendible obligations.

Security* An instrument issued in bearer form or registered form; commonly dealt in on securities exchanges or markets or commonly recognized in any area in which it is issued or dealt in as a medium for investment; one of a class or series of instruments; evidences a share, a participation or other interest in property or in an enterprise or evidences an obligation of the issuer.

Security agreement* Creates or provides for a security interest.

Security interest* An interest in personal property or fixtures that secures payment or performance of an obligation.

Self-help* In the law of secured transactions, this term describes the creditor's attempt to take possession of collateral without the court's assistance.

Sell To negotiate or make arrangement for a sale. A sale is an executed contract, a result of the process of selling.

Separation of powers The doctrine that the legislative, executive, and judicial branches of government function independently of one another and that each branch serves as a check on the others.

Servant A person employed by another and subject to the direction and control of the employer in performance of his duties.

Setoff A matter of defense, called a cross-complaint, used by the defendant for the purpose of making a demand on the plaintiff. It arises out of contract but is independent and unconnected with the cause of action set out in the complaint. *See* Counterclaims and Recoupment.

Settle* Under Article 4—Bank Deposits and Collections, settle means to pay in cash, by clearinghouse settlement, in a charge or credit or by remittance or otherwise as instructed. A settlement may be either provisional or final.

Settlement A concept applicable in agency relationships when the principal is undisclosed. By paying (or settling with) the agent, the principal is relieved of liability to the third party. This third party will look to the agent for performance of their agreement.

Severable contract A contract in which the performance is divisible. Two or more parts may be set over against each other. Items and prices may be apportioned to each other without relation to the full performance of all of its parts.

Shareholders (stockholders) Persons whose names appear on the books of a corporation as owners of shares of stock and who are entitled to participate in the management and control of the corporation.

Share of stock A proportional part of the rights in the management and assets of a corporation. It is a chose in action. The certificate is the evidence of the share.

Silent partner A partner who has no voice in the management of the partnership.

Situs "Place, situation." The place where a thing is located. The situs of personal property is the domicile of the owner. The situs of land is the state or county where it is located.

Slander An oral utterance that tends to injure the reputation of another. *See* Libel.

Small claims court A court with jurisdiction to hear cases involving a limited amount of money. The jurisdictional amount varies among the states and local communities.

Special agent In agency relationships, an agent with a limited amount of specific authority. This agent usually has instructions to accomplish one specific task.

Special appearance The appearance in court of a person through his attorney for a limited purpose only. A court does not get jurisdiction over a person by special appearance.

Special verdict The jury finds the facts only, leaving it to the court to apply the law and draw the conclusion as to the proper disposition of the case.

Specific performance A remedy in personam in equity that compels performance of a contract to be substantial enough to do justice among the parties. A person who fails to obey a writ for specific performance may be put in jail by the equity judge for contempt of court. The remedy applies to contracts involving real property. In the absence of unique goods or peculiar circumstances, damages generally are an adequate remedy for breach of contracts involving personal property.

Standing to sue The doctrine that requires the plaintiff in a lawsuit to have a sufficient legal interest in the subject matter of the case.

Stare decisis "Stand by the decision." The law should adhere to decided cases. *See* Precedent.

Statute A law passed by the legislative body of a state.

Statutes of limitations Laws that exist for the purpose of bringing to an end old claims. Because witnesses die, memory fails, papers are lost, and the evidence becomes inadequate, stale claims are barred. Such statutes are called statutes of repose. Within a certain period of time, action on claims must be brought; otherwise, they are barred. The period varies from six months to twenty years.

Status quo The conditions or state of affairs at a given time.

Stay In the bankruptcy law, this occurs upon the entry of an order of relief. This order prevents all creditors from taking any action to collect debts owed by the protected debtor.

Stock dividend New shares of its own stock issued as a dividend by a corporation to its shareholders, in order to transfer retained earnings to capital stock.

Stock split A readjustment of the financial plan of a corporation, whereby each existing share of stock is split into new shares, usually with a lowering of par value.

Stock warrant A certificate that gives the holder the right to subscribe for and purchase, at a stated price, a given number of shares of stock in a corporation.

Stoppage in transit Upon learning of the insolvency of a buyer of goods, the seller has the right to stop the goods in transit and hold them as security for the purchase price. The right is an extension of the unpaid seller's lien.

Strict foreclosure The agreement by the creditor and debtor to allow the creditor to retain possession of the debtor's property in satisfaction of the creditor's claim.

Strict liability The doctrine under which a party may be required to respond in tort damages, without regard to that party's use of due care.

Subordinate In the case of a mortgage or other security interest, the mortgagee may agree to make his mortgage inferior to another mortgage or interest.

Subpoena A process issued out of a court requiring the attendance of a witness at a trial.

Subrogation The substitution of one person in another's place, whether as a creditor or as the possessor of any lawful right, so that the substituted person may succeed to the rights, remedies, or proceeds of the claim. It rests in equity on the theory that a party who is compelled to pay a debt for which another is liable should be vested with all the rights the creditor has against the debtor. For example: an insurance company pays Y for damage to Y's cat, caused by Z's negligent act. The insurance company will be subrogated to Y's cause of action against Z.

Subsequent purchaser* A person who takes a security other than by original issue.

Substantial performance The complete performance of all the essential elements of a contract. The only permissible omissions or derivations are those that are trivial, inadvertent, and inconsequential. Such performance will not justify repudiation. Compensation for defects may be substituted for actual performance.

Substantive law Law that regulates and controls the rights and duties of all persons in society. In contradistinction to the term *adjective law,* which means the rules of court procedure or remedial law, which prescribe the methods by which substantive law is enforced.

Succession The transfer by operation of law of all rights and obligations of a deceased person to those who are entitled to them.

Summary judgment A judicial determination that no genuine factual dispute exists and that one party to the lawsuit is entitled to judgment as a matter of law.

Summons A writ issued by a court to the sheriff, directing him to notify the defendant that the plaintiff claims to have a cause of action against the defendant and that he is required to answer. If the defendant does not answer, judgment will be taken by default.

Supremacy Clause Article VI, U.S. Constitution, which states that the Constitution, laws, and treaties of the United States shall be the "supreme law of the land" and shall take precedence over conflicting state laws.

Surety A person who agrees to become liable to the creditor for the debtor's obligation in the event the debtor fails to perform as promised.

Suretyship The legal relationship whereby one person becomes a surety for the benefit of the creditor and debtor.

Suspends payments* Under Article 4—Bank Deposits and Collections, with respect to a bank this means that it has been closed by order of the supervisory authorities, that a public officer has been appointed to take it over, or that it ceases or refuses to make payments in the ordinary course of business.

Tangible Describes property that is physical in character and capable of being moved. A debt is intangible, but a promissory note evidencing such debt is tangible. *See* Chattel; Chose in action.

Tenancy The interest in property that a tenant acquired from a landlord by a lease. It may be at will or for a term. It is an interest in land.

Tenancy by the entireties Property acquired by husband and wife whereby upon the death of one, the survivor takes the whole property. The tenancy exists in only a few states. The husband and wife are both vested with the whole estate, so that the survivor takes no new title upon death of the other but remains in possession of the whole as originally granted. For the legal effect of such estate, the state statute should be consulted. *See* Joint tenants.

Tenancy in common The most usual method of two or more persons owning property at the same time. None of the formalities or unities required for other specialized forms of co-ownership are essential for this method.

Tenant The person to whom a lease is made. A lessee.

Tender To offer and produce money in satisfaction of a debt or obligation and express to the creditor a willingness to pay.

Tender of delivery* The seller must put and hold conforming goods at the buyer's disposition and give the buyer any notification reasonably necessary to enable him to take delivery.

Termination In the law of business organizations, this event occurs when the winding up or liquidation is completed. In essence, this is the end of the organization and its business. This term also applies to the destruction of an agency or employment relationship.

Testamentary capacity A person is said to have testamentary capacity when he understands the nature of his business and the value of his property, knows those persons who are natural objects of his bounty, and comprehends the manner in which he has provided for the distribution of his property.

Testator A male who has died leaving a will. A female is a testatrix.

Testimony Statements made by a witness under oath or affirmation in a legal proceeding.

Title This word has limited or broad meaning. tangible and intangible, against all other persons, he may be said to have the complete title thereto. The aggregate of legal relations concerning property is the title. The term is used to describe the means by which a person exercises control and dominion over property. A trustee has a limited title. *See* Possession.

Tort "Twisted" or wrong. A wrongful act committed by one person against another person or his property. It is the breach of a legal duty imposed by law other than by contract. X assaults Y, thus committing a tort. *See* Duty; Right.

Tortfeasor One who commits a tort.

Trade fixtures Personal property placed upon, or annexed to, land leased by a tenant for the purpose of carrying on a trade or business during the term of the lease. Such property is generally to be removed at the end of the term, providing removal will not destroy or injure the premises. Trade fixtures include showcases, shelving, racks, machinery, and the like.

Trademark No complete definition can be given for a trademark. Generally it is any sign, symbol, mark, word, or arrangement of words in the form of a label adopted and used by a manufacturer or distributor to designate his particular goods, and which no other person has the legal right to use. Originally, the design or trademark indicated origin, but today it is used more as an advertising mechanism.

Traffic court A court with jurisdiction to hear cases involving violations of the state and local traffic laws.

Transfer In its broadest sense, the word means the act by which an owner sets over or delivers his right, title, and interest in property to another person. A "bill of sale" to personal property is evidence of a transfer.

Treason The offense of attempting by overt acts to overthrow the government of the state to which the offender owes allegiance; or of betraying the state into the hands of a foreign power.

Treasury stock Stock of a corporation that has been issued by the corporation for value but is later returned to the corporation by way of gift or purchase or otherwise. It may be returned to the trustees of a corporation for the purpose of sale.

Treble damages An award of damages allowable under some statutes equal to three times the amount found by the jury to be a single recovery.

Trespass An injury to the person, property, or rights of another person committed by actual force and violence or under such circumstances that the law will infer that the injury was caused by force or violence.

Trust A relationship between persons by which one holds property for the use and benefit of another. The relationship is called fiduciary. Such rights are enforced in a court of equity. The person trusted is called a trustee. The person for whose benefit the property is held is called a beneficiary or "cestui que trust.

Trustee (generally) A person who is entrusted with the management and control of another's property and estate. A person occupying a fiduciary position. An executor, an administrator, a guardian.

Trustee in bankruptcy An agent of the court authorized to liquidate the assets of the bankrupt, protect them, and bring them to the court for final distribution for the benefit of the bankrupt and all the creditors.

Truth-in-lending A federal law that requires disclosure of total finance charges and the annual percentage rate for credit in order that borrowers may be able to shop for credit.

Tying contract Ties the sales of one piece of property (real or personal) to the sale or lease of another item of property.

Ultra vires "Beyond power." The acts of a corporation are ultra vires when they are beyond the power or capacity of the corporation as granted by the state in its charter.

Unauthorized* Refers to a signature or indorsement made without actual, implied, or apparent authority. Includes a forgery.

Unconscionable In the law of contracts, provisions that are oppressive, overreaching, or shocking to the conscience.

Unfair competition The imitation, by design, of the goods of another, for the purpose of palming them off on the public, misleading it, and inducing it to buy goods made by the imitator. Includes misrepresentation and deceit; thus, such conduct is fraudulent not only to competitors but to the public.

Unilateral contract A promise for an act or an act for a promise, a single enforceable promise. C promises B $10 if B will mow C's lawn. B mows the lawn. C's promise, now binding, is a unilateral contract. *See* Bilateral contract.

Usage of trade* Any practice or method of dealing so regularly observed in a place, vocation, or trade that observance may justly be expected in the transaction in question. The existence and scope of such usage are to be proved as facts. If it is established that such a usage is embodied in a written trade code or similar writing, the interpretation of the writing is for the court.

Usurious A contract is usurious if made for a loan of money at a rate of interest in excess of that permitted by statute.

Utter "Put out or pass off." To utter a check is to offer it to another in payment of a debt. To "utter a forged writing" means to put such writing in circulation, knowing of the falsity of the instrument, with the intent to injure another.

Value* Except as otherwise provided with respect to negotiable instruments and bank collections, a person gives "value" for rights if he acquires them (a) in return for a binding commitment to extend credit or for the extension of immediately available credit, whether or not drawn upon and whether or not a chargeback is provided for in the event of difficulties in collection; or (b) as security for, or in, total or partial satisfaction of a preexisting claim; or (c) by accepting delivery pursuant to a preexisting contract for purchase; or (d) generally, in return for any consideration sufficient to support a simple contract.

Vendee A purchaser of property. Generally, the purchaser of real property. A buyer is usually a purchaser of chattels.

Vendor The seller of property, usually real property. The word *seller* is used with personal property.

Vendor's lien An unpaid seller's right to hold possession of property until he has recovered the purchase price.

Venire To come into court, a writ used to summon potential jurors.

Venue The geographical area over which a court presides. Venue designates the county in which the action is tried. Change of venue means to move to another county.

Verdict The decision of a jury, reported to the court, on matters properly submitted to the jury for consideration.

Vertical merger A merger of corporations, one corporation being the supplier of the other.

Void Has no legal effect. A contract that is void is a nullity and confers no rights or duties.

Voidable That which is valid until one party, who has the power of avoidance, exercises such power. An infant has the power of avoidance of his contract. A defrauded party has the power to avoid his contract. Such contract is voidable.

Voir dire Preliminary examination of a prospective juror.

Voting trust Two or more persons owning stock with voting powers divorce those voting rights from ownership but retain to all intents and purposes the ownership in themselves and transfer the voting rights to trustees in whom voting rights of all depositors in the trust are pooled.

Wager A relationship between persons by which they agree that a certain sum of money or thing owned by one of them will be paid or delivered to the other upon the happening of an uncertain event, which event is not within the control of the parties and rests upon chance.

Waive (verb) To "waive" at law is to relinquish or give up intentionally a known right or to do an act that is inconsistent with the claiming of a known right.

Waiver (noun) The intentional relinquishment or giving up of a known right. It may be done by express words or conduct that involves any acts inconsistent with an intention to claim the right. Such conduct creates an estoppel on the part of the claimant. *See* Estoppel.

Warehouseman* A person engaged in the business of storing goods for hire.

Warehouse receipt* Issued by a person engaged in the business of storing goods for hire.

Warehouse receipt An instrument showing that the signer has in his possession certain described goods for storage. It obligates the signer, the warehouseman, to deliver the goods to a specified person or to his order or bearer upon the return of the instrument. Consult Uniform Warehouse Receipts Act.

Warrant (noun) An order in writing in the name of the state, signed by a magistrate, directed to an officer, commanding him to arrest a person. (verb) To guarantee, to answer for, to assure that a state of facts exists.

Warranty An undertaking, either expressed or implied, that a certain fact regarding the subject matter of a contract is presently true or will be true. The word has particular application in the law of sales of chattels. It relates to title and quality. Warranty should be distinguished from *guaranty,* which means a contract or promise by one person to answer for the performance of another.

Warranty of fitness for a particular purpose* An implied promise by a seller of goods that arises when a buyer explains the special needs and relies on the seller's advice.

Warranty of merchantability* A promise implied in a sale of goods by merchants: that the goods are reasonably fit for the general purpose for which they are sold.

Waste Damage to the real property, so that its value as security is impaired.

Watered stock Corporate stock issued by a corporation for property at an overvaluation, or stock issued for which the corporation receives nothing in payment.

Will (testament) The formal instrument by which a person makes disposition of his property, to take effect upon his death.

Winding up The process of liquidating a business organization.

Working capital The amount of cash necessary for the convenient and safe transaction of present business.

Workers' compensation A plan for compensating employees for occupational disease, accidental injury, and death suffered in connection with employment.

Writ An instrument in writing, under seal in the name of the state, issued out of a court of justice at the commencement of, or during, a legal proceeding; directed to an officer of the court, commanding him to do some act or requiring some person to refrain from doing some act pertinent or relative to the cause being tried.

Writ of certiorari A discretionary proceeding by which an appellate court may review the ruling of an inferior tribunal.

Writ of *habeas corpus* A court order to one holding custody of another, to produce that individual before the court for the purpose of determining whether such custody is proper.

Yellow-dog contract A worker agrees not to join a union and to be discharged if he breaches the contract.

Zoning ordinance Passed by a city council by virtue of police power. Regulates and prescribes the kind of buildings, residences, or businesses that shall be built and used in different parts of a city.

Photo Credits

Chapter 1: iStockphoto, 1; iStockphoto, 3; iStockphoto, 5; iStockphoto, 6; iStockphoto, 16; iStockphoto, 21.

Chapter 2: iStockphoto, 25; iStockphoto, 28; Associated Press, 29; iStockphoto, 32; iStockphoto, 33; Associated Press, 35.

Chapter 3: Shutterstock images, 41; iStockphoto, iStockphoto 43; 44; iStockphoto, 46; Shutterstock images, 50; iStockphoto, 51.

Chapter 4: iStockphoto, 61; iStockphoto, 63; iStockphoto, 67; iStockphoto, 69; iStockphoto, 71.

Chapter 5: Shutterstock images; 75; Shutterstock images; 78; iStockphoto, 82; Library of Congress, 85; Associated Press, 87; iStockphoto, 88; iStockphoto, 92.

Chapter 6: iStockphoto, 99; Associated Press, 101; Associated Press, 106; iStockphoto, 108; iStockphoto, 111; iStockphoto, 115.

Chapter 7: Dreamstime, 123; iStockphoto, 126; iStockphoto, 129; iStockphoto, 130; iStockphoto, 131.

Chapter 8: Associated Press, 139; iStockphoto, 143; iStockphoto, 146; iStockphoto, 147; iStockphoto, 150.

Chapter 9: iStockphoto, 155; iStockphoto, 159; iStockphoto, 161; iStockphoto, 169; iStockphoto, 172; iStockphoto, 173.

Chapter 10: iStockphoto, 181; iStockphoto, 190; iStockphoto, 191; iStockphoto, 194; iStockphoto, 195; iStockphoto, 198.

Chapter 11: Associated Press, 203; iStockphoto, 205; iStockphoto, 206; iStockphoto, 209; iStockphoto, 213; Associated Press, 214; iStockphoto, 215.

Chapter 12: iStockphoto, 221; iStockphoto, 224; iStockphoto, 225; iStockphoto, 232 (top); iStockphoto, 232 (bottom); iStockphoto, 236.

Chapter 13: iStockphoto, 243; iStockphoto, 245; iStockphoto, 250; iStockphoto, 251; iStockphoto, 256; iStockphoto, 258; iStockphoto, 259.

Chapter 14: iStockphoto, 267; iStockphoto, 269; iStockphoto, 271; iStockphoto, 279; iStockphoto, 282.

Chapter 15: iStockphoto, 289; iStockphoto, 291; iStockphoto, 296; iStockphoto, 297; iStockphoto, 301; iStockphoto, 303.

Chapter 16: iStockphoto, 307; iStockphoto, 310; iStockphoto, 313 (top); iStockphoto, 313 (bottom); iStockphoto, 317; iStockphoto, 320.

Chapter 17: iStockphoto, 325; iStockphoto, 327; iStockphoto, 329; iStockphoto, 333; iStockphoto, 337; iStockphoto, 338.

Chapter 18: iStockphoto, 343; iStockphoto, 346; iStockphoto, 349; iStockphoto, 352; iStockphoto, 353; iStockphoto, 354.

Chapter 19: iStockphoto, 361; iStockphoto, 365; iStockphoto, 369; iStockphoto, 370; iStockphoto, 375; iStockphoto, 376.

Chapter 20: iStockphoto, 385; iStockphoto, 386; iStockphoto, 388; iStockphoto, 391; iStockphoto, 392; iStockphoto, 397

Chapter 21: iStockphoto, 403; iStockphoto, 405; iStockphoto, 408; iStockphoto, 410; iStockphoto, 413; iStockphoto, 419.

Chapter 22: iStockphoto, 427; iStockphoto, 430; iStockphoto, 433; iStockphoto, 436; iStockphoto, 437; iStockphoto, 438.

Chapter 23: Shutterstock, 443; iStockphoto, 446; iStockphoto, 448; iStockphoto, 450; iStockphoto, 452; iStockphoto, 454.

Chapter 24: iStockphoto, 461; Associated Press, 463; iStockphoto, 467; Associated Press, 470; iStockphoto, 472; iStockphoto, 476.

Chapter 25: Associated Press, 483; iStockphoto, 486; Associated Press, 491; iStockphoto, 494; iStockphoto, 495; iStockphoto, 496.

Chapter 26: iStockphoto, 503; iStockphoto, 506; iStockphoto, 509; iStockphoto, 510; iStockphoto, 513; iStockphoto, 518.

Chapter 27: iStockphoto, 525; iStockphoto, 529; iStockphoto, 530; iStockphoto, 534; iStockphoto, 535; iStockphoto, 539.

Chapter 28: iStockphoto, 545; iStockphoto, 547; iStockphoto, 549; iStockphoto, 556; iStockphoto, 560; iStockphoto, 567.

Chapter 29: iStockphoto, 577; iStockphoto, 579; Associated Press, 581; iStockphoto, 584; iStockphoto, 587; iStockphoto, 590.

Chapter 30: iStockphoto, 599; iStockphoto, 601; iStockphoto, 607; iStockphoto, 610; iStockphoto, 615.

Chapter 31: iStockphoto, 625; iStockphoto, 629; iStockphoto, 630; iStockphoto, 631; iStockphoto, 633 (top); iStockphoto, 633 (bottom).

Chapter 32: Shutterstock, 639; Associated Press, 643; iStockphoto, 646; iStockphoto, 652; iStockphoto, 653; iStockphoto, 657.

Chapter 33: iStockphoto, 663; iStockphoto, 665; iStockphoto, 669; iStockphoto, 670; iStockphoto, 673; iStockphoto, 677.

Chapter 34: iStockphoto, 685; iStockphoto, 688; iStockphoto, 690; iStockphoto, 692; iStockphoto, 693; iStockphoto, 696;

Chapter 35: iStockphoto, 705; iStockphoto, 707; iStockphoto, 710; iStockphoto, 712; iStockphoto, 714.

Chapter 36: iStockphoto, 723; iStockphoto, 725; iStockphoto, 729; iStockphoto, 730; iStockphoto, 736.

Chapter 37: iStockphoto, 743; iStockphoto, 745; iStockphoto, 748; iStockphoto, 749; iStockphoto, 760; iStockphoto, 763.

Chapter 38: iStockphoto, 777; iStockphoto, 780; iStockphoto, 782; iStockphoto, 783; iStockphoto, 794.

Chapter 39: iStockphoto, 805; iStockphoto, 814; iStockphoto, 818; iStockphoto, 820; iStockphoto, 827.

Chapter 40: iStockphoto, 833; iStockphoto, 835; iStockphoto, 837; Associated Press, 840; iStockphoto, 843; iStockphoto, 846; iStockphoto, 850.

Chapter 41: iStockphoto, 857; Associated Press, 862; iStockphoto, 864; iStockphoto, 869; iStockphoto, 874; Associated Press, 877.

Chapter 42: iStockphoto, 883; iStockphoto, 887; iStockphoto, 889; iStockphoto, 893; iStockphoto, 895; iStockphoto, 897.

Chapter 43: Associated Press, 903; iStockphoto, 905; iStockphoto, 906; iStockphoto, 911; iStockphoto, 913; iStockphoto, 915.

Appendix A: iStockphoto, 919

Index

E

F

J

K

L

M